Annotated Teacher's Edition

Prentice Hall
LITERATURE
Timeless Voices, Timeless Themes

PLATINUM

ISBN 0-13-434864-8

2 3 4 5 6 7 8 9 10   02 01 00 99 98

PRENTICE HALL
Simon & Schuster Education Group

Prentice Hall
LITERATURE
Timeless Voices, Timeless Themes

What's special about *Prentice Hall Literature: Timeless Voices, Timeless Themes?*

This exciting new program sets a new standard in quality language arts instructional materials. No other literature program provides a more complete blend of classic and contemporary literature; such an extensive array of motivating, real-world connections; such consistent and comprehensive instruction in communication skills; or such a flexible array of teaching materials.

The program also includes a library of longer works and technology in the form of literature videodiscs, audiocassettes of selections, and CD-ROM software. Use the materials you want in the medium that is most convenient for you to address your students' needs.

◆ **A unique, flexible organization**
Prentice Hall Literature: Timeless Voices, Timeless Themes is the first literature program that lets you choose a thematic approach, a genre-based organization, or a combination of the two.

◆ **Strong real-world connections make literature relevant to students**
Prentice Hall Literature: Timeless Voices, Timeless Themes provides features that make all literature, including the classics, relevant to today's students.

◆ **A new level of skills instruction**
Prentice Hall Literature: Timeless Voices, Timeless Themes is the only program to provide instruction in all of the following skills with *every selection*:

Reading Strategies	Literary Elements and Forms
Writing	Vocabulary
Grammar	Critical Thinking
Visual Literacy	Speaking and Listening

◆ **Teaching support that you can customize to your needs**
A wide array of print and technology resources make it easy for you to customize instruction to meet the needs of all students.

A unique, flexible organization *fits any teaching approach.*

The Gold and Platinum levels of *Prentice Hall Literature: Timeless Voices, Timeless Themes* let you choose a thematic approach, a genre-based approach, or a combination of the two. Each book is organized into five thematic units, followed by five genre-based units. If you prefer a strictly thematic or a purely genre-based approach, however, you can use one of the alternative tables of contents:

- complete contents by theme
- complete contents by genre

The Platinum level also offers a contents of literature from around the world.

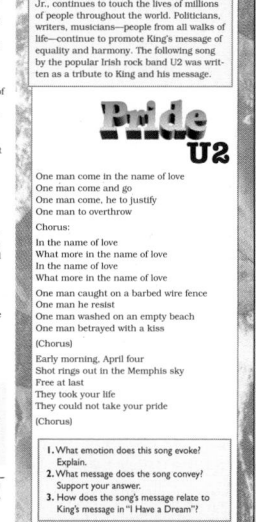

. . . I say to you today, my friends, that in spite of the difficulties and frustrations of the moment I still have a dream. It is a dream deeply rooted in the American dream.

I have a dream that one day this nation will rise up and live out the true meaning of its creed: "We hold these truths to be self-evident; that all men are created equal."

I have a dream that one day on the red hills of Georgia the sons of former slaves and the sons of former slaveowners will be able to sit down together at the table of brotherhood.

I have a dream that one day even the state of Mississippi, a desert state sweltering with the heat of injustice and oppression, will be transformed into an oasis of freedom and justice.

I have a dream that my four little children will one day live in a nation where they will not be judged by the color of their skin but by the content of their character.

I have a dream today.

I have a dream that one day the state of Alabama, whose governor's lips are presently dripping with the words of interposition and nullification,[1] will be transformed into a situation where little black boys and black girls will be able to join hands with little white boys and white girls and walk together as sisters and brothers.

I have a dream today.

I have a dream that one day every valley shall be exalted, every hill and mountain shall be made low, the rough places will be made plains,

1. Interposition (in´ tər pə zish´ ən) and **nullification** (nuf´ ə fi kā´ shən): Disputed doctrine that a state can reject federal laws considered to be violations of its rights.

◆ Build Vocabulary

creed (krēd) *n.:* Statement of belief

oppression (ə presh´ ən) *n.:* Keeping others down by the unjust use of power

oasis (ō ā´ sis) *n.:* Fertile place in the desert

exalted (eg zôlt´ əd) *v.:* Lifted up

◄ **Critical Viewing** What does this photograph tell you about the importance of Dr. King's message to those who heard his speech? [Draw Conclusions]

CONNECTIONS TO TODAY'S WORLD

Years after his death, Martin Luther King, Jr., continues to touch the lives of millions of people throughout the world. Politicians, writers, musicians—people from all walks of life—continue to promote King's message of equality and harmony. The following song by the popular Irish rock band U2 was written as a tribute to King and his message.

Pride
U2

One man come in the name of love
One man come and go
One man come, he to justify
One man to overthrow

Chorus:
In the name of love
What more in the name of love
In the name of love
What more in the name of love

One man caught on a barbed wire fence
One man he resist
One man washed on an empty beach
One man betrayed with a kiss

(Chorus)

Early morning, April four
Shot rings out in the Memphis sky
Free at last
They took your life
They could not take your pride

(Chorus)

1. What emotion does this song evoke? Explain.
2. What message does the song convey? Support your answer.
3. How does the song's message relate to King's message in "I Have a Dream"?

I Have a Dream ◆ 141

Strong real-world connections

Each unit includes a Connections to Today's World feature that links classic literature to high-interest contemporary writings, including songs, sports articles, cartoons, and Internet Web sites. The program also provides Beyond Literature features that lead students into an exploration of careers, communities, and other subject areas.

Comprehensive skills instruction with every selection

Prentice Hall Literature: Timeless Voices, Timeless Themes is the only literature program to provide instruction in all language arts skills with *every selection*. The following instructional options are provided before, during, and after each selection. Choose the ones that best fit your curricular goals.

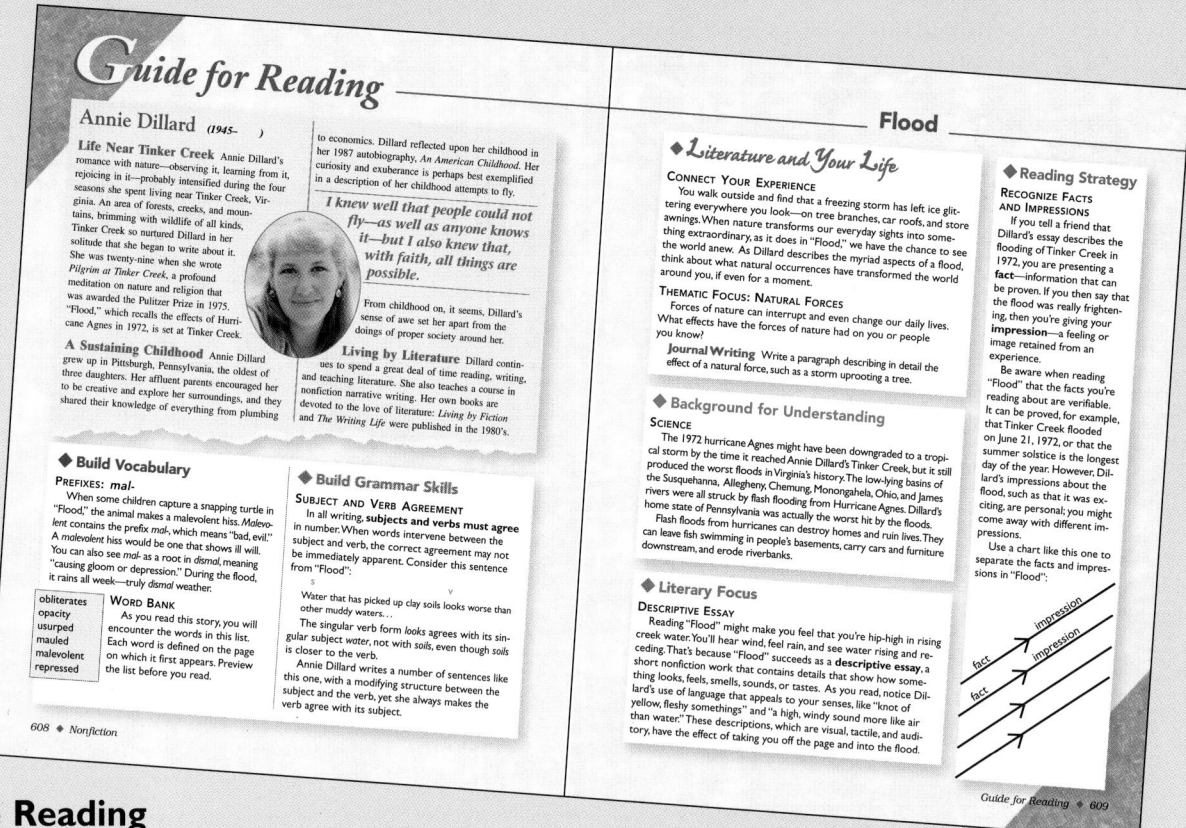

Before Reading

Engage your students and prepare them to read each selection through the unparalleled prereading support offered in the **Guide for Reading**.

◆ **An extensive author biography** brings the author to life for students.

◆ **Build Vocabulary** previews new words and teaches a vocabulary building strategy.

◆ **Build Grammar Skills** provides instruction in a grammar skill modeled in the selection.

◆ **Literature and Your Life** captures students' interest by linking the literature to their own experiences.

◆ **Background for Understanding** provides context related to history, science, culture, and more.

◆ **Reading Strategy** helps students read more critically and with a higher level of comprehension.

◆ **Literary Focus** teaches a literary form or element.

During Reading

To help students through the selection, *Prentice Hall Literature: Timeless Voices, Timeless Themes* offers the following support:

◆ **Reading Strategy** prompts support comprehension and guide students in using the strategy introduced before the selection.

> ◆ **Reading Strategy**
> Is this a fact or an impression? How do you know?

◆ **Literary Focus** prompts help students see how the literary element is illustrated in specific passages.

> ◆ **Literary Focus**
> In what specific ways is this passage typical of a descriptive essay?

◆ **Literature and Your Life** prompts help students connect details in the selection to their lives.

After Reading

Assess students' understanding and **extend** their learning through the **Guide for Responding** after each selection. Additional instruction and practice are provided for <u>all of the skills</u> introduced before the literature.

◆ **Literature and Your Life** promotes reader response and thematic connections.

☑ **Check Your Comprehension** questions assess students' literal understanding of the selection.

◆ **Critical Thinking** questions assess students' ability to use higher-level thinking skills to construct meaning.

◆ **Reading Strategy** assesses students' mastery of the reading strategy.

◆ **Literary Focus** reinforces students' understanding of the literary element.

◆ **Build Vocabulary** checks students' mastery of both the vocabulary strategy and the words used in the selection, often in an SAT-style format.

◆ **Build Grammar Skills** provides reteaching and assessment with practice activities and a writing application.

Build Your Portfolio provides a wealth of activities for students to demonstrate their understanding.

📁 **Idea Bank** provides:
- Three writing activities keyed to varying performance levels
- Two speaking and listening activities
- Two projects, often linked to cross-curricular topics

📁 **Writing Mini-Lesson** provides step-by-step writing process instruction and focuses students on developing a specific writing skill.

Skills Workshops provide additional in-depth skills instruction.

Writing Process Workshops provide detailed step-by-step writing process instruction in all modes of writing.

- Provides 20 opportunities for extended writing projects
- Linked to the end-of-selection Writing Mini-Lesson through the Writing Skills Focus sections; enables students to build on skills they've already learned

Two **Applying Language Skills** mini-lessons accompany each Writing Process Workshop to provide additional grammar instruction right at point-of-use.

Real-World Reading Skills Workshops help students build reading skills essential to success in careers and in daily life.

- 20 lessons in each book

Speaking and Listening Workshops provide instruction and practice in real-life communication skills.

Extended Reading Opportunities provide a wide range of suggestions for extended reading, including titles in the *Prentice Hall Literature Library*.

The Annotated Teacher's Edition provides flexible teaching pathways and customized strategies to meet your curricular goals and your students' individual needs.

Following are just a few of the many features:

Customize notes provide tips and strategies for addressing the needs of various student populations: Less Proficient Readers, More Advanced Students, English Language Learners, Visual/Spatial Learners, and so on.

Interest Grabber notes at the beginning of every selection provide a quick activity or teaching strategy for piquing students' interest.

One-Minute Insight provides a summary and an explanation of the selection's underlying meaning.

Preparing for Standardized Tests shows you how to connect skills instruction to a standardized test format.

Beyond the Selection notes with every selection provide **Internet Links** to appropriate Web sites.

Other notes include:

Humanities Notes

Cross-Curricular Connections

Cultural Connections

Beyond the Classroom (Career and Community Connections)

Literary Focus

Reading Strategy

Build Grammar Skills

Build Vocabulary

Enrichment

Check Your Comprehension

Comprehension Check

A wealth of options for reteaching, extension, and assessment

Teacher Resources

Selection Support: Skills Development

Practice pages reinforce the skills taught with each selection:

◆ **Build Vocabulary** includes practice activities in standardized test formats.

◆ **Build Grammar Skills** includes practice activities and a writing application.

◆ **Reading Strategy** often provides graphic organizers to aid students as they read the selection.

◆ **Literary Focus** reinforces literary concepts.

Beyond Literature

◆ Cross Curricular, Career, and Community Connections

Daily Language Practice

Brief daily activities, ready for easy class presentation

Art Transparencies

20 full-color transparencies

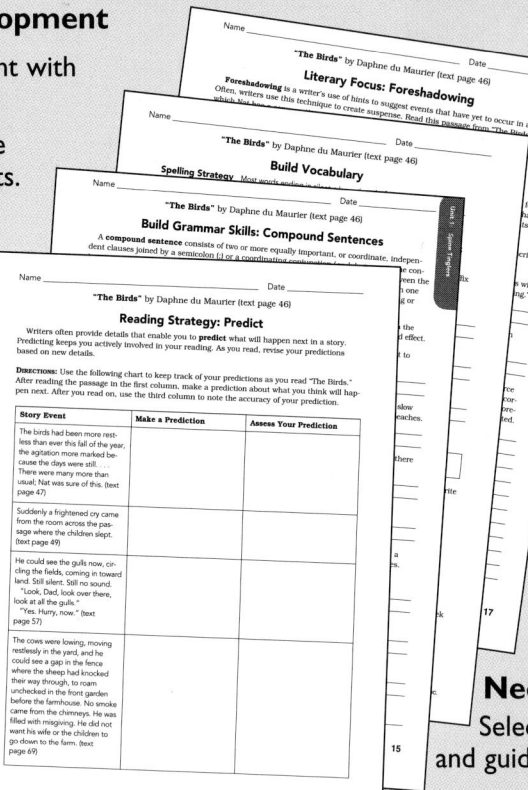

Formal Assessment

◆ **Selection Tests** assess all skills objectives and include essay questions geared to varying performance levels.

◆ **Unit Tests** assess mastery of unit skills objectives in a standardized-test format.

◆ **Assessment Resources Software** allows you to easily customize tests to performance levels or curricular goals.

Alternative Assessment

Alternative assessment activities, rubrics, portfolio forms, peer and parental assessment support, and much more

Strategies for Diverse Student Needs

Selection summaries in English and Spanish and guided support for every selection

Professional Development

Professional articles on a wide range of topics

Writing and Language Transparencies

◆ Provides over 100 transparencies for writing and grammar instruction

◆ Complete writing models for various types of writing—ranging from reports to persuasive essays—including rough drafts, revised drafts, and proofread drafts

◆ Graphic organizers for support of both writing and reading

◆ Daily Language Practice overheads that make it easy to provide five-minute activities to improve language skills

Extend your students' appreciation of fine literature.

Prentice Hall Literature Library

◆ 24 titles to choose from

◆ Special hardcovers with a beautiful design for attractiveness and durability

◆ Uncut editions so students enjoy complete works

◆ Classic novels by honored writers

◆ Great drama, including additional Shakespeare offerings

◆ Literature collections featuring writings from specific regions, cultures, or genre

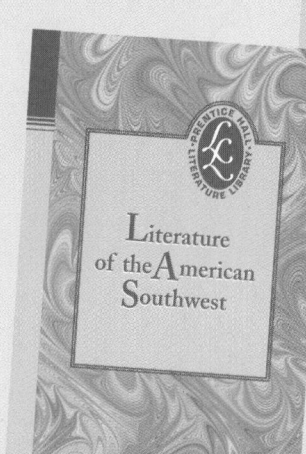

Study Guides for each title provide expert teaching support with summaries, teaching strategies, and more.

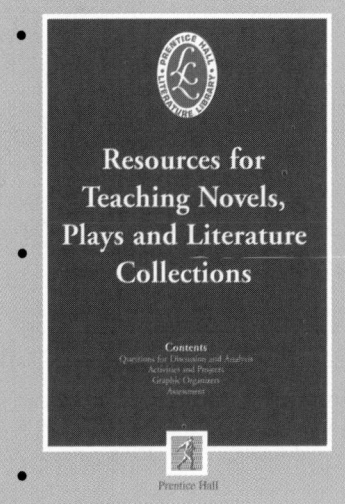

Resources for Teaching Novels, Plays, and Literature Collections provides a wealth of teaching materials and assessment aids for use with any of the titles in our library. Includes transparencies, graphic organizers, and tests.

A wide range of quality technology enhances and extends literature instruction.

Listening to Literature Audiocassettes

Use these complete, unabridged recordings of selections in *Prentice Hall Literature: Timeless Voices, Timeless Themes* to bring the literature to life and to meet the diverse needs and learning styles of your students. Includes <u>all of the selections</u> in the program.

◆ Motivate auditory learners

◆ Help less proficient readers

◆ Aid English language learners

Looking at Literature Videodiscs and Videotapes

Full-motion video segments provide a wide range of support for the literature—from student response to historical context to connections to today's world.

◆ Motivate students

◆ Build background

◆ Establish relevance

◆ Encourage class discussion of the literature

Resource Pro and Literature Database CD-ROM

Imagine a complete Teaching Resources, a customizable Lesson Planner, and a wide range of additional literature selections that fits in your hand! With this CD-ROM, you can customize lesson plans at the touch of a button. You can also review, edit, and print an entire year's worth of blackline masters and other teaching support materials. In addition, more than 100 supplemental literature selections are provided for every grade level.

Narration
Revising and Editing Self-Revision

Prewriting Notes Writing Notebook Editing Tools Handbook Show Help

Play the video to hear an editing tip from Isabel Allende.

Turn your draft into a polished piece of writing by carefully revising it. Strengthen your plot, round out your characters, and sharpen your settings. Also, if your narrative has a theme or message, make sure it is evident by the story's end.

For help, click the following:

Complete a Self-Evaluation Checklist.
Use a Character Trait Word Bin.
Use a Sensory Word Bin.
Check for anachronisms in your dialogue.
Revise your narrative for style.
See a revised student model.

Writing Hints   Challenge
Activity Drawer

Revising Your Narrative

Drafting   Map   Peer Revision

Writer's Solution

Writer's Solution, Prentice Hall's award-winning interactive writing instruction program, has been fully integrated into *Prentice Hall Literature: Timeless Voices, Timeless Themes*. Components include:

◆ Writing Lab CD-ROM provides interactive tutorials on the major modes of writing, including Response to Literature.

◆ Language Lab CD-ROM provides self-directed instruction and practice in grammar, usage, and mechanics.

◆ Writers at Work videodisc and videotape bring real writers into the classroom.

◆ Writer's Toolkit networked software provides tools and activities for all stages of writing.

Formal Assessment CD-ROM

All selection tests and unit tests are available on software so you can customize assessment for your students. The software is also available on floppy disk for Windows and Macintosh. The software enables you to:

◆ Customize tests to ability levels

◆ Customize tests by skills objectives

◆ Administer tests on-line in the computer lab

Literature CD-ROM Library

Multimedia presentations; hyperlinks to glossaries, indexes, and encyclopedias; and complete, on-line testing are just some of the outstanding features on these interactive CD-ROMs. Titles include the following:

◆ How to Read and Understand Poetry

◆ How to Read and Understand Drama

◆ The Time, Life, and Works of Shakespeare

◆ The History of American Literature, Part 1

◆ The History of American Literature, Part 2

◆ Greek Myths and Legends

Internet Home Page

Visit the Prentice Hall Web site at **phschool.com** for features that support *Prentice Hall Literature: Timeless Voices, Timeless Themes*:

◆ Visit literary sites through our updated Links.

◆ Share ideas through our Faculty Forum electronic bulletin board.

◆ Take part in special events such as electronic dialogues with notable authors.

Netscape - [Prentice Hall School]

File Edit View Go Bookmarks Options Directory Window Help

PRENTICE HALL School   *Dinner Workshops*
Write Now / Site Map

Foreign Language
Language Arts
Mathematics
Science & Health
Social Studies

Products and Services
Faculty FORUM
Editor's Picks
Sales Rep Locator
Professional Development

SIMON & SCHUSTER

Look for the Prentice Hall booth at NMSA in Indianapolis fr

Selection	Reading	Literary Elements/Forms	Vocabulary	Grammar
"Contents of the Dead Man's Pocket," Jack Finney, SE p. 2 Reading Level: Average	• Reading for Success: Literal Comprehension Strategies, SE pp. 4, 19; TR Selection Support, pp. 3–4 • Model, SE pp. 5–18 • Sequence Events, TR Str. for Diverse St. Needs, p. 1	• Suspense, SE pp. 3, 19; TR Selection Support, p. 5	• Word Roots: *-term-*, SE pp. 2, 19; TR Selection Support, p. 1 Word Bank: convoluted, p. 7; grimace, deftness, imperceptibly, p. 11; reveling, p. 13; interminable, p. 15	• Possessive *its* vs. Contraction *it's*, SE pp. 2, 19; TR Selection Support, p. 2 • WS Language Lab CD-ROM, Capitalization and Punctuation • WS Gram. Pr. Book, p. 110
"The Final Assault," Sir Edmund Hillary; "The Dream Comes True," Tenzing Norgay, SE p. 22 Reading Levels: Challenging, Challenging	• Distinguish Fact From Opinion, SE pp. 23, 42; TR Selection Support, p. 8 • Outline Main Idea and Supporting Details, TR Str. for Diverse St. Needs, p. 2	• Author's Perspective, SE pp. 23, 42; TR Selection Support, p. 9	• Word Roots: *-voc-*, SE pp. 22, 42; TR Selection Support, p. 6 Word Bank: precipitous, discernible, belay, p. 28; encroaching, p. 31; undulations, vociferous, p. 34	• Compound Predicates, SE pp. 22, 42; TR Selection Support, p. 7 • WS Language Lab CD-ROM, Subject/Verb Agreement • WS Gram. Pr. Book, pp. 26–29
"The Monkey's Paw," W. W. Jacobs; "The Bridegroom," Alexander Pushkin, SE p. 44 Reading Levels: Average, Average	• Predict Outcomes, SE pp. 45, 58; TR Selection Support, p. 12 • Recognize Cause and Effect, TR Str. for Diverse St. Needs, p. 3	• Foreshadowing, SE pp. 45, 58; TR Selection Support, p. 13	• Word Roots: *-cred-*, SE pp. 44, 58; TR Selection Support, p. 10 Word Bank: doughty, p. 46; maligned, credulity, p. 49; prosaic, avaricious, furtively, p. 50; fusillade, p. 53; foreboding, p. 54; tumult, p. 56	• Regular and Irregular Verb Forms, SE pp. 44, 58; TR Selection Support, p. 11 • WS Language Lab CD-ROM, Verb Tense • WS Gram. Pr. Book, pp. 67–69
from ***A Walk to the Jetty,*** **Jamaica Kincaid,** SE p. 60 Reading Level: Average	• Make Inferences, SE pp. 61, 69; TR Selection Support, p. 16 • Identify Characters, TR Str. for Diverse St. Needs, p. 4	• Flashback, SE pp. 61, 69; TR Selection Support, p. 17	• Word Roots: *-stup-*, SE pp. 60, 69; TR Selection Support, p. 14 Word Bank: loomed, apprenticed, p. 62; raked, stupor, p. 68	• Clauses, SE pp. 60, 69; TR Selection Support, p. 15 • WS Gram. Pr. Book, pp. 51–58
"The Masque of the Red Death," Edgar Allan Poe, SE p. 76 Reading Level: Challenging	• Context Clues, SE pp. 77, 84; TR Selection Support, p. 20 • Paraphrase, TR Str. for Diverse St. Needs, p. 5	• Symbols, SE pp. 77, 84; TR Selection Support, p. 21	• Suffixes: *-tion,* SE pp. 76, 84; TR Selection Support, p. 18 Word Bank: august, p. 78; piquancy, arabesque, p. 81; cessation, disapprobation, habiliments, p. 82	• Subject-Verb Agreement, SE pp. 76, 84; TR Selection Support, p. 19 • WS Language Lab CD-ROM, Subject/Verb Agreement • WS Gram. Pr. Book, pp. 80–82
"Fear," Gabriela Mistral; "The street," Octavio Paz; "Spring and All," William Carlos Williams, SE p. 86 Reading Levels: Average, Challenging, Average	• Form a Mental Image, SE pp. 87, 92; TR Selection Support, p. 24 • Restate Poetry as Prose, TR Str. for Diverse St. Needs, p. 6	• Imagery, SE pp. 87, 92; TR Selection Support, p. 25	• Suffixes: *-less,* SE pp. 86, 92; TR Selection Support, p. 22 Word Bank: contagious, lifeless, clarity, stark, profound, p. 91	• Pronouns and Antecedents, SE pp. 86, 92; TR Selection Support, p. 23 • WS Language Lab CD-ROM, Pronoun and Antecedent • WS Gram. Pr. Book, p. 83
"Two Friends," Guy de Maupassant; "Damon and Pythias," myth retold by William F. Russell, SE p. 94 Reading Levels: Average, Easy	• Significant Details, SE pp. 95, 106; TR Selection Support, p. 28 • Identify Chain of Events, TR Str. for Diverse St. Needs, p. 7	• Climax, SE pp. 95, 106; TR Selection Support, p. 29	• Word Roots: *-tain-*, SE pp. 94, 106; TR Selection Support, p. 26 Word Bank: ardent, vernal, p. 96; jauntiness, p. 98; dire, p. 102; detained, impediments, hindrances, annals, p. 104	• Appositives, SE pp. 94, 106; TR Selection Support, p. 27 • WS Language Lab CD-ROM, Commas • WS Gram. Pr. Book, p. 40

Writing	Speaking and Listening	Projects	Assessment	Technology
• Annotated Drawing, New Story Titles, Credo, SE p. 20 • Mini-Lesson: Cliffhanger Scene [Grab and Hold Audience's Attention], SE p. 20 • Epitaph, Advice Letter, Suspense, TR Alt. Assess., p. 1	• Role Play, School Speech, SE p. 20 • Mini-Lesson: School Speech, Role Play, ATE p. 10 and 15 • Ballad, TR Alt. Assess., p. 1	• Risks of Everyday Life, Changing Technology, SE p. 20 • Scrapbook, Proposal, TR Alt. Assess., p. 1	• Selection Test, TR Formal Assessment, pp. 1–3; Assess. Res. Software • Drama Rubric [for Mini-Lesson], TR Alt. Assess., p. 112 • TR Alt. Assess., p. 1	• "The Contents of the Dead Man's Pocket," LL Audiocassettes • WS Writing Lab CD-ROM, Narration Tutorial; Wr. at Work Videodisc, Ch. 2
• Book Jacket, Article on Everest, Mountain's Eye View, SE p. 43 • Mini-Lesson: Hall-of-Fame Placards [Transitions], SE p. 43 • Letter, Intrapersonal Reflection, TR Alt. Assess., p. 2	• Advice for Future Climbers, Oral Report, SE p. 43 • Mini-Lesson: Oral Report, ATE p. 34 • Debate, TR Alt. Assess., p. 2	• Everest Statistics, Video Game Design, SE p. 43 • Activity Log, Scale Drawing, Triptych, TR Alt. Assess., p. 2	• Selection Test, TR Formal Assessment, pp. 4–6; Assess. Res. Software • Description Rubric [for Mini-Lesson], TR Alt. Assess., p. 100 • TR Alt. Assess., p. 2	• "The Final Assault," "The Dream Comes True," LL Audiocassettes • Looking at Lit., Ch. 1 • WS Writing Lab CD-ROM, Description Tutorial; Wr. at Work Videodisc, Ch. 1
• Headlines, Warning Label, Proposal, SE p. 59 • Mini-Lesson: Yearbook Prediction [Transitions to Show Cause and Effect], SE p. 59 • Nonverbal Communication, Fateful Essay, Three Sensible Wishes, TR Alt. Assess., p. 3	• Television Interview, Dramatic Monologue, SE p. 59 • Mini-Lesson: Being Tactful; Television Interview, ATE pp. 50, 54 • Wish Charade, TR Alt. Assess., p. 3	• A Monkey's Paw Poll, Poster Showing Fortuna, SE p. 59 • Dramatic Enactment, Missing Poster, TR Alt. Assess., p. 3	• Selection Test, TR Formal Assessment, pp. 7–9; Assess. Res. Software • Cause-and-Effect Rubric [for Mini-Lesson], TR Alt. Assess., p. 105 • TR Alt. Assess., p. 3	• "The Monkey's Paw," "The Bridegroom," LL Audiocassettes • WS Writing Lab CD-ROM, Narration Tutorial
• Packing List, Letter of Introduction, Description, SE p. 70 • Mini-Lesson: How-to Manual [Clear Explanation of Procedures], SE p. 70 • Letter, Intrapersonal Reflection, TR Alt. Assess., p. 4	• Telephone Interview, Persuasive Speech, SE p. 70 • Mini-Lesson: Conducting an Interview, ATE p. 67 • Reality Check, TR Alt. Assess., p. 4	• The Statistics of a Decision, Map of Annie's Walk, SE p. 70 • Capital Tour, Climate Comparison, Farewell Snapshot, TR Alt. Assess., p. 4	• Selection Test, TR Formal Assessment, pp. 10–12; Assess. Res. Software • How-To Process Explanation Rubric [for Mini-Lesson], TR Alt. Assess., p. 103 • TR Alt. Assess., p. 4	• from A Walk to the Jetty, LL Audiocassettes • WS Writing Lab CD-ROM, Exposition Tutorial; Wr. at Work Videodisc, Ch. 3
• Invitation, Description, Report, SE p. 85 • Mini-Lesson: Proposal [Demonstrate the Benefits of an Idea], SE p. 85 • Story Summary, Personality Portrait, Pro-Con Argument, TR Alt. Assess., p. 5	• Press Conference, Radio Script, SE p. 85 • Mini-Lesson: Radio Script, ATE p. 80	• Costume Design, Multimedia Presentation, SE p. 85 • Musical Score, Set Design, TR Alt. Assessment, p. 5	• Selection Test, TR Formal Assessment, pp. 13–15; Assess. Res. Software • Persuasion Rubric [for Mini-Lesson], TR Alt. Assess., p. 105 • TR Alt. Assess., p. 5	• "The Masque of the Red Death," LL Audiocassettes • WS Writing Lab CD-ROM, Persuasion Tutorial; Wr. at Work Videodisc, Ch. 4
• Letter to a Poet, Poem, Short Story, SE p. 93 • Mini-Lesson: Anecdote [Cause-and-Effect], SE p. 93 • Dream Description, Journal Entry, Differing Perspectives, TR Alt. Assess., p. 6	• Oral Interpretation, Speech, SE p. 93 • Mini-Lesson: Speech, ATE p. 90 • Color Report, Monologue, Letting Go, TR Alt. Assess., p. 6	• Scientific Diagram, Dance, SE p. 93 • Science Report: Quarantine, TR Alt. Assess., p. 6	• Selection Test, TR Formal Assessment, pp. 16–18; Assess. Res. Software • Narrative Based on Personal Experience Rubric [for Mini-Lesson], TR Alt. Assess., p. 96 • TR Alt. Assess., p. 6	• "Fear," "The street," Spring and All," LL Audiocassettes • WS Writing Lab CD-ROM, Narration
• Epitaph, Yearbook Profiles, Officer's Report, SE p. 107 • Mini-Lesson: Extended Definition [Examples], SE p. 107 • Images of Friendship, Comparing and Contrasting Characters, Reflection, Letter to the Editor, TR Alt. Assess., p. 7	• Role Play, Humorous Monologue, SE p. 107 • Mini-Lesson: Role Play, ATE p. 100 • Myth, TR Alt. Assess., p. 7	• Friendship Collage, Brochure for a Friendship Film Festival, SE p. 107 • Report on Prussia, Song Lyrics, TR Alt. Assess., p. 7	• Selection Test, TR Formal Assessment, pp. 19–21; Assess. Res. Software • Definition/Classification Rubric [for Mini-Lesson], TR Alt. Assess., p. 99 • TR Alt. Assess., p. 7	• "Two Friends," "Damon and Pythias" LL Audiocassettes • WS Writing Lab CD-ROM, Exposition

Program Planner   Unit 2 Striving for Success

Selection	Reading	Literary Elements/Forms	Vocabulary	Grammar
from *In Commemoration: One Million Volumes*, Rudolfo A. Anaya, SE p. 116 Reading Level: Average	• Reading for Success: Interactive Reading Strategies, SE pp. 118, 125; TR Selection Support, pp. 32–33 • Model, SE pp. 119–124 • Summarize, TR Str. for Diverse St. Needs, p. 8	• Author's Purpose, SE pp. 117, 125; TR Selection Support, p. 34	• Prefixes: *in-*, SE pp. 116, 125; TR Selection Support, p. 30 Word Bank: induced, p. 119; inherent, litany, dilapidated, satiated, p. 121; enthralls, labyrinth, p. 123; poignant, termination, p. 124	• Action Verbs and Linking Verbs, SE pp. 116, 125; TR Selection Support, p. 31 • WS Language Lab CD-ROM, Eight Parts of Speech • WS Gram. Pr. Book, p. 11
"How Much Land Does a Man Need?," Leo Tolstoy, SE p. 128 Reading Level: Average	• Predict Based on Character Traits, SE pp. 129, 144; TR Selection Support, p. 37 • Identify Character Traits, TR Str. for Diverse St. Needs, p. 9	• Parable, SE pp. 129, 144; TR Selection Support, p. 38	• Related Words, SE pp. 128, 144; TR Select. Support, p. 35 Word Bank: piqued, disparaged, p. 131; forbore, aggrieved, p. 133; sheaf, arable, fallow, p. 135	• Possessive Nouns, SE pp. 128, 144; TR Selection Support, p. 36 • WS Gram. Pr. Book, p. 110
"Success . . ." and **"I dwell . . . ,"** Emily Dickinson; **"Uncoiling,"** Pat Mora; **"Columbus,"** Vassar Miller, SE p. 146 Reading Levels: Average, Challenging, Challenging, Average	• Make Inferences, SE pp. 147, 152; TR Selection Support, p. 41 • Explain Poetic Phrases, TR Str. for Diverse St. Needs, p. 10	• Stated and Implied Themes in Poetry, SE pp. 147, 152; TR Selection Support, p. 42	• Prefixes: *-im*, SE pp. 146, 152; TR Selection Support, p. 39 Word Bank: impregnable, p. 149; thrall, vertigo, p. 151	• Subject and Verb Agreement, SE pp. 146, 152; TR Selection Support, p. 40 • WS Language Lab CD-ROM, Subject/Verb Agreement • WS Gram. Pr. Book, pp. 80–86
from *My Left Foot*, Christy Brown, SE p. 154 Reading Level: Average	• Identify Author's Purpose, SE pp. 155, 162; TR Selection Support, p. 45 • Identify Main Idea and Supporting Details, TR Str. for Diverse St. Needs, p. 11	• Significant Moment, SE pp. 155, 162; TR Selection Support, p. 46	• Word Roots: *-vol-*, SE pp. 154, 162; TR Selection Support, p. 43 Word Bank: impertinence, conviction, p. 157; inert, contention, p. 158; volition, taut, p. 160	• Active and Passive Voice, SE pp. 154, 162; TR Selection Support, p. 44 • WS Language Lab CD-ROM, Active and Passive Voice • WS Gram. Pr. Book, pp. 74–75
"A Visit to Grandmother," William Melvin Kelley, SE p. 164 Reading Level: Easy	• Clarify, SE pp. 165, 175; TR Selection Support, p. 49 • Respond to Characters' Actions, TR Str. for Diverse St. Needs, p. 12	• Characterization, SE pp. 165, 175; TR Selection Support, p. 50	• Word Origins: *ventured*, SE pp. 164, 175; TR Selection Support, p. 47 Word Bank: ventured, p. 167; indulgence, grimacing, p. 168; lacquered, p. 174	• Pronoun Case, SE pp. 164, 175; TR Selection Support, p. 48 • WS Language Lab CD-ROM, Pronoun Case • WS Gram. Pr. Book, pp. 76–79
"Mowing" and **"After Apple-Picking,"** Robert Frost; **"Style"** and **"At Harvesttime,"** Maya Angelou, SE p. 182 Reading Levels: Average, Average, Easy, Easy	• Interpret, SE pp. 183, 190; TR Selection Support, p. 53 • Compare and Contrast Images, TR Str. for Diverse St. Needs, p. 13	• Tone, SE pp. 183, 190; TR Selection Support, p. 54	• Spelling: *-ough*, SE pp. 182, 190; TR Selection Support, p. 51 Word Bank: bough, trough, p. 187; manifestation, disparaging, judicious, gibe, admonition, immutable, potency, p. 188	• Participles as Adjectives, SE pp. 182, 190; TR Selection Support, p. 52 • WS Gram. Pr. Book, p. 41
"The Apple Tree," Katherine Mansfield, SE p. 192 Reading Level: Average	• Question, SE pp. 193, 198; TR Selection Support, p. 57 • Prepare a Readers' Theater, TR Str. for Diverse St. Needs, p. 14	• Allusion, SE pp. 193, 198; TR Selection Support, p. 58	• Word Origins: Words From Myths, SE pp. 192, 198; TR Selection Support, p. 55 Word Bank: paddocks, p. 195; exquisite, bouquet, jovial, p. 196	• Punctuation, SE pp. 192, 198; TR Select. Support, p. 56 • WS Language Lab CD-ROM, Semicolons, Colons, and Quotation Marks • WS Gram. Pr. Book, pp. 104–106
"Africa," David Diop; **"Old Song;"** *The Analects*, Confucius; **"All,"** Bei Dao; **"Also All,"** Shu Ting, SE p. 200 Reading Levels: Challenging, Average, Average, Challenging, Challenging	• Relate to What You Know, SE pp. 201, 208; TR Selection Support, p. 61 • Explain Comparisons TR Str. for Diverse St. Needs, p. 15	• Aphorisms, SE pp. 201, 208; TR Selection Support, p. 62	• Suffixes: *-ment*, SE pp. 200, 208; TR Selection Support, p. 59 Word Bank: impetuous, p. 202; chastisements, p. 204; lamentation, p. 206	• Infinitives and Infinitive Phrases, SE pp. 200, 208; TR Selection Support, p. 60 • WS Gram. Pr. Book, p. 46

KEY: SE: Student Edition;   ATE: Annotated Teacher's Edition;   TR: Teaching Resources;   LL: Listening to Literature;   WS: Writer's Solution

Writing	Speaking and Listening	Projects	Assessment	Technology
• Library Dedication, Article, Directions, SE p. 126 • Mini-Lesson: Reading Journal [Level of Formality], SE p. 126 • Article, Prediction, Travel Guide, TR Alt. Assess., p. 8	• Storytelling Performance, Panel Discussion, SE p. 126 • Mini-Lesson: Storytelling Performance, ATE p. 122 • Cultural Report, Technical Report, Panel Discussion, TR Alt. Assess., p. 8	• Library Poster, Library Survey, SE p. 126 • Display, TR Alt. Assess., p. 8	• Selection Test, TR Formal Assessment, pp. 26–28; Assess. Res. Software • Response to Literature Rubric [for Mini-Lesson], TR Alt. Assess., p. 110 • TR Alt. Assess., p. 8	• from *In Commemoration: One Million Volumes*, LL Audiocassettes • Looking at Lit., Ch. 2 • WS Writing Lab CD-ROM Response to Literature
• Newspaper Article, Land Advertisement, Parable, SE p. 145 • Mini-Lesson: Video Script [Clear Explanation], SE p. 145 • Personal Obstacle, Essay, TR Alt. Assess., p. 9	• Update the Story, Eulogy, SE p. 145 • Mini-Lesson: Eulogy, ATE p. 142 • Conversation With the Devil, TR Alt. Assess., p. 9	• Map of Russia, Scale Diagram of Pahom's Field, SE p. 145 • Land-Cost Graph, Contemporary Tales of Greed, TR Alt. Assess., p. 9	• Selection Test, TR Formal Assessment, pp. 29–31; Assess. Res. Software • Drama Rubric [for Mini-Lesson], TR Alt. Assess., p. 109 • TR Alt. Assess., p. 9	• "How Much Land Does a Man Need?," LL Audiocassettes • WS Writing Lab CD-ROM, Creative Writing Tutorial; Wr. at Work Videodisc, Ch. 8
• Letter, Advertisement, Parody of a Poem, SE p. 153 • Mini-Lesson: Submission Letter [Elaboration], SE p. 153 • Achievement Log, Personification, Thesis, Comparison, Elegy, TR Alt. Assess., p. 10	• Informal Debate, Panel Discussion, SE p. 153 • Mini-Lesson: Informal Debate, ATE p. 149	• Round Earth Demonstration, Oral Report, SE p. 153 • Wind Dance, Architectural Sketches, TR Alt. Assess., p. 10	• Selection Test, TR Formal Assessment, pp. 32–34; Assess. Res. Software • Business Letter Rubric [for Mini-Lesson], TR Alt. Assess., p. 113 • TR Alt. Assess., p. 10	• "Success. . .," "I dwell in . . .," "Uncoiling," "Columbus . . .," LL Audiocassettes • WS Writing Lab CD-ROM, Practical and Technical Writing Tutorial; Wr. at Work Videodisc, Ch. 8
• Mother's Day Card, Movie Review, Story, SE p. 163 • Mini-Lesson: Narrative [Causes and Effects], SE p. 163 • Task Breakdown, Article, Book Jacket, TR Alt. Assess., p. 11	• Role Play, Speech, SE p. 163 • Mini-Lesson: Speech, ATE p. 157 • Persuasive Speech, TR Alt. Assess., p. 11	• Chart on Cerebral Palsy, Christy Brown Timeline, SE p. 163 • Graphic Organizer, Bill of Rights, Artistic Interpretation, TR Alt. Assess., p. 11	• Selection Test, TR Formal Assessment, pp. 35–37; Assess. Res. Software • Personal Narrative Rubric [for Mini-Lesson], TR Alt. Assess., p. 96 • TR Alt. Assess., p. 11	• from *My Left Foot*, LL Audiocassettes • WS Writing Lab CD-ROM, Narration Tutorial
• Letter, News Report, Alternative Ending, SE p. 176 • Mini-Lesson: Firsthand Biography [Examples], SE p. 176 • Expressions, Conflict Journal, Prediction, First Chapter, TR Alt. Assess., p. 12	• Casting Discussion, Oral Anecdote, SE p. 176 • Mini-Lesson: Casting Discussion, ATE p. 173 • Dinner Conversation, Debate, TR Alt. Assess., p. 12	• Conflict-Resolution Workshop, Cultural Comparisons Chart, SE p. 176 • Family Tree Presentation, TR Alt. Assess., p. 12	• Selection Test, TR Formal Assessment, pp. 38-40; Assess. Res. Software • Personal Narrative Rubric [for Mini-Lesson], TR Alt. Assess., p. 96 • TR Alt. Assess., p. 12	• "A Visit to Grandmother," LL Audiocassettes • WS Writing Lab CD-ROM, Narration Tutorial
• Description, Essay, Advice Column, SE p. 191 • Mini-Lesson: Application Letter [Support], SE p. 191 • Intrapersonal Reflection, Letter of Advice, Poem, Essay, TR Alt. Assess., p. 13	• Speech, Role Play, SE p. 191 • Mini-Lesson: Role Play, ATE p. 186 • Skits, TR Alt. Assess., p. 13	• Farming Update, Food Source, SE p. 191 • Career Perspectives, Poetry Collection, TR Alt. Assess., p. 13	• Selection Test, TR Formal Assessment, pp. 41–43; Assess. Res. Software • Résumé/Cover Letter Rubric [for Mini-Lesson], TR Alt. Assess., p. 114 • TR Alt. Assess., p. 13	• "Mowing," "After Apple-Picking," "Style, "At Harvest-time," LL Audiocassettes • WS Writing Lab CD-ROM, Practical Writing Tutorial
• Summary, Narrative, Alternative Ending, SE p. 199 • Mini-Lesson: Retell a Story [Show, Don't Tell], SE p. 199 • Analysis, Poem, Essay, TR Alt. Assess., p. 14	• Dramatic Reading, Monologue, SE p. 199 • Mini-Lesson: Monologue, ATE p. 196 • Oral Report, TR Alt. Assess., p. 14	• Travel Brochure, Map, SE p. 199 • Scientific Illustration, Timeline, Cookbook, TR Alt. Assess., p. 14	• Selection Test, TR Formal Assessment, pp. 44-46; Assess. Res. Software • Fictional Narrative Rubric [for Mini-Lesson], TR Alt. Assess, p. 95 • TR Alt. Assess., p. 14	• "The Apple Tree," LL Audiocassettes • WS Writing Lab CD-ROM, Narration Tutorial; Wr. at Work Videodisc, Ch. 2
• Letter, Poem, SE p. 209 • Mini-Lesson: Calendar [Brevity and Clarity], SE p. 209 • Credo, Rebuttal, Journal, TR Alt. Assess., p. 15	• Oral Interpretation, Interview, SE p. 209 • Mini-Lesson: Oral Interpretation, ATE p. 205 • Non-Western Music Report, Aphorism Play List, TR Alt. Assess., p. 15	• Tiananmen Square Presentation, Collage, SE p. 209 • History Table, Relativity Map, TR Alt. Assess., p. 15	• Selection Test, TR Formal Assessment, pp. 47–49; Assess. Res. Software • Expression Rubric [for Mini-Lesson], TR Alt. Assess., p. 94 • TR Alt. Assess., p. 15	• "Africa," "Old Song," from *The Analects*, "All," "Also All," LL Audiocassettes • WS Writing Lab CD-ROM, Creative Writing Tutorial; Wr. at Work Videodisc, Ch. 6

Program Planner   Unit 3 Clashing Forces

Selection	Reading	Literary Elements/Forms	Vocabulary	Grammar
"Through the Tunnel," Doris Lessing, SE p. 218 Reading Level: Average	• Reading for Success: Interactive Reading Strategies, SE pp. 220, 229; TR Selection Support, pp. 65–66 • Model, SE pp. 221–228 • Form a Mental Image, TR Str. for Diverse St. Needs, p. 16	• Internal Conflict, SE pp. 219, 229; TR Selection Support, p. 67	• Word Roots: -lum-, SE pp. 218, 229; TR Selection Support, p. 63 Word Bank: contrition, p. 221; promontories, luminous, supplication, p. 223; frond, p. 225; convulsive, p. 227; gout, p. 228	• Participial Phrases, SE pp. 218, 229; TR Selection Support, p. 64 • WS Gram. Pr. Book, p. 41
"The Dog That Bit People," James Thurber, SE p. 232 Reading Level: Average	• Form Mental Images, SE pp. 233, 240; TR Selection Support, p. 70 • Break Down Sentences, TR Str. for Diverse St. Needs, p. 17	• Humorous Essay, SE pp. 233, 240; TR Selection Support, p. 71	• Prefixes: epi-, SE pp. 232, 240; TR Selection Support, p. 68 Word Bank: incredulity, choleric, p. 235; irascible, jangle, p. 236; indignant, epitaph, p. 239	• Correct use of like and as if, SE pp. 232, 240; TR Selection Support, p. 69
"Conscientious Objector," Edna St. Vincent Millay; **"A Man,"** Nina Cassian; **"The Weary Blues,"** Langston Hughes; **"Jazz Fantasia,"** Carl Sandburg, SE p. 242 Reading Levels: Challenging, Easy, Challenging, Challenging	• Respond to Images and Ideas, SE pp. 243, 248; TR Selection Support, p. 74 • Translate Music Terms, TR Str. for Diverse St. Needs, p. 18	• Tone, SE pp. 243, 248; TR Selection Support, p. 75	• Word Roots: -chol-, SE pp. 242, 248; TR Selection Support, p. 72 Word Bank: reap, p. 245; pallor, melancholy, p. 246	• Use of shall and will, SE pp. 242, 248; TR Selection Support, p. 73
"Like the Sun," R.K. Narayan; **"Tell all the Truth but tell it slant—,"** Emily Dickinson, SE p. 250 Reading Levels: Average, Average	• Identify Consequences of Actions, SE pp. 251, 255; TR Selection Support, p. 78 • Identify Chain of Events, TR Str. for Diverse St. Needs, p. 19	• Irony, SE pp. 251, 255; TR Selection Support, p. 79	• Word Roots: -gratis-, SE pp. 250, 255; TR Selection Support, p. 76 Word Bank: essence, tempering, shirked, incessantly, ingratiating, stupefied, p. 253; scrutinized, p. 254	• Comparative and Superlative Forms, SE pp. 250, 255; TR Selection Support, p. 77 • WS Language Lab CD-ROM, Forms of Comparison • WS Gram. Pr. Book, pp. 86–88
"Hearts and Hands, " O. Henry; **"The Fish,"** Elizabeth Bishop, SE p. 262 Reading Levels: Easy, Easy	• Predict Story Events, SE pp. 263, 268; TR Selection Support, p. 82 • Explain Comparisons, TR Str. for Diverse St. Needs, p. 20	• Surprise Ending, SE pp. 263, 268; TR Selection Support, p. 83	• Prefixes: counter-, SE pp. 262, 268; TR Selection Support, p. 80 Word Bank: influx, forestalled, counterfeiting, sidled, p. 264; venerable, infested, sullen, p. 266	• Coordinate Adjectives, SE pp. 262, 268; TR Selection Support, p. 81
from **Desert Exile,** Yoshiko Uchida; **"Remarks Upon Signing a Proclamation . . .,"** SE p. 270 Reading Levels: Average, Average	• Prior Knowledge, SE pp. 271, 280; TR Selection Support, p. 86 • Analyze Author's Purpose, TR Str. for Diverse St. Needs, p. 21	• Writer's Purpose, SE pp. 271, 280; TR Selection Support, p. 87	• Word Roots: -curs-, SE pp. 270, 280; TR Selection Support, p. 84 Word Bank: cursory, euphemism, p. 272; adept, destitute, unwieldy, communal, p. 275; conspicuous, p. 277; assuage, p. 278	• Adjective Clauses, SE pp. 270, 280; TR Selection Support, p. 85 • WS Gram. Pr. Book, p. 51
"The Cabuliwallah," Rabindranath Tagore, SE p. 282 Reading Level: Average	• Engage Your Senses, SE pp. 283, 292; TR Selection Support, p. 90 • Identify Characters, TR Str. for Diverse St. Needs, p. 22	• Relationships Between Characters, SE pp. 283, 292; TR Selection Support, p. 91	• Word Roots: -jud-, SE pp. 282, 292; TR Selection Support, p. 88 Word Bank: precarious, impending, judicious, euphemism, imploring, p. 287; fettered, sordid, pervaded, p. 288	• Pronoun and Antecedent Agreement, SE pp. 282, 292; TR Selection Support, p. 89 • WS Language Lab CD-ROM, Pronouns and Antecedents • WS Gram. Pr. Book, p. 83

KEY: SE: Student Edition;   ATE: Annotated Teacher's Edition;   TR: Teaching Resources;   LL: Listening to Literature;   WS: Writer's Solution

Writing	Speaking and Listening	Projects	Assessment	Technology
• Water Safety Rules, Letter, Observation, SE p. 230 • Mini-Lesson: Travel Brochure [Persuasive Tone], SE p. 230 • Intrapersonal Reflection, Character Analysis, TR Alt. Assess., p. 16	• Account of an Outdoor Adventure, Dialogue, SE p. 230 • Mini-Lesson: Account of an Outdoor Adventure, ATE p. 224	• Collage, Movie Score, SE p. 230 • Pro-Con Chart, Model, Suspense Diagram, How-to Pamphlet, Body Inventory, TR Alt. Assess., p. 16	• Selection Test, TR Formal Assessment, pp. 54-56; Assess. Res. Software • Description Rubric [for Mini-Lesson], TR Alt. Assess., p. 97 • TR Alt. Assess., p. 16	• "Through the Tunnel," LL Audiocassettes • WS Writing Lab CD-ROM, Description Tutorial; Wr. at Work Videodisc, Ch. 1
• Description, News Story, Persuasive Letter, SE p. 241 • Mini-Lesson: Animal Anecdote [Vivid Verbs], SE p. 241 • Description, Police Report, Character Sketch, Intrapersonal Reflection, List, Limerick, Comparison, TR Alt. Assess., p. 17	• Pet Talk, Pantomime, SE p. 241 • Mini-Lesson: Pet Talk, ATE p. 236	• Wanted Poster, Breed Chart, SE p. 241	• Selection Test, TR Formal Assessment, pp. 57–59; Assess. Res. Software • Fictional Narrative Rubric [for Mini-Lesson], TR Alt. Assess., p. 95 • TR Alt. Assess., p. 17	• "The Dog That Bit People," LL Audiocassettes • WS Writing Lab CD-ROM, Narration Tutorial; Wr. at Work Videodisc, Ch. 2
• Newspaper Headlines, Interview, Song Lyrics, SE p. 249 • Mini-Lesson: Press Release [Appropriate Language], SE p. 249 • Jazz Report, C.O. Report, Death Report, TR Alt. Assess., p. 18	• Music Panel, Dramatic Reading, SE p. 249 • Mini-Lesson: Dramatic Reading, ATE p. 245 • Population Analysis, Presentation, TR Alt. Assess., p. 18	• Graphic Design, Music Timeline, SE p. 249 • Essay, Drawing/Painting, TR Alt. Assess., p. 18	• Selection Test, TR Formal Assessment, pp. 60–62; Assess. Res. Software • Persuasion Rubric [for Mini-Lesson], TR Alt. Assess., p. 105 • TR Alt. Assess., p. 18	• "Conscientious Objector," "A Man," "The Weary Blues," "Jazz Fantasia," LL Audiocassettes • WS Writing Lab CD-ROM, Persuasion Tutorial; Wr. at Work Videodisc, Ch. 4 • Lit. CD-ROMs, Reading Poetry
• Advice Column, Guidelines, Fairy Tale, SE p. 256 • Mini-Lesson: Review of a Song [Supporting Details], SE p. 256 • Reflection, Comparison, Essay, Day of Truth, TR Alt. Assess., p. 19	• Oral Argument, Debate, SE p. 256 • Children's Lesson, TR Alt. Assess., p. 19	• Indian Folk Songs, Map, SE p. 256 • Fictional Town, Truth Study, TR Alt. Assess., p. 19	• Selection Test, TR Formal Assessment, pp. 63–65; Assess. Res. Software • Evaluation/Review Rubric [for Mini-Lesson], TR Alt. Assess., p. 104 • TR Alt. Assess., p. 19	• "Like the Sun," "Tell all the Truth but tell it slant—," LL Audiocassettes • Looking at Lit., Ch. 3 • WS Writing Lab CD-ROM, Response to Literature Tutorial
• Monologue, Opening Scene, Speech, SE p. 269 • Wr. Mini-Lesson: Letter to the Editor [Elaboration], SE p. 269 • Remote Remembrances, Poem, Continuation, TR Alt. Assess., p. 20	• Casting Discussion, Sound Effects Tape, SE p. 269 • Drama, Oral Report, TR Alt. Assess., p. 20	• Money Chart, Opening Credits, SE p. 269 • Anatomical Drawing, Historical Investigation, TR Alt. Assess., p. 20	• Selection Test, TR Formal Assess., pp. 66–68; Assess. Res. Software • Persuasion Rubric [for Mini-Lesson], TR Alt. Assess., p. 105 • TR Alt. Assess., p. 20	• "Hearts and Hands," "The Fish," LL Audiocassettes • WS Writing Lab CD-ROM, Persuasion Tutorial • Lit. CD-ROMs, How to Read and Understand Poetry
• Letter to a Friend, Monologue, Dear Editor, SE p. 281 • Mini-Lesson: WRA Camp Report [Accuracy], SE p. 281 • Rules of Conduct, Speech Writing, Nonfiction Organization, TR Alt. Assess., p. 21	• Lawyer's Argument, Oral Interpretation, SE p. 281 • Mini-Lesson: Lawyer's Argument, ATE p. 275 • Debate, TR Alt. Assess., p. 21	Interview, Meet the Press, SE p. 281 • Stamp design, Public Recognition, Photo Montage, TR Alt. Assess., p. 21	• Selection Test, TR Formal Assessment, pp. 69–71; Assess. Res. Software • Research Report Rubric [for Mini-Lesson], TR Alt. Assess. p. 106 • TR Alt. Assess., p. 21	• from _Desert Exile_, "Remarks Upon Signing a Proclamation . . .," LL Audiocassettes • WS Writing Lab CD-ROM, Research Tutorial; Wr. at Work Videodisc, Ch. 5
• Description, Character's Journal Entry, Letter to the Embassy, SE p. 293 • Mini-Lesson: Firsthand Biography [Logical Organization], SE p. 293 • Diary Entry, Letter From Prison, TR Alt. Assess., p. 22	• Courtroom Speech, Oral Interpretation, SE p. 293 • Mini-Lesson: Courtroom Speech, ATE p. 289 • Oral Presentation, Wedding Music, TR Alt. Assess., p. 22	• Timeline, Sketch, SE p. 293 • Sensory Detail Web, Comparison-Contrast Chart, Mixed-Media Portrait, TR Alt. Assess., p. 96	• Selection Test, TR Formal Assessment, pp. 72–74; Assess. Res. Software • Narrative Based on Personal Experience Rubric [for Mini-Lesson], TR Alt. Assess., p. 96 • TR Alt. Assess., p. 22	• "The Cabuliwallah," LL Audiocassettes • Looking at Lit., Ch. 3 • WS Writing Lab CD-ROM, Narration Tutorial

Program Planner   Unit 4 Turning Points

Selection	Reading	Literary Elements/Forms	Vocabulary	Grammar
from **Speak, Memory,** **Vladimir Nabokov,** SE p. 302 Reading Level: Average	• Reading for Success: Strategies for Reading Critically, SE pp. 304, 309; TR Selection Support, pp. 94–95 • Model, SE pp. 305–308 • Simplifying Word Order, TR Str. for Diverse St. Needs, p. 23	• Personal Narrative, SE pp. 303, 309; TR Selection Support, p. 96	• Prefixes: pro-, SE pp. 302, 309; TR Selection Support, p. 92 Word Bank: procession, p. 305; proficiency, laborious, portentously, limpid, p. 306	• Dashes, SE pp. 302, 309; TR Selection Support, p. 93 • WS Gram. Pr. Book, p. 107
"With All Flags Flying," **Anne Tyler,** SE p. 312 Reading Level: Easy	• Judge a Character's Decision, SE pp. 313, 322; TR Selection Support, p. 99 • Classify Descriptive Details, TR Str. for Diverse St. Needs, p. 24	• Characters as Symbols, SE pp. 313, 322; TR Selection Support, p. 100	• Prefixes: mono-, SE pp. 312, 322; TR Selection Support, p. 97 Word Bank: appurtenances, conspicuous, p. 316; doddering, monosyllabic, p. 319	• Past Participial Phrases, SE pp. 312, 322; TR Selection Support, p. 98 • WS Gram. Pr. Book, p. 41
"The Bridge," Leopold Staff; **"The Old Stoic," Emily** **Brontë; "I Am Not One of** **Those Who Left the Land,"** **Anna Akhmatova; "Speech** **During the Invasion of** **Constantinople," Empress** **Theodora,** SE p. 324 Reading Levels: Average, Challenging, Challenging, Average	• Author's Perspective, SE pp. 325, 331; TR Selection Support, p. 103 • Interpret Poetic Images, TR Str. for Diverse St. Needs, p. 25	• Dramatic Situation, SE pp. 325, 331; TR Selection Support, p. 104	• Word Roots: -dom-, SE pp. 324, 331; TR Selection Support, p. 101 Word Bank: implore, p. 327; timorous, indomitable, p. 329	• Negatives and Double Negatives, SE pp. 324, 331; TR Selection Support, p. 102 • WS Gram. Pr. Book, p. 90
"The Good Deed," Pearl S. **Buck,** SE p. 338 Reading Level: Average	• Make Inferences About Character, SE pp. 339, 354; TR Selection Support, p. 107 • Respond to Characters' Actions, TR Str. for Diverse St. Needs, p. 26	• Static and Dynamic Characters, SE pp. 339, 354; TR Selection Support, p. 108	• Word Roots: -pel-, SE pp. 338, 354; TR Selection Support, p. 105 Word Bank: contemplatively, p. 341; revere, compelled, p. 342; abashed, p. 344; repressed, indignantly, p. 346; assailed, p. 348; expedition, conferred, p. 350	• Adverb Clauses, SE pp. 338, 354; TR Selection Support, p. 106 • WS Language Lab CD-ROM, Problems with Modifiers and Varying Sentence Structure • WS Gram. Pr. Book, p. 52
"Thoughts of Hanoi," **Nguyen Thi Vinh; "Pride,"** **Dahlia Ravikovitch; "Auto** **Wreck," Karl Shapiro;** **"Before the Law," Franz** **Kafka,** SE p. 362 Reading Levels: Challenging, Easy, Average, Challenging	• Evaluate a Writer's Message, SE pp. 363, 370; TR Selection Support, p. 111 • Identify Key Ideas, TR Str. for Diverse St. Needs, p. 27	• Theme, SE pp. 363, 370; TR Selection Support, p. 112	• Word Roots: -sat-, SE pp. 362, 370; TR Selection Support, p. 109 Word Bank: deranged, convalescents, banal, expedient, p. 367; importunity, contemplation, insatiable, p. 369	• Present Participial Phrases, SE pp. 362, 370; TR Selection Support, p. 110 • WS Language Lab CD-ROM, Misplaced Modifiers • WS Gram. Pr. Book, pp. 41–43

Writing	Speaking and Listening	Projects	Assessment	Technology
• On-line Message, Children's Story, The Author's World, SE p. 310 • Mini-Lesson: Memory of a Milestone [Sensory Details], SE p. 310 • Letter, Personal Narrative, TR Alt. Assess., p. 23	• Memory Exchange, Oral Presentation, SE p. 310 • Mini-Lesson: Oral Presentation, ATE p. 307 • Oral Reading, TR Alt. Assess., p. 23	• Multimedia Presentation, Illustration, SE p. 310 • Book Cover, Book List, Reading Statistics, Landscape at Dusk, TR Alt. Assess., p. 23	• Selection Test, TR Formal Assessment, pp. 79-81; Assess. Res. Software • Narrative Based on Personal Experience Rubric [for Mini-Lesson], TR Alt. Assess., p. 96 • TR Alt. Assess., p. 23	• from Speak, Memory, LL Audiocassettes • WS Writing Lab CD-ROM, Narration Tutorial; Wr. at Work Videodisc, Ch. 2
• Essay on Growing Old, Letter From Mr. Carpenter, Alternative Ending, SE p. 323 • Mini-Lesson: Dialogue With an Older Person [Appropriate Language for Purpose], SE p. 323 • Scrapbook, Old Age Plan, Business Memo, TR Alt. Assess., p. 24	• Soundtrack, Debate, SE p. 323 • Mini-Lesson: Debate, ATE p. 317 • Dialogue, One-Act Play, TR Alt. Assess., p. 24	• Volunteer at a Nursing Home, Service for the Elderly, SE p. 323 • Population Projection, Advertisement, TR Alt. Assess., p. 24	• Selection Test, TR Formal Assessment, pp. 82–84; Assess. Res. Software • Drama Rubric [for Mini-Lesson], TR Alt. Assess., p. 109 • TR Alt. Assess., p. 24	• "With All Flags Flying," LL Audiocassettes • WS Writing Lab CD-ROM, Creative Writing Tutorial; Wr. at Work Videodisc, Ch. 6
• Summaries, News Commentary, Compare-and-Contrast Essay, SE p. 332 • Mini-Lesson: Poem About a Turning Point [Figurative Language], SE p. 332 • Letter to Emily, Report on Russia, Journal Entry, TR Alt. Assess., p. 25	• Speech, Role Play, SE p. 332 • Mini-Lesson: Speech, ATE p. 328 • Top Five List, Presentation—A Nation Surrounded, TR Alt. Assess., p. 25	• Timeline, Collage, SE p. 332 • Travel Brochure—Ancient Rome, Drama—The Empress Rises, TR Alt. Assess., p. 25	• Selection Test, TR Formal Assessment, pp. 85–87; Assess. Res. Software • Poetry Rubric [for Mini-Lesson], TR Alt. Assess., p. 108 • TR Alt. Assess., p. 25	• "The Bridge," "The Old Stoic," "I Am Not One of Those Who Left the Land," "Speech During the Invasion of Constantinople," LL Audiocassettes • WS Writing Lab CD-ROM, Creative Writing Tutorial; Wr. at Work Videodisc, Ch. 6
• Letters, Story Segment, Newsletter, SE p. 355 • Mini-Lesson: Award Speech on a Character [Create a Main Impression], SE p. 355 • Good Deeds, Reflections on Home, Sequel, Personal Essay, TR Alt. Assess., p. 26	• Unrehearsed Speech, Radio Interview, SE p. 355 • Mini-Lesson: Radio Interview, ATE p. 348 • Dramatic Monologue, TR Alt. Assess., p. 26	• Multimedia Presentation, Timeline, SE p. 355 • Presentation, Day of Good Deeds, TR Alt. Assess., p. 26	• Selection Test, TR Formal Assessment, pp. 88–90; Assess. Res. Software • Classification Rubric [for Mini-Lesson], TR Alt. Assess., p. 99 • TR Alt. Assess., p. 26	• "The Good Deed," LL Audiocassettes • WS Writing Lab CD-ROM, Exposition Tutorial; Wr. at Work Videodisc, Ch. 3
• Interview, Visitor's Guide, Allegory, SE p. 371 • Mini-Lesson: Letter to the Editor [Elaboration to Make Writing Personal], SE p. 371 • Thoughts on Friendship, Compare and Contrast, Alternative Theme, TR Alt. Assess., p. 27	• Telephone Conversation, Improvisational Skit, SE p. 371 • Mini-Lesson: Telephone Conversation, ATE p. 366 • Interpretive Reading, TR Alt. Assess., p. 27	• Two Maps, Auto Safety Presentation, SE p. 371 • Choreography, Artistic Representation, "First on the Scene" Pamphlet, TR Alt. Assess., p. 27	• Selection Test, TR Formal Assess., pp. 91–93; Assess. Res. Software • Persuasion Rubric [for Mini-Lesson], TR Alt. Assess., p. 105 • TR Alt. Assess., p. 27	• "Thoughts of Hanoi," "Pride," "Auto Wreck," "Before the Law," LL Audiocassettes • Looking at Lit., Ch. 4 • WS Writing Lab CD-ROM, Persuasion

Program Planner   Unit 5 Expanding Horizons

Selection	Reading	Literary Elements/Forms	Vocabulary	Grammar
"The Widow and the Parrot," Virginia Woolf, SE p. 380 Reading Level: Easy	• Reading for Success: Strategies for Reading Fiction, SE pp. 382, 391; TR Selection Support, pp. 115–116 • Model, SE pp. 383–390 • Identify Predictions, TR Str. for Diverse St. Needs, p. 28	• Motivation, SE pp. 381, 391; TR Selection Support, p. 117	• Related Words: Forms of *sagacity*, SE pp. 380, 391; TR Selection Support, p. 113 Word Bank: ford, dilapidated, p. 385; sovereigns, sagacity, p. 389	• Correct Use of Adjectives and Adverbs, SE pp. 380, 391; TR Selection Support, p. 114 • WS Language Lab CD-ROM, Eight Parts of Speech • WS Gram. Pr. Book, p. 19
"Civil Peace," Chinua **Achebe,** SE p. 394 Reading Level: Challenging	• Prior Knowledge, SE pp. 395, 402; TR Selection Support, p. 120 • Understand Dialect, TR Str. for Diverse St. Needs, p. 29	• Key Statement, SE pp. 395, 402; TR Selection Support, p. 121	• Related Words: Forms of *Disreputable*, SE pp. 394, 402; TR Selection Support, p. 118 Word Bank: inestimable, disreputable, amenable, p. 396; edifice, destitute, p. 398; imperious, p. 399; commiserate, p. 400	• Past and Past Perfect Tenses, SE pp. 394, 402; TR Selection Support, p. 119 • WS Language Lab CD-ROM, Verb Tense • WS Gram. Pr. Book, pp. 67–71
"The Bean Eaters," Gwendolyn Brooks; **"How to React to Familiar Faces,"** Umberto Eco, SE p. 404 Reading Levels: Easy, Easy	• Respond to Connotations, SE pp. 405, 410; TR Selection Support, p. 124 • Compare and Contrast Images, TR Str. for Diverse St. Needs, p. 30	• Tone, SE pp. 405, 410; TR Selection Support, p. 125	• Word Roots: -ami-, SE pp. 404, 410; TR Selection Support, p. 122 Word Bank: expound, syndrome, amiably, protagonist, p. 409	• Pronoun Agreement With an Indefinite Antecedent, SE pp. 404, 410; TR Selection Support, p. 123 • WS Language Lab CD-ROM, Pronouns and Antecedents • WS Gram. Pr. Book, p. 83
"A Picture From the Past: Emily Dickinson," Reynolds **Price; "What Makes a Degas a Degas?"** Richard **Mühlberger,** SE p. 412 Reading Levels: Average, Average	• Relate Text and Pictures, SE pp. 413, 419; TR Selection Support, p. 128 • Question Author's Purpose, TR Str. for Diverse St. Needs, p. 31	• Analytical Essay, SE pp. 413, 419; TR Selection Support, p. 129	• Word Roots: -cent-, SE pp. 412, 419; TR Selection Support, p. 126 Word Bank: titanic, centenarian, austere, p. 415; lacquered, p. 417	• Compound Sentences, SE pp. 412, 419; TR Selection Support, p. 127 • WS Language Lab CD-ROM, Varying Sentence Structure • WS Gram. Pr. Book, pp. 120–121
"The Orphan Boy and the Elk Dog," Blackfeet myth, SE p. 426 Reading Level: Average	• Identify With a Character, SE pp. 427, 436; TR Selection Support, p. 132 • Prepare a Reader's Theater, TR Str. for Diverse St. Needs, p. 32	• Myth, SE pp. 427, 436; TR Selection Support, p. 133	• Word Groups: Homographs, SE pp. 426, 436; TR Selection Support, p. 130 Word Bank: refuse, p. 429; surpassed, p. 431; emanating, relish, p. 432; stifle, p. 434	• Commonly Confused Words: *accept* and *except*, SE pp. 426, 436; TR Selection Support, p. 131
"The Street of the Cañon," Josephina Niggli, SE p. 438 Reading Level: Easy	• Predict, SE pp. 439, 446; TR Selection Support, p. 136 • Use a Chain of Events Organizer, TR Str. for Diverse St. Needs, p. 33	• Point of View, SE pp. 439, 446; TR Selection Support, p. 137	• Suffixes: -ly, SE pp. 438, 446; TR Selection Support, p. 134 Word Bank: officious, mottled, p. 441; nonchalantly, audaciously, imperiously, plausibility, p. 443	• Commas in a Series, SE pp. 438, 446; TR Selection Support, p. 135 • WS Language Lab CD-ROM, Commas • WS Gram. Pr. Book, pp. 99–101
"A Storm in the Mountains," Alexander Solzhenitsyn; **"In the Orchard,"** Henrik Ibsen; **"A Tree Telling of Orpheus,"** Denise Levertov, SE p. 448 Reading Levels: Average, Average, Challenging	• Engage the Senses, SE pp. 449, 458; TR Selection Support, p. 140 • Form a Mental Image, TR Str. for Diverse St. Needs, p. 34	• Speaker, SE pp. 449, 458; TR Selection Support, p. 141	• Borrowed Words: Latin Terms, SE pp. 448, 458; TR Selection Support, p. 138 Word Bank: terra firma, p. 450; sultry, p. 451; asunder, p. 456	• Correct use of *like* and *as*, SE pp. 448, 458; TR Selection Support, p. 139

Writing	Speaking and Listening	Projects	Assessment	Technology
• Character Sketch, Review, Health Report, SE p. 392 • Mini-Lesson: Will [Logical Organization], SE p. 392 • Report, Point-of-View Study, Essay, Proposal, TR Alt. Assess., p. 28	• Debate, Dialogue Between Person and Pet, SE p. 392 • Mini-Lessons: Debate, ATE p. 385, Dialogue Between Person and Pet, ATE p. 389 • Role Play, TR Alt. Assess., p. 28	• Conversion Chart, Area Map, SE p. 392 • Plot Diagram, Animal Behavior Chart, TR Alt. Assess., p. 28	• Selection Test, TR Formal Assessment, pp. 98–100; Assess. Res. Software • Classification Rubric [for Mini-Lesson], TR Alt. Assess., p. 99 • TR Alt. Assess., p. 28	• "The Widow and the Parrot," LL Audiocassettes • Looking at Lit., Ch. 5 • WS Writing Lab CD-ROM, Exposition Tutorial; Wr. at Work Videodisc, Ch. 3
• Interview, Article, Poem, SE p. 403 • Mini-Lesson: Annotated Map [Brevity and Clarity], SE p. 403 • Pamphlet, Letter, Documentary, Cultural Sketch, Observation, TR Alt. Assess., p. 29	• Reworking a Dialogue Proverbs Presentation, SE p. 403 • Mini-Lesson: Reworking a Dialogue, ATE p. 398	• Collage, Scenic Sketches, SE p. 403 • Comparison-Contrast Chart, Timeline, TR Alt. Assess., p. 29	• Selection Test, TR Formal Assessment, pp. 101–103; Assess. Res. Software • Definition/Classification Rubric [for Mini-Lesson], TR Alt. Assess., p. 99 • TR Alt. Assess., p. 29	• "Civil Peace," LL Audiocassettes • WS Writing Lab CD-ROM, Exposition Tutorial
• Interview, Dialogue, Techno-Reaction, SE p. 411 • Mini-Lesson: Introduction of Talk-Show Guest [Audience Knowledge], SE p. 411 • Eulogy, Narrative, Letter, Contract, TR Alt. Assess., p. 30	• Comic Scene, Debate, SE p. 411 • Mini-Lesson: Debate, ATE p. 408 • Monologue, Interview and Article, TR Alt. Assess., p. 30	• Drawing, Celebrity Home Page, SE p. 411	• Selection Test, TR Formal Assessment, pp. 104–106; Assess. Res. Software • Description Rubric [for Mini-Lesson], TR Alt. Assess., p. 97 • TR Alt. Assess., p. 30	• "The Bean Eaters," "How to React to Familiar Faces," LL Audiocassettes • WS Writing Lab CD-ROM, Description Tutorial; Wr. at Work Videodisc, Ch. 1
• Exhibit Promotion, Photo Essay, Art Analysis, SE p. 420 • Mini-Lesson: Museum Placard [Anticipation of Questions], SE p. 420 • Poem, Journal Entry, Portrait Narration, Tour Guide, TR Alt. Assess., p. 31	• Poetry Reading, Art Narration, SE p. 420 • Mini-Lesson: Art Narration, ATE p. 417	• Painting and Poetry Exhibit, Art Exchange, SE p. 420 • Daguerrotype History, Painting, Analysis, TR Alt. Assess., p. 31	• Selection Test, TR Formal Assessment, pp. 107–109; Assess. Res. Software • Classification Rubric [for Mini-Lesson], TR Alt. Assess., p. 99 • TR Alt. Assess., p. 31	• "A Picture From the Past: Emily Dickinson," "What Makes a Degas a Degas?" LL Audiocassettes • WS Writing Lab CD-ROM, Exposition Tutorial; Wr. at Work Videodisc, Ch. 3
• Speech, Dialogue, Description of a Mystery Animal, SE p. 437 • Mini-Lesson: Retelling of a Myth [Clear Beginning, Middle, and End], SE p. 437 • Journal, Reflection, Myth, Story, TR Alt. Assess., p. 32	• Debate, Retell a Myth, SE p. 437 • Mini-Lesson: Debate, ATE p. 434 • Animals and People, TR Alt. Assess., p. 32	• Animal Population Graph, Storyboard Mural, SE p. 437 • Mythical Board Game, Map, TR Alt. Assess., p. 32	• Selection Test, TR Formal Assessment, pp. 110–112; Assess. Res. Software • Fictional Narrative Rubric [for Mini-Lesson], TR Alt. Assess., p. 95 • TR Alt. Assess., p. 32	• "The Orphan Boy and the Elk Dog," LL Audiocassettes • WS Writing Lab CD-ROM, Narration Tutorial; Wr. at Work Videodisc, Ch. 2
• Postcard, Legend, Compare and Contrast, SE p. 447 • Mini-Lesson: Song [Connotation], SE p. 447 • Suspense, Celebration Scene, Alternate Ending, Essay, TR Alt. Assess., p. 33	• Dialogue, Debate, SE p. 447 • Mini-Lesson: Dialogue, ATE p. 444 • Interview, TR Alt. Assess., p. 33	• Sketch, Photo Essay, SE p. 447 • Social Dance, Conflict Reso-lution, TR Alt. Assess., p. 33	• Selection Test, TR Formal Assessment, pp. 113–115 Assess. Res. Software • Poetry Rubric [for Mini-Lesson], TR Alt. Assess., p. 108 • TR Alt. Assess., p. 33	• "The Street of the Cañon," LL Audiocassettes • WS Writing Lab CD-ROM, Creative Writing Tutorial; Wr. at Work Videodisc, Ch. 6
• Description, Film Treatment, Biographical Sketch, SE p. 459 • Mini-Lesson: Monologue [Grab Readers' Attention], SE p. 459 • Journal, Rebuttal, TR Alt. Assess., p. 34	• Speech, Interview, SE p. 459 • Mini-Lesson: Interview, ATE p. 451 • Instrumentation Report, TR Alt. Assess., p. 34	• Presentation of Ancient Instrument, Multimedia Project, SE p. 459 • Cycle Poster, Drawing, Accompaniment, Interpretive Dance, TR Alt. Assess., p. 34	• Selection Test, TR Formal Assessment, pp. 116–118; Assess. Res. Software • Fictional Narrative Rubric [for Mini-Lesson], TR Alt. Assess., p. 95 • TR Alt. Assess., p. 34	• "A Storm in the Mountains," "In the Orchard," "A Tree Telling of Orpheus," LL Audiocassettes • WS Writing Lab CD-ROM, Narration Tutorial

Program Planner Unit 6 Short Stories

Selection	Reading	Literary Elements/Forms	Vocabulary	Grammar
"The Open Window," Saki, SE p. 468 Reading Level: Average	• Reading for Success: Strategies for Constructing Meaning, SE pp. 470, 475; TR Selection Support, pp. 144–145 • Model, SE pp. 471–474 • Identifying Story Elements, TR Str. for Diverse St. Needs, p. 35	• Plot Structure, SE pp. 469, 475; TR Selection Support, p. 146	• Word Origins: Words From Names, SE pp. 468, 475; TR Selection Support, p. 142 Word Bank: delusion, p. 472; imminent, mackintosh, pariah, p. 474	• Placement of *only* and *just*, SE pp. 468, 475; TR Selection Support, p. 143 • WS Language Lab CD-ROM, Misplaced Modifiers Lesson • WS Gram. Pr. Book, pp. 61–63
"Leiningen Versus the Ants," **Carl Stephenson,** SE p. 478 Reading Level: Average	• Predict Based on Plot Details, SE pp. 479, 496; TR Selection Support, p. 149 • Identifying Chain of Events, TR Str. for Diverse St. Needs, p. 36	• Conflict, SE pp. 479, 496; TR Selection Support, p. 150	• Borrowed Words: Latin Plural Forms, SE pp. 478, 496; TR Selection Support, p. 147 Word Bank: peons, p. 483; flout, weir, p. 485; provender, p. 487; alluvium, fomentations, p. 495	• Correct Use of Apostrophes, SE pp. 478, 496; TR Selection Support, p. 148 • WS Gram. Pr. Book, pp. 110–111
"By the Waters of Babylon," **Stephen Vincent Benét,** SE p. 498 Reading Level: Challenging	• Draw Conclusions, SE pp. 499, 510; TR Selection Support, p. 153 • Sequence Events, TR Str. for Diverse St. Needs, p. 37	• First-Person Point of View, SE pp. 499, 510; TR Selection Support, p. 154	• Word Groups: Conjunctive Adverbs, SE pp. 498, 510; TR Selection Support, p. 151 Word Bank: purified, p. 500; bowels, p. 503; moreover, nevertheless, p. 506	• Subordination, SE pp. 498, 510; TR Selection Support, p. 152 • WS Gram. Pr. Book, pp. 51–52
"A Problem," Anton **Chekhov; "Luck,"** Mark **Twain,** SE p. 512 Reading Levels: Average, Average	• Make Inferences About Character, SE pp. 513, 525; TR Selection Support, p. 157 • Analyze Character's Behavior, TR Str. for Diverse St. Needs, p. 38	• Static and Dynamic Characters, SE pp. 513, 525; TR Selection Support, p. 158	• Word Roots: -ver-, SE pp. 512, 525; TR Selection Support, p. 155 Word Bank: taciturn, rheumatic, p. 515; vestibule, p. 519; zenith, countenance, veracity, p. 520; guileless, prodigious, sublimity, p. 522	• Restrictive and Nonrestrictive Adjective Clauses, SE pp. 512, 525; TR Selection Support, p. 156
"There Will Come Soft Rains," Ray Bradbury; **"The Garden of Stubborn Cats,"** Italo Calvino, SE p. 532 Reading Levels: Average, Average	• Clarify, SE pp. 533, 548; TR Selection Support, p. 161 • Form a Mental Image, TR Str. for Diverse St. Needs, p. 39	• Setting, SE pp. 533, 548; TR Selection Support, p. 162	• Word Origins: Words From Myths, SE pp. 532, 548; TR Selection Support, p. 159 Word Bank: warrens, p. 535; titanic, paranoia, tremulous, p. 536; psychopathic, p. 539; supernal, itinerary, p. 541; transoms, rank, p. 543; scrimmage, p. 545; indigence, p. 546	• Commonly Confused Words: *lie* and *lay*, SE pp. 532, 548; TR Selection Support, p. 160 • WS Gram. Pr. Book, p. 91
"The Princess and All the Kingdom," Pär Lagerkvist; **"The Censors,"** Luisa **Valenzuela,** SE p. 550 Reading Levels: Easy, Average	• Challenge the Writer's Message, SE pp. 551, 558; TR Selection Support, p. 165 • Identify Key Ideas, TR Str. for Diverse St. Needs, p. 40	• Universal Themes, SE pp. 551, 558; TR Selection Support, p. 166	• Word Roots: -ultra-, SE pp. 550, 558; TR Selection Support, p. 163 Word Bank: ardent, venerable, sordid, p. 553; ulterior, staidness, p. 556	• *Who* and *Whom* in Adjective Clauses, SE pp. 550, 558; TR Selection Support, p. 164 • WS Language Lab CD-ROM, Pronoun Case • WS Gram. Pr. Book, p. 79

Writing	Speaking and Listening	Projects	Assessment	Technology
• Letter, Diary, Story, SE p. 476 • Mini-Lesson: Study Notes: Summary [Transitions That Show Time], SE p. 476 • "Nice Division" Lists, Description of Social Customs, Tall Tale, Personal Essay, TR Alt. Assess., p. 35	• Tape Recording, Storytelling, SE p. 476 • Mini-Lesson: Storytelling, ATE p. 472 • Role Play, Poem of Introduction, TR Alt. Assess., p. 35	• Music, Comic Strip, SE p. 476 • Vacation Plan, TR Alt. Assess., p. 35	• Selection Test, TR Formal Assessment, pp. 123–125; Assess. Res. Software • Summary Rubric [for Mini-Lesson], TR Alt. Assess., p. 98 • TR Alt. Assess., p. 35	• "The Open Widow," LL Audiocassettes • WS Writing Lab CD-ROM, Exposition Tutorial
• Letter to the Editor, Change the Disaster, News Report, SE p. 497 • Mini-Lesson: Movie Scene [Climax and Resolution], SE p. 497 • Natural Medicine, Point of View, Bias Analysis, Special Effects, Action Plan, TR Alt. Assess., p. 36	• Motivational Speech, The Author's Motive, SE p. 497 • Mini-Lesson: Motivational Speech, ATE p. 482 • Tall Tale, TR Alt. Assess., p. 36	• Map of the Plantation, Disaster Relief, SE p. 497 • Character Wheel, TR Alt. Assess., p. 36	• Selection Test, TR Formal Assessment, pp. 126–128; Assess. Res. Software • Drama Rubric [for Mini-Lesson], TR Alt. Assess., p. 109 • TR Alt. Assess., p. 36	• "Leiningen Versus the Ants," LL Audiocassettes • WS Writing Lab CD-ROM, Creative Writing Tutorial
• Postcard, Publicity Release, Poem, SE p. 511 • Mini-Lesson: Description From Another Vantage Point [Consistent Point of View], SE p. 511 • Wilderness Survival Kit, Intrapersonal Reflection, Hypotheses, TR Alt. Assess., p. 37	• Radio Interview, Oral Presentation, SE p. 511 • Mini-Lessons: Radio Interview, ATE p. 502, Oral Presentation, ATE p. 506 • Storytelling, TR Alt. Assess., p. 37	• Tourism Poster, Storyboard, SE p. 511 • Travel Plan, Chart, Story Graph, TR Alt. Assess., p. 37	• Selection Test, TR Formal Assessment, pp. 129–131; Assess. Res. Software • Description Rubric [for Wr. Mini-Lesson], TR Alt. Assess., p. 97 • TR Alt. Assess., p. 37	• "By the Waters of Babylon," LL Audiocassettes • WS Writing Lab CD-ROM, Description Tutorial; Wr. at Work Videodisc, Ch. 1
• Invitation, Journal Entry, Story Ending, SE p. 526 • Mini-Lesson: Telephone Conversation [Realistic Dialogue], SE p. 526 • Reflection, Definition, Comparison-Contrast, Biography, TR Alt. Assess., p. 38	• Monologue, Roundtable Discussion, SE p. 526 • Mini-Lesson: Roundtable Discussion, ATE p. 518 • Judgment, TR Alt. Assess., p. 38	• Period Presentation, Multimedia Biography, SE p. 526 • Portrait, Song for Sasha, TR Alt. Assess., p. 38	• Selection Test, TR Formal Assessment, pp. 132–134; Assess. Res. Software • Drama Rubric [for Mini-Lesson], TR Alt. Assess., p. 109 • TR Alt. Assess., p. 38	• "A Problem," "Luck," LL Audiocassettes • WS Writing Lab CD-ROM, Creative Writing Tutorial; Wr. at Work Videodisc, Ch. 2
• Schedule, Speculation, Science Fiction Story, SE p. 549 • Mini-Lesson: Advertisement for a New Technology [Consider the Knowledge Level of Your Audience], SE p. 549 • Cat Journal, TR Alt. Assess., p. 39	• Inanimate Dialogue, Persuasive Argument, SE p. 549 • Mini-Lessons: Inanimate Dialogue, ATE p. 538, Persuasive Argument, ATE p. 544 • Debate, Technology Report, TR Alt. Assess., p. 39	• Painting Presentation, Floor Plan, SE p. 549 • City Plan, Time Capsule, Sounds of a Day, Population Graph, TR Alt. Assess., p. 39	• Selection Test, TR Formal Assessment, pp. 135–137; Assess. Res. Software • Persuasion Rubric [for Mini-Lesson], TR Alt. Assess., p. 105 • TR Alt. Assess., p. 39	• "There Will Come Soft Rains," "The Garden of Stubborn Cats," LL Audiocassettes • Looking at Lit., Ch. 6 • WS Writing Lab CD-ROM, Persuasion Tutorial; Wr. at Work Videodisc, Ch. 4
• Letter to Juan, The Censor, Princess With a Point of View, SE p. 559 • Mini-Lesson: Letter to an Elected Official [Correct Format], SE p. 559 • Sequel, Building Design, Front-Page Story, TR Alt. Assess., p. 40	• Debate, Improvised Speech, SE p. 559 • Mini-Lesson: Improvised Speech, ATE p. 553 • Monologue, TR Alt. Assess., p. 40	• Music Collection, Internet Research, SE p. 559 • Flow Chart, Informational Poster, Children's Fairy Tale, TR Alt. Assess., p. 40	• Selection Test, TR Formal Assessment, pp. 138–140; Assess. Res. Software • Persuasion Rubric [for Mini-Lesson], TR Alt. Assess., p. 105 • TR Alt. Assess., p. 40	• "The Princess and All the Kingdom," "The Censors," LL Audiocassettes • WS Writing Lab CD-ROM, Persuasion Tutorial; Wr. at Work Videodisc, Ch. 4

Program Planner   Unit 7 Nonfiction

Selection	Reading	Literary Elements/Forms	Vocabulary	Grammar
"The Marginal World," **Rachel Carson,** SE p. 568 Reading Level: Average	• Reading for Success: Strategies for Reading Nonfiction, SE pp. 570, 577; TR Selection Support, pp. 169–170 • Model, SE pp. 571–576 • Identify Main Idea and Supporting Details, TR Str. for Diverse St. Needs, p. 41	• Expository Essay, SE pp. 569, 577; TR Selection Support, p. 171	• Suffixes: -able, SE pp. 568, 577; TR Selection Support, p. 167 Word Bank: mutable, p. 571; ephemeral, p. 572; primeval, essence, marginal, p. 575; subjectively, manifestations, cosmic, p. 576	• Linking Verbs and Subject Complements, SE pp. 568, 577; TR Selection Support, p. 168 • WS Language Lab CD-ROM, Eight Parts of Speech • WS Gram. Pr. Book, p. 33
from ***The Way to Rainy Mountain,*** **N. Scott Momaday;** "The One Great **Heart," Alexander Solzhenitsyn;** "Keep Memory **Alive," Elie Wiesel,** SE p. 580 Reading Levels: Average, Challenging, Challenging	• Analyze the Author's Purpose, SE pp. 581, 592; TR Selection Support, p. 174 • Summarize Main Idea, TR Str. for Diverse St. Needs, p. 42	• Reflective and Persuasive Essays, SE pp. 581, 592; TR Selection Support, p. 175	• Related Words: Forms of *Reciprocity,* SE pp. 580, 592; TR Selection Support, p. 171 Word Bank: engender, tenuous, p. 585; reciprocity, p. 587; assimilate, inexorably, oratory, p. 588; transcends, p. 591	• Capitalization of Proper Nouns and Adjectives, SE pp. 580, 592; TR Selection Support, p. 172 • WS Language Lab CD-ROM, Problems with Capitalization • WS Gram. Pr. Book, pp. 93–94
"A Child's Christmas in Wales," Dylan Thomas; "Marian Anderson: Famous **Concert Singer," Langston Hughes,** SE p. 594 Reading Levels: Average, Average	• Recognize the Author's Attitude, SE pp. 595, 606; TR Selection Support, p. 178 • Question Author's Purpose, TR Str. for Diverse St. Needs, p. 43	• Biography and Autobiography, SE pp. 595, 606; TR Selection Support, p. 179	• Word Groups: Musical Words, SE pp. 594, 606; TR Selection Support, p. 176 Word Bank: sidle, prey, wallowed, p. 597; crocheted, p. 598; brittle, trod, forlorn, p. 601; arias, staunch, p. 603; repertoire, p. 605	• Restrictive and Nonrestrictive Appositives, SE pp. 594, 606; TR Selection Support, p. 177 • WS Language Lab CD-ROM, Commas • WS Gram. Pr. Book, p. 40
"Flood," Annie Dillard, SE p. 608 Reading Level: Average	• Recognize Facts and Impressions, SE pp. 609, 617; TR Selection Support, p. 182 • Classify Descriptive Details, TR Str. for Diverse St. Needs, p. 44	• Descriptive Essay, SE pp. 609, 617; TR Selection Support, p. 183	• Prefixes: mal-, SE pp. 608, 617; TR Selection Support, p. 180 Word Bank: obliterates, opacity, usurped, p. 612; mauled, malevolent, repressed, p. 614	• Subject and Verb Agreement, SE pp. 608, 617; TR Selection Support, p. 181 • WS Language Lab CD-ROM, Subject/Verb Agreement • WS Gram. Pr. Book, pp. 80–82
"Star Wars: A Trip to a Far Galaxy That's Fun and Funny . . . ," Vincent Canby; "Star Wars: Breakthrough **Film Still Has the Force," Roger Ebert,** SE p. 624 Reading Levels: Average, Easy	• Identify Evidence, SE pp. 625, 634; TR Selection Support, p. 186 • Recognizing Allusions, TR Str. for Diverse St. Needs, p. 45	• Critical Review, SE pp. 625, 634; TR Selection Support, p. 187	• Connotations, SE pp. 624, 634; TR Selection Support, p. 184 Word Bank: apotheosis, eclectic, facetiousness, adroit, p. 627; piously, condescension, p. 628; watershed, synthesis, p. 629; fastidious, p. 631; effete, laconic, p. 633	• Parenthetical Interrupters, SE pp. 624, 634; TR Selection Support, p. 185 • WS Language Lab CD-ROM, Commas • WS Gram. Pr. Book, pp. 99–101
"Mothers and Daughters," Tillie Olsen and Estelle Jussim, SE p. 636 Reading Level: Average	• Reading Strategy: Interpret Pictures, SE pp. 637, 644; TR Selection Support, p. 190 • Summarize Observations, TR Str. for Diverse St. Needs, p. 46	• Visual Essay, SE pp. 637, 644; TR Selection Support, p. 191	• Related Words: Words Describing Color, SE pp. 636, 644; TR Selection Support, p. 188 Word Bank: hue, sullenness, rapture, p. 639; fervor, p. 640; implicit, p. 642	• Semicolons in a Series, SE pp. 636, 644; TR Selection Support, p. 189 • WS Language Lab CD-ROM, Semicolons, Colons, and Quotation Marks • WS Gram. Pr. Book, pp. 102–103
"Imitating Nature's Mineral Artistry," Paul O'Neil; "Work **That Counts," Ernesto Ruelas Inzunza,** SE p. 646 Reading Levels: Challenging, Easy	• Relate Diagrams to Text, SE pp. 647, 654; TR Selection Support, p. 194 • Translate Technical Terms, TR Str. for Diverse St. Needs, p. 47	• Technical Article, SE pp. 647, 654; TR Selection Support, p. 195	• Prefixes: syn-, SE pp. 646, 654; TR Select. Support, p. 192 Word Bank: synthetic, constituents, synthesized, metamorphosis, p. 649; divulge, saturated, fortuitous, vigilance, p. 650; myriad, topography, p. 652	• Varied Sentence Beginnings: Adverb Phrases, SE pp. 646, 654; TR Selection Support, p. 193 • WS Language Lab CD-ROM, Varying Sentence Structure • WS Gram. Pr. Book, pp. 121–123

KEY: SE: Student Edition;   ATE: Annotated Teacher's Edition;   TR: Teaching Resources;   LL: Listening to Literature;   WS: Writer's Solution

Writing	Speaking and Listening	Projects	Assessment	Technology
• Letter, Nature Report, Essay, SE p. 578 • Mini-Lesson: Proposal for a Documentary [Transitions], SE p. 578 • Bibliography, Cause-and-Effect Essay, Nature Essay, TR Alt. Assess., p. 41	• Poetry Reading, Conservation Speech, SE p. 578 • Mini-Lesson: Poetry Reading, ATE p. 573 • Dialogue, Ocean Music, TR Alt. Assess., p. 41	• Art Exhibit, The Living Sea, SE p. 578 • Audubon Exhibit, Comparison-Contrast Chart, TR Alt. Assess., p. 41	• Selection Test, TR Formal Assessment, pp. 145–147; Assess. Res. Software • Description Rubric [for Mini-Lesson], TR Alt. Assess., p. 97 • TR Alt. Assess., p. 41	• "The Marginal World," LL Audiocassettes • WS Writing Lab CD-ROM, Description Tutorial
• Review Letter, Report, Creation Myth, SE p. 593 • Mini-Lesson: Speech [Emphasis], SE p. 593 • Reflective Essay, Transcript, Letter of Recommendation, Article, TR Alt. Assess., p. 42	• Persuasive Speech, Myth Reading, SE p. 593 • Mini-Lesson: Persuasive Speech, ATE p. 588 • Public Service Announcement, Oral Report, TR Alt. Assess., p. 42	• Native American Dances, Writers-in-Prison, SE p. 593 • American Scenes, TR Alt. Assess., p. 42	• Selection Test, TR Formal Assessment, pp. 148–150; Assess. Res. Software • Persuasion Rubric [for Mini-Lesson], TR Alt. Assess., p. 105 • TR Alt. Assess., p. 42	• from The Way to Rainy Mountain, "The One Great Heart," "Keep Memory Alive," LL Audiocassettes • Looking at Lit., Ch. 7 • WS Writing Lab CD-ROM, Persuasion Tutorial
• Holiday, Memory, Biography, SE p. 607 • Mini-Lesson: Letter to Yourself in Twenty Years [Logical Organization], SE p. 607 • List, Journal, Letter, Review, TR Alt. Assess., p. 43	• Memory Music, Marian Anderson Recording, SE p. 607 • Mini-Lesson: Analyzing a Recording, ATE p. 603 • Dramatic Readings, TR Alt. Assess., p. 43	• Greeting Card, Multimedia Presentation, SE p. 607 • Children's Production, Music Study, TR Alt. Assess., p. 43	• Selection Test, TR Formal Assessment, pp. 151–153; Assess. Res. Software • Fictional Narrative Rubric [for Mini-Lesson], TR Alt. Assess., p. 95 • TR Alt. Assess., p. 43	• "A Child's Christmas in Wales," "Marian Anderson: Famous Concert Singer," LL Audiocassettes • WS Writing Lab CD-ROM, Narration Tutorial; Wr. at Work Videodisc, Ch. 2
• Descriptive Paragraph, Storm Journal, Fable, SE p. 618 • Mini-Lesson: Radio Call-In Transcript [Sensory Language], SE p. 618 • Description, Journal, Essay, Description, TR Alt. Assess., p. 44	• Storm Report, Talk-Show Interview, SE p. 618 • Mini-Lesson: Storm Report, ATE p. 613 • Poem, TR Alt. Assess., p. 44	• Hurricane Chart, Food-Chain Presentation, SE p. 618 • Storm Study, Painting, TR Alt. Assess., p. 44	• Selection Test, TR Formal Assessment, pp. 154–156; Assess. Res. Software • Description Rubric [for Mini-Lesson], TR Alt. Assess., p. 97 • TR Alt. Assess., p. 44	• "Flood," LL Audiocassettes • WS Writing Lab CD-ROM, Description Tutorial
• Press Release, Speech, Interview, SE p. 635 • Mini-Lesson: Movie Review [Examples], SE p. 635 • Reference Search, TR Alt. Assess., p. 45	• Star Wars Recording, Skit, SE p. 635 • Mini-Lesson: Star Wars Recording, ATE p. 627, Skit, ATE p. 630 • Debate, Play List, TR Alt. Assess., p. 45	• Movie Collage, Science-Fiction Exhibit, SE p. 635 • Review Critique, Wanted Poster, Box Office Graph, Scene Re-enactment, TR Alt. Assess., p. 45	• Selection Test, TR Formal Assessment, pp. 157–159; Assess. Res. Software • Evaluation/Review Rubric [for Mini-Lesson], TR Alt. Assess., p. 104 • TR Alt. Assess., p. 45	• "Star Wars: A Trip to a Far Galaxy That's Fun and Funny . . .," "Star Wars: Breakthrough Film Still Has the Force," LL Audiocassettes • WS Writing Lab CD-ROM, Response to Literature Tutorial; Wr. at Work Videodisc, Ch. 7
• Descriptive Paragraph, Interview, Poem, SE p. 645 • Mini-Lesson: Introduction to an Art Exhibit [Elaboration], SE p. 645 • Letter, Advice Column, Metaphor, Intrapersonal Reflection, TR Alt. Assess., p. 46	• Award Panel, Dramatic Reading, SE p. 645 • Mini-Lesson: Award Panel, ATE p. 641	• Parent-and-Child Encyclopedia, Parent-and-Child Video, SE p. 645 • Mood Palette, Soundtrack, Dance, TR Alt. Assess., p. 46	• Selection Test, TR Formal Assessment, pp. 160–162; Assess. Res. Software • Definition/Classification Rubric [for Mini-Lesson], TR Alt. Assessment, p. 99 • TR Alt. Assess., p. 46	• "Mothers & Daughters," LL Audiocassettes • WS Writing Lab CD-ROM, Exposition Tutorial
• Persuasive Letter, Essay, Technical Article, SE p. 655 • Mini-Lesson: Product Description [Precise Details], SE p. 655 • Dream Job, Outline, TR Alt. Assess., p. 47	• Bird-Cast, Oral Demonstration, SE p. 655 • Mini-Lesson: Oral Demonstration, ATE p. 651 • Diagram Analysis, Career Profile, Interview, TR Alt. Assess., p. 47	• Conservation Update, Diamond Weighing, SE p. 655 • Diamond Sources, Heat Pictograph, TR Alt. Assess., p. 47	• Selection Test, TR Formal Assessment, pp. 163–165; Assess. Res. Software • Description Rubric [for Mini-Lesson], TR Alt. Assess., p. 97 • TR Alt. Assess., p. 47	• "Imitating Nature's Mineral Artistry," "Work That Counts," LL Audiocassettes • WS Writing Lab CD-ROM, Description Tutorial; Wr. at Work Videodisc, Ch. 1

Program Planner   Unit 8 Drama

Selection	Reading	Literary Elements/Forms	Vocabulary	Grammar
Antigone, **Prologue Through Scene 2, Sophocles,** SE p. 668 Reading Level: Average	• Question the Characters' Motives, SE pp. 669, 683; TR Selection Support, p. 198 • Write Headlines, TR Str. for Diverse St. Needs, p. 48	• Protagonist and Antagonist, SE pp. 669, 683; TR Selection Support, p. 199	• Prefixes: *trans-,* SE pp. 668, 683; TR Selection Support, p. 196 Word Bank: sated, p. 674; anarchists, sententiously, p. 676; sultry, p. 678; transcends, p. 682	• Coordinating Conjunctions, SE pp. 668, 683; TR Selection Support, p. 197 • WS Language Lab CD-ROM, Eight Parts of Speech • WS Gram. Pr. Book, pp. 22 and 120
Antigone, **Scenes 3 Through 5, Sophocles,** SE p. 684 Reading Level: Average	• Identify With a Character, SE pp. 684, 699; TR Selection Support, p. 202 • Paraphrase Dialogue, TR Str. for Diverse St. Needs, p. 49	• Tragic Character, SE pp. 684, 699; TR Selection Support, p. 203	• Word Roots: *-chor-,* SE pp. 684, 699; TR Selection Support, p. 200 Word Bank: deference, p. 685; vile, p. 686; piety, blasphemy, p. 688; lamentation, p. 690; chorister, p. 694	• Pronoun Case in Incomplete Clauses, SE pp. 684, 699; TR Selection Support, p. 201 • WS Language Lab CD-ROM, Special Problems with Agreement
The Tragedy of Julius Caesar, **Act I, William Shakespeare,** p. 710 Reading Level: Challenging	• Use Text Aids, SE pp. 711, 731; TR Selection Support, p. 206 • Predict Events, TR Str. for Diverse St. Needs, p. 50	• Exposition in Drama, SE pp. 711, 731; TR Selection Support, p. 207	• Related Words: Forms of *Portent,* SE pp. 711, 731; TR Selection Support, p. 204 Word Bank: replication, p. 715; spare, p. 721; infirmity, p. 724; surly, portentous, prodigious, p. 727	• The Subjunctive Mood, SE pp. 711, 731; TR Selection Support, p. 205
The Tragedy of Julius Caesar, **Act II, William Shakespeare,** p. 732 Reading Level:Challenging	• Read Blank Verse, SE pp. 732, 749; TR Selection Support, p. 210 • Analyze Characters, TR Str. for Diverse St. Needs, p. 51	• Blank Verse, SE pp. 732, 749; TR Selection Support, p. 211	• Word Roots: *-spir-,* SE pp. 732, 749; TR Selection Support, p. 208 Word Bank: augmented, entreated, conspiracy, p. 735; resolution, p. 736; exploit, p. 742; imminent, p. 744	• Commonly Confused Words: *affect* and *effect,* SE pp. 732, 749; TR Selection Support, p. 209
The Tragedy of Julius Caesar, **Act III, William Shakespeare,** p. 750 Reading Level: Challenging	• Paraphrase, SE pp. 750, 771; TR Selection Support, p. 214 • Recognize Cause and Effect, TR Str. for Diverse St. Needs, p. 52	• Dramatic Speeches, SE pp. 750, 771; TR Selection Support, p. 215	• Word Roots: *-ora-,* SE pp. 750, 771; TR Selection Support, p. 212 Word Bank: suit, p. 751; spurn, confounded, mutiny, p. 753; malice, p. 756; oration, discourse, p. 758; vile, p. 761	• Parallel Structure, SE pp. 750, 771; TR Selection Support, p. 213 • WS Gram. Pr. Book, p. 64
The Tragedy of Julius Caesar, **Act IV, William Shakespeare,** p. 772 Reading Level: Challenging	• Read Between the Lines, SE pp. 772, 787; TR Selection Support, p. 218 • Prepare a Readers' Theater, TR Str. for Diverse St. Needs, p. 53	• Conflict in Drama, SE pp. 772, 787; TR Selection Support, p. 219	• Word Roots: *-phil-,* SE pp. 772, 787; TR Selection Support, p. 216 Word Bank: legacies, slanderous, p. 773; covert, p. 775; chastisement, p. 777; philosophy, p. 781	• Noun Clauses, SE pp. 772, 787; TR Selection Support, p. 217 • WS Gram. Pr. Book, p. 53
The Tragedy of Julius Caesar, **Act V, William Shakespeare,** p. 788 Reading Level: Challenging	• Identify Cause and Effect, SE pp. 788, 802; TR Selection Support, p. 222 • Use a Story Map Organizer, TR Str. for Diverse St. Needs, p. 54	• Tragedy, SE pp. 788, 802; TR Selection Support, p. 223	• Prefixes: *mis-,* SE pp. 788, 802; TR Selection Support, p. 220 Word Bank: presage, ensign, consorted, demeanor, p. 793; disconsolate, p. 795; misconstrued, p. 796; envy, p. 801	• Words of Direct Address, SE pp. 788, 802; TR Selection Support, p. 221

Writing	Speaking and Listening	Projects	Assessment	Technology
• Newspaper Article, Letter, SE p. 683 • Interpersonal Reflection, Modern Reworking, Gender-Role Analysis, TR Alt. Assess., p. 48	• Readers Theater, SE p. 683 • Mini-Lesson: Readers' Theater, ATE p. 677	• Character Wheels, Playbill, Pro-Con Chart, Song, TR Alt. Assess., p. 48	• Selection Test, TR Formal Assessment, pp. 170–172; Assess. Res. Software • TR Alt. Assess., p. 48	• *Antigone*, Prol.–Sc. 2, LL Audiocassettes • Looking at Lit., Ch. 8 • WS Language Lab CD-ROM, Eight Parts of Speech Tutorial
• Introduction, Final Speech, Editorial, SE p. 700 • Mini-Lesson: Scene of Conflict [Format], SE p. 700 • Diary Entry, Alternative Ending, TR Alt. Assess., p. 49	• Mock Trial, Film Response, SE p. 700 • Mini-Lesson: Mock Trial, ATE p. 691 • Debate, Charades, TR Alt. Assess., p. 49	• Multimedia Presentation, SE p. 700 • Plot Diagram, Sympathy Ratings, Set Design, TR Alt. Assess., p. 49	• Selection Test, TR Formal Assessment, pp. 173–175; Assess. Res. Software • Drama Rubric [for Mini-Lesson], TR Alt. Assess., p. 109 • TR Alt. Assess., p. 49	• *Antigone*, Sc. 3–5, LL Audiocassettes • WS Writing Lab CD-ROM, Creative Writing Tutorial
• Journal Entry, Speech, SE p. 731 • Film Review, Character Sketches, TR Alt. Assess., p. 50	• Enactment, SE p. 731 • Mini-Lesson: Enacting an Improvised Scene, ATE p. 723	• Political Cartoon, Biography, Stage Directions, Tour Brochure, Billboard, TR Alt. Assess., p. 50	• Selection Test, TR Formal Assessment, pp. 176–178; Assess. Res. Software • TR Alt. Assess., p. 50	• *The Tragedy of Julius Caesar*, Act I, LL Audiocassettes • Lit. CD-ROMs, How to Read and Understand Drama
• Editorial, Monologue, SE p. 749 • Correspondence, Journal Entry, Comparison, TR Alt. Assess., p. 51	• Debate, SE p. 749 • Mini-Lesson: Debate, ATE p. 746 • Assassination Report, TR Alt. Assess., p. 51	• Map of Rome, Bill of Rights, Drawing, TR Alt. Assess., p. 51	• Selection Test, TR Formal Assessment, pp. 179–181; Assess. Res. Software • TR Alt. Assess., p. 51	• *The Tragedy of Julius Caesar*, Act II, LL Audiocassettes • Lit. CD-ROMs, How to Read and Understand Drama
• Obituary, Reaction to Speeches, SE p. 771 • Outline, Motivation, Script, TR Alt. Assess., p. 52	• Background Music, SE p. 771 • Mini-Lesson: Background Music, ATE p. 754 • Oration, Public Address, TR Alt. Assess., p. 52	• Magazine Cover, Survey, TR Alt. Assess., p. 52	• Selection Test, TR Formal Assessment, pp. 182–184; Assess. Res. Software • TR Alt. Assess., p. 52	• *The Tragedy of Julius Caesar*, Act III, LL Audiocassettes • Lit. CD-ROMs, The Time, Life, and Works of Shakespeare
• Character Profile, Rewrite a Scene, SE p. 787 • Letter, Journal Entry, Ghost Story, Personal Essay, TR Alt. Assess., p. 53	• Musical Score, SE p. 787 • Mini-Lesson: Musical Score, ATE p. 777 • Scene, TR Alt. Assess., p. 53	• Tragic Hero Poem or Essay, Map, TR Alt. Assess., p. 53	• Selection Test, TR Formal Assessment, pp. 185–187; Assess. Res. Software • TR Alt. Assess., p. 53	• *The Tragedy of Julius Caesar*, Act IV, LL Audiocassettes • Lit. CD-ROMs, The Time, Life, and Works of Shakespeare
• Epitaph, Response, Take a Side, SE p. 803 • Mini-Lesson: Speech [Connotation], SE p. 803 • Character Description, Journal Entry, Speech, Newspaper Article, TR Alt. Assess., p. 54	• Sound Effects, Respond to Shakespearean English, SE p. 803 • Mini-Lessons: Respond to Shakespearean English, ATE p. 794, Sound Effects, ATE p. 797 • Dramatic Monologue, TR Alt. Assess., p. 54	• Model of the Globe, Elizabethan Faire, SE p. 803 • Constitution, Poster, TR Alt. Assess., p. 54	• Selection Test, TR Formal Assessment, pp. 188–190; Assess. Res. Software • Persuasion Rubric [for Mini-Lesson], TR Alt. Assess., p. 105 • TR Alt. Assess., p. 54	• *The Tragedy of Julius Caesar*, Act V, LL Audiocassettes • Lit. CD-ROMs, The Time, Life, and Works of Shakespeare

Program Planner   Unit 9 Poetry

Selection	Reading	Literary Elements/Forms	Vocabulary	Grammar
"The Stolen Child," William Butler Yeats, SE p. 812 Reading Level: Average	• Reading for Success: Strategies for Reading Poetry, SE pp. 814, 819; TR Selection Support, pp. 226–227 • Model, SE pp. 815–816 • Restate Poetry as Prose, TR Str. for Diverse St. Needs, p. 55	• Atmosphere, SE pp. 813, 819; TR Selection Support, p. 228	• Words With Multiple Meanings, SE pp. 812, 819; TR Selection Support, p. 224 Word Bank: herons, glosses, p. 815; slumbering, p. 816	• Inverted Word Order, SE pp. 812, 819; TR Selection Support, p. 225 • WS Language Lab CD-ROM, Special Problems in Agreement • WS Gram. Pr. Book, p. 121
"In Flanders Fields," John McCrae; **"The Kraken,"** Alfred, Lord Tennyson; **"Reapers,"** Jean Toomer; **"Meeting at Night,"** Robert Browning; **"Prayer of First Dancers,"** Navajo, SE p. 822 Reading Levels: Average, Challenging, Average, Challenging, Easy	• Listen, SE pp. 823, 830; TR Selection Support, p. 231 • Identify Key Ideas, TR Str. for Diverse St. Needs, p. 56	• Musical Devices, SE pp. 823, 830; TR Selection Support, p. 232	• Prefixes: mil-, SE pp. 822, 830; TR Selection Support, p. 229 Word Bank: abysmal, millennial, p. 825	• Concrete and Abstract Nouns, SE pp. 822, 830; TR Selection Support, p. 230 • WS Language Lab CD-ROM, Types of Nouns • WS Gram. Pr. Book, pp. 5–6
"The Wind—tapped like a tired Man," Emily Dickinson; **"A Pace Like That,"** Yehuda Amichai; **"Metaphor,"** Eve Merriam; **"Right Hand,"** Philip Fried, SE p. 832 Reading Levels: Average, Challenging, Easy, Average	• Paraphrase, SE pp. 833, 839; TR Selection Support, p. 235 • Recognize Similes, TR Str. for Diverse St. Needs, p. 57	• Figurative Language, SE pp. 833, 839; TR Selection Support, p. 236	• Word Roots: -tac-, SE pp. 832, 839; TR Selection Support, p. 233 Word Bank: countenance, tremulous, flurriedly, p. 834; decipher, p. 835; taciturn, eloquent, guttural, diffused, garrulity, p. 838	• Elliptical Clauses, SE pp. 832, 839; TR Selection Support, p. 234
"La Belle Dame sans Merci," John Keats; **"Danny Deever,"** Rudyard Kipling, SE p. 846 Reading Levels: Average, Average	• Identify the Speaker, SE pp. 847, 852; TR Selection Support, p. 239 • Prepare a Readers' Theater, TR Str. for Diverse St. Needs, p. 58	• Narrative and Dramatic Poetry, SE pp. 847, 852; TR Selection Support, p. 240	• Word Roots: -journ-, SE pp. 846, 852; TR Selection Support, p. 237 Word Bank: sedge, thrall, sojourn, p. 849; whimpers, quickstep, p. 850	• Hyphens, SE pp. 846, 852; TR Selection Support, p. 238 • WS Gram. Pr. Book, p. 109
"The Guitar," Federico García Lorca; **"Making a Fist,"** Naomi Shihab Nye; **"Jade Flower Palace,"** Tu Fu; **"The Moon at the Fortified Pass,"** Li Po; **"What Are Friends For,"** Rosellen Brown; **"Some Like Poetry,"** Wisława Szymborska, SE p. 854 Reading Levels: Average, Easy, Challenging, Challenging, Easy, Average	• Read in Sentences, SE pp. 855, 862; TR Selection Support, p. 243 • Recognize Unusual Comparisons, TR Str. for Diverse St. Needs, p. 59	• Lyric Poetry, SE pp. 855, 862; TR Selection Support, p. 244	• Word Roots: -path-, SE pp. 854, 862; TR Selection Support, p. 241 Word Bank: monotonously, p. 856; pathos, wistful, p. 858	• Adjectival Modifiers, SE pp. 854, 862; TR Selection Support, p. 242 • WS Gram. Pr. Book, p. 51
Sonnet 18, William Shakespeare; **"The Waking,"** Theodore Roethke; Tanka, Ki no Tsurayuki & Priest Jakuren; Haiku, Bashō & Issa, SE p. 864 Reading Levels: Challenging, Easy, Challenging, Challenging, Easy, Average	• Envision the Imagery, SE pp. 865, 870; TR Selection Support, p. 247 • Identify Sensory Words, TR Str. for Diverse St. Needs, p. 60	• Poetic Forms, SE pp. 865, 870; TR Selection Support, p. 248	• Related Words: Forms of *Temperate*, SE pp. 864, 870; TR Selection Support, p. 245 Word Bank: temperate, p. 866	• Noun Clauses, SE pp. 864, 870; TR Selection Support, p. 246 • WS Language Lab CD-ROM, Varying Sentence Structure • WS Gram. Pr. Book, p. 53

Writing	Speaking and Listening	Projects	Assessment	Technology
• Idea Bank: Journal Entry, Editorial, Alternate Chorus, SE p. 820 • Mini-Lesson: Crime Report [Clear, Consistent Purpose], SE p. 820 • Fairy Tale, Rebuttal, TR Alt. Assess., p. 55	• Paired Reading, Folk Music, SE p. 820 • Mini-Lesson: Folk Music, ATE p. 817 • Rebuttal, Folktale, TR Alt. Assess., p. 55	• Irish Writers Timeline, Encyclopedia of Folklore, SE p. 820 • Irish Music, Sketch, Panel Discussion, TR Alt. Assess., p. 55	• Selection Test, TR Formal Assessment, pp. 195–197; Assess. Res. Software • Technical Description/ Explanation Rubric [for Mini-Lesson], TR Alt. Assess., p. 115 • TR Alt. Assess., p. 55	• "The Stolen Child," LL Audiocassettes • Lit. CD-ROMs, How to Read and Understand Poetry; Feature 2 • WS Writing Lab CD-ROM, Practical Writing; Wr. at Work Videodisc, Ch. 8
• Idea Bank: Letter to Editor, City Chant, Musical Devices, SE p. 831 • Mini-Lesson: Proposal for a Poetry Anthology [Specific Examples], SE p. 831 • Journal Entry, Description, Onomatopoeia Poem, "Meeting at Night" Scene, TR Alt. Assess., p. 56	• Medieval Chants, Oral Report, SE p. 831 • Mini-Lesson: Oral Report, ATE p. 826 • "Prayer of First Dancers" Listening to Poems, TR Alt. Assess., p. 56	• Creatures Across Cultures, World War I, SE p. 831 • Myth, TR Alt. Assess., p. 56	• Selection Test, TR Formal Assessment, pp. 198–200; Assess. Res. Software • Description Rubric [for Mini-Lesson], TR Alt. Assess., p. 97 • TR Alt. Assess., p. 56	• "In Flanders Fields," "The Kraken," "Reapers," "Meeting at Night," "Prayer of First Dancers," LL Audiocassettes • Looking at Lit., Ch. 9 • WS Writing Lab CD-ROM, Description Tutorial • Lit. CD-ROMs, How to Read and Understand Poetry; Features 8 and 10
• Idea Bank: Most Admired, Perfect Day Directions, Metaphor Poem, SE p. 840 • Mini-Lesson: Character Creation [Consistent Focus], SE p. 840 • Morning Description, Biographical Poem, Personification Poem, Personal Essay, TR Alt. Assess., p. 57	• Wind Interview, Dialogue, SE p. 840 • Mini-Lesson: Dialogue, ATE p. 837 • Discussion, Presentation, TR Alt. Assess., p. 57	• Visual Biography, Hurricane Statistics, SE p. 840 • Illustration, TR Alt. Assess., p. 57	• Selection Test, TR Formal Assessment, pp. 201–203; Assess. Res. Software • Description Rubric [for Mini-Lesson], TR Alt. Assess., p. 97 • TR Alt. Assess., p. 57	• "The Wind—tapped like a tired Man," "A Pace Like That," "Metaphor," "Right Hand," LL Audiocassettes • WS Writing Lab CD-ROM, Description Tutorial
• Idea Bank: Diary Entry, Letter to the Knight, Mock Narrative, SE p. 853 • Mini-Lesson: News Bulletin Based on Poem [Climax and Resolution], SE p. 853 • Journal Entry, Eulogy, Comparison, TR Alt. Assess., p. 58	• Oral Reading, Story in Music, SE p. 853 • Mini-Lesson: Story in Music, ATE p. 850 • Oral Report, Debate, TR Alt. Assess., p. 58	• Dialect Chart, Art, SE p. 853 • Sound Track, Rank Chart, TR Alt. Assess., p. 58	• Selection Test, TR Formal Assessment, pp. 204–206; Assess. Res. Software • Summary Rubric [for Mini-Lesson], TR Alt. Assess., p. 98 • TR Alt. Assess., p. 58	• "La Belle Dame sans Merci," "Danny Deever," LL Audio-cassettes • WS Writing Lab CD-ROM, Narration Tutorial • Lit. CD-ROMs, How to Read and Understand Poetry; Feature 4
• Idea Bank: Remembrance, Statement Poem, Story, SE p. 863 • Mini-Lesson: Lyric Poem [Setting and Mood], SE p. 863 • Letter, Intrapersonal Response, Hypothesis, TR Alt. Assess., p. 59	• Reading to Music, Newscast, SE p. 863 • Mini-Lesson: Newscast, ATE p. 859	• Painting/Drawing, Profile of a People, SE p. 863 • Cluster Diagram, Advice Booklet, Mood Graph, Interpretive Dance, TR Alt. Assess., p. 59	• Selection Test, TR Formal Assessment, pp. 207–209; Assess. Res. Software • Poetry Rubric [for Mini-Lesson], TR Alt. Assess., p. 108 • TR Alt. Assess., p. 59	• "The Guitar," "Making a Fist," "Jade Flower Palace," "The Moon at the Fortified Pass," "What Are Friends For," "Some Like Poetry," LL Audiocassettes • WS Writing Lab CD-ROM, Creative Writing Tutorial; Wr. at Work Videodisc, Ch. 6
• Idea Bank: Villanelle Opener, Haiku, Essay, SE p. 871 • Mini-Lesson: Consumer Report of Poetic Forms [Grab Readers' Attention], SE p. 871 • Paraphrase, Debate, Translation, TR Alt. Assess., p. 60	• Rhyme Scheme, Poetry Reading, SE p. 871 • Mini-Lesson: Poetry Reading, ATE p. 867 • Clapping, TR Alt. Assess., p. 60	• Oral Report, Japanese Poetry, SE p. 871 • Venn Diagram, Concentration, Snapshots, TR Alt. Assess., p. 60	• Selection Test, TR Formal Assessment, pp. 210–212; Assess. Res. Software • Comparison/Contrast and Technical Description/ Explanation Rubrics [for Mini-Lesson] TR Alt. Assess., pp. 103, 115 • TR Alt. Assess., p. 60	• Sonnet 18, "The Waking," Tanka, Haiku, LL Audio-cassettes • Lit. CD-ROMs, How to Read and Understand Poetry; Feature 10 • WS Writing Lab CD-ROM, Exposition Tutorial

Program Planner Unit 10 Epics and Legends

Selection	Reading	Literary Elements/Forms	Vocabulary	Grammar
from *Don Quixote,* Miguel de Cervantes, SE p. 882 Reading Level: Average	• Compare and Contrast, SE pp. 883, 890; TR Selection Support, p. 251 • Selection, SE pp. 884–889 • Analyze Characters' Behavior, TR Str. for Diverse St. Needs, p. 61	• Parody, SE pp. 883, 890; TR Selection Support, p. 252	• Word Roots: *-son-*, SE pp. 882, 890; TR Selection Support, p. 249 Word Bank: lucidity, adulation, interminable, p. 885; affable, sallying, requisite, sonorous, veracious, vanquish, extolled, p. 886	• Gerunds and Gerund Phrases, SE pp. 882, 890; TR Selection Support, p. 250 • WS Gram. Pr. Book, pp. 44–45
"Morte d'Arthur," Alfred, Lord Tennyson; "Arthur Becomes King of Britain," T. H. White, SE p. 892 Reading Levels: Challenging, Average	• Recognize an Author's Attitude, SE pp. 893, 915; TR Selection Support, p. 255 • Paraphrase Dialogue, TR Str. for Diverse St. Needs, p. 62	• Legend, SE pp. 893, 915; TR Selection Support, p. 256	• Suffixes: *-ous*, SE pp. 892, 915; TR Selection Support, p. 253 Word Bank: lamentation, p. 900; swarthy, p. 902; stickler, p. 904; sumptuous, p. 909; palfrey, p. 911	• Subjunctive Mood, SE pp. 892, 915; TR Selection Support, p. 254
"Rama's Initiation" from the *Ramayana,* R. K. Narayan, SE p. 922 Reading Level: Challenging	• Make Inferences About Culture, SE pp. 923, 930; TR Selection Support, p. 259 • Identify Epic Elements, TR Str. for Diverse St. Needs, p. 63	• The Epic Hero, SE pp. 923, 930; TR Selection Support, p. 260	• Word Roots: *-min-*, SE pp. 922, 930; TR Selection Support, p. 257 Word Bank: austerities, decrepitude, sublime, august, p. 925; secular, obeisance, exuberance, diminutive, p. 927; esoteric, p. 928	• Restrictive and Nonrestrictive Appositives, SE pp. 922, 930; TR Selection Support, p. 258 • WS Language Lab CD-ROM, Commas • WS Gram. Pr. Book, p. 40
from *Sundiata: An Epic of Old Mali,* D. T. Niane, SE p. 932 Reading Level: Average	• Storyteller's Purpose, SE pp. 933, 940; TR Selection Support, p. 263 • Connect with Hero's Conflict, TR Str. for Diverse St. Needs, p. 64	• Epic Conflict, SE pp. 933, 940; TR Selection Support, p. 264	• Word Roots: *-firm-*, SE pp. 932, 940; TR Selection Support, p. 261 Word Bank: fathom, taciturn, malicious, infirmity, innuendo, diabolical, estranged, p. 935; affront, p. 939	• Sentence Variety, SE pp. 932, 940; TR Selection Support, p. 262 • WS Language Lab CD-ROM, Varying Sentence Structure and Varying Sentence Length • WS Gram. Pr. Book, pp. 121–123

KEY: SE: Student Edition;   ATE: Annotated Teacher's Edition;   TR: Teaching Resources;   LL: Listening to Literature;   WS: Writer's Solution

Writing	Speaking and Listening	Projects	Assessment	Technology
• Idea Bank: Definition of a Hero, Don Quixote in America, Create a Scene, SE p. 891 • Mini-Lesson: Sketch of a Comic Hero [Clear and Logical Organization], SE p. 891 • Postcard From Sancho, Continuation, Want Ad for a Squire, TR Alt. Assess., p. 61	• Role Play, Musical, SE p. 891 • Mini-Lesson: Role Play, ATE p. 888 • Technology Report, Committee Meeting, TR Alt. Assess., p. 61	• Cartoon, Visual Essay, SE p. 891 • Media List, Casting Call, TR Alt. Assess., p. 61	• Selection Test, TR Formal Assessment, pp. 217-219; Assess. Res. Software • Description Rubric [for Mini-Lesson], TR Alt. Assess., p. 97 • TR Alt. Assess., p. 61	• from Don Quixote, LL Audiocassettes • WS Writing Lab CD-ROM, Description Tutorial; Wr. at Work Videodisc, Ch. 1
• Idea Bank: List, Epic Essay, Local Legends, SE p. 916 • Mini-Lesson: Letter of Recommendation [Clear and Consistent Purpose], SE p. 916 • Thoughts on Destiny, Book Review, Modern-Day Arthur, TR Alt. Assess., p. 62	• Music, Oral Reading, SE p. 916 • Mini-Lesson: Oral Reading, ATE p. 896 • Social History, Dramatization, TR Alt. Assess., p. 62	• Art, Feudalism Chart, SE p. 916 • Compare and Contrast, Travel Brochure, TR Alt. Assess., p. 62	• Selection Test, TR Formal Assessment, pp. 220–222; Assess. Res. Software • Business Letter/Memo Rubric [for Mini-Lesson], TR Alt. Assess., p. 113 • TR Alt. Assess,, p. 62	• "Morte d'Arthur," "Arthur Becomes King of Britain," LL Audiocassettes • Looking at Lit., Ch. 10 • WS Writing Lab CD-ROM, Practical and Technical Writing Tutorial
• Idea Bank: Letter, Personal Narrative, Opening Argument, SE p. 931 • Mini-Lesson: Script Treatment Proposal [Appropriate Language for Your Purpose], SE p. 931 • Letter, Skills Description, Sequel, Mentor, TR Alt. Assess., p. 63	• Oral Tales, Indian Music, SE p. 931 • Mini-Lesson: Oral Tales, ATE p. 925 • Mantra, Pantomime, TR Alt. Assess., p. 63	• Painting, Dance, SE p. 931 • Comparison-Contrast Chart, TR Alt. Assess., p. 63	• Selection Test, TR Formal Assessment, pp. 223–225; Assess. Res. Software • Description Rubric [for Mini-Lesson], TR Alt. Assess., p. 97 • TR Alt. Assess., p. 63	• "Rama's Initiation" from the Ramayana, LL Audiocassettes • WS Writing Lab CD-ROM, Description Tutorial
• Idea Bank: News Article, Writing in the Heroic Tradition, Critical Evaluation, SE p. 941 • Mini-Lesson: Storytelling Notes [Audience Knowledge], SE p. 941 • Reflection, Legacy List, Short Story, Personal Essay, TR Alt. Assess., p. 64	• Oral Tales, Role Play, SE p. 941 • Mini-Lesson: Oral Tales, ATE p. 938 • Reading of Sundiata, TR Alt. Assess., p. 64	• Documentary, Herb Research, SE p. 941 • Hero Mural, Wildlife Map, TR Alt. Assess., p. 64	• Selection Test, TR Formal Assessment, pp. 226–228; Assess. Res. Software • Fictional Narrative Rubric [for Mini-Lesson], TR Alt. Assess., p. 95 • TR Alt. Assess., p. 64	• from Sundiata: An Epic of Old Mali, LL Audiocassettes • WS Writing Lab CD-ROM, Narration Tutorial; Wr. at Work Videodisc, Ch. 2

Skills Workshops

Unit	Writing Process Workshops	Applying Language Skills	Real-World Reading Skills Workshops	Speaking and Listening Workshops
On the Edge	How-to Instructions, p. 71 Problem-and-Solution Essay, p. 108	Transitions to Show Time; Pronouns and Antecedents, pp. 72, 73 Sentence Fragments; Coordination and Subordination, pp. 109, 110	Evaluating Persuasive Messages, p. 74 Evaluating Advertisements, p. 111	Resisting Persuasion, p. 112
Striving for Success	User's Manual, p. 177 Timed-Test Essay, p. 210	Exact Nouns; Subject-Verb Agreement, pp. 178, 179 Standard and Informal English; Placement of Modifiers, pp. 211, 212	Reading for Specific Information, p. 180 Reading an Application, p. 213	Job Interview, p. 214
Clashing Forces	Editorial, p. 257 Position Paper, p. 294	Active and Passive Voice; "Loaded" Words, pp. 258, 259 Unity and Coherence; Appositives, pp. 295, 296	Understanding a Writer's Purpose, p. 260 Challenge What You Read, p. 297	Expressing Disagreement, p. 298
Turning Points	Description, p. 333 Reflective Essay, p. 372	Figurative Language; Precise Nouns, pp. 334, 335 Misplaced and Dangling Modifiers; Vivid Adjectives and Adverbs, pp. 373, 374	Reading Manuals, p. 336 Reading Product Labels, p. 375	Following Oral Directions, p. 376
Expanding Horizons	Oral Presentation of Research, p. 421 Firsthand Biography, p. 460	Direct and Indirect Quotations; Varying Sentence Structure, pp. 422, 423 Quotation Marks; Vivid Verbs, pp. 461, 462	Evaluating Sources of Information, p. 424 Breaking Down Difficult Text, p. 463	Making an Introduction, p. 464
Short Stories	Short Story, p. 527 Persuasive Essay, p. 560	Verb Tense; Proper Nouns, pp. 528, 529 Types of Sentences; Parallel Structure, pp. 561, 562	Reading Novels and Extended Works, p. 530 Building Research Skills, p. 563	Evaluating Movies, p. 564
Nonfiction	Comparison and Contrast Essay, p. 619 Consumer Report, p. 656	Commas; Forms of Comparison, pp. 620, 621 Eliminating Unnecessary Words; Infinitives and Infinitive Phrases, pp. 657, 658	Using Heads and Text Structure, p. 622 Recognizing Bias, p. 659	Viewing Television Reports Critically, p. 660
Drama	Video Script, p. 701 Critical Evaluation, p. 804	Spoken and Written Language; Punctuating Words of Direct Address, pp. 702, 703 Quotation Marks and Underlining; Capitalization, pp. 805, 806	Sorting Information on the Internet, p. 704 Adjust Your Reading Rate, p. 807	Telephone Conversation, p. 808
Poetry	Literary Analysis, p. 841 Narrative Poem, p. 872	Run-on Sentences; Adjective Clauses, pp. 842, 843 Punctuating Poetry; Problems With Modifiers, pp. 873, 874	Using Visual Clues, p. 844 Reading Directions, p. 875	Body Language, p. 876
Epics and Legends	Research Paper, p. 917 Multimedia Presentation, p. 946	Topic Sentence and Support; Citing Sources, pp. 918, 919 Semicolons and Colons; Concise Language, pp. 947, 948	Reading Charts, p. 920 Reading a Map, p. 949	Running a Meeting, p. 950

Prentice Hall
LITERATURE
Timeless Voices, Timeless Themes

Copper

Bronze

Silver

Gold

Platinum

The American Experience

The British Tradition

PROGRAM ADVISORS

The program advisors provided ongoing input throughout the development of Prentice Hall Literature: Timeless Voices, Timeless Themes. *Their valuable insights ensure that the perspectives of the teachers throughout the country are represented within this literature series.*

Diane Cappillo
Language Arts Department Chair
Barbara Goleman Senior High School
Miami, Florida
Facilitator at the University of Miami/Dade County Public Schools Summer Writing Institute. Past president of the Dade County Council of Teachers of English.

Anita Clay
English Instructor
Gateway Institute of Technology
St. Louis, Missouri
Former supervisory positions: Middle School Team Leader Chairman, High School English Department; Coordinator, Effective and Efficient School; Coordinator, Writing Across the Curriculum Project.

Nancy M. Fahner
Language Arts Instructor
Charlotte High School
Charlotte, Michigan
Recipient of Charlotte Teacher of the Year Award 1992. Currently working on School-to-Work Curriculum Development.

Terri Fields
Language Arts and Communication Arts Teacher, Author
Sunnyslope High School
Phoenix, Arizona
Recipient of both Arizona Teacher of the Year and U.S. WEST Outstanding Arizona Teacher awards. Member of the Northern Arizona University Center for Excellence in Education Advisory Council. First place award for educational writing from National Federation of Press Women.

Argelia Arizpe Guadarrama
Secondary Curriculum Coordinator
Phar–San Juan–Alamo Independent School District
San Juan, Texas
Recognized by Texas Education Agency for work on Texas Assessment of Academic Skills. Recipient of National Recognition of Positive Avenues for Student Success Program.

V. Pauline Hodges, Ph.D.
Teacher and Educational Consultant
Forgan High School
Forgan, Oklahoma
Formerly Language Arts Coordinator
Jefferson County, Colorado
Denver Professor in English Education/Reading, Colorado State University. President-elect of the National Rural Education Association. Recipient of Oklahoma Foundation for Excellence Award for Secondary Teaching 1993 and Outstanding Educator Award from the Colorado Language Arts Society.

Jennifer Huntress
Secondary Language Arts Coordinator
Putnam City Schools
Oklahoma City, Oklahoma
National trainer for writing evaluation, curriculum integration, and alternative assessment strategies. Instructor of language arts methods classes at Oklahoma City University.

Angelique McMath Jordan
English Teacher
Dunwoody High School
Dunwoody, Georgia
*Teacher of the Year at Dunwoody
High School, 1991.*

Nancy L. Monroe
English and Speed Reading Teacher
Bolton High School
Alexandria, Louisiana
*Past president of the Rapides Council of
Teachers of English and the Louisiana Council
of Teachers. National Advanced Placement
Consultant.*

Rosemary A. Naab
English Chairperson
Ryan High School
Archdiocese of Philadelphia
Philadelphia, Pennsylvania
*English Curriculum Committee.
Awarded Curriculum Quill Award by the Archdiocese
of Philadelphia for the development of effective strate-
gies for the teaching of writing and the integration of
technology and writing.*

Ann Okamura
English Teacher
Laguna Creek High School
Elk Grove, California
*Participant of the College Board
Pacesetters Program. Formerly K–12
District Resource Specialist in Writing,
Foreign Languages, Lay Readers,
District Writing, Competency Assessment,
and the Elk Grove Writing Project.*

*A fellow in the San Joaquin Valley Writing
Project and California Literature Project.*

Jonathan L. Schatz
English Teacher/Team Leader
Tappan Zee High School
Orangeburg, New York
*Creator of a literacy program to assist students
with reading in all content areas.*

John Scott
English Teacher
Hampton High School
Hampton, Virginia
*Recipient of the Folger Shakespeare Library
Renaissance Forum Award. Master Teacher
in Shakespeare who produces workshops for
professional development at the local, state,
and national levels. Selected to participate in four
National Endowment for the Humanities teacher
programs.*

Ken Spurlock
Assistant Principal
Boone County High School
Florence, Kentucky
*Former English Teacher at Holmes High School
and district writing supervisor. Past president of
Kentucky Council of Teachers of English.*

iv

Prentice Hall
LITERATURE
Timeless Voices, Timeless Themes

PLATINUM

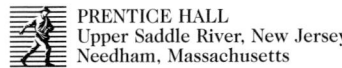

PRENTICE HALL
Upper Saddle River, New Jersey
Needham, Massachusetts

ISBN 0-13-434057-4

2 3 4 5 6 7 8 9 10 02 01 00 99 98

 PRENTICE HALL
Simon & Schuster Education Group

STAFF CREDITS FOR PRENTICE HALL LITERATURE

(in alphabetical order)

Advertising and Promotion: Judy Goldstein, Carol Leslie, Rip Odell, Rob Richman, Ann Shea

Business Office: Emily Heins

Design: Laura Jane Bird, Sarah Carroll, Annemarie Franklin, Monduane Harris, Jim O'Shea, AnnMarie Roselli, Gerry Schrenk

Director of Language Arts: Douglas McCollum

Editorial: Ellen Bowler, Pam Cardiff, Megan Chill, Barbara W. Coe, Donna C. DiCuffa, Elisa Mui Eiger, Amy E. Fleming, Philip Fried, Rebecca Z. Graziano, James S. Jeglikowski, Jacqueline M. Regan

Electronic Publishing: Gregory Myers, Cleasta Wilburn

Manufacturing: Katherine Clarke, Rhett Conklin

Market Research: Eileen Friend, Joan McCulley

Marketing: Glenn E. Bell, Jean Faillace, Belinda Loh

Media Resources: Martha Conway, Libby Forsyth, Melanie Jones, Vickie Menanteaux, Maureen Raymond, Melissa Shustyk, Keirsten Wallace

National Language Arts Consultants: Linda Alexander, Kelly Ford, Karen Massey, Gail Witt

Permissions: Doris Robinson

PrePress Production: Kathryn Dix, William J. Hanna

Production: Christina Burghard, Holly Gordon, Elizabeth Torjussen

Technology: Rick Hickox

Art/Photograph Credits begin on p. 990.

ACKNOWLEDGMENTS

Grateful acknowledgment is made to the following for copyrighted material:

Rudolfo Anaya
"In Commemoration: One Million Volumes" by Rudolfo Anaya, from *A Million Stars: The Millionth Acquisition for the University of New Mexico General Library*, edited by Connie Capers Thorsen (Albuquerque: The University of New Mexico General Library, 1981). Reprinted by permission of the author.

Aperture Foundation, Inc.
"Mothers and Daughters" from *Mothers and Daughters* by Tillie Olsen with Julie Olsen Edwards and Estelle Jussim. Copyright © 1987 by Aperture Foundation, Inc.

(Acknowledgments continue on p. 994)

Looking at Universal Themes

On the Edge

Contents ◆ *vii*

Unit 2

Looking at Universal Themes

Striving for Success

Looking at Universal Themes

Clashing Forces

Unit 4

Looking at Universal Themes

Turning Points

x ◆ *Contents*

Looking at Universal Themes

Expanding Horizons

Unit

6

Short Stories

Contents ◆ *xiii*

Unit 8

Drama

Poetry

Contents ◆ *xv*

Complete Contents by Genre

Complete Contents by Genre

POETRY (CONTINUED)

DRAMA

Complete Contents by Genre

NONFICTION

EPICS, LEGENDS, AND MYTHS

Complete Contents by Theme

LEGACIES

THE NATURAL WORLD

Complete Contents by Theme

Complete Contents by Theme

Complete Contents by Theme

ON THE EDGE

Literature from Around the World*

* not including selections from the United States

Literature from Around the World* (continued)

* not including selections from the United States

Prentice Hall

LITERATURE
Timeless Voices, Timeless Themes

Planning Instruction and Assessment

Unit Objectives

1. To read selections in different genres that develop the theme of Unit 1, "On the Edge"
2. To apply a variety of reading strategies, particularly literal comprehension strategies, appropriate for reading these selections
3. To recognize literary elements used in these selections
4. To increase vocabulary
5. To learn elements of grammar and usage
6. To write in a variety of modes and about situations based on the selections
7. To develop speaking and listening skills, by doing proposed activities

Meeting the Objectives

With each selection you will find instructional material and portfolio opportunities through which students can meet these objectives. Further, you will find additional practice pages for reading strategies, literary elements, vocabulary, and grammar in the **Selection Support** booklet in the Teaching Resources box.

Setting Goals Work with your students at the beginning of the unit to set goals for unit outcomes. Plan what skills and concepts you wish students to acquire. You may individualize according to students' performance levels or learning modalities.

Portfolios You may have students keep portfolios of their work or of their work in progress. The activities and prompts on the Build Your Portfolio page of each selection provide opportunities for students to apply the concepts presented with the selection.

Guardrail/Ocean, Woody Gwyn

 Humanities: Art

Guardrail/Ocean by Woody Gwyn.
    Born in west Texas, Gwyn frequently combines natural vistas with highways, road signs, underpasses, and other symptoms of humanity's encroachment on the natural world. His earlier works tended to comment ironically on such human invasions of nature; however, his later paintings are less ironic and create formal and thematic connections between nature and the artifices of humanity. For example, in *Guardrail/Ocean* a kind of balance has been achieved between the natural and nonnatural: The curve of the rail and the road harmonize with the serenity of the ocean. While the vertical posts on the rail menacingly suggest teeth biting into the land, the weathered rust marks on the guardrail suggest that nature is claiming it, making it as moral as any living creature. The whole painting seems balanced on the edge between two worlds, natural and human, as well as between two moods: the serene beauty of the seascape, on the one hand, and, on the other, an uneasy sense of being perched on an unstable vantage point.

    Have your students link the art to the theme of Unit 1, "On the Edge," by answering the following question:
If you were standing at this guardrail on the edge between highway and sea, what emotions would you feel, and why? *They might feel frightened by the danger of the situation.*

On the Edge

Your heart pounds, your brow perspires, your stomach is in knots—like riding a rollercoaster, reading suspenseful literature can be nerve-wracking, even frightening, but always exciting. The stories, poems, and essays you are about to read in this unit will take you to the edge—and beyond. You'll hang perilously from a narrow ledge, travel to the top of the world, and be greeted by Death's terrifying messenger. By the end, you'll feel as if you've gone along on the most dangerous but delightfully daring ride of your life!

◆ 1

Assessing Student Progress

Tools that are available to measure the degree to which students meet the unit objectives are listed here.

Informal Assessment

The questions on the Guide for Responding sections are a first level of response to the concepts and skills presented with the selection. Students' responses are a brief, informal measure of their grasp of the material. Their responses on this level can indicate where further instruction and practice are needed. You may then follow up with the practice pages in the *Selection Support* booklet.

You will find literature and reading guides in the *Alternative Assessment* booklet, which you may give students on an individual basis for informal assessment of their performance.

Formal Assessment

In the *Formal Assessment* booklet, you will find selection tests and a unit test.

Selection Tests The selection tests measure comprehension and skills acquisition for each selection or group of selections.

Unit Test The unit test, which calls on students to read a passage of literature they have not previously seen, applies the unit skills on a broader level. The Critical Reading section measures Unit Objectives 1, 2, and 3. The Vocabulary and Grammar section measures Objectives 4 and 5. The Essay section measures Objectives 1 and 6. Both the Critical Reading and the Grammar sections use formats similar to those found on many standardized tests.

Alternative Assessment

Portfolios As you review individual pieces or the collected work in students' portfolios, you will find assessment sheets available in the portfolio section of the *Alternative Assessment* booklet.

Scoring Rubrics You will find scoring rubrics for writing modes in the *Alternative Assessment* booklet. You can apply these to Writing Mini-Lessons and to Writing Process Workshop lessons.

Speaking and Listening The *Alternative Assessment* booklet contains assessment sheets for speaking and listening activities.

Learning Modalities The *Alternative Assessment* booklet contains activities that appeal to different learning styles. You may use these as an alternative measurement of students' growth.

Guide for Reading

1. To read, comprehend, and interpret a short story
2. To relate a story to personal experience
3. To use literal comprehension strategies to read for success
4. To identify suspense
5. To build vocabulary in context and learn the root *-term*
6. To discriminate between the possessive *its* and the contraction *it's*
7. To write a Cliffhanger Scene From a Movie that grabs and holds an audience's attention
8. To respond to the story through writing, speaking and listening, and projects

SKILLS INSTRUCTION

Vocabulary:
Word Roots: *-term-*
Grammar:
Possessive *Its* vs. Contraction *It's*
Reading for Success:
Literal Comprehension Strategies
Literary Focus:
Suspense

Writing:
Grab and Hold Your Audience's Attention
Speaking and Listening:
School Speech; Role Play (teacher edition)
Critical Viewing:
Interpret; Draw Conclusions

PORTFOLIO OPPORTUNITIES

Writing: Annotated Drawing; New Titles for the Story; Credo
Writing Mini-Lesson: Cliffhanger Scene From a Movie
Speaking and Listening: Role Play; School Speech
Projects: Risks of Everyday Life; Changing Technology

More About the Author
Most of Jack Finney's work is a blend of science-fiction, nostalgia, mystery, and criticism of modern life. He brought his interest in time travel to a number of works, *Time and Again* being the most famous. Finney carefully researched the time periods about which he wrote. The novel *Time and Again* contains actual photographs, sketches, and quotations from newspapers of the late nineteenth century.

Jack Finney *(1911–1995)*

Jack Finney combines fantastic events and realistic characters in his fascinating, and sometimes frightening, tales.

Finney's short story "The Body Snatchers" inspired the popular horror film The Invasion of the Body Snatchers.

A Brilliant Beginning In 1946, Finney worked for an advertising agency and dreamed of becoming a writer. He began to realize his dream when he entered his first short story in a contest sponsored by a magazine—and won! Not long afterward, Finney took his wife and two children to Marin County, California, and started to concentrate more seriously on writing.

Impossible Links With the Past He continued to combine real and imaginary details in his fiction, often writing about time travel. In many of his tales, the hero escapes from the present into a simpler and calmer time in the past. For example, his novel *Time and Again* is about a man who participates in an experiment to travel back to the nineteenth century. Once there, he falls in love with a woman and chooses to spend his life with her in the nineteenth century.

Finney's concern with time, and escaping from it, is reflected in the titles of some of his works: "About Time" (1986) and *From Time to Time*, the long-awaited sequel to *Time and Again*.

"Contents of the Dead Man's Pocket" is not about time travel. However, it does show how a single step can take a man out of his ordinary life and into another dimension.

◆ Build Vocabulary

WORD ROOTS: *-term-*
In this story, a character describes a series of movie previews as *interminable*. The root *-term-* means "end," and as you probably know, the prefix *in-* means "not" or "without." You can combine these meanings to figure out that *interminable* means "without end" or "seemingly endless."

convoluted
grimace
deftness
imperceptibly
reveling
interminable

WORD BANK
As you read "Contents of the Dead Man's Pocket," you will encounter the words on this list. Each word is defined on the page where it first appears. Preview the list before you read and look for another *-term-* word in the story: *determined.*

◆ Build Grammar Skills

POSSESSIVE *ITS* VS. CONTRACTION *IT'S*
In "Contents of the Dead Man's Pocket," you will see both *it's* and *its*—two forms of the pronoun *it* that are sometimes confused:

Contraction: It's just that I hate you to miss this movie . . .

Possessive: He . . . stared at the yellow paper . . . hoping he could follow its course to the street . . .

It's is a **contraction,** an abbreviation for *it is*. As in other contractions, the apostrophe replaces a missing letter; here, the letter replaced is *i*.

Its is the **possessive** form of the pronoun *it*, showing that something belongs to the noun for which the pronoun stands. That noun is *paper* in the example from the story.

Prentice Hall Literature Program Resources

REINFORCE / RETEACH / EXTEND
Selection Support Pages
Build Vocabulary: Word Roots: *-term-*, p. 1
Build Grammar Skills: Possessive *Its* vs. Contraction *It's*, p. 2
Reading for Success: Literal Comprehension Strategies, pp. 3–4
Literary Focus: Suspense, p. 5
Strategies for Diverse Student Needs, p. 5

Formal Assessment Selection Test, pp. 1–3; Assessment Resources Software
Alternative Assessment, p. 5
Resource Pro CD-ROM
"Contents of the Dead Man's Pocket"—includes all resource material and customizable lesson plan
Listening to Literature Audiocassettes
"Contents of the Dead Man's Pocket"

Contents of the Dead Man's Pocket

◆ *Literature and Your Life*

CONNECT YOUR EXPERIENCE

Living means taking chances—not foolish ones, as your teachers and parents correctly warn against. However, even crossing the street means taking a small chance. You constantly take all kinds of everyday risks, such as trying out for a team, approaching someone you like, and making an effort to succeed in school. This story is about a man who takes a more dramatic and foolish risk, based on a moment's impulse.

Journal Writing In your journal, briefly list some everyday risks you have taken. Remember that they shouldn't involve life-threatening situations. Anything you do that can fail involves a risk.

THEMATIC FOCUS: ON THE EDGE

The central character in this story risks everything for what he has written on a sheet of paper. A single step takes him to the edge of death and forces him to ask: What is really important in life?

◆ Background for Understanding

CULTURE

Not only will this story take you out on the edge; it will also take you back in time to the 1950's. In the mid-twentieth century, there were no photocopiers or computers, and most people still worked on typewriters or laboriously wrote things out in longhand. As a result, a single document was often unique. Losing it meant losing it forever.

Documents may have been one-of-a-kind in the 1950's, but time seemed to stretch out. For example, movies were often double features, combining two major films with previews and cartoons and lasting four or five hours.

These facts about the 1950's may seem unrelated, but they both add to the tension of the story.

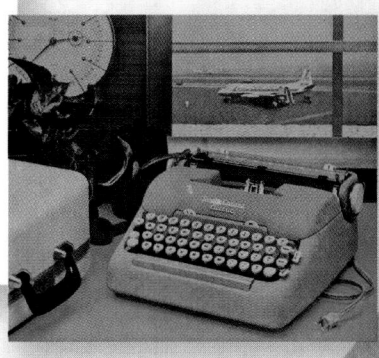

◆ Literary Focus

SUSPENSE

Another word for the tension and nervous uncertainty that some stories can create is **suspense.** This feeling keeps you wondering about the outcome of events, guessing, and turning pages. Often the uncertainty comes from a dangerous choice that you must live through with a character.

In this story, for example, a man wonders whether to pursue a piece of paper onto a narrow building ledge high above the street. Notice how Finney forces you to ponder this choice with the character, make it, and then experience the consequences.

Guide for Reading ◆ 3

✎ Preparing for Standardized Tests

Grammar and Language Portions of some standardized tests call on students to identify usage errors in passages of writing. The types of errors in such passages include the incorrect use of *its* and *it's*. Have students practice applying the instruction in the Build Grammar Skills section by completing the following sample test item in which they are called on to identify which part of a sentence contains an error.

When a government loses the support of it's
(A)   (B)

people, it will sometimes resort to taking
(C)
violent measures to suppress dissent and
(D)
retain control.
(E)

Lead students to see that the correct answer to this item is (B). *It's* should be replaced by *its*. For additional practice, use the Build Grammar Skills page in **Selection Support** (p. 2).

The Reading for Success page in each unit presents a set of problem-solving procedures to help readers understand authors' words and ideas on multiple levels. Good readers develop a bank of strategies from which they can draw as needed.

Unit I introduces strategies for literal comprehension. It is important for students to understand a work on its literal level before they apply higher-level critical thinking strategies. These strategies for literal comprehension give readers an approach for attacking text on a surface level—understanding, vocabulary, sentence structure, and sometimes complex language.

These strategies for literal comprehension are modeled with "Contents of the Dead Man's Pocket." An example of the thinking process involved in applying one of these strategies is shown in each green box.

How to Use the Reading for Success Pages

- Introduce the literal comprehension strategies, presenting each as a problem-solving procedure. Be sure students understand what each strategy involves and under what circumstances to apply it.

- Before students read the story, have them preview it, looking at the annotations in the green boxes that model the strategies.

- To reinforce these strategies after students have read "Contents . . . ," have students do the Reading for Success page in **Selection Support** (pp. 9–10). These pages gives students an opportunity to read a selection and practice strategies for literal comprehension by writing their own annotations.

Reading for Success

Literal Comprehension Strategies

With any piece of literature—from fiction to poetry—your first goal in reading is to understand what the writer is saying. Some writers have a clear, direct style that is easy to understand, but others may write in a way that is less clear. However, there are strategies you can apply to help you understand even complex writing.

Reread or read ahead.

▶ Reread a sentence or a paragraph to find the connections among the words.

▶ Read ahead—a word or detail you don't understand may become clear further on.

Use context clues.

Context refers to the words, phrases, and sentences that surround a word. Look for clues in the context to help you figure out the meaning of an unknown word. For example, you might be unfamiliar with the word *muffled* in the following sentence from "Contents of the Dead Man's Pocket."

Her voice was *muffled*, and he knew her head and shoulders were in the bedroom closet.

The context clue that "her head and shoulders were in the bedroom closet" suggests the reason that her voice was muffled, that is, "quieted" or "softened and blurred."

Break down confusing sentences.

▶ Read sentences in logical sections, not word by word.

▶ Determine the subject of each sentence (what the sentence is about). Then read to see what the rest of the sentence says about the subject.

Restate for understanding.

▶ Paraphrase, or restate a sentence or a paragraph in your own words.

▶ Summarize at appropriate points; review and state the main points of what has happened. Notice story details that seem to be important. Try to fit them into your picture of what is happening.

As you read the following story by Jack Finney, look at the notes in the boxes. These notes demonstrate how to apply these strategies to a work of literature.

4 ◆ *On the Edge*

Reading Strategies: Support and Reinforcement
Appropriate Reading Strategies Students are given a reading strategy to apply when reading each selection. In those selections where surface language may be challenging, students are given one of these literal comprehension strategies.

Reading Prompts To encourage application of the given reading strategy, there are occasional prompts, within green boxes, at appropriate and significant points.

In addition, there are red boxes prompting application of the Literary Focus concept and maroon boxes prompting students to connect with their lives.

Using the Boxed Annotations and Prompts
The material in the green, red, and maroon boxes along the sides of selections is intended to help students apply the literary element and the reading strategy and to make a connection with their lives.

You may use the boxed material in several ways:

- Have students pause when they come to a box and respond to its prompt before they continue reading.

- Urge students to read through the selection ignoring the boxes. After they have read the selection completely, they may go back and review the selection, responding to the prompts.

Contents of the Dead Man's Pocket

Jack Finney

A t the little living-room desk Tom Benecke rolled two sheets of flimsy[1] and a heavier top sheet, carbon paper sandwiched between them, into his portable. Interoffice Memo, the top sheet was headed, and he typed tomorrow's date just below this;

> **Read ahead** to see that several of the words in this paragraph—*flimsy, carbon paper,* and *portable*—are connected to typing.

then he glanced at a creased yellow sheet, covered with his own handwriting, beside the typewriter. "Hot in here," he muttered to himself. Then, from the short hallway at his back, he heard the muffled clang of wire coat hangers in the bedroom closet, and at this reminder of what his wife was doing he thought: Hot, no—guilty conscience.

He got up, shoving his hands into the back pockets of his gray wash slacks, stepped to the living-room window beside the desk and stood breathing on the glass, watching the expanding circle of mist, staring down through the autumn night at Lexington Avenue, eleven stories below. He was a tall, lean, dark-haired young man in a pullover sweater, who looked as though he had played not football, probably, but basketball in college. Now he placed the heels of his hands against the top edge of the lower window frame and shoved upward. But as usual the window didn't budge, and he had to lower his hands and then shoot them hard upward to jolt the window open a few inches. He dusted his hands, muttering.

But still he didn't begin his work. He crossed the room to the hallway entrance and, leaning against the doorjamb, hands shoved into his back pockets again, he called, "Clare?" When his wife answered, he said, "Sure you don't mind going alone?"

---

1. **flimsy** (flim´ zē) *n.*: Thin typing paper for making carbon copies.

▲ Critical Viewing How does this photograph suggest suspense and danger? [Interpret]

Contents of the Dead Man's Pocket ◆ 5

5

"No." Her voice was muffled, and he knew her head and shoulders were in the bedroom closet. Then the tap of her high heels sounded on the wood floor and she appeared at the end of the little hallway, wearing a slip, both hands raised to one ear, clipping on an earring. She smiled at him—a slender, very pretty girl with light brown, almost blonde, hair—her prettiness emphasized by the pleasant nature that showed in her face. "It's just that I hate you to miss this movie; you wanted to see it too."

"Yeah, I know." He ran his fingers through his hair. "Got to get this done though."

She nodded, accepting this. Then, glancing at the desk across the living room, she said, "You work too much, though, Tom—and too hard."

He smiled. "You won't mind though, will you, when the money comes rolling in and I'm known as the Boy Wizard of Wholesale Groceries?"

"I guess not." She smiled and turned back toward the bedroom.

Tom sat at his desk again; then a few moments later Clare appeared, dressed and ready to leave. "Just after seven," she said. "I can make the beginning of the first feature."

He walked to the front-door closet to help her on with her coat. He kissed her then and, for an instant, holding her close, smelling the perfume she had used, he was tempted to go with her; it was not actually true that he had to work tonight, though he very much wanted to. This was his own project, unannounced as yet in his office, and it could be postponed. But then they won't see it till Monday, he thought once again, and if I give it to the boss tomorrow he might read it over the weekend . . . "Have a good time," he said aloud. He opened the door for her, feeling the air from the building hallway, smelling faintly of floor wax, stream gently past his face.

He watched her walk down the hall, flicked a hand in response as she waved, and then he started to close the door, but it resisted for a moment. As the door opening narrowed, the current of warm air from the hallway, channeled through this smaller opening now, suddenly rushed past him with accelerated force. Behind him he heard the slap of the window curtains against the wall and the sound of paper fluttering from his desk, and he had to push to close the door.

Turning, he saw a sheet of white paper drifting to the floor in a series of arcs, and another sheet, yellow, moving toward the window, caught in the dying current flowing through the narrow opening. As he watched, the paper struck the bottom edge of the window and hung there for an instant, plastered against the glass and wood. Then as the moving air stilled completely the curtains swinging back from the wall to hang free again, he saw the yellow sheet drop to the window ledge and slide over out of sight.

He ran across the room, grasped the bottom edge of the window and tugged, staring through the glass. He saw the yellow sheet, dimly now in the darkness outside, lying on the ornamental ledge a yard below the window. Even as he watched, it was moving, scraping slowly along the ledge, pushed by the breeze that pressed steadily against the building wall. He heaved on the window with all his strength and it shot open with a bang, the window weight rattling in the casing. But the paper was past

> **Break down** this sentence to identify the series of events: First Tom waves to his wife. Then he starts to close the door. The door resists.

6 ◆ *On the Edge*

6

his reach and, leaning out into the night, he watched it scud steadily along the ledge to the south, half plastered against the building wall. Above the muffled sound of the street traffic far below, he could hear the dry scrape of its movement, like a leaf on the pavement.

The living room of the next apartment to the south projected a yard or more farther out toward the street than this one; because of this the Beneckes paid seven and a half dollars less rent than their neighbors. And now the yellow sheet, sliding along the stone ledge, nearly invisible in the night, was stopped by the projecting blank wall of the next apartment. It lay motionless, then, in the corner formed by the two walls—a good five yards away, pressed firmly against the ornate corner ornament of the ledge, by the breeze that moved past Tom Benecke's face

He knelt at the window and stared at the yellow paper for a full minute or more, waiting for it to move, to slide off the ledge and fall, hoping he could follow its course to the street, and then hurry down in the elevator and retrieve it. But it didn't move, and then he saw that the paper was caught firmly between a projection of the <u>convoluted</u> corner ornament and the ledge. He thought about the poker from the fireplace, then the broom, then the mop—discarding each thought as it occurred to him. There was nothing in the apartment long enough to reach that paper.

It was hard for him to understand that he actually had to abandon it—it was ridiculous—and he began to curse. Of all the papers on his desk,

◆ **Build Vocabulary**

convoluted (kän′ və lōot′ id) *adj.*: Intricate; twisted

why did it have to be this one in particular! On four long Saturday afternoons he had stood in supermarkets counting the people who passed certain displays, and the results were scribbled on that yellow sheet. From stacks of trade publications, gone over page by page in snatched half hours at work and during evenings at home, he had copied facts, quotations, and figures onto that sheet. And he had carried it with him to the Public Library on Fifth Avenue, where he'd spent a dozen lunch hours and early evenings adding more. All were needed to support and lend authority to his idea for a new grocery-store display method; without them his idea was a mere opinion. And there they all lay, in his own improvised short-hand—countless hours of work—out there on the ledge.

> **Summarize** the four sentences beginning with "On four long Saturday afternoons." The results of hours of work are written on the paper. Without the paper, Tom cannot present his idea to his boss.

For many seconds he believed he was going to abandon the yellow sheet, that there was nothing else to do. The work could be duplicated. But it would take two months, and the time to present this idea was now, for use in the spring displays. He struck his fist on the window ledge. Then he shrugged. Even though his plan were adopted, he told himself, it wouldn't bring him a raise in pay—not immediately, anyway, or as a direct result. It won't bring me a promotion either, he argued—not of itself.

But just the same, and he couldn't escape the thought, this and other independent projects, some already done and others planned for the future, would gradually mark him out from the score of other young men in

Contents of the Dead Man's Pocket ◆ 7

◆ **Critical Thinking**

❸ **Infer** Ask students: How has Tom been spending his free time? What does this imply about his attitude toward life at this point in the story? *Tom has been compiling statistics and doing research during his free time. His attitude toward life seems to be that one should apply oneself relentlessly in order to get ahead.*

Comprehension Check ☑

❹ What is on this yellow paper? How is it written? *The yellow paper contains Tom's ideas for the plan he was developing with all the supporting information that he had been researching for months.*

◆ **Literary Focus**

❺ **Suspense** Ask students how Tom's indecision builds suspense. *As Tom reviews all his work, what it means to him, and what the loss of it would mean, the reader wonders what action he will take.*

Beyond the Classroom

Career Connection

Retailing and Marketing In this story, Tom Benecke compiles facts and figures to create a more efficient grocery-store display. Retailers maximize sales through a variety of methods. For example, grocery retailers place "impulse purchase" items such as candy bars and magazines in checkout aisles where customers wait in line. Some companies hire people to go into grocery stores and hand out free samples of their products. Let students know that people who special-

ize in marketing plan and implement these selling strategies. Companies that sell everything from books to cars have marketing departments. Students can compare special displays at retailers to discover what makes displays effective. If they think a career in marketing would interest them, have them research the preparation required for an entry-level position.

Community Connection

Architecture Point out the architectural

details that prove important to the plot, such as the "ornate corner ornaments" and "narrow ledge" on the building. The very height of the apartment buildings in New York City is also crucial to the story's suspense. Guide students to notice the architectural details that distinguish the buildings in their area, such as tile roofs. Then have students speculate how the architectural details in this story might change if the story were set in their community.

① Draw Conclusions Ask students: Why is getting the paper back so important to Tom? *The paper is crucial because it can help him distinguish himself from all the other young men in the company.*

◆ Reading for Success

② Use Context Clues Have students use context clues to infer the meaning of *infinite* in this sentence. *The context clues are the situation itself ("he brought out his other leg") and the word* care. *Tom is doing something very dangerous, so he would be taking* extremely great *care. Students might be able to infer that* infinite *means "boundless" or "limitless," but* extremely great *or* very great *will unlock the meaning of the sentence.*

Customize for
Visual/Spatial Learners

Have visual/spatial learners set up a demonstration or explanation for the class of the difficulty of walking on a ledge that's only twelve inches wide.

---

his company. They were the way to change from a name on the payroll to a name in the minds of the company officials. They were the beginning of the long, long climb to where he was determined to be, at the very top. And he knew he was going out there in the darkness, after the yellow sheet fifteen feet beyond his reach.

① By a kind of instinct, he instantly began making his intention acceptable to himself by laughing at it. The mental picture of himself sidling along the ledge outside was absurd—it was actually comical—and he smiled. He imagined himself describing it; it would make a good story at the office and, it occurred to him, would add a special interest and importance to his memorandum, which would do it no harm at all.

> The **context clue** that Tom would be out on the ledge indicates that *sidling* probably describes the way he would move—sideways and very slowly.

To simply go out and get his paper was an easy task—he could be back here with it in less than two minutes—and he knew he wasn't deceiving himself. The ledge, he saw, measuring it with his eye, was about as wide as the length of his shoe, and perfectly flat. And every fifth row of brick in the face of the building, he remembered—leaning out, he verified this—was indented half an inch, enough for the tips of his fingers, enough to maintain balance easily. It occurred to him that if this ledge and wall were only a yard aboveground—as he knelt at the window staring out, this thought was the final confirmation of his intention—he could move along the ledge indefinitely.

> **Break down** the sentence beginning with "It occurred to him." Read it without the words set off by dashes. Then reread it to include the interrupting thought.

On a sudden impulse, he got to his feet, walked to the front closet and took out an old tweed jacket; it would be cold outside. He put it on and buttoned it as he crossed the room rapidly toward the open window. In the back of his mind he knew he'd better hurry and get this over with before he thought too much, and at the window he didn't allow himself to hesitate.

He swung a leg over the sill, then felt for and found the ledge a yard below the window with his foot. Gripping the bottom of the window frame very tightly and carefully, he slowly ducked his head under it, feeling on his face the sudden change from the warm air of the room to the chill outside. With infinite care he brought out **②** his other leg, his mind concentrating on what he was doing. Then he slowly stood erect. Most of the putty, dried out and brittle, had dropped off the bottom edging of the window frame, he found, and the flat wooden edging provided a good gripping surface, a half inch or more deep, for the tips of his fingers.

Now, balanced easily and firmly, he stood on the ledge outside in the slight, chill breeze, eleven stories above the street, staring into his own lighted apartment, odd and different-seeming now.

First his right hand, then his left, he carefully shifted his fingertip grip from the puttyless window edging to an indented row of bricks directly to his right. It was hard to take the first shuffling sideways step then—to make himself move—and the fear stirred in his stomach, but he did it, again by not allowing himself time to think. And now—with his chest, stomach, and the left side of his face pressed against the rough cold brick —his lighted apartment was suddenly

---

 Beyond the Classroom

Career Connection

Physical Education At the beginning of the story, the author notes that Tom "looked as though he had played not football, probably, but basketball in college" (see page 5). From this, we can infer that Tom is athletic with a tall, thin build. His college experience as a basketball player would likely have given him the equilibrium he needed to maintain his balance on the narrow ledge. In addition, he would have the training to remain somewhat calm in tense situations.

Tom has not made his career in sports, but many young men and women who are interested in sports and are gifted athletes pursue careers in physical education. Have students interested in careers in sports consider this option. They can interview a physical education teacher at your school to find out how she or he prepared for this career. Encourage students to report to the class what they have learned.

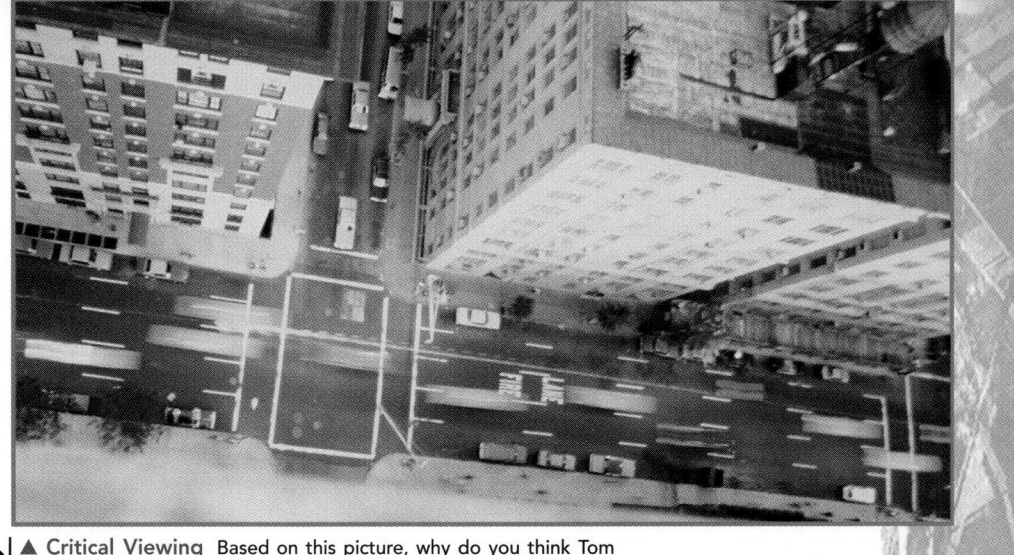

▶Critical Viewing◀

❸ Draw Conclusions Students may suggest that looking down makes Tom feel terrified and panicky. Responses should focus on the height of the buildings and the dizzying view of the street below.

Customize for
More Advanced Students
Have more advanced readers explain why the author includes scenes like this, showing Tom as confident and ignoring the danger of the situation. *By minimizing the suspense now, the author increases his opportunity to build the suspense to greater peaks later in the story.*

Customize for
Visual/Spatial Learners
Encourage these students to use the photograph on this page to help them visualize what Tom is experiencing. Have them consider what the photograph adds to the details that Finney provides in his story. How does viewing the photograph compare to envisioning the situation while reading? *Students may respond that viewing the photograph evokes a more powerful response in them because it calls to mind experiences in which they looked down from a great height.*

❸ ▲ Critical Viewing Based on this picture, why do you think Tom should or shouldn't look down? Explain. [Draw Conclusions]

gone, and it was much darker out here than he had thought.

Without pause he continued—right foot, left foot, right foot, left—his shoe soles shuffling and scraping along the rough stone, never lifting from it, fingers sliding along the exposed edging of brick. He moved on the balls of his feet, heels lifted slightly; the ledge was not quite as wide as he'd expected. But leaning slightly inward toward the face of the building and pressed against it, he could feel his balance firm and secure, and moving along the ledge was quite as easy as he had thought it would be. He could hear the buttons of his jacket scraping steadily along the rough bricks and feel them catch momentarily, tugging a little, at each mortared crack. He simply did not permit himself to look down, though the compulsion to do

> **Context clues** can help you figure out the meaning of *compulsion*. Because Tom will not permit himself to look down, you can figure out that "compulsion to do so" means he wants to. His fear and the danger are clues that the word *compulsion* conveys some intensity.

so never left him; nor did he allow himself actually to think. Mechanically—right foot, left foot, over and again—he shuffled along crabwise, watching the projecting wall ahead loom steadily closer . . .

Then he reached it, and, at the corner—he'd decided how he was going to pick up the paper—he lifted his right foot and placed it carefully on the ledge that ran along the projecting wall at a right angle to the ledge on which his other foot rested. And now, facing the building, he stood in the corner formed by the two walls, one foot on the ledging of each, a hand on the shoulder-high indentation of each wall. His forehead was pressed directly into the corner against the cold bricks, and now he carefully lowered first one hand, then the other, perhaps a foot farther down, to the next indentation in the rows of bricks.

Very slowly, sliding his forehead down the trough of the brick corner and bending his knees, he lowered his body toward the paper lying between

Contents of the Dead Man's Pocket ◆ 9

 Humanities: Photography

Have students consider how photographs like this one can capture a scene or a moment in time in a way that motion video cannot. While motion video can capture action over a period of time, a photograph preserves a single moment and draws viewers into the scene, sparking personal connections and associations. Encourage students to study the details of this photograph and to use their observations to help them answer the following questions:

1. How might your reaction to viewing video footage of this scene be different from viewing the photograph? *Encourage students to explain their answers.*

2. What might you notice in the video that you don't notice in the photograph? *Students may note that they would get a* *stronger sense of motion from viewing the video.*

3. What do you notice in the photograph that you would probably miss in the video? *Students may respond that they would not notice specific cars in the video.*

Draw students' attention to the risk Tom is taking. Ask if they think the risk is worth the reward if he succeeds. What about if he fails? Parallel Tom's experience here to some of the less dangerous risks that students have taken.

◆ Reading for Success

❶ Summarize At this point, have students summarize the story from the beginning to the point at which Tom retrieves the paper. Encourage them to include all important details to form a picture of what has happened. Ask students to predict what will happen, now that Tom appears to have achieved his goal.

◆ Critical Thinking

❷ Analyze Have students analyze how Tom's emotions in this scene may affect his ability to get off the ledge safely. *Students may say that Tom's panic might make him fall. When he was feeling more confident, he didn't have these problems.*

Customize for
Less Proficient Readers

Be sure students understand that the author is speaking figuratively, not literally, at the bottom of the first column, when he describes the "instantaneous explosion of absolute terror" that Tom experiences. Only Tom can hear the "explosion" that roars through his head. There is no actual explosion.

his outstretched feet. Again he lowered his fingerholds another foot and bent his knees still more, thigh muscles taut, his forehead sliding and bumping down the brick V. Half squatting now, he dropped his left hand to the next indentation and then slowly reached with his right hand toward the paper between his feet.

He couldn't quite touch it, and his knees now were pressed against the wall; he could bend them no farther. But by ducking his head another inch lower, the top of his head now pressed against the bricks, he lowered his right shoulder and his fingers had the paper by a corner, pulling it loose. At the same instant he saw, between his legs and far below, Lexington Avenue stretched out for miles ahead.

> **Read ahead.** In the next paragraph, Tom's mental picture of himself makes clear how dangerous his physical position is.

He saw, in that instant, the Loew's theater sign, blocks ahead past Fiftieth Street; the miles of traffic signals, all green now; the lights of cars and street lamps; countless neon signs; and the moving black dots of people. And a violent instantaneous explosion of absolute terror roared through him. For a motionless instant he saw himself externally—bent practically double, balanced on this narrow ledge, nearly half his body projecting out above the street far below—and he began to tremble violently, panic flaring through his mind and muscles, and he felt the blood rush from the surface of his skin.

In the fractional moment before horror paralyzed him, as he stared between his legs at that terrible length of street far beneath him, a fragment of his mind raised his body in a spasmodic jerk to an upright position again, but so violently that his head scraped hard against the wall, bounc-

ing off it, and his body swayed outward to the knife edge of balance, and he very nearly plunged backward and fell. Then he was leaning far into the corner again, squeezing and pushing into it, not only his face but his chest and stomach, his back arching; and his fingertips clung with all the pressure of his pulling arms to the shoulder-high half-inch indentation in the bricks.

He was more than trembling now; his whole body was racked with a violent shuddering beyond control, his eyes squeezed so tightly shut it was painful, though he was past awareness of that. His teeth were exposed in a frozen <u>grimace</u>, the strength draining like water from his knees and calves. It was extremely likely, he knew, that he would faint, to slump down along the wall, his face scraping, and then drop backward, a limp weight, out into nothing. And to save his life he concentrated on holding onto consciousness, drawing deliberate deep breaths of cold air into his lungs, fighting to keep his senses aware.

Then he knew that he would not faint, but he could neither stop shaking nor open his eyes. He stood where he was, breathing deeply, trying to hold back the terror of the glimpse he had had of what lay below him; and he knew he had made a mistake in not making himself stare down at the street, getting used to it and accepting it, when he had first stepped out onto the ledge.

It was impossible to walk back. He simply could not do it. He couldn't bring himself to make the slightest movement. The strength

> **Paraphrase** this paragraph about what has happened to Tom: Tom didn't prepare himself for how high up he would be, so when he accidentally looked down at the street, he became so frightened that he couldn't move.

10 ◆ On the Edge

 Speaking and Listening Mini-Lesson

School Speech: Critical Listening

This mini-lesson extends the Speaking and Listening activity in the Idea Bank on p. 20.

Introduce the Concept Point out that when they are listening to speeches, students should evaluate the arguments the speaker presents on the basis of their own knowledge and how well the speaker presents and supports his or her points.

Develop Background Before students listen to the school speech, give them these

guidelines to follow:

1. Identify the speaker's main idea. Focus on the introduction and conclusion of the speech, where the speaker's main idea is often stated or restated.
2. Look for clear organization, logical reasoning, and evidence that support the speaker's main points.
3. Keep an open mind.
4. Summarize the speaker's main points.

Apply the Information Have students

apply these criteria to listen critically to the speeches.

Assess the Outcome Students should be able to answer the following:

1. What was the speaker's main idea, and how well did he or she support it?
2. How was the speech organized, and how did that organization affect my understanding of the speech?
3. What important new idea or attitude did I take away from the speech?

was gone from his legs; his shivering hands—numb, cold and desperately rigid—had lost all <u>deftness</u>; his easy ability to move and balance was gone. Within a step or two, if he tried to move, he knew that he would stumble clumsily and fall.

Seconds passed, with the chill faint wind pressing the side of his face, and he could hear the toned-down volume of the street traffic far beneath him. Again and again it slowed and then stopped, almost to silence; then presently, even this high, he would hear the click of the traffic signals and the subdued roar of the cars starting up again. During a lull in the street sounds, he called out. Then he was shouting "*Help!*" so loudly it rasped his throat. But he felt the steady pressure of the wind, moving between his face and the blank wall, snatch up his cries as he uttered them, and he knew they must sound directionless and distant. And he remembered how habitually, here in New York, he himself heard and ignored shouts in the night. If anyone heard him, there was no sign of it, and presently Tom Benecke knew he had to try moving; there was nothing else he could do.

Eyes squeezed shut, he watched scenes in his mind like scraps of motion-picture film—he could not stop them. He saw himself stumbling suddenly sideways as he crept along the ledge and saw his upper body arc outward, arms flailing. He saw a dangling shoestring caught between the ledge and the sole of his other shoe, saw a foot start to move, to be stopped with a jerk, and felt his balance leaving him. He saw himself falling with a terrible speed as his body revolved in the air, knees clutched tight to his chest, eyes squeezed shut, moaning softly.

Out of utter necessity, knowing

that any of these thoughts might be reality in the very next seconds, he was slowly able to shut his mind against every thought but what he now began to do. With fear-soaked slowness, he slid his left foot an inch or two toward his own impossibly distant window. Then he slid the fingers of his shivering left hand a corresponding distance. For a moment he could not bring himself to lift his right foot from one ledge to the other; then he did it, and became aware of the harsh exhalation of air from his throat and realized that he was panting. As his right hand, then, began to slide along the brick edging, he was astonished to feel the yellow paper pressed to the bricks underneath his stiff fingers, and he uttered a terrible, abrupt bark that might have been a laugh or a moan. He opened his mouth and took the paper in his teeth, pulling it out from under his fingers.

By a kind of trick—by concentrating his entire mind on first his left foot, then his left hand, then the other foot, then the other hand—he was able to move, almost <u>imperceptibly</u>, trembling steadily, very nearly without thought. But he could feel the terrible strength of the pent-up horror on just the other side of the flimsy barrier he had erected in his mind; and he knew that if it broke through he would lose this thin artificial control of his body.

During one slow step he tried keeping his eyes closed; it made him feel

◆ Build Vocabulary

grimace (grĭ´ məs) *n.*: Twisted facial expression

deftness (deft´ nis) *n.*: Skillfulness

imperceptibly (im pər sep´ tə blē) *adv.*: In such a slight way as to be almost unnoticeable

◆ Critical Thinking

❸ Analyze Have students analyze Tom in terms of his response to the pressure he feels here. *Some students may realize that the pressure Tom is under has caused him to feel paralyzed; they may take his loss of control as a normal response to a dangerous situation. Other students may think that a stronger character would be able to master his body's response to terror.*

Customize for
Interpersonal Learners
Invite interpersonal learners, students who communicate especially well with other people, to explain what they might say to Tom to calm him in this situation.

Listening to Literature Audiocassettes To reinforce the terror of Tom's situation, you may wish to play the audiocassette recording of this portion of Finney's story as students follow along in their texts.

►Critical Viewing◄

1 Connect Students may suggest that the lit lamps, pictures, and filled bookshelves in the apartments all suggest comfort and security.

◆ Build Grammar Skills

2 Possessive *Its* vs. Contraction *It's* Have students explain how they know that *its* is a possessive pronoun rather than a contraction. Then ask students to identify the noun that the possessive pronoun *its* stands for. *Students should be able to tell that its is not a contraction because it has no apostrophe. The pronoun stands for the noun* apartment *and shows that the apartment possesses something— "unbelievable security."*

Customize for
Visual/Spatial Learners

Encourage these students to use this photograph to help them appreciate what Tom is picturing in his mind. You may even want to have them contrast this photograph with the one on page 9 to make it easier for them to understand what Finney describes at the end of this page. Ask: If they were in Tom's place, how would the contrast between the two scenes affect them? *Students may respond that the contrast would cause them to be overcome with panic or a sense of despair.*

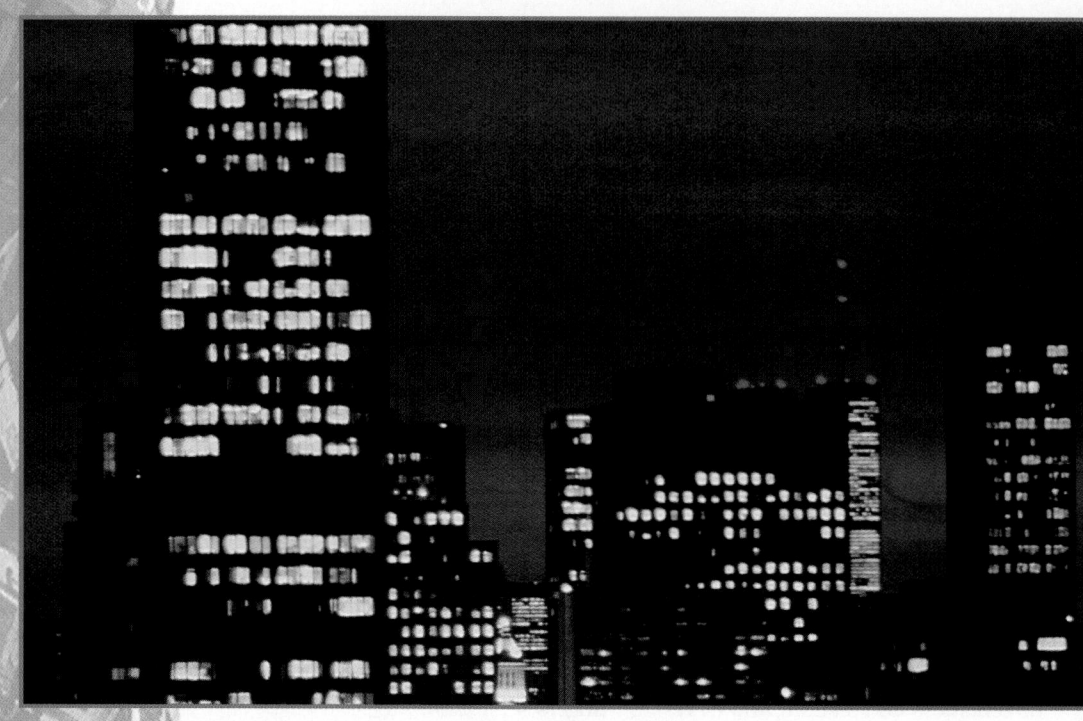

1 ▲ Critical Viewing In what ways does this picture help you appreciate Tom's feelings on the ledge? [Connect]

safer, shutting him off a little from the fearful reality of where he was. Then a sudden rush of giddiness swept over him and he had to open his eyes wide, staring sideways at the cold rough brick and angled lines of mortar, his cheek tight against the building. He kept his eyes open then, knowing that if he once let them flick outward, to stare for an instant at the lighted windows across the street, he would be past help.

He didn't know how many dozens of tiny sidling steps he had taken, his chest, belly, and face pressed to the wall; but he knew the slender hold he was keeping on his mind and body was going to break. He had a sudden mental picture of his apartment on just the other side of this wall—warm, cheerful, incredibly spacious. And he **2** saw himself striding through it, lying down on the floor on his back, arms spread wide, <u>reveling</u> in its unbeliev- **2** able security.

The impossible remoteness of this utter safety, the contrast between it and where he now stood, was more than he could bear. And the barrier broke then, and the fear of the awful height he stood on coursed through his nerves and muscles.

> **Context clues** help you understand the full meaning of *striding*. Because Tom is envisioning a relief from what he is experiencing, *striding* is probably walking fast and confidently, or the opposite of the careful, cautious movement he is using on the ledge.

A fraction of his mind knew he was going to fall, and he began taking rapid blind steps with no feeling of **3** what he was doing, sidling with a

12 ◆ *On the Edge*

it closed and his wrists struck the sill and were jarred off. ❹

For a single moment he knelt, knee bones against stone on the very edge of the ledge, body swaying and touching nowhere else, fighting for balance. Then he lost it, his shoulders plunging backward, and he flung his arms forward, his hands smashing against the window casing on either side; and—his body moving backward—his fingers clutched the narrow wood stripping of the upper pane.

For an instant he hung suspended between balance and falling, his fingertips pressed onto the quarter-inch wood strips. Then, with utmost delicacy, with a focused concentration of all his senses, he increased even further the strain on his fingertips hooked to these slim edgings of wood. Elbows slowly bending, he began to draw the full weight of his upper body forward, knowing that the instant his fingers slipped off these quarter-inch strips he'd plunge backward and be falling. Elbows imperceptibly bending, body shaking with the strain, the sweat starting from his forehead in great sudden drops, he pulled, his entire being and thought concentrated in his fingertips. Then suddenly, the strain slackened and ended, his chest touching the window sill, and he was kneeling on the ledge, his forehead pressed to the glass of the closed window.

Dropping his palms to the sill, he stared into his living room—at the red-brown davenport[2] across the room, and a magazine he had left there; at the pictures on the walls and the gray rug; the entrance to the hallway; and at his papers, typewriter and desk, not two feet from his nose. All was as he had left it—this was past all belief—only a few minutes before.

❸ clumsy desperate swiftness, fingers scrabbling along the brick, almost hopelessly resigned to the sudden backward pull and swift motion outward and down. Then his moving left hand slid onto not brick but sheer emptiness, an impossible gap in the face of the wall, and he stumbled.

His right foot smashed into his left anklebone; he staggered sideways, began falling, and the claw of his hand cracked against glass and wood, slid down it, and his fingertips were pressed hard on the puttyless edging of his window. His right hand smacked gropingly beside it as he fell to his knees; and, under the full ❹ weight and direct downward pull of his sagging body, the open window dropped shudderingly in its frame till

◆ **Build Vocabulary**
reveling (rev′ əl in) v.: Taking great pleasure

2. **davenport** (dav′ ən pôrt) n.: Couch.

 Contents of the Dead Man's Pocket ◆ 13

◆ **Reading for Success**

❸ **Break Down Confusing Sentences** Have students break down this long sentence into logical parts. Lead them to identify both subjects and predicates of this compound sentence. Then have them tell what Tom knew, how he reacted to what he knew, and to what Tom was "almost hopelessly resigned." *Students might break down the sentence as follows: "A fraction of his mind knew he was going to fall,/and he began taking rapid blind steps with no feeling of what he was doing,/sidling with a clumsy desperate swiftness,/fingers scrabbling along the brick,/almost hopelessly resigned to the sudden backward pull and swift motion outward and down." The first complete subject and predicate are "A fraction of his mind" and "knew he was going to fall"; the second complete subject and predicate are "he" and "began taking rapid blind steps with no feeling of what he was doing." Tom was almost hopelessly resigned to the fact that he will fall. The remaining phrases are all modifiers describing his actions and feelings.*

◆ **Literary Focus**

❹ **Suspense** Have students explain how this incident increases the story's tension and builds suspense. *Just when Tom appears to be safe, his avenue of escape—the window—is slammed shut. Further, Tom's "wrists struck the sill and were jarred off," suggesting that he will plunge off the ledge to his death.*

Workplace Skills Mini-Lesson

Concentration

Introduce the Concept Ask students to identify the personal qualities that help Tom through his ordeal. What does Tom tell himself to do each time he feels he may fall? Guide students to appreciate Tom's power of concentration. Tom's ability to concentrate on the task at hand and filter out anything that would distract him enables him to think clearly and make decisions that may save his life.

Develop Background Ask students when concentration is important for them. For example, what distractions do they have to filter out in order to concentrate on homework or studying for a test? How does their power of concentration help them to perform in sports or music? Lead students to recognize that the ability to concentrate is important for virtually all jobs, including students' part-time or summer jobs.

Apply the Information Have students give themselves concentration tests. They should set aside one hour to concentrate fully on a book, a job, a basketball game, etc. Afterward, have them list the distractions they avoided.

Assess the Outcome In groups, have students talk about their concentration tests and evaluate their own powers of concentration. Have them list the personal strategies they used for canceling out distractions and focusing on the task at hand.

His head moved, and in faint reflection from the glass before him he saw the yellow paper clenched in his front teeth. Lifting a hand from the sill he took it from his mouth; the moistened corner parted from the paper, and he spat it out.

For a moment, in the light from the living room, he stared wonderingly at the yellow sheet in his hand and then crushed it into the side pocket of his jacket.

He couldn't open the window. It had been pulled not completely closed, but its lower edge was below the level of the outside sill; there was no room to get his fingers underneath it. Between the upper sash and the lower was a gap not wide enough—reaching up, he tried—to get his fingers into; he couldn't push it open. The upper window panel, he knew from long experience, was impossible to move, frozen tight with dried paint.

Very carefully observing his balance, the fingertips of his left hand again hooked to the narrow stripping of the window casing, he drew back his right hand, palm facing the glass, and then struck the glass with the heel of his hand.

His arm rebounded from the pane, his body tottering, and he knew he didn't dare strike a harder blow.

But in the security and relief of his new position, he simply smiled; with only a sheet of glass between him and the room just before him, it was not possible that there wasn't a way past it. Eyes narrowing, he thought for a few moments about what to do. Then his eyes widened, for nothing occurred to him. But still he felt calm: the trembling, he realized, had stopped. At the back of his mind there still lay the thought that once he was again in his home, he could give release to his feelings. He actually

would lie on the floor, rolling, clenching tufts of the rug in his hands. He would literally run across the room, free to move as he liked, jumping on the floor, testing and reveling in its absolute security, letting the relief flood through him, draining the fear from his mind and body. His yearning for this was astonishingly intense, and somehow he understood that he had better keep this feeling at bay.

He took a half dollar from his pocket and struck it against the pane, but without any hope that the glass would break and with very little disappointment when it did not. After a few moments of thought he drew his leg up onto the ledge and picked loose the knot of his shoelace. He slipped off the shoe and, holding it across the instep, drew back his arm as far as he dared and struck the leather heel against the glass. The pane rattled, but he knew he'd been a long way from breaking it. His foot was cold and he slipped the shoe back on. He shouted again experimentally, and then once more, but there was no answer.

The realization suddenly struck him that he might have to wait here till Clare came home, and for a moment the thought was funny. He could see Clare opening the front door, withdrawing her key from the lock, closing the door behind her, and then glancing up to see him crouched on the other side of the window. He could see her rush across the room, face astounded and frightened, and hear himself shouting instructions: "Never mind how I got here! Just open the wind—" She couldn't open it, he remembered, she'd never been able to; she'd always had to call him. She'd have to get the building superintendent or a neighbor, and he pictured himself smiling and answering their questions as he

3 climbed in. "I just wanted to get a breath of fresh air, so—"

He couldn't possibly wait here till Clare came home. It was the second feature she'd wanted to see, and she'd left in time to see the first. She'd be another three hours or—He glanced **4** at his watch; Clare had been gone eight minutes. It wasn't possible, but only eight minutes ago he had kissed his wife goodbye. She wasn't even at the theater yet!

It would be four hours before she could possibly be home, and he tried to picture himself kneeling out here, fingertips hooked to these narrow strippings, while first one movie, preceded by a slow listing of credits, began, developed, reached its climax and then finally ended. There'd be a **5** newsreel next, maybe, and then an animated cartoon, and then <u>interminable</u> scenes from coming pictures. And then, once more, the beginning of a full-length picture—while all the time he hung out here in the night.

He might possibly get to his feet, but he was afraid to try. Already his legs were cramped, his thigh muscles tired; his knees hurt, his feet felt numb and his hands were stiff. He couldn't possibly stay out here for four hours, or anywhere near it. Long before that his legs and arms would give out; he would be forced to try changing his position often—stiffly, clumsily, his coordination and strength gone—and he would fall. Quite realistically, he knew that he would fall; no one could stay out here on this ledge for four hours.

> **Break down** the parts of this sentence to identify the cause and effect. The effect is that he will fall. The beginning of the sentence explains that his movements will cause him to fall. The words set off by dashes describe his movements.

A dozen windows in the apartment building across the street were lighted. Looking over his shoulder, he could see the top of a man's head behind the newspaper he was reading; in another window he saw the blue-gray flicker of a television screen. No more than twenty-odd yards from his back were scores of people, and if just one of them would walk idly to his window and glance out. . . . For some moments he stared over his shoulder at the lighted rectangles, waiting. But no one appeared. The man reading his paper turned a page and then continued his reading. A figure passed another of the windows and was immediately gone.

In the inside pocket of his jacket he found a little sheaf of papers, and he pulled one out and looked at it in the light from the living room. It was an old letter, an advertisement of some sort; his name and address, in purple ink, were on a label pasted to the envelope. Gripping one end of the envelope in his teeth, he twisted it into a tight curl. From his shirt pocket he brought out a book of matches. He didn't dare let go the casing with both hands, but, with the twist of paper in his teeth, he opened the matchbook with his free hand; then he bent one of the matches in two without tearing it from the folder, its red-tipped end now touching the striking surface. With his thumb, he rubbed the red tip across the striking area.

He did it again, then again, and still again, pressing harder each time, and the match suddenly flared, burning his thumb. But he kept it alight, cupping the matchbook in his hand and shielding it with his body. He held the flame to the paper in his

6

7

◆ **Build Vocabulary**

interminable (in tur´ mi nə bəl) *adj.*: Seemingly endless

Contents of the Dead Man's Pocket ◆ 15

◆ **Critical Thinking**

4 Synthesize Remind students that Jack Finney's stories are famous for their concern with time. Have students analyze how the author makes eight minutes seem like hours. Then have them analyze the effect of the time distortion here. *Finney makes a short time seem endless by describing every single detail of Tom's actions and every thought that goes through his mind. Students may say that Finney distorts time to create suspense. It seems that readers will never find out what happens to Tom in the end.*

5 Clarification Point out that a "newsreel" was a short motion picture presenting current events, similar to today's TV news. Although regular TV broadcasts began in 1939, very few people had TV sets at that time. It was not until 1952, when the FCC announced a plan for more than 2,000 TV stations, that sales of televisions soared and the TV news began to replace newsreels.

◆ **Reading for Success**

6 Use Context Clues Ask students to identify the "lighted rectangles" in this passage. Point out that often the meaning of an unclear word or phrase is found right in the sentence. Have them find a word that could correspond to "lighted rectangles." *Students should be able to identify the "lighted rectangles" as windows of apartment buildings, using the context clue "window."*

◆ **Build Grammar Skills**

7 Possessive *Its* vs. Contraction *It's* Ask students whether *its* is a possessive pronoun or a contraction. Direct them to give reasons for their response. *Its is a possessive pronoun. The "red-tipped end" belongs to "it," the match.*

Speaking and Listening Mini-Lesson

Role Play

This mini-lesson supports the Speaking and Listening activity in the Idea Bank on page 20.

Introduce the Concept Explain that role-playing involves assuming a character's personality to interpret his behavior.

Develop Background Before students begin, have them explore the following ways to make their skits realistic:
1. Analyze their character to make sure their role-play will be consistent with

their character's personality and behavior. They might want to complete a cluster map detailing character traits and behaviors before they begin.
2. Vary the expression in their voices to convey their character.
3. Use body language to reveal the character.
4. Listen to each other—as Tom and Clare would.

Apply the Information Students might rehearse the meeting between Tom and Clare using these guidelines. They can then present

their role-played meeting to the class.

Assess the Outcome Audience members can write a brief review of each role-play. In their reviews they should assess the following points:
1. How true to personality each character seemed
2. How effectively each student used body language in his or her role
3. The pace and style of each student's delivery

15

◆ **Critical Thinking**

1 **Connect** Ask students why no one would be able to identify Tom's body. Then have students link Tom's realization here with his earlier career goals. *There is nothing on Tom to identify him—only the paper with the cryptic notes. Tom begins to realize the emptiness of his driving ambition; he doesn't want to be defined only by his career.*

◆ **Reading for Success**

2 **Reread** At this point, encourage students to reread to understand why Tom feels that his life has been wasted. They should go back to the beginning of the story to remind themselves of how important the yellow paper was to Tom; then contrast his feelings now.

◆ **Critical Thinking**

3 **Interpert** What does the phrase *"contents of the dead man's pockets"* signify for Tom now? *He puts the emphasis on dead man, and realizes that if he did die, his life would have been wasted because he didn't enjoy what he had while he was alive.*

mouth till it caught. Then he snuffed out the match flame with his thumb and forefinger, careless of the burn, and replaced the book in his pocket. Taking the paper twist in his hand, he held it flame down, watching the flame crawl up the paper, till it flared bright. Then he held it behind him over the street, moving it from side to side, watching it over his shoulder, the flame flickering and guttering in the wind.

There were three letters in his pocket and he lighted each of them, holding each till the flame touched his hand and then dropping it to the street below. At one point, watching over his shoulder while the last of the letters burned, he saw the man across the street put down his paper and stand—even seeming, to Tom, to glance toward his window. But when he moved, it was only to walk across the room and disappear from sight.

There were a dozen coins in Tom Benecke's pocket and he dropped them, three or four at a time. But if they struck anyone, or if anyone noticed their falling, no one connected them with their source, and no one glanced upward.

His arms had begun to tremble from the steady strain of clinging to this narrow perch, and he did not know what to do now and was terribly frightened. Clinging to the window stripping with one hand, he again searched his pockets. But now—he had left his wallet on his dresser when he'd changed clothes—there was nothing left but the yellow sheet. It occurred to him irrelevantly that his death on the sidewalk below would be an eternal mystery; the window closed—why, how, and from where could he have fallen? No one would be able to identify his body for a time, either— the thought was somehow unbearable

and increased his fear. All they'd find in his pockets would be the yellow sheet. *Contents of the dead man's pockets, he thought, one sheet of paper bearing penciled notations— incomprehensible.*

He understood fully that he might actually be going to die; his arms, maintaining his balance on the ledge, were trembling steadily now. And it occurred to him then with all the force of a revelation that, if he fell, all he was ever going to have out of life he would then, abruptly, have had. Nothing, then, could ever be changed; and nothing more—no least experience or pleasure—could ever be added to his life. He wished, then, that he had not allowed his wife to go off by herself tonight—and on similar nights. He thought of all the evenings he had spent away from her, working; and he regretted them. He thought wonderingly of his fierce ambition and of the direction his life had taken; he thought of the hours he'd spent by himself, filling the yellow sheet that had brought him out here. *Contents of the dead man's pockets, he thought with sudden fierce anger, a wasted life.*

He was simply not going to cling here till he slipped and fell; he told himself that now. There was one last thing he could try; he had been aware of it for some moments, refusing to think about it, but now he faced it. Kneeling here on the ledge, the fingertips of one hand pressed to the narrow strip of wood, he could, he knew, draw his other hand back a yard perhaps, fist clenched tight, doing it very slowly till he sensed the outer limit of

Paraphrase the two sentences beginning with "All they'd find" to understand a central point in the story: As Tom imagines his death, he realizes that the only thing people will find in his pockets is a meaningless scrap of paper.

balance, then, as hard as he was able from the distance, he could drive his fist forward against the glass. If it broke, his fist smashing through, he was safe; he might cut himself badly, and probably would, but with his arm inside the room, he would be secure. But if the glass did not break, the rebound, flinging his arm back, would topple him off the ledge. He was certain of that.

He tested his plan. The fingers of his left hand clawlike on the little stripping, he drew back his other fist until his body began teetering backward. But he had no leverage now—he could feel that there would be no force to his swing—and he moved his fist slowly forward till he rocked forward on his knees again and could sense that his swing would carry its greatest force. Glancing down, however, measuring the distance from his fist to the glass, he saw that it was less than two feet.

It occurred to him that he could raise his arm over his head, to bring it down against the glass. But, experimenting in slow motion, he knew it would be an awkward blow without the force of a driving punch, and not nearly enough to break the glass.

Facing the window, he had to drive a blow from the shoulder, he knew now, at a distance of less than two feet; and he did not know whether it would break through the heavy glass. It might; he could picture it happening, he could feel it in the nerves of his arm. And it might not; he could feel that too—feel his fist striking this glass and being instantaneously flung back by the unbreaking pane, feel the fingers of his other hand breaking loose, nails scraping along the casing as he fell.

He waited, arm drawn back, fist balled, but in no hurry to strike; this pause, he knew, might be an extension of his life. And to live even a few seconds longer, he felt, even out here on this ledge in the night, was infinitely better than to die a moment earlier than he had to. His arm grew tired, and he brought it down and rested it.

Then he knew that it was time to make the attempt. He could not kneel here hesitating indefinitely till he lost all courage to act, waiting till he slipped off the ledge. Again he drew back his arm, knowing this time that he would not bring it down till he struck. His elbow protruding over Lexington Avenue far below, the fingers of his other hand pressed down bloodlessly tight against the narrow stripping, he waited, feeling the sick tenseness and terrible excitement building. It grew and swelled toward the moment of action, his nerves tautening. He thought of Clare—just a wordless, yearning thought—and then drew his arm back just a bit more, fist so tight his fingers pained him, and knowing he was going to do it. Then with full power, with every last scrap of strength he could bring to bear, he shot his arm forward toward the glass, and he said, *"Clare!"*

He heard the sound, felt the blow, felt himself falling forward, and his hand closed on the living-room curtains, the shards and fragments of glass showering onto the floor. And then, kneeling there on the ledge, an arm thrust into the room up to the shoulder, he began picking away the protruding slivers and great wedges of glass from the window frame, tossing them in onto the rug. And, as he grasped the edges of the empty window frame and climbed into his home, he was grinning in triumph.

He did not lie down on the floor or run through the apartment, as he had promised himself; even in the first few

Contents of the Dead Man's Pocket ◆ 17

◆ **Reading for Success**

4 Paraphrase Invite students to paraphrase this passage to clarify its meaning. Remind students that paraphrase means restating in their own words. *Paraphrases should include Tom's effort to figure out a way to achieve the greatest power from his swing. Example paraphrase: Because of Tom's position, he knew he would not be able to swing his fist far enough to break the window. He tried it out and saw that he was right— he had only two feet to swing his fist.*

Customize for
Bodily/Kinesthetic Learners
Students who process information through motion may wish to pantomime this scene for classmates. Encourage students to use their posture, stance, and facial expressions to convey Tom's tension and fear.

Customize for
Musical/Rhythmic Learners
Students comfortable with oral interpretation can read this passage aloud to the class, using tone, pitch, and volume to capture the tension and suspense.

Cross-Curricular Connection: Social Studies

Here, Tom realizes that he has only one way to save his life: He must break the glass in the window. Tom weighs his chances of punching through the glass without having the rebound fling his arm back and topple him off the ledge.

In his calculations, Tom is dealing with the science of *physics*, which concerns itself with the fundamental elements of the universe, the forces they exert on each other, and the results produced by these forces.

The ancient Babylonians, Egyptians, and early Mesoamericans observed the motions of the planets. The Greek mathematician Archimedes designed devices to deal with force and motion, such as the lever. It was not until 1665, however, that English mathematician Sir Isaac Newton stated the principles of mechanics. The subsequent development of physics owes much to Newton's laws of motion. Have interested students research how Newton's laws of motion, notably the second and third, affect Tom's chances of success.

17

◆ Critical Thinking

❶ Draw Conclusions Judging from Tom's actions, what does the piece of paper mean to him now? *Tom has realized what's really important in his his life and what's not. The piece of paper and what it represented now mean little to him.*

◆ Critical Thinking

❷ Synthesize Challenge students to explain why Tom immediately went to find his wife. *Tom realizes that he has wasted too much of his life in isolation, and perhaps in vanity, because of his fierce ambition.*

Customize for
More Advanced Students
Have students discuss with a group how Tom's climb to retrieve the paper symbolizes his career goals.
Tom must climb across the face of the building just as he is trying to climb the "ladder of success." As he risks his life to climb along the ledge, he risks his happiness and possibly his marriage by his determination to climb the "corporate ladder."

Reinforce and Extend

Answers

◆ *Literature and Your Life*
Reader's Response Students may say that they agreed with Tom's choice to stay at home and work, but disagreed with his choice to go out to the ledge.

Thematic Focus Students may say that by taking risks and succeeding, they learn more about what's important to them.

☑ Check Your Comprehension
1. Tom goes out on the ledge to retrieve a paper that was blown out by the wind.
2. Tom creeps up to the paper, retrieves it, creeps back, falls against the window and accidentally forces it shut, sets letters on fire to attract attention, and finally breaks the window.
3. Clare had been gone for eight minutes.
4. He breaks the window.
5. Tom laughs when the yellow paper soars out the window.

---

❶ moments it seemed to him natural and normal that he should be where he was. He simply turned to his desk, pulled the crumpled yellow sheet from his pocket and laid it down where it had been, smoothing it out; then he absently laid a pencil across it to weight it down. He shook his head wonderingly, and turned to walk toward the closet.

❷ There he got out his topcoat and hat and, without waiting to put them on, opened the front door and stepped out, to go find his wife. He turned to ❷ pull the door closed and the warm air from the hall rushed through the narrow opening again. As he saw the yellow paper, the pencil flying, scooped off the desk and, unimpeded by the glassless window, sail out into the night and out of his life, Tom Benecke burst into laughter and then closed the door behind him.

> The meaning of *unimpeded* will become clear when you read the rest of the sentence.

◆ *Guide for Responding*

◆ *Literature and Your Life*

Reader's Response At what points in the story did you agree with Tom's choices? When did you disagree with his choices?

Thematic Focus Not all risks are as dramatic or dangerous as the risk Tom took. How do everyday risks, like trying out for a team or auditioning for a play, help you understand what's important to you?

☑ Check Your Comprehension
1. Why does Tom go out on the ledge?
2. Briefly summarize what Tom does on the ledge before he manages to get back in.
3. About how much time elapses from Clare's departure to when Tom is kneeling on the ledge, trying to break the window?
4. How does Tom succeed in getting back into his apartment?
5. What event causes Tom to laugh at the end of the story?

18 ◆ On the Edge

Beyond Literature

Math Connection

Statistics in Business Tom Benecke collects statistics to support his idea for a new grocery-store display method. Statistics play an important role in countless businesses. Collecting data through surveys and samples and then analyzing the data is essential to everything from test marketing a new cola to creating a safer automobile for the public. Economists and meteorologists use statistical techniques to predict future economic and weather conditions. How do statistics help to ensure the success of a product?

 Beyond the Selection

FURTHER READING
Other Works by Jack Finney
5 Against the House
The Body Snatchers
Time and Again

Other Works About Risk Taking
Greek myths: *Phaethon, Daedalus and Icarus, Prometheus*
Kon Tiki, Thor Heyerdahl

We suggest that you preview these works before recommending them to students.

INTERNET
You and your students may find additional information about Jack Finney on the Internet. We suggest the following site:
http://www.catch22.com/~espana/ SFAuthors/SFF/Finney,Jack.html

Please be aware, however, that the site may have changed from the time we published this information. We *strongly recommend* that you preview the site before you send students to it.

Guide for Responding (continued)

◆ Critical Thinking

INTERPRET
1. Why does Tom risk his life for a piece of paper? **[Draw Conclusions]**
2. Give three examples of how Tom's thoughts and feelings affect his ability to get off the ledge. **[Analyze]**
3. Contrast Tom's attitude toward life at the beginning of the story with his attitude at the end. **[Compare and Contrast]**

APPLY
4. What changes, if any, will Tom make in his life as a result of this experience? Explain. **[Apply]**

EXTEND
5. In the end, Tom regrets risking his life for his job.
   (a) In what kinds of jobs is it routine to risk one's life? (b) Why are some people attracted to these jobs? **[Career Link]**

◆ Reading for Success

LITERAL COMPREHENSION STRATEGIES
Review the reading strategies and the notes showing how to understand what a writer is saying. Then apply the strategies to answer the following.
1. Paraphrase the paragraph that begins "His right foot smashed" on page 13.
2. Break down the sentence that begins "Then, with utmost delicacy" on page 13.
3. Use context clues to identify the meaning of *incomprehensible* on page 16.

◆ Literary Focus

SUSPENSE
In this story, Finney creates the feeling of uncertainty called **suspense** by keeping you guessing whether Tom will fall.
1. Find a passage describing Tom's thoughts and actions on the ledge and explain how Finney keeps you uncertain about the outcome.
2. How does the suspense in the story make you feel closer to Tom?
3. Why does the suspense make you more likely to think about what is really important in life?

◆ Build Vocabulary

USING THE ROOT -term-
Knowing that the root -term- means "end," answer the following questions in your notebook.
1. When do you hand in a *term* paper?
2. How would you *terminate* a conversation?
3. Why did Tom's time on the ledge seem *interminable*?
4. How was Tom's decision nearly a *terminal* one?

USING THE WORD BANK
On your paper, write the word whose meaning is closest to the meaning of the word from the Word Bank.
1. convoluted: (a) boisterous, (b) twisted, (c) greedy
2. grimace: (a) sneer, (b) buffoon, (c) sadness
3. deftness: (a) foolishness, (b) clumsiness, (c) skill
4. imperceptibly: (a) obviously, (b) visually, (c) unnoticeably
5. reveling: (a) mourning, (b) enjoying, (c) showing

◆ Build Grammar Skills

POSSESSIVE *ITS* VS. CONTRACTION *IT'S*
Two forms of the pronoun it that are sometimes confused are the **possessive** *its,* meaning "belonging to it," and the **contraction** *it's,* which stands for "it is."

Practice On your paper, rewrite each sentence using *its* or *it's*.
1. (Its, It's) amazing that there was ever a time when people did not own computers.
2. "(Its, It's) cold out here!" Tom exclaimed as he stepped out onto the ledge.
3. A pigeon landed on the ledge and turned (its, it's) back on Tom.
4. Tom saw the paper and could hear the muffled scrape of (its, it's) movement along the ledge.
5. Tom's wife saw the paper but did not understand (its, it's) significance.

Writing Application Write a brief description of the behavior of a pet or another animal. Use both *its* and *it's* in your description.

Using the Word Bank
1. b 2. a 3. c 4. c 5. b

◆ Build Grammar Skills
1. It's; 2. It's; 3. its; 4. its; 5. its

✍ Writer's Solution
For additional instruction and practice, use the lesson in the **Language Lab CD-ROM** on punctuation and the page on apostrophes (p. 110) in the *Writer's Solution Grammar Practice Book*.

Answers
◆ Critical Thinking
1. The paper contains information that represents a chance to advance in his workplace.
2. Tom's worrying and fretting cause his legs to cramp, trembling to overtake his body, and strength to leave his limbs.
3. At the beginning of the story, Tom thinks getting ahead is the most important thing in life, while at the end he comes to realize that the enjoyment of his wife's company is more important.
4. Students might say that Tom will now work less or with less ambition and seriousness and devote more time to what he really values.
5. (a) Police officers, firefighters, and rescue workers are some who routinely risk their lives. (b) Perhaps they feel the rewards of saving lives justify the risk; perhaps they like performing heroic acts.

◆ Reading for Success
1. Tom stumbled, and in using the window to break his fall, he pulled the window shut.
2. Tom is the subject of the sentence. "He increased even further the strain on his fingertips" (he pressed harder) is the predicate.
3. "Penciled notations" is a context clue that points to the meaning of *incomprehensible*—not clear.

◆ Literary Focus
1. The passage on page 14, beginning with "The realization . . .," lets the reader know that Clare will not be home any time soon to help Tom off the ledge.
2. Tom's fear makes him vulnerable and more human.
3. The suspense has a way of compressing time to make you look at life with a special clarity.

◆ Build Vocabulary
Using the Word Root -term-
1. You hand in a term paper at the end of a term.
2. You would terminate a conversation by ending it.
3. Tom's time on the ledge seemed as if it would never end.
4. Tom's life could have ended with one misstep.

19

Idea Bank

Customizing for
Performance Levels

Following are suggestions for matching Idea Bank topics with your students' performance levels:

Less Advanced Students: 1, 4, 6
Average Students: 2, 4, 7
More Advanced Students: 3, 5

Customizing for
Learning Modalities

Following are suggestions for matching Idea Bank topics with your students' learning modalities:

Visual/Spatial: 1, 6
Verbal/Linguistic: 4, 5
Logical/Mathematical: 7

Writing Mini-Lesson

Refer students to the Writing Handbook, page 965, for instruction on the writing process, and page 968 for further information on creative writing.

Writer's Solution

Writers at Work Videodisc

Have students view the videodisc segment (Ch. 2) featuring Maxine Hong Kingston to spark classroom discussion of narrative writing. Have students discuss what Kingston says about mood and atmosphere in stories.

Play frames 11644 to 20980

Writing Lab CD-ROM

Have students complete the tutorial on Narration. Follow these steps:
1. Have students use the Word Bins activities to gather details of setting and character.
2. Have students draft on computer.
3. Have students use the Self-Evaluation Checklist to help them revise.

Sourcebook

Have students use Chapter 2, Narration (pp. 30–56), for additional support. The chapter includes an annotated student model of a detective story (p. 56).

Build Your Portfolio

Idea Bank

Writing

1. **Annotated Drawing** Using details from the story, draw the ledge on which Tom is caught. Then write brief notes on the drawing that explain Tom's movements away from and back to the window. **[Art Link]**

2. **New Titles for the Story** Choose three possible titles for the story, in addition to "Contents of the Dead Man's Pocket." Describe the pluses and minuses of each choice.

3. **Credo** This story may have led you to reconsider what's important to you in life. Write a credo, a statement that summarizes what you believe or value most.

Speaking and Listening

4. **Role Play** Suppose that Tom runs into Clare as he's walking out the door at the story's end. With a partner, role-play a dialogue between Tom and Clare. Have Tom explain what has happened, and have Clare respond. **[Performing Arts Link]**

5. **School Speech** Prepare a speech for your classmates in which you warn them about the dangers of making sudden decisions to do physically risky things. **[Performing Arts Link]**

Projects

6. **Risks of Everyday Life** Going out on a ledge is foolish, but you face more common risks everyday. Design a poster that presents tips for minimizing a risk such as a sports injury. **[Art Link]**

7. **Changing Technology** Create a timeline that shows when photocopiers and personal computers were introduced to the market and how quickly they caught on. **[Science Link; Art Link]**

Writing Mini-Lesson

Cliffhanger Scene From a Movie

Tom's sidling dance across the ledge is as suspenseful as any movie's cliffhanger scene. Write your own "cliffhanger" with a dangerous setting that includes one or more characters, sound effects, and dialogue. To make your scene successful, grab viewers' attention and keep them involved in the action.

Writing Skills Focus: Grab and Hold Your Audience's Attention

Whether you write a cliffhanger scene, a story, or a how-to essay, it's important to grab and hold your audience's attention. Finney grabs your attention before you even start reading with the title of his story: "Contents of the Dead Man's Pocket." Although the story itself begins with a very ordinary moment, the title keeps you wondering when a crime or accident will occur.

At the beginning of your scene, you can hook your audience with an exciting image or event.

Prewriting Choose a setting or situation that will keep viewers on the edge of their seats. Examples: a high-speed train derailment, a person hanging from a ledge fifty stories up, or a jumbo jet that is about to crash.

Drafting The filmmaker Alfred Hitchcock once said that an audience will never forgive you if you endanger a star's life for a period of time and then let him or her die. Be sure that your star is rescued in the end.

Revising In reviewing your scene, add camera shots that heighten the uncertainty and suspense. For example, as someone clings to a ledge, zoom in on his or her whitening knuckles. Then move the camera back for a shot that shows exactly what could happen if the person let go.

✓ ASSESSMENT OPTIONS

Formal Assessment, Selection Test, pp. 1–3, and Assessment Resources Software. The selection test is designed so that it can be easily customized to the performance levels of your students.
Alternative Assessment, p. 1, includes options for less advanced students, more advanced students, interpersonal learners, musical/rhythmic learners, verbal/linguistic learners, and visual/spatial learners.

PORTFOLIO ASSESSMENT
Use the following rubrics in the *Alternative Assessment* booklet to assess student writing:
Annotated Drawing: Process Explanation Rubric, p. 100
New Titles for the Story: Description Rubric, p. 97
Credo: Summary Rubric, p. 97
Writing Mini-Lesson: Drama Rubric, p. 109

PART 1 *Daring Decisions*

Le Modele Vivant, Rene Magritte, Christie's Images

One-Minute Planning Guide

The selections in this section encompass a wide range of suspenseful and challenging situations in which people make daring decisions or deal with the result of them. In "The Final Assault" Edmund Hillary gives his view of the decisions he and Tenzing Norgay faced in their push to the summit of Mt. Everest. In "The Dream Comes True" Norgay describes his reflections on the experience. The selections are paired with an excerpt from Jon Krakauer's *Into Thin Air*, an account of the 1996 disaster on Everest. "The Monkey's Paw" is a classic tale of horror that describes what happens when people decide not to heed a mysterious warning. "The Bridegroom" is a narrative poem that tells the tale of a bride-to-be's horrible dream and what it reveals. Part 1 ends with Jamaica Kincaid's "A Walk to the Jetty." This selection describes the anxiety a young girl feels as she walks for the last time down the streets of her town on the island of Antigua.

Customize for
Varying Student Needs
When assigning the selections in Part 1, keep in mind the following factors:

"The Final Assault"; "The Dream Comes True"
- Together, a long selection (17 pp.)
- The prose is dense in places and filled with technical terms

"The Monkey's Paw"
- A brief short story that should be of high interest to most students

"The Bridegroom"
- Elements of nineteenth-century Russian culture may need further explaining

from "A Walk to the Jetty"
- Contains long paragraphs that may give less proficient readers trouble

 Humanities: Art

Le Modele Vivant by René Magritte.
   Belgian painter René Magritte (1898–1967) was one of the leading artists of the Surrealist movement in the early twentieth century. Arising from the period's awakening of interest in the human unconscious, Surrealist art combined elements of realism and fantasy in an attempt to explore the mysteries of the unconscious. Surrealist artists like Magritte created dreamlike images to startle the viewer and express the irrational side of human experience.

Magritte was drawn to the surreal, and his paintings of the mysterious, bizarre, and inexplicable were often rendered in a concretely detailed style.
   Le Modele Vivant (The Living Model), with its wavy door and baseboard, seems to offer a portal to a warped world in which normally inanimate objects are, to say the least, bent into strange shapes and, given the title, perhaps are not inanimate at all. Help students notice that the floorboards are not wavy; it is as if this wall represents the inter-

section between our everyday, normal world and a new dimension.
   Have your students link the painting to the theme of Part 1, "Daring Decisions," by answering the following question.
If you were following someone through this door, what questions would cross your mind as you decided whether or not to open it? *Sample answers: Why is the door wavy? Is it alive? Who or what is on the other side? Will I be stepping into another dimension? Is it dangerous?*

21

OBJECTIVES

1. To read, comprehend, and interpret non-fiction personal narratives
2. To relate nonfiction narratives to personal experience
3. To distinguish fact from opinion
4. To identify author's perspective
5. To build vocabulary in context and learn the word root -voc-
6. To identify compound predicates
7. To write Hall-of-Fame placards using transitions to show time
8. To respond to the narratives through writing, speaking and listening, and projects

SKILLS INSTRUCTION

Vocabulary: Word Roots: -voc-
Grammar: Compound Predicates
Reading Strategy: Distinguish Fact From Opinion
Literary Focus: Author's Perspective

Writing: Transitions to Show Time
Speaking and Listening: Oral Report (teacher edition)
Critical Viewing: Draw Conclusions; Analyze; Interpret; Analyze; Speculate; Infer; Connect

PORTFOLIO OPPORTUNITIES

Writing: Book Jacket; Article on Everest; Mountain's Eye View
Writing Mini-Lesson: Hall-of-Fame Placards
Speaking and Listening: Advice for Future Climbers; Oral Report
Projects: Everest Statistics; Video Game Design

More About the Authors

Sir Edmund Hillary did not conquer Everest the first time he tried. He made it part way to the summit in 1951 and 1952 before succeeding in 1953. Later searches for even more challenging adventures led him to Antarctica in 1957 and 1958, and up a 27,824-foot mountain in 1960 to see how high humans could go without oxygen.

Tenzing Norgay made six tries to climb to the summit of Mt. Everest before he succeeded. After his success, he returned to live with his family and became the field director of training at the Himalayan Mountaineering Institute. He became known as Tiger of the Snows after his world-renowned climb.

Guide for Reading

Sir Edmund Hillary
(1919–)

Few people can claim they have stood on top of the world—and only one man can claim to have been there first. That person is Sir Edmund Hillary. Although he shares the glory of his achievement with climbing partner Tenzing Norgay, Hillary was the first person to reach the summit of Mount Everest in Nepal, 29,028 feet above sea level—the highest spot on Earth.

Hillary has said of himself, "I've moved from being a child who dreamed a lot and read a lot of books about adventure, to actually getting involved in things like mountaineering, and then becoming a reasonably competent mountaineer. . . ." These are humble words for a man who has climbed the Swiss Alps and conquered eleven different peaks of over 20,000 feet in the Himalayas of Tibet and Nepal.

Tenzing Norgay (1914–1986)

At 11:30 on the morning of May 29, 1953, Tenzing Norgay changed the course of his destiny—and began a journey toward international fame. At that moment, he and Edmund Hillary stood on the summit of Mount Everest in Nepal—a place where no man or woman had ever stood before and where few have stood since!

Norgay was born into a family of Sherpa farmers—Nepalese people of Tibetan descent. Norgay started guiding climbers at the age of fourteen. In 1953, he joined a Mount Everest expedition led by Sir John Hunt. Although all the other members of the expedition eventually turned back, Norgay and Hillary struggled on and fulfilled their dream of being the first men ever to reach the summit.

◆ Build Vocabulary

WORD ROOTS: -voc-

Edmund Hillary recalls that upon reaching the summit of Mount Everest, he felt "a satisfaction less *vociferous* but more powerful than [he] had ever felt on a mountain top before." *Vociferous* contains the word root -voc-, which means "speak" or "say." The meaning of the root seems to indicate that something that is *vociferous* speaks out. This meaning is close to the actual definition, which is "loud or noisy in making one's feelings known." It is understandable that Hillary and Norgay would be too tired for a *vociferous* celebration after climbing over 29,000 feet!

precipitous
discernible
belay
encroaching
undulations
vociferous

WORD BANK

Before you read, preview this list of words from the selections.

◆ Build Grammar Skills

COMPOUND PREDICATES

A **compound predicate** consists of two or more verbs or verb phrases (a main verb plus a helping verb) that share the same subject. Compound predicates enable the writer to include a lot of action in a single sentence without having to repeat the subject. In the following example from "The Final Assault," Hillary links two related climbing actions by using a compound predicate to combine them in a single sentence.

```
 S   V                          V
```
I <u>swung</u> my ice axe and <u>started</u> chipping a line of steps upward . . .

As you read "The Final Assault" and "The Dream Comes True," notice the authors' frequent use of compound predicates to describe related or sequential actions.

22 ◆ On the Edge

 Prentice Hall Literature Program Resources

REINFORCE / RETEACH / EXTEND

Selection Support Pages
Build Vocabulary: Word Roots: -voc-, p. 6
Build Grammar Skills: Compound Predicates, p. 7
Reading Strategy: Distinguish Fact From Opinion, p. 8
Literary Focus: Author's Perspective, p. 9
Strategies for Diverse Student Needs, p. 2
Beyond Literature
Cross-Curricular Connection: Physical Education, p. 2

Formal Assessment Selection Test, pp. 4–6; Assessment Resources Software
Alternative Assessment, p. 2
Resource Pro CD-R∅M
"The Final Assault" and "The Dream Comes True"
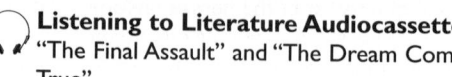 **Listening to Literature Audiocassettes**
"The Final Assault" and "The Dream Comes True"
 Looking at Literature Videodisc
Chapter 1

The Final Assault ◆ The Dream Comes True

◆ Literature and Your Life

CONNECT YOUR EXPERIENCE
Whether you are training to improve your race time or studying to get an *A* on your final exam, you may have to convince yourself that your goal is worth the effort required to reach it. When Hillary doubted his ability to reach the top of Everest, he said to himself, "Ed, my boy, this is Everest—you've got to push it a bit."

THEMATIC FOCUS: DARING DECISIONS
As you read these two men's accounts of the dangers they faced in their quest to stand on the highest point on the planet, you may ask yourself, "Where do I find what it takes to reach the top?"

Journal Writing Describe a time when you had to struggle to achieve a goal or complete a task. How did you keep yourself motivated to make the effort required to meet the goal?

◆ Background for Understanding

MATH
The temperature on the day of Hillary and Norgay's historic achievement—twenty degrees *below zero*—was colder than anything you have probably experienced. Read the graph to contrast the temperature with others that may be more familiar to you.

Think about the ways the extreme temperature would make Hillary's and Norgay's climb more difficult.

Average Temperatures (in May)

New York, Chicago, Los Angeles, Dallas, Everest

◆ Literary Focus

AUTHOR'S PERSPECTIVE
When you read a novel, a poem, a magazine, or even a newspaper article, you get the point of view of one person: the author. How the author views and interprets the events that he or she sees, hears, or experiences personally is the **author's perspective**. In these two accounts of the ascent of Everest, each man's report is influenced by his own beliefs and assumptions. To identify each author's perspective, pay close attention to the details and events they choose to present and the descriptive words they use.

◆ Reading Strategy

DISTINGUISH FACT FROM OPINION
Many people have died attempting to reach the summit of Everest. That's a **fact**—a statement that can be proved true or false by evidence. Mountain climbing is an exciting sport. That's an **opinion**—a statement that can be *supported* by facts but is not itself a fact.

When you read works of nonfiction, determine whether the author's statements are facts or opinions by asking yourself, "Can this statement be proved true or false by evidence?" If the answer is yes, the statement is a fact; if no, it is an opinion.

By distinguishing fact from opinion, you can form your own opinions and understanding of an event or idea, rather than simply accepting what the author wants you to believe. As you read, use a chart like the one below to separate facts from opinions in these accounts.

Facts	Opinions

Guide for Reading ◆ 23

A great way to engage your students' interest and help them appreciate the enormity of Hillary and Norgay's accomplishment is to play a segment of the film adaptation of Jon Krakauer's book *Into Thin Air* (available on videotape from your local store) depicting a recent tragic climbing expedition on Mt. Everest in which several people lost their lives. You may want to choose a segment toward the end of the film, when the members of the party are trapped at top of the mountain by a violent storm. Have students discuss what the film reveals about the dangers of climbing Everest. Then have them imagine what it might have been like to have been one of the first people to climb the mountain. Tell them that they are about to find out.

Customize for
Less Proficient Readers
Help less proficient readers understand that these two narratives describe the same journey as seen through the eyes of two different people. Students may benefit from noting the opinions each writer expresses about his experience.

Customize for
More Advanced Students
Encourage more advanced students to compare and contrast the two perspectives offered in the narratives. Urge them to make inferences about the personalities of the writers based on the details each writer includes, excludes, or emphasizes.

Customize for
English Language Learners
English language learners (and other students as well) might be unfamiliar with words relating to mountain climbing. Help these students define words such as *crampons, cornice, summit,* and *precipice.*

Preparing for Standardized Tests

Reading and Vocabulary The Reading Strategy for this selection is to distinguish fact from opinion. Many standardized tests require students to use this skill in reading comprehension passages. Say the following sentences, and ask students to identify each as a fact or an opinion and give reasons for their answer: "Most people would jump at the chance to climb Mt. Everest." *opinion; the writer has made a generalization that can't be supported* "Before Hillary and Norgay's climb, many

people tried but failed to reach the Summit of Everest." *fact: can be proven*

Once students have finished the selection, have them practice applying the reading strategy to a standardized test format by working in groups to develop sample test questions based on passages from the selection. For example, they might develop a question that asks, "Which of the following details from the passage is an opinion?"

One-Minute Insight No two people perceive the same experience alike, as these narratives clearly illustrate. In telling the story of the first successful climb to the summit of Mt. Everest, Sir Edmund Hillary focuses on his achievement and the difficulties his guide experienced. His guide, Tenzing Norgay, provides his perspective in "The Dream Comes True" (see page 36). The differences in perspectives will give students both a full interpretation of the climb and a glimpse into the characters of the two climbers.

Looking at Literature Videodisc To provide students with background and to motivate them to read these selections, play Chapter 1 of the videodisc. The footage and the description of Mt. Everest will give students a sense of the stark beauty of the Himalayas as well as the physical challenges of high-altitude climbing. Discuss what motivates people to take on such challenges.

Chapter 1

24   *On the Edge*

Block Scheduling Strategies

Consider these suggestions to take advantage of extended class time:

- Have students work in groups to discuss the Thematic Focus question in Literature and Your Life on page 23. Groups can list character traits as well as outside resources, then compare their lists with other class lists.

- After students have read the two narratives, encourage them to debate their responses to the two narratives from the Reader's Response in Literature and Your Life on page 41. Students who prefer Hillary's account can present their reasons, and those who like Norgay's version can give their reasons.

- Have students work in pairs to complete and discuss the Critical Thinking questions on pages 35 and 41.

- Suggest that students work in groups of three to write their Articles on Everest in the Idea Bank on page 43. One student can write an editorial, one can write a news article, and one can write a profile of the climbers.

The Final Assault

from High Adventure
Edmund Hillary

I watched our support party disappear down the ridge and then turned to examine our campsite more closely. It wasn't really much of a place. Above us was a rock cliff—black and craggy, but at least devoid of loose stones to fall on us. From the foot of the cliff a little snow slope ran at an easy angle for eight or nine feet to the top of the steep and exposed South Face of the mountain. This little slope was to be our campsite. It was certainly far from flat and it was going to need a lot of work on it before we could possibly pitch a tent. We carefully moved all the gear to one side and then set to work with our ice axes to remove the surface snow off a reasonably large area. Ten inches down, we struck rock, and after an hour's hard work we had cleared an area about eight feet long and six feet wide. The slope underneath was made up of stones and rubble all firmly glued together with ice. This was much harder going. With the picks on our ice axes we chopped away at the slope, prizing out the separate stones and scraping away the rubble. But our progress was very slow. We weren't using any oxygen at all, but we found we could work very hard indeed for periods of ten minutes or so. Then we'd have to stop and have a short rest. With the debris we chopped out of the slope we tried to build up the platform on the downhill side, but almost invariably saw it collapse and go roaring down over the bluffs below. At times we were buffeted[1] by wind and snow, yet we worked doggedly on, knowing that our tent was our only

---

1. **buffeted** (buf´ it əd) *v.*: Beaten back as by repeated blows.

◄ **Critical Viewing** What can you conclude about Hillary based on his desire to conquer mountains like these? **[Draw Conclusions]** ❷

The Final Assault 25

 Humanities: Photography

This dramatic photograph shows the mountain range that includes Mt. Everest. The photograph presents both the majesty and the menace of the mountains. The awesome spectacle suggests both why humans want to conquer it and the formidable challenge required to do so.

Use these questions for discussion:
1. What can you conclude about the weather in these mountains from the photograph? *It is cold, stormy, and changeable.*

2. What effect does the play of light and shadow in the photograph have? *It makes the mountains look both threatening and beautiful.*
3. What feelings does this photo invoke in you? *Answers may include fear, awe, or an appreciation for the tremendous beauty of this jagged peak.*

◆ Build Grammar Skills

❶ Compound Predicates Have students identify the two verbs in the compound predicate and discuss the effect the compound predicate has on the narrative. *The two verbs are crawled and stood; the compound predicate links the actions and helps show how difficult movement was.*

◆ Critical Thinking

❷ Infer Ask students: What does this passage reveal about the importance of oxygen at these heights? *It shows that oxygen is vital to the climbers' physical and mental endurance; without sufficient oxygen, humans can't perform as well as they normally would.*

◆ Literary Focus

❸ Author's Perspective The author speaks commendably about Norgay and describes Norgay's movements as he saw them.

▶Critical Viewing◀

❹ Analyze Because the mountain is much steeper closer to the summit (and therefore more arduous for climbers), it is necessary for Camps 8 and 9 to be spaced closer together than Camps 3 and 4, which are on a less steep part of the mountain. In addition, students may note that the air is much thinner toward the top, making it difficult for climbers to travel even short distances.

---

chance of survival against the rigors of the night.

❶ At 6:30 A.M. we crawled slowly out of the tent and stood on our little ledge. Already the upper part of the mountain was bathed in sunlight. It looked warm and inviting, but our ledge was dark and cold. We lifted our oxygen onto our backs and slowly connected up the tubes to our face masks. My thirty-pound load seemed to crush me downward and stifled all ❷ enthusiasm, but when I turned on the oxygen and breathed it deeply, the burden seemed to lighten and the old urge to get to grips with the mountain came back. We strapped on our crampons[2] and tied on our nylon rope, grasped our ice axes, and were ready to go.

2. **crampons** (kram´ pənz) *n*.: Pair of spiked iron plates fastened on climbers' shoes to prevent slipping.

I looked at the way ahead. From our tent very steep slopes covered with deep powder snow led up to a prominent snow shoulder on the southeast ridge about a hundred feet above our heads. The slopes were in the shade and breaking trail was going to be cold work. Still a little worried about my boots, I asked Tenzing to lead off. Always willing to do his share, and more than his share if necessary, Tenzing scrambled past me and tackled the slope. With powerful thrusts of his legs he

◆ Literary Focus
Which details in this paragraph suggest that it is told from Hillary's perspective? ❸

▼ **Critical Viewing** Why do you think Camps 8 and 9 are so close together compared with Camps 3 and 4? **[Analyze]** ❹

EVEREST
29,028 feet
SUMMIT
SOUTH SUMMIT
CAMP 9
LHOTSE
27,890 feet
NUPTSE
25,680 feet
South Column
CAMP 8
Geneva Spur
CAMP 7
CAMP 6
CAMP 5
Western CWM
CAMP 4
Ice Fall
CAMP 3
CAMP 2
KHUMBU GLACIER
BASE CAMP

The Final Assault

Hillary and Norgay's 1953 expedition to the summit of Mt. Everest

26 ◆ On the Edge

Humanities: Map

This map shows the heights of the mountains and the locations of the camps Hillary and Norgay made as they ascended Mt. Everest.

Use these questions for discussion:

1. What can you learn from this map that you could not learn from an ordinary photograph? *This map shows the relative heights of the three mountains, the shape and terrain of the three mountains, and the route the climbers took.*

2. Why did the climbers follow such a circuitous route to the summit? *They had to find a safe and accessible route to ascend the mountain.*

3. What features does this map have that other maps you've seen do not share? *Students may note that the map has a three-dimensional quality and is very colorful and lifelike.*

forced his way up in knee-deep snow. I gathered in the rope and followed along behind him.

We were climbing out over the tremendous South Face of the mountain and below us snow chutes and rock ribs plummeted thousands of feet down to the Western Cwm.[3] Starting in the morning straight on to exposed climbing is always trying on the nerves and this was no exception. In imagination I could feel my heavy load dragging me backward down the great slopes below; I seemed clumsy and unstable and my breath was hurried and uneven. But Tenzing was pursuing an irresistible course up the slope and I didn't have time to think too much. My muscles soon warmed up to their work, my nerves relaxed, and I dropped into the old climbing rhythm and followed steadily up his tracks. As we gained a little height we moved into the rays of the sun, and although we could feel no appreciable warmth, we were greatly encouraged by its presence. Taking no rests, Tenzing plowed his way up through the deep snow and led out onto the snow shoulder. We were now at a height of 28,000 feet. Towering directly above our heads was the South Summit—steep and formidable. And to the right were the enormous cornices of the summit ridge. We still had a long way to go.

Ahead of us the ridge was sharp and narrow but rose at an easy angle. I felt warm and strong now, so took over the lead. First I investigated the ridge with my ice ax. On the sharp crest of the ridge and on the right-hand side loose powder snow was lying dangerously over hard ice. Any attempt to climb on this would only produce an unpleasant slide down toward the Kangshung Glacier. But the left-hand slope was better—it was still rather steep, but it had a firm surface of wind-blown powder snow into which our crampons would bite readily.

❺ Taking every care, I moved along onto the left-hand side of the ridge. Everything seemed perfectly safe. With increased confidence I took another step. Next moment I was almost thrown off balance as the wind crust suddenly

gave way and I sank through it up to my knee. It took me a little while to regain my breath. Then I gradually pulled my leg out of the hole. I was almost upright again when the wind crust under the other foot gave way and I sank back with both legs enveloped in soft loose snow to the knees. It was the mountaineer's curse—breakable crust. I forced my way along. Sometimes for a few careful steps I was on the surface, but usually the crust would break at the critical moment and I'd be up to my knees again. Though it was tiring and exasperating work, I felt I had plenty of strength in reserve. For half an hour I continued on in this uncomfortable fashion, with the violent balancing movement I was having to make completely destroying rhythm and breath. It was a great relief when the snow condition improved and I was able to stay on the surface. I still kept down on the steep slopes on the left of the ridge, but plunged ahead and climbed steadily upward. I came over a small crest and saw in front of me a tiny hollow on the ridge. And in this hollow lay two oxygen bottles almost completely covered with snow. It was Evans and Bourdillon's[4] dump.

I rushed forward into the hollow and knelt **❻** beside them. Wrenching one of the bottles out of its frozen bed, I wiped the snow off its dial— it showed a thousand pounds pressure—it was nearly a third full of oxygen. I checked the other—it was the same. This was great news. It meant that the oxygen we were carrying on our backs only had to get us back to these bottles instead of right down to the South Col. It gave us more than another hour of endurance. I explained this to Tenzing through my oxygen mask. I don't think he understood, but he realized I was pleased about something and nodded enthusiastically.

I led off again. I knew there was plenty of **❽** hard work ahead and Tenzing could save his energies for that. The ridge climbed on upward rather more steeply now and then broadened

---

3. **Western Cwm** (ko͞om) *n.*: Steep, hollow hole in Everest's mountainside, made by glacial erosion.

4. **Evans and Bourdillon:** Mountain climbers who attempted unsuccessfully to ascend Mount Everest in 1951.

The Final Assault ◆ 27

Cross-Curricular Connection: Science

Point out the author's mention, on this page, of an "unpleasant slide down toward the Kangshung Glacier." Also, have students locate the Khumbu Glacier on the map on page 26. Explain that a glacier is a huge mass of ice that actually moves, flowing very slowly—less than 1 foot per day. Glaciers form in very high mountains, such as Mt. Everest. The low temperatures in these places cause large amounts of snow to build up and turn into ice, up to 10,000 feet thick. The glacier shown on page 26 is a *valley glacier*—a long, narrow "river" of ice that fills a high mountain valley.

Glaciers begin to form when more snow falls during the winter than melts and evaporates in summer. The excess snow gradually builds up in layers. Its increasing weight compresses the snow underneath into dense crystals of ice. The ice becomes so thick and heavy that the pull of gravity causes it to move downhill, while more ice layers continue to form at the top.

Glaciers can be seen in the United States in Alaska, on Mt. Rainier in Washington, and in Glacier National Park in Montana.

out and shot up at a sharp angle to the foot of the enormous slope running up to the South Summit. I crossed over onto the right-hand side of the ridge and found the snow was firm there. I started chipping a long line of steps up to the foot of the great slope. Here we stamped out a platform for ourselves and I checked our oxygen. Everything seemed to be going well. I had a little more oxygen left than Tenzing, which meant I was obtaining a slightly lower flow rate from my set, but it wasn't enough to matter and there was nothing I could do about it anyway.

❶ Ahead of us was a really formidable problem and I stood in my steps and looked at it. Rising from our feet was an enormous slope slanting steeply down onto the <u>precipitous</u> East Face of Everest and climbing up with appalling steepness to the South Summit of the mountain 400 feet above us. The left-hand side of the slope was a most unsavory mixture of steep loose rock and snow, which my New Zealand training immediately regarded with grave suspicion, but which in actual fact the rock-climbing Britons, Evans and Bourdillon, had ascended in much trepidation when on the first assault. The only other route was up the snow itself, and still fairly <u>discernible</u> here and there were traces of the track made by the first assault party, who had come down it in preference to their line of ascent up the rocks. The snow route it was for us! There looked to be some tough work ahead, and as Tenzing had been taking it easy for a while I hardheartedly waved him through. With his first six steps I realized that the work ❷ was going to be much harder than I had thought. His first two steps were on top of the snow, the third

was up to his ankles, and by the sixth he was up to his hips. But almost lying against the steep slope, he drove himself onward, plowing a track directly upward. Even following in his steps was hard work, for the loose snow refused to pack into safe steps. After a long and valiant spell he was plainly in need of a rest, so I took over.

Immediately I realized that we were on dangerous ground. On this very steep slope the snow was soft and deep with little coherence. My ice ax shaft sank into it without any support and we had no form of a <u>belay</u>. The only factor that made it at all possible to progress was a thin crust of frozen snow which tied the whole slope together. But this crust was a poor support. I was forcing my way upward, plunging deep steps through it, when suddenly with a dull breaking noise an area of crust all around me about six feet in diameter broke off into large sections and slid with me back through three or four steps. And then I stopped; but the crust, gathering speed, slithered on out of sight. It was a nasty shock. My whole training told me that the slope was exceedingly dangerous, but at the same time I

◆ **Build Vocabulary**

precipitous (prē sip´ ə təs) *adj.*: Steep

discernible (di zurn´ i bəl) *adj.*: Recognizable; noticeable

belay (bi lā´) *n.*: Rope support

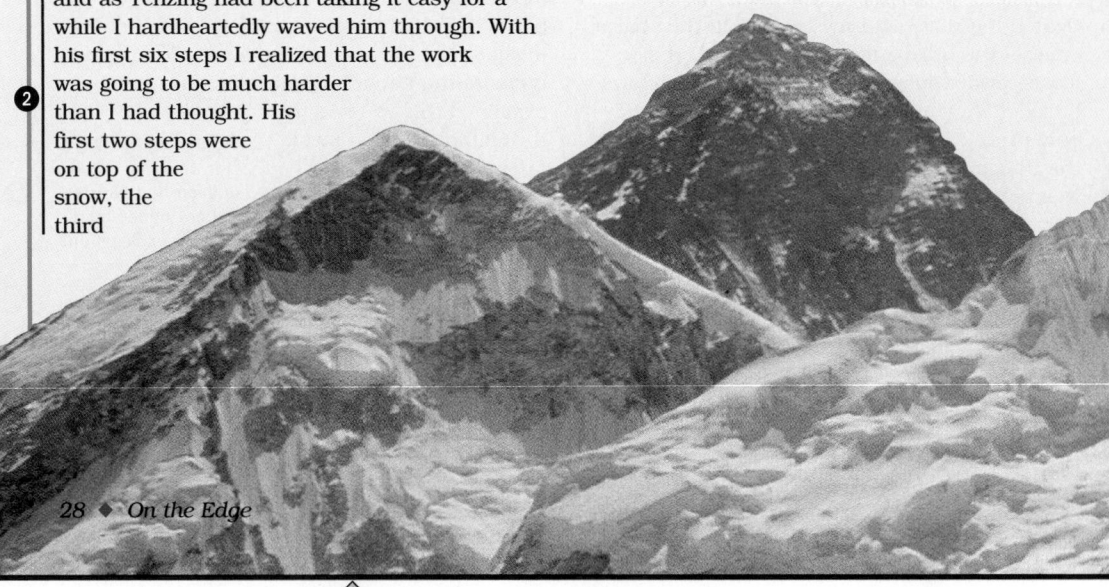

28 ◆ *On the Edge*

◆ **Beyond the Classroom**

Community Connection
Outdoor Challenges Not many communities boast a 29,000-foot mountain to climb, but many do have outdoor challenges such as mountains, rivers, rock walls, caves, and so on. Cities, too, can offer outdoor challenges in parks and outly-

ing areas. Discuss with students the challenges offered by the natural world in your community and encourage them to share stories of any such challenges they have undertaken. Have them compare their feelings of accomplishment with Hillary's and Norgay's.

was saying to myself, "Ed, my boy, this is Everest—you've got to push it a bit harder!" My solar plexus was tight with fear as I plowed on. Halfway up I stopped, exhausted. I could look down 10,000 feet between my legs and I have never felt more insecure. Anxiously I waved Tenzing up to me.

"What do you think of it, Tenzing?" And the immediate response, "Very bad, very dangerous!" "Do you think we should go on?" and there came the familiar reply that never helped you much but never let you down: "Just as you wish!" I waved him on to take a turn at leading. Changing the lead much more frequently now, we made our unhappy way upward, sometimes sliding back and wiping out half a dozen steps and never feeling confident that at any moment the whole slope might not avalanche. In the hope of some sort of a belay we traversed a little toward the rocks but found no help in their smooth holdless surface. We plunged on upward. And then I noticed that, a little above us, the left-hand rock ridge turned into snow and the snow looked firm and safe. Laboriously and carefully we climbed across some steep rock and I sank my ice ax shaft into the snow of the ridge. It went firm and hard. The pleasure of this safe belay after all the uncertainty below was like a reprieve to a condemned man.

Strength flowed into my limbs and I could feel my tense nerves and muscles relaxing. I swung my ice ax at the slope and started chipping a line of steps upward—it was very steep but seemed so gloriously safe. Tenzing, an inexpert but enthusiastic step cutter, took a turn and chopped a haphazard line of steps up another pitch. We were making fast time now and the slope was starting to ease off. Tenzing gallantly waved me through and with a growing feeling of excitement I cramponed up some firm slopes to the rounded top of the South Summit. It was only 9 A.M.

With intense interest I looked at the vital ridge leading to the summit—the ridge about which Evans and Bourdillon had made such gloomy forecasts. At first glance it was an exceedingly impressive and indeed a frightening sight. In the narrow crest of this ridge, the basic rock of the mountain had a thin capping of snow and ice—ice that reached out over the East Face in enormous cornices,[5] overhanging and treacherous, and only waiting for the careless foot of the mountaineer to break off and crash

◆ **Literary Focus**
How might Hillary's assessment of Norgay's climbing skills differ from Norgay's perspective?

---

5. **cornices** (kôr′ nis əs) *n.*: Layers of ice and snow projecting over the top of a ridge.

◆ *Literature and Your Life*

Toward the beginning of this page, Hillary remarks, "I could look down 10,000 feet between my legs and I have never felt more insecure." Draw students' attention to Hillary's observations. Then have them share their own experiences with heights. For example, they may have been to the top of a skyscraper, or they may have had experiences of their own on tall mountains. How did their reactions compare to Hillary's? *Students may respond that, like Hillary, they experienced fear when they looked down from a great height.* Considering their reactions to heights, would they ever consider climbing a tall mountain? Why or why not? *Many students may respond that they would have no desire to climb a tall mountain such as Everest.*

◆ **Literary Focus**

❸ **Author's Perspective** Ask students to describe how Hillary views Mt. Everest. What does this reveal about his character? *He sees Everest as a challenge and as something he can control. He is adventurous and confident.*

◆ **Critical Thinking**

❹ **Draw Conclusions** Ask students why they think Hillary asked Norgay's opinion of the situation. Does he like the answer Norgay gives? *He wanted to verify his own feelings of fear and anxiety. He liked the answer because it allowed him to make the decision.*

◆ **Literary Focus**

❺ **Author's Perspective** Norgay probably considers himself as good a step cutter as anyone else.

◆ Critical Thinking

❶ Make Judgments Have students determine whether the difference in the amount of oxygen the two men had left was significant. *The amount was not significant; Norgay had a little less than Hillary.*

◆ Reading Strategy

❷ Distinguish Fact From Opinion It is Hillary's opinion that the ledge is safe. Although he forms this opinion on the basis of his mountain-climbing experience, it is not a fact that can be proven.

Customize for
Logical/Mathematical Learners

Have these students work out the mathematical equations on this page. Exactly how long will the oxygen last the climbers?

Customize for
Less Proficient Readers

Less proficient readers might need help understanding why Hillary was so excited at this point in the narrative. Explain that the hard, crystalline snow was strong enough to support steps that he could cut, easing the ascent.

10,000 feet into the Kangshung Glacier. And from the cornices the snow dropped steeply to the left to merge with the enormous rock bluffs which towered 8,000 feet above the Western Cwm. It was impressive all right! But as I looked, my fears started to lift a little. Surely I could see a route there? For this snow slope on the left, although very steep and exposed, was practically continuous for the first half of the ridge, although in places the great cornices reached hungrily across. If we could make a route along that snow slope we could go quite a distance at least.

With a feeling almost of relief I set to work with my ice ax and cut a platform for myself just down off the top of the South Summit. Tenzing did the same, and then we removed our oxygen sets and sat down. The day was still remarkably fine and we felt no discomfort through our thick layers of clothing from either wind or cold. We had a drink out of Tenzing's water bottle and then I checked our oxygen supplies. Tenzing's bottle was practically exhausted, but mine still had a little in it. As well as this we each had a full bottle. I decided that the difficulties ahead would demand as light a weight on our backs as possible, so determined to use only the full bottles. I removed Tenzing's empty bottle and my nearly empty one and laid them in the snow. With particular care I connected up our last bottles and tested to see that they were working efficiently. The needles on the dials were steady on 3,300 pounds per square inch pressure—they were very full bottles, holding just over 800 liters of oxygen each. At 3 liters a minute we consumed 180 liters an hour, and this meant a total endurance of nearly 4 1/2 hours. This didn't seem much for the problems ahead, but I was determined if necessary to cut down to 2 liters a minute for the homeward trip.

I was greatly encouraged to find how, even at 28,700 feet and with no oxygen, I could work out slowly but clearly the problems of mental arithmetic that the oxygen supply demanded. A correct answer was imperative—any mistake could well mean a trip with no return. But we had no time to waste. I stood up and took a series of photographs in every direction, then

thrust my camera back to its warm home inside my clothing. I heaved my now pleasantly light oxygen load onto my back and connected up my tubes. I did the same for Tenzing and we were ready to go. I asked Tenzing to belay me and then with a growing air of excitement I cut a broad and safe line of steps down to the snow saddle below the South Summit. I wanted an easy route when we came back up here weak and tired. Tenzing came down the steps and joined me and then belayed[6] once again.

I moved along onto the steep snow slope on the left side of the ridge. With the first blow of my ice ax my excitement increased. The snow—to my astonishment—was crystalline and hard. A couple of rhythmical blows of the ice ax produced a step that was big enough even for our oversize high-altitude boots. But best of all, the steps were strong and safe. A little conscious of the great drops beneath me, I chopped a line of steps for the full length of the rope—forty feet—and then forced the shaft of my ice ax firmly into the snow. It made a fine belay and I looped the rope around it. I waved to Tenzing to join me, and as he moved slowly and carefully along the steps I took in the rope as I went on cutting steps. It was exhilarating work—the summit ridge of Everest, the crisp snow, and the smooth, easy blows of the ice ax all combined to make me feel a greater sense of power than I had ever felt at great altitudes before. I went on cutting for rope length after rope length.

We were now approaching a point where one of the great cornices was encroaching onto our slope. We'd have to go down to the rocks to avoid it. I cut a line of steps steeply down the slope to a small ledge on top of the rocks. There wasn't much room, but it made a reasonably safe stance. I waved to Tenzing to join me. As he came down to me I realized there was something wrong with him. I had been so absorbed in the technical problems of the ridge that I hadn't thought much about Tenzing

> ◆ **Reading Strategy**
> Is it a fact or an opinion that the ledge is "safe"?

---

6. **belayed** (bi lād´) *v.*: Supported by a rope.

30 ◆ On the Edge

 Cross-Curricular Connection: Geography

The Himalayan Mountains Explain to students that the Himalayan Mountains were formed 27 to 70 million years ago, when two continental plates crashed together. The mountain system extends for about 1,500 miles through Pakistan, India, China, Nepal, Sikkim, Bhutan, and Tibet. The system is still relatively young and suffers frequent earthquakes. Much of the area is uninhabited. Have students locate the Himalayan Mountains on a world map or a map of Asia. Encourage them to find photographs of these mountains in library reference books, travel magazines, or on the Internet.

except for a vague feeling that he seemed to move along the steps with unnecessary slowness. But now it was quite obvious that he was not only moving extremely slowly but was breathing quickly and with difficulty and was in considerable distress. I immediately suspected his oxygen set and helped him down onto the ledge so that I could examine it. The first thing I noticed was that from the outlet of his face mask there were hanging some long icicles. I

▲ **Critical Viewing** What feelings are revealed in the expressions on Hillary's and Norgay's faces? [Interpret]

looked at it more closely and found that the outlet tube—about two inches in diameter—was almost completely blocked up with ice. This was preventing Tenzing from exhaling freely and must have made it extremely unpleasant for him. Fortunately the outlet tube was made of rubber, and by manipulating this with my hand I was able to release all of the ice and let it fall out. The valves started operating and Tenzing was given immediate relief. Just as a check I examined my own set and found that it, too, had partly frozen up in the outlet tube, but not sufficiently to have affected me a great deal. I removed the ice out of it without a great deal of trouble. Automatically I looked at our pressure gauges—just over 2,900 pounds (2,900 pounds was just over 700 liters; 180 into 700 was

◆ **Build Vocabulary**
encroaching (en krōch´ in) v.: Trespassing or intruding

about 4)—we had nearly four hours' endurance left. That meant we weren't going badly.

I looked at the route ahead. This next piece wasn't going to be easy. Our rock ledge was perched right on top of the enormous bluff running down into the Western Cwm. In fact, almost under my feet, I could see the dirty patch on the floor of the cwm which I knew was Camp IV. In a sudden urge to escape our isolation I waved and shouted, then as suddenly stopped as I realized my foolishness. Against the vast expanse of Everest, 8,000 feet above them, we'd be quite invisible to the best binoculars. I turned back to the problem ahead. The rock was far too steep to attempt to drop down and go around this pitch. The only thing to do was to try and shuffle along the ledge and cut handholds in the bulging ice that was trying to push me off it. Held on a tight rope by Tenzing, I cut a few handholds and then thrust my ice ax as hard as I could into the solid snow and ice. Using this to take my weight, I moved quickly along the ledge. It proved easier than I had anticipated. A few more handholds, another quick swing across them, and I was able to cut a line of steps up onto a safe slope and chop out a roomy terrace from which to belay Tenzing as he climbed up to me.

We were now fast approaching the most formidable obstacle on the ridge—a great rock step. This step had always been visible in aerial photographs and in 1951 on the Everest

---

❸ **Clarification** Point out that as Hillary and Norgay breathed through the tubes the cold made the moisture in their breath freeze inside the tube, blocking their airways.

▶Critical Viewing◀

❹ **Interpret** Students might indicate that Norgay's expression is of "delight," as Hillary indicated, while Hillary's expression is more subdued, but proud, as he also indicated.

◆ **Build Grammar Skills**

❺ **Compound Predicates** Have students identify the two verbs in the main clause of this sentence. Ask them why Hillary performed these two actions. *The verbs are* waved *and* shouted; *he suddenly realized how completely alone he and Tenzing were.*

Customize for
Visual/Spatial Learners
Have these students use this photograph, which shows the two climbers after their success on Everest, to help them picture Hillary and Norgay and to enhance their appreciation of the characters of the two climbers. Have them compare the expressions on Norgay and Hillary's faces. Which of them looks more at ease? Why? *Norgay looks more relaxed, perhaps because his feelings about conquering Everest are more straightforward.* Ask: Do the two men look as if they are friends? Explain. *Answers should touch on the awkwardness of their body language and the fact that they are not looking at each other.*

Customize for
Visual/Spatial Learners

Encourage these students to study the details of the photograph on this page and to use them to enhance their appreciation for the challenges that Hillary and Norgay faced as they completed their ascent. Draw their attention to the steepness of the face. Ask: How does the photograph help to illustrate the dangers that the two climbers faced? *Students should note such features as the steep cliffs and the snow and ice.*

▶Critical Viewing◀

❶ **Analyze** The sheer sides and the steepness suggest the difficulties of the climb; the border of clouds suggests the dangers of lack of oxygen.

❷ **Clarification** Explain that the climbers' protective clothing is important because, even though the weather on Everest is good, the temperature is very low and the wind is strong, blowing ice at dangerously high speeds. The clothing provides warmth and protection from eye and skin damage.

◆ *Literature and Your Life*

❸ Students' answers will vary but should focus on the various manifestations of fear when faced with a challenge, and the ability to overcome that fear.

❶ ▲ Critical Viewing What elements in this photograph suggest the dangers of climbing? [Analyze]

Reconnaissance we had seen it quite clearly with glasses from Thyangboche. We had always thought of it as the obstacle on the ridge which could well spell defeat. I cut a line of steps across the last snow slope and then commenced traversing[7] over a steep rock slab that led to the foot of the great step. The holds were small and hard to see and I brushed my snow glasses away from ❷ my eyes. Immediately I was blinded by a bitter wind sweeping across the ridge and laden with particles of ice. I hastily replaced my glasses and blinked away the ice and tears until I could see again. But it made me realize how efficient was our clothing in protecting us from the rigors of even a fine day at 29,000 feet. Still half-blinded, I

7. **traversing** (trə vʉrs´ iŋ) v.: Crossing.

climbed across the slab and then dropped down into a tiny snow hollow at the foot the step. And here Tenzing slowly joined me.

I looked anxiously up at the rocks. Planted squarely across the ridge in a vertical bluff, they looked extremely difficult, and I knew that our strength and ability to climb steep rock at this altitude would be severely limited. I examined the route out to the left. By dropping fifty or a hundred feet over steep slabs, we might be able to get around the bottom of the bluff, but there was no indication that we'd be able to climb back onto the ridge again. And to lose any height now might be fatal. Search as I could, I was unable to see an easy route up to the step or in fact any route at all. Finally, in desperation, I examined the

◆ *Literature and Your Life*

Compare Hillary's feelings of anxiety and fear with your own when faced with a difficult challenge.

❸

32 ◆ *On the Edge*

 Humanities: Photography

This photograph shows the peaks of the highest Himalayan mountains above a layer of clouds. The view emphasizes the height of the peaks and presents a strong reminder of the difficulties and dangers of the problems associated with reduced oxygen at such altitudes.

Use these questions for discussion:

1. How does the photograph emphasize the height of the mountains? *By showing the clouds below the peaks, which makes it seem as if the mountains reach into the sky.*

2. Imagine climbing above the cloud line. How would you feel? *Students may respond that they'd feel courageous, fearful, proud, disoriented, or anxious.*

3. What makes photographs of mountain peaks beautiful and captivating? *Students may note that photographs can capture scenes that few people can witness firsthand.*

CONNECTIONS TO TODAY'S WORLD

In April 1996, writer and climber Jon Krakauer signed on as a client of an Everest expedition to report on the growing commercialization of Everest. As he horrifyingly discovered, climbing in the Himalayas is just as dangerous today as it was in Hillary's and Norgay's day.

from Into Thin Air

Jon Krakauer

Straddling the top of the world, one foot in Tibet and the other in Nepal, I cleared the ice from my oxygen mask, hunched a shoulder against the wind, and stared absently at the vast sweep of earth below. I understood on some dim, detached level that it was a spectacular sight. I'd been fantasizing about this moment, and the release of emotion that would accompany it, for many months. But now that I was finally here, standing on the summit of Mount Everest, I just couldn't summon the energy to care.

It was the afternoon of May 10. I hadn't slept in 57 hours. The only food I'd been able to force down over the preceding three days was a bowl of Ramen soup and a handful of peanut M&M's. Weeks of violent coughing had left me with two separated ribs, making it excruciatingly painful to breathe. Twenty-nine thousand twenty-eight feet up in the troposphere, there was so little oxygen reaching my brain that my mental capacity was that of a slow child. Under the circumstances, I was incapable of feeling anything but cold and tired.

* * *

I snapped four quick photos of Harris and Bourkeev [two guides] striking summit poses, and then turned and started down. My watch read 1:17 P.M. All told, I'd spent less than five minutes on the roof of the world.

After a few steps, I paused to take another photo, this one looking down the Southeast Ridge, the route we had ascended. Training my lens on a pair of climbers approaching the summit, I saw something that until this moment had escaped my attention. To the south, where the sky had been perfectly clear just an hour earlier, a blanket of clouds now hid Pumori, Ama Dablam, and the other lesser peaks surrounding Everest.

Days later—after six bodies had been found, after the search for two others had been abandoned, after surgeons had amputated the gangrenous right hand of my teammate Beck Weathers—people would ask why, if the weather had begun to deteriorate, had climbers on the upper mountain not heeded the signs? Why did veteran Himalayan guides keep moving upward, leading a gaggle of amateurs, each of whom had paid as much as $65,000 to be ushered safely up Everest, into an apparent death trap?

* * *

Climbers, as a species, are simply not distinguished by an excess of common sense. And that holds especially true for Everest climbers: When presented with a chance to reach the planet's highest summit, people are surprisingly quick to abandon prudence altogether.

> Compare and contrast Krakauer's expedition to Hillary and Norgay's.

Connections to Today's World

Journalist Jon Krakauer was one of the survivors of a disastrous attempt on Everest in May 1996. He published his account of that trip in *Into Thin Air*. In these passages from his account of the tragic expedition, students will see that although technology and human knowledge may have advanced in the forty-three years between Hillary and Norgay's historic climb and Krakauer's expedition, the beautiful Mt. Everest remains as formidable—and as dangerous—as ever.

Reading this segment will help students to appreciate the enormity of Hillary and Norgay's accomplishment and stir debate about whether or not people who are not professional climbers should attempt to climb a peak as challenging as Everest. In addition, the segment should help enhance students' appreciation for the awesome power of nature. To ensure that students grasp this fact, make sure that they understand that the climbers were killed as a result of an incredibly violent and unforgiving storm that appeared virtually without warning.

Customize for
More Advanced Students
Encourage these students to extend their exploration of the dangers of Mt. Everest by reading the rest of Krakauer's book and sharing their reactions with the rest of the class.

Answer
In Krakauer's expedition, there were more climbers in the party, and the mortality rate was higher. Students might recognize that, unlike Hillary and Norgay's expedition, his was a commercial expedition involving amateurs.

◆ **Reading Strategy**

❶ Distinguish Fact From Opinion Ask students if Hillary really knows that he will get to the top. *He does not know; this is just his opinion.*

◆ **Literary Focus**

❷ Author's Perspective The description is entirely from Hillary's point of view, and he describes things as he would have seen them.

◆ **Critical Thinking**

❸ Infer Ask students to infer what the climbers are experiencing from Hillary's description of Norgay's movements. *They are approaching exhaustion; Norgay's slow movements hint that he is very tired and perhaps low on oxygen.*

right-hand end of the bluff. Attached to this and overhanging the precipitous East Face was a large cornice. This cornice, in preparation for its inevitable crash down the mountainside, had started to lose its grip on the rock and a long narrow vertical crack had been formed between the rock and the ice. The crack was large enough to take the human frame, and though it offered little security it was at least a route. I quickly made up my mind—Tenzing had an excellent belay and we must be near the top—it was worth a try.

Before attempting the pitch I produced my camera once again. I had no confidence that I would be able to climb this crack and with a surge of competitive pride which unfortunately afflicts even mountaineers I determined to have proof that at least we had reached a good deal higher than the South Summit. I took a few photographs and then made another rapid check of the oxygen—2,500 pounds pressure (2,550 from 3,300 leaves 750; 750 is about 2/9; 2/9 off 800 liters leaves about 600 liters; 600 divided by 180 is nearly 3 1/2. Three and a half hours to go. I examined Tenzing's belay to make sure it was a good one and then slowly crawled inside the crack.

In front of me was the rock wall, vertical but with a few promising holds. Behind me was the ice wall of the cornice, glittering and hard but cracked and there. I took a hold on the rock in front and then jammed one of my crampons hard into the ice behind. Leaning back with my oxygen set on the ice, I slowly levered myself upward. Searching feverishly with my spare boot, I found a tiny ledge on the rock and took some of the weight off my other leg. Leaning back on the cornice, I fought to regain my breath. Constantly at the back of my mind was the fear that the cornice might break off, and my nerves were taut with suspense. But slowly I forced my way up—wriggling and jamming and using every little hold. In one place I managed to force my ice ax into a crack in the ice, and this gave me the necessary purchase to get over a holdless stretch. And then I found a solid foothold in a hollow in the ice and next moment I was reaching over the top of the rock and pulling myself to

safety. The rope came tight—its forty feet had been barely enough.

I lay on the little rock ledge panting furiously. Gradually it dawned on me that I was up the step and I felt a glow of pride and determination that completely subdued my temporary feeling of weakness. For the first time on the whole expedition I really knew I was going to get to the top. "It will have to be pretty tough to stop us now" was my thought. But I couldn't entirely ignore the feeling of astonishment and wonder that I'd been able to get up such a difficulty at 29,000 feet even with oxygen.

When I was breathing more evenly I stood and, leaning over the edge, waved to Tenzing to come up. He moved into the crack and I gathered in the rope and took some of his weight. Then he, in turn, commenced to struggle and jam and force his way up until I was able to pull him to safety—gasping for breath. We rested for a moment. Above us the ridge continued on as before—enormous overhanging cornices on the right and steep snow slopes on the left running down to the rock bluffs. But the angle of the snow slopes was easing off. I went on chipping a line of steps, but thought it safe enough for us to move together in order to save time. The ridge rose up in a great series of snakelike undulations which bore away to the right, each one concealing the next. I had no idea where the top was. I'd cut a line of steps around the side of one undulation and another would come into view. We were getting desperately tired now and Tenzing was going very slowly. I'd been cutting steps for almost two hours and my back and arms were starting to tire. I tried cramponing along the slope without cutting steps, but my feet slipped uncomfortably down the slope. I went on cutting. We seemed to have been going for a very long time and my confidence was fast

❶

◆ **Literary Focus**
Which details in this paragraph reveal that it is told from Hillary's perspective?

❷

❸

◆ **Build Vocabulary**
undulations (un′ dyoo lā′ shənz) *n.*: Waves
vociferous (vō sif′ ər əs) *adj.*: Loud; noisy

34 ◆ On the Edge

Speaking and Listening Mini-Lesson

Oral Report
This mini-lesson supports the Speaking and Listening activity in the Idea Bank on p. 43.

Introduce the Concept Remind students that, like a written report, an oral report needs to be clearly organized, and its central idea should be clear from the beginning. Have them brainstorm for aspects of mountain climbing that they might report on, drawing on the narratives for such ideas as climbing on ice and the use of oxygen.

Develop Background Encourage students to use library materials such as encyclopedias and reference books to find information on their topics. They should take notes and arrange their notes into an outline. Those students who would be uncomfortable delivering a report from an outline can write out their reports.

Apply the Information Encourage students to include visual aids such as maps, charts, or photos, to add interest. When

they have prepared and practiced, have students present their reports to the class.

Assess the Outcome Have students assess their own and others' reports in terms of (a) the organization of the information and (b) how well the central idea was presented and supported. You might have students use the Self and Peer Assessment sheets for a speech, pages 117 and 118 in *Alternative Assessment.*

evaporating. Bump followed bump with maddening regularity. A patch of shingle barred our way and I climbed dully up it and started cutting steps around another bump. And then I realized that this was the last bump, for ahead of me the ridge dropped steeply away in a great corniced curve, and out in the distance I could see the pastel shades and fleecy clouds of the highlands of Tibet.

To my right a slender snow ridge climbed up to a snowy dome about forty feet above our heads. But all the way along the ridge the thought had haunted me that the summit might be the crest of a cornice. It was too late to take risks now. I asked Tenzing to belay me strongly and I started cutting a cautious line of steps up the ridge. Peering from side to side and thrusting with my ice ax, I tried to discover a possible cornice, but everything seemed solid and firm. I waved Tenzing up to me. A few more whacks of the ice ax, a few very weary steps, and we were on the summit of Everest.

It was 11:30 A.M. My first sensation was one of relief—relief that the long grind was over; that the summit had been reached before our oxygen supplies had dropped to a critical level; and relief that in the end the mountain had been kind to us in having a pleasantly rounded cone for its summit instead of a fearsome and unapproachable cornice. But mixed with the relief was a vague sense of astonishment that I could have been the lucky one to attain the ambition of so many brave and determined climbers. It seemed difficult at first to grasp that we'd got there. I was too tired and too conscious of the long way down to safety really to feel any great elation. But as the fact of our success thrust itself more clearly into my mind I felt a quiet glow of satisfaction spread through my body—a satisfaction less <u>vociferous</u> but more powerful than I had ever felt on a mountaintop before. I turned and looked at Tenzing. Even beneath his oxygen mask and the icicles hanging from his hair I could see his infectious grin of sheer delight.

❹

Guide for Responding

◆ Literature and Your Life

Reader's Response How did you feel when Hillary and Norgay finally reached the summit of Everest? Explain your reaction.

Thematic Focus Norgay and Hillary possessed certain qualities that helped them reach the top. What character traits are needed to face a difficult challenge?

Group Discussion As a group, discuss why people are so interested in conquering mountains, raging rivers, and other wilderness challenges. Also, discuss whether or not you would try to climb to the summit of a mountain and why you would or would not.

☑ Check Your Comprehension

1. Summarize the events leading up to the reaching of the summit on the final day of climbing.
2. What does Hillary find in the snow? Why is it such a helpful discovery?
3. At what time do Hillary and Norgay reach the summit?

◆ Critical Thinking

INTERPRET
1. Why does Hillary continually mention the progress and condition of his partner? **[Infer]**
2. Do you think Norgay's oxygen situation was as critical as Hillary made it seem? Explain your answer. **[Make a Judgment]**
APPLY
3. After reading about the effort and energy required to conquer Everest, why do you think two men from such different backgrounds are able to help each other succeed? **[Speculate]**

The Final Assault ◆ 35

Cross-Curricular Connection: Social Studies

The Sherpas Explain to students that the Sherpas are a distinct ethnic group of Nepal. They live in the North in the high valleys and are accustomed to high altitudes, which made them very popular as guides for Himalayan climbs. Many Sherpas make a living growing potatoes, wheat, and barley and herding goats, yaks, and sheep. Some students may recall having seen a television advertisement highlighting the capabilities of the Internet in which a Sherpa advertises his service through his own Web site.

◆ **Literary Focus**

❶ **Author's Perspective** Ask students what perspective Norgay brings to the conquering of Mt. Everest. *Tenzing presents a focus on the mountain as a force; he also is responding to Hillary's account.*

◆ **Reading Strategy**

❷ **Distinguish Fact From Opinion** This is Norgay's opinion of what Hillary has said. In fact, Norgay even directly states that he is presenting an opinion.

▶ **Critical Viewing** ◀

❸ **Infer** The photo was probably taken at the end of the adventure; the men look tired and weathered. At the same time, however, they look as if they are relieved and have a sense of accomplishment.

The Dream Comes True
from The Tiger of the Snows

Tenzing Norgay

Written in collaboration with James Ramsey Ullman

▲ Critical Viewing Do you think this photo was taken at the beginning or end of the climb? Explain. [Infer] ❸

From the south summit we first had to go down a little. Then up, up, up. All the time the danger was that the snow would slip, or that we would get too far out on a cornice that would then break away; so we moved just one at a time, taking turns going ahead, while the second one wrapped the rope around his ax and fixed the ax in the snow as an anchor. The weather was still fine. We were not too tired. But every so often, as had happened all the way, we would have trouble breathing and have to stop and clear away the ice that kept forming in the tubes of our oxygen sets. In regard to this, I must say in all honesty that I do not think Hillary is quite fair in the story he later told, indicating that I had more trouble than he with breathing and that without his help I might have been in serious difficulty. In my opinion our difficulties were the same—and luckily never too great—and we each helped and were helped by the other in equal measure.

❷ ◆ **Reading Strategy** Is this statement a fact or an opinion?

Anyhow, after each short stop we kept going, twisting always higher along the ridge between the cornices and the precipices. And at last we came to what might be the last big obstacle below the top. This was a cliff of rock rising straight up out of the ridge and blocking it off, and we had already known about it from aerial photographs and from seeing it through binoculars from Thyangboche.[1] Now it was a question of how to get over or around it, and we could find only one possible way. This was along a steep, narrow gap between one side of the rock and the inner

---

1. **Thyangboche** (tän bō´ chā): Village in Nepal.

36 ◆ *On the Edge*

---

side of an adjoining cornice, and Hillary, now going first, worked his way up it, slowly and carefully, to a sort of platform above. While climbing, he had to press backwards with his feet against the cornice, and I belayed him from below as strongly as I could, for there was great danger of the ice giving way. Luckily, however, it did not. Hillary got up safely to the top of the rock and then held the rope while I came after.

Here again I must be honest and say that I do not feel his account, as told in *The Conquest of Everest*, is wholly accurate. For one thing, he has written that this gap up the rock wall was about forty feet high, but in my judgment it was little more than fifteen. Also, he gives the impression that it was only he who really climbed it on his own, and that he then practically pulled me, so that I "finally collapsed exhausted at the top, like a giant fish when it has just been hauled from the sea after a terrible struggle." Since then I have heard plenty about that "fish," and I admit I do not like it. For it is the plain truth that no one pulled or hauled me up the gap. I climbed it myself, just as Hillary had done; and if he was protecting me with the rope while I was doing it, this was no more than I had done for him. In speaking of this I must make one thing very plain. Hillary is my friend. He is a fine climber and a fine man, and I am proud to have gone with him to the top of Everest. But I do feel that in his story of our final climb he is not quite fair to me;

> ◆ **Literary Focus**
> How does Norgay's perspective differ from Hillary's? ❺

❻

The Dream Comes True ◆ 37

▶Critical Viewing◀

❹ **Speculate** Answers should mention Norgay's love and respect for the mountain helped him. He also needed knowledge of the mountain, weather, and climbing techniques, and he needed the ability to "read" the mountain.

◆ **Literary Focus**

❺ **Author's Perspective** Norgay feels that the rock wall was smaller than Hillary thought. He also believed that his climbing was as energetic as Hillary's.

◆ **Critical Thinking**

❻ **Make Judgments** Ask students which version of the story they believe, Hillary's or Norgay's. Have them give reasons for their responses. *Some students may believe Hillary because he has little reason to lie; others may feel Norgay is truthful because Hillary may have been trying to make himself look heroic.*

Customize for
Less Proficient Readers
Draw these students' attention to the last sentence—"We were partners."—in the first paragraph. Point out that this sentence sums up one of the key points of Norgay's account. Urge students to look carefully for other sentences that appear at the beginnings or ends of paragraphs and seem to sum up main ideas. Tell students that looking closely at opening and closing sentences is an effective reading strategy to help them improve comprehension.

◆ *Literature and Your Life*

❶ Answers might focus on feelings of hurt and anger and methods of bringing the truth to light.

▶Critical Viewing◀

❷ **Infer** Answers might mention feelings of accomplishment, awe, exhaustion, excitement, and fear.

◆ **Build Grammar Skills**

❸ **Compound Predicates** Have students identify the compound predicate in this sentence. *"I pick up two small stones and put them in my pocket."* The verbs are pick and put.

that all the way through he indicates that when things went well it was his doing and when things went badly it was mine. For this is simply not true. Nowhere do I make the suggestion that I could have climbed Everest by myself; and I do not think Hillary should suggest that he could have, or that I could not have done it without his help. All the way up and down we helped, and were helped by, each other—and that was the way it should be. But we were not leader and led. We were partners.

> ◆ *Literature and Your Life*
> How would you respond to false accusations or rumors that were being spread about you?

On top of the rock cliff we rested again. Certainly, after the climb up the gap we were both a bit breathless, but after some slow pulls at the oxygen I am feeling fine. I look up; the top is very close now; and my heart thumps with excitement and joy. Then we are on our way again. Climbing again. There are

38 ◆ On the Edge

▲ **Critical Viewing** Describe how Hillary and Norgay must have felt as they looked ahead and back from this point. [Infer]

still the cornices on our right and the precipice on our left, but the ridge is now less steep. It is only a row of snowy humps, one beyond the other, one higher than the other. But we are still afraid of the cornices and, instead of following the ridge all the way, cut over to the left, where there is now a long snow slope above the precipice. About a hundred feet below the top we come to the highest bare rocks. There is enough almost level space here for two tents, and I wonder if men will ever camp in this place, so near the summit of the earth. I pick up two small stones and put them in my pocket to bring back to the world below. Then the rocks, too, are beneath us. We are back among the snowy humps. They are curving off to the right, and each time we pass one I wonder, "Is the next the last one? Is the

 Humanities: Photography

Nepal: Mt. Everest by Paul Keel.
  This photograph shows the peak of Everest from part way up the slope. Use these questions for discussion:
1. Why do you think the photographer chose to position the photo so that Mt. Everest is in that particular spot? *Mt. Everest is in front so it*

looks even bigger, and by showing the other peaks, the photographer allows the viewer to compare its size.
2. How does Everest's peak compare with the other peaks in the photograph? *It is higher and more jagged, giving it a threatening appearance.*

next the last?" Finally we reach a place where we can see past the humps, and beyond them is the great open sky and brown plains. We are looking down the far side of the mountain upon Tibet. Ahead of us now is only one more hump—the last hump. It is not a pinnacle. The way to it is an easy snow slope, wide enough for two men to go side by side. About thirty feet away we stop for a minute and look up. Then we go on. . . .

I have thought much about what I will say now: of how Hillary and I reached the summit of Everest. Later, when we came down from the mountain, there was much foolish talk about who got there first. Some said it was I, some Hillary. Some that only one of us got there—or neither. Still others that one of us had to drag the other up. All this was nonsense. And in Katmandu,[2] to put a stop to such talk Hillary and I signed a statement in which we said, "we reached the summit almost together." We hoped this would be the end of it. But it was not the end. People kept on asking questions and making up stories. They pointed to the "almost" and said, "What does that mean?" Mountaineers understand that there is no sense to such a question; that when two men are on the same rope they are *together*, and that is all there is to it. But other people did not understand. In India and Nepal, I am sorry to say, there has been great pressure on me to say that I reached the summit before Hillary. And all over the world I am asked, "Who got there first? Who got there first?"

Again I say: it is a foolish question. The answer means nothing. And yet it is a question that has been asked so often—that has caused so much talk and doubt and misunderstanding—that I feel, after long thought, that the answer must be given. As will be clear, it is not for my own sake that I give it. Nor is it for Hillary's. It is for the sake of Everest—the prestige of Everest—and for the generations who will come after us. "Why," they will say, "should there be a mystery to

◆ **Literary Focus**
Which details indicate that the account is told from Norgay's perspective?

this thing? Is there something to be ashamed of? To be hidden? Why can we not know the truth?" . . . Very well: now they will know the truth. Everest is too great, too precious, for anything but the truth.

A little below the summit Hillary and I stopped. We looked up. Then we went on. The rope that joined us was thirty feet long, but I held most of it in loops in my hand, so that there was only about six feet between us. I was not thinking of "first" and "second." I did not say to myself, "There is a golden apple up there. I will push Hillary aside and run for it." We went on slowly, steadily. And then we were there. Hillary stepped on top first. And I stepped up after him.

So there it is: the answer to the "great mystery." And if, after all the talk and argument, the answer seems quiet and simple, I can only say that that is as it should be. Many of my own people, I know, will be disappointed at it. They have given a great and false importance to the idea that it must be I who was "first." These people have been good and wonderful to me, and I owe them much. But I owe more to Everest—and to the truth. If it is a discredit to me that I was a step behind Hillary, then I must live with that discredit. But I do not think it was that. Nor do I think that, in the end, it will bring discredit on me that I tell the story. Over and over again I have asked myself, "What will future generations think of us if we allow the facts of our achievement to stay shrouded in mystery? Will they not feel ashamed of us—two comrades in life and death—who have something to hide from the world?" And each time I asked it the answer was the same: "Only the truth is good enough for the future. Only the truth is good enough for Everest."

Now the truth is told. And I am ready to be judged by it.

We stepped up. We were there. The dream had come true. . . .

What we did first was what all climbers do when they reach the top of their mountain. We shook hands. But this was not enough for Everest. I waved my arms in the air and then threw them around Hillary, and we thumped each other on the back until, even with the

2. **Katmandu** (kät´män dōō´): Capital of Nepal.

The Dream Comes True ◆ 39

◆ **Literary Focus**

❹ **Author's Perspective** This account of who reached the top of Everest first describes Norgay's thoughts on the matter and reflects Norgay's feelings about the mountain.

◆ **Critical Thinking**

❺ **Draw Conclusions** Ask students why Norgay feels it is important to tell the truth about what happened at the summit. *He respects the mountain and feels its greatness deserves a truthful account.*

◆ **Literary Focus**

❻ **Author's Perspective** Have students summarize Norgay's view of the issue. *Norgay states that Hillary stepped first on the peak of Everest. He feels that it's important that everyone know the truth, regardless of how people will receive it.*

◆◆◆ **Beyond the Classroom**

Career Connection

Guides Tenzing Norgay worked as a guide for mountain climbers in the Himalayas. He was suited for the work because he knew the mountains and their dangers and he was accustomed to living at high altitudes. Many people who love the outdoors hold jobs as guides in the United States. Some take people on adventurous treks, such as river rafting, rock climbing, or sailing. Others lead hunting or fishing parties in wilder-

ness areas. Still others conduct nature walks, pointing out wildflowers, birds, and trees. Interested students can research what a guide needs to know and what training would benefit a guide. They can explore the organizations that employ guides, such as the National Park Service and private and local organizations, and learn what each type of organization requires of its guides.

◀ **Critical Viewing** How does this image reflect the climbers' triumph? **1** [Connect]

oxygen, we were almost breathless. Then we looked around. It was eleven-thirty in the morning, the sun was shining, and the sky was the deepest blue I have ever seen. Only a gentle breeze was blowing, coming from the direction of Tibet, and the plume of snow that always blows from Everest's summit was very small. Looking down the far side of the mountain, I could see all the familiar landmarks from the earlier expeditions: the Rongbuk Monastery, the town of Shekar Dzong, the Kharta Valley, the Rongbuk and East Rongbuk Glaciers, the North Col, the place near the northeast ridge where we had made Camp Six in 1938. Then, turning, I looked down the long way we ourselves had come: past the south summit, the long ridge, the South Col; onto the Western Cwm, the icefall, the Khumbu Glacier; all the way down to Thyangboche and on to the valleys and hills of my homeland.

Beyond them, and around us on every side, were the great Himalayas, stretching away through Nepal and Tibet. For the closer peaks—giants like Lhotse, Nuptse and Makalu—you now had to look sharply downward to see their summits. And farther away, the whole sweep of the greatest range on earth—even Kangchenjunga[3] itself—seemed only like little bumps under the spreading sky. It was such a sight as I had never

3. **Kangchenjunga** (kän´ chen jσσn´ gə): Third highest mountain in the world, lies near Mount Everest.

40 ◆ *On the Edge*

seen before and would never see again: wild, wonderful and terrible. But terror was not what I felt. I loved the mountains too well for that. I loved Everest too well. At that great moment for which I had waited all my life my mountain did not seem to me a lifeless thing of rock and ice, but warm and friendly and living. She was a mother hen, and the other mountains were chicks under her wings. I too, I felt, had only to spread my own wings to cover and shelter the brood that I loved.

We turned off our oxygen. Even there on top of the world it was possible to live without it, so long as we were not exerting ourselves. We cleared away the ice that had formed on our masks, and I popped a bit of sweet into my mouth. Then we replaced the masks. But we did not turn on the oxygen again until we were ready to leave the top. Hillary took out his camera, which he had been carrying under his clothing to keep it from freezing, and I unwound the four flags from around my ax. They were tied together on a string, which was fastened to the blade of the ax, and now I held the ax up and Hillary took my picture. Actually he took three, and I think it was lucky, in those difficult conditions, that one came out so well. The order of the flags from top to bottom was United Nations, British, Nepalese, Indian; and the same sort of people who have made trouble in other ways have tried to find political meaning in this too. All I can say is that on Everest I was not thinking about politics. If I had been, I suppose I would have put the Indian or Nepalese flag highest—though that in itself would have been a bad problem for me. As it is, I am glad that the U.N. flag was on top. For I like to think that our victory was not only for ourselves—not only for our own nations—but for all men everywhere.

Guide for Responding

◆ Literature and Your Life

Reader's Response Whose account of climbing Everest was more appealing to you—Hillary's or Norgay's? Why?

Thematic Focus Hillary and Norgay spent many years preparing themselves mentally and physically for the climb of their lives. Discuss ways in which you prepare yourself—mentally and physically—for a challenging task.

Role Play With a partner, take turns role-playing a conversation with Tenzing Norgay. Ask him questions about his preparation and attitude and how they helped him conquer Everest. Also, ask his advice on how you can prepare yourself for challenges you face.

☑ Check Your Comprehension

1. What qualities does Norgay possess that helped contribute to his success?
2. Who does Norgay say reached the summit first?
3. What do Norgay and Hillary do when they reach the top of Everest?

◆ Critical Thinking

INTERPRET

1. Why is Norgay so bothered by the comparison Hillary makes between Norgay and a "giant fish"? **[Connect]**
2. (a) Why do you think Norgay is so concerned with the "prestige of Everest"? (b) What does he mean by "Everest and the truth"? **[Analyze]**

EVALUATE

3. Norgay calls Hillary his friend at the beginning of this excerpt. Do you think that was a sincere compliment? Why or why not? **[Evaluate]**
4. What does Norgay's account of the Everest ascent reveal about the two men? **[Draw Conclusions]**

The Dream Comes True ◆ 41

Reinforce and Extend

Answers

◆ Literature and Your Life

Reader's Response Some students might answer Hillary's because it was more detailed about the climb itself. Others might prefer Norgay's.

Thematic Focus Some students might say they prepare themselves for a challenge by working out and getting into shape, or by studying if their challenge is some kind of test.

☑ Check Your Comprehension

1. He possesses determination, courage, patriotism, and a great love for Everest.
2. Norgay said that Hillary stepped up first.
3. They shake hands, pat each other on the back, and then remove their oxygen.

◆ Critical Thinking

1. One acceptable answer is Norgay is so upset because he considered himself Hillary's equal climbing partner.
2. (a) He is concerned with the "prestige of Everest" because he grew up in the foothills of Everest and wants to preserve its mystique. (b) He wants the truth to be known about who stepped up first to put an end to the questions and also to assert that it is an insignificant matter.
3. Some students might suggest that Norgay believed Hillary to be his friend and that is why he was so hurt by his account of Everest.
4. Norgay's account reveals that there was tension between the two men.

Beyond the Selection

FURTHER READING

Other Works by Hillary and Norgay
High Adventure, Sir Edmund Hillary
After Everest, Tenzing Norgay

Other Works About Reaching the Top
The Shining Mountain: Two Men on Changabang's West Wall, Peter Boardman
The Spirit of St. Louis, Charles A. Lindbergh
Into Thin Air, Jon Krakauer
We suggest that you preview these works before recommending them to students.

INTERNET

You and your students may find additional information about these authors and Mt. Everest on the Internet. We suggest the following sites. Please be aware, however, that sites may have changed from the time we published this information. For wonderful photographs and a guide to what it feels like to climb Mt. Everest, go to **http://www.1997everest.com/**
We *strongly recommend* that you preview the site before you send students to it.

◆ Reading Strategy

1. Hillary states a fact that he found oxygen tanks, and an opinion that Norgay was in distress during the climb. Norgay states the fact that Hillary was the first to reach the summit and the opinion that it is not important who reached the top first.
2. It is an opinion because it cannot be proven.
3. The two men have different accounts of whether or not Norgay was in distress as he climbed, and on whether or not they were equal partners.

◆ Literary Focus

1. Hillary's account includes these details: Norgay was an "inexpert step cutter"; Norgay was in "considerable distress" toward the end of the climb; Norgay had no idea why finding the oxygen tanks is positive.
2. Norgay's account includes (1) that he and Hillary were equal partners and that Hillary could not have climbed Everest alone; (2) that it is not important who reached the summit first; it was still a joint effort.
3. Hillary's excitement is more controlled and internal, while Norgay shows more joy.
4. Someone who was not involved would have a broader perspective—perhaps focusing on the challenge of the environment rather than on either climber's views.

◆ Build Vocabulary

Using the Word Root -voc-
1. vocal: of or pertaining to the voice
2. vocabulary: the words a person knows and uses
3. vocalist: singer

Using the Word Bank
1. b   2. a   3. a   4. c   5. b   6. c

Guide for Responding (continued)

◆ Reading Strategy

DISTINGUISHING FACT FROM OPINION

Norgay and Hillary include many **facts**—statements that can be proven—in their accounts of the climb up Everest. They also include their **opinions**, statements that can be supported but not proved. For instance, Norgay supports his statement that Hillary was not quite fair with examples from Hillary's writing. However, since the statement cannot be proved true or false by evidence, it is an opinion.

1. Identify one fact and one opinion that each climber states about the other.
2. Hillary calls Norgay "an inexpert but enthusiastic step cutter." Explain whether this statement is a fact or an opinion.
3. List two examples of the writers' different opinions about the same events.

◆ Literary Focus

AUTHOR'S PERSPECTIVE

Like most nonfiction works, "The Final Assault" and "The Dream Comes True" are each told from one **author's perspective**—the presentation of events that reflects the author's personal outlook and recollection of the experience. For example, from Hillary's perspective, Norgay often struggled and needed Hillary's help during their ascent of Everest. However, from Norgay's perspective, the climbers helped each other equally.

1. List three details in the account told from Hillary's perspective that are not included in the account told from Norgay's perspective.
2. List two details in the account told from Norgay's perspective that are not included in the account told from Hillary's perspective.
3. Compare the two writers' perspectives on the final moment of the climb—reaching the summit.
4. In what ways might an account of Hillary and Norgay's expedition written by someone who was not involved in the expedition be different from these first-person accounts?

◆ Build Vocabulary

USING THE ROOT -voc-

The root -voc- means "speak" or "say." Define each of these words. Explain how the definition of each word is related to "speaking" or "saying."

1. vocal   2. vocabulary   3. vocalist

USING THE WORD BANK

Write the letter of the word that is the best synonym, or closest meaning, of the first word.
1. precipitous: (a) rainy, (b) steep, (c) noisy
2. discernible: (a) visible, (b) agreeable, (c) ornery
3. belay: (a) support, (b) hindrance, (c) alcove
4. encroaching: (a) growing, (b) helping, (c) invading
5. undulations: (a) holes, (b) waves, (c) shivers
6. vociferous: (a) timid, (b) uneventful, (c) loud

◆ Build Grammar Skills

COMPOUND PREDICATES

A **compound predicate** consists of two or more verbs or verb phrases that share the same subject and are joined by a conjunction.

Practice On your paper, copy the following sentences. Then write S over each subject and V over each verb in the compound predicates.
1. Hillary chipped away at ice, secured his rope support, and hoisted himself up to the next level.
2. Making their way up the mountain, they sometimes slid back, sometimes changed leads, and always hoped they would conquer Everest.
3. Norgay checked his oxygen level, paused to adjust his backpack, and then trudged on.

Writing Application Combine the following sentences, using compound predicates.
1. Hillary and Norgay cleared away ice and rocks. They pitched a tent. They prepared their gear for the following day.
2. Hillary waited for Norgay to catch his breath. He also helped him secure his oxygen mask. Then Hillary paved a trail for Norgay to follow.

◆ Build Grammar Skills

1. *Subject:* Hillary; *verbs:* chipped, secured, hoisted
2. *Subject:* they; *verbs:* slid, changed, hoped
3. *Subject:* Norgay; *verbs:* checked, paused, trudged

Writing Application

1. Hillary and Norgay cleared away ice and rocks, pitched their tent, and prepared their gear for the following day.
2. Hillary waited for Norgay to catch his breath, helped him secure his oxygen mask, and paved a trail for Norgay to follow.

✎ Writer's Solution

For additional instruction and practice, use the lesson in the **Language Lab CD-ROM** on Subject and Verb Agreement and the pages on Subjects and Verbs (pp. 26–29) in the *Writer's Solution Grammar Practice Book.*

Build Your Portfolio

 ## Idea Bank

Writing

1. **Book Jacket** Write a summary for the back-cover of either Hillary's or Norgay's book. Highlight a gripping scene or suspenseful moment to entice your readers to read the book.

2. **Article on Everest** Write a newspaper article about the first successful Everest climb based on what you learned from Hillary's and Norgay's accounts. Include an attention-grabbing headline.

3. **Mountain's Eye View** Write a description of what you think the world looks like from the top of Everest based on the descriptions you read about in the selections.

Speaking and Listening

4. **Advice for Future Climbers** Drawing from the details in one or both of the selections, prepare a brief talk in which you provide advice to aspiring climbers. Present your talk to the class.

5. **Oral Report** Using information in these selections and facts that you gather through research, prepare and present a brief oral report on an aspect of mountain climbing. **[Science Link]**

Projects

6. **Everest Statistics** Create a chart illustrating some statistics related to Mount Everest. For example, how many people have attempted to climb it, and how many have succeeded? How many have died trying? **[Math Link]**

7. **Video Game Design** Design the graphics for a video game based on this story. Present your ideas in a series of sketches. Show what the game screens will look like, how the players will move, and where the hazards will be. **[Art Link]**

 ## Writing Mini-Lesson

Hall-of-Fame Placards

Choose your favorite sport—it doesn't have to be mountain climbing—and write **placards**—display cards that briefly describe a player's achievements, statistics, and accomplishment—for your favorite players. The following tip will help you indicate the time order of events.

Writing Skills Focus: Transitions to Show Time

When writing your placards, use **transitions to show time.** Transitional words that show time include *first, next, finally, before, after, later,* and *at the same time.*

Tenzing Norgay uses transitions to show what happened first and next as he recalls his famous climb:

> From the south summit we *first* had to go down a little. *Then* up, up, up.

As you draft, use transitions to show the order of events and achievements you jotted down in prewriting. Check for clear transitions when you revise.

Prewriting Begin by making individual lists for each athlete, recording his or her statistics, achievements, and any interesting anecdotes you may discover. Choose only the most significant statistics and facts and arrange them in time order.

Drafting As you draft each placard, be sure to write your facts and statistics using transitions to show time. For example, you might start by saying "First ___?___ did ___?___. Then ___?___. Finally ___?___ capped his career off with ___?___."

Revising Have a friend read your placards and see if the time relations are clear. If not, you may need to insert transitions where your readers may get confused.

 ## Idea Bank

Customizing for *Performance Levels*

Following are suggestions for matching Idea Bank topics with your students' performance levels:
- Less Advanced Students: 1, 4
- Average Students: 2, 4, 6, 7
- More Advanced Students: 3, 5

Customizing for *Learning Modalities*

Following are suggestions for matching Idea Bank topics with your students' learning modalities:
- Visual/Spatial: 3, 6, 7
- Verbal/Linguistic: 4, 5
- Logical/Mathematical: 6

 ## Writing Mini-Lesson

Refer students to the Writing Handbook, page 965, for instruction on the writing process, and page 967 for further information on description.

 ## Writer's Solution

Writers at Work Videodisc

Have students view the videodisc segment (Ch. 1) featuring Colleen McElroy to see some techniques for descriptive writing. Have students discuss the points McElroy makes about the elements of good description.

Play frames 335 to 9140

Writing Lab CD-ROM

Have students complete the tutorial on Description. Follow these steps:
1. Have students browse through the word bin for character trait words to use on their placards.
2. Have students draft on computer.
3. Invite pairs of students to answer the questions of a peer evaluation checklist to help them evaluate each other's placards.

Sourcebook

Have students use Chapter 1, Description (pp. 1–24), for additional support. The chapter includes an annotated student model of a remembrance (p. 24).

✓ ASSESSMENT OPTIONS

Formal Assessment, Selection Test, pp. 4–6, and Assessment Resources Software. The selection test is designed so that it can be easily customized to the performance levels of your students.
Alternative Assessment, p. 2, includes options for less advanced students, more advanced students, logical/mathematical learners, visual/spatial learners, bodily/kinesthetic learners, and intrapersonal learners.

PORTFOLIO ASSESSMENT
Use the following rubrics in the **Alternative Assessment** booklet to assess student writing:
Book Jacket: Process Summary Rubric, p. 98
Article on Everest: Description Rubric, p. 97
Mountain's Eye View: Description Rubric, p. 97
Writing Mini-Lesson: Description Rubric, p. 97

Guide for Reading

1. To read, comprehend, and interpret a story
2. To relate a story to personal experience
3. To predict outcomes in a story and poem
4. To identify foreshadowing
5. To build vocabulary in context and learn the word root -cred-
6. To develop skill in using regular and irregular verb forms
7. To write a yearbook prediction using transitions to show cause and effect
8. To respond to the story through writing, speaking and listening, and projects

SKILLS INSTRUCTION

Vocabulary:
Word Roots: cred-

Grammar:
Regular and Irregular Verb Forms

Literary Focus:
Foreshadowing

Reading Strategy:
Predict Outcomes

Writing:
Transitions to Show Cause and Effect

Speaking and Listening:
Television Interview (teacher edition)

Critical Viewing:
Infer

PORTFOLIO OPPORTUNITIES

Writing: Newspaper Headlines; Warning Label; Paw Proposal

Writing Mini-Lesson: Yearbook Prediction

Speaking and Listening: Television Interview; Dramatic Monologue

Projects: A Monkey's Paw Poll; Poster Showing Fortuna

More About the Authors

Although **W. W. Jacobs** is most often remembered today for his horror classic "The Monkey's Paw," in his own time, he was considered a master of the humorous story. Like "The Monkey's Paw," his comic tales frequently had surprise endings, catching readers off-guard and provoking unexpected laughter.

Alexander Pushkin's ideas were considered so dangerous that Czar Nicholas I himself served as the censor of Pushkin's work.

W. W. Jacobs *(1863–1943)*

As a boy, W. W. Jacobs traveled around the world without ever leaving his home in London, England. He didn't travel via the Internet or even by reading about other places. Instead, he soaked up tales of adventure told by sailors he met at the dockside house where he lived with his father.

The tales that Jacobs heard as a child shaped the stories he wrote as an adult—stories in which everyday life is disrupted by strange and fantastic events.

"The Monkey's Paw" is his most famous tale of suspense and the supernatural. First published in 1902, it was made into a successful one-act play a year later.

One reason for the story's popularity is that it hardly seems like a story that someone wrote. It is more like an age-old tale made up by no one in particular and told around a campfire at night.

Alexander Pushkin *(1799–1837)*

This father of modern Russian literature is more like an adventurous teenager than a settled "father." Although born into the nobility, he had great sympathy for poor Russian peasants and criticized the absolute power and corruption of the government. His dangerous opinions and friendships got him banished to a remote part of Russia and later to his family's estate.

In literature, too, he was a rebel. His poems express his democratic ideas and draw on themes from folklore, the oral literature of the people. "The Bridegroom," for example, is like a literary version of a song passed on by word of mouth.

Pushkin's own death was like an incident from a folk tale or ballad. Resettled in the capital city of St. Petersburg, he was as hotheaded as ever and died after being wounded in a duel.

◆ Build Vocabulary

WORD ROOTS: -cred-

In "The Monkey's Paw," a character smiles "shamefacedly at his own credulity." The meaning of the word root -cred- is "believe"; *credulity* means "a tendency to believe something too quickly."

WORD BANK

doughty
maligned
credulity
prosaic
avaricious
furtively
fusillade
foreboding
tumult

As you read these selections, you will encounter the words on this list. Each word is defined on the page where it first appears. Preview the list before you read.

◆ Build Grammar Skills

REGULAR AND IRREGULAR VERB FORMS

A verb has four basic forms known as principal parts: the present (also known as the infinitive), the present participle, the past, and the past participle. All verbs form the present participle by adding -ing to the present form. **Regular** verbs form their past and past participles by adding -d or -ed to the present form. Other verbs are **irregular**; they form their past and past participles in some other way.

Regular: ...the fire *burned* brightly

Irregular: ...said Mr. White, the old man *rose* ...

It is important to know the irregular forms so that you can use them correctly.

 Prentice Hall Literature Program Resources

REINFORCE / RETEACH / EXTEND

Selection Support
Build Vocabulary: Word Roots: -cred-, p. 10
Build Grammar Skills: Regular and Irregular Verb Forms, p. 11
Reading Strategy: Predict Outcomes, p. 12
Literary Focus: Foreshadowing, p. 13

Strategies for Diverse Student Needs, p. 3.

Beyond Literature
Cross-Curricular Connection: Community Action, p. 3

Formal Assessment Selection Test, pp. 7–9; Assessment Resources Software

Alternative Assessment, p. 3

Writing and Language Transparencies
Daily Language Practice Week 2, p. 113

Resource Pro CD-ROM
"The Monkey's Paw"—includes all resource materials and customizable lesson plan

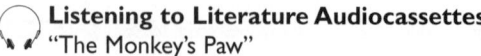 **Listening to Literature Audiocassettes**
"The Monkey's Paw"

The Monkey's Paw ◆ The Bridegroom

◆ Literature and Your Life

CONNECT YOUR EXPERIENCE

Fate, chance, and *luck* are words that hint at mysterious forces out of your control. Your team, for example, might seem fated to win a championship, as if the result were written down beforehand.

Choice, will, and *determination* are opposite kinds of words. They suggest that you can control the outcome of events. If you're losing in any situation, the answer is to get determined, figure out the problems, and make some choices.

The characters in this story and poem believe that they *can* choose the future. You'll soon see whether or not they get the future they choose.

Journal Writing Describe a situation whose outcome seemed to be decided by fate, luck, or chance. Then describe a situation that you influenced through your own choices.

THEMATIC FOCUS: DARING DECISIONS

This story and poem will help you think about the power you have to influence events.

◆ Background for Understanding

CULTURE

The concept of fate—a force that determines the outcome of events before they occur—plays a key role in "The Monkey's Paw." Ancient peoples sometimes worshiped fate in the form of one or more goddesses. The ancient Greeks, for example, pictured fate as three goddesses, weavers of human destiny: Clotho (klō´ thō), who spun the thread of life; Lachesis (lak´ i sis), who measured it out; and Atropos (a´ trə päs), who cut it.

◆ Literary Focus

FORESHADOWING

Writers determine the outcome of *all* the events in the little worlds they create. They keep you interested in what will happen by giving you hints, called **foreshadowing**, of future events. If you find these hints, you'll have the fun of almost knowing what the future will bring.

To find the foreshadowing in "The Monkey's Paw," listen more carefully than the White family does to the sergeant major's tale. In reading "The Bridegroom," find clues to future events in Natasha's changing reactions to her suitor.

◆ Reading Strategy

PREDICT OUTCOMES

You can use a writer's hints at future events to **predict outcomes** or to make educated guesses about what will happen in a story or poem. Your predictions will keep you involved in the world the author creates as you read on to see whether you were correct.

In predicting the outcome of "The Monkey's Paw," remember that warnings sometimes turn out to be true—even if characters disregard them. To figure out what will happen in "The Bridegroom," think about who is coming to Natasha's wedding. One guest is a clue to her plans.

As you read, jot down predictions in a chart like this one. Note predictions in one column and the actual outcome in the other.

Predictions	Actual Outcome

Engage your students' attention by writing these story details on the chalkboard:

Who: An elderly man and wife and their son.

Where: An isolated house near a factory.

What: A guest carries a monkey's paw in his pocket.

Invite volunteers to tell impromptu scary stories using and embellishing these details. Urge students to notice as they read how W. W. Jacobs uses the same details in "The Monkey's Paw."

(You could try the same with these details from "The Bridegroom":
Who: A young, unmarried woman.
Where: A village in Russia years ago.
What: A mysterious bridegroom comes to claim the young woman.)

Customize for
Less Proficient Readers
To help less proficient readers through "The Monkey's Paw," have them follow along in their text as they listen to the recording of the selection. "The Bridegroom" can be a mystifying poem, at first reading. Pair students up to try to make sense of it together by questioning reasons for characters' words and actions.

 Listening to Literature Audiocassettes

Customize for
More Advanced Students
Foreshadowing plays an important role in "The Monkey's Paw." Invite these students to imagine they are directing a movie version of the story. Have them meet in a group to discuss which moments of foreshadowing they consider the most important in the story and how would they capture those moments on film.

Customize for
English Language Learners
The long dialogue scene that opens "The Monkey's Paw" offers an opportunity for developing oral reading skills in a natural way. Organize groups of three to read the scene aloud. Include at least one native speaker in each group.

Preparing for Standardized Tests

Grammar and Language Alert students to the fact that portions of standardized tests may call on them to be able to recognize errors in the use of regular or irregular verbs. For example, students might be given a passage such as the following and asked to identify the underlined portion that contains an error.

It was one of the greatest disasters that anyone
                (A)   (B)
could remember. By the time the fire had ended,
                        (C)

twenty buildings had burnt to the ground.
        (D)   (E)

Before introducing the Build Grammar Skills lesson, write the passage on the board. Lead students to see that the correct answer is *(E)*, because *burn* is a regular verb with a past participle of *burned*. For additional practice, use the Build Grammar Skills page on Regular and Irregular Verb Forms (p. 11) in **Selection Support**.

⏱ **One-Minute Insight** "The Monkey's Paw" is a chilling version of the "three-wishes" tale told the world over. Like many renditions of the tale, it offers lessons in morality, but it distinguishes itself from other three-wishes tales through its aura of terror and suspense. Students will be taken on an emotional roller-coaster ride as the Whites are pushed to the brink of desperation, trying to reverse their wish and bring their son back from the dead.

❶ **Clarification** Explain that "Hark at the wind" is a British phrase meaning "listen to the wind." Remind students that the author was British. Then point out that the story is set in England around 1900 and that students will encounter other British words and phrases throughout.

◆ **Reading Strategy**

❷ **Predict Outcomes** Elicit responses like the following: *The gloomy setting suggests that something unpleasant might happen. The eerie isolation of the Whites' house further hints that the family may become cut off from society or parted from one another.*

◆ **Critical Thinking**

❸ **Infer** Ask students: What is the meaning behind the knowing glance between the mother and son? *The mother and son are acknowledging that the mother has just humored Mr. White. She has assumed his diatribe was set off by his failure to win at chess.*

❹ **Clarification** "Tut" is a sound made by sucking in breath and is an expression of disapproval or disbelief. Ask students: What is Mrs. White expressing disapproval about? *She's probably expressing disapproval that the new arrival is complaining about the weather and road conditions to an unnecessary degree.*

❺ **Clarification** India was a colony of Great Britain from the late 1770's to 1947. See the Cross-Curricular Connection on page 48.

The Monkey's Paw

W. W. Jacobs

I

Without, the night was cold and wet, but in the small parlor of Laburnum Villa the blinds were drawn and the fire burned brightly. Father and son were at chess, the former, who possessed ideas about the game involving radical changes, putting his king into such sharp and unnecessary perils that it even provoked comment from the white-haired old lady knitting placidly by the fire.

"Hark at the wind," said Mr. White, who, having seen a fatal mistake after it was too late, was amiably desirous of preventing his son from seeing it.

"I'm listening," said the latter, grimly surveying the board as he stretched out his hand. "Check."[1]

I should hardly think that he'd come tonight," said his father, with his hand poised over the board.

"Mate,"[2] replied the son.

"That's the worst of living so far out," bawled Mr. White, with sudden and unlooked-for violence; "of all the beastly, slushy, out-of-the-way places to live in, this is the worst. Pathway's a bog, and the road's a torrent. I don't know what people are thinking about. I suppose because only two houses on the road are let, they think it doesn't matter."

"Never mind, dear," said his wife, soothingly; "perhaps you'll win the next one."

Mr. White looked up sharply, just in time to intercept a knowing glance between mother and son. The words died away on his lips, and

◆ **Reading Strategy**
What predictions can you make about this story based on the gloomy setting?

1. **check** *n.*: Chess move that threatens to capture the king.
2. **mate** *n.*: Checkmate, a chess move in which the king is captured and the game is over.

46 ◆ On the Edge

he hid a guilty grin in his thin gray beard.

"There he is," said Herbert White, as the gate banged to loudly and heavy footsteps came toward the door.

The old man rose with hospitable haste, and opening the door, was heard condoling with the new arrival. The new arrival also condoled with himself, so that Mrs. White said, "Tut, tut!" and coughed gently as her husband entered the room, followed by a tall, burly man, beady of eye and rubicund of visage.[3]

"Sergeant Major Morris," he said, introducing him.

The sergeant major shook hands, and taking the proffered seat by the fire, watched contentedly while his host got out tumblers and stood a small copper kettle on the fire.

At the third glass his eyes got brighter, and he began to talk, the little family circle regarding with eager interest this visitor from distant parts, as he squared his broad shoulders in the chair and spoke of wild scenes and doughty deeds; of wars and plagues and strange peoples.

"Twenty-one years of it," said Mr. White, nodding at his wife and son. "When he went away he was a slip of a youth in the warehouse. Now look at him."

"He don't look to have taken much harm," said Mrs. White, politely.

"I'd like to go to India myself," said the old man, "just to look round a bit, you know."

"Better where you are," said the sergeant major, shaking his head. He put down the empty glass, and sighing softly, shook it again.

3. **rubicund** (roo′ bi kund′) **of visage** (viz′ ij) *adj.*: Having a red complexion.

◆ **Build Vocabulary**
doughty (dout′ ē) *adj.*: Brave; valiant

Block Scheduling Strategies

Consider these suggestions to take advantage of extended class time:

• After students have completed the journal activity in Literature and Your Life and read the Background for Understanding (see page 45), have a brief class discussion about the concept of fate. Elicit opinions about the role of fate in our lives.

• Use the Daily Language Practice sentences for Week 2, on page 118 of *Writing and Language Transparencies.*

• Encourage interested students to locate British

words and phrases in the story and provide their American English equivalents. Examples include: "at chess," "hark at the wind," "only two houses on the road are let," and so on.

• Have students complete the Writing Mini-Lesson on page 59.

• Challenge motivated students to explore the Internet for Web sites with information about classic horror stories. Ask your Internet researchers to share what they've learned with the class.

The Monkey's Paw ♦ 47

▶Critical Viewing◀

Infer Ask students to determine the attitude of each character toward the monkey's paw, based on the expression on his or her face in this illustration. *Mrs. White appears to be skeptical; Mr. White seems interested, as he was interested in the exotic aspects of India; Herbert seems to be a little aloof and disinterested; and Sergeant Major Morris seems to have a knowing, almost warning, attitude.*

Enrichment The number three is prevalent in tales from all over the world. Whether it is three wishes, three bears, or three musketeers, the number three seems to have a special significance in the beliefs and superstitions of various cultures. To some, three represents father, mother, and child—meaning life itself. To others, three represents the earth, the sea, and the sky—meaning the unity and harmony of nature. Still others believe the number to be unlucky—"Bad things happen in threes."

Have students offer additional examples of beliefs in threes. You might have them cooperatively explore the issue further. Assign small groups a part of the world to research for beliefs about the number three. For example, one group could explore stories from Africa, while another investigates stories from Asia.

47

❶ Clarification A fakir is someone who is believed to be able to cast spells and work wonders.

◆ Literary Focus

❷ Foreshadowing Ask students: How does this warning about fate foreshadow a possible disaster? *Sergeant Major Morris's words are a clear warning that interfering with fate by making wishes on the monkey's paw will bring unhappiness or misfortune.*

◆ *Literature and Your Life*

❸ Ask students to jot down what they would do with the three wishes. Encourage them to keep their lists and to look them over later in their reading to see if they would change them.

Customize for
Less Proficient Readers

Draw these students' attention to Sergeant Major Morris's warnings about the monkey's paw. Lead them to see that this is a key detail that they should consider when making predictions about the story's outcome.

"I should like to see those old temples and ❶ fakirs and jugglers," said the old man. "What was that you started telling me the other day about a monkey's paw or something, Morris?"

"Nothing," said the soldier, hastily. "Leastways nothing worth hearing."

"Monkey's paw?" said Mrs. White, curiously.

"Well, it's just a bit of what you might call magic, perhaps," said the sergeant major, offhandedly.

His three listeners leaned forward eagerly. The visitor absent-mindedly put his empty glass to his lips and then set it down again. His host filled it for him.

"To look at," said the sergeant major, fumbling in his pocket, "it's just an ordinary little paw, dried to a mummy."

He took something out of his pocket and proffered it. Mrs. White drew back with a grimace, but her son, taking it, examined it curiously.

"And what is there special about it?" inquired Mr. White as he took it from his son, and having examined it, placed it upon the table.

"It had a spell put on it by an old fakir," said the sergeant major, "a very holy man.

❷ "He wanted to show that fate ruled people's lives, and that those who interfered with it did so to their sorrow. He put a spell on it so that three separate men could each have three wishes from it."

His manner was so impressive that his hearers were conscious that their light laughter jarred somewhat.

"Well, why don't you have three, sir?" said Herbert White, cleverly.

The soldier regarded him in the way that middle age is wont to regard presumptuous youth. "I have," he said, quietly, and his blotchy face whitened.

"And did you really have the three wishes granted?" asked Mrs. White.

"I did," said the sergeant major, and his glass tapped against his strong teeth.

"And has anybody else wished?" persisted the old lady.

"The first man had his three wishes, yes,"

was the reply; "I don't know what the first two were, but the third was for death. That's how I got the paw."

His tones were so grave that a hush fell upon the group.

"If you've had your three wishes, it's no good to you now, then, Morris," said the old man at last. "What do you keep it for?"

The soldier shook his head. "Fancy, I suppose," he said, slowly. "I did have some idea of selling it, but I don't think I will. It has caused enough mischief already. Besides, people won't buy. They think it's a fairy tale, some of them, and those who do think anything of it want to try it first and pay me afterward."

"If you could have another three wishes," said the old man, eyeing him keenly, "would you have them?"

"I don't know, said the other. "I don't know."

He took the paw, and dangling it between his forefinger and thumb, suddenly threw it upon the fire. White, with a slight cry, stooped down and snatched it off.

"Better let it burn," said the soldier, solemnly.

"If you don't want it, Morris," said the other, "give it to me."

"I won't," said his friend doggedly. "I threw it on the fire. If you keep it, don't blame me for what happens. Pitch it on the fire again, like a sensible man."

The other shook his head and examined his new possession closely. "How do you do it?" he inquired.

"Hold it up in your right hand and wish aloud," said the sergeant major, "but I warn you of the consequences."

"Sounds like the *Arabian Nights*,"[4] said Mrs. White, as she rose and began to set the supper. "Don't you think you might wish for four pairs of hands for me?"

Her husband drew the talisman from his pocket, and then all three burst into laughter

◆ *Literature and Your Life*
How would you change the future if you could have three wishes?

❸

---

4. *Arabian Nights*: Collection of stories from the ancient Near East.

Cross-Curricular Connection: Social Studies

From the late 1700's until it became an independent nation in 1947, India was a colony of Great Britain. Because India's culture was so different from that of England, the English had a great fascination with India. During the colonial period, many British government officials and soldiers—like Sergeant Major Morris in "The Monkey's Paw"—lived and worked in India. Through letters and visits back home, these officials and soldiers passed on information—and misinformation—

about India to their fellow British citizens. Before long, India became a symbol of the mysterious and exotic. Its reputation for mystery and magic is suggested in "The Monkey's Paw" when Mr. White says, "I should like to see those old temples and fakirs and jugglers." Have students discuss the connection between India's reputation and the Whites' fascination with and belief in the monkey's paw.

as the sergeant major, with a look of alarm on his face, caught him by the arm. "If you must wish," he said, gruffly, "wish for something sensible."

Mr. White dropped it back in his pocket, and placing chairs, motioned his friend to the table. In the business of supper the talisman was partly forgotten, and afterward the three sat listening in an enthralled fashion to a second installment of the soldier's adventures in India.

"If the tale about the monkey's paw is not more truthful than those he has been telling us," said Herbert, as the door closed behind their guest, just in time for him to catch the last train, "we shan't make much out of it."

"Did you give him anything for it, Father?" inquired Mrs. White, regarding her husband closely.

"A trifle," said he, coloring slightly. "He didn't want it, but I made him take it. And he pressed me again to throw it away."

4 "Likely," said Herbert, with pretended horror. "Why, we're going to be rich, and famous and happy. Wish to be an emperor, Father, to begin with; then you can't be bossed around."

He darted round the table, pursued by the <u>maligned</u> Mrs. White armed with an antimacassar.[5]

5 Mr. White took the paw from his pocket and eyed it dubiously. "I don't know what to wish for, and that's a fact," he said, slowly. "It seems to me I've got all I want."

"If you only cleared the house, you'd be quite happy, wouldn't you?" said Herbert, with his hand on his shoulder. "Well, wish for two hundred pounds,[6] then; that'll just do it."

His father, smiling shamefacedly at his own <u>credulity</u>, held up the talisman, as his son, with a solemn face somewhat marred by a wink at his mother, sat down at the piano and struck a few impressive chords.

"I wish for two hundred pounds," said the old man distinctly.

A fine crash from the piano greeted the words, interrupted by a shuddering cry from the old man. His wife and son ran toward him.

"It moved," he cried, with a glance of disgust at the object as it lay on the floor. "As I wished it twisted in my hand like a snake."

"Well, I don't see the money," said his son as he picked it up and placed it on the table, "and I bet I never shall."

"It must have been your fancy, Father," said his wife, regarding him anxiously.

He shook his head. "Never mind, though; there's no harm done, but it gave me a shock all the same."

They sat down by the fire again while the two men finished their pipes. Outside, the wind was higher than ever, and the old man started nervously at the sound of a door banging upstairs. A silence unusual and depressing settled upon all three, which lasted until the old couple rose to retire for the night.

"I expect you'll find the cash tied up in a big bag in the middle of your bed," said Herbert, as he bade them good night, "and something horrible squatting up on top of the wardrobe watching you as you pocket your ill-gotten gains."

Herbert sat alone in the darkness, gazing at the dying fire, and seeing faces in it. The last face was so horrible and so simian[7] that he gazed at it in amazement. It got so vivid that, with a little uneasy laugh, he felt on the table for a glass containing a little water to throw over it. His hand grasped the monkey's paw, and with a little shiver he wiped his hand on his coat and went up to bed.

---

7. **simian** *adj.*: Monkeylike.

◆ **Build Vocabulary**

maligned (mə līnd´) *adj.*: Spoken ill of

credulity (krə dōō´ lə tē) *n.*: Tendency to believe too readily

---

5. **antimacassar** (an´ ti mə kas´ ər) *n.*: Small cover on the arms or back of a chair or sofa to prevent soiling.
6. **pounds** *n.*: English money.

The Monkey's Paw ◆ 49

Beyond the Classroom

Career Connection

Armed Services In this tale, Sergeant Major Morris is a soldier who has served in the British armed forces in India. Some readers might say that the formal and informal education Morris gained by traveling the world in service to his country has made him the worldliest and wisest character in the story.

Ask interested students to research the armed services of the United States and the career and educational opportunities they offer. Encourage students to use the Internet and to investigate the recruiting offices in your area. Ask these students to share their findings with the class.

Community Connection

Streets and Highways Remind students that Mr. White complains about the conditions of the roads that lead to his house: "Pathway's a bog, and the road's a torrent."

Invite students to imagine they work for the department of streets and highways in your area. What problems and dangerous conditions can they identify? How can these conditions be improved? Encourage students to find out how local authorities ordinarily maintain roads and what they plan to do about the problems students have identified.

◆ Critical Thinking

❶ Analyze Ask students: What does this exchange among the three family members reveal about each one? *Mrs. White shows common sense. Herbert appears to be carefree and a little silly. Mr. White is gullible and hopes, almost blindly, that the monkey's paw will work.*

◆ Literary Focus

❷ Foreshadowing Point out that Mrs. White's remark referring to Herbert's remarks at dinner is an ironic foreshadowing. Ask students what it might foreshadow. *Some students may be able to guess that Herbert won't be home for dinner as the wish is fulfilled. If they are unable to see that outcome at this point, have them look back to this statement after they have completed reading this section.*

◆ Reading Strategy

❸ Predict Outcomes Possible answers from students include: *The stranger has bad news of some sort— perhaps about Sergeant Major Morris, Herbert, the monkey's paw, the Whites' house, or the money wished for.*

II

In the brightness of the wintry sun next morning as it streamed over the breakfast table Herbert laughed at his fears. There was an air of <u>prosaic</u> wholesomeness about the room which it had lacked on the previous night, and the dirty, shriveled little paw was pitched on the sideboard with a carelessness which betokened no great belief in its virtues.

"I suppose all old soldiers are the same," said Mrs. White. "The idea of our listening to such nonsense! How could wishes be granted in these days? And if they could, how could two hundred pounds hurt you, Father?"

"Might drop on his head from the sky," said the frivolous Herbert.

"Morris said the things happened so naturally," said his father, "that you might if you so wished attribute it to coincidence."

"Well, don't break into the money before I come back," said Herbert, as he rose from the table. "I'm afraid it'll turn you into a mean, <u>avaricious</u> man, and we shall have to disown you."

His mother laughed, and following him to the door, watched him down the road, and, returning to the breakfast table, was very happy at the expense of her husband's credulity. All of which did not prevent her from scurrying to the door at the postman's knock, nor prevent her from referring somewhat shortly to retired sergeant majors of bibulous habits when she found that the post brought a tailor's bill.

"Herbert will have some more of his funny remarks, I expect, when he comes home," she said, as they sat at dinner.

"I dare say," said Mr. White, "but for all that, the thing moved in my hand; that I'll swear to."

"You thought it did," said the old lady soothingly.

"I say it did," replied the other. "There was no thought about it; I had just—What's the matter?"

His wife made no reply. She was watching the mysterious movements of a man outside, who, peering in an undecided fashion at the house, appeared to be trying to make up his mind to enter. In mental connection with the

two hundred pounds, she noticed that the stranger was well dressed, and wore a silk hat of glossy newness. Three times he paused at the gate, and then walked on again. The fourth time he stood with his hand upon it, and then with sudden resolution flung it open and walked up the path. Mrs. White at the same moment placed her hands behind her, and hurriedly unfastening the strings of her apron, put that useful article of apparel beneath the cushion of her chair.

She brought the stranger, who seemed ill at ease, into the room. He gazed at her <u>furtively</u>, and listened in a preoccupied fashion as the old lady apologized for the appearance of the room, and her husband's coat, a garment which he usually reserved for the garden. She then waited patiently for him to broach his business, but he was at first strangely silent.

> ◆ **Reading Strategy** Predict why the stranger has come calling on the Whites.

"I—was asked to call," he said at last, and stooped and picked a piece of cotton from his trousers. "I come from 'Maw and Meggins.'"

The old lady started. "Is anything the matter?" she asked, breathlessly. "Has anything happened to Herbert? What is it? What is it?"

Her husband interposed. "There, there, mother," he said, hastily. "Sit down, and don't jump to conclusions. You've not brought bad news, I'm sure, sir," and he eyed the other wistfully.

"I'm sorry—" began the visitor.

"Is he hurt?" demanded the mother, wildly.

The visitor bowed in assent. "Badly hurt," he said quietly, "but he is not in any pain."

"Oh, thank God!" said the old woman, clasping her hands. "Thank God for that! Thank—"

She broke off suddenly as the sinister meaning of the assurance dawned upon her and she saw the awful confirmation of her fears in the

◆ Build Vocabulary

prosaic (prō zā′ ik) *adj.*: Commonplace; ordinary
avaricious (av′ ə rish′ əs) *adj.*: Greedy for riches
furtively (fʉr′ tiv lē) *adv.*: Secretly; stealthily

50 ◆ *On the Edge*

Speaking and Listening Mini-Lesson

Being Tactful

Introduce the Concept Remind students that the quality of tact is the ability to appreciate the delicacy of a situation and to do or say the most suitable thing. Invite a volunteer to read aloud the passage from "The Monkey's Paw" on page 50 that begins "She brought the stranger" and ends at the bottom of the page. Have them discuss whether or not the stranger showed tact in the way he announced the bad news.

Develop Background Through discussion, guide students to come up with a list of situations in which tact might be important and tactful approaches to each situation. Lists might include the following:

- When delivering negative criticism, also stress the positive of a situation.
- Deliver bad news in a sensitive and delicate way.

Apply the Information Ask students how they would use tact to deal with the

following situation: A classmate is not contributing to a team project in which all students will receive the same grade.

Form small groups to discuss the situation and come up with a tactful solution.

Assess the Outcome Use these questions to evaluate students' tactful solutions: Did they try to gain cooperation from the student without hurting his or her feelings? Did they make sure the student knew that his or her contribution would be valued?

other's averted face. She caught her breath, and turning to her husband, laid her trembling old hand upon his. There was a long silence.

"He was caught in the machinery," said the visitor at length, in a low voice.

"Caught in the machinery," repeated Mr. White, in a dazed fashion, "yes."

He sat staring blankly out at the window, and taking his wife's hand between his own, pressed it as he had been wont to do in their old courting days nearly forty years before.

"He was the only one left to us," he said, turning gently to the visitor. "It is hard."

The other coughed, and, rising, walked slowly to the window. "The firm wished me to convey their sincere sympathy with you in your great loss," he said, without looking round. "I beg that you will understand I am only their servant and merely obeying orders."

There was no reply; the old woman's face was white, her eyes staring, and her breath inaudible; on the husband's face was a look such as his friend the sergeant might have carried into his first action.

"I was to say that Maw and Meggins disclaim all responsibility," continued the other. "They admit no liability at all, but in consideration of your son's services they wish to present you with a certain sum as compensation."

Mr. White dropped his wife's hand, and rising to his feet, gazed with a look of horror at his visitor. His dry lips shaped the words, "How much?"

"Two hundred pounds," was the answer.

Unconscious of his wife's shriek, the old man smiled faintly, put out his hands like a sightless man, and dropped, a senseless heap, to the floor.

III

In the huge new cemetery, some two miles distant, the old people buried their dead, and came back to a house steeped in shadow and silence. It was all over so quickly that at first they could hardly realize it, and remained in a state of expectation as though of something else to happen—something else which was to lighten this load, too heavy for old hearts to bear.

But the days passed, and expectation gave place to resignation—the hopeless resignation of the old, sometimes miscalled apathy. Sometimes they hardly exchanged a word, for now they had nothing to talk about, and their days were long to weariness.

It was about a week after that the old man, waking suddenly in the night, stretched out his hand and found himself alone. The room was in darkness, and the sound of subdued weeping came from the window. He raised himself in bed and listened.

"Come back," he said, tenderly. "You will be cold."

"It is colder for my son," said the old woman, and wept afresh.

The sound of her sobs died away on his ears. The bed was warm, and his eyes heavy with sleep. He dozed fitfully, and then slept until a sudden wild cry from his wife awoke him with a start.

"The paw!" she cried wildly. "The monkey's paw!"

He started up in alarm. "Where? Where is it? What's the matter?"

She came stumbling across the room toward him. "I want it," she said quietly. "You've not destroyed it?"

"It's in the parlor, on the bracket," he replied, marveling. "Why?"

She cried and laughed together, and bending over, kissed his cheek.

The Monkey's Paw ◆ 51

◆ **Reading Strategy**

4 **Predict Outcomes** Ask students to review the predictions they had made about the stranger's news. How close did they come to predicting correctly, and on what did they base their predictions? *Some students may say they predicted the bad news would be about Herbert because Herbert was the only family member missing and because his mother had already alluded to his return.*

◆ *Literature and Your Life*

5 Ask students: After seeing Mr. White's wish come true in a horrible way, would you change your three wishes? How? *Students might revise their wishes to make them more inconsequential, or say they would rather not wish at all.*

◆ **Build Grammar Skills**

6 **Regular and Irregular Verb Forms** Have students identify the three verbs in this sentence. Ask students: What is the present tense of each verb? Which of the verbs is regular in form and which are irregular? *dozed/doze—regular; slept/sleep—irregular; awoke/awake—irregular*

Cultural Connection

Cultural Connection

The theme of wishing comes up again and again in the folk lore of different cultures. One common variation features characters who have three wishes and who use them so foolishly that in the end their lives do not change for the better. In a Jewish folk tale from Eastern Europe, a man is helped by a magical wishing ring, but he nearly dies when he reveals its existence to others. An Ancient Chinese tale tells of the mother of heaven who tries to grant everyone's wishes, but who only causes more problems.

Proverbs about wishing also reveal something of the culture from which they come. The French, for example, have the following saying: "After the act, wishing is in vain." The Italians say, "With wishing comes grieving." The Chinese warn, "Be careful what you wish for; you may get it."

Students might find more folk tales about wishing and speculate about why wishing is such a common theme.

◆ Literary Focus

1 Foreshadowing Elicit such responses as the following: *Because the result of the first wish was so disastrous, it seems likely that the results of the other wishes might be just as bad or worse. Or the following wishes might be more wisely made and successful now that the Whites know the danger of the monkey's paw.*

◆ Critical Thinking

2 Compare and Contrast Ask students: How have Mr. and Mrs. White's attitudes toward the monkey's paw changed since Sergeant Major Morris first introduced them to it? *Mrs. White now desperately believes in it, as Mr. White originally did; and Mr. White no longer wants to have anything to do with it.*

◆ Critical Thinking

3 Analyze What in this description creates suspense? *Suspense is created as the reader wonders whether wishing on the monkey's paw again can really bring Herbert back, and if he comes back, in what kind of condition he will be. Readers also wonder if Mr. White will really make the wish.*

◆ Critical Thinking

4 Infer Why would Mr. White be afraid of his wife? *He seems to fear her almost unnatural obsession with wishing on the monkey's paw as a way to bring their son back. He's afraid of what might really happen.*

◆ Critical Thinking

5 Analyze Ask students to identify the words and details that create suspense in these paragraphs. *The following words or details contribute to the suspense: their silent expectant waiting and the ticking of the clock and other sounds; Mr. White's going downstairs in the dark; the knock on the door and its repetition.*

Listening to Literature Audiocassettes To help students appreciate the final horrifying effects in the story, play the audiocassette from the paragraph that begins "Neither spoke, but lay silently listening to the ticking of the clock" to the end.

"I only just thought of it," she said hysterically. "Why didn't I think of it before? Why didn't *you* think of it?"

"Think of what?" he questioned.

"The other two wishes," she replied rapidly. "We've only had one."

"Was not that enough?" he demanded, fiercely.

"No," she cried triumphantly; "we'll have one more. Go down and get it quickly, and wish our boy alive again."

> **◆ Literary Focus**
> How might the outcome of the first wish foreshadow that of the other two wishes?

The man sat up in bed and flung the bedclothes from his quaking limbs. "You are mad!" he cried, aghast.

"Get it," she panted; "get it quickly, and wish— Oh, my boy, my boy!"

Her husband struck a match and lit the candle. "Get back to bed," he said unsteadily. "You don't know what you are saying."

"We had the first wish granted," said the old woman feverishly; "why not the second?"

"A coincidence," stammered the old man.

"Go and get it and wish," cried his wife, quivering with excitement.

The old man turned and regarded her, and his voice shook. "He has been dead ten days, and besides he—I would not tell you else, but—I could only recognize him by his clothing. If he was too terrible for you to see then, how now?"

"Bring him back," cried the old woman, and dragged him toward the door. "Do you think I fear the child I have nursed?"

He went down in the darkness, and felt his way to the parlor, and then to the mantelpiece. The talisman was in its place, and a horrible fear that the unspoken wish might bring his mutilated son before him ere he could escape from the room seized upon him, and he caught his breath as he found that he had lost the direction of the door. His brow cold with sweat, he felt his way round the table, and groped along the wall until he found himself in the small passage with the unwholesome thing in his hand.

Even his wife's face seemed changed as he entered the room. It was white and expectant, and to his fears seemed to have an unnatural look upon it. He was afraid of her.

"*Wish!*" she cried, in a strong voice.

"It is foolish and wicked," he faltered.

"*Wish!*" repeated his wife.

He raised his hand. "I wish my son alive again."

The talisman fell to the floor, and he regarded it fearfully. Then he sank trembling into a chair as the old woman, with burning eyes, walked to the window and raised the blind.

He sat until he was chilled with the cold, glancing occasionally at the figure of the old woman peering through the window. The candle-end, which had burned below the rim of the china candlestick, was throwing pulsating shadows on the ceiling and walls, until, with a flicker larger than the rest, it expired. The old man, with an unspeakable sense of relief at the failure of the talisman, crept back to his bed, and a minute or two afterward the old woman came silently and apathetically beside him.

Neither spoke, but lay silently listening to the ticking of the clock. A stair creaked, and a squeaky mouse scurried noisily through the wall. The darkness was oppressive, and after lying for some time screwing up his courage, he took the box of matches, and striking one, went downstairs for a candle.

At the foot of the stairs the match went out, and he paused to strike another; and at the same moment a knock so quiet and stealthy as to be scarcely audible, sounded on the front door.

The matches fell from his hand and spilled in the passage. He stood motionless, his breath suspended until the knock was repeated. Then he turned and fled swiftly back to his room, and closed the door behind him. A third knock sounded through the house.

"*What's that?*" cried the old woman, starting up.

"A rat," said the old man in shaking tones—"a rat. It passed me on the stairs."

His wife sat up in bed listening. A loud knock resounded through the house.

"It's Herbert!" she screamed. "It's Herbert!"

52 ◆ On the Edge

Beyond the Selection

FURTHER READING

Other Works by W. W. Jacobs
The Lady of the Barge (collection in which "The Monkey's Paw" first appeared)
Short Cruises
Sailor's Knots

Other Works With the Theme of the Power of Wishes
"Gift of the Magi," O. Henry
"The Necklace," Guy de Maupassant
"The Third Wish," Joan Aiken

She ran to the door, but her husband was before her, and catching her by the arm, held her tightly.

"What are you going to do?" he whispered hoarsely.

"It's my boy; it's Herbert!" she cried, struggling mechanically. "I forgot it was two miles away. What are you holding me for? Let go. I must open the door."

"Don't let it in," cried the old man, trembling.

"You're afraid of your own son," she cried struggling. "Let me go. I'm coming Herbert; I'm coming."

There was another knock, and another. The old woman with a sudden wrench broke free and ran from the room. Her husband followed to the landing, and called after her appealingly as she hurried downstairs. He heard the chain rattle back and the bottom bolt drawn slowly and stiffly from the socket. Then the old woman's voice, strained and panting.

"The bolt," she cried, loudly. "Come down. I can't reach it."

But her husband was on his hands and knees groping wildly on the floor in search of the paw. If he could only find it before the thing outside got in. A perfect <u>fusillade</u> of knocks reverberated through the house, and he heard the scraping of a chair as his wife put it down in the passage against the door. He heard the creaking of the bolt as it came slowly back, and at the same moment he found the monkey's paw, and frantically breathed his third and last wish.

The knocking ceased suddenly, although the echoes of it were still in the house. He heard the chair drawn back and the door opened. A cold wind rushed up the staircase, and a long loud wail of disappointment and misery from his wife gave him courage to run down to her side, and then to the gate beyond. The street lamp flickering opposite shone on a quiet and deserted road.

◆ Build Vocabulary

fusillade (fyo͞o´ sə lād´) *n.*: Something that is like the rapid firing of many firearms

---

Guide for Responding

◆ *Literature and Your Life*

Reader's Response What was the most frightening moment of the story? Why?

Thematic Focus Contrast the wishes made by the Whites with wishes that you work to fulfill. In what way are both these types of wishes daring?

☑ Check Your Comprehension

1. Summarize the story that the sergeant major tells the Whites.
2. In what way is Mr. White's first wish fulfilled?
3. Describe Mr. White's next two wishes and how they are fulfilled.
4. How does the story end?

◆ Critical Thinking

INTERPRET

1. How does the opening setting of the cold, wet night and the warm, cozy fire set the mood? [Analyze]
2. Contrast the reactions of mother, father, and son to the paw as the story progresses. [Compare and Contrast]
3. Would things have turned out better if Mr. and Mrs. White had phrased the second wish more carefully? Explain. [Infer]
4. What do the events of the story seem to indicate about "fate"? [Draw Conclusions]

APPLY

5. After reading the story, what would you do if you were granted three wishes? Why? [Speculate]

The Monkey's Paw ◆ 53

"The Bridegroom" is a variation on the familiar folk motif of a worthy young person standing up to declare independence and becoming heroic by doing so. It raises questions about fate, wishes, and particularly about making choices for yourself.

◆ Reading Strategy

❶ Predict Outcomes Ask students to predict what Natasha will tell her parents in response to their questions. *Natasha might tell her parents that she ran away to be by herself or to meet a boyfriend. She might also say she was abducted. Or she might say nothing at all.*

◆ Literary Focus

❷ Foreshadowing Have students explain what the word *foreboding* suggests about the events that will follow. *The word foreboding means "an omen or prediction of coming evil"; the parents' fear of the future is a powerful clue that there will be trouble ahead.*

◆ Critical Thinking

❸ Analyze Characters Ask students: What does Natasha's silence say about her? *Natasha's silence suggests that she is strong, independent, and perhaps considerate of her parents' feelings, not wishing to hurt them, or that there is something she feels she cannot tell them.*

The Bridegroom

Alexander Pushkin
Translated by D. M. Thomas

❶   For three days Natasha,
    The merchant's daughter,
    Was missing. The third night,
    She ran in, distraught.
5   Her father and mother
    Plied her with questions.
    She did not hear them,
    She could hardly breathe.

❷   Stricken with foreboding
10 They pleaded, got angry,
    But still she was silent;
    At last they gave up.
    Natasha's cheeks regained
    Their rosy color.
15 And cheerfully again
    She sat with her sisters.

    Once at the shingle-gate
    She sat with her friends
    —And a swift troika[1]
20 Flashed by before them;
    A handsome young man
    Stood driving the horses;
    Snow and mud went flying,
    Splashing the girls.

25 He gazed as he flew past,
    And Natasha gazed.
    He flew on. Natasha froze.

---

1. troika (troi′ kə) *n.*: Russian carriage or sleigh drawn by a specially trained team of three horses abreast.

54 ◆ On the Edge

    Headlong she ran home.
    "It was he! It was he!"
30 She cried. "I know it!
    I recognized him! Papa,
    Mama, save me from him!"

    Full of grief and fear,
    They shake their heads, sighing.
35 Her father says: "My child,
    Tell me everything.
    If someone has harmed you,
    Tell us . . . even a hint."
    She weeps again and
40 Her lips remain sealed. ❸

    The next morning, the old
    Matchmaking woman
    Unexpectedly calls and
    Sings the girl's praises;
45 Says to the father: "You
    Have the goods and I
    A buyer for them:
    A handsome young man.

    "He bows low to no one,
50 He lives like a lord
    With no debts nor worries;

◆ Build Vocabulary
foreboding (fôr bōd′ iŋ) *n.*: Feeling that something bad will happen

---

Speaking and Listening Mini-Lesson

Television Interview
This mini-lesson supports the Speaking and Listening activity in the Idea Bank on page 59.

Introduce the Concept Have students review TV interviews they've seen and identify the purpose, procedures, and other details that they remember.

Develop Background Suggest that students prepare their role-playing interviews with the following points in mind:
Good interview questions

• often begin with the words *who, what, where, when, why,* and *how*.
• are short and to the point.

A good interviewer
• listens attentively without interjecting personal opinions.
• does not ask overly personal questions.
• asks for further clarification if necessary.

A good interviewee
• answers questions directly and generously.

• responds to the main point of the question.

Apply the Information When students feel prepared, have them conduct their role-played interviews for the class.

Assess the Outcome You and your students may evaluate the interviews on the basis of these questions: Were the interview questions appropriate and concise? Did the interviewer exhibit good listening skills? Were the interviewee's responses focused?

The Lights of Marriage, Marc Chagall, Kunsthaus, Zurich

▲ Critical Viewing What might you infer about Natasha's marriage based on this painting? [Infer] **⑤**

He's rich and he's generous,
Says he will give his bride,
On their wedding-day,
55   A fox-fur coat, a pearl,
Gold rings, brocaded[2] dresses.

"Yesterday, out driving,
He saw your Natasha;
Shall we shake hands
❹ 60   And get her to church?"
The woman starts to eat
A pie, and talks in riddles,
While the poor girl
Does not know where to look.

65   "Agreed," says her father;
"Go in happiness
To the altar, Natasha;
It's dull for you here;
A swallow should not spend
70   All its time singing,
It's time for you to build
A nest for your children."

Natasha leaned against
The wall and tried
75   To speak—but found herself
Sobbing; she was shuddering
And laughing. The matchmaker
Poured out a cup of water,

---

2. **brocaded** (brō kād′ əd) *adj.*: Woven, raised design in a cloth.

The Bridegroom ◆ 55

Customize for
Visual/Spatial Learners
Encourage these students to take some time to study the details in the Chagall painting either before or after they read the poem. Then have them note ways in which the painting adds to or changes their impressions of the poem. Urge them to share their observations with classmates.

Customize for
Less Proficient Readers
To help these students follow the story that Pushkin presents, instruct them to read the poem in sentences, rather than pausing at the end of each line. In addition, you may want to encourage them to pause at the end of each stanza, to summarize the events and details that it presents.

◆ *Literature and Your Life*

❹ Encourage students to think about how they would feel if others made major life decisions for them.

▶Critical Viewing◀

❺ **Infer** The strange, surrealistic quality of the painting suggests that Natasha's marriage will be less than perfect. Students may also note the distracted, disturbed look of the bride, who, like Natasha, seems to have more than a simple wedding on her mind.

 Humanities: Art

The Lights of Marriage by Marc Chagall.
This painting by Marc Chagall (1887–1985) depicts a wedding scene that is suggestive of the wedding scene described in "The Bridegroom."
Chagall was born in Russia and educated as a painter in Paris. His paintings are distinguished by deeply colored landscapes in which people, objects, and animals fly and float in dreamlike fantasy. His work is asso-ciated with Surrealism and Cubism, two schools of painting that gave the world new, nonrealistic ways of looking at itself.
Use these questions for discussion:
1. How is the mood of the painting similar to the mood of Natasha's wedding? *Just as the painting creates a mysterious tension in the viewer with its unexplained human and animal figures flying about, so Natasha's wedding is unsettling to the* *guests and the reader with its vivid description of a mysterious, violent dream and its melodramatic revelation and conclusion.*
2. Natasha is the focus of the story. Who is the focus of the painting? Provide evidence to support your answer. *The bride is the focus of the painting, too. The painter accomplishes this by placing the bride in the center of the painting and by using light and detail to draw our eye to the bride.*

Gave her some to drink,
80 Splashed some in her face.

Her parents are distressed.
Then Natasha recovered,
❶ And calmly she said:
"Your will be done. Call
85 My bridegroom to the feast,
Bake loaves for the whole world,
Brew sweet mead[3] and call
The law to the feast."

"Of course, Natasha, angel!
90 You know we'd give our lives
To make you happy!"
They bake and they brew;
The worthy guests come,
The bride is led to the feast,
95 Her maids sing and weep;
Then horses and a sledge[4]

With the groom—and all sit.
The glasses ring and clatter,
The toasting-cup is passed

100 From hand to hand in <u>tumult</u>,
The guests are drunk.

BRIDEGROOM
"Friends, why is my fair bride
Sad, why is she not
Feasting and serving?"

105 The bride answers the groom:
"I will tell you why
As best I can. My soul
❷ Knows no rest, day and night
I weep; an evil dream
110 Oppresses me." Her father
Says: "My dear child, tell us
What your dream is."

"I dreamed," she says, "that I
Went into a forest,
115 It was late and dark;

---

3. **mead** (mēd) *n.*: Drink made of fermented honey and water.
4. **sledge** *n.*: Sleigh.

56 ◆ On the Edge

The moon was faintly
Shining behind a cloud;
I strayed from the path;
Nothing stirred except
120 The tops of the pine-trees.

"And suddenly, as if
I was awake, I saw
A hut. I approach the hut
And knock at the door
125 —Silence. A prayer on my lips
I open the door and enter.
A candle burns. All
Is silver and gold."

BRIDEGROOM
"What is bad about that?
130 It promises wealth."

BRIDE
"Wait, sir, I've not finished.
Silently I gazed
On the silver and gold,
The cloths, the rugs, the silks,
135 From Novgorod,[5] and I
Was lost in wonder.

"Then I heard a shout
And a clatter of hoofs . . .
Someone has driven up
140 To the porch. Quickly
I slammed the door and hid
Behind the stove. Now
I hear many voices . . .
Twelve young men come in,

145 "And with them is a girl,
Pure and beautiful.
They've taken no notice
Of the ikons,[6] they sit ❸

---

5. **Novgorod**: City in the northwestern part of Russia.
6. **ikons** (ī känz′) *n.*: Images of Jesus, Mary, a saint, or another sacred Christian religious figure.

◆ Build Vocabulary

tumult (tōō′ mult) *n.*: Noisy commotion

---

3 150 To the table without
Praying or taking off
Their hats. At the head,
The eldest brother,
At his right, the youngest;
155 At his left, the girl.
Shouts, laughs, drunken clamor . . . "

BRIDEGROOM
"That betokens merriment."

BRIDE
4 "Wait, sir, I've not finished.
The drunken din goes on
And grows louder still.
160 Only the girl is sad.

"She sits silent, neither
Eating nor drinking;
But sheds tears in plenty;
The eldest brother

165 Takes his knife and, whistling,
Sharpens it; seizing her by
The hair he kills her
And cuts off her right hand."

"Why," says the groom, "this
170 Is nonsense! Believe me,
My love, your dream is not evil."
She looks him in the eyes.
"And from whose hand
Does this ring come?"

175 The bride said. The whole throng
Rose in the silence.

With a clatter the ring
Falls, and rolls along
The floor. The groom blanches,
180 Trembles. Confusion . . .
"Seize him!" the law commands.
He's bound, judged, put to death.
Natasha is famous! **5**
Our song at an end.

Literary Focus

4 **Foreshadowing** Ask students what the repetition of this line suggests about events to follow. *The repetition of this line demonstrates Natasha's strength and determination and foreshadows her ultimate victory.*

Literature and Your Life

5 Natasha took a risk, which resulted in her achieving fame. Encourage students to think about a risk they have taken and how the situation turned out. Did the risk accomplish what they had hoped? How do they feel when they look back at the risk-taking behavior now?

Reinforce and Extend

Answers

Literature and Your Life

Reader's Response Many students will say that they admire Natasha because she showed independence and resourcefulness in carrying through her plan to expose the bridegroom.

Thematic Focus Students might say that the events of the poem prove that the power of choice can vanquish the power of fate in some instances.

☑ **Check Your Comprehension**

1. Natasha disappears for three days.
2. She sees a man drive by in a carriage, whom she recognizes as the man she witnessed murdering a woman as twelve brothers looked on.
3. At first she is upset, then she resigns herself to the marriage.
4. She tells the guests at the wedding that she had a horrible dream, and as the dream unfolds, she reveals the killer to be her husband.

Critical Thinking

1. She had gone into the forest, and when it became late and dark, she entered a cottage. When people came, she hid behind the stove and probably witnessed the murder she later describes.
2. She probably felt she couldn't tell them because they probably would not believe she witnessed a murder, or she didn't want to upset them.

Guide for Responding

Literature and Your Life

Reader's Response Do you admire Natasha? Why or why not?

Thematic Focus What does the poem suggest about the power of choice versus that of chance or fate?

Connection to Music Name a modern song or ballad that, like "The Bridegroom," tells about a daring decision. Then briefly summarize the story told in the song.

☑ **Check Your Comprehension**

1. What unexplained event occurs at the very beginning of the poem?
2. What upsets Natasha when she's sitting with her friends at the gate?
3. Describe her changing reactions to the marriage.
4. Summarize the events of the wedding.

◆ Critical Thinking

INTERPRET

1. Where was Natasha during the three days she was missing? **[Infer]**
2. Why does she refuse to reveal where she was to her parents? **[Analyze]**
3. What accounts for her changing reactions to the marriage? **[Infer]**
4. Do you think Natasha had the evil dream she describes? Explain. **[Interpret]**
5. How does Natasha's behavior at the beginning of the poem contrast with her behavior at the end? **[Compare and Contrast]**
6. Why does Natasha become famous? **[Draw Conclusions]**

EVALUATE

7. Is the title of the poem effective in grabbing your attention and hinting at the poem's story? Explain. **[Criticize]**

APPLY

8. Would the story have happened the same way in our times? Why or why not? **[Hypothesize]**

The Bridegroom ◆ 57

---

3. Possibly she felt resigned and felt that she would be safe in confronting the bridegroom as a murderer with all of her family and friends surrounding her.
4. Probably not; she probably used the dream rather than make an outright accusation.
5. At the beginning of the poem, Natasha is terrified and timid, by the end, she bravely confronts the murderer.
6. She becomes famous because her bravery led to the arrest of a murderer.
7. Students might say the simplicity of the title hints at something much more complex and ominous.
8. Students might recognize that although arranged marriages are not common in our country today, they do occur in other cultures—the story might be more likely to happen in another culture.

Answers

◆ Reading Strategy

1. Her sudden decision to have the wedding probably coincides with her plan to expose the murderer; she probably refuses food or drink for fear of being poisoned; her tale of the evil dream predicts her exposure of the murderer.

2. (1) The sergeant major doesn't want to talk about the paw. (2) The sergeant wanted to burn the paw. (3) Herbert sees a simian face in the fire.

◆ Literary Focus

1. It foreshadows Herbert's horrible death.

2. It is an example of foreshadowing because of its ironic truth: He dies before the money is received.

3. Her reaction of terror indicated she knew him or something about him, and that knowledge foreshadows the events to come.

4. It foreshadows her intent to reveal the murderer and the eventual arrest of the bridegroom.

◆ Build Vocabulary

Using the Word Root -cred-
1. *incredible*—unbelievable;
2. *credible*—capable of being believed;
3. *credentials*—qualifications that make a person believable; 4. *credulity*—a disposition to believe too readily; 5. *credit*—belief in the truth of someone or something

Using the Word Bank
1. c   2. b   3. a   4. c   5. a   6. b
7. a   8. c

◆ Build Grammar Skills

1. seen;   2. became;   3. known;
4. saw;   5. knew

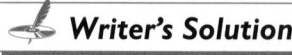 **Writer's Solution**

For additional instruction and practice, use the lesson in the **Language Lab CD-ROM** on Verb Tenses and the pages on Verb Tenses (pp. 67–69) in the *Writer's Solution Grammar Practice Book*.

Guide for Responding (continued)

◆ Reading Strategy

PREDICT OUTCOMES

Reading in "The Bridegroom" that Natasha invites "the whole world" and "the law" to her wedding, you may wonder why she singles out someone who enforces the law. This clue helps you **predict the outcome** of the story because it suggests that Natasha plans to capture a criminal.

1. Explain how each of these other details helps you predict the outcome of "The Bridegroom": Natasha's sudden decision to have the wedding; her refusal to eat and drink at the wedding; and her tale of "an evil dream."

2. List three clues from "The Monkey's Paw" that suggest the paw will bring sorrow to the Whites. Give reasons for your choices.

◆ Literary Focus

FORESHADOWING

In the story and the poem, hints at future events, called **foreshadowing**, give you glimpses of what will happen that make you want to find out more. Sometimes these hints give a general sense of what will come. Other times, they can be linked to specific occurrences, although you may not understand the connection until much later.

For example, in "The Monkey's Paw," Herbert says that "something horrible squatting up on top of the wardrobe" will watch his father pocket the wished-for money. This hint suggests that frightening events are in store but leaves you guessing about what they are. Later you find out that Herbert's image also foreshadows something specific.

1. What exactly does the horrible squatting thing foreshadow?

2. Why is Herbert's statement that he'll never see the money an example of foreshadowing?

3. In "The Bridegroom," why is Natasha's first reaction to the "handsome young man" an example of foreshadowing?

4. Natasha invites "the law" to her wedding. What specific later event does this invitation foreshadow?

◆ Build Vocabulary

USING THE ROOT -cred-

Knowing that the root -cred- means "to believe," use a form of the word *believe* in defining each of these words:

1. incredible   3. credentials   5. credit (noun)
2. credible   4. credulity

USING THE WORD BANK

On your paper, write the word whose meaning is closest to that of the first word:

1. doughty: (a) exhausted, (b) sarcastic, (c) brave
2. maligned: (a) flattered, (b) slandered, (c) underlined
3. credulity: (a) gullibility, (b) disbelief, (c) futility
4. prosaic: (a) unusual, (b) essential, (c) ordinary
5. avaricious: (a) greedy, (b) generous, (c) stubborn
6. fusillade: (a) handful, (b) barrage, (c) shot
7. foreboding: (a) forewarning, (b) hindsight, (c) unawareness
8. tumult: (a) boredom, (b) order, (c) commotion

◆ Build Grammar Skills

REGULAR AND IRREGULAR VERBS

Irregular verbs, like the ones in the following chart, form their past and past participles in a variety of ways.

Practice Choose a form of the given irregular verb to complete the sentences.

Present	Past	Past Participle
know	knew	known
see	saw	seen
become	became	become

1. The sergeant major had ____?____ what happened to people who used the monkey's paw. (see)
2. Mr. White ____?____ fascinated with the monkey's paw. (become)
3. The Whites could not have ____?____ the terrible result of their wishes. (know)
4. Natasha ____?____ a sight that terrified her. (see)
5. Natasha's tale revealed what she ____?____. (know)

Build Your Portfolio

Idea Bank

Writing

1. **Newspaper Headlines** For each selection, write two headlines that would entice people to read the sensational story. An example of such a headline might be "Bridegroom in Big Trouble."

2. **Warning Label** Write a warning label for the monkey's paw. Caution users to wish carefully and include a list of possible consequences for those who do not heed your warning.

3. **Paw Proposal** The Whites have given you the monkey's paw. Write a persuasive letter to a government leader suggesting how the paw could be used for the public good. **[Social Studies Link]**

Speaking and Listening

4. **Television Interview** With a partner, role-play an interview between Natasha from "The Bridegroom" and a television reporter. Focus on Natasha's three-day absence and her plans for confronting the criminal. **[Media Link]**

5. **Dramatic Monologue** Imagine the bridegroom in prison, awaiting execution. Write a dramatic monologue for him, a speech he gives to a silent listener explaining *his* side of the story. **[Performing Arts Link]**

Projects

6. **A Monkey's Paw Poll** List ten possible wishes, ranging from such things as a shopping spree at the mall to a new school library. Use the list as a class survey and record your results on a bar graph or a pie chart. **[Math Link]**

7. **Poster Showing Fortuna** Research Fortuna, the ancient goddess of fortune. Then create a poster illustrating what you've learned about her. **[Social Studies Link; Art Link]**

Writing Mini-Lesson

Yearbook Prediction

Choose a wish you have for your own future. Then write a yearbook prediction for yourself based on this wish. Show the cause-and-effect relationships that would be involved in making your wish a reality.

> **Writing Skills Focus:**
> **Transitions to Show Cause and Effect**
> You'll need to use **transitions to show cause and effect**—words and phrases that show how one thing brings about another—when writing a how-to essay, a prediction, or a short story. Such transitions include words like *because*, *as a result*, and *consequently*. Jacobs uses one of these words in "The Monkey's Paw" to show how a situation influences people's thoughts:
>
>   transition   cause
> "I suppose *because* only two houses on the road
>   effect
> are let, they think it doesn't matter."

Prewriting Make an imaginary timeline showing how today's interests and abilities can lead you step by step to tomorrow's opportunities. In addition, list cause-and-effect transition words you can draw on as you draft and revise your prediction.

Drafting Refer to your cause-and-effect word list as you write, using transitions to show how one event brings about another.

Revising Reread your prediction and add transitions to clarify any vague cause-and-effect relationships. Also, be sure you've used the correct forms of any irregular verbs.

    For more on regular and irregular verb forms, see Build Grammar Skills on pages 44 and 58.

Idea Bank

Customizing for *Performance Levels*
Following are suggestions for matching Idea Bank topics with your students' performance levels:
    Less Advanced Students: 1, 4
    Average Students: 2, 4, 6, 7
    More Advanced Students: 3, 5

Customizing for *Learning Modalities*
Following are suggestions for matching Idea Bank topics with your students' learning modalities:
    Visual/Spatial: 7
    Verbal/Linguistic: 4,5
    Logical/Mathematical: 6
    Interpersonal: 4

Writing Mini-Lesson
Refer students to the Writing Handbook, page 965, for instruction on the writing process, and page 967 for further information on cause-and-effect relationships.

Writer's Solution

Writing Lab CD-ROM
Have students complete the tutorial on Narration. Follow these steps:
1. Have students use the Storyline Diagram to help them develop their plots.
2. Have students draft on computer.
3. Have students use the Self-Evaluation Checklist to help them revise.

Sourcebook
Have students use Chapter 2, Narration (pp. 30–56), for additional support. The chapter includes an annotated student model of a story (p. 56).

✓ ASSESSMENT OPTIONS

Formal Assessment, Selection Test, pp. 7–9, and Assessment Resources Software. The selection test is designed so that it can be easily customized to the performance levels of your students. *Alternative Assessment,* p. 3, includes options for less advanced students, more advanced students, verbal/linguistic learners, logical/mathematical learners, bodily/kinesthetic learners, interpersonal learners, and visual/spatial learners.

PORTFOLIO ASSESSMENT
Use the following rubrics in the *Alternative Assessment* booklet to assess student writing:
Newspaper Headlines: Summary Rubric, p. 98
Warning Label: Process Explanation Rubric, p.100
Paw Proposal: Persuasion Rubric, p. 105
Writing Mini-Lesson: Cause-and-Effect Rubric, p. 102

*G*uide for Reading

OBJECTIVES

1. To read, comprehend, and interpret a story
2. To relate a story to personal experience
3. To make inferences
4. To identify flashbacks
5. To build vocabulary in context and learn the word root *-stup-*
6. To identify independent and subordinate clauses
7. To write a how-to manual for new students, including a clear explanation of procedures
8. To respond to the story through writing, speaking and listening, and projects

SKILLS INSTRUCTION

Vocabulary:
Word Roots: *-stup-*

Grammar:
Clauses

Reading Strategy:
Make Inferences

Literary Focus:
Flashback

Writing:
Clear Explanation of Procedures

Speaking and Listening:
Conducting an Interview (teacher edition)

Critical Viewing:
Interpret, Analyze

PORTFOLIO OPPORTUNITIES

Writing: Annie's Packing List; Letter of Introduction; Description of Antigua for the Internet

Writing Mini-Lesson: Writing a How-to Manual for New Students

Speaking and Listening: Telephone Interview; Persuasive Speech

Projects: Statistics Chart; Map

More About the Author

Jamaica Kincaid once told a newspaper reporter: "Everyone thought I had a way with words, but it came out as a sharp tongue. No one expected anything from me at all. Had I just sunk in the cracks it would not have been noted." Kincaid did not slip through the cracks, however. She became a writer for *The New Yorker* and a successful novelist and short-story writer.

Jamaica Kincaid (1949–   )

Imagine leaving everyone and everything that is familiar to you and moving to a foreign country on your own. That is exactly what this writer did.

At the age of sixteen, Jamaica Kincaid set off into the unknown.

She left her home in Antigua to take a job caring for the children of a family in New York.

A Changing Family Situation

She was born Elaine Potter Richardson on the West Indian island of Antigua. Although she grew up in a home without electricity or running water, Kincaid's early childhood was a happy one because of her deep connection with her mother. As a teen however, she yearned for a life of her own.

She moved to America, held a series of unskilled jobs, and made an unsuccessful attempt to get a college degree. Despite setbacks, she entered the New York publishing world and soon was writing articles for teen magazines. She also adopted the pen name Jamaica Kincaid, a symbol of her new, independent self.

Literary Success Jamaica Kincaid has won acclaim for her autobiographical novels *Annie John* and *Lucy*. These works focus on the complex relationship between a mother and daughter and how it changes, sometimes painfully.

"A Walk to the Jetty" is the conclusion to *Annie John*. It describes the narrator's last walk through her childhood world, as she prepares to leave her native island.

◆ Build Vocabulary

WORD ROOTS: *-stup-*

In "A Walk to the Jetty," the main character shakes herself as if waking herself "out of a *stupor.*" The word *stupor* contains the root *-stup-*, which means "to be stunned or amazed." Knowing this meaning, you can figure out that *stupor* means "a state in which the mind is stunned."

WORD BANK

loomed
apprenticed
raked
stupor

As you read the excerpt from "A Walk to the Jetty," you will encounter the words on this list. Each word is defined on the page where it first appears. Preview the list before you read.

◆ Build Grammar Skills

CLAUSES

Clauses are groups of words with both a subject and a verb. An **independent clause** can stand by itself as a sentence, and a sentence can contain more than one independent clause. A **subordinate clause** cannot stand alone. It must be linked with an independent clause to form a sentence.

Kinkaid uses both types of clauses:

subordinate clause	independent clause
S V	S V
When we were all on board,	the launch headed out to sea.

60 ◆ On the Edge

Prentice Hall Literature Program Resources

REINFORCE / RETEACH / EXTEND

Selection Support Pages
Build Vocabulary: Word Roots: *-stup-*, p. 14
Build Grammar Skills: Clauses, p. 15
Literary Focus: Flashback, p. 17
Reading Strategy: Make Inferences, p. 16

Strategies for Diverse Student Needs, p. 4

Beyond Literature
Cross-Curricular Connection: Social Studies. p. 4

Formal Assessment Selection Test, pp. 10–12; Assessment Resources Software
Alternative Assessment, p. 4

Resource Pro CD-R*O*M
"A Walk to the Jetty"—includes all resource materials and customizable lesson plans

Listening to Literature Audiocassettes
"A Walk to the Jetty"

from A Walk to the Jetty

◆ *Literature and Your Life*

CONNECT YOUR EXPERIENCE

One day you might move away from home to go to college, join the military, or live on your own. Preparing to leave, you may be flooded with memories. A little keepsake may recall a store that your family often visited. A battered volleyball may remind you of a field where you played with friends.

The teenage girl in this story is about to leave her island home, and her walk to the harbor is along a road of bittersweet memories.

Journal Writing Jot down some of the things you would miss most if you were leaving home.

THEMATIC FOCUS: DARING DECISIONS

On the verge of being an adult, the young woman in this story leaves her home and says goodbye to her childhood self.

◆ Background for Understanding

HISTORY

Antigua is the island home that Annie John, the main character in this story, is leaving. It is also the place where the author herself grew up. Antigua became a British colony in the seventeenth century and won its independence in 1981. As a result of the long-term British presence on the island, Antiguans speak English, use the British monetary system, and play British games such as cricket.

Early on, the British discovered that the island's tropical climate was ideal for growing sugar cane. Until 1834 when they abolished slavery, the British brought enslaved Africans to work on the island's sugar plantations. Most Antiguans, like Annie John and the author herself, are descendants of these Africans.

◆ Literary Focus

FLASHBACK

A **flashback** is a section of a literary work that interrupts the sequence of events to relate an event from an earlier time. Writers often use flashbacks to show what motivates a character or to reveal something about a character's past in a dramatic way.

In this story, you learn about Annie John's childhood through a series of flashbacks triggered by familiar sights as she walks through town. These flashbacks hint at the reasons for Annie's departure.

◆ Reading Strategy

MAKE INFERENCES

As you read a story, you can **make inferences**—reach conclusions—about characters based on their speech, thoughts, and actions. These inferences help you better understand who the characters are and why they behave as they do.

In "A Walk to the Jetty," both present actions and flashbacks can serve as a basis for inferences. At the beginning of the story, for example, a flashback shows you how proud Annie's mother was when her five-year-old daughter went on an errand alone. From this detail, you can infer that Annie and her mother were very close.

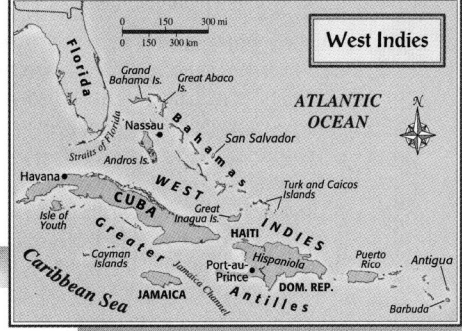

West Indies

Guide for Reading ◆ 61

Invite students to picture themselves in the following situation: They are sixteen years old and they are leaving their country and their family to begin life in another country. Help students to generate a class list of the feelings that might surround the circumstances you describe, such as fear of the unknown, excitement, and a sense of insecurity. Generate a brief discussion about ways students could help themselves overcome fears and maximize the positive aspects of this situation. Tell the class that Annie John in the selection they are about to read left her native Antigua as a teenager. In this story, she shares her thoughts and feelings as she heads off for a new life in a new land.

Customize for
Less Proficient Readers
These readers may be unfamiliar with cues that signal a flashback. Before they read, tell them to watch for passages in which the narrator suddenly thinks or "flashes" back to an earlier time. Point out an example of a sentence that signals a flashback: "I was five years old when I first walked on this road."

Customize for
More Advanced Students
Students skilled at making inferences can model this process for others. Tell them to watch for places in the story that hint at what kinds of relationships Annie has with her mother and father.

Customize for
English Language Learners
Students from the West Indies can share their knowledge of these islands. Other immigrants may be unfamiliar with the Britishisms *chemist* (druggist, pharmacist), *cricket* (a game with some resemblance to baseball), and *sixpence* (a unit of money). Use the footnotes in the story to clarify these terms before students read.

Preparing for Standardized Tests

Reading and Vocabulary Making inferences is a skill that is key to success on reading comprehension items on the verbal portions of standardized tests. For practice in this skill, help students generate a list of details about Annie, her father, and her mother, and use these as evidence to make inferences about each character. For example, from the detail that Annie John wanted to weep when passing the library, students can infer that she is a lover of books. For reinforcement, use the Reading Strategy page in *Selection Support* (p. 16).

Grammar and Language Many standardized tests require students to write an essay. Tell students that the ability to use independent and subordinate clauses effectively to express ideas in their own writing will help students construct better and more varied sentences when they write these essays. For practice with clauses, use the Build Grammar Skills page in *Selection Support* (p. 15).

Fear, excitement, nostalgia, resentment, confusion, regret—this autobiographical story captures all the complex emotions a young adult can feel when taking the first tentative steps toward independence. For Annie John, the emotions associated with leaving home are complicated by her conflicted relationship with her mother and her island home, as well as her need to rise above the low expectations for girls in her culture. Students will find much to identify with in this poignant leaving-home story.

❶ Clarification Point out that some ports are too shallow to accommodate large ships, so passengers must be ferried out to the ships, which drop anchor in deep water.

◆ Literature and Your Life

❷ Point out Annie's feelings of self-consciousness about walking along between her parents. Have students write in their journals about a time they might have worried about being perceived as a small child when in the company of their parent(s) or guardian(s). Have them analyze how this feeling is connected to a growing sense of independence.

◆ Reading Strategy

❸ Infer Students may say that Miss Dulcie's treatment of Annie shows a lack of respect for the girl's feelings and intelligence. The woman's low expectations for Annie and her critical, fault-finding attitude may have been typical of the way adults treated Annie.

◆ Critical Thinking

❹ Interpret Ask what the narrator means by "the dustheap of my life."
The narrator considers the experiences with Miss Dulcie as something to be discarded—in "the dustheap."

from A Walk to the Jetty

from Annie John

Jamaica Kincaid

My mother had arranged with a stevedore[1] to take my trunk to the jetty ahead of me. At ten o'clock on the dot, I was dressed, and we set off for the jetty. An hour after that, I would board a launch that would take me out to sea, where I then would board the ship. Starting out, as if for old time's sake and without giving it a thought, we lined up in the old way: I walking between my mother and my father. I loomed way above my father and could see the top of his head. We must have made a strange sight: a grown girl all dressed up in the middle of a morning, in the middle of the week, walking in step in the middle between her two parents, for people we didn't know stared at us. It was all of half an hour's walk from our house to the jetty, but I was passing through most of the years of my life. We passed by the house where Miss Dulcie, the seamstress that I had been apprenticed to for a time, lived, and just as I was passing by, a wave of bad feeling for her came over me, because I suddenly remembered that the months I spent with her all she had me do was sweep the floor, which was always full of threads and pins and needles, and I never seemed to sweep it clean enough to please her. Then she would send me to the store to buy buttons or thread, though I was only allowed to do this if I was given a sample of the button or thread, and then she would find fault even though they were an exact match of the samples she had given me. And all the while she said to me, "A girl like you will never learn to sew properly, you know." At the time, I don't suppose I minded it, because it was customary to treat the first-year apprentice with such scorn, but now I placed on the dustheap of my life Miss Dulcie and everything that I had had to do with her.

◆ **Reading Strategy**
How does this first reminiscence of childhood help you infer why Annie might be leaving the island?

◆ Build Vocabulary

loomed (lōōmd) *v.*: Appeared in a large or threatening form

apprenticed (ə pren′ tist) *v.*: Assigned to work a specified length of time in a craft or trade in return for instruction

1. **stevedore** (stē′ və dôr) *n.*: Person whose job is loading and unloading ships.

62 ◆ On the Edge

Block Scheduling Strategies

Consider these suggestions to take advantage of extended class time:

- Introduce the reading strategy. You may wish to use the Reading Strategy page from **Selection Support** (p. 16) to give students practice in making inferences before they read the story.
- Give students the Cross-Curricular Connection, from **Beyond Literature** (p. 4). Have them do the map activity to build background on Antigua.
- Encourage students to research information about Antigua and the West Indies on the Internet.

- After students have read the selection, facilitate (or choose a student to facilitate) a panel discussion on the role of girls and women in Antigua versus the United States. Encourage West Indian students to lend their expertise to the discussion.
- Have students complete the Writing Mini-Lesson on page 70. First they can meet in small groups to brainstorm for ideas and procedures to include in their manual. Then each person can choose one procedure to break down into steps.

San Antonio de Oriente (detail), José Antonio Velásquez, Museum of Modern Art of Latin America, Washington, D.C.

▲ Critical Viewing In what ways does this picture
evoke a small-town feel? **[Interpret]**

from *A Walk to the Jetty* ◆ 63

Customize for
Bodily/Kinesthetic Learners
To help these students infer Annie's
feelings, have them role-play one of
the flashbacks or the final scene in
which Annie boards the ship and says
good-bye to her parents. After the
role-plays, have students tell what
emotions they think each character
in the scene was feeling.

Customize for
Visual/Spatial Learners
Encourage these students to use the
painting on this page to help them
envision the story's setting. Have
them note the colorfulness of the
landscape that is depicted, and draw
their attention to the many flowers.
Point out that the lush vegetation is
typical of a tropical landscape.

►Critical Viewing◄
❺ **Interpret** Students may say that
the photograph conveys a small-town
feel because it depicts a landscape
with few buildings, people, or vehicles, that the town is surrounded by
nature, and that the church seems to
be the focus of the town.

☙ Humanities: Art

San Antonio de Oriente (detail) by José
Antonio Velásquez.

This painting depicts a quiet Honduran
village in a setting similar to the one Jamaica
Kincaid—and her character Annie John—
decided to leave.

The primitivist painter José Antonio
Velásquez has painted many pictures depicting San Antonio de Oriente, a small town in
the Latin American country of Honduras.
His paintings allow viewers to identify the

charming and humble reality of small
Honduran towns—and of small towns the
world over. In this painting, the rhythmic
patterns of the tiles, flowers, and stone
walls are offset by the smooth solid planes
of white walls of the buildings and the colorful wash hung on a line in the foreground.

Use these questions for discussion:
1. What mood, or feeling, does the painting
   convey to you? *Responses may range from
   peaceful, quiet, serene, unhurried, and relax-*

ing to lazy and boring
2. Why might a young person who grew up
   in such a setting choose to leave it as he
   or she reaches adulthood? *Responses may
   include a desire for a more exciting, busy
   life; desire for economic opportunities not
   available here but available only in metropolitan areas; desire to be in touch with
   technological progress and popular culture;
   desire to meet a wider variety of people.*

63

◆ Literary Focus

❶ Flashback Students may mention the three pennies, the little basket, the freshly ironed yellow dress printed with acrobats, the smell of Annie's mother's talcum powder, the scene on the can of talcum powder, the name of the talcum powder, her mother's tears of pride and joy at Annie's return, her being swooped up in her mother's arms, and her mother's proud words at Annie's accomplishments.

◆ Critical Thinking

❷ Analyze Ask students what this vivid memory suggests about Annie's childhood relationship with her mother. *Students may say that Annie and her mother had a close, affectionate relationship, that Annie's mother was proud of her young daughter's growing independence, and that her mother's pride in her meant a great deal to Annie.*

◆ Build Grammar Skills

❸ Clauses Have students identify the independent and subordinate clauses in the two sentences beginning "Once, when she had mumps" and "I don't know how." *Once I went to visit her against my mother's wishes—independent; when she had mumps—subordinate; we sat on her bed and ate the cure of roasted, buttered sweet potatoes—independent; that had been placed on her swollen jaw—subordinate; I don't know—independent; how my mother found out about it—subordinate; I don't know how—independent, she put an end to our friendship—independent.*

◆ *Literature and Your Life*

❹ Ask students if they can remember an instance when, like Annie John, they argued with their parent(s) over an article of clothing. What are some reasons parents and children argue over clothing? *Students might say that parents' ideas about clothes don't often match theirs. Parents might perceive their children's independent taste in clothing as a sign they are growing away from them; parents sometimes disagree with or don't understand the important role clothes play in gaining social acceptance.*

We were soon on the road that I had taken to school, to church, to Sunday school, to choir practice, to Brownie meetings, to Girl Guide meetings, to meet a friend. I was five years old when I first walked on this road unaccompanied by someone to hold my hand. My mother had placed three pennies in my little basket, which was a duplicate of her bigger basket, and sent me to the chemist's shop to buy a pennyworth of senna leaves, a pennyworth of eucalyptus leaves, and a pennyworth of camphor.[2] She then instructed me on what side of the road to walk, where to make a turn, where to cross, how to look carefully before I crossed, and if I met anyone that I knew to politely pass greetings and keep on my way. I was wearing a freshly ironed yellow dress that had printed on it scenes of acrobats flying through the air and swinging on a trapeze. I had just had a bath, and after it, instead of powdering me with my baby-smelling talcum powder, my mother had, as a special favor, let me use her own talcum powder, which smelled quite perfumy and came in a can that had painted on it people going out to dinner in nineteenth-century London and was called Mazie. How it pleased me to walk out the door and bend my head down to sniff at myself and see that I smelled just like my mother. I went to the chemist's shop, and he had to come from behind the counter and bend down to hear what it was that I wanted to buy, my voice was so little and timid then. I went back just the way I had come, and when I walked into the yard and presented my basket with its three packages to my mother, her eyes filled with tears and she swooped me up and held me high in the air and said that I was wonderful and good

> **◆ Literary Focus**
> What details in this flashback help you to picture in your mind Annie's first walk?

and that there would never be anybody better. If I had just conquered Persia, she couldn't have been more proud of me.

We passed by our church—the church in which I had been christened and received[3] and had sung in the junior choir. We passed by a house in which a girl I used to like and was sure I couldn't live without had lived. Once, when she had mumps, I went to visit her against my mother's wishes, and we sat on her bed and ate the cure of roasted, buttered sweet potatoes that had been placed on her swollen jaws, held there by a piece of white cloth. I don't know how, but my mother found out about it, and I don't know how, but she put an end to our friendship. Shortly after, the girl moved with her family across the sea to somewhere else. We passed the doll store, where I would go with my mother when I was little and point out the doll I wanted that year for Christmas. We passed the store where I bought the much-fought-over shoes I wore to church to be received in. We passed the bank. On my sixth birthday, I was given, among other things, the present of a sixpence.[4] My mother and I then went to this bank, and with the sixpence I opened my own savings account. I was given a little gray book with my name in big letters on it, and in the balance column it said "6d." Every Saturday morning after that, I was given a sixpence—later a shilling, and later a two-and-sixpence piece—and I would take it to the bank for deposit. I had never been allowed to withdraw even a farthing from my bank account until just a few weeks before I was to leave; then the whole account was closed out, and I received from the bank the sum of six pounds ten shillings and two and a half pence.

---

2. **chemist's shop . . . camphor** (kam′ fər): The first phrase is a British term for a pharmacy. The items mentioned are small amounts of plant matter to be used in remedies.

3. **received** *v.*: Accepted into the congregation as a mature Christian.
4. **sixpence** *n.*: A monetary unit in the British commonwealth, worth six pennies (not of the same value as the pennies in United States currency). A shilling is worth two sixpence, a two-and-sixpence is two and one-half shillings, that is, two shillings and one sixpence. A pound is worth twenty shillings. A farthing is a "fourthing": one fourth of a penny.

64 ◆ *On the Edge*

Cross-Curricular Connection: Social Studies

Like Annie John, an increasing number of young people from islands in the West Indies have emigrated to Europe and North America in search of better opportunities. In the 1980's, for example, 17 percent of the population of the islands of Antigua and Barbados legally emigrated to North America. Often, these immigrants are young professionals, such as doctors, nurses, teachers, and writers. Have students speculate on what effects a tiny island nation might experience when an increasing number of its young people, particularly those who are skilled and trained in professions, leave.

We passed the office of the doctor who told my mother three times that I did not need glasses, that if my eyes were feeling weak a glass of carrot juice a day would make them strong again. This happened when I was eight. And so every day at recess I would run to my school gate and meet my mother, who was waiting for me with a glass of juice from carrots she had just grated and then squeezed, and I would drink it and then run back to meet my chums. I knew there was nothing at all wrong with my eyes, but I had recently read a story in *The Schoolgirl's Own Annual* in which the heroine, a girl a few years older than I was then, cut such a figure to my mind with the way she was always adjusting her small, round, horn-rimmed glasses that I felt I must have a pair exactly like them. When it became clear that I didn't need glasses, I began to complain about the glare of the sun being too much for my eyes, and I walked around with my hands shielding them—especially in my mother's presence. My mother then bought for me a

pair of sunglasses with the exact horn-rimmed frames I wanted, and how I enjoyed the gestures of blowing on the lenses, wiping them with the hem of my uniform, adjusting the glasses when they slipped down my nose, and just removing them from their case and putting them on. In three weeks, I grew tired of them and they found a nice resting place in a drawer, along with some other things that at one time or another I couldn't live without.

We passed the store that sold only grooming aids, all imported from England. This store had in it a large porcelain dog—white, with black spots all over and a red ribbon of satin tied around its neck. The dog sat in front of a white porcelain bowl that was always filled with fresh water, and it sat in such a way that it looked as if it had just taken a long drink. When I was a small child, I would ask my mother, if ever we were near this store, to please take me to see the dog, and I would stand in front of it, bent over slightly, my hands resting on my knees, and stare at it and stare at it. I

Port de la Saline, Haiti, Lois Mailou Jones

▲ **Critical Viewing** The people in this painting are setting out on unique adventures. Explain how you can be surrounded by people sharing a similar experience and yet still be alone. **[Analyze]**

from *A Walk to the Jetty* ◆ 65

Customize for
Less Proficient Readers
Check these students' comprehension by having them summarize the events leading up to this point in the story. Then encourage them to make predictions about how the story will turn out. Urge them to record their predictions, and revise them as they proceed through the story.

◆ **Critical Thinking**

❺ **Evaluate** Ask students what this episode about the carrot juice and Annie's demand for glasses reveals about the personalities of Annie and her mother and their relationship. *Students may say that the episode shows that Annie is imaginative, impressionable, determined, and changeable. Her mother seems devoted to Annie's needs and desires and is eager to please her when possible.*

▶**Critical Viewing**◀

❻ **Analyze** Students may say that an experience such as setting out on an adventure can arouse feelings such as fear of the unknown or sadness at leaving loved ones. These feelings can cause people to withdraw into their own memories of the past or their fantasies about the future, rather than relating to the other people sharing their current experience.

Humanities: Art

Port de la Saline, Haiti, by Lois Mailou Jones.

This painting depicts a busy wharf in the Caribbean island nation of Haiti. Its vivid primary colors and repeated angular forms suggest a busy, bustling place. The geometric shapes of the clouds, sails, and foreground objects speak of the artist's ties to Cubism and fascination with African textile patterns. The port suggests a connection with other parts of the world, a connection that Annie

John is about to make.

Lois Mailou Jones was born in Boston in 1905. She has enjoyed a consistently successful career as a painter, teacher, book illustrator, and textile designer. In 1945, James Lane, then curator of painting at the National Gallery of Art in Washington, D.C., said of Jones's work, "It is all, in the best sense of the word, happy art."

Use these questions for discussion:
1. How does the mood of this scene compare with that of the art on page 61? *The mood of this piece is bustling, vibrant, and exciting, unlike the calm mood of the earlier work.*
2. What feelings might a child growing up in an otherwise serene island have about visiting the island's busy harbor? *The child might find the bustling harbor exciting or frightening. Seeing the boats arrive from faraway places might make the child curious and eager to see what those places were like.*

◆ Reading Strategy

❶ Infer Students may say that the library was important to Annie because it was important to her mother, and she wanted to be close to her mother and be like her mother. They may also say that the books in the library allowed the curious girl a view of a wider world outside her island home and that she was a young person with a vivid imagination who loved books.

❷ Clarification Make sure students understand that a jetty is a platform or other structure projecting out into a harbor to influence the current or tide or protect a harbor or shoreline. A jetty may connect to a wharf, where boats can pull alongside to pick up or discharge passengers and cargo.

◆ Critical Thinking

❸ Interpret Ask how the narrator's description of physical sensations suggests an emotional state. *The increased heartbeat and open mouth reflect her nervousness and anticipation.*

◆ Critical Thinking

❹ Compare and Contrast Have students compare and contrast Annie's childhood feelings about being in her father's company with those feelings she has expressed about being in her mother's company. *As a child, Annie felt very intimate with her mother and comfortable sharing the experiences and feelings of her mother's world. In contrast, she finds her father's conversation difficult to understand and identify with because it is not "personal."*

◆ Literary Focus

❺ Flashback In what specific way is this flashback relevant to the action on the jetty now? *Students might say that the fact that this childhood fear returns as she is about to leave home is significant because now—as then—she fears her uncertain, unknown future.*

---

thought this dog more beautiful and more real than any actual dog I had ever seen or any actual dog I would ever see. I must have outgrown my interest in the dog, for when it disappeared I never asked what became of it. We passed the library, and if there was anything on this walk that I might have wept over leaving, this most surely would have been the thing. My mother had been a member of the library long before I was born. And since she took me everywhere with her when I was quite little, when she went to the library she took me along there, too. I would sit in her lap very quietly as she read books that she did not want to take home with her. I could not read the words yet, but just the way they looked on the page was interesting to me. Once, a book she was reading had a large picture of a man in it, and when I asked her who he was she told me that he was Louis Pasteur[5] and that the book was about his life. It stuck in my mind, because she said it was because of him that she boiled my milk to purify it before I was allowed to drink it, that it was his idea, and that that was why the process was called pasteurization. One of the things I had put away in my mother's old trunk in which she kept all my childhood things was my library card. At that moment, I owed sevenpence in overdue fees.

As I passed by all these places, it was as if I were in a dream, for I didn't notice the people coming and going in and out of them, I didn't feel my feet touch ground, I didn't even feel my own body—I just saw these places as if they were hanging in the air, not having top or bottom, and as if I had gone in and out of them all in the same moment. The sun was bright; the sky was blue and just above my head. We then arrived at the jetty.

> ◆ **Reading Strategy**
> Infer why the library is such an important part of Annie's childhood.

5. **Louis Pasteur** (Pas tʉr´) (1822–1895): The French chemist and bacteriologist who developed the process (pasteurization) for using heat to kill disease-causing bacteria in milk.

66 ◆ *On the Edge*

My heart now beat fast, and no matter how hard I tried, I couldn't keep my mouth from falling open and my nostrils from spreading to the ends of my face. My old fear of slipping between the boards of the jetty and falling into the dark-green water where the dark-green eels lived came over me. When my father's stomach started to go bad, the doctor had recommended a walk every evening right after he ate his dinner. Sometimes he would take me with him. When he took me with him, we usually went to the jetty, and there he would sit and talk to the night watchman about cricket[6] or some other thing that didn't interest me, because it was not personal; they didn't talk about their wives, or their children, or their parents, or about any of their likes and dislikes. They talked about things in such a strange way, and I didn't see what they found funny, but sometimes they made each other laugh so much that their guffaws would bound out to sea and send back an echo. I was always sorry when we got to the jetty and saw that the night watchman on duty was the one he enjoyed speaking to; it was like being locked up in a book filled with numbers and diagrams and what-ifs. For the thing about not being able to understand and enjoy what they were saying was I had nothing to take my mind off my fear of slipping in between the boards of the jetty.

Now, too, I had nothing to take my mind off what was happening to me. My mother and my father—I was leaving them forever. My home on an island—I was leaving it forever. What to make of everything? I felt a familiar hollow space inside. I felt I was being held down against my will. I felt I was burning up from head to toe. I felt that someone was tearing me up into little pieces and soon I would be able to see all the little pieces as they floated out into nothing in the deep blue sea. I didn't know whether to laugh or cry. I could see that it would be

6. **cricket** *n.*: A British game, similar to baseball, but played with a flat bat and eleven players on each team.

 Beyond the Classroom

Community Connection

Personal Landmarks As Annie walks to the jetty, she passes community landmarks that remind her of her childhood. Every community is identifiable by landmarks, some obvious and well known, others taken for granted by residents and almost overlooked. Have students consider the general landmarks in their community—those places that stand out, like public buildings, parks, or monuments. Then have them brainstorm for a list of "personal landmarks" in their community, places that hold special memories for them or that played an important part in their growing up. Have each student make a map or drawing, or write a description of his or her personal landmarks, labeling each place with a caption that explains its importance.

66

better not to think too clearly about any one thing. The launch was being made ready to take me, along with some other passengers, out to the ship that was anchored in the sea. My father paid our fares, and we joined a line of people waiting to board. My mother checked my bag to make sure that I had my passport, the money she had given me, and a sheet of paper placed between some pages in my Bible on which were written the names of the relatives—people I had not known existed—with whom I would live in England. Across from the jetty was a wharf, and some stevedores were loading and unloading barges. I don't know why seeing that struck me so, but suddenly a wave of strong feeling came over me, and my heart swelled with a great gladness as the words "I shall never see this again" spilled inside me. But then, just as quickly, my heart shriveled up and the words "I shall never see this again" stabbed at me. I don't know what stopped me from falling in a heap at my parents' feet.

When we were all on board, the launch headed out to sea. Away from the jetty, the water became the customary blue, and the launch left a wide path in it that looked like a road. I passed by sounds and smells that were so familiar that I had long ago stopped paying any attention to them. But now here they were, and the ever-present "I shall never see this again" bobbed up and down inside me. There was the sound of the seagull diving down into the water and coming up with something silverish in its mouth. There was the smell of the sea and the sight of small pieces of rubbish floating around in it. There were boats filled with fishermen coming in early. There was the sound of their voices as they shouted greetings to each other. There was the hot sun, there was the blue sea, there was the blue sky. Not very far away, there was the white sand of the shore, with the run-down houses all crowded in next to each other, for in some places only poor people lived near the shore. I was seated in the launch between my parents, and when I realized that I was

gripping their hands tightly I glanced quickly to see if they were looking at me with scorn, for I felt sure that they must have known of my never-see-this-again feelings. But instead my father kissed me on the forehead and my mother kissed me on the mouth, and they both gave over their hands to me, so that I could grip them as much as I wanted. I was on the verge of feeling that it had all been a mistake, but I remembered that I wasn't a child anymore, and that now when I made up my mind about something I had to see it through. At that moment, we came to the ship, and that was that.

The goodbyes had to be quick, the captain said. My mother introduced herself to him and then introduced me. She told him to keep an eye on me, for I had never gone this far away from home on my own. She gave him a letter to pass on to the captain of the next ship that I would board in Barbados.[7] They walked me to my cabin, a small space that I would share with someone else—a woman I did not know. I had never before slept in a room with someone I did not know. My father kissed me goodbye and told me to be good and to write home often. After he said this, he looked at me, then looked at the floor and swung his left foot, then looked at me again. I could see that he wanted to say something else, something that he had never said to me before, but then he just turned and walked away. My mother said, "Well," and then she threw her arms around me. Big tears streamed down her face, and it must have been that—for I could not bear to see my mother cry—which started me crying, too. She then tightened

◆ **Reading Strategy**
What can you infer about Annie's relationship with her mother based on the fact that she cannot breathe because her mother squeezes her so tightly?

---

7. **Barbados** (bär bā´ dōs): The easternmost island in the West Indies; southeast of Antigua.

from *A Walk to the Jetty* ◆ 67

◆ **Critical Thinking**

6 Interpret Ask students: Why do the words "I shall never see this again" first cause Annie's heart to swell with gladness and then shrivel up? *She has intensely mixed emotions about leaving the people and places she has known since her childhood. Although her childhood world feels confining and she longs for wider experience and opportunities, she also loves much of her past and fears her uncertain future.*

◆ **Critical Thinking**

7 Analyze Ask students how Annie's parents surprise her when she grips their hands on the launch. What does this scene suggest about Annie's relationships with both her parents? *She expects them to scorn her for her weakness, but instead they kiss her and offer their hands to her. Students may say that until this moment Annie was unaware how much both her parents love her and how much she depends on them.*

◆ **Critical Thinking**

8 Analyze What do you think Annie's father wanted to say to her that he had never said before? *He wanted to say he loved her.*

◆ **Reading Strategy**

9 Make Inferences Students may say Annie feels that her mother is overprotective and that her mother's love sometimes feels stifling, holding her back from her own independent life.

🎙 **Speaking and Listening Mini-Lesson**

Conducting an Interview

This mini-lesson supports the Speaking and Listening activity in the Idea Bank on page 70.

Introduce the Concept Tell students that an interview is an opportunity to ask a knowledgeable person a series of focused questions. An interview is an excellent way to gather firsthand, practical information.

Develop Background Help students prepare for their interview by giving them these pointers:

- Students should develop a list of specific questions to ask. What particular concerns do they have about traveling on their own?
- Students should be prepared to ask follow-up questions.
- Encourage students to take notes or tape the interview.

Apply the Information Help groups of students to locate a travel agent to interview. Have them schedule their telephone interview for a time that is convenient for

the travel agent and then carry out the telephone interview. As the interviewee answers their question, they should take notes. When they have finished, they should share the information they received with the class.

Assess the Outcome Evaluate the success of the interviews with these questions: (1) What valuable tips for traveling did they gain? (2) What important information did follow-up questions elicit? (3) What did they learn about conducting an interview?

◆ Critical Thinking

❶ Support Ask students how this last image reinforces one of the themes of the selection. *The image reinforces her growing separation from her mother.*

Reinforce and Extend

Answers

◆ *Literature and Your Life*

Reader's Response Students may admire Annie for leaving home because she was looking to better herself.

Thematic Focus Students may suggest pursuing a new interest or forging new friendships.

☑ Check Your Comprehension

1. The places that remind Annie of her childhood are Miss Dulcie's house, the chemist's shop, the church, the doll store, the bank, the doctor's office, the store that sold grooming aids.
2. Miss Dulcie's house conjures her unhappy days as a seamstress apprentice; the chemist's shop makes her think of first walk alone; the church calls up her christening and the choir; the doll store makes her think of her Christmas dolls; the bank brings back memories of opening her savings account; the doctor's office makes her recall her longing for eyeglasses; the grooming store makes her think of the porcelain dog in the window.
3. Annie has mixed feelings about leaving home. She is happy to be independent, but at the same time, sad to leave home.
4. Annie's mother clutches Annie tightly and sobs during the farewell. Annie's father looks as if he has something important to say, then walks away.

her arms around me and held me to her close, so that I felt that I couldn't breathe. With that, my tears dried up and I was suddenly on my guard. "What does she want now?" I said to myself. Still holding me close to her, she said, in a voice that <u>raked</u> across my skin, "It doesn't matter what you do or where you go, I'll always be your mother and this will always be your home."

I dragged myself away from her and backed off a little, and then I shook myself, as if to wake myself out of a <u>stupor</u>. We looked at each other for a long time with smiles on our faces, but I know the opposite of that was in my heart. As if responding to some invisible cue, we both said, at the very same moment, "Well." Then my mother turned around and walked out the cabin door. I stood there for I don't know how long, and then I remembered that it was customary to stand on deck and wave to your relatives who were returning to shore. From the deck, I could not see my father, but I could see my mother facing the

ship, her eyes searching to pick me out. I removed from my bag a red cotton handkerchief that she had earlier given me for this purpose, and I waved it wildly in the air. Recognizing me immediately, she waved back just as wildly, and we continued to do this until she became just a dot in the matchbox-size launch swallowed up in the big blue sea.

❶

I went back to my cabin and lay down on my berth. Everything trembled as if it had a spring at its very center. I could hear the small waves lap-lapping around the ship. They made an unexpected sound, as if a vessel filled with liquid had been placed on its side and now was slowly emptying out.

◆ Build Vocabulary

raked (rākd) *v.*: Scratched or scraped, as with a rake

stupor (stoō′ per) *n.*: Mental dullness, as if drugged

Guide for Responding

◆ *Literature and Your Life*

Reader's Response Do you admire Annie for leaving home? Why or why not?

Thematic Focus There are many quieter ways of showing independence than a dramatic departure from home. Tell about a quiet way in which you have shown greater maturity and independence.

Timeline On a timeline showing the next five years, indicate some of the steps you will take to achieve an important goal.

☑ Check Your Comprehension

1. Identify four of the places that remind Annie of episodes from her childhood.
2. Briefly summarize the memory that each of these places calls up.
3. What are Annie's feelings about leaving home?
4. Describe how her mother and father say goodbye.

68 ◆ On the Edge

Beyond Literature

Geography Connection

The Landscape and Climate of Antigua White sand beaches, spectacular coral reefs, and an average temperature of 80 degrees make Antigua a popular vacation spot. There are 365 beaches on Antigua—one for each day of the year! Antigua is about 14 miles long and 11 miles wide, covering 108 square miles. With an average rainfall of only 40 inches per year, Antigua is one of the sunniest eastern Caribbean islands. While this is welcome news for tourists, for the people who live on Antigua year-round, droughts can be devastating to their property and livelihood. Why do you think islands are such popular tourist spots?

 Beyond the Selection

FURTHER READING

Other Works by Jamaica Kincaid
Annie John, Lucy, The Autobiography of My Mother

Other Works About Growing Up and Leaving Home
The Beggar Maid and Other Stories, Alice Munro
Black Ice, Lorene Cary
I Know Why the Caged Bird Sings, Maya Angelou
We suggest that you preview these works before recommending them to students.

INTERNET

For more information on Jamaica Kincaid, we suggest that you and your students visit the following site on the Internet. Please be aware, however, that sites may have changed from the time we published this information. **http://www. Salon1999.com./05/ features/ kincaid.html**
We *strongly recommend* that you preview the site before you send students to it.

Guide for Responding (continued)

◆ Critical Thinking

INTERPRET

1. In what way is Annie walking through time as well as through space? [Infer]
2. Why does Annie reexperience her old fear of falling through the boards of the jetty? [Infer]
3. Compare Annie's relationship with her father with the one she has with her mother. [Compare and Contrast]
4. Describe Annie's response to leaving the island. [Interpret]

APPLY

5. Will Annie be successful in her new life? Why or why not? [Hypothesize]

EXTEND

6. Although Annie disliked it, an apprentice situation could have advantages. Name three trades that could be best learned this way. [Career Link]

◆ Reading Strategy

MAKE INFERENCES

Annie's mother hugs Annie so tightly that she can hardly breathe. From this painful embrace and Annie's response to it, you can **infer** that Annie sometimes feels trapped by her mother.

Use the following details to make inferences about Annie's relationship with her father.

1. His conversation with the watchman didn't interest her "because it was not personal."
2. As they part, he wants "to say . . . something he had never said . . . before," but then he walks away.

◆ Literary Focus

FLASHBACK

This story is told mainly through **flashbacks,** journeys back into time. These flashbacks help you understand how Annie developed, but their precise details also make the past come alive.

1. Find two other flashbacks and explain how the author uses precise details to make them vivid.
2. What do the flashbacks suggest about Annie's reasons for leaving home?

◆ Build Vocabulary

USING THE ROOT -stup-

Knowing that -stup- means "to be stunned or amazed," choose the letter of the best synonym for each of the numbered words containing -stup-.

1. stupefy: (a) entertain, (b) numb, (c) revive
2. stupendous: (a) astonishing, (b) excessive, (c) ridiculous
3. stupefaction: (a) alertness, (b) satisfaction, (c) bewilderment

USING THE WORD BANK

On your paper, complete each sentence with the most appropriate word from the Word Bank:

1. Annie had been ____?____ to a rude and stern seamstress.
2. Annie ____?____ above her father and could see the top of his head.
3. Annie complained that her mother's voice ____?____ across her skin.
4. For a moment, staring at her mother, Annie was in a ____?____.

◆ Build Grammar Skills

CLAUSES

A **clause** is a group of words that contains both a subject and a verb. An **independent clause** can stand alone as a sentence, but a **subordinate clause** cannot.

Practice Identify the independent and subordinate clauses in these sentences from the story.

1. If I had just conquered Persia, she couldn't have been more proud of me.
2. We passed the bank.
3. We then arrived at the jetty.
4. My father paid our fares, and we joined a line of people waiting to board.
5. She told him to keep an eye on me, for I had never gone this far away from home on my own.

Writing Application Write a paragraph describing places that are special to you. Include at least three sentences that contain subordinate clauses.

from A Walk to the Jetty ◆ 69

Answers

◆ Critical Thinking

1. As she walks, Annie is going back to scenes from her childhood and forward to a new life.
2. Annie's fear reflects her apprehension about leaving home.
3. Annie's relationship with her father is constrained, while the relationship with her mother is affectionate and mutually dependent.
4. Her response to leaving home is bittersweet; she's torn between the need to strike out on her own and her attachment to childhood experiences.
5. Some students will say that although luck will play a role in Annie's future, her determination and curiosity will serve her well in her new life.
6. Examples of trades in which people could benefit from an apprenticeship include electrician, carpenter, hair stylist, salesperson.

◆ Reading Strategy

1. Since Annie responds to the personal, you can infer her relationship with her father is remote.
2. You can infer that this lost opportunity to make a connection leaves both Annie and her father feeling sad; the incident reinforces their communication difficulties.

◆ Literary Focus

1. Possible flashbacks include the apprenticeship with Miss Dulcie, brought alive by details such as sweeping needles off the floor, and Annie's walk to the chemist, brought alive by details such as the smell of her mother's talcum powder and Annie's dress with acrobats on it.
2. Some students will say the flashbacks suggest that Annie was overprotected and that her life in Antigua had its limitations; therefore, she wanted to leave home.

◆ Build Grammar Skills

1. If I had just conquered Persia—*subordinate*; she couldn't have been more proud of me—*independent*
2. We passed the bank—*independent*
3. We then arrived at the jetty—*independent*
4. My father paid our fares—*independent*; we joined a line of people waiting to board—*independent*
5. She told him to keep an eye on me—*independent*; I had never gone this far away from home on my own—*independent*

✒ Writer's Solution

For additional instruction and practice, use the lesson in the **Language Lab CD-ROM** on clauses and use the pages on clauses (pp. 51–58) in the *Writer's Solution Grammar Practice Book.*

◆ Build Vocabulary

Using the Word Root -stup-
1. b 2. a 3. c

Using the Word Bank
1. apprenticed; 2. loomed;
3. raked; 4. stupor

69

Idea Bank

Customizing for
Performance Levels

Following are suggestions for matching Idea Bank topics with your students' performance levels:

Less Advanced Students: 1, 4
Average Students: 2, 5, 7
More Advanced Students: 3, 6

Customizing for
Learning Modalities

Following are suggestions for matching Idea Bank topics with your students' learning modalities:

Visual/Spatial: 7
Verbal/Linguistic: 4, 5
Logical/Mathematical: 6
Interpersonal: 4

Writing Mini-Lesson

Refer students to the Writing Handbook, page 965, for instruction on the writing process, and page 967 for further information on expository writing.

Writers at Work Videodisc

Have students view the videodisc segment (Ch. 3) featuring Rudolfo Anaya to spark class discussion of expository writing. Have students discuss what Anaya says about commitment to a subject.

Play frames 22803 to 32243

Writing Lab CD-ROM

Have students complete the tutorial on Expository Writing. Follow these steps:

1. Students can view a video clip to learn more about how to write how-to instructions.
2. Invite students to complete a notecard activity to enter details for their how-to manual.
3. Have students draft on computer.
4. Have students use the Revision Checker for transition words.

Sourcebook

Have students use Chapter 3, Exposition (pp. 63–89), for additional support. The chapter includes an annotated student model of a problem-and-solution essay (p. 89).

Build Your Portfolio

Idea Bank

Writing

1. **Annie's Packing List** Create a list of items that Annie might have packed for her journey to England.

2. **Letter of Introduction** As Annie John, write a letter of introduction to an English family or business, offering a brief biography and a description of your skills. **[Career Link]**

3. **Description of Antigua for the Internet** Write a description of Antigua for an Internet Home Page. Describe Antigua's attractions so that Internet surfers will want to visit the island. **[Media Link; Social Studies Link]**

Speaking and Listening

4. **Telephone Interview** Like Annie John, you may soon be making a trip on your own. Interview a local travel agent by phone to learn some of the dos and don'ts for the teenage traveler.

5. **Persuasive Speech** One way in which teenagers can travel abroad is to participate in exchange programs. Write a persuasive speech that convinces listeners that your school should participate in such a program. **[Social Studies Link]**

Projects

6. **The Statistics of a Decision** Create a chart that shows the numbers of high-school graduates who move out of state to pursue education or job opportunities. **[Social Studies Link; Math Link]**

7. **Map of Annie's Walk** Using details from the story and your own imagination, create a map showing Annie's walk to the jetty. Include all the landmarks mentioned in the story. **[Art Link]**

Writing Mini-Lesson

How-to Manual for New Students

Write a how-to manual for new students in your school. Include tips, advice, and amusing anecdotes. As you cover everything from lunchroom behavior to test taking, be sure to explain clearly any procedures new students must follow.

Writing Skills Focus: Clear Explanation of Procedures

Problem-solution essays and informative speeches also require a clear explanation of procedures. Even short stories may contain such explanations, as this example from "A Walk to the Jetty" proves.

Model From the Story

My mother . . . instructed me on what side of the road to walk, where to make a turn, where to cross, how to look carefully before I crossed, and if I met anyone that I knew to politely pass greetings and keep on my way.

Your explanation won't be designed for a five-year-old, but like this one it will contain all the necessary details. Also, you can develop your explanation at every stage of the writing process.

Prewriting Brainstorm for items to include in your how-to manual. Then identify the items you will actually include. After identifying the procedures you'll explain, break them down into steps.

Drafting Begin by drafting the most important procedures and explain them as clearly as possible. For example, don't just say, "Join a team." Give the steps involved in trying out for a team.

Revising Have a classmate read your explanations of procedures and determine whether or not they're clear and concise. Where appropriate, add or clarify steps in a procedure to ensure that your manual will be useful to a newcomer.

✓ ASSESSMENT OPTIONS

Formal Assessment, Selection Test, pp. 10–12, and Assessment Resources Software. The selection test is designed so that it can be easily customized to the performance levels of your students.
Alternative Assessment, p. 4, includes options for less advanced students, more advanced students, logical/mathematical learners, verbal/linguistic learners, and visual/spatial learners.

PORTFOLIO ASSESSMENT
Use the following rubrics in the *Alternative Assessment* booklet to assess student writing:
Annie's Packing List: Definition/Classification Rubric, p. 99
Letter of Introduction: Résumé/Cover Letter Rubric, p. 114
Description of Antigua for the Internet: Description Rubric, p. 97
Writing Mini-Lesson: How-to/Process Explanation Rubric, p. 100

Writing Process Workshop

How-to Instructions

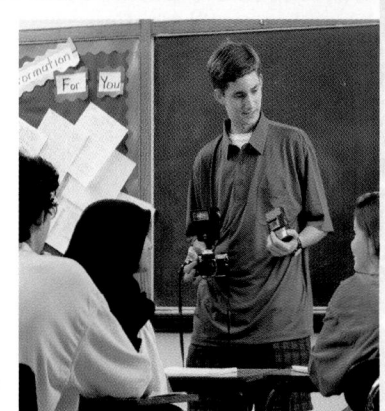

How-to instructions explain the steps involved in doing a particular activity or process. Write a set of instructions for something you know how to do—for example, hit a baseball or install a new game on your computer. Your instructions will help your readers perform the process—even if they are unfamiliar with it.

The following skills, introduced in this section's Writing Mini-Lessons, will help you write clear how-to instructions.

Writing Skills Focus

▶ **Give a clear explanation** of the procedures involved. Start by writing down the most important procedures and then explaining the steps within each procedure. (See p. 70.)

▶ **Use transitions to show time.** Words such as *first, next,* and *finally* will make the sequence of steps that you are describing more logical. (See p. 43.)

▶ **Use transitions to show cause-and-effect relationships.** Words and phrases such as *as a result, because,* and *in order to* will let the reader clearly understand how one action will bring about another. (See p. 57.)

Edmund Hillary uses these skills as he describes the laborious ascent up Mt. Everest.

MODEL FROM LITERATURE

from "The Final Assault" by Edmund Hillary

I took a hold on the rock in front and then jammed one of my crampons into the hard ice behind. Leaning back with my oxygen set on the ice, I slowly levered myself upward. ② Searching feverishly with my spare boot, I found a tiny ledge on the rock and took some of the weight off of my other leg. I slowly forced my way up—wriggling and jamming and using every little hold. In one place I managed to force my ice axe into a crack in the ice, and this gave me the necessary purchase to get over a holdless stretch.

① The phrase *and then* indicates a transition in time that makes the sequence easier to follow.

② Hillary clearly explains the steps involved in his struggle up the rock wall.

③ This sentence describes a clear cause-and-effect relationship.

Beyond the Classroom

Career Connection

Tell students that they will frequently come across written instructions for completing a task and may someday be asked to write such instructions themselves. Careers that may involve such a task range from a technical writer who writes instruction manuals to a person working at a foundation or for a member of Congress, writing instructions that tell how to change people's attitude on a particular subject.

Have students think about how-to instructions that they've come across that strike them as poorly or expertly written. Invite them to describe the problems with weak real-life examples and to suggest ways to improve them.

Develop Student Writing

Prewriting

To help students choose a topic, you might suggest that they think about unusual activities that might be fun for others to learn, and jot them down on separate slips of paper. For example, students may write "How to Play Bagpipes," "How to Draw an Animated Cartoon," and "How to Care for a Pet Iguana." Have students place their topics in a bin. Other students then pick topics at random.

Customize for
English Language Learners

Students learning English may have trouble with specialized vocabulary that relates to their topic. Once students have chosen a topic, define any specialized words that you think they might need. For example, if a student chooses "How to Play a Saxophone," define such words as *reed, blow, beat, bass, treble,* and any other musical words you think the student might need.

Customize for
Less Proficient Writers

These students may benefit from using a transition word bin, listing any transition words they might use, before they begin to draft.

Customize for
More Advanced Students

Challenge these students to write on a topic about which they know nothing at all. Doing so will enhance their research skills, vocabulary, and general knowledge.

 Writer's Solution

Writing Lab CD-ROM
The Gathering Details section of the tutorial on Exposition includes the screen Identifying Important Details. Have students consult this screen to help them streamline their instructions and weed out any unnecessary information.

Drafting

Encourage students to draft their how-to instructions in a single sitting, without pausing to labor over a word choice or to correct grammatical errors. Once students have completed a draft, they can go back into their work and make extensive revisions.

APPLYING LANGUAGE SKILLS:
Transitions to Show Time

Transition words that show time will make the sequence of steps that you are describing obvious.

Transition Words:

first	second	next
last	then	finally
after	before	soon
third	fourth	later
after a while		following
simultaneously		
at the same time		

Practice On your paper, add transition words to show time to the following passage. Crack two eggs in a bowl. Whip the eggs. Pour into a preheated frying pan. Turn over the eggs with a spatula.

Writing Application As you draft your how-to instructions, use transition words to show time in order to make the sequence of steps you are describing logical.

Writer's Solution Connection
Writing Lab

To help you narrow your topic, see the screen entitled Focusing Your Topic. You'll find it in the Writing Lab tutorial on Exposition.

72 ◆ On the Edge

Prewriting

Choose a Topic Think about a skill or activity that interests you, that you know well, and that is complicated to the extent that a person could not learn it simply by watching. It could be a hobby, such as building model airplanes or origami. You can also choose one of the topics below.

> **Topic Ideas**
> - Setting up an aquarium
> - Skateboarding
> - Collecting crystals
> - Starting a vegetable garden
> - Training a pet to perform a trick

Focus Your Topic Once you've chosen your topic, make sure you'll be able to give complete instructions within the planned length of your paper. The example below shows how one student narrowed his topic.

Using a Camera

Taking Pictures

Loading Film

Organize Details in Categories Make lists of details for each of the following: materials, safety factors, steps in the process.

Drafting

Make Your Writing Clear and Brief As you write, assume that readers know little or nothing about your topic. Write your explanation in easy-to-understand terms. Avoid using specialized vocabulary that readers might not understand. Show how one step or event leads to another by using transition words to indicate the cause-and-effect relationships.

Anticipate Problems At some time, you may have encountered problems doing the activity you're now explaining. If you had a problem, there's a good chance others will as well. Mention possible problems that the reader may have, and show how to solve them.

Applying Language Skills

Transitions to Show Time
Remind students that transitions such as *first, next,* and *finally* are especially important in how-to instructions. They not only make the instructions flow more smoothly but are crucial for a proper understanding.

Answers

1. *First,* crack two eggs in a bowl. *Next,* whip the eggs, *then* pour into a preheated frying pan. *Last,* turn over the eggs with a spatula.

 Writer's Solution

For additional instruction and practice, have students complete the **Language Lab CD-ROM** lesson on Unity and Coherence in Paragraphs.

Revising

Use a Checklist Review the Writing Skills Focus on p. 71. Use the items as a checklist to evaluate and revise your observation.

▶ Have I given a clear explanation of the procedures involved?

Include any steps you may have forgotten to mention in the first draft.

▶ Have I used transitions to show cause-and-effect relationships?

Add words or phrases such as because, as a result, consequently, *and so on, to make the relationships between cause and effect clear to the reader.*

▶ Have I used transitions to show time?

Add words such as first, simultaneously, at the same time, *and so on, to describe a logical sequence of events.*

REVISION MODEL
Fixing a Flat Tire

First let all the air out of the tire. ① *Then remove the entire tire from the bicycle.* Separate the tire from the rim, revealing the tube inside. ② *Next,* using a dull knife or a spoon, take the tube out of the metal rim and reinflate it. Place the tube in a pan of water and gently squeeze. ③ ~~Keep your hair out of the water.~~ Look for tiny bubbles on the tube. When you see them, you've found the puncture.

① The writer adds an important step in the process, using a transition to show time order.

② The writer adds a transition word.

③ The writer deletes an unnecessary sentence.

Publishing and Presenting

Demonstration Hold a demonstration of your how-to instructions. Here are some tips for presenting your writing.

▶ Create charts or diagrams to aid your presentation.

▶ Use index cards to keep your information organized and handy.

▶ Print out finished copies of your instructions so your listeners can refer to them during your presentation.

▶ Leave time for questions.

APPLYING LANGUAGE SKILLS: Pronouns

Pronouns—words that take the place of nouns—help writers avoid repeating the same nouns over and over. For a pronoun to make sense, however, its antecedent—the noun or nouns it replaces—must be clear. All personal pronouns, such as *he, she, it, they,* and *we,* must have clear antecedents.

Example:

Make sure that your oxygen tank has all of its valves working properly.
antecedent   pronoun

Practice On your paper, circle the pronoun and its antecedent.

1. Edmund Hillary stopped to check his oxygen.
2. Make sure that your partner has both of his or her hands on the ice axe.

Writing Application Review your how-to instructions, and make sure that all of the pronouns have clear antecedents.

Writer's Solution Connection
Language Lab

For more practice with pronouns, complete the Language Lab lesson on Pronouns and Antecedents.

Revising

You may have students work with peer editors to revise their how-to instructions. Have peer reviewers use the revision checklist to review. Tell the peer reviewers to offer specific, concrete suggestions for improvement rather than general criticism.

Publishing

If students choose not to share their instructions, have them ask themselves these questions to help them reflect on the assignment:

• What parts did I enjoy the most? The least?

• What did this writing experience teach me about the topic? What else would I like to learn about it?

Reinforce and Extend

Review the Writing Guidelines
After students have completed their papers, review the characteristics of how-to instructions. Encourage students to come up with additional criteria for an interesting short story based on what they learned through completing the assignment.

Applying Language Skills
Answers
1. Edmund Hillary stopped to check his oxygen. Pronoun: *his.* Antecedent: *Edmund Hillary.*
2. Make sure that your partner has both of his or her hands on the ice axe. Pronouns: *his, her.* Antecedent: *partner.*

Writer's Solution

For additional instruction and practice, have students complete the **Language Lab CD-ROM** lessons on Pronouns and Antecedents or Pronoun Case and the practice pages in the *Writer's Solution Grammar Practice Book* (pp. 76–79).

✓ ASSESSMENT		4	3	2	1
PORTFOLIO ASSESSMENT Use the rubric on How-to/ Process Explanation in the *Alternative Assessment* booklet (p. 100) to assess students' writing. Add these criteria to customize the rubric to this assignment.	**Transitional Words**	Transitions to show time and cause-effect relationships are used effectively.	Transitions to show time and cause-effect relationships are used.	Transition words are few.	Transition words are almost completely absent.
	Pronouns	There are no mistakes with pronoun case. All antecedents are clear.	There are minor mistakes with pronoun case and antecedents.	There are noticeable mistakes with pronoun case, as well as misplaced and dangling modifiers.	There are frequent mistakes with pronoun case as well as numerous misplaced and dangling modifiers.

Students will be familiar with persuasive writing—first and foremost from advertisements on television and radio and in print. Inform students that the ability to evaluate persuasive messages is increasingly important in our consumer-driven society.

Customize for
English Language Learners

Students learning English may have trouble with words in the sample persuasive message, including, but not limited to, *proposed, inhabit, defenseless, inevitably, displaced, unsuspecting,* and *disruption.* Explain the meanings of these words and the connotations of such words as *defenseless* and why the writer would use such a word in a persuasive essay.

Apply the Strategy

After students have answered the questions, have them think of a controversial issue in their school or community. Have them discuss various sides of the issue and then look for examples of reverse psychology and emotional appeals.

Answers

1. The writer employs the following persuasive techniques: appeals to the reader's emotions through loaded words and phrases ("defenseless animals"), reverse psychology ("For those of you unmoved by the disruption of wildlife"), and appeals to intellect (taxes will be raised $400 per year; traffic will increase on the weekends).

2. The writer uses the following points to support his or her claim that the pool is a mistake: plants will be destroyed, animals will be displaced, taxes and weekend traffic will increase.

3. Students should not be persuaded by this poorly reasoned and supported appeal.

Evaluating Persuasive Messages

Real-World Reading Skills Workshop

Strategies for Success

When your little brother whines to come along with you and your friends, he has something in common with this poster recruiting Red Cross volunteers. They are both trying, in different ways, to persuade you to take an action. An editorial in the newspaper may appeal to your reason to get you to take a stand on a certain issue. A charity's request for a donation will more likely appeal to your emotions. The following guidelines will help you evaluate

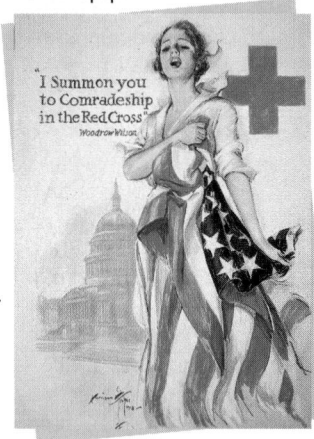

persuasive messages and the techniques through which they are presented.

Identify Persuasive Techniques First, identify the persuasive technique. For instance, is the request for a donation appealing to your sense of compassion or guilt? Is the editorial offering sound reasons, or is it trying to stir up fears? The following persuasive techniques are common in persuasive writing:

▶ Using enticing slogans and/or images to get the reader or viewer to buy a product
▶ Appealing to the reader's emotions
▶ Appealing to the reader's intellect or sense of reason
▶ Using reverse psychology ("You don't want to wear these shades—they're probably too cool for you.")

Evaluate the Message and the Technique
Advertisers and salespeople will try to appeal to your emotions, but you must consider your needs and the soundness of their arguments before agreeing to purchase anything or to take an action.

When you are being persuaded, evaluate whether the persuasive message and technique are appropriate for the situation.

Apply the Strategy

Look at this editorial and evaluate the message and techniques the writer uses against the construction of a swimming pool.

> To Whom It May Concern:
>
> Constructing the proposed new pool would be a huge mistake for our town. Plants would be destroyed, and wildlife that inhabit the park would be driven from their homes. Defenseless animals would inevitably starve or be killed by automobiles as they wander the streets searching for new homes. The displaced animals would also be a serious traffic hazard to unsuspecting motorists.
>
> For those of you who are unmoved by the disruption of our wildlife, think about the increase in taxes. Each resident's taxes must be raised by $400 for the first year in order to pay for the pool's construction. Also, traffic to our small town would increase during weekends and holidays due to the out-of-towners coming to use the pool.
>
> Please write to town hall and tell them that you DO NOT support the construction of the New Valley Swim Club.

1. What techniques does the writer employ?
2. What evidence supports the writer's claim?
3. Would you be persuaded by this editorial? Why or why not?

PART 2 *Dangerous Destinies*

Untitled, Rob Day/SIS

Dangerous Destinies ◆ 75

This section's selections emphasize the dangers, real and imagined, in our destinies. In "The Masque of the Red Death" destiny takes the form of a horrible plague to which the sequestered nobles of Middle Ages Europe find they are not immune. The "fear" described in the poem of the same name is a fear of not raising a daughter well. The fear in the poem "The street" is the fear of following and being followed by a nameless, faceless foe. The poem "Spring and All," meanwhile, describes the delicate rebirth of the natural world in a cold, harsh environment. The danger in "Two Friends" is very real indeed—the Prussian soldiers who patrol the outskirts of Paris during the Franco-Prussian War. The two friends who encounter this danger find it has fatal consequences. The section ends on a positive note, in "Damon and Pythias." This retelling of the classical Greek myth tells how two friends are able to evade death through their unswerving loyalty to each other.

Customize for
Varying Student Needs
When assigning the selections in this part to your students, keep in mind the following factors:

"The Masque of the Red Death"
• A classic short story whose nine-tenth-century prose may be challenging, especially for less proficient readers
• The macabre subject matter will appeal to students.

"Fear"; The street"; "Spring and All"
• Three short poems
• Vivid imagery and short stanzas make these poems accessible to students

"Two Friends"
• A medium-length short story (6 pp.) with a shocking ending

"Damon and Pythias"
• A very brief selection (3 pp.)
• Simple vocabulary and style make it accessible to most students

 Humanities: Art

Untitled by Rob Day.
Born and raised in Indiana, and staunchly committed to staying there, Rob Day has become an extremely successful illustrator of magazine and newspaper articles, having created works for such publications as *Sports Illustrated, Business Week,* and *Rolling Stone.* Day began to draw as a small child and first thought of a career in art under the encouragement of his junior-high-school art teacher. After graduating from the Herron School of Art, he began to submit his work to publishers.

His combination of a dreamlike tone and realistic style won him almost instantaneous success as a graphic illustrator.

Have your students link the painting to the theme of Part 2, "Dangerous Destinies," by answering the following:
Make up a story idea to explain how the man got there. *Sample answers: The man climbed up from below but has reached a point where he cannot go any higher; the man fell from his business class seat in an airplane and slid down the cliff to this spot.*

Guide for Reading

OBJECTIVES

1. To read, comprehend, and interpret a short story
2. To relate a story to personal experience
3. To use context clues to define unfamiliar words
4. To recognize symbols
5. To build vocabulary in context and learn the suffix *-tion*
6. To develop skill in identifying subject-verb agreement
7. To write a proposal for a team symbol, demonstrating the benefits of the idea
8. To respond to the story through writing, speaking and listening, and projects

SKILLS INSTRUCTION

Vocabulary: Suffixes: *-tion*

Grammar: Subject-Verb Agreement

Reading Strategy: Context Clues

Literary Focus: Symbols

Writing: Demonstrating Benefits

Speaking and Listening: Radio Script (teacher edition)

Critical Viewing: Analyze

PORTFOLIO OPPORTUNITIES

Writing: Invitation; Description; Research Report

Writing Mini-Lesson: Proposal for a Team Symbol

Speaking and Listening: Press Conference; Radio Script

Projects: Costume Design; Multimedia Presentation

More About the Author
Because Edgar Allan Poe's life was disappointing in many ways, he escaped into a fantasy world in his imagination. Though his stories are horrifying, they are also strangely compelling. As one critic has written, "He dreams aloud, and we witness the extraordinary adventures he took pleasure in inventing because he was not allowed to live them. His heroes are projections of his real and secret self."

Edgar Allan Poe *(1809–1849)*

The early American author Edgar Allan Poe died childless, but today he is credited with numerous literary grandchildren and great-grandchildren.

Included among Poe's literary "descendants" are Stephen King and Sir Arthur Conan Doyle.

In fact, the author who set the standards for the modern horror story and detective story, Poe has influenced literally thousands of writers.

A Troubled Childhood Poe was born in Boston, Massachusetts, to a family of impoverished traveling actors. Within a year, his father had deserted the family and his mother had died.

Young Edgar was raised, but never formally adopted, by Mr. and Mrs. John Allan in Richmond, Virginia. As he grew up, Poe got into conflicts with his adoptive father. In 1827, for example, Poe had to withdraw from the University of Virginia because of gambling debts that Allan refused to pay.

Success and Failure and Success In 1833, Poe entered a group of stories and a poem in a Baltimore literary contest. One of the stories, "MS. Found in a Bottle," won the fiction prize.

Although Poe's stories and poems continued to win recognition, his writing did not bring him financial success. In 1849, two years after the death of his beloved wife, Virginia, Poe died poor and alone.

Today the works of this solitary figure—stories like "The Tell-Tale Heart" and poems like "The Raven"—attract crowds of readers. You can join Poe's enormous "family" too as you enter the frightening but fascinating world of "The Masque of the Red Death."

◆ Build Vocabulary

SUFFIXES: *-tion*

At one point in the story, there comes "an uneasy *cessation* of all things"—all activity ceases. The word *cessation* is built on *cease* with the suffix *-tion*, which means "the act of." Therefore, the word *cessation* literally means "the act of ceasing."

The suffix *-tion* makes a noun of the word to which it is added. It is a very common suffix. The Word Bank also contains the word *disapprobation*, which means "the act of disapprobating," or disapproving.

august
piquancy
arabesque
cessation
disapprobation
habiliments

WORD BANK

Before you read, preview this list of words from the selection.

◆ Build Grammar Skills

SUBJECT-VERB AGREEMENT

A verb must **agree** with its subject in number (singular or plural), even when the subject comes after the verb, rather than before it.

In describing the palace in this story, Poe often lists details in sentences beginning with *there* followed by the verb *is* or *was* (singular) or *are* or *were* (plural). Notice how the verb agrees with the subject that follows it:

Singular Subject and Verb:

There was a sharp turn at every twenty yards . . .

Plural Subject and Verb:

There were arabesque figures . . .

76 ◆ On the Edge

Prentice Hall Literature Program Resources

REINFORCE / RETEACH / EXTEND

Selection Support Pages
Build Vocabulary: Suffixes: *-tion*, p. 18
Build Grammar Skills: Subject-Verb Agreement, p. 19
Reading Strategy: Context Clues, p. 20
Literary Focus: Symbols, p. 21

Strategies for Diverse Student Needs, p. 5

Beyond Literature
Cross-Curricular Connection: Science, p. 5

Formal Assessment Selection Test, pp. 13–15;

Assessment Resources Software

Alternative Assessment, p. 5

Writing and Language Transparencies
Daily Language Practice, Weeks 8 and 9, pp. 119 and 120 (also hard copy)

Resource Pro CD-ROM
"The Masque of the Red Death"—includes all resource material and customizable lesson plan

Listening to Literature Audiocassettes
"The Masque of the Red Death"

The Masque of the Red Death

◆ *Literature and Your Life*

CONNECT YOUR EXPERIENCE

Some celebrities go to great lengths to shield themselves from the world, building elaborate homes with grounds protected by gates and guards. Inside these compounds, they can create a fantasy world filled with every luxury money can buy.

Like one of these celebrities, the prince in this story builds a palace where he can live out all his fantasies and escape from the sufferings of his subjects and the disease that ravages his country.

Journal Writing As a celebrity, plan what you would include in your magnificent dream house.

THEMATIC FOCUS: DANGEROUS DESTINIES

As you read about Prince Prospero's attempt to escape from the "Red Death," ask yourself: Can money and power buy safety?

◆ Background for Understanding

HISTORY

It seemed that no one was safe in medieval Europe. In the 1300's and 1400's, a plague known as the Black Death swept across the continent, killing 25 million people. Most of the afflicted died within three to five days after the first symptoms appeared. Again, in 1665, an outbreak of the plague ravaged the city of London.

For Poe and others living in the early nineteenth century, these outbreaks were a haunting historical memory. In addition, diseases like influenza, cholera, and typhoid were an ever-present threat. The "Red Death" is a plague Poe invented for his story, but it is based on historical and timeless fear.

◆ Literary Focus

SYMBOLS

If you wanted to create a **symbol** for the disease Poe calls the "Red Death"—a person, place, event, or thing that represented it— you might describe a skeleton in a red cape. Writers often use concrete symbols like this to help readers *experience* the meaning of a general idea, like "disease" or "safety."

Poe's story is filled with symbols. The prince, his fantastic masquerade ball, the plague raging in the kingdom—all these things seem to stand for more than themselves. Ask yourself what they could mean.

◆ Reading Strategy

CONTEXT CLUES

If you were invited to a masquerade, you'd use **context clues**—hints from the surroundings—to figure out what to wear. Such hints might include the purpose of the party, instructions on the invitation, and the dress plans of other guests. In a similar way, you can figure out the meanings of unfamiliar words by using context clues in surrounding sentences.

As you read the story, identify context clues to define unfamiliar words. Look at the example from the following passage:

> . . . All these and security were within. Without was the Red Death.
>
> It was toward the close of the fifth or sixth month of his *seclusion*, and while the pestilence raged most furious abroad . . .

Unfamiliar word: *seclusion*
Words similar in meaning: *within*
Words opposite in meaning: *without*
Probable meaning of seclusion: *Keeping inside, hiding*

Guide for Reading ◆ 77

Interest Grabber Have students imagine themselves in this situation: They are living in Europe in the 1300's. A plague called the Black Death threatens the lives of millions. They have been invited to embark on a plague-free ship until the epidemic dies out. However, some members of their families and many of their friends are not invited. How would they handle this dilemma?

Use students' comments as a springboard to discuss the plague and Poe's use of it as backdrop for a tale of anxiety and horror. In Poe's story, the Black Death becomes the Red Death.

Customize for *Less Proficient Readers*

To help less proficient readers deal with the sophisticated vocabulary and sentence structure in this story, have them follow along in their text as they listen to the recording of the selection. Then guide them to determine the meaning of a word from context as they read, looking for unfamiliar words and using the surrounding context clues to define them.

🎧 Listening to Literature Audiocassettes

Customize for *More Advanced Students*

Have your more advanced students read this story as an allegory, a story intended to be read entirely on a symbolic level. In an allegorical story, the characters, settings, and events are intended to have meanings independent of the surface story. For example, the palace in "The Masque of the Red Death" may stand for the entire world. Your more advanced students can try to determine the symbolic lesson about life being told in this tale.

Customize for *English Language Learners*

The difficult vocabulary and long, complicated sentences in this story may cause comprehension problems for these students. Model the process of defining unfamiliar words by using context clues. Then guide students to break down sentences.

Preparing for Standardized Tests

Reading and Vocabulary Practice using context clues will improve students' performance on reading comprehension items on the verbal portions of standardized tests. Guide students through the process of using context clues to unlock word meaning. Write the following on the chalkboard: ". . . a gigantic wall clock of ebony. Its *pendulum* swung. . . ." Elicit from students that the word *its* refers to *wall clock*, and that the unfamiliar word (*pendulum*) is associated with something that swings. Using these context clues, students can figure out that *pendulum* means "a weight that swings back and forth, often used to regulate clocks." Students can also use the Reading Strategy page in *Selection Support* (p. 20) to practice this skill.

Grammar and Language In English usage sections and writing sections of tests, students are required to apply the concept of agreement. Students may be asked to choose the correct verb to complete a sentence, as in the following:

There (was, were) three people waiting. *were*

They may also be required to apply correct agreement in a revision portion of a standardized test.

One-Minute Insight In addition to being a chilling horror story, this selection is a brilliant portrayal of the vanity of the rich and powerful and their illusions of invulnerability. Prince Prospero, the main character, believes he can save himself and a select few from the plague that is menacing the rest of society. In the story's climax, Prospero learns that wealth and privilege will not spare him from the grip of death.

◆ Reading Strategy

❶ Context Clues Ask students to explain how the sequence "seizure, progress and termination" is a context clue that can help them figure out the meaning of *termination*. Encourage them to then define *termination*. *Because the sequence refers to a deadly disease, seizure would mean the onset or beginning of the disease, progress would refer to the stages of the disease from beginning to end, and termination, coming last in the sequence, would therefore mean the end of the disease.*

◆ Critical Thinking

❷ Deduce Ask students: What kind of person is Prince Prospero? How does Poe play on Prospero's name? *The prince is wealthy, happy, and not particularly concerned about the pestilence devastating his land. His name suggests "prosperity."*

◆ Literary Focus

❸ Symbol Students should take into account details that suggest how carefully the prince planned the wall to make sure it was strong and would protect him from the disease outside: "gates of iron," "welded bolts." Their reasoning should lead them to conclude the following: *The wall represents the efforts of the rich and powerful to shield themselves from the dangers faced by ordinary people.*

◆ Critical Thinking

❹ Interpret Ask students: From the courtiers' point of view, why was it folly to grieve or to think? *They felt that since there was nothing they could do about the Red Death, there was nothing to be gained from grieving for those who lost their lives to it.*

78

The Masque[1] of the Red Death

Edgar Allan Poe

The "Red Death" had long devastated the country. No pestilence had ever been so fatal, or so hideous. Blood was its Avatar[2] and its seal—the redness and the horror of blood. There were sharp pains, and sudden dizziness, and then profuse bleeding at the pores, with dissolution. The scarlet stains upon the body and especially upon the face of the victim, were the pest ban which shut him out from the aid and from the sympathy of his fellow men. And the whole **❶** seizure, progress and termination of the disease, were the incidents of half an hour.

❷ But the Prince Prospero was happy and dauntless and sagacious. When his dominions were half depopulated, he summoned to his presence a thousand hale and lighthearted friends from among the knights and dames of his court, and with these retired to the deep seclusion of one of his castellated abbeys.[3] This was an extensive and magnificent structure, the creation of the prince's own eccentric yet august taste. A strong and lofty wall girdled it in. This wall had gates of iron. The courtiers, having entered, brought furnaces and massy[4] hammers and welded the bolts. They resolved to leave means neither of ingress or egress[5] to the sudden impulses of despair or frenzy from within. The abbey was amply provisioned. With such precautions the courtiers might bid defiance to contagion. The external world could take care of itself. In the meantime it was folly to grieve, or to think. The prince had provided all the appliances of

◆ Literary Focus
What could the wall symbolize?
❸

❹

---

1. **masque** (mask) *n*.: Costume ball or masquerade theme.
2. **Avatar** (av´ ə tär) *n*.: Symbol or manifestation of an unseen force.

3. **castellated** (kas´ tə lā´ tid) **abbeys** (ab´ ez): Monasteries or convents with castlelike towers.
4. **massy** (mas´ ē) *adj*.: Massive or large.
5. **ingress** (in´ gres) or **egress** (ē´ gres): Entering or leaving.

◆ Build Vocabulary
august (ô gust´) *adj*.: Imposing and magnificent

78   *On the Edge*

Block Scheduling Strategies

Consider these suggestions to take advantage of extended class time:

- Have students complete the journal activity in Literature and Your Life (p. 77) and read their entries aloud to the class.
- Introduce the reading strategy. To give students practice, have them do the Reading Strategy page (p. 20) in **Selection Support.**
- Use the Daily Language Practice sentences for Weeks 8 and 9, in the Teaching Resources and in the **Writing and Language Transparencies.**

- Interested students can use a computer program or grid paper to design a layout of the floor plan in Prince Prospero's castle.
- Set aside class time for students to perform the radio script they write for the Speaking and Listening activity or share their multimedia presentation (both on page 85).
- Have students complete the Writing Mini-Lesson on page 85. While some students draft and revise the proposal, others can sketch designs of the symbol and choose the best one.

pleasure. There were buffoons, there were improvisatori,[6] there were ballet dancers, there were musicians, there was Beauty, there was wine. All these and security were within. Without was the "Red Death."

It was toward the close of the fifth or sixth month of his seclusion, and while the pestilence raged most furiously abroad, that the Prince Prospero entertained his thousand friends at a masked ball of the most unusual magnificence.

It was a voluptuous scene, that masquerade. But first let me tell of the rooms in which it was held. There were seven—an imperial suite. In many palaces, however, such suites form a long and straight vista, while the folding doors slide back nearly to the walls on either hand, so that the view of the whole extent is scarcely impeded. Here the case was very different; as might have been expected from the duke's love of the bizarre. The apartments were so irregularly disposed that the vision embraced but little more than one at a time. There was a sharp turn at every twenty or thirty yards, and at each turn a novel effect. To the right and left, in the middle of each wall, a tall and narrow Gothic window looked out upon a closed corridor which

---

6. **improvisatori** (im′ prə vē zə tôr ē) *n.:* Poets who improvise, or create verses without previous thought.

pursued the windings of the suite. These windows were of stained glass whose color varied in accordance with the prevailing hue of the decorations of the chamber into which it opened. That at the eastern extremity was hung, for example, in blue—and vividly blue were its windows. The second chamber was purple in its ornaments and tapestries, and here the panes were purple. The third was green throughout, and so were the casements. The fourth was furnished and lighted with orange—the fifth with white—the sixth with violet. The seventh apartment was closely shrouded in black velvet tapestries that hung all over the ceiling
and down
the

The Masque of the Red Death ♦ 79

♦ **Literary Focus**

5 Symbols Have students discuss the different kinds of people whom Prospero has invited to the security of the abbey. Collectively, whom do they represent? *Prospero's guests include two categories of people: his friends, who are knights and ladies, and a variety of people to entertain them and provide for their needs. They represent the privileged class.*

♦ **Build Grammar Skills**

6 Subject-Verb Agreement Call students' attention to the series of clauses beginning "there were" and "there was." Have them explain why some clauses use the verb *was* and some use *were*. *The singular verb was agrees with the singular subjects "Beauty" and "wine." The plural verb were agrees with the plural subjects "buffoons," "improvisatori," "ballet dancers," and "musicians."*

♦ **Literary Focus**

7 Symbols Point out that the number seven is often considered significant. Lead students to see that seven apartments may represent the seven deadly sins: pride, lust, envy, anger, covetousness, gluttony, and sloth. These sins might be related to the pleasures of the masked ball.

♦ **Reading Strategy**

8 Context Clues Have students infer the meaning of the word *impeded* from the context of the sentence. *When rooms are lined up in sequence and the doors between them slide back to the walls, a person's view is not impeded, that is, "interfered with" or "slowed down."*

♦ **Literary Focus**

9 Symbols Engage students in a discussion of the symbolism of colors. Ask what the color of each apartment might mean. *Possible responses: Blue represents water, coolness, wisdom and the intellect, and the sky. Purple seems to be a color of royalty, and therefore suggests power. Green, associated with nature, often symbolizes growth and life. Orange may suggest midday—the high noon of existence, the harvest, or fire and destruction. White generally symbolizes purity. Violet symbolizes memory or knowledge, sorrow and mourning. Black generally represents gloom and death.*

Beyond the Classroom

Career Connection
Architecture/Construction Visual/spatial learners who were able to imagine the castle chambers in this story may be interested in a career in architecture or construction. Encourage students to visit the architecture department of a nearby college or university to learn more about preparing for careers in this field. Let students know that architects and construction workers often work side by side. Invite students to interview a construction worker about his or

her job or visit a building under construction.

Community Connection
Containing Contagious Diseases The prince seeks to isolate himself and his friends from the Red Death. Have students contact your local Red Cross or public health hotline to get information on what contagious diseases are of concern to health-care workers in your community. Have them find out what preventive measures are recommended to stop the spread of the disease.

◆ Literary Focus

1 Symbols Ask students what the black room with blood-red window panes might represent. *This room probably represents death.*

◆ Critical Thinking

2 Analyze Have students describe the lighting in the rooms—especially the last room. What effect does the lighting have on the guests? What feeling or quality does Poe create in this passage? *The only light comes from fires opposite each window, which produce glare and "gaudy and fantastic appearances." The light in the last room reflects off blood-red panes, and the effect is "ghastly in the extreme." It produces a wild look on the guests' faces and makes them want to stay out of the last room. Poe creates feelings of horror as the surroundings take on a fantastic, nightmarish quality.*

◆ Literary Focus

3 Symbols Ask students what the clock represents. *The clock represents time and specifically the limited time remaining in their lives. As it strikes each hour, it serves as a reminder and a warning that death is always near.*

Literature and Your Life

4 Students may say the prince's revel reminds them of today's celebrity parties because it takes place in a lavish setting in which exotic entertainment is provided. They may add that most celebrities probably do not try to create such ghastly effects.

◆ Critical Thinking

5 Speculate Why does Poe try to create doubt in the reader's mind about whether the prince is sane? *He wants to keep the reader on edge about what exactly is going on and what will happen next.*

---

1 walls, falling in heavy folds upon a carpet of the same material and hue. But in this chamber only, the color of the windows failed to correspond with the decorations. The panes here were scarlet—a deep blood color. Now in no one of the seven apartments was there any lamp or candelabrum amid the profusion of golden ornaments that lay scattered to and fro or depended from the roof. There was no light of any kind emanating from lamp or candle within the suite of chambers. But in the corridors that followed the suite, there stood, opposite to each window, a heavy tripod, bearing a brazier[7] of fire **2** that projected its rays through the tinted glass and so glaringly illumined the room. And thus were produced a multitude of gaudy and fantastic appearances. But in the western or black chamber the effect of the firelight that streamed upon the dark hangings through the blood-tinted panes, was ghastly in the extreme, and produced so wild a look upon the countenances of those who entered, that there were few of the company bold enough to set foot within its precincts at all.

It was in this apartment, also, that there stood against the western wall a gigantic clock of ebony. Its pendulum swung to and fro with a dull, heavy, monotonous clang; and when the minute-hand made the circuit of the face, and the hour was to be stricken, there came from the brazen lungs of the clock a sound which was clear and loud and deep and exceedingly musical, but of so peculiar a note and emphasis that, **3** at each lapse of an hour, the musicians of the orchestra were constrained to pause, momentarily, in their performance, to hearken to the sound; and thus the waltzers perforce ceased their evolutions; and there was a brief disconcert of the whole gay company; and, while the chimes of the clock yet rang, it was observed that the giddiest grew pale, and the more aged and sedate passed their hands over their brows as if in confused

---

7. **brazier** (brā´ zhər) *n.*: Metal pan or bowl to hold burning coals or charcoal.

80 ◆ *On the Edge*

reverie or meditation. But when the echoes had fully ceased, a light laughter at once pervaded the assembly; the musicians looked at each other and smiled as if at their own nervousness and folly, and made whispering vows, each to the other, that the next chiming of the clock should produce in them no similar emotion; and then, after the lapse of sixty minutes, (which embrace three thousand and six hundred seconds of the Time that flies), there came yet another chiming of the clock, and then were the same disconcert and tremulousness and meditation as before.

But, in spite of these things, it was a gay and magnificent revel. The tastes of the duke were peculiar. He had a fine eye for colors and effects. He disregarded the decora[8] of mere fashion. His plans were bold and fiery, and his conceptions glowed with barbaric luster. There are some who would have thought him mad. His followers felt that he was **5**

◆ *Literature and Your Life*
Connect the prince's revel with what you've read and heard about celebrity parties of today. **4**

---

8. **decora** (da kôr´ ə) *n.*: Requirements of good taste.

♦ **Build Grammar Skills**

❻ **Subject-Verb Agreement**
Have students justify the use of the verb *were* in these three sentences. *Each sentence has a plural subject requiring a plural verb. The first sentence has a compound subject: glare, glitter, and piquancy. The subject of the second sentence is the word* figures. *The subject of the third is* fancies.

♦ **Reading Strategy**

❼ **Context Clues** Students will find both *hue* and *tinted* further in this column and recognize that *hue* refers to color.

♦ **Critical Thinking**

❽ **Infer** Ask students what the striking of the ebony clock might foreshadow. Have them explain their responses. *Students should grasp that the striking of the clock foreshadows the death of the dancers. Reasoning leading to this inference should include the color of the clock (ebony, or black), the color of the room (black velvet), and the silence as the clock is striking.*

Customize for
More Advanced Students
Ask students: What could be the significance of the clock's "muffled peal"? What might the clock be trying to "say"? *Lead students to suggest that the sound of the clock is a warning to the dancers, who persist in their decadent revels while the common people are suffering and dying.*

---

❺ not. It was necessary to hear and see and touch him to be *sure* that he was not.

He had directed, in great part, the movable embellishments of the seven chambers, upon occasion of this great fête; and it was his own guiding taste which had given character to the masqueraders. Be sure they were grotesque. ❻ There were much glare and glitter and piquancy and phantasm—much of what has been since seen in *Hernani*.[9] There were arabesque figures with unsuited limbs and appointments. There were delirious fancies such as the madman fashions. There was much of the beautiful, much of the wanton, much of the bizarre, something of the terrible, and not a little of that which might have excited disgust. To and fro in the seven chambers there stalked, in fact, a multitude of dreams. And these—the dreams—writhed in and

---

9. *Hernani:* Extravagant drama by the French author Victor Hugo.

♦ **Build Vocabulary**

piquancy (pē´ kən sē) *n.*: Pleasantly sharp quality
arabesque (ar´ ə besk´) *adj.*: Elaborately designed

---

about, taking hue from the rooms, and causing the wild music of the orchestra to seem as the echo of their steps. And, anon, there strikes the ebony clock which stands in the hall of the velvet. And then, for a moment, all is still, and all is silent save the voice of the clock. The dreams are stiff-frozen as they stand. But the echoes of the chime die away—they have endured but an instant—and a light, half-subdued laughter floats after them as they depart. And now again the music swells, and the dreams live, and writhe to and fro more merrily than ever, taking hue from the many-tinted windows through which stream the rays from the tripods. But to the chamber which lies most westwardly of the seven, there are now none of the maskers who venture; for the night is waning away; and there flows a ruddier light through the blood-colored panes; and the blackness of the sable drapery appalls; and to him whose foot falls upon the sable carpet, there comes from the near clock of ebony a muffled peal more solemnly emphatic than any which reaches *their* ears who

♦ **Reading Strategy**
Read ahead to find *tinted*, a context clue that will help you determine the meaning of *hue*.

The Masque of the Red Death ♦ 81

Humanities: Music

Several classical composers have written orchestral works with a mood of horror or the fantastic. Portions of these works might make good music for a performance of a radio script based on the story. Encourage students to listen to recordings of the following works to find music for the dance at the Prince's ball:
Hector Berlioz, *Symphonie Fantastique*, Opus 14
Paul Dukas, *The Sorcerer's Apprentice*
Igor Stravinsky, *Le Sacre du Printemps*
    Students might also consider movie soundtracks such as John Williams's score for the movie *Dracula.*

Cultural Connection

Point out to students that the word *masque* comes from the Italian word *maschera,* used to describe any covering for the face. *Masque* is also used to describe a form of drama, based on allegorical themes, common in Renaissance England, as well as masquerade balls and other court entertainments.

    Explain to your students that wearing masks is an ancient practice. Greek and Roman actors wore masks to conceal their identity as well as to direct their voice toward the stage. Masks are also used in Japanese Noh plays and in a popular

Italian dramatic form known as the pantomime. Ask students what the purpose of wearing a mask might be. Does it give the actor more freedom of expression? What are some of the limitations of wearing a mask?

    In Poe's timeless world, party-goers dress up in costumes and masks. Poe describes the abbey as grotesque and strangely imaginary. After students have read the story, ask them what such a place might stand for. Is Poe's description satiric? To what extent do the prince's abbey and the masque come to stand for the imagination itself?

① Analyze The story has a mood of horror and ghastliness. The same mood is conveyed through the eerie images of death in the painting. The faces are contorted in ghastly expressions of suffering or glee.

◆ Literary Focus

② Symbols Details that indicate that the uninvited guest represents death include the fact that the figure is shrouded like a corpse and that it wears a mask that resembles a stiffened corpse. His clothes are dabbled in blood, and his face is marked with the red markings of the Red Death.

◆ Reading Strategy

③ Context Clues Have students use context clues to figure out the meaning of the words *visage* and *countenance*. *Both are synonyms for the word face. The contexts "mask concealed the visage" and "resemble the countenance of" suggest the meanings.*

④ Clarify Make sure students understand that the word *convulsed* means "taken over by a violent, uncontrollable contraction of the muscles, shaken or agitated with spasms."

Customize for
More Advanced Students
Point out that several terms in this story are no longer in common usage, such as *castellated abbeys* and *improvisatori*. Challenge these students to identify anachronistic terms in the story and gather in groups to discuss what they know about these terms and the times and places with which they might be associated.

---

indulge in the more remote gaieties of the other apartments.

But these other apartments were densely crowded, and in them beat feverishly the heart of life. And the revel went whirlingly on, until at length there commenced the sounding of midnight upon the clock. And then the music ceased, as I have told; and the evolutions of the waltzers were quieted; and there was an uneasy cessation of all things as before. But now there were twelve strokes to be sounded by the bell of the clock; and thus it happened, perhaps, that more of thought crept, with more of time, into the meditations of the thoughtful among those who reveled. And thus, too, it happened, perhaps, that before the last echoes of the last chime had utterly sunk into silence, there were many individuals in the crowd who had found leisure to become aware of the presence of a masked figure which had arrested the attention of no single individual before. And the rumor of this new presence having spread itself whisperingly around, there arose at length from the whole company a buzz, or murmur, expressive of disapprobation and surprise—then, finally, of terror, of horror, and of disgust.

In an assembly of phantasms such as I have painted, it may well be supposed that no ordinary appearance could have excited such sensation. In truth the masquerade license of the night was nearly unlimited; but the figure in question had out-Heroded Herod,[10] and gone beyond the bounds of even the prince's indefinite decorum. There are chords in the hearts of the most reckless which cannot be touched

---

10. **out-Heroded Herod:** Behaved excessively, just as King Herod did. In the Bible, Herod slaughtered innocent babies, hoping to kill Jesus.

▲ **Critical Viewing** How is the mood of "The **①** Masque of the Red Death" reflected in the details in this painting? [Analyze]

Les Masques et la Mort 1897, © Estate of James Ensor/VAGA, New York, 1993

---

without emotion. Even with the utterly lost, to whom life and death are equally jests, there are matters of which no jest can be made. The whole company, indeed, seemed now deeply to feel that in the costume and bearing of the stranger neither wit nor propriety existed. The figure was tall and gaunt, and shrouded from head to foot in the habiliments of the grave. The mask which concealed the visage was made so nearly to resemble the countenance of a stiffened corpse that the closest scrutiny must have had difficulty in detecting the cheat. And yet all this might have been endured, if not approved, by the mad revelers around. But the mummer[11] had gone so far as to assume the type of the Red Death. His vesture was dabbled in blood—and his broad brow, with all the features of the face, was besprinkled with the scarlet horror.

When the eyes of Prince Prospero fell upon this spectral image (which with a slow and solemn movement, as if more fully to sustain its role, stalked to and fro among the waltzers) he was seen to be convulsed, in the first moment **④**

---

11. **mummer** n.: Masked and costumed person who acts out pantomimes.

◆ Literary Focus
What details in the following description help you understand the symbolism of the new guest?

②

③

◆ Build Vocabulary

cessation (se sā′ shən) n.: Stopping, either forever or for some time

disapprobation (dis ap′ rə bā′ shən) n.: Disapproval

habiliments (hə bil′ ə mənts) n.: Clothing

Humanities: Art

Les Masques et la Mort (Masks and Death), 1897, by James Ensor.

This piece of art depicts frightening masks reminiscent of those in Poe's story.

James Ensor (1860–1949) was a Belgian artist whose paintings are filled with tortured images of skeletons and masked figures. He found inspiration in the fantastic and morbid literature of Poe. Although Ensor did not name his work for a Poe story, it is not difficult to surmise that "The Masque of the Red Death" inspired it.

Use these questions for discussion:

1. What details in the facial expressions of the masks make them especially horrifying?
   Students should cite the hollow eyes, the misshapen mouths and the contorted expressions.

2. The title of the painting, "Les Masques et la Mort," is French for "Masks and Death." Ask students to conjecture why Death is smiling in the painting, whereas the masks all have contorted faces. *Students might agree that no mask can compete with death. No matter how frightening humans may try to appear, Death knows it will have "the last laugh."*

with a strong shudder either of terror or distaste; but, in the next, his brow reddened with rage.

"Who dares?" he demanded hoarsely of the courtiers who stood near him—"who dares insult us with this blasphemous mockery? Seize him and unmask him—that we may know whom we have to hang at sunrise, from the battlements!"

It was in the eastern or blue chamber in which stood the Prince Prospero as he uttered these words. They rang throughout the seven rooms loudly and clearly—for the prince was a bold and robust man, and the music had become hushed at the waving of his hand.

It was in the blue room where stood the prince, with a group of pale courtiers by his side. At first, as he spoke, there was a slight rushing movement of this group in the direction of the intruder, who at the moment was also near at hand, and now, with deliberate and stately step, made closer approach to the speaker. But from a certain nameless awe with which the mad assumptions of the mummer had inspired the whole party, there were found none who put forth hand to seize him; so that, unimpeded, he passed within a yard of the prince's person; and, while the vast assembly, as if with one impulse, shrank from the centers of the rooms to the walls, he made his way uninterruptedly, but with the same solemn and measured step which had distinguished him from the first, through the blue chamber to the purple—through the purple to the green—through the green to the orange—through this again to the white—and even thence to the violet, ere a decided movement had been made to arrest him. It was then, however, that the Prince Prospero, maddening with rage and the shame of his own momentary cowardice, rushed hurriedly through the six chambers, while none followed him on account of a deadly terror that had seized upon all. He bore aloft a drawn dagger, and had approached, in rapid impetuosity, to within three or four feet of the retreating figure, when the latter, having attained the extremity of the velvet apartment, turned suddenly and confronted his pursuer. There was a sharp cry—and the dagger dropped gleaming upon the sable carpet, upon which, instantly afterwards, fell prostrate in death the Prince Prospero. Then, summoning the wild courage of despair, a throng of the revelers at once threw themselves into the black apartment, and, seizing the mummer, whose tall figure stood erect and motionless within the shadow of the ebony clock, gasped in unutterable horror at finding the grave cerements[12] and corpselike mask which they handled with so violent a rudeness, untenanted by any tangible form.

And now was acknowledged the presence of the Red Death. He had come like a thief in the night. And one by one dropped the revelers in the blood-bedewed halls of their revel, and died each in the despairing posture of his fall. And the life of the ebony clock went out with that of the last of the gay. And the flames of the tripods expired. And Darkness and Decay and the Red Death held illimitable dominion over all.

12. **cerements** (ser′ ə mənts) *n*.: Wrappings or shroud.

---

❺
❻
❼

◆ **Critical Thinking**

❺ **Interpret** Point out to students that the uninvited guest is able to pass "unimpeded" through the party. Ask how this fact helps convey the meaning of the story. *Like the uninvited guest, contagious disease is unstoppable and does not spare victims on the basis of their social status.*

◆ **Literary Focus**

❻ **Symbols** Ask students which symbols in these two lines represent death. *Symbols of death include the stopping of the clock and the extinguishing of the flames.*

◆ **Critical Thinking**

❼ **Evaluate** Ask students what makes this final statement so effective. *The statement makes clear that Death, with Darkness and Decay, is the ruler in the end. Try as they might, humans have no influence over Death.*

Reinforce and Extend

Answers

◆ *Literature and Your Life*

Reader's Response Some students might say they would like to be his friend because he is a reveler and very imaginative.

Thematic Focus Some students might say that Prospero's attempt to escape his destiny is admirable because he tries to resist fate.

☑ **Check Your Comprehension**

1. They retreat to the palace to try and hide from the Red Death.
2. Answers should include that there were seven rooms, all situated at different angles, that they were of different colors and contained different decorations and windows.
3. The uninvited stranger is "tall and gaunt," wrapped in "habiliments of the grave," and wearing a mask that resembled a corpse.
4. Prince Prospero convulses when he sees the uninvited guest. He later pursues the uninvited guest with a knife through the chambers. The uninvited guest kills Prospero; the revelers unmask the guest and find he is the Red Death.

Guide for Responding

◆ *Literature and Your Life*

Reader's Response Would you have liked Prince Prospero as a friend? Why or why not?

Thematic Focus What, if anything, is admirable about the prince's attempt to escape from his destiny? Give reasons for your answer.

Sketch Do a quick drawing of the symbolic stranger who crashes Prince Prospero's masquerade.

☑ **Check Your Comprehension**

1. Why do Prince Prospero and his followers retreat to one of his abbeys?
2. Briefly describe the series of rooms in which the prince entertains his guests.
3. Describe the uninvited guest.
4. Summarize the events that follow the uninvited guest's arrival.

The Masque of the Red Death ◆ 83

Beyond the Selection

FURTHER READING

Other Works by Edgar Allan Poe
"The Pit and the Pendulum"
"The Cask of Amontillado"
"The Raven"

Other Works With the Theme of Searching for Safety
"An Occurrence at Owl Creek Bridge," Ambrose Bierce

We suggest that you preview these works before recommending them to your students.

INTERNET

For more information on Edgar Allan Poe and his work, we suggest the following sites on the Internet. Please be aware, however, that sites may have changed from the time we published this information.
http://www.cais.com/webweave/poe. html
http://www.comnet.ca/~forrest/index.html

We *strongly recommend* that you preview the sites before you send students to them.

◆ Critical Thinking

1. Outside the palace there is death and despair. Inside the palace there is life and merriment. However, outside the abbey, there is no frantic denial of suffering and dying; inside there is total denial.

2. He is concerned only with himself and his well-being; he seems to think he's invincible.

3. He conveys the message that no one, no matter how privileged or grand, can vanquish death.

4. Students might suggest that the old-fashioned language adds an air of distant formality.

5. Most students will probably feel that Poe would agree with the quotation.

◆ Reading Strategy

Students should explain that because they know that *tinted* means "colored," they can infer from context that *hue* is a synonym for *color*.

◆ Literary Focus

1. The uninvited guest—Unstoppable disease and death
2. The clock—Passing time that brings death
3. The prince's abbey—An illusion of safety

◆ Build Vocabulary

Using the Suffix *-tion*

1. *decoration*—the quality of being decorated
2. *creation*—the act of creating
3. *desperation*—the state of being desperate
4. *termination*—the act of ending

Using the Word Bank

1. They perceived him as august.
2. The costumes were arabesque.
3. The uninvited guest wore habiliments.
4. The food had the quality of piquancy.
5. He viewed those who didn't enjoy his ball with disapprobation.
6. When the clock struck the hour there was a cessation of life.

◆ Build Grammar Skills

1. plague; was
2. costumes, music, dancing; were
3. windows; are
4. people; are
5. way; isn't

Guide for Responding (continued)

◆ Critical Thinking

INTERPRET

1. Contrast life outside the prince's abbey with life inside it. **[Compare and Contrast]**
2. Why does the prince think he'll be able to escape the plague? **[Infer]**
3. What message does Poe convey through the prince's unsuccessful battle with the intruder? **[Interpret]**

EVALUATE

4. Does Poe's old-fashioned language add to the chilling mood and dreamlike atmosphere of the tale? Why or why not? **[Criticize]**

APPLY

5. An Italian writer declared, "Every tiny part of us cries out against the idea of dying, and hopes to live forever." How would Poe have responded to this quotation? **[Hypothesize]**

◆ Reading Strategy

CONTEXT CLUES

Context clues—hints in the surrounding passage—can help you figure out the meaning of unfamiliar words in the story.

Explain how the context clues give hints to the meaning of the italicized word: "These windows were of stained glass whose color varied in accordance with the prevailing *hue* of the decorations . . ."

◆ Literary Focus

SYMBOLS

Many people, places, and objects in Poe's tale are **symbols** that stand for more than themselves, adding layers of meaning to the story. On your paper, connect the symbol in Column A with the idea it symbolizes in Column B.

Column A	Column B
1. The uninvited guest	a. An illusion of safety
2. The clock	b. Unstoppable disease and death
3. The prince's abbey	c. Passing time that brings death

◆ Build Vocabulary

USING THE SUFFIX *-tion*

Use the meaning of the suffix *-tion* ("act or quality of") to define each of these words:

1. decoration   3. desperation
2. creation   4. termination

USING THE WORD BANK

On your paper, answer each question with a sentence that contains a word from the Word Bank. (Use each word once.)

1. How did the guests perceive the prince?
2. Describe the guests' costumes.
3. What was the uninvited guest wearing?
4. Describe the food that was probably served at the ball.
5. How did the prince view anyone who didn't enjoy his ball?
6. What happened when the clock struck the hour?

◆ Build Grammar Skills

SUBJECT AND VERB AGREEMENT

Poe emphasizes things rather than actions by beginning sentences with *there*, reversing subject and verb, and using forms of the verb *be: is, was* (singular); *are, were* (plural).

> When you begin sentences with *there*, remember that the **verb** must agree with the subject that follows it.

Practice Identify the subject in each sentence, then choose the verb that agrees with it.

1. There (was, were) a horrible plague devastating the kingdom.
2. There (was, were) costumes, music, and dancing at the masque.
3. There (is, are) beautiful windows of stained glass in the abbey.
4. There (is, are) people in every room but the last.
5. There (isn't, aren't) any way to escape the uninvited guest.

✎ Writer's Solution

For additional instruction and practice, use the lesson in the **Language Lab CD-ROM** on Subject and Verb Agreement and the pages on Subject and Verb Agreement (pp. 80–82) in the *Writer's Solution Grammar Practice Book*.

Build Your Portfolio

 ## Idea Bank

Writing

1. Invitation to the Prince's Masquerade
Write and design an invitation to Prince Prospero's masquerade. Style the invitation in keeping with the party as Poe describes it. **[Art Link]**

2. Description of a Modern Masquerade
Prince Prospero was inventive, but he didn't have the benefit of modern technology. Describe the party he could have thrown with up-to-date lighting and sound equipment.

3. Report on the Black Plague Research and report on the Black Plague that threatened Europe in the fourteenth century. Include the symptoms of the disease, the speed with which it spread, and its effect on society. **[Social Studies Link; Science Link]**

Speaking and Listening

4. Press Conference With a small group, role-play a press conference in which reporters ask the prince about the masquerade and the plague. **[Social Studies Link]**

5. Radio Script Write a radio script for a scene from "The Masque of the Red Death." Include dialogue, music, and sound effects. **[Media Link; Performing Arts Link]**

Projects

6. Costume Design Sketch out a costume you could wear to Prince Prospero's masquerade, indicating colors and fabrics. **[Art Link]**

7. Multimedia Presentation Give a multimedia presentation on an event that involves masks and costumes, like the Venice carnival. If possible, include slides and sound effects. **[Art Link; Social Studies Link]**

 ## Writing Mini-Lesson

Proposal for a Team Symbol

In "The Masque of the Red Death," Poe's symbols stress the dark side of life. However, you see symbols every day that communicate a positive message about a group, an idea, a product, or a team. Keeping these in mind, propose a symbol for a school athletic team or for a professional team.

Writing Skills Focus: Demonstrate the Benefits of an Idea

Make your proposal convincing by demonstrating the benefits of your idea. Here, for example, are some benefits of using a lightning bolt as a team symbol:

- It will inspire the team with a sense of power.
- It will increase team pride.
- It will make a striking visual image on team jerseys.

After listing such benefits, support them by explaining *how* the lightning bolt will inspire the team, *why* it will boost pride, and *why* a strong visual image is important.

Prewriting Create a chart with several benefits categories, such as inspiration for team, inspiration for fans, and visual appeal. After choosing a symbol, note on the chart how it will benefit the team in each category.

Drafting Begin your proposal with a vivid description of the symbol. Then, referring to the chart you created, explain specifically how the symbol will benefit the team.

Revising Read your draft as if you were on the panel evaluating the pluses and minuses of the proposed symbol. If there are not enough pluses, you may want to include additional benefits that the symbol will bring.

The Masque of the Red Death ♦ 85

 ## Idea Bank

Customizing for *Performance Levels*
Following are suggestions for matching Idea Bank topics with your students' performance levels:
    Less Advanced Students: 1, 6
    Average Students: 2, 4, 5, 7
    More Advanced Students: 3

Customizing for *Learning Modalities*
Following are suggestions for matching Idea Bank topics with your students' learning modalities:
    Visual/Spatial: 1, 6, 7
    Verbal/Linguistic: 4, 5, 7
    Logical/Mathematical: 3

 ## Writing Mini-Lesson

Refer students to the Writing Handbook, page 965, for instruction on the writing process, and page 968 for further information on persuasive writing.

Writer's Solution

Writers at Work Videodisc
Have students view the videodisc segment (Ch. 4) featuring Sayu Bhojwani to see and hear some tips on how to interest readers in a subject. Have students discuss what Bhojwani says about how persuasive writing differs from other forms of writing.

Play frames 33643 to 43235

Writing Lab CD-ROM
Have students complete the tutorial on Persuasive Writing. Follow these steps:
1. Have students use the Note Cards activity to help them gather details.
2. Have students draft on computer.
3. Have students use the Self-Evaluation Checklist to help them revise.

Sourcebook
Have students use Chapter 4, Persuasion (pp. 97–122), for additional support. The chapter includes an annotated student model of a persuasive letter (p. 122).

✓ ASSESSMENT OPTIONS

Formal Assessment, Selection Test, pp. 13–15, and Assessment Resources Software. The selection test is designed so that it can be easily customized to the performance levels of your students. ***Alternative Assessment,*** p. 5, includes options for less advanced students, more advanced students, musical/rhythmic learners, visual/spatial learners, and logical/mathematical learners.

PORTFOLIO ASSESSMENT
Use the following rubrics in the ***Alternative Assessment*** booklet to assess student writing:
Invitation to the Prince's Masquerade: Expression Rubric, p. 94
Description of a Modern Masquerade: Description Rubric, p. 97
Report on the Black Plague: Research Report Rubric, p. 106

Guide for Reading

OBJECTIVES

1. To read, comprehend, and interpret a group of poems
2. To relate a group of poems to personal experience
3. To form mental images in response to poetry
4. To identify imagery
5. To build vocabulary in context and learn the suffix -less
6. To identify pronouns and their antecedents
7. To write an anecdote about a challenge using cause-and-effect relationships
8. To respond to the poems through writing, speaking and listening, and projects

SKILLS INSTRUCTION

Vocabulary:
Suffixes: -less
Grammar:
Pronouns and Antecedents
Reading Strategy:
Form a Mental Image
Literary Focus:
Imagery

Writing:
Cause-and-Effect Relationships
Speaking and Listening:
Speech (teacher edition)
Critical Viewing:
Draw Conclusions; Connect

PORTFOLIO OPPORTUNITIES

Writing: Letter to a Poet; Poem; Short Story Based on a Poem
Writing Mini-Lesson: Anecdote About a Challenge
Speaking and Listening: Oral Interpretation; Speech
Projects: Scientific Diagram; Dance

Gabriela Mistral (1889–1957)

Most fifteen-year-olds do not have full-time jobs but at fifteen, Gabriela Mistral (gä brē ä´ lä mē sträl´) was a full-time grade-school teacher in her native Chile. When Mistral (whose real name is Lucila Godoy Alcayaga) began publishing her poetry, she tried a variety of pen names, eventually settling on Gabriela Mistral.

In 1945, Mistral became the first woman poet and the first Latin American to receive the Nobel Prize in Literature.

Octavio Paz (1914–)

The Mexican poet Octavio Paz (ok täv´ yō päs) has probably been to more unusual places and seen more interesting things than almost any writer alive. His wide-ranging travel is matched by the freedom of his imagination. Paz's poetry has universal appeal, and in 1990 he received the Nobel Prize in Literature. For all the acclaim he has won and places he has traveled, however, Paz remains deeply committed to his Mexican heritage.

William Carlos Williams (1883–1963)

Most people would agree that being a doctor is a full-time job. William Carlos Williams was both a doctor and a poet. When asked how he managed his double career, he replied that he treated his patients like poems and his poems like patients.

Williams believed that Americans should write about the details in the world around them. That's why the road in "Spring and All" is a local route that he often took to see patients.

◆ Build Vocabulary

SUFFIXES: -less
Williams describes early spring as "lifeless." Knowing that the suffix -less means "without," you can figure out that lifeless means "without life."

WORD BANK
As you read the poems, you will encounter the words on this list. Each word is defined on the page where it first appears. Preview the list before you read. Also, look for other words with the suffix -less, like leafless and doorless.

contagious
lifeless
clarity
stark
profound

◆ Build Grammar Skills

PRONOUNS AND ANTECEDENTS
A pronoun's **antecedent** is the noun or pronoun to which it refers. An antecedent can come before or after the pronoun, can be in another sentence, and might be more than one word. In poetry, an antecedent may be on a different line, as in the following example from "The street":

antecedent
Someone behind me also stepping on
            pronoun
stones, leaves:/if I slow down, *he* slows

As you read "Fear," however, you'll notice that the pronoun *them* has no antecedent. Think about why the poet leaves it out.

More About the Authors

A prominent advocate for school reform, **Gabriela Mistral** became director of Chile's primary and secondary schools. In poems like "Fear," she expressed her deeply personal hopes and thoughts regarding children.

Octavio Paz's poetry has been acclaimed for its moving exploration of the individual's search for identity. In "The street," the poet turns an unflinching eye toward this search and the anxiety that often accompanies it.

William Carlos Williams brought remarkable emotional honesty to his poetry. Fellow poet Randall Jarrell wrote: "There is no optimistic blindness in Williams, though there is . . . a stubborn or invincible joyousness."

Prentice Hall Literature Program Resources

REINFORCE / RETEACH / EXTEND
Selection Support Pages
Build Vocabulary: Suffixes: -less, p. 22
Build Grammar Skills: Pronouns and Antecedents, p. 23
Reading Strategy: Form a Mental Image, p. 24
Literary Focus: Imagery, p. 25
Strategies for Diverse Student Needs, p. 6
Beyond Literature
Humanities Connection: Fine Art for "Spring and All," p. 6

Formal Assessment Selection Test, pp. 16–18
Alternative Assessment, p. 6
Writing and Language Transparencies,
Writing Process Model 3: Personal Narrative, pp. 17–23
Resource Pro CD-ROM
"The street"; "Fear"; "Spring and All"—includes all resource materials and customizable lesson plans
Listening to Literature Audiocassettes
"The street"; "Fear"; "Spring and All"

Fear ◆ The street ◆ Spring and All

◆ *Literature and Your Life*

CONNECT YOUR EXPERIENCE
As you grow older, you face new and sometimes difficult experiences. You may have to overcome your shyness to make a presentation to the class, or you may have to sacrifice time with friends to work at an after-school job. Without experiences like these, however, you'd remain the same person throughout your life—never changing, never growing.

Like you, the subjects in these poems must face difficult and frightening challenges.

THEMATIC FOCUS: DANGEROUS DESTINIES
These selections about challenges and change raise the question "What kind of courage does it take to live in an uncertain world?"

Journal Writing In the center of a sunburst diagram like the one shown, note a challenge you are facing. Along the rays projecting from it, briefly describe the rewards and difficulties associated with this challenge.

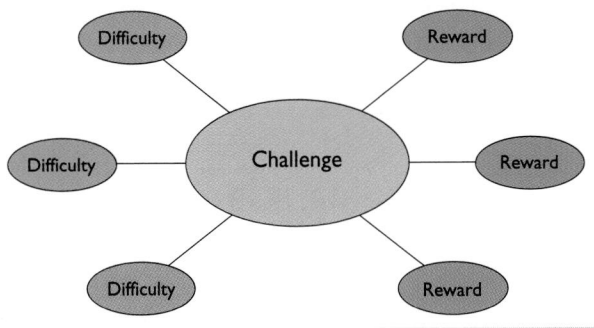

◆ Background for Understanding

LITERATURE
Translators face an especially difficult challenge; they must carry the meaning of a poem or story from one language to another. This job is difficult because a word in one language can often be translated by several possible words in another.

For example, the word *niña* in the Spanish original of Mistral's poem "Fear" could be translated as "child" or "little girl." Those translating "Fear" must make many such choices. As a result, different translators may write different versions of a poem or story.

◆ Literary Focus

IMAGERY
No matter what language they speak, people can all understand the language of the senses. For that reason, the element of a poem that is often easiest to appreciate is its **imagery**, the descriptive language that re-creates sensory experiences.

You can begin to enter the world each poem describes by identifying its imagery. In reading "Spring and All," for example, notice the sensory language the poet uses to describe the sky, the earth, and the plants of early spring.

◆ Reading Strategy

FORM A MENTAL IMAGE
Reading a poem is like having a conversation. As you hear someone speak, you often **form a mental image**, a picture in your mind, of what that person is saying. In the same way, you can picture in your mind what these poets are saying.

Enter the mysterious world of "The street," for example, by forming an image of the "dark and doorless" street that Paz describes. Glimpse the speaker in the "blackness" as he stumbles, falls, and rises.

Guide for Reading ◆ 87

Interest Grabber

Present students with magazine or other pictures that might inspire the feelings suggested by these poems: parting of people, which might suggest abandonment; a bleak and desolate street at night that would arouse fear; or the burst of new life that is spring. Encourage students to share their impressions of these pictures. Then explain that, like pictures, the images in poems bring forth our deepest emotions and make these emotions concrete. As they read the three poems, invite students to open their minds and look for ways in which one thing is transformed into another through the power of imagery.

Customize for
Less Proficient Readers
Reassure these students by acknowledging that poems often make for challenging reading. Suggest that students identify particularly difficult passages as they read. Then, in small-group settings, use these passages to model helpful strategies, such as paraphrasing and breaking down sentences.

Customize for
More Advanced Students
Have these students find a poem written in a foreign language that they are studying. Challenge them to translate all or part of the poem into English, with the help of a bilingual dictionary.

Customize for
English Language Learners
Two of these poems are written by Latin American poets whose work might be familiar to some Spanish-speaking students. Ask these students to form small groups to select and translate a passage of one of the poems into Spanish, and then discuss the difference between English and Spanish versions. Have other English language learners pair up to help each other work through difficult passages of all the poems.

 Preparing for Standardized Tests

Grammar and Language Alert students to the fact that language sections of standardized tests will often call on them to identify sentence errors, including errors in pronoun-antecedent agreement—a skill closely tied to what is taught in the Build Grammar Skills section of this lesson. To help students apply what they learn about pronouns and antecedents to a standardized test format, have them complete the following sample test item by identifying which of the underlined words or phrases contains an error.

It is <u>considered appropriate</u> for <u>a guest to thank</u>
(A)   (B)   (C)
<u>their</u> host by sending <u>a card or a small</u> gift.
(D)   (E)

Lead students to see that the correct answer is (D), because the plural pronoun *their* does not agree in number with its singular antecedent.

One-Minute Insight

Although diverse in style and subject matter, these poems have one thing in common: Each explores a significant challenge or uncertainty that people face in life. In "Fear," a mother worries that her little girl might grow apart from her. In "The street," a man struggles with basic questions such as: Who am I? Where am I going?

Customize for
Visual/Spatial Learners

Point out that illustrators translate words into pictures. Have visual/spatial learners choose one of the poems and create one or more illustrations based on the imagery in it, or just explain how they would illustrate the poems.

◆ Literary Focus

❶ Imagery What imagery does the poet use in these lines? How does this imagery add to the idea that the speaker is expressing? *Imagery includes "swallow," "straw bed," "nest in the eaves." Students may say that the imagery emphasizes the idea that the speaker does not want her little girl to be away from her; the imagery conjures up a vivid picture.*

◆ Critical Thinking

❷ Infer Based on these lines, what inferences can you make about the speaker's fears and hopes? *The speaker fears that her little girl may not always be as close to her as she is today; she hopes that her little girl will always be able to express her joy freely.*

◆ Build Grammar Skills

❸ Pronouns and Antecedents Have students identify the noun from the preceding stanza to which the pronoun *her* refers. *girl.*

▶ Critical Viewing ◀

❹ Draw Conclusions Students will probably connect the fear of the woman in the painting to that of the speaker in the poem. Based on the evidence that the mother in the painting appears worried and is clinging to her child, students might conclude she fears the dangers of the world and wants to protect her child from these dangers.

88

Fear

Gabriela Mistral
Translated by **Doris Dana**

Woman With Child, Pablo Picasso, Museo Picasso, Barcelona, Spain

❶
I don't want them to turn
my little girl into a swallow.
She would fly far away into the sky
and never fly again to my straw bed,
5   or she would nest in the eaves[1]
where I could not comb her hair.
I don't want them to turn
my little girl into a swallow.

❷
I don't want them to make
10   my little girl a princess.
In tiny golden slippers
how could she play on the meadow?
And when night came, no longer
would she sleep at my side.
15   I don't want them to make
my little girl a princess.

❸
And even less do I want them
one day to make her queen.
They would put her on a throne
20   where I could not go to see her.
And when nighttime came
I could never rock her . . .
I don't want them to make
my little girl a queen!

---

1. **eaves** (ēvz) *n.*: The lower edge or edges of a roof, usually projecting beyond the sides of a building.

▲ **Critical Viewing** What might the mother in this painting fear? Explain your answer. [**Draw Conclusions**] ❹

88 ◆ *On the Edge*

Block Scheduling Strategies

Consider these suggestions to take advantage of extended class time:

• Have students meet in small groups to discuss the question in the Thematic Focus section of Literature and Your Life on page 87. Then have compare the ideas charted on their sunburst diagrams.

• Direct pairs of students to brainstorm for a list of images that they think evoke fear. After discussing the significance of the images on their lists, students can compare them with some of

the images that call up fear in these poems, such as "a long and silent street."

• Have students listen to the poems on the Listening to Literature audiocassette. Then guide them to practice and present oral interpretations of the poems, as suggested in the Speaking and Listening section of the Idea Bank.

• Have students complete the Writing Mini-Lesson on page 93. As a prewriting activity, invite volunteers to share interesting or amusing anecdotes about challenges they have faced.

The street

Octavio Paz
Translated by *Muriel Rukeyser*

A long and silent street.
I walk in blackness and I stumble and fall
and rise, and I walk blind, my feet
stepping on silent stones and dry leaves.
5 Someone behind me also stepping on
     stones, leaves:
if I slow down, he slows;
if I run, he runs, I turn: nobody.

Everything dark and doorless.
Turning and turning among these corners
10 which lead forever to the street
where nobody waits for, nobody follows me,
where I pursue a man who stumbles
and rises and says when he sees me: nobody.

Guide for Responding

◆ Literature and Your Life

Reader's Response Did you want to comfort the speakers in these poems? Why or why not?

Thematic Focus Briefly describe the challenges that each speaker faces.

☑ Check Your Comprehension

1. Who is the speaker in "Fear"?
2. Describe three fears the speaker has.
3. What happens in the first stanza of "The street"? The second?

◆ Critical Thinking

INTERPRET

1. Find three details that give "Fear" the quality of a fairy tale and explain your choices. **[Support]**
2. In "Fear" what is the common element in each of the fears the speaker expresses? **[Draw Conclusions]**
3. Show how there are two speakers in "The street" and explain who they are. **[Interpret]**
4. In what ways does "The street" resemble a nightmare? **[Compare and Contrast]**
5. Compare and contrast the fears of the speaker in "Fear" with the fears expressed in "The street." **[Compare and Contrast]**

APPLY

6. Describe a situation that could lead up to the speech in "Fear." For example, how might the mother's speech be a response to fairy tales she has just told her daughter? **[Hypothesize]**

EXTEND

7. Mistral begins the first two stanzas of "Fear" with the words "I don't want." Imagine that you are Mistral. Name two other things you don't want. **[Relate]**

Fear/The street ◆ 89

◆ Literary Focus

❺ Imagery Lead students to identify specific images in this passage, such as "long and silent street," "dry leaves," and "someone behind me also stepping." Encourage them to comment on the senses that these images appeal to, as well as the overall impression that they create. *The images appeal to the senses of sight, hearing, and touch. Students may say that the overall impression is one of being lost.*

◆ Build Vocabulary

❻ Suffixes: -less Ask students to identify the word that contains the suffix -less and tell the meaning of the word. *The word is doorless; it means "without doors."*

◆ Reading Strategy

❼ Form a Mental Image Invite students to form a mental image in response to these words. What does their image suggest about the larger meaning of the poem? *Students may compare the image of "turning and turning among these corners" to being caught in a maze—suggesting that the poem deals with the feelings of entrapment in general.*

Reinforce and Extend

Answers

◆ Literature and Your Life

Reader's Response Some students may want to comfort the speakers with whom they sympathize.

Thematic Focus The mother in "Fear" faces the challenge of guarding her little girl from certain dangers in the world; the speaker of "The street" faces the challenge of discovering his own identity.

☑ Check Your Comprehension

1. The speaker is a mother.
2. She fears her daughter will be turned into a swallow, a princess, and a queen.
3. In the first stanza the speaker walks blindly down a street, hears someone behind him, turns to see no one. In the second stanza the speaker pursues a phantom who is himself.

(Answers continued on p. 91)

✦ Humanities: Art

Woman With Child by Pablo Picasso.
   Both highly imaginative and prolific, Pablo Picasso (1881–1973) contributed inestimably to the development of modern art in the twentieth century. Picasso was born in Malaga, Spain, and began painting seriously at the age of fourteen. A master of both realistic and abstract styles, he explored such deeply human themes as love, war, and loneliness. His interpretations of these themes were sometimes tender and sometimes confrontational.

Use these questions for discussion:

1. How would you describe the feelings that the mother shows for her child in both the painting and the poem? *Students may describe her feelings as loving, caring, or protective.*
2. What details in the painting suggest that, like the speaker in the poem, the woman has fears and worries regarding her child? *Students may point out the far-off look in her eyes and the protective hand she has placed on the child's shoulder.*

One-Minute Insight In "Spring and All," the speaker finds that birth and renewal may be as difficult as they are joyous.

◆ **Literary Focus**

❶ **Imagery** Which images do students find particularly powerful in these opening lines? How would they describe the overall scene that these images create? *Some students may name images such as "cold wind," "waste of broad muddy fields," and "standing water," which paint a picture of a cold, stagnant, unwelcoming spot. Others may find the image of the "contagious hospital" powerful because it is surprising and somewhat mysterious at this point.*

◆ **Build Grammar Skills**

❷ **Pronouns and Antecedents** Point out the pronouns *they* and *them*. Remind students that the antecedents of pronouns sometimes follow those pronouns, as is the case with *they* and *them* in these lines. Have students find the noun(s) to which these pronouns refer. *The antecedent is the objects— including the grass and the wildcarrot leaf—in lines 21–23.*

◆ **Reading Strategy**

❸ **Form a Mental Image** Point out the image of the "stiff curl of wildcarrot leaf." What other images does this bring to mind? What ideas about spring does it suggest? *Students may be reminded of a tightly coiled spring—which is full of tension and potential energy, just as the season spring is. The might also suggest a spiral design.*

▶**Critical Viewing**◀

❹ **Connect** Students who feel that the artist shares Williams's vision may point out that both the poem and the art communicate the two-sided nature of spring. Williams does so through contrasting images of life-lessness and reawakening, while the artist does so by combining subdued colors with traditional symbols of spring.

90

Spring and All

William Carlos Williams

By the road to the <u>contagious</u> hospital
under the surge of the blue
mottled clouds driven from the
northeast—a cold wind. Beyond, the
5   waste of broad, muddy fields
brown with dried weeds, standing and fallen

❶   patches of standing water
the scattering of tall trees

All along the road the reddish
10   purplish, forked, upstanding, twiggy
stuff of bushes and small trees
with dead, brown leaves under them
leafless vines—

<u>Lifeless</u> in appearance, sluggish
15   dazed spring approaches—

❷   They enter the new world naked,
cold, uncertain of all
save that they enter. All about them
the cold, familiar wind—

20   Now the grass, tomorrow
❸   the stiff curl of wildcarrot leaf
One by one objects are defined—
It quickens: <u>clarity</u>, outline of leaf

But now the <u>stark</u> dignity of
25   entrance—Still, the <u>profound</u> change
has come upon them: rooted, they
grip down and begin to awaken

❹ ▶ **Critical Viewing** Do you think this artist shares Williams's vision of spring? Support your answer. **[Connect]**

90 ◆ On the Edge

 Speaking and Listening Mini-Lesson

Speech
This mini-lesson supports the Speaking and Listening activity in the Idea Bank on page 93.
Introduce the Concept Point out that a speech should capture an audience's attention with a strong or catchy opening and then keep the audience engaged by presenting a series of interesting and clearly expressed ideas.
Develop Background Discuss the approaches students might take to convey the drama of a given season. Lead them to consider the following:

• Bold imagery: Use language to help listeners picture specific details.
• Personal recollections: Capture audience attention by giving a strong example of how a season makes them feel—and why.

Apply the Information Have students prepare their speeches, rehearse them, and deliver them to the class.

Assess the Outcome You may have students use the Peer Assessment sheet for a Speaker/ Speech (p. 119) in *Alternative Assessment*.

Untitled, David Gaz

Guide for Responding

◆ Literature and Your Life

Reader's Response How do the images in this poem compare to your images of spring?

Thematic Focus What details in lines 16–19 suggest that birth can be a dangerous destiny? Explain.

Sketch Make a quick line drawing of an image you like in this poem.

☑ Check Your Comprehension

1. What does the speaker see in the sky and on the earth?
2. Summarize the speaker's description of the approach of spring.

◆ Critical Thinking

INTERPRET

1. Why do you think the poet sets a spring scene near a hospital? **[Infer]**
2. Pointing to words like *defined, clarity,* and *awaken,* explain what the coming of spring means to this poet. **[Interpret]**

APPLY

3. How might this poet describe another season like fall or winter? **[Hypothesize]**

◆ Build Vocabulary

contagious (kən tā′ jəs) *adj.:* Spread by direct or indirect contact

lifeless (līf′ lis) *adj.:* Without life

clarity (klar′ ə tē) *n.:* The quality or condition of being clear

stark (stärk) *adj.:* Bare; plain

profound (prō found′) *adj.:* Deep

Spring and All ◆ 91

 Beyond the Selection

FURTHER READING

Other Works by the Featured Poets
Tenderness, Gabriela Mistral (collection of poems)
A Draft of Shadows and Other Poems, Paz
Spring and All, William Carlos Williams

Other Works With the Theme of Struggling With Uncertainty
"Prayer for my Daughter," William Butler Yeats
"The Road Not Taken," Robert Frost
   We suggest that you preview these works before recommending them to students.

INTERNET

You may find more information on these poets and their work on the Internet. We suggest the following sites. Please be aware that sites may have changed from the time we published this information. For more on Mistral, go to **http://www.netsrq.com/~dbois/ mistral.htm/** For more on Williams, go to **http://www. charm.net/~brooklyn/People/ WilliamCarlosWilliams.html/**
   We *strongly recommend* that you preview the sites before you send students to them.

Reinforce and Extend

Answers

◆ Critical Thinking (p. 89)

1. Details include a princess, golden slippers, a queen, and a throne—all of which are associated with fairy tales involving royalty, such as *Cinderella.*
2. The common element of the fears is that the daughter will become independent.
3. The two speakers are the man who is being pursued and the pursuer—actually one person.
4. "The street" is like a nightmare because it shows being trapped in a situation that keeps going around in circles.
5. Students may mention that both poems evoke fears of being alone and finding one's own identity in the world.
6. Students might describe a situation in which the mother imagines her daughter swept away by romantic love or by worldly temptations.
7. Suggestions should follow the central idea of the mother fearing her daughter's separation from her.

◆ Literature and Your Life

Reader's Response If students live in a place with definite seasonal cycles they may mention such signs of spring such as crocuses budding or rain storms.

Thematic Focus Students should mention "naked," "cold," and "uncertain of all." These images suggest the vulnerability of the newborn.

☑ Check Your Comprehension

1. He sees mottled clouds in the sky and muddy fields, dry weeds, patches of standing water, and leafless vines on Earth.
2. The speaker notices new grass growing and wildcarrot leaf as nature grows clearer.

◆ Critical Thinking

1. A plant faces danger trying to survive, just as patients may struggle to survive in a hospital.
2. Spring is an awakening because it is a time of rebirth and renewal for plants, trees, and nature.
3. One acceptable response is that fall is a time of nature shrinking and folding in on itself and winter is a time of harshness.

◆ Reading Strategy

1. Students may say they formed a mental image of footsteps, the sound of breathing or whispers, or a shadowy figure in pursuit.
2. The little girl can be pictured as a swallow, a princess, and a queen.
3. The road is bleak, colorless, and lifeless.

◆ Build Grammar Skills

1. with dead brown leaves under them. (bushes and small trees)
2. if I slow down, he slows (someone)
3. and rises and says when he sees me: nobody (a man)
4. She would fly far away into the sky (girl or my little girl)
5. And even less do I want them/ one day to make her a queen. (girl or my little girl)

◆ Literary Focus

1. (a) Students will probably cite lines 1–6 because *cold wind* evokes the sense of touch and *the blue mottled clouds* and *muddy fields brown with dry weeds* call upon sight and touch (dry). (b) The description in this passage seems to imply the danger that spring will never come to enliven the dead scene.
2. Possible imagery includes the daughter being turned into a swallow and flying off and the daughter's long hair being combed by her mother.
3. Possible answer is the imagery of rooted plants gripping down and beginning to "awaken" in "Spring and All."

◆ Build Vocabulary

Using the Suffix -*less*
1. a   2. b   3. c   4. c

Using the Word Bank
1. contagious;   2. clarity;   3. lifeless;
4. profound;   5. stark

 Writer's Solution

For additional instruction and practice, use the lesson in the **Language Lab CD-ROM** on Pronoun Usage and the pages on Pronoun and Antecedent Agreement (p. 83) in the *Writer's Solution Grammar Practice Book.*

Guide for Responding (continued)

◆ Reading Strategy

FORM A MENTAL IMAGE

If you **form a mental image** of the scene in "The street," you can better experience the speaker's fear. You'll "hear" the silence, "walk blind" through the "blackness," and feel the footsteps on the "stones and dry leaves."

1. As you read "The street," what mental image did you form of the "Someone" who pursues the speaker?
2. Describe three different ways you can picture the little girl in "Fear."
3. Briefly describe your picture of "the road to the contagious hospital" in "Spring and All."

◆ Build Grammar Skills

PRONOUNS AND ANTECEDENTS

In "Fear" the speaker refers several times to *them,* a pronoun without an antecedent. By leaving out the antecedent, the poet creates a sense of mystery about *them.* Similarly, in "Spring and All," the pronoun *It* in line 23 doesn't have a clear antecedent and mysteriously refers to all of nature's rebirth. In your own writing, however, you'll want every pronoun to refer clearly to an antecedent.

> An **antecedent** is a noun or pronoun to which a pronoun refers.

Practice Copy these lines from the poems. Find the underlined pronoun's antecedent in the poem and then write it next to the line you've copied.

1. with dead, brown leaves under them ("Spring and All," line 12)
2. if I slow down, he slows ("The street," line 7)
3. and rises and says when he sees me: nobody. ("The street," line 13)
4. She would fly far away into the sky ("Fear," line 3)
5. And even less do I want them/one day to make her a queen. ("Fear," lines 17 and 18)

◆ Literary Focus

IMAGERY

These poets use **imagery**—language that re-creates sensory experiences—to enhance your appreciation of the dangers and difficulties they describe. In "Spring and All," for example, words that appeal to the sense of touch—"naked,/cold"; "grip down"—stress the difficulty of nature's rebirth in spring.

1. (a) Find a passage in "Spring and All" that re-creates experiences of both touch and sight. (b) Explain how this passage helps you appreciate the danger or uncertainty of spring.
2. Explain how two sensory descriptions in "Fear" help you understand the speaker's anxiety about losing her daughter.
3. Which sensory description in these poems creates the most vivid image of a struggle? Explain.

◆ Build Vocabulary

USING THE SUFFIX -*less*

Knowing that the suffix -*less* means "without," choose the letter of the word that is the best antonym, or opposite, of the first word.

1. odorless: (a) fragrant, (b) scentless, (c) pale
2. restless: (a) excited, (b) relaxed, (c) upset
3. speechless: (a) wordless, (b) mute, (c) talkative
4. sleepless: (a) alert, (b) annoyed, (c) drowsy

USING THE WORD BANK

On your paper, write the word from the Word Bank that will make the relationship between the second pair of words similar to the relationship between the first pair. Use each word only once.

1. Sickly is to ill as infectious is to ___?___ .
2. Darkness is to gloom as clearness is to ___?___ .
3. Alive is to lively as dead is to ___?___ .
4. Shallow is to superficial as deep is to ___?___ .
5. Costumed is to naked as adorned is to ___?___ .

Build Your Portfolio

 Idea Bank

Writing

1. **Letter to a Poet** Respond to one of the poems by writing a letter to the poet. Tell how the poem made you feel and which images helped you share the experience the poet describes.

2. **Poem** Write your own poem about a struggle or challenge using imagery that will help your readers share the experience.

3. **Short Story Based on a Poem** Turn one of these poems into a short story. Expand on the situation in the poem by showing, for example, why the man in "The street" is running or how the speaker in "Fear" brings up her daughter.

Speaking and Listening

4. **Oral Interpretation** Practice reading one of these poems aloud. Experiment with your tone of voice, the speed with which you read, and the words you stress. Then perform the poem for the class. **[Performing Arts Link]**

5. **Speech** The speaker in "Spring and All" vividly describes the drama of early spring. Write a speech in which you emphasize the drama and uncertainty of another season. Then deliver your speech to the class. **[Performing Arts Link]**

Projects

6. **Scientific Diagram** The speaker in "Spring and All" describes the rebirth of plants in spring as a struggle. Create a scientific diagram showing what happens to a plant in late winter and early spring. **[Science Link; Art Link]**

7. **Dance** Create a two-person dance that communicates the action and mood of "The street." Perform your dance for the class. **[Performing Arts Link]**

 Writing Mini-Lesson

Anecdote About a Challenge

Draw on your own experience to tell an **anecdote**—an interesting or amusing story—about a challenge. The following tip will help you clarify the cause-and-effect relationships in your anecdote.

Writing Skills Focus: Cause-and-Effect Relationships

Whether you're writing an anecdote, a remembrance, or a problem-and-solution essay, you must show how one event or condition (the cause) brings about another (the effect). Even a poem like "The street" describes cause-and-effect relationships:

> **Cause**: Dark street
> **Effect**: Speaker stumbles
> **Cause**: Speaker stumbles
> **Effect**: Speaker falls

In planning, writing, and revising your anecdote, show the cause-and-effect relationships among events.

Prewriting To find a topic for an anecdote, think about a mistake you have made, like showing up at the wrong time for an appointment. Jot down some amusing consequences that resulted from the error.

Drafting You can create humor in your account by showing how silly causes lead to ridiculous effects at an ever-quickening pace.

Revising In reviewing your draft, clarify any cause-and-effect relationships that are unclear by using words like *as a result, consequently,* and *because.* Also, be sure that each pronoun you use has an easily identifiable antecedent.

For more on pronouns and antecedents, see Build Grammar Skills on pages 86 and 92.

Fear/The street/Spring and All ♦ 93

 Idea Bank

Customizing for *Performance Levels*
Following are suggestions for matching Idea Bank topics with your students' performance levels:
Less Advanced Students: 1, 4
Average Students: 2, 4, 5, 7
More Advanced Students: 3, 6

Customizing for *Learning Modalities*
Following are suggestions for matching Idea Bank topics with your students' learning modalities:
Visual/Spatial: 6
Verbal/Linguistic: 4, 5, 7
Logical/Mathematical: 6
Bodily/Kinesthetic: 7

 Writing Mini-Lesson
Refer students to the Writing Handbook, page 965, for instruction on the writing process, and page 967 for further information on narrative writing.

Writing and Language Transparencies Writing Process Model 3 takes students through the stages of writing a personal narrative. You might introduce the Writing Mini-Lesson by showing the transparencies of the process and having students notice and discuss the features of the narrative. Alternatively, you could use the transparencies to guide students through the revision process of the anecdotes.

Writer's Solution

Writing Lab CD-ROM
Have students complete the tutorial on Narration. Follow these steps:
1. Encourage students to use a Storyline Diagram to help them develop their plots.
2. Have students draft on computer.
3. Have students use the Revision Checkers to help them revise.

Sourcebook
Have students use Chapter 2, Narration (pp. 31–56), for additional support. The chapter includes an annotated student model of a story (p. 56).

✓ ASSESSMENT OPTIONS

Formal Assessment, Selection Test, pp. 16–18, and Assessment Resources Software. The selection test is designed so that it can be easily customized to the performance levels of your students. *Alternative Assessment,* p. 6, includes options for less advanced students, more advanced students, visual/spatial learners, verbal/linguistic learners, intrapersonal and bodily/kinesthetic learners.

PORTFOLIO ASSESSMENT
Use the following rubrics in the *Alternative Assessment* booklet to assess student writing:
Letter to a Poet: Expression Rubric, p. 94
Poem: Poetry Rubric, p. 108
Short Story Based on a Poem: Fiction Narrative Rubric, p. 95

*G*uide for Reading

OBJECTIVES

1. To read, comprehend, and interpret a story and a myth
2. To relate a story and a myth to personal experience
3. To recognize significant details
4. To identify the climax of a story
5. To build vocabulary in context and learn the word root *-tain-*
6. To recognize and use appositives
7. To write an extended definition of friendship using concrete examples
8. To respond to the story and the myth through writing, speaking and listening, and projects

SKILLS INSTRUCTION

Vocabulary:
Word Roots: *-tain-*

Grammar:
Appositives

Reading Strategy:
Significant Details

Literary Focus:
Climax

Writing:
Concrete Examples

Speaking and Listening:
Role Play (teacher edition)

Critical Viewing:
Contrast; Draw Conclusions; Infer

PORTFOLIO OPPORTUNITIES

Writing: Epitaph for Damon and Pythias; Yearbook Profiles; Report of the Prussian Officer

Writing Mini-Lesson: Extended Definition of Friendship

Speaking and Listening: Role Play; Humorous Monologue

Projects: Friendship Collage; Brochure for a Friendship Film Festival

More About the Authors
During his lifetime, **Guy de Maupassant** was probably the world's best-known writer of short stories. Today, along with such writers as Anton Chekhov, O. Henry, and Ernest Hemingway, he is still considered one of the all-time greats of the genre.
William F. Russell became interested in the timeless lessons that myths like "Damon and Pythias" have to teach while he was working on a doctorate degree in education. Reflected in the title of one of his books—*Classic Myths to Read Aloud*—is his belief that these stories are meant to be shared among family members and friends.

Guy de Maupassant
(1850–1893)

The modern short stories of Guy de Maupassant (g d§ m p s n¨) are filled with fascinating details of nineteenth-century life. Forces such as a person's family, surroundings, physical makeup, and personality determine the outcome of events.

Born into an aristocratic family, Maupassant was apparently destined for success. As a young man, he was a talented writer and won the attention of famous authors. Soon he was famous in his own right.

Then, as he might have described it in one of his own stories, his weaknesses caught up with him. Troubled by health problems, he died in his early forties. Yet he left a "fortune" to every future reader: 300 short stories.

About Myths

"Damon and Pythias" is a myth—a fictional story about gods or heroes. Myths may be ancient imaginary stories, but they explain real phenomena. They answer the most basic questions about the world and the human heart: How did this mountain come to be? Why is this flower purple? Who were the truest friends that ever lived? We read myths today because they offer timeless answers to timeless questions.

William F. Russell (1945–   )

William F. Russell has retold this and many other myths so that modern readers can appreciate their universal messages. He is also the author of a widely read newspaper column on education.

◆ Build Vocabulary

WORD ROOTS: *-tain-*
In "Damon and Pythias," Pythias is "detained far longer in his task than he had imagined." Knowing that Pythias has not returned and that the root *-tain-* means "to hold," you can figure out that *detained* means "held back."

| ardent |
| vernal |
| jauntiness |
| dire |
| detained |
| impediments |
| hindrances |
| annals |

WORD BANK
As you read "Damon and Pythias" and "Two Friends," you will encounter these words. Each word is defined on the page where it first appears. Preview the list before you read.

◆ Build Grammar Skills

APPOSITIVES
Maupassant gives details about characters by using **appositives**—nouns or noun phrases that are placed near another noun or pronoun to explain it:

> … M. Morissot, *watchmaker by trade but local militiaman for the time being,* stopped short …

The italicized appositive quickly explains both Morissot's usual trade and his military duties during the war. If Maupassant had provided these details in a separate sentence, he would have slowed down the pace of his story. Instead, he includes the appositive, separating it by commas because it is not essential to the meaning.

94 ◆ *On the Edge*

Prentice Hall Literature Program Resources

REINFORCE / RETEACH / EXTEND

Selection Support Pages
Build Vocabulary: Word Roots: *-tain-*, p. 26
Build Grammar Skills: Appositives, p. 27
Reading Strategy: Significant Details, p. 28
Literary Focus: Climax, p. 29

Strategies for Diverse Student Needs, p. 7

Beyond Literature
Cross-Curricular Connection: Social Studies: *Rules of Warfare,* p. 7

Art Transparencies 11 and 12, pp. 47–53

Formal Assessment Selection Test, pp. 19–21; Assessment Resources Software

Alternative Assessment, p. 7

Writing and Language Transparencies
Writing Process Model 4: Extended Definition, pp. 25–28

Resource Pro CD-ROM
"Two Friends"; "Damon and Pythias"—includes all resource materials and customizable lesson plan

 Listening to Literature Audiocassettes
"Two Friends"; "Damon and Pythias"

Two Friends ◆ Damon and Pythias

◆ *Literature and Your Life*

CONNECT YOUR EXPERIENCE
Mathematics says that if you share something with another person, you each have less than the total amount. Friendship proves this statement wrong. If you share a dream, a joke, or a story with a friend, it increases in value—and you both get to keep it.

"Damon and Pythias" and "Two Friends" show the value of friendship. They also show how life can test friendship.

Journal Writing Jot down some of the qualities that you look for in a friend. Then tell why each of these qualities is important to you.

THEMATIC FOCUS: DANGEROUS DESTINIES
In this ancient myth and modern short story, friends get into dangerous situations. As the tension mounts, you may wonder whether the friendship—and the friends—will survive.

◆ Background for Understanding

CULTURE
Stories about friends appear not only in books. The ancient Greeks placed such a high value on friendship that they advertised it in skywriting. They made the legendary friends and brothers Castor and Pollux into stars and included them in the constellation we call Gemini ("the twins").

Look for these ancient friends in today's night sky, close to the Big Dipper.

◆ Literary Focus

CLIMAX
The **climax** of a story, especially one in which friends are tested, is the point at which the tension is greatest. It is also the point at which the outcome is about to be revealed. In some stories, the tension increases gradually, leading to a climax that you know is coming. In other stories, the climax arrives suddenly and unexpectedly.

"Damon and Pythias" and "Two Friends" show two different ways of building toward a climax. As you read each tale, decide whether the moment of greatest tension is expected or is unexpected.

◆ Reading Strategy

SIGNIFICANT DETAILS
Significant details in a story often hint at how events may turn out. Sometimes these details have to do with character traits—human qualities that help to determine the outcome of events. Other times, these details are events in the world that surround the characters.

As you read "Damon and Pythias," jot down details about the characters themselves; then ask yourself how these details might influence what happens. For "Two Friends," notice significant details in the surroundings, even if they seem to be off in the distance. Then consider how things that were distant may suddenly become all too close.

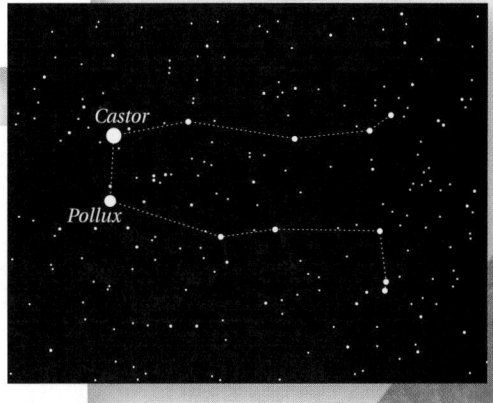

Castor

Pollux

Guide for Reading ◆ 95

Interest Grabber To capture students' interest, ask them to name and discuss a Hall of Fame with which they are familiar, such as a sports or rock-and-roll Hall of Fame. Elicit a list of the personal qualities of people elected to these Halls of Fame. Then have them imagine a Friendship Hall of Fame that honors the world's closest and noblest friendships. What special qualities would a Friendship Hall of Fame honor? Let students know that both of the stories in this selection pay tribute to unique friendships. As students read, they might recognize aspects of their own friendships.

Customize for
Less Proficient Readers
The early part of the narrative in "Two Friends" moves back and forth in time. Help less proficient readers identify the passages that represent flashbacks by calling their attention to such signal phrases as "some days" and "on a spring morning."

Customize for
More Advanced Students
More advanced students can contrast Russell's direct style of storytelling with Maupassant's indirect one. For example, they might contrast the ways in which Dionysius and the Prussian officer, both cruel characters, are described and revealed.

Customize for
English Language Learners
To help these students with challenging vocabulary, particularly in Maupassant's descriptions of nature, pair them with native speakers. The partners can work together to use context clues to determine the meanings of such words as *ruddy, gilded,* and *draught.*

Customize for
Logical/Mathematical Learners
Have these students choose one of the stories and design a flowchart or other graphic that displays significant details and their relationship to the climax.

Preparing for Standardized Tests

Reading and Vocabulary A sound knowledge of word roots will enable students to improve performance on vocabulary and reading comprehension items on the verbal portions of standardized tests. The Build Vocabulary lesson focuses on learning word meaning through the use of the root *-tain-*. For additional practice, use the Build Vocabulary page in **Selection Support** (p. 26).

Grammar and Language Portions of some standardized tests require students to write essays. Explain that using appositives—nouns or phrases that explain another noun or pronoun—

demonstrates maturity in their writing. Write these two examples on the chalkboard:
1. Athena often intervened in human affairs. Athena was the Greek goddess of wisdom.
2. Athena, the Greek goddess of wisdom, often intervened in human affairs.

Have students point out the appositive (Athena, the Greek goddess of wisdom) and analyze why the second example is more fluid than the first. Remind them to use appositives in their writing whenever they wish to clarify a noun or pronoun or to add an important detail about it.

One-Minute Insight

In this story, Morissot (mô' rē sō) and Sauvage (sō' va...) try to conduct their friendship in a business-as-usual manner against the backdrop of the Franco-Prussian War. War perplexes and disgusts these two characters, and they wish only to recapture the simple pleasures they shared before war changed their lives. When they are captured by the enemy, they must choose between honor and survival. Students will probably recall times in which their own friendships have been challenged by self-interest.

◆ **Critical Thinking**

❶ **Infer** What inferences can you make about narrator's attitude toward the Franco-Prussian War based on this opening description? *The narrator seems more concerned with the suffering that it caused— evidenced particularly by his mention of the sparrows—than with the issues it was fought to determine.*

◆ **Build Grammar Skills**

❷ **Appositives** Have students identify the appositive in this sentence. *The appositive is a riverside acquaintance.* What noun does this appositive explain? *It is in apposition to M. Sauvage.*

◆ **Build Grammar Skills**

❸ **Appositives** Point out that this sentence is unusual in that it contains three appositives. Have students identify the noun that *M. Sauvage,* the first of these appositives, explains. *The appositives all explain* man. *Then have them identify the remaining two appositives that provide information about M. Sauvage. The remaining appositives are a* haberdasher *and* another ardent fisherman.

Two Friends

Guy de Maupassant
Translated by Gordon R. Silber

The following story is set during the Franco-Prussian War. Beginning on July 19, 1870, the war had resulted from the Prussian prime minister Otto von Bismarck's belief that a war with France would strengthen the bond between the German states, along with French emperor Napoleon III's feeling that a successful conflict with Prussia would help him to gain support among the French people. As it turned out, the French army was no match for the German forces. After a series of victories, one of which ended in the capture of Napoleon III, the German army established a blockade around Paris on September 19, 1870. Led by a provisional government, Paris managed to hold out until January 28, 1871, though the city's inhabitants were plagued by famine and a sense of hopelessness. As Maupassant's story begins, the city is on the verge of surrender.

❶ Paris was blockaded, starved, in its death agony. Sparrows were becoming scarcer and scarcer on the rooftops and the sewers were being depopulated. One ate whatever one could get.

As he was strolling sadly along the outer boulevard one bright January

◆ **Build Vocabulary**

ardent (ärd′ ənt) *adj.*: Intensely enthusiastic or devoted

vernal (vʉrn′ əl) *adj.*: Springlike

96 ◆ *On the Edge*

morning, his hands in his trousers pockets and his stomach empty, M.[1] Morissot, watchmaker by trade but local militiaman for the time being, stopped short before a fellow militiaman whom he recognized as a friend. It was M. Sauvage, a riverside acquaintance. ❷

Every Sunday, before the war, Morissot left at dawn, a bamboo pole in his hand, a tin box on his back. He would take the Argenteuil railroad, get off at Colombes, and walk to Marante Island. As soon as he arrived at this ideal spot he would start to fish; he fished until nightfall.

Every Sunday he would meet a stout, jovial little man, M. Sauvage, a haberdasher[2] in Rue Notre-Dame-de-Lorette, another ardent fisherman. Often ❸ they spent half a day side by side, line in hand and feet dangling above the current. Inevitably they had struck up a friendship.

Some days they did not speak. Sometimes they did; but they understood one another admirably without saying anything because they had similar tastes and responded to their surroundings in exactly the same way.

On a spring morning, toward ten o'clock, when the young sun was drawing up from the tranquil stream wisps of haze which floated off in the direction of the current and was pouring down its vernal warmth on the backs of the two fanatical anglers,[3] Morissot would sometimes say to

---

1. **M.:** Abbreviation for *Monsieur* (mə syö′), or "Mister" or "Sir" (French).
2. **haberdasher** (hab′ ər dash′ ər) *n.*: Person who is in the business of selling men's clothing.
3. **anglers** (aŋ′ glərz) *n.*: People who fish.

Block Scheduling Strategies

Consider these suggestions to take advantage of extended class time:

• Use the Interest Grabber note on this page to introduce the subject of friendship. Then have students complete the journal activity in Literature and Your Life on p. 95.

• Introduce the literary element, climax. To reinforce this concept, have students answer the Literary Focus questions on p. 106 after they read, and follow up with the Literary Focus page in *Selection Support* (p. 29).

• Ask students to work in pairs to complete the Critical Thinking questions on pp. 101 and 105.

• As preparation for creating a brochure for a friendship film festival (see p. 107), have pairs of students come up with a list of movies that have treated friendship in a special way. Next to each entry, they should jot down the message about friendship that the movie presented.

• Have students complete the Writing Mini-Lesson on p. 107. Have them look for concrete examples in "Two Friends" and "Damon and Pythias."

The Anglers, Georges Seurat, Musée National d'Art Moderne, Troyes, France

his neighbor, "Nice, isn't it?" and M. Sauvage would answer, "There's nothing like it." And that was enough for them to understand and appreciate each other.

◆ Literature and Your Life
❹ Does their friendship remind you of one of your own friendships?

On an autumn afternoon, when the sky, reddened by the setting sun, cast reflections of its scarlet clouds on the water, made the whole river crimson, lighted up the horizon, made the two friends look as ruddy as fire, and gilded the trees which were already brown and beginning to tremble with a wintery shiver, M. Sauvage would look at Morissot with a smile and say, "Fine sight!" And Morissot, awed, would answer, "It's better than the city, isn't it?" without taking his eyes from his float.

❺ As soon as they recognized one another they shook hands energetically, touched at meeting under such changed circumstances. M. Sauvage, with a sigh, grumbled, "What

▲ Critical Viewing Compare this painting with the description in the story of an autumn afternoon. [Compare and Contrast] ❻

goings-on!" Morissot groaned dismally, "And what weather! This is the first fine day of the year." ❺

The sky was, in fact, blue and brilliant.

They started to walk side by side, absent-minded and sad. Morissot went on, "And fishing! Ah! Nothing but a pleasant memory."

"When'll we get back to it?" asked M. Sauvage.

They went into a little café and had an absinthe,[4] then resumed their stroll along the sidewalks.

Morissot stopped suddenly, "How about another, eh?" M. Sauvage agreed, "If you want." And they entered another wine shop.

On leaving they felt giddy, muddled, as one does after drinking on an empty stomach. It was mild. A caressing breeze touched ▼

4. **absinthe** (ab´ sinth) n.: Type of liqueur.

Two Friends ◆ 97

Customize for
Less Proficient Readers
Make sure that these students have read the background information on page 96 and that they are aware that Morissot and Sauvage have been kept from their fishing expeditions by the war. Have them consider why the war might prevent them from engaging in leisure activities such as fishing. *They should recognize that if the two men were to go fishing, they would be in extreme danger because enemy forces surround the city.*

◆ *Literature and Your Life*
❹ Sauvage and Morissot communicate with each other easily and naturally; as they enjoy the beautiful sunset, they are able to share their responses without having to say much. Students may describe similar experiences they have had while enjoying a sight in nature, a movie, or a sports event with a friend.

◆ **Critical Thinking**
❺ **Infer** What does this exchange reveal about the two friends' attitude toward the war? *Students may point out that both regret the way it has disrupted normal life. They may also note that, while the war has affected both men, they do not seem to feel completely overwhelmed by it at this point in the story.*

▶ **Critical Viewing** ◀
❻ **Compare and Contrast**
Students may describe the mood of the painting as peaceful, calm, or idyllic. The two men are sitting together companionably, as do Morissot and Sauvage in the story, exchanging few words.

 Humanities: Art

The Anglers, 1883, by Georges Seurat.
This oil painting captures the idyllic pleasures of a fishing trip.

French artist Georges Seurat (1859–1891) was a contemporary of Guy de Maupassant. Many of Seurat's works, including *The Anglers,* were heavily influenced by impressionism—a style of painting that used loose brush strokes and dabs of rich color to capture fleeting moments in nature and everyday life.

Use these questions for discussion:
1. In this painting, Seurat uses light and color to convey a special mood. What words might you use to describe the light in this painting and the mood it helps to convey? *Possible response: The light on the pond is soft and shimmering, presenting a contrast to the shadowy figures of the fishermen. The light conveys a mood of tranquillity.*

2. How does the picture that Maupassant "paints" add to your understanding of the two friends? *Students may respond that it helps readers understand the love of nature and fishing that they share.*

Encourage these students to use the painting on this page to help them visualize the story's foreign setting—which may seem incredibly remote to them. Have them note the ways in which the countryside in the painting differs from the area in which they live. Then have them look for details in the painting that add to the details provided in the story. Encourage them to share their observations with classmates.

◆ Critical Thinking

❶ Infer Have students discuss what leads the two men to decide to go fishing again. Is it a wise decision? *They have been discussing their pleasant memories of fishing. After several drinks, their desire to fish overcomes their concern about the circumstances. Students may suggest that it's not a wise decision, because of the blockade by the Prussian soldiers.*

Comprehension Check ☑

❷ Why would the two men need a pass to travel to the island? *The area is under the control of the French army, which is monitoring all comings and goings as a security measure.*

▶ Critical Viewing ◀

❸ Draw Conclusions Some students may say that the painting was selected because it evokes the normal, peaceful times that the friends are trying to recapture by going on their fishing trip. Others may say that the trees and land in the painting are reminiscent of the "bare cherry trees" and "colorless fields" that Morissot and Sauvage see; in this respect, the painting evokes the eerie stillness of the wartime landscape.

◆ Reading Strategy

❹ Significant Details Elicit the following responses: *Apparently, the people who live in the area have fled; this suggests that an attack by the Prussians is a very real possibility.*

Les Maisons Cabassud à la Ville D'Avray, Camille Corot

their faces.

The warm air completed what the absinthe had begun. M. Sauvage stopped. "Suppose we went?"

"Went where?"

"Fishing, of course."

"But where?"

❶ "Why, on our island. The French outposts are near Colombes. I know Colonel Dumoulin; they'll let us pass without any trouble."

Morissot trembled with eagerness: "Done! I'm with you." And they went off to get their tackle.

❷ An hour later they were walking side by side on the highway. They reached the villa which the Colonel occupied. He smiled at their request and gave his consent to their whim. They started off again, armed with a pass.

Soon they passed the outposts, went through the abandoned village of

98 ◆ *On the Edge*

▲ **Critical Viewing** This painting does not suggest the horror or hardships of war. What aspects of this story does it illustrate? [Draw Conclusions] ❸

Colombes, and reached the edge of the little vineyards which slope toward the Seine. It was about eleven.

Opposite, the village of Argenteuil seemed dead. The heights of Orgemont and Sannois dominated the whole countryside. The broad plain which stretches as far as Nanterre was empty, absolutely empty, with its bare cherry trees and its colorless fields.

Pointing up to the heights, M. Sauvage

◆ **Reading Strategy**
What might this emptiness suggest about the possible danger? ❹

◆ **Build Vocabulary**
jauntiness (jônt′ ē nis) *n.:* Carefree attitude

Humanities: Art

Les Maisons Cabassud à la Ville D'Avray (The Cabassud Houses in the Town of Avray) by Camille Corot.

During his long, distinguished career, French artist Camille Corot (1796–1875) became known primarily as a landscape painter. Classically trained, Corot traveled throughout Europe, painting pastures, mountainsides, and villages. His early landscapes were rendered in a highly detailed and highly realistic style. Later, he adopted the softer, more romantic style represented by *Les Maisons Cabassud*.

Use these questions for discussion:
1. What elements in the painting convey a sense of harmony and peacefulness? *Students may point to the harmony between the color of the ground and the earthy colors of the buildings and to the small, unhurried human figures.*
2. Like Morissot and Sauvage, Corot—also a Parisian—was drawn to rural places. What do students think city-dwellers find most appealing about the country? *Responses may include the opportunity to observe nature; the slower pace of life.*

murmured, "The Prussians are up there!" And a feeling of uneasiness paralyzed the two friends as they faced this deserted region.

"The Prussians!" They had never seen any, but for months they had felt their presence—around Paris, ruining France, pillaging, massacring, starving the country, invisible and all-powerful. And a kind of superstitious terror was superimposed on the hatred which they felt for this unknown and victorious people.

Morissot stammered, "Say, suppose we met some of them?"

His Parisian jauntiness coming to the surface in spite of everything, M. Sauvage answered, "We'll offer them some fish."

But they hesitated to venture into the country, frightened by the silence all about them.

Finally M. Sauvage pulled himself together: "Come on! On our way! But let's go carefully." And they climbed over into a vineyard, bent double, crawling, taking advantage of the vines to conceal themselves, watching, listening.

A stretch of bare ground had to be crossed to reach the edge of the river. They began to run, and when they reached the bank they plunged down among the dry reeds.

Morissot glued his ear to the ground and listened for sounds of anyone walking in the vicinity. He heard nothing. They were indeed alone, all alone.

Reassured, they started to fish.

Opposite them Marante Island, deserted, hid them from the other bank. The little building which had housed a restaurant was shut up and looked as if it had been abandoned for years.

❺ M. Sauvage caught the first gudgeon.[5] Morissot got the second, and from then on they pulled in their lines every minute or two with a silvery little fish squirming on the end, a truly miraculous draught.

Skillfully they slipped the fish into a sack made of fine net which they had hung

in the water at their feet. And happiness pervaded their whole being, the happiness which seizes upon you when you regain a cherished pleasure of which you have long been deprived. **❺**

The good sun was pouring down its warmth on their backs. They heard nothing more; they no longer thought about anything at all; they forgot about the rest of the world—they were fishing!

But suddenly a dull sound which seemed to come from under ground made the earth tremble. The cannon were beginning.

Morissot turned and saw, over the bank to the left, the great silhouette of Mount Valérien wearing a white plume on its brow, powdersmoke which it had just spit out. **❻**

And almost at once a second puff of smoke rolled from the summit, and a few seconds after the roar still another explosion was heard.

Then more followed, and time after time the mountain belched forth death-dealing breath, breathed out milky-white vapor which rose slowly in the calm sky and formed a cloud above the summit.

◆ **Reading Strategy** Why might this description of the mountain be a significant detail? **❼**

M. Sauvage shrugged his shoulders. "There they go again," he said.

As he sat anxiously watching his float bob up and down, Morissot was suddenly seized by the wrath which a peace-loving man will feel toward madmen who fight, and grumbled, "Folks sure are stupid to kill one another like that."

M. Sauvage answered, "They're worse than animals."

And Morissot, who had just pulled in a bleak, went on, "And to think that it will always be like this as long as there are governments."

M. Sauvage stopped him: "The Republic[6] wouldn't have declared war—"

---

5. **gudgeon** (guj´ en) *n.*: Small European freshwater fish.

6. **The Republic:** The provisional republican government that assumed control when Napoleon III was captured by the Prussians.

Two Friends ◆ 99

◆ **Critical Thinking**

❺ Analyze Encourage students to comment on this description of the pleasures of fishing. How does this passage help the reader understand Maupassant's attitude toward war? *Elicit the following responses: Through this tender description, the author suggests that everyday life and its simple pleasures are precious. By vividly reminding us of these pleasures, the author makes the miseries of war seem even more painful.*

◆ **Build Grammar Skills**

❻ Appositives Have students identify the appositive in this sentence along with the noun that it explains. *appositive: powdersmoke which it had just spit out; noun: plume*

◆ **Reading Strategy**

❼ Significant Details Students may say that the cannon fire smoke coming from the mountain suggests that the war will intrude on the friends' peaceful day.

Cross-Curricular Connection: Social Studies

Where in the world is the territory that used to be called Prussia? Students may become curious about this former European power as they read "Two Friends."

During most of the 1800's, the country we know as Germany was not a unified nation but rather a loose confederation of states. The largest and most powerful of these states was the kingdom of Prussia. In 1871, after Prussia had fought and defeated France in the Franco-Prussian War, the German states unified to form the German

empire, with King Wilhelm I of Prussia as its *kaiser,* or emperor.

Following Germany's defeat in World Wars I and II, large portions of Prussia were ceded to Russia and Poland. In 1947, what remained of German Prussia was legally abolished as an administrative district.

Have students find a historic map of Prussia in an encyclopedia or other reference source. What still-famous city was the kingdom's capital? *Berlin was the capital.*

◆ Literary Focus

❶ Climax Do students think that this passage signals the beginning of the story's climax? Why or why not? *Possible responses: Yes—whereas earlier details hinted at danger, the danger becomes very concrete at this moment. Now that Sauvage and Morissot have been captured, the story's outcome is about to be revealed.*

◆ Literary Focus

❷ Climax Students should note that the officer informs the friends in a cold, matter-of-fact manner that they will die in five minutes if they do not reveal the password. The chilling quality of this news adds to the urgency and suddenness of the climax.

◆ Reading Strategy

❸ Significant Details Point out that the detail about the cannon fire has appeared twice before. Have students compare and contrast the effect that the detail has here with its effect earlier in the story. *Possible responses: Earlier, the "thunder" acted as a reminder of the war and of surrounding danger. Here it heightens the tension of the story's climax; it emphasizes that the war has caught up with Morissot and Sauvage.*

Comprehension Check ☑

❹ Why does the officer take each of the men aside? *He thinks that each is more likely to give up the password if his friend isn't present; in this way, he is trying to break down the friends' sense of honor and loyalty.*

Morissot interrupted: "Under kings you have war abroad; under the Republic you have war at home."

And they started a leisurely discussion, unraveling great political problems with the sane reasonableness of easygoing, limited individuals, and found themselves in agreement on the point that men would never be free. And Mount Valérien thundered unceasingly, demolishing French homes with its cannon, crushing out lives, putting an end to the dreams which many had dreamt, the joys which many had been waiting for, the happiness which many had hoped for, planting in wives' hearts, in maidens' hearts, in mothers' hearts, over there, in other lands, sufferings which would never end.

"That's life for you," opined M. Sauvage.

"You'd better say 'That's death for you,'" laughed Morissot.

❶ But they shuddered in terror when they realized that someone had just come up behind them, and looking around they saw four men standing almost at their elbows, four tall men, armed and bearded, dressed like liveried[7] servants, with flat caps on their heads, pointing rifles at them.

The two fish lines dropped from their hands and floated off down stream.

In a few seconds they were seized, trussed up, carried off, thrown into a rowboat and taken over to the island.

And behind the building which they had thought deserted they saw a score of German soldiers.

A kind of hairy giant who was seated astride a chair smoking a porcelain pipe asked them in excellent French: "Well, gentlemen, have you had good fishing?"

Then a soldier put down at the officer's feet the sack full of fish which he had carefully brought along. The Prussian smiled: "Aha! I see that it didn't go badly. But we have to talk about another little matter. Listen to me and don't get excited.

"As far as I am concerned, you are two

---

7. **liveried** (liv´ ər ēd) *adj.*: Uniformed.

100 ◆ On the Edge

---

spies sent to keep an eye on me. I catch you and I shoot you. You were pretending to fish in order to conceal your business. You have fallen into my hands, so much the worse for you. War is like that.

"But—since you came out past the outposts you have, of course, the password to return. Tell me that password and I will pardon you."

The two friends, side by side, pale, kept silent. A slight nervous trembling shook their hands.

The officer went on: "No one will ever know. You will go back placidly. The secret will disappear with you. If you refuse, it is immediate death. Choose."

They stood motionless, mouths shut.

The Prussian quietly went on, stretching out his hand toward the stream: "Remember that within five minutes you will be at the bottom of that river. Within five minutes! You have relatives, of course?"

Mount Valérien kept thundering. ❸

The two fishermen stood silent. The German gave orders in his own language. Then he moved his chair so as not to be near the prisoners and twelve men took their places, twenty paces distant, rifles grounded.

The officer went on: "I give you one minute, not two seconds more."

Then he rose suddenly, approached the two Frenchmen, took Morissot by the arm, dragged him aside, whispered to him, "Quick, the password? Your friend won't know. I'll pretend to relent."

Morissot answered not a word.

The Prussian drew M. Sauvage aside and put the same question.

M. Sauvage did not answer.

They stood side by side again.

And the officer began to give commands. The soldiers raised their rifles.

Then Morissot's glance happened to fall on the sack full of gudgeons which was lying on the grass a few steps away.

> ◆ **Literary Focus**
> How does the officer's calm manner add to the tension? ❷

Speaking and Listening Mini-Lesson

Role Play

This mini-lesson supports the Speaking and Listening activity in the Idea Bank on page 107.

Introduce the Concept Point out that in a role play students step into the shoes of characters, and it is important that they be true to those characters.

Develop Background Before students begin their role-playing, have them explore and discuss the characters' states of mind at this crucial moment. Lead students to consider:

- Would the two men be completely certain of their choice, or would they feel some doubt?
- What reasons would they have for revealing the password? What reasons would they have for refusing?

Apply the Information Have pairs of students practice their conversations and then perform them for the class.

Assess the Outcome Evaluate the conversations based on the following criterion: Were the ideas expressed true to the characters?

A ray of sunshine made the little heap of still squirming fish gleam. And he almost weakened. In spite of his efforts his eyes filled with tears.

He stammered, "Farewell, Monsieur Sauvage."

M. Sauvage answered, "Farewell, Monsieur Morissot."

They shook hands, trembling from head to foot with a shudder which they could not control.

The officer shouted, "Fire!"

The twelve shots rang out together.

M. Sauvage fell straight forward, like a log. Morissot, who was taller, tottered, half turned, and fell crosswise on top of his comrade, face up, as the blood spurted from his torn shirt.

The German gave more orders.

His men scattered, then returned with rope and stones which they tied to the dead men's feet. Then they carried them to the bank.

Mount Valérien continued to roar, its summit hidden now in a mountainous cloud of smoke.

Two soldiers took Morissot by the head and the feet, two others seized M. Sauvage. They swung the bodies for a moment then let go. They described an arc and plunged into the river feet first, for the weights made them seem to be standing upright.

There was a splash, the water trembled, then grew calm, while tiny wavelets spread to both shores.

A little blood remained on the surface.

The officer, still calm, said in a low voice: "Now the fish will have their turn."

And he went back to the house.

And all at once he caught sight of the sack of gudgeons in the grass. He picked it up, looked at it, smiled, shouted, "Wilhelm!"

A soldier in a white apron ran out. And the Prussian threw him the catch of the two and said: "Fry these little animals right away while they are still alive. They will be delicious."

Then he lighted his pipe again.

Guide for Responding

◆ Literature and Your Life

Reader's Response Were you shocked by the outcome of the story? Why or why not?

Thematic Focus In this story, is it friendship itself that leads the two men into danger and finally to death? Explain.

Farewell Note As Morissot or Sauvage, write a brief farewell note to your family before you are executed.

☑ Check Your Comprehension

1. How does the wartime situation in Paris affect the Sunday habits of Morissot and Sauvage?
2. How do they succeed for a while in defying the war?
3. What surprise do they encounter?
4. How does a final choice they have to make lead to the end of the story?

◆ Critical Thinking

INTERPRET
1. What causes the two friends to try fishing again? **[Infer]**
2. (a) Find two details of the men's journey to the island that might give readers an uneasy feeling. (b) Explain your choices. **[Infer]**
3. What message does Maupassant convey by showing how war breaks in on the peacefulness of fishing? **[Synthesize]**

EVALUATE
4. Is it effective to end the story with the Prussian officer's order to cook the fish? Explain. In answering, consider what this detail does or does not add to the central idea of the story. **[Assess]**

APPLY
5. What does this story suggest about the effects of modern warfare on everyday life? **[Generalize]**

◆ Critical Thinking

1. Giddiness from the wine and the warm weather tempts them to try fishing again.
2. (a) Students might cite the emptiness of the landscape and the abandoned restaurant building. (b) Both these details suggest people had left the area because it is dangerous.
3. A possible answer is that simple, daily pleasures can-

not be taken for granted; war destroys citizens' right to relax.
4. One acceptable answer is that the incident reinforces the shocking nature of events, and also emphasizes the activity of fishing at the heart of the story.
5. The story shows that even the simplest human activities become prohibited in times of war.

◆ Critical Thinking

⑤ Analyze Ask students how they would characterize the two men's behavior in their final moments. *Possible response: Even in the face of death, the men remained true to their friendship; neither betrays the other.*

◆ Critical Thinking

⑥ Identify Character Traits What traits do the Prussian officer's words and actions reveal? Is his behavior here consistent with his behavior earlier in the story? *Responses may include: The officer is clearly unaffected by the deaths he himself ordered and thus shows himself to be callous and cold-blooded. His behavior is consistent with the cold-blooded way in which he treated Morissot and Sauvage when they were captured.*

⑦ Enrichment Help students to see the irony of this sequence of events. The two friends, who were going to eat their fish, will presumably now be eaten by fish. Meanwhile the Prussian officer, who has had the two friends executed (as they trembled and squirmed like fish), has now given orders to have the fish fried while they are still alive. Students can note the parallels between the fate of the two men and the fate of the fish.

Reinforce and Extend

Answers
◆ Literature and Your Life

Reader's Response Some students might say they did not expect the two friends to die for the honor of their country after discussing the folly of war.

Thematic Focus It is not the friendship itself, but the sense of honor of each man.

☑ Check Your Comprehension

1. They have to forgo fishing because of the war.
2. They decide to go fishing at their old spot despite the war.
3. They encounter cannon fire and soldiers with rifles upon them.
4. Their decision to keep the password to themselves leads to their execution.

One-Minute Insight In the myth "Damon and Pythias," two friends prove that they are willing to lay down their lives for each other. Students may be challenged to apply the standards of loyalty brought out in these stories to their own friendships.

◆ **Reading Strategy**

❶ Significant Details The author stresses the friends' unwavering trust and their belief in each other's honesty.

◆ **Build Grammar Skills**

❷ Appositives Have students identify the appositive in this sentence as well as the noun that it explains. *The word Dionysius is in apposition to the noun tyrant.*

◆ **Critical Thinking**

❸ Infer What inferences can students make about Pythias based on this passage? *Possible responses: He is loyal to his family as well as his friends; he places the needs of others above his own.*

▶ **Critical Viewing** ◀

❹ Infer Inferences may include the following: Damon, the figure whose hands are tied, is loyal, brave, and noble; these traits are revealed by his willingness to die for his friend. Pythias, the figure who is stepping forward, is equally loyal, brave, and noble; these traits are revealed by his willingness to be put to death in order to save Damon.

Damon and Pythias

Retold by William F. Russell, Ed.D.

Damon and Pythias were two noble young men who lived on the island of Sicily in a city called Syracuse. They were such close companions and were so devoted to each other that all the people of the city admired them as the highest examples of true friendship. Each trusted the other so completely that nobody could ever have persuaded one that the other had been unfaithful or dishonest, even if that had been the case.

Now it happened that Syracuse was, at that time, ruled by a famous tyrant named Dionysius, who had gained the throne for himself through treachery, and who from then on flaunted his power by behaving cruelly to his own subjects and to all strangers and enemies who were so unfortunate as to fall into his clutches. This tyrant, Dionysius, was so unjustly cruel that once, when he awoke from a restless sleep during which he dreamt that a certain man in the town had attempted to kill him, he immediately had that man put to death.

It happened that Pythias had, quite unjustly, been accused by Dionysius of trying to overthrow him, and for this supposed crime of treason Pythias was sentenced by the king to die. Try as he might, Pythias could not prove his innocence to the king's satisfaction, and so, all hope now lost, the noble youth asked only for a few days' freedom so that he could settle his business affairs and see to it that his relatives would be cared for after he was executed. Dionysius, the hardhearted tyrant, however, would not believe Pythias's promise to return and would not allow him to leave unless he left behind him a hostage, someone who would be put to death in his place if he should fail to return within the stated time.

Pythias immediately thought of his friend Damon, and he unhesitatingly sent for him in this hour of <u>dire</u> necessity, never thinking for a moment that his trusty

◆ **Reading Strategy**
❶ What details of the friendship are stressed?

◆ **Build Vocabulary**
dire (dīr) *adj.*: Calling for quick action; urgent

▶ **Critical Viewing** What does this picture reveal about the characters of Damon and Pythias? [Infer] **❹**

Damon and Pythias

Customize for
Visual/Spatial Learners
Because this engraving directly illustrates a scene from the myth, it provides an excellent opportunity for visual/spatial learners to utilize their ability to absorb visual details to enhance their understanding of the story. Have them carefully study the details of the engraving and consider how the depiction of the events and the characters compares to the way in which they envision them as they read the selection. Encourage them to share their observations with classmates.

Customize for
Bodily/Kinesthetic Learners
Ask these students to describe the body language of Damon, Pythias, and Dionysius in this picture and how—in each case—that body language communicates what a character is feeling. *Possible answers: Damon is leaning toward his friend and his eyes express his relief, although not surprise, that Pythias has returned; Pythias' sense of urgency is conveyed through his outstretched hand, as well as his flowing hair and robe, which indicate his speed; Dionysius appears shocked.*

◊ **Humanities: Art**

Damon and Pythias (engraving), artist unknown.

An engraving is a picture printed from an image that has been cut into a metal plate. This engraving illustrates the climactic moment in which Pythias appears to save Damon, to the surprise of the tyrant Dionysius and the cheers of the crowd.

Use these questions for discussion:

1. Call students' attention to the artist's use of diagonals. Have them identify various diagonal elements in the composition. *Elements include the executioner's arm and sword; the upper half of Damon's body; the outstretched arms of Pythias, Dionysius, and the spectator in the lower left corner; the line that extends from the executioner's shoulder to Pythias' robe.*

2. What effect do all these diagonals create? In what way is this effect appropriate for the climax of the story? *Students may say that the lines convey movement and action; the climax is the point at which the action is most intense.*

103

◆ Critical Thinking

❶ Infer What does Damon's reply to the king reveal? What does it suggest about the outcome of the story? *He is sincere in the commitment he made to his friend. At this point it seems inevitable that one of the two friends will be put to death.*

◆ Build Vocabulary

❷ Word Roots: -tain- Ask students to explain the relationship between the meaning of the word *detained* and the meaning of the word root *-tain-. Detained means "kept in custody." The meaning of the word root -tain- is "hold." To keep someone is custody is to hold him or her in custody.*

◆ Literary Focus

❸ Climax Possible responses: The details add to the suspense because although the reader might trust Pythias' loyalty to his friend, it begins to look like he will not be able to fulfill his promise and Damon will be put to death—a very disappointing climax to the story.

companion would refuse his request. Nor did he, for Damon hastened straightaway to the palace—much to the amazement of King Dionysius—and gladly offered to be held hostage for his friend, in spite of the dangerous condition that had been attached to this favor. Therefore, Pythias was permitted to settle his earthly affairs before departing to the Land of the Shades,[1] while Damon remained behind in the dungeon, the captive of the tyrant Dionysius.

After Pythias had been released. Dionysius asked Damon if he did not feel afraid, for Pythias might very well take advantage of the opportunity he had been given and simply not return at all, and then he, Damon, would be executed in his place. But Damon replied at once with a willing smile: "There is no need for me to feel afraid, O King, since I have perfect faith in the word of my true friend, and I know that he will certainly return before the appointed time—unless, of course, he dies or is held captive by some evil force. Even so, even should the noble Pythias be captured and held against his will, it would be an honor for me to die in his place."

Such devotion and perfect faith as this was unheard of to the friendless tyrant; still, though he could not help admiring the true nobility of his captive, he nevertheless determined that Damon should certainly be put to death should Pythias not return by the appointed time.

And, as the Fates would have it, by a strange turn of events, Pythias was detained far longer in his task than he had imagined. Though he never for a single minute intended to evade the sentence of death to which he had been so unjustly

committed, Pythias met with several accidents and unavoidable delays. Now his time was running out and he had yet to overcome the many impediments that had been placed in his path. At last he succeeded in clearing away all the hindrances, and he sped back the many miles to the palace of the king, his heart almost bursting with grief and fear that he might arrive too late.

Meanwhile, when the last day of the allotted time arrived, Dionysius commanded that the place of execution should be readied at once, since he was still ruthlessly determined that if one of his victims escaped him, the other should not. And so, entering the chamber in which Damon was confined, he began to utter words of sarcastic pity for the "foolish faith," as he termed it, that the young man of Syracuse had in his friend.

In reply, however, Damon merely smiled, since, in spite of the fact that the eleventh hour had already arrived, he still believed that his lifelong companion would not fail him. Even when, a short time later, he was actually led out to the site of his execution, his serenity remained the same.

Great excitement stirred the crowd that had gathered to witness the execution, for all the people had heard of the bargain that had been struck between the two friends.

◆ Literary Focus

How do these details add to the tension of the climax?

❸

---

1. **Land of the Shades:** Mythical place where people go when they die.

◆ Build Vocabulary

detained (dē tānd´) *v.*: Kept in custody

impediments (im pēd´ ə məntz) *n.*: Something standing in the way of something else

hindrances (hin´ drəns əz) *n.*: People or things in the way; obstacles

annals (an´ əlz) *n.*: Historical records or chronicles; history

104 ◆ On the Edge

 Beyond the Selection

FURTHER READING

Other Works by the Featured Authors
"The Necklace," Guy de Maupassant
"The Piece of String," Guy de Maupassant
Classic Myths to Read Aloud, William F. Russell

Other Works With the Theme of Tests of Friendship
"A Child's Heart," Herman Hesse
A Separate Peace, John Knowles
   We suggest that you preview these works before recommending them to students.

INTERNET

You and your students may find additional information about Guy de Maupassant on the Internet. We suggest the following site. Please be aware, however, that the site may have changed from the time we published this information.

   To access stories by Guy de Maupassant in English, go to **http://lib.univ-fcomte.fr/PEOPLE/selva/Maupassant.html**

   We *strongly recommend* that you preview the site before you send students to it.

There was much sobbing and cries of sympathy were heard all around as the captive was brought out, though he himself somehow retained complete composure even at this moment of darkest danger.

Presently the excitement grew more intense still as a swift runner could be seen approaching the palace courtyard at an astonishing speed, and wild shrieks of relief and joy went up as Pythias, breathless and exhausted, rushed headlong through the crowd and flung himself into the arms of his beloved friend, sobbing with relief that he had, by the grace of the gods, arrived in time to save Damon's life.

❹ This final exhibition of devoted love and faithfulness was more than even the stony heart of Dionysius, the tyrant, could resist. As the throng of spectators melted into tears at the companions' embrace, the king approached the pair and declared that Pythias was hereby pardoned and his death sentence canceled. In addition, he begged the pair to allow him to become their friend, to try to be as much a friend to them both as they had shown each other to be.

Thus did the two friends of Syracuse, by the faithful love they bore to each other, conquer the hard heart of a tyrant king, and in the annals of true friendship there are no more honored names than those of Damon and Pythias—for no person can do more than be willing to lay down his life for the sake of his friend.

❹

◆ *Literature and Your Life*
When have you observed that friendship can be contagious?

❺

◆ **Critical Thinking**

❹ **Relate** Ask students if they think that modern readers share the admiration that the tyrant and the crowd show for Damon and Pythias. If so, what does this demonstrate about the meaning of friendship? *Students may say that people today can appreciate the two friends as much as the ancient Greeks did—showing that trust and loyalty are still the essentials of true friendship.*

◆ *Literature and Your Life*

❺ Some students might say that observing the warmth and closeness of a particular relationship has inspired them to want to join that friendship or give and get more out of a growing friendship of their own.

Reinforce and Extend

Answers
◆ *Literature and Your Life*
Reader's Response Students will probably cite the point at which "he had yet to overcome the many impediments that had been placed in his path."

Thematic Focus Example incidents should show how students gave advice or provided the practical help that made a difference in their friend's life

☑ **Check Your Comprehension**
1. Damon and Pythias had the reputation of being noble and loyal, while Dionysius was considered treacherous and power hungry.
2. Pythias needs Damon's help while he goes to settle his affairs befo:e he is executed. Damon stays in his cell to guarantee his return.
3. Dionysius is so touched by the unselfishness of the two friends that he spares Pythias' life.

Guide for Responding

◆ *Literature and Your Life*

Reader's Response At what point in the story were you most nervous about the return of Pythias? Explain.

Thematic Focus You may not have risked your life for a friend, as Damon does in this tale. However, you've probably helped friends who were in danger of failing a test, not making a team, or doing the wrong thing in a social situation. Choose one such incident and tell how you came through for your friend.

☑ **Check Your Comprehension**
1. As the story begins, what reputations do Damon, Pythias, and Dionysius have in Syracuse?
2. What are the events leading up to the execution scene at the end?
3. How does the outcome of the story affect the king?

◆ **Critical Thinking**

INTERPRET
1. Give two examples of how Damon and Pythias are "noble" in ways other than their birth. **[Infer]**
2. Compare and contrast Dionysius's behavior at the beginning and end of the story. **[Compare and Contrast]**
3. Why isn't Damon afraid as he waits for Pythias? **[Infer]**
4. What universal message does this myth teach? **[Interpret]**
EVALUATE
5. Remembering what you know about tyrants—both ancient and modern—decide whether the king's change of heart is realistic. **[Evaluate]**
APPLY
6. Could a friendship like the one between Damon and Pythias exist in our own times? Why or why not? **[Relate]**

◆ **Critical Thinking**
1. Possible examples: Pythias' willingness to die although he had been wrongly accused; Damon's readiness to die in his friend's place; Pythias' return to his own execution.
2. Dionysius' behavior at the beginning of the story is cold-blooded and cruel, while at the end he acts justly because he has been warmed by the friendship of Pythias and Damon.
3. Damon isn't afraid while he waits for Pythias, because he has faith that his friend will return.
4. One acceptable response is that you should always stand by your friends.
5. Students may answer that it is not realistic; tyrants usually do not have sudden changes of heart.
6. Students might say that the dramatic events that tested Pythias and Damon's friendship are not likely to occur in daily life today, but that in times of war there might be similar circumstances.

◆ Reading Strategy

1. The powdersmoke is significant because it indicates cannon fire nearby.
2. They both detest war and fighting and have expressed moral values.
3. Damon is probably happy for the opportunity to have his loyalty to Pythias tested.

◆ Literary Focus

1. The climax in "Two Friends" occurs when the two friends are shot after refusing to betray each other. The conflict and suspense in the plot had led up to this moment.
2. Three hints include needing a pass to enter the war zone; the landscape and buildings on the way to the river had been abandoned; smoke from cannon fire. A reader might overlook these hints because they are woven into the story as the friends were having a good time.
3. The climax in "Damon and Pythias" comes when Pythias returned just in time and the king spared both their lives.
4. Some students might find surprising climaxes more exciting; others will find expected climaxes more satisfying.

◆ Build Vocabulary

Using the Root -tain-
1. *contain*—to be able to hold
2. *retain*—to hold in one's possession
3. *maintain*—to carry on

Using the Word Bank
1. b 2. c 3. c 4. b 5. a 6. c 7. a

◆ Build Grammar Skills

Practice
1. Damon and Pythias
2. a shy man
3. a man of honor

Writing Application
1. This tyrant, Dionysius, was so unjustly cruel that he had many men put to death.
2. However, Dionysius, a hardhearted tyrant, would not believe Pythias' promise.
3. Morissot, a watchman by trade but a local militiaman for the time being, stopped short before a fellow militiaman.

Guide for Responding (continued)

◆ Reading Strategy

SIGNIFICANT DETAILS
Paying close attention to the **significant details** in these stories helps you guess the fate of characters. Among the most important details in the two selections are the descriptions of the friendship of Damon and Pythias in the myth and background details of the war in "Two Friends." Because Damon and Pythias are so "devoted," their friendship is more likely to survive a test. In "Two Friends," however, the strange "silence all about" Morissot and Sauvage near the river suggests that they may not survive their little outing.

1. In "Two Friends," what is significant about the "powdersmoke" that Morissot and Sauvage see on the mountain?
2. What details about the two men in "Two Friends" might lead you to believe that they will not betray each other?
3. How is Damon's gladness about being a "hostage" a significant detail?

◆ Literary Focus

CLIMAX
"Damon and Pythias" builds up to its **climax**— the moment of greatest tension—like an imaginary drumroll that gets louder and louder. Detail after detail, from the imprisoning of Damon to the delay of Pythias, add to this drumroll as the expected climax approaches.

In "Two Friends," however, the climax comes unexpectedly. The drumming of cannon seems part of the background, a noise in a faraway war that does not concern the friends. Suddenly, the distant war comes close, in the form of a Prussian officer with the power of life and death.

1. What is the climax in "Two Friends"? Give reasons for your answer.
2. In "Two Friends," Maupassant hints at the climax even though it arrives with a shocking suddenness. Find three of these hints; then tell why a reader might overlook them.
3. Identify the climax in "Damon and Pythias" and explain your choice.
4. Which type of climax do you prefer—expected or unexpected? Why?

◆ Build Vocabulary

USING THE ROOT -tain-
Knowing that the root *-tain-* means "to hold," write definitions for the following words:

1. contain   2. retain   3. maintain

USING THE WORD BANK
On your paper, write the letter of the word that is the antonym—opposite in meaning—of the first word:
1. dire: (a) urgent, (b) unimportant, (c) alive
2. detained: (a) restrained, (b) studied, (c) released
3. impediments: (a) footwear, (b) obstacles, (c) supports
4. hindrances: (a) fronts, (b) aids, (c) lances
5. ardent: (a) indifferent, (b) confident, (c) intent
6. vernal: (a) mild, (b) angry, (c) wintry
7. jauntiness: (a) seriousness, (b) lightheartedness, (c) reluctance

◆ Build Grammar Skills

APPOSITIVES
By including information in appositives, the authors of "Damon and Pythias" and "Two Friends" avoid putting each new fact in a separate sentence.

> **Appositives** are nouns or noun phrases placed near another noun or pronoun to explain it.

Practice Identify the appositives in the following sentences.
1. The faithful friends Damon and Pythias won over the tyrant.
2. Morissot, a shy man, grew bolder as he drank absinthe.
3. The Prussian officer, a man of honor, insisted on executing the friends.

Writing Application Combine each pair of sentences by using appositives.
1. This tyrant was so unjustly cruel that he had many men put to death. This tyrant was named Dionysius.
2. Dionysius, however, would not believe Pythias' promise. Dionysius was a hardhearted tyrant.
3. Morissot stopped short before a fellow militiaman. Morissot was a watchmaker by trade but local militiaman for the time being.

✎ Writer's Solution

For additional instruction and practice, use the lesson in the **Language Lab CD-ROM** on Commas—and the pages on appositives and appositive phrases in the *Writer's Solution Grammar Practice Book* (p. 40).

Build Your Portfolio

Idea Bank

Writing

1. **Epitaph for Damon and Pythias** Write a few words to be carved into a stone that will stand above the graves of Damon and Pythias. **[Art Link]**

2. **Yearbook Profiles** Write yearbook profiles for yourself and a good friend. Include information about your accomplishments and preferences.

3. **Report of the Prussian Officer** As the Prussian officer in "Two Friends," write a report for your superior on the execution of Morissot and Sauvage. Include such details as where you discovered them, what they were doing, and why you had them shot. **[Social Studies Link]**

Speaking and Listening

4. **Role Play** With a partner, role-play a conversation between the two friends in Maupassant's story, discussing whether or not you should give away the password. **[Performing Arts Link]**

5. **Humorous Monologue** Write and deliver a funny speech about a friend. Purposely exaggerate your friend's ordinary experiences, pretending that they're dangerous adventures. **[Performing Arts Link]**

Projects

6. **Friendship Collage** Create a collage of pictures from magazines, ticket stubs, photographs, and other items that "illustrate" an adventure you've had with a friend. **[Art Link]**

7. **Brochure for a Friendship Film Festival** Choose three movies about friendship to be included in a brochure for a "Friendship Film Festival." Create a brochure describing why each film is included in the festival. **[Media Link]**

Writing Mini-Lesson

Extended Definition of Friendship

Use your own ideas and feelings as well as events in "Damon and Pythias" and "Two Friends" to write an extended definition of friendship. Unlike a dry dictionary definition, your extended definition will illustrate your ideas with concrete examples of friends and their behavior from your own experience, literature, the movies, and television.

Writing Skills Focus: Concrete Examples

Use **concrete examples** to support your ideas when writing an extended definition, a problem-and-solution essay, or an editorial. Such examples even help to make a short story more vivid. Maupassant, for example, begins "Two Friends" with a general statement and then brings it to life with two concrete examples:

Model From the Story

Paris was blockaded, starved, in its death agony. *Sparrows were becoming scarcer and scarcer on the rooftops* and *the sewers were being depopulated.*

Jot down concrete examples of friendship as you plan your extended definition, and refer to them as you draft and revise it.

Prewriting Start with a two-column chart. In the left column, write general ideas about friendship. In the right column, describe a concrete example that supports each idea.

Drafting Use the left column of your chart to write a general definition of friendship. Then choose the best examples from the right column to make that definition more vivid.

Revising Illustrate each general point you make about friendship with a concrete example. Where necessary, describe the actions that show what friends do for each other and how they express their devotion.

Two Friends/Damon and Pythias ◆ 107

Idea Bank

Customizing for
Performance Levels
Following are suggestions for matching Idea Bank topics with your students' performance levels:
   Less Advanced Students: 1, 6
   Average Students: 2, 4, 5, 7
   More Advanced Students: 3

Customizing for
Learning Modalities
Following are suggestions for matching Idea Bank topics with your students' learning modalities:
   Visual/Spatial: 1, 6
   Verbal/Linguistic: 4, 5, 7

Writing Mini-Lesson

Refer students to the Writing Handbook, page 965, for instruction on the writing process. For additional or alternative extended definition assignments, see Art Transparencies 11 and 12.

Writing and Language Transparencies Use the set of transparencies for Writing Process Model 4 (pp. 25–28) to provide a model for an extended definition and to guide students through the writing process.

Writer's Solution

Writing Lab CD-ROM
Have students complete the tutorial on Expositon. Follow these steps:
1. Have them look at the audio-annotated model organized by order of importance.
2. Ask them to complete a note card activity to help them organize their ideas.
3. Have students draft on computer.
4. Encourage students to use the Self-Evaluation Checklist to help them revise.

Sourcebook
Have students use Chapter 3, Exposition (pp. 63–89), for additional support.

✓ ASSESSMENT OPTIONS

Formal Assessment, Selection Test, pp. 19–21, and Assessment Resources Software. The selection test is designed so that it can be easily customized to the performance levels of your students.
Alternative Assessment, p. 7, includes options for less advanced students, more advanced students, verbal/linguistic learners, logical/mathematical learners, visual/spatial learners, and musical/rhythmic learners.

PORTFOLIO ASSESSMENT
Use the following rubrics in the *Alternative Assessment* booklet to assess student writing:
Epitaph for Damon and Pythias: Expression Rubric, p. 94
Yearbook Profiles: Narrative Based on Personal Experience Rubric, p. 96
Report of the Prussian Officer: Summary Rubric, p. 98

Before students begin, review the following key characteristics of a problem-and-solution essay:

- It identifies a problem or obstacle and then offers some sort of resolution.

- It begins with a clear statement of the problem and then follows a reasoned and logical path to its solution.

You may want to distribute the scoring rubric for Problem-Solution (p. 102 in *Alternative Assessment*) to make students aware before they begin of the criteria on which they will be evaluated. See the suggestions on page 110 for how you can customize the rubric for this workshop.

 ### Writer's Solution

Writers at Work Videodisc

To introduce students to the key elements and show them how Rudolfo Anaya uses them in his expository writing, play the videodisc segment on Exposition (Ch. 2). Have students discuss what Anaya says about the way he gets his ideas across.

Play frames 22803 to 32243

Writing Lab CD-ROM

You may want to have them work on the tutorial on Exposition to complete all or part of their problem-and-solution essays. Follow these steps:

1. Have students review the interactive model of a problem-and-solution essay.
2. Suggest that students complete the self-interview activity to find out what problems or issues are important to them.
3. Have students draft on computer.
4. Suggest students use a revision checker for unity and coherence.
5. Have students use the revision checker for homophones.

Sourcebook

Students can find additional support, including topic ideas, models, audience and purpose profiles, and graphic organizers, in the chapter on Exposition (pp. 62–95).

Problem-and-Solution Essay | Writing Process Workshop

Air pollution . . . information overload . . . can't concentrate on schoolwork . . . Everywhere you turn, there are problems! What can you do about it? One thing you can do is write a **problem-and-solution essay.** In a problem-and-solution essay, you identify a problem, then lay out a plan for solving that problem. In the course of the essay, you explain the strategy for solving the problem, as well as the steps required to solve it. For this type of essay to work, it's important that a solution to the problem exists.

The following skills, introduced in this section's Writing Mini-Lessons, will help you write an effective problem-and-solution essay.

Writing Skills Focus

▶ As you explain your solution, **show the benefits of your proposal.** Few will be willing to accept your proposed solution to the problem if they do not know the benefits of it. (See p. 85.)

▶ Every problem has both a cause and an effect. Make sure you clearly **show cause-and-effect relationships**—how one event or condition brings about another. (See p. 93.)

James Thurber puts these skills to humorous use as he explains how his family tried to deal with a troublesome dog.

MODEL FROM LITERATURE

from "The Dog That Bit People" by James Thurber

. . . Muggs used to spend practically all of his time outdoors. . . . ① It was hard to get him to come in and as a result the garbage man, the iceman, and the laundry man wouldn't come near the house. ② We had to haul the garbage down to the corner, take the laundry out and bring it back, and meet the iceman a block from home. After this had gone on for some time ③ we hit on an ingenious arrangement for getting the dog in the house . . . Thunder frightened him out of his senses . . . So we fixed up a thunder machine [to scare him inside.] ④

① Here, the writer reveals his particular problem: The biting dog won't come inside.

② Further details emphasize the importance of the problem.

③ The writer signals that a solution to the problem is coming.

④ The solution to the problem is given here: a thunder machine.

108 ◆ *On the Edge*

 ## Beyond the Classroom

Career Connection

Students should have little difficulty thinking of problems to write about in their essays. Remind students that no matter what career they eventually choose, they will be confronted with problems either directly and indirectly and be required to offer a plausible solution to them. Suggest to politically inclined students that they think of problems such as poverty and welfare that are frequently in the news. Scientifically minded students may be inclined to tackle problems such as pollution or ozone depletion. Suggest to mathematically inclined students that they look at the business section of a newspaper to find articles about business or financial problems for which they might suggest solutions.

Prewriting

Choose an Interesting Topic Choose a problem that interests you and about which you have an opinion. If you're having trouble thinking of one, use a problems-and-solutions chart like the one below to help you.

Problems	Solutions
overdevelopment	zoning restrictions
pollution	recycling
elderly	retirement communities
loneliness	friends
obesity	exercise and a good diet

Focus Decide whether your problem is too broad to explain a solution in the time and space you are given. If your problem has too many parts or aspects to it, decide on just one part to examine. For example, instead of discussing all the problems associated with illiteracy, discuss illiteracy in your community and how your school could do its part in setting up tutoring programs.

Drafting

Show the Benefits of Your Proposed Solution As you draft your proposed solution, show your readers why your suggestions are the most logical or beneficial. Explain how the steps you recommend will lead to a solution of the problem, and emphasize the positive effects of solving the problem.

Show Cause-and-Effect Relationships People are more likely to follow your advice if you show how their actions will bring about these positive effects. Make the cause-and-effect relationships clear in your proposed solution.

> People often ask me how to lose weight. I used to give them detailed explanations about calories and the body's ability to use fuel. Now I give a simple answer—to lose weight, eat less and exercise more.

Here the writer has clearly identified the causes (eating less, exercising more) and the effect (losing weight).

Applying Language Skills: Sentence Fragments

A sentence fragment lacks a subject or a verb or simply does not express a complete thought. Always try to express your ideas in complete sentences, which contain a subject and a verb and express a complete thought.

Sentence Fragment:
While almost everyone likes to eat sweets.

Complete Sentence:
While almost everyone likes to eat sweets, you need to eat healthy foods to stay slim.

Practice On your paper, rewrite the following fragments as complete sentences.

1. Because our rivers are polluted.
2. Exercising on a daily basis.

Writing Application Check your problem-and-solution essay to make sure that all of your sentences are complete.

Writer's Solution Connection Language Lab

For more practice on fixing sentence fragments, complete the Language Lab lesson on Run-on Sentences and Fragments.

Writing Process Workshop ◆ 109

Prewriting

Students may enjoy writing about a problem they or their family solved in an ingenious way. They can talk with family members to recall tricky but comical situations and the welcome solutions. Alternatively, students can use their findings as the basis for a humorous set of how-to instructions (see page 71).

Customize for
English Language Learners
Encourage these students to think about a problem with which they are familiar in their native country. They will feel more confident writing about something they know better than other students. Help them with any specialized vocabulary for the topic they choose.

Customize for
Less Proficient Writers
Encourage these students to write about a problem that affects them personally, such as budgeting one's time efficiently or tackling some other problem around the house. If they are familiar with the subject matter they will be able to concentrate more fully on the techniques of writing.

Customize for
More Advanced Students
Challenge these students to write about a larger issue that they will have to do research on, such as a major political, scientific, or social issue.

Writer's Solution

Writing Lab CD-ROM
Have students review the Tips on Gathering Details and Conducting Library Research screens in the Gathering Details section of the Writing Lab tutorial on Exposition.

Drafting

Encourage students to draft their problem-and-solution essay in a single sitting, without pausing to labor over single words or grammatical errors. Once students have completed a draft, they can go back into their work and make extensive revisions.

Applying Language Skills

Sentence Fragments Remind students that while they may speak in fragments, they are unacceptable for a piece of formal writing.

Suggested Answers
1. Because our rivers are polluted, we must not swim or fish in them.
2. Exercising on a daily basis not only builds muscles and strengthens your heart; it also significantly reduces stress.

Writer's Solution

For additional instruction and practice, have students complete the **Language Lab CD-ROM** lesson on Fragments and Run-on Sentences and the practice page 59 in the *Writer's Solution Grammar Practice Book.*

Revising

Reading a piece aloud can help a writer or editor hear stiff language, overused words, choppy sentences, disjointed paragraphs, or other errors. This approach works well for partners. The peer editor can read a draft aloud as the writer listens for spots where revisions are needed; roles can be reversed.

Publishing

In addition to publishing on-line, some students may want to present their essays orally. Arrange for a time and place for students to give oral presentations of their papers. Have them post a notice on a bulletin board inviting people to attend the reading.

Applying Language Skills
Answers
1. Grapefruits help you lose weight <u>because they speed up your metabolism and also contain lots of water.</u>
2. <u>Although it may at first be difficult to maintain</u>, a healthy diet has many benefits.

 Writer's Solution

For additional instruction and practice, have students complete the **Language Lab CD-ROM** lesson on Varying Sentence Structure and the practice page 121 in the *Writer's Solution Grammar Practice Book*.

Reinforce and Extend

Review the Writing Guidelines
After students have completed their papers, review the characteristics of problem-and-solution essays. Encourage students to come up with additional criteria for an interesting short story based on what they learned through the assignment.

APPLYING LANGUAGE SKILLS: Subordination

Use subordination to vary your sentences. Subordinating conjunctions such as *because, since, while,* and *though* link a subordinate clause (a clause of less importance) to a main clause.

Example: subordinate clause
<u>Because we have an addiction to junk food</u>, many of us find it difficult to lose weight.

Practice On your paper, underline the subordinate clauses in the following sentences.

1. Grapefruits help you to lose weight because they speed up your metabolism and also contain lots of water.
2. Although it may at first be difficult to maintain, a healthy diet has many benefits.

Writing Application Review your essay. Look for places where subordinate clauses would make your sentence structure more interesting.

Writer's Solution Connection Writing Lab

For more tips on how to be a peer reviewer, look at the tips for peer reviewers in the Writing Lab tutorial on Exposition.

Revising

Use a Checklist Make sure that the following are true for your paper.
► Your opening sentences lead logically into your topic.
► You identify a problem and suggest a solution.
► You clearly show the relationships between causes and effects. Your instructions show how the reader's actions can bring about a desired effect.
► Your essay grabs and keeps the reader's interest.

Use a Peer Reviewer A classmate can often point out weaknesses that you may have missed. Ask one of your classmates to read your paper and comment on it.

If you are the peer reviewer, make sure that you offer your criticism in a positive way. This will ensure that your comments are put to good use instead of causing resentment.

Negative Comment	**Positive Comment**
This is totally unorganized!	Reorganize your points so that the reader can follow them more easily.

REVISION MODEL

① *Because*
We don't think about how our actions affect the future. Many of us don't do our part to conserve natural resources.
② *If*   *gasoline use and air pollution will be reduced*
People should drive in carpools.

① The writer combines two sentences by making one a subordinate clause. The subordinating conjunction *because* clarifies the cause-and-effect relationship.
② The writer adds details that show the benefits of his suggestion.

Publishing

Publish Your Paper On-Line No matter what your topic is, there's bound to be a site related to it on the World Wide Web. Consult with an experienced Internet user to post your paper on the appropriate Web site.

✓ ASSESSMENT		4	3	2	1
PORTFOLIO ASSESSMENT Use the rubric on Description in *Problem-Solution* (p. 97) to assess students' writing. Add these criteria to customize the rubric to this assignment.	**Sentence Fragments**	There are no sentence fragments or run-on sentences.	There are one or two sentence fragments or run-on sentences.	There are noticeable sentence fragments or run-on sentences.	There are so many sentence fragments or run-on sentences that understanding of the piece is impaired.
	Subordination	The essay contains a perfect mix of sentence structures including subordinate clauses.	The essay contains different sentence structures and subordination.	The essay could clearly use more subordination and/or sentence variety.	Subordination and sentence variety are nonexistent; grammar is atrocious and shows an utter lack of effort.

Real-World Reading Skills Workshop

Evaluating Advertisements

Strategies for Success

Radio, television, magazines, billboards—the world bombards you with advertisements. Advertisers try to persuade you that you absolutely cannot live without Supersonic sneakers or a Mega-Monster video game, and they will say almost anything to get you to buy, do, or believe something. Whether you hear, see, or read ads, you need to evaluate the claims before you respond to them.

Evaluate the Advertisements As you evaluate the message of an ad, keep in mind the advertiser's primary goal: to entice you to buy its product. An advertiser will try to convince you that its product is the most delicious, that its spot remover is the most effective, that its automobile is the ultimate status symbol, or that its dog food will make your dog a champion. It is up to you to decide whether the claims are valid. When you respond to an ad, you should do so carefully and thoughtfully. Do not be lured by excessive claims. For instance, a shampoo can make your hair clean; but if the ad suggests you will also become more popular, beware. Make a decision based on your needs and on facts in the ad, not on opinions or excessive claims.

As you evaluate an advertisement, ask yourself the following questions:

> ▶ Is the ad making excessive claims about its product?
> ▶ Does the ad consist of concrete facts or statements of opinion?
> ▶ Do I have a need for this product?

To Buy or Not to Buy Once you've evaluated the advertisement, decide whether you accept the ad's claims. If you do, then you may decide to purchase the product. If, however, you do not accept the claims, you will probably not buy the product.

Apply the Strategy

Evaluate the ad below.

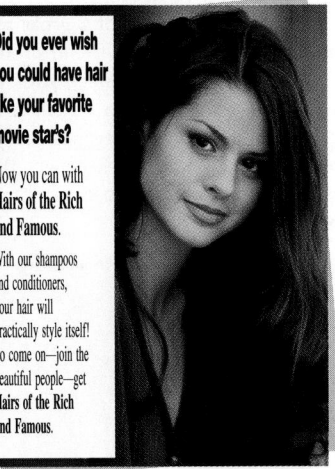

Did you ever wish you could have hair like your favorite movie star's?

Now you can with **Hairs of the Rich and Famous.**

With our shampoos and conditioners, your hair will practically style itself! So come on—join the beautiful people—get **Hairs of the Rich and Famous.**

1. What claim is the advertiser making?
2. How does the ad attempt to influence you? What does it promise?
3. How does the ad support its claims?
4. Does the product's purpose match your needs?
5. Would you buy this product based on the ad? Explain.

✔ *Here are other situations in which it's important to evaluate advertisements:*
> ▶ *Products that have to do with safety (e.g., smoke alarms, child seats, and so on)*
> ▶ *People or groups promising a service (e.g., health-care organizations, lawyers, banks)*
> ▶ *Public service announcements*

Real-World Reading Skills Workshop ◆ *111*

111

Remind students that learning how to say "no" is an important skill that will serve them well both personally and professionally for the rest of their lives. Not being able to say "no" when necessary can lead to dissatisfaction at work and in relationships. Easy as it may sound, however, some may find it difficult to learn to say "no" and can benefit from practice.

Customize for
English Language Learners

Students who are uncomfortable with English may be shy about saying no for fear of offending the other person or feeling inadequate about their language use. Remind these students that their lack of English ability is not indicative of any deficiency.

Suggested Answers

1. Suggested responses should include trying to persuade the other students to consider the consequences of their actions. If the students still persist, the lone student might explain to his or her friends that he or she is not obligated to give a reason for his or her refusal to go along, and that if they respect him or her as a person, they will respect his or her decision.

2. A good way to deal with phone solicitors is to say something politely to the effect of "I'm sorry, but I can't do that now," and repeat it as necessary.

3. If a student is shy about revealing a fact that can be embarrassing to teenagers—say, that he or she is frightened by scary movies—he or she can make a general comment such as "I'm not crazy about those kinds of movies," which gets the point across without revealing any personal details.

Resisting Persuasion

Speaking and Listening Workshop

You and your best friend are headed to the movies, but you can't seem to agree on which film to see. Your idea of a great movie is a romantic comedy, but your friend prefers action films. You want to consider your friend's wishes, but you don't want to be talked into another special-effects extravaganza. Keep your own needs in mind when others try to persuade you. Be willing to compromise, but don't be a pushover.

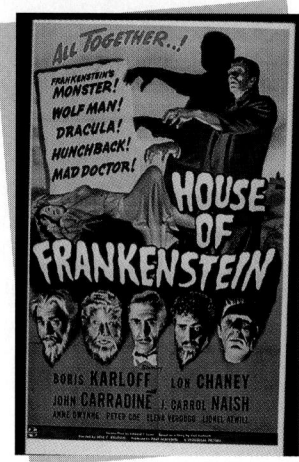

Tips for Resisting Persuasion

✔ If you want to resist persuasion but not offend the persuader, follow these strategies:
- ▶ Be firm, but polite, in your resistance.
- ▶ Remember that salespeople do not necessarily have your best interests at heart and may not always be telling the truth.
- ▶ If the persuader is a friend or family member and the request is reasonable, offer a compromise.

Looking Out for Your Best Interests

The next time you are choosing a movie to see, think about what you can say to resist your friend's persuasion.

Friend:	*Great! That new action movie opens today! Let's go see that. I love action movies!*
You:	*We just saw an action movie last weekend. Why don't we see* Two of Hearts *instead? I've been wanting to see that.*
Friend:	*But the action movie got good reviews, and I've been dying to see it!*
You:	*I'm really not interested in an action film tonight. How about seeing* Two of Hearts *today, and you can choose the movie next time?*

Apply the Strategies

With a partner, role-play these situations. Work out a confident, polite refusal to the following persuasion attempts:

1. A group of friends have decided to skip school for the day. They are trying to persuade you to go along, but you don't want to risk getting caught by school officials or being punished by your parents. How do you respond to your friends' persuasive efforts?

2. A phone solicitor is trying to persuade you to donate $25 to the Save the Iguana Foundation. You'd like to, but you really can't afford such a sum. What will you say to the solicitor?

3. Your two friends want to see the latest horror film, but scary movies give you nightmares. How will you resist their persuasion and come up with a film you'd all enjoy seeing?

112 ◆ On the Edge

Extended Reading Opportunities

These books are full of suspense, adventure, and danger. They will keep you "on the edge" until you've read the final page.

Suggested Titles

Lord of the Flies
William Golding

William Golding's exciting and terrifying story has been a favorite of high-school and college students since it was first published in 1954. A plane crashes on a tropical island in the Pacific, stranding a group of six- to twelve-year-old boys from a private school. The boys' society quickly degenerates into a nightmarish power struggle brought on by their own darkest fears and impulses. Vivid yet compact, the story moves swiftly to its fiery conclusion.

The Man Eater of Malgudi
R. K. Narayan

Like many of Narayan's stories, this tale takes place in the fictional Indian town of Malgudi. Nataraj, the main character, owns a small printing press in the town and has never had any enemies. Things change abruptly when an unruly taxidermist named Vasu moves into his attic, bringing with him a jungle's worth of stuffed animals. In the end, Nataraj dares to confront his intimidating tenant. Share the suspense as Nataraj waits to see the results of his daring decision.

Watership Down
Richard Adams

This is the exciting story of the journey of a group of rabbits forced to leave their home and search for a new warren amid the scenic and beautiful English countryside. Their journey is fraught with danger from foxes, weasels, humans, and most of all, other rabbits. Hardly a children's story, Richard Adams's tale shows us the world from a rabbit's point of view, at the same time making keen observations about humans and our relationship to each other and nature.

Other Possibilities

The Great Train Robbery   Michael Crichton
The Hound of the Baskervilles   Sir Arthur Conan Doyle
Tiger of the Snows   Tenzing Norgay with
                                   James Ramsey Ullman

Planning Students' Extended Reading

All the works on this page are good choices for extending the theme of Unit 1, "On the Edge." The following information may help you choose which to assign.

Customize for *Varying Student Needs*

When assigning these works to your students, keep in mind the following factors:

- *Lord of the Flies* is a contemporary classic with a strong interest level. However, the novel does include sensitive issues listed below.
- *Man-Eater of Malgudi* is a longer novel that is a good introduction to the culture of India.
- *Watership Down* is another high-interest contemporary classic.

Sensitive Issues

Lord of the Flies contains some violence that results in death. It also contains religious imagery (Simon is like a Christ figure) and sexual imagery (in the scene in which the pig is killed).

Literature Study Guides

A Literature Study Guide is available for *Lord of the Flies*. It includes section summaries, discussion questions, and activities.

Resources for Teaching Novels, Plays and Literature Collections

This booklet contains graphic organizers, teaching strategies, and transparencies that will be invaluable in teaching any of these novels.

Planning Instruction and Assessment

Unit Objectives

1. To read selections in different genres that develop the theme of Unit 2, "Striving for Success"
2. To apply a variety of reading strategies, particularly interactive reading strategies, appropriate for these selections
3. To recognize literary elements used in these selections
4. To increase vocabulary
5. To learn elements of grammar and usage
6. To write in a variety of modes and about situations based on the selections
7. To develop speaking and listening skills, by doing proposed activities

Meeting the Objectives

With each selection, you will find instructional material and portfolio opportunities through which students can meet these objectives. Further, you will find additional practice pages for reading strategies, literary elements, vocabulary, and grammar in the **Selection Support** booklet in the Teaching Resources box.

Setting Goals Work with your students at the beginning of the unit to set goals for unit outcomes. Plan what skills and concepts you wish students to acquire. You may individualize according to students' performance levels or learning modalities.

Portfolios You may have students keep portfolios of their work or of their work in progress. The activities and prompts on the Build Your Portfolio page of each selection provide opportunities for students to apply the concepts presented with the selection.

Steps to the Steps, Brad Holland

🎵 Humanities: Art

Steps to the Steps by Brad Holland.

In his early twenties, Brad Holland began writing and drawing for underground newspapers; he has since created covers for such mainstream publications as *The New Yorker, Newsweek,* and *U.S. News and World Report.* In 1981 Holland designed a U.S. postage stamp of Chief Crazy Horse and also produced a 10-by-30-foot mural for the United Nations Building in New York.

1. Imagine that the man on the steps has climbed a long way already. How do you think he feels about seeing the next set of steps? *Possible answers: He might feel discouraged that he is facing a much greater challenge; he might feel proud of having gotten so far; he might be thinking about how to climb these tall steps.*

2. Imagine that the steps you see represent stages on the way to success in some field, such as scientific discovery or athletics or the performing arts. What would be the goal at the very top of the steps? *Possible answers: For scientific discovery, the ultimate goal might be the discovery of a cure for cancer or of life on other planets; for athletics, the goal might be a world championship or Olympic gold medal; for performing arts, the goal might be an award such as an Oscar or the highest salary in films or critical acclaim.*

UNIT 2

Striving for Success

Yyou will strive to reach many goals in life—getting your driver's license, graduating from high school, establishing a successful career, starting a family—and along the way you may have to overcome many obstacles. Let these poems, stories, and essays inspire you to strive for success and accomplish your goals. Share the determination and fear, the disappointment and hope of people from a wide variety of times and places.

◆ 115

OBJECTIVES

1. To read, comprehend, and interpret an essay
2. To relate an essay to personal experience
3. To use interactive reading strategies
4. To identify the author's purpose
5. To develop vocabulary in context and learn the prefix *in-*
6. To recognize action and linking verbs
7. To write a reading journal using an appropriate level of formality
8. To respond to the essay through writing, speaking and listening, and projects

SKILLS INSTRUCTION

Vocabulary:
Prefixes: *in-*
Grammar:
Action and Linking Verbs
Reading for Success:
Interactive Reading
Literary Focus:
Author's Purpose

Writing:
Level of Formality
Speaking and Listening:
Storytelling Performance (teacher edition)
Critical Viewing:
Interpret; Infer

PORTFOLIO OPPORTUNITIES

Writing: Library Dedication; Informational Article; Directions
Writing Mini-Lesson: Reading Journal
Speaking and Listening: Storytelling Performance; Library Panel Discussion
Projects: Library Poster; Library Survey

More About the Author

"Much is in the blood," Rudolfo Anaya has said, "because the blood has memory, memory that has been imprinted, encoded, from the past—whispers of the blood are stories." Anaya's writing reflects this respect for the mystical stories of the Spanish oral tradition as well as for the land and the people of his native New Mexico.

Guide for Reading

Rudolfo Anaya (1937–)

The deep blue sky stretching as far as the eye can see to the horizon . . . the dry, red soil dotted with patches of brown grass and green cacti . . . the sweet smell of sagebrush wafting in the air. . . . This is New Mexico, the land that Rudolfo Anaya has called home his entire life, the land that has nurtured his imagination and given birth to his stories.

The Wisdom of the *Cuentos*

Anaya was born in the rural village of Pastura in 1937. His poems, short stories, novels, and articles reflect his Mexican American heritage. As a child, Anaya listened to the *cuentos* of his people—stories that had been passed down from generation to generation. Listening to these *cuentos* set Anaya's imagination on fire, and he knew he wanted to be a writer. Anaya feels a strong connection with the past in his personal life and in his work as a writer. He says, "The oral tradition of telling stories was part of my culture."

> *The old legends and the myths of the people, the whispers of the blood draw us to our past.*

Bless Me, Ultima In 1972, while he was a high-school English teacher, Anaya wrote *Bless Me, Ultima*, a coming-of-age novel set in New Mexico. The book received immediate praise and has sold over 300,000 copies. Anaya later became a professor of writing and literature at the University of New Mexico. In 1993, he retired so he could write full time. He says, "Writing novels seems to be the medium which allows me to bring together all the questions I ask about life."

◆ Build Vocabulary

PREFIXES: *in-*

When Rudolfo Anaya was a child, ancient tales *induced* him to become a writer. His love for these stories was *inherent*. You will encounter the words *induced* and *inherent* in this essay. The prefix *in-* can mean "not" or "into." In both these words, the prefix *in-* means "into." *Induced* means "led into" or "caused." The prefix *in-* also contributes to the definition of *inherent*, which means "inborn."

WORD BANK

induced
inherent
litany
dilapidated
satiated
enthralls
labyrinth
poignant
fomentation

Before you read, preview this list of words from the essay.

◆ Build Grammar Skills

ACTION VERBS AND LINKING VERBS

The two main categories of verbs are **action verbs** (verbs that express physical or mental action) and **linking verbs** (verbs that express a state of being and tell what the subject is by linking it to one or more words that further describe or identify it).

In "One Million Volumes," Anaya describes a memory of his grandfather with an action verb:

> Then he would *whisper* his favorite riddle.

The action verb *whisper* expresses a physical action and creates a vivid sensory image.

Linking verbs connect the subject with other words that describe or identify it:

> I *was* fortunate.

The adjective *fortunate* describes the subject, *I,* and is linked to it by the linking verb *was.*

116 ◆ *Striving for Success*

 Prentice Hall Literature Program Resources

REINFORCE / RETEACH / EXTEND

Selection Support Pages
Build Vocabulary: Prefixes, *in-,* p. 30
Build Grammar Skills: Action and Linking Verbs, p. 31
Reading for Success: Interactive Reading, pp. 32–33
Literary Focus: Author's Purpose, p. 34

Strategies for Diverse Student Needs, p. 8

Beyond Literature
Community Connection: The Library, p. 8

Formal Assessment Selection Test, pp. 26–28;
Assessment Resources Software

Alternative Assessment, p. 8

Writing and Language Transparencies
Writing Process Model 8: Interpreting a Work of Literature, pp. 53–59

Resource Pro CD-ROM
"In Commemoration . . ."—includes all resource materials and customizable lesson plan

 Listening to Literature Audiocassettes
"In Commemoration: One Million Volumes"

 Looking at Literature Videodisc
"In Commemoration: One Million Volumes"

from *In Commemoration:*
One Million Volumes

◆ Literature and Your Life

CONNECT YOUR EXPERIENCE

Do you remember when you were a child and you turned ten years old? Remember how it felt to be in "double digits"? At the time, it may have seemed like a significant milestone. Three years later, you were finally in "the teens." Throughout our lives, we remember specific dates, events, and numbers. They act as markers of progress, showing us how far we've come and giving us an opportunity to reflect what we've learned. In this essay Rudolfo Anaya celebrates his university's library for reaching the one-millionth book mark. He uses the milestone as an occasion to reflect on the importance of libraries, books, and words in general.

THEMATIC FOCUS: STRIVING FOR SUCCESS

In his essay, Anaya not only honors his university's library but explains how the words and ideas housed in libraries have helped him reach goals in his life. Ask yourself how his vision of a library compares with your own.

Journal Writing Anaya describes a library as "a warm place that reflects the needs and aspirations of the people." List ten titles (of real books or books you would like to see written) that would reflect your needs and aspirations.

◆ Background for Understanding

MATH

When Anaya entered the University of New Mexico's library for the first time, he was astounded at the size of it compared with his neighborhood library. There are other libraries even larger, containing more books than any person could read in a lifetime. Use this graph to get a sense of the size of several well-known libraries. These vast collections house, as Anaya marvels, "Books on every imaginable subject, in every field, a history of the thought of the world … the collective memory of all mankind at my fingertips."

◆ Literary Focus

AUTHOR'S PURPOSE

The **author's purpose** is his or her reason for writing. For example, Anaya's general purpose is to share ideas. Other general purposes include persuading readers or explaining how to do something. Determine Anaya's specific purpose by noticing the kinds of details he includes, the direct statements he makes, and his attitude toward his subject.

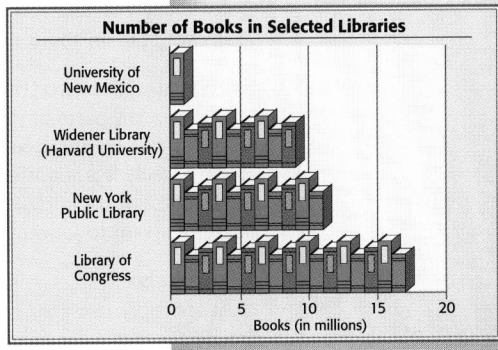

Number of Books in Selected Libraries

University of New Mexico; Widener Library (Harvard University); New York Public Library; Library of Congress. Books (in millions) 0 5 10 15 20

Guide for Reading ◆ 117

 Preparing for Standardized Tests

Reading and Vocabulary The Build Vocabulary lesson for this selection focuses on the prefix *in-*. Understanding the meaning of this prefix will help students infer the meanings of unfamiliar words on vocabulary and reading comprehension items on the verbal portions of standardized tests. For additional practice, use the Build Vocabulary page in *Selection Support* (p. 30).

Grammar and Language Write on the chalkboard this question: *Is it true that most libraries now offer consumers Internet access?* Ask students to identify the verbs in the sentence. *is; offer*

Guide them to explain the difference between the verbs. (*Is* a linking verb because it expresses a state of being, and *offer* is an action verb because it expresses a mental action.) Let students know that some standardized tests will require them to identify whether a verb is an action or linking verb. The Build Grammar Skills lesson for this selection will help students perform successfully on such items. For additional practice, use the Build Grammar Skills page on Action and Linking Verbs in *Selection Support* (p. 31).

Interest Grabber Ask students to take out a piece of paper and write down the first things that come to mind when you say "library." Guide them to think about *everything* associated with a library, not just books and computers. What do the rooms of the library look like; with whom do students usually go to the library; what do they do there? What mood does a library call up for them? After volunteers share their writing, encourage students to compare their impressions of libraries with those of Rudolfo Anaya as they read this selection.

Customize for
Less Proficient Readers
Anaya does not directly state his purpose for writing—to celebrate the acquisition of the University of New Mexico Library's millionth book—at the outset of his essay. Make sure these students understand the milestone that has inspired Anaya to write this essay. Ask them to look closely for references to this event as they read the essay.

Customize for
More Advanced Students
Encourage these students to analyze how Anaya achieves links between his topic—the million books in the library—and details such as the million stars and the cuentos. Have them explain in their journals why the author links these elements, if they think he does so successfully, and why or why not.

Customize for
Logical/Mathematical Learners
On the board, write the figures for one million, a hundred million, and a "million million." Invite students to think of logical items that might be indicated by these numbers, such as a million books, a million dollars, a hundred million people, a million million stars. Encourage interested students to make graphs, like the one shown on this page, comparing other large collections.

117

The Reading for Success page in each unit presents a set of problem-solving procedures to help readers understand authors' words and ideas on multiple levels. Good readers develop a bank of strategies from which they can draw as needed.

Unit 2 introduces strategies for interactive reading. Interactive strategies get students actively involved in their reading. The process of interacting with text while reading is an important factor in students' constructing of meaning from the text.

These strategies for interactive reading are modeled with "One Million Volumes." An example of the thinking process involved in applying one of these strategies is shown in each green box.

How to Use the Reading for Success Page

- Introduce the interactive reading strategies, presenting each as a means of enhancing the reading experience for maximum retention and enjoyment. Be sure students understand what each strategy involves and under what circumstances to apply it.

- Before students read the essay, have them preview it, looking at the annotations in the green boxes that model the strategies.

- To reinforce these strategies after students have read "One Million Volumes," have students do the Reading for Success pages in *Selection Support,* pp. 32–33. This activity gives students an opportunity to read a selection and practice interactive reading strategies by writing their own annotations.

Reading for Success

Interactive Reading Strategies

You wouldn't stand in front of a video game and just watch it like a movie, would you? Of course not! Video games are interactive—your choices affect the way the game turns out. Like a video game, reading is also interactive. It's a process by which you get involved with the ideas, images, events, and information presented in the text. The more involved you are, the richer your understanding is.

Apply the following strategies to interact with what you read:

Set a purpose.

Decide *why* you are reading a piece. You may read for enjoyment, for information, or to consider new ideas. For example, Anaya's essay can help you look at libraries in a new way. Set a purpose to discover a new perspective on libraries; then look for details that help you achieve this purpose.

Use your prior knowledge.

Keep in mind what you already know—in this case, what you know about libraries. Use that knowledge to make connections with what the author is saying. You may find details in the text that confirm opinions you already have, as well as details that change your opinions.

Question.

Don't accept everything you read at face value. Ask yourself questions about why certain information is included or how a fact or idea fits in with what you've already read. Look for answers to your questions as you read on. Questioning will help you recognize the relationships between ideas and form your own opinion about the work.

Clarify details and information.

Clear up any parts of the work that you don't understand. The best way to do this is to read ahead for more information or read back to review what you've already learned. Another technique is to represent information visually. For instance, you can clarify Anaya's picture of the ideal library by making a cluster diagram to jot down key words that describe his feelings and opinions.

Summarize.

At appropriate places, review and state the main points of the author. Notice details that seem important. Try to fit them into your picture of what the author is saying.

As you read "One Million Volumes," look at the notes in the boxes. These notes demonstrate how to apply the above strategies to a work of literature.

Reading Strategies: Support and Reinforcement

Appropriate Reading Strategies Students are given a reading strategy to apply in reading each selection. In appropriate selections, students are given an interactive reading strategy. In other selections a strategy is suggested that is appropriate to the selection.

Reading Prompts To encourage application of the given reading strategy, there are occasional prompts, within green boxes, at appropriate and significant points.

In addition, there are red boxes prompting application of the Literary Focus concept and maroon boxes prompting students to connect with their lives.

Using the Boxed Annotations and Prompts

The material in the green, red, and maroon boxes along the sides of selections is intended to help students apply the literary element and the reading strategy and to make a connection with their lives.

You may use the boxed material in these ways:

- Have students pause when they come to a box and respond to its prompt before they continue reading.

- Urge students to read through the selection ignoring the boxes. After they have read the selection completely, they may go back and review the selection, responding to the prompts.

from In Commemoration:

ONE MILLION VOLUMES

Rudolfo A. Anaya

A million volumes.

A magic number.

A million books to read, to look at, to hold in one's hand, to learn, to dream. . . .

I have always known there were at least a million stars. In the summer evenings when I was a child, we, all the children of the neighborhood, sat outside under the stars and listened to the stories of the old ones, los

> Clarify the Spanish phrases by reading ahead and looking at the footnotes.

viejitos.[1] The stories of the old people taught us to wonder and imagine. Their adivinanzas[2] induced the stirring of our first questioning, our early learning.

I remember my grandfather raising his hand and pointing to the swirl of the Milky Way which swept over us. Then he would whisper his favorite riddle:

Hay un hombre con tanto dinero
Que no lo puede contar

1. **los viejitos** (lôs´ byā hē´ tôs)
2. **adivinanzas** (a thē vē nan´ sas) *n.*: Riddles.

Una mujer con una sábana tan grande
Que no la puede doblar.

There is a man with so much money
He cannot count it
A woman with a bedspread so large
She cannot fold it

We knew the million stars were the coins of the Lord, and the heavens were the bedspread of his mother, and in our minds the sky was a million miles wide. A hundred million. Infinite. Stuff for the imagination. And what was more important, the teachings of the old ones made us see that we were bound to the infinity of that cosmic dance of life which swept around us. Their teachings created in us a thirst for knowledge. Can this library with its million volumes bestow that same inspiration?

I was fortunate to have had those old and

◆ **Build Vocabulary**

induced (in dōost´) *v.*: Caused

from In Commemoration: One Million Volumes ◆ 119

Develop Understanding

One-Minute Insight When the University of New Mexico Library acquires its one millionth book, Rudolfo Anaya uses the occasion to reflect upon the great importance of libraries as places that stimulate and nurture free thought. What makes this essay especially unique is that Anaya draws a connection between books and the many people and stories that opened his childhood mind to the natural and intellectual world.

Looking at Literature Videodisc To provide background and insight into the author of "In Commemoration: One Million Volumes," play Chapter 2 of the videodisc. In this interview, Rudolfo Anaya discusses his love of reading and how it inspired him to write about a New Mexico library that had just acquired its millionth book.

◆ **Reading for Success**

❶ Question Ask students what question they are asking themselves at this point in the essay. Suggest they keep their questions in mind until they are answered. *Students may say they are wondering how the author will connect the two ideas he has raised so far: books and the stories and riddles of los viejitos.*

◆ **Reading for Success**

❷ Set a Purpose Have students set their preliminary purpose for reading. Let them know they may add to or revise this purpose later. *For now, students' purpose is to find out how the author will answer this question.*

Block Scheduling Strategies

Consider these suggestions to take advantage of extended class time:

• Have students complete the journal activity under Literature and Your Life on page 117. As a class, make a list of the books chosen. Under each title, have a volunteer write the type of book—such as adventure story or how-to book—as well as its specific purpose—for example, to entertain. Then invite students to discuss how books help us meet our needs.

• With students, read Literary Focus: Author's Purpose on page 117. Let them know that Anaya's general purpose was to share ideas with his audience—people assembled to celebrate the acquisition of a library's one millionth volume. Lead a discussion with students about how audience affects a writer's purpose. Encourage them to suggest how Anaya's purpose might have changed to adjust to these audiences: a group of primary school children *Anaya might have stressed humor or entertainment in his purpose;* a group of people who never used libraries *Anaya's purpose would probably be more persuasive.* Have students suggest other audience and purpose matches for Anaya's essay.

• Have students work in groups to answer the Critical Thinking questions on p. 125.

• Encourage students to begin their Reading Journals on page 126 before they read the essay. They can continue them afterward.

❶ Infer Ask students what Anaya means by the "power inherent in each volume." *The stories and riddles of the old people had the power to inspire and teach; books have that same power.*

♦ **Build Grammar Skills**

❷ Action and Linking Verbs Have students identify the action verbs and the linking verbs in this sentence. *Action verbs: spoke, came; linking verbs: were, were.*

▶**Critical Viewing**◀

❸ Interpret The painting suggests that books have the power to open the universe to readers.

♦ **Reading for Success**

❹ Use Prior Knowledge Ask students if Anaya's grandfather's statement about books, "[Words] hold joy, and they are a deadly power if misused" confirms an opinion they already held, and why or why not. *Students may say they have already thought about the power of words and relate an event they experienced or observed that shows the power of words to bestow pleasure or pain.*

---

wise viejitos as guides into the world of nature and knowledge. They taught me with their stories; they taught me the magic of words. Now the words lie captured in ink, but the magic is still there, the power inherent in each volume. Now with book in hand we can participate in the wisdom of mankind.

Each person moves from innocence through rites of passage into the knowledge of the world, and so I entered the world of school in search of the magic in the words. The sounds were no longer the soft sounds of Spanish which my grandfather spoke; the words were in English, and with each new awareness came my first steps toward a million volumes. I, who was used to reading my oraciones en español[3] while I sat in the kitchen and answered the litany to the slap of my mother's tortillas,[4] I now stumbled from sound to word to groups of words, head throbbing, painfully

Orion, 1984, Martin Wong, Exit Art Gallery, New York

aware that each new sound took me deeper into the maze of the new language. Oh, how I clutched the hands of my new guides then!

Learn, my mother encouraged me, learn. Be as wise as your grandfather. He could speak many languages. He could speak to the birds and the animals of the field.

Yes, I remember the cuentos[5] of my grandfather, the stories of the people. Words are a way, he said, they hold joy, and they are a deadly power if misused. I clung to each syllable which lisped from his tobacco-stained lips. That was the winter the snow came, he would say, it piled high and we lost many sheep and cattle, and the trees groaned and broke with its weight. I looked across the llano[6] and saw the raging blizzard, the awful destruction of that winter which was imbedded in our people's mind.

And the following summer, he would say, the grass of the llano grew so high we

Question how the *cuentos* connect to Anaya's message about libraries. As you read on, you will find that one connection is the power of words to inspire.

Critical Viewing What does the painting on this page suggest about the power of books? [Interpret] ▲

3. **oraciones en español** (ô ra syôn′ ās en es pa nyōl′): Spanish for "prayers in Spanish."
4. **tortillas** (tôr tē′ yəs) *n.*: Thin, flat, round cakes of unleavened cornmeal.

5. **cuentos** (kwen′ tôs) *n.*: Stories.
6. **llano** (ya′ nō) *n.*: Plain.

120 ♦ *Striving for Success*

Humanities: Art

Orion, 1984, by Martin Wong.

Martin Wong (1946–) is a self-taught painter whose work was originally inspired by the graffiti art in his San Francisco neighborhood. Now living in New York City, he is well-known for his stark paintings of the urban struggles.

Several motifs regularly occur in Martin Wong's paintings. Among them, the gold picture frames and constellations in a night sky are most prevalent. The painting *Orion* fea-

tures both of these. The frame containing the constellation is circular, perhaps suggesting the mystical and infinite qualities of the geometric shape. The stack of books gives reference to Orion. By their juxtaposition to the constellation and their containment within the golden circle, they assume an importance out of reality.

You might read aloud the inscription around the painting or have a student do so. Then use these questions for discussion:

1. Suppose Anaya had quoted Wong's inscription. How might he connect that quotation to his own ideas about books and stories? *He might say that stories are so powerful, the mythical Orion means more to us than some real-life conquerors.*
2. What is similar about the way Anaya and Wong see books? *Both see that books inspire us to appreciate and connect to natural wonders, such as stars and constellations.*

couldn't see the top of the sheep. And I would look and see what was once clean and pure and green. I could see a million sheep and the pastores[7] caring for them, as I now care for the million words that pasture in my mind.

But a million books? How can we see a million books? I don't mean just the books lining the shelves here at the University of New Mexico Library, not just the fine worn covers, the intriguing titles; how can we see the worlds that lie waiting in each book? A million worlds. A million million worlds. And the beauty of it is that each world is related to the next, as was taught to us by the old ones. Perhaps it is easier for a child to see. Perhaps it is easier for a child to ask: How many stars are there in the sky? How many leaves in the trees of the river? How many blades of grass in the llano? How many dreams in a night of dreams?

So I worked my way into the world of books, but here is the paradox, a book at once quenches the thirst of the imagination and ignites new fires. I learned that as I visited the library of my childhood, the Santa Rosa Library. It was only a dusty room in those days, a room sitting atop the town's fire department, which was comprised of one dilapidated fire truck used by the town's volunteers only in the direst emergencies. But in that small room I found my shelter and retreat. If there were a hundred books there we were fortunate,

6 Question what this paradox means. How can something quench thirst *and* start fires? As you continue to read, you will discover that books quenched Anaya's thirst for knowledge but lit the fires of curiosity.

but to me there were a million volumes. I trembled in awe when I first entered that library, because I realized that if the books held as much magic as the words of the old ones, then indeed this was a room full of power.

Miss Pansy, the librarian, became my new guide. She fed me books as any mother would nurture her child. She brought me book after book, and I consumed them all. Saturday afternoons disappeared as the time of day dissolved into the time of distant worlds. In a world that occupied most of my other schoolmates with games, I took the time to read. I was a librarian's dream. My tattered library card was my ticket into the same worlds my grandfather had known, worlds of magic that fed the imagination.

You can **summarize** Anaya's Saturday afternoon in the following way: He read all day, lost track of time, then, at the end of the day, he raced home across the river that used to frighten him.

Late in the afternoon, when I was satiated with reading, when I could no longer hold in my soul the characters that crowded there, I heard the call of the llano, the real world of my father's ranchito, the solid, warm world of my mother's kitchen. Then to the surprise and bewilderment of Miss Pansy, I

8

◆ **Build Vocabulary**

inherent (in hir´ ənt) *adj.*: Inborn; existing in naturally and inseparably

litany (lit´ ən ē) *n.*: Series of responsive religious readings

dilapidated (di lap´ ə dā´ tid) *adj.*: Broken down

satiated (sā´ shē ā tid) *adj.*: Having had enough; full

---

7. **pastores** (pas tō´ rās) *n.*: Shepherds.

◆ **Literary Focus**

5 **Author's Purpose** Ask students how this passage serves Anaya's purpose in this essay—to communicate to readers how books can inspire readers. Have them cite the phrase that encapsulates his purpose. *The phrase that captures his purpose is "the worlds that lie waiting in each book."*

◆ **Critical Thinking**

6 **Relate** Ask students for other examples of something that "quenches the thirst of the imagination and ignites new fires." *Students might say that this is true of most activities you enjoy, such as listening to a favorite kind of music, exchanging anecdotes with friends, or even playing a sport.*

◆ **Build Grammar Skills**

7 **Action and Linking Verbs** Have students identify the action verbs and the linking verbs in these two sentences. Have them explain how each kind of verb functions in the sentence. *Action verb:* found; *linking verbs:* were, were. *In both cases,* were *links the subject of the verb to something that further describes it.* Found *in this sentence, expresses both mental and physical action.*

◆ *Literature and Your Life*

8 Invite students to relate their own experiences with being lost in an imaginary world and then coming back into the real world. In what kinds of experiences do they tend to get most absorbed? *Students might cite reading, playing music, listening to an involved anecdote, watching movies or videotapes, playing video games, or being involved in an individual sport such as running.*

Cross-Curricular Connection: Math

Anaya refers to "millions," "hundreds of millions," and a "million million." Mathematicians have a variety of names for very large numbers. For example, a "thousand million" is also known as a *billion*. A "thousand billion" or a "million million" is known as a *trillion*. Continuing in that vein are the numbers *quintillion, sextillion, septillion, octillion,* and *nonillion*.

Invite students to write these numbers and count the number of zeros in each.

(A *million* is a one followed by six zeros; a *nonillion* is a one followed by thirty zeros.) Then introduce them to the concept of a *googol*: the number one followed by one hundred zeros. An even larger number is the *googolplex*: the number one followed by a googol of zeros. The googol was a concept developed by U. S. mathematician Edward Kasner (1879–1955), who based the name on a child's word.

Another way of writing large numbers is with the use of exponents. Thus, 10^2 represents 10 times 10, or 100, or a one with two zeros after it.

Encourage students to express one million, and "a million million," both in figures and as exponents.

◆ Critical Thinking

❶ Speculate Anaya says that the word *freedom* must reflect what a library's collection is all about. Invite students to analyze that statement further by speculating about the collection of a library in a society that exercises censorship. *Students might say the collection would be smaller, would reflect the political views of one group, would not contain books that expressed views contrary to those that the group held.*

◆ Critical Thinking

❷ Connect Ask students how preserving and using the literature of other cultures can help preserve and regenerate one's own culture. *Students may say that by becoming aware of how other people see things, we become more aware of the views of our own cultures. Students may also point out that many cultures deal with universal issues, so that learning about another culture may reinforce one's own beliefs.*

◆ Reading for Success

❸ Question With students, question why Anaya is telling about this part of his childhood in this essay. Is it relevant? *Students may point out that the author is trying to show the ways in which libraries are exciting places, and that reading and writing can be connected to real-world values such as friendship, love, and even earning money.*

> These ideas will help you achieve your **purpose** for reading this essay—to discover a new perspective on libraries.

would rush out and race down the streets of our town, books tucked under my shirt, in my pockets, clutched tightly to my breast. Mad with the insanity of books, I would cross the river to get home, shouting my crazy challenge even at la Llorona,[8] and that poor spirit of so many frightening cuentos would wither and withdraw. She was no match for me.

Those of you who have felt the same exhilaration from reading—or from love—will know about what I'm speaking. Alas, the people of the town could only shake their heads and pity my mother. At least one of her sons was a bit touched. Perhaps they were right, for few will trade a snug reality to float on words to other worlds.

❶ And now there are a million volumes for us to read here at the University of New Mexico Library. Books on every imaginable subject, in every field, a history of the thought of the world which we must keep free of censorship, because we treasure our freedoms. It is the word *freedom* which eventually must reflect what this collection, or the collection of any library, is all about. We know that as we preserve and use the literature of all cultures, we preserve and **❷** regenerate our own. The old ones knew and taught me this. They eagerly read the few newspapers that were available. They kept their diaries, they wrote décimas[9] and cuentos, and they survived on their oral stories and traditions.

---

8. la Llorona (la yô rō′ na): Spirit of many stories, famous for shouting and crying for her lost love.
9. décimas (dā′ sē mas) *n.*: Ten-line stanzas.

Another time, another library. I entered Albuquerque[10] High School Library prepared to study, because that's where we spent our study time. For better or for worse, I received my first contracts as a writer there. It was a place where budding lovers spent most of their time writing notes to each other, and when my friends who didn't have the gift of words found out I could turn a phrase I quickly had all the business I could do. I wrote poetic love notes for a dime apiece and thus worked my way through high school. And there were fringe benefits, because the young women knew very well who was writing the sweet words, and many a heart I was supposed to capture fell in love with me. And so, a library is also a place where love begins.

A library should be the heart of a city. With its storehouse of knowledge, it liberates, informs, teaches, and <u>enthralls</u>. A library indeed should be the cultural center of any city. Amidst the bustle of work and commerce, the great libraries of the world have provided a sanctuary where scholars and common man alike come to enlarge and clarify knowledge, to read and reflect in quiet solitude.

---

10. Albuquerque (al′ bə kʉr′ kē): City in central New Mexico.

> Use your **prior knowledge** to connect your own experience with libraries to Anaya's high-school library experiences.

❸

◆ Build Vocabulary
enthralls (en thrôlz′) *v.*: Captivates; fascinates
labyrinth (lab′ ə rinth) *n.*: Maze

 Speaking and Listening Mini-Lesson

Storytelling Performance
This mini-lesson supports the Speaking and Listening activity in the Idea Bank on page 126.

Introduce the Concept Let students know that when people perform stories they use a range of acting techniques to bring their story to life. Have students recall situations in which they enjoyed listening to someone perform a story.

Develop Background With students, list the qualities that make an effective storytelling performance. The list should include knowing the story well, using different voices for different characters, pacing, facial and vocal expression, humor, and gestures.

Apply the Information Have students work in pairs or small groups to develop and rehearse their stories. If possible, have them perform for younger children; if not, for the class or for other groups.

Assess the Outcome Encourage students to discuss their experiences as a class. Were their stories well-paced? Did students use facial, bodily, and vocal expression to the story's advantage? Why or why not? You may wish to have students use the Peer Assessment sheets for Oral Interpretation or Dramatic Performance in *Alternative Assessment* (pp. 120, 121).

I knew a place like this, I spent many hours in the old library on Central Avenue and Edith Street. But my world was growing, and quite by accident I wandered up the hill to enroll in the University of New Mexico. And what a surprise lay in store for me. The libraries of my childhood paled in comparison to this new wealth of books housed in Zimmerman Library. Here there were stack after stack of books, and ample space and time to wander aimlessly in this labyrinth of new frontiers.

I had known the communal memory of my people through the newspapers and few books my grandfather read to me and through the rich oral tradition handed down by the old ones; now I discovered the collective memory of all mankind at my fingertips. I had only to reach for the books that laid all history bare. Here I could converse with the writers from every culture on earth, old and new, and at the same time I began my personal odyssey, which would add a few books to

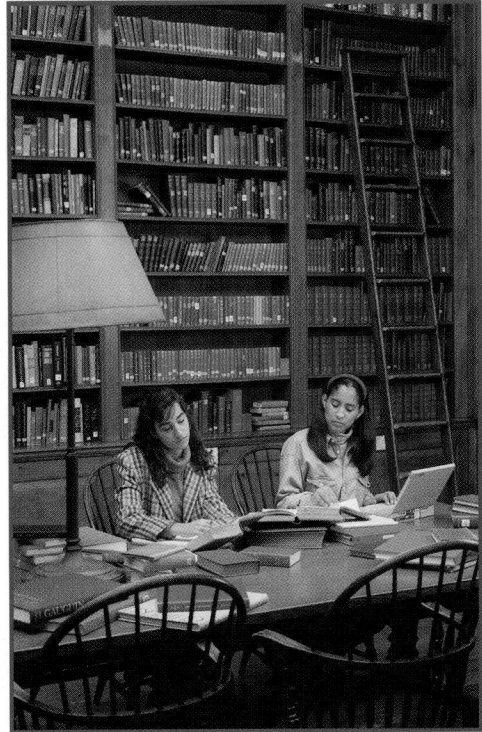

▲ **Critical Viewing** How do you think the two women in this photograph feel about libraries? [Infer]

the collection which in 1981 would come to house a million volumes.

Those were exciting times. Around me swirled the busy world of the university, in many respects an alien world. Like many fellow undergraduates, I sought refuge in the library. My haven during those student university years was the reading room of the west wing of the old library. There I found peace. The carved vigas[11] decorating the ceiling, the solid wooden tables and chairs and the warm adobe color of the stucco were things with which I was familiar. There I felt comfortable. With books scattered around me, I could read and doze and dream. I took my breaks in the warm sun of the portal, where I ate my tortilla sandwiches, which I carried in my brown paper bag. There, with friends, I sipped coffee as we talked of changing the world and exchanged idealistic dreams.

11. **vigas** (bē′ gas) *n.*: Roof beams.

from *In Commemoration: One Million Volumes* ◆ 123

Beyond the Classroom

Career Connection
Library Science In this essay, Anaya describes a number of different kinds of libraries: his one-room local library, his high school library, and the huge university library that eventually acquires one million volumes. Each of these libraries had a system for ordering and cataloging books, so that library patrons could find what they were looking for, or so that the librarian could help a visitor find a particular book or piece of information.

A trained librarian learns different systems of cataloging books, such as the Dewey Decimal system (used in most small libraries) and the Library of Congress system (used in most larger libraries). Most libraries now offer materials besides books: audio- and videotapes, CDs, electronic resources, and the computers by which to access electronic files. Invite students to interview a school, community, or university librarian to find out about library ordering systems, the various skills and duties of a librarian, and the training necessary to become a librarian.

◆ Critical Thinking

❶ Compare What elements are shared by the village *resolana* and the library? *Both are places where people meet and pass on knowledge. The library provides an ongoing "conversation" about anything one finds of interest.*

Reinforce and Extend

Customize for
Less Proficient Readers
Invite students to review the essay, looking for three answers that Anaya offers for the question "Why are libraries important?" *Sample answers: "because they connect us to our culture," "they stimulate our imaginations," "they are places of love," "they are havens and places of refuge," "they help make us free," and "they are places of debate and research."*

Answers
◆ *Literature and Your Life*

Reader's Response Encourage students to think of nonfiction as well as fiction. Guide them toward discussion of new ideas and insights gained from reading.

Thematic Focus Students might say that libraries help people by providing access to a wide range of literature and research material. They might also mention library programs such as literacy and children's programs. Many libraries also provide access to the Internet.

☑ Check Your Comprehension

1. Anaya compares a million books to stars, worlds, leaves, blades of grass, and dreams.
2. Anaya's interest in learning was ignited by the stories of the old ones that he listened to as a child.
3. He learned to love reading as a child in the Santa Rosa library.
4. The old ones preserved and regenerated their culture through cuentos, the stories of the people.
5. Anaya's memories include visiting the Santa Rosa library atop the city's fire department, and its librarian, Miss Pansy; writing love notes on behalf of his friends at his high school library; seeking refuge in the Zimmerman Library at the University of New Mexico.

124

> You can **summarize** Anaya's essay with the following points: Anaya's love of words comes from a rich storytelling tradition; his love of stories, books, and learning grew in libraries; he sees libraries as havens, gathering places, and storehouses of knowledge.

❶ That is a rich and pleasant time in my memory. No matter how far across the world I find myself in the future, how deep in the creation of worlds with words, I shall keep the simple and <u>poignant</u> memories of those days. The sun set golden on the ocher walls, and the green pine trees and the blue spruce, sacred trees to our people, whispered in the breeze. I remembered my grandfather meeting with the old men of the village in the resolana[12] of one of the men's homes, or against the wall of the church on Sundays, and I remembered the things they said. Later,

---

12. **resolana** (rä sô lä´ na) *n.*: Place for enjoying the sun.

alone, dreaming against the sun-warmed wall of the library, I continued that discourse in my mind.

Yes, the library is a place where people should gather. It is a place for research, reading, and for the quiet <u>fomentation</u> of ideas, but because it houses the collective memory of our race, it should also be a place where present issues are discussed and debated and researched in order for us to gain the knowledge and insight to create a better future. The library should be a warm place that reflects the needs and aspirations of the people.

◆ Build Vocabulary

poignant (poin´ yənt) *adj.*: Emotionally moving
fomentation (fō men tā´ shən) *n.*: Incitement; a stirring up

---

Guide for Responding

◆ *Literature and Your Life*

Reader's Response Anaya appeals to people who have "felt the same exhilaration from reading" as he has felt. What reading has exhilarated you? Why?

Thematic Focus In his essay, Anaya describes how libraries help individuals and societies to succeed by being places where "scholars and common man alike come to enlarge and clarify knowledge, to read and reflect in quiet solitude." How would you describe how libraries help people?

Activity Create a floor plan of your vision of the perfect library. Make the sections different sizes and label them—sports, history, poetry—to show what you think should be the largest sections.

☑ Check Your Comprehension

1. Name three things that Anaya compares to "a million volumes."
2. What ignited Anaya's passion for learning?
3. How and when did Anaya come to love words and reading?
4. How did the "old ones" of Anaya's childhood preserve and regenerate their culture?
5. Summarize three of Anaya's library memories.

124 ◆ Striving for Success

 Beyond the Selection

FURTHER READING

Other Works by Rudolfo Anaya
Bless Me, Ultima
Heart of Aztlan
Tortuga

Other Works With the Theme of Striving for Success
Crystal, Walter Dean Myers
To Be Young, Gifted, and Black, Lorraine Hansberry
We suggest that you preview these works before recommending them to students.

INTERNET

You and your students may find additional information about Rudolfo Anaya on the Internet. We suggest the following site. Please be aware, however, that the site may have changed from the time we published this information.

For information about Rudolfo Anaya, go to **http://www.unm.edu/~wrtgsw/anaya.html**

We *strongly recommend* that you preview this and related sites before you send students to them.

Guide for Responding (continued)

◆ Critical Thinking

INTERPRET

1. What does Anaya mean when he says that "a book at once quenches the thirst of the imagination and ignites new fires"? [Interpret]
2. Why does Anaya associate libraries with freedom? [Connect]
3. In what ways do books and reading help preserve a culture? [Draw Conclusions]

APPLY

4. Anaya says that a library should "reflect the needs and aspirations of the people." What specific needs and aspirations do you think your library should reflect? [Relate]

EXTEND

5. List three works of literature that inspired you or helped you reach a goal, and explain how they did so. [Literature Link]

◆ Reading for Success

INTERACTIVE READING STRATEGIES

Review the reading strategies and notes showing how to read interactively. Then apply those strategies to answer the following questions.

1. Explain how Anaya's feelings about the stories of the old people reinforce the message of his essay.
2. List one question you asked yourself while reading and explain how you answered it.

◆ Literary Focus

AUTHOR'S PURPOSE

Anaya wrote this essay as a speech to be delivered on the occasion of a library's acquiring its one-millionth volume. In general, the **author's purpose**—his reason for writing—is to share his ideas with the group that has gathered to celebrate the event. The information he presents helps him achieve his specific purpose of acknowledging the importance of libraries in linking the wisdom of the past to the goals of the future.

1. Identify two details that Anaya includes to illustrate how libraries can help children.
2. Find one direct statement that helped you recognize Anaya's specific purpose.

◆ Build Vocabulary

USING THE PREFIX in-

In your notebook, write an antonym for each word below that begins with the prefix in-, meaning "in" or "into."

1. inhale   2. include   3. internal

USING THE WORD BANK

In your notebook, describe what each of the following would be like.

1. dilapidated car
2. meal that left you satiated
3. book that enthralls
4. poem like a litany
5. fomentation of ideas
6. poignant movie scene
7. inherent quality of cats
8. labyrinth of hallways
9. speech that induces sleep

◆ Build Grammar Skills

ACTION VERBS AND LINKING VERBS

Common linking verbs include the following: *become, seem, appear, feel, look, taste, smell, sound, stay, remain, grow,* and *be* (including the forms *am, is, are, was,* and *were*). Some of these can also be used as action verbs. If you can replace the verb with a form of *be* and the sentence still makes sense, the verb is probably a linking verb.

> **Action verbs** express physical or mental action.
> **Linking verbs** express a state of being and tell what the subject is by linking it to one or more words that further describe or identify it.

Practice Copy each of the following sentences in your notebook. Underline the verbs. Then identify the verb as an action verb *(V)* or a linking verb *(LV)*.

1. Anaya feels exhilarated by the power of words.
2. The people of his village told him stories.
3. His love for stories grew in the library.
4. In college, he grew eager to learn even more.
5. He delivered this speech at his alma mater.

from In Commemoration: One Million Volumes ◆ 125

Answers

◆ Critical Thinking

1. In books, we find the answers to the questions that intrigue us. We also find new ideas that spark our curiosity.
2. Anaya associates libraries with freedom because libraries represent ideas from many points of view in their uncensored collections.
3. Books are the written record of a culture. They transcend barriers of time and space and keep the thoughts and customs of a culture alive.
4. The library might reflect the need to know more about culture and heritage, practical skills, and career opportunity information. It might reflect aspirations to improve oneself or become a professional or skilled worker.
5. Selections in Units 1 and 2 that students might suggest include: "The Final Assault," "The Dream Comes True," "from My Left Foot." "Mowing," and "After Apple-Picking."

◆ Reading for Success

1. Both the stories of the old people and libraries serve to preserve culture and heritage. They both value the power of the word.
2. A possible response is that students questioned how Anaya would connect his childhood memories to his love for books; when they read on, they found the connections and went back in the text to confirm them.

◆ Literary Focus

1. Libraries can help children by providing refuge and introducing them to the power of stories.
2. A sample direct statement is "Now with book in hand we can participate in the wisdom of mankind."

◆ Build Vocabulary

Using the Prefix in-
1. exhale; 2. exclude; 3. external

Using the Word Bank
1. A dilapidated car would be a broken down car.
2. A meal that left you satiated would leave you full.
3. A book that enthralls you is a book that captivates or fascinates you.
4. A poem like a litany would be one with a series of repetitive responses.
5. A fomentation of ideas is like a stirring up of ideas.
6. A poignant movie scene is an emotionally moving one.
7. An inherent quality of cats is their inborn grace.
8. A labyrinth of hallways is like a maze of hallways.
9. A speech that induces sleep is a speech that causes someone to sleep.

◆ Build Grammar Skills

1. Anaya feels exhilarated by the power of words. (LV)
2. The people of his village told him stories. (V)
3. His love for stories grew in the library. (V)
4. In college, he grew eager to learn even more. (LV)
5. He delivered this speech at his alma mater. (V)

✎ Writer's Solution

For additional instruction and practice, use the lesson in the **Language Lab CD-ROM** on Eight Parts of Speech and the page on Action Verbs and Linking Verbs (p. 11) in the *Writer's Solution Grammar Practice Book.*

Idea Bank

Customizing for *Performance Levels*

Following are suggestions for matching Idea Bank topics with your students' performance levels:

Less Advanced Students: 1, 4, 6
Average Students: 2, 5, 7
More Advanced Students: 3

Customizing for *Learning Modalities*

Following are suggestions for matching Idea Bank topics with your students' learning modalities:

Visual/Spatial: 6
Logical/Mathematical: 3, 7
Bodily/Kinesthetic: 4
Verbal/Linguistic: 2, 4, 5

Writing Mini-Lesson

Refer students to the Writing Handbook, page 965, for instruction on the writing process, and page 969 for further information on response to literature.

Writing and Language Transparencies

Use Writing Process Model 8: Interpreting a Work of Literature (pp. 53–59) to provide pointers on how to respond to literature.

Writer's Solution

Writers at Work Videodisc

Have students view the videodisc segment (Ch. 7) featuring Miquel Algarín to spark a class discussion on the importance of responding to works of literature.

Play frames 22209 to 31154

Writing Lab CD-ROM

Have students complete the tutorial on Response to Literature. Follow these steps:

1. Direct students to use the Sunburst Diagram to organize details.
2. Have them use an Evaluation Word Bin for precise modifiers.
3. Have them get a video tip from Miquel Algarín on revising a draft.

Sourcebook

Have students use Chapter 7, Response to Literature (pp. 195–221), for additional support. The chapter includes an annotated student model of a response to a Shakespeare play (p. 221).

126

*B*uild *Y*our *P*ortfolio

Idea Bank

Writing

1. **Library Dedication** Based on the ideas Anaya has shared and your own opinions, write a brief statement, to be read at the dedication of a newly opened library, about the value of libraries.

2. **Informational Article** Find out what resources (besides books) and activities are available to the public at your local library. Present your findings in a brief article for your school or local newspaper. **[Community Link]**

3. **Directions** Write step-by-step directions for how to use a technological tool, such as a CD-ROM guide to periodicals or an electronic card catalog. **[Technology Link]**

Speaking and Listening

4. **Storytelling Performance** Choose a story you liked when you were a child. Practice telling it aloud with expression, using gestures and facial expressions. If possible, perform your story for a group of young children. **[Performing Arts Link]**

5. **Library Panel Discussion** Have a group discussion in which each group member gives reasons why his or her favorite books should be included in the school library. Present your reasons to the class.

Projects

6. **Library Poster** Libraries frequently display posters that promote the benefits of reading. Create your own reading promotion poster. Display the poster in your classroom.

7. **Library Survey** Ask your school librarian what percentage of the school's library books are fiction, nonfiction, poetry, and drama. Represent the percentages on a chart or graph. **[Math Link]**

Writing Mini-Lesson

Reading Journal

One way to explore the ideas you find in books is to respond to them in writing. For one week, keep a **reading journal**—a record of your thoughts and feelings about what you read and how the issues or topics apply to your life. The following tips will help you record your ideas in the most appropriate style.

Writing Skills Focus: Level of Formality

Whether you're writing a letter to a company, a report for school, or a journal entry, take time to consider the **level of formality** you should use.

Because you are the audience for your journal, you want to capture your thoughts in your own natural voice. For a journal, it is appropriate to use informal English—the "everyday" English that we speak. Feel free to use contractions and slang—but the standard rules of grammar, punctuation, and spelling still apply.

Use informal English to capture the natural sound of speech in your journal.

Prewriting While you are reading, keep your journal handy so you can jot down your reactions to specific passages and ideas. Sketch characters and settings and record quotations you want to remember.

Drafting Write each full entry as if you were speaking to a friend. Expand your notes into full sentences written in the language and informal style of your everyday speech. Explain why you do or do not like or agree with what you read.

Revising In a personal journal, you don't need to revise as extensively as you would if someone else were going to read it. You may want to look over your entries, however, and add a few more details or reword a sentence to better express your thoughts.

✓ ASSESSMENT OPTIONS

Formal Assessment, Selection Test, pp. 26–28, and Assessment Resources Software. The selection test is designed so that it can be easily customized to the performance levels of your students. **Alternative Assessment,** p. 8, includes options for less advanced students, more advanced students, logical/mathematical learners, verbal/linguistic learners, interpersonal learners, and visual/spatial learners.

PORTFOLIO ASSESSMENT

Use the following rubrics in the **Alternative Assessment** booklet to assess student writing:
Library Dedication: Persuasion Rubric, p. 105
Informational Article: Explanation Rubric, p. 115
Directions: How-to Explanation Rubric, p. 100

PART **1** *Overcoming Obstacles*

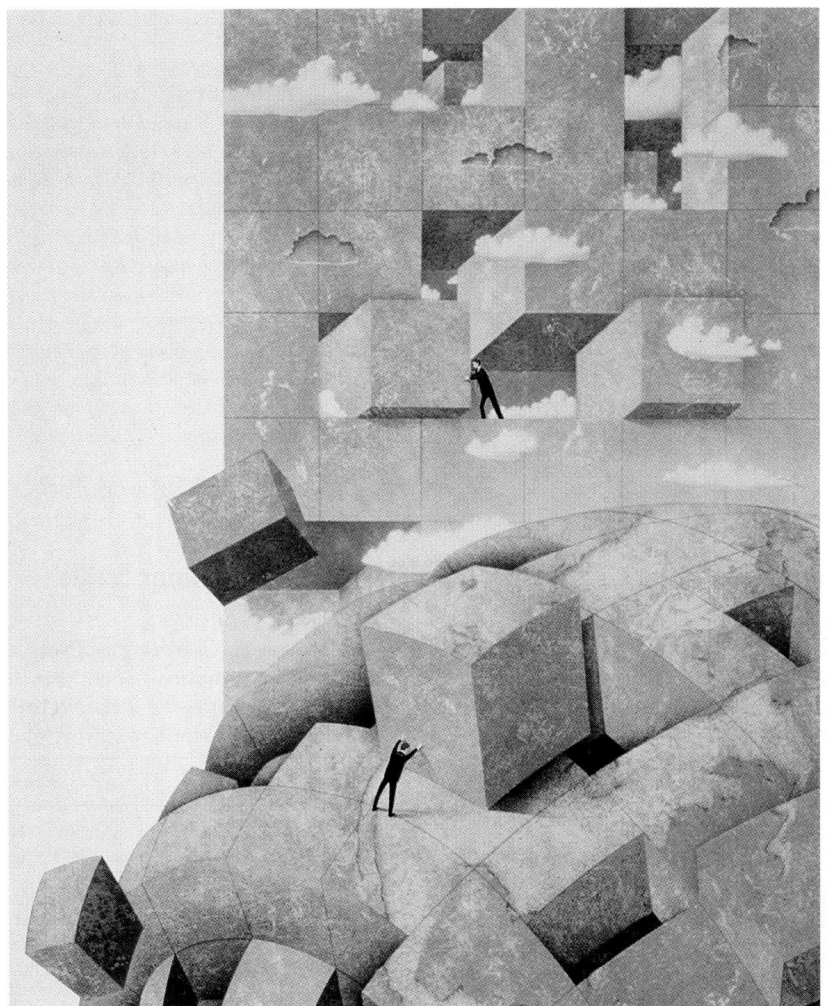

Earth and Sky Puzzle, Curtis Parker/SIS

Overcoming Obstacles ◆ 127

One-Minute Planning Guide

The selections in this section deal with people's trying to overcome obstacles. In "How Much Land Does a Man Need?" a Russian farmer assumes that the obstacle is his lack of land, though he finds out too late it is his own greed. The poems "Success is counted sweetest," "I dwell in Possibility—," "Uncoiling," and "Columbus Dying" deal with success and failure. In the excerpt from *My Left Foot,* Christy Brown overcomes the obstacles of his cerebral palsy and the attitudes of others. In "A Visit to Grandmother," a man must overcome what he perceives to be his mother's unequal treatment of him and a sibling.

Customize for *Varying Student Needs*

When assigning the selections in this part to students, keep in mind the following factors:

"How Much Land Does a Man Need?"
• A longer selection (13 pp.)
• Less proficient readers may need to read in sections

"Success is counted sweetest," "I dwell in Possibility—," "Uncoiling," "Columbus Dying"
• Four brief poems

from *My Left Foot*
• Connection to popular film will interest students

"A Visit to Grandmother"
• Story will be accessible to most students

 Humanities: Art

Earth and Sky Puzzle by Curtis Parker.

Parker, who operated his own design studio before becoming a commercial artist, is known as a "thinking person's illustrator." He uses acrylic paints to create images with appealing textures that engage the viewer in intriguing visual puzzles that recall the works of M. C. Escher.

Earth and Sky Puzzle combines recognizable concrete images with abstract geometric ones. Help students notice the way the painting resembles a three-dimensional puzzle. Encourage them to speculate what the completed puzzle should look like as well as to speculate about where the various loose pieces might belong.

Help students link the painting to the theme of Part 1, "Overcoming Obstacles," with the following questions:

1. What do you think the figures in this painting are trying to do? *Possible answers: They are trying to put the pieces of* *the puzzle together so that they form the earth and sky; they are trying to move the pieces of the puzzle around to change the appearance of earth and sky.*

2. What particular obstacles do the various figures have to deal with? *Possible answers: They have to move pieces larger than themselves; they have to figure out where the pieces go; the pieces might fall out of the sky and off of the earth; the figures could lose their footing and fall.*

127

OBJECTIVES

1. To read, comprehend, and interpret a parable
2. To relate a parable to personal experience
3. To predict based on character traits
4. To identify characteristics of a parable
5. To use words in different contexts
6. To use possessive noun forms correctly
7. To write a video script with clear explanations of procedures
8. To respond to the parable through writing, speaking and listening, and projects

SKILLS INSTRUCTION

Vocabulary:
Words in Other Contexts

Grammar:
Possessive Nouns

Reading Strategy:
Predict Based on Character Traits

Literary Focus:
Parable

Writing: Clear Explanation of Procedure

Speaking and Listening:
Eulogy (teacher edition)

Critical Viewing:
Speculate; Interpret; Connect

PORTFOLIO OPPORTUNITIES

Writing: Newspaper Article; Land Advertisement; Parable

Writing Mini-Lesson: Video Script

Speaking and Listening: Update the Story; Eulogy

Projects: Map of Russia; Scale Diagram of Pahom's Field

More About the Author

Leo Tolstoy is known both as a great novelist and a master of the short story. As a young man he spent some time in the army and while still there he published his first works—a set of autobiographical novels. Following his religious conversion, Tolstoy disowned his earlier writings, including *War and Peace* and *Anna Karenina,* and determined that art had value only if it took a strong moral stance. His later work, of which "How Much Land Does a Man Need?" is an example, is marked by a plain narrative style.

Guide for Reading

Leo Tolstoy (1828–1910)

Leo Tolstoy is remembered almost as much for his unusual lifestyle as he is for his literary achievements.

Tolstoy's life reads like a Cinderella story in reverse. He was born rich and died poor.

After inheriting the wealth and power of his family's estate at the age of nineteen, he opened a school for peasant children and tried somewhat unsuccessfully to improve the lives of the serfs who were bound to the estate.

One Wife, Two Masterpieces, Thirteen Children
When he was thirty-four, Tolstoy married an intelligent, headstrong woman named Sonya Baers. She energetically supported his writing, copying by hand his long, nearly indecipherable manuscript for the mammoth novel *War and Peace* nine times, by candlelight, so that it could be sent to publishers. At the same time, she found time to manage Tolstoy's estate and raise thirteen children.

Tolstoy's other masterpiece is *Anna Karenina*, a tragic love story. While working on the novel, Tolstoy began to question the meaning of life and the inevitability of death.

A Personal Crisis
After *Anna Karenina* was published in installments from 1875 to 1877, Tolstoy suffered a spiritual crisis. He created his own religion, took up shoemaking, became a vegetarian, and stopped drinking and smoking. He handed over the copyrights to all of his works produced before 1881 to his wife and attempted to be as self-sufficient as possible. He often wore peasant's clothes and worked in the fields. His actions placed a great strain on his marriage and eventually forced him to leave home. In 1910, he died at an obscure railroad station.

◆ Build Vocabulary

WORDS IN OTHER CONTEXTS: LAND-RELATED WORDS

As the title of Tolstoy's story suggests, many of the words you will encounter in this story describe land. Some of these words, such as *fallow*, which means "not cultivated," can be used in other contexts as well. *Fallow* can refer to land left uncultivated and to a mind that is uncultivated or inactive.

WORD BANK

piqued
disparaged
forbore
aggrieved
sheaf
arable
fallow

As you read you will encounter the words on this list. Each word is defined on the page where it first appears. Preview the list before you read, and look for more land-related words, such as *sowed,* that can be used in other contexts.

◆ Build Grammar Skills

POSSESSIVE NOUNS

In this story about owning land, you will see many **possessive nouns**—nouns that show ownership, belonging, or another close relationship. The chart shows how to form possessive nouns.

Rules for Possessive Forms of Nouns	Examples
To form the possessive of singular nouns, add an apostrophe and s.	• Pahom's field • sun's rays
To form the possessive of plural nouns that end in s, just add an apostrophe.	• peasants' complaints • three days' work
To form the possessive of plural nouns that do not end in s, add an apostrophe and s.	• women's conversation • people's land

Notice other examples of these possessive forms of nouns in Tolstoy's story.

Prentice Hall Literature Program Resources

REINFORCE / RETEACH / EXTEND

Selection Support Pages
Build Vocabulary: Using Words in Other Contexts, p. 35
Build Grammar Skills: Possessive Nouns, p. 36
Reading Strategy: Predict Based on Character Traits, p. 37
Literary Focus: Parable, p. 38

Strategies for Diverse Student Needs, p. 9

Beyond Literature
Cross-Curricular Connection: Social Studies, p. 9

Formal Assessment Selection Test, pp. 29–31; Assessment Resources Software

Alternative Assessment, p. 9

Resource Pro CD-ROM
"How Much Land Does a Man Need?"—includes all resource materials and customizable lesson plan

 Listening to Literature Audiocassettes
"How Much Land Does a Man Need?"

How Much Land Does a Man Need?

◆ *Literature and Your Life*

CONNECT YOUR EXPERIENCE

Just one more... just a little longer... just a little farther—almost everyone has used one of these phrases at one time or another. For instance, you yourself have probably felt that you could have done better on that last test if you had had just a little longer!

The events in this Russian tale illustrate the universal truth that "a little more" is *never* enough.

THEMATIC FOCUS: OVERCOMING OBSTACLES

Tolstoy's story illustrates the old proverb, "The more you have, the more you want." As you read this story, ask yourself, How much is enough?

◆ Background for Understanding

HISTORY

From the sixteenth century to the mid-nineteenth century, Russian peasants were bound by law to work land they could rent but not own. They grew food they couldn't eat, cultivated crops they couldn't sell, and worked to exhaustion to make a profit for the landowner. Peasants could be bought and sold with the land they lived on. This story is set after the laws had been changed to allow ordinary people to own land. Because of the old laws, however, land is more than just property. Land ownership represents the ability to control one's own destiny.

It is not a coincidence that Tolstoy uses land to explore the question "How much is enough?" He uses an image that was close to the heart of every Russian.

◆ Literary Focus

PARABLE

Tolstoy's story is not simply a tale about land. It is a **parable**, a simple, brief narrative that teaches a lesson by using characters and events to stand for abstract ideas or moral qualities.

This parable focuses on Pahom, a Russian peasant who feels that all his problems would be solved if he had enough land. Through Pahom's actions, the story explores the question "How much land is enough land?" Think about the lesson that this parable teaches, a lesson concerning the difference between *need* and *greed*.

◆ Reading Strategy

PREDICT BASED ON CHARACTER TRAITS

When you read stories that teach a lesson, you can usually **predict** the outcome before you actually read what happens. In such stories, casual remarks and small details are filled with meaning and hint at future events. Clouds on the horizon can foretell a thunderstorm; a minor dispute between neighbors can be an early sign of a bitter feud.

In "How Much Land Does a Man Need?" the peasant Pahom's wife says to her wealthier sister, "Though you often earn more than you need, you're very likely to lose all you have." This statement hints at the lesson to come. Pahom's response to the conversation between the two women reveals character traits that will help you predict how he will act in the story.

Guide for Reading ◆ 129

Preparing for Standardized Tests

Vocabulary The Build Vocabulary lesson focuses on using land-related words in other contexts. Practice using the same word in different contexts will help prepare students for the reading comprehension, analogies, and sentence completion sections of standardized tests. For additional practice, use the Build Vocabulary page in *Selection Support*, p. 35.

Grammar and Language Some standardized tests require students to locate incorrect words in a passage. These words are often possessive nouns that are missing apostrophes or use apostrophes incorrectly. Write this passage on the chalkboard, telling students it contains three possessive nouns that need to be correctly punctuated:

> Leo Tolstoys novels have captured peoples imaginations and gained readers loyalty for generations. *Leo Tolstoy's novels have captured people's imaginations and gained readers' loyalty for generations.*

After students have placed apostrophes correctly, point out that *Tolstoy's* is a posses- sive singular noun, *people's* is a possessive plural noun that does not end in *s*, and *readers'* is a possessive noun that ends in *s*.

The Build Grammar Skills lesson for this selection, which reviews possessive nouns, will help students improve their performance on such test items. For additional practice, use the Build Grammar Skills page on Possessive Nouns in *Selection Support* (p. 36).

How Much *Land* Does a Man Need?

Leo Tolstoy

Translated by Louise and Aylmer Maude

One-Minute Insight This parable illuminates Tolstoy's sentiments about the perils of private ownership. A peasant named Pahom seeks to acquire more and more land. He rejects the advantages of cooperative ownership and finds fault with each new land acquisition until, far from his home, he at last dies in a final, desperate grasp for even more land.

Tolstoy would have approved of the peasants' owning the land jointly. It is owning private property, this story tells us, that encourages individual greed.

▶**Critical Viewing**◀

❶ **Speculate** *Students are likely to suggest that the peasants want to gain more control over their lives so they won't be beholden to landowners, that they want to feel a pride in ownership, that they generally want to improve their prospects for the future and to be able to provide better for their material needs.*

Customize for
Logical/Mathematical Learners

Pahom's land acquisition grows by leaps and bounds. Have these students create a diagram or graph showing how his holdings increase as the story progresses.

Rest During the Harvest, Alexander Morosov, Tretyakov Gallery, Moscow, Russia

❶ ▲ **Critical Viewing** Why do you think people like the peasants in this picture place great importance on owning land? [Speculate]

130 ◆ *Striving for Success*

Humanities: Art

Rest During the Harvest (detail) by Alexander Morosov.

This painting depicts peasants taking a break from their labor. It might be set in the region of Bryansk, a province of Russia from which the painter Alexander Morosov comes.

Use these questions for discussion:

1. What might the people in this picture have in common? *Possible responses: They are tied to working a landowner's farm; they are all members of the peasant class.*

2. What are some advantages and disadvantages of tending land that you do not own? *Possible advantages: You aren't burdened with the responsibility of ownership; you are free to enjoy simple pleasures. Possible disadvantages: There is no opportunity to better yourself; there is no incentive to do an excellent job.*

1

An elder sister came to visit her younger sister in the country. The elder was married to a shopkeeper in town, the younger to a peasant in the village. As the sisters sat over their tea talking, the elder began to boast of the advantages of town life, saying how comfortably they lived there, how well they dressed, what fine clothes her children wore, what good things they ate and drank, and how she went to the theater, promenades,[1] and entertainments.

The younger sister was piqued, and in turn disparaged the life of a shopkeeper, and stood up for that of a peasant.

"I wouldn't change my way of life for yours," said she. "We may live roughly, but at least we're free from worry. You live in better style than we do, but though you often earn more than you need, you're very likely to lose all you have. You know the proverb, 'Loss and gain are brothers twain.'[2] It often happens that people who're wealthy one day are begging their bread the next. Our way is safer. Though a peasant's life is not a rich one, it's long. We'll never grow rich, but we'll always have enough to eat."

---

1. **promenades** (präm´ ə nädz) *n.*: Balls or formal dances.
2. **twain** (twān) *n.*: Two.

◆ Build Vocabulary

piqued (pēkt) *v.*: Offended

disparaged (di spar´ ijd) *v.*: Spoke slightly of; belittled

The elder sister said sneeringly:

"Enough? Yes, if you like to share with the pigs and the calves! What do you know of elegance or manners! However much your good man may slave, you'll die as you live—in a dung heap—and your children the same."

"Well, what of that?" replied the younger sister. "Of course our work is rough and hard. But on the other hand, it's sure, and we need not bow to anyone. But you, in your towns, are surrounded by temptations; today all may be right, but tomorrow the Evil One may tempt your husband with cards, wine, or women, and all will go to ruin. Don't such things happen often enough?"

Pahom, the master of the house, was lying on the top of the stove and he listened to the women's chatter.

"It is perfectly true," thought he. "Busy as we are from childhood tilling mother earth, we peasants have no time to let any nonsense settle in our heads. Our only trouble is that we haven't land enough. If I had plenty of land, I shouldn't fear the Devil himself!"

The women finished their tea, chatted a while about dress, and then cleared away the tea things and lay down to sleep.

But the Devil had been sitting behind the stove and had heard all that had been said. He was pleased that the peasant's wife had led her husband into boasting and that he had said that if he had plenty of land he would not fear the Devil himself.

"All right," thought the Devil. "We'll have a tussle. I'll give you land

How Much Land Does a Man Need? ◆ 131

❶ enough; and by means of the land I'll get you into my power."

2

Close to the village there lived a lady, a small landowner who had an estate of about three hundred acres. She had always lived on good terms with the peasants until she engaged as her manager an old soldier, who took to burdening the people with fines. However careful Pahom tried to be, it happened again and again that now a horse of his got among the lady's oats, now a cow strayed into her garden, now his calves found their way into her meadows—and he always had to pay a fine.

Pahom paid up, but grumbled, and, going home in a temper, was rough with his family. All through that summer Pahom had much trouble because of this manager, and he was actually glad when winter came and the cattle had to be stabled. Though he grudged the fodder when they could no longer graze on the pasture land, at least he was free from anxiety about them.

In the winter the news got about that the lady was going to sell her land and that the keeper of the inn on the high road was bargaining for it. When the peasants heard this they were very much alarmed.

"Well," thought they, "if the innkeeper gets the land, he'll worry us with fines worse than the lady's manager. We all depend on that estate."

So the peasants went on behalf of their village council and asked the lady not to sell the land to the innkeeper, offering her a better price for it themselves. The lady agreed to let them have it. Then the peasants tried to arrange for the village council to buy the whole estate, so that it might be held by them all in common. They met twice to discuss it, but could not settle the matter;

❷ the Evil One sowed discord among them and they could not agree. So they decided to buy the land individually, each according to his means; and the lady agreed to this plan as she had to the other.

Presently Pahom heard that a neighbor of his was buying fifty acres, and that the lady had consented to accept one half in cash and to wait a year for the other half. Pahom felt envious.

"Look at that," thought he, "the land is all being sold, and I'll get none of it." So he spoke to his wife.

"Other people are buying," said he, "and we must also buy twenty acres or so. Life is becoming impossible. That manager is simply crushing us with his fines."

❸ So they put their heads together and considered how they could manage to buy it. They had one hundred rubles[3] laid by. They sold a colt and one half of their bees, hired out one of their sons as a farmhand and took his wages in advance, borrowed the rest from a brother-in-law, and so scraped together half the purchase money.

Having done this, Pahom chose a farm of forty acres, some of it wooded, and went to the lady to bargain for it. They came to an agreement, and he shook hands with her upon it and paid her a deposit in advance. Then they went to town and signed the deeds, he paying half the price down, and undertaking to pay the remainder within two years.

❹ **◆ Reading Strategy** Based on what you know about Pahom's character, predict whether he will be happy now.

❺ So now Pahom had land of his own. He borrowed seed and sowed it on the land he had bought. The harvest was a

---
3. **rubles** (rōō′ bəlz) *n.*: Russian money.

Beyond the Classroom

Community Connection
Council Person The village council before which the peasants appear is much like village, town, and city councils today. In the United States, councilmen and councilwomen are elected officials. Although being a councilperson can be a full-time position in smaller municipalities, they usually hold other jobs as well.

Suggest that students learn who their city or town council members are. In a small town, one of them may agree to be interviewed about how to become a member of the council and what the council does.

⑤ good one, and within a year he had managed to pay off his debts both to the lady and to his brother-in-law. So he became a landowner, plowing and sowing his own land, making hay on his own land, cutting his own trees, and feeding his cattle on his own pasture. When he went out to plow his fields, or to look at his growing corn, or at his grass meadows, his heart would fill with joy. The grass that grew and the flowers that bloomed there seemed to him unlike any that grew elsewhere. **⑥** Formerly, when he had passed by that land, it had appeared the same as any other land, but now it seemed quite different.

3

So Pahom was well contented, and everything would have been right if the neighboring peasants would only not have trespassed on his wheatfields and meadows. He appealed to them most civilly, but they still went on: now the herdsmen would let the village cows stray into his meadows, then horses from the night pasture would get among his corn. Pahom turned them out again and again, and forgave their owners, and for a long time he <u>forbore</u> to prosecute anyone. But at last he lost patience and complained to the District Court. He knew it was the peasants' want of land, and no evil intent on their part, that caused the trouble, but he thought:

"I can't go on overlooking it, or they'll destroy all I have. They must be taught a lesson."

⑦ So he had them up, gave them one lesson, and then another, and two or three of the peasants were fined. After a time Pahom's neighbors began to bear him a grudge for this, and would now and then let their cattle onto his land on purpose. One peasant even got into Pahom's wood at night and cut down five young lime trees for their bark. Pahom, passing

through the wood one day, noticed something white. He came nearer and saw the stripped trunks lying on the ground, and close by stood the stumps where the trees had been. Pahom was furious.

"If he'd only cut one here and there it would have been bad enough," thought Pahom, "but the rascal has actually cut down a whole clump. If I could only find out who did this, I'd get even with him."

He racked his brains as to who it could be. Finally he decided: "It must be Simon—no one else could have done it." So he went to Simon's homestead to have a look around, but he found nothing and only had an angry scene. However, he now felt more certain than ever that Simon had done it, and he lodged a complaint. Simon was summoned. The case was tried, and retried, and at the end of it all Simon was acquitted, there being no evidence against him. Pahom felt still more <u>aggrieved</u>, and let his anger loose upon the Elders and the Judges. **⑧**

"You let thieves grease your palms," said he. "If you were honest folk yourselves you wouldn't let a thief go free."

So Pahom quarreled with the judges and with his neighbors. Threats to burn his hut began to be uttered. So though Pahom had more land, his place in the community was much worse than before.

About this time a rumor got about that many people were moving to new parts.

"There's no need for me to leave my land," thought Pahom. "But some of the others may leave our village and then

⑨

> ◆ **Literary Focus**
> How do Pahom's experiences begin to teach a lesson about greed?

> ◆ **Build Vocabulary**
> **forbore** (fôr bôr′) v.: Refrained from
> **aggrieved** (ə grēvd′) v.: Wronged

How Much Land Does a Man Need? ◆ 133

Beyond the Classroom

Community Connection

Mortgages Pahom buys his forty-acre farm by scraping together half the purchase price and agreeing to pay the remainder within two years. Today, most home buyers apply to a local bank for a *mortgage.* The buyer pays a certain amount of the asking price—for example, 10 or 15 percent. Then the bank lends the buyer the money

for the rest, to be paid back with interest over a period of years.

Interested students might inquire at local banks about current interest rates. Have them find out the total cost of a specified mortgage—say, $50,000 or $100,000—over a given time period—fifteen, twenty, or thirty years.

❶ Using Words in Other Contexts: Land-Related Words
Point out the word *sheaf*, which means "a bundle of cut stalks of grain." Explain that the word may be used to refer to a variety of items that are bundled together. Ask: What would a *sheaf* of paper look like?
It would be a stack of paper bound together.

◆ *Literature and Your Life*

❷ Students may reveal that they get angry or upset. Or they may take a more philosophical attitude and reason that they will not miss out on the next good thing.

◆ Critical Thinking

❸ Evaluate The use of communal land is typical of many agrarian societies. Usually, a section of land was set aside on which everyone in a village might graze cattle or plant a garden. Ask students to briefly evaluate the pros and cons of such a system.
Some students might say the system is a good one because it is equitable, allows everyone to be productive, and fosters self-esteem; others might argue the system is rigid and does not allow people to get ahead on their own or to be independent.

❹ Clarification The phrase *stood treat to the Elders* involves a rare connotation for *treat*—"negotiation." This meaning for the word *treat* is related to the word *treaty*. Ask: What did Pahom do when he "stood treat"? *He negotiated with the chiefs of the village.*

---

there'd be more room for us. I'd take over their land myself and make my estates somewhat bigger. I could then live more at ease. As it is, I'm still too cramped to be comfortable."

One day Pahom was sitting at home when a peasant, passing through the village, happened to drop in. He was allowed to stay the night, and supper was given him. Pahom had a talk with this peasant and asked him where he came from. The stranger answered that he came from beyond the Volga,[4] where he had been working. One word led to another, and the man went on to say that many people were settling in those parts. He told how some people from his village had settled there. They had joined the community there and had had twenty-five acres per man granted them. The land was so good, he said, that the rye sown on it grew as high as a horse, and so thick that five cuts of a sickle made a **❶ sheaf.** One peasant, he said, had brought nothing with him but his bare hands, and now he had six horses and two cows of his own.

Pahom's heart kindled with desire.

"Why should I suffer in this narrow hole, if one can live so well elsewhere?" he thought. "I'll sell my land and my homestead here, and with the money I'll start afresh over there and get everything new. In this crowded place one is always having trouble. But I must first go and find out all about it myself."

Toward summer he got ready and started out. He went down the Volga on a steamer to Samara,[5] then walked

> ◆ *Literature and Your Life*
> ❷ How do you react when you feel you're missing out on a good thing?

---

4. **Volga** (väl´ gə): The major river in western Russia.
5. **Samara** (Sə ma´ rə): City in eastern Russia.

---

another three hundred miles on foot, and at last reached the place. It was just as the stranger had said. The peasants had plenty of land: every man had twenty-five acres of communal land given him for his use, and anyone who had money could buy, besides, at a ruble and a half an acre, as much good freehold land[6] as he wanted. **❸**

Having found out all he wished to know, Pahom returned home as autumn came on, and began selling off his belongings. He sold his land at a profit, sold his homestead and all his cattle, and withdrew from membership in the village. He only waited till the spring, and then started with his family for the new settlement.

4

As soon as Pahom and his family reached their new abode, he applied for admission into the council of a large village. He stood treat to the Elders and obtained the necessary documents. Five shares of communal land were given him for his own and his sons' use: that is to say—125 acres (not all together, but in different fields) besides the use of the communal pasture. Pahom put up the buildings he needed and bought cattle. Of the communal land alone he had three times as much as at his former home, and the land was good wheat land. He was ten times better off than he had been. He had plenty of arable land and pasturage, and could keep as many head of cattle as he liked.

At first, in the bustle of building and settling down, Pahom was pleased with it all, but when he got used to it he began to think that even here he hadn't enough land. The first year he sowed wheat on his share of the communal land and had

---

6. **freehold land:** Privately owned land that the owner can lease to others for a fee.

Cross-Curricular Connection: Science

The practices of rotating crops and of sowing wheat for one or two years and then allowing the field to lie fallow until it is covered with grass have a scientific justification. Certain crops, such as wheat and corn, leach nutrients from soil. Other crops, such as alfalfa or soybeans, can reconstitute the soil, making it ready for planting grain again. By rotating crops from year to year, farmers can increase the productivity of their cropland. Sometimes farmers let the land "rest," so they do not plant it, and let it just lie fallow.

Students might like to speculate on how greed might make a farmer sacrifice productivity over time. If a farmer were shortsighted and planted grain year after year in hopes of making the best profit, eventually the grain crop would fail because the soil would be barren.

Cornfield at Ewell, c. 1846 (detail), William Holman Hunt, Tate Gallery, London

Customize for

English Language Learners

5 Use simpler language to explain this passage. Words like sowing (planting) virgin (unplanted) and let (rent) may cause confusion because English language learners may not have encountered these words in the context in which they are used here.

▶ **Critical Viewing** ◀

6 Speculate Students' answers may include the following: *He may be overwhelmed by the work he has to do, or he may feel pride in the success of the crop he has produced.*

◆ Literary Focus

7 Parable Ask students to relate the story so far to this proverb: "The grass is always greener on the other side of the fence." *Even when he has a lot of land and a fine crop, Pahom is not satisfied. Here, his problem is that the wheat is too far from town. He thinks there's a better way to do his farming.*

Customize for

Less Proficient Readers

8 These readers may have difficulty distinguishing between the land Pahom now holds and freehold land. However, they should be able to identify the main idea of this passage: Once again, Pahom thinks others are doing better than he is and thinks he needs more land.

a good crop. He wanted to go on sowing wheat, but had not enough communal land for the purpose, and what he had already used was not available, for in those parts wheat is sown only on virgin soil or on <u>fallow</u> land. It is sown for one or two years, and then the land lies fallow till it is again overgrown with steppe grass. There were many who wanted such land, and there was not enough for all, so that people quarreled about it. Those who were better off wanted it for

5

◆ Build Vocabulary

sheaf (shēf) *n.*: Bundle of grain

arable (ar´ ə bəl) *adj.*: Suitable for growing crops

fallow (fal´ ō) *adj.*: Plowed, but not planted

▲ **Critical Viewing** What might be going through the mind of the person tending to this land? **[Speculate]** **6**

growing wheat, and those who were poor wanted it to let to dealers, so that they might raise money to pay their taxes. Pahom wanted to sow more wheat, so he rented land from a dealer for a year. He sowed much wheat and had a fine crop, but the land was too far from the village—the wheat had to be carted more than ten miles. After a time Pahom noticed that some peasant dealers were living on separate farms and were growing wealthy, and he thought:

"If I were to buy some freehold land and have a homestead on it, it would be a different thing altogether. Then it

5

7
8

How Much Land Does a Man Need? ◆ 135

🎵 **Humanities: Art**

Cornfield at Ewell (detail), c. 1846, by William Holman Hunt.

This landscape depicts a large field of grain similar to those Pahom would have cultivated in Russia. The artist, William Holman Hunt, was a member of the Pre-Raphaelite Brotherhood in England, a group of artists and poets who held to Renaissance standards and ideals in art. They strove to portray nature in a way that demonstrated both its detail and its simplicity.

Use these questions for discussion:
1. What quality does this field have that might appeal to Pahom? *Students might mention its vastness or its potential productivity.*
2. Do you think this is an appropriate illustration for this story? Explain. *Students may say that its content—a lone man in vast expanse of land—suits the story well.*

◆ Reading Strategy

① Predict Based on Character Traits Students may say that Pahom is never satisfied and that he is stubborn—traits that will clearly lead him to a fall.

Customize for
Less Proficient Readers

② Length and unusual idioms may make this sentence particularly difficult to comprehend. Ask a volunteer to paraphrase it. *In the third year, Pahom and a dealer rented some land from some peasants. They had already plowed it up, but the peasants argued with them and took them to court, so all their work was wasted.*

◆ Build Grammar Skills

③ Possessive Nouns Students may not realize that phrases such as *one hundred rubles' worth* are possessive. Point out that the phrase could also be expressed as "the worth of one hundred rubles." Then have volunteers write the following phrases on the board, punctuating them correctly: *ten dollars' worth, a lifetime's worth, seven weeks' worth.*

◆ Literary Focus

④ Parable As Pahom's actions indicate, one of the lessons this story teaches is that the more people have, the more they want. Ask students to agree or disagree with this view. *Some students may agree, and cite examples. Others may disagree, not having a basis for seeing the statement as true.*

⑤ Enrichment The Bashkirs live "far away" from Pahom's present home, but their land is still in Europe, not Asia. Pahom is moving eastward (somewhat like America's westward-moving pioneers) in search of cheaper and more abundant land.

Customize for
Visual/Spatial Learners

These students might enjoy looking at a topographical map of Russia to get a sense of the vast distances Pahom covered in his quest for land. Ask them to find some of the points of reference in the story: the Volga, the Samara, and the plains or steppes

---

would all be fine and close together."

The question of buying freehold land recurred to him again and again.

He went on in the same way for three years, renting land and sowing wheat. The seasons turned out well and the crops were good, so that he began to lay by money. He might have gone on living contentedly, but he grew tired of having to rent other people's land every year and having to scramble for it. Wherever there was good land to be had, the peasants would rush for it and it was taken up at once, so that unless you were sharp about it, you got none. It happened in the third year that he and a dealer together rented a piece of pasture land from some peasants, and they had already plowed it up, when there was some dispute and the peasants went to law about it, and things fell out so that the labor was all lost.

> ◆ **Reading Strategy**
> ① What are you learning about Pahom's personality?

"If it were my own land," thought Pahom, "I should be independent, and there wouldn't be all this unpleasantness."

So Pahom began looking out for land which he could buy, and he came across a peasant who had bought thirteen hundred acres, but having got into difficulties was willing to sell again cheap. Pahom bargained and haggled with him, and at last they settled the price at fifteen hundred rubles, part in cash and part to be paid later. They had all but clinched the matter when a passing dealer happened to stop at Pahom's one day to get feed for his horses. He drank tea with Pahom, and they had a talk. The dealer said that he was just returning from the land of the Bashkirs,[7] far

---

7. **Bashkirs** (bash kirz'): Nomadic people who live in the plains of southwestern Russia.

---

away, where he had bought thirteen thousand acres of land, all for a thousand rubles. Pahom questioned him further, and the dealer said:

"All one has to do is to make friends with the chiefs. I gave away about one hundred rubles' worth of silk robes and carpets, besides a case of tea, and I gave wine to those who would drink it; and I got the land for less than three kopecks[8] an acre." And he showed Pahom the title deed, saying:

"The land lies near a river, and the whole steppe is virgin soil."

Pahom plied him with questions, and the dealer said:

"There's more land there than you could cover if you walked a year, and it all belongs to the Bashkirs. They're as simple as sheep, and land can be got almost for nothing."

"There, now," thought Pahom, "with my one thousand rubles, why should I get only thirteen hundred acres, and saddle myself with a debt besides? If I take it out there, I can get more than ten times as much for my money."

5

Pahom inquired how to get to the place, and as soon as the grain dealer had left him, he prepared to go there himself. He left his wife to look after the homestead, and started on his journey, taking his hired man with him. They stopped at a town on their way and bought a case of tea, some wine, and other presents, as the grain dealer had advised.

On and on they went until they had gone more than three hundred miles, and on the seventh day they came to a place where the Bashkirs had pitched their round tents. It was all just as the dealer had said. The people lived on the

---

8. **kopecks** (kō´ peks) *n.*: Russian money, equal to one hundredth of a ruble.

---

136 ◆ Striving for Success

The Hay Harvest, Boris Kustodiev, St. Petersburg, Russia

❻ Interpret Students may say that owning a lot of land involves the responsibility and work of maintaining it and keeping it productive. To do so, an owner may need to employ other people.

◆ **Critical Thinking**

❼ Infer Let students know the Bashkirs are nomads, people traveling from place to place in search of food, water, and grazing land. Based on this passage, ask students what might be Pahom's opinion about the Bashkir men. *Students will probably say that because Pahom places such value on land ownership he does not respect the men.*

❽ Clarification Tell students that Pahom needs an interpreter because the Bashkirs, who are a Muslim people, speak a Turkic language.

◆ **Critical Thinking**

❾ Infer Ask students what inferences they can make about Bashkir culture, based on details in this passage and in earlier passages. *The Bashkirs are probably a nomadic people, since they don't live in tents or place much importance on land ownership. They are probably a peaceful people, since they welcome Pahom without hostility. Based on their treatment of Pahom—bringing him to one of the best tents and giving him cushions and tea, they probably place great importance on hospitality, even to strangers.*

❻ ▲ Critical Viewing Based on this painting, what do you learn about the responsibility of owning a lot of land? [Interpret]

steppe,[9] by a river, in felt-covered tents. They neither tilled the ground nor ate bread. Their cattle and horses grazed in herds on the steppe. The colts were tethered behind the tents, and the mares were driven to them twice a day. The mares were milked, and from the milk kumiss[10] was made. It was the women who prepared the kumiss, and they also **❼** made cheese. As far as the men were

concerned, drinking kumiss and tea, eating mutton, and playing on their pipes was all they cared about. They were all stout and merry, and all the summer long they never thought of doing any work. They were quite ignorant, and knew no Russian, but were good-natured enough. **❼**

As soon as they saw Pahom, they came out of their tents and gathered around the visitor. An interpreter was found, and Pahom told them he had come about some land. The Bashkirs seemed very glad; they took Pahom and led him into one of the best tents, where they made him sit on some down cushions placed on a carpet, while they sat around him. They gave him some tea **❽** **❾**

9. steppe (step) *n.*: High grassland of central Asia.
10. kumiss (k$\overline{oo}$′ mis) *n.*: Mare's milk that has been fermented and is used as a drink.

How Much Land Does a Man Need? ◆ 137

Humanities: Art

The Hay Harvest by Boris Kustodiev.

The Russian peasants harvesting hay in this painting are very much like those that Tolstoy might have seen in the countryside where he lived.

Boris Kustodiev (1878–1933) is not well known today, but in his day he was famous for his brightly colored paintings of country and small-town life. Popular in the Soviet Union in the early twentieth century, Kustodiev's paintings celebrated Soviet ideals.

Use these questions for discussion:
1. Does this painting have a joyous or a somber mood? Which specific part of the story would

it best illustrate? *The line of the path and the river give the painting a feeling of lively, joyous motion. The women seem happy working the land together. The painting depicts what life could have been like for Pahom and the other peasants if they had bought land together.*

2. What does this painting tell you about the life of a peasant in Russia? *It indicates that life involved hard work but perhaps that community feeling was strong.*

137

**Listening to Literature
Audiocassettes** The conversation between Pahom and the
Bashkirs demonstrates Pahom's
obsessive nature and is a good point
at which to introduce the audiocassette recording of this selection. Play
this section of the selection to the
whole class and then have them read
through to the end.

Comprehension Check ☑

❶ Why might these nomads find
Pahom's request amusing? *Nomads do
not own land in the traditional sense;
they simply use what they find and
move on.*

❷ Clarification Make sure that
students understand that a deed is
a legal document that grants title for
a piece of land to the deed holder.
When Pahom says this will "make it
secure," he means that it will protect
him from other people's claims on
the land.

❸ Clarification Tell students that
in earlier times very few people in
tribes such as the Bashkirs could
write. They might have a single *scribe*,
or person with writing skills, to take
care of all their written tasks.

and kumiss, and had a sheep killed, and
gave him mutton to eat. Pahom took
presents out of his cart and distributed
them among the Bashkirs, and divided
the tea amongst them. The Bashkirs
were delighted. They talked a great deal
among themselves and then told the
interpreter what to say.

"They wish to tell you," said the interpreter, "that they like you and that it's
our custom to do all we can to please a
guest and to repay him for his gifts. You
have given us presents, now tell us
which of the things we possess please
you best, that we may present them to
you."

"What pleases me best here,"
answered Pahom, "is your land. Our
land is crowded and the soil is worn out,
but you have plenty of land, and it is
good land. I never saw the likes of it."

❶ The interpreter told the Bashkirs what
Pahom had said. They talked among
themselves for a while. Pahom could not
understand what they were saying, but
saw that they were much amused and
heard them shout and laugh. Then they
were silent and looked at Pahom while
the interpreter said:

"They wish me to tell you that in
return for your presents they will gladly
give you as much land as you want. You
have only to point it out with your hand
and it is yours."

The Bashkirs talked again for a while
and began to dispute. Pahom asked
what they were disputing about, and the
interpreter told him that some of them
thought they ought to ask their chief
about the land and not act in his
absence, while others thought there was
no need to wait for his return.

6

While the Bashkirs were disputing, a
man in a large fox-fur cap appeared on
the scene. They all became silent and

rose to their feet. The interpreter said:
"This is our chief himself."

Pahom immediately fetched the best
dressing gown and five pounds of tea,
and offered these to the chief. The chief
accepted them and seated himself in the
place of honor. The Bashkirs at once
began telling him something. The chief
listened for a while, then made a sign
with his head for them to be silent, and
addressing himself to Pahom, said in
Russian:

"Well, so be it. Choose whatever piece
of land you like; we have plenty of it."

"How can I take as much as I like?"
thought Pahom. "I must get a deed to
make it secure, or else they may say: 'It
is yours,' and afterward may take it
away again."

❷ "Thank you for your kind words," he
said aloud. "You have much land, and I
only want a little. But I should like to be
sure which portion is mine. Could it not
be measured and made over to me? Life
and death are in God's hands. You good
people give it to me, but your children
might wish to take it back again."

"You are quite right," said the chief.
"We will make it over to you."

"I heard that a dealer had been here,"
continued Pahom, "and that you gave
him a little land, too, and signed title
deeds to that effect. I should like to have
it done in the same way."

The chief understood.

❸ "Yes," replied he, "that can be done
quite easily. We have a scribe, and we
will go to town with you and have the
deed properly sealed."

"And what will be the price?" asked
Pahom.

"Our price is always the same: one
thousand rubles a day."

Pahom did not understand.

"A day? What measure is that? How
many acres would that be?"

138 ◆ *Striving for Success*

Beyond the Classroom

Career Connection

Interpreting English language learners may not
have considered that their bilingual skills may be
useful in the workplace.

Point out the role of the interpreter in this
story. He listens to both sides and translates
what the people are saying. He is equally fluent
in Russian and in the language of the Bashkirs.

Have students list skills that a good interpreter should have. *Besides facility with languages,
interpreters must have tact, good listening skills, good
speaking skills, and so on.*

Then let students work in pairs to decide
what kinds of businesses or services might use
interpreters and for what reasons. Are there any
local businesses or individuals who might hire a
student as an interpreter? Ask them to formulate
their ideas as a list and then present their lists to
the class. Write new ideas on the board as they
are mentioned. Point out the variety of places
where bilingual students might use their skills as
interpreters.

"We do not know how to reckon it out," said the chief. "We sell it by the day. As much as you can go around on your feet in a day is yours, and the price is one thousand rubles a day."

Pahom was surprised.

4 "But in a day you can get around a large tract of land," he said.

The chief laughed.

"It will all be yours!" said he. "But there is one condition: If you don't return on the same day to the spot whence you started, your money is lost."

"But how am I to mark the way that I have gone?"

"Why, we shall go to any spot you like and stay there. You must start from that spot and make your round, taking a spade with you. Wherever you think necessary, make a mark. At every turning, **5** dig a hole and pile up the turf; then afterward we will go around with a plow from hole to hole. You may make as large a circuit as you please, but before the sun sets you must return to the place you started from. All the land you cover will be yours."

Pahom was delighted. It was decided to start early next morning. They talked a while, and after drinking some more kumiss and eating some more mutton, they had tea again, and then the night came on. They gave Pahom a featherbed to sleep on, and the Bashkirs dispersed for the night, promising to assemble the next morning at daybreak and ride out before sunrise to the appointed spot.

7

Pahom lay on the featherbed, but could not sleep. He kept thinking about the land.

"What a large tract I'll mark off!" thought he, "I can easily do thirty-five **6** miles in a day. The days are long now, and within a circuit of thirty-five miles what a lot of land there will be! I'll sell the poorer land or let it to peasants, but I'll pick out the best and farm it myself. I'll buy two ox teams and hire two more laborers. About a hundred and fifty acres shall be plowland, and I'll pasture cattle on the rest."

Pahom lay awake all night and dozed off only just before dawn. Hardly were his eyes closed when he had a dream. He thought he was lying in that same tent and heard somebody chuckling outside. He wondered who it could be, and rose and went out, and he saw the Bashkir chief sitting in front of the tent holding his sides and rolling about with laughter. Going nearer to the chief, Pahom asked: "What are you laughing at?" But he saw that it was no longer the chief but the grain dealer who had recently stopped at his house and had told him about the land. Just as Pahom was going to ask: "Have you been here long?" he saw that it was not the dealer, but the peasant who had come up from the Volga long ago, to Pahom's old home. Then he saw that it was not the peasant either, but the Devil himself with hoofs and horns, sitting there and chuckling, and before him lay a man, prostrate on the ground, barefooted, with only trousers and a shirt on. And Pahom dreamed that he looked more attentively to see what sort of man it was lying there, and he saw that the man was dead, and that it was himself. Horror-struck, he awoke.

> ◆ **Reading Strategy**
> How does this dream help you predict what will happen? **7**

"What things one dreams about!" thought he.

Looking around he saw through the open door that the dawn was breaking.

"It's time to wake them up," thought he. "We ought to be starting."

He got up, roused his man (who was sleeping in his cart), bade him harness,

4 Predict Based on Character Traits Have students recall Pahom's behavior thus far and predict how he will proceed as he measures his land according to the Bashkirs' rules. *He will probably be greedy and try to obtain as much as he can.*

◆ **Build Vocabulary**

5 Using Words in Other Contexts: Land-Related Words Have students use context clues to infer the meaning of the word *turf*. *Turf refers to a clump of sod or dirt.* Explain that *turf* may also be used casually to mean a piece of territory claimed by a person or group. Ask: How are these two meanings of *turf* related? *Both have to do with land.*

6 Enrichment Thirty-five miles is a very long distance to walk in one day. Tell students that if Pahom does walk that far—forming a square with 8.75 miles on each side—he will acquire 76.5 square miles of land, or 48,960 acres.

◆ **Reading Strategy**

7 Predict Based on Character Traits Elicit the following: *Pahom's dream foreshadows his death; the presence of the Devil seems to indicate that Pahom's greed will lead to his destruction.*

▶Critical Viewing◀

1 Connect Elicit the following: *The photograph shows a vast expanse of land that seems never to end. The endless quality reflects the theme of never having enough. There will always be more land to acquire.*

2 Analyze Ask students what is revealed by the Bashkirs' ability to remain in the same spot for an entire day. Do they think that Pahom would be able to do this? Why or why not? *Suggested response: The Bashkirs are patient and don't seem overly concerned with material things. Pahom would probably not be able to do this. He is impatient and eager to do work that he sees as gainful.*

◆ *Literature and Your Life*

3 Students might say that they feel excited and overwhelmed or that they can feel greed building up inside them. Some students may add that because they can have as much as they want, their desire decreases.

Customize for
English Language Learners
A few idioms on this page may need clarification for English language learners. Have native English speakers assist their classmates by restating the following in their own words: *It's high time* and *Dawn was beginning to kindle.* The phrases mean *the time has come* and *the sky was turning the color of fire.*

Customize for
Less Proficient Readers
Before they begin reading this page, tell students to note when Pahom turns the three corners to form the sides of his new property. This will help them keep track of his progress.

1 ▲ Critical Viewing How does the setting in this picture relate to the theme of this parable? [Connect]

and went to call the Bashkirs.

"It's time to go to the steppe to measure the land," he said.

The Bashkirs rose and assembled, and the chief came, too. Then they began drinking kumiss again, and offered Pahom some tea, but he would not wait.

"If we are to go, let's go. It's high time," said he.

8

2 The Bashkirs got ready and they all started; some mounted on horses and some in carts. Pahom drove in his own small cart with his servant and took a spade with him. When they reached the steppe, the red dawn was beginning to kindle. They ascended a hillock (called by the Bashkirs a shikhan) and, dismounting from their carts and their horses, gathered in one spot. The chief came up to Pahom and, stretching out his arm toward the plain:

"See," said he, "all this, as far as your eye can reach, is ours. You may have any part of it you like."

Pahom's eyes glistened: it was all virgin soil, as flat as the palm of your hand, as black as the seed of a poppy, and in the hollows different kinds of grasses grew breast-high.

2

◆ *Literature and Your Life*
How do you feel when someone offers you as much as you want of something?

3

140 ◆ *Striving for Success*

 Humanities: Photography

Road in Field by D. Brookover.

This photograph of a road winding away in a field of grain illustrates the principle of *linear perspective*. To create the illusion of three-dimensionality, objects appear smaller as they recede into the distance, and lines that seem parallel actually converge at a vanishing point on the horizon. This vision of land as far as the eye can see would have tempted Pahom.

Use these questions for discussion:

1. How do you think this scene would have made Pahom feel? *Students may say he would have become excited at the prospect of trying to buy this land, or they might say he would have felt envy because he did not own it.*

2. How would you react to owning such a vast tract of land? *Some students may think they would enjoy the feeling of ownership; others may think life would be lonely.*

The chief took off his fox-fur cap, placed it on the ground, and said:

"This will be the mark. Start from here, and return here again. All the land you go around shall be yours."

Pahom took out his money and put it on the cap. Then he took off his outer coat, remaining in his sleeveless undercoat. He unfastened his girdle and tied it tight below his stomach, put a little bag of bread into the breast of his coat, and, tying a flask of water to his girdle,[11] he drew up the tops of his boots, took the spade from his man, and stood ready to start. He considered for some moments which way he had better go—it was tempting everywhere.

"No matter," he concluded, "I'll go toward the rising sun."

He turned his face to the east, stretched himself, and waited for the sun to appear above the rim.

"I must lose no time," he thought, "and it's easier walking while it's still cool."

The sun's rays had hardly flashed above the horizon when Pahom, carrying the spade over his shoulder, went down into the steppe.

Pahom started walking neither slowly nor quickly. After having gone a thousand yards he stopped, dug a hole, and placed pieces of turf one on another to make it more visible. Then he went on; and now that he had walked off his stiffness he quickened his pace. After a while he dug another hole.

Pahom looked back. The hillock could be distinctly seen in the sunlight, with the people on it, and the glittering iron rims of the cartwheels. At a rough guess Pahom concluded that he had walked three miles. It was growing warmer; he took off his undercoat, slung it across his shoulder, and went on again. It had

11. **girdle** (gurd´ əl) *n.:* Belt or sash.

grown quite warm now; he looked at the sun—it was time to think of breakfast.

"The first shift is done, but there are four in a day, and it's too soon yet to turn. But I'll just take off my boots," said he to himself.

He sat down, took off his boots, stuck them into his girdle, and went on. It was easy walking now.

"I'll go on for another three miles," thought he, "and then turn to the left. This spot is so fine that it would be a pity to lose it. The further one goes, the better the land seems."

He went straight on for a while, and when he looked around, the hillock was scarcely visible and the people on it looked like black ants, and he could just see something glistening there in the sun.

"Ah," thought Pahom, "I have gone far enough in this direction; it's time to turn. Besides, I'm in a regular sweat, and very thirsty."

He stopped, dug a large hole, and heaped up pieces of turf. Next he untied his flask, had a drink, and then turned sharply to the left. He went on and on; the grass was high, and it was very hot.

Pahom began to grow tired: he looked at the sun and saw that it was noon.

"Well," he thought, "I must have a rest."

He sat down, and ate some bread and drank some water; but he did not lie down, thinking that if he did he might fall asleep. After sitting a little while, he went on again. At first he walked easily; the food had strengthened him; but it had become terribly hot and he felt sleepy. Still he went on, thinking: "An hour to suffer, a lifetime to live."

He went a long way in this direction also, and was about to turn to the left again, when he perceived a damp hollow:

How Much Land Does a Man Need? ◆ 141

◆ **Critical Thinking**

4 **Infer** Ask students how they think Pahom is feeling at this point in the story. How can they tell? *Pahom is feeling optimistic. He is ready to go, and starts out in the direction of the rising sun—a symbol for hope. They might also say he is feeling greedy, "it was tempting everywhere."*

◆ **Literary Focus**

5 **Connect** Have students contemplate how this passage relates to the message that Tolstoy is trying to convey. *The passage conveys Pahom's inability to restrain his greed.*

Comprehension Check ☑

6 To make sure students understand that Pahom is following the instructions he was given by the chief, ask them why Pahom digs a hole and heaps up pieces of turf. *That is how the chief told him to mark his turnings.*

◆ **Critical Thinking**

7 **Infer** Have students discuss how Pahom's observation might foreshadow the outcome of the story. *Suggested response: The comment "a lifetime to live" is an ironic foreshadowing because Pahom is not going to live to enjoy the land.*

141

◆ Reading Strategy

❶ Predict Based on Character Traits Students will probably predict that, based on his character and past actions in this parable, Pahom will try to include more land.

◆ Literary Focus

❷ Parable Pahom now sees the error of his ways, but he is still unable to stop. Ask: Has Pahom learned a lesson from this experience? How do you know? *Students will probably say that Pahom has not learned a lesson. Although he now recognizes that his greed has made him foolish and hasty, he is not yet willing to make the necessary sacrifices to save himself. He is trying to beat the odds to make it back on time to claim his land.*

◆ Critical Thinking

❸ Infer Have students discuss what the Bashkirs would be likely to think of Pahom's actions. *Suggested response: They probably think he's very foolish. Most likely they don't understand why owning this land is so important to him.*

Customize for
More Advanced Students

Have these students consider why the author causes his main character to suffer the way he does. *This is a moralistic parable, and the author wants to underscore Pahom's fall in grasping for more than he needs.*

◆ **Reading Strategy**
❶ Based on Pahom's character, predict whether he will try to include any more land.

"It would be a pity to leave that out," he thought. "Flax would do well there." So he went on past the hollow and dug a hole on the other side of it before he made a sharp turn. Pahom looked toward the hillock. The heat made the air hazy: it seemed to be quivering, and through the haze the people on the hillock could scarcely be seen.

"Ah," thought Pahom, "I have made the sides too long; I must make this one shorter." And he went along the third side, stepping faster. He looked at the sun: it was nearly halfway to the horizon, and he had not yet done two miles of the third side of the square. He was still ten miles from the goal.

"No," he thought, "though it will make my land lopsided, I must hurry back in a straight line now. I might go too far, and as it is I have a great deal of land."

So Pahom hurriedly dug a hole and turned straight toward the hillock.

9

Pahom went straight toward the hillock, but he now walked with difficulty. He was exhausted from the heat, his bare feet were cut and bruised, and his legs began to fail. He longed to rest, but it was impossible if he meant to get back before sunset. The sun waits for no man, and it was sinking lower and lower.

"Oh, Lord," he thought, "if only I have not blundered trying for too much! What if I am too late?"

He looked toward the hillock and at the sun. He was still far from his goal, and the sun was already near the rim of the sky.

Pahom walked on and on; it was very hard walking, but he went quicker and quicker. He pressed on, but was still far from the place. He began running, threw

away his coat, his boots, his flask, and his cap, and kept only the spade which he used as a support.

"What am I to do?" he thought again. "I've grasped too much and ruined the whole affair. I can't get there before the sun sets."

And this fear made him still more breathless. Pahom kept on running; his trousers stuck to him, and his mouth was parched. His breast was working like a blacksmith's bellows, his heart was beating like a hammer, and his legs were giving way as if they did not belong to him. Pahom was seized with terror lest he should die of the strain.

Though afraid of death, he could not stop.

"After having run all that way they will call me a fool if I stop now," thought he.

And he ran on and on, and drew near and heard the Bashkirs yelling and shouting to him, and their cries inflamed his heart still more. He gathered his last strength and ran on.

The sun was close to the rim of the sky and, cloaked in mist, looked large, and red as blood. Now, yes, now, it was about to set! The sun was quite low, but he was also quite near his goal. Pahom could already see the people on the hillock waving their arms to make him hurry. He could see the fox-fur cap on the ground and the money in it, and the chief sitting on the ground holding his sides. And Pahom remembered his dream.

"There's plenty of land," thought he, "but will God let me live on it? I have lost my life, I have lost my life! Never will I reach that spot!"

Pahom looked at the sun, which had reached the earth: one side of it had already disappeared. With all his remaining strength he rushed on, bending his body forward so that his legs could hardly follow fast enough to keep

---

Speaking and Listening Mini-Lesson

Eulogy

This mini-lesson supports the Speaking and Listening activity in the Idea Bank on p. 145.

Introduce the Concept Explain that a eulogy is a tribute that is often read aloud or spoken at a funeral by someone who knew the deceased well.

Develop Background Remind students that a eulogy says positive things to celebrate the life of the deceased. Encourage students to:

- work in pairs to brainstorm for positive things to say about Pahom.
- point out that Pahom's example provided a lesson from which others can learn.
- recall an incident that particularly illustrates an aspect of Pahom's personality.

Apply the Information Have students work individually to write eulogies for Pahom. Suggest that they practice delivering their eulogies before presenting them orally to the class.

Assess the Outcome Evaluate the eulogies based on content and delivery. Did the eulogy include examples that illustrated Pahom's personality? Was it delivered in language and tone appropriate to the occasion? Have students use Peer Assessment: Speaker/Speech (p. 121) in *Alternative Assessment* for guidance on evaluating one another's speeches.

him from falling. Just as he reached the hillock it suddenly grew dark. He looked up—the sun had already set!

He gave a cry: "All my labor has been in vain," thought he, and was about to stop, but he heard the Bashkirs still shouting and remembered that though to him, from below, the sun seemed to have set, they on the hillock could still see it. He took a long breath and ran up the hillock. It was still light there. He reached the top and saw the cap. Before it sat the chief, laughing and holding his sides. Again Pahom remembered his dream, and he uttered a cry: his legs gave way beneath him, he fell forward and reached the cap with his hands.

"Ah, that's a fine fellow!" exclaimed the chief. "He has gained much land!"

Pahom's servant came running up and tried to raise him, but he saw that blood was flowing from his mouth. Pahom was dead.

The Bashkirs clicked their tongues to show their pity.

His servant picked up the spade and dug a grave long enough for Pahom to lie in, and buried him in it.

Six feet from his head to his toes was all he needed.

◆ **Literary Focus**
What lesson do you learn from Pahom's experiences?

❹

❺

Guide for Responding

◆ Literature and Your Life

Reader's Response Do you sympathize with Pahom? Why or why not?

Thematic Focus Ultimately, Pahom pays for "success" with his life. What price are you willing to pay for success?

Group Discussion Like Pahom, many people find themselves always wanting something *more* to make them happy. With a group of classmates, brainstorm for a list of reasons why some people are dissatisfied with what they have.

☑ Check Your Comprehension

1. What does Pahom believe is the only trouble that peasants face?
2. How does Pahom come to buy his first parcel of land?
3. List three problems Pahom experiences as he increases his land holdings.
4. How do the Bashkirs determine how much land a man can own?
5. Briefly summarize what happens on the last day of Pahom's life.

Beyond Literature

History Connection

Russia in the Twentieth Century In 1922, Russia became part of the newly established Union of Soviet Socialist Republics (USSR), better known as the Soviet Union. The Soviet Union initially consisted of four republics, with the Russian Republic being the strongest and most influential one. The Soviet Union gained further territory after World War II, under Joseph Stalin's rule. Increasing disillusionment with communism and demands for greater freedoms led to the eventual defeat of Communist party rule and the dissolution of the Soviet Union in 1991. Throughout the Soviet era and the years that followed, Russia has remained a highly agricultural society, like the one depicted in the story. Conduct research to find out how Russia is adapting to a changing economic climate in an increasingly industrial and technological world.

How Much Land Does a Man Need? ◆ 143

Beyond the Selection

FURTHER READING

Other Works by Leo Tolstoy
"The Death of Ivan Ilyich"
"Master and Man"

Other Works With the Theme of Greed
A Christmas Carol, Charles Dickens
The story of King Midas, Greek myth
We suggest that you preview these works before recommending them to your students.

INTERNET

Students can learn more about the author and his work at the following Web sites. Please be aware that sites may have changed from the time we published this information.
http://www. he.net/~works/tolstoy/life.html
http://www.ece. arizona.edu/~melcher/ moscow/tolstoy.html
We *strongly recommend* that you preview sites before sending students to them.

◆ Literary Focus

❹ **Parable** Students might say they learned the lesson that greed does not bring satisfaction, and that it can lead a person to isolation and even tragedy.

◆ Critical Thinking

❺ **Analyze** Remind students that irony is a literary technique that involves amusing contradictions. Ask students why this ending is ironic. *It is ironic because Pahom desired more and more land, and yet it took so little land to lay him to rest.*

Enrichment Tolstoy's story echoes the biblical parable of the rich fool (Luke 12:16–20). Bring in a copy of the Bible and read this parable to the class. Then have students discuss the parallels between the biblical parable and Tolstoy's story.

Reinforce and Extend

Answers

◆ Literature and Your Life

Reader's Response Some students might sympathize with Pahom for having lost a sense of community during his quest for more land; others might feel he deserves his fate.

Thematic Focus Possible responses include sacrificing material things or missing out on certain pleasurable activities.

☑ Check Your Comprehension

1. Pahom believes the only trouble that peasants face is that they don't have enough land.
2. He buys forty acres from the landlady by paying her a deposit and undertaking to pay the remainder within two years.
3. Peasants keep trespassing on his land, someone cuts down five young lime trees, his land is too far from the town market, he can't grow wheat on fallow fields.
4. A man can own as much land as he can walk around in one day. The price for one day's walk is one thousand rubles.
5. In his greed, Pahom walks so much of the land he cannot get back in time to own it. Although he does arrive before sunset, he dies from the effort.

143

◆ Critical Thinking

1. At first he's grateful for it, but then he begins to resent peasants trespassing on his land. At the same time, he grows greedy for more land.

2. Pahom believes in deeds and the exclusive rights of ownership, while the nomadic Bashkirs believe in communal sharing of the land.

3. The last sentence answers the title question by saying a man needs only enough land in which to be buried.

4. Some students will say many people are tempted by greed and would behave as Pahom did; others would say that most people have more control over themselves.

5. (a) Students may suggest characters from myths or fairy tales, such as King Midas or the farmer whose goose laid the golden eggs. (b) These characters usually lose everything.

◆ Reading Strategy

1. He quickens his pace to cover more ground; he takes off his boots to walk more comfortably; he goes past a hollow and digs a hole on the other side of it even though he should have turned.

2. Students may find the ending satisfying in that it points up the futility of Pahom's ambitions.

◆ Literary Focus

1. The lesson is that greed does not end in satisfaction.

2. A possible response is that "How Much Land Does a Man Need?" could be used to teach humility and to illustrate the futility of living a materialistic existence.

◆ Build Vocabulary

Using Words in Other Contexts
1. sheaf; 2. fallow

Using the Word Bank
1. arable; 2. disparaged;
3. aggrieved; 4. piqued

◆ Build Grammar Skills

1. Pahom's heart kindled with desire.
2. He gave away about a hundred rubles' worth of silk robes and carpets.
3. It was the Bashkirs' custom to sell land by the day.
4. The chief's real identity is

Guide for Responding (continued)

◆ Critical Thinking

INTERPRET
1. How and why does Pahom's attitude toward his first plot of land change? **[Analyze]**
2. How do Pahom's and the Bashkirs' attitudes toward landownership differ? **[Compare and Contrast]**
3. How does the last sentence in the story reflect the message that answers the title question? **[Connect]**

EVALUATE
4. Explain whether you think that most people would behave as Pahom does if they were put in his situation. **[Make a Judgment]**

EXTEND
5. (a) Name one other character you know from literature who, like Pahom, is never satisfied with what he or she has. (b) What happens to this character? **[Literature Link]**

◆ Reading Strategy

PREDICT BASED ON CHARACTER TRAITS
Based on Pahom's greed, you were probably able to **predict**—make an educated guess—that he would try to wrestle a large parcel of land from the Bashkirs.
1. Identify two things Pahom said or did that helped you predict he would try to take more land than he should have from the Bashkirs.
2. Did you find this ending satisfying? Surprising? Explain.

◆ Literary Focus

PARABLE
Tolstoy's story of ownership and greed is classified as a **parable,** a special type of story that teaches a lesson.
1. What is the lesson that Tolstoy's parable teaches?
2. Parables are often used as a means of religious instruction. How might "How Much Land Does a Man Need?" be used for this purpose?

◆ Build Vocabulary

USING WORDS IN OTHER CONTEXTS
Words that have very specific meanings in one context often have a broader meaning in a broader context. For instance, in the context of land cultivation, *sheaf* refers to a bundle of grain stalks. In a broader context, *sheaf* is also used to describe any collection of things gathered together—such as a *sheaf* of paper.

Choose a word from the Word Bank to complete each sentence.
1. The landowner stormed into the house, holding a ____?____ of bills in his hand.
2. His mind has gone ____?____ ; he hasn't read a book in a month.

USING THE WORD BANK
Choose the word from the Word Bank that best fits each sentence. Write the complete sentence in your notebook.
1. Although the area used to be a desert, irrigation made the land ____?____ .
2. Pahom's sister-in-law ____?____ the country ways.
3. The ____?____ peasants complained to the landowner.
4. Pahom was ____?____ by his neighbor's inconsiderate behavior.

◆ Build Grammar Skills

POSSESSIVE NOUNS
The **possessive** form of a noun or pronoun shows ownership, belonging, or another close relationship.

Practice Copy the following sentences in your notebook, using the possessive form of the noun in parentheses.
1. (Pahom) heart kindled with desire.
2. He gave away about one hundred (rubles) worth of silk robes and carpets.
3. It was the (Bashkirs) custom to sell land by the day.
4. The (chief) real identity is revealed at the end of the story.

revealed at the end of the story.

 Writer's Solution

For additional instruction and practice, use the page on Apostrophes (p. 110) in the *Writer's Solution Grammar Practice Book.*

*B*uild *Y*our *P*ortfolio

Idea Bank

Writing

1. **Newspaper Article** Write a news article that reports the events leading up to Pahom's death. You may include quotations from other characters who knew or met Pahom. **[Career Link]**

2. **Land Advertisement** Write an advertisement for a piece of property or a building near your home. Focus on good points, such as beautiful views or access to shopping malls. **[Career Link]**

3. **Parable** Using "How Much Land Does a Man Need?" as a model, write a contemporary parable. Choose a lesson you think would help people today. Teach your lesson by focusing on the actions of one or two main characters.

Speaking and Listening

4. **Update the Story** With a small group, improvise a scene from an updated version of this story. Perform your scene for the class. **[Performing Arts Link]**

5. **Eulogy** Prepare a eulogy—a speech about a person who has died—for Pahom. Look back at the story to recall some facts about his life. Deliver your eulogy to the class.

Projects

6. **Map of Russia** Make a map of Russia. On the map, label the various geographic regions and peoples—including the Bashkirs—that live in each region. **[Social Studies Link]**

7. **Scale Diagram of Pahom's Field** Create a scale diagram that shows the dimensions of Pahom's field. Use one-half inch to represent a mile. You may need to convert some measurements from the story into miles before you create your diagram. **[Math Link]**

Writing Mini-Lesson

Video Script

Have you ever read a story and thought, "That would make a great movie"? Now's your chance to try your hand at making one. Choose any of parts one through nine from "How Much Land Does a Man Need?" and write a **video script** for that part. The following tip will ensure that your video turns out as you envision it.

Writing Skills Focus: Clear Explanation of Procedure

A good video script gives a **clear explanation** of everything that will be seen and heard. If you want the camera to show a scene moving from left to right, state those directions clearly. Explain how you see settings, action, sounds, music, and spoken words working together. The following technical terms will help you explain your ideas clearly.

long shot: view from a distance, showing one or more people and the background
close-up: shot of a single person or object
pan: move the camera across the scene
zoom: adjust from a long shot to a close-up using a single lens
cut: move directly from one shot to another
audio dub: sound added to the video
voice-over: comment or narration by an unseen person

Prewriting Create a storyboard—a rough sketch of each scene in your video. Then decide how you will make the visual transition from one image to another.

Drafting Describe what will be heard as well as what will be seen. Use technical terms to explain clearly how the parts of the video script work together.

Revising Compare your draft with your storyboards. If your script does not have a clear explanation of each shot you mapped out, add the necessary instructions.

How Much Land Does a Man Need? ◆ 145

Customizing for
Performance Levels
Following are suggestions for matching Idea Bank topics with your students' performance levels:
    Less Advanced Students: 2, 4
    Average Students: 1, 5, 6
    More Advanced Students: 3, 7

Customizing for
Learning Modalities
Following are suggestions for matching Idea Bank topics with your students' learning modalities:
    Visual/Spatial: 6, 7
    Logical/Mathematical: 7
    Verbal/Linguistic: 3, 4, 5

 Writing Mini-Lesson

Refer students to the Writing Handbook, page 965, for instruction on the writing process, and page 969 for further information on drama.

 Writer's Solution

Writers at Work Videodisc
Have students view the videodisc segment (Ch. 8) featuring Larry Cataldo to hear some tips for writing clear explanations. Have students discuss how these tips can be applied to writing their video scripts.

Play frames 33166 to 42350

Writing Lab CD-ROM
Have students complete the tutorial on Creative Writing. Follow these steps:
1. Tell students to use the Story Line Diagram to map out plot elements.
2. Encourage them to view examples of dialogue in an audio-annotated Writing Model.
3. Allow time for drafting on the computer.
4. Direct students to complete the Peer Evaluation Checklists for drama.

Sourcebook
Have students use Chapter 6, Creative Writing (pp. 166–193), for additional support. The chapter includes an annotated student model of a script (p. 171).

✓ ASSESSMENT OPTIONS

Formal Assessment, Selection Test, pp. 29–31, and Assessment Resources Software. The selection test is designed so that it can be easily customized to the performance levels of your students. *Alternative Assessment,* p. 9, includes options for less advanced students, more advanced students, logical/mathematical learners, verbal/linguistic learners, bodily/kinesthetic learners, and visual/spatial learners.

PORTFOLIO ASSESSMENT
Use the following rubrics in the *Alternative Assessment* booklet to assess student writing:
Newspaper Article: Summary Rubric, p. 98
Land Advertisement: Persuasion Rubric, p. 105
Parable: Expression Rubric, p. 94

Guide for Reading

OBJECTIVES

1. To read, comprehend, and interpret poetry
2. To relate poetry to personal experience
3. To make inferences while reading poems
4. To identify stated and implied themes in poetry
5. To build vocabulary in context and learn the prefix *im-*
6. To recognize and apply subject and verb agreement
7. To write a submission letter using elaboration to give information
8. To respond to poetry through writing, speaking and listening, and projects

SKILLS INSTRUCTION

Vocabulary:
Prefixes: *im-*

Grammar:
Subject and Verb Agreement

Reading Strategy:
Make Inferences

Literary Focus:
Stated and Implied Theme in Poetry

Writing:
Elaboration to Give Information

Speaking and Listening:
Informal Debate (teacher edition)

Critical Viewing:
Analyze; Compare

PORTFOLIO OPPORTUNITIES

Writing: Letter to a Poet; Advertisement; Parody of a Poem

Writing Mini-Lesson: Submission Letter

Speaking and Listening: Informal Debate; Panel Discussion

Projects: Round Earth Demonstration; Oral Report

More About the Authors

Emily Dickinson's closest companions were her older brother and younger sister. In her youth, Dickinson went to school at Amherst Academy and Mount Holyoke Female Seminary.

Pat Mora has worked as a high school and college teacher, a college administrator, and the director of a museum. She has said, "I write, in part, because Hispanic perspectives need to be part of our literary heritage . . . [and] because I am fascinated by the pleasure and power of words."

Vassar Miller has said that poetry, like all art, "can transform the pain and ugliness of life into joy and beauty."

Emily Dickinson (1830–1886)

Like secret messages in a time capsule, many of Emily Dickinson's poems remained undiscovered and unread by the public during her lifetime. She wrote 1,775 poems, yet only seven were published—anonymously—before she died. Today, however, she is generally regarded as one of the greatest American poets.

Although she lived her life in virtual isolation, she explored the world through her poetry. The extent of Dickinson's talent was not widely recognized until 1955, when a complete, unedited edition of her poems was published.

Pat Mora (1942–)

Pat Mora is fascinated by borders. She herself was born and raised in El Paso, near the border that separates Mexico and the United States. During her childhood, she sometimes felt that living on the United States side of the border separated her not just from Mexico, but from her Mexican heritage and culture.

As an adult, she encourages today's young people to cross borders, feeling pride in their heritage but also appreciating cultural diversity. Her own Hispanic background is an important part of her writing.

Vassar Miller (1924–)

Vassar Miller's father probably didn't realize he was creating a world-class writer when he brought home a typewriter from his office! Yet his daughter—who typed her first poems on that secondhand typewriter—was once nominated for a Pulitzer Prize and was inducted into the Texas Women's Hall of Fame in 1997.

Miller has had cerebral palsy since birth. The faith and courage that have helped her face her physical challenges are apparent in her work. In addition to books of her own poetry, she has published *Despite This Flesh,* an anthology of poetry and stories about the disabled.

146 ◆ *Striving for Success*

◆ Build Vocabulary

PREFIXES: *im-*

In "I dwell in Possibility—", Emily Dickinson uses the word *impregnable*. *Impregnable* begins with the prefix *im-* (a variation of *in-*), which usually means "not." The meaning of *impregnable* is "not conquerable" or "not able to be captured."

WORD BANK

As you read these poems, you will encounter the words on this list. Each word is defined on the page where it first appears. Preview the list before you read.

impregnable
thrall
vertigo

◆ Build Grammar Skills

SUBJECT AND VERB AGREEMENT

Although poetry is different from other forms of writing, some basic rules still apply. One of these rules is **subject and verb agreement**—using a verb form that agrees in number (singular or plural) with its subject. Notice how the verbs change form in these examples:

Singular: A river *leaps.*
She *sighs.*

Plural: Rivers *leap.*
They *sigh.*

In each of these poems, notice that the verbs agree with their subjects.

Prentice Hall Literature Program Resources

REINFORCE / RETEACH / EXTEND

Selection Support Pages
Build Vocabulary: Prefixes: *im-*, p. 39
Build Grammar Skills: Subject/Verb Agreement, p. 40
Reading Strategy: Make Inferences, p. 41
Literary Focus: Stated and Implied Theme, p. 42

Strategies for Diverse Student Needs, p. 10

Beyond Literature Humanities Connection: Impressionist Art, p. 10

Formal Assessment Selection Test, pp. 32–34; Assessment Resources Software

Alternative Assessment, p. 10

Resource Pro CD-ROM
"Success is counted sweetest," "I dwell in Possibility—," "Uncoiling," "Columbus Dying"—includes all resource materials and customizable lesson plan

Writing and Language Transparencies,
Writing Process Model 9: Business Letter, pp. 61–64

Listening to Literature Audiocassettes
"Success is counted sweetest," "I dwell in Possibility—," "Uncoiling," "Columbus Dying"

Success is counted sweetest
◆ I dwell in Possibility— ◆
Uncoiling ◆ Columbus Dying

◆ *Literature and Your Life*

CONNECT YOUR EXPERIENCE

Every day, you make judgments about your experiences: worth it or not worth it, success or failure. Like you, the three poets in this group explore the positive and negative feelings that accompany the big and small struggles in life.

THEMATIC FOCUS: OVERCOMING OBSTACLES

The speakers in these four poems describe facing and overcoming obstacles. Each poem, however, will give you a unique answer to the question, "What does it take to succeed?"

Journal Writing In the center of a reaction wheel like the one shown, write a success you have recently had. In the outer sections of the circle, record the feelings you had as you worked to overcome obstacles to that success.

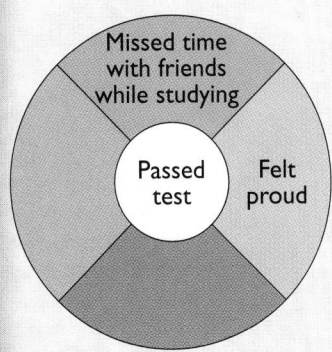

◆ Background for Understanding

LITERATURE

A person sprawled across a couch tells you he is relaxed without saying a word. Poems, too, can communicate through "body language." Some poems "sprawl" across the page, while others "sit" properly.

In a traditional poem, lines are grouped into stanzas, and new lines always begin at the left margin. In other poems, the shape of the poem on the page suggests an action, object, or idea. Three poems in this group have a traditional appearance. One, however, "Uncoiling," may surprise you with the way its appearance reflects the action named in the title.

◆ Literary Focus

STATED AND IMPLIED THEMES IN POETRY

Poems, like most works of literature, convey a **theme**—a central idea, concern, or message about life. In some poems, the theme is directly **stated.** In other poems, the theme is **implied**—the message is suggested, not stated. An implied theme may be revealed through events, the actions of a character, a speaker's words and attitude, or the details a poet chooses to include.

One of these Emily Dickinson poems has a stated theme: "Success is counted sweetest / By those who ne'er succeed." You must figure out the implied themes of the other poems in this group.

◆ Reading Strategy

MAKE INFERENCES

Like a letter from a friend, a poem brings you a message. To get the message, you may need to **make inferences**—reach conclusions based on evidence. You can infer the message of a poem, when it is not stated, from specific details and images.

For example, when you begin reading "Columbus Dying," you will encounter images of sick, starving sailors. From these images you can infer that this poem is not about the glory of Columbus's voyage. Use the other images and details in these poems to make inferences about their meanings.

Read aloud or write on the chalkboard the first two lines of Dickinson's first poem, "Success is counted sweetest/By those who ne'er succeed." Ask students to imagine that this is a motto written on a T-shirt or a bumper sticker. After discussing the meaning of these lines— that success is most glorified when it is most elusive—ask students if they agree or disagree with the motto, and why. You might also ask them for their own definitions of success. Let them know that each of these poems focuses on an aspect of success students may not have considered before.

Customize for
Less Proficient Readers

To ensure literal comprehension, review the "story" of each poem with less proficient readers. Encourage them to read each poem, then tell a partner, in their own words, what is happening in the poem.

Customize for
More Advanced Students

Invite more advanced students to compare the different styles of the three poets. For example, they might compare Emily Dickinson's and Vassar Miller's use of rhyme, or Vassar Miller's and Pat Mora's use of imagery.

Customize for
English Language Learners

Have English language learners listen to the recording as they follow in their books. Then have them pair with native speakers to take turns reading the poems aloud to each other.

Listening to Literature
Audiocassettes

Customize for
Musical/Rhythmic Learners

Encourage these learners to read the poems aloud several times, focusing on how slight differences in stress, tone of voice, or rhythm can bring out different nuances of feeling and meaning in the poems.

 ## Preparing for Standardized Tests

The ability to make inferences is a valuable reading skill, which students must apply in reading comprehension and critical reading items on standardized tests. For additional practice, use the Reading Strategy page in *Selection Support*, p. 41.

Grammar and Language Standardized tests may require identifying and correcting sentences whose subjects and verbs do not agree:

The hive of bees are buzzing loudly. *Incorrect; the singular verb* is *is required to agree with the singular subject* hive.

The sounds of the river is soothing. *Incorrect; the plural verb* are *is required to agree with the plural subject* sounds.

This lesson's Build Grammar Skills will help improve students' performance on such items. For more practice, use the Build Grammar Skills page on Subject-Verb Agreement, p. 40, in *Selection Support.*

One-Minute Insight

Emily Dickinson takes an ironic view of success. In "Success is counted sweetest," success is fully understood only by those to whom it is denied. In "I dwell in Possibility—," the poet paints a picture of a recluse who has attained no worldly trappings of success, yet feels successful. These poems should encourage students to look at success from a more psychological and personal perspective.

◆ Literary Focus

❶ Stated and Implied Theme Ask students if these two lines reveal a stated or an implied theme, and to tell the theme in their own words. *It is a stated theme. A possible rewording is, "People who don't succeed are the ones who best know how sweet success can be."*

◆ Build Grammar Skills

❷ Subject and Verb Agreement Ask students to identify the subject and verb in this sentence and explain why the two agree in number. *The subject is* <u>success</u> *and the verb is* <u>is</u>. *The singular subject requires the singular form of the verb.*

❸ Clarification Point out that "purple" is the color of victory, that "Host" means a large number (in this case, of soldiers), and that taking "the Flag" is what a victorious troop does in battle.

◆ Reading Strategy

❹ Make Inferences Ask students what the image "forbidden ear" suggests about the dying soldier, and how this image contributes to the meaning of the poem. *Students may say that "forbidden ear" suggests that the soldier is not permitted to know victory. It is an image that makes his sense of defeat all the harsher.*

►Critical Viewing◄

❺ Analyze *Some may think that a person who owns a house with a garden like this must be successful. Students who notice the transparent figure sitting on the bench may see the sitting figure as dwelling "in possibility." The scene around her may be a possibility in her imagination.*

148

Success is counted sweetest

Emily Dickinson

❶ Success is counted sweetest
❷ By those who ne'er succeed.
To comprehend a nectar[1]
Requires sorest need.

5 ❸ Not one of all the purple Host
Who took the Flag today
Can tell the definition
So clear of Victory

As he defeated—dying—
10 On whose forbidden ear
The distant strains of triumph ❹
Burst agonized and clear!

---

1. nectar (nek´ tər) *n.*: Something delicious to drink.

The Terrace at Meric, 1867, Frédéric Bazille, Cincinnati Museum of Art

▲ **Critical Viewing** What details in this painting suggest success or possibility? **[Analyze]** ❺

148 ◆ *Striving for Success*

Block Scheduling Strategies

Consider these suggestions to take advantage of extended class time:

- Introduce the prefix *im-*, then use the Build Vocabulary page in *Selection Support* (p. 39).
- Direct students to read and complete the activity on Impressionist Art. In small groups, they can discuss their ideas about Impressionism. They might also enjoy comparing and contrasting this style of painting to the poet's use of language in these selections.
- Let students work in small groups to answer the Critical Thinking questions on pages 149 and 151.

- Encourage students to work in small groups to prepare for the informal debate in the Speaking and Listening activity on page 153. Suggest they brainstorm for a list of examples from life, literature, or the movies that prove or disprove the wisdom of the two lines from "Success is counted sweetest."
- To assess their understanding of the poems, have students take the multiple-choice portion of the Selection Test, *Formal Assessment,* p. 32. You may wish to assign the test essay for homework.

I dwell in Possibility—

Emily Dickinson

I dwell in Possibility—
A fairer House than Prose—
More numerous of Windows—
Superior—for Doors—

5   Of Chambers as the Cedars—
Impregnable of Eye—
And for an Everlasting Roof—
The Gambrels[1] of the Sky—

Of Visiters[2]—the fairest—
10 For Occupation—This—
   The spreading wide my narrow Hands
   To gather Paradise—

1. **Gambrels:** Angled windows.
2. **Visiters:** Visitors.

◆ Build Vocabulary

Impregnable (im preg´ nə bəl) *adj.*:
Unconquerable; not able to be captured

Guide for Responding

◆ *Literature and Your Life*

Reader's Response With whom would you most like to share these poems? Why?

Thematic Focus Dickinson overcomes the obstacles of the "ordinary" world by using her imagination. Why do you think imagination is such a powerful positive force?

Journal Writing Make a list of ways in which imagination enriches your everyday experiences.

☑ Check Your Comprehension

1. To whom does success seem most sweet?
2. What thing does Dickinson use to represent "Possibility"?

◆ Critical Thinking

INTERPRET
1. Why does success seem sweeter to someone who has not achieved it? **[Interpret]**
2. Explain how the gesture the poet described in the last two lines of "I dwell in Possibility—" illustrates the statement she makes in the first two lines. **[Connect]**

EVALUATE
3. How much influence do you think imagination has on your approach to life? Decide whether Dickinson overstates the importance of imagination. **[Assess]**

APPLY
4. Which poem do you find easier to relate to your own life? Why? **[Relate]**

Success is counted sweetest/I dwell in Possibility— ◆ 149

◆ Critical Thinking

6 Interpret Invite students to explain the meaning of these lines. *Students might say that while the actual scope of the speaker's life is narrow, the workings of her imagination make her experience seem broad.*

Reinforce and Extend

Answers

◆ *Literature and Your Life*

Reader's Response Encourage students to describe the personalities of the individual they identify.

Thematic Focus Students may suggest that imagination allows people to envision positive outcomes.

☑ Check Your Comprehension

1. Success seems most sweet to people who do not succeed.
2. Dickinson uses a house with many windows and doors to represent possibility.

◆ Critical Thinking

1. Success seems sweeter to people who haven't achieved it because they build it up in their minds.
2. By spreading wide her narrow hands to gather Paradise, the speaker is confirming the ideas stated in the first two lines; her "real" world is small but her "possible" world is large.
3. Some students will say their imaginations help them create things or imagine their futures; others might say that Dickinson's emphasis on the life of the imagination promotes unsociable behavior.
4. Students who strive to succeed might choose "Success is counted sweetest," while students who tend toward introspection might choose "I dwell in Possibility—."

Speaking and Listening Mini-Lesson

Informal Debate

This mini-lesson supports the Speaking and Listening activity in the Idea Bank on p. 153.
Introduce the Concept Explain that an informal debate has fewer rules and guidelines than a formal debate. However, it is still important for students to represent their ideas and opinions clearly, and to support them with solid examples. Two rules of thumb follow:
1. Don't assert an opinion or disagree with anyone else's opinion unless you have specific evidence to support your point.
2. Be polite. Give each idea expressed serious consideration.

Develop Background As a class, review the literal meaning of Dickinson's statement. Brain-storm for some general examples of people who have not succeeded and yet wish for success, such as a defeated athlete, an actor who does not get a part, or an ambitious worker who fails to get promoted.

Apply the Information Form students into groups. They should develop specific and relevant examples for the side they are supporting. Then they should conduct their informal debates.

Assess the Outcome As a group, discuss the experience. What new insights into success and failure did students gain? To evaluate their listening skills during the informal debate, have them use the Listening Self-Assessment (p. 124) in the *Alternative Assessment* booklet.

One-Minute Insight

In some ways, these poems represent the dark side of success. Pat Mora's hurricane has "successfully" destroyed all in its path; Vassar Miller shows that in succeeding, Columbus lost his most precious possession—his faith in the meaning of life.

◆ Reading Strategy

① **Make Inferences** Ask students to suppose they didn't know that the poem is about a tornado. Which details would they use as clues? *Students might point out that a tornado might blow branches against a window, be characterized by dark clouds and lightning, and blow hawks and butterflies around.*

◆ Build Grammar Skills

② **Subject and Verb Agreement** Have students identify the subject and verb in this stanza. Have them explain why the two agree. *The subject (plural) is boulders; the verb is retreat.*

◆ Literary Focus

③ **Stated and Implied Theme** Ask students to identify the poem's implied theme and explain how it is revealed in this passage. *Students might say that the implied theme is one of destruction. The images of frightened women and the tornado blowing itself out into "sound" reveal the poem's theme.*

◆ Critical Thinking

④ **Analyze** Invite students to describe the poem's shape and discuss how it relates to the poem's meaning. *Students will probably point out that the poem is shaped like a tornado, extending the reader's experience from verbal to visual.*

▶Critical Viewing◀

⑤ **Compare** Students might point out that both the poem and the photograph portray a tornado as dark, coiled, and uncoiling. The photograph, however, shows only the tornado against the sky, whereas the poem shows the effects that the tornado has on human beings.

150

Uncoiling
Pat Mora

①
With thorns, she scratches
   on my window, tosses her hair dark with rain,
      snares lightning, cholla,[1] hawks, butterfly
         swarms in the tangles.

5 She sighs clouds,
    head thrown back, eyes closed, roars
          and rivers leap,

②
boulders retreat like crabs
into themselves.

10 She spews gusts and thunder,
    spooks pale women who scurry to
      lock doors, windows
         when her tumbleweed skirt starts its spin.

They sing lace lullabies
15 **③** so their children won't hear
④   her uncoiling
       through her lips, howling
        leaves off trees, flesh
          off bones, until she becomes

20 sound, spins herself
    to sleep, sand stinging her ankles,
      whirring into her raw skin like stars.

---

1. **cholla** (chōl′ yä) *n.*: Spiny shrub found in the southwestern United States and Mexico.

▲ **Critical Viewing** Compare the mood of this photograph with the mood of Mora's poem. [Compare] **⑤**

150 ◆ *Striving for Success*

Cross-Curricular Connection: Science

Most tornadoes form between a layer of cool, dry air from the north and warm, humid air from the south. Warm air naturally rises, while cool air sinks. When the warm air rises, more warm air rushes in to replace it, causing winds. The inrushing air also rises. If the warm air rises very rapidly, it may begin to rotate. The rotating air then forms into the funnel shape of a tornado. In the United States, tornadoes are most common in the Midwest in the spring months.

Invite students to do research on tornadoes as well as on related storms: monsoons, cyclones, and hurricanes. Interested students might find out what causes the different storms, why they occur in some places and not others, what type of damage they may cause, and how people take precautions against them. Students can share their information with the class by presenting oral reports. Encourage students to bring in photographs, drawings, and other visual aids.

Columbus Dying
Vassar Miller

His men in fever, scabs, and hunger pains—
He found a world and put to scorn his scorners.
Yet having learned the living sea contains
No dragons gnawing on drowned sailors' brains,
5   He missed the angels guarding the four corners, ●6
And begged that he be buried with his chains.
In token that he'd sworn to serve as thrall
His vision of men creeping to and fro,
Gum-footed flies glued to a spinning ball.
10 Whether they tumble off earth's edge or crawl ●7
Till dropped dead in their tracks from vertigo,
He deemed would make no difference at all.

◆ Build Vocabulary

thrall (thrôl) *n.*: Servant; slave

vertigo (vur′ ti gō) *n.*: Dizzy, confused state of mind

Guide for Responding

◆ Literature and Your Life

Reader's Response How do you feel after reading these poems? Why do you feel as you do?

Thematic Focus As Columbus does in the poem, you may sometimes question whether a particular goal is as important as you originally thought it was. How do you decide when the price is too high?

✓ Check Your Comprehension

1. Identify three outcomes of the wind's actions in "Uncoiling."
2. What happens to the sailors on Columbus's ship?
3. Why does Columbus ask to be buried in chains?

◆ Critical Thinking

INTERPRET

1. Explain how the shape of the poem "Uncoiling" reflects the title. **[Connect]**
2. Describe Columbus's attitude toward his own achievement. **[Interpret]**

EVALUATE

3. How convincing do you find this portrait of Columbus? Why? **[Assess]**

APPLY

4. How does the image of Columbus in this poem compare with the historical picture of him? **[Apply]**

Uncoiling/Columbus Dying ◆ 151

---

6 Clarify Explain that although Columbus found there were no monsters in the sea, he also discovered that there were no angels guarding the world's four corners, as people used to believe.

◆ Critical Thinking

7 Interpret Work with the class to understand the poet's meaning in this passage. What makes no difference? *Columbus no longer cares whether the world is flat (tumbling off the edge) or round (dropping from motion sickness).*

Reinforce and Extend

Answers

◆ Literature and Your Life

Reader's Response Students might say they feel saddened because the poems speak of destruction and human disappointment.

Thematic Focus Students might decide that the price is too high when they see they are struggling to attain something they no longer value.

✓ Check Your Comprehension

1. The boulders "retreat like crabs"; women lock doors and windows and sing lullabies to their children; leaves fall off trees and "flesh off bones" (people are killed).
2. The sailors get sick, starve, or drown.
3. He asks to be buried with chains because he discovered that no angels guard the earth.

◆ Critical Thinking

1. The shape resembles a spiral.
2. Columbus is scornful of his achievement and finds it meaningless.
3. Some students may not believe that Columbus would be as despairing as the poem portrays him.
4. Students will probably say that the poem differs from what they have learned about Columbus.

Beyond the Selection

FURTHER READING

Other Works by the Poets

"The Soul Selects Her Own Society," Emily Dickinson
Borders, Pat Mora
Wage War on Silence, Vassar Miller

Other Works About Striving for Success

My Name Is Asher Lev, Chaim Potok
Tell Me if the Lovers Are Losers, Cynthia Voight

   We suggest that you preview these works before recommending them to students.

INTERNET

Students may visit the following Web sites for information about the poets and their poems. Addresses may have changed since we published this information.

   Emily Dickinson: **http://english.cla.umn.edu/ Course web/1017/Emily dickinson/home**

   Pat Mora: **http://www.herald.com/liv_art/ books/docs/023698.htm**

   We *strongly recommend* that you preview sites before you send students to them.

◆ Reading Strategy

1. The images "forbidden ear," "distant strains of triumph," and "burst agonized" lead the reader to infer that the speaker's sympathy is with the loser.
2. You can infer that the speaker equates her imaginary world with paradise.
3. You can infer that he finds his conception of the world as round to be comical.
4. The speaker might think the pale women are nervous or easily timid.

◆ Literary Focus

1. (a) Possible restatement: People envy and glorify success when they themselves are not successful. (b) The battle images make the theme clearer because the contrast between success and failure is so distinct.
2. (a) The theme of "Uncoiling" is destruction; of "I dwell in Possibility—," the joys of the imagination. (b) Students might say that in each poem, the poet uses images and events (e.g., "gather Paradise"; "howling/leaves off trees, flesh/off bones") from which the reader can infer the theme.

◆ Build Vocabulary

Using the Prefix im-
1. impassable—not passable
2. immobile—not mobile or not able to move
3. impossible—not possible
4. impatient—not patient

Using the Word Bank
1. true; 2. false; 3. false

◆ Build Grammar Skills

Practice
1. The rooms of "Possibility" have many windows. (rooms—plural)
2. Columbus's men are tired and hungry. (men—plural)
3. The wind stings my face. (wind—singular)
4. The people who fail are the ones who know how sweet success is. (people—plural)
5. The women scurry back to their houses. (women—plural)

Guide for Responding (continued)

◆ Reading Strategy

MAKE INFERENCES
By **making inferences**—reaching conclusions based on evidence—you can discover the rich meaning in each line of these poems. The image of the wind roaring with her head thrown back in "Uncoiling," for instance, suggests freedom and awesome power. From positive images like this one, you can infer that the speaker's fear of the force of the wind is mixed with admiration.

1. What images help you infer the speaker's sympathy for the loser in "Success is counted sweetest"?
2. The word "Paradise" is used in the last line of "I dwell in Possibility—." What can you infer from this about the speaker's feelings about imagination?
3. In "Columbus Dying," people are described as "Gum-footed flies glued to a spinning ball." What does this detail help you infer about Columbus's feelings about proving the Earth is not flat?
4. What inference can you make concerning the speaker's opinion of the "pale women" in "Uncoiling," based on her description of their fearful actions?

◆ Literary Focus

STATED AND IMPLIED THEMES IN POETRY
The **theme**—the central idea, concern, or purpose—is partly stated in the title of "Success is counted sweetest." You have to explore a little further to discover the **implied theme** of "Columbus Dying." Columbus's indifference to his own achievement, described in the last lines, suggests that the poem's message is that his success came at too high a price.

1. The theme of "Success is counted sweetest" is stated. (a) Restate it in your own words. (b) Explain how the battle images help make the theme clearer.
2. (a) What is the implied theme of "Uncoiling" and "I dwell in Possibility—"? (b) Explain how specific details, characters, events, or actions helped you determine the theme of each poem.

◆ Build Vocabulary

USING THE PREFIX im-
The prefix im- (a variation of the prefix in-) usually means "not." On your paper, explain how the meaning "not" works into the definition of each word.

1. impassable
2. immobile
3. impossible
4. impatient

USING THE WORD BANK
Copy the following sentences in your notebook. Next to each, write *true* or *false*.
1. A king would most likely want his castle to be *impregnable*.
2. Most people would jump at the chance to become a *thrall*.
3. A person with *vertigo* would make an especially good tight-rope walker.

◆ Build Grammar Skills

SUBJECT AND VERB AGREEMENT
These poets play with the appearances and structures of their poems. Dickinson sprinkles her poems with dashes; Mora spreads the words out on the page to create the shape of a whirlwind. All verbs, however, agree with their subjects.

Practice Write the following sentences on your paper. Label the subject as singular or plural, and choose the correct verb form to complete the sentence.

> **Subject-verb agreement:**
> A verb changes form to agree in number (singular or plural) with its subject.

1. The rooms of "Possibility" (has, have) many windows.
2. Columbus's men (is, are) tired and hungry.
3. The wind (stings, sting) my face.
4. The people who fail (is, are) the ones who know how sweet success is.
5. The women (scurries, scurry) back to their houses.

✎ **Writer's Solution**

For additional instruction and practice, use the lesson in the **Language Lab CD-ROM** on Subject-Verb Agreement and the pages on agreement (pp. 80–86) in the *Writer's Solution Grammar Practice Book*.

Build Your Portfolio

 ## Idea Bank

Writing

1. Letter to a Poet Write a letter to one of these poets, responding to the theme of her poem. Explain whether you agree or disagree with her message and why.

2. Advertisement Write an advertisement that highlights the qualities of one of these poems. **[Career Link]**

3. Parody of a Poem Choose one of the poems in this group and write a parody—an imitation that exaggerates or distorts the language, images, or theme of the poem.

Speaking and Listening

4. Informal Debate In a small group, debate the assertion "Success is counted sweetest/By those who ne'er succeed." Use situations from life, literature, or the movies to demonstrate the truth or falsity of the poem's theme.

5. Panel Discussion Role-play a panel discussion that might take place among the three poets in this group. Have someone act as a moderator leading a discussion about the nature of success.

Projects

6. Round Earth Demonstration Columbus's voyage changed the way people view the world. Create a model that demonstrates something we now know about the Earth; for instance, that the sun rises and sets because the Earth rotates. Demonstrate your model in class. **[Science Link]**

7. Oral Report Prepare an oral report about the living conditions on Columbus's ships. Use visual aids, such as diagrams or charts, to illustrate some of your explanations. Present your report to the class. **[Social Studies Link]**

 ## Writing Mini-Lesson

Submission Letter

When poets or other writers send their work to a magazine or journal, they usually accompany it with a **submission letter** explaining why the work is appropriate for the particular publication. As one of the poets in this group, write a submission letter that would accompany one of these poems. The following hints will help you explain in detail why the editor should publish your work.

> #### Writing Skills Focus:
> #### Elaboration to Give Information
>
> Use **elaboration**—details and examples—to give the editor more information about you and your work. For example, don't just say your poem will interest readers; point out a striking image or idea from the poem.

Prewriting Brainstorm for a list of reasons you think the poem should be published. Avoid vague words like *nice* and *good*. They don't give enough information to distinguish your poem from any other.

Drafting Organize the letter around the main points you have identified. Elaborate on each point by quoting from your work or describing a section of it.

Revising Review your letter and identify the example or detail that elaborates on each point you wish to make. If you come across a point that does not have an example or detail, elaborate on the point by adding one.

Proofread your work and check especially for subject-verb agreement.

For more on subject and verb agreement, see Build Grammar Skills on pp. 146 and 152.

 ## Idea Bank

Customizing for *Performance Levels*

Following are suggestions for matching Idea Bank topics with your students' performance levels:

Less Advanced Students: 1, 4
Average Students: 2, 5,
More Advanced Students: 3, 6, 7

Customizing for *Learning Modalities*

Following are suggestions for matching Idea Bank topics with your students' learning modalities:

Visual/Spatial: 6, 7
Verbal/Linguistic: 3, 4, 5, 7

 ## Writing Mini-Lesson

Refer students to the Writing Handbook, page 965, for instruction on the writing process, and page 969 for further information on practical writing.

Writing and Language Transparencies Before students work on their business letters, use Writing Process Model 9, pp. 61–64, showing a draft and revision of a business letter.

 ### Writer's Solution

Writers at Work Videodisc
Have students view the videodisc segment (Ch. 8) featuring Larry Cataldo to spark a class discussion on various applications of practical writing.

Chapter 8

Writing Lab CD-ROM
Have students complete the tutorial on Practical Writing. Follow these steps:

1. Direct students to look at audio-annotated examples of writings for different audiences.
2. Have them use an outliner to help organize their points.
3. Encourage them to use the interactive subject and verb agreement instruction in Proofreading.

Sourcebook
Refer students to Chapter 8, Practical and Technical Writing (pp. 229–257), for additional support. The chapter includes an annotated student model of a process essay (p. 257).

✓ ASSESSMENT OPTIONS

Formal Assessment, Selection Test, pp. 32–34, and Assessment Resources Software. The selection test is designed so that it can be easily customized to the performance levels of your students. *Alternative Assessment,* p.10, includes options for less advanced students, more advanced students, bodily/kinesthetic learners, musical/rhythmic learners, visual/spatial learners, logical/mathematical learners, and verbal/linguistic learners.

PORTFOLIO ASSESSMENT
Use the following rubrics in the *Alternative Assessment* booklet to assess student writing:
Letter to a Poet: Response to Literature Rubric, p.113
Advertisement: Poetry Rubric, p.108
Parody of a Poem: Poetry Rubric, p.111

Guide for Reading

OBJECTIVES

1. To read, comprehend, and interpret a personal narrative
2. To relate a narrative to personal experience
3. To identify the author's purpose in a personal narrative
4. To identify a significant moment in a narrative
5. To build vocabulary in context and learn the word root *-vol-*
6. To distinguish between active and passive voice
7. To write a personal narrative using a clear explanation of cause and effect
8. To respond to a personal narrative through writing, speaking and listening, and projects

SKILLS INSTRUCTION

Vocabulary:
Word Roots: *-vol-*

Grammar:
Active and Passive Voice

Reading Strategy:
Author's Purpose

Literary Focus:
Significant Moment

Writing:
Clear Explanation of Cause and Effect

Speaking and Listening:
Speech (teacher edition)

Critical Viewing:
Interpret; Connect

PORTFOLIO OPPORTUNITIES

Writing: Mother's Day Card; Movie Review; Different Point of View

Writing Mini-Lesson: Personal Narrative

Speaking and Listening: Role Play; Speech

Projects: Chart; Timeline

More About the Author

At twenty-one, Christy Brown wrote the autobiographical *My Left Foot*, but—despite its great popularity—he was not entirely happy with the book. He later stated that it was "the kind of book they expected a cripple to write, too sentimental, too corny." In *Down All the Days*, a novel that took him fifteen years to complete, Brown fictionalized his life. Brown referred to this work as "just a slice of life, a very raw slice of life." His "slice of life" was a best-seller that was translated into fourteen languages—a remarkable achievement for a man once assumed to be mentally retarded.

Christy Brown (1932–1981)

He was trapped in a body that he could not control, surrounded by people but unbearably alone. These problems would crush most adults, but Christy Brown faced and overcame these obstacles when he was only a child.

The tenth of twenty-two children, Christy Brown was born in Dublin, Ireland, in 1932. His father was a bricklayer, a profession that usually—but not always—brought in enough money to support the family. When money was scarce, his mother often took odd jobs in addition to raising the children.

A Difficult Birth, a Difficult Life

Born with cerebral palsy, Brown had no control over most of his limbs, could not talk, and had to be fed by hand. Many people assumed he was mentally retarded until one day he grabbed a piece of chalk with his left foot and scrawled the letter A. This action proved his intelligence and changed his life completely.

Christy Brown recalls, "I was tormented, revolted at the very thought that I had been made different—cruelly different—from other people."

> "... I was soon to realize that it was this very affliction ... that was to bring a strange beauty into my life."

His Left Foot

When he was ten years old, he started to paint, also with his left foot. He later grew tired of painting and started to write. He wrote the manuscript for *My Left Foot* with a pencil that he held with his left big toe. Later, he taught himself to type and wrote the novel *Down All the Days*, which became a bestseller in Ireland. He also wrote three more novels and a collection of poetry. In 1989, his life became the basis for the popular and critically acclaimed film *My Left Foot,* which introduced the rest of the world to this incredible man.

◆ Build Vocabulary

WORD ROOTS: *-vol-*

A dramatic moment in *My Left Foot* occurs when the author's left foot, apparently by its own volition, grabs a piece of chalk out of his sister's hand. The root of *volition* is *-vol-,* which comes from Latin and means "wish" or "will." *Volition* is "the act of using the will": Brown's foot apparently grabs the piece of chalk by its own free will.

impertinence
conviction
inert
contention
volition
taut

WORD BANK

As you read you will encounter the words in the boxed list. Each word is defined on the page where it first appears. Preview the list before you read. Look for other words in the story, such as *involuntary,* that have the root *-vol-.*

◆ Build Grammar Skills

ACTIVE AND PASSIVE VOICE

A verb is in the **active voice** when the subject of the sentence performs the action. A verb is in the **passive voice** when the action is performed on the subject. When the performer of an action is not known or is not important, the writer uses the passive voice.

Christy Brown uses both the active and passive voice in his narrative.

Active Voice: Mother *decided* there and then to take matters into her own hands.

Passive Voice: In a moment, everything *was* changed.

Brown uses the active voice more than the passive. Notice how this creates a sense of action and purpose in his narrative.

154 ◆ Striving for Success

 Prentice Hall Literature Program Resources

REINFORCE / RETEACH / EXTEND

Selection Support Pages
Build Vocabulary: Word Roots: *-vol-*, p. 43
Build Grammar Skills: Active and Passive Voice, p. 44
Reading Strategy: Author's Purpose, p. 45
Literary Focus: Significant Moment, p. 46

Strategies for Diverse Student Needs, p. 11

Beyond Literature
Community Connection: Accommodating the Physically Challenged, p. 11

Formal Assessment Selection Test, pp. 35–37;

Assessment Resources Software

Alternative Assessment, p. 11

Writing and Language Transparencies
Writing Process Model 3: Personal Narrative, pp. 17–23

Resource Pro CD-ROM
"My Left Foot"—includes all resource materials and customizable lesson plan

Listening to Literature Audiocassettes
"My Left Foot"

from My Left Foot

◆ Literature and Your Life

CONNECT YOUR EXPERIENCE

Suppose you were kept after school every day for five years. Every day you would watch your friends run off to participate in sports, work at after-school jobs, or just sit around and talk to one another while you remained trapped in the detention classroom.

If you can imagine these five years of detention, you can begin to understand how Christy Brown might have felt. Able to think and feel emotions just like everyone else, Brown was trapped inside a body he couldn't control.

THEMATIC FOCUS: OVERCOMING OBSTACLES

This inspiring account of Christy Brown's first step in dealing with an enormous personal challenge may lead you to ask yourself, "What qualities must a person have to overcome great obstacles?"

Journal Writing List people you know or have seen in the news who have met great personal challenges. For each person, list a quality that has helped him or her achieve success.

◆ Background for Understanding

SCIENCE

Christy Brown was born with a disorder known as cerebral palsy. People who suffer from cerebral palsy have difficulty controlling their limbs, facial expressions, or both. The condition may be barely noticeable or extremely severe, as in Christy Brown's case. While some people with the condition are mentally retarded, others, such as Christy Brown, have average or above-average intelligence.

◆ Literary Focus

SIGNIFICANT MOMENT

If someone asked you to describe every moment of yesterday, you probably couldn't do it. Not every moment seems important. When you read a nonfiction account, the writer usually focuses on a **significant moment**—a moment that is a turning point, or a moment of discovery.

In this excerpt from his autobiography, Christy Brown describes the moment when he proved to his family that his physical disability had not affected his brain. In a single moment, Brown demonstrated his intelligence and changed the course of his life forever.

◆ Reading Strategy

IDENTIFY AUTHOR'S PURPOSE

When you speak, you usually have a reason. Maybe you want to share information, make someone laugh, or express a new idea you've had. When an author writes, he or she has a **purpose,** a reason for writing. This purpose might be to influence you to take a position on an issue, to act in a certain way, or to make you laugh or think. The purpose shapes the writer's choice of language and use of details. Notice the details that Christy Brown chooses to tell you. Determine his purpose for writing his autobiography.

Guide for Reading ◆ 155

This personal narrative proves inspirational on two levels. It shows how the love and faith of Christy Brown's mother enhanced his full development. Her faith was fully justified by Christy himself, a boy—and then a man—who determined he must be taken seriously. Through the nurturing atmosphere his mother created and his own drive to express himself truthfully, Christy overcame the limits of his cerebral palsy to become an artist and a writer of merit. Students may recognize aspects of his story in the lives of people they know.

◆ Build Grammar Skills

❶ Active and Passive Voice
Point out that Brown begins this narrative with a verb in the passive voice: "*I was born . . .*" Ask students to explain why the passive is appropriate in this context, and why the active voice would not be appropriate. *The passive voice is used when the performer of the action is either not known or not important. In this sentence, the subject of the sentence, "I," is the focal point, not Christy's mother. The emphasis of the sentence would be on the mother if the sentence had been written, "My mother gave birth to me . . ."—a less effective choice.*

❷ Clarification Students might be confused by the word *steel* in the phrase "leaving thirteen steel to hold the family fort." Tell them that *steel* is used to mean "strong" in this context.

---

from
My Left Foot

Christy Brown

❶ I was born in the Rotunda Hospital on June 5th, 1932. There were nine children before me and twelve after me, so I myself belong to the middle group. Out of this total of twenty-two, seventeen lived, but four died in infancy, leaving thirteen steel to hold the family fort. **❷**

Mine was a difficult birth, I am told. Both mother and son almost died. A whole army of relations queued up[1] outside the hospital until the small hours of the morning, waiting for news and praying furiously that it would be good.

After my birth mother was sent to recuperate for some weeks and I was kept in the hospital while she was away. I remained there for some time, without name, for I wasn't baptized until my mother was well enough to bring me to church.

It was mother who first saw that there was something wrong with me. I was about four

months old at the time. She noticed that my head had a habit of falling backward whenever she tried to feed me. She attempted to correct this by placing her hand on the back of my neck to keep it steady. But when she took it away back it would drop again. That was the first warning sign. Then she became aware of other defects as I got older. She saw that my hands were clenched nearly all of the time and were inclined to twine behind my back; my mouth couldn't grasp the teat of the bottle because even at that early age my jaws would either lock together tightly, so that it was impossible for her to open them, or they would suddenly become limp and fall loose, dragging my whole mouth to one side.[2] At six months I could not sit up without having a mountain of pillows around me; at twelve months it was the same.

---

1. **queued** (kyo͞od) **up:** Joined a line of people.

2. **my hands . . . dragging my whole mouth to one side:** Characteristic behavior of a person with severe cerebral palsy, a condition sometimes caused by lack of oxygen to the brain during birth. It often occurs as a result of a difficult childbirth.

156 ◆ Striving for Success

Block Scheduling Strategies

Consider these suggestions to take advantage of extended class time:

• Have students read the Background for Understanding. Encourage them to exchange ideas about ways in which people can cope with the limitations imposed by cerebral palsy. (Students may wish to visit the Web site of the United Cerebral Palsy Association at http://www.ucpa.org/)

• To prepare students to answer the Literary Focus questions in Guide for Responding,

have them gather in small groups to discuss the characteristics of a significant moment. Give students copies of the Literary Focus practice page in **Selection Support,** p. 46, for reinforcement.

• Have students complete Build Grammar Skills: Active and Passive Voice on page 162. After they have finished the activity, suggest that they return to the narrative to see if they can notice a pattern of Brown's use of active or passive voice.

• Direct students to work on their personal narratives (Writing Mini-Lesson on p. 163). Begin by having them brainstorm for a list of the type of incidents or events that are apt to be memorable in someone's life.

Very worried by this, mother told my father her fears, and they decided to seek medical advice without any further delay. I was a little over a year old when they began to take me to hospitals and clinics, convinced that there was something definitely wrong with me, something which they could not understand or name, but which was very real and disturbing.

Almost every doctor who saw and examined me labeled me a very interesting but also a hopeless case. Many told mother very gently that I was mentally defective and would remain so. That was a hard blow to a young mother who had already reared five healthy children. The doctors were so very sure of themselves that mother's faith in me seemed almost an impertinence. They assured her that nothing could be done for me.

She refused to accept this truth, the inevitable truth—as it then seemed—that I was beyond cure, beyond saving, even beyond hope. She could not and would not believe that I was an imbecile, as the doctors told her. She had nothing in the world to go by, not a scrap of evidence to support her conviction that, though my body was crippled, my mind was not. In spite of all the doctors and specialists told her, she would not agree. I don't believe she knew why—she just knew without feeling the smallest shade of doubt.

Finding that the doctors could not help in any way beyond telling her not to place her trust in me, or, in other words, to forget I was a human creature, rather to regard me as just something to be fed and washed and then put away again, mother decided there and then to take matters into her own hands. I was *her* child, and therefore part of the family. No matter how dull and incapable I might grow up to be, she was determined to treat me on the

❸

◆ **Reading Strategy**
What do you think is Brown's **purpose** in focusing so strongly on his mother's belief that he was not hopeless?

❹

❺

same plane as the others, and not as the "queer one" in the back room who was never spoken of when there were visitors present.

That was a momentous decision as far as my future life was concerned. It meant that I would always have my mother on my side to help me fight all the battles that were to come, and to inspire me with new strength when I

◆ **Build Vocabulary**
impertinence (im purt´ ən əns) *n.*: Inappropriate, rude action
conviction (kən vik´ shən) *n.*: Strong belief

▲ **Critical Viewing** Look at this still from the movie *My Left Foot.* Describe the feelings the actress playing Christy's mother is showing in her expression. [Interpret]

❻

from *My Left Foot* ◆ 157

◆ **Build Grammar Skills**
❸ **Active and Passive Voice** Ask students to analyze the use of active and passive voice in the sentence, "They assured her that nothing could be done for me." *"Assured" is in the active voice; they—the doctors—are the performers of the action. "Could be done" is passive voice; the performer of the action is unknown or not specified.*

◆ **Reading Strategy**
❹ **Author's Purpose** Elicit from students that even though it seems that the doctors are right, Christy wants his readers to know the extent of his mother's faith in him. His purpose is probably both to emphasize her strong and loving nature and also to begin to show how she would influence his development.

◆ **Critical Thinking**
❺ **Draw Conclusions** Ask students: Why do the doctors want Brown's mother to forget that he is a human creature? *Students should realize that according to the thinking about cerebral palsy and its effects at the time, people with this disease were thought to be incapable of just about all levels of human functioning. It was also incorrectly assumed that mental function was minimal in all cases; the doctor thought he was acting in Christy's mother's best interest by encouraging her not to work on her son's development.*

▶**Critical Viewing**◀
❻ **Interpret** *Christy's mother's position behind Christy symbolizes that she "stands behind" him, or supports him. Her facial expression shows pride in her son and happiness for him.*

Speaking and Listening Mini-Lesson

Speech
This mini-lesson supports the Speaking and Listening activity in the Idea Bank on page 163.
Introduce the Concept Remind students that speeches convey emotion through vocal inflection, facial expression, and gesture.
Develop Background As students prepare their speeches, have them consider these issues:

• Christy is intelligent. He has been observing and thinking even though he hasn't been speaking.
• Christy is five years old. Most five-year-olds can speak fluently, but their vocabulary and the complexity of their sentences are limited.
• Christy's audience is his family.
Apply the Information Students should plan and write their speeches, expressing

what they think Christy's main message would be.

Assess the Outcome Have students use Peer Assessment: Speaker/Speech on page 121 of the *Alternative Assessment* booklet to help them evaluate how well one another's speeches express the importance and emotion of this significant moment in Christy's life.

Develop Understanding

◆ Reading Strategy

❶ Author's Purpose Ask how this detail serves Brown's purpose in creating an inspiring portrait of his mother. *It is even more difficult to maintain faith and hope without the support of one's friends and relatives.*

◆ Literary Focus

❷ Significant Moment Ask students how the author starts here to build toward the significant moment of the narrative—the moment in which he will prove that his mother was right. *Students should grasp that by saying that his mother "was so successful," Brown is preparing the reader for the significant moment.*

◆ Reading Strategy

❸ Author's Purpose Ask students what they think is the author's purpose in describing how unappealing he must have been as a young child. *Including these details underscores his mother's strength, love, and faith. She never let Christy's disabilities shake her confidence.*

◆ Build Vocabulary

❹ Word Roots: -vol- Point out the adverb *involuntarily.* Ask students how knowing the meaning of the root *-vol-* can help determine the meaning of the word. *If both the word root -vol- and the prefix in- are familiar, the meaning of the word—"without willing," or "unintentionally"—can be deduced.*

◆ Literary Focus

❺ Significant Moment Students should recognize that Mrs. Brown is beginning to wonder if they might be right.

❶ was almost beaten. But it wasn't easy for her because now the relatives and friends had decided otherwise. They contended that I should be taken kindly, sympathetically, but not seriously. That would be a mistake. "For your own sake," they told her, "don't look to this boy as you would to the others; it would only break your heart in the end." Luckily for me, mother and father held out against the lot of them. But mother wasn't content just to say that I was not an idiot, ❷ she set out to prove it, not because of any rigid sense of duty, but out of love. That is why she was so successful.

At this time she had the five other children to look after besides the "difficult one," though as yet it was not by any means a full house. They were my brothers, Jim, Tony and Paddy, and my two sisters, Lily and Mona, all of them very young, just a year or so between each of them, so that they were almost exactly like steps of stairs.

Four years rolled by and I was now five, and still as helpless as a newly-born baby. While my father was out at bricklaying earning our bread and butter for us, mother was slowly, patiently pulling down the wall, brick by brick, that seemed to thrust itself between me and the other children, slowly, patiently penetrating beyond the thick curtain that hung over my mind, separating it from theirs. It was hard, heart-breaking work, for often all she got from me in return was a vague smile and perhaps a faint gurgle. I could not speak or even mumble, nor could I sit up without support on my own, let alone take steps. But I wasn't <u>inert</u> or motionless. I ❸ seemed, indeed, to be convulsed with movement, wild, stiff, snakelike movement that never left me, except in sleep. My fingers twisted and twitched continually, my arms twined backwards and would often shoot out suddenly this way and that, and my head lolled and sagged sideways. I was a queer, crooked little fellow.

Mother tells me how one day she had been sitting with me for hours in an upstairs room, showing me pictures out of a great big storybook that I had got from Santa Claus last Christmas and telling me the names of different animals and flowers that were in them, trying without success to get me to repeat them. This had gone on for hours while she talked and laughed with me. Then at the end of it she leaned over me and said gently into my ear:

"Did you like it, Chris? Did you like the bears and the monkeys and all the lovely flowers? Nod your head for yes, like a good boy."

But I could make no sign that I had understood her. Her face was bent over mine hopefully. Suddenly, involuntarily, my queer hand reached up and grasped one of the dark curls ❹ that fell in a thick cluster about her neck. Gently she loosened the clenched fingers, though some dark strands were still clutched between them.

Then she turned away from my curious stare and left the room, crying. The door closed behind her. It all seemed hopeless. It looked as though there was some justification for my relatives' <u>contention</u> that I was an idiot and beyond help.

> ◆ **Literary Focus** ❺
> What is the significance of this moment?

They now spoke of an institution.

"Never!" said my mother almost fiercely, when this was suggested to her. "I know my boy is not an idiot. It is his body that is shattered, not his mind. I'm sure of that."

Sure? Yet inwardly, she prayed God would give her some proof of her faith. She knew it

◆ Build Vocabulary

inert (i nʉrt′) *adj.:* Lacking the power to move; inactive

contention (kən ten′ shən) *n.:* Statement that one argues for

---

🏰 Beyond the Classroom

Career Connection

Developmental Psychology Christy's mother suspected that something was wrong with her son when he was four months old. Explain to students that infants and children develop in predictable stages, conquering one developmental task before moving on to another.

Developmental psychologists are people who study children's development in such areas as appropriately expressing needs, reasoning ability, and language acquisition. Have students gather information about the stages of child development and developmental psychologists and make a chart with their findings.

Community Connection

Parking Spaces Various laws require that a certain number of parking spaces within a public parking lot be clearly marked and reserved for people who have parking permits that designate them as physically challenged. Interested students might like to survey a busy parking lot and investigate questions such as these:

• How many spaces are set aside? What percent?

• How many cars use the spaces? Do they all have special permits?

• Are these spaces conveniently located near ramps?

• In what other ways do public spaces provide for the needs of the physically challenged?

Students can make a chart with their results.

was one thing to believe but quite another thing to prove.

I was now five, and still I showed no real sign of intelligence. I showed no apparent interest in things except with my toes—more especially those of my left foot. Although my natural habits were clean I could not aid myself, but in this respect my father took care of me. I used to lie on my back all the time in the kitchen or, on bright warm days, out in the garden, a little bundle of crooked muscles and twisted nerves, surrounded by a family that loved me and hoped for me and that made me part of their own warmth and humanity. I was lonely, imprisoned in a world of my own, unable to communicate with others, cut off, separated from them as though a glass wall stood between my existence and theirs, thrusting me

beyond the sphere of their lives and activities. I longed to run about and play with the rest, but I was unable to break loose from my bondage.

Then, suddenly, it happened! In a moment everything was changed, my future life molded into a definite shape, my mother's faith in me rewarded and her secret fear changed into open triumph.

It happened so quickly, so simply after all

◆ **Literature and Your Life**

How would you feel if you were unable to communicate with your family or friends?
7

8

▼ **Critical Viewing** This scene from the movie shows Christy as an adult with his mother. How does this picture reinforce what you have learned about them in the narrative? **[Connect]**
9

from My Left Foot ◆ 159

◆ **Critical Thinking**

6 **Speculate** In what ways did the fact that Christy Brown was part of a loving, caring family help him? *Suggested response: His physical needs were attended to and he received attention. He was therefore able to focus his mind and spirit on finding a way to communicate.*

◆ **Literature and Your Life**

7 Accept all reasonable responses. Students are likely to say that they would feel lonely, frustrated, and isolated.

◆ **Literary Focus**

8 **Significant Moment** Ask students how Brown indicates that he is about to reveal the significant moment. *Brown's assertion that "... in a moment everything was changed indicates the importance of what is about to happen.*

▶**Critical Viewing**◀

9 **Connect** Students should recognize the mood, or feeling, of the photograph as caring, compassionate, or loving. The mother's hand on her son's face and the proximity of their heads indicates closeness and caring.

Customize for
English Language Learners
Use visual images from advertisements, art books, and posters to show these students in a concrete way what is meant by figureative language. Discuss the images, then ask students to explain some of the images in Brown's narrative. *The images all highlight Brown's sense of isolation.*

Develop Understanding

◆ Literary Focus

➊ Significant Moment Point out the description of the weather and the setting. Ask students: *Why does Brown describe the scene in such precise descriptive detail? Possible responses: Because this was such a significant moment in his life, Brown wants the reader to know that he, as the silent child, was actually aware of all that was going on around him. Also, Brown, as the adult writer, wants to set the stage and draw out the suspense as the reader awaits the significant happening.*

➋ Listening to Literature This would be a good point at which to play the audiocassette recording. Students can hear the description of the significant moment along with the significance of the title.

🎧 **Listening to Literature Audiocassettes**

➌ Clarification Some students, especially English language learners, might be confused by the use of the word *impolitely* in reference to Christy's taking the chalk out of his sister's hand. Tell students that Brown uses the word to inject humor into a tension-filled situation. No one was concerned with manners in the midst of such a significant event.

Comprehension Check ☑

➍ Why does the mother stop walking? *She was not in the room when Christy took the chalk, but as soon as she enters the room she realizes something important has happened because everyone is quiet and staring at Christy.*

➊ the years of waiting and uncertainty, that I can see and feel the whole scene as if it had happened last week. It was the afternoon of a cold, gray December day. The streets outside glistened with snow; the white sparkling flakes stuck and melted on the window-panes and hung on the boughs of the trees like molten silver. The wind howled dismally, whipping up little whirling columns of snow that rose and fell at every fresh gust. And over all, the dull, murky sky stretched like a dark canopy, a vast infinity of grayness.

Inside, all the family were gathered round the big kitchen fire that lit up the little room with a warm glow and made giant shadows dance on the walls and ceiling.

In a corner Mona and Paddy were sitting huddled together, a few torn school primers³ before them. They were writing down little sums on to an old chipped slate, using a bright piece of yellow chalk. I was close to them, propped up by a few pillows against the wall, watching.

It was the chalk that attracted me so much. It was a long, slender stick of vivid yellow. I had never seen anything like it before, and it showed up so well against the black surface of the slate that I was fascinated by it as much as if it had been a stick of gold.

➋ Suddenly, I wanted desperately to do what my sister was doing. Then—without thinking or knowing exactly what I was doing, I reached out and took the stick of chalk out of my sister's hand—*with my left foot.*

I do not know why I used my left foot to do this. It is a puzzle to many people as well as to myself, for, although I had displayed a curious interest in my toes at an early age, I had never attempted before this to use either of my feet in any way. They could have been as useless to me as were my hands. That day, however, my left foot, apparently by its own <u>volition</u>, reached

➌ out and very impolitely took the chalk out of my sister's hand.

---

3. primers (prim´ ərz): Small books for teaching young children reading, writing, and arithmetic.

---

 held it tightly between my toes, and, acting on an impulse, made a wild sort of scribble with it on the slate. Next moment I stopped, a bit dazed, surprised, looking down at the stick of yellow chalk stuck between my toes, not knowing what to do with it next, hardly knowing how it got there. Then I looked up and became aware that everyone had stopped talking and was staring at me silently. Nobody stirred. Mona, her black curls framing her chubby little face, stared at me with great big eyes and open mouth. Across the open hearth,⁴ his face lit by flames, sat my father, leaning forward, hands outspread on his knees, his shoulders tense. I felt the sweat break out on my forehead.

y mother came in from the pantry with a steaming pot in her hand. She stopped midway between the table and the fire, feeling the tension flowing ➍ through the room. She followed their stare and saw me, in the corner. Her eyes looked from my face down to my foot, with the chalk gripped between my toes. She put down the pot.

Then she crossed over to me and knelt down beside me, as she had done so many times before.

"I'll show you what to do with it, Chris," she said, very slowly and in a queer, jerky way, her face flushed as if with some inner excitement.

Taking another piece of chalk from Mona, she hesitated, then very deliberately drew, on the floor in front of me, the single letter "A."

"Copy that," she said, looking steadily at me. "Copy it, Christy."

I couldn't.

I looked about me, looked around at the

◆ Build Vocabulary

volition (vō lish´ ən) *n.*: The act of using the will

taut (tôt) *adj.*: High-strung; tense

---

4. hearth: Fireplace.

---

faces that were turned toward me, tense, excited faces that were at that moment frozen, immobile, eager, waiting for a miracle in their midst.

The stillness was profound. The room was full of flame and shadow that danced before my eyes and lulled my <u>taut</u> nerves into a sort of waking sleep. I could hear the sound of the water-tap dripping in the pantry, the loud ticking of the clock on the mantelshelf, and the soft hiss and crackle of the logs on the open hearth.

I tried again. I put out my foot and made a wild jerking stab with the chalk which produced a very crooked line and nothing more. Mother held the slate steady for me.

"Try again, Chris," she whispered in my ear. "Again."

I did. I stiffened my body and put my left foot out again, for the third time. I drew one side of the letter. I drew half the other side. Then the stick of chalk broke and I was left with a stump. I wanted to fling it away and give up. Then I felt my mother's hand on my shoulder. I tried once more. Out went my foot. I shook, I sweated and strained every muscle.

My hands were so tightly clenched that my fingernails bit into the flesh. I set my teeth so hard that I nearly pierced my lower lip. Everything in the room swam till the faces around me were mere patches of white. But—I drew it—*the letter "A."* There it was on the floor before me. Shaky, with awkward, wobbly sides and a very uneven center line. But it *was* the letter "A." I looked up. I saw my mother's face for a moment, tears on her cheeks. Then my father stooped down and hoisted me on to his shoulder.

I had done it! It had started—the thing that was to give my mind its chance of expressing itself. True, I couldn't speak with my lips, but now I would speak through something more lasting than spoken words—written words.

That one letter, scrawled on the floor with a broken bit of yellow chalk gripped between my toes, was my road to a new world, my key to mental freedom. It was to provide a source of relaxation to the tense, taut thing that was me, which panted for expression behind a twisted mouth.

5

◆ **Literary Focus**
Why is the outcome of this event so significant?

6

Guide for Responding

◆ *Literature and Your Life*

Reader's Response Which person do you admire most in this piece? Why?

Thematic Focus What qualities enabled Christy Brown—and his mother—to overcome his isolation?

Group Discussion With a group of classmates, discuss factors other than a physical disability that might create a sense of isolation.

☑ **Check Your Comprehension**

1. What were the first signs that there was something wrong with Christy?
2. What was the doctors' conclusion about Christy's case?
3. How does Christy's mother respond to the doctors' diagnosis?
4. How did Christy's brothers and sisters treat him?
5. What did Christy do that changed other people's impression of him?

from *My Left Foot* ◆ 161

Beyond the Selection

FURTHER READING

Other Works by Christy Brown
Down All the Days (novel)
Come Softly to My Wake: The Poems of Christy Brown

Other Works With the Theme of Facing Personal Challenge
The Miracle Worker, William Gibson
Flowers for Algernon, Daniel Keyes
   We suggest that you preview these works before recommending them to students.

INTERNET

Students may find additional information about *My Left Foot* at the following site. Please be aware, however, that sites may have changed since the time we published this information.

   For reviews of the film *My Left Foot* and links to resources about cerebral palsy, go to:
http://curry.edschool.virginia.edu/go/cise/ose /information/film/left/html

   We *strongly recommend* that you preview this and related sites before you send students to them.

◆ **Critical Thinking**

5 Speculate Point out that Christy does not succeed immediately in copying the letter "A." Ask students to speculate about what Christy was feeling during this event, and why. *Students may speculate that Christy felt extremely tense as he tried to provide evidence of his intelligence. He was probably aware that this was his one chance to prove himself. If he failed, he would not gain his family's serious attention again.*

◆ **Literary Focus**

6 Significant Moment Students should recognize the following: *This is the first time anyone in the family knows for sure that Christy can learn and that his cerebral palsy does not affect him mentally. It means he has a future.*

Reinforce and Extend

Answers
◆ *Literature and Your Life*

Reader's Response Some students might admire Christy because his determination and talent caused him to override his physical limitation; others might say his mother because her patience and faith were an inspiration.

Thematic Focus Responses include determination, the ability to stand up against popular opinion, optimism, and courage.

☑ **Check Your Comprehension**

1. Christy could not hold his head up when he should have been able to; his hands were clenched all the time; he could not control his jaw movements; he could not sit up.
2. The doctors concluded Christy's case was hopeless.
3. Christy's mother ignores the doctors' advice. She takes matters into her own hands.
4. Christy's brothers and sisters treated him sympathetically, but they did not take him seriously.
5. He used his left foot to write the letter "A" on a slate.

◆ Critical Thinking

1. He was frustrated.
2. Possible answers include the obstacle of being labeled a hopeless case; the disregard of most of his family; his mother's attention to the competing demands of his brothers and sisters.
3. He was able to convince people that he had intelligence.
4. Examples will probably center on others not recognizing the strengths, talents, and abilities of people who are in some way physically challenged.
5. Mrs. Brown's belief in her son contributed in a major way to Christy's ability to flourish.

◆ Reading Strategy

1. Mrs. Brown overcame these obstacles: (1) doctors' hopeless prognoses for Christy; (2) friends and relatives' opinion that he should be institutionalized; (3) the demands of a large family without financial resources.
2. Possible statements include: "mother decided there and then to take matters into her own hands"; "It meant that I would always have my mother to inspire me with new strength when I was almost beaten."
3. Students' answers might acknowledge that the excerpt from *My Left Foot* reveals Christy's profound indebtedness to his mother and the courageous way in which she raised him.

◆ Literary Focus

1. Details leading up to the significant moment include Mrs. Brown's blind conviction in her son's mental abilities and Christy's own frustration at not being able to signal that he understood his mother.
2. Three details that emphasize the significant moment are (1) Mrs. Brown asking Christy to copy her letter "A"; (2) the stillness in the room as everyone watched; (3) Christy's tremendous concentration—his tightly clenched hands, the room swimming.

Guide for Responding (continued)

◆ Critical Thinking

INTERPRET
1. Explain how Christy feels about being unable to respond to his mother's questions. [Infer]
2. List two obstacles in addition to his physical disability that Christy has to overcome. [Deduce]
3. Explain the significance of the incident with the chalk. [Draw Conclusions]

APPLY
4. Describe another situation in which a physically challenged person has had to deal with the ignorance or misunderstanding of others. [Synthesize]

EVALUATE
5. How did Christy's mother's belief in her son affect Christy's life? [Evaluate]

◆ Reading Strategy

IDENTIFY AUTHOR'S PURPOSE
Christy Brown uses language and includes details that best accomplish his **purpose,** his reason for writing. For instance, the many examples he includes of his mother's refusal to give up on him support his purpose to inspire—her strength in the face of obstacles is an example of courage and perseverance.
1. List three obstacles that Brown's mother overcomes.
2. Identify a direct statement in which Brown expresses his mother's strength.
3. In your own words, describe the impact Brown's mother had on his life.

◆ Literary Focus

SIGNIFICANT MOMENT
When Christy Brown drew the letter *A*, his life was instantly transformed. He builds toward this **significant moment,** the moment of discovery, throughout his narrative.
1. Identify two details in the early part of the narrative that indicate the deep significance of this moment.
2. List three specific details that Brown includes to give emphasis to this moment.

◆ Build Vocabulary

USING THE WORD ROOT -vol-
Knowing that the root of *volition* is *-vol-,* which means "wish" or "will," write the following items in your notebook and fill in the blanks.
1. Volition: act of using one's ___?___
2. Volunteer: person who is ___?___ to help
3. Benevolent: ___?___ to do good

USING THE WORD BANK
On your paper, respond to the following items:
1. An *inert* ingredient is (a) important, (b) strong, (c) inactive.
2. A *taut* rope is (a) tight, (b) loose, (c) uncut.
3. A person with strong *convictions* (a) gives up easily, (b) stands by her beliefs, (c) is intelligent.
4. What response would an *impertinent* person most likely get from others? (a) attraction, (b) boredom, (c) anger
5. Who would most likely make a *contention*? (a) a doctor, (b) a lawyer, (c) a minister

◆ Build Grammar Skills

ACTIVE AND PASSIVE VOICE
A verb is in the **active voice** when the subject of the sentence performs the action. A verb is in the **passive voice** when the action is performed on the subject.

Practice Determine whether the verb or verbs in the following sentences are in the active or passive voice.
1. After my birth, mother was sent home to recuperate for some weeks, and I was kept in the hospital.
2. I reached out and took the stick of chalk out of my sister's hand.

Writing Application Rewrite the following sentences in your notebook. Change each sentence from the passive voice to the active voice.
1. The room was filled with noise.
2. The piece of chalk was taken out of my hands by mother.
3. I was called a hopeless case by doctors.

◆ Build Vocabulary

Using the Word Root -vol-
1. will; 2. willing; 3. wishing

Using the Word Bank
1. c 2. a 3. b 4. c 5. b

◆ Build Grammar Skills

Practice
1. passive; 2. active

Writing Application
1. Noise filled the room.
2. Mother took the piece of chalk out of my hands.
3. Doctors called me a hopeless case.

✒ Writer's Solution

For additional instruction and practice, use the lesson in the **Language Lab CD-ROM** on Active and Passive Voice and the pages on Active and Passive Voice (pp. 74–75) in the *Writer's Solution Grammar Practice Book.*

Build Your Portfolio

 ## Idea Bank

Writing

1. **Mother's Day Card** Write a Mother's Day card from Christy to his mother, acknowledging all she has done for him.

2. **Movie Review** Watch the film *My Left Foot* and write a review of it. In your review, discuss how well the film portrays the incident you have just read about. **[Media Link; Performing Arts Link]**

3. **Story From the Mother's Point of View** Most of the events in this section of Christy Brown's autobiography also concern his mother. Rewrite this chapter of Brown's autobiography from the point of view of Christy's mother.

Speaking and Listening

4. **Role Play** Role-play a conversation between one of Christy's doctors and Christy's mother. Base your words and actions on what you've learned in the story. **[Performing Arts Link]**

5. **Speech** Suppose that Christy could clearly express his thoughts and feelings after writing the *A*. Improvise a speech that, under these circumstances, he might have spoken to his family. **[Performing Arts Link]**

Projects

6. **Chart on Cerebral Palsy** Create a poster with an awareness chart that outlines the symptoms and causes of cerebral palsy and the number of people in the United States who have it. **[Science Link; Art Link]**

7. **Christy Brown Timeline** Research other significant moments in Christy Brown's life. Create a timeline that shows these events in chronological order.

Writing Mini-Lesson

Personal Narrative

Choose a memorable moment from your own life and write a **personal narrative** about it, letting your feelings about events shape the way you tell your story. These tips will help you show why these events were significant:

Writing Skills Focus: Clear Explanation of Causes and Effects

A clear explanation of causes and effects is important in personal narratives, process explanations, and test essays. Such an explanation of causes and effects involves showing how one event or condition brings about another.

Notice, for example, how Christy Brown clearly demonstrates the cause-and-effect relationship between his mother's decision to treat him normally and his own sense of strength.

Prewriting Once you have identified the events to be included in your narrative, map out the relationship between them visually.

Drafting Refer to your prewriting notes to make sure you are connecting related events. Use terms like *because, consequently, as a result,* and *so* to show cause-and-effect relationships.

Revising Have a partner read your draft. Ask him or her to identify any places where you have not clearly established the cause-and-effect relationship between events. If necessary, add the words and phrases that will clarify the relationship. Also, clarify cause-and-effect links by changing the passive voice to the active voice.

For more on the active and passive voice, see Build Grammar Skills on pp. 154 and 162.

from My Left Foot ◆ 163

 ## Idea Bank

Customizing for *Performance Levels*

Following are suggestions for matching Idea Bank topics with your students' performance levels:

Less Advanced Students: 1, 4
Average Students: 2, 5, 6
More Advanced Students: 3, 7

Customizing for *Learning Modalities*

Following are suggestions for matching Idea Bank topics with your students' learning modalities:

Visual/Spatial: 2, 6
Verbal/Linguistic: 3, 4, 5
Logical/Mathematical: 7
Bodily/Kinesthetic: 2

 ## Writing Mini-Lesson

Refer students to the Writing Handbook, page 965, for instruction on the writing process, and page 967 for further information on narrative writing.

Writing and Language Transparencies Use Writing Model 3: Personal Narrative (pp. 17–23) to help students shape their personal narratives in the Writing Mini-Lesson.

 ## Writer's Solution

Writing Lab CD-ROM

Have students complete the tutorial on Narration. Follow these steps:

1. Have students use the Inspirations for Narration to help them choose a topic for their personal narratives.

2. Have them read tips for peer revision to help them work productively with a peer reviewer.

3. Suggest that students use tips for publishing to get pointers for publishing in print or on-line.

Sourcebook

Have students use Chapter 2, Narration (pp. 31–56), for additional support. The chapter includes a professional model of a personal narrative (p. 36).

✓ ASSESSMENT OPTIONS

Formal Assessment, Selection Test, pp. 35–37, and Assessment Resources Software. The selection test is designed so that it can be easily customized to the performance levels of your students.

Alternative Assessment, p. 11, includes options for less advanced students, more advanced students, visual/spatial learners, interpersonal and verbal/linguistic learners.

PORTFOLIO ASSESSMENT

Use the following rubrics in the *Alternative Assessment* booklet to assess student writing:
Mother's Day Card: Description Rubric, p. 100
Movie Review: Evaluation/Review Rubric, p. 107
Story From the Mother's Point of View: Fiction Narrative Rubric, p. 98

Guide for Reading

OBJECTIVES

1. To read, comprehend, and interpret a short story
2. To relate a story to personal experience
3. To clarify to facilitate comprehension
4. To distinguish between direct and indirect characterization
5. To build vocabulary in context and learn the word origin for *venture*
6. To use correct pronoun case
7. To write a firsthand biography providing examples
8. To respond to the story through writing, speaking and listening, and projects

SKILLS INSTRUCTION

Vocabulary:
Word Origins: *ventured*

Grammar:
Pronoun Case

Reading Strategy:
Clarify

Literary Focus:
Characterization

Writing:
Provide Examples

Speaking and Listening:
Casting Discussion (teacher edition)

Critical Viewing:
Analyze; Compare and Contrast; Connect

PORTFOLIO OPPORTUNITIES

Writing: Letter to Charles's Mother; News Report; Alternative Ending
Writing Mini-Lesson: Firsthand Biography
Speaking and Listening: Casting Discussion; Oral Anecdote
Projects: Conflict-Resolution Workshop; Cultural Comparisons Chart

More About the Author
William Melvin Kelley knows about marching to a different drummer. His high school record as an outstanding student, captain of the track team, and student council president got him admitted to Harvard, where he planned to study law—until he discovered writing. As a result, in the middle of his senior year, he flunked all his courses *except* writing, and was invited to take a year off. He never returned. He had found his drummer.

William Melvin Kelley
(1937–   )

Some people think they have all the answers. William Melvin Kelley, on the other hand, is a man of questions. He says, "I am not a sociologist or a politician or a spokesman. Such people try to give answers. A writer, I think, should ask questions."

Marching to His Own Beat
Kelley's questions about his own life have rarely found their answers in conformity. The title of his first book—*A Different Drummer*—reflects his belief in the importance of individuality. The title is based on the words of the nineteenth-century philosopher Henry David Thoreau, who said, "If a man does not keep pace with his companions, perhaps it is because he hears a different drummer. Let him step to the music which he hears, however measured or far away."

A Question of Individuals Kelley's stories focus on the problems of individual characters, some of them black.

> *"A Visit to Grandmother" focuses on an age-old problem—a conflict between parent and child.*

In this story, Kelley shows the drama of one family's search for answers to questions about pain in the past and acceptance in the present.

◆ Build Vocabulary

WORD ORIGINS: *ventured*

In this story, you will encounter the word *ventured*. Its similarity to the word *adventure* is no coincidence; both words come from the Latin *aventura,* which means "a happening." An adventure is usually a happening that involves some risk or excitement; *ventured* means taking a risk.

Tracing the origins of words often helps you understand the meaning of unfamiliar words by revealing their relationships to words you already know.

WORD BANK

As you read, you will encounter the words in this list. Each word is defined on the page where it first appears. Preview this list of words from the story.

ventured
indulgence
grimacing
lacquered

◆ Build Grammar Skills

PRONOUN CASE

William Melvin Kelley, like other writers, uses pronouns to avoid unnecessary repetition in his writing. His writing is clear because he uses the correct form of a pronoun, depending on its use in the sentence.

Pronoun case refers to the different forms that a pronoun takes to indicate its function in a sentence.

Subjective case pronouns—*I, we, you, she, it, they*—are used when the pronoun performs the action or renames the subject.

She let him go . . .

The objective case—*me, us, you, him, he, it, they*—is used when the pronoun receives the action of the verb or is the object of a preposition.

I swapped *him* for that old chair.

Prentice Hall Literature Program Resources

REINFORCE / RETEACH / EXTEND

Selection Support Pages
Build Vocabulary: Word Origins: *ventured*, p. 57
Build Grammar Skills: Pronoun Case, p. 48
Reading Strategy: Clarify, p. 49
Literary Focus: Characterization, p. 50

Strategies for Diverse Student Needs, p. 12

Beyond Literature
Career Connection: Performing Arts, p. 12

Formal Assessment Selection Test, pp. 38–40;
Assessment Resources Software

Alternative Assessment, p. 11

Writing and Language Transparencies
Writing Process Model 2: Biographical Profile,
pp. 13–16

Resource Pro CD-ROM
"A Visit to Grandmother"—includes all resource materials and customizable lesson plan

Listening to Literature Audiocassettes
"A Visit to Grandmother"

A Visit to Grandmother

◆ Literature and Your Life

CONNECT YOUR EXPERIENCE

It doesn't matter whether a family has two members or ten—misunderstandings are common. Disagreements can be healthy, however, when they lead people to work out their differences. Through a confrontation, the family members in "A Visit to Grandmother" gain a better understanding of one another.

Journal Writing Use a Venn diagram like the one shown to explore both sides of a misunderstanding you've had with a friend or family member. Use the center area to show areas of agreement that helped you reach a common ground.

My Side | My Brother's Side

He bothers my friends and me. / We both like football. / He wants to hang out with us.
He never leaves us alone. / He says we never include him.

Common ground: We can share some activities like football games; other times he'll leave us alone.

THEMATIC FOCUS: OVERCOMING OBSTACLES

The events in this story may help you answer the question, "What happens when people don't communicate with one another?"

◆ Background for Understanding

CULTURE

In "A Visit to Grandmother," one character sweet-talks his mother into taking a hair-raising ride with a wild horse and a borrowed buggy. Today, a character might suggest a spin around the block in a new car, but in the late 1920's the automobile was just beginning its conquest of the American road. In parts of the rural South, where this story takes place, the horse and buggy was not just transportation; it was as much of a status symbol as a convertible or a hot rod.

◆ Literary Focus

CHARACTERIZATION

Sometimes writers use **direct characterization**, directly telling you about the character's personality. More frequently, a writer uses **indirect characterization**, revealing personality traits through the character's thoughts, words, and actions, and through other characters' comments. Kelley uses indirect characterization to show one character's kindness: "When people ventured timidly into his office, it took only a few words from him to make them relax, and even laugh."

Notice the other thoughts, actions, and reactions, as well as the direct statements, that bring the characters in this story to life.

◆ Reading Strategy

CLARIFY

To avoid misunderstandings when you read, **clarify**—check your understanding of—any parts of the story you don't understand. The best way to do this is to read ahead for more information or read back to review what you have already learned. For example, you might want to review details of the setting, clarify the relationships among the characters, or look back at the details of a key event.

One technique you can use to help you clarify relationships among characters and events is to represent them visually.

As you meet the members of the Dunford family, you may want to sketch out a rough family tree, to clarify how the characters are related to one another, or a timeline that clarifies the order of events in the family's past.

Guide for Reading ◆ 165

Ask students to name a book they've read or TV show or film they've seen that dealt with a problem between a parent or guardian and a teenager. Encourage students to share their thoughts about the book or show and to explain how the conflict did—or didn't—get resolved. Did students agree with the resolution? Point out that some parent-child conflicts reach on into adulthood, when the "child" already has children of his or her own. Tell students that this kind of conflict is at the heart of "A Visit to Grandmother."

Customize for
Less Proficient Readers
Less proficient readers might have difficulty with the dialect in which some of the dialogue in this selection is written. Listen to the story on **Listening to Literature Audiocassettes** as they follow the text will aid their comprehension.

Customize for
More Advanced Students
Suggest that more advanced students choose a section of the story and rewrite it to reflect the point of view of the grandmother. Advise them to use the characterizations presented in the story, but as seen from the grandmother's first-person perspective.

Customize for
English Language Learners
Point out that the dialogue is written as informal speech and is often not standard English. Assist these students in restating these ideas in standard English.

Preparing for Standardized Tests

Grammar and Language Write the following sentences on the chalkboard, and ask students to choose the correct pronoun and identify its case—subjective or objective.

1. Divide the work equally between you and (I, me). *me—objective*
2. Sara and (he, him) went to see the fireworks. *he—subjective*

Let students know that in the first sentence the correct choice, *me*, serves as the object of the preposition *between*. In the second sentence, the subjective pronoun *he* is correct because *he* is part of the compound subject of the sentence, *Sara and he*. Some standardized tests may require students to select the correct pronoun case to complete a sentence and to understand the distinction between subjective and objective case in pronouns. Using pronoun case correctly will also improve students performance on the essay portions of standardized tests. The Build Grammar Skills lesson for this selection focuses on pronoun case. For additional practice, use the Build Grammar Skills page on Pronoun Case (p. 48) in **Selection Support**.

165

One-Minute Insight This story shows how old grievances and tensions within a family can survive through the years, affecting even the most capable and accomplished people. Dr. Charles Dunford has achieved much in his life and has applied his intelligence, determination, and empathy to serve others. Yet even as an adult, he is not exempt from the emotional burdens of sibling rivalry and feelings of rejection. When his bitter feelings finally emerge, the result is a shock to his family, including his admiring son.

Customize for
Visual/Spatial Learners

Have these students preview the illustrations on pages 166, 169, and 172. Ask them what expectations these pictures create about the characters and their way of life.

A Visit to Grandmother

William Melvin Kelley

166   *Striving for Success*

Block Scheduling Strategies

Consider these suggestions to take advantage of extended class time:

- Have students listen to all or part of the selection on audiocassette, and discuss the characters of the grandmother and Dr. Dunford, based on what they hear as well as what they have read.

- Give students practice with correct pronoun case by having them do the Build Grammar Skills exercise on page 175, and the Build Grammar Skills page from *Selection Support,* p. 48.

- Introduce students to direct and indirect characterization. Have them read the Literary Focus information on page 165 and follow up with the questions on page 175. You may also give them the Literary Focus page from *Selection Support* for reinforcement.

- Help students to complete the Alternate Ending to the story in the Idea Bank on page 176. Before they begin, ask them to make a comparison chart on which they note thoughts, words, and actions that reveal each brother's personality traits.

- Direct students to complete the Writing Mini-Lesson on page 176. Before students start writing, guide them through the drafts in the Writing Process Model 2: Biographical Profile (pp. 13–16).

Springtime Rain, 1975, Ogden M. Pleissner

❶ **Characterization** Ask students to find examples of both indirect and direct characterization in this paragraph. Have them explain the examples they choose. *Chig's thoughts about his father's kindness and ability to set people at ease are examples of indirect characterization. The author then uses direct characterization to tell that Dr. Dunford cared about people.*

◆ **Critical Thinking**

❷ **Infer** Ask students: What do the words "in a far too offhand way" suggest? *These words suggest that Dr. Dunford was not really being offhand—that he had planned to make this visit all along; his announcement to his son sounds rehearsed.*

▶**Critical Viewing**◀

❸ **Analyze** Elicit responses such as the following: The setting is bleak; there is a humble tin-roofed house on a post foundation situated on a barren piece of land. Smoke comes from the chimney, indicating that people are at home. The figure on the bicycle might be visiting and the people huddled under the umbrella might be members of the household.

Chig knew something was wrong the instant his father kissed her. He had always known his father to be the warmest of men, a man so kind that when people <u>ventured</u> timidly into his office, it took only a few words from him to make them relax, and even laugh. Doctor Charles Dunford cared about people. ❶

But when he had bent to kiss the old lady's black face, something new and almost ugly had come into his eyes: fear, uncertainty, sadness, and perhaps even hatred.

Ten days before in New York, Chig's father had decided suddenly he wanted to go to Nashville to attend his college class reunion, twenty years out. Both Chig's brother and sister, Peter and Connie, were packing for camp and besides were too young for such an affair. But Chig was seventeen, had nothing to do that summer, and his father asked if he would like to go along. His father had given him additional reasons: "All my running buddies got their diplomas and were snapped up by them crafty young gals, and had kids within a year—now all those kids, some of them gals, are your age."

The reunion had lasted a week. As they packed for home, his father, in a far too offhand way, had suggested they visit Chig's grandmother. "We this close. We might as well drop in on her and my brothers." ❷

So, instead of going north, they had gone farther south, had just entered her house. And Chig had a suspicion now that the reunion had

◆ **Build Vocabulary**

ventured (ven´ chərd) *v.:* Took a risk

 Critical Viewing Describe this setting as if you are speaking to someone who has never seen it. **[Analyze]** ❸

A Visit to Grandmother ◆ 167

Springtime Rain, 1975, Ogden M. Pleissner.

Ogden Pleissner was as comfortable in New York City as he was in rural settings such as the one shown here. He traveled to Europe when he worked for the War Department during World War II, sketching battle scenes quickly and under dangerous conditions.

In addition to capturing the "essence" of a scene, Pleissner is known as a superb

draftsman. He shows this skill in the balanced composition and perfect perspective of his work. The form and emotion of his human figures is also admired by many critics.

Have students analyze the painting on this page, looking for evidence of these strengths in Pleissner's work. Use these questions for discussion:

1. Why do you think Pleissner paints the scene from an angle, rather than head-on? *The angle gives a more immediate, real-*

istic feel to the scene, as if the viewer is entering the scene. In addition, the angle of the building adds depth and balance to the composition.

2. How does Pleissner make the people seem realistic and capture their human qualities? *The postures of the people, and their placement outside the building, make it seem as if they have been caught in a candid, unguarded moment.*

◆ Literary Focus

❶ Characterization Dr. Dunford's refusal to discuss members of his family suggests negative feelings about them.

❷ Clarification Point out that when Dr. Dunford was growing up segregation was a fact of life in the South. Public education facilities for African Americans were inferior in quality and far less available than those for white students.

◆ Critical Thinking

❸ Infer Ask students what they can infer about Chig's grandmother from these lines. *Students will probably say they can infer that Chig's grandmother's eyesight is extremely poor or that she is nearly blind.*

◆ Reading Strategy

❹ Clarify Ask students how they can clarify the relationship between Dr. Dunford and his mother. *Readers can look back to find that Dr. Dunford left home at an early age and that he was reluctant to tell his son they were going to visit his mother. They can use these details and the fact that the mother never hears from Charles to conclude that something is amiss between them.*

◆ Critical Thinking

❺ Infer Ask students why they think Dr. Dunford's voice cracks. *Students may answer that he is showing the strain of a difficult moment, that even though he has had a troubled relationship with his mother, it is still important to him that she meet his son, of whom he is proud.*

---

been only an excuse to drive south, that his father had been heading to this house all the time.

His father had never talked much about his

> ◆ **Literary Focus**
> What does this detail indirectly reveal about Chig's father's feelings?

❶

family, with the exception of his brother, GL, who seemed part con man, part practical joker and part Don Juan;[1] he had spoken of GL with the kind of <u>indulgence</u> he would have shown a cute, but ill-behaved and potentially dangerous, five-year-old.

Chig's father had left home when he was fifteen. When asked why, he would answer: "I wanted to go to school. They didn't have a Negro high school at home, so I went up to Knoxville and lived with a cousin and went to school."

❷

They had been met at the door by Aunt Rose, GL's wife, and ushered into the living room. The old lady had looked up from her seat by the window. Aunt Rose stood between the visitors.

The old lady eyed his father. "Rose, who that? Rose?" She squinted. She looked like a doll, made of black straw, the wrinkles in her face running in one direction like the head of a broom. Her hair was white and coarse and grew out straight from her head. Her eyes were brown—the whites, too, seemed light brown— and were hidden behind thick glasses, which remained somehow on a tiny nose. "That Hiram?" That was another of his father's brothers. "No, it ain't Hiram; too big for Hiram." She turned then to Chig. "Now that man, he look like Eleanor, Charles's wife, but Charles wouldn't never send my grandson to see me. I never even hear from Charles." She stopped again.

❸

❹

---

1. **Don Juan** (dän´ wän´): An idle, immoral nobleman who enjoyed a great appeal for women.

168 ◆ Striving for Success

His father had never talked much about his family . . .

"It Charles, Mama. That who it is." Aunt Rose, between them, led them closer. "It Charles come all the way from New York to see you, and brung little Charles with him."

The old lady stared up at them. "Charles? Rose, that really Charles?" She turned away, and reached for a handkerchief in the pocket of her clean, ironed, flowered housecoat, and wiped her eyes. "God have mercy, Charles." She spread her arms up to him, and he bent down and kissed her cheek. That was when Chig saw his face, <u>grimacing</u>. She hugged him; Chig watched the muscles in her arms as they tightened around his father's neck. She half rose out of her chair. "How are you, son?"

Chig could not hear his father's answer.

She let him go, and fell back into her chair, grabbing the arms. Her hands were as dark as the wood, and seemed to become part of it. "Now, who that standing there? Who that man?"

"That's one of your grandsons, Mama." His father's voice cracked. "Charles Dunford, junior. You saw him once, when he was a baby, in Chicago. He's grown now."

❺

"I can see that, boy!" She looked at Chig squarely. "Come here, son, and kiss me once." He did. "What they call you? Charles too?"

"No, ma'am, they call me Chig."

She smiled. She had all her teeth, but they were too perfect to be her own. "That's good. Can't have two boys answering to Charles in the same house. Won't nobody at all come. So you that little boy. You don't remember me, do

---

◆ **Build Vocabulary**

indulgence (in dul´ jəns) *n.*: Leniency; forgiveness

grimacing (grim´ əs in) *v.*: Making a twisted or distorted facial expression

---

Cultural Connection

Notable African American Colleges

Because of the official segregation that existed during the early part of the twentieth century, Chig's father had to leave the South to get a high school education. He returned south, however, for his college education, probably to attend one of the several noted colleges set up for the higher education of African American students.

Morehouse College is a small liberal arts college that has such renowned alumni as Dr. Martin Luther King, Jr., Olympic athlete Edwin Moses, filmmaker Spike Lee, and a number of congressmen and federal judges.

Other African American colleges with outstanding reputations include Spelman College in Atlanta, Georgia, Howard University in Washington, D.C., and Booker T. Washington's alma mater, Hampton University in Hampton, Virginia.

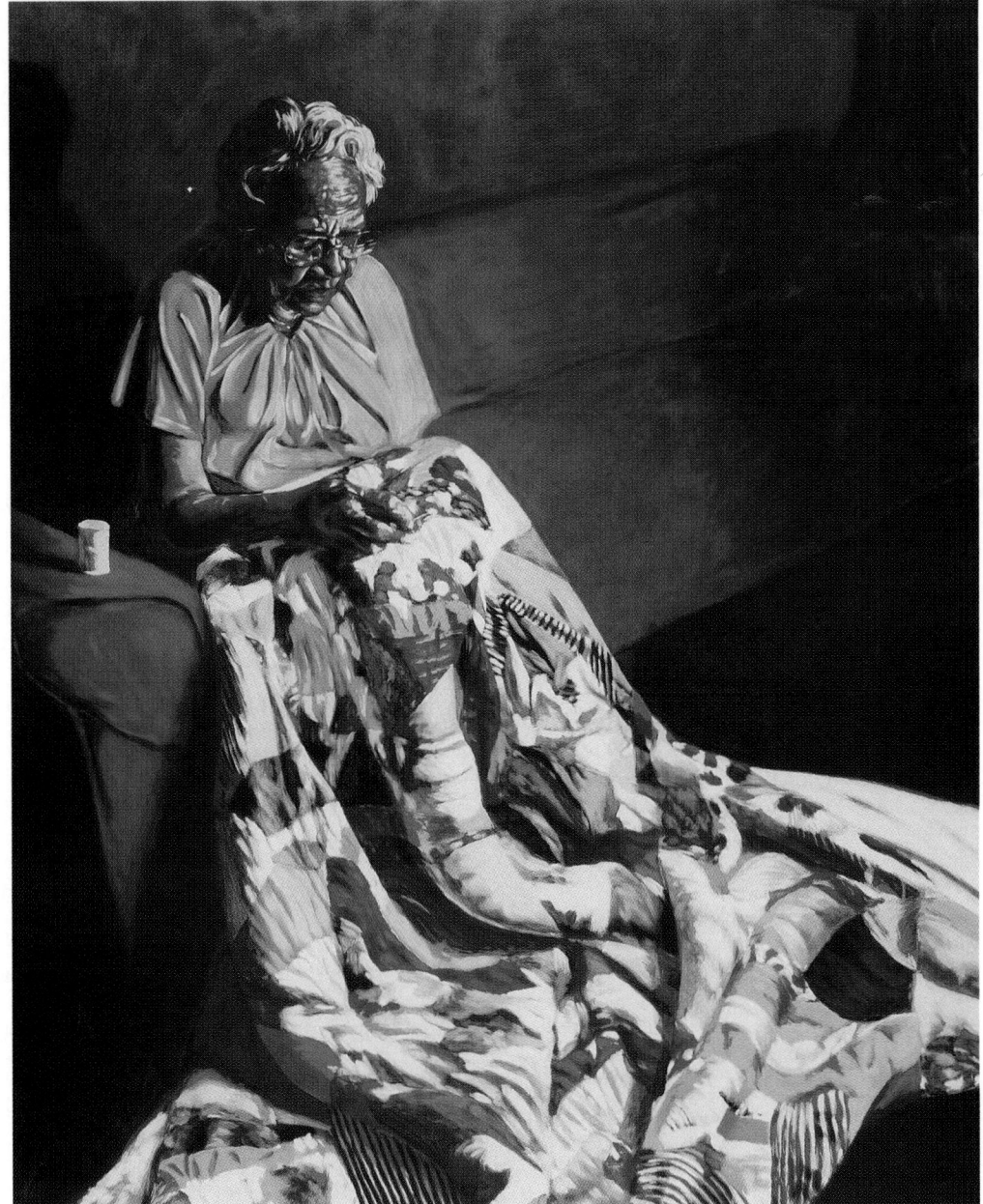

Strong Steady Hands, Alonzo Adams

▲ **Critical Viewing** Compare and contrast the woman in this picture with Chig's grandmother. **[Compare and Contrast]** ⑥

❻ **Compare and Contrast** Elicit responses such as the following: *Although the woman in the painting is an elderly African American woman, like the grandmother in the story, she looks different from Charles's mother. Her hair is more manageable and, most significant, her eyesight is good enough to enable her to do needlework.*

Customize for
Visual/Spatial Learners
Encourage these students to describe in detail how their mental images of the grandmother contrast with the woman in the picture. Then ask them to use what they know about the grandmother to explore these two characters further. Eyesight allowing, would the grandmother in the story be likely to quilt? Why or why not?

Listening to Literature Audiocassettes Play the recording of this portion of the story to help students appreciate the sound and flavor of the dialect. Explain to students that although we use standard English for formal speaking and writing, people generally use a more colloquial English for conversations with friends and family. This informal speech varies from region to region. In this story, characters use a Southern dialect. Ask students to listen, and then to explain what the dialect adds to the story. *The dialect makes the characters seem more like real people from a real place.*

Humanities: Art

Strong Steady Hands by Alonzo Adams.
   This serigraph—a print made by the silkscreen process—shows an African American woman working on an elaborate quilt.
   Alonzo Adams was born in Harlem in New York City in 1961. As a painter, he specializes in capturing everyday scenes associated with contemporary black life. Students might be interested to know that Bill Cosby, the Rev. Jesse Jackson, Maya Angelou, and former Senator Bill Bradley all own works by Adams.

Use these questions for discussion:
1. What personal quality might the woman in the picture share with the grandmother in the story? *Students may say that the woman in the painting shows strength and patience in being able to finish a difficult task. The grandmother in the story shows strength when she tells Chig she doesn't need help.*
2. How would the painting be different without the quilt? *Students might say that the quilt is what makes the painting beautiful. Without it, the painting would be dark and dull.*

◆ **Reading Strategy**

❶ Clarify *The phrase "those boys" implies that Hiram is another of Mama's sons. For verification, students can also look back at the following passage on page 168: "'That Hiram?' That was another of his father's brothers."*

◆ **Literary Focus**

❷ Characterization Ask students how the grandmother's own words characterize her in this passage. *Students may say that she shows herself to be strong or tough.*

◆ **Critical Thinking**

❸ Infer Ask students what they infer from the observation that Dr. Dunford's wife would sit and not speak for long periods. *Students may answer that Dr. Dunford's wife is calm and can focus on a task.*

◆ **Reading Strategy**

❹ Clarify Ask students to think back to what they know of Dr. Dunford's character and suggest why this situation might be especially difficult for him. *Students may answer that it must be very difficult for Dr. Dunford—a successful and independent professional—to feel reduced to a child in his mother's presence.*

◆ **Literary Focus**

❺ Characterization Ask students to give their ideas about GL's character, based on what they have read about him. *Students may say that GL seems unpredictable and immature on the one hand, but charming and fun-filled on the other.*

---

you. I used to take you to church in Chicago, and you'd get up and hop in time to the music. You studying to be a preacher?"

"No, ma'am. I don't think so. I might be a lawyer."

"You'll be an honest one, won't you?"

"I'll try."

"Trying ain't enough! You be honest, you hear? Promise me. You be honest like your daddy."

"All right. I promise."

"Good. Rose, where's GL at? Where's that thief? He gone again?"

"I don't know, Mama." Aunt Rose looked embarrassed. "He say he was going by the store. He'll be back."

"Well, then where's Hiram? You call up those boys, and get them over here—now! You got enough to eat? Let me go see." She started to get up. Chig reached out his hand. She shook him off. "What they tell you about me, Chig? They tell you I'm all laid up? Don't believe it. They don't know nothing about old ladies. When I want help, I'll let you know. Only time I'll need help getting anywheres is when I dies and they lift me into the ground."

❶ ◆ **Reading Strategy**
What clues help you clarify who Grandma is talking about?

She was standing now, her back and shoulders straight. She came only to Chig's chest. She squinted up at him. "You eat much? Your daddy ate like two men."

"Yes, ma'am."

❸ "That's good. That means you ain't nervous. Your mama, she ain't nervous. I remember that. In Chicago, she'd sit down by a window all afternoon and never say nothing, just knit." She smiled. "Let me see what we got to eat."

"I'll do that, Mama." Aunt Rose spoke softly. "You haven't seen Charles in a long time. You sit and talk."

The old lady squinted at her. "You can do the cooking if you promise it ain't because you think I can't."

Aunt Rose chuckled. "I know you can do it, Mama."

"All right. I'll just sit and talk a spell." She

sat again and arranged her skirt around her short legs.

Chig did most of the talking, told all about himself before she asked. His father spoke only when he was spoken to, and then, only one word at a time, as if by coming back home, he had become a small boy again, sitting in the parlor while his mother spoke with her guests.

When Uncle Hiram and Mae, his wife, came they sat down to eat. Chig did not have to ask about Uncle GL's absence; Aunt Rose volunteered an explanation: "Can't never tell where the man is at. One Thursday morning he left here and next thing we knew, he was calling from Chicago, saying he went up to see Joe Louis[2] fight. He'll be here though; he ain't as young and footloose as he used to be." Chig's father had mentioned driving down that GL was about five years older than he was, nearly fifty.

Uncle Hiram was somewhat smaller than Chig's father; his short-cropped kinky hair was half gray, half black. One spot, just off his forehead, was totally white. Later, Chig found out it had been that way since he was twenty. Mae (Chig could not bring himself to call her Aunt) was a good deal younger than Hiram, pretty enough so that Chig would have looked at her twice on the street. She was a honey-colored woman, with long eyelashes. She was wearing a white sheath.

At dinner, Chig and his father sat on one side, opposite Uncle Hiram and Mae; his grandmother and Aunt Rose sat at the ends. The food was good; there was a lot and Chig ate a lot. All through the meal, they talked about the family as it had been thirty years before, and particularly about the young GL. Mae and Chig asked questions; the old lady answered; Aunt Rose directed the discussion, steering the old lady onto the best stories; Chig's father laughed from time to time; Uncle Hiram ate.

"Why don't you tell them about the horse, Mama?" Aunt Rose, over Chig's weak protest,

---

2. **Joe Louis:** U.S. boxer (1914–1981) and the world heavyweight champion from 1937 to 1949.

Cross-Curricular Connection: History

Dr. Dunford tells Chig that he left his hometown at fifteen because there was no high school for African American students. In 1896, the Supreme Court made a ruling in the case of *Plessy v. Ferguson* that segregation did not violate the constitutional rights of African Americans, provided that schools and other facilities were separate but equal. Despite this stipulation, schools and other public facilities for the segregated races were separate but *unequal*. In some cases, small

towns did not even have high schools for African Americans.

Plessy v. Ferguson was overturned by the landmark 1954 Supreme Court decision, *Brown v. the Board of Education*, where the court ruled that all school segregation was unconstitutional. This eliminated school segregation by law. However, segregated school systems and their inequities stayed in place in much of the country for many years afterward.

was spooning mashed potatoes onto his plate. "There now, Chig."

"I'm trying to think." The old lady was holding her fork halfway to her mouth, looking at them over her glasses. "Oh, you talking about that crazy horse GL brung home that time."

6 "That's right, Mama." Aunt Rose nodded and slid another slice of white meat on Chig's plate.

Mae started to giggle. "Oh, I've heard this. This is funny, Chig."

The old lady put down her fork and began: Well, GL went out of the house one day with an old, no-good chair I wanted him to take over to the church for a bazaar, and he met up with this man who'd just brung in some horses from out West. Now, I reckon you can expect one swindler to be in every town, but you don't rightly think there'll be two, and God forbid they should ever meet—but they did, GL and his chair, this man and his horses. Well, I wished I'd-a been there; there must-a been some mighty high-powered talking going on. That man with his horses, he told GL them horses was half-Arab, half-Indian, and GL told that man the chair was an antique he'd stole from some rich white folks. So they swapped. Well, I was a-looking out the window and seen GL dragging this animal to the house. It looked pretty gentle and its eyes was most closed and its feet was shuffling.

"GL, where'd you get that thing?" I says.

"I swapped him for that old chair, Mama," he says. "And made myself a bargain. This is even better than Papa's horse."

Well, I'm a-looking at this horse and noticing how he be looking more and more wide awake every minute, sort of warming up like a teakettle until, I swears to you, that horse is blowing steam out its nose.

His father spoke only when he was spoken to, and then, only one word at a time.

"Come on, Mama," GL says, "come on and I'll take you for a ride." Now George, my husband, God rest his tired soul, he'd brung home this white folks' buggy which had a busted wheel and fixed it and was to take it back that day and GL says: "Come on, Mama, we'll use this fine buggy and take us a ride."

"GL," I says, "no, we ain't. Them white folks'll burn us alive if we use their buggy. You just take that horse right on back." You see, I was sure that boy'd come by that animal ungainly.

"Mama, I can't take him back," GL says.

"Why not?" I says.

"Because I don't rightly know where that man is at," GL says.

"Oh," I says. "Well, then I reckon we stuck with it." And I turned around to go back into the house because it was getting late, near dinner time, and I was cooking for ten.

"Mama," GL says to my back. "Mama, ain't you coming for a ride with me?"

"Go on, boy. You ain't getting me inside kicking range of that animal." I was eying that beast and it was boiling hotter all the time. I reckon maybe that man had drugged it. "That horse is wild, GL," I says.

"No, he ain't. He ain't. That man say he is buggy and saddle broke and as sweet as the inside of a apple."

My oldest girl, Essie, had-a come out on the porch and she says: "Go on, Mama. I'll cook. You ain't been out the house in weeks."

"Sure, come on, Mama," GL says. "There ain't nothing to be fidgety about. This horse is gentle as a rose petal." And just then that animal snorts so hard it sets up a little dust storm around its feet.

"Yes, Mama," Essie says, "you can see he gentle." Well, I looked at Essie and then at that

7

8

A Visit to Grandmother ◆ 171

◆ **Literary Focus**

6 Characterization Ask students: What can you tell about GL from the fact that the family loves to tell stories about him? *Even though GL is still thought of as naughty, everyone is fond of him and finds him entertaining and charming.*

◆ **Critical Thinking**

7 Draw Conclusions Ask students what this exchange between Mama and GL might lead them to believe about GL and how he got the horse. What details point to their conclusion? *Students will probably conclude that GL either got the horse by deception or stole it. Mama's assertion that GL had "come by that horse ungainly" leads to this conclusion. Also, the fact that GL says he doesn't know where the man is indicates he either swindled him or is lying altogether and stole the horse.*

Comprehension Check ☑

8 What does Grandmother suspect has been done to the horse, and for what purpose? *She thinks it was given a sedative to quiet it, but it actually has not been broken.*

🎧 **Listening to Literature Audiocassettes** Play the recording of this portion of the story either before students read or as they read along. Discuss with students the elements that add to the interest and excitement of listening to this story. *Elements include the comments and interruptions from family members, the dialogue the mother uses as she tells the tale, and the mother's side comments about the action.*

Beyond the Classroom

Life and Workplace Skills

The difference between GL and Chig's father demonstrates the difference between someone who thinks ahead and someone who doesn't. Although GL is charming and funny, he doesn't appear to have set any goals for his life. Chig's father, on the other hand, set goals for his education and followed through on them in spite of the obstacle of segregation. Tell students that planning ahead and setting goals are important skills in life and in the workplace. Part of thinking ahead is

considering all the possible outcomes in a situation, not just the ones you would like to have happen. Allow time for students to work in small groups and brainstorm for possible outcomes to GL's taking his mother out for a buggy ride. Have groups share their answers, then suggest how they would have approached the situation by thinking ahead or planning for potential problems.

After students have analyzed GL's situation, have them identify goals of their own and use the same strategies to explore the possible outcomes and necessary steps.

1 Connect The title of this collage, "Spring Fever," emphasizes the "released" feeling that is evoked in this picture by people coming out of doors, the horse outside, and the bright green plant in the foreground.

◆ Build Grammar Skills

2 Pronoun Case Have students determine whether the word me in this sentence is objective or subjective case. Ask them to explain their answers. *Students should know that me is objective because it receives the action of the verb made.*

◆ Literary Focus

3 Characterization Ask students what this part of the story shows about GL. *Students may say that GL, despite his mischievous nature, is charming and knows how to use his charm to win affection.*

Spring Fever, 1978. From the Profile Part I: The Twenties series (Mecklenburg County). Collage on board, 7 x 9 3/8" Private Collection © Romare Bearden Foundation/Licensed by VAGA, New York, NY

1 ▲ **Critical Viewing** How does the title of this painting contribute to the mood it evokes? **[Connect]**

horse because I didn't think we could be looking at the same animal. I should-a figured how Essie's eyes ain't never been so good.

"Come on, Mama," GL says.

"All right," I says. So I stood on the porch and watched GL hitching that horse up to the white folks' buggy. For a while there, the animal was pretty quiet, pawing a little, but not much. And I was feeling a little better about riding with GL behind that crazy-looking horse. I could see how GL was happy I was going with him. He was scurrying around that animal buckling buckles and strapping straps, all the time smiling, and that made me feel good.

Then he was finished, and I must say, that horse looked mighty fine hitched to that buggy and I knew anybody what climbed up there

would look pretty good too. GL came around and stood at the bottom of the steps, and took off his hat and bowed and said: "Madam," and reached out his hand to me and I was feeling real elegant like a fine lady. He helped me up to the seat and then got up beside me and we moved out down our alley. And I remember how black folks come out on their porches and shook their heads, saying: "Lord now, will you look at Eva Dunford, the fine lady! Don't she look good sitting up there!" And I pretended not to hear and sat up straight and proud.

We rode on through the center of town, up Market Street, and all the way out where Hiram is living now, which in them days was all woods, there not being even a farm in sight and that's when that horse must-a first realized

 Humanities: Art

Spring Fever, 1978, by Romare Bearden.

Bearden (1912?–1988) was one of the most accomplished artists of his time. He was born in Charlotte, North Carolina, but grew up in New York City, where his mother was a newspaper editor. Many of the great African American artists of the Harlem Renaissance visited his home. For some time Bearden painted in an abstract, cubist style, but he experienced his greatest

artistic success when he shifted to collage in the 1960's. Notice that despite the strong abstract element in *Spring Fever*, Bearden manages to make the people and horses seem alive.

Use the following questions for discussion:
1. How do you feel when you look at *Spring Fever*? How did Bearden create the mood of the work? *The mood seems to be rather relaxed and quiet. Bearden cre-*

ates this mood by the colors, particularly the purple of the sky, and by the stillness of the figures.

2. Explain in what ways this art reflects the characters or setting of "A Visit to Grandmother." *The figures in the scene might represent Grandmother and one of her sons, but the scene depicted seems much more calm than any of the scenes in this story.*

he weren't at all broke or tame or maybe thought he was back out West again, and started to gallop.

"GL," I says, "now you ain't joking with your mama, is you? Because if you is, I'll strap you purple if I live through this."

Well, GL was pulling on the reins with all his meager strength, and yelling, "Whoa, you. Say now, whoa!" He turned to me just long enough to say, "I ain't fooling with you, Mama. Honest!"

I reckon that animal weren't too satisfied with the road, because it made a sharp right turn just then, down into a gulley and struck out across a hilly meadow. "Mama," GL yells. "Mama, do something!"

I didn't know what to do, but I figured I had to do something so I stood up, hopped down onto the horse's back and pulled it to a stop. Don't ask me how I did that; I reckon it was that I was a mother and my baby asked me to do something, is all.

I didn't know what to do, but I figured I had to do something...

◆ Literary Focus
What does this paragraph reveal about the relationship between Grandma and GL?

"Well, we walked that animal all the way home; sometimes I had to club it over the nose with my fist to make it come, but we made it, GL and me. You remember how tired we was, Charles?"

"I wasn't here at the time." Chig turned to his father and found his face completely blank, without even a trace of a smile or a laugh.

"Well, of course you was, son. That happened in . . . in . . . it was a hot summer that year and—"

"I left here in June of that year. You wrote me about it."

The old lady stared past Chig at him. They all turned to him; Uncle Hiram looked up from his plate.

"Then you don't remember how we all laughed?"

"No, I don't, Mama. And I probably wouldn't have laughed. I don't think it was funny." They were staring into each other's eyes.

"Why not, Charles?"

"Because in the first place, the horse was gained by fraud. And in the second place, both of you might have been seriously injured or even killed." He broke off their stare and spoke to himself more than to any of them:

"And if I'd done it, you would've beaten me good for it."

"Pardon?" The old lady had not heard him; only Chig had heard.

Chig's father sat up straight as if preparing to debate. "I said that if I had done it, if I had done just exactly what GL did, you would have beaten me good for it, Mama." He was looking at her again.

"Why you say that, son?" She was leaning toward him.

"Don't you know? Tell the truth. It can't hurt me now." His voice cracked, but only once. "If GL and I did something wrong, you'd beat me first and then be too tired to beat him. At dinner, he'd always get seconds and I wouldn't. You'd do things with him, like ride in that buggy, but if I wanted you to do something with me, you were always too busy." He paused and considered whether to say what he finally did say: "I cried when I left here. Nobody loved me, Mama. I cried all the way up to Knoxville. That was the last time I ever cried in my life."

"Oh, Charles." She started to get up, to come around the table to him.

He stopped her. "It's too late."

"But you don't understand."

"What don't I understand? I understood

A Visit to Grandmother ◆ 173

◆ **Literary Focus**

④ Characterization Elicit responses such as the following: *She refers to GL as her baby. She still saw him as an immature child in need of protection, and was willing to risk injury to save him.*

◆ **Reading Strategy**

⑤ Clarify Point out that we are finally about to find out what is really bothering Charles. Suggest they look back in the story for places where the author suggests that Charles has a troubled relationship with his mother. Then have them read a bit further to understand the source of the trouble. *Students will soon clarify that Charles was jealous of his brother because he thought their mother favored him.*

Customize for
Bodily Kinesthetic Learners
Allow time for these students to sit in a group, simulating the arrangement of family members around the dinner table. Have group members read the parts, noting the facial expressions and gestures they might use as they act out this scene. Ask students why they use these movements. *Students might scowl, pound the table, stand, or cover their faces with their hands. Encourage students to identify the emotion behind each of these expressions and gestures.*

Speaking and Listening Mini-Lesson

Casting Discussion

This mini-lesson supports the Speaking and Listening activity in the Idea Bank on page 176.

Introduce the Concept Talk with students about how actors are chosen for a film. First casting directors meet to talk about how the characters should look and behave. They can then choose appropriate actors. Explain that the class will form small groups to discuss casting a movie based on the story.

Develop Background The groups should jot down their thoughts about each character.

Encourage students to draw upon the mental images they formed as they read the story.

Apply the Information Using their notes, the group can choose actors they have seen in films and television who best fit the roles as they conceive them. They should give reasons for each casting decision they propose.

Assess the Outcome The groups can compare their cast lists and share the reasoning for their choices. Have students assess how imagining real actors in the parts of the characters affects their appreciation of the story.

◆ Critical Thinking

❶ Make Judgments Ask students if they find this explanation reasonable. Have them back up their opinions with evidence from the story. *Some students may cite the story about the horse as evidence that the mother really did love GL better. Some may cite her remarks about Charles's honesty as evidence that she loved both her sons equally, but for different reasons.*

◆ Critical Thinking

❷ Make Judgments Ask students if they think Charles's accusation is true. *Some students may believe that it is true; others may think Charles is now voicing childish fears and jealousies that had another basis.*

◆ Literary Focus

❸ Characterization Charles's words and abrupt departure from the table reveal the depth of his sense of rejection, even after the passage of thirty years.

Reinforce and Extend

Answers

◆ Literature and Your Life

Reader's Response Some students might sympathize with the grandmother because she is now the object of her son's withheld anger. Others may sympathize with Charles for his unfair treatment as a child, or with Chig, who has been dragged into the conflict.

Thematic Focus Communication difficulties can lead family members to grow remote from one another, to get into trouble, or to become deceitful.

☑ Check Your Comprehension

1. He says they are close by so they may as well visit her.
2. He went to Knoxville so he could attend high school.
3. He is silent and unamused.
4. She said she gave all of them what they needed most.
5. GL arrives immediately after the confrontation.

---

then; I understand now."

Tears now traveled down the lines in her face, but when she spoke, her voice was clear. "I thought you knew. I had ten children. I had to give all of them what they needed most." She nodded. "I paid more mind to GL. I had to. GL could-a ended up swinging if I hadn't. But you was smarter. You was more growed up than GL when you was five and he was ten, and I tried to show you that by letting you do what you wanted to do."

"That's not true, Mama. You know it. GL was light-skinned and had good hair and looked almost white and you loved him for that."

"Charles, no. No, son. I didn't love any one of you more than any other."

"That can't be true." His father was standing now, his fists clenched tight. "Admit it, Mama . . . please!" Chig looked at him, shocked; the man was actually crying.

"It may not-a been right what I done, but I ain't no liar." Chig knew she did not really understand what had happened, what he wanted

of her. "I'm not lying to you, Charles."

Chig's father had gone pale. He spoke very softly. "You're about thirty years too late, Mama." He bolted from the table. Silverware and dishes rang and jumped. Chig heard him hurrying up to their room.

They sat in silence for awhile and then heard a key in the front door. A man with a new, lacquered straw hat came in. He was wearing brown and white two-tone shoes with very pointed toes and a white summer suit. "Say now! Man! I heard my brother was in town. Where he at? Where that rascal?"

He stood in the doorway, smiling broadly, an engaging, open, friendly smile, the innocent smile of a five-year-old.

◆ Literary Focus
What do Charles's actions tell you about him?

◆ Build Vocabulary

lacquered (lak´ ərd) *adj.*: Coated with varnish made from shellac or resin

---

Guide for Responding

◆ Literature and Your Life

Reader's Response With which character in the story do you sympathize? Explain.

Thematic Focus When family members do not communicate, small misunderstandings can grow into big problems. What are some of the other possible effects of not discussing problems as they arise?

Group Discussion With a partner, role-play a conversation that might occur between Charles and GL or Charles and Chig after the confrontation between Charles and his mother.

☑ Check Your Comprehension

1. What is the reason Chig's father, Charles, gives for visiting Chig's grandmother?
2. What reason does Charles give for leaving home when he was fifteen?
3. How does Charles react to Mama's story about the horse?
4. How does Mama explain the different ways she treated her children?
5. Who arrives immediately after the confrontation between Charles and his mother?

174 ◆ *Striving for Success*

Beyond the Selection

FURTHER READING

Other Works by William Melvin Kelley
A Different Drummer
Dancers on the Shore (stories)

Other Works About Families
Barrio Boy, Ernesto Galarza
My Father Sits in the Dark, Jerome Weidman
    We suggest that you preview these works before recommending them to students.

INTERNET

You and your students may find additional information about William Melvin Kelley on the Internet. Sites may have changed since we published this information.

    To read a review of Kelley's novel *A Drop of Patience*, go to **http://www.wwnorton.com/ecco/884601.htm**

    We *strongly recommend* that you preview this and related sites before you send students to them.

Guide for Responding (continued)

◆ Critical Thinking

INTERPRET
1. Describe Charles's attitude toward GL. **[Interpret]**
2. Give two reasons that Charles has not visited his mother in so long. **[Analyze]**
3. What has drawn Charles back to his mother now? **[Infer]**
4. What do you think Charles's relationship with his mother will be like in the future? **[Draw Conclusions]**

APPLY
5. Identify two ways to clear up misunderstandings. **[Apply]**

EXTEND
6. Describe the qualities you think are important in a person whose career involves guiding other people to communicate and resolve their differences. **[Career Link]**

◆ Reading Strategy

CLARIFY
You may have felt confused by the force of Charles's emotions until you were able to **clarify** the reasons for his feelings.
1. Explain how you clarified two ideas or relationships that were not at first clear to you.
2. How you would help someone clarify the problem Charles has with his mother and brother?

◆ Literary Focus

CHARACTERIZATION
Kelley uses **direct characterization** when he states, "Doctor Charles Dunford cared about people." With **indirect characterization**, the author allows you to discover what a character is like through the dialogue and action of the character or through other characters' comments.
1. Explain three things you learned about GL indirectly.
2. Identify one thing you learned about a character through direct characterization and one thing you learned through indirect characterization.

◆ Build Vocabulary

USING WORD ORIGINS
Use a dictionary to look up the origins of the following words. Then explain how each pair is related in meaning.
1. navigate, navy
2. pose, position
3. material, matter

USING THE WORD BANK
Read each book title below. On your paper, write the word from the Word Bank that you would most expect to find in that book.
1. *A History of Japanese Enamels*
2. *Smile! Dr. Bill's Guide to Being Happy*
3. *The Church in Europe*, A.D. *984–1517*
4. *Business Risks in the Twenty-first Century*

◆ Build Grammar Skills

PRONOUN CASE
The **subjective case** is used when a pronoun is the subject or renames the subject. The **objective case** is used when the pronoun is a direct object or the object of a preposition.

Practice Copy the following sentences in your notebook. Replace the noun or nouns in parentheses with the correct form of a pronoun.
1. Charles had never talked much about (Charles's) family.
2. (Charles) spoke very softly.
3. (Grandmother) had to give all of (the children in the family) what they needed most.
4. (Mae, Grandma, and Chig) sat down to supper.

Writing Application Rewrite the following passage, correcting the pronoun usage errors. Continue the passage with two more sentences that contain pronouns.

> Charles felt that his mother loved GL more than he. Him and GL were very different. I would have felt bad if it happened to I.

A Visit to Grandmother ◆ 175

◆ Build Vocabulary

Using Word Origins
1. *navigate* and *navy* derive from the Latin *navigāre*—to manage a ship.
2. *pose* and *position* derive from the Latin *pōnere*—to place.
3. *material* and *matter* derive from the Latin *materia*—matter.

Using the Word Bank
1. lacquered; 2. grimacing;
3. indulgence; 4. ventured

◆ Build Grammar Skills

Practice
1. Charles had never talked much about <u>his</u> family.
2. <u>He</u> spoke very softly.
3. <u>She</u> had to give all of <u>them</u> what they needed most.
4. <u>They</u> sat down to supper.

Writing Application
Charles felt that his mother loved GL more than <u>him</u>. He and GL were very different. I would have felt bad if it happened to <u>me</u>.

 Writer's Solution

For additional instruction and practice, use the lesson in the **Language Lab CD-ROM** on Pronoun case and the pages on the Cases of Pronouns (pp. 76–79) in the *Writer's Solution Grammar Practice Book.*

◆ Critical Thinking
1. Charles is indulgent of GL but does not seem to respect him.
2. Charles has not visited his mother because he has been busy developing his career and raising his family. A second reason is that he has harbored resentment towards her.
3. Students might say Charles's mother is getting older and even though Charles feels anger toward her, he probably wants to see her again and clear the air.
4. Perhaps Charles and his mother will come to some sort of understanding and reestablish contact.
5. Possible ways to clear up misunderstandings include (1) paying particular attention to the other person's point of view and (2) finding a compromise between two positions.
6. A person who guides others in conflict resolution should be objective, empathetic, and tactful.

◆ Reading Strategy
1. Students' examples should indicate that they clarified information by looking back to review details of setting, characterization, or key events; looking ahead for more information; creating a family tree or timeline to keep track of characters and events.
2. Students might suggest they would highlight past events that contributed to the problem, such as Charles being beaten when his brother was not.

◆ Literary Focus
1. Possible responses are: (1) GL has a love of mischief; (2) he is irresponsible; (3) he knows how to charm and manipulate his mother.
2. Students might say they learned that Charles cared about people through direct characterization. They learned through indirect characterization—such as Charles grimacing when he kisses his mother—that Charles harbors resentment towards his mother.

Idea Bank

Customizing for
Performance Levels

Following are suggestions for matching Idea Bank topics with your students' performance levels:

Less Advanced Students: 1, 4
Average Students: 2, 5, 6
More Advanced Students: 3, 7

Customizing for
Learning Modalities

Following are suggestions for matching Idea Bank topics with your students' learning modalities:

Logical/Mathematical: 7
Verbal/Linguistic: 2, 4, 5
Interpersonal: 4, 6

Writing Mini-Lesson

Refer students to the Writing Handbook, page 965, for instruction on the writing process, and page 967 for further information on narrative writing.

Writing and Language Transparencies Use Writing Process Model 2: Biographical Profile (pp. 13–16) to help students draft and revise their firsthand biographies.

Writer's Solution

Writing Lab CD-ROM

Have students complete the tutorial on Narration. Follow these steps:

1. Encourage students to view video tips on narrative elements.
2. Use the word bins to help them select transition words that communicate relationships.
3. Use a proofreading checklist to locate possible errors in their drafts.

Build Your Portfolio

Idea Bank

Writing

1. **Letter to Charles's Mother** Put yourself in Charles's place and write a letter to Mama about your feelings. Base your letter on what you know about Charles from the story.

2. **News Report** Write a news report about the incident with the horse from the objective point of view of a newspaper reporter. Base your report on the facts you learn from the story.

3. **Alternative Ending** This story ends abruptly after Charles rushes from the table. Write an alternative ending to the story that has Charles staying to meet his brother.

Speaking and Listening

4. **Casting Discussion** With a group of classmates, choose actors to play the roles in a movie version of this story. Present and explain your recommendations to the class. **[Media Link]**

5. **Oral Anecdote** Choose a humorous or exciting incident from your own life as the subject of an anecdote—a brief story—and practice telling it aloud. Present your anecdote to the class.

Projects

6. **Conflict-Resolution Workshop** Plan activities for a conflict-resolution workshop that could teach people like Charles and his mother strategies for working out their differences. Lead a small group of classmates through one activity.

7. **Cultural Comparisons Chart** Create a chart that compares how family members relate to one another in three different world cultures. Address issues such as interaction with extended family, activities families share, and responsibilities of children and adults. **[Social Studies Link]**

Writing Mini-Lesson

Firsthand Biography

Flip through a mental scrapbook of the individuals who have played special roles in your life and have influenced your understanding of yourself and the world around you. These people might include relatives, friends, teachers, or other adults whom you admire. Choose one of these people and write a firsthand biography—a story about the life or an important episode in the life of a person with whom you have had direct experiences. Include personal insights that show the close relationship between you and your subject. The following tips will explain how to highlight the significance of the events you include.

Writing Skills Focus: Provide Examples

Provide examples of events or actions that demonstrate the qualities of your subject and capture your relationship with him or her. For example, if you wish to point out that your subject is compassionate, you might include a description of a time when he or she worked in a food kitchen to feed the homeless. Use transitions such as *for example* and *for instance* to introduce your examples.

Prewriting Write your subject's name on a sheet of paper. Around the person's name, write down the words and phrases that capture his or her significant characteristics. Around each of the characteristics, jot down examples.

Drafting For each characteristic you want to highlight, include at least one example that demonstrates that quality in your subject. Use words that show the connection between the characteristic and the example.

Revising Review your firsthand biography and add examples of events or actions that will clarify the points you want to make about the subject.

✓ ASSESSMENT OPTIONS

Formal Assessment, Selection Test, pp. 38–40, and Assessment Resources Software. The selection test is designed so that it can be easily customized to the performance levels of your students. *Alternative Assessment*, p. 12, includes options for less advanced students, more advanced students, verbal/linguistic learners, bodily/kinesthetic learners, logical/mathematical learners, and visual/spatial learners.

PORTFOLIO ASSESSMENT

Use the following rubrics in the *Alternative Assessment* booklet to assess student writing:
Letter to Charles's Mother: Description Rubric, p. 97
News Report: Evaluation/Review Rubric, p. 104
Alternative Ending: Summary Rubric, p. 98

Writing Process Workshop

User's Manual

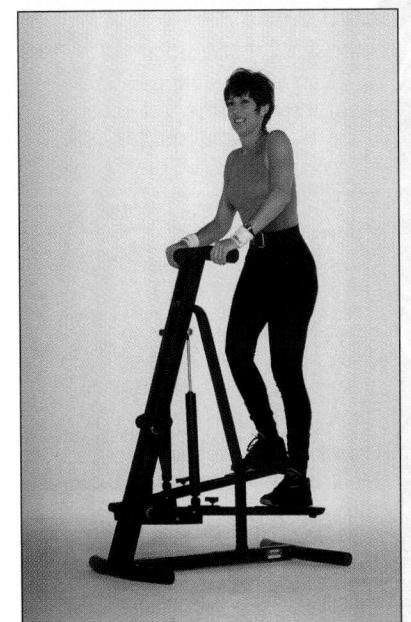

A **user's manual** explains how to operate a tool, a vehicle, an appliance, or other device. A good user's manual conveys specific and often technical information in as few words as possible. The explanations may be supported by visual aids that condense information into a small space. Lists or headings can also call attention to various points or steps.

The following skills, introduced in this section's Writing Mini-Lessons, will help you write a user's manual about any product.

Writing Skills Focus

▶ **Give a clear explanation** of any procedures involved. A well-written user's manual is one in which directions are easy to follow. (See p. 145.)

▶ **Elaborate on certain steps** to give more information. Provide details that tell why or how the step is performed. Give examples when appropriate. (See p. 153.)

▶ **Clearly explain each cause and effect**—show how one action or condition brings about another. (See p. 163.)

▶ **Use transition words,** such as *first* or *next,* to describe the required sequence.

The following user's manual for the StairWalker 2000™ exercise machine demonstrates these skills.

MODEL

① Before you start using your new Stair-Walker 2000™, first adjust the steps to fit your height. Next ② set resistance and speed to your desired settings.

Refer to the chart below to find the proper resistance setting, speed, and length of time for your workouts:

GOAL	RESISTANCE	AVG. SPEED	TIME ③
Max. Fat Burn	1, 2, 3	90 steps per min.	30 min.
Max. Tone	4, 5, 6	80 steps per min.	20–30 min.
Max. Strength	7, 8	90 steps per min.	10–20 min.

BURNING FAT: If you exercise at a low resistance setting for a sustained period of time, you will burn fat. ④

① These sentences explain the procedure for the user to follow.

② Transition words such as *before, first,* and *next* clarify the order of steps in the procedure.

③ This chart elaborates on setting resistance and speed. It also presents a great deal of information in a small space.

④ Here the writer clearly shows a cause-and-effect relationship.

◆ Beyond the Classroom

Career Connection

Tell students that regardless of what they do in their lives, they are likely to find themselves relying frequently on practical and technical writing, both as a writer and as a reader. Filling out a form, writing a memo, reading a user's manual for a recently bought product, and writing a job-application letter are all examples of practical and technical writing that they are all likely to engage in at some time in their lives.

Prepare and Engage

Establish Writing Guidelines
Before students begin, review the following key characteristics of a user's manual:

• It opens with a brief overview of the product or item.

• It provides detailed information and instruction about the product or item.

• It uses various visual devices to illustrate details.

You may want to distribute the Scoring Rubric for Technical Description/Explanation in *Alternative Assessment* (p. 116) to alert students to the criteria on which they will be evaluated. See the suggestions on page 179 for customizing the rubric for this workshop.

Refer students to the Writing Handbook, page 965, for instruction in the writing process, and page 969 for further information on practical and technical writing.

✒ Writer's Solution

Writers at Work Videodisc
To introduce students to the key elements and show them how auto mechanic Larry Cataldo uses technical writing in his work, play the videodisc segment on Practical and Technical Writing (Ch. 8). Have students discuss what Cataldo says about the kind of writing he does at work.

Play frames 33166 to 42350

Writing Lab CD-ROM
If your students have access to computers, you may want to have them work on the tutorial on Practical and Technical Writing to complete all or part of their user's manuals. Follow these steps:

1. Have students review the interactive model of a user's manual.

2. Have students draft on computer.

3. Suggest that students consult the screen on formatting technical writing.

Sourcebook
Students can find additional support, including topic ideas, models, audience and purpose profiles, and graphic organizers, in the chapter on Practical and Technical Writing (pp. 228–262).

177

Prewriting

In a typical day, students may operate several machines without even thinking about it. For example, they might wake up to an alarm clock, use a microwave oven or toaster oven to cook breakfast, and use a telephone before they leave for school. Have students make a list of these everyday devices and consider how they would explain their operation to someone using them for the first time. Have them choose one of the devices as the subject of a user's manual.

Customize for
English Language Learners

Students learning English may not know the vocabulary related to their topics. Once they have decided on a topic, make a list of the words they are likely to need to describe it. Give them the list and have them find the words in a bilingual dictionary.

Customize for
Less Proficient Writers

These students may benefit from writing each important component or step in the process of operating a device on a notecard. They can then arrange the cards chronologically, spatially, in order of importance, or however they think best for writing the manual.

Customize for
More Advanced Students

Challenge these students to write about something they know little about and will have to research before explaining.

 Writer's Solution

Writing Lab CD-ROM

The Gathering Details section of the tutorial on Practical and Technical Writing includes a screen on using visual aids. Have students consult this screen to help them work with visual aids such as graphs, charts, and pictures, and incorporate them into their user's manuals.

Drafting

Encourage students to include visuals in their drafts and to write their drafts quickly.

APPLYING LANGUAGE SKILLS: Exact Nouns

Make your explanation as clear as possible by using exact nouns. An exact noun is the most specific or precise noun for the given situation.

Vague Nouns:
Using a tool, unscrew the thing on the front of your VCR.

Exact Nouns:
Using a Phillips screwdriver, unscrew the aluminum cover on the control panel of your VCR.

Practice On your paper, replace the vague nouns with exact nouns in the following sentence.

> To turn on your device, first plug the thing into the nearest spot on your wall and turn the round object.

Writing Application As you draft your user's manual, use exact nouns to help your reader precisely visualize the steps.

Writer's Solution Connection Writing Lab

To help you choose a topic for your user's manual, refer to the following activity in the Writing Lab tutorial on Practical/Technical Writing: Using Phrases to Find a Topic.

Prewriting

Choose a Topic Ideas for a user's manual may stem from recreational activities or from items in the classroom or home. For instance, creating guidelines for a personal fitness program or describing how to use an electronic device are great topics for a user's manual. Choose a topic that you find interesting or relevant.

Use different combinations of these words and phrases to spark an idea for writing a user's manual.

Combinations	
Making	a bird feeder
Building	a guitar
Programming	an answering machine
Maintaining	a remote control device
Using	a fish tank

Is Your Topic Too Broad? Make sure that your topic is narrow enough to cover in a short paper. Below, see how one student narrowed his topic.

Broad	Narrow	Narrower
Operating a VCR	Remote taping	Setting the clock on your VCR

Drafting

Choose the Right Format Headings, lists, and charts can make your user's manual clear, concise, and effective. For example, a list will call out separate points in a direct and easy-to-read way. You can incorporate these features in your first draft or add them while revising.

Create Visual Aids Visual aids can be an important part of a user's manual. They can convey significant information in only a few words. Look over your draft to see where a visual aid will fit. If you use a visual aid, consider labeling parts.

Tape Deck

Function Controls

12:00 PM — Clock

Applying Language Skills

Exact Nouns Explain to students that precise language is important in technical writing because an imprecise or vague word can make it impossible to follow directions properly.

Suggested Answer
Practice

To turn on your DVD player, first plug the AC cord into the nearest wall outlet, and turn the large round dial on the front right marked "ON/VOL."

 Writer's Solution

For additional instruction and practice, have students see the lesson on Exact Nouns in the *Sourcebook*, pp. 258–259.

Revising

Test Your Manual The most important aspect of your user's manual is to describe accurately the steps to perform a function. Precisely follow the steps you have outlined, and see whether they work. Add information you may have left out.

Use a Checklist Refer again to the Writing Skills Focus on p. 177, and use those and the following items as a checklist to evaluate and revise your user's manual.

▶ Have you given a clear explanation of the procedure?
  Fill in any details you may have forgotten when you drafted the manual.

▶ Have you elaborated on your information?
  Add a picture or graph to make your manual easier to understand.

▶ Have you clearly explained causes and effects?
  Make sure you demonstrate the effect of each action.

▶ Have you used transition words?
  Add words such as first, next, and finally in places where they will clarify the steps you describe.

REVISION MODEL

Press the "action" button on the ①~~thing you hold in your hand.~~ ①remote control.

②Next, press
~~Press~~ the "down" arrow until the word "clock" is highlighted.

③This will put the VCR in "clock" mode.
Now you're ready to set the clock.

① *The writer replaces a vague term with an exact noun.*
② *The writer adds a transition word.*
③ *The writer adds an explanation of cause and effect.*

Publishing

Demonstration Booth A demonstration booth will allow you to showcase your talent as a writer, as well as your talent for assembling visuals and products in a creative way.

▶ Get permission from your teacher or librarian to set up a booth.
▶ Inside the booth, display a finished copy of your user's manual.
▶ Post charts, diagrams, and other visuals on the wall of the booth.
▶ If possible, include a working model so that visitors can actually follow your instructions.

APPLYING LANGUAGE SKILLS: Subject and Verb Agreement

Make sure that all your verbs agree in number with their subjects. Number means that a word is either singular or plural. Verbs change form to agree with their subjects. A subject and verb agree when both are singular or both are plural.

Incorrect:
The action button control all the programming functions.

Correct:
The action button controls all the programming functions.

Practice On your paper, make the verb agree with the subject in the following sentences.

1. The dial on each of the meters inform you of your progress.

2. Many people who have a stairwalker exercises every day.

Writing Application Review your user's manual to make sure that all subjects and verbs agree in number.

Writer's Solution Connection Language Lab

For more practice with subject and verb agreement, complete the Language Lab lesson on Agreement in Number.

Revising

Have students work with peer editors to revise their work. Have the peer editor read the user's manual and judge whether he or she can adequately understand its contents. Make sure that peer editors offer constructive comments rather than just general criticism.

Publishing

Tell students that even if they do not wish to share their user's manuals with a wider audience at this time, they should keep them for reference and possibly to incorporate into a longer piece of writing at a later time.

Reinforce and Extend

Review the Writing Guidelines
After students have completed their papers, review the characteristics of a user's manual. Encourage students to come up with additional criteria for a user's manual based on what they learned through completing the assignment.

Applying Language Skills

Subject and Verb Agreement
Explain to students that the number of the subject determines the number of the verb, not the other way around.

Answers
1. The dial on each of the meters informs you of your progress.
2. Many people who have a stairwalker exercise every day.

 Writer's Solution

For additional instruction and practice, have students complete the **Language Lab CD-ROM** lesson on Subject-Verb Agreement and the practice pages 80–82 in the *Writer's Solution Grammar Practice Book*.

✓ ASSESSMENT		4	3	2	1
PORTFOLIO ASSESSMENT Use the rubric on Technical Description/Explanation in the *Alternative Assessment* booklet (p. 115) to assess the students' writing. Add these criteria to customize the rubric to this assignment.	**Exact Nouns**	All nouns are exact and the best noun for each situation.	Most nouns are exact and descriptive.	There are both exact nouns and vague nouns that should be replaced.	Most nouns are vague and provide little description.
	Subject-Verb Agreement	All verbs agree with their subjects; grammar is flawless.	Almost all verbs agree with their subjects; grammar is good.	Subject-verb agreement is acceptable, but there are noticeable errors.	Numerous errors in subject-verb agreement render the piece difficult to understand and read.

Students will be familiar with reading to find specific information from their social studies and history assignments. Point out that such critical reading skills will serve them well both in college doing research reports and in the outside world reading and/or analyzing anything from business reports to long, itemized bills to tax forms.

Customize for
Less Proficient Readers

Remind these students that the prose in history and reference books is often denser than that of works of literature and should thus be read at a slower pace. Rereading sentences, paragraphs, and entire chapters should not be seen as a sign of weakness but rather a necessity to understand the selection completely.

Apply the Strategy

Have students scan the entire sample so that they know what to expect. This should become a habit for reading such texts. Then have them read the selection as many times as necessary to acquire a full understanding of it.

Answers

1. The Indus Valley is located in South Asia on the Indian subcontinent. The first sentence of the section entitled Geography: The Indian Subcontinent reveals this information.
2. The three major geographic zones of the Indian subcontinent are the well-watered northern plain, the dry triangular Deccan plateau, and the coastal plains flanking the Deccan. The section Three Regions gives this information.
3. The monsoons affect Indian life by bringing rain that is desperately needed to water crops. A late monsoon could mean starvation. The section The Monsoons gives this information.
4. Section 3, Early Civilization in China, would be the place to look for information about rulers of northern China in 1027 B.C.

Reading for Specific Information

Real-World Reading Skills Workshop

Strategies for Success

Your social studies homework requires you to answer questions about cities of the Indus Valley. You have your social studies book; now you just have to find the specific information you need to answer the questions. Use the following strategies to find specific information in a textbook or other reference.

Early Civilizations in India and China

Chapter Outline
1. Cities of the Indus Valley
2. Kingdoms of the Ganges
3. Early Civilization in China

Cities of the Indus Valley

In 1922, archaeologists made a startling discovery. While digging in the Indus River valley, they unearthed bricks, small statues, and other artifacts. They soon realized that they had uncovered a "lost civilization." They had found the cities of the Indus Valley.

Geography:
The Indian Subcontinent

The Indus Valley is located in the region known as South Asia or the subcontinent of India. The Indian subcontinent is a huge, wedge-shaped peninsula extending into the Indian Ocean. Towering snow-covered mountain ranges arc across the northern border of the subcontinent.

Three regions. The Indian subcontinent is divided into three major zones. They are the well-watered northern plain, the dry triangular Deccan plateau, and the coastal plains on either side of the Deccan.

The monsoons. Today, as in the past, a defining feature of Indian life is the monsoon. In late May or early June, the wet summer monsoon blows from the southwest. These winds pick up moisture over the Indian Ocean and then drench the land with daily downpours. Each year, people welcome the rain that is desperately needed to water the crops. If the rains are late, famine and starvation may occur.

Use the Table of Contents and the Index
The table of contents may list a topic that is broader than your specific needs, but it will get you close. For example, information about the Indus Valley might be listed in the chapter

entitled "Early Civilizations in India and China." An index lists very specific topics. For example, if you know the names of one of the cities, you could look it up in the index and find the exact page on which information about that city appears.

Scan Subheads and Key Words Scan the pages for subheads or key words that refer, or are related to, your topic. For example, if you want to find the location of the Indus Valley, scan the subheads until you find one that refers to geography or neighboring countries.

Apply the Strategy

Scan the information in the sample textbook page to the left to answer these questions.

1. Where is the Indus Valley located? Which words helped you find this information?
2. Describe the three major zones of the Indian subcontinent. Which words helped you find the section with this information?
3. Describe how the monsoon affects Indian life. How did you find this information?
4. In which section of this chapter would you begin looking for information about rulers of northern China in 1027 B.C.?

✔ You may also read for specific information
▶ Newspapers and magazines
▶ Almanacs
▶ Encyclopedias

PART 2 *Reaching a Goal*

One-Minute Planning Guide

The selections in this section are about striving for goals. "Mowing," and "After Apple Picking," deal with concrete physical goals. In "Style," and "At Harvesttime," Maya Angelou describes principles toward which all people should strive. In "The Apple Tree," the father's goal is to harvest the fruit of a beautiful apple tree, but finds that the apples are not what he expected. The poem "Africa" figuratively describes the struggle for liberty, while "Biko" describes the fatal consequences of one man who struggled for liberty. The African "Old Song" and the selections from *The Analects* offer advice for living successfully. The Chinese poems "All" and "Also All" describe the despair and subsequent hope after the Tienanmen Square massacre.

Customize for
Varying Student Needs
When assigning the selections in this part to your students, keep in mind the following factors:

"Mowing"; "After Apple Picking"
• Two poems from a well-known, high-interest author

"Style"; "At Harvesttime"
• Two very short essays
• Well-known author

"The Apple Tree"
• A brief story with easy vocabulary and an accessible plot

"Africa"; "Old Song"; "Biko"; from *The Analects;* "All"; "Also All"
• "Biko" has connection to popular song and artist (Peter Gabriel)

"All" and "Also All" have connection to social studies (Tiananmen Square)

Reaching a Goal ◆ 181

Humanities: Art

Untitled by Bart Forbes.

Bart Forbes has created posters and prints and has designed over twenty commemorative postage stamps, including the 1988 Olympic stamps, as well as the Lou Gehrig and Jesse Owens stamps. Forbes was appointed the official artist of the 1988 Olympics in Seoul, Korea.

Encourage students to notice the warm colors, somewhat unexpected in a painting of a snowy scene. Realistically, they might be reflections of the sunset; however, the strongest red tones in the center of the skier's chest might suggest the pumping of his heart.

Help students link the painting to the theme of Part 2, Reaching a Goal, by answering the following questions:

1. **What do you think this skier is feeling?** *Possible answers: He is feeling nervous about the success of his jump; he is proud, knowing he has jumped farther than ever.*

2. **How do you think the painter feels about the goal of achieving a perfect ski jump?** *The painter shows that he values this goal highly in the following details: the skier's disciplined posture; the Olympic insignia on his chest, indicating the highest level of competition; the beautiful natural backdrop against which the skier seems to fly like a bird; the pleasing combination of warm earth tones and the cool slate blues.*

181

Guide for Reading

OBJECTIVES

1. To read, comprehend, and interpret selections of poetry and prose
2. To relate the selections to personal experience
3. To interpret images in poetry and prose
4. To identify tone
5. To build vocabulary in context and learn the pronunciation of words ending in -ough
6. To recognize participles as adjectives
7. To write a letter of application using supporting details
8. To respond to the selections through writing, speaking and listening, and projects

SKILLS INSTRUCTION

Vocabulary:
Spelling vs. Pronunciation: -ough

Grammar:
Participles as Adjectives

Reading Strategy:
Interpret

Literary Focus:
Tone

Writing:
Supporting Details

Speaking and Listening:
Role Play (teacher edition)

Critical Viewing:
Compare

PORTFOLIO OPPORTUNITIES

Writing: Description; Essay; Advice Column

Writing Mini-Lesson: Application Letter

Speaking and Listening: Speech; Role Play

Projects: Farming Update; Food Source

More About the Authors

On a blustery and snowy day in January of 1961, in Washington, D.C., **Robert Frost** was thrust into the limelight when he read his poem "The Gift Outright" at the inauguration of President John F. Kennedy. Millions of TV viewers were thus introduced to one of America's greatest poets.

On another very cold day thirty-two years later, **Maya Angelou** gave a stirring recitation of her poem "On the Pulse of Morning" at Bill Clinton's 1993 presidential inauguration. Angelou is the author of eleven best-selling books, in addition to being an accomplished singer and actress.

Robert Frost (1874–1963)

Frost was born in San Francisco but moved to New England, his family's original home, when he was eleven. In his youth, he worked as a farmer, editor, and schoolteacher, absorbing the ebb and flow of New England life that would form the themes for many of his poems.

In 1912, Frost moved to England, where he met the famous poets Ezra Pound and William Butler Yeats. Encouraged by their praise, he published his first volume of poetry, entitled *A Boy's Will*, in 1913. Frost went on to become one of the most successful and prolific poets the country has ever known, winning numerous awards, including four Pulitzer Prizes.

Maya Angelou (1928–   )

Maya Angelou was born Marguerite Johnson in St. Louis, Missouri. She and her older brother were raised by their grandmother in Stamps, Arkansas. She records the experiences of her childhood in her autobiography, *I Know Why the Caged Bird Sings*.

In her adult life, she achieved success as a singer and actress, a civil rights worker, and a writer of nonfiction, fiction, poetry, and plays. "Style" and "At Harvesttime" are from *Wouldn't Take Nothin' for My Journey Now*, a collection of essays in which she shares her reflections on life.

◆ Build Vocabulary

SPELLING VS. PRONUNCIATION: –ough

In "After Apple-Picking," Robert Frost notices that there may be a few "Apples [he] didn't pick upon some bough." If you don't know the pronunciation of *bough*, you learn it as soon as you read the next line: it rhymes with *now*. Further down, he ends another line with the word *trough*, which rhymes with *off* three lines up. Still other words ending in *-ough* have an $\overline{oo}$ sound—*through*, for example. Think of other words that end in *-ough*. How do you pronounce them?

bough
trough
manifestation
disparaging
judicious
admonition
immutable
potency

WORD BANK

Before you read, preview this list of words from the poems and essays.

◆ Build Grammar Skills

PARTICIPLES AS ADJECTIVES

As Robert Frost describes cutting the long grass in "Mowing," he mentions his "long scythe whispering to the ground." If your teacher asked you to assign a part of speech to each word in that phrase, what would you put for *whispering*? If you answered participle, you'd be correct.

A **participle** is a word formed from a verb that modifies a noun or a pronoun. Participles fit into two groups: present or past. Present participles always end in *-ing*. Past participles usually end in *-ed* or *-d*, but they may also have irregular endings, such as *-t* and *-en*.

Present: . . . from the *drinking* trough

Past: *Magnified* apples appear . . .

Notice how participles add detail to these poems and essays.

182 ◆ *Striving for Success*

Prentice Hall Literature Program Resources

REINFORCE / RETEACH / EXTEND

Selection Support Pages
Build Vocabulary: Spelling vs. Pronunciation: -ough, p. 51
Build Grammar Skills: Participles as Adjectives, p. 52
Reading Strategy: Interpret, p. 53
Literary Focus: Tone, p. 54

Strategies for Diverse Student Needs, p. 13

Beyond Literature
Career Connection: Farming, p. 13

Formal Assessment Selection Test, pp. 41–43; Assessment Resources Software

Alternative Assessment, p. 13

Writing and Language Transparencies
Writing Process Model 9: Business Letter, pp. 61–64

Resource Pro CD-ROM
"Mowing," "After Apple-Picking," "Style," "At Harvesttime"—includes all resource material and customizable lesson plans

 Listening to Literature Audiocassettes
"Mowing," "After Apple-Picking," "Style," "At Harvesttime"

Mowing ◆ After Apple-Picking
Style ◆ At Harvesttime

◆ Literature and Your Life

CONNECT YOUR EXPERIENCE
When you plant a marigold seed, you don't expect a daisy to sprout, do you? In life, as in gardening, what you put into an experience usually affects what you get out of it. The poems and essays in this group remind you that success requires effort.

Journal Writing Write down your recollection of a particularly difficult job that, when finished, gave you a great deal of satisfaction.

THEMATIC FOCUS: REACHING A GOAL
The ideas explored in these poems and essays will help you consider the question, "How do my attitudes and actions affect my chances for success?"

◆ Background for Understanding

CULTURE
Most of Robert Frost's poems take place among the rolling pastures, dark woods, and clear streams of rural New England. Life in New England is dictated to a great extent by the ebb and flow of the four seasons. Winters in New England last from mid-November to early April and are marked by long nights and snowy days. Spring is damp and cool, with misty mornings. Summer days are long and hot, but the nights are often comfortable. Autumn, however, is when New England shows its true colors. Autumn is harvest time, time to go to work picking apples amid an array of brilliant red and orange and yellow leaves falling all around.

◆ Literary Focus

TONE
When the speaker in "Mowing" talks about "the earnest love that laid the swale in rows," he shows a respectful attitude toward his work. The attitude of the speaker or author toward his or her subject in a literary work is known as the **tone**. The tone may be, among other things, serious or casual, distant or personal, angry or humorous. You can determine the tone of a work by looking carefully at the writer's choice of words.

◆ Reading Strategy

INTERPRET
These poems and essays contain distinct images. In "Mowing," we see the image of a sharp blade slicing through the long grass. In "After Apple-Picking," we are presented with an image of "ten thousand thousand" apples. Writers use images such as these to create a mood, or feeling, and to convey the underlying meaning.

As a reader, part of your job is to **interpret** these images, to understand what the images represent and how they contribute to the work's mood or meaning. For instance, in "Mowing," the image of the lone whispering scythe creates a mood of solitude and tranquillity and captures the rhythm and progress of outdoor work. Think about the images you encounter in these works. What associations do the images call to mind? What feelings or emotions do the images spark? What are the speakers' attitudes toward the images? What point or message do the writers convey beyond the literal words? Answering these questions will help you interpret the images and delve into their underlying meanings.

Guide for Reading ◆ 183

 Interest Grabber

To prepare students to read the poems and essays, write on the chalkboard: "You reap what you sow." If necessary, clarify for students that *reap* means "to obtain a result" and *sow* means "to scatter seed for growing." Have them discuss both the literal and figurative meaning of this sentence. Then, to help them apply it directly to their lives, begin a two-column chart on the chalkboard. Label the left column *Sow* and write "works in a video store" and "misses three play rehearsals." Label the right column *Reap* and write "earns money for a computer" and "forgets lines on stage." Lead students to see the relationship between "reaping" and "sowing." After students have added examples to the list, tell them to keep this saying in mind as they read these selections.

Customize for
Less Proficient Readers
The Frost poems include some long sentences. Pair these students with stronger readers who can help them break down and paraphrase some of the more complicated sentences to grasp their literal meaning.

Customize for
More Advanced Students
Introduce to these students the term, *explication of text,* telling them that it refers to the analysis of a literary work in great detail, finally explaining the underlying meaning as a whole. Have them write an explication of one of the Frost poems in the selection. (For those studying French, you might add that the term comes originally from the French *explication de texte.*)

Customize for
English Language Learners
Listening to the recordings on the **Listening to Literature Audiocassette** will help these students understand the sense of the poems as they follow along in their texts.

Customize for
Musical/Rhythmic Learners
Have these students work together to plan choral readings of the poems. As they practice, they should agree on the rhythm of lines and the words or syllables to be stressed.

Preparing for Standardized Tests

Reading The ability to interpret the meaning of a piece of literature is a sophisticated reading skill, one that students can apply to their benefit on reading comprehension and critical reading portions of standardized tests. Interpreting requires that students be able to recognize a number of literary techniques and understand how they work together to suggest a meaning. In addition to the Reading Strategy questions on page 190, students can practice interpretation with the Reading Strategy page in **Selection Support,** p. 53.

Grammar and Language Because participles are verb forms, students may confuse them with verbs in a sentence even when they are acting as adjectives. The distinction is important in grammar application items on standardized tests and also in revision items in which students must choose the best solution for a problem or error in writing. For further practice, use the Build Grammar Skills page on Participles as Adjectives in **Selection Support,** p. 52.

One-Minute Insight Both these poems celebrate "the sweetest dream that labor knows" by focusing on the physicality of mowing and of harvesting. In "Mowing" the scythe with which the speaker mows seems itself to be a sentient being, whispering and communicating with the land. In "After Apple-Picking" the reader feels the exhaustion of the speaker who has just worked hard to harvest apples before the long winter sets in.

◆ Critical Thinking

❶ Infer Ask students why the personified scythe "whispered and did not speak." *Students might say that if the scythe was commenting to the ground about "the lack of sound," it was being respectful of that silence by whispering instead of talking aloud.*

◆ Reading Strategy

❷ Interpret Ask students what they think the scythe whispered. Tell them to consider lines 9 and 10 and line 13 for their interpretations. *Based on previous lines, some students may say that the scythe was simply whispering about its work, or loving its work. Accept all reasonable responses.*

Mowing
Robert Frost

There was never a sound beside the wood but one,
And that was my long scythe[1] whispering to the ground.
What was it it whispered? I knew not well myself;
Perhaps it was something about the heat of the sun,
5   Something, perhaps, about the lack of sound— **❶**
And that was why it whispered and did not speak.
It was no dream of the gift of idle hours,
Or easy gold at the hand of fay[2] or elf:
Anything more than the truth would have seemed too weak
10 To the earnest love that laid the swale[3] in rows,
Not without feeble-pointed spikes of flowers
(Pale orchises),[4] and scared a bright green snake.
The fact is the sweetest dream that labor knows.
My long scythe whispered and left the hay to make. **❷**

---

1. **scythe** (si*th*) *n.*: Slightly curved blade at the end of a long handle, used for cutting grass.
2. **fay** (fā) *n.*: Fairy.
3. **swale** (swāl) *n.*: Low-lying marshland.
4. **orchises** (ôr′ kis iz) *n.*: Orchids.

184 ◆ *Striving for Success*

Block Scheduling Strategies

Consider these suggestions to take advantage of extended class time:

• Before students add examples to the chalkboard chart for the Interest Grabber activity on page 183, have them gather in groups to exchange thoughts. Remind them that when a person reaps, he or she plants a seed, and that to sow means to obtain results from that planting. Tell them that the examples on the board shows a logical relationship between "reaping" and "sowing."

• Have students listen to the four selections on audiocassette; then have students read them to themselves or to partners.

• Introduce the concept of tone. Students may read about it in Literary Focus on page 183 and then answer the questions on page 190. You may follow up with Literary Focus page in *Selection Support* (p. 54).

• Ask students to write about their attitudes toward work in their journals. After

they have read the Frost poems, have them write a quick response comparing their attitudes to those of the speakers.

• Suggest that students work in small groups on the Build Grammar Skills section on page 190 and the practice page from *Selection Support* (p. 52).

• Direct students to choose one of the writing activities from the Idea Bank on page 191.

The Mowers, Sir George Clausen, Usher Art Gallery, Lincoln, Great Britain/The Bridgeman Art Library, London

 ▲ Critical Viewing Compare Frost's description of mowing with the artist's visual description. [Compare]

❸ **Compare** Students may respond that in the poem, the mower is solitary, but Clausen's painting shows several men working together. The action of mowing with a scythe is depicted in both. The trees in the background could be the wood beside the "swale" in the poem. Some students may say that the mood in both is tranquil, and the figures in the painting seem to be "listening" to the whisperings of their scythes.

Customize for
Visual/Spatial Learners
You might wish to have these students relate the movement of the clothes of the men in the foreground of *The Mowers* to that of the painting as a whole. *Students should observe how the curves of the men's flowing clothes echo the curves or diagonals of the scythe's handle, the grass, and the bending trees and grass.*

Mowing ◆ 185

🎵 **Humanities: Art**

The Mowers by Sir George Clausen.
   Sir George Clausen (1852–1944) was an English painter who liked to paint landscapes and bucolic scenes. In this painting, workers mow a peaceful meadow, much like the one in Frost's poem.
   Use these questions for discussion:
1. Looking carefully at the motion of the mowers, describe the sound you think the scythe might make. *The scythe probably makes a swishing or whispering sound as it moves through the grass.*

2. Jean-François Millet and Vincent Van Gogh are among many artists who have painted laborers mowing or sowing. Why do you think this is an appealing painting subject? *Students might say that the subject allows painters to show human anatomy in motion or that artists might paint laborers as a way that pays homage to the importance of honest physical labor.*

◆ Literary Focus

❶ Tone Ask students to describe the tone in the opening of this poem. *The detailed description of work partly done and the long sentences suggest a tone of weariness. This tone is reinforced by the speaker's statement that he or she is done with apple picking now.*

◆ Reading Strategy

❷ Interpret Ask students what lines 9–13 tell them about the weather. *The weather is getting cold. The temperature has dropped below 32 degrees—the "pane of glass" in the drinking trough that morning was actually a sheet of ice.*

◆ Build Grammar Skills

❸ Participles as Adjectives Have students identify the participial phrase in line 20 and identify the noun phrase it modifies. *The participial phrase is showing clear and the noun phrase it modifies is fleck of russet.*

◆ Critical Thinking

❹ Infer Ask students to explain the inference they make here. *The speaker has been working so long, and feels so overworked that he continues to hear the sounds of the apples even after the work is done.*

After Apple-Picking

Robert Frost

My long two-pointed ladder's sticking through a tree
Toward heaven still,
And there's a barrel that I didn't fill
❶ Beside it, and there may be two or three
5 Apples I didn't pick upon some <u>bough</u>.
But I am done with apple-picking now.
Essence of winter sleep is on the night,
The scent of apples: I am drowsing off.
I cannot rub the strangeness from my sight
10 I got from looking through a pane of glass
❷ I skimmed this morning from the drinking <u>trough</u>
And held against the world of hoary[1] grass.
It melted, and I let it fall and break.
But I was well
15 Upon my way to sleep before it fell,
And I could tell
What form my dreaming was about to take.
Magnified apples appear and disappear,
Stem end and blossom end,
❸ 20 And every fleck of russet[2] showing clear.
My instep arch not only keeps the ache,
It keeps the pressure of a ladder-round.
I feel the ladder sway as the boughs bend.
And I keep hearing from the cellar bin
❹ 25 The rumbling sound
Of load on load of apples coming in.

---

1. **hoary** (hō′ rē) *adj.*: Gray or white with age.
2. **russet** (rus′ it) *n.*: Strong reddish-brown color; type of winter apple having rough, reddish-brown skin.

Speaking and Listening Mini-Lesson

Role Play

This mini-lesson supports the Speaking and Listening activity in the Idea Bank on page 191.

Introduce the Concept Remind students that the speakers in both poems are involved in hard, physical labor. Both probably have strong feelings about the kind of work they do.

Develop Background To role-play the speakers, students will need to have a sense of each speaker. Have students discuss the attitude of each speaker. Lead them to realize that the speaker in "Mowing" seems more content than the one in "After Apple-Picking" who might be too tired to appreciate all that he has accomplished.

Apply the Information Students can work with a partner, each taking the role of one of the speakers, to work out a realistic conversation. You might suggest that they practice the conversation until they feel comfortable. Then they can present the conversations before the class.

Assess the Outcome Have students evaluate each pair's performance by answering the following questions:
1. Did each student faithfully represent the personality of his or her speaker?
2. Did each student communicate his or her speaker's thoughts clearly?

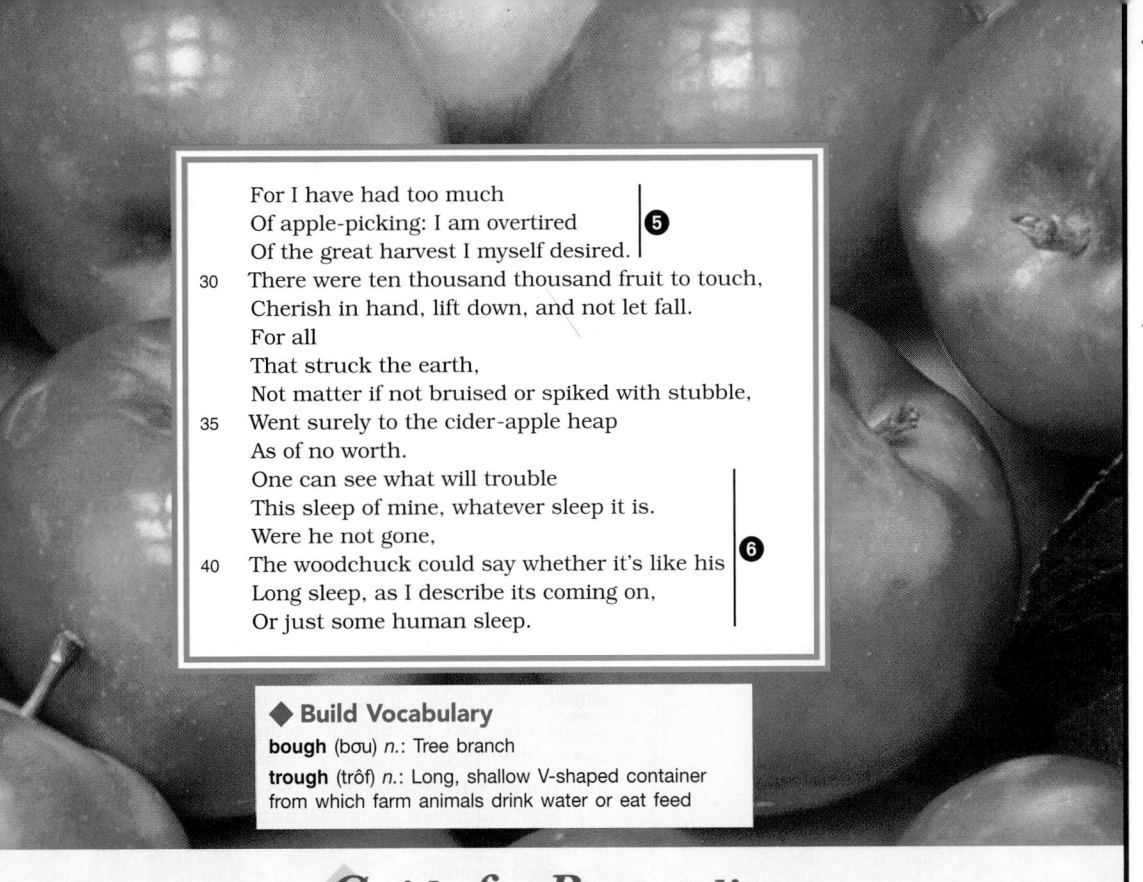

For I have had too much
Of apple-picking: I am overtired
Of the great harvest I myself desired. **⑤**
30 There were ten thousand thousand fruit to touch,
Cherish in hand, lift down, and not let fall.
For all
That struck the earth,
Not matter if not bruised or spiked with stubble,
35 Went surely to the cider-apple heap
As of no worth.
One can see what will trouble
This sleep of mine, whatever sleep it is.
Were he not gone,
40 The woodchuck could say whether it's like his **⑥**
Long sleep, as I describe its coming on,
Or just some human sleep.

◆ Build Vocabulary

bough (bou) *n.*: Tree branch

trough (trôf) *n.*: Long, shallow V-shaped container from which farm animals drink water or eat feed

Guide for Responding

◆ *Literature and Your Life*

Reader's Response What personal experiences do these poems call to mind?

Thematic Focus Why do you think it is sometimes hard for people to stop thinking about a job they've just completed?

☑ Check Your Comprehension

1. In "Mowing," what is the one sound the speaker hears?
2. What does the speaker of "Mowing" say is "the sweetest dream that labor knows"?
3. (a) In "After Apple-Picking," what pictures flash through the speaker's mind as he drifts off to sleep? (b) What sensations does he feel? (c) What does he hear?

◆ Critical Thinking

INTERPRET
1. Why is the setting of "Mowing" important? **[Support]**
2. (a) In "After Apple-Picking," how would you describe the speaker's condition? (b) What is the cause of his condition? **[Deduce]**

APPLY
3. How do the feelings a person experiences after completing a physical task, such as picking apples, compare with those one experiences after completing a mental task, such as homework? **[Distinguish]**

EXTEND
4. What are some of the advantages and disadvantages of jobs that require working outdoors? **[Career Link]**

After Apple-Picking ◆ 187

◆ Critical Thinking

⑤ Infer Ask students what they can determine about the speaker from his words in lines 27–29. *A possible response is that the speaker might be a person who "bites off more than he can chew"—realizes he has taken on more than he can accomplish.*

◆ Literary Focus

⑥ Tone Have students describe the speaker's tone in these lines. *The tone seems to reflect what the speaker is saying; it communicates a feeling of profound tiredness.*

Reinforce and Extend

Answers

◆ *Literature and Your Life*

Reader's Response Students might recall a particular time in which they exerted themselves in physical labor.

Thematic Focus A possible response is that when people get involved in consuming work it is hard to leave it behind.

☑ Check Your Comprehension

1. He hears his scythe "whispering to the ground."
2. The simple "fact" of work being done is the sweetest dream that labor knows.
3. (a) Magnified apples appeared and disappeared; (b) his instep aches; he feels the ladder-round pressure; (c) he hears apples rumbling into the cellar bin.

◆ Critical Thinking

1. The setting is important because the silence of the wood and the work that is being done there are central to the meaning of the poem.
2. (a) The speaker is spent and exhausted; (b) He feels this way because he has worked very hard to help harvest apples.
3. Responses may include: a physical task might cause bodily pain or exhaustion while a mental task does not; someone could feel satisfied or energized after a physical task and stimulated after a mental task.
4. Advantages include physical movement and enjoyment of good weather; disadvantages include exposure to rain and snow or possibly dangerous conditions.

187

"Style" and "At Harvesttime" examine and expand upon the theme of the saying "You reap what you sow." Angelou says that those who cultivate and remain true to their unique styles can successfully deal with most situations in life.

◆ Build Grammar Skills

❶ Participles as Adjectives
There are two participles in this sentence. Have students identify them. *developed; accomplished* Ask students which participle is used as an adjective. *The participle accomplished is an adjective; it modifies the noun teacher. The other participle is part of the verb phrase "can be developed."*

◆ Literary Focus

❷ Tone Ask students: What is the tone of this passage? *Responses suggest that the tone is serious because the author is teaching the reader something she considers important; others may suggest that the tone is humorous because the image of a robin with peacock feathers is funny.*

STYLE
MAYA ANGELOU

Wind on the Water, Richard McDermott Miller

Content is of great importance, but we must not underrate the value of style. That is, attention must be paid to not only what is said but how it is said; to what we wear, as well as how we wear it. In fact, we should be aware of all we do and of how we do all that we do.

Manners and a respect for style can be developed if one is eager and has an accomplished teacher. On the other hand, any observant person can acquire the same results without a teacher simply by carefully watching the steady march of the human parade. ❶

Never try to take the manners of another as your own, for the theft will be immediately evident and the thief will appear as ridiculous as a robin with peacock feathers hastily stuck on. Style is as unique and nontransferable and perfectly personal as a fingerprint. It is wise to take the time to develop one's own way of being, increasing those things one does well and eliminating the elements in one's character which can hinder and diminish the good personality. ❷

Any person who has charm and some confidence can move in and through societies ranging from the most privileged to the most needy. Style allows the person to appear neither inferior in one location nor superior in the other. Good manners and tolerance, which are the highest <u>manifestation</u> of style, can often transform disaster into good fortune. Many people utter insults or <u>disparaging</u> remarks without thinking, but a wise or stylish person takes the time to consider the positive as well as negative possibilities in each situation. The <u>judicious</u> response to a gibe can disarm the rude person, removing the power to injure.

This is not another <u>admonition</u> to turn the other cheek, although I do think that that can be an effective ploy on certain occasions. Rather, this is an encouragement to meet adverse situations with the intent and style to control them. Falling into an entanglement with brutes will usually result in nothing more conclusive than a stimulated nervous system and an upset digestive tract.

◆ Build Vocabulary

manifestation (man′ ə fes tā′ shən) *n.*: Something that is made clear or plainly revealed

disparaging (di spar′ ij iŋ) *adj.*: Belittling; showing contempt for

judicious (jo͞o dish′ əs) *adj.*: Showing good judgment; wise and careful

gibe (jīb) *v.*: Jeer; taunt

admonition (ad′ mə nish′ ən) *n.*: Warning; mild reprimand

immutable (im myo͞ot′ ə bəl) *adj.*: Unchangeable

potency (pōt′ ən sē) *n.*: Power

188 ◆ *Striving for Success*

Beyond the Classroom

Career Connection

Landscape Architecture Many high school students earn money from the land by mowing lawns, raking leaves, shoveling snow, and so on. An interest in mowing can lead to a career in landscape architecture. A landscape architect may design anything from a backyard garden to the grounds of a corporate park. Have students investigate what a landscape architect does and the qualifications necessary to become one.

Suggest that they present their research in a report with pictures, if possible.

Community Connection

Local Growing Apples, referred to in "After Apple-Picking" and tomatoes, in "Harvesttime," are hardy crops that grow in many areas of the United States. Have students consider the following questions and then make an illustrated chart showing kinds of crops grown in the regions in

which they live.

• Do apples grow in your region? If so, where, and what kinds of apples?

• Is other produce grown in your region? If so, what fruits and vegetables are among the local crops? If produce is not grown in your region, where does it come from?

AT HARVESTTIME
MAYA ANGELOU

There is an <u>immutable</u> life principle with which many people will quarrel.

Although nature has proven season in and season out that if the thing that is planted bears at all, it will yield more of itself, there are those who seem certain that if they plant tomato seeds, at harvesttime they can reap onions.

Too many times for comfort I have expected to reap good when I know I have sown evil. My lame excuse is that I have not always known that actions can only reproduce themselves, or rather, I have not always allowed myself to be aware of that knowledge. Now, after years of observation and enough courage to admit what I have observed, I try to plant peace if I do not want discord; to plant loyalty and honesty if I want to avoid betrayal and lies.

Of course, there is no absolute assurance that those things I plant will always fall upon arable land and will take root and grow, nor can I know if another cultivator did not leave contrary seeds before I arrived. I do know, however, that if I leave little to chance, if I am careful about the kinds of seeds I plant, about their <u>potency</u> and nature, I can, within reason, trust my expectations.

③
④

Guide for Responding

◆ Literature and Your Life

Reader's Response With whom would you like to share these essays? Why?

☑ Check Your Comprehension

1. In "At Harvesttime," what does Maya Angelou suggest is a life principle that cannot be changed?
2. Why does Angelou say she sometimes expected to "reap good when [she] sowed evil"?
3. In the essay "Style," what two qualities are identified as the greatest proof of style?

◆ Critical Thinking

INTERPRET
1. Explain the meaning of the title "At Harvesttime." **[Interpret]**
2. In what ways can style help you achieve success? **[Analyze]**

EXTEND
3. Identify a character in literature who would benefit from the advice in one of these essays. Explain your choice **[Literature Link]**

Style/At Harvesttime ◆ 189

Beyond the Selection

FURTHER READING

Other Works by Robert Frost
"The Road Not Taken"
"Stopping by Woods on a Snowy Evening"
"Birches"

Other Works by Maya Angelou
I Know Why the Caged Bird Sings
I Shall Not Be Moved
Wouldn't Take Nothing for My Journey Now

We suggest that you preview these works before recommending them to students.

INTERNET

Students may learn more about these poets at the following Web sites. Please be aware that sites may have changed since we published this information.

For Frost quotations, go to **http://www.chesco. com/artman/frost.html**

For more information about Maya Angelou, go to **http://ucaswww.mem.uc.edu/worldfest/MayaPage. html**

We *strongly recommend* that you preview this and related sites before you send students to them.

◆ Reading Strategy

1. (a) He respects his work. (b) Students may be influenced to interpret the poem as a celebration of work.
2. (a) The speaker is exhausted. (b) Students may interpret the poem as one which takes a realistic look at the difficulty of labor.
3. The images reinforce Angelou's point about the relationship between actions and consequences.
4. Students might mention the image of the robin with peacock feathers to represent someone trying to imitate another's style.

◆ Literary Focus

1. (a) The tone is respectful. (b) The words "earnest love" and "sweetest dream that labor knows" convey that respect.
2. (a) Students may say that the tone is one of exhaustion. (b) The tone is communicated by "I am drowsing off," "My instep arch . . . keeps the ache," "sleep."
3. Students might find the tone of these essays to be either preachy or wise.

◆ Build Vocabulary

Using -ough
1. b   2. c   3. a

Using the Word Bank
1. admonition;   2. potency;
3. immutable;   4. judicious;
5. manifestation;   6. disparaging;
7. bough;   8. trough

◆ Build Grammar Skills

Practice
1. whispering;   2. rumbling;
3. accomplished;   4. disparaging;
5. stimulated

Writing Application
Sample answers:
1. picked;   2. exhausted;
3. bending;   4. fallen;   5. experienced

 Writer's Solution

For additional instruction and practice, use the lesson on Participial, Gerund, and Infinitive Phrases (pp. 264–265) in the *Sourcebook* and the page on participles and participial phrases (p. 41) in the *Writer's Solution Grammar Practice Book.*

Guide for Responding (continued)

◆ Reading Strategy

INTERPRET

Writers like Robert Frost and Maya Angelou use images to create a feeling and convey meaning. You can **interpret** these images by examining the feelings and attitudes associated with them.
1. (a) How does the speaker in "Mowing" feel about his work? (b) How do his feelings affect your interpretations of the poem?
2. (a) How does the speaker in "After Apple-Picking" feel at the end of the day? (b) How do his feelings affect your interpretations of the poem?
3. How do the images of planting and harvesting help you understand the message in "At Harvesttime"?
4. What images would you use to communicate the message of "Style" to someone who hasn't read it?

◆ Literary Focus

TONE

The words that a writer uses convey a specific **tone**—the speaker's or author's attitude toward the subject. Often, the tone is an important clue to the work's meaning.
1. (a) How would you describe the tone of "Mowing"? (b) What words and phrases are most helpful in determining this tone?
2. (a) What is the tone of "After Apple-Picking"? (b) What words convey this tone?
3. What word would you use to describe the tone of the essays "At Harvesttime" and "Style"?

Beyond Literature

Career Connection

Careers in Agriculture Career opportunities in agriculture are available in such diverse areas as science, business, and education. For example, scientists and engineers work together to improve methods and machinery. Business people buy and sell crops and other agricultural products. Agricultural educators teach new methods for protecting crops and livestock from disease. What kind of career in agriculture would interest you most?

◆ Build Vocabulary

USING -ough

Match the word from Column A to the rhyming word in Column B.

Column A	**Column B**
1. bough	a. dough
2. trough	b. plough
3. though	c. cough

USING THE WORD BANK

On your paper, write a synonym from the Word Bank for each numbered word.

1. warning	5. evidence
2. power	6. critical
3. unchangeable	7. branch
4. wise	8. tub

◆ Build Grammar Skills

PARTICIPLES

A **participle** is a verb form that can modify a noun or pronoun. Frost uses participles to add details that bring his images to life. Participles fall into two categories: present (always end in -ing) and past (usually end in -ed but may have an irregular ending).

Practice In your notebook, write the participle that modifies the following words from "Mowing," "After Apple-Picking," and "Style."
1. scythe ("Mowing": line 2)
2. sound ("After Apple-Picking": line 25)
3. teacher ("Style": paragraph 2)
4. remarks ("Style": paragraph 4)
5. nervous system ("Style": paragraph 5)

Writing Application Add a participle to each sentence to modify the noun in italics.
1. The *apples* are thrown on the cider heap.
2. The *worker* cannot stop thinking about the harvest.
3. The *branches* almost touch the ground.
4. The *fruit* fills the bin.
5. The *men* work faster than the boys.

Build Your Portfolio

 ## Idea Bank

Writing Description

1. **Description** Write a paragraph describing a job that gives you satisfaction. Include details that will help your readers share the experience.

2. **Essay** The speakers in "Mowing" and "After Apple-Picking" are at two different stages of work. Write a brief essay in which you contrast the feelings and attitudes of the two speakers.

3. **Advice Column** "At Harvesttime" and "Style" offer good advice for people of any age. Write an advice column with at least two letters from readers asking advice on situations related to Angelou's ideas. Use the ideas in the essays as a basis for answering the letters.

Speaking and Listening

4. **Speech** Practice reading one of the essays as a speech. Experiment with pauses, volume, and tone of voice. Deliver your speech to the class.

5. **Role Play** With a partner, role-play a conversation between the speakers in "At Harvesttime" and "After Apple-Picking." Have them compare the nature of their work and their reactions to it.

Projects

6. **Farming Update** Technology has dramatically changed the way farmers work. Create a timeline that shows the impact of technology on a specific area of agriculture during the past ten decades. [Technology Link]

7. **Food Source** Choose one of your favorite foods and find out what work is involved in producing it. Discover how it travels, what happens to it, and what it's combined with before it reaches your table. Present your findings to the class.

 ## Writing Mini-Lesson

Application Letter for a Summer Job

In his poems, Robert Frost talks about what it's like to work outside. If you've never had a job where you've worked in nature, a summer job might be a good place to start. Write a letter of application for a summer job in the great outdoors. The following tips will help you support your claim that you are qualified for the job.

Writing Skills Focus: Support With Details

A prospective employer will not hire you just because you *say* you can do the job. You will have to **support** your claim with details. For example, if you claim to work well with children, support your claim with details, such as your two years of babysitting experience and the fact that you have two younger brothers.

Brainstorm for details before you begin writing, and incorporate them in your draft. As you revise, make sure you have used enough details to support your points.

Prewriting First, identify the qualities that are required for the job. Then, brainstorm for details that show you have these qualities.

Drafting Organize your letter so that each of your points is supported clearly. One way to organize is to begin each paragraph with a general statement and then support the statement with details in the body of the paragraph.

Revising Ask a partner to read your letter and identify any claims you have not supported. Add details to support these areas.

 ## Idea Bank

Customizing for
Performance Levels
Following are suggestions for matching Idea Bank topics with your students' performance levels:
Less Advanced Students: 1, 5
Average Students: 2, 3, 4, 6
More Advanced Students: 7

Customizing for
Learning Modalities
Following are suggestions for matching Idea Bank topics with your students' learning modalities:
Visual/Spatial: 6
Interpersonal: 3
Verbal/Linguistic: 4, 5

 ## Writing Mini-Lesson

Refer students to the Writing Handbook, page 965, for instruction on the writing process, and page 969 for further information on practical writing.

Writing and Language Transparencies Use Writing Process Model 9: Business Letter, pp 61–64, to guide students through annotated drafts of a business letter.

 ## Writer's Solution

Writing Lab CD-ROM
Have students complete the tutorial on Practical Writing. Follow these steps:
1. Have them use a details checklist to help them include appropriate supporting details in their application letter.
2. Encourage them to use the revision checker for vague language to help them determine if their language is concrete enough.

Sourcebook
Have students use Chapter 8, Practical and Technical Writing (pp. 229–257), for additional support.

✓ ASSESSMENT OPTIONS

Formal Assessment, Selection Test, pp. 41–43, and Assessment Resources Software. The selection test is designed so that it can be easily customized to the performance levels of your students.
Alternative Assessment, p.13, includes options for less advanced students, more advanced students, verbal/linguistic learners, interpersonal learners, visual/spatial learners, and bodily/kinesthetic learners.

PORTFOLIO ASSESSMENT
Use the following rubrics in the *Alternative Assessment* booklet to assess student writing:
Description: Description Rubric, p. 97
Essay: Comparison and Contrast Rubric, p. 103
Advice Column: Expression Rubric, p. 94

Guide for Reading

OBJECTIVES

1. To read, comprehend, and interpret a story
2. To relate a story to personal experience
3. To ask questions while reading
4. To identify allusions
5. To build vocabulary in context and learn the words from myths
6. To punctuate dialogue
7. To retell a story, focusing on showing, not telling
8. To respond to the story through writing, speaking and listening, and projects

SKILLS INSTRUCTION

Vocabulary:
Word Origins:
Words From Myths

Grammar:
Punctuating
Dialogue

Reading Strategy:
Question

Literary Focus:
Allusion

Writing:
Show, Don't Tell

Speaking and Listening:
Monologue From
Father's Point of
View (teacher edition)

Critical Viewing:
Deduce

PORTFOLIO OPPORTUNITIES

Writing: Summary of the Story; Personal Narrative; Alternative Ending

Writing Mini-Lesson: Retelling a Story

Speaking and Listening: Dramatic Reading; Monologue From Father's Point of View

Projects: Travel Brochure; Map

More About the Author
Katherine Mansfield stated that suffering was the gift that had taught her to look on the world with love. She brings her own experiences and insight derived from tragic events, personal loss, deep passion, and physical illness to her stories. The charm or silliness of her characters is tempered by the sorrows they are bound to encounter: pain, fear, and loneliness.

Katherine Mansfield
(1888–1923)

Today, short stories are one of the most popular and respected forms of writing. However, one hundred years ago, plays, poetry, and novels were considered the highest forms of literary expression. One of the authors who helped increase our appreciation of the short story was Katherine Mansfield.

Mansfield is credited by critics for helping to refine and advance the art of the short story.

From the Edge to the Center
Mansfield was born in Wellington, the capital of New Zealand. Believing that Wellington was too remote a place for someone with literary aspirations, Mansfield moved to London while still in her teens.

Although London was a vibrant literary center that was home to many of the world's finest writers, it seemed cold and impersonal to Mansfield. Her sense of disillusionment with life in London is reflected in her early stories.

From Death, Inspiration In 1915, she received a sudden shock. Her brother, a soldier in the British army, died in the trenches in World War I. This tragic event led Mansfield to the conclusion that she had neglected her roots, and she began to write stories, including "The Apple Tree," based on her childhood in New Zealand.

Tragically, Mansfield's life was cut short by disease. After contracting tuberculosis, she spent her last few years in and out of clinics and hospitals in France and Italy, before the disease claimed her life in 1923.

◆ Build Vocabulary

WORD ORIGINS: WORDS FROM MYTHS

Myths are fictional tales that explain the actions of gods or the causes of natural phenomena. Many English words come from Greek and Roman myths. For example, the word *jovial,* which appears in this story, comes from the name Jove, another name for Jupiter, the ruler of the Roman gods. The planet Jupiter is named for him, and it was once believed that people born under the sign of Jupiter (Jove) were playful and merry. The word *jovial* describes these qualities: a jovial mood, a jovial man.

WORD BANK

paddocks
exquisite
bouquet
jovial

Before you read, preview this list of words from the story.

◆ Build Grammar Skills

PUNCTUATION OF DIALOGUE

Mansfield uses **dialogue**—conversation between characters—to bring her characters to life and advance the action of her story. You will notice that she follows these rules for formatting and **punctuating** the dialogue:

• A speaker's exact words are enclosed in quotation marks.
• Commas separate quotations from words that identify the speaker. The comma always appears before the quotation mark.
• A new paragraph begins each time the speaker changes.
• When a paragraph ends while a character is still speaking, quotation marks *do not* appear at the end of that paragraph. However, quotation marks do appear at the beginning of the new paragraph.

Prentice Hall Literature Program Resources

REINFORCE / RETEACH / EXTEND

Selection Support Pages
Build Vocabulary: Words From Myths, p. 55
Build Grammar Skills: Punctuating Dialogue, p. 56
Reading Strategy: Question, p. 57
Literary Focus: Allusion, p. 58

Strategies for Diverse Student Needs, p. 14

Beyond Literature
Cross-Curricular Connection: Plant Science, p. 14

Formal Assessment Selection Test, pp. 44–46;
Assessment Resources Software

Alternative Assessment, p. 14

Resource Pro CD-ROM
"The Apple Tree"—includes all resource materials and customizable lesson plan

Listening to Literature Audiocassettes
"The Apple Tree"

The Apple Tree

◆ *Literature and Your Life*

CONNECT YOUR EXPERIENCE

If you've ever spent a long time waiting in anticipation of something, then you know how the characters in "The Apple Tree" feel. Based on your own experiences, try to predict whether the anticipated event will live up to the characters' expectations.

Journal Writing Think of something for which you spent a long time waiting. In your journal, write about whether the outcome was worth the wait.

THEMATIC FOCUS: REACHING A GOAL

As you read this story of a man and his children's painful, mouth-watering anticipation, you may ask yourself, What things in life are worth waiting for?

◆ Background for Understanding

LITERATURE

In this story, a man discovers a special apple tree he has never noticed in his orchard before. He tells his children that eating the fruit of this tree is forbidden. "The Apple Tree" is only one of a vast number of literary works inspired by biblical stories.

This story may sound familiar. It is a variation of the biblical account of Adam and Eve. The Bible relates that Adam and Eve were forbidden by God to eat the fruit (traditionally represented as an apple) of a tree in the center of the garden. Adam and Eve *do* eat the fruit, and they are consequently banished from the Garden of Eden.

◆ Literary Focus

ALLUSION

Katherine Mansfield's reference to the forbidden tree is an **allusion**, a reference to a well-known person, place, event, literary work, or work of art. Writers most frequently make allusions to the Bible, Greek or Roman mythology, or Shakespeare's plays, but they may also allude to current events, popular culture, or other fields of interest to readers. Recognizing allusions will help you better understand and appreciate literature, because allusions often hint at the underlying meaning of a literary work.

◆ Reading Strategy

QUESTION

Writers almost never spell out the significance of each detail or each character's actions. Instead, it's left up to the reader to ask questions and to look for answers. When you **question** as you read, you ask yourself about the meaning of events, character's actions, and key details. Why does a character act the way he or she does? Does a specific detail of the setting have an underlying meaning?

Keep your questions in mind as you read ahead. Try to piece together details that will enable you to answer them. For example, you might gather information about a character's background that will help you answer a question about his or her behavior.

Apple Plenty, 1970, Herbert Shuptrine

To capture students' interest, draw two simple signs on the chalkboard: "Private: Keep Out" and "Authorized Personnel Only." Encourage students to exchange information about where and when they have encountered such signs. Ask: What did you imagine was behind the signs? Did you ever find out? What is the effect of making something "off-limits" or forbidden? After discussing the effect of classifying something as "forbidden," tell students that "The Apple Tree" centers on a "forbidden" fruit—the apple. Students will have a chance to compare their own reactions to forbidden situations to those of the characters in this story.

Customize for
Less Proficient Readers

On the surface this is a very simple story. Work with these students to help them understand the building of the theme as the story progresses. They might pause after each page, for example, and summarize its most important idea before continuing.

Customize for
More Advanced Students

Invite more advanced students to read other stories that center on something forbidden, such as the stories of Pandora from Greek mythology or the story of Bluebeard. Have them analyze how something forbidden affects each main character.

Customize for
English Language Learners

Explain to these students that they will encounter the idiom "Don't bolt it" (footnote 5) in the story. *Bolt* literally means "a sudden dash." "Don't bolt it" means "don't eat your food in a sudden dash." These students will also benefit from reading along as they listen to the recording on **Listening to Literature Audiocassettes.**

Customize for
Interpersonal Learners

Have these students role-play a private conversation between the children after they have been told to stay away from the apple tree. Role-plays should stress how the admonition makes each character feel.

 Preparing for Standardized Tests

Reading The Reading Strategy focuses on asking questions to understand plot and character development, recognize cause and effect, envision the setting, analyze details. Students can apply this interactive strategy to any reading comprehension items on the verbal portions of standardized tests. For additional practice, use the Reading Strategy page in **Selection Support,** p. 57.

Grammar and Language Portions of some standardized tests require students to punctuate dialogue correctly, as in the following item:

Which of the following is correct? *(A)*

(A) "I've never been so disgusted in my life," he said.

(B) "I've never been so disgusted in my life" he said.

(C) "I've never been so disgusted in my life, he said."

The Build Grammar Skills lesson for this selection focuses on punctuating dialogue. For additional practice, use the Build Grammar Skills page on punctuating dialogue in **Selection Support,** p. 56.

Develop Understanding

One-Minute Insight

On its literal level, this is the story of how anticipation is rewarded—literally—with bitter disappointment. The children's disappointment at how terrible the "magnificent" apple tastes is matched only by their desire to shield their father from disappointment. Read as an "Adam-and-Eve" story, the children, as the biblical characters, ultimately find that the forbidden fruit is bitter. Even though the children in this story have permission to taste the fruit, they are driven like Adam and Eve from the innocence of childhood as they witness the foolishness of their respected father.

Humanities: Art

Orchard With Flowering Fruit Trees, Springtime, Pontoise, 1877, by Camille Pissarro.

This painting captures the delicate light and colors of springtime, reminiscent of the season of anticipation in which the characters in this story await the fruit of an apple tree.

Camille Pissarro (1830–1903) was a French impressionist painter, the only painter to exhibit in all eight of the Impressionist group exhibitions of 1874 to 1886. Landscapes, often with peasant figures, were his main subjects. The blossoms on the fruit trees in this painting radiate light and illuminate the orchard. As Mansfield's story focuses in on a fleeting event in everyday life, this painting captures a spring day— one of nature's fleeting moments.

After reading the first page of the story, students can discuss the following questions:

1. From the details in the painting and the title of the selection, what can you predict about this story? *Students may say that the plot will revolve around an apple tree; that there is something special or mysterious about a particular tree.*

2. How is the orchard in the picture different from the second orchard described in the story? *The orchard in the story is more remote than the one in the picture—there would probably be no building or buildings in sight. Also, the grass in the picture is not as long as the grass described in the story.*

Block Scheduling Strategies

Consider these suggestions to take advantage of extended class time:

- Have students read the Background for Understanding. Elaborate on the story as necessary for your class.
- Ask students to recall allusions in their recent reading. For example, did they read a review of a film that alluded to another film, or a work of literature? Did they understand the allusion? If so, how did the allusion affect or change their understanding of the selection? Use the Literary

Focus page on Allusions in **Selection Support** (p. 58).

- Have students work with a partner to develop responses to the Critical Thinking questions.
- Encourage students to share orally the stories they have retold in the Writing Mini-Lesson.
- Have students complete the multiple-choice portion of the Selection Test (p. 44) in the **Formal Assessment** booklet. You may wish to assign the test essay for this selection as homework.

The Apple Tree

Katherine Mansfield

There were two orchards belonging to the old house. One, that we called the "wild" orchard, lay beyond the vegetable garden; it was planted with bitter cherries and damsons[1] and transparent yellow plums. For some reason it lay under a cloud; we never played there, we did not even trouble to pick up the fallen fruit; and there, every Monday morning, to the round open space in the middle, the servant girl and the washerwoman carried the wet linen—Grandmother's nightdresses, Father's striped shirts, the hired man's cotton trousers and the servant girl's "dreadfully vulgar" salmon-pink flannelette drawers jigged and slapped in horrid familiarity. But the other orchard, far away and hidden from the house, lay at the foot of a little hill and stretched right over to the edge of the paddocks—to the clumps of wattles[2] bobbing yellow in the bright sun and the blue gums with their streaming sickle-shaped leaves. There, under the fruit trees, the grass grew so thick and coarse that it tangled and knotted in your shoes as you walked, and even on the hottest day it was damp to touch when you stopped and parted it this way and that, looking for windfalls—the apples marked with a bird's beak, the big bruised pears, the quinces,[3] so good to eat with a pinch of salt, but so delicious to smell that you could not bite for sniffing. . . .

One year the orchard had its Forbidden Tree. It was an apple tree discovered by Father and a friend during an after-dinner prowl one Sunday afternoon.

◆ **Literary Focus**
What allusion does the author make here?

---

1. **damsons** (dam′ zənz) *n.*: Small purple plums.

◀ Critical Viewing What season is shown in this picture? What details reveal the season? [Deduce]

◆ **Build Vocabulary**
paddocks (pad′ əks) *n.*: Small enclosed fields

---

2. **wattles** (wät′ əlz) *n.*: Small flowering trees.
3. **quinces** (kwins′ iz) *n.*: Hard greenish-yellow apple-shaped fruit.

The Apple Tree ◆ 195

Humanities: Art

Apple Plenty by Herbert Shuptrine.
The basket of ripe apples, nestled in the autumn grass, suggests the bounty of apples. Such a heartwarming picture is probably what Father in this story expects from his tree.

Have students examine the way in which the basket of apples is presented to the viewer. Use these questions for discussion:

1. How does its central position in the painting reflect the importance placed on the "rare" apple tree in the English farmer's life? *The central position suggests the focus that Father places*

on the apples while he is anticipating their harvest.

2. Are these apples a fair representation of the crimson apples which the narrator describes? *On the outside these apples match the narrator's description; however, the insides of these are probably sweet and crisp, not like the apples in this story.*

3. If students were to pick a theme for this picture, what would it be—harvest time, abandonment, nature's bounty, or what other theme? *Students might justify any of the suggested themes or supply another. Request reasons for their choices.*

◆ Critical Thinking

❶ Infer Why does the father act as if he knows what the visitor is talking about? *The father does not want to appear to be ignorant, especially in front of his children.*

◆ Build Grammar Skills

❷ Punctuate Dialogue Ask students to explain why the quotation marks and commas appear where they do in this sentence. Have them explain why a new paragraph begins with the word, "They're." *The quotation marks enclose what the characters are actually saying; the commas separate the dialogue from words that identify the speaker; the new paragraph indicates that the speaker has changed.*

◆ Reading Strategy

❸ Question Ask students: Why does the father issue this warning? How will answering this question help you to understand the story? *Students may say that the father issues the warning because he now thinks the tree is valuable. By answering this question, students can predict that the father's new conception of the tree will affect future events.*

◆ *Literature and Your Life*

❹ Point out that sometimes taking a particular walk or route becomes a custom for people. Ask: Do you have a customary route? What is special about it and its landmarks? *Students can describe the routes they take to get to special places and the associations they make with landmarks along the way.*

◆ Reading Strategy

❺ Question The father feels that the unique qualities he has discovered in the apple tree reflect on his own character; he takes pride in the tree as if it were his personal accomplishment.

◆ Critical Thinking

❻ Infer Ask students: Why do you think Bogey stood with his scratched knees pressed together and his hands behind his back? *Students may say he is trying to hide his scratched knees from his father, and trying to imitate his father, who also stands with his hands behind his back.*

"Great Scott!" said the friend, lighting upon it with every appearance of admiring astonishment: "Isn't that a—?" And a rich, splendid name settled like an unknown bird on the tree.

❶ "Yes, I believe it is," said Father lightly. He knew nothing whatever about the names of fruit trees.

"Great Scott!" said the friend again: "They're wonderful apples. Nothing like 'em—and you're going to have a tiptop crop. Marvelous apples! You can't beat 'em!"

"No, they're very fine—very fine," said Father carelessly, but looking upon the tree with new and lively interest.

❷ "They're rare—they're very rare. Hardly ever see 'em in England nowadays," said the visitor and set a seal on Father's delight. For Father was a self-made man and the price he had to pay for everything was so huge and so painful that nothing rang so sweet to him as to hear his purchase praised. He was young and sensitive still. He still wondered whether in the deepest sense he got his money's worth. He still had hours when he walked up and down in the moonlight half deciding to "chuck this confounded rushing to the office every day—and clear out—clear out once and for all." And now to discover that he'd a valuable apple tree thrown in with the orchard—an apple tree that this Johnny from England positively envied!

❸ "Don't touch that tree! Do you hear me, children!" said he, bland and firm; and when the guest had gone, with quite another voice and manner:

"If I catch either of you touching those apples you shall not only go to bed—you

◆ Build Vocabulary

exquisite (eks´ kwi zit) *adj.*: Delicately beautiful

bouquet (bōō kā´) *n.*: Fragrance

jovial (jō´ vē əl) *adj.*: Full of good humor

---

shall each have a good sound whipping." Which merely added to its magnificence.

❹ Every Sunday morning after church Father, with Bogey and me tailing after, walked through the flower garden, down the violet path, past the lace-bark tree, past the white rose and syringa⁴ bushes, and down the hill to the orchard. The apple tree seemed to have been miraculously warned of its high honor, standing apart from its fellows, bending a little under its rich clusters, fluttering its polished leaves, important and exquisite before Father's awful eye. His heart swelled to the sight—we knew his heart swelled. He put his hands behind his back and screwed

> ### ◆ Reading Strategy
> **❺** Why is the father so excited about the apple tree?

up his eyes in the way he had. There it stood—the accidental thing—the thing that no one had been aware of when the hard bargain was driven. It hadn't been counted in, hadn't in a way been paid for. If the house had been burned to the ground at that time it would have meant less to him than the destruction of his tree. And how **❻** we played up to him, Bogey and I,—Bogey with his scratched knees pressed together, his hands behind his back, too, and a round cap on his head with "H.M.S. Thunderbolt" printed across it.

The apples turned from pale green to yellow; then they had deep pink stripes painted on them, and then the pink melted all over the yellow, reddened, and spread into a fine clear crimson.

At last the day came when Father took out of his waistcoat pocket a little pearl penknife. He reached up. Very slowly and very carefully he picked two apples growing on a bough.

"Why, they're warm," cried Father in amazement. "They're wonderful apples!

---

4. **syringa** (sə riŋ´ gə) *n.*: Hardy shrub with tiny, fragrant flowers, also known as lilac.

Speaking and Listening Mini-Lesson

Monologue From Father's Point of View

This mini-lesson supports the Speaking and Listening activity in the Idea Bank on page 199.

Introduce the Concept Remind students that in a monologue—a speech made by one person—a character reveals his or her truest feelings. Students should give the father the opportunity to tell events as he sees them.

Develop Background Students can brainstorm for a list of characteristics that describe the father and then decide which part of the story they want to relate from his point of view. The father might

be thinking about ways to impress the visitor, how eager he is to taste the ripe fruit—or how foolish he feels at the end of the story.

Apply the Information Have students create their monologues with the father's character traits in mind. Suggest that they put themselves in his place and imagine his thoughts and feelings.

Assess the Outcome Have students use the Peer Assessment: Speech (p. 119) of the *Alternative Assessment* booklet to help them evaluate each others' and their own monologues.

Tiptop! Marvelous!" he echoed. He rolled them over in his hands.

"Look at that!" he said. "Not a spot—not a blemish!" And he walked through the orchard with Bogey and me stumbling after, to a tree stump under the wattles. We sat, one on either side of Father. He laid one apple down, opened the penknife and neatly and beautifully cut the other in half.

"Look at that!" he exclaimed.

"Father!" we cried, dutiful but really enthusiastic, too. For the lovely red color had bitten right through the white flesh of the apple; it was pink to the shiny black pips lying so justly in their scaly pods. It looked as though the apple had been dipped in wine.

"Never seen *that* before," said Father.

"You won't find an apple like that in a hurry!" He put it to his nose and pronounced an unfamiliar word. "Bouquet. What a bouquet!" And then he handed to Bogey one half, to me the other.

"Don't *bolt* it!"[5] said he. It was agony to give even so much away. I knew it, while I took mine humbly and humbly Bogey took his.

Then he divided the second with the same neat beautiful little cut of the pearl knife.

I kept my eyes on Bogey. Together we took a bite. Our mouths were full of a floury stuff, a hard, faintly bitter skin—a horrible taste of something dry. . . .

"Well?" asked Father, very jovial. He had cut his two halves into quarters and was taking out the little pods. "Well?" ❼

Bogey and I stared at each other, chewing desperately. In that second of chewing and swallowing a long silent conversation passed between us—and a strange meaning smile. We swallowed. We edged near Father, just touching him. ❽

"Perfect," we lied. "Perfect—Father! Simply lovely!" ❾

But it was no use. Father spat his out and never went near the apple tree again.

---

5. **Don't bolt it:** Don't eat it all in one bite.

Guide for Responding

◆ *Literature and Your Life*

Reader's Response Were you surprised by the ending? Why or why not?

Thematic Focus Why do you think that eagerly anticipated events so often fail to live up to people's expectations?

Group Discussion With a small group, discuss why the children mislead their father about the taste of the apple. What would each of you have done in that situation? Why?

☑ Check Your Comprehension

1. What does the friend from England tell the father about the apple tree?
2. How does the father treat the tree after his friend's revelation?
3. Describe the apples' appearance.
4. Explain how the apples' taste compares with the characters' expectations.

The Apple Tree ◆ 197

 Beyond the Selection

FURTHER READING

Other Works by Katherine Mansfield
"The Dolls' House"
"Her First Ball"
The Garden Party: Katherine Mansfield's New Zealand Stories—Stories illustrated with color plates by New Zealand artists

We suggest that you preview these works before recommending them to students.

INTERNET

Students may find additional information about the Katherine Mansfield on the Internet. Please be aware that sites may have changed from the time we published this information:
http://www.buffnet.net./~starmist/ kmansfld/kmansfld.htm
http://www.futurenet.co.uk/Penguin/ Books/01401888000.html

We *strongly recommend* that you preview these sites before you send students to them.

197

Answers

◆ Critical Thinking

1. He is easily convinced because he does not know anything about apple trees and is all too ready to believe he has a special one.
2. The first hint was probably the color inside the apple.
3. The children are afraid to disappoint and humiliate their father.
4. They learn not to build up expectations so high, particularly on the basis of someone else's opinion.
5. The need for approval might cause people to use poor judgment in attaching value to some things.
6. Students might suggest the jobs of politician or salesperson.

◆ Reading Strategy

1. Students' main question might be: Why is it so important to the father to have something rare and valuable?
2. Students might observe that the father needs the approval of others, including his children.

◆ Literary Focus

1. The story mentions the Forbidden Tree, an allusion to tree of knowledge; father cautions the children not to touch "that tree"—an allusion to God's forbidding Adam and Eve to eat from the tree of knowledge.
2. The tree in the biblical story represents worldly experience. In this story the tree stands for the value or prestige people seek.
3. By comparing the children with Adam and Eve, students can better understand the children's loss of innocence at the end.

◆ Build Vocabulary

Using Words From Myths
1. c 2. a 3. b

Using the Word Bank
1. c 2. b 3. a 4. a

◆ Build Grammar Skills

Practice
"Great Scott!" said the friend, lighting upon it with every appearance of admiring astonishment: "Isn't that a—?" And a rich splendid name settled like an unknown bird on the tree.

"Yes, I believe it is," said Father lightly. He knew nothing whatever about the names of fruit trees.

198

Guide for Responding (continued)

◆ Critical Thinking

INTERPRET
1. Why is the father so easily convinced by his friend that the tree produces wonderful apples? **[Infer]**
2. What are the first hints that the taste of the apples might not live up to expectations? **[Infer]**
3. Why do the children mislead their father about the taste of the apple? **[Infer]**
4. What lesson do the father and the children learn? **[Draw Conclusions]**

APPLY
5. How do image and public approval play a role in determining the worth of some of the things we value? **[Apply]**

EXTEND
6. What are some careers in which public opinion influences how a person performs his or her job? **[Career Link]**

◆ Reading Strategy

QUESTION
After you've finished reading a literary work, reflect on the **questions** that came to mind as you read. Answer any unresolved questions by piecing together details from the work and, if necessary, going back into the text.
1. What is the main question that came to mind about the father's behavior?
2. After reading the story, how would you answer that question?

◆ Literary Focus

ALLUSION
In "The Apple Tree," Katherine Mansfield makes an **allusion** to the biblical story of Adam and Eve.
1. Point out two references in "The Apple Tree" to the biblical story.
2. How does "The Apple Tree" differ from the biblical story?
3. How does knowing the biblical story of Adam and Eve increase your understanding and appreciation of "The Apple Tree"?

198 ◆ Striving for Success

◆ Build Vocabulary

USING WORDS FROM MYTHS
Use the clues below to match each word with the letter of its definition.

Clues From Greek Mythology

Pan: minor god who lived in wild places and sometimes frightened travelers
Chaos: formless confusion that existed before the Earth or the gods appeared
Lethe: river of forgetfulness that separates the worlds of the living and the dead

1. lethal ____?____   **a.** completely confused and disordered
2. chaotic ____?____   **b.** sudden, hysterical fear
3. panic ____?____   **c.** deadly

USING THE WORD BANK
On your paper, write the word or phrase whose meaning is closest to that of the first word:
1. jovial: (a) simple, (b) wealthy, (c) merry
2. paddock: (a) marsh, (b) pasture, (c) grove
3. exquisite: (a) superb, (b) favorable, (c) fragrant
4. bouquet: (a) smell, (b) collection, (c) roses

◆ Build Grammar Skills

PUNCTUATION OF DIALOGUE
You can picture Mansfield's characters interacting with one another because of her extensive use of **dialogue**—characters' conversations written as if quoted word for word.

Practice Copy the following passage from "The Apple Tree" and punctuate it correctly.

Great Scott! said the friend, lighting upon it with every appearance of admiring astonishment: Isn't that a—? And a rich, splendid name settled like an unknown bird on the tree. Yes, I believe it is, said Father lightly. He knew nothing whatever about the names of fruit trees.

Writing Application Re-create a recent conversation that you've had with a friend or family member in a brief passage of written dialogue. Punctuate your passage correctly.

✎ **Writer's Solution**

For additional instruction and practice, use the pages on Quotation Marks and Direct Quotations (pp. 104–106) in the *Writer's Solution Grammar Practice Book*.

Build Your Portfolio

 Idea Bank

Writing

1. **Summary of the Story** Write a summary of "The Apple Tree" to appear in *Short Story Digest* magazine. Keep the summary as brief as possible, but include all the key events from the story.

2. **Personal Narrative** Recall a time when an anticipated event didn't live up to your expectations. Then write a personal narrative in which you re-create the experience and tell what you learned from it.

3. **Alternative Ending** Write an alternative ending to the story in which you explore the possibility of what might have happened had the apples tasted better.

Speaking and Listening

4. **Dramatic Reading** With three classmates, give a dramatic reading of "The Apple Tree" in front of your classmates. Have one person be the narrator, one the father, one the father's friend, and one the boy. **[Performing Arts Link]**

5. **Monologue From Father's Point of View** Prepare a monologue in which you tell the story from the father's point of view. Show his anticipation and disappointment. Perform your monologue for the class. **[Performing Arts Link]**

Projects

6. **Travel Brochure** Make a travel brochure for New Zealand, Mansfield's native land. Include text and pictures that give information about geography, culture, and climate. **[Social Studies Link]**

7. **Map** Use details from the story and your imagination to create a map of the father's property. Show the locations of the two orchards and of the "Forbidden Tree." **[Social Studies Link]**

 Writing Mini-Lesson

Retelling a Story

On one level, "The Apple Tree" is a retelling of the biblical story of Adam and Eve from the Bible. Choose a story that you can retell. It can be from any number of sources: the Bible, classical mythology, even current events. Retell the story, giving it a new setting or other unique twist.

Writing Skills Focus: Show Don't Tell

Add interest to your story by **showing** readers your setting and characters rather than simply telling about them. Katherine Mansfield doesn't say the apple is beautiful, she shows its beauty with specific details.

> . . . the lovely red color had bitten right through the white flesh of the apple; it was pink to the shiny black pips lying so justly in their scaly pods. It looked as though the apple had been dipped in wine.

Prewriting Make your retelling unique. For example, you may want to recast *Romeo and Juliet* in modern times in your community. Then list the key elements of the work or event you're adapting.

Drafting Organize events in a logical order; time order is probably best. Present the key elements of the original work in a way that readers will recognize. Also, use dialogue as much as possible to make your characters come alive.

Revising After you've finished your draft, put it aside for a day or two. Then review it with a critical eye. Add descriptive details or actions for characters that show (rather than tell) what you want readers to know.

The Apple Tree ◆ 199

Guide for Reading

More About the Authors

All the writers in this section have been committed to making the world a better place.

David Diop's work has helped give voice to the struggle for cultural identity and political autonomy.

The traditional song and the teachings of **Confucius** advocate moderation, self-control, strong moral character, and dignity; his teachings offer guidelines for ethical reform and have influenced rulers in Asian nations for centuries.

Bei Dao and **Shu Ting** offer two views of contemporary China, both of which acknowledge the high price of liberty.

David Diop (1927–1960)

David Diop published only one volume of poetry before his life was tragically cut short in a plane crash. That one book, *Hammerblows*, reflects Diop's rejection of colonialism in Africa.

Diop was born in France, but his roots were in the region that became the West African nation of Senegal. His poem "Africa" captures the power and dignity of a continent struggling against oppression.

Confucius (551?–479? B.C.)

One man's ideas have influenced the pattern of Chinese life for more than two thousand years. That man is Confucius, a scholar from Shandong province in northeast China. In all his teachings, Confucius emphasized the importance of moral conduct.

Confucius' moral teachings have had a profound impact on Chinese life and have influenced the lives of many people in a number of other countries as well.

Bei Dao (1949–)

Born two months before the founding of the People's Republic of China in October 1949, Bei Dao seemed destined for a successful government career. However, he dropped out of school and joined the Red Guards, a movement of teenagers seeking to revitalize the Chinese Revolution. When he became disillusioned with the violent tactics of this movement, he turned to writing poetry. Soon his poems, including "All," became rallying cries for those who wanted China to become more democratic. He has lived outside China since 1989, when Chinese leaders ordered the massacre of protesting students in Tiananmen Square.

Shu Ting (1952–)

As a teenager, Shu Ting was forced by political events to leave Beijing and live in a small peasant village. She gained fame as a poet while still in her twenties. She won China's National Poetry Award in 1981 and 1983.

◆ Build Vocabulary

SUFFIXES: -ment

In the excerpt from *The Analects*, you will encounter the word *chastisements*. The suffix -*ment* can help you figure out that this word is the noun form of the verb *chastise*, which means "punish." *Chastisements*, then, are "punishments."

WORD BANK

Before you read, preview this list of words from the selections. As you read, look for other words—like *treatment* and *improvement*—that end with -*ment*.

> impetuous
> chastisements
> lamentation

◆ Build Grammar Skills

INFINITIVES AND INFINITIVE PHRASES

An **infinitive** is the base form of a verb, usually preceded by *to*; it can be used as a noun, an adjective, or an adverb. An **infinitive phrase** is an infinitive with modifiers or complements (words that complete the meaning of the verb), all acting together as a single part of speech.

The following line from "Old Song" contains two infinitive phrases: *To be alive* is a noun; it is the subject of the sentence. *To hear this song* is an adverb modifying *alive*.

To be alive to hear this song is a victory.

Africa ◆ Old Song
from The Analects ◆ All ◆ Also All

◆ *Literature and Your Life*

CONNECT YOUR EXPERIENCE

Advice—you can't escape it. You get it from teachers, parents, and friends—even from talk show hosts. People love to tell you what you should do or think. Authors are no different. They want to communicate what they have learned about life.

These writers may not give you the same advice, but that's understandable because they come from different places and eras. Think about what they say and suggest about life's goals.

THEMATIC FOCUS: REACHING A GOAL

Each of these works offers a different answer to the question, "How do we measure the success of a life?"

Journal Writing Make a cluster diagram to map out what you think are the ingredients of a successful life.

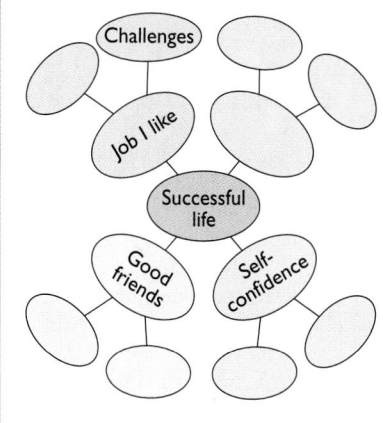

◆ Background for Understanding

CULTURE

If success is measured by time, "Old Song" and the sayings of Confucius are a success. These works have survived for thousands of years, passed down from generation to generation.

Many African societies did not preserve their wisdom and stories on paper. Instead, they developed a rich oral tradition. In each village, elders passed on wisdom in the form of sayings, stories, and poems like "Old Song."

No writings from Confucius' own hand exist today. *The Analects*, or collected sayings of Confucius, were also preserved orally and compiled in writing long after his death.

◆ Literary Focus

APHORISMS

The ideas of Confucius have endured partly because they were expressed as **aphorisms**—brief sayings that express a basic truth. Many cultures pass on truths in the form of aphorisms, like gifts handed from one generation to another.

All the pieces in this grouping contain aphorisms. Look for these brief sayings. Then read them thoughtfully, as if you were slowly unwrapping a gift sent to you across many miles or years.

◆ Reading Strategy

RELATE TO WHAT YOU KNOW

The best way to judge advice is to think about how it applies to your own situation. The best way to understand a writer's words is by **relating** them to what you know—finding something in your own experience that helps you understand and evaluate them.

These selections come from distant parts of the globe, Africa and China. When you first read them, you may think, "Interesting, but what does this have to do with me?" Look closely, and you'll discover that their themes are universal. Consider their messages about survival, hope, dignity, and morality. Then apply these messages to your own experience.

Guide for Reading ◆ 201

Preparing for Standardized Tests

Grammar and Writing Portions of some standardized tests require students to identify infinitives and infinitive phrases and to determine if they serve as nouns, adjectives, or adverbs. Write the following sentences on the chalkboard. Ask students to identify the infinitive or infinitive phrase in each and to identify its role in the sentence:

1. To write poems is sometimes a political act. *To write poems—infinitive phrase; it serves as the subject (noun).*

2. She has the capacity to influence people. *to influence people—infinitive phrase; it serves as an adjective modifying capacity.*

3. To clarify her point, she gives an example. *To clarify her point—infinitive phrase; it serves as an adverb modifying gives.*

The Build Grammar Skills lesson for this selection, which focuses on this topic, will help students with such items. Skill with using infinitives and infinitive phrases correctly will also improve performances on the essay portions of standardized tests. For additional practice, use the Build Grammar Skills page on Infinitives and Infinitive Phrases (p. 60) in **Selection Support**.

These writings offer a range of valuable insights intended to guide, caution, inspire, and ignite. The poem by David Diop searches for roots and renewal; the traditional song offers quiet, steady strength; the sayings of Confucius provide sound advice. Whereas the poem by Bei Dao reflects resignation, the poem by Shu Ting responds by offering hope. Voices from ancient times unite with contemporary voices to reflect on life's struggles and its triumphs.

◆ **Reading Strategy**

❶ **Relate to What You Know** Ask students to think about people in their families. Did their ancestors have to overcome hardship or oppression? How did their ancestors' struggle for success affect students' lives? *Students can share family stories or write in their journals about how they have been influenced by their past.*

◆ **Critical Thinking**

❷ **Infer** Ask students if the speaker is praising or criticizing Africa. How do they know? *The speaker is criticizing Africa for saying "yes" to oppression for so long. The speaker uses images reminiscent of slavery ("the trembling back striped red") to chide Africa for its submissiveness.*

◆ **Critical Thinking**

❸ **Infer** Ask students: Who is the solemn answering voice? Why does it call the speaker "child"? *Students may think the solemn voice is the speaker's mother, the spirit of Africa, the spirit of the speaker's ancestors. All these could appropriately call the speaker "child."*

▶ **Critical Viewing** ◀

❹ **Synthesize** The painting shows Africans working together, and "Africa" says that African people will work together, "with patience and stubbornness." The painting shows people handing fish to each other. "Old Song" celebrates traditions that are handed down from one generation to the next.

Africa

David Diop

Translated by Ulli Beier

to my Mother

❶ Africa my Africa
Africa of proud warriors in the ancestral
  savannahs[1]
Africa my grandmother sings of
Beside her distant river
5 I have never seen you
But my gaze is full of your blood
Your black blood spilt over the fields
The blood of your sweat
The sweat of your toil
10 The toil of slavery
The slavery of your children
Africa, tell me Africa,
Are you the back that bends
Lies down under the weight of humbleness?
❷ 15 The trembling back striped red
That says yes to the sjambok[2] on the roads
  of noon?
Solemnly a voice answers me
"Impetuous child, that young and sturdy tree
That tree that grows
20 There splendidly alone among white and
  faded flowers
❸ Is Africa, your Africa. It puts forth new
  shoots
With patience and stubbornness puts forth
  new shoots
Slowly its fruits grow to have
The bitter taste of liberty."

---

1. **savannahs** (sə vanˈəz) *n.*: Tropical grassland containing scattered trees.
2. **sjambok** (jamˈbôk) *n.*: Whip.

◆ **Build Vocabulary**

impetuous (im pechˈ oo əs) *adj.*: Impulsive; passionate

▲ **Critical Viewing** Discuss how this painting reflects the thoughts conveyed in both poems. [Synthesize] ❹

Traditional Yam Harvest, John Malinga, LAMU,

Old Song

traditional

Do not seek too much fame,
but do not seek obscurity.
Be proud.
But do not remind the world of your deeds.
5 Excel when you must,
but do not excel the world.
Many heroes are not yet born,
many have already died.
To be alive to hear this song is a victory.

 Block Scheduling Strategies

Consider these suggestions to take advantage of extended class time:

• Have students make a cluster diagram, like the one shown on page 201, as a journal activity about a successful life.

• Together with students, read Background for Understanding on page 201. Lead a brief discussion in which students compare and contrast the qualities of orally based literature, such as "Old Song" and the analects of Confucius, with those of original written literature.

• Ask students to provide specific examples of how a teenager in today's world could live in accordance with the advice in "Old Song." Students could respond through a class discussion or in their journals.

• Let students work in small groups to answer the Critical Thinking questions on pages 203 and 205.

CONNECTIONS TO TODAY'S WORLD

Until the 1990's, the right to vote and equal access to schools and public facilities were denied to South Africa's black majority.

However, mounting international pressure helped bring an end to **apartheid**—South Africa's system of forced segregation. Among the many voices to speak out against apartheid were musicians such as Peter Gabriel, who wrote the following song of tribute to Stephen Biko, a pioneer in the struggle against apartheid. Biko was killed by police in 1977.

1. Like poetry, song lyrics use a variety of sound devices, such as rhyme and repetition, to create a rhythmical effect and emphasize meaning. Explain how Gabriel uses rhyme and repetition in "Biko."
2. Look at lines 17–20. (a) In what way do they resemble an aphorism? (b) Explain what they mean in terms of the struggle for justice.
3. Explain how the last line of Bei Dao's poem— "every death reverberates forever"—is similar in meaning to lines 17–20 of this song.

BIKO
Peter Gabriel

September '77
Port Elizabeth weather fine
It was business as usual
In police room 619
5   Oh Biko, Biko, because Biko
Oh Biko, Biko, because Biko
Yihla Moja, Yihla Moja
—The man is dead

When I try to sleep at night
10 I can only dream in red
The outside world is black and white
With only one colour dead
Oh Biko, Biko, because Biko
Oh Biko, Biko, because Biko
15 Yihla Moja, Yihla Moja
—The man is dead

You can blow out a candle
But you can't blow out a fire
Once the flames begin to catch
20 The wind will blow it higher
Oh Biko, Biko, because Biko
Yihla Moja, Yihla Moja
—The man is dead

And the eyes of the world are
25   watching now
        watching now

Connections to Today's World

More About the Author The work Peter Gabriel did with African musicians in producing the film *Biko* inspired him to launch the World of Music, Arts, and Dance (WOMAD), an organization dedicated to preserving traditional arts through performances, education, special projects, and recordings.

Thematic Focus

More than twenty years after his violent death, Stephen Biko's commitment to the principles of justice and equality are still inspiring generations of young people.

Answers

1. Rhyme and repetition emphasize Biko's name and give the song a chantlike quality.
2. (a) These lines express a basic truth in a pithy way. (b) As the struggle for justice gains more supporters, it feeds on itself and gets stronger.
3. Both the lines in the poem and the lines in the song indicate that actions have consequences.

Reinforce and Extend

Answers
◆ *Literature and Your Life*

Reader's Response Some students might cite "Africa" because of its strong tone; others might prefer the quiet power of "Old Song."

Thematic Focus Students may say that failure can cause determined people to strive harder for success.

☑ **Check Your Comprehension**

1. The speaker of "Africa" asks if the country is meant to be treated as a slave.
2. Do not seek too much fame, but don't seek to be unknown, either.

◆ Critical Thinking

1. The speaker is troubled that Africa has martyred itself by accepting the oppression of its people.
2. "The bitter taste of liberty" means that liberty is won at human cost.
3. "Old Song" has the more hopeful message, because it celebrates living in an honest, humble way.

Guide for Responding

◆ *Literature and Your Life*

Reader's Response Which poem did you find more powerful? Why?

Thematic Focus These poems suggest that success can rise out of failure. Explain why you agree or disagree.

☑ **Check Your Comprehension**

1. What question does the speaker of "Africa" ask?
2. What advice about fame is found in "Old Song"?

◆ Critical Thinking

INTERPRET
1. What troubles the speaker of "Africa" and causes him to ask his question? **[Infer]**
2. Explain the meaning of the final line of "Africa." **[Interpret]**
EVALUATE
3. Which of these poems has the more hopeful message? Explain. **[Make a Judgment]**

Africa/Old Song/Biko ◆ 203

🎵 Cross-Curricular Connection: Social Studies

David Diop's poem speaks of the oppression African people have suffered under colonial rule and apartheid governmental systems. The following historical background about West Africa, the location of Diop's homeland, Senegal, will enrich students' reading experience:

In the late 1800's, the French government looked to Africa as a potential source of much-needed land, resources, and human power. As French colonial rule spread, the African people were subjugated and exploited. Colonial rule has

slowly been replaced by independence, but French dominance in many West African countries is still evident, and economic and educational opportunities are still far from equal. The people of post-colonial Africa remain faced with the challenge of overcoming the legacy of exploitation and re-establishing their cultural identities.

Have students discuss how the hardships of regaining independence are reflected in Diop's poem and what Confucius might have said about French rule on the rich continent of Africa.

❶ **Generalize** Judging from these lines, ask students to indicate if Confucius advocates humility, ambitiousness, or greed in human relations, and to explain their response. *He advocates humility; it takes a sense of humility to "remain unsoured even though one's merits are unrecognized."*

◆ **Literary Focus**

❷ **Aphorisms** Have students use modern language to express this idea— "to have kindly feelings towards everyone but seek the intimacy of the Good"—as an aphorism. *Sample response: Treat everyone respectfully, but pursue the most worthy as friends.*

◆ **Critical Thinking**

❸ **Analyze Cause and Effect** Ask: According to Confucius, what kind of leadership will have the best results, and why? *Confucius advocates using moral leadership and being consistent in order to govern most effectively. He indicates that this approach to leadership will increase people's self-respect and make them more governable.*

▶ **Critical Viewing** ◀

❹ **Deduce** His elaborate and rich-looking clothing, his venerable beard, and all suggest a respected position. Students might also suggest that the decorations on the clothing, and perhaps even some of the items of clothing, have symbolic significance.

---

from *The Analects*
Confucius

Translated by Arthur Waley

The Master[1] said, To learn and at due times to repeat what one has learnt, is that not after all[2] a pleasure? That friends should come to one from afar, is this not after all delightful? To remain unsoured even though one's merits are unrecognized by others, is that not after all what is expected of a gentleman?

The Master said, A young man's duty is to behave well to his parents at home and to his elders abroad, to be cautious in giving promises and punctual in keeping them, to have kindly feelings towards everyone, but seek the intimacy of the Good. If, when all that is done, he has any energy to spare, then let him study the polite arts.[3]

The Master said, (the good man) does not grieve that other people do not recognize his merits. His only anxiety is lest he should fail to recognize theirs.

The Master said, He who rules by moral force is like the pole-star,[4] which remains in its place while all the lesser stars do homage to it.

The Master said, If out of three hundred Songs[5] I had to take one phrase to cover all my teaching, I would say, "Let there be no evil in your thoughts."

The Master said, Govern the people by regulations, keep order among them by <u>chastisements</u>, and they will flee from you, and lose all self-respect. Govern them by moral force, keep order among them by ritual, and they will keep their self-respect and come to you of their own accord.

---

1. **The Master:** Confucius.
2. **after all:** Even though one does not hold public office.
3. **the polite arts:** Such activities as reciting from *The Book of Songs*, practicing archery, and learning proper behavior.
4. **pole-star:** Polaris, the North Star.
5. **three hundred Songs:** Poems in *The Book of Songs*.

▲ **Critical Viewing** What clues in this picture indicate that Confucius held a respected position in his society? [Deduce]

◆ **Build Vocabulary**
chastisements (chas tiz′ mintz) *n.*: Punishments

 Workplace Skills Mini-Lesson

Setting and Meeting Goals

Introduce the Concept Discuss the idea that success in any area almost always hinges on setting and meeting goals. Reaching goals requires dedication and discipline, whether you are determined to improve your backhand or help people to achieve equality.

Develop Background Have students recall the advice in *The Analects* of Confucius. Suggest that they jot down a list of possible ways to apply the wisdom of Confucius to everyday achievement.

Apply the Information Using their list of ideas, students can write up a set of goals that they wish to achieve. What steps will they take to ensure success? How can they use the strength of Confucius' teachings to inspire them when the going gets tough? Encourage students to put their ideas in a chart that shows a step-by-step plan for success.

Assess the Outcome Have students share their charts with the group. Discuss which goals are realistic, and guide students to find ways to revise unrealistic goals so that they can be met successfully.

Meng Wu Po[6] asked about the treatment of parents. The Master said, Behave in such a way that your father and mother have no anxiety about you, except concerning your health.

The Master said, A gentleman can see a question from all sides without bias. The small man is biased and can see a question only from one side.

The Master said, Yu[7] shall I teach you what knowledge is? When you know a thing, to recognize that you know it, and when you do not know a thing, to recognize that you do not know it. That is knowledge.

The Master said, High office filled by men of narrow views, ritual performed without reverence, the forms of mourning observed without grief—these are things I cannot bear to see!

The Master said, In the presence of a good man, think all the time how you may learn to equal him. In the presence of a bad man, turn your gaze within!

The Master said, In old days a man kept a hold on his words, fearing the disgrace that would ensue should he himself fail to keep pace with them.

The Master said, A gentleman covets the reputation of being slow in word but prompt in deed.

The Master said, In old days men studied for the sake of self-improvement; nowadays men study in order to impress other people.

The Master said, A gentleman is ashamed to let his words outrun his deeds.

The Master said, He who will not worry about what is far off will soon find something worse than worry close at hand.

The Master said, To demand much from oneself and little from others is the way (for a ruler) to banish discontent.

6. **Meng Wu Po** (muŋ wōō bō): The son of one of Confucius' disciples.
7. **Yu** (yōō): Tzu-lu, one of Confucius' disciples.

Guide for Responding

◆ *Literature and Your Life*

Reader's Response If you had lived in China during the time of Confucius, do you think you would have been drawn to him and his ideas? Explain.

Thematic Focus According to Confucius, what attributes make a successful leader?

Group Discussion With a group, discuss how well some leaders of today fit Confucius' model of a successful leader.

☑ **Check Your Comprehension**

1. How does Confucius believe people should behave toward their parents?
2. What does Confucius believe knowledge is?

◆ Critical Thinking

INTERPRET
1. What does Confucius mean when he says that a ruler should govern by "moral force"? **[Interpret]**
2. Give two examples from these passages that show that Confucius attaches great importance to humility. **[Support]**

APPLY
3. Which of Confucius' ideas do you think you could apply to your own life? Explain. **[Apply]**

EXTEND
4. Which of Confucius' ideas do you think today's politicians should practice to gain more respect from voters? **[Social Studies Link]**

from *The Analects* ◆ 205

⑤ Clarification Be sure students understand that Confucius, the Master, is teaching a group of students. Have them identify Meng Wu Po as being one of the students participating in the discussion.

◆ Reading Strategy

⑥ Relate to What You Know How do students apply this aphorism in their own lives? *Encourage them to suggest compromise measures that will allow them some freedom and reassure parents at the same time.*

◆ Build Grammar Skills

⑦ Infinitive and Infinitive Phrases Have students identify the infinitives in the paragraph and name their function in the sentence. *The infinitives are* to demand *(subject) and* to banish *(adjective).*

Reinforce and Extend

Answers

◆ *Literature and Your Life*

Reader's Response Some students may say they would have been drawn to Confucius and his ideas because he showed basic wisdom and serenity.

Thematic Focus A successful leader is one who governs by modeling moral standards.

☑ **Check Your Comprehension**

1. Young people should behave well toward their parents.
2. Knowledge is recognizing that you know a thing and recognizing that you do not know a thing.

◆ Critical Thinking

1. Governing by moral force means governing by strong moral principles, not through force.
2. Examples could be Confucius' definition of knowledge and his idea that a person should not grieve if his merits are not recognized.
3. Possible response: I could treat everyone with respect while choosing my friends with care.
4. Students will probably cite Confucius' idea about governing with moral force.

Speaking and Listening Mini-Lesson

Oral Interpretation
This mini-lesson supports the Speaking and Listening activity in the Idea Bank on page 209.

Introduce the Concept Have students choose one of the poems for an oral presentation. Remind them that oral interpretation means reading it in a way that expresses its meaning.

Develop Background Each student should paraphrase each line to ensure a solid understanding of the text. Then students can discuss with partners how their readings can convey the poets' meanings. Have students copy their poems on paper, adding margin notes to remind themselves how to read each line.

Apply the Information Have students practice reading their poems before delivering their oral presentation.

Assess the Outcome Have students discuss what they discovered about the poems as they prepared their own presentations and listened to those of their classmates. What made presentations especially effective? Students might use the Peer Assessment page for Oral Interpretation (p. 120) in *Alternative Assessment.*

▶Critical Viewing◀

❶ Speculate Students may suggest that they hope to find inspiration or a sense of personal balance. Or, they hope to gain a sense of humility.

◆ **Reading Strategy**

❷ Relate to What You Know Have students write in their journals about a time when a person might feel so sad that "all joys [seemed] grave." What keeps a person going in such circumstances? *Students can write about insights and methods for continuing to move forward.*

◆ *Literature and Your Life*

❸ Have students discuss what advice Bei Dao would give to someone striving for success. *Students can share their ideas; based on the content of the poem, Bei Dao's advice is likely to be cautionary.*

Old Trees by Cold Waterfall, 1470–1559, Wen Zhengming, The Los Angeles County Museum of Art

▲ **Critical Viewing** What might these people be hoping to find in this natural setting? **[Speculate]** ❶

All

Bei Dao

Translated by Donald Finkel and Xueliang Chen

All is fated,
all cloudy,

all an endless beginning,
all a search for what vanishes,

5   all joys grave,
all griefs tearless, ❷

every speech a repetition,
every meeting a first encounter,

all love buried in the heart,
10   all history prisoned in a dream,

all hope hedged with doubt,
all faith drowned in <u>lamentation</u>. ❸

Every explosion heralds an instant of stillness,
every death reverberates forever.

◆ **Build Vocabulary**
lamentation (la mən tā´ shən) *n.:* Act of crying out in grief; wailing

---

Humanities: Art

Old Trees by Cold Waterfall by Wen Zhengming.

Chinese landscape painting follows an orderly set of rules in keeping with the teachings of Confucius. Mountains, streams, rocks, and trees are delicately executed with only minimal brush strokes to convey mood, atmosphere, and distance; human figures are kept small to reinforce the grandeur of nature.

Wen Zhengming (1470–1559) was a Ming dynasty painter who was revered as the ideal scholar-artist. After a career as a government official and a historian, he decided to abandon his city position. He retired to the country, and for the last thirty years of his life devoted himself to painting, poetry, and calligraphy.

Have students look at the painting and discuss the following questions:

1. Suppose Confucius is the teacher depicted in this painting. What might he be telling his pupil? *Encourage students to use details of the painting, The Analects, and their imaginations to create aphorisms to go with the painting.*

2. Why would the Master in the painting choose to conduct his "lesson" outdoors, instead of inside a house or school? *Students might say that teaching outdoors allows the Master to use objects in nature and natural phenomena to support his ideas.*

Also All

In answer to Bei Dao's "All"

Shu Ting

Translated by Donald Finkel
and Jinsheng Yi

4 Not all trees are felled by storms.
Not every seed finds barren soil.
Not all the wings of dream are broken,
nor is all affection doomed
5 to wither in a desolate heart.

No, not all is as you say.

Not all flames consume themselves,
shedding no light on other lives.
Not all stars announce the night
10 and never dawn. Not every song
will drift past every ear and heart.

No, not all is as you say.

Not every cry for help is silenced,
nor every loss beyond recall.
15 Not every chasm spells disaster.
Not only the weak will be brought
   to their knees,
nor every soul be trodden under.

It won't all end in tears and blood.
Today is heavy with tomorrow—
20 the future was planted yesterday.
5 Hope is a burden all of us shoulder
though we might stumble under the load.

Guide for Responding

◆ Literature and Your Life

Reader's Response If you could ask either of these poets a question, what would you ask? Why?

Thematic Focus Judging from these poems, do you think either of these poets believes in striving to overcome obstacles? Explain.

☑ Check Your Comprehension

1. Summarize what the poet says in "All."
2. Summarize the speaker's view of life in "Also All."

◆ Critical Thinking

INTERPRET

1. What effect does the repetition have on the feeling that "All" calls up? **[Analyze]**
2. Explain how the last two lines of "All" suggest the possibility of hope. **[Interpret]**
3. List three details in "Also All" that indicate Shu Ting's optimism is difficult to maintain. **[Analyze]**

APPLY

4. Bei Dao's poem "All" is a response to political events in China. What events in American news today might inspire someone to write a poem like this? Explain. **[Hypothesize]**
5. Describe a situation in which a person—either someone you know or someone in the news—showed courage and perseverance when all hope seemed lost. **[Relate]**

EXTEND

6. "Also All" was written in response to Bei Dao's poem "All." (a) What is Shu Ting's interpretation of the poem she is answering? (b) Explain how lines 19 and 20 express her disagreement with "All." **[Literature Link]**

All/Also All ◆ 207

◆ Build Grammar Skills

4 Infinitives and Infinitive Phrases Have students identify the infinitive phrase in the stanza and its part of speech and function in the sentence. *The infinitive phrase is to wither in a desolate heart. It serves as a noun, the complement of the participle doomed.*

◆ Critical Thinking

5 Compare and Contrast Have students contrast what Shu Ting says to what Bei Dao says. *Bei Dao says that life is hopeless; Shu Ting disagrees. She says, "Hope is a burden all of us shoulder."*

Reinforce and Extend

Answers

◆ Literature and Your Life

Reader's Response Students might say they would ask Bei Dao why he is so pessimistic, because they don't agree with his world view.

Thematic Focus Students may say that Shu Ting probably believes in striving to overcome obstacles because she has a positive attitude.

☑ Check Your Comprehension

1. Sorrow overwhelms joy.
2. There is reason to have hope for the future.

◆ Critical Thinking

1. The repetition seems to emphasize the feeling of doom in this poem.
2. The last two lines seem to suggest it is everyone's responsibility to keep up hope.
3. She calls today "heavy"; she calls hope "a burden"; she indicates that sometimes we will stumble (or fail to keep up hope).
4. Possible examples are news of epidemics or wars.
5. Appropriate examples will show how the person's optimism and determination helped him or her to overcome the obstacles.
6. (a) Shu Ting interprets the poem she is answering as one that expresses complete desolation; (b) The two lines indicate that the lessons we learn accumulate through the years.

Beyond the Selection

FURTHER READING
"Vultures," David Diop
"The Renegade," David Diop
Old Snow, Bei Dao

Related Works
"Never Tell Me Again," Francis Bebey
"To David Diop," Paulin Joachim
Cry Freedom (film about Stephen Biko)

   We suggest that you preview these works before recommending them to students.

INTERNET
   For more information about Diop go to **http://www.uflib.ufl.edu/hss/africana/diop.html**
   For information on Stephen Biko, go to **http://www.usnews.com/usnews/issue/10wrbr.htm**
   To read an interview with Bei Dao, go to **http://philo.ucdavis.edu/~txie/faculty/faculty.htm**
   Please be aware that sites may have changed from the time we published this information. We *strongly recommend* that you preview these sites before you send students to them.

Answers

◆ Reading Strategy

1. Students' comparisons might highlight the wise tone of the advice from both sources.
2. Possible response: I "turned my gaze within" by examining my own character when I met someone I didn't respect.
3. Students might say that mood plays a major role in people's attitudes, thus one day they may feel as the poet does in "All," and another day adapt the attitude expressed in "Also All."

◆ Literary Focus

1. Because aphorisms express a lot in a few words, they are more memorable than longer explanations.
2. The basic truth that it is important to be humble is expressed in both Confucius' sayings and in the poem "Old Song."
3. Example aphorism: Past mistakes can be turned to future triumphs.

◆ Build Vocabulary

Using the Suffix -ment
1. statement;   2. replacement;
3. commandment;   4. assignment

Using the Word Bank
1. b   2. c   3. a

◆ Build Grammar Skills

Practice
1. To learn and at due times to repeat what one has learnt, is that not after all a pleasure?
2. To remain unsoured even though one's merits are unrecognized by others, is that not after all what is expected of a gentleman?
3. The Master said, A young man's duty is to behave well to his parents and to his elders abroad, to be cautious in giving promises and punctual in keeping them, to have kindly feelings towards everyone, but [to] seek the intimacy of the Good.

✎ **Writer's Solution**

For additional instruction and practice, use the page on Infinitives and Infinitive Phrases (p. 46) in the *Writer's Solution Grammar Practice Book*.

Guide for Responding (continued)

◆ Reading Strategy

RELATE TO WHAT YOU KNOW
    Relating what these writers say to your own experience will help you to find meaning in their work.
1. Compare the advice in "Old Song" with some advice you have received from an older relative or friend.
2. Describe an experience in your life in which one of Confucius' principles was illustrated.
3. Explain how one person might be able to experience the feelings expressed in both "All" and "Also All."

◆ Literary Focus

APHORISMS
    The authors of these pieces use **aphorisms**—brief sayings that illustrate a basic truth.
1. How do aphorisms illustrate the expression "Less is more"?
2. Identify one basic truth expressed in both the sayings of Confucius and "Old Song."
3. Write your own aphorism that expresses a basic truth found in "Also All."

Beyond Literature

Social Studies Connection

The Effects of Colonialism in Africa
Europeans began colonizing Africa in the late 1700's. By 1914, only Ethiopia and Liberia remained independent from European control. As World War II ended, independence movements gained strength in Africa. Today, Africa is a continent of more than fifty independent nations. The legacy of colonialism, however, lives on. New national boundaries, established in the 1950's and 1960's, were artificial creations of colonial powers. They included many rival ethnic groups. In addition, many new nations are small, with fewer than 10 million people. These nations have difficulty meeting the economic needs of their people. Find out more about the negative and positive effects of colonialism in Africa. Create a chart to display in your classroom.

◆ Build Vocabulary

USING THE SUFFIX -ment
    The suffix -ment indicates the noun form of the word to which it is attached. Use the suffix -ment to create a noun for each of the following examples:

1. To state your opinion is to make a ____?____ .
2. You replace something with a ____?____ .
3. A ruler commands with a ____?____ .
4. A teacher assigns an ____?____ .

USING THE WORD BANK
    In your notebook, write the antonym for each word from the Word Bank:
1. impetuous: (a) lively, (b) careful, (c) wise
2. lamentation: (a) despair, (b) interest, (c) rejoicing
3. chastisements: (a) rewards, (b) orders, (c) duties

◆ Build Grammar Skills

INFINITIVES AND INFINITIVE PHRASES
    Writers of aphorisms, like Confucius, often use infinitives to express universal ideas. The infinitive form gives the action being described a timeless flavor.

Practice Copy each sentence in your notebook. Underline the infinitives or the infinitive phrases.
1. To learn and at due times to repeat what one has learnt, is that not after all a pleasure?
2. To remain unsoured even though one's merits are unrecognized by others, is that not after all what is expected of a gentleman?
3. The Master said, A young man's duty is to behave well to his parents and to his elders abroad, to be cautious in giving promises and punctual in keeping them, to have kindly feelings towards everyone, but seek the intimacy of the Good.

Infinitives, which are the base forms of verbs and usually begin with the word *to*, can be used as nouns, adjectives, or adverbs. **Infinitive phrases** include an infinitive with its modifiers and complements (words that complete the meaning of the verb), all acting as a single part of speech.

Build Your Portfolio

 ## Idea Bank

Writing

1. **Letter to an Author** Write a letter to an author from this group. In your letter, explain why you agree or disagree with his or her ideas.

2. **Life Poem** Each writer expresses his or her view of life. Write a poem in which you express your view of life. Use images and examples from your own experience to express your ideas.

3. **Comparing and Contrasting Poems** Shu Ting wrote "Also All" as a rebuttal to Bei Dao's "All." Write a short essay in which you evaluate which poem makes a better case.

Speaking and Listening

4. **Oral Interpretation** Practice reading one of these works aloud. Vary the tone and speed of your voice for emphasis. Perform your reading for the class. **[Performing Arts Link]**

5. **Interview** With a partner, role-play an interview with one of the writers in this group. Develop questions about the author's views and experiences. Base your answers on what you've learned from their works and biographies.

Projects

6. **Tiananmen Square Presentation** "All" and "Also All" are responses to political events in China during the 1980's. In April 1989, students took over Tiananmen Square. Find out more about this event and give a presentation on it for your class. **[Social Studies Link]**

7. **Collage** Assemble a number of images with words from one of these works at the center. Find images in newspapers, magazines, and personal photos that reflect the ideas expressed. Display your collage in the classroom. **[Art Link]**

 ## Writing Mini-Lesson

Aphorism Calendar

Aphorisms are meant to be useful in daily life. What better way to make them a part of your daily life than by putting them in a calendar? Create your own aphorism calendar by making up one brief saying for each month of the year. The following tips will help you state your ideas concisely.

Writing Skills Focus: Brevity and Clarity

Like written directions and essays on tests, aphorisms are best when they are **brief and clear**. In the following example, Confucius clearly states a basic principle of conduct in just two sentences:

> The Master said, A gentleman can see a question from all sides without bias. The small man is biased and can see a question only from one side.

This aphorism can be easily remembered and understood. As you plan, draft, and revise your calendar, use the fewest words possible to convey your ideas clearly.

Prewriting Brainstorm for single words that name qualities you admire in a person. Then briefly describe examples of each quality in action.

Drafting Refer to your prewriting notes as an inspiration for your twelve aphorisms. For example, you might write, "Courage is ___?___" and then use your description of someone's courageous action to help fill in the blank. Convey as much information as you can in few words.

Revising Revise each aphorism and eliminate any words that do not add to the meaning. However, ask a classmate to read your abbreviated sayings, and determine whether or not they are clear.

Africa/Old Song/Biko/from The Analects/All/Also All ◆ 209

 ## Idea Bank

Customizing for *Performance Levels*

Following are suggestions for matching Idea Bank topics with your students' performance levels:

- Less Advanced Students: 1, 4
- Average Students: 2, 5, 7
- More Advanced Students: 3, 6

Customizing for *Learning Modalities*

Following are suggestions for matching Idea Bank topics with your students' learning modalities:

- Visual/Spatial: 7
- Bodily/Kinesthetic: 4
- Verbal/Linguistic: 4, 5
- Logical/Mathematical: 3

 ## Writing Mini-Lesson

Refer students to the Writing Handbook, page 965, for instruction on the writing process.

 ## Writer's Solution

Writers at Work Videodisc

Have students view the videodisc segment (Ch. 6) featuring Naomi Shihab Nye to get them thinking about how aphorisms, like other forms of creative writing, can inspire people.

Play frames 11043 to 20512

Writing Lab CD-ROM

Have students complete the tutorial on Creative Writing. Follow these steps:

1. Have them consult a word bin to help them select vivid words expressing emotions.
2. Encourage them to view video tips for peer editors and then work with a peer to revise their aphorisms for clarity.

Sourcebook

Have students use Chapter 6, Creative Writing (pp. 165–189), for additional support.

✓ ASSESSMENT OPTIONS

Formal Assessment, Selection Test, pp. 47–49, and Assessment Resources Software. The selection test is designed so that it can be easily customized to the performance levels of your students. ***Alternative Assessment,*** p.15, includes options for less advanced students, more advanced students, logical/mathematical learners, visual/spatial learners, musical/rhythmic learners, interpersonal learners, intrapersonal learners, and verbal/linguistic learners.

PORTFOLIO ASSESSMENT

Use the following rubrics in the ***Alternative Assessment*** booklet to assess student writing:
Letter to an Author: Expression Rubric, p. 94
Life Poem: Poetry Rubric, p. 108
Comparing and Contrasting Poems: Comparison and Contrast Rubric, p. 103

Establish Writing Guidelines

Before students begin, review the following key characteristics of a timed-test essay:

- The essay should have an introduction, body, and conclusion.
- The introduction should let readers know what the essay will be about by offering a thesis statement that responds to the essay's question.
- The body should be organized into paragraphs that express a main idea supporting the thesis statement. Each main idea should be supported by examples or other details in the paragraph.
- The conclusion should rephrase the thesis and sum up the main points of the essay.

You may want to distribute a scoring rubric for a timed-test essay (see page 212) to make students aware before they begin of the criteria on which they will be evaluated.

Refer students to the Writing Handbook, page 965, for guidance in the writing process.

 Writer's Solution

You might give students the following pages from the *Writer's Solution Grammar Practice Book:*

p. 148: Preparing Answers to Essay Exams
p. 167: Reading and Test-Taking Skills
p. 168: Test-Taking Skills

Writing Lab CD-ROM

If your students have access to computers, you may want to have them work on the tutorial on Practical and Technical Writing to complete parts of their timed-test essays. Follow these steps:

1. Have students review the interactive model of a timed-test essay.
2. Have students use an outliner to organize their essays.
3. Have students draft on computer.
4. Suggest that students consult the screen on revising a timed-test essay.

Sourcebook

Students can find additional support, including topic ideas, models, audience and purpose profiles, and graphic organizers, in the chapter on Practical and Technical Writing (pp. 228–262).

Timed-Test Essay — Writing Process Workshop

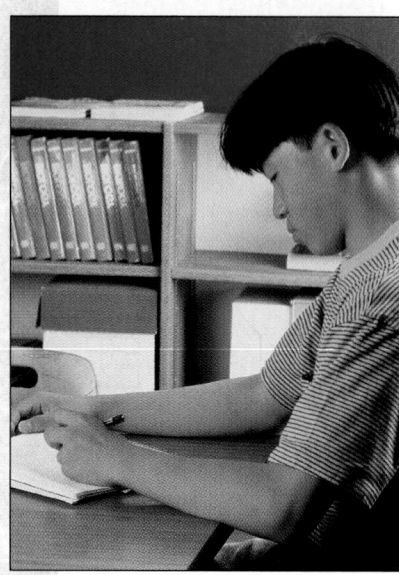

Tests are one way to measure how successfully you have learned something. A timed-test essay is an essay on a test that you must complete within a certain time limit.

The following skills, introduced in this section's Writing Mini-Lessons, will help you write an effective test essay when you have time limits.

Writing Skills Focus

▶ **Support** any assertions you make with details. For instance, if you say "*Silas Marner* is a good book," say *why* it is as well. (See p. 191.)
▶ **Show, don't tell,** the features or qualities of your topic. Offer examples, summarize events, or cite facts. (See p. 199.)
▶ **Be brief and clear.** Since your time is limited, say only what is essential to your topic. (See p. 209.)

The following excerpt from an essay about the theme of "How Much Land Does a Man Need?" shows these skills.

MODEL

① The writer gets right to the point in the first paragraph.

② Here, the writer backs up his assertion with a direct example from the text.

③ This brief, clear paragraph offers another assertion and example.

Although, as Leo Tolstoy makes painfully clear, six feet of land is all a man needs, the theme of "How Much Land Does a Man Need?" is that no matter how much a person has, he or she will always want more. ①

In the beginning of the story, Pahom muses that if he had plenty of land, he wouldn't even fear the Devil. ② Yet as soon as he acquires the old woman's land, he finds he has the same problems as before. Once more, he thinks the only solution for his problems is to get even more land.

Later in the story, after Pahom has moved to another town and acquired three times as much land as at his former home, he still finds he is not satisfied, ③ even though he was much better off than he had been before....

210 ◆ *Striving for Success*

 Beyond the Classroom

Tell students that writing under the pressure of a deadline is nearly as common in the "real" world as it is in school. Even if they never take another test after they leave high school or college, they may be called upon to compose a piece of writing or to do some other task under pressure, whether on a job application or as part of a job itself. Being able to organize and elucidate one's thoughts quickly and clearly is a valuable benefit they will receive from the agonizing hours writing timed-test essays.

Prewriting

Clarify the Topic Usually on an essay test, the topic is assigned to you. When you are given a topic, make sure that you know exactly what the question requires you to write, so you won't get off track. For practice, choose one of the following topics related to the selections in this unit.

Topic Choices

1. Compare and contrast the messages in "Mowing" and "After Apple-Picking." Support your points with details from both selections.

2. Choose the selection from this unit that you feel communicates the most valuable message about success. Explain the message, and apply it to a real-life situation.

Plan Your Time Imagine that you have twenty minutes to complete your essay. Quickly plan out your time. Allow a few minutes to gather and organize your thoughts, a large chunk of time to draft your essay, and a few minutes to make quick revisions.

Plan the Points You Will Elaborate Make a list of the main ideas you will introduce in your essay. Under each main idea, note the supporting details you will offer. This preparation will prevent you from wasting time and space on irrelevant details.

Drafting

Get Started As soon as you've organized your main ideas and details, begin drafting. Use an objective tone, and organize your points logically. Present your main idea in the introduction of your essay. Follow that with the body of your essay, in which you state and develop your ideas.

Support Your Points Each paragraph should either directly or indirectly support your main idea. Within each paragraph, make sure that each supporting sentence either directly or indirectly supports the topic sentence of the paragraph. Finish your essay with a conclusion, in which you restate your main idea or make a general observation about it. You may also wish to end by including an intriguing question or challenge to the reader.

Applying Language Skills: Standard and Informal English

A timed-test essay should be written in standard English. Standard English uses an objective tone and correct usage, contains no slang, avoids contractions, and often uses long sentences with varied structures.

Informal English:
The Japanese are totally crazy about baseball.

Standard English:
Baseball is extremely popular in Japan.

Practice On your paper, rewrite the following passage in standard English.

> Some people are grossed out by sushi, but they're crazy! It totally rules.

Writing Application Check your essay to make sure that it is written in standard English and follows the above guidelines.

Writer's Solution Connection Writing Lab

For more help on writing a timed-test essay, see Drafting a Timed-Test Essay in the Writing Lab tutorial on Practical/Technical Writing.

Prewriting

Since students will only have a few moments to organize their thoughts on a timed-test essay, a good exercise would be to give them practice essay questions such as the two on this page and then tell them they have two minutes to organize their thoughts into a brief, concise outline.

Customize for
English Language Learners
Vocabulary will be the biggest hurdle facing these students. Since they will not have time to consult a dictionary, tell these students to use simple language with which they are familiar. They should not spend too much time on grammar and spelling, but should not ignore it altogether either.

Customize for
Less Proficient Writers
Encourage these students to take a few moments to make an outline before they begin to write so that their essays will be as organized as possible.

Writer's Solution

Writing Lab CD-ROM
The Organizing Details and Information section of the tutorial on Practical and Technical Writing includes a screen on organizing a timed-test essay. Have students consult this screen to help them learn how to organize their essays quickly and efficiently.

Drafting

Students should draft their timed-test essays in a single sitting, without pausing to labor over a single word or to correct a grammatical error. Once students have completed a draft, they may have a brief opportunity to go back into their work and make revisions.

Applying Language Skills
Standard and Informal English Explain to students that they should use standard, formal English when writing a timed-test essay. They should avoid informal phrases, contractions, and above all, slang.

Suggested Answer
Although some people find sushi hard to stomach, I disagree. I find it quite delicious.

 Writer's Solution

For additional instruction and practice, have students complete practice page 66, The Varieties of English, in the *Writer's Solution Grammar Practice Book*.

Revising

Emphasize that students should use their time to revise serious errors and omissions.

 Writer's Solution

Writing Lab CD-ROM
The proofreading checklist in the Proofreading section of the tutorial on Practical and Technical Writing will help students quickly check their essays.

Publishing

Tell students that even if they do not wish to share their essays at this time, they might want to hold on to them and use them as reference for later writing projects.

Reinforce and Extend

After students have completed their papers, encourage them to come up with additional criteria for a timed-test essay based on what they learned through completing the assignment.

Applying Language Skills

Placement of Modifiers Remind students that correctly placed modifiers are vital not only for stylistic reasons but also for a clear meaning. Misplaced or dangling modifiers can damage an otherwise perfect essay.

Answer
Each year, millions of Americans between the ages of seventeen and sixty-six enter blood centers to donate blood.

 Writer's Solution

For additional instruction and practice, have students complete the **Language Lab CD-ROM** lesson on Problems With Modifiers.

APPLYING LANGUAGE SKILLS: Placement of Modifiers

Make sure that all of your modifiers—your adjectives, adverbs, and modifying phrases—are in the proper place in each sentence.

Misplaced Modifier:
A red cross on a white field became the symbol of the Red Cross, which was a reversal of the Swiss flag.

Correctly Placed Modifier:
A red cross on a white field, which was a reversal of the Swiss flag, became the symbol of the Red Cross.

Practice On your paper, rewrite the following sentence so that the modifying phrase is in the proper place.

Each year, millions of Americans enter blood centers between the ages of 17 and 66 to donate blood.

Writing Application Review your essay, and make sure that all of your modifiers are correctly placed.

Writer's Solution Connection Language Lab

For more practice with placement of modifiers, complete the Language Lab lesson on Misplaced Modifiers.

212 ◆ Striving for Success

Revising

Check Quickly Because time is limited during this type of essay, you'll have only a few moments in which to review and polish your writing. Look through the tips that follow, and use them as a guide to revise your essay.

▶ Reread the essay question to make sure you've addressed it.
▶ Skim the introduction and conclusion to make sure they match; in other words, make sure you haven't drifted from your original topic.
▶ Review the points you've made. Add supporting details where needed. Delete irrelevant information.
▶ Make sure that you use standard English in your paper. Take out any slang terms and any unnecessary contractions. Check your spelling and grammar.

REVISION MODEL

The computer industry is extremely important to the
① most populous ②
economy of California, our biggest state. I love playing

Myst on my computer, but I've never been able to figure
③ The companies of "Silicon Valley" alone employ more than 20,000 people.
out how to get past the final stage.

① The student made this sentence more accurate.
② The student deleted this irrelevant sentence.
③ The student added this example to back up her assertion in the first sentence.

Publishing

Share Your Paper Because the information in timed-test essays is organized and compact, the essays are good records of what you've learned. Here are some ideas for sharing your work.
▶ Start a portfolio of essays.
▶ Use the essay as the basis for a research paper.
▶ Ask your teacher for feedback and ways to improve your writing on future tests.

✓ ASSESSMENT		4	3	2	1
PORTFOLIO ASSESSMENT Use the rubric to assess students' writing.	**Organization**	The writing is clearly and consistently organized. All assertions are backed up by facts or examples.	The writing is clearly organized. Most assertions are backed up by facts or examples.	The writing has some organization, but needs improvement. Assertions need more evidence to back them up.	The writing is completely unorganized. Assertions have no support.
	Grammar, Usage, Spelling, and Mechanics	There are few or no errors. Word choice is appropriate for subject and audience.	There are minor errors. Word choice is usually appropriate for subject and audience. The observation includes some precise details.	There are numerous errors. Word choice may be inappropriate for subject and audience. The writer consistently uses vague verbs.	Numerous errors hinder comprehension. Word choice shows little understanding of subject or audience.

Real-World Reading Skills Workshop

Reading an Application

Driver's license applications, job applications, college applications—you'll be surprised by the number of applications you encounter as you go through life! Whenever you fill out an application, it's important to read and follow the instructions carefully, because filling it out incorrectly can result in missed opportunities.

Familiarize Yourself Start by skimming the entire application. Knowing the sections will help you determine how much detail is required in each section. Identify information you need to complete the application—such as your social security number or telephone numbers of references.

Get Specific Make sure you are clear about information the application requires. Read every line carefully, and follow directions. Look for restrictions and conditions in the application. For example, the reference section of a job application might not allow family members as references. Once you are familiar with the layout and content of the application, write clearly in the spaces provided.

Apply the Strategy

Answer the following questions about the job application shown below.

APPLICATION FOR EMPLOYMENT

Name (Last, First, Middle)

Address (Street and number, City, State, Zip)

Home Phone   School or Business Phone   Social Security Number

Please describe the position you are seeking.

Education
Schools attended
Current level of education
Scholastic honors and awards
Interests and activities

Employment Experience List all employment in the past three years, beginning with your most recent position.

Office Skills
Word Processing: ☐ Yes ☐ No   Typing: ☐ Yes ☐ No (w.p.m.)
List all computer programs you can use.

References Please give the names, addresses, and telephone numbers of two references (note: references cannot be relatives).

1. What information or numbers will you need to complete this application?
2. In which section will you include information about your hobbies?
3. Which sections limit your answer with restrictions or conditions? What are the restrictions or conditions?

Tell students that filling out applications is a necessity in today's world. Emphasize the importance of filling them out carefully—completely and correctly. An application creates an impression of the person who fills it out. It's important to make a good impression.

Answers

1. The applicant will need his or her name, address, home and school/business phone, social security number, as well as the names, addresses, and phone numbers of references.
2. In the Education section the applicant will include information about his or her hobbies.
3. The Employment Experience section limits the employment to the last three years. The References section restricts references to non-family members.

Introduce the Strategy

Remind students that interviewing for a job is one thing that all of them will almost certainly have to do at least one time in their lives, and probably many times. Since a job interview can often determine the course of a person's career, its importance should not be underestimated.

Apply the Strategy

In addition to the strategies listed, tell students that they should learn the interviewer's full name and title before they leave and write a brief thank-you note to the interviewer as soon as they get home.

Answers

1. Important traits to display at such an interview would be technical expertise and the ability to work with others.
2. Important traits to show at such an interview would be cheerfulness and organizational ability.
3. Important traits to show at such an interview would be cheerfulness, enthusiasm, and responsibility.

Speaking and Listening Workshop

Job Interview

If you haven't done so already, you may soon apply for your first job and go on your first job interview. Whether you're looking for an after-school job, a summer job, or your first full-time job, the impression you make during your job interview will determine whether you are offered the position.

Make a Good Impression First impressions are important. Create a good one by arriving on time and being dressed appropriately. During the interview, be aware of the nonverbal messages you send through body language, eye contact, and gestures. Maintain eye contact with your interviewer; don't look around the room as if you're uninterested or avoiding answering questions. Positive body language, such as a firm handshake and good posture, will suggest that you are self-assured, confident, and capable. Speak clearly and loudly enough, and avoid using slang or clichés.

Throughout, listen attentively to your interviewer. Answer the questions asked, and listen for cues about what is important. You might use these cues to ask follow-up questions.

Strategies for a Successful Job Interview

✔ *If you want to make a good impression during your interview, remember these strategies:*
- ▶ *Arrive on time and dressed neatly*
- ▶ *Speak clearly, confidently, and positively about yourself and what you will bring to your new position*
- ▶ *Take your time answering questions, to make sure you answer completely*
- ▶ *Ask questions about the position to show your interest in the company*

Apply the Strategies

With a partner, role-play these situations. Using the tips above, make a good impression at the following job interviews:

1. An interview at a local television show to help with teleprompting, set construction, and setting up camera equipment.
2. An interview at a doctor's office for administrative work.
3. An interview for a position as a baby sitter.

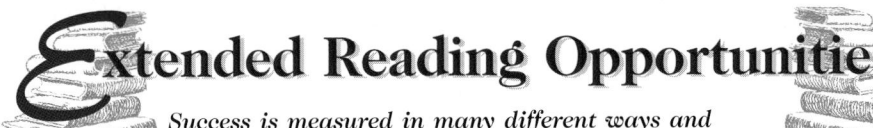Extended Reading Opportunities

Success is measured in many different ways and achieved through a variety of efforts. The books suggested here will help you explore "success" through the struggles and triumphs of real and fictional people.

Suggested Titles

Literature From Around the World
Published by Prentice Hall

A collection of short stories, poems, and essays, this anthology includes the most respected writers of the twentieth century and the past. Works of authors from around the world deal with the universal themes of success, personal challenges, and overcoming obstacles.

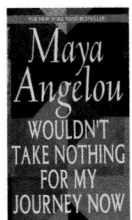

Wouldn't Take Nothing for My Journey Now
Maya Angelou

A collection of inspirational essays, *Wouldn't Take Nothing for My Journey Now* celebrates life and discusses developing one's full potential in today's world. In the personal, informal tone of an autobiography, Maya Angelou discusses her own experiences and then draws universal lessons from them.

Silas Marner
George Eliot

The hero of George Eliot's story is an extremely near-sighted linen weaver in nineteenth-century England. Accused unjustly of theft, Marner becomes a recluse for fifteen years, hoarding the gold that he earns from his trade. When circumstances deprive him of that as well, Silas must end his long reclusiveness. Having lost everything he once held dear, he finds all of his chances for redemption hinge on a little orphan girl with golden hair.

Other Possibilities

The Last Unicorn   Peter S. Beagle
Shoeless Joe   W. P. Kinsella
Grass Roots and Schoolyards   Nelson Campbell, Editor
Flowers for Algernon   Daniel Keyes

Planning Students' Extended Reading

All of the works listed on this page extend the theme of Striving for Success. The following information may help you choose which to assign.

Customize for
Varying Student Needs

When assigning the selections in this part to your students, keep in mind the following factors:

• *Literature From Around the World* contains a variety of selections in translation. They vary in length and accessibility. You may choose from among them or use the entire book.

• *Wouldn't Take Nothing for My Journey Now* is a high-interest selection from a well-respected contemporary author. It is divided into short, manageable chapters and will be of special interest to female students.

• *Silas Marner* is an acknowledged classic. Being a Victorian novel, it is long, and will require a longer time commitment.

Literature Study Guides

Literature study guides are available for *Silas Marner* and *Literature From Around the World*. These guides include summaries, discussion questions, and activities.

Customize for
Special Needs

To meet the needs of your special needs students (grades 5–6 reading level), you may want to consider using *Silas Marner* from Globe Fearon's Adapted Classics series.

Planning Instruction and Assessment

Unit Objectives

1. To read selections in different genres that develop the theme of Clashing Forces
2. To apply a variety of reading strategies, particularly literal comprehension strategies, appropriate for reading these selections
3. To recognize literary elements used in these selections
4. To increase vocabulary
5. To learn elements of grammar and usage
6. To write in a variety of modes and about situations based on the selections
7. To develop speaking and listening skills, by doing proposed activities

Meeting the Objectives

With each selection, you will find instructional material and portfolio opportunities through which students can meet these objectives. Further, you will find additional practice pages for reading strategies, literary elements, vocabulary, and grammar in the **Selection Support** booklet in the Teaching Resources box.

Setting Goals Work with your students at the beginning of the unit to set goals for unit outcomes. Plan what skills and concepts you wish students to acquire. You may individualize according to students' performance levels or learning modalities.

Portfolios You may have students keep portfolios of their work or of their work in progress. The activities and prompts on the Build Your Portfolio page of each selection provide opportunities for students to apply the concepts presented with the selection.

The Deluge, 1920, Winifred Knights, Tate Gallery, London, Great Britain

Humanities: Art

The Deluge by Winifred Knights.

Ask someone to define *deluge*, and then encourage students to identify the details in this art that depict a flood *(the half-submerged houses; the men waist-deep in water; the girl being pulled out of the water to the roof)*. Help students see that the people's stylized postures give the art an abstract, formal quality. It is almost as if the artist is depicting a ballet about a flood, rather than real people fleeing real floodwaters.

Have your students link the art to the theme of Unit 3, "Clashing Forces," by answering the following questions:

1. Does the abstract quality of the painting add to or detract from the sense of the people's struggle to escape the flood? Why? *Sample answers: The abstract quality adds to the sense of the people's struggle because it is so stark, focusing on the bodies straining to escape; the abstract quality takes away from the struggle because it makes it* *look graceful and orderly, like a dance.*

2. Focus on one of the people portrayed here. Invent some circumstances for that person—who he or she is, who or what is being left behind, what hopes and fears the person experiences. *Sample answer: The man pulling the little girl up is her father, working with her mother to save their child; he had thought she was with them, but fell behind and almost got swept away in the water.*

216

Clashing Forces

There are many clashing forces in life—good versus evil, right versus wrong, man versus nature. The stories, poems, and essays you're about to read share one common theme: They all deal with the clashing forces that we encounter in life. Turn the page to see how real people and fictional characters respond to—and often overcome— obstacles and injustices.

♦ 217

Assessing Student Progress

The following tools are available to measure the degree to which students meet the unit objectives:

Informal Assessment

The questions on the Guide for Responding sections are a first level of response to the concepts and skills presented with the selection. Students' responses are a brief informal measure of their grasp of the material. Their responses on this level can indicate where further instruction and practice are needed. You may then follow up with the practice pages in the *Selection Support* booklet.

You will find literature and reading guides in the *Alternative Assessment* booklet, which you may give students on an individual basis for informal assessment of their performance.

Formal Assessment

In the *Formal Assessment* booklet, you will find selection tests and a unit test.

Selection Tests The selection tests measure comprehension and skills acquisition for each selection or group of selections.

Unit Test The unit test applies the unit skills on a broader level. The Critical Reading section measures Unit Objectives 1, 2, and 3. The Vocabulary and Grammar section measures Objectives 4 and 5. The Essay section measures Objectives 1 and 6.

Alternative Assessment

Portfolios As you review individual pieces or the collected work in students' portfolios, you will find assessment sheets available in the portfolio section of the *Alternative Assessment* booklet.

Scoring Rubrics You will find scoring rubrics for writing modes in the *Alternative Assessment* booklet. You can apply these to Writing Mini-Lessons and to Writing Process Workshop lessons.

Speaking and Listening The *Alternative Assessment* booklet contains assessment sheets for speaking and listening activities.

Learning Modalities The *Alternative Assessment* booklet contains activities that appeal to different learning styles. You may use these as an alternative measurement of students' growth.

OBJECTIVES

1. To read, comprehend and interpret a story
2. To relate a story to personal experience
3. To use interactive reading strategies to read for success
4. To identify internal conflict
5. To build vocabulary in context and learn the word root -lum-
6. To recognize participial phrases
7. To write a travel brochure using persuasive tone
8. To respond to the story through writing, speaking and listening, and projects

SKILLS INSTRUCTION

Vocabulary:
The Word Root -lum-

Grammar:
Participial Phrases

Reading for Success

Strategies:
Interactive Reading

Literary Focus:
Internal Conflict

Writing:
Persuasive Tone

Speaking and Listening:
Account of an Outdoor Adventure (teacher edition)

Critical Viewing:
Analyze; Compare and Contrast; Speculate

PORTFOLIO OPPORTUNITIES

Writing: Water Safety Rules; Letter; Observation

Writing Mini-Lesson: Travel Brochure

Speaking and Listening: Account of an Outdoor Adventure; Dialogue

Projects: Collage; Movie Score

More About the Author

During Doris Lessing's childhood, books were an escape from the confining restrictions imposed on her by her mother. Some of the authors that nurtured Lessing's early imagination were Charles Dickens, Walter Scott, R. L. Stevenson, and Rudyard Kipling, and later, D. H. Lawrence, Leo Tolstoy, and Feodor Dostoevsky. Before becoming a writer, Lessing worked as a nursemaid and as a telephone operator. She published her first novel in 1949 and was nominated for the Nobel Prize for Literature in 1996.

*G*uide for Reading

Doris Lessing (1919–)

Some writers shy away from controversy; Doris Lessing, however, seems to invite it. When her novel *The Golden Notebook* appeared in 1962, she was accused of being a "man-hater" because of the resentment and anger toward men that some of her female characters expressed. Lessing has also written about the conflicts between cultures, focusing especially on the conflicts between Europeans and Africans.

Growing up in Africa
Doris May Taylor was born on October 22, 1919, in Persia (now Iran). In 1925, enticed by the prospect of getting rich by farming maize, her father moved the family to the colony of Rhodesia (now Zimbabwe) in southern Africa. There, Lessing began to observe how, under colonialism, Europeans displaced Africans from their land and ignored their traditions.

From Outcast to Hero
In 1949, Lessing published her first novel, *The Grass Is Singing*. In this and her later novels, Lessing highlights the injustices suffered by black Africans at the hands of white colonials. Her strong views provoked a strong reaction.

In 1956, Lessing was declared a "prohibited alien" by the governments of Southern Rhodesia and South Africa.

Ironically, when apartheid ended in South Africa in 1995, she was welcomed back as a hero—for writing about the very topics for which she was banished earlier.

A Different Kind of Conflict
In this story, Lessing doesn't write about the conflicts between men and women or between cultures. Instead, she describes the struggle going on in the mind of a boy.

◆ Build Vocabulary

WORD ROOTS: -lum-
In this story, you will encounter the word *luminous*. The word root -lum- comes from the Latin *lumen*, meaning "light." Knowing this root can help you figure out that words that contain the root -lum- are related to light. *Luminous* means "giving off light."

WORD BANK
contrition
promontories
luminous
supplication
frond
convulsive
gout

As you read this story, you will encounter the words on this list. Each word is defined on the page where it first appears. Preview the list before you read.

◆ Build Grammar Skills

PARTICIPIAL PHRASES
"Going to the shore on the first morning of the vacation, the young English boy stopped at a turning of the path ..." So begins "Through the Tunnel"—with a participial phrase. A **participial phrase** consists of a participle (a verb form ending in -*ing*, -*ed*, or an irregular ending) plus any other words that go with it. Participial phrases function as adjectives.

The participial phrase "Going to the shore on the first morning of the vacation," beginning with the present participle *going*, acts as an adjective modifying "boy." Lessing varies her sentence structure and creates vivid pictures of the characters and setting in this story by using participial phrases.

218 ◆ *Clashing Forces*

Prentice Hall Literature Program Resources

REINFORCE / RETEACH / EXTEND

Selection Support Pages
Build Vocabulary: The Word Root -lum-, p. 63
Build Grammar Skills: Participial Phrases, p. 64
Reading for Success: Interactive Reading Strategies, p. 65
Literary Focus: Internal Conflict, p. 67

Writing and Language Transparencies
Herringbone Organizer, p. 75–77

Strategies for Diverse Student Needs, p. 16

Beyond Literature
Cross-Curricular Connection: Physical Education, p. 16

Formal Assessment Selection Test, pp. 54–56; Assessment Resources Software

Alternative Assessment, p. 16

Resource Pro CD-ROM
"Through the Tunnel"—includes all resource materials and customizable lesson plan

Through the Tunnel

◆ *Literature and Your Life*

CONNECT YOUR EXPERIENCE

When you set personal goals, you challenge yourself, push yourself to see just how far you can go. Whether or not you succeed, you learn something about yourself. The boy in Lessing's story gives himself a physical challenge that requires all his courage to meet.

Journal Writing Write about a challenge you have successfully met—either physical, emotional, or intellectual. List the steps you took to accomplish your goal.

THEMATIC FOCUS: CLASHING FORCES

In this story, a boy chooses to take on an underwater challenge despite his inner fear of failure. How do you think success or failure to meet a challenge changes a person?

◆ Background for Understanding

SCIENCE

Oxygen, which your body needs on a regular basis, is an important, but relatively small, part of the air you breathe. Depriving the brain of oxygen can quickly cause dizziness and, if prolonged, brain damage. However, you don't usually have to think about breathing. Special cells, called chemoreceptors, sense the oxygen and carbon dioxide levels in your blood. These cells then send out signals that quicken or slow the rate of breathing as necessary.

Jerry, the young boy in this story, deprives his body of oxygen, pushing the limit of how long he can hold his breath. His self-testing makes for interesting reading, but it is not something you should imitate.

How much oxygen is in the air you breathe?

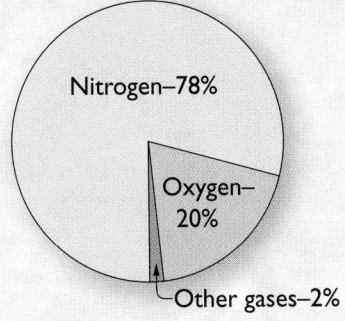

Nitrogen–78%

Oxygen–20%

Other gases–2%

◆ Literary Focus

INTERNAL CONFLICT

The personal challenge that Jerry, the character in "Through the Tunnel," sets for himself involves an **internal conflict**—a struggle within a character over opposing feelings, beliefs, or needs. Jerry's struggle with his opposing feelings about this enormous and frightening challenge he faces results in a gripping story.

Use a graphic organizer like the one shown to explore Jerry's opposing feelings.

Jerry's Feelings

Wants to go to bay → ← Doesn't want to hurt mother's feelings

→ ←

→ ←

Interest Grabber Students will relate to the way time seems to expand during Jerry's physical ordeal. Have students close their eyes. Tell them to keep their eyes closed and raise their hands when they think two minutes have passed. Most students will raise their hands before the time has elapsed. Point out to students that a boy in this story will spend that much time in a dark, frightening place, holding his breath and facing a great physical challenge. Lead a discussion of how these factors might affect a person's perception of time.

Customize for *Less Proficient Readers*

As an aid to literal comprehension, have these students pay particular attention to the Reading for Success strategy, Form Mental Images. Suggest that they pause frequently while reading to form images in their minds of what is happening in the story. Use the Form a Mental Image page in the ***Strategies for Diverse Student Needs*** booklet, p. 16.

Customize for *More Advanced Students*

Tell these students that "Through the Tunnel," like many pieces of fiction, focuses on an important event in the coming of age, or emotional growth, of a young character. This event is sometimes referred to as a "rite of passage." Have students think in these terms as they read "Through the Tunnel" and look for symbols of Jerry's rite of passage in the story.

Customize for *English Language Learners*

Remind these students to use the art with the story to help them picture the setting and action. Also, have them read along as they listen to the **Listening to Literature Audiocassettes.**

Customize for *Interpersonal Learners*

These students will benefit by paying particular attention to the Reading for Success strategy, Question, with regard to the more subtle details of characterization in the story. Suggest they pause at intervals while reading to ask themselves questions concerning not only Jerry's motivation, but Jerry's mother's motives as well.

Preparing for Standardized Tests

Reading and Vocabulary The Build Vocabulary Skills lesson focuses on the word root *-lum-*, as in *illumination, luminous*. Students can use knowledge of word roots when choosing correct definitions on verbal portions of standardized tests. Knowing word roots will also help students choose the best answers for sentence completions that offer unfamiliar words as choices. For more practice, use the Build Vocabulary page in *Selection Support*, p. 63.

Grammar and Language Understanding how participial phrases add information to a sentence and variety to a paragraph will help students on sections of standardized tests that require them to improve sentences or paragraphs. The Build Grammar Skills lesson for this story focuses on identifying participial phrases and the nouns they modify. For additional practice, use the Build Grammar Skills page on Participial Phrases, p. 64, in *Selection Support*.

The Reading for Success page in each unit presents a set of problem-solving procedures to help readers understand authors' words and ideas on multiple levels. Good readers develop a bank of strategies from which they can draw as needed.

Unit 3 introduces strategies for interactive reading. Interacting with the text helps readers make meaning from a work in the context of their own experience, knowledge, and ideas. These strategies for interactive reading give students an approach for becoming involved with the text by envisioning details, considering the significance of events, and responding to characters, events, and ideas.

These strategies for interactive reading are modeled with "Through the Tunnel." Each green box shows an example of the thinking process involved in applying one of these strategies.

How to Use the Reading for Success Page

- Introduce the interactive reading strategies, presenting each as a problem-solving procedure. Be sure students understand what each strategy involves and under what circumstances to apply it.

- Before students read the story, have them preview it, looking at the annotations in the green boxes that model the strategies.

- To reinforce these strategies after students have read "Through the Tunnel," have students do the Reading for Success page in *Selection Support,* p. 65. This page gives students an opportunity to read a selection and practice strategies for interactive reading by writing their own annotations.

Reading for Success

Interactive Reading Strategies

Reading is interactive. When you interact with the words on each page, you can really feel the sights and sounds of new worlds. Otherwise, if you just sit back and passively look at the words, it's like going on a field trip and never getting off the bus!

When you read, apply the following strategies to help you interact with the text:

Predict.

What do you think will happen? Why? Look for hints in the story that seem to suggest a certain outcome. As you read on, you will see whether your predictions are correct.

Use your prior knowledge.

No matter how different a character, subject matter, opinion, or situation is from what you are familiar with, chances are you will be able to relate to certain aspects of the character or experience. If a character goes to the beach, think about a trip to the beach you may have taken. This technique will give you a mental picture of what is happening and help you relate to the character better.

Question.

What questions come to mind as you are reading? For example, why do the characters act as they do? What causes events to happen? Why does the writer include certain information? Look for answers to your questions as you read.

Form mental images.

Use details from the selection you are reading to create pictures in your mind. As you read along, change your picture as the story unfolds and your understanding grows. If you find yourself confused, try to state your confusion. Use your visualization to clarify whatever hasn't been clear to you.

Respond.

Think about what the selection means. What does it say to you? What feelings does it evoke in you? What has the selection added to your understanding of people and of life in general?

As you read the following story by Doris Lessing, look at the notes along the margins. These notes demonstrate how to apply these strategies to a work of literature.

Reading Strategies: Support and Reinforcement

Appropriate Reading Strategies Students are given a reading strategy to apply in reading each selection. In selections where students' understanding will be especially enhanced by making connections to their own experiences and knowledge, one of these interactive reading strategies is suggested. In other selections, a strategy is suggested that is appropriate to the selection.

Reading Prompts To encourage application of the given reading strategy, there are occasional prompts, within green boxes, at appropriate and significant points.

In addition, there are red boxes prompting application of the Literary Focus concept and maroon boxes prompting students to connect with their lives.

Using the Boxed Annotations and Prompts The material in the green, red, and maroon boxes along the sides of selections is intended to help students apply the literary element and the reading strategy and to make a connection with their lives.

You may use the boxed material in several ways:

- Have students pause when they come to a box and respond to its prompt before they continue reading.

- After students have read the selection completely, they can review the selection in groups, discussing their responses to the prompts.

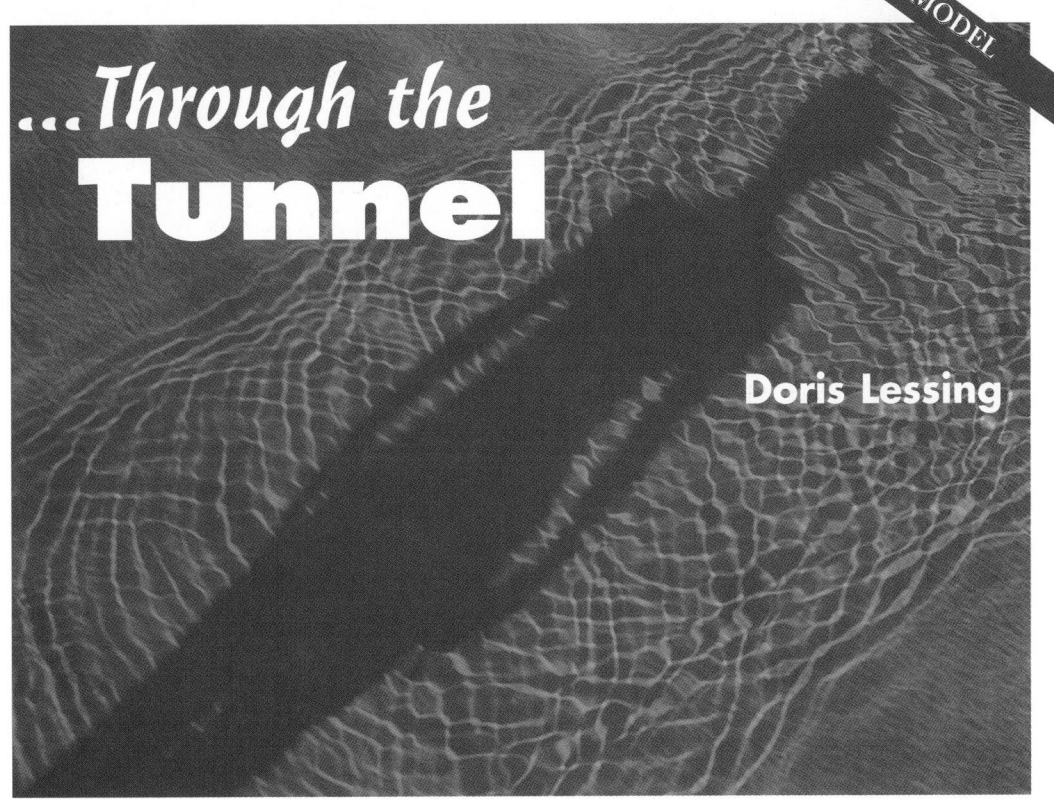

...Through the Tunnel

Doris Lessing

MODEL

① ▲ Critical Viewing How does the use of shadows and light affect the mood of this photograph? [Analyze]

---

② Going to the shore on the first morning of the vacation, the young English boy stopped at a turning of the path and looked down at a wild and rocky bay, and then over to the crowded beach he knew so well from other years. His mother walked on in front of him, carrying a bright striped bag in one hand. Her other arm, swinging loose, was very white in the sun. The boy watched that white, naked arm, and turned his eyes, which had a frown behind them, toward the bay and back again to his mother. When she felt he was not with her, she swung around. "Oh, there you are, Jerry!" she said. She looked impatient, then smiled. "Why, darling, would you rather not come with

me? Would you rather—" She frowned, conscientiously worrying over what amusements he might secretly be longing for, which she had been too busy or too careless to imagine. He was very familiar with that anxious, apologetic smile. <u>Contrition</u> sent him running after her. And yet, as he ran, he looked back over his shoulder at the wild bay; and all morning, as he played on the safe beach,

③

> This detail helps you **predict** that something will happen at the bay.

④

◆ **Build Vocabulary**

contrition (kən trish′ ən) *n*.: Feeling of remorse for having done something wrong

Through the Tunnel ◆ 221

Block Scheduling Strategies

Consider these suggestions to take advantage of extended class time:

- Have students preview the work in small groups, focusing on the visuals and answering the Critical Viewing questions on pages 221 and 225.
- Introduce the Reading for Success strategies. As students read, have them notice the annotations that model the strategies. Then have students apply the interactive reading strategies by completing the Reading for Success page in *Selection Support*, p. 65.

- After all students have read the story, have them break into groups to explore the group discussion suggestion on page 228.
- Complete the Literary Focus on page 229 as a class. Then have students work independently to complete the Literary Focus page on Internal Conflict in *Selection Support*, p. 67.
- Use the Speaking and Listening Mini-Lesson (p. 224) to support the Speaking and Listening activity on page 230.

Develop Understanding

One-Minute Insight In "Through the Tunnel," Doris Lessing establishes a level of tension that increases with every heart-pounding moment. The story reaches beyond suspense, however, to make profound points about a boy's conflict between love for his mother and desire for independence. For the boy, making the perilous journey through a dark underwater tunnel and breaking through to the light on the other end is an important rite of passage that helps him reconcile these two forces.

►Critical Viewing◄

① **Analyze** Some students may suggest that the highlighted ripples on the water seem to be ensnaring the shaded human figure in a tangled web. Some may say the dark shaded figure, contrasted with the bright blue water, creates an air of mystery.

◆ Reading for Success

② **Form Mental Images** Ask a volunteer to read this first sentence aloud while the other students concentrate on picturing the setting. Ask students to describe the setting in their own words. *Suggested response: There is a path going down a hill to the beach. If you look down on one side you see a typical ocean beach, crowded with swimmers and sunbathers. If you look down on the other side you see a bay. It is wild and rocky, and totally deserted.*

◆ Build Grammar Skills

③ **Participial Phrases** Have students identify the participial phrase "conscientiously worrying over what amusements he might secretly be longing for." Ask them what noun the phrase modifies. *she.* Point out that by relating the phrase to the noun it modifies, students can clarify the significance of the information in the phrase.

◆ Reading for Success

④ **Predict** Have students speculate about what will come of the boy's interest in the "wild bay." *Students will probably say that the boy will return to the bay; some may say that something bad will happen when he does, based on the description of the bay as "wild," in contrast to "the safe beach."*

221

① Internal Conflict Ask students to identify the opposing feelings with which Jerry and his mother are struggling. *Jerry wants to go to the bay but doesn't want to worry his mother or leave her alone. Jerry's mother wants Jerry to be safe, but she doesn't want to baby him or hold him back.*

◆ Reading for Success

② Form a Mental Image Ask students which details help them imagine the scene. What details do they add in their mental pictures? *Students can identify details such as red-brown rocks, bluish green fringed with white, and inlets of rough, sharp rocks; they may add details such as the feel of wind or sunshine or the sound of the water.*

►Critical Viewing◄

③ Compare and Contrast Students may say that the beach in the painting is less crowded than the one in the story. They may add more people and a woman sitting on a yellow towel or wearing a yellow bathing suit, sitting under an orange beach umbrella. They might also add the ocean and waves.

◆ Build Grammar Skills

④ Participial Phrases Have students identify the participial phrase that modifies *he* in this sentence. Ask what information the phrase adds to the sentence. *The phrase is "relieved at being sure she was there." The phrase provides information about the boy's conflicted feelings about his mother: He wants independence, but he wants to be close to his mother as well.*

---

he was thinking of it.

Next morning, when it was time for the routine of swimming and sunbathing, his mother said, "Are you tired of the usual beach, Jerry? Would you like to go somewhere else?"

> **Use your prior knowledge** by relating Jerry's reaction to a time when you've hidden your feelings to avoid hurting someone else's feelings.

"Oh, no!" he said quickly, smiling at her out of that unfailing impulse of contrition—a sort of chivalry. Yet, walking down the path with her, he blurted out, "I'd like to go and have a look at those rocks down there."

① She gave the idea her attention. It was a wild-looking place, and there was no one there; but she said, "Of course, Jerry. When you've had enough, come to the big beach. Or just go straight back to the villa, if you like." She walked away, that bare arm, now slightly reddened from yesterday's sun, swinging. And he almost ran after her again, feeling it unbearable that she should go by herself, but he did not.

She was thinking, Of course he's old enough to be safe without me. Have I been keeping him too close? He mustn't feel he ought to be with me. I must be careful.

He was an only child, eleven years old. She was a widow. She was determined to be neither possessive nor lacking in devotion. She went worrying off to her beach.

As for Jerry, once he saw that his mother had gained her beach, he began the steep descent to the bay. From where he was, high up among red-brown rocks, it was a scoop of moving bluish green fringed with white. As he went lower, he saw that it spread among small <u>promontories</u> and inlets of rough, sharp rock,

②
> Use these sensory details—sharp rocks, vivid blue sea, and the sound of water—to **form a mental image** of this beautiful, isolated place.

and the crisping, lapping surface showed stains of purple and darker blue. Finally, as he ran sliding and scraping down the last few yards, he saw an edge of white surf and the shallow, <u>luminous</u> movement of water over white sand, and,

▲ **Critical Viewing** Compare the details of this painting with the way you envisioned the "big beach" in the story. [Compare and Contrast] **③**

beyond that, a solid, heavy blue.

He ran straight into the water and began swimming. He was a good swimmer. He went out fast over the gleaming sand, over a middle region where rocks lay like discolored monsters under the surface, and then he was in the real sea—a warm sea where irregular cold currents from the deep water shocked his limbs.

When he was so far out that he could look back not only on the little bay but past the promontory that was between it and the big beach, he floated on the buoyant surface and looked for his mother. There she was, a speck of yellow under an umbrella that looked like a slice of orange peel. He swam back to shore, relieved at being sure she was there, but all at once very lonely. **④**

On the edge of a small cape that marked the

 Humanities: Art

The Beach Treat by Suzanne Nagler.

Suzanne Nagler's painting of a beach scene is, in some ways, similar to the description of the beach in the story. Even the artist's use of childlike primary colors emphasizes the safe, peaceful quality of this place.

Use the following questions for discussion:

1. What details in the painting give an impression of safety and tranquillity? *Possible observations include the following: the building that could be a*

home or a life guard station gives a sense of permanence; phone lines link the remoteness of the beach to the rest of the world.

2. What important element of a beach scene is missing in this painting? Why do you think the artist omitted it? *Encourage students to note that the ocean is missing. Suggest that the vastness and the motion of the sea would not contribute to the feelings of stability and calm of the beach scene.*

The Beach Treat (detail), Suzanne Nagler

side of the bay away from the promontory was a loose scatter of rocks. Above them, some boys were stripping off their clothes. They came running, naked, down to the rocks. The English boy swam toward them, but kept his distance at a stone's throw. They were of that coast; all of them were burned smooth dark brown and speaking a language he did not understand. To be with them, of them, was a craving that filled his whole body. He swam a little closer; they turned and watched him with narrowed, alert dark eyes. Then one smiled and waved. It was enough. In a minute, he had swum in and was on the rocks beside them, smiling with a desperate, nervous <u>supplication</u>. They shouted cheerful greetings at him; and then, as he preserved his nervous, uncomprehending smile, they understood that he was a foreigner strayed from his own beach, and they proceeded to forget him. But he was happy. He

was with them.

They began diving again and again from a high point into a well of blue sea between rough, pointed rocks. After they had dived and come up, they swam around, hauled themselves up, and waited their turn to dive again. They were big boys—men, to Jerry. He dived, and they watched him; and when he swam around to take his place, they made way for him. He felt he was accepted and he dived again, carefully, proud of himself. **❺**

Soon the biggest of the boys poised himself, shot down into the water, and did not come up. The others stood about, watching. Jerry, after waiting for the sleek brown head to appear, let out a yell of warning; they looked at him idly and turned their eyes back toward the water. **❻** After a long time, the boy came up on the other side of a big dark rock, letting the air out of his lungs in a sputtering gasp and a shout of triumph. Immediately the rest of them dived in. One moment, the morning seemed full of chattering boys; the next, the air and the surface of the water were empty. But through the heavy blue, dark shapes could be seen moving and groping.

Jerry dived, shot past the school of underwater swimmers, saw a black wall of rock looming at him, touched it, and bobbed up at once to the surface, where the wall was a low barrier he could see across. There was no one visible; under him, in the water, the dim shapes of the swimmers had disappeared. Then one, and then another of the boys came up on the far side of the barrier of rock, and he understood that they had swum through some gap or hole in it. He plunged down again. He could see nothing through the stinging salt water but the blank rock. When he came up the boys were all on the diving rock, preparing to attempt the feat again. And now, in a panic of

◆ Build Vocabulary

promontories (präm´ ən tôr´ ēz) *n.*: High places extending out over a body of water

luminous (lōō´ mə nəs) *adj.*: Giving off light

supplication (sup´ lə kā´ shən) *n.*: The act of asking humbly and earnestly

Through the Tunnel ◆ 223

◆ Literary Focus

❺ Internal Conflict Point out to students that Jerry's interaction with these older boys highlights his desire to grow up and be independent of his mother. Tell students to notice how Jerry's actions in the next few paragraphs highlight his childlike side.

◆ Reading for Success

❻ Question Wonder with students why the author includes this information. Jerry is feeling accepted by the boys. How do they feel about him? *The fact that the boys "looked at him idly and turned their eyes back toward the water" implies that they do not, in fact, accept Jerry. They are behaving indifferently, at best—possibly even in a hostile manner.*

Customize for
English Language Learners
Help English language learners list words to identify the range of emotions that Jerry experiences during his encounter with the boys: *nervous, happy, accepted, proud, worried, surprised, confused.*

Customize for
More Advanced Learners
Have more advanced students describe Jerry's encounter with the boys from the older boys' point of view.

Cross-Curricular Connection: Social Studies

Sea caves are formed by the action of the waves against a rock face. Rock is eroded away particle by particle, forming an irregular chamber; a tunnel is formed when erosion breaks through the other side of the rock, creating a passageway.

Cave study—speleology—and cave exploration—spelunking—are pursued worldwide by specialists and enthusiasts who follow strict

guidelines for safety. Efforts to map the world's most intricate cave systems are ongoing. (See Internet resources for related web sites to visit.)

Have students discuss the inherent dangers in exploring an underwater cave or tunnel. Ask students how their knowledge or impression of caves and tunnels and their own fears add to the suspense of the story.

❶ Question Ask students how they would have responded to Jerry if they had been one of the big boys. What would they think about his actions, and how would they react?

Responses may range from wanting to ignore Jerry to feeling sorry for him, to trying to include him.

◆ **Reading for Success**

❷ Use Prior Knowledge Ask students how fear, anticipation, and other strong emotions affect their perception of time. Based on their experiences, do students think the older boys are underwater a dangerously long time or does Jerry only perceive the time to be too long?

Students will probably say that strong emotions can make time seem to pass more quickly or more slowly. For this reason, Jerry probably feels as if the older boys are under water a longer time than they actually are.

◆ **Critical Thinking**

❸ Compare and Contrast Have students compare Jerry's attitude toward his mother in this passage with his treatment of her earlier.

Students may say that Jerry is acting selfishly and childishly. Because he has been hurt, he is now obsessed with his own needs and feelings, whereas before he was thoughtful of hers.

◆ **Reading Strategy**

❹ Form Mental Images Encourage students to form a mental image based on this passage. Then ask them to identify the words that helped them form their images. *Sample answers: "shining white sand, rippled firm and hard," "two grayish shapes," "dart forward, swerve off," "the water sparkled as if sequins were dropping through it," "like swimming in flaked silver."*

---

failure, he yelled up, in English, "Look at me! Look!" and he began splashing and kicking in the water like a foolish dog.

They looked down gravely, frowning. He knew the frown. At moments of failure, when

> **❶ Question** why Jerry might be acting this way. Is he trying to get attention?

he clowned to claim his mother's attention, it was with just this grave, embarrassed inspection that she rewarded him.

Through his hot shame, feeling the pleading grin on his face like a scar that he could never remove, he looked up at the group of big brown boys on the rock and shouted, *"Bonjour! Merci! Au revoir! Monsieur, monsieur!"*[1] while he hooked his fingers round his ears and waggled them.

Water surged into his mouth; he choked, sank, came up. The rock, lately weighted with boys, seemed to rear up out of the water as their weight was removed. They were flying down past him, now, into the water; the air was full of falling bodies. Then the rock was empty in the hot sunlight. He counted one, two, three. . . .

At fifty, he was terrified. They must all be drowning beneath him, in the watery caves of the rock! At a hundred, he stared around him at the empty hillside, wondering if he should yell for help. He counted faster, faster, to hurry them up, to bring them to the surface quickly, to drown them quickly—anything rather than the terror of counting on and on into the blue emptiness of the morning. And then, at a hundred and sixty, the water beyond the rock was full of boys blowing like brown whales. They swam back to the shore without a look at him.

He climbed back to the diving rock and sat down, feeling the hot roughness of it under his thighs. The boys were gathering up their bits of clothing and running off along the shore to an-

> Think about how you would **respond** to this situation.

other promontory. They were leaving to get away from him. He cried openly, fists in his eyes. There was

---

1. **Bonjour!** . . . **monsieur!** (bōn zhōōr . . . mə syö´): Babbling of commonly known French words: "Hello! Thank you! Goodbye! Sir, sir!"

224 ◆ Clashing Forces

---

no one to see him, and he cried himself out.

It seemed to him that a long time had passed, and he swam out to where he could see his mother. Yes, she was still there, a yellow spot under an orange umbrella. He swam back to the big rock, climbed up, and dived into the blue pool among the fanged and angry boulders. Down he went, until he touched the wall of rock again. But the salt was so painful in his eyes that he could not see.

> Use these sensory details to **form a mental image** of how difficult it is to swim in this place.

He came to the surface, swam to shore and went back to the villa to wait for his mother. Soon she walked slowly up the path, swinging her striped bag, the flushed, naked arm dangling beside her. "I want some swimming goggles," he panted, defiant and beseeching.

She gave him a patient, inquisitive look as she said casually, "Well, of course, darling."

But now, now, now! He must have them this minute, and no other time. He nagged and pestered until she went with him to a shop. As soon as she had bought the goggles, he grabbed them from her hand as if she were going to claim them for herself, and was off, running down the steep path to the bay.

Jerry swam out to the big barrier rock, adjusted the goggles, and dived. The impact of the water broke the rubber-enclosed vacuum, and the goggles came loose. He understood that he must swim down to the base of the rock from the surface of the water. He fixed the goggles tight and firm, filled his lungs, and floated, face down, on the water. Now he could see. It was as if he had eyes of a different kind—fish eyes that showed everything clear and delicate and wavering in the bright water.

Under him, six or seven feet down, was a floor of perfectly clean, shining white sand, rippled firm and hard by the tides. Two grayish shapes steered there, like long, rounded pieces of wood or slate. They were fish. He saw them nose toward each other, poise motionless, make a dart forward, swerve off, and come around again. It was like a water dance. A few inches above them the water sparkled as if

---

Speaking and Listening Mini-Lesson

Account of an Outdoor Adventure

This mini-lesson supports the Speaking and Listening activity in the Idea Bank on page 230.

Introduce the Concept Discuss with the class what makes an outdoor-adventure account interesting. Students may suggest that suspense and physical challenges are what make adventure accounts gripping. Call students' attention to the passages in the story that use descriptive language such as "fanged and angry boulders" and narrative elements

that build suspense such as "He counted faster, faster, to hurry them up, to bring them to the surface quickly. . . ."

Develop Background Students can relate an actual experience or invent an adventure. Allow time for students to outline ideas for their presentations.

Apply the Information Based on their outlines, students can prepare their presentations. Encourage students to include props (such as climbing ropes or snowshoes) and

graphics, such as snapshots or magazine pictures and maps.

Assess the Outcome Each student's account should incorporate the techniques discussed and modeled when the concept was introduced (elements of suspense, descriptive details that highlight the physical challenge). Also evaluate the appropriateness and effectiveness of any props.

The Diver, Dennis Angel

▲ **Critical Viewing** How do you think this diver feels? [Speculate]

---

sequins were dropping through it. Fish again—myriads of minute fish, the length of his fingernail, were drifting through the water, and in a moment he could feel the innumerable tiny touches of them against his limbs. It was like swimming in flaked silver. The great rock the big boys had swum through rose sheer out of the white sand—black, tufted lightly with greenish weed. He could see no gap in it. He swam down to its base.

Again and again he rose, took a big chestful of air, and went down. Again and again he groped over the surface of the rock, feeling it, almost hugging it in the desperate need to find the entrance. And then, once, while he was clinging to the black wall, his knees came up and he

> This discovery will help you **predict** that upcoming plot events will be related to the tunnel.

shot his feet out forward and they met no obstacle. He had found the hole.

He gained the surface, clambered about the stones that littered the barrier rock until he found a big one, and, with this in his arms, let himself down over the side of the rock. He dropped, with the weight, straight to the sandy floor. Clinging tight to the anchor of stone, he lay on his side and looked in under the dark shelf at the place where his feet had gone. He could see the hole. It was an irregular, dark gap; but he could not see deep into it. He let go of his anchor, clung with his hands to the edges of the hole, and tried to push himself in.

He got his head in, found his shoulders jammed, moved them in sidewise, and was inside as far as his waist. He could see nothing ahead. Something soft and clammy touched his mouth; he saw a dark <u>frond</u> moving against the grayish rock, and panic filled him. He thought of octopuses, of clinging weed. He pushed himself out backward and caught a glimpse, as he retreated, of a harmless tentacle of seaweed drifting in the mouth of the tunnel. But it was enough. He reached the sunlight, swam to shore, and lay on the diving rock. He looked down into the blue well of water. He knew he must find his way through that cave, or hole, or tunnel, and out the other side.

First, he thought, he must learn to control his breathing. He let himself down into the water with another big stone in his arms, so that he could lie effortlessly on the bottom of the sea. He counted. One, two, three. He counted steadily. He could hear the movement of blood in his chest. Fifty-one, fifty-two. . . . His chest was hurting. He let go of the rock and went up into the air. He saw that the sun was low. He rushed to the villa and found his mother at her supper. She said only "Did you enjoy yourself?" and he said "Yes."

All night the boy dreamed of the water-filled cave in the rock, and as soon as breakfast was over he went to the bay.

◆ **Build Vocabulary**

frond (fränd) *n.*: Leaflike shoot of seaweed

Through the Tunnel ◆ 225

▶**Critical Viewing**◀

❺ **Speculate** As students respond to the question, have them discuss the mental preparation and concentration required to perform any difficult physical feat. Discuss also the effect of the artist's setting the diver against a vast expanse of sea and sky. *Students may suggest that the diver feels exhilarated and free, proud and triumphant. Others may speculate that the diver feels isolated and fearful. Many students will suggest a combination of fear and excitement.*

Customize for
Visual/Spatial Learners
Have visual/spatial learners use the details of the tunnel description to create a diagram or sketch of the underwater scene.

◆ *Literature and Your Life*

❻ Have students discuss Jerry's resolve to find his way through the tunnel, the steps he decides to take, and the goals he sets for himself. Have students share physical goals that they have set for themselves, such as learning a skill or training for a sport. How are their approaches to goal-setting similar to Jerry's? How are they different?

 Humanities: Art

The Diver by Dennis Angel.

Dennis Angel received a Master of Fine Arts degree from Indiana University, Bloomington, in 1988. He has taught at several universities and has exhibited his paintings all over the United States.

In this painting, the scene is fantastic, but the grace and daring of the diver are very real. By blurring the distinction between sea and sky, the artist places the focus on the diver and the dive, capturing the moments when the diver hangs in midair before success or failure is determined.

Use the following questions for discussion:
1. Is this a realistic scene or a fantasy scene? *The scene is fantastic. The diver seems to hang in midair; the pool seems to be set in the middle of nowhere; the diver's position is more like a bird's than a person's.*
2. What does the diver in the painting have in common with Jerry in the story? *Both are executing a feat of daring; both are about to pass through a dark, mysterious opening under the water; perhaps neither one knows if he or she will succeed or even survive.*

❶ Clarification Explain that water pressure increases as a person dives deeper. The increased pressure can cause small blood vessels in the nose to burst and cause nosebleeds.

◆ Literary Focus

❷ Internal Conflict Ask students to describe the emotional extremes that Jerry is experiencing. Why is he waiting? Why does the author call his persistence "unchildlike"? *Jerry feels ready to try swimming through the tunnel but is forcing himself to wait with "controlled impatience." He is waiting because he wants to be certain he will succeed. His persistence is unchildlike because most children do not exhibit this much self-control.* Challenge students to compare Jerry's "unchildlike" behavior now with his behavior when he asked his mother to buy the swim goggles. To what do they attribute this change? *Jerry is acting in a much more mature way now. His new goal may be helping him to grow up.*

◆ Build Grammar Skills

❸ Participial Phrases Have students identify the participial phrase that modifies *words*. Ask students what purpose the phrase serves. *The participial phrase is "authorized by the clock." Its purpose is to show that Jerry could hold his breath for exactly two minutes—not approximately.*

◆ Critical Thinking

❹ Make a Judgment Have students discuss the pros and cons of Jerry's decision. *Pros include a sense of accomplishment, pride in overcoming fear, meeting a goal. Cons include potential failure, injury, or death.*

---

❶ That night, his nose bled badly. For hours he had been underwater, learning to hold his breath, and now he felt weak and dizzy. His mother said, "I shouldn't overdo things, darling, if I were you."

That day and the next, Jerry exercised his lungs as if everything, the whole of his life, all that he would become, depended upon it. Again his nose bled at night, and his mother insisted on his coming with her the next day. It was a torment to him to waste a day of his careful self-training, but he stayed with her on that other beach, which now seemed a place for small children, a place where his mother might lie safe in the sun. It was not his beach.

He did not ask for permission, on the following day, to go to his beach. He went, before his mother could consider the complicated rights and wrongs of the matter. A day's rest, he discovered, had improved his count by ten. The big boys had made the passage while he counted a hundred and sixty. He had been counting fast, in his fright. Probably now, if he tried, he could get through that long tunnel, **❷** but he was not going to try yet. A curious, most unchildlike persistence, a controlled impatience, made him wait. In the meantime, he lay underwater on the white sand, littered now by stones he had brought down from the upper air, and studied the entrance to the tunnel. He knew every jut and corner of it, as far as it was possible to see. It was as if he already felt its sharpness about his shoulders.

He sat by the clock in the villa, when his mother was not near, and checked his time. He was incredulous and then proud to find he could hold his breath without strain for two minutes. The words "two minutes," authorized **❸** by the clock, brought close the adventure that was so necessary to him.

In another four days, his mother said casually one morning, they must go home. On the day before they left, he would do it. He would do it if it killed him, he said defiantly to himself. But two days before they were to leave—a day of triumph when he increased his count by fifteen—his nose bled so badly that he turned dizzy and had to lie limply over the big rock

like a bit of seaweed, watching the thick red blood flow onto the rock and trickle slowly down to the sea. He was frightened. Supposing he turned dizzy in the tunnel? Supposing he died there, trapped? Supposing—his head went around, in the hot sun, and he almost gave up. He thought he would return to the house and lie down, and next summer, perhaps, when he had another year's growth in him—*then* he would go through the hole.

The next paragraph provides the answer to the **question** of whether or not Jerry will go through the tunnel.

But even after he had made the decision, or thought he had, he found himself sitting up on the rock and looking down into the water; and he knew that now, this moment, when his nose had only just stopped bleeding, when his head was still sore and throbbing—this was the moment when he would try. If he did not do it now, he never would. He was trembling with fear that he would not go; and he was trembling with horror at that long, long tunnel under the rock, under the sea. Even in the open sunlight, the barrier rock seemed very wide and very heavy; tons of rock pressed down on where he would go. If he died there, he would **❹** lie until one day—perhaps not before next year—those big boys would swim into it and find it blocked.

He put on his goggles, fitted them tight, tested the vacuum. His hands were shaking. Then he chose the biggest stone he could carry and slipped over the edge of the rock until half of him was in the cool, enclosing water and half in the hot sun. He looked up once at the empty sky, filled his lungs once, twice, and then sank fast to the bottom with the stone. He let it go and began to count. He took the edges of the hole in his hands and drew himself into it, wriggling his shoulders in sidewise as he remembered he must, kicking himself along with his feet.

Soon he was clear inside. He was in a small rockbound hole filled with yellowish-gray water. The water was pushing him up against the **❺** roof. The roof was sharp and pained his back. He pulled himself along with his hands—fast,

226 ◆ *Clashing Forces*

✎ Workplace Skills Mini-Lesson

Setting and Meeting Goals

Introduce the Concept Jerry set a goal for himself and then challenged himself to meet it. Setting your own personal goals and finding a systematic way of meeting them are essential life and workplace skills. Goals students might wish to achieve include improving a grade in a particular subject, earning a spot on a team, or getting a part in a school play. Job related goals that students might consider include improving

keyboard skills or learning to operate a new piece of equipment such as a copier.

Develop Background Ask students to identify other goals they might set for themselves. Point out to students that many goals are actually the final product of a set of smaller goals. Use the Herringbone graphic organizer transparency, *Writing and Language Transparencies,* pp. 75–77, to model how one of the student-suggested goals might be broken down into smaller

goals or steps.

Apply the Information Distribute copies of the Herringbone organizer. Have students break individual goals into steps.

Assess the Outcome Evaluate how well the students have identified the sequence or combination of events or skills that will lead to their goals. Encourage pairs of students to evaluate each other on how well they identified the steps they would need to take to meet their goals.

fast—and used his legs as levers. His head knocked against something; a sharp pain dizzied him. Fifty, fifty-one, fifty-two. . . . He was without light, and the water seemed to press upon him with the weight of rock. Seventy-one, seventy-two. . . . There was no strain on his lungs. He felt like an inflated balloon, his lungs were so light and easy, but his head was pulsing.

He was being continually pressed against the sharp roof, which felt slimy as well as sharp. Again he thought of octopuses, and wondered if the tunnel might be filled with weed that could tangle him. He gave himself a panicky, <u>convulsive</u> kick forward, ducked his head, and swam. His feet and hands moved freely, as if in open water. The hole must have widened out. He thought he must be swimming fast, and he was frightened of banging his head if the tunnel narrowed.

A hundred, a hundred and one. . . . The water paled. Victory filled him. His lungs were beginning to hurt. A few more strokes and he would be out. He was counting wildly; he said a hundred and fifteen, and then, a long time later, a hundred and fifteen again. The water was a clear jewel-green all around him. Then he saw, above his head, a crack running up through the rock. Sunlight was falling through it, showing the clean, dark rock of the tunnel, a single mussel shell, and darkness ahead.

He was at the end of what he could do. He looked up at the crack as if it were filled with air and not water, as if he could put his mouth to it to draw in air. A hundred and fifteen, he heard himself say inside his head—but he had said that long ago. He must go on into the

Coast Scene, Isles of Shoals, 1901, Childe Hassam, The Metropolitan Museum of Art

▲ **Critical Viewing** Does this picture make you think of Jerry's beach or his mother's? Explain. **[Compare and Contrast]** **8**

blackness ahead, or he would drown. His head was swelling, his lungs cracking. A hundred and fifteen, a hundred and fifteen pounded through his head, and he feebly clutched at rocks in the dark, pulling himself forward, leaving the brief space of sunlit water behind. He felt he was dying. He was no longer quite conscious. He struggled on in the darkness between lapses into unconsciousness. An immense, swelling pain filled his head, and then the darkness cracked with an explosion of green light. His hands, groping forward, met nothing; and his feet, kicking back, propelled him out into the open sea. **9**

He drifted to the surface, his face turned up to the air. He was gasping like a fish. He felt he

◆ **Build Vocabulary**

convulsive (kən vul´ siv) *adj.:* Marked by an involuntary muscular contraction

Through the Tunnel ◆ 227

 Humanities: Art

Coast Scene, Isles of Shoals, 1901, by Childe Hassam.

American-born Childe Hassam established himself as a key figure in the French Impressionist movement of the late nineteenth century. His goal as a painter was to capture sunlight and its effect on the landscape. His paintings are noted for their sparkling radiance.

In this painting, the sunlit rocks look inviting and the sea appears to be calm, but the dark recesses of the churning water meeting the rocks in the foreground add an element of danger to the scene, while the deep blue of the water underscores the mystery of what is unseen.

Have students study the painting and then discuss the following question:

From which rock in the painting might the boys have dived? Which rock could be the one with the underwater tunnel? *Encourage students to support answers with details from the painting.*

Customize for
Body/Kinesthetic Learners
Suggest to these students that the Reading for Success strategy, Form Mental Images, can apply not only to visual images but to body-and-movement images as well. For example, for the underwater scenes, students can not only picture the scene visually, but "feel" it as well—as if they, themselves, were swimming in the tunnel.

◆ **Reading for Success**

5 Use Your Prior Knowledge
Even though students are not likely to have had an experience like Jerry's, many will have prior knowledge of what it is like to be in a situation that requires courage and some daring. Based on their experience, ask students to explain some of the emotions Jerry might be feeling. *Students might say that Jerry feels excited and determined but scared.*

◆ **Reading for Success**

6 Question Guide students to question why Lessing made them think Jerry was nearly out of the tunnel, then surprised them by letting them know they—and Jerry—were wrong. *Students should grasp that this is a technique for building tension, increasing suspense, building to a climax.*

◆ **Reading for Success**

7 Question Ask students if they think there is any chance that the author will let her main character die at the end of the story. If not, lead them to question where the suspense comes from in this passage. *Students should grasp that the suspense comes from identifying with the character. Jerry himself doesn't know if he will make it through the tunnel, and the reader shares Jerry's suspense.*

▶**Critical Viewing**◀

8 Compare and Contrast The beach seems more like Jerry's beach. Like Jerry's beach, the scene in the picture is wild and isolated, surrounded by rocks and rough places. In contrast, Jerry's mother's beach is a stretch of smooth sand dotted with people.

◆ **Build Grammar Skills**

9 Participial Phrases Have students identify the participial phrases that modify *hands* and *feet* in the sentence. *The phrase groping forward modifies hands; kicking back modifies feet.*

227

◆ Literary Focus

❶ Internal Conflict Ask students how this sentence is one indication of how Jerry's internal conflict has been resolved. *The fact that Jerry no longer wants or needs the approval of the older boys indicates a newfound independence and maturity.*

Reinforce and Extend

Use the *Beyond Literature* Cross-Curricular page on Physical Education (p. 16) to help students relate Jerry's physical challenge to a high-interest topic.

Answers

◆ Literature and Your Life

Reader's Response While many students may feel that Jerry's experience has helped him mature and become more independent, others may point out that he should not have taken on a challenge that could have cost him his life.

Thematic Focus Jerry has matured, learned patience, and achieved a measure of independence.

☑ Check Your Comprehension

1. While Jerry's mother is concerned for his safety, she is also worried that she may be overprotective.
2. (a) Jerry's encounter with the local boys begins well; they seem to accept him because he is able to dive along with them. When he begins clowning immaturely, they move on to get away from him. (b) Jerry is devastated by the change in the boys' attitude. His determination to do what they do is strengthened by their rejection.
3. Jerry prepares by getting goggles, checking the cave opening, and practicing holding his breath.
4. The tunnel is smaller than he thought, and much longer. When he thinks he has reached the end, he discovers he is only seeing light through a crack in the cave. Just when he thinks he can't go any further, he finally emerges into the open sea and pulls himself to safety on the big rock.
5. He sits quietly alone for a while and then goes back to the villa.

---

would sink now and drown; he could not swim the few feet back to the rock. Then he was clutching it and pulling himself up on to it. He lay face down, gasping. He could see nothing but a red-veined, clotted dark. His eyes must have burst, he thought; they were full of blood. He tore off his goggles and a <u>gout</u> of blood went into the sea. His nose was bleeding, and the blood had filled the goggles.

He scooped up handfuls of water from the cool, salty sea, to splash on his face, and did not know whether it was blood or salt water he tasted. After a time, his heart quieted, his eyes cleared, and he sat up. He could see the local ❶ boys diving and playing half a mile away. He did not want them. He wanted nothing but to get back home and lie down.

In a short while, Jerry swam to shore and climbed slowly up the path to the villa. He flung himself on his bed and slept, waking at the sound of feet on the path outside. His mother was coming back. He rushed to the bathroom, thinking she must not see his face with bloodstains, or tearstains, on it. He came out of the bathroom and met her as she walked into the villa, smiling, her eyes lighting up.

"Have a nice morning?" she asked, laying her hand on his warm brown shoulder a moment.

"Oh, yes, thank you," he said.

"You look a bit pale." And then, sharp and anxious, "How did you bang your head?"

"Oh, just banged it," he told her.

She looked at him closely. He was strained; his eyes were glazed-looking. She was worried. And then she said to herself, Oh, don't fuss! Nothing can happen. He can swim like a fish.

They sat down to lunch together.

"Mummy," he said, "I can stay under water for two minutes—three minutes, at least." It came bursting out of him.

"Can you, darling?" she said. "Well, I shouldn't overdo it. I don't think you ought to swim any more today."

She was ready for a battle of wills, but he gave in at once. It was no longer of the least importance to go to the bay.

> ◆ **Build Vocabulary**
> **gout** (gout) *n.*: Spurt; splash; glob

Guide for Responding

◆ Literature and Your Life

Reader's Response Do you think Jerry's victory is worth the pain and risks entailed? Why or why not?

Thematic Focus How has Jerry changed as a result of his success?

Group Discussion As a group, discuss the guidelines you could use to determine whether a test or challenge involves too great a physical risk. Also discuss how you can gracefully avoid taking risks that are too great.

☑ Check Your Comprehension

1. What concerns does Jerry's mother have about raising him?
2. (a) Describe Jerry's encounter with the local boys. (b) What effect does it have on him?
3. How does Jerry prepare for his task?
4. Briefly summarize how Jerry finally swims through the tunnel.
5. What happens after Jerry passes the test he sets for himself?

228 ◆ *Clashing Forces*

 Beyond the Selection

FURTHER READING

Other Works by Doris Lessing
"No Witchcraft for Sale" (1964)
Going Home—nonfiction (1968)

Other Works on the Theme of Clashing Forces
Red Badge of Courage, Stephen Crane
Diary of a Young Girl, Anne Frank
We suggest that you preview these works before recommending them to students.

INTERNET

Please be aware that sites may have changed since we published this information. Students can find out more about Doris Lessing at the following Web site: **http://tile.net/lessing/index.html**

Students can find out more about caves and cave diving at the following Web site: **http://www. caves.org/~cds**

We *strongly recommend* that you preview these sites before sending students to them.

Guide for Responding (continued)

◆ Critical Thinking

INTERPRET

1. (a) Describe Jerry's relationship with his mother at the beginning of the story. (b) How does it change by the story's end? Support your answer with examples. **[Analyze]**
2. What must Jerry prove to himself by swimming through the tunnel? **[Infer]**
3. At the end of the story, why is going to the bay "no longer of the least importance" to Jerry? **[Draw Conclusions]**

APPLY

4. Why do many young people set up situations in which they test themselves, as Jerry does? Give examples. **[Speculate]**

EXTEND

5. What jobs require people to meet physical challenges on a regular basis? What are the rewards of some of these jobs? **[Career Link]**

◆ Reading for Success

INTERACTIVE READING STRATEGIES

Review the reading strategies and notes showing how to read interactively. Then apply those strategies to answer the following questions.

1. What hints enable you to predict when Jerry will make his attempt?
2. What words help you form a mental image of Jerry's passage through the tunnel?
3. What does Jerry's experience with the tunnel tell you about the nature of growing up?

◆ Literary Focus

INTERNAL CONFLICT

A conflict involves a struggle between opposing forces. An **internal conflict** involves a character in conflict with himself. Jerry's internal conflict begins as he experiences "a craving that filled his whole body" to be one of the local boys who swim through the tunnel.

1. What are the two opposing forces in the internal conflict?
2. How does the physical challenge make the internal conflict more exciting?

◆ Build Vocabulary

USING THE ROOT -lum-

Knowing that the word root -lum- means light, define the -lum- words that appear in the following sentences.

1. The astronomer observed the *luminous* planet.
2. The torches *illuminate* the cave passage.
3. The scientist studied the *luminosity* of the star.
4. The great scientist is considered a *luminary* of our time.

USING THE WORD BANK

On your paper, write the word from the Word Bank that is the best synonym for each of the following words.

1. spurt
2. shining
3. ridges
4. remorse
5. leaf
6. begging
7. shaking violently

◆ Build Grammar Skills

PARTICIPIAL PHRASES

Doris Lessing uses a variety of sentence elements to keep "Through the Tunnel" moving as swiftly as Jerry through the underwater cave. One element she uses frequently is the participial phrase.

> A **participial phrase** consists of a present or past participle (a verb form ending in *-ing, -ed,* or an irregular ending) and any other words that go with it. Participles function as adjectives.

Practice Copy the following sentences in your notebook. Underline each participial phrase and circle the noun it modifies. Each participial phrase begins with a present participle.

1. His mother walked on in front of him, carrying a bright striped bag.
2. Her other arm, swinging loose, was very white in the sun.
3. The boy came up, letting the air out of his lungs.
4. Walking down the path with her, he blurted out, "I'd like to go and have a look at those rocks."

Through the Tunnel ◆ 229

◆ Build Vocabulary

Using the Root -lum-
1. shining
2. light up, fill with light
3. light, quality of light
4. shining person, a star

Using the Word Bank
1. gout; 2. luminous;
3. promontories; 4. contrition;
5. frond; 6. supplication;
7. convulsive

◆ Build Grammar Skills
1. *Carrying a bright striped bag* modifies *mother*.
2. *Swinging loose* modifies *arm*.
3. *Letting the air out of his lungs* modifies *boy*.
4. *Walking down the path* modifies *he*.

 Writer's Solution

For additional instruction and practice, use the *Writer's Solution Grammar Practice Book* page on Participles and Participial Phrases, p. 41

Answers

◆ Critical Thinking

1. (a) Jerry's relationship with his mother is close, but in some ways suffocating. (b) By the end of the story, Jerry doesn't feel it is necessary to challenge his mother to prove his independence.
2. Jerry originally wants to prove that he can do what the older boys do. His goal in the end, however, is to prove that he can overcome his own fear.
3. Jerry has proved to himself that he has courage and strength.
4. Students may suggest that, like Jerry, young people feel the need to do something that proves they are strong, mature, or "cool." Some examples may be positive, such as learning to drive or overcoming stage fright to try out for a play. Encourage students to distinguish between healthy and unhealthy challenges.
5. Jobs such as firefighter, construction worker, police officer, and soldier in the armed forces require people to meet physical challenges in the course of their work. Rewards include the satisfaction of meeting a physical challenge, working outdoors, and using strength to help others.

◆ Reading for Success

1. Jerry's mother's announcement that they will leave in four days is one hint that Jerry will soon make his attempt. Another hint is the internal debate that Jerry has with himself.
2. The words yellowish-gray water, blackness, darkness, and jewel-green help readers form a mental image of what Jerry sees. Sharp pain, inflated balloon, head pulsing, slimy, lungs cracking, and feebly clutching are words that help readers form a mental image of what Jerry feels.
3. Students may say that like Jerry's experience in the tunnel, growing up sometimes involves fear, pain, disappointment, and struggle.

◆ Literary Focus

1. The two main forces in Jerry's internal conflict are his fear and his desire to accomplish his goal.
2. Jerry's internal conflict is intensified for readers by the knowledge that some of the dangers he fears are real possibilities.

229

Idea Bank

Customizing for
Learning Modalities

Following are suggestions for matching Idea Bank topics with your students' learning modalities:

- Kinesthetic: 1, 4, 6
- Visual/Spatial: 6
- Verbal/Lingustic: 2, 3, 5
- Musical/Rhythmic: 7

Customizing for
Performance Levels

- Less Advanced Students: 1, 5, 6
- Average Students: 2, 4, 5, 7
- More Advanced Students: 3, 7

Writing Mini-Lesson

Refer students to the Writing Handbook, page 965 for instruction on the writing process, page 967 for further information on description, and page 968 for further information on persuasion.

Writer's Solution

Writing Lab CD-ROM

Have students complete the tutorial on Description. Follow these steps:

1. Encourage students to preview the criteria for a travel brochure.
2. Suggest that they use the audio-annotated model of a travel brochure.
3. Have students draft on the computer.
4. Tell them to use the Proofreading guidelines for checking for misplaced modifiers.

Sourcebook

Have students use Chapter 1, Description (pp. 1–25), for additional support. The chapter includes in-depth instruction on gathering details (p. 18) and details to use for different purposes (p. 17).

Build Your Portfolio

Idea Bank

Writing

1. **Water Safety Rules** Jerry is lucky to have survived the dangers of his underwater challenge. Write a list of water safety rules that wiser swimmers should follow. **[Physical Education Link]**

2. **Letter** As Jerry, write a letter to one of your friends at home, describing your accomplishment. Describe your thoughts and feelings before, during, and after your swim.

3. **Observation** Jerry first wants to swim through the tunnel in order to win acceptance from the local boys. Using your own experience, write an observation showing how peer pressure affects people's actions and decisions.

Speaking and Listening

4. **Account of an Outdoor Adventure** Give an oral presentation about an outdoor adventure you have had or would like to experience. Use visuals or props to enliven your presentation.

5. **Dialogue** Imagine that another boy has discovered Jerry's plan and wants to talk him out of it. Role-play the dialogue that might take place between the two boys. **[Performing Arts Link]**

Projects

6. **Collage** Doris Lessing uses vivid words to describe the setting of this story. Create your own vivid image of the setting in the form of a collage. Incorporate a variety of artistic media and found objects, such as sand, fabric, and shells. **[Art Link]**

7. **Movie Score** Use songs you know to create a musical score for a film version of this story. Choose different songs for different scenes. Play your choices for the class. **[Music Link]**

Writing Mini-Lesson

Travel Brochure

Choose a vacation place that you have visited or would like to visit and write a travel brochure about it. Packing a lot of information into a small space, use descriptions and colorful images to attract tourists. Provide specific details about things to do and sights to see. The following tip will help you convince readers that your destination is a worthwhile place to visit.

Writing Skills Focus: Persuasive Tone

Persuasive essays use a **persuasive tone**—they take a positive attitude toward the ideas and actions they want readers to accept. Here's how you can achieve a persuasive tone:

- Use words that appeal to readers' senses: *soft, tropical breezes.*
- Convey your own enthusiasm for activities: *a fun-filled afternoon of shopping.*
- Stress the benefits of a place or a plan: *For only a few dollars more, you can . . .*

Prewriting Consider what your readers may desire in a travel destination. Depending on the place you choose, you may want to highlight physical beauty, comfort, historical interest, or activities.

Drafting As you write, introduce your main points with phrases that create appealing images ("Leave the world behind . . .") or compelling reasons ("It's worth an extra day just to . . ."). Don't expect your readers to accept your claims at face value. Support each point you make with details and examples.

Revising Ask a partner to read your brochure to see if he or she would like to visit the place you describe. If not, add descriptions or details that would help persuade your partner to visit the place.

✓ ASSESSMENT OPTIONS

Formal Assessment, Selection Test, pp. 54–56, and Assessment Resources Software. The selection test is designed so that it can be easily customized to the ability levels of your students.

Alternative Assessment, p. 16, includes options for less advanced students, more advanced students, logical/mathematical learners and bodily/kinesthetic learning.

PORTFOLIO ASSESSMENT

Use the following rubrics in the *Alternative Assessment* booklet to assess students' writing:
Water Safety Rules: How-To/Process Explanation Rubric, p. 100
Letter: Expression Rubric, p. 94
Observation: Cause-and-Effect Rubric, p. 102
Writing Mini-Lesson: Description Rubric, p. 97

PART 1 *Personal Challenges*

Woman Dragging Key to Keyhole, Brad Holland

One-Minute Planning Guide

The selections in Part 1 offer a variety of perspectives on personal challenges. "The Dog That Bit People" chronicles the humorous challenges of owning a problem dog. In "Conscientious Objector" and "A Man" the speakers describe a positive approach to dealing with choices and challenges. "The Weary Blues" and "Jazz Fantasia" show how music can inspire an individual. "Like the Sun" is a humorous perspective on the challenge of telling the truth, while "Tell all the Truth but tell it slant—" deals with the same theme in a more serious tone.

Customize for
Varying Student Needs
When assigning the selections in this part to your students, keep in mind the following factors:

"The Dog That Bit People"
• A high-interest short story

"Conscientious Objector"
• Contains allusions with which some students may need help

"A Man "
• A short poem with easy-to-understand symbolism

"The Weary Blues" and "Jazz Fantasia"
• Poems that use dialect and slang
  "Like the Sun"
• Vocabulary is more difficult than in other selections
• Terms specific to Indian culture will need to be explained

"Tell all the Truth but tell it slant—"
• A short poem

Humanities: Art

Woman Dragging Key to Keyhole by Brad Holland.

Brad Holland has been a professional artist since the age of 17. He has since created covers for such mainstream publications as *The New Yorker, Newsweek, The Atlantic Monthly,* and *U.S. News and World Report.*

Call students' attention to the very realistic way in which the artist has painted the key, down to the discolorations and rubbed spots on the metal. Invite them to contrast such details with the other, less representational aspects of the painting—the mysterious looming dark space, the fact that the key is as large as the woman but nowhere near a match for the size of that mysterious keyhole, the sketchiness of the area where the woman stands, the way the woman herself is faceless and almost blends into the keyhole.

Help students link the painting to the theme of Part 1, Personal Challenges, by answering the following questions:

1. What might the huge, dark space of the keyhole represent? *The keyhole might represent the unknown future or a problem the woman has to face.*
2. What might the artist be suggesting by making the key the woman drags very large but still much smaller than the keyhole? *The artist might be suggesting that we have resources to deal with our problems, but the problem often seems—and sometimes is—greater than our resources.*

231

OBJECTIVES

1. To read, comprehend, and interpret a humorous essay
2. To relate an essay to personal experience
3. To form mental images to enhance appreciation
4. To recognize techniques used in a humorous essay
5. To build vocabulary in context and learn the prefix *epi-*
6. To distinguish the correct use of *like* and *as if*
7. To write an animal anecdote using vivid verbs
8. To respond to the essay through writing, speaking and listening, and projects

SKILLS INSTRUCTION

Vocabulary:
The Prefix *epi-*
Grammar:
Correct Use of *Like* and *As If*
Reading Strategy:
Form Mental Images

Literary Focus:
Humorous Essay
Writing:
Vivid Verbs
Speaking and Listening:
Holding a Radio Show (teacher edition)

PORTFOLIO OPPORTUNITIES

Writing: Lost Dog Description; News Story; Persuasive Letter to Mother
Writing Mini-Lesson: Animal Anecdote
Speaking and Listening: Pet Talk; Pantomime
Projects: Wanted Poster; Dog Breed Chart

More About the Author

In addition to books, essays, and cartoons for adults, James Thurber also created memorable books for children. *The Thirteen Clocks* (1950) and *The Wonderful O* (1957) are two of his most famous children's books.

Thurber's problems with his vision started with a childhood accident that cost him an eye. He often explained that the distinctive style of his line drawings evolved from his inability to see small details.

Guide for Reading

James Thurber (1894–1961)

From Carol Burnett to Jerry Seinfeld, today's popular comedians make millions of people laugh by finding the humor in everyday life. Writer James Thurber helped lay the groundwork for this kind of comedy back in the 1920's.

Thurber made people laugh by poking fun at pesky pets, stressed-out spouses, and misplaced valuables.

From Clerk to Cartoonist

Thurber was born in Columbus, Ohio. He never completed college, leaving to become a clerk in the U.S. State Department. Soon, however, Thurber turned to writing and cartooning. Much of his early work appeared in *The New Yorker*. His cartoons of frightened men, menacing women, wicked children, and silent, observing animals delighted readers across the country.

Whimsical Style Thurber's whimsical, comedic style fills his autobiography, *My Life and Hard Times* (1933), with laughter and comic richness. In "The Dog That Bit People," which comes from this book, Thurber creates a likeable but hysterical character who also happens to be a dog.

Although Thurber left *The New Yorker* staff in 1933, he remained a leading contributor. In 1940, failing eyesight forced him to decrease his drawing. By 1952, when he became almost totally blind, he had to give it up altogether. He still continued, however, to contribute articles to numerous magazines.

Other works by James Thurber include *Fables for Our Time* (1940), *The Male Animal* (1941), and "The Secret Life of Walter Mitty."

◆ Build Vocabulary

PREFIXES: *epi-*
In this selection, you will encounter the word *epitaph*. The prefix *epi-* can mean "upon," "outside," "among," or "above." Knowing this definition gives you a clue to the meaning of *epitaph*—an inscription on a tomb or gravestone.

WORD BANK
incredulity
choleric
irascible
jangle
indignant
epitaph

As you read this essay, you will encounter the words on this list. Each word is defined on the page where it first appears. Preview the list before you read.

◆ Build Grammar Skills

CORRECT USE OF *LIKE* AND *AS IF*
Even though he writes in an informal style, Thurber follows the rules of good usage, including using **like** and **as if** correctly. Although it's a common mistake, *like* cannot be used in place of *as if*.

Like is used to introduce a prepositional phrase—a preposition and a noun or pronoun.

Muggs could read him *like* a book.

As if is used to introduce a subordinate clause—a group of words that contains a subject and a verb but cannot stand alone as a sentence.

He always acted *as if* he thought I wasn't one of the family.

232 ◆ *Clashing Forces*

Prentice Hall Literature Program Resources

REINFORCE / RETEACH / EXTEND

Selection Support Pages
Build Vocabulary: The Prefix *epi-*, p. 68
Build Grammar Skills: *Like* and *As If*, p. 69
Reading Strategy: Form Mental Images, p. 70
Literary Focus: Humorous Essay, p. 71

Strategies for Diverse Student Needs, p. 17

Beyond Literature
Career Connection: Humor Columnist, p. 17

Formal Assessment Selection Test, pp. 57–58; Assessment Resources Software

Alternative Assessment, p. 17

Resource Pro CD-ROM
"The Dog That Bit People"—includes all resource material and customizable lesson plan

 Listening to Literature Audiocassettes
"The Dog That Bit People"

The Dog That Bit People

◆ *Literature and Your Life*

CONNECT YOUR EXPERIENCE

You may not think of yourself as a comedian—but you've probably made people laugh! In some way, we are all comedians. We all share stories and experiences with friends or relatives, exaggerating details to get a bigger laugh from our audience.

By giving a little twist of the ridiculous to your stories, you are following in the footsteps of comic writers like James Thurber. In this essay, he makes an irritable family pet into an unforgettable character.

Journal Writing Jot down several amusing real-life situations that, although they were not funny at the time, would make amusing stories.

THEMATIC FOCUS: PERSONAL CHALLENGES

In "The Dog That Bit People," James Thurber uses humor to lighten the seriousness of having a "challenging" pet. What does his essay reveal about the use of humor to help ease a conflict?

◆ Background for Understanding

ART

James Thurber enjoyed a dual career as a writer and a cartoonist. Indeed, the lines of his drawings, as you can see, are as whimsical as the lines of his prose.

Thurber created nearly 500 cartoons—sketchy scribbles of men, women, children, and animals, especially dogs. People related to these cartoons. They felt as if they *knew* Thurber's overworked guy at the office or his angry woman filing a complaint with the police department.

In "The Dog That Bit People," James Thurber's cartoons combine with his prose to depict Muggs and his long list of "victims."

◆ Literary Focus

HUMOROUS ESSAY

A **humorous essay** is a nonfiction composition that presents the author's thoughts on a subject in an amusing way. This light-hearted approach is intended to make the reader laugh.

A writer may create humor in an essay by describing a ridiculous situation in a serious way or by using exaggeration. Thurber uses anecdotes—brief stories about an event—to create humor in his essay about the vicious dog Muggs.

◆ Reading Strategy

FORM MENTAL IMAGES

All comic writers are cartoonists whether or not they draw. They create humorous pictures with words. You can help them create these pictures by **forming mental images** of the silly situations they describe.

Don't just read this essay as words on the page. Think of it as a verbal cartoon. Picture the expressions on people's faces. See the dog chewing up the morning paper. By the end of this essay, you should have created a mental comic book.

Lots of People Reported Our Dog to the Police, James Thurber

Guide for Reading ◆ 233

Interest Grabber Have students brainstorm for a list of their favorite animated and live comedy shows. Ask students to describe the type of humor in each show and to identify some of the techniques used to achieve the humor. Students might suggest such elements as exaggeration, sight gags, and word play. Guide students to present specific examples from each show. Then have students use the title and the introductory illustrations to predict how Thurber will create humor in this essay.

Customize for
Less Proficient Readers
Guide less proficient readers in identifying the individual ideas expressed in some of Thurber's longer, more complex sentences. Use the Break Down Sentences page in the *Strategies for Diverse Student Needs,* p. 17.

Customize for
More Advanced Students
These students can try telling portions of the essay from Muggs's or the mother's point of view. Comparing their retellings with the original will help them analyze the effect of Thurber's choice of narrator and point of view on the essay's particular type of humor.

Customize for
English Language Learners
Students may recognize some words but not understand them as they are used in this narrative. Help students clarify the meaning in context of words such as *miniature* (small dog), *garage* (repair shop), *good side* (in favor), and *humor* (attitude).

Customize for
Visual/Spatial Learners
Have these students preview the drawings on pages 235 and 237. What do these cartoons reveal about the essay's topic and tone?

 Preparing for Standardized Tests

Reading and Vocabulary By teaching students how to use their knowledge of the prefix *epi-* to define new words, the Build Vocabulary lesson will help students improve their scores on both reading comprehension and vocabulary items on the verbal portions of standardized tests. For more practice, use the Build Vocabulary page in *Selection Support*, p. 68.

Grammar and Language The usage items that appear in the verbal portions of some standardized tests may require students to recognize incorrect usage in sentences. The Build Grammar Skills lesson teaches the correct use of *like* and *as if*. This skill can help students improve their performance on English usage items on standardized tests. Students may also apply this skill in revision items on tests, in which they must choose the best revision of a sentence containing an error with these words. For additional practice, use the Build Grammar Skills page in *Selection Support*, p. 69.

Thurber uses exaggeration and contrast to achieve humor in this series of bad-dog anecdotes, but this master comic has other tricks up his sleeve as well. In addition, he uses understatement, irony, absurdity, and digression to keep his readers chuckling. Thurber's wry anecdotes will help students see that humor is a combination of keen observation of details and a unique style of reporting those details.

Customize for
Less Proficient Readers
Help students identify the three related ideas expressed in the opening sentence: (1) Thurber has had a lot of dogs. (2) Most of Thurber's dogs have given him more pleasure than trouble. (3) The Airedale named Muggs gave him more trouble than pleasure.

◆ **Literary Focus**

❶ **Humorous Essay** Ask students how Thurber creates humor in this portion of the essay. *He creates humor through exaggeration, claiming that Muggs gave him more trouble than fifty-five or more other dogs. Then Thurber digresses with long, involved sentences in which each detail increases the absurdity of the situation.*

◆ **Reading Strategy**

❷ **Form Mental Images** Have students visualize the scene described in this passage and invite them to verbalize what is funny about the mental images they form. *Lead students to grasp that the humor in this description comes from the absurdity of the mental image and the juxtaposition of images. The sight of a person holding a fancy green parasol over a poodle wearing a bib is unusual enough, but the humor is heightened when Thurber adds the tough garage men.*

◆ *Literature and Your Life*

❸ Lead a discussion of why it can sometimes be helpful to laugh at oneself. Elicit from students examples of how the embarrassment or aggravation of certain situations can be alleviated with humor.

The Dog That Bit People

James Thurber

Probably no one man should have as many dogs in his life as I have had, but there was more pleasure than distress in them for me except in the case of an Airedale[1] named Muggs. He gave me more trouble than all the other fifty-four or-five put together, although my moment of keenest embarrassment was the time a Scotch terrier named Jeannie, who had just had six puppies in the clothes closet of a fourth floor apartment in New York, had the unexpected seventh and last at the corner of Eleventh Street and Fifth Avenue during a walk she had insisted on taking. Then, too, there was the prize winning French poodle, a great big black poodle—none of your little, untroublesome white miniatures—who got sick riding in the rumble seat[2] of a car with me on her way to the Greenwich Dog Show. She had a red rubber bib tucked around her throat and, since a rain storm came up when we were halfway through the Bronx, I had to hold over her a small green umbrella, really more of a parasol. The rain beat down fearfully and suddenly the driver of the car drove into a big garage, filled with mechanics. It happened so quickly that I forgot to put the umbrella down and I will always remember, with sickening distress, the look of <u>incredulity</u> mixed with hatred that came over the face of the particular hardened garage man that came over to see what we wanted, when he took a look at me and the poodle. All garage men, and people of that intolerant stripe, hate poodles with their curious hair

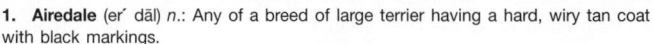

1. **Airedale** (er´ dāl) *n.*: Any of a breed of large terrier having a hard, wiry tan coat with black markings.
2. **rumble seat:** In some earlier automobiles, an open seat in the rear, behind the roofed seat, which could be folded shut when not in use.

Block Scheduling Strategies

Consider these suggestions to take advantage of extended class time:

• Introduce the selection by playing a portion of the essay on the Listening to Literature audio-cassette.

• Introduce the Build Grammar Skills topic—the correct use of *like* and *as if* (p. 232). After students have completed the exercise on p. 240, pairs of students can create dialogues showing how to use *like* and *as if* correctly.

• Have more advanced students identify examples of irony, understatement, and digression and average students identify examples of exaggeration and describing a ridiculous situation in a serious way. Meanwhile, you can work with less proficient readers and English language learners to break down sentences and complete *Strategies for Diverse Student Needs*, p. 17.

• Discussion groups can share their answers to the Reader's Response and Thematic Focus portions of the Guide for Responding, p. 239.

Nobody Knew Exactly What Was the Matter with Him

Nobody Knew Exactly What Was the Matter With Him, James Thurber

cut, especially the pom-poms that you got to leave on their hips if you expect the dogs to win a prize.

But the Airedale, as I have said, was the worst of all my dogs. He really wasn't my dog, as a matter of fact: I came home from a vacation one summer to find that my brother Roy had bought him while I was away. A big, burly, <u>choleric</u> dog, he always acted as if he thought I wasn't one of the family. There was a slight advantage in being one of the family, for he didn't bite the family as often as he bit strangers. Still, in the years that we had him he bit everybody but mother, and he made a pass at her once but missed. That was during the month when we suddenly had mice, and Muggs refused to do anything about them. Nobody ever

had mice exactly like the mice we had that month. They acted like pet mice, almost like mice somebody had trained. They were so friendly that one night when mother entertained at dinner the Friraliras, a club she and my father had belonged to for twenty years, she put down a lot of little dishes with food in them on the pantry floor so that the mice would be satisfied with that and wouldn't come into the dining room. Muggs stayed out in the pantry with the mice, lying on the floor,

The Dog That Bit People ◆ 235

◆ Literary Focus

❶ Humorous Essay Students should mention that the exaggerated tameness of the mice highlights Muggs's unwillingness to do anything to help his human family. Thurber is strengthening the humorous impression that the household is run for Muggs's convenience.

◆ Critical Thinking

❷ Making Inferences Ask students what they can infer from this detail. *Readers can infer that Thurber's mother felt affection for Muggs, because she made excuses for him. Her feelings are probably the reason the family doesn't get rid of Muggs.*

◆ Literary Focus

❸ Humorous Essay Ask students what effect Thurber achieves by including details such as the exact location where Major Moberly fired at Muggs or the Congressman's astrological sign. *Including precise, realistic details in this absurd anecdote makes it sound serious—and therefore, even funnier.*

◆ Build Grammar Skills

❹ *Like* and *As If* Have students explain why Thurber uses the word *like* rather than the phrase *as if* here. Challenge them to change the sentence so that *as if* would be correct. *Thurber uses* like *to introduce the prepositional phrase "like a book." As* if *could introduce the subordinate clause "as if he were a book,"* if *the sentence were rewritten.*

◆ Reading Strategy

❺ Form Mental Images Students should identify these words and details: the modifiers *moodily, brass, vicious,* precise nouns *grapefruit, leap, fire screen,* and participial phrases *scattering dishes, spilling the coffee.*

◆ Critical Thinking

❻ Draw Conclusions Ask students: Why is Mother forever defending Muggs? *Based on the information in this paragraph and inferences they have made earlier in the essay, students should conclude that Mother defends Muggs's behavior because she loves him.*

> **◆ Literary Focus**
> Explain how the exaggeration of the tameness of the mice adds humor to this scene.

❶

growling to himself—not at the mice, but about all the people in the next room that he would have liked to get at. Mother slipped out into the pantry once to see how everything was going. Everything was going fine. It made her so mad to see Muggs lying there, oblivious of the mice—they came running up to her—that she slapped him and he slashed at her, but didn't make it. He was sorry immediately, mother said. He was always sorry, she said, after he bit someone, but we could not understand how she figured this out. He didn't act sorry.

❷
Mother used to send a box of candy every Christmas to the people the Airedale bit. The list finally contained forty or more names. Nobody could understand why we didn't get rid of the dog. I didn't understand it very well myself, but we didn't get rid of him. I think that one or two people tried to poison Muggs—he acted poisoned once in a while—and old Major Moberly fired at him once with his service revolver near the Seneca Hotel in East Broad Street—but Muggs lived to be almost eleven years old and even when he could hardly get around he bit a Congressman who had called to see my father on business. My mother had never liked the Congressman—she said the signs of his horoscope showed he couldn't be trusted (he was Saturn with the moon in Virgo)—but she sent him a box of candy that Christmas. He sent it right back, probably because he suspected it was trick candy. Mother persuaded herself it was all for the best that the dog had bitten him, even though father lost an important business association because of it. "I wouldn't be associated with such a man," mother said, "Muggs could read him like a book."

❸

❹

We used to take turns feeding Muggs to be on his good side, but that didn't always work. He was never in a very good humor, even after a meal. Nobody knew exactly what was the

matter with him, but whatever it was it made him <u>irascible</u>, especially in the mornings. Roy never felt very well in the morning, either, especially before breakfast, and once when he came downstairs and found that Muggs had moodily chewed up the morning paper he hit him in the face with a grapefruit and then jumped up on the dining room table, scattering dishes and silverware and spilling the coffee. Muggs' first free leap carried him all the way across the table and into a brass fire screen in front of the gas grate but he was back on his feet in a moment and in the end he got Roy and gave him a pretty vicious bite in the leg. Then he was all over it; he never bit anyone more than once at a time. Mother always mentioned that as an argument in his favor; she said he had a quick temper but that he didn't hold a grudge. She was forever defending him. I think she liked him because he wasn't well. "He's not strong," she would say, pityingly, but that was inaccurate; he may not have been well but he was terribly strong.

> **◆ Reading Strategy**
> Identify the details that help you form a mental picture of this scene.

❺

❻

One time my mother went to the Chittenden Hotel to call on a woman mental healer who was lecturing in Columbus on the subject of "Harmonious Vibrations." She wanted to find out if it was possible to get harmonious vibrations into a dog. "He's a large tan-colored Airedale," mother explained. The woman said that she had never treated a dog but she advised my mother to hold the thought that he did not bite and would not bite. Mother was holding the thought the very next morning when Muggs got

◆ Build Vocabulary
irascible (i ras´ ə bəl) *adj.*: Easily angered; quick-tempered
jangle (jaŋ´ gəl) *n.*: Discord; harsh sounds

236 ◆ Clashing Forces

Speaking and Listening Mini-Lesson

Pet Talk
This mini-lesson supports the Speaking and Listening activity in the Idea Bank on page 241.

Introduce the Concept Students will prepare a radio talk show in which listeners call in with questions about their pets and a panel answers the questions. Their radio show will be assessed on the accuracy and clarity of their answers.

Develop Background Guide students toward resources that will help them find accurate answers to their questions. Suggest that they look

for information on the Internet, interview veterinarians and animal trainers if possible.

Apply the Information Based on what they discover through research, students may wish to modify or add questions. Tell students to prepare a script that gives the order of questions and to make sure that the panel is well prepared to answer the questions agreed upon.

Assess the Outcome Assess the radio show based on evidence of research, accuracy of information, and clarity of presentation.

Muggs at His Meals Was an Unusual Sight, James Thurber

◆ **Literary Focus**

❽ **Humorous Essay** Call students' attention to the contrast between the result Thurber's mother expects and the result she gets. Explain that this kind of irony is frequently used in humorous essays.

◆ *Literature and Your Life*

❾ Ask students how they think Thurber was feeling when he had this experience. Why do they think he is able to tell it as a humorous anecdote now? *Students will say that Thurber felt a mixture of fear and anger when he had the experience, but that the fact that he didn't get hurt badly after all and the time that has passed have enabled him to take a humorous view of the event.*

Customize for
Bodily/Kinesthetic Learners
Have these students hold a bag of books or some other heavy object at arm's length to help them appreciate the difficulty Thurber has keeping the dog off the floor.

Customize for
Visual/Spatial Learners
Have students discuss the appeal of visual humor and slapstick comedy. Have them identify the elements of visual humor they find in this description. *Examples include the image of Thurber holding a snarling dog by the tail, Thurber being surprised by the dog as he comes down the back stairs, and Thurber crashing to the floor.*

❼❽ the iceman but she blamed that slip-up on the iceman. "If you didn't think he would bite you, he wouldn't," mother told him. He stomped out of the house in a terrible <u>jangle</u> of vibrations.

❾ One morning when Muggs bit me slightly, more or less in passing, I reached down and grabbed his short stumpy tail and hoisted him into the air. It was a foolhardy thing to do and the last time I saw my mother, about six months ago, she said she didn't know what possessed me. I don't either, except that I was pretty mad. As long as I held the dog off the floor by his tail he couldn't get at me, but he twisted and jerked so, snarling all the time, that I realized I couldn't hold him that way very long. I carried him to the kitchen and flung him onto the floor and shut the door on him just as he crashed against it. But I forgot about the backstairs. Muggs went up the backstairs and down the frontstairs and had me cornered in the living room. I managed to get up onto the mantelpiece above the fireplace, but it gave way and came down with a tremendous crash throwing a large marble clock, several vases, and myself heavily to the floor. Muggs was so alarmed by the racket that when I picked myself up he had disappeared. We couldn't find him anywhere, although we whistled and ❾

🎼 **Humanities: Art**

Muggs at His Meals, 1933, by James Thurber.

This cartoon shows Muggs eating his dinner at a table, as described in the essay. Through simple lines and basic forms, Thurber captures the essence of the humorous situation. The dog's turned head and annoyed expression hint that a confrontation is about to occur.

Use these questions for discussion:

1. What does Muggs' posture suggest about his personality? *Muggs is guarding his food. His posture conveys his combative personality.*

2. How does this picture support what you've learned about Muggs from reading the essay? *The essay indicates that the family made special accommodations for Muggs because of his irritable personality. The picture shows him eating at a table, probably another special accommodation the family has made.*

shouted, until old Mrs. Detweiler called after
dinner that night. Muggs had bitten her once,
in the leg, and she came into the living room
only after we assured her that Muggs had run
away. She had just seated herself when, with a
great growling and scratching of claws, Muggs
emerged from under a davenport[3] where he had
been quietly hiding all the time, and bit her
again. Mother examined the bite and put
arnica[4] on it and told Mrs. Detweiler that
it was only a bruise. "He just bumped
you," she said. But Mrs. Detweiler left the
house in a nasty state of mind.

> ◆ **Literary Focus**
> How does this anec-
> dote highlight the
> ridiculousness of
> Mother's defense of
> Muggs?

Lots of people reported
our Airedale to the police
but my father held a mu-
nicipal office at the time
and was on friendly terms
with the police. Even so,
the cops had been out a
couple of times—once when Muggs bit Mrs.
Rufus Sturtevant and again when he bit
Lieutenant-Governor Malloy—but mother
told them that it hadn't been Muggs' fault
but the fault of the people who were bitten. "When he starts for them, they
scream," she explained, "and that excites
him." The cops suggested that it might be
a good idea to tie the dog up, but mother
said that it mortified him to be tied up and
that he wouldn't eat when he was tied up.

Muggs at his meals was an unusual
sight. Because of the fact that if you
reached toward the floor he would bite
you, we usually put his food plate on
top of an old kitchen table with a bench
alongside the table. Muggs would stand
on the bench and eat. I remember that
my mother's Uncle Horatio, who boasted
that he was the third man up Missionary

---

3. **davenport** (dav´ en pôrt´) *n.*: Large couch or
sofa.
4. **arnica** (är´ ni kə) *n.*: Preparation made from certain
plants, once used for treating sprains, bruises, and so
forth.

Ridge,[5] was splutteringly indignant when he
found out that we fed the dog on a table because we were afraid to put his plate on the
floor. He said he wasn't afraid of any dog that
ever lived and that he would put the dog's plate
on the floor if we would give it to him. Roy said
that if Uncle Horatio had fed Muggs on the
ground just before the battle he would have
been the first man up Missionary Ridge. Uncle
Horatio was furious. "Bring him in! Bring him
in now!" he shouted. "I'll feed the—on the
floor!" Roy was all for giving him a chance, but
my father wouldn't hear of it. He said that
Muggs had already been fed. "I'll feed him
again!" bawled Uncle Horatio. We had quite a
time quieting him.

In his last year Muggs used to spend practically all of his time outdoors. He didn't like to
stay in the house for some reason or other—
perhaps it held too many unpleasant memories
for him. Anyway, it was hard to get him to
come in and as a result the garbage man, the
iceman, and the laundryman wouldn't come
near the house. We had to haul the garbage
down to the corner, take the laundry out and
bring it back, and meet the iceman a block
from home. After this had gone on for some
time we hit on an ingenious arrangement for
getting the dog in the house so that we could
lock him up while the gas meter was read, and
so on. Muggs was afraid of only one thing, an
electrical storm. Thunder and lightning frightened him out of his senses (I think he thought
a storm had broken the day the mantelpiece
fell). He would rush into the house and hide
under a bed or in a clothes closet. So we fixed
up a thunder machine out of a long narrow
piece of sheet iron with a wooden handle on
one end. Mother would shake this vigorously
when she wanted to get Muggs into the house.
It made an excellent imitation of thunder, but I
suppose it was the most roundabout system for

---

5. **Missionary Ridge:** Hill south of Chattanooga, Tennessee, that was the site of a Civil War battle.

Cross-Curricular Connection: Social Studies

Generally considered the first domesticated animals, dogs have coexisted with humans as pets
and working partners through the ages in nearly
all cultures. Originally, there were only a few
species of *Canis familiaris*; through selective breed-
ing, nearly 150 breeds exist today. The smallest dogs
weigh less than two pounds; the largest ones tip
the scales at over 200 pounds.

In addition to providing companionship, dogs
fulfill many other functions today. For example,
dogs often work with police officers on patrol

duty. Some breeds of dogs, such as collies, are
herders; huskies draw transport sleds in the
Arctic; others, notably golden retrievers, aid the
visually impaired and hearing impaired.

Have students work in small groups to discuss
the care and training of dogs kept as family pets.
Students should consider proper food, bedding,
exercise, training, and affectionate care. Have
them consider how they would cope with the
problems of owning a dog like Muggs.

running a household that was ever devised. It took a lot out of mother.

A few months before Muggs died, he got to "seeing things." He would rise slowly from the floor, growling low, and stalk stiff-legged and menacing toward nothing at all. Sometimes the Thing would be just a little to the right or left of a visitor. Once a Fuller Brush salesman got hysterics. Muggs came wandering into the room like Hamlet[6] following his father's ghost. His eyes were fixed on a spot just to the left of the Fuller Brush man, who stood it until Muggs was about three slow, creeping paces from him. Then he shouted. Muggs wavered on past him into the hallway grumbling to himself but the Fuller man went on shouting. I think mother had to throw a pan of cold water on him before he stopped. That was the way she used to stop us boys when we got into fights.

Muggs died quite suddenly one night. Mother wanted to bury him in the family lot under a marble stone with some such inscription as "Flights of angels sing thee to thy rest" but we persuaded her it was against the law. In the end we just put up a smooth board above his grave along a lonely road. On the board I wrote with an indelible pencil "Cave Canem."[7] Mother was quite pleased with the simple classic dignity of the old Latin epitaph.

---

6. **Hamlet:** The tragic hero of the play *Hamlet* by William Shakespeare. Hamlet follows his father's ghost and learns that his father, a Danish king, had been murdered by Hamlet's uncle Claudius.

7. **Cave Canem** (kä´ vā kä´ nem): Latin for "Beware the dog."

◆ **Build Vocabulary**

indignant (in dig´ nǝnt) *adj.*: Feeling or expressing anger or scorn, especially at an injustice

epitaph (ep´ ǝ taf´) *n.*: Inscription on a tomb or gravestone

Guide for Responding

◆ *Literature and Your Life*

Reader's Response Which one of Muggs's escapades did you find most amusing? Why?

Thematic Focus James Thurber uses humor to lighten the seriousness of his dog's behavioral problems. Tell about an incident in which you used humor to ease a conflict or lighten a moment in your life.

Sketch Do a quick, humorous drawing of Muggs attacking his latest victim.

☑ Check Your Comprehension

1. Who is the only person in Thurber's family never bitten by Muggs?
2. Briefly summarize the anecdote about Muggs and the mice.
3. Describe Thurber's "foolhardy" experience with Muggs.
4. Describe how Muggs eats his meals. Why does he eat this way?
5. Tell what Muggs does in his last year.

The Dog That Bit People ◆ 239

Beyond the Selection

FURTHER READING

Other Works by James Thurber
The Owl in the Attic and Other Perplexities
The Middle-Aged Man on the Flying Trapeze

Other Works About Animals and Conflict
Whitefang, Jack London
"Growltiger's Last Stand," T. S. Eliot
We suggest that you preview these works before recommending them to your students.

INTERNET
Students can read excerpts from Thurber's *Fables for Our Time* at the following Internet address. (Please be aware that sites may have changed since we published this information.)
http://www.escape.com/~tansal/Authors/Thurber/index.htm
We *strongly recommend* that you preview this site before sending students to it.

239

◆ Critical Thinking

1. Muggs is a cranky, temperamental, spoiled dog.
2. Thurber tolerates Muggs, his brother Roy is less patient with Muggs, Uncle Horatio is aggressively disapproving of Muggs, Mother is loving and forgiving toward Muggs.
3. The family probably doesn't get rid of Muggs because Mother loves him.
4. Students should include specific examples of exaggeration, contrast, or describing something ridiculous in a serious way. Some students may suggest additional details that Thurber could have included to enhance the humor.
5. Students might suggest that school scheduling problems, vacations, or an outing with friends could be subjects for a humorous anecdote.

◆ Reading Strategy

1. Details include the grapefruit, the scattered dishes and silverware, and the crashing fire screen.
2. Details include *large*, *tan-colored*, *stumpy tail*, and *stiff-legged*.
3. Students should support their answers with examples of specific nouns, modifiers, vivid verbs, or phrases that provide the details that help them form a mental image.

◆ Literary Focus

1. Thurber's exaggerations include the reaction of the garage men to the poodle and the reactions of Roy and Uncle Horatio to Muggs's behavior. Through exaggeration he creates verbal caricatures, making the facts bigger than life to make them funnier.
2. Thurber describes the family's method for getting Muggs into the house as if he were explaining an ordinary household routine. Explaining this ridiculous activity in a serious, matter-of-fact way highlights just how ridiculous the activity is.

Guide for Responding (continued)

◆ Critical Thinking

INTERPRET

1. Describe the portrait of Muggs that Thurber paints. **[Infer]**
2. How do different family members react to the dog? **[Compare and Contrast]**
3. Why doesn't the family get rid of Muggs? **[Draw Conclusions]**

EVALUATE

4. Choose one of Thurber's stories about Muggs and rate how well Thurber conveys its humor. **[Evaluate]**

APPLY

5. Thurber describes an aspect of his home life in a humorous way. What other aspects of daily life could be the subject of a humorous essay? **[Relate]**

◆ Reading Strategy

FORM MENTAL IMAGES

The details in Thurber's story help you **form a mental image**—a picture in your mind—of Muggs and his escapades. You "see" the fear in the eyes of Mrs. Detweiler, "hear" the clash of the sheet iron that scares Muggs, and "feel" sharp teeth biting at your leg.

1. What details help you form a mental image of Roy's reaction to the chewed up newspaper? Explain.
2. Find three details that help you picture Muggs.
3. Which mental picture inspired by this essay is most vivid? Why?

◆ Literary Focus

HUMOROUS ESSAY

In his **humorous essay,** Thurber transforms everyday events into an amusing series of stories. He conveys humor by exaggerating actions and reactions and by treating silly things seriously. For example, he exaggerates Uncle Horatio's response to Muggs's eating habits to create a ridiculous picture of a "heroic" uncle defying a ferocious dog.

1. Explain how Thurber uses exaggeration to make his readers laugh.
2. Show how Thurber creates humor by treating a silly situation as if it were serious.

◆ Build Vocabulary

USING THE PREFIX *epi-*

The prefix *epi-* can mean "upon," "outside," "over," or "among." Explain how one or another of these meanings contributes to the definition of each of these words:

1. epitaph   4. epidemic
2. epidermis   5. epilogue
3. epicenter

USING THE WORD BANK

In your notebook, write a word from Column B next to its synonym from Column A.

Column A	Column B
1. irascible	a. disbelief
2. indignant	b. cranky
3. choleric	c. upset
4. incredulity	d. hot-headed
5. epitaph	e. vibration
6. jangle	f. inscription

◆ Build Grammar Skills

CORRECT USE OF *LIKE* AND *AS IF*

Thurber avoids the common usage error of using *like* in place of *as if*. As a preposition, *like* can be combined with a noun or pronoun to make a comparison. *As if* is used to introduce a subordinate clause (a group of words that contains a subject and a verb but cannot stand alone as a sentence).

Practice Complete the following sentences using *like* or *as if*.

1. Muggs behaved ____?____ he had been abused as a puppy.
2. Mother treated Muggs ____?____ a member of the family.
3. When Muggs chewed up the paper, Roy reacted ____?____ he had destroyed a rare manuscript.
4. Thurber thought Muggs was ____?____ a spoiled child.
5. Readers feel ____?____ they know Muggs and his family.

◆ Build Vocabulary

Using the Prefix *epi-*

1. An epitaph is written *upon* a tombstone.
2. The epidermis covers *over* a body.
3. The epicenter is the spot on the earth's surface directly *above* the origin of an earthquake.
4. An epidemic is a disease the spreads quickly *among* many individuals.
5. An epilogue is added *on* to the rest of a play or novel.

Using the Word Bank

1. b or d
2. c
3. b or d
4. a
5. f
6. e

◆ Build Grammar Skills

1. as if
2. like
3. as if
4. like
5. as if

Build Your Portfolio

 ## Idea Bank

Writing

1. **Lost Dog Description** Imagine Muggs is your dog and you have lost him. Write a description of him for a poster to help get him back.

2. **News Story** Write a news article about the neighborhood's quest to put a stop to Muggs's menacing ways. Answer the five standard "W" questions (*who, what, when, where,* and *why*) in your news story. **[Career Link]**

3. **Persuasive Letter to Mother** Write a letter to Mother persuading her to send Muggs for obedience training. Remind her of his past attacks and present her with success stories of pets who have attended obedience school.

Speaking and Listening

4. **Pet Talk** With a group, create a radio show called *Pet Talk.* Have some group members "call in" problems about pets and have others give advice. **[Media Link; Performing Arts Link]**

5. **Pantomime** Using only hand gestures, facial expressions, and exaggerated physical reactions, present a scene from this essay to your classmates that will bring the humor and absurdity of the situation to life for your audience. **[Performing Arts Link]**

Projects

6. **Wanted Poster** Create a "wanted" poster that features Muggs's "mug" as your subject. State Muggs's crime, physical features, and notable characteristics. **[Art Link]**

7. **Dog Breed Chart** Research the traits of several different dog breeds. Then create a chart that illustrates the characteristics of each breed. **[Science Link]**

 ## Writing Mini-Lesson

Animal Anecdote

Like Thurber, many people find humor in the behavior of animals. Write an **anecdote**—a brief account about a humorous or strange event—about an animal you've known or observed. The following tips will help you bring the situation to life.

Writing Skills Focus: Vivid Verbs

Vivid verbs will add humor to your anecdote by creating specific pictures in the minds of your readers. Notice, for example, how Thurber uses vivid verbs in this description: "I reached down and grabbed his short stumpy tail and hoisted him into the air." Yet this passage would have fallen flat if Thurber had merely written "I picked up the dog."

Incorporate vivid verbs into all the phases of your writing.

Prewriting Brainstorm for a variety of vivid verbs to describe your animal's traits and actions. For instance, *run* can be expressed more specifically as *gallop, sprint, flee, scurry,* and *dash.* Outline the sequence of events in your anecdote and jot down notes about the characters you want to include.

Drafting Exaggerate physical features and personality traits with very specific and lively verbs. Thurber exaggerates his uncle's anger by saying he "bawled" rather than "yelled."

Revising Have a partner read your anecdote and point out places where more detail would help him or her form a mental picture. Add detail by replacing general verbs with more vivid ones. Also, in describing your animal and its actions, make sure you have used *like* and *as if* correctly.

For more on *like* and *as if,* see Build Grammar Skills on pp. 232 and 240.

The Dog That Bit People ◆ 241

 ## Idea Bank
Customizing for *Learning Modalities*
Following are suggestions for matching Idea Bank topics with your students' learning modalities:
- Interpersonal: 4
- Verbal/Linguistic: 1, 2, 3, 4
- Bodily/Kinesthetic: 5
- Visual/Spatial: 6, 7

Customizing for *Performance Levels*
Following are suggestions for matching the Idea Bank topics with your students' ability levels:
- Less Advanced: 1, 5, 6
- Average: 2, 4, 5, 6, 7
- More Advanced: 3, 4, 7

 ## Writing Mini-Lesson
Refer students to the Writing Handbook, page 965, for instruction on the writing process and page 967 for further information on Anecdote.

 ## Writer's Solution

Writers at Work Videodisc
Have students view the videodisc segment (Ch. 2) featuring writer Maxine Hong Kingston talking about the importance of setting, dialogue, and atmosphere. Point out to students that these elements can be used to enhance the humor of their anecdotes.

Play frames 18612 to 19873

Writing Lab CD-ROM
Have students complete the tutorial on Narration. Follow these steps.
1. Use the Character Traits Word Bins to develop character
2. Have students use the Audio-annotated Literary Models in the Drafting section to consider ways of organizing their anecdotes.
3. Encourage students to use the Self-evaluation checklist before submitting their completed anecdotes.

Sourcebook
Have students use Chapter 2, Narration (pp. 30–61), for additional support. The chapter includes in-depth instruction on developing characters (pp. 48 and 51).

✓ ASSESSMENT OPTIONS

Formal Assessment, Selection Test, pp. 57–58, and Assessment Resources Software. The selection test is designed so that it can be easily customized to the ability levels of your students.

Alternative Assessment, p. 17, includes options for more advanced students, less advanced students, logical/mathematical learners, visual/spatial learners, verbal/linguistic learners, and musical/rhythmic learners.

PORTFOLIO ASSESSMENT
Use the following rubrics in the *Alternative Assessment* booklet to assess student writing:
Lost Dog Description: Description Rubric, p. 97
New Story: Fictional Narrative Rubric, p. 95
Persuasive Letter to Mother: Persuasion Rubric, p. 105
Writing Mini-Lesson: Fictional Narrative Rubric, p. 95

OBJECTIVES

1. To read, comprehend, and interpret poems
2. To relate poems to personal experience
3. To respond to images and ideas
4. To recognize tone
5. To build vocabulary in context and learn the word root *-chol-*
6. To distinguish between the use of *shall* and *will*
7. To write a press release for a CD using appropriate language for an audience
8. To respond to the poems through writing, speaking and listening, and projects

SKILLS INSTRUCTION

Vocabulary:
The word root *-chol-*

Grammar:
Use of *shall* and *will*

Reading Strategy:
Respond to Images and Ideas

Literature:
Tone

Writing:
Appropriate Language for an Audience

Speaking and Listening:
Dramatic Reading (teacher edition)

Critical Viewing:
Support; Infer; Compare and Contrast

PORTFOLIO OPPORTUNITIES

Writing: Newspaper Headlines; Interview; Song Lyrics

Writing Mini-Lesson: Press Release for a Favorite CD

Speaking and Listening: Music Panel; Dramatic Reading

Projects: Graphic Design; Music Timeline

More About the Authors

In 1985, while a visiting professor at New York University, **Nina Cassian** found that it would be unsafe for her to return to Romania, then under Communist rule. New York is now her home.

As a young woman, **Edna St. Vincent Millay** acted with the Provincetown Players, a group credited with promoting a revitalization of American theater after World War I.

Langston Hughes wrote newspaper sketches, stories, novels, plays, and scripts for radio and film.

When **Carl Sandburg's** *Chicago Poems* was first published, he was at first criticized harshly for his "gutter naturalism."

*G*uide for Reading

Nina Cassian (1924–   )

Poet Nina Cassian, gymnast Nadia Comaneci, and mythical figure Dracula have something in common. They're all from Romania! Cassian studied music at the Bucharest Conservatory of Music in Romania and is a past Romanian State Prize Poet Laureate. Today she lives and works in New York City.

Edna St. Vincent Millay (1892–1950)

Actress, popular poet, foreign correspondent, and isolated writer—all these words describe Edna St. Vincent Millay, yet none captures her completely. She wrote and spoke her mind on controversial issues from women's rights to political freedom. Her opinions brought her public praise and public scorn. She retired from public life in 1925, moved to a farm, and wrote lyrical poems until her death.

Langston Hughes (1901–1967)

Langston Hughes makes music with words the way a blues musician plays notes on the saxophone. About poetry, he has said: "It is the human soul entire, squeezed like a lemon or lime, drop by drop, into atomic words." Hughes read both Walt Whitman and Carl Sandburg as a high-school student, and he was especially influenced by Carl Sandburg's "Jazz Fantasia," published in 1919.

Carl Sandburg (1876–1960)

Carl Sandburg once said that some poetry was perfect only in form, "all dressed up with nowhere to go." The poetry of Carl Sandburg may have been dressed only in blue jeans, but it went everywhere and spoke in the voice of everyday people. That same voice came through in this poet's Pulitzer Prize-winning biography of Lincoln.

◆ Build Vocabulary

WORD ROOTS: *-chol-*

In "The Weary Blues," we hear a voice with a *melancholy* tone. The word root *-chol-* refers to bile, a digestive fluid that was once believed to be one of the four "humors," or bodily fluids governing health and disposition. *Melancholy,* which means literally "black bile," supposedly caused depression and irritability. It's easy to understand how *melancholy* came to mean "sad" or "depressed."

WORD BANK

As you read these poems, you will encounter the words on this list. Each word is defined on the page where it first appears. Preview the list before you read.

reap
pallor
melancholy

◆ Build Grammar Skills

USE OF *SHALL* AND *WILL*

When Millay writes, "I shall die, but that is all that I shall do for Death," *shall* gives special emphasis to the speaker's determination to avoid assisting Death.

At one time **shall** was used when expressing future actions in the first person (*I, we*) and *will* for the second (*you*) and third person (*he, she, it, they*). Today *will* is the accepted form for first, second, and third person future and *shall* is used—as Millay does—to emphasize determination or indicate that something *must* happen.

Notice how these poets choose to use *shall* or *will* in their poems, depending on whether or not they want to create emphasis.

Prentice Hall Literature Program Resources

REINFORCE / RETEACH / EXTEND

Selection Support Pages
Build Vocabulary: The Word Root *-chol-*, p. 72
Build Grammar Skills: Use of *Shall* and *Will*, p. 73
Reading Strategy: Respond to Images and Ideas, p. 74
Literary Focus: Tone, p. 75

Strategies for Diverse Student Needs, p. 18

Beyond Literature
Cross-Curricular Connection: Music, p. 18

Formal Assessment Selection Test, pp. 60–62; Assessment Resources Software

Alternative Assessment, p. 18

Resource Pro CD-ROM
"A Man," "Conscientious Objector," "The Weary Blues," "Jazz Fantasia"— includes all resource materials and customizable lesson plan

Listening to Literature Audiocassettes
"Conscientious Objector," "A Man," "The Weary Blues," "Jazz Fantasia"

Literature CD-ROM
Reading Poetry

Conscientious Objector ◆ A Man
The Weary Blues ◆ Jazz Fantasia

Interest Grabber Tell students that a conscientious objector is a person who, for reasons of conscience, refuses to take part in warfare. Then play the Listening to Literature audiocassette recording "Conscientious Objector." Tell students to listen for the examples Millay offers of ways that some people collaborate with death. Then ask students to suggest examples from recent history and current events. Point out the poems in this group are affirmations of life and hopefulness. Tell students to look for the way each poet celebrates life.

◆ *Literature and Your Life*

CONNECT YOUR EXPERIENCE

You're walking along and you hear your favorite song through the open window of a passing car. Most likely, it influences how you feel and what you're thinking. Music of any kind can call forth an emotional response. The sounds, rhythms, and lyrics stir memories and call up feelings.

Two of these poems focus specifically on types of music, but all the poets express their ideas through the music of words.

Journal Writing Write a few sentences explaining how one of your favorite songs inspires you to face life's challenges.

THEMATIC FOCUS: PERSONAL CHALLENGES

Music helps two of the speakers in these poems to face life's challenges by lifting their spirits. Music is just one answer to the question, "Where do we find the strength to face challenges?"

◆ Background for Understanding

MUSIC

Two of these poems deal with specific musical forms. The music called the blues originated as folk music of African Americans. Early blues was characterized by mournful vocals and repetitive lyrics that told a story. Instruments, particularly guitars, were added to imitate and accompany the vocalists.

Jazz, which developed from blues, has been called the only art form to originate in the United States. Both Hughes and Sandburg capture the spontaneity and originality of these distinctly American forms of music.

◆ Literary Focus

TONE

A singer's attitude affects your response to a song. Similarly, your response to poems is influenced by the **tone** of the poem, the attitude the poet takes toward the poem's subject. In song or in conversation, a person conveys a certain attitude mainly through tone of voice. Usually, poets can't speak their poems for you. They must convey attitudes by choosing precise words and specific images.

In reading these poems, look for the words that communicate the poet's attitude. Sandburg, for example, conveys his enthusiasm for jazz with vivid verbs like *sob* and *batter*.

◆ Reading Strategy

RESPOND TO IMAGES AND IDEAS

Whether you're discussing the great lyrics on your favorite CD or which poems you like and dislike, you are sharing a response. When you **respond to images and ideas** in poetry, you are reacting to the sensory descriptions and thoughts in a poem.

As you read these poems, respond to them with your whole self—your mind, your heart, and your senses. You don't need to be an expert on jazz, for example, to respond to Sandburg's instruction to jazz musicians:

> "Moan like an autumn wind high in the lonesome treetops, ..."

Just hear the "autumn wind" and remember what it's like to be lonesome.

Guide for Reading ◆ 243

Customize for
Less Proficient Readers
To aid literal comprehension, encourage students to preview the Check Your Comprehension questions before reading each poem. These questions will give students a focus around which to organize the details of each poem.

Customize for
More Advanced Students
Have students determine which of the poems uses the following as the dominant figure of speech: metaphor (*"A Man"*), personification (*"Conscientious Objector"*), onomatopoeia (*"Jazz Fantasia"*). Which poem makes the least use of figurative language, but makes the most of rhythm and rhyme? (*"The Weary Blues"*)

Customize for
English Language Learners
Help these students understand the dialect and musical expressions in "The Weary Blues" and "Jazz Fantasia."

Customize for
Musical/Rhythmic Learners
Have these students read the poems aloud to hear the rhythms and sound patterns in each poem.

✎ Preparing for Standardized Tests

Reading and Vocabulary The Build Vocabulary lesson for these selections focuses on the word root *-chol-*. Practice with using word roots to determine meaning will improve students' performance on vocabulary and comprehension items on the verbal portions of standardized tests. For additional practice, use the Build Vocabulary page in **Selection Support**, p. 72.

Some standardized tests ask students to complete analogies in the following way:

Choose the pair that *best* expresses a relationship

similar to the one expressed by the capitalized pair. *(A) a real animal and a mythical one.*

GOAT: UNICORN (A) horse: dragon,
(B) ram: bull,   (C) sheep: dog,
(D) mountain: milk,   (E) fox: wolf

The vocabulary exercises at the end of the group of poems require students to complete analogies using the words they have learned in context. Practicing this kind of exercise will improve students' ability to identify relationships between words and ideas.

In "Conscientious Objector," the proud, determined speaker refuses to cooperate in any way—passive or active—with the forces of death. Through allusions and figurative language, Millay communicates a timeless portrait of an individual who accepts that evil forces exist in the world, but refuses to surrender to them.

◆ Literary Focus

① Tone Ask students to identify the ways that the poet immediately establishes a serious, determined tone. *The directness of the statement and the use of the word* shall *give the opening line a serious tone, as if the speaker is making a proclamation.*

◆ Build Grammar Skills

② Use of *Shall* and *Will* Point out the emphasis the poet creates by using the word *shall*.

③ Clarification Cuba, an island country in the West Indies, has a long history of struggle for independence and social reform. In the early part of the twentieth century the government's lack of interest in the plight of the lower classes led to violent uprisings. The Balkans are located in the southeast corner of Europe. Throughout history, this region has been plagued with ethnic conflicts and political dispute. The bloody Balkan wars at the beginning of the twentieth century and the high tension prior to World War I earned the area the name "the powder keg of Europe."

◆ Reading Strategy

④ Respond to Images and Ideas Ask students how these images communicate the poet's message about death. *These images suggest that the poet associates fear and oppression with death.*

Conscientious Objector

Edna St. Vincent Millay

①
② I shall die, but that is all that I shall do for Death.

I hear him leading his horse out of the stall; I hear the clatter on the barn-floor.
③ He is in haste; he has business in Cuba, business in the Balkans, many calls to make this morning.
But I will not hold the bridle while he cinches the girth.[1]
5 And he may mount by himself: I will not give him a leg up.

Though he flick my shoulders with his whip, I will not tell him which way the fox ran.
④ With his hoof on my breast, I will not tell him where the black boy hides in the swamp.
I shall die, but that is all that I shall do for Death; I am not on his pay-roll.

I will not tell him the whereabouts of my friends nor of my enemies either.
10 Though he promise me much, I will not map him the route to any man's door.

Am I a spy in the land of the living, that I should deliver men to Death?
Brother, the password and the plans of our city are safe with me; never through me
Shall you be overcome.

---

1. **bridle . . . cinches . . . girth:** *n., v., n.:* Terms that apply to horses. Harness; fastens on; band put around the belly of a horse for holding a saddle.

◆ Block Scheduling Strategies

Consider these suggestions to take advantage of extended class time:

- Have students share their explanations from the Journal Writing activity (p. 243) about how songs can inspire people to face life's challenges. Ask students to identify some specific images and ideas from songs that they find inspiring.

- Introduce the literary concept of tone. Have students read the Literary Focus on tone on page 243 and answer the

questions on page 248. **Selection Support**, p. 75. Use the Literature CD-ROM Reading Poetry feature 5, to prepare students to read these works.

- As a class, discuss the Music Connection, p. 248, and complete the activity on listening to the blues. Follow up by allowing students to complete the Cross-Curricular page on which students complete a comparison and contrast chart on jazz and the blues. (**Beyond Literature**, p. 18)

- Have students work together in small groups to discuss the Reading Strategy questions (p. 248). Which images were most vivid? Which ideas were the most compelling?

- Assign specific research tasks to individual students and combine their findings to complete the Music Timeline activity, p. 249, as a class.

A Man

Nina Cassian
Translated by Roy MacGregor-Hastie

While fighting for his country, he lost an arm
and was suddenly afraid:
"From now on, I shall only be able to do
    things by halves.
I shall <u>reap</u> half a harvest.

5 I shall be able to play either the tune
or the accompaniment on the piano,
but never both parts together.
I shall be able to bang with only one fist
on doors, and worst of all
10 I shall only be able to half hold
my love close to me.
There will be things I cannot do at all,
applaud for example,
at shows where everyone applauds."

15 From that moment on, he set himself to do
everything with twice as much enthusiasm.
And where the arm had been torn away
a wing grew.

◆ **Build Vocabulary**
reap (rēp) *v.*: Gather

▲ **Critical Viewing** What details in this picture reflect the sentiments of the man in these poems? **[Support]**

❺ **Respond to Images and Ideas** Discuss how the inability to applaud isolates the speaker more than the other adjustments he mentions. *The speaker is able to participate to some degree in other activities but there is no way to applaud partially.*

▶**Critical Viewing**◀

❻ **Support** The upward flight of the bird reflects the freedom of the speaker in "Conscientious Objector" and the hopefulness of the man at the end of Nina Cassian's poem. The wind or air currents pushing against the bird suggest that freedom and hopefulness require effort.

Reinforce and Extend

Answers

Reader's Response Students may suggest that the speakers would admire each other's determination and optimism.

Thematic Focus Some people are intimidated by challenges, some are inspired by them.

☑ **Check Your Comprehension**
1. The man lost an arm.
2. The speaker will not help Death prepare for his journey. The speaker will not betray friends or enemies. Some students may give more literal answers from the poem, such as holding the bridle, or telling where the fox ran.

◆ **Critical Thinking**
1. The image of a wing ends the poem on an upbeat note.
2. Death is a greater enemy.
3. People can refuse to cooperate with Death in their everyday lives by avoiding unhealthy practices and substances, by not accepting injustice or cruelty, and by being aware of world events.
4. Optimism, determination, patience, and compassion are important qualities for a person working with the physically challenged.

Guide for Responding

◆ Literature and Your Life

Reader's Response How do you think the speakers of these poems would feel about each other?

Thematic Focus Challenges call forth emotional responses from these speakers. What are some other responses people have to challenges?

☑ **Check Your Comprehension**
1. What happened to the man in "A Man" when he was "fighting for his country"?
2. In "Conscientious Objector," what are two things the speaker will not do?

◆ Critical Thinking

INTERPRET
1. Why do you think the poet chooses the image of a wing to end "A Man"? **[Interpret]**
2. Why do you think the speaker in "Conscientious Objector" will not tell the whereabouts even of enemies? **[Speculate]**

APPLY
3. In what ways can ordinary people refuse to "cooperate with Death" in their day-to-day lives? **[Relate]**

EXTEND
4. What qualities are important for physical therapists or counselors who work with the physically challenged? **[Career Link]**

Conscientious Objector/A Man ◆ 245

Speaking and Listening Mini-Lesson

Dramatic Reading
This mini-lesson supports the Speaking and Listening activity in the Idea Bank on page 249.

Introduce the Concept Introduce the term "oral interpretation," bringing out that a reader's interpretation of a poem is communicated by her or his performance. Refer students to the Speaking and Listening Handbook, p. 100, for more information on oral interpretation.

Develop Background Have students copy the poems they choose into their notebooks. Guide

them in marking the copy to indicate words to be stressed, places to pause, and sections to read more emphatically or softly.

Apply the Information Have students practice their performances with partners and then deliver their oral interpretations to the class.

Assess the Outcome Use the Oral Interpretation peer assessment page in *Alternative Assessment*, p. 119

One-Minute Insight

Hughes captures the languid repetition and syncopation of the blues by using long sentences punctuated with shorter ones. The repeated ō and o͞o sounds echo the crooning of a blues singer. Like a story within a story, the poem conveys the "blues" of the life of a blues musician.

◆ Reading Strategy

❶ Respond to Images and Ideas Ask students what they see, hear, and feel based on this section. *Students may say they hear soft, slow singing and piano music. They may see an African American man singing and swaying in the dim light. Some students may say they feel the swaying sensation created by the music and the man's motion.*

◆ Literary Focus

❷ Tone Ask students which words convey a melancholy tone. Why do they think the poet chose this tone for this poem? *Words that convey a melancholy tone include* poor piano, moan, rickety stool, *and* sad raggy tune. *The melancholy tone echoes the melancholy tone of the blues music that is the subject of the poem.*

Customize for *Musical/Rhythmic Learners*

Have musical/rhythmic learners sway while they read the poem aloud. Ask them how the length of the lines and the tone of the words affect their motion. *Students may suggest that the long lines and melancholy tone lead to a slow, relaxed swaying motion.*

▶Critical Viewing◀

❸ Infer The relaxed poses and smiling faces of the people, and the prominence of the instruments in the picture indicate that these musicians enjoy playing the blues.

Customize for *Logical/Mathematical Learners*

Have logical/mathematical learners compare and contrast Sandburg's and Hughes's poems, noting how the music styles described are alike and how they are different. Students can organize their ideas in a chart.

The Weary Blues

Langston Hughes

❶
Droning a drowsy syncopated[1] tune,
Rocking back and forth to a mellow croon,
    I heard a Negro play.
Down on Lenox Avenue the other night
5 By the pale dull <u>pallor</u> of an old gas light
    He did a lazy sway. . . .
    He did a lazy sway. . . .
To the tune o' those Weary Blues.
With his ebony hands on each ivory key
10 He made that poor piano moan with
    melody.
    O Blues!
❷ Swaying to and fro on his rickety stool
He played that sad raggy tune like a
    musical fool.
    Sweet Blues!

---

1. **syncopated** (siŋ´ kə pā´ tid) *adj.*: With rhythm shifted stressing beats that are ordinarily weak.

15 Coming from a black man's soul.
    O Blues!
In a deep song voice with a <u>melancholy</u>
    tone
I heard that Negro sing, that old piano
    moan—
    "Ain't got nobody in all this world,
20   Ain't got nobody but ma self.
    I's gwine to quit ma frownin'
    And put ma troubles on the shelf."
Thump, thump, thump, went his foot on
    the floor.
He played a few chords then he sang
    some more—
25   "I got the Weary Blues
    And I can't be satisfied.
    Got the Weary Blues
    And can't be satisfied—
    I ain't happy no mo'
30   And I wish that I had died."
And far into the night he crooned that
    tune.
The stars went out and so did the moon.
The singer stopped playing and went to
    bed
While the Weary Blues echoed through
    his head.
35 He slept like a rock or a man that's
    dead.

◀ **Critical Viewing** How can you tell that these musicians enjoy playing the blues? [Infer] ❸

◆ Build Vocabulary

pallor (pal´ ər) *n.*: Lack of color; unnatural paleness
melancholy (mel´ ən käl´ ē) *adj.*: Sad and depressed

246 ◆ *Clashing Forces*

 Humanities: Art

Solo/Interval, 1987, by Romare Bearden.
Although he was born more than a decade after Langston Hughes, Romare Bearden (1912–1988), like Hughes and the writers and artists of the Harlem Renaissance, focuses on themes from African American life and culture. Many of his works, including *Solo/Interval,* are collages, combinations of paper, magazine cutouts, paint, and photographs.

Bearden received the National Medal of Arts in 1987.

Use the following question for discussion: Why is collage a good technique to employ in depicting a jazz man? *Both collage and jazz allow the artist a certain amount of freedom and room to improvise. Like music, collage combines individual parts to create a unified composition.*

246

Jazz Fantasia

Carl Sandburg

❹

Drum on your drums, batter on your banjoes,
sob on the long cool winding saxophones.
Go to it, O jazzmen.

5 Sling your knuckles on the bottoms of the happy
tin pans, let your trombones ooze, and go husha-
husha-hush with the slippery sand-paper.

Moan like an autumn wind high in the lonesome treetops,
moan soft like you wanted somebody terrible, cry like a
racing car slipping away from a motorcycle cop,
10 bang-bang! you jazzmen, bang altogether drums, traps,
banjoes, horns, tin cans—make two people fight on the
top of a stairway and scratch each other's eyes in a
clinch[1] tumbling down the stairs.

Can[2] the rough stuff . . . now a Mississippi steamboat
15 pushes up the night river with a hoo-hoo-hoo-oo . . . and
the green lanterns calling to the high soft stars . . . a red
moon rides on the humps of the low river hills . . . go to it,
O jazzmen.

---

1. **clinch** (klinch) *n*.: Slang for embrace.
2. **can**: Slang for stop.

Autumn Lamp (Guitar player), 1983, Romare Bearden, From the Mecklenburg Autumn Series, Oil with collage, 40" x 31", Private collection, ©1997 Romare Bearden Foundation/Licensed by VAGA, New York, New York

Critical Viewing Compare and contrast the musicians in the paintings by Romare Bearden on these pages. **[Compare and Contrast]** **❺**

One-Minute Insight Sandburg combines slang and musical expressions to create a unique, jumpy rhythm that echoes the energetic rhythms of jazz.

◆ Literary Focus

❹ Tone Which words and expressions indicate Sandburg's attitude toward his subject? *Expressive words such as* drum, batter, sob, sling, *and* ooze *indicate Sandburg's enjoyment of the sounds of the music.*

▶Critical Viewing◀

❺ Compare and Contrast The trumpet player is more elegantly dressed, the colors in his clothes are varied and jewel-like. The guitar player is dressed casually; in his picture, most of the color is primary colors (yellow and blue, which occasionally overlap to make green).

Reinforce and Extend

Answers
◆ *Literature and Your Life*

Reader's Response Some students may prefer the relaxed, bittersweet music described by Hughes while others may lean toward the energetic variations described by Sandburg.

Thematic Focus Students will probably respond that a positive attitude helps people meet challenges more effectively than if they approach a challenge with a negative attitude.

☑ Check Your Comprehension
1. Sandburg describes jazz.
2. Hughes describes the blues.

◆ Critical Thinking
1. Jazz is a mix of instruments played with energy and passion.
2. The piano player/singer is a talented persistent man who is resigned to a difficult life.
3. Students may say that Hughes captures the feeling of the blues in the varied line lengths, the melancholy words, and the images of the singer swaying and crooning. Sandburg expresses the sound of jazz with onomatopoeic words like husha-husha, and hoo-hoo-hoo.

Guide for Responding

◆ *Literature and Your Life*

Reader's Response Would you rather listen to the music described in "The Weary Blues" or in "Jazz Fantasia"? Why?

Thematic Focus Both these poems describe a musical "attitude," or mood. How does attitude affect the way people face challenges?

☑ Check Your Comprehension
1. What kind of music does Sandburg describe?
2. What kind of music does Hughes describe?

◆ Critical Thinking

INTERPRET
1. Using Sandburg's images as a source of information, write a brief definition of jazz. **[Interpret]**
2. Describe the personality of the piano player and singer in "The Weary Blues." **[Draw Conclusions]**

EVALUATE
3. Rate how well each poet captures the feeling of the music he describes. Support your answer with examples from the poems. **[Evaluate]**

The Weary Blues / Jazz Fantasia ◆ 247

Beyond the Selection

FURTHER READING

Other Works by the Poets
Call Yourself Alive?, Nina Cassian
Selected Poems of Langston Hughes
Selected Poems of Edna St. Vincent Millay
The Complete Poems of Carl Sandburg

RELATED WORKS
Moment's Notice: Jazz in Poetry and Prose, edited by Art Lange and Nathaniel Mackey
We suggest that you preview these works before recommending them to students.

INTERNET
Students can find out more about the poets featured in this section at the following Web sites. Please be aware that sites may have changed since we published this information.

Hughes: **http://ie.uwindsor.ca/jazz/hughes. html**
Millay: **http://www.millaycolony.org/ednabio. html**
Sandburg: **http://www.lis.uiuc.edu/~roberts/ carlpage.htm**

We *strongly recommend* that you preview these sites before sending students to them.

247

◆ Reading Strategy

1. Some students will respond most to the image of the wing. Some may respond to the individual examples of fears expressed by the man.

2. Most students will probably think that "A Man" expresses the most upbeat ideas and that "Jazz Fantasia" has the most upbeat images of music and enjoyment.

3. Students should include in their answers reasons based on the rhythms and instruments mentioned in the poems.

◆ Literary Focus

1. The wing conveys the positive tone of "A Man." It suggests that the man will "fly," that he will rise above his difficulties.

2. "The Weary Blues" has a relaxed, easygoing tone. Details include the swaying of the musician, the repetition of words and sounds, and words like *droning* and *drowsy*.

3. Some words that indicate the tone of "Jazz Fantasia" include *sob, happy, moan, tumbling*. These words indicate the intensity of the poet's feelings about jazz.

Beyond Literature

Music Connection Use the Comparison and Contrast Organizer in *Writing and Language Transparencies*, p. 95, on the overhead projector to complete the Beyond Literature activity on this page as a class. Alternatively, distribute copies of the organizer and have students complete the activity independently.

◆ Build Vocabulary

1. A choleric person is quick-tempered and has a negative outlook.

2. Melancholy is a sad feeling or mood.

3. Cholera is related to physical health; it is an intestinal disease.

4. Too much cholesterol can cause physical health problems.

5. Choler is anger, believed in the past to be caused by too much bile in the system.

Using the Word Bank

1. reap; 2. melancholy; 3. pallor

Guide for Responding (continued)

◆ Reading Strategy

RESPOND TO IMAGES AND IDEAS

Your own experience and knowledge influence the way you **respond to the images and ideas** in these poems. In "A Man," the image of a wing may call up a sense of freedom or possibility.

1. To which image in "A Man" do you respond most strongly? Why?

2. Which poem did you feel had the most upbeat images and ideas? Explain.

3. Do the descriptions in "Jazz Fantasia" and "The Weary Blues" make you want to listen to these forms of music? Why or why not?

◆ Literary Focus

TONE

Tone—a speaker's attitude toward the subject—helps convey a poem's meaning and creates an effect on its audience. For instance, the speaker's attitude in "Conscientious Objector" is dignified. This gives the poem a serious, purposeful tone.

1. What image helps to convey the positive tone of "A Man"? Explain.

2. Describe the tone of "The Weary Blues." Support your answer with details from the poem.

3. Identify three words that indicate the tone of "Jazz Fantasia." Explain.

Beyond Literature

Music Connection

The Blues Now one of the most recognizable types of music worldwide, the music known as the blues has come a long way from its roots along the rural back byways of the Mississippi Delta. It has influenced musical forms as varied as jazz, rock-and-roll, rhythm and blues, and soul music.

Activity Listen to a blues recording by B. B. King, such as "The Thrill Is Gone," and compare it to a selection of your favorite music. Create a chart showing similarities and differences in lyrics, types of instruments, and tempo.

◆ Build Vocabulary

USING THE ROOT -chol-

Using your knowledge of the root -chol- (and a dictionary if necessary), explain how each of the following words containing the root -chol- relates to physical health, outlook, or mood.

1. choleric   4. cholesterol

2. melancholy   5. choler

3. cholera

USING THE WORD BANK

For each of the following, notice that the second word of the first pair is a characteristic or result of the first word. In your notebook, write the word from the Word Bank that best completes the second word pair.

1. *Spring* is to *plant* as *autumn* is to ____?____.

2. *Good luck* is to *joy* as *bad luck* is to ____?____.

3. *Happiness* is to *smile* as *sickness* is to ____?____.

◆ Build Grammar Skills

USE OF SHALL AND WILL

At one time, **shall** was used to express future actions in the first person. **Will** was used for the second and third person. Today, the difference between *shall* and *will* is no longer a question of correct usage but a question of emphasis. *Shall* indicates determination or compulsion.

Practice Copy the following sentences in your notebook. Complete each sentence with *shall* or *will* and explain why you made your choice.

1. They (will, shall) never surrender.

2. Mary (will, shall) call you later.

3. I (will, shall) never harm a living creature.

4. She (will, shall) meet us at the store.

5. Her inspiring words (will, shall) not soon be forgotten.

◆ Build Grammar Skills

1. shall
2. will
3. shall
4. will
5. shall

Build Your Portfolio

Idea Bank

Writing

1. Newspaper Headlines Write a headline for each poem in this group that expresses the main idea of the poem and grabs the reader's interest. For instance, the headline for "A Man" might read "Hope Helps Man Grow Wings."

2. Interview Write an interview with the speaker of one of these poems. Base your questions on your response to the poem; base the speaker's response on the tone and content of the poem.

3. Song Lyrics Sandburg and Hughes write about music that helps them and others face some of life's challenges. Write song lyrics about a challenge you have faced. **[Music Link]**

Speaking and Listening

4. Music Panel With a small group, listen to a variety of songs and nonvocal pieces. (Group members may each choose one for the group to hear.) After listening, discuss what you liked or disliked about each of the pieces. Create a chart recording your responses. **[Music Link]**

5. Dramatic Reading Prepare a dramatic reading of one of these poems. Decide how you will use volume and tempo to help you express the tone of the poem. **[Performing Arts Link]**

Projects

6. Graphic Design Design a CD cover for the music described in "The Weary Blues" or "Jazz Fantasia." You can either sketch your design or write out the description. **[Art Link]**

7. Music Timeline Create a music timeline that indicates a major event in each of the past ten decades and the music that was popular at the time. **[Music Link]**

Writing Mini-Lesson

Press Release for a Favorite CD

Certain lines and phrases in Carl Sandburg's "Jazz Fantasia" could be used in a brief promotional statement (a press release) for a jazz CD. Write a **press release** for your favorite CD, explaining what the music is, who created it, why it's good, and when the CD will be available. The following tips will help you choose the right language to communicate with your readers.

Writing Skills Focus: Appropriate Language for the Audience

In almost every type of writing, including press releases and position papers, you must use **appropriate language for the audience.** You can assume, for example, that your readers probably know something about the style of music or the group featured on the CD. Their interest in the music means they have a basic vocabulary they share with others interested in this type of music. In "The Weary Blues," Hughes includes words like *syncopated, croon,* and *ivory key* that would be clear to any lover of the blues.

Before you begin writing, think about the words and phrases you usually use when you talk about the music you are describing. Keep them in mind as you draft and revise.

Prewriting Discuss the CD with a partner who shares your enthusiasm for it. As you speak, jot down expressions and words you use to describe what you like about the music and the musicians.

Drafting Write as if you were convincing a friend to buy this CD. Use the words and phrases that you jotted down before you began writing.

Revising Show your press release to several people. Ask them what catches their interest most and if it appears early enough in the press release. If not, consider moving it to the first paragraph.

Idea Bank

Customizing for *Learning Modalities*

Following are suggestions for matching Idea Bank topics with your students' learning modalities.

Musical/Rhythmic: 4, 5
Verbal/Linguistic: 5
Interpersonal: 4, 5
Intrapersonal: 6, 7
Visual/Spatial: 6, 7
Mathematical/Logical: 4, 7

Customizing for *Performance Levels*

Following are suggestions for matching the Idea Bank topics with your students' ability levels.

Less Advanced: 1, 4, 6
Average: 2, 4, 5, 6, 7
More Advanced: 3, 4, 5, 7

Writing Mini-Lesson

Refer students to the Writing Handbook on page 965 for instruction on the writing process, and page 968 for further information on persuasion.

Writer's at Work Videodisc

Play the videodisc segment (Ch. 4) featuring Sayu Bhojwani, who writes promotional pieces for the Asia Society. Tell students to use her tips for connecting with an audience while writing their press releases.

Play frames 33643 to 43235

Writing Lab CD-ROM

Have students complete the following steps in the tutorial on Persuasion.

1. In the prewriting section, play the video clip and use the audio-annotated models that demonstrate the importance of using appropriate language.
2. Use the cluster diagram to organize main idea and details.
3. In the publishing and presenting section, view the tips for presenting an ad.

Sourcebook

Use Chapter 4, Persuasion (pp. 97–123), for additional support. The chapter includes in-depth instruction on writing for different audiences (p. 113).

✓ ASSESSMENT OPTIONS

Formal Assessment, Selection Test, pp. 60–61, and Assessment Resources Software.
Alternative Assessment, p. 18, includes options for less advanced students, more advanced students, musical/rhythmic learners, interpersonal learners, visual/spatial learners, and verbal/linguistic learners.

PORTFOLIO ASSESSMENT
Use the following rubrics in the *Alternative Assessment* booklet to assess student writing and activities:
Song Lyrics: Expression Rubric, p. 94
Dramatic Reading: Poetry Rubric, p. 108
Writing Mini-Lesson: Persuasion Rubric, p. 105

Guide for Reading

OBJECTIVES

1. To read, comprehend, and interpret a short story and poem
2. To relate a story and poem to personal experience
3. To identify the consequences of characters' actions
4. To recognize irony
5. To build vocabulary in context and learn the word root *-gratis-*
6. To use comparative and superlative forms correctly
7. To write a review of a song with supporting details
8. To respond to the story through writing, speaking and listening, and projects

SKILLS INSTRUCTION

Vocabulary:
The Word Root *-gratis-*

Grammar:
Comparative and Superlative Forms

Reading Strategy:
Identify Consequences of Actions

Literary Focus:
Irony

Writing:
Supporting Details

Critical Viewing:
Interpret

PORTFOLIO OPPORTUNITIES

Writing: Advice Column; Guidelines; Fairy Tale
Writing Mini-Lesson: Review of a Song
Speaking and Listening: Oral Argument, Debate
Projects: Indian Folk Songs; Map

More About the Authors

Like Sekhar in the story, **Narayan** was a village school teacher. He is now, perhaps, the best-known Indian writing in English today. For his skill with characterization, he has been compared to such writers as Chekhov and Isaac Bashevis Singer.

Emily Dickinson, famous as America's first "modern" poet, was as reclusive as Narayan is sociable. Dickinson, who lived from 1830–1886, was a vivacious and affectionate child, but soon retreated to her room, and would see no one for most of her life.

R. K. Narayan (1906–)

If the Indian writer R. K. Narayan lived in your city or town, he might turn it on its head to create an imaginary place full of characters that would make you smile in recognition.

Narayan's own town, Mysore, probably served as the basis for his fictional town of Malgudi, a place full of eccentric characters who find themselves in peculiar situations.

Imaginary Town Writers sometimes devise special settings for the cast of characters that pass through their books, and Narayan has done this with Malgudi. "Malgudi was an earth-shaking discovery for me, because I had no mind for facts and things like that, which would be necessary in writing about . . . any real place." Narayan's fictional south Indian town of Malgudi has seen so many changes and human dramas that it almost seems like a character itself.

Narayan's Languages R. K. Narayan, whose initials stand for Rasipuram Kirshnaswamy, speaks both the Indian language Tamil and English—but he writes all his fiction in English. As a child, he was also taught traditional Indian melodies and prayers in Sanskrit. As an adult, Narayan went on to translate from Sanskrit the ancient Indian epic *Mahabharata*, a poem consisting of more than 90,000 pairs of rhyming lines!

Literary Forms R. K. Narayan has written extensively in several forms: novels, short stories, essays, and travel books among them.

If you want to find out more about the life of R. K. Narayan, you might be interested in reading his memoir, *My Days*. His best-known novels include *Swami and Friends* (1935), *The English Teacher* (1945), and *The Painter of Signs* (1976).

◆ Build Vocabulary

WORD ROOTS: *-gratis-*
In "Like the Sun," you will learn that Sekhar's boss behaves in an ingratiating way. Knowing that the word root *-gratis-* comes from a Latin word meaning "pleasing" or "a favor," you can figure out that being *ingratiating* means "trying to please."

WORD BANK

| essence |
| tempering |
| shirked |
| incessantly |
| ingratiating |
| stupefied |
| scrutinized |

As you read "Like the Sun," you will encounter the words on this list. Each word is defined on the page where it first appears. Preview the list before you read, and identify any words that are already familiar to you. In your notebook, write what you think they mean.

◆ Build Grammar Skills

COMPARATIVE AND SUPERLATIVE FORMS
When writers compare two things, they use the **comparative form** of an adjective. To compare more than two things, they use the **superlative form**.

Comparative Form: No judge delivering a sentence felt *more pained* and *hopeless*.

In comparing a story character with one other person, the author uses the comparative form of the adjectives *pained* and *hopeless*. The comparative of these adjectives is formed by using *more* with them.

Superlative Form: Sekhar felt the *greatest* pity for him.

The author implies that of all the pity there is to feel, the character Sekhar feels the most. Therefore, the author uses *greatest*, the superlative form of the adjective *great*.

Prentice Hall Literature Program Resources

REINFORCE / RETEACH / EXTEND

Selection Support Pages
Build Vocabulary: The Word Root *-gratis-*, p. 76
Build Grammar Skills: Comparative and Superlative Forms, p. 77
Reading Strategy: Consequences of Actions, p. 78
Literary Focus: Irony, p. 79

Strategies for Diverse Student Needs, p. 19

Beyond Literature
Cross-Curricular Connection: Science, p. 19

Formal Assessment Selection Test, pp. 63–65;

Assessment Resources Software

Alternative Assessment, p. 19

Writing and Language Transparencies
Cause and Effect Graphic Organizer, p. 99

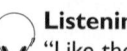
Listening to Literature Audiocassettes
"Like the Sun"

Looking at Literature Videodisc
"Like the Sun"

Resource Pro CD-ROM
"Like the Sun"—includes all resource material and customizable lesson plan

Like the Sun
◆ Tell all the Truth but tell it slant— ◆

◆ *Literature and Your Life*

CONNECT YOUR EXPERIENCE

Your closest friend just gave a less-than-impressive performance in the class play and asks for your honest response. Do you reveal your true opinion or do you spare your friend's feelings?

You're not alone with this dilemma. The matter of whether to tell the whole, unvarnished truth has troubled people throughout the ages. Follow Sekhar, the main character in this story, as he decides how to deal with the truth—at least for a day.

Journal Writing Briefly note what might happen if everyone told the truth all the time.

THEMATIC FOCUS: PERSONAL CHALLENGES

In different ways, Narayan's story and Dickinson's poem both pose this challenging question: Is it better to tell the absolute truth or to modify it for the sake of getting along with others?

◆ Background for Understanding

MUSIC

"Like the Sun" features the performance of a song, and this is not surprising, because song is at the root of south Indian music. The headmaster in the story sings an alapana—the introductory section of a piece of music—and then goes on to sing a song written by Thyagaraja (1767–1847), a composer who strongly influenced the music of south India. The region's biggest music festival, in fact, is named after Thyagaraja.

You'll notice, too, that the headmaster sings to the accompaniment of a drum and a violin. The violin is widely used in southern Indian music, and percussion instruments include the double-headed drum known as *mridangam* and the *ghatam*, a clay pot that the player may sometimes toss into the air.

◆ Literary Focus

IRONY

Irony is the literary technique that involves surprising, interesting, or amusing contradictions at work. These differences can result from clashes between what a character believes and what is actually the case. Irony might also result from clashes between what a character expects to happen and what actually happens.

By focusing on the clash between the main character's ideals and the real situation, you'll understand the irony of this tale.

◆ Reading Strategy

IDENTIFY CONSEQUENCES OF ACTIONS

In life you must experience directly the **consequences of your actions**—the results of what you do. The advantage of reading a story, however, is that you can sit safe and sound in a chair and watch the consequences of someone else's actions unfold.

"Like the Sun" is a perfect story with which to observe the relationship between action and consequences. Sekhar makes an important decision right off, a decision that just seems to invite consequences. Filling out a graphic organizer like the following will help you connect Sekhar's actions and their results.

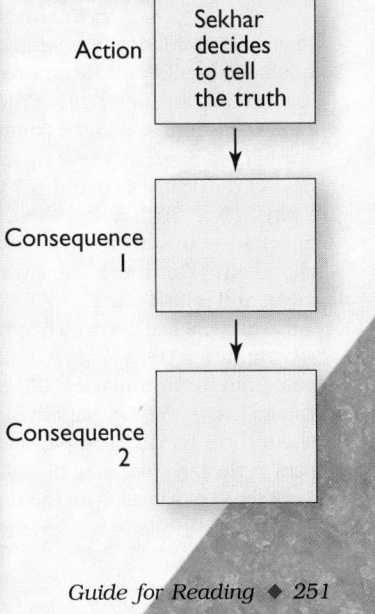

Guide for Reading ◆ 251

Customize for
Less Proficient Readers
To help students understand the story's irony, have them complete a chart like this one as they read:

	What Sekhar expects	What happens
1.		
2.		
3.		

Customize for
More Advanced Students
Invite these students to discuss Narayan's style with partners or in a group. Suggest that they pay particular attention to his use of figurative language.

Customize for
Interpersonal Learners
Allow time for these students to discuss their reactions to the different situations Sekhar finds himself in as a result of his decision. Students might role-play some of these situations and extend the dialogue to explore character's feelings and responses.

Customize for
English Language Learners
Preview the Build Vocabulary boxes and footnotes with these students. In addition, check students' knowledge of the following challenging words: *resolve, wince, colleagues, scrawls, sermonized, engaged, inclinations,* and *consolation* on page 252; *medley, assailed,* and *sullen* on page 253; and *apprehensive* on page 254. Some words, like *wince, scrawls, assailed, sullen,* and *apprehensive* may be demonstrated with actions and facial expression. For the others, substitute simpler terms. For example, substitute *co-worker* for *colleague, assortment* for *medley.*

 Preparing for Standardized Tests

Reading and Vocabulary The Reading Strategy for this selection focuses on identifying the consequences of actions. Students can apply this skill in the critical reading portions of some standardized tests, which often involve answering questions about cause-and-effect relationships. For additional practice, use the Reading Strategy page in *Selection Support*, p. 78.

Grammar and Language Some standardized tests ask students to identify sentence errors, as in the following example. *A; more difficult*

Sekhar had the <u>more difficult</u> job of all.
            A
He wanted to tell the truth, but this task was <u>more painful</u> than he thought it would be.
        B
In most cases, it would have been <u>easier</u>
                 C
to bend the truth.

The Build Grammar Skills lesson for this story focuses on the correct use of comparative and superlative forms. For additional practice, use the Build Grammar Skills page in *Selection Support*, p. 77.

When Sekhar decides to tell the whole truth for one day, he hurts his wife's feelings, alienates a colleague, and insults his headmaster. Through the experiences of the main character in this story, Narayan explores the question of whether it is possible or wise to tell the unvarnished truth at all times.

◆ **Reading Strategy**

❶ Consequences of Actions
Elicit the following: *Students should note that Sekhar's decision to be candid has made his wife feel bad.*

◆ **Critical Thinking**

❷ Infer What can students infer from Sekhar's procrastination? *Sekhar's procrastination indicates that he tries to avoid or put off unpleasant tasks. This would seem to indicate that if telling the absolute truth becomes unpleasant, he will be unable to continue for long.*

◆ *Literature and Your Life*

❸ Students might have been asked to comment on a friend's performance in an athletic event or concert. Ask them how they responded to what they considered a poor performance. *Guide students to distinguish between examples of constructive criticism, hurtful criticism, and tempered truth.*

◆ **Critical Thinking**

❹ Analyze Have students analyze why, at this point in the story, Narayan has the headmaster tell Sekhar that he has spent a fortune on his music. *The headmaster's remark shows how important his music is to him and how difficult it will be for Sekhar to be critical.*

Like the Sun

R. K. Narayan

Truth, Sekhar reflected, is like the sun. I suppose no human being can ever look it straight in the face without blinking or being dazed. He realized that, morning till night, the essence of human relationships consisted in tempering truth so that it might not shock. This day he set apart as a unique day—at least one day in the year we must give and take absolute Truth whatever may happen. Otherwise life is not worth living. The day ahead seemed to him full of possibilities. He told no one of his experiment. It was a quiet resolve, a secret pact between him and eternity.

The very first test came while his wife served him his morning meal. He showed hesitation over a titbit, which she had thought was her culinary[1] masterpiece. She asked, "Why, isn't it good?" At other times he would have said, considering her feelings in the matter, "I feel full up, that's all." But today he said, "It isn't good. I'm unable to swallow it." He saw her wince and said to himself, Can't be helped. Truth is like the sun.

His next trial was in the common room when one of his colleagues came up and said, "Did you hear of the death of so-and-so? Don't you think it a pity?" "No," Sekhar answered. "He was such a fine man—" the other began. But Sekhar cut him short with: "Far from it. He always struck me as a mean and selfish brute."

 During the last period when he was teaching geography for Third Form A, Sekhar received a note from the headmaster: "Please see me before you go home." Sekhar said to himself: It must be about these horrible test papers. A hundred papers in the boys' scrawls; he had shirked this work for weeks, feeling all the time as if a sword

◆ **Reading Strategy**
❶ What is the first consequence of Sekhar's "pact" with "eternity"?

were hanging over his head.

The bell rang, and the boys burst out of the class.

Sekhar paused for a moment outside the headmaster's room to button up his coat; that was another subject the headmaster always sermonized about.

He stepped in with a very polite "Good evening, sir."

The headmaster looked up at him in a very friendly manner and asked, "Are you free this evening?"

Sekhar replied, "Just some outing which I have promised the children at home—"

"Well, you can take them out another day. Come home with me now."

"Oh. . . yes, sir, certainly. . ." And then he added timidly, "anything special, sir?"

"Yes," replied the headmaster, smiling to himself. . . "You didn't know my weakness for music?"

"Oh, yes, sir. . ."

"I've been learning and practicing secretly, and now I want you to hear me this evening. I've engaged a drummer and a violinist to accompany me—this is the first time I'm doing it full-dress,[2] and I want your opinion. I know it will be valuable."

Sekhar's taste in music was well known. He was one of the most dreaded music critics in the town. But he never anticipated his musical inclinations would lead him to this trial. . . . "Rather a surprise for you, isn't it?" asked the headmaster. "I've spent a fortune on it behind closed doors. . . ." They started for the headmaster's house. "God hasn't given me a child, but at least let him not deny me the consolation of music," the headmaster said, pathetically, as they walked. He incessantly chattered about music: how he began one day out of sheer boredom; how his teacher at

---

1. **culinary** (kyōō′ lə ner′ ē) *adj.*: Having to do with cooking or the kitchen.

2. **full-dress:** Complete in every respect.

◆ **Block Scheduling Strategies**

Consider these suggestions to take advantage of extended class time:

• Allow time for students to complete the journal activity in Literature and Your Life (p. 251) before introducing the "Interest Grabber" discussion (p. 251).

• Expand on the Background provided on page 251 by using the Looking at Literature Videodisc, Chapter 3, which features Indian music and dance.

Play frames 11043 to 20512

• Introduce the literary concept of irony. As a class, complete the Literary Focus page on irony in *Selection Support*, p. 79. After reading the story, students can work independently or in small groups to answer the Literary Focus questions on page 255.

• Model the use of an action-consequence

chart like the one on page 251, or use the Cause and Effect Graphic Organizer in *Writing and Language Transparencies*, p. 99.

• To prepare students for the Writing Mini-Lesson (p. 256), allow students to bring in examples of songs to play for their classmates as possible topics for reviews. Lead a class discussion on what elements students might consider in their reviews. Then have students complete the Writing Mini-Lesson.

▲ Critical Viewing Describe the personality the artist has given the sun. [Interpret]

Face in Sun, Hal Lose, Stock Illustration Source, Inc.

first laughed at him and then gave him hope; how his ambition in life was to forget himself in music.

At home the headmaster proved very ingratiating. He sat Sekhar on a red silk carpet, set before him several dishes of delicacies, and fussed over him as if he were a son-in-law of the house. He even said, "Well, you must listen with a free mind. Don't worry about these test papers."

◆ **Build Vocabulary**

essence (es´ əns) *n.*: The crucial element or basis

tempering (tem´ pə riŋ) *adj.*: Modifying or adjusting

shirked (shûrkt) *v.*: Neglected or avoided

incessantly (in ses´ ənt lē) *adv.*: Endlessly; constantly

ingratiating (in grā´ shē āt´ iŋ) *adj.*: Bringing into favor

stupefied (stoo´ pə fīd´) *adj.*: Dazed; stunned

He added half humorously, "I will give you a week's time."

"Make it ten days, sir," Sekhar pleaded.

"All right, granted," the headmaster said generously. Sekhar felt really relieved now—he would attack them at the rate of ten a day and get rid of the nuisance.

The headmaster lighted incense sticks. "Just to create the right atmosphere," he explained. A drummer and a violinist, already seated on a Rangoon mat, were waiting for him. The headmaster sat down between them like a professional at a concert, cleared his throat and began an alapana,[3] and paused to ask, "Isn't it good Kalyani?"[4] Sekhar pretended not to have heard the question. The headmaster went on to sing a full song composed by Thyagaraja and followed it with two more. All the time the headmaster was singing, Sekhar went on commenting within himself, He croaks like a dozen frogs. He is bellowing like a buffalo. Now he sounds like loose window shutters in a storm.

The incense sticks burnt low. Sekhar's head throbbed with the medley of sounds that had assailed his eardrums for a couple of hours now. He felt half stupefied. The headmaster had gone nearly hoarse, when he paused to ask, "Shall I go on?" Sekhar replied, "Please don't, sir; I think this will do. . . ." The headmaster looked stunned. His face was beaded with perspiration. Sekhar felt the greatest pity for him. But he felt he could not help it. No judge delivering a sentence felt more pained and helpless. Sekhar noticed that the headmaster's wife peeped in from the kitchen, with eager curiosity. The drummer and the violinist put away their burdens with an air of relief. The headmaster removed his spectacles, mopped his brow, and asked, "Now, come out with your opinion."

"Can't I give it tomorrow, sir?" Sekhar asked tentatively.

"No. I want it immediately—your frank opinion. Was it good?"

"No, sir. . ." Sekhar replied.

"Oh! . . . Is there any use continuing my

---

3. **alapana:** Improvisational Indian music in the classical style.
4. **Kalyani:** Traditional Indian folk songs.

Like the Sun ◆ 253

▶Critical Viewing◀

❺ **Interpret** The arched eyebrows and big eyes suggest that this sun is observant and watchful. The smile suggests that the sun is amused by what it sees. Suggest to students that the sun's expression reflects that of a detached observer who might be chuckling at poor Sekhar's misadventures with the truth.

◆ **Critical Thinking**

❻ **Predict** Discuss how the headmaster is making a huge fuss over Sekhar. Ask students what they predict will happen. Will the headmaster's playing be good or bad? If bad, what will Sekhar say, after being treated so well? How will the headmaster react? *Most students will think that the author is setting the scene for the headmaster to play badly, posing a problem for Sekhar. Some may predict he will criticize the headmaster's playing, making the headmaster angry; others may think the headmaster will accept Sekhar's criticism without anger; still others may predict that Sekhar will not tell the truth.*

◆ **Build Grammar Skills**

❼ **Comparative and Superlative Forms** Ask students to identify the comparative and superlative forms in this section and explain why each is used. *The comparative form is "more pained." It is used because Sekhar is being compared to only one other person, a judge delivering sentence. The superlative form is "greatest." It is used because this pity is being compared to all the other pity it would be possible to feel.*

Cross-Curricular Connection: Science

The sun is about 150 million kilometers away from the Earth. The sun is not unusual compared to other stars in the universe. It is a medium-sized, middle-aged yellow star approximately 4.6 billion years old. Without the sun, there would be no life on Earth.

The angle at which the sun's rays strike the surface of the Earth is not the same everywhere on the planet. At the equator (the imaginary line that separates the Earth into two halves), the sun is nearly overhead.

There, its rays strike the Earth at a ninety degree angle all year long. At a ninety-degree angle, the sun's rays are most direct and result in the greatest heat. Temperatures at the equator have been known to reach 130 degrees Fahrenheit. The farther away from the equator an area is, the smaller the angle becomes at which the rays hit. As the angle becomes smaller, the rays become less direct. The result is less heat and lower temperatures.

Ask students to explain why the sun is a good metaphor for truth. *Like the sun, the truth is necessary, but can be overwhelming if it is too direct.*

Explain, in terms of the sun's rays, Emily Dickinson's line "tell it slant." *Like the sun's rays, the truth is less intense or damaging when it is less direct.*

◆ Literary Focus

❷ Irony At the beginning of the story, Sekhar felt a day of telling the truth was "full of possibilities." In contrast, by the end of the day, his truth telling appears to have destroyed his possibilities.

◆ Reading Strategy

❸ Identify Consequences of Actions Ask students to identify the positive and negative consequences of Sekhar's truth telling so far. Were any outcomes positive? *Sekhar's actions have hurt and angered his wife, upset a colleague, made Sekhar uncomfortable, and hurt the headmaster's feelings. Some students may point out that Sekhar won't have to keep eating the food he doesn't like and the headmaster won't keep wasting money on music lessons.*

Reinforce and Extend

Answers
◆ Literature and Your Life

Reader's Response Students will probably reply that telling the absolute truth all day would be difficult and uncomfortable.

Thematic Focus A person might become concerned that he or she was bending the truth more and more, or a person might tell the truth all day if protecting someone else's feelings would lead to larger problems later.

☑ Check Your Comprehension
1. He decided to tell the absolute truth for one complete day.
2. The headmaster wanted to get Sekhar's opinion of his music.
3. Sekhar decided that of all the consequences he might have suffered, grading 100 test papers in one day was not that bad.
4. She compares the truth to light.

254

Tell all the Truth but tell it slant—
Emily Dickinson

❶

Tell all the Truth but tell it slant—
Success in Circuit lies
Too bright for our infirm Delight
The Truth's superb surprise
5   As Lightning to the Children eased
With explanation kind
The Truth must dazzle gradually
Or every man be blind—

lessons?"

"Absolutely none, sir. . ." Sekhar said with his voice trembling. He felt very unhappy that he could not speak more soothingly. Truth, he reflected, required as much strength to give as to receive.

All the way home he felt worried. He felt that his official life was not going to be smooth sailing hereafter. There were questions of

❷ **◆ Literary Focus**
Notice the clash between Sekhar's noble view and the situation to which it has brought him.

◆ Build Vocabulary
scrutinized (skr$\overline{oo}$t′ ən īzd′) *v.*: Looked at carefully; examined closely

increment and confirmation[5] and so on, all depending upon the headmaster's goodwill. All kinds of worries seemed to be in store for him. . . . Did not Harischandra[6] lose his throne, wife, child, because he would speak nothing less than the absolute Truth whatever happened?

At home his wife served him with a sullen face. He knew she was still angry with him for his remark of the morning. Two casualties for today, Sekhar said to himself. If I practice it for a week, I don't think I shall have a single friend left.

He received a call from the headmaster in his classroom next day. He went up apprehensively.

"Your suggestion was useful. I have paid off the music master. No one would tell me the truth about my music all these days. Why such antics at my age! Thank you. By the way, what about those test papers?"

"You gave me ten days, sir, for correcting them."

"Oh, I've reconsidered it. I must positively have them here tomorrow. . . ." A hundred papers in a day! That meant all night's sitting up! "Give me a couple of days, sir . . ."

"No. I must have them tomorrow morning. And remember, every paper must be thoroughly scrutinized."

"Yes, sir," Sekhar said, feeling that sitting up all night with a hundred test papers was a small price to pay for the luxury of practicing Truth.

❸

5. **increment and confirmation:** Salary increase and job security.
6. **Harishchandra** (hə rish chən′ drə): Legendary Hindu king who was the subject of many Indian stories. His name has come to symbolize truth and integrity.

Guide for Responding

◆ Literature and Your Life

Reader's Response Would you find telling the truth all day, as Sekhar does in this story, to be pleasurable? Why, or why not?

Thematic Focus Give a reason why a person might set himself or herself the personal challenge of telling the absolute truth for one day.

☑ Check Your Comprehension

1. What experiment did Sekhar set for himself at the beginning of the story?
2. For what reason did the headmaster want to meet with Sekhar?
3. What was Sekhar's response to having to grade 100 test papers in a day?
4. What comparison does Dickinson use to describe Truth?

254 ◆ Clashing Forces

Beyond the Selection

FURTHER READING
Other Works by R. K. Narayan
A Horse and Two Goats (stories)
An Astrologer's Day and Other Stories
Malgudi Days
Malgudi Landscapes: The Best of R. K. Narayan

Other Works With the Theme of Clashing Forces
"By Any Other Name," Santha Rama Rau
"Street Cries," Sarojini Naidu
     We suggest that you preview these works before recommending them to students.

INTERNET
Please be aware that sites may have changed since we published this information.
     For a profile of R. K. Narayan and a list of his books, students can visit the following Internet address: **http://www.cis,upenn. edu/~anoop/ narayan/narayan.html**
     We *strongly recommend* that you preview this site before sending students to it.

Guide for Responding (continued)

◆ Critical Thinking

INTERPRET
1. What effect does the headmaster's remark that he has spent a fortune on his music have on the story? **[Analyze]**
2. The phrase "luxury of practicing Truth" appears at the end of the story. How can truth be a luxury? **[Interpret]**

EVALUATE
3. Was Sekhar brave or foolish to tell the truth all day? Why? **[Make a Judgment]**

APPLY
4. Describe a situation in which you might "temper the truth." **[Interpret]**

◆ Reading Strategy

IDENTIFY CONSEQUENCES OF ACTIONS
This story is somewhat unusual in that all its key events are so clearly the **consequences** of a single decision: Sekhar's vow to tell the truth all day.
1. Identify two consequences that follow as a result of Sekhar's truthfulness about the headmaster's performance.
2. In describing the consequences of his vow, Sekhar calls them "casualties." Why?
3. Is Sekhar right in predicting that if he keeps telling the truth, he won't have a single friend left? Why or why not?

◆ Literary Focus

IRONY
The central **irony** in this story is the clash between Sekhar's idealistic expectations and what actually occurs. For example, telling the absolute truth as Sekhar vows to do, seems to be a noble goal. However, this vow leads to bad feelings. At breakfast, Sekhar's wife winces when he criticizes her cooking. The conflict between noble ideal and disappointing result is what creates irony.
1. What do you think Sekhar believes might happen as a result of his poor review of the headmaster's performance?
2. What is ironic about the headmaster's actual reaction to the criticism?

◆ Build Vocabulary

USING THE ROOT -gratis-
Use your knowledge of the root -gratis-, which means "pleasing" or "a favor," to define these words.
1. grateful
2. gratitude
3. ingrate
4. gratis
5. gratuitous

USING THE WORD BANK
Write the paragraph on your paper and fill in the blanks with words from the Word Bank. Use each word just once.

The ___?___ of Sekhar's vow was to tell the truth. This one day at least, he was not in favor of ___?___ truth to protect people's feelings. ___?___ throughout the day, he ___?___ no opportunity of telling his wife and colleagues exactly what he thought. As they ___?___ Sekhar's behavior, many of his colleagues were ___?___. They expected Sekhar to be more ___?___.

◆ Build Grammar Skills

COMPARATIVE AND SUPERLATIVE FORMS
Almost all one-syllable adjectives and some two-syllable adjectives use -er to form the **comparative** and -est to form the **superlative**. Many adjectives of two or more syllables use the words *more* or *most*, respectively, for comparative and superlative forms.

Practice In your notebook, write the correct form of the adjective from the choices given in parentheses.
1. Sekhar didn't say whether he liked one of the headmaster's songs (better, best) than the other.
2. If Sekhar had told the headmaster his music was the (more fine, most fine, finer, finest) he'd ever heard, the story would have had a different ending.
3. Sekhar would have told a (more temperate, most temperate, temperater, temperatest) truth the next day.

Writing Application Write a paragraph in which you compare Sekhar and the headmaster. Use at least two each of the comparative and the superlative forms of adjectives.

Like the Sun/Tell all the Truth but tell it slant— ◆ 255

Using the Word Bank
The essence of Sekhar's vow was to tell the truth. This one day at least, he was not in favor of tempering the truth to protect people's feelings. Incessantly through the day, he shirked no opportunity of telling his wife and colleagues exactly what he thought. As they scrutinized Sekhar's behavior, many of his colleagues were stupefied. They expected Sekhar to be more ingratiating.

◆ Build Grammar Skills
1. better; 2. finest;
3. more temperate

✒ Writer's Solution

For additional instruction and practice, use the lesson in the **Language Lab CD-ROM** on Forms of Comparison. For more practice, use the Recognizing Degrees of Comparison and Using Comparative and Superlative Degrees pages in the *Writer's Solution Grammar Practice Book*, pp. 86 and 88.

Answers
◆ Critical Thinking
1. The headmaster's remark gives some justification for Sekhar to tell him the absolute truth.
2. If the price of something is more than a person can afford, the person considers that thing a luxury. Sekhar's experiences show that the price of telling the truth can be high.
3. Students should base their answers on the range of Sekhar's experiences not just on one or two.
4. Situations might include ones in which another person's feelings might be hurt without any constructive effect or situations in which telling the absolute truth would cause harm.

◆ Reading Strategy
1. The headmaster quits his music lessons and Sekhar must correct the papers overnight instead of within ten days.
2. Most of the consequences were negative.
3. Based on people's reactions to the truth, Sekhar is probably correct. Even when hearing the truth is constructive, people often resent the person who tells it to them.

◆ Literary Focus
1. Sekhar thinks he will be fired or demoted.
2. While Sekhar fears the headmaster will be angry, the headmaster actually appreciates that someone has stopped him from wasting his money. In another ironic twist, however, his gratitude does not extend to allowing Sekhar the extra time for the test papers.

◆ Build Vocabulary
Using the Root -gratis-
1. Grateful is thankful for a favor.
2. Gratitude is the feeling of thankfulness you have when someone does you a favor.
3. An ingrate is someone who does not appreciate a favor.
4. Something done gratis is done as a favor.
5. Something that is gratuitous is extra—outside what is required—thrown in as a favor.

255

Idea Bank

Customizing for
Learning Modalities

Following are suggestions for matching Idea Bank topics with your students' learning modalities:

    Interpersonal: 4, 5
    Verbal/Linguistic: 4, 5, 6
    Musical/Rhythmic: 6
    Visual/Spatial: 7

Customizing for
Performance Levels

Following are suggestions for matching the Idea Bank topics with your students' ability levels:

    Less Advanced: 1, 5
    Average: 2, 4, 7
    More Advanced: 3, 4, 6, 7

Writing Mini-Lesson

Refer students to the Writing Handbook, p. 965, for instruction on the writing process, and page 969 for further information on reviews.

Writer's Solution

Have students complete the Response to Literature Tutorial. Follow these steps:

1. Tell students to use the Topic Web to organize subtopics and details that relate to their response to the song.
2. Encourage them to use the Evaluation Word Bins to choose suitable and precise adjectives and adverbs.
3. Have students draft on computer.
4. Suggest that they use the Language Variety Checker to find places to revise and eliminate repeated words.

Sourcebook

Have students use Chapter 7, Response to Literature (pp. 194–227), for additional support. The chapter includes in-depth instruction on using evaluative modifiers (p. 217).

*B*uild *Y*our *P*ortfolio

Idea Bank

Writing

1. **Advice Column** Write an advice column response to tenth-grader Dara. Should Dara tell her friend, who can't carry a tune, not to try out for the school musical? Give reasons for your answer.

2. **Guidelines** You and your classmates will be exchanging ideas and editing one another's papers throughout the year. Write a set of guidelines for telling the truth in a useful, constructive way.

3. **Fairy Tale** Write a fairy tale about a teenager who must tell the truth in every situation. Set your fairy tale in ancient or modern times.

Speaking and Listening

4. **Oral Argument** Suppose that Sekhar was fired for telling the truth. As his attorney, prepare and deliver an oral argument summing up why he has been unfairly treated and why he should be re-hired. **[Social Studies Link]**

5. **Debate** With a small group, debate the question of whether it is better to reveal the truth fully in social interactions or to soften it in some way. **[Social Studies Link; Performing Arts Link]**

Projects

6. **Indian Folk Songs** The term *Kalyani* refers to traditional Indian folk songs. Find out more about Kalyani and present your findings to the class. If possible, play a recording of Kalyani as part of your presentation. **[Music Link]**

7. **Map** Draw a map of southern India that shows Madras, where Narayan was born, and Mysore, which served as the basis for Narayan's fictional Malgudi. **[Social Studies Link]**

Writing Mini-Lesson

Review of a Song

Sekhar had to give an oral review of his headmaster's song. In writing, a **review** is an article giving a critical evaluation of a work of art. Use your knowledge of music to write a review of a song. Address your review to readers of a popular music magazine and win their confidence by clearly supporting your opinions with reasons.

Writing Skills Focus: Supporting Details

When writing a review, a research paper, or an editorial, use **supporting details**—facts, statistics, examples, or reasons—to persuade readers that your assertions are true.

Suppose, for example, that you write this topic sentence: "The lyrics of the song have particular meaning for teenagers living in the city." Your readers are going to ask themselves why this is the case. To answer that question, you can provide a supporting detail: "The lyrics of the song focus on what it feels like to be alone on a crowded city street."

Prewriting Create an outline for your review. For each paragraph, come up with a topic sentence and at least two supporting details to back it up.

    I. Paragraph topic sentence

        A. Supporting detail

        B. Supporting detail

Drafting Your details should support the point in your topic sentence by clarifying, explaining, or giving an example.

Revising Show your review to a friend or writing partner. Ask whether your supporting details fit with their topic sentences. If any supporting details seem unclear, rewrite them to establish a clear connection to the main idea of your paragraph.

✓ ASSESSMENT OPTIONS

Formal Assessment, Selection Test, pp. 63–65, and Assessment Resources Software. The selection test is designed so that it can be easily customized to the ability levels of your students. *Alternative Assessment*, p. 19, includes options for less advanced students, more advanced students, verbal/linguistic learners, visual/spatial learners, logical/mathematical learners, interpersonal learners, and bodily/kinesthetic learners.

PORTFOLIO ASSESSMENT
Use the following rubrics in the *Alternative Assessment* booklet to evaluate student writing
Advice Column: Problem Solution Rubric, p. 101
Guidelines: Process Explanation, p. 100
Fairy Tale Fictional Narrative Rubric, p. 95
Writing Mini-Lesson: Evaluation/Review Rubric, p. 104

Writing Process Workshop

Editorial

Where there is conflict, there are opinions. Like people, publications have their own opinions on issues. An **editorial** is a piece of persuasive writing, found in newspapers and magazines, that is written by the editor or editors of the publication about a current issue. In an editorial, the writer states the publication's viewpoint and tries to persuade readers to agree with it.

Write an editorial stating your viewpoint on an issue. The following skills, introduced in this section's Writing Mini-Lessons, will help you write an effective editorial.

Writing Skills Focus

▶ **Use the appropriate language** for your audience. If your readers will be your classmates, use vocabulary that will be familiar to them. (See p. 249.)

▶ **Use supporting details** to back up any assertions that you make. (See p. 256.)

▶ **Use a persuasive tone.** Use words that appeal to the readers' senses, convey enthusiasm for your idea, and stress the idea's benefits. (See p. 230.)

▶ **Use vivid verbs.** These will create specific pictures in your readers' minds. (See p. 241.)

The following editorial uses these skills to convince readers of the importance of teaching typing in school.

WRITING MODEL

We are alarmed ① that despite America's continuing move toward electronic communication, many American schools today do not teach typing.

It is ② incomprehensible that our educational establishment spends billions of dollars to purchase computers, yet does not teach students how to type quickly so they can obtain the maximum benefit from these machines. Our schools require driver education so that students will drive ③ safely, but many do not teach typing so their students will work more efficiently at computers and be much better prepared for college and the work world.④

① Alarmed is a vivid verb that sets an urgent tone for the editorial.

② Words such as *incomprehensible* set a persuasive tone by showing the writer's strong feelings about the issue.

③ Here the writer uses a supporting detail to back up his argument.

④ The writer uses language that doesn't talk down to readers or insult their intelligence.

Writing Process Workshop ◆ 257

Beyond the Classroom

Career Connection

Current Events Tell students interested in journalism or current events that they may someday be called upon or wish to write an editorial. To write a good editorial, it is important to keep aware of current events and know what the important issues are. Tell them that the best-written editorial will not be effective if it does not concern an important or current issue.

Encourage students to do research to find out the variety of jobs available in the field of journalism. Have them make a chart showing the educational requirements, starting salaries, and job responsibilities for each position.

Prepare and Engage

Establish Writing Guidelines
Before students begin, review these characteristics of an editorial:

- It is written by the editor or editors of a publication, states the publication's viewpoint, and tries to persuade readers to agree with that viewpoint.

- It concerns a current issue that is important to the community or readers of the periodical.

You may want to distribute the scoring rubric for Persuasion in *Alternative Assessment* (p. 105) to make students aware before they begin of the criteria on which they will be evaluated. See the suggestion on page 259 for additional points with which to customize the rubric for this workshop assignment.

Writers at Work Videodisc
To introduce students to the key elements of persuasive writing and show them how Sayu Bhojwani of the Asia Society in New York City incorporates them into her fund-raising writing, play the videodisc segment on Persuasion (Ch. 4).

Play frames 3 to 9933

Writing Lab CD-ROM
If your students have access to computers, you may want to have them work on the tutorial on Persuasion to complete all or part of their editorials. Follow these steps:
1. Have students review the interactive model of an editorial.
2. Suggest students use an Issue Wheel to help find an appropriate topic.
3. Have students draft on computer.
4. Suggest that students use a Transition Word Bin.
5. Have students complete the Proofreading checklist.

Sourcebook
Students can find additional support, including topic ideas, models, audience and purpose profiles, and graphic organizers, in the chapter on Persuasion (pp. 96–127).

Connection to Literature To see examples of persuasive essays that share many of the characteristics of an editorial, refer students to Alexander Solzhenitsyn's Nobel Lecture (p. 587) and Elie Wiesel's "Keep Memory Alive" (p. 590).

257

Prewriting

Once students have decided their topics, encourage them to do some research at the library using reference books, magazines, or newspapers to acquire facts that they can use to support the arguments they make in their editorials.

Customize for
English Language Learners

These students may benefit from using a Persuasion Word Bin to help them find the proper words for their editorials.

Customize for
Less Proficient Writers

These students may benefit from using a Pros and Cons Chart to organize their information. They should refer to this chart while drafting.

 Writer's Solution

Writing Lab CD-ROM

The Considering Audience and Purpose section of the tutorial on Persuasion contains the screen Getting the Opposition on Your Side. Students can consult this screen to sharpen their persuasive techniques before they begin drafting.

Writing Process Workshop

APPLYING LANGUAGE SKILLS: Active and Passive Voice

Excessive use of the **passive voice** makes writing flat, wordy, and hard to follow. The **active voice** is generally more lively, concise, and easier to understand.

Passive Voice:

Citizens are endangered by the current condition of our town's streets.

Active Voice:

The current condition of our town's streets endangers our citizens.

Practice On your paper, rewrite the following sentences in the active voice.

1. Midwestern farmlands were devastated by the 1996 floods.

2. Crops were destroyed by the flood waters.

Writing Application As you draft your editorial, use active-voice verbs to keep your writing lively and easy to read.

Writer's Solution Connection
Language Lab

For more practice with active-voice verbs, complete the Language Lab lesson on Active and Passive Voice.

Prewriting

Choose a Topic A good way to choose a topic for an editorial is to sit with a group of classmates and brainstorm for a list of important issues in your community or school. Some people's opinions might be focused on crime; others', on pollution. Jot down notes as group members express their ideas, and refer to your notes for topics for your editorial.

Is Your Topic Too Broad? You can't effectively cover a large issue in a short piece of persuasive writing. Consider all the things you want to say about your topic. Do you think you can deal adequately with all the different parts of your topic? If not, narrow your topic so that you can focus on a more specific aspect of it.

Narrowing Your Topic		
Broad	**Narrow**	**Narrower**
Sports	Funding for high-school sports	Men's and women's sports should receive equal funds
Politics	Presidential elections	Presidents should be elected for a single six-year term

Drafting

Avoid Faulty Logic As you write, avoid the following types of faulty logic and unreasonable statements:

Overgeneralization: Nobody likes the present lunch menu.
Improved: The cafeteria staff has heard dozens of complaints about the lunch menu this month.

Circular reasoning: Movies are popular because many people attend them.
Improved: Movies are popular because people love to be entertained by good stories.

Bandwagon appeal: All of the most attractive people exercise regularly.
Improved: People who exercise regularly improve their strength and stamina.

Either/Or arguments: Either we adopt a curfew, or the gangs will run wild.
Improved: If we don't adopt a curfew, it will be harder to keep our neighborhood safe and manageable.

Applying Language Skills
Active and Passive Voice

Explain to students that the active voice should be used in almost all situations. In general, the only appropriate use of the passive voice in persuasive writing is if the actor is clearly unknown or less important than the act itself.

Answers

1. The 1996 floods devastated midwestern farmlands.
2. The flood waters destroyed crops.

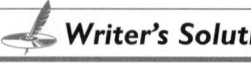 **Writer's Solution**

For additional instruction and practice, have students complete the **Language Lab CD-ROM** lesson on Active and Passive Voice and practice page 74 in the *Writer's Solution Grammar Practice Book*.

Revising

Use a Checklist Review the Writing Skills Focus on p. 257, and use the points as a checklist to evaluate and revise your editorial.

▶ Have you used language appropriate for your audience?

Define any difficult terms or use more sophisticated language if appropriate.

▶ Have you used supporting details?

Back up each assertion with a fact or detail that supports it.

▶ Have you used a persuasive tone?

Convey a sense of enthusiasm or urgency regarding your idea or position.

▶ Have you used vivid verbs?

Replace any general verbs with vivid ones that will help your readers picture what you are trying to say.

REVISION MODEL

① must
We should make shops accessible to people with
② does the law require it
disabilities. Not only is it proper jurisprudence, but so does
③ People with disabilities need food, clothing, and personal items just as
everyone else does.
common sense.

① The word *must* is more persuasive than *should*.

② The writer replaces an unnecessarily difficult term with a simpler, more direct one.

③ The writer adds this supporting detail.

Proofreading

Use a Proofreading Checklist ✔

✔ Make sure you have no spelling or punctuation errors.

✔ Correct run-on sentences or sentence fragments.

✔ Replace the passive voice with the active voice.

✔ Eliminate loaded words.

Publishing

Send a Letter to the Editor By adding an introduction and changing a few words, you can turn your editorial into a letter to the editor. After you turn your editorial into a letter to the editor, mail it to the editor of your school or local newspaper.

APPLYING LANGUAGE SKILLS: "Loaded" Words

Avoid "loaded" words—words with strong connotations—that will influence your readers' judgment by appealing to their fears or prejudices rather than their good sense.

Loaded Word:
Unfortunately, in England soccer attracts a rowdy audience.

Unbiased:
English police frequently have to break up fights among members of the audience at soccer matches.

Practice On your paper, rewrite the following sentence, removing any loaded words.

Security should bounce the punks from the stadium.

Writing Application Review your editorial to make sure you have eliminated loaded words.

Writer's Solution Connection
Writing Lab

To learn more about loaded language, see the section on Drafting in the Persuasion tutorial in the Writing Lab.

Writing Process Workshop ◆ 259

Revising

After students have written a draft, have them review the logic to be sure that they have built support that is logical and reasonable.

Writer's Solution

Writing Lab CD-ROM
The Proofreading section of the tutorial on Persuasion contains the screen About Active and Passive Voice. Have students consult this screen to make sure they have used active-voice verbs where appropriate.

Publishing

Students who choose not to share their editorials with others should be encouraged to keep them as an example of persuasive writing that they can refer to later.

Applying Language Skills

"Loaded" Words Remind students that loaded words attempt to manipulate feelings, fears, or prejudices rather than persuade by reason and logic.

Suggested Answer
Security should eject rowdy fans from the stadium.

Writer's Solution

For additional practice, have students complete the practice page 74 on Active and Passive Voice in the *Writer's Solution Grammar Practice Book*.

Reinforce and Extend

Review the Writing Guidelines
After students have completed their papers, review the characteristics of an editorial. Encourage students to come up with additional criteria for an editorial based on what they learned through completing the assignment.

✓ ASSESSMENT		4	3	2	1
PORTFOLIO ASSESSMENT Use the rubric on Persuasion in the *Alternative Assessment* booklet (p. 105) to assess students' writing. Add these criteria to customize the rubric to this assignment.	**Active Voice**	Verbs are in the active voice except in cases where the passive is clearly acceptable.	Most verbs are in the active voice.	Most verbs are in the active voice, but there are some improper passive-voice verbs.	A large number of passive-voice verbs make the piece tedious to read.
	Loaded Words	The editorial contains no inappropriate loaded words. The argument uses reason, not emotional appeals.	The editorial avoids loaded words; the argument appeals to the reader's reason rather than emotions.	The editorial contains many loaded words; the argument appeals more to emotions than to reason.	The editorial is fraught with loaded words; the argument appeals primarily to the reader's emotions.

259

Introduce the Strategy

Tell students that everything is written for a purpose. Once they understand what that purpose is, they can read more critically and with greater comprehension of important details.

Customize for
English Language Learners

These students may have trouble with the following important vocabulary words: *indictment, lawful, mockery, downright, ballot.* Explain to these students the importance of the word *we*—that in this case it refers specifically to men and women—in the second paragraph.

Apply the Strategy

Have students read Susan B. Anthony's speech closely, more than once if necessary. Ask them what they think the most important parts of the passage are.

Suggested Answers

1. Her purpose was to convince both men and woman that women deserve the right to vote.
2. One possible answer: The Constitution explicitly says "We the people . . . in order to . . . secure the blessings of liberty . . . do establish this Constitution for the United States of America." Since the word "we" implies women as well as men, women should not be denied the most basic tool for securing their liberty and freedom—that tool being the right to vote.
3. One possible answer: Since Anthony's purpose is to persuade, a reader would be careful to scrutinize closely her reasoning and support.

Strategies for Success

Common purposes for writing are these: to entertain, to inform, to right a wrong, or to persuade. The writer's purpose, or combination of purposes, for any particular work affects the writer's choice of details and writing style. For this reason, a writer's purpose affects the meaning you take from a work.

What's the Point? When you pick up something to read, ask yourself what its purpose, or point, is. For a textbook, the writer's purpose is to inform, so you should read carefully and closely. On the other hand, the purpose of a humorous essay is to entertain, so you will read to appreciate the humor. If a writer's purpose is to persuade you, you will approach the work skeptically and check that the writer supports his or her statements and claims. In these ways, a writer's purpose affects not only the meaning you take from a work, but the way you read it.

Susan B. Anthony

✔ *Here are other situations in which understanding a writer's purpose can be helpful:*
▶ Reading a pamphlet you've been handed on the street
▶ Reading a product label

Apply the Strategy

Imagine that you lived in the late 1800's when Susan B. Anthony, a leader in the women's rights movement, gave this speech defending her constitutional right to vote.

Friends and Fellow Citizens:

I stand before you tonight under indictment for the alleged crime of having voted at the last Presidential election, without having a lawful right to vote. It shall be my work this evening to prove to you that, in thus voting, I not only committed no crime, but instead, simply exercised my citizen's rights guaranteed to me and all United States citizens by the national Constitution, beyond the power of any state to deny. "We the people of the United States, in order to form a more perfect union, establish justice, insure domestic tranquillity, provide for the common defense, promote the general welfare, and secure the blessings of liberty to ourselves and our posterity, do ordain and establish this Constitution for the United States of America." It was we, the people; not we, the white male citizens; nor yet we, the male citizens; but we, the whole people who formed the Union. And we formed it, not to give the blessings of liberty, but to secure them; not to the half of ourselves and the half of our posterity, but to the whole people, women as well as men. And it is a downright mockery to talk to women of their enjoyment of the blessings of liberty while they are denied the use of the only means of securing them provided by this democratic-republican government—the ballot. . . .

---

1. What do you think was Susan B. Anthony's purpose for writing this speech?
2. What meaning do you take from the work?
3. How does Anthony's purpose affect the way you read the speech?

PART 2 *Struggling for Justice*

Hands, Gerald Bustomante/Stock Illustration Source

Struggling for Justice ◆ 261

The selections in Part 2 deal with people and groups struggling for personal and public justice. "Hearts and Hands" and "The Fish" will help students see how compassion is a form of justice. The excerpt from "Desert Exile" and Gerald Ford's "Remarks Upon Signing a Proclamation Concerning Japanese American Internment During World War II" give a personal and a public perspective on basic human rights. "The Cabuliwallah" is a bittersweet story that shows how time can be the cruelest thief of all. This theme is reinforced in the Connections to Today's World feature, "Yesterday."

Customize for
Varying Student Needs
When assigning the selections in this part to your students, keep in mind the following factors:

"Hearts and Hands"
• A very short short story

"The Fish"
• An easy-to-understand poem
• Some students may need assistance with vocabulary

from "Desert Exile" and "Remarks Upon Signing a Proclamation"
• Students will need to understand context of selections before reading

"The Cabuliwallah "
• A long short story
• Cultural references may need to be explained
• Vocabulary is more difficult than in other selections

"Yesterday"
• High-interest song lyrics connecting theme to music

 Humanities: Art

Hands, by Gerald Bustomante.

Ask students to count how many hands or near-complete hands (as opposed to just fingertips) are in the artwork and to tally how many of those hands are right versus left hands. *There are eighteen hands: six right hands, twelve left hands*

Help students link the artwork to the theme of Part 2, Struggling for Justice, by answering the following questions:

1. Do you think the hands are cooperating with one another or opposing one another, and why? Sample answer: *Students who see the hands as cooperating might point to the way the fingers are outstretched, as opposed to clenched in fists, as well as the fact that many of the hands overlap. Students who see the hands as opposing one another might note that none of the hands grasps another and the out-stretched fingers could be regarded as pushing other hands away or reaching for something the other hands want.*

2. Give this work a different title, one using the word *hands* to make some comment about society or human nature. *Sample answer: "Helping Hands"; "The Right Hand Doesn't Know What the Left Hand Is Doing"; "Many Hands Make Light Work."*

Guide for Reading

More About the Authors
William Sydney Porter (O. Henry) left school when he was fifteen years old and traveled around the country for five years before he took the ill-fated job as a bank teller in Texas. He was one of the first to perfect the technique of the surprise ending. Like Charles Dickens, he concentrates on ordinary people. He wrote tales set in the eastern United States, the Southwest, and Latin America. "The Gift of the Magi" and "The Ransom of Red Chief" are his most famous stories.

Elizabeth Bishop is known for her razor-sharp precision of language, for the strong emotional quality of her work, and the sense of strangeness that can underlie even ordinary events in her poems. In addition to poetry, Bishop also wrote short stories.

O. Henry (1862–1910)

A criminal turned storyteller, O. Henry (real name: William Sydney Porter) stole the show when it came to surprise endings.

William Sydney Porter was born in Greensboro, North Carolina. He had the amazing ability to identify with the common man, but his own life was anything but ordinary. He moved to Texas at the age of twenty-four and tried a number of unrelated jobs, including ranch hand, cartoonist, and bank teller. While working as a bank teller, he was accused (and eventually convicted) of embezzling funds. In prison, he took up writing short stories under the now famous pen name O. Henry.

Elizabeth Bishop (1911–1979)

A childhood friend of Elizabeth Bishop once said, "We all knew with no doubt whatsoever that she was a genius." Based on Bishop's accomplishments, it's hard to argue with her friend's assessment.

Bishop was born and raised in Massachusetts, but she loved to travel and spent many years living in Brazil. In 1945, she entered a poetry contest along with 800 other contestants—and she won! As a result, her first book, *North and South,* was published. "The Fish" was one of the poems in that first book.

By the time she died, Bishop had won virtually every poetry prize in the United States at least once, including the Pulitzer in 1956.

◆ Build Vocabulary

PREFIXES: *counter-*

One of the characters in "Hearts and Hands" is being taken to prison for counterfeiting. *Counterfeiting* begins with the prefix *counter-*, which means "in opposition." *Counterfeiting* (in this story, making fake money) means making something that is "in opposition" to what it seems—an imitation made to deceive.

WORD BANK

As you read this story, you will encounter the words on this list. Each word is defined on the page where it first appears. Preview the list before you read. Identify any words you think you know already.

| influx |
| forestalled |
| counterfeiting |
| sidled |
| venerable |
| infested |
| sullen |

◆ Build Grammar Skills

COORDINATE ADJECTIVES

Writers use adjectives to describe characters, settings, and images. When they use **coordinate adjectives**—two or more adjectives of equal rank that separately modify the same noun—the adjectives are separated by commas.

The order of coordinate adjectives can be changed without altering the meaning of the sentence or sounding incorrect. For example, when O. Henry describes a character's voice as "full, sweet, and deliberate," he could have arranged the adjectives in any order—the adjectives are coordinate.

In Bishop's description of the "five old pieces of fish-line" in a fish's jaw, on the other hand, the adjectives "five" and "old" are not coordinate—their order cannot be reversed. A comma is not used between adjectives that are not coordinate.

262 ◆ *Clashing Forces*

Prentice Hall Literature Program Resources

REINFORCE / RETEACH / EXTEND

Selection Support Pages
Build Vocabulary: The Prefix *counter-*, p. 80
Build Grammar Skills: Coordinate Adjectives, p. 81
Reading Strategy: Predict Story Events, p. 82
Literary Focus: Surprise Ending, p. 83

Strategies for Diverse Student Needs, p. 20

Beyond Literature
Community Connection: Random Acts of Kindness, p. 20

Formal Assessment Selection Test, pp. 66–68;

Assessment Resources Software

Alternative Assessment, p. 20

Writing and Language Transparencies
Writing Process Model 9, Business Letter, pp. 61–64

Resource Pro CD-ROM
"Hearts and Hands," "The Fish"—includes all resource material and customizable lesson plan

Literature CD-ROM
How to Read and Understand Poetry

 Listening to Literature Audiocassette
"Hearts and Hands," "The Fish"

◆ *Literature and Your Life*

CONNECT YOUR EXPERIENCE

When your best friend tells you a sad story about a difficult time he or she is going through, you probably don't respond by telling your latest success story. It's easy to feel sympathy for a friend—but compassion isn't limited to people we know. When there are news reports of an abandoned animal or a lost child, people from all over the country respond with calls to help or donations of money. Even if you can't help personally, you feel compassion for the sufferer.

Journal Writing Write about a compassionate act that you have witnessed or heard about.

THEMATIC FOCUS: STRUGGLING FOR JUSTICE

The actions of the characters in this story and this poem may surprise you. Their compassion offers a unique answer to the question, "What is 'justice'?"

◆ Background for Understanding

THE STORY BEHIND THE STORY

It's no surprise if you feel compassion for the prisoner when you read "Hearts and Hands." O. Henry deliberately creates sympathy for the prisoner—perhaps because he himself was one.

While working as a bank teller, William Sydney Porter (later to be known as O. Henry) was accused of embezzling funds. He denied the accusations and fled to Honduras. A year later, he returned to Texas to visit his sick wife and was arrested. He spent three years in a penitentiary in Columbus, Ohio. The story "Hearts and Hands" may have been inspired by his own journey to prison.

◆ Literary Focus

SURPRISE ENDING

Sometimes you can predict the ending of a story while you are reading it. At other times, you can't tell for certain how the story will be resolved, but the ending seems in all ways the logical outcome of the events. Some stories, however, have **surprise endings**—twists at the end that you did not expect. Authors build up to surprise endings by misleading you. No matter how surprising an ending is, however, it must be believable. Therefore, the author plants clues throughout that lead to the final outcome.

Pay attention to the details in the story and the poem that hint at the unexpected, but logical, outcomes.

◆ Reading Strategy

PREDICT STORY EVENTS

You can predict whether or not it will rain by looking at the sky. You can **predict story events** in much the same way—you make an educated guess based on what you know about the characters, the situation, and the logical pattern that many stories seem to follow.

No matter how logical your predictions, you may need to revise them as new information is presented. Just as a new cloud in an otherwise clear sky might change your prediction about the weather, new circumstances introduced by the author may lead you to change your predictions about story events.

Use a chart like the one shown to record and check your predictions.

Prediction	Reason	Actual Outcome

Guide for Reading ◆ 263

Show video of magicians such as Siegfried and Roy or David Copperfield performing an illusion in which something or someone is exchanged for another. (If you have any amateur magicians in your class, invite them to perform an illusion live for the class.) Lead students to see that an illusion is like a surprise ending. When the curtain is whisked away, you see a person where a tiger used to be, or a quarter appears from behind your ear when you expect it to be in the magician's hand. Tell students that the selections they are about to read are like magic tricks. When the writers "whisk away the curtain" to reveal the ending, readers may not see what they expect to see.

Customize for
More Advanced Students
Encourage these students to speculate on the reasons behind characters' actions. As students read, have them take notes for a "character history" that explains how each character develops the personality shown in the selection. Tell students to pay special attention to the dialogue between Mr. Easton and Miss Fairchild.

Customize for
Less Proficient Readers
Have students pause frequently to review important details and visualize the action. Give students specific points at which to make their predictions and guide them in supporting their predictions with details they've discovered in the story so far.

Customize for
English Language Learners
Ask these students to find the punctuation that will help them identify complete sentences in the poem. Then assist students in restating the sentences in simpler terms.

Customize for
Visual/Spatial Learners
These students can make a timeline of events and significant details in the story and poem, using either stick figures or brief descriptions.

Preparing for Standardized Tests

Reading and Vocabulary The Build Vocabulary lesson that accompanies these selections will help students define words that begin with the prefix *counter-*.

Vocabulary development is the key to success for synonym, analogy, sentence completion, and reading comprehension questions on the verbal portions of standardized tests. For additional practice, use the Build Vocabulary page in **Selection Support**, p. 80.

Grammar and Language The usage/mechanics portions of some standardized tests include a section of questions that cover internal and end-of-sentence punctuation. The Build Grammar Skills lesson for this selection focuses on the use of commas with coordinate adjectives. For additional practice, use the Build Grammar Skills page on Coordinate Adjectives, p. 81.

"Hearts and Hands" tells the story of a brief encounter between three characters on a train. Through dialogue, O. Henry hints at a past conflict between one young man and the young woman. At the end of the story, we realize that the real conflict, which is not between the young man and the young woman, is very much in the present, and that what characters say doesn't always reveal who they are.

◆ Build Grammar Skills

❶ Coordinate Adjectives Have students explain why O. Henry doesn't separate the adjectives "two" and "young" with commas yet does separate the adjectives "bold" and "frank" with commas. *The first pair are not coordinate, so their order cannot be switched without losing meaning. ("Young two men" doesn't make sense.) The second pair, in contrast, are coordinate, so they are separated by commas ("frank, bold countenance" still makes sense).*

◆ Reading Strategy

❷ Predict Story Events Guide students to recognize that Easton's embarrassment is a clue that there is something he doesn't want the young woman to know. Students' predictions can springboard from this inference.

◆ Build Vocabulary

❸ The Prefix *counter-* In context, most students will probably identify counterfeiting as creating fake money. Discuss the way in which counterfeit money is "in opposition" to real money.

◆ Critical Thinking

❹ Draw Conclusions Based on this conversation, have students draw conclusions about the past relationship of Easton and Miss Fairchild. *The conversation suggests that at one time, Easton was interested in Miss Fairchild romantically, but that he was without money and status and thought she preferred an ambassador (who probably had money).*

264

Hearts and Hands

O. HENRY

❶ At Denver there was an <u>influx</u> of passengers into the coaches on the eastbound B. & M. express. In one coach there sat a very pretty young woman dressed in elegant taste and surrounded by all the luxurious comforts of an experienced traveler. Among the newcomers were two young men, one of handsome presence with a bold, frank countenance and manner; the other a ruffled, glum-faced person, heavily built and roughly dressed. The two were handcuffed together.

As they passed down the aisle of the coach the only vacant seat offered was a reversed one facing the attractive young woman. Here the linked couple seated themselves. The young woman's glance fell upon them with a distant, swift disinterest; then with a lovely smile brightening her countenance and a tender pink tingeing her rounded cheeks, she held out a little gray-gloved hand. When she spoke her voice, full, sweet, and deliberate, proclaimed that its owner was accustomed to speak and be heard.

"Well, Mr. Easton, if you *will* make me speak first, I suppose I must. Don't you ever recognize old friends when you meet them in the West?"

> ◆ **Reading Strategy**
> What prediction do you make based on Easton's embarrassment?

❷ The younger man roused himself sharply at the sound of her voice, seemed to struggle with a slight embarrassment which he threw off instantly, and then clasped her fingers with his left hand.

"It's Miss Fairchild," he said, with a smile. "I'll ask you to excuse the other hand; it's otherwise engaged just at present."

He slightly raised his right hand, bound at the wrist by the shining "bracelet" to the left one of his companion. The glad look in the girl's eyes slowly changed to a bewildered horror. The glow faded from her cheeks. Her lips parted in a vague, relaxing distress. Easton, with a little laugh, as if amused, was about to speak again when the other <u>forestalled</u> him. The glum-faced man had been watching the girl's countenance with veiled glances from his keen, shrewd eyes.

❸ "You'll excuse me for speaking, miss, but I see you're acquainted with the marshal here. If you'll ask him to speak a word for me when we get to the pen he'll do it, and it'll make things easier for me there. He's taking me to Leavenworth prison. It's seven years for <u>counterfeiting</u>."

"Oh!" said the girl, with a deep <u>breath</u> and returning color. "So that is what you are doing out here? A marshal!"

❹ "My dear Miss Fairchild," said Easton, calmly, "I had to do something. Money has a way of taking wings unto itself, and you know it takes money to keep step with our crowd in Washington. I saw this opening in the West, and—well, a marshalship isn't quite as high a position as that of ambassador, but—"

"The ambassador," said the girl, warmly,

◆ Build Vocabulary

influx (in´ fluks) *n.*: A coming in

forestalled (fôr stôld´) *v.*: Prevented by having done something ahead of time

counterfeiting (koun´ tər fit´ iŋ) *v.*: Making imitation money to pass off as real money

sidled (sī´ dəld) *v.*: Moved sideways

264 ◆ Clashing Forces

Block Scheduling Strategies

Consider these suggestions to take advantage of extended class time:

- Use the Community Connection page on Random Acts of Kindness in the **Beyond Literature** booklet, p. 20. This activity can supplement the Literature and Your Life journal writing activity (p. 263).
- Preview the vocabulary list on page 262 as a class. Ask volunteers to identify words they think they know and share definitions. Guide students to check the accuracy of each definition by looking at the Build Vocabulary box on

the page where the word appears.

- Introduce the Reading Strategy, and model the use of the chart on page 263 for predicting events and checking predictions. You may use the Grid Organizer in the **Writing and Language Transparencies,** p. 79, to demonstrate.
- Link "Hearts and Hands" to math skills by having small groups of students work in class to complete the Money Chart project on page 269.
- Have students complete the Writing Mini-Lesson (p. 269), perhaps using a tape recorder during the interview.

❹ "doesn't call any more. He needn't ever have done so. You ought to know that. And so now you are one of these dashing Western heroes, and you ride and shoot and go into all kinds of dangers. That's different from the Washington life. You have been missed from the old crowd."

The girl's eyes, fascinated, went back, widening a little, to rest upon the glittering handcuffs.

"Don't you worry about them, miss," said the other man. "All marshals handcuff themselves to their prisoners to keep them from getting away. Mr. Easton knows his business."

"Will we see you again soon in Washington?" asked the girl.

"Not soon, I think," said Easton. "My butterfly days are over, I fear."

"I love the West," said the girl irrelevantly. Her eyes were shining softly. She looked away out the car window. She began to speak truly and simply, without the gloss of style and manner: "Mamma and I spent the summer in Denver. She went home a week ago because father was slightly ill. I could live and be happy in the West. I think the air here agrees with me. Money isn't everything. But people always misunderstand things and remain stupid—"

"Say, Mr. Marshal," growled the glum-faced man. "This isn't quite fair. Haven't had a smoke all day. Haven't you talked long enough? Take me in the smoker now, won't you? I'm half dead for a pipe."

The bound travelers rose to their feet, Easton with the same slow smile on his face.

"I can't deny a petition for tobacco," he said lightly. "It's the one friend of the unfortunate. Goodbye, Miss Fairchild. Duty calls, you know." He held out his hand for a farewell.

"It's too bad you are not going East," she said, reclothing herself with manner and style. "But you must go on to Leavenworth, I suppose?"

"Yes," said Easton. "I must go on to Leavenworth."

The two men sidled down the aisle into the smoker.

The two passengers in a seat nearby had heard most of the conversation. Said one of them: "That marshal's a good sort of chap. Some of these Western fellows are all right."

"Pretty young to hold an office like that, isn't he?" asked the other.

"Young!" exclaimed the first speaker, "why— Oh! didn't you catch on? Say—did you ever know an officer to handcuff a prisoner to his *right* hand?" ❺

Guide for Responding

◆ *Literature and Your Life*

Reader's Response Would you have bailed Mr. Easton out of his uncomfortable situation? Explain.

Thematic Focus How does the marshal's compassionate act broaden the definition of justice?

☑ **Check Your Comprehension**

1. Why did the two handcuffed men sit across from Miss Fairchild?
2. How do Miss Fairchild and Mr. Easton know each other?

◆ **Critical Thinking**

INTERPRET
1. Why does the marshal deceive Miss Fairchild? **[Speculate]**
2. Explain what role "hearts" and "hands" play. **[Analyze]**

EXTEND
3. Do you think compassion is a necessary quality for a person who works in law enforcement or the justice system? Why or why not? **[Career Link]**

Hearts and Hands ◆ 265

 Beyond the Classroom

Career Connection

Law Enforcement Police officers help to keep peace and order in a community. They prevent criminal acts, enforce the law, and arrest people who break the law. They also perform services to aid people who are in trouble. Most police officers are required to be high school graduates. For more information, students can write to obtain the Police Employment Guide, Sam Houston State University, Huntsville TX, 77340.

Corrections officers see to the safekeeping of people who have been arrested and are awaiting trial or who have been sentenced to serve time in correctional institutions. Corrections officers maintain order and enforce the rules in their institutions. They may serve as guards inside prisons, on towers, and at gates to prevent escapes. Most correctional officers are expected to have a high school diploma or its equivalent. For more information, students can write to American Correctional Association, 4321 Hartwick Road L-208, College Park, MD 20740.

Please be aware that addresses may have changed since this information was published.

265

One-Minute Insight

At the opening of this poem, the conflict seems to be resolved—the fish is caught. As the poem continues, the speaker reveals an internal conflict that leads to an outcome readers may not expect.

◆ Critical Thinking

❶ Infer Ask students what they can infer about the fish from details such as "ancient wallpaper" and "stained and lost through age." *The fish is very old. He has survived what appears to be a difficult life.*

◆ Reading Strategy

❷ Predict Events Encourage students to predict what the speaker will do with the fish. *This section indicates that the speaker is thinking about filleting the fish. Some students may interpret this passage as the speaker's reflection on the fish's living organs, and that this reflection will lead to feeling compassion for the fish.*

◆ Critical Thinking

❸ Make Inferences Ask students why Bishop wants the reader to know that the fish didn't return the speaker's stare. How might this make the speaker feel? *Students may say that the fish doesn't care about being caught and is not interested in the speaker at all. This might make the speaker feel unimportant.*

◆ Build Grammar Skills

❹ Coordinate Adjectives Ask students why Bishop puts commas between the adjectives "grim, wet, and weaponlike" but not between "five old." *The first three adjectives are coordinate. The second pair are not coordinate (their order cannot be switched without losing their meaning).*

◆ Reading Strategy

❺ Predict Events Have students make a logical guess about the poem's outcome. *Students might guess that the speaker will let the fish go because she feels compassion for the pain it has suffered in the past or respect for the fish who has eluded being caught so many times.*

The Fish

Elizabeth Bishop

I caught a tremendous fish
and held him beside the boat
half out of water, with my hook
fast in a corner of his mouth.
5 He didn't fight.
He hadn't fought at all.
He hung a grunting weight,
battered and <u>venerable</u>
and homely. Here and there
10 his brown skin hung in strips
like ancient wallpaper,
❶ and its pattern of darker brown
was like wallpaper:
shapes like full-blown roses
15 stained and lost through age.
He was speckled with barnacles,
fine rosettes of lime,
and <u>infested</u>
with tiny white sea-lice,
20 and underneath two or three
rags of green weed hung down.
While his gills were breathing in
the terrible oxygen
—the frightening gills,
25 fresh and crisp with blood,
that can cut so badly—
I thought of the coarse white flesh
packed in like feathers,
❷ the big bones and the little bones,
30 the dramatic reds and blacks
of his shiny entrails,[1]

and the pink swim-bladder[2] ❷
like a big peony.
I looked into his eyes
35 which were far larger than mine
but shallower, and yellowed,
the irises backed and packed
with tarnished tinfoil ❸
seen through the lenses
40 of old scratched isinglass.[3]
They shifted a little, but not
to return my stare.
—It was more like the tipping
of an object toward the light.
45 I admired his <u>sullen</u> face,
the mechanism of his jaw,
and then I saw
that from his lower lip
—if you could call it a lip— ❹
50 grim, wet, and weaponlike, ❺
hung five old pieces of fish-line,

---

1. **entrails** (en´ trālz) *n*.: Intestines; guts.

2. **swim-bladder:** Gas-filled sac that keeps a fish from sinking.
3. **isinglass** (ī´ zin glas´) *n*.: Semitransparent substance obtained from fish bladders and sometimes used for windows.

◆ Build Vocabulary

venerable (ven´ ər ə bəl) *adj*.: Worthy of respect or reverence by reason of age, character, or position

infested (in fest´ id) *adj*.: Overrun by

sullen (sul´ ən) *adj*.: Gloomy; sad

266 ◆ *Clashing Forces*

Cross-Curricular Connection: Science

Scientists have identified about 30,000 species of fish—a greater number than in any other class of vertebrates. Fish are found in nearly every body of salt and fresh water around the world. The greatest number of species, however, is found in the tropical waters of the Indian Ocean and southwest Pacific Ocean.

Fish is one of the most important sources of protein for humans, and most of the fish caught in the oceans and in fresh water are used for food.

Fish is also a key ingredient of nitrogen-based fertilizers, dietary supplements rich in vitamin D, and a form of gelatin.

Have students find out which types of fish live in bodies of fresh or salt water in their region. Suggest they learn how these fish are caught and possibly marketed.

or four and a wire leader
with the swivel still attached,
with all their five big hooks
55 grown firmly in his mouth.
A green line, frayed at the end
where he broke it, two heavier lines
and a fine black thread
still crimped from the strain and snap
60 when it broke and he got away.
Like medals with their ribbons
frayed and wavering,
a five-haired beard of wisdom
trailing from his aching jaw.
65 I stared and stared
6 and victory filled up
the little rented boat,
from the pool of bilge[4]
where oil had spread a rainbow
70 around the rusted engine
to the bailer rusted orange,

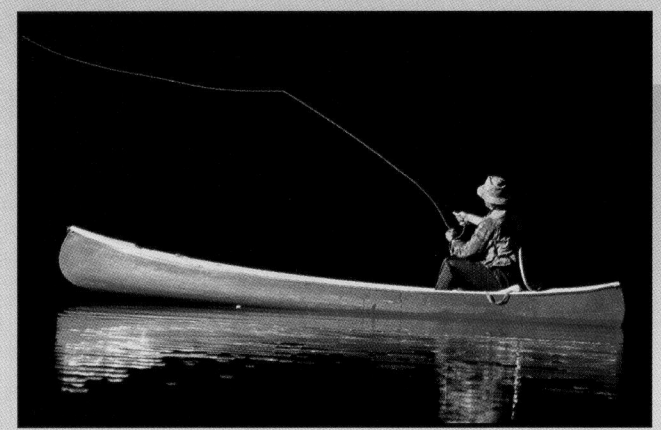

▲ **Critical Viewing** Based on this picture, why do you think many people enjoy fishing? **[Draw Conclusions]**

the sun-cracked thwarts,[5]
the oarlocks on their strings,
the gunnels[6]—until everything
75 was rainbow, rainbow, rainbow!
And I let the fish go.

---

4. **bilge** (bilj) *n.*: Dirty water in the bottom of a boat.

5. **thwarts** (*th*wôrts) *n.*: Rowers' seats lying across a boat.
6. **gunnels** (gun´ əlz) *n.*: Upper edges of the sides of a boat.

Guide for Responding

◆ *Literature and Your Life*

Reader's Response Would you have let the fish go? Explain.

Thematic Focus How do the fish's past conflicts affect the speaker?

☑ **Check Your Comprehension**

1. What does the speaker find in the lower lip of the fish?
2. Explain what the speaker does with the fish.

◆ **Critical Thinking**

INTERPRET
1. Why didn't the fish fight against being caught? **[Infer]**
APPLY
2. Explain how compassion can be a sign of strength. **[Relate]**
3. How well do you think Bishop's poem captures the nature of compassion? Explain. **[Make a Judgment]**

The Fish ◆ 267

Beyond the Selection

FURTHER READING
Other Works by O. Henry
The Four Million (short stories)
The Gentle Grafter (short stories)
Other Works by Elizabeth Bishop
North and South (poems)
Other Works About Clashing Forces
"After Twenty Years," O. Henry
"The Old Man and the Sea," Ernest Hemingway
    We suggest that you preview these works before recommending them to students.

INTERNET
Students can learn more about O. Henry at the following Web site: **http://www.ci.austin.tx.us/parks/ohenry.htm**
    For a look into O. Henry's life, students can visit **http://www.dcr.state.nc.us/NC/NCSITES/GREENSBO/O_HENRY.HTM**
    We *strongly suggest* that you preview these Web sites before sending students to them. Please be aware that addresses may have changed since this information was published.

◆ **Critical Thinking**

6 Interpret Ask students what the poet means by "victory filled up the little boat." To whose victory does she refer—the speaker's or the fish's? *Students may say that the victory is the fish's because it has so many "medals" and battle scars. Some may say that the speaker feels victorious, having caught such a venerable fish.*

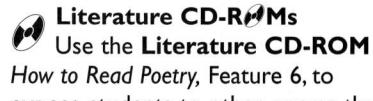
Reinforce and Extend

Literature CD-ROMs
Use the **Literature CD-ROM** *How to Read Poetry*, Feature 6, to expose students to other poems that explore the themes of moral choices.

Answers
◆ *Literature and Your Life*

Reader's Response Some students may feel that, like the speaker, they would have felt admiration for the fish and released it. Others may say they would not release it, feeling that the fish is an even more valuable "prize" because it has eluded so many other anglers.

Thematic Focus Because the fish has successfully survived so many battles, the speaker doesn't feel it would be just to end his life being caught.

☑ **Check Your Comprehension**
1. The speaker finds four or five pieces of fish line and five hooks in the fish's jaw.
2. The speaker holds the fish up and examines him, then releases him.

◆ **Critical Thinking**
1. The fish may not have fought against getting caught because he was old and tired, or because he realized the hopelessness of his situation.
2. A person who shows compassion is strong enough not to have to prove his or her strength.
3. Students may feel that catching the fish in the first place is contrary to the concept of compassion. Others may see the speaker's change of heart as a perfect example of compassion.

Answers

◆ Reading Strategy

1. The way the young woman brightens up helps you predict that the young woman knows one of the men.
2. Mr. Easton's reaction confirms the past acquaintance between the young woman and Mr. Easton. In addition, it indicates that he is worried about what she thinks of him.
3. Mr. Easton's embarrassment and ironic way of speaking are clues that can help you predict that Mr. Easton is not who he seems to be.
4. Some students will have predicted that the speaker would take the fish home as a prize, or to eat it. Other students may have predicted the actual outcome of the fish's release.

◆ Literary Focus

1. Until very near the end of the story, it seems as if Mr. Easton and Miss Fairchild may renew their relationship.
2. Students should identify the specific detail that gave them the final clue to Easton's identity.
3. Mr. Easton's embarrassment, his comment that money takes wing, and his easy acceptance of the "prisoner's" request to leave the car are clues that he is not really the marshal.
4. Students should explain how details from the poem led to their realization that the speaker would release the fish.
5. The rough appearance and manner of Mr. Easton's companion contribute to the surprise when it is revealed that he is the marshal. The excitement the speaker feels at having caught the fish contributes to the surprise when the speaker releases the fish.

◆ Build Vocabulary

Using the Prefix counter-

1. Counterclockwise is the opposite direction from the way a clock moves.
2. Counterproductive is the opposite of productive, or constructive, action.
3. A counterbalance is a weight or force placed in opposition so that it balances another weight.
4. Counterpoint is something (often a melody or an argument) set up to contrast or be opposite to another thing.

Guide for Responding (continued)

◆ Reading Strategy

PREDICT STORY EVENTS

Many stories seem to follow a logical pattern that helps you **predict story events**—that is, to make educated guesses about what will happen. In "Hearts and Hands," for instance, when the two handcuffed men board the train, you can predict that they will somehow become involved with the young woman. As you learn more about the characters and the situation, you can make more specific, and usually more accurate, predictions.

1. In "Hearts and Hands," what prediction can you make based on the young woman's reaction when she sees the two men?
2. How does Mr. Easton's reaction to the young woman affect your prediction?
3. Why might you expect that Mr. Easton and the other man are not exactly who they claim to be?
4. In "The Fish," what did you predict the speaker would do after catching the fish? Why?

◆ Literary Focus

SURPRISE ENDING

Stories, like life, can sometimes surprise you. A **surprise ending** is an unexpected twist at the end of a story. O. Henry is known for his surprise endings, and many readers try to outsmart him by looking for his clues to the real ending. In "Hearts and Hands," the fact that Mr. Easton has the handcuff on his right hand is one such clue. Elizabeth Bishop also gives a surprising twist to the end of her poem by having the speaker do the opposite of what you would expect.

1. What ending are you led to expect as you read "Hearts and Hands"?
2. At what point in the story did you realize that Mr. Easton was not the marshal?
3. Point out at least three things in Mr. Easton's words and behavior that provide clues to the real ending.
4. At what point did you first suspect that the speaker in "The Fish" would release the catch?
5. What quality or personality trait contributed to the surprise ending in the story and the poem?

◆ Build Vocabulary

USING THE PREFIX counter-

Knowing that the prefix *counter-* means "in opposition," explain how *opposite* contributes to the meaning of each of the following words.

1. counterclockwise   3. counterbalance
2. counterproductive   4. counterpoint

USING THE WORD BANK

Choose the best word from the Word Bank to complete each sentence.

1. The fish was ___?___ with lice.
2. The marshal ___?___ an embarrassing situation.
3. The prisoner ___?___ toward the door.
4. An ___?___ of people hid them from view.
5. The ___?___ man never looked up.
6. O. Henry's crime was embezzlement, not ___?___.

◆ Build Grammar Skills

COORDINATE ADJECTIVES

The order of coordinate adjectives can be reversed without changing the meaning of the description or sounding awkward. O. Henry uses coordinate adjectives when he describes Mr. Easton's "*bold, frank* countenance."

> **Coordinate adjectives** are adjectives of equal rank that separately modify a noun.

Practice Copy the following sentences in your notebook. Put commas between any coordinate adjectives.

1. The embarrassed young man didn't speak.
2. The thoughtful compassionate marshal helped him out.
3. The ugly battered fish didn't fight.
4. The little rented boat was full of rainbows.

Writing Application Use coordinate adjectives to add details to each of the following sentences.

1. The train pulled out of the station.
2. The woman looked at the men.
3. The marshal and the prisoner walked away.

Using the Word Bank

1. infested;   2. forestalled;
3. sidled;   4. influx;
5. sullen;   6. counterfeiting

◆ Build Grammar Skills

Practice

1. The embarrassed young man didn't speak. *no change*
2. The thoughtful, compassionate marshal helped him out.

3. The ugly, battered fish didn't fight.
4. The little rented boat was full of rainbows. *no change*

Writing Application

Suggested answers:

1. The *fast, powerful* train pulled out of the *noisy, crowded* station.
2. The *pleasant, gentle* woman looked at the two *scruffy, ragged* men.
3. The *thoughtful, compassionate* marshal and the *angry, sullen* prisoner walked away.

Build Your Portfolio

Idea Bank

Writing

1. **Monologue** Write a brief monologue—a speech to be delivered by a single character—in which the marshal explains why he pretended to be the criminal. **[Performing Arts Link]**

2. **Opening Scene** Write an opening scene for a sequel to "Hearts and Hands" in which Mr. Easton and Miss Fairchild meet after Mr. Easton is released from prison.

3. **Speech** Write a speech expressing where you stand on the balance between conserving natural areas for recreation (such as fishing and boating) and developing industry and housing. **[Science Link]**

Speaking and Listening

4. **Casting Discussion** With a group, discuss actors who could play the roles in "Hearts and Hands." Reach a consensus and present your recommendations and reasons to the class.

5. **Sound Effects Tape** Create a sound-effects tape to play behind a dramatic reading of "The Fish." Experiment with ways of creating the sound of a boat rocking in the water, a fishing line being reeled, and a fish slipping back into the water.

Projects

6. **Money Chart** O. Henry's counterfeiting character created fake money—money that had no value. Create a chart that shows the value of a U.S. dollar in comparison with the currency from two other countries. Write a brief explanation to go with your chart. **[Math Link; Social Studies Link]**

7. **Opening Credits** Create a set of images that you would show behind the opening credits of a movie of "Hearts and Hands." Choose images that will set the scene for the events that follow.

Writing Mini-Lesson

Letter to the Editor

Many compassionate acts—such as those of the marshal and the speaker in "The Fish"—go unnoticed or unacknowledged. Write a letter to the editor of your local newspaper about a person in your community that you feel deserves to be acknowledged for his or her compassion or charitable deeds. The following tips will help you create a convincing portrait of the person you wish to acknowledge.

Writing Skills Focus: Elaboration

Don't just *say* that the subject of your letter deserves recognition for a compassionate act—*prove it!* **Elaborate** with details, examples, and facts to support your claim. Describe the actions that led you to choose this person as the subject of your letter. If appropriate, offer statistics, such as number of hours of volunteer work. The more specific and factual you are, the more compelling your letter will be. Look for ways to elaborate as you draft and revise.

Prewriting Interview the person you are writing about or talk to people who know your subject. Personal conversations will allow you to ask questions and obtain more detailed information about the person.

Drafting Organize your letter around several key points. As you draft, include the details you've discovered to support each of the points you make.

Revising Reread your draft and identify at least one fact, example, or detail that supports each main point. If you cannot identify at least one detail supporting each main point, add a detail or example that elaborates on your general statement.

Hearts and Hands/The Fish ◆ 269

✓ ASSESSMENT OPTIONS

Formal Assessment, Selection Test, pp. 66–67, and on Assessment Resources Software. The selection test is designed so that it can be easily customized to the ability levels of your students. *Alternative Assessment,* p. 20, includes options for less advanced students, more advanced students, visual/spatial learners, verbal/linguistic learners, and logical/mathematical learners.

PORTFOLIO ASSESSMENT
Use the following rubrics in the *Alternative Assessment* booklet to assess students' writing
Monologue: Expression Rubric, p. 94
Opening Scene: Drama Rubric, p. 107
Speech: Persuasion Rubric, p. 105
Writing Mini-Lesson: Persuasion Rubric, p. 105 and Business Letter Rubric, p. 113

Guide for Reading

1. To read, comprehend, and interpret a narrative and a speech
2. To relate a narrative and a speech to personal experience
3. To apply prior knowledge to a selection
4. To identify a writer's purpose
5. To build vocabulary in context and learn the word root *-curs-*
6. To recognize and use adjective clauses
7. To write a research report with accuracy
8. To respond to the selections through writing, speaking and listening, and projects

SKILLS INSTRUCTION

Vocabulary:
Word Roots: *-curs-*

Grammar:
Adjective Clauses

Reading Strategy:
Prior Knowledge

Literary Focus:
Writer's Purpose

Writing:
Accuracy

Speaking and Listening:
Lawyer's Argument (teacher edition)

Critical Viewing:
Interpret; Analyze; Draw Conclusions

PORTFOLIO OPPORTUNITIES

Writing: Letter to a Friend; Monologue; Dear Editor

Writing Mini-Lesson: WRA Camp Report

Speaking and Listening: Lawyer's Argument; Oral Interpretation

Projects: Interview; Meet the Press

More About the Authors

Yoshiko Uchida completed her first short stories at the age of ten. A visit to Japan when she was twelve, and her later internment in the WRA camps, helped her develop a strong sense of her Japanese ancestry, which is felt in much of her writing.

After **Gerald Ford** left the White House, he lectured, served on the board of directors for several companies, and wrote his autobiography, *A Time to Heal*, published in 1979.

Yoshiko Uchida *(1921–1992)*

There was nothing unusual about Yoshiko Uchida's life until she and her family had to give up their comfortable home in Berkeley, California, and move into a stable.

In 1941, while Uchida was a student at the University of California, Japan attacked the United States naval base at Pearl Harbor. Under mounting political pressure, President Franklin Roosevelt ordered all Japanese Americans placed in camps administered by the Wartime Relocation Agency (WRA). Uchida and her family were taken first to Tanforan Racetrack near San Francisco, where they actually lived in a stable, and then to a camp in Utah.

After her release, Uchida went on to attend Smith College and became a teacher and an award-winning author of more than thirty books. In this excerpt from her book *Desert Exile: The Uprooting of a Japanese-American Family* Uchida tells how her family coped with life in a WRA camp.

Gerald Ford *(1913–   )*

As a young man, Gerald Ford turned down the chance to play professional football for the Detroit Lions and the Green Bay Packers, choosing instead to study law at Yale University.

Ford graduated from Yale Law School in 1941. He practiced law briefly but soon entered politics, serving in the House of Representatives for nearly twenty-five years.

In 1973, Ford replaced the resigning vice president, Spiro Agnew. When President Nixon resigned his office eight months later, Ford became the first president of the United States who had not been elected either president or vice president.

In 1976—more than thirty years after World War II ended—President Ford issued a public apology for the way Japanese Americans had been treated by their government.

◆ Build Vocabulary

WORD ROOTS: *-curs-*

In Uchida's narrative, you learn that she and her family receive a *cursory* medical check. Knowing that the word root *-curs-* comes from the Latin word meaning "to run," you may be able to guess that *cursory* means "run through rapidly and without care."

WORD BANK

cursory
euphemism
adept
destitute
unwieldy
communal
conspicuous
assuage

As you read this story, you will encounter the words on this list. Each word is defined on the page where it first appears. Preview the list before you read.

◆ Build Grammar Skills

ADJECTIVE CLAUSES

Uchida makes her writing concise and varied by using **adjective clauses**—groups of words that contain a subject and verb, modify a noun or pronoun, and begin with *who, that, what, whom,* or *which*.

For example, in the following sentence, Uchida tells us that friends found them and that these friends had arrived earlier. She makes one of these ideas an adjective clause that begins with *who* and modifies *friends*:

Fortunately, some friends *who had arrived earlier* found us. . . .

Look for other adjective clauses in Uchida's narrative and in Ford's speech, and notice that they add information to sentences in an economical way.

270 ◆ Clashing Forces

Prentice Hall Literature Program Resources

REINFORCE / RETEACH / EXTEND

Selection Support Pages
Build Vocabulary: Word Roots: *-curs-*, p. 84
Build Grammar Skills: Adjective Clauses, p. 85
Reading Strategy: Prior Knowledge, p. 86
Literary Focus: Writer's Purpose, p. 87

Strategies for Diverse Student Needs, p. 21

Beyond Literature Media Connection: Japanese American Internment, p. 21

Formal Assessment Selection Test, pp. 69–71; Assessment Resources Software

Alternative Assessment, p. 21

Writing and Language Transparencies
Outline, p. 103
Context Chart, p. 107

Resource Pro CD-ROM
"Desert Exile," "Remarks Upon Signing a Proclamation . . ."—includes all resource material and customizable lesson plan

Listening to Literature Audiocassettes
"Desert Exile," "Remarks Upon Signing a Proclamation . . ."

◆ from Desert Exile ◆
Remarks Upon Signing a Proclamation . . .

◆ *Literature and Your Life*

CONNECT YOUR EXPERIENCE
Although it's unfair, people often judge by appearances rather than actions. Some people may form their opinion of you based on what they think of your clothes, your hairstyle, or some other aspect of your physical appearance. As this narrative and speech demonstrate, in 1942, thousands of Americans were judged by their appearance. They were wrongly imprisoned simply because they "looked like the enemy."

Journal Writing Describe a situation in which you were judged by your appearance instead of by your actions.

THEMATIC FOCUS: STRUGGLING FOR JUSTICE
In this account, you read about innocent people who became political prisoners. Why do you think President Ford's public apology was such an important moment in our nation's history?

◆ Background for Understanding

HISTORY
During the 1940's, many Japanese Americans were imprisoned in camps run by the Wartime Relocation Agency (WRA). As this graph shows, two thirds of those imprisoned in 1942 were United States citizens. (About 33,000 Japanese Americans volunteered for the armed forces and fought courageously.) Many others had lived in the United States for years but had been barred from becoming citizens by a 1924 federal law.

After the war, the Japanese American Citizens League struggled to have the government pay the former prisoners for their lost property. In 1988, Congress finally agreed to pay the surviving Japanese Americans $1.25 billion for their losses.

◆ Literary Focus

WRITER'S PURPOSE
Writers often have **purposes**—reasons for writing—such as these: to entertain, to inform, or to persuade. The purpose or combination of purposes for any work affects the writer's choice of details and writing style. Uchida wants to inform readers about the WRA camps, so she includes details of day-to-day life in the camps. President Ford's purpose is to acknowledge officially that an injustice was done to Japanese Americans. He uses formal language appropriate for a historic speech.

◆ Reading Strategy

PRIOR KNOWLEDGE
Whether you're reading a story about a young person like yourself or a narrative about an event in history, you can use **prior knowledge**— what you already know about the subject—to help you understand what you are reading.

As you read Uchida's narrative and Ford's speech, make connections between what each author is saying and your own experience. You will also need to keep in mind the background information about WRA camps during World War II. You may find details in the narrative and the speech that confirm opinions you already have, as well as details that change your opinions.

Population of WRA Camps

Guide for Reading ◆ 271

Interest Grabber Ask students to imagine the following situation: One day you are ordered out of your home and school and told you must go and live in a camp with other people whose families came originally from the same country as yours. Your parents have to leave their jobs, and you have to leave your home, school, and friends to live in a place that is crowded and uncomfortable. It's like being in prison. Have them tell how they respond to this situation. After discussion, make sure students know that the United States Government actually forced thousands of Japanese Americans into internment camps during World War II. Have students discuss whether a similar situation could ever arise in the United States today.

Customize for
Less Proficient Readers
Less proficient readers might benefit from using their prior knowledge about the thoughts and feelings of teenagers. Suggest that they pause after reading each paragraph and consider how they would feel if they were in the writer's position.

Customize for
English Language Learners
These students may be confused by the dual references to "apartment" and "stall" and other euphemisms that are used in Uchida's description of the camps. Help these students identify the literal meaning of these references.

Customize for
Verbal/Linguistic Learners
Students who learn best through language can think about why Uchida wanted to write about such a devastating event as the internment of her family. Have them consider how writing about the event may have helped the author deal with it.

Preparing for Standardized Tests

Reading and Vocabulary The Build Vocabulary lesson for this selection focuses on the word root -curs- and the words that are built from that root. By recognizing and defining word roots, students can improve performance on vocabulary and reading comprehension items on verbal portions of standardized tests. For additional practice, use the Build Vocabulary page in **Selection Support**, p. 84.

Grammar and Language The Build Grammar Skills lesson for this selection focuses on adjective clauses. Knowing how adjective clauses function will improve students' performance on revision and essay portions of standardized tests. For additional practice, use the Build Grammar Skills page on Adjective Clauses, p. 85, in **Selection Support.**

One-Minute Insight This narrative describes one family's experiences in one of the Japanese American internment camps of the 1940's. The speech following the narrative is an apology for the treatment of Japanese Americans in these camps. Read together, they give a personal and a public perspective on an episode in American history.

◆ **Literary Focus**

❶ **Writer's Purpose** Have students note that in this passage Uchida begins to fulfill her purpose to inform readers about what happened to Japanese Americans during World War II. Ask them to list the details they learn in the first two paragraphs. *The internees were transported by bus; there were hundreds of people in the camp; they were fenced in; they were bored; they were not treated with respect, they had to live in a barrack.*

◆ **Critical Thinking**

❷ **Analyze** Have students determine what these details about the writer's mother tell them about her character. *She is a traditional, conservative woman who believes in proper manners and does not adapt well to change.*

◆ **Reading Strategy**

❸ **Use Prior Knowledge** Have students refer to the graph on page 271 to get a sense of the total number of people who were in WRA camps across the country. Guide students to see that the 8,000 Uchida refers to here is just a small portion of the total number.

from Desert Exile:
The Uprooting of a Japanese-American Family

Yoshiko Uchida

A s the bus pulled up to the grand-stand, I could see hundreds of Japanese Americans jammed along the fence that lined the track. These people had arrived a few days earlier and were now watching for the arrival of friends or had come to while away the empty hours that had suddenly been thrust upon them.

❶ As soon as we got off the bus, we were directed to an area beneath the grandstand where we registered and filled out a series of forms. Our baggage was inspected for contraband,[1] a <u>cursory</u> medical check made, and our living quarters assigned. We were to be housed in Barrack 16, Apartment 40. Fortunately, some friends who had arrived earlier found us and offered to help us locate our quarters.

It had rained the day before and the hundreds of people who had trampled on the track had turned it into a miserable mass of slippery

mud. We made our way on it carefully, helping my mother who was dressed just as she would have been to go to church. She wore a hat, gloves, her good coat, and her Sunday shoes, because she would not have thought of venturing outside our house dressed in any other way.

❷ Everywhere there were black tar-papered barracks[2] that had been hastily erected to house the 8,000 Japanese Americans of the area who had been uprooted from their homes. Barrack 16, however, was not among them, and we couldn't find it until we had traveled

❸

---

1. **contraband** (kän´ trə band´) *n.:* Smuggled goods.

2. **barracks** (bar´ əks) *n.:* Large, plain, often temporary housing.

◆ **Build Vocabulary**

cursory (kʉr´ sə rē) *adj.:* Superficial; done rapidly with little attention to detail

euphemism (yōō´ fə miz´ əm) *n.:* Word or phrase substituted for a more offensive word or phrase

---

Block Scheduling Strategies

Consider these suggestions to take advantage of extended class time:

• Introduce the Reading Strategy on page 271. Encourage volunteers to share what they know about World War II and Japanese American internment. As a class, read the Background for Understanding on page 271 and discuss the population graph. Follow up by having students complete the Cross-Curricular Connection

page on Japanese American Internment in *Beyond Literature,* p. 21.

• Use the Context Chart in *Writing and Language Transparencies,* p. 107. As a class, complete a Context Chart for each selection to set them in their respective historical and cultural contexts.

• Allow time for students to work in groups to discuss each writer's purpose and to complete the Literary Focus page

on Writer's Purpose in *Selection Support,* p. 87.

• Allow some class time for students to work on the Writing Mini-Lesson (p. 281) in class. Provide instruction on citing sources and guide students in using an outline to organize their information. Use the Outline in *Writing and Language Transparencies,* p. 103, to model the making of an outline.

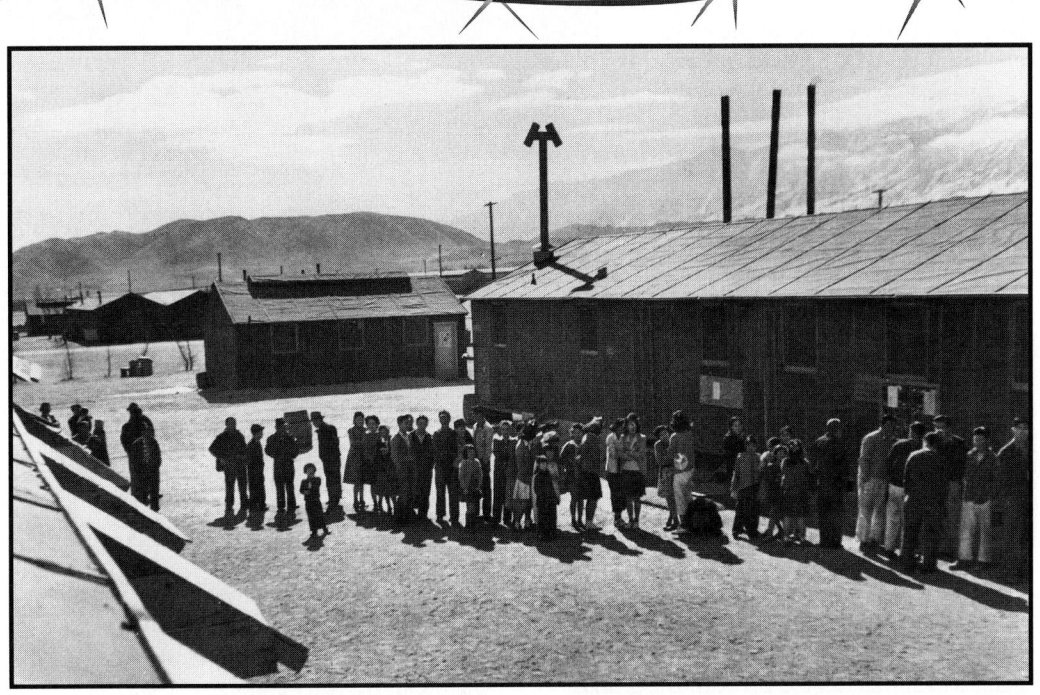

◆ **Literary Focus**

❹ **Writer's Purpose** What purpose do these details help Uchida fulfill? *These details help Uchida achieve her purpose of informing readers about the deplorable conditions of the camps.*

▶**Critical Viewing**◀

❺ **Interpret** Based on the lines of people shown in the picture and the desolate setting, students may interpret that waiting for food and supplies, overcrowding, and boredom will be some of the hardships faced at the camp.

Customize for
Visual Learners
Encourage students to create diagrams or sketches that will help them visualize the setup of the stalls in which the internees are expected to live.

Customize for
Less Proficient Readers
In addition to the Build Vocabulary, less proficient readers may need help with the following words on this page: *eucalyptus, ludicrous, ventilation.* You might bring in a sample of eucalyptus. Assist students in using context clues to determine the meaning of *ludicrous* and *ventilation.*

half the length of the track and gone beyond it to the northern rim of the racetrack compound.

Finally one of our friends called out, "There it is, beyond that row of eucalyptus trees." Barrack 16 was not a barrack at all, but a long stable raised a few feet off the ground with a broad ramp the horses had used to reach their stalls. Each stall was now numbered, and ours was number 40. That the stalls should have been called "apartments" was a euphemism so ludicrous it was comical.

When we reached stall number 40, we pushed open the narrow door and looked uneasily into the vacant darkness. The stall was about ten by twenty feet and empty except for three folded Army cots lying on the floor. Dust, dirt, and wood shavings covered the linoleum that had been laid over manure-covered boards, the smell of horses hung in the air, and

▲ **Critical Viewing** This photograph shows Japanese Americans in a WRA camp. What do you think will be some of the hardships of life in such a camp? [Interpret] ❺

the whitened corpses of many insects still clung to the hastily white-washed walls. ❹

High on either side of the entrance were two small windows which were our only source of daylight. The stall was divided into two sections by Dutch doors[3] worn down by teeth marks, and each stall in the stable was separated from the adjoining one only by rough partitions that stopped a foot short of the sloping roof. The space, while perhaps a good source of ventilation for the horses, deprived us of all but visual privacy, and we couldn't even

---

3. **Dutch doors:** Doors split across the middle so the top and bottom halves can be opened separately.

from *Desert Exile* ◆ 273

Cross-Curricular Connection: Social Studies

Japanese Houses Explain to students that the arrangement of traditional Japanese homes stresses space, light, simplicity, and harmony of form. The rooms are divided by sliding screens made of wood and paper or glass. The floors are covered by *tatami*, woven grass mats. Bedding is hidden in closets during the day, and furniture is minimal. Often a home includes an alcove with a flower

arrangement and a hanging scroll. Ask students why people used to this sort of home would find the internment camps especially difficult to bear. *The contrast between the simple, spacious elegance of a traditional Japanese home and the crowded squalor of the stalls would make living in the stalls an especially difficult adjustment.*

◆ Reading Strategy

❶ Use Prior Knowledge Based on what they know about the reasons for the internment, why do students think the internees were brought in before everything was prepared? *As public sentiment against the Japanese Americans increased, pressure to move them into the camps faster probably led to many being brought to inadequately prepared facilities.*

◆ Literary Focus

❷ Writer's Purpose Guide students to see that Uchida includes these details to communicate the feelings of the internees about the conditions they endured.

▶ Critical Viewing ◀

❸ Analyze Call students' attention to the tags on each of the individuals in this picture. Elicit from students that the individual identity of these people has been reduced to a name or number on a tag.

◆ *Literature and Your Life*

❹ Ask students how they would react in this situation. *Students may respond to the depressing setting, to the unsanitary serving methods, or to the unappetizing menu.*

◆ Critical Thinking

❺ Infer What effect do the details of the living conditions have on the internees? *Suggested response: Their living conditions have so depressed the internees that they cannot even make polite small talk.*

be sure of that because of the crevices and knotholes in the dividing walls.

Because our friends had already spent a day as residents of Tanforan, they had become <u>adept</u> at scrounging for necessities. One found a broom and swept the floor for us. Two of the boys went to the barracks where mattresses were being issued, stuffed the ticking with straw themselves, and came back with three for our cots.

❶ Nothing in the camp was ready. Everything was only half-finished. I wondered how much the nation's security would have been threatened had the Army permitted us to remain in our homes a few more days until the camps were adequately prepared for occupancy by families.

By the time we had cleaned out the stall and set up the cots, it was time for supper. Somehow, in all the confusion, we had not had lunch, so I was eager to get to the main mess hall,[4] which was located beneath the grandstand.

The sun was going down as we started along the muddy track, and a cold, piercing wind swept in from the bay. When we arrived, there were six long weaving lines of people waiting to get into the mess hall. We took our place at the end of one of them, each of us clutching a plate and silverware borrowed from friends who had already received their baggage.

Shivering in the cold, we pressed close together trying to shield Mama from the wind. As we stood in what seemed a breadline for the <u>destitute</u>, I felt degraded, humiliated, and overwhelmed with a longing for home. And I saw the unutterable sadness on my mother's face.

> **◆ Literary Focus**
> **❷** What is Uchida's purpose in revealing her feelings about standing in the line?

---
4. **mess hall:** Room or building where a group regularly meets for meals.

▲ **Critical Viewing** What detail in this picture indicates that people in WRA camps were not viewed as individuals? [Analyze] **❸**

This was only the first of many lines we were to endure, and we soon discovered that waiting in line was as inevitable a part of Tanforan as the north wind that swept in from the bay stirring up all the dust and litter of the camp.

Once we got inside the gloomy cavernous mess hall, I saw hundreds of people eating at wooden picnic tables, while those who had already eaten were shuffling aimlessly over the wet cement floor. When I reached the serving table and held out my plate, a cook reached into a dishpan full of canned sausages and dropped two onto my plate with his fingers. Another man gave me a boiled potato and a piece of butterless bread. **❹**

With 5,000 people to be fed, there were few unoccupied tables, so we separated from our friends and shared a table with an elderly man and a young family with two crying babies. No one at the table spoke to us, and even Mama could seem to find no friendly word to offer as she normally would have done. We tried to eat, but the food wouldn't go down. **❺**

"Let's get out of here," my sister suggested.

We decided it would be better to go back to

our barrack than to linger in the depressing confusion of the mess hall. It had grown dark by now and since Tanforan had no lights for nighttime occupancy, we had to pick our way carefully down the slippery track.

Once back in our stall, we found it no less depressing, for there was only a single electric light bulb dangling from the ceiling, and a one-inch crevice at the top of the north wall admitted a steady draft of the cold night air. We sat huddled on our cots, bundled in our coats, too cold and miserable even to talk. My sister and I worried about Mama, for she wasn't strong and had recently been troubled with neuralgia,[5] which could easily be aggravated by the cold. She in turn was worrying about us, and of course we all worried and wondered about Papa.

Suddenly we heard the sound of a truck stopping outside.

"Hey, Uchida! Apartment 40!" a boy shouted.

I rushed to the door and found the baggage boys trying to heave our enormous "camp bundle" over the railing that fronted our stall.

"What ya got in here anyway?" they shouted good-naturedly as they struggled with the unwieldy bundle. "It's the biggest thing we got on our truck!"

I grinned, embarrassed, but I could hardly wait to get out our belongings. My sister and I fumbled to undo all the knots we had tied into the rope around our bundle that morning and eagerly pulled out the familiar objects from home.

We unpacked our blankets, pillows, sheets, tea kettle, and, most welcome of all, our electric hot plate. I ran to the nearest washroom to fill the kettle with water, while Mama and Kay made up the Army cots with our bedding. Once we hooked up the hot plate and put the kettle on to boil, we felt better. We sat close to its warmth, holding our hands toward it as

5. **neuralgia** (nŏŏ ral′ jə) *n.*: Pain along the path of a nerve.

though it were our fireplace at home.

Before long some friends came by to see us, bringing with them the only gift they had—a box of dried prunes. Even the day before, we wouldn't have given the prunes a second glance, but now they were as welcome as the boxes of Maskey's chocolate my father used to bring home from San Francisco.

Mama managed to make some tea for our friends, and we sat around our steaming kettle, munching gratefully on our prunes. We spent much of the evening talking about food and the lack of it, a concern that grew obsessive over the next few weeks, when we were constantly hungry.

Our stable consisted of twenty-five stalls facing north which were back to back with an equal number facing south, so we were surrounded on three sides. Living in our stable were an assortment of people— mostly small family units—that included an artist, my father's barber and his wife, a dentist and his wife, an elderly retired couple, a group of Kibei bachelors (Japanese born in the United States but educated in Japan), an insurance salesman and his wife, and a widow with two daughters. To say that we all became intimately acquainted would be an understatement. It was, in fact, communal living, with semi-private cubicles provided only for sleeping.

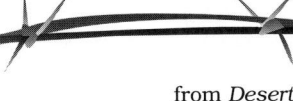

◆ *Literature and Your Life*

Discuss how you would feel if faced with the same uprooting and imprisonment that these teens dealt with.

◆ **Build Vocabulary**

adept (ə dept′) *adj.*: Expert; highly skilled

destitute (des′ tə tōōt) *n.*: Those living in poverty

unwieldy (un wēl′ dē) *adj.*: Hard to manage because of shape or weight

communal (käm yōō′ nəl) *adj.*: Shared by the community

from *Desert Exile* ◆ 275

◆ **Critical Thinking**

❻ **Draw Conclusions** Based on what they have learned and inferred so far, ask students to draw conclusions about the effect that imprisonment has on the mother's physical and emotional state. *Physically, she might suffer from cold and exhaustion. Emotionally, the worry and crude conditions might depress her.*

◆ **Reading Strategy**

❼ **Prior Knowledge** Ask students to think about the effects of hunger on people. Why did the writer compare the prunes they received to chocolate? *The food that Tanforan offered was so bad, and the Uchidas were so hungry, that the prunes were a real treat to them.*

◆ *Literature and Your Life*

❽ Most answers will focus on feelings of confusion, anger, depression, and fear students might experience.

Speaking and Listening Mini-Lesson

Lawyer's Argument

This mini-lesson supports the Speaking and Listening activity in the Idea Bank on page 281.

Introduce the Concept As a class, discuss what happened to the Uchida family. Elicit from students why they think it should not have happened.

Develop Background Encourage students to read Amendments 5 and 14 to the United States Constitution to discover exactly which of the Japanese Americans' rights were violated. They can use this information to support their

arguments. Students might also focus on the conditions of the internment camps and the loss of jobs, homes, and lifestyles.

Apply the Information Have students integrate the background information into their arguments. Encourage students to practice their arguments before giving them for the group.

Assess the Outcome Encourage students to evaluate one another's arguments using the Peer Assessment Speaker/Speech Guide in *Alternative Assessment,* p. 118.

❶ **Writer's Purpose** Ask students why they think the wrier included this statement about family life. *She wanted to show that internment had an effect on families as well as on individuals.*

▶**Critical Viewing**◀

❷ **Draw Conclusions** The small overnight cases that the people in the picture carry indicate that they did not have time to gather many belongings. The worried expressions on the faces of the people in line and the impatient expressions on the faces of the soldiers are another indication that these people are moving in a hurry.

◆ **Critical Thinking**

❸ **Relate** Encourage students to think about how difficult circumstances can lead to friendship. *Students may recall friends they made during the difficult first weeks of starting a new school or while at camp, or learning the ropes of an after-school job.*

◆ **Critical Thinking**

❹ **Make Judgments** Ask students why the army didn't provide privacy for the Japanese Americans. *Students may say that the Army was used to housing soldiers or because of prejudice against Japanese Americans the Army didn't want to make them comfortable. Some students may observe that the larger a group becomes, the more difficult it is to accommodate the need for privacy.*

▲ **Critical Viewing** What details indicate that these people were forced to leave their homes in a hurry? [Draw Conclusions]

Our neighbors on one side spent much of their time playing cards, and at all hours of the day we could hear the sound of cards being shuffled and money changing hands. Our other neighbors had a teenage son who spent most of the day with his friends, coming home to his stall at night only after his parents were asleep. Family life began to show signs of strain almost immediately, not only in the next stall but throughout the entire camp.

One Sunday our neighbor's son fell asleep in the rear of his stall with the door bolted from inside. When his parents came home from church, no amount of shouting or banging on the door could awaken the boy.

"Our stupid son has locked us out," they explained, coming to us for help.

I climbed up on my cot and considered

pouring water on him over the partition, for I knew he slept just on the other side of it. Instead I dangled a broom over the partition and poked and prodded with it, shouting, "Wake up! Wake up!" until the boy finally bestirred himself and let his parents in. We became good friends with our neighbors after that.

About one hundred feet from our stable were two latrines and two washrooms for our section of camp, one each for men and women. The latrines were crude wooden structures containing eight toilets, separated by partitions, but having no doors. The washrooms were divided into two sections. In the front section was a

Workplace Skills Mini-Lesson

Resolving Conflicts

Introduce the Concept The ability to resolve conflicts was an important skill in the internment camps. It is an important skill in the workplace as well.

Develop Background Have students identify and discuss conflicts that may arise in a workplace. Introduce these conflict situations: scheduling conflicts, interaction with angry customers, and disagreements over responsibilities. Allow time for students to

work in groups and discuss ways to resolve these conflicts. Suggest appropriate conflict resolution strategies such as the following:

• Communicate your feelings and needs clearly and calmly.

• Listen to the other person and restate your understanding of what he or she said.

• Be willing to compromise and consider other viewpoints.

Apply the Information Have students role-play each conflict situation using the skills discussed to bring the conflicts to resolution.

Assess the Outcome Encourage students to evaluate one another's resolutions. Ask them to consider if any of their solutions would have helped the families in the internment camp.

long tin trough spaced with spigots of hot and cold water where we washed our faces and brushed our teeth. To the rear were eight showers, also separated by partitions but lacking doors or curtains. The showers were difficult to adjust and we either got scalded by torrents of hot water or shocked by an icy blast of cold. Most of the Issei[6] were unaccustomed to showers, having known the luxury of soaking in deep pine-scented tubs during their years in Japan, and found the showers virtually impossible to use.

Our card-playing neighbor scoured the camp for a container that might serve as a tub, and eventually found a large wooden barrel. She rolled it to the showers, filled it with warm water, and then climbed in for a pleasant and leisurely soak. The greatest compliment she could offer anyone was the use of her private tub.

The lack of privacy in the latrines and showers was an embarrassing hardship especially for the older women, and many would take newspapers to hold over their faces or squares of cloth to tack up for their own private curtain. The Army, obviously ill-equipped to build living quarters for women and children, had made no attempt to introduce even the most common of life's civilities into these camps for us.

During the first few weeks of camp life everything was erratic and in short supply. Hot water appeared only sporadically, and the minute it was available, everyone ran for the showers or the laundry. We had to be clever and quick just to keep clean, and my sister and I often

---

6. **Issei:** Japanese who emigrated to the United States after 1907. They were not granted citizenship until 1952.

◆ **Build Vocabulary**

conspicuous (kən spik′ yoō əs) *adj.*: Easy to see

---

walked a mile to the other end of the camp where hot water was in better supply, in order to boost our morale with a hot shower.

Even toilet paper was at a premium, for new rolls would disappear as soon as they were placed in the latrines. The shock of the evacuation compounded by the short supply of every necessity brought out the baser instincts of the internees,[7] and there was little inclination for anyone to feel responsible for anyone else. In the early days, at least, it was everyone for himself or herself.

One morning I saw some women emptying bed pans into the troughs where we washed our faces. The sight was enough to turn my stomach, and my mother quickly made several large signs in Japanese cautioning people against such unsanitary practices. We posted them in conspicuous spots in the washroom and hoped for the best.

Across from the latrines was a double barrack, one containing laundry tubs and the other equipped with clotheslines and ironing boards. Because there were so many families with young children, the laundry tubs were in constant use. The hot water was often gone by 9:00 A.M., and many women got up at 3:00 and 4:00 in the morning to do their wash, all of which, including sheets, had to be done entirely by hand.

We found it difficult to get to the laundry by 9:00 A.M., and by then every tub was taken and there were long lines of people with bags of dirty laundry waiting behind each one. When we finally got to a tub, there was no more hot water. Then we would leave my mother to hold the tub while my sister and I rushed to the washroom where there was a better supply and carried back bucketfuls of hot water as everyone else learned to do. By the time we had

---

7. **internees** (in′ turn′ ēz′) *n.*: Prisoners, especially during wartime.

---

from Desert Exile ◆ 277

⑤ Clarification Tell students that *Issei* refers to Japanese people who were born in Japan. Refer students to the graph on page 271 to clarify that almost twice as many internees were born in the United States (*Nisei* and *Sonsei*) as were born in Japan.

◆ **Literary Focus**

⑥ Writer's Purpose Point out that Uchida highlights the poor conditions of the camp by concentrating on basic needs to which most people can relate: food, privacy, and cleanliness.

◆ **Critical Thinking**

⑦ Make a Judgment Ask students whether they agree that difficult conditions bring out the worst in people. *Some students may say that difficult conditions bring out the best in people, as evidenced by examples of cooperation and kindness Uchida has offered earlier in the narrative. Other students may say that the toilet paper example illustrates that difficult situations bring out the worst in people. Encourage students to offer examples from current events and literature as well as citing examples from the story.*

◆ **Build Grammar Skills**

⑧ Adjective Clauses Have students locate the adjective clause in this sentence. How does the clause add to the impact of the statement? *The adjective clause is "where we washed our faces"; it modifies troughs. The clause makes the emptying of the bedpans more horrifying.*

◆ *Literature and Your Life*

⑨ Have students compare the Uchidas' laundry with the way students' families do their laundry. Whether students have washers in their own homes and apartments or go to the Laundromat, most will agree that they do not face the same difficulties as the Uchidas in getting their laundry done.

 Cross-Curricular Connection: Social Studies

Wartime Relocation Agency Camps In the early 1940's, most Japanese Americans lived on the West Coast or in Hawaii. Many of those on the West Coast were successful farmers or business people. For years, they had faced prejudice, in part because of their success.

After Pearl Harbor, many people on the West Coast questioned the loyalty of Japanese Americans. Japanese Americans, they said, might act as spies and help Japan invade the United States. No evidence of disloyalty existed. Nonetheless, President Roosevelt agreed to move

Japanese Americans to inland camps set up by the Wartime Relocation Agency. Approximately 120,000 Japanese Americans were forced to sell their homes and businesses at great loss.

Years later, Americans began to recognize the injustice that had been done to Japanese Americans. Congress reviewed the government's wartime policy toward Japanese Americans. Lawmakers admitted that they could not right the wrong that had been done. They did however, approve a payment of $20,000 dollars to every survivor of the camps.

❶ Writer's Purpose Ask students for what purpose Uchida may have included this information about her non-Japanese friends. *She may have wanted readers to know that the government's distrust of Japanese Americans was not shared by all non-Japanese.*

◆ *Literature and Your Life*

❷ Point out to students that Uchida is citing as luxuries conditions and food items that students probably take for granted such as soap for washing dishes and an occasional lettuce salad for dinner.

◆ **Reading Strategy**

❸ Prior Knowledge Students have already learned that if the internees don't rush around they are likely to miss out on something.

◆ **Critical Thinking**

❹ Analyze Have these students consider why the Uchidas' friends helped them in the camp. Why were they not giving in to their basic instincts? *Students may suggest that difficult situations such as the Uchidas' are complex—they bring out people's baser instincts and also their more noble ones. The same person who ran to be first in line at the mess hall may give someone else part of her or his meal a few minutes later.*

◆ **Critical Thinking**

❺ Make Inferences Have students consider why the Uchidas worked so hard to make their dreadful "apartment" comfortable and homelike. *The more like home they could make their stall, the more "normal" they would feel and the less unbearable it would be to endure the harsh conditions at the camp.*

---

finally hung our laundry on lines outside our stall, we were too exhausted to do much else for the rest of the day.

For four days after our arrival we continued to go to the main mess hall for all our meals. My sister and I usually missed breakfast because we were assigned to the early shift and we simply couldn't get there by 7:00 A.M. Dinner was at 4:45 P.M., which was a terrible hour, but not a major problem, as we were always hungry. Meals were uniformly bad and skimpy, with an abundance of starches such as beans and bread. I wrote to my non-Japanese friends in Berkeley shamelessly asking them to send us food, and they obliged with large cartons of cookies, nuts, dried fruit, and jams.

We looked forward with much anticipation to the opening of a half dozen smaller mess halls located throughout the camp. But when ours finally opened, we discovered that the preparation of smaller quantities had absolutely no effect on the quality of the food. We went eagerly to our new mess hall only to be confronted at our first meal with chili con carne, corn, and butterless bread. To <u>assuage</u> our disappointment, a friend and I went to the main mess hall which was still in operation, to see if it had anything better. Much to our amazement and delight, we found small lettuce salads, the first fresh vegetables we had seen in many days. We ate ravenously and exercised enormous self-control not to go back for second and third helpings.

The food improved gradually, and by the time we left Tanforan five months later, we had fried chicken and ice cream for Sunday dinner. By July tubs of soapy water were installed at the mess hall exits so we could wash our plates and utensils on the way out. Being slow eaters, however, we usually found the dishwater tepid and dirty by the time we reached the tubs, and we often rewashed our dishes in the washroom.

Most internees got into the habit of rushing for everything. They ran to the mess halls to be first in line, they dashed inside for the best tables and then rushed through their meals to get to the washtubs before the suds ran out.

The three of us, however, seemed to be at the end of every line that formed and somehow never managed to be first for anything.

One of the first things we all did at Tanforan was to make our living quarters as comfortable as possible. A pile of scrap lumber in one corner of camp melted away like snow on a hot day as residents salvaged whatever they could to make shelves and crude pieces of furniture to supplement the Army cots. They also made ingenious containers for carrying their dishes to the mess halls, with handles and lids that grew more and more elaborate in a sort of unspoken competition.

Because of my father's absence, our friends helped us in camp, just as they had in Berkeley, and we relied on them to put up shelves and build a crude table and two benches for us. We put our new camp furniture in the front half of our stall, which was our "living room," and put our three cots in the dark windowless rear section, which we promptly dubbed "the dungeon." We ordered some print fabric by mail and sewed curtains by hand to hang at our windows and to cover our shelves. Each new addition to our stall made it seem a little more like home.

One afternoon about a week after we had arrived at Tanforan, a messenger from the administration building appeared with a telegram for us. It was from my father, telling us he had been released on parole from Montana and would be able to join us soon in camp. Papa was coming home. The wonderful news had come like an unexpected gift, but even as we hugged each other in joy, we didn't quite dare believe it until we actually saw him. . . .

◆ **Reading Strategy**
How does your prior knowledge about the harsh living conditions in the camps help explain why internees might be constantly rushing around?

◆ **Build Vocabulary**
assuage (ə swāj´) *v.*: Calm; pacify

Beyond the Classroom

Community Connection

Volunteering Remind students that people in the camp community helped the Uchidas, making furniture for them and putting up shelves. Point out that volunteering is a way to help others in local communities. People can volunteer for many different jobs, from helping older people, to cleaning up public areas, to working with children. Point out to students that, in addition to helping others in their communities, volunteers gain valuable experience that can be listed on résumés and applications for paid positions. Organizational skills, dependability, the ability to deal with the public are just a few work skills that can be developed in volunteer situations. Interested students can find out about volunteering opportunities in their community by using the Yellow Pages or contacting a local Voluntary Action Center.

Remarks Upon Signing a Proclamation Concerning Japanese American Internment During World War II

Gerald Ford February 19, 1976

February 19 is the anniversary of a very, very sad day in American history. It was on that date in 1942 that Executive Order 9066 was issued resulting in the uprooting of many, many loyal Americans. Over 100,000 persons of Japanese ancestry were removed from their homes, detained in special camps, and eventually relocated.

We now know what we should have known then—not only was that evacuation wrong but Japanese Americans were and are loyal Americans. On the battlefield and at home the names of Japanese Americans have been and continue to be written in America's history for the sacrifices and the contributions they have made to the well-being and to the security of this, our common Nation.

Executive Order 9066 ceased to be effective at the end of World War II. Because there was no formal statement of its termination, there remains some concern among Japanese Americans that there yet may be some life in that obsolete document. The proclamation [4417] that I am signing here today should remove all doubt on that matter.

I call upon the American people to affirm with me the unhyphenated American promise that we have learned from the tragedy of that long ago experience—forever to treasure liberty and justice for each individual American and resolve that this kind of error shall never be made again.

Guide for Responding

◆ *Literature and Your Life*

Reader's Response Were you surprised by Uchida's description of life in the camp? Tell why or why not.

Thematic Focus What forces came into conflict in the creation of WRA camps?

Group Discussion With a small group, list three reasons why people tend to judge others by their appearance rather than by their actions.

☑ Check Your Comprehension

1. What was "Barrack 16"?
2. How did one of the Uchidas' neighbors cope with the lack of bathtubs at Tanforan?
3. Why did President Ford choose February 19 to give his speech and to sign Proclamation 4417?
4. What did Proclamation 4417 do?

◆ Critical Thinking

INTERPRET

1. Is the camp prepared for the arrival of prisoners when the Uchidas arrive? Explain. **[Draw Conclusions]**
2. Why do you think Executive Order 9066 was never formally revoked? **[Speculate]**

EVALUATE

3. President Ford describes the imprisonment of Japanese Americans as an "error." Does that seem accurate to you? Why or why not? **[Assess]**

EXTEND

4. What do the conditions at the camp suggest about the government's attitude toward Japanese Americans? Do you think other groups would have been treated the same way? **[Social Studies Link]**

Remarks Upon Signing a Proclamation . . . ◆ 279

◆ Literary Focus

6 Writer's Purpose How does this sentence help establish the purpose of Ford's speech? *By calling it a sad day and identifying it as the anniversary of Executive Order 9066, Ford indicates that his purpose is to acknowledge the wrong that has been done.*

Reinforce and Extend

Answers

◆ *Literature and Your Life*

Reader's Response Encourage students to identify the specific reasons why they were or were not surprised.

Thematic Focus Fear and prejudice came into conflict with the basic human rights of Japanese Americans.

☑ Check Your Comprehension

1. Barrack 16 was a stable that had been minimally modified to provide shelter for the internees.
2. The neighbor scrounged around for an empty barrel and filled it with water from the showers.
3. February 19 is the anniversary of the signing of the executive order that resulted in Japanese American internment.
4. Proclamation 4417 publicly acknowledged the injustice of Japanese American internment and formally terminated Executive Order 9066.

◆ Critical Thinking

1. The camp is not prepared for the arrival of prisoners as evidenced by the overcrowded conditions, the sporadic supply of hot water and the shortage of supplies.
2. Students may suggest that Executive Order 9066 was never revoked because people assumed that internment would not be enforced again.
3. Most students will respond based on whether or not they think the word *error* is strong enough.
4. The conditions at the camp suggest that the government did not view the Japanese Americans as citizens or individuals. History shows that although the United States was also at war with Germany and Italy, German Americans and Italian Americans were not treated as traitors.

Beyond the Selection

FURTHER READING

Other Works by Yoshiko Uchida
The Sea of Gold and Other Tales from Japan
Journey to Topaz
Journey Home

Other Works About Clashing Forces
Voices from the Camps, Larry Dane Brimner
We Were Not Like Other People, Ephriam Sevela

We suggest that you preview these works before recommending them to your students.

INTERNET

Students can read the introduction to Yoshiko Uchida's short story, "The Bracelet" at the following address: **http://www.mca.com/putnam/ books/bracelet_ph/book.html**

Please be aware that the address may have changed since this information was published. We *strongly recommend* that you preview the site before sending students to it.

Answers

◆ Reading Strategy

1. Students may draw on the information presented in Background for Understanding, p. 271, from movies, plays, or novels on the subject, as well as from what they may have learned in social studies classes or at home.

2. Students will probably say they thought of examples of conditions in the camp as described by Uchida while they read Ford's speech.

3. Some students may say that the narrative gave them a deeper understanding of the conditions in the camps. Others may say that the speech helped them realize some of the underlying reasons people reacted as they did.

◆ Build Vocabulary

Using the Root -curs-
1. a   2. c   3. b

Using the Word Bank

1. A euphemism used for the WRA centers is "camps."

2. In order to get what they needed, the prisoners needed to be skillful, or adept, at scrounging.

3. A destitute, or poverty stricken, person might steal or beg to assuage, or calm, his or her hunger.

4. The Uchidas would not have brought unwieldy furniture to camp because it would have been difficult to transport.

5. A difficult adjustment to communal living is learning to deal with less privacy than one would have living in a private residence.

6. A thief wouldn't want to be conspicuous because he or she wouldn't want to be noticed while committing a crime.

◆ Literary Focus

1. The stalls are dirty, drafty, and not very private. The meals are not healthful or plentiful, the hot water for washing dishes and bathing is scarce.

2. History books would probably not contain details about how the internees dealt with the lack of privacy, or the feelings of frustration and humiliation.

3. The formal, dignified style of Ford's speech indicates the importance of the issue and the official nature of the acknowledgment.

4. The number of the executive order, the number of the proclamation, and the formal

280

Guide for Responding (continued)

◆ Reading Strategy

PRIOR KNOWLEDGE

Your **prior knowledge**—what you already knew about WRA camps—may have influenced your understanding of and reaction to this narrative and speech. What you read may also have influenced what you thought you knew about the subject.

1. What did you know about WRA camps before you read the excerpt from "Desert Exile"?

2. What did you learn in one of these pieces that you thought about while you read the other?

3. Explain how your ideas about WRA camps did or did not change as a result of reading these two works.

◆ Build Vocabulary

USING THE ROOT -curs-

Knowing that the word root -curs- means "to run," match each word in Column A with its description in Column B.

Column A	Column B
1. cursory	a. quickly done
2. cursor	b. handwriting in which the letters run together
3. cursive	c. movable light that runs across a computer screen

USING THE WORD BANK

Answer the following questions in your notebook.

1. What is a *euphemism* used for the WRA centers?
2. Why did the prisoners become *adept* at scrounging necessities?
3. What might a *destitute* person do to *assuage* his or her hunger?
4. Would the Uchidas bring *unwieldy* furniture to the camp?
5. What do you think would be the most difficult adjustment to *communal* living?
6. Why wouldn't a thief want to be *conspicuous*?

280 ◆ Clashing Forces

◆ Literary Focus

WRITER'S PURPOSE

Ford and Uchida both write about the WRA camps, but each writer's **purpose**—reason for writing—was different. Uchida's purpose is to create a personal record of her experience to help others understand what it was like to live in the camp. Ford's purpose was to create a historical record acknowledging the injustice of the camps.

1. Identify three details in the excerpt from "Desert Exile" that give you a personal glimpse of life inside the camp.

2. Identify one detail in Uchida's narrative that you would not find in a history book.

3. Explain how the style of Ford's speech helps him accomplish his purpose.

4. Identify one detail that Ford includes for the sake of history that would not be included in a personal account. Explain your choice.

◆ Build Grammar Skills

ADJECTIVE CLAUSES

An **adjective clause** is a group of words that contains a subject and a verb, modifies a noun or pronoun, and begins with a word like *who, that,* or *which.*

Practice Copy the following sentences in your notebook. Underline the adjective clause in each. Draw an arrow from the clause to the noun it modifies.

1. People who had trampled on the track had turned it into a slippery mess.

2. On either side of the entrance were two small windows which were our only source of daylight.

3. The proclamation that I am signing here today should remove all doubt.

Writing Application In your notebook, combine each pair of sentences by turning one of them into an adjective clause.

1. Uchida wrote about WRA camps. Uchida experienced life in the camp firsthand.

2. Ford's speech was made in 1976. Ford's speech acknowledged a government mistake.

3. Uchida described the food. The food was served in the mess hall.

---

request to the public would probably not be found in a personal account. Students may explain that these details would not help the writer of a personal account communicate the day-to-day experience of living in one of the camps.

◆ Build Grammar Skills

1. The clause "who had trampled on the track" modifies people.

2. The clause "which were our only source of daylight" modifies windows.

3. The clause "that I am signing here today" modifies proclamation.

Writing Application

Suggested answers:
1. Uchida, who experienced life in the camp firsthand, wrote about WRA camps.

2. Ford's speech, which he made in 1976, acknowledged a government mistake.

3. Uchida described the food that was served in the mess hall.

Writer's Solution

For additional instruction and practice, use the *Writer's Solution Grammar Practice Book* page on adjective clauses, p. 51.

Build Your Portfolio

Idea Bank

Writing

1. **Letter to a Friend** As Uchida, write a letter to one of your friends back in Berkeley describing conditions in the camp and your feelings about being there.

2. **Monologue** Write a brief monologue in which a guard at one of the camps tells how he or she feels about the imprisonment of innocent people.

3. **Dear Editor** Imagine that you were a teenager in 1942. Write a letter to the editor in which you express your views on the imprisonment of Japanese Americans.

Speaking and Listening

4. **Lawyer's Argument** As a lawyer during World War II, prepare an argument you could present in court to defend a Japanese American family against unlawful imprisonment. Then perform your defense for the class. **[Social Studies Link; Performing Arts Link]**

5. **Oral Interpretation** Pretend that you are President Ford and rehearse the 1976 speech. Then give the speech in class.

Projects

6. **Interview** Interview someone who lived during World War II or read another firsthand account of someone's experiences during this time. Share what you learn in an oral presentation to your class.

7. **Meet the Press** After a president gives a speech, reporters often have the chance to ask questions. Act out the press conference that might have taken place after President Ford's speech. **[Social Studies Link; Performing Arts Link]**

from *Desert Exile/Remarks Upon Signing a Proclamation . . .* ♦ 281

Writing Mini-Lesson

WRA Camp Report

Yoshiko Uchida describes only one of the many places where Japanese Americans were held. Write a **research report** that describes conditions at other WRA camps during World War II.

Writing Skills Focus: Accuracy

When you use facts to support a point in a research report, on a test, or in a position paper, **accuracy** is essential. Often you'll find more than one version of the facts and have to decide which one is more likely to be correct. President Ford says

> Over 100,000 persons of Japanese ancestry were removed from their homes, detained in special camps, and eventually relocated.

The Japanese American Citizens League says the total was closer to 120,000.

It is important to cite several sources in order to ensure accuracy in your research paper. Be accurate in your notetaking as well as your writing. When you revise, check facts again.

Prewriting Use books about World War II to compile facts and figures about the many WRA centers set up for Japanese Americans during the war. Refer to several sources to ensure the accuracy of your facts.

Drafting As you draft, include specific details you learned from your research about the other WRA camps and explain how they compare with Uchida's description. Don't include any facts you are unable to verify.

Revising As you revise your report, double-check all facts and figures mentioned in your draft with your original notes. If necessary, qualify statements with words like *approximately, nearly,* and *more than.*

Idea Bank

Customizing for
Learning Modalities
Following are suggestions for matching Idea Bank topics with your students' learning modalities:
Verbal/Linguistic: 4, 5, 6
Interpersonal: 6, 7
Bodily/Kinesthetic: 4, 7

Customizing for
Performance Levels
Following are suggestions for matching the Idea Bank topics with your students' ability levels.
Less Advanced: 1, 5, 7
Average: 2, 4, 7
More Advanced: 3, 5, 6

Writing Mini-Lesson

Refer students to the Writing Handbook, page 965 for instruction in the writing process, and page 968 for more information on research writing.

Use the Outline in *Writing and Language Transparencies* to model one way students can organize their information before drafting.

Writer's Solution

Writers at Work Videodisc
Use the Research Writing segment (Ch. 5) of the videodisc in which N. Scott Momaday discusses his research techniques.

Play frames 3 to 9933

Writing Lab CD-ROM
Have students complete the Research tutorial. Follow these steps:
1. Complete the Audience Profile activity.
2. Use the interactive KWL chart to focus research needs.
3. Use the Timeline, Chain of Events Organizer, or the Notecards Activity to organize information on the computer.
4. Draft on the computer.
5. Review the audio-annotated student models before revising your report.

Sourcebook
Have students use Chapter 5, Research Writing (pp. 128–163). The chapter includes in-depth instruction on organizing information (pp. 150–153).

✓ ASSESSMENT OPTIONS

Formal Assessment, Selection Test, pp. 69–70, and in Assessment Resources Software.
Alternative Assessment, p. 21, includes options for less advanced students, more advanced students, verbal/linguistic learners, visual/spatial learners, and logical/mathematical learners.

PORTFOLIO ASSESSMENT
Use the following rubrics to assess student writing and activities.
Letter to a Friend: Expressive Writing Rubric, p. 94
Monologue: Drama Rubric, p. 109
Dear Editor: Business Letter Rubric, p. 113
Writing Mini-Lesson: Research Report Rubric, p. 106

Guide for Reading

1. To read, comprehend, and interpret a story
2. To relate a story to personal experience
3. To engage the senses in reading
4. To identify relationships between characters
5. To build vocabulary in context and learn the word root -*jud*-
6. To make pronouns agree with their antecedents
7. To write a firsthand biography with logical organization
8. To respond to the story through writing, speaking and listening, and projects

SKILLS INSTRUCTION

Vocabulary:
Word Roots: -*jud*-
Grammar:
Pronoun-
Antecedent
Agreement
Reading Strategy:
Engage Your Senses
Literary Focus:
Relationships
Between
Characters

Writing:
Logical
Organization
Speaking and Listening:
Courtroom Speech (teacher edition)
Critical Viewing:
Connect; Speculate

PORTFOLIO OPPORTUNITIES

Writing: Description; Character's Journal Entry; Letter to the Embassy
Writing Mini-Lesson: Firsthand Biography
Speaking and Listening: Courtroom Speech; Oral Interpretation
Projects: Timeline; Sketch

More About the Author

Rabindranath Tagore grew up in a large extended family, with sometimes as many as 200 relatives living in the house. These relatives included painters, writers, and musicians. Tagore's father furthered his education by taking him on a trip to the Himalayas where he taught his son Sanskrit, English, and astronomy, and gave him instruction in Hindu religion. At the age of 14, Tagore gave his first public recitation of his poetry. He went on to write more than 100,000 lines of poetry in his long career.

Rabindranath Tagore
(1861–1941)

Rabindranath Tagore spent his life fighting for India's independence—but his weapon was a pen, not a sword or a gun. Six years after his death, Tagore's dream came true: India won its independence.

A Man of Many Talents
Tagore was a very diverse man. He was a poet, short-story writer, novelist, playwright, philosopher, and an accomplished painter and composer. He composed more than 4,000 songs, including India's national anthem.

A Man of Principles Tagore was deeply disturbed by the poverty and other hardships faced by millions of Indians. He was also troubled by the British army's use of force to suppress any type of protest by the Indian people. (Britain ruled India at the time.) He took action in response to the problems he saw.

> *Tagore turned down a knighthood as a protest against the injustices of British rule in India.*

Although Tagore died in 1941 at the age of 80, his work continues to grow in popularity throughout the world. In honor of his work as a writer, Tagore received the Nobel Prize for Literature in 1913. He was the first Indian to win this award.

◆ Build Vocabulary

WORD ROOTS: -*jud*-
In this selection, you will encounter the word *judicious*. The word root -*jud*-, which means "judge," gives you a clue that *judicious* means "showing good judgment," or "common sense."

WORD BANK

precarious
impending
judicious
euphemism
imploring
fettered
sordid
pervaded

As you read "The Cabuliwallah," you will encounter the words on this list. Each word is defined on the page where it first appears. Preview the list before you read. With a partner, explain the meanings of any words you think you already know.

◆ Build Grammar Skills

PRONOUN AND ANTECEDENT AGREEMENT
Pronouns help writers avoid repeating the same nouns over and over. For a pronoun to make sense, however, it must **agree** with its **antecedent** (the noun or pronoun it replaces) in **number** (singular or plural) and **gender** (masculine, feminine, or neuter).

Notice the pronouns in these examples:

...the two *friends* so far apart in age would subside into *their* old language and *their* old jokes...

(The plural pronoun *their* refers to the plural antecedent *friends*.)

I cannot tell what my *daughter*'s feelings were at the sight of this *man,* but *she* began to call *him* loudly.

(The singular feminine pronoun *she* refers to the singular feminine noun *daughter;* the singular masculine pronoun *him* refers to the singular masculine noun *man.*)

Prentice Hall Literature Program Resources

REINFORCE / RETEACH / EXTEND

Selection Support Pages
Build Vocabulary: Word Roots: -*jud*-, p. 88
Build Grammar Skills: Pronoun-Antecedent Agreement, p. 89
Reading Strategy: Engage Your Senses, p. 90
Literary Focus: Character Relationships, p. 91

Strategies for Diverse Student Needs, p. 22

Beyond Literature
Multicultural Connection: Wedding Customs, p. 22

Formal Assessment Selection Test, pp. 72–74;

Assessment Resources Software

Alternative Assessment, p. 22

Writing and Language Transparencies
Writing Process Model 2: Biographical Profile, p. 13

Resource Pro CD-ROM
"The Cabuliwallah"—includes all resource material and customizable lesson plan

 Looking at Literature Videodisc
Chapter 3, Indian Music and Dance

 Listening to Literature Audiocassettes
"The Cabuliwallah"

The Cabuliwallah

◆ *Literature and Your Life*

CONNECT YOUR EXPERIENCE

Your memory records people from your past like snapshots in a scrapbook. When you don't see or hear from someone for a long time, that person becomes "frozen" on the film of your memory. A childhood friend who moved away remains five years old in your mind, although he or she would be attending high school now.

The main character in this story experiences a conflict created by such a "time freeze."

Journal Writing Describe someone you used to know who is "frozen" on the film of your memory. What do you think that person is like now?

THEMATIC FOCUS: STRUGGLING FOR JUSTICE

In this story, clashing forces send a man to prison, separating him from his family and friends for eight years. You may find yourself questioning whether his punishment fits his crime.

◆ Background for Understanding

CULTURE

The Cabuliwallah in this story is a kind of traveling salesman. The Indian word *wallah* means "salesman"; the *Cabuli*wallah is the "salesman from Cabul" (Kabul, the capital of Afghanistan).

People travel from their homes to live and work temporarily in other countries for a variety of reasons. Frequently, these "guest workers" come to a country with greater economic opportunities, working hard and living poorly so they can send money to loved ones at home. The Cabuliwallah travels from Afghanistan to India, returning home once a year to visit his wife and daughter.

◆ Literary Focus

RELATIONSHIPS BETWEEN CHARACTERS

You can learn a lot about a person by the company he or she keeps. Similarly, in a short story you can learn a lot by examining the **relationships between characters**—the interactions and feelings that pass between the people in the story. For instance, in "The Cabuliwallah" a little girl grows up and grows away from her childhood friend who has been gone for eight years. The changes in the way she responds to him reveal important changes in her character.

◆ Reading Strategy

ENGAGE YOUR SENSES

People say "a picture is worth a thousand words," but pictures show you only how something looks. You can't *hear* a picture of a bell or *taste* a picture of an orange. When you read a short story, **engage your senses**—use the details of sight, sound, taste, smell, and touch to fully experience the richness of the characters and the setting. For example, when Tagore describes the sound of his daughter's laughter and the feel of sunshine on his face, draw on your own memories to try to experience these sensations yourself.

Use a sensory details chart to record the variety of sensory details that bring this story to life.

Sight	Sound	Touch	Taste	Smell
	Daughter's laughter	Sunshine on his face		

Guide for Reading ◆ 283

Play a recording of the Beatles song "Yesterday," featured in the Connections to Today's World, page 288. Ask students what they think the lyrics say about the nature of relationships. Then direct students' attention to the song lyrics and the questions on page 288 and the picture on page 289. Lead a discussion in which students discuss ways people and relationships change. Tell students that "The Cabuliwallah" provides another perspective on the changing nature of relationships.

Customize for
Less Proficient Readers
To help less proficient readers understand the story, encourage them to make a chart showing the relationships among these characters: the narrator and his daughter, the narrator and the Cabuliwallah, Mini (the daughter) and the Cabuliwallah, and so on. They can note how the relationships change as the story progresses.

Customize for
More Advanced Students
More advanced students might enjoy noting how the sensory descriptions in the story give a sense of a culture different from their own. What sensory details reflect the culture of the narrator?

Customize for
English Language Learners
English language learners might benefit from listing and defining words that refer to items from the narrator's culture, such as *turban*, *bamboo*, and *sari*.

Preparing for Standardized Tests

Grammar and Language The grammar and usage section of some standardized tests requires students to identify and explain correct pronoun usage in a passage like the following:

> Some years ago, the theory was rampant that after the age of about 40, the average researcher began losing *their* creative spark.

Is the author's use of the pronoun *their* appropriate? *(C)*

(A) Yes, because the pronoun is inclusive.

(B) Yes, the pronoun shows agreement and gives emphasis to "average researcher."

(C) No, the pronoun "their" does not agree in number with "researcher."

(D) No, the pronoun "their" should not be used in formal writing.

The Build Grammar Skills lesson for this selection focuses on pronoun-antecedent agreement. Practice with making pronouns agree with their antecedents will help students identify errors and know why they are incorrect. For additional practice, use the Build Grammar Skills page on Pronoun-Antecedent Agreement, p. 89, in **Selection Support.**

One-Minute Insight

This short story is set in India and describes a culture and customs very different from the culture in the United States. However, it treats themes that are universal: the love of fathers for their daughters, and the ways that relationships change as people change. In the beginning of the story, the narrator considers the Cabuliwallah very different from himself, but by the story's end, he realized that the similarities between them are more important than the differences.

◆ Literary Focus

❶ Relationships Between Characters Have students describe the relationship between father and daughter at the beginning of the story as open, communicative, and comfortable.

❷ Enrichment Explain to students that, while the official language of India is Hindi, only about half the people speak it. In fact, there are fourteen major languages, more than 150 minor ones, and more than 700 dialects spoken in India. The most widely spoken language has two different alphabets. Written one way, it is called Hindi, and written the other way, it is called Urdu. Bengali, Gujariti, Kashmiri, and Punjabi are only a few of the other languages spoken in India. Most people who live in the same state speak the same language.

◆ Reading Strategy

❸ Engage Your Senses To what senses does the writer appeal in these lines? *The writer appeals to the senses of sight and hearing.*

▶ Critical Viewing ◀

❹ Connect The busy, chaotic scene reflects the feeling of energy in the author's description of Mini. The scene suggests the lively variety that might draw a child of Mini's temperament to look out the window.

The Cabuliwallah

Rabindranath Tagore

Translated From the Bengali Language

❶ Mini, my five-year-old daughter, cannot live without chattering. I really believe that in all her life she has not wasted one minute in silence. Her mother is often vexed at this and would stop her prattle, but I do not. To see Mini quiet is unnatural, and I cannot bear it for long. Because of this, our conversations are always lively.

One morning, for instance, when I was in the midst of the seventeenth chapter of my new novel, Mini stole into the room and, putting her hand into mine, said: "Father! Ramdayal the doorkeeper calls a crow a krow! He doesn't know anything, does he?"

❷ Before I could explain the language differences in this country, she was on the trace of another subject. "What do you think, Father? Shola says there is an elephant in the clouds, blowing water out of his trunk, and that is why it rains!"

The child had seated herself at my feet near the table and was playing softly, drumming on her knees. I was hard at work on my seventeenth chapter, where Pratap Singh, the hero, had just caught Kanchanlata, the heroine, in his arms and was about to escape with her by the third-story window of the castle, when all of a sudden Mini left her play and ran to the window, crying "A Cabuliwallah! a Cabuliwallah!" Sure enough, in the street below was a Cabuliwallah passing slowly along. He ❸ wore the loose, soiled clothing of his people, and a tall turban; there was a bag on his back, and he carried boxes of grapes in his hand.

I cannot tell what my daughter's feelings were at the sight of this man, but she began to call him loudly. Ah, I thought, he will come in, and my seventeenth chapter will never be

---

❹ **Critical Viewing** How does this market scene reflect the mood at ▶ the beginning of "The Cabuliwallah"? [Connect]

284 ♦ Clashing Forces

Block Scheduling Strategies

Consider these suggestions to take advantage of extended class time:

- Use the Journal Activity from Literature and Your Life on page 283 as a lead-in to introduce the Literary Focus, Relationships Between Characters. Point out to students that like real people, as characters grow and change, so do their relationships with others.

- Use the Cross-Curricular Connections notes on the Caste System (p. 285) and Afghanistan and Britain (p. 286) to provide students with additional background.

- Share with students the Career Connection note on p. 287.

- Use the *Beyond Literature* feature, p. 291, to expand students' understanding of the story's setting and develop their map-reading skills.

- Allow time for students to meet in groups and discuss the Connections to Today's World feature on page 288.

- Have the class work in groups to create the Timeline from the Idea Bank on page 293.

The Cabuliwallah   285

Have these students describe the sounds that might accompany the scene in this photograph. *Answers may include shouting voices, music, and the sounds of wagons and motor vehicles.* Encourage students to add details of sight, sound, touch, taste, and smell to their sensory details chart, based on what they see in the photograph.

Cross-Curricular Connection: Social Studies

The Caste System Explain to students that the caste system is a class system in Hindu society. The top caste is the *Brahman*, or priest, caste. Below that are the *Kshatriyas*, or warriors, the *Vaisyas*, who are merchants and bankers, and the *Sudras*, artisans and laborers. Each of these broad divisions has many subdivisions—perhaps as many as 3,000 in all. There are also the untouchables, people in the lowest social group. The caste system was abolished in India in 1950, but discrimination against the untouchables is still a problem. Tell students that Tagore's own caste was *pirali brahman*—one of the brahman castes.

❶ Relationships Between Characters Ask students why Mini decides to make friends with the Cabuliwallah. *She has found an adult who will listen to her and isn't too busy to spend time with her.*

◆ Critical Thinking

❷ Make Inferences Why is Mini's mother shocked that Mini took money from the Cabuliwallah? *Mini's mother does not understand the relationship between Mini and the Cabuliwallah. Also, the Cabuliwallah is from a lower and poorer class than Mini's.*

◆ Critical Thinking

❸ Speculate Ask students to offer reasons why the Cabuliwallah enjoys talking to Mini so much. *Some students may say that, because the Cabuliwallah travels all the time, he has no friends and is lonely. Other students may suggest that the Cabuliwallah likes children or that spending time with Mini allows him to laugh and be silly.*

Customize for
Less Proficient Readers

❹ Students who have trouble identifying the relationships between characters should examine the exchange about the elephant to understand the relationship between the Cabuliwallah and Mini. The private joke emphasizes that these two have found in each other a quality they do not find in other people.

---

finished! At this exact moment the Cabuliwallah turned and looked up at the child. When she saw this, she was overcome by terror, fled to her mother's protection, and disappeared. She had a blind belief that inside the bag which the big man carried were two or three children like herself. Meanwhile, the peddler entered my doorway and greeted me with a smiling face.

So <u>precarious</u> was the position of my hero and my heroine that my first impulse was to stop and buy something, especially since Mini had called to the man. I made some small purchases, and a conversation began about Abdurrahman, the Russians, the English, and the frontier policy.[1]

As he was about to leave, he asked: "And where is the little girl, sir?"

I, thinking that Mini must get rid of her false fear, had her brought out. She stood by my chair, watching the Cabuliwallah and his bag. He offered her nuts and raisins, but she would not be tempted and only clung closer to me, with all her doubts increased. This was their first meeting.

❶ One morning, however, not many days later, as I was leaving the house, I was startled to find Mini seated on a bench by the door, laughing and talking with the great Cabuliwallah at her feet. In all her life, it appeared, my small daughter had never found so patient a listener, except for her father. Already the corner of her little sari[2] was stuffed with almonds and raisins, gifts from her visitor. "Why did you give her those?" I said and, taking out an eight-anna piece,[3] handed it to him. The man accepted the money without delay, and slipped it into his pocket.

❷ Alas, on my return an hour later, I found the unfortunate coin had made twice its own worth of trouble. The Cabuliwallah had given it to

---

1. **Abdurrahman . . . policy:** Political issues between Great Britain and Afghanistan at the time of the story.
2. **sari** (sä´ rē) *n.*: Garment worn by a Hindu woman, which consists of a long piece of cloth worn wrapped around the body, with one end forming an ankle-length skirt and the other end draped over one shoulder and, sometimes, around the head.
3. **eight-anna piece:** Coin formerly used in India.

Mini, and her mother, seeing the bright round object, had pounced on the child with: "Where did you get that eight-anna piece?"

❷

"The Cabuliwallah gave it to me," said Mini cheerfully.

"The Cabuliwallah gave it to you!" cried her mother much shocked. "O Mini! how could you take it from him?"

Entering at this moment, I saved her from <u>impending</u> disaster and proceeded to make my own inquiries. I found that it was not the first or the second time the two had met. The Cabuliwallah had overcome the child's first terror by a <u>judicious</u> bribery of nuts and almonds, and the two were now great friends.

They had many quaint jokes which afforded them a great deal of amusement. Seated in front of him, and looking with all her tiny dignity on his gigantic frame, Mini would ripple her face with laughter and begin "O Cabuliwallah! Cabuliwallah! what have you got in your bag?"

❸
❹

He would reply in the nasal accents of a mountaineer: "An elephant!" Not much cause for merriment, perhaps, but how they both enjoyed their joke! And for me, this child's talk with a grown-up man always had in it something strangely fascinating.

Then the Cabuliwallah, not to be caught behind, would take his turn with: "Well, little one, and when are you going to the father-in-law's house?"[4]

Now most small Bengali[5] maidens have heard long ago about the father-in-law's house, but we, being a little modern, had kept these things from our child, and at this question Mini must have been a trifle bewildered. But she would not show it and with instant composure replied: "Are you going there?"

Among men of the Cabuliwallah's class, however, it is well-known that the words "father-in-law's house" have a double meaning. It is a <u>euphemism</u> for jail, the place where we are well cared for at no expense. The sturdy peddler

---

4. **father-in-law's house:** An expression meaning "getting married."
5. **Bengali:** Of or from Bengal, a region of eastern India and, now, Bangladesh.

Cross-Curricular Connection: Social Studies

Afghanistan and Britain Explain to students that Afghanistan became a united state in 1747. In the 1800's, Britain wanted to protect India, which it controlled, from the Russians, but Afghanistan wanted the British off their frontier. Afghanistan engaged in two wars with the British, one in 1839 and one in 1878. In 1893 Shah Abdur Rahman Khan negotiated a treaty defining the boundary between Afghanistan and Pakistan, and an uneasy peace was maintained until World War I. In 1919, there was a third Afghan War, and with the treaty following it, the British gave up their interests in Afghanistan. Point out that the story takes place during the rule of Abdur Rahman; ask students what the narrator and the Cabuliwallah would have discussed.

would take my daughter's question in this sense. "Ah," he would say, shaking his fist at an invisible policeman, "I will thrash my father-in-law!" Hearing this, and picturing the poor, uncomfortable relative, Mini would go into peals of laughter, joined by her formidable friend.

These were autumn mornings, the time of year when kings of old went forth to conquest; and I, never stirring from my corner in Calcutta,[6] would let my mind wander over the whole world. At the very name of another country, my heart would go out to it, and at the sight of a foreigner in the streets, I would fall to weaving a network of dreams: the mountains, the glens,[7] the forests of his distant homeland with a cottage in its setting, and the free and independent life of faraway wilds. Perhaps these scenes of travel pass in my imagination all the more vividly because I lead a vegetable existence such that a call to travel would fall upon me like a thunderbolt. In the presence of this Cabuliwallah I was immediately transported to the foot of mountains, with narrow defiles[8] twisting in and out amongst their towering, arid peaks. I could see the string of camels bearing merchandise, and the company of turbaned merchants carrying queer old firearms, and some of their spears down toward the plains. I could see—but at this point Mini's mother would intervene, imploring me to "beware of that man."

Unfortunately Mini's mother is a very timid lady. Whenever she hears a noise in the street or sees people coming toward the house, she always jumps to the conclusion that they are either thieves, drunkards, snakes, tigers, malaria, cockroaches, caterpillars, or an English sailor. Even after all these years of experience, she is not able to overcome her terror. Thus she was full of doubts about the Cabuliwallah and used to beg me to keep a

◆ **Reading Strategy**
To which sense or senses does this paragraph appeal?

5

6. **Calcutta:** Large city in eastern India.
7. **glens** (glenz) *n.*: Valleys.
8. **defiles** (de fils´) *n.*: Deep, narrow mountain passes.

watchful eye on him.

I tried to gently laugh her fear away, but then she would turn on me seriously and ask solemn questions.

Were children never kidnapped?

Was it, then, not true that there was slavery in Cabul?

Was it so very absurd that this big man should be able to carry off a tiny child?

I told her that, though not impossible, it was highly improbable. But this was not enough, and her dread persisted. As her suspicion was unfounded, however, it did not seem right to forbid the man to come to the house, and his familiarity went unchecked.

Once a year, in the middle of January, Rahmun the Cabuliwallah was in the habit of returning to his country, and as the time approached, he would be very busy going from house to house collecting his debts. This year, however, he always found time to come and see Mini. It would have seemed to an outsider that there was some conspiracy between them, for when he could not come in the morning, he would appear in the evening.

Even to me it was a little startling now and then, to suddenly surprise this tall, loose-garmented man of bags in the corner of a dark room; but when Mini would run in, smiling, with her "O Cabuliwallah! Cabuliwallah!" and the two friends so far apart in age would subside into their old language and their old jokes, I felt reassured.

One morning, a few days

6

◆ **Literary Focus**
What does this sentence suggest about the father's feelings toward the Cabuliwallah?

7

◆ **Build Vocabulary**
precarious (prē ker´ ē əs) *adj.*: Dangerously lacking in security or stability

impending (im pen´ diŋ) *adj.*: About to happen

judicious (jōō dish´ əs) *adj.*: Exhibiting sound judgment or common sense

euphemism (yōō´ fə miz´ əm) *n.*: Word or phrase substituted for a more offensive word or phrase

imploring (im plôr´ iŋ) *v.*: Asking or begging

The Cabuliwallah ◆ 287

 Beyond the Classroom

Career Connection
Salesperson The Cabuliwallah is a sort of salesperson who was once common even in the United States—one who sold goods door-to-door or in a marketplace. Today, many salespeople work in stores or offices; some work over the telephone as telemarketers; and some visit customers at customers' places of business. Salespeople past and present need certain traits and skills to be successful: enthusiasm and knowledge about their product, a friendly and respectful manner toward customers, and an ability to make people trust them and relax around them. Discuss with students whether the Cabuliwallah possesses these characteristics and skills, and whether he would be a successful salesperson today.

Connections to Today's World

Thematic Focus Like the speaker in the song, by the end of the story, the Cabuliwallah and Mini's father will both feel that time has passed quickly and changed an important relationship in their lives. The Beatles themselves are an example of how people change and grow apart over time. Due to artistic, business, and personal differences the musicians began experimenting with independent projects in the late 1960's. Although "Yesterday" was ultimately recorded as a Beatles song, it was originally recorded by Paul McCartney alone. In 1970, the group broke up and the band members moved on to perform as soloists or to lead other groups.

Answer

Mini's father might sing this song as an expression of his sadness over losing his "little girl," and the change in Mini's attitude from the easy closeness of a child to the awkward distance of a young woman about to become married. The Cabuliwallah might sing the song about Mini for the same reasons, or he might sing it about his own daughter.

◆ Reading Strategy

❶ Engage Your Senses Ask students to which senses this description appeals. What impression does it give the reader? *The contrast between the chill in the air and the warmth of the sun appeals to the sense of touch.*

CONNECTIONS TO TODAY'S WORLD

The Cabuliwallah and Mini's father both discover that the passage of time changes relationships. This theme of changing relationships is common in songs as well as in literature. The song "Yesterday" by The Beatles deals with this theme.

The Beatles—George Harrison, John Lennon, Paul McCartney, and Ringo Starr—burst onto the American music scene in 1962 with their hit "Love Me Do." Although their early musical style was influenced by such American rock artists as Chuck Berry, Buddy Holly, and the Everly Brothers, the Beatles gave a new direction to rock-and-roll in the middle and late sixties. Earlier rock music was based mostly on rhythm—a strong beat— but The Beatles emphasized melody, complex chord progressions, and imaginative and meaningful lyrics. The Beatles also incorporated Indian instruments into their music. This ballad, from their later years, is one of their most popular.

YESTERDAY
Paul McCartney

Yesterday, all my troubles seemed so far away
Now it looks as though they're here to stay
Oh, I believe in yesterday

Suddenly, I'm not half the man I used to be
There's a shadow hanging over me
Oh, yesterday came suddenly

Why she had to go I don't know, she wouldn't say
I said something wrong, now I long for yesterday

Yesterday, love was such an easy game to play
Now I need a place to hide away
Oh, I believe in yesterday

Why she had to go I don't know, she wouldn't say
I said something wrong, now I long for yesterday

Yesterday, love was such and easy game to play
Now I need a place to hide away
Oh, I believe in yesterday.

---

1. If this song were sung by a character in "The Cabuliwallah," with who would sing it? Explain.
2. How does the mood of the song compare and contrast with the mood of the story?

---

before he had made up his mind to go, I was correcting my proof sheets[9] in my study. It was chilly weather. Through the window the rays of the sun touched my feet, and the slight warmth was very welcome. It was almost eight o'clock, and the early pedestrians were returning home with their heads covered. All at once I heard an uproar in the street and, looking out, saw Rahmun bound and being led away between two policemen, followed by a crowd of curious

---

9. **proof sheets:** Copies of a typeset manuscript on which changes or corrections are made by the author or an editor.

---

boys. There were bloodstains on the clothes of the Cabuliwallah, and one of the policemen carried a knife. Hurrying out, I stopped them and inquired what it all meant. Partly from one, partly from another, I gathered that a certain neighbor had owed the peddler something for a

◆ Build Vocabulary

fettered (fet′ ərd) *adj.:* Restrained, as with a chain

sordid (sôr′ did) *adj.:* Filthy or dirty

pervaded (pər vād′ id) *v.:* Spread throughout; filled

288 ◆ *Clashing Forces*

Cross-Curricular Connection: Social Studies

Afghan Dress Explain that in the cities nowadays, most Afghans wear western clothing. However, in the villages, they still dress as they did in the Cabuliwallah's time. The men wear long shirts over baggy pants. In the summer they wear cotton shawls, while in the winter they wear heavy coats called *chapans.* Most wear turbans wound around caps, or in cold weather a lambskin cap. The women wear long dresses with long sleeves over baggy pants. Their ankle bands can be beautifully embroidered. Most wear the *chador,* a cloth draped over the hair. In public, until 1959, women wore a *chaderi,* a long garment like a sack that covered them completely. Point out which of these garments the man in the photo on page 289 is wearing, and which the Cabuliwallah might have worn.

Rampuri shawl[10] but had falsely denied having bought it, and that in the course of the quarrel Rahmun had struck him. Now, in the heat of his excitement, the prisoner began calling his enemy all sorts of names. Suddenly, from a verandah of my house my little Mini appeared, with her usual exclamation: "O Cabuliwallah! Cabuliwallah!" Rahmun's face lighted up as he turned to her. He had no bag under his arm today, so she could not discuss the elephant with him. She at once therefore proceeded to the next question: "Are you going to the father-in-law's house?" Rahmun laughed and said: "Just where I am going, little one!" Then seeing that the reply did not amuse the child, he held up his fettered hands. "Ah," he said, "I would have thrashed that old father-in-law, but my hands are bound!"

On a charge of murderous assault, Rahmun was sentenced to many years of imprisonment.

Time passed, and he was forgotten. The accustomed work in the accustomed place was ours, and the thought of the once free mountaineer spending his years in prison seldom occurred to us. Even my lighthearted Mini, I am ashamed to say, forgot her old friend. New companions filled her life. As she grew older, she spent more of her time with girls, so much in fact that she came no more to her father's room. I was scarcely on speaking terms with her.

Many years passed. It was autumn once again, and we had made arrangements for Mini's marriage; it was to take place during the Puja holidays.[11] With the goddess Durga returning to her seasonal home in Mount Kailas, the light of our home was also to

10. **Rampuri shawl:** Shawl from Rampur, India. Such shawls are the finest in India because of the quality of the fabric.

11. **Puja holidays:** Great Hindu festival (also called Durgapuja) that honors Durga, a war goddess. It is a time for family reunions and other gatherings, as well as religious ceremonies.

▶ Critical Viewing What details of this man's appearance do you think five-year-old Mini would notice? [Speculate]

depart, leaving our house in shadows.

The morning was bright. After the rains, there was a sense of cleanness in the air, and the rays of the sun looked like pure gold; so bright that they radiated even to the sordid brick walls of our Calcutta lanes. Since early dawn, the wedding pipes had been sounding, and at each beat my own heart throbbed. The wailing tune, Bhairavi,[12] seemed to intensify my pain at the approaching separation. My Mini was to be married tonight.

From early morning, noise and bustle pervaded the house. In the courtyard the canopy had to be slung on its bamboo poles; the tinkling chandeliers should be hung in

12. **Bhairavi** (bī′ rə vē): The name of a particular tune. It is a happy piece of music and is associated with joyous events.

The Cabuliwallah ◆ 289

◆ Literary Focus

❶ Relationships Between Characters Encourage students to notice that time and events have changed the Cabuliwallah's appearance and manner and Mini's father's reaction to him.

◆ Literary Focus

❷ Relationships Between Characters Discuss with students the reasons that Mini will probably not respond to the Cabuliwallah in the same way she did when she was a child. *She has become more quiet and reserved even with her father and she will no longer be influenced by jokes and treats. As a young woman, she will probably pay more attention to appearances than she did as a child.*

◆ *Literature and Your Life*

❸ Guide students to recognize that while appearances change over time, the types of details people notice also change as they get older. For this reason, a person may seem different than students remember due to changes in themselves as well as in the person.

Customize for
Logical/Mathematical Learners

Have these students use the map on page 291 to appreciate just how far the Cabuliwallah was from his home and family during his imprisonment and while he worked as a fruit seller.

---

each room and verandah; there was great hurry and excitement. I was sitting in my study, looking through the accounts, when someone entered, saluting respectfully, and stood before me. It was Rahmun the Cabuliwallah, and at first I did not recognize him. He had no bag, nor the long hair, nor the same vigor that he used to have. But he smiled, and I knew him again.

❶ "When did you come, Rahmun?" I asked him.

"Last evening," he said, "I was released from jail."

The words struck harsh upon my ears. I had never talked with anyone who had wounded his fellowman, and my heart shrank when I realized this, for I felt that the day would have been better omened if he had not turned up.

"There are ceremonies going on," I said, "and I am busy. Could you perhaps come another day?"

At once he turned to go; but as he reached the door, he hesitated and said: "May I not see the little one, sir, for a moment?" It was his belief that Mini was still the same. He had pic-
❷ tured her running to him as she used to do, calling "O Cabuliwallah! Cabuliwallah!" He had imagined that they would laugh and talk together, just as in the past. In fact, in memory of those former days he had brought, carefully wrapped up in paper, a few almonds and raisins and grapes, somehow obtained from a countryman—his own little fund was gone.

I said again: "There is a ceremony in the house, and you will not be able to see anyone today."

The man's face fell. He looked wistfully at me for a moment, said "Good morning," and went out.

I felt a little sorry, and would have called him back, but saw that he was returning of his own accord. He came close up to me, holding out his offerings, and said: "I brought these few things, sir, for the little one. Will you give them to her?"

I took them and was going to pay him, but he caught my hand and said: "You are very kind, sir! Keep me in your recollection; do not offer me money! You have a little girl; I too have

one like her in my own home. I thought of my own and brought fruits to your child, not to make a profit for myself."

Saying this, he put his hand inside his big loose robe and brought out a small dirty piece of paper. With great care he unfolded this and smoothed it out with both hands on my table. It bore the impression of a little hand, not a photograph, not a drawing. The impression of an ink-smeared hand laid flat on the paper. This touch of his own little daughter had been always on his heart, as he had come year after year to Calcutta to sell his wares in the streets.

Tears came to my eyes. I forgot that he was a poor Cabuli fruit seller, while I was—but no, was I more than he? He was also a father.

That impression of the hand of his little Parbati in her distant mountain home reminded me of my own little Mini, and I immediately sent for her from the inner apartment. Many excuses were raised, but I would not listen. Clad in the red silk of her wedding day, with the sandal paste[13] on her forehead, and adorned as a young bride, Mini came and stood bashfully before me.

The Cabuliwallah was staggered at the sight of her. There was no hope of reviving their old friendship. At last he smiled and said: "Little one, are you going to your father-in-law's house?"

But Mini now understood the meaning of the word "father-in-law," and she could not reply to him as in the past. She flushed at the question and stood before him with her bride's face looking down.

> ◆ *Literature and Your Life*
>
> Discuss a time when you saw someone after many years who did not look as you remembered.

I remembered the day when the Cabuliwallah and my Mini first met, and I felt sad. When she had gone, Rahmun heaved a deep sigh and sat down on the floor. The idea had suddenly come to him that his daughter also must have grown up during this long time, and that he

13. **sandal paste:** Paste made from sandalwood sawdust mixed with water and used as a liquid makeup that gives the skin a paler appearance.

Cross-Curricular Connection: Music

Indian Music The narrator refers to the "wedding pipes," an important part of the Indian wedding ceremony. Explain that music is important in many aspects of Indian life. A formal tradition of music has been developed in India for over 2,000 years. There are two main styles of music, one practiced in the North, on stringed instruments such as the sitar and wind instruments such as the bamboo flute. The other style is practiced in the South, often on the *vina*, or violin, the reed pipe, and the drum called the *mrindanga*. Point out that

the pipes the narrator referred to might have been the reed pipe, or *nagasvaram*. Use the **Looking at Literature Videodisc** Chapter 3, featuring Indian music and dance, to provide students with samples of Indian music.

🎵 **Looking at Literature Videodisc**

Chapter 3

would have to make friends with her all over again. Surely he would not find her as he used to know her; besides, what might have happened to her in these eight years?

The marriage pipes sounded, and the mild autumn sun streamed around us. But Rahmun sat in the little Calcutta lane and saw before him the barren mountains of Afghanistan.

I took out a bank note and gave it to him, saying: "Go back to your own daughter, Rahmun, in your own country, and may the happiness of your meeting bring good fortune to my child!"

After giving this gift, I had to eliminate some of the festivities. I could not have the electric lights, nor the military band, and the ladies of the house were saddened. But to me the wedding feast was brighter because of the thought that in a distant land a long-lost father met again with his only child.

Beyond Literature

Social Studies Connection

India and Its People India is the second largest country in the world in population. In fact, nearly one out of every six people in the world lives in India! A country of vast differences, India's land includes a desert, jungles, broad plains, the tallest mountain system in the world, and one of the world's rainiest areas. The map shows the diversity of physical features in India. The people of India belong to many different ethnic groups, religions, and caste systems—or social classes. They speak sixteen major languages and more than 1,000 minor languages and dialects.

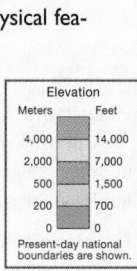

Guide for Responding

◆ *Literature and Your Life*

Reader's Response With which character do you identify most? Why?

Thematic Focus The Cabuliwallah loses eight years of his life and eight years of his daughter's life. His experiences may have led you to question the justice of his situation.

☑ **Check Your Comprehension**

1. What is Mini's relationship with her mother? With her father?
2. Why is Mini afraid of the Cabuliwallah at first?
3. What are the two meanings of "the father-in-law's house"?
4. What is Mini's father's final act of kindness and justice to Rahmun the Cabuliwallah?

The Cabuliwallah ◆ 291

Beyond the Selection

FURTHER READING

Other Works by Rabindranath Tagore
A Poet's Tale
The Hungry Stones and Other Stories
Glimpses of Bengal

Other Works With the Theme of Clashing Forces
Letters from the Inside, John Marsden
Somewhere in the Darkness, Walter Dean Myers

We recommend that you preview these titles before suggesting them to students.

INTERNET

A collection of Tagore's poems is available at the following Internet address: **http://www.genius. net/indolink/poetry/tgorPref.html**

For conversations between Tagore and Einstein and H. G. Wells, visit **http://www.c.s.brock-port.edu/~smitra/tagore.html**

Please be aware that the addresses may have changed since this information was published. We *strongly recommend* that you preview the sites before sending students to them.

Answers

◆ Critical Thinking

1. (a) Mini and the Cabuliwallah develop a close relationship; they both enjoy laughing with and talking to each other. (b) Each gets attention from the other that they do not get from other people.
2. Mini has become more reserved and self-conscious in the years of the Cabuliwallah's absence.
3. Mini feels awkward because she cannot interact with the Cabuliwallah on the level that she used to do.
4. It is sometimes awkward to see someone you haven't seen in a long time because interests and attitudes that you once had in common may have changed.
5. Students should explain their answers with details from the story such as the extenuating circumstances of the Cabuliwallah's crime, the feelings Mini's father has for his daughter, and the sadness Rahmun feels at being separated from his daughter.

◆ Reading Strategy

1. The childlike chattering and the musical laughter are two sounds students might associate with Mini as a little girl.
2. Sensory details that help students imagine the Cabuliwallah include the sight of his loose, soiled clothing, his tall turban, the taste of the grapes he carries and the fruits and nuts he brings to Mini, and the sound of his nasal voice telling jokes to Mini.

◆ Literary Focus

1. (a) Mini's relationship with the Cabuliwallah before he is arrested is comfortable and merry. (b) Her reaction to him on her wedding day is awkward and uncomfortable.
2. Mini's relationship with her father has changed in that she used to share every thought that entered her head with him; now she has some private thoughts.
3. Mini's father is able to relate his own feelings and experiences as a father to the pain the Cabuliwallah must feel at being separated from his own daughter.

Guide for Responding (continued)

◆ Critical Thinking

INTERPRET

1. (a) Why do Mini and the Cabuliwallah develop such a close relationship? (b) What does each gain from the other? **[Infer]**
2. In what ways do you think Mini has changed in the eight years of the Cabuliwallah's absence? **[Speculate]**
3. Why do you think Mini acts so reserved with the Cabuliwallah when she sees him again? **[Hypothesize]**

APPLY

4. Why is it sometimes awkward to see someone you haven't seen in a long time? **[Relate]**

EVALUATE

5. Do you believe Mini's father acted appropriately toward the Cabuliwallah at the end of the story? Why or why not? **[Make a Judgment]**

◆ Reading Strategy

ENGAGE YOUR SENSES

Tagore provides many details to help you **engage your senses** to fully experience his characters and setting.

1. What are two sounds associated with Mini as a young girl?
2. Identify three sensory details that helped you imagine the Cabuliwallah.

◆ Literary Focus

RELATIONSHIPS BETWEEN CHARACTERS

Important changes in the characters of Mini and her father are revealed in their **relationships** to each other and to the Cabuliwallah.

1. (a) Describe Mini's relationship with the Cabuliwallah before he is arrested. (b) Describe her reaction to him when he returns on her wedding day.
2. Explain how Mini's relationship with her father has changed.
3. Why does Mini's father feel such a close relationship to the Cabuliwallah at the end of the story?

◆ Build Vocabulary

USING THE ROOT *-jud-*

Knowing that the word root *-jud-* means "judge," match the word in Column A with its definition in Column B.

Column A	Column B
1. judicial	a. a judgment or opinion formed before the facts are known
2. prejudice	b. showing sound judgment
3. judicious	c. belonging to or related to judges and law courts

USING THE WORD BANK

In your notebook, match each numbered word from the Word Bank to the letter of its antonym, the word most opposite in meaning.

1. sordid	a. safe
2. imploring	b. distant
3. precarious	c. clean
4. impending	d. blunt statement
5. euphemism	e. refusing
6. fettered	f. free
7. pervaded	g. emptied

◆ Build Grammar Skills

PRONOUN AND ANTECEDENT AGREEMENT

A **pronoun** must agree with its **antecedent** in number (singular or plural) and gender (masculine, feminine, or neuter).

Practice In your notebook, copy the following sentences from the story. Circle each pronoun and draw an arrow to its antecedent. Then label each pronoun as masculine, feminine, or neuter and as singular or plural.

1. Mini, my five-year-old daughter, cannot live without chattering. I really believe that in all her life she has not wasted one minute in silence.
2. The man accepted the money without delay, and slipped it into his pocket.
3. Whenever Mini's mother sees people in the street, she thinks they are thieves.

◆ Build Vocabulary

Using the Root *-jud-*
1. c   2. a   3. b

Using the Word Bank
1. d   2. f   3. b   4. c   5. e
6. a   7. h   8. g   9. i

◆ Build Grammar Skills

1. "Her" and "she" refer to Mini (feminine singular).
2. "His" refers to "man" (masculine singular); "it" refers to "money" (neuter).
3. "She" refers to Mini's mother (feminine singular); "they" refers to "people" (plural).

Writer's Solution

For additional instruction and practice, use the **Language Lab CD-ROM** lesson on Pronouns and Antecedents. You can also use the *Writer's Solution Grammar Practice Book* page on Pronoun and Antecedent Agreement, p. 83.

Build Your Portfolio

 ## Idea Bank

Writing

1. Description Describe a place that could be the setting for a short story about an episode from your childhood. Include sensory details that will help your readers experience the setting.

2. Character's Journal Entry As the Cabuliwallah, write a journal entry that expresses your thoughts and feelings about the events of the wedding day.

3. Letter to the Embassy Write a letter to the Indian embassy requesting information about the history and culture of the country. Use a business-letter format. **[Social Studies Link]**

Speaking and Listening

4. Courtroom Speech As the Cabuliwallah's lawyer, give a speech recommending that the Cabuliwallah be given a light sentence for his crime. In your speech, refer to the circumstances of his life and the character traits you have discovered in the story.

5. Oral Interpretation Find a story from Indian mythology. Practice reading the story aloud, using an expressive voice. Then read the story to the class.

Projects

6. Timeline Create a timeline that shows key events in India's fight for independence. Illustrate your timeline with copies of photos from magazines, newspapers, or books. **[Social Studies Link]**

7. Sketch Using any medium (pencil, ink, or paint), draw what you think the Cabuliwallah looks like at the beginning of the story. **[Art Link]**

Writing Mini-Lesson

Firsthand Biography

Tagore describes his characters so well that readers almost feel as if they've met them in person! Write a firsthand biography of someone you do know. A **firsthand biography** tells about the life of a person with whom the writer is personally acquainted. This close relationship allows for personal insights that are not found in biographies based solely on research. The following tips will help you create a biography that reads smoothly and carries the reader along from idea to idea.

Writing Skills Focus: Logical Organization

Your firsthand biography should have a logical, consistent overall **order**. Chronological order (time order) and order of importance are both good choices for a firsthand biography.

If you want to tell the events in the order in which they happened, use chronological order. Begin with events from the subject's childhood and work your way up to the present day.

If you want to stress what you think are the person's most important qualities, arrange the details you include around each important quality you want to illustrate. Present the details in order of importance.

Prewriting Talk with the subject of your biography. Ask him or her to identify some significant events. Take careful notes during your discussion. Then arrange your notes into an outline.

Drafting Add details to the bare bones of your biography. Where you include the details depends on the kind of organization you choose.

Revising Compare your draft with your outline to ensure that you've used a consistent organization. In addition, look for places where you can add transitions to make the organization more clear.

The Cabuliwallah ◆ 293

 ## Idea Bank
Customizing for
Learning Modalities
Following are suggestions for matching Idea Bank topics with your students' learning modalities:
  Verbal/Linguistic: 4, 5
  Logical/Mathematical: 6
  Visual/Spatial: 6, 7

Customizing for
Performance Levels
Following are suggestions for matching the Idea Bank topics with your students' ability levels:
  Less Advanced: 1, 5, 7
  Average: 2, 4, 6, 7
  More Advanced: 3, 4, 6

Writing Mini-Lesson

Refer students to the Writing Handbook, page 965, for instruction on the writing process, and page 967 for more information on a firsthand biography.

Writing Lab CD-ROM
The tutorial on Narration will help students create their firsthand biography. Have them follow these steps:
1. Use the Character Trait and Sensory Details word bins to gather details with which they can describe their subject and the setting.
2. Use the Chain of Events Organizer to map the sequence of events in the firsthand biography.
3. Draft on the computer.
4. Use the Transitions Word Checker and Revision Checkers for passive voice, language variety, sentence openers, and sentence length.

Sourcebook
Have students use Chapter 2, Narration (pp. 31–57), for additional support.

✓ ASSESSMENT OPTIONS

Formal Assessment, Selection Test, pp. 72–73, and Assessment Resources Software. The selection test is designed so that it can be easily customized to the ability levels of your students.
Alternative Assessment, p. 22, includes options for less advanced students, more advanced students, visual/spatial learners, logical/mathematical learners, and verbal/linguistic learners.

PORTFOLIO ASSESSMENT
Use the following rubrics in *Alternative Assessment* to assess student writing:
Description: Description Rubric, p. 97
Character's Journal Entry: Expressive Writing Rubric, p. 94
Letter to the Embassy: Business Letter Rubric, p. 113
Writing Mini-Lesson: Narrative Based on Personal Experience Rubric, p. 96

Establish Writing Guidelines

Before students begin, review the following key characteristics of a position paper:

- It aims to persuade readers to accept the writer's view on a controversial issue.
- The position presented is supported with evidence.
- In many cases, it is written to a person with the power to shape policy related to the issue.

You may want to distribute the scoring rubric for Persuasion (p. 105 in *Alternative Assessment*) to make students aware before they begin of the criteria on which they will be evaluated. See the suggestions on page 296 for ways to customize the rubric for this workshop.

Refer students to the Writing Handbook, p. 965, for instruction in the writing process, and page 968 for further information on persuasion.

 Writer's Solution

Writers at Work Videodisc

To introduce students to the key elements of persuasive writing and show them how Sayu Bhojwani uses them in her writing, play the videodisc segment on Persuasion (Ch. 4). Have students discuss the ways in which persuasive writing differs from other writing.

Play frames 34707 to 44369

Writing Lab CD-ROM

If your students have access to computers, you may want to have them work on the tutorial on Persuasion to complete all or part of their position papers. Follow these steps:

1. Have students review the interactive model of a position paper.
2. Suggest that students complete the Interviewing Yourself activity to find out what problems or issues are important to them.
3. Have students draft on computers.
4. Suggest students use a revision checker for sentence openers.
5. Have students use the revision checker for double comparisons.

Sourcebook

Students can find additional support, including audience profiles and graphic organizers, in the chapter on Persuasion (pp. 96–127).

Position Paper

Writing Process Workshop

If you had a strong opinion about a controversial issue, you'd want to let others know about it. One way to do this is to write a **position paper**. In a position paper, the writer attempts to persuade the reader to accept his or her viewpoint on a controversial issue. In many cases, position papers are written for an audience, such as a town council, with the power to shape policy related to the issue.

Write a position paper on an issue that's important to you. The following skills, introduced in this section's Writing Mini-Lessons, will help you write a persuasive position paper.

Writing Skills Focus

▶ **Elaborate** with details, examples, and facts to support your claim. The more specific and factual you are, the more compelling your argument will be. (See p. 269.)

▶ **Use a logical organization** for your paper. Order of importance, cause and effect, pro and con, and compare and contrast are all good methods of organization. (See p. 293.)

▶ **Be accurate.** Use care in expressing your ideas—avoid words like *all* and *never* unless you know they are true. (See p. 281.)

The following excerpt uses these skills to argue a point persuasively: Youths need more training to drive safely.

① The writer uses statistics to support her position.

② The writer cites a reliable source of information to back up her example.

MODEL

New drivers under the age of twenty-one should be required to take at least thirty hours of formal driver training. ① Drivers age twenty-one and under make up less than 10 percent of the driving population, yet they represent nearly 20 percent of Americans killed in auto accidents.

A study by the University of North Carolina's Highway Safety Research Center ② suggests that a major reason so many young people are involved in accidents is that they are inadequately prepared . . .

294 ◆ *Clashing Forces*

 Cross-Curricular Connection: Social Studies

Point out that current events provide a wealth of controversial issues that students may plumb for their position papers. A perusal through a week's worth of daily papers or a few issues of a national newsmagazine should reveal any number of social issues they may want to tackle. Remind students that writing such papers will help them clarify their ideas as they logically think through their own views on an issue. This practice will help them in the future whether or not they write more position papers.

Prewriting

Choose Your Topic You'll find many ideas for a position paper in newspapers and magazines. Scan the contents of a newspaper or magazine. Do any issues or current events especially engage your interests or emotions? What issues make you want to write to a government official or other leader? Jot down your reactions to various stories or photographs. Then review your notes and choose a topic. Write your topic as a statement of your position.

Know Your Audience Knowing the identity of the audience you're trying to persuade is essential. Use the following questions to help identify your audience.

► Who is your audience? Your peers? Teachers? Experts on the topic?

► How old are the people in your audience? Are they younger than, older than, or the same age as you?

► What is your audience's view on the position you'll argue? If it's an opposing view, what counterarguments can you devise?

► What parts of your subject might especially interest your audience? How can you make these parts stand out?

As you draft your position paper, you can make your points address the concerns of the audience you've identified.

Drafting

Distinguish Fact From Opinion Facts are statements that can be proven true by research or direct observation. Opinions are statements of belief that can be supported, but not proven, with facts. As you draft, use facts to support your opinions. Notice how the following facts support opinions:

Opinions	Facts
This is a responsible newspaper.	This newspaper won a Pulitzer Prize.
Americans eat too much fat.	The average American diet is 40 percent fat.
We need more pet shelters.	Last year, more than 600 stray animals were destroyed because shelters had no room for them.

APPLYING LANGUAGE SKILLS: Unity and Coherence

Good writing has **unity** (it focuses on one thought at a time) and **coherence** (the ideas are arranged in an orderly fashion).

Not Unified or Coherent:
Jazz, pop, and rock are all legitimate forms of music. Sting is my favorite musician. I don't think the Grammy Awards always go to the best musicians, however...

Unified and Coherent:
Although they have their critics, the Grammy Awards today honor a spectrum of musical talent far broader than they did when they originated in 1959. For example...

Writing Application Check your essay to make sure that you focus on a single topic and that your ideas within the essay are coherently arranged.

Writer's Solution Connection Writing Lab

To help you choose a topic, refer to the Inspirations for Persuasion in the Writing Lab tutorial on Persuasion.

Prewriting

You may want to have students brainstorm in small groups to find additional topic ideas. Remind them that any topic that inspires different viewpoints is a valid one for a position paper.

Customize for
More Advanced Students
Challenge these students to take a position that is the opposite of what they believe. This will force them to broaden their thinking and reassess their own opinions even more closely.

 Writer's Solution

Writing Lab CD-ROM
To help them conduct research for their position papers, have students consult the screen Detecting Bias in Sources in the Organizing Details section of the tutorial on Persuasion.

Drafting

Encourage students to build their positions as they draft. They may include both facts and opinions as long as they use both appropriately. Remind them that they should not present opinions as facts.

Applying Language Skills

Unity and Coherence
Explain to students that it is important that a unified and coherent essay present an argument more effectively.

 Writer's Solution

For additional instruction and practice, have students complete the **Language Lab CD-ROM** lesson on Unity and Coherence.

Revising

Encourage students to work with peers to revise and proofread their papers.

Writing Lab CD-ROM

The Persuasion Word Bin in the Revising and Editing section of the tutorial on Persuasion will help students add the right persuasive and transitional words to their drafts.

Publishing

Encourage students to send their papers to a policy maker. For more information, consult Prentice Hall on the World Wide Web at **http://www.phschool.com.**

Applying Language Skills

Appositives Explain to students that appositives always explain nouns. They are useful when the writer wants to add or clarify information without using too many words.

Answers
1. Mahmoud
2. the most dangerous accidents

 Writer's Solution

For additional instruction and practice, have students complete practice page 40 on Appositives and Appositive Phrases in the *Writer's Solution Grammar Practice Book.*

Reinforce and Extend

Review the Writing Guidelines Encourage students to come up with additional criteria for an interesting position paper based on what they learned through completing the assignment.

APPLYING LANGUAGE SKILLS: Appositives

An **appositive** is a noun or pronoun placed near another noun or pronoun to identify or provide more information about it.

My main mode of transportation, my car, is not very reliable.

Here, *my car* identifies the writer's main mode of transportation.

Use appositives to add details and specifics to your position paper. For example, don't just say "drivers under twenty-one," say "drivers under twenty-one, *the majority of drivers in our state,* account for . . ."

Practice On your paper, identify the appositives in the following sentences.
1. My friend Mahmoud was born in Cairo.
2. Head-on collisions, the most dangerous accidents, are on the rise.

Writing Application Review your position paper, adding appositives where they would strengthen your writing.

Writer's Solution Connection Language Lab

For more practice with appositives, complete the Language Lab lesson on Varying Sentence Structure.

296 ◆ *Clashing Forces*

Revising

Use a Self-Evaluation Checklist Review your draft and answer the following questions about it.

▶ Do you elaborate on assertions with facts and statistics?
Add facts where necessary to make your argument more compelling.

▶ Are your facts and statistics accurate?
Check with at least two sources to make sure that the integrity of your information cannot be challenged.

▶ Is your organization coherent?
Make sure that your paragraphs and sentences within each paragraph follow a logical and easy-to-understand organizational plan.

▶ Have you checked your spelling and grammar?

REVISION MODEL

① *In countries where formal driver education is mandated, teen driver fatalities are significantly lower.*
∧For any driver under 21, formal driver education should be required. In addition, there should be a lower limit of the number of points, from the current 10, ② 12 a driver is allowed to collect before his or her license is suspended.

① *The writer strengthens her argument with a fact that supports her position.*
② *The writer changes this inaccurate information.*

Publishing

Deliver a Persuasive Speech One way to publish your position paper is by presenting it as a speech. Use these tips to guide you as you present your speech:
▶ Practice several times on your own.
▶ Mark places that you want to emphasize.
▶ Speak slowly and clearly.
▶ Allow your voice to rise and fall naturally.
▶ Speak loudly enough to be heard.
▶ Look directly at your audience or the camera.

✓ ASSESSMENT		4	3	2	1
PORTFOLIO ASSESSMENT Use the rubric on Persuasion in the *Alternative Assessment* booklet (p. 105) to assess the students' writing. Add these criteria to customize the rubric to this assignment.	**Elaboration**	The writer elaborates all important claims with specific facts, details, or examples.	The writer elaborates most important claims with facts, details, or examples.	The writer elaborates some claims with facts and examples, but stronger support is needed.	The writer provides little or no details, facts, or examples to support any of his or her claims.
	Unity and Coherence	The paper has a clear thesis statement, which each paragraph directly supports. Transitions are used effectively.	The paper has a thesis statement that is supported by most of the body paragraphs. Transitions are used.	Thesis statement is unclear. Body paragraphs provide some support. Better transitions are needed.	The paper has no thesis statement. Body paragraphs provide scant support. Transitions are lacking.

Real-World Reading Skills Workshop

Challenge What You Read

Strategies for Success

Imagine what the world would be like if people believed everything that they read in print. The tabloids (newspapers with many pictures and sensational, often unreliable, stories) would have us believe that aliens are taking over the world, that eating ice cream can make you smarter, and that Elvis Presley is alive and well. Whether you're reading a tabloid newspaper or a campaign letter from a politician, you must challenge what you read and decide whether or not the writer's statements are reliable.

Check It Out If you were shopping for a CD player, would you take the first one the salesperson showed you? Probably not. Careful shoppers ask questions, check the way a product performs, and look at all the options. In the same way, careful readers ask questions, check the logic behind a statement, and consider alternatives to a writer's statements. Put every statement under a mental microscope until it becomes a habit.

Be Critical Be ready to question a writer's assertions. The following questions provide some points on which you can challenge what you read:

▶ What is the writer's motive? If you read surprising sensational statements in a supermarket tabloid, the motive is probably to sell copies of the paper.

▶ What about the truth of the statements? Reliable journalism presents reasonable, researched, and supported stories. Unreliable journalism, however, may present questionable stories under sensational headlines. If you see statements that seem unrealistic or unreasonable, do not accept them unless you can verify their truth.

▶ Does the writer have a bias? A bias is an inclination to favor a particular point of view. Good journalism is unbiased; it does not take a point of view.

▶ Does the writer use logical reasoning in presenting the information? Look for faulty logic, in which the writer overgeneralizes or makes unsupported statements.

Apply the Strategies

You've probably seen headlines like these as you waited in line at the supermarket. Tabloids are notorious for sensationalizing news and stretching the truth. Apply the strategies for challenging a text as you study these attention-grabbing headlines.

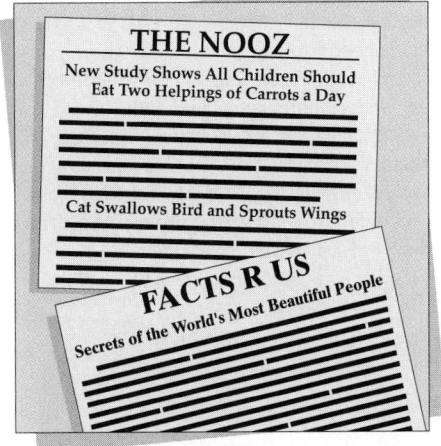

1. What is one problem with the statement: "New study shows that all children should eat two helpings of carrots a day"?
2. What questions would you ask about the claims in the article entitled "Secrets of the World's Most Beautiful People"?
3. In which articles would you challenge the writer's motives and the truth of the statements?

You are not always going to agree with other people's opinions and suggestions, but it is up to you to decide when to express your disagreement. Sometimes, expressing disagreement can cause tension between you and the person with whom you are disagreeing. It's important to learn how to express disagreement constructively and in a way that will not alienate others.

Presenting Your Case If you disagree with a person's comments, opinions, or actions, express your disagreement in a way that makes your position known without offending or upsetting others. Suppose your friends think that the legal driving age should be changed from sixteen or seventeen to fourteen. You feel, however, that fourteen-year-olds lack the maturity needed for such an awesome responsibility, and furthermore, you know plenty of sixteen- and seventeen-year-olds who aren't mature enough to drive. In expressing your disagreement, present your position in a calm, clear voice. Arguing with people will only cause them to defend their own position more firmly, and they will fail to see your point.

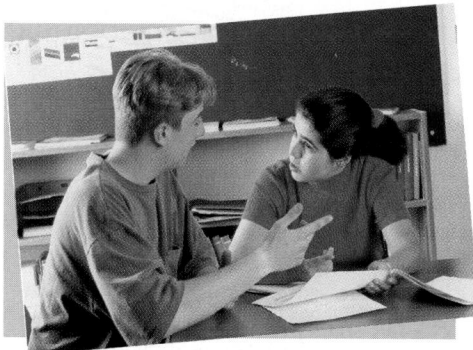

Expressing Disagreement Successfully To express your disagreement in an intelligent and effective way, follow these strategies:

▶ Use a clear, respectful tone, while remaining assertive as you make and support your point.

▶ Present specific reasons why you disagree.

▶ Offer evidence, if available, to support your disagreement. For example, if you were expressing disagreement about the legal driving age, you could cite the statistic that drivers age twenty-one and under make up less than 10 percent of the driving population, yet they represent nearly 20 percent of Americans killed in auto accidents.

▶ Do not raise your voice or get upset when expressing disagreement. Doing so will only cause tension between you and the person with whom you are disagreeing.

Apply the Strategies

With a partner, role-play these situations. Express your disagreement clearly and convincingly:

1. You and your best friend disagree over what movie to see. How would you express your disagreement?

2. Your sister borrows your clothes without asking you first and sees nothing wrong with doing so. What would you say to her to express your disagreement with her actions?

3. One person in your science lab makes decisions and plans projects without consulting the rest of the group. What would you say to this person to get him or her to listen to input from the rest of the group?

298 ◆ *Clashing Forces*

Extended Reading Opportunities

Conflict and its resolution persists as one of the most enduring themes in literature. The following selections show clashing forces in a variety of settings and situations.

Suggested Titles

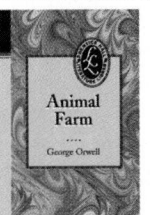

The Red Badge of Courage
Stephen Crane

Stephen Crane's classic about the Civil War ushered in a new era of war stories: Rather than narrating an epic about victory and defeat in battle, *The Red Badge of Courage* follows the personal reactions of one soldier, a young, idealistic farm boy named Henry Fleming. Swept suddenly into the heat of battle, Henry must confront his own fears and make a decision between cowardice and courage that may well cost him his life.

Cry, the Beloved Country
Alan Paton

This story, considered the greatest novel ever to come out of South Africa, concerns the unlikely relationship that develops between two men. A black pastor from a rural village, who journeys to the city of Johannesburg to find his sister and son, and a cold-hearted white man find themselves on the opposite sides of a tragic event. The two men discover their races and families have more in common than they ever could have imagined.

Animal Farm
George Orwell

A simple tale with a powerful message about revolution, *Animal Farm* tells the story of the beasts of Manor Farm. Suffering hunger and neglect at the hands of Mr. Jones, the animals rebel, drive the farmer and his wife off the land, and set up their own society where "All animals are equal." Equality, however, means different things to different animals. To their dismay, the animals soon find that "some animals are more equal than others."

Other Possibilities

Farewell to Manzanar	Jeanne Wakatsuki Houston
War of the Worlds	H. G. Wells
The Chosen	Chaim Potok
One Day in the Life of Ivan Denisovich	Alexander Solzhenitsyn

Planning Students' Extended Reading

All works listed on this page extend the theme of Clashing Forces. The following information may help you choose which to assign.

Customize for *Varying Students Needs*

When assigning these works to your students, keep in mind the following factors:

- The prose of *Red Badge of Courage* is older and may be challenging to some students, though the novel itself is short.
- *Cry, the Beloved Country* is a longer novel that will require a longer time commitment.
- *Animal Farm* is a short, high-interest novel that can supplement students' learning about the Russian Revolution.

Literature Study Guides

Literature study guides are available for the three suggested titles. These guides include selection summaries, discussion questions, and activities.

Resources for Teaching Novels and Plays
This resource contains graphic organizers, teaching strategies, and transparencies that will be invaluable in teaching any of these novels.

Customize for *Special Needs*

To meet the needs of your special needs students (grades 3 and 4 reading level), you may want to consider using *The Red Badge of Courage* from Globe Fearon's Pacemaker Classics series.

Planning Instruction and Assessment

Unit Objectives

1. To read selections in different genres that develop the theme Turning Points
2. To apply a variety of reading strategies, particularly literal comprehension strategies, appropriate for reading these selections
3. To recognize literary elements used in these selections
4. To increase vocabulary
5. To learn elements of grammar and usage
6. To write in a variety of modes and about situations based on the selections
7. To develop speaking and listening skills, by doing proposed activities

Meeting the Objectives

With each selection, you will find instructional material and portfolio opportunities through which students can meet these objectives. Further, you will find additional practice pages for reading strategies, literary elements, vocabulary, and grammar in the *Selection Support* booklet in the Teaching Resources box.

Setting Goals

Work with your students at the beginning of the unit to set goals for unit outcomes. Plan what skills and concepts you wish students to acquire. You may individualize according to students' performance levels or learning modalities.

Portfolios

You may have students keep portfolios of their work or of their work in progress. The activities and prompts on the Build Your Portfolio page of each selection provide opportunities for students to apply the concepts presented with the selection.

Summer Breeze, Alice Dalton Brown, Fischbach Gallery, New York

 Humanities: Art

Summer Breeze, 1995, by Alice Dalton Brown.

Alice Dalton Brown has made a specialty of painting Victorian houses, usually in summer (like the house suggested in *Summer Breeze*), experimenting with different kinds of light and times of day.

You can use *Summer Breeze* to help students develop a sense of the way a painter incorporates mood and formal design elements into an apparently realistic picture. Have your students link the art to the theme of Unit 4, "Turning Points," by answering the following questions:

1. What mood does the painting create? Cite details that support your answer. *Most students will say that the painting creates a hopeful mood, citing the sunny sky, the breeze blowing in the window, the delicate grace of the room, the summery land-scape; students sensing an ominous mood may cite the eerie shadow on the wall and the emptiness of the room.*

2. What details in the painting suggest a change or turning point to you? *Students will probably mention the breeze blowing in the window, suggesting a change in weather. Some may also suggest that the bareness of the room makes it look as if someone has just moved out or is about to move in.*

300

UNIT 4

Turning Points

Turning points can be exciting and frightening. Windows of opportunity open briefly and life-changing decisions must be made. Stories, poems, and essays can show you how some people approach these fateful moments. Share the anticipation and anxiety of the writers and characters in this unit as they deal with the chances and challenges that change their lives.

◆ *301*

Assessing Student Progress

The following tools are available to measure the degree to which students meet the unit objectives:

Informal Assessment

The questions on the Guide for Responding sections are a first level of response to the concepts and skills presented with the selection. Students' responses are a brief informal measure of their grasp of the material. Their responses on this level can indicate where further instruction and practice are needed. You may then follow up with the practice pages in the **Selection Support** booklet.

You will find literature and reading guides in the **Alternative Assessment** booklet, which you may give students on an individual basis for informal assessment of their performance.

Formal Assessment

In the **Formal Assessment** booklet, you will find selection tests and a unit test.

Selection Tests The selection tests measure comprehension and skills acquisition for each selection or group of selections.

Unit Test The unit test, which calls on students to read a passage of literature they have not previously seen, applies the unit skills on a broader level. The Critical Reading section measures Unit Objectives 1, 2, and 3. The Vocabulary and Grammar section measures Objectives 4 and 5. The Essay section measures Objectives 1 and 6.

Both the Critical Reading and the Vocabulary and Grammar sections use formats similar to those found on many standardized tests, including the SAT.

Alternative Assessment

Portfolios As you review individual pieces or the collected work in students' portfolios, you will find assessment sheets available in the portfolio section of the **Alternative Assessment** booklet.

Scoring Rubrics You will find scoring rubrics for writing modes in the **Alternative Assessment** booklet. You can apply these to Writing Mini-Lessons and to Writing Process Workshop lessons.

Speaking and Listening The **Alternative Assessment** booklet contains assessment sheets for speaking and listening activities.

Learning Modalities The **Alternative Assessment** contains activities that appeal to different learning styles. You may use these as an alternative measurement of students' growth.

Guide for Reading

OBJECTIVES

1. To read, comprehend, and interpret a personal narrative

2. To relate a personal narrative to personal experience

3. To use critical reading strategies to read for success

4. To identify a personal narrative

5. To build vocabulary in context and learn the prefix *pro-*

6. To understand the use of dashes

7. To write a memory of a milestone using sensory details

8. To respond to the personal narrative through writing, speaking and listening, and projects

SKILLS INSTRUCTION

Vocabulary:
Prefixes: *pro-*

Grammar:
Dashes

Reading for Success:
Reading Critically

Literary Focus:
Personal Narrative

Writing:
Sensory Details

Speaking and Listening:
Oral Presentation (teacher edition)

Critical Viewing:
Connect

PORTFOLIO OPPORTUNITIES

Writing: On-line Message; Children's Story; The Author's World

Writing Mini-Lesson: Memory of a Milestone

Speaking and Listening: Memory Exchange; Oral Presentation

Projects: Multimedia Presentation; Illustration

More About the Author
Vladimir Nabokov's career as a writer can be split into two distinct phases: one during his European exile, when he wrote in Russian, and one starting in the late 1930's and continuing throughout his life in the United States, when he wrote in English. He also translated his Russian works into English, effectively rewriting and revising them stylistically.

Vladimir Nabokov (1899–1977)

Besides being a novelist, a poet, and a translator, Russian-born Vladimir Nabokov was a passionate butterfly collector. Some critics have said that Nabokov, who wrote in both Russian and English, treated words like butterflies: each a rare, colorful specimen pinned to the page.

Early Success Nabokov was born into an upper-class but politically liberal Russian family from St. Petersburg. He quickly became, in his own words, "a perfectly normal trilingual child." His languages were Russian, French, and English. By the time he was fifteen years old, he had published his first volume of Russian verse.

Early Tragedy The Russian Revolution of 1917 drove the Nabokovs into exile, and Vladimir finished his education at an English university. There, in 1922, he learned the tragic news that his father had been assassinated while shielding another man at a political gathering. Nabokov's great affection for his father and equally great feeling of loss are evident in his autobiography.

From Exile to Citizenship Nabokov spent years in Europe, living away from his native Russia. In 1940, he had to flee Hitler's Germany. He moved his wife and young son to the United States, where he taught at various universities. In 1945, he became a citizen of this country.

Literary Achievements From his early teens until his death, Nabokov was a committed writer. His carefully constructed and playful novels include *Bend Sinister* (1947), *Pnin* (1957), and *Ada* (1969). He also won acclaim for his autobiography, *Speak, Memory* (1967), whose title shows the importance of memory for this writer. Not only words but memories were the rare, fluttering specimens of this literary butterfly collector.

◆ Build Vocabulary

PREFIXES: *pro-*
In this personal narrative, you will encounter the word *procession.* Knowing that the prefix *pro-* often means "before in place or time" or "moving forward," you can figure out the part that it plays in the word *procession*, which means "a number of persons or things moving forward."

procession
proficiency
laborious
portentously
limpid

WORD BANK
As you read this excerpt from *Speak, Memory*, you will encounter the words on this list. Work together with a group of classmates to write sentences containing as many of the words as you can. If necessary, use a dictionary to help you.

◆ Build Grammar Skills

DASHES
Throughout this selection, Nabokov uses **dashes**—punctuation marks that create longer pauses than commas do. Used in pairs, dashes separate material that would interrupt the flow of the thought:

The kind of Russian family to which I belonged—a kind now extinct—had, among other virtues ...

Used singly, dashes can announce an example or definition or can signal an abrupt change of mood:

Summer *soomerki*—the lovely Russian word for dusk.

For Nabokov, dashes—and the information they set off—are like little notes with further background. They help him explain and bring you in to the lost world of his childhood.

302 ◆ *Turning Points*

Prentice Hall Literature Program Resources

REINFORCE / RETEACH / EXTEND

Selection Support Pages
Build Vocabulary: Prefixes: *pro-,* p. 92
Build Grammar Skills: Dashes, p. 93
Reading for Success: Reading Critically, pp. 94–95
Literary Focus: Personal Narrative, p. 96

Strategies for Diverse Student Needs, p. 23

Beyond Literature
Cross-Curricular Connection: Geography, p. 23

Formal Assessment Selection Test, pp. 79–81; Assessment Resources Software.

Alternative Assessment, p. 23

Writing and Language Transparencies
Writing Process Model 3: Personal Narrative, pp. 17–23

Resource Pro CD-ROM
"Speak, Memory"—includes all resource material and customizable lesson plan

 Listening to Literature Audiocassettes "Speak, Memory"

from Speak, Memory

◆ *Literature and Your Life*

CONNECT YOUR EXPERIENCE

Just think, no two people have read the exact same books, articles, and stories in their lifetime. The special combination of books you have read contributes uniquely to your personality.

In this section of his autobiography, Nabokov fondly recalls his first reading experiences—he learned to read English before Russian, his native language!

Journal Writing Jot down some impressions of your first reading experiences.

THEMATIC FOCUS: TURNING POINTS

Learning to read is a turning point in most people's lives. This narrative asks (and gives one answer to) the question: How does what you read affect your life?

◆ Background for Understanding

THE STORY BEHIND THE STORY

People write in order to preserve what might otherwise be lost. Nabokov's autobiography preserves the upper-class life with loving parents that was snatched from his hands by the Russian Revolution of 1917. (In this picture, you see Vladimir, age seven, with his beloved father.)

Nabokov was a teenager when his family was forced to leave Russia. From the graced life of his childhood, he took a few belongings and a million precise memories—some of which he shares in this excerpt from his autobiography. The life he lost became the life he could never forget.

◆ Literary Focus

PERSONAL NARRATIVE

This episode from a larger autobiography of Vladimir Nabokov's life is a **personal narrative**—a true story about a memorable person, event, or situation in the writer's life. Writers tell such narratives from the first-person point of view. They also hint at or state directly the meaning of this chapter in their lives. In his narrative, Nabokov captures memories of childhood reading just as he netted butterflies. He closes in on some fluttering early impressions, traps them, pins them down, and examines them in a clear light.

Use a graphic organizer like the one shown to jot down details that help you share Nabokov's memories.

- Schoolroom
  - Caterpillars
  - Sunlight

Memories

- Breakfast
  - Bread and butter
  - Golden syrup

Guide for Reading ◆ 303

Preparing for Standardized Tests

Reading and Vocabulary The Build Vocabulary lesson for this selection focuses on recognizing meanings of words that contain the prefix *pro-*. Students can apply this skill when working on vocabulary, reading comprehension, and verbal reasoning items on standardized tests. For additional practice, use the Build Vocabulary page in *Selection Support,* p. 92.

The Reading for Success strategies will help improve students' peformance on the critical reading portions of standardized tests. The ability

to recognize an author's purpose and bias and to differentiate between fact and opinion are tested by asking a series of questions after reading a passage. By learning to evaluate a writer's points and judge the work as a whole, students will enhance their ability to respond to evaluative questions about a passage. Each of the skills is presented on the Reading for Success page in the Student Edition, p. 304. For further practice, have students use the Reading for Success pages in *Selection Support,* pp. 94–95.

The Reading for Success page in each unit presents a set of problem-solving procedures to help readers understand authors' words and ideas on multiple levels. Good readers develop a bank of strategies from which they can draw as needed.

Unit 4 introduces strategies for reading critically. These strategies give readers an approach for examining text on a critical level. By using these strategies as they read, students will gain a higher-level understanding and appreciation of the selection.

These strategies for reading critically are modeled with the excerpt from *Speak, Memory.* Each green box shows an example of the thinking process involved in applying one of these strategies.

How to Use the Reading for Success Page

- Introduce the strategies for reading critically, presenting each as a problem-solving procedure. Be sure students understand what each strategy involves and under what circumstances to apply it.

- Before students read the story, have them preview it, looking at the annotations in the green boxes that model the strategies.

- To reinforce these strategies after students have read the excerpt from *Speak, Memory,* have students do the Reading for Success pages in *Selection Support,* pp. 94–95. This activity gives students an opportunity to read a selection and practice strategies for reading critically by writing their own annotations.

Reading for Success

Strategies for Reading Critically

When you read a work that presents an individual's perspective or ideas on a subject, it is a good idea to read the work critically. When you read critically, you examine and question the writer's ideas, especially in light of his or her purpose. You also evaluate the information the writer includes (or doesn't include) as support, and you form a judgment about the content and quality of the work. Here are specific strategies to help you read critically.

Recognize the author's purpose and bias.

The author's purpose is his or her reason for writing, such as to inform, entertain, or persuade. An author might have more than one purpose. In a personal narrative, for example, an author might want to inform *and* entertain.

Writers often write from a particular bias—a point of view influenced by their experience. It's important to be aware of any factors that might bias a writer's opinion. For example, Nabokov's aristocratic background certainly influenced his attitude toward the Russian Revolution.

Distinguish fact from opinion.

A fact is information that can be proved true or false. An opinion cannot be proved true or false. Nabokov's statement that he "learned to read English before … Russian" is a fact. However, when he describes children's book characters as "wan-faced, big-limbed, silent nitwits," he's expressing an opinion.

Some forms of literature, including personal narratives, contain both fact and opinion. However, it's always important to be able to tell the two apart.

Evaluate the writer's points or statements.

Evaluating involves making a critical judgment. Ask questions like these:
▶ Does the writer present facts that are true?
▶ Does the writer support opinions with sound reasons?
▶ Does the writer's background or experience qualify him or her to make such a statement?

Judge the writer's work.

As you judge the work in its totality, ask yourself questions like these:
▶ Do the statements follow logically?
▶ Is the material clearly organized?
▶ Are the writer's points interesting and well supported?
▶ Did the piece hold my interest or stimulate me throughout my reading?

As you read this excerpt from *Speak, Memory* by Vladimir Nabokov, look at the notes in the boxes. These notes demonstrate how to apply these strategies to a work of literature.

Reading Strategies: Support and Reinforcement

Appropriate Reading Strategies Students are given a reading strategy to apply in reading each selection in this unit. As appropriate, students are given a critical reading strategy. In other selections a strategy is suggested that is appropriate to the selection.

Reading Prompts To encourage application of the given reading strategy, there are occasional prompts, within green boxes, at appropriate and significant points.

In addition, there are red boxes prompting application of the Literary Focus concept and maroon boxes prompting students to connect with their lives.

Using the Boxed Annotations and Prompts

The material in the green, red, and maroon boxes along the sides of selections is intended to help students apply the literary element and the reading strategy and to make a connection with their lives.

You may use the boxed material in these ways:

- Have students pause when they come to a box and respond to its prompt before they continue reading.

- Urge students to read through the selection ignoring the boxes. After they have read the selection completely, they may go back and review the selection, responding to the prompts.

from Speak, Memory

Vladimir Nabokov

1

The kind of Russian family to which I belonged—a kind now extinct—had, among other virtues, a traditional leaning toward the comfortable products of Anglo-Saxon civilization. Pears' Soap, tar-black when dry, topaz-like when held to the light between wet fingers, took care of one's morning bath. Pleasant was the decreasing weight of the English collapsible tub when it was made to protrude a rubber underlip and disgorge its frothy contents into the slop pail. "We could not improve the cream, so we improved the tube," said the English toothpaste. At breakfast, Golden Syrup imported from London would entwist with its glowing coils the revolving spoon from which enough of it had slithered onto a piece of Russian bread and butter. All sorts of snug, mellow things came in a steady procession from the English Shop on Nevski Avenue: fruitcakes, smelling salts, playing cards, picture puzzles, striped blazers, talcum-white tennis balls.

I learned to read English before I could read Russian. My first English friends were four simple souls in my grammar—Ben, Dan, Sam and Ned. There used to be a great deal of fuss about their identities and whereabouts—"Who is Ben?" "He is Dan," "Sam is in bed," and so on. Although it all remained rather stiff and patchy (the compiler was handicapped by having to employ—for the initial lessons, at least—words of not more than three letters), my imagination somehow managed to obtain the necessary data. Wan-faced, big-limbed, silent nitwits, proud in the possession of certain tools ("Ben has an axe"), they now drift with a slow-motioned slouch across the remotest backdrop of memory; and, akin to the mad alphabet of an optician's chart, the grammar-book lettering looms again before me.

The schoolroom was drenched with sunlight. In a sweating glass jar, several spiny

> These details show that Nabokov came from an aristocratic background, which helps explain his **bias** about the characters in his books.

> It is a **fact** that Nabokov learned to read English before he could read Russian, but it was Nabokov's **opinion** that the text of his grammar book was "stiff and patchy."

◆ Build Vocabulary

procession (prō sesh´ ən) n.: Number of persons or things moving forward in an orderly or formal way

---

Develop Understanding

One-Minute Insight

In this excerpt from *Speak, Memory*, Vladimir Nabokov blends memories, sensory impressions, and historical facts to create a unique autobiographical reflection. The excerpt focuses primarily on Nabokov's early memories of books—those his mother read to him and those he first learned to read on his own. These experiences had a profound effect on Nabokov, helping to develop an enduring love for language.

◆ Reading for Success

❶ Distinguish Fact From Opinion Ask students to identify the detail in this opening sentence that is the author's opinion. *It is an opinion that the "traditional leaning toward the comfortable products of Anglo-Saxon civilization" is a virtue.*

◆ Reading for Success

❷ Judge the Writer's Work Ask students what criteria they would use to judge this passage. *Students might point out such elements as the language and choice of details as well as the use of sensory images, such as "glowing coils," or vivid verbs, such as "slithered." They might also point to the author's use of syntax—or arrangement of sentence parts—as a criteria for judging the passage.*

◆ Reading for Success

❸ Evaluate Writer's Statements Have students explain whether the writer's background qualifies him to judge the writing in his grammar as "stiff and patchy." *Yes; the writer is a respected author who even as a child would probably be a good judge of writing as "stiff and patchy."*

Block Scheduling Strategies

Consider these suggestions to take advantage of extended class time:

• Together with students, read The Story Behind the Story in Background for Understanding on page 303. Let students know that the Nabokov family was forced into exile because Nabokov's father was a liberal politician who opposed the Bolshevik government that came into power in 1917. Encourage students to suggest other circumstances in which

people might have to flee their native lands.

• Introduce the Critical Reading Strategies. Discuss the kinds of reading situations that call for critical reading. Encourage students to look at the annotations that model the strategies. To give students more practice, you can follow up with the Reading for Success in **Selection Support,** pp. 94–95.

• Have students work in groups to complete the Critical Thinking questions on page 309. Encourage them to compare and discuss their suggestions for books or stories Nabokov would have enjoyed as a child.

• Direct students to complete the Writing Mini-Lesson (p. 310). Before students start writing, guide them through the drafts in the Writing Process Model 3: Personal Narrative, pp. 17–23.

305

caterpillars were feeding on nettle[1] leaves (and ejecting interesting, barrel-shaped pellets of olive-green grass). The oilcloth that covered the round table smelled of glue. Miss Clayton smelled of Miss Clayton. Fantastically, gloriously, the blood-colored alcohol of the outside thermometer had

---

1. **nettle** (net´ əl) *n.*: Any of various other stinging or spiny plants.

◆ **Build Vocabulary**

proficiency (prō fish´ ən sē) *n.*: Expertise

❷ laborious (lə bôr´ ē əs) *adj.*: Involving or calling for much hard work; difficult

❸ portentously (pôr ten´ təs lē) *adv.*: Ominously; scarily

limpid (lim´ pid) *adj.*: Perfectly clear; transparent

▲ **Critical Viewing** What details in this picture reflect the feelings Nabokov associates with reading? **[Connect]** **❶**

risen to 24° Réaumur (86° Fahrenheit) in the shade. Through the window one could see kerchiefed peasant girls weeding a garden path on their hands and knees or gently raking the sun-mottled sand. (The happy days when they would be cleaning streets and digging canals for the State were still beyond the horizon.) Golden orioles in the greenery emitted their four brilliant notes: dee-del-dee-O! **❹**

Ned lumbered past the window in a fair impersonation of the gardener's mate Ivan (who was to become in 1918 a member of the local Soviet). On later pages longer words appeared; and at the very end of the

 Beyond the Classroom

❺ Analyze Cause and Effect Ask students how the writer's understanding of the sentences in his grammar book affected his life. *His excitement at understanding and at the thought that someday he too might write may have pushed him toward his career as a writer.*

◆ **Build Grammar Skills**

❻ Dashes Ask students to explain the purpose the dashes in this passage serve. Why did the author use them? *They set off words that specify the term* everything, *thereby completing the author's description of the Russian dusk. The dashes signal to the reader that it is necessary to pause when reading this clarifying information.*

◆ **Reading for Success**

❼ Judge the Writer's Work Ask students to determine if the two parts of this statement—the part about his mother's ringed hand and the part about émigré life—have a logical connection. *Students should recognize that the author is saying that the ring his mother wore was later sold to pay for their life in exile. Although it may not appear so at first, the two thoughts are logically connected.*

◆ **Critical Thinking**

❽ Connect Ask students how this memory reflects Nabokov's statement that his type of family is "extinct." *Just as the chivalrous knights and maidens of his tales no longer exist, so his family and its habits are no more.*

> Here, the **author's purpose** is to emphasize the profound effect learning to read had on him as a child and how it has continued with him throughout adulthood.

brown, inkstained volume, a real, sensible story unfolded its adult sentences ("One day Ted said to Ann: Let us—"), the little reader's ultimate triumph and reward. I was

❺ thrilled by the thought that some day I might attain such <u>proficiency</u>. The magic has endured, and whenever a grammar book comes my way, I instantly turn to the last page to enjoy a forbidden glimpse of the <u>laborious</u> student's future, of that promised land where, at last, words are meant to mean what they mean.

2

Summer *soomerki*—the lovely Russian word for dusk. Time: a dim point in the first decade of this unpopular century. Place: latitude[2] 59° north from your equator, longitude[3] 100° east from my writing hand. The day would take hours to fade,

❻ and everything—sky, tall flowers, still water—would be kept in a state of infinite vesperal[4] suspense, deepened rather than resolved by the doleful moo of a cow in a distant meadow or by the still more moving cry that came from some bird beyond the lower course of the river, where the vast expanse of a misty-blue sphagnum[5] bog, because of its mystery and remoteness, the Rukavishnikov children had baptized America.

In the drawing room of our country house, before going to bed, I would often be read to in English by my mother. As

she came to a particularly dramatic passage, where the hero was about to encounter some strange, perhaps fatal danger, her voice would slow down, her words would be spaced <u>portentously</u>, and before turning the page she would place upon it her hand, with its familiar pigeon-blood ruby and diamond ring (within the <u>limpid</u> facets of which, had I been a better crystal-gazer, I might have seen a room, people, lights, trees in the rain—a whole period of émigré life for which that ring was to pay).

There were tales about knights whose terrific but wonderfully aseptic[6] wounds were bathed by damsels in grottoes.[7] From a windswept clifftop, a medieval maiden with flying hair and a youth in hose gazed at the round Isles of the Blessed. In "Misunderstood," the fate of Humphrey used to bring a more specialized lump to one's throat than anything in Dickens or Daudet[8] (great devisers of lumps), while a shamelessly allegorical story, "Beyond the Blue Mountains," dealing with two pairs of little travelers—good Clover and Cowslip, bad Buttercup and Daisy—contained enough exciting details to make one forget its "message."

There were also those large, flat, glossy picture books. I particularly liked the blue-coated, red-trousered, coal-black

> **Evaluate** Nabokov's description and feeling about the "lovely" summer dusk: His supporting details create a soft, warm, and satisfying time of day that ended with his mother reading to him.

> Nabokov expresses the **opinion** that stories about knights were better than the works he read by Dickens or Daudet.

---

2. **latitude** (lat′ ə tōōd) *n.*: Angular distance, measured in degrees, north or south from the equator.
3. **longitude** (län′ jə tōōd) *n.*: Distance east or west on the Earth's surface, measured as an arc of the equator.
4. **vesperal** (ves′ pər əl) *adj.*: Eveninglike.
5. **sphagnum** (sfag′ nəm) *n.*: Highly absorbent, spongelike, grayish peat mosses found in bogs.

6. **aseptic** (ā sep′ tik) *adj.*: Free from or keeping away disease-producing microorganisms.
7. **grottoes** (grät′ ōz) *n.*: Caves.
8. **Dickens** (dik′ ənz) **or Daudet** (dō dā′): Charles Dickens and Alphonse Daudet, nineteenth-century novelists who sympathized with common people.

from Speak, Memory ◆ 307

Speaking and Listening Mini-Lesson

Oral Presentation

This mini-lesson supports the Speaking and Listening activity in the Idea Bank on page 310.

Introduce the Concept Have students think about a book that had meaning for them when they were younger. In choosing, remind them to think about the book's characters, language, and illustrations.

Develop Background Encourage students to make a list of the elements of the book that

most affected them, and why, for example:
1. Most memorable character: funny grandmother who gives advice to all the kids in the neighborhood
2. Language—no compound or complex sentences created a strange, lulling rhythm
3. Tone—moralistic, but humorous, too

Apply the Information Working from their notes, students can present the book to the class. Remind them to use sensory

details, as Nabokov did, so their audience will "see" the book as they did.

Assess the Outcome Students can use the following questions as criteria to evaluate one another's presentations:
1. What did the presenter like most—and least—about the book?
2. Did his or her descriptions appeal to the senses?
3. Was the presentation clearly organized, with a logical connection between points?

❶ Personal Narrative Ask students how Nabokov links the stories he reads with details from his life in this passage. What effect does the link have on the narrative? *He associates the frightened expression on the face of Sarah, a book character, with the expressions of little girls he encountered at children's parties, making the narrative all the more personal.*

◆ **Critical Thinking**

❷ Draw Conclusions Ask students why they think the writer had been envious of the solo balloonist. *He wanted to be part of the soloist's adventure, even though it was dangerous.*

Reinforce and Extend

Answers

◆ *Literature and Your Life*

Reader's Response Students' comparisons should consider such elements as characterization, style of language and of illustrations, and tone.

Thematic Focus Being able to read opens up a whole new realm of possibilities.

☑ **Check Your Comprehension**

1. The author's first friends were Ben, Dan, Sam, and Ned—children's book characters.
2. The author's impressions were that his friends were "wan-faced, big-limbed, silent nitwits."
3. The author turns to the last page of a grammar because he wants to see what the future will hold for the student who reads it.
4. The author remembers "the Golliwog and his harem" for their funny clothes and their adventurous spirits and merrymaking.

Golliwogg, with underclothes buttons for eyes, and his meager harem of five wooden dolls. By the illegal method of cutting themselves frocks out of the American flag (Peg taking the motherly stripes, Sarah Jane the pretty stars) two of the dolls acquired a certain soft femininity, once their neutral articulations had been clothed. The Twins (Meg and Weg) and the Midget remained stark naked and, consequently, sexless.

We see them in the dead of night stealing out of doors to sling snowballs at one another until the chimes of a remote clock ("But Hark!" comments the rhymed text) send them back to their toybox in the nursery. A rude jack-in-the-box shoots out, frightening my lovely Sarah, and that picture I heartily disliked because it reminded me of children's parties at which this or that graceful little girl, who had bewitched me, happened to pinch her finger or hurt her knee, and would forthwith expand into a purple-faced goblin, all wrinkles and bawling mouth. Another time they went on a bicycle journey and were captured by cannibals; our unsuspecting

travelers had been quenching their thirst at a palm-fringed pool when the tom-toms sounded. Over the shoulder of my past I admire again the crucial picture: the Golliwogg, still on his knees by the pool but no longer drinking; his hair stands on end and the normal black of his face has changed to a weird ashen hue. There was also the motorcar book (Sarah Jane, always my favorite, sporting a long green veil), with the usual sequel—crutches and bandaged heads.

And, yes—the airship. Yards and yards of yellow silk went to make it, and an additional tiny balloon was provided for the sole use of the fortunate Midget. At the immense altitude to which the ship reached, the aeronauts huddled together for warmth while the lost little soloist, still the object of my intense envy notwithstanding his plight, drifted into an abyss of frost and stars—alone.

> **Judge** whether Nabokov has successfully presented the pleasure and satisfaction of his learning to read.

Guide for Responding

◆ *Literature and Your Life*

Reader's Response Compare the earliest books and stories you read with those that Nabokov read as a boy.

Thematic Focus Explain why learning to read might be considered a turning point.

Group Discussion In a small group, discuss how the characters in your first reading books did—or did not—reflect life at the time.

☑ **Check Your Comprehension**

1. Who were the author's "first English friends," and where did they come from?
2. What were the author's impressions of his first English friends?
3. Why does the author now always turn to the last page of a "grammar" (student's first reader)?
4. Summarize the author's impressions of the "Golliwog and his harem."

308 ◆ *Turning Points*

🕮 Beyond the Selection

FURTHER READING

Other Works by Vladimir Nabokov
Pnin (novel)
Nabokov's Dozen (short stories)
Glory (novel)

Other Works With the Theme of Turning Points
My Life, Helen Keller
Up From Slavery, Frederick Douglass
Out of Africa, Isak Dinesen
We suggest that you preview these works before recommending them to students.

INTERNET
Your students can find information about Nabokov at the following site. Please be aware that sites may have changed since we published this information.
http://www.libraries.psu.edu/iasweb/nabokov/hsintro.html
We *strongly recommend* that you preview the site before you send students to it.

Guide for Responding (continued)

◆ Critical Thinking

INTERPRET

1. Why does Nabokov say the kind of family to which he belonged is "now extinct"? [Speculate]
2. What does Nabokov intend for you to know about his mother's ruby and diamond ring? [Draw Conclusions]
3. Nabokov was strongly affected by the books of his childhood. Support this statement with evidence from the selection. [Support]
4. What was the author's purpose in writing these particular impressions of his childhood? [Infer]

APPLY

5. Recommend a book or story that you think Nabokov would have liked. Give reasons for your recommendation. [Apply]

EXTEND

6. What are some reasons that people would use products imported from another country, as the Nabokovs did? [Social Studies Link]

◆ Reading For Success

STRATEGIES FOR READING CRITICALLY

Apply the strategies and the notes showing how to read critically to answer the following questions.

1. Give an example of an opinion from this essay and explain how you know it's an opinion.
2. Explain how the first sentence of Nabokov's narrative reflects the bias of an upper-class Russian.
3. What do you think was the author's purpose in recording these impressions of his early reading?

◆ Literary Focus

PERSONAL NARRATIVE

Nabokov's essay is a **personal narrative**—a true story drawn from his own life and told in the first person.

1. How does the first sentence indicate that this work is a personal narrative?
2. Find two details that help you see the characters Ben, Dan, Sam, and Ned.
3. Show how Nabokov appeals to every sense except taste in his description of the schoolroom.

◆ Build Vocabulary

USING THE PREFIX pro-

In the following words, the prefix pro- means "before in place or time" or "moving forward." Match each pro- word with the correct definition.

1. proceed   a. drive forward
2. projection   b. something read before a drama
3. prologue   c. go forward
4. propel   d. a look ahead

USING THE WORD BANK

On your paper, fill in the blanks with words from the Word Bank. Use each word only once.

Nabokov offers a ___?___ of sensory details, rendered with ___?___ . The author is accurate without being ___?___ . You can almost see the ___?___ facets of his mother's jewels and hear how she ___?___ lowers her voice.

◆ Build Grammar Skills

DASHES

As Nabokov introduces you to his childhood world, he uses **dashes** to set off interrupting or clarifying phrases, to show an unfinished thought, and to introduce a final word that changes or emphasizes thought.

Practice In your notebook, write the following sentences, adding two dashes where necessary to set off interrupting phrases or sentences, or one dash to signal a clarification or shift in thought.

1. A biography of Nabokov the first major one in years shows the relationship between his life and work.
2. You can read about Nabokov his life, work, and travels in reference sources on world authors.
3. Nabokov spent many years in France and Germany impoverished.
4. Everyone knows Nabokov's favorite hobby butterfly collecting.
5. Nabokov not popular with all readers is greatly respected by those who call themselves his fans.

from Speak Memory ◆ 309

Answers

◆ Critical Thinking

1. The economy and government in Russia at the time Nabokov was writing were very different from those of his childhood.
2. He intends for you to know that she sold the ring to support the family in exile.
3. Students may cite the very fact that Nabokov remembered the names Ben, Dan, Sam, and Ned, or that he was attached to the character Sarah Jane from a series picture book.
4. Nabokov might have wanted to preserve recollections from a life that is "now extinct."
5. Students should support their recommendations with details they observed about Nabokov's character or his reading taste.
6. Students might observe that some countries import products they don't have the resources to produce, or they might say that consumers like to try goods that come from different cultures.

◆ Reading for Success

1. An example might be "Summer *soomerki*—the lovely Russian word for dusk." It can't be proven that this is a lovely word.
2. To say that a taste for products of Anglo-Saxon civilization is a virtue implies that those products are superior—a cultural bias.
3. His purpose might have been to entertain and to share memories with which readers could identify.

◆ Literary Focus

1. The first sentence uses the first-person point of view.
2. Possible details include that these characters were proud in their possession of tools, that they were silent and "dim-witted."
3. "Drenched with sunlight" appeals to both sight and touch; the oilcloth smelling of glue appeals to smell; the chirps of the golden orioles appeals to sound.

◆ Build Vocabulary

Using the Prefix pro-

1. c   2. d   3. b   4. a

Using the Word Bank

Nabokov offers a <u>procession</u> of sensory details rendered with <u>proficiency</u>. The author is accurate without being <u>laborious</u>. You can almost see

---

the <u>limpid</u> facets of his mother's jewels and hear how she <u>portentously</u> lowers her voice.

◆ Build Grammar Skills

Practice

1. A biography of Nabokov—the first major one in years—shows the relationship between his life and work.
2. You can read about Nabokov—his life, work, and travels—in reference sources on world authors.
3. Nabokov spent many years in France and Germany—impoverished.
4. Everyone knows Nabokov's favorite hobby—butterfly collecting.
5. Nabokov—not popular with all readers—is greatly respected by those who call themselves his fans.

✎ Writer's Solution

For additional instruction and practice, use the lesson in the **Language Lab CD-ROM** on mechanics and the pages on Dashes and Parentheses, page 107 in the *Writer's Solution Grammar Practice Book.*

Idea Bank

Customizing for
Performance Levels

Following are suggestions for matching Idea Bank topics with your students' performance levels:

Less Advanced Students: 1, 4
Average Students: 2, 5, 7
More Advanced Students: 3, 6

Customizing for
Learning Modalities

Following are suggestions for matching Idea Bank topics with your students' learning modalities:

Visual/Spatial: 7
Bodily/Kinesthetic: 4
Verbal/Linguistic: 4, 5
Logical/Mathematical: 3

Writing Mini-Lesson

Refer students to the Writing Handbook, page 965, for instruction on the writing process, and page 967 for further information on narrative writing.

Writing and Language Transparencies Use Writing Process Model 3: Personal Narrative, pp. 17–23, to model tips for drafting a narrative.

Writer's Solution

Writers at Work Videodisc

Have students view the videodisc segment for Chapter 2 in which Maxine Hong Kingston talks about developing narrative elements.

Play frames 18612 to 19873

Writing Lab CD-ROM

Have students complete the tutorial on Narration. Follow these steps:
1. Have students consult an audio-annotated slide show on drafting. They will hear helpful tips for developing a narrative.
2. Suggest that students use Word Bins to select sensory words to help make their memories of a milestone come alive for their readers.

Sourcebook

Have students use Chapter 2, Narration (pp. 31–56), for additional support.

Build Your Portfolio

Idea Bank

Writing

1. **On-line Message** Write a message about this excerpt from Nabokov's *Speak, Memory* to send to an on-line reader's circle. Tell why you liked or disliked the it. Support your opinion.

2. **Children's Story** Make up characters like Nabokov's Golliwog and friends and write a story about them that children would enjoy reading.

3. **The Author's World** Write a description of the world Nabokov lost when he left Russia as a teenager. Use details from *Speak, Memory*, as well as an encyclopedia and books on early twentieth-century Russia. **[Social Studies Link]**

Speaking and Listening

4. **Memory Exchange** In a small group, exchange stories about some of your most important achievements as young children—for example, learning to read, swim, or travel by yourself. Record your stories on tape or tell them to the class. **[Performing Arts Link]**

5. **Oral Presentation** Give a presentation to your class on a children's book that meant a great deal to you. Following Nabokov's lead, describe the characters and events of the book so that your listeners will see them. **[Art Link]**

Projects

6. **Multimedia Presentation** Using film clips, recordings, pictures from books, and quotations from authors, give a presentation on the Russian Revolution of 1917. **[Social Studies Link]**

7. **Illustration** Choose one of Nabokov's detailed descriptions and illustrate it with a drawing or painting. **[Art Link]**

Writing Mini-Lesson

Memory of a Milestone

Nabokov describes how he learned to read English. Choose a milestone (significant event) from your life and write a **narrative** about your memory of it. You might describe learning to swim, moving to a new home, or graduating from school. Tell readers not only what happened, but why it was important. Help them understand its importance by using sensory details to make events come alive.

> **Writing Skills Focus: Sensory Details**
> **Sensory details**—details that appeal to the senses—are important in stories, personal narratives, and descriptions of all kinds. Nabokov begins his personal narrative with details that appeal both to the eye and to the sense of touch:
>
> Pears' Soap, tar-black when dry, topaz-like when held to the light between wet fingers, took care of one's morning bath.
>
> The sensory details help you experience this long-lost bath as he did himself. Even before you draft your narrative, begin gathering sensory details you can use.

Prewriting In gathering sensory details, pay special attention to the often neglected senses of smell, touch, and taste.

Drafting Sometimes you can suggest how important a milestone was by showing someone else's reaction to it. For example, you might show how catching your first fish won you the respect of your brothers and sisters.

Revising Ask a classmate whether it's clear why the event was a milestone. If not, add sensory details to make the description more vivid, or include a statement explaining the importance of what happened.

✓ ASSESSMENT OPTIONS

Formal Assessment, Selection Test, pp. 79–81, and Assessment Resources Software. The selection test is designed so that it can be easily customized to the performance levels of your students. **Alternative Assessment,** p. 23, includes options for less advanced students, more advanced students, verbal/linguistic learners, logical/mathematical learners, bodily/kinesthetic learners, and visual spatial learners.

PORTFOLIO ASSESSMENT
Use the following rubrics in the **Alternative Assessment** booklet to assess student writing:
On-line Message: Expression Rubric, p. 94
Children's Story: Fiction Narrative Rubric, p. 95
The Author's World: Description Rubric, p. 97

PART **1**   *Working It Out*

 Untitled, David Wilcox, The Newborn Group

Working It Out ◆ *311*

One-Minute Planning Guide

The selections in this part show characters working out a variety of problematic situations. The main character in "With All Flags Flying" is an eighty-two-year-old man who decides to move into a nursing home. The narrator of the poem "The Bridge" describes his indecision and fear about crossing a treacherous bridge. The narrator of Emily Brontë's "The Old Stoic," meanwhile, asks for the courage to endure her final days before death. The tone of Anna Akhmatova's "I Am Not One of Those Who Left the Land" is one of defiance and victory after having survived the violence of the Russian Revolution. The selection ends with Roman Empress Theodora's rousing "Speech During the Invasion of Constantinople," in which she exhorts her timid husband and advisors to remain in Constantinople and fight rather than flee and live in exile and ignominy.

Customize for
Varying Student Needs
When assigning the selections in this part to your students, keep in mind the following factors:

"With All Flags Flying"
• A medium-length short story (7 pp.)

"The Bridge"; The Old Stoic"; "I Am Not One of Those Who Left the Land"
• Three very short poems

Speech During the Invasion of Constantinople
• A short speech
• Will be accessible to students

Humanities: Art

Untitled by David Wilcox.

Born in 1943 in Kansas City, Missouri, David Wilcox has created illustrations for magazines, movie posters, and book covers, and his clients include a number of corporations and mainstream publications.

Encourage students to describe what seems to be going on in the painting. Once they have established the representational circumstances of the painting, have them look at its formal elements: the fact that the empty spot in the bridge lines up with the mountain peak in the distance, dividing the picture into right and left halves. Encourage them to notice the unrealistic landscape—the small, lollipop-like trees, the succession of hills—as well as other unrealistic touches, such as the facelessness of the people and fact that they are doing heavy manual labor in what appear to be business clothes.

Help students link the art to the theme of Part 1, "Working It Out," by answering the following questions:

1. Normally, people building a bridge would not be dressed in suits. The clothing hints that the bridge-building here is meant as a metaphor. What might it stand for? *Possible answers include working to make a better society or cooperating to accomplish a goal in the business world.*

2. Does the group appear to be cooperating successfully? What tensions might be present among them? *Most students will feel that the group is cooperating; possible tensions might arise from the fact that three men are pulling, while only one is pushing.*

311

OBJECTIVES

1. To read, comprehend, and interpret a short story
2. To relate a story to personal experience
3. To judge a character's decision in a story
4. To identify characters as symbols
5. To build vocabulary in context and learn the prefix *mono-*
6. To recognize and use past participial phrases
7. To write a dialogue using appropriate language for purpose
8. To respond to the story through writing, speaking and listening, and projects

SKILLS INSTRUCTION

Vocabulary:
Prefixes: *mono-*

Grammar:
Past Participial Phrases

Reading Strategy:
Judge a Character's Decision

Literary Focus:
Characters as Symbols

Writing:
Appropriate Language for Purpose

Speaking and Listening:
Debate (teacher edition)

Critical Viewing:
Analyze; Infer

PORTFOLIO OPPORTUNITIES

Writing: Essay on Growing Old; Letter From Mr. Carpenter; Alternative Ending

Writing Mini-Lesson: Writing a Dialogue With an Older Person

Speaking and Listening: Soundtrack; Debate

Projects: Volunteer at a Nursing Home; Service for the Elderly

More About the Author

Anne Tyler is interested in choices that people make and the factors that influence their decisions. She has said, "Who hasn't had the urge to up and leave at some point, packing no more than a tooth-brush? . . . It seems to me that the proper choice varies from one person to the next, and even from one moment to the next."

Guide for Reading

Anne Tyler (1941–)

At an age when most people are thinking about prom dates and getting their driver's licenses, Anne Tyler was already in college, majoring in Russian.

Tyler began her college career at Duke University at age sixteen and graduated at nineteen!

Early Achiever Born in Minneapolis, Minnesota, Anne Tyler moved frequently with her family during childhood. She lived in many communities in the South and the Midwest. After Duke, she went on to do graduate work in Russian studies at Columbia University. Tyler wrote her first novel, *If Morning Ever Comes*, at the age of twenty-

two and has been writing full time since 1965.

In her works, Tyler draws heavily from her personal experiences. Many of her stories and novels, including "With All Flags Flying," are set in Baltimore, Maryland, where she has lived since 1967. The characters and events in her work are often drawn from her encounters with real people and from her daily observations.

Acclaim and Awards Anne Tyler's tales about the lives of ordinary people have won her widespread critical acclaim. Tyler is a member of the American Academy and Institute of Arts and Letters and the recipient of the 1988 Pulitzer Prize for her novel *Breathing Lessons*. Many of her novels, including *Dinner at the Homesick Restaurant* (1982), *The Accidental Tourist* (1985), and *Saint Maybe* (1991), have been bestsellers.

◆ Build Vocabulary

PREFIXES: *mono–*

In this story, an old man gives *monosyllabic* answers to his granddaughter's questions. The prefix *mono-* means "one." A *monosyllabic* word, therefore, is a word with one syllable. The main character answers his granddaughter in words of one syllable.

WORD BANK

appurtenances
conspicuous
doddering
monosyllabic

As you read, you will encounter the words on this list. Each word is defined on the page where it first appears. Preview the list before you read.

◆ Build Grammar Skills

PAST PARTICIPIAL PHRASES

In this story, Anne Tyler incorporates detailed information into many of her sentences using participial phrases formed with past participles. A past participle is a form of a verb that usually ends in *-ed* but may also have an irregular ending such as *-t* or *-en*. A **past participial phrase** consists of a past participle and its modifiers and complements. Participles and participial phrases act as adjectives. In this sentence, the italicized participial phrase modifies the noun *weeds*:

"The bank was covered with small, crawling weeds, *planted especially by young men with scientific training in how to prevent soil erosion*."

312 ◆ *Turning Points*

Prentice Hall Literature Program Resources

REINFORCE / RETEACH / EXTEND

Selection Support Pages
Build Vocabulary Worksheet: Prefixes: *mono-*, p. 97
Build Grammar Skills: Past Participial Phrases, p. 98
Reading Strategy: Judge a Character's Decision, p. 99
Literary Focus: Characters as Symbols, p. 100

Strategies for Diverse Student Needs, p. 24

Beyond Literature
Community Connection: Caring for the Elderly, p. 24

Formal Assessment Selection Test, pp. 82–84; Assessment Resources Software

Alternative Assessment, p. 24

Resource Pro CD-ROM
"With All Flags Flying"—includes all resource materials and customizable lesson plan

Listening to Literature Audiocassettes
"With All Flags Flying"

With All Flags Flying

◆ Literature and Your Life

CONNECT YOUR EXPERIENCE

At each stage in your life, you have to make decisions. Some decisions, like choosing between spending your money on clothes or on a movie, have minimal consequences. Occasionally, you have to make a more significant and difficult decision, such as choosing a college. This story focuses on one character's life-changing decision.

Journal Writing Jot down your memories of some tough decisions you've made. On what did you base these decisions?

THEMATIC FOCUS: WORKING IT OUT

This selection shows how one man works out his own answer to the question, "Where am I going?"

◆ Background for Understanding

CULTURE

As life expectancies rise, the question of how the elderly are cared for in a society becomes an increasingly important issue. In many societies around the world, elderly adults do not have to decide where to live when they can no longer care for themselves because they already live in an extended family that tends to their needs. For example, in some countries in Africa and Asia, it is common to have three or even four generations of one family living under the same roof. In Japan it is traditionally the duty of the oldest son to care for his parents. Many older American parents, however, do not live with their adult children. When an elderly family member can no longer live alone, life-changing decisions must be made.

◆ Literary Focus

CHARACTERS AS SYMBOLS

Sometimes the characters in a story are just that: characters, and nothing else. Other times, writers use **characters as symbols**—that is, a character represents an idea, belief, or feeling. You can figure out what a character represents by looking for especially strong character traits or a consistent pattern of behavior. For example, if a particular character always has a cheerful outlook despite repeated tragedies, that character may represent optimism.

Examine the individual characters in "With All Flags Flying" and think about what some of them might represent.

◆ Reading Strategy

JUDGE A CHARACTER'S DECISION

In this story, Mr. Carpenter, the main character, makes a decision that will change his entire life. As you read this story, **judge the main character's decision**. Using the facts at hand, assess whether the decision he makes is the best one.

To judge a decision fairly, you have to look at it from many angles. Consider what would have happened had the character acted differently. Look to see what other options may have been available. Try to find out the character's motive—why does he or she act in this way? What were the reasons behind his or her action? The answers to these questions will help you make an informed judgment on the character's decision.

Life Expectancy in Selected Countries

Age (in years), bar graph showing M and F for Bolivia, Burkina-Fasso, France, Japan, U.S.

Source: *The World Almanac, 1997*

Ask students to imagine themselves at the following ages: twenty, thirty, forty, sixty, eighty. What will they look like? What will they be doing? To whom would they be close? Focus students' attention on the age of eighty. What are some problems people that age have to face? What do students hope for themselves at that age? Suggest that they base their thoughts on an older person they know or have known. Tell them Anne Tyler's story ponders some of these same questions. Like most good fiction, it both comes up with answers and poses more questions.

Customize for
Less Proficient Readers

To help these students attach symbolic meanings to some of the characters in the story, have them make a chart like this one, and fill it in as they read:

Name of Character:

His/Her Belief:

His/Her Feelings:

His/Her Pattern of Behavior:

After studying their chart, students can write the main quality the character symbolizes.

Customize for
More Advanced Students

Suggest that, in addition to identifying characters as symbols, these students probe deeper to find smaller symbols—the motorcycle, contents of the brown bag—that stand for aspects of Mr. Carpenter's character. They can keep a list of symbols as they read.

Customize for
English Language Learners

Clarify for these students such words and references as "old folks' home," "Fig Newtons," and "teeny-bopper."

Customize for
Interpersonal Learners

Have interpersonal learners improvise a conversation between Clara and her father in which Clara convinces the old man to stay with her, rather than go to the old folks' home.

✎ Preparing for Standardized Tests

Reading and Vocabulary The Build Vocabulary Skills lesson focuses on using the prefix *mono-* to determine word meaning in words such as *monotonous* and *monopoly*. Students can apply this skill when matching words with definitions or choosing correct spellings on standardized tests. For additional practice, use the Build Vocabulary page in **Selection Support,** p. 97.

Grammar and Language Portions of some standardized tests require students to identify past participial phrases and the words they modi-

fy. Write the following sentence on the chalkboard, and provide practice in this skill by asking students to identify the past participial phrase and the word it modifies:

The dog stared at the table heaped with Thanksgiving food. *heaped with Thanksgiving food; table*

The Build Grammar Skills lesson for this selection focuses on this topic. For additional practice, use the Build Grammar Skills page on Past Participial Phrases, p. 98, in **Selection Support.**

Develop Understanding

►Critical Viewing◄

❶ **Analyze** Elicit a response similar to this: *The road itself suggests the idea of change ahead. The color of the grass and trees suggests that the season is changing from summer to fall.*

Route 6, Eastham, 1941, Edward Hopper, Sheldon Swope Art Museum, Terre Haute, Indiana

▲ **Critical Viewing** What details in this painting suggest that this story will deal with changes? [Analyze]

314 ◆ *Turning Points*

With All Flags Flying

Anne Tyler

Weakness was what got him in the end. He had been expecting something more definite—chest pains, a stroke, arthritis—but it was only weakness that put a finish to his living alone. A numbness in his head, an airy feeling when he walked. A wateriness in his bones that made it an effort to pick up his coffee cup in the morning. He waited some days for it to go away, but it never did. And meanwhile the dust piled up in corners; the refrigerator wheezed and creaked for want of defrosting. Weeds grew around his rosebushes.

He was awake and dressed at six o'clock on a Saturday morning, with the patchwork quilt pulled up neatly over the mattress. From the kitchen cabinet he took a hunk of bread and two Fig Newtons, which he dropped into a paper bag. He was wearing a brown suit that he had bought on sale in 1944, a white T-shirt and copper-toed work boots. These and his other set of underwear, which he put in the paper bag along with a razor, were all the clothes he took with him. Then he rolled down the top of the bag and stuck it under his arm, and stood in the middle of the kitchen staring around him for a moment.

The house had only two rooms, but he owned it—the last scrap of the farm that he had sold off years ago. It

Route 6, Eastham (detail), Edward Hopper, Sheldon Swope Art Museum, Terre Haute, Indiana

With All Flags Flying ◆ 315

🎼 Humanities: Art

Route 6, Eastham, 1941, by Edward Hopper.

The painting depicts a farm seen from across a highway. The absence of human and animal figures along with the scale of the houses in relation to the road and sky evokes a feeling of remoteness, emptiness, or loneliness.

Edward Hopper (1882–1967) was an American painter born in Nyack, New York. Hopper lived in New York City and worked

as a commercial artist and illustrator for many years before he concentrated fully on painting after he was forty.

Use the following questions for discussion:

1. How does the painting help you understand the kind of life the old man has been living? *Students can discuss the isolation of the farmhouse and outbuildings and the desolation of the highway leading away.*

2. Compare the painting with the description of the old man's house in this story. *In the story, the house is very small, with only two rooms. The rest of the farm has been sold. In the painting, the large farmhouse and outbuildings are intact. Still, students should recognize the painting reflects the mood of the story.*

1 Infer Ask students why the man didn't mind having "a thousand appurtenances" when he had a wife and children, but now considers even his few possessions too much. *Lead students to see that the man is giving up his grasp on life. "Worldly" possessions symbolize ties to the world, which he is preparing to leave behind. On a more literal level, students might also suggest that the man is overwhelmed by the prospect of caring for so many things.*

▶**Critical Viewing**◀

2 Infer Students might judge from the man's expression that he was feeling calm, but perhaps also sad and resigned.

◆ **Build Grammar Skills**

3 Past Participial Phrases Have students identify the past participial phrase in this sentence. Have them name the participle and the noun the phrase modifies. *The past participial phrase is "clenched tight upon the paper bag." The past participle in the phrase is "clenched." The phrase modifies the noun "fingers."*

◆ **Reading Strategy**

4 Judge a Character's Decision By now, students should have an idea of where Mr. Carpenter is going— either to a nursing home or to stay with a relative. Ask: If this man considers this his "last free day," why is he leaving his home? *Students should grasp that the man has accepted that he no longer has the strength to take care of himself.*

Customize for
English Language Learners
English language learners may have trouble with the homophones in this story. Team them with native speakers who can help clarify the two meanings of words on this page such as *suit, bank, buckled, stretches, limp, temples.* Be sure they understand the correct meaning in the given context and other possible meanings.

316

---

stood in a hollow of dying trees beside a super-highway in Baltimore County. All it held was a few sticks of furniture, a change of clothes, a skillet and a set of dishes. Also odds and ends, which disturbed him. If his inventory were complete, he would have to include six clothes-pins, a salt and a pepper shaker, a broken-toothed comb, a cheap ballpoint pen—oh, on and on, past logical numbers. Why should he be so cluttered? He was eighty-two years old. **1** He had grown from an infant owning nothing to a family man with a wife, five children, every-day and Sunday china and a thousand appurtenances, down at last to solitary old age and the bare essentials again, but not bare enough to suit him. Only what he needed surrounded him. Was it possible he needed so much?

Now he had the brown paper bag; that was all. It was the one satisfaction in a day he had been dreading for years.

He left the house without another glance, heading up the steep bank toward the super-highway. The bank was covered with small, crawling weeds planted especially by young men with scientific training in how to prevent soil erosion. Twice his knees buckled. He had to sit and rest, bracing himself against the slope of the bank. The scientific weeds, seen from close up, looked straggly and gnarled. He sifted dry earth through his fingers without thinking, concentrating only on steadying his breath and calming the twitching muscles in his legs.

Once on the superhighway, which was fairly

▲ **2 Critical Viewing** How do you think this man was feeling when this picture was taken? **[Infer]**

316 ◆ *Turning Points*

---

level, he could walk for longer stretches of time. He kept his head down and his fingers clenched tight upon the paper bag, which was growing limp and damp now. Sweat rolled down the back of his neck, fell in drops from his temples. When he had been walking maybe half an hour he had to sit down again for a **3** rest. A black motorcycle buzzed up from behind and stopped a few feet away from him. The driver was young and shabby, with hair so long that it drizzled out beneath the back of his helmet.

"Give you a lift, if you like," he said. "You going somewhere?"

"Just into Baltimore."

"Hop on."

He shifted the paper bag to the space beneath his arm, put on the white helmet he was handed and climbed on behind the driver. For safety he took a clutch of the boy's shirt, tightly at first and then more loosely when he saw there was no danger. Except for the helmet, he was perfectly comfortable. He felt his face cooling and stiffening in the wind, his body learning to lean gracefully with the tilt of the motorcycle as it swooped from lane to lane. It was a fine way to **4** spend his last free day.

Half an hour later they were on the outskirts of Baltimore, stopped at the first traffic light.

◆ **Build Vocabulary**

appurtenances (ə purt′ ən əns ez) *n.*: Accessories
conspicuous (kən spik′ yoo əs) *adj.*: Attracting attention by being unexpected

---

 Humanities: Photograph

Resident of Valle Verde Retirement Home
by Bill Aron.

The photographic portrait on this page shows an elderly man sitting on a chair with a lamp in the background. In the lines of the man's face and body, the artist has captured the passivity and acceptance that sometimes comes with old age.

Use the following questions for discussion:
1. How would you compare the man in this picture with your mental image of Mr. Carpenter? *Students can share their ideas about how the man in this picture is the same as or different from their*

image of Mr. Carpenter. They might say the man in the picture seems more complaisant than they imagine Mr. Carpenter to be—he has a mild or pleasant facial expression that students might not associate with the story character.

2. Which details in the portrait make you think that the man may be experiencing the same weakness that the old man in the story is feeling? *Students may cite the man's position in the chair, the way he holds his head, the position of his hands.*

The boy turned his head and shouted, "Whereabouts did you plan on going?"

"I'm visiting my daughter, on Belvedere near Charles Street."

"I'll drop you off, then," the boy said. "I'm passing right by there."

◆ Literary Focus
What might the boy on the motorcycle symbolize?

The light changed, the motor roared. Now that they were in traffic, he felt more conspicuous, but not in a bad way. People in their automobiles seemed sealed in, overprotected; men in large trucks must envy the way the motorcycle looped in and out, hornetlike, stripped to the bare essentials of a motor and two wheels. By tugs at the boy's shirt and single words shouted into the wind he directed him to his daughter's house, but he was sorry to have the ride over so quickly.

His daughter had married a salesman and lived in a plain, square stone house that the old man approved of. There were sneakers and a football in the front yard, signs of a large, happy family. A bicycle lay in the driveway. The motorcycle stopped just inches from it. "Here we are," the boy said.

"Well, I surely do thank you."

He climbed off, fearing for one second that his legs would give way beneath him and spoil everything that had gone before. But no, they held steady. He took off the helmet and handed it to the boy, who waved and roared off. It was a really magnificent roar, ear-dazzling. He turned toward the house, beaming in spite of himself, with his head feeling cool and light now that the helmet was gone. And there was his daughter on the front porch, laughing. "Daddy, what on *earth*?" she said. "Have you turned into a teeny-bopper?" Whatever that was. She came rushing down the steps to hug him—a plump, happy-looking woman in an apron. She was getting on toward fifty now. Her hands were like her mother's, swollen and veined. Gray had started dusting her hair.

"You never *told* us," she said. "Did you ride all this way on a motorcycle? Oh, why didn't you find a telephone and call? I would have come. How long can you stay for?"

"Now . . . " he said, starting toward the house. He was thinking of the best way to put it. "I came to a decision. I won't be living alone any more. I want to go to an old folks' home. That's what I *want*," he said, stopping on the grass so she would be sure to get it clear. "I don't want to live with you—I want an old folks' home." Then he was afraid he had worded it too strongly. "It's nice *visiting* you, of course," he said.

"Why, Daddy, you know we always asked you to come and live with us."

"I know that, but I decided on an old folks' home."

"We couldn't do that. We won't even talk about it."

"Clara, my mind is made up."

Then in the doorway a new thought hit her, and she suddenly turned around. "Are you sick?" she said. "You always said you would live alone as long as health allowed."

"I'm not up to that any more," he said.

"What is it? Are you having some kind of pain?"

"I just decided, that's all," he said. "What I *will* rely on you for is the arrangements with the home. I know it's a trouble."

"We'll talk about that later," Clara said. And she firmed the corners of her mouth exactly the way her mother used to do when she hadn't won an argument but wasn't planning to lose it yet either.

In the kitchen he had a glass of milk, good and cold, and the hunk of bread and the two Fig Newtons from his paper bag. Clara wanted to make him a big breakfast, but there was no sense wasting what he had brought. He munched on the dry bread and washed it down with milk, meanwhile staring at the Fig Newtons, which lay on the smoothed-out bag. They were the worse for their ride—squashed and pathetic looking, the edges worn down and crumbling. They seemed to have come from somewhere long ago and far away. "Here, now, we've got cookies I baked only yesterday," Clara said; but he said, "No, no," and ate the Fig Newtons, whose warmth on his tongue filled him with a vague, sad feeling deeper than

With All Flags Flying ◆ 317

◆ Literary Focus

❺ Characters as Symbols Elicit responses such as the following: *The motorcyclist represents freedom, a sense of abandon, or energy.*

◆ Reading Strategy

❻ Judge a Character's Decision Have students discuss whether the old man seems to have thought his decision through carefully. *He seems to have anticipated his daughter's objections, and his determination suggests that his decision was well thought out.*

◆ Critical Thinking

❼ Analyze Ask students why they think that Tyler included this reference to Clara's mother. *Students might say that the reference to Clara's mother—Mr. Carpenter's deceased wife—was meant to evoke Mr. Carpenter's younger days, and perhaps remind the reader that it might be difficult for Mr. Carpenter to see his wife reflected in his daughter.*

◆ Build Grammar Skills

❽ Past Participial Phrases Have students identify the two past participial phrases in this sentence. Which nouns or pronouns do they modify? Which past participle is irregular? *The two past participial phrases are "squashed and pathetic looking," which modifies the pronoun "they" (the Fig Newtons), and "worn down and crumbling," which modifies the noun "edges." "Worn" is irregular.*

Speaking and Listening Mini-Lesson

Debate

This mini-lesson supports the second Speaking and Listening activity in the Idea Bank on page 323.

Introduce the Concept Briefly explain the rules of formal debate to the class (or refer students to the entry on Debate in the Speaking and Listening Handbook, on page 978). One team supports the "pro" side and the other the "con" side of the statement: *Mr. Carpenter made the right decision.* Team members take turns expressing their opinions and supporting them with facts from the story and from experience. Then team members take turns "rebutting" or arguing points made by their opponents.

Develop Background Have team members work together to brainstorm for the pros or cons of the old man's decision, taking into account other options that he could have chosen.

Apply the Information Assign a time frame for students to make their opening arguments. Follow with a shorter time for rebuttals. Remind students to pace themselves and to make sure to include their strongest arguments.

Assess the Outcome Have students evaluate the debate using these criteria: Were opinions presented clearly? Were they well supported with facts and with examples from real life? Were rebuttal arguments strong and to the point?

◆ Literary Focus

❶ Characters as Symbols
Encourage students to speculate about the qualities Francie represents in this story, and in particular in Mr. Carpenter's life. *Students might suggest she represents honesty, openness, and innocence.*

◆ Reading Strategy

❷ Judge a Character's Decision
Ask why students think he has rejected the idea of living with family members. *Students may say he does not want to be taken care of like a child; he does not want to be a burden.*

◆ Reading Strategy

❸ Judge a Character's Decision
Students should respond that in addition to considering moving into a nursing home, he could have lived with any one of his children.

◆ Critical Thinking

❹ Infer Ask students: What kind of impression is the old man trying to make on his daughter and her family? Why is he working so hard to make this impression? *The old man wants to make the impression that he is still in control of his life. He does not want to be taken care of by his family. He doesn't want to be a burden to them, but more important, he wants to remain independent in his own eyes. He is holding on to his pride and dignity.*

---

homesickness. "In my house," he said, "I left things a little messy. I hate to ask it of you, but I didn't manage to straighten up any."

"Don't even think about it," Clara said. "I'll take out a suitcase tomorrow and clean everything up. I'll bring it all back."

"I don't want it. Take it to the poor people."

"Don't want any of it? But, Daddy—"

He didn't try explaining it to her. He finished his lunch in silence and then let him lead him upstairs to the guest room.

Clara had five boys and a girl, the oldest twenty. During the morning as they passed one by one through the house on their way to other places, they heard of his arrival and trooped up to see him. They were fine children, all of them, but it was the girl he enjoyed the most. Francie. She was only thirteen, too young yet to know how to hide what she felt. And what she felt was always about love, it seemed: whom she just loved, who she hoped loved her back. Who was just a darling. Had thirteen-year-olds been so aware of love in the old days? He didn't know and didn't care; all he had to do with Francie was sit smiling in an armchair and listen. There was a new boy in the neighborhood who walked his English sheepdog past her yard every morning, looking toward her house. Was it because of her, or did the dog just like to go that way? When he telephoned her brother Donnie, was he hoping for her to answer? And when she did answer, did he want her to talk a minute or hand the receiver straight to Donnie? But what would she say to him, anyway? Oh, all her questions had to do with where she might find love, and everything she said made the old man wince and love her more. She left in the middle of a sentence, knocking against a doorknob as she flew from the room, an unlovable-looking tangle of blond hair and braces and scrapes and Band-Aids. After she was gone the room seemed too empty, as if she had accidentally torn part of it away in her flight.

Getting into an old folks' home was hard. Not only because of lack of good homes, high expenses, waiting lists; it was harder yet to talk his family into letting

him go. His son-in-law argued with him every evening, his round, kind face anxious and questioning across the supper table. "Is it that you think you're not welcome here? You are, you know. You were one of the reasons we bought this big house." His grandchildren when they talked to him had a kind of urgency in their voices, as if they were trying to impress him with their acceptance of him. His other daughters called long distance from all across the country and begged him to come to them if he wouldn't stay with Clara. They had room, or they

◆ **Reading Strategy**
Evaluate the man's options.

would make room; he had no idea what homes for the aged were like these days. To all of them he gave the same answer: "I've made my decision." He was proud of them for asking, though. All his children had turned out so well, every last one of them. They were good, strong women with happy families, and they had never given him a moment's worry. He was luckier than he had a right to be. He had felt lucky all his life, dangerously lucky, cursed by luck; it had seemed some disaster must be waiting to even things up. But the luck had held. When his wife died it was at a late age, sparing her the pain she would have had to face, and his life had continued in its steady, reasonable pattern with no more sorrow than any other man's. His final lot was to weaken, to crumble and to die—only a secret disaster, not the one he had been expecting.

He walked two blocks daily, fighting off the weakness. He shelled peas for Clara and mended little household articles, which gave him an excuse to sit. Nobody noticed how he arranged to climb the stairs only once a day, at bedtime. When he had empty time he chose a chair without rockers, one that would not be a symbol of age and weariness and lack of work. He rose every morning at six and stayed in his room a full hour, giving his legs enough warning to face the day ahead. Never once did he disgrace himself by falling down in front of people. He dropped nothing more important than a spoon or a fork.

318 ◆ Turning Points

◆ Beyond the Classroom

Making Decisions

Introduce the Concept Making good decisions requires the ability to assess a situation from a variety of angles. This ability is an important workplace skill for any job students may hold.

Develop Background Talk with the class about jobs students have or might have in the future. Ask them what sorts of decisions they might make about these jobs. How can

knowing all the options of a particular work situation help students to make good decisions on the job? *The more options they are aware of, the more likely they will be to find and pursue an opportunity.*

Apply the Information Present the following hypothetical situation: If your boss told you that in six months you could move from the job of stocking CDs to the job of selling them, what information would you

want to know? *Possible responses: What skills would I need for the new position; how could I acquire those skills; what would be the difference in pay and hours; what other opportunities might be available to me?*

Assess the Outcome Have students share their decision-making questions. Discuss which questions are the most helpful and why, and what further questions would help them make an informed decision.

Meanwhile the wheels were turning; his name was on a waiting list. Not that that meant anything, Clara said. "When it comes right down to driving you out there, I just won't let you go," she told him. "But I'm hoping you won't carry things that far. Daddy, won't you put a stop to this foolishness?"

He hardly listened. He had chosen long ago what kind of old age he would have; everyone does. Most, he thought, were weak, and chose to be loved at any cost. He had seen women turn soft and sad, anxious to please, and had watched with pity and impatience their losing battles. And he had once known a schoolteacher, no weakling at all, who said straight out that when she grew old she would finally eat all she wanted and grow fat without worry. He admired that—a simple plan, dependent on no one. "I'll sit in an armchair," she had said, "with a lady's magazine in my lap and a box of homemade fudge on the lampstand. I'll get as fat as I like and nobody will give a hang." The schoolteacher was thin and pale, with a kind of stooped, sloping figure that was popular at the time. He had lost track of her long ago, but he liked to think that she had kept her word. He imagined her fifty years later, cozy and fat in a puffy chair, with one hand moving constantly between her mouth and the candy plate. If she had died young or changed her mind or put off her eating till another decade, he didn't want to hear about it.

He had chosen independence. Nothing else had even occurred to him. He had lived to himself, existed on less money than his family would ever guess, raised his own vegetables and refused all gifts but an occasional tin of coffee. And now he would sign himself into the old folks' home and enter on his own two feet, relying only on the impersonal care of nurses and cleaning women. He could have chosen to die alone of neglect, but for his daughters that would have been a burden too—a different kind of burden, much worse. He was sensible enough to see that.

Meanwhile, all he had to do was to look as busy as possible in a chair without rockers and hold fast against his family. Oh, they gave him no peace. Some of their attacks were obvious—the arguments with his son-in-law over the supper table—and some were subtle; you had to be on your guard every minute for those. Francie, for instance, asking him questions about what she called the "olden days." Inviting him to sink unnoticing into doddering reminiscence. "Did I see Granny ever? I don't remember her. Did she like me? What kind of person was she?" He stood his ground, gave monosyllabic answers. It was easier than he had expected. For him, middle age tempted up more memories. Nowadays events had telescoped. The separate agonies and worries—the long, hard births of each of his children, the youngest daughter's

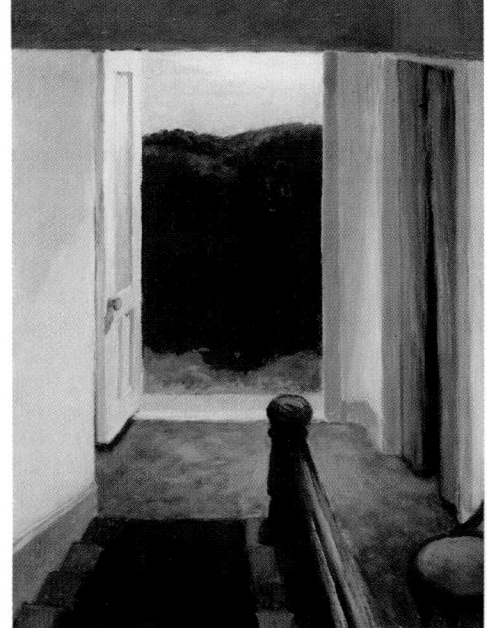

Stairway, Edward Hopper, Whitney Museum of American Art

▲ **Critical Viewing** Explain how this picture symbolizes choice. [Analyze]

◆ **Build Vocabulary**

doddering (däd′ ər iŋ) *adj.*: Shaky, tottering, or senile

monosyllabic (mon′ ō si lab′ ik) *adj.*: Having only one syllable

With All Flags Flying ◆ 319

◆ Reading Strategy

❶ Judge a Character's Decision
Ask students how they feel about the man's apparent disregard for his daughter's feelings. Under what conditions might they support a decision that hurts another person's feelings? *Students may wish the old man would change his mind and stay with Clara for a "happy ending," but they might also recognize that even though he is temporarily hurting his daughter's feelings, he is mastering his own fate, a choice that under certain circumstances justifies hurting someone else's feelings.*

◆ Critical Thinking

❷ Infer Why does the old man insist on giving all the answers himself? *He wants to show the world and himself that he is independent. He wants to be respected and to maintain his self-respect.*

◆ Build Grammar Skills

❸ Past Participial Phrases Have students identify the past participial phrases and the words they modify in the paragraph. *The phrases are "deadened by carpeting," which modifies "corridor," and "flooded with sunlight," which modifies "room."*

◆ Critical Thinking

❹ Interpret Ask students: In what way is Mr. Carpenter being "generous"? What victory has he "won"? *He knows that his daughter feels hurt because her father will not accept anything from her. He is being generous by letting her know he will accept her help now. His victory is his success in asserting his will over the objections of his children.*

chronic childhood earaches, his wife's last illness—were smoothed now into a single, summing-up sentence: He was a widowed farmer with five daughters, all married, twenty grandchildren and three great-grandchildren. "Your grandmother was a fine woman," he told Francie; "just fine." Then he shut up.

Francie, not knowing that she had been spared, sulked and peeled a strip of sunburned skin from her nose.

Clara cried all the way to the home. She was the one who was driving; it made him nervous. One of her hands on the steering wheel held a balled-up tissue, which she had stopped using. She let tears run unchecked down her face and drove jerkily with a great deal of brake-slamming and gear-gnashing.

"Clara, I wish you wouldn't take on so," he told her. "There's no need to be sad over *me*."

❶ "I'm not sad so much as mad," Clara said. "I feel like this is something you're doing *to* me, just throwing away what I give. Oh, why do you have to be so stubborn? It's still not too late to change your mind."

The old man kept silent. On his right sat Francie, chewing a thumbnail and scowling out the window, her usual self except for the unexplainable presence of her other hand in his, tight as wire. Periodically she muttered a number: she was counting red convertibles, and had been for days. When she reached a hundred, the next boy she saw would be her true love.

He figured that was probably the reason she had come on this trip—a greater exposure to red convertibles.

Whatever happened to DeSotos?[1] Didn't there use to be a car called a roadster?[2]

They parked in the U-shaped driveway in front of the home, under the shade of a poplar tree. If he had had his way, he would have arrived by motorcycle, but he made the best of it—picked up his underwear sack from between his feet, climbed the front steps ramrod-

---

1. **DeSotos** (də sō′ tōz): Models of a car in the 1950's.
2. **roadster** (rōd′ stər) *n.*: Early sportscar with an open cab.

320 ◆ Turning Points

straight. They were met by a smiling woman in blue who had to check his name on a file and ask more questions. He made sure to give all the answers himself, overriding Clara when necessary. Meanwhile Francie spun on one squeaky sneaker heel and examined the hall, a cavernous, polished square with old-fashioned parlors on either side of it. A few old people were on the plush couches, and a nurse sat idle beside a lady in a wheelchair.

They went up a creaking elevator to the second floor and down a long, dark corridor deadened by carpeting. The lady in blue, still carrying a sheaf of files, knocked at number 213. Then she flung the door open on a narrow green room flooded with sunlight.

"Mr. Pond," she said, "this is Mr. Carpenter. I hope you'll get on well together."

Mr. Pond was one of those men who run to fat and baldness in old age. He sat in a rocking chair with a gilt-edged Bible on his knees.

"How-do," he said. "Mighty nice to meet you."

They shook hands cautiously, with the women ringing them like mothers asking their children to play nicely with each other. "Ordinarily I sleep in the bed by the window," said Mr. Pond, "but I don't hold it in much importance. You can take your pick."

"Anything will do," the old man said.

Clara was dry-eyed now. She looked frightened.

"You'd best be getting on back now," he told her. "Don't you worry about me. I'll let you know," he said, suddenly generous now that he had won, "if there is anything I need."

Clara nodded and kissed his cheek. Francie kept her face turned away, but she hugged him tightly, and then she looked up at him as she stepped back. Her eyebrows were tilted as if she were about to ask him one of her questions. Was it her the boy with the sheepdog came for? Did he care when she answered the telephone?

They left, shutting the door with a gentle click. The old man made a great business out of settling his underwear and razor in a bureau drawer, smoothing out the paper bag and folding it, placing it in the next drawer down.

"Didn't bring much," said Mr. Pond, one

Cross-Curricular Connection: Social Studies

Mr. Carpenter has five children, but we don't know how many sisters and brothers he has, or who his parents or grandparents were. Genealogy could tell us. Genealogy is the study of people's links to a network of close relatives and ancestors.

Genealogy can be pursued through primary and secondary sources. Family photo albums, oral accounts of personal history or favorite family stories, letters and diaries, newspaper clippings,

and public records provide information that can reveal marvelous tales, surprises, and puzzles.

Have students conduct interviews with family members—whether they are biological, adoptive, or foster—to plot family trees. Interested students can pursue as many branches as they wish, including those of step-families. Have them collect stories about their grandparents through anecdote or interview and share them with the group.

thumb marking his page in the Bible.

"I don't need much."

"Go on—take the bed by the window. You'll feel better after awhile."

"I *wanted* to come," the old man said.

"That there window is a front one. If you look out, you can see your folks leave."

He slid between the bed and the window and looked out. No reason not to. Clara and Francie were just climbing into the car, the sun lacquering the tops of their heads. Clara was blowing her nose with a dot of tissue.

"*Now* they cry," said Mr. Pond, although he had not risen to look out himself. "Later they'll buy themselves a milkshake to celebrate."

"I wanted to come. I made them bring me."

"And so they did. *I* didn't want to come. My son wanted to put me here—his wife was expecting. And so he did. It all works out the same in the end."

"Well, I could have stayed with one of my daughters," the old man said. "But I'm not like some I have known. Hanging around making burdens of themselves, hoping to be loved. Not me."

"If you don't care about being loved," said Mr. Pond, "how come it would bother you to be a burden?"

Then he opened the Bible again, at the place where his thumb had been all the time and went back to reading.

The old man sat on the edge of the bed, watching the tail of Clara's car flash as sharp and hard as a jewel around the bend of the road. Then, with nobody to watch that mattered, he let his shoulders slump and eased himself out of his suit coat, which he folded over the foot of the bed. He slid his suspenders down and let them dangle at his waist. He took off his copper-toed work boots and set them on the floor neatly side by side. And although it was only noon, he lay down full-length on top of the bedspread. Whiskery lines ran across the plaster of the ceiling high above him. There was a cracking sound in the mattress when he moved; it must be covered with something waterproof.

The tiredness in his head was as vague and restless as anger; the weakness in his knees made him feel as if he had just finished some exhausting exercise. He lay watching the plaster cracks settle themselves into pictures, listening to the silent, neuter voice in his mind form the words he had grown accustomed to hearing now: Let me not give in at the end. Let me continue gracefully till the moment of my defeat. Let Lollie Simpson be alive somewhere even as I lie on my bed; let her be eating homemade fudge in an overstuffed armchair and growing fatter and fatter.

Guide for Responding

◆ Literature and Your Life

Reader's Response What do you think will be most important to you in your old age? Explain.

Thematic Focus The onset of old age marks a turning point in any person's life. What are some concrete things that a person can do to maintain his or her dignity through this difficult stage?

Group Discussion The ancient philosopher Buddha once said, "He who always greets and constantly reveres the aged, four things will increase in him: life, beauty, happiness, power." As a group, discuss whether you find this statement to be true.

☑ Check Your Comprehension

1. Why does Mr. Carpenter decide not to live alone anymore?
2. How does he plan to live the rest of his life?
3. How does Mr. Carpenter's family feel about his plan?
4. What obstacles does Mr. Carpenter encounter?
5. Explain whether Mr. Carpenter is able to carry out his plan.

With All Flags Flying ◆ 321

Beyond the Selection

FURTHER READING
Other Works by Anne Tyler
Ladder of Years
Dinner at the Homesick Restaurant
Searching for Caleb

Related Works
Cold Sassy Tree, Olive Burns
"You Are Old, Father William," Lewis Carroll

We suggest that you preview these works before recommending them to students.

INTERNET
Your students can find more information on the Internet. We suggest the following sites. Please be aware, however, that sites may have changed from the time we published this information.

For more information on Anne Tyler, visit **http:// www.randomhouse.com/vintage/ read/ladder/ladder.html** or **http://web.aacpl. lib.md. us/dsakers/tylera.htm**

We *strongly recommend* that you preview the sites before you send students to them.

◆ Literary Focus

❺ **Characters as Symbols** Ask students to explain what Mr. Pond might represent in the story, and to give reasons for their answers. *Students may say that Mr. Pond represents the bitterness that can sometimes come with old age. Because he feels unloved and rejected, he assumes that everyone else feels the same.*

◆ Critical Thinking

❻ **Interpret** Ask students why Mr. Carpenter hopes that Lollie Simpson is alive and growing fat from eating fudge. *Although exhausted, he is proud of his victory. He wishes the same victory to others: that, until they die, they will make their own choices and live by their own decisions.*

Reinforce and Extend

Answers
◆ *Literature and Your Life*

Reader's Response Students might say that, like Mr. Carpenter in Tyler's story, independence will be important to them. They might also cite good health, financial security, the capacity to enjoy life.

Thematic Focus Students might recognize the importance of planning ahead and keeping informed about options in order to make an informed and independent decision.

☑ Check Your Comprehension

1. He feels he's too weak to take care of himself and his home.
2. He plans to go to an old age home.
3. His family is unhappy about his plan; they want to take care of him.
4. It is hard to get into the old age home, and it is hard for Mr. Carpenter to talk his family into letting him go.
5. Mr. Carpenter is able to carry out his plan by overriding his family's objections and not allowing himself to get too comfortable in their home.

Answers

◆ Critical Thinking

1. Mr. Carpenter wants only the most essential possessions. He reflects on having needed so much—two sets of china and a "thousand appurtenances"—when he was younger.
2. He loves his family and does not want to burden them; he also wants to be his own master.
3. Mr. Carpenter is relieved; Mr. Pond is bitter.
4. Students might interpret the title "With All Flags Flying" to represent Mr. Carpenter's victory in determining his own fate.
5. Responses might cover a spectrum: Our society does well by providing Social Security and other benefits for the elderly, but does not encourage enough respect for the elderly.
6. Students might say they learned that it is important to be faithful to your principles up to the end of your life.

◆ Reading Strategy

1. He does not want to burden his family; he wants to maintain his dignity.
2. He could have lived with any one of his daughters and their families, or he could have lived alone—neglecting himself.
3. Some students will sympathize with Mr. Carpenter's need to claim his psychological independence; others will wish he had stayed in the more personal atmosphere of family.

◆ Literary Focus

1. Clara represents security, conventionality, a sense of responsibility, and generosity.
2. Lollie Simpson represents willful and joyful independence.
3. Mr. Pond represents bitterness and loneliness.

◆ Build Vocabulary

Using the Prefix mono-
1. c 2. b 3. a

Using the Word Bank
1. c 2. d 3. a 4. b

Guide for Responding (continued)

◆ Critical Thinking

INTERPRET
1. Using examples from the story, describe Mr. Carpenter's attitude about material possessions. **[Analyze]**
2. Why is Mr. Carpenter so determined not to move in with his daughter and her family? **[Infer]**
3. How does Mr. Carpenter's attitude about the nursing home compare with Mr. Pond's? **[Compare and Contrast]**
4. What is the significance of the story's title? **[Draw Conclusions]**

EVALUATE
5. How well do you think our society cares for the elderly? Explain. **[Evaluate]**

APPLY
6. What can you learn from this story that might help you at some point in your life? **[Apply]**

◆ Reading Strategy

JUDGE A CHARACTER'S DECISION
When you **judge a character's decision,** such as Mr. Carpenter's decision to enter the nursing home, consider the reasons for the decision, the alternatives, and the consequences of the decision.
1. What are the reasons for Mr. Carpenter's decision?
2. What other options were available to him?
3. Do you think Mr. Carpenter made the right decision? Explain.

◆ Literary Focus

CHARACTERS AS SYMBOLS
Writers often get their message across by using **characters as symbols.** For instance, Tyler uses Mr. Carpenter to represent *all* elderly people who fear the loss of dignity and independence.

What do you think each of the following characters represents?
1. Clara
2. Lollie Simpson (the teacher)
3. Mr. Pond

◆ Build Vocabulary

USING THE PREFIX mono–
Knowing that the prefix mono- means "one," match each word from Column A with its definition in Column B.

Column A	Column B
1. monopoly	a. Having no variety
2. monocle	b. Eyeglass for one eye only
3. monotonous	c. Exclusive control over a commodity or service

USING THE WORD BANK
On your paper match each word with the word most nearly opposite in meaning.

1. appurtenances	a. firm
2. conspicuous	b. long-winded
3. doddering	c. necessities
4. monosyllabic	d. hidden

◆ Build Grammar Skills

PAST PARTICIPIAL PHRASES
Anne Tyler uses past participial phrases to pack her sentences full of details about Mr. Carpenter, his family, and his surroundings.

> A **past participial phrase** consists of a past participle along with its modifiers and complements.

Practice Copy the following sentences in your notebook. Underline each participial phrase and circle the noun it modifies.
1. The scientific weeds, seen from close up, looked straggly and gnarled.
2. They were on the outskirts of Baltimore, stopped at a red light.
3. Men in large trucks must envy the way the motorcycle looped in and out, hornetlike, stripped to the bare essentials of a motor and two wheels.
4. By tugs at the boy's shirt and single words shouted into the wind he directed him.

◆ Build Grammar Skills
Practice
1. The scientific weeds, <u>seen from close up,</u> looked straggly and gnarled. (modifies weeds)
2. They were on the outskirts of Baltimore, <u>stopped at a red light.</u> (modifies They)
3. Men in large trucks must envy the way the motorcycle looped in and out, hornetlike, <u>stripped to the bare essentials of a motor and two wheels.</u> (modifies motorcycle)
4. By tugs at the boy's shirt and single words <u>shouted into the wind</u> he directed him. (modifies words)

 Writer's Solution

For additional instruction and practice, use the page on Participles and Participial Phrases, p. 41, in the *Writer's Solution Grammar Practice Book*.

Build Your Portfolio

Idea Bank

Writing

1. **Essay on Growing Old** What kinds of activities would you like to do when you're old? Write a brief description on how you would ideally spend your "autumn years."

2. **Letter From Mr. Carpenter** Pretend that you are Mr. Carpenter and you've just moved into the nursing home. Write a letter to your family, explaining in detail your reasons for moving.

3. **Alternative Ending** What do you think the story would be like if Mr. Carpenter had decided to live with his daughter? Write an alternative ending exploring this possibility.

Speaking and Listening

4. **Soundtrack** Create a soundtrack for a dramatic adaptation of the story. Make a mix tape of songs that relate to various themes of the story. Indicate where in the story each song would appear. **[Music Link]**

5. **Debate** Split the class into two teams and debate whether Mr. Carpenter made the best decision in entering the nursing home. Use examples from the story and real life to back up any assertions you make.

Projects

6. **Volunteer at a Nursing Home** Volunteer in a local nursing home or retirement home for a day. Compare what you learned about the people in the home with what your classmates observed in the people they met. **[Community Link]**

7. **Service for the Elderly** With a group of classmates, outline a plan for providing a service for the elderly. Include how you aim to provide the service and what the estimated cost would be.

Writing Mini-Lesson

Dialogue With an Older Person

A crucial part of any story is good dialogue. In "With All Flags Flying," there are a number of dialogues between Mr. Carpenter, the main character, and people who are younger than he is. Using these examples from the story as inspiration, write a **dialogue** involving an older person and someone younger, possibly the older person's son or daughter. You can either use two of the characters from the story or make up two of your own.

Writing Skills Focus: Appropriate Language for Purpose

One purpose of dialogue is to bring characters to life. Use **appropriate language for your purpose**—make sure the words and phrases you use are consistent with the age and personality of the character. For example, when Mr. Carpenter says, "Well, I surely do thank you," his courteously formal speech pattern is consistent with the character Tyler has created.

Prewriting First, come up with a topic for your dialogue. Focus on an important decision in the older person's life. Then brainstorm for a list of expressions that an older person might use—or talk to an older person and jot down the phrases that he or she says. These phrases will make your dialogue sound more realistic.

Drafting As you write your dialogue, strive to make the speech as natural as possible. Remember that most people use contractions and speak informally in conversation. Copy these natural speech patterns in your dialogue.

Revising Read your draft aloud—if possible, with another person. Does the dialogue sound realistic? Sometimes changing just a few words will fix it. Use language that is consistent and accurately reflects how a person of that age would speak.

With All Flags Flying ◆ 323

Idea Bank

Customizing for
Performance Levels
Following are suggestions for matching Idea Bank topics with your students' performance levels:
Less Advanced Students: 1, 6
Average Students: 2, 4
More Advanced Students: 3, 5, 7

Customizing for
Learning Modalities
Following are suggestions for matching Idea Bank topics with your students' learning modalities:
Musical/Rhythmic: 4
Interpersonal: 6
Verbal/Linguistic: 4, 5
Logical/Mathematical: 7

Writing Mini-Lesson

Refer students to the Writing Handbook, page 965, for instruction on the writing process, and page 968 for further information on creative writing.

Writer's Solution

Writers at Work Videodisc
Have students view the videodisc segment for Chapter 6 in which Naomi Shihab Nye talks about drafting. Discuss with students the reasons why she likes to "begin quickly."

Play frames 14950 to 17080

Writing Lab CD-ROM
Have students complete the tutorial on Creative Writing. Follow these steps:
1. Have students use interactive tips on purpose to get advice on techniques that can help them tailor their language to their purpose in their dialogues.
2. Direct students to view the video tips for peer editors to learn the benefits of revising their dialogues with a peer.

Sourcebook
Have students use Chapter 6, Creative Writing (pp. 165–189), for additional support. The chapter includes an annotated student model of a lyric poem (p. 189).

✓ ASSESSMENT OPTIONS

Formal Assessment, Selection Test, pp. 82–84, and Assessment Resources Software. The selection test is designed so that it can be easily customized to the performance levels of your students.
Alternative Assessment, p. 24, includes options for less advanced students, more advanced students, visual/spatial and bodily/kinesthetic learners.

PORTFOLIO ASSESSMENT
Use the following rubrics in the *Alternative Assessment* booklet to assess student writing:
Essay on Growing Old: Description Rubric, p. 97
Letter From Mr. Carpenter: Problem/Solution Rubric, p. 101
Alternative Ending: Fiction Narrative Rubric, p. 95

OBJECTIVES

1. To read, comprehend, and interpret a poem and speech
2. To relate a poem and speech to personal experience
3. To analyze author's perspective
4. To identify a dramatic situation
5. To build vocabulary in context and learn the word root -dom-
6. To recognize negatives and avoid double negatives
7. To write a poem about a turning point using figurative language
8. To respond to the poems and a speech through writing, speaking and listening, and projects

SKILLS INSTRUCTION

Vocabulary:
Word Roots: -dom-

Grammar:
Negatives and Double Negatives

Reading Strategy:
Author's Perspective

Literary Focus:
Dramatic Situation

Writing: Figurative Language

Speaking and Listening: Speech (teacher edition)

Critical Viewing: Analyze; Speculate; Connect

PORTFOLIO OPPORTUNITIES

Writing: Summaries; News Commentary; Compare-and-Contrast Essay

Writing Mini-Lesson: Poem About a Turning Point

Speaking and Listening: Speech; Role Play

Projects: Timeline; Collage

More About the Authors

Leopold Staff published his first poems when he was in his early twenties and continued writing until he was in his late seventies.

When **Emily Brontë** began writing, she used a pseudonym because at the time it was not respectable for women to publish their writing.

Anna Akhmatova did not write about politics until her son Lev was arrested. Then she published poems exalting Stalin in an attempt to free her son. Later still, she wrote and published poems criticizing the Russian Revolution.

Theodora was a mime and actress before she met Justinian. Because she was so intelligent and cultured, Emperor Justinian allowed her to share the throne.

Guide for Reading

Leopold Staff (1878–1957)

Leopold Staff loved the quiet moments of life: marveling at the beauty of nature or musing on the glories of long-past civilizations. The miracle of Staff's poetry is that he kept true to those concerns despite the times in which he lived. Poland was a major battleground during both World War I and World War II, yet during that same period Staff and a group of other poets revitalized Polish literature.

Emily Brontë (1818–1848)

To have one famous writer in a family is unusual, but having three is extraordinary! The Brontë sisters—Emily, Charlotte, and Ann—were all successful novelists. They grew up in Yorkshire, England, in a landscape of bleak, windswept hills. When Emily was eighteen years old, she and her two sisters published a book of their poems. Just two years later, they each published novels. Emily's was *Wuthering Heights,* a classic story of love and revenge.

Anna Akhmatova (1889–1966)

Anna Akhmatova published her first poetry at the age of eighteen. She survived the most tumultuous events of modern times: two world wars, the Russian Revolution of 1917, and the reign of terror of dictator Joseph Stalin. Through it all, Akhmatova's poetry celebrated the personal heroism she prized above everything else.

Empress Theodora (c. 502–548)

Theodora and her husband, the emperor Justinian, ruled the eastern Roman empire early in the sixth century. She is mostly remembered for a single action: When a rebellion broke out against her and her husband, she persuaded her husband to defend their palace in Constantinople, rather than try to escape.

324 ◆ Turning Points

◆ Build Vocabulary

WORD ROOTS: -dom-

The time: A.D. 532. The place: Rome, the emperor's palace. The main character: The *indomitable* Empress Theodora. The word *indomitable* contains the Latin root -*dom-*, which means "to rule." Add the prefix *in-,* meaning "not," and you might guess that the meaning of *indomitable* is "unrulable," which is close to the actual meaning "not easily defeated."

implore
timorous
indomitable

WORD BANK

Before you read, preview this list of words from the selections.

◆ Build Grammar Skills

NEGATIVES AND DOUBLE NEGATIVES

The Roman empress Theodora cries out in her speech, "... may I never see the day when those who meet me do not call me empress." In this dramatic request, she uses two **negatives**—words or word parts that deny or mean "no." In former times, two negatives may have been used to make a point emphatically, but today it is incorrect to use a **double negative**—two negatives that express the same "no." For instance, it would be incorrect to say "... may I *not never* see the day ..."

⬥ Prentice Hall Literature Program Resources

REINFORCE / RETEACH / EXTEND

Selection Support Pages
Build Vocabulary: Word Roots: -dom-, p. 101
Build Grammar Skills: Negatives and Double Negatives, p. 102
Reading Strategy: Author's Perspective, p. 103
Literary Focus: Dramatic Situation, p. 104

Strategies for Diverse Student Needs, p. 25

Beyond Literature
Humanities Connection: What Is Courage? p. 25

Formal Assessment Selection Test, pp. 85–87;

Assessment Resources Software.

Alternative Assessment, p. 25

Resource Pro CD-ROM
"The Bridge," "The Old Stoic," "I Am Not One of Those Who Left the Land," "Speech During the Invasion of Constantinople"—includes all resource material and customizable lesson plan

Listening to Literature Audiocassette
"The Bridge," "The Old Stoic," "I Am Not One of Those Who Left the Land," "Speech During the Invasion of Constantinople"

The Bridge ◆ The Old Stoic
◆ I Am Not One of Those Who Left the Land ◆
Speech During the Invasion of Constantinople

◆ *Literature and Your Life*

CONNECT YOUR EXPERIENCE

Life is filled with situations in which we're forced to make tough decisions. It might involve something as simple as deciding to try out for the school play despite having terrible stage fright. In the following selections, however, you'll encounter characters who show the courage to make decisions that could be a matter of life or death.

Journal Writing Jot down your memories about the toughest decision you've faced. What was the outcome?

THEMATIC FOCUS: WORKING IT OUT

These selections may set you thinking about decisions you've made or fears you've overcome.

◆ Background for Understanding

HISTORY

In 532, citizens of the eastern Roman empire rebelled against Emperor Justinian and Empress Theodora. When rebels stormed the castle, Theodora encouraged her husband to face their attackers rather than flee. As it turned out, Justinian and Theodora survived.

Fourteen centuries later, in the early 1900's, Russia was torn by civil war. Many Russians emigrated to Germany and France. The poet Anna Akhmatova, however, refused to go, even after her husband was executed and her son put in jail.

◆ Literary Focus

DRAMATIC SITUATION

The life-and-death conditions under which Empress Theodora makes her speech create a gripping backdrop for her impassioned words. This **dramatic situation**—the circumstances and conflicts that form the focal point of a literary work—provides a context that helps you understand the full significance of Theodora's words.

The dramatic situation of Akhmatova's poem arises from the circumstances of the civil war in Russia. Due to food shortages, riots, strikes, and political oppression, many of Akhmatova's friends and neighbors fled the country. The dramatic situation gives you a framework in which you can appreciate the courage of her decision.

◆ Reading Strategy

AUTHOR'S PERSPECTIVE

If you've just lost a game, the account you give will be very different from the story told by the winner. The details that are included in a piece of literature depend on the **author's perspective**—his or her outlook on the subject.

Often, writers hint at or directly reveal their perspective. For example, Akhmatova indicates her perspective in the opening lines of her poem:

> I am not one of those who
> left the land/to the mercy
> of its enemies.

In other cases, however, it is left up to the reader to determine the author's perspective by looking closely at the use of words to see what attitude the words convey. To fully understand an author's perspective, it is sometimes necessary to go beyond the text and gather information about the historical or social context in which the work was written.

Guide for Reading ◆ 325

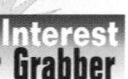
Interest Grabber Write on the chalkboard the following words: *money, love, fame, freedom, power.* Ask students why they think these are "big" themes—ones that have attracted writers from ancient to present times. Lead students to see that although each of these goals might be desirable, each can lead to conflicts that test people. Ask students to suggest some negative and positive results that might come from attaining each goal listed on the board. *Possibilities: money: greed/generosity; love: jealousy/fulfillment: fame: loss of privacy/excitement; freedom: chaos/independence; power: exploiting people/helping people.* Tell students that the writers in this grouping highlight some rewards and conflicts connected to these universal themes.

Customize for
Less Proficient Readers
To help these students understand the selections, go over difficult vocabulary before they read, defining words such as "esteem" and "endure" in "The Old Stoic"; "fragile" and "wavered" in "The Bridge," "felon" and "wormwood" in "I Am Not One . . . ," and "convention" in "Speech During the Invasion of Constantinople."

Customize for
English Language Learners
Students learning English may be confused by the word order and sentence structure in the first two poems. For "The Old Stoic," work with them to rephrase the lines with inverted word order (Riches I hold in light esteem; *I hold riches in light esteem.*) For "The Bridge," help them rephrase the first sentence so that "That I would cross that bridge," immediately follows, "I didn't believe."

Customize for
Intrapersonal Learners
Point out that poetry often reflects the poet's deep feelings. Encourage students to think about what Brontë, Staff, and Akhmatova were feeling when they wrote their poems.

Preparing for Standardized Tests

Grammar and Language Students can apply what they learn about double negatives to both writing and grammar sections of standardized tests. In grammar sections, students might be called on to identify and correct a double negative when revising a passage from a rough draft. To help prepare students to do this, write the following sentence on the chalkboard:

Since no spectators came to watch my team practice, I won't never invite all my friends again.

Ask students to identify the double negative in the sentence. *The double negative is* won't never. How would they revise the sentence to eliminate the double negative? *"I won't ever invite all my friends again" or "I will never invite all my friends again."* For additional practice, use the Build Grammar Skills page on Negatives and Double Negatives in **Selection Support,** p. 102.

One-Minute Insight

"The Bridge" metaphorically describes the anxiety and fear associated with life's risks and change. Staff had to cross the bridge of the dangers and difficulties of wartime Poland, but people of any time can relate his theme to changes in their own lives.

Customize for
English Language Learners

Students who are learning English may have difficulty with the following expressions: "but a dream" (only a dream), "laugh to scorn" (laugh at), "'Tis all that I implore" (It is all I ask). Before these students read, you might want to explain these expressions to them.

◆ Literary Focus

❶ Dramatic Situation Ask students to describe the dramatic situation that forms the framework for the poem. *The speaker is recalling standing on the bank of a wide, dangerous river, trying to muster the courage to cross a bridge that looks as if it might not hold him.*

◆ *Literature and Your Life*

❷ Turning Points Ask students if they have ever faced a situation that, similar to the bridge in this poem, seemed like a difficult and dangerous crossing to a new life. *Answers should focus on the idea of change as a bridge.*

◆ Reading Strategy

❸ Author's Perspective Ask students how the author's perspective changes from the beginning to the end of the poem. *At the beginning of the poem the perspective is that of a person trying to muster the courage to take an important step in life. At the end, the perspective is that of a person who has taken the step successfully, but, as before, still sees the step as being difficult and dangerous.*

THE BRIDGE

Leopold Staff

❶ I didn't believe,
Standing on the bank of a river
Which was wide and swift,
That I would cross that bridge
❷ 5 Plaited[1] from thin, fragile reeds
Fastened with bast.[2]
I walked delicately as a butterfly
And heavily as an elephant,
I walked surely as a dancer
10 And wavered like a blind man.
I didn't believe that I would cross that bridge,
❸ And now that I am standing on the other side,
I don't believe I crossed it.

---

1. **plaited** (plāt´ əd) *adj.*: Braided; woven.
2. **bast** (bast) *n.*: Inner bark of trees.

326 ◆ *Turning Points*

Block Scheduling Strategies

Consider these suggestions to take advantage of extended class time:

- Introduce the concept of author's perspective. Have students read the Reading Strategy on page 325. After they have read these selections, they can answer the Reading Strategy questions on p. 331. If you wish, you can follow up with the Reading Strategy practice, p. 103, in **Selection Support.**

- Have students explore the idea of courage with the **Beyond Literature** activity on page 25.

- Students can work in pairs to complete the Role Play in the Idea Bank on page 332. If possible, have them tape record or videotape their role-playing.

- Encourage students to complete the Writing Mini-Lesson on page 332. Before they write their poems, have them work in pairs to create mental images using figurative language.

- Use Activity 7, p. 25, in **Alternative Assessment:** Presentation—A Nation Surrounded.

The Old Stoic
Emily Brontë

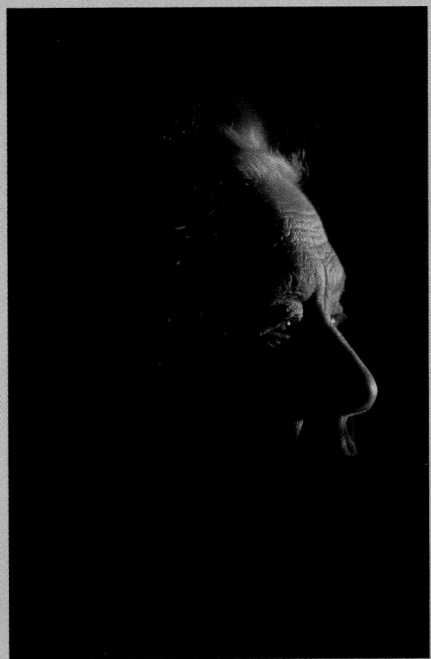

◄ **Critical Viewing** In what ways does this woman's expression suggest courage? [Analyze] **④**

Riches I hold in light esteem,
And love I laugh to scorn;
And lust of fame was but a dream
That vanished with the morn:

5 And if I pray, the only prayer
That moves my lips for me
Is, "Leave the heart that now I bear, **⑤**
And give me liberty!"

Yes, as my swift days near their goal, **⑥**
10 'Tis all that I implore—
Through life and death a chainless soul, **⑦**
With courage to endure.

◆ **Build Vocabulary**

implore (im plôr´) v.: Plead; ask for earnestly

The Bridge/The Old Stoic ◆ 327

One-Minute Insight In "The Old Stoic" Brontë celebrates the freedom of facing the future unafraid. Her wish is not for material wealth or for fame but for internal courage and a strong life spirit.

▶**Critical Viewing**◀

④ Analyze Possible response: Her gaze is steady, and her expression is one of determination.

◆ **Critical Thinking**

⑤ Interpret Ask students why the speaker doesn't think fame is important. *By calling "lust of fame" a ". . . dream/That vanished with the morn," she means that fame is something to dream about briefly, not a lasting value.*

◆ **Reading Strategy**

⑥ Author's Perspective Have students analyze this line to determine the author's perspective. Ask how the speaker's main points in this poem might have been different if she had written from a different perspective. *By "as my swift days near their goal," the speaker means, "as I grow older and nearer to the end of my life." The speaker is writing from a perspective of growing older. Perhaps a speaker writing from the perspective of youth would value riches, fame, and love more than this speaker.*

◆ **Critical Thinking**

⑦ Draw Conclusions Ask students to name the two things the speaker thinks are most important. *The speaker thinks freedom and courage are the most important things.*

 Beyond the Classroom

Community Connection
Volunteering With the Elderly The speaker of Emily Brontë's "The Old Stoic," an elderly woman, has lived long enough to know with some certainty what she values in life. Explain to students that elderly people are bound to have a different perspective from young people on the principles that have lasting value. Suggest that they spend some time volunteering in a retirement village, senior center, or other setting where elderly people gather. While volunteering, students might like to put together an oral history project in which several elderly people identify the most important values in their lives and tell how they came to embrace these values. To help students focus their oral history questions, make these suggestions:

1. Show Emily Brontë's poem "The Old Stoic" to interview subjects and ask if they agree with its emphasis on independence and courage as important values. How did they come to their views?

2. Encourage interview subjects to identify three guiding principles in their lives and to talk about why those principles are important.

Students can record their interviews and compile them into a class oral history project.

Akhmatova's poem illustrates how poets often use their art as a means of political expression. In this poem, Akhmatova suggests that in times of trouble, securing personal safety is not worth sacrificing national identity. She feels those who stay and face the dangers will emerge on the other side with fewer regrets and more pride than those who left their country in its time of need.

◆ Background for Understanding

❶ History Help students understand this reference by telling them that many of the upper classes in Russia became exiles in countries such as England and France to avoid execution by the Revolutionary forces. Ask: Who are the "enemies" the speaker refers to in line 2? *The speaker thinks the Revolutionaries were enemies of Russia.*

◆ Literary Focus

❷ Dramatic Situation Ask students to explain the "murk of conflagration" to which the poet refers. *It is the horror of revolution and its aftermath, which resulted in the deaths of thousands and the destruction of a way of life.*

◆ Reading Strategy

❸ Author's Perspective Have students explain what the poet, from the perspective of an anti-Revolutionary, thinks will happen to those who engineered the Revolution. *She says "the reckoning will be made"; she feels that the Revolution is temporary and those responsible will be punished.*

►Critical Viewing◄

❹ Speculate The people on the train may be fleeing oppression.

I Am Not One of Those Who Left the Land

Anna Akhmatova
Translated by Stanley Kunitz

❶ I am not one of those who left the land
to the mercy of its enemies.
Their flattery leaves me cold,
my songs are not for them to praise.

5   But I pity the exile's lot.
Like a felon, like a man half-dead,
dark is your path, wanderer;
wormwood infects your foreign bread.

❷ 10 But here, in the murk of conflagration,[1]
where scarcely a friend is left to know,
we, the survivors, do not flinch
from anything, not from a single blow.

❸ Surely the reckoning will be made
after the passing of this cloud.
15 We are the people without tears,
straighter than you . . . more proud . . .

---

1. **conflagration** (kän′ flə grā′ shən) *n.*: Destructive fire.

---

❹ ▼ **Critical Viewing** Why do you think these people are on this train? **[Speculate]**

◈ Speaking and Listening Mini-Lesson

Speech

This mini-lesson supports the Speaking and Listening activity in the Idea Bank on page 332.

Introduce the Concept Have students review the elements of a successful speech: strong points or opinions, reasons or facts to support opinions, body language and vocal intonation to emphasize strongest points.

Develop Background Before students

begin writing their speeches, suggest that they consider the following questions:

• Why does Theodora say it is intolerable for a ruler to be a fugitive? Is this true?

• What could realistically be accomplished by remaining behind?

• How far do a ruler's responsibilities extend?

Apply the Information Students can prepare speeches that address the questions in

Develop Background, or they can argue other points—stated or unstated—related to Theodora's position. Give students an opportunity to practice their speeches before presenting them to the class.

Assess the Outcome When students are finished delivering their speeches, have them use the Peer Assessment page for a Speech on page 118 of *Alternative Assessment* to help them evaluate the effectiveness of their speeches.

Speech During the Invasion of Constantinople

Empress Theodora

In his collection of historical speeches, Lend Me Your Ears, William Safire wrote the following introduction to Empress Theodora's inspirational words.

❧

Roman Emperor Justinian, on January 18 of the year 532, was certain he was about to be overthrown by rebel leader Hypatius and killed. A fast galley waited at the palace's private harbor to take him and Empress Theodora to safety in Thrace. His <u>timorous</u> advisers persuaded him that the rebellion could not be stopped and that the way out for the imperial couple was flight. As the panicky leader made for the door, the <u>indomitable</u> empress rose from her throne and delivered a brief speech that kept her husband in Rome and led to the slaughter of the rebels.

❻

▲ Critical Viewing This picture shows a strong, triumphant Theodora. Identify details in the speech that reflect these qualities. **[Connect]**

❺

◆ Build Vocabulary

timorous (tim′ ər es) *adj.*: Full of fear; timid

indomitable (in däm′ it ə bəl) *adj.*: Not easily defeated

One-Minute Insight

This inspirational speech by Empress Theodora expresses a universal theme, based on specific historical circumstances. Faced with almost certain death at the hands of invaders, Theodora halts the panicky evacuation of government leaders with her proud words. Her speech carries a message of courage and integrity that applies far beyond the historical events that prompted it.

▶ Critical Viewing ◀

❺ **Connect** Students might respond as follows: *Although the Empress Theodora stands in the background of the picture, she assumes a confident, authoritative pose. While others seem to be responding to dramatic events, the empress seems to represent reasoned calm and wisdom.*

◆ Background for Understanding

❻ **History** Explain to students that Theodora's speech was given during a riot staged by two political groups called the Blues and the Greens. These groups disagreed on religious beliefs and on Justinian's political appointments. They set up a new emperor who might have overthrown the Justinian's empire if it had not been for Theodora's speech.

🎼 Humanities: Art

Illustration for Speech During the Invasion of Constantinople.

In this piece of art, the Emperor Justinian is receiving a supplicant. Behind him stands the Empress Theodora.

Use these questions to spark a discussion:

1. The artist has chosen to make the figures in the foreground darker than those in the background. What effect does this have? *Some students might say that although the figures in the foreground are more detailed and darker, the eye is drawn to the contrasting, more broadly sketched Theodora in the background.*

2. How is Theodora's speech different from the way she is portrayed in the picture? *In the picture, she is seen behind Justinian, while in the speech the reader pictures her alone or in the foreground of a scene.*

3. Do you think the illustration represents Theodora truthfully? *Possible answer: Yes; though she is placed behind the throne, she very possibly was a "power behind the throne"—one whose influence was subtle but great.*

◆ Literary Focus

❶ Dramatic Situation To what dramatic situation is Theodora referring to when she says "the present occasion" and "extreme danger"? *She is referring to the riot and attempted takeover of the government.*

◆ Reading Strategy

❷ Author's Perspective How is the author's perspective reflected here? *The author implies that she believes it would be better to die than to give up the empire.*

Reinforce and Extend

Answers
◆ *Literature and Your Life*

Reader's Response Students may answer this question by relating the concerns of the poems—the value of riches, fame, courage, freedom, and love—to incidents from their own lives.

Thematic Focus Turning points call upon people to make decisions that might have great consequences for their own and other lives; this requires courage.

☑ **Check Your Comprehension**

1. The speaker is surprised that he has crossed the bridge.
2. The speaker values independence and courage.
3. The speaker thinks those who fled Russia acted in a cowardly and faithless manner.
4. She has a matter-of-fact view of death: "It is impossible for a person . . . not to die."

◆ Critical Thinking

1. The speaker knows the bridge is fragile and doesn't seem to think himself capable of the necessary maneuvers to cross it successfully.
2. As the speaker has grown older she has seen that love and fame are elusive.
3. Many students will recognize that staying to live in difficult circumstances is the more courageous choice because it involves standing up for one's principles.
4. Possible response: Stand up for what you believe in, even if you risk unpopularity.

---

❶ My lords, the present occasion is too serious to allow me to follow the convention that a woman should not speak in a man's council. Those whose interests are threatened by extreme danger should think only of the wisest course of action, not of conventions.

In my opinion, flight is not the right course, even if it should bring us to safety. It is impossible for a person, having been born into this world, not to die; but for one who has reigned it is intolerable to be a fugitive. May I never be **❷** deprived of this purple robe, and may I never see the day when those who meet me do not call me empress.

If you wish to save yourself, my lord, there is no difficulty. We are rich; over there is the sea, and yonder are the ships. Yet reflect for a moment whether, when you have once escaped to a place of security, you would not gladly exchange such safety for death. As for me, I agree with the adage that the royal purple is the noblest shroud.

Beyond Literature

Social Studies Connection

Byzantine Empire At the height of its power in the fifth century A.D., the Byzantine empire (also known as the East Roman empire) included parts of southern and eastern Europe, as well as parts of northern Africa and the Middle East. Christianity, Greek culture, and Roman customs flourished in the empire, which served as a link between ancient and modern European civilization. From A.D. 527 to 565, the Byzantine empire was ruled by Emperor Justinian.

Activity Use an encyclopedia to find the extent of Justinian's empire. On a copy of a contemporary world map, indicate the areas he ruled.

Guide for Responding

◆ *Literature and Your Life*

Reader's Response What personal experiences do these works call to mind?
Thematic Focus Why is courage required at turning points?

☑ **Check Your Comprehension**

1. What surprises the speaker in "The Bridge"?
2. What does the speaker in "The Old Stoic" value?
3. In "I Am Not One of Those . . . ," what is the speaker's attitude toward those who fled Russia?
4. How does the Empress Theodora feel about dying?

◆ Critical Thinking

INTERPRET
1. Why doesn't the speaker in "The Bridge" think he can cross the bridge? **[Speculate]**
2. Why doesn't the speaker in "The Old Stoic" care for love and fame? **[Infer]**

EVALUATE
3. Do you think it is more courageous to face the dangers of traveling across a continent and an ocean or to stay and live in difficult and dangerous circumstances? **[Apply]**

APPLY
4. What advice do you think the speaker of each poem would give to you and your friends? **[Generalize]**

 Beyond the Selection

FURTHER READING

Other Works by the Authors
Wuthering Heights, Emily Brontë
Wyklina, Leopold Staff
Requiem, Anna Akhmatova

Other Works About Turning Points
Cry the Beloved Country, Alan Paton
Children of the Fox, Jill Paton Walsh

We suggest that you preview these works before recommending them to students.

INTERNET

Students can visit the following Web sites for information. Please be aware that sites may have changed since we published this information.

For Emily Bronte go to **http://www.buckinghamgate.com/events/features/emily/emily.html**

For Anna Akhmatova go to **http://www.odessit.com/namegal/english/ahmatova.htm**

We *strongly recommend* that you preview the sites before you send students to them.

Guide for Responding (continued)

◆ Reading Strategy

AUTHOR'S PERSPECTIVE

Understanding the historical context of Anna Akhmatova's poem "I Am Not One of Those Who Left the Land" helps you identify the **author's perspective**—the viewpoint from which the poem is written. An author's perspective affects the details that are included in the work, as well as the way an event or idea is presented. For instance, Akhmatova's reference to the wormwood in foreign bread reflects her deep love for her country as well as her disapproval of those who would leave.

1. Leopold Staff lived through some of the most devastating events in history. What details in Staff's poem indicate that he has lived through dangerous times?
2. Empress Theodora's speech is made from the perspective of royalty. What details are included that might not be included in a speech by one of the common people during the invasion?
3. Identify two details in Akhmatova's poem that indicate she opposes the rulers of her country.

◆ Literary Focus

DRAMATIC SITUATION

The **dramatic situation**—the circumstances and events that provide the context of a work of literature—of Akhmatova's poem is the turmoil of civil war in Russia. For Empress Theodora's speech, the dramatic situation is the rebellion that threatens the lives of the empress and her husband.

1. Theodora makes her speech just as she and Justinian are about to board a ship and sail to Thrace. How does this detail add to the drama of her remarks?
2. Akhmatova stayed in Russia in the "murk of conflagration" while others fled. How do the circumstances surrounding her decision make her situation more dramatic?
3. Leopold Staff's poem was written in the aftermath of the tremendous devastation that Poland suffered during World War II. How does knowing this affect your understanding of the poem?

◆ Build Vocabulary

USING THE ROOT -dom-

Fill in the blanks to complete the meanings of these words that include the root -dom-, meaning "to rule."

1. domineer: ___?___ in a harsh or arrogant way
2. domain: the area that is ___?___
3. dominant: ___?___ over another

USING THE WORD BANK

On your paper, complete the following word pairs with words from the Word Bank.

1. Courageous is to hero as ___?___ is to ruler.
2. Devour is to eat as ___?___ is to ask.
3. Enraged is to joyful as ___?___ is to brave.

◆ Build Grammar Skills

NEGATIVES AND DOUBLE NEGATIVES

Negatives are words or word parts that deny or mean "no." Some examples of negatives include *no, not* (and contractions with *n't*), *never, none, nobody, no one, nothing, nowhere, neither, barely, scarcely,* and *hardly.* Using a **double negative**—two negative words where only one is needed—is incorrect.

Practice Identify which of the following sentences use double negatives and which use negatives correctly. Correct the double negatives you identify.

1. Although Empress Theodora did not leave, she was not killed during the rebellion.
2. Staff's poem tells of a man who didn't believe he could never get across a bridge.
3. Hardly none of Akhmatova's friends remained in Russia.
4. Brontë does not care for riches and she does not care for fame.

Writing Application In your notebook, rewrite each of these sentences using only one negative.

1. Those who meet me don't never call me empress.
2. Scarcely no friends are left to know.
3. We do not flinch from nothing.
4. I didn't believe in nothing.
5. She wasn't scared of no one.

Answers

◆ Reading Strategy

1. This poem suggests that he lived through difficult times by referring to the river (his life) as "wide and swift," and by describing the way to cross it (get through his life) as "fragile." Sometimes he had to "walk delicately" or "waver."
2. The empress refers to herself as "one who has reigned." She says "we are rich" and alludes to the adage that "the royal purple is the noblest shroud." All these details relate to her perspective as an empress.
3. The first detail is that she speaks up against the convention of "not speaking in a man's council." Another detail is her assertion that one who reigns cannot be a fugitive.

◆ Literary Focus

1. The timing of the empress's remarks make them all the more dramatic; it is late to suggest an altogether contrary course of action.
2. The circumstances surrounding Akhmatova's decision show that she has taken the least popular—and therefore more dramatic—course of action.
3. Knowing that Staff lived through events that devastated Poland makes his survival all the more dramatic.

◆ Build Vocabulary

Using the Root -dom-
1. Rule; 2. ruled; 3. ruling

Using the Word Bank
1. indomitable; 2. implore;
3. timorous

◆ Build Grammar Skills

Practice
1. correct
2. incorrect: Staff's poem tells of a man who didn't believe he could <u>ever</u> get across a bridge.
3. incorrect. Hardly <u>any</u> of Akhmatova's friends remained in Russia.
4. correct

Writing Application
1. Those who meet me don't ever call me empress.
2. Scarcely any friends are left to know.
3. We do not flinch from anything.
4. I didn't believe in anything.
5. She wasn't scared of anyone.

✎ Writer's Solution

For additional instruction and practice, use the lesson in the lesson in the **Language Lab CD-ROM** on avoiding double negatives and page 90 on Negative Sentences in the *Writer's Solution Grammar Practice Book.*

Idea Bank
Customizing for
Performance Levels

Following are suggestions for matching Idea Bank topics with your students' performance levels:

Less Advanced Students: 1, 7
Average Students: 2, 4, 6
More Advanced Students: 3, 5

Customizing for
Learning Modalities

Following are suggestions for matching Idea Bank topics with your students' learning modalities:

Visual/Spatial: 6, 7
Interpersonal: 5
Verbal/Linguistic: 2, 4, 5

Writing Mini-Lesson

Refer students to the Writing Handbook, page 966, for instruction on the writing process, and page 968 for further information on creative writing.

Writer's Solution

Writers at Work Videodisc

Have students view the videodisc segment for Ch. 6 in which Naomi Shihab Nye talks about gathering details for creative writing. Discuss with student what Nye means when she says that poetry isn't "primarily a mental experience."

Play frames 20514 to 20978

Writing Lab CD-ROM

Have students complete the tutorial on Creative Writing. Follow these steps:

1. Have students use Word Bins for poetry to help them choose sensory words and rhyming words for their poems.

2. Suggest that students consult interactive instruction on poetic structures. Here they can learn the meanings of *couplet, tercet, quatrain, cinquain, sestet, heptastich, octave, sonnet,* and *haiku.* Suggest that students might try writing their poems about a turning point in one of these forms.

Build Your Portfolio

Idea Bank

Writing

1. **Summaries** Write a summary of each of these works that captures the key details.

2. **News Commentary** Write a commentary that a newscaster might give following Empress Theodora's speech. Summarize what she said and discuss the impact that the speech may have.

3. **Compare-and-Contrast Essay** Write an essay in which you compare and contrast Anna Akhmatova's poem with Empress Theodora's speech. Look at similarities and differences in the attitudes of the speakers, the situations they face, and the character traits they exhibit.

Speaking and Listening

4. **Speech** Give a short speech in which you answer Empress Theodora and try to persuade Emperor Justinian and his aides that the wiser course of action is to board the ship and sail to safety in Thrace. Deliver your speech to the class. **[Performing Arts Link]**

5. **Role Play** Role-play a conversation between Akhmatova and someone who chose to leave Russia. Use what you learn in the poem and in the background on p. 325 as the basis for the discussion.

Projects

6. **Timeline** Several of these works are written in response to specific historical events. Using information gathered through research, create a timeline that captures the events surrounding one of these works. **[Social Studies Link]**

7. **Collage** Create a collage of visual images, quotations, and found objects that captures the ideas expressed in one of these works. **[Art Link]**

Writing Mini-Lesson

Poem About a Turning Point

Each of these works captures the thoughts of a person making a choice—facing a turning point. Write a **poem** about a turning point in your own life. You might write about a social or political issue that affects your life (as Akhmatova does), or you might write about a personal choice. Use the following tip to help you communicate your ideas.

Writing Skills Focus:
Figurative Language

Words such as *happy* or *sad* and other abstract language—language that refers to things that cannot be experienced with the senses—can mean something different to every person. By connecting abstract words to concrete images, however, you can help readers identify with what you're describing. The best way to do this is to use **figurative language**—writing not meant to be interpreted literally. For example, Leopold Staff uses figurative language when he describes a period of life as a fragile bridge. The specific type of figurative language that Staff uses is a **metaphor**—a comparison in which one thing is described as if it were another. You can also use **similes**—comparisons between dissimilar things using the word *like* or *as.*

Prewriting Choose the experience on which you will focus. Then brainstorm for a list of images you can use to help capture your feelings associated with the experience.

Drafting Don't overload your poem with a wide variety of images. Choose a small number that are related, and use them as the focus of your poem.

Revising Read your poem to a friend. Get feedback about how you can improve the wording or strengthen the images in your poem.

✓ ASSESSMENT OPTIONS

Formal Assessment, Selection Test, pp. 85–87, and Assessment Resources Software. The selection test is designed so that it can be easily customized to the performance levels of your students. *Alternative Assessment,* p. 25, includes options for less advanced students, more advanced students, intrapersonal learners, verbal/linguistic learners, bodily/kinesthetic learners, interpersonal learners, and visual/spatial learners.

PORTFOLIO ASSESSMENT
Use the following rubrics in the *Alternative Assessment* booklet to assess student writing:
Summaries: Summary Rubric, p. 98
News Commentary: Summary Rubric, p. 98
Compare-and-Contrast Essay: Comparison and Contrast Rubric, p. 103

Writing Process Workshop

Description

Much of the pleasure we take in the world around us comes through our senses. We observe the beauties of nature, listen to music, enjoy the feel of comfortable clothing, and taste and smell our favorite foods. **Description** is writing that captures the sensory pleasures in the world using precise details to show the way something looks, tastes, smells, sounds, or feels. Effective description re-creates a scene or an image so that readers can perceive it for themselves.

The following skills, introduced in this section's Writing Mini-Lessons, will help you write an effective descriptive essay.

Writing Skills Focus

▶ **Use sensory details**—words that appeal to the five senses. (See p. 310.)

▶ **Use appropriate language** for your purpose. (See p. 323.)

▶ **Use figurative language** such as metaphors, similes, or personification. (See p. 332.)

▶ **Make abstract terms concrete.** Connect abstract terms, such as *delicate* or *powerful,* to concrete images, such as a *butterfly* or a *freight train.*

Anne Tyler uses these skills to describe one man's experience with old age.

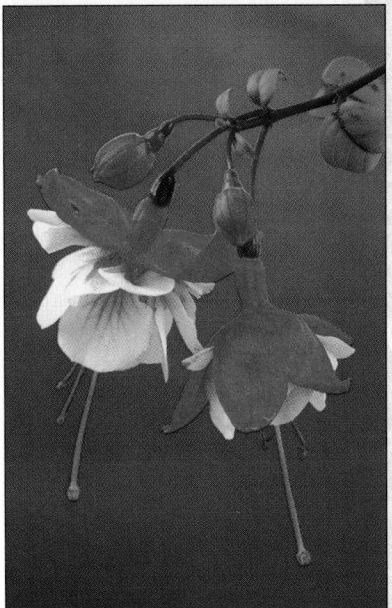

MODEL FROM LITERATURE

from "With All Flags Flying" by Anne Tyler

① Weakness was what got him in the end. He had been expecting something more definite—chest pains, a stroke, arthritis—but it was only weakness that put a finish to his living alone. ② A numbness in his head, an airy feeling when he walked. ③ A wateriness in his bones that made it an effort to pick up his coffee cup in the morning. He waited some days for it to go away, but it never did. And meanwhile the dust piled up in the corners; the refrigerator wheezed and creaked ④ for want of defrosting. Weeds grew around his rosebushes.

① The author's language is simple and direct, appropriate for a short story.

② *Numbness* appeals to the sense of touch.

③ The writer connects the abstract term *weakness* to the concrete images of air and water.

④ The words *wheezed* and *creaked* appeal to the sense of hearing.

Writing Process Workshop ◆ 333

Develop Student Writing

Prewriting

Once students have decided on a topic, you might want to tell them to make a chart with the five senses and then list any sensory words or details that come to mind pertaining to their topic. They can refer to the list while drafting.

You might have them use the grid organizer, which you can find in the *Writing and Language Transparencies,* pp. 79–81, to create a sensory language chart.

Customize for
English Language Learners

English language learners might find this assignment more manageable if they describe something they can see, rather than describing something from memory. You might suggest that they bring in somthing to describe, or you might use one of the art transparencies, which you can project for students to look at while drafting. Consider Art Transparency 12 or Art Transparency 20 in *Art Transparencies,* pp. 51 and 83.

Customize for
More Advanced Students

Challenge these students to write a description of something from a professional's point of view. For example, a student might describe the last inning of a championship baseball game from the point of view of the home plate umpire.

 Writer's Solution

Writing Lab CD-ROM

Sensory, Color, Places, and Character Trait word bins in the Gathering Details section of the tutorial on Description contain exhaustive lists of words. Students should consult these lists to help them find the most descriptive words and phrases for their topics.

Drafting

Encourage students to refer to their sensory language charts in include the appropriate words and details in their drafts. Remind them that they don't have to include every detail, only those that create the impression that they want.

APPLYING LANGUAGE SKILLS: Figurative Language

Figurative language is not meant to be taken literally; it's usually used to state or imply a comparison of two unlike things.

Simile:
The taxi moved like a python through the evening traffic.

Metaphor:
In the evening traffic, the taxi was a slithering python.

Personification:
The taxi moved in and out of traffic, cleverly weaving a fabric in the night.

Practice On your paper, add figurative language to the following passage.

It was a hot day. The sun shone brightly. The riverbed was dry. I walked slowly down the road.

Writing Application Use figurative language to make your descriptive essay more vivid.

Writer's Solution Connection
Writing Lab

For more examples of topics for descriptive writing, see the Inspirations for Description in the Description tutorial in the Writing Lab.

334 ◆ Turning Points

Prewriting

Choose a Topic Choose a topic that you find interesting enough to describe in detail. Memorable people, remarkable places, unusual events, and intriguing objects or ideas all make great topics for description. Use the following chart to help you choose a topic.

If you're considering...	Then try this ...
A remarkable place	Think about cities, regions, or countries you've visited or would like to visit.
A memorable person	Make a list of five distinct groups of people; for example, Sports Heroes or People From Mythology. Write down people for each category, and choose one.
An idea description	Consider subjects that interest you at school.

Consider Your Purpose How do you want your description to affect the people who read it? Your purpose will shape your tone, word choice, and details. For example, if your purpose is to encourage people to visit a place, you'll want to provide attractive details and use positively charged words and phrases, such as *breathtaking views* or *pleasant climate year-round.* On the other hand, if your purpose is to describe a trip that you didn't enjoy, you will focus on unpleasant details and use words and phrases with negative connotations, such as *dismal, gloomy weather,* or *surly, abusive waiters.*

Drafting

Organize Your Draft Choose the right method of organization for your topic. You may choose **chronological order** and place details in the order in which they happened in time. If you use chronological order, include transitional terms, such as *before, next,* and *a few minutes later.*

If you use **spatial order,** you place details as they appear in some physical relationship to one another. To make spatial order clear, use directional terms, such as *next to, in the center,* or *on the right.*

If you present ideas in **order of importance,** you place details from most important to least important or vice versa.

Applying Language Skills

Figurative Language Tell students that figurative language will enliven their descriptions, making them more fun to read and more memorable.

Suggested Answer

The day was so hot the tar on the roads bubbled and dripped like molten lava. The sun was a spotlight focused on me. The dry riverbed shrank further behind its dusty stones. Like a desert tortoise, I slowly ambled down the road.

 Writer's Solution

For additional instruction and practice, have students complete the **Language Lab CD-ROM** lesson on Figurative Language.

Revising

Have a Peer Review Your Work Team up with a classmate to review each other's work. Ask your peer reviewer to read your description once straight through to get a general impression. Then, he or she should read it a second time and jot down notes indicating what is strong about the description, pointing out areas that need clarification and offering constructive criticism with specific suggestions for improvement. Use the following questions to guide your peer reviewer:

▶ What is the central impression of the description? Does the language contribute to the impression?

▶ Is the description vivid? Where can I add sensory details or precise nouns?

▶ Where can I use figurative language to make comparisons more vivid?

▶ Is the imagery effective? How can I improve these details to make them more vivid or interesting?

REVISION MODEL

I save everything. Nothing ever goes into the garbage

without my rapt contemplation over whether or not I

am throwing away something meaningful. My drawers₍₁₎ *overflow*

₍₂₎ *ticket stubs, playbills, old letters, and photographs*
are filled to the brim with junk that would be worthless to

₍₃₎ *packrat, storing up memories like food for the cold winter.*
anybody else. I am a saver, a collector of memories.

① *The writer adds the precise word* overflow.

② *These sensory details clarify the vague term* junk.

③ *The writer adds a metaphor and a simile to compare himself to an image of a creature famous for saving things.*

Publishing

▶ **Create a Class Anthology** Working with classmates, gather your writings into a book of descriptions. Include a cover, title, and table of contents. Artistically talented students might also add illustrations.

▶ **Post Your Work On-Line** The Internet has many sites where you can post your writing. For a list of sites that publish student work, visit Prentice Hall at http://www.phschool.com.

APPLYING LANGUAGE SKILLS: Precise Nouns

Vague or general nouns will make your description less effective and more difficult for your readers to envision. Use **precise nouns** to give your readers a vivid and accurate picture of what you are describing.

Vague Nouns:
building, food, animal, ballplayer

More Specific Nouns:
library, pasta, reptile, shortstop

Precise Nouns:
Ridgewood Public Library, ziti, crocodile, Derek Jeter

Practice Replace the vague nouns with precise ones in the following sentences.

1. I bought my friend a piece of colored jewelry with an animal on it.

2. A vehicle passed the place where the man stood.

Writing Application Review your description. Replace any vague nouns with precise ones.

Writer's Solution Connection Language Lab

For more practice with precise nouns, complete the Language Lab lesson on Exact Nouns.

Revising

Encourage students to work with peer reviewers. Have the peer reviewer concentrate on sensory details and vivid imagery, and look for abstract images that can be converted to concrete terms.

Publishing

In addition to the suggestions presented in the Student Edition, students may also wish to read their descriptions aloud to background music. Students who do not wish to share their descriptions with other students should be encouraged to save them for future reference.

Reinforce and Extend

Review the Writing Guidelines After students have completed their papers, review the characteristics of description. Encourage students to come up with additional criteria for an interesting description based on what they learned through completing the assignment.

Applying Language Skills

Precise Nouns Tell students that using precise nouns is especially important in a description. Rather than loading up and weighing down their descriptions with adjectives and adverbs, they should concentrate on using the most precise nouns to describe people, places, things, and ideas.

Suggested Answers
1. I bought Amy a silver necklace with a lizard on it.
2. A bus passed the corner where the construction worker stood.

 Writer's Solution

For additional instruction and practice, have students complete the **Language Lab CD-ROM** lesson on Writing With Nouns and Verbs.

✓ ASSESSMENT		4	3	2	1
PORTFOLIO ASSESSMENT Use the rubric on Description in *Alternative Assessment* (p. 97) to assess students' writing. Add these criteria to customize the rubric to this assignment.	**Figurative Language**	The description uses figurative language effectively.	The description contains some figurative language.	There is little figurative language, but the description could use more.	There is no figurative language.
	Precise Nouns	All nouns are both precise and well chosen for each situation.	Most nouns are precise.	There are some precise nouns but also a number of vague nouns. Adjectives are overused.	Most nouns are vague and undescriptive, and/or the piece is weighed down by too many adjectives.

335

Students will already be familiar with user's manuals from electronic products they may have bought or received, as well as other products such as certain sporting goods or outdoor gear. Ask how many of them read the user's manuals for the products. Explain to them that reading a user's manual is a small investment of time that more often than not pays off with the time saved later.

Customize for
Visual/Spatial Learners

These students may benefit from seeing an actual keyboard or a picture of one and labeling each key appropriately.

Apply the Strategy

Answers

1. A keyboard diagram can be found on page 10.
2. Shift-F6 (pressing the shift and F6 keys simultaneously) boldfaces a word.
3. Shift-F5 allows the user to change margins.
4. To cut and paste material, first highlight the text to be cut by holding the button on the mouse down and dragging the mouse until the desired portion is highlighted. Then press shift-F7. Next, direct the mouse to the part of the document where you want to insert the text and click the mouse once so that the cursor appears. Then press shift-F5.

Reading Manuals

Real-World Reading Skills Workshop

Strategies for Success

You just purchased a new VCR, and you're ready to connect it to your television set. The first thing to do is to open the user's manual. Manuals provide assembly and operating instructions or user information, usually about equipment or appliances but often about organization or systems, like a college or a community's resources. They often include diagrams, photographs, charts, or other visual aids to illustrate the written material.

Look Over the Manual Become acquainted with the manual's organization and contents. These tips will help you use the manual efficiently:

▶ Review the table of contents for an overview of the manual.
▶ Turn to the index for a detailed alphabetical listing of topics.
▶ Read the instructions or information thoroughly.
▶ Refer to diagrams, charts, and maps as you use the manual.
▶ Look for a toll-free number to call if you have any questions.

✔ Here are other situations in which reading a manual is useful:
▶ Assembling or operating electronic equipment
▶ Gathering information on a college
▶ Acquainting yourself with the features of a product
▶ Identifying resources in your community

Identify Your Needs First, identify the information you need from the manual. For example, if you are using a manual to set up a piece of equipment, you will need assembly instructions. If you want to know where your car's spare tire is stored, do a quick search in the table of contents of your car owner's manual. Focus your search to meet your needs.

Apply the Strategy

You just got a new computer and can't wait to try out its many features. Refer to this manual to answer the questions that follow:

• Getting Started on Your PC

Everything you need to know to make the most of your new computer is in this handy PC manual. This chart gives you the keys you will need to perform common functions. Refer to page 10 for a keyboard diagram.

Common Commands

shift-F1: Italicize type
shift-F2: All CAPS
shift-F3: Margins (when screen appears, enter desired column widths for left, right, top, and bottom)
shift-F4: Undo
shift-F5: Boldface type
shift-F6: Cut text (first you must highlight the text you want to cut by holding your mouse down and dragging until the end of text)
shift-F7: Paste text (direct your mouse to the part of your document where you want to paste text in and then click so that cursor appears)

---

1. Where in the manual can you find a diagram of the keyboard?
2. Which command allows you to boldface a word?
3. Which command allows you to change the margins in your document?
4. How do you cut and paste material from one part of your document to another?

PART **2** *Fateful Moments*

Man Catching Shooting Sun, James Endicott,
Stock Illustration Source, Inc.

Fateful Moments ◆ 337

One-Minute Planning Guide

The selections in this part show people dealing with important or fateful moments and events that shape their lives. In Pearl S. Buck's "The Good Deed," an elderly Chinese woman finds new worth for herself by arranging a meeting between two younger people. Frank Deford's article "The Greatest Ever" lists the men he considers the fifty greatest basketball players of all time, as well as the qualities that make them special. Michael Jordan gives his own take on what it means to be the greatest in "Rare Air: Michael on Michael." The author of "Thoughts of Hanoi" remembers her city before it was destroyed by war, while in "Pride" the poet discusses how pride can lead to a point at which a person cracks like a rock. "Auto Wreck" describes the horrifying moments after an auto accident. The section ends with "Before the Law," Franz Kafka's description of the futility of trying to alter fate.

Customize for
Varying Student Needs
When assigning the selections in this part to your students, keep in mind the following factors:
"The Good Deed"
• A longer story (14 pp.)
• Its subject matter may be unfamiliar to many students

"The Greatest Ever"; "Rare Air"
• Very brief, high-interest topic and author
• Accessible to most students

"Thoughts of Hanoi"; "Pride"; "Auto Wreck"
• Diverse subject matter will be of interest

"Before the Law"
• Difficult vocabulary and sentence structure will be challenging for many students

---

♪ Humanities: Art

Man Catching Shooting Sun by James Endicott.

Born in 1946, James Endicott has been a freelance illustrator all his adult life.

Have students establish the surface premise of the art: A man standing on a high, narrow promontory, with a paper or banner streaming from his right hand, appears to be reaching his left hand to catch the most colorful of the many stars shooting in the sky. Help students to recognize the fantasy elements in the painting, the most striking of

which is the man catching the shooting star; others include the sheer quantity of simultaneously shooting stars; the flat, cut-out quality of the man; the strangely curvy promontory on which he stands; the mysterious item that streams from his right hand.

Help students link the artwork to the theme of Part 2, "Fateful Moments," by answering the following questions:
1. Does the art suggest whether it is good or bad to catch a shooting star, and what elements in the picture lead you to think

so? *Most students will say that the art suggests it is a good thing to catch the shooting star, since the man has safely reached a high place and catches the star gracefully. The star itself seems to be something special—more colorful than the others.*
2. What "fateful" event might catching a shooting star represent? *Sample answers: It might suggest unexpected success in a long pursuit or reaching for an ultimately unattainable dream.*

337

Guide for Reading

1. To read, comprehend, and interpret a story
2. To relate a story to personal experience
3. To make inferences about character
4. To identify static and dynamic characters
5. To build vocabulary in context and learn the word root -pel-
6. To recognize and use adverb clauses
7. To write an award speech on a character that creates a main impression
8. To respond to the story through writing, speaking and listening, and projects

SKILLS INSTRUCTION

Vocabulary:
Word Roots: -pel-

Grammar:
Adverb Clauses

Reading Strategy:
Make Inferences About Character

Literary Focus:
Static and Dynamic Characters

Writing:
Create a Main Impression

Speaking and Listening:
Radio Interview (teacher edition)

PORTFOLIO OPPORTUNITIES

Writing: Letters; Story Segment; Newsletter

Writing Mini-Lesson: Award Speech on a Character

Speaking and Listening: Unrehearsed Speech; Radio Interview

Projects: Multimedia Presentation; Timeline

More About the Author
Pearl S. Buck's 1954 autobiography, *My Several Worlds*, is a reflection on her diverse and eventful career as well as on her American and Chinese upbringing. In addition to being a Nobel Prize-winning author, Buck was an activist for women's rights, civil rights, and cross-cultural understanding. Among her many achievements in public life was the founding of the first international adoption agency.

Pearl S. Buck (1892–1973)

Pearl Buck's novel *The Good Earth* not only won her a Pulitzer Prize, but also earned her $50,000 for the movie rights (which was a record sum at the time). In addition, the female lead in *The Good Earth* won an Academy Award for best actress.

Living in Two Worlds Most of Buck's work, including the novel *The Good Earth* and the story "The Good Deed," focuses on China, its people, and its traditions. Although Buck was born to American parents in West Virginia, she spent most of her first forty years in China. Her father was a missionary in the Chinese countryside, and she and her sister grew up speaking both Chinese and English and playing with Chinese friends.

Buck married an American who taught at the university in Nanking, and she became an English teacher in local high schools. Because of circumstances in China and her personal life, she began spending extended periods of time in the United States

Life as a Writer By the late 1930's, Chinese politics as well as an impending divorce from her husband brought Pearl Buck back to the United States permanently. She decided to support herself and her daughter by writing, and her first book was published to some acclaim. Her next book, *The Good Earth*, made her an overnight success. It also influenced American thinking about China and Chinese culture, erasing many old, untrue stereotypes. In 1938, Buck became the first woman to win the Nobel Prize for Literature.

◆ Build Vocabulary

WORD ROOTS: -pel-

As recently as fifty years ago, young men and women in China had their spouses chosen for them by their elders. Whether or not they loved the other person, they were *compelled* to marry that person. The verb *compel* includes the root *-pel-*, which means "drive" or "push." The root *-pel-* helps you determine that the word *compel* means "to push to do something." The idea of being compelled to marry someone is an important factor in this story.

contemplatively
revere
compelled
abashed
repressed
indignantly
assailed
expedition
conferred

WORD BANK

As you read this story, you will encounter the words on this list. Each word is defined on the page where it first appears. Preview the list before you read.

◆ Build Grammar Skills

ADVERB CLAUSES

An **adverb clause** is a subordinate clause—a group of words that contains a subject and a verb but cannot stand by itself as a complete sentence—that modifies a verb, an adjective, or an adverb. Adverb clauses clarify information in other clauses by telling *where, when, why, how, to what extent,* or *under what conditions* actions occur. Adverb clauses are introduced by subordinating conjunctions such as *when, whenever, where, although, because, since, if, as,* and *while.*

main clause | adv. clause
She took up that magazine when her daughter-in-law came in . . .

In this example from "The Good Deed," the adverb clause clarifies *when* the old woman took up the magazine.

Prentice Hall Literature Program Resources

REINFORCE / RETEACH / EXTEND

Selection Support Pages
Build Vocabulary: Word Roots: -pel-, p. 105
Build Grammar Skills: Adverb Clauses, p. 106
Reading Strategy: Make Inferences About Character, p. 107
Literary Focus: Static and Dynamic Characters, p. 108

Strategies for Diverse Student Needs, p. 26

Beyond Literature
Multicultural Connection: *Dating Customs,* p. 26

Formal Assessment Selection Test, pp. 88–90; Assessment Resources Software

Alternative Assessment, p. 26

Resource Pro CD-ROM
"The Good Deed"—includes all resource materials and customizable lesson plan

Listening to Literature Audiocassette
"The Good Deed"

The Good Deed

◆ *Literature and Your Life*

CONNECT YOUR EXPERIENCE

Starting a new school, joining a new club, moving to a new neighborhood—you might feel uncertainty in any of these situations. Just imagine how uncertain Mrs. Pan, the central character in this story, must feel after moving away from China late in her life to live with her son in New York City.

THEMATIC FOCUS: FATEFUL MOMENTS

For Mrs. Pan, moving to New York City is a major turning point that opens the door to a new life. As you read, you may find yourself thinking about how moving to a distant place would change your life.

Journal Writing Mrs. Pan eventually makes adjustments that help her enjoy her new life. Make a list of ways that you can help yourself deal with a new situation and even enjoy the experience.

◆ Background for Understanding

CULTURE

In "The Good Deed," an elderly Chinese woman tries to arrange a marriage between two young Chinese Americans. Arranged marriages are a tradition in China as well as in many other countries. Parents choose their children's spouse; then they engage in negotiations with the parents of the prospective bride or groom. In modern China, many young people choose marriage partners based on common interests and mutual attraction, but arranged marriages still do take place, especially in the countryside.

◆ Literary Focus

STATIC AND DYNAMIC CHARACTERS

Adjusting to life in a new home is likely to bring about important changes in a character. These experiences help the person to change and grow. A character that changes during the course of a literary work is known as a **dynamic character**. The changes dynamic characters undergo affect their attitudes and beliefs. A **static character** does not change.

Notice the changes in the characters—especially in Mrs. Pan—in "The Good Deed." Think about how the change helps her grow.

◆ Reading Strategy

MAKE INFERENCES ABOUT CHARACTER

Writers rarely announce that a character is changing or state directly that a character is happy or sad. Instead, you must **make inferences**—logical assumptions—about the characters based on what they say and how they act. For example, young Mr. Pan saves his money and risks his life to help his mother escape from the dangers she faces in China to come to live safely with him. Buck never writes the words "Mr. Pan loves his mother," but based on the evidence, you can infer that he does.

Use a graphic organizer like the one shown below to record your observations and make inferences about the characters.

Words	Actions
	He risks his life to help her escape from China.

Inference
Mr. Pan loves his mother.

Customize for
Less Proficient Readers

Less proficient readers may have a hard time sustaining their effort through the length of this story. Also, certain details, such as the many views of marriage expressed along the way, may puzzle less proficient readers. Break the story into sections and assign by sections. Thus, students can find success in completing smaller reading tasks. Have them summarize the plot as they complete each section.

Customize for
More Advanced Students

Encourage these students to gather information on Chinese culture and political history as they read. Interested students can find out in greater detail the political events that caused old Mrs. Pan to emigrate to the United States.

Customize for
English Language Learners

Suggest that English language learners listen to the audiocassette as they follow in their texts. Have them work with native speakers who can jot down the words they don't understand and, after the recording, clarify those words for them. Students who are fluent in Chinese dialects might want to translate simple sentences or passages for the rest of the class.

Customize for
Visual/Spatial Learners

Have these students devise a graphic organizer that they can use to note changes in Mrs. Pan, a dynamic character. Invite the students to share their finished charts with the class.

✎ Preparing for Standardized Tests

Reading and Vocabulary Proficiency in determining word meaning from recognizable roots and affixes will enable students to improve performance on both reading comprehension and vocabulary items. The Build Vocabulary lesson for this story focuses on learning word meaning through the use of the word root -pel-, meaning to "drive" or "push." For additional practice, use the Build Vocabulary page in *Selection Support*, p. 105.

Grammar and Language Portions of some tests require students to write essays in which they express ideas completely and precisely. The use of adverb clauses can make a piece of information more complete and precise.

You might also point out that the use of adverb clauses can contribute to sentence variety. The Build Grammar Skills lesson for this selection focuses on this topic. For additional practice, use the Build Grammar Skills page on Adverb Clauses, p. 106, in *Selection Support*.

One-Minute Insight

Through her good deed, the old woman in this story joins the traditional to the modern. When her son brings her from China to New York, Mrs. Pan at first feels profoundly homesick. Her spirits lift, however, once she discovers and sets a purpose for herself: to arrange a satisfactory marriage for Lili Yang, the only young person who has taken the time to speak to Mrs. Pan in her own language. The matchmaking effort proves successful not only for the young people involved but for Mrs. Pan, who discovers she can make a mark in her newly adopted country without abandoning the ways of her cherished homeland.

Comprehension Check ☑

1 What has Mr. Pan done to help his mother? Why did he take this action? *He brought her from China to New York. Her life was in danger because of political changes in China.*

◆ Reading Strategy

2 **Make Inferences About Character** What do the words Mrs. Pan tells her son reveal about her feelings and thoughts? *Some students may say that Mrs. Pan's words reveal how acutely homesick and unhappy she is. Others may say that they reveal her stubbornness or resentment—she suggests she would rather die than live in New York.*

►Critical Viewing◄

3 **Connect** Students might say that judging by the women's traditional style of dress, they seem closer to old Mrs. Pan's experience than to her son's.

The Good Deed

Pearl S. Buck

Mr. Pan was worried about his mother. He had been worried about her when she was in China, and now he was worried about her in New York, although he had thought that once he got her out of his ancestral village in the province of Szechuen and safely away from the local bullies, who took over when the distant government fell, his anxieties would be ended. To this end he had risked his own life and paid out large sums of sound American money, and he felt that day when he saw her on the wharf, a tiny, dazed little old woman, in a lavender silk coat and black skirt, that now they would live happily together, he and his wife, their four small children and his beloved mother, in the huge safety of the American city.

It soon became clear, however, that safety was not enough for old Mrs. Pan. She did not even appreciate the fact, which he repeated again and again, that had she remained in the village, she would now have been dead, because she was the widow of the large landowner who had been his father and therefore deserved death in the eyes of the rowdies in power.

Old Mrs. Pan listened to this without reply, but her eyes, looking very large in her small withered face, were haunted with homesickness.

"There are many things worse than death, especially at my age," she replied at last, when again her son reminded her of her good fortune in being where she was.

He became impassioned when she said this. He struck his breast with his clenched fists and he shouted, "Could I have forgiven myself if I had allowed you to die? Would the ghost of my father have given me rest?"

"I doubt his ghost would have traveled over such a wide sea," she replied. "That man was

▶ **Critical Viewing** Do these women seem closer to Mr. Pan's experience or to his mother's? [Connect]

340 ◆ Turning Points

◆ Block Scheduling Strategies

Consider these suggestions to take advantage of extended class time:

- Have students complete the journal activity in Literature and Your Life (p. 339). Then have them meet in small groups to discuss their lists.
- Introduce and reinforce the Build Grammar Skills lesson on pages 338 and 354 by leading a brief discussion on the function of adverb clauses—to provide more information and add specificity to sentences.

Then encourage students to find further examples of adverb clauses in the story and in their own pieces of writing.

- Ask small groups of students to select por-tions of the story to act out. Then have them listen to the selection on audiocassette so that they can model their portrayals of the characters on the readers' portrayals.
- Introduce the concept of static and dynamic characters. Have them read the

Literary Focus on page 339. After reading have them answer the Literary Focus questions on page 354. You may follow up with the Literary Focus page on Dynamic Character in **Selection Support,** p. 108.

- Have students work in discussion groups to answer the Critical Thinking questions (p. 354.)
- Have students complete the Writing Mini-Lesson (p. 355).

◆ **Reading Strategy**

④ Make Inferences About Character What can students tell about Mrs. Pan from her remarks about the water? *Responses may include these: She finds it difficult to let go of her memories; because she feels that she does not belong in New York, nothing there seems right to her.*

Mother and Daughter: Leaf from a Manchu family album, Unidentified artist, The Metropolitan Museum of Art

always afraid of the water."

Yet there was nothing that Mr. Pan and his wife did not try to do for his mother in order to make her happy. They prepared the food that she had once enjoyed, but she was now beyond the age of pleasure in food, and she had no appetite. She touched one dish and another with the ends of her ivory chopsticks,[1] which she had brought with her from her home, and she thanked them prettily. "It is all good," she said, "but the water is not the same as our village water; it tastes of metal and not of earth, and so the flavor is not the same. Please allow the children to eat it."

She was afraid of the children. They went to an American school and they spoke English very well and Chinese very badly, and since she could speak no English, it distressed her to hear her own language maltreated by their careless tongues. For a time she tried to coax them to a few lessons, or she told them stories, to which they were too busy to listen. Instead they preferred to look at the moving pictures in the box that stood on a table in the living room. She gave them up finally and merely watched them <u>contemplatively</u> when they were in the same room with her and was glad when they were gone. She liked her son's wife. She did not understand how there could be a Chinese woman who had never been in China, but such her son's wife was. When her son was away, she could not say to her daughter-in-law, "Do you remember how the willows grew over the

---

1. ivory chopsticks: Thin pair of sticks used as eating utensils.

◆ **Build Vocabulary**

contemplatively (kən tem′ plā tiv lē) *adv.:* In a thoughtful or studious way

---

The Good Deed ◆ 341

◆ **Build Grammar Skills**

⑤ Adverb Clauses Have students identify the two adverb clauses in this sentence and tell what words or phrases these adverb clauses modify. *"When they were in the same room with her" modifies* watched *and "when they were gone" modifies* glad.

Customize for
Less Proficient Readers
Since much of this story reflects Mrs. Pan's perspective, students may have difficulty with some of the descriptions. Guide students to understand that the moving pictures in the box describes a television, and that a Chinese woman who had never been to China is a woman of Chinese heritage who was brought up in America.

Humanities: Art

Mother and Daughter, Leaf from a Manchu family album.

Manchu warriors frequently invaded China in the 1600's. They conquered northern China in 1644 and remained the ruling dynasty in China until 1912.

In the illustration, the Manchu mother and daughter are both posed in a stiff and formal manner. While Mrs. Pan in "The Good Deed" lives in the United States in modern times, she clings to the traditional formal ways of her native China.

Use these questions for discussion:
1. What might the striking similarity between mother and daughter indicate about the old Manchu culture? Would Mrs. Pan approve or disapprove of this cultural trait? *Children were expected to emulate their parents rather than develop their own individual styles Mrs. Pan would have approved.*
2. Is Lili more like the daughter in the illustration, or a modern American daughter? Explain. *Lili is an independent young woman, yet she respects traditional Chinese culture.*

❶ Interpret Ask students: What do you think Mr. Pan means when he says that the children were not taught as he was in China? Why is this difficult for Mrs. Pan to accept? *Mr. Pan seems to be making an excuse for lax discipline, implying that Americans don't value the kind of discipline he had. To Mrs. Pan, children's lack of obedience is unimaginable and unacceptable.*

❷ Infer Point out that feeling lonely and useless is the most difficult aspect of Mrs. Pan's new life. Based on this information, what can students assume about the life she left behind in China? *Students should infer that Mrs. Pan's life was busy and productive.*

◆ *Literature and Your Life*

❸ Ask students if they think they might have feelings similar to Mrs. Pan's if they moved to a distant place. If so, in what ways? *Some students may say that they would miss their friends, neighbors, and community. Others may say that, like Mrs. Pan, they would miss the ease and independence that come with knowing how things are done in a familiar place.*

◆ Reading Strategy

❹ Make Inferences About Character What inference can students make about Mr. Pan from this conversation? *Inferences may include that he cares deeply about his mother's well-being and that he has a sensitive understanding of her needs.*

◆ Critical Thinking

❺ Interpret Ask students what point they think the author is making. *Students should note that Mrs. Pan and her daughter-in-law react very differently to what is probably an American fashion magazine, revealing that their tastes reflect cultural differences.*

gate?" For her son's wife had no such memories. She had grown up here in the city and she did not even hear its noise. At the same time, though she was so foreign, she was very kind to the old lady, and she spoke to her always in a gentle voice, however she might shout at the children, who were often disobedient.

The disobedience of the children was another grief to old Mrs. Pan. She did not understand how it was that four children could all be disobedient, for this meant that they had never been taught to obey their parents and <u>revere</u> their elders, which are the first lessons a child should learn.

"How is it," she once asked her son, "that the children do not know how to obey?"

❶ Mr. Pan had laughed, though uncomfortably. "Here in America the children are not taught as we were in China," he explained.

"But my grandchildren are Chinese nevertheless," old Mrs. Pan said in some astonishment.

"They are always with Americans," Mr. Pan explained. "It is very difficult to teach them."

Old Mrs. Pan did not understand, for Chinese and Americans are different beings, one on the west side of the sea and one on the east, and the sea is always between. Therefore, why should they not continue to live apart even in the same city? She felt in her heart that the children should be kept at home and taught those things which must be learned, but she said nothing. She felt lonely and there was no one who under-

❷ stood the things she felt and she was quite use-

❸ less. That was the most difficult thing: She was of no use here. She could not even remember which spout the hot water came from and which brought the cold. Sometimes she turned on one and then the other, until her son's wife came in briskly and said, "Let me, Mother."

So she gave up and sat uselessly all day, not by the window, because the machines and the many people frightened her. She sat where she could not see out; she looked at a few books, and day by day she grew thinner and thinner until Mr. Pan was concerned beyond endurance.

❹ One day he said to his wife, "Sophia, we must do something for my mother. There is no use in saving her from death in our village if she dies

here in the city. Do you see how thin her hands are?"

"I have seen," his good young wife said. "But what can we do?"

"Is there no woman you know who can speak Chinese with her?" Mr. Pan asked. "She needs to **❹** have someone to whom she can talk about the village and all the things she knows. She cannot talk to you because you can only speak English, and I am too busy making our living to sit and listen to her."

Young Mrs. Pan considered. "I have a friend," she said at last, "a schoolmate whose family <u>compelled</u> her to speak Chinese. Now she is a social worker here in the city. She visits families in Chinatown and this is her work. I will call her up and ask her to spend some time here so that our old mother can be happy enough to eat again."

"Do so," Mr. Pan said.

That very morning, when Mr. Pan was gone, young Mrs. Pan made the call and found her friend, Lili Yang, and she explained everything to her.

"We are really in very much trouble," she said finally. "His mother is thinner every day, and she is so afraid she will die here. She has made us promise that we will not bury her in foreign soil but will send her coffin back to the ancestral village. We have promised, but can we keep this promise, Lili? Yet I am so afraid, because I think she will die, and Billy will think he must keep his promise and he will try to take the coffin back and then he will be killed. Please help us, Lili."

Lili Yang promised and within a few days she came to the apartment and young Mrs. Pan led her into the inner room, which was old Mrs. Pan's room and where she always sat, wrapped in her satin coat and holding a magazine at whose pictures she did not care to look. She took **❺** up that magazine when her daughter-in-law came in, because she did not want to hurt her feelings, but the pictures frightened her. The

◆ Build Vocabulary

revere (ri vir′) *v.*: Regard with deep respect and love
compelled (kəm peld′) *v.*: Forced to do something

342 ◆ *Turning Points*

Cross-Curricular Connection: Social Studies

"The Good Deed" is set against a backdrop of decades of political instability, civil war, and revolution in China.

In 1912, China's last emperor gave up his throne following a prolonged popular uprising. Over the years that followed, the new Nationalist party government was besieged by troubles as foreign powers, provincial warlords, and a growing Communist movement all struggled to gain control of all or parts of the country. Finally, in 1949, Communist

forces drove Nationalist forces from power. It is during the years immediately after this Communist takeover—while the party was consolidating its control over China—that Mrs. Pan fled the country to join her son in the United States.

- Challenge students to find a detail in the story (other than the references to the political situation in China) that helps establish when it is set. *The Pan children*

watch television; television sets became common in households during the 1950's.

- Have students research and report on the following leaders and their roles in the history of twentieth-century China: Sun Yat-sen; Chiang Kai-shek; Mao Zedong.

- Encourage students to gather information on current political and economic conditions in China and report their findings to the class.

women looked bold and evil, their bosoms bare, and sometimes they wore only a little silk stuff over their legs and this shocked her. She wondered that her son's wife would put such a magazine into her hands, but she did not ask questions. There would have been no end to them had she once begun, and the ways of foreigners did not interest her. Most of the time she sat silent and still, her head sunk on her breast, dreaming of the village, the big house there where she and her husband had lived together with his parents and where their children were born. She knew that the village had fallen into the hands of their enemies and that strangers lived in the house, but she hoped even so that the land was tilled.[2] All that she remembered was the way it had been when she was a young woman and before the evil had come to pass.

She heard now her daughter-in-law's voice, "Mother, this is a friend. She is Miss Lili Yang. She has come to see you."

Old Mrs. Pan remembered her manners. She tried to rise but Lili took her hands and begged her to keep seated.

6 "You must not rise to one so much younger," she exclaimed.

Old Mrs. Pan lifted her head. "You speak such good Chinese!"

"I was taught by my parents," Lili said. She sat down on a chair near the old lady.

Mrs. Pan leaned forward and put her hand on Lili's knee. "Have you been in our own country?" she asked eagerly.

Lili shook her head. "This is my sorrow. I have not and I want to know about it. I have come here to listen to you tell me."

"Excuse me," young Mrs. Pan said, "I must prepare the dinner for the family."

She knew that the village had fallen into the hands of their enemies . . .

She slipped away so that the two could be alone and old Mrs. Pan looked after her sadly. "She never wishes to hear; she is always busy."

"You must remember in this country we have no servants," Lili reminded her gently.

"Yes," old Mrs. Pan said, "and why not? I have told my son it is not fitting to have my daughter-in-law cooking and washing in the kitchen. We should have at least three servants: one for me, one for the children and one to clean and cook. At home we had many more but here we have only a few rooms."

Lili did not try to explain. "Everything is different here and let us not talk about it," she said. "Let us talk about your home and the village. I want to know how it looks and what goes on there."

Old Mrs. Pan was delighted. She smoothed the gray satin of her coat as it lay on her knees and she began.

"You must know that our village lies in a wide valley from which the mountains rise as sharply as tiger's teeth."

7

"Is it so?" Lili said, making a voice of wonder.

"It is, and the village is not a small one. On the contrary, the walls encircle more than one thousand souls, all of whom are relatives of our family."

"A large family," Lili said.

"It is," old Mrs. Pan said, "and my son's father was the head of it. We lived in a house with seventy rooms. It was in the midst of the village. We had gardens in the courtyards. My own garden contained also a pool wherein are aged goldfish, very fat. I fed them millet[3] and they knew me."

8

"How amusing." Lili saw with pleasure that the old lady's cheeks were faintly pink and that her large beautiful eyes were beginning to shine and glow. "And how many years did you live there, Ancient One?"

---

2. **tilled** (tild) *v.*: Plowed and fertilized to be ready for planting.

3. **millet** (mil´ it) *n.*: Food grain.

The Good Deed ◆ 343

◆ **Reading Strategy**

6 Make Inferences About Character What inferences can students make about Lili, based on her first words to Mrs. Pan? *Suggested responses: She is respectful and courteous; she has an understanding of Chinese customs.*

◆ **Literary Focus**

7 Static and Dynamic Characters Ask students whether they think Mrs. Pan shows signs of change in this part of her conversation with Lili. *Some students may say yes—whereas Mrs. Pan was unhappy and listless before, she is now delighted and animated; others may say no—her delight in talking about her village shows that she continues to have more interest in her old life than in her new one.*

◆ **Critical Thinking**

8 Infer Ask: What does this description reveal about Mrs. Pan and her life in China? How does it help you to understand her character? *Suggested response: The description reveals that Mrs. Pan and her family lived a wealthy and comfortable life. Knowing what she has lost makes it easier to understand her difficulty in and her resistance to adjusting to life in the United States*

Customize for
English Language Learners
Remind students that Lili and Mrs. Pan are supposed to be speaking in Chinese. "Ancient One" is Buck's translation of a respectful title that someone like Lili would have used when addressing the elderly woman.

Cross-Curricular Connection: Social Studies/Geography

Build students' interest in world geography by asking the following "trick" question: "Is China the world's largest country? Vote yes or no." After students have voted, explain that either answer could be considered correct, depending on what is meant by "largest." With a population of over one billion, China is the largest country in terms of population. In terms of land area, it is the third largest, after Russia and Canada.

Follow up by pointing out references to places within China in the story. These include *Szechuen,* the province where Mrs. Pan's ancestral village is located, *Shantung,* the province that is the ancestral home of the Lim family, and the cities of *Canton, Hangchow,* and *Soochow.* Have students locate each of these places on a map of China.

You might help students find the cities by providing these hints: Canton is near the southern coast of China; Hangchow and Soochow are near the city of Shanghai.

◆ Reading Strategy

❶ Make Inferences About Character From her remark "I cannot be responsible for what other persons do, but I must be responsible for my own kind," students can infer that Mrs. Pan is responsible, lives by her sense of morality, and is community-minded.

◆ Literary Focus

❷ Static and Dynamic Characters Ask: Do Mrs. Pan's words signal a change in her attitude or behavior? Why or why not?
Students may say that there is a change; she is taking action rather than withdrawing from life; she is taking an interest in something other than her past; she is now at least admitting to the reality of living in a foreign country.

◆ Critical Thinking

❸ Compare and Contrast Have students use this passage to compare and contrast Mrs. Pan's view of the Chinese customs and traditions with Lili's view. *Students may point out that Mrs. Pan has an absolute belief in the customs; Lili seems sympathetic to the customs and the values they represent, but she also accepts that things are done differently in the United States.*

Customize for
More Advanced Students
Have more advanced students look back over the story to find examples of details or events related from one character's point of view. *Possibilities include "moving pictures in a box"— a television set from Mrs. Pan's point of view—and "bullies" and "rowdies"— those in power in China from Mr. Pan's point of view.*

"I went there as a bride. I was seventeen." She looked at Lili, questioning, "How old are you?"

Lili smiled, somewhat ashamed, "I am twenty-seven."

Mrs. Pan was shocked. "Twenty-seven? But my son's wife called you Miss."

"I am not married," Lili confessed.

Mrs. Pan was instantly concerned. "How is this?" she asked. "Are your parents dead?"

"They are dead," Lili said, "but it is not their fault that I am not married."

Old Mrs. Pan would not agree to this. She shook her head with decision. "It is the duty of the parents to arrange the marriage of the children. When death approached, they should have attended to this for you. Now who is left to perform the task? Have you brothers?"

"No," Lili said, "I am an only child. But please don't worry yourself, Madame Pan. I am earning my own living and there are many young women like me in this country."

Old Mrs. Pan was dignified about this. "I cannot be responsible for what other persons do, but I must be responsible for my own kind," she declared. "Allow me to know the names of the suitable persons who can arrange your marriage. I will stand in the place of your mother. We are all in a foreign country now and we must keep together and the old must help the young in these important matters."

Lili was kind and she knew that Mrs. Pan meant kindness. "Dear Madame Pan," she said. "Marriage in America is very different from marriage in China. Here the young people choose their own mates."

"Why do you not choose, then?" Mrs. Pan said with some spirit.

Lili Yang looked <u>abashed</u>. "Perhaps it would be better for me to say that only the young men choose. It is they who must ask the young women."

"What do the young women do?" Mrs. Pan inquired.

"They wait," Lili confessed.

"And if they are not asked?"

> **◆ Reading Strategy**
> ❶
> ❷
> What do Mrs. Pan's words reveal about her character?

"They continue to wait," Lili said gently.

"How long?" Mrs. Pan demanded.

"As long as they live."

Old Mrs. Pan was profoundly shocked. "Do you tell me that there is no person who arranges such matters when it is necessary?"

"Such an arrangement is not thought of here," Lili told her.

"And they allow their women to remain unmarried?" Mrs. Pan exclaimed. "Are there also sons who do not marry?"

"Here men do not marry unless they wish to do so."

Mrs. Pan was even more shocked. "How can this be?" she asked. "Of course, men will not marry unless they are compelled to do so to provide grandchildren for the family. It is necessary to make laws and create customs so that a man who will not marry is denounced as an unfilial[4] son and one who does not fulfill his duty to his ancestors."

"Here the ancestors are forgotten and parents are not important," Lili said unwillingly.

"What a country is this," Mrs. Pan exclaimed. "How can such a country endure?"

Lili did not reply. Old Mrs. Pan had unknowingly touched upon a wound in her heart. No man had ever asked her to marry him. Yet above all else she would like to be married and to have children. She was a good social worker, and the head of the Children's Bureau sometimes told her that he would not know what to do without her and she must never leave them, for then there would be no one to serve the people in Chinatown. She did not wish to leave except to be married, but how could she find a husband? She looked down at her hands, clasped in her lap, and thought that if she had been in her own country, if her father had not come here as a young man and married here, she would have been in China and by now the mother of many children. Instead what would

❸

---

4. **unfilial** (un fil´ ē əl) *adj.*: Without the devotion of a son or daughter.

◆ Build Vocabulary
abashed (ə bashd´) *adj.*: Embarrassed

Beyond the Classroom

Career Connection

Social Work The character Lili Yang in this story is a social worker, and she works for the city's Children's Bureau; she serves the people of Chinatown by visiting families who need help.

The type of work that Lili does is known as casework, and her field is known as family and child welfare. Caseworkers in this field may help families in need obtain financial assistance or medical care. They may also counsel people on

family issues such as child care, education, and adoption.

Have interested students gather more information about social work. Some students might report on other settings, such as hospitals, retirement communities, and homeless shelters, that employ social workers. Other students might contact a school of social work for information about higher education and career opportunities in this field.

become of her? She would grow older and older, and twenty-seven was already old, and at last hope must die. She knew several American girls quite well; they liked her, and she knew that they faced the same fate. They, too, were waiting. They tried very hard; they went in summer to hotels and in winter to ski lodges, where men gathered and were at leisure enough to think about them, and in confidence they told one another of their efforts. They compared their experiences and they asked anxious questions. "Do you think men like talkative women or quiet ones?" "Do you think men like lipstick or none?" Such questions they asked of one another and who could answer them? If a girl succeeded in winning a proposal from a man, then all the other girls envied her and asked her special questions and immediately she became someone above them all, a successful woman. The job which had once been so valuable then became worthless and it was given away easily and gladly. But how could she explain this to old Mrs. Pan?

Meanwhile Mrs. Pan had been studying Lili's face carefully and with thought. This was not a pretty girl. Her face was too flat, and her mouth was large. She looked

4 like a girl from Canton and not from Hangchow or Soochow. But she had nice skin, and her eyes, though small, were kind. She was the sort of girl, Mrs. Pan could see, who would make an excellent wife and a good mother, but certainly she was one for whom a marriage must be arranged. She was a decent, plain, good girl and, left to herself, Mrs. Pan could predict, nothing at all would happen. She would wither away like a dying flower.

Old Mrs. Pan forgot herself and for the first time since she had been hurried away from the village without even being allowed to stop and

see that the salted cabbage, drying on ropes across the big courtyard, was brought in for the winter. She had been compelled to leave it there and she had often thought of it with regret. She could have brought some with her had she known it was not to be had here. But there it was, and it was only one thing among others that she had left undone. Many people depended upon her and she had left them, because her son compelled her, and she was not used to this idleness that was killing her day by day.

Now as she looked at Lili's kind, ugly face it occurred to her that here there was something she could do. She could find a husband for this good girl, and it would be counted for merit when she went to heaven. A good deed is a good deed, whether one is in China or in America, for the same heaven stretches above all.

Yes, she grieved in the secret places of her heart . . .

She patted Lili's clasped hands. "Do not grieve anymore," she said tenderly. "I will arrange everything."

"I am not grieving," Lili said.

"Of course, you are," Mrs. Pan retorted. "I see you are a true woman, and women grieve when they are not wed so that they can have children. You are grieving for your children."

Lili could not deny it. She would have been ashamed to confess to any other person except this old Chinese lady who might have been her grandmother. She bent her head and bit her lip; she let a tear or two fall upon her hands. Then she nodded. Yes, she grieved in the secret places of her heart, in the darkness of the lonely nights, when she thought of the empty future of her life.

"Do not grieve," old Mrs. Pan was saying, "I will arrange it; I will do it."

It was so comforting a murmur that Lili could not bear it. She said, "I came to comfort you, but it is you who comfort me." Then she got up and

5

6

◆ **Critical Thinking**

5 **Interpret** Encourage students to paraphrase Mrs. Pan's observation about a good deed. Then have them comment on its significance. *Paraphrases should resemble this: Helping others is important, no matter where you live; kindness is universally recognized. Students may note that, for the first time, Mrs. Pan sees a common thread in American and Chinese life. They may also note that Mrs. Pan's observation is reflected in the story's title.*

◆ **Build Grammar Skills**

6 **Adverb Clauses** Have students identify the adverb clause that appears in this sentence. Also have them identify the word that it modifies. *The adverb phrase is "when she thought of the empty future of her life." It modifies the verb grieved.*

 Workplace Skills Mini-Lesson

Sensitivity to Others

This mini-lesson is designed to help students explore the value of interpersonal skills, including sensitivity to others, in a variety of work situations.

Introduce the Concept Have students briefly discuss some ways in which Lili Yang shows sensitivity and empathy when she is with Mrs. Pan. Point out that these "people skills" are of central importance in her job as a social worker.

Develop Background Lead students to see that sensitivity to others is essential in any job that deals directly with people. Have students brainstorm to name examples of summer or part-time jobs that fit this description (such as camp counselor and supermarket cashier). Then have them discuss how sensitivity to others might come into play in these roles.

Apply the Information Have pairs of students role-play a situation in which they

show sensitivity as part of an everyday work situation. Alternatively, they could role-play another interaction between Lili Yang and Mrs. Pan that demonstrates the positive results of showing sensitivity.

Assess the Outcome In a class discussion, have students share what they learned as a result of their role-playing.

◆ Literary Focus

❶ Static and Dynamic Characters Have students explain the reason behind the change in Mrs. Pan. Elicit the following response: *She now feels that she has a purpose in life.*

❷ Clarify Help students to understand Mrs. Pan's remarks to her son about arranged marriages by letting them know that arrangements were taken very seriously; go-betweens were sometimes involved, and the bride's and groom's entire families played important roles. Suggest that students review earlier parts of the story to gather more facts and details about traditionally arranged marriages.

◆ Critical Thinking

❸ Infer What does the fact that Mr. Pan and Sophia fell in love but then allowed their marriage to be arranged indicate about them and their attitude toward traditional Chinese culture? *Suggested response: It shows that they respected their elders and traditional customs.*

---

went out of the room quickly because she did not want to sob aloud. She was unseen, for young Mrs. Pan had gone to market and the children were at school, and Lili went away telling herself that it was all absurd, that an old woman from the middle of China who could not speak a word of English would not be able to change this American world, even for her.

Old Mrs. Pan could scarcely wait for her son to come home at noon. She declined to join the family at the table, saying that she must speak to her son first.

❶ When he came in, he saw at once that she was changed. She held up her head and she spoke to him sharply when he came into the room, as though it was her house and not his in which they now were.

"Let the children eat first," she commanded, "I shall need time to talk with you and I am not hungry."

He <u>repressed</u> his inclination to tell her that he was hungry and that he must get back to the office. Something in her look made it impossible for him to be disobedient to her. He went away and gave the children direction and then returned.

"Yes, my mother," he said, seating himself on a small and uncomfortable chair.

Then she related to him with much detail and repetition what had happened that morning; she declared with indignation that she had never before heard of a country where no marriages were arranged for the young, leaving to them the most important event of their lives and that at a time when their judgment was still unripe, and a mistake could bring disaster upon the whole family.

❷ "Your own marriage," she reminded him, "was arranged by your father with great care, two families knowing each other well. Even though you and my daughter-in-law were distant in this country, yet we met her parents through a suitable go-between, and her uncle here stood in her father's place, and your father's friend in place of your father, and so it was all done according to custom though so far away."

❸ Mr. Pan did not have the heart to tell his mother that he and his wife Sophia had fallen in love first, and then, out of kindness to their

elders, had allowed the marriage to be arranged for them as though they were not in love, and as though, indeed, they did not know each other. They were both young people of heart, and although it would have been much easier to be married in the American fashion, they considered their elders.

❸

"What has all this to do with us now, my mother?" he asked.

"This is what is to do," she replied with spirit. "A nice, ugly girl of our own people came here today to see me. She is twenty-seven years old and she is not married. What will become of her?"

"Do you mean Lili Yang?" her son asked.

"I do," she replied. "When I heard that she has no way of being married because, according to the custom of this country, she must wait for a man to ask her—"

Old Mrs. Pan broke off and gazed at her son with horrified eyes.

"What now?" he asked.

"Suppose the only man who asks is one who is not at all suitable?"

"It is quite possible that it often happens thus," her son said, trying not to laugh.

"Then she has no choice," old Mrs. Pan said <u>indignantly</u>. "She can only remain unmarried or accept one who is unsuitable."

"Here she has no choice," Mr. Pan agreed, "unless she is very pretty, my mother, when several men may ask and then she has choice." It was on the tip of his tongue to tell how at least six young men had proposed to his Sophia, thereby distressing him continually until he was finally chosen, but he thought better of it. Would it not be very hard to explain so much to his old mother, and could she understand? He doubted it. Nevertheless, he felt it necessary at least to make one point.

"Something must be said for the man also, my mother. Sometimes he asks a girl who will not have him, because she chooses another,

◆ Build Vocabulary

repressed (ri presd´) *v.*: Held back or restrained

indignantly (in dig´ nənt lē) *adv.*: Feeling anger as a reaction to ungratefulness

346 ◆ *Turning Points*

Cross-Curricular Connection: Social Studies

Arranged Marriages

Throughout history, in many cultures, the practice of arranging marriages has enabled families or countries to create advantageous social, economic, or political ties. Rulers often arranged marriages between their sons and daughters and the relative of a rival nation. In this way, they hoped to ensure peaceful relations between the two countries.

Arranged marriage is not a practice restricted to royalty. As Mrs. Pan explains in this story, arranged marriages were once common in China. Although today many young people choose whom

they will marry, parents still might arrange a marriage; this practice is more common in rural areas. In Japan, also, arranged marriages were more common in the past than they are today, but some marriages are still arranged. In some cases, the bride and groom might not even meet before the wedding. In India, marriages are usually arranged by the parents, but the young person has the right to reject any arrangement. As the Pans discuss in this story, there are advantages and disadvantages to both arranged marriages and allowing young people to choose whom they will marry.

and then his sufferings are intense. Unless he wishes to remain unmarried he must ask a second girl, who is not the first one. Here also is some injustice."

Old Mrs. Pan listened to this attentively and then declared, "It is all barbarous.[5] Certainly it is very embarrassing to be compelled to speak of these matters, man and woman, face to face. They should be spared; others should speak for them."

She considered for a few seconds and then she said with fresh indignation, "And what woman can change the appearance her ancestors have given her? Because she is not pretty is she less a woman? Are not her feelings like any woman's; is it not her right to have husband and home and children? It is well-known that men have no wisdom in such matters; they believe that a woman's face is all she has, forgetting that everything else is the same. They gather about the pretty woman, who is surfeited with them,[6] and leave alone the good woman. And I do not know why heaven has created ugly women always good but so it is, whether here or in our own country, but what man is wise enough to know that? Therefore his wife should be chosen for him, so that the family is not burdened with his follies."

Mr. Pan allowed all this to be said and then he inquired, "What is on your mind, my mother?"

Old Mrs. Pan leaned toward him and lifted her forefinger. "This is what I command you to do for me, my son. I myself will find a husband for this good girl of our people. She is helpless and alone. But I know no one; I am a stranger, and I must depend upon you. In your business there must be young men. Inquire of them and see who

. . . *he saw at once that she was changed.*

stands for them, so that we can arrange a meeting between them and me; I will stand for the girl's mother. I promised it."

Now Mr. Pan laughed heartily. "Oh, my mother!" he cried. "You are too kind, but it cannot be done. They would laugh at me, and do you believe that Lili Yang herself would like such an arrangement? I think she would not. She has been an American too long."

Old Mrs. Pan would not yield, however, and in the end he was compelled to promise that he would see what he could do. Upon this promise she consented to eat her meal, and he led her out, her right hand resting upon his left wrist. The children were gone and they had a quiet meal together, and after it she said she felt that she would sleep.

This was good news, for she had not slept well since she came, and young Mrs. Pan led her into the bedroom and helped her to lie down and placed a thin quilt over her.

When young Mrs. Pan went back to the small dining room where her husband waited to tell her what his mother had said, she listened thoughtfully.

"It is absurd," her husband said, "but what shall we do to satisfy my mother? She sees it as a good deed if she can find a husband for Lili Yang."

Here his wife surprised him. "I can see some good in it myself," she declared. "I have often felt for Lili. It is a problem, and our mother is right to see it as such. It is not only Lili—it is a problem here for all young women, especially if they are not pretty." She looked quizzically at her husband for a moment and then said, "I too used to worry when I was very young, lest I should not find a husband for myself. It is a great burden for a young woman. It would be nice to have someone else arrange the matter."

5. **barbarous** (bär′ bə rəs) *adj.*: Uncivilized.
6. **is surfeited** (surˊ fit əd) **with them:** Has had enough of them.

The Good Deed ◆ 347

Comprehension Check ☑

❹ Have students summarize the argument against American-style marriages that Mrs. Pan makes here. *She argues that men make the mistake of valuing women's looks over their inner qualities; in her view, such "follies" lead to unsound marriages.*

◆ **Critical Thinking**

❺ **Evaluate** Ask students whether they agree or disagree with Mr. Pan's opinion that Lili would not appreciate an arranged meeting. Encourage them to support their responses. *Students who agree may cite the reason Mr. Pan himself gives—"She has been in America too long." Those who disagree may cite the fact that earlier in the story, Lili was deeply moved by Mrs. Pan's talk of marriage and tradition.*

◆ **Reading Strategy**

❻ **Make Inferences About Character** Ask students what they can tell about the young Mrs. Pan from her remarks. *Students will probably infer from her remarks that Mrs. Pan is sensitive and empathetic; she can reach beyond her own circumstance to imagine the experience of someone else and judge it unfair.*

Customize for
Less Proficient Readers
Mrs. Pan uses a formal speech pattern and choice of words that may challenge less proficient readers. Assist these students in previewing some of the words on this page that are not commonly used in conversation. Use the footnotes to clarify *barbarous* and *surfeited*. Discuss with students synonyms for words like *compelled, inquire, follies.* You may wish to follow up by having students role-play or summarize the conversation in their own words.

◆ Critical Thinking

❶ Compare and Contrast Have students analyze this passage and describe how marriage is the same and different in China and in the United States. *Responses may include this: Unhappy or unsuccessful marriages exist in both places, but in the United States such marriages frequently end in divorce.*

▶Critical Viewing◀

❷ Compare Students may say that, like the stores they are used to, the store in the photo draws customers in with an attractive and colorful display of items.

◆ Literary Focus

❸ Static and Dynamic Characters *For the first time, old Mrs. Pan is making a change in her behavior; by opening the curtains to the outside world, she is exhibiting curiosity about her new environment.*

▲ **Critical Viewing** How would you compare this Chinese store with the stores in which you shop? [Compare] ❷

❶ "Remember," he told her, "how often in the old country the wrong men are arranged for and how often the young men leave home because they do not like the wives their parents choose for them."

"Well, so do they here," she said pertly. "Divorce, divorce, divorce!"

"Come, come," he told her. "It is not so bad."

"It is very bad for women," she insisted. "When there is divorce here, then she is thrown out of the family. The ties are broken. But in the old country, it is the man who leaves home and the woman stays on, for she is still the daughter-in-law and her children will belong to the family, and however far away the man wants to go, she has her place and she is safe."

Mr. Pan looked at his watch. "It is late and I must go to the office."

"Oh, your office," young Mrs. Pan said in an uppish[7] voice, "what would you do without it?"

They did not know it but their voices roused old Mrs. Pan in the bedroom, and she opened her eyes. She could not understand what they said for they spoke in English, but she understood

that there was an argument. She sat up on the bed to listen, then she heard the door slam and she knew her son was gone. She was about to lie down again when it occurred to her that it would be interesting to look out of the window to the street and see what young men there were coming to and from. One did not choose men from the street, of course, but still she could see what their looks were.

She got up and tidied her hair and tottered on her small feet over to the window and opening the curtains a little she gazed into the street really for the first time since she came.

◆ **Literary Focus**
How do Mrs. Pan's actions indicate the beginning of a change in her character? ❸

◆ **Build Vocabulary**
assailed (ə sāld´) *v.:* Attacked physically

---

7. **uppish:** Haughty or arrogant.

348 ◆ *Turning Points*

 Speaking and Listening Mini-Lesson

Radio Interview

This mini-lesson supports the Speaking and Listening activity in the Idea Bank on page 355.

Introduce the Concept Point out to students that it is beginning to come clear that old Mrs. Pan is a dynamic character, capable of changing to accommodate new circumstances. Have students offer reasons why old Mrs. Pan would make a particularly good subject for a radio interview.

Develop Background Before students prepare their interviews, suggest that they work to develop two kinds of questions. Specifically, the interviewer will need to do the following:

• Start the interview by asking a few basic questions, such as "Why did you come to this country?"

• Ask questions that follow up on interesting aspects of Mrs. Pan's story.

Apply the Information Have students

prepare, practice, and perform their interviews. Encourage them to ask both questions they have formulated and ones that come naturally to mind as the interview progresses.

Assess the Outcome Have students evaluate their own and their classmates' interviews according to the following criteria: How effectively did the interviewer probe Mrs. Pan for interesting and fresh information? How well did the interviewer listen to and follow up on Mrs. Pan's responses?

She was pleased to see many Chinese men, some of them young. It was still not late, and they loitered in the sunshine before going back to work, talking and laughing and looking happy. It was interesting to her to watch them, keeping in mind Lili Yang and thinking to herself that it might be this one or that one, although still one did not choose men from the street. She stood so long that at last she became tired and she pulled a small chair to the window and kept looking through the parted curtain.

Here her daughter-in-law saw her a little later, when she opened the door to see if her mother-in-law was awake, but she did not speak. She looked at the little satin-clad figure, and went away again, wondering why it was that the old lady found it pleasant today to look out of the window when every other day she had refused the same pleasure.

It became a pastime for old Mrs. Pan to look out of the window every day from then on. Gradually she came to know some of the young men, not by name but by their faces and by the way they walked by her window, never, of course looking up at her, until one day a certain young man did look up and smile. It was a warm day, and she had asked that the window be opened, which until now she had not allowed, for fear she might be <u>assailed</u> by the foreign winds and made ill. Today, however, was near to summer, she felt the room airless and she longed for freshness.

After this the young man habitually smiled when he passed or nodded his head. She was too old to have it mean anything but courtesy and so bit by bit she allowed herself to make a gesture of her hand in return. It was evident that he belonged in a china shop across the narrow street. She watched him go in and come out; she watched him stand at the door in his shirt sleeves on a fine day and talk and laugh, showing, as she observed, strong white teeth set off by two gold ones. Evidently he made money. She did not believe he was married, for she saw an old man who must be his father, who smoked a water pipe, and now and then an elderly woman, perhaps his mother, and a younger brother, but there was no young woman.

She began after some weeks of watching to fix upon this young man as a husband for Lili. But who could be the go-between except her own son?

She confided her plans one night to him, and, as always, he listened to her with courtesy and concealed amusement. "But the young man, my mother, is the son of Mr. Lim, who is the richest man on our street."

"That is nothing against him," she declared.

"No, but he will not submit to an arrangement, my mother. He is a college graduate. He is only spending the summer at home in the shop to help his father."

"Lili Yang has also been to school."

"I know, my mother, but, you see, the young man will want to choose his own wife, and it will not be someone who looks like Lili Yang. It will be someone who—"

He broke off and made a gesture which suggested curled hair, a fine figure and an air. Mrs. Pan watched him with disgust. "You are like all these other men, though you are my son," she said and dismissed him sternly.

Nevertheless, she thought over what he had said when she went back to the window. The young man was standing on the street picking his fine teeth and laughing at friends who passed, the sun shining on his glistening black hair. It was true he did not look at all obedient; it was perhaps true that he was no more wise than other men and so saw only what a girl's face was. She wished that she could speak to him, but that, of course, was impossible. Unless—

She drew in a long breath. Unless she went downstairs and out into that street and crossed it and entered the shop, pretending that she came to buy something! If she did this, she could speak to him. But what would she say, and who would help her cross the street? She did not want to tell her son or her son's wife, for they would suspect her and laugh. They teased her often even now about her purpose, and Lili was so embarrassed by their laughter that she did not want to come anymore.

Old Mrs. Pan reflected on the difficulty of her position as a lady in a barbarous and strange country. Then she thought of her eldest grandson, Johnnie. On Saturday, when her son was at

◆ Literary Focus

❹ Static and Dynamic Characters Encourage students to compare the detail about Mrs. Pan's longing for fresh air with the earlier detail about her dislike of the water in New York. In what way do these details, considered together, reveal a change in Mrs. Pan? *Earlier, she rejected anything that did not remind her of home; now she seems more in harmony with her new surroundings.*

◆ Reading Strategy

❺ Make Inferences About Character Point out that Mrs. Pan makes inferences about the young man she has been watching. Have students identify these inferences as well as the "evidence" Mrs. Pan used to make them. *Mrs. Pan infers that the young man has money and that he is unmarried. The evidence she uses is his gold teeth and the fact that no one resembling a wife dropped by to see him.*

◆ Critical Thinking

❻ Analyze Cause and Effect Ask students to explain the basis upon which Mr. Pan assumes that Mr. Lim will not submit to an arranged marriage. *Students should recognize that Mr. Pan assumes that because Mr. Lim has a bright future and is eligible he has no reason to submit to an arranged marriage.*

◆ Critical Thinking

❼ Analyze Why is the thought of going downstairs and out into the street so terrifying to Mrs. Pan? *Suggested response: She is still afraid of her new environment and of the way people behave.*

◆ Critical Thinking

❽ Connect Have students summarize some of the reasons Mrs. Pan has for calling this country "barbarous." *She feels that people are undisciplined, unmannered, and ignorant of the proper ways of doing things.*

Beyond the Classroom

Career Connection

Retail Sales Like the young man in the story, some students may wish to consider jobs in retail sales. Sales people are required to dress neatly and be well groomed. Some types of sales will require specialized knowledge, but good communication skills and the ability to deal with all kinds of people are probably the most important assets in any retail position. Math skills are also helpful in most retail sales jobs.

Retail positions are available in a wide variety of areas. Automobiles, clothing, food, flowers, electronics, and music are just a few of the areas that employ salespeople. Salespeople can sometimes advance to the position of manager. A manager must have patience and good organizational skills. Students should be aware that a high school diploma and further education in retailing and merchandising will improve their chances to advance to this level. Students who think they might enjoy working in retail can talk to salespeople about their responsibilities and perhaps even take part-time positions after school.

◆ Literary Focus

❶ Static and Dynamic Characters *Mrs. Pan's plan to venture outside marks a significant change in her behavior and attitude. She is overcoming her fear and suspicions of the world outside her window as well as her earlier feelings of "uselessness."*

◆ Build Grammar Skills

❷ Adverb Clauses Have students find two adverb clauses in this sentence and tell how they add to the sentence. *The clauses are because he was a man and because she was not ill. Both answer the question why.*

◆ Critical Thinking

❸ Compare and Contrast What qualities does young Mr. Lim have in common with Lili? *Like Lili he speaks good Chinese, and he is courteous and respectful toward Mrs. Pan.*

Comprehension Check ☑

❹ Ask students to explain why Mrs. Pan is glad to see the young Mr. Lim is "not too handsome." *This makes him a better match for Lili, who is not beautiful.*

◆ Critical Thinking

❺ Compare and Contrast Ask students what similarities they see between the way Mrs. Pan responds to young Mr. Lim and way she responded to Lili. *Students should note that in both cases she feels comfortable talking about her past and about her feelings about living in a strange new place.*

◆ Critical Thinking

❻ Evaluate Ask students if they agree or disagree with Mrs. Pan's major points in this passage, and to explain why. *Many students will disagree that "beauty in a woman made virtue unlikely" and that plain women are grateful to their husbands for marrying them. Some students might state that Mrs. Pan's point of view is sexist, but also recognize that it emerges from her cultural background.*

> **◆ Literary Focus**
> **❶** How is this event an example of what happens to a dynamic character?

his office and her son's wife was at the market, she could coax Johnnie to lead her across the street to the china shop; she would pay him some money, and in the shop she would say he was looking for two bowls to match some that had been broken. It would be an <u>expedition</u>, but she might speak to the young man and tell him—what should she tell him? That must first be planned.

This was only Thursday and she had only two days to prepare. She was very restless during those two days, and she could not eat. Mr. Pan spoke of a doctor whom she indignantly refused to see, because he was a man and also because she was not ill. But Saturday came at last and everything came about as she planned. Her son went away, and then her son's wife, and she crept downstairs with much effort to the sidewalk where her grandson was playing marbles and beckoned him to her. The child was terrified to see her there and came at once, and she pressed a coin into his palm and pointed across the street with her cane.

❷ "Lead me there," she commanded and, shutting her eyes tightly, she put her hand on his shoulder and allowed him to lead her to the shop. Then to her dismay he left her and ran back to play and she stood wavering on the threshold, feeling dizzy, and the young man saw her and came hurrying toward her. To her joy he spoke good Chinese, and the words fell sweetly upon her old ears.

❸ "Ancient One, Ancient One," he chided[8] her kindly. "Come in and sit down. It is too much for you."

He led her inside the cool, dark shop and she sat down on a bamboo chair.

"I came to look for two bowls," she said faintly.

---

8. **chided** (chīd´ əd) *v.*: Gently scolded.

◆ Build Vocabulary

expedition (eks´ pə dish´ ən) *n.*: Journey or voyage for a definite purpose

conferred (kən furd´) *v.*: Granted or bestowed

"Tell me the pattern and I will get them for you," he said. "Are they blue willow pattern or the thousand flowers?"

"Thousand flowers," she said in the same faint voice, "but I do not wish to disturb you."

❸ "I am here to be disturbed," he replied with the utmost courtesy.

He brought out some bowls and set them on a small table before her and she fell to talking with him. He was very pleasant; his rather large face was shining with kindness and he laughed easily. Now that she saw him close, she was glad to notice that he was not too handsome; his nose and mouth were big, and he had big hands and feet.

❹ "You look like a countryman," she said. "Where is your ancestral home?"

"It is in the province of Shantung," he replied, "and there are not many of us here."

"That explains why you are so tall," she said. "These people from Canton are small. We of Szechuen are also big and our language is yours. I cannot understand the people of Canton."

From this they fell to talking of their own country, which he had never seen, and she told him about the village and how her son's father had left it many years ago to do business here in this foreign country and how he had sent for their son and then how she had been compelled to flee because the country was in fragments and torn between many leaders. When she had told this much, she found herself telling him how difficult it was to live here and how strange the city was to her and how she would never have looked out of the window had it not been for the sake of Lili Yang.

❺ "Who is Lili Yang?" he asked.

Old Mrs. Pan did not answer him directly. That would not have been suitable. One does not speak of a reputable young woman to any man, not even one as good as this one. Instead she began a long speech about the virtues of young women who were not pretty, and how beauty in a woman made virtue unlikely, and how a woman not beautiful was always grateful to her husband and did not consider that she had done him a favor by the marriage, but rather that it was he who <u>conferred</u> the favor, so that she served him

❻

Beyond the Classroom

Community Connection
Resources for Recent Immigrants Ask students to suppose that old Mrs. Pan lives in your community. After a period of adjustment, she wishes to learn English and to learn more about practical aspects of life in her new country.

Encourage students to consult resources such as the library, community newspapers, and the Internet to find out the names and specific services of some local organizations and institutions that might assist recent immigrants like Mrs. Pan.

You might also have students find out if any of the local services provide volunteer opportunities. For example, does a local English language program have a need for tutors? Suggest that students write detailed descriptions of any volunteer opportunities they learn about and post their descriptions in your classroom or another area of your school.

---

far better than she could have done were she beautiful.

To all this the young man listened, his small eyes twinkling with laughter.

"I take it that this Lili Yang is not beautiful," he said.

Old Mrs. Pan looked astonished. "I did not say so," she replied with spirit. "I will not say she is beautiful and I will not say she is ugly. What is beautiful to one is not so to another. Suppose you see her sometime for yourself, and then we will discuss it."

"Discuss what?" he demanded.

"Whether she is beautiful."

Suddenly she felt that she had come to a point and that she had better go home. It was enough for the first visit. She chose two bowls and paid for them and while he wrapped them up she waited in silence, for to say too much is worse than to say too little.

When the bowls were wrapped, the young man said courteously, "Let me lead you across the street, Ancient One."

❼ So, putting her right hand on his left wrist, she let him lead her across and this time she did not shut her eyes, and she came home again feeling that she had been a long way and had accomplished much. When her daughter-in-law came home she said quite easily, "I went across the street and bought these two bowls."

Young Mrs. Pan opened her eyes wide. "My mother, how could you go alone?"

"I did not go alone," old Mrs. Pan said tranquilly. "My grandson led me across and young Mr. Lim brought me back."

Each had spoken in her own language with helpful gestures.

❽ Young Mrs. Pan was astonished and she said no more until her husband came home, when she told him. He laughed a great deal and said,

"Do not interfere with our old one. She is enjoying herself. It is good for her."

But all the time he knew what his mother was doing and he joined in it without her knowledge. That is to say, he telephoned the same afternoon from his office to Miss Lili Yang, and when she answered, he said, "Please come and see my old mother again. She asks after you every day. Your visit did her much good."

Lili Yang promised, not for today but for a week hence, and when Mr. Pan went home he told his mother carelessly, as though it were nothing, that Lili Yang had called him up to say she was coming again next week.

Old Mrs. Pan heard this with secret excitement. She had not gone out again, but every day young Mr. Lim nodded to her and smiled, and once he sent her a small gift of fresh ginger root. She made up her mind slowly but she made it up well. When Lili Yang came again, she would ask her to take her to the china shop, pretending that she wanted to buy something, and she would introduce the two to each other; that much she would do. It was too much, but, after all, these were modern times, and this was a barbarous country, where it did not matter greatly whether the old customs were kept or not. The important thing was to find a husband for Lili, who was already twenty-seven years old.

So it all came about, and when Lili walked into her room the next week, while the fine weather still held, old Mrs. Pan greeted her with smiles. She seized Lili's small hand and noticed that the hand was very soft and pretty, as the hands of most plain-faced girls are, the gods being kind to such women and giving them pretty bodies when they see that ancestors have not bestowed pretty faces.

❿ "Do not take off your foreign hat," she told Lili. "I wish to go across the street to that shop and

. . . these were modern times, and this was a barbarous country . . .

❾

The Good Deed ♦ 351

◆ **Literary Focus**

❼ **Static and Dynamic Characters** Ask students to explain in specific terms why the following detail reveals that Mrs. Pan is a dynamic character: "this time she did not shut her eyes." *A possible response is that by opening her eyes to the world around her Mrs. Pan shows that her attitude about her new home is beginning to change; she is becoming more open and curious. This significant change in attitude marks her as a dynamic character.*

◆ **Build Grammar Skills**

❽ **Adverb Clauses** Point out the two adverb clauses in this sentence. Help students see that the adverb clause *until her husband came home* modifies *said* and that the adverb clause *when she told him* modifies *came,* the verb in the first adverb clause. Both adverb clauses answer the question *when.*

◆ **Literary Focus**

❾ **Static and Dynamic Characters** Have students explain the change in Mrs. Pan that this passage reveals. *Students should note her new willingness to adjust to modern times and a "barbarous country"; that is, she is adjusting her ways in response to her new situation.*

◆ **Build Grammar Skills**

❿ **Adverb Clauses** Ask students to identify the adverb clauses in this sentence. *The clauses are as the hands of most plain-faced girls are and when they see that the ancestors . . . Also have students identify the word that each clause modifies. The first clause modifies soft and pretty; the second clause modifies the participle giving.*

Customize for
Bodily Kinesthetic Learners
Ask these students to identify some physical reactions to stress. These may include trembling, increased heart rate, and sweaty palms. Tell students to relate Mrs. Pan's adventure to some challenge they have faced that produced these physical reactions. For Mrs. Pan, crossing the street to go to the shop was a feat of daring.

◆ **Critical Thinking**

❶ **Analyze** Ask students: What is ironic about this passage? *Suggested response: Lili is unaware of Mrs. Pan's real reason for wanting to go to the shop, which is to have Lili meet young Mr. Lim.*

◆ **Reading Strategy**

❷ **Make Inferences About Character** Lili blushes in response to young Mr. Lim's gallant compliment and frank gaze. From this, students may infer that she is feeling shy and nervous.

▶ **Critical Viewing** ◀

❸ **Speculate** Students might imagine that these two people, like Mr. Lim and Mrs. Pan in a previous scene, are talking about their own country.

◆ **Critical Thinking**

❹ **Infer** Ask students why Mrs. Pan is so cautious when talking about marriage. *Students may infer that she is wary of customs in this country and doesn't know if Mr. Lim will be open to her matchmaking plan.*

buy some dishes as a gift for my son's wife. She is very kind to me."

❶ Lili Yang was pleased to see the old lady so changed and cheerful and in all innocence she agreed and they went across the street and into the shop. Today there were customers, and old Mr. Lim was there too, as well as his son. He was a tall, withered man, and he wore a small beard under his chin. When he saw old Mrs. Pan he stopped what he was doing and brought her a chair to sit upon while she waited. As soon as his customer was gone, he introduced himself, saying that he knew her son.

"My son has told me of your honored visit last week," he said. "Please come inside and have some tea. I will have my son bring the dishes, and you can look at them in quiet. It is too noisy here."

She accepted his courtesy, and in a few minutes young Mr. Lim came back to the inner room with the dishes while a servant brought tea.

Old Mrs. Pan did not introduce Lili Yang, for it was not well to embarrass a woman, but young Mr. Lim boldly introduced himself, in English.

"Are you Miss Lili Yang?" he asked. "I am James Lim."

"How did you know my name?" Lili asked, astonished.

"I have met you before, not face to face, but through Mrs. Pan," he said, his small eyes twinkling. "She has told me more about you than she knows."

Lili blushed. "Mrs. Pan is so old-fashioned," she murmured. "You must not believe her."

"I shall only believe what I see for myself," he said gallantly. He looked at her frankly and Lili kept blushing. Old Mrs. Pan had not done her justice, he thought. The young woman had a nice, round face, the sort of face he liked. She was shy, and he liked that also. It was something new.

❷ ◆ **Reading Strategy**
What can you infer about Lili from the way she acts?

Meanwhile old Mrs. Pan watched all this with

▲ **Critical Viewing** What do you think these people are saying? [Speculate] ❸

amazement. So this was the way it was: The young man began speaking immediately, and the young woman blushed. She wished that she knew what they were saying but perhaps it was better that she did not know.

She turned to old Mr. Lim, who was sitting across the square table sipping tea. At least here ❹ she could do her duty. "I hear your son is not married," she said in a tentative way.

"Not yet," Mr. Lim said. "He wants first to finish learning how to be a Western doctor."

"How old is he?" Mrs. Pan inquired.

"He is twenty-eight. It is very old but he did not make up his mind for some years, and the learning is long."

"Miss Lili Yang is twenty-seven," Mrs. Pan said in the same tentative voice.

The young people were still talking in English and not listening to them. Lili was telling James Lim about her work and about old Mrs. Pan. She was not blushing anymore; she had forgotten, it seemed, that he was a young man and she a young woman. Suddenly she stopped and blushed again. A woman was supposed to let a man talk about himself, not about her.

"Tell me about your work," she said. "I wanted to be a doctor, too, but it cost too much."

"I can't tell you here," he said. "There are customers waiting in the shop and it will take a long time. Let me come to see you, may I? I could come on Sunday when the shop is closed. Or we could take a ride on one of the riverboats. Will you? The weather is so fine."

"I have never been on a riverboat," she said. "It would be delightful."

She forgot her work and remembered that he was a young man and that she was a young woman. She liked his big face and the way his black hair fell back from his forehead and she knew that a day on the river could be a day in heaven.

The customers were getting impatient. They began to call out and he got up. "Next Sunday," he said in a low voice. "Let's start early. I'll be at the wharf at nine o'clock."

"We do not know each other," she said, reluctant and yet eager. Would he think she was too eager?

He laughed. "You see my respectable father, and I know old Mrs. Pan very well. Let them guarantee us."

He hurried away, and old Mrs. Pan said immediately to Lili, "I have chosen these four dishes. Please take them and have them wrapped. Then we will go home."

Lili obeyed, and when she was gone, old Mrs. Pan leaned toward old Mr. Lim.

"I wanted to get her out of the way," she said in a low and important voice. "Now, while she is gone, what do you say? Shall we arrange a match? We do not need a go-between. I stand as her mother, let us say, and you are his father. We must have their horoscopes read, of course, but just between us, it looks as though it is suitable, does it not?"

Mr. Lim wagged his head. "If you recommend her, Honorable Old Lady, why not?"

Why not, indeed? After all, things were not so different here, after all.

"What day is convenient for you?" she asked.

"Shall we say Sunday?" old Mr. Lim suggested.

"Why not?" she replied. "All days are good, when one performs a good deed, and what is better than to arrange a marriage?"

"Nothing is better," old Mr. Lim agreed. "Of all good deeds under heaven, it is the best."

They fell silent, both pleased with themselves, while they waited.

❺

Guide for Responding

◆ Literature and Your Life

Reader's Response How do you think this experience will affect Mrs. Pan's life in the United States in the future?

Thematic Focus What, for you, is the most fateful moment in this story about Mrs. Pan? Why?

Group Discussion With a few other students, discuss ways in which the experience of a new immigrant student in your school could be made easier and more comfortable. List your ideas and share them with the other groups in the class.

☑ Check Your Comprehension

1. In the beginning of the story, why can't Mrs. Pan sleep or eat properly?
2. What important idea does Mrs. Pan come up with when she meets Lili Yang?
3. What are two reasons why Mrs. Pan goes to the shop across the street?
4. What is the outcome of Mrs. Pan's visits to the shop across the street?

The Good Deed ◆ 353

◆ Critical Thinking

❺ Interpret How does the date that Mr. Lim proposes represent a blend of old and new ways? *Students should note that young Mr. Lim reminds Lili that they have the older people's blessing. They should also note that it is equally true that the date was arranged in the old, traditional way and that the young people, who were truly interested in each other, arranged it on their own.*

Reinforce and Extend

Answers
◆ Literature and Your Life

Reader's Response Students might answer that the successful match-making experience might open doors for Mrs. Pan, making her more outgoing and happy.

Thematic Focus Possible fateful moments include these: She first decides to make a match for Lili, she first spots Mr. Lim; she pulls back the curtain; she ventures across the street.

☑ Check Your Comprehension

1. She is homesick.
2. She gets the idea of making a marriage match for Lili.
3. She came to buy two bowls and to see young Mr. Lim for herself.
4. Ultimately young Mr. Lim and Lili meet and arrange to go out on a date.

Beyond the Selection

FURTHER READING

Other Works by Pearl S. Buck
The Good Earth
Dragon Seed
China as I See It

Other Works With the Theme of Moving to a New Place
Yellow Raft in Blue Water, Michael Dorris
Giants of the Earth, Ole Rolvaag
We suggest that you preview these works before recommending them to students.

INTERNET

The Internet provides an excellent opportunity for students to learn more about Pearl S. Buck and her work. Encourage students to visit the following Web site for information. Please be aware, however, that the site may have changed from the time we published this information.
http://www.cup.org/Books/conn/pearl.html
    We *strongly recommend* that you preview the site before you send students to it.

353

Answers

◆ Critical Thinking

1. She feels displaced and useless in her new country. Her depression causes her to eat and sleep poorly.
2. Lili and Mrs. Pan both respect their heritage; Lili is more modern.
3. She can discuss her old country and both men show traditional respect for her.
4. Choosing one's own mate clashes with the custom of arranged marriages. Both cultures respect family bonds.
5. Students might say it is important to combine old and new ways, for example, reading classic literature but also using the Internet.
6. Students might think people should be free to choose their own partners; they may think that arranged marriages for religious or economic purposes are appropriate.

◆ Reading Strategy

1. Young Mrs. Pan is kind, respectful, and to some extent, traditional.
2. Lili is empathetic and sensitive and is respectful of her elders.
3. (a) They are interested in each other. (b) They plan a date.

◆ Literary Focus

1. Old Mr. Lim and young Mrs. Pan are static characters: their behavior and attitudes do not change.
2. She leaves the apartment and cheers up.
3. At the beginning of the story she is depressed, homesick, and unwilling to adapt; by the end she is more open and optimistic and has begun to reach out to others.

◆ Build Vocabulary

Using the Root -pel-
1. c   2. b   3. a

Using the Word Bank
1. *Contemplatively*—thoughtfully; *contemptuously*—scornfully
2. *Compel*—force to do something; *ask*—to make a request
3. *Abashed*—embarrassed; *ashamed*—disgraced
4. *Repressed*—held back; *impressed*—affected the mind favorably
5. *Revere*—regard with deep respect; *respect*—admire or honor
6. *Indignantly*—angrily reacting to something that is not right; *insistently*—demandingly
7. *Assail*—to attack physically; *assist*—to help

Guide for Responding (continued)

◆ Critical Thinking

INTERPRET
1. Identify the causes of old Mrs. Pan's depression. How does her depression affect her physical health? **[Analyze]**
2. In what ways are Lili and Mrs. Pan similar? How are they different? **[Compare and Contrast]**
3. Why does Mrs. Pan enjoy her conversations with old Mr. Lim and his son? **[Draw a Conclusion]**
4. In what ways does the story reveal a clash of cultures? In what ways does it reveal similarities between cultures? **[Deduce]**

APPLY
5. Do you think it is important for people to hold on to the old as well as the new? Use details from life to support your answer. **[Apply]**

EVALUATE
6. In what situations, if any, would arranged marriages be appropriate in modern American society? Explain. **[Make a Judgment]**

◆ Reading Strategy

MAKE INFERENCES ABOUT CHARACTER
You can learn a lot about characters by **making inferences**—logical assumptions—about them based on their words, thoughts, and actions.
1. What can you infer about young Mrs. Pan based on the fact that old Mrs. Pan likes her?
2. What can you infer about Lili based on her treatment of Mrs. Pan?
3. (a) What inferences can you make about Lili's and Mr. Lim's feelings about each other? (b) On what did you base your inferences?

◆ Literary Focus

STATIC AND DYNAMIC CHARACTERS
Mrs. Pan is a **dynamic character**, a character who changes during the course of a literary work. **Static characters** do not change.
1. Identify two static characters in this story. Explain.
2. What actions does Mrs. Pan take that show you she is changing?
3. How is Mrs. Pan's character different at the end of the story from her character at the beginning?

354 ◆ Turning Points

◆ Build Vocabulary

USING THE ROOT -pel-
Knowing that the root *-pel-* means "to drive" or "to push," match each word that contains the root with its definition.

1. repel   a. drive forward
2. expel   b. drive out
3. propel   c. push away

USING THE WORD BANK
Explain the difference between the following pairs of words.

1. contemplatively, contemptuously
2. expedition, expedite
3. abashed, ashamed
4. repressed, impressed
5. revere, respect
6. indignantly, insistently
7. assail, assist
8. conferred, inferred

◆ Build Grammar Skills

ADVERB CLAUSES
Pearl S. Buck frequently uses adverb clauses to tell *where, when, why, how, to what extent,* or *under what conditions* the actions in the story occur.

> An **adverb clause** is a subordinate clause—a group of words that contains a subject and a verb but cannot stand alone—that modifies a verb, an adjective, or an adverb.

Practice Copy the following sentences into your notebook. Underline the adverb clause and circle the word it modifies.
1. Mrs. Pan worried because Lili was not married.
2. Mr. Pan listened when his mother revealed her plan.
3. Mrs. Pan watched while they talked.

Writing Application Add one or more adverb clauses to make each sentence more specific and informative.
1. Mrs. Pan decided to cross the street.
2. Mrs. Pan's daughter-in-law spoke slowly to Mrs. Pan.
3. Young Mr. Lim met Lili Yang.

---

8. *Conferred*—granted or bestowed; *inferred*—made logical assumptions

◆ Build Grammar Skills

Practice
1. Mrs. Pan (worried) because Lili was not married.
2. Mr. Pan (listened) when his mother revealed her plan.
3. Mrs. Pan (watched) while they talked.

Writing Application
Sample sentences:
1. Mrs. Pan decided to cross the street when she saw the young Mr. Lim.
2. Mrs. Pan's daughter-in-law spoke slowly to Mrs. Pan because she wanted to be clearly understood.
3. Young Mr. Lim met Lili Yang after Mrs. Pan made certain arrangements.

 Writer's Solution

For additional instruction and practice, use the lesson in the **Language Lab CD-ROM** on Varying Sentence Structure and page 52 on Adverb Clauses in the *Writer's Solution Grammar Practice Book.*

Build Your Portfolio

Idea Bank

Writing

1. **Letters** Write two letters from old Mrs. Pan to a friend who still lives in China. In the first letter, tell how you felt when you first arrived in the United States. In the second letter, explain how you felt after introducing Lili and James.

2. **Story Segment** Write a continuation of this story, telling of another adventure in which Mrs. Pan adjusts to an aspect of life in the United States.

3. **Newsletter** Create a newsletter that tells about events and services that would help a recent immigrant, like Mrs. Pan, to adjust to life in your community. **[Social Studies Link]**

Speaking and Listening

4. **Unrehearsed Speech** When James asks Mrs. Pan about Lili Yang, she launches into an unrehearsed speech. Have a partner ask your opinion on an issue and speak for a full minute on the topic.

5. **Radio Interview** Imagine that old Mrs. Pan is interviewed for a radio program about the experiences of recent immigrants. With a partner, develop questions and responses. Perform your interview for the class. **[Performing Arts Link]**

Projects

6. **Multimedia Presentation** Give a multimedia presentation that focuses on Chinese culture and traditions. Include in your presentation art, photos, maps, music, and, if possible, food. **[Social Studies Link]**

7. **Timeline** Create a timeline of the events in "The Good Deed." You may choose to represent the events as a series of quotations from the story, as illustrations, or in some other way.

Writing Mini-Lesson

Award Speech on a Character

Any number of characters from "The Good Deed" could win a community award for helping others in their Chinese American community in New York City. Write a brief **speech** introducing a story character to whom you would give an award. In your speech, identify the award, the character, and the reasons he or she is receiving the award. The following tips will help you create a clear picture of your award winner.

> **Writing Skills Focus: Create a Main Impression**
> **Create a main impression** that makes clear to your audience why the character is winning an award. First identify a quality—such as kindness, determination, or courage—that you would like your audience to recognize in the character. Then support this impression by sharing appropriate accomplishments, anecdotes, and insights.

Prewriting After you have decided on a character and an award, brainstorm for a list of qualities that relate to the award. Choose the quality you feel is strongest in the character and list accomplishments and experiences that demonstrate this quality.

Drafting You don't have to begin your speech by identifying your character. You may want to start building the impression first, naming the award, and then revealing the name of your character. However you choose to organize your speech, be sure to include details that are related only to the award and contribute to your main impression.

Revising Ask a partner to read your draft and identify the main impression he or she has of the character after reading your speech of introduction. Ask your partner how you can strengthen the main impression you want to create.

The Good Deed ◆ 355

Idea Bank

Customizing for *Performance Levels*
Following are suggestions for matching Idea Bank topics with your students' performance levels:

    Less Advanced Students: 1, 7
    Average Students: 2, 4, 6
    More Advanced Students: 3, 5

Customizing for *Learning Modalities*
Following are suggestions for matching Idea Bank topics with your students' learning modalities:

    Visual/Spatial: 6, 7
    Interpersonal: 5
    Verbal/Linguistic: 4, 5
    Logical/Mathematical: 7

Writing Mini-Lesson
Refer students to the Writing Handbook, page 965, for instruction on the writing process, and page 967 for further information on exposition.

Writer's Solution

Writers at Work Videodisc
Have students view the videodisc segment for Ch. 3 in which Rudolfo Anaya talks about keeping an audience in mind. Discuss with students which of Anaya's techniques for capturing an audience would work best for their award speech, and why.

Play frames 23159 to 33243

Writing Lab CD-ROM
Have students complete the tutorial on Exposition. Follow these steps:
1. Have students use the cluster diagram tool to help them identify the main impression they want to create about their character. This tool will also help them to identify and organize the accomplishments, anecdotes, and insights that support the main impression.
2. Suggest that students use the revision checker for language variety to help them spot repeated words in their speeches. They can then revise to correct this problem.

Sourcebook
Have students use Chapter 3, Exposition (pp. 63–89), for additional support.

✓ ASSESSMENT OPTIONS

Formal Assessment, Selection Test, pp. 88–90, and Assessment Resources Software. The selection test is designed so that it can be easily customized to the performance levels of your students.

Alternative Assessment, p. 26, includes options for less advanced students, more advanced students, verbal/linguistic learners, visual/spatial learners, logical/mathematical learners, and bodily/kinesthetic learners.

PORTFOLIO ASSESSMENT
Use the following rubrics in the *Alternative Assessment* booklet to assess student writing:
Letters: Comparison and Contrast Rubric, p. 103
Story Segment: Fiction Narrative Rubric p. 95
Newsletter: Technical Description Rubric, p. 115

CONNECTIONS TO TODAY'S WORLD

NBA at Fifty: The Greatest Ever
Frank Deford

from Rare Air
Michael Jordan

OBJECTIVES

1. To read, comprehend, and interpret two essays
2. To relate the essays to personal experience
3. To respond to the essays through writing, speaking and listening, and projects

SKILLS INSTRUCTION

Speaking and Listening:
Television Interview

Critical Viewing:
Analyze, Speculate, Connect

PORTFOLIO OPPORTUNITIES

Writing: Hall-of-Fame Placard; Sports Poem; Fitness Is Fundamental
Speaking and Listening: Television Interview
Project: Virtual Reality One on One

Thematic Connection

Fateful Moments Have students identify the fateful moment in Pearl Buck's story "The Good Deed," and compare it with the impact of the first Knicks' game. *The fateful moment occurs when Mrs. Pan helps Lili. Both turning points have far-reaching consequences: Mrs. Pan's successful match probably leads to marriage for Lili and a renewed sense of purpose for herself, and the first Knicks' game leads to great success for the NBA.*

◆ Background for Understanding

Professional basketball debuted in 1896, when a group of players charged admission to cover the cost of renting a court in Trenton, New Jersey. From the proceeds, each player got $15; the captain got a bonus of $1!

More About the Authors

Frank Deford Did you ever wonder about the people behind the scenes who show us the true excitement of sports—the sportswriters? Deford is one of the best. Colleague Doug Looney calls Deford an elegant, eloquent writer, the best writer ever at *Sports Illustrated*.

Michael Jordan Jordan holds the all-time NBA playoff record for the most points scored in a single game—63! He has the league's highest-scoring average, too. Jordan was the NBA's most valuable player in 1991, 1992, and 1993.

Thematic Connection

FATEFUL MOMENTS

Often we don't know a moment is fateful until after it occurs. For example, no one could have imagined how successful the National Basketball Association (NBA) would become when the first game between the New York Knicks tipped off on November 1, 1946.

Today, an NBA ticket is one of the hottest tickets in town! In celebration of fifty successful years, the NBA announced a list of the "50 Greatest Players," identifying the biggest superstars from 1947 to 1997.

The following selections capture some results of that fateful moment when the first NBA game was held. In "NBA at Fifty: The Greatest Ever," sportswriter Frank Deford introduces you to fifty basketball superstars who have each created their share of unforgettable moments. The excerpt from *Rare Air* gives an insight from one of those players, Michael Jordan.

THE BIRTH OF THE NBA

The first professional basketball league was the six-team National League, formed in 1898. Other leagues, including the National Basketball League (NBL) and the Basketball Association of America (BAA), were formed in the 1930's and 1940's. However, it wasn't until November 1946 that the first NBA game was played. Today, basketball's popularity is at an all-time high. Superstars of the 1980's and 1990's—like Michael Jordan, Larry Bird, Magic Johnson, and Shaquille O'Neal—sent attendance and television ratings soaring into the record books. Individually and collectively, the fifty players on this list are all responsible for turning basketball into one of the most popular professional and recreational sports in the world.

FRANK DEFORD (1938–)

Frank Deford has been voted "Sportswriter of the Year" six times! This Baltimore native has written for *Sports Illustrated*, *Newsweek*, National Public Radio and ESPN Radio. Deford is also the author of eleven books—including his famous football novel *Everybody's All-American*, which was made into a movie.

MICHAEL JORDAN (1963–)

Amazingly, basketball superstar Michael Jordan was cut from his high-school team in his sophomore year! Jordan made the high-school team in his junior year and quickly became its star player. Today, Jordan has established himself as one of the greatest basketball players of all time. He has led his team to numerous NBA championships and has won many individual awards, including Most Valuable Player of the Year and Defensive Player of the Year.

NBA at Fifty: The Greatest Ever

Frank Deford

Sports is perhaps the only entertainment where we actually expect the best to be succeeded by someone better. If you suggested that anyone today could surpass Beethoven, or Shakespeare, or Caruso or Michelangelo, you'd be laughed at. But we accept it that athletes are always improving—and, of all sports, basketball seems to advance the most dramatically.

In that sense, basketball is like modern technology or science. But, in fact, it is quite the reverse. It is *not* improved technique which primarily makes for improved basketball players.

Rather, the best players—the stars on this list of the 50 greatest players in NBA history—are originals. They are unique and idiosyncratic.

 Perhaps it's not fair to compare other sports, but, really, Mark McGwire swings for a home run pretty much exactly like Babe Ruth did 70 years ago. And John Elway throws a pass in the same magic way as Johnny Unitas or Sammy Baugh.

But the best basketball players seem to have invented themselves. The first time I saw big George Mikan, when I was a boy, or when I saw Elgin Baylor turning a horizontal move into a vertical one, or when I saw Earl Monroe yo-yoing at a little black college called Winston-Salem State, I just instinctively recognized that what I was seeing was seminal and pure. For lack of a better word . . . yes, it

The Fifty Greatest Players In NBA History 1947–1997

Kareem Abdul-Jabbar	Karl Malone
Nate Archibald	Moses Malone
Paul Arizin	Pete Maravich
Charles Barkley	Kevin McHale
Rick Barry	George Mikan
Elgin Baylor	Earl Monroe
Dave Bing	Hakeem Olajuwon
Larry Bird	Shaquille O'Neal
Wilt Chamberlain	Robert Parish
Bob Cousy	Bob Pettit
Dave Cowens	Scottie Pippen
Billy Cunningham	Willis Reed
Dave DeBusschere	Oscar Robertson
Clyde Drexler	David Robinson
Julius Erving	Bill Russell
Patrick Ewing	Dolph Schayes
Walt Frazier	Bill Sharman
George Gervin	John Stockton
Hal Greer	Isiah Thomas
John Havlicek	Nate Thurmond
Elvin Hayes	Wes Unseld
Earvin Johnson	Bill Walton
Sam Jones	Jerry West
Michael Jordan	Lenny Wilkens
Jerry Lucas	James Worthy

NBA at Fifty: The Greatest Ever ◆ 357

Interest Grabber To capture students' interest, ask them to suppose they are putting together a basketball team that they hope will go all the way to the top. What qualities would they look for in individual players? Invite students to rank ten qualities they think a professional athlete should have from most to least important. Here are some qualities to consider: *strong character, good attitude, individuality, intelligence, focus, speed, shooting ability, discipline, ball handling skills,* and *team spirit.* Let students know that in reading these essays they will have the opportunity to see what a major sportswriter and a basketball superstar think are the most winning qualities in a player.

Customize for
English Language Learners
Some of these students may not be familiar with the basketball jargon sprinkled throughout these essays. Help them to "translate" terms such as *yo-yoing* (moving from one position to another repeatedly) and *get to the hole* (get to an opening in the other team's defensive formation).

Customize for
More Advanced Students
Challenge more advanced learners to evaluate the *tone* of Deford's essay. Help students first isolate terms such as *blessed by God, superiority,* and *majesty* to identify Deford's worshipful tone. Ask students to consider whether Deford's reverent tone fits his subject matter, and why or why not.

Develop Understanding

◆ Critical Thinking
❶ Compare and Contrast Have students summarize the difference Deford finds between the best basketball players and the best football and baseball players. *He finds the best basketball players to be unique while the best football and baseball players do not distinguish themselves through their unique or individual styles.*

◆ Beyond the Classroom

Career Connection
Sportswriter In addition to writing articles and books on sports, Deford is a sports analyst on the radio.

Have interested students gather information about the requirements for a career as a sportswriter or sportscaster. Students can start by locating the biographies of famous sportswriters and sportscasters. They can also request catalogues from colleges and universities that have journalism programs.

Community Connection
Sports Areas Most communities have an area designated for sports, whether the area is a high-school gym, a park with a baseball diamond and basketball hoops, or a major sports arena that is the home of a professional team. Encourage students to visit their local sports areas and jot down its best and worst features. Students can later gather in small groups to compare their lists and make recommendations for how their sports areas could be improved.

◆ Critical Thinking

❶ Infer Ask students to explain why Deford would recognize the best moves of the players he mentions even if he could not see their features. *He would recognize their best moves because each of them has a particularly individual style of play.*

❷ Clarification Although he does not like having attention called to it, Michael Jordan is well-known for sticking out his tongue in concentration. Discuss with students that Deford is making the point that details like this are not as apparent in sports such as football or hockey, in which players heads and often faces are covered with helmets or face guards. Deford also says that basketball players "perform so close to us." Discuss with students how television brings players of all sports closer to the spectators.

❸ Assess Ask students to weigh the importance of a single player or participant in any sport or group effort. Do students agree with Deford's assertion that in basketball particularly one player can be extraoridinarily important? *Some students may agree, based on the statistic he cites, others may feel that in all team sports, victories and defeats are a group responsibility.*

▶Critical Viewing◀

❹ Analyze Details students might mention include Larry Bird's unique dribbling style, Shaquille O'Neal's look of concentration.

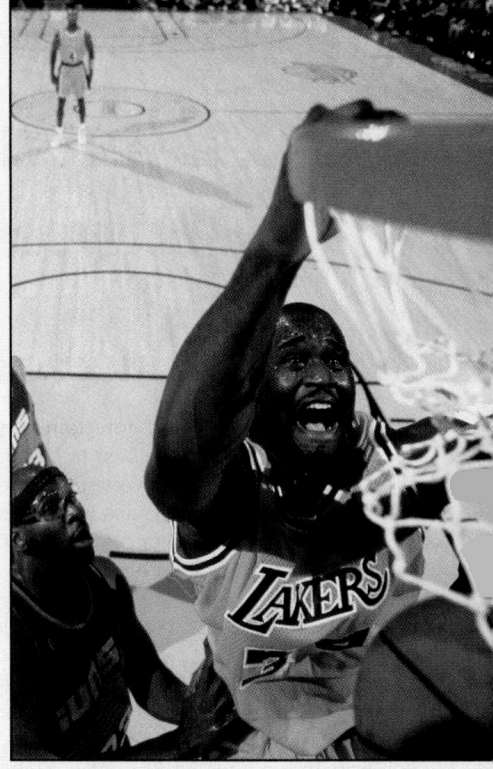

CONNECTIONS TO TODAY'S WORLD

was genius.

And most all of the 50 players selected are, in the Latin, *sui generis*—one of a kind. Put most of them in silhouette, and tell them to put on their best move, and I will recognize them. That's The Big O, that's Dr. J, that's Kareem, that's Magic, that's Larry. It may be 30 years later, and while much of the sport may have improved altogether, nobody yet can put a shot softly off the glass like Sam Jones did. Trust me.

But, of course, it is not just their moves that distinguish the basketball elite. We feel like we know basketball players, for they perform so close to us. They have faces, not uniforms. They have expressions, not numbers. We even know one tongue! There are 50 *people* on this list. Fifty friends.

Most of them can also be identified as win-

ners. One player can mean so much in this sport, that there is an inordinately high correlation between personal superiority and team victory. Indeed, of the 50, 38 played on NBA championship teams—and six of those who haven't won are still playing. Only three of the 50 never made the Finals. That's no accident.

The 50 are blessed by God with talent and possessed of their own desire and discipline. They are intelligent, most all of them and as extraordinary as they are, they know how to subjugate their own skill to their team.

But above all, to each his own special majest —which is why I think of these 50 more as artists than as athletes.

◀ **Critical Viewing** What details in these pictures of Larry Bird and Shaquille O'Neal show that they have the qualities Deford describes? [**Analyze**]

358 ◆ *Turning Points*

Speaking and Listening Mini-Lesson

Television Interview

This mini-lesson supports the Speaking and Listening activity in the Idea Bank on page 361.

Introduce the Concept Let students know that the key to a successful interview is preparation. An interviewer should have a basic understanding of the subject's field; he or she should brush up on special terms or issues related to that field; he or she should have a list of prepared questions.

Develop Background Before students stage their interviews, have them prepare questions using these guidelines:

- Questions that can't be answered with *yes* or *no* get better responses. These questions often begin with *who, what, when, where, why,* or *how.*

- Be prepared to ask follow-up questions to clarify confusing points or get more detail.

- Keep in mind the knowledge level of your audience.

Apply the Information Have students use these guidelines as they conduct their interviews. Remind them to make sure the subject is finished speaking before asking another question or making a comment.

Assess the Outcome Pairs of students can evaluate each other's interviews by answering these questions: How well suited were questions to audience knowledge level? How well prepared was the interviewer?

FROM Rare Air:

Michael on Michael

Michael Jordan

I always felt I could shoot. When I came out of college everyone said, "He can't shoot the jumper." I never had to. I could penetrate zones in college. And teams played me one-on-one at North Carolina. They never double-teamed me. I always had a quick enough first step to get to the hole. I never looked to be aggressive offensively in college because I was playing in a system and I was learning the game.

That was the education I got from Dean Smith. Coming out of high school, I had all the ability in the world but I didn't know the game. Dean taught me the game, when to apply speed, how to use your quickness, when to use that first step, or how to apply certain skills in certain situations. I gained all that knowledge so that when I got to the pros, it was just a matter of applying the information.

A lot of people say Dean Smith held me to under 20 points a game.

▲ Critical Viewing What do you think is going through the mind of the person trying to guard Michael Jordan in this photograph? [Speculate]

NBA at Fifty: The Greatest Ever/from Rare Air: Michael on Michael ◆ 359

◆ **Critical Thinking**

❺ **Clarify** Encourage students to use context clues to try to clarify these technical terms. Ask students what resources they might use to check their assumptions. *Students might use a book on basketball, a related site on the Internet, or they might ask a fellow student or a family member who follows basketball.* Then ask students who are particularly knowledgeable about basketball and its terminology to define the following terms for the class: *shoot the jumper; penetrate zones; double-teamed me.*

◆ **Critical Thinking**

❻ **Compare and Contrast** Have students compare Jordan's athleticism before and after his work with Dean Smith. *Before his work with Smith, Jordan was talented but unformed; after Smith, Jordan was able to combine his talent with the concrete skills Smith taught him to become a much better athlete.*

▶ **Critical Viewing** ◀

❼ **Speculate** Students might suggest that the guard is probably unhappy and frustrated because Jordan is outmaneuvering him.

Cross-Curricular Connection: Physical Education

The History of Basketball

James Naismith, a physical education instructor at what is now Springfield College, invented the game of basketball in 1891. He created the game to provide a challenging team sport that could be played indoors during the winter months. The first game was played with a soccer ball, and players tried to shoot the ball into a peach basket attached to the gym's balcony railing, about ten feet above the floor. The original rules were first published in the school's newspaper in 1892. The game quickly became popular, and some modifications followed: Metal hoops were replaced with net bags in 1893 and larger basketballs replaced the soccer balls; the backboard was added in 1894; bottomless nets were introduced in 1913.

The first intercollegiate basketball game using five-man teams was played between the University of Chicago and the University of Iowa. The game was played in Iowa City, Iowa, on January 16, 1896. The University of Chicago defeated the University of Iowa, with a score of 15–12.

◆ Critical Thinking

❶ Evaluate Michael Jordan claims that ability is the least important requirement for success as a professional basketball player. Have students debate this issue, relating their opinions now to the ranking they prepared in the beginning of this lesson.

◆ Critical Thinking

❷ Interpret Ask: What do you think Jordan means when he uses the word *heart* in this sentence?
Interpretations might include these: He means generosity toward himself and other players; he means to be focused, or to have your whole heart in what you're doing; he means a strong enough love of the game to carry him through tough situations.

▶Critical Viewing◀

❸ Connect Students might suggest the following: *Jordan looks highly focused, he's looking directly at the ball; a viewer can conclude that he has his whole heart in what he is doing.*

ONNECTIONS TO TODAY'S WORLD

Dean Smith gave me the knowledge to score 37 points a game and that's something people don't understand.

• • • •

❶ If I was looking for players I would want around me, I'd look for quickness, heart, and strong fundamentals. Ability comes last. If you've got a good mind for the game, you can overcome the lack of ability in certain areas.

Look at Larry Bird. He's a prime example. He was slow. He couldn't jump that well. He had good hands, good ball handling and shooting skills. But he was very smart. He could outthink his opponents and he had a big heart.

❷ Heart is probably the biggest key to success in basketball at this level. There are a lot of players who pass through the NBA with the ability, but they don't have the heart or the intelligence to get the job done. That's the divider, always has been.

Give me four guys of average ability with strong fundamentals and big hearts and I'll take my chances every time. Big games come down to those two things. The team that executes is usually the team that reaches inside for that little extra. I want those kinds of guys with me.

▲ **Critical Viewing** How does this picture of Michael Jordan show what it means to have heart? [**Connect**]

360 ◆ *Turning Points*

Cross-Curricular Connection: Social Studies

How is a basketball made? An official NBA ball starts with a piece of top-grade cow-hide, prepared by a tanning process (a process that turns cowhide into leather) that goes back to the days of cave-dwellers. The hide is then imprinted with tiny pebbles to give it the right texture. The inner part of the ball is created from a molded form wound with 6,890 feet of glue-coated nylon thread. The leather covering is glued to the inner part and then put under 140 pounds of pressure to force out any air bubbles. A finished regulation ball

must measure between 29 ½ and 29 ⅞ inches around. It is inflated to an air pressure of 7 ½ to 8 ½ pounds per square inch. Official NBA balls are "highly guarded": if they end up in the stands, spectators are not allowed to take them home!

• Discuss with students why it might be important for all teams to play with a special, regulation ball.

• Have students who play basketball compare the balls they play with to the official NBA basketball.

Thematic Connection

TURNING POINTS

Basketball has come a long way since its early days of soccer balls and peach baskets. The creation of the NBA marked a turning point in the popularity of basketball because it introduced the world to this little-known sport. Since the establishment of the NBA, the league has grown immensely in popularity, and basketball is rapidly becoming the most popular sport in the world.

1. How does breaking a scoring or most-games-played record serve as a turning point in basketball history?
2. Frank Deford states that in sports, people "expect the best to be succeeded by someone better." Do you agree with this statement, or do you believe that some records will never be broken?
3. What do the fateful moments in a basketball game have in common with the fateful moments in a short story or novel?

Idea Bank

Writing

1. **Hall-of-Fame Placard** Imagine that you work for a sports hall of fame, and write a description of your favorite athlete to appear beside his or her picture. In your placards, include vivid descriptive details that capture the players' contributions to the game.

2. **Sports Poem** A number of memorable poems, stories, and novels have been written about sports. Write a poem about your favorite sport or athlete.

3. **Fitness Is Fundamental** All the athletes mentioned in Deford's article had to train vigorously to be in top physical condition. Write a brief report in which you stress the value of a regular exercise routine. **[Science Link]**

Speaking and Listening

4. **Television Interview** Work with a partner to stage an interview with a famous athlete. One of you should assume the role of reporter and the other should take on the role of the athlete. Ask and answer questions that you've always wanted to ask the athlete. Present your interview to your classmates. **[Performing Arts Link]**

Project

5. **Virtual Reality One on One** Imagine that you can create your ideal virtual reality video game that enables players to go one on one with their favorite basketball player. Describe the computer graphics, sound effects, and details of your game. If possible, provide sketches of what the screen will look like. **[Art Link]**

NBA at Fifty: The Greatest Ever/from Rare Air: Michael on Michael ◆ 361

Beyond the Selection

FURTHER READING
Other Work by Frank Deford
Alex: The Life of a Child

Other Works About Turning Points in Sports
I Am Third by Gale Sayers
Comeback Stars of Pro Sports by Nathan Aaseng
Shoeless Joe by W. P. Kinsella
Hoops by Walter Dean Myers

We suggest that you preview these works before recommending them to students.

INTERNET
Students can learn more at the following Web sites. Please be aware, however, that these sites may have changed from the time we published this information.

For background about Deford and his thoughts on sports and sportswriters today, go to: **http://bon.boulder.co.us/campuspress/Deford.html**

For information about Jordan, go to: **http//www.evansville.net/~lhess/Jordan23.html**

We *strongly recommend* that you preview the sites before you send students to them.

Reinforce and Extend

Answers
Thematic Connection

1. Breaking a scoring record is a turning point because it sets a new benchmark for success; breaking a most-games-played record represents a turning point in the career of the player by marking the length and success of his or her career.

2. Some students may agree with this statement because better training and equipment, as well as sports psychology, are factors that contribute to ever-greater accomplishments; students who disagree might say that an athlete's capacity is finite, that perhaps people just have the perception that current athletes are better than past ones.

3. In both a basketball game and in a short story, fateful moments affect consequences. For example, in Buck's story, Mrs. Pan's decision to make a match resulted in a major change in Lili's life. Likewise, in basketball, a fateful moment like missing a key shot in a close game could result in the loss of the game.

 Idea Bank
Customizing for
Performance Levels
Following are suggestions for matching Idea Bank topics with your students' performance levels:
Less Advanced Students: 1
Average Students: 2, 3, 4
More Advanced Students: 5

Guide for Reading

1. To read, comprehend, and interpret poems and a story
2. To relate poems and a story to personal experience
3. To evaluate a writer's message in poems and a story
4. To identify theme
5. To build vocabulary in context and learn the word root -*sat*-
6. To recognize and use present participial phrases
7. To write a letter to the editor using elaboration to make writing personal
8. To respond to the story through writing, speaking and listening, and projects

SKILLS INSTRUCTION

Vocabulary:
Word Roots: -*sat*-
Grammar:
Present Participial Phrases
Reading Strategy:
Evaluate a Writer's Message
Literary Focus:
Theme

Writing:
Elaboration to Make Writing Personal
Speaking and Listening:
Telephone Conversation; Improvisational Skit (Teacher's Edition)
Critical Viewing:
Analyze

PORTFOLIO OPPORTUNITIES

Writing: Interview; Visitor's Guide; Allegory
Writing Mini-Lesson: Letter to the Editor
Speaking and Listening: Telephone Conversation; Improvisational Skit
Projects: Two Maps; Auto Safety Presentation

Nguyen Thi Vinh *(1924–   )*

A prominent writer in Saigon (Vietnam) before the Communist takeover in 1975, Nguyen Thi Vinh has written novels, poems, and short stories, as well as being an editor and a publishing executive. Her collection *The Poetry of Nguyen Thi Vinh* was published in 1973. She remained in Vietnam for eight years after the fall of Saigon, but then joined her family in Norway, as a refugee.

Dahlia Ravikovitch *(1936–   )*

The intensely personal poems of this Israeli author also use images of history, religion, and mythology. A native of Tel Aviv, Dahlia Ravikovitch has translated the poetry of William Butler Yeats and T. S. Eliot. In turn, two of her books, *Dress of Fire* and *The Window*, have been translated into English.

Karl Shapiro *(1913–   )*

American poet Karl Shapiro has been a college professor, a critic, and an editor, as well as a Pulitzer Prize-winning poet. Shapiro has said that he would like to see the elimination "of the line between poetry and prose." The harsh realism of "Auto Wreck" reflects Shapiro's preferred poetic style.

Franz Kafka *(1883–1924)*

In his will, the Czech writer Franz Kafka asked that all his unpublished literary works be burned and all others be allowed to go out of print. Fortunately, his wishes were ignored, and much of Kafka's major work was published after his death.

Kafka's writing reflects the anxiety and alienation that has pervaded much of twentieth-century society. "Before the Law" is an allegory—a narrative in which the actions of characters represent abstract ideas and moral principles.

◆ Build Vocabulary

WORD ROOTS: -*sat*-
Have you ever wanted something so badly that you kept asking and asking for it? You might say that your desire was *insatiable*. *Insatiable* has as its root -*sat*- and comes from the Latin *satiare* meaning "to fill entirely." An *insatiable* desire, curiosity, or appetite, therefore, is one that cannot be filled.

WORD BANK
Before you read, preview this list of words from the selections.

deranged
convalescents
banal
expedient
importunity
contemplation
insatiable

◆ Build Grammar Skills

PRESENT PARTICIPIAL PHRASES
A **present participial phrase** consists of a present participle—a verb form ending in -*ing*—plus any other words that go with it. Participial phrases function as adjectives.

Nguyen Thi Vihn writes these lines in "Thoughts of Hanoi":

> jubilant voices of children
> *stumbling through the alphabet,*

The participial phrase *stumbling through the alphabet* modifies *children*. It identifies *what kind* of children.

Notice other participial phrases that these writers use to add detail to their work.

More About the Authors

During the day, **Franz Kafka** worked as a lawyer for an insurance company; at night he wrote feverishly. However Kafka might have felt about his daily work, it is documented that he was well liked by the people with whom he worked.

In his essays, **Karl Shapiro** expresses opposition to rules for making or judging art.

Nguyen Thi Vinh writes short stories as well as poetry.

Dahlia Ravikovitch has translated children's literature written in English, including *Mary Poppins* and *Cinderella,* into Hebrew.

Thoughts of Hanoi ◆ Pride
Auto Wreck ◆ Before the Law

◆ *Literature and Your Life*

CONNECT YOUR EXPERIENCE

If you could control all the events that affect your life, you'd win every game and pass every test. Sometimes, however, life throws a curve ball: Your team forfeits the game because half the players have the flu, or the science test includes a section of questions you weren't expecting. These selections show how people respond to circumstances that are (or seem to be) beyond their control.

THEMATIC FOCUS: FATEFUL MOMENTS

These selections show how specific events become fateful moments that change a person's life forever. The different ways the speakers deal with these events may lead you to examine how you respond to events that seem to be out of your control.

Journal Writing Jot down ideas for adjusting to circumstances you cannot change, taking action on circumstances you can change, and knowing the difference between the two.

◆ Background for Understanding

VIETNAM

Nguyen Thi Vinh writes about her home country, Vietnam, which was torn apart by a long and bloody war that lasted from just after the end of World War II until 1974. A 1954 treaty led to the division of the country into South Vietnam, which was supported by the United States, and North Vietnam, which was controlled by a Communist government. With support from the North Vietnamese, guerrillas called Viet Cong fought to overthrow South Vietnam. To support South Vietnam, the United States sent hundreds of thousands of troops to Vietnam. Ultimately, however, the Americans withdrew. In 1974, the North Vietnamese routed the South Vietnamese army, and in 1976 Hanoi became the capital of Vietnam.

◆ Literary Focus

THEME

The **theme** of a work is its central meaning—the comment the writer is making about human life and values. For example, the central message of "Pride" is that just as a hidden crack in a rock can eventually cause the rock to crumble, so a hidden hurt or problem in a person can eventually cause the person to "crack." By writing about how weather and other conditions cause rocks to crack, Ravikovitch communicates an insight about people without directly stating it.

◆ Reading Strategy

EVALUATE A WRITER'S MESSAGE

You walk out of a movie theater discussing the movie you just saw with your friends. As you evaluate it, you consider a variety of questions. Did the movie have a point? Did the plot make sense? You can examine literature in a similar way. You **evaluate a writer's message** by first identifying the message and then judging whether the message is valid—that is, whether it makes sense and is well supported. You can evaluate a message without necessarily agreeing or disagreeing with it.

In the poem "Pride," Dahlia Ravikovitch communicates a message about how difficulties and troubles affect people. Your evaluation of her message will rate how well you think she communicates and supports her message. Identify the message in each of the other selections. Then use a graphic organizer like the one shown to help you evaluate the message.

Guide for Reading ◆ 363

Thoughts of Hanoi
Nguyen Thi Vinh

Translated by Nguyen Ngoc Bich With Burton Raffel and W. S. Merwin

The night is deep and chill
as in early autumn. Pitchblack,
it thickens after each lightning flash.
I dream of Hanoi:
5   Co-ngu[1] Road
❶ ten years of separation
the way back sliced by a frontier of hatred.
I want to bury the past
to burn the future
10 still I yearn
still I fear
those endless nights
waiting for dawn.

❷ Brother,
15 how is Hang Dao[2] now?
How is Ngoc Son[3] temple?
Do the trains still run
each day from Hanoi
to the neighboring towns?
20 To Bac-ninh, Cam-giang, Yen-bai,[4]
the small villages, islands
of brown thatch in a lush green sea?

---

1. **Co-ngu** (cô gōō)
2. **Hang Dao** (häŋ dou)
3. **Ngoc Son** (nōk sōn)
4. **Bac-ninh** (bäk nin), **Cam-giang** (cäm giän), **Yen-bai** (ēŋ bī)

Peacefulness, Tran Nguyen Dan, Indochina Arts Project

364   ◆   *Turning Points*

Block Scheduling Strategies

The girls
25   bright eyes
                 ruddy cheeks
           four-piece dresses
                 raven-bill scarves
           sowing harvesting
                 spinning weaving
30   all year round,
       the boys
           plowing
                 transplanting
           in the fields
35   in their shops
           running across
                 the meadow at evening
           to fly kites
                 and sing alternating songs.

40   Stainless blue sky,
           jubilant voices of children
       stumbling through the alphabet,
           village graybeards strolling to the
                 temple,
       grandmothers basking in twilight sun,
45   chewing betel leaves
       while the children run—

                                    Brother,
                                    how is all that now?   ❸
                                    Or is it obsolete?
50   Are you like me,
                                    reliving the past,
                                    imagining the future?
                                    Do you count me as a friend
                                    or am I the enemy in your eyes?
55   Brother, I am afraid
                                    that one day I'll be with the March-
                                          North Army
                                    meeting you on your way to the South.
                                    I might be the one to shoot you then   ❹
                                    or you me
60   but please
                                    not with hatred.
                                    For don't you remember how it was,
                                    you and I in school together,
                                    plotting our lives together?
65   Those roots go deep!

                                    Brother, we are men,
                                    conscious of more
                                    than material needs.
                                    How can this happen to us   ❺
70   my friend
                                    my foe?

Guide for Responding

◆ *Literature and Your Life*

Reader's Response Explain a situation in which someone you thought of as a "foe" became a friend.

Thematic Focus What are some turning points that could change friends into enemies or enemies into friends?

☑ Check Your Comprehension

1. What is probably the speaker's hometown?
2. What does the speaker remember the "village graybeards" doing?

◆ Critical Thinking

INTERPRET
1. Why would the speaker wonder if the daily life he describes is now obsolete? **[Analyze]**

EVALUATE
2. Do you think it's possible to shoot someone "not with hatred" in war? Explain. **[Make a Judgment]**

EXTEND
3. How might the situation described in the poem compare with others in history? Explain. **[Social Studies Link]**

Thoughts of Hanoi ◆ 365

◆ Critical Thinking

❸ Analyze Cause and Effect
Have students analyze the causes and effects of the changes Vietnam experienced, as alluded to in the lines **48–49.** *War and foreign influence have caused a change in the traditional way of life.*

Comprehension Check ☑

❹ Ask students what the speaker is afraid of. *The speaker fears that one day he/she will have to kill a fellow countryman because of war within Vietnam.*

◆ Reading Strategy

❺ Evaluate a Writer's Message
Have students explain how this stanza relates to the writer's message. *The writer's message concerns the war's focus on land and power. The writer suggests that friendship and family are what really matter.*

Reinforce and Extend

Answers
◆ *Literature and Your Life*

Reader's Response Students might describe a time when a miscommunication was cleared up and an enemy became a friend.

Thematic Focus Turning points that could change enemies into friends include coming to an enemy's aid when he or she is in trouble or discovering a mutual interest. Turning points that could change friends into enemies include an act of betrayal, such as breaking a confidence.

☑ Check Your Comprehension
1. Hanoi is probably the speaker's hometown.
2. The speaker remembers them strolling to the temple.

◆ Critical Thinking
1. As a result of the war, so much has changed that the daily life he describes could be obsolete.
2. Students might say that it is possible to shoot someone "not without hatred" because a soldier might feel he or she is fighting for a cause, not against a person.
3. Students might cite other wars or clashes between groups that divide people who had been peaceful among themselves.

One-Minute Insight The tone of these two poems shows that turning points can come upon one slowly ("Pride") or with a terrible and stunning suddenness. ("Auto Wreck")

◆ **Critical Thinking**

❶ **Interpret** Have students explain what the author means by pride in this passage. *The poet means the kind of pride that makes people hide their painful feelings; that makes people stop themselves from crying because they are ashamed to show weakness.*

◆ **Critical Thinking**

❷ **Deduce** Ask students what the seal represents in the poem. *The seal stands for the last straw; not necessarily the worst thing that happens to a person, but the one that completes the crack that was there all along.*

◆ **Critical Thinking**

❸ **Infer** Ask students to infer how the rocks in this poem are like people. *Students might suggest that with people, as with rocks, a crack that starts out small can turn into a complete break under pressure.*

Pride

Dahlia Ravikovitch

Translated by Chana Bloch and Ariel Bloch

> I tell you, even rocks crack,
> and not because of age.
> For years they lie on their backs
> in the heat and the cold,
> 5 so many years,
> it almost seems peaceful.
> ❶ They don't move, so the cracks stay hidden.
> A kind of pride.
> Years pass over them, waiting.
> 10 Whoever is going to shatter them
> hasn't come yet.
> And so the moss flourishes, the seaweed
> whips around,
> the sea pushes through and rolls back—
> 15 the rocks seem motionless.
> ❷ Till a little seal comes to rub against them,
> comes and goes away.
> And suddenly the rock has an open wound.
> ❸ I told you, when rocks break, it happens by surprise.
> 20 And people, too.

366 ◆ *Turning Points*

Speaking and Listening Mini-Lesson

Telephone Conversation

This mini-lesson supports the first Speaking and Listening activity in the Idea Bank on page 371.

Introduce the Concept Have students discuss the benefits and limits of conversations that are held on the telephone. Ask how these benefits and limits would affect the conversation they will role-play.

Develop Background Have students pair up with partners and decide which partner will be the "you" and which will be the speaker of the poem. Ask them to jot down their thoughts about the kinds of circumstances that can cause friends to become enemies.

Apply the Information The student playing "you" can use his or her notes as a basis to answer the last question the speaker asks. After "you" gives an answer, partners can have a free exchange of ideas.

Assess the Outcome Have students discuss how the activity helped them to evaluate the writer's message in "Thoughts of Hanoi."

Auto Wreck

Karl Shapiro

Its quick soft silver bell beating, beating,
And down the dark one ruby flare
Pulsing out red light like an artery,
The ambulance at top speed floating down
5 Past beacons and illuminated clocks
Wings in a heavy curve, dips down,
And brakes speed, entering the crowd.
The doors leap open, emptying light;
Stretchers are laid out, the mangled lifted
10 And stowed into the little hospital.
Then the bell, breaking the hush, tolls once,
And the ambulance with its terrible cargo
Rocking, slightly rocking, moves away,
As the doors, an afterthought, are closed.

15 We are deranged, walking among the cops
Who sweep glass and are large and composed.
One is still making notes under the light.
One with a bucket douches ponds of blood
Into the street and gutter.
20 One hangs lanterns on the wrecks that cling,
Empty husks of locusts, to iron poles.

Our throats were tight as tourniquets,[1]
Our feet were bound with splints, but now,
Like convalescents intimate and gauche,[2]
25 We speak through sickly smiles and warn
With the stubborn saw of common sense,
The grim joke and the banal resolution.
The traffic moves around with care,
But we remain, touching a wound
30 That opens to our richest horror.
Already old, the question Who shall die?
Becomes unspoken Who is innocent?
For death in war is done by hands;
Suicide has cause and stillbirth, logic;
35 And cancer, simple as a flower, blooms.
But this invites the occult mind,
Cancels our physics with a sneer,
And spatters all we knew of denouement[3]
Across the expedient and wicked stones.

◆ Build Vocabulary

deranged (də rānjd´) *adj.*: Unsettled

convalescents (kän´ və les´ ənts) *n.*: People who are recovering from illness

banal (bā´ nəl) *adj.*: Dull or stale because of overuse

expedient (ek spē´ dē´ ənt) *adj.*: Convenient

---

1. **tourniquets** (tʉr´ nə ketz) *n.*: Bandages to stop bleeding by compressing a blood vessel.
2. **gauche** (gōsh) *adj.*: Awkward.
3. **denouement** (dā´ nü män´) *n.*: Outcome or the end.

✦ Beyond the Classroom

Career Connection: Paramedics

Behind the scenes of "Auto Wreck," paramedics were probably hard at work, trying to save lives and administer emergency care as the ambulance sped to the hospital. These specialized paramedics, known as emergency medical technicians, or EMTs, are at the pulse of emergency medicine; their efforts have saved thousands of lives. Let students know that the term *paramedic* originated during the Korean War. Military medical technicians were parachuted into locations where they were urgently needed—a paramedic was a medical corpsman who was also a trained parachutist.

Have interested students gather more information about paramedics. Some students might report on the different kinds of paramedics, such as physicians' assistants, EMTs, and veterinary technicians. Other students might contact a college or vocational program to find out specifically what is required to train for and be successful in these fields. Students might wish to contribute articles and research information on this field to a class career file.

Insight This parable describes the frustration and lost opportunity of a man waiting his turn to be allowed through a door. Students can read this on several levels, recognizing the message that sometimes a person must trigger a turning point through his or her own action rather than waiting for something to happen.

▶ Critical Viewing◀

❶ **Analyze** Students might observe that the figure, viewed from behind, seems without identity, that the long shadow cast by the building gives the scene a forlorn look, and that the starkness of the scene in general suggests isolation.

◆ **Critical Thinking**

❷ **Speculate** Ask students: What might happen if the man goes through the gateway? *Students may say he will meet even greater obstacles than the first doorkeeper; he may find what he is seeking from the Law; he may never find justice; he may even be killed.*

Enigma of the Hour, 1912, Giorgio de Chirico, Coll. Mattioli, Milan, Italy© Foundation Giorgio de Chirico/Licensed by VAGA, New York, NY

◀ Critical Viewin
What details in the
picture on this pag
indicate a sense o
isolation? [Analyze

Before the Law

Franz Kafka
Translated by Willa and Edwin Muir

Before the Law stands a doorkeeper. To this doorkeeper there comes a man from the country and prays for admittance to the Law. But the doorkeeper says that he cannot grant admittance at the moment. The man thinks it over and then asks if he will be allowed in later. "It is possible," says the doorkeeper, "but not at the moment." Since the gate stands open, as usual, and the doorkeeper steps to one side, the man stoops to peer through the gateway into the interior. Observing that, the doorkeeper laughs and says: "If you are so drawn to it, just try to go in despite my veto.[1] But take note: I am powerful. And I am only the least of the doorkeepers. From hall to hall there is one doorkeeper after another, each more powerful than the last. The third doorkeeper is already so terrible that even I cannot bear to look at him." These are difficulties the man from the country has not expected; the Law, he thinks, should surely be accessible at all times and to everyone, but as he now takes a closer look at the doorkeeper in his fur coat, with his big sharp nose and long, thin, black Tartar[2] beard, he decides that it is better to wait

---

1. **veto** (vē´ tō) *n.*: An order prohibiting some proposed or intended act.
2. **Tartar** (tär´ tər): Member of a Turkic people living in a region of European Russia.

 Humanities: Art

Enigma of the Hour, 1912, by Giorgio de Chirico.
In this painting, a figure stands before a facade of arches with the face of a clock above. The identity of the figure, the place, the historical period, and the significance of the clock are all unclear.

Giorgio de Chirico was an Italian painter, born in Greece in 1888. Chirico's earlier paintings communicate a sense of reality very different from ordinary experience, and for that reason he is considered a forerunner of the Surrealist movement of the early 1920's.

Use the following questions for discussion:
1. How does the mood of this painting reflect the mood of Kafka's story? *Both are mysterious. The people and places in both are outside of ordinary reality. Both invite speculation and interpretation.*
2. How can you connect the clock in the painting to the theme of the story? *Students may say the clock may reflect the idea that time runs out for the man in the story.*

until he gets permission to enter. The door-keeper gives him a stool and lets him sit down at one side of the door. There he sits for days and years. He makes many attempts to be admitted, and wearies the doorkeeper by his <u>importunity</u>. The doorkeeper frequently has little interviews with him, asking him questions about his home and many other things, but the questions are put indifferently, as great lords put them, and always finish with the statement that he cannot be let in yet. The man, who has furnished himself with many things for his journey, sacrifices all he has, however valuable, to bribe the door-keeper. The doorkeeper accepts everything, but always with the remark: "I am only taking it to keep you from thinking you have omitted anything." During these many years the man fixes his attention almost continuously on the door-keeper. He forgets the other doorkeepers, and this one seems to him the sole obstacle prevent-ing access to the Law. He curses his bad luck, in his early years boldly and loudly; later, as he grows old, he only grumbles to himself. He be-comes childish, and since in his yearlong <u>contemplation</u> of the doorkeeper he has come to know even the fleas in his fur collar, he begs the fleas as well to help him and to change the door-keeper's mind. At length his eyesight begins to fail, and he does not know whether the world is really darker or whether his eyes are only de-ceiving him. Yet in his darkness he is now aware

of a radiance that streams inextinguishable from the gateway of the Law. Now he has not very long to live. Before he dies, all his experiences in these long years gather themselves in his head to one point, a question he has not yet asked the doorkeeper. He waves him nearer, since he can no longer raise his stiffening body. The door-keeper has to bend low toward him, for the dif-ference in height between them has altered much to the man's disadvantage. "What do you want to know now?" asks the doorkeeper; "you are <u>insatiable</u>." "Everyone strives to reach the Law," says the man, "so how does it happen that for all these many years no one but myself has ever begged for admittance?" The doorkeeper recognizes that the man has reached his end, and, to let his failing senses catch the words, roars in his ear: "No one else could ever be admitted here, since this gate was made only for you. I am now going to shut it."

◆ **Reading Strategy**
What do you think the message of this piece is?
④

◆ **Build Vocabulary**

importunity (im´ pôr to͞on´ i tē) *n.*: Persistence in requesting or demanding

contemplation (kän´ tem plā´ shən) *n.*: Thoughtful inspection; study

insatiable (in sā´ shə bəl) *adj.*: Cannot be satisfied; constantly wanting more

◆ **Critical Thinking**
③ **Interpret** Ask students to ex-plain why the doorkeeper gives this response after he accepts the bribes. *Students will probably recognize that the doorkeeper is serving himself, and really won't do anything.*

◆ **Reading Strategy**
④ **Evaluate a Writer's Message** Responses might include that a per-son who sits and waits for justice to come to him will never obtain it. However, the person who demands justice, who is not afraid to stand up for his rights, may have a chance.

Reinforce and Extend

Answers

◆ *Literature and Your Life*

Reader's Response Sample alter-native titles are "The Final Blow" ("Pride"); "Shock" ("Auto Wreck"); "The Gatekeeper and the Man" ("Before the Law").

Thematic Focus Together, these works suggest that turning points can be subtle, as in "Pride," or sudden and violent, as in "Auto Wreck."

☑ **Check Your Comprehension**

1. A seal rubs up against them.
2. The speaker asks, "Who shall die?" "Who is innocent?"
3. The gate was made only for the man.

◆ **Critical Thinking**

1. Possible responses: the seal repre-sents the "last straw" that causes a person to crack.
2. Possible responses: Yes, sometimes people die for a cause or as an end to suffering; or no, all death is random.
3. Students should compare works in terms of content and tone.

Guide for Responding

◆ *Literature and Your Life*

Reader's Response Suggest another title that you think would fit one of these selections.

Thematic Focus What do these works say about turning points?

☑ **Check Your Comprehension**

1. In "Pride," what causes the rocks to crack?
2. What questions does the speaker of "Auto Wreck" ask?
3. Why has no one else begged admittance to the Law in "Before the Law"?

◆ **Critical Thinking**

INTERPRET
1. What does the seal represent in "Pride"? **[Apply]**

APPLY
2. Do you agree with the speaker in "Auto Wreck" that some forms of death seem to have a pur-pose? **[Apply]**

EXTEND
3. Compare these works to other stories or po-ems you have read that treat the theme of love, pride, or justice. **[Literature Link]**

Before the Law ◆ 369

 Speaking and Listening Mini-Lesson

Improvisational Skit
This mini-lesson supports the second Speaking and Listening activity in the Idea Bank on page 371.

Introduce the Concept Let students know that in an improvisation actors are called upon to act out a situation with no rehearsal and little or no planning. Therefore, they need to be spontaneous.

Develop Background Before students perform their improvisational skits, present these guidelines:

• Relax and focus your body and awareness on the activity.
• Use gestures, expressions, posture, and movement to reveal *who* you are, *what* you are doing, and *where* you are.
• Respond in character to what the other person says and does.

Apply the Information Give partners five minutes to come up with a quick plan for their approach. Then have them improvise a skit.

Assess the Outcome Have students eval-uate their own performances in terms of how effectively they communicated the situation between the man and the gatekeeper and how effectively they created an impression of the characters.

Answers

◆ Reading Strategy

1. Events like auto accidents defy logic and order.
2. Encourage students to support their answers with reasons.
3. Most students will feel that the message is clearly communicated.

◆ Literary Focus

1. Example: Individual friendships can be destroyed by political divisions.
2. The message is communicated through images: the rock (pride) and the seal (final pressure).
3. He uses the images "pulsing out red light like an artery," "throats tight as tourniquets."
4. Sample response: "frustrated." The feeling suggests that Kafka's theme relates to futility.

◆ Build Vocabulary

Using the Word Root -sat-
1. fill; 2. fill; 3. fully

Using the Word Bank
Example sentences:
1. The salesperson called over and over, showing *importunity*.
2. He sat in deep *contemplation*.
3. She has an *insatiable* appetite.
4. Bob's thoughts became *deranged*.
5. The *convalescents* healed.
6. His observations are *banal*.
7. This method is *expedient*.

◆ Build Grammar Skills

Practice
1. . . . (flare) Pulsing out a red light . . .
2. (doors) emptying light
3. (We,) walking among the cops
4. Observing that, (doorkeeper)
5. (graybeards,) strolling to the temple

Writing Application
1. Sitting at the gate, the man cannot enter.
2. The gatekeeper guards the gate, keeping the man out.
3. Waiting a long time, the man grew old.

 ## Writer's Solution

For additional instruction and practice, use the lessons in the **Language Lab CD-ROM** on Misplaced Modifiers and pp. 41–43 on Participles and Participial Phrases in the *Writer's Solution Grammar Practice Book.*

Guide for Responding (continued)

◆ Reading Strategy

EVALUATE A WRITER'S MESSAGE

You **evaluate a writer's message** by identifying the message, rating its validity, and examining the examples and support the writer offers.

For example, in "Thoughts of Hanoi" the questions the speaker asks are a clue that the message of the work deals with change. As you read, examine the details and examples to evaluate the message.

1. Identify the message in "Auto Wreck."
2. Explain whether you think the message in "Pride" is valid.
3. How clearly does Thi Vinh communicate her message in "Thoughts of Hanoi"? Give reasons to support your opinion.

◆ Literary Focus

THEME

The **theme** of a work is its central meaning—the comment the writer is making about human life and values.

1. In your own words, state the theme of "Thoughts of Hanoi."
2. Explain how Ravikovitch communicates the theme of "Pride" without directly stating it.
3. What images does Shapiro use to communicate his theme in "Auto Wreck"?
4. What word would you use to describe the feeling you get after reading "Before the Law"? How does this feeling give you a clue to Kafka's theme?

 Beyond Literature

Social Studies Connection

The Geography of Vietnam A tropical country in Southeast Asia, Vietnam extends south from China in a long, narrow S-curve. North and Central Vietnam are mountainous regions interspersed with coastal lowlands, while South Vietnam lies very close to sea level.
Activity On a map of Vietnam locate the major cities of Hanoi and Ho Chi Minh City, the Mekong and Red River Deltas, and the Annamite mountain range.

◆ Build Vocabulary

USING THE ROOT -sat-

On your paper, complete the meanings of these words that include the root -sat-.
1. satisfy: _____?_____ one's needs or expectations
2. satiate: to completely _____?_____
3. saturate: to cause to be soaked _____?_____

USING THE WORD BANK

On your paper, write sentences using the words from the Word Bank as directed.
1. Describe an action, using the word *importunity*.
2. Describe a library, using the word *contemplation*.
3. Describe a person, using the word *insatiable*.
4. Describe a character, using the word *deranged*.
5. Use the word *convalescents* in a sentence about a hospital.
6. Use the word *banal* in a sentence from a book review.
7. Use the word *expedient* in an advertisement.

◆ Build Grammar Skills

PRESENT PARTICIPIAL PHRASES

A **present participial phrase** consists of a present participle (a verb form ending in -ing) plus any other words that go with it. Participial phrases function as adjectives in sentences.

Practice Copy the following examples on to your paper. Underline the present participial phrase and circle the word it modifies.
1. . . . one ruby flare/Pulsing out a red light . . .
2. The doors leap open, emptying light;
3. We are deranged, walking among the cops
4. Observing that, the doorkeeper laughs . . .
5. . . . village graybeards strolling to the temple,

Writing Application Combine each pair of sentences by making one of them a present participial phrase.
1. The man sits at the gate. The man cannot enter.
2. The gatekeeper guards the gate. The gatekeeper keeps the man out.
3. The man grew old. The man waited a long time.

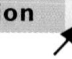 **Beyond the Selection**

FURTHER READING

Other Works by the Authors
Metamorphosis by Franz Kafka
The Dome of Sunday by Karl Shapiro
Two Sisters by Nguyen Thi Vinh

Other Works About Turning Points
Ethan Frome, Edith Wharton
The Joy Luck Club, Amy Tan

We suggest that you preview these works before recommending them to students.

INTERNET

To learn more about Franz Kafka, go to **http//www. levity.com/corduroy/kafka.htm**

To access an interview with Karl Shapiro, go to **http:// www.wilmington.net/arts/ poets**

For other works by Vietnamese women, go to **http:// globetrotter.berkeley.edu/GlobalGender/sea.lit.html**

Please be aware sites may have changed since we published this information.

We *strongly recommend* that you preview the sites before you send students to them.

Build Your Portfolio

Idea Bank

Writing

1. **Interview** Prepare a list of interview questions for Nguyen Thi Vinh. Focus six or eight questions around the author's life before and after the Vietnam War.

2. **Visitor's Guide** Research Kafka's birthplace in Prague, capital of the Czech Republic. Write a one-page visitor's guide highlighting the interesting aspects of the famous writer's home.

3. **Allegory** Write an allegory—a narrative in which the actions of characters represent abstract ideas or moral principles. First decide upon your message, then develop characters and a plot.

Speaking and Listening

4. **Telephone Conversation** Suppose you are the "you" in "Thoughts of Hanoi." Call the speaker of the poem and answer the last question he asks.

5. **Improvisational Skit** With a partner, perform an improvisational skit—a skit without preparation—based on a conversation between the man and the gatekeeper from "Before the Law." Make your skit humorous.

Projects

6. **Two Maps** On a computer or by hand, create two maps of Vietnam—one before the Communist takeover in 1974 and one after it. For both maps, label capital cities. **[Social Studies Link; Art Link; Technology Link]**

7. **Auto Safety Presentation** "Auto Wreck" introduces us to the grim realities of car crashes. Create a chart or other visual aid that shows some of the important auto safety legislation your state has passed since you were born.

Writing Mini-Lesson

Letter to the Editor

Write a **letter to the editor** of the local paper expressing your concerns about an issue such as auto safety. Your letter will give statistics and pose several recommendations on how people can reduce the likelihood of being in an auto accident. However, you don't want your letter to be all blunt statistics and cold, hard facts. The following tip will help you give your writing that personal touch.

Writing Skills Focus: Elaboration to Make Writing Personal

Make a connection with your audience by providing personal examples. For instance, if you make the point that not enough people wear their seat belts for local trips, you can elaborate by adding that you almost made this mistake when you were riding with your uncle—and later you were sure glad he made you buckle up when he slammed on the brakes to avoid hitting a raccoon. Use examples from your own experience sparingly and only when they really "drive" home your point.

Prewriting Go to the library, use the Internet, or call your local police precinct to find out where you can get the latest statistics on car accidents. Jot down your ideas about personal experiences that illustrate the same point as the statistics.

Drafting Choose the most dramatic personal anecdotes to include with your draft. Support the points you make with these anecdotes by citing the statistics that show your experience is not unique.

Revising Reread your draft. Look for places where you can elaborate with a personal anecdote or a human interest story that will make your point more immediate for your audience.

Thoughts of Hanoi/Pride/Auto Wreck/Before the Law ◆ 371

Idea Bank

Customizing for *Performance Levels*

Following are suggestions for matching Idea Bank topics with your students' performance levels:

Less Advanced Students: 1, 4
Average Students: 2, 5
More Advanced Students: 3, 6, 7

Customizing for *Learning Modalities*

Following are suggestions for matching Idea Bank topics with your students' learning modalities:

Visual/Spatial: 6, 7
Interpersonal: 4
Verbal/Linguistic: 4, 5
Logical/Mathematical: 7

Writing Mini-Lesson

Refer students to the Writing Handbook, page 965, for instruction on the writing process, and page 969 for further information on practical writing.

Writer's Solution

Writers at Work Videodisc

Have students view the videodisc segment for Ch. 8 in which Larry Cataldo discusses techniques he uses to organize ideas. Ask students how they can apply his techniques. Discuss with students which of Cataldo's techniques for capturing an audience would work best for their award speech, and why.

Play frames 23159 to 33243

Writing Lab CD-ROM

Have students complete the tutorial on Practical Writing. Follow these steps:

1. Have students use the notecard activity to help them arrange their points and examples in order of importance.

2. Suggest that students use the transition word checker to highlight transition words so they can see whether then have show relationships that indicate logical order.

Sourcebook

Have students use Chapter 8, Practical and Technical Writing (pp. 229–257), for additional support. The chapter includes an annotated student model of a process essay (p. 257).

✓ ASSESSMENT OPTIONS

Formal Assessment, Selection Test, pp. 91–93, and Assessment Resources Software. The selection test is designed so that it can be easily customized to the performance levels of your students. *Alternative Assessment,* p. 27, includes options for less advanced students, more advanced students, musical/rhythmic learners, bodily/kinesthetic learners, visual/spatial learners, interpersonal learners, and logical/mathematical learners.

PORTFOLIO ASSESSMENT

Use the following rubrics in the *Alternative Assessment* booklet to assess student writing:
Interview: Response to Literature Rubric, p. 110
Visitor's Guide: Description Rubric p. 97
Allegory: Fiction Narrative Rubric, p. 95

Establish Writing Guidelines

Before students begin, review the following key characteristics of a reflective essay:

- It describes the effect of a past event or person on the writer's life
- It maintains a consistent mood.
- It is usually written from the first-person point of view.

After you've discussed reflective essays, work with students to develop a rubric for scoring their essays. See the suggestions on page 374 for points to include in the rubric.

Refer students to the Writing Handbook, page 965, for instruction in the writing process.

Connect to Literature You might have students look again at *Speak, Memory* (p. 305) by Vladimir Nabokov, which is a reflective essay.

 Writer's Solution

Writers at Work Videodisc If you encourage students to use description in their position papers, you might show them how Colleen McElroy uses descriptive elements in her writing. Play the videodisc segment on Description (Ch. 1). Have students discuss how McElroy draws forth on her own images to call forth images for readers.

Play frames 335 to 10062

Writing Lab CD-ROM

If your students have access to computers, you may want to have them work on the tutorial on Description if they are including description in their reflective essays. Follow these steps:

1. Have students review the interactive model of a reflective essay.
2. Have students listen to tips from authors for writing for different audiences.
3. Have students draft on computer.
4. Suggest students review the screen on Making Point of View consistent.

Sourcebook

Students can find additional support, including topic ideas, models, audience and purpose profiles, and graphic organizers, in the chapter on Description (pp. 1–29).

| Reflective Essay | Writing Process Workshop |

A **reflective essay** describes your thoughts and feelings about a person, place, or memorable event. It may be anchored in a specific moment in the past, but it can also be a reflection upon an event or trend that you notice in the present. An effective reflective essay uses vivid details and figurative language to capture not only physical appearances but also your emotional responses.

The following skills, introduced in this section's Writing Mini-Lesson, will help you write an effective reflective essay.

Writing Skills Focus

▶ **Create a main impression** that you would like to instill in the reader of your reflective essay. For example, if you would like to establish a sentimental mood, use words and phrases such as, *as I fondly remember.* (See p. 355.)

▶ **Elaborate to make your writing personal**. For instance, if you say that summer is your favorite season, give an example of something that happened one particular summer. (See p. 369.)

▶ **Record your final insight** by stating the effect this memory had on you and what you learned or discovered from it.

The following excerpt from "Speak, Memory" shows how Vladimir Nabokov uses these skills.

① The phrase *lovely Russian word for dusk* gives the essay a personal, reflective tone.

② The writer elaborates on how much he loved the summers of his youth by giving concrete examples of the sights and sounds of those remote summer evenings.

MODEL FROM LITERATURE

from "Speak, Memory" by Vladimir Nabokov

Summer *soomerki*—the lovely Russian word for dusk. ① Time: a dim point in the first decade of this unpopular century. Place: latitude 59° north from your equator, longitude 100° east from my writing hand. The day would take hours to fade, and everything—sky, tall flowers, still water—would be kept in a state of infinite vesperal suspense, deepened rather than resolved by the doleful moo of a cow in a distant meadow ② or by the still more moving cry that came from some bird beyond the lower course of the river.

372 ◆ *Turning Points*

 Cross-Curricular Connection: Art

Just as a painting uses imagery to capture a particular scene or moment in time, so a reflective essay uses words to accomplish the same task. Point out to students that, just as an artist brings his or her own feelings, thoughts, and responses to bear on the visual representation of an object, so will their own feelings, thoughts, and responses affect their representation of an event as presented in a reflective essay. For a concrete example of this concept, place Art Transparency 17 on an overhead projector. Point out to students that the art shows a variety of interpretations of what is recognizably the same shape. The triangle is shown in a fragmented way, in a fluid way, in a colorful way, in a crisp, clear way, and also with blurred edges. Discuss with students the feelings that might lead to different interpretations and representations of an event.

Prewriting

Choose Your Topic: What Triggers a Memory? Does the smell of burning leaves or perfume or nutmeg recall an _ experience that you had years ago? Does hearing an "oldie" on the radio remind you of an incident from your childhood? Focus on different sensory stimuli that you encounter in the world around you, and jot down past experiences that these tastes, smells, sounds, sights, and physical sensations bring to mind. Then choose one experience on which you can reflect in your essay.

Use a Word Bin As you gather details for your reflective essay, think about how you want to portray your subject. What kinds of words will you use to describe it? How will you describe its color or the way it sounds? Make a list of words that describe how your subject looks, sounds, feels, tastes, and smells, but also include words that conjure feelings and suggest opinions. The following word bin shows examples of various sensory words.

Sensory Words				
Sight	**Sound**	**Smell**	**Taste**	**Touch**
sunny	musical	flowery	spicy	smooth
glistening	humming	pungent	salty	knotted
glowing	whining	musty	zesty	wet
murky	melodic	ripe	bitter	sandy

Drafting

Create a Main Impression As you draft your reflective essay, focus on conveying a particular impression of your topic. Include enough sensory details to support your main impression. Study the following example:

Topic: A fireworks display from a July 4th celebration when I was younger

Main Impression: The fireworks display was an unforgettable presentation of energy, excitement, and color.

Include: Descriptions of vibrant colors, the sounds of the fireworks exploding, the smells of popcorn and cotton candy, the feel of the wet grass or hard pavement under your feet, the joy of witnessing this grand historical event.

APPLYING LANGUAGE SKILLS: Misplaced and Dangling Modifiers

Misplaced modifiers (phrases or clauses placed so that they seem to modify something other than what they are meant to modify) and **dangling modifiers** (modifying phrases that don't really modify anything) make your writing confusing.

Misplaced Modifier:
My house is on Cedar Avenue, which has a huge red front door.

Corrected:
My house, which has a huge red front door, is on Cedar Avenue.

Practice Rewrite the sentences, correcting misplaced or dangling modifiers.

1. Watching the sunset, dusk was beautiful.

2. He realized the mistake he had made after a few minutes.

Writing Application Correct any misplaced or dangling modifiers in your essay.

Writer's Solution Connection Writing Lab

For more on sensory words, use the Sensory Language Word Bin in the Drafting section of the Writing Lab tutorial on Description.

Prewriting

Students may benefit from using a topic web to narrow their topics. Have them list their broad topic at the top of the web and divide that topic into two or more subtopics. Then have them divide those subtopics further into subtopics. Then they should be able to find a narrowed topic for their essays.

Customize for
More Advanced Students
Challenge these students to present their reflective essays in creative ways, such as in copy for a newspaper, or as information that a witness to a crime might give to a police officer.

Writer's Solution

Writing Lab CD-ROM
The Drafting section of the tutorial on Description contains Sensory, Colors, Places, and Character Traits word bins. Have students consult these lists of words before or while they draft to make their essays more descriptive and concise.

Drafting

Remind students to include only details and information that contribute to the impression they want to create.

Applying Language Skills
Misplaced and Dangling Modifiers Explain to students that they should be extra careful of misplaced and dangling modifiers in their reflective essays, since they will probably be using a lot of modifiers in their pieces.

Suggested Answers

1. Watching the sunset, *I thought* dusk was beautiful.

2. *After a few minutes,* he realized the mistake he had made.

Writer's Solution

For additional instruction and practice, have students complete the **Language Lab CD-ROM** lesson on Problems With Modifiers and practice page 61 on Misplaced and Dangling Modifiers in the *Writer's Solution Grammar Practice Book.*

Revising

- Have students team up with peer editors as they revise. Have the peer editors use these guidelines:
- Does the essay have a vivid and memorable mood?
- Is the writing personal and detailed?
- Is there a clear insight that the writer gained from the experience?

 Writer's Solution

Writing Lab CD-ROM

The revising and editing section of the tutorial on Description contains the following strategies for self-revision:
- A video of author Colleen McElroy's thoughts on revising.
- Revision checkers for vague adjectives and sentence length.
- Audio-annotated instruction of a first and revised draft.

Publishing

Encourage students to save their essays for possible incorporation into a longer work.

Reinforce and Extend

Review the Writing Guidelines.
After students have completed their papers, review the characteristics of a reflective essay. Encourage students to come up with additional criteria for an interesting reflective essay based on what they learned through completing the assignment.

Applying Language Skills

 Writer's Solution

For additional instruction and practice, have students complete page 116 on Choosing Precise Words in the *Writer's Solution Grammar Practice Book*.

Applying Language Skills: Vivid Adjectives and Adverbs

Avoid vague adjectives whose meanings have become imprecise or unclear. Instead, use **vivid adjectives and adverbs**. These will make your writing more colorful and interesting to read.

Vague:
Our Sunday brunch is great. My mom's good bread tastes good.

Vivid:
Our Sunday brunch is eagerly awaited. My mom's home-baked bread tastes heavenly.

Practice On your paper, replace the vague adjectives and adverbs in the following sentence with vivid ones.

Last spring was really nice. The flowers were pretty and the weather was fine.

Writing Application Review your reflective essay and replace any vague adjectives and adverbs with vivid ones.

Writer's Solution Connection
Language Lab

For more practice with vivid adjectives and adverbs, complete the Language Lab lesson on Vivid Adjectives and Adverbs.

Revising

Revise With a Fresh Mind After you've finished drafting your reflective essay, put it aside for a while before revising it. It's best to approach your writing with a fresh mind; you're more likely to see areas where you can make improvements. You might also try reading your essay aloud. Hearing your writing can help you pinpoint aspects that need revising.

Proofreading

Use a Proofreading Checklist Make sure you can answer yes to each of the following questions:
▶ Have you spelled all words correctly?
▶ Have you used contractions correctly?
▶ Have you corrected misplaced or dangling modifiers?
▶ Have you used words that appeal to the five senses to evoke vivid images?
▶ Have you avoided run-on sentences and sentence fragments?

REVISION MODEL

When autumn leaves begin to fall, my mind returns to ① *sadly*
② *There, I used to set my blanket down in*
the cool sand and listen to the waves crashing against the shore.
my favorite summer spot: the beach in the early morning.

I can still hear the seagulls calling to each other, and

if I close my eyes, I can sometimes smell the salty air.

① *The writer adds the word* sadly *to convey an impression of longing and loss.*
② *The writer adds this sentence to elaborate on why the beach is such a memorable place to her.*

Publishing

Read Your Description Aloud to Background Music Choose music that would go best with your essay, and play it as you read your essay aloud.

Bulletin Board Display With classmates, post your reflective essays on a bulletin board. Decide on a theme for the board, as well as a visual organization plan that will make the essays appealing.

✓ ASSESSMENT		4	3	2	1
PORTFOLIO ASSESSMENT Use this rubric to assess the students' writing.	**Modifiers**	All modifiers are vivid and precise. There are no misplaced or dangling modifiers.	Most modifiers are vivid and precise. No misplaced or dangling modifiers.	Many modifiers are vague and could be improved. Misplaced or dangling modifiers are noticeable.	Most modifiers are vague. Incorrect placement of modifiers impairs understanding.
	Impression	The piece creates a vivid mood that remains with the reader. Writing is personal and clearly shows the impression the subject left on the writer.	The piece has a definite mood. The writing has a personal touch.	The mood of the piece could be better defined. The writer elaborates a little on the topic, but it needs to be developed more.	There is no distinct mood. There is little or no elaboration that tells why the subject is important to the writer.

Real-World Reading Skills Workshop

Reading Product Labels

Strategies for Success

Labels show up on many of the things you touch every day. You may tend to ignore product labels, but they actually contain useful—and sometimes essential—information. Take a look at the labels in your clothes or on your food packages. They provide substantial information you need to know when you purchase or use a product.

Why Read Product Labels? Following are some important reasons to pay attention to product labels:

- ▶ If you are under any dietary restrictions or have food allergies, it is essential that you read the list of ingredients in food products. The order of the ingredients tells you the relative amounts of each.
- ▶ Products work best when you use them as directed. For example, you must thoroughly shake many paints and cleaners before using them.

- ▶ Proper care—"dry cleaning only," for example—keeps clothing and other articles in the best condition and may prolong their life.
- ▶ Labels give warnings about who should not use the product. Labels on medicine also warn about side effects or dosage for young children.
- ▶ Addresses or phone numbers provide a source for assistance or questions.

Apply the Strategy

Look at the product label below to find out how to use the paint.

Application: Stir thoroughly before use. Apply to clean, dry surface by brush, roller, flat applicator, or spray. Allow two hours final drying time if the surface is porous and four hours if the surface is sealed. Double coating is recommended.

USE ONLY WITH ADEQUATE VENTILATION.

KEEP OUT OF REACH OF CHILDREN.

KEEP FROM FREEZING.

PAINT

1. What preparations should you make before you begin to paint?
2. What materials do you need?
3. What is the best way to apply the paint? How many coats are recommended?
4. What warnings are on the product label?

✔ It's important to read the following product labels:
- ▶ Nutritional labels on food
- ▶ Care labels in clothing
- ▶ Safety warnings on cleaning supplies, electrical appliances, and power tools
- ▶ Allergy warnings on health and beauty aids

Real-World Reading Skills Workshop ◆ 375

Introduce the Strategy

Students will be familiar with product labels from many products they find about the house, from detergent to bug spray to shampoo. Remind them that because product labels often include important and not always obvious safety information, it is important to read and understand them.

Customize for
English Language Learners
These students may have trouble with the often specialized and difficult vocabulary found on product labels. Remind them that the important warnings and messages on labels are often accompanied by signs or symbols intended to adequately convey the message.

Apply the Strategy

Answers
1. Before painting, the user should clean and dry the surface to be painted and stir the paint thoroughly.
2. The user will need a brush, roller, flat applicator, or spray.
3. The best way to apply the paint is with the aforementioned applicators. Two coats are recommended.
4. There are three warnings on the label: Use with adequate ventilation, keep out of the reach of children, and keep from freezing.

Tell students that receiving oral directions to a place is something that they will have to do in countless situations over the course of their lives. Listening carefully the first time to acquire the necessary details is a vital and often-ignored communication skill.

Customize for
Visual/Spatial Learners

Remind these students that they can use line drawings and simple pictures as part of their notes. In taking notes on how to get from one place to another, these students may benefit from using line drawings to show where to turn and to identify important landmarks. Arrows, circles, and stars can also help these learners to highlight the most significant parts of the directions.

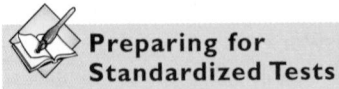

Preparing for
Standardized Tests

This practice will serve students well when they take standardized tests in which they must follow oral directions closely.

Following Oral Directions

Speaking and Listening Workshop

When a new friend gives you directions to her house over the phone or a teacher gives you instructions before a test, you're getting directions orally. Oral directions are more critical than written ones because you have only one chance to get them right.

Listen Up The most important thing to remember when receiving oral directions is to listen carefully. Focus on hearing and remembering important details. If you are unclear on any part of the directions, ask for that portion of the directions to be repeated. Otherwise, when you actually carry out the directions, you may find yourself lost or confused.

Repeat What You Hear Repeat the directions to the person who gave them. Doing so will ensure that you have heard the directions carefully.

Tips for Listening to Oral Directions

✔ *Getting correct directions is the first step in ensuring that you arrive at your destination or achieve your goal. When listening to oral directions, keep these points in mind:*

▶ *Listen attentively and carefully.*

▶ *Repeat what you have heard.*

▶ *If steps must be followed in a certain order, be sure you understand that order.*

▶ *Ask questions to clarify any part of the oral directions that are confusing or unclear.*

▶ *Take notes as the person gives the directions; do not rely on your memory.*

▶ *If you are getting directions to a place, ask for visual identification markers to locate key points along the way.*

Apply the Strategies

With a partner, role-play these situations:

1. Take turns giving each other oral directions on how to get from one part of your school to another. After you have followed the directions, discuss with your partner how successful each of you was in both giving and receiving oral directions.

2. Dictate directions to a place that both you and your partner know. Do not identify the place. Have your partner mentally follow your directions and identify the place.

Extended Reading Opportunities

These longer works about the theme of turning points are filled with irony and inspiration.

Suggested Titles

Latino Literature
Published by Prentice Hall

This collection includes the finest essays, poems, and fiction by modern Latino authors. Gary Soto, Sandra Cisneros, and Gabriel García Márquez, among others share their works that deal with life's challenges and choices.

Of Mice and Men
John Steinbeck

John Steinbeck's classic story tells of the unforgettable friendship between two California migrant workers: Lenny, a simple-minded kind-hearted man, and George, a headstrong determined man who is also devoted to protecting Lenny. The two friends set out to acquire a farm of their own, but a tragic turn of events brings an unexpected end to their dreams.

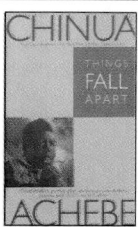

Things Fall Apart
Chinua Achebe

This story by one of Africa's most famous and respected novelists tells the tale of Okonkwo, a wealthy and powerful man from a rural Nigerian village named Umuofia. From the first sentence of the novel, Achebe envelops us in the sights and sounds of the traditional African village. Achebe's voice is both loving and critical of the traditional culture—a culture that starts to fall apart when it runs headlong into European colonialism.

Other Possibilities

A Separate Peace   John Knowles
All Quiet on the Western Front   Erich Maria Remarque
Les Miserables   Victor Hugo

Planning Students' Extended Reading

All of the works listed on this page extend the theme of Unit 4, "Turning Points." The following information may help you choose which to assign:

Customize for
Varying Student Needs

When assigning the selections in this part to your students, keep in mind the following factors:

- *Of Mice and Men* is a modern classic that is short and high interest.
- *Things Fall Apart* is probably the most famous contemporary African novel. It is medium length and fast moving.

Literature Study Guides

Literature study guides are available for *Latino Literature, Of Mice and Men,* and *Things Fall Apart.* These guides include section summaries, discussion questions, and activities.

Resources for Teaching Novels and Plays

This resource guide contains graphic organizers, teaching strategies, and transparencies that will be invaluable in teaching any of these novels.

Sensitive Issues

Things Fall Apart contains some issues and references that you may find sensitive in your classroom. For example, the roles and attitudes of men and women in Ibo society may seem sexist. The novel also contains some frank conversations among the Ibo about sexual matters. Finally, the treatment of the Ibo and Christian religions may be troublesome to some students who hold strong Christian beliefs.

Planning Instruction and Assessment

Unit Objectives

1. To read selections in different genres that develop the theme of Expanding Horizons
2. To apply a variety of reading strategies, particularly Strategies for Reading Fiction, appropriate for reading these selections
3. To recognize literary elements used in these selections
4. To increase vocabulary
5. To learn elements of grammar and style
6. To write in a variety of modes and about situations based on the selections
7. To develop speaking and listening skills by doing proposed activities

Meeting the Objectives

With each selection, you will find instructional material and portfolio opportunities through which students can meet these objectives. Further, you will find additional practice pages for reading strategies, literary elements, vocabulary, and grammar in the **Selection Support** booklet in the Teaching Resources box.

Setting Goals Work with your students at the beginning of the unit to set goals for unit outcomes. Plan what skills and concepts you wish students to acquire. You may individualize according to students' performance levels or learning modalities.

Portfolios You may have students keep portfolios of their work or of their work in progress. The activities and prompts on the Build Your Portfolio page of each selection provide opportunities for students to apply the concepts presented with the selection.

Torn in Transit, John Haberle, Brandywine River Museum

 Humanities: Art

Torn in Transit by John Haberle, 1890–95.

Help students examine the multiple levels of meaning of this painting. Ask students about the title; it refers to the tickets shown and to the package, whose torn edges are seen around the perimeter of the landscape. The painting might be interpreted as a comment on the way human traffic tends to despoil nature; the work might also be interpreted as expressing the opposite idea—that nature cannot be tidily contained, despite human efforts to do so.

Help students link the artwork to the theme of Unit 5, "Expanding Horizons," by answering the following questions:

1. Has the painter made the landscape seem an intimidating or an inviting place, and how? *Most students will probably say that the landscape seems inviting because it is so beautiful; some students might find the mountains challenging and the water potentially treacherous.*

2. What effect does the cord tied around the landscape create? *The cord makes you realize that this is a picture of a landscape, since you can see the cord's shadow on the painting. Some students may say that the cord constricts the landscape, impinging on its freedom, while others may say that the landscape appears about to burst the straining cord.*

378

UNIT 5

Expanding Horizons

New places, new ideas, new friends—every new experience expands your horizons. Your world becomes larger when you consider new ways of seeing and doing. Through the stories, poems, and essays in this unit, you will travel from Nigeria to England, meeting a kindly old widow, celebrities, and a band of thieves. Your horizons will expand with a variety of new experiences and interesting people.

Assessing Student Progress

The following tools are available to measure the degree to which students meet the unit objectives:

Informal Assessment

The questions on the Guide for Responding sections are a first level of response to the concepts and skills presented with the selection. Students' responses are a brief informal measure of their grasp of the material. Their responses on this level can indicate where further instruction and practice are needed. You may then follow up with the practice pages in the *Selection Support* booklet.

You will find literature and reading guides in the *Alternative Assessment* booklet, which you may give students on an individual basis for informal assessment of their performance.

Formal Assessment

In the *Formal Assessment* booklet, you will find selection tests and part tests.

Selection Tests The selection tests measure comprehension and skills acquisition for each selection or group of selections.

Part Tests Each part test, which calls on students to read a passage of literature they have not previously seen, applies the unit skills on a broader level. The Critical Reading section measures Unit Objectives 1, 2, and 3. The Vocabulary and Grammar section measures Objectives 4 and 5. The Essay section measures Objectives 1 and 6. Both the Critical Reading and Vocabulary and Grammar section use formats similar to those found on many standardized tests, including the SAT.

◆ *379*

Alternative Assessment

Portfolios As you review individual pieces or the collected work in students' portfolios, you will find assessment sheets available in the portfolio section of the *Alternative Assessment* booklet.

Scoring Rubrics You will find scoring rubrics for writing modes in the *Alternative Assessment* booklet. You can apply these to Writing Mini-Lessons and to Writing Process Workshop lessons.

Speaking and Listening The *Alternative Assessment* booklet contains assessment sheets for speaking and listening activities.

Learning Modalities The *Alternative Assessment* booklet contains activities that appeal to different learning styles. You may use these as an alternative measurement of students' growth.

OBJECTIVES

1. To read, comprehend, and interpret a short story
2. To relate a story to personal experience
3. To use strategies for reading fiction to read for success
4. To identify motivation
5. To build vocabulary in context and learn forms of *sagacity*
6. To use adjectives and adverbs correctly
7. To write a last will and testament using logical organization
8. To respond to the story through writing, speaking and listening, and projects

SKILLS INSTRUCTION

Vocabulary:
Related Words:
Forms of *sagacity*

Grammar:
Correct Use of
Adjectives and
Adverbs

Reading for Success:
Strategies for
Reading Fiction

Literary Focus:
Motivation

Writing:
Logical
Organization

Speaking and Listening:
Informal Debate
(teacher edition)

Critical Viewing:
Predict; Infer

PORTFOLIO OPPORTUNITIES

Writing: Character Sketch; Review; Health Report

Writing Mini-Lesson: Last Will and Testament

Speaking and Listening: Informal Debate; Dialogue Between Person and Pet

Projects: Conversion Chart; Area Map

More About the Author

Virginia Woolf suffered for most of her life from manic depression, an illness that is now often easily diagnosed and treated with medication. In Woolf's day, however, no treatment existed. She had nervous breakdowns in 1913 and 1915; nevertheless, her writing greatly influenced the current of literary experimentation known as stream of consciousness.

*G*uide for Reading

Virginia Woolf (1882–1941)

Breaking free from her prim and proper upbringing, Virginia Woolf overcame sexism and stereotypes to become one of the most influential shapers of contemporary modern fiction.

Virginia Woolf (born Virginia Stephen) was brought up in a family of old-fashioned Victorians. Her father, Leslie Stephen, saw to it that his daughter grew up surrounded by books. He also introduced her to a number of writers in person. By the age of twenty-three, Virginia began contributing reviews to the Literary Supplement of *The Times of London*.

Meeting of the Minds In 1912, Virginia married Leonard Woolf, author and social reformer, with whom she founded the Hogarth Press. Their house in London became an informal meeting place for some of the more important thinkers of the era, including writers E. M. Forster and Katherine Mansfield, art critic Roger Fry, and economist John Maynard Keynes.

A Matter of Principle Virginia Woolf's intellectual and privileged social background allowed her liberal beliefs to flourish. She resented the sexism and corruption of English universities and other aspects of male-dominated Victorian England.

Virginia Woolf's sensitivity to the abuse of women's rights led to her refusal of honorary degrees from several universities.

Stream of Novels After her first two novels, Woolf began to experiment with "stream of consciousness," a narrative technique that presents thoughts as if they are coming directly from a character's mind. Woolf continued to refine her fluid, inward-looking style in the novels *Mrs. Dalloway* (1925), *To the Lighthouse* (1927), and *The Waves* (1931). Unlike many of her works, "The Widow and the Parrot" has a traditional narrative form.

◆ Build Vocabulary

RELATED WORDS: FORMS OF *SAGACITY*

In this story, you will encounter an unusual parrot—a parrot of great sagacity. *Sagacity* and its related words come from the Latin word *sagax*, which means "keen" or "acute." *Sagacity* means "wisdom," or "keen judgment." A *sage* is a person who has keen judgment—a wise person. *Sagacious*, on the other hand, describes a person or thing, such as a decision that shows good judgment.

WORD BANK

ford
dilapidated
sovereigns
sagacity

As you read, you will encounter the words on this list. Each word is defined on the page where it first appears. Preview the list before you read.

◆ Build Grammar Skills

CORRECT USE OF ADJECTIVES AND ADVERBS

Do not confuse the use of **adjectives** and **adverbs.** Remember that adjectives modify nouns and adverbs modify verbs, adjectives, and other adverbs. A common mistake is the use of an adjective to modify a verb, whereas an adverb is correct.

Notice the correct use of the adjective *slow* and the adverb *slowly* in these sentences from "The Widow and the Parrot."

. . . her progress was very *slow* indeed.

(The predicate adjective *slow* modifies the subject *progress*.)

At the best of times she walked *slowly*.

(The adverb *slowly* modifies the verb *walked*. The adjective *slow* would be incorrect here.)

380 ◆ Expanding Horizons

Prentice Hall Literature Program Resources

REINFORCE / RETEACH / EXTEND

Selection Support Pages
Build Vocabulary: Forms of *sagacity*, p. 113
Build Grammar Skills: Correct Use of Adjectives and Adverbs, p. 114
Reading for Success: Strategies for Reading Fiction, pp. 115–116
Literary Focus: Motivation, p. 117

Strategies for Diverse Student Needs, p. 28

Beyond Literature, Career Connection:
Veterinary Science, p. 28

Formal Assessment
Selection Test, pp. 98–100

Alternative Assessment, p. 28

Resource Pro CD-R⊘M
"The Widow and the Parrot"—includes all resource material and customizable lesson plans

 Listening to Literature Audiocassettes
"The Widow and the Parrot"

 Looking at Literature Videodisc,
"The Widow and the Parrot"

The Widow and the Parrot

◆ *Literature and Your Life*

CONNECT YOUR EXPERIENCE

If you've ever had a pet, you know that the bond between people and animals can be a strong one. The woman in this story has a strong connection with animals. Her kindness and devotion to animals change her life for the better.

Journal Writing Describe a time when it seemed that your pet was trying to tell you something or communicate something to you. For example, you may have a pet who reminds you of feeding times by scratching at the pantry at the same time every day. If you've never had a pet, describe an unusual exchange between a person and an animal that you witnessed on television or at a zoo.

THEMATIC FOCUS: EXPANDING HORIZONS

The woman and the parrot in this story communicate as if the parrot were human. As you read this story, ask yourself what animals can teach us.

◆ Background for Understanding

LANGUAGE

You wouldn't expect to understand someone who speaks a language you don't know, but you would probably expect to understand someone who speaks English. You might be surprised to find that someone who speaks "American English" might, in fact, have difficulty understanding some words and expressions in "British English."

In "The Widow and the Parrot," Mrs. Gage mentions *pounds sterling* and *solicitors*. Although an American might think of *pounds* as weight and *solicitors* as salespeople, a resident of Great Britain thinks of *pounds* as British money (shown below) and *solicitors* as lawyers.

◆ Literary Focus

MOTIVATION

Detectives in mystery stories are always looking for the motive for a crime. However, you don't have to be a detective to want to know a character's **motivation**—the reason for his or her actions or words. Understanding why characters act as they do will help you understand story events. For instance, in "The Widow and the Parrot," a rich old man leaves all his wealth to a sister he hasn't seen in years. This action is understandable when you consider the man's possible motive: He may have been sorry that he didn't help her during his lifetime.

Use a chart like the one shown here to explore the motives behind the actions of the characters in this story.

Motive
Sorrow that he hasn't been in touch

Action
Leaves money to sister

Action

Action

Guide for Reading ◆ 381

Ask students what they would do if they suddenly learned they had won or inherited a million dollars. Would they continue their lives much as they are living them now? Would they make any significant changes? What would they buy? Would they give any money away? After discussing what students would do if they received such an unexpected piece of good fortune, tell them they are about to read a story about a poor person who is told she inherits a large fortune.

Customize for
Less Proficient Readers
These students can benefit from breaking the plot of the story into scenes. Have students work together to list the scenes in the story that advance the plot, as if in a play version of the story.

Customize for
More Advanced Students
Tell students that Mrs. Gage is an unusual character for Virginia Woolf—most of Woolf's characters are upper-class intellectuals. However, Mrs. Gage clearly has some qualities the author admires. As they read, have students reflect on the reasons Woolf might have created this particular character to be the heroine of her story.

Customize for
English Language Learners
An occasional "Britishism" or unusual idiom such as "sovereign," "wealth of the Indies," or "half a crown" in this story may pose problems for English language learners. Explain these unfamiliar phrases as needed. Remind students that they can often determine meanings from context.

Customize for
Visual/Spatial Learners
As they read the story, have students graph and label the main character's highs and lows. For example, the line graph might begin at zero as the story opens, spring upward as Mrs. Gage reads the letter from Sussex, and drop as she visits her brother's house for the first time. Reviewing the graph will help students recall the plot of the story.

Preparing for Standardized Tests

Reading and Vocabulary Understanding related forms of a word can help students identify unfamiliar words in reading comprehension sections as well as vocabulary sections of standardized tests. The Build Vocabulary lesson focuses on words related to *sagacity*. Knowing any of these words can help students decode other related words, such as *sage*. For additional practice, use the Build Vocabulary page in **Selection Support**, p. 113.

Grammar and Language The sentence error section of the PSAT and SAT II standardized tests

asks students to recognize errors in sentences. Test items often include identifying misused adjectives and adverbs, as in the following example:

    She walked <u>slow</u> to the bus stop. <u>Slowly</u>
          A   B
    she sat down on the hard bench. *A*

The grammar lesson for this selection focuses on this skill. For additional practice, use the Build Grammar Skills page on Correct Use of Adjectives and Adverbs, p. 114, in **Selection Support**.

The Reading for Success page in each unit presents a set of problem-solving procedures to help readers understand authors' words and ideas on multiple levels. Good readers develop a bank of strategies from which they can draw as needed.

Unit 5 focuses on strategies for reading fiction. For students to enjoy a work of fiction it is important to apply strategies that will enhance their understanding and appreciation of an author's craft.

These strategies for reading fiction are modeled with "The Widow and the Parrot." Each green box shows an example of the thinking process involved in applying one of these strategies.

How to Use the Reading for Success Page

- Introduce the strategies, presenting each as a problem solving procedure. Be sure students understand what each strategy involves and under what circumstances to apply it.

- Before students read the story, have them preview it, looking at the annotations in the green boxes that model the strategies.

- To reinforce these strategies after students have read "The Widow and the Parrot," have students do the Reading for Success pages in *Selection Support,* pp. 115–116. This activity gives students an opportunity to read a selection and practice the strategies for reading fiction by writing their own annotations.

Reading for Success

Strategies for Reading Fiction

Suppose you could visit a new and exciting place each week—you can if you read works of fiction! Reading fiction allows you to explore unfamiliar places and unusual worlds.

Just as mapping out a strategy for a vacation helps ensure a pleasant trip, applying effective strategies as you read fiction helps you understand and enjoy what you are reading. When you read fiction, use the following strategies:

Predict what will happen or what the author will say.

As you read, ask yourself what might happen. You may base a prediction on your own experience in a similar situation or on information that has been provided in the text. Continue to make predictions as you read.

Identify with a character or the situation.

Identify with a character or the situation in your reading. Put yourself in the place of the character and experience his or her thoughts, feelings, and so on. Ask yourself how you would handle the situation.

Envision the setting and the action.

Use details from the story to create a picture in your mind, as if you were watching the story unfold on the big screen. For example, see the house that your character lives in. Is it big or small? How is it decorated? As you read along, envision the action and revise the images in your mind as events unfold.

Make inferences.

Writers don't always tell you everything directly. You have to make inferences to arrive at ideas that writers suggest but don't say. You make an inference by considering the details that the writer includes or doesn't include. Sometimes it's also helpful to "read between the lines"—to look beyond the literal meaning of the words to obtain a full picture of what the author means.

Draw conclusions.

A conclusion is a general statement that you can make and explain by reasons or that you can support with details from the text. A series of inferences can lead you to a conclusion.

Respond.

Think about what the story means. What feelings does it evoke in you? What has the story added to your understanding of people and of life in general?

As you read the following story by Virginia Woolf, look at the notes in the boxes. These notes demonstrate how to apply these strategies to a work of fiction.

Reading Strategies: Support and Reinforcement

Appropriate Reading Strategies Students are given a reading strategy to apply in reading each selection. For example, students may be asked to identify with a character or situation in a selection where character is central to the story.

Reading Prompts To encourage application of the given reading strategy, there are occasional prompts, within green boxes, at appropriate and significant points. In addition, there are red boxes prompting application of the Literary Focus concept and maroon boxes prompting students to connect with their lives.

Using the Boxed Annotations and Prompts

The material in the green, red, and maroon boxes along the sides of selections is intended to help students apply the literary element and the reading strategy and to make a connection with their lives.

You may use the boxed material in these ways:

- Have students pause when they come to a box and respond to its prompt before they continue reading.

- Urge students to read through the selection ignoring the boxes. After they have read the selection completely, they may go back and review the selection, responding to the prompts.

The Widow and the Parrot

Virginia Woolf

One-Minute Insight

Kindly old Mrs. Gage gains an inheritance from her brother, but the miserly old man hides it where it cannot be found. After a series of apparent disasters, Mrs. Gage's kindness to her brother's beloved parrot leads her to discover the missing fortune. The story ends happily, as the heroine's goodness to animals is rewarded with her finding the inheritance.

►Critical Viewing◄

❶ Predict Students may note that the title implies that a parrot will be a main character in the story.

◆ **Reading for Success**

❷ Predict What Will Happen Point out this introduction to Mrs. Gage. Ask: What do you know about Mrs. Gage so far? What makes you think the letter is important? *She is old, lame, and poor. The appearance of the letter at the end of the first paragraph indicates that it will influence the plot in an important way.*

❸ Clarification The phrase "lawk a mussy" is a dialect form of "Lord have mercy." Ask: What does the author's use of this phrase tell you about the character? *Her speech indicates that she is not from the upper class and is probably not very well educated.*

Some fifty years ago Mrs. Gage, an elderly widow, was sitting in her cottage in a village called Spilsby in Yorkshire. Although lame and rather shortsighted she was doing her best to mend a pair of clogs, for she had only a few shillings a week to live on. As she hammered at the clog, the postman opened the door and threw a letter into her lap. ❷

It bore the address "Messrs. Stagg and Beetle, 67 High Street, Lewes, Sussex."

Mrs. Gage opened it and read:

"Dear Madam: We have the honor to inform you of the death of your brother Mr. Joseph Brand."

"Lawk a mussy," said Mrs. Gage. "Old brother Joseph gone at last!" ❸

"He has left you his entire property," the letter went on, "which consists of a dwelling house, stable, cucumber frames, mangles, wheelbarrows, etc., etc., in the village of Rodmell, near Lewes. He also bequeaths to you his entire fortune; Viz: £3,000. (three thousand pounds[1]) sterling."

> You might **predict** that there will be obstacles to Mrs. Gage's getting this inheritance.

 ▲ Critical Viewing What role might a parrot like this one play in the story? [Predict]

---

1. **three thousand pounds:** This amount of British money was worth about $15,000 at the time of the story.

The Widow and the Parrot ◆ 383

Consider these suggestions to take advantage of extended class time:

- Have students complete the journal activity in Literature and Your Life (p. 381) and discuss their entries with the class.
- Introduce the Reading for Success strategies for reading fiction. As they read, encourage students to look at the annotations that model the strategies. For more practice, give them the Reading for

Success pages in *Selection Support*, pp. 115–116.

- As you review the information in Background for Understanding (p. 381), have students mention any other British expressions with which they are familiar; for example, *boot* for trunk of a car, *pram* for baby carriage, *flat* for apartment, and *lorry* for truck.

- Have students work in small groups to discuss their answers to the Critical Thinking Questions (p. 391).
- Before students complete the Writing Mini-Lesson (p. 392), have them brainstorm for a list of story characters who might leave money, property, or advice in a will. Students may select from the class list or use ideas of their own as they prepare their last will and testament.

① Make Inferences Ask students: What does the fact that Mrs. Gage is devoted to animals even though she is poor tell you about her personality? *That she would sacrifice for her dog shows that she has a kind, unselfish nature. Some students, however, may say that some people who are devoted to animals do not show the same concern for fellow humans. Students should be encouraged to read on to find if this is true of Mrs. Gage or not.*

◆ **Reading for Success**

② Envision the Setting This description shows very clearly what the ford was like. Have students describe the ford in their own words. *Students may say that it is a shallow, rocky path across the wide river.*

◆ **Reading for Success**

③ Draw Conclusions Ask students to think back to the beginning of the story when they learn that Mrs. Gage is devoted to her dog. Have them combine what they learned about Mrs. Gage's personality with this description of her with the parrot and draw a conclusion about her personality. *It should now be evident that she is a kind, sensitive person.*

◆ **Critical Thinking**

④ Identify Character Traits Ask students: Would you say Mrs. Gage is an optimist or a pessimist? Why? *She is an optimist; even though part of her inheritance has come to nothing, she is able to focus on the other part.*

Mrs. Gage almost fell into the fire with joy. She had not seen her brother for many years, and, as he did not even acknowledge the Christmas card which she sent him every year, she thought that his miserly habits, well known to her from childhood, made him grudge even a penny stamp for a reply.

But now it had all turned out to her advantage. With three thousand pounds, to say nothing of house, etc., etc., she and her family could live in great luxury for ever. She determined that she must visit Rodmell at once. The village clergyman, the Rev. Samuel Tallboys, lent her two pound ten, to pay her fare, and by next day all preparations for her journey were complete. The most important of these was the care of her dog Shag during her absence, for in spite of her poverty she was devoted to animals, and often went short herself rather than stint her dog of his bone.

She reached Lewes late on Tuesday night. In those days, I must tell you, there was no bridge over the river at Southease, nor had the road to Newhaven yet been made. To reach Rodmell it was necessary to cross the river Ouse by a <u>ford</u>, traces of which still exist, but this could only be attempted at low tide, when the stones on the riverbed appeared above the water. Mr. Stacey, the farmer, was going to Rodmell in his cart, and he kindly offered to take Mrs. Gage with him. They reached Rodmell about nine o'clock on a November night and Mr. Stacey obligingly pointed out to Mrs. Gage the house at the end of the village which had been left her by her brother. Mrs. Gage knocked at the door. There was no answer. She knocked again. A very strange high voice shrieked out "Not at home." She was so much taken aback that if she had not heard footsteps coming she would have run away. However, the door was opened by an old village woman, by name Mrs. Ford.

"Who was that shrieking out 'Not at home'?" said Mrs. Gage.

"Drat the bird!" said Mrs. Ford very peevishly, pointing to a large gray parrot. "He almost screams my head off. There he sits all day humped up on his perch like a monument screeching 'Not at home' if ever you go near his perch." He was a very handsome bird, as Mrs. Gage could see; but his feathers were sadly neglected. "Perhaps he is unhappy, or he may be hungry," she said. But Mrs. Ford said it was temper merely; he was a seaman's parrot and had learnt his language in the east. However, she added, Mr. Joseph was very fond of him, had called him James; and, it was said, talked to him as if he were a rational being. Mrs. Ford soon left. Mrs. Gage at once went to her box and fetched some sugar which she had with her and offered it to the parrot, saying in a very kind tone that she meant him no harm, but was his old master's sister, come to take possession of the house, and she would see to it that he was as happy as a bird could be. Taking a lantern she next went round the house to see what sort of property her brother had left her. It was a bitter disappointment. There were holes in all the carpets. The bottoms of the chairs had fallen out. Rats ran along the mantelpiece. There were large toadstools growing through the kitchen floor. There was not a stick of furniture worth seven pence halfpenny; and Mrs. Gage only cheered herself by thinking of the three thousand pounds that lay safe and snug in Lewes Bank.

She determined to set off to Lewes next day in order to claim her money from

> You can **infer** that Joseph, despite his miserliness, seemed to be good to his parrot.

> You might **predict** that Mrs. Gage's kindness to the parrot will have a positive effect.

> Details such as the holes in the carpets and the rats on the floor help you **envision** the house.

Cross-Curricular Connection: Science

Mrs. Gage found toadstools growing through the kitchen floor. Point out to students that toadstools are inedible forms of mushrooms. These are fungi consisting of two parts: a mycelium (stem) and a fruiting body (the umbrella-shaped top). Mushrooms vary greatly in size and color, rising from about ¾ of an inch to about 15 inches in height and ranging from whites and yellows to blue, violet, green, red, and black. Many species of mushroom live on decaying matter, although some live on living organisms such as trees and plants. In some instances the mushroom causes no harm to its host; however, many such growths are parasitic and will destroy the host plant.

Ask students what the presence of toadstools indicates about the house Mrs. Gage has inherited. *Students should note that the toadstools are feeding on the decaying matter of the floor of the house.* Suggest that interested students research species of mushroom that can be described as toadstools.

Messrs. Stagg and Beetle the solicitors,[2] and then to return home as quick as she could. Mr. Stacey, who was going in to market with some fine Berkshire pigs, again offered to take her with him, and told her some terrible stories of young people who had been drowned through trying to cross the river at high tide, as they drove. A great disappointment was in store for the poor old woman directly she got in to Mr. Stagg's office.

"Pray take a seat, Madam," he said, looking very solemn and grunting slightly. "The fact is," he went on, "that you must prepare to face some very disagreeable news. Since I wrote to you I have gone carefully through Mr. Brand's papers. I regret to say that I can find no trace whatever of the three thousand pounds. Mr. Beetle, my partner, went himself to Rodmell and searched the premises with the utmost care. He found absolutely nothing—no gold, silver, or valuables of any kind—except a fine gray parrot which I advise you to sell for whatever he will fetch. His language, Benjamin Beetle said, is very extreme. But that is neither here nor there. I much fear you have had your journey for nothing. The premises are <u>dilapidated</u>; and of course our expenses are considerable." Here he stopped, and Mrs. Gage well knew that he wished her to go. She was almost crazy with disappointment. Not only had she borrowed two pound ten from the Rev. Samuel Tallboys, but she would return home absolutely empty handed, for the parrot James would have to be sold to pay her fare. It was raining hard, but Mr. Stagg did not press her to stay, and she was too beside herself with sorrow to care what she did. In spite of the rain she started to walk back to Rodmell across the meadows.

Mrs. Gage, as I have already said, was lame in her right leg. At the best of times she walked

> Because you know Mrs. Gage's feelings and expectations, you can **identify** with her great disappointment.

slowly, and now, what with her disappointment and the mud on the bank, her progress was very slow indeed. As she plodded along, the day grew darker and darker, until it was as much as she could do to keep on the raised path by the river side. You might have heard her grumbling as she walked, and complaining of her crafty brother Joseph, who had put her to all this trouble "Express," she said, "to plague me. He was always a cruel little boy when we were children," she went on. "He liked worrying the poor insects, and I've known him trim a hairy caterpillar with a pair of scissors before my very eyes. He was such a miserly varmint too. He used to hide his pocket money in a tree, and if anyone gave him a piece of iced cake for tea, he cut the sugar off and kept it for his supper. I make no doubt he's all aflame at this very moment in fire, but what's the comfort of that to me?" she asked, and indeed it was very little comfort, for she ran slap into a great cow which was coming along the bank, and rolled over and over in the mud.

She picked herself up as best she could and trudged on again. It seemed to her that she had been walking for hours. It was now pitch dark and she could scarcely see her own hand before her nose. Suddenly she bethought her of Farmer Stacey's words about the ford. "Lawk a mussy," she said, "however shall I find my way across? If the tide's in, I shall step into deep water and be swept out to sea in a jiffy! Many's the couple that been drowned here; to say nothing of horses, carts, herds of cattle, and stacks of hay."

Indeed what with the dark and the mud she had got herself into a pretty pickle. She could

> You can **predict** that Mrs. Gage will be overcome by obstacles or that something unforeseen will happen to turn events around.

◆ **Build Vocabulary**

ford (fôrd) *n.*: Shallow place in a stream or river, where people can cross

dilapidated (di lap´ ə dāt´ id) *adj.*: Fallen into a shabby and neglected state

The Widow and the Parrot ◆ 385

Customize for
Less Proficient Readers
Have volunteers summarize Mr. Stagg's remarks to Mrs. Gage. *It appears that the three thousand pounds Mrs. Gage expected are nowhere to be found. The only thing of worth she has inherited is the parrot.*

◆ **Reading for Success**

❺ **Identify With a Character or the Situation** Have students think about times when they have been so disappointed that they didn't care what they did. Ask: Why does your identification with Mrs. Gage's despair make you want to read on? *Students may say that they hope that something good will happen to her.*

◆ **Build Grammar Skills**

❻ **Correct Use of Adjectives and Adverbs** Ask students to identify and explain Mrs. Gage's grammar error in this passage. What part of speech is *express*? Which word does it modify? Which word should she have used instead? *Mrs. Gage has used the adjective* express *to modify the verb* put*. She should have used the adverb* expressly.

◆ **Critical Thinking**

❼ **Compare and Contrast** Have students compare and contrast Mrs. Gage and her brother Joseph as children. How did Mrs. Gage, as a child, feel about her brother's treatment of insects? Would Mrs. Gage have been cruel to any animal? Would she have been miserly or generous? *From what readers already know and from the words "worrying," "poor," and "before my very eyes," readers should know that Mrs. Gage disapproved of her brother's treatment of insects. While Joseph was miserly with his pocket money, readers can assume that Mrs. Gage was generous, based on their knowledge that she has done with less food herself in order to feed her dog.*

Speaking and Listening Mini-Lesson

Informal Debate
This mini-lesson supports the first Speaking and Listening activity in the Idea Bank on page 392.

Introduce the Concept Have volunteers explain what a debate is: an oral presentation in which two sides of an issue are discussed and evaluated. Point out that the purpose of a debate is to persuade others to share your side's opinion. Refer students to the Speaking and Listening Handbook, p. 978, for further clarification of debate.

Develop Background Divide the class into two teams: one team will argue in favor of studying animal behavior; one will argue against it.
Suggest that each team research to find facts, statistics, and examples to support their position. Then they should try to anticipate the other side's arguments and plan how to answer them.

Apply the Information Have the teams take turns presenting their arguments. Allow time for teams to refute or argue each point as it is raised.

Assess the Outcome Assess the debate by answering these questions:
• Were points presented convincingly?
• Were points supported with facts, examples, and statistics?
• Were arguments refuted logically?

◆ **Reading for Success**

❶ Predict What Will Happen or What the Author Will Say Mrs. Gage's fate appears bleak indeed. Ask students: Based on your experience reading similar stories, you would most likely predict that Mrs. Gage will neither drown nor freeze to death. Why? *Students may say that she seems to be a good woman, and they doubt whether the author will allow her to die without some reward for her goodness. They may also say that she is the main character, and if she dies, the story will end pointlessly.*

◆ **Build Vocabulary**

❷ Related Words: Forms of *Sagacity* Like *sagacity*, *monstrosity* is a noun with an *-ity* ending. Have students identify the forms of *monstrosity* that parallel *sagacious* and *sage*. *The words are* monstrous *and* monster.

◆ **Reading for Success**

❸ Draw Conclusions Have students identify the hints in previous paragraphs that lead them to conclude that the mysterious light is not a comet but Mrs. Gage's burning house. *The village of Rodmell was lit up, the light shot up into the sky, the brother's house was described as being "at the end of the village."*

hardly see the river itself, let alone tell whether she had reached the ford or not. No lights were visible anywhere, for, as you may be aware, there is no cottage or house on that side of the river nearer than Asheham House, lately the seat of Mr. Leonard Woolf. It seemed that there was nothing for it but to sit down and wait for the morning. But at her age, with the rheumatics in her system, she might well die of cold. On the other hand, if she tried to cross the river it was almost certain that she would be drowned. So miserable was her state that she would gladly have changed places with one of the cows in the field. No more wretched old woman could have been found in the whole county of Sussex; standing on the river bank, not knowing whether to sit or to swim, or merely to roll over in the grass, wet though it was, and sleep or freeze to death, as her fate decided.

> **❶** You can **infer** that, in her disappointment and in the face of these obstacles, Mrs. Gage has given up hope.

At that moment a wonderful thing happened. An enormous light shot up into the sky, like a gigantic torch, lighting up every blade of grass, and showing her the ford not twenty yards away. It was low tide, and the crossing would be an easy matter if only the light did not go out before she had got over.

> **❷** You can **identify** with Mrs. Gage's feeling of relief.

❷ "It must be a comet or some such wonderful monstrosity," she said as she hobbled across. She could see the village of Rodmell brilliantly lit up in front of her.

"Bless and save us!" she cried out. "There's a house on fire—thanks be to the Lord"—for she reckoned that it would take some minutes at least to burn a house down, and in that time she would be well on her way to the village.

"It's an ill wind that blows nobody any good," she said as she hobbled along the Roman road. Sure enough, she could see every inch of the way, and was almost in the village street when for the first time it struck her: "Perhaps it's my own house that's blazing to cinders before my very eyes!" **❸**

She was perfectly right.

A small boy in his nightgown came capering up to her and cried out, "Come and see old Joseph Brand's house ablaze!"

Cross-Curricular Connection: Geography

Students may be surprised that a river can be affected by tides. The river Ouse flows into the North Sea to the east of England at a bay called The Wash. For many miles upstream, the ocean tides control the river's depth. Similarly, in New York State, the mouth of the Hudson River, where it empties into the Atlantic Ocean, is east of New York City. The Hudson is tidal—and salty—for more than 20 miles north of its mouth. A name for the part of a river whose waters mix with ocean water is *estuary*.

Explain to students that tides are controlled primarily by the gravitational pull of the moon. At any time of day, there are always two points on Earth that are at high tide: the point directly facing the moon and the point facing directly away from the moon.

▲ **Critical Viewing** How do you think Mrs. Gage felt at seeing a sight like this and learning that it was her own house? [Infer]

④

All the villagers were standing in a ring round the house handing buckets of water which were filled from the well in Monk's house kitchen, and throwing them on the flames. But the fire had got a strong hold, and just as Mrs. Gage arrived, the roof fell in.

"Has anybody saved the parrot?" she cried.

"Be thankful you're not inside yourself, Madam," said the Rev. James Hawkesford, the clergyman. "Do not worry for the dumb creatures. I make no doubt the parrot was mercifully suffocated on his perch."

⑤

But Mrs. Gage was determined to see for herself. She had to be held back by the village people, who remarked that she must be crazy to hazard her life for a bird.

⑤

"Poor old woman," said Mrs. Ford, "she has lost all her property, save one old wooden box, with her night things in it. No doubt we should be crazed in her place too."

So saying, Mrs. Ford took Mrs. Gage by the hand and led her off to her own cottage, where she was to sleep the night. The fire was now extinguished, and everybody went home to bed. But poor Mrs. Gage could not sleep. She tossed and tumbled thinking of her miserable state, and wondering how she could get back to Yorkshire and pay the Rev. Samuel Tallboys the money she owed him. At the same time she was even more grieved to think of the fate of the poor parrot James. She had taken a liking to the bird, and thought that he must have an affectionate heart to mourn so deeply for the death of old Joseph Brand, who had never done a kindness to any human creature. It was a terrible death for an innocent bird, she thought; and if only she had been in time, she would have risked her own life to save his.

⑥

She was lying in bed thinking these thoughts when a slight tap at the window made her start. The tap was repeated three times over. Mrs. Gage got out of bed as quickly as she could and went to the window. There, to her utmost surprise, sitting on the window ledge, was an enormous parrot. The rain had stopped and it was a fine moonlight night. She was greatly alarmed at first, but soon recognized the gray parrot,

The Widow and the Parrot ◆ 387

Beyond the Classroom

◆ Reading for Success

❶ Envision the Setting and the Action Have students close their eyes and imagine the parrot's actions as a volunteer reads this sentence aloud. Ask students to identify how the author makes the parrot's actions come alive. *She uses specific action verbs and descriptive phrases.*

◆ Literary Focus

❷ Motivation Have students consider what they know about Mrs. Gage's character. Ask: What motivates Mrs. Gage to follow the parrot? *She likes the animal and thinks he's intelligent; she treats him with as much respect as she would a human being. She may be motivated by her respect for him or by simple curiosity.*

◆ Build Grammar Skills

❸ Correct Use of Adjectives and Adverbs The author uses adverbs throughout the story to make the action clear. Have students identify the adverbs that end in *-ly* in these sentences and tell which verbs they modify. What would happen if the adverbs were omitted? *Soothingly modifies "said"; violently modifies "repeated." Without these modifiers, the way Mrs. Gage spoke and the way the bird acted would be less clear.*

◆ Reading for Success

❹ Make Inferences Previously, Mrs. Gage did not understand what the bird meant by his squawking. Why does Mrs. Gage now understand the parrot? *She has paid close attention to his actions, which seem to have some logic to them.*

You can **infer** that the writer has respect for the intelligence of animals.

❶ James, and was overcome with joy at his escape. She opened the window, stroked his head several times, and told him to come in. The parrot replied by gently shaking his head from side to side, then flew to the ground, walked away a few steps, looked back as if to see whether Mrs. Gage were coming, and then returned to the window sill, where she stood in amazement.

"The creature has more meaning in its acts than we humans know," she said to herself. "Very well, James," she said aloud, talking to him as though he were a human being, "I'll take your word for it. Only wait a moment while I make myself decent."

❷ So saying she pinned on a large apron, crept as lightly as possible downstairs, and let herself out without rousing Mrs. Ford.

The parrot James was evidently satisfied. He now hopped briskly a few yards ahead of her in the direction of the burnt house. Mrs. Gage followed as fast as she could. The parrot hopped, as if he knew his way perfectly, round to the back of the house, where the kitchen had originally been. Nothing now remained of it except the brick floor, which was still

dripping with the water which had been thrown to put out the fire. Mrs. Gage stood still in amazement while James hopped about, pecking here and there, as if he were testing the bricks with his beak. It was a very uncanny sight, and had not Mrs. Gage been in the habit of living with animals, she would have lost her head, very likely, and hobbled back home. But stranger things yet were to happen. All this time the parrot had not said a word. He suddenly got into a state of the greatest excitement, fluttering his wings, tapping the floor repeatedly with his beak, and crying so shrilly, "Not at home! Not at home!" that Mrs. Gage feared that the whole village would be roused.

Judging from the way Woolf has described Joseph, you can probably **predict** what's under the bricks.

"Don't take on so, James; you'll hurt yourself," she said soothingly. But he repeated his ❸ attack on the bricks more violently than ever.

"Whatever can be the meaning of it?" said Mrs. Gage, looking carefully at the kitchen floor. The moonlight was bright enough to show her a slight unevenness in the laying of the bricks, as if they had been taken up and then relaid not quite flat with the others. She had fastened her apron with a large safety pin, and she now prized this pin between the bricks and found that they were only loosely laid together. Very soon she had taken one up in her hands. No sooner had she done this than the parrot hopped onto the brick next to it, and, tapping it smartly with ❹ his beak, cried, "Not at home!" which Mrs. Gage understood to mean that she was to move it. So they went on taking up the bricks in the moonlight until they had laid bare a space some six feet by four and a half. This the parrot seemed to think was enough. But what was to be done next?

388 ◆ *Expanding Horizons*

🏳 **Cross-Curricular Connection: Science**

Tell the class that James the parrot is a member of a large family of birds found chiefly in warm, tropical regions. They are popular as pets because they become affectionate and tame and can be taught to "talk." The demand for these birds in the United States led to problems in capturing and importing them. Today, most states outlaw the sale of imported parrots and allow only birds bred in captivity to be sold.

There are more than 300 species of parrots, about half of which are found in Central and

South America. Most parrots have colorful feathers. Since James is gray, he may be an African gray parrot like the one in the photograph that accompanies this selection.

Have interested students find out more about parrots and the laws that protect them. Visual/spatial learners may enjoy collecting photographs and drawings and labeling different species for a visual presentation.

Mrs. Gage now rested, and determined to be guided entirely by the behavior of the parrot James. She was not allowed to rest for long. After scratching about in the sandy foundations for a few minutes, as you may have seen a hen scratch in the sand with her claws, he unearthed what at first looked like a round lump of yellowish stone. His excitement became so intense that Mrs. Gage now went to his help. To her amazement she found that the whole space which they had uncovered was packed with long rolls of these round yellow stones, so neatly laid together that it was quite a job to move them. But what could they be? And for what purpose had they been hidden here? It was not until they had removed the entire layer on the top, and next a piece of oilcloth which lay beneath them, that a most miraculous sight was displayed before their eyes—there, in row after row, beautifully polished, and shining brightly in the moonlight, were thousands of brand new <u>sovereigns</u>!

5

This, then, was the miser's hiding place; and he had made sure that no one would detect it by taking two extraordinary precautions. In the first place, as was proved later, he had built a kitchen range over the spot where his treasure lay hid, so that unless the fire had destroyed it, no one could have guessed its existence; and secondly he had coated the top layer of sovereigns with some sticky substance, then rolled them in the earth, so that if by any chance one had been laid bare no one would have suspected that it was anything but a pebble such as you may see for yourself any day in the garden. Thus, it was only by the extraordinary coincidence of the fire and the parrot's <u>sagacity</u> that old Joseph's craft was defeated.

> From the parrot's actions, you can **infer** that he wants to help Mrs. Gage.

6

Mrs. Gage and the parrot now worked hard and removed the whole hoard—which

numbered three thousand pieces, neither more nor less—placing them in her apron which was spread upon the ground. As the three thousandth coin was placed on the top of the pile, the parrot flew up into the air in triumph and alighted very gently on the top of Mrs. Gage's head. It was in this fashion that they returned to Mrs. Ford's cottage, at a very slow pace, for Mrs. Gage was lame, as I have said, and now she was almost weighted to the ground by the contents of her apron. But she reached her room without anyone knowing of her visit to the ruined house.

Next day she returned to Yorkshire. Mr. Stacey once more drove her into Lewes and was rather surprised to find how heavy Mrs. Gage's wooden box had become. But he was a quiet sort of man, and merely concluded that the kind people of Rodmell had given her a few odds and ends to console her for the dreadful

◆ Build Vocabulary

sovereigns (säv′ rənz) *n.*: British gold coins worth one pound each

sagacity (sə gas′ ə tē) *n.*: Wisdom

The Widow and the Parrot ◆ 389

◆ Literary Focus

5 Motivation Ask students to speculate on the motivation that led Mrs. Gage's brother to hide the coins. *He may have been too miserly to let anyone know he had the money and too mistrustful to leave it where it might be stolen.*

6 Clarification The word *craft* has a variety of meanings; among them are "skill," "trickery," and "occupation." Have students explain how they know which of those three meanings is intended here. *"Trickery" is the intended meaning; the old man was crafty, or devious, not artistically skilled or employed.*

Looking at Literature Videodisc To provide a connection for the theme of the bond between humans and their pets, play Chapter 5 of the videodisc. This segment focuses on an organization that brings animals into convalescent homes and rest homes to enrich the lives of the sick and the elderly. Have students discuss how the parrot and the dog Shag have enriched Mrs. Gage's life. Students may discuss the importance of pets and other animals in their own lives as well.

Chapter 5

Speaking and Listening Mini-Lesson

Dialogue Between Person and Pet

This mini-lesson supports the second Speaking and Listening activity in the Idea Bank on page 392.

Introduce the Concept Ask students who have or know pets what they wish they could ask their animal friends, if pets could only speak. Invite them to pair up and role-play a conversation between Mrs. Gage and James the parrot.

Develop Background Before students begin their conversations, have them brainstorm for what the parrot might have to say and how Mrs. Gage would answer him. Have them consider these questions:

- What would James have to say about his life with Joseph?
- How would James explain the fire?
- How would James feel about Joseph's death?
- How would James feel about Mrs. Gage?

Apply the Information With this background, students should be able to let their imaginations guide them in improvised conversations between Mrs. Gage and James the parrot.

Assess the Outcome Have students discuss how this activity enriched their appreciation of the story. You may want to have students use the Peer Assessment: Dramatic Performance page in *Alternative Assessment*, p. 120, to assess this activity.

❶ Respond Ask students how this ending makes them feel, and why. Do they think that good people are rewarded in real life, or only in fiction? *Students may say that they like the ending because Mrs. Gage is rewarded for being good and kind. Opinions may vary as to whether or not the ending is realistic.*

◆ **Literary Focus**

❷ Motivation Have students consider what they know about Mrs. Gage's character and hypothesize about why she might have kept this story secret until she was on her deathbed. *Mrs. Gage was not the sort of person to try to impress others with her wealth. She probably wanted to live as simply as before without a lot of fuss being made over her.*

Reinforce and Extend

Answers
◆ *Literature and Your Life*

Reader's Response Students should list their responses in order of importance.

Thematic Focus Students may wish to discuss whether the goodness and kindness had a cause-and-effect relationship to the outcome.

☑ **Check Your Comprehension**

1. Mrs. Gage is living in poverty, so the news of inherited wealth was good news indeed.
2. The house is worthless and the promised inheritance is not to be found.
3. Mrs. Gage faces the obstacles of fatigue and darkness, plus the danger of drowning in the river.
4. The burning of the house prompts Mrs. Gage's concern for the parrot's fate; the parrot leads her to the buried treasure.
5. Mrs. Gage believes that the parrot's actions were her reward for her kindness to animals.

390

---

loss of all her property in the fire. Out of sheer goodness of heart Mr. Stacey offered to buy the parrot off her for half a crown; but Mrs. Gage refused his offer with such indignation, saying that she would not sell the bird for all the wealth of the Indies, that he concluded that the old woman had been crazed by her troubles.

❶ It now only remains to be said that Mrs. Gage got back to Spilsby in safety; took her black box to the Bank; and lived with James the parrot and her dog Shag in great comfort and happiness to a very great age.

❷ It was not till she lay on her deathbed that she told the clergyman (the son of the Rev. Samuel Tallboys) the whole story, adding that she was quite sure that the house had been burnt on purpose by the parrot James, who, being aware of her danger on the river bank, flew into the scullery, and upset the oil stove which was keeping some scraps warm for her dinner. By this act, he not only saved her from drowning, but brought to light the three thousand pounds, which could have been found in no other manner. Such, she said, is the reward of kindness to animals.

The clergyman thought that she was wandering in her mind. But it is certain that the very moment the breath was out of her body, James the parrot shrieked out, "Not at home! Not at home!" and fell off his perch stone dead. The dog Shag had died some years previously.

Visitors to Rodmell may still see the ruins of the house, which was burnt down fifty years ago, and it is commonly said that if you visit it in the moonlight you may hear a parrot tapping with his beak upon the brick floor, while others have seen an old woman sitting there in a white apron.

> You can **respond** to a general statement like the one Mrs. Gage makes about kindness to animals by agreeing or disagreeing with it.

Guide for Responding

◆ *Literature and Your Life*

Reader's Response What would you do with a $15,000 inheritance?

Thematic Focus Mrs. Gage's life was forever changed because of her goodness and kindness. What good quality in you or someone you know has brought about a positive change in your life?

Group Discussion Mrs. Gage continued to lead a simple, unselfish life, even after inheriting a large sum of money. Take turns discussing if and how you think a significant inheritance would change your life.

☑ **Check Your Comprehension**

1. Why is the news Mrs. Gage receives at the beginning of the story so welcome?
2. In what two ways does the inheritance from her brother prove disappointing?
3. What obstacles does Mrs. Gage face as she returns to Rodmell from Mr. Stagg's office?
4. Summarize the series of events that reverses Mrs. Gage's fortune.
5. At the end of the story, to what does Mrs. Gage attribute her good fortune?

 Beyond the Selection

FURTHER READING

Other Works by Virginia Woolf
A Room of One's Own
Haunted House and Other Short Stories

Other Works About Communication With Animals
Shiloh, Phyllis Reynolds Naylor
When Elephants Weep, Susan McCarthy and Jeffrey Moussaieff Masson

We suggest that you preview these works before recommending them to students.

INTERNET

Biographical information about Virginia Woolf can be found at **http://www.biography.com/biography/read/reviews/vwoolf.html** A useful list of links to other sites related to Virginia Woolf is at **http://199.185.130.85/orlando/woolf.html**

Please be aware, however, that sites may have changed from the time we published this information. We *strongly recommend* that you preview the sites before you send students to them.

◆ Critical Thinking

INTERPRET

1. How does Mrs. Gage show her concern for animals? **[Analyze]**
2. What can you infer about Mrs. Gage's relationship with her brother based on her comments about his will? **[Infer]**
3. Describe Mrs. Gage's personality. Support your answer with examples from the story. **[Support]**

EVALUATE

4. Do you think Mrs. Gage's good fortune is a reward, or is it merely a coincidence? Explain your answer. **[Make a Judgment]**

APPLY

5. Are there more benefits or disadvantages to elderly people having pets? Explain. **[Generalize]**

◆ Reading for Success

STRATEGIES FOR READING FICTION

Review the reading strategies and notes showing how to read fiction. Then apply those strategies to answer the following questions.

1. What predictions did you make about Mrs. Gage's inheritance? Which predictions did you change before you reached the end of the story?
2. What words does the author use to help you envision the unfolding action?
3. What can you infer about Joseph from the measures he took to hide his fortune?
4. Relate two scenes in the story in which you particularly identified with Mrs. Gage. Explain why.

◆ Literary Focus

MOTIVATION

A character's **motivation** is the reason for his or her actions or words. Identifying characters' motives will help you understand story events.

1. What motivates Mrs. Gage to be kind to the parrot?
2. Why do you think the parrot helps Mrs. Gage?
3. Using examples from the story, explain how a character's motivation may bring about unexpected results.

◆ Build Vocabulary

USING FORMS OF *SAGACITY*

On your paper, write sentences that indicate that you understand these forms of the word *sagacity*.

1. Describe a decision that shows sagacity.
2. Identify a sagacious person you know.
3. Offer a piece of sage advice.

USING THE WORD BANK

On your paper, answer the following questions.

1. If you ford a river, do you cross it on a bridge?
2. Would most people want to move into a dilapidated house?
3. Where might you be if you reached into your pocket and pulled out a sovereign?
4. People of what professions are known for their sagacity?

◆ Build Grammar Skills

CORRECT USE OF ADJECTIVES AND ADVERBS

Do not confuse **adjectives** and **adverbs.** Use adjectives to modify nouns, and use adverbs to modify verbs, adjectives, and other adverbs.

Practice Copy the following sentences on your paper, completing each with the correct adjective or adverb. Circle the word it modifies and label that word's part of speech.

1. He was a very handsome bird, but his feathers were (sad, sadly) neglected.
2. "Drat that bird," said Mrs. Ford (peevish, peevishly).
3. Mrs. Gage walked (slow, slowly) across the fields.
4. The parrot, James, hopped (brisk, briskly) a few yards ahead of her towards the burnt house.
5. His excitement became so (intense, intensely) that Mrs. Gage now went to his help.

Writing Application Write several sentences in which you correctly use the following adjectives and adverbs: *quick, quickly; safe, safely.*

The Widow and the Parrot ◆ 391

◆ Critical Thinking

1. She arranges care for her dog and feeds the neglected parrot.
2. Mrs. Gage has been ill treated by her brother but has nevertheless extended her hand in friendship.
3. Students should note her kindness to animals, her acceptance of her circumstances, and her refusal to lay blame on others.
4. Students may see the bequeathed inheritance as penance by Mrs. Gage's brother for his evil ways and thereby support the idea of the good fortune as a reward.
5. Students may cite studies that have shown how pets enhance the lives of the elderly by providing companionship and help.

◆ Reading for Success

1. Students who predicted that the inheritance was fake will have revised their predictions; those who predicted it was legitimate had their predictions confirmed.
2. The ford in Mrs. Gage's rocky road is described as follows: "the stones of the riverbed appeared above the water"; the house is seen by lantern light as having "holes in all the carpets"; "bottoms of all the chairs . . . fallen out"; "large toadstools growing through the kitchen floor."
3. Joseph is so miserly that he hid his fortune so thoroughly that it would take the destruction of his house to discover it.
4. Students may identify with her elation at hearing the good news of her inheritance as well as with her resignation when it seems that she has been the victim of a hoax. They may also relate to her concern for the parrot, her fears at being alone on a dark journey, and her courage in trusting the parrot to lead her to an interesting discovery.

◆ Literary Focus

1. Mrs. Gage feels sorry for the parrot.
2. The parrot recognizes Mrs. Gage's kindness and repays her in kind.
3. Students may cite Mrs. Gage's trust in the parrot as bringing the unexpected consequence of discovering the fortune.

◆ Build Vocabulary

Using Forms of *Sagacity*

1. Students may say that avoiding substance abuse shows sagacity.
2. Students may name a teacher, a parent or relative, or a wise neighbor.
3. Accept reasonable responses.

Using the Word Bank

1. No; 2. No
3. You would most likely be in Great Britain.
4. Teachers and professors, counselors and psychiatrists are known for their sagacity.

◆ Build Grammar Skills

1. sadly; 2. peevishly;
3. slowly; 4. briskly;
5. intense

✎ *Writer's Solution*

For additional instruction and practice, use the lesson in the **Language Lab CD-ROM** on the Eight Parts of Speech and the practice page Adjective or Adverb? in the *Writer's Solution Grammar Practice Book,* p. 19.

Idea Bank

Customizing for
Performance Levels

Following are suggestions for matching Idea Bank topics with your students' performance levels:

Less Advanced Students: 1, 4, 7
Average Students: 2, 4, 6
More Advanced Students: 3, 5

Customizing for
Learning Modalities

Following are suggestions for matching Idea Bank topics with your students' learning modalities:

Verbal/Linguistic: 2, 4, 5
Logical/Mathematical: 6
Visual/Spatial: 7

Writing Mini-Lesson

Refer students to the Writing Handbook, page 965, for instruction on the writing process, and page 967 for further information on exposition.

Writing and Language Transparencies Students may use the Grid Organizer, p. 80, to organize their last will and testament. In the first column they can list the items they wish to bequeath; in the second, the intended recipient.

 Writer's Solution

Writers at Work Videodisc

Have students view the videodisc segment (Ch. 3) featuring Rudolfo Anaya to see how he organizes his material. Have students discuss how they might outline their last will and testaments.

Play frames 28660 to 29650

Writing Lab CD-ROM

Have students complete the tutorial on Exposition. Follow these steps:
1. Have students use the interactive instruction on gathering details.
2. Students may draft on computer.
3. Suggest that students use the revision checker for language variety in revising their last will and testament.

Sourcebook

Have students use Chapter 3, Exposition (pp. 62–95), for additional support.

392

Build Your Portfolio

Idea Bank

Writing Ideas

1. **Character Sketch** The parrot in this story has a unique and strong personality. Write a character sketch of an animal you would use as a character in a short story.

2. **Review** Imagine that you have been assigned to create a "Best Short Stories" Home Page on the Internet. Write a brief review of "The Widow and the Parrot" that will make Web-surfers want to read the story. **[Technology Link]**

3. **Health Report** Studies have shown that owning a pet can reduce stress. Do research to find specific information about the relationship between pets and stress reduction. Write a brief report explaining your findings. **[Science Link]**

Speaking and Listening

4. **Informal Debate** Like Mrs. Gage, some people feel that much can be learned from the study of animal behavior. Divide your class into two groups that take opposing sides on whether or not the study of animals is important.

5. **Dialogue Between Person and Pet** With a partner, take turns playing the role of James and Mrs. Gage. Allow James to say everything he's wanted to say to Mrs. Gage.

Projects

6. **Conversion Chart** Suppose you inherited 3,000 pounds—you'd want to know how that translated into dollars! Create a conversion chart showing pounds sterling to dollars. **[Math Link]**

7. **Area Map** Create a map of the setting of this story—where you envision the house, village, and river. Base your map on the details provided in the story. **[Art Link; Social Studies Link]**

392 ◆ Expanding Horizons

Writing Mini-Lesson

Last Will and Testament

Readers learn about Mrs. Ford's brother, in part, from the contents of his will and the possessions he leaves behind when he dies. Write a revealing **last will and testament** for a character from another fictional work. List possessions that indicate what was important to the character. Use the following tip to help you organize your character's last will and testament:

**Writing Skills Focus:
Logical Organization**

Your character's last will and testament will flow more smoothly and be easier to understand if you use a **logical organization**—an arrangement that shows clear relationships among ideas. For example, you might choose order of importance and present the most important details first, followed by the less significant ones. If you choose part-to-whole organization, arrange your details into categories, such as money, property, and advice.

Prewriting Before you begin drafting your character's last will and testament, jot down your ideas on note cards. Write a single thought on each card. Then, experiment with different ways of grouping your ideas until you find the most logical organization.

Drafting Begin your character's last will and testament by stating his or her overall wishes. Then, present the details of the character's will—specifically, what should go to whom. Follow a consistent organization throughout the will and testament.

Revising As you revise your character's last will and testament, be sure that you have used a logical organization. Read over your draft to be sure that every item was addressed in detail. Add transitions if necessary to show how ideas are related.

✓ ASSESSMENT OPTIONS

Formal Assessment, Selection Test, pp. 98–100, and Assessment Resources Software. The selection test is designed so that it can be easily customized to the performance levels of your students.
Alternative Assessment, p. 28, includes options for less advanced students, more advanced students, logical/mathematical learners, intrapersonal learners, verbal/linguistic learners, bodily/kinesthetic learners, and interpersonal learners.

PORTFOLIO ASSESSMENT
Use the following rubrics in the *Alternative Assessment* booklet to assess student writing:
Character Sketch: Description Rubric, p. 97
Review: Evaluation/Review Rubric, p. 104
Health Report: Research Report/Paper Rubric, p. 106
Writing Mini-Lesson: Expression Rubric, p. 94

PART **1** *A World of People*

Mingling, Diana Ong

A World of People ◆ 393

One-Minute Planning Guide

The selections in this part show the variety of people and situations from around the world. The section opens with Chinua Achebe's "Civil Peace," a short story about a man who is robbed during the Biafran War in Nigeria. "The Bean Eaters" is a poem that describes the monotonous lives of faceless, nameless characters, while Paul Simon's "Old Friends" explores how friendships expand our horizons. Umberto Eco's "How to React to Familiar Faces" talks about the disorienting feeling that comes with seeing a famous person. Finally, "A Picture from the Past: Emily Dickinson," and "What Makes a Degas a Degas?" discuss the role photographs and paintings have in opening up new worlds for us.

Customize for
Varying Student Needs
When assigning the selections in this part to your students, keep in mind the following factors:

"Civil Peace"
• Contains dialect that may be difficult for some students to understand

"The Bean Eaters"
• Short poem by a well-known writer
• Vocabulary accessible to all ability levels

"Old Friends"
• Popular music by a contemporary artist

"How to React to Familiar Faces"
• High interest topic of celebrities
• Appealing to interpersonal learners

"A Picture from the Past: Emily Dickinson"; "What Makes a Degas a Degas?"
• Very short nonfiction
• Appealing to visual/spatial learners

 Humanities: Art

Mingling by Diana Ong.
　Encourage students to enumerate as many kinds of "mingling" as they can see in this painting—for example, the mingling of colors, the overlapping of heads, the blending of heads and upper bodies, and so on. Discuss the artist's technique of using white to outline and define spaces which are filled in with multi-colored scribbled lines. Encourage students to talk about how color influences the mood of the painting.

You might explain that some color analysts say that shades of yellow are associated with optimism.
　Help students link the artwork to the theme of this section, "A World of People," by answering the following questions:
1. How does the artist emphasize what people have in common? How does she emphasize their differences? *She emphasizes what people share by using the same scribbling technique and the same combina-*

tions of colors for all the heads. She emphasizes their differences by boldly defining heads and features.

2. Imagine that this work were untitled, and that you were asked to provide a title with the word "people" in it. What would you come up with? *Sample answers: People Talking; People Face to Face to Face; People Who Need People; Too Many People? How Do People Get Along?*

OBJECTIVES

1. To read, comprehend, and interpret a short story
2. To relate a story to personal experience
3. To apply prior knowledge in reading
4. To identify and interpret key statements
5. To build vocabulary in context and learn related words: forms of *disreputable*
6. To recognize and use past and past perfect tenses
7. To write annotations for a map of Nigeria using brevity and clarity
8. To respond to the story through writing, speaking and listening, and projects

SKILLS INSTRUCTION

Vocabulary:
Related Words: Forms of *disreputable*

Grammar:
Past and Past Perfect Tenses

Reading Strategy:
Prior Knowledge

Literary Focus:
Key Statement

Writing:
Brevity and Clarity

Speaking and Listening:
Reworking a Dialogue (teacher edition)

Critical Viewing:
Infer; Interpret

PORTFOLIO OPPORTUNITIES

Writing: News Interview; Human-Interest Article; Poem

Writing Mini-Lesson: Annotated Map of Nigeria

Speaking and Listening: Reworking a Dialogue; Proverbs Presentation

Projects: Collage; Scenic Sketches

More About the Author

A prolific writer, Chinua Achebe is considered one of Nigeria's finest novelists. His first novel, *Things Fall Apart*, was so successful that it was adapted for the stage, radio, and television. Although Achebe writes in English, his work is steeped in the African tradition. In fact, Achebe translates Ibo proverbs into English and makes them part of his stories. Achebe states: "Among the Ibo the art of conversation is regarded very highly, and proverbs are the palm-oil with which words are eaten."

Guide for Reading

Chinua Achebe (1930–)

During civil war in his homeland of Nigeria, Chinua Achebe (chin wä´ ə cheb´ ā) survived the bombing of his house. He fled the town, leaving behind a book in press at the publishing company he had formed with his friend, poet Christopher Okigbo. That book was *How the Leopard Got His Claws,* Achebe's parable about Nigeria. Okigbo died in the war, and when Achebe returned, the Citadel Press was demolished. There remained only one copy of the proofs of the book, which someone had managed to save.

Early Life Born in the Ibo village of Ogibi, Nigeria, Achebe was brought up with both the traditional values of the Ibo people as well as English and Western values. He feels that stories are a way to preserve the traditional values that are so important to him.

> "Stories are not just meant to make people smile . . . our life depends on them."

Achebe has also been influenced by his experiences with war and its aftermath.

Professional Life Achebe has directed a radio station, taught in universities, and involved himself in local Nigerian politics as a diplomat. His greatest success, however, has been as a novelist. His novels, including *Things Fall Apart* (1958) and *Anthills of the Savannah* (1988), convey the tragic history of tribal Africa's encounter with European power.

◆ Build Vocabulary

RELATED WORDS: FORMS OF *DISREPUTABLE*

You can increase your vocabulary by learning other forms of a particular word. For example, in this story, you will encounter the word *disreputable,* which means "not respectable" and refers to the filthy clothes that one character wears. Using other forms of *disreputable,* you might describe a disreputable person as someone who has a bad *reputation,* a person of ill *repute,* or someone who has fallen into *disrepute.* The words *reputation, repute, disrepute,* and *disreputable* are all related because they contain the word root *-reput-,* which means "to be regarded."

inestimable
disreputable
amenable
edifice
destitute
imperious
commiserate

WORD BANK

As you read this story, you will encounter the words on this list. Each word is defined on the page where it first appears. Preview the list before you read.

◆ Build Grammar Skills

PAST AND PAST PERFECT TENSES

The **past tense** of a verb indicates that an action took place prior to the present.

The **past perfect tense** indicates a past action that was completed before another action that took place in the past. It is formed with *had* and the past participle of a verb (the form ending in *-ed* or an irregular ending such as *-n* or *-t*).

In the following sentence from the story, the past perfect *had started* indicates that the water began running before the other past actions.

       past   past
. . . he . . . *bought* fresh palm-wine which he *mixed*

               past perfect
. . . with the water which *had* recently *started* running again . . .

Notice other places in the story where Achebe uses the past and past perfect tenses to indicate the relationship between past events.

394 ◆ *Expanding Horizons*

Prentice Hall Literature Program Resources

REINFORCE / RETEACH / EXTEND

Selection Support Pages
Build Vocabulary: Related Words: Forms of *Disreputable*, p. 118
Build Grammar Skills: Past and Past Perfect Tenses, p. 119
Reading Strategy: Prior Knowledge, p. 120
Literary Focus: Key Statement, p. 121

Strategies for Diverse Student Needs, p. 29

Beyond Literature
Cross-Curricular Connection: Geography, p. 29

Formal Assessment
Selection Test, pp. 101–103
Alternative Assessment, p. 29

Writing and Language Transparencies
Herringbone Organizer, p. 76

Resource Pro CD-ROM
"Civil Peace"—includes all resource material and customizable lesson plan

 Listening to Literature Audiocassettes

Civil Peace

◆ *Literature and Your Life*

CONNECT YOUR EXPERIENCE

Different factors, such as your outlook or your circumstances, influence the way you respond to a loss: If you lose the last five dollars you had for this month, your reaction will probably be stronger than if you lose five dollars the day before you get paid for your after-school job.

The main character in this story faces several difficulties and losses more serious than five dollars, yet he tries to keep a positive attitude.

Journal Writing What strategies do you use to keep a positive attitude?

THEMATIC FOCUS: A WORLD OF PEOPLE

The changes in the world of the main character broaden his horizons, but they also create difficulty. His experiences may lead you to ask yourself, "How do I deal with the difficulties of change?"

◆ Background for Understanding

HISTORY

In the late 1800's, the British annexed lands in west Africa, eventually setting up the colony of Nigeria. Local rulers resisted British domination, and in 1960, Nigeria finally achieved independence.

Religious, economic, and ethnic divisions flared after independence. The Ibo in the southeast felt that the Muslim Huasa-Fulani of the north dominated Nigeria. The Ibo seceded from Nigeria, setting up the independent Republic of Biafra. A brutal civil war followed, and in 1970, a defeated Biafra rejoined Nigeria. "Civil Peace" takes place in the aftermath of this civil war.

◆ Literary Focus

KEY STATEMENT

Just as a key unlocks a door, **key statements** unlock the meaning of a story. Key statements often go beyond the events of a particular story and point to a general truth about life. Chinua Achebe uses repetition to emphasize several key statements in "Civil Peace." These keys can help you unlock the meaning behind the tale. Use a graphic organizer like the one shown to identify and explore the meaning of key statements in "Civil Peace."

◆ Reading Strategy

PRIOR KNOWLEDGE

When a story takes you to another country or introduces you to unfamiliar people and places, you may feel the need for a "guide." Your **prior knowledge**—what you already know and can relate to—can guide you in understanding the new experiences and ideas.

In "Civil Peace," Achebe tells about a man in a particular historical situation—a man returning home after the civil war in Nigeria. Even if you have not lived through a war, you can use your prior knowledge of coping with loss and gain to understand the man's experiences.

Key Statement	Possible Meaning
Happy survival	

Guide for Reading ◆ 395

Play a video segment from a documentary or show pictures of a disaster area after such events as a flood, an earthquake, or a war. Ask students: What would be their first concerns if they found themselves in such a disaster area? Have students make a list of the first steps they would take. After students have compiled a list, tell them to read the story and find out how the characters in the story dealt with a similar disaster.

Customize for
Less Proficient Readers
Suggest to these students that, as they read, they make a list of the things that Jonathan Iwegbu considers a "miracle." Such a list can help them understand the main character's outlook on life.

Customize for
More Advanced Students
Have these students consider the following question as they read: Besides a positive outlook, what other character traits does Jonathan Iwegbu possess? Have students jot down notes for a character description of Jonathan.

Customize for
English Language Learners
This story contains unfamiliar vocabulary, unexpected phrasing, and difficult dialect. To help these students, have them follow along in their text as they listen to the **Listening to Literature Audiocassettes** recording of the selection. Pause the recording after particularly puzzling passages and explain the meanings of the passages written in dialect.

Customize for
Intrapersonal Learners
Have these students keep a "reflective journal" as they read the story. Encourage them to write their thoughts and feelings each time Jonathan Iwegbu states, "Nothing puzzles God."

Preparing for Standardized Tests

Reading The Literary Focus lesson for this selection, Key Statement, asks students to interpret key words and phrases in the story. This skill is useful for students in answering reading comprehension questions on standardized tests, such as the SAT, where students are offered several statements about a passage and are asked to select the one that best describes the passage. For additional practice, use the Literary Focus page in *Selection Support*, p. 121.

Grammar and Language In the grammar and usage sections of standardized tests, students are

sometimes asked to select verbs that correctly complete a sentence, as in the following: *(A)*

Sherri _____ the CD that she _____ at lunch.

(A) played, had bought (B) played, will buy
(C) played, buys (D) had played, bought
Understanding the relationship between past and past perfect tenses can help students answer these questions. The Build Grammar Skills lesson focuses on this topic. For more practice, use Build Grammar Skills: Past and Past Perfect Tenses, p. 119, in *Selection Support*.

One-Minute Insight

"If life gives you lemons, make lemonade." This expression sums up the main character's ability to make the best of the difficult situations thrust upon him by a chaotic, lawless post-civil war society. Having survived with most of his family intact, Jonathan Iwegbu realizes that flexibility is the key to success. If one business doesn't work, another one might. Even when thieves threaten his family and steal his money, Jonathan shows that a positive mental attitude helps one to adapt to change and loss.

◆ Literary Focus

❶ Key Statement Ask students what they think the greeting "Happy survival" means and why it is used. Then have students predict, on the basis of this opening paragraph, whether or not Jonathan will have a "happy survival." *"Happy survival" is the equivalent of our "hello" or, "hi." It is used because people were so happy to have survived the war. This optimistic key statement sets the tone for the rest of the story, in which Jonathan looks at the positive aspect of all situations. Students may predict a happy survival for Jonathan.*

◆ Critical Thinking

❷ Identify Character Traits Ask students what they have learned about Jonathan from the opening paragraph. *He has a positive attitude, recognizes the important things in life, and also delights in the less important things.*

Civil Peace

Chinua Achebe

❶ Jonathan Iwegbu counted himself extraordinarily lucky. "Happy survival!" meant so much more to him than just a current fashion of greeting old friends in the first hazy days of peace. It went deep to his heart. He had come out of the war with five **❷** inestimable blessings—his head, his wife Maria's head and the heads of three out of their four children. As a bonus he also had his old bicycle—a miracle too but naturally not to be compared to the safety of five human heads.

The bicycle had a little history of its own. One day at the height of the war it was commandeered "for urgent military action." Hard as its loss would have been to him he would still have let it go without a thought had he not had some doubts about the genuineness of the officer. It wasn't his disreputable rags, nor the toes peeping out of one blue and one brown canvas shoe, nor yet the two stars of his rank done obviously in a hurry in biro,[1] that troubled Jonathan; many good and heroic soldiers looked the same or worse. It was rather a certain lack of grip and firmness in **❸** his manner. So Jonathan, suspecting he might

---

1. **biro** (bir′ ō) *n.*: Ballpoint pen.

◆ Build Vocabulary

inestimable (in es′ tə mə bəl) *adj.*: Priceless; beyond measure

disreputable (dis rep′ yo͞o tə bəl) *adj.*: Not respectable

amenable (ə mē′ nə bəl) *adj.*: Responsive; open

✦ Block Scheduling Strategies

Consider these suggestions to take advantage of extended class time:

• Have students preview the story by reading Beyond Literature on page 401. Then have them complete the Cross-Curricular Connection: Geography page in **Beyond the Literature**, p. 29, to learn about the setting of the story.

• Students may also benefit from researching the history of Nigeria before reading the selection to give them a better under-

standing of the story's setting. Suggest that they look for maps and atlases in encyclopedias or on the Internet.

• Have students use the chart on page 395 to focus on key statements in the story. They may work with partners to complete the questions on page 402 and the Literary Focus page in **Selection Support**, p. 121.

• After students have read the selection, have them listen to the part of the audio-

cassette recording that contains the scene with the thieves. Discuss how listening to the dialogue affects their understanding of what the thief and his accomplices are demanding.

• Since the dialect in the story may present difficulties, have students work with partners on Speaking and Listening: Reworking a Dialogue (p. 403). Invite several pairs of students to present their interpretations to the class.

3 Clarification This sentence about the bicycle may be confusing to students. Explain that Jonathan had money with which he was planning to buy firewood. He planned to give the firewood to his wife, who would exchange it for stock-fish and corn meal from camp officials. Instead, he used the money to "persuade" the soldier not to confiscate his bicycle. Point out that the "camp" is a refugee camp for Biafrans who had fled their homes.

▶**Critical Viewing**◀

4 Infer Students may observe that the landscape appears vast and rugged. As there are no automobiles visible, animals and bicycles would be the most likely forms of transportation.

◆**Literary Focus**

5 Key Statement This is the first of several times that Jonathan says, "Nothing puzzles God." Ask students what they think he means by this statement. *Students may suggest that the statement means that people don't always have to understand the reason why something happens. Some may extend their interpretation to suggest that, as Jonathan does, people should accept that there probably is a reason for everything, even when we don't understand it or recognize it.*

◀ Critical Viewing
Why would a bicycle be important to Jonathan, who lives in a landscape like the one shown? [Infer] **4**

3 be <u>amenable</u> to influence, rummaged in his raffia bag and produced the two pounds with which he had been going to buy firewood which his wife, Maria, retailed to camp officials for extra stock-fish and corn meal, and got his bicycle back. That night he buried it in the little clearing in the bush where the dead of the camp, including his own youngest son, were

buried. When he dug it up again a year later after the surrender all it needed was a little palm-oil greasing. "Nothing puzzles God," he said in wonder. **5**

He put it to immediate use as a taxi and accumulated a small pile of Biafran[2] money

2. **Biafran** (bē ăf′ rən) *adj.*: From the east part of the Gulf of Guinea on the west coast of Africa.

 Workplace Skills Mini-Lesson

Positive Attitude
This mini-lesson supports the value of developing a positive attitude.

Introduce the Concept Have students discuss the effect Jonathan's positive attitude has on his life.

Develop Background Students who work at part-time jobs might have noticed that co-workers (or even they themselves) often complain about their jobs. Discuss

how excessive complaining can make a situation seem worse than it is, while concentrating on positive aspects can make the same situation seem better.

Apply the Information Share these negative thoughts with students. Have them determine how to make them more positive:

• My job pays only $4.75 an hour.
• They make me sweep the floor when I'm not working at a register.

• We have to wear nerdy-looking uniforms instead of our own clothes.

Have students suggest how they might apply positive thinking to real-life situations.

Assess the Outcome Assess students' ability to apply the skill by the number and quality of suggestions they make for additional situations. Ask students to explain why a positive attitude would be beneficial in the situations they suggest.

◆ Critical Thinking

❶ Identify Character Traits Ask students: What does Jonathan's starting a taxi service tell you about his attitude toward life? *Students should recognize that Jonathan has a positive attitude, is ambitious, and is resourceful because he uses what little he has to make a better life for himself and his family.*

◆ Critical Thinking

❷ Identify Character Traits Ask students: What is Jonathan's attitude toward the condition of his home? How might someone else react when faced with the same situation? *His attitude is positive; he is both grateful and happy that the house is salvageable. Responses regarding other possible reactions might indicate that some people would be angry, upset, or discouraged about the missing doors and windows and the damaged roof.*

◆ Build Grammar Skills

❸ Past and Past Perfect Tenses Have students identify the past tense and past perfect tense verbs in this sentence. Ask them to explain the use of the past perfect tense. *Past: took, bought, mixed, opened; past perfect: had started; the water "had recently started running" before any of the other past actions occurred.*

◆ Critical Thinking

❹ Infer Draw attention to the contrast between the other ex-miners and Jonathan. Why might some of these ex-miners have no place to go? Why aren't they as resourceful as Jonathan? *Their homes were probably destroyed in the war; they may not be as resourceful as Jonathan, but even if they were, it would be harder for them to start up in business because they have no homes. Jonathan is well-off compared to these men.*

---

ferrying camp officials and their families across the four-mile stretch to the nearest tarred road. His standard charge per trip was six pounds and those who had the money were only glad to be rid of some of it in this way. At the end of a ❶ fortnight[3] he had made a small fortune of one hundred and fifteen pounds.

Then he made the journey to Enugu and found another miracle waiting for him. It was unbelievable. He rubbed his eyes and looked again and it was still standing there before him. But, needless to say, even that monumental blessing must be accounted also totally inferior to the five heads in the family. This newest miracle was his little house in Ogui Overside. Indeed nothing puzzles God! Only two houses away a huge concrete <u>edifice</u> some wealthy contractor had put up just before the war was a ❷ mountain of rubble. And here was Jonathan's little zinc house of no regrets built with mud blocks quite intact! Of course the doors and windows were missing and five sheets off the roof. But what was that? And anyhow he had returned to Enugu early enough to pick up bits of old zinc and wood and soggy sheets of cardboard lying around the neighborhood before thousands more came out of their forest holes looking for the same things. He got a <u>destitute</u> carpenter with one old hammer, a blunt plane and a few bent and rusty nails in his tool bag to turn this assortment of wood, paper and metal into door and window shutters for five Nigerian shillings or fifty Biafran pounds. He paid the pounds, and moved in with his overjoyed family carrying five heads on their shoulders.

His children picked mangoes near the military cemetery and sold them to soldiers' wives for a few pennies—real pennies this time—and his wife started making breakfast akara balls[4]

---

3. **fortnight** (fôrt′ nit) *n.*: Two weeks.
4. **akara** (ə kär′ ə) **balls:** Balls made of cooked yams.

◆ Build Vocabulary

edifice (ed′ i fis) *n.*: Building

destitute (des′ tə tōōt′) *adj.*: Poverty stricken; in great need

398 ◆ Expanding Horizons

---

for neighbors in a hurry to start life again. With his family earnings he took his bicycle to the villages around and bought fresh palm-wine which he mixed generously in his rooms with the water which had recently started running again in the public tap down the road, and opened up a bar for soldiers and other lucky people with good money.

At first he went daily, then every other day and finally once a week, to the offices of the Coal Corporation where he used to be a miner, to find out what was what. The only thing he did find out in the end was that that little house of his was even a greater blessing than he had thought. Some of his fellow ex-miners who had nowhere to return at the end of the day's waiting just slept outside the doors of the offices and cooked what meal they could scrounge together in Bournvita tins. As the weeks lengthened and still nobody could say what was what Jonathan discontinued his weekly visits altogether and faced his palm-wine bar. ❹

But nothing puzzles God. Came the day of the windfall when after five days of endless scuffles in queues[5] and counterqueues in the sun outside the Treasury he had twenty pounds counted into his palms as exgratia[6] award for the rebel money he had turned in. It was like Christmas for him and for many others like him when the payments began. They called it (since few could manage its proper official name) *egg-rasher*. ❼

As soon as the pound notes were placed in his palm Jonathan simply closed it tight over them and buried fist and money inside his trouser pocket. He had to be extra careful because he had seen a man a couple of days earlier collapse into near-madness in an instant before that oceanic crowd because no sooner had he got his twenty pounds than some heartless ruffian picked it off him. Though it was not

---

5. **queues** (kyōōz) *n.*: Lines.
6. **ex gratia** (eks grä′ shē ə): As a favor.

◆ Literary Focus

How does the key statement that begins this paragraph capture the spirit of Jonathan's attitude toward good and bad events?

Speaking and Listening Mini-Lesson

Reworking a Dialogue

This mini-lesson supports the Speaking and Listening activity in the Idea Bank on page 403.

Introduce the Concept Remind students that there are many regional dialects of English even within the United States. For example, depending on where they live, people may refer to soft drinks as *soda*, *tonic*, or *pop*.

Develop Background Have students discuss why the dialect in the story might be difficult to understand. Lead students to recognize these points:

- Some words and phrases are unfamiliar.
- The word order in the sentence does not follow the normal English pattern.

Apply the Information Remind students that they can use context to figure out the meanings of words and sentences. Reading

aloud can help, as well. Have students work in pairs to rewrite the dialogue.

Assess the Outcome Have students read their dialogues to the class. Encourage listeners to evaluate the dialogues on the basis of how well they made sense within the context of the story. Students may use the Peer Assessment: Dramatic Performance page in *Alternative Assessment*, p. 120.

right that a man in such an extremity of agony should be blamed yet many in the queues that day were able to remark quietly at the victim's carelessness, especially after he pulled out the innards of his pocket and revealed a hole in it big enough to pass a thief's head. But of course he had insisted that the money had been in the other pocket, pulling it out too to show its comparative wholeness. So one had to be careful.

Jonathan soon transferred the money to his left hand and pocket so as to leave his right free for shaking hands should the need arise, though by fixing his gaze at such an elevation as to miss all approaching human faces he made sure that the need did not arise, until he got home.

He was normally a heavy sleeper but that night he heard all the neighborhood noises die down one after another. Even the night watchman who knocked the hour on some metal somewhere in the distance had fallen silent after knocking one o'clock. That must have been the last thought in Jonathan's mind before he was finally carried away himself. He couldn't have been gone for long, though, when he was violently awakened again.

"Who is knocking?" whispered his wife lying beside him on the floor.

"I don't know," he whispered back breathlessly.

The second time the knocking came it was so

▲ **Critical Viewing** What is the effect of this extreme close-up photo? [Interpret] ❿

loud and <u>imperious</u> that the rickety old door could have fallen down.

"Who is knocking?" he asked them, his voice parched and trembling.

"Na tief-man and him people," came the cool reply. "Make you hopen de door."[7] This was followed by the heaviest knocking of all.

Maria was the first to raise the alarm, then he followed and all their children.

---

7. **"Na tief-man . . . hopen de door":** The man is speaking a dialect of English that includes some word forms and grammar of his own language. He is saying, "I am not a thief with my accomplices. Open the door." As you read the rest of the story, read aloud when characters speak this way and try to figure out what they are saying.

Civil Peace ◆ 399

❽

◆ **Reading Strategy**
How does your prior knowledge of anxiety help you understand Jonathan's experience here?

◆ **Build Vocabulary**
imperious (im pir´ ē əs) *adj.*: Commanding; powerful

◆ **Literary Focus**
❺ **Key Statement** Jonathan is resilient, undaunted by setbacks; he accepts the good and the bad; he believes that all is for the good, even if human beings cannot see the reasons.

◆ **Build Grammar Skills**
❻ **Past and Past Perfect Tenses** Have students identify the past form of the verb *have* and past perfect form of the verb *turn* in this passage. Ask them to explain the use of the past perfect. *Past:* had; *past perfect:* had *turned (in); Jonathan had turned in the rebel money before receiving the twenty pounds "ex-gratia."*

❼ **Clarification** Be sure students recognize that "egg-rasher" is the Nigerians' pronunciation of "ex-gratia."

❽ Because of the difficult dialect in the passage that follows, this is a good time to play the audiocassette recording. The inflections of the speakers' voices can help students understand the meaning of the dialogue.

 Listening to Literature Audiocassettes

◆ **Reading Strategy**
❾ **Prior Knowledge** Students should recognize that anxiety can cause behavioral changes and sleeplessness. Jonathan does not look at people on the way home and even when he is safe at home, he has difficulty falling asleep.

▶**Critical Viewing**◀
❿ **Interpret** Students may suggest that the close-up forces the viewer to look at the man's expression and share in his feelings.

 Beyond the Classroom

Career Connection
Law Enforcement Lawlessness and chaos often characterize a society in the aftermath of war. As they read on, students will see that restoration of law enforcement by ethical and well-trained law-enforcement officers is necessary for life to go on in any reasonable, orderly way.

Students interested in a career in law enforcement can do research to find out what kind of background is necessary to

become an officer of the law. Some questions students might consider include the following:
• How does one apply to become a police officer?
• Is a college education necessary?
• How does one become a detective or an FBI agent?

Community Connection
Local Security When the thieves appeared at Jonathan's house, he and his family tried to scare them away by loudly calling for help. In the United States today, most people are security-minded. What do people do to protect their homes, businesses, and vehicles? Have interested students find out about anti-theft devices common in your community.

❶ Clarification If students seem confused by this passage, tell them that the Iwegbu family has neither a telephone nor a sophisticated security system. This is the family's way of calling for help.

❷ Clarification Point out that the leader is saying "We'll help you a little. Now, everybody!" Then the thieves, imitating the previous chant of the Iwegbu family, all call for the police and neighbors, to show how little they are impressed by the Iwegbus' calls for help.

◆ **Critical Thinking**

❸ Make Inferences Ask students if they think it is normal for thieves to have so little fear of apprehension and punishment that they would make fun of a threat to call soldiers and police. What is the cause of this strange situation? *Students should understand that chaos and lawlessness often follow war. In a peaceful society, an active police force is a deterrent to crime.*

◆ **Critical Thinking**

❹ Interpret Point out that the thief says that the civil war is over; now "civil peace." Ask: What is ironic about the thief's statement? *The civil war was between two political entities. Now that the war is over, people expect to live in peace, but instead, the people are now faced with a new threat from their fellow citizens.*

Comprehension Check ☑

❺ What reason does the thief give for stealing Jonathan's money? *The thief says perhaps Jonathan does not have plenty of money but he and his cohorts themselves have none; therefore, Jonathan should give them his money.*

"Police-o! Thieves-o! Neighbors-o! Police-o! We are lost! We are dead! Neighbors, are you asleep? Wake up! Police-o!"

❶ This went on for a long time and then stopped suddenly. Perhaps they had scared the thief away. There was total silence. But only for a short while.

"You done finish?" asked the voice outside. "Make we help you small. Oya, everybody!"

❷ *"Police-o! Tief-man-so! Neighbors-o! we done loss-o! Police-o! . . ."*

There were at least five other voices besides the leader's.

Jonathan and his family were now completely paralyzed by terror. Maria and the children sobbed inaudibly like lost souls. Jonathan groaned continuously.

The silence that followed the thieves' alarm vibrated horribly. Jonathan all but begged their leader to speak again and be done with it.

"My frien," said he at long last, "we don try our best for call dem but I tink say dem all done sleep-o . . . So wetin we go do now? Sometaim you wan call soja? Or you wan make we call **❸** dem for you? Soja better pass police. No be so?"

"Na so!" replied his men. Jonathan thought he heard even more voices now than before and groaned heavily. His legs were sagging under him and his throat felt like sandpaper.

"My frien, why you no de talk again. I de ask you say you wan make we call soja?"

"No."

"Awrighto. Now make we talk business. We no be bad tief. We no like for make trouble. **❹** Trouble done finish. War done finish and all the katakata wey de for inside. No Civil War again. This time na Civil Peace. No be so?"

"Na so!" answered the horrible chorus.

"What do you want from me? I am a poor man. Everything I had went with this war. Why do you come to me? You know people who have money. We . . ."

◆ **Build Vocabulary**

commiserate (kə miz´ ər āt´) *v.*: Sympathize; share suffering

---

"Awright! We know say you no get plenty money. But we sef no get even anini. So dere- **❺** fore make you open dis window and give us one hundred pound and we go commot. Orderwise we de come for inside now to show you guitar-boy like dis . . ."

A volley of automatic fire rang through the sky. Maria and the children began to weep aloud again.

"Ah, missisi de cry again. No need for dat. We done talk say we na good tief. We just take our small money and go nwayorly. No molest. Abi we de molest?"

"At all!" sang the chorus.

"My friends," began Jonathan hoarsely. "I hear what you say and I thank you. If I had one hundred pounds . . ."

"Lookia my frien, no be play we come play for your house. If we make mistake and step for in-side you no go like am-o. So derefore . . ."

"To God who made me; if you come inside and find one hundred pounds, take it and shoot me and shoot my wife and children. I swear to God. The only money I have in this life is this twenty-pounds *egg-rasher* they gave me today . . ."

"Ok. Time de go. Make you open dis window and bring the twenty pound. We go manage am like dat."

There were now loud murmurs of dissent among the chorus: "Na lie de man de lie; e get **❻** plenty money . . . Make we go inside and search properly well . . . Wetin be twenty pound? . . ."

"Shurrup!" rang the leader's voice like a lone shot in the sky and silenced the murmuring at once. "Are you dere? Bring the money quick!"

"I am coming," said Jonathan fumbling in the darkness with the key of the small wooden box he kept by his side on the mat.

At the first sign of light as neighbors and others assembled to <u>commiserate</u> with him he was already strapping his five-gallon demijohn[8] to his bicycle carrier and his wife, sweating in the open fire, was turning over akara balls in a

---

8. **demijohn** (dem´ i jän´) *n.*: Large bottle.

Cross-Curricular Connection: Science

The story mentions palm oil, which Jonathan uses to grease his bicycle, and palm wine, which he sells at his bar. Explain that palms are important in tropical regions, such as Nigeria, because they provide people with food, clothing, and building materials. There are more than 2,600 different kinds of palm trees throughout the world, varying greatly in size and the kind of flowers, leaves, and fruits they produce. Widely used food products made from palm trees include dried coconut meat, soap, salad oils, margarine, dates, and sago, a starch taken from palm trunks. Other palm products include baskets and chair bottoms, woven from strips of palm leaves, and furniture made from the stems of the rattan palm.

Have interested students find out more about palm trees and their products. After students have collected their information, reserve some time for them to share with the class what they discovered.

wide clay bowl of boiling oil. In the corner his eldest son was rinsing out dregs of yesterday's palm-wine from old beer bottles.

❼ "I count it as nothing," he told his sympathizers, his eyes on the rope he was tying. "What is egg-rasher? Did I depend on it last week? Or is it greater than other things that went with the war? I say, let *egg-rasher* perish in the flames! Let it go where everything else has gone. Nothing puzzles God." **❼**

Beyond Literature

Geography Connection

The Changing Boundaries in Africa

In 1945, four European powers—Britain, France, Belgium, and Portugal—controlled almost all of Africa. However, a great liberation took place in Africa following World War II. Slowly at first, and then with increasing speed, the people of Africa regained their independence. In the struggle for independence, some nations, like Nigeria, have experienced internal difficulties.

Activity Trace this map, and draw additional lines to show the boundaries created (and lost) in the civil war in Nigeria.

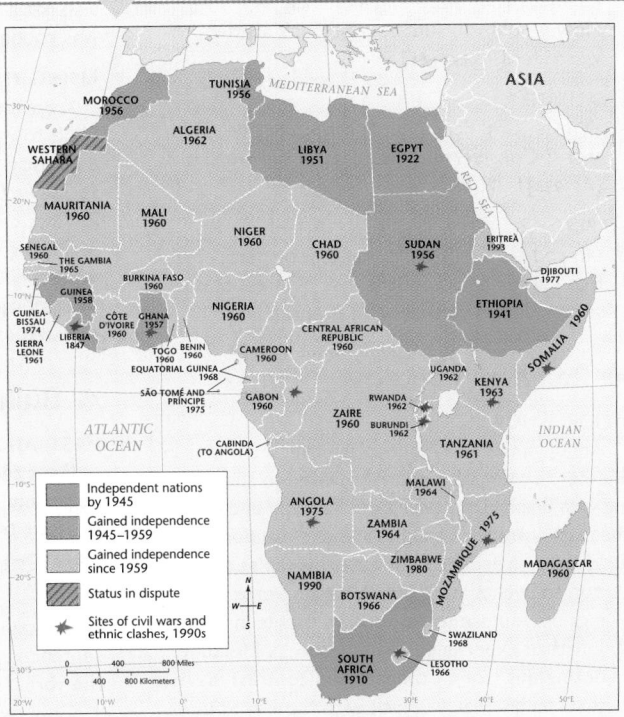

Guide for Responding

◆ Literature and Your Life

Reader's Response In what ways do you identify with Jonathan? Explain.

Thematic Focus Did reading about Jonathan's experiences make you feel more or less connected to people in Nigeria? Explain.

☑ Check Your Comprehension

1. What does Jonathan Iwegbu count as his greatest blessings? For what else is he grateful?
2. How does Jonathan earn money?
3. How do Jonathan and his family behave after their money is stolen?

Civil Peace ◆ 401

Beyond the Selection

FURTHER READING

Other Works by Chinua Achebe
Things Fall Apart
Christmas in Biafra, and Other Poems
Girls at War

Other Works With the Theme of the Difficulties of Change
Two Moons In August, Martha Brooks
Daniel's Story, Carol Matas

We suggest that you preview these works before recommending them to students.

INTERNET

For more Nigerian proverbs translated by Chinua Achebe, suggest that students go to **http://www.bemorecreative.com/one/890.htm**

Please be aware, however, that sites may have changed from the time we published this information. We *strongly recommend* that you preview the sites before you send students to them.

401

◆ Critical Thinking

1. The war destroyed people's homes and possessions and killed people, including one of Jonathan's children.
2. The thief feels he can just take what he wants; Jonathan knows how to create what he wants by working for it.
3. Jonathan is optimistic, trusting, and peaceful.
4. The peace between Jonathan and the thieves is achieved in a civilized manner, without resorting to violence.
5. Students may argue that rich people have so much they can easily accept the loss of some of their possessions. Others may say that although poor people may be accustomed to loss, they may value what little they have and grieve for its loss.

◆ Reading Strategy

1. Students may cite such sayings as "A penny saved is a penny earned" or "Never put off 'til tomorrow what you can do today."
2. Most students will admit that they may become upset by setbacks more easily than Jonathan is.

◆ Literary Focus

1. This key statement reflects Jonathan's optimism and happiness in just being alive.
2. The proverb states the philosophy that underlies Jonathan's trust that all will work out for the best.

◆ Build Vocabulary

Using Forms of *Disreputable*

1. reputed; reputation; disreputable

Using the Word Bank

1. edifice; 2. imperious;
3. commiserate; 4. amenable;
5. destitute; 6. inestimable

◆ Build Grammar Skills

1. past perfect tense: had put; past tense: was
2. past perfect tense: had returned; past tense: came
3. past tense: was; past perfect tense: had thought
4. past tense: pulled, revealed; past perfect tense: had insisted, had been

Guide for Responding (continued)

◆ Critical Thinking

INTERPRET

1. How did the war affect the lives of people like Jonathan? **[Infer]**
2. Compare and contrast the attitude toward money of the leader of the thieves with that of Jonathan. **[Compare and Contrast]**
3. How would you sum up Jonathan's attitude toward life? **[Interpret]**

EVALUATE

4. Why is "Civil Peace" an appropriate title for this story? Consider the meanings of the word *civil*. **[Assess]**

APPLY

5. Do you think it is easier for a poor person or a rich person to accept the loss of material possessions? Explain your answer. **[Generalize]**

◆ Reading Strategy

PRIOR KNOWLEDGE

Although this story takes place after a civil war in another country, your **prior knowledge** about dealing with unexpected events can help you understand the main character's experiences and reactions.

1. Jonathan frequently quotes proverbs as a reaction to events in his life. What proverbs or sayings do you use to respond to events in your life?
2. Jonathan experiences several turns of fortune during this story. Compare and contrast his reactions to his changing luck with the way you respond to life's ups and downs.

◆ Literary Focus

KEY STATEMENTS

Chinua Achebe makes use of a proverb that has been important in Ibo life. This proverb also acts as a **key statement** that throws light on the central meaning of his story.

1. What does the key saying, "Happy survival!" reveal about Jonathan's values?
2. Why do you think the proverb "Nothing puzzles God" is repeated in the story? How does it help reveal the story's message about life?

◆ Build Vocabulary

USING FORMS OF *DISREPUTABLE*

Write the sentences below in your notebook and fill in the blanks with *disreputable, reputation,* or *reputed.*

Jonathan is ___?___ to be a careful man. He also has a ___?___ for honesty. Unfortunately, he was robbed by some ___?___ men.

USING THE WORD BANK

Copy the following book titles in your notebook. Next to each title, write the word from the Word Bank that you would expect to find in the book.
1. *The Architecture of Frank Lloyd Wright*
2. *Kings and Queens of the World*
3. *Sharing Your Pain*
4. *Getting Others to Agree*
5. *The Causes of Poverty*
6. *Jewels and Gemstones*

◆ Build Grammar Skills

PAST AND PAST PERFECT TENSES

Past tense indicates an action or condition that began and ended at a given time in the past. **Past perfect tense** (formed with *had* plus a past participle) shows an action or condition that was completed when another past action began.

Practice In your notebook, copy each of these sentences. Circle the past tense verbs and underline the verbs in the past perfect tense.
1. Only two houses away a huge concrete edifice some wealthy contractor had put up before the war was a mountain of rubble.
2. ...he had returned to Enugu early enough ...before thousands more came out of their forest holes ...
3. ...that little house of his was even a greater blessing than he had thought.
4. ...he pulled out the innards of his pocket and revealed a hole in it.... But of course he had insisted that the money had been in the other pocket ...
5. This went on for a long time and then stopped suddenly. Perhaps they had scared the thief away.

5. past tense: went, stopped; past perfect tense: had scared

✎ Writer's Solution

For additional instruction and practice, use the lesson in the **Language Lab CD-ROM** on Verb Tense and the pages on tenses of verbs, pp. 67–71 in the *Writer's Solution Grammar Practice Book.*

Build Your Portfolio

 Idea Bank

Writing

1. **News Interview** Create a list of five interview questions a reporter covering the aftermath of the civil war might ask Jonathan. Based on details in the story, write Jonathan's answers to the questions. **[Social Studies Link]**

2. **Human-Interest Article** Use the events described in the story to write a human-interest article about one family's experiences after the civil war.

3. **Poem** Write a short poem expressing some thoughts or feelings that the story "Civil Peace" evoked in you.

Speaking and Listening

4. **Reworking a Dialogue** Rewrite the dialogue between the thieves and Jonathan in language that is familiar to you. With a partner, read the dialogue aloud. **[Performing Arts Link]**

5. **Proverbs Presentation** With a panel of "experts," collect a number of proverbs and sayings. Present the origins and applications of each and speculate why the saying has survived the test of time.

Projects

6. **Collage** Create a collage composed of magazine pictures, your own artwork, poems, music, and words that shows your interpretation of the proverb, "Nothing puzzles God." **[Art Link]**

7. **Scenic Sketches** Sketch the settings for several scenes of a movie version of "Civil Peace." Possible scenes to include are Jonathan's home, the road to Enugu, and the outside of the Treasury. **[Art Link]**

 Writing Mini-Lesson

Annotated Map of Nigeria

The setting of this story is Nigeria, a country of great diversity and political and social change. Create an **annotated map** of Nigeria to instruct readers about significant features of the landscape, ethnic diversity, and types of industry. The annotations you write will give essential information about each aspect of Nigeria you decide to include. The following tip will help you in preparing your annotations.

> ### Writing Skills Focus: Brevity and Clarity
>
> When you need to convey a great deal of information in a small space, **brevity and clarity** (being brief and being clear) are especially important. Bulleted lists, numbered sentences, and charts are a few ways you can communicate important information in a small space. Annotations that you write in sentence form should be brief and to the point.

Prewriting Brainstorm for a list of topics you think will help someone better understand the story. For instance, the regions in which different ethnic groups live would give insight into the causes and boundaries of the civil war.

Drafting Put numbers on the map to locate the area to which each annotation refers. Then write your annotations. Try to avoid making the map too crowded, but include the facts that will be most helpful to readers.

Revising Look back at the biography of Achebe and the story. See if there is any information that you could present that would further enhance reading. Review each of your annotations to make sure they are not only short but clear.

Civil Peace ◆ 403

 Idea Bank
Customizing for
Performance Levels
Following are suggestions for matching the Idea Bank topics with your students' performance levels:
Less Advanced Students: 1, 5, 6
Average Students: 2, 4, 7
More Advanced Students: 3, 5

Customizing for
Learning Modalities
Following are suggestions for matching Idea Bank topics with your students' learning modalities:
Verbal/Linguistic: 1, 2, 3, 4, 5
Visual/Spatial: 6, 7

 Writing Mini-Lesson

Refer students to the Writing Handbook, page 965, for instruction on the writing process, and page 967 for further information on exposition.

Writing and Language Transparencies Students may use the Herringbone Organizer, p. 76, to list and organize the information for their annotated maps before marking labels on the map.

Writing Lab CD-ROM
Have students complete the tutorial on Exposition. Follow these steps:
1. Students can use the Questionnaire to help them gather details for their annotated maps.
2. Students may work in pairs to use the interactive instruction on conducting library research.
3. Have students draft their annotations on computer.
4. Students can use the guidelines for sharing reports with a group when presenting their annotated maps.
Allow approximately 90 minutes of class time to complete these steps.

Sourcebook
Have students use Chapter 3, Exposition (pp. 62–95), for additional support. The chapter includes specific instructions on organizing details (pp. 82–83).

✓ ASSESSMENT OPTIONS

Formal Assessment, Selection Test, pp. 101–103, and Assessment Resources Software. The selection test is designed so that it can be easily customized to the performance levels of your students.
Alternative Assessment, p. 29, includes options for less advanced students, more advanced students, bodily/kinesthetic learners, intrapersonal learners, logical/mathematical learners, and verbal/linguistic learners.

PORTFOLIO ASSESSMENT
Use the following rubrics in the *Alternative Assessment* booklet to assess student writing:
News Interview: Expression Rubric, p. 94
Human-Interest Article: Fictional Narrative Rubric, p. 95
Poem: Poetry Rubric, p. 108
Writing Mini-Lesson: Technical Description/ Explanation Rubric, p. 115

OBJECTIVES

1. To read, comprehend, and interpret a poem and an essay
2. To relate a poem and an essay to personal experience
3. To respond to connotations and images
4. To identify tone
5. To build vocabulary in context and learn the word root *-ami-*
6. To develop skill in using pronouns that agree with indefinite antecedents
7. To write an introduction of a talk show guest that takes audience knowledge into account
8. To respond to the literature through writing, speaking and listening, and projects

SKILLS INSTRUCTION

Vocabulary:
Word Roots: *-ami-*
Grammar:
Pronoun Agreement with an Indefinite Antecedent
Reading Strategy:
Respond to Connotations
Literary Focus:
Tone

Writing:
Audience Knowledge
Speaking and Listening:
Debate (teacher edition)
Critical Viewing:
Analyze; Hypothesize

PORTFOLIO OPPORTUNITIES

Writing: Fan Magazine Interview; Dialogue; Techno-Reaction
Writing Mini-Lesson: Introduction of Talk Show Guest
Speaking and Listening: Comic Scene; Debate
Projects: Drawing; Celebrity Home Page

More About the Authors

Like "The Bean Eaters," most of **Gwendolyn Brooks's** poems explore the forces that shape people's lives—both from within and without. Her major themes deal with the way people face—and often overcome—adversities such as poverty and prejudice.

"How to React to Familiar Faces" is not the only piece of social commentary with a "How-to" title that **Umberto Eco** has written. This piece is from a collection entitled *How to Travel with a Salmon and Other Essays*, which includes such other short works as "How to Eat in Flight."

*G*uide for Reading

Gwendolyn Brooks *(1917–   )*

If there is such a thing as a "born writer," Gwendolyn Brooks must be one. She began to write at age seven and published her first poem, "Eventide," at the age of seventeen.

In many of her poems, Brooks explores the struggles and dreams of African Americans. She won the Pulitzer Prize (the first African American to do so) for her 1949 collection of poetry, *Annie Allen*. She has received numerous other honors, including the title Poet Laureate of Illinois (1968) and an appointment as poetry consultant to the Library of Congress (1985–1986).

Umberto Eco *(1932–   )*

Umberto Eco's personal library is larger than some school libraries—holding more than 30,000 volumes! His extensive library is just one indication of the Italian author's strong interest in all forms of communication. At the University of Bologna in Italy he teaches Semiotics, the study of communication through signs and symbols. He is also an avid follower of the information revolution taking place on the Internet. Eco achieved an international audience with his 1981 novel, *The Name of the Rose*, a suspenseful tale of murder in a Benedictine monastery.

◆ Build Vocabulary

WORD ROOTS: *-ami-*

In "How to React to Familiar Faces" you will encounter the word *amiably*, meaning "in a friendly way." The Latin word root *-ami-*, meaning "friend," appears in the French word for friend (*ami*) and in the Spanish words for friend (*amigo, amiga*). In English, *-ami-* is the root of several words related to friendship, such as *amiably, amenable, amity,* and *amicable.*

WORD BANK

As you read this poem and essay, you will encounter the words on this list. Each word is defined on the page where it first appears. Preview the list before you read.

expound
syndrome
amiably
protagonist

◆ Build Grammar Skills

PRONOUN AGREEMENT WITH AN INDEFINITE ANTECEDENT

A pronoun's **antecedent** is the noun or pronoun to which the pronoun refers. A pronoun must agree in number (singular or plural) and gender (feminine or masculine) with its antecedent. Sometimes the gender or the number of the antecedent may not be known. For instance, in his essay, Eco says:

…we don't speak of *this person* in a loud voice when *he* or *she* can overhear.

Because the antecedent, *this person*, is singular but of unknown gender, Eco use the singular *he* or *she* to refer to the antecedent.

A common mistake is to use the word *they* in this situation; however, *they* is plural, so it does not agree with the singular antecedent.

Prentice Hall Literature Program Resources

REINFORCE / RETEACH / EXTEND

Selection Support Pages
Build Vocabulary: Word Roots: *-ami-*, p. 122
Build Grammar Skills: Pronoun Agreement with Indefinite Antecedent, p. 123
Reading Strategy: Respond to Connotations, p. 124
Literary Focus: Tone, p. 125

Strategies for Diverse Student Needs, p. 30

Beyond Literature Art of Portraiture, p. 30

Formal Assessment Selection Test, pp.104–106; Assessment Resources Software

Alternative Assessment, p. 30

Writing and Language Transparencies
Writing Process Model 2, Biographical Profile, pp. 13–16, Art Transparency 1

Resource Pro CD-ROM
"The Bean Eaters," "How to React to Familiar Faces"—includes all resource materials and customizable lesson plan

 Listening to Literature Audiocassettes
"The Bean Eaters," "How to React to Familiar Faces"

◆ The Bean Eaters ◆
How to React to Familiar Faces

◆ *Literature and Your Life*

CONNECT YOUR EXPERIENCE

Although you've never met your favorite movie actor, chances are you know his or her age, likes and dislikes, and hobbies. With television and film delivering people into our living rooms, it's easy to feel as if you know celebrities. This poem and essay provide a contrast between the very public life of famous people and the very personal details of ordinary people who might live near you.

THEMATIC FOCUS: A WORLD OF PEOPLE

These selections give you a glimpse of famous people and anonymous lives. Both the people you know and those who enter your life through books and film can expand your horizons.

Journal Writing Jot down details about a famous or not-so-famous person who has made a favorable impression on you.

◆ Background for Understanding

ENTERTAINMENT

Umberto Eco was born in 1932, so the entertainment names he's familiar with may not be familiar to you. Then again, they might be. The following information identifies the people to whom Eco refers in his essay.

The film actor Anthony Quinn was born in Chihuahua, Mexico, in 1916. After years of being stereotyped in such roles as a Mexican bandit and an Indian warrior, Quinn eventually achieved international fame, winning two Academy Awards. Charlton Heston is an American actor. Johnny Carson was the host of *The Tonight Show* for thirty years, until 1992. Oprah Winfrey has been one of the most successful talk-show hosts in history.

Journal Writing Think about a character—from a book, movie, or television show—that you feel you really know. Describe the character's qualities that seem most familiar to you.

◆ Literary Focus

TONE

Each of these literary selections has a distinct **tone**—that is, an attitude toward its readers and its subject matter. A writer's tone may be formal or informal, friendly or distant, personal or impersonal. For example, Eco's tone is lighthearted and amusing. His attitude toward his subject and his readers is good-natured.

◆ Reading Strategy

RESPOND TO CONNOTATIONS

When you see a familiar face, you respond based on the associations you have with that person. In a similar way, you **respond** to connotations (associations that go beyond a word's literal definition) based on your personal experience. For example, in reading "The Bean Eaters," you probably create an image in your mind of the two people—what they look like and what they are wearing. The title "The Bean Eaters" refers literally to people who eat beans. Yet the phrase connotes simplicity and poverty.

Be prepared to take some words in literary works beyond their everyday meanings; these words tap you on the shoulder as if to say, "Hey, don't I remind you of something else?"

Anthony Quinn

Guide for Reading ◆ 405

People Magazine... Us ...The Tonight Show ...

Brainstorm with students to name some of the many magazines and TV shows that focus on celebrities. Discuss with students the fascination people have for these subjects. Ask them why "ordinary people" are less likely to be subject to media attention. Tell them that the selections they will read offer some interesting insights on this topic.

Customize for
Less Proficient Readers

Less proficient readers may need extra help in identifying the distinct tone of each piece. Help students by highlighting specific passages for them to consider. Ask such guiding questions as: Is the attitude expressed here light-hearted or serious? Joyous or sad? Formal or informal?

Customize for
More Advanced Students

Encourage more advanced students to compare and contrast aspects of the two selections. For example, how would they identify the common thread that runs through each one? How is Eco's tone different from that of Gwendolyn Brooks?

Customize for
English Language Learners

You might use Eco's essay as an opportunity for students to share knowledge and ideas about popular culture. For example, students might describe some of the movies that the stars mentioned in the piece have appeared in; students of different cultures might inform classmates about the familiar faces in the popular cultures of their countries.

Customize for
Interpersonal Learners

Have these students evaluate the attitude toward people that each of the authors expresses. Suggest that they work with partners to role-play an interview with Brooks and Eco to demonstrate these attitudes to classmates.

✎ Preparing for Standardized Tests

Grammar and Language Portions of some standardized tests require students to demonstrate their mastery of grammar and usage. Students may be asked to choose the best word to complete a sentence as in this example:

Everyone should bring _____ favorite book.

(A) their (B) his or her (C) its *(B)*

The Build Grammar Skills lesson for this selection focuses on pronoun agreement with an indefinite antecedent. Understanding pronoun antecedent agreement will improve students' performance on sentence completion items testing grammar and usage skills. For additional practice, use the Build Grammar Skills page on Pronoun Agreement with Indefinite Antecedent, p. 123, in **Selection Support**.

405

These selections explore the lives of people, both ordinary and extraordinary, and how we view them. Poet Gwendolyn Brooks vividly evokes the texture of everyday lives and helps us glimpse the sensitive realities that lie beneath surface images.

◆ Reading Strategy

❶ Respond to Connotations
Encourage students to comment on the connotations of "plain chipware," "plain and creaking wood," and "tin flatware." *Connotations include simplicity, homeyness, inexpensiveness, poverty.* Then invite students to discuss the connotations of "this old yellow pair." *Students may say that the description evokes the quality of being worn out but comfortable.*

◆ Critical Thinking

❷ Interpret Ask students what two aspects of the people's lives Brooks contrasts in these lines. Also have students comment on the larger meaning of this contrast. *Brooks contrasts the pair's ordinary, day-to-day existence with the accumulated richness of their lives; she shows that these seemingly ordinary lives are full of complexity and meaning.*

◆ Literary Focus

❸ Tone Ask students to describe the tone of the poem. Encourage them to cite specific phrases or images that support their responses. *Students may describe the tone as sympathetic, straightforward, and slightly sad or bittersweet.*

►Critical Viewing◄

❹ Analyze The plain plate and fork are serviceable and practical; the beans are common and everyday.

406

The Bean Eaters

Gwendolyn Brooks

❶ They eat beans mostly, this old yellow pair.
Dinner is a casual affair.
Plain chipware on a plain and creaking wood,
Tin flatware.

5   Two who are Mostly Good.
Two who have lived their day,
But keep on putting on their clothes
And putting things away.
❷

❸ And remembering . . .
10   Remembering, with twinklings and twinges,
As they lean over the beans in their rented back room
     that is full of beads and receipts and dolls
     and cloths,tobacco crumbs, vases and fringes.

▲ **Critical Viewing** In what ways do these pictures suggest the simplicity of the old couple's lives? **❹** [**Analyze**]

406 ◆ Expanding Horizons

Block Scheduling Strategies

Consider these suggestions to take advantage of extended class time:

• Play a recording of Paul Simon's song, "Old Friends." Have students read the lyrics and answer the questions in the Connections to Today's World on page 407.

• Have students complete the activities on Tone on page 410 and the Literary Focus page in **Selection Support,** p. 125.

• Use Art Transparency 1 to introduce "How to React to Familiar Faces." You might have stu-

dents do one of the optional activities accompanying the transparency.

• Have students complete the page on the Art of Portraiture in **Beyond Literature,** p. 30, and compare their responses to the portrait of Anthony Quinn on page 408.

• Students may work in discussion groups to identify and explore words and images that have powerful connotations in the works in this section. Then have students answer the Reading Strategy questions (p. 410).

Old Friends

Paul Simon

Old Friends,
Old Friends
Sat on their park bench
Like bookends.
5 A newspaper blown through the grass
Falls on the round toes
Of the high shoes
Of the Old Friends.

Old Friends,
10 Winter companions,
The old men
Lost in their overcoats,
Waiting for the sunset.
The sounds of the city,
15 Sifting through the trees,
Settle like dust
On the shoulders
Of the old friends.

Can you imagine us
20 Years from today,
Sharing a park bench quietly?
How terribly strange
To be seventy.

Old Friends,
25 Memory brushes the same years.
Silently sharing the same fears. . . .

CONNECTIONS TO TODAY'S WORLD

In the late 1960's, singer/songwriter Paul Simon recorded this song with Art Garfunkel, who was his partner at that time. In this song, Paul Simon looks at the friendship of anonymous elderly people. Like the couple in "The Bean Eaters," these old friends show how our everyday relationships expand the horizons of our world.

1. Describe the qualities of the friendship shown in these lyrics.
2. Based on the thoughts he expresses here, how much importance do you think celebrity Paul Simon places on fame?

Guide for Responding

◆ Literature and Your Life

Reader's Response If you could meet the people in "The Bean Eaters," what would you ask them about their memories?

Thematic Focus In what ways do people like the pair in "The Bean Eaters" enrich the world?

☑ **Check Your Comprehension**

1. Who is the subject of "The Bean Eaters"?
2. How do they spend most of their time?

◆ Critical Thinking

INTERPRET
1. Identify two details that indicate the couple in the poem are not rich. **[Deduce]**
2. Which details lead you to believe that they share many memories? Explain. **[Draw Conclusions]**

APPLY
3. Do you think the people in this poem are happy? Explain. **[Hypothesize]**

Thematic Focus They have stores of memories that others will appreciate when they are shared.

☑ **Check Your Comprehension**

1. The subject is an old couple who live together in a rented room.
2. They spend their time reminiscing about people, places, and things from their past.

◆ Critical Thinking

1. Details that indicate the old pair's poverty include "plain and creaking wood" and "rented back room."
2. The phrase "twinklings and twinges" suggests that the pair share many memories.
3. The couple is happy enough to care for themselves and share their memories with each other.

Connections to Today's World

About the Author Paul Simon wrote and recorded such hits as "Kodachrome" and "Still Crazy After All These Years." During the 1980's, he explored international styles and rhythms. His musical experimentation resulted in two highly successful albums: *Graceland,* on which he collaborated with several black South African musicians, and *Rhythms of the Saints,* on which he collaborated with some of Brazil's leading musicians. Simon collaborated with Derek Walcott on the 1997 Broadway musical *The Capeman.*

Thematic Connection

Have students compare the importance of memories in the song and the poem, "The Bean Eaters." *The role is similar. In "The Bean Eaters," the two people have "lived their day." By "putting on their clothes/And putting things away," they go through the motions of life, but the story of their lives is over, preserved in the "beads and receipts and dolls and clothes/tobacco crumbs, vases and fringes." In the song, the two friends sit passively while life goes on around them. Their memories are "all that's left."*

◆ Critical Thinking

Compare and Contrast Ask students: How is the tone of "Old Friends" similar to or different from that of "The Bean Eaters"? *Students may say that the tone is similar—it is sympathetic and somewhat melancholy.*

Answers to Connections to Today's World

1. The friends are seventy years old, quiet, thoughtful, and fearful.
2. Suggested responses: He places little importance on fame—the song suggests that friendship and personal memories are the most important things in life.

Reinforce and Extend

Answers

◆ Literature and Your Life

Reader's Response Students might ask them about their work, their friends and family, and their hobbies.

407

One-Minute Insight Author and social critic Umberto Eco humorously analyzes the effects of the media on the way people react to celebrities. In a lighthearted tone, he raises questions on a serious theme.

Art Transparency Place Art Transparency 1, *Bauhaus Stairway*, on the overhead projector. As students look at the art, have them discuss the issue of familiarity and anonymity among people.

◆ **Literary Focus**

❶ **Tone** Have students describe the tone of this passage. Encourage them to cite specific phrases or offer explanations in support of their descriptions. *Students may describe the tone as humorous. In support, they many point out that Eco exaggerates in a humorous way when he writes, "It was too late to flee"; and "I might as well make the first move."*

▶ **Critical Viewing** ◀

❷ **Hypothesize** Students may say he is reacting to a greeting from an acquaintance or a fan; his expression seems pleased.

◆ *Literature and Your Life*

❸ Ask students if they agree with Eco's statement. If not, why not?

How to React to Familiar Faces

Umberto Eco

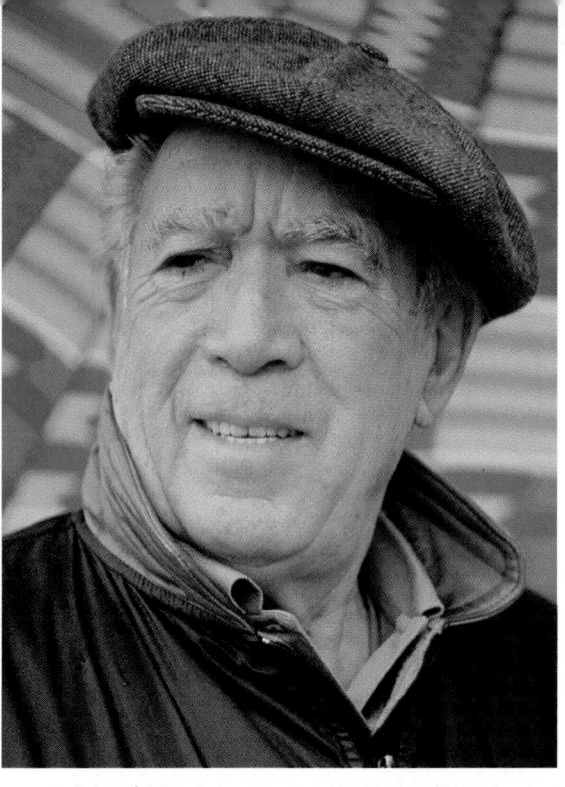

▲ **Critical Viewing** This photograph is of the movie star Anthony Quinn. What do you think he is reacting to in this picture? [Hypothesize] ❷

A few months ago, as I was strolling in New York, I saw, at a distance, a man I knew very well heading in my direction. The trouble was that I couldn't remember his name or where I had met him. This is one of those sensations you encounter especially when, in a foreign city, you run into someone you met back home, or vice versa. A face out of context creates confusion. Still, that face was so familiar that, I felt, I should certainly stop, greet him, converse; perhaps he would immediately respond, "My dear Umberto, how are you?" or "Were you able to do that thing you were telling me ❶ about?" And I would be at a total loss. It was too late to flee. He was still looking at the opposite side of the street, but now he was beginning to turn his eyes towards me. I might as well make the first move; I would wave and then, from his voice, his first remarks, I would try to guess his identity.

We were now only a few feet from each other,

I was just about to break into a broad, radiant smile, when suddenly I recognized him. It was Anthony Quinn. Naturally, I had never met him in my life, nor he me. In a thousandth of a second I was able to check myself, and I walked past him, my eyes staring into space.

Afterwards, reflecting on this incident, I realized how totally normal it was. Once before, in a restaurant, I had glimpsed Charlton Heston and had felt an impulse to say hello. These faces inhabit our memory; watching the screen, we spend so many hours with them that they ❸ are as familiar to us as our relatives', even more so. You can be a student of mass communication, debate the effects of reality, or the confusion between the real and the imagined, and expound the way some people fall permanently into this confusion; but still you are not immune to the syndrome. And there is worse.

I have received confidences from people who,

Speaking and Listening Mini-Lesson

Debate

This mini-lesson supports the Speaking and Listening activity in the Idea Bank on page 411.

Introduce the Concept Point out that in a debate, two teams present opposing viewpoints on a subject. The teams then take turns "rebutting," or arguing against, their opponents' presentations. (See the Speaking and Listening Handbook, p. 978.)

Develop Background Before students

debate the question of whether or not publicity is part of the "job" of being a celebrity, encourage them to think about both sides of the question. For example:

• Celebrities owe their success to the public—therefore, they should do all they can to attract and please fans.

• Most celebrities owe their success to hard work in a certain field, such as acting or sports—they shouldn't have to give up their privacy to please fans.

Apply the Information The opposing teams can develop these and other arguments to support their side. Then they can present their positions in debate format.

Assess the Outcome After the debate, ask: Were the arguments clear and focused? Which position was more persuasive? What could students have done to make their arguments more persuasive? Use the answers to these questions to assess students' performance.

appearing fairly frequently on TV, have been subjected to the mass media over a certain period of time. I'm not talking about Johnny Carson or Oprah Winfrey, but public figures, experts who have participated in panel discussions often enough to become recognizable. All of them complain of the same disagreeable experience. Now, as a rule, when we see someone we don't know personally, we don't stare into his or her face at length, we don't point out the person to the friend at our side, we don't speak of this person in a loud voice when he or she can overhear. Such behavior would be rude, even—if carried too far—aggressive. But the same people who would never point to a customer at a counter and remark to a friend that the man is wearing a smart tie behave quite differently with famous faces.

My guinea pigs insist that, at a newsstand, in the tobacconist's, as they are boarding a train or entering a restaurant toilet, they encounter others who, among themselves, say aloud, "Look there's X." "Are you sure?" "Of course I'm sure. It's X, I tell you." And they continue their conversation <u>amiably</u>, while X hears them, and they don't care if he hears them: it's as if he didn't exist.

Such people are confused by the fact that a <u>protagonist</u> of the mass media's imaginary world should abruptly enter real life, but at the same time they behave in the presence of the real person as if he still belonged to the world of images, as if he were on a screen, or in a weekly picture magazine. As if they were speaking in his absence.

I might as well have grabbed Anthony Quinn by the lapel, dragged him to a phone booth, and called a friend to say, "Talk about coincidence! I've run into Anthony Quinn. And you know something? He seems real!" (After which I would throw Quinn aside and go on about my business.)

The mass media first convinced us that the imaginary was real, and now they are convincing us that the real is imaginary; and the more reality the TV screen shows us, the more cinematic our everyday world becomes.

◆ Build Vocabulary

expound (eks pound´) *v.*: Explain in detail

syndrome (sin´ drōm) *n.*: Group of signs that occur together and may form a pattern

amiably (ā´ mē ə blē) *adv.*: In a cheerful, friendly way

protagonist (prō tag´ ə nist´) *n.*: Main character; person who plays a leading part

Guide for Responding

◆ *Literature and Your Life*

Reader's Response Do you react to celebrities in the way Umberto describes? Explain.

Thematic Focus Which celebrities interest you? Why?

☑ Check Your Comprehension

1. What celebrity does the author see in New York?
2. What reaction does Eco say most people have to celebrities?
3. Why does Eco say people react as they do?

◆ Critical Thinking

INTERPRET

1. How do you think Eco feels about the way people react to celebrities? **[Interpret]**
2. Explain how the title of the essay relates to its message. **[Connect]**
3. Explain Eco's understanding of the role the media plays in our reaction to and attitude toward famous people. **[Analyze]**

APPLY

4. Based on Eco's observations, do you think you would like to be famous? Why or why not? **[Relate]**

How to React to Familiar Faces ◆ 409

  Beyond the Selection

FURTHER READING

Other Works by the Authors
Annie Allen, Gwendolyn Brooks
The Name of the Rose, Umberto Eco

Other Works About Individuals
Working, Studs Terkel
"Richard Cory," Edwin Arlington Robinson
Our Town, Thornton Wilder
We suggest that you preview these works before recommending them to students.

INTERNET

Students can use the Internet to learn more about the writers Gwendolyn Brooks: **http://www.wilmington.net/arts/poets/brooks.html**

Umberto Eco: **http://www1.geocites.com/Athens/6642/index.html**

Paul Simon: **http://www.connix.com/~rdrie/Frames/simon/history.html**

Please be aware, that sites may have changed since we published this information. We *strongly recommend* that you preview the sites before you send students to them.

409

► Reading Strategy

1. The connotation is simplicity.
2. (a) They alliteratively suggest the pleasures and pain of memory. (b) The poet suggests the two extremes of memory—the positive and negative aspects.
3. Encourage students to explain whether the connotations affected their response in a positive or negative manner.

◆ Build Vocabulary

Using the Root -ami-

1. An amiable approach would be accompanied by a smile.
2. You might have said, "Thanks for meeting with me" and "I appreciate your interest."
3. Students may suggest good communication.
4. Some students may be willing to accept shorter vacations if they occur at more frequent intervals. Others may argue that they need a long vacation to rest from the pressure of academic work.

Using the Word Bank

1. A bibliophile may expound on the importance of reading.
2. You usually act amicably to your parents and friends.
3. Descriptions should include personality traits as well as physical details.
4. Students may find it humorous that they all need a "wake-up" activity in order to pay attention on Monday mornings.

◆ Literary Focus

1. (a) Brooks appears to be warmly sympathetic to the couple. (b) Phrases that reflect her attitude include *casual, Mostly Good,* and *remembering with twinklings and twinges.*
2. A humorous tone is reflected in statements such as "It was too late to flee," and "My guinea pigs insist that. . . ."
3. Brooks reveals a positive and empathetic attitude toward people often disparaged; Eco pokes fun at those who dehumanize the celebrities of mass media.

◆ Build Grammar Skills

1. Anyone . . . should buy his or her . . . .
2. Several could have reserved their. . . .
3. One person thought he or she. . . .
4. All . . . had seats, and they. . . .

Guide for Responding (continued)

◆ Reading Strategy

RESPOND TO CONNOTATIONS

You might find yourself relating more to one of these selections than to another. Your personal experience and the associations you have with particular words influence your response to the images and connotations in each selection.

1. Keeping in mind the subject of "The Bean Eaters," what is the connotation of "plain chipware" and "tin flatware"?
2. (a) How do you respond to the words "twinklings" and "twinges" in "The Bean Eaters"? (b) What do you think the poet was trying to convey with each of these words?
3. To which image in "How to React to Familiar Faces" do you respond most strongly? What connotations create the image for you?

◆ Build Vocabulary

USING THE ROOT -ami-

Knowing that the root -ami- means "friend," respond to the following questions in your notebook.

1. Would a person approach you amiably wearing a smile or a frown?
2. You've just finished meeting with the principal, and you parted amicably. Write the last two things you might have said to each other.
3. Write one suggestion for fostering amity between students and teachers.
4. Explain why you would or would not be amenable to shorter vacations.

USING THE WORD BANK

On your paper, respond to the following items.

1. What kind of person might expound on the importance of reading?
2. Name a person to whom you usually act amiably.
3. Describe the protagonist in your favorite movie or book.
4. Describe a humorous syndrome that might affect students early on a Monday morning.

◆ Literary Focus

TONE

The **tone** of a literary work is the writer's attitude toward the readers and toward the subject. In the poem "The Bean Eaters," Gwendolyn Brooks presents you with two people in a room. Her tone is as intimate as her subject matter, but some readers will find it lonely, too. In his social commentary "How to React to Familiar Faces," Eco's purpose is to reveal a common human behavior, and his tone is suitably objective. It is also a bit wry, or humorous.

1. (a) How do you think Brooks feels about the people in her poem "The Bean Eaters"? (b) List two details that help you identify her attitude toward the people.
2. Find two statements in "How to React to Familiar Faces" that reflect a humorous tone.
3. Compare and contrast the tone of "The Bean Eaters" with the tone of "How to React to Familiar Faces."

◆ Build Grammar Skills

PRONOUN AGREEMENT WITH AN INDEFINITE ANTECEDENT

Singular pronouns must be used to refer to **indefinite antecedents** such as *someone, anyone,* and *everybody.* If the gender is unknown, it's best to use a combination of two singular personal pronouns such as *he or she* or *his or her.* When words like *all* or *several* are antecedents, they require a plural word to refer to them.

Practice In your notebook, write the pronoun that agrees with its indefinite antecedent in each of the following sentences:

1. Anyone who wants a seat to hear Gwendolyn Brooks read should buy (their, his, her, his or her) ticket early.
2. Several could have reserved (their, his or her) seats earlier.
3. One person thought (he, she, they, he or she) would have to stand for the reading.
4. All who called ahead had seats, and (they, he or she, he, she) were grateful.

✎ Writer's Solution

For additional instruction and practice, use the lesson in the **Language Lab CD-ROM** on Pronouns and Antecedents and the page on Pronoun and Antecedent Agreement, p. 83 in the *Writer's Solution Grammar Practice Book.*

Build Your Portfolio

Idea Bank

Writing

1. **Fan Magazine Interview** Write five questions you would ask your favorite celebrity in an interview. Write an answer to one of the questions, as if you were the celebrity.

2. **Dialogue** Write a brief dialogue that might occur between the man and the woman in the poem "The Bean Eaters."

3. **Techno-Reaction** Write your reaction to some effect of technology, such as doing business on the World Wide Web or making friends on Internet chat lines. **[Technology Link]**

Speaking and Listening

4. **Comic Scene** With a group of classmates, enact a scene in which several teenagers recognize their favorite music star in front of them in line at the music store's cash register. **[Performing Arts Link]**

5. **Debate** Divide into teams to debate this statement: Publicity is part of the "job" of being a celebrity. Support your position with sound reasoning. **[Social Studies Link]**

Projects

6. **Drawing** Using the medium of your choice (color pencils, markers, charcoal), draw a picture of the room and couple described in "The Bean Eaters." Try to capture the tone of the poem in your drawing. **[Art Link]**

7. **Celebrity Home Page** Design a home page for one of the celebrities Eco mentions in his nonfiction piece. Choose visuals and suggest topics and links. **[Technology Link]**

Writing Mini-Lesson

Introduction of Talk-Show Guest

Although celebrities are usually well known to the public, talk-show hosts often introduce them in a way that builds up audience interest. Write an **introduction** for a celebrity guest you would like to interview on a talk show. Keep your audience in mind as you prepare your introduction.

Writing Skills Focus: Audience Knowledge

Finding details about your celebrity that haven't already been published or broadcast may be difficult. Your audience will probably already know a great deal about the guest, so choose details that show the person in a light the audience doesn't normally view him or her.

For example, if your guest is a movie actor, listing all of his or her movies will probably not add to **audience knowledge.** Instead, name just one or two recent projects, then focus on an anecdote that will draw audience attention to an aspect of the celebrity's personality that isn't usually considered.

Prewriting Focus on listing details that will build interest in the aspect that you want to highlight. For instance, if you want to show how hardworking a movie actor is, you might plan to include details about the difficult conditions during the making of his or her last movie, such as filming during the hurricane season or sixteen-hour filming sessions.

Drafting Keep your introduction brief. Include just enough details to heighten your audience's interest and draw them into the interview that will follow.

Revising Read your draft aloud to a partner. Ask him or her to identify the most and least interesting details. Revise your draft based on your partner's suggestions.

The Bean Eaters/How to React to Familiar Faces ◆ 411

Guide for Reading

OBJECTIVES

1. To read, comprehend, and interpret essays

2. To relate essays to personal experience

3. To relate text and pictures

4. To recognize the features of analytical essays

5. To build vocabulary in context and learn the word root -cent-

6. To develop skill in using compound sentences

7. To write a museum placard that anticipates viewers' questions

8. To respond to the essays through writing, speaking and listening, and projects

SKILLS INSTRUCTION

Vocabulary:
Word Roots: -cent-

Grammar:
Compound Sentences

Reading Strategy:
Relate Text and Pictures

Literary Focus:
Analytical Essay

Writing:
Anticipation of Questions

Speaking and Listening:
Art Narration (teacher edition)

Critical Viewing:
Infer; Apply; Interpret

PORTFOLIO OPPORTUNITIES

Writing: Exhibit Promotion; Photo Essay; Art Analysis

Writing Mini-Lesson: Museum Placard

Speaking and Listening: Poetry Reading; Art Narration

Projects: Painting and Poetry Exhibit; Art Exchange

More About the Authors

Reynolds Price's talent as a young writer won him a scholarship to Duke University and a Rhodes Scholarship, upon graduation, to study at Oxford University. After Oxford, he was offered and accepted a teaching position at Duke, cementing his ties to the North Carolina of his childhood. Price's childhood memories of summer camp are the basis of his novel, *The Tongues of Angels*.

Richard Mühlberger, the author of "What Makes a Degas a Degas," writes extensively on art and artists. Among his other books are *Christmas Story: Told Through Paintings,* and *What Makes a Monet a Monet?*

Reynolds Price (1933–)

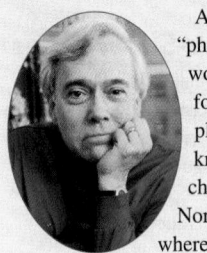

American author Reynolds Price "photographs" his characters with words. He is known for his talent for characterization, creating people that readers feel they have known all their lives. Most of his characters are drawn from the North Carolina cotton country where Price was raised.

Although best known for his novels—including *A Long and Happy Life* and *A Generous Man*, as well as his short stories—Price works in a variety of genres. He has published essays, poetry, and a memoir in addition to his fiction works.

In this essay, Reynolds Price uses his keen perception of characters to analyze the character of the very private American author Emily Dickinson.

Richard Mühlberger (1938–)

You're most likely to find Richard Mühlberger's nonfiction in museum shops. In his book *What Makes a Degas a Degas?* he makes the work of a famous French artist understandable to the ordinary reader and viewer. In this essay, he analyzes two works of the nineteenth-century French painter Edgar Degas. Many of Degas's paintings show scenes that might have been captured by a hidden camera. They depict people in unguarded moments and sometimes show them in awkward positions. Degas studied art in both Paris and Italy. He intended to become a painter of historical scenes, but he soon turned to modern subjects. He became part of an artistic movement known as Impressionism, whose followers focused on capturing a momentary glimpse of a subject.

◆ Build Vocabulary

WORD ROOTS: -cent-

Have you ever seen a *centenarian*? That's not some kind of monster with the head of a man and the body of a horse, but a person who is at least one hundred years old. An important clue to the meaning of the word *centenarian* is the word root -cent-, which means "hundred." What other words can you think of that contain the root -cent-?

WORD BANK

Before you read, preview this list of words from the essays. Several of the words may already be familiar to you. Discuss the words with a partner, and jot down what you think the words mean.

| titanic |
| centenarian |
| austere |
| lacquered |

◆ Build Grammar Skills

COMPOUND SENTENCES

Both Reynolds Price and Richard Mühlberger use compound sentences to provide information about their subjects. A **compound sentence** consists of two or more equally important, or coordinate, independent clauses. (An independent clause is a group of words with a subject and a verb that can stand alone as a sentence.) The clauses may be joined by a coordinating conjunction such as *and, but,* or *or,* or by a semicolon (;). Look at these examples:

> Subscribers to the Opéra were allowed backstage in the theater, *and* some took advantage of this access to pester dancers.

> The Impressionists painted out of doors; Degas preferred working in his studio.

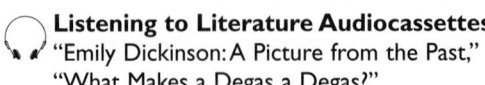

Prentice Hall Literature Program Resources

REINFORCE / RETEACH / EXTEND

Selection Support Pages
Build Vocabulary: Word Roots: -cent-, p. 126
Build Grammar Skills: Compound Sentences, p. 127
Reading Strategy: Relate Text and Pictures, p. 128
Literary Focus: Analytical Essay, p. 129

Strategies for Diverse Student Needs, p. 31

Beyond Literature
Humanities Connection: Art and Photography, p. 31

Formal Assessment Selection Test, pp. 107–109;
Assessment Resources Software

Alternative Assessment, p. 31

Writing and Language Transparencies
Grid organizer, p. 80; Cubing organizer, p. 88

Resource Pro CD-R⌀M
"Emily Dickinson: A Picture from the Past" and "What Makes a Degas a Degas?"—includes all resource materials and customizable lesson plan

 Listening to Literature Audiocassettes
"Emily Dickinson: A Picture from the Past," "What Makes a Degas a Degas?"

A Picture From the Past: Emily Dickinson
◆ What Makes a Degas a Degas? ◆

 Interest Grabber Use the picture on page 413 and display other optical illusions to generate discussion on the difference between looking and seeing. Ask students to suggest reasons that people's eyes can be fooled. Elicit from students that what people expect to see affects their perceptions. Ask students to describe their expectations of what they will see in the pictures with the essays, based on the titles. Have students preview the pictures, jotting down details they notice. Tell students that the essays that analyze the pictures may help readers notice details they did not expect to see.

◆ *Literature and Your Life*

CONNECT YOUR EXPERIENCE

Your eye doctor tests your vision by having you read an eye chart, but a hidden picture puzzle like the one on this page tests how much you really *see*. Look carefully at this picture to find the young woman *and* the old woman. (Hint: The young woman's ear is the old woman's eye.) To find the hidden pictures, you have to do more than just look, you have to notice details that might not be immediately apparent. The authors of these two essays will help you notice the "hidden" details in a photograph and in two pieces of art.

Journal Writing In your journal, describe another activity that requires you to see, not just to look.

THEMATIC FOCUS: A WORLD OF PEOPLE

Looking at things in a new way can expand your horizons. These two essays will help you analyze pictures and see the significance of details you might otherwise have overlooked.

◆ Background for Understanding

HUMANITIES

Think about photographs that have caught your eye in a magazine, newspaper, or exhibit. In addition to the pleasure they bring or the curiosity they satisfy, photographs help us learn about people from different places, at different points in time. Far-off people and places can appear right before our eyes.

Paintings also have the power to transport viewers to distant places and to earlier periods in history. In fact, paintings and other works of art provide our only visual records of what life was like in the centuries before photography was invented.

◆ Literary Focus

ANALYTICAL ESSAY

Finding out how something works (or why it has stopped working) often involves taking the thing apart. A mechanic working on a car engine will take out parts of the engine to examine them and make sure they are working together properly. In an **analytical essay,** the author breaks down a large idea into parts, helping the reader to understand how the parts fit together and what they mean as a whole. The authors of these two essays analyze pictures. By focusing on details, they will increase your appreciation for the whole picture.

◆ Reading Strategy

RELATE TEXT AND PICTURES

Movies have dialogue and comic strips often need captions. Sometimes, pictures and words are meant to go together. Together, they communicate a meaning that neither can convey alone.

Relate the text to the pictures in these essays; pause to look at the pictures and notice the details being described and interpreted. Compare the writers' interpretations of the pictures with your own impressions.

For instance, in the essay "A Picture From the Past: Emily Dickinson," the author presents a detailed analysis of a specific picture, and the essay about Degas includes a detailed description of two of his paintings. Their insights enhance your appreciation of what you see.

Guide for Reading ◆ 413

Customize for
Less Proficient Readers
These essays require readers to move back and forth between pictures and text. Suggest to these students that they use a placeholder—a finger or the eraser end of a pencil—to keep their place in the text, before changing their focus from words to pictures.

Customize for
More Advanced Students
Reynolds Price describes Emily Dickinson in great detail. After students have read both essays, challenge them to write a description of one of the Degas dancers in the style of Reynolds Price.

Customize for
English Language Learners
Preview the pictures with these students, having students describe in their own words what they see in the pictures. Guide students as they read the essays to locate the portions of the picture being described.

Customize for
Visual/Spatial Learners
Have these students preview the art on pages 414, 417, and 418. Before they begin reading, have them jot down what they believe are the important aspects of the pictures. Encourage them to compare their notes with the points in the essays.

 ### Preparing for Standardized Tests

Reading and Vocabulary The Build Vocabulary lesson for this selection focuses on the meaning of the root *-cent-*. This is a very common root; students' knowledge of this word root can improve their performance on vocabulary items on standardized tests. For additional practice, use Build Vocabulary: Using the Root *-cent-*, p. 126 in *Selection Support.*

Grammar and Language Students sometimes have difficulty distinguishing between a compound sentence and a simple sentence that has compound parts. Understanding the difference will

help them punctuate sentences correctly. In examples like the following, students must choose which sentence is punctuated incorrectly. *(A)*

(A) Kris put on her ballet shoes, and warmed up.
(B) The girls filed in, and the teacher followed.
(C) The dancers took their places; the music began.

The Build Grammar Skills lesson focuses on compound sentences. For more practice, use Build Grammar Skills: Compound Sentences, p. 127 in *Selection Support.*

One-Minute Insight

In this essay, Reynolds Price describes an image of Emily Dickinson and speculates on what the image reveals about the poet's personality and life. His analysis of the image raises questions about perpetions and appearances.

◆ Build Vocabulary

❶ Word Roots: -cent- Have students identify the word that has the root -cent-. *The word is* century. *Ask:* How is the root meaning reflected in the meaning of the word century? How can knowing the meaning of the root help you determine the meaning of the word? -Cent- *means* hundred; *there are one hundred years in a century.*

◆ Critical Thinking

❷ Make Judgments Ask students if they can tell whether this negative physical description of the subject of the photograph is an indication of the author's feelings about her. How can they find out? *Students should note that reading ahead will answer this question.*

Humanities: Art

Emily Dickinson, daguerreotype, 1847 or 1848.

The first popular method of photography was daguerreotype, named after Louis J. M. Daguerre, the Frenchman who perfected the process in 1837. Daguerreotype portraits required the subject to remain still for a long period of time, resulting in the very formal style seen in this image of Emily Dickinson.

Use these questions for discussion:
1. Why might Emily Dickinson have chosen to have a book in the picture? *The book draws attention to the literary aspect of her life.*
2. What is the purpose of a posed portrait as opposed to a photo of a person engaged in some activity? *Students may say that a posed portrait is more formal or that it seems more important as a record of a person's life.*

A Picture From the Past: Emily Dickinson

Reynolds Price

▲ **Critical Viewing** What can you infer about Emily Dickinson based on this photograph? **[Infer]**

Sorting the effects of an ancient aunt, in the wake of her death in the family homeplace or a merciless cell in an old-folks corral, you still might find such a picture and a face. The table drawers of middle-class America were once stuffed with them. No name, no date, no indication of why it's been saved to turn up now like a pebble from Mars in the glare of our world, where pictures of faces assail us at every glance and turn—assaulted children, the baffled old, the sleek in-betweeners.

❶ A daguerreotype[1] the size of a calling card, hazed with the passage of more than a century; yet for all the immobility forced on the hapless sitter by a primitive process, it rides as lightly in your hand as a fragment of undoubted life, still pulsing. A homely girl with oddly dead eyes, set too far apart and flat as the eyes **❷** of a stunned fish in your stagnant bowl—or could she be warming to the verge of a blush and a big-toothed smile? A lopsided face, bigger on her right; a skewed part in **❸** the dark horsehair above the high forehead, unmatched eyebrows, a

1. **daguerreotype** (də ger′ ō tīp′) *n.*: Photographic image made by chemically treating a flat, thin piece of metal.

414 ◆ *Expanding Horizons*

Block Scheduling Strategies

Consider these suggestions to take advantage of extended class time:

• Have students discuss the hidden picture puzzle on page 413. Then have them complete the journal activity and talk over their ideas before they read the essays.

• Introduce the Literary Focus on page 413. When students have read the selections they can answer the Literary Focus questions on page 419. You may also use the page on Analytical Essay in **Selection Support**, p. 129.

• Have students apply the Reading Strategy, Relate Text to Pictures, as they read. Then have them work in small groups to complete the Reading Strategy activity on page 419. Suggest each group appoint a Presenter to share the group's responses with the other groups.

• Give students the opportunity to research pieces of art before they begin the Writing Mini-Lesson on page 420. After they have chosen the art, encourage them to anticipate and list questions others might have.

③ fleshy nose, unpainted bruised lips, an ample
④ chin and a tall strong neck.

The hair, the ribbon around the neck, the sensible rough-knuckled hands and the complicated clinging dress date her to the midst of the 19th century. She's lasted somewhere between 16 and 20 years. Will she die shortly after this moment—consumption or childbirth—or will she endure through <u>titanic</u> throes and the ambush of pleasure to be your great-great-grandmother, say, or the maiden great-aunt your father remembers as a <u>centenarian</u> in his boyhood, a smuggler of priceless news to children—the secrets of solitude in the heart of the family but only on the rim, the watchful outrider?

⑤ None of those—no prior known option. Once

this closely held girlhood ended, and the path ahead found no one waiting, she mastered solitude patiently as any rogue lioness, though she haunted her home's back room and kitchen (a sensible cook). Through the chilling or broiling hours in her upstairs room with the white door ajar on a chattering mother, an <u>austere</u> father, a loyal, silly sister, she wrote 1,800 lyrics—some clear as hill water, some dark as oak gall[2]—that stand her yet, with no rival but Whitman,[2] at the head of our poetry: maiden aunt after all, our own Cassandra,[3] presiding mother of all this staggering nation still spooked as cubs by the mere glimpse of loneliness, that steady diet she ate by the hour all her lean years.

⑤

⑥

---

2. **Whitman:** Walt Whitman (1819–1892). Recognized as one of the most gifted American poets. Both he and Dickinson wrote poetry that was different from the standard poetry of their times.
3. **Cassandra:** In Greek mythology, Cassandra was a prophetess whose predictions were always correct but never believed. Her name is used to refer to any prophet of doom.

◆ Build Vocabulary

titanic (tī tan´ ik) *adj.*: Huge and powerful

centenarian (sen´ tə ner´ ē ən) *n.*: Person who is at least one hundred years old

austere (ô stir´) *adj.*: Severe; stern

Guide for Responding

◆ *Literature and Your Life*

Reader's Response What detail in the essay or photograph did you find most surprising?

Thematic Focus How do you enlarge your world by thinking about someone you know only from a picture?

☑ Check Your Comprehension

1. To what does Price compare old pictures?
2. Describe Dickinson's appearance.

◆ Critical Thinking

INTERPRET

1. How do you think Price feels about Dickinson? Explain. **[Infer]**
2. What is the main impression Price gives of Dickinson? Support your answer with details. **[Synthesize]**

APPLY

3. How much do you think people judge you by your appearance? **[Relate]**

EVALUATE

4. How well do you think Price interprets the picture of Emily Dickinson? **[Make a Judgment]**

A Picture From the Past: Emily Dickinson ◆ 415

415

One-Minute Insight In this essay, Richard Mühlberger analyzes Edgar Degas's painting style and points out the techniques he used to bring immediacy and the illusion of reality to his work.

Customize for
Logical/Mathematical Learners

Have these students make a chart to compare and contrast the two paintings by Degas. They may use the Grid organizer in *Writing and Language Transparencies*, p. 80.

◆ **Reading Strategy**

❶ **Relate Text and Pictures** Have students match each detail in this passage with details in the painting. Ask: Would you describe the painting in the same way or differently? *Students' descriptions would probably be similar to the author's.*

◆ **Critical Thinking**

❷ **Compare and Contrast** Ask students: How would you compare and contrast the way Mühlberger describes this painting with the way Price describes the photograph of Emily Dickinson? *Students should note that Mühlberger's description is much more objective. He sticks to the details, while Price offers more of his own interpretation.*

◆ **Literary Focus**

❸ **Analytical Essay** Ask students: Without having read this passage, would you have noticed the *composition* of the painting—the blocks of color and the relationship of lines and shapes? How can reading an analysis of a work of art affect your perception of the work? *Students should note that the analysis brings out details in the painting that viewers might not notice. Noticing such details can enrich a viewer's experience of the painting.*

What Makes a DEGAS a DEGAS?

Richard Mühlberger

DANCERS, PINK AND GREEN

Degas's famous ballet paintings witness his enthusiasm for dance and his intimacy with the private backstage areas of the Paris Opéra, the huge complex where the ballet made its home. He was equally familiar with the theater's more public boxes and stalls, where he watched many performances. During his lifetime, he produced about fifteen hundred drawings, prints, pastels, and oil paintings with ballet themes.

In *Dancers, Pink and Green*, each ballerina is caught in a characteristic pose as she waits to go on the stage. One stretches and flexes her foot. Another secures her hair, while a third is almost hidden. The fourth dancer, who looks at her shoulder strap as she adjusts it, holds a pose that was a favorite of the artist and one he used in many paintings. An upright beam separates her from the fifth ballerina, who also turns her head but in the opposite direction, full of anticipation. Above her in the distance are the box seats, which Degas simplified into a stack of six red and orange rectangles along the edge of the canvas. The vertical beam the ballerina is touching extends to the

top and the bottom of the painting. The multicolored vertical shapes behind the dancers represent a large, painted landscape used as a backdrop for one of the dances. It will provide an immaterial, dreamworld quality to the performance, as it does to the painting.

Subscribers to the Opéra were allowed backstage in the theater, and some took advantage of this access to pester dancers. On the far side of the tall wood column is the partial silhouette of a large man in a top hat. He seems to be trying to keep out of the way, but his protruding profile overlaps a ballerina. None of the dancers pay attention to him. They also ignore one another, for this scene represents the tense moments just before the curtain rises.

Degas discovered that with oil paints he could achieve the same fresh feeling conveyed with pastels. Although this painting took the same amount of time to finish as many of his others and was designed and executed in his studio, Degas wanted to make it look as though it had been executed quickly, backstage. To do this, he imitated the marks of a charcoal pencil with his brush, making narrow black lines that edge the dancers' bodies and costumes. Next, he used

> **WHAT MAKES A DEGAS A DEGAS?**
> Notice the following techniques as you look at the paintings by Degas:
> - As if viewing it from above, Degas tipped the stage upward to keep figures from blocking one another.
> - Degas used patches of brilliant color to increase the feeling of movement.
> - Degas cut figures off at the edge of the canvas, creating a candid effect.
> - Degas used large, open spaces to move the eye deep into the picture.

416 ◆ *Expanding Horizons*

Humanities: Art

Dancers, Pink and Green by Edgar Degas.

Hillaire Germain Edgar Degas (1834–1917) was born in Paris of wealthy parents. He spent much time in Italy studying painters of the Italian Renaissance. Back in France, he came under the influence of the Impressionist movement and, influenced by painters Gustave Courbet and Edouard Manet, began to concentrate on scenes from everyday life.

This piece of art is one of Degas's many paintings of ballet dancers. Most of Degas's ballet pic-

tures were painted from the early 1870's to the early 1880's. Degas tried to capture the idea that ballet is work; sometimes dancers look tired or bored. In this painting, the body positions of the dancers reflect strength and energy as well as grace and delicacy.

Use this question for discussion:

If you had read the essay but never seen the painting, would you imagine it as it is or differently? Explain. *Students should make specific references to details in the art.*

Dancers, Pink and Green, Edgar Degas, Metropolitan Museum of Art

◎
◎

◎

◎

▲ Critical Viewing Which of Degas's techniques can you identify in this painting? [Apply]

◎

his own innovation of simulating the matte finish of pastels by taking the sheen out of oil paint, then filling in the sketchy "charcoal" outlines of his figures with a limited range of colors. The colors he used for the dancers extend to the floor and the background. The technique gives the impression that he applied the colors hastily while standing in the wings watching the dancers get ready.

The results of Degas's experiments could have been executed much more quickly had he used pastels instead of oils. What Degas wanted, however, was to make paint look spontaneous. This

was part of his life-long quest: to make viewers feel that they were right there, beside him.

CARRIAGE AT THE RACES

Paul Valpinçon was Degas's best friend in school and remained close to the artist all his life. Degas was a frequent visitor to his country house in Normandy, the northwest region of France, a long journey from Paris. Degas thought that the Normandy countryside was "exactly like England," and the beautiful horse farms there inspired him to paint equestrian subjects. During a visit in 1869, however, Degas found horses secondary to Paul Valpinçon's infant son, Henri. This becomes apparent by looking at the painting *Carriage at the Races.*

At first, Degas's composition seems lopsided. In one corner are the largest and darkest objects, a pair of horses and a carriage. Against the lacquered body of the carriage, the creamy white tones of the passengers stand out. They are framed by the dark colors rather than overwhelmed by them.

◆ Build Vocabulary

lacquered (lak´ ərd) *adj.*: Covered in tough, adherent varnish

What Makes a Degas a Degas? ◆ 417

▶Critical Viewing◀

❹ Apply Students should list the view from above that keep figures from blocking one another, the patches of brilliant color that suggest movment, the cutoff figure at right, and the pole that obstructs the dancer in the center.

◆ Critical Thinking

❺ Connect Ideas Ask students to identify passages in the essay that support this statement. *Students might include the poses of the dancers, the presence of man with the top hat, and Degas's painting technique.*

◆ Critical Thinking

❻ Identify Character Traits Ask: What does the final paragraph tell you about Degas? *He was an innovator; he looked for new ways to achieve a desired effect.*

◆ Build Grammar Skills

❼ Compound Sentences Ask students if this is a compound sentence. Have them explain their answers. *This sentence has a compound predicate, but it is not a compound sentence because it has only one subject— "Paul Valpinçon."*

◆ Build Grammar Skills

❽ Compound Sentences Have students identify the parts of this compound sentence: the two independent clauses, and the subject of each clause. Ask them why the comma is placed where it is. *The subjects of the independent clauses in this compound sentence are "Degas" and "horse farms." A comma is always placed inside quotation marks.*

 Speaking and Listening Mini-Lesson

Art Narration

This mini-lesson supports the second Speaking and Listening activity in the Idea Bank on page 420.

Introduce the Concept Tell students that they will use their imaginations to invent a story about a scene evoked by a work of art. Point out that pictures, as well as words, can tell a story.

Develop Background Before students begin their story, have them think about

what makes an interesting story. Lead them to consider these points:

- The story can be told by a narrator who is viewing the scene or in the first person by one of the people in the painting.
- The story may focus on one or more "main characters."
- A plot that includes a conflict that needs to be resolved will make the story more interesting.

Apply the Information As students plan and develop their stories, have them try to

incorporate as many of the painting's details as they can. When they present their story, remind them to show a picture of the painting and to speak clearly and expressively.

Assess the Outcome Students can evaluate the narrations on the basis of how well they correlate with the art, as well as on how well they are performed. Use the Peer Assessment: Dramatic Performance page in *Alternative Assessment,* p. 120, to evaluate the narrations.

◆ Reading Strategy

① **Relate Text and Pictures** As students read this passage, have them identify each detail in the painting. Ask them which elements of the composition the essay helped them to notice. *Students may mention the lopsided first impression the painting makes, the pair of horses and the carriage in one corner, the creamy white tones of the passengers standing out against the dark body of the carriage.*

◆ Literary Focus

② **Analytical Essay** Have students locate, in the essay, the larger idea that the details in this passage support. *The larger idea is, "Degas found horses secondary to Paul Valpinçon's infant son, Henri." The details in this passage demonstrate how Degas made the baby the center of attention.*

Humanities: Art

Carriage at the Races, 1872, by Edgar Degas.

This oil on canvas painting was done before most of Degas's ballet paintings. Ask students to use a method similar to Mühlberger's to analyze the painting and answer the following question:

How does the use of color and shading in the sky help point out the mother and child as the central focus of the painting? *At the center of the painting, the blue of the sky changes to creamy white; the bright area of white blends with the umbrella, almost forming an arrow pointing the mother and child, also clothed in white.*

►Critical Viewing◄

③ **Interpret** The painting focuses on a family in a carriage, with an infant at the center, shaded from the bright sunlight by a white umbrella. A team of horses seems to be moving the carriage off the canvas to the right.

◆ Critical Thinking

④ **Support** Have students identify Mühlberger's support, in this section of the essay, for his point that Degas wanted his paintings to be intimate, immediate, and realistic. *Degas showed only part of the horses and carriage in the painting.*

418

Degas placed a cream-colored umbrella in the middle of the painting above some of the figures in the carriage. Near it, balanced on the back of the driver's seat, is a **①** black bulldog. Paul **②** Valpinçon himself is the driver. Both Paul and the dog are gazing at the baby, who lies in the shade of the umbrella. With pink, dimpled knees, Henri, not yet a year old, sprawls on the lap of his nurse while his mother looks on.

IDEAS FROM THE EXOTIC, OLD, AND NEW

Degas always enjoyed looking at art. One of the thrills of his school years was being allowed to inspect the great paintings in the collection of Paul Valpinçon's father. Throughout his life, the artist drew inspiration from the masterpieces in the Louvre in Paris, one of the greatest museums in the world. He also found ideas in Japanese prints. They were considered cheap, disposable souvenirs in Japan, but were treasured by artists and others in the West as highly original, fascinating works of art. Photographs,

Carriage at the Races, Edgar Degas, Museum of Fine Arts, Boston

▲ Critical Viewing Describe this painting to someone who has not seen it. [Interpret] **③**

then newly invented, also suggested to Degas ways of varying his paintings. He eventually became an enthusiastic photographer himself.

In *Carriage at the Races,* the way in which the horses and carriage are cut off recalls figures in photographs and Japanese prints. For Degas, showing only part of a subject made his paintings more intimate, immediate, and realistic. He wanted viewers to see the scene as if they were actually there. **④**

Guide for Responding

◆ *Literature and Your Life*

Reader's Response Would you like to see more of the work of Edgar Degas? Why or why not?

Thematic Focus How can the work of artists like Degas expand our view of the world?

☑ Check Your Comprehension

1. What kinds of scenes did Degas paint?
2. What kind of effect did Degas hope to achieve in his paintings?

418 ◆ Expanding Horizons

◆ Critical Thinking

INTERPRET
1. Do you think Degas was a follower or a leader? Why? **[Infer]**

APPLY
2. Which of the two paintings better illustrates the points Mühlberger makes about Degas's work? Why? **[Make a Judgment]**

EXTEND
3. In his later years, Degas took up photography. What qualities in his paintings indicate he might be a good photographer? **[Career Link]**

Reinforce and Extend

Answers

◆ *Literature and Your Life*

Reader's Response Students should support their opinions with specific reasons.

Thematic Focus Degas brings into focus people in situations not usually open to public view.

☑ Check Your Comprehension

1. Degas painted performers in candid, "off-camera" moments.

2. He hoped to achieve an immediacy and intimacy with his subjects.

◆ Critical Thinking

1. Degas was a follower in imitating the effects of pastel artists and photographers; he was a leader in creating similar effects in oils.
2. *Dancers, Pink and Green* illustrates the candid immediacy of Degas's art. *Carriage at the Races* appears more posed.
3. Degas knows how to line up his subjects to create a pleasing effect. This quality also creates an effective photograph.

Guide for Responding (continued)

◆ Reading Strategy

RELATE TEXT AND PICTURES

To fully understand these essays, you need to **relate the text to the pictures** the writers describe. For example, when Richard Mühlberger describes how Degas outlines the figures with imitation charcoal pencil lines, you should be able to look at the painting of the dancers and actually see the effect of this technique.

1. Explain whether you think Price's conclusions about Dickinson are supported by the details in the picture.
2. In "What Makes a Degas a Degas?" Mühlberger describes characteristics of Degas's work. Identify details from the paintings that illustrate three of these characteristics.

◆ Literary Focus

ANALYTICAL ESSAYS

In an **analytical essay,** an author breaks a big idea down into its smaller pieces. The authors of these two essays focus point by point on the details of pictures. In doing so, they give you a broader understanding of the whole image.

1. (a) On which details of Emily Dickinson's appearance does Price focus? (b) What personality traits does he relate to these details?
2. (a) What does Mühlberger say is Degas's lifelong quest? (b) What techniques does Mühlberger identify that helped Degas achieve his goal?

Beyond Literature

Humanities Connection

Degas and the Impressionists Although Edgar Degas is considered one of the Impressionist painters, he did not share their enthusiasm for light and color. Instead, he focused on composition, drawing, and form. He created many sculptures to study form and body movement. These "practice works" made Degas one of the most important sculptors in modern times. Find pictures of some of Degas's sculptures, and compare them with his paintings.

◆ Build Vocabulary

USING THE ROOT -cent-

Knowing that the root *-cent-* means "hundred," match each word with its definition.

1. centigrade   a. hundredth anniversary
2. century   b. one one-hundredth of a meter
3. centennial   c. period of one hundred years
4. centimeter   d. temperature scale in which one hundred degrees represents the boiling point of water

USING THE WORD BANK

Complete each of the numbered items by writing a word from the Word Bank on your paper.

1. Judges are often ___?___.
2. Critics might use the word ___?___ to describe a huge new blockbuster movie.
3. You might find a ___?___ item in a fine gift shop.
4. The ___?___ remembered historic events we had only read about.

◆ Build Grammar Skills

COMPOUND SENTENCES

In these essays, the authors convey a great deal of information in **compound sentences**—sentences that consist of two or more equally important independent clauses.

Practice Combine each pair of sentences into a compound sentence. Use a coordinating conjunction or semicolon to join them.

1. Emily Dickinson lived a lonely life. She produced more than 1,800 poems.
2. Her picture raises questions. It gives only a glimpse of her personality.

Writing Application Rewrite the following paragraph, combining independent clauses into compound sentences.

> Degas enjoyed looking at art. He drew his inspirations from the masterpieces in the Louvre. He found ideas in Japanese art, too. The prints he admired were considered cheap disposable souvenirs in Japan. They were treasured by Degas and other artists in the West.

A Picture From the Past: Emily Dickinson/What Makes a Degas a Degas? ◆ 419

 Beyond the Selection

FURTHER READING

Other Works by the Authors
Good Hearts, Reynolds Price
What Makes a Raphael a Raphael? Richard Mühlberger

Other Works With the Theme of Seeing, Not Just Looking
Hidden Pictures, Linda Bolton
That's the Way I See It, David Hockney
We suggest that you preview these works before recommending them to students.

INTERNET

For information about Emily Dickinson students can visit the following Web site: **http://www.gis.net/~mtf/related.htm**

To see more paintings by Degas, suggest students visit **http://who.inet.jpmorgan:com/CorpInfo/Perspectives/Degas/1-Degas_frames.html**

Please be aware that sites may have changed since we published this information. We *strongly recommend* that you preview the sites before you send students to them.

Answers
◆ Reading Strategy

1. Price's interpretation is supported by details from the picture, but it is not the only interpretation.
2. In *Dancers, Pink and Green* Degas's candid style is revealed in the cut-off figure whose back is to the viewer; his spontaneous quality is captured in the un-synchronized movements of the dancers. *Carriage at the Races* captures Degas's photographic style.

◆ Literary Focus

1. (a) Price describes Dickinson's wide-set eyes, strong neck, large chin, and rough hands. (b) He relates them to strength and solitude.
2. (a) Degas's quest is to place the viewer in immediate contact with his subject. (b) Elements of Degas's paintings that contribute to its effect of spontaneity are the matte finish and limited range of colors of his oils, and his choice of off-center composition.

◆ Build Vocabulary

Using the Root *-cent-*
1. d   2. c   3. a   4. b

Using the Word Bank
1. austere;   2. titanic;
3. lacquered;   4. centenarian

◆ Build Grammar Skills

Sample sentences:
1. Emily Dickinson lived a lonely life, but she produced more than 1,800 poems.
2. Her picture raises questions, and it gives only a glimpse of her personality.

Writing Application
Degas enjoyed looking at art, and he drew inspiration from the masterpieces in the Louvre. He found ideas in Japanese art too, but the prints he admired were considered cheap, disposable souvenirs in Japan. They were treasured by Degas and other artists in the West.

 Writer's Solution

For additional instruction and practice, use the pages on Sentence Combining and Varying Your Sentences, pp. 120–121 in the *Writer's Solution Grammar Practice Book.*

Build Your Portfolio

 ## Idea Bank

Writing

1. **Exhibit Promotion** Write a paragraph to appear on a poster promoting an exhibit of Edgar Degas's work. Include details that raise audience interest and give highlights of the exhibit. **[Art Link]**

2. **Photo Essay** Put together a series of photographs that provide insights into your personality or the personality of someone close to you. Write a caption for each photograph.

3. **Art Analysis** Choose another painting or photograph of a person and analyze it using one of these essays as your model. **[Art Link]**

Speaking and Listening

4. **Poetry Reading** The best way to learn about Emily Dickinson is through her poetry. Find one or more Dickinson poems to read aloud to the class. Then lead a discussion about what each poem reveals about her.

5. **Art Narration** Choose a painting that you like by Degas. From the images in the painting, make up a story about what was happening at the time it was painted. Tell the story aloud to the class. **[Performing Arts Link]**

Projects

6. **Painting and Poetry Exhibit** Find an Emily Dickinson poem you like and create a drawing, painting, or collage to accompany it. Display your artwork with the poem. **[Art Link]**

7. **Art Exchange** With a small group, organize an art exhibit of famous paintings, with each group member selecting one entry. Display the paintings and hold a question-and-answer session in which your group explains its choices.

 ## Writing Mini-Lesson

Museum Placard

Write a **placard**—a small informational card—that might be displayed beside a favorite painting or sculpture in a museum. Include basic information about the painting, such as the date, title, and painter. Write a few sentences that would help a reader appreciate the images and ideas that originally guided the artist's hand.

Writing Skills Focus:
Anticipation of Questions

The information that you provide on your placard will influence the way people view the work of art. By **anticipating questions** that viewers might ask, you can decide what information to include. For instance, someone viewing *Dancers, Pink and Green* might wonder where Degas got his inspiration. Therefore, on a placard for this painting, you might mention that he went to the Opéra regularly in order to observe and sketch the dancers. However, you probably wouldn't mention that Degas had brothers who lived in New Orleans, because that doesn't answer any questions about the painting.

Prewriting Choose a piece of art you like. Then brainstorm for a list of questions viewers might have. Choose one or two questions to answer that will give the most insight into the painting or sculpture.

Drafting The basic information, such as title, date, and artist, should be easy for the viewer to locate. Write this information clearly at the top of the placard. Then write a short paragraph including other interesting facts about the work.

Revising Exchange your placard with a partner. Ask your partner if the information is clearly presented. Revise where necessary to clarify.

✓ ASSESSMENT OPTIONS

Formal Assessment, Selection Test, pp. 107–109, and Assessment Resources Software. The selection test is designed so that it can be easily customized to the performance levels of your students.
Alternative Assessment, p. 31, includes options for less advanced students, more advanced students, verbal/linguistic learners, visual/spatial learners, and logical/mathematical learners.

PORTFOLIO ASSESSMENT
Use the following rubrics in the *Alternative Assessment* booklet to assess student writing:
Exhibit Promotion: Persuasion Rubric, p. 105
Photo Essay: Expression Rubric, p. 94
Art Analysis: Evaluation/Review Rubric, p. 104
Writing Mini-Lesson: Description Rubric, p. 97

Writing Process Workshop

Oral Presentation of Research

One way to make a research paper come alive is to give an **oral presentation of your research**. Giving an oral presentation is much like teaching a class: You'll be educating your listeners about what you've discovered through your research.

The following skills, introduced in this section's Writing Mini-Lessons, will help you prepare and give an effective oral presentation of your research.

Writing Skills Focus

▶ **Use logical organization.** Organizations such as order of importance, chronological, and compare/contrast will help your listeners follow your report. (See p. 392.)

▶ **Anticipate questions** that your listeners will have about your topic. (See p. 420.)

▶ **Consider audience knowledge.** Think about what the audience might know about your topic, and try to teach them something new. (See p. 411.)

▶ **Be brief and clear.** Stick to the main topic so that your listeners' interest and attention don't wander. (See p. 403.)

▶ **Use visual aids,** such as maps, graphs, and photos.

In the following passage from a presentation about the Assyrian empire, the speaker uses these skills.

Assyrian and Persian Empires

Assyrian empire about 625 B.C.	Persian empire about 500 B.C.
▲ Assyrian capitals	▲ Persian capitals

MODEL

After Ashurbanipal died in 631 B.C., internal troubles broke out, and the Assyrian empire declined and failed. Babylonia became independent and in 626 B.C. established its eleventh and last dynasty, called the Chaldean dynasty. ① By 615 B.C. all of the Sumer and Akkad had been liberated and the Medes had invaded Assyria and marched to Nineveh. ② By the end of 612 B.C., Assyria's enemies had destroyed its three main cities, shown on the map: ③ Ashur, the religious hub; Nineveh, the administrative center; and Nimrud, the military headquarters. ④

① The speaker uses clear, chronological organization.

② The speaker is brief and keeps to the point.

③ The speaker uses a map to illustrate his subject.

④ By further explaining the significance of the three main cities, the speaker both anticipates a listener's question and teaches the audience something new.

◆ **Beyond the Classroom**

Career Connection

Presentations Tell students that giving an oral presentation of research they have conducted is a common practice in the business and professional world. For example, analysts frequently give oral reports on companies or industries they have been studying. Consultants give presentations to companies in order to solicit their business and as a part of their work. Politicians give presentations in order to sway voters to agree with them on an issue, while lawyers and lobbyists give presentations to those same politicians in order to sway *them* to vote a particular way. Teachers give oral presentations to their classes every day.

Prepare and Engage

Establish Writing Guidelines

Before students begin, review the following key characteristics of an oral presentation of research:

- The presentation should be organized logically, so that the audience can follow it without difficulty.
- The presenter should anticipate questions and leave time for them after the presentation.
- The presenter should speak loudly and clearly, and use visual aids if possible.
- If feasible, the presenter should use visual aids.

You may want to distribute the scoring rubric for Research Report/Paper (p. 106 in *Alternative Assessment*) to make students aware before they begin of the criteria on which they will be evaluated. See the suggestions on page 423 for customizing the rubric for this workshop.

Refer students to the Writing Handbook, page 965, for instruction in the writing process, and page 968 for further information on research writing.

Writing Lab CD-ROM

If your students have access to computers, you may want to have them work on the tutorial on Research to complete all or part of their oral presentations of research. Follow these steps:

1. Students can use the Research Paper Topic Bin to select a topic.
2. Review the Video tips from writers on audience.
3. Have students draft on computer.
4. Suggest students use the interactive instruction on improving content.
5. Use the tips on presenting work orally.

Sourcebook

Students can find additional support, including topic ideas, models, audience and purpose profiles, and graphic organizers, in the chapter on Research Writing (pp. 128–163).

Develop Student Writing

Prewriting

Have students brainstorm in groups for topic ideas. Some broad areas where they may begin include important people or events from the past, current events, other cities or countries, or the world of sports or entertainment. If students choose one of these broad areas, they must then narrow it further to find a suitable topic.

Customize for
English Language Learners

Once these students have chosen a topic, have them analyze it in terms of *Who? What? Where? When?* and, if appropriate, *Why?* and *How?* Have the students answer these questions and have the answers form the outline for the presentation. Students might also benefit from using the Cubing organizer, which is available in *Writing and Language Transparencies,* pp. 87–90.

Customize for
More Advanced Students

Challenge these students to give an oral presentation on a historical figure whom they do not admire, or on a controversial event, such as the decision to drop atomic bombs on Japan during World War II, or on an event that had a negative impact on society.

 Writer's Solution

Writing Lab CD-ROM

The Considering Audience and Purpose section of the tutorial on Research Writing helps students tailor their work to different purposes and audiences. Have students consult these screens to help focus their presentations on a specific audience.

Drafting

Encourage students to refer to their outline or notes as they draft their oral presentations of research. Remind them to keep their audience and purpose in mind. Have them pay particular attention to writing a strong introduction and following up with an effective conclusion. Once students have completed a draft, they can go back and make revisions.

422

APPLYING LANGUAGE SKILLS: Direct and Indirect Quotations

A **direct quotation** represents the exact speech of a person. The words are enclosed in quotation marks.

Direct Quotation:

The secretary general said, "Unchecked population growth is an environmental time bomb."

An indirect quotation reports the general meaning of a person's words and does not require quotation marks.

Indirect Quotation:

The secretary general said that rapid population growth is a serious problem.

Writing Application Vary your use of direct and indirect quotations in your presentation. Quote directly when the speaker's words are especially powerful. Use indirect quotations to lend weight to general information.

Writer's Solution Connection
Writing Lab

For more help finding a topic, see Choosing a Topic: Inspirations for Research. You'll find it in the Writing Lab tutorial on Research Writing.

422 ◆ *Expanding Horizons*

Prewriting

Choose a Topic Choose a topic that you find interesting and for which there is adequate source information. The following suggestions may help you if you're having trouble thinking of a topic.

Topic Ideas

- **Oral Report on a Southeast Asian Country** With a combined population of more than 452 million people, the ten nations that make up Southeast Asia offer a wealth of information. Choose one nation, and prepare a report on an aspect of its history or culture.
- **The Environment** Choose a process or practice that aims to protect the environment, such as building jetties to prevent beach erosion, and evaluate whether or not such a process is effective.
- **Current Events** Choose a topic that has been in the news lately. Prepare a report that informs the audience of the important aspects of the topic, and then make your own comments about it.

Find Reliable Sources It's extremely important that the information in your research report be accurate. There are numerous sources of reliable and current information. (See the Research Handbook, p. 982, for suggestions.) It's also important to evaluate your sources. (For strategies to evaluate sources, see p. 424.) Use at least three sources to find information.

Plan Visual Aids When you're giving an oral presentation, you'll feel more comfortable referring to visual aids, and your audience will probably grasp your points better. Consider using any of the following:

▶ **Maps** can clarify historical information.
▶ **Graphs** can represent changes over time.
▶ **Diagrams** can show the relationship of parts to a whole.
▶ **Charts** can help show comparison/contrast relationships.

Drafting

Use Note Cards Draft your presentation based on notes from your research. Writing out your presentation will ensure that you include all necessary information and that you organize it in a way that's easy to follow.

Applying Language Skills
Direct and Indirect Quotations

Tell students that using direct quotations will enliven their oral presentations by making them more direct and personal, and will also lend the reports an air of authority.

 Writer's Solution

For additional instruction and practice, have students complete the **Language Lab CD-ROM** lesson on Semicolons, Colons, and Quotation Marks and practice page 104 on Quotation Marks and Direct Quotations in the *Writer's Solution Grammar Practice Book.*

Revising

Read Your Work Aloud After you've finished drafting, read your presentation aloud. Listen for movement from one point to another. Make sure your important ideas are emphasized and do not get lost in your presentation. Revise any parts that do not flow naturally. Also, organize your research notes in an order that will be easy for you to refer to during the presentation, or prepare a set of brief notes, based on your draft, to guide you as you give your presentation. Your notes will serve as cues for visual aids and reminders of quotations you plan to use.

Do a Dry Run Before your presentation, rehearse in front of family members or a friend, before a video camera, or in front of a mirror. This will help you improve your speaking form and calm any jitters you may have about speaking in front of others.

REVISION MODEL

Since the introduction of CD technology ① in 1983 , the music industry has increased sales ~~quite a bit~~ ② 100 million dollars annually . The new technology created consumer demand in nearly every category ③ —from classical to jazz, rock, and rap . The instant popularity of CDs created a revolution in how music is delivered.

① This date answers a potential question from the audience.

② The writer replaced this vague term with an exact figure from her research.

③ These examples help define "every category."

Publishing

Give Your Oral Presentation Refer to your note cards as you make your presentation, but be as familiar as possible with your draft so that your presentation will be credible and engaging.

▶ When you speak, **vary the sentence structure** to include a mix of simple, compound, and complex sentences.

▶ **Refer to your visual aids** to support your findings and maintain audience interest.

▶ **Speak loudly** enough so that everyone can hear you.

▶ **Be prepared** to answer questions at the end of the report.

APPLYING LANGUAGE SKILLS: Varying Sentence Structure

If your sentences are all simple sentences of the same length, your report will be very monotonous. **Vary your sentence structure** in order to make your presentation more interesting.

Same Sentence Structure:
Lacrosse was originally a Native American game. It was played on the east coast. Games were violent. They often lasted two or more days.

Varied Sentence Structure:
Lacrosse was originally a Native American game played on the east coast. Games, which were sometimes violent, often lasted two or more days.

Writing Application Review your report before you present it. Make sure that your sentence structure is varied. If it is not, add transitions and subordinate clauses to make the sentences more interesting.

Writer's Solution Connection Language Lab

For more practice with sentence structures, complete the Language Lab lesson on Varying Sentence Structure.

Revising

Have students do a dry run of their presentations with peer reviewers before they present them to the class. Giving a practice presentation will reveal rough spots that need revising. Peer reviewers should offer concrete suggestions and constructive criticism.

Publishing

Before giving their oral presentations, suggest that students practice them at least once in front of family members or on videotape.

Applying Language Skills

Varying Sentence Structure
Though students will probably consult notecards as they give their presentations, they should be reminded to vary their sentences as they speak. Using only simple sentences or one type of sentence will probably bore the audience.

Writer's Solution

For additional instruction and practice, have students complete the **Language Lab CD-ROM** lesson on Varying Sentence Structure and the practice page 121 on Varying Your Sentences in the *Writer's Solution Grammar Practice Book*.

Reinforce and Extend

Review the Writing Guidelines
After students have completed their papers, review the characteristics of an oral presentation of research. Encourage students to come up with additional criteria for an interesting oral presentation based on what they learned through completing the assignment.

✓ ASSESSMENT		4	3	2	1
PORTFOLIO ASSESSMENT Use the rubric on Research Report/Paper in the *Alternative Assessment* booklet (p. 106) to assess the students' writing. Add these criteria to customize the rubric to this assignment.	**Research**	The research is thorough and accurate and explores the topic fully.	The research is accurate, and explores the topic adequately.	Research lacks sufficient depth and may be questionable in one or two instances.	Research is clearly inadequate; accuracy is suspect.
	Presentation	Student speaks loudly and clearly, using appropriate vocal expression to keep audience interested. Visuals are compelling and clearly augment the report.	Student speaks loudly and clearly enough to be understood. Visuals are used.	Student should speak louder or more clearly, and/or vary vocal expression to retain interest. Visuals are inadequate or irrelevant.	Student is unable to be heard. Visuals are not used or not related to the subject matter.

Real-World Reading Skills Workshop

Introduce the Strategy

With the wealth of information available for research, including the Internet, it becomes ever more important to scrutinize that information closely and evaluate its appropriateness for writing purposes. Students should be urged to validate the information they find by looking for supporting information in other sources.

Apply the Strategy

Answers

1. The *Washington Post* article would be preferable, since it is specifically about the relationship between cats and people.

2. The *Washington Post* article would be preferable because the topic is closer to that of the research paper and it is much newer, so the research would be more current.

3. The title *Cat Fancy* suggests a relationship between cats and people, so that book would be preferable.

Strategies for Success

Research is a major part of writing a report. (See the Research Handbook, beginning on p. 982, for suggestions about sources of information.) As you undertake your research, you may find yourself poring through books, magazines, encyclopedias, and other materials that may have information on your topic. Before you plunge into writing, evaluate your sources of information to determine which resources will provide the best information.

Consider the Source Before choosing a source, investigate the author of the text. Is he or she an expert on the subject? Look in the book for biographical information that tells the author's qualifications.

Consider the Date Check to see when a book was published. (You can usually find the date on the page following the title page.) The information in older works might be outdated, especially if the subjects are science or social studies. For example, if you were researching information on Germany today and used a book from 1987, it would refer to East Germany and West Germany, but it would not include information about the reunification of Germany since the Berlin Wall came down in 1989. The information would not be current.

Apply the Strategy

You are writing a research paper on the relationship between cats and their owners. Look at the sources available to you as you answer the questions that follow:

The World Book Encyclopedia, Volume C, © 1998

Cats: Creatures of Wonder, by Lori Rigby, © 1960 by Roan Publishing

"New Research on Cat–People Connection," *The Washington Post,* February 5, 1998

"Cats Have Feelings Too," *Milford Daily News,* November 8, 1975

Cat Fancy by Dr. R. Gonzales, © 1998 by Prentice Hall

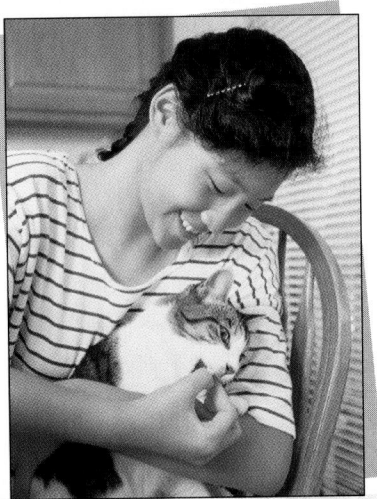

1. Which would you prefer to use—the encyclopedia or *The Washington Post* article? Why?

2. Which of the two newspapers would you prefer to use? Why?

3. Which of the two books would you prefer to use? Why?

✔ Here are other situations in which it is helpful to evaluate sources of information:
▶ Reading newspaper editorials
▶ Investigating a rumor
▶ Reading two articles on the same topic

PART **2** *A Larger World*

Waiting for Will, 1986, Janet Fish

One-Minute
Planning Guide

The selections in Part 2 describe the adventures and thoughts of people from across cultures and across generations. "The Orphan Boy and the Elk Dog" tells how the Blackfeet got horses. "The Street of the Cañon," set in a small village in old Mexico, tells about young woman's encounter with a mysterious stranger. Alexander Solzhenitsyn's essay "A Storm in the Mountains" vividly describes a terrifying storm that swamped the author and his companions in the Caucasus mountains. Henrik Ibsen's poem "In the Orchard," describes nature at its most calm and pastoral. The section ends with Denise Levertov's poem "A Tree Telling of Orpheus," which describes the ancient Greek musician's beautiful music from the point of view of one of the trees persuaded to uproot itself and dance.

Customize for
Varying Student Needs
When assigning the selections in this part to your students, keep in mind the following factors:

"The Orphan Boy and the Elk Dog"
• Subject matter may be remote for some students

"The Street of the Cañon"
• A medium-length short story
• Accessible to all ability levels

"A Storm in the Mountains"; "In the Orchard"
• Two short selections
• Language is more difficult than that in other selections

"A Tree Telling of Orpheus"
• A longer narrative poem
• An echo of a classical Greek myth

Humanities: Art

Waiting for Will, 1986, by Janet Fish.
Born in 1938, New Englander Janet Fish hails from several generations of artists. She is known for her bright, glowing paintings; although her subjects are usually still lifes, her paintings seem to be full of movement.

Direct students' attention to the contrast between the foreground and background in *Waiting for Will.* The foreground is full of pattern and color, mostly warm golds and roses, with a few contrasting blue and green notes. The cool blues and greens take over completely in the background, and the whole painting is almost neatly divided into two horizontal halves by the yellow railing.

Help students link the artwork to the theme of this part, "A Larger World," by answering the following questions:
1. This painting has two definite halves: the table in the foreground, and the green and blue landscape in the background. What is the atmosphere of each? *The*
foreground, with its clutter and bright colors has a warm, inviting, cheerful atmosphere; the landscape, with its cool colors and cloudy sky, has a dreamy, pensive atmosphere.

2. Why might the person in this painting have turned away from the table to gaze at the hills? *Sample answer: The woman, who might be the artist, might be thinking about "Will," or waiting for inspiration.*

Guide for Reading

OBJECTIVES

1. To read, comprehend, and interpret a myth
2. To relate a myth to personal experience
3. To identify with a character
4. To identify myth
5. To build vocabulary in context and learn to recognize homographs
6. To develop distinguish the commonly confused words *accept* and *except*
7. To write a retelling of a myth with a clear beginning, middle, and end
8. To respond to the myth through writing, speaking and listening, and projects

SKILLS INSTRUCTION

Vocabulary:
Word Groups:
Homographs
Grammar:
Commonly
Confused Words:
accept and *except*
Reading Strategy:
Identify With a
Character

Literary Focus:
Myth
Writing: Retelling
of a Myth
**Speaking and
Listening:** Debate
(teacher edition)
Critical Viewing:
Draw Conclusions;
Infer; Interpret

PORTFOLIO OPPORTUNITIES

Writing: Speech; Dialogue; Description of a Mystery Animal
Writing Mini-Lesson: Retelling of a Myth
Speaking and Listening: Debate; Retell a Myth
Projects: Animal Population Graph; Storyboard Mural

More About the Blackfeet

These Native Americans are one of three closely related groups that speak the Algonkian language. During the first half of the nineteenth century, their territory stretched from northern Saskatchewan, south into Missouri. They were a powerful force on the northwestern plains, following the buffalo and hunting. When the buffalo were nearly exterminated in the early 1880's the Blackfeet were forced to turn to farming and cattle ranching.

Blackfeet

The Blackfeet are one of the many Native American nations that have lived on the Great Plains of North America. Like other Plains Indians, the Blackfeet had no horses before the 1600's. Once they discovered these strange creatures, however, they quickly recognized their value.

The Shoshone (another group of Plains Indians) had herds of horses before the Blackfeet did. One daring Blackfeet, who may have been the inspiration for the "orphan boy" in this myth, slipped into a Shoshone camp with his companions, untied four horses, and led them away. To the amazed Blackfeet, these animals looked like elk-sized dogs.

In time, the Blackfeet became skillful riders. Because they could travel farther and faster than before, they raised fewer crops and hunted more. They made larger tipis because the strong horses could easily pull the folded tipis from one encampment to the next. Slowly, horses transformed the Blackfeet way of life.

Today, the Blackfeet live on reservations in Montana and in Canada. (Those in Canada usually go by the name Black*foot*.) Although they are no longer a nomadic people following buffalo, traditional stories like "The Orphan Boy and the Elk Dog" reflect the importance of the horse to their culture.

◆ Build Vocabulary

WORD GROUPS: HOMOGRAPHS

In this story you will meet an orphan boy who is forced to eat things he finds in the *refuse* heaps. *Refuse* is a **homograph**—a word with the same spelling as another but with a different meaning and pronunciation. For example, *refuse* (ref' yo͞oz) in this myth is a noun meaning "garbage." *Refuse* (ri fyo͞oz') is a verb that means "to reject."

When you encounter a homograph such as *refuse,* the context in which it appears will give you clues to its meaning. Use a dictionary, if necessary, to confirm the correct pronunciation.

refuse
surpassed
emanating
relish
stifle

WORD BANK

Before you read, preview this list of words from the myth.

◆ Build Grammar Skills

**COMMONLY CONFUSED WORDS:
ACCEPT AND EXCEPT**

In this Blackfeet myth, you will encounter the words **accept** and **except.** These words are often confused because they have a similar spelling and sound. *Accept* is a verb meaning "to receive" or "to agree with." *Except* is usually a preposition meaning "not including," but it is sometimes a verb meaning "to leave out."

Notice the correct use of *accept* and *except* in these sentences from "The Orphan Boy and the Elk Dog":

"*Accept* these wonderful Elk Dogs as my gift."

...no one *except* his grandfather knew where and for what purpose.

426 ◆ *Expanding Horizons*

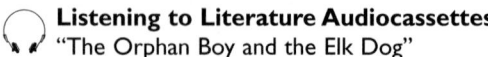

Prentice Hall Literature Program Resources

REINFORCE / RETEACH / EXTEND

Selection Support Pages
Build Vocabulary: Word Groups: Homographs, p. 130
Build Grammar Skills: Commonly Confused Words: *accept* and *except,* p. 131
Reading Strategy: Identify with a Character, p. 132
Literary Focus: Myth, p. 133

Strategies for Diverse Student Needs, p. 32

Beyond Literature
Cultural Connection: The Role of the Horse, p. 32

Formal Assessment Selection Test, pp. 110–113;

Assessment Resources Software

Alternative Assessment, p. 32

Writing and Language Transparencies
Story Map, pp. 83–86

Resource Pro CD-ROM
"The Orphan Boy and the Elk Dog"—includes all resource materials and customizable lesson plan.

Listening to Literature Audiocassettes
"The Orphan Boy and the Elk Dog"

The Orphan Boy and the Elk Dog

◆ *Literature and Your Life*

CONNECT YOUR EXPERIENCE

When you need to go somewhere, you have many choices about how you will travel. Depending on where you're going, you might take a bus, a car, a train, or an airplane. Trips to the mall would be a lot less frequent if there were no cars or buses. In fact, without cars and buses, malls probably wouldn't exist, because people couldn't get to them easily or often enough to keep so many stores in business. Transportation influences the way people live. Big changes in transportation mean big changes in lifestyle.

THEMATIC FOCUS: A LARGER WORLD

As a new form of transportation, horses changed the Blackfeet world! Thinking about the impact of horses on Blackfeet society may start you wondering, "How does modern transportation make my world larger or smaller?"

Journal Writing Explain how your life would be different without a particular form of transportation—such as cars.

◆ Background for Understanding

HISTORY

At one time, most Plains Indians were farmers who lived in semi-permanent villages. They sent out hunting parties that pursued buffalo and other animals—on foot. Agriculture, however, was their main source of food.

During the 1600's, the Plains Indians' way of life changed. The Indians captured and tamed wild horses descended from herds the Spanish had brought to the Americas. On horseback, the Indians could travel farther and faster. Hunting replaced farming as the Plains Indians became better hunters. They moved often to follow the herds of buffalo. Large tipis and other belongings could easily be carried on a travois—a sledge pulled by a horse.

◆ Literary Focus

MYTH

Myths are traditional stories passed down from generation to generation, characteristically involving immortal beings. Myths attempt to explain natural phenomena, the origin of humans, the customs or institutions of a people, or events beyond people's control. Indirectly, myths teach the values and ideals of a culture.

"The Orphan Boy and the Elk Dog" is a myth that offers an explanation of how the Blackfeet came to have horses.

◆ Reading Strategy

IDENTIFY WITH A CHARACTER

The main character in this story dives into a pond and discovers a fantastic world beneath the surface. One way you can dive into a work of literature is to **identify with a character**—put yourself in the character's place and share his or her thoughts, feelings, problems, adventures, and so on.

In "The Orphan Boy and the Elk Dog," you will travel with an outcast Native American boy who becomes a triumphant hero. You will experience his difficulties and his successes. Throughout the story, think about what you might say, do, or think in the situation.

Following the Buffalo Run, Charles M. Russell, Amon Carter Museum, Fort Worth, Texas

Guide for Reading ◆ 427

Interest Grabber Read the following passage aloud to students:

"... he boldly jumped into the water. To his surprise, he found it did not make him wet, that it parted before him, that he could breathe and see."

Ask students to tell from what kind of story they think this excerpt comes. On the chalkboard, list the qualities they might expect to find in such a story. *Possible responses: magic, adventure, symbolic meaning.* Have students predict where the hero of this story might be going and what he might find beneath the surface of the water. Then have them read the myth, "The Orphan Boy and the Elk Dog."

Customize for
Less Proficient Readers
Suggest that students imagine the myth as a movie and divide it into scenes, jotting down a brief summary of what happens in each scene.

Customize for
More Advanced Students
Invite students to point out story elements that this myth has in common with other myths or traditional tales they have read; for example, an underwater world ("The Little Mermaid"), a quest with difficult obstacles to overcome (the Grail legends), increasingly bigger obstacles ("The Tinder Box"), magical objects ("Aladdin"), an order to "never look back" (Orpheus, Lot).

Customize for
English Language Learners
Have these students preview the Check Your Comprehension questions on page 435 before they read and answer them as they read. Suggest they look for key words in the text to find answers, and avoid getting stuck on unfamiliar words.

Customize for
Visual/Spatial Learners
Suggest that students make a storyboard of significant scenes in the myth.

▶Critical Viewing◀

Interpret Ask students: What is happening in this painting? *Students can infer from the title that the Native American people on horseback are hunting buffalo.*

Preparing for Standardized Tests

Reading and Vocabulary Recognizing words that are homographs can help students in answering vocabulary items on standardized tests. For example, knowing that *entrance* can be a noun meaning "place to enter" as well as a verb meaning "fascinate" can help answer the following analogy question:

fascinate : entrance :: (B)
(A) bank : vault (B) catalog : classify

The Build Vocabulary lesson focuses on homographs. For additional practice, use the Build Vocabulary page in **Selection Support**, p. 130.

Grammar and Language Commonly confused words are often found as alternatives on fill-in or multiple-choice questions such as the following:

I could not (accept, except) the invitation.
accept

Recognizing the correct word for the context will help students improve their scores on standardized tests. The Build Grammar Skills lesson for this selection focuses on this topic. For additional practice, use the Build Grammar Skills page on Commonly Confused Words: *Accept* and *Except*, p.131, in **Selection Support.**

Develop Understanding

One-Minute Insight So important were horses to the Plains Indians, that the explanation for how these animals came into their possession is an integral part of their cultural history. According to this myth, a young man who had been an outcast went on a dangerous quest to prove himself to his people and to prove his own self-worth. By a feat of courage and daring, and aided by magic, he returned with horses, or "Elk Dogs," which changed and improved the lives of his people. This myth, in addition to explaining an important aspect of life for the Blackfeet, conveys important cultural values through the relationship of the young man to the old chief who adopted him: courage, respect for elders, generosity, and compassion.

▶Critical Viewing◀

❶ Draw Conclusions The Native American man may be standing sentry, watching for threats of attack; or he may be hunting, searching for game.

Customize for
Visual/Spatial Learners
Have these students infer what the story may be about from the image of the young man and horse in the painting. *Students may infer that the story will be about Indians and horses in a beautiful natural setting.*

The Color of Sun, Howard Terpning, The Greenwich Workshop, Inc.

▲ Critical Viewing What do you think this Native American man is seeing or searching for? [Draw Conclusions]

428 ◆ *Expanding Horizons*

Humanities: Art

The Color of Sun by Howard Terpning.

This painting shows a young Plains Indian brave riding a horse with bow and arrow strapped behind. The horse nuzzles the spring flowers as the brave scans the horizon. The horse's piebald coloring serves as effective camouflage against the dappled woodland background.

Use these questions for discussion:
1. In what ways might a brave like the young man in the painting identify with Long Arrow? *He* *might see himself as a brave adventurer aiding his people; he might share Long Arrow's love of horses.*

2. Based on the composition of the painting, how did the artist make the youth look brave and heroic? *The young man and his horse take up most of the canvas; the brave's face is radiant with light; the horse and rider appear arrested in a moment of calm, awaiting action.*

The Orphan Boy and the Elk Dog

Native American (Blackfeet)

In the days when people had only dogs to carry their bundles, two orphan children, a boy and his sister, were having a hard time. The boy was deaf, and because he could not understand what people said, they thought him foolish and dull-witted. Even his relatives wanted nothing to do with him. The name he had been given at birth, while his parents still lived, was Long Arrow. Now he was like a beaten, mangy dog, the kind who hungrily roams outside a camp, circling it from afar, smelling the good meat boiling in the kettles but never coming close for fear of being kicked. Only his sister, who was bright and beautiful, loved him.

Then the sister was adopted by a family from another camp, people who were attracted by her good looks and pleasing ways. Though they wanted her for a daughter, they certainly did not want the awkward, stupid boy. And so they took away the only person who cared about him, and the orphan boy was left to fend for himself. He lived on scraps thrown to the dogs and things he found on the <u>refuse</u> heaps. He dressed in remnants of skins and frayed robes discarded by the poorest people. At night he bedded down in a grass-lined dugout, like an animal in its den.

Eventually the game was hunted out near the camp that the boy regarded as his, and the people decided to move. The lodges were taken down, belongings were packed into rawhide bags and put on dog travois, and the village departed. "Stay here," they told the boy. "We don't want your kind coming with us."

For two or three days the boy fed on scraps the people had left behind, but he knew he would starve if he stayed. He had to join his people, whether they liked it or not. He followed their tracks, frantic that he would lose them, and crying at the same time. Soon the sweat was running down his skinny body. As he was stumbling, running, panting, something suddenly snapped in his left ear with a sound like a small crack, and a wormlike substance came out of that ear. All at once on his left side he could hear birdsongs for the first time. He took this wormlike thing in his left hand and hurried on. Then there was a snap in his right ear and a wormlike thing came out of it, and on his right side he could hear the rushing waters of a stream. His hearing was restored! And it was razor-sharp—he could make out the rustling of a tiny mouse in dry leaves a good

◆ Build Vocabulary

refuse (ref′ yo͞oz) *n.*: Anything thrown away as useless

◆ Reading Strategy

Identify with Long Arrow by thinking of times in your life when you felt excluded.

The Orphan Boy and the Elk Dog ◆ 429

◆ Critical Thinking

❷ Compare and Contrast Point out that like all myths, this story takes place in a far-off time. Have students compare and contrast the way deaf people are treated in modern society. *Students may say that modern society also discriminates against the physically challenged, but they should note that many steps have been taken to end discrimination.*

◆ Build Vocabulary

❸ Homographs Ask students to identify the part of speech for the word *close* in this sentence. Then have them think of a homograph and its part of speech. *In this sentence, close is an adverb modifying coming. Close can also be a verb when pronounced differently and serving a different function in a sentence.*

◆ Reading Strategy

❹ Identify With a Character Students may say that although they have not been as cruelly abandoned as Long Arrow, they understand what it feels like to be snubbed or rejected and can generalize from that experience.

Comprehension Check ☑

❺ What is happening to Long Arrow's ear? *A blockage is falling out, enabling him to hear. Some may think the event is realistic, others magical.*

 Block Scheduling Strategies

Consider these suggestions to take advantage of extended class time:

- Build background with the **Beyond the Literature** page, Cultural Connection: The Role of the Horse in Different Cultures, p. 32.

- Introduce the concept of Myth by reading with students the Literary Focus paragraph on page 427. After students have read the selection, have them answer the Literary Focus questions on page 436 and complete the page on Myth in **Selection Support**, p.133.

- Students may listen to all or part of the myth on audiocassette. Reminding students that myths were originally oral tales, invite them to compare and contrast the experience of hearing the myth with that of reading it.

- Have students work on the Critical Thinking questions (p. 436) in small discussion groups.

- Encourage students to form pairs or small groups to select and work on a project from the Idea Bank on page 437.

- Have students complete the Writing Mini-Lesson (p. 437). Before they prewrite individually, have groups brainstorm for myths they know. Then have students use the Story map organizer in **Writing and Language Transparencies**, p. 84, to plan their myth.

Listening to Literature Audiocassettes The entrance of the chief, and his later discussions with his wife and with Long Arrow on this page and page 431 make dramatic listening. Invite students to discuss how the oral reading helps define the three characters for them.

◆ Literary Focus

1 Myth Students may say that the sharpness of his hearing gives him a kind of super-power; or, that the experience of having been magically healed of a disability sets him off as special.

◆ Reading Strategy

2 Identify With a Character Ask students to imagine how they would feel if they had to catch up all at once with what their peers had learned long ago. (English Language Learners may in fact feel that way.) Discuss whether this is easy or hard for Long Arrow, and how students relate to his achievement.

◆ Build Grammar Skills

3 Commonly Confused Words Referring to the phrase, "Good Running's wife accepted him," ask students whether Good Running's wife took Long Arrow in or left him out. *She took him in.* Ask them to name the similar-sounding word that would mean that she left him out. *Excepted*

◆ Critical Thinking

4 Analyze Character Ask students how Long Arrow's ambition to do something special is connected to his unusual early life. *Because he was once ostracized, he now feels he must prove his worth both to those who ostracized him and to himself.*

distance away. The orphan boy laughed and was happy for the first time in his life. With renewed courage he followed the trail his people had made.

In the meantime the village had settled into its new place. Men were already out hunting. Thus the boy came upon Good Running, a kindly old chief, butchering a fat buffalo cow he had just killed. When the chief saw the boy, he said to himself, "Here comes that poor good-for-nothing boy. It was wrong to abandon him." To the boy Good Running said "Rest here, grandson, you're sweaty and covered with dust. Here, have some tripe."[1]

> ◆ **Literary Focus**
> How might the events in the preceding paragraph contribute to Long Arrow's eventual hero status?

❶

The boy wolfed down the meat. He was not used to hearing and talking yet, but his eyes were alert and Good Running also noticed a change in his manner. "This boy," the chief said to himself, "is neither stupid nor crazy." He gave the orphan a piece of the hump meat, then a piece of liver, then a piece of raw kidney, and at last the very best kind of meat—a slice of tongue. The more the old man looked at the boy, the more he liked him. On the spur of the moment he said, "Grandson, I'm going to adopt you; there's a place for you in my tipi. And I'm going to make you into a good hunter and warrior." The boy wept, this time for joy. Good Running said, "They called you a stupid, crazy boy, but now that I think of it, the name you were given at birth is Long Arrow. I'll see that people call you by your right name. Now come along."

---

1. **tripe** (trip) *n.*: Part of the stomach of an ox or cow when used as food.

He grew up into a fine young hunter, tall and good-looking in the quilled buckskin outfit the chief's wife made for him.

The chief's wife was not pleased. "Why do you put this burden on me," she said, "bringing into our lodge this good-for-nothing, this slow-witted crazy boy? Maybe you're a little slow-witted and crazy yourself!"

"Woman, keep talking like that and I'll beat you! This boy isn't slow or crazy; he's a good boy, and I have taken him for my grandson. Look—he's barefooted. Hurry up, and make a pair of moccasins for him, and if you don't do it well I'll take a stick to you."

Good Running's wife grumbled but did as she was told. Her husband was a kind man, but when aroused, his anger was great.

So a new life began for Long Arrow. He had to learn to speak and to understand well, and to catch up on all the things a boy should know. He was a fast learner and soon surpassed other boys his age in knowledge and skills. At last even Good Running's wife accepted him. **❷** **❸**

He grew up into a fine young hunter, tall and good-looking in the quilled buckskin outfit the chief's wife made for him. He helped his grandfather in everything and became a staff for Good Running to lean on. But he was lonely, for most people in the camp could not forget that Long Arrow had once been an outcast. "Grandfather," he said one day, "I want to do something to make you proud and show people that you were wise to adopt me. What can I do?" **❹**

Good Running answered, "Someday you will be a chief and do great things."

"But what's a great thing I could do now, Grandfather?"

The chief thought for a long time. "Maybe I shouldn't tell you this," he said. "I love you and don't want to lose you. But on winter nights, men talk of powerful spirit people living

430 ◆ Expanding Horizons

Cross-Curricular Connection: Social Studies

The Blackfeet traditionally occupied a large area east of the Rocky Mountains, with the present-day Yellowstone Park as its southern border and present-day Edmonton, Alberta, Canada, as its northern border. In addition to hunting, Blackfeet raised tobacco and trapped beaver; they traded furs for weapons, tools, and other goods. They were known for their beautiful craftwork—their tipis,

clothing, weapons, and riding equipment were of exceptional design. They dyed their moccasins black; hence the name Blackfeet.

Invite students to do research to compare and contrast Blackfeet culture with at least one other Plains culture and at least one mountain or seaboard Native American culture.

430

at the bottom of a faraway lake. Down in that lake the spirit people keep mystery animals who do their work for them. These animals are larger than a great elk, but they carry the burdens of the spirit people like dogs. So they're called Pono-Kamita—Elk Dogs. They are said to be swift, strong, gentle, and beautiful beyond imagination. Every fourth generation, one of our young warriors has gone to find these spirit folk and bring back an Elk Dog for us. But none of our brave young men has ever returned."

◆ **Reading Strategy**
Why might people want to do great deeds for those they love?

"Grandfather, I'm not afraid. I'll go and find the Elk Dog."

"Grandson, first learn to be a man. Learn the right prayers and ceremonies. Be brave. Be generous and open-handed. Pity the old and the fatherless, and let the holy men of the tribe find a medicine for you which will protect you on your dangerous journey. We will begin by purifying you in the sweat bath."

So Long Arrow was purified with the white steam of the sweat lodge. He was taught how to use the pipe, and how to pray to the Great Mystery Power. The tribe's holy men gave him a medicine and made for him a shield with designs on it to ward off danger.

Then one morning, without telling anybody, Good Running loaded his best travois dog with all the things Long Arrow would need for traveling. The chief gave him his medicine, his shield, and his own fine bow and, just as the sun came up, went with his grandson to the edge of the camp to purify him with

Crow Lodge of Twenty-five Buffalo Skins, George Catlin, National Museum of American Art, Washington, D.C.

▲ Critical Viewing What do you imagine life might be like living in such a vulnerable setting? [Infer] ❽

sweet-smelling cedar smoke. Long Arrow left unheard and unseen by anyone else. After a while some people noticed that he was gone, but no one except his grandfather knew where and for what purpose.

Following Good Running's advice, Long Arrow wandered southward. On the fourth day of his journey he came to a small pond, where a strange man was standing as if waiting for him. "Why have you come here?" the stranger asked.

"I have come to find the mysterious Elk Dog."

"Ah, there I cannot help you," said the man, who was the spirit of the pond. "But if you travel further south, four-times-four days, you might chance upon a bigger lake and there meet one of my uncles. Possibly he might talk to you; then again, he might not. That's all I can tell you."

Long Arrow thanked the man, who went down to the bottom of the pond, where he lived.

Long Arrow wandered on, walking for long hours and taking little time for rest. Through deep canyons and over high mountains he went, wearing out his moccasins and enduring

◆ **Build Vocabulary**
surpassed (sər past′) *v.*: Went beyond; excelled

◆ **Reading Strategy**

❺ **Identify With a Character** Students might conclude that people want to give benefits to people they love, or, that people want to merit being loved in return.

◆ **Critical Thinking**

❻ **Analyze** In the conversation between Long Arrow and Good Running, several qualities of a Blackfeet hero are stated or implied. Ask students to point them out. *Qualities include fearlessness, knowledge of prayers and ceremonies, generosity, pity for the weak, respect for the elders of the tribe.*

◆ **Build Grammar Skills**

❼ **Homographs** Ask students to differentiate the two words that are spelled *bow* but pronounced differently. *A noun referring to a weapon that shoots arrows, and a verb meaning "to bend at the waist."* Note that *bow,* meaning a kind of knot, is not a homograph with *bow,* meaning a weapon that shoots arrows, since they are pronounced identically.

▶ **Critical Viewing** ◀

❽ **Infer** Accept a variety of answers, such as "exciting," "adventurous," "dangerous," "mobile," "free."

Customize for
Less Proficient Readers

❾ Ask students how many days Long Arrow must travel further south. *Sixteen.* Help students recognize the repeated pattern of Long Arrow's journey: four days to one lake, then four-times-four (four squared) days to another lake.

The Orphan Boy and the Elk Dog ◆ 431

 Humanities: Art

Crow Lodge of Twenty-five Buffalo Skins, 1832–1833, by George Catlin.

This painting documents a domestic scene centered on the tipi. The Crow are a Plains hunting people who lived along the Yellowstone River. They call themselves *Absaroka,* or "bird people."

George Catlin (1796–1872) was an American painter famous for his portrayal of Native Americans. From 1830 to 1836 he lived among Native Americans, recording their lives in a colorful, realistic style. After unsuccessful attempts to sell his paintings, he traveled to England and France

in 1839 with more than 500 paintings and a group of Native Americans. Abroad, he found the success he sought.

Use these questions for discussion:
1. What elements of the myth can you find in this painting? *The tipi, dog, weapons, man and woman working are all mentioned in the myth.*
2. How would life in a tipi differ from your life? *Among reasonable responses is that camping out in a tipi provides a closeness to nature that isn't possible in a house or an apartment building.*

❶ Analyze Ask students how Long Arrow's encounter with the tall spirit man helps Long Arrow. *Students may say that it boosts his self-esteem to be accepted by a powerful spirit who rejects most other humans.*

▶**Critical Viewing**◀

❷ Interpret The thin outlines and modulated tones of the horses and the landscape give the animals a mystical, shimmery quality like the "gamboling," "wonderful" animals of the myth.

◆ **Critical Thinking**

❸ Interpret Ask students how Long Arrow's early life might have prepared him to withstand his journey. *As a child, he had to fend for himself, including sleeping alone in the open and scavenging for food.*

Wild Horses at Play, 1834–37, George Catlin, National Museum of American Art, Washington, D.C.

cold and heat, hunger and thirst.

Finally Long Arrow approached a big lake surrounded by steep pine-covered hills. There he came face to face with a tall man, fierce and scowling and twice the height of most humans. This stranger carried a long lance with a heavy spearpoint made of shining flint. "Young one," he growled, "why did you come here?"

"I came to find the mysterious Elk Dog."

The stranger, who was the spirit of the lake, stuck his face right into Long Arrow's and shook his mighty lance. "Little one, aren't you afraid of me?" he snarled.

❶ "No, I am not," answered Long Arrow, smiling.

The tall spirit man gave a hideous grin, which was his way of being friendly. "I like small humans who aren't afraid," he said, "but I can't help you. Perhaps our grandfather will take the trouble to listen to you. More likely he won't. Walk south for four-times-four days, and maybe you'll find him. But probably you won't." With that the tall spirit turned his back

432 ◆ *Expanding Horizons*

▲ **Critical Viewing** What mood or feeling does the artist invoke through his use of subtle color and shadow? How is this feeling conveyed in the story? [Interpret] ❷

on Long Arrow and went to the bottom of the lake, where he lived.

Long Arrow walked on for another four-times-four days, sleeping and resting little. By now he staggered and stumbled in his weakness, and his dog was not much better off. At last he came to the biggest lake he had ever seen, surrounded by towering snow-capped peaks and waterfalls of ice. This time there was nobody to receive him. As a matter of fact, there seemed to be no living thing around. "This must be the Great Mystery Lake," thought Long Arrow. Exhausted, he fell down ❸

◆ **Build Vocabulary**

emanating (em′ ə nāt′ ıŋ) *v.*: Coming forth
relish (rel′ ish) *n.*: Pleasure and enjoyment

 Humanities: Art

Wild Horses at Play, 1834–1837, by George Catlin.

This landscape painting shows a herd of horses gamboling on the prairie in the foreground, overseen by the mountain peak in the middle of the canvas. Large areas of uninterrupted land and sky give the painting a feeling of open space and freedom.

Tell students that "wild" horses in North America, sometimes called mustangs, are actually the escaped descendants of domesticated horses

brought by the Spanish in the 1500's. True wild horses had become extinct on this continent thousands of years earlier.

Use these questions for discussion:
1. If, like Long Arrow's people, you had never seen a horse before, what might you think of these animals? *It would be reasonable to think of them as a kind of large dog or elk-like animal.*
2. Which scene in the myth could this painting illustrate? *The painting could illustrate the scene in which Long Arrow first sees the Elk Dogs.*

upon the shortgrass meadow by the lake, fell down among the wild flowers, and went to sleep with his tired dog curled up at his feet.

When Long Arrow awoke, the sun was already high. He opened his eyes and saw a beautiful child standing before him, a boy in a dazzling white buckskin robe decorated with porcupine quills of many colors. The boy said, "We have been expecting you for a long time. My grandfather invites you to his lodge. Follow me."

Telling his dog to wait, Long Arrow took his medicine shield and his grandfather's bow and went with the wonderful child. They came to the edge of the lake. The spirit boy pointed to the water and said, "My grandfather's lodge is down there. Come." The child turned himself into a kingfisher and dove straight to the bottom.

❹

Afraid, Long Arrow thought, "How can I follow him and not be drowned?" But then he said to himself, "I knew all the time that this would not be easy. In setting out to find the Elk Dog, I already threw my life away." And he boldly jumped into the water. To his surprise, he found it did not make him wet, that it parted before him, that he could breathe and see. He touched the lake's sandy bottom. It sloped down, down toward a center point.

Long Arrow descended this slope until he came to a small flat valley. In the middle of it stood a large tipi of tanned buffalo hide. The images of two strange animals were drawn on it in sacred vermilion[2] paint. A kingfisher perched high on the top of the tipi flew down and turned again into the beautiful boy, who

◆ Literary Focus
Keep in mind Long Arrow's bravery in this scene, as it will be rewarded later.

❺

❻

---

2. **vermilion** (vər mil′ yən) n.: Bright red.

... some strange animals, unlike any the young man had ever seen, were galloping and gamboling ...

said, "Welcome. Enter my grandfather's lodge."

Long Arrow followed the spirit boy inside. In the back at the seat of honor sat a black-robed old man with flowing white hair and such power emanating from him that Long Arrow felt himself in the presence of a truly Great One. The holy man welcomed Long Arrow and offered him food. The man's wife came in bringing dishes of buffalo hump, liver, tongues, delicious chunks of deer meat, the roasted flesh of strange, tasty water birds, and meat pounded together with berries, chokecherries, and kidney fat. Famished after his long journey, Long Arrow ate with relish. Yet he still looked around to admire the furnishings of the tipi, the painted inner curtain, the many medicine shields, wonderfully wrought weapons, shirts and robes decorated with porcupine quills in rainbow colors, beautifully painted rawhide containers filled with wonderful things, and much else that dazzled him.

After Long Arrow had stilled his hunger, the old spirit chief filled the pipe and passed it to his guest. They smoked, praying silently. After a while the old man said, "Some came before you from time to time, but they were always afraid of the deep water, and so they went away with empty hands. But you, grandson, were brave enough to plunge in, and therefore you are chosen to receive a wonderful gift to carry back to your people. Now, go outside with my grandson."

❼

The beautiful boy took Long Arrow to a meadow on which some strange animals, unlike any the young man had ever seen, were galloping and gamboling, neighing and nickering. They were truly wonderful to look at, with their glossy coats fine as a maiden's hair, their long manes and tails streaming in the wind.

❽
❾

The Orphan Boy and the Elk Dog ◆ 433

◆ **Build Vocabulary**

❹ **Homographs** Point out the word *dove* in this sentence. Have students pronounce it and identify its part of speech. Then ask them to name a homograph for *dove*. *Dove is a verb; a homograph is the noun, "dove," a bird.*

◆ **Literary Focus**

❺ **Myth** Ask students what personal quality allows Long Arrow to enter the lake. Then ask what external phenomenon helps Long Arrow. *The personal quality is courage; the external phenomenon is magic.*

❻ **Clarification** A kingfisher is a bird usually found in the tropics or subtropics. It is brightly colored, with a crested head and a long powerful beak. There are several varieties—the American varieties are fishing birds, while some other varieties live in forests.

◆ **Reading Strategy**

❼ **Identify With a Character** Invite students to imagine how they would feel in Long Arrow's situation. *They would probably feel proud, happy, excited.*

Comprehension Check ☑

❽ What kind of animal is it? *It is the horse.*

◆ **Build Vocabulary**

❾ **Homographs** Have students note the word *wind* in this sentence and identify its part of speech. Then ask them to name a differently pronounced word that is spelled "wind." *Wind, in this sentence, is a noun. The homograph* wind *is a verb meaning to twist or turn.*

🖐 **Workplace Skills Mini-Lesson**

Following a Procedure

Introduce the Concept In making his journey, Long Arrow had to listen to, remember, and follow procedures at several points: when his grandfather gave him advice, when the stranger at the pond directed him to the lake, when the tall spirit directed him to another lake, and when the old spirit chief gave him gifts and instructed him on how to catch the Elk Dogs. Have

students reread the relevant passages and summarize the procedures Long Arrow followed.

Develop Background Ask students to think of procedures they must follow either at a job, at a recreational activity, or in a school activity. Have students write a list of steps for performing one such procedure.

Apply the Information Have students work in pairs, each partner reciting his or

her procedures list to the other. The partner then repeats the steps of the procedure from memory. Partners should then switch roles and repeat the process.

Assess the Outcome Ask students to assess how well they and their partners recalled the procedures step by step.

◆ Build Vocabulary

❶ Homographs Ask students which homograph is used here, the noun meaning "garbage" or the verb meaning "to reject." *It is the verb.*

◆ Build Grammar Skills

❷ Commonly Confused Words Ask students to choose the correct word to fill in the blank in the following sentence: He could not (accept, except) such as lavish gift.

Customize for
More Advanced Students
Point out the repeated use of the number four in this myth: Long Arrow travels four days, then four times four days, then stays under the lake four days. Invite students to discuss the purpose of this motif. *Accept reasonable answers: four might have a mystical meaning in Blackfeet culture; the repetition lends unity to the myth.*

◆ Literary Focus

❸ Myth Students should note the presence of magical helpers, the encounter with a powerful spirit, the granting of magical aids to the hero, and the hero's successful return from a quest.

Customize for
More Advanced Students
Ask students where else in literature or myth they have seen the command not to look back. *The story of Lot's wife in Genesis, and the Greek myth of Orpheus and Eurydice.*

Now rearing, now nuzzling, they looked at Long Arrow with gentle eyes which belied their fiery appearance.

"At last," thought Long Arrow, "here they are before my own eyes, the Pono-Kamita, the Elk Dogs!"

"Watch me," said the mystery boy, "so that you learn to do what I am doing." Gracefully and without effort, the boy swung himself onto the back of a jet-black Elk Dog with a high, arched neck. Larger than any elk Long Arrow had ever come across, the animal carried the boy all over the meadow swiftly as the wind. Then the boy returned, jumped off his mount, and said, "Now you try it." A little timidly Long Arrow climbed up on the beautiful Elk Dog's back. Seemingly regarding him as feather-light, it took off like a flying arrow. The young man felt himself soaring through the air as a bird does, and experienced a happiness greater even than the joy he had felt when Good Running had adopted him as a grandson.

When they had finished riding the Elk Dogs, the spirit boy said to Long Arrow, "Young hunter from the land above the waters, I want you to have what you have come for. Listen to me. You may have noticed that my grandfather wears a black medicine robe as long as a woman's dress, and that he is always trying to hide his feet. Try to get a glimpse of them, for if you do, he can refuse you nothing. He will then tell you to ask him for a gift, and you must ask for these three things: his rainbow-colored quilled belt, his black medicine robe, and a herd of these animals which you seem to like."

Long Arrow thanked him and vowed to follow his advice. For four days the young man stayed in the spirit chief's lodge, where he ate well and often went out riding on the Elk Dogs. But try as he would, he could never get a look at the old man's feet. The spirit chief always kept them carefully covered. Then on the morning of the fourth day, the old one was walking out of the tipi when his medicine robe caught in the entrance flap. As the robe opened, Long Arrow caught a glimpse of a leg and one foot. He was awed to see that it was not a human limb at all, but the glossy leg and

434 ◆ Expanding Horizons

firm hoof of an Elk Dog! He could not <u>stifle</u> a cry of surprise, and the old man looked over his shoulder and saw that his leg and hoof were exposed. The chief seemed a little embarrassed, but shrugged and said, "I tried to hide this, but you must have been fated to see it. Look, both of my feet are those of an Elk Dog. You may as well ask me for a gift. Don't be timid; tell me what you want."

Long Arrow spoke boldly: "I want three things: your belt of rainbow colors, your black medicine robe, and your herd of Elk Dogs."

❷

"Well, so you're really not timid at all!" said the old man. "You ask for a lot, and I'll give it to you, except that you cannot have all my Elk Dogs; I'll give you half of them. Now I must tell you that my black medicine robe and my many-colored belt have Elk Dog magic in them. Always wear the robe when you try to catch Elk Dogs; then they can't get away from you. On quiet nights, if you listen closely to the belt, you will hear the Elk Dog dance song and Elk Dog prayers. You must learn them. And I will give you one more magic gift: this long rope woven from the hair of a white buffalo bull. With it you will never fail to catch whichever Elk Dog you want."

> ◆ **Literary Focus**
> What elements does this myth have in common with other myths you've read?

❸

The spirit chief presented him with the gifts and said, "Now you must leave. At first the Elk Dogs will not follow you. Keep the medicine robe and the magic belt on at all times, and walk for four days toward the north. Never look back—always look to the north. On the fourth day the Elk Dogs will come up beside you on the left. Still don't look back. But after they have overtaken you, catch one with the rope of white buffalo hair and ride him home. Don't lose the black robe, or you will lose the Elk Dogs and never catch them again."

Long Arrow listened carefully so that he would remember. Then the old spirit chief had

◆ Build Vocabulary
stifle (stī′ fəl) *v.*: Hold back

🖋 Speaking and Listening Mini-Lesson

Debate
This Mini-Lesson supports the first Speaking and Listening activity in the Idea Bank on page 437.

Introduce the Concept Debates were an important feature in the political life of many Native American peoples. Remind students that in debating they do not necessarily have to argue for the side with which they agree. They should plan their arguments based on facts and details from the story and form

their arguments to anticipate the arguments of the other side. Refer students to the Speaking and Listening Handbook, p. 978, for more information on Debate.

Develop Background Form teams of two or three students. Before they debate, have teams reread the myth and takes notes on any points they feel might bear on Long Arrow's potential as a chief. They should then make an outline of their arguments and anticipated counter-arguments.

Apply the Information After rehearsing their arguments, have students debate Long Arrow's fitness as chief.

Assess the Outcome Evaluate the debates according to the following criteria:
1. Were the arguments clear and well-supported?
2. Were the counter-arguments reasonable and well expressed?
3. Which team was more convincing in its presentation?

434

his wife make up a big pack of food, almost too heavy for Long Arrow to carry, and the young man took leave of his generous spirit host. The mysterious boy once again turned himself into a kingfisher and led Long Arrow to the surface of the lake, where his faithful dog greeted him joyfully. Long Arrow fed the dog, put his pack of food on the travois, and started walking north.

On the fourth day the Elk Dogs came up on his left side, as the spirit chief had foretold. Long Arrow snared the black one with the arched neck to ride, and he caught another to carry the pack of food. They galloped swiftly on, the dog barking at the big Elk Dogs' heels.

When Long Arrow arrived at last in his village, the people were afraid and hid. They did not recognize him astride his beautiful Elk Dog but took him for a monster, half man and half animal. Long Arrow kept calling, "Grandfather Good Running, it's your grandson. I've come back bringing Elk Dogs!"

Recognizing the voice, Good Running came out of hiding and wept for joy, because he had given Long Arrow up for lost. Then all the others emerged from their hiding places to admire the wonderful new animals.

Long Arrow said, "My grandfather and grandmother who adopted me, I can never repay you for your kindness. Accept these wonderful Elk Dogs as my gift. Now we no longer need to be humble footsloggers, because these animals will carry us swiftly everywhere we want to go. Now buffalo hunting will be easy. Now our tipis will be larger, our possessions will be greater, because an Elk Dog travois can carry a load ten times bigger than that of a dog. Take them, my grandparents. I shall keep for myself only this black male and this black female, which will grow into a fine herd."

"You have indeed done something great, grandson," said Good Running, and he spoke true. The people became the bold riders of the Plains and soon could hardly imagine how they had existed without these wonderful animals.

After some time Good Running, rich and honored by all, said to Long Arrow, "Grandson, lead us to the Great Mystery Lake so we can camp by its shores. Let's visit the spirit chief and the wondrous boy; maybe they will give us more of their power and magic gifts."

Long Arrow led the people southward and again found the Great Mystery Lake. But the waters would no longer part for him, nor would any of the kingfishers they saw turn into a boy. Nor, gazing down into the crystal-clear water, could they discover people, Elk Dogs, or a tipi. There was nothing in the lake but a few fish.

◆ **Reading Strategy**

❹ **Identify With a Character** Ask students how they would feel if they were Long Arrow, returning home with his horses. *They would probably feel triumphant, finally accepted as valuable by the whole tribe.*

◆ **Literary Focus**

❺ **Myth** Have students explain how this paragraph conveys the qualities of a myth. *Students may say that a myth helps to explain how something real came to be; once the reality has been created, the magic that created it ceases to function.*

Reinforce and Extend

Answers
◆ *Literature and Your Life*

Reader's Response Adventurous students could respond to the journey as to an exciting wilderness trek.

Thematic Focus Students may identify an inventor, such as Thomas Edison, a political or social force, such as Dr. Martin Luther King, Jr., or an artist, writer, or musician.

☑ **Check Your Comprehension**

1. Long Arrow is disabled by his inability to hear, and people think he is stupid.
2. The old chief, Good Running, adopts the boy.
3. He doesn't want to lose the boy to a dangerous quest.
4. Summaries should include the purification of the sweat lodge, the spirit of the pond, the spirit of the lake, the boy of the Great Mystery Lake, the Great One of the underwater lodge, and the gift of the Elk Dogs, followed by the return north with the Elk Dogs.

Guide for Responding

◆ *Literature and Your Life*

Reader's Response Would you have wanted to travel with Long Arrow? Why or why not?

Thematic Focus Long Arrow brought back a great gift to his people, which changed the way they lived. Who in the last one hundred years do you feel has given modern American society a gift that has had a positive impact?

☑ **Check Your Comprehension**

1. Why do the villagers shun Long Arrow at the beginning of the story?
2. Who takes pity on Long Arrow and why?
3. Why is the chief reluctant to tell Long Arrow about the Elk Dogs?
4. Summarize Long Arrow's journey to and from the Great Mystery Lake.

The Orphan Boy and the Elk Dog ◆ 435

 Beyond the Selection

FURTHER READING

Other Native American Myths
American Indian Myths and Legends, edited by Richard Erdoes and Alfonso Ortiz
The Winged Serpent: American Indian Prose and Poetry, edited by Margot Astrov
They Dance in the Sky: Native American Star Myths, Jean Guard Monroe and Ray A. Williamson

Other Works About Transportation Expanding Our Horizons
The Spirit of St. Louis, Charles A. Lindbergh
The Right Stuff, Tom Wolfe
Life on the Mississippi, Mark Twain

We suggest that you preview these works before recommending them to students.

INTERNET
You and your students may visit the following Web sites for more information about the Blackfeet
http://users.aol.com/Donh523/navapage/blackfee.htm
http://itrc29.itrc.umt.edu/indianinfo/blackfeet.htm

Please be aware, however, that sites may have changed from the time we published this information. We *strongly recommend* that you preview the sites before you send students to them.

◆ Critical Thinking

1. Courage and determination keep Long Arrow on his quest.
2. Long Arrow discovers his own strength and identity.
3. Most students will say the use of horses for the tribe is the greatest benefit; others may say that the tribe's acceptance of Long Arrow is the greatest benefit.
4. Special educational facilities and technological equipment to enhance auditory capabilities are available for the hearing-impaired today.

◆ Reading Strategy

1. Students should consider whether they have the courage to set out on an unknown path.
2. He must have felt proud and happy.

◆ Literary Focus

1. Long Arrow endures extreme hardships on his journey and experiences magical powers in his descent to the underwater lodge of the Elk Dog. These qualities make him seem "larger than life."
2. The Blackfeet use steam sweat baths and cedar smoke for purification; they have a holy man who dispenses medicine; they revere the horse or Elk Dog.

◆ Build Vocabulary

Using Homographs

1. I refuse to accept your criticism. She placed her garbage in the refuse container.
2. I am content to read at the beach. What is the content of that jar?
3. He stood in the entrance to the tipi, brooding. Puzzles and mysteries entrance my brother for hours on end.
4. Bow to your elders to show respect. String your bow tight to shoot your arrow straight.

Using the Word Bank

1. S 2. S 3. A 4. A 5. S

◆ Build Grammar Skills

1. accept; 2. accepted; 3. except;
4. except; 5. accepted

◆ Critical Thinking

INTERPRET

1. What qualities help Long Arrow overcome the obstacles he faces during his journey? **[Infer]**
2. Long Arrow's journey was beneficial to his people because he brought back horses. In what ways was his journey beneficial to himself as an individual? **[Analyze]**

EVALUATE

3. What do you think is the most important result of Long Arrow's journey? Why? **[Assess]**

APPLY

4. The people of Long Arrow's village made no accommodation for Long Arrow's disability at the beginning of the story. In what ways does our society make accommodations for physical disabilities? In what ways can we improve? **[Relate]**

◆ Reading Strategy

IDENTIFY WITH A CHARACTER

In reading "The Orphan Boy and the Elk Dog," you **identify** with Long Arrow. That means you share his experiences and feelings. As you do, you consider what you would have done and felt in his place.

1. If you were Long Arrow, would you have undertaken the journey to find the Elk Dogs? Why or why not?
2. How do you think Long Arrow felt when he returned with the Elk Dogs?

◆ Literary Focus

MYTH

Myths are ancient stories that generally involve immortal or "larger-than-life" characters. These stories explain the mysteries of nature or the customs of a people. Often, details in a myth reveal the values and customs of the culture.

1. What qualities make Long Arrow seem "larger than life"?
2. Identify three details about Blackfeet culture that are revealed in this myth.

◆ Build Vocabulary

USING HOMOGRAPHS

On your paper, write two sentences for each homograph, showing its two different meanings.

1. refuse   3. entrance

2. content   4. bow

USING THE WORD BANK

On your paper, write S if the pair of words are synonyms and A if the pair are antonyms.

1. refuse, garbage
2. surpassed, exceeded
3. emanating, suppressing
4. relish, loathe
5. stifle, smother

◆ Build Grammar Skills

COMMONLY CONFUSED WORDS: ACCEPT AND EXCEPT

Accept is a verb meaning "to receive" or "to agree with." **Except** is a preposition meaning "not including," but it is sometimes a verb meaning "to leave out." These words are commonly confused, because although they have different meanings, they have a similar look and sound.

Practice Choose the word that correctly completes each sentence.
1. Will you (accept, except) these moccasins?
2. He (accepted, excepted) a ride on an Elk Dog.
3. All (accept, except) Long Arrow returned.
4. The holy man looked normal (accept, except) for his leg and foot.
5. The holy man offered gifts, and Long Arrow (accepted, excepted) them.

Writing Application Write a single sentence in which you use both *accept* and *except* correctly.

Build Your Portfolio

Idea Bank

Writing

1. **Speech** Write a brief statement that Long Arrow might make to the villagers when he returns with the Elk Dogs.

2. **Dialogue** Write a dialogue that might occur between Long Arrow and the Chief when they reach the Great Mystery Lake at the end of the myth and discover only fish in the lake.

3. **Description of a Mystery Animal** Horses were at first such a mystery to the Blackfeet that they could describe them only by using words for familiar animals. Describe an animal as if you had never seen it before and didn't know its name. Compare its features with those of other animals that have similar features. **[Science Link]**

Speaking and Listening

4. **Debate** With other students, debate whether or not Long Arrow will make a good future chief for the Blackfeet. Use story details to argue and support your view.

5. **Retell a Myth** Retell this myth in your own words. Use tone of voice and facial expressions to make your telling exciting. **[Performing Arts Link]**

Projects

6. **Animal Population Graph** Buffalo were important to the Blackfeet, but their numbers have declined since the late nineteenth century. Create a bar graph that shows the changes in the buffalo population in the United States since 1850. **[Math Link; Science Link]**

7. **Storyboard Mural** Create a mural of scenes that show the major events of "The Orphan Boy" in order. Look at the pictures that accompany the myth to get ideas about color and style. **[Art Link]**

Writing Mini-Lesson

Retelling of a Myth

"The Orphan Boy and the Elk Dog" has been retold many times over many generations. When you **retell a myth**, you use your own words and style to tell a tale that already exists.

Think of a myth you already know and retell it in your own words. The following tip will help you organize the events of your myth.

Writing Skills Focus: Clear Beginning, Middle, and End

A myth, like any other good story, needs a **clear beginning, middle,** and **end** in order to make sense. In the beginning of your retelling, include important details about the setting. When and where does it take place? Introduce the main characters, then the conflict or problem that the characters face. In the middle, as the tale develops, present events in a logical order, such as time order. As you bring the tale to a close, tell how the conflict is worked out.

Prewriting Create a story map to organize the retelling of your myth. Include these categories: title, setting, character names and descriptions, conflict description, and events that develop and resolve the conflict.

Drafting Use your story map to create a clear beginning, logical development for the middle, and an effective end. Inject your retelling with clear, lively language. To do this, use active verbs and specific nouns.

Revising Read your draft to a small group of classmates. See whether they can summarize your story correctly. If there are places where group members become confused, add details or transitional words to indicate the connections among events.

The Orphan Boy and the Elk Dog ◆ 437

 Idea Bank

Customizing for *Performance Levels*
Following are suggestions for matching Idea Bank topics with your students' performance levels:
Less Advanced Students: 1, 5, 7
Average Students: 2, 4, 6
More Advanced Students: 3, 4, 6

Customizing for *Learning Modalities*
Following are suggestions for matching Idea Bank topics with your students' learning modalities:
Visual/Spatial: 3, 6, 7
Verbal/Linguistic: 1, 4, 5
Logical/Mathematical: 6

Writing Mini-Lesson

Refer students to the Writing Handbook, page 965, for instruction on the writing process, and page 967 for further information on narration.

Writing and Language Transparencies Students may use the Story Map, pp. 83–86, to organize their retelling of a myth.

Writer's Solution

Writers at Work Videodisc
Have students view the videodisc segment (Ch. 2) featuring Maxine Hong Kingston to see how she develops narrative elements. Have students discuss how they can use these techniques in writing their narrations.

Play frames 18612 to 19873

Writing Lab CD-ROM
Have students complete the tutorial on Narration. Follow these steps:
1. Students may use the Photo Storyboard activity to suggest a story line.
2. Have students draft on computer.
3. Students may use the interactive tips on ending a narrative.
4. Suggest that students use the homophone checker in revising their work.

Sourcebook
Have students use Chapter 2, Narration (pp. 30–61), for additional support. The chapter includes detailed instruction on organizing a narrative (pp. 50–51).

✓ ASSESSMENT OPTIONS

Formal Assessment, Selection Test, pp. 110–112, and Assessment Resources Software. The selection test is designed so that it can be easily customized to the performance levels of your students.
Alternative Assessment, p. 32, includes options for less advanced students, more advanced students, verbal/linguistic learners, visual/spatial learners, and logical mathematic learners.

PORTFOLIO ASSESSMENT
Use the following rubrics in the *Alternative Assessment* booklet to assess student writing:
Speech: Expression Rubric, p. 94
Dialogue: Fictional Narrative Rubric, p. 95
Description of a Mystery Animal: Description Rubric, p. 97
Writing Mini-Lesson: Fictional Narrative Rubric, p. 95

OBJECTIVES

1. To read, comprehend, and interpret a story
2. To relate a story to personal experience
3. To predict story events
4. To identify third-person point of view
5. To build vocabulary in context and learn the suffix -ly
6. To use commas correctly in a series
7. To write a song for a moment in the story, including words that carry specific connotations
8. To respond to the story through writing, speaking and listening, and projects

SKILLS INSTRUCTION

Vocabulary:
Suffixes: -ly

Grammar:
Commas in a Series

Reading Strategy:
Predict

Literary Focus:
Point of View

Writing:
Connotation

Speaking and Listening:
Dialogue (teacher edition)

Critical Viewing:
Infer; Analyze

PORTFOLIO OPPORTUNITIES

Writing: Postcard; Legend; Compare and Contrast

Writing Mini-Lesson: Song for a Moment in the Story

Speaking and Listening: Dialogue; Debate

Projects: Sketch; Photo Essay

More About the Author

Josephina Niggli's *Mexican Village* was a landmark: published in 1945, it was the first literary work by a Mexican American to achieve widespread success among the general reading public in the United States. The ten stories in the collection not only share a common setting but also feature recurrent characters—most of whom live in the village of Hidalgo, a place that plays a key role in "The Street of the Cañon."

*G*uide for Reading

Josephina Niggli (1910–   )

When Josephina Niggli was just a child, she and her family fled their native Mexico to escape the turmoil of the Mexican Revolution. They settled in San Antonio, Texas, where Niggli grew up.

From Texas to Hollywood Niggli was educated at home until she reached high school. Her first book of poems was published shortly after her high-school graduation. After college, she began writing and producing plays, and later, movie scripts.

> *Niggli spent two years in Hollywood as a screenwriter.*

Niggli's background in drama has served her well in her prose works. Her dialogue is believable, and her skill at describing a setting enables the reader to picture the scene as if it were on stage.

Cultural Influences Although she left Mexico at a young age, Niggli carried the richness of her Mexican culture with her to the United States. In 1945, she published *Mexican Village,* a collection of ten stories, all set in the Sabinas Valley of northern Mexico. In these stories, she shows a talent for capturing the local color—the details of life in this valley.

Daring Heroes As a child, she heard exciting stories of the fearless heroes Pancho Villa and Emiliano Zapata, who fought for reform during the Mexican Revolution. Pepe Gonzalez, the main character in "The Street of Cañon," exhibits the same daring, romantic nature as these daring, romantic figures.

◆ Build Vocabulary

SUFFIXES: -ly

The suffix -ly is one of the most common in English. Most, but not all, words that end in -ly are adverbs. An adverb is a word that modifies a verb, adjective, or another adverb. Josephina Niggli uses adverbs to make her writing more descriptive. When one of her characters *nonchalantly* enters a room, for instance, you can picture the person's walk as he tries to enter the room without being noticed.

WORD BANK

officious
mottled
nonchalantly
audaciously
imperiously
plausibility

As you read "The Street of the Cañon," you will encounter the words on this list. Each word is defined on the page where it first appears. Preview the list before you read.

◆ Build Grammar Skills

COMMAS IN A SERIES

A **comma** can make a big difference in the clarity of your writing. Separating three or more items in a series is one way that commas make writing clear.

. . . the air was hot with the too-sweet perfume of gardenias, tuberoses, and the pungent scent of close-packed humanity.

In this sentence, commas separate the three details that describe what the room is hot with. Notice that Niggli uses a comma before the coordinating conjunction *and,* which joins the last two items.

If the items in the series are already separated by conjunctions (such as *and* or *or*), commas are not necessary.

There were yellow cheese *and* white cheese *and* curded cheese from cow's milk.

438 ◆ *Expanding Horizons*

Prentice Hall Literature Program Resources

REINFORCE / RETEACH / EXTEND

Selection Support Pages
Build Vocabulary: Suffixes: -ly, p. 134
Build Grammar Skills: Commas in a Series, p. 135
Reading Strategy: Predict, p. 136
Literary Focus: Point of View, p. 137

Strategies for Diverse Student Needs, p. 33

Beyond Literature
Community Connection, p. 33

Formal Assessment Selection Test, pp. 113–115;

Assessment Resources Software

Alternative Assessment, p. 33

Writing and Language Transparencies
Analysis Map, pp. 71–73

Resource Pro CD-R♦M
"The Street of the Cañon"—includes all resource materials and customizable lesson plan

Listening to Literature Audiocassettes
"The Street of the Cañon"

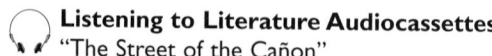

The Street of the Cañon

◆ Literature and Your Life

CONNECT YOUR EXPERIENCE

Celebrations acknowledge significant occasions. Some celebrations, such as a Fourth of July picnic or a town parade, are public. Others, such as a wedding or birthday party, are personal. In this story, a young woman named Sarita celebrates her birthday. The celebration has elements of a public event, however, as Sarita's father throws a fiesta to which the whole town is invited.

Journal Writing Describe the last celebration you attended, and tell what made it special.

THEMATIC FOCUS: A LARGER WORLD

Celebrations unite you with other people who also honor the same event or a person. How does celebrating with others enlarge your world?

◆ Background for Understanding

CULTURE

Courtship and marriage customs play an important role in this story. In Mexico, there are many different marriage customs, depending on the region of Mexico. In most groups, however, a young man seeking to marry must ask permission of the young woman's family elders. In some regions, however, the parents arrange a match. Marriages typically take place within the community. In the town of San Juan Iglesias, the Mexican village in which this story is set, "to walk around the plaza with a girl" is a sign of engagement.

◆ Literary Focus

POINT OF VIEW

Imagine a new kind of microscope that allows you to see into someone's mind and examine his or her thoughts and feelings. Actually, writers give you this kind of look into fictional characters' minds. They do it through **point of view** in a story—the vantage point from which the story is told. The point of view determines what you as a reader know.

When a story is told from a **limited third-person** point of view, what you know is limited to the thoughts and feelings of one character. If the point of view is all-knowing, or **omniscient**, the writer allows you to share the thoughts and feelings of more than one character. This is the point of view of "The Street of the Cañon." Niggli allows us to peek into the minds of several characters, and she reveals some details that even the characters don't know!

◆ Reading Strategy

PREDICT

Your baseball team is up against a team that has lost their last three games because their best players are injured. You can probably predict that your team will win. You can **predict story events** in much the same way—you make an educated guess based on what you know about the characters, the situation, and the logical pattern that many stories seem to follow.

No matter how logical your predictions, however, you may need to revise them as new information is revealed. If the injured players from the other team were suddenly able to play, you might reconsider your prediction. Similarly, new circumstances introduced by the author may lead you to change your predictions about story events.

Use a chart like the one shown to keep track of your predictions and how they change as you read this story.

Question	Clues	Prediction
Who is the stranger?		
What does he have tightly clutched to his side?		
Why is he going to San Juan Iglesias?		
Why would the townspeople turn on him if they recognized him?		

Guide for Reading ◆ 439

Preparing for Standardized Tests

Reading In reading comprehension passages on standardized tests it is important to identify the point of view of a writer in order to understand how to evaluate the information presented. In this story, the omniscient point of view colors readers' responses to the characters. For additional practice with this concept, use the Literary Focus page in *Selection Support,* p. 137.

Grammar and Language Portions of some tests require students to demonstrate their mastery of grammar, usage, and punctuation. Students

may be asked to identify correct punctuation in sentences such as the following: *(B)*

I brought bread cheese, and fruit.

(A) bread cheese and fruit; (B) bread, cheese, and fruit; (C) no error

The Build Grammar Skills lesson focuses on this topic. For additional practice, use the Build Grammar Skills page on Commas in a Series, p. 135, in *Selection Support.*

439

Josephina Niggli uses changing perspectives to full advantage in this tale of intrigue, local color, and local legend. The story's omniscient narrator sets the scene: A stranger makes his way to Sarita Calderon's eighteenth-birthday celebration, carrying a mysterious package. Gradually, pieces of the puzzle—in the forms of conversations, glimpses into the stranger's and Sarita's thoughts, and further insights from the narrator—come together. It becomes clear that the stranger is Pepe Gonzalez—a notoriously daring young "devil" from a rival town. What remains intriguingly unclear, however, are Pepe's intentions toward Sarita—does he charm his way into her heart because he genuinely wishes to marry her, or is winning her affection merely another daring adventure on his part?

◆ Critical Thinking

❶ Analyze Call students' attention to the details the author uses to describe the man's movements. What can students tell about him based on this description? *Responses may include that he has something to hide or that he has a secret purpose. Students should note that the man clutches the package tightly and acts in a way that suggests that he is sneaking into town.*

◆ Build Vocabulary

❷ Suffixes: -ly Point out the suffix *-ly* in the word tightly. Ask: What part of speech is this word? *It is an adverb.* What word does it modify? *It modifies the verb* clutched.

The Street of the Cañon

from Mexican Village

Josephina Niggli

It was May, the flowering thorn was sweet in the air, and the village of San Juan Iglesias in the Valley of the Three Marys was celebrating. The long dark streets were empty because all of the people, from the lowest-paid cowboy to the mayor, were helping Don Roméo Calderón celebrate his daughter's eighteenth birthday.

On the other side of the town, where the Cañon Road led across the mountains to the Sabinas Valley, a tall slender man, a package clutched tightly against his side, slipped from shadow to shadow. Once a dog barked, and the man's black suit merged into the blackness of a wall. But no voice called out, and after a moment he slid into the narrow, dirt-packed street again.

The moonlight touched his shoulder and spilled across his narrow hips. He was young, no more than twenty-five, and his black curly head was bare. He walked swiftly along, heading

▲ **Critical Viewing** What time period do you think this painting depicts? What details suggest the time period? [Infer] ❸

always for the distant sound of guitar and flute. If he met anyone now, who could say from which direction he had come? He might be a trader from Monterrey, or a buyer of cow's milk from farther north in the Valley of the Three Marys. Who would guess that an Hidalgo[1] man dared to walk alone in the moonlit streets of San Juan Iglesias? ❹

Carefully adjusting his flat package so that it was not too prominent, he squared his shoulders and walked jauntily across the street to the laughter-filled house. Little boys packed in the doorway made way for him, smiling and nodding to him. The long, narrow room with the orchestra at one end was filled with ❺

---
1. **Hidalgo** (ē dal′ gō) *adj.*: Nearby village.

440 ◆ *Expanding Horizons*

Block Scheduling Strategies

Consider these suggestions to take advantage of extended class time:

- Use the Daily Language Practice for Week 6, which is based on "The Street of the Cañon," p. 117 in *Writing and Language Transparencies.*
- Students may work with a partner to complete a Prediction Chart like the one on page 439 as they read. Have pairs compare their charts with other pairs when they have finished reading the story.

- Introduce the Literary Focus, Point of View, by reading with students the paragraphs on page 439. Have students preview the Literary Focus questions on page 446 before they read. After they have read the story they may work in groups to answer the questions and do the page on Point of View in *Selection Support,* p. 137.
- To help students understand the context of the story, have students work in groups

to complete the activity page in *Beyond Literature:* Community Connection: Social Dancing, p. 33.

- Have students complete the Writing Mini-Lesson (p. 447). Before students get started, have them review the story to find and discuss words within it that have rich connotations. You may wish to have them use the Analysis Map, p. 72 in *Writing and Language Transparencies,* to analyze the connotations of words.

whirling dancers. Rigid-backed chaperones were gossiping together, seated in their straight chairs against the plaster walls. Over the scene was the yellow glow of kerosene lanterns, and the air was hot with the too-sweet perfume of gardenias, tuberoses, and the pungent scent of close-packed humanity.

The man in the doorway, while trying to appear at ease, was carefully examining every smiling face. If just one person recognized him, the room would turn on him like a den of snarling mountain cats, but so far all the laughter-dancing eyes were friendly.

Suddenly a plump, officious little man, his round cheeks glistening with perspiration, pushed his way through the crowd. His voice, many times too large for his small body, boomed at the man in the doorway. "Welcome, stranger, welcome to our house." Thrusting his arm through the stranger's, and almost dislodging the package, he started to lead the way through the maze of dancers. "Come and drink a toast to my daughter—to my beautiful Sarita. She is eighteen this night."

In the square patio the gentle breeze ruffled the pink and white oleander bushes. A long table set up on sawhorses held loaves of flaky crusted French bread, stacks of thin, delicate tortillas, plates of barbecued beef, and long red rolls of spicy sausages. But most of all there were cheeses, for the Three Marys was a cheese-eating valley. There were yellow cheese and white cheese and curded cheese from cow's milk. There was even a flat white cake of goat cheese from distant

...ango (detail), Gentilz, The Alamo Library

Linares, a delicacy too expensive for any but feast days.

To set off this feast were bottles of beer floating in ice-filled tin tubs, and another table was covered with bottles of mescal, of tequila, of maguey wine.

Don Roméo Calderón thrust a glass of tequila into the stranger's hand. "Drink, friend, to the prettiest girl in San Juan. As pretty as my fine fighting cocks, she is. On her wedding day she takes to her man, and may she find him soon, the best fighter in my flock. Drink deep, friend. Even the rivers flow with wine."

The Hidalgo man laughed and raised his glass high. "May the earth be always fertile beneath her feet."

Someone called to Don Roméo that more guests were arriving, and with a final delighted pat on the stranger's shoulder, the little man scurried away. As the young fellow smiled after his retreating host, his eyes caught and held another pair of eyes—laughing black eyes set in a young girl's face. The last time he had seen that face it had been white and tense with rage, and the lips clenched tight to prevent an outgushing stream of angry words. That had been in February, and she had worn a white lace shawl over her hair. Now it was May, and a gardenia was a splash of white in the glossy dark braids. The moonlight had mottled his face that February night, and he knew that she did not recognize him. He grinned impudently back at her, and her eyes widened, then slid sideways to one of the chaperones. The fan in her small hand snapped shut. She tapped its parchment tip against her mouth and slipped away to join the dancing couples in the front room. The gestures of a fan translate into a coded language on the frontier. The stranger raised one eyebrow as he

♦ **Build Vocabulary**

officious (ə fish′ əs) *adj.*: Overly ready to serve

mottled (mät′ əld) *adj.*: Marked with spots of different shades

The Street of the Cañon ♦ 441

►**Critical Viewing**◄

❸ **Infer** Students may say that based on the partygoers' elaborate, old-fashioned costumes, the painting depicts a time about a hundred years ago.

◆ **Literary Focus**

❹ **Point of View** Ask students to explain how this passage illustrates the third-person point of view. *Students should observe that Niggli lets us in on the mysterious man's thoughts as he makes his way through the village.*

◆ *Literature and Your Life*

❺ Have students compare the celebration described here to those they have attended or heard about. *Students may describe weddings or other celebrations they have attended that, like the celebration in the story, featured musicians, guests of all ages, and lively, festive atmospheres.*

◆ **Reading Strategy**

❻ **Predict** Encourage students to make predictions about the reasons the guests might have for turning on the stranger. What clue or clues did students use to make their predictions? *Students should note that the only clues revealed so far are that the stranger is from Hidalgo and that someone from Hidalgo would not normally dare to be seen in San Juan Iglesias. This indicates some sort of hostility between the two towns.*

◆ **Reading Strategy**

❼ **Predict** Ask students whether the information in this passage affects the predictions they made about the reasons for the grudge between the two towns. In what way? *Students should note that they can now revise their predictions—an event in which Sarita was in some way involved had something to do with the hostilities. Students should also note that the nature of the event is yet to be revealed.*

◆ **Build Vocabulary**

❽ **Suffixes: -ly** Point out the suffix -ly in impudently. Ask students what part of speech this word is and what word it modifies. *It is an adverb; it modifies grinned.* You might also ask which word in the Word Bank is close in meaning to impudently. *The word is audaciously.*

🎵 **Humanities: Art**

Fandango (detail), by Theodore Gentilz.

The paintings of the renowned Texas artist Theodore Gentilz (1819–1906) can be seen at the Alamo and Witte museums in San Antonio, Texas. In this painting, the artist captures the drama and color of a Spanish *baile,* or festive dance.

Use these questions for discussion:

1. In addition to the partygoers' costumes, what details in the painting suggest that this celebration takes place in a past era? *Students may cite the candlelight in the room and the old-fashioned dance being performed, in which a man holds a candle in one hand and his partner's hand in the other.*

2. What details in the story suggest that the party that the stranger attends takes place in the not-too-recent past? *Details include the kerosene lamps that light Don Romeo's house; the presence of chaperones; and the importance of traditional social customs, such as walking around the plaza to announce an engagement.*

❶ What is the meaning of Sarita's gesture? *She wants the stranger to follow her to the front room, where the dancing is taking place.*

◆ Critical Thinking

❷ **Infer** What inferences can students make about the stranger's personality from the way he behaves toward the old lady and from her reaction to him? *He is a smooth, suave character; he knows how to charm people to get his way.*

◆ Reading Strategy

❸ **Predict** Students should note that the song that the stranger requested is associated with the town of Hidalgo. Predictions may include these: The stranger plans to reveal that he is from Hidalgo; he plans to shock the guests.

❶ interpreted the signal.

But he did not move toward her at once. Instead, he inched slowly back against the table. No one was behind him, and his hands quickly unfastened the package he had been guarding so long. Then he <u>nonchalantly</u> walked into the front room.

The girl was sitting close to a chaperone. As he came up to her he swerved slightly toward the bushy-browed old lady.

"Your servant, señora. I kiss your hands and feet."

The chaperone stared at him in astonishment. Such fine manners were not common to the town of San Juan Iglesias.

"Eh, you're a stranger," she said. "I thought so."

"But a stranger no longer, señora, now that I have met you." He bent over her, so close she could smell the faint fragrance of talcum on his **❷** freshly shaven cheek.

"Will you dance the *parada* with me?"

This request startled her eyes into popping open beneath the heavy brows. "So, my young rooster, would you flirt with me, and I old enough to be your grandmother?"

"Can you show me a prettier woman to flirt with in the Valley of the Three Marys?" he asked <u>audaciously</u>.

She grinned at him and turned toward the girl at her side. "This young fool wants to meet you, my child."

The girl blushed to the roots of her hair and shyly lowered her white lids. The old woman laughed aloud.

"Go out and dance, the two of you. A man clever enough to pat the sheep has a right to play with the lamb."

The next moment they had joined the circle of dancers and Sarita was trying to control her laughter.

"She is the worst dragon in San Juan. And how easily you won her!"

"What is a dragon," he asked <u>imperiously</u>, "when I longed to dance with you?"

"Ay," she retorted, "you have a quick tongue. I think you are a dangerous man."

In answer he drew her closer to him, and turned her toward the orchestra. As he reached the chief violinist he called out, "Play the *Virgencita*, 'The Shy Young Maiden.'"

The violinist's mouth opened in soundless surprise. The girl in his arms said sharply, "You heard him, the *Borachita*, 'The Little Drunken Girl.'"

With a relieved grin, the violinist tapped his music stand with his bow, and the music swung into the sad farewell of a man to his sweetheart:

Farewell, my little drunken one,
I must go to the capital
To serve the master
Who makes me weep for my return.

The stranger frowned down at her. "Is this a joke, señorita?" he asked coldly.

"No," she whispered, looking about her quickly to see if the incident had been observed. "But the *Virgencita* is the favorite song of Hidalgo, a village on the other side of the mountains in the next valley. The people of Hidalgo and San Juan Iglesias do not speak."

"That is a stupid thing," said the man from Hidalgo as he swung her around in a large turn. "Is not music free as air? Why should one town own the rights to a song?"

The girl shuddered slightly. "Those people from Hidalgo—they are wicked monsters. Can you guess what they did not six months since?"

The man started to point out that the space of time from February to May was three months, but he thought it better not to appear too wise. "Did these Hidalgo monsters frighten you, señorita? If they did, I personally will kill them all."

She moved closer against him and tilted her face until her mouth was close to his ear. "They **❹**

◆ **Reading Strategy**
Make a prediction about the stranger, based on his actions.

❸

442 ◆ Expanding Horizons

Cross-Curricular Connection: Social Studies

The history of early twentieth-century Mexico is marked by political turbulence as well as legendary exploits. As noted in the Guide for Reading, Josephina Niggli and her family fled the country shortly after the Mexican Revolution of 1910; years later, as a writer, Niggli would be inspired by the colorful stories she had heard about two famous rebel leaders, Pancho Villa and Emiliano Zapata.

Villa and Zapata were leaders of two of the revolutionary bands that formed across Mexico to bring down the dictatorship of General Porfirio Diaz. In the years that followed, each led one of the many rival factions that opposed the presidents who assumed power in the wake of the Revolution. Zapata, an Indian, demanded more far-reaching land reforms. Villa became the notorious leader of a band of outlaws.

Have students do research to learn more about Villa, Zapata, and the Mexican Revolution.

attempted to steal the bones of Don Rómolo Balderas."

"Is it possible?" He made his eyes grow round and his lips purse up in disdain. "Surely not that! Why, all the world knows that Don Rómolo Balderas was the greatest historian in the entire Republic. Every school child reads his books. Wise men from Quintana Roo to the Río Bravo bow their heads in admiration to his name. What a wicked thing to do!" He hoped his virtuous tone was not too virtuous for <u>plausibility</u>, but she did not seem to notice.

"It is true! In the night they came. Three devils!"

"Young devils, I hope."

"Young or old, who cares? They were devils. The blacksmith surprised them even as they were opening the grave. He raised such a shout that all of San Juan rushed to his aid, for they were fighting, I can tell you. Especially one of them—their leader."

"And who was he?"

"You have heard of him doubtless. A proper wild one named Pepe Gonzalez."

"And what happened to them?"

"They had horses and got away, but one, I think, was hurt."

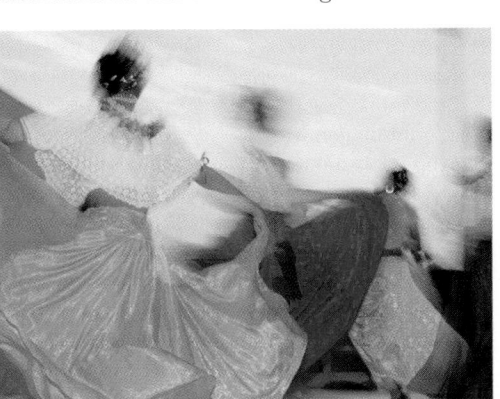

▲ **Critical Viewing** How do the style and arrangement of figures in this photograph suggest a celebration? **[Analyze]**

◆ **Build Vocabulary**

nonchalantly (nän´ shə länt´ lē) *adv.:* Casually; indifferently

audaciously (ô dā´ shəs lē) *adv.:* In a bold manner

imperiously (im pir´ ē əs lē) *adv.:* Arrogantly

plausibility (plô´ zə bil´ ə tē) *n.:* Believability

T he Hidalgo man twisted his mouth remembering how Rubén the candymaker had ridden across the whitewashed line high on the cañon trail that marked the division between the Three Marys' and the Sabinas' sides of the mountains, and then had fallen in a faint from his saddle because his left arm was broken. There was no candy in Hidalgo for six weeks, and the entire Sabinas Valley resented that broken arm as fiercely as did Rubén.

The stranger tightened his arm in reflexed anger about Sarita's waist as she said, "All the world knows that the men of Hidalgo are sons of the mountain witches."

"But even devils are shy of disturbing the honored dead," he said gravely.

"'Don Rómolo was born in our village,' Hidalgo says. 'His bones belong to us.' Well, anyone in the valley can tell you he died in San Juan Iglesias, and here his bones will stay! Is that not proper? Is that not right?"

To keep from answering, he guided her through an intricate dance pattern that led them past the patio door. Over her head he could see two men and a woman staring with amazement at the open package on the table.

His eyes on the patio, he asked blandly, "You say the leader was one Pepe Gonzalez? The name seems to have a familiar sound."

"But naturally. He has a talent." She tossed her head and stepped away from him as the music stopped. It was a dance of two *paradas*. He

The Street of the Cañon ◆ 443

◆ **Literary Focus**
What clues do the stranger's memories provide about his identity?

6

7

8

9

❶ Predict Have students predict what is in the package, which is now open on the table. Ask them to connect the package with the conversation between Sarita and the stranger.

Students should note that the stranger is probably Pepe Gonzalez—the daring and colorful character who led the attempt to recover Don Rómolo's bones. Some students may connect the placement of the package to the "talent for doing the impossible" mentioned in the conversation.

◆ Critical Thinking

❷ Speculate Point out that both Sarita and the stranger know that "to walk around the plaza with a girl means a wedding." Have students speculate on the stranger's motives for asking Sarita to do so with him.

Some students may say that the stranger—Pepe Gonzalez—fell in love with Sarita when he saw her three months ago and has returned to court her in a characteristically bold way. Others may say that he is toying with her affections as part of a plan to get even with the people of San Juan Iglesias.

◆ Build Grammar Skills

❸ Commas in a Series Have students identify the sentence that contains three items in a series. *The sentence contains these three items: Such flavor, such texture, such whiteness.* **How are the items punctuated?** *They are separated by commas.*

◆ Reading Strategy

❹ Predict Students should note that the contents of the package has been discovered; the stranger has probably left because he does not want to be identified and caught.

---

slipped his hand through her arm and guided her into place in the large oval of parading couples. Twice around the room and the orchestra would play again.

"A talent?" he prompted.

"For doing the impossible. When all the world says a thing cannot be done, he does it to prove the world wrong. Why, he climbed to the top of the Prow, and not even the long vanished Joaquín Castillo had ever climbed that mountain before. And this same Pepe caught a mountain lion with nothing to aid him but a rope and his two bare hands."

"He doesn't sound such a bad friend," protested the stranger, slipping his arm around her waist as the music began to play the merry song of the soap bubbles:

> Pretty bubbles of a thousand colors
> That ride on the wind
> And break as swiftly
> As a lover's heart.

The events in the patio were claiming his attention. Little by little he edged her closer to the door. The group at the table had considerably enlarged. There was a low murmur of excitement from the crowd.

"What has happened?" asked Sarita, attracted by the noise.

"There seems to be something wrong at the table," he answered, while trying to peer over the heads of the people in front of him. Realizing that this might be the last moment of peace he would have that evening, he bent toward her.

"If I come back on Sunday, will you walk around the plaza with me?"

She was startled into exclaiming, "Ay, no! "

"Please. Just once around."

"And you think I'd walk more than once with you, señor, even if you were no stranger? In San Juan Iglesias, to walk around the plaza with a girl means a wedding."

"Ha, and you think that is common to San Juan alone? Even the devils of Hidalgo respect

that law." He added hastily at her puzzled upward glance. "And so they do in all the villages." To cover his lapse he said softly, "I don't even know your name."

A mischievous grin crinkled the corners of her eyes. "Nor do I know yours, señor. Strangers do not often walk the streets of San Juan."

Before he could answer, the chattering in the patio swelled to louder proportions. Don Roméo's voice lay on top, like thick cream on milk. "I tell you it is a jewel of a cheese. Such flavor, such texture, such whiteness. It is a jewel of a cheese."

"What has happened?" Sarita asked of a woman at her elbow.

"A fine goat's cheese appeared as if by magic on the table. No one knows where it came from."

"Probably an extra one from Linares," snorted a fat bald man on the right.

"Linares never made such a cheese as this," said the woman decisively.

"Silence!" roared Don Roméo. "Old Tio[2] Daniel would speak a word to us."

A great hand of silence closed down over the mouths of the people. The girl was standing on tiptoe trying vainly to see what was happening. She was hardly aware of the stranger's whispering voice although she remembered the words that he said. "Sunday night—once around the plaza."

She did not realize that he had moved away, leaving a gap that was quickly filled by the blacksmith.

Old Tio Daniel's voice was a shrill squeak, and his thin, stringy neck jutted forth from his body like a turtle's from its shell. "This is no cheese from Linares," he said with authority, his mouth sucking in over his toothless gums between

◆ **Reading Strategy**
Predict why the stranger has left.

his sentences. "Years ago, when the great Don Rómolo Balderas was still alive, we had such

2. **Tio** (tē´ ō): Spanish for uncle

Speaking and Listening Mini-Lesson

Dialogue

This mini-lesson supports the first Speaking and Listening activity in the Idea Bank on page 449.

Introduce the Concept Remind students that, by the end of the story, Sarita learns that the stranger who had asked her to walk around the plaza was actually the notorious Pepe Gonzalez. The dialogue, or conversation between the two characters, will pick up where the story ends.

Develop Background Before students prepare their dialogues, have them explore and discuss the following:

• How might knowing Pepe's true identity affect Sarita's feelings and attitude toward him?

• What were Pepe's real intentions regarding Sarita? Had he really fallen in love with her, or was he only trying to live up to his reputation for "doing the impossible" by courting her?

Apply the Information Once students have decided on answers to both of these questions, they can plan to act out what might happen next between Pepe and Sarita.

Assess the Outcome After each performance, ask: Was the dialogue true to the story? Did it effectively reveal the characters' thoughts and feelings? Students may use the Peer Assessment: Dramatic Performance page in *Alternative Assessment,* p. 120, to evaluate the dialogues.

cheese as this—ay, in those days we had it. But after he died and was buried in our own sainted ground, as was right and proper . . ."

"Yes, yes," muttered voices in the crowd. He glared at the interruption. As soon as there was silence again, he continued:

"After he died, we had it no more. Shall I tell you why?"

"Tell us, Tío Daniel," said the voices humbly.

"Because it is made in Hidalgo!"

The sound of a waterfall, the sound of a wind in a narrow cañon, and the sound of an angry crowd are much the same. There were no distinct words, but the sound was enough.

"Are you certain, Tío?" boomed Don Roméo.

"As certain as I am that a donkey has long ears. The people of Hidalgo have been famous for generations for making cheese like this—especially that wicked one, that owner of a cheese factory, Timotéo Gonzalez, father to Pepe, the wild one, whom we have good cause to remember."

"We do, we do," came the sigh of assurance.

"But on the whole northern frontier there are no vats like his to produce so fine a product. Ask the people of Chihuahua, of Sonora. Ask the man on the bridge at Laredo, or the man in his boat at Tampico, 'Hola, friend, who makes the finest goat cheese?' And the answer will always be the same, 'Don Timotéo of Hidalgo.'"

It was the blacksmith who asked the great question. "Then where did that cheese come from, and we haters of Hidalgo these ten long years?"

No voice said, "The stranger," but with one fluid movement every head in the patio turned toward the girl in the doorway. She also turned, her eyes wide with something that she realized to her own amazement was more apprehension than anger.

But the stranger was not in the room. When the angry, muttering men pushed through to the street, the stranger was not on the plaza. He was not anywhere in sight. A few of the more religious crossed themselves for fear that the Devil had walked in their midst. "Who was he?" one voice asked another. But Sarita, who was meekly listening to a lecture from Don Roméo on the propriety of dancing with strangers, did not have to ask. She had a strong suspicion that she had danced that night within the circling arm of Pepe Gonzalez.

◆ **Literary Focus**
Why do you think the author reveals the stranger's identity through the thoughts of Sarita?

Guide for Responding

◆ Literature and Your Life

Reader's Response Based on this excerpt, would you like to read more of *Mexican Village?* Why or why not?

Thematic Focus In this story, a family celebration expands a young girl's horizons by showing her that people are not always who they seem to be. How can participating in town and family celebrations expand your horizons?

☑ Check Your Comprehension

1. What kind of welcome does Pepe Gonzalez receive?
2. What two things does Pepe set out to do at the party?
3. What outrageous deed had men from Hidalgo attempted in San Juan Iglesias three months previously?
4. What causes an uproar among the guests?

The Street of the Cañon ◆ 445

 Beyond the Selection

FURTHER READING
Other Works by Josephina Niggli
Mexican Village
Mexican Folk Plays
This is Villa!
A Miracle for Mexico

Other Works About Cultural Heritage
I Dream a World, Brian Lanker
Talking Leaves, Craig Lesley, ed.
    We suggest that you preview these works before recommending them to students.

INTERNET
For an essay on teaching Chicano literature that includes a discussion of Niggli's work, go to **http://www.georgetown.edu/tamlit/essays/chicano.html**
    For a timeline of Chicano culture and history, go to **http://www.pbs.org.chicano/19211940.html**
    Please be aware, however, that sites may have changed from the time we published this information. We *strongly recommend* that you preview the sites before you send students to them.

Answers

◆ Critical Thinking

1. His behavior suggests that he has something to hide.
2. He is bold, humorous, caring, and just.
3. Gonzalez wants to remind the people of San Juan Iglesias of the fine quality of the Hidalgo cheese, to upset the festivities by infiltrating as a spy, and to prove again that he has accomplished the impossible.
4. Gonzalez saw the festivities as an opportunity to prove himself and a challenge to his enemies.
5. The relationship has the potential to heal the rift between the two communities; it also has the potential to bring disaster to them. Students should support their speculations with specific reasons.

◆ Reading Strategy

1. Students may have suspected that he meant to do harm to the festivities.
2. They could predict his identity from the direction he was taking on the Street of the Cañon and from his hiding in the shadows.
3. His charm and pleasure at the festivities suggested that he was not there to harm anyone.

◆ Literary Focus

1. The stranger knows that her viewpoint on the proper location of Don Rómolo's grave differs from his.
2. Sarita is thinking about her feelings for the stranger who she has now learned is her enemy.
3. Niggli may want readers to see that the potential for healing the rift between two warring towns lies in personal relationships.

◆ Build Vocabulary

Using the Suffix -ly
1. generously; 2. timidly;
3. confidently

Using the Word Bank
1. Pepe Gonzalez behaves audaciously.
2. A cheetah's coat is mottled.
3. You would act nonchalantly if you saw someone was embarrassed and didn't want to make them feel worse.

4. Advertisements gain plausibility by including testimonials and statistics that support their claims.
5. Officious people are unpleasant to work with because they behave as if they know everything but they don't.
6. Pepe and perhaps Don Roméo act imperiously in the story.

Guide for Responding (continued)

◆ Critical Thinking

INTERPRET
1. What does Pepe Gonzalez's caution in arriving in the village suggest about his motives? **[Draw Conclusions]**
2. Describe Gonzalez's personality. **[Infer]**
3. Give three reasons Pepe Gonzalez might have had for leaving the cheese. **[Infer]**

EVALUATE
4. Do you think Pepe Gonzalez was wise to go to Sarita's party when doing so posed such a great danger to him? Explain. **[Make a Judgment]**

APPLY
5. What do you think will happen now between Pepe and Sarita and between the two villages? Give your reasons for making those predictions. **[Speculate]**

◆ Reading Strategy

PREDICT
Review the story and your process of making **predictions.** Evaluate the reasons you made certain predictions and whether you revised them when new information was revealed.
1. What predictions did you make about the stranger when he first arrived?
2. What details helped you predict his identity?
3. What details led you to revise, or at least reconsider, a prediction?

◆ Literary Focus

POINT OF VIEW
A story told from a **third-person point of view** is told by an outside observer. "The Street of the Cañon" is told in third-person omniscient point of view—the narrator, who is all knowing, allows readers to know the thoughts and feelings of more than one character.
1. What are the stranger's thoughts when Sarita talks about the people of Hidalgo?
2. What is Sarita thinking at the end of the story?
3. Why do you think Niggli wants readers to know the thoughts and feelings of both Sarita and Pepe Gonzalez?

◆ Build Vocabulary

USING THE SUFFIX -ly
Add -ly to the following words to make them adverbs. Then, on your paper, complete the following sentences with one of the adverbs you created.

confident   timid   generous

1. She gave ____?____, keeping hardly any for herself.
2. The nervous men entered the room ____?____.
3. The champ smiled ____?____ at his weaker opponent.

USING THE WORD BANK
In your notebook, write your response to each of the numbered items.
1. Which character from the story behaves audaciously?
2. Name an animal whose coat is mottled.
3. Describe a situation in which you would try to act nonchalantly.
4. What types of details give an advertisement plausibility?
5. Would you want to work with an officious person? Why or why not?
6. Which character or characters from the story behave imperiously?

◆ Build Grammar Skills

COMMAS IN A SERIES
When you list three or more items in a series, separate them with commas to make your meaning clear. A series may be a series of words, a series of phrases, or a series of clauses.

Practice In your notebook, copy the following sentences. Insert commas to separate each of the items in the series.
1. A table held loaves of bread stacks of tortillas and plates of beef.
2. Sarita nodded smiled and turned away.
3. The sound of a waterfall the sound of a wind in a narrow cañon and the sound of an angry crowd are much the same.

Writing Application In a paragraph or two, describe a celebration you've attended. Include at least two series. Punctuate the series.

◆ Build Grammar Skills

1. A table held loaves of bread, stacks of tortillas, and plates of beef.
2. Sarita nodded, smiled, and turned away.
3. The sound of a waterfall, the sound of a wind in a narrow cañon, and the sound of an angry crowd are much the same.

✎ Writer's Solution

For additional instruction and practice, use the lesson in the **Language Lab CD-ROM** on Commas and the pages on commas, pp. 99–101 in the *Writer's Solution Grammar Practice Book.*

Build Your Portfolio

Idea Bank

Writing

1. Postcard Write a postcard home to your family describing your recent visit to San Juan Iglesias. Use sensory details to help your family envision the town.

2. Legend Pepe Gonzalez's feats quickly became legendary among the people of San Juan Iglesias. Write a legend about a person who performed a heroic feat. Base your legend on a news story you read or something impressive done by a friend.

3. Compare and Contrast In an essay, compare and contrast Pepe Gonzalez with another hero you know—real or fictional. Present readers with specific examples of the legends and feats surrounding your hero.

Speaking and Listening

4. Dialogue With a partner, take turns being Sarita and Pepe when they meet in the plaza now that Sarita is aware of Pepe's identity.

5. Debate Break into two teams to debate the question from the story, "Is not music free as air?" Develop your arguments around current issues related to the censorship and rating of music.

Projects

6. Sketch Choose your favorite scene in the story and illustrate it. In your illustration, try to convey the same sense of mystery that Niggli creates in her writing. **[Art Link]**

7. Photo Essay Collect photographs of Mexico from travel magazines and brochures. Organize your photos around a theme or a message. Arrange the photos and display them.

Writing Mini-Lesson

Song for a Moment in the Story

Music is an important part of the celebration in this story. Imagine that you are a playwright who wants to turn this story into a musical. Select a moment in the story and write the **lyrics** to a song that would be sung in your musical.

As you plan and write the song lyrics, keep these points in mind:

Writing Skills Focus: Connotation

All writers, whether consciously or unconsciously, select words to convey a certain message or elicit a particular feeling or emotion. A word's **connotation** is the set of associations that the word calls to mind. For example, most people would prefer a "vintage automobile" to a "used car." A word's connotation can be positive, negative, or neutral.

Prewriting Reread the story, keeping an eye out for scenes that would be suitable for a song. For example, you might identify the opening scene or the scene where Sarita and Pepe dance. After you've selected a scene for your song, think about whether you want your scene to be happy, sad, or funny. Then jot down words that elicit the specific connotations that you are trying to convey.

Drafting As you write the lyrics to your song, capture the actions and mood of the moment in the story. Include some of the words you jotted down.

Revising Reread your draft. Make sure you've used words with connotations that will elicit the feelings you desire. If necessary, add details that strengthen the song's connection with the actions and mood of the moment in the story.

The Street of the Cañon ♦ 447

OBJECTIVES

1. To read, comprehend, and interpret a description and two poems
2. To relate a description and poems to personal experience
3. To engage the senses in reading
4. To identify the speaker
5. To build vocabulary in context and learn Latin terms used in English
6. To use *like* and *as* correctly
7. To write a monologue that grabs the readers' attention
8. To respond to the descriptive monologue and poems through writing, speaking and listening, and projects

SKILLS INSTRUCTION

Vocabulary:
Borrowed Words: Latin Terms

Grammar:
Correct Use of *Like* and *As*

Reading Strategy:
Engage the Senses

Literary Focus:
Speaker

Writing:
Grab Readers' Attention

Speaking and Listening:
Interview

Critical Viewing:
Connect; Analyze

PORTFOLIO OPPORTUNITIES

Writing: Description; Film Treatment; Biographical Sketch

Writing Mini-Lesson: Monologue Spoken by a Plant or Animal

Speaking and Listening: Speech; Interview

Projects: Presentation of Ancient Instrument; Multimedia Project

More About the Authors
Alexander Solzhenitsyn, exiled for treason by the Soviet Union in 1970, had his citizenship revoked in 1974. He lived in Switzerland for about two years and then settled in the United States in 1976.

Although **Henrik Ibsen** began his writing career as a poet, it was his plays that made him famous. In fact, he is known as the father of modern drama for introducing modern social problems into his plays in a realistic way.

Denise Levertov, born in Essex, England, was educated chiefly at home by her mother and the Schools Programs of British television. She emigrated to the United States and became a citizen in 1955.

Guide for Reading

Alexander Solzhenitsyn (1918–   )

Born in the Soviet Union, Alexander Solzhenitsyn (sōl´zhə nēt´sin) began to write poetry while imprisoned in a labor camp for the crime of criticizing Communist leader Joseph Stalin in 1945. His first book, *A Day in the Life of Ivan Denisovitch*—the story of an inmate in a Soviet labor camp—brought its author instant recognition, but its publication was banned in the Soviet Union. Despite his 1970 Nobel Prize for Literature, Solzhenitsyn was tried for treason and exiled after the publication in Paris of parts of *The Gulag Archipelago*. Only since 1991 has his work been available to the people of his homeland.

Henrik Ibsen (1828–1906)

It all started with poetry for Henrik Ibsen. Isolated on a small farm near the port town of Skien, Norway, young Henrik turned for solace to writing poetry. His first successful play, *Brand*, was in fact originally written as a narrative poem. It was his plays, however, that made him famous. His emphasis on character rather than the contrived plots that were popular at the time resulted in realistic plays such as *A Doll's House* and *Hedda Gabler*.

Denise Levertov (1923–1998)

When Denise Levertov moved to the United States from England in 1948, she became associated with the Black Mountain School, an experimental community of writers, painters, musicians, and dancers that thrived from 1933 to 1956. The Black Mountain poets, Levertov among them, began to change the rigid view of how a poem should read and look. Levertov has published a great many volumes of poetry, including *Relearning the Alphabet,* the 1966 collection in which "A Tree Telling of Orpheus" first appeared.

448 ◆ Expanding Horizons

◆ Build Vocabulary

BORROWED WORDS: LATIN TERMS
When Alexander Solzhenitsyn describes the terror of being caught in a violent thunderstorm while in the mountains, he mentions that, for only a second, he and his companions felt as if they were on *terra firma. Terra firma* (which means "solid earth") is one of many Latin phrases that have found their way unchanged into modern English.

WORD BANK
Before you read, preview this list of words from the selections.

terra firma
sultry
asunder

◆ Build Grammar Skills

CORRECT USE OF *LIKE* AND *AS*
A common usage error is to use *like* when we mean *as.*

Like, a preposition meaning "similar to" introduces a prepositional phrase—a preposition and a noun or pronoun.

Like the arrows of Sabaoth, the lightning flashes . . .

As, a subordinating conjunction, introduces a subordinate clause—a group of words that contains a subject and a verb but that cannot stand alone as a sentence.

. . . we forgot to be afraid of the lightning, the thunder, and the downpour, just *as* [not *like*] a droplet in the ocean has no fear of a hurricane.

Prentice Hall Literature Program Resources

REINFORCE / RETEACH / EXTEND
Selection Support Pages
Build Vocabulary: Latin Terms, p. 138
Build Grammar Skills: *Like* and *As,* p. 139
Reading Strategy: Engage the Senses, p. 140
Literary Focus: Speaker, p. 141

Strategies for Diverse Student Needs, p. 34

Beyond Literature
Career Connection: Meteorology, p. 34

Formal Assessment Selection Test, pp. 116–118; Assessment Resources Software

Alternative Assessment, p. 34

Writing and Language Transparencies
Writing Process Model 1, Reflective Essay, pp. 5–11

Resource Pro CD-ROM
"A Storm in the Mountains," "In the Orchard," "A Tree Telling of Orpheus"—includes all resource materials and customizable lesson plan

Listening to Literature Audiocassettes
"A Storm in the Mountains," "In the Orchard," "A Tree Telling of Orpheus"

A Storm in the Mountains ◆ In the Orchard
◆ A Tree Telling of Orpheus ◆

◆ *Literature and Your Life*

CONNECT YOUR EXPERIENCE

You dim the lights, put on your headphones, and pop in your favorite CD. That's it—you're taken to a place all its own, beyond the pressures of the daily world, a place that seems to be music itself.

The selections in this group show the transforming powers of nature and music. Connect with the sensations described and imagine what it feels like to be in the place the poet is writing about.

THEMATIC FOCUS: A LARGER WORLD

As you explore the beauties and the power of nature through these selections, you will expand your view of the natural world.

Journal Writing Write three sentences describing the last time you paused to examine something in nature. What was it, and how did it make you feel?

◆ Background for Understanding

LITERATURE

"A Tree Telling of Orpheus" is Denise Levertov's interpretation of the classic Orpheus myth. Orpheus' skill on the lyre (an ancient stringed instrument) was so great and his voice was so beautiful that trees were said to uproot themselves and follow him, rivers stopped flowing to listen to him, and wild beasts were made gentle by his music. In her *Mythology,* Edith Hamilton quotes one of the great Roman writers:

> In the deep still woods upon the Thracian mountains
> Orpheus with his singing lyre led the trees,
> Led the wild beasts of the wilderness.

◆ Literary Focus

SPEAKER

Each of these selections has a **speaker,** the imaginary voice assumed by the writer of a work. The speaker is the character—the poet, person, animal, or object—who says the work.

These selections present a range of speakers, each with a distinct personality. To enrich your understanding of what is being said, consider who might be speaking in each of these works and what you can tell about each speaker.

◆ Reading Strategy

ENGAGE THE SENSES

To fully appreciate poems with sensory images, you need to **engage your senses** as you read. This means allowing the poem to speak not just to your mind, but to your eyes, ears, and senses of touch, taste, and smell. For example, when the speaker of "In the Orchard" says "Brothers! there is better music / In the singing of the birds," he is counting on your sense of hearing (and your memory) to re-create the sound of that singing so you can experience and be moved by the image.

To help you engage your senses as you read, construct a chart, like the one below, of the five senses. Fill in as many sensory details as you can.

	"Storm"	"Orchard"	"Tree"
Sight			
Sound			
Smell			
Taste			
Touch			

Guide for Reading ◆ 449

Interest Grabber Read aloud the following passage from Alexander Solzhenitsyn's "A Storm in the Mountains": "It caught us one pitch-black night at the foot of the pass. We crawled out of our tents and ran for shelter as it came towards us over the ridge." Ask students to conjecture about what "It" might be. As they suggest possibilities, list them on the chalkboard. Tell them that the passage describes a storm in the mountains. Then have students brainstorm to make a list of comparisons they might use for different kinds of weather. *Responses may include a lamb, a dervish, a windbag, and so on.* Tell them that each of the selections they will read views nature as an entity with a life and voice of its own.

Customize for
More Advanced Students

The writers in this section have all used literature to explore social issues: political oppression (Solzhenitsyn), equality for women (Ibsen), and world peace (Levertov). Have more advanced students compile an anthology of poetry and other writings that explore social issues or current events that have particular meaning for them.

Customize for
English Language Learners

Use context clues and pictures to help these students determine the meaning of unfamiliar vocabulary such as *serpentine, primal, warblers, fruitage, sapling,* and *felled.*

Customize for
Visual/Spatial Learners

Encourage visual/spatial learners to picture the landscapes suggested by the descriptive language in one of the works in this selection and draw or collect photographs that illustrate them. They may use details they list in the sensory details chart on page 449.

Preparing for Standardized Tests

Reading and Vocabulary The Build Vocabulary lesson for this selection focuses on borrowed Latin Terms in English. Understanding Latin terms can help students in vocabulary and reading comprehension items on standardized tests, where they may come across terms such as *terra firma, incognito,* or *curriculum vitae.* For additional practice, use the Build Vocabulary page in **Selection Support,** p. 138.

Grammar and Language The Sentence Error portions of some standardized tests, such as the

SAT II, require students to recognize correct use of *like* and *as,* as in this example:

> Clouds veiled the moon like a filmy curtain covers a window. *(A)*
> (A) as a filmy curtain draws across the sky
> (B) like a window is covered by a filmy curtain
> (C) as a filmy curtain, which covers a window

The Build Grammar Skills lesson for this selection focuses on this topic. For additional practice, use the Build Grammar Skills page on Correct Use of *Like* and *As,* p. 139, in **Selection Support.**

Develop Understanding

One-Minute Insight The selections in this group explore different aspects of nature. In "A Storm in the Mountains," Solzhenitsyn describes a raging storm so overwhelming that individuals surrender to it, transcending their fear to feel at one with the powerful phenomenon—and with all of nature.

◆ Literary Focus

❶ Speaker Ask students what information is revealed about the speaker in this first paragraph. *Readers can tell that the speaker is camping outdoors in a tent, and that he or she is not alone, since the first-person plural pronouns we, us, and our are used.*

◆ Critical Thinking

❷ Interpret Have students rephrase this sentence to express, in their own words, what the speaker is seeing. If they are not sure, have them read the next paragraph before answering. *The speaker is seeing tall trees and mountain peaks illuminated only for a split second when a bolt of lightning flashes.*

◆ Reading Strategy

❸ Engage the Senses Ask students which senses they engage in reading this passage. *The sound of thunder engages the sense of hearing; the lightning flashes engage the sense of sight.*

◆ Build Grammar Skills

❹ Correct Use of *Like* and *As* Point out the word *like* in this passage. Ask students to explain why it is used here rather than *as*. *"Like a living thing" is a prepositional phrase, not a subordinate clause with a subject and verb.*

◆ Build Grammar Skills

❺ Correct Use of *Like* and *As* Have students identify the subordinate clause in this passage. Ask them to find the subordinating conjunction. Then ask why *as* is used here instead of *like*. *The subordinate clause is "just as a droplet in the ocean has no fear of a hurricane." The subordinating conjunction is as.*

450

A Storm in the Mountains

Alexander Solzhenitsyn
Translated by Michael Glenny

❶ It caught us one pitch-black night at the foot of the pass. We crawled out of our tents and ran for shelter as it came towards us over the ridge.

Everything was black—no peaks, no valleys, no horizon to be seen, only the searing flashes of lightning separating darkness from light, and the gigantic peaks of Belaya-Kaya and Djuguturlyuchat[1] looming up out of the night. The huge black pine trees around us seemed as high as the mountains themselves. For a split

❷ second we felt ourselves on terra firma; then once more everything would be plunged into darkness and chaos.

The lightning moved on, brilliant light alternating with pitch blackness, flashing white, then pink, then violet, the mountains and pines always springing back in the same place, their hugeness filling us with awe; yet when they disappeared we could not believe that they had ever existed.

The voice of the thunder filled the gorge,

❸ drowning the ceaseless roar of the rivers. Like the arrows of Sabaoth,[2] the lightning flashes rained down on the peaks, then split up into serpentine streams as though bursting into

❹ spray against the rock face, or striking and then shattering like a living thing.

As for us, we forgot to be afraid of the lightning, the thunder, and the downpour, just as a droplet

❺ in the ocean has no fear of a hurricane. Insignificant yet grateful, we became part of this world—a primal world in creation before our eyes.

---

1. **Belaya-Kaya** (bye lǐ′ə kǐ′ə) **and Djuguturlyuchat** (djōō gōō toor lyōō′ chət): Russian mountains.
2. **Sabaoth** (sab′ ā äth′): Biblical word for "armies."

◆ Build Vocabulary

terra firma (ter′ ə fur′ mə): Latin for "solid earth."

450 ◆ Expanding Horizons

Block Scheduling Strategies

Consider these suggestions to take advantage of extended class time:

- Have students listen to the audiocassette "A Storm in the Mountains," focusing on how the tension builds throughout and then releases in the last paragraph.
- To have students engage their senses as they read, refer them to the Reading Strategy explained on page 449. Have them complete a sensory image chart like the one on page 449.
- Have students work in groups to answer the

Reading Strategy questions on page 458.

- Introduce the concept of speaker. As students read, have them consider who the speaker is in each selection. You may follow up with the Literary Focus: Speaker page in **Selection Support,** p. 141.
- Have students complete the Writing Mini-Lesson on page 459. Before they get started, have a class discussion about the authors' use of sensory details. Suggest students use sensory details in their monologues.

In the Orchard

Henrik Ibsen
Translated by Sir Edmund Gosse

In the sunny orchard closes,[1]
  While the warblers sing and swing,
Care not whether blustering Autumn
  Break the promises of Spring!

5 Rose and white, the apple blossom
  Hides you from the sultry sky—
Let it flutter, blown and scatter'd,
  On the meadows by-and-by!

Will you ask about the fruitage
10 In the season of the flowers?
Will you murmur, will you question,
  Count the run of weary hours?
Will you let the scarecrow clapping
  Drown all happy sounds and words?
15 Brothers! there is better music
  In the singing of the birds.

From your heavy-laden garden
  Will you hunt the mellow thrush;
He will play you for protection
20 With his crown-song's liquid rush.
O but you will win the bargain,

Though your fruit be spare and late,
For remember Time is flying
  And will shut the garden gate.

25 With my living, with my singing,
  I will tear the hedges down.
Sweep the grass and heap the blossom!
  Let it shrivel, pale and brown!
Swing the wicket![2] Sheep and cattle,
30 Let them graze among the best!
I broke off the flowers; what matter
  Who may revel with the rest?

---

1. **closes:** Enclosed place, as a farmyard.
2. **wicket:** Small door or gate.

◆ Build Vocabulary

sultry (sul ́ trē) *adj.*: Oppressively hot and moist; sweltering

---

▲ Critical Viewing Explain how the photograph on this page suggests the speaker's sense of celebration. [Connect]

A Storm in the Mountains/In the Orchard ◆ 451

One-Minute Insight Ibsen uses the seasons spring and autumn as symbols of youth and old age—and ultimately, death. His poem urges readers to enjoy the budding blossoms of spring without thinking about the withered leaves of fall.

◆ Literary Focus

6 Speaker Point out to students that the first stanza of the poem is an imperative sentence. What is the speaker telling readers not to do? What does this tell about the speaker? *The speaker is telling readers not to let thoughts of autumn ruin their enjoyment of spring; in other words, not to let worrying about the future spoil enjoyment of the present. The speaker is someone who feels qualified to give advice about life—perhaps an older person or a philosopher.*

◆ Reading Strategy

7 Engage the Senses Have students identify the sense engaged by these lines. *These lines engage the sense of sight.*

◆ Critical Thinking

8 Interpret Ask students to identify in this passage symbols of spring and symbols of autumn or late summer. *Symbols of spring are "flowers" and "singing of the birds"; symbols of autumn/late summer are "fruitage" and "scarecrow."*

◆ Reading Strategy

9 Engage the Senses Ask students to identify the lines in this stanza that engage the sense of hearing. *"He will play you for protection/With his crown-song's liquid rush."*

◆ Critical Thinking

10 Interpret Ask students: What does the garden represent? What happens when the gate is shut? *The garden represents life, youth, happiness; death shuts the gate when life has ended.*

► Critical Viewing ◄

11 Connect The lavish profusion of daffodils and apple blossoms suggests the speaker's message to celebrate life in its fullness.

Speaking and Listening Mini-Lesson

Interview

This mini-lesson supports the second Speaking and Listening activity in the Idea Bank on page 459.

Introduce the Concept Establish that a good interviewer avoids questions that can be answered by "yes" or "no." The best questions begin with "Who," "What," "Where," "When," "Why," and "How."

Develop Background Suggest that students re-read "A Storm in the Mountains," putting themselves in the speaker's place. As they plan the

questions and answers, suggest they consider questions like the following:
Who was there when the storm broke out? What did they do? What did they see? How did they feel?

Apply the Information Have partners work together to create questions and answers and then stage the interview for the class.

Assess the Outcome Have students use page 118 in *Alternative Assessment*, Peer Assessment: Speaker/Speech.

One-Minute Insight Denise Levertov uses the point of view of a tree to describe the stirrings of the emotions created by the music of nature. Through a metaphor based on ancient mythology she presents an enchanted view of nature.

◆ **Literary Focus**

❶ Speaker Have students read this passage and identify the speaker of the poem. *The speaker is a tree, as indicated by the words, "the leaves of my brothers remained outstretched. . . ."*

◆ **Reading Strategy**

❷ Engage the Senses Ask students: Which of your senses is engaged by these lines? Which words appeal to this sense? *The words and phrases "tingle," "fire," and "drying and curling" appeal to the sense of touch.*

◆ **Build Grammar Skills**

❸ Correct Use of *Like* and *As* Point out the two uses of the word *like* in this passage and ask students to explain its function. *"Like the beaked face of a bird" and "like a flower's" are prepositional phrases. Like correctly functions as a preposition in these situations.*

❹ Clarification Point out that the tree sees Orpheus with his lyre. Explain that in Greek mythology, Orpheus was the son of Oeagrus, the king of Thrace, and Calliope, the muse of epic poetry. Apollo, the god of the sun and also the god of music, gave Orpheus a lyre, and the music he played on it could enchant wild beasts and make trees and rocks dance.

◆ **Critical Thinking**

❺ Analyze Ask students: What is the speaker describing? Why do you think Levertov chose to describe it in this way? What is the ripple? *The words, "From this,/when he touched it, and from his voice/. . . came the ripple" let the reader know the speaker is describing a stringed musical instrument (a lyre). "Some cut branch" and "strands of a vine" refer to the frame and strings of the instrument. Levertov is describing the instrument as it might be seen from the point of view of a tree. The "ripple" is music.*

A Tree Telling of Orpheus

Denise Levertov

White dawn. Stillness.　　When the rippling began
　　I took it for sea-wind, coming to our valley with rumors
　　of salt, of treeless horizons. But the white fog
didn't stir; the leaves of my brothers remained outstretched,
5 unmoving.
　　　　　　Yet the rippling drew nearer—and then
my own outermost branches began to tingle, almost as if
fire had been lit below them, too close, and their twig-tips
were drying and curling.
　　　　　　Yet I was not afraid, only
10 　　　　　　deeply alert.

I was the first to see him, for I grew
　　　　　out on the pasture slope, beyond the forest.
He was a man, it seemed: the two
15 moving stems, the short trunk, the two
arm-branches, flexible, each with five leafless
　　　　　　　　　　twigs at their ends,
and the head that's crowned by brown or gold grass,
bearing a face not like the beaked face of a bird,
20 　　　　more like a flower's.
　　　　　　　　　　He carried a burden made of
some cut branch bent while it was green,
strands of a vine tight-stretched across it. From this,
when he touched it, and from his voice
25 which unlike the wind's voice had no need of our
leaves and branches to complete its sound,
　　　　　　　　　came the ripple,
But it was now no longer a ripple (he had come near and
stopped in my first shadow) it was a wave that bathed me
30 　　　　　as if rain
　　　　　　　　　rose from below and around me
　　　　　instead of falling.
And what I felt was no longer a dry tingling:

452 ◆ Expanding Horizons

▲ **Critical Viewing** What details in this photo indicate the dance described in the poem? [Analyze]

Cultural Connection

Greek Mythology
Tell students the story of Orpheus.

After the death of his young wife Eurydice, Orpheus did what no other mortal had ever done—he descended to the underworld and, by charming Hades, the lord of the dead, with his enchanting music, convinced him to allow Eurydice to return to the world of the living. Orpheus was permitted to lead Euridyice out of the underworld, but was not to look back at her. Because he was so eager to make sure Eurydice was behind him, he looked back a moment too soon, and she was lost forever.

Grief stricken, Orpheus wandered through the wild country of Thrace, always playing his lyre, the rocks and trees his only companions. When a band of Maenads (followers of Dionysus, god of wine in Greek mythology) became frenzied by his music, they killed Orpheus and flung his head into a river. The Muses buried Orpheus' body at the foot of Mount Olympus, but his head and his lyre were carried across the sea.

A Tree Telling of Orpheus ◆ 453

▶Critical Viewing◀

❻ Analyze Students may point out features of the tree that reflect movement, such as the sinewy look of the trunk and the graceful, arm-like lines of the branches.

Customize for
Less Proficient Readers
Have these students make a list of words that describe the tree's feelings as they are revealed in the poem. They may then organize these words in a flow chart to indicate the changes as they evolve in the poem.

Customize for
Visual/Spatial Learners
These students may benefit from creating a story board for the poem, chronicling the scenes in the tree's "story."

♦ Humanities: Photography

Photographs of trees illustrate this poem. Students can identify details of the photographs that evoke the shape or movement of a dancing human body. For example, the photograph on this page can help them picture the trees in motion.

Use the following questions for discussion.

1. What features of these trees in the photographs give them the appearance of movement and life? *Students can describe the curve of the branches, the interplay of light and shadow, and the contrasting textures.*

2. How do the photographs of real trees influence your feelings about the poem? How does the effect of photographs differ from that of illustrations? *Students may say that having real trees as a visual reference helps them visualize what is happening in the poem. They may say photographs were a better choice than illustrations, because the real trees make the poem seem more real.*

453

◆ **Build Grammar Skills**

❶ **Correct Use of *Like* and *As***
Have students identify the subordinate clause introduced by the conjunction *as*. *The clause is "as he sang."*

◆ **Reading Strategy**

❷ **Engage the Senses** Ask students: How does the poet blend two senses in these lines? *Levertov blends the sense of touch with the sense of hearing by mentioning the tree's bark (skin) and music in the same stanza.*

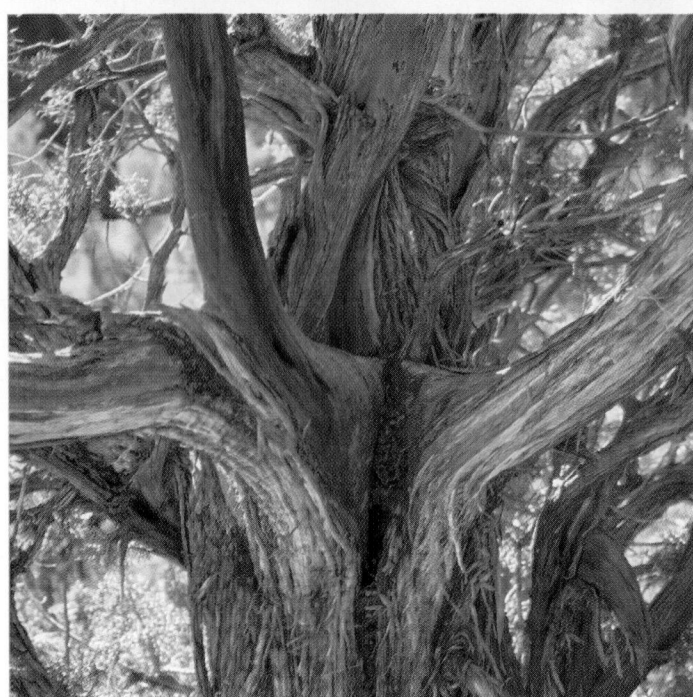

> ❶ I seemed to be singing as he sang, I seemed to know
> 35   what the lark knows; all my sap
>   was mounting towards the sun that by now
>   had risen, the mist was rising, the grass
> was drying, yet my roots felt music moisten them
> deep under earth.
>
> 40   He came still closer, leaned on my trunk:
> ❷   the bark thrilled like a leaf still-folded.
> Music! There was no twig of me not
>   trembling with joy and fear.
>
> Then as he sang
> 45 it was no longer sounds only that made the music:
> he spoke, and as no tree listens I listened, and language
>   came into my roots
>   out of the earth,
>   into my bark
> 50   out of the air,
>   into the pores of my greenest shoots
>   gently as dew
> and there was no word he sang but I knew its meaning.

454 ◆ *Expanding Horizons*

 Cross-Curricular Connection: Art

Orpheus

Explain to students that the image of Orpheus with his lyre is a favorite subject in classical art. He is often pictured with other mythological figures, such as Bacchus, the Roman god of wine, and the Bacchantes, women who followed Bacchus. (Equivalents in Greek mythology are Dionysus and Maenads.)

Have students look for examples of Orpheus in art in fine art resource materials in a library. They may collect illustrations and make a presention of them to the class.

Have students use questions like these to prompt discussion:

1. Why do you think the artist chose to depict Orpheus at this moment? *Students may say that the moment something is*

about to happen is more tense than the moment it does happen.

2. How would you compare the image of Orpheus in a painting with that of the poem? *A tree in the painting could be the tree in the poem; Orpheus playing his lyre could be leading the trees in their dance.*

He told of journeys,
        of where sun and moon go while we stand in dark,
    of an earth-journey he dreamed he would take some day
55 deeper than roots . . .
He told of the dreams of man, wars, passions, griefs,
      and I, a tree, understood words—ah, it seemed
60 my thick bark would split like a sapling's that
               grew too fast in the spring
when a late frost wounds it.

                       Fire he sang,
that trees fear, and I, a tree, rejoiced in its flames.
65 New buds broke forth from me though it was full summer.
     As though his lyre[1] (now I knew its name)
       were both frost and fire, its chords flamed
up to the crown of me.
           I was seed again.
70   I was fern in the swamp.
               I was coal.

And at the heart of my wood
(so close I was to becoming man or a god)
     there was a kind of silence, a kind of sickness,
75   something akin to what men call boredom,
                       something

(the poem descended a scale, a stream over stones)
      that gives to a candle a coldness
         in the midst of its burning, he said.

80 It was then,
      when in the blaze of his power that
             reached me and changed me
     I thought I should fall my length,
that the singer began
85   to leave me.   Slowly
    moved from my noon shadow
                to open light,
words leaping and dancing over his shoulders
back to me
90   rivery sweep of lyre-tones becoming
slowly again
      ripple.
And I
     in terror ↓

---

1. **lyre** (līr) *n*.: Small stringed instrument of the harp family, used by the ancient Greeks to accompany singers.

A Tree Telling of Orpheus ◆ 455

Cross-Curricular Connection: Music

Music History

When students think of music, they may focus on their favorite CDs or Top 40 radio station without considering how powerful a force music can be. Music plays a central role in cultures worldwide and may be used to educate and inspire as well as to entertain.

For example, music was seen as a powerful tool during the French revolution.

Agents of the new regime traveled through the countryside, teaching schoolchildren short, patriotic tunes that were easy to sing. When huge groups gathered in the streets for political rallies, there was no public address system; the politicians relied on the singing of the children to spread the word and tap emotions to sway the population.

Hymns, chants, folk songs, work songs, lullabies, and nursery rhymes have all been used to pass along information, share ideas, teach morals, define political ideology, and forge cultural ties.

Invite students to explore the power of music in "A Tree Telling of Orpheus" and the role it has played in their own lives. Have them consider these questions: What songs do they all know? What songs explore the history they share? How do these songs shape the way they see the world?

❶ Ask what the speaker is moved to do, inspired by Orpheus' music. *The tree uproots itself to follow Orpheus and is joined by the other trees of the forest.*

◆ Reading Strategy

❷ Engage the Senses Point out how, once again, Levertov blends the senses of touch and hearing. Ask students: Which parts of this passage engage the sense of touch? Which engage the sense of hearing? *References to pain, to wrenching, tearing, and pulling engage the sense of touch. "But the music! The music reached us" engages the sense of hearing.*

◆ *Literature and Your Life*

❸ Ask students to connect their own lives to the poem by thinking of music that makes them feel like dancing, or at least tapping a foot and moving to the rhythm.

◆ Literary Focus

❹ Speaker Ask students to estimate how old the speaker of the poem is. How can they tell from this passage? *Orpheus led the trees to a grassy knoll. When he left them there, they took root, creating what is now an "ancient grove," implying that the tree is now very old, or ancient.*

95   but not in doubt of
                 what I must do
in anguish, in haste,
            wrenched from the earth root after root,
the soil heaving and cracking, the moss tearing <u>asunder</u>—
100 and behind me the others: my brothers
forgotten since dawn. In the forest
they too had heard,
and were pulling their roots in pain
out of a thousand years' layers of dead leaves,
105   rolling the rocks away,
               breaking themselves
                     out of
                 their depths.
You would have thought we would lose the sound of the lyre,
110   of the singing
so dreadful the storm-sounds were, where there was no storm,
           no wind but the rush of our
        branches moving, our trunks breasting the air.
           But the music!
115   The music reached us.

Clumsily,
        stumbling over our own roots,
               rustling our leaves
                  in answer,
120 we moved, we followed.
All day we followed, up hill and down.
            We learned to dance,
for he would stop, where the ground was flat,
              and words he said
125 taught us to leap and to wind in and out
around one another   in figures   the lyre's measure designed.
The singer
        laughed till he wept to see us, he was so glad.
                At sunset
130 we came to this place I stand in, this knoll[2]
with its ancient grove that was bare grass then.
        In the last light of the day his song became
farewell.
        He stilled our longing.
135   He sang our sun-dried roots back into earth,
watered them: all-night rain of music so quiet
           we could almost
        not hear it in the

---

2. **knoll** (nōl) *n.*: Mound.

◆ Build Vocabulary
asunder (ə sun′ dər) *adv.*: Into pieces or parts

456 ◆ *Expanding Horizons*

Beyond the Selection

FURTHER READING

Other Work by the Authors
One Day in the Life of Ivan Denisovitch, Alexander Solzhenitsyn
The First Circle, Alexander Solzhenitsyn
A Doll's House, Henrik Ibsen
Peer Gynt, Henrik Ibsen
The Cold Spring, and Other Poems, Denise Levertov
Footprints, Denise Levertov

Other Works About the Beauty and Power of Nature
Pilgrim at Tinker Creek, Annie Dillard
The Sea Around Us, Rachel Carson
"Birches," Robert Frost
"Ode to the West Wind," Percy Bysshe Shelley
"To Autumn," John Keats
    We suggest that you preview these works before recommending them to students.

moonless dark.

140　By dawn he was gone.

　　　　　　　　We have stood here since,

in our new life.

　　　　We have waited.

　　　　　　　　　　He does not return.

145　It is said he made his earth-journey, and lost

what he sought.

　　　　It is said they felled him

and cut up his limbs for firewood.

　　　　　　　　　　And it is said

150　his head still sang and was swept out to sea singing.

Perhaps he will not return.

　　　　　　　　But what we have lived

comes back to us.

　　　　We see more.

155　　　　　　　　We feel, as our rings increase,

something that lifts our branches, that stretches our furthest

　　　　　　　　　　　　　　　　　leaf-tips

further.

　　　　The wind, the birds,

160　　　　　　　　　do not sound poorer but clearer,

recalling our agony, and the way we danced.

The music!

❺

❺ Clarification Explain that Orpheus' "earth-journey" was his journey to the underworld to rescue Eurydice; the rest of the passage refers to Orpheus' death, according to the myth, at the hands of the Maenads, or Bacchantes.

Guide for Responding

◆ Literature and Your Life

Reader's Response Which selection gives you the most unexpected view of nature? Explain.

Thematic Focus How do these views of nature broaden the way you look at the natural world?

☑ Check Your Comprehension

1. Describe the setting of "A Storm in the Mountains."
2. In which season is "In the Orchard" set? How do you know?
3. By what power does Orpheus lead the trees?
4. What does the tree say happens to Orpheus?

◆ Critical Thinking
INTERPRET

1. Why does the speaker in "A Storm ..." feel on terra firma for only a split second? **[Interpret]**
2. Explain the significance of the scarecrow in the second stanza of "In the Orchard." **[Interpret]**
3. How well does Ibsen's use of sensory images communicate the meaning of "In the Orchard"? **[Assess]**
4. What details in "A Tree ..." indicate that Orpheus is making music? **[Synthesize]**
5. What lasting effect does Orpheus have on the trees? **[Infer]**

EXTEND

6. Explain how one of these poems might be used in a public-service announcement about protecting the environment. **[Career Link]**

A Tree Telling of Orpheus ◆ 457

Reinforce and Extend

Answers
◆ Literature and Your Life

Reader's Response Students may say that "A Tree Telling of Orpheus" is the most unusual in its combination of mythology and a tree speaking. Others may say that the personified "Storm in the Mountains" is the more unusual.

Thematic Focus Viewing a subject from different perspectives broadens your understanding of it.

☑ Check Your Comprehension

1. The setting is the foot of a mountain pass, or the narrow valley between high-peaked mountains.
2. "In the Orchard" is set in spring, when the apple trees are in blossom.
3. Orpheus leads the tree by the power of his singing and playing on his lute.
4. He was killed and his head was swept out to sea, singing.

◆ Critical Thinking

1. Only when the lightning illuminates his surroundings does he experience the earth beneath him.
2. The scarecrow is an image of the coming winter, the end of the fruiting season and also death.
3. Most students will feel the images effectively convey the meaning of growth and death.
4. The references to voice and singing indicate that Orpheus is making music.
5. The trees are more alive than they were before they heard the music.
6. Students may cite any of the poems to argue for preserving nature.

Beyond the Selection

INTERNET

Students can explore the following Web sites to learn more about the writers and their work: Solzhenitsyn: **http://www.empirenet.com/ ~rdaeley/authors/solzhenitsyn.html** Ibsen: **http://odin.edp.no/ud/nornytt/ibsen. html** Levertov: **http://www.keplers.com/theme16. shtml**

The following Web sites are for further exploration of the Orpheus myth: **http://cdr.stanford. edu/PENS/pandp/vonkrogh/5704.html http://cdr.stanford.edu/PENS/pandp/lam/ 10451.html**

　Please be aware, however, that sites may have changed from the time we published this information. We *strongly recommend* that you preview the sites before you send students to them.

◆ Reading Strategy

1. They call upon sight and touch.
2. The image of time flying and shutting the gate underscores the "seize the day" theme.
3. The image of the coldness in the candle (a combination of touch and sight) effectively suggests the lifelessness of the sickness of boredom, from which Orpheus' song has rescued the grove of trees.

◆ Build Vocabulary

Using Latin Terms
1. ad hoc; 2. caveat emptor;
3. de facto; 4. status quo

Using the Word Bank
1. High humidity and temperatures in the region will produce sultry weather for the next few days.
2. The tremor split highways and buildings asunder.
3. View the magnificent volcano from terra firma in our earth-quake-proof lodge.

◆ Literary Focus

1. The speaker is addressing a gardener or worker in an orchard who is concerned with the produce rather than the beauty of the garden.
2. The speaker could be the poet or the wind, as in "With my living, with my singing" and "I broke off the flowers...."
3. The image of a tree so moved as to uproot itself and dance is a dramatic metaphor for the power of passion.

◆ Build Grammar Skills

1. as; 2. like; 3. like; 4. as; 5. as

Writing Application
1. The leaves ripple in the wind as waves do in the ocean.
2. Orpheus' trees move to the sound of his music like teenagers flock to a rock concert.

Guide for Responding (continued)

◆ Reading Strategy

ENGAGE YOUR SENSES
Sensory details in a poem or a description allow you to enter a work completely. **Engaging your senses** as you read helps you to experience the sights, sounds, smells, textures, and tastes. For example, images such as "a wave that bathed me/as if rain/rose from below and around me" from "A Tree Telling of Orpheus" draw upon your sense of touch to coax you into experiencing the sensation just as the tree did.

1. What two senses do Solzhenitsyn's words "the searing flashes of lightning" call upon?
2. Which image in "In the Orchard" made you most "sense the meaning" of the poem, and why?
3. From your chart, choose a sensory detail from the poem "A Tree Telling of Orpheus," and explain why it is important to the poem.

◆ Build Vocabulary Skills

USING LATIN TERMS
The following list gives some Latin terms, and their English definitions, that have found their way, unchanged, into English. Fill in the blanks below with the correct Latin term.
   ad hoc: for a specific purpose
   caveat emptor: let the buyer beware
   status quo: the existing state of things
   de facto: in reality
1. The school board assembled a(an) ___?___ committee to handle budget issues.
2. A good slogan for those who purchase items from street vendors might be ___?___.
3. Though Kim was editor of the school paper, everyone knew that Ms. Lao was the ___?___ editor.
4. The rest of the group decided it would be easier to maintain the ___?___

USING THE WORD BANK
On your paper, respond to the numbered sentences using words from the Word Bank.
1. Write a weather forecast using the word *sultry.*
2. Use the word *asunder* to describe the effects of an earthquake.
3. Use the term *terra firma* in a passage from a travel journal.

◆ Literary Focus

SPEAKER
Even with no conversation, poems can sometimes seem like a dialogue between the **speaker,** or voice telling the poem, and the person (or thing) being addressed. Often a poet chooses to speak directly to you, the reader, but sometimes he or she will speak to a character or object in the poem.
1. Whom is the speaker addressing in "In the Orchard"? Give evidence from the poem to support your answer.
2. Among the following, who is the most likely speaker of "In the Orchard"—a tree, the wind, the poet, a song? Explain your choice.
3. For what reason might Levertov have had a tree be the speaker of "A Tree Telling of Orpheus"?

◆ Build Grammar Skills

CORRECT USE OF *LIKE* AND *AS*
Both *like* and *as* can be used in making comparisons. When writing, use *like* as the preposition in a prepositional phrase that compares one thing with another. Do not use *like* as a conjunction to introduce a subordinate clause (a group of words that contains a subject and a verb but cannot stand alone as a sentence).

Practice Write these sentences in your notebook, replacing the blanks with *like* or *as.*
1. ... my own outermost branches began to tingle, almost ___?___ if/fire had been lit below them ...
2. ... the bark thrilled ___?___ a leaf still-folded.
3. ... it seemed my thick bark would split ___?___ a sapling's ...
4. ... into the pores of my greenest shoots/ gently ___?___ dew ...
5. The poet wrote ___?___ a tree would speak.

Writing Application On your paper, follow the directions to write a sentence for each numbered item. Use the word indicated in parentheses.
1. Compare the way the wind moves with the way the ocean moves. (as)
2. Compare Orpheus' effect on the trees with the way people react to music stars today. (like)

Build Your Portfolio

 ## Idea Bank

Writing

1. **Description** From the point of view of a third-person observer, write a description of a tree in a severe storm. Use strong images to engage your readers' senses.

2. **Film Treatment** You are pitching a three-scene film based on the myth of Orpheus to a film producer. Describe what will happen in each scene.

3. **Biographical Sketch** Write a biographical sketch on Russian writer Alexander Solzhenitsyn.

Speaking and Listening

4. **Speech** Deliver a brief speech in which you introduce Nobel Prize-winner Alexander Solzhenitsyn to an audience. **[Social Studies Link]**

5. **Interview** With a partner, role-play a television interview with the speaker of "A Storm in the Mountains." Ask questions about the speaker's observations and feelings about events described in the work. **[Performing Arts Link]**

Projects

6. **Presentation of Ancient Instrument** The lyre that Orpheus plays is one of the world's most ancient stringed instruments. Create a diagram that shows the construction of a lyre. If possible, find recordings of lyre music to play for the class. **[Social Studies Link; Music Link]**

7. **Multimedia Project** The Black Mountain School, which Denise Levertov attended, had an exceptional influence on the development of the arts in America. Gather materials—audio- and videotapes, poems, photos—and give a multimedia presentation about this school. **[Art Link]**

 ## Writing Mini-Lesson

Monologue Spoken by a Plant or Animal

A **monologue** is a long speech delivered by one person, without interruption from other people. A monologue may be spoken in the presence of others and may or may not reveal what the speaker really thinks or feels. "A Tree Telling of Orpheus" could be read as a monologue by a tree. Open your imagination and write a monologue from the perspective of a plant or an animal.

Writing Skills Focus: Grab Readers' Attention

Don't bury your most stylish line or interesting fact deep within your monologue. Your audience might walk out before you get to it! **Grab** their **attention** with a strong, controversial statement, a joke, or an exceptionally curious fact. Here's the beginning of a monologue spoken by a queen ant to its worker ants:

> You pay homage to me every hour of your miserable, sniveling lives, but do you think my life is a bed of roses?

This disagreeable speaker immediately raises a question in your mind: Why is her life not a "bed of roses"?

Prewriting Establish a speaker and a situation. After all, your plant or animal must speak *about* something. Decide what the speaker wants to say about the situation, and jot down main points or key phrases.

Drafting In the monologue, your speaker will respond to a situation in its life; it should do so with emotion. Through its emotion, your speaker will communicate its personality and attitude to the audience.

Revising Ask a classmate whether the beginning of your monologue is attention-grabbing, if the "voice" of your speaker is consistent throughout, and if the speaker's emotion is communicated. If necessary, go back and revise to strengthen these areas.

A Storm in the Mountains/In the Orchard/A Tree Telling of Orpheus ◆ 459

 ## Idea Bank

Customizing for *Performance Levels*
Following are suggestions for matching Idea Bank topics with your students' performance levels:
Less Advanced Students: 1, 5, 7
Average Students: 2, 4, 6
More Advanced Students: 3, 4, 6

Customizing for *Learning Modalities*
Following are suggestions for matching Idea Bank topics with your students' learning modalities:
Visual/Spatial: 1, 2, 7
Verbal/Linguistic: 3, 4, 5
Musical/Rhythmic: 6

 ## Writing Mini-Lesson

Refer students to the Writing Handbook, page 965, for instruction on the writing process, and page 967 for further information on Creative Writing

Writing and Language Transparencies Use the Writing Process Model 1: Reflective Essay to guide students through the writing process.

 ## Writer's Solution

Writing Lab CD-ROM
Have students complete the tutorial on Creative Writing. Follow these steps:
1. Encourage students to use the word bin featuring words that describe emotional responses.
2. Allow time for students to draft on the computer.
3. Tell students to review the tips for peer reviewing.
4. Suggest that students use the Guidelines for Publishing and Presenting to help them plan a presentation of their monologue.

Sourcebook
Have students use Chapter 6, Creative Writing (pp. 164–193), for additional support. The chapter includes specific instruction on using vivid verbs (p. 192).

✓ ASSESSMENT OPTIONS

Formal Assessment, Selection Test, pp. 116–118, and Assessment Resources Software. The selection test is designed so that it can be easily customized to the performance levels of your students. *Alternative Assessment,* p. 34, includes options for less advanced students, more advanced students, visual/spatial learners, musical/rhythmic learners, interpersonal learners, and bodily/kinesthetic learners.

PORTFOLIO ASSESSMENT
Use the following rubrics in the *Alternative Assessment* booklet to assess student writing:
Description: Description Rubric, p. 97
Film Treatment: Summary Rubric, p. 98
Biographical Sketch: Description Rubric, p. 97
Writing Mini-Lesson: Fictional Narrative Rubric, p. 95

Before students begin, review the following key characteristics of a firsthand biography:

- It is a narrative about a person with whom the writer has had direct experience. This person is called the subject.

- Although the narrative can be about the entire life of the subject, it usually focuses on one particular incident.

- The relationship between the writer and his or her subject allows for personal insights not found in biographies based solely on research.

You may want to create a scoring rubric for a firsthand biography using the General Rubric, p. 93 in *Alternative Assessment,* to make students aware before they begin of the criteria on which they will be evaluated. You may include the additional points outlined on page 462.

Refer students to the Writing Handbook, page 965, for instruction in the writing process, and page 967 for further information on narration.

Writing Lab CD-ROM

If your students have access to computers, you may want to have them work on the tutorial on Narration to complete all or part of their firsthand biographies. Follow these steps:
1. Have students review the interactive model of a firsthand biography.
2. Students can look at the examples written for different audiences.
3. Have students draft on the computer.
4. Suggest students use the language variety checker.
5. Have students review the Proofreading Checklist.

Sourcebook

Students can find additional support, including topic ideas, models, audience and purpose profiles, and graphic organizers, in the chapter on Narration (pp. 30–61).

Firsthand Biography

Writing Process Workshop

In this unit, you've met some interesting characters—both fictional and real—from dashing Pepe Gonzalez to the famous Anthony Quinn. Choose someone you know, and write a **firsthand biography** of him or her. A firsthand biography is a narrative about a person—the subject—with whom you have had direct experience. A firsthand biography can be about the entire life of the subject or it may focus on an important episode or period in the subject's life. Your relationship with your subject should give you insights not found in biographies based solely on research.

The following skills, introduced in this section's Writing Mini-Lessons, will help you write an interesting firsthand biography.

Writing Skills Focus

▶ **Grab your reader's attention** at the beginning with a startling quotation or interesting anecdote. (See p. 459.)
▶ Like other stories, a biography should have a **beginning, middle,** and **end.** (See p. 437.)
▶ **Choose words with appropriate connotations**. For example, when describing a person, the word *skinny* has a different connotation from the word *lean*.(See p. 447.)

The following excerpt from Truman Capote's *A Christmas Story* illustrates these skills.

MODEL FROM LITERATURE

from *A Christmas Memory* by Truman Capote

① The connotation of the phrase *pitifully hunched* creates sympathy by conjuring up the image of a frail, old woman.

② When the writer says that "We are each other's best friend," he grabs the reader's attention, since the ages of the two are so far apart.

She is wearing tennis shoes and a shapeless gray sweater over a summery calico dress. She is small and sprightly, like a bantam hen; but due to a long youthful illness her shoulders are pitifully hunched ①. Her face is remarkable—not unlike Lincoln's, craggy like that, and tinted by the sun and wind; but it is delicate too, finely boned, and her eyes are sherry-colored and timid. "Oh my," she exclaims, her breath smoking the windowpane, "it's fruitcake weather!"

The person to whom she is speaking is myself. I am seven; she is sixty-something. We are each other's best friend. ②

460 ◆ *Expanding Horizons*

Cross-Curricular Connection: Social Studies

Students can use their firsthand biographies to explore larger social issues as well. For example, if a student is writing about a friend from South Africa, he or she might also discuss apartheid and how it affected the subject's life. Closer to home, if a student is writing about an adult who happened to have lost his or her job recently, the student may wish to explore briefly such issues as corporate downsizing or factory closings caused by the changing American economy.

Prewriting

Choose a Topic Think about a person whom you admire. It might be a close friend, a student or teacher you admire, a favorite relative, or someone who has done something interesting. Make a list of several possibilities, and then consider which one you know best. Choose that person as the subject of your firsthand biography.

Consider Your Audience Before you begin to write, think about the people for whom you are writing. Consider your audience's interests and background, and make sure your details and language are appropriate for such an audience. The following checklist will help you define your audience:

▶ Who are your readers—classmates, relatives, or a teacher?

▶ How much does your audience know about your subject?

▶ Is your audience familiar with words or phrases that your subject may use or have used?

▶ If you wish to convey a message, how do you think your readers will feel about it?

Drafting

Reveal Your Subject You can reveal important aspects of your subject's personality or life either directly or indirectly. When you reveal the character of your subject directly, you openly state the personality traits of the subject. To reveal your subject's character indirectly, present his or her own thoughts, words, or actions. Use direct quotations and vivid verbs to reveal your character's personality more effectively. Look at the following two examples:

Direct

Tom is a very competitive person. He always wants to have the highest score. He is rude to anyone who scores higher than he does.

Indirect

Last week I ran into Tom at the mall. My smile of greeting froze on my face when he said, "Hey Brad! What's the big idea? Since when did you become the brilliant math student? How did you get a better score than I did?" I had expected Tom to be upset. He's been known to sulk for days if he doesn't get the highest score on an exam.

APPLYING LANGUAGE SKILLS: Quotation Marks

You'll probably want to use **quotations** in your firsthand biography. Make sure that you punctuate all of your direct quotations correctly.

• Use quotation marks to set off the exact words of a speaker.

• Place commas and periods inside final quotation marks.

• Start a new paragraph when the speaker changes.

Practice On your paper, punctuate the following dialogue correctly.

I can't believe Mike isn't here yet said Frank. Me neither, replied Bob. He was supposed to be here an hour ago. Where could he be? You got me, answered Frank.

Writing Application Include direct quotations in your firsthand biography. Punctuate them correctly.

Writer's Solution Connection Language Lab

For more practice with quotation marks, complete the Language Lab lesson on Quotation Marks, Colons, and Semicolons.

Prewriting

To help students choose a subject, have them think of a person whom they admire, perhaps a close friend, a teacher, relative, or other interesting person they know. Have each student make a list of several possibilities and then decide which person is most interesting. That person would be a good subject for the firsthand biography.

Customize for *English Language Learners*

Because these students may have trouble with verb tenses, encourage them to write their firsthand biography in the historical present. This will make the task more manageable as well as make their writing more immediate.

 Writer's Solution

Writing Lab CD-ROM

The Character Trait Word Bin in the Developing Narrative Elements section of the tutorial on Narration will help students find words to describe their subject.

Drafting

Encourage students to begin their drafts of their firsthand biographies with a colorful image or anecdote to set the tone of their narrative. Then have them organize the details about the person in a meaningful way as they draft. They should consider which point will make an effective ending and build toward it. Once students have completed a draft, they can go back and revise to make their biographies more interesting.

Applying Language Skills
Quotation Marks

Remind students that their firsthand biographies will be much more immediate and lively if they use direct quotations. Make sure they know how to punctuate those quotations correctly.

Answers

"I can't believe Mike isn't here yet," said Frank. "Me neither," replied Bob. "He was supposed to be here an hour ago. Where could he be?" "You got me," answered Frank.

 Writer's Solution

For additional instruction and practice, have students complete the **Language Lab CD-ROM** lesson on Semicolons, Colons, and Quotation Marks and practice pages 104–105 on punctuating quotations in the *Writer's Solution Grammar Practice Book*.

Revising

Writing Lab CD-ROM
The Revising and Editing section of the tutorial on Narration contains the following screens to help students revise their firsthand biographies:
• Character trait word bin
• Using details of setting to enhance mood
• Transition word bin

Publishing

In addition to the publishing suggestions, students may also wish to consider publishing in a student newspaper or national literary magazine that publishes student writing. For more information, visit Prentice Hall on the World Wide Web at **http://www. phschool.com.**

Applying Language Skills
Suggested Answer
Last week the temperature *skyrocketed* to 95°. The morning sun *shone* brightly as John *rode* to my house on his bike.

For additional instruction and practice, have students complete the **Language Lab CD-ROM** lesson on Choosing Words: Writing With Nouns and Verbs.

Reinforce and Extend

Review the Writing Guidelines
After students have completed their papers, review the characteristics of a firsthand biography. Encourage students to come up with additional criteria for an interesting firsthand biography, based on what they learned through completing the assignment.

APPLYING LANGUAGE SKILLS: Vivid Verbs

Good writers use **vivid verbs** to make their writing clear and precise. A vivid verb describes an action in a strong, exact manner.

Vague Verbs:
Rows of books and trophies <u>are</u> on John's shelves. Posters <u>are</u> on his wall. On his desk <u>is</u> a small totem-pole.

Vivid Verbs:
Rows of books and trophies <u>clutter</u> John's shelves. Posters <u>decorate</u> his wall. On his desk <u>stands</u> a small totem pole.

Practice On your paper, replace the vague verbs in the following sentence with vivid ones.

The weather was hot last week. The morning sun was bright as John came up to my house on his bike.

Writing Application Review your firsthand biography and replace vague, weak verbs with vivid ones.

Writer's Solution Connection
Writing Lab

To see more ideas for publishing your firsthand biography, refer to Publishing and Presenting in the Writing Lab tutorial on Narration.

Revising

Read Your Firsthand Biography Aloud A good revising technique is to read your work aloud. If you find parts difficult to read aloud, chances are a reader will also have trouble reading and understanding it. Work on making those areas smooth and clear.

Proofreading

Use a Proofreading Checklist Use the following checklist to make sure your draft is free of errors in grammar, spelling, and punctuation:
▶ Have you punctuated all dialogue correctly?
▶ Does each sentence end with the appropriate punctuation?
▶ Have you spelled all words correctly, including homophones such as *your* and *you're*?
▶ If you're using a computer, did you check that you didn't accidentally substitute one small word for another, such as *and* for *an* or *of* for *or*?

REVISION MODEL

① *"Belay on! Climb when ready!"* ② *those words,* ③ *stared*
When I heard Lynn shout I took a big gulp, looked up at

③ *stepped*
the rope snaking into the distance above me, and moved

out onto the blank rock face.

① The writer adds this direct quotation to make the situation more lifelike.
② This addition is needed to clarify the connection to the direct quotation.
③ The writer replaces these vague verbs with vivid ones.

Publishing

Publish On-Line On-line magazines, Usenet news groups, and electronic bulletin boards are just a few of the options for publishing your writing on the World Wide Web. For more information, consult Prentice Hall on the Web at http://www.phschool.com.

✓ ASSESSMENT		4	3	2	1
PORTFOLIO ASSESSMENT Use the following criteria to assess students' firsthand biographies.	**Organization**	The biography has a clear beginning, middle, and end. It contains relevant personal thoughts and insights.	The biography has a beginning, middle, and end. It contains personal thoughts and insights.	The biography lacks a clear beginning or end. It contains personal comment but may require more elaboration.	The biography lacks both a narrative structure and personal comments.
	Elements of Narration	The biography is compelling. Transitions make the order clear; the writer uses the first-person point of view consistently.	The biography is interesting. Transitions are used, though they may be repetitive. The writer uses the first-person point of view.	The biography is readable. More transitions are needed; point of view may shift from first- to third-person.	The biography is confusing and difficult to read. Transitions are lacking; point of view continually shifts.

Real-World Reading Skills Workshop

Breaking Down Difficult Text

Strategies for Success

If you've read a play by William Shakespeare, an article in a technical publication, or complex how-to instructions, then you know that sometimes English can look like a foreign language! A writer's vocabulary or sentence structure can make written text appear difficult, but a systematic plan can help you penetrate difficult text. The way to approach this kind of text is to break it down, part by part, into understandable chunks.

Clues to Comprehension Before you begin reading, note the title—it gives the first clue as to the content of the selection. Then look for other items, like a summary section, that will help you understand the main points of the selection. Finally, notice how the work is broken up into chapters, stanzas, or paragraphs. If these have titles or headings, read them too for clues to the content.

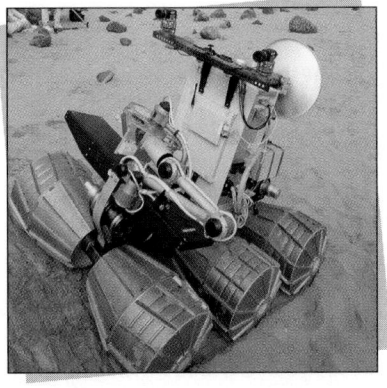

One Section at a Time Read the section heads, highlighted words, footnotes, and glosses (notes in the side columns). Read sentences in sections, breaking them where commas or other punctuation appears. Read the entire text once for general meaning. Then go back and reread those parts you didn't fully understand.

Apply the Strategies

Read this portion of an article, using the strategies to break down the text. Then answer the questions that follow.

Robotics: Japanese Researchers Look to the Twenty-first Century
Robotics Assembly Lines Advances

Since the 1970's, the Japanese have been leaders in making and using robotic structures to increase productivity on the assembly lines at car manufacturing plants. In particular, the new robots are intended for jobs that are dangerous or for which there is a shortage of workers.

Computer-Aided Manufacturing

In the field of CAD/CAM,[1] scientists are attempting to design a new structure that will not only create such things as integrated circuits, but will perform even more intricate work. In their attempt to refine CIM[2] processes, they will begin to create increasingly autonomous robots. These robots will be equipped with vision and touch senses and will be able to share learned data.

[1] CAD/CAM: Computer-aided design; Computer-aided manufacturing
[2] CIM: Computer-integrated manufacturing

1. How is the text divided? What did you learn about the article from the title and subtitles?
2. What specific topic does the author discuss in each paragraph?
3. What does CAD/CAM mean? How did you find out?
4. Which vocabulary words were you able to figure out from context? Which did you need to look up in a dictionary?

Remind students that it's a matter of common courtesy to introduce the people with whom you are speaking. Ask students if they were ever with a friend who met someone he or she knew, and the friend started talking with the new person without introducing the student. Have students explain how they felt in that situation.

Customize for
Intrapersonal Learners

Introverted students may have difficulty with this exercise. Tell them that performing a task such as making introductions becomes easier each time one does it, eventually becoming a habit.

Customize for
English Language Learners

Use this opportunity to teach English words indicating relationships between people. Encourage English language learners to practice introductions using indicators such as *my friend, my brother,* and *our teacher.* You may wish to allow time for these students to share with the class words from their own language that indicate the same relationships.

If you've ever stood by uncomfortably as your friend spoke to another person you didn't know, then you can appreciate the importance of making introductions. Introductions are a way to present two people to each other. Making introductions is a valuable social skill. Your friends and acquaintances will appreciate your willingness and ability to introduce them to people they don't know when the situation requires it. Use the following guidelines when you make an introduction.

Exchanging Names An introduction is like a presentation—you present one person to another. In general, you present a younger person to an adult, then the adult to the younger person. For instance, "Mom, this is my friend Sarah," then "Sarah, this is my mother, Mrs. DiCuffa." You can use a phrase such as, "I'd like you to meet . . ." or "Let me introduce you to . . ." In a more formal or professional setting, you should state the full names of the people you are introducing. It also helps to include an identifier or an explanation of relationship. For example, "Mr. Marcus, this is my friend Aldo Royce. He is interested in working here at the video store."

Make a Connection People like to feel that they have common interests or situations, so when you make an introduction, mention a connection between the people you are introducing. For example, "Bob, Frank plays the drums in a band, just as you do." By making a connection, you will put the people at ease and give them a subject for conversation.

Tips For Making an Introduction

✔ *When making an introduction, follow these strategies:*
  ▶ Introduce each person to the other by name. If you are introducing a young person to an adult, present the younger person to the older person.
  ▶ In a formal or professional setting, state the full name of each person you introduce.
  ▶ If possible, make a connection between the people you are introducing so that they will feel more comfortable together.
  ▶ Speak clearly.

Apply the Strategies

In groups of three or four, role-play these situations. Work out an appropriate introduction for each situation based on the strategies in the Tips above:

1. Introduce your childhood friend visiting from another town to several of your high-school friends.
2. Introduce your new boyfriend or girlfriend to your parents.
3. Introduce your boss at the television station where you work to a potential intern.

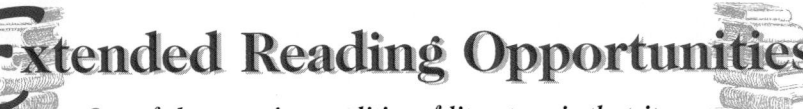

Extended Reading Opportunities

One of the amazing qualities of literature is that it can take you to new places and introduce you to new experiences. These selections will help you expand your own horizons.

Suggested Titles

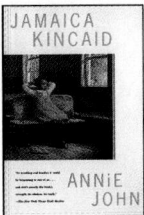

Annie John
Jamaica Kincaid

Annie John is a series of eight short stories that describe the title character's childhood and adolescence on the Caribbean island of Antigua. Told in the hypnotic voice of the young schoolgirl, the stories vividly describe the mischief of her childhood, the tension of her adolescence, and the eventual separation from her homeland.

Oliver Twist
Charles Dickens

Oliver Twist depicts the poverty, crime, and working conditions of nineteenth-century London. The hero of the tale is a young orphan named Oliver Twist who is expelled from the workhouse in which he was born, for the grave crime of asking for more porridge. Kidnapped by a gang of thugs and forced to take part in a burglary, Oliver experiences many close brushes with the dark criminal underbelly of London before being rescued by the wealthy Mr. Brownlow.

African American Literature
Published by Prentice Hall

This collection of poems, short stories, and essays will introduce you to the finest African American literature—from folk tales to contemporary fiction. Authors include Maya Angelou, Langston Hughes, Paul Laurence Dunbar, and others. Each of these African American authors explores the ways in which people expand their horizons.

Other Possibilities

I Heard the Owl Call My Name	Margaret Craven
Kon Tiki	Thor Heyerdahl
Never Cry Wolf	Farley Mowatt
Paris in the Twentieth Century	Jules Verne
The Good Earth	Pearl Buck
The Jungle	Upton Sinclair

Customize for *Special Needs*

To meet the needs of your special needs students you may want to consider using the cassette recording and study guide of *Oliver Twist* from Globe Fearon's Pacemaker Classic series.

Planning Students' Extended Reading

All of the works listed on this page extend the theme of Expanding Horizons. The following may help you choose which to assign.

Customize for *Varying Student Needs*

When assigning these works to your students, keep in mind the following factors:

- *Annie John* presents Jamaica Kincaid's candid reminiscences about growing up in the Caribbean feeling oppressed and eventually leaving for a life of greater freedom in England.

- *Oliver Twist*, Dickens's classic, reveals the sordid underworld of the slums of London in the late nineteenth century. Less proficient readers will find the reading difficult. Musical/rhythmic learners may connect through the songs from the musical *Oliver*, which was based on the novel.

- The anthology *African American Literature* is a collection of fine examples of the work of celebrated black American authors. Because this contains a number of selections of varied length and accessibility, you can choose those selections that are most appropriate for your students.

Sensitive Issues
Annie John contains frank observations about a young person's experience with death, separation, emotional illness, and parent-child conflict. You may want to guide students through these sensitive issues.

Resources for Teaching Novels, Plays, and Literature Collections
In addition to graphic organizers, teaching strategies, and transparencies that will be invaluable in teaching any of these novels, this booklet includes formal tests for and support materials for the anthology *African American Literature* and other featured works in the *Prentice Hall Literature Library*.

465

Planning Instruction and Assessment

Unit Objectives

1. To read short stories that illustrate different elements of the genre
2. To apply a variety of reading strategies, particularly those appropriate for reading fiction
3. To recognize literary elements used in these selections
4. To increase vocabulary
5. To learn elements of grammar and style
6. To write in a variety of modes and about situations based on the selections
7. To develop speaking and listening skills, by doing proposed activities

Meeting the Objectives

With each selection, you will find instructional material and portfolio opportunities through which students can meet these objectives. Further, you will find additional practice pages for reading strategies, literary elements, vocabulary, and grammar in the **Selection Support** booklet in the Teaching Resources box.

Setting Goals Work with your students at the beginning of the unit to set goals for unit outcomes. Plan what skills and concepts you wish students to acquire. You may individualize according to students' performance levels or learning modalities.

Portfolios You may have students keep portfolios of their work or of their work in progress. The activities and prompts on the Build Your Portfolio page of each selection provide opportunities for students to apply the concepts presented with the selection.

Final Departure, Lisa Learner

 Humanities: Art

Final Departure by Lisa Learner.

Help students establish the literal reality portrayed in this artwork. It shows a terminal, probably a platform for boarding trains or buses, covered by a barrel roof that lets in the sunlight. The artist draws a great deal of attention to the structure of the building and has chosen an unusual perspective, from the steps going up to the platform.

Help students link the artwork to the focus of Unit 6, "The Short Story," by answering the following questions:

1. In what ways might reading a story be like getting on board a train, bus, or plane? *The story takes us to new places; it has its own direction; it presents many images.*

2. Why would a train or bus station or an airport be a good place to set the beginning of a story? *A train or bus station or airport is full of many different individuals, each with a strong reason for being there; it can be a setting for homecomings and leave-takings; it also is a large area with many potentially mysterious spaces, as shown here.*

3. What could a story titled "Final Departure" be about? *It could be a realistic story about someone leaving home for good; the title could also refer figuratively to death.*

Short Stories

As long as people have had language, they have had stories—stories of the hunt, stories of battles, stories of romance, mystery, and adventure. There are no limits to the places short stories can take you. In a realistic short story, you might share the experiences of someone like yourself, while in a science-fiction short story, you might travel to a future world. No matter where you go or whom you meet, however, you can be sure your brief encounter will enrich your life.

◆ 467

Assessing Student Progress

The following tools are available to measure the degree to which students meet the unit objectives:

Informal Assessment

The questions on the Guide for Responding sections are a first level of response to the concepts and skills presented with the selection. Students' responses are a brief informal measure of their grasp of the material. Their responses on this level can indicate where further instruction and practice are needed. You may then follow up with the practice pages in the *Selection Support* booklet.

You will find literature and reading guides in the *Alternative Assessment* booklet, which you may give students on an individual basis for informal assessment of their performance.

Formal Assessment

In the *Formal Assessment* booklet, you will find selection tests and part tests.

Selection Tests The selection tests measure comprehension and skills acquisition for each selection or group of selections.

Part Tests Each part test, which calls on students to read a passage of literature they have not previously seen, applies the unit skills on a broader level. The Critical Reading section measures Unit Objectives 1, 2, and 3. The Vocabulary and Grammar section measures Objectives 4 and 5. The Essay section measures Objectives 1 and 6. Both the Critical Reading and Vocabulary and Grammar section use formats similar to those found on many standardized tests, including the SAT.

Alternative Assessment

Portfolios As you review individual pieces or the collected work in students' portfolios, you will find assessment sheets available in the portfolio section of the *Alternative Assessment* booklet.

Scoring Rubrics You will find scoring rubrics for writing modes in the *Alternative Assessment* booklet. You can apply these to Writing Mini-Lessons and to Writing Process Workshop lessons.

Speaking and Listening The *Alternative Assessment* booklet contains assessment sheets for speaking and listening activities.

Learning Modalities The *Alternative Assessment* booklet contains activities that appeal to different learning styles. You may use these as an alternative measurement of students' growth.

Guide for Reading

OBJECTIVES

1. To read, comprehend, and interpret a short story
2. To relate a story to personal experience
3. To use strategies for constructing meaning to read for success
4. To identify plot structure
5. To build vocabulary in context and recognize word origins: words from names
6. To recognize appropriate placement of *only* and *just*
7. To write a summary using transitions that show time
8. To respond to the story through writing, speaking and listening, and projects

SKILLS INSTRUCTION

Vocabulary:
Word Origins: Words From Names

Grammar:
Placement of Only and Just

Reading for Success:
Strategies for Constructing Meaning

Literary Focus:
Plot Structure

Writing:
Transitions That Show Time

Speaking and Listening:
Storytelling (teacher edition)

Critical Viewing:
Infer; Compare and Contrast

PORTFOLIO OPPORTUNITIES

Writing: Letter; Diary; Story
Writing Mini-Lesson: Summary
Speaking and Listening: Tape Recording; Storytelling
Projects: Music; Comic Strip

More About the Author

Hector Hugh Munro and his two siblings grew up in their grandmother's house. One of their greatest pleasures was reading or being read to. Among their favorite stories was *Alice in Wonderland*, which proved to be an influence on the adult Saki. When Saki was 26, he began writing political satires for London's *Westminster Gazette*. The public figures in the stories were illustrated as characters from *Alice in Wonderland!* The satires were so popular that they were collected and published in 1902 as *The Westminster Alice*.

Saki (1870–1916)

Long before celebrities of today started using single names, the writer Saki made his one name famous. Saki is the pen name of Hector Hugh Munro, born to British parents in Akyab, Burma, which was a British colony at that time.

A Struggle to Survive When Saki was born, a doctor told his parents that their son had little chance of reaching adulthood. Although he did live, his mother died when he was only two years old. He was sent to England to be raised by two aunts and his grandmother. Saki based many of the characters in his work on family members, particularly his two aunts. Throughout his life, Saki was plagued with illnesses.

At the age of twenty-three, he returned to Burma to join the military police, but only one year later contracted a severe case of malaria that forced him to return to England. There, he began his writing career, penning political satires for several newspapers.

Stories With a Twist Although Saki began by writing nonfiction, he is most famous for his fiction, especially his short stories. These tales, including "The Open Window," are noted for both their wit and humor as well as for their surprise endings. Curiously, the story of Saki's own life ends with an ironic twist. After surviving childhood diseases and a bout with malaria, Saki was killed at the age of forty-five by a sniper's bullet during World War I.

◆ Build Vocabulary

WORD ORIGINS: WORDS FROM NAMES

One of the characters in "The Open Window" carries a white mackintosh, or waterproof raincoat, over his shoulder. *Mackintosh* is a word that derives from the name of an actual person—Charles *Macintosh* (1766–1843), a Scottish chemist who invented waterproof clothing by soaking layers of cloth in rubber.

WORD BANK

delusion
imminent
mackintosh
pariah

As you read, you will encounter the words on this list. Each word is defined on the page where it first appears. Preview the list before you read.

◆ Build Grammar Skills

PLACEMENT OF ONLY AND JUST

Certain modifiers, such as *only* and *just*, should be placed immediately before the words they modify. If they are not, the intended meaning may be unclear. In the following example from the story, notice the placement of *only*.

> ...he was conscious that his hostess was giving him *only* a fragment of her attention...

In this example, *only* modifies *a fragment*. If you change the placement of *only*, the meaning of the sentence changes:

> He was conscious that his hostess was giving *only* him a fragment of her attention...

Now, *only* modifies *him* and gives the sentence an entirely new meaning.

Prentice Hall Literature Program Resources

REINFORCE / RETEACH / EXTEND

Selection Support Pages
Build Vocabulary: Word Origins: Words From Names, p. 142
Build Grammar Skills: Placement of *Only* and *Just*, p. 143
Reading for Success: Strategies for Constructing Meaning, p. 144
Literary Focus: Plot Structure, p. 146

Strategies for Diverse Student Needs, p. 35

Beyond Literature

Career Connection: Letter of Recommendation, p. 35

Formal Assessment Selection Test, pp. 123–125; Assessment Resources Software

Alternative Assessment, p. 35

Writing and Language Transparencies
Outline Organizer, pp. 103–106

Resource Pro CD-ROM
"The Open Window"—includes all resource materials and customizable lesson plan

Listening to Literature Audiocassettes "The Open Window"

The Open Window

◆ *Literature and Your Life*

CONNECT YOUR EXPERIENCE

The popularity of horror movies indicates that many people enjoy fictional stories that shock, frighten, or surprise. Not everyone enjoys a terrifying tale, however. For some, stories of romance or humor are more entertaining. In "The Open Window," two characters have very different feelings about the same tale: It horrifies one yet amuses the other.

Journal Writing Make a list of your five favorite stories and your five favorite movies. Look for a pattern in the types of entertainment you enjoy.

THEMATIC FOCUS: DANGEROUS DESTINIES

Imagination plays an important role in the destinies of the characters in this story. The events in this story may lead you to wonder whether a person's imagination can be too vivid!

◆ Literary Focus

PLOT STRUCTURE

Plot is the sequence of events that make up a story. The plot usually begins with an exposition, which introduces the setting, characters, and basic situation. An inciting incident often introduces the story's central conflict, or problem. The conflict then develops in the rising action until it reaches a high point of interest or suspense—the climax. The climax is followed by the resolution of the conflict or the end of the story. Use a plot diagram, like the one shown here, to note the plot elements of "The Open Window."

◆ Background for Understanding

CULTURE

During the time that this story is set—around the beginning of the twentieth century—people with money and land enjoyed a life of leisure in which social connections were very important. A person was judged as much on his or her acquaintances and family background as on his or her personality and accomplishments. To make new acquaintances, people often presented themselves through letters of introduction—a kind of social letter of recommendation. Mr. Nuttel, a character in this story, arrives at the country home of a "friend of a friend" with just such a letter.

Interest Grabber Draw students into the story by reading the following passage aloud:

> The child was staring out through the open window with dazed horror in her eyes. In a chill shock of nameless fear Framton swung around in his seat and looked in the same direction.

Have students discuss what kind of story they would expect this quotation to come from. *Students may respond: a horror story; a ghost story.* Tell them to read "The Open Window" to find out.

Customize for *Less Proficient Readers*

Since this story has many short paragraphs and a great deal of dialogue, it is ideal for oral reading. Have students form a Read Around Circle. The first student reads the first paragraph, the second student the second paragraph, and so on. When everyone in the circle has read a paragraph, the first student begins again.

Customize for *More Advanced Students*

Tell students that Saki's stories are known for their surprise endings. As students read, have them take notes to help them predict the ending.

Customize for *English Language Learners*

Help these students paraphrase sections of dialogue that are peppered with unfamiliar "Britishisms" such as *rectory, moor,* and *bound.*

Customize for *Interpersonal Learners*

Encourage these students to imagine they are in the room with Vera, observing her as she interacts with Mr. Nuttel. Suggest they jot down what they can determine about her personality from her words and actions.

✎ Preparing for Standardized Tests

Grammar and Language Placing modifiers correctly is essential to clear, precise writing. Students may encounter items such as the following on standardized tests:

Which sentence states that no more than four people attended the picnic? *(C)*

(A) Four people came to the only picnic in the park.

(B) Four people only came to the picnic in the park.

(C) Only four people came to the picnic in the park.

The Build Grammar Skills lesson for this selection will help students know that sentence C is correct because the modifier *only* is placed immediately before the word *four.*

You can also have students use Build Grammar Skills: Placement of *Only* and *Just,* p.143, in **Selection Support.**

The Reading for Success page in each unit presents a set of problem-solving procedures to help readers understand authors' words and ideas on multiple levels. Good readers develop a bank of strategies from which they can draw as needed.

Unit 6 introduces strategies for constructing meaning. It is important for students to go beyond the literal comprehension level in order to apply higher-level critical thinking strategies. These strategies for constructing meaning help readers achieve a higher level of reading comprehension—making inferences, drawing conclusions, interpreting information and identifying relationships, and recognizing an author's purpose.

These strategies for constructing meaning are modeled with "The Open Window." Each green box shows an example of the thinking process involved in applying one of these strategies.

How to Use the Reading for Success Page

- Introduce the strategies for constructing meaning, presenting each as a problem-solving procedure. Be sure students understand what each strategy involves and under what circumstances to apply it.

- Before students read the story, have them preview it, looking at the annotations in the green boxes that model the strategies.

- To reinforce these strategies after students have read "The Open Window," have students do the Reading for Success pages in *Selection Support,* pp. 144–145. These pages give students an opportunity to read a selection and practice these strategies by writing their own annotations.

Reading for Success

Strategies for Constructing Meaning

In order to understand a piece of writing fully, you must do more than simply comprehend the writer's words. You have to go a step further and put the words and ideas together in your own mind. Why did the author write it? What idea does he or she want to convey? What does the work mean to you? In looking for answers to questions like these, you construct the meaning that the work has for you.

Use these strategies to help you construct meaning:

Make inferences.

Writers don't always tell you everything directly. You have to make inferences to arrive at ideas that writers suggest but don't say. You make an inference by considering the details that the writer includes or doesn't include. Sometimes it's also helpful to "read between the lines." This means looking beyond the literal meaning of the words to obtain a full picture of what the author means.

Draw conclusions.

A conclusion is a general statement that you can make and explain by reasons or that you can support with details from the text. A series of inferences can lead you to a conclusion.

Interpret the information.

Interpret, or explain the meaning or significance of, what you read. When you interpret, you also explain the importance of what the author is saying.

Identify relationships in the text.

Identify the various relationships in the story. For example, look for the causes and effects of important actions, keep clear in your mind the sequence of events, and identify which events are of greater or lesser importance. This will help you get the "nuts and bolts" of the story down and let you devote your energy to more challenging tasks, such as finding out the theme.

Compare and contrast the ideas.

Compare and contrast ideas in the work with other ideas in the same work or with ideas that are already familiar to you. For example, you might look for ways in which an experience described in an essay is similar to something you've done or different from anything you've heard of or experienced.

Recognize the writer's purpose.

A writer's purpose will influence the details he or she chooses to present. This factor can affect the meaning that you take from a work.

As you read "The Open Window," look at the notes in the boxes. These notes demonstrate how to apply these strategies to a piece of literature.

Reading Strategies: Support and Reinforcement

Appropriate Reading Strategies Students are given a reading strategy to apply in reading each selection. For example, students will be asked to draw conclusions in a selection where a writer has an implied message. In other selections a strategy is suggested that is appropriate to the selection.

Reading Prompts To encourage application of the given reading strategy, there are occasional prompts, within green boxes, at appropriate and significant points.

In addition, there are red boxes prompting application of the Literary Focus concept and maroon boxes prompting students to connect with their lives.

Using the Boxed Annotations and Prompts

The material in the green, red, and maroon boxes along the sides of selections is intended to help students apply the literary element and the reading strategy and to make a connection with their lives. You may use the boxed material in several ways:

- Have students pause when they come to a box and respond to its prompt before they continue reading.

- Urge students to read through the selection ignoring the boxes. After they have read the selection completely, they may go back and review the selection, responding to the prompts.

Nelli Kabel, Gari Melchers

The Open Window
Saki

❶ "My aunt will be down presently, Mr. Nuttel," said a very self-possessed young lady of fifteen; "in the meantime you must try and put up with me."

Framton Nuttel endeavored to say the correct something that should duly flatter the niece of the moment without unduly

---

❷ ▲ Critical Viewing Based on her posture, expression, and surroundings, what is your impression of the girl in the painting? [Infer]

discounting the aunt that was to come. ❶ Privately he doubted more than ever whether these formal visits on a succession of total strangers would do much towards helping the nerve cure which he was supposed to be undergoing.

"I know how it will

> The details in this passage **identify** Mr. Nuttel's reason for being here. During the time in which this story is set, a common prescription for a "nervous condition" was rest and clean country air.

The Open Window ◆ 471

MODEL

Develop Understanding

One-Minute Insight
This story celebrates the power a good storyteller can have over a susceptible audience. Fifteen-year-old Vera is bright, poised, and imaginative—with a wry sense of humor. When she meets the nervous Mr. Nuttel, she quickly determines he is the perfect victim and plays a little joke on him, with spectacular results. She tells Nuttel a story so tragic and convincing that she has him believing in ghosts—and seeing them as well. When faced with explaining the man's odd behavior to her aunt, she invents an equally bizarre story, making her aunt the next unsuspecting victim.

◆ Critical Thinking

❶ **Interpret** Ask students: What do you know about Vera and Framton after reading this passage? *Vera's words and the author's description of her indicate that she is self-assured and talkative. Framton Nuttel appears is a worrier, unsure of himself and uncomfortable in social situations.*

▶Critical Viewing◀

❷ **Infer** From her posture and facial expression, the young woman in the painting appears poised and in command of the situation; her clothing and surroundings—artwork and freshly cut flowers—suggest wealth.

Humanities: Art

Nellie Kabel by Gari Melchers.
Gari Melchers (1860–1932) was an American painter whose work focused on human figures and faces. His best known work is a portrait of President Theodore Roosevelt, painted in 1906.

Use these questions for discussion:
1. Would you imagine the young woman in the painting to be shy or self-confident? Which of her features helped you form your opinion? *The subject of the painting seems confident. Her straightforward gaze and her relaxed, open posture create this impression.*
2. When you learn more about Vera, decide if you think this painting is a good illustration for the story and explain why. *The subject appears to have character traits similar to Vera's—self-confidence and a mischievous streak.*

Block Scheduling Strategies

Consider these suggestions to take advantage of extended class time:

- Begin by introducing the Reading for Success strategies for Constructing Meaning. After students have read the story, have them work in small groups to complete the Reading for Success activity on page 475. For more practice, give students the Reading for Success pages in **Selection Support,** pp. 144–145.
- Use the Daily Language Practice activities for Week 10, based on "The Open Window," p. 121

in *Writing and Language Transparencies.*

- Direct students to the plot diagram on page 469. Suggest that as they read "The Open Window" they look for and identify the plot elements noted on the diagram. You may wish to give them the Story Map blackline master in *Writing and Language Transparencies,* p. 84.
- Have students meet in discussion groups to answer the Critical Thinking questions (p. 475).
- Have students work together on one of the projects in the Idea Bank on page 476.

① Make Inferences Draw students' attention to Framton's remembered conversation with his sister. Ask: What does this conversation tell you about Framton Nuttel? *Since his sister believed that he would never attempt to meet people on his own, Framton is probably an introvert with a passive personality.*

◆ Reading for Success

② Interpret the Information Ask students: Might you interpret Vera's questions in some way other than mere polite conversation? *The choice of the word* pursued, *rather than* asked, *suggests that Vera might be probing for information about what Framton knows and does not know about local people and her aunt.*

③ Clarification In order for Vera's story to make sense, students need to understand that a French window is really a door with glass panes—a door that people can use to walk in and out of a room or house.

◆ Reading for Success

④ Make Inferences Ask students what earlier clue lets the careful reader infer that the story might not be true. Give them a moment to look back over the text to find the clue. *The clue that the story might not be true is the earlier mention of "masculine habitation." If the aunt is a widow and her brothers are dead, men would probably not be living in the house.*

① be," his sister had said when he was preparing to migrate to this rural retreat; "you will bury yourself down there and not speak to a living soul, and your nerves will be worse than ever from moping. I shall just give you letters of introduction to all the people I know there. Some of them, as far as I can remember, were quite nice."

Framton wondered whether Mrs. Sappleton, the lady to whom he was presenting one of the letters of introduction, came into the nice division.

"Do you know many of the people round here?" asked the niece, when she judged that they had had sufficient silent communion.

"Hardly a soul," said Framton. "My sister was staying here, at the rectory, you know, some four years ago, and she gave me letters of introduction to some of the people here."

② He made the last statement in a tone of distinct regret.

"Then you know practically nothing about my aunt?" pursued the self-possessed young lady.

"Only her name and address," admitted the caller. He was wondering whether Mrs. Sappleton was in the married or widowed state. An undefinable something about the room seemed to suggest masculine habitation.

"Her great tragedy happened just three years ago," said the child; "that would be since your sister's time."

"Her tragedy?" asked Framton; somehow in this restful country spot tragedies seemed out of place.

③ "You may wonder why we keep that window wide open on an October afternoon," said the niece, indicating a large French window that opened on to a lawn.

"It is quite warm for the time of the year,"

> When the author says that "something about the room seemed to suggest masculine habitation," you can **infer** that men live there.

◆ **Build Vocabulary**

delusion (di lōō´ zhən) *n.*: False belief held in spite of evidence to the contrary

said Framton; "but has that window got anything to do with the tragedy?"

"Out through that window, three years ago to a day, her husband and her two young brothers went off for their day's shooting. They never came back. In crossing the moor to their favorite snipe-shooting ground[1] they were all three engulfed in a treacherous piece of bog. It had been that dreadful wet summer, you know, and places that were safe in other years gave way suddenly without warning. Their bodies were never recovered. That was the dreadful part of it." Here the child's voice lost its self-possessed note and became falteringly human. "Poor aunt always thinks that they will come back some day, they and the little brown spaniel that was lost with them, and walk in at that window just as they used to do. That is why the window is kept open every evening till it is quite dusk. Poor dear aunt, she has often told me how they went out, her husband with his white waterproof coat over his arm, and Ronnie, her youngest brother, singing, 'Bertie, why do you bound?' as he always did to tease her, because she said it got on her nerves. Do you know, sometimes on still, quiet evenings like this, I almost get a creepy feeling that they will walk in through that window—"

④ She broke off with a little shudder. It was a relief to Framton when the aunt bustled into the room with a whirl of apologies for being late in making her appearance.

"I hope Vera has been amusing you?" she said.

"She has been very interesting," said Framton.

"I hope you don't mind the open window," said Mrs. Sappleton briskly; "my husband and brothers will be home directly from shooting, and they always come in this way. They've been out for snipe in the marshes today, so they'll make a fine mess over my poor carpets. So like you menfolk, isn't it?"

⑤ She rattled on cheerfully about the shooting and the scarcity of birds, and the prospects for duck in the winter. To Framton, it was all

---

1. **snipe-shooting ground:** Area for hunting snipe—wading birds who live chiefly in marshy places and have long, flexible bills.

Speaking and Listening Mini-Lesson

Storytelling
This mini-lesson supports the Speaking and Listening activity in the Idea Bank on page 476.

Introduce the Concept Vera is an engaging storyteller. Have students discuss what she does to make her stories sound believable.

Develop Background Have students review Vera's story before they determine what details they would like to add. As

students develop their ideas, remind them to consider the following points about storytelling:

- The details in a story should interest the audience.
- Details in a story should create "mind pictures" for the audience.
- A storyteller should use pauses and facial expressions to help get meaning across.

Apply the Information Using these hints about storytelling, students should plan their

stories and then practice their delivery.

Assess the Outcome Have students assess their own stories and those of their classmates on the basis of how convincing or believable they are. To evaluate the presentations, students may use the pages for Self-Assessment: Speech (p. 117) or Peer Assessment: Oral Interpretation (p. 119) in *Alternative Assessment.*

The Hunters, Gari Melchers, Private collection

▲ **Critical Viewing** How is this picture similar to and different from the scene Vera describes? **6** [Compare and Contrast]

purely horrible. He made a desperate but only partially successful effort to turn the talk on to a less ghastly topic; he was conscious that his hostess was giving him only a fragment of her attention, and her eyes were constantly straying past him to the open window and the lawn beyond. It was certainly an unfortunate coincidence that he should have paid his visit on this tragic anniversary.

"The doctors agree in ordering me complete rest, an absence of mental excitement, and avoidance of anything in the nature of violent physical exercise," announced Framton, who labored under the tolerably wide-spread <u>delusion</u> that total strangers and chance acquaintances are hungry for the least detail of one's ailments and infirmities, their cause and cure. "On the matter of diet they are not so much in agreement," he continued.

"No?" said Mrs. Sappleton, in a voice which ↓

❺ Compare and Contrast Ideas
Now that students have met Vera's aunt, Mrs. Sappleton, ask: How does your view of Mrs. Sappleton compare or contrast with what Vera has told Framton about her? *Students should recognize that the facts in Mrs. Sappleton's hunting story agree with Vera's story; but in speaking to Framton earlier, Vera referred sympathetically to her "poor" aunt. Mrs. Sappleton does not seem to fit that description, with her brisk, cheerful tone ("She rattled on cheerfully . . .") and her offhand mention of the "menfolk."*

▶Critical Viewing◀

❻ Compare and Contrast
Students should recognize that Mr. Nuttel essentially sees the scene that Vera described to him in her story—the hunters with their guns and dogs. In the story, there was one more hunter and only one dog. Also, it is winter rather than fall in the painting, and the white coat is not shown.

Humanities: Art

The Hunters by Gari Melchers.
   Julius Gari Melchers (1860–1932) was born in Detroit, Michigan. The scene Vera describes to Framton is quite similar to this one. By using sharply contrasting colors and letting the figures occupy the central foreground, the artist creates as vivid and striking a visual scene as Vera creates a verbal one.
   Use these questions for discussion:

1. How does the artist draw your attention to the men and the animals? *The men and the animals are delineated with bold colors. The colors of the background are muted grays and off-white.*
2. Imagine how Framton would feel if he saw this scene from the window at this point in the story. What would he do or say? *Students may conjecture that he would scream, run out of the house, or have a nervous breakdown.*

Listening to Literature Audiocassettes Play the audiocassette so that students can hear the climax of the story.

◆ Build Grammar Skills

❶ Placement of *Only* and *Just*
Ask students where else the "only" could be placed without changing the meaning of the sentence. *It could be placed after yawn to modify the prepositional phrase at the last moment.*

◆ Reading for Success

❷ Recognize the Writer's Purpose Ask: Why does the writer include the detail, "don't they look as if they were muddy up to the eyes"? *The phrase recalls Vera's description of how the men died in a bog.*

◆ Reading for Success

❸ Draw Conclusions Ask: What can you conclude from Framton's behavior? *He believes Vera's story.*

◆ Reading for Success

❹ Identify Relationships in Text
Ask students to identify the relationship between this story of Vera's and the one she told Framton. *This story suggests Vera doesn't have evil intentions but just likes to amuse herself in this way.*

Reinforce and Extend

Answers
◆ Literature and Your Life

Reader's Response Students might say Nuttel would simply express horror at what he thought to be ghosts.

Thematic Focus Students who share Vera's sense of humor might answer yes; those who feel Vera acted cruelly may answer no.

☑ Check Your Comprehension

1. (a) Nuttel is living in the country to calm a nervous condition. (b) He is visiting the Sappletons at his sister's suggestion.
2. Vera says that her aunt expects her dead husband and brothers to return through the window.
3. Three men who fit Vera's descriptions come in through the window. Nuttel thinks they are ghosts.
4. She says that Nuttel told her that, due to a horrifying experience in India, he is terrified of dogs.

474

---

❶ You can **interpret** Mrs. Sappleton's yawn to mean she is bored.

only replaced a yawn at the last moment. Then she suddenly brightened into alert attention—but not to what Framton was saying.

❷ "Here they are at last!" she cried. "Just in time for tea, and don't they look as if they were muddy up to the eyes!"

Framton shivered slightly and turned towards the niece with a look intended to convey sympathetic comprehension. The child was staring out through the open window with dazed horror in her eyes. In a chill shock of nameless fear Framton swung round in his seat and looked in the same direction.

In the deepening twilight three figures were walking across the lawn towards the window; they all carried guns under their arms, and one of them was additionally burdened with a white coat hung over his shoulders. A tired brown spaniel kept close at their heels. Noiselessly they neared the house, and then a hoarse young voice chanted out of the dusk: "I said, Bertie, why do you bound?"

◆ Build Vocabulary

imminent (im´ ən ənt) *adj.*: Likely to happen soon; threatening

mackintosh (mak´ in täsh´) *n.*: Waterproof raincoat

pariah (pə rī´ ə) *adj.*: Despised; outcast

Framton grabbed wildly at his stick and hat; the hall door, the gravel drive, and the front gate were dimly noted stages in his headlong retreat. A cyclist coming along the road had to run into the hedge to avoid <u>imminent</u> collision.

❸

"Here we are, my dear," said the bearer of the white <u>mackintosh</u>, coming in through the window; "fairly muddy, but most of it's dry. Who was that who bolted out as we came up?"

"A most extraordinary man, a Mr. Nuttel," said Mrs. Sappleton; "could only talk about his illnesses, and dashed off without a word of goodbye or apology when you arrived. One would think he had seen a ghost."

"I expect it was the spaniel," said the niece calmly; "he told me he had a horror of dogs. He was once hunted into a cemetery somewhere on the banks of the Ganges[2] by a pack of <u>pariah</u> dogs, and had to spend the night in a newly dug grave with the creatures snarling and grinning and foaming just above him. Enough to make anyone lose their nerve."

> Vera's made-up story gives you a final clue from which you can **draw the conclusion** that her story about her uncle and cousins was false.

❹

Romance at short notice was her specialty.

---

2. **Ganges** (gan´ jēz): River in northern India and Bangladesh.

Guide for Responding

◆ Literature and Your Life

Reader's Response If you were Mr. Nuttel, what would you have said to Vera as the men came through the window?

Thematic Focus Would you ever tell such a tale to a newcomer? Why or why not?

Activity Based on what you know about Nuttel, write a letter of introduction for him. You may wish to write the letter as Nuttel's sister.

☑ Check Your Comprehension

1. (a) For what reason is Framton Nuttel living in the country? (b) Why is he visiting the Sappletons?
2. How does Vera explain the open window?
3. Explain what causes Nuttel to rush from the house so suddenly.
4. How does Vera explain Nuttel's departure?

474 ◆ Short Stories

Beyond the Selection

FURTHER READING

Other Works by Saki
"The Interlopers"
"The Square Egg"

Other Works With the Theme of Imagination
"The Catbird Seat," James Thurber
"The Veldt," Ray Bradbury

We suggest that you preview these works before recommending them to students.

INTERNET

You can find additional information about Saki on the Internet. We suggest the following sites:
For a biography of Saki, go to **http://www.crl.com/%7Esubir/saki/bio.html**
For a bibliography of Saki's works, go to **http://www.crl.com/~subir/saki/bib.html**

Please be aware, however, that sites may have changed since we published this information. We *strongly recommend* that you preview the sites before you send students to them.

Guide for Responding (continued)

◆ Critical Thinking

INTERPRET

1. Contrast the personalities of Framton and Vera. What personality traits of Framton make him susceptible to her story? **[Contrast]**

2. At what point could you begin to suspect that Vera is telling a story? Give evidence from the story that shows her intent. **[Deduce]**

3. Explain how this story can be thought of as having a double ending. **[Interpret]**

4. Saki concludes the story with the statement "Romance at short notice was her specialty." Explain the meaning of romance. **[Interpret]**

EVALUATE

5. Do you think the story's ending is effective? Why or why not? **[Criticize]**

APPLY

6. Explain how a person's expectations can lead him or her to misunderstand or misinterpret obvious facts. **[Generalize]**

◆ Reading for Success

STRATEGIES FOR CONSTRUCTING MEANING

Review the reading strategies and notes showing how to construct meaning from what you read. Then apply the strategies to answer the following.

1. What is the effect of combining Mr. Nuttel's condition with Vera's mischievous nature?

2. What details and clues lead you to conclude that Vera's tale is fiction and not reality?

3. What can you infer about Vera's character from the way she treats Mr. Nuttel?

◆ Literary Focus

PLOT STRUCTURE

The **plot structure** is the sequence of a story's events.

1. What are two events that lead up to the climax of the story?

2. What is the climax of the story?

3. What are two events that lead to the resolution, or end of the story?

◆ Build Vocabulary

USING WORDS FROM NAMES

English contains some words that derive from the name of a person. On your paper, match the following words with the definition and description of the person from whose name they derive.

1. boycott   **a.** a nonconformist; from a Texas rancher who refused to brand his cattle

2. draconian   **b.** to protest by refusing to use; from a nineteenth-century Irish land agent who refused to lower his rents

3. maverick   **c.** someone who willfully destroys property; from a Germanic tribe from the Dark Ages of Europe

4. vandal   **d.** severe; from a harsh Athenian lawgiver

USING THE WORD BANK

On your paper, write the word from the Word Bank described in each sentence.

1. This would be handy in the rain.
2. Nobody wants to be one of these.
3. This keeps you from seeing reality.
4. If you drive recklessly, having an accident is this.

◆ Build Grammar Skills

PLACEMENT OF *ONLY* AND *JUST*

The placement of modifying words can affect the meaning of a sentence. For example, when the placement of the word *just* or *only* is changed, the meaning of a sentence changes.

Practice In your notebook, explain how the different placement of the word *just* or *only* changes the meaning of the following sentences.

1. (a) Mr. Nuttel could *only* talk about his illnesses.
   (b) Mr. Nuttel could talk about *only* his illnesses.

2. (a) I shall give *just* you letters of introduction to all the people I know there.
   (b) I shall give you *just* letters of introduction to all the people I know there.

The Open Window ◆ 475

✎ **Writer's Solution**

For additional instruction and practice, use the lesson in the **Language Lab CD-ROM** on Misplaced Modifiers and the pages on Misplaced and Dangling Modifiers, pp. 61–63, in the *Writer's Solution Grammar Practice Book*.

475

Idea Bank
Customizing for
Performance Levels

Following are suggestions for matching Idea Bank topics with your students' performance levels:

Less Advanced Students: 1, 4, 6
Average Students: 2, 4, 7
More Advanced Students: 3, 5

Customizing for
Learning Modalities

Following are suggestions for matching Idea Bank topics with your students' learning modalities:

Verbal/Linguistic: 1, 2, 3, 4, 5
Musical/Rhythmic: 6
Visual/Spatial: 7
Interpersonal: 5

Writing Mini-Lesson

Refer students to the Writing Handbook, page 965, for instruction on the writing process, and page 967 for further information on exposition.

Writing and Language Transparencies Have students use the Outline organizer, pp. 103–106, to organize their summaries.

Writing Lab CD-ROM
Have students complete the tutorial on Exposition. Follow these steps:
1. Students can use the timeline to arrange details of their summary chronologically.
2. Use the computer for drafting.
3. Have students use the interactive Self-Evaluation checklist for summaries.

Allow approximately 60 minutes of class time to complete these steps.

Sourcebook
Have students use Chapter 3, Exposition (pp. 62–95), for additional support.

Build Your Portfolio

Idea Bank

Writing

1. **Letter** As Mr. Nuttel, write a letter to your sister. Tell her what happened at Mrs. Sappleton's and how the incident has affected your nervous condition.

2. **Diary** Write a diary entry from Vera's point of view, describing Nuttel's reactions to her trick.

3. **Story** Vera creates stories that contain real elements. Write another story that Vera might tell about the open window if the story were set in your city or town. Include real elements about life where you live.

Speaking and Listening

4. **Tape Recording** With classmates, record a reading of this story. In your recording, experiment with different tones (sarcastic, sincere, surprised, regretful, and so on) as you read the dialogue, and see how the different tones affect the story's meaning.

5. **Storytelling** Practice telling the tale that Vera tells. Use the details Vera provides, and add some of your own that make the story seem more real. Use pauses and facial expressions to make your telling believable. Tell the story to the class.

Projects

6. **Music** Find music that would be appropriate background for one scene in the story. Play the music for the class while you read the scene. Then explain why you chose it. **[Music Link]**

7. **Comic Strip** Illustrate key moments from the story in comic-strip form. Show characters' thoughts as well as their words. **[Art Link]**

Writing Mini-Lesson

Study Notes: Summary

When you **summarize**, you condense something longer into a few sentences or a paragraph. Vera's story about the open window is, in a sense, a summary of what could have been a longer, more detailed story. When writing a summary of a short story, you should include the key events of the story's plot. As you plan and write your summary, keep this point in mind:

**Writing Skills Focus:
Transitions That Show Time**

When summarizing, it's important to indicate which events happened before others. **Transitions that show time** order include *first, then, next, afterward, at that time, before, earlier, immediately, in the past, later, now, soon, when,* and so on. These words indicate how one event is related to another in time.

Prewriting Reread "The Open Window." As you read, jot down the key events in the order in which they occur and the people involved. If you made a plot map earlier, you can use that to help you. At this stage, you can simply make a list of the events on a plot map, timeline, or in outline form.

Drafting Using the diagram you created, draft a summary of the story. Develop each key event into a sentence or two. Use transitional words to show readers the relationships between the events as they occurred over time.

Revising Reread your draft. Make sure you captured all the key events and people in your summary. Add any important details you may have forgotten, as well as transitional words and phrases that show time order. If you have used the modifiers *only* and *just*, check that they are placed correctly. For more on the placement of *only* and *just*, see pp. 468 and 475.

✓ ASSESSMENT OPTIONS

Formal Assessment, Selection Test, pp. 123–125, and Assessment Resources Software. The selection test is designed so that it can be easily customized to the performance levels of your students.

Alternative Assessment, p. 35, includes options for less advanced students, more advanced students, verbal/linguistic learners, visual/spatial learners, bodily/kinesthetic learners, and musical/rhythmic learners.

PORTFOLIO ASSESSMENT
Use the following rubrics in the *Alternative Assessment* booklet to assess student writing:
Letter: Expression Rubric, p. 94
Diary: Description Rubric, p. 97
Story: Fictional Narrative Rubric, p. 95
Writing Mini-Lesson: Summary Rubric, p. 98

PART **1** *Plot, Character, and Point of View*

Abstract Puzzle of Woman Assembling Self,
Paul Micich

Plot, Character, and Point of View ◆ 477

One-Minute
Planning Guide

The selections in this part are stories that have strong elements of plot, character, and point of view. The section opens with Carl Stephenson's "Leiningen and the Ants," a short story about a man whose intelligence and will are pitted against an infestation of killer ants. "By the Waters of Babylon" is Stephen Vincent Benét's poetic story told from the viewpoint of a future dweller on our planet. Anton Chekhov's "A Problem" and Mark Twain's "Luck" reveal the peculiarities of memorable characters.

Customize for
Varying Student Needs
When assigning the selections in this part to your students, keep in mind the following factors:

"Leiningen and the Ants"
• Contains violence in the struggle of man against nature.
• High interest for visual/spatial learners.

"By the Waters of Babylon"
• Students need to follow clues carefully to unravel the mystery of the story.

"A Problem"
• Through conversations, subtle qualities of character and issues are revealed.

"Luck"
• Difficult reading, but highly humorous satire.
• Some stilted language, used for comic effect.

 Humanities: Art

Abstract Puzzle of Woman Assembling Self by Paul Micich.

Ask students to explain what they see here in light of the title of the artwork. They should notice that the puzzle is incomplete; encourage them to describe what is most clear, what is partly clear, and what is missing from the puzzle.

Help students link the artwork to the focus of Part 1—Plot, Character, Point of View—by answering the following questions:

1. The eyes are thought to be the feature that most reveals the inner person. What explanations can you give for the fact that all the woman's features are at least partly visible except for her eyes? *If the woman is "assembling herself," the inner person, as shown in her eyes, may be the part of her that remains most mysterious or difficult to see. She might be unwilling to reveal that part of herself, or she may not know herself well enough to have "assembled" that part yet.*

2. In what way is the woman gradually assembling herself doing the same thing a writer of stories does? *A story writer creates characters out of details that are gradually revealed to an audience.*

477

Guide for Reading

OBJECTIVES

1. To read, comprehend, and interpret a short story
2. To relate a short story to personal experience
3. To predict based on plot details in a story
4. To identify conflict in plot
5. To build vocabulary in context and learn borrowed words: Latin plural forms
6. To use apostrophes correctly
7. To write a movie scene with a climax and resolution
8. To respond to the short story through writing, speaking and listening, and projects

SKILLS INSTRUCTION

Vocabulary:
Borrowed Words: Latin Plural Forms

Grammar:
Correct Use of Apostrophes

Reading Strategy:
Predict Based on Plot Details

Literary Focus:
Conflict

Writing:
Climax and Resolution

Speaking and Listening:
Motivational Speech (teacher edition)

Critical Viewing:
Draw Conclusions; Speculate; Connect

PORTFOLIO OPPORTUNITIES

Writing: Letter to the Editor; Change the Disaster; News Report

Writing Mini-Lesson: Movie Scene

Speaking and Listening: Motivational Speech; The Author's Motive

Projects: Map of the Plantation; Disaster Relief

More About the Author

Carl Stephenson's story "Leiningen Versus the Ants" has achieved the status of a classic, even though it is his only published story. The story's riveting suspense and portrayal of human courage in the ultimate conflict of man versus nature make it a timeless literary contribution.

Carl Stephenson (1886–1954)

Although Carl Stephenson was born and lived his entire life in Germany, he vividly captures the torrid atmosphere and raw wilderness of the jungles of Brazil in "Leiningen Versus the Ants." This short story has been widely read and included in numerous anthologies since it was first published in *Esquire* magazine in 1938. It was also adapted for a radio program entitled "Suspense," starring Vincent Price, and made into a film entitled "The Naked Jungle," starring Charlton Heston as Leiningen.

Shying away from the spotlight, Stephenson insisted that "Leiningen Versus the Ants" be the only story of his to be published during his lifetime.

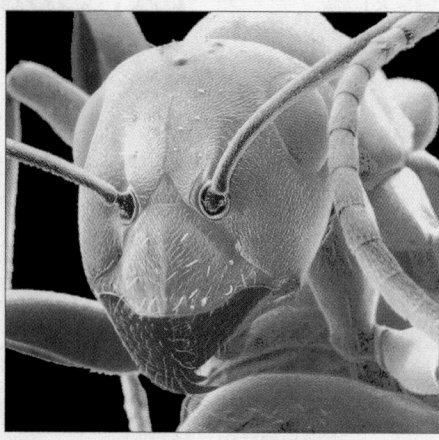

◆ Build Vocabulary

BORROWED WORDS: LATIN PLURAL FORMS

As a group of ants are swept down a river in this story, the author refers to them as "an *alluvium* of ants." *Alluvium* is a word borrowed from Latin that means "material, such as sand or gravel, swept along by water." Because *alluvium* comes directly from Latin, it retains its Latin plural form: *alluvia.* There are other words in English that behave the same way: *data* is the plural form of *datum.* When you use *data,* therefore, you are always referring to more than one *datum.*

WORD BANK
peons
flout
weir
provender
alluvium
fomentations

As you read "Leiningen Versus the Ants," you will encounter the words on this list. Each word is defined on the page where it first appears. Preview the list before you read.

◆ Build Grammar Skills

CORRECT USE OF APOSTROPHES

While reading "Leiningen Versus the Ants," you'll see several instances where the author uses apostrophes. An **apostrophe** (') is a punctuation mark used to show possession and contraction.

Apostrophes are used to form possessives as follows: To make a singular noun possessive, an apostrophe and *s* are added: *Leiningen's* word.

To make a plural noun possessive, an apostrophe is added after the *s*: *Indians'* trust.

When apostrophes are used to form contractions, the apostrophe indicates where letters are omitted. In the following example, the apostrophe indicates that the *i* from *is* has been omitted.

... *there's* no reason ...

Apostrophes are *not* used to form plurals:
ten *miles* wide
nothing but *ants*

 Prentice Hall Literature Program Resources

REINFORCE / RETEACH / EXTEND

Selection Support Pages
Build Vocabulary: Borrowed Words, p. 147
Build Grammar Skills: Correct Use of Apostrophes, p. 148
Reading Strategy: Predict Based on Plot Details, p. 149
Literary Focus: Conflict, p. 150

Strategies for Diverse Student Needs, p. 36

Beyond Literature Cross-Curricular Connection: Science, p. 36

Formal Assessment Selection Test, pp. 126–128; Assessment Resource Software

Alternative Assessment, p. 36

Writing and Language Transparencies Story Map, pp. 83–86

Resource Pro CD-ROM
"Leiningen Versus the Ants"—includes all resource materials and customizable lesson plan

Listening to Literature Audiocassettes
"Leiningen Versus the Ants"

Leiningen Versus the Ants

◆ Literature and Your Life

CONNECT YOUR EXPERIENCE

Nature can be a terrifying enemy. Hurricanes, tornadoes, and violent thunderstorms are just a few of the natural phenomena that can do serious damage. Compare these familiar catastrophes with the one that the main character in this story, Leiningen, faces.

Journal Writing Imagine you have just learned that your community is in the path of a tornado or hurricane. What would you do? Write about steps you and your neighbors would take to avert disaster.

THEMATIC FOCUS: PERSONAL CHALLENGES

Leiningen uses a variety of tactics to try to overcome a seemingly invincible foe. What do you think are the most important attributes a person needs to succeed against overpowering odds?

◆ Background for Understanding

SCIENCE

Scientists divide the army ants that invade Stephenson's story into two groups. *Legionary ants* live in South America, while *driver ants* haunt the jungles of central Africa. Army ant colonies may have anywhere from ten thousand to more than one million members. The colonies travel across the land in narrow columns, killing anything unlucky enough to get in their path—usually other insects, but occasionally small mammals or lizards. A colony usually hunts for a few weeks, then rests for a few weeks, often clinging together in one giant mass. Imagine stumbling upon *that* on a stroll through the forest!

◆ Literary Focus

CONFLICT

A story almost always contains a **conflict**—a struggle between opposing forces. The conflict can be internal or external. An **internal conflict** takes place within a character, as he or she struggles with opposing feelings, beliefs, or needs. An **external conflict** occurs between two or more characters or between a character and a natural force. The main character in this story faces an external conflict as he struggles to protect his home from an onslaught of army ants.

◆ Reading Strategy

PREDICT BASED ON PLOT DETAILS

You're watching the latest thriller when the main character hears a noise outside. As she steps into the darkness you think "No!" Based on what has already happened in the story, and the formula that movies like this seem to follow, you can **predict** that something scary is about to happen.

Stories, too, follow a pattern that helps you predict what is going to happen. Your predictions may be based on details that you pick up from the story, as well as on the expectations you have about stories in general.

As this story opens, we learn that an army of flesh-eating ants is headed toward the main character's plantation. Because there would be no story without a problem, you can predict that the ants will get close enough to be a real threat to the plantation. Details revealed in the story will enable you to make more specific predictions. Keep track of your predictions with a chart like the one shown.

Prediction	Reason	Outcome

Guide for Reading ◆ 479

Interest Grabber Ask students if they have seen horror movies in which the "monster" was an insect or insects. If they were making such a movie, which insect would they choose to be the monster? *Students may cite spiders, locusts, cockroaches, etc.*

Point out that the story they are about to read, "Leiningen Versus the Ants," first published in 1938, was made into a horror movie entitled "The Naked Jungle," starring Charlton Heston, a famous movie star. Have students speculate about the kind of ant that would be the more dramatic in the film—a monster ant or a giant mass of small, deadly ants.

Customize for
Less Proficient Readers
Have these students complete the prediction chart (p. 479) as they read. Suggest that they pause at intervals during the story to check the predictions they have made and revise the predictions, if necessary.

Customize for
More Advanced Students
More advanced students can be challenged to think about the internal conflict that Leiningen faces throughout the story, in addition to the external one. What forces are at war in him? Which force wins?

Customize for
English Language Learners
Point out to English language learners that many words from British English are used in the story. Explain words such as *petrol* (gas), *blighters* (mean or contemptible people or creatures), and *torches* (flashlights).

Customize for
Visual/Spatial Learners
Visual/spatial learners might plot out a map of the plantation that shows the advance of the ants as the story progresses.

Preparing for Standardized Tests

Grammar and Language Correct use of apostrophes may be tested on the usage/mechanics portion of standardized tests such as the ACT or SAT. For example, students may be asked to identify the error in a sentence such as the following: *(A)*

The four boy's back packs hold everything
    A   B

they will need for three days of hiking
         C

in the wilderness. No error
      D   E

The Build Grammar Skills lesson for this selection focuses on the correct use of apostrophes to show possession and mark contractions. Have students read Build Grammar Skills on page 478 and answer the Build Grammar Skills questions on page 496. For additional practice, use the Build Grammar Skills page on Correct Use of Apostrophes, in **Selection Support,** p. 148.

479

One-Minute Insight

"Leiningen Versus the Ants" is a story in the long tradition of "man against nature" fiction. Leiningen is convinced that his superior intelligence will enable him to win the war against the voracious army of ants that attacks his plantation. He has planned long and carefully, but the battle insects prove to be persistent and resourceful. In the end, human intelligence and courage win out—but not by much. Leiningen shows bravado at the finale, but he has also learned humility in the face of nature's devastating threats.

Customize for
Visual/Spatial Learners

Direct these students to infer from the photograph what the story may be about. *Students may say that there will be giant ants in the story.*

Customize for
English Language Learners

Review with students these expressions in the third paragraph of the story: "Decent of you" *Kind of you;* "give me the tip" *warn me;* "do a bunk" *evacuate, or leave.* Have students be alert for other idiomatic expressions that may not be familiar.

Leiningen Versus the Ants

Carl Stephenson

480 ◆ *Short Stories*

Block Scheduling Strategies

Consider these suggestions to take advantage of extended class time:

- Build background with the Cross-Curricular Connection: Science page in *Beyond Literature*, p. 36.
- Have students work in pairs to complete the Journal Activity in Literature and Your Life on page 479. Pairs can form groups to discuss their disaster plans.
- Introduce the Reading Strategy, Predict Based on Plot Details. As students read,

encourage them to watch for details in the story that help readers predict the outcome. Suggest they complete a chart such as the one on page 479 as they read.

- Use the Literary Focus paragraph on page 479 to introduce the concept of conflict in a story, referring to familiar stories to clarify the distinction between internal and external conflict. After reading, have students answer the Literary Focus questions on page 496 and follow up with the Literary Focus:

Conflict page in *Selection Support*, p. 150.

- Interested students can do further research into the habits of army ants discussed in Background for Understanding on page 479. Encourage them to present their findings to the class.
- Have students work in groups to complete the Disaster Relief project in Build Your Portfolio on page 497. If their area has been involved in a disaster, they might wish to focus specifically on that event.

1 "Unless they alter their course, and there's no reason why they should, they'll reach your plantation in two days at the latest."

Leiningen sucked placidly at a cigar about the size of a corn cob and for a few seconds gazed without answering at the agitated District Commissioner. Then he took the cigar from his lips and leaned slightly forward. With his bristling gray hair, bulky nose, and lucid eyes, he had the look of an aging and shabby eagle.

"Decent of you," he murmured, "paddling all this way just to give me the tip. But you're pulling my leg, of course, when you say I must do a bunk. Why, even a herd of saurians[1] couldn't drive me from this plantation of mine."

The Brazilian official threw up lean and lanky arms and clawed the air with wildly distended fingers. "Leiningen!" he shouted, "you're insane! They're not creatures you can fight—they're an elemental—an 'act of God'! Ten miles long, two miles wide—ants, nothing but ants! And every single one of them a fiend from hell; before you can spit three times they'll eat a full-grown buffalo to the bones. I tell you if you don't clear out at once there'll be nothing left of you but a skeleton picked as clean as your own plantation."

Leiningen grinned. "Act of God, my eye! Anyway, I'm not going to run for it just because an elemental's on the way. And don't think I'm the kind of fathead who tries to fend off lightning with his fists, either. I use my intelligence, old man. With me, the brain isn't a second blind gut;[2] I know what it's there for. When I began **2** this model farm and plantation three years ago, I took into account all that could conceivably happen to it. And now I'm ready for anything and everything—including your ants."

The Brazilian rose heavily to his feet. "I've done my best," he gasped. "Your obstinacy endangers not only yourself, but the lives of your four hundred workers. You don't know these ants!"

---

1. **saurians** (sôr´ ē enz) *n.*: Lizardlike animals.
2. **blind gut:** Reference to the appendix, which may have no function.

Leiningen accompanied him down to the river, where the government launch was moored. The vessel cast off. As it moved downstream, the exclamation mark neared the rail and began waving arms frantically. Long after the launch had disappeared round the bend, Leiningen thought he could still hear that dimming, imploring voice. "You don't know them, I tell you! *You don't know them!*"

But the reported enemy was by no means unfamiliar to the planter. Before he started work on his settlement, he had lived long enough in the country to see for himself the fearful devastations sometimes wrought by these ravenous insects in their campaigns for food. But since then he had planned measures of defense accordingly, and these, he was convinced, were in every way adequate to withstand the approaching peril.

Moreover, during his three years as planter, Leiningen had met and defeated drought, flood, plague, and all other "acts of God" which had come against him—unlike his fellow settlers in the district, who had made little or no resistance. This unbroken success he attributed solely to the observance of his lifelong motto: *The human brain needs only to become fully aware of its powers to conquer even the elements.* Dullards reeled senselessly and aimlessly into the abyss; cranks, however brilliant, lost their heads when circumstances suddenly altered or accelerated and ran into stone walls; **3** sluggards drifted with the current until they were caught in whirlpools and dragged under. But such disasters, Leiningen contended, merely strengthened his argument that intelligence, directed aright, invariably makes man the master of his fate.

Yes, Leiningen had always known how to grapple with life. Even here, in this Brazilian wilderness, his brain had triumphed over every difficulty and danger it had so far encountered. First he had vanquished primal forces by cunning and organization, then he had enlisted the resources of modern science to increase miraculously the yield of his plantation. And now he was sure he would prove more than a match for the "irresistible" ants.

Leiningen Versus the Ants ◆ 481

◆ **Reading Strategy**

1 Predict Based on Plot Details Ask students to use information from the title and the opening photograph to predict what the speaker is describing. *He is describing the movement of vicious ants.*

◆ **Critical Thinking**

2 Infer Have students determine what they can tell about Leiningen's personality, based on his response to the official. *He is proud and very self-assured.*

◆ **Critical Thinking**

3 Make a Judgment Ask students if they think Leiningen is correct when he says that the human brain can conquer the elements. *Sample answers: No; the elements cannot always be predicted and can foil even the best-laid plans. Yes; the human intellect is powerful when used wisely.*

Cross-Curricular Connection: Geography

Brazil Point out to students that the landscape of Brazil, where "Leiningen Versus the Ants" is set, is varied. In the Northeast Region is a coastal plain and high plateaus. The Central and Southern Plateau Region is fertile and includes large coffee plantations. The Amazon Region is located in the North, and includes tropical rain forest and mountains. Most of the inhabitants of Brazil live in the plateaus, where the cities of São Paulo and Rio de Janeiro are located.

Give students the opportunity to look at a map of Brazil that shows geographical features and have them decide in what region the story probably takes place and what is probably grown on the plantation. *coffee* If possible, provide pictures from an Atlas or geography text that show coffee plantations in the Southern Plateau Region.

As students read the story, have them notice clues to the geographical features and animal and plant life of this region of Brazil.

◆ Critical Thinking

❶ Draw Conclusions Ask students what aspect of Leiningen's character makes his workers trust him so completely. *His utter self-confidence gives the workers confidence in him.*

◆ Reading Strategy

❷ Predict Based on Plot Details The ants must be very fierce to frighten the animals into a stampede.

◆ Literary Focus

❸ Conflict Have students identify the type of conflict in these paragraphs and name the two opposing sides. *The conflict is external, between the ants and the people of the plantation.*

◆ Reading Strategy

❹ Predict Based on Plot Details Ask students if they agree with Leiningen's opinion that the petrol would be impassable. *Sample answer: No; Leiningen appears overconfident and will probably underestimate the ants.*

---

❶ That same evening however, Leiningen assembled his workers. He had no intention of waiting till the news reached their ears from other sources. Most of them had been born in the district; the cry, "The ants are coming!" was to them an imperative signal for instant, panic-stricken flight, a spring for life itself. But so great was the Indians' trust in Leiningen, in Leiningen's word, and in Leiningen's wisdom, that they received his curt tidings, and his orders for the imminent struggle, with the calmness with which they were given. They waited, unafraid, alert, as if for the beginning of a new game or hunt which he had just described to them. The ants were indeed mighty, but not so mighty as the boss. Let them come!

They came at noon the second day. Their approach was announced by the wild unrest of the horses, scarcely controllable now either in stall or under rider, scenting from afar a vapor instinct with horror.

❷ ◆ **Reading Strategy** What can you predict about the ants based on the behavior of the animals?

It was announced by a stampede of animals, timid and savage, hurtling past each other; jaguars and pumas flashing by nimble stags of the pampas;[3] bulky tapirs, no longer hunters, themselves hunted, outpacing fleet kinkajous; maddened herds of cattle, heads lowered, nostrils snorting, rushing through tribes of loping monkeys, chattering in a dementia[4] of terror; then followed the creeping and springing denizens of bush and steppe, big and little rodents, snakes, and lizards.

Pell-mell the rabble swarmed down the hill to the plantation, scattered right and left before the barrier of the water-filled ditch, then sped onwards to the river, where, again hindered, they fled along its banks out of sight.

This water-filled ditch was one of the defense measures which Leiningen had long since prepared against the advent of the ants. It encompassed three sides of the plantation like a huge horseshoe. Twelve feet across, but not very deep, when dry it could hardly be described as

---

3. **pampas** (pam′ pəz) *n.*: South American grassland.
4. **dementia** (di men′ shə) *n.*: Insanity or madness.

---

an obstacle to either man or beast. But the ends of the "horseshoe" ran into the river which formed the northern boundary, and fourth side, of the plantation. And at the end nearer the house and outbuildings in the middle of the plantation, Leiningen had constructed a dam by means of which water from the river could be diverted into the ditch.

So now, by opening the dam, he was able to fling an imposing girdle of water, a huge quadrilateral with the river as its base, completely around the plantation, like the moat encircling a medieval city. Unless the ants were clever enough to build rafts, they had no hope of reaching the plantation, Leiningen concluded.

❸ The twelve-foot water ditch seemed to afford in itself all the security needed. But while awaiting the arrival of the ants, Leiningen made a further improvement. The western section of the ditch ran along the edge of a tamarind wood,[5] and the branches of some great trees reached over the water. Leiningen now had them lopped so that ants could not descend from them within the "moat."

The women and children, then the herds of cattle, were escorted by <u>peons</u> on rafts over the river, to remain on the other side in absolute safety until the plunderers had departed. Leiningen gave this instruction, not because he believed the noncombatants were in any danger, but in order to avoid hampering the efficiency of the defenders.

❹ Finally, he made a careful inspection of the "inner moat"—a smaller ditch lined with concrete, which extended around the hill on which stood the ranch house, barns, stables, and other buildings. Into this concrete ditch emptied the inflow pipes from three great petrol[6] tanks. If by some miracle the ants managed to cross the water and reach the plantation, this "rampart of petrol" would be an absolutely impassable protection for the besieged and their dwellings and stock. Such, at least, was Leiningen's opinion.

He stationed his men at irregular distances

---

5. **tamarind** (tam′ ə rind) **wood:** Grove of leafy trees found in the tropics.
6. **petrol** (pet′ rəl) *adj.*: Gasoline.

◆ Speaking and Listening Mini-Lesson

Motivational Speech

This mini-lesson supports the Speaking and Listening activity in the Idea Bank on page 497.

Introduce the Concept A motivational speech encourages a group of people to act in a certain way. The speaker should use strong persuasive language, as well as facial expressions and body language to support his or her ideas.

Develop Background Ask students to identify the persuasive language Leiningen uses to motivate his workers. Have them think about these questions:

- What character traits do the workers admire in Leiningen?
- What emotions does Leiningen appeal to as he addresses the workers?
- What words does he use to inspire trust?

Apply the Information Encourage students to use tactics similar to Leiningen's in their speeches.

Assess the Outcome Students can base their evaluations of their classmates' speeches on the strength of their persuasive language. Students might also use Peer Assessment: Speaker/Speech in *Alternative Assessment,* p. 118.

along the water ditch, the first line of defense. Then he lay down in his hammock and puffed drowsily away at his pipe until a peon came with the report that the ants had been observed far away in the south.

Leiningen mounted his horse, which at the feel of its master seemed to forget its uneasiness, and rode leisurely in the direction of the threatening offensive. The southern stretch of ditch—the upper side of the quadrilateral—was nearly three miles long; from its center one could survey the entire countryside. This was destined to be the scene of the outbreak of war between Leiningen's brain and twenty square miles of life-destroying ants.

It was a sight one could never forget. Over the range of hills, as far as eye could see, crept a darkening hem, ever longer and broader, until the shadow spread across the slope from east to west, then downward, downward, uncannily swift, and all the green herbage of that wide vista was being mown as by a giant sickle, leaving only the vast moving shadow, extending, deepening, and moving rapidly nearer.

When Leiningen's men, behind their barrier of water, perceived the approach of the long-expected foe, they gave vent to their suspense in screams and imprecations. But as the distance began to lessen between the "sons of hell" and the water ditch, they relapsed into silence. Before the advance of that awe-inspiring throng, their belief in the powers of the boss began to steadily dwindle.

Even Leiningen himself, who had ridden up just in time to restore their loss of heart by a display of unshakable calm, even he could not free himself from a qualm of malaise. Yonder were thousands of millions of voracious jaws bearing down upon him and only a suddenly

◆ **Build Vocabulary**

peons (pē´ änz) *n*.: Laborers

▼ Critical Viewing What does this picture suggest will happen to those who get too close to the ants? [Draw Conclusions] **❼**

 Leiningen Versus the Ants ◆ 483

insignificant, narrow ditch lay between him and his men and being gnawed to the bones "before you can spit three times."

Hadn't his brain for once taken on more than it could manage? If the blighters decided to rush the ditch, fill it to the brim with their corpses, there'd still be more than enough to destroy every trace of that cranium of his. The planter's chin jutted; they hadn't got him yet, and he'd see to it they never would. While he could think at all, he'd <u>flout</u> both death and the devil.

The hostile army was approaching in perfect formation; no human battalions, however well drilled, could ever hope to rival the precision of that advance. Along a front that moved forward as uniformly as a straight line, the ants drew nearer and nearer to the water ditch. Then, when they learned through their scouts the nature of the obstacle, the two outlying wings of the army detached themselves from the main body and marched down the western and eastern sides of the ditch.

This surrounding maneuver took rather more than an hour to accomplish; no doubt the ants expected that at some point they would find a crossing.

During this outflanking movement by the wings, the army on the center and southern front remained still. The besieged were therefore able to contemplate at their leisure the thumb-long, reddish-black, long-legged insects; some of the Indians believed they could see, too, intent on them, the brilliant, cold eyes, and the razor-edged mandibles,[7] of this host of infinity.

It is not easy for the average person to imagine that an animal, not to mention an insect, can *think*. But now both the brain of Leiningen and the brains of the Indians began to stir with the unpleasant foreboding that inside every single one of that deluge of insects dwelled a thought. And that thought was: Ditch or no ditch, we'll get to your flesh!

Not until four o'clock did the wings reach the "horseshoe" ends of the ditch, only to find these ran into the great river. Through some kind of

---

7. **mandibles** (man´ də bəlz) *n.:* Biting jaws.

secret telegraphy, the report must then have flashed very swiftly indeed along the entire enemy line. And Leiningen, riding—no longer casually—along his side of the ditch, noticed by energetic and widespread movements of troops that for some unknown reason the news of the check had its greatest effect on the southern front, where the main army was massed. Perhaps the failure to find a way over the ditch was persuading the ants to withdraw from the plantation in search of spoils more easily attainable.

An immense flood of ants, about a hundred yards in width, was pouring in a glimmering black cataract down the far slope of the ditch. Many thousands were already drowning in the sluggish creeping flow, but they were followed by troop after troop, who clambered over their sinking comrades, and then themselves served as dying bridges to the reserves hurrying on in their rear.

Shoals of ants were being carried away by the current into the middle of the ditch, where gradually they broke asunder and then, exhausted by their struggles, vanished below the surface. Nevertheless, the wavering, floundering hundred-yard front was remorselessly if slowly advancing toward the besieged on the other bank. Leiningen had been wrong when he supposed the enemy would first have to fill the ditch with their bodies before they could cross: instead, they merely needed to act as stepping-stones, as they swam and sank, to the hordes ever pressing onwards from behind.

Near Leiningen a few mounted herdsmen awaited his orders. He sent one to the <u>weir</u>— the river must be dammed more strongly to increase the speed and power of the water coursing through the ditch.

A second peon was dispatched to the outhouses to bring spades and petrol sprinklers. A third rode away to summon to the zone of the offensive all the men, except the observation posts, on the nearby sections of the ditch, which were not yet actively threatened.

The ants were getting across far more quickly than Leiningen would have deemed possible. Impelled by the mighty cascade behind them, they struggled nearer and nearer to the inner

---

Cultural Connection

Insect Plagues

One of the most common themes of insect plagues in world folklore is that of the locust, a small type of grasshopper that travels in swarms, eating all vegetation in its path. Plagues of locusts are mentioned in the Bible and by the ancient Greeks, who thought the little insects were mythological monsters. Special ceremonies to drive away the feared locusts exist in Dahomey (West Africa), India, and Syria, where the people simply make as much noise as possible to deter an oncoming swarm. The locust is also a symbol of death and destruction for many Native Americans, especially among the Yurok and Wiyot groups.

Have students explore other plagues that appear in the folk literature and history of different cultures or in such works as the Bible.

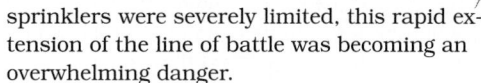

bank. The momentum of the attack was so great that neither the tardy flow of the stream nor its downward pull could exert its proper force; and into the gap left by every submerging insect, hastened forward a dozen more.

When reinforcements reached Leiningen, the invaders were halfway over. The planter had to admit to himself that it was only by a stroke of luck for him that the ants were attempting the crossing on a relatively short front: had they assaulted simultaneously along the entire length of the ditch, the outlook for the defenders would have been black indeed.

Even as it was, it could hardly be described as rosy, though the planter seemed quite unaware that death in a gruesome form was drawing closer and closer. As the war between his brain and the "act of God" reached its climax, the very shadow of annihilation began to pale to Leiningen, who now felt like a champion in a new Olympic game, a gigantic and thrilling contest, from which he was determined to emerge victor. Such, indeed, was his aura of confidence that the Indians forgot their fear of the peril only a yard or two away; under the planter's supervision, they began fervidly digging up to the edge of the bank and throwing clods of earth and spadefuls of sand into the midst of the hostile fleet.

The petrol sprinklers, hitherto used to destroy pests and blights on the plantation, were also brought into action. Streams of evil-reeking oil now soared and fell over an enemy already in disorder through the bombardment of earth and sand.

The ants responded to these vigorous and successful measures of defense by further developments of their offensive. Entire clumps of huddling insects began to roll down the opposite bank into the water. At the same time, Leiningen noticed that the ants were now attacking along an ever-widening front. As the numbers both of his men and his petrol

◆ **Build Vocabulary**

flout (flout) *v.*: Show open contempt

weir (wēr) *n.*: Low dam

sprinklers were severely limited, this rapid extension of the line of battle was becoming an overwhelming danger.

To add to his difficulties, the very clods of earth they flung into that black floating carpet often whirled fragments toward the defenders' side, and here and there dark ribbons were already mounting the inner bank. True, wherever a man saw these they could still be driven back into the water by spadefuls of earth or jets of petrol. But the file of defenders was too sparse and scattered to hold off at all points these landing parties, and though the peons toiled like mad men, their plight became momently more perilous.

One man struck with his spade at an enemy clump, did not draw it back quickly enough from the water; in a trice the wooden haft swarmed with upward scurrying insects. With a curse, he dropped the spade into the ditch; too late, they were already on his body. They lost no time; wherever they encountered bare flesh they bit deeply; a few, bigger than the rest, carried in their hindquarters a sting which injected a burning and paralyzing venom. Screaming, frantic with pain, the peon danced and twirled like a dervish.[8]

Realizing that another such casualty, yes, perhaps this alone, might plunge his men into confusion and destroy their morale, Leiningen roared in a bellow louder than the yells of the victim: "Into the petrol, idiot! Douse your paws in the petrol!" The dervish ceased his pirouette as if transfixed, then tore off his shirt and plunged his arm and the ants hanging to it up to the shoulder in one of the large open tins of petrol. But even then the fierce mandibles did not slacken; another peon had to help him squash and detach each separate insect.

Distracted by the episode, some defenders had turned away from the ditch. And now

◆ *Literature and Your Life*

How do Leiningen's observations about morale in an emergency apply to less drastic situations?

---

8. **dervish** (dәr´ vish) *n.*: One who performs a ritual Muslim whirling dance.

Leiningen Versus the Ants ◆ 485

◆ **Critical Thinking**

❺ Analyze Character Ask students what Leiningen's new attitude tells them about his character. *He is unwilling or unable to consider defeat, is highly competitive, and is blinded by his own determination. He sees life as a game.*

◆ *Literature and Your Life*

❻ Students will recognize the importance of morale in sports teamwork as well as in firefighting and disaster rescue operations.

cries of fury, a thudding of spades, and a wild trampling to and fro, showed that the ants had made full use of the interval, though luckily only a few had managed to get across. The men set to work again desperately with the barrage of earth and sand. Meanwhile an old Indian, who acted as medicine man to the plantation workers, gave the bitten peon a drink he had prepared some hours before, which, he claimed, possessed the virtue of dissolving and weakening ants' venom.

❶ Leiningen surveyed his position. A dispassionate observer would have estimated the odds against him at a thousand to one. But then such an onlooker would have reckoned only by what he saw—the advance of myriad battalions of ants against the futile efforts of a few defenders—and not by the unseen activity that can go on in a man's brain.

For Leiningen had not erred when he decided he would fight elemental with elemental. The water in the ditch was beginning to rise; the stronger damming of the river was making itself apparent.

Visibly the swiftness and power of the masses of water increased, swirling into quicker and quicker movement its living black surface, dispersing its pattern, carrying away more and more of it on the hastening current.

Victory had been snatched from the very jaws of defeat. With a hysterical shout of joy, the peons feverishly intensified their bombardment of earth clods and sand.

And now the wide cataract down the opposite bank was thinning and ceasing, as if the ants were becoming aware that they could not

---

▼ **Critical Viewing** What do you think Leiningen and his assistant are discussing here? **[Speculate]** ❷

 486 ◆ *Short Stories*

Cross-Curricular Connection: Social Studies

Medicine Men Medicine men, or shamans, have been found in cultures all over the world. These powerful men were believed to communicate with the spirit world. People believed that they helped make hunts successful and they foresaw the future. Above all, medicine men were healers. They assisted at births and deaths, and in many cultures they were the only doctors available. Their knowledge of local medicinal plants made it possible for them to treat many injuries and illnesses successfully. Have students consider how the Brazilian medicine man's knowledge might help Leiningen.

attain their aim. They were scurrying back up the slope to safety.

All the troops so far hurled into the ditch had been sacrificed in vain. Drowned and floundering insects eddied in thousands along the flow, while Indians running on the bank destroyed every swimmer that reached the side.

Not until the ditch curved toward the east did the scattered ranks assemble again in a coherent mass. And now, exhausted and half-numbed, they were in no condition to ascend the bank. Fusillades of clods drove them round the bend toward the mouth of the ditch and then into the river, wherein they vanished without leaving a trace.

The news ran swiftly along the entire chain of outposts, and soon a long scattered line of laughing men could be seen hastening along the ditch toward the scene of victory.

For once they seemed to have lost all their native reserve, for it was in wild abandon now they celebrated the triumph—as if there were no longer thousands of millions of merciless, cold and hungry eyes watching them from the opposite bank, watching and waiting.

The sun sank behind the rim of the tamarind wood and twilight deepened into night. It was not only hoped but expected that the ants would remain quiet until dawn. But to defeat any forlorn attempt at a crossing, the flow of water through the ditch was powerfully increased by opening the dam still further.

In spite of this impregnable barrier, Leiningen was not yet altogether convinced that the ants would not venture another surprise attack. He ordered his men to camp along the bank overnight. He also detailed parties of them to patrol the ditch in two of his motor cars and ceaselessly to illuminate the surface of the water with headlights and electric torches.

After having taken all the precautions he deemed necessary, the farmer ate his supper with considerable appetite and went to bed. His slumbers were in no wise disturbed by the memory of the waiting, live, twenty square miles.

Dawn found a thoroughly refreshed and active Leiningen riding along the edge of the ditch. The planter saw before him a motionless and unaltered throng of besiegers. He studied the wide belt of water between them and the plantation, and for a moment almost regretted that the fight had ended so soon and so simply. In the comforting, matter-of-fact light of morning, it seemed to him now that the ants hadn't the ghost of a chance to cross the ditch. Even if they plunged headlong into it on all three fronts at once, the force of the now powerful current would inevitably sweep them away. He had got quite a thrill out of the fight—a pity it was already over.

He rode along the eastern and southern sections of the ditch and found everything in order. He reached the western section, opposite the tamarind wood, and here, contrary to the other battle fronts, he found the enemy very busy indeed. The trunks and branches of the trees and the creepers of the lianas,[9] on the far bank of the ditch, fairly swarmed with industrious insects. But instead of eating the leaves there and then, they were merely gnawing through the stalks, so that a thick green shower fell steadily to the ground.

No doubt they were victualing columns sent out to obtain provender for the rest of the army. The discovery did not surprise Leiningen. He did not need to be told that ants are intelligent, that certain species even use others as milch cows, watchdogs, and slaves. He was well aware of their power of adaptation, their sense of discipline, their marvelous talent for organization.

His belief that a foray to supply the army was in progress was strengthened when he saw the leaves that fell to the ground being dragged to the troops waiting outside the wood. Then all at once he realized the aim that rain of green was intended to serve.

◆ **Build Vocabulary**
provender (präv´ ən dər) n.: Food

9. **lianas** (lē ä´ nəz) n.: Climbing vines found in the tropics.

Leiningen Versus the Ants ◆ 487

◆ **Reading Strategy**

❸ **Predict Based on Plot Details** Ask students if they think the men have really vanquished the ants. *Sample answer: No; the ants will regroup and try another strategy. Students can use their experience with other stories to know that if the ants were vanquished at this point, the story would be over.*

◆ **Reading Strategy**

❹ **Predict Based on Plot Details** Have students think of a way the ants might cross the wide belt of water. *Sample answer: They could cross on a raft or a bridge of debris. Accept any reasonable predictions.*

◆ **Critical Thinking**

❺ **Draw Conclusions** What do students think the ants plan to do with the creepers of the lianas? Are the ants acting intelligently or simply using instinct? *They plan to use them to float across the water. It seems that the ants are now matching their ingenuity and intelligence against Leiningen's.*

◆ **Background for Understanding**

❻ **Science** Explain to students that army ants, like other ants, live in highly structured societies. Each colony has a queen, whose job is to reproduce, and legions of workers that perform the various tasks that are necessary to maintain the colony. Although real army ants are not quite as destructive as the author portrays, they are well-organized, carnivorous creatures that can cause great damage.

◆ **Beyond the Classroom**

Community Connection
Insect Threats Many communities face threats from insects—though, unlike Leiningen's ants, they are rarely threats to the inhabitants' lives. Some midwestern areas live through periodic infestations of locusts. Fruit-growing communities have pests that eat fruit. Many areas are infested with tent caterpillars or gypsy moths, or suffer from disease-carrying ticks or mosquitoes. Have students look into the insect pests that bother their community to find out how they threaten the area and what can be done to control them.

◆ Critical Thinking

❶ Connect Have students connect Macbeth's fate to the fate suggested for Leiningen. *Macbeth misinterpreted a prophecy and believed he was invulnerable; Leiningen's belief in the invulnerability of his fortifications is about to be tested.*

◆ Critical Thinking

❷ Infer Ask students what Leiningen's curiosity about the stag reveals about him. *He is a bit cold-blooded, and he has very little fear. He is also curious.*

◆ Literary Focus

❸ Conflict The ants will probably find a way to ride out the water surges and cross the ditch. It is still too soon in the story for the ants to be finally defeated.

Customize for
More Advanced Students

Students can be challenged to note how Leiningen's attitude toward the ants has changed. Point out that now his battle has taken on the epic proportions of a struggle between good and evil, and he has cast himself as the proponent of good. Have students discuss evidence for this change and why it has occurred.

---

❶ Each single leaf, pulled or pushed by dozens of toiling insects, was borne straight to the edge of the ditch. Even as Macbeth watched the approach of Birnam Wood in the hands of his enemies,[10] Leiningen saw the tamarind wood move nearer and nearer in the mandibles of the ants. Unlike the fey Scot, however, he did not lose his nerve; no witches had prophesied his doom,[11] and if they had he would have slept just as soundly. All the same, he was forced to admit to himself that the situation was now far more ominous than that of the day before.

He had thought it impossible for the ants to build rafts for themselves—well, here they were, coming in thousands, more than enough to bridge the ditch. Leaves after leaves rustled down the slope to the water, where the current drew them away from the bank and carried them into midstream. And every single leaf carried several ants. This time the farmer did not trust to the alacrity of his messengers. He galloped away, leaning from his saddle and yelling orders as he rushed past outpost after outpost: "Bring petrol pumps to the southwest front! Issue spades to every man along the line facing the wood!" And arrived at the eastern and southern sections, he dispatched every man except the observation posts to the menaced west.

Then, as he rode past the stretch where the ants had failed to cross the day before, he witnessed a brief but impressive scene. Down the slope of the distant hill there came toward him a singular being, writhing rather than running, an animal-like blackened statue with a shapeless head and four quivering feet that knuckled under almost ceaselessly. When the creature reached the far bank of the ditch and collapsed opposite Leiningen, he recognized it as a pampas stag, covered over and over with ants.

It had strayed near the zone of the army. As usual, they had attacked its eyes first. Blinded,

---

10. **Macbeth . . . enemies:** In William Shakespeare's play *Macbeth*, soldiers carried boughs from Birnam Wood to hide behind as they attacked a castle.
11. **fey** (fā) **Scot . . . doom:** "Fey Scot" refers to Macbeth, whose death was foretold by three witches.

---

it had reeled in the madness of hideous torment straight into the ranks of its persecutors, and now the beast swayed to and fro in its death agony.

With a shot from his rifle Leiningen put it out of its misery. Then he pulled out his watch. He hadn't a second to lose, but for life itself he could not have denied his curiosity the satisfaction of knowing how long the ants would take—for personal reasons, so to speak. After six minutes the white polished bones alone remained. That's how he himself would look before you can—Leiningen spat once, and put spurs to his horse. ❷

The sporting zest with which the excitement of the novel contest had inspired him the day before had now vanished; in its place was a cold and violent purpose. He would send these vermin back to the hell where they belonged, somehow, anyhow. Yes, but how was indeed the question; as things stood at present it looked as if the devils would raze him and his men from the earth instead. He had underestimated the might of the enemy; he really would have to bestir himself if he hoped to outwit them.

The biggest danger now, he decided, was the point where the western section of the ditch curved southward. And arrived there, he found his worst expectations justified. The very power of the current had huddled the leaves and their crews of ants so close together at the bend that the bridge was almost ready.

True, streams of petrol and clumps of earth still prevented a landing. But the number of floating leaves was increasing ever more swiftly. It could not be long now before a stretch of water a mile in length was decked by a green pontoon over which the ants could rush in millions.

Leiningen galloped to the weir. The damming of the river was controlled by a wheel on its bank. The planter ordered the man at the wheel first to lower the water in the ditch almost to vanishing point, next to wait a moment, then suddenly to

◆ **Literary Focus** Predict whether this strategy will be successful. ❸

Cross-Curricular Connection: Social Studies

Farming in Brazil Explain to students that the interior of Brazil is a harsh region, with scarce grazing land and poor soil. Farmers there raise small crops of beans, corn, and cotton. On the coastal plains of the Northeast, there are cacao bean, sugar cane, and tobacco farms. In the Central and Southern Plateaus, where Leiningen's plantation is probably located, coffee is the largest crop. Farmers also grow potatoes, sugar cane, rice, and wheat.

let the river in again. This maneuver of lowering and raising the surface, of decreasing then increasing the flow of water through the ditch, was to be repeated over and over again until further notice.

This tactic was at first successful. The water in the ditch sank, and with it the film of leaves. The green fleet nearly reached the bed and the troops on the far bank swarmed down the slope to it. Then a violent flow of water at the original depth raced through the ditch, overwhelming leaves and ants, and sweeping them along.

This intermittent rapid flushing prevented just in time the almost completed fording of the ditch. But it also flung here and there squads of the enemy vanguard simultaneously up the inner bank. These seemed to know their duty only too well, and lost no time accomplishing it. The air rang with the curses of bitten Indians. They had removed their shirts and pants to detect the quicker the upward-hastening insects; when they saw one, they crushed it; and fortunately the onslaught as yet was only by skirmishers.

Again and again, the water sank and rose, carrying leaves and drowned ants away with it. It lowered once more nearly to its bed; but this time the exhausted defenders waited in vain for the flush of destruction. Leiningen sensed disaster; something must have gone wrong with the machinery of the dam. Then a sweating peon tore up to him:

"They're over!"

While the besieged were concentrating upon the defense of the stretch opposite the wood, the seemingly unaffected line beyond the wood had become the theater of decisive action. Here the defenders' front was sparse and scattered; everyone who could be spared had hurried away to the south.

Just as the man at the weir had lowered the water almost to the bed of the ditch, the ants on a wide front began another attempt at a direct crossing like that of the preceding day. Into the emptied bed poured an irresistible throng. Rushing across the ditch, they attained the inner bank before the Indians fully grasped the situation. Their frantic screams dumbfounded the man at the weir. Before he could direct the river anew into the safeguarding bed he saw himself surrounded by raging ants. He ran like the others, ran for his life.

When Leiningen heard this, he knew the plantation was doomed. He wasted no time bemoaning the inevitable. For as long as there was the slightest chance of success, he had stood his ground; and now any further resistance was both useless and dangerous. He fired three revolver shots into the air—the prearranged signal for his men to retreat instantly within the "inner moat." Then he rode toward the ranch house.

This was two miles from the point of invasion. There was therefore time enough to prepare the second line of defense against the advent of the ants. Of the three great petrol cisterns near the house, one had already been half emptied by the constant withdrawals needed for the pumps during the fight at the water ditch. The remaining petrol in it was now drawn off through underground pipes into the concrete trench which encircled the ranch house and its outbuildings.

And there, drifting in twos and threes, Leiningen's men reached him. Most of them were obviously trying to preserve an air of calm and indifference, belied, however, by their restless glances and knitted brows. One could see their belief in a favorable outcome of the struggle was already considerably shaken.

The planter called his peons around him.

"Well, lads," he began, "we've lost the first round. But we'll smash the beggars yet, don't you worry. Anyone who thinks otherwise can draw his pay here and now and push off. There are rafts enough and to spare on the river and plenty of time still to reach 'em."

Not a man stirred.

Leiningen acknowledged his silent vote of confidence with a laugh that was half a grunt. "That's the stuff, lads. Too bad if you'd missed the rest of the show, eh? Well, the fun won't start till morning. Once these blighters turn

These students may benefit from having Leiningen's plan outlined to them. Explain that there are two lines of defense for the plantation, and that the men have had to retreat from the first line. The second line is much nearer to the house; retreating there means that the ants will destroy the crops grown on the plantation.

◆ **Critical Thinking**

❹ **Draw Conclusions** Ask students what the workers now realize about their situation. *They can now see that they are in mortal danger, a fact that their faith in Leiningen has kept them from knowing.*

◆ **Build Grammar Skills**

❺ **Correct Use of Apostrophes** Have students identify the words in these paragraphs that use apostrophes. Ask them whether the apostrophes indicate contractions or possessives; for the contractions, have them state the words that have been joined or shortened. *They are all contractions:* we've *for "we have,"* we'll *for "we will,"* 'em *for "them," and* that's *for "that is."*

Leiningen Versus the Ants ◆ 489

tail, there'll be plenty of work for everyone and higher wages all round. And now run along and get something to eat; you've earned it all right."

In the excitement of the fight the greater part of the day had passed without the men once pausing to snatch a bite. Now that the ants were for the time being out of sight, and the "wall of petrol" gave a stronger feeling of security, hungry stomachs began to assert their claims.

The bridges over the concrete ditch were removed. Here and there solitary ants had reached the ditch; they gazed at the petrol meditatively, then scurried back again. Apparently they had little interest at the moment for what lay beyond the evil-reeking barrier, the abundant spoils of the plantation were the main attraction. Soon the trees, shrubs and beds for miles around were hulled with ants zealously gobbling the yield of long weary months of strenuous toil.

As twilight began to fall, a cordon of ants marched around the petrol trench, but as yet made no move toward its brink. Leiningen posted sentries with headlights and electric torches, then withdrew to his office, and began to reckon up his losses. He estimated these as large, but, in comparison with his bank balance, by no means unbearable. He worked out in some detail a scheme of intensive cultivation which would enable him, before very long, to more than compensate himself for the damage now being wrought to his crops. It was with a contented mind that he finally betook himself to bed where he slept deeply until dawn, undisturbed by any thought that next day little more might be left of him than a glistening skeleton.

He rose with the sun and went out on the flat roof of his house. And a scene like one from Dante[12] lay around him; for miles in every direction there was nothing but a black, glittering multitude, a multitude of rested, sated, but nonetheless voracious ants; yes, look as far as one might, one could see nothing but that rustling black throng, except in the north,

where the great river drew a boundary they could not hope to pass. But even the high stone breakwater, along the bank of the river, which Leiningen had built as a defense against inundations, was, like the paths, the shorn trees and shrubs, the ground itself, black with ants.

So their greed was not glutted in razing that vast plantation? Not by a long chalk; they were all the more eager now on a rich and certain booty—four hundred men, numerous horses, and bursting granaries.

At first it seemed that the petrol trench would serve its purpose. The besiegers sensed the peril of swimming it, and made no move to plunge blindly over its brink. Instead they devised a better maneuver; they began to collect shreds of bark, twigs and dried leaves and dropped these into the petrol. Everything green, which could have been similarly used, had long since been eaten. After a time, though, a long procession could be seen bringing from the west the tamarind leaves used as rafts the day before.

Since the petrol, unlike the water in the outer ditch, was perfectly still, the refuse stayed where it was thrown. It was several hours before the ants succeeded in covering an appreciable part of the surface. At length, however, they were ready to proceed to a direct attack.

Their storm troops swarmed down the concrete side, scrambled over the supporting surface of twigs and leaves, and impelled these over the few remaining streaks of open petrol until they reached the other side. Then they began to climb up this to make straight for the helpless garrison.

During the entire offensive, the planter sat peacefully, watching them with interest, but not stirring a muscle. Moreover, he had ordered his men not to disturb in any way whatever the advancing horde. So they squatted listlessly along the bank of the ditch and waited for a sign from the boss.

The petrol was now covered with ants. A few had climbed the inner concrete wall and were scurrying toward the defenders.

---

12. Dante (dän´ tā): Italian poet (1265–1321) who wrote *The Divine Comedy*, describing the horrors of hell.

490 ◆ *Short Stories*

Beyond the Classroom

Career Connection

Workplace Leadership Point out to students that showing leadership in the workplace can help them achieve their goals. Invite students to describe a workplace situation in which they would be required to show leadership qualities. Have them consider these questions:

• What qualities does a leader need?
• How can a leader promote confidence in his or her workers?
• What aspects of a situation does a leader need

to consider?

With their answers to these questions, students can create a realistic workplace situation in which they could identify leadership qualities. Have them write down their situations.

Students can exchange their written situations and judge the qualities and actions their classmates have outlined. As a final discussion, they can note which of the qualities they have chosen are qualities Leiningen possesses, and whether they, as leaders, would have made the choices Leiningen made.

"Everyone back from the ditch!" roared Leiningen. The men rushed away, without the slightest idea of his plan. He stooped forward and cautiously dropped into the ditch a stone which split the floating carpet and its living freight, to reveal a gleaming patch of petrol. A match spurted, sank down to the oily surface—Leiningen sprang back; in a flash a towering rampart of fire encompassed the garrison.

❸ This spectacular and instant repulse threw the Indians into ecstasy. They applauded, yelled and stamped. Had it not been for the awe in which they held their boss, they would infallibly have carried him shoulder high.

It was some time before the petrol burned down to the bed of the ditch, and the wall of smoke and flame began to lower. The ants had retreated in a wide circle from the devastation, and innumerable charred fragments along the outer bank showed that the flames had spread from the holocaust in the ditch well into the ranks beyond, where they had wrought havoc far and wide.

❹ Yet the perseverance of the ants was by no means broken; indeed, each setback seemed only to whet it. The concrete cooled, the flicker of the dying flames wavered and vanished, petrol from the second tank poured into the trench—and the ants marched forward anew to the attack.

The foregoing scene repeated itself in every detail, except that on this occasion less time was needed to bridge the ditch, for the petrol was now already filmed by a layer of ash. Once again they withdrew; once again petrol flowed into the ditch. Would the creatures never learn that their self-sacrifice was utterly senseless? It really was senseless, wasn't it? Yes, of course it was senseless—provided the defenders had an *unlimited* supply of petrol.

When Leiningen reached this stage of reasoning, he felt for the first time since the arrival of the ants that his confidence was deserting him. His skin began to creep; he loosened his collar. Once the devils were over the trench there wasn't a chance for him and his men. What a prospect, to be eaten alive like that!

For the third time the flames immolated the attacking troops, and burned down to extinction. Yet the ants were coming on again as if nothing had happened. And meanwhile Leiningen had made a discovery that chilled him to the bone—petrol was no longer flowing into the ditch. Something must be blocking the outflow pipe of the third and last cistern—a snake or a dead rat? Whatever it was, the ants could be held off no longer, unless petrol could by some method be led from the cistern into the ditch.

Then Leiningen remembered that in an outhouse nearby were two old disused fire engines. The peons dragged them out of the shed, connected their pumps to the cistern, uncoiled and laid the hose. They were just in time to aim a stream of petrol at a column of ants that had already crossed and drive them back down the incline into the ditch. Once more an oily girdle surrounded the garrison, once more it was possible to hold the position—for the moment.

It was obvious, however, that this last resource meant only the postponement of defeat and death. A few of the peons fell on their knees and began to pray; others, shrieking insanely, fired their revolvers at the black, advancing masses, as if they felt their despair was pitiful enough to sway fate itself to mercy.

> ◆ **Literary Focus**
> What other elements besides ants influence the external conflict?

❺

At length, two of the men's nerves broke: Leiningen saw a naked Indian leap over the north side of the petrol trench, quickly followed by a second. They sprinted with incredible speed toward the river. But their fleetness did not save them; long before they could attain the rafts, the enemy covered their bodies from head to foot.

In the agony of their torment, both sprang blindly into the wide river, where enemies no less sinister awaited them. Wild screams of mortal anguish informed the breathless onlookers that crocodiles and sword-toothed piranhas were no less ravenous than ants, and

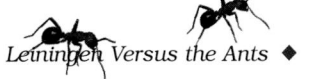
Leiningen Versus the Ants ◆ 491

◆ **Critical Thinking**

❸ Draw Conclusions Ask students how the Indians feel about Leiningen, and why. *They respect him, admire him, and think of him as almost superhuman. His calmness and determination makes him seem powerful.*

◆ **Literary Focus**

❹ Conflict Ask: What effect does the conflict with Leiningen seem to have on the ants? *It appears to make them more determined to advance—just as it makes Leiningen more determined to halt them.*

◆ **Literary Focus**

❺ Conflict Students may cite the presence of crocodiles and piranhas in the water, rendering the water unusable for refuge. The dwindling supply of petrol also influences the external conflict.

◆ **Critical Thinking**

❶ Analyze Character Ask students why they think Leiningen is able to keep developing new ideas to repel the ants. *He has trained himself to analyze a situation carefully and thoroughly. His mind keeps working logically, and he never panics, even in an emergency.*

◆ **Build Grammar Skills**

❷ Correct Use of Apostrophes Have students note the words that are contractions in this paragraph and tell what words were joined to make each one. *The contractions are I'm for "I am," That'll for "that will," and I've for "I have."*

◆ **Critical Thinking**

❸ Make a Judgment Ask students what Leiningen's elaborate preparations reveal about him. *He is thorough and thinks things through, and he plans to survive his trip to the dam.*

even nimbler in reaching their prey.

In spite of this bloody warning, more and more men showed they were making up their minds to run the blockade. Anything, even a fight midstream against alligators, seemed better than powerlessly waiting for death to come and slowly consume their living bodies.

Leiningen flogged his brain till it reeled. Was there nothing on earth could sweep this devils' spawn back into the hell from which it came?

Then out of the inferno of his bewilderment rose a terrifying inspiration. Yes, one hope remained, and one alone. It might be possible to dam the great river completely, so that its waters would fill not only the water ditch but overflow into the entire gigantic "saucer" of land in which lay the plantation.

The far bank of the river was too high for the waters to escape that way. The stone breakwater ran between the river and the plantation; its only gaps occurred where the "horseshoe" ends of the water ditch passed into the river. So its waters would not only be forced to inundate into the plantation, they would also be held there by the breakwater until they rose to its own high level. In half an hour, perhaps even earlier, the plantation and its hostile army of occupation would be flooded.

The ranch house and outbuildings stood upon rising ground. Their foundations were higher than the breakwater, so the flood would not reach them. And any remaining ants trying to ascend the slope could be repulsed by petrol.

It was possible—yes, if one could only get to the dam! A distance of nearly two miles lay between the ranch house and the weir—two miles of ants. Those two peons had managed only a fifth of that distance at the cost of their lives. Was there an Indian daring enough after that to run the gauntlet five times as far? Hardly likely; and if there were, his prospect of getting back was almost nil.

No, there was only one thing for it, he'd have to make the attempt himself; he might just as well be running as sitting still, anyway, when the ants finally got him. Besides, there *was* a bit of a chance. Perhaps the ants weren't so almighty, after all; perhaps he had allowed the

mass suggestion of that evil black throng to hypnotize him, just as a snake fascinates and overpowers.

The ants were building their bridges. Leiningen got up on a chair. "Hey, lads, listen to me!" he cried. Slowly and listlessly, from all sides of the trench, the men began to shuffle toward him, the apathy of death already stamped on their faces.

"Listen, lads!" he shouted. "You're frightened of those beggars, but I'm proud of you. There's still a chance to save our lives—by flooding the plantation from the river. Now one of you might manage to get as far as the weir—but he'd never come back. Well, I'm not going to let you try it; if I did, I'd be worse than one of those ants. No, I called the tune, and now I'm going to pay the piper.

"The moment I'm over the ditch, set fire to the petrol. That'll allow time for the flood to do the trick. Then all you have to do is to wait here all snug and quiet till I'm back. Yes, I'm coming back, trust me"—he grinned—"when I've finished my slimming cure."

He pulled on high leather boots, drew heavy gauntlets over his hands, and stuffed the spaces between breeches and boots, gauntlets and arms, shirt and neck, with rags soaked in petrol. With close-fitting mosquito goggles he shielded his eyes, knowing too well the ants' dodge of first robbing their victim of sight. Finally, he plugged his nostrils and ears with cottonwool, and let the peons drench his clothes with petrol.

He was about to set off when the old Indian medicine man came up to him; he had a wondrous salve, he said, prepared from a species of chafer[13] whose odor was intolerable to ants. Yes, this odor protected these chafers from the attacks of even the most murderous ants. The Indian smeared the boss's boots, his gauntlets, and his face over and over with the extract.

Leiningen then remembered the paralyzing effect of ants' venom, and the Indian gave him a gourd full of the medicine he had administered to the bitten peon at the water ditch.

---

13. **chafer** (chāf´ er) *n*.: Insect that feeds on plants.

492 ◆ *Short Stories*

Cross-Curricular Connection: Science

Animals of Brazilian Rivers Point out that the largest river in Brazil is the Amazon, which is home to a vast number of species of animals. Other rivers in the area would support the same wildlife, which includes the small but vicious piranha, which will attack any animal in the water; electric eels; giant anacondas; crocodiles; and freshwater stingrays. There are other less

fearsome animals as well, such as the pirarucu, reputed to be the best and biggest freshwater fish in the world, and the giant catfish. Ask students why in "Leiningen Versus the Ants" only the dangerous river inhabitants are mentioned. *Students should observe that only the dangerous animals contribute to the conflict in the story.*

▲ **Critical Viewing** Imagine yourself in this situation. What would you need to do to survive? [**Connect**]

The planter drank it down without noticing its bitter taste; his mind was already at the weir.

He started off toward the northwest corner of the trench. With a bound he was over—and among the ants.

The beleaguered garrison had no opportunity to watch Leiningen's race against death. The ants were climbing the inner bank again—the lurid ring of petrol blazed aloft. For the fourth time that day the reflection from the fire shone on the sweating faces of the imprisoned

men, and on the reddish-black cuirasses[14] of their oppressors. The red and blue, dark-edged flames leaped vividly now, celebrating what? The funeral pyre of the four hundred, or of the hosts of destruction?

Leiningen ran. He ran in long, equal strides, with only one thought, one sensation, in his being—he *must* get through. He dodged all trees and shrubs; except for the split seconds his soles touched the ground, the ants should have no opportunity to alight on him. That they

---

14. **cuirasses** (kwi ras´ ez) *n.*: Body armor; here, the ants' outer bodies.

○ **Listening to Literature Audiocassettes** This may be a good time to play the recording of "Leiningen Versus the Ants," since the suspense and action in the story are building to a climax.

►**Critical Viewing**◄

❹ **Connect** Students may say you would need to keep moving, cover your skin as completely as possible, and get to safety quickly.

❺ **Clarification** Make sure students understand that the "four hundred" are the people on the plantation, while the "hosts of destruction" are the ants.

Cross-Curricular Connection: Health

Poisonous Animal Bites Point out to students that Leiningen's ants aren't the only animals with poisonous, or even fatal, bites. Spiders such as the black widow, tarantula, or brown spider can administer dangerous or even fatal bites. Mosquitoes can transmit diseases such as malaria and dengue fever that, if untreated, can kill. Some ticks transmit Lyme disease; bee stings, if the victim is allergic to them, can result in shock and death. Rattlesnakes and copperheads can kill with their venomous bites. Even mammals such as raccoons, skunks, and bats can transmit rabies, an infectious disease that is fatal, if untreated. Remind students that these animals present relatively minor threats because they do not travel in huge packs, as the ants do.

◆ Reading Strategy

❶ Predict Based on Plot Details
Have students predict whether they think Leiningen will die at this point. *Suggested answer: No. Based on what we know of his determination, he will triumph over his own weakness.*

◆ Critical Thinking

❷ Draw Conclusions Ask students why they think Leiningen was able to rise again and go on. Until now, he has relied on his intellect. What is he relying on now? *When Leiningen recalls the horrifying death of the deer, his instinct for survival forces him to get to his feet and continue.*

would get to him soon, despite the salve on his boots, the petrol on his clothes, he realized only too well, but he knew even more surely that he must, and that he would, get to the weir.

Apparently the salve was some use after all: not until he had reached halfway did he feel ants under his clothes, and a few on his face. Mechanically, in his stride, he struck at them, scarcely conscious of their bites. He saw he was drawing appreciably nearer the weir—the distance grew less and less—sank to five hundred—three—two—hundred yards.

Then he was at the weir and gripping the ant-hulled wheel. Hardly had he seized it when a horde of infuriated ants flowed over his hands, arms, and shoulders. He started the wheel—before it turned once on its axis the swarm covered his face. Leiningen strained like a madman, his lips pressed tight; if he opened them to draw breath . . .

He turned and turned; slowly the dam lowered until it reached the bed of the river. Already the water was overflowing the ditch. Another minute, and the river was pouring through the nearby gap in the breakwater. The flooding of the plantation had begun.

Leiningen let go the wheel. Now, for the first time, he realized he was coated from head to foot with a layer of ants. In spite of the petrol, his clothes were full of them, several had got to his body or were clinging to his face. Now that he had completed his task, he felt the smart raging over his flesh from the bites of sawing and piercing insects.

Frantic with pain, he almost plunged into the river. To be ripped and slashed to shreds by piranhas? Already he was running the return journey, knocking ants from his gloves and jacket, brushing them from his bloodied face, squashing them to death under his clothes.

One of the creatures bit him just below the rim of his goggles; he managed to tear it away, but the agony of the bite and its etching acid drilled into the eye nerves; he saw now through circles of fire into a milky mist, then he ran for a time almost blinded, knowing that if he once tripped and fell. . . . The old Indian's brew

didn't seem much good; it weakened the poison a bit, but didn't get rid of it. His heart pounded as if it would burst; blood roared in his ears; a giant's fist battered his lungs.

Then he could see again, but the burning girdle of petrol appeared infinitely far away; he could not last half that distance. Swift-changing pictures flashed through his head, episodes in his life, while in another part of his brain a cool and impartial onlooker informed this ant-blurred, gasping, exhausted bundle named Leiningen that such a rushing panorama of scenes from one's past is seen only in the moment before death.

A stone in the path . . . too weak to avoid it . . . the planter stumbled and collapsed. He tried to rise . . . he must be pinned under a rock . . . it was impossible . . . the slightest movement was impossible. . . .

Then all at once he saw, starkly clear and huge, and, right before his eyes, furred with ants, towering and swaying in its death agony, the pampas stag. In six minutes—gnawed to the bones. He *couldn't* die like that! And something outside him seemed to drag him to his feet. He tottered. He began to stagger forward again.

Through the blazing ring hurtled an apparition which, as soon as it reached the ground on the inner side, fell full length and did not move. Leiningen, at the moment he made that leap through the flames, lost consciousness for the first time in his life. As he lay there, with glazing eyes and lacerated face, he appeared a man returned from the grave. The peons rushed to him, stripped off his clothes, tore away the ants from a body that seemed almost one open wound; in some places the bones were showing. They carried him into the ranch house.

As the curtain of flames lowered, one could see in place of the illimitable host of ants an extensive vista of water. The thwarted river had swept over the plantation, carrying with it the entire army. The water had collected and mounted in the great "saucer," while the ants had in vain attempted to reach the hill on which stood the ranch house. The girdle of flames held them back.

And so, imprisoned between water and fire, they had been delivered into the annihilation that was their god. And near the farther mouth of the water ditch, where the stone mole had its second gap, the ocean swept the lost battalions into the river, to vanish forever.

The ring of fire dwindled as the water mounted to the petrol trench and quenched the dimming flames. The inundation rose higher and higher: because its outflow was impeded by the timber and underbrush it had carried along with it, its surface required some time to reach the top of the high stone breakwater and discharge over it the rest of the shattered army.

It swelled over ant-stippled shrubs and bushes, until it washed against the foot of the knoll whereon the besieged had taken refuge. For a while an <u>alluvium</u> of ants tried again and again to attain the dry land, only to be repulsed by streams of petrol back into the merciless flood.

Leiningen lay on his bed, his body swathed from head to foot in bandages. With <u>fomentations</u> and salves, they had managed to stop the bleeding, and had dressed his many wounds. Now they thronged around him, one question in every face. Would he recover? "He won't die," said the old man who had bandaged

him, "if he doesn't want to."

The planter opened his eyes. "Everything in order?" he asked.

"They're gone," said his nurse. He held out to his master a gourd full of a powerful sleeping-draft. Leiningen gulped it down.

"I told you I'd come back," he murmured, "even if I am a bit streamlined."

◆ Build Vocabulary

alluvium (ə lōō´ vē əm) *n.*: Material such as sand or gravel deposited by moving water

fomentations (fō´ mən tā´ shənz) *n.*: Applications of warm, moist substances in the treatment of an injury

---

Beyond Literature

Media Connection

The Naked Jungle The vivid descriptions and exciting action in "Leiningen Versus the Ants" inspired movie makers at Paramount Pictures to create a film based on Stephenson's short story. The film version, starring Charlton Heston, was released in 1954 with the title *The Naked Jungle*. The photos you see in the story are stills from the movie. Screenwriters Ranald MacDougall, Ben Maddow, and Philip Yordan expanded the cast of characters, adding a wife for Leiningen and increasing the roles of two plantation workers. They also added several more "close calls" to the plot. Why do you think the screenwriters made some of these changes? What changes might you make if you were doing a movie version of this story?

Guide for Responding

◆ *Literature and Your Life*

Reader's Response Put yourself in Leiningen's place. What would you have done differently? Why?

Thematic Focus What attributes do you think helped Leiningen overcome the ants? Why?

☑ Check Your Comprehension

1. What threat do the ants pose to Leiningen?
2. At what point in the story does it first seem that Leiningen has snatched victory "from the very jaws of defeat"? How do the ants recover?
3. How does Leiningen finally defeat the ants?

Leiningen Versus the Ants ◆ 495

---

❸ Conflict Leiningen has won the battle. Suggest to students that in most conflicts, the winner pays a price for victory. Ask students: What has been the price of Leiningen's victory? Was the victory worth the price? *He has sacrificed several lives and lost much of the plantation. Some students may think the victory was not worth the price, since if Leiningen and his people had evacuated in the first place, all lives would have been saved. Others will think that it was worth the price to prove that the human mind and spirit can triumph over anything.*

Reinforce and Extend

Answers

◆ *Literature and Your Life*

Reader's Response Students may say they would have been less confident that they could save themselves in the conflict with the ants.

Thematic Focus Students may cite Leiningen's determination and ingenuity. Without determination, he would have given up; without ingenuity he would have been defeated.

☑ Check Your Comprehension

1. The ants threaten to destroy his plantation and kill him and his workers.
2. It first appears that Leiningen will defeat the ants when they can't find a way to cross the moat. However, the ants create "rafts" to ferry themselves across.
3. He lowers the dam to allow the river to flood the plantation. The flood waters of the river carry away the ants.

Beyond the Selection

FURTHER READING

Other Works with the Theme of Clashing Forces
Hour of the Wolf, Patricia Calvert
"The Most Dangerous Game," Richard Connell
Hatchet, Gary Paulsen
"The Open Boat," Stephen Crane
Lost in the Barrens, Farley Mowat
The Old Man and the Sea, Ernest Hemingway
Kon Tiki, Thor Heyerdahl
  We suggest that you preview these works before recommending them to students.

INTERNET

You and your students may not find information about Carl Stephenson on the Internet, as "Leiningen and the Ants" is his only published work. However, students who are interested in discovering more about ants and how they live can visit the following Web site: **http://science.coe.4wf.edu/SH/curr/insects/ants.htm**
    Please be aware, however, that the site may have changed since we published this information. We *strongly recommend* that you preview the site before you send students to it.

Answers

◆ Critical Thinking

1. It is his nature to fight back rather than surrender; he enjoys the challenge to his intelligence and ingenuity; he has worked very hard to build his plantation.
2. (a) The qualities that equip Leiningen to fight the ants include intelligence, courage, self-confidence, determination, and experience. (b) His self-confidence leads him to put the lives of others in danger.
3. The ants use each other as bridges and cut leaves to make rafts. Overall, they demonstrate an ability to adapt, discipline, and organize.
4. Leiningen's instinct for survival forces him up when he sees the stag eaten by the ants.
5. Some students may say that Leiningen was justified because the plantation was the peons' home, too, and the peons did not stand a chance out in the open against the ants. Others may think that he was wrong to risk the lives of others to satisfy his own need for victory.
6. Students who have read stories or novels set in wartime featuring disaster situations may have titles to suggest.

◆ Reading Strategy

1. Leiningen's resolve not to die as the stag does suggests a resolve that won't be defeated.
2. Some may say that making predictions increases the suspense of a story by keeping readers guessing whether their predictions will prove valid. Others may enjoy a mental duel with the author as they try to discover his or her intentions.

◆ Literary Focus

1. The two opposing forces are Leiningen and the ants.
2. Leiningen's internal conflict is between his fear of the ants and his determination to defeat them.
3. The peons experience an internal conflict between their loyalty to and dependence on Leiningen and their desire to flee the plantation.

---

*G*uide for Responding (continued)

◆ Critical Thinking

INTERPRET

1. Why do you think Leiningen is so determined to stay and fight the ants? **[Infer]**
2. (a) What qualities do you think make Leiningen well equipped to fight the ants? (b) What qualities might make him dangerous to others? **[Analyze]**
3. What behavior of the ants makes them appear to be intelligent beings? **[Interpret]**
4. After Leiningen stumbles and falls on the way back from the river, is it his intellect that forces him to get up or his natural instinct? Explain. **[Distinguish]**

EVALUATE

5. By staying to fight the ants, Leiningen risks others' lives as well as his own. Do you think he was justified? Why or why not? **[Make a Judgment]**

EXTEND

6. What other examples from literature can you recall in which a character has to make a decision upon which others' lives depend? Compare them with this tale. **[Literature Link]**

◆ Reading Strategy

PREDICT BASED ON PLOT DETAILS

As the plot of an action-filled story like this develops, you continue to **predict based on new details.**

1. What hints indicate how the war against the ants will end?
2. How can predicting increase your enjoyment of a story?

◆ Literary Focus

CONFLICT

The **conflicts** in this tale are both **internal**—within a character—and **external**—between a character and an outside force.

1. What are the two opposing forces in the external conflict?
2. What is Leiningen's internal conflict?
3. Which characters besides Leiningen experience an internal conflict? What is that conflict?

◆ Build Vocabulary

USING LATIN PLURAL FORMS

Some words in English, such as *alluvium*, that are borrowed from Latin retain their Latin plural forms. Words from Latin change endings as follows to form plurals:

- *-um* becomes *-a*
- *-us* becomes *-i*
- *-a* becomes *-ae*

On your paper, write the plural forms of each of the following words.

1. datum   3. focus   5. octopus
2. curriculum 4. medium   6. antenna

USING THE WORD BANK

On your paper, complete the following analogies using the words from the Word Bank. Fill in the blank with the word that best completes each comparison.

1. *Water* is to *plants* as ____?____ is to *ants*.
2. *Ignore* is to *rule* as ____?____ is to *law*.
3. *Bandage* is to *cut* as ____?____ is to *river*.
4. *Sawdust* is to *chainsaw* as ____?____ is to *current*.
5. *Employee* is to *manager* as ____?____ is to *master*.
6. *Detergent* is to *clothing* as ____?____ is to *injury*.

◆ Build Grammar Skills

CORRECT USE OF APOSTROPHES

Apostrophes are used to form possessives and contractions. They are not used to form plurals. To make a singular noun possessive, add an apostrophe and an *s*. To make a plural noun possessive, add an apostrophe after the *s* or, if the plural does not end in *s*, add an apostrophe and an *s*.

Practice Copy the following sentences on your paper, and add apostrophes in the proper places.

1. Finally, two of the mens nerves broke.
2. Here the defenders front was sparse.
3. "Well, lads," he began, "theres no shame in leaving."
4. Hadnt his brain for once taken on more than it could manage?
5. The workers watched, thinking, "Hes not going to make it."
6. Leiningens bandages covered the ants damage.

◆ Build Vocabulary

1. data;   2. curricula;
3. foci;   4. media;
5. octopi;   6. antennae

Using the Word Bank
1. provender;   2. flout;
3. weir;   4. alluvium;
5. peon;   6. fomentations

◆ Build Grammar Skills

1. Finally, two of the men's nerves broke.

2. Here the defenders' front was sparse.
3. "Well, lads," he began, "there's no shame in leaving."
4. Hadn't his brain for once taken on more than it could manage?
5. The workers watched, thinking, "He's not going to make it."
6. Leiningen's bandages covered the ants' damage.

Writer's Solution

For additional instruction and practice, use pages 110–111 on Apostrophes in the *Writer's Solution Grammar Practice Book.*

Build Your Portfolio

Idea Bank

Writing

1. **Letter to the Editor** Leiningen is not able to defeat the ants single-handedly. Think of a situation in which people you know have tried to solve a problem through a group effort. Describe their actions in a letter to the editor of your local paper.

2. **Change the Disaster** How would the story be different if Leiningen's foe were a volcano rather than ants? Write a brief summary of the story as it would change if you change the enemy.

3. **News Report** Imagine that you are a reporter covering Leiningen's war against the ants. Write the story in 250 words or less.

Speaking and Listening

4. **Motivational Speech** Review the motivational tactics Leiningen uses on his workers. Then develop your own speech to raise morale and inspire courage in the frightened peons.

5. **The Author's Motive** As a group, discuss why Carl Stephenson may have decided to write this story as well as why he decided not to publish any others.

Projects

6. **Map of the Plantation** Based on Stephenson's description, draw a map of Leiningen's plantation. On your map, use symbols and lines to show the measures of defense taken and the distance the ants advanced at each stage. **[Art Link]**

7. **Disaster Relief** Contact an agency such as the American Red Cross to find out how and what kind of aid is supplied to communities affected by natural disasters. **[Social Studies Link]**

Writing Mini-Lesson

Movie Scene

Carl Stephenson's tale of terror has all the ingredients of a blockbuster movie: exotic locale, heroic main character, terrifying villain. Write a script for a movie scene of the final action-packed moment—the climax and resolution—of the soon-to-be-released thriller.

Write a screenplay of the scene with dialogue and a description of the actors' movements. Also include camera angles and other directions to the film crew.

> #### Writing Skills Focus: Climax and Resolution
>
> The conflict is the central part of the plot of any story. Your conflict should be both believable and serious enough so that a solution is not readily apparent. Following the **climax,** or high point of the conflict, the **resolution** shows how the problems and tension are worked out. Make sure that your resolution ties up any "loose ends" of the plot.

Prewriting Reread the end of the story, jotting down crucial actions and words of the story's high point. Brainstorm for visual details that will add to the suspense of the climax.

Drafting Begin your scene with a striking image that will capture the mood you want to portray. For example, a close-up of Leiningen's face followed by a shot of the millions of ants he must soon face will establish a mood of suspense. Refer to your notes as you draft the scene to remind yourself of details that will translate into vivid on-screen images.

Revising Reread your draft, pretending that you are an actor who will use the screenplay. Would you understand everything you must do based only on the screenplay? Fill in any gaps in the action, dialogue, and directions.

Leiningen Versus the Ants ◆ 497

Idea Bank

Customizing for
Performance Levels

Following are suggestions for matching Idea Bank topics with your students' performance levels:

   Less Advanced Students: 1, 6, 7
   Average Students: 2, 4, 6
   More Advanced Students: 3, 4, 5

Customizing for
Learning Modalities

Following are suggestions for matching Idea Bank topics with your students' learning modalities:

   Verbal/Linguistic: 1, 2, 3, 4, 5
   Visual/Spatial: 6
   Logical/Mathematical: 7

Writing Mini-Lesson

Refer students to the Writing Handbook, page 965, for instruction on the writing process, and pages 968–969 for further information on creative writing: drama.

Writing and Language Transparencies Have students use the Story Map blackline master, p. 84, to help them organize the details for their movie scripts.

Writing Lab CD-ROM
Have students complete the tutorial on Creative Writing. Follow these steps:

1. Students can use the interactive tips on purpose to learn about techniques that can help them.
2. Have students review video clips about gathering details for drama.
3. Suggest that students use the audio-annotated writing models for drama.
4. Have students draft on computer.
5. Students can use the proofreading checklist for drama to revise their drafts.

Allow approximately 120 minutes of class time to complete these steps.

Sourcebook
Have students use Chapter 6, Creative Writing (pp. 164–193), for additional support. The chapter includes a model from literature of a dramatic scene (p. 168).

✓ ASSESSMENT OPTIONS

Formal Assessment, Selection Test, pp. 126–128, and Assessment Resources Software. The selection test is designed so that it can be easily customized to the performance levels of your students.
Alternative Assessment, p. 36, includes options for less advanced students, more advanced students, bodily/kinesthetic learners, verbal/linguistic learners, visual/spatial learners, and logical/mathematic learners.

PORTFOLIO ASSESSMENT
Use the following rubrics in *Alternative Assessment* to assess student writing:
Letter to the Editor: Persuasion Rubric, p. 105
Change the Disaster: Summary Rubric, p. 98
News Report: Research/Report Rubric, p. 106
Writing Mini-Lesson: Drama Rubric, p. 109

497

Guide for Reading

OBJECTIVES

1. To read, comprehend, and interpret a story
2. To relate a story to personal experience
3. To draw conclusions while reading a story
4. To identify first-person point of view
5. To build vocabulary in context and understand conjunctive adverbs
6. To understand and identify subordination in sentences
7. To write a description from another vantage point, maintaining a consistent point of view
8. To respond to the story through writing, speaking and listening, and projects

SKILLS INSTRUCTION

Vocabulary:
Words Groups:
Conjunctive
Adverbs
Grammar:
Subordination
Reading Strategy:
Draw Conclusions
Literary Focus:
First-Person Point
of View

Writing:
Consistent Point
of View
**Speaking and
Listening:**
Radio Interview;
Oral Presentation
(teacher edition)
Critical Viewing:
Relate; Analyze

PORTFOLIO OPPORTUNITIES

Writing: Post Card; Publicity Release; Poem

Speaking and Listening: Radio Interview; Oral Presentation

Projects: Tourism Poster; Storyboard

More About the Author
Stephen Vincent Benét was not the only literary member of his family. His brother, William Rose Benét, wrote poems on American themes. His sister, Laura, wrote novels and biography. Stephen Vincent Benét wrote scripts for two motion pictures, including a film biography of Abraham Lincoln, directed by D. W. Griffith. One of his stories was used as the basis for one of the most popular movie musicals ever made, *Seven Brides for Seven Brothers*.

Stephen Vincent Benét
(1898–1943)

When a clock strikes thirteen, you can expect strange things to happen. "By the Waters of Babylon" first appeared in a story collection by Stephen Vincent Benét with just that title—*Thirteen O'Clock* (1937).

Proud American Born in Bethlehem, Pennsylvania, Benét grew up listening to his father's evening poetry readings. As a young man, he took time off from his studies at Yale University to serve in the State Department during World War I. (His poor eyesight prevented him from serving in the army.) Much of Benét's work centers on American history and the establishment of American ideals.

A Poet at Heart Benét considered himself a poet first and foremost. His interest in American history and folklore, in addition to his interest in the ballad form, influenced his epic poem, *John Brown's Body*, which won a Pulitzer Prize in 1929. (He was awarded another Pulitzer, after his death, for the first part of an unfinished American epic, *Western Star*.)

Though he preferred poetry, Benét also achieved success writing short stories. His best-known short story, "The Devil and Daniel Webster," was the basis for a play, an opera, and a motion picture.

"By the Waters of Babylon" actually began as a poem, which Benét then transformed into a short story called "The Place of the Gods." He later changed the title while preparing *Thirteen O'Clock* for publication.

◆ Build Vocabulary

WORD GROUPS: CONJUNCTIVE ADVERBS

In this story, the main character encounters a dog "as big as a wolf." He lists a number of reasons for not killing the dog, and he ends by saying *"Moreover, night was falling." Moreover* is a special type of adverb called a conjunctive adverb. **Conjunctive adverbs** show a relationship between ideas and often connect independent clauses. *Moreover* indicates that the idea that follows (night was falling) is in addition to what has come before. Other conjunctive adverbs include *nevertheless, finally, therefore,* and *however.*

WORD BANK

purified
bowels
moreover
nevertheless

Preview this list of words from the story. Look for familiar word parts and discuss with a partner how they can help you determine the meaning of the whole word.

◆ Build Grammar Skills

SUBORDINATION

Subordination is the process by which writers connect two unequal but related ideas in a complex sentence. The subordinate (less important) idea limits, develops, describes, or adds meaning to the main idea. For instance, in the following sentence from the story, the subordinate (adverb) clause clarifies under what circumstances the idea in the main clause occurs.

We do not even say its name *though we know its name.*

The less important idea is introduced with the subordinate conjunction *though.* Other words that indicate the relationship between main clauses and subordinate clauses include subordinating conjunctions like *after, because, while, unless, when, if,* and *than,* as well as relative pronouns like *who, which,* and *that.*

 Prentice Hall Literature Program Resources

REINFORCE / RETEACH / EXTEND

Selection Support Pages:
Build Vocabulary: Word Groups, p. 151
Build Grammar Skills: Subordination, p. 152
Reading Strategy: Draw Conclusions, p. 153
Literary Focus: First-Person Point of View, p. 154

Strategies for Diverse Students Needs, p. 37

Beyond Literature
Cross-Curricular Connection: Social Studies, p. 37

Formal Assessment Selection Test, pp. 129–131; Assessment Resources Software

Alternative Assessment, p. 37

Writing and Language Transparencies
Comparison and Contrast Organizer, pp. 95–97

Resource Pro CD-ROM
"By the Waters of Babylon"—includes all resource materials and customizable lesson plan

 Listening to Literature Audiocassettes
"By the Waters of Babylon"

By the Waters of Babylon

◆ *Literature and Your Life*

CONNECT YOUR EXPERIENCE
The crumbling buildings you see when you look at pictures of ancient civilizations were once schools, theaters, and places of business. As they do today, people of the past worked, learned, and socialized. Someday in the future, people may look at the ruins of the buildings of today and try to imagine the kind of people who lived here.

Journal Writing Describe a public building in your neighborhood that would tell a good story of your community to future generations.

THEMATIC FOCUS: TO THE FUTURE
The main character in "By the Waters of Babylon" explores the ruins of a once mighty civilization. This story raises the question, "What story will our society tell to the future?"

◆ Background for Understanding

LITERATURE
The title "By the Waters of Babylon" is an allusion to Psalm 137 in the Bible, in which the Israelites, held captive in Babylon, wept over their lost homeland, Zion.

> By the rivers of Babylon, there we sat down, yea, we wept, when we remembered Zion . . .

When you read "By the Waters of Babylon," consider how these lines from the psalm relate to the story.

◆ Literary Focus

FIRST-PERSON POINT OF VIEW
The information you receive when you hear or read a story is influenced by the point of view of the storyteller. **Point of view** is the position or perspective from which the events of a story are seen. When the author uses **first-person** point of view, the narrator is a character who participates in the events and tells the story using the first-person pronoun *I*. You the reader "see" the events of the story through the eyes and mind of this first-person narrator.

The "I" in "By the Waters of Babylon" is John, who introduces himself in the following way: "I am the son of a priest. I have been in the Dead Places near us . . . at first, I was afraid." Because John tells the story, you see, feel, and know only what John sees, feels, and knows.

◆ Reading Strategy

DRAW CONCLUSIONS
When an author gives you details about settings, events, and characters, you use those details along with your logic to **draw conclusions** about what is happening, where it's happening, and why. Sometimes an author creates a sense of mystery by presenting only a few details at a time. As each new detail is revealed, you combine it with others to draw conclusions

At the beginning of "By the Waters of Babylon," the narrator presents these mysterious details:

> It is forbidden to go to any of the Dead Places except to search for metal . . . It is forbidden to cross the great river and look upon the place that was the Place of the Gods . . . it is there that there are the ashes of the Great Burning.

As the story continues, you will learn more details that will help you draw conclusions about the Dead Places, why it is forbidden to go there, and what events led to the Great Burning.

Interest Grabber Ask students to imagine that they are exploring an empty building and they come upon the following scene:

> "He was sitting in his chair, by the window. . . and, for the first moment, I thought he was alive. Then I saw the skin on the back of his hand—it was like dry leather."

Ask students to tell what their reaction would be to this discovery. Then tell students that the narrator of this story relates his adventures as he explores a place where danger and other frightening discoveries like this one lie in wait.

Customize for
Less Proficient Readers
Have these students keep lists of clues that help answer the questions: Who are the gods in the story? Where is the "Place of the Gods"? Suggest that each time they come to a clue that might help them find an answer, they write it down. As more clues accumulate, they can begin to draw conclusions.

Customize for
More Advanced Students
The author of this story gives his narrator a style of speech meant to sound more primitive than contemporary English. To analyze this style, have students rewrite short passages of John's monologue in a more contemporary style and compare their rewritten passages with the original.

Customize for
English Language Learners
Alert these students that, in this story, the character tells his story using language that is neither standard English nor modern colloquial speech. Students should take notes as they read and list phrases or references that need explanation. Pause at the end of a page or a section to explain the confusing passages.

Customize for
Intrapersonal Learners
Encourage students to think, as they read, about the inner qualities that make John, the hero of "By the Waters of Babylon," a person of destiny in his community. Suggest they note their thoughts in their journals.

 Preparing for Standardized Tests

Reading Students can improve their scores on the reading comprehension portions of standardized tests by applying the Reading Strategy for this selection, Draw Conclusions. Both the ACT and SAT tests, for example, require students to draw appropriate conclusions based on passages they read. After students have answered the Reading Strategy questions on page 510, give them the Draw Conclusions page in *Selection Support,* p. 153.

Grammar and Language Subordination is an essential skill for students to master in order to express complex ideas in clear, coherent, fluent sentences. Applying the skill by completing the Build Grammar Skills activity on page 510 and reinforcing it with the Build Grammar Skills page in *Selection Support,* p. 152, will help students improve their writing as well as their scores on essay sections of standardized tests.

One-Minute Insight John's people are the survivors of our own civilization after it is destroyed in a war. They know little of that civilization, and call its ruins "Places of the Gods." John's hunger for knowledge drives him to enter the forbidden ruins and learn the secrets of the "gods." John, the son of a priest, will reveal what he has learned. Will his people embark on a path toward their own destruction—or avoid the mistakes of the past? The story is a warning that unless we use technology wisely, we may destroy civilization.

◆ Reading Strategy

❶ Draw Conclusions Ask students: What are the "Dead Places"? What was the "Great Burning"? Who are the gods? *Students might guess that the "Dead Places" are houses that contain dead people, that the Great Burning was a great explosion, and that the gods are people from a former civilization. Accept all reasonable answers.*

◆ Build Vocabulary

❷ Conjunctive Adverbs Ask students to identify the conjunctive adverb in this sentence and explain the relationship between the ideas it connects. *The adverb* nevertheless *contrasts the idea that the narrator touched the metal with the idea that his brothers would not have touched it.*

◆ Build Grammar Skills

❸ Subordination Ask students to identify the main and subodinate clauses in this sentence. Have them explain how the subordinate limits the idea in the main clause. *The main clause is "he punished me more strictly than my brothers." The subordinate clause is "when I boasted or wept without a reason." The subordinate clause tells under what circumstances his father punished him.*

◆ Reading Strategy

❹ Draw Conclusions Ask students what they can conclude about the narrator's people. *Students can conclude that these people are primitive; only the priests know simple first aid techniques, and only people of the priestly class learn how to read.*

500

By the Waters of Babylon

Stephen Vincent Benét

❶ The north and the west and the south are good hunting ground, but it is forbidden to go east. It is forbidden to go to any of the Dead Places except to search for metal, and then he who touches the metal must be a priest or the son of a priest. Afterwards, both the man and the metal must be <u>purified</u>! These are the rules and the laws: they are well made. It is forbidden to cross the great river and look upon the place that was the Place of the Gods—this is most strictly forbidden. We do not even say its name though we know its name. It is there that spirits live, and demons—it is there that there are the ashes of the Great Burning. These things are forbidden—they have been forbidden since the beginning of time.

My father is a priest; I am the son of a priest. I have been in the Dead Places near us, with my father—at first, I was afraid. When my father went into the house to search for the metal, I stood by the door and my heart felt small and weak. It was a dead man's house, a spirit house. It did not have the smell of man, though there were old bones in a corner. But it is not fitting that a priest's son should show fear. I looked at the bones in the shadow and kept my voice still.

Then my father came out with the metal —a good, strong piece. He looked at me with both eyes but I had not run away. He gave me the metal to hold—I took it and did not die. So he knew that I was truly his son and would be a priest in my time. That was when I was very young—nevertheless, my brothers would not **❷** have done it, though they are good hunters. After that, they gave me the good piece of meat and the warm corner by the fire. My father watched over me—he was glad that I should be a priest. But when I boasted or wept without a reason, he punished me more strictly than my **❸** brothers. That was right.

After a time, I myself was allowed to go into the dead houses and search for metal. So I learned the ways of those houses—and if I saw bones, I was no longer afraid. The bones are light and old—sometimes they will fall into dust if you touch them. But that is a great sin.

I was taught the chants and the spells—I was taught how to stop the running of blood from a wound and many secrets. A priest must know many secrets—that was what my father **❹** said. If the hunters think we do all things by chants and spells, they may believe so—it does not hurt them. I was taught how to read in the

◆ Build Vocabulary

purified (py‌oor´ ə fid) *v.*: Cleansed; made pure.

▶ **Critical Viewing** How does this picture of a city fit into your ideas of a future world? [Relate]

500 ◆ Short Stories

Block Scheduling Strategies

Consider these suggestions to take advantage of extended class time:

• Introduce the Reading Strategy, Draw Conclusions, on page 499. Encourage students to note the details in the story that help them draw conclusions about facts the author does not directly reveal.

• After students have read the first few paragraphs of the story, direct their attention to the concept of the first-person point of view. Have them read the Literary Focus on page 499.

• After students have read the story, they can work in pairs to answer the Literary Focus questions on page 510. For more practice, follow up with the Literary Focus page in *Selection Support,* p. 154.

• Have students work in groups on the Community Connection activity in *Beyond Literature* on page 509. Creating a visitors' guide for community landmarks will help students connect their own experience with Benét's story.

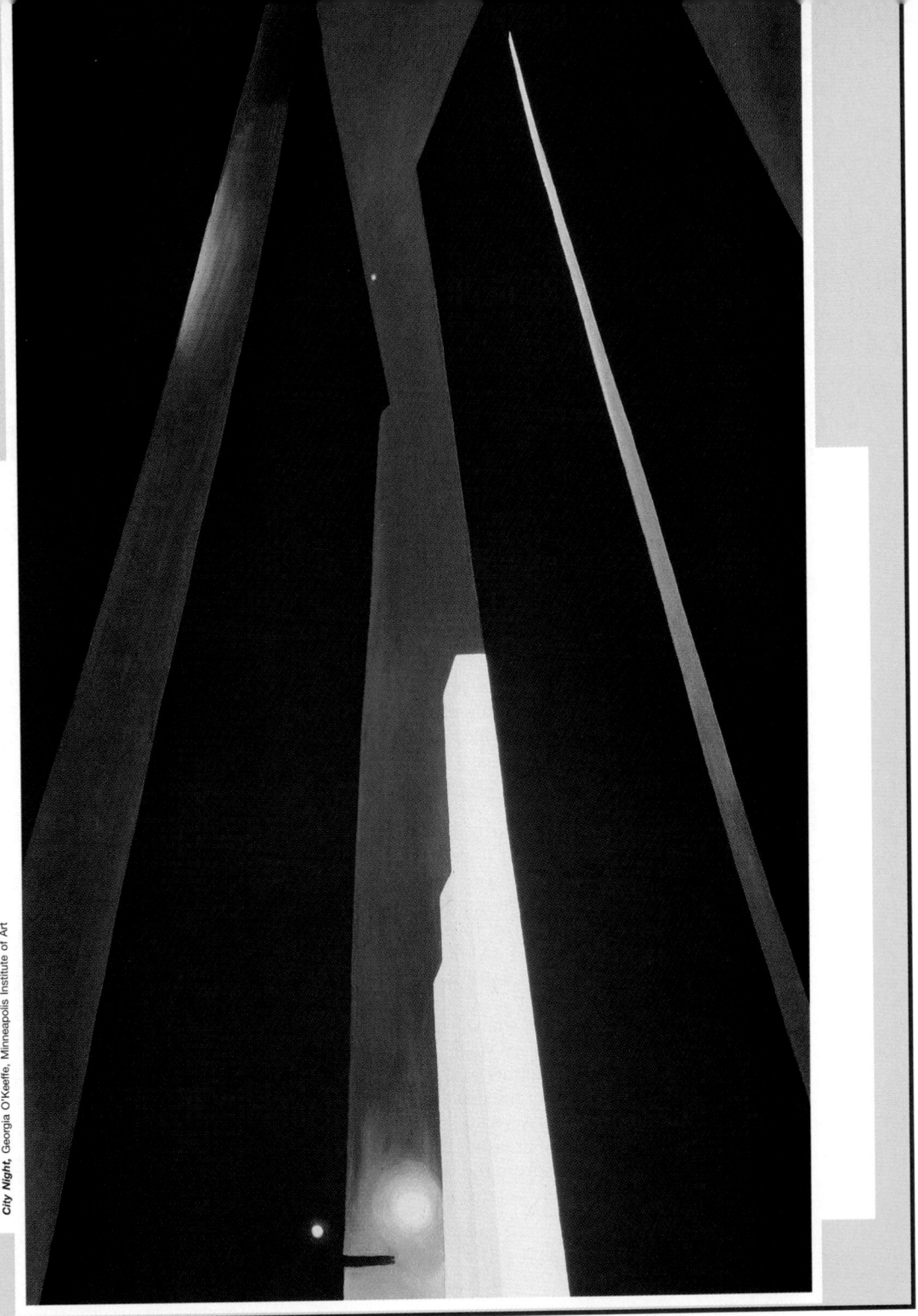

City Night, Georgia O'Keeffe, Minneapolis Institute of Art

City Night, 1926, by Georgia O'Keeffe.

Georgia O'Keeffe (1887–1986) is considered one of the foremost twentieth-century American artists. The greater part of her life and work is associated with the American Southwest, particularly New Mexico. However, this painting of towering monolithic skyscrapers illuminated by the moon is typical of O'Keeffe's cityscapes, as it features a geometric design with no human figures.

Use these questions for discussion:
1. What clue does this painting give you about the forbidden "Place of the Gods"?
   The painting, "City Night," could be a clue that the "Place of the Gods" is really a city. Students may speculate about the city and why it is forbidden.
2. How does the mood of the painting reflect the mood of the beginning of the story? *Students may say that the beginning of the story is mysterious because so much is left unexplained—Place of the Gods, Dead Places, the Great Burning. The painting reflects this mood because it, too, looks mysterious and eerie.*

◆ Build Grammar Skills

❶ Subordination Ask students to identify the main and subordinate clauses in this sentence. Ask: What information does the subordinate idea add to the main idea? *The main clause begins, "I came to my father and said...." The subordinate clause is "When I was a man at last." The subordinate clause answers the question "When?"*

◆ Reading Strategy

❷ Draw Conclusions Ask students what they think the narrator's intentions may be based on this passage. Ask: Which words lead you to draw your conclusion? *While the narrator agrees with his father, the words, "...it was my voice that spoke and not my spirit," may lead students to believe that he intends to explore the forbidden places.*

◆ Critical Thinking

❸ Infer Ask students: What does the father mean by dreams that "eat you up"? Why will the boy become a great priest if he is not eaten up by his dreams? *By dreams that "eat you up," the father might mean dreams that are too big for the boy because they become obsessions and lead him into danger. If he is not eaten up by his dreams, the boy will become a great priest because he will return from his journey with new and powerful knowledge that he will use for the good of his people.*

I went fasting, as is the law. My body hurt but not my heart. When the dawn came, I was out of sight. . . .

old books and how to make the old writings—that was hard and took a long time. My knowledge made me happy—it was like a fire in my heart. Most of all, I liked to hear of the Old Days and the stories of the gods. I asked myself many questions that I could not answer, but it was good to ask them. At night, I would lie awake and listen to the wind—it seemed to me that it was the voice of the gods as they flew through the air.

We are not ignorant like the Forest People—our women spin wool on the wheel, our priests wear a white robe. We do not eat grubs from the tree, we have not forgotten the old writings, although they are hard to understand. Nevertheless, my knowledge and my lack of knowledge burned in me—I wished to know more. When I was a man at last, I came to my father and said, "It is time for me to go on my journey. Give me your leave."

❶

He looked at me for a long time, stroking his beard, then he said at last, "Yes. It is time." That night, in the house of the priesthood, I asked for and received purification. My body hurt but my spirit was a cool stone. It was my father himself who questioned me about my dreams.

He bade me look into the smoke of the fire and see—I saw and told what I saw. It was what I have always seen—a river, and, beyond it, a great Dead Place and in it the gods walking. I have always thought about that. His eyes were stern when I told him—he was no longer my father but a priest. He said, "This is a strong dream."

"It is mine," I said, while the smoke waved and my head felt light. They were singing the Star song in the outer chamber and it was like the buzzing of bees in my head.

He asked me how the gods were dressed and I told him how they were dressed. We know how they were dressed from the book, but I saw them as if they were before me.

When I had finished, he threw the sticks three times and studied them as they fell.

"This is a very strong dream," he said. "It may eat you up."

"I am not afraid," I said and looked at him with both eyes. My voice sounded thin in my ears but that was because of the smoke.

He touched me on the breast and the forehead. He gave me the bow and the three arrows.

"Take them," he said. "It is forbidden to travel east. It is forbidden to cross the river. It is forbidden to go to the Place of the Gods. All these things are forbidden."

"All these things are forbidden," I said, but it was my voice that spoke and not my spirit. He looked at me again.

❷

"My son," he said. "Once I had young dreams. If your dreams do not eat you up, you may be a great priest. If they eat you, you are still my son. Now go on your journey."

❸

I went fasting, as is the law. My body hurt but not my heart. When the dawn came, I was out of sight of the village. I prayed and purified myself, waiting for a sign. The sign was an eagle. It flew east.

Sometimes signs are sent by bad spirits. I waited again on the flat rock, fasting, taking no food. I was very still—I could feel the sky above me and the earth beneath. I waited till the sun was beginning to sink. Then three deer passed in the valley, going east—they did not wind me or see me. There was a white fawn with them—a very great sign.

I followed them, at a distance, waiting for what would happen. My heart was troubled about going east, yet I knew that I must go. My head hummed with my fasting—I did not even see the panther spring upon the white fawn. But, before I knew it, the bow was in my hand. I shouted and the panther lifted his head from the fawn. It is not easy to kill a panther with one arrow but the arrow

502 ◆ *Short Stories*

Speaking and Listening Mini-Lesson

Radio Interview

This mini-lesson supports the Speaking and Listening activity in the Idea Bank on page 511.

Introduce the Concept In a radio interview, a professional interviewer asks a guest questions, the answers to which will be of interest to listeners.

Develop Background Ask students to describe radio interviews they have heard. What makes a radio interview interesting?

In preparing, students might consider these points:

- Interview questions that elicit the most interesting answers begin with *Who, What, Where, When, Why,* and *How.* These questions are least likely to be answered by "yes" or "no."

- John may not want to reveal certain information to his people.

- John might have a particular message he

wants to deliver to his people.

Apply the Information The interviews can be performed for the class or recorded on audiocassette.

Assess the Outcome Have students evaluate their own interviews on the basis of how well the interviewer was able to elicit answers other than "yes" or "no" answers. Use the Self-Assessment: Speech page in *Alternative Assessment*, p. 117.

went through his eye and into his brain. He died as he tried to spring—he rolled over, tearing at the ground. Then I knew I was meant to go east—I knew that was my journey. When the night came, I made my fire and roasted meat.

It is eight suns' journey to the east and a man passes by many Dead Places. The Forest People are afraid of them but I am not. Once I made my fire on the edge of a Dead Place at night and, next morning, in the dead house, I found a good knife, little rusted. That was small to what came afterward, but it made my heart feel big. Always when I looked for game, it was in front of my arrow, and twice I passed hunting parties of the Forest People without their knowing. So I knew my magic was strong and my journey clean, in spite of the law.

Toward the setting of the eighth sun, I came to the banks of the great river. It was half-a-day's journey after I had left the god-road—we do not use the god-roads now for they are falling apart into great blocks of stone, and the forest is safer going. A long way off, I had seen the water through trees but the trees were thick. At last, I came out upon an open place at the top of a cliff. There was the great river below, like a giant in the sun. It is very long, very wide. It could eat all the streams we know and still be thirsty. Its name is Ou-dis-sun, the Sacred, the Long. No man of my tribe had seen it, not even my father, the priest. It was magic and I prayed.

Then I raised my eyes and looked south. It was there, the Place of the Gods.

How can I tell what it was like—you do not know. It was there, in the red light, and they were too big to be houses. It was there with the red light upon it, mighty and ruined. I knew that in another moment the gods would see me. I covered my eyes with my hands and crept back into the forest.

Surely, that was enough to do, and live. Surely it was enough to spend the night upon the cliff. The Forest People themselves do not come near. Yet, all through the night, I knew that I should have to cross the river and walk in the places of the gods, although the gods ate me up. My magic did not help me at all and yet there was a fire in my bowels, a fire in my mind. When the sun rose, I thought, "My journey has been clean. Now I will go home from my journey." But, even as I thought so, I knew I could not. If I went to the place of the gods, I would surely die, but, if I did not go, I could never be at peace with my spirit again. It is better to lose one's life than one's spirit, if one is a priest and the son of a priest.

Nevertheless, as I made the raft, the tears ran out of my eyes. The Forest People could have killed me without fight, if they had come upon me then, but they did not come. When the raft was made, I said the sayings for the dead and painted myself for death. My heart was cold as a frog and my knees like water, but the burning in my mind would not let me have peace. As I pushed the raft from the shore, I began my death song—I had the right. It was a fine song.

"I am John, son of John," I sang.
  "My people are the Hill People.
  They are the men.
I go into the Dead Places but I am not slain.
I take the metal from the Dead Places

◆ **Build Vocabulary**

bowels (bou′ əlz) *n.*: Intestines; guts

The Forest People could have killed me without fight, if they had come upon me then, but they did not come.

By the Waters of Babylon ◆ 503

◆ *Literature and Your Life*

How is the knife John finds similar to the kinds of things we study to learn about ancient civilizations?

Cross-Curricular Connection: Geography

The Hudson River—which John calls "Ou-dis-sun"—is a major waterway. It originates in New York's Adirondack Mountains and flows 315 miles (510 km), emptying into New York Bay and the Atlantic Ocean at New York City. It is navigable by ocean-going vessels as far north as Albany. The New York State Barge Canal links the river to the Great Lakes. Among the points of interest on the Hudson are the United States Military Academy at West Point and Sing Sing Prison on the lower east bank.

The beauty of the Hudson inspired the famous Hudson River school of nineteenth-century American painters. One of the river's most beautiful and imposing landmarks is the Palisades, a line of sheer cliffs, on the west bank of the lower Hudson, that rise as high as 550 feet (165 m). It is from these cliffs that John first sees the Place of the Dead.

Have students discuss how his first glimpse of the feared Place of the Dead from such a vantage point might have affected John.

Have these students characterize this "song" of John. *Students may observe that John's song, with its repeated cry of "E-yah," suggests a Native American song. The author may be suggesting that John's people are similar to members of early Native American groups.*

◆ **Reading Strategy**

❶ **Draw Conclusions** John has described "god roads" as made of stone and in disrepair. He sees god roads that spanned the river, but now hang down like "broken vines" (cables). God roads must be paved roads and bridges.

◆ **Critical Thinking**

❷ **Infer** Ask students: After learning that the ground does not burn forever and that the island is not covered with fogs and enchantments, what might John start thinking about the other tales he has heard? How could these thoughts make John a better priest? *John might start to think that other tales are not true either. John can be a better priest by dispelling some of the fears that prevented his people from exploring the places of the gods.*

◆ **Reading Strategy**

❸ **Draw Conclusions** Have students add the information in this passage to other clues in the story to draw a conclusion (or confirm a conclusion already drawn) about the "high towers of the gods" and about the gods themselves. Who were they? *Many students will put the information together to conclude that the high towers are skyscrapers; John is in a big city after it has been destroyed, perhaps by war ("The Great Burning"). The gods are really the people who lived there.*

Never have I been so alone . . .
There was no strength in my knowledge anymore . . .

but I am not blasted.
I travel upon the god-roads and am not afraid. E-yah! I have killed the panther, I have killed the fawn!
E-yah! I have come to the great river. No man has come there before.
It is forbidden to go east, but I have gone, forbidden to go on the great river, but I am there.
Open your hearts, you spirits, and hear my song.
Now I go to the Place of the Gods, I shall not return.
My body is painted for death and my limbs weak, but my heart is big as I go to the Place of the Gods!"

All the same, when I came to the Place of the Gods, I was afraid, afraid. The current of the great river is very strong—it gripped my raft with its hands. That was magic, for the river itself is wide and calm. I could feel evil spirits about me, in the bright morning; I could feel their breath on my neck as I was swept down the stream. Never have I been so much alone—I tried to think of my knowledge, but it was a squirrel's heap of winter nuts. There was no strength in my knowledge any more, and I felt small and naked as a new-hatched bird—alone upon the great river, the servant of the gods.

Yet, after a while, my eyes were opened and I saw. I saw both banks of the river—I saw that once there had been god-roads across it, though now they were broken and fallen like broken vines. Very great they were, and wonderful and broken—broken in the time of the Great Burning when the fire fell out of the sky. And always the cur-

◆ **Reading Strategy**
Put John's description together with the other things he's seen and found to draw a conclusion about the "god roads."

rent took me nearer to the Place of the Gods, and the huge ruins rose before my eyes.

I do not know the customs of rivers—we are the People of the Hills. I tried to guide my raft with the pole but it spun around. I thought the river meant to take me past the Place of the Gods and out into the Bitter Water of the legends. I grew angry then—my heart felt strong. I said aloud, "I am a priest and the son of a priest!" The gods heard me—they showed me how to paddle with the pole on one side of the raft. The current changed itself—I drew near to the Place of the Gods.

When I was very near, my raft struck and turned over. I can swim in our lakes—I swam to the shore. There was a great spike of rusted metal sticking out into the river—I hauled myself up upon it and sat there, panting. I had saved my bow and two arrows and the knife I found in the Dead Place but that was all. My raft went whirling downstream toward the Bitter Water. I looked after it, and thought if it had trod me under, at least I would be safely dead. Nevertheless, when I had dried my bow-string and restrung it, I walked forward to the Place of the Gods.

It felt like ground underfoot; it did not burn me. It is not true what some of the tales say, that the ground there burns forever, for I have been there. Here and there were the marks and stains of the Great Burning, on the ruins, that is true. But they were old marks and old stains. It is not true either, what some of our priests say, that it is an island covered with fogs and enchantments. It is not. It is a great Dead Place—greater than any Dead Place we know. Everywhere in it there are god-roads, though most are cracked and broken. Everywhere there are the ruins of the high

504 ◆ *Short Stories*

Cross-Curricular Connection: Social Studies

The Dead Place that John explores is the ruins of Manhattan in New York City. Many people think of Manhattan and New York City as one and the same, though New York City has four other boroughs—the Bronx, Brooklyn, Queens, and Staten Island. However, Manhattan remains the cultural and commercial heart of the city. The 1990 census estimated Manhattan's population at almost 1,500,000, with a population density of about 67,615 per square mile (26,097 per sq. km.).

Manhattan is a world capital for theater, music, and the other arts. The shops, such as those along Fifth Avenue, are equally renowned. It is a financial capital, as well; the New York Stock Exchange, on Wall Street, is among the most important such institutions.

Discuss with students the effect of having Manhattan serve as the location of the Place of the Gods in this selection. A great urban center is now in ruins.

Red Hills and Bones, Georgia O'Keeffe, Philadelphia Museum of Art, The Alfred Stieglitz Collection

◀ Critical Viewing
What details in this painting indicate lifelessness? [Analyze]
❽

❸ towers of the gods.

How shall I tell what I saw? I went carefully, my strung bow in my hand, my skin ready for danger. There should have been the wailings of spirits and the shrieks of demons, but there were not. It was very ❹ silent and sunny where I had landed—the wind and the rain and the birds that drop seeds had done their work—the grass grew in the cracks of the broken stone. It is a fair island—no wonder the gods built there. If I ❺ had come there, a god, I also would have built.

How shall I tell what I saw? The towers are not all broken—here and there one still ❻ stands, like a great tree in a forest, and the birds nest high. But the towers themselves look blind, for the gods are gone. I saw a fish-hawk, catching fish in the river. I saw a little dance of white butterflies over a great heap of broken stones and columns. I went there and looked about me—there was a carved stone with cut-letters, broken in half. I can read letters but I could not understand these. They said UBTREAS. There was ❼ also the shattered image of a man or a god. It had been made of white stone and he wore his hair tied back like a woman's. His name was ASHING, as I read on the cracked

half of a stone. I thought it wise to pray to ASHING, though I do not know that god.

How shall I tell what I saw? There was no smell of man left, on stone or metal. Nor were there many trees in that wilderness of stone. There are many pigeons, nesting and dropping in the towers—the gods must have loved them, or, perhaps, they used them for sacrifices. There are wild cats that roam the god-roads, green-eyed, unafraid of man. At night they wail like demons but they are not ❾ demons. The wild dogs are more dangerous, for they hunt in a pack, but them I did not meet till later. Everywhere there are the carved stones carved with magical numbers or words.

I went North—I did not try to hide myself. When a god or a demon saw me, then I would die, but meanwhile I was no longer afraid. My hunger for knowledge burned in me—there was so much that I could not understand. After awhile, I knew that my belly ❿ was hungry. I could have hunted for my meat, but I did not hunt. It is known that the gods did not hunt as we do—they got their food from enchanted boxes and jars. Sometimes these are still found in the Dead Places—once, when I was a child and foolish, I opened such a jar and tasted it and

By the Waters of Babylon ◆ 505

Red Hills and Bones, 1941, by Georgia O'Keeffe.

In 1929, Georgia O'Keeffe first visited New Mexico, and lived there from 1949 on. From her first visit, she made increasing use of southwestern motifs in her work. Animal bones were frequent subjects, as in *Red Hills and Bones.* O'Keeffe's attention to detail makes the painting seem realistic, but the subject matter and perspective gives a surreal quality.

Use these questions for discussion:

1. Do you think this is an appropriate illustration for the story? *Students may say that the painting gives the impression of a "dead place," even though it is of a desert rather than a city.*

2. How would you describe the mood of the painting? How does the artist create that mood? *Students may say the mood is lonely, desolate, eerie. The artist creates this mood by using only earth tones, and including no human or animal figures.*

◆ **Reading Strategy**

❹ **Draw Conclusions** Ask students: What information in this passage can help you begin to draw a conclusion about the name of the city? *The information that the city is built on a "fair island" may help some students conclude that John is on Manhattan Island in New York City.*

◆ **Build Grammar Skills**

❺ **Subordination** Ask students to identify the main and subordinate clauses in this sentence and to explain how the subordinate clause qualifies the main clause. *The main clause is, "I also would have built"; the subordinate clause is "If I had come there, a god." The subordinate clause clarifies the circumstances under which the idea in the main clause would have occurred.*

◆ **Critical Thinking**

❻ **Synthesize** Ask students to decide whether this story takes place in the present, past, or future. How do they know? *Great buildings have been destroyed, but John's people do not know how to build these things. Therefore, the story must take place in the future after a more advanced civilization has been destroyed.*

Comprehension Check ☑

❼ Explain that "UBTREAS" refers to the Manhattan Subtreasury Building and the statue is of George Washington.

▶Critical Viewing◀

❽ **Analyze** Details indicating lifelessness include the bones, the dry landscape, and the red clay with no plants growing in it.

◆ **Reading Strategy**

❾ **Draw Conclusions** Ask students to explain where the wild cats and dogs most likely came from. *The dogs and cats are probably descendants of pets kept by residents of what became the Dead Place.*

◆ **Literary Focus**

❿ **First-Person Point of View** Have students observe the effect of the point of view on the passage. *Students may say that the author adds a dimension of humor when he has John observe that our food came not from hunting but "from enchanted boxes and jars."*

505

❶ Clarification Explain that John is in Grand Central Terminal in New York City. The ceiling of the main concourse there is painted with stars forming well-known constellations. The tunnels are subway tunnels. This information confirms that John is in Manhattan.

◆ Reading Strategy

❷ Draw Conclusions Ask students to use what they already know from experience along with this description to draw a conclusion about the kind of place John found the food and drink. What might the drink have been? *Students may say that John found food and drink in an old market, and that the drink probably contained alcohol.*

◆ Reading Strategy

❸ Draw Conclusions Have students explain where John finds himself in this passage. *He is on an upper floor of an apartment building, in a hallway between the elevator door and a door to an apartment.*

I had long gone past what was forbidden, and I entered the likeliest towers . . .

found the food sweet. But my father found out and punished me for it strictly, for, often, that food is death. Now, though, I had long gone past what was forbidden, and I entered the likeliest towers, looking for the food of the gods.

❶ I found it at last in the ruins of a great temple in the mid-city. A mighty temple it must have been, for the roof was painted like the sky at night with its stars—that much I could see, though the colors were faint and dim. It went down into great caves and tunnels—perhaps they kept their slaves there. But when I started to climb down, I heard the squeaking of rats, so I did not go—rats are unclean, and there must have been many tribes of them, from the squeaking. But near there, I found food, in the heart of a ruin, behind a door that still ❷ opened. I ate only the fruits from the jars—they had a very sweet taste. There was drink, too, in bottles of glass—the drink of the gods was strong and made my head swim. After I had eaten and drunk, I slept on the top of a stone, my bow at my side.

When I woke, the sun was low. Looking down from where I lay, I saw a dog sitting on his haunches. His tongue was hanging out of his mouth; he looked as if he were laughing. He was a big dog, with a gray-brown coat, as big as a wolf. I sprang up and shouted at him but he did not move—he just sat there as if he were laughing. I did not like that. When I reached for a stone to throw, he moved swiftly out of the way of the stone. He was not afraid of me; he looked at me as if I were meat. No doubt I could have killed him with an arrow, but I did not know if there were others. Moreover, night was falling.

I looked about me—not far away there was a great, broken god-road, leading North. The towers were high enough, but not so high, and while many of the dead-

houses were wrecked, there were some that stood. I went toward this god-road, keeping to the heights of the ruins, while the dog followed. When I had reached the god-road, I saw that there were others behind him. If I had slept later, they would have come upon me asleep and torn out my throat. As it was, they were sure enough of me; they did not hurry. When I went into the dead-house, they kept watch at the entrance—doubtless they thought they would have a fine hunt. But a dog cannot open a door and I knew, from the books, that the gods did not like to live on the ground but on high.

I had just found a door I could open when the dogs decided to rush. Ha! They were surprised when I shut the door in their faces—it was a good door, of strong metal. I could hear their foolish baying beyond it, but I did not stop to answer them. I was in darkness—I found stairs and climbed. There were many stairs, turning around till my head was dizzy. At the top was another door—I found the knob and opened it. I was in a long small chamber—on one side of it was a bronze door that could not be opened, for it had no handle. Perhaps there was a magic word to open it, but I did not have the ❸ word. I turned to the door in the opposite side of the wall. The lock of it was broken and I opened it and went in.

Within, there was a place of great riches. The god who lived there must have been a powerful god. The first room was a small anteroom—I waited there for some time, telling the spirits of the place that I came in peace and not as a robber. When it seemed to me that they had had time to hear me, I

◆ Build Vocabulary

moreover (môr ō′ vər) *adv.*: In addition to; further

nevertheless (nev′ ər the les′) *adv.*: In spite of that; however

506 ◆ *Short Stories*

Speaking and Listening Mini-Lesson

Oral Presentation

This mini-lesson supports the Speaking and Listening activity in the Idea Bank on page 511.

Introduce the Concept With the class, discuss techniques for making an oral presentation interesting. Include such techniques as beginning with an interest-grabbing sentence, using lively, vivid language, and using visual aids.

Develop Background Once students have topics, they should check to see that their reports answer these questions:

- When and where did the culture flourish?
- What artifacts of the civilization have been found?
- What do we know of how these people lived?
- What connection exists between their culture and ours?

Apply the Information Before presenting their reports to the class, students can pair off and practice, using their partners' suggestions to polish their delivery and clarify the material, if necessary.

Assess the Outcome Have students evaluate the presentations for accuracy of content and effectiveness of presentation. Use the Peer Assessment: Speaker/Speech page in *Alternative Assessment,* p. 118.

went on. Ah, what riches! Few, even, of the windows had been broken—it was all as it had been. The great windows that looked over the city had not been broken at all though they were dusty and streaked with many years. There were coverings on the floors, the colors not greatly faded, and the chairs were soft and deep. There were pictures upon the walls, very strange, very wonderful—I remember one of a bunch of flowers in a jar—if you came close to it, you could see nothing but bits of color, but if you stood away from it, the flowers might have been picked yesterday. It made my heart feel strange to look at this picture—and to look at the figure of a bird, in some hard clay, on a table and see it so like our birds. Everywhere there were books and writings, many in tongues that I could not read. The god who lived there must have been a wise god and full of knowledge. I felt I had right there, as I sought knowledge also.

Nevertheless, it was strange. There was a washing-place but no water—perhaps the gods washed in air. There was a cooking-place but no wood, and though there was a machine to cook food, there was no place to put fire in it. Nor were there candles or lamps—there were things that looked like lamps but they had neither oil nor wick. All these things were magic, but I touched them and lived—the magic had gone out of them. Let me tell one thing to show. In the washing-place, a thing said "Hot" but it was not hot to the touch—another thing said "Cold" but it was not cold. This must have been a strong magic but the magic was gone. I do not understand—they had ways I wish that I knew.

It was close and dry and dusty in their house of the gods. I have said the magic was gone but that is not true—it had gone from the magic things but it had not gone from the place. I felt the spirits about me, weighing upon me. Nor had I ever slept in a Dead Place before—and yet, tonight, I must sleep there. When I thought of it, my tongue felt dry in my throat, in spite of my wish for knowledge. Almost I would have gone down again and faced the dogs, but I did not.

I had not gone through all the rooms when the darkness fell. When it fell, I went back to the big room looking over the city and made fire. There was a place to make fire and a box with wood in it, though I do not think they cooked there. I wrapped myself in a floor-covering and slept in front of the fire—I was very tired.

Now I tell what is very strong magic. I woke in the midst of the night. When I woke, the fire had gone out and I was cold. It seemed to me that all around me there were whisperings and voices. I closed my eyes to shut them out. Some will say that I slept again, but I do not think that I slept. I could feel the spirits drawing my spirit out of my body as a fish is drawn on a line. Why should I lie about it? I am a priest and the son of a priest. If there are spirits, as they say, in the small Dead Places near us, what spirits must there not be in that great Place of the Gods? And would not they wish to speak? After such long years? I know that I felt myself drawn as a fish is drawn on a line. I had stepped out of my body—I could see my body asleep in front of the cold fire, but it was not I. I was drawn to look out upon the city of the gods.

It should have been dark, for it was night, but it was not dark. Everywhere there were lights—lines of light—circles and blurs of light—ten thousand torches would not have been the same. The sky itself was alight—you could barely see the stars for the glow in the sky. I thought to myself "This is strong magic" and trembled. There was a roaring in my ears like the rushing of rivers. Then my eyes grew used to the light and my ears to the sound. I knew that I was seeing the city as it had been when the gods were alive.

◆ **Literary Focus**
How does the first-person point of view affect this description? What questions do you have about John's situation?

By the Waters of Babylon ◆ 507

◆ **Literary Focus**
❹ First-Person Point of View
Invite students to discuss how a third-person narrator would describe this room. Why does the author have John describe it in this way? *A third-person narrator might say, "The carpets on the floors" instead of "coverings on the floors"; "The people who lived there," rather than "The god who lived there." John, however, speaks from the point of view of someone who has never seen carpeted floors and who still believes that the people of the city were gods. The description lets us see ourselves from John's point of view.*

◆ **Literary Focus**
❺ First-Person Point of View
Ask students: What is the effect of the first-person point of view in this paragraph? *John describes modern appliances—a sink, a stove, lamps—from the point of view of a person who cannot see how they work. He explains everything he does not understand by "magic."*

◆ **Build Grammar Skills**
❻ Subordination Ask students to identify the main and subordinate clauses in this sentence. Have them explain how the subordinate clause adds meaning to the main idea. *The main clause is "It seemed to me"; the subordinate clause is, "that all around me there were whisperings and voices." The subordinate clause adds meaning by answering the question "what?"*

◆ **Literary Focus**
❼ First-Person Point of View
The author uses the first-person point of view to describe what is real to him but only imagined by the character. John imagines what the city once looked like when it was alive with light and sound.

Beyond the Classroom

Career Connection
Intellectual Curiosity Ask students what traits set John off from most of his community. Elicit the fact that John's intellectual curiosity is so strong that not even fear of death can keep him from exploring the unknown.

Ask students to suggest fields in which such curiosity would be an asset. Science is clearly one. It could also lead a historian to unearth evidence that sheds new light on the past. It could help

writers develop new ways of expressing thoughts and feelings. Have students brainstorm for other fields in which intellectual curiosity would be valued.

Have interested students do research on jobs requiring such curiosity. Their research could take the form of interviews, surveys, explorations, or observations, in addition to reading.

Have students discuss what they learned and their experiences researching their topics.

❶ Make sure students understand that John is having a vision of the city as it was before it was destroyed.

◆ Critical Thinking

❷ **Interpret** Ask students what John thought would have happened if the "gods" had not destroyed themselves by war. Do students agree? *John says, "...their wisdom could not but grow until all was peace." John thinks that, if given the chance, the "gods" would have used their wisdom to ensure world peace. Whether or not students agree, they should back up their opinions with facts.*

◆ Critical Thinking

❸ **Synthesize** Ask students how John's vision can be interpreted as a warning. *John's vision is a warning that war can end in annihilation. (While the description sounds like a nuclear attack, the first atom bomb was not exploded until 1945. Benét would have been referring to massive bombing.)*

◆ Critical Thinking

❹ **Infer** Ask students why they think John weeps. *Students may say that he weeps over the loss of life, or over the idea that such a miraculous and beautiful place could be destroyed by the same knowledge that had built it in the first place.*

◆ Critical Thinking

❺ **Analyze** Ask students to tell why this passage is ironic. *John sees the "magic" as being wonderful. He doesn't yet comprehend that it was the "magic" that caused the destruction.*

---

❶ That was a sight indeed—yes, that was a sight: I could not have seen it in the body— my body would have died. Everywhere went the gods, on foot and in chariots—there were gods beyond number and counting and their chariots blocked the streets. They had turned night to day for their pleasure— they did not sleep with the sun. The noise of their coming and going was the noise of many waters. It was magic what they could do—it was magic what they did.

I looked out of another window—the great vines of their bridges were mended and the god-roads went East and West. Restless, restless, were the gods and always in motion! They burrowed tunnels under rivers— they flew in the air. With unbelievable tools they did giant works—no part of the earth was safe from them, for, if they wished for a thing, they summoned it from the other side of the world. And always, as they labored and rested, as they feasted and made love, there was a drum in their ears—the pulse of the giant city, beating and beating like a man's heart.

❷ Were they happy? What is happiness to the gods? They were great, they were mighty, they were wonderful and terrible. As I looked upon them and their magic, I felt like a child—but a little more, it seemed to me, and they would pull down the moon from the sky. I saw them with wisdom beyond wisdom and knowledge beyond knowledge. And yet not all they did was well done—even I could see that—and yet their wisdom could not but grow until all was peace.

❸ Then I saw their fate come upon them and that was terrible past speech. It came upon them as they walked the streets of their city. I have been in the fights with the Forest People—I have seen men die. But this was not like that. When gods war with gods, they use weapons we do not know. It was fire falling out of the sky and a mist that poisoned. It was the time of the Great Burning and the Destruction. They ran about like ants in the streets of their city—

poor gods, poor gods! Then the towers began to fall. A few escaped—yes, a few. The legends tell it. But, even after the city had become a Dead Place, for many years the poison was still in the ground. I saw it happen, I saw the last of them die. It was darkness over the broken city, and I wept. **❹**

All this, I saw. I saw it as I have told it, though not in the body. When I woke in the morning, I was hungry, but I did not think first of my hunger, for my heart was perplexed and confused. I knew the reason for the Dead Places but I did not see why it had happened. It seemed to me it should not have happened, with all the magic they had. **❺** I went through the house looking for an answer. There was so much in the house I could not understand—and yet I am a priest and the son of a priest. It was like being on one side of the great river, at night, with no light to show the way.

Then I saw the dead god. He was sitting in his chair, by the window, in a room I had not entered before and, for the first moment, I thought that he was alive. Then I saw the skin on the back of his hand—it was like dry leather. The room was shut, hot and dry—no doubt that had kept him as he was. At first I was afraid to approach him— then the fear left me. He was sitting looking out over the city—he was dressed in the clothes of the gods. His age was neither young nor old—I could not tell his age. But there was wisdom in his face and great sadness. You could see that he would have not run away. He had sat at his window, watching his city die—then he himself had died. But it is better to lose one's life than one's spirit—and you could see from the face that his spirit had not been lost. I knew, that, if I touched him, he would fall into dust—and yet, there was something unconquered in the face.

That is all of my story, for then I knew he was a man—I knew then that they had been men, neither gods nor demons. It is a great knowledge, hard to tell and believe. They were men—they went a dark road, but they were men. I had no fear after that—I had no fear going home, though twice I fought off the dogs and once I was hunted for two days by the Forest People. When I saw my father again, I prayed and was purified. He touched my lips and my breast, he said, "You went away a boy. You come back a man and a priest." I said, "Father, they were men! I have been in the Place of the Gods and seen it! Now slay me, if it is the law— but still I know they were men."

He looked at me out of both eyes. He said, "The law is not always the same shape—you have done what you have done. I could not have done it in my time but you come after me. Tell!"

I told and he listened. After that, I wished to tell all the people but he showed me otherwise. He said, "Truth is a hard deer to hunt. If you eat too much truth at once, you may die of the truth. It was not idly that our fathers forbade the Dead Places." He was **⑥** right—it is better the truth should come little by little. I have learned that, being a priest. Perhaps, in the old days, they ate knowledge too fast.

Nevertheless, we make a beginning. It is not for the metal alone we go to the Dead Places now—there are the books and the **⑦** writings. They are hard to learn. And the magic tools are broken—but we can look at them and wonder. At least, we make a beginning. And, when I am chief priest we

shall go beyond the great river. We shall go to the Place of the Gods—the place newyork—not one man but a company. We shall look for the images of the gods and find the god ASHING and the others—the gods Lincoln and Biltmore[1] and Moses.[2] But they were men who built the city, not gods or demons. They were men. I remember the dead man's face. They were men who were here before us. We must build again. **⑦**

1. **Biltmore:** A hotel in New York City.
2. **Moses:** Robert Moses, former New York City municipal official who oversaw many large construction projects.

Beyond Literature

Community Connection

Landmarks and Monuments In this story, John encounters the Subtreasury building and a statue of George Washington—two landmarks in New York City. Most cities have special places, buildings, or statues. For example, Seattle has the Space Needle, New York City has the Empire State Building, and San Francisco has the Golden Gate Bridge. Smaller communities also have their landmarks and monuments that are famous locally.

Activity Create a visitors' guide for one of the landmarks mentioned here or for a landmark or monument in your community.

Guide for Responding

◆ Literature and Your Life

Reader's Response John's father says, "Perhaps, in the old days, they ate knowledge too fast." In your opinion, does our society "eat knowledge too fast"? Explain your answer.

Thematic Focus What warning is Benét giving about the future?

☑ Check Your Comprehension

1. Why does John set out on his journey? Why is John's journey unusual?
2. Describe three things John sees in the Place of the Gods.

By the Waters of Babylon ◆ 509

Beyond the Selection

FURTHER READING

Other Works on the Theme of Ruined Civilizations

"Ozymandias," Percy Bysshe Shelley
The Planet of the Apes, Pierre Boulle
"The Stars Look Down," Isaac Asimov

We suggest that you preview these works before recommending them to students.

INTERNET

The Internet provides many sites where interested students can find out more about Stephen Vincent Benét and his work. One Web site that provides several examples of his poetry can be found at: **http://ftp.lexmark.com/data/poem/benet01. html**

Please be aware, however, that sites may have changed from the time we published this information. We *strongly recommend* that you preview the site before you send students to it.

509

◆ Critical Thinking

1. For John, the journey means becoming a man. For his people it is an opportunity to build again.
2. John's father wants the truth to be revealed gradually.
3. The title refers to Psalm 137, in which the Israelites, captured by the Babylonians, weep for their lost homeland. It is appropriate for this story to appear in a collection called *Thirteen O'Clock* because that hour, like the events in this story, has not yet occurred.
4. Some students might say that avoidance may occur by not eating knowledge so fast. Others may say that people always repeat the mistakes of the past.
5. Students may cite ancient Egypt, Greece, Rome, Machu Picchu, or other past civilizations. Encourage students to research these civilizations.

◆ Reading Strategy

1. The Great Burning was the destruction of the city by bombs during a war.
2. The Place of the Gods is New York City after its destruction. Clues include the river's name, Ou-dis-sun; broken signs with names like the Subtreasury Building; and, the reference to "the place new york."

◆ Literary Focus

1. The first-person point of view allows the reader to explore the mysterious ruins as John does. It also allows the reader to see over John's shoulder, because the details enable readers to solve the mystery before John does.
2. The narrator reveals that he thinks the people of the past were great, but that they made mistakes that ended in their destruction.

◆ Build Vocabulary

1. Our life raft was sinking; therefore, we donned our life vests.
2. The elders had forbidden me to enter the Place of the Gods; nevertheless, curiosity pushed me onward.
3. I needed to find shelter soon: night was falling; moreover, the wolves would soon be out.

510

Guide for Responding (continued)

◆ Critical Thinking

INTERPRET

1. What significance does the journey have for John and his people? **[Draw Conclusions]**
2. Explain why John's father wants to keep secret what John has learned about the Place of the Gods. **[Speculate]**
3. Explain the title of this story. Why is it appropriate that this story would appear in a collection called *Thirteen O'Clock?* **[Connect]**

APPLY

4. How do you think John's people can best avoid repeating the mistakes that led to the destruction of civilization in the past? **[Solve]**

EXTEND

5. What other places do you know that are ruins of a past civilization? What do you imagine life in those places was like ? **[Social Studies Link]**

◆ Reading Strategy

DRAW CONCLUSIONS

You **draw conclusions** based on facts and details given in a story. When John describes the "god-roads" that are fallen and broken like vines, you can put this detail together with the other facts you have learned to draw the conclusion that he is looking at the ruins of suspension bridges.

1. What is the Great Burning? Why and how did it happen?
2. What is the Place of the Gods? What details led you to your conclusion?

◆ Literary Focus

FIRST-PERSON POINT OF VIEW

In a story told in the **first-person point of view,** the narrator tells what he or she thinks, feels, and observes. The narrator's attitudes and experiences shape the story, and, in turn, the readers' view of what happens, and why, is shaped by the narrator's perspective.

1. Identify two ways that the first-person point of view adds to the mystery of this story.
2. What does the narrator reveal about his feelings toward the past?

◆ Build Vocabulary

USING CONJUNCTIVE ADVERBS

Conjunctive adverbs are words like *moreover, nevertheless,* and *therefore* that act as conjunctions. They act as adverbs in the clauses in which they appear, but they also link clauses or sentences and clarify the relation between them. On your paper, copy the following sentences, completing them with one of these conjunctive adverbs: *nevertheless, therefore,* or *moreover.*

1. Our life raft was sinking; ____?____, we donned our life vests.
2. The elders had forbidden me to enter the Place of the Gods; ____?____, curiosity pushed me onward.
3. I needed to find shelter soon: night was falling; ____?____, the wolves would soon be out.

USING THE WORD BANK

On your paper, answer the following questions using the words from the Word Bank.

1. Which would be referred to as the *bowels* of a city: the streets, subways, or skyscrapers?
2. What is an example of something you can buy that has been *purified*?

◆ Build Grammar Skills

SUBORDINATION

Writers use **subordination** when they connect unequal but related ideas in a complex sentence. The subordinate (less important) idea limits, develops, describes, or adds meaning to the main idea.

Practice Copy the following sentences in your notebook. Underline the subordinate clause, and explain why it is less important than the idea in the main clause.

1. It was my father himself who questioned me about my dreams.
2. ...he who touches the metal must be a priest or the son of a priest.
3. When my father went into the house to search for the metal, I stood by the door ...
4. John entered the building because the dogs were chasing him.
5. After he ate and drank, he went to sleep.

Using the Word Bank

1. The subways are the *bowels* of a city.
2. Water can be *purified.*

◆ Build Grammar Skills

1. It was my father himself <u>who questioned me about my dreams.</u> The subordinate clause adds meaning to the main clause.
2. ... he <u>who touches the metal</u> must be a priest or

the son of a priest. The subordinate clause limits the subject, *he.*

3. <u>When my father went into the house to search for the metal,</u> I stood by the door ...The subordinate clause adds information.
4. John entered the building <u>because the dogs were chasing him.</u> The subordinate clause develops the main idea.

5. <u>After he ate and drank,</u> he went to sleep. The subordinate clause answers the question *when.*

 Writer's Solution

For additional instruction and practice, use pages 51–52 on Adjective and Adverb Clauses and page 124 on Making Clear Connections in the *Writer's Solution Grammar Practice Book.*

Build Your Portfolio

Idea Bank

Writing

1. **Postcard** As John, write a postcard to your family or a friend after a visit to the Place of the Gods. Include details about what you see, hear, smell, taste, or touch in this mysterious place.

2. **Publicity Release** Imagine that John visits various locations among the People of the Hills and speaks about his recent experiences. Write a publicity release to be distributed shortly before one of his visits. Include details that will give people information about him and raise interest in his experiences.

3. **Poem** Write a poem John might compose to express his thoughts and feelings about what he experienced during his journey.

Speaking and Listening

4. **Radio Interview** With a partner, improvise a one-minute scene in which one of you plays the role of a radio news reporter and one plays the role of John, who has just arrived home from his journey. **[Performing Arts Link]**

5. **Oral Presentation** Prepare an oral presentation on a lost civilization. Find pictures of ruins of the civilization. Present a report to the class, using the pictures to illustrate your points. **[Social Studies Link]**

Projects

6. **Tourism Poster** Although New York City is in ruins in this story, it is one of the most vibrant, busy cities in the world. Create a tourism poster advertising some highlights of the "Big Apple."

7. **Storyboard** Choose a scene from this story and create a storyboard of it for the film version of "By the Waters of Babylon." **[Art Link]**

Writing Mini-Lesson

Description From Another Vantage Point

You learn about the Place of the Gods from John's thoughts, feelings, and experience. What if you were a fly on a wall and could see John enter a building in the Place of the Gods? Your vantage point, or perspective, would be vastly different from a person's because of your size and concerns about life.

Write a **description** of a familiar place from another vantage point. For example, you could describe your house from the perspective of your dog or your television set.

Writing Skills Focus: Consistent Point of View

Whether you're writing a description, a speech, or a short story, it is important to keep your point of view consistent. In "By the Waters of Babylon," Benét maintains a **consistent point of view**; throughout the story, he reveals only what John could know. In your description, you will reveal only what can be observed from the perspective of the animal or the object you choose to be.

Prewriting Look carefully at the place you are describing from your new vantage point. Jot down only what can be observed, not what you yourself know.

Drafting Describe the place in terms that your animal or object might use. For instance, if cars are zooming past, don't refer to them as cars, describe their sound, smell, and action. Include your reactions to your subject as well as your observations of it.

Revising Reread your draft, looking for places where you have included information you know rather than details that can be observed. Eliminate any details that interfere with a consistent point of view.

By the Waters of Babylon ◆ 511

Idea Bank

Customizing for *Performance Levels*
Following are suggestions for matching Idea Bank topics with your students' performance levels:
    Less Advanced Students: 1, 4, 7
    Average Students: 2, 4, 6
    More Advanced Students: 3, 5

Customizing for *Learning Modalities*
Following are suggestions for matching Idea Bank topics with your students' learning modalities:
    Verbal/Linguistic: 1, 2, 3, 4, 5
    Bodily/Kinesthetic: 4
    Visual/Spatial: 6, 7

Writing Mini-Lesson

Refer students to the Writing Handbook, page 965, for instruction on the writing process, and page 967 for further information on description.

Writing and Language Transparencies Have students use the Comparison and Contrast organizer, pp. 95–97, to record differences between the original perspective and the vantage point of their description.

Writer's Solution

Writing Lab CD-ROM
Have students complete the tutorial on Description. Follow these steps:
1. Have students use the interactive instruction in using different organizational plans.
2. Students can use the annotated writing models to help them choose a specific point of view.
3. Students should draft their descriptions on computer.
4. Have them use the assessment criteria to help them revise their drafts.

Allow approximately 90 minutes of class time to complete these steps.

Sourcebook
Have students use Chapter 1, Description (pp. 1–29), for additional support. The chapter includes writing models of spatial order and order of importance (p. 20).

Prepare and Engage

OBJECTIVES

1. To read, comprehend, and interpret two stories
2. To relate two stories to personal experience
3. To make inferences about character
4. To identify static and dynamic characters
5. To build vocabulary in context and learn the word root -ver-
6. To punctuate restrictive and nonrestrictive adjective clauses correctly
7. To write a telephone conversation using realistic dialogue
8. To respond to the stories through writing, speaking and listening, and projects

SKILLS INSTRUCTION

Vocabulary:
Word Roots: -ver-

Grammar:
Restrictive and Nonrestrictive Adjective Clauses

Reading Strategy:
Make Inferences About Character

Literary Focus:
Static and Dynamic Characters

Writing:
Realistic Dialogue

Speaking and Listening:
Roundtable Discussion (teacher edition)

Critical Viewing:
Connect; Compare and Contrast; Draw Conclusions; Support

PORTFOLIO OPPORTUNITIES

Writing: Invitation; Journal Entry; Story Ending
Writing Mini-Lesson: Telephone Conversation
Speaking and Listening: Monologue; Roundtable Discussion
Projects: Period Presentation; Multimedia Biography

More About the Authors

Anton Chekhov greatly influenced the style of modern fiction and drama. In most of his serious stories and plays, Chekhov captures the inner lives of his characters by focusing on their thoughts and the mood and atmosphere surrounding them rather than on plot and external action.

Mark Twain is widely regarded as the greatest humorist in American literature. Although be began his writing career during his years of adventure in the American west, he penned most of his greatest works from the comfort of his home in cultured and civilized Hartford, Connecticut.

512

Guide for Reading

Anton Chekhov (1860–1904)

Anton Chekhov was born in the small coastal town of Taganrog in southern Russia. After the failure of his father's grocery business, his family moved to Moscow. Chekhov continued his schooling in Taganrog, then moved to Moscow to be with his family and to enroll in medical school. While a medical student, he wrote comic sketches and light short stories to earn money to help support his family. Although he suffered from tuberculosis, Chekhov continued to write until he died. *The Cherry Orchard,* one of his most famous plays, was written during the last year of his life.

Athough his reputation did not extend outside of Russia during his lifetime, since his death he has come to be regarded as one of the finest short-story writers the world has ever produced.

Mark Twain (1835–1910)

Like actors or musicians, writers sometimes take new names, called pen names. Mark Twain is the pen name of Samuel Langhorne Clemens, one of America's greatest writers. He was born in Florida, Missouri, and grew up in nearby Hannibal. He drew on his boyhood experiences for many of the characters and incidents that appear in his work.

Twain's formal education ended early. After he left school, he learned the printing trade. At various times, he worked as a printer and a riverboat pilot, prospected for gold, and gave lectures around the world. His pen name is from the cry of Mississippi River boatmen: "By the mark, twain!" assessing the river as two fathoms deep. His two most widely read novels are *The Adventures of Tom Sawyer* (1876) and *The Adventures of Huckleberry Finn* (1885).

◆ Build Vocabulary

WORD ROOTS: -ver-

The narrator of Mark Twain's "Luck" describes another character as a "man of strict *veracity*." The word *veracity* means "truthfulness; honesty." Its root is -ver-, which comes from the Latin *verax,* meaning "speaking truly." The root -ver- is used in other words as well: to *verify* something is to see whether it's true. A *verdict* is a judgment that, ideally, reflects the truth.

USING THE WORD BANK

taciturn
rheumatic
vestibule
zenith
countenance
veracity
guileless
prodigious
sublimity

As you read, you will encounter the words on this list. Each word is defined on the page where it first appears. Preview the list before you read. With a partner, define any words or word parts that you already know.

◆ Build Grammar Skills

RESTRICTIVE AND NONRESTRICTIVE ADJECTIVE CLAUSES

Adjective clauses modify nouns or pronouns. An adjective clause is **restrictive** when it is necessary to complete the meaning of the noun or pronoun it modifies. It is not set off with a comma:

Orders were given *that no one was to be admitted.*

A **nonrestrictive clause** adds details that are not necessary to the meaning of the sentence, and it is set off with commas:

. . . and by the advice of kind-hearted Ivan Markovitch, his uncle, *who was taking his part,* he sat meekly in the hall by the door leading to the study . . .

Prentice Hall Literature Program Resources

REINFORCE / RETEACH / EXTEND

Selection Support Pages
Build Vocabulary: Word Roots: -ver-, p. 155
Build Grammar Skills: Restrictive and Nonrestrictive Adjective Clauses, p. 156
Reading Strategy: Make Inferences, p. 157
Literary Focus: Static and Dynamic Characters, p. 158

Strategies for Diverse Student Needs, p. 38

Beyond Literature
Humanities Connection: Personal Honor, p. 38

Formal Assessment Selection Test, pp. 132–134; Assessment Resources Software

Alternative Assessment, p. 38

Writing and Language Transparencies
Comparison and Contrast Organizer, pp. 95–98

Resource Pro CD-ROM
"A Problem," "Luck"—includes all resource materials and customizable lesson plan

 Listening to Literature Audiocassettes
"A Problem," "Luck"

A Problem ◆ Luck

◆ Literature and Your Life

Have you ever met a person who turned out to be different from what you had expected? A person's outside appearance often disguises the true feelings and thoughts of a person. In each of these stories, you may be surprised to find that what you see and hear does not always reflect what lies behind the actions and words of the main characters.

THEMATIC FOCUS: FACING THE CONSEQUENCES

After you've read these stories, you may have a new answer to the question "Do people make choices based on the potential consequences of their actions?

Journal Writing Jot down some notes about possible consequences you might experience as a result of a choice you make.

◆ Background for Understanding

CULTURE

People's lifestyles reflect their culture or country. The aristocracy (people born to ruling families) of England, where Mark Twain's "Luck" takes place, have more formal habits than English working people. The same situation existed in Russia, where Anton Chekhov lived and wrote, before the Communist revolution of 1917. For these groups of people, as well as for the wealthy business classes, appearance and honor often meant more than the truth of how each person felt, thought, and behaved.

◆ Literary Focus

STATIC AND DYNAMIC CHARACTERS

Characters are the people or animals who take part in the action of a work of fiction. Characters can be classified as either static or dynamic. **Static characters** do not change during the course of a story. They remain the same no matter what happens to them. **Dynamic characters** change and usually learn something as a result of the events of the story. The changes they undergo affect their attitudes, beliefs, or behavior.

◆ Reading Strategy

MAKE INFERENCES ABOUT CHARACTER

When you meet new people, you form opinions about them based on their words and actions and, sometimes, on what others tell you about them. When you put those clues together to form an idea about a person, you **make inferences** about his or her personality, beliefs, or qualities. You get to know fictional characters in a similar way. Their actions and words provide clues from which you make inferences about them. Use a graphic organizer like the one shown to make inferences about the characters in these stories.

Colonel says Sasha won't reform → Sasha has disappointed his uncle before.

Words   **Inference**   **Actions**

Guide for Reading ◆ 513

Customize for
Less Proficient Readers
Both stories contain long and complex sentences that may pose difficulty for these students. Using examples from one or both of the stories, model how to break such sentences down into smaller parts. Remind students to use punctuation marks as well as signal words such as *if, that,* and *so* as clues to the logic of the sentence.

Customize for
More Advanced Students
Encourage more advanced students to contrast the two stories in terms of tone, style, and theme. Which writer's style did they prefer, and why?

Customize for
English Language Learners
Expressions such as "touched to the quick," and "It was food and drink to me" are likely to confuse some students for whom English is a second language. Encourage these students to question any unfamiliar idioms or old-fashioned expressions they encounter in the stories.

Customize for
Interpersonal Learners
Have these students work together in small groups. Each group member can focus on one character in each story, reading aloud the character's words and leading others in a discussion of the character's role, traits, and motives.

Preparing for Standardized Tests

Grammar and Language Correctly identifying and punctuating restrictive and nonrestrictive adjective clauses presents difficulty for many students. The explanations and examples in the Build Grammar Skills lesson for this selection will help them master this often problematic skill.

Tests such as the ACT and PSAT include questions that require students to detect errors in usage and mechanics. Students may be asked to determine whether a sentence that contains a restrictive or nonrestrictive adjective clause is correctly punctuated, as in this example:

The <u>movie, that we wanted to see,</u> was sold out. *(B)*

(A) movie, that we wanted to see,
(B) movie that we wanted to see
(C) movie that we wanted, to see

The Build Grammar Skills will help students understand that B is correct because the adjective clause *that we wanted to see* should not be set off by commas, as it is necessary to the meaning. For additional practice, use the Build Grammar Skills page on Restrictive and Nonrestrictive Adjective Clauses in **Selection Support,** p. 156.

One-Minute Insight

In "A Problem," three uncles grapple with the question of what to do about their errant nephew Sasha. Instead of welcoming their decision to be lenient as an opportunity to mend his ways, however, Sasha seizes it as an opportunity to continue in his irresponsible habits, with just one difference—he has gained self-knowledge. He now sees how he can manipulate his relatives and avoid facing up to the consequences he deserves. The story raises important questions about forgiveness and responsibility.

◆ Critical Thinking

❶ **Analyze** What do these details suggest about the problem that the Uskov family faces? *They suggest the problem is a serious one; it could lead to embarrassment or shame for the entire family.*

▶Critical Viewing◀

❷ **Connect** The posture of the man in the picture makes him look stiff and stern. The fact that his head is turned away from the viewer creates a cold and impersonal impression. Therefore, students may say they would not want to go to this man for help.

A Problem

Anton Chekhov

Translated by Constance Garnett

❶ The strictest measures were taken that the Uskovs' family secret might not leak out and become generally known. Half of the servants were sent off to the theater or the circus; the other half were sitting in the kitchen and not allowed to leave it. Orders were given that no one was to be admitted. The wife of the Colonel, her sister, and the governess, though they had been initiated into the secret, kept up a pretense of knowing nothing; they sat in the dining room and did not show themselves in the drawing room or the hall.

Sasha Uskov, the young man of twenty-five who was the cause of all the commotion, had arrived some time before, and by the advice of kind-hearted Ivan Markovitch, his uncle, who was taking his part, he sat meekly in the hall by the door leading to the study, and prepared himself to make an open, candid explanation.

The other side of the door, in the study, a family council was being

❷ ▶ **Critical Viewing** If you were in Sasha's situation, would you want to go to this man for help? Why or why not? [Connect]

Man on a Balcony, Boulevard Haussmann, 1880, Gustave Caillebotte, Art Resource, N

◆ Block Scheduling Strategies

Consider these suggestions to take advantage of extended class time:

- Introduce the Literary Focus, Static and Dynamic Characters. Ask students to name familiar characters who exemplify both types. After reading the story, students can answer the Literary Focus questions on page 525 and complete the Literary Focus page in *Selection Support,* p. 158.

- As students read, have them pay special attention to the Reading Strategy, Make

Inferences About Character. Encourage them to use a chart such as the one on page 513 to record and explain the inferences they make about the characters in the story.

- Have students listen to the stories on the audiocassette. Suggest that they listen for details that tell whether or not the main characters change as the stories unfold.

- Have students complete the Writing Mini-Lesson on page 526. As a prewriting activ-

ity, have a class discussion on the dialogue in "A Problem" and "Luck." Do students think the dialogue realistically reflects the way people talked in the late nineteenth century? How might they update some of the dialogue to reflect the way people talk today?

- Use the Humanities Connection: Personal Honor page in *Beyond Literature,* p. 38, to help students synthesize their response to the stories.

held. The subject under discussion was an exceedingly disagreeable and delicate one. Sasha Uskov had cashed at one of the banks a false promissory note,[1] and it had become due for payment three days before, and now his two paternal uncles and Ivan Markovitch, the brother of his dead mother, were deciding the question whether they should pay the money and save the family honor, or wash their hands of it and leave the case to go to trial.

To outsiders who have no personal interest in the matter such questions seem simple; for those who are so unfortunate as to have to decide them in earnest they are extremely difficult. The uncles had been talking for a long time, but the problem seemed no nearer decision.

"My friends!" said the uncle who was a colonel, and there was a note of exhaustion and bitterness in his voice. "Who says that family honor is a mere convention? I don't say that at all. I am only warning you against a false view; I am pointing out the possibility of an unpardonable mistake. How can you fail to see it? I am not speaking Chinese; I am speaking Russian!"

"My dear fellow, we do understand," Ivan Markovitch protested mildly.

"How can you understand if you say that I don't believe in family honor? I repeat once more; fa-mil-y ho-nor false-ly un-der-stood is a prejudice! Falsely understood! That's what I say: whatever may be the motives for screening a scoundrel, whoever he may be, and helping him to escape punishment, it is contrary to law and unworthy of a gentleman. It's not saving the family honor; it's civic cowardice! Take the army, for instance. . . . The honor of the army is more precious to us than any other honor, yet we don't screen our guilty members, but condemn them. And does the honor of the army suffer in consequence? Quite the opposite!"

The other paternal uncle, an official in the Treasury, a <u>taciturn</u>, dull-witted, and <u>rheumatic</u> man, sat silent, or spoke only of

---

1. **promissory note:** Written promise to pay a certain sum of money on demand; an IOU.

the fact that the Uskovs' name would get into the newspapers if the case went for trial. His opinion was that the case ought to be hushed up from the first and not become public property; but, apart from publicity in the newspapers, he advanced no other argument in support of this opinion.

The maternal uncle, kind-hearted Ivan Markovitch, spoke smoothly, softly, and with a tremor in his voice. He began with saying that youth has its rights and its peculiar temptations. Which of us has not been young, and who has not been led astray? To say nothing of ordinary mortals, even great men have not escaped errors and mistakes in their youth. Take, for instance, the biography of great writers. Did not every one of them gamble, drink, and draw down upon himself the anger of right-thinking people in his young days? If Sasha's error bordered upon crime, they must remember that Sasha had received practically no education; he had been expelled from the high school in the fifth class; he had lost his parents in early childhood, and so had been left at the tenderest age without guidance and good, benevolent influences. He was nervous, excitable, had no firm ground under his feet, and, above all, he had been unlucky. Even if he were guilty, anyway he deserved indulgence and the sympathy of all compassionate souls. He ought, of course, to be punished, but he was punished as it was by his conscience and the agonies he was enduring now while awaiting the sentence of his relations. The comparison with the army made by the Colonel was delightful, and did credit to his lofty intelligence; his appeal to their feeling of public

> ◆ **Reading Strategy**
> What inferences can you make about Ivan Markovitch based on his speech?

◆ **Build Vocabulary**

taciturn (ta′ sə tərn) *adj.*: Preferring not to talk; uncommunicative; silent

rheumatic (rü ma′ tik) *adj.*: Suffering from a disease of the joints; able to move only with great pain

A Problem ◆ 515

Comprehension Check ☑

❸ Have students explain in their own words what Sasha did to bring trouble upon himself and his family. *He forged an IOU and cashed it at a bank; if the money that he received is not paid back, he will be charged with a crime.*

◆ **Build Grammar Skills**

❹ **Restrictive and Nonrestrictive Adjective Clauses** Point out the restrictive adjective clause *who was a colonel.* To show students why this clause is restrictive, have them read the sentence without it. Ask: Why is the clause necessary? *The clause identifies the particular uncle who is speaking.*

◆ **Critical Thinking**

❺ **Contrast** Have students contrast the views of the two paternal uncles. How does each one's notion of family honor affect his opinion about how to treat Sasha? *The uncle who is with the treasury is concerned with family honor in the sense of keeping up appearances. The uncle who was a colonel regards this approach to family honor as a false and mistaken one—he believes that covering up another person's wrongdoing is dishonorable, no matter what the circumstances.*

◆ **Reading Strategy**

❻ **Infer** Markovitch is kind-hearted and forgiving. His comments about Sasha show that he has an understanding, compassionate nature.

🎼 **Humanities: Art**

Man on a Balcony, Boulevard Haussman, 1880, by Gustave Caillebotte.

This man's posture appears stiff and stern, and his face is turned away from the viewer, depersonalizing the figure and creating an air of mystery.

Caillebotte is best known as an art patron and collector. During the late 1800's, he helped organize the exhibits that introduced the works of such Impressionists as Monet,

Manet, and Renoir. Caillebotte's own works were also exhibited at some of these shows. Use these questions for discussion:

1. In what ways does the setting in the painting reflect the setting of "A Problem"? *The man's elegant clothing and surroundings suggest that he is in an expensive home or apartment in town; "A Problem" takes place in the city home of an aristocratic family.*

2. Which character in the story does the figure in the painting resemble? Why? *The painting depicts an older man, apparently deep in thought. Students may say that he could be either the uncle who is a former colonel or Ivan Markovitch, Sasha's maternal uncle.*

515

516

Comprehension Check ☑

❶ What does Ivan Markovitch, Sasha's maternal uncle, think that the family should do about Sasha? *He feels that the family should forgive Sasha and repay the debt that he incurred.*

◆ **Literary Focus**

❷ **Static and Dynamic Characters** Remind students that a static character does not change during the course of a story. Then have them identify Sasha's attitude toward his misdeed at this point. Encourage them to be aware of whether or not Sasha changes as the story progresses. *Students should note that at this point, Sasha feels neither ashamed nor guilty about cashing the false promissory note.*

◆ *Literature and Your Life*

❸ Students may say that they felt helpless and frustrated because they were not in control of what would happen to them; they may say they felt anxious and worried about what the other person would do or decide.

---

duty spoke for the chivalry of his soul, but they must not forget that in each individual the citizen is closely linked with the Christian. . . .

❶ "Shall we be false to civic duty," Ivan Markovitch exclaimed passionately, "if instead of punishing an erring boy we hold out to him a helping hand?"

Ivan Markovitch talked further of family honor. He had not the honor to belong to the Uskov family himself, but he knew their distinguished family went back to the thirteenth century; he did not forget for a minute, either, that his precious, beloved sister had been the wife of one of the representatives of that name. In short, the family was dear to him for many reasons, and he refused to admit the idea that, for the sake of a paltry fifteen hundred rubles,[2] a blot should be cast on the escutcheon[3] that was beyond all price. If all the motives he had brought forward were not sufficiently convincing, he, Ivan Markovitch, in conclusion, begged his listeners to ask themselves what was meant by crime? Crime is an immoral act founded upon ill-will. But is the will of man free? Philosophy has not yet given a positive answer to that question. Different views were held by the learned. The latest school of Lombroso,[4] for instance, denies the freedom of the will, and considers every crime as the product of the purely anatomical peculiarities of the individual.

"Ivan Markovitch," said the Colonel, in a voice of entreaty, "we are talking seriously about an important matter, and you bring in Lombroso, you clever fellow. Think a little, what are you saying all this for? Can you imagine that all your thunderings and rhetoric will furnish an answer to the question?"

❷ Sasha Uskov sat at the door and listened. He felt neither terror, shame, nor depression, but

2. **rubles** (rōō´ bəlz) *n.*: Russian unit of currency.
3. **escutcheon** (is kə´ chən) *n.*: Shield on which a coat of arms is displayed.
4. **Lombroso:** Cesare Lombroso, (1836–1909), an Italian physician and criminologist who believed that a criminal was a distinct human type, with specific physical and mental deviations, and that a criminal tendency was the result of hereditary factors.

516 ◆ *Short Stories*

only weariness and inward emptiness. It seemed to him that it made absolutely no difference to him whether they forgave him or not; he had come here to hear his sentence and to explain himself simply because kind-hearted Ivan Markovitch had begged him to do so. He was not afraid of the future. It made no difference to him where he was: here in the hall, in prison, or in Siberia.

"If Siberia, then let it be Siberia, damn it all!"

He was sick of life and found it insufferably hard. He was inextricably involved in debt; he

◆ *Literature and Your Life*

Connect this story to a time in your life when your future was in someone else's hands. What was the dominant emotion you felt?

❷

◆ **Beyond the Classroom**

Career Connection: Criminology

While arguing for leniency for Sasha, Ivan Markovitch brings up the latest theories of *criminology*—the scientific study of crime and criminal behavior. Although the particular ideas that this Chekhov character cites have long been out of fashion, criminology remains an important field of social science.

Among the questions that modern criminologists study are the causes of crime, the nature of criminal organizations, how to prevent crime, and how to rehabilitate convicted criminals. Criminologists may work within the criminal justice system, or they may teach and conduct studies within a college or university setting.

Have students gather more information on criminology and report their findings to the class. For example, students may focus on how the work of a criminologist differs from that of a *criminalist*—a person versed in criminal law or a psychiatrist dealing with criminality. They may also report on why some background in criminology is important for lawyers, judges, and others who work in the criminal justice system.

had not a farthing[5] in his pocket; his family had become detestable to him; he would have to part from his friends and his women sooner or later, as they had begun to be too contemptuous of his sponging on them. The future looked black.

Sasha was indifferent, and was only disturbed by one circumstance; the other side of the door they were calling him a scoundrel and a criminal. Every minute he was on the point of jumping up, bursting into the study and shouting in answer to the detestable metallic voice of the Colonel:

"You are lying!"

"Criminal" is a dreadful word—that is what

---

5. **farthing** (fär´ thing) *n.*: Coin of little value.

murderers, thieves, robbers are; in fact, wicked and morally hopeless people. And Sasha was very far from being all that. . . . It was true he owed a great deal and did not pay his debts. But debt is not a crime, and it is unusual for a man not to be in debt. The Colonel and Ivan Markovitch were both in debt. . . .

"What have I done wrong besides?" Sasha wondered.

He had discounted a forged note. But all the young men he knew did the same. Handrikov and Von Burst always forged IOU's from their parents or friends when their allowances were not paid at the regular time, and then when they got their money from home they redeemed them before they became due. Sasha had done the same, but had not redeemed the IOU because he had not got the money which Handrikov had promised to lend him. He was not to blame; it was the fault of circumstances. It was true that the use of another person's signature was considered reprehensible; but, still, it was not a crime but a generally accepted dodge, an ugly formality which injured no one and was quite harmless, for in forging the Colonel's signature Sasha had had no intention of causing anybody damage or loss.

"No, it doesn't mean that I am a criminal . . ." thought Sasha. "And it's not in my character to bring myself to commit a crime. I am soft, emotional. . . . When I have the money I help the poor. . . ."

Sasha was musing after this fashion while they went on talking the other side of the door.

"But, my friends, this is endless," the Colonel declared, getting excited. "Suppose we were to forgive him and pay the money. You know he would not give up leading a dissipated life, squandering money, making debts, going to our tailors and ordering suits in our names! Can you guarantee that this will be his last prank?

◄ **Critical Viewing** The ruble is the Russian monetary unit. How are these rubles similar to and different from other money, such as American dollars? **[Compare and Contrast]**

⑤

A Problem ◆ 517

◆ **Reading Strategy**

❹ **Make Inferences About Character** Encourage students to describe Sasha's line of reasoning in their own words. Then have them make inferences about his character and personality traits based on these thoughts. *Students should point out that Sasha makes numerous excuses for his behavior. They may infer that he generally does not take responsibility for his actions or that he does not have a basic sense of the difference between right and wrong.*

▶ **Critical Viewing** ◄

❺ **Compare and Contrast** Sample answer: The ruble is apparently more colorful and more ornate than American dollars.

❶ Static and Dynamic Characters Students should note the following: Neither the Colonel nor Ivan Markovitch shows changes in personality traits, attitudes, or beliefs. Neither seems to be learning or growing.

◆ **Build Grammar Skills**

❷ Restrictive and Nonrestrictive Adjective Clauses Point out the adjective clause *that were rolling down her cheeks,* which modifies the noun *tears.* Ask students if the clause is restrictive or nonrestrictive and have them explain their answers. *The clause is restrictive; it adds necessary information to the noun, and it is not set off by commas.*

◆ **Build Grammar Skills**

❸ Restrictive and Nonrestrictive Adjective Clauses Have students identify the restrictive adjective clause in this sentence. *The clause is "who had moved him to such wrath." What noun does it modify? It modifies person.*

As far as I am concerned, I have no faith whatever in his reforming!"

The official of the Treasury muttered something in reply; after him Ivan Markovitch began talking blandly and suavely again. The Colonel moved his chair impatiently and drowned the other's words with his detestable metallic voice. At last the door opened and Ivan Markovitch came out of the study; there were patches of red on his cleanshaven face.

"Come along," he said, taking Sasha by the hand. "Come and speak frankly from your heart. Without pride, my dear boy, humbly and from your heart."

> ◆ **Literary Focus**
> ❶ Explain the ways in which the Colonel and Ivan Markovitch are static characters.

Sasha went into the study. The official of the Treasury was sitting down; the Colonel was standing before the table with one hand in his pocket and one knee on a chair. It was smoky and stifling in the study. Sasha did not look at the official or the Colonel; he felt suddenly ashamed and uncomfortable. He looked uneasily at Ivan Markovitch and muttered:

"I'll pay it . . . I'll give it back. . . ."

"What did you expect when you discounted the IOU?" he heard a metallic voice.

"I . . . Handrikov promised to lend me the money before now."

Sasha could say no more. He went out of the study and sat down again on the chair near the door. He would have been glad to go away altogether at once, but he was choking with hatred and he awfully wanted to remain, to tear the Colonel to pieces, to say something rude to him. He sat trying to think of something violent and effective to say to his hated uncle, and at that moment a woman's figure, shrouded in the twilight, appeared at the drawing room door. It was the Colonel's wife. She beckoned Sasha to her, and, wringing her hands, said, weeping:

"*Alexandre*, I know you don't like me, but . . . listen to me; listen, I beg you. . . . But, my dear, how can this have happened? Why, it's awful, awful! For goodness' sake, beg them, defend

yourself, entreat them."

Sasha looked at her quivering shoulders, at the big tears that were rolling down her cheeks, heard behind his back the hollow, nervous voices of worried and exhausted people, and shrugged his shoulders. He had not in the least expected that his aristocratic relations would raise such a tempest over a paltry fifteen hundred rubles! He could not understand her tears nor the quiver of their voices.

An hour later he heard that the Colonel was getting the best of it; the uncles were finally inclining to let the case go for trial.

"The matter's settled," said the Colonel, sighing. "Enough."

After this decision all the uncles, even the emphatic Colonel, became noticeably depressed. A silence followed.

"Merciful Heavens!" signed Ivan Markovitch. "My poor sister!"

And he began saying in a subdued voice that most likely his sister, Sasha's mother, was present unseen in the study at that moment. He felt in his soul how the unhappy, saintly woman was weeping, grieving, and begging for her boy. For the sake of her peace beyond the grave, they ought to spare Sasha.

The sound of a muffled sob was heard. Ivan Markovitch was weeping and muttering something which it was impossible to catch through the door. The Colonel got up and paced from corner to corner. The long conversation began over again.

But then the clock in the drawing room struck two. The family council was over. To avoid seeing the person who had moved him to such wrath, the Colonel went from the study, not into the hall, but into the <u>vestibule</u>. . . . Ivan Markovitch came out into the hall. . . . He was agitated and rubbing his hands joyfully. His tear-stained eyes looked good-humored and his mouth was twisted into a smile.

"Capital," he said to Sasha. "Thank God! You can go home, my dear, and sleep tranquilly. We have decided to pay the sum, but on condition that you repent and come with me tomorrow

---

Speaking and Listening Mini-Lesson

Roundtable Discussion
This mini-lesson supports the Speaking and Listening activity in the Idea Bank on page 526.

Introduce the Concept A roundtable discussion is an informal group discussion on a specific topic. The group may or may not select a leader. Point out that students will discuss how the basic question raised in each story applies to our own times.

Develop Background Before students

break into small groups, have them identify some of the specific questions and issues they might explore. Possibilities include:

• What choices does Sasha in "A Problem" make? What consequences might these choices lead to?

• How do the choices that the clergyman and Scoresby make in "Luck" differ? In what way does each character experience different consequences?

• What kind of person would be the modern

equivalent of Sasha? Of the clergyman? Of Scoresby?

Apply the Information Have students explore these and similar questions in groups, then present their summaries to the class.

Assess the Outcome Have students evaluate their discussions on the basis of the following criteria: (1) Was the summary clear? (2) Was there evidence of reasoned discussion of the issue? (3) Were specific applications made to modern times?

into the country and set to work."

A minute later Ivan Markovitch and Sasha in their greatcoats and caps were going down the stairs. The uncle was muttering something edifying. Sasha did not listen, but felt as though some uneasy weight were gradually slipping off his shoulders. They had forgiven him; he was free! A gust of joy sprang up within him and sent a sweet chill to his heart. He longed to breathe, to move swiftly, to live! Glancing at the street lamps and the black sky, he remembered that Von Burst was celebrating his name day[6] that evening at the "Bear," and again a rush of joy flooded his soul. . . .

"I am going!" he decided.

But then he remembered he had not a farthing, that the companions he was going to would despise him at once for his empty pockets. He must get hold of some money, come what may!

"Uncle, lend me a hundred rubles," he said to Ivan Markovitch.

His uncle, surprised, looked into his face and backed against a lamppost.

"Give it to me," said Sasha, shifting impatiently from one foot to the other and beginning

---

6. **name day:** Feast day of the saint after whom a person is named.

to pant. "Uncle, I entreat you, give me a hundred rubles."

His face worked; he trembled, and seemed on the point of attacking his uncle. . . .

"Won't you?" he kept asking, seeing that his uncle was still amazed and did not understand. "Listen. If you don't, I'll give myself up tomorrow! I won't let you pay the IOU! I'll present another false note tomorrow!"

Petrified, muttering something incoherent in his horror, Ivan Markovitch took a hundred-ruble note out of his pocketbook and gave it to Sasha. The young man took it and walked rapidly away from him. . . .

Taking a sledge,[7] Sasha grew calmer, and felt a rush of joy within him again. The "rights of youth" of which kind-hearted Ivan Markovitch had spoken at the family council woke up and asserted themselves. Sasha pictured the drinking party before him, and, among the bottles, the women, and his friends, the thought flashed through his mind:

"Now I see that I am a criminal; yes, I am a criminal."

---

7. **sledge** (slej) *n.*: Strong, heavy sled.

◆ **Build Vocabulary**

vestibule (ves´ tə byül) *n.*: Small entrance hall or room

◆ **Critical Thinking**

❺ **Interpret** Ask students why Ivan Markovitch is horrified by Sasha's words. *He suddenly realizes that Sasha has no intention of repenting; he is shocked by Sasha's shamelessness and ingratitude.*

Reinforce and Extend

Answers

◆ *Literature and Your Life*

Reader's Response Some students may sympathize with Ivan Markovitch because his trust and kindness are betrayed by his nephew. Others may feel that Sasha is deeply troubled and needs help.

Thematic Focus Sasha has not been made to face the consequences of his actions and therefore will continue his "criminal" activity.

☑ **Check Your Comprehension**

1. Sasha needs help because he has cashed a false promissory note at the bank, and it has come due for payment. If his family doesn't cover the debt, Sasha will be tried in court, convicted, and probably sent to debtor's prison.
2. He reminds the other relatives that Sasha is young, uneducated, and an orphan, and should therefore be treated with leniency.

Guide for Responding

◆ *Literature and Your Life*

Reader's Response With whom in this story do you sympathize? Why?

Thematic Focus What point about choices and consequences is demonstrated by Sasha's experiences?

☑ **Check Your Comprehension**

1. Why does Sasha need help?
2. How does Uncle Ivan convince the other uncles to help Sasha?

◆ **Critical Thinking**

INTERPRET

1. Why do you think most of the relatives don't want to help Sasha? **[Speculate]**
2. Why do you think Sasha wrote a note he knew he could not honor? **[Infer]**

EVALUATE

3. Do you think Uncle Ivan's attitude helps or harms Sasha? Explain. **[Make a Judgment]**

APPLY

4. What would you have done if you were one of Sasha's uncles? **[Relate]**

A Problem ◆ 519

◆ **Critical Thinking**

1. Most of the relatives believe Sasha will never reform and will continue to disgrace the family name.
2. Sasha was playing financial roulette, believing he could cover one debt with another loan. He is behaving irresponsibly.
3. Some students may say that, ultimately, Uncle Ivan's kindness may help Sasha to reform; others will say that Uncle Ivan is simply enabling Sasha to continue his irresponsible ways.
4. Encourage students to think carefully about the effect their actions would have on Sasha. What will help Sasha more—letting him "off the hook" or forcing him to face the consequences of his actions?

One-Minute Insight

In "Luck," a clergyman describes how he attempted to protect a military man from his own blundering ways—from the time the man was a cadet to his battlefield experience in the Crimean War. Due to luck, however, every situation in which the military man found himself seemed to work in his favor. Finally, the man became a renowned and highly decorated military leader. The reader has every reason to believe that the man will continue through life as the fortunate fool that he is.

◆ Build Grammar Skills

❶ Restrictive and Nonrestrictive Adjective Clauses Have students identify the restrictive adjective clause in the sentence beginning, "There sat the . . . " Ask: How is the clause punctuated? What noun does it modify? *The clause "whom I had heard of . . . that day" is essential to the meaning and would not have a comma in front of it if the nonessential phrase "in actual flesh" were deleted, together with its surrounding commas. The clause modifies man.*

◆ Critical Thinking

❷ Support Have students explain in their own words how the narrator feels about Scoresby. Encourage them to cite specific details or phrases in support of their answers. *Students should note that the narrator has enormous admiration for Scoresby; they may cite such phrases as "whom I had heard of so many thousand times," "forever celebrated," "that demigod," and so on.*

LUCK Mark Twain

It was at a banquet in London in honor of one of the two or three conspicuously illustrious[1] English military names of this generation. For reasons which will presently appear, I will withhold his real name and titles, and call him Lieutenant-General Lord Arthur Scoresby, V.C., K.C.B., etc., etc., etc. What a fascination there is in a renowned name! There sat the man, in actual flesh, whom I had heard of so many thousands of times since that day, thirty years before, when his name shot suddenly to the <u>zenith</u> from a Crimean battlefield,[2] to remain forever celebrated. It was food and drink to me to look, and look, and look at that demigod; scanning, searching, noting: the quietness, the reserve, the noble gravity of his <u>countenance</u>; the simple honesty that expressed itself all over him; the sweet unconsciousness of his greatness—unconsciousness of the hundreds of admiring eyes fastened upon him, unconsciousness of the deep, loving, sincere worship welling out of the breasts

---

1. **conspicuously** (kən spik´ yōō wəs lē) **illustrious** (il us´ trē əs): Outstandingly famous.
2. **Crimean** (krī mē´ ən) **battlefield:** Place of battle during the Crimean War (1854–1856), in which Russia was defeated in trying to dominate southeastern Europe.

◆ Build Vocabulary

zenith (zē´ nith) *n.*: Highest point

countenance (koun´ tə nəns) *n.*: Expression on a person's face

veracity (və ras´ ə tē) *n.*: Truthfulness; honesty

Scotland Forever, Elizabeth Butler, Leeds City Art Galleries

Cross-Curricular Connection: Social Studies

Florence Nightingale Through a series of unlikely events Arthur Scoresby becomes a hero of the Crimean War, in which Great Britain, allied with France, Turkey, and the Italian kingdom of Sardinia, fought against Russia. Students may be interested to learn that a famous nineteenth-century woman—Florence Nightingale—was a real-life hero of that war.

In 1854, while Nightingale was working as the superintendent of a women's hospital in London, the Secretary of War asked her to travel to the Crimea and take charge of nursing for the allied troops. The conditions she found there were wretched and appalling, but she and her staff of nurses did much to improve army hospitals and save lives. As a result of her work, Nightingale became a world-famous expert on field medicine—the care of sick and wounded soldiers; several years later, during the American Civil War, she advised the United States on the operation and administration of military hospitals.

Have students do research to learn more about Florence Nightingale's life and her contributions to modern medicine.

of those people and flowing toward him.

The clergyman at my left was an old acquaintance of mine—clergyman now, but had spent the first half of his life in the camp and field, and as an instructor in the military school at Woolwich. Just at the moment I have been talking about, a veiled and singular light glimmered in his eyes, and he leaned down and muttered confidentially to me—indicating the hero of the banquet with a gesture:

"Privately—he's an absolute fool."

This verdict was a great surprise to me. If its subject had been Napoleon,[3] or Socrates,[4] or Solomon,[5] my astonishment could not have been greater. Two things I was well aware of: that the Reverend was a man of strict <u>veracity</u>,

3. **Napoleon** (nə pō′ lē ən): Napoleon Bonaparte (1769–1821), French military leader and emperor of France from 1804 to 1815.
4. **Socrates** (säk′ rə tēz′): Athenian philosopher and teacher (470?–399 B.C.).
5. **Solomon** (säl′ ə mən): In the Bible, the King of Israel who built the first temple and was noted for his wisdom.

❸ ▼ Critical Viewing Based on this painting, would you rather be a good soldier or a lucky one? Explain. [Draw Conclusions]

►Critical Viewing◄
❸ **Draw Conclusions** Students may prefer being a good soldier because there is more personal satisfaction in being good at something than being lucky; other students, however, may point out that lucky soldiers are not wounded or killed and may be rewarded for some things for which they did not have to work.

Luck ◆ 521

 Humanities: Art

Scotland Forever, 1881, by Elizabeth Butler.

Elizabeth Butler's vividly realistic and patriotic depictions of battle and military life made her one of the most successful painters in Victorian England. Queen Victoria herself was a great admirer of Butler's works and bought a Butler painting entitled *Calling the Roll After an Engagement, Crimea* for her own collection.

Use these questions for discussion:

1. What elements in the painting convey a sense of movement and action? *Elements include the* soldiers with raised swords in the foreground; the turbulent, rolling clouds and gunsmoke; and the point of view, in which the horses appear to charge directly toward the viewer.

2. Which side of Scoresby does the painting reflect—the "public" Scoresby or the "real" Scoresby, known only by the clergyman and the narrator? Explain. *Students should note that the painting reflects the public Scoresby—that is, the one who is regarded as a brilliant military hero.*

◆ Reading Strategy

❶ Make Inferences Have students use this passage to make inferences about the clergyman's character and his motives for helping young Scoresby. *Inferences may include: He is caring and soft-hearted; he helps Scoresby out of kindness.*

◆ Build Vocabulary

❷ Word Roots: -ver- Point out that *veritably* contains the word root *-ver-*, which comes from the Latin *verax*, meaning "speaking truly." Have students use this information as well as context clues to determine the meaning of *veritably*. *It means* truly.

◆ Build Grammar Skills

❸ Restrictive and Nonrestrictive Adjective Clauses Point out the nonrestrictive adjective clause *who knew a thousand times more than he.* Ask students what noun it modifies. How is it punctuated? *It modifies others; it is set off by commas.*

Comprehension Check ☑

❹ How is Scoresby's performance on the mathematics exam similar to his performance on the history exam? *In both cases he did outstandingly well due to a "strangely lucky accident"—the questions that the clergyman drilled him on turned out to be the very ones that appeared on the exams.*

---

and that his judgment of men was good. Therefore I knew, beyond doubt or question, that the world was mistaken about this hero: he *was* a fool. So I meant to find out, at a convenient moment, how the Reverend, all solitary and alone, had discovered the secret.

Some days later the opportunity came, and this is what the Reverend told me:

About forty years ago I was an instructor in the military academy at Woolwich. I was present in one of the sections when young Scoresby underwent his preliminary examination. I was touched to the quick with pity; for the rest of the class answered up brightly and handsomely, while he—why, dear me, he didn't know *anything*, so to speak. He was evidently good, and sweet, and lovable, and guileless; and so it was exceedingly painful to see him stand there, as serene as a graven image, and deliver himself of answers which were veritably miraculous for stupidity and ignorance. All the compassion in me was aroused in his behalf. I said to myself, when he comes to be examined again, he will be flung over, of course; so it will be simply a harmless act of charity to ease his fall as much as I can. I took him aside, and found that he knew a little of Caesar's history;[6] and as he didn't know anything else, I went to work and drilled him like a galley slave on a certain line of stock questions concerning Caesar which I knew would be used. If you'll believe me, he went through with flying colors on examination day! He went through on that purely superficial "cram," and got compliments too, while others, who knew a thousand times

---

6. **Caesar's** (sē´ zərz) **history:** Account of Julius Caesar (100?–44 B.C.), Roman emperor from 49 to 44 B.C.

◆ Build Vocabulary

guileless (gīl´ lis) *adj.*: Without slyness or cunning; frank

prodigious (prə dij´ əs) *adj.*: Enormous

sublimity (sə blim´ ə tē) *n.*: A noble or exalted state

---

more than he, got plucked. By some strangely lucky accident—an accident not likely to happen twice in a century—he was asked no question outside of the narrow limits of his drill.

It was stupefying. Well, all through his course I stood by him, with something of the sentiment which a mother feels for a crippled child; and he always saved himself—just by miracle, apparently.

Now of course the thing that would expose him and kill him at last was mathematics. I resolved to make his death as easy as I could; so I drilled him and crammed him, and crammed him and drilled him, just on the line of questions which the examiners would be most likely to use, and then launched him on his fate. Well, sir, try to conceive of the result: to my consternation he took the first prize! And with it he got a perfect ovation in the way of compliments.

Sleep? There was no more sleep for me for a week. My conscience tortured me day and night. What I had done I had done purely through charity, and only to ease the poor youth's fall—I never had dreamed of any such preposterous result as the thing that had happened. I felt as guilty and miserable as the creator of Frankenstein. Here was a woodenhead whom I had put in the way of glittering promotions and prodigious responsibilities, and but one thing could happen: he and his responsibilities would all go to ruin together at the first opportunity.

The Crimean War had just broken out. Of course there had to be a war, I said to myself: we couldn't have peace and give this donkey a chance to die before he is found out. I waited for the earthquake. It came. And it made me reel when it did come. He was actually gazetted[7] to a captaincy in a marching regiment! Better men grow old and gray in the service before they climb to a sublimity like that. And who could ever have foreseen that they would go and put such a load of responsibility on such green and inadequate shoulders?

---

7. **gazetted** (gə zet´ əd) *v.*: Officially promoted.

I could just barely have stood it if they had made him a cornet;[8] but a captain—think of it! I thought my hair would turn white.

Consider what I did—I who so loved repose and inaction. I said to myself, I am responsible to the country for this, and I must go along with him and protect the country against him as far as I can. So I took my poor little capital that I had saved up through years of work and grinding economy, and went with a sigh and bought a cornetcy in his regiment, and away we went to the field.

And there—oh dear, it was awful. Blunders?—why, he never did anything *but* blunder. But, you see, nobody was in the fellow's secret—everybody had him focused wrong, and necessarily misinterpreted his performance every time—consequently they took his idiotic blunders for inspirations of genius; they did, honestly! His mildest blunders were enough to make a man in his right mind cry; and they did make me cry—and rage and rave too, privately. And the thing that kept me always in a sweat of apprehension was the fact that every fresh blunder he made increased the luster of his reputation! I kept saying to myself, he'll get so high, that when discovery does finally come, it will be like the sun falling out of the sky.

He went right along up, from grade to grade, over the dead bodies of his superiors, until at last, in the hottest moment of the battle of * * * * down went our colonel, and my heart jumped into my mouth, for Scoresby was next in rank! Now for it, said I;

8. **cornet** (kôr net´) *n.*: British cavalry officer who carried his troop's flag.

we'll all land in Sheol[9] in ten minutes, sure.

The battle was awfully hot: the allies were steadily giving way all over the field. Our regiment occupied a position that was vital; a blunder now must be destruction. At this crucial moment, what does this immortal fool do but detach the regiment from its place and order a charge over a neighboring hill where

9. **Sheol** (shē´ ol) *n.*: In the Bible, a place in the depths of the Earth where the dead are thought to dwell.

▲ Critical Viewing Does this man look like a good leader? Explain why or why not. [Support] ❽

Luck ◆ 523

Comprehension Check ☑

❶ In what way is the battle that the clergyman describes an example of another "lucky accident" in Scoresby's career? *The Russians mistake the English charge mindlessly led by Scoresby for a massive, well-planned attack.*

◆ Literary Focus

❷ Static and Dynamic Characters Ask students: Is Scoresby a static character or a dynamic character at this point? *Scoresby is static; he is still making mistakes that turn out right.*

◆ Critical Thinking

❸ Analyze Why does the clergyman tell the truth about Scoresby? *He can no longer hold in his sense of frustration and amazement.*

Reinforce and Extend

Answers
◆ Literature and Your Life

Reader's Response Some students may want to ask Scoresby to what he attributes his success.

Thematic Focus Ever since he chose to help Scoresby, he has felt responsible for him.

☑ Check Your Comprehension

1. He describes Scoresby as a fool.
2. He helps Scoresby with history and math, and joins Scoresby's regiment to help him in battle.
3. Scoresby is asked only questions to which he knows the answers on his examinations; he is made a captain in the army; his blunders in the war are taken for genius.
4. Scoresby wins a stunning military victory as a result of mistaking his right hand for his left.

◆ Critical Thinking

1. The narrator admires Scoresby; the clergyman thinks he is a fool.
2. He finds Scoresby "lovable," but pities him for being such a fool.
3. The clergyman feels that other people are his responsibility. Scoresby simply accepts his good fortune.
4. Students should include evidence from the story as support.
5. Encourage students to support their opinions with concrete examples from their own experience.

524

---

there wasn't a suggestion of an enemy. "There you go!" I said to myself; "this *is* the end at last."

And away we did go, and were over the shoulder of the hill before the insane movement could be discovered and stopped. And what did we find? An entire and unsuspected Russian army in reserve! And what happened? We were eaten up? That is necessarily what would have happened in ninety-nine cases out of a hundred. But no, those Russians argued that no single regiment would come browsing around there at such a time. It must be the entire English army, and that the sly Russian game was detected and blocked; so they turned tail, and away they went, pell-mell, over the hill and down into the field, in wild confusion, and we after them; they themselves broke the solid Russian center in the field, and tore through, and in no time there was the most tremendous rout you ever saw, and the defeat of the allies was turned into a sweeping and splendid victory! Marshal Canrobert looked on, dizzy with astonishment, admiration, and delight; and sent right off for Scoresby, and hugged him, and decorated him on the field, in presence of all the armies!

And what was Scoresby's blunder that time? Merely the mistaking his right hand for his left—that was all. An order had come to him to fall back and support our right; and instead, he fell *forward* and went over the hill to the left. But the name he won that day as a marvelous military genius filled the world with his glory, and that glory will never fade while history books last.

He is just as good and sweet and lovable and unpretending as a man can be, but he doesn't know enough to come in when it rains. Now that is absolutely true. He is the supremest fool in the universe; and until half an hour ago nobody knew it but himself and me. He has been pursued, day by day and year by year, by a most phenomenal and astonishing luckiness. He has been a shining soldier in all our wars for a generation; he has littered his whole military life with blunders, and yet has never committed one that didn't make him a knight or a baronet or a lord or something. Look at his breast; why, he is just clothed in domestic and foreign decorations. Well, sir, every one of them is the record of some shouting stupidity or other; and taken together, they are proof that the very best thing in all this world that can befall a man is to be born lucky. I say again, as I said at the banquet, Scoresby's an absolute fool.

Guide for Responding

◆ Literature and Your Life

Reader's Response If you could ask Scoresby about his experiences, what would you ask him?

Thematic Focus What is a consequence the clergyman experiences based on a choice he made when he was a teacher?

☑ Check Your Comprehension

1. How does the clergyman describe Scoresby?
2. Describe two things the clergyman does to help Scoresby.
3. Summarize the series of lucky events that put Scoresby in a position of leadership.
4. How does Scoresby achieve his "greatest victory"?

◆ Critical Thinking
INTERPRET

1. How does the narrator's first impression of Scoresby contrast with the view of him given by the clergyman? **[Distinguish]**
2. Why does the clergyman help Scoresby? **[Speculate]**
3. Compare and contrast Scoresby and the clergyman. **[Compare and Contrast]**
4. Do you agree with the clergyman that Scoresby is a fool? Explain your answer. In what way is the clergyman also a fool? **[Draw Conclusions]**

APPLY

5. What role do you think luck plays in a person's success? Support your opinion with examples. **[Defend]**

524 ◆ Short Stories

Beyond the Selection

FURTHER READING

Other Works by the Authors
"The Duel," Anton Chekhov
"The Celebrated Jumping Frog of Calaveras County," Mark Twain

Other Works with the Theme of Choices and Consequences
"The Road Not Taken," Robert Frost
"The Necklace," Guy De Maupassant

We suggest that you preview these works before recommending them to students.

INTERNET

Students can visit the following Web sites to learn more about Chekhov and Twain.

For more on Chekhov, go to **http://www.winnipeg. Freenet.mb.ca/~vbu053/Anton_Chekhov.html**

For information about Twain's life and works, go to **http://www.literature.org/works/Mark-Twain**

Please be aware, however, that sites may have changed since we published this information. We *strongly recommend* that you preview the sites before you send students to them.

Guide for Reponding (continued)

◆ Literary Focus

STATIC AND DYNAMIC CHARACTERS

Some characters in stories can be classified as **static characters**—that is, characters that do not change during the course of the story. Others are **dynamic characters**—characters whose attitudes, beliefs, or personality traits change as a result of the story events. In these stories, both of the focal characters are static.

1. Describe the behavior that led to Sasha Uskov's troubles in "A Problem." Describe the way he behaves at the end of the story.
2. Compare Arthur Scoresby's character traits at the beginning of "Luck" and at the end.
3. Explain why Scoresby and Sasha Uskov are both static characters.

◆ Build Vocabulary

USING THE ROOT -ver-

The root -ver- comes from the Latin verax and means "speaking truly." It forms the basis of a number of English words whose meaning relates to the idea of truth. On your paper, match each numbered word with its corresponding definition.

1. veritable   **a.** a truth
2. verisimilitude   **b.** the appearance of being true
3. verity   **c.** actual; in fact

USING THE WORD BANK

On your paper, answer the following questions.

1. What's another word for the *zenith* of success?
2. What type of *countenance* does a clown typically display?
3. Should politicians have *veracity*? Why or why not?
4. How successful would a *guileless* burglar be?
5. True or false: The grasshopper is a *prodigious* creature.
6. Name a type of person who would be said to be in a position of *sublimity*.
7. Which career would most fit a *taciturn* person: violinist, teacher, or stand-up comedian?
8. Would a *rheumatic* person be good at sports? Why or why not?
9. What kind of furniture might fit in a *vestibule*?

◆ Reading Strategy

MAKE INFERENCES ABOUT CHARACTER

You can apply logic to the evidence provided by each author to make inferences about the personalities of characters in "Luck" and "A Problem." For example, when the Colonel in "A Problem" declares about his nephew, "I have no faith whatever in his reforming," you can infer that he has disappointed his family more than once.

1. What do you infer about Sasha's character when he asks his uncle for money at the end of the story?
2. What inferences can you make about Scoresby based on the fact that all his advancements are a result of blunders?

◆ Build Grammar Skills

RESTRICTIVE AND NONRESTRICTIVE ADJECTIVE CLAUSES

A **restrictive adjective clause** is not set off by commas because it is necessary to complete the meaning of the noun or pronoun it modifies. A **nonrestrictive adjective clause** is set off by commas. It provides additional but not necessary information.

Practice Copy the following sentences in your notebook. Underline the adjective clause in each. Then tell whether it is restrictive or nonrestrictive.
1. "My friends!" said the uncle who was a colonel …
2. For reasons which will presently appear, I will withhold my name.
3. Others, who knew a thousand times more than he, got plucked.

Writing Application Write the following sentences in your notebook, supplying adjective clauses where there are blank spaces.

Sasha's uncle ____?____ said he would help. He offered to pay the notes ____?____ . Sasha wanted to go to the party ____?____ . He asked his uncle for money ____?____ . The uncle was shocked that his nephew ____?____ would be so ungrateful.

◆ Literary Focus

1. Sasha's recklessness and lack of responsibility lead to his troubles. At the end of the story, he recklessly betrays his uncle's trust.
2. Scoreby is the same lucky blunderer throughout.
3. Scoresby starts out and ends up a fool. Although Sasha's lack of morality is revealed at the end of the story, he has never had a sense of morality or responsibility.

◆ Build Vocabulary

Using the Root -ver-
1. c 2. b 3. a

Using the Word Bank
1. Another word for *zenith* is height.
2. A clown usually displays a happy or comical *countenance*.
3. Politicians should have *veracity*; they should be honest.
4. A *guileless* burglar, without tricks, would be unsuccessful.
5. False; a grasshopper is small.
6. A happy and successful person would be in a position of *sublimity*.
7. A *taciturn* person would be more fit to be a violinist than a teacher or a comedian.
8. A *rheumatic* person would be stiff, rather than agile, and therefore not good at sports.

◆ Reading Strategy

1. Sasha has no moral sense.
2. Scoresby is lucky.

◆ Build Grammar Skills

1. "My friends!" said the uncle who was a colonel … ; restrictive
2. For reasons which will presently appear, I will withhold my name; restrictive
3. Others, who knew a thousand times more than he, got plucked; nonrestrictive

Writing Application

Sample answers: Sasha's uncle, who was sympathetic, said he would help. He offered to pay the notes that Sasha owed. Sasha wanted to go to the party that was being held that night. He asked his uncle for money, which he needed for the party. The uncle was shocked that his nephew, whom he had just helped, would be so ungrateful.

Idea Bank

Customizing for
Performance Levels

Following are suggestions for matching Idea Bank topics with your students' performance levels:

    Less Advanced Students: 1, 4, 6
    Average Students: 2, 4, 7
    More Advanced Students: 3, 5

Customizing for
Learning Modalities

Following are suggestions for matching Idea Bank topics with your students' learning modalities:

    Verbal/Linguistic: 1, 2, 3, 4, 5
    Visual/Spatial: 6, 7

Writing Mini-Lesson

Refer students to the Writing Handbook, page 965, for instruction on the writing process, and page 968 for information on creative writing.

Writing and Language Transparencies Students can use the Comparison and Contrast organizer blackline master, p. 97, to list points of agreement and disagreement in their conversations.

Writer's Solution

Writers at Work Videodisc
Have students view the videodisc segment from Chapter 2 featuring Maxine Hong Kingston to see how she develops narrative elements.

Play frames 18612 to 19873

Writing Lab CD-ROM
Have students complete the tutorial on Creative Writing. Follow these steps:

1. Have students watch the video clip about gathering details for drama.
2. Students should draft on computer.
3. Students can use the proofreading checklist for drama to guide them in revising their conversations.

Allow approximately 90 minutes of class time to complete these steps.

Sourcebook
Have students use Chapter 6, Creative Writing (pp. 164–193), for additional support. The chapter includes instruction on writing dialogue (p. 185).

526

Build Your Portfolio

Idea Bank

Writing

1. **Invitation** Write the invitation the narrator and clergyman from "Luck" might have received to attend the banquet in honor of Arthur Scoresby.

2. **Journal Entry** Write an entry in Sasha Uskov's journal from the day before his family met to discuss the promissory note he took out and failed to pay back on time.

3. **Story Ending** Write a new story ending for either "Luck" or "A Problem" that shows one major character changing as a result of the events in the original story.

Speaking and Listening

4. **Monologue** As the clergyman in "Luck," describe the character of Arthur Scoresby aloud to a partner. Base your description on details from the story.

5. **Roundtable Discussion** With three other students, discuss how the messages about choices and consequences in these stories apply to modern times. Present a summary of your conclusions to the rest of the class.

Projects

6. **Period Presentation** Find pictures in books or specialty magazines that show how people dressed and lived in the mid to late 1800's. Make a presentation of those pictures or create your own drawings based on your research. **[Art Link; Social Studies Link]**

7. **Multimedia Biography** Create a multimedia biography of Twain or Chekhov. Use maps to show where they lived and the settings they wrote about. Record yourself reading a passage from the author's writing. **[Art Link; Social Studies Link]**

526 ◆ *Short Stories*

Writing Mini-Lesson

Telephone Conversation

Even though each of these stories takes place before the telephone was invented, it is possible to imagine updated versions of each story, in which the conversations take place on a telephone. When a person talks on a telephone, the language used reflects that person's unique personality.

Choose a subject from one of these stories, and write a **telephone conversation**. Use the kind of language contemporary people would use when talking on the phone.

Writing Skills: Realistic Dialogue

Realistic dialogue reflects the language people really use when they talk with one another. The dialogue in "Luck" and "A Problem" reflects the way people talked in the settings for those stories, the late nineteenth century. For your telephone conversation, choose and arrange words to convey the ideas and feelings each person might use in a real phone conversation.

Prewriting Once you decide on the two characters and subject of the telephone conversation, jot down specific quotations that reveal important characteristics or the speaking style of each speaker. Then list other words and phrases that each character might use.

Drafting Write the conversation, making it as believable as you can. Include the quotations and other phrases you wrote down for each speaker. You may even want to include stage directions in parentheses or brackets; for instance (*Coughs before answering*).

Revising Read your dialogue aloud with a partner. Listen to make sure each speaker responds to the other. If a sentence or word does not sound realistic, go back to your prewriting notes to find the appropriate language, or just rewrite it based on the way people speak.

✓ ASSESSMENT OPTIONS

Formal Assessment, Selection Test, pp. 132–134, and Assessment Resources Software. The selection test is designed so that it can be easily customized to the performance levels of your students.
Alternative Assessment, p. 38, includes options for less advanced students, more advanced students, visual/spatial learners, verbal/linguistic learners, musical/rhythmic learners, logical/mathematical, and interpersonal learners.

PORTFOLIO ASSESSMENT
Use the following rubrics in the *Alternative Assessment* booklet to assess student writing:
Invitation: General Rubric, p. 93
Journal Entry: Fictional Narrative Rubric, p. 95
Story Ending: Fictional Narrative Rubric, p. 95
Writing Mini-Lesson: Drama Rubric, p. 109

Writing Process Workshop

Short Story

Short stories can be surprising, thrilling, thoughtful, or mysterious. However, short stories have certain elements in common: They create a single, powerful impression, have a limited number of characters and settings, and center on a conflict that is usually resolved by the story's end.

Write your own short story. The following skills, introduced in this section's Writing Mini-Lessons, will help you write your story.

Writing Skills Focus

▶ **Use transitions to show time,** such as *later, next,* and *after that,* to keep the plot flowing smoothly. (See p. 476.)

▶ Develop your plot so that it leads to a **climax,** or high point of tension, and then have a **resolution,** in which the conflict is settled. (See p. 497.)

▶ Bring your characters to life through **realistic dialogue.** Read your dialogue aloud to see how it sounds. (See p. 526.)

▶ Keep a **consistent point of view**—either first person or third person—throughout the story. (See p. 511.)

In the following excerpt, the author uses these skills to heighten the conflict in the story.

MODEL FROM LITERATURE

from *Leiningen Versus the Ants* by Carl Stephenson

"Unless they alter their course, and there's no reason why they should, they'll reach your plantation in two days at the latest." ①

Leiningen sucked placidly at a cigar about the size of a corn cob and for a few seconds ② gazed without answering the agitated District Commissioner. Then he took the cigar from his lips and leaned slightly forward. With his bristling gray hair, bulky nose, and lucid eyes, he had the look of an aging and shabby eagle. ③

"Decent of you," ④ he murmured, "paddling all this way just to give me the tip.

① The author wastes no time in setting up the story's conflict.

② The transition *for a few seconds* shows time passing.

③ The writer uses third-person point of view.

④ The dialogue is realistic and reveals the personalities of the characters.

Writing Process Workshop ◆ 527

Cross-Curricular Connection: Science

One of the most popular genres of fiction is science fiction, fiction that blends traditional narrative techniques with a fascination with the inventions, discoveries and world of science. Although many science fiction tales suffer from stiff prose that relegates them to second-rate status in the literary world, tales by authors such as Jules Verne, H. G. Wells, Isaac Asimov, and Ray Bradbury have been accepted into the greater canon of literature. Other authors such as Arthur C. Clarke, Ursula K. LeGuin, Frank Herbert, and Robert Heinlein have also achieved prestige in the literary world. You might encourage students with a predilection for math and/or science to take advantage of their interest in those fields and have them consider writing a science fiction story.

Prepare and Engage

Establish Writing Guidelines

Before students begin, review the following key characteristics of a short story:

- It is a brief fictional narrative.
- It creates a powerful impression through few characters.
- Its main character faces a conflict.
- Its narrator is usually an outside persona who refers to the characters as *he* or *she.*

You may want to distribute the scoring rubric for a Fictional Narrative (p. 95 in **Alternative Assessment**) to make students aware before they begin of the criteria on which they will be evaluated. See the suggestions on page 529 for how you can customize the rubric for this workshop. Refer students to the Writing Handbook, page 965, for instruction on the writing process, and page 967 for further information on narration.

✎ Writer's Solution

Writers at Work Videodisc To introduce students to the key elements of a short story and learn how author Maxine Hong Kingston uses them in her writing, play the videodisc segment on Narration (Ch. 2). Have students discuss what Kingston says about how a story itself can shape a narrative.

Play frames 11644 to 20980

Writing Lab CD-ROM

If your students have access to computers, you may want to have them work on the tutorial on Narration to complete all or part of their short stories. Follow these steps:

1. Have students view the interactive model of a short story.
2. Suggest that students use a photo storyboard for plot ideas.
3. Have students draft on the computer.
4. Suggest students consult the screen on tightening suspense.
5. Have students consult the screen on punctuating dialogue.

Sourcebook

Students can find additional support, including topic ideas, models, audience and purpose profiles, and graphic organizers, in the chapter on Narration (pp. 30–61).

527

Develop Student Writing

Prewriting

As students prepare to write their stories, some may be under the impression that a short story differs from a novel only in terms of length. Remind them that short stories themselves can vary greatly in length and that the fundamental difference between stories and novels is that stories are less complex in plot and character development than novels.

Customize for
English Language Learners

These students may confuse homonyms such as *there* and *their*, and *to, too,* and *two*. Explain the differences among these words before the students begin drafting.

Customize for
Less Proficient Writers

If these students are having difficulty thinking of a plot, encourage them to write about an incident in their own lives. Make sure they write in the third-person.

 Writer's Solution

Writing Lab CD-ROM

The Developing Narrative Elements section of the tutorial on Narration contains a Story Line diagram. Encourage students to use this screen to outline the plot elements of their stories, including exposition, inciting incident, rising action, climax, falling action, and resolution.

Drafting

Suggest that students plan out their short stories, beginning with a dramatic opening incident and building to a high point or climax. Encourage them to draft without concern for grammatical or other errors. Once students have completed a draft, they can go back into their work and make extensive revisions.

APPLYING LANGUAGE SKILLS: Verb Tense

Verbs have different forms to show time. These forms are called **tenses**. Use appropriate verb tenses when referring to different periods of time. For example, use the present tense for action in the present and use past tenses for actions that have already happened.

Wrong Tense:

Long before the detective met Mendoza, he <u>hears</u> about him.

Correct Tense:

Long before the detective met Mendoza, he <u>had heard</u> about him.

Practice On your paper, rewrite the following passage using correct verb tenses:

1. John remembers when covered bridges dot the countryside.
2. He continues to search for clues, since the mystery was still not solved.

Writing Application Check the tenses in your short story.

Writer's Solution Connection
Writing Lab

For more examples of topics for short stories, see the Inspirations for Narration in the Narration tutorial in the Writing Lab.

Prewriting

Choose a Topic A good way to think of an idea for a short story is to create a Plot Word Bin like the one below. Make two lists, the first one containing potential main characters, the second containing potential conflicts. Mix and match the two until you come up with a suitable conflict.

Plot Word Bin	
Characters	**Conflicts**
Detective	Missing diamond
Young doctor	Terminal illness
Recent immigrant	Crisis of conscience
Biologist	Environmental disaster
Reporter	Political scandal

Develop the Plot The plot is the sequence of events in your narrative. Begin the plot with an exposition that introduces the setting and characters. Then introduce the conflict. Develop the conflict with rising suspense and action until you reach the climax, or high point of tension. Finally, resolve the conflict and tie up any loose ends in the plot. Use a story line diagram like the one shown to help you plan the plot.

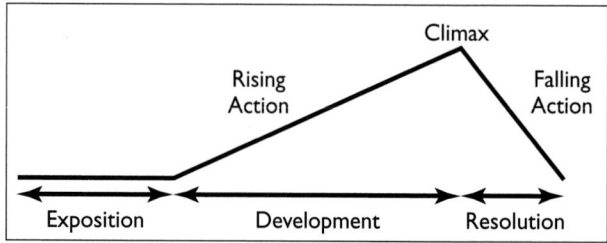

Drafting

Beginning Starting can be the hardest part of writing a short story. The simplest way to tell a story is to present the events in chronological order. You may want to start with a flashback, in the middle of the situation, and go back and fill in the details. You could also begin with a scene of dialogue that introduces the characters or conflict.

Ending A good ending to your narrative is as important as a good beginning. The ending should resolve the conflict, end the suspense, and tie up any loose strings in the plot. It should also be logically consistent with the preceding events.

Applying Language Skills

Verb Tense When writing short stories in particular, students may have trouble shifting between the present and past tenses. Remind them that they should probably use the past tense for most of the narration. Dialogue, of course, can be any tense. Remind them also to use the past perfect tense to describe a past action that occurred before another past action.

Answers

1. John remembers (*remembered* also acceptable) when covered bridges *dotted* the countryside.
2. He *continued* to search for clues, since the mystery *had* still not *been solved*. (*was still not solved* also acceptable)

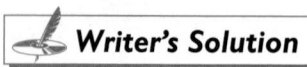 **Writer's Solution**

For additional instruction and practice, have students complete the **Language Lab CD-ROM** lesson on Verb Tense and the practice page 67 in the *Writer's Solution Grammar Practice Book*.

Revising

Use a Checklist A first draft is not a final product. To make it into something wonderful, you need to trim, shape, and polish it. Use the following checklist to help you revise your writing.

▶ What can you do to make the plot or conflict clearer? *Insert changes that would make the plot more logical or would help make the rising action more suspenseful. Add transitions where necessary.*

▶ What can you do to make the characters more realistic? *Add dialogue to bring them to life.*

▶ Who is telling the story? Is this point of view consistent throughout the story?

▶ What language would make your writing more vivid or precise? *Replace weak verbs with vivid ones and vague nouns with exact ones.*

▶ What changes would vary the length and structure of your sentences?

REVISION MODEL

① "P.L. Patterson, private investigator." ⨍
"Hello?" she said. "Mrs. Patterson, I'm glad I reached
② The voice on the line was
you." ⌃said a masculine and sophisticated voice. "My

name is Mr. Chamberlain. Some jewels belonging to

my family were stolen last night. I'd like you to come

by as soon as possible." ③

① *The new dialogue reveals a direct, confident character.*
② *This change makes the sentence structure more interesting.*
③ *Here, the writer sets up the conflict.*

Publishing

Consider a Live Audience Reading a short story aloud is a great way to share it with others. Keep the following points in mind when reading before others: Read slowly and clearly, make eye contact with your audience, vary your volume and tone for emphasis, and take on the personalities of your characters when you read dialogue.

APPLYING LANGUAGE SKILLS: Proper Nouns

Proper nouns, which are always capitalized, name individual people, places, or things. Proper nouns are the most exact nouns.

Common Nouns:
author, lake, war, mountain

Proper Nouns:
Ernest Hemingway, Lake Malawi, World War II, Mt. Kenya

Practice On your paper, replace the following common nouns with proper nouns.

city	book
language	car
river	country
actress	politician
album	gem

Writing Application Review your short story. Look for places where replacing a common noun with a proper noun will make your story more vivid.

Writer's Solution Connection Language Lab

For more practice with proper nouns, complete the Language Lab lesson on Types of Nouns.

Revising

Have students read their stories aloud to find awkward passages.

Writer's Solution

Writing Lab CD-ROM
Students can use the following tools for revising their short stories:

• Proofreading checklist
• Audio-annotated guides for revising dialogue
• Verb-tense checker
• Audio-annotated student model

Publishing

If students do not wish to share their short stories, suggest that they keep them for possible incorporation into a longer work.

Proper Nouns Remind students that proper nouns convey a sense of precision and exactness.

Suggested Answers
Bangkok	*Moby Dick*
Tamil	Corvette
the Amazon	Nepal
Meryl Streep	Bill Clinton
Abbey Road	the Hope Diamond

Writer's Solution

Have students complete the **Language Lab CD-ROM** lesson on Types of Nouns and the practice page 93 in the *Writer's Solution Grammar Practice Book.*

Reinforce and Extend

Review the Writing Guidelines Encourage students to come up with additional criteria for interesting short stories based on what they learned.

Connect to Literature Have students read and study some of the short stories in this book.

✓ ASSESSMENT		4	3	2	1
PORTFOLIO ASSESSMENT Use the rubric on Fictional Narrative in the *Alternative Assessment* booklet (p. 95) to assess the students' writing. Add these criteria to customize the rubric to this assignment.	**Transitions**	Transitions are used effectively to keep the plot moving.	Transitions are used.	More transitions are needed.	Transitions are not used at all; the story suffers significantly as a result.
	Verb Tense	All verb tenses are used correctly. There are no shifts in tense.	There are a few shifts in verb tense.	There are noticeable shifts in verb tense.	There are so many shifts in verb tense that understanding is impaired.

529

When it comes to reading novels, students will generally fall into one of three categories: avid readers who enjoy the act of reading; those who read occasionally when it suits their fancy; and those who despise reading and never read anything that is not assigned to them. The first group will need little or no impetus to justify their reading. The other two groups will benefit from these strategies. In addition to concentrating on these strategies *while* they read, encourage these students to set a time *when* they will read. For example, suggest that they take an hour each day usually devoted to television and read a book just for fun instead.

Customize for
Less Proficient Readers

Tell these students that reading a novel is intrinsically better than watching television since it allows the reader to use his or her imagination. Suggest that they look for titles that are not too challenging, but will be fun instead. Moreover, reading for half an hour before they go to bed is a great way to relax the body and mind and sleep better.

Answers

1. These two paragraphs suggest that two things happened fifteen years ago that were of critical importance. Because a war is mentioned, that may be important as well.
2. The narrator's specifically wanting to see a couple of "fearful sites" suggests that he has come to confront some of the ghosts of his past or finally hold himself accountable for some past actions.
3. Because the narrator immediately starts talking about events "fifteen years before," that suggests that the structure of the novel will be a long flashback or series of flashbacks.

Reading Novels and Other Extended Works

Real-World Reading Skills Workshop

Strategies for Success

Reading a novel or other extended work requires a different approach from the one you use when reading a short story or a poem. First of all, you will probably read a novel over a period of time, rather than in one sitting. If you're reading it for an assignment, plan to read sections regularly so that you're finished by the assigned date. If you're reading for yourself, you can read at your own pace.

Use the following strategies to read novels and other extended works successfully.

Break It Down Most extended works are divided into small, manageable parts. If you are reading a nonfiction book, preview the book's organization by examining the table of contents. Flip through the pages to get an overview of the material covered. Within chapters, there may be further divisions, such as italicized or bulleted smaller sections. If you are reading a novel, preview the chapters. Do they have titles, and if so, what do the titles suggest about the chapter contents?

✔ Use the strategies you have learned to read other types of extended works, including:
▶ Multi-part magazine articles
▶ Instruction manuals and textbooks
▶ Biographies and autobiographies

Make Predictions Use chapters and sections to stop and think about what you have read. Ask yourself: "What was that chapter about?" Make predictions about what you think might happen.

Look Back When you're reading a work over a longer period of time, you need to remember more characters, more information, and the relationships between characters and events. If you need to, don't hesitate to go back and reread earlier sections or scenes. Rereading will reinforce your understanding of the work.

Apply the Strategy

Use the strategies to answer the questions that follow the excerpt from the first chapter of *A Separate Peace*.

from *A Separate Peace* by John Knowles
Chapter 1

I went back to the Devon School not long ago, and found it looking oddly newer than when I was a student there fifteen years before. It seemed more sedate than I remembered, with narrower windows and shinier woodwork, as though a coat of varnish had been put over everything for better preservation. But, of course, fifteen years before there had been a war going on. Perhaps the school wasn't as well kept up in those day; perhaps varnish, along with everything else, had gone to war. . .

There were a couple of places now which I wanted to see. Both were fearful sites, and that was why I wanted to see them. So after lunch at the Devon Inn I walked back toward the school. It was a raw, nondescript time of year, toward the end of November, the kind of wet, self-pitying November day when every speck of dirt stands out clearly. . ."

1. What details from these paragraphs do you think will be important later on in the story?
2. Why do you think the speaker has returned to his old school?
3. What can you conclude about the organization of this novel?

PART 2 *Setting and Theme*

Couple and Ship, Keith Lo Bue,
Stock Illustration Source, Inc.

Setting and Theme ♦ 531

One-Minute Planning Guide

The selections in this part are stories that are strong in the elements of setting and theme. The part opens with Ray Bradbury's "There Will Come Soft Rains," in which the setting itself is the focus of the story. Italo Calvino's "The Garden of Stubborn Cats" also creates an unforgettable setting, in which cats face off against encroaching development. Pär Lagerkvist conveys a memorable theme about the burdens of responsibility in the fable-like "The Princess and All the Kingdom"; Luisa Valenzuela comments on the ills of oppressive regimes in "The Censors."

Customize for
Varying Student Needs
When assigning the selections in this part to your students, keep in mind the following factors:

"There Will Come Soft Rains"
• Some technical terms may pose problems for English language learners.

"The Garden of Stubborn Cats"
• The plot may be difficult to follow for less proficient readers.

"The Princess and All the Kingdom"
• The point of the story is expressed so simply that some students may miss it.

"The Censors"
• The operations of the bureaucracy may be difficult for some students to understand.

 Humanities: Art

Couple and Ship by Keith LoBue.
The style of this art recalls the art deco advertisements of the 1920's and 1930's; in addition, the clothing of the man and woman and their luggage evoke that period, when people who traveled overseas more typically traveled on ocean liners than on airplanes. Elicit the effect created by the artist's use of black, which sets off the heads of the man and woman as well as the upper part of the ship. Encourage students to discuss the effect of the artist's stylization here—the lack of detail, the solid blocks of color, as well as his rather theatrical (as opposed to naturalistic) use of light; the whole work is deliberately artificial, giving an air of glamour and mystery to the scene.

Help students link the artwork to the focus of this part, Setting and Theme, by answering the following questions:

1. If this art were used to illustrate a story, what ideas about travel might the picture suggest? *It might suggest that travel is exciting; that it is a diversion for wealthy people, since the couple is well-dressed; that people who travel entrust themselves to unknown and powerful forces, like the huge black ship.*

2. Suggest an idea for a story based on this artwork. *Sample answer: The couple are a pair of international spies who pose as a wealthy, leisured couple during the 1930's; they travel a great deal (the well-stamped suitcase). This time they are rushing to board a ship that will take them to China to look for a missing diplomat.*

531

*G*uide for Reading

OBJECTIVES

1. To read, comprehend, and interpret two short stories
2. To relate stories to personal experience
3. To clarify details in a story
4. To analyze the settings of two stories
5. To build vocabulary in context and learn words from Greek myths
6. To distinguish between the commonly confused words *lie* and *lay*
7. To write an advertisement for a new technology, considering the knowledge level of the audience
8. To respond to the story through writing, speaking and listening, and projects

SKILLS INSTRUCTION

Vocabulary:
Word Origins:
Words from Myths
Grammar:
Commonly
Confused Words:
Lie and *Lay*
Reading Strategy:
Clarify
Literary Focus:
Setting
Writing: Consider
the Knowledge
Level of Your
Audience

**Speaking and
Listening:**
Inanimate
Dialogue;
Persuasive
Argument
(teacher edition)
Critical Viewing:
Connect; Compare
and Contrast;
Interpret

PORTFOLIO OPPORTUNITIES

Writing: Schedule; Speculation; Science Fiction Story
Writing Mini-Lesson: Writing an Advertisement for a New Technology
Speaking and Listening: Inanimate Dialogue; Persuasive Argument
Projects: Painting Presentation, Floor Plan

More About the Authors

In two of **Ray Bradbury's** best-known works, *The Martian Chronicles* and *Fahrenheit 451*, he uses a setting in the future for a thoughtful criticism of American society. *The Martian Chronicles* reflects Americans' fear of nuclear war. *Fahrenheit 451* is a disturbing portrait of the consequences of censorship.

To **Italo Calvino**, a sense of home is connected to language: "Everything can change but not the language that we carry inside," he says.

Ray Bradbury *(1920–)*

Many of science-fiction writer Ray Bradbury's stories are set on Mars, but one of his books "lives" on the moon! Dandelion Crater on the moon is named for Bradbury's book *Dandelion Wine*.

Bradbury is one of the world's most celebrated science-fiction writers. He was born in Waukegan, Illinois, and grew up along the western shores of Lake Michigan. He began reading the stories of Edgar Allan Poe as a child and also developed a fascination with horror movies and fantasy— especially futuristic fantasy. In many of his stories, including "There Will Come Soft Rains," Bradbury explores the consequences of future technological growth.

Italo Calvino *(1923–1985)*

Italo Calvino was born in Cuba, but as a young boy, he moved with his family to Italy. He settled in Turin after fighting in the Italian Resistance during World War II. Two of his works of fiction, *The Path to the Nest of Spiders* and *Adam, One Afternoon,* were in fact inspired by his participation in the Resistance.

Calvino is best known for having edited a monumental collection of fables. According to his theory, the "fable formula," which involves a child in the woods or a knight fighting beasts, is the scheme for all human stories. One fable element that can be found in almost all of Calvino's fiction is the tension between character and environment. You will see this conflict between characters and environment in "The Garden of Stubborn Cats."

◆ Build Vocabulary

WORD ORIGINS: WORDS FROM MYTHS

In "There Will Come Soft Rains," Ray Bradbury describes "one *titanic* instant." *Titanic* comes from the classical myths of ancient Greece. The Titans were a race of giants who ruled the world long before the gods. They were overthrown by the Olympians, led by Zeus, who assumed dominion over the world after defeating the Titans. Because the Titans were giants with great strength, the word *titanic* describes something of great size or power. The "titanic instant" in this story is a powerful moment.

warrens
titanic
paranoia
tremulous
psychopathic
supernal
itinerary
transoms
rank
scrimmage
indigence

WORD BANK

Before you read, preview this list of words from the story. Write the words in two columns: words you know and words you need to learn.

◆ Build Grammar Skills

COMMONLY CONFUSED WORDS: *LIE* AND *LAY*

Because *lie* and *lay* seem similar, and because the past tense of *lie* is *lay*, these verbs are often confused. In fact, they have two different meanings and uses. *Lay* means "to put or set (something) down," and it usually takes a direct object. Its principal parts are *lay, laying, laid,* and *laid.*

dir. obj.
...he ... *laid* his place among the packing-cases ...

Lie means "to recline." Its principal parts are *lie, lying, lay,* and *lain.* *Lie* does not take a direct object.

... dry leaves *lay* everywhere under the boughs ...

Prentice Hall Literature Program Resources

REINFORCE / RETEACH / EXTEND

Selection Support Pages
Build Vocabulary: Word Origins, p. 159
Build Grammar Skills: Lie and Lay, p. 160
Reading Strategy: Clarify, p. 161
Literary Focus: Setting, p. 162

Strategies for Diverse Student Needs, p. 39

Beyond Literature
Community Connection: Automation, p. 39

Formal Assessment Selection Test, pp. 135–137;
Assessment Resources Software

Alternative Assessment, p. 39

Writing and Language Transparencies
Writing Process Model 7, pp. 45–51

Resource Pro CD-ROM
"There Will Come Soft Rains," "The Garden of Stubborn Cats"—includes all resource materials

Listening to Literature Audiocassettes
"There Will Come Soft Rains," "The Garden of Stubborn Cats"

Looking at Literature Videodisc
"There Will Come Soft Rains"

◆ There Will Come Soft Rains ◆
The Garden of Stubborn Cats

◆ *Literature and Your Life*

CONNECT YOUR EXPERIENCE

You've exchanged hundreds of e-mails with your best friend. Suddenly, something seems missing—your best friend. You're starting to forget what he or she looks and sounds like because all you have to do to communicate is press "send." Situations like this call your attention to the fact that advances in technology have disadvantages as well as advantages.

THEMATIC FOCUS: TO THE FUTURE

These two stories highlight the need to examine the effects of progress as we move into the future.

Journal Writing Create a chart showing the pros and cons of a technological advance in this century, such as airplanes or transatlantic communication.

◆ Background for Understanding

TECHNOLOGY

Automation is the use of machines to perform tasks that require a decision. Some familiar uses of automation are thermostats that "decide" when to turn the heat on and off in a home and traffic lights that change based on the amount of traffic that passes through. Automation allows machines to perform tasks that are too boring or dangerous for people to do. The house of the future in "There Will Come Soft Rains" has an impressive level of automation. As more and more areas of business and personal life become automated, people continue to evaluate the effects of automation on society.

◆ Literary Focus

SETTING

All stories have a **setting**—the time and place of the action—but authors sometimes emphasize a particular aspect of a setting to help bring out their theme. For example, time is of the greatest importance in "There Will Come Soft Rains" because everything that happens hinges on the fact that the story is set in the future.

In "The Garden of Stubborn Cats," place is the more important feature of the setting. Readers can join Marcovaldo, as he follows a cat around the city, getting a new perspective on familiar locations. Use a chart like the one shown to record details that help you identify and understand the setting of each story.

◆ Reading Strategy

CLARIFY

To avoid misunderstandings when you read, **clarify** any parts of the story you don't understand. The best way to do this is to read ahead for more information or read back to review what you have already learned. For example, you might want to review details of the setting, clarify the relationships among the characters, or look back at the details of a key event.

As both of these stories develop, you may come to places that are not completely clear. At these points, stop, look back or ahead, and put details together to clarify the events.

	Rains	Cats
Time Details		
Place Details		
Unusual Perspective Details		

Guide for Reading ◆ 533

Interest Grabber Have students anticipate technological developments by describing a typical day in the life of someone living fifty years from now. For example, what kind of gadgets would be available for preparing breakfast and what kinds of transportation would take the person to work? Ask students to brainstorm for technological developments as you go through a day from morning to afternoon. Then tell them that each of these stories deals with the consequences of technology.

Customize for
Less Proficient Readers
These students may need help understanding what is happening in each story. Read the first pages aloud, and use the Reading Strategy prompts on pages 536 and 543 to help students clarify what is going on.

Customize for
More Advanced Students
Challenge these students to infer the message of the stories as they read. Have them compare and contrast the views of the two stories toward technological "progress."

Customize for
English Language Learners
Before these students begin reading, make sure they are familiar with words such as *robot, electric eye,* and *radioactive,* which are important to the meaning of "There Will Come Soft Rains"; and *demolition, condominium, penthouses,* and *tabby,* which are important in "The Garden of Stubborn Cats."

Customize for
Musical/Rhythmic Learners
Listening to the tones and rhythms of the house's automated voice and robots will help these students imagine the setting of "There Will Come Soft Rains." Have these students weigh the positive and negative aspects of audiovisual technology as it may some day be applied in the home environment.

Preparing for Standardized Tests

Reading and Vocabulary The Reading Strategy for this selection focuses on clarifying details in a story, an important critical reading skill tested on standardized tests such as the SAT. Students may be given a passage followed by a set of questions to answer based on what is stated or implied in the passage. Answering the Literary Focus questions on page 548 and completing the Reading Strategy page in *Selection Support,* p. 161, will help students perform better on such standardized test items.

Grammar and Language Understanding the difference between the words *lie* and *lay* and being able to use these words correctly in sentences will help students on essay sections of standardized tests. Mastering this skill, targeted in the Build Grammar Skills lesson for this selection, will also improve students' performance on tests that require them to identify errors in sentences. For more practice, use the Build Grammar Skills page on Commonly Confused Words: Lie and Lay, p. 160, in *Selection Support.*

There Will Come Soft Rains
Ray Bradbury

With no human characters, this story is an ironic reflection on the strengths and weaknesses of human nature. It is also a warning about the limits and dangers of technology. The same technical wizardry that enables people of the future to create a fully automated house is also responsible for the creation of the nuclear weapons that destroy the human race. What use is all our cleverness, Bradbury seems to ask, without the wisdom to use it wisely and the humility to accept our vulnerable position in the universe?

▶Critical Viewing◀

❶ **Predict** Students should recognize that fallout after a nuclear explosion contains a deadly, radioactive "soft rain." The story may take place at that future time.

▲ Critical Viewing Based on the title of the story and this painting, make a prediction about the subject of the story. [Predict]

534 ◆ Short Stories

Block Scheduling Strategies

Consider these suggestions for taking advantage of extended class time:

• Introduce the literary element, Setting, by having students read the Literary Focus on page 533. As students read, encourage them to be aware of the importance of setting in each story. After reading, they can answer the Literary Focus questions on page 548 and complete the Literary Focus page in *Selection Support,* p. 162.

• Introduce the Reading Strategy, Clarify. As students read, encourage them to look ahead and review what they have already read in order to clarify details of plot, character, and setting. Have them practice the strategy by answering the Reading Strategy questions on page 548, and follow up with the Reading Strategy page in *Selection Support,* p. 161.

• Have students complete the Writing Mini-Lesson (p. 549). Before they get started,

have them study print ads for computers and other technological items in several different magazines. Have them discuss how the language and information in the ads are designed to appeal to different audiences.

• As a follow-up activity, invite students to choose one of the projects on page 549—Painting Presentation or Floor Plan.

Bikini, 1987, Vernon Fisher, Krannert Art Museum

◆ **Reading Strategy**

❷ Clarify Ask students why the house might be empty. What explanation can they offer for the phrase "as if it were afraid that nobody would"? *Students might speculate that the owners are away on vacation, have moved away, or have been called out on an emergency. The phrase suggests a more ominous explanation.*

I n the living room the voice-clock sang, *Tick-tock, seven o'clock, time to get up, time to get up, seven o'clock!* as if it were afraid that nobody would. The morning house lay empty. The clock ticked on, repeating and repeating its sounds into the emptiness. *Seven-nine, breakfast time, seven-nine!*

In the kitchen the breakfast stove gave a hissing sigh and ejected from its warm interior eight pieces of perfectly browned toast, eight eggs sunnyside up, sixteen slices of bacon, two coffees, and two cool glasses of milk.

"Today is August 4, 2026," said a second voice from the kitchen ceiling, "in the city of Allendale, California." It repeated the date three times for memory's sake. "Today is Mr. Featherstone's birthday. Today is the anniversary of Tilita's marriage. Insurance is payable, as are the water, gas, and light bills."

Somewhere in the walls, relays clicked, memory tapes glided under electric eyes.

Eight-one, tick-tock, eight-one o'clock, off to school, off to work, run, run, eight one! But no doors slammed, no carpets took the soft tread of rubber heels. It was raining outside. The weather box on the front door sang quietly: "Rain, rain, go away; rubbers, raincoats for today . . ." And the rain tapped on the empty house, echoing.

Outside, the garage chimed and lifted its door to reveal the waiting car. After a long wait the door swung down again.

At eight-thirty the eggs were shriveled and the toast was like stone. An aluminum wedge scraped them into the sink, where hot water whirled them down a metal throat which digested and flushed them away to the distant sea. The dirty dishes were dropped into a hot washer and emerged twinkling dry.

Nine-fifteen, sang the clock, *time to clean*.

Out of <u>warrens</u> in the wall, tiny robot mice darted. The rooms were acrawl with the small cleaning animals, all rubber and metal. They thudded against chairs, whirling their mustached runners, kneading the rug nap, sucking gently at hidden dust. Then, like mysterious invaders, they popped into their burrows. Their pink electric eyes faded. The house was clean.

Ten o'clock. The sun came out from behind the rain. The

◆ **Build Vocabulary**

warrens (wôr´ ənz) *n.*: Mazelike passages

◆ **Literary Focus**

❸ Setting Ask students if any details from this paragraph are familiar features of houses today. Then ask what all the details taken together might suggest about the time when the story takes place. *Although some people today have computerized calendars that remind them of important events, most do not have a talking house or stoves that automatically prepare meals. The details suggest that the story is set in the future.*

There Will Come Soft Rains ◆ 535

 Humanities: Art

Bikini, 1987, by Vernon Fisher.

This photo shows the aftermath of a nuclear explosion on the Pacific island of Bikini, where the United States once tested its nuclear weapons. Vernon Fisher has worked as a photographer for newspapers in California and for magazines such as *Sports Illustrated, People,* and *Outside.* In his work he has covered breaking news stories, as well as sports events.

Use these questions for discussion:
1. What characteristic feature of a nuclear explosion can you see in the picture? *The mushroom*

cloud is characteristic of a nuclear explosion.

2. What do you know about the immediate and long-term effects of a nuclear bomb? *Immediate effects include deadly firestorms; long-term effects include radioactive fallout, deadly particles that continue to fall from the sky days after the explosion.*

3. How might the title of this story refer to these effects? *The "soft rains" of the title might refer to radioactive fallout from a nuclear bomb.*

❶ Clarify The details in this paragraph, taken together with those in the previous paragraph, suggest that the city has been destroyed by an atomic bomb or other nuclear weapon. The people who lived in the house were outside in their yard, caught unawares, when the bomb went off. Clues include "a city of rubble and ashes," "radioactive glow," the charring of the walls, and the radioactive silhouettes of the family members burned onto the walls of the house.

▶ **Critical Viewing** ◀

❷ Compare and Contrast Like the house in the story, the one in the picture looks empty and desolate. It stands alone in an eerie red glow, similar to how students might imagine the last surviving house of a nuclear war to stand. Students may say the house is unlike the one they envision in the story because it looks old-fashioned, rather than futuristic. It does not look like a house that would be equipped with automated devices. The picture also does not show the charring and the radioactive silhouettes mentioned in the story.

house stood alone in a city of rubble and ashes. This was the one house left standing. At night the ruined city gave off a radioactive glow which could be seen for miles.

Ten-fifteen. The garden sprinklers whirled up in golden founts, filling the soft morning air with scatterings of brightness. The water pelted window-panes, running down the charred west side where the house had been burned evenly free of its white paint. The entire west face of the house was black, save for five places. Here the silhouette in paint of a man mowing a lawn. Here, as in a photograph, a woman bent to pick flowers. Still farther over, their images burned on wood in one <u>titanic</u> instant, a small boy, hands flung into the air; higher up, the image of a thrown ball, and opposite him a girl, hands raised to catch a ball which never came down.

◆ **Reading Strategy** ❶ Use the details in this paragraph to clarify the situation of the story.

The five spots of paint—the man, the woman, the children, the ball—remained. The rest was a thin charcoaled layer.

The gentle-sprinkler rain filled the garden with falling light.

Until this day, how well the house had kept its peace. How carefully it had inquired, "Who goes there? What's the password?" and, getting no answer from lonely foxes and whining cats, it had shut up its windows and drawn shades in an old-maidenly preoccupation with self-protection which bordered on a mechanical <u>paranoia</u>.

It quivered at each sound, the house did. If a sparrow brushed a window, the shade snapped up. The bird, startled, flew off! No, not even a

◆ **Build Vocabulary**

titanic (tī tan´ ik) *adj.*: Having great power

paranoia (par´ ə noi´ ə) *n.*: Mental disorder characterized by delusions of persecution

tremulous (trem´ yōō ləs) *adj.*: Trembling; quivering

The Body of a House, #1 of 8, ©1993, Robert Beckman

▲ Critical Viewing How does the house in this picture compare with the house in the story? [Compare and Contrast]

bird must touch the house!

The house was an altar with ten thousand attendants, big, small, servicing, attending, in choirs. But the gods had gone away, and the ritual of the religion continued senselessly, uselessly.

Twelve noon.

A dog whined, shivering, on the front porch.

The front door recognized the dog voice and opened. The dog, once huge and fleshy, but now gone to bone and covered with sores, moved in and through the house, tracking mud. Behind it whirred angry mice, angry at having to pick up mud, angry at inconvenience.

For not a leaf fragment blew under the door but what the wall panels flipped open and the

Cross-Curricular Connection: Social Studies

The world's first nuclear weapon was an atomic bomb developed by the United States. It was first tested by scientists in New Mexico in July of 1945, and a few weeks later it was used to bomb the Japanese cities of Hiroshima and Nagasaki, near the end of World War II. After the war, the United States and several other countries built thousands of nuclear weapons, many times more than enough to destroy each other. As these weapons proliferated, so did people's fears of a possible nuclear war. As tensions between the United States and the Soviet Union escalated during the Cold War, which lasted through the 1980's, American newspapers and magazines warned citizens of the dire consequences that might follow a nuclear attack. In this story Bradbury projects the fears of his own time onto an indefinite future setting.

Have students discuss whether fears of nuclear war still play an important part in American life today. Ask what has happened since this story was written to increase or decrease such fears.

copper scrap rats flashed swiftly out. The offending dust, hair, or paper, seized in miniature steel jaws, was raced back to the burrows. There, down tubes which fed into the cellar, it was dropped into the sighing vent of an incinerator which sat like evil Baal[1] in a dark corner.

The dog ran upstairs, hysterically yelping to each door, at last realizing, as the house realized, that only silence was here.

It sniffed the air and scratched the kitchen door. Behind the door, the stove was making pancakes which filled the house with a rich baked odor and the scent of maple syrup.

❸ The dog frothed at the mouth, lying at the door, sniffing, its eyes turned to fire. It ran wildly in circles, biting at its tail, spun in a frenzy, and died. It lay in the parlor for an hour.

Two o'clock, sang a voice.

Delicately sensing decay at last, the regiments of mice hummed out as softly as blown gray leaves in an electrical wind.

Two-fifteen.

The dog was gone.

In the cellar, the incinerator glowed suddenly and a whirl of sparks leaped up the chimney.

Two thirty-five.

❹ Bridge tables sprouted from patio walls. Playing cards fluttered onto pads in a shower of pips. Glasses manifested on an oaken bench with egg-salad sandwiches. Music played.

But the tables were silent and the cards untouched.

At four o'clock the tables folded like great butterflies back through the paneled walls.

Four-thirty.

The nursery walls glowed.

Animals took shape: yellow giraffes, blue lions, pink antelopes, lilac panthers cavorting[2] in crystal substance. The walls were glass. They looked out upon color and fantasy. Hidden films clocked through well-oiled sprockets, and the walls lived. The nursery floor was woven to resemble a crisp, cereal meadow. Over this ran aluminum roaches and iron crickets, and in the hot still air butterflies of delicate red tissue

---

1. **Baal** (bā´ əl): An ancient Phoenician and Canaanite deity.
2. **cavorting** (kə vôrt´ ing) v.: Leaping or prancing about.

---

wavered among the sharp aroma of animal spoors![3] There was the sound like a great matted yellow hive of bees within a dark bellows, the lazy bumble of a purring lion. And there was the patter of okapi[4] feet and the murmur of a fresh jungle rain, like other hoofs, falling upon the summer-starched grass. Now the walls dissolved into distances of parched weed, mile on mile, and warm endless sky. The animals drew away into thorn brakes and water holes.

It was the children's hour.

Five o'clock. The bath filled with clear hot water.

Six, seven, eight o'clock. The dinner dishes manipulated like magic tricks, and in the study a *click.* In the hearth a fire now blazed up warmly.

◆ **Literary Focus**
What do the details in this section tell you about the time period of the setting?

❺

Nine o'clock. The beds warmed their hidden circuits, for nights were cool here.

Nine-five. A voice spoke from the study ceiling: "Mrs. McClellan, which poem would you like this evening?"

The house was silent.

The voice said at last, "Since you express no preference, I shall select a poem at random." Quiet music rose to back the voice. "Sara Teasdale. As I recall, your favorite. . . ."

*There will come soft rains and the smell of
  the ground,
And swallows circling with their shimmering
  sound;*

*And frogs in the pools singing at night,
And wild plum trees in* tremulous *white;*

*Robins will wear their feathery fire,
Whistling their whims on a low fence-wire;*

*And not one will know of the war, not one
Will care at last when it is done.*

❻

---

3. **spoors** (spōrz) n.: Droppings of wild animals.
4. **okapi** (ō kä´ pē) n.: African animal related to the giraffe but with a much shorter neck.

There Will Come Soft Rains ◆ 537

◆ **Build Grammar Skills**

❸ Commonly Confused Words: Lie and Lay Ask students why the words *lying* and *lay* are correct in these two sentences. *Both words are principal parts of the verb* lie, *meaning "recline," the meaning needed here. Lay, in the second sentence, is used as the past tense of* lie, *rather than as the present tense of the verb* lay.

◆ *Literature and Your Life*

❹ Ask students if they have any machines in their own homes that continue turning on and off even when no one is home. Then ask why the house might prepare bridge tables and a lunch, even though no people are there. *Students are probably familiar with programmable devices such as VCRs, automated lighting systems, clock radios, and alarms. The house in the story has been programmed to provide certain functions at different times of day, to suit the usual routines of the people who once lived there.*

◆ **Literary Focus**

❺ Setting The details suggest a future world in which the walls of a child's room are equipped with amazing multimedia equipment that can create the illusion of being in a jungle.

◆ **Critical Thinking**

❻ Apply Ask students how the words of this poem can be applied to the story. *The title of the story is taken from the first line of the poem: "There will come soft rains." The poem describes the natural world continuing unawares, even after a war, much as the mechanical house continues functioning after a nuclear war.*

Humanities: Art

The Body of a House, #1 of 8, and The Body of a House, #6 of 8, 1993, by Robert Beckmann.

The painting on page 536 is the first of a series of eight large oil paintings depicting the successive stages of destruction of a house during a nuclear explosion. (Painting #6 of 8 is on page 538.) The paintings are based on actual film footage shot during the test of a nuclear weapon in Nevada in 1953. The original paintings are eight feet long and

nearly six feet high. The monumental size and stark realism of these paintings dramatize the destructiveness of a nuclear explosion.

Robert Beckmann has worked with students as an artist in the schools in Nevada and has also completed murals for many buildings in Nevada and Colorado.

Use these questions for discussion:

1. Why does the house look so completely alone and uninhabited? *Students may say that there is no vegetation, no human or animal figures, no sign of a car, a road or driveway, no curtains in the windows.*

2. What effect would the other paintings have on the first of the series? (Students should look at painting #6 on the next page before they answer.) *Students might say that knowing the fate of the house adds drama to the first painting in the series.*

3. What destructive element does the second painting call to mind? *It suggests destruction by fire or a bomb.*

Looking at Literature Videodisc To provide background for understanding the theme of the story, play Chapter 6 of the videodisc. This segment provides a history of the invention of nuclear power and how it has been used. Have students discuss the positive and negative contributions of nuclear power. Ask students: Why is nuclear energy a popular topic for stories, poems, and film?

►Critical Viewing◄

❶ Connect Suggested response: The painting is dominated by wild splotches of red and black, suggesting the destructive effects of a fire or the firestorms associated with a nuclear explosion such as the one that occurred before this story begins.

◆ **Critical Thinking**

❷ Make a Judgment Ask students which lines of the poem could serve as the story's theme, or message. *"Not one would mind, neither bird nor tree/If mankind perished utterly."*

Comprehension Check ☑

❸ How does the fire start in the house? *The wind knocks a tree bough through the kitchen window. Flammable cleaning liquid spills over the stove and ignites. The fire is fed by the wind coming through the windows broken by the heat.*

Customize for *Logical/Mathematical Learners*

Ask these students to note the illogical details that contribute to the house's destruction. *Students should note that tree branches should be kept pruned away from windows and that cleaning solvents should never be stored near a stove.*

The Body of a House, #6 of 8, ©1993, Robert Beckman

❶ ▲ Critical Viewing Use the details in this picture to envision the events that occur before this story begins. [Connect]

❷
Not one would mind, neither bird nor tree,
If mankind perished utterly;

And Spring herself, when she woke at dawn
Would scarcely know that we were gone."

The fire burned on the stone hearth. The empty chairs faced each other between the silent walls, and the music played.

At ten o'clock the house began to die.
The wind blew. A falling tree bough crashed through the kitchen window. Cleaning solvent, bottled, shattered over the stove. The room was ablaze in an instant!

❸ "Fire!" screamed a voice. The house lights flashed, water pumps shot water from the ceilings. But the solvent spread on the linoleum, licking, eating, under the kitchen door, while the voices took it up in chorus: "Fire, fire, fire!"

The house tried to save itself. Doors sprang tightly shut, but the windows were broken by the heat and the wind blew and sucked upon the fire.

The house gave ground as the fire in ten billion angry sparks moved with flaming ease from room to room and then up the stairs. While scurrying water rats squeaked from the walls, pistoled their water, and ran for more. And the wall sprays let down showers of mechanical rain.

But too late. Somewhere, sighing, a pump shrugged to a stop. The quenching rain ceased. The reserve water supply which had filled baths and washed dishes for many quiet days was gone.

The fire crackled up the stairs. It fed upon Picassos and Matisses[5] in the upper halls, like delicacies, baking off the oily flesh, tenderly crisping the canvases into black shavings.

Now the fire lay in beds, stood in windows, changed the colors of drapes!
And then, reinforcements.
From attic trapdoors, blind robot faces peered down with faucet mouths gushing green chemical.

The fire backed off, as even an elephant must at the sight of a dead snake. Now there were twenty snakes whipping over the floor, killing the fire with a clear cold venom of green froth.

But the fire was clever. It had sent flame outside the house, up through the attic to the pumps there. An explosion! The attic brain which directed the pumps was shattered into bronze shrapnel on the beams.

The fire rushed back into every closet and felt of the clothes hung there.

The house shuddered, oak bone on bone, its bared skeleton cringing from the heat, its wire, its nerves revealed as if a surgeon had torn the skin off to let the red veins and capillaries quiver in the scalded air. Help, help! Fire! Run, run! Heat snapped mirrors like the first brittle winter

5. **Picassos** (pi kä′ sōz) **and Matisses** (mä tēs′ ez): Works by the painters Pablo Picasso and Henri Matisse.

538 ◆ Short Stories

 Speaking and Listening Mini-Lesson

Inanimate Dialogue
This mini-lesson supports the Speaking and Listening activity in the Idea Bank on page 549.

Introduce the Concept Tell students that a writer must try to imagine the attitudes and personalities of characters in order to write good dialogue.

Develop Background Before students begin their role-plays, have them work in pairs to list all the appliances in the story and choose two appliances that might have an interesting conversation. Then have each partner quickwrite a brief description of the interests and personality each appliance might have.

Apply the Information Have each pair of students choose a topic for their appliances to discuss and role-play what each appliance might have to say on this topic, as well as the feelings they might express for each other. Have different pairs of students perform their role-plays for the class.

Assess the Outcome Have the class compare different interpretations of the same appliances and evaluate which role-play is most convincing. Students may use the Peer Assessment: Dramatic Performance page in **Alternative Assessment,** p. 120, to evaluate the performances.

ice. And the voices wailed Fire, fire, run, run, like a tragic nursery rhyme, a dozen voices, high, low, like children dying in a forest, alone, alone. And the voices fading as the wires popped their sheathings like hot chestnuts. One, two, three, four, five voices died.

In the nursery the jungle burned. Blue lions roared, purple giraffes bounded off. The panthers ran in circles, changing color, and ten million animals, running before the fire, vanished off toward a distant steaming river. . . .

Ten more voices died. In the last instant under the fire avalanche, other choruses, oblivious, could be heard announcing the time, playing music, cutting the lawn by remote-control mower, or setting an umbrella frantically out and in the slamming and opening front door, a thousand things happening, like a clock shop when each clock strikes the hour insanely before or after the other, a scene of maniac confusion, yet unity; singing, screaming, a few last cleaning mice darting bravely out to carry the horrid ashes away! And one voice, with sublime disregard for the situation, read poetry aloud in the fiery study, until all the film spools burned, until all the wires withered and the circuits cracked.

The fire burst the house and let it slam flat down, puffing out skirts of spark and smoke.

In the kitchen, an instant before the rain of fire and timber, the stove could be seen making breakfasts at a <u>psychopathic</u> rate, ten dozen eggs, six loaves of toast, twenty dozen bacon strips, which, eaten by fire, started the stove working again, hysterically hissing!

The crash. The attic smashing into kitchen and parlor. The parlor into cellar, cellar into subcellar. Deep freeze, armchair, film tapes, circuits, beds, and all like skeletons thrown in a cluttered mound deep under.

Smoke and silence. A great quantity of smoke.

Dawn showed faintly in the east. Among the ruins, one wall stood alone. Within the wall, a last voice said, over and over again and again, even as the sun rose to shine upon the heaped rubble and steam:

"Today is August 5, 2026, today is August 5, 2026, today is . . ."

④

◆ Build Vocabulary

psychopathic (sī′ kō path′ ik) *adj.*: With a dangerous mental disorder

Guide for Responding

◆ *Literature and Your Life*

Reader's Response Does the picture presented in this story fit with your idea of a future world? Why, or why not?

Thematic Focus Based on what you've read in this story, how do you think Bradbury views our legacy to the future?

☑ **Check Your Comprehension**

1. List five functions the house performs.
2. What happened to the occupants of the house, and how do you know?
3. Describe the final hours of the house.

◆ Critical Thinking

INTERPRET
1. Why do you think Bradbury chose to have the house broadcast the poem? **[Speculate]**
2. Compare the house—both in its normal operations and in its final hours—to a human. **[Compare]**
3. Explain this story's message. **[Infer]**

APPLY
4. What qualities make this story different from others you know that deal with the future? **[Distinguish]**

EVALUATE
5. How possible do you think the future described in this story is? **[Make a Judgment]**

There Will Come Soft Rains ◆ 539

One-Minute Insight In this story, an Italian worker named Marcovaldo begins to become aware of cats and their pathways through a city. He discovers an old villa in a seedy garden where they congregate and resist the efforts of construction workers to build a new structure. For Calvino, the cats symbolize nature's mysterious, persistent presence even in a busy city. They also symbolize nature's resistance to human aims and designs.

◆ **Reading Strategy**

❶ Clarify Ask students what the author means by this opening sentence. Have them look ahead to find information about the setting that clarifies the meaning of the sentence. *From "... the streets are uninterruptedly overrun" through "... on the roof-tiles" describes the city of men; from "But in this vertical city ..." to "... the ancient cat population still scurries" describes the city of cats. The two exist within the same boundaries, but are completely different; neither city is inhabitable by the population of the other.*

◆ **Literary Focus**

❷ Setting Ask students: Which details in this passage help you visualize the setting of the "city of men"? *Details include heavy traffic everywhere, apartment buildings and skyscrapers over every inch of land; there is no grass or gardens because the earth is covered with concrete.*

The Garden of Stubborn Cats

Italo Calvino Translated by William Weaver

❶ The city of cats and the city of men exist one inside the other, but they are not the same city. Few cats recall the time when there was no distinction: the streets and squares of men were also streets and squares of cats, and the lawns, courtyards, balconies, and fountains: you lived in a broad and various space. But for several generations now domestic felines have been prisoners of an uninhabitable city: the streets are uninterruptedly **❷** overrun by the mortal traffic of cat-crushing automobiles; in every square foot of terrain where once a garden extended or a vacant lot or the ruins of an old demolition, now condominiums loom up, welfare housing, brand-new skyscrapers; every entrance is crammed with parked cars; the courtyards, one by one, have been roofed by reinforced concrete and transformed into garages or movie houses or storerooms or workshops. And where a rolling plateau of low roofs once extended, copings,[1] terraces, water tanks, balconies, skylights, corrugated-iron sheds, now one general superstructure rises wherever structures can rise; the intermediate differences in height, between the low ground of the street and the supernal heaven of the penthouses, disappear; the cat of a recent litter seeks in vain the itinerary of its **❷**

---

1. **copings** (kō′ piŋz) *n.*: Top layers of masonry walls.

540 ◆ *Short Stories*

 Humanities: Art

Cats in Art.

Because of their mysterious nature, their sensitivity to light and sound, and their skill as night-time hunters, cats have been credited with supernatural powers in many cultures and have even been worshipped as gods in some. The ancient Egyptians, for example, produced many statues of cats in honor of their cat-goddess, Bastet. Later, cats were associated with witches in European cultures. Today, images of cats show our mixed feelings about these creatures. They are sometimes depicted as cute, cuddly balls of fluff and sometimes as mysterious, predatory hunters.

Use these questions for discussion:
1. How well do the pictures of cats shown in this selection reflect your own feelings about these animals? Explain. *Students who love cats' cozy furriness may prefer the images on pages 540, 541, and 544; those who stress their mysterious, predatory natures may point to the art on page 542.*

2. In your opinion, why are some people cat-lovers while others are dog-lovers? *Cats are independent, solitary hunters, while dogs may seem more friendly to and dependent on humans. People vary in their preferences for these qualities.*

fathers, the point from which to make the soft leap from balustrade to cornice to drainpipe, or for the quick climb on the roof-tiles.

But in this vertical city, in this compressed city where all voids tend to fill up and every block of cement tends to mingle with other blocks of cement, a kind of counter-city opens, a negative city, that consists of empty slices between wall and wall, of the minimal distances ordained by the building regulations between two constructions, between the rear of one construction and the rear of the next; it is a city of cavities, wells, air conduits, driveways, inner yards, accesses to basements, like a network of dry canals on a planet of stucco and tar, and it is through this network, grazing the walls, that the ancient cat population still scurries.

❸ ◆ Literary Focus
What details in this paragraph help you envision the setting?

On occasion, to pass the time, Marcovaldo would follow a cat. It was during the work-break, between noon and three, when all the personnel except Marcovaldo went home to eat, and he—who brought his lunch in his bag—laid his place among the packing-cases in the warehouse, chewed his snack, smoked a half-cigar, and wandered around, alone and idle, waiting for work to resume. In those hours, a cat that peeped in at a window was always welcome company, and a guide for new explorations. He had made friends with a tabby, well fed, a blue ribbon around its neck, surely living with some well-to-do family. This tabby shared with Marcovaldo the habit of an afternoon stroll right after lunch; and naturally a friendship sprang up.

Following his tabby friend, Marcovaldo had started looking at places as if through the round eyes of a cat and even if these places were the usual environs of his firm he saw them in a different light, as settings for cattish stories, with connections practicable only by light, velvety paws. Though from the outside the neighborhood seemed poor in cats, every day on his rounds Marcovaldo made the acquaintance of some new face, and a miau, a hiss, a stiffening of fur on an arched back was enough for him to sense ties and intrigues and rivalries among them. At those moments he thought he had already penetrated the secrecy of the felines' society: and then he felt himself scrutinized by pupils that became slits, under the surveillance of the antennae of taut whiskers, and all the cats around him sat impassive as sphinxes, the pink triangles of their noses convergent on the black triangles of their lips, and the only things that moved were the tips of the ears, with a vibrant jerk like radar. They reached the end of a narrow passage, between squalid blank walls; and, looking around, Marcovaldo saw that the cats that had led him this far had vanished, all of them together, no telling in which direction, even his tabby friend, and they had left him alone. Their realm had territories, ceremonies, customs that it was not yet granted to him to discover.

On the other hand, from the cat city there opened unsuspected peepholes onto the city of men: and one day the same tabby led him to discover the great Biarritz Restaurant.

Anyone wishing to see the Biarritz Restaurant had only to assume the posture of a cat, that is, proceed on all fours. Cat and man, in this fashion, walked around a kind of dome, at whose foot some low, rectangular little windows opened. Following the tabby's example,

◆ **Build Vocabulary**
supernal (sə pʉrn´ əl) *adj.*: Celestial or divine
itinerary (ī tin´ ər er´ ē) *n.*: Route

The Garden of Stubborn Cats ◆ 541

◆ **Literary Focus**

❸ **Setting** Students may cite details such as ". . . every block of cement tends to mingle with other blocks of cement," "empty slices between wall and wall," "cavities, wells, air conduits, driveways, inner yards, accesses to basements," and the simile "like a network of dry canals on a planet of stucco and tar."

Comprehension Check ☑

❹ Make sure students understand what is going on here and in the rest of the story: Marcovaldo, a warehouse worker, has three hours off for lunch—point out to students that in Italy and some other countries it is customary to take such a long break at midday and to return home—and he has decided to use the time to follow a cat around the city. If students need help, suggest they go back to the left-hand column on this page to find details that clarify what Marcovaldo is doing.

◆ **Build Vocabulary**

❺ **Word Origins: Words From Myths** Tell students that *sphinx* is a word derived from Greek mythology. In Greek myths the sphinx was a winged monster with a lion's body and the head of a woman. The sphinx killed anyone who could not answer its mysterious riddles. The word also came to be applied to ancient Egyptian statues with the body of a lion and the head of a man. Today the word *sphinx* is used to describe any unknowable, mysterious person or thing.

Marcovaldo looked down. They were <u>transoms</u> through which the luxurious hall received air and light. To the sound of gypsy violins, partridges and quails swirled by on silver dishes balanced by the white-gloved fingers of waiters in tailcoats. Or, more precisely, above the partridges and quails the dishes whirled, and above the dishes the white gloves, and poised on the waiters' patent-leather shoes, the gleaming parquet floor,[2] from which hung dwarf potted palms and tablecloths and crystal and buckets like bells with the champagne bottle for their clapper: everything was turned upside-down because Marcovaldo, for fear of being seen, wouldn't stick his head inside the window and confined himself to looking at the reversed reflection of the room in the tilted pane.

But it was not so much the windows of the dining-room as those of the kitchens that interested the cat: looking through the former you saw, distant and somehow transfigured, what in the kitchens presented itself—quite concrete and within paw's reach—as a plucked bird or a

2. **parquet** (pär kā´) **floor:** Floor with inlaid woodwork in geometric forms.

Schrödinger's Cat, Elizabeth Knight, New York Academy of Sciences

 ▲ Critical Viewing What qualities of cats are captured in this picture? [Interpret]

542 ◆ Short Stories

fresh fish. And it was toward the kitchens, in fact, that the tabby wanted to lead Marcovaldo, either through a gesture of altruistic friendship or else because it counted on the man's help for one of its raids. Marcovaldo, however, was reluctant to leave his belvedere[3] over the main room: first as he was fascinated by the luxury of the place, and then because something down there had riveted his attention. To such an extent that, overcoming his fear of being seen, he kept peeking in, with his head in the transom.

In the midst of the room, directly under that pane, there was a little glass fish tank, a kind of aquarium, where some fat trout were swimming. A special customer approached, a man with a shiny bald pate, black suit, black beard. An old waiter in tailcoat followed him, carrying a little net as if he were going to catch butterflies. The gentleman in black looked at the trout with a grave, intent air; then he raised one hand and with a slow, solemn gesture singled out a fish. The waiter dipped the net into the tank, pursued the appointed trout, captured it, headed for the kitchens, holding out in front of him, like a lance, the net in which the fish wriggled. The gentleman in black, solemn as a magistrate who has handed down a capital sentence, went to take his seat and wait for the return of the trout, sauteed "à la meunière."[4]

If I found a way to drop a line from up here and make one of those trout bite, Marcovaldo thought, I couldn't be accused of theft; at worst, of fishing in an unauthorized place. And ignoring the miaus

3. **belvedere** (bel´ və dir´) *n.:* Open, roofed gallery in an upper story, built for giving a view of the scenery.
4. **sauteed "à la meunière"** (sô tād´ à lä mə nyer´): Fish prepared by being rolled in flour, fried in butter, and sprinkled with lemon juice and chopped parsley.

◈ **Beyond the Classroom**

Career Connection

Urban Planning The situation in this story reflects the consequences of allowing developers to build wherever they wish, with no regard for the environmental impact of their construction. In many cities today, urban planners are responsible for balancing a community's need for progress and economic development with the need for a healthy environment that respects the natural world. Have students research this topic and find examples of cities that have successfully balanced these two opposing forces.

Community Connection

Visiting Animal Shelters In many cities and towns, the Society for the Prevention of Cruelty to Animals maintains animal shelters for abandoned pets, educates the public about pet ownership, and ensures the enforcement of laws protecting animals from cruel treatment. Have students visit a local animal shelter and report to the class on what is done in your community to ensure proper treatment of cats and other pets.

that called him toward the kitchens, he went to collect his fishing tackle.

Nobody in the crowded dining room of the Biarritz saw the long, fine line, armed with hook and bait, as it slowly dropped into the tank. The fish saw the bait, and flung themselves on it. In the fray one trout managed to bite the worm: and immediately it began to rise, rise, emerge from the water, a silvery flash, it darted up high, over the laid tables and the trolleys of hors d'oeuvres,[5] over the blue flames of the crêpes Suzette,[6] until it vanished into the heavens of the transom.

Marcovaldo had yanked the rod with the brisk snap of the expert fisherman, so the fish landed behind his back. The trout had barely touched the ground when the cat sprang. What little life the trout still had was lost between the tabby's teeth. Marcovaldo, who had abandoned his line at that moment to run and grab the fish, saw it snatched from under his nose, hook and all. He was quick to put one foot on the rod, but the snatch had been so strong that the rod was all the man had left, while the tabby ran off with the fish, pulling the line after it. Treacherous kitty! It had vanished.

But this time it wouldn't escape him: there was that long line trailing after him and showing the way he had taken. Though he had lost sight of the cat, Marcovaldo followed the end of the line: there it was, running along a wall; it climbed a parapet, wound through a doorway, was swallowed up by a basement . . . Marcovaldo, venturing into more and more cattish places, climbed roofs, straddled railings, always managed to catch a glimpse—perhaps only a second before it disappeared—of that moving trace that indicated a thief's path.

Now the line played out down a sidewalk, in the midst of the traffic, and Marcovaldo, running after it, almost managed to grab it. He

◆ Reading Strategy
❸ What information in this paragraph helps you clarify the title of this story?

flung himself down on his belly: there, he grabbed it! He managed to seize one end of the line before it slipped between the bars of a gate.

Beyond a half-rusted gate and two bits of wall buried under climbing plants, there was a little rank garden, with a small, abandoned-looking building at the far end of it. A carpet of dry leaves covered the path, and dry leaves lay everywhere under the boughs of the two plane-trees, forming actually some little mounds in the yard. A layer of leaves was yellowing in the green water of a pool. Enormous buildings rose all around, skyscrapers with thousands of windows, like so many eyes trained disapprovingly on that little square patch with two trees, a few tiles, and all those yellow leaves, surviving right in the middle of an area of great traffic.

And in this garden, perched on the capitals and balustrades,[7] lying on the dry leaves of the flowerbeds, climbing on the trunks of the trees or on the drainpipes, motionless on their four paws, their tails making a question-mark, seated to wash their faces, there were tiger cats, black cats, white cats, calico cats, tabbies, angoras, Persians, house cats and stray cats, perfumed cats and mangy cats. Marcovaldo realized he had finally reached the heart of the cats' realm, their secret island. And, in his emotion, he almost forgot his fish.

It had remained, that fish, hanging by the line from the branch of a tree, out of reach of the cats' leaps; it must have dropped from its kidnapper's mouth at some clumsy movement, perhaps as it was defended from the others, or perhaps displayed as an extraordinary prize. The line had got tangled, and Marcovaldo, tug as he would, couldn't manage to yank it loose. A furious battle had meanwhile been joined among the cats, to reach that unreachable fish, or rather, to win the right to try and reach it. Each wanted to prevent the others from

---

7. **capitals and balustrades** (bal´ əs trāds): Top parts of columns and railings, respectively.

◆ **Build Vocabulary**

transoms (tran´ səmz) n.: Small windows

rank (raŋk) adj.: Growing vigorously and coarsely

---

5. **hors d'oeuvres** (ôr dʉrvz´) n.: Appetizers served at the beginning of a meal.
6. **crêpes Suzette** (krăp´ soo zet´): Thin pancakes rolled or folded in a hot orange-flavored sauce and usually served in flaming brandy.

◆ **Reading Strategy**

❸ **Clarify** The title mentions "stubborn cats"; the cat Marcovaldo is pursuing is stubborn in its refusal to yield the stolen trout.

◆ **Literary Focus**

❹ **Setting** Ask students why the windows of the skyscrapers might seem to look "disapprovingly" on the little rank garden. *The garden is one of the few areas of the city where a little bit of nature still remains, unconquered by urban development.*

◆ **Build Grammar Skills**

❺ **Commonly Confused Words: *Lie* and *Lay*** Ask students why the word *lying* is correct here. *The meaning of lie is "to recline," the meaning needed here. The word laying, on the other hand, means "putting or setting something down" and usually requires a direct object.*

◆ **Build Vocabulary**

❻ **Word Origins: Words From Mythology** Tell students that the word *furious* is related to the word *fury*. In Greek mythology the Furies were avenging goddesses who inflicted plagues and other punishments on people. *Furious* means "angry," "intense," or "raging."

❶ **Clarify** Ask students if they can guess to whom the two yellow, skinny hands belong. Encourage them to read the rest of this page to find out. *They belong to the Marchesa.*

Comprehension Check ☑

❷ Why do the developers want the Marchesa's land? Why does she refuse to sell it? *The developers want to build modern skyscrapers on the land; it's very valuable because it's the last undeveloped space in the downtown area. The Marchesa wants to hold onto the land because she's old and doesn't want to give up her home.*

🎧 **Listening to Literature Audiocassettes** This is a good spot to play the audiocassette recording of the story. Students can listen to the neighbors' arguments about the fate of the Marchesa's land and decide for themselves which side of the argument sounds most convincing.

---

leaping: they hurled themselves on one another, they tangled in midair, they rolled around clutching each other, and finally a general war broke out in a whirl of dry, crackling leaves.

After many futile yanks, Marcovaldo now felt the line was free, but he took care not to pull it: the trout would have fallen right in the midst of that infuriated scrimmage of felines.

It was at this moment that, from the top of the walls of the gardens, a strange rain began to fall: fish-bones, heads, tails, even bits of lung and lights. Immediately the cats' attention was distracted from the suspended trout and they flung themselves on the new delicacies. To Marcovaldo, this seemed the right moment to ❶ pull the line and regain his fish. But, before he had time to act, from a blind of the little villa, two yellow, skinny hands darted out: one was brandishing scissors; the other, a frying pan. The hand with the scissors was raised above the trout, the hand with the frying pan was thrust under it. The scissors cut the line, the trout fell into the pan; hands, scissors and pan withdrew, the blind closed: all in the space of a second. Marcovaldo was totally bewildered.

"Are you also a cat lover?" A voice at his back made him turn round. He was surrounded by little old women, some of them ancient, wearing old-fashioned hats on their heads; others, younger, but with the look of spinsters; and all were carrying in their hands or their bags packages of leftover meat or fish, and some even had little pans of milk. "Will you help me throw this package over the fence, for those poor creatures?"

All the ladies, cat lovers, gathered at this hour around the garden of dry leaves to take the food to their protégés.[8]

"Can you tell me why they are all here, these cats?" Marcovaldo inquired.

"Where else could they go? This garden is all they have left! Cats come here from other neighborhoods, too, from miles and miles around . . ."

8. **protégés** (prōt´ ə zhāz´) *n.*: Those guided and helped by another.

544 ◆ *Short Stories*

"And birds, as well," another lady added. "They're forced to live by the hundreds and hundreds on these few trees . . ."

"And the frogs, they're all in that pool, and at night they never stop croaking . . . You can hear them even on the eighth floor of the buildings around here."

"Who does this villa belong to anyway?" Marcovaldo asked. Now, outside the gate, there weren't just the cat-loving ladies but also other people: the man from the gas pump opposite, the apprentices from a mechanic's shop, the postman, the grocer, some passers-by. And none of them, men and women, had to be asked twice: all wanted to have their say, as always when a mysterious and controversial subject comes up.

"It belongs to a Marchesa.[9] She lives there, but you never see her . . ."

"She's been offered millions and millions, by developers, for this little patch of land, but she won't sell . . ."

"What would she do with millions, an old woman all alone in the world? She wants to hold on to her house, even if it's falling to pieces, rather than be forced to move . . ." ❷

"It's the only undeveloped bit of land in the downtown area . . . Its value goes up every year . . . They've made her offers—"

"Offers! That's not all. Threats, intimidation, persecution . . . You don't know the half of it! Those contractors!"

"But she holds out. She's held out for years . . ."

"She's a saint. Without her, where would those poor animals go?"

"A lot she cares about the animals, the old miser! Have you ever seen her give them anything to eat?"

"How can she feed the cats when she doesn't have food for herself? She's the last descendant of a ruined family!"

"She hates cats! I've seen her chasing them and hitting them with an umbrella!"

"Because they were tearing up her flowerbeds!"

9. **Marchesa** (mär kā´ zä): Title of an Italian noble-woman.

🔪 **Speaking and Listening Mini-Lesson**

Persuasive Argument

This mini-lesson supports the Speaking and Listening activity in the Idea Bank on page 549.

Introduce the Concept Tell students that the purpose of a persuasive argument is to influence the thoughts and actions of those who read or hear the argument. A persuasive argument should be well-reasoned and planned to appeal to a particular audience.

Develop Background Lead students to consider the following points:

- A persuasive argument uses reasons that appeal to the needs and concerns of the listener.
- Each reason is supported with evidence that the listener can understand.
- A persuasive argument should use words that are forceful but not insulting to the listener.

Apply the Information Have students make a list of reasons and facts they might use to appeal to the Marchesa. Then have them draft their arguments, using words that will present each reason as forcefully and respectfully as possible.

Assess the Outcome Invite students to evaluate each others' arguments on the basis of how well they have supported each point. Use the Peer Assessment: Speaker/Speech page in *Alternative Assessment,* p. 118.

CONNECTIONS TO TODAY'S WORLD

It might surprise you to learn that Jim Davis, creator of Garfield—one of the world's most famous and beloved cats—has no cats. His wife is allergic to the furry felines!

When Davis created Garfield in 1978, he never imagined the phenomenal success that would follow. Garfield is the most widely syndicated Sunday comic in the United States, and worldwide it has more than 220 million daily readers. In addition to the daily and Sunday comics, Davis has written dozens of Garfield books, a CBS television series, and thirteen prime-time specials.

1. What qualities does Garfield have in common with the cats in "Garden of Stubborn Cats"?
2. Compare the way Calvino and Davis portray the relationship between humans and cats.
3. Why do you think this cartoon cat is so popular?

"What flowerbeds? I've never seen anything in this garden but a great crop of weeds!"

Marcovaldo realized that with regard to the old Marchesa opinions were sharply divided: some saw her as an angelic being, others as an egoist and a miser.

"It's the same with the birds; she never gives them a crumb!"

"She gives them hospitality. Isn't that plenty?"

"Like she gives the mosquitoes, you mean. They all come from here, from that pool. In the summertime the mosquitoes eat us alive, and it's all the fault of that Marchesa!"

"And the mice? This villa is a mine of mice. Under the dead leaves they have their burrows, and at night they come out . . ."

"As far as the mice go, the cats take care of them . . ."

"Oh, you and your cats! If we had to rely on them . . ."

"Why? Have you got something to say against cats?"

Here the discussion degenerated into a general quarrel.

"The authorities should do something: confiscate the villa!" one man cried.

"What gives them the right?" another protested.

"In a modern neighborhood like ours, a mouse-nest like this . . . it should be forbidden . . ."

❸

"Why, I picked my apartment precisely because it overlooked this little bit of green . . ."

"Green, hell! Think of the fine skyscraper they could build here!"

Marcovaldo would have liked to add something of his own, but he couldn't get a word in. Finally, all in one breath, he exclaimed: "The Marchesa stole a trout from me!"

The unexpected news supplied fresh ammunition to the old woman's enemies,

◆ **Build Vocabulary**

scrimmage (skrim′ ij) *n.*: Rough-and-tumble fight

The Garden of Stubborn Cats ◆ 545

Connections to Today's World

More About the Author
Jim Davis was born in Marion, Indiana, in 1945. He had asthma as a child and was forced to spend hours in bed. That is when he first began drawing cartoons. To find out more, students can visit the Garfield Web site at **http://www.garfield.com/ paws/jimdavis**. Please be aware that sites may have changed since we published this information. Also, we *strongly recommend* that you preview sites before sending students to them.

Genre Connection
Ask students if they think cartoons, as well as stories, can communicate serious messages about such issues as the relationship between people and animals. Have them cite evidence from cartoons they have seen to support their point of view.

Customize for
Visual/Spatial Learners
Have these students compare the image of Garfield the cat shown on this page with the photographs of cats shown throughout the story. How are the images similar? How are they different? *In both the cartoon and the photos, cats are shown as creatures with strong, independent, dominating personalities. The photos emphasize the mysterious implications of these qualities, while the cartoon emphasizes the amusing implications of them.*

◆ Critical Thinking

❸ **Draw Conclusions** Ask students what opposing forces the two groups of neighbors represent. What does each side want? *The two groups of neighbors represent the two opposing forces in the story—nature and technology. The neighbors who want the "little bit of green" to remain represent the force of nature; the ones who would rather have a skyscraper represent the force of "progress" and technology.*

◆ **Critical Thinking**

❷ **Draw Conclusions** Ask what side, if any, the Marchesa is on—the side that wants to preserve the garden or the side that wants a skyscraper instead. *The Marchesa is not on either side. She doesn't care about the cats or the garden; she just wants to stay in her own house and not be bothered. She will complain only when either side affects her as an individual. Students may say she represents self-interest.*

◆ *Literature and Your Life*

❸ Students who prefer preserving the natural world over progress and development may cheer the cats on and be glad they are stopping the developers. Students who believe progress and development are important may feel that the cats should be removed.

◆ **Build Vocabulary**

❹ **Word Origins: Words From Myths** Tell students that the word *demon* is derived from the Greek *daimon* or *daemon*. In Greek mythology the daemons were supernatural beings with powers between those of gods and people. The word gradually came to mean "evil spirit."

---

❶ but her defenders exploited it as proof of the indigence to which the unfortunate noblewoman was reduced. Both sides agreed that Marcovaldo should go and knock at her door to demand an explanation.

It wasn't clear whether the gate was locked or unlocked; in any case, it opened, after a push, with a mournful creak. Marcovaldo picked his way among the leaves and cats, climbed the steps to the porch, knocked hard at the entrance.

At a window (the very one where the frying pan had appeared), the blind was raised slightly and in one corner a round, pale blue eye was seen, and a clump of hair dyed an undefinable color, and a dry skinny hand. A voice was heard, asking: "Who is it? Who's at the door?" the words accompanied by a cloud smelling of fried oil.

"It's me, Marchesa. The trout man," Marcovaldo explained. "I don't mean to trouble you. I only wanted to tell you, in case you didn't know, that the trout was stolen from me, by that cat, and I'm the one who caught it. In fact the line . . ."

"Those cats! It's always those cats . . . " the Marchesa said, from behind the shutter, with a shrill, somewhat nasal voice. "All my troubles come from the cats! Nobody knows what I go through! Prisoner night and day of those horrid beasts! And with all the refuse people throw over the walls, to spite me!"

"But my trout . . ."

❷ "Your trout! What am I supposed to know about your trout!" The Marchesa's voice became almost a scream, as if she wanted to drown out the sizzle of oil in the pan, which came through the window along with the aroma of fried fish. "How can I make sense of anything, with all the stuff that rains into my house?"

"I understand, but did you take the trout or didn't you?"

"When I think of all the damage I

◆ **Build Vocabulary**
indigence (in´ di jəns) *n.:* Poverty

546 ◆ *Short Stories*

---

suffer because of the cats! Ah, fine state of affairs! I'm not responsible for anything! I can't tell you what I've lost! Thanks to those cats, who've occupied house and garden for years! My life at the mercy of those animals! Go and find the owners! Make them pay damages! Damages? A whole life destroyed! A prisoner here, unable to move a step!"

"Excuse me for asking: but who's forcing you to stay?"

From the crack in the blind there appeared sometimes a round, pale blue eye, sometimes a mouth with two protruding teeth; for a moment the whole face was visible, and to Marcovaldo it seemed, bewilderingly, the face of a cat.

"They keep me prisoner, they do, those cats! Oh, I'd be glad to leave! What wouldn't I give for a little apartment all my own, in a nice clean modern building! But I can't go out . . . They follow me, they block my path, they trip me up!" The voice became a whisper, as if to confide a secret. "They're afraid I'll sell the lot . . . They won't leave me . . . won't allow me . . . When the builders come to offer me a contract, you should see them, those cats! They get in the way, pull out their claws; they even chased a lawyer off! Once I had the contract right here, I was about to sign it, and they dived in through the window, knocked over the inkwell, tore up all the pages . . ."

❸ ◆ *Literature and Your Life*
How do your opinions about progress and development affect your reaction to the cats' actions?

All of a sudden Marcovaldo remembered the time, the shipping department, the boss. He tiptoed off over the dried leaves, as the voice continued to come through the slats of the blind, enfolded in that cloud apparently from the oil of a frying pan. "They even scratched me . . . I still have the scar . . . All alone here at the mercy of these demons . . ."

❹ Winter came. A blossoming of white flakes decked the branches and capitals and the cats' tails. Under the snow, the dry leaves dissolved into mush. The cats were rarely seen, the cat lovers even less; the packages of fish-bones were consigned only to cats who came to the door. Nobody, for quite a while, had seen anything of the Marchesa. No smoke came now from the chimneypot of the villa.

One snowy day, the garden was again full of cats, who had returned as if it were spring, and they were miauing as if on a moonlight night. The neighbors realized that something had happened: they went and knocked at the Marchesa's door. She didn't answer: she was dead.

In the spring, instead of the garden, there was a huge building site that a contractor had set up. The steam shovels dug down to great depths to make room for the foundations, cement poured into the iron armatures, a very high crane passed beams to the workmen who

were making the scaffoldings. But how could they get on with their work? Cats walked along all the planks, they made bricks fall and upset buckets of mortar, they fought in the midst of the piles of sand. When you started to raise an armature, you found a cat perched on top of it, hissing fiercely. More treacherous pusses climbed onto the masons' backs as if to purr, and there was no getting rid of them. And the birds continued making their nests in all the trestles,[10] the cab of the crane looked like an aviary . . . And you couldn't dip up a bucket of water that wasn't full of frogs, croaking and hopping . . .

❺

---

10. **trestles** (tres´ əlz) *n*.: Frameworks of vertical or slanting beams and crosspieces.

◆ **Critical Thinking**

❺ **Predict** Ask students if they predict the skyscraper will be finished. What seems to be happening? *Some students may say that nature will never stop the "wheels of progress"; others will say that in the end, nature is the stronger force and will prevail.*

Reinforce and Extend

Answers

◆ *Literature and Your Life*

Reader's Response According to the Marchesa, she is trapped because the cats thwart her attempts to sell or even to leave the villa.

Thematic Focus Some students may think they will be destroyed; others may agree with Calvino, that they will prevail.

Journal Writing Students may observe that cats can resume their wild state and survive even in paved, overbuilt city environments.

☑ **Check Your Comprehension**

1. The "negative city" consists of the in-between spaces that the cats inhabit.
2. He follows the cat first out of curiosity; later he chases it to retrieve the trout.
3. The tabby leads him to the Garden of Stubborn Cats, where he finds the city's concentration of wildlife.
4. The wildlife of the garden is hampering the construction effort.

◆ **Critical Thinking**

1. They represent anti-natural forces.
2. Her supporters think she is helping the cats by preserving an area where they can live; her critics observe her adversarial relationship with the cats.
3. The opposing forces in the story are technology and nature. Nature prevails at the end, with animals subverting the builders' efforts.
4. Marcovaldo tells himself that he is not stealing the trout because the trout would voluntarily take his bait. Students may see Marcovaldo's reasoning as rationalization for stealing.
5. Urban students may see similarities; rural students may not.

Guide for Responding

◆ *Literature and Your Life*

Reader's Response What is your impression of the Marchesa's circumstances in this story? Was she trapped or not? Explain.

Thematic Focus Speculate on what will happen to street animals, such as the cats in the story, in the world of our future.

Journal Writing Write a paragraph explaining what the cats represent in this story.

☑ **Check Your Comprehension**

1. What is the "negative city," and how is it created?
2. Why does Marcovaldo follow the cat?
3. Where does the tabby ultimately lead Marcovaldo, and what does Marcovaldo find there?
4. Describe the situation at the end of the story.

◆ **Critical Thinking**

INTERPRET
1. What do the developers represent in this story?
2. Explain why the Marchesa's supporters believe she is helping the cats and her critics think she is not. **[Infer; Compare and Contrast]**
3. What are the opposing forces in this story, and which prevails? Support your answer with evidence from the story. **[Draw Conclusions]**

EVALUATE
4. Evaluate Marcovaldo's thought "I couldn't be accused of theft; at worst, of fishing in an unauthorized place." **[Assess]**

EXTEND
5. Compare the buildings in the city of this story to buildings in the place where you live. **[Social Studies Link]**

The Garden of Stubborn Cats ◆ 547

Beyond the Selection

FURTHER READING
Other Works by the Authors
Dandelion Wine, Ray Bradbury
The Golden Apples of the Sun, Ray Bradbury
Something Wicked This Way Comes, Ray Bradbury
Marcovaldo or the Seasons in the City, Italo Calvino
Italian Folktales, Italo Calvino

Other Works About the Future
"The Fun They Had," Isaac Asimov
   We suggest that you preview these works before recommending them to students.

INTERNET
For more on Bradbury, see: **http://www.on-ramp.com/johnston/bradbury.html**; **http://www.catch22.com/~espana/SF Authors/SFB/Bradbury**
   For Calvino, see: **http://userwww.service.emory.edu/~mpajare/calauto.html**
   Sites may have changed since we published this information. We *strongly recommend* that you preview the sites before you send students to them.

◆ Reading Strategy

1. Students may have been confused by the absence of people, the futuristic setting, and all the futuristic appliances. Once the narrator says "this was the one house left standing," the setting becomes clear.
2. The dog's sores indicate exposure to radioactivity.
3. Some students may find the final clue in the silhouettes of the family against the charred wall of the house; others will find the explanation in the poem by Sara Teasdale.
4. Examples include the "network" through which "the ancient cat population still scurries," the "territories, ceremonies, customs" that belong to the realm of cats, and the "unsuspected peepholes onto the city of men" used by the cats.

◆ Literary Focus

1. (a) Details that alert readers that "There Will Come Soft Rains" occurs in the future include the automated breakfast; the date, "August 4, 2026"; and the robot cleaning-mice. (b) Bradbury's purpose is to warn humans of what could happen if nuclear weapons are permitted to proliferate. To make his warning effective, he envisions a future as it could be if the warning goes unheeded.
2. Students should describe an automated world in which humans do little for themselves and are totally dependent on technology.
3. (a) Marcovaldo's city is so overpopulated and built up that practically no traces of nature are left. (b) The setting is bad for cats and other animals because their lives are endangered by threats such as "cat-crushing automobiles," but it is good for them because they can exist in their own "city of cats" where they live a life independent of humans.
4. (a) In the city, building and technology seem to have obliterated nature, while in the garden, nature seems to be going wild. (b) The wildness of the garden suggests that nature resists human effort to destroy it.

◆ Build Vocabulary

1. *Tantalize* means "tempt": Tantalus was tempted by the food and drink he could not reach.

◆ Reading Strategy

CLARIFY

You may have felt confused by the events that occurred in either of the stories until you were able to **clarify**—make clear—the reasons particular events unfolded.

1. Identify two details of the situation in "There Will Come Soft Rains" that were unclear to you at the beginning of the story. Explain how you clarified these details.
2. How did the condition of the dog in "There Will Come Soft Rains" help you clarify the situation?
3. What was the final clue that allowed you to understand what had happened in "There Will Come Soft Rains"?
4. "The Garden of Stubborn Cats" opens with the statement "The city of cats and the city of men exist one inside the other, but they are not the same city." Identify three details that helped you clarify that statement.

◆ Literary Focus

SETTING

Both of these stories use **setting** as a significant element that contributes to their purposes. The events and the message in "There Will Come Soft Rains" are connected to the future. Time is the most important aspect of the setting.

Calvino presents his setting of a city within a city from an unusual perspective. Marcovaldo discovers places and things he wouldn't have known if he didn't follow his feline friends.

1. (a) Identify three details that alert you that "There Will Come Soft Rains" occurs in the future. (b) Why is this future setting essential to Bradbury's purpose?
2. Describe the future as it is presented in "There Will Come Soft Rains."
3. (a) Describe the city where Marcovaldo lives. (b) Why is this a good or a bad setting for cats and other animals?
4. (a) Contrast the city with the garden Marcovaldo discovers. (b) How does this contrast reinforce the message of the story?

◆ Build Vocabulary

USING WORDS FROM MYTHS

Look up each of the italicized words in a dictionary. On your paper, give the meaning of the word and explain how it relates to the mythological character from which it comes.

1. *tantalize:* from Tantalus, a man for whom food and drink were always out of reach
2. *odyssey:* from Odysseus, a hero who underwent a long and dangerous journey
3. *mercurial:* from Mercury, the speedy messenger god

USING THE WORD BANK

On your paper, write the word from the Word Bank suggested by each sentence.

1. You might use this word when planning a trip.
2. Rabbits live in these.
3. It would be tough to squeeze through one of these to escape a burning building.
4. Ending this is a societal problem.
5. Frequent run-ins with the law could give you this.
6. You'd use this word in astronomy.
7. An encounter with a bear would make you this.
8. This word describes weeds or an odor.
9. A thunderstorm is this.
10. People who are this are usually in hospitals.
11. You might get hurt in this activity.

◆ Build Grammar Skills

COMMONLY CONFUSED WORDS: *LIE* AND *LAY*

Lie means to rest or recline. Its principal parts are *lying, lay,* and *lain. Lay* means to set down, and its principal parts are *laying, laid,* and *laid.*

Practice Write the following sentences into your notebook, and circle the appropriate word.

1. The hungry dog is (lying, laying) at the door.
2. It (lies, lays) there waiting for someone to feed it.
3. Marcovaldo (lies, lays) the fish down.
4. When Marcovaldo arrived at the garden, cats were (lying, laying) everywhere.
5. The old woman of the house went to (lie, lay) down on her bed.

2. *Odyssey* means "long journey": Odysseus went on a long journey.
3. *Mercurial* means "unpredictable, quickly changing": Mercury traveled swiftly from one place to another.

Using the Word Bank

1. itinerary; 2. warrens;
3. transoms; 4. indigence;
5. paranoia; 6. supernal;
7. tremulous; 8. rank;
9. titanic; 10. psychopathic

◆ Build Grammar Skills

1. The hungry dog is <u>lying</u> at the door.
2. It <u>lies</u> there waiting for someone to feed it.
3. Marcovaldo <u>lays</u> the fish down, and the cat steals it.
4. When Marcovaldo arrived at the garden, cats were <u>lying</u> everywhere.
5. The old woman of the house went to <u>lie</u> down on her bed.

 Writer's Solution

For additional instruction and practice, use the page on Sixty Common Usage Problems (p. 91) in the *Writer's Solution Grammar Practice Book.*

548

Build Your Portfolio

Idea Bank

Writing

1. **Schedule** Write a schedule for the house in Bradbury's story. On it, record the house's duties for each of the twenty-four hours. Use duties from the story, and add some of your own.

2. **Speculation** Write three paragraphs in which you speculate what your life might be like in the year 2026, the year in which Bradbury's story ends.

3. **Science-Fiction Story** "The Garden of Stubborn Cats" shows how the cats have gained control of a small section of their city. Write a continuation of the story, in which the construction workers give up and the cats gain more control.

Speaking and Listening

4. **Inanimate Dialogue** Suppose the appliances in "There Will Come Soft Rains" could talk. Would they have similar interests? Role-play dialogue between two inanimate objects from the story.

5. **Persuasive Argument** As Marcovaldo, try to convince the Marchesa of the merits of staying in her villa and cultivating her garden. Support your argument with reasons. Present your argument to the class.

Projects

6. **Painting Presentation** Find out about the paintings of Picasso and Matisse—artists mentioned in Bradbury's story. Using books or photocopies, present your findings. **[Art Link]**

7. **Floor Plan** Draw a floor plan to scale—one inch for one yard—of your ideal house of the future. Briefly describe special features. **[Math Link]**

Writing Mini-Lesson

Advertisement for a New Technology

You've just discovered a great new technology, and you want to tell the world about it. It could be anything—from a way to grow tearless onions to a robot that interacts with human beings. The important thing is that you get your message across. Write an **advertisement** that describes the new technology, persuades your audience they need it, and provides ordering information.

> **Writing Skills Focus: Consider the Knowledge Level of Your Audience**
>
> Whether you're writing an advertisement, a short story, or a magazine article, you'll need to consider what your audience knows, Once you've determined the **knowledge level** of your audience, write for that level. For example, for an audience of people who've had no exposure to computers, define even simple computer terms. If you write at the knowledge level of your audience, you have a better chance of keeping their interest.

Prewriting Create and fill out a questionnaire to identify the characteristics of your audience. Provide information under headings such as Age Range, Education Level, Specialized Training, Technology, Buying Habits, and so on.

Drafting Write directly to your target audience—the people to whom you are trying to sell your product. They'll be more likely to buy your product if you address their needs in terms and language they can understand.

Revising Get feedback on your ad from someone whose knowledge level is close to that of your target audience. Define any technological terms that are unclear. Add any missing details about the function or advantages of your product.

 Idea Bank

Customizing for *Performance Levels*
Following are suggestions for matching Idea Bank topics with your students' performance levels:
Less Advanced Students: 1, 4, 7
Average Students: 2, 4, 6
More Advanced Students: 3, 5, 6

Customizing for *Learning Modalities*
Following are suggestions for matching Idea Bank topics with your students' learning modalities:
Logical/Mathematical: 1, 2, 5, 7
Visual/Spatial: 6, 7
Verbal/Linguistic: 1, 2, 3, 4, 5

 Writing Mini-Lesson

Refer students to the Writing Handbook, page 965, for instruction on the writing process, and page 968 for more on persuasion.

Writing and Language Transparencies Use the Writing Process Model 7: Persuasive Essay, pp. 45–51, to guide students through the writing process.

Writer's Solution

Writers at Work Videodisc
Have students view the videodisc segment (Ch. 4) featuring Sayu Bhojwani to see how she uses persuasion in her work.

Play frames 33643 to 43235

Writing Lab CD-ROM
Have students complete the tutorial on Persuasion. Follow these steps:
1. Students can view the annotated model on supporting a persuasive argument.
2. Suggest that they use the interactive instruction on choosing persuasive strategies.
3. Have students complete an Audience Profile.
4. Students should draft on computer.
5. Have them consider the tips for creating an ad when revising and editing their drafts.

Allow approximately 120 minutes of class time to complete these steps.

Sourcebook
Chapter 4, Persuasion (pp. 96–127), includes a writing model of an advertisement (p. 101).

✓ ASSESSMENT OPTIONS

Formal Assessment, Selection Test, pp. 135–137, and Assessment Resources Software. The selection test is designed so that it can be easily customized to the performance levels of your students.
Alternative Assessment, p. 39, includes options for less advanced students, more advanced students, interpersonal learners, verbal/linguistic learners, musical/rhythmic learners, logical/mathematical learners and visual/spatial learners.

PORTFOLIO ASSESSMENT
Use the following rubrics in the ***Alternative Assessment*** booklet to assess student writing:
Schedule: Technical Description/Explanation Rubric, p. 115
Speculation: Expression Rubric, p. 94
Science-Fiction Story: Fictional Narrative Rubric, p. 95
Writing Mini-Lesson: Persuasion Rubric, p. 105

*G*uide for Reading

1. To read, comprehend, and interpret short stories
2. To relate stories to personal experience
3. To build comprehension by challenging the writer's message
4. To identify universal themes
5. To build vocabulary in context and learn the word root *-ultra-*
6. To develop skill in using *who* and *whom* in adjective clauses
7. To write a letter to an elected official using the correct format
8. To respond to the stories through writing, speaking and listening, and projects

SKILLS INSTRUCTION

Vocabulary:
Word Roots: *-ultra-*

Grammar:
Who and *Whom* in Adjective Clauses

Reading Strategy:
Challenge the Writer's Message

Literary Focus:
Universal Themes

Writing:
Correct Letter Format

Speaking and Listening:
Improvised Speech (teacher edition)

Critical Viewing:
Deduce; Analyze

PORTFOLIO OPPORTUNITIES

Writing: Letter to Juan; The Censor; Princess With a Point of View

Writing Mini-Lesson: Letter to an Elected Official

Speaking and Listening: Debate; Improvised Speech

Projects: Music Collection; Internet Research

More About the Authors
Pär Lagerkvist is considered one of the major Swedish writers of the first half of the twentieth century. One of his most unusual works is the play *Let Man Live.* It focuses on people's willingness always to condemn others. With the publication of his 1944 novel *The Dwarf,* he had his first bestseller in Sweden, but it was not until the 1950 publication of *Barabbas* that he achieved international success.

Luisa Valenzuela is a writer of short stories and novels. One of her works, *Black Novel (With Argentines),* draws on her knowledge and experiences of life in New York as an exile by choice from Argentina.

Pär Lagerkvist *(1891–1974)*

Swedish writer Pär Lagerkvist (pär lä´ gər kvist´) did not achieve much public recognition until late in his career. Finally, however, when he was sixty, he won the most distinguished prize of all literary awards: the Nobel Prize.

Many Questions This Nobel Prize-winning writer was born the son of a railway worker. Unlike many of the inhabitants of his town, he received a university education, which led him to question many of his family's traditional beliefs. Because of his uncertainty, Lagerkvist's early work is pessimistic.

A Ray of Hope Although he continued to struggle with his beliefs, Lagerkvist's work gradually grew more optimistic. He reached a major turning point when he completed *The Triumph Over Life,* in which he expresses his growing faith in humanity.

Luisa Valenzuela *(1938–   )*

Born in Buenos Aires, the capital of Argentina, Luisa Valenzuela has lived in places as diverse as New York City and Tepotzlán, Mexico, a little village with cobblestone streets where people still speak the ancient Aztec language. Because she was married to a French sailor, she lived for a time in Normandy and Paris. Valenzuela travels to extremes in some of her work as well. She changes spellings, creates new words and uses many puns.

Defender of Rights Like many other Latin American writers, Valenzuela writes novels and stories that are very political. Having lived through a repressive regime herself, she is a strong defender of human rights and an active member of several international human rights organizations. "The Censors" shows one aspect of the repressions she has experienced.

◆ Build Vocabulary

WORD ROOTS: *-ultra-*
In "The Censors," a young man with an *ulterior* motive applies for a job. *Ulterior* means "undisclosed; beyond what is stated." An ulterior motive, therefore, is a reason beyond the one that you tell others.

Ulterior comes from the Latin word *ultra,* which means "further; beyond." In English, *ultra* also takes the forms *ulter* and *ulti.* Other common words with this root include *ultrasonic,* "faster than (or "beyond") the speed of sound," and *ultimate,* "the farthest or last."

WORD BANK

ardent	As you read, you will encounter the
venerable	words on this list. Each word is defined
sordid	on the page where it first appears. Pre-
ulterior	view the list before you read, and look
staidness	for the words in the story.

550 ◆ Short Stories

◆ Build Grammar Skills

WHO AND WHOM IN ADJECTIVE CLAUSES
Adjective clauses, also known as relative clauses, modify nouns or pronouns and begin with a relative pronoun. When choosing between the relative pronouns **who** and **whom** to introduce an adjective clause, use the following rules.

Use *who* if it is the subject of the clause:

      subject
Mariana, *who* must finally feel safe there . . .

Use *whom* if it is a direct object or the object of a preposition in the clause.

        dir. obj.
I have fought merely to win her *whom* I love, . . .

Prentice Hall Literature Program Resources

REINFORCE / RETEACH / EXTEND

Selection Support Pages
Build Vocabulary: Word Roots: *-ultra-*, p. 163
Build Grammar Skills: *Who* and *Whom* in Adjective Clauses, p. 164
Reading Strategy: Challenge the Writer's Message, p. 165
Literary Focus: Universal Themes, p. 166

Strategies for Diverse Student Needs, p. 40

Beyond Literature
Cross-Curricular Connection: Social Studies, p. 40

Formal Assessment Selection Test, pp. 138–140

Alternative Assessment, p. 40

Writing and Language Transparencies
Business Letter, pp. 61–64

Resource Pro CD-R*O***M**
"The Princess and All the Kingdom," "The Censors"—includes all resource materials and customizable lesson plan

Listening to Literature Audiocassettes
"The Princess and All the Kingdom," "The Censors"

The Princess and All the Kingdom
◆ The Censors ◆

◆ *Literature and Your Life*

CONNECT YOUR EXPERIENCE

Have you ever fought for something and then found out you got more than you had bargained for? Both of these stories are about people who believe they are pursuing noble intentions but find themselves in circumstances that are very different from those they had imagined.

Journal Writing Describe a situation in which your good intentions led to an unforeseen or even disastrous consequence.

THEMATIC FOCUS: FACING THE CONSEQUENCES

The events in these stories raise questions about how much control individuals have over the outcomes of their actions.

◆ Background for Understanding

HISTORY

Like the United States, Argentina, the setting of "The Censors," is a country with a high standard of living and a long tradition of immigration from all parts of the world. Unlike the United States, however, Argentina does not have a well-established tradition of democracy. Consequently, it has suffered for many years under colonialism and military dictatorships. In the 1970's, a military regime took power and brutally hunted down suspected political foes. Luisa Valenzuela spent many of those years in self-imposed exile. Although democracy has now been restored, many Argentineans are still traumatized by the events of the "Dirty War" in which thousands of people lost their lives.

◆ Literary Focus

UNIVERSAL THEMES

From Argentina to Alaska, from Zurich to Zaire, it would be difficult to find a place where fairy tales are not told. One reason that fairy tales continue to be told to generation after generation of children around the world is that they deal with **universal themes**—messages that are relevant to people of almost any place or time—such as courage, love, and honor. "The Princess and All the Kingdom" uses a fairy-tale format to communicate a message about happiness and responsibility. The short story "The Censors" does not take the familiar fairy-tale form, but it does deal with the universal themes of power and fear.

◆ Reading Strategy

CHALLENGE THE WRITER'S MESSAGE

When you see a television commercial that implies you'll be able to jump as high as an NBA star if you just buy a particular brand of sneakers, do you go right out and buy a pair of the advertised footwear? If you're thinking critically, you'll **challenge the message** behind the advertisement.

Use the same critical mindset when you're reading. Look for the writer's message. Sometimes the writer states the message openly—either through the voice of a narrator or through one of the characters. In these cases, it's easy to recognize the message.

In other stories, the message is implied—often through the actions of the main character. In stories like these, try to state the message in your own words. Then ask yourself, "Does this hold true in real life, or am I being sold a pair of magical sneakers?"

Guide for Reading ◆ 551

Interest Grabber Have students look at the dramatic piece of art on page 555 and read the title, "Restricted Man." Ask them to conjecture about the subject of the work. What is the artist's message? *The person appears trapped inside a cement box. The artist may be depicting political repression.* Ask students what kind of traps people find themselves in. Then have them predict what the theme might be in the stories they will read.

Customize for
Less Proficient Readers
To be sure these students comprehend the meaning, have them work in pairs to read the selections. Suggest they pause after each paragraph and take turns summarizing the content.

Customize for
More Advanced Students
An important element in both stories is irony. Have students define the three main types of irony—verbal, situational, and dramatic—and determine which type of irony is most prevalent in each story. Students should support their choices with examples from each story.

Customize for
English Language Learners
These students can benefit from using the Story Map organizer in **Writing and Language Transparencies,** p. 84, to chart the events of the plots as they read. When they finish reading, they can use their maps to support their ideas about the theme of each story.

Customize for
Visual/Spatial and Intrapersonal Learners
Have these students look at the title and illustration at the start of each story. Invite them to write a short journal entry that summarizes their predictions about each story, based on the illustration. When they have finished reading, have them write another journal entry that evaluates their predictions.

Preparing for Standardized Tests

Grammar and Language Understanding the correct uses of the relative pronouns *who* and *whom* will help students improve their performance on essay sections of standardized tests, including tests such as the ACT college entrance exam, which tests usage and mechanics skills. Such tests may require students to choose between *who* and *whom* to complete a sentence, as in this example:

(Who, Whom) do you like better? *Whom*
The Build Grammar Skills lesson for this selection focuses on the correct use of *who* and *whom* in adjective clauses. For more practice in making this distinction, use Build Grammar Skills: *Who and Whom* in Adjective Clauses, p. 164, in **Selection Support.**

There is a saying, "Be careful what you wish for, because you just might get it." These words of wisdom could apply to the main character in "The Princess and All the Kingdom." In this story, the prince yearns for the lovely princess and fights bravely to win her. To his surprise and initial dismay, he also wins the entire kingdom—with all its problems and responsibilities. The story suggests therefore that even in our victorious moments—perhaps most in our victorious moments—we cannot evade responsibility.

🎵 Humanities: Art

View of the Ile de la Cité, Paris, by Jehan Fouquet.

This piece of art illustrates a scene from a medieval kingdom. The stylized buildings with their turrets, towers, and banners evoke a fairy-tale kingdom like the one in "The Princess and All the Kingdom."

Jehan Fouquet (c. 1420–1481) was probably the first French painter to win international renown. Having traveled to Rome in the mid-1400's, he learned Italian theories of perspective and architecture. When he returned to France, he became court painter to Louis XI. Best known for his miniatures and panel paintings, Fouquet demonstrated an appreciation of landscape and perspective.

Use this question for discussion: How does this painting influence your expectations about the story?

Students should note that the work evokes tales of chivalry and knights in armor. They should be expecting to read a fairy tale or fantasy.

THE PRINCESS AND ALL THE Kingdom

Pär Lagerkvist
Translated by Alan Blair

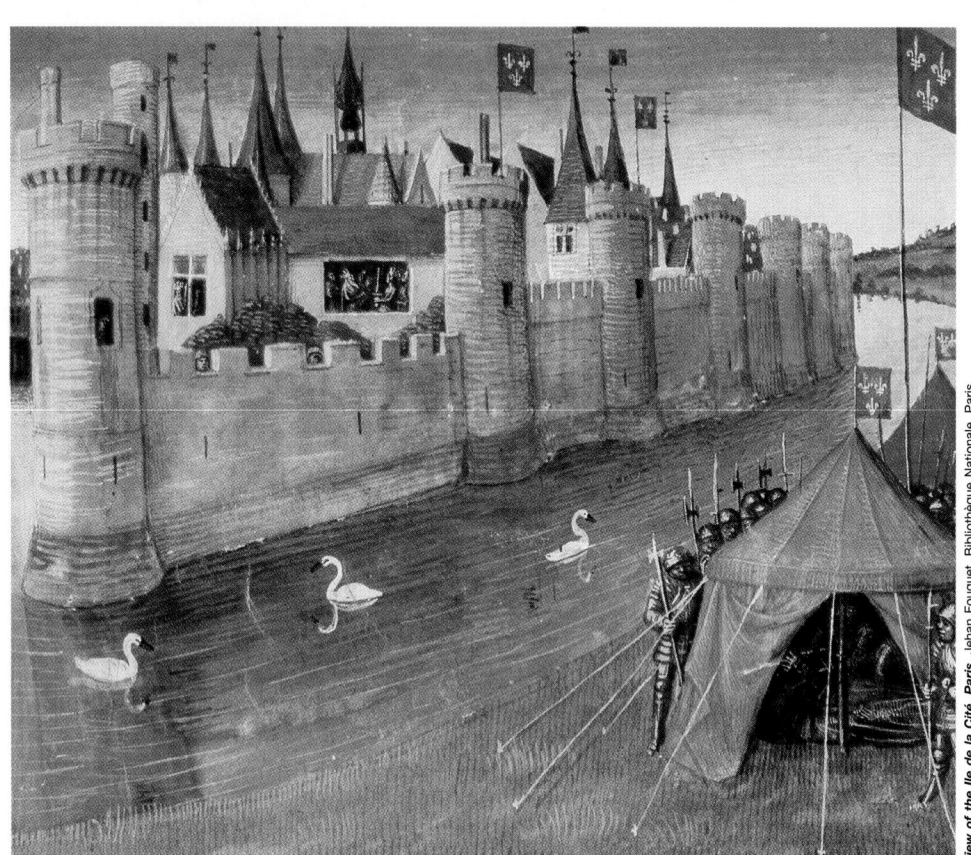

View of the Ile de la Cité, Paris, Jehan Fouquet, Bibliothèque Nationale, Paris

▲ **Critical Viewing** What clues does this painting give you about the style and content of the story you are about to read? **[Deduce]**

552 ◆ *Short Stories*

Once upon a time there was a prince, who went out to fight in order to win the princess whose beauty was greater than all others' and whom he loved above everything. He dared his life, he battled his way step by step through the country, ravaging it; nothing could stop him. He bled from his wounds but merely cast himself from one fight to the next, the most valiant nobleman to be seen and with a shield as pure as his own young features. At last he stood outside the city where the princess lived in her royal castle. It could not hold out against him and had to beg for mercy. The gates were thrown open; he rode in as conqueror.

When the princess saw how proud and handsome he was and thought of how he had dared his life for her sake, she could not withstand his power but gave him her hand. He knelt and covered it with <u>ardent</u> kisses. "Look, my bride, now I have won you!" he exclaimed, radiant with happiness. "Look, everything I have fought for, now I have won it!"

And he commanded that their wedding should take place this same day. The whole city decked itself out for the festival and the wedding was celebrated with rejoicing, pomp, and splendor.

When in the evening he went to enter the princess's bedchamber, he was met outside by the aged chancellor, a <u>venerable</u> man. Bowing his snow-white head, he tendered the keys of the kingdom and the crown of gold and precious stones to the young conqueror.

"Lord, here are the keys of the kingdom which open the treasuries where everything that now belongs to you is kept."

The prince frowned.

"What is that you say, old man? I do not want your keys. I have not fought for <u>sordid</u> gain. I have fought merely to win her whom I love, to win that which for me is the only costly thing on earth."

The old man replied, "This, too, you have won, lord. And you cannot set it aside. Now you must administer and look after it."

"Do you not understand what I say? Do you not understand that one can fight, can conquer, without asking any reward other than one's happiness—not fame and gold, not land and power on earth? Well, then, I have conquered but ask for nothing, only to live happily with what, for me, is the only thing of value in life."

"Yes, lord, you have conquered. You have fought your way forward as the bravest of the brave, you have shrunk from nothing, the land lies ravaged where you have passed by. You have won your happiness. But, lord, others have been robbed of theirs. You have conquered, and therefore everything now belongs to you. It is a big land, fertile and impoverished, mighty and laid waste, full of riches and need, full of joy and sorrow, and all is now yours. For he who has won the princess and happiness, to him also belongs this land where she was born; he shall govern and cherish it."

The prince stood there glowering and fingering the hilt of his sword uneasily.

"I am the prince of happiness, nothing else!" he burst out. "Don't want to be anything else. If you get in my way, then I have my trusty sword."

But the old man put out his hand soothingly and the young man's arm sank. He looked at him searchingly, with a wise man's calm.

"Lord, you are no longer a prince," he said gently. "You are a king."

And lifting the crown with his aged hands, he put it on the other's head.

When the young ruler felt it on his brow he stood silent and moved, more erect than before. And gravely, with his head crowned for power on earth, he went in to his beloved to share her bed.

♦ **Literature and Your Life**

Contrast the prince's situation with a time when you acquired something you wanted only to find there were unforeseen conditions attached.

♦ **Build Vocabulary**

ardent (är′ dənt) *adj.*: Warm or intense in feeling

venerable (ven′ ər ə bəl) *adj.*: Worthy of respect by reason of age and dignity, character, or position

sordid (sôr′ did) *adj.*: Dirty; filthy

The Princess and All the Kingdom ♦ 553

♦ **Build Grammar Skills**

❶ *Who* and *Whom* in **Adjective Clauses** The opening sentence contains examples of both *who* and *whom* in adjective clauses. Have students explain why each relative pronoun is used correctly. *Who is the subject of the verb* went. *Whom is the direct object of the verb* loved.

♦ **Literary Focus**

❷ **Universal Themes** In most fairy tales, an obstacle stands in the way of the prince and princess being united. Ask: What is the obstacle? *The passage suggests that the prince's new responsibilities are an obstacle.*

♦ **Critical Thinking**

❸ **Infer** Ask students what they think is the real reason the prince doesn't want the keys. Is he really being noble, or is there another reason? *The prince thinks he is being noble, but he is really reacting to the chancellor's words, "Now you must administer and look after it." The prince wants to live "happily ever after" with the beautiful fairy-tale princess, but he doesn't want to face the responsibilities of running a real kingdom.*

♦ *Literature and Your Life*

❹ Similar situations include the following: When students of driving age are allowed to use the family car, they are often asked to do family errands as well; students who have pets have to take care of them as well as play with them.

♦ **Critical Thinking**

❺ **Infer** Ask: How does the chancellor feel toward the prince? Explain. *Responses can include: The chancellor feels compassion for the prince because he knows he is young and hasn't yet learned how difficult life can be; the chancellor knows he must be firm with the prince or he will never accept responsibility.*

♦ **Reading Strategy**

❻ **Challenge the Writer's Message** Ask students: What does the crown symbolize? How does wearing the crown change the prince? *The crown symbolizes the responsibilities a king takes for his land and people. The prince is changed from a spoiled child to a mature young man.*

Speaking and Listening Mini-Lesson

Improvised Speech

This mini-lesson supports the second Speaking and Listening activity in the Idea Bank on page 559.

Introduce the Concept Review that an improvised speech is not written out in advance. However, the speechmaker should take a few moments to plan what she or he will say.

Develop Background Have students imagine themselves as the new King. Have them consider the following points before they speak:

• The land is big, fertile, full of riches and joy.

• The land is also laid waste, impoverished and full of sorrow.

Apply the Information Students should think about what the waiting populace will want to hear; then, give their speeches in a voice with appropriate expression.

Assess the Outcome Have students evaluate the speeches based on the following criteria: (1) Did the speaker use a kingly manner of speaking? (2) Were the points appropriate for the king to make? (3) Was the speech well organized?

The Censors

Luisa Valenzuela
Translated by David Unger

Restricted Man, 1961, © Jerry Uelsmann, Collection of the Center for Creative Photography, Tucson, Arizona

❶ Poor Juan! One day they caught him with his guard down before he could even realize that what he had taken as a stroke of luck was really one of fate's dirty tricks. These things happen the minute you're careless, as one often is. Juancito let happiness—a feeling you can't trust—get the better of him when he received from a confidential source Mariana's new address in Paris and knew that she hadn't forgotten him. Without thinking twice, he sat down at his table and wrote her a letter. *The* letter that now keeps his mind off his job during the day and won't let him sleep at night (what had he scrawled, what had he put on that sheet of paper he sent to Mariana?).

Juan knows there won't be a problem with the letter's contents, that it's irreproachable, harmless. But what about the rest? He knows that they examine, sniff, feel, and read between the lines of each and every letter, and check its tiniest comma and most accidental stain. He knows that all letters pass from hand to hand and go through all sorts of tests in the huge censorship offices and that, in the end, very few continue on their way. Usually it takes months, even years, if there aren't any snags; all this time the freedom, maybe even the life, of both sender and receiver is in jeopardy. And that's why Juan's so troubled: thinking that something might happen to Mariana because of his letters. Of all people, Mariana, who must finally feel safe there where she always dreamt she'd live. But he knows that the *Censor's* ❷ *Secret Command* operates all over the world and cashes in on the discount in air fares; there's nothing to stop them from going as far as that hidden Paris neighborhood, kidnapping Mariana, and returning to their cozy homes, certain of having fulfilled their noble mission.

Well, you've got to beat them to the punch, do what everyone tries to do: sabotage the machinery, throw sand in its gears, get to the bottom of the problem so as to stop it.

This was Juan's sound plan when he, like many others, applied for a censor's job—not because he had a calling or needed a job: no, he ❸ applied simply to intercept his own letter, a consoling albeit unoriginal idea. He was hired immediately, for each day more and more censors were needed and no one would bother to check on his references.

554 ◆ *Short Stories*

Cross-Curricular Connection: Social Studies

Argentina Even though "The Censor" could take place in any oppressive state, the author's nationality suggests that she probably intended the setting to be Argentina. The movie *Evita,* starring Madonna, brought a part of Argentina's history into the public eye. To begin a discussion about Argentina, you might draw on students' knowledge of the movie or the musical, and then direct the discussion into some of the geographical

as-pects of the country. For example, Argentina is the second largest country in South America, occupying most of the southern portion of the continent. Since it is so large, the landscape varies greatly, from the Andes Mountain regions to the barren plateau of Patagonia to the fertile plain called the Pampas. Ironically, Argentina's name comes from the Latin word for silver, but Argentina lacks the precious metal.

Interested students might like to form a small group to find out more about Argentina. Some students might focus on the geography of the country and create a map. Other students might focus on the political history and construct a time line of the leaders and military regimes. Still others might focus on the economic development and make a poster showing the country's major products.

▲ **Critical Viewing** In what ways does this art suggest fear and repression? [Analyze]

The Censors ◆ 555

Humanities: Art

Restricted Man, 1961, by Jerry Uelsmann.
   This photograph portrays how a man like Juan probably feels.
   Photographer Jerry Uelsmann (1934–   ) received his M.F.A. from Indiana University in 1960 and immediately began teaching photography at the University of Florida. His work has been exhibited in more than 100 shows in the United States and around the world. He has published six books of photography and his work can be found on display in museums as diverse as the Metropolitan Museum of Art in New York and the Tokyo Metropolitan Museum of Photography.
   Use these questions for discussion:
• What is the man in the photograph doing? *He is looking out through an opening in some stone. A similar adjacent opening is almost completely covered.*
• What, do you think, does Uelsmann want you to know about the man? *The man has* "tunnel" vision; he is as rigid and unmoving as the stone.*
• Why is this photograph appropriate for "The Censors"? *Juan has tunnel vision; he is obsessed first with finding the letter and later with being the most cunning censor. He refuses to do anything not related to his job and becomes rigid in his quest to be the perfect censor.*

◆ Critical Thinking

❶ Analyze Ask: What do you know about Juan from his reaction when he is sent to Section K?

Students might say that Juan is losing touch with reality because he is so obsessed with worrying about his letter that he does not recognize the real danger in screening letters for explosives.

◆ Critical Thinking

❷ Evaluate Draw students' attention to Juan's response to the union organizer. Ask: What are Juan's motives in reporting the man? Should Juan be proud of his promotion? Why or why not? *Juan reports the organizer to favorably impress his superiors. His words to himself as he leaves his boss's office tell the reader that Juan knows his motive was self-serving. Therefore, he should not be proud of his promotion, especially because the union organizer probably lost his job and perhaps his life.*

Comprehension Check ☑

❸ What was Juan's noble mission that is beginning to blur? *His noble mission was to intercept his letter to Mariana so that no harm would come to her. Now he is beginning to enjoy the work for its own sake.*

◆ Literary Focus

❹ Universal Themes Students may mention people who become so involved in a work project that they put its importance ahead of their families, or people who can't put the office behind them while they are on vacation, or people who lie or cheat to get ahead.

❺ Interpret Have students consider the sentence, "We don't know if this made him happy." Ask: How could the narrator, who seems to have known everything about Juan's innermost thoughts up until now, not know if promotion made Juan happy? *Perhaps the narrator is implying that Juan is acting less and less like a reasonable person, and so his state of mind can't be assessed.*

🎧 **Listening to Literature Audiocassettes** By listening to a reading of "The Censor," students will receive the full benefit of the storyteller's inflections, beginning with the opening words, "Poor Juan!"

<u>Ulterior</u> motives couldn't be overlooked by the *Censorship Division*, but they needn't be too strict with those who applied. They knew how hard it would be for the poor guys to find the letter they wanted and even if they did, what's a letter or two when the new censor would snap up so many others? That's how Juan managed to join the *Post Office's Censorship Division*, with a certain goal in mind.

The building had a festive air on the outside that contrasted with its inner <u>staidness</u>. Little by little, Juan was absorbed by his job, and he felt at peace since he was doing everything he could to get his letter for Mariana. He didn't even worry when, in his first month, he was sent to *Section K* where envelopes are very carefully screened for explosives.

It's true that on the third day, a fellow worker had his right hand blown off by a letter, but the division chief claimed it was sheer negligence on the victim's part. Juan and the other employees were allowed to go back to their work, though feeling less secure. After work, one of them tried to organize a strike to demand higher wages for unhealthy work, but Juan didn't join in; after thinking it over, he reported the man to his superiors and thus got promoted.

◆ Build Vocabulary

ulterior (ul tir′ ē ər) *adj.*: Undisclosed; beyond what is openly stated

staidness (stād′ nəs) *n.*: State of being settled or resistant to change

---

Well, you've got to beat them to the punch, do what everyone tries to do: sabotage the machinery . . .

You don't form a habit by doing something once, he told himself as he left his boss's office. And when he was transferred to *Section F*, where letters are carefully checked for poison dust, he felt he had climbed a rung in the ladder.

By working hard, he quickly reached *Section E* where the job became more interesting, for he could now read and analyze the letters' contents. Here he could even hope to get hold of his letter, which, judging by the time that had elapsed, had gone through the other sections and was probably floating around in this one.

Soon his work became so absorbing that his noble mission blurred in his mind. Day after day he crossed out whole paragraphs in red ink, pitilessly chucking many letters into the censored basket. These were horrible days when he was shocked by the subtle and conniving ways employed by people to pass on subversive messages; his instincts were so sharp that he found behind a simple "the weather's unsettled" or "prices continue to soar" the wavering hand of someone secretly scheming to overthrow the Government.

His zeal brought him swift promotion. We don't know if this made him happy. Very few letters reached him in *Section B*—only a handful passed the other hurdles—so he read them over and over again, passed them under a

◆ Literary Focus
The theme of someone's becoming so caught up in his work that he loses sight of his original mission is universal. Explain how.

---

556 ◆ Short Stories

◈ **Beyond the Classroom**

Career Connection
Postal Workers When Juan mailed his letter, it made a detour through his city's Post Office Censorship Division. Without such a detour, what would have happened to his letter? Although much of today's mail service is automated, postal workers are still needed to keep the mail flowing. Have interested students research United States Postal Service jobs and report their findings to the class. For example, students could investigate the following: educational requirements, application process, career opportunities, and pay and benefits.

Community Connection
Local Mail Service Where do students mail their letters? Where do they, or their parents, buy stamps? How do students receive their mail? The answers to these questions can vary greatly. Encourage students to do a survey that answers the three questions above. After students have compiled the results of their survey, they might like to discuss the results with someone who has lived in the community for more than ten or fifteen years to see how services have changed.

magnifying glass, searched for microprint with an electronic microscope, and tuned his sense of smell so that he was beat by the time he made it home. He'd barely manage to warm up his soup, eat some fruit, and fall into bed, satisfied with having done his duty. Only his darling mother worried, but she couldn't get him back on the right track. She'd say, though it wasn't always true: Lola called, she's at the bar with the girls, they miss you, they're waiting for you. Or else she'd leave a bottle of red wine on the table. But Juan wouldn't overdo it: any distraction could make him lose his edge, and the perfect censor had to be alert, keen, attentive, and sharp to nab cheats. He had a truly patriotic task, both self-denying and uplifting.

His basket for censored letters became the best fed as well as the most cunning basket in the whole *Censorship Division*. He was about to congratulate himself for having finally discovered his true mission, when his letter to Mariana reached his hands. Naturally, he censored it without regret. And just as naturally, he couldn't stop them from executing him the following morning, another victim of his devotion to his work.

Guide for Responding

◆ *Literature and Your Life*

Reader's Response Do you think the prince's prize was worth the price in "The Princess and All the Kingdom"?

Thematic Focus In both of these stories, the universal theme of power shows the great responsibilities that come with power.

☑ Check Your Comprehension

1. In "The Princess and All the Kingdom," in addition to the princess's hand in marriage, what else does the prince receive?
2. In "The Censors," why does Juan seek a job as a censor?
3. What happens to Juan at the end of "The Censors"?

◆ Critical Thinking

INTERPRET
1. In "The Princess and All the Kingdom," why do you think the prince had to fight in order to win the princess? **[Speculate]**
2. In "The Princess and All the Kingdom," how do the attitudes of the aged chancellor and the prince contrast with each other? **[Compare and Contrast]**
3. In "The Censors," why does Juan's attitude change? **[Draw Conclusions]**
4. What is your opinion of Juan in "The Censors"? Support your opinion with examples from the story. **[Support]**

APPLY
5. To what types of situations in the real world do you think that the themes of these stories could be applied? **[Apply]**

The Censors ◆ 557

Beyond the Selection

FURTHER READING

Other Works by the Authors
"A Hero's Death," Pär Lagerkvist
"Open Door," Luisa Valenzuela

Other Works With the Theme of Accepting Responsibility
We Are All Guilty, Kingsley Amis
One of the Boys, Scott Johnson
    We suggest that you preview these works before recommending them to students.

INTERNET

The Internet provides opportunities for students to learn more about the authors.
    For information and works by Pär Lagerkvist, go to **http://heml.passagen.se/iblis/lagrkvst.html**
    For a review of Luisa Valenzuela's *Black Novel (With Argentines)*, go to **http://lenti.med.umn. edu/~ernesto/Criticas/Cri_BlackNovel.html**
    Sites may have changed since we published this information. We *strongly recommend* that you preview the sites before students go to them.

◆ Reading Strategy

1. Teenagers are apt to view life in this way until they learn to accept the consequences of their actions.
2. Students may cite the stories of lottery winners who go bankrupt after spending their money.
3. Juan's pride in and devotion to his job causes him to forget his original purpose.
4. Some students may argue that Juan is too exaggerated to be a believable character. Others may observe that power is capable of making such changes in a person.

◆ Literary Focus

1. (a) Students may point to historical situations where a military victory forced the conquering nation to provide protection and rule for the vanquished. (b) Sample examples: Students who win elections must run their organizations; the suitor to the rich girl must spend money on her to keep her interest.
2. The simplicity of the plot and the uncomplicated nature of its characters makes the fairy tale an effective vehicle for conveying a theme.
3. "The Censors" illustrates that power corrupts.
4. Sample response: In attempting to avenge a real wrong, people may take the law into their own hands.

◆ Build Vocabulary

Using the Root -ultra-
1. c   2. a   3. b

Using the Word Bank
1. d   2. c   3. a   4. b   5. e

◆ Build Grammar Skills

1. who;   2. whom;   3. who;   4. who;
5. whom

 Writer's Solution

For additional instruction and practice, use the lesson in the **Language Lab CD-ROM** on Pronoun Case and the page on Special Problems With Pronouns (p. 79) in the *Writer's Solution Grammar Practice Book*.

558

Guide for Responding (continued)

◆ Reading Strategy

CHALLENGE THE WRITER'S MESSAGE

When you read critically, you **challenge the writer's message**—you test what the writer says or implies against your own experiences and opinions.

1. The prince wanted happiness without responsibility. Explain why you agree or disagree that some people approach life in a similar way.
2. Through the voice of the Chancellor, Lagerkvist states that happiness and responsibility are tied together, that every prize has a price. Explain why you agree or disagree with this idea.
3. In "The Censors," how does Juan's fast rise through the ranks of the Censorship Division relate to his downfall?
4. Did you find the changes in Juan's attitude believable or not? Explain.

◆ Literary Focus

UNIVERSAL THEMES

Though these two stories differ in style and subject matter, both have **universal themes**—timeless messages that apply to the lives of people all over the world.

1. (a) Explain how the message of "The Princess and All the Kingdom" could apply to a ruler of any country. (b) Explain how the message could apply to you and your friends.
2. What features of a fairy tale make it an effective form for communicating a theme?
3. State the theme of "The Censors" in your own words.
4. Juan sets out to beat the system of censorship that he feels is oppressive and unjust. In the end, he becomes one of the most aggressive censors. Describe another situation in which someone might become a part of a problem he or she originally tried to solve.

◆ Build Vocabulary

USING THE ROOT -ultra-

Many English words contain the root -ultra-, which means "further; beyond." On your paper, match each word with its correct definition.

1. ultraviolet   **a.** a final offer or demand
2. ultimatum   **b.** finally
3. ultimately   **c.** having wavelengths that are shorter than those of violet light

USING THE WORD BANK

On your paper, match each word from the Word Bank with its closest synonym.

1. ardent   **a.** filthy
2. venerable   **b.** hidden
3. sordid   **c.** revered
4. ulterior   **d.** zealous
5. staidness   **e.** stuffiness

◆ Build Grammar Skills

WHO AND WHOM IN ADJECTIVE CLAUSES

In informal speech, some people may not distinguish between *who* and *whom*. In formal writing and speaking, however, it is important to use these words correctly.

> Use **who** as the subject of a clause. Use **whom** as a direct or indirect object or as an object of a preposition.

Practice Write the following sentences on your paper, choosing the correct word from the parentheses.

1. There once was a prince (who, whom) fought to win the heart of a beautiful princess.
2. The prince did not care for riches; he wanted to be with the princess (who, whom) he loved so much.
3. The chancellor, (who, whom) was a patient man, informed the prince of his new responsibilities.
4. It was Juan (who, whom) became a censor for his own letter.
5. Juan knew (who, whom) the authorities wanted.

Build Your Portfolio

 ## Idea Bank

Writing

1. Letter to Juan All we know about the mysterious character Mariana in "The Censors" is that she is in Paris, perhaps to escape the dictatorship of her country. Write a letter from her to Juan, explaining her reasons for leaving her country.

2. The Censor Choose a partner and write each other a simple postcard, such as you would write while on vacation. Then, exchange cards and pretend that you are censors in a dictatorship. Based on what you've read in "The Censors," find three suspicious details and explain why you chose them.

3. Princess With a Point of View Write and perform a short monologue for the princess in "The Princess and All the Kingdom," in which she expresses *her* opinions on war, victory, love and responsibility. **[Performing Arts Link]**

Speaking and Listening

4. Debate Form two opposing groups to debate both sides of a censorship/free speech issue from current events.

5. Improvised Speech As the prince who has just become a king, give your first speech to the crowd outside the palace.

Projects

6. Music Collection Plan a CD based on the theme of freedom versus responsibility. List the names of popular songs you would include on the CD. **[Performing Arts Link]**

7. Internet Research Use the Internet to locate information on groups whose purpose is the advancement of human rights. Create a chart that shows your findings on at least two groups. **[Social Studies Link; Technology Link]**

 ## Writing Mini-Lesson

Letter to an Elected Official

In "The Censors," Juan, like the author Luisa Valenzuela, had the misfortune of living under a dictatorship. In a democracy, government officials, who are often elected, must be responsive to the needs of the citizens. Write a letter to an elected official about a public issue that matters to you.

Writing Skills Focus: Correct Format

When you write a letter to a government official, you should use the format, or style, of a standard business letter.

> Your Address
> Date
>
> Inside Address:
> Name of Official
> Department
> Address
>
> Greeting:
>
> Body of letter
>
> Closing,
> Your Signature
> Your Typed Name

Prewriting Find the information you need to complete the inside address. Then make notes on the points you want to make in your letter.

Drafting In the body of your letter, state the problem and explain the action you want the official to take.

Revising Review your letter and eliminate any slang words or colloquial expressions. Check your spelling and grammar—especially your use of *who* and *whom*. For more on the correct use of *who* and *whom*, see pp. 550 and 558.

 ## Idea Bank

Customizing for *Performance Levels*

Following are suggestions for matching Idea Bank topics with your students' performance levels:

Less Advanced Students: 1, 4, 6, 7
Average Students: 2, 5, 6, 7
More Advanced Students: 3, 7

Customizing for *Learning Modalities*

Following are suggestions for matching Idea Bank topics with your students' learning modalities:

Bodily/Kinesthetic: 3, 5
Verbal/Linguistic: 1, 2, 3, 4, 5
Musical/Rhythmic: 6
Logical/Mathematical: 2, 7

 ## Writing Mini-Lesson

Refer students to the Writing Handbook, page 965, for instruction on the writing process, and page 968 for further information on persuasion.

You may use the Writing Process Model of a Business Letter in *Writing and Language Transparencies,* pp. 61–64, to guide students through the writing process.

 ## Writer's Solution

Writers at Work Videodisc

Have students view the videodisc segment (Ch. 4) featuring Sayu Bhojwani to see how she chooses words carefully and conveys information accurately in writing proposals. Have students discuss how they can apply her ideas to writing to elected officials.

Play frames 39679 to 41420

Writing Lab CD-ROM

Have students complete the tutorial on Persuasion. Follow these steps:

1. Have students use the Pros and Cons Chart to evaluate their arguments.
2. Students should draft on computer.
3. Have them review the tips for including ideas in a letter.

Allow approximately 90 minutes of class time to complete these steps.

Sourcebook

Have students use Chapter 4, Persuasion (pp. 96–127), for additional support. The chapter includes a model of a Letter to the Editor (p. 102).

✓ ASSESSMENT OPTIONS

Formal Assessment, Selection Test, pp. 138–140, and Assessment Resources Software. The selection test is designed so that it can be easily customized to the performance levels of your students.
Alternative Assessment, p. 40, includes options for less advanced students, more advanced students, verbal/linguistic learners, visual/spatial learners, and intrapersonal learners.

PORTFOLIO ASSESSMENT

Use the following rubrics in the **Alternative Assessment** booklet to assess student writing:
Letter to Juan: Fictional Narrative Rubric, p. 95
The Censor: Evaluation/Review Rubric, p. 104
Princess With a Point of View: Expression Rubric, p. 94
Writing Mini-Lesson: Persuasion Rubric, p. 105

Establish Writing Guidelines

Before students begin, review the following key characteristics of a persuasive essay:

- It aims to convince an audience to accept a position on an issue.
- Persuasive essays appear frequently in newspapers and magazines.

You may want to distribute the scoring rubric for Persuasion (p. 105 in the **Alternative Assessment** booklet) to make students aware before they begin of the criteria on which they will be evaluated. See the suggestions on page 562 for how you can customize the rubric to this workshop.

Refer students to the Writing Handbook, page 965, for instruction in the writing process, and page 968 for further information on persuasion.

 Writer's Solution

Writers at Work Videodisc

To introduce students to the key elements of persuasion and show them how Asia Society worker Sayu Bhojwani uses them in her proposal writing, play the videodisc segment on Persuasion (Ch. 4).

Play frames 33643 to 43235

Writing Lab CD-ROM

If your students have access to computers, you may want to have them work on the tutorial on Persuasion to complete all or part of their persuasive essays. Follow these steps:

1. Suggest that students review the interactive model of a persuasive essay.
2. Have students look at the examples of purposes for persuasive writing.
3. Students should draft on the computer.
4. For help revising drafts, students can use the screen Adding Supporting Details.
5. Suggest students use the Persuasion Word Bin to strengthen their drafts.

Sourcebook

Students can find additional support, including topic ideas, models, audience and purpose profiles, and graphic organizers, in the chapter on Persuasion (pp. 96–127).

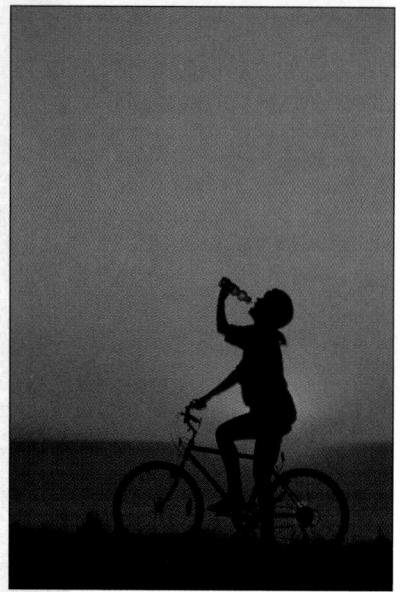

Persuasive Essay

Writing Process Workshop

You may have noticed one character persuading another in the short stories in this section. Persuasion can take place informally or formally. A **persuasive essay** is a formal opportunity to convince an audience to think or act in a certain way.

Develop a persuasive essay in which you convince readers to accept your position on an issue that is important to you. The following skills, introduced in this section's Writing Mini-Lessons, will help you develop your persuasive essay.

Writing Skills Focus

▶ **Consider what your audience knows.** If you write at the knowledge level of your audience, you have a better chance of persuading them to accept your position. For instance, if your topic is state-to-state driving laws and your audience has little knowledge of them, make sure you let them know the facts. (See p. 549.)

▶ **Use the proper format.** A persuasive essay should first present your position, develop an argument with evidence to support that position, bring up counterarguments and then counter those arguments, and conclude with a summary or restatement. (See p. 559.)

The following excerpt from an article that recommends cycling and in-line skating at night demonstrates these skills.

① The writer mentions a possible problem with her argument and then offers reasons countering it.

② The writer backs up her original assertion with further examples.

③ The writer assumes that the audience has had experience cycling during the day but not at night, so she starts with a basic safety precaution.

MODEL

Most people automatically assume that bicycling at night is dangerous. After all, it's dark, and most decent people are safely off the streets.

① As it happens, most cars are also off the streets, which is one of the great attractions of night riding—or night in-line skating, for that matter. There are other appealing factors, too. ② You don't have to get up at 5 A.M. to get in a workout and you can enjoy the cool night air.

We are not, for obvious reasons, suggesting you go alone. Traveling with a buddy or two both increases your visibility and deters would-be harassers. . . . ③

560 ◆ Short Stories

 Beyond the Classroom

Career Connection

Tell students that people in your community may routinely write persuasive essays as part of their work. Have students look for examples of persuasive essays in print and broadcast media. For example, they might find a letter to a newspaper editor stressing the need for road repair. Students can also find persuasive writing in advertisement posters on buses and trains, in political campaign messages, and on the Internet. Have students find a persuasive essay and analyze it, asking themselves whom the essay attempts to persuade, what its message is, and how successful they think it is.

Prewriting

Choose a Topic Think of issues that are important to you. You may want to browse through magazines and newspapers to look for ideas, or you may choose one of the following topics.

> ### Topic Ideas
> - School should be in session year-round
> - Channel One should not have advertising
> - Ticket brokers should be outlawed
> - High-school newspapers should be censored

Anticipate Readers' Questions Once you've chosen your topic, clarify the position that you will present in your essay. Then list potential objections and questions about that position. For example, if your essay presents an argument that zoos are cruel and should be closed, you might list these questions as issues that your opponents would raise and that you must address:

- ▶ What will happen to the animals currently in zoos?
- ▶ What alternatives are there to educate people about animals?
- ▶ What arguments are there in favor of zoos?

Gather Strong Evidence Using the questions and objections you listed as a starting point, gather evidence—facts, statistics, and reasons—to support your argument. This may require research, either in the library or on the Internet.

Drafting

Appeal to Your Audience As you write, always keep your readers in mind. Use formal, respectful language, and address each concern you think your readers may have. Also, keep your audience's knowledge level in mind as you draft.

Present Strong Support for Your Argument Use the evidence you've gathered to support each point you make. Your argument is only as strong as the support you offer.

Use a Persuasive Tone Carefully choose your words and phrases to make readers eager to agree with your views. When discussing zoos, for example, you might mention the "cold iron bars" and the "harsh fluorescent light" of the cages.

APPLYING LANGUAGE SKILLS: Types of Sentences

To enliven your writing, use different **types of sentences**, including simple sentences (a subject and verb), compound sentences (two independent clauses connected by a conjunction), and complex sentences (a main clause and one or more subordinate clauses).

Simple Sentence:
Seventy percent of the student body reads the school paper.

Compound Sentence:
The articles educate students on current events, and the columns entertain students and teachers alike.

Complex Sentence:
Because some people were upset by a few recent articles, they are calling for the paper to be censored.

Writing Application Make sure that your persuasive essay has a variety of sentence structures.

Writer's Solution Connection Writing Lab

To tailor your writing for a specific audience, complete the Audience Profile in the Writing Lab tutorial on Persuasion.

Prewriting
To help students find topics for their persuasive essays, have them work in small groups to brainstorm for a list of the most important issues in the school, home, and community. Have one student be the notetaker. Students can use the notes from the session as possible topics for essays.

Customize for
English Language Learners
These students may have trouble with *would* and *should,* words they will probably want to use in a persuasive essay. Explain to them that *would* is used to express a wish or customary action. (Would that I had listened! I would ride the same bus every day.) *Should* expresses a condition or obligation. (If he should stay. We should go in order to meet her.)

 Writer's Solution

Writing Lab CD-ROM
Before students begin drafting, have them consult the screen on deciding what type of organization to use in the Organizing Details and Information section of the tutorial on Persuasion.

Drafting
Encourage students to draft their persuasive essays in a single sitting, without pausing to labor over a single word or to correct a grammatical error. Once students have completed a draft, they'll have an opportunity to go back into their work and make extensive revisions.

Applying Language Skills

Types of Sentences Tell students that their essays will be much more interesting—and persuasive—if they vary their sentence types to include simple, compound, and complex sentences.

 Writer's Solution

For additional instruction and practice, have students complete the **Language Lab CD-ROM** lesson on Varying Sentence Structure and the practice pages 121–123 on Varying Your Sentences in the *Writer's Solution Grammar Practice Book.*

Applying Language Skills

Parallel Structure Tell students that using parallel structure will make their essays easier to read and therefore more persuasive.

Answers
Suggested response:
At Yellowstone you can ride a bike, or take a hike.

 Writer's Solution

Have students complete the **Language Lab CD-ROM** lesson on Eliminating Unnecessary Words and the practice pages 64–65 on Faulty Parallelism in the *Writer's Solution Grammar Practice Book.*

Revising

Have the peer reviewer poke holes in the argument. The writer can then use these criticisms when revising the essay.

 Writer's Solution

Writing Lab CD-ROM
The Revising and Editing section of the tutorial on Persuasion contains a Persuasion Word Bin. Have students consult this resource.

Publishing

Encourage students to discuss their essays with readers, especially those with different views.

Reinforce and Extend

Review the Writing Guidelines
Review the characteristics of a persuasive essay. Encourage students to come up with additional criteria.

Connection to Literature Unit 7, Nonfiction, contains two persuasive essays (p. 587 and p. 590).

Applying Language Skills: Parallel Structure

Use **parallel structure,** or similar grammatical form, to express similar ideas. The similarity in form helps readers recognize the similarity in content and makes the writing easier to remember.

Not Parallel:
In the Rocky Mountains, avalanches are one threat, and you also have to watch out for flash floods.

Parallel:
In the Rocky Mountains, avalanches are one threat, *while flash floods are another.*

Practice On your paper, correct the faulty parallelism in the following sentence.

At Yellowstone you can take a bike ride, and hiking is fun, too.

Writing Application Review your persuasive essay, and look for places where you can use parallel structure.

Writer's Solution Connection Language Lab

For more practice with parallel structure, complete the Language Lab lesson on Varying Sentence Structure.

Revising

Hold a Peer Conference Share your draft with a classmate, and get some feedback. Use the comments as guidelines for revising your essay. Ask your peer these questions:
- ▶ Have I anticipated all my readers' questions?
- ▶ How well have I appealed to my audience?
- ▶ How persuasive is the tone in my writing?

REVISION MODEL

What advantages would a student gain by working at a job after a day of school? ①One disadvantage might be that the student would not be able to keep up with his or her school work. On the other hand, the The student may feel more independent as a result of having new ②adult responsibilities ③ On the whole, I believe the advantages outweigh the disadvantages. and a little extra money.

① The writer deletes this line, which strays from his topic sentence.

② The writer replaces the word <u>new</u> with the more precise <u>adult.</u>

③ This sentence completes the essay.

Publishing

- ▶ **Classroom** Invite classmates to read your persuasive essay. Encourage them to share their opinions.
- ▶ **Newspaper** Send your essay to your school or local newspaper as a letter to the editor.
- ▶ **Internet** Post your essay on a bulletin board or class Web site. See what responses you receive.

✓ ASSESSMENT		4	3	2	1
PORTFOLIO ASSESSMENT Use the rubric on Persuasion in the *Alternative Assessment* booklet (p. 105) to assess students' writing. Add these criteria to customize the rubric to this assignment.	**Sentence Variety**	Writing includes an outstanding mix of simple, compound, and complex sentences. Essay flows naturally from one point to the next.	Writing includes a mix of simple, compound, and complex sentences. Essay flows from one point to the next.	Writing varies types of sentences only occasionally; more variety is needed. Essay is slightly monotonous.	One type of sentence predominates, making the essay awkward and hindering the flow of ideas.
	Parallelism	Parallelism is used to help drive the important points home.	Parallelism is used occasionally.	Parallelism is not used; sentences are otherwise clear.	Parallelism is not used; sentences contain unnecessary words and phrases.

Real-World Reading Skills Workshop

Building Research Skills

Strategies for Success

You've done research for term papers and class projects, so you probably already know how to use basic sources such as an encyclopedia. (If you wish to review the use of basic sources, turn to the Research Handbook on p. 982.) There are many other resources available that, although they may require a little extra time to master, will reward you with in-depth information on some of the most obscure topics.

Surf the Net The Internet provides Home Pages on almost every conceivable topic. Evaluate the source before you use it as an authority on a topic, as anyone with access to the Internet can create a Home Page.

Make the Government Work for You The state and federal governments can provide a great deal of useful information. Demographics, voting patterns, and explanations of legislation are just a few of the types of information available. Government organizations also publish pamphlets on topics ranging from starting your own business to nutritional studies.

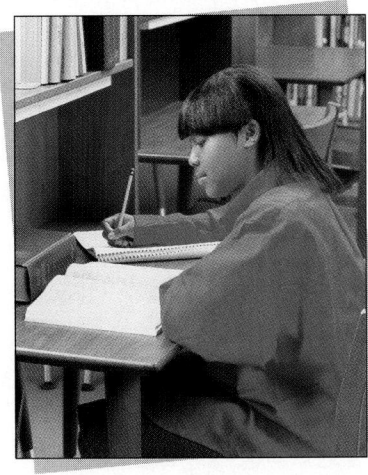

Keeping It Local Your community has many research resources available, too. Ask a librarian to show you how to use the *Readers' Guide to Periodical Literature,* which lists magazine articles by topic and tells you where to find them. While you're in the library, use an electronic card catalog to do a subject search. You may also wish to call or write your local government, requesting information on the topic you're researching.

Ask Questions Another way to build your research skills is to ask questions about the topic you are researching and, if possible, interview an expert on the topic. Use the Yellow Pages to find organizations or companies that might help you in your research. Call to inquire about literature that can be sent to you, or ask to speak to a person who may be able to answer your questions.

Apply the Strategy

Explain how you would do research for each of the following situations. Be specific about which sources you would use and why.

1. You want to learn about famous mountain climbers for an oral report.
2. You want to create a chart comparing the unemployment statistics for 1991 and 1995.
3. You want information on defensive driving to improve your driving safety.

✔ Here are other situations in which it's important to evaluate the persuasive message:
- ▶ Political campaigns
- ▶ Sales messages
- ▶ Product information

Introduce the Strategy

Students will be familiar with research from the essays they have had to write for social studies and history classes. Many of them will be familiar with the resources of the World Wide Web, though not necessarily for research purposes. Explain to students that the ability to get good information quickly will help them not only with term papers, but also with performing tasks such as finding out at the last moment about a company with which you have a job interview.

Customize for
English Language Learners

Emphasize to these students that being persistent and asking lots of questions are more important than having a perfect command of the English language.

Apply the Strategy

Answers

1. A library catalog or the World Wide Web would be excellent sources of information. Executing a keyword search using the term "mountain climber" would turn up a number of articles or sites devoted to the sport and its more famous practitioners.
2. The Bureau of Labor and Statistics in Washington, D. C., would be the best source for this information.
3. The local Department of Motor Vehicles would probably have the most pertinent and up-to-date materials for this topic.

Speaking and Listening Workshop

Introduce the Strategy

Movies are the most popular purely entertainment medium in the country, so students will no doubt have seen many movies—probably more than books they have read—and will have opinions on all or most of them. Explain to students that once they start viewing movies with a critical eye, they may begin to reevaluate films they had previously liked and better appreciate those quality films that they do like.

Apply the Strategy

Answers

Good evaluations will take into account the following factors: development and depth of characters, quality of dialogue, development and believability of plot, quality of acting, and quality of sound and cinematography.

Thumbs up, thumbs down . . . almost everyone understands these movie ratings. However, rating a movie isn't as simple as saying it was good or bad. When you judge a movie, you should look closely at its treatment of various elements—characters, acting, plot, visuals, special effects—and evaluate the quality of each element. A movie that is a "zero" in plot believability may be a "ten" in special effects. The following strategies will help you to evaluate movies.

Set Criteria Set criteria by which to judge the movie. As you watch the performances, ask yourself: Are the characters believable? Is the acting convincing? Is the dialogue realistic? Are plot events logical for this type of movie? Should any scenes be longer or shorter? Are the special effects original?

Apply the Strategies

1. You are a film critic on your local cable channel. Evaluate a film stating what you liked and disliked about it.
2. Evaluate a movie you've seen in one of your classes. Discuss with a partner whether or not it was an engaging film and why.
3. Rent a film and watch it with a friend or family member. Then present a "movie review," evaluating it for your class. Conclude with your decision whether or not to give the film the "thumbs up."

Tips for Evaluating Movies

▶ Avoid reading film reviews before you go to the movies. Film reviews sometimes reveal plot surprises, and they may influence your opinions and evaluation of the film.

▶ Arrive on time at the theater. It is difficult to give a fair or accurate evaluation of a film if you miss the first fifteen minutes. Similarly, if you are watching a video, try to watch the movie in its entirety, even if that means unplugging the phone for a few hours.

▶ Be specific. When you respond to the dialogue, be clear in your mind whether it is the writing or the acting that is influencing your opinion.

▶ Ask yourself questions about what you liked and disliked. Were the characters and story line engaging? Why or why not? Did you find the plot and characters believable? Why or why not?

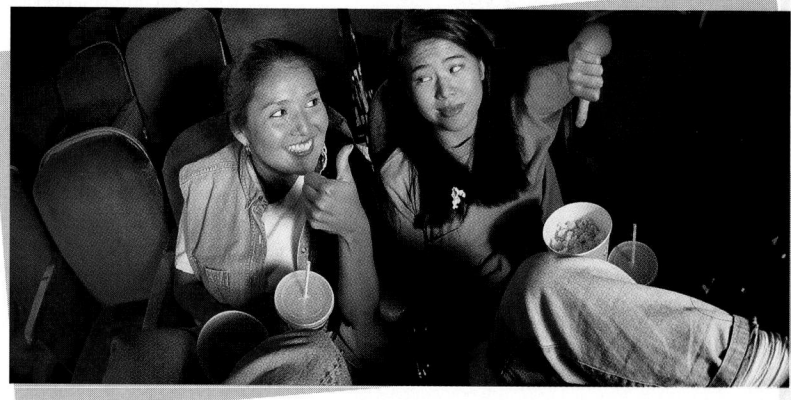

Extended Reading Opportunities

Brevity, clarity, vivid imagery: These are the common characteristics of short stories. The following collections of short stories will help you further appreciate this popular genre.

Suggested Titles

Great Modern European Short Stories
Douglas and Sylvia Angus, Editors

This anthology features modern classics by such noted European authors as Anton Chekhov, James Joyce, Joseph Conrad, D. H. Lawrence, Jean-Paul Sartre, Albert Camus, Franz Kafka, Isaac Bashevis Singer, Katherine Mansfield, and W. Somerset Maugham. In these brief works of fiction, the authors explore topics and themes that are relevent in any time and place.

Space Opera: An Anthology of Way-Back-When Futures
Brian W. Aldiss, Editor

This anthology features works by Isaac Asimov, George Griffiths, and Philip K. Dick, and others. These masters of the science-fiction genre offer a variety of perspectives on where technology is taking us and what the future holds.

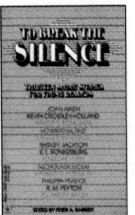

To Break the Silence
Peter A. Barnett, Editor

This collection of short stories deals with issues and themes of interest to teens. These works of short fiction depict realistic characters in stories about friendship, challenges, and courage. Written by celebrated British and American authors, the stories entertain and enrich while offering insights into the elements of short fiction. Authors include Joan Aiken, Langston Hughes, and Phillipa Pearce.

Other Possibilities

Other Voices, Other Vistas: Short Stories From Africa, China, India, Japan, and Latin America

Barbara Solomon, Editor

The Eye of the Heart

Barbara Howes, Editor

The Death of Ivan Ilych and Other Stories

Leo Tolstoy

Planning Students' Extended Reading

All of the works listed on this page are good choices for short stories. Following is some information that may help you choose which to teach.

Customize for
Varying Student Needs

When assigning the selections in this part to your students, keep in mind the following factors:

- *Great Modern European Short Stories* has many challenging works by acknowledged masters that students are likely to encounter in college. It is more appropriate for more advanced students.

- *Space Opera: An Anthology of Way-Back-When Futures* will appeal to fans of science fiction.

- The stories in *To Break the Silence* deal with specifically teenage issues, and would be a good choice for students who may not like to read.

Planning Instruction and Assessment

Unit Objectives

1. To read a variety of types of non-fiction
2. To apply a variety of reading strategies appropriate for reading nonfiction
3. To recognize literary elements used in these selections
4. To increase vocabulary
5. To learn elements of grammar and usage
6. To write in a variety of modes and about situations based on the selections
7. To develop speaking and listening skills by doing proposed activities

Meeting the Objectives

With each selection, you will find instructional material and portfolio opportunities through which students can meet these objectives. Further, you will find additional practice pages for reading strategies, literary elements, vocabulary, and grammar in the **Selection Support** booklet in the Teaching Resources box.

Setting Goals Work with your students at the beginning of the unit to set goals for unit outcomes. Plan what skills and concepts you wish students to acquire. You may individualize according to students' performance levels or learning modalities.

Portfolios You may have students keep portfolios of their work or of their work in progress. The activities and prompts on the Build Your Portfolio page of each selection provide opportunities for students to apply the concepts presented with the selection.

The Last Painter on Earth, 1983, James Doolin, Koplin Gallery, Los Angeles, California

Humanities: Art

The Last Painter on Earth, 1983, by James Doolin.

Ask students to apply the title to what they see in the painting. They should understand that the shadow represents a painter at his easel, and that the landscape is meant to suggest a post-cataclysmic vision of Earth, an Earth more like the moon or Mars. The light looks as if the sun is setting, so the painter may be trying to catch the last light of day. Encourage students to recognize the futuristic or fantastic quality to the painting, in contrast to a standard self-portrait or landscape.

Help students link the art to the focus of Unit 7, "Nonfiction," by answering the following questions:

1. In what ways is this painting like a persuasive essay? *By showing a barren Earth, the painting argues in favor of protecting the environment or against nuclear weapons.*

2. Why might "the last painter on Earth" continue to paint, and what might he be painting? *The last painter on Earth might continue to paint to take his mind off his loneliness, or because he wants to leave a record of what he sees, or because he finds this strange landscape compelling to paint. He might be painting this eerily beautiful landscape or painting a greener, populated one from memory.*

Nonfiction

Nonfiction introduces you to a wide variety of real people and places—some that are familiar to you and some that are far from your experience. Through the essays, biographies, and articles in this section, you can enjoy new experiences, consider new ideas, and learn new concepts.

Assessing Student Progress

The following tools are available to measure the degree to which students meet the unit objectives:

Informal Assessment

The questions on the Guide for Responding sections are a first level of response to the concepts and skills presented with the selection. Students' responses are a brief informal measure of their grasp of the material. Their responses on this level can indicate where further instruction and practice are needed. You may then follow up with the practice pages in the *Selection Support* booklet.

You will find literature and reading guides in the *Alternative Assessment* booklet, which you may give students on an individual basis for informal assessment of their performance.

Formal Assessment

In the *Formal Assessment* booklet, you will find selection tests and part tests.

Selection Tests The selection tests measure comprehension and skills acquisition for each selection or group of selections.

Part Tests Each part test applies the unit skills on a broader level. The Critical Reading section measures Unit Objectives 1, 2, and 3. The Vocabulary and Grammar section measures Objectives 4 and 5. The Essay section measures Objectives 1 and 6.

♦ 567

Alternative Assessment

Portfolios As you review individual pieces or the collected work in students' portfolios, you will find assessment sheets available in the portfolio section of the *Alternative Assessment* booklet.

Scoring Rubrics You will find scoring rubrics for writing modes in the *Alternative Assessment* booklet. You can apply these to Writing Mini-Lessons and to Writing Process Workshop lessons.

Speaking and Listening The *Alternative Assessment* booklet contains assessment sheets for speaking and listening activities.

Learning Modalities The *Alternative Assessment* contains activities that appeal to different learning styles. You may use these as an alternative measurement of students' growth.

Guide for Reading

OBJECTIVES

1. To read, comprehend, and interpret an essay
2. To relate an essay to personal experience
3. To use strategies for reading nonfiction to read for success
4. To recognize features of an expository essay
5. To build vocabulary in context and learn the suffix *-able*
6. To recognize linking verbs and subject complements
7. To write a proposal for a nature documentary using transitions to show comparisons
8. To respond to the essay through writing, speaking and listening, and projects

SKILLS INSTRUCTION

Vocabulary:
Suffixes: *-able*

Grammar:
Linking Verbs and Subject Complements

Reading for Success:
Strategies for Reading Nonfiction

Literary Focus:
Expository Essay

Writing:
Transitions to Show Comparisons

Speaking and Listening:
Poetry Reading (teacher edition)

Critical Viewing:
Speculate; Evaluate; Analyze; Connect; Compare and Contrast

PORTFOLIO OPPORTUNITIES

Writing: Letter; Nature Report; Cause-and-Effect Essay

Writing Mini-Lesson: Proposal for a Nature Documentary

Speaking and Listening: Poetry Reading; Conservation Speech

Projects: Art Exhibit; The Living Sea

More About the Author

Rachel Carson's love of trees and flowers stemmed from her childhood on a large property filled with orchards, fields, and forests in the Allegheny Valley of Pennsylvania. Carson's mother helped foster her interest in books and writing as well as her love for animals. Although she majored in zoology in college, Carson always knew she would combine her three loves and write books about nature.

Rachel Carson (1907–1964)

Rachel Carson was successful in combining the two compelling interests of her life—nature and writing—into a career that spanned nearly a half century.

Nature's Inspiration Born in Springdale, Pennsylvania, Carson was a naturalist who specialized in marine biology—the study of sea life. Carson spent several summers during college at the Woods Hole Oceanographic Institution in Massachusetts. She later observed, "I am sure that the genesis of *The Sea Around Us* (1951) belongs to that first year at Woods Hole, when I began storing away facts about the sea—facts discovered in scientific literature or by personal observation and experience."

Environmental Crusader In her writing, Carson stressed the interrelation of all living things and the dependence of human welfare on natural processes.

In *Silent Spring* (1962), her most controversial book, Carson drew attention to the horrors and possible disaster resulting from wasteful and destructive uses of pesticides. *Silent Spring* caused such an uproar that it prompted President Kennedy to announce a federal investigation and helped launch the modern environmental movement.

Awards and Accolades Rachel Carson's writing helped lead to the establishment of the Environmental Protection Agency (EPA) in 1970 and to an overall environmental awareness. She received numerous honors and awards, including a National Book Award for *The Sea Around Us*, and honorary degrees in both science and literature.

At the time of her death in 1964, Carson was in the process of finishing her revisions of *The Sense of Wonder*, a book that enables children to share some of her love and enjoyment of nature.

◆ Build Vocabulary

SUFFIXES: *-able*

Rachel Carson calls the "marginal world"—the area where the land and sea meet—a *mutable* region. *Mutable* combines the root *-mut-*, meaning "change," with the suffix *-able*, meaning "that can or will be." A *mutable* region therefore is one that "can or is able to change." *Mutable* appropriately describes the edge of the sea, where the crashing surf and changing tides ensure that nothing remains in one state for long.

mutable
ephemeral
primeval
essence
marginal
subjectively
manifestations
cosmic

WORD BANK

Before you read, preview this list of words from the selection.

◆ Build Grammar Skills

LINKING VERBS AND SUBJECT COMPLEMENTS

In her descriptions of the "marginal world," Carson frequently uses sentences with linking verbs and subject complements. **Linking verbs** express a state of being rather than action. They link the subject with a **subject complement**—a noun, pronoun or adjective that identifies or elaborates on the subject.

                 s   lv   sc
The *edge* of the sea *is* a strange and beautiful *place*.

The link between a subject and a subject complement is so close that the sentence is like an equation: subject = complement. This pattern is effective for making descriptive statements.

Prentice Hall Literature Program Resources

REINFORCE / RETEACH / EXTEND

Selection Support Pages
Build Vocabulary: Suffixes: *-able,* p. 167
Build Grammar Skills: Linking Verbs and Subject Complements, p. 168
Reading for Success: Strategies for Reading Nonfiction, pp. 169–170
Literary Focus: Expository Essay, p. 171

Strategies for Diverse Student Needs, p. 41

Beyond Literature Cross Curricular Connection: *Science: Marine Biology,* p. 41

Formal Assessment Selection Test, pp. 145–147; Assessment Resources Software

Alternative Assessment, p. 41

Writing and Language Transparencies
Comparison-and-Contrast Organizer, pp. 96–98

Daily Language Practice Week 20, p. 131

Resource Pro CD-ROM
"The Marginal World"—includes all resource materials and customizable lesson plan

 Listening to Literature Audiocassettes
"The Marginal World"

The Marginal World

◆ *Literature and Your Life*

CONNECT YOUR EXPERIENCE

What place has special meaning for you? Perhaps a walk along the rocky shore holds fond memories of childhood vacations, or the local park in your town reminds you of good times with your friends. For Rachel Carson, the author of "The Marginal World," the edge of the sea is a special place of beauty and wonder.

Journal Writing Jot down your fondest memories of a place that has special meaning for you. What made it so special? What did you learn or gain from going there?

THEMATIC FOCUS: IN AWE OF NATURE

As a scientist specializing in marine biology, Rachel Carson spent her life preserving our living Earth. Her essay provides some answers to the question, "Why should people care for the environment?"

◆ Background for Understanding

SCIENCE

In "The Marginal World," Rachel Carson describes the intertidal zone of the ocean—the zone between the high and low tide marks. Animals and organisms that live in this area must adapt to very changeable, and often harsh, conditions—periodic exposure to air and sun, changes in temperature, rain that dilutes salt water, evaporation that increases the salt level of tidal pools, and wave action.

Despite these changing conditions, many organisms thrive here because they adapt to the tidal actions by burrowing in sand, by living in tidal pools or crevices of rocks, or by living within a protective shell.

The adaptability and survival of these organisms is crucial to the survival of other sea-dwelling creatures—and even to human survival. This diverse food chain that begins with tiny microorganisms is a crucial system that acts as a lifeline for countless species.

◆ Literary Focus

EXPOSITORY ESSAY

An **expository essay** is a piece of short nonfiction writing that informs by explaining, defining, or interpreting an idea, an event, or a process. Writers may develop expository essays in many ways, including analyzing, interpreting, or classifying information; giving illustrations; comparing and contrasting ideas; or presenting causes and effects.

In "The Marginal World," Rachel Carson uses examples to illustrate her points, classifies the different types of life found on the sea's edge, and explains the cause-and-effect relationships that affect the survival of these plants and animals. She organizes her observations by focusing on different places at different times of day.

Use a chart like the one shown to jot down details about each time and place.

Time and Place	Observations

Interest Grabber Have students look at the palms of their hands. To make the point that life exists on both visible and microscopic levels, show them a picture of skin cells from a science book or magazine. Suggest that looking at living things at a microscopic level can reveal whole new worlds. Rachel Carson uses this close focus to observe what happens in the place she calls "the marginal world"—that ever-changing sliver of space between land and sea. Where we might simply see a strip of sand, her close focus allows us to see that this limited space teems with animal and plant life.

Customize for
Less Proficient Readers
Help these students to identify the main ideas of the first two paragraphs. Discuss how other ideas in the paragraphs relate to these main ideas. Encourage them to look for the link between main and supporting ideas in each paragraph of "The Marginal World."

Customize for
More Advanced Students
Ask students to pay attention to the author's style as they read. What stylistic qualities differentiate this expository essay from other science writing they have read? What techniques does Carson borrow from poetry or fiction?

Customize for
English Language Learners
Use maps, pictures, and diagrams to illustrate specialized vocabulary found in this selection. For instance, English language learners may need a visual reference for terms such as *sediments, continental margins, niche, basin, tentacle, flats,* and *cove.*

Customize for
Logical/Mathematical Learners
These students might enjoy working together to create a classification chart of the animal and plant life in "The Marginal World." (For example, the phylum *Mollusca* includes the species lobster and ghost crab.) Encourage them to display their chart for classmates.

✎ Preparing for Standardized Tests

Reading and Vocabulary The five Reading for Success strategies presented with this selection will help students with reading comprehension items on standardized tests. Students are often called upon to identify the main idea and their supporting ideas in nonfiction passages; in this selection they will practice applying these strategies. For additional practice, use Reading for Success Strategies: Strategies for Reading Nonfiction, in **Selection Support,** pp. 169–170.

Understanding how a suffix such as *-able* changes the part of speech of a word can help

students apply meaning in vocabulary items or reading comprehension items. For additional practice, use the Build Vocabulary page in **Selection Support,** p. 167.

Grammar and Language The grammar focus for this lesson is linking verbs and subject complements. Understanding these functions will help students on the grammar and usage items for standardized tests. For additional practice, use the Build Grammar Skills page on Linking Verbs and Subject Complements, p. 168, in **Selection Support.**

The Reading for Success page in each unit presents a set of problem-solving procedures to help readers understand authors' words and ideas on multiple levels. Good readers develop a bank of strategies from which they can draw as needed.

Unit 7 introduces strategies for reading nonfiction. These strategies give readers an approach for breaking down and understanding concepts, support, and structure in nonfiction text. By using these strategies as they read, students will be better able to analyze and evaluate the nonfiction material.

These strategies for reading nonfiction are modeled with "The Marginal World." Each green box shows an example of the thinking process involved in applying one of these strategies.

How to Use the Reading for Success Page

- Introduce the strategies for reading nonfiction, presenting each as a problem-solving procedure. Be sure students understand what each strategy involves and under what circumstances to apply it.

- Before students read the essay, have them preview it, looking at the annotations in the green boxes that model the strategies.

- To reinforce these strategies after students have read "The Marginal World," have students do the Reading for Success pages in *Selection Support,* pp. 169–170. This activity gives students an opportunity to read a selection and practice strategies for reading nonfiction by writing their own annotations.

Reading for Success

Strategies for Reading Nonfiction

Probably the majority of what you read is nonfiction—your textbooks, newspaper and magazine articles, information on the Internet. Reading nonfiction can open doors to new worlds, introduce you to interesting people, and help you to look at ideas and events in new ways. Because most nonfiction deals with information, concepts, or ideas, you will benefit from strategies that help you analyze it.

Recognize the author's purpose.

Consider *why* the author is writing. What ideas or information does the author want to convey, or how does he or she want you to respond to this piece of writing? By being aware of the author's purpose, you can read with the same purpose and accept the writer's ideas, or you can be prepared to question what the writer is saying.

Identify the author's main points.

Sort out the main points the writer is making. If you're reading a textbook or news article, use the heads to help you identify the important points.

Identify support for the author's points.

Notice how the writer supports the points he or she makes. The author's reasoning and evidence should be believable and should lead you to understand and accept the points. If you find the support unsatisfactory, you may not accept the writer's ideas.

Recognize patterns of organization.

Noticing how the material is presented and developed can help you understand it. The writer may present material in a number of ways: explaining events chronologically, building up ideas in order of importance, comparing and contrasting ideas or things, showing the effects of causes, and so on.

Vary your reading rate.

You may read different kinds of nonfiction material at different rates, depending on your own purpose. When you're reading information that you need to remember, read slowly and attentively, perhaps even pausing to jot down notes. If you're looking for a fact or a single piece of information, you may want to skim very quickly, not trying to remember everything but looking only for the information you need.

As you read the following work of nonfiction by Rachel Carson, look at the notes in the boxes. These notes demonstrate how to apply the above strategies to a piece of literature.

Reading Strategies: Support and Reinforcement

Appropriate Reading Strategies Students are given a reading strategy to apply in reading each selection. All of the reading strategies in this unit apply to aspects of nonfiction. In other selections a strategy is suggested that is appropriate to the selection.

Reading Prompts To encourage application of the given reading strategy, there are occasional prompts, within green boxes, at appropriate and significant points. In addition, there are red boxes prompting application of the Literary Focus concept and maroon boxes prompting students to connect with their lives.

Using the Boxed Annotations and Prompts

The material in the green, red, and maroon boxes along the sides of selections is intended to help students apply the literary element and the reading strategy and to make a connection with their lives.

You may use the boxed material in these ways:

- Have students pause when they come to a box and respond to its prompt before they continue reading.

- Urge students to read through the selection ignoring the boxes. After they have read the selection completely, they may go back and review the selection, responding to the prompts.

The Marginal World

Rachel Carson

The edge of the sea is a strange and beautiful place. All through the long history of Earth it has been an area of unrest where waves have broken heavily against the land, where the tides have pressed forward over the continents, receded, and then returned. For no two successive days is the shoreline precisely the same. Not only do the tides advance and retreat in their eternal rhythms, but the level of the sea itself is never at rest. It rises or falls as the glaciers melt or grow, as the floor of the deep ocean basins shifts under its increasing load of sediments, or as the earth's crust along the continental margins warps up or down in adjustment to strain and tension. Today a little more land may belong to the sea, tomorrow a little less. Always the edge of

◆ **Build Vocabulary**

mutable (my$\overline{oo}$t′ ə bəl) *adj.*: Capable of change

▲ Critical Viewing How does this photo support Carson's feelings about the sea? [Speculate] ❶

the sea remains an elusive and indefinable boundary. ❷

The shore has a dual nature, changing with the swing of the tides, belonging now to the land, now to the sea. On the ebb tide it knows the harsh extremes of the land world, being exposed to heat and cold, to wind, to rain and drying sun. On the flood tide it is a water world, returning briefly to the relative stability of the open sea. ❸

Only the most hardy and adaptable can survive in a region so mutable, yet the area

---

Develop Understanding

One-Minute Insight Although Carson imparts a great deal of scientific knowledge about tidal zones in her essay, the main focus is philosophical. In language that is more often poetic than scientific, Carson describes the sights, sounds, and feelings that contribute to her appreciation of this delicate and changeable region.

By presenting three different sections of the "marginal world" at three different times of day, Carson leads readers to recognize the beauty and interdependence of all life forms.

▶ Critical Viewing ◀

❶ **Speculate** The photograph focuses on one small and beautiful detail in nature; it seems to echo the awe and respect that Carson feels for the natural world of the sea.

◆ **Build Vocabulary**

❷ **Suffixes: -able** Have students determine the meaning of *indefinable* by combining the meaning of the prefix *in-* (without), the word root *-defin-* (determine; define) and the suffix *-able*. *Students should suggest "without ability to determine or define" or "unable to be defined."*

◆ **Reading for Success**

❸ **Recognize Patterns of Organization** Carson describes the dual nature of the shore, organizing her paragraph around the comparison. Ask students what two things are being compared. *The shore at ebb tide is compared to the shore at flood tide.*

Block Scheduling Strategies

Consider these suggestions to take advantage of extended class time:

- Have students complete the journal activity in Literature and Your Life (p. 569) and share their memories with the class.
- Together with students, review the information in Background for Understanding (p. 569). Give students the opportunity to explain in detail what they may have learned in science or biology class (or from other sources) about the food

chain—both in the sea and on land.

- Introduce the Reading for Success strategies for nonfiction. Remind students that they can effectively apply these strategies to all nonfiction selections they read. For more practice, students can use the Reading for Success page in **Selection Support,** pp. 169–170.
- Have students work in small groups to discuss their answers to the Critical Thinking Questions (p. 576).

- To help students complete the Writing Mini-Lesson (p. 578), show them the ***Writing and Language Transparencies:*** Comparison-and-Contrast Organizer, pp. 96–98. They can use this organizer to help them define and clarify points being compared. This activity will prepare them for the Writing Skills Focus: Transitions to Show Comparisons.

❶ Here Carson explores a place she especially loves. Have students share experiences they have had with places that they consider "exquisitely" beautiful. They might refer to the journal entries they wrote under Literature and Your Life on page 569.

▶ **Critical Viewing** ◀

❷ Evaluate Students may appreciate the strange beauty of the light filtering down through the water in this picture of a kelp forest. However, some students may point out that this is a picture of underwater sea life, rather than of the shore life or cave pool that Carson describes.

◆ **Build Grammar Skills**

❸ Linking Verbs and Subject Complements Ask students to identify the three linking verbs in this passage. Have them identify the subject and complement of each linking verb. Finally, ask students to determine the part of speech for each complement. *Linking verbs: was, were, was; subjects: sky, water and air, moon; complements: full (adj,) pallid (adj,) disc (noun).*

> Carson's **main point** is that the creatures who have adapted to life at the edge of the sea have a unique strength and beauty.

between the tide lines is crowded with plants and animals. In this difficult world of the shore, life displays its enormous toughness and vitality by occupying almost every conceivable niche. Visibly, it carpets the intertidal rocks; or half hidden, it descends into fissures and crevices, or hides under boulders, or lurks in the wet gloom of sea caves. Invisibly, where the casual observer would say there is no life, it lies deep in the sand, in burrows and tubes and passageways. It tunnels into solid rock and bores into peat and clay. It encrusts weeds or drifting spars[1] or the hard, chitinous[2] shell of a lobster. It exists minutely, as the film of bacteria that spreads over a rock surface or a wharf piling; as spheres of protozoa, small as pinpricks, sparkling at the surface of the sea; and as Lilliputian[3] beings swimming through dark pools that lie between the grains of sand.

The shore is an ancient world, for as long as there has been an earth and sea there has been this place of the

> This reflection suggests that the author's **purpose** is to explain the world at the edge of the sea in such a way that readers will gain an awareness of its beauty and feel a connection with nature.

meeting of land and water. Yet it is a world that keeps alive the sense of continuing creation and of the relentless drive of life. Each time that I enter it, I gain some new awareness of its beauty and its deeper meanings, sensing that intricate fabric of life by which one creature is linked with another, and each with its surroundings.

❶ In my thoughts of the shore, one place stands apart for its revelation of exquisite beauty. It is a pool hidden within a cave that one can visit only rarely and briefly when the lowest of the year's low tides fall below it, and

---

1. **spars** (spärs) *n.*: Masts, booms, or other supports for sails.
2. **chitinous** (kĭ′ tən əs) *adj.*: Of a material which forms the tough outer covering of insects, crustaceans, and so on.
3. **Lilliputian** (lil′ ə pyoo′ shən) *adj.*: Tiny and thus like the tiny people who inhabit Lilliput in the book *Gulliver's Travels* by Jonathan Swift.

▲ **Critical Viewing** How well does this photo capture the strange beauty Carson describes? [Evaluate] **❷**

perhaps from that very fact it acquires some of its special beauty. Choosing such a tide, I hoped for a glimpse of the pool. The ebb was to fall early in the morning. I knew that if the wind held from the northwest and no interfering swell ran in from a distant storm the level of the sea should drop below the entrance to the pool. There had been sudden ominous showers in the night, with rain like handfuls of gravel flung on the roof. When I looked out into the early morning the sky was full of a gray dawn light but the sun had not yet risen. Water and air were pallid. Across the bay the moon was a luminous disc in the western sky, suspended above the dim line of distant shore—the full August moon, drawing the tide to the low, low levels of the threshold of the alien sea world. As I watched, a gull flew by, above the spruces. Its **❸**

◆ **Build Vocabulary**

ephemeral (i fem′ ə rəl) *adj.*: Passing quickly

Beyond the Classroom

Career Connection
Oceanographer The study of the sea, oceanography, is broken into four spheres of study. Geological oceanographers study the rocks and minerals of the sea floor. Biological oceanographers study marine life. Chemical oceanographers study sea water's chemical makeup and the effect of those chemicals on the ocean environment. Physical oceanographers study currents, tides, and the movement of water.

Have students suggest aspects of the marginal world described by Carson that might interest each type of oceanographer. For example, a physical oceanographer might be interested in measuring the difference between ebb and flood tides.

Community Connection
Protected Wetlands The marginal world described by Carson is threatened by pollution, excessive building along shorelines, and erosion due to destruction of plant life.

Many shores and other wetlands, such as swamps and bogs, are now protected, which means that laws exist to prevent their destruction.

Students may know of protected wetlands in your area. Have volunteers describe any such wetlands they have visited. Alternatively, suggest that students research how the protection of wetlands during the last two decades has affected the survival of specific bird and animal species.

breast was rosy with the light of the unrisen sun. The day was, after all, to be fair.

Later, as I stood above the tide near the entrance to the pool, the promise of that rosy light was sustained. From the base of the steep wall of rock on which I stood, a moss-covered ledge jutted seaward into deep water. In the surge at the rim of the ledge the dark fronds of oarweeds swayed, smooth and gleaming as leather. The projecting ledge was the path to the small hidden cave and its pool. Occasionally a swell, stronger than the rest, rolled smoothly over the rim and broke in foam against the cliff. But the intervals between such swells were long enough to admit me to the ledge and long enough for a glimpse of that fairy pool, so seldom and so briefly exposed.

And so I knelt on the wet carpet of sea moss and looked back into the dark cavern that held the pool in a shallow basin. The floor of the cave was only a few inches below the roof, and a mirror had been created in which all that grew on the ceiling was reflected in the still water below.

Under water that was clear as glass the pool was carpeted with green sponge. Gray patches of sea squirts[4] glistened on the ceiling and colonies of soft coral[5] were a pale apricot color. In the moment when I looked into the cave a little elfin starfish hung down, suspended by the merest thread, perhaps by only a single tube foot. It reached down to touch its own reflection, so perfectly delineated that there might have been, not one starfish, but two. The beauty of the reflected

> Carson **supports her main point** by describing the strength and beauty of a starfish clinging to a ledge of the cave.

▲ Critical Viewing What characteristics of the crab have helped it survive living in the harsh sea? [Analyze] ❹

4. **sea squirts:** Sac-shaped water animals with tough outer coverings.
5. **coral** (kôr´ əl) *n*.: Animals with tentacles at the top of tubelike bodies.

images and of the limpid[6] pool itself was the poignant[7] beauty of things that are ephemeral, existing only until the sea should return to fill the little cave.

Whenever I go down into this magical zone of the low water of the spring tides, I look for the most delicately beautiful of all the shore's inhabitants—flowers that are not plant but animal, blooming on the threshold of the deeper sea. In that fairy cave I was not disappointed. Hanging from its roof were the pendent[8] flowers of the hydroid Tubularia, pale pink, fringed and delicate as the wind flower. Here were creatures so exquisitely fashioned that they seemed unreal, their beauty too fragile to exist in a world of crushing force. Yet every detail was functionally useful, every stalk and hydranth[9] and petallike tentacle fashioned for dealing with

> With this example, Carson **supports her main point:** that the creatures at the edge of the sea have strength as well as beauty.

the realities of existence. I knew that they were merely waiting, in that moment of the tide's ebbing, for the return of the sea. Then in the rush of water, in the surge of surf and the pressure of the incoming tide, the delicate flower heads would stir with life. They would sway on their slender stalks, and their long tentacles would sweep the returning water, finding in it all that they needed for life.

And so in that enchanted place on the threshold of the sea the realities that possessed my mind were far from those of the land world I had left an hour before. In a different way the same sense of remoteness and of a world apart came to me in a twilight hour on a great beach on the coast of Georgia. I had come down after sunset and walked far out over sands that lay wet and gleaming, to the very

6. **limpid** (lim´ pid) *adj*.: Clear.
7. **poignant** (poin´ yənt) *adj*.: Emotionally moving.
8. **pendent** (pen´ dənt) *adj*.: Hanging.
9. **hydranth** (hī´ dranth) *n*.: Feeding structure.

❺

Customize for
Musical/Rhythmic Learners
Carson's descriptions of the sea often call to mind aspects of music: *rush of water, surge of surf, pressure of incoming tides.* Suggest that these students find descriptions in the selection that remind them of music. In a small group, they can compare and contrast the sounds of the sea to music. They might also want to create their own musical descriptions of the sea.

▶Critical Viewing◀

❹ **Analyze** Students may mention that the crab's hard outer shell protects it, and its legs move it across the rocky and sandy sea bottom.

♦ **Literary Focus**

❺ **Expository Essay** Point out the way in which Carson ends one description and moves directly into another. Ask: How does the author use comparison to make a transition in time and place in her essay? *She remarks that the same sense of remoteness came to her in both places, but in different ways.*

◆◆◆ **Speaking and Listening Mini-Lesson**

Poetry Reading
This mini-lesson supports the Speaking and Listening activity in the Idea Bank on page 578.

Introduce the Concept Tell students that of all the literary forms, poetry is perhaps the best for reading aloud because much of it uses musical devices such as rhythm and rhyme, alliteration, consonance and assonance. Successful poetry readers know how to pace their tone and emphasize certain

passages to bring out their musical qualities.

Develop Background Suggest that students find two or three poems about the ocean or the tides and then read them aloud to themselves to help determine which they would to recite for the class. You might recommend "The Tide Rises, The Tide Falls" by Henry Wordsworth Longfellow or George Gordon, Lord Byron's "Apostrophe to the Ocean" from *Childe Harold's Pilgrimage*.

Apply the Information Ask students to

practice their recitation before delivering it to the class. Allow time for students to present their readings to the class.

Assess the Outcome Have students evaluate their own readings by answering these questions: Did I speak clearly and fluently? Did I use my voice to bring out its emotion and musicality?

You may also have students use the Peer Assessment sheet for Oral Interpretation, page 119 in *Alternative Assessment*.

edge of the retreating sea. Looking back across that immense flat, crossed by winding, waterfilled gullies and here and there holding shallow pools left by the tide, I was filled with awareness that this intertidal area, although abandoned briefly and rhythmically by the sea, is always reclaimed by the rising tide. There at the edge of low water the beach with its reminders of the land seemed far away. The only sounds were those of the wind and the sea and the birds. There was one sound of wind moving over water, and another of water sliding over the sand and tumbling down the faces of its own wave forms. The flats were astir with birds, and the voice of the willet[10] rang insistently. One of them stood at the edge of the water and gave its loud, urgent cry; an answer came from far up the beach and the two birds flew to join each other.

The flats took on a mysterious quality as dusk approached and the last evening light was reflected from the scattered pools and creeks. Then birds became only dark shadows, with no color discernible. Sanderlings[11] scurried across the beach like little ghosts, and here and there the darker forms of the willets stood out. Often I could come very close to them before they would start up in alarm—the sanderlings running, the willets flying up, crying. Black skimmers[12] flew along the ocean's edge silhouetted

10. **willet** (wil′ it) *n.*: Large, gray and white, long-legged wading bird.
11. **Sanderlings:** Small, gray and white birds found on sandy beaches.
12. **skimmers:** Long-winged sea birds.

 Critical Viewing How might the photographer's purpose be similar to Carson's? [Connect]

against the dull, metallic gleam, or they went flitting above the sand like large, dimly seen moths. Sometimes they "skimmed" the winding creeks of tidal water, where little spreading surface ripples marked the presence of small fish.

The shore at night is a different world, in which the very darkness that hides the distractions of daylight brings into sharper focus the elemental realities. Once, exploring the night beach, I surprised a small ghost crab in the searching beam of my torch. He was lying in a pit he had dug just above the surf, as though watching the sea and waiting. The blackness of the night possessed water, air, and beach. It was the darkness of an older world, before Man. There was no sound but the all-enveloping, primeval sounds of wind blowing over water and sand, and of waves crashing on the beach. There was no other visible life—just one small crab near the sea. I have seen hundreds of ghost crabs in other settings, but suddenly I was filled with the odd sensation that for the first time I knew the creature in its own world—that I understood, as never before, the essence of its being. In that moment time was suspended; the world to which I belonged did not exist and I might have been an onlooker from outer space. The little crab alone with the sea became a symbol that stood for life itself—for the delicate, destructible, yet incredibly vital force that somehow holds its place amid the harsh realities of the inorganic world.

The sense of creation comes with memories

Cross-Curricular Connection: Science

Crustaceans Crustaceans such as crabs are among the oldest forms of life. Scientists believe that life began in the sea, and that sea creatures, in the process of evolution, gradually adapted themselves to life on land.

All crustaceans are covered by exoskeletons—bony shells. Most live in the ocean, but some live in fresh water, such as lakes and ponds, and a few live on land. Crabs, lobsters, and shrimp seem more similar to insects than to some other mollusks such as clams or octopuses. Students might like to use reference books to learn more about the features of crustaceans to determine their similarities to insects.

of a southern coast, where the sea and the mangroves,[13] working together, are building a wilderness of thousands of small islands off the southwestern coast of Florida, separated from each other by a tortuous[14] pattern of bays, lagoons, and narrow waterways, I remember a winter day when the sky was blue and drenched with sunlight; though there was no wind one was conscious of flowing air like cold clear crystal. I had landed on the surf-washed tip of one of those islands, and then worked my way around to the sheltered bay side. There I found the tide far out, exposing the broad mud flat of a cove bordered by the mangroves with their twisted branches, their glossy leaves, and their long prop roots reaching down, grasping and holding the mud, building the land out a little more, then again a little more.

> By **organizing** her essay around different examples of the edge of the sea at different times of day, Carson can share with readers the wide variety of life to be found at the edge of the sea.

The mud flats were strewn with the shells of that small, exquisitely colored mollusk,[15] the rose tellin, looking like scattered petals of pink roses. There must have been a colony nearby, living buried just under the surface of the mud. At first the only creature visible was a small heron in gray and rusty plumage—a reddish egret that waded across the flat with the stealthy, hesitant movements of its kind. But other land creatures had been there, for a line of fresh tracks wound in and out among the mangrove roots, marking the path of a raccoon feeding on the oysters that gripped the supporting roots with projections from their shells. Soon I found the tracks of a shore bird, probably a sanderling, and followed them a little; then they turned toward the water and were lost, for the tide had erased them and made them as though they had never been.

13. **mangroves** (maŋ´ grōvs) *n*.: Tropical trees that grow in swampy ground with spreading branches that send down roots and thus form more trunks.
14. **tortuous** (tôr´ chōō wəs) *adj*.: Full of twists and turns.
15. **mollusk** (mäl´ əsk) *n*.: One of a large group of soft-bodied animals with shells, including clams and snails.

Looking out over the cove I felt a strong sense of the interchangeability of land and sea in this marginal world of the shore, and of the links between the life of the two. There was also an awareness of the past and of the continuing flow of time, obliterating much that had gone before, as the sea had that morning washed away the tracks of the bird.

The sequence and meaning of the drift of time were quietly summarized in the existence of hundreds of small snails—the mangrove periwinkles—browsing on the branches and roots of the trees. Once their ancestors had been sea dwellers, bound to the salt waters by every tie of their life processes. Little by little over the thousands and millions of years the ties had been broken, the snails had adjusted themselves to life out of water, and now today they were living many feet above the tide to which they only occasionally returned. And perhaps, who could say how many ages hence, there would be in their descendants not even this gesture of remembrance for the sea.

> Here, Carson reinforces her **purpose**, to create in the reader a feeling of connection with nature.

The spiral shells of other snails—these quite minute[16]—left winding tracks on the mud as they moved about in search of food. They were horn shells, and when I saw them I had a nostalgic moment when I wished I might see what Audubon[17] saw, a century and more ago. For such little horn shells were the food of the flamingo, once so numerous on this coast, and when I half closed

16. **minute** (mī nōōt´) *adj*.: Tiny.
17. **Audubon** (ôd´ ə bän´): John James Audubon (1785–1851), a famous ornithologist, naturalist, and painter famed for his paintings of North American birds.

◆ **Build Vocabulary**

primeval (prī mē´ vəl) *adj*.: Ancient or primitive
essence (es´ əns) *n*.: Real nature of something
marginal (mär´ jən əl) *adj*.: Occupying the borderland of a stable area

◆ **Reading for Success**

❹ **Identify Support for the Author's Points** In this section, the author explains *how* the marginal world can remind us of creation. Ask: How does this description support her main idea? *She shows how the mangroves build the land, creating it from the sea.*

◆ **Reading for Success**

❺ **Identify the Author's Main Points** Have students summarize the main idea in this paragraph. Let them know that they will not find one sentence that states the main idea—they will have to pull the main idea from several sentences. *One of the things we can learn by studying the marginal world is that even when the shore looks empty and barren, close observation reveals that life exists there.*

◆ **Critical Thinking**

❻ **Generalize** Ask students: What broader meaning about life does the author see in the snails' movement from sea to land? *The snails adaptation to a land environment over millions of years represents the force of evolution. It lets us know that we are connected to forms of life that came before us on the evolutionary scale and probably to life in the sea. It also indicates that evolution will continue, changing living things even more.*

❼ **Clarification** Explain that Carson mentions Audubon here, not only because he lived a century ago when flamingos were more numerous than they are today, but also because he was known as a keen observer of nature. Ask: What do you suppose has happened to the flamingos? *They may have been run out of the groves by hunting, pollution, or many other causes.*

The Marginal World ◆ 575

Workplace Skills Mini-Lesson

Powers of Observation

The observational skills Carson applies to the world of tide pools are vital for a zoologist but useful for other workers as well.

Introduce the Concept Discuss what it means to have acute powers of observation: to notice details, to pay close attention, to be aware of things that others might miss.

Develop Background Review some ways that students use powers of observation in their lives; for example, to find their way along an unfamiliar route or to notice that a friend got his or her hair trimmed.

Apply the Information Have students list three summer jobs they might like to have and explain how powers of observation might help them to succeed in each one. For example, as a lifeguard, they would have to be very observant of all the people and activity in or near the water.

Assess the Outcome Have volunteers share their ideas aloud. As a group, decide which of the described jobs requires the most acute powers of observation. Suggest that they write in their journals several techniques they might use to improve their powers of observation before applying for such jobs.

① Compare and Contrast
Students might observe that the leaves appear more translucent than plants that grow on land, and that they are more delicate in both color and texture than land plants.

◆ **Reading for Success**

② Vary Your Reading Rate
Suggest that students reread this sentence, slowing down to improve their understanding. Have them then paraphrase the author's statement. *Possible answer: The flamingos disappeared only a short while ago; sometimes a special occasion or place reminds us to think about the significance of time.*

◆ **Reading for Success**

③ Identify the Author's Main Point Ask students to explain why this is an important sentence. How is it related to the author's main point? *Her main point is that we can learn much by studying the sea. This sentence states that the sea is more than beautiful—it is meaningful; that is, there is meaning to be gained from studying it.*

Reinforce and Extend

Answers
◆ *Literature and Your Life*

Reader's Response Students could name any aspect of nature—underwater life, stars and planets, woodland life. They should give reasons for their choices.

Thematic Focus Students might say that this essay deepened their understanding of the interrelatedness of life forms.

☑ **Check Your Comprehension**
1. She describes a pool in a cave at dawn.
2. She sees a starfish suspended from the ceiling and reflected in the pool.
3. She sees the edge of the low waters where many birds dwell; the shore at night and a single crab; an island off the southwest coast of Florida where she sees the mollusk, rose tellin.

576

① ▲ **Critical Viewing** How does this plant differ from plants that grow on land? [Compare and Contrast]

② my eyes I could almost imagine a flock of these magnificent flame birds feeding in that cove, filling it with their color. It was a mere yesterday in the life of the earth that they were there; in nature, time and space are relative matters, perhaps most truly perceived <u>subjectively</u> in occasional flashes of insight, sparked by such a magical hour and place.

There is a common thread that links these scenes and memories—the spectacle of life in all its varied <u>manifestations</u> as it has appeared, evolved, and sometimes died out. Underlying the beauty of the spectacle there is meaning and significance. It is the elusiveness of that meaning that haunts us, that sends us again and again into the natural world where the key to the riddle is hidden. It sends us back to the edge of the sea, where the drama of life played its first scene on earth and perhaps even its prelude; where the forces of evolution are at work today, as they have been since the appearance of what we know as life; and where the spectacle of living creatures faced by the <u>cosmic</u> realities of their world is crystal clear. **③**

◆ **Build Vocabulary**
subjectively (səb jek´ tiv lē) *adv.*: Personally
manifestations (man´ ə fes tā shənz) *n.*: Appearances or evidence
cosmic (käz´ mik) *adj.*: Relating to the universe

Guide for Responding

◆ *Literature and Your Life*

Reader's Response What aspects of nature intrigue you?
Thematic Focus What have you learned about nature from reading this essay?
Nature Walk Visit a natural setting near your home or school. Identify three details you would describe to Carson.

☑ **Check Your Comprehension**

1. What time and special place does Carson describe first?
2. What special beauty does Carson find in this first place?
3. Summarize the other times, places, and experiences Carson describes.

Beyond Literature

Science Connection

Pesticides and the Environment
When *Silent Spring* was first published, many people criticized Carson as "hysterical." Today, however, we know that we must consider the impact of pesticides on all aspects of the natural world. For instance, DDT, which was once widely used for pest control, also affects animals and people that eat plants sprayed with DDT. The use of DDT is now banned in the United States.
Activity Find out more about the effects of DDT on people and wildlife and the reasons its use was banned in the United States.

 Beyond the Selection

FURTHER READING
Other Works by Rachel Carson
The Edge of the Sea
Silent Spring
Other Works With the Theme of Nature
Capturing Nature, John James Audubon
The Living Sea, Jacques-Yves Cousteau
Gentle Wilderness: The Sierra Nevada, John Muir
 We suggest that you preview these works before recommending them to students.

INTERNET
Students can learn more about Rachel Carson and her work at the following Web site on the Internet. Please be aware, however, that the site may have changed from the time we published this information.
http://www.teleport.com/~megaines/carson.htm
 An ecologically-minded newsletter based on Carson's life and work is located at **http://www. rachelcarson.org/newslett.html**
 We *strongly recommend* that you preview the sites before you send students to them.

Guide for Responding (continued)

◆ Critical Thinking

INTERPRET
1. Explain Carson's statement, "The shore has a dual nature." **[Interpret]**
2. What broader meaning about life does the "marginal world" Carson describes help you to see? **[Interpret]**
3. Think of another title for this essay—one that states the meaning of the essay for you. **[Connect]**

EVALUATE
4. Compare the three different locations described in the essay. What are their similarities and differences? **[Compare and Contrast]**

APPLY
5. What other places could help you experience the interconnectedness of life? **[Relate]**

◆ Reading for Success

STRATEGIES FOR READING NONFICTION
Review the reading strategies and notes showing how to read nonfiction. Then apply those strategies to answer the following questions.
1. What is the author's main purpose in writing this essay?
2. (a) What three points does the author make about the sea and the creatures who inhabit it? (b) Explain how Carson supports each point.

◆ Literary Focus

EXPOSITORY ESSAY
An **expository essay** explains a concept, event, or process. In presenting information about life at the edge of the ocean, Carson explains the way plants and animals adapt to the changing environment.
1. Identify three reasons that Carson provides about why the level of the sea changes.
2. Explain the differences Carson identifies between the shore at night and the shore in daylight.
3. Summarize the main points Carson makes about the "marginal world."

◆ Build Vocabulary

USING THE SUFFIX -able
The suffix -able means "capable of being." When added to the root of a word, it indicates the "ability" to do, provide, or be something.
On your paper, match each word ending in -able with the noun most closely associated with it.
1. perishable   **a.** truth
2. comfortable   **b.** couch
3. believable   **c.** food

USING THE WORD BANK
For each of the following pairs of words, write S on your paper if the words are synonyms and A if they are antonyms.
1. essence, heart
2. manifestations, forms
3. marginal, borderline
4. mutable, solid
5. subjectively, disinterestedly
6. cosmic, earthly
7. ephemeral, short-lived
8. primeval, contemporary

◆ Build Grammar Skills

LINKING VERBS AND SUBJECT COMPLEMENTS
Rachel Carson uses **subject complements** following **linking verbs** to describe life where the earth and sea come together.

> A **subject complement** is a noun, pronoun, or adjective that identifes or elaborates on the subject.

Practice Copy each sentence onto your paper. Label the linking verb in each sentence, then draw an arrow from the subject complement to the subject.
1. The projecting ledge was the path to the small hidden cave and its pool.
2. The shore is an ancient world . . .
3. For such little horn shells were the food of the flamingo . . .
4. . . . the moon was a luminous disc in the western sky . . .
5. . . . it is a world that keeps alive many creatures . . .

◆ Build Grammar Skills

Practice
1. The projecting ledge *was* the path to the small hidden cave and its pool.
2. The shore *is* an ancient world. . . .
3. For such little horns *were* the food of the flamingo.
4. the moon *was* a luminous disc in the western sky. . . .
5. . . . it *is* a world that keeps alive many creatures. . . .

✎ Writer's Solution

For additional instruction and practice, use the lesson in the **Language Lab CD-ROM** on Eight Parts of Speech to get information on linking verbs and page 33 on Subject Complements in the *Writer's Solution Grammar Practice Book.*

Answers
◆ Critical Thinking
1. The shore is the meeting place between land and sea—its dual nature includes elements of both.
2. Carson communicates the broader meaning that all in nature is related—to each other and to past and future times.
3. Suggested titles: "Marine Life, Then and Now," "Changing Life on the Shore."
4. They are all part of shore life, but the locales and life they support differ: the cave pool has sponge, sea squirts, coral, and star fish; the beach in Georgia has willets, sanderlings, and other birds; the island off the coast of Florida has various kinds of mollusk.
5. Students might suggest forests, canyons, fields, or mountain areas.

◆ Reading for Success
1. Students might mention one of several possibilities: to show the interconnectedness of life forms, to communicate respect for shore life, to support her ideas as a conservationist.
2. Carson makes these points: (1) Life forms at the shore are enduring. Carson supports this with examples. (2) The shore is beautiful. Carson describes different locales at different times of day. (3) We can learn by studying the sea. Carson gives many examples of current and extinct species teaching us lessons about life.

◆ Literary Focus
1. The level of the sea rises and falls as glaciers melt or grow, as the ocean shifts, or as the earth's crust changes.
2. Whereas the daylight reveals different life forms and is filled with sounds of birds, the dark is quiet and so black that water, air, and beach seem to blend together.
3. The marginal world is beautiful; it teems with life that is strong and enduring; the forms of life support one another.

◆ Build Vocabulary
Using the Suffix -able
1. c   2. b   3. a

Using the Word Bank
1. s   2. s   3. s   4. a   5. a   6. a   7. s   8. a

Idea Bank

Customizing for
Performance Levels

Following are suggestions for matching Idea Bank topics with your students' performance levels:

Less Advanced Students: 1, 4, 6
Average Students: 2, 5, 7
More Advanced Students: 3

Customizing for
Learning Modalities

Following are suggestions for matching Idea Bank topics with your students' learning modalities:

Visual/Spatial: 6, 7
Verbal/Linguistic: 4, 5
Rhythmic/Musical: 4
Logical/Mathematical: 3

Writing Mini-Lesson

Refer students to the Writing Handbook, page 965, for instruction on the writing process, and page 967 for further information on description. Use the transparency for a Comparison-and-Contrast Organizer in *Writing and Language Transparencies* to help students identify comparisons in their proposals.

Writing Lab CD-ROM

Have students complete the tutorial on Description. Follow these steps:

1. Have students use the cluster diagram tool to connect details to the main idea of their proposals.
2. Suggest that students use the revision checker to find any vague or overused adjectives in the drafts of their proposals.

Sourcebook

Have students use Chapter 1, Description (pp. 1–24), for additional support. The chapter includes an annotated student model of a remembrance (p. 24).

Build Your Portfolio

Idea Bank

Writing

1. **Letter** Imagine that you have been invited to accompany Rachel Carson on a nature excursion. Write a letter home to your family describing what you have seen and heard.

2. **Nature Report** Research at a library and write a report on an aspect of nature that you find interesting—a sunset, a blooming flower, a hawk's hunting habits. **[Science Link]**

3. **Cause-and-Effect Essay** Write a cause-and-effect essay on how the sea has eroded rocks and shorelines over the past thousands of years. **[Science Link]**

Speaking and Listening

4. **Poetry Reading** Oceans and rivers have long been an inspiration to writers and poets. Choose and recite a poem about the ocean or the tides to your class.

5. **Conservation Speech** Continue Rachel Carson's crusade. Plan and deliver a persuasive speech urging your classmates to help preserve a natural resource about which you are concerned. Include in your speech specific suggestions for actions your listeners can take.

Projects

6. **Art Exhibit** Create a classroom display with photographs and sketches that capture the magical or mysterious quality of the shore. Use a quotation from "The Marginal World" as a caption for each picture. **[Art Link]**

7. **The Living Sea** Use natural objects, photos, video, and music to give a multimedia presentation about the beauty of the ocean to your class. **[Science Link]**

Writing Mini-Lesson

Proposal for a Nature Documentary

The descriptive passages about the unpredictable sea in "The Marginal World" lend themselves to spectacular documentary footage! Write a **proposal** for a nature documentary for a science television program. Your documentary can be about any element of nature that interests you. Your proposal will present your plan for the documentary, summarizing the content and pointing out any special features that it will include. You will probably want to make comparisons in your documentary. The following tip will help you to do that effectively.

> **Writing Skills Focus: Transitions to Show Comparisons**
>
> As you draft your proposal, use **transitional words**—such as *like, likewise, in contrast, similarly, nevertheless,* and *in the same way*—to show comparisons.
>
> Rachel Carson uses a transition to compare birds to moths: "Black skimmers flew along the ocean's edge . . . *like* large, dimly seen moths."

Prewriting Decide on a topic for your documentary and then list all the elements you'll capture on film, including scenery and sounds. Jot down comparisons that you will use to show the similarities or differences between two items.

Drafting Use vivid descriptions to make your proposal appealing. Include a summary of an especially exciting or beautiful scene you plan to include. Indicate similarities between scenes and ideas with transitional words.

Revising Look over your proposal. Add transitions where necessary. Ask a partner to read your proposal to make sure it is clear and engaging.

✓ ASSESSMENT OPTIONS

Formal Assessment, Selection Test, pp. 145–147, and Assessment Resources Software. The selection test is designed so that it can be easily customized to the performance levels of your students.
Alternative Assessment, p. 41, includes options for less advanced students, more advanced students, verbal/linguistic learners, interpersonal learners, musical/rhythmic learners, and visual/spatial learners, logical/mathematical learners.

PORTFOLIO ASSESSMENT
Use the following rubrics in the *Alternative Assessment* booklet to assess student writing:
Letter: Description Rubric, p. 97
Nature Report: Research Report Rubric p. 106
Cause-and-Effect Essay: Cause-and-Effect Rubric p. 102

PART 1 *Biographies and Personal Accounts*

Cover, 1980, John Hall, Art Gallery of Hamilton, Canada

Biographies and Personal Accounts ◆ 579

One-Minute Planning Guide

The essays in Part I are all biographical or personal in content. They illustrate different types of essays. In "The Way to Rainy Mountain," Momaday reflects on the value of his grandmother's life and culture. Alexander Solzhenitsyn's Nobel Lecture makes a persuasive case for the solidarity of world writers against oppression, and Elie Wiesel in "Keep Memory Alive" makes a persuasive plea that readers not forget the horrors of the Holocaust. In "A Child's Christmas in Wales," Dylan Thomas remembers his childhood Christmas experiences. Langston Hughes offers a biographical portrait of the great opera singer Marian Anderson. In "Flood," a descriptive essay, Annie Dillard provides personal observations on a local flood.

Customizing for *Varying Student Needs*
The following factors may guide you in assigning the selections in this part.

"The Way to Rainy Mountain"
• Narrative, descriptive structure is accessible

Nobel Lecture; "Keep Memory Alive"
• The essays are brief, but concepts are more challenging

"A Child's Christmas in Wales"
• Somewhat complex descriptive language may challenge less proficient readers or English language learners
• Humorous, narrative incidents make the essay appealing

"Marian Anderson: Famous Concert Singer"
• Short essay (four pages)
• Easily understandable language

"Flood"
• Language is straightforward, but the lack of narrative structure may make the essay hard for some students to follow.

 Humanities: Art

Cover, 1980, by John Hall.

Encourage students to appreciate the self-referential aspects of this painting, which is a little like a visual riddle or joke. Help them see that the painting is most likely a self-portrait, since the man above the word "COVER" seems to be working intently in what looks like an artist's studio. Ask students to try to decipher the black painted letters on the dark gray background, just above the word "COVER." *They are upside down, but probably spell "cover."* Help them to understand that the central, square part of this painting is supposed to represent a protective cover for another painting that is wrapped up like a present to someone.

Help students link the artwork to the focus of Part I, "Biographies and Personal Accounts," by answering the following questions:

1. If this is a self-portrait, what ideas about the artist does it give you? *It suggests that he is witty and likes to hide things, that he gets very caught up in his work and probably thinks his work is more important than he is.*

2. This is a painting that has very realistic details and almost looks like a photograph. In what ways might it be similar to a personal account of an actual event? *It works with reality but does something personal and imaginative with it.*

579

*G*uide for Reading

OBJECTIVES

1. To read, comprehend, and interpret essays
2. To relate essays to personal experience
3. To analyze author's purpose
4. To recognize features of reflective and persuasive essays
5. To build vocabulary in context and learn forms of *reciprocity*
6. To develop skill in capitalizing proper nouns and adjectives
7. To write an acceptance speech using placement for emphasis
8. To respond to the essays through writing, speaking and listening, and projects

SKILLS INSTRUCTION

Vocabulary:
Related Words:
Forms of *Reciprocity*
Grammar:
Capitalization of
Proper Nouns and
Adjectives
Reading Strategy:
Analyze the
Author's Purpose
Literary Focus:
Reflective and

Persuasive Essays
Writing:
Placement for
Emphasis
**Speaking and
Listening:**
Persuasive Speech
(teacher edition)
Critical Viewing:
Relate, Draw
Conclusions,
Connect

PORTFOLIO OPPORTUNITIES

Writing: Letter; Report; Creation Myth
Writing Mini-Lesson: Acceptance Speech
Speaking and Listening: Persuasive Speech; Myth Reading
Projects: Native American Dances; Writers-in-Prison

More About the Authors

N. Scott Momaday's personal creative spirit is the bear, a force that he says guards his power to write. Momaday has written a poem called "The Bear," and his book, *House Made of Dawn* contains many stories about bears, in which bears are both healers and enemies.

Alexander Solzhenitsyn's writings on the prison system of the former Soviet Union were informed by personal experience. In 1945, he was falsely accused of a political crime and spent eight years in the labor camps he writes about in *The Gulag Archipelago.*

Elie Wiesel believes that harm to any single person's dignity harms all of humankind. His response is to protest and protect others through writing.

N. Scott Momaday *(1934–   )*

A Kiowa Indian, N. Scott Momaday's interest in Native American culture and history began as a child, when he lived on several Indian reservations where his parents taught. Momaday earned a doctoral degree from Stanford University, where he now teaches English. His first novel, *House Made of Dawn,* was awarded a Pulitzer Prize. *The Way to Rainy Mountain* includes his impressions of contemporary Kiowa culture and world view, as well as their history and legends.

Alexander Solzhenitsyn *(1918–   )*

A dissident is one who departs from established opinion, and the Russian writer Alexander Solzhenitsyn has been a dissident his whole literary life. His first book, *A Day in the Life of Ivan Denisovitch*—the story of an inmate in a Soviet labor camp—was banned in the Soviet Union. Solzhenitsyn was tried for treason and exiled after the publication in Paris of parts of *The Gulag Archipelago.* Only since 1991 has his work been available to the people of his homeland. This excerpt from his Nobel Prize acceptance speech, reflects on what it means to be part of a great world literature.

Elie Wiesel *(1928–   )*

The Romanian-born teacher, philosopher, and writer Elie Wiesel was deported to the Nazi death camp at Auschwitz at age sixteen. His parents and sister were killed, and he was forced into slave labor at Buchenwald, another Nazi death camp. After surviving the war, Wiesel studied in France and moved to the United States in 1956. In his first book, *Night,* Wiesel recounts the horrors of his experiences at the hands of the Nazis.

Elie Wiesel has been awarded the Congressional Gold Medal of Achievement and the Nobel Peace Prize. He delivered the speech here in 1986, in acceptance of that prize.

580 ◆ *Nonfiction*

◆ Build Vocabulary

RELATED WORDS: FORMS OF *RECIPROCITY*

"Today," Alexander Solzhenitsyn writes, "there is an almost instant *reciprocity*" between the writers of one country and the readers and writers of another. The word *reciprocity,* which means a "mutual action or dependence," has several forms. As the adjective *reciprocal,* it means "something done in response to something else" or simply, "mutual." As the verb *reciprocate,* it means "to do in return."

WORD BANK

Before you read, preview this list of words from the selections.

engender
tenuous
reciprocity
assimilate
inexorably
oratory
transcends

◆ Build Grammar Skills

CAPITALIZATION OF PROPER NOUNS AND ADJECTIVES

In these selections, you'll see many **proper nouns and adjectives**. All proper nouns and proper adjectives begin with capital letters. Proper nouns name specific places, people, and things.

Name of Place: Rainy Mountain
Name of Region: the West
Name of Group: the Kiowas
Name of Thing: Nobel Prize

Proper adjectives are adjectives made from proper nouns. For instance, the following examples come from the proper nouns the *West* and *Europe:*

Western writers
European writers

Prentice Hall Literature Program Resources

REINFORCE / RETEACH / EXTEND

Selection Support Pages
Build Vocabulary: Forms of *Reciprocity*, p. 172
Build Grammar Skills: Capitalization of Proper Nouns and Adjectives, p. 173
Reading Strategy: Author's Purpose, p. 174
Literary Focus: Reflective and Persuasive Essays, p. 175

Strategies for Diverse Student Needs, p. 42

Beyond Literature Art, p. 42

Formal Assessment Selection Test, pp. 148–150; Assessment Resources Software

Alternative Assessment, p. 42

Resource Pro CD-ROM
"The Way to Rainy Mountain," Nobel Lecture, "Keep Memory Alive"—includes all resource material and customizable lesson plan

Listening to Literature Audiocassettes
"The Way to Rainy Mountain," Nobel Lecture, "Keep Memory Alive"

Looking at Literature Videodisc
Chapter 7: "The Way to Rainy Mountain"

from The Way to Rainy Mountain
◆ *from* Nobel Lecture ◆ Keep Memory Alive ◆

◆ *Literature and Your Life*

CONNECT YOUR EXPERIENCE

We all have memories, and we cherish those that are most important to us. Writers often relive their most vivid or important memories by recording them. These three works of literature are the records of three authors' recollections and reflections on important events in their lives.

THEMATIC FOCUS: FROM THE PAST

Memoirists and historic novelists, among others, reflect on the past in their writing. What do writers gain by reflecting on the past?

Journal Writing Jot down two or three memories that have stayed with you since childhood.

◆ Background for Understanding

LITERATURE

One of the highest honors a writer can receive is to be awarded the Nobel Prize for Literature. The Nobel Prizes—which include awards in physics, chemistry, medicine, literature, and peace—were established by a Swede, Alfred Nobel, the inventor of dynamite. Wanting to be associated not with destruction but with peace, Nobel set up a fund to finance annual achievement and peace awards.

Both Alexander Solzhenitsyn and Elie Wiesel were awarded Nobel Prizes—Solzhenitsyn for literature and Wiesel for peace.

◆ Literary Focus

REFLECTIVE AND PERSUASIVE ESSAYS

In a **reflective essay,** an author shares his or her thoughts about an idea or a personal experience. In the excerpt from *The Way to Rainy Mountain,* Momaday reflects on the death of his grandmother and the passing of the Kiowa culture.

A **persuasive essay** attempts to convince readers to adopt a particular opinion or course of action. Solzhenitsyn's and Wiesel's speeches use persuasive language and sound reasons to convince you that their ideas are worth embracing.

◆ Reading Strategy

ANALYZE THE AUTHOR'S PURPOSE

An **author's purpose** is the reason he or she is writing; for example, to inform or to entertain. N. Scott Momaday has a dual purpose in writing—to honor his grandmother's memory and to inform you about a culture that has been largely lost. The other two authors in this group, Solzhenitsyn and Wiesel, have the purpose of persuading you to adopt their opinion or point of view.

Each author's purpose comes with a set of criteria by which you can measure its success. For example, with a persuasive piece, ask yourself: Is it well-reasoned? Are the author's arguments supported by facts when appropriate? Does the author use persuasive language effectively?

Momaday's purpose is broader, and it can be analyzed according to each of its aims. Ask yourself: Have I gotten to know Momaday's grandmother in the way he intended? Did I gain interesting or useful information about the Kiowa Indian culture?

Answering questions like these will help you to formulate your own questions and make your own determination about the success of an author's purpose.

Preparing for Standardized Tests

Reading and Vocabulary Vocabulary development is based in part on recognizing related forms of words. The Build Vocabulary lesson for these selections focuses on forms of the word *reciprocity.* Students can generalize their understanding of related words and apply this skill when working with verbal reasoning and vocabulary items on standardized tests. For additional practice, use the Build Vocabulary page in *Selection Support,* p. 172.

Critical Reading portions of standardized tests require students to evaluate a writer's position or assertion. Understanding and analyzing a writer's purpose will help students make sound judgments about the writer's work. The Reading Strategy for this selection focuses on analyzing an author's purpose. For further instruction and practice, use the Reading Strategy page in *Selection Support,* p. 174.

One-Minute Insight Like all the essays in this grouping, "The Way to Rainy Mountain" focuses on the importance of memory in understanding the lessons of the past. In this essay, N. Scott Momaday weaves together his love for tradition, nature, and community to give his message a particular essence—the spiritual essence of the Kiowa.

Looking at Literature Videodisc To provide background and insight into the author of *The Way to Rainy Mountain,* play Chapter 7 of the videodisc. In this interview, N. Scott Momaday describes the importance of researching the people and places he writes about in *The Way to Rainy Mountain.* Have students discuss why research is so important for writing nonfiction.

Chapter 7

▶**Critical Viewing**◀

❶ **Relate** The body language of the Native American men in this painting expresses a variety of emotions: The man crouching on the right seems stern and serious; the man in the black hat next to him seems thoughtful; the pose of the older man in the center expresses resistance or stubbornness. Students might also note the man turning away in the background; perhaps he is indifferent. As a whole, this group seems serious.

from *The Way to* RAINY MOUNTAIN *N. Scott Momaday*

Old Ones Talking, R. Brownell McGrew, Courtesy of the artist

❶ ▲ **Critical Viewing** Describe three emotions or attitudes you see depicted in this painting. [Relate]

582 ◆ Nonfiction

Block Scheduling Strategies

Consider these suggestions to take advantage of extended class time:

• Introduce types of essays, and indicate that these essays are examples of reflective and persuasive essays. Have students read the Literary Focus on page 581 and, after reading the essays, answer the Literary Focus questions on page 592.

• You may wish to break the class into three groups and assign each group to read and analyze one essay. Have groups

prepare a brief presentation in which they "teach" their essay to the other groups, with special attention to the features of the essay type and the authors' purposes. Students can evaluate one another's presentations after reading all three essays.

• After students have read the selection, review the questions posed in the Reading Strategy feature on page 581. Do students feel they now know Momaday's grandmother? Was the information on the

Kiowa useful and significant? How would they describe Momaday's overall purpose in writing, and did he achieve his purpose?

• Direct students to work in discussion groups to answer the Critical Thinking questions on pages 586, 589, and 591.

• Some students can develop the Report in the Idea Bank on page 593. Encourage them to include information on other groups that suffered repression in the Soviet Union of the 1940's and 1950's.

582

A single knoll rises out of the plain in Oklahoma, north and west of the Wichita Range.[1] For my people, the Kiowas, it is an old landmark, and they gave it the name Rainy Mountain. The hardest weather in the world is there. Winter brings blizzards, hot tornadic winds arise in the spring, and in summer the prairie is an anvil's edge.[2] The grass turns brittle and brown, and it cracks beneath your feet. There are green belts along the rivers and creeks, linear groves of hickory and pecan, willow and witch hazel. At a distance in July or August the steaming foliage seems almost to writhe[3] in fire. Great green and yellow grasshoppers are everywhere in the tall grass, popping up like corn to sting the flesh, and tortoises crawl about on the red earth, going nowhere in the plenty of time. Loneliness is an aspect of the land. All things in the plain are isolate; there is no confusion of objects in the eye, but *one* hill or *one* tree or *one* man. To look upon that landscape in the early morning, with the sun at your back, is to lose the sense of proportion. Your imagination comes to life, and this, you think, is where Creation was begun.

I returned to Rainy Mountain in July. My grandmother had died in the spring, and I wanted to be at her grave. She had lived to be very old and at last infirm.[4] Her only living daughter was with her when she died, and I was told that in death her face was that of a child.

◆ **Reading Strategy**
Why do you think Momaday included this detail?

I like to think of her as a child. When she was born, the Kiowas were living the last great moment of their history. For more than a hundred years they had controlled the open range from the Smoky Hill River to the Red, from the headwaters of the Canadian to the fork of the Arkansas and Cimarron. In alliance with the Comanches, they had ruled the whole of the southern Plains.

1. **Wichita** (wich ə tô´) **Range:** Mountain range in southwestern Oklahoma.
2. **anvil's edge:** Edge of the iron or steel block on which metal objects are hammered into shape.
3. **writhe** (rīth) *v.:* Twist in pain and agony.
4. **infirm** (in furm´) *adj.:* Weak; feeble.

War was their sacred business, and they were among the finest horsemen the world has ever known. But warfare for the Kiowas was preeminently a matter of disposition rather than of survival, and they never understood the grim, unrelenting advance of the U.S. Cavalry. When at last, divided and ill-provisioned, they were driven onto the Staked Plains in the cold rains of autumn, they fell into panic. In Palo Duro Canyon they abandoned their crucial stores to pillage[5] and had nothing then but their lives. In order to save themselves, they surrendered to the soldiers at Fort Sill and were imprisoned in the old stone corral that now stands as a military museum. My grandmother was spared the humiliation of those high gray walls by eight or ten years, but she must have known from birth the affliction of defeat, the dark brooding of old warriors.

Her name was Aho, and she belonged to the last culture to evolve in North America. Her forebears came down from the high country in western Montana nearly three centuries ago. They were a mountain people, a mysterious tribe of hunters whose language has never been positively classified in any major group. In the late seventeenth century they began a long migration to the south and east. It was a journey toward the dawn, and it led to a golden age. Along the way the Kiowas were befriended by the Crows, who gave them the culture and religion of the Plains. They acquired horses, and their ancient nomadic spirit was suddenly free of the ground. They acquired Tai-me, the sacred Sun Dance doll, from that moment the object and symbol of their worship, and so shared in the divinity of the sun. Not least, they acquired the sense of destiny, therefore courage and pride. When they entered upon the southern Plains they had been transformed. No longer were they slaves to the simple necessity of survival; they were a lordly and dangerous society of fighters and thieves, hunters and priests of the sun. According to their origin myth, they entered the world through a hollow log. From one point of view, their migration was the fruit of an old prophecy,

5. **pillage** (pil´ ij) *n.:* Act of robbing and destroying, especially during wartime.

from *The Way to Rainy Mountain* ◆ 583

Fan, Kiowa ca. 1900, Philbrook Art Center, Tulsa, Oklahoma

◆ **Literary Focus**
❷ **Reflective Essays** Ask: What characteristics in this paragraph indicate that it is part of a reflective essay? *The writer is describing a scene from his own past. His language is descriptive, and he includes his own thoughts and feelings about what he observes, as in "Loneliness is an aspect of the land."*

◆ **Reading Strategy**
❸ **Analyze the Author's Purpose** By saying that in death his grandmother's face was the face of a child, Momaday is revealing an aspect of her personality—her innocence—and arousing the reader's curiosity about his grandmother.

◆ **Build Grammar Skills**
❹ **Capitalization of Proper Nouns and Adjectives** Point out that the word *red*, which is not a proper adjective by itself, is capitalized in this sentence. Ask students to draw a conclusion about why *red* is capitalized here. *Students will probably guess that Red is part of the name of a place. This is correct; red becomes a proper adjective as part of the name Red River.*

◆ **Reading Strategy**
❺ **Analyze the Author's Purpose** Ask students why they think the author includes the information that the Kiowa's language has never been positively classified. *He is emphasizing the group's uniqueness to make it seem even more tragic that their traditions are fading away.*

🎵 **Humanities: Art**

Old Ones Talking by R. Brownell McGrew.
R. Brownell McGrew is a Native American artist who often focuses on Native American life as the subject of his paintings.

This painting depicts a group of Native American men gathered in the woods. The golden light of the sun through the trees illuminates the background and reflects off the colorful tones of the men's clothing, as it does off the ground and tree trunks, making the men seem a part of the natural surroundings and emphasizing the feeling of oneness with nature that comes forth in Momaday's piece.

Use these questions for discussion:
1. What specific aspects of their clothing suggest that the men in this painting are caught between native traditional and mainstream cultures? *Their jeans, shirts, and hats are items of contemporary western clothing, while their beads and jewelry and the hair of the man in the background are part of the customary dress of their American Indian tradition.*

2. How does the painting remind you of the description Momaday gives of the old warlords who visit his grandmother? *The men wear black hats and bright shirts; they have strips of cloth wound around their hair.*

❶ Analyze the Author's Purpose
Have students determine why the author includes this detail about the mountains in his essay. *The detail shows how much the Kiowa valued freedom; they preferred to be in an open environment where they could see the horizon, rather than enclosed by forests and mountains. This adds to the reader's knowledge about Momaday's people and their lives.*

◆ *Literature and Your Life*

❷ Ask students if there is a place in nature that makes them feel the "awful quiet" that Momaday mentions here. *Answers should focus on places that evoke a feeling of awe and a sense of the past.*

Humanities: Art

Annie Old Crow by James Bama.

This painting of a Native American woman, done in the style of a portrait, seems to convey a quiet dignity. Have students note the jewelry and the decorative elements in the woman's braids and on her dress. You might have students discuss the strengths and weaknesses the portrait seems to reveal.

Use these questions for discussion:

1. How are the struggles that the author's grandmother faced throughout her lifetime reflected in this woman's face? *The face shows many wrinkles, which seem to indicate a difficult life. Her expression seems to be one of acceptance or resignation.*

2. Are the traits shown in this painting similar to those demonstrated by the grandmother in the essay? *The woman in this painting shows strength, great age, and some sadness, but her bearing shows dignity. All of these qualities are those of the grandmother in the essay.*

for indeed they emerged from a sunless world.

Although my grandmother lived out her long life in the shadow of Rainy Mountain, the immense landscape of the continental interior lay like memory in her blood. She could tell of the Crows, whom she had never seen, and of the Black Hills, where she had never been. I wanted to see in reality what she had seen more perfectly in the mind's eye, and traveled fifteen hundred miles to begin my pilgrimage.

Yellowstone,[6] it seemed to me, was the top of the world, a region of deep lakes and dark timber, canyons and waterfalls. But, beautiful as it is, one might have the sense of confinement there. The skyline in all directions is close at hand, the high wall of the woods and deep cleavages of shade. There is a per- fect freedom in the mountains, but it belongs to the eagle and the elk, the badger and the bear. The Kiowas reckoned their stature by the distance they could see, and they were bent and blind in the wilderness.

Descending eastward, the highland meadows are a stairway to the plain. In July the inland slope of the Rockies is luxuriant with flax and buckwheat, stonecrop and larkspur. The earth unfolds and the limit of the land recedes. Clusters of trees, and animals grazing far in the distance, cause the vision to reach away and wonder to build upon the mind. The sun follows a longer course in the day, and the sky is immense beyond all comparison. The great billowing clouds that sail upon it are shadows that move upon the brain like water, dividing light. Farther down, in the land of the Crows and Blackfeet, the plain is yellow. Sweet clover takes hold of the hills and bends upon itself to cover and seal the soil. There the Kiowas paused on their way; they had come to the place where they must change their lives. The sun is at home on the plains. Precisely there does it have the certain character of a god. When the Kiowas came to the land of the Crows, they could see the dark lees of the hills at dawn across the Bighorn

6. **Yellowstone:** Yellowstone National Park, mostly in northwestern Wyoming but including narrow strips in southern Montana and eastern Idaho.

584 ◆ Nonfiction

River, the profusion of light on the grain shelves, the oldest deity ranging after the solstices. Not yet would they veer southward to the caldron[7] of the land that lay below; they must wean their blood from the northern winter and hold the mountains a while longer in their view. They bore Tai-me in procession to the east.

A dark mist lay over the Black Hills, and the land was like iron. At the top of a ridge I caught sight of Devil's Tower upthrust against the gray sky as if in the birth of time the core of the earth had broken through its crust and the motion of the world was begun. There are things in nature that <u>engender</u> an awful quiet in the heart of man; Devil's Tower is one of them. Two centuries ago, because they could not do otherwise, the Kiowas made a legend at the base of the rock. My grandmother said:

Eight children were there at play, seven sisters and their brother. Suddenly the boy was struck dumb; he trembled and began to run upon his hands and feet. His fingers became claws, and his body was covered with fur. Directly there was a bear where the boy had been. The sisters were terrified; they ran, and the bear after them. They came to the stump of a great tree, and the tree spoke to them. It bade them climb upon it, and as they did so it began to rise in the air. The bear came to kill them, but they were just beyond its reach. It reared against the tree and scored the bark all around with its claws. The seven sisters were borne into the sky, and they became the stars of the Big Dipper.

From that moment, and so long as the legend lives, the Kiowas have kinsmen in the night sky. Whatever they were in the mountains, they could be no more. However <u>tenuous</u> their well-being, however much they had suffered and would suffer again, they had found a way out of the wilderness.

My grandmother had a reverence for the sun, a holy regard that now is all but gone out of mankind. There was a wariness in her, and an

7. **caldron** (kôl′ drən) *n.*: Heat like that of a boiling kettle.

Annie Old Crow, James Bama, Courtesy of the Artist

 ### Cross-Curricular Connection: Social Studies

The Kiowa Explain to students that the Kiowa Indians lived in the southern plains of North America. Buffalo hunters, they lived in lodges made of skin that they could transport easily from place to place. They vigorously—and often violently—protested white settlement in their territory and were hostile to settlers until 1875. After many Kiowa leaders were imprisoned and their horses taken, the Kiowa retreated to a reservation in southwestern Oklahoma, where they now number around 5,000.

Community Connection
Regional Native Americans Suggest that students find out what Native American group lived—or still lives—in their area. What contributions did they make to the area? What signs—such as place names—suggest their influence on the community? What was their relationship with white settlers in the area? Interested students can present their findings to the class.

ancient awe. She was a Christian in her later years, but she had come a long way about, and she never forgot her birthright. As a child she had been to the Sun Dances; she had taken part in those annual rites, and by them she had learned the restoration of her people in the presence of Tai-me. She was about seven when the last Kiowa Sun Dance was held in 1887 on the Washita River above Rainy Mountain Creek. The buffalo were gone. In order to consummate the ancient sacrifice—to impale the head of a buffalo bull upon the medicine tree—a delegation of old men journeyed into Texas, there to beg and barter for an animal from the Goodnight herd. She was ten when the Kiowas came together for the last time as a living Sun Dance culture. They could find no buffalo; they had to hang an old hide from the sacred tree. Before the dance could begin, a company of soldiers rode out from Fort Sill under orders to disperse the tribe. Forbidden without cause the essential act of their faith, having seen the wild herds slaughtered and left to rot upon the ground, the Kiowas backed away forever from the medicine tree. That was July 20, 1890, at the great bend of the Washita. My grandmother was there.

3 Without bitterness, and for as long as she lived, she bore a vision of deicide.[8]

Now that I can have her only in memory, I see my grandmother in the several postures that were peculiar to her: standing at the wood stove on a winter morning and turning meat in a great iron skillet; sitting at the south window, bent above her beadwork, and afterwards, when her vision failed, looking down for a long time into the fold of her hands; going out upon a cane, very slowly as she did when the

◆ **Literary Focus**
How do Momaday's recollections of his grandmother reflect his feelings for her?
4

◆ **Build Vocabulary**

engender (in jen′ dər) v.: Bring about; cause; produce

tenuous (ten′ yoo wəs) adj.: Slight; flimsy; not substantial or strong

weight of age came upon her; praying. I remember her most often at prayer. She made long, rambling prayers out of suffering and hope, having seen many things. I was never sure that I had the right to hear, so exclusive were they of all mere custom and company. The last time I

5

saw her she prayed standing by the side of her bed at night, naked to the waist, the light of a kerosene lamp moving upon her dark skin. Her long, black hair, always drawn and braided in the day, lay upon her shoulders and against her breasts like a shawl. I do not speak Kiowa, and I never understood her prayers, but there was something inherently sad in the sound, some merest hesitation upon the syllables of sorrow. She began in a high and descending pitch, exhausting her breath to silence; then again and again—and always the same intensity of effort, of something that is, and is not, like urgency in the human voice. Transported so in the dancing light among the shadows of her room, she seemed beyond the reach of time. But that was illusion; I think I knew then that I should not see her again.

6

Houses are like sentinels in the plain, old keepers of the weather watch. There, in a very little while, wood takes on the appearance of great age. All colors wear soon away in the wind and rain, and then the wood is burned gray and the grain appears and the nails turn red with rust. The windowpanes are black and opaque; you imagine there is nothing within, and indeed there are many ghosts, bones given up to the land. They stand here and there against the sky, and you approach them for a longer time than you expect. They belong in the distance; it is their domain.

Once there was a lot of sound in my grandmother's house, a lot of coming and going, feasting and talk. The summers there were full of excitement and reunion. The Kiowas are a summer people; they abide the cold and keep to themselves, but when the season turns and the land becomes warm and vital they cannot hold still; an old love of going returns upon them. The aged visitors who came to my grandmother's

Pouch, Kiowa ca. 1890–1910, New York State Historical Association, Cooperstown

8. **deicide** (dē′ ə sīd′) n.: Killing of a god.

from The Way to Rainy Mountain ◆ 585

◆ **Critical Thinking**

3 **Infer** Ask students how they think the ending of the Sun Dance affected Momaday and his grandmother. *His grandmother remembers it "Without bitterness," but the author appears to resent that the Kiowas were "Forbidden without cause the essential act of their faith, . . ."*

◆ **Literary Focus**

4 **Reflective Essay** The details Momaday chooses to describe his grandmother—such as her attention to her work and her prayers—indicate his respect and affection for her.

◆ **Reading Strategy**

5 **Analyze the Author's Purpose** Have students determine why the author reveals these details about his grandmother. *His strongest memories are of her at prayer. Her prayers reflected all the things she saw and suffered in her life; they were an essential part of her, and Momaday is showing respect for her privacy.*

◆ **Critical Thinking**

6 **Interpret** Ask students: What does Momaday mean by saying his grandmother ". . . seemed beyond the reach of time"? Why was that an illusion? *When she was praying, his grandmother seemed more like a symbol than an individual, and therefore as if she would not die; however, that was an illusion—she was mortal, and she did die.*

Cross-Curricular Connection: Art

Native American Beadwork Tell students that in the early 1800's, traders introduced glass beads to the Native Americans. Decorating in beads gradually replaced porcupine quill work. Women usually sewed beads onto buckskin clothing or bags, but some groups developed weaving techniques. The bead designs were mostly geometric, though around the turn of the century floral patterns became popular. The Cheyenne were known for creating sacred designs in beads; their decora-

tions on cradle boards and moccasins symbolized protection and long life.

Interested students might enjoy finding out more about the meaning and technique of beadwork in different Native American groups, particularly the beadwork of the Kiowa. Suggest that students try some of the beadwork designs themselves. They can start by trying to work out a design on a T-shirt.

❶ Analyze the Author's Purpose
Ask students: What is Momaday's purpose in reflecting back in this passage? *The author is comparing the liveliness and warmth of the meetings of elders to the silence and loneliness he now senses in his grandmother's rooms.*

◆ **Literary Focus**

❷ Reflective Essay Ask students: Why does the author look back at his grandmother's grave? Why does he then come away? *The author feels he is breaking with his past, and he still feels drawn to it; he is able to come away because he realizes that he will always have the past in his memory.*

Reinforce and Extend

Answers
◆ Literature and Your Life

Reader's Response Students might be interested in exploring their cultural roots so that they can find out more about their personal identity.

Thematic Focus By reflecting on the past, students can put present-day events into perspective.

☑ **Check Your Comprehension**
1. They made up a legend to explain Devil's Tower.
2. Possible activities include feasting and talking, reminiscing, cooking, prayer meetings, the cousins playing together.

◆ Critical Thinking

1. Momaday is paying homage to the lost way of life of the Kiowa and specifically to the life of his grandmother.
2. Students might suggest that Momaday's reflection about the cricket could also apply to the Kiowa—that the spirit of the culture lives on in eternity.
3. Students should see that Momaday's life has bridged two cultures—Kiowa and mainstream contemporary American—much more than did his grandmother's life.

---

house when I was a child were made of lean and leather, and they bore themselves upright. They wore great black hats and bright ample shirts that shook in the wind. They rubbed fat upon their hair and wound their braids with strips of colored cloth. Some of them painted their faces and carried the scars of old and cherished enmities. They were an old council of warlords, come to remind and be reminded of who they were. **❶** Their wives and daughters served them well. The women might indulge themselves; gossip was at once the mark and compensation of their servitude. They made loud and elaborate talk among themselves, full of jest and gesture, fright and false alarm. They went abroad in fringed and flowered shawls, bright beadwork and German silver. They were at home in the kitchen, and they prepared meals that were banquets.

There were frequent prayer meetings, and great nocturnal feasts. When I was a child I played with my cousins outside, where the lamplight fell upon the ground and the singing of the old people rose up around us and carried away into the darkness. There were a lot of good things to eat, a lot of laughter and surprise. And afterwards, when the quiet returned, I lay down with my grandmother and could hear the frogs away by the river and feel the motion of the air.

Now there is a funeral silence in the rooms, the endless wake of some final word. The walls have closed in upon my grandmother's house.

When I returned to it in mourning, I saw for the first time in my life how small it was. It was late at night, and there was a white moon, nearly full. I sat for a long time on the stone steps by the kitchen door. From there I could see out across the land; I could see the long row of trees by the creek, the low light upon the rolling plains, and the stars of the Big Dipper. Once I looked at the moon and caught sight of a strange thing. A cricket had perched upon the handrail, only a few inches away from me. My line of vision was such that the creature filled the moon like a fossil. It had gone there, I thought, to live and die, for there, of all places, was its small definition made whole and eternal. A warm wind rose up and purled[9] like the longing within me.

The next morning I awoke at dawn and went out on the dirt road to Rainy Mountain. It was already hot, and the grasshoppers began to fill the air. Still, it was early in the morning, and the birds sang out of the shadows. The long yellow grass on the mountain shone in the bright light, and a scissortail[10] hied above the land. There, where it ought to be, at the end of a long and legendary way, was my grandmother's grave. Here and there on the dark stones were ancestral names. Looking back once, I saw the mountain and came away. **❷**

---

9. **purled** (purld) *v.*: Moved in ripples or with a murmuring sound; swirled.
10. **scissortail** (siz′ ər tāl′) *n.*: Pale gray and pink variety of flycatcher.

Guide for Responding

◆ Literature and Your Life

Reader's Response Would you be interested in searching out the roots of your culture in the way Momaday does? Explain.

Thematic Focus How can reflecting upon the past help you to understand yourself?

☑ **Check Your Comprehension**
1. What natural phenomenon did the Kiowa make up a legend to explain?
2. Describe two activities at Momaday's grandmother's house in the summer.

◆ Critical Thinking
INTERPRET
1. To what and to whom is Momaday paying homage in this piece? **[Infer]**
2. Describe the personality of Momaday's grandmother based on the details in the essay. **[Synthesize]**
3. What does the appearance of the cricket at the end of the essay signify about the Kiowa culture? **[Draw Conclusions]**
APPLY
4. How do you think Momaday's life differs from his grandmother's? **[Speculate]**

Beyond the Classroom

Community Connection
Community Feasts Momaday describes great nighttime feasts that his grandmother's friends held. Discuss with students what community feasts are held in their area. Are there Fourth of July picnics, church suppers, or feasts featuring the food of a particular cultural group? Talk about the reasons for having such celebrations and why people enjoy them. Have students compare feasts in their community to the feasts the author describes. To help them with their comparisons, use these questions:

1. What other activities take place at the community feasts you have attended or that you know about? What is the significance of these activities?
2. In what specific ways does the food served at these celebrations relate to the heritage of the people involved?

from # Nobel Lecture

Alexander Solzhenitsyn
Translated by F. D. Reeve

❸ I am, however, encouraged by a keen sense of WORLD LITERATURE as the one great heart that beats for the cares and misfortunes of our world, even though each corner sees and experiences them in a different way.

In past times, also, besides age-old national literatures there existed a concept of world literature as the link between the summits of national literatures and as the aggregate[1] of reciprocal literary influences. But there was a time lag: readers and writers came to know foreign writers only belatedly, sometimes centuries later, so that mutual influences were delayed and the network of national literary high points was visible not to contemporaries but to later generations.

Today, between writers of one country and the readers and writers of another, there is an almost instantaneous reciprocity as I myself know. My books, unpublished, alas, in my own country, despite hasty and often bad translations have quickly found a responsive world **❹** readership. Critical analysis of them has been

undertaken by such leading Western writers as Heinrich Böll.[2] During all these recent years, **❹** when both my work and my freedom did not collapse, when against the laws of gravity they held on seemingly in thin air, seemingly ON NOTHING, on the invisible, mute surface tension of sympathetic people, with warm gratitude I learned, to my complete surprise, of the support of the world's writing fraternity. On my fiftieth birthday I was astounded to receive greetings from well-known European writers. No pressure put on me now passed unnoticed. During the dangerous weeks when I was being expelled from the Writers' Union,[3] THE PROTECTIVE WALL put forward by the prominent writers of the world saved me from worse persecution,

---

2. **Heinrich Böll** (hin riH böl): German novelist (1917–1985) and winner of the Nobel Prize for Literature.
3. **the Writers Union:** Official Soviet writers' organization.

◆ **Build Vocabulary**

reciprocity (res′ ə präs′ ə tē) *n.*: Mutual action; dependence

---

1. **aggregate** (ag′ rə git) *adj.*: Group of things gathered together and considered a whole.

from *Nobel Lecture* ◆ 587

▲ **Critical Viewing** These stamps from various countries honor writers. What do they suggest about the importance of writers? [Draw Conclusions] ❸

and Norwegian writers and artists hospitably prepared shelter for me in the event that I was exiled from my country. Finally, my being nominated for a Nobel Prize was originated not in the land where I live and write but by François Mauriac[4] and his colleagues. Afterward, national writers' organizations expressed unanimous support for me.

As I have understood it and experienced it myself, world literature is no longer an abstraction or a generalized concept invented by literary critics, but a common body and common spirit, a living, heartfelt unity reflecting the growing spiritual unity of mankind. State borders still turn crimson, heated red-hot by electric fences and machine-gun fire; some ministries of internal affairs still suppose that literature is "an internal affair" of the countries under their jurisdiction; and newspaper headlines still herald, "They have no right to interfere in our internal affairs!" Meanwhile, no such thing as INTERNAL AFFAIRS remains on our crowded Earth. Mankind's salvation lies exclusively in everyone's making everything his business, in the people of the East being anything but indifferent to what is thought in the West, and in the people of the West being anything

> ◆ **Literary Focus**
> ❶ What point does Solzhenitsyn want readers to support or accept?

---

4. **François Mauriac** (frän swá′ mô ryàk′): French novelist and essayist (1885–1970).

◆ **Build Vocabulary**

assimilate (ə sim′ ə lāt′) *v.*: To absorb into a greater body

inexorably (in eks′ ə rə blē) *adv.*: Certainly

oratory (ôr′ ə tôr′ ē) *n.*: Skill in public speaking

588 ◆ *Nonfiction*

but indifferent to what happens in the East. Literature, one of the most sensitive and responsive tools of human existence, has been the first to pick up, adopt, and <u>assimilate</u> this sense of the growing unity of mankind. I therefore confidently turn to the world literature of the present, to hundreds of friends whom I have not met face to face and perhaps never will see.

My friends! Let us try to be helpful, if we are worth anything. In our own countries, torn by differences among parties, movements, castes, and groups, who for ages past has been not the dividing but the uniting force? This, essentially, is the position of writers, spokesmen of a national language, of the chief tie binding the nation, the very soil which the people inhabit, and, in fortunate circumstances, the nation's spirit too.

I think that world literature has the power in these frightening times to help mankind see itself accurately despite what is advocated by partisans[5] and by parties. It has the power to transmit the condensed experience of one region to another, so that different scales of values are combined, and so that one people accurately and concisely knows the true history of another with a power of recognition and acute awareness as if it had lived through that history itself—and could thus be spared repeating old mistakes. At the same time, perhaps we ourselves may succeed in developing our own

---

5. **partisans** (pärt′ ə zənz): Unreasoning; emotional supporters of a party or viewpoint.

 Speaking and Listening Mini-Lesson

Persuasive Speech

This mini-lesson supports the Speaking and Listening activity in the Idea Bank on page 593.

Introduce the Concept Have students talk about persuasive speeches they have heard or read. Discuss the techniques the speakers used to make their points—such as persuasive language and emphasizing their strongest points—and whether these techniques were effective.

Develop Background Have each student choose an issue to explore. Encourage them to think about effective ways to convince their audiences to share their opinions. Have them ask themselves these questions:

• What do I want to convince my audience to do or think?

• What reasons can I give my audience for agreeing with me?

• What objections might my audience raise? How can I counter these objections?

Apply the Information Using the answers to the questions, students can write their speeches. Remind them to use language their audience will respond to and understand.

Assess the Outcome You and the students can assess the effectiveness of the speeches with the Scoring Rubric for Persuasion and the Self and Peer Assessment sheets for a speech, pages 105, 117, and 118 in *Alternative Assessment*.

588

WORLDWIDE VIEW, like any man, with the center of the eye seeing what is nearby but the periphery[6] of vision taking in what is happening in the rest of the world. We will make correlations[7] and maintain worldwide standards.

Who, if not writers, are to condemn their own unsuccessful governments (in some states this is the easiest way to make a living; everyone who is not too lazy does it) as well as society itself, whether for its cowardly humiliation or for its self-satisfied weakness, or the lightheaded escapades of the young, or the youthful pirates brandishing knives?

We will be told: What can literature do against the pitiless onslaught of naked violence? Let us not forget that violence does not and cannot flourish by itself; it is inevitably intertwined with LYING. Between them there is the closest, the most profound and natural bond: nothing screens violence except lies, and the only way lies can hold out is by violence. Whoever has once announced violence as his METHOD must inexorably choose lying as his PRINCIPLE. At birth, violence behaves openly and even proudly. But as soon as it becomes stronger and firmly established, it senses the thinning of the air around it and cannot go on without befogging itself in lies, coating itself with lying's sugary oratory. It does not always

or necessarily go straight for the gullet; usually it demands of its victims only allegiance to the lie, only complicity in the lie.

The simple act of an ordinary courageous man is not to take part, not to support lies! Let *that* come into the world and even reign over it, but not through me. Writers and artists can do more: they can VANQUISH LIES! In the struggle against lies, art has always won and always will. Conspicuously, incontestably for everyone. Lies can stand up against much in the world, but not against art.

Once lies have been dispelled, the repulsive nakedness of violence will be exposed—and hollow violence will collapse.

That, my friends, is why I think we can help the world in its red-hot hour: not by the naysaying of having no armaments, not by abandoning oneself to the carefree life, but by going into battle!

In Russian, proverbs about TRUTH are favorites. They persistently express the considerable, bitter, grim experience of the people, often astonishingly:

ONE WORD OF TRUTH OUTWEIGHS THE WORLD.

On such a seemingly fantastic violation of the law of the conservation of mass and energy[8] are based both my own activities and my appeal to the writers of the whole world.

---

6. **periphery** (pə rif′ ə rē) n.: Boundary; perimeter.
7. **correlations** (kôr ə lā′ shənz) n.: Relationships; connections.

8. **the law of conservation of mass and energy:** This law states that in any physical or chemical change, neither mass nor energy can be lost.

Guide for Responding

◆ Literature and Your Life

Reader's Response Tell how a work of literature has helped you to understand the values and traditions of different people.

Thematic Focus How can reflecting on other people's experiences help you understand yourself?

☑ Check Your Comprehension

1. To what does the "one great heart" refer?
2. What does Solzhenitsyn believe writers and artists can do?

◆ Critical Thinking

INTERPRET

1. What connection does Solzhenitsyn see between lies and violence? **[Analyze]**
2. What is the meaning of the Russian proverb that Solzhenitsyn quotes? **[Interpret]**

APPLY

3. How well do you think Solzhenitsyn supports his statement that "no such thing as INTERNAL AFFAIRS remains on our crowded Earth"? **[Judge]**
4. Explain why you agree or disagree with the statement "Lies can stand up against much in the world, but not against art." **[Assess]**

from *Nobel Lecture* ◆ 589

589

Keep Memory Alive

Elie Wiesel

▶Critical Viewing◀

❶ Connect The boy in the picture looks apprehensive, or even frightened. If you combine the picture with the title "Keep Memory Alive," you wonder what the boy went through, and why it is important to remember the experience.

Customize for
Less Proficient Readers
Prepare these students by explaining that Wiesel, the speaker, will hold an imaginary dialogue with himself as a youth. Ask students to identify movies or television programs they have seen in which this device has been used, and to describe the purpose or effect.

▲ **Critical Viewing** What emotion do you read on this boy's face? How does it relate to the title of this essay? **[Connect]**

🇩🇪 **Cross-Curricular Connection: Social Studies**

Nazi Concentration Camps Explain that as early as 1933, Nazi leaders set up concentration camps where Jews, Communists, Gypsies, and others who the Nazi party felt did not exemplify pure Germans were imprisoned. By the time World War II started, more than 20,000 people were imprisoned in these camps. The numbers grew tremendously over the next six years. Inmates were worked to death; the sick were killed; Nazi doctors performed experiments on healthy individuals. Millions of camp victims were gassed or shot to death, and millions more died from sickness, overwork, starvation, and brutality.

Discuss with the class why Elie Wiesel feels it is so important to keep such horrifying memories alive. Why would it be wrong for people to put these terrible visions out of their minds? By remembering the horrors that human beings have committed against others, perhaps we can prevent such horrors from occurring in the present and future—or stand up in protest against violations of human rights when they do occur.

It is with a profound sense of humility that I accept the honor you have chosen to bestow upon me. I know: your choice transcends me. This both frightens and pleases me.

It frightens me because I wonder: do I have the right to represent the multitudes who have perished? Do I have the right to accept this great honor on their behalf? I do not. That would be presumptuous. No one may speak for the dead, no one may interpret their mutilated dreams and visions.

❷ It pleases me because I may say that this honor belongs to all the survivors and their children, and through us, to the Jewish people with whose destiny I have always identified.

I remember: it happened yesterday or eternities ago. A young Jewish boy discovered the kingdom of night. I remember his bewilderment, I remember his anguish. It all happened
❸ so fast. The ghetto. The deportation.[1] The sealed cattle car. The fiery altar upon which

the history of our people and the future of mankind were meant to be sacrificed.

I remember: he asked his father: "Can this be true? This is the 20th century, not the Middle Ages. Who would allow such crimes to be committed? How could the world remain silent?"

And now the boy is turning to me: "Tell me," he asks. "What have you done with my future? What have you done with your life?"

And I tell him that I have tried. That I have tried to keep memory alive, that I have tried to fight those who would forget. Because if we forget, we are guilty, we are accomplices.

And then I explained to him how naive we were, that the world did know and remain silent. And that is why I swore never to be silent whenever and wherever human beings endure suffering and humiliation. We must always take sides. Neutrality helps the oppressor, never the victim. Silence encourages the tormentor, never the tormented.

❹

---

1. **deportation** (dē′ pôr tā′ shən) n.: Expulsion from a country.

◆ **Build Vocabulary**

transcends (tran sendz′) v.: Surpasses; exceeds

Guide for Responding

◆ *Literature and Your Life*

Reader's Response Describe a situation today in which silently witnessing might do harm.

Thematic Focus Have you ever reflected on the past in order to keep a lesson in your mind? Explain.

Group Discussion Discuss with several classmates what you know about the Holocaust, where you got your information, and what you can do to "keep memory alive."

☑ Check Your Comprehension

1. What right, or claim, does Wiesel question?
2. Why is the boy incredulous as he's being deported?
3. What does Wiesel call those who deliberately forget the Holocaust?

◆ Critical Thinking

INTERPRET
1. Why does Wiesel use the term "the fiery altar"? **[Interpret]**
2. What is Wiesel's purpose in having his boy self talk to his man self? **[Speculate; Synthesize]**
3. At the end of the piece, of what crime does Wiesel accuse the world, and how did this crime affect his future actions? **[Draw Conclusions]**

APPLY
4. Name two or three atrocities throughout history that were silently witnessed by some. **[Relate]**

EXTEND
5. What are some careers that might involve themselves with keeping historical memories alive? Explain your answer. **[Career Link]**

Keep Memory Alive ◆ 591

Answers

◆ Reading Strategy

1. The strong family ties of the Kiowas is one of the reasons Momaday wants to memorialize his grandmother.
2. Knowing something about the oppressive Communist regime would help students to understand not only Solzhenitsyn's message, but his sense of urgency (or purpose) in writing it.

◆ Build Vocabulary

Using Forms of *Reciprocity*
1. reciprocal; 2. reciprocity;
3. reciprocate; 4. reciprocation

Using the Word Bank
1. tenuous; 2. assimilate; 3. reciprocity; 4. oratory; 5. transcends; 6. inexorably; 7. engender

◆ Literary Focus

1. (a) He loves and respects his grandmother; (b) He respects the Kiowa's unique culture and heritage and regrets their loss.
2. He uses the death of his grandmother as a metaphor for the death of the Kiowa's traditions and heritage.
3. Students should cite appropriate reasons supporting Solzhenitsyn's argument.
4. Allow time for students to compare and evaluate their choices.

◆ Build Grammar Skills

1. The last Sun Dance was held on the Washita River above Rainy Mountain Creek.
2. In July the inland slope of the Rockies is luxuriant.
3. The route stretched from Montana to the plains of Kansas and Oklahoma.
4. The Royal Swedish Academy of Sciences awarded the Jewish writer Elie Wiesel a Nobel Prize for his contributions to world peace.
5. The writer Solzhenitsyn was surprised to receive greetings from European writers.

 Writer's Solution

For additional instruction and practice, use the Problems with Capitalization lesson in the **Language Lab CD-ROM** and pages 93–94 on Rules for Capitalization in the *Writer's Solution Grammar Practice Book*.

Guide for Responding *(continued)*

◆ Reading Strategy

ANALYZE THE AUTHOR'S PURPOSE

In these essays, Solzhenitsyn and Wiesel wrote to persuade and Momaday wrote to share his reflections on his grandmother and the culture of the Kiowas. Your own background knowledge and involvement in what you're reading can help you to understand an author's purpose.

1. Family ties among Kiowa Indians are very tight. How does this fact affect Momaday's purpose in writing?
2. Why would knowing some twentieth-century Russian history help you to understand Solzhenitsyn's purpose in writing?

◆ Build Vocabulary

USING FORMS OF *RECIPROCITY*

Words such as *reciprocity* have other forms—nouns, adjectives, adverbs, or verbs. On your paper, complete each sentence with a form of *reciprocity*.

a. reciprocity   b. reciprocal
c. reciprocate   d. reciprocation

1. Pen pals have a ___?___ arrangement.
2. The worldwide response to Solzhenitsyn's writing demonstrates the ___?___ between writers and readers.
3. Although his situation did not allow him to ___?___, he appreciated the support of other writers.
4. Now, in ___?___, he acknowledges their help in his acceptance speech.

USING THE WORD BANK

On your paper, write the word from the Word Bank that is suggested by each song title.
1. *Hanging by a Thread*
2. *(You Know) I Fit Right In*
3. *Give and Take*
4. *Speaking for Myself*
5. *My Love Is Higher Than the Sky*
6. *Without a Doubt (It Has to Be)*
7. *You've Created This Feeling*

◆ Literary Focus

REFLECTIVE AND PERSUASIVE ESSAYS

Your own ideas, experiences, and opinions affect the way you respond to Momaday's reflections in the excerpt from *The Way to Rainy Mountain* and the arguments in the persuasive essays by Solzhenitsyn and Wiesel.

1. (a) How does Momaday feel about his grandmother? (b) How does he feel about Kiowa culture?
2. How do Momaday's reflections on the death of his grandmother help him communicate a message about his Kiowa culture?
3. Analyze how well Solzhenitsyn argues his premise that world literature belongs to the world and not to a single country. What reasons does he give?
4. In your opinion, what is the most persuasive sentence in "Keep Memory Alive"? Explain your choice.

◆ Build Grammar Skills

CAPITALIZATION OF PROPER NOUNS AND ADJECTIVES

All **proper nouns** and **proper adjectives** begin with capital letters.

Practice Rewrite the following sentences, capitalizing the proper nouns and adjectives in each.
1. The last sun dance was held on the washita river above rainy mountain creek.
2. In july the inland slope of the rockies is luxuriant.
3. The route stretched from montana to the plains of kansas and oklahoma.
4. The royal swedish academy of sciences awarded the jewish writer Elie Wiesel a nobel prize for his contributions to world peace.
5. The writer solzhenitsyn was surprised to receive greetings from european writers.

Writing Application Write a paragraph describing your achievements that would qualify you for a prize. Use at least two proper nouns and two proper adjectives.

 Beyond the Selection

FURTHER READING

Other Works by the Authors
The Ancient Child, N. Scott Momaday
One Day in the Life of Ivan Denisovich, Alexander Solzhenitsyn
Night, Elie Wiesel

Other Works About the Past
The Diary of a Young Girl, Anne Frank
The Wall, John Hersey

We suggest that you preview these works before recommending them to students.

INTERNET

Students can learn more at the following Web sites. Please be aware that addresses may have changed.

For N. Scott Momaday: **http://www.ipl.org/cgi/ref/native/browse.pl/A50**

For Alexander Solzhenitsyn: **http://www.empirenet.com/~rdaeley/authors/solzhenitsyn.html**

For Elie Wiesel: **http://members.aol.com/KatharenaE/private/Philo/Wiesel/wiesel.html**

We *strongly recommend* that you preview the sites before you send students to them.

Build Your Portfolio

 Idea Bank

Writing

1. **Letter** Write a persuasive letter to convince a friend of the importance of remembering the Holocaust.

2. **Report** Write a two-page report on Communist Russia during the time Solzhenitsyn's work was being repressed, beginning in the 1940's. Emphasize the climate that resulted in the repression of writers' works.

3. **Creation Myth** The excerpt from *The Way to Rainy Mountain* includes a Kiowa myth that explains a rock formation in the Black Hills. Write a brief myth of your own to explain the origins of something—such as telling how the Big Dipper or another natural phenomenon came to be.

Speaking and Listening

4. **Persuasive Speech** Choose an issue, such as whether gyms should be open at night, and give a five-minute speech persuading your audience to feel as you do. **[Performing Arts Link]**

5. **Myth Reading** Find a collection of myths from the Kiowa or another Native American culture. Read your favorite aloud to classmates, recording it if possible. **[Social Studies Link]**

Projects

6. **Native American Dances** In a small group, research the ritual dances of four Native American groups, including the Kiowa Sun Dance. Explain the dances to your class. **[Social Studies Link; Performing Arts Link]**

7. **Writers-in-Prison** Contact a human rights organization or search the Internet to find out about writers who, like Solzhenitsyn, have been imprisoned as a result of what they write. **[Social Studies Link]**

 Writing Mini-Lesson

Acceptance Speech

The Nobel Prize acceptance speeches of Solzhenitsyn and Wiesel have been read by people around the world. Write an acceptance speech for the award of your dreams. The achievement is up to you, but this is your chance to address yourself to the largest possible audience. Organize your speech around a strong and meaningful main point.

Writing Skills Focus: Placement for Emphasis

In a speech or persuasive essay, the placement of ideas affects a reader's response to them. The last line of Elie Wiesel's speech—"Silence encourages the tormentor, never the tormented"—has tremendous staying power. Had he begun with this line, it might not have been as effective, because Wiesel needed to provide information to lead up to it. Arrange your ideas in an order that is clear and logical and that emphasizes the most important points. You may, like Wiesel, choose to place your most important points at the end of your speech to make a strong final impression.

Prewriting What will be your most important point? Write a list of possible points, then cross out points that seem weaker or difficult to handle in the form of a speech.

Drafting As you draft, keep in mind the final point you plan to make. Lead up to it with examples, facts, or relevant details.

Revising Read your speech aloud to yourself. Is your key point placed effectively? Make any necessary changes to improve the effectiveness of your speech. Check also that all proper nouns and adjectives are capitalized.

For more on capitalization of proper nouns and adjectives, see pp. 580 and 592.

from *The Way to Rainy Mountain*/from *Nobel Lecture*/*Keep Memory Alive* ◆ 593

 Idea Bank

Customizing for
Performance Levels

Following are suggestions for matching Idea Bank topics with your students' performance levels:

Less Advanced Students: 1, 4, 6
Average Students: 2, 5, 7
More Advanced Students: 3

Customizing for
Learning Modalities

Following are suggestions for matching Idea Bank topics with your students' learning modalities:

Visual/Spatial: 6, 7
Verbal/Linguistic: 4, 5
Rhythmic/Musical: 4
Logical/Mathematical: 3

Writing Mini-Lesson

Refer students to the Writing Handbook, page 965, for instruction on the writing process, and page 968 for further information on persuasion.

Writing Lab CD-ROM

In writing their acceptance speeches, students may make a point persuasively. Have students complete the tutorial on Persuasion. Follow these steps:

1. Have students consult an annotated model on supporting a persuasive argument.

2. Suggest that students also go to the annotated example of exploiting an emotional reaction for ideas to give emotional appeal to a persuasive argument.

3. Ask students to use the notecard activity and drag cards into different positions to organize their ideas.

Sourcebook

Have students use Chapter 4, Persuasion (pp. 97–122), for additional support. The chapter includes an annotated model of a persuasive speech (p. 104).

✓ ASSESSMENT OPTIONS

Formal Assessment, Selection Test, pp. 148–150, and Assessment Resources Software. The selection test is designed so that it can be easily customized to the performance levels of your students.
Alternative Assessment, p. 42, includes options for less advanced students, more advanced students, verbal/linguistic learners, visual/spatial learners, and musical/rhythmic learners.

PORTFOLIO ASSESSMENT
Use the following rubrics in the *Alternative Assessment* booklet to assess student writing:
Letter: Persuasion Rubric, p. 105
Report: Research Report Rubric p. 106
Creation Myth: Fictional Narrative Rubric p. 95

OBJECTIVES

1. To read, comprehend, and interpret a biography and an autobiography
2. To relate a biography and an autobiography to personal experience
3. To recognize the author's attitude
4. To identify elements of biography and autobiography
5. To build vocabulary in context and learn musical words
6. To recognize and correctly punctuate restrictive and nonrestrictive appositives
7. To write a letter using logical organization
8. To respond to the biography and the autobiography through writing, speaking and listening, and projects

SKILLS INSTRUCTION

Vocabulary:
Musical Words

Grammar:
Restrictive and Nonrestrictive Appositives

Reading Strategy:
Recognize Author's Attitude

Literary Focus:
Biography and Autobiography

Writing:
Logical Organization

Speaking and Listening:
Analyzing a Recording (teacher edition)

Critical Viewing:
Draw Conclusions; Assess; Analyze

PORTFOLIO OPPORTUNITIES

Writing: Essay: Your Favorite Holiday; Memory from Childhood; Biography

Writing Mini-Lesson: Letter to Yourself in Twenty Years

Speaking and Listening: Memory Music; Marian Anderson Recording

Projects: Greeting Card; Multimedia Presentation

More About the Authors

Dylan Thomas was in love with the sound of language. Even his prose works display appreciation of the sound of language through poetic devices such as alliteration, onomatopoeia, and rhythm.

Langston Hughes was an inspiration and mentor to many poets in Africa, the Caribbean, and the United States. Hughes said in an interview for *The Nation* (1926), "We younger Negro artists who create now intend to express our individual dark skinned selves without fear or shame...."

Guide for Reading

Dylan Thomas *(1914–1953)*

Some people spend years trying to figure out what they want to do with their lives. Dylan Thomas, however, wanted to be a poet ever since he was a small child.

A Brief Life Thomas was born in the picturesque seaside village of Swansea, Wales. In the poem "Fern Hill" (1946), he fondly evokes the memories of his early childhood.

Thomas's first book of poetry was published when he moved to London at the age of twenty. Recent research indicates that all his poems—at least the first drafts—were completed by the time he was twenty-one years old! His poetry readings in England and the United States brought him popular appeal, but little income. Poverty and a stormy private life took their toll, and Thomas died in New York at the age of thirty-nine.

Langston Hughes *(1902–1967)*

Langston Hughes traveled to places as far and wide as Africa, Europe, the Soviet Union (now Russia), China, and Japan, and he lived in Paris and Italy.

Renaissance Man Although Hughes traveled widely, his work is associated mostly with the Harlem Renaissance —a period when some of America's finest writers, artists, and musicians centered in Harlem, New York, brought previously unrecognized aspects of the African American experience into the spotlight. Hughes, for instance, used the rhythm and mood of jazz and blues in his poetry. He has been called the poet laureate of the Harlem Renaissance, but he also wrote nonfiction, novels, and plays, as well as at least twenty scripts for opera, radio, and film.

◆ Build Vocabulary

WORD GROUPS: MUSICAL WORDS

The world of music has its own vocabulary of specific "musical" terms. One such word, which you will encounter in Hughes's account of Marian Anderson, is *aria*. An *aria* is a melody in an opera, usually for a solo voice with instrumental accompaniment. Another word he uses is *repertoire*, a French word that refers to a group of songs that a musician or singer knows well and is always ready to perform. Marian Anderson had a number of *arias* in her *repertoire*.

sidle
prey
wallowed
crocheted
brittle
trod
forlorn
arias
staunch
repertoire

WORD BANK

Before you read, preview this list of words from the selections. Some may already be familiar to you. In your notebook, write all the words and jot down the meanings of those you know.

◆ Build Grammar Skills

RESTRICTIVE AND NONRESTRICTIVE APPOSITIVES

An **appositive** is a noun or pronoun placed near another noun or pronoun to provide more information about it. An appositive phrase contains the appositive and any words that modify it.

Appositives are either restrictive or nonrestrictive. A **restrictive appositive** is essential to the meaning of the sentence and is not set off by commas.

...I was in Mrs. Prothero's garden...with her son *Jim*.

The appositive *Jim* is restrictive. It is necessary to identify which son.

A **nonrestrictive appositive** is not essential and is set off by commas.

...a famous group of Negro singers, *the Fisk Jubilee Singers*, had already carried the spirituals.

This appositive adds detail to the sentence, but it is not essential to the sentence's meaning.

594 ◆ Nonfiction

Prentice Hall Literature Program Resources

REINFORCE / RETEACH / EXTEND

Selection Support Pages
Build Vocabulary: Musical Words, p. 176
Build Grammar Skills: Restrictive and Nonrestrictive Appositives, p. 177
Reading Strategy: Recognize Author's Attitude, p. 178

Literary Focus: Biography/Autobiography, p. 179

Strategies for Diverse Student Needs, p. 43

Beyond Literature Career Connection: Music, p. 43

Formal Assessment Selection Test, pp. 151–153;

Assessment Resources Software

Alternative Assessment, p. 43

Writing and Language Transparencies
Daily Language Practice, Week 16, p. 127

Art Transparency, 20

Resource Pro CD-R⊘M "A Child's Christmas in Wales," "Marian Anderson,"—includes all resource materials and customizable lesson plan

Listening to Literature Audiocassettes "A Child's Christmas in Wales," "Marian Anderson"

◆ A Child's Christmas in Wales ◆
Marian Anderson: Famous Concert Singer

◆ *Literature and Your Life*

CONNECT YOUR EXPERIENCE

Our remembrances take shape around people, places, and events from our past because they have a special significance. In "A Child's Christmas in Wales," Dylan Thomas shares memories of a holiday in his childhood home. Langston Hughes's account of Marion Anderson makes it possible for generations of readers to "remember" her.

THEMATIC FOCUS: FROM THE PAST

These two selections show two kinds of legacies—one personal, one public. What do you think is the value of reflecting on the past?

Journal Writing Write a short autobiographical account based on a person, place, or event that you remember fondly.

◆ Background for Understanding

HISTORY

That Marian Anderson (an African American woman living before the civil rights movements of the 1950's and 1960's) achieved the level of success she did is a remarkable achievement. Because of racial prejudice in the United States, Anderson and a number of other African American musicians and artists of the same era were unable to achieve the level of recognition of their white counterparts and went to Europe to find fame. Even after she achieved international recognition, Anderson was not permitted to sing in certain public places in the United States because of her race.

◆ Literary Focus

BIOGRAPHY AND AUTOBIOGRAPHY

A **biography** is an account of a person's life written by another individual. In many biographies, the major events and accomplishments of the subject's life are covered in chronological order. The biographer gathers information from sources such as letters, diaries, and interviews with the subject or people who knew the subject, and then weaves together and interprets the information.

An **autobiography,** on the other hand, is a person's own account of his or her life. The writer of an autobiography can share personal thoughts and feelings and may comment on the effects of certain events on his or her life. Dylan Thomas shares events from his life in his autobiographical account, "A Child's Christmas in Wales."

◆ Reading Strategy

RECOGNIZE THE AUTHOR'S ATTITUDE

Both biographers and autobiographers have a particular attitude toward their subjects. Once you recognize the **author's attitude** you'll be able to read with better understanding.

The author's attitude is the way he or she feels about the subject. This attitude is reflected in the way the author interprets the events of the subject's life. If the author admires and respects the subject, for example, then the author will present the details of the subject's life in such a way that you, the reader, will also admire and respect the subject.

In an autobiographical account, if the author remembers an event fondly or humorously or sadly, then you will feel that way too.

To recognize an author's attitude, notice the details and events the author chooses to present, and think about the message the author conveys— either directly or indirectly— through this information.

Preparing for Standardized Tests

Grammar and Language In portions of standardized tests where students are asked to select the correctly punctuated sentence, some sentences with restrictive and nonrestrictive appositives will be among the items. Write the following sentences on the chalkboard. Ask students to choose the one that is correctly punctuated and to give reasons for their choice.

(A) My cousin, Kyle, has two sisters.
(B) Kyle O'Brien, my favorite cousin, is here.

Sentence *B* is correctly punctuated. It contains a nonrestrictive appositive, which is not essential to the meaning of the sentence and should be set off by commas. (Sentence A may be correct if the speaker has only one cousin, Kyle.)

The Build Grammar Skills lesson for this selection focuses on this topic. For more practice, use the Build Grammar Skills page on Restrictive and Nonrestrictive Appositives, p. 177, in *Selection Support.*

"A Child's Christmas in Wales" evokes the enchantment that holiday celebrations hold for children. In this famous work, the voice of the adult Dylan Thomas describes childhood Christmases, blended and transfigured by the magic of memory. With fondness and nostalgia, he recalls the activities, sensory details, and people he associates with this holiday.

Customizing for
Intrapersonal Learners

These students may experience a sense of personal connection with the feelings and attitudes Thomas conveys in this autobiographical piece. As they read, encourage them to pause and reflect on events from their own past that arouse feelings similar to those that Thomas describes. They can record these feelings in their journals to later use them as a basis for their own remembrances.

◆ Critical Thinking

❶ Interpret Let students know that Thomas is making the point that family stories tend to get exaggerated and mixed up. Ask students to explain why this might be so. *Events from the past tend to overlap in our memories and blur together; sometimes people exaggerate events to create a humorous or dramatic effect on listeners.*

A Child's Christmas
in
Wales

Dylan Thomas

❶ One Christmas was so much like another, in those years around the sea-town corner now and out of all sound except the distant speaking of the voices I sometimes hear a moment before sleep, that I can never remember whether it snowed for six days and six nights when I was twelve or whether it snowed for twelve days and twelve nights when I was six. All the Christmases roll down toward the **❶**

The Whistle (tinted), Fritz Eichenberg etching, © Fritz Eichenberg Trust/Licensed by VAGA, New York, NY

596 ◆ *Nonfiction*

Consider these suggestions to take advantage of extended class time:

• Introduce the concepts of biography and autobiography. After students have read these essays, have them answer the Literary Focus questions on page 606. You may follow up with the Literary Focus page in *Selection Support,* p. 179.

• Have students listen to all or part of the selections on audiocassette. You may want to play "A Child's Christmas in Wales" in portions over several days to give students a chance to accustom themselves to the work's poetic language and improve their comprehension.

• Expand upon the Reading Strategy by encouraging volunteers to identify the author's attitude in literary works they have read recently, and to explain how they arrived at their conclusion.

• Use *Daily Language Practice* for Week 16. You may want to use the transparency on the overhead projector and have students write the sentences correctly, or you may dictate the sentences and have students write them.

• Set aside class time for students to present their Memory Music selections from the Speaking and Listening Activities (p. 607) or their Multimedia Presentations from the Projects in the Idea Bank (p. 607).

two-tongued sea, like a cold and headlong moon bundling down the sky that was our street; and they stop at the rim of the ice-edged, fish-freezing waves, and I plunge my hands in the snow and bring out whatever I can find. In goes my hand into that wool-white bell-tongued ball of holidays resting at the rim of the carol-singing seas, and out come Mrs. Prothero and the firemen.

It was on the afternoon of the day of Christmas Eve, and I was in Mrs. Prothero's garden, waiting for cats, with her son Jim. It was snowing. It was always snowing at Christmas. December, in my memory, is white as Lapland, though there were no reindeers. But there were cats. Patient, cold and callous, our hands wrapped in socks, we waited to snowball the cats. Sleek and long as jaguars and horrible-whiskered, spitting and snarling, they would slink and <u>sidle</u> over the white back-garden walls, and the lynx-eyed hunters, Jim and I, furcapped and moccasined trappers from Hudson Bay,[1] off Mumbles Road, would hurl our deadly snowballs at the green of their eyes. The wise cats never appeared. We were so still, Eskimo-footed arctic marksmen in the muffling silence of the eternal snows—eternal, ever since Wednesday—that we never heard Mrs. Prothero's first cry from her igloo at the bottom of the garden. Or, if we heard it at all, it was, to us, like the far-off challenge of our enemy and <u>prey</u>, the neighbor's polar cat. But soon the voice grew louder. "Fire!" cried Mrs. Prothero, and she beat the dinner-gong.

And we ran down the garden, with the snowballs in our arms, toward the house; and smoke, indeed, was pouring out of the dining room, and the gong was bombilating,[2] and Mrs. Prothero was announcing ruin like a town crier in Pompeii.[3] This was better than all the cats in Wales standing on the wall in a row. We bounded into the house, laden with snowballs, and stopped at the open door of the smoke-filled room.

Something was burning all right; perhaps it

was Mr. Prothero, who always slept there after midday dinner with a newspaper over his face. But he was standing in the middle of the room, saying "A fine Christmas!" and smacking at the smoke with a slipper.

"Call the fire brigade," cried Mrs. Prothero as she beat the gong.

"They won't be there," said Mr. Prothero, "it's Christmas."

There was no fire to be seen, only clouds of smoke and Mr. Prothero standing in the middle of them, waving his slipper as though he were conducting.

"Do something," he said.

And we threw all our snowballs into the smoke—I think we missed Mr. Prothero—and ran out of the house to the telephone box.

"Let's call the police as well," Jim said.

"And the ambulance."

"And Ernie Jenkins, he likes fires."

But we only called the fire brigade, and soon the fire engine came and three tall men in helmets brought a hose into the house and Mr. Prothero got out just in time before they turned it on. Nobody could have had a noisier Christmas Eve. And when the firemen turned off the hose and were standing in the wet, smoky room, Jim's aunt, Miss Prothero, came downstairs and peered in at them. Jim and I waited, very quietly, to hear what she would say to them. She said the right thing, always. She looked at the three tall firemen in their shining helmets, standing among the smoke and cinders and dissolving snowballs, and she said: "Would you like anything to read?"

Years and years and years ago, when I was a boy, when there were wolves in Wales, and birds the color of red-flannel petticoats whisked past the harp-shaped hills, when we sang and <u>wallowed</u> all night and day in caves that smelt

---

1. **Hudson Bay:** Inland sea in northeastern Canada.
2. **bombilating** (bäm´ be lāt in) *v.:* Making a buzzing, droning sound as though a bomb were approaching.
3. **Pompeii** (päm pā´): City in Italy that was destroyed by the eruption of Mount Vesuvius in A.D. 79.

◀ Critical Viewing Based on this picture, what kind of characters do you expect to find in Thomas's childhood memory? [Draw Conclusions]

◆ **Literary Focus**
Notice how Thomas reveals details in this passage that only someone who was present would know.

◆ **Build Vocabulary**

sidle (sī´ del) *v.:* Move sideways in a sneaky manner

prey (prā) *n.:* Animal hunted and killed for food

wallowed (wäl´ ōd) *v.:* Enjoyed completely; took great pleasure

A Child's Christmas in Wales ◆ 597

◆ **Build Grammar Skills**

❷ **Restrictive and Nonrestrictive Appositives** Ask students why the words "Jim and I" are set off by commas. What information do they add to the noun "hunters"? *The words Jim and I form a nonrestrictive appositive phrase. Because the appositive phrase is not essential, it is set off by commas. The phrase tells who the "lynx-eyed hunters" are.*

❸ **Clarify** If necessary, explain that Mrs. Prothero doesn't really live in an igloo. Thomas is describing events as the boys envisioned them in their imaginations, while they were pretending to be Eskimo hunters.

◆ **Reading Strategy**

❹ **Recognize the Author's Attitude** Ask students what attitude Thomas takes toward the fire in Mrs. Prothero's house. Then ask which details in the passage hint at his feelings. *Thomas is amused by the incident. Whimsical phrases such "bombilating," "like a town crier in Pompeii," and "better than all the cats in Wales standing on the wall in a row" suggest he finds the incidents funny and that he looks back fondly upon them.*

▶Critical Viewing◀

❺ **Draw Conclusions** Elicit responses such as the following: *Based on the expressions on the boys' faces, the memory might include boys who are mischievous and rambunctious.*

◆ **Literary Focus**

❻ **Biography and Autobiography** Point out details such as "three tall men in helmets," "Mr. Prothero got out just in time," and Miss Prothero's question "Would you like anything to read?"

Cross-Curricular Connection: Social Studies

Wales is a principality located west of England. Along with England, Scotland, and Northern Ireland, it makes up the United Kingdom, or Great Britain. The Welsh have their own ancient language, but Welsh citizens are bilingual, speaking English as well.

Wales is bounded on the north by the Irish Sea, on the west by St. George's Channel (across which lies the country of Ireland), and on the south by the Bristol Channel. Wales has a maritime climate with heavy annual precipitation of rain and snow. Dylan Thomas was born in the southern seaport town of Swansea, a large industrial center where coal mined in the north is used in the manufacture of steel.

Have students discuss how living on the Welsh seacoast influenced Dylan Thomas's childhood experiences and memories.

❶ Clarify Explain that although Wales is part of the United Kingdom and governed by England, the Welsh have fought many battles throughout history to resist English rule.

Comprehension Check ☑

❷ Who might the small boy be? He might be a youngster who is listening while the narrator reminisces, or he might be a fantasized boy in the narrator's imagination.

◆ Critical Thinking

❸ Infer Ask students why the narrator tells the boy that the snows of his childhood were different from the snows of today. *Possible response: People tend to exaggerate memories from their childhood because the world seems more intense and extreme from a child's point of view.*

►Critical Viewing◄

❹ Assess Students should notice the relaxed body positions and facial expressions of the four figures. The soft light, the homey furnishings, and the sampler reading "GOD BLESS OUR HOME" create the comforting mood described in Thomas's piece.

---

❶ like Sunday afternoons in damp front farmhouse parlors, and we chased, with the jawbones of deacons, the English and the bears, before the motor car, before the wheel, before the duchess-faced horse, when we rode the daft[4] and happy hills bareback, it snowed and it snowed. But here a small boy says: "It snowed last year, too. I made a snowman and my

❷ brother knocked it down and I knocked my brother down and then we had tea."

"But that was not the same snow," I say. "Our snow was not only shaken from whitewash buckets down the sky, it came shawling[5] out of the ground and swam and drifted out of the arms and hands

❸ and bodies of the trees; snow grew overnight on the roofs of the houses like a pure and grandfather moss, minutely white-ivied the walls and settled on the postman, opening the gate, like a dumb, numb thunderstorm of white, torn Christmas cards."

"Were there postmen then, too?"

"With sprinkling eyes and wind-cherried noses, on spread, frozen feet they crunched up to the doors and mittened on them manfully. But all that the children could hear was a ringing of bells."

"You mean that the postman went rat-a-tat-tat and the doors rang?"

"I mean that the bells that the children could hear were inside them."

"I only hear thunder sometimes, never bells."

"There were church bells, too."

"Inside them?"

"No, no, no, in the bat-black, snow-white belfries, tugged by bishops and storks. And they rang their tidings over the bandaged town, over

4. **daft:** Silly; foolish.
5. **shawling:** Draping like a shawl.

598 ◆ Nonfiction

● the frozen foam of the powder and ice-cream hills, over the crackling sea. It seemed that all the churches boomed for joy under my window: and the weathercocks crew for Christmas, on our fence."

"Get back to the postmen."

"They were just ordinary postmen, fond of walking and dogs and Christmas and the snow. They knocked on the doors with blue knuckles. . . ."

"Ours has got a black knocker. . . ."

"And then they stood on the white Welcome mat in the little, drifted porches and huffed and puffed, making ghosts with their breath, and jogged from foot to foot like small boys wanting to go out."

The Aunts (tinted), Fritz Eichenberg etching, © Fritz Eichenberg Trust/Licensed by VAGA, New York, NY

▲ **Critical Viewing** How well does this picture capture
❹ the atmosphere of the holiday Thomas describes?
[Assess]

"And then the presents?"

"And then the Presents, after the Christmas box. And the cold postman, with a rose on his button-nose, tingled down the tea-tray-slithered run of the chilly glinting hill. He went in his ice-bound boots like a man on fishmonger's slabs.[6] He wagged his bag like a frozen camel's hump, dizzily turned the corner on one foot, and was gone."

"Get back to the Presents."

"There were the Useful Presents: engulfing mufflers of the old coach days, and mittens made for giant sloths;[7] zebra scarfs of a

6. **fishmonger's slabs:** Flat, slimy surface on which fish are displayed for sale.
7. **sloths** (slôths) *n.*: Two-toed mammals that hang from trees.

◆ Build Vocabulary

crocheted (krō shād´) *v.*: Made with thread or yarn woven with hooked needles

---

🎵 Humanities: Art

The Whistle and **The Aunts** by Fritz Eichenberg.

The German artist Fritz Eichenberg has illustrated many classic children's books, including Jonathan Swift's *Gulliver's Travels* and the modern classic *Black Beauty,* by Anne Sewell. Born in Cologne, Germany, Eichenberg traveled as a young man and eventually settled in Tuckahoe, New York.

These highly rendered ink drawings depict two scenes described in Thomas's autobiographical work. In both illustrations, Eichenberg's cartoonish faces capture perfectly the boys and aunts Dylan describes—loving and cozy characters.

Use these questions for discussion:
1. Why did the artist depict the two boys as looking exactly alike? *In the text Thomas says the other boy is "the spit of myself," meaning he looks the same. The physical resemblance also suggests the common cocky attitude the two boys share, as*

well as their similar Christmas experiences.

2. Which aspects of the scene shown in "The Aunts" suggests a setting in the past? Which aspect of the scene might be the same as in a contemporary holiday illustration? *The clothing, hairstyles, and room furnishings suggest a past setting. The child playing among relatives is common to all times.*

substance like silky gum that could be tug-o'-warred down to the galoshes;[8] blinding tam-o'-shanters[9] like patchwork tea cozies[10] and bunny-suited busbies[11] and balaclavas[12] for victims of head-shrinking tribes; from aunts who always wore wool next to the skin there were mustached and rasping vests that made you wonder why the aunts had any skin left at all; and once I had a little <u>crocheted</u> nose bag from an aunt now, alas, no longer whinnying with us. And pictureless books in which small boys, though warned with quotations not to, *would* skate on Farmer Giles' pond and did and drowned; and books that told me everything about the wasp, except why."

"Go on to the Useless Presents."

"Bags of moist and many-colored jelly babies[13] and a folded flag and a false nose and a tram-conductor's cap[14] and a machine that punched tickets and rang a bell; never a catapult;[15] once, by mistake that no one could explain, a little hatchet; and a celluloid duck that made, when you pressed it, a most unducklike sound, a mewing moo that an ambitious cat might make who wished to be a cow; and a painting book in which I could make the grass, the trees, the sea and the animals any color I pleased, and still the dazzling sky-blue sheep are grazing in the red field under the rainbow-billed and peagreen birds. Hard-boileds, toffee, fudge and allsorts, crunches, cracknels, humbugs, glaciers, marzipan, and butterwelsh[16] for the Welsh. And troops of bright tin soldiers who, if they could not fight, could always run. And Snakes-and-Families and Happy

Ladders.[17] And Easy Hobbi-Games for Little Engineers, complete with instructions. Oh, easy for Leonardo![18] And a whistle to make the dogs bark to wake up the old man next door to make him beat on the wall with his stick to shake our picture off the wall. And a packet of cigarettes: you put one in your mouth and you stood at the corner of the street and you waited for hours, in vain, for an old lady to scold you for smoking a cigarette, and then with a smirk you ate it. And then it was breakfast under the balloons."

◆ **Reading Strategy**
What is the author's attitude toward the Useful Presents? The Useless Presents?
❺

"Were there Uncles, like in our house?"

"There are always Uncles at Christmas. The same Uncles. And on Christmas mornings, with dog-disturbing whistle and sugar fags,[19] I would scour the swatched town for the news of the little world, and find always a dead bird by the white Post Office or by the deserted swings; perhaps a robin, all but one of his fires out. Men and women wading or scooping back from chapel, with taproom noses and wind-bussed cheeks, all albinos,[20] huddled their stiff black jarring feathers against the irreligious snow. Mistletoe hung

❻

The Aunts (detail and tint), Fritz Eichenberg etching.
© Fritz Eichenberg Trust/Licensed by VAGA, New York, NY

8. **galoshes** (gə läsh′ əz) *n.:* Rubber overshoes or boots.
9. **tam-o'-shanters:** Scottish caps.
10. **tea cozies:** Knitted or padded covers placed over a teapot to keep the contents warm.
11. **busbies** (buz′ bēz): Tall fur hats worn as part of the full-dress uniforms of guardsmen in the British army.
12. **balaclavas** (bäl′ ə klä′ vez): Knitted helmets with an opening for the nose and eyes.
13. **jelly babies:** Candies in the shape of babies.
14. **tram conductor's cap:** Streetcar or trolley car operator's cap.
15. **catapult** (kat′ ə pult′): Ancient military machine for throwing or shooting stones or spears; slingshot.
16. **hard-boileds . . . butterwelsh:** Various kinds of

17. **Snakes-and-Families and Happy Ladders:** Games, the names of which Dylan Thomas mixes up on purpose. The games are actually Snakes-and-Ladders and Happy Families.
18. **Leonardo:** Leonardo da Vinci (1452–1519), an Italian painter, sculptor, architect, engineer, and scientist.
19. **sugar fags:** Candy cigarettes.
20. **albinos** (al bī′ nōz): People who because of a genetic factor have unusually pale skin and white hair.

A Child's Christmas in Wales ◆ 599

◆ **Reading Strategy**

❺ **Recognize the Author's Attitude** Elicit responses such as the following: *Like a child, Thomas still finds the "Useful Presents" uninteresting and silly. On the other hand, he still feels a sense of wonder, enchantment, and delight as he remembers the "Useless Presents," the favorite toys of his childhood.*

◆ **Literary Focus**

❻ **Biography and Autobiography** Ask: In what ways do the details in this passage add to the autobiography? *The vivid details help readers to imagine exactly what life was like in Thomas's town at Christmas. The details enable readers to put themselves in the boy's place. They may also evoke readers' own memories of Christmas.*

Customize for
Visual Spatial Learners
Encourage these students to compare the details of the pictures that accompany the text to the text itself. Tell students that because the pictures were created specifically for this story, they should be able to identify significant details in the pictures that reflect Thomas's recollections.

Cross-Curricular Connection: Art

Use Art Transparency 20 to illustrate for students how an artist can uses images and impressions to create a sense of "memory." Place the transparency on the overhead projector. Ask students to identify the objects in the picture that are often associated with, or that suggest, memory or the past. *Mirrors, with their reflective properties, suggest looking back. The clock, as a timepiece, could represent the passage of time. The empty room suggests events that have passed or people that have left. The train suggests moving on, leaving something behind.*

Then ask students to explain how these objects and the way they are represented might relate to the title. *The crisp, neat arrangement suggests a suspended moment, a moment transfixed in time.* Finally, have students discuss how memory creates a sense of time transfixed, as in Thomas's recollection of Christmases past. *Like the artist, Thomas combines several images and, in his memory, seems to suspend them. The boy in his memory does not grow older, even though the man who remembers him does.*

The Whistle (detail and tint), Fritz Eichenberg etching, © Fritz Eichenberg Trust/Licensed by VAGA, New York, NY

❶ from the gas brackets[21] in all the front parlors; there was sherry and walnuts and bottled beer and crackers by the dessert-spoons; and cats in their fur-abouts watched the fires; and the high-heaped fire spat, all ready for the chestnuts and the mulling pokers. Some few large men sat in the front parlors, without their collars, Uncles almost certainly, trying their new cigars, holding them out judiciously at arms' length, returning them to their mouths, coughing, then holding them out again as though waiting for the explosion; and some few small aunts, not wanted in the kitchen, nor anywhere else for that matter, sat on the very edges of their chairs, poised and <u>brittle,</u> afraid to break, like faded cups and saucers."

Not many those mornings <u>trod</u> the piling streets: an old man always, fawn-bowlered,[22] yellow-gloved and, at this time of year, with spats[23] of snow, would take his constitutional[24] to the white bowling green and back, as he would take it wet or fine on Christmas Day or Dooms-day; sometimes two hale young men, with big pipes blazing, no overcoats and wind-blown scarfs, would trudge, unspeaking, down to the <u>forlorn</u> sea, to work up an appetite, to blow away the fumes, who knows, to walk into the waves until nothing of them was left but the two curling smoke clouds of their inextinguishable briars.[25] Then I would be slap-dashing home, the gravy smell of the dinners of others, the bird smell, the brandy, the pudding and mince, coiling up to my ❷ nostrils, when out of a snow-clogged side lane would come a boy the spit of myself, with a pink-tipped cigarette and the violet past of a black eye, cocky as a bullfinch, leering all to himself. I hated him on sight and sound, and would be about to put my dog whistle to my lips and blow him off the face of Christmas when suddenly he, with a violet wink, put *his* whistle to *his* lips and blew so stridently, so high, so exquisitely loud,

---

21. **gas brackets:** Wall fixtures for gas lights.
22. **fawn-bowlered:** Tan-hatted.
23. **spats:** Coverings for the instep and ankle.
24. **constitutional:** Walk taken for one's health.
25. **briars:** Pipes.

600 ◆ *Nonfiction*

● that gobbling faces, their cheeks bulged with goose, would press against their tinseled windows, the whole length of the white echoing street. For dinner we had turkey and blazing pudding, and after dinner the Uncles sat in front of the fire, loosened all buttons, put their large moist hands over their watch chains, groaned a little and slept. Mothers, aunts and sisters scuttled to and fro, bearing tureens.[26] Auntie Bessie, who had already been frightened, twice, by a clock-work mouse, whimpered at the sideboard and had some elderberry wine. The dog was sick. Auntie Dosie had to have three as-pirins, but Auntie Hannah, who liked port, stood in the middle of the snowbound back yard, singing like a big-bosomed thrush. I would blow up balloons to see how big they would blow up to; and, when they burst, which they all did, the Uncles jumped and rumbled. In the rich and heavy afternoon, the Uncles breathing like dol-phins and the snow descending, I would sit among festoons[27] and Chinese lanterns and nib-ble dates and try to make a model man-o'-war[28] following the Instructions for Little Engineers, and produce what might be mistaken for a sea-going tramcar.

Or I would go out, my bright new boots squeaking, into the white world, on to the sea-ward hill, to call on Jim and Dan and Jack and to pad through the still streets, leaving huge deep footprints on the hidden pavements.

"I bet people will think there's been hippos."

"What would you do if you saw a hippo coming down our street?"

"I'd go like this, bang! I'd throw him over the railings and roll him down the hill and then I'd tickle him under the ear and he'd wag his tail."

"What would you do if you saw *two* hippos?"

● Iron-flanked and bellowing he-hippos clanked and battered through the scudding snow toward us as we passed Mr. Daniel's house.

---

26. **tureens** (too rēnz′): Deep dishes with covers.
27. **festoons:** Wreaths and garlands.
28. **man-o'-war:** Warship.

Cross-Curricular Connection: Social Studies

Winter Holidays Since ancient times many cultures around the world have celebrated holidays around the winter solstice, the longest night of the year. Today, some of the best-known mid-winter holidays are Christmas, in which Christians celebrate the birth of the Infant Jesus; Hanukkah, in which Jews commemorate the rededication of the Temple of Jerusalem in ancient times; and Kwanzaa, a festival in which African Americans celebrate their African heritage.

Suggest that students compare traditional holidays from different cultures and religions by completing a chart of several different winter holidays. They can note facts under the following categories: Event Celebrated; Food; Dress; Customs; Decorations; Games or Activities.

"Let's post Mr. Daniel a snowball through his letter box."

"Let's write things in the snow."

"Let's write, 'Mr. Daniel looks like a spaniel' all over his lawn."

Or we walked on the white shore. "Can the fishes see it's snowing?"

The silent one-clouded heavens drifted on to the sea. Now we were snow-blind travelers lost on the north hills, and vast dewlapped[29] dogs, with flasks round their necks, ambled and shambled up to us, baying "Excelsior."[30] We returned home through the poor streets where only a few children fumbled with bare red fingers in the wheel-rutted snow and cat-called after us, their voices fading away, as we trudged uphill, into the cries of the dock birds and the hooting of ships out in the whirling bay. And then, at tea the recovered Uncles would be jolly; and the ice cake loomed in the center of the table like a marble grave. Auntie Hannah laced her tea with rum, because it was only once a year.

Bring out the tall tales now that we told by the fire as the gaslight bubbled like a diver. Ghosts whooed like owls in the long nights when I dared not look over my shoulder; animals lurked in the cubbyhole under the stairs where the gas meter ticked. And I remember that we went singing carols once, when there wasn't the shaving of a moon to light the flying streets. At the end of a long road was a drive that led to a large house, and we stumbled up the darkness of the drive that night, each one of us afraid, each one holding a stone in his hand in case, and all of us too brave to say a word. The wind through the trees made noises as of old and unpleasant and maybe webfooted men wheezing in caves. We reached the black bulk of the house.

"What shall we give them? Hark the Herald?"

"No," Jack said, "Good King Wenceslas. I'll count three."

One, two, three, and we began to sing, our voices high and seemingly distant in the snow-felted darkness round the house that was occupied by nobody we knew. We stood close together, near the dark door.

> Good King Wenceslas
> looked out
> On the Feast of Stephen . . .

And then a small, dry voice, like the voice of someone who has not spoken for a long time, joined our singing: a small, dry, eggshell voice from the other side of the door: a small dry voice through the keyhole. And when we stopped running we were outside *our* house; the front room was lovely; balloons floated under the hot-water-bottle-gulping gas; everything was good again and shone over the town.

"Perhaps it was a ghost," Jim said.

"Perhaps it was trolls,"[31] Dan said, who was always reading.

"Let's go in and see if there's any jelly left," Jack said. And we did that.

Always on Christmas night there was music. An uncle played the fiddle, a cousin sang "Cherry Ripe," and another uncle sang "Drake's Drum." It was very warm in the little house. Auntie Hannah, who had got on to the parsnip wine, sang a song about Bleeding Hearts and Death, and then another in which she said her heart was like a Bird's Nest; and then everybody laughed again; and then I went to bed. Looking through my bedroom window, out into the moonlight and the unending smoke-colored snow, I could see the lights in the windows of all the other houses on our hill and hear the music rising from them up the long, steadily falling night. I turned the gas down, I got into bed. I said some words to the close and holy darkness, and then I slept.

---

31. **trolls:** Mythical Scandinavian beings.

---

29. **dewlapped:** Having loose folds of skin hanging from the throat.

30. **Excelsior** (ek sel′ sē ôr′): Latin phrase meaning "onward and upward."

◆ **Build Vocabulary**

brittle (brit′ əl) *adj.*: Stiff and unbending; easily broken or shattered

trod (träd) *v.*: Walked

forlorn (fər lôrn′) *adj.*: Abandoned; deserted

◆ *Literature and Your Life*

5 Ask students if families still tell each other ghost stories and other tall tales at holiday gatherings. Then ask what activities have often replaced such storytelling. *Many students will say that TV shows, videos, video games, and computer games have replaced storytelling at family gatherings.*

Customize for
English Language Learners

6 Have students who are familiar with the customs of Christmas caroling explain these customs to those who are not. If they know the carols mentioned here, have them sing them or say their lyrics for English language learners in the class. In turn, these students can sing Christmas or holiday songs in their native languages.

◆ **Critical Thinking**

7 Interpret Ask students to describe the mood the last sentence of the selection conveys. *Students might describe a mood of contentment, peace, holiness, or mystery.*

A Child's Christmas in Wales ◆ 601

"Marian Anderson: Famous Concert Singer," by Langston Hughes, is an account of how the great African American singer overcame racial bias to become one of the world's most renowned and revered artists. Hughes's attitude toward his subject is one of admiration and esteem.

❶ **Clarification** Explain to students that, at the time this biographical account was written, the terms *Negro* and *colored* were the acceptable terms for *African Americans*. (You might want to lead a brief discussion about how the different terms reflect the social attitudes of their times.)

◆ **Literary Focus**

❷ **Biography and Autobiography** Ask students why Hughes includes this information about other African American performers in a biographical piece on Marian Anderson. *The information sets the scene by establishing the status and stereotypes of African American singers at the time Anderson was growing up. It also heightens the significance of her accomplishments.*

Marian Anderson: Famous Concert Singer

Langston Hughes

❶ hen Marian Anderson was born in a little red brick house in Philadelphia, a famous group of Negro singers, the Fisk Jubilee Singers, had already carried the spirituals all over Europe. And a colored woman billed as "Black Patti" had become famous on variety programs as a singer of both folk songs and the classics. Both Negro and white minstrels had popularized American songs. The all-Negro musical comedies of Bert Williams and George Walker had been successful on Broadway. But no well-trained colored singers performing the great songs of Schubert, Handel, and the other masters, or the arias from famous operas, had become successful on the concert stage. And most people thought of Negro vocalists only in connection with spirituals. Roland Hayes[1] and Marian Anderson were the first to become famous enough to break this stereotype.

Marian Anderson's mother was a staunch church worker who loved to croon the hymns

---

1. **Roland Hayes** (1887–1977): Famous African American tenor in the United States.

602 ◆ *Nonfiction*

Cross-Curricular Connection: Music

Spirituals are folk songs that were sung by enslaved African Americans, expressing their desire for freedom in terms of Christian images. The blues—from which rhythm and blues, jazz, and rock and roll were all derived—is another form of folk music that originated with African Americans. Classical music, on the other hand, is a European tradition of music in which individual composers wrote musical works according to formal rules. Writing and performing this kind of music requires extensive training and education in musical notation and theory.

Marian Anderson was a skilled performer of classical as well as folk music. Share with students recordings of various types of vocal music from your library: spirituals, the blues, jazz, and opera. Have students compare and contrast performance styles and the emotional impact of the various types of vocal music.

of her faith about the house, as did the aunt who came to live with them when Marian's father died. Both parents were from Virginia. Marian's mother had been a schoolteacher there, and her father a farm boy. Shortly after they moved to Philadelphia where three daughters were born, the father died, and the mother went to work at Wanamaker's department store. But she saw to it that her children attended school and church regularly. The father had been an usher in the Union Baptist Church, so the congregation took an interest in his three little girls. Marian was the oldest and, before she was eight, singing in the Sunday school choir, she had already learned a great many hymns and spirituals by heart.

One day Marian saw an old violin in a pawn-shop window marked $3.45. She set her mind on that violin, and began to save the nickels and dimes neighbors would give her for scrubbing their white front steps—the kind of stone steps so characteristic of Philadelphia and Baltimore houses—until she had $3.00. The pawnshop man let her take the violin at a reduced price. Marian never became very good on the violin. A few years later her mother bought a piano, so the child forgot all about it in favor of their newer instrument. By that time, too, her unusual singing voice had attracted the attention of her choir master, and at the age of fourteen she was promoted to a place in the main church choir. There she learned all four parts of all the hymns and anthems and could easily fill in anywhere from bass to soprano.

Sensing that she had exceptional musical talent, some of the church members began to raise money so that she might have singing lessons. But her first teacher, a colored woman, refused to accept any pay for instructing so talented a child. So the church folks put their money into a trust fund called "Marian Anderson's Future," banking it until the time came for her to have advanced training. Meanwhile, Marian attended South Philadelphia High School for Girls and took part in various group concerts, usually doing the solo parts. When she was fifteen she

◀ Critical Viewing In what ways does this photograph illustrate the qualities Langston Hughes describes? [Analyze]

sang a group of songs alone at a Sunday School Convention in Harrisburg and word of her talent began to spread about the state. When she was graduated from high school, the Philadelphia Choral Society, a Negro group, sponsored her further study and secured for her one of the best local teachers. Then in 1925 she journeyed to New York to take part, with three hundred other young singers, in the New York Philharmonic Competitions, where she won first place, and appeared with the orchestra at Lewisohn Stadium.

This appearance was given wide publicity, but very few lucrative engagements came in, so Marian continued to study. A Town Hall concert was arranged for her in New York, but it was unsuccessful. Meanwhile, she kept on singing with various choral groups, and herself gave concerts in churches and at some of the Negro colleges until, in 1930, a Rosenald Fellowship made European study possible. During her first year abroad she made her debut in Berlin. A prominent Scandinavian concert manager read of this concert, but was attracted more by the name, Anderson, than by what the critics said about her voice. "Ah," he said, "a Negro singer with a Swedish name! She is bound to be a success in Scandinavia." He sent two of his friends to Germany to hear her, one of them being Kosti Vehanen who shortly became her accompanist and remained with her for many years.

Sure enough, Marian Anderson did become a great success in the Scandinavian countries, where she learned to sing in both Finnish and Swedish, and her first concert tour of Europe became a critical triumph. When she came back home to America, she gave several programs and appeared as soloist with the famous Hall Johnson Choir, but without financial success. However, the Scandinavian people, who had fallen in love with her, kept asking her to come back there. So, in 1933, she went again to Europe for 142 concerts in Norway, Sweden, Denmark, and Finland. She was decorated by the King of Denmark and the King of Sweden.

◆ Build Vocabulary

arias (är′ ē əz) n.: Melodies in an opera, especially for solo voice with instrumental accompaniment

staunch (stônch) adj.: Steadfast; loyal

Marian Anderson: Famous Concert Singer ◆ 603

◆ Reading Strategy

❸ Recognize the Author's Attitude Ask students: What attitude can you infer towards Anderson in this passage? Upon what evidence do you make your inference? *Hughes probably considers even her behavior as a child to be admirable. By using the phrase "she set her mind," Hughes conveys that Anderson was a determined person.*

◆ Build Vocabulary

❹ Musical Words Ask students who have sung in choruses to explain what the *bass* and *soprano* parts of choral music are. Then ask what a *solo* part is. *The bass part is the one with the lowest notes, sung by male singers; the soprano part has the highest notes and is usually sung by female singers. A solo part is one in which one singer performs alone. A solo is usually awarded to one of the best singers in the group.*

▶Critical Viewing◀

❺ Analyze Elicit responses such as the following: *The singer appears in a very dignified, confident pose worthy of admiration. The respectful look that the accompanist is giving Anderson echoes this attitude.*

◆ Build Grammar Skills

❻ Restrictive and Nonrestrictive Appositives Ask students why the phrase "a Negro group" is set off by commas. *It is a nonrestrictive appositive, giving further information about the Philadelphia Choral Society. Because the information in the appositive is not essential to the meaning of the sentence, it is set off with commas.*

◆ Critical Thinking

❼ Infer Ask students why they think Marian Anderson has to go to Europe to achieve her first major success. *Racial prejudice and stereotypes in the United States make it difficult for an American audience to accept an African American who sings classical music.*

Speaking and Listening Mini-Lesson

Analyze a Marian Anderson Performance

This mini-lesson supports the Speaking and Listening activity in the Idea Bank on page 607.

Introduce the Concept Tell students that just as there are specific elements they can analyze in works of literature, there are also specific elements they can analyze in a vocal performance.

Develop Background Lead students to an understanding of some of the musical elements involved in a classical vocal performance:
• dynamic range—from loud to soft

• pitch range—from high notes to low
• emotional range—Can the artist express the feelings of sad songs as well as happy ones?

Apply the Information If students cannot find a Marian Anderson recording, they can analyze the recording of another classical singer. Have them prepare their charts using the elements described above.

Assess the Outcome Have groups compare their charts, and support their responses with examples from the recording.

◆ **Literary Focus**

❶ **Biography and Autobiography**
Elicit responses such as the following: *Hughes chose to include this incident because it demonstrates admirable qualities in Marian Anderson's character: her courage, dignity, pride, and sense of responsibility to her audience.*

◆ **Literary Focus**

❷ **Biography and Autobiography**
Ask students to identify possible sources of the facts in this paragraph and to explain why so many facts are included here. *Possible sources of the facts are newspapers, record companies, the singer herself, or her managers and publicity spokespeople. The facts are included to support the main idea of the paragraph: that Marian Anderson became one of the most popular and most honored singers in the nation and the world.*

◆ **Reading Strategy**

❸ **Recognize the Author's Attitude** Ask students why the author probably chose to describe these events. What can they infer is Hughes's attitude about the events he describes? *Hughes thought it was important for his readers to know that Anderson, despite her prominence, experienced racial prejudice. Students can infer that Hughes's attitude towards these injustices was one of anger or disgust.*

Sibelius[2] dedicated a song to her. And the following spring she made her debut in Paris where she was so well received that she had to give three concerts that season at the Salle Gaveau.[3] Great successes followed in all the European capitals. In 1935 the famous conductor, Arturo Toscanini, listened to her sing at Salzburg.[4] He said, "What I heard today one is privileged to hear only once in a hundred years." It was in Europe that Marian Anderson began to be acclaimed by critics as "the greatest singer in the world."

 hen Marian Anderson again returned to America, she was a seasoned artist. News of her tremendous European successes had preceded her, so a big New York concert was planned. But a few days before she arrived at New York, in a storm on the liner crossing the Atlantic, Marian fell and broke her ankle. She refused to allow this to interfere with her concert, however, nor did she even want people to know about it. She wore a very long evening gown that night so that no one could see the plaster cast on her leg. She propped herself in a curve of the piano before the curtains parted, and gave her New York concert standing on one foot! The next day Howard Taubman wrote enthusiastically in *The New York Times*:

> Marian Anderson has returned to her native land one of the great singers of our time. . . . There is no doubt of it, she was mistress of all she surveyed. . . . It was music making that proved too deep for words.

A coast-to-coast American tour followed. And, from that season on, Marian Anderson has been one of our country's favorite singers, rated, according to *Variety*,[5] among the top ten

◆ **Literary Focus**
❶ Why do you think Hughes chose to include this incident in Marion Anderson's biography?

2. **Sibelius** (si bā′ lē ōōs): Jean Sibelius (1865–1957), a Finnish composer.
3. **Salle Gaveau** (sal ga vō′): Concert hall in Paris, France.
4. **Salzburg:** City in Austria noted for its music festivals.
5. *Variety:* Show-business newspaper.

604 ◆ *Nonfiction*

of the concert stage who earn over $100,000 a year. Miss Anderson has sung with the great symphony orchestras, and appeared on all the major radio and television networks many times, being a particular favorite with the millions of listeners to the Ford Hour. During the years she has returned often to Europe for concerts, and among the numerous honors accorded her abroad was a request for a command performance before the King and Queen of England, and a decoration from the government of Finland. Her concerts in South America and Asia have been as successful as those elsewhere. Since 1935 she has averaged over one hundred programs a year in cities as far apart as Vienna, Buenos Aires, Moscow, and Tokyo. Her recordings have sold millions of copies around the world. She has been invited more than once to sing at the White House. She has appeared in concert at the Paris Opera and at the Metropolitan Opera House in New York. Several colleges have granted her honorary degrees, and in 1944 Smith College made her a Doctor of Music.

In spite of all this, as a Negro, Marian Anderson has not been immune from those aspects of racial segregation which affect most traveling artists of color in the United States. In his book, *Marian Anderson*, her longtime accompanist, Vehanen, tells of hotel accommodations being denied her, and service in dining rooms often refused. Once after a concert in a Southern city, Vehanen writes that some white friends drove Marian to the railroad station and took her into the main waiting room. But a policeman ran them out, since Negroes were not allowed in that part of the station. Then they went into the smaller waiting room marked, COLORED. But again they were ejected, because *white* people were not permitted in the cubby hole allotted to Negroes. So they all had to stand on the platform until the train arrived.

The most dramatic incident of prejudice in all Marian Anderson's career occurred in 1939 when the Daughters of the American Revolution, who own Constitution Hall in Washington, refused to allow her to sing there. The newspapers headlined this and many Americans were outraged. In protest a committee of prominent

❷

❸

◆ **Beyond the Classroom**

Career Connection
Music Langston Hughes's piece on Marian Anderson brings out that the great singer was accomplished in several musical genres, including spiritual and classical singing. Discuss with students the different roles open to those with musical talent and training, or ability and knowledge. These roles include performer, composer (one who creates music), lyricist (one who writes the lyrics for songs) arranger (one who resets music for different instruments or voices), producer (one who supervises the production of

music), and sound engineer (one who manages the recording equipment). Lead students to see that several important fields use musicians in these roles, that they can be employed in the film, record, or advertising industries, as well as by companies who create multimedia products.

Interested students might research careers in music to find out what educational background and preparation is required for the roles discussed. Suggest that they contact a music department of a local college or search the Internet to get more information.

people, including a number of great artists and distinguished figures in the government, was formed. Through the efforts of this committee, Marian Anderson sang in Washington, anyway—before the statue of Abraham Lincoln—to one of the largest crowds ever to hear a singer at one time in the history of the world. Seventy-five thousand people stood in the open air on a cold clear Easter Sunday afternoon to hear her. And millions more listened to Marian Anderson that day over the radio or heard her in the newsreels that recorded the event. Harold Ickes, then Secretary of the Interior, presented Miss Anderson to that enormous audience standing in the plaza to pay honor, as he said, not only to a great singer, but to the basic ideals of democracy and equality.

In 1943 Marian Anderson married Orpheus H. Fisher, an architect, and settled down—between tours—in a beautiful country house in Connecticut where she rehearses new songs to add to her already vast <u>repertoire</u>. Sometimes her neighbors across the fields can hear the rich warm voice that covers three octaves

singing in English, French, Finnish, or German. And sometimes they hear in the New England air that old Negro spiritual, "Honor, honor unto the dying Lamb. . . ."

Friends say that Marian Anderson has invested her money in real estate and in government bonds. Certainly, throughout her career, she has lived very simply, traveled without a maid or secretary, and carried her own sewing machine along by train, ship, or plane to mend her gowns. When in 1941 in Philadelphia she was awarded the coveted Bok Award for outstanding public service, the $10,000 that came with the medallion she used to establish a trust fund for "talented American artists without regard to race or creed." Now, each year from this fund promising young musicians receive scholarships.

◆ **Reading Strategy**

What attitude toward Marian Anderson is shown by the details given in this paragraph?

④

◆ **Build Vocabulary**

repertoire (rep′ ə twär) *n.*: Stock of songs that a singer knows and is ready to perform

---

Guide for Responding

◆ *Literature and Your Life*

Reader's Response If you could meet one person from Hughes's or Thomas's essay, whom would you choose? Why?

Thematic Focus How can something like Hughes's or Thomas's essay, which concentrate on the past, still be relevant in today's world?

☑ **Check Your Comprehension**

1. In "A Child's Christmas in Wales," how did Jim and Dylan respond to the fire at Prothero's house?
2. Decribe three events in Thomas's recollections of Christmas.
3. How did Marian Anderson's congregation help her?
4. What difficulties did Anderson face traveling in the United States?

◆ **Critical Thinking**

INTERPRET
1. What details indicate that "A Child's Christmas in Wales" is a childhood memory narrated by an adult? **[Analyze]**
2. In what ways was Christmas for the children different from Christmas for the adults? **[Contrast]**
3. Why was it so difficult for Marian Anderson to gain success in the United States? **[Interpret]**
4. What can you learn about Anderson from the way she chooses to spend the money given with the Bok Award? **[Draw Conclusions]**

APPLY
5. Why do people's memories tend to blend together and exaggerate the past? **[Relate]**

EXTEND
6. What other performers have overcome obstacles to achieve success? **[Career Link]**

Marian Anderson: Famous Concert Singer ◆ 605

 Beyond the Selection

FURTHER READING

Other Works by Dylan Thomas
"Fern Hill," "Poem in October"

Other Works by Langston Hughes
"Harriet Tubman: The Moses of Her People,"

Other Works About Special Memories
"A Christmas Memory," Truman Capote
"Women," Alice Walker

We suggest that you preview these works before recommending them to students.

INTERNET

Students can learn more at the following sites on the Internet. Please be aware that the sites may have changed since we published this information.
Dylan Thomas: **http://www.cord.edu./homepages/pjlerohl/DYLAN.html**
Black History Web site: **http://www.interlog.com/~csteele/flavour.htmlz**

We *strongly recommend* that you preview the sites before you send students to them.

◆ **Reading Strategy**

❹ **Recognize the Author's Attitude** Elicit responses such as the following: *The author shows admiration for Anderson's simplicity, humility, and generosity.*

Reinforce and Extend

Answers

◆ *Literature and Your Life*

Reader's Response Students might chose the character of Dylan Thomas as a boy or Marian Anderson. Both, in different ways, showed great spirit.

Thematic Focus Although people in the past had different kinds of experiences than they do today, they have basic human feelings in common.

☑ **Check Your Comprehension**

1. They ran to the house with their snowballs to put out the fire.
2. Possible events: getting Useful and Useless presents; eating turkey dinner; telling stories; caroling
3. They raised money to pay for her musical training.
4. Anderson encountered racial prejudice: She was sometimes refused rooms or service in hotels.

◆ **Critical Thinking**

1. In the first paragraph Thomas says he can never remember how long it snowed, indicating he's writing about a long time ago. All adventures of the "we" characters are adventures of little boys.
2. The children were excited and full of mischief; the adults were more disinterested and weary.
3. Her career in the United States was stalled by racial prejudice; people did not accept an African American who sang classical music.
4. Anderson was extremely generous in wanting young musicians to have an easier time than she had.
5. Memories blend and become exaggerated because time affects people's perceptions.
6. Sample response: Christopher Reeve, an actor who has gone on to direct films after being disabled by a spinal chord injury.

605

Answers

◆ Literary Focus

1. (a) Thomas wants to share his experience of a particular and warm childhood. (b) He remembers details such as the kinds of presents exchanged with great clarity.

2. Incidents that reveal Anderson's character include her saving money to buy the second-hand violin and her performing with a broken ankle.

3. (a) He has emphasized aspects of her career and the obstacles she met in achieving success. (b) He has left out mention of her personal life—her life outside music.

◆ Build Vocabulary

Using Musical Words
1. c   2. a   3. b

Using the Word Bank
1. g   2. a   3. h   4. f   5. e   6. d
7. b   8. c

◆ Reading Strategy

1. (a) Thomas finds many events in his childhood amusing. (b) He characterizes the people in his childhood in such a way as to make them seem humorous.

2. Hughes shows his admiration of Anderson by stressing her professionalism—such as performing with a broken ankle—and her generous nature—setting up a fund for young musicians.

◆ Build Grammar Skills

Practice
1. *Jim*—restrictive; 2. *Mabel*—nonrestrictive; 3. *an African American woman*—nonrestrictive; 4. *Orpheus H. Fisher*—restrictive

Writing Application
1. Marion Anderson, <u>beloved singer</u>, toured Europe. (nonrestrictive)
2. The writer <u>Langston Hughes</u> admired Marian Anderson. (restrictive)
3. Dylan Thomas, <u>a famous writer</u>, shares his Christmas memories. (nonrestrictive)

Guide for Responding (continued)

◆ Literary Focus

BIOGRAPHY AND AUTOBIOGRAPHY

In an **autobiography,** the author may include details that would never be known through the research of a biographer. Dylan Thomas reveals details about his childhood that only he would know. In Langston Hughes's **biography** of Marion Anderson, he provides factual information about her life while emphasizing certain aspects of her character.

1. (a) Why do you think Thomas tells this memory of his childhood? (b) What details in "A Child's Christmas in Wales" support your opinion?

2. What incidents in "Marian Anderson: Famous Concert Singer" reveal Anderson's character?

3. (a) What aspects of Anderson's life has the author emphasized? (b) What has he left out?

◆ Build Vocabulary

USING MUSICAL WORDS

Like law, medicine, and other disciplines, music has a vocabulary all its own. On your paper, match each of the following words with its definition.

1. soprano   **a.** sing in a soft, often sentimental, manner
2. croon   **b.** song of praise or devotion
3. anthem   **c.** highest vocal range for a woman or boy singer

USING THE WORD BANK

On your paper, match each word from the Word Bank with the animal, person, or thing that is most closely associated with that word.

1. staunch   **a.** burglar
2. sidle   **b.** shoes
3. prey   **c.** lost child
4. wallowed   **d.** twigs
5. crocheted   **e.** sweater
6. brittle   **f.** pig
7. trod   **g.** friend
8. forlorn   **h.** hunter

◆ Reading Strategy

RECOGNIZE AUTHOR'S ATTITUDE

The **attitude** that a biographer or autobiographer has toward his or her subject is reflected in the way that the author presents information about that person.

1. (a) What is Dylan Thomas's attitude about the events in his childhood related in "A Child's Christmas in Wales"? (b) What details convey his attitude?

2. What details in "Marian Anderson: Famous Concert Singer" indicate that Hughes admires his subject?

◆ Build Grammar Skills

RESTRICTIVE AND NONRESTRICTIVE APPOSITIVES

Appositives and appositive phrases provide more information about the noun they are placed near. Appositives can be either restrictive or nonrestrictive. A **restrictive appositive** is essential to the meaning of the sentence and is not set off by commas. A **nonrestrictive appositive** is not essential and is set off by commas.

Practice Locate the appositive or appositive phrase in each sentence and identify it as restrictive or nonrestrictive.

1. I was in Mrs. Prothero's garden, waiting for cats, with her son Jim.
2. Jim's only aunt, Mabel, was staying with his family.
3. Marian Anderson's first teacher, an African American woman, refused to accept any pay for instructing so talented a child.
4. In 1943, Marian Anderson married the architect Orpheus H. Fisher and settled down in Connecticut.

Writing Application Rewrite each sentence on your paper, highlighting the appositive or appositve phrase and indicating whether it is restrictive or nonrestrictive. Include commas where necessary.

1. Marion Anderson beloved singer toured Europe.
2. The writer Langston Hughes admired Marion Anderson.
3. Dylan Thomas a famous writer shares his Christmas memories.

 Writer's Solution

For additional instruction and practice, use the lesson in the **Language Lab CD-ROM** on Commas to get information on how to punctuate appositives and page 40 on Appositives and Appositive Phrases in the *Writer's Solution Grammar Practice Book.*

Build Your Portfolio

Idea Bank

Writing

1. **Your Favorite Holiday** Write an essay about your favorite holiday. Describe how you typically spend this day and why it is so special to you.

2. **Memory From Childhood** Choose a memory from your childhood. Write down what you can recall, then interview others who are part of the memory. Write an account of the event, noting how others' recollections differ from yours.

3. **Biography** Write a biography of someone you know. Make a list of your subject's qualities and accomplishments. Then describe an incident from his or her life that best highlights those traits.

Speaking and Listening

4. **Memory Music** With a group of classmates, choose songs that call to mind special memories. Choose an order for the songs, prepare a brief introduction that explains your choices, and present your selections to the class. **[Music Link]**

5. **Marian Anderson Recording** Find one of Marian Anderson's recordings in a library and listen to it. Make a chart analyzing her singing. **[Music Link]**

Projects

6. **Greeting Card** Design a greeting card for a holiday that you celebrate. On the card, illustrate the customs and traditions common to that holiday. Inside, write a message that captures the spirit of the holiday. **[Art Link]**

7. **Multimedia Presentation** Choose an individual who has excelled in a field such as art or athletics. Give a multimedia presentation that shows the obstacles your subject had to overcome and how he or she has enriched that field.

Writing Mini-Lesson

Letter to Yourself in Twenty Years

Consider your life as an ongoing biography. It's easy to remember where you were and what you were doing a few years ago. It's far more challenging to think where you'll be and what you'll be doing twenty years from now. Perhaps you will be married and raising a family. You may be living in another city, or even another country. The possibilities are endless. Write a **letter to yourself**, to be opened in twenty years. In the letter, mention some of the high and low points of your life right now, and then discuss your dreams. Seal the letter and write on the envelope "To be opened in the year 20__."

Writing Skills Focus: Logical Organization

Choose a **logical method of organization** for your letter. You might organize it chronologically, starting in the present and gradually chronicling your projected achievements through the years. You might compare and contrast your life now with the life you would like twenty years from now. You might organize in order of importance, discussing what's most important to you now and what may seem less or more important as time passes.

Prewriting Make a two-column chart that shows your interests and abilities now (left column) and where these interests and abilities might lead you (right column). After creating your chart, choose an organization plan appropriate for your letter.

Drafting Use a personal, conversational tone for your letter—you are writing to yourself. Refer to your chart, including the details you think will most influence your future.

Revising Look back over your draft to see if there's anything you've left out. Make sure that you've been honest in your letter—remember, the only person you're trying to impress is yourself.

A Child's Christmas in Wales/Marian Anderson: Famous Concert Singer ◆ 607

Idea Bank

Customizing for
Performance Levels
Following are suggestions for matching Idea Bank topics with your students' performance levels:

Less Advanced Students: 1, 4, 6
Average Students: 2
More Advanced Students: 3, 5, 7

Customizing for
Learning Modalities
Following are suggestions for matching Idea Bank topics with your students' learning modalities:

Visual/Spatial: 6, 7
Verbal/Linguistic: 4,
Rhythmic/Musical: 4, 5

Writing Mini-Lesson

Refer students to the Writing Handbook, page 965, for instruction on the writing process, and page 967 for further information on narration.

Writing Lab CD-ROM
To develop their letters, have students complete the tutorial on Narration. Follow these steps:

1. Have students consult interactive tips for accomplishing a purpose.
2. Refer students to the Chain of Events tool to help them organize their letters to themselves in twenty years.
3. Have students use the Revision Checker for sentence length and passive voice.

Sourcebook
Have students use Chapter 2, Narration (pp. 31–56), for additional support.

✓ ASSESSMENT OPTIONS

Formal Assessment, Selection Test, pp. 151–153, and Assessment Resources Software. The selection test is designed so that it can be easily customized to the performance levels of your students.
Alternative Assessment, p. 43, includes options for less advanced students, more advanced students, verbal/linguistic learners, bodily/kinesthetic learners, visual/spatial learners, and musical/rhythmic learners.

PORTFOLIO ASSESSMENT
Use the following rubrics in the *Alternative Assessment* booklet to assess student writing:
Your Favorite Holiday: Description Rubric, p. 97
Memory From Childhood: Narrative Based on Personal Experience Rubric, p. 96
Biography: Description Rubric, p. 97

Guide for Reading

OBJECTIVES

1. To read, comprehend, and interpret a descriptive essay
2. To relate a descriptive essay to personal experience
3. To recognize facts and impressions in an essay
4. To identify features of a descriptive essay
5. To build vocabulary in context and learn the prefix *mal-*
6. To make verbs agree with subjects when words intervene between subject and verb
7. To write a radio call-in transcript using sensory language
8. To respond to the essay through writing, speaking and listening, and projects

SKILLS INSTRUCTION

Vocabulary:
Prefixes: *mal-*

Grammar:
Subject-Verb Agreement

Reading Strategy:
Recognize Facts and Impressions

Literary Focus:

Descriptive Essay

Writing:
Sensory Language

Speaking and Listening:
Storm Report (teacher edition)

Critical Viewing:
Support

PORTFOLIO OPPORTUNITIES

Writing: Descriptive Paragraph; Storm Journal; Fable

Writing Mini-Lesson: Radio Call-In Transcript

Speaking and Listening: Storm Report; Talk Show Interview

Projects: Hurricane Chart; Food Chain Presentation

More About the Author
Annie Dillard's time at Tinker Creek followed a nearly fatal attack of pneumonia in 1971. After she recovered, Dillard felt the need to experience life more fully. She spent most of her time outdoors, walking and camping. When she was inside, she spent most of her time reading. Dillard started writing about Tinker Creek in a journal. When it reached more than twenty volumes, she transferred the journal to note cards. It took her about eight months of full-time writing to turn the note cards into the well-crafted *Pilgrim at Tinker Creek*.

Annie Dillard (1945–   )

Life Near Tinker Creek Annie Dillard's romance with nature—observing it, learning from it, rejoicing in it—probably intensified during the four seasons she spent living near Tinker Creek, Virginia. An area of forests, creeks, and mountains, brimming with wildlife of all kinds, Tinker Creek so nurtured Dillard in her solitude that she began to write about it. She was twenty-nine when she wrote *Pilgrim at Tinker Creek*, a profound meditation on nature and religion that was awarded the Pulitzer Prize in 1975. "Flood," which recalls the effects of Hurricane Agnes in 1972, is set at Tinker Creek.

A Sustaining Childhood Annie Dillard grew up in Pittsburgh, Pennsylvania, the oldest of three daughters. Her affluent parents encouraged her to be creative and explore her surroundings, and they shared their knowledge of everything from plumbing to economics. Dillard reflected upon her childhood in her 1987 autobiography, *An American Childhood*. Her curiosity and exuberance is perhaps best exemplified in a description of her childhood attempts to fly.

> *I knew well that people could not fly—as well as anyone knows it—but I also knew that, with faith, all things are possible.*

From childhood on, it seems, Dillard's sense of awe set her apart from the doings of proper society around her.

Living by Literature Dillard continues to spend a great deal of time reading, writing, and teaching literature. She also teaches a course in nonfiction narrative writing. Her own books are devoted to the love of literature: *Living by Fiction* and *The Writing Life* were published in the 1980's.

◆ Build Vocabulary

PREFIXES: *mal-*

When some children capture a snapping turtle in "Flood," the animal makes a malevolent hiss. *Malevolent* contains the prefix *mal-*, which means "bad, evil." A *malevolent* hiss would be one that shows ill will. You can also see *mal-* as a root in *dismal*, meaning "causing gloom or depression." During the flood, it rains all week—truly *dismal* weather.

WORD BANK
obliterates
opacity
usurped
mauled
malevolent
repressed

WORD BANK

As you read this story, you will encounter the words in this list. Each word is defined on the page on which it first appears. Preview the list before you read.

◆ Build Grammar Skills

SUBJECT AND VERB AGREEMENT

In all writing, **subjects and verbs must agree** in number. When words intervene between the subject and verb, the correct agreement may not be immediately apparent. Consider this sentence from "Flood":

> s   v
> Water that has picked up clay soils looks worse than other muddy waters...

The singular verb form *looks* agrees with its singular subject *water*, not with *soils*, even though *soils* is closer to the verb.

Annie Dillard writes a number of sentences like this one, with a modifying structure between the subject and the verb, yet she always makes the verb agree with its subject.

608 ◆ *Nonfiction*

 Prentice Hall Literature Program Resources

REINFORCE / RETEACH / EXTEND

Selection Support Pages
Build Vocabulary: Prefixes: *mal-*, p. 180
Build Grammar Skills: Subject-Verb Agreement, p. 181
Reading Strategy: Recognize Facts and Impressions, p. 182
Literary Focus: Descriptive Essay, p. 183

Strategies for Diverse Student Needs, p. 44

Beyond Literature Community Connection: *Flood Control,* p. 44

Formal Assessment Selection Test, pp. 154–156; Assessment Resources Software

Alternative Assessment, p. 44

Resource Pro CD-R⊘M
"Flood"—includes all resource materials and customizable lesson plan.

 Listening to Literature Audiocassettes "Flood"

Flood

◆ Literature and Your Life

CONNECT YOUR EXPERIENCE

You walk outside and find that a freezing storm has left ice glittering everywhere you look—on tree branches, car roofs, and store awnings. When nature transforms our everyday sights into something extraordinary, as it does in "Flood," we have the chance to see the world anew. As Dillard describes the myriad aspects of a flood, think about what natural occurrences have transformed the world around you, if even for a moment.

THEMATIC FOCUS: NATURAL FORCES

Forces of nature can interrupt and even change our daily lives. What effects have the forces of nature had on you or people you know?

Journal Writing Write a paragraph describing in detail the effect of a natural force, such as a storm uprooting a tree.

◆ Background for Understanding

SCIENCE

The 1972 hurricane Agnes might have been downgraded to a tropical storm by the time it reached Annie Dillard's Tinker Creek, but it still produced the worst floods in Virginia's history. The low-lying basins of the Susquehanna, Allegheny, Chemung, Monongahela, Ohio, and James rivers were all struck by flash flooding from Hurricane Agnes. Dillard's home state of Pennsylvania was actually the worst hit by the floods.

Flash floods from hurricanes can destroy homes and ruin lives. They can leave fish swimming in people's basements, carry cars and furniture downstream, and erode riverbanks.

◆ Literary Focus

DESCRIPTIVE ESSAY

Reading "Flood" might make you feel that you're hip-high in rising creek water. You'll hear wind, feel rain, and see water rising and receding. That's because "Flood" succeeds as a **descriptive essay**, a short nonfiction work that contains details that show how something looks, feels, smells, sounds, or tastes. As you read, notice Dillard's use of language that appeals to your senses, like "knot of yellow, fleshy somethings" and "a high, windy sound more like air than water." These descriptions, which are visual, tactile, and auditory, have the effect of taking you off the page and into the flood.

◆ Reading Strategy

RECOGNIZE FACTS AND IMPRESSIONS

If you tell a friend that Dillard's essay describes the flooding of Tinker Creek in 1972, you are presenting a **fact**—information that can be proven. If you then say that the flood was really frightening, then you're giving your **impression**—a feeling or image retained from an experience.

Be aware when reading "Flood" that the facts you're reading about are verifiable. It can be proved, for example, that Tinker Creek flooded on June 21, 1972, or that the summer solstice is the longest day of the year. However, Dillard's impressions about the flood, such as that it was exciting, are personal; you might come away with different impressions.

Use a chart like this one to separate the facts and impressions in "Flood":

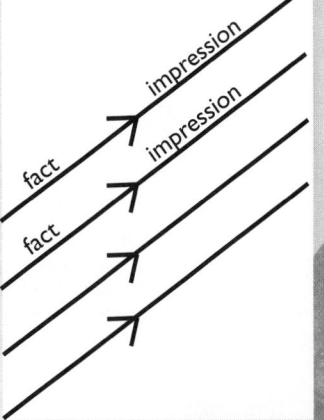

Guide for Reading ◆ 609

Preparing for Standardized Tests

Reading and Vocabulary The Build Vocabulary lesson for this selection focuses on using the prefix *mal-* to determine the meaning of words such as *malevolent*. Students can apply their word-building skills when matching words with correct definitions on standardized tests. For additional practice, use the Build Vocabulary page in *Selection Support,* p. 180.

Grammar and Language Portions of some standardized tests require students to identify correct subject-verb agreement, as in the following:

The people waiting in line (was, <u>were</u>) growing impatient.

The set of dishes (are, <u>is</u>) in the cupboard.

Students may also be asked to apply the concept of subject-verb agreement in revision items on standardized tests. The Build Grammar Skills lesson for this selection focuses on this topic. For additional practice, use the Build Grammar Skills page on Subject-Verb Agreement, p. 181, in *Selection Support.*

One-Minute Insight Annie Dillard's recollection of the Tinker Creek flood is sparked by a watchful, uneasy feeling brought on by a June rain. As the account of the flood unfolds, tension rises. The landscape undergoes a dramatic change as a small creek becomes a roiling river that snatches everything in its path and transforms the landscape into an other-worldly waterscape—complete with waves and waterfalls. For the people in the area, the flood is frightening, but it also holds a certain fascination. When it is over and the waters begin to recede, people take up their normal lives once again. Dillard's account of the flood gives readers a glimpse of both nature's power and how people respond to its assault by helping one another.

Customize for
Musical/Rhythmic Learners

Ask these students to describe how sound effects and background music contribute to their appreciation of movie scenes. Then, encourage these students to think of background music and sound effects as they read Dillard's vivid descriptions. Have students pause occasionally in their reading to explain the effects they would use in different sections and how these effects would enhance the scene.

610 ◆ Nonfiction

FLOOD

Block Scheduling Strategies

Consider these suggestions to take advantage of extended class time:

- Introduce the descriptive essay. Have students read the Literary Focus on page 609. After reading "Flood," have them answer the Literary Focus questions on page 617. You may also have them do the Literary Focus page in **Selection Support,** p. 183.
- Have students work together in small groups to discuss the Critical Thinking questions on page 617.

- Have students read excerpts from *Pilgrim at Tinker Creek* to gain further insight about the area and Dillard's ties to it.
- Help prepare students to complete the **Beyond Literature** activity (p. 44), Community Connection: *Flood Control.* Discuss with them dams they have seen or know about. To help them form opinions to answer the **Beyond Literature** questions, suggest that students use reference books or the Internet to research dams

and flood control.

- Encourage students to work together to evaluate and enhance your school or community disaster-preparedness plan.
- In prewriting for the Writing Mini-Lesson on page 618, have students work together to brainstorm for words and phrases that describe a hurricane. Then have them complete the lesson on their own.

ANNIE DILLARD

It's summer. We had some deep spring sunshine about a month ago, in a drought; the nights were cold. It's been gray sporadically, but not oppressively, and rainy for a week, and I would think: When is the real hot stuff coming, the mind-melting weeding weather? It was rainy again this morning, the same spring rain, and then this afternoon a different rain came: a pounding, three-minute shower. And when it was over, the cloud dissolved to haze. I can't see Tinker Mountain. It's summer now: the heat is on. It's summer now all summer long.

The season changed two hours ago. Will my life change as well? This is a time for resolutions, revolutions. The animals are going wild. I must have seen ten rabbits in as many minutes. Baltimore orioles are here; brown thrashers seem to be nesting down by Tinker Creek across the road. The coot is still around, big as a Thanksgiving turkey, and as careless; it doesn't even glance at a barking dog.

The creek's up. When the rain stopped today I walked across the road to the downed log by the steer crossing. The steers were across the creek, a black clot on a distant hill. High water had touched my log, the log I sit on, and dumped a smooth slope of muck in its lee. The water itself was an opaque pale green, like pulverized jade, still high and very fast, lightless, like no earthly water. A dog I've never seen before, thin as death, was flushing rabbits.

A knot of yellow, fleshy somethings had grown up by the log. They didn't seem to have either proper stems or proper flowers, but instead only blind,

◀ Critical Viewing Do you think the physical damage or the emotional damage brought on by a natural disaster like this flood is harder to overcome? [Support]

Flood ◆ *611*

◆ *Literature and Your Life*

❶ Ask students what changes signal summer to them. What do they watch for as the season changes? *Students can share their ideas and observations. Encourage them to focus on sights, smells, sounds.*

◆ **Literary Focus**

❷ **Descriptive Essay** Ask students to identify the senses to which the author appeals in this passage. How do the sensory descriptions affect the mood in this passage? *The passage appeals to the senses of touch and sight. The sensory details "black clot," "a smooth slope of muck," "opaque pale green, like pulverized jade," "lightless, like no earthly water," and "thin as death" create an ominous mood.*

▶Critical Viewing◀

❸ **Support** Students may say that the physical damage is shocking and immediate; the emotional damage may linger long after the physical damage is repaired, as people try to rebuild their lives and come to terms with what they have lost.

◆ **Literary Focus**

❶ **Descriptive Essay** Ask students which sensory details in this passage create an ominous feeling. *Students should note: "strangely empty," "so steamy I could barely see," "dead tan mud," "horny orange roots," "roots hung, an empty net in air, clutching an incongruous light bulb," "four jays flew around me very slowly, acting generally odd."*

◆ *Literature and Your Life*

❷ Point out that Dillard's apprehension is due in part to realizing that it is the anniversary of Hurricane Agnes. Ask students why anniversaries of memorable or devastating events are significant for people. *Students will probably realize that anniversaries of such events tend to bring the events to the forefront of people's minds. For some people, such anniversaries seem to suggest that the experience could be repeated.*

❸ **Clarification** If necessary, explain that hurricane season runs from May 15–November 30 each year. Hurricanes that occur during the season are named alphabetically.

◆ **Reading Strategy**

❹ **Recognize Facts and Impressions** Students should note the following: *That the creek is out of its four-foot banks is a verifiable fact. The rest of the information is based on Dillard's own impressions; for example, "The high creek doesn't look like our creek," "the high creek obliterates everything in flat opacity," and "It looks like somebody else's creek . . ." are personal impressions of the author that cannot be measured or verified.*

---

featureless growth, like etiolated[1] potato sprouts in a root cellar. I tried to dig one up from the crumbly soil, but they all apparently grew from a single, well-rooted corm, so I let them go.

Still, the day had an air of menace. A broken whiskey bottle by the log, the brown tip of a snake's tail disappearing between two rocks on the hill at my back, the rabbit the dog nearly caught, the rabies I knew was in the county, the bees who kept unaccountably fumbling at my forehead with their furred feet . . .

❶ I headed over to the new woods by the creek, the motorbike woods. They were strangely empty. The air was so steamy I could barely see. The ravine separating the woods from the field had filled during high water, and a dead tan mud clogged it now. The horny orange roots of one tree on the ravine's jagged bank had been stripped of soil; now the roots hung, an empty net in the air, clutching an incongruous light bulb stranded by receding waters. For the entire time that I walked in the woods, four jays flew around me very slowly, acting generally odd, and screaming on two held notes. There wasn't a breath of wind.

Coming out of the woods, I heard loud shots; they reverberated ominously in the damp air. But when I walked up the road, I saw what it was, and the dread quality of the whole afternoon vanished at once. It was a couple of garbage trucks, huge trash compacters humped like armadillos, and they were making their engines backfire to impress my neighbors' pretty daughters, high school girls who had just been let off the school bus. The long-haired girls strayed into giggling clumps at the corner of the road; the garbage trucks sped away gloriously, as if they had been the Tarleton twins on thoroughbreds cantering away from the gates of Tara.[2] In the distance a white vapor was rising from the waters of Carvin's Cove and catching in trailing tufts in the mountains' sides. I

1. **etoliated** (ē′ tē ə lāt′ id) *adj.* Made pale and unhealthy.
2. **Tarleton twins . . . Tara:** Two suitors who try to win the love of Scarlett, the main character in *Gone With the Wind*.

---

stood on my own porch, exhilarated, unwilling to go indoors.

❷ It was just this time last year that we had the flood. It was Hurricane Agnes, really, but by the time it got here, the weather bureau had demoted it to a tropical storm. I see by a clipping I saved that the date was June twenty-first, the solstice, midsummer's night, the longest daylight of the year; but I didn't notice it at the time. Everything was so exciting, and so very dark. All it did was rain. It rained, and the creek started to rise. The creek, naturally, rises every time it rains; this didn't seem any different. But it kept raining, and, that morning of the twenty-first, the creek kept rising. ❸

hat morning I'm standing at my kitchen window. Tinker Creek is out of its four-foot banks, way out, and it's still coming. The high creek doesn't look like our creek. Our creek splashes transparently over a jumble of rocks; the high creek <u>obliterates</u> everything in flat <u>opacity</u>. It looks like somebody else's creek that has <u>usurped</u> or eaten our creek and is roving frantically to escape, big and ugly, like a blacksnake caught in a kitchen drawer. The color is foul, a rusty cream. Water that has picked up clay soils looks worse than other muddy waters, because the particles of clay are so fine; they spread out and cloud the water so that you can't see light through even an inch of it in a drinking glass.

◆ **Reading Strategy**
Is this a fact or an impression? How do you know? ❹

Everything looks different. Where my eye is used to depth, I see the flat water, near, too

---

◆ **Build Vocabulary**

obliterates (ə blit′ ə rāts′) *v.:* Destroys; erases without a trace
opacity (ō pas′ ə tē) *n.:* Quality of not letting light pass through
usurped (yo͞o surpt′) *v.:* Taken power over; held by force

◆ **Beyond the Classroom**

Community Connection

Disaster Preparedness The efforts and expertise of many different people, agencies, and organizations come into play when a disaster strikes. Cooperation, quick response, and up-to-the-minute information is critical when coping with a disaster. Professionals and volunteers need to work together to implement safety measures, evacuate people in immediate danger, treat the injured, and orchestrate the clean-up. Smooth operation of these measures can mean the difference between life and death.

Have students find out about the many people in their community who help ensure the safety of the population when a disaster hits: utility workers, fire fighters, police, volunteer ambulance drivers, paramedics, and so on. Interested students can work in small groups to write a disaster short story scene—a scene in which all these people work together successfully to respond to an emergency.

near. I see trees I never noticed before, the black verticals of their rainsoaked trunks standing out of the pale water like pilings for a rotted dock. The stillness of grassy banks and stony ledges is gone; I see rushing, a wild sweep and hurry in one direction, as swift and compelling as a waterfall. The Atkins kids are out in their tiny rain gear, staring at the monster creek. It's risen up to their gates; the neighbors are gathering; I go out.

I hear a roar, a high windy sound more like air than like water, like the run-together whaps of a helicopter's propeller after the engine is off, a high million rushings. The air smells damp and acrid, like fuel oil, or insecticide. It's raining.

I'm in no danger; my house is high. I hurry down the road to the bridge. Neighbors who have barely seen each other all winter are there, shaking their heads. Few have ever seen it before: the water is *over* the bridge. Even when I see the bridge now, which I do every day, I still can't believe it: the water was *over* the bridge, a foot or two over the bridge, which at normal times is eleven feet above the surface

of the creek.

Now the water is receding slightly; someone has produced empty metal drums, which we roll to the bridge and set up in a square to keep cars from trying to cross. It takes a bit of nerve even to stand on the bridge; the flood has ripped away a wedge of concrete that buttressed the bridge on the bank. Now one corner of the bridge hangs apparently unsupported while water hurls in an arch just inches below.

It's hard to take it all in, it's all so new. I look at the creek at my feet. It smashes under the bridge like a fist, but there is no end to its force; it hurtles down as far as I can see till it lurches round the bend, filling the valley, flattening, mashing, pushed, wider and faster, till it fills my brain.

It's like a dragon. Maybe it's because the bridge we are on is chancy, but I notice that no one can help imagining himself washed overboard, and gauging his chances for survival. You couldn't live. Mark Spitz couldn't live. The water arches where the bridge's supports at the banks prevent its

Flood ◆ 613

Speaking and Listening Mini-Lesson

Storm Report
This mini-lesson supports the first Speaking and Listening activity in the Idea Bank on page 618.

Introduce the Concept Discuss with students times when TV shows they were watching were interrupted by a winter storm warning, tornado watch, hurricane warning, or other extreme weather warning. Talk about the purpose of such warnings.

Develop Background Have students discuss the kinds of information that will be useful to local residents as the storm approaches such as,

the expected severity of the storm, precautions residents should take, and community evacuation procedures, if necessary.

Apply the Information Students can put together their two-minute broadcasts. Suggest that they focus on giving an initial report, updating information, or providing eyewitness coverage of the storm as it hits.

Assess the Outcome Have students evaluate the broadcasts based on overall presentation and descriptive details. What made the most convincing reports successful?

◆ Build Grammar Skills

❺ Subject-Verb Agreement Ask students to identify the subject and verb in the clause, "The stillness of grassy banks and stony ledges is gone." Have them explain why the verb is singular. Discuss why the words "banks" and "ledges" might cause some confusion in determining subject-verb agreement. *Subject: stillness; verb: is. The verb is singular because it agrees with the singular subject "stillness." The plural nouns "banks" and "ledges" might confuse the issue because they are closer to the verb than the subject is.*

◆ Literary Focus

❻ Descriptive Essay Have students identify the sensory images in the paragraph. *Dillard describes the sound of the water and the smell of the air.*

◆ Reading Strategy

❼ Recognize Facts and Impressions Ask students to identify the facts in this passage and to explain how they can distinguish them from impressions. *These facts are in the paragraph: The neighbors are shaking their heads, the water is a foot or two over the bridge, the bridge is normally eleven feet above the surface of the creek. These facts can be verified by observation or measurement.*

❽ Clarification Point out that U.S. swimmer Mark Spitz won seven gold medals at the 1972 Summer Olympics. Dillard's reference indicates that even the greatest swimmer could not survive.

❶ Descriptive Essay Students should note the following: *Dillard packs this passage with vivid visual images. For example, the floodwater looks "like dirty lace," the earth "moves backwards, rises and swells," the land looks "as though it were not solid and real at all, but painted on a scroll . . ."*

◆ **Critical Thinking**

❷ Analyze Ask students: Why do you think Dillard chose these particular objects to imagine floating down the creek? *Dillard made the objects as diverse as possible to create a bizarre impression.*

◆ **Build Grammar Skills**

❸ Subject-Verb Agreement Ask students to identify the subject and verb in this sentence and explain why the verb is singular even though the word "eggs" is plural. *Subject: hill; verb: is. The verb is singular to agree with the singular subject, "hill." The plural word "eggs" is not the subject, even though it is closer to the verb.*

Customize for
Interpersonal Learners
Allow time for these students to discuss Dillard's description and share their own impressions of floods based on experience or scenes from television news or movies. Encourage students to jot down details and ideas that help them envision the flood Dillard describes.

614

---

enormous volume from going wide, forcing it to go high; that arch drives down like a diving whale, and would butt you on the bottom. "You'd never know what hit you," one of the men says. But if you survived that part and managed to surface . . . ? How fast can you live? You'd need a windshield. You couldn't keep your head up; the water under the surface is fastest. You'd spin around like a sock in a clothes dryer. You couldn't grab onto a tree trunk without leaving that arm behind. No, you couldn't live. And if they ever found you, your gut would be solid red clay.

It's all I can do to stand. I feel dizzy, drawn, <u>mauled</u>. Below me the floodwater roils to a violent froth that looks like dirty lace, a lace that continuously explodes before my eyes. If I look away, the earth moves backwards, rises and swells, from the fixing of my eyes at one spot

> ◆ **Literary Focus**
> ❶ In what specific ways is this passage typical of a descriptive essay?

against the motion of the flood. All the familiar land looks as though it were not solid and real at all, but painted on a scroll like a backdrop, and that unrolled scroll has been shaken, so the earth sways and the air roars.

Everything imaginable is zipping by, almost too fast to see. If I stand on the bridge and look downstream, I get dizzy; but if I look upstream, I feel as though I am looking up the business end of an avalanche. There are dolls, split wood and kindling, dead fledgling songbirds, bottles, whole bushes and trees, rakes and garden gloves. Wooden, rough-hewn railroad ties charge by faster than any express. Lattice fencing bobs along, and a wooden picket gate. There are so many white plastic gallon milk jugs that when the flood ultimately recedes, they are left on the grassy banks looking from a distance like a flock of white geese.

I expect to see anything at all. In this one way, the creek is more like itself when it floods than at any other time: mediating, bringing things down. I wouldn't be at all surprised to

see John Paul Jones coming round the bend, standing on the deck of the *Bon Homme Richard*, or Amelia Earhart waving gaily from the cockpit of her floating Lockheed. Why not a cello, a basket of breadfruit, a casket of antique coins? Here comes the Franklin expedition on snowshoes, and the three magi, plus camels, afloat on a canopied barge!

T he whole world is in flood, the land as well as the water. Water streams down the trunks of trees, drips from hat-brims, courses across roads. The whole earth seems to slide like sand down a chute; water pouring over the least slope leaves the grass flattened, silver side up, pointing downstream. Everywhere windfall and flotsam twigs and leafy boughs, wood from woodpiles, bottles, and saturated straw spatter the ground or streak it in curving windrows. Tomatoes in flat gardens are literally floating in mud; they look as though they have been dropped whole into a boiling, brown-gravy stew. The level of the water table is at the top of the toe of my shoes. Pale muddy water lies on the flat so that it all but drowns the grass; it looks like a hideous parody of a light snow on the field, with only the dark tips of the grass blades visible.

When I look across the street, I can't believe my eyes. Right behind the road's shoulder are waves, waves whipped in rhythmically peaking scallops, racing downstream. The hill where I watched the praying mantis lay her eggs is a waterfall that splashes into a brown ocean. I can't even remember where the creek usually runs—it is everywhere now. My log is gone for sure, I think—but in fact, I discover later, it holds, rammed between growing trees. Only the cable suspending the steers' fence is visible,

◆ **Build Vocabulary**
mauled (môld) *adj.:* Roughly or clumsily handled
malevolent (mə lev´ ə lənt´) *adj.:* Intended as evil or harmful
repressed (ri prest´) Held back; restrained

614 ◆ *Nonfiction*

Workplace Skills Mini-Lesson

Being Prepared

Introduce the Concept Make the point that people who have prepared for natural disasters by storing canned food and keeping flashlights and first-aid kits on hand are often able to get through a disaster with the least amount of trouble. Ask students how the habit of preparing in advance for problems in general could make an employee an especially valuable asset.

Develop Background Discuss the kinds of jobs for which advance preparation for problems would be important. For example, a baby sitter

should have a list of emergency telephone numbers and information concerning where first-aid supplies can be found.

Apply the Information Have students list two or three jobs for which being prepared is particularly important, then note specific measures they would take to be prepared in those jobs.

Assess the Outcome Have students assess each other's lists on the basis of how appropriate each measure of preparation is to the job they listed. Which were the best preparation measures suggested, and why?

and not the fence itself; the steers' pasture is entirely in flood, a brown river. The river leaps its banks and smashes into the woods where the motorbikes go, devastating all but the sturdiest trees. The water is so deep and wide it seems as though you could navigate the *Queen Mary* in it, clear to Tinker Mountain.

What do animals do in these floods? I see a drowned muskrat go by like he's flying, but they all couldn't die; the water rises after every hard rain, and the creek is still full of muskrats. This flood is higher than their raised sleeping platforms in the banks; they must just race for high ground and hold on. Where do the fish go, and what do they do? Presumably their gills can filter oxygen out of this muck, but I don't know how. They must hide from the current behind any barriers they can find, and fast for a few days. They must: otherwise we'd have no fish; they'd all be in the Atlantic Ocean. What about herons and kingfishers, say? They can't see to eat. It usually seems to me that when I see any animal, its business is urgent enough that it couldn't easily be suspended for forty-eight hours. Crayfish, frogs, snails, rotifers? Most things must simply die. They couldn't live. Then I suppose that when the water goes down and clears, the survivors have a field day with no competition. But you'd think the bottom would be knocked out of the food chain—the whole pyramid would have no base plankton, and it would crumble, or crash with a thud. Maybe enough spores and larvae and eggs are constantly being borne down from slower upstream waters to repopulate . . . I don't know.

Some little children have discovered a snapping turtle as big as a tray. It's hard to believe that this creek could support a predator that size: its shell is a foot and a half across, and its head extends a good seven inches beyond the shell. When the children—in the company of a shrunken terrier—approach it on the bank, the snapper rears up on its thick front legs and hisses very impressively. I had read earlier that

since turtles' shells are rigid, they don't have bellows lungs; they have to gulp for air. And, also since their shells are rigid, there's only room for so much inside, so when they are frightened and planning a retreat, they have to expel air from their lungs to make room for head and feet—hence the <u>malevolent</u> hiss.

The next time I look, I see that the children have somehow maneuvered the snapper into a washtub. They're waving a broom handle at it in hopes that it will snap the wood like a matchstick, but the creature will not deign to oblige. The kids are crushed; all their lives they've heard that this is the one thing you do with a snapping turtle—you shove a broom handle near it, and it "snaps it like a matchstick." It's nature's way; it's sure-fire. But the turtle is having none of it. It avoids the broom handle with an air of patiently <u>repressed</u> rage. They let it go, and it beelines down the bank, dives unhesitatingly into the swirling floodwater, and that's the last we see of it.

A cheer comes up from the crowd on the bridge. The truck is here with a pump for the Bowerys' basement, hooray! We roll away the metal drums, the truck makes it over the bridge, to my amazement—the crowd cheers again. State police cruise by; everything's fine here; downstream people are in trouble. The bridge over by the Bings' on Tinker Creek looks like it's about to go. There's a tree trunk wedged against its railing, and a section of concrete is out. The Bings are away, and a young couple is living there, "taking care of the house." What can they do? The husband drove to work that morning as usual; a few hours later, his wife was evacuated from the front door in a *motorboat*.

 walk to the Bings'. Most of the people who are on our bridge eventually end up over there; it's just down the road. We straggle along in the rain, gathering a crowd. The men who work away from home are here, too; their wives have telephoned them at work this morning to say that the creek is rising fast,

Flood ◆ 615

Cross-Curricular Connection: Science

The devastation caused by flooding can be extreme, and the effect on the environment can be long term. Common causes of river floods include too much rain at one time, as at Tinker Creek, and sudden melting of snow and ice. Under such conditions, rivers may receive more than ten times as much water as their beds can hold. Heavy rains produce flash floods if the rains cause small rivers or streams, such as Tinker Creek, to rise suddenly and overflow. Flash floods occur chiefly in mountainous areas and do not allow much time for people to be warned of danger.

Since 1936, a year of bad floods, the U.S. government has spent billions of dollars to prevent and control floods. Flood control involves building dams to store water and channels to allow it to flow quickly to the sea. It also involves various embankments to hold back river or sea waters, such as dikes, flood walls, and levees. These embankments help keep water off the land.

In addition, the National Weather Service has a network of river forecast centers and local district offices whose function it is to track the state of rivers and provide flood warnings, if necessary.

❶ Students may suggest that basic tasks, such as cutting down a tree, are made extraordinarily difficult by the flood waters.

◆ Critical Thinking

❷ Interpret In what way is this meeting representative of how people behave in crisis situations? *The narrator and the young man "pull together" so that each can pass on the narrow wall without falling. Once the problem has been solved, they continue on their separate ways. This represents the way people "pull together" and cooperate during an emergency, then go back to their usual, more isolated lives afterward.*

◆ Critical Thinking

❸ Infer What evidence does Dillard give to show that things are returning to normal? *Students should note that people are relaxing, children are playing, the atmosphere is not charged with dread and tension, as it was when the creek was rising.*

Reinforce and Extend

Answers
◆ *Literature and Your Life*

Reader's Response Some students might say their impression would be one of fear; others might say they would find the flood exhilarating.

Thematic Focus Encourage students to verify the facts they've learned by checking another source.

☑ **Check Your Comprehension**

1. It's out of its four-foot banks; the color is rusty.
2. The water's arches would knock people down; the water under the surface is so fast a person couldn't keep his/her head up.
3. Dolls, wood, bushes and trees, rakes, garden gloves, railroad ties, fencing, and plastic jugs rush by.
4. Dillard worries that they won't find food.
5. Dillard heads home because the water is going down and the danger is past.

---

and they'd better get home while the gettin's good.

There's a big crowd already there; everybody knows that the Bings' is low. The creek is coming in the recreation-room windows; it's halfway up the garage door. Later that day people will haul out everything salvageable and try to dry it: books, rugs, furniture—the lower level was filled from floor to ceiling. Now on this bridge a road crew is trying to chop away the wedged tree trunk with a long-handled ax. The handle isn't so long that they don't have to stand on the bridge, in Tinker Creek. I walk along a low brick wall that was built to retain the creek away from the house at high water. The wall holds just fine, but now that the creek's receding, it's retaining water around the house. On the wall I can walk right out into the flood and stand in the middle of it. Now on the return trip I meet a young man who's going in the opposite direction. The wall is one brick wide; we can't pass. So we clasp hands and lean out backwards over the turbulent water; our feet interlace like teeth on a zipper, we pull together, stand, and continue on our ways. The kids have spotted a rattlesnake draping itself out of harm's way in a bush; now they all want to walk over the brick wall to the bush, to get bitten by the snake.

 ◆ *Literature and Your Life*
In what ways does the flood transform ordinary actions into extraordinary events?

The little Atkins kids are here, and they are hopping up and down. I wonder if I hopped up and down, would the bridge go? I could stand at the railing as at the railing of a steamboat, shouting deliriously, "Mark three! Quarter-less-three! Half twain! Quarter twain! . . ." as the current bore the broken bridge out of sight around the bend before she sank. . . .

Everyone else is standing around. Some of the women are carrying curious plastic umbrellas that look like diving bells—umbrellas they don't put up, but on; they don't get under, but in. They can see out dimly, like goldfish in bowls. Their voices from within sound distant, but with an underlying cheerfulness that plainly acknowledges, "Isn't this ridiculous?" Some of the men are wearing their fishing hats. Others duck their heads under folded newspapers held not very high in an effort to compromise between keeping their heads dry and letting rain run up their sleeves. Following some form of courtesy, I guess, they lower these newspapers when they speak with you, and squint politely into the rain.

Women are bringing coffee in mugs to the road crew. They've barely made a dent in the tree trunk, and they're giving up. It's a job for power tools; the water's going down anyway, and the danger is past. Some kid starts doing tricks on a skateboard; I head home. **❸**

Guide for Responding

◆ *Literature and Your Life*

Reader's Response What do you think would have been your immediate impression on first seeing the flood? Explain.

Thematic Focus In what specific ways does this piece add to your knowledge about natural forces and their effects?

Floods Scrapbook Gather pictures (from books, magazines, or the Internet) of historic floods worldwide. Annotate the pictures with important facts, such as the causes and environmental effects of the flood.

☑ **Check Your Comprehension**

1. What is different about Tinker Creek the morning before the flood?
2. What are some reasons that someone wouldn't survive in the flood waters?
3. What are some things that rush by in the water?
4. For what reason is Dillard concerned about the creatures who will survive the flood?
5. Why does Dillard eventually head home?

Beyond the Selection

FURTHER READING

Other Works by Annie Dillard
An American Childhood
The Living

Other Works About Natural Forces
The Johnstown Flood, David McCullough
The Sea Wolf, Jack London
K2, Triumph and Tragedy, Jim Curran
   We suggest that you preview these works before recommending them to students.

INTERNET

Students can learn more about Annie Dillard and her work at the following Web sites. Please be aware that the sites may have changed. **http://www.well.com/USer/elliotts/smse_dillard.html**
   Students can find out more about floods and hurricanes at the following Web sites:
http://water.USgs.gov/
http://www.nhc.noaa.gov/index.html
   We *strongly recommend* that you preview the sites before you send students to them.

Guide for Responding (continued)

◆ Critical Thinking

INTERPRET

1. What does the fact that Dillard stood on the bridge tell you about her character? Explain. **[Infer]**
2. Speculate about why Dillard lists the people and things she wouldn't be surprised to see floating down the creek. **[Speculate]**
3. What feelings about nature do you think Dillard wants you to take away from her piece? Explain. **[Draw Conclusions]**

APPLY

4. Defend the following statement with examples from "Flood": Natural disasters bring people together. **[Defend]**

EXTEND

5. Describe the role of at least three kinds of professionals and volunteers who respond to natural disasters. **[Career Link]**

◆ Reading Strategy

RECOGNIZE FACTS AND IMPRESSIONS

Recognizing a fact is a straightforward matter—a **fact** is provable. An **impression**, though, reflects an author's personal feelings.

1. Find evidence that Dillard's knowledge of history and religion contributed to her impressions of the flood.
2. Analyze this sentence in terms of fact and impression: "The steers were across the creek, a black clot on a distant hill."

◆ Literary Focus

DESCRIPTIVE ESSAY

A **descriptive essay** is a short nonfiction work that provides concrete and sensory details so that you can clearly and easily envision the subject. A flood caused by a hurricane, while potentially horrible in real life, makes an excellent descriptive subject because it is full of sensory experiences.

1. Which of Dillard's descriptions best makes you feel you are at the flood? Why?
2. Find examples of language that appeals to each of the five senses.

◆ Build Vocabulary

USING THE PREFIX mal-

The prefix mal- means "bad, evil." On your paper, match each word with its appropriate definition.

1. malice   **a.** criminal
2. malefactor   **b.** to fail to work properly
3. malfunction   **c.** desire to do harm to others

USING THE WORD BANK

On your paper, write the letter of the word that is the best antonym, or opposite, of the first word.

1. obliterates: (a) annihilates, (b) builds, (c) kills
2. usurped: (a) conquered, (b) swamped, (c) released
3. repressed: (a) freed, (b) oppressed, (c) bound
4. opacity: (a) depth, (b) translucence, (c) intelligence
5. mauled: (a) attacked, (b) smeared, (c) protected
6. malevolent: (a) corrupt, (b) injurious, (c) helpful

◆ Build Grammar Skills

SUBJECT AND VERB AGREEMENT

Verbs must **agree** in number with their **subjects**, even when words intervene between the subject and verb. Don't be misled into making the verb agree with a noun that is closer but that is not the subject:

> When flood *waters* caused by a hurricane finally *recede* they can leave dead wildlife in their wake.

In this sentence, the plural verb form *recede* agrees with the plural subject *waters*. You should not make the verb agree with *hurricane,* even though *hurricane* is closer to the verb.

Practice Rewrite each of the following sentences so that their verbs agree in number with their subjects.

1. Neighbors who have barely seen each other all winter is there.
2. Most of the people who are on our bridge eventually ends up over there.
3. The hill where I watched the praying mantis lay her eggs are a waterfall that splashes.
4. The stillness of grassy banks and stony ledges are gone.

Flood ◆ 617

◆ Build Grammar Skills

Practice

1. Neighbors who have barely seen each other <u>are</u> there.
2. Most of the people who are on our bridge eventually <u>end</u> up over there.
3. The hill where I watched the praying mantis lay her eggs <u>is</u> a waterfall that splashes.
4. The stillness of grassy banks and stony ledges <u>is</u> gone.

✎ Writer's Solution

For additional instruction and practice, use the Subject-Verb Agreement lesson in the **Language Lab CD-ROM** and pages 80–82 on Subject-Verb Agreement in the *Writer's Solution Grammar Practice Book.*

617

Idea Bank

Customizing for
Performance Levels

Following are suggestions for matching Idea Bank topics with your students' performance levels:

Less Advanced Students: 1
Average Students: 2, 4, 5
More Advanced Students: 3, 6

Customizing for
Learning Modalities

Following are suggestions for matching Idea Bank topics with your students' learning modalities:

Visual/Spatial: 2
Verbal/Linguistic: 4, 5
Logical/Mathematical: 6, 7

Writing Mini-Lesson

Refer students to the Writing Handbook, page 965, for instruction on the writing process and page 967 for further information on narration.

Writing Lab CD-ROM

Have students complete the tutorial on Description. Follow these steps:

1. Suggest that students use the cluster diagram to record details of their impressions.
2. Encourage students to use the Sensory Word Bin to discover additional descriptive words.
3. Allow time for students to draft on the computer.
4. Have students use Revision Checker for vague or overused adjectives.

Sourcebook

Have students use Chapter 1, Description (pp. 1–29) for additional support. The lesson includes specific instruction on gathering details (p. 18).

Build Your Portfolio

Idea Bank

Writing

1. **Descriptive Paragraph** What was the best food you ever tasted or the best song you ever heard? Using sensory language, write a paragraph describing a "best."

2. **Storm Journal** Write a three-paragraph factual or imaginary journal entry describing a major storm whipping through your neighborhood.

3. **Fable** Write a fable, set at the Tinker Creek flood, that features the animals and fish Dillard mentions. Remember, a fable is a brief story that usually has a moral.

Speaking and Listening

4. **Storm Report** A hurricane with 120-mile-an-hour winds is moving up the coast. As a broadcast meteorologist, give a two-minute warning and description of the storm.

5. **Talk-Show Interview** With a partner, prepare and present an interview between a television talk-show host and Annie Dillard about what it was like to be present at the flood at Tinker Creek.

Projects

6. **Hurricane Chart** Gather information on the worst hurricanes in history. Organize your findings (such as locale, deaths, and property damage toll) in a chart.

7. **Food-Chain Presentation** Dillard says that plankton, microscopic plants and animals, are the start of the food chain. Research information about the food chain at a creek. Organize your findings into a presentation in which you provide descriptions and pictures.

Writing Mini-Lesson

Radio Call-In Transcript

Write a **transcript** of a radio call-in show. A transcript is a written record of the dialogue. Here's your situation: A hurricane is traveling up the East Coast at sixteen miles an hour. Part of Florida is devastated. The hurricane just hit Georgia, and it's on its way to South Carolina. Write a transcript of a conversation between the show's host and a caller from each of these states. What they say is up to you, but make sure to convey their feelings and impressions.

> **Writing Skills Focus:**
> **Sensory Language**
>
> Describe the many sensory experiences of a hurricane so that others will feel they're on the scene. Use action verbs (*roar*) and figurative language (*looking from the distance like a flock of white geese*) that evoke the senses.

Prewriting Use a chart like this one to jot down words or phrases appropriate for describing a hurricane.

Visual	Auditory	Tactile	Olfactory (smell)	Taste

Drafting When writing, remember that the callers are likely to mention verifiable facts (amount of damage) along with their personal impressions of the storm. Include both in your transcript.

Revising Read your transcript aloud to a partner. Make sure that it flows naturally, as dialogue should. Also be sure that you have used sensory language in your transcript to convey the chaos and destruction caused by the hurricane.

✓ ASSESSMENT OPTIONS

Formal Assessment, Selection Test, pp. 154–156, and Assessment Resources Software. The selection test is designed so that it can be easily customized to the performance levels of your students.
Alternative Assessment, p. 44 includes options for less advanced students, more advanced students, interpersonal learners, verbal/linguistic learners, logical/mathematical learners, and visual/spatial learners.

PORTFOLIO ASSESSMENT
Use the following rubrics in the *Alternative Assessment* booklet to assess student writing:
Descriptive Paragraph: Description Rubric, p. 97
Storm Journal: Description Rubric, p. 97
Fable: Fiction Narrative Rubric, p. 95
Writing Mini-Lesson: Description Rubric, p. 97

Writing Process Workshop

Comparison-and-Contrast Essay

In the selections in this section, you probably saw similarities and differences in the ways in which writers view their identities, nature, jobs, and even movies.

A **comparison-and-contrast essay** is a brief written exploration of the similarities and differences between two (or more) things. Using the skills listed below—which were introduced in this section's Writing Mini-Lessons—write a comparison-and-contrast essay on a topic that interests you.

Writing Skills Focus

▶ **Choose a logical method of organization.** Decide whether your subject is best suited for point-by-point organization or subject-by-subject organization. (See p. 607.)

▶ **Use sensory language.** Words and phrases that appeal to one of the five senses help your readers vividly experience what you're comparing and contrasting. (See p. 618.)

▶ **Use transitions** such as *likewise, similarly, nevertheless,* and *in contrast* to indicate the relationships between ideas. (See p. 578.)

In the following excerpt, author Rachel Carson uses these skills to compare the shore under two different tides.

MODEL FROM LITERATURE

from The Marginal World by Rachel Carson

The shore has a dual nature, changing with the swing of the tides, belonging now to the land, now to the sea. ① On the ebb tide it knows the harsh extremes of the land world, being exposed to the heat and cold, to wind, to rain, and drying sun. ② On the flood tide it is a water world, returning briefly to the stability of the open sea.

Only the most hardy and adaptable can survive in a region so mutable, ③ *yet* the area between the tides is crowded with plants and animals.

① Carson first describes the conditions at low tide, then she describes the conditions at high tide.

② The writer includes sensory details of *heat, cold, wind, rain* and *drying sun.*

③ The transition <u>yet</u> indicates the contrast between the lack of life one would expect in this harsh environment and the abundance of life forms that exists there.

Establish Writing Guidelines

Before students begin, review the following key characteristics of a comparison-and-contrast essay:

- It explores similarities and differences between two items.
- It focuses on one subject or detail at a time, then moves on to another.

You may want to distribute the scoring rubric for Comparison/Contrast (p. 103 in *Alternative Assessment*) to make students aware before they begin of the criteria on which they will be evaluated. See the suggestions on page 621 for additional points with which you can customize the rubric for this workshop.

Refer students to the Writing Handbook, page 965, for instruction in the writing process, and page 967 for further information on comparison and contrast.

 Writer's Solution

Writing Lab CD-ROM

If your students have access to computers, you may want to have them work on the tutorial on Exposition to complete all or part of their comparison-and-contrast essays. Follow these steps:

1. Have students view the interactive model of a comparison-and-contrast essay.
2. Suggest that students use a Venn diagram to organize their details.
3. Have students draft on the computer.
4. Have students use the screen Checking Your Paragraphs for organization.
5. Have students use the Proofreading checklist.

Sourcebook

Students can find additional support for a comparison-and-contrast essay, including topic ideas, models, audience and purpose profiles, and graphic organizers, in the chapter on Exposition (pp. 62–95).

Connect to Literature Refer students to Rachel Carson's *The Marginal World* (p. 571). The essay contains examples of comparison and contrast.

 ### Cross-Curricular Connection: Social Studies

Suggest that students look to other disciplines for a topic for a comparison-and-contrast essay. For example, scientifically inclined students can write essays comparing and contrasting the methods used to produce electricity, such as coal, hydro-electric, and nuclear. Students interested in social studies might compare the cultures of two nations or the reliance on public transportation in New York, Chicago, and Los Angeles. Students interested in physical education can compare the effects on the cardiovascular system of swimming, jogging, and cross-country skiing. Mechanically inclined students may want to compare and contrast the mechanical differences between automatic and manual transmissions.

Develop Student Writing

Remind students that their comparison-and-contrast essays have a purpose beyond comparing and contrasting two items. For example, after their comparison, they might draw a conclusion about one or both of the items for the purpose of informing or persuading an audience.

Customize for
English Language Learners

You might give these students a mini-lesson on the comparative and superlative forms, which they will likely use in their essays. Explain to them the differences between *more* and *most,* as well as *-er* and *-est.* You might use the page on degrees of comparison, p. 86, in the *Writer's Solution Grammar Practice Book.*

 Writer's Solution

Writing Lab CD-ROM

The Gathering Details and Organizing Details and Information sections of the tutorial on Exposition contain the following screens that will help students in writing their comparison-and-contrast essays:

• Answering questions about your topic
• Identifying important details
• Examples of details ordered by comparison and contrast
• Venn diagram

Writing and Language Transparencies

Have students use the Comparison and Contrast Organizer, pp. 95–96, to develop and organize details for their essays.

Drafting

Point out to students that they need to balance the details of comparison or contrast that they present in their essays. For every detail that they present about item A, they should present a corresponding detail about item B. They may arrange these details in either of two ways:

• Follow each point about item A with a corresponding point about item B.
• Group all of the details about item A together and then all of those about item B.

Applying Language Skills:
Commas

Use **commas** correctly in your essay. Too few commas cause confusion, while too many make writing choppy and slow. The following are some common uses of commas:

To Separate Items in a Series:
ghost crabs, herons, starfish . . .

To Set Off Interrupting Words:
The shore, however, . . .

To Separate Clauses in a Compound Sentence:
The tide is low, and I can reach the cave.

Practice On your paper, place commas correctly in the following sentences:

1. Parrotfish struggle to survive in the competitive environment of the coral reef but their strong jaws give them an advantage.
2. There are many life forms within the coral reef, including starfish coral sea squirts fronds and Tubularia.

Writing Application Review your use of commas in your essay. Revise when necessary.

Writer's Solution Connection
Writing Lab

For help organizing your essay, use the Organizing and Ordering Details section of the Exposition tutorial in the Writing Lab.

620 ◆ *Nonfiction*

Prewriting

Brainstorm to Find a Topic With a small group of classmates, brainstorm to come up with possible topics. Consider topics such as actors, musicians, athletes, cities, television programs, and so on. List the ideas your group offers, then choose the topic that you find most interesting.

Decide on Your Purpose After choosing a topic, decide on the reason for your comparison. It might be one of the following reasons:

▶ **To inform** readers about your two subjects
▶ **To persuade** readers to accept a specific point of view related to the two subjects
▶ **To entertain** your audience by making an unlikely or unusual comparison

Once you've decided on your purpose, gather details that will help you achieve your purpose.

Keep Your Audience in Mind Identify your audience. Then keep the answers to questions such as these in mind as you gather details and write your essay:

▶ How old are my readers?
▶ What type of language will appeal to them?
▶ What might they already know about my topic?
▶ What might they not know that I should explain?

Organize Your Details Before you begin writing, use a Venn diagram like the one below to help organize your details. Write similarities in the space where the circles overlap, and note the differences in the outer sections of the circles.

Venn Diagram

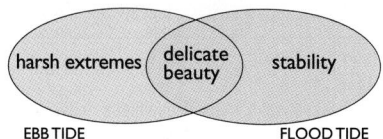

Drafting

Use Comparison-and-Contrast Organization There are two basic types of comparison-and-contrast organization: point-by-point and subject-by-subject. In point-by-point organization, each aspect of your subject is discussed in turn. For example, you might compare and contrast tape players and CD players in terms of cost, availability, and convenience of use.

In a subject-by-subject comparison, you would discuss all the features of one kind of player first and then discuss the features of the second kind.

Applying Language Skills

Commas Explain to students that while the use of commas may seem simple and self-evident, their importance should not be ignored. Too many, too few, or misplaced commas could result in misreading or confusion.

Answers

1. Parrotfish struggle to survive in the competitive environment of the coral reef, but their strong jaws give them an advantage.
2. There are many life forms within the coral reef, including starfish, coral, sea squirts, fronds, and Tubularia.

 Writer's Solution

For additional instruction and practice, have students complete the **Language Lab CD-ROM** lesson on Commas and practice pages 99–101 on commas in the *Writer's Solution Grammar Practice Book.*

Give Specific Examples Be specific about the ways in which your subjects are alike and different. For example, if you are comparing and contrasting life in a desert region and life in a polar region, offer details showing how the climate specifically affects things such as shelter, diet, and general health. Also include similarities and differences in the sensory details.

Revising

Use a Checklist Refer to the Writing Skills Focus on p. 619, and use the items as a checklist to evaluate and revise your comparison-and-contrast essay. Ask yourself the following questions and make revisions as necessary.

▶ Have I used transitions to show comparisons?
▶ Have I organized my points logically?
▶ Have I used sensory language?

REVISION MODEL

When you're choosing whether to buy cassettes or CDs you ① , should consider several factors. Cassette tapes are
② er
cheapest. Time and use, however, deteriorate the tape.
③ on the other hand,
CDs, will not deteriorate in quality.

① The writer adds a comma to make the sentence clear.
② This writer corrects this comparison.
③ The writer adds this transitional phrase to make the essay flow smoothly.

Publishing

Post Your Writing Electronically You can reach a large audience by posting your writing on the Internet for users interested in your subject. Consult with an experienced Internet user or visit Prentice Hall on the World Wide Web at http://phschool.com.

Give an Oral Presentation Arrange with a teacher or librarian for a time and place to give an oral reading of your paper. Then post a notice on a bulletin board, inviting people to attend the reading. In the notice, make the subject of your paper clear. During the reading, speak clearly and maintain eye contact with the audience. Leave time at the end for questions and answers.

APPLYING LANGUAGE SKILLS: Forms of Comparison

Make sure you use the proper **forms of comparison** for adjectives and adverbs. Use the basic, or positive, form to modify another word, the comparative form to compare two things, and the superlative form to compare more than two things.

Positive Form:
slow, sunny, humid, bad

Comparative Form:
slower, sunnier, more humid, worse

Superlative Form:
slowest, sunniest, most humid, worst

Practice On your paper, correct the forms of comparison in the following sentences.

1. Of the two cars, Jack's was fastest.
2. Of all the cars, mine was the more colorful.

Writing Application Review your essay, checking that you have used the proper forms of comparison for all modifiers.

Writer's Solution Connection Language Lab

For more practice with comparisons, complete the Language Lab lesson on Forms of Comparison.

Revising

Encourage students to review their prewriting notes to check that they have included the details they planned.

Writer's Solution

Writing Lab CD-ROM

Students can use the following tools in the Revising and Editing section of the tutorial on Exposition for revising their essays:

• Interactive Evaluation Checklists
• Revision Checkers for transition words and language variety
• Audio-annotated student model

Publishing

Students may wish to consider incorporating their comparison-and-contrast essay into a larger work, such as a persuasive speech or a visitor's guide. Discuss with students appropriate options based on their topics.

Applying Language Skills

Forms of Comparison Students will most likely use comparative and superlative forms frequently in their comparison-and-contrast essays. Make sure they understand the correct use and forms before drafting.

Answers

1. Of the two cars, Jack's was the *faster.*
2. Of all the cars, mine was the *most* colorful.

Writer's Solution

For additional instruction and practice, have students complete the **Language Lab CD-ROM** lesson on Forms of Comparison and the practice page 86 on Degrees of Comparison in the *Writer's Solution Grammar Practice Book.*

✓ ASSESSMENT		4	3	2	1
PORTFOLIO ASSESSMENT Use the rubric on Comparison/Contrast in the *Alternative Assessment* booklet (p. 103) to assess students' writing. Add these criteria to customize the rubric to this assignment.	**Sensory Words**	Frequent, vivid sensory words significantly enrich the effectiveness of the essay.	Sensory words are used.	A few sensory words are used, but more are needed.	Sensory words are absent; the essay is dull and vague.
	Forms of Comparison	The comparative and superlative forms are used correctly.	Comparative and superlative forms are mostly correct.	There are a number of mistakes with the comparative and superlative forms.	Incorrect use of the comparative and superlative forms impairs understanding.

Students will recognize heads, sub-heads, and sidebars from textbooks, magazines, and newspapers. Tell them that understanding how such structures are used to organize text will help them do research and find important pieces of information quickly and efficiently.

Customize for
Less Proficient Readers

Have these students preview the questions about heads and text structure. Point out to students that these questions will help them recognize how to use heads and text structure to mentally organize details.

Customize for
Visual/Spatial Learners

Encourage these students to use heads as the basis for a chart on which they can list details while they read.

Answers

1. The general idea of the article is that certain fruits and vegetables contain properties essential for good health.
2. The sections *Broccoli Is Key, Garlic Power,* and *Bananas About Bananas* give more information about *Vegetables and More.*
3. An outline may resemble the following:

I. Vegetables and More
   A. Broccoli
   B. Garlic
   C. Bananas
II. The Nutrition Habit
   A. Make a Plan
   B. Guidelines for Healthy Eating
      1. five servings of fruits and vegetables
      2. healthy snacks
      3. limited fat and oil

Using Heads and Text Structure

Real-World Reading Skills Workshop

Strategies for Success

When you look at articles in newspapers and magazines or the pages of nonfiction books—including your textbooks, notice the way that the text appears on the pages. (You can use this page as an example.) You will notice some of the following features:

- ▶ Heads in bold or colored type
- ▶ Lists
- ▶ Sections set off in boxes
- ▶ Sidebars

Articles and books are designed with these features to help you read, remember, and work with the material. Take advantage of the structure to master the content.

Preview Heads Headings indicate the main topic of a section. Scan the heads to get an overview of the content of the article or chapter. Knowing the main topics and general organization will help you process the information in each section efficiently.

Identify Relationships The size or color of a head is usually a clue to the section's relationship to other sections. For example, three subheads under a main head indicate that the information in those sections supports or explains the idea or topic expressed in the main head. Heads of equal size usually indicate ideas of equal weight.

Look at Set Off Material Pay attention to any material that is set apart from the rest of the text, such as a list, a box, a sidebar, or any words or sections pulled out and displayed. This material is set off so that you will notice it.

> ✔ Here are other situations in which you can use heads and text structure:
> ▶ Extended encyclopedia entries
> ▶ Textbooks
> ▶ World Wide Web pages

Apply the Strategy

Use the heads and text structure to help you answer the questions about this sample page.

VEGETABLES and MORE

In a recent study by the O'Brien Institute of Nutrition, nutritionists have found . . .

Broccoli Is Key
Broccoli is a wonderful source of nutrition because it contains substantial amounts of calcium and vitamin A, known cancer-fighting agents. By eating 1/2 cup of broccoli a day, . . .

Garlic Power
Garlic was worshiped by the ancient Egyptians and chewed by Greek Olympian athletes. It is also good for zapping bacteria, keeping your heart healthy, warding off coughs and colds, . . .

Bananas About Bananas
Bananas are an excellent source of potassium. Potassium has been found to . . .

The Nutrition Habit

Make a Plan
Consistency is the key to good health through nutrition. Start with a plan that will be easy for you to follow. . . .

Guidelines for Healthy Eating
The following guidelines will help you get on the right nutritional track:
- Eat five servings of fruits and vegetables daily
- Choose healthy snacks
- Limit the use of fats and oils

1. Scan the heads. What is your general idea of the article?
2. Which sections give more detail about "Vegetables and More"?
3. Make an outline of this article based on the heads and subheads.

PART 2 *Visual Essays and Workplace Writing*

Time & Memory Series, Nydia Preede, Courtesy of the artist

Visual Essays and Workplace Writing ◆ 623

The essays in this section represent the types of nonfiction students are likely to encounter in everyday reading. The two reviews of the *Star Wars* films appeared in newspapers. The visual essay "Mothers and Daughters" represents photographers' interpretations of relationships. "Imitating Nature's Mineral Artistry" explains a technical subject, with diagrams; it provides practice in reading scientific material. "Work That Counts" is a reflective description of work in the field of ornithology.

Customize for
Varying Student Needs
When assigning the selections in this part, be aware of these factors:

Star Wars reviews
- Two brief, high interest

"Mothers and Daughters"
- Visual essay with engaging photographs
- The accompanying text includes some abstract concepts

"These Are Days"
- High-interest popular song

"Nature's Mineral Artistry"
- Contains technical descriptions, which may be challenging for some
- Diagrams may appeal to visual learners

"Work That Counts"
- Fairly easy reading
- Short

 Humanities: Art

Time & Memory Series by Nydia Preede.

Explain that this work combines paint and collage, with scraps of paper glued to the canvas. Ask students to find elements that occur on the scraps of paper and also in the painted portions of the work (for example, the graph lines, the rectangular shapes). Ask them what words they can find in the work *"Words, Sounds, and Images" in the lower right; "Time" in the center; "and Memory" a few inches below.* Explain that this is an abstract work; explores the forms of things, how they look, rather than re-creating recognizable people, places, and things on canvas.

Help students link the artwork to the focus of Part 2, "Visual Essays and Workplace Writing," by answering the following questions:

1. What images in the artwork remind you of an office? *Office images include the graphs, the scraps of paper, the printed words.*

2. What idea about time and memory does this work help to communicate, and what elements of the work communicate this idea to you? *Sample answer: With its deep blue and green background, the artwork makes me think that memories are fragments, some clear, some unclear, floating in a kind of river of time.*

623

OBJECTIVES

1. To read, comprehend, and interpret critical reviews
2. To relate critical reviews to personal experience
3. To identify evidence in critical reviews
4. To recognize features of a critical review
5. To build vocabulary in context and recognize connotations
6. To recognize parenthetical interrupters
7. To write a movie review using specific examples
8. To respond to the story through writing, speaking and listening, and projects

SKILLS INSTRUCTION

Vocabulary:
Connotations

Grammar:
Parenthetical
Interrupters

Reading Strategy:
Identify Evidence

Literary Focus:
Critical Review

Writing:
Specific Examples

**Speaking and
Listening:**
Star Wars
Recording, Skit
(teacher edition)

Critical Viewing:
Compare; Analyze;
Speculate

PORTFOLIO OPPORTUNITIES

Writing: Press release; Speech; Interview

Writing Mini-Lesson: Movie Review

Speaking and Listening: Star Wars
Recording; Skit

Projects: Collage; Science-Fiction Exhibit

More About the Authors

Vincent Canby's reviews have long been an influential factor in determining whether new movies will be hits; few reviewers are quoted more often in ads for new films.

In addition to writing critical film reviews for newspapers, **Roger Ebert** is also the author of several books, including the annually revised *Video Companion,* featuring capsule reviews of more than a thousand films available on videocassette.

Guide for Reading

Vincent Canby (1924–)

If you were looking for all the news fit to print about movies between 1969 and 1993, you would have, no doubt, read the film reviews written by the lead film critic of *The New York Times*, Vincent Canby. In addition to theater and film reviews, he has also written the play *After All* (1981) and the novel *Unnatural Scenery* (1979). He continues to produce movie reviews as the Sunday drama critic for *The New York Times*.

Roger Ebert (1942–)

Thumbs up, thumbs down. These symbols for movies worth seeing or avoiding were made popular by the duo of Siskel and Ebert, Chicago-based movie reviewers and co-hosts of their own television program. Roger Ebert's reviews appear in the *Chicago Sun-Times* and two hundred other newspapers around the country. He has won two Pulitzer Prizes for his work. About movie viewing he has said: "The audience: In the dark, lined up facing the screen. The light comes from behind their heads—from back there where dreams come true."

◆ Build Vocabulary

CONNOTATIONS

In his review of the re-released 1997 version of *Star Wars*, Roger Ebert describes Han Solo, the character portrayed by Harrison Ford, as "laconic." The denotation, or dictionary definition, of *laconic* is "using few words to express thoughts." In this case, *laconic* has a connotation as well. A connotation is what a word suggests or implies. A *laconic* character is a person who not only uses few words, but usually does so almost impolitely because he or she understands the uselessness of idle chatter.

apotheosis
eclectic
facetiousness
adroit
piously
condescension
watershed
synthesis
fastidious
effete
laconic

WORD BANK

As you read these reviews, you will encounter the words in this list. Each word is defined on the page where it first appears. Preview the list before you read, and look for each word as it appears in the reviews.

624 ◆ Nonfiction

◆ Build Grammar Skills

PARENTHETICAL INTERRUPTERS

As if they are having an informal conversation about a movie, reviewers add side remarks that interrupt the main flow of a sentence. These remarks are **parenthetical interrupters**—expressions that comment on or give additional information about the main part of a sentence. Because they interrupt the main idea, they are set off from the rest of the sentence with commas.

Look at these sentences from the movie reviews of *Star Wars* by Vincent Canby and Roger Ebert. The parenthetical interrupters are italicized:

All of these works, *of course,* had earlier left their marks . . .

Those who analyze its philosophy do so, *I imagine,* with a smile in their minds.

As you read these reviews, notice how such remarks make you feel that the reviewers are engaged in a conversation with you.

Prentice Hall Literature Program Resources

REINFORCE / RETEACH / EXTEND

Selection Support:
Build Vocabulary: Connotations, p. 184
Build Grammar Skills: Parenthetical Interrupters, p. 185
Reading Strategy: Identify Evidence, p. 186
Literary Focus: Critical Review, p. 187

Strategies for Diverse Students Needs, p. 45

Beyond Literature Media Connection: Classic Films, p. 45

Formal Assessment Selection Test, p. 157; Assessment Resources Software

Alternative Assessment, p. 45

Writing and Language Transparencies

Resource Pro CD-R⊘M
"Star Wars—a Trip to a Far Galaxy"; "Star Wars—Breakthrough Film"—includes all resource materials and customizable lesson plan.

 Listening to Literature Audiocassettes
"Star Wars—a Trip to a Far Galaxy"; "Star Wars—Breakthrough Film"

Star Wars: A Trip to the Galaxy That's Fun and Funny . . .
◆ Star Wars: Breakthrough Film Still Has the Force ◆

◆ *Literature and Your Life*

CONNECT YOUR EXPERIENCE

You're sitting in a crowded movie theater. The houselights dim. The audience, once chattering away, falls silent. As the projector cackles and the screen in front of you bursts into sight and sound, you feel a tinge of excitement and anticipation.

Sometimes a film is so bad that you feel that you've wasted both your time and money. Other times, you're pleasantly surprised. Occasionally, a film comes along that completely surpasses any expectations you may have had and redefines the movie-going experience for you. For millions of people, *Star Wars* was just such a film.

THEMATIC FOCUS: TO THE FUTURE

What movie have you seen recently that you think will still be popular twenty years from now? Why?

Journal Writing Imagine that a Hollywood studio has given you an unlimited budget to produce and direct a film. What kind of film would you make, and why?

◆ Background for Understanding

CULTURE

If you travel down a long road, certain landmarks—say, a mountain, gorge, or building—will at once jump out at you and remain in your memory long after the trip has ended. These landmarks help define the road and put it in perspective. In a similar way, movies and other art forms become cultural landmarks for entire generations. From the moment in 1977 when *Star Wars* first opened, it became a landmark in the lives of people who were old enough to go see it at the movie theater. These reviews will help you understand why *Star Wars* is considered a landmark in cinema.

◆ Literary Focus

CRITICAL REVIEW

If you see a terrific movie, you might try to persuade a friend to go see it. Film critics provide this service for millions of newspaper readers every day. Reviewers, using evidence to support any claims, aim to convince you to follow their recommendation. They write **critical reviews** in which they discuss the various elements of a film and recommend that you see it—or not see it. Critical reviews tend to be persuasive.

◆ Reading Strategy

IDENTIFY EVIDENCE

When you read a piece that is intended to persuade you, it is important that you identify the evidence the writer uses to support his or her claims. **Evidence** may be facts, statistics, observations, examples, and statements from authorities that support the writer's opinion.

Look to identify evidence that supports the claims each reviewer makes. You might use a chart like the one below. Then determine whether or not there is enough evidence to support the claim.

Claim	Evidence
	✓
	✓
	✓
	✓
	✓
	✓
	✓
	✓
	✓

Guide for Reading ◆ 625

✎ Preparing for Standardized Tests

Reading and Vocabulary Recognizing connotations of words will help students improve their performance on the analogy portions of standardized tests. The Build Vocabulary Lesson for this selection focuses on word connotations. For additional practice, use the Build Vocabulary page in *Selection Support,* p. 184

The Critical Reading portion of many standardized tests requires students to locate the support or evidence a writer offers for points made within a nonfiction passage. The Reading Strategy for this selection is Identify Evidence. Identifying the evidence in these two reviews will develop students' ability to read nonfiction critically. For additional practice, use the Reading Strategy page on Identifying Evidence, p. 186, in *Selection Support.*

One-Minute Insight

In language that is exciting and enthusiasitic, Vincent Canby reviews the first film in the *Star Wars* trilogy. He balances summary with evaluation, demonstrasting for students the qualities of an effective review. In addition to offering an opinion on the movie itself, Canby analyzes the reasons why the characters and situations may be appealing to audiences.

Enrichment The almost human droids shown on this page are creations of George Lucas's imagination, but less sophisticated robots have long since emerged from science fiction into the real world. Point out to students other aspects of modern technology were "predicted" in fiction before they became a reality. Have interested students find out more about some of the inventions and innovations that appear in the work of Jules Verne and Edward Everett Hale.

STAR WARS

—A TRIP TO A FAR GALAXY THAT'S FUN AND FUNNY . . .

Vincent Canby

from The New York Times, May 26, 1977

626   *Nonfiction*

Block Scheduling Strategies

Consider these suggestions to take advantage of extended class time:

- Have students complete the journal activity in Literature and Your Life (p. 625), and form small groups to discuss what kinds of films they would choose to make, and why.
- Encourage students to prepare a Reading Strategy chart like the one on page 625. Keeping a chart like this will help them answer the Reading Strategy questions on page 634.
- Have students evaluate whether there is enough evidence to back up the reviewers' claims, and whether the evidence they present is persuasive.
- Have students work in discussion groups to answer the Critical Thinking questions (pp. 628 and 633).
- Have students look for and read other examples of film criticism, on the Internet or at the library, before or after they read the selection.
- Allow classtime for students to write their own movie reviews by completing the Writing Mini-Lesson on page 635.

"Star Wars," George Lucas's first film since his terrifically successful "American Graffiti," is the movie that the teen-agers in "American Graffiti" would have broken their necks to see. It's also the movie that's going to entertain a lot of contemporary folk who have a soft spot for the virtually ritualized manners of comic-book adventure.

"Star Wars," which opened yesterday[1] at the Astor Plaza, Orpheum and other theaters, is the most elaborate, most expensive, most beautiful movie serial ever made. It's both an **apotheosis** of "Flash Gordon" serials and a witty critique that makes associations with a variety of literature that is nothing if not **eclectic**: "Quo Vadis?", "Buck Rogers," "Ivanhoe," "Superman," "The Wizard of Oz," "The Gospel According to St. Matthew," the legend of King Arthur and the knights of the Round Table.

All of these works, of course, had earlier left their marks on the kind of science-fiction comic strips that Mr. Lucas, the writer as well as director of "Star Wars," here remembers with affection of such cheerfulness that he avoids **facetiousness**. The way definitely not to approach "Star Wars," though, is to expect a film of cosmic implications or to footnote it with so many references that one anticipates it as if it were a literary duty. It's fun and funny.

The time, according to the opening credit card, is "a long time ago" and the setting "a galaxy far far away," which gives Mr. Lucas and his associates total freedom to come up with their own landscapes, housing, vehicles, weapons, religion, politics—all of which are variations on the familiar.

When the film opens, dark times have fallen upon the galactal empire once ruled, we are given to believe, from a kind of space-age Camelot. Against these evil tyrants there is, in progress, a rebellion led by a certain Princess

---

1. **which opened yesterday:** Wednesday, May 25, 1977.

◀ Critical Viewing In what ways do R2-D2 and C-3PO remind you of Laurel and Hardy? [Compare]

Leia Organa, a pretty round-faced young woman of old-fashioned pluck who, before you can catch your breath, has been captured by the guardians of the empire. Their object is to retrieve some secret plans that can be the empire's undoing.

That's about all the plot that anyone of voting age should be required to keep track of. The story of "Star Wars" could be written on the head of a pin and still leave room for the Bible. It is, rather, a breathless succession of escapes, pursuits, dangerous missions, unexpected encounters, with each one ending in some kind of defeat until the final one.

These adventures involve, among others, an ever-optimistic young man named Luke Skywalker (Mark Hamill), who is innocent without being naïve; Han Solo (Harrison Ford), a freebooting freelance, space-ship captain who goes where he can make the most money, and an old mystic named Ben Kenobi (Alec Guinness), one of the last of the Old Guard, a fellow in possession of what's called "the force," a mixture of what appears to be ESP and early Christian faith.

Accompanying these three as they set out to liberate the princess and restore justice to the empire are a pair of Laurel-and-Hardyish robots. The thin one, who looks like a sort of brass woodman, talks in the polished phrases of a valet ("I'm **adroit** but I'm not very knowledgeable"), while the squat one, shaped like a portable washing machine, who is the one with the knowledge, simply squeaks and blinks his

◆ **Reading Strategy**
What evidence does Canby give to support his claim that the film is "fun and funny"?

◆ **Build Vocabulary**

apotheosis (ə päth´ ē ō´ sis) n.: Glorification of a person or thing; raising of something to the status of a god

eclectic (ek lek´ tik) adj.: Composed of material from various sources

facetiousness (fə sē´ shəs nəs) n.: Act of making jokes at an inappropriate time

adroit (ə droit´) adj.: Clever

Speaking and Listening Mini-Lesson

Star Wars Recording

This mini-lesson supports the first Speaking and Listening activity in the Idea Bank on page 635.

Introduce the Concept Lead a discussion in which the class analyzes the music in one scene from *Star Wars*. Then tell students they will be applying the same strategies in their presentations.

Develop Background Have students consider the following questions as they prepare their talks: What is the mood of the scene? How do the volume, pace, and rhythm of the music reflect

the mood of that scene? Is the music used in other scenes in the film, and if so, what do the scenes have in common?

Apply the Information Have students work in small groups to develop their talks. Suggest that they limit presentations to five minutes.

Assess the Outcome Hold a discussion in which students talk about the effect of the presentations on their appreciation for this music and the film. Do they appreciate the score more since hearing the talks? Why or why not?

---

❶ **Clarify** *Quo Vadis?* (1896) is a novel by Henryk Sienkiewicz about Rome under Emperor Nero. *Ivanhoe* (1817), by Sir Walter Scott, is a historical novel about the struggles between the Normans and Saxons in medieval England.

◆ **Critical Thinking**

❷ **Draw Conclusions** Ask students what Canby seems to be saying about Star Wars by linking it to such a wide range of earlier film classics. *By tying Star Wars to film classics, Canby shows that it has a timeless quality and that it may well become a classic itself.*

◆ **Build Vocabulary**

❸ **Connotations** Ask students to suggest connotations for the word *footnote*, and ask why Canby may have chosen the word. *Making footnotes is a scholarly activity. Canby implies that viewers should not approach the movie as though they were doing scholarly work.*

▶ **Critical Viewing** ◀

❹ **Make Comparisons** The physical contrast between the robots is reminiscent of Laurel and Hardy.

◆ **Reading Strategy**

❺ **Identify Evidence** Students can point to the following: *The links the author makes with such popular fiction serials as Flash Gordon and Buck Rogers, and with the comic book hero Superman. Students can also refer to the simple plot, the many action sequences, and the happy ending.*

Customize for
English Language Learners
❻ Point out that ESP stands for Extra-Sensory Perception, meaning the power to read minds and perceive things that cannot be detected by use of sight, hearing, or the other senses.

◆ **Build Vocabulary**

❼ **Connotations** Ask students what the author wants to convey by using the term, *Laurel-and-Hardyish*. *By invoking Laurel and Hardy, a slapstick comedy team, Canby indicates that the robots are intended to be comic. This term definitely carries a connotation of funny or buffoonish.*

◆ Literary Focus

❶ Critical Review Have students identify the persuasive language in this passage and point out Canby's supporting evidence. *Persuasive language includes* stars, incredible, *and* fondness. *Canby often supports his points with examples of the special effects and the elaborate settings.*

Reinforce and Extend

Answers

◆ *Literature and Your Life*

Reader's Response Most students would probably say they would enjoy it because Canby has made the movie seem very exciting.

Thematic Focus There are elements that evoke the past, such as princesses, and ones that suggest the future, such as androids.

☑ Check Your Comprehension

1. *Star Wars* was inspired by old-fashioned comic books and serial movies.
2. Princess Leia leads a rebellion against hostile forces in her galactic empire while the guardians of the empire try to retrieve some secret plan.
3. The true stars are the production designers and the special effects people.

◆ Critical Thinking

1. Young children will judge the film strictly on its entertainment value.
2. Yes, he says it is "fun and funny."
3. Canby rates special effects as most important, followed by plot. He considered acting least important.
4. Students might mention objectivity, a facility with language, and a wide knowledge of film.

---

lights. They are the year's best new comedy team.

In opposition to these good guys are the imperial forces led by someone called the Grand Moff Tarkin (Peter Cushing) and his executive assistant, Lord Darth Vader (David Prowse), a former student of Ben Kenobi who elected to leave heaven sometime before to join the evil ones.

 The true stars of "Star Wars" are John Barry, who was responsible for the production design, and the people who were responsible for the incredible special effects—space ships, explosions of stars, space battles, hand-to-hand combat with what appear to be lethal neon swords. I have a particular fondness for the look of the interior of a gigantic satellite called the Death Star, a place full of the kind of waste space one finds today only in old Fifth Avenue mansions and public libraries.

There's also a very funny sequence in a low-life bar on a remote planet, a frontierlike establishment where they serve customers who look like turtles, apes, pythons and

various amalgams of same, but draw the line at robots. Says the bartender <u>piously</u>: "We don't serve *their* kind here."

It's difficult to judge the performances in a film like this. I suspect that much of the time the actors had to perform with special effects that were later added in the laboratory. Yet everyone treats his material with the proper combination of solemnity and good humor that avoids <u>condescension</u>. One of Mr. Lucas's particular achievements is the manner in which he is able to recall the tackiness of the old comic strips and serials he loves without making a movie that is, itself, tacky. "Star Wars" is good enough to convince the most skeptical 8-year-old sci-fi buff, who is the toughest critic.

◆ Build Vocabulary

piously (pī´ əs lē) *adv.*: With actual or pretended religious devotion

condescension (kän´ di sen´ shən) *n.*: Looking down upon; regarding as below one's dignity

---

Guide for Responding

◆ *Literature and Your Life*

Reader's Response Do you think you would enjoy this movie based on Canby's review?
Thematic Focus How does *Star Wars* combine the past and the future?

☑ Check Your Comprehension

1. What are two sources that inspired *Star Wars*?
2. Summarize the plot elements of *Star Wars* that Canby identifies as all you "should be required to keep track of."
3. According to Canby, who are the "true stars" of *Star Wars*?

◆ Critical Thinking

INTERPRET
1. Why do you think Canby considers an "8-year-old sci-fi buff" the toughest critic of *Star Wars*? **[Speculate]**
2. Did Canby enjoy watching *Star Wars*? Explain. **[Infer]**
3. Explain how each of these elements affects Canby's evaluation of the film: acting, plot, special effects. **[Evaluate]**

EXTEND
4. What three skills do you think are important for a movie reviewer to have to judge movies well and to write interesting reviews? **[Career Link]**

♫ Humanities: Film

At the end of the century, the American inventor Thomas Edison devised the *kinetoscope,* the first successful machine for showing motion pictures. In 1903, *The Great Train Robbery* appeared; it was the first movie with a plot—and the first western. Shot in New Jersey, it was three minutes long.

Movies quickly grew longer, more ambitious, and more popular. Until 1927, they were silent; theater musicians provided the only accompaniment. Instead of spoken dialogue, films had printed titles between scenes.

In 1927, the first film with a sound track made its debut: The *Jazz Singer,* starring Al Jolson. Overnight, the movies switched to sound, and many actors whose voices recorded poorly (or whose voices did not match their screen personalities) saw their careers come to abrupt ends.

Today, motion pictures are a huge worldwide industry, whose stars are often better known than heads of government.

Interested students can do further research about the history of films.

Star Wars

Breakthrough Film Still Has the Force

Roger Ebert
Of the *Chicago Sun-Times*

from *The Oakland Press*,
Friday, January 31, 1997

To see "Star Wars" again after 20 years is to revisit a place in the mind. George Lucas' space epic has colonized our imaginations, and it is hard to stand back and see it simply as a motion picture because it has so completely become part of our memories. It's as goofy as a children's tale, as shallow as an old Saturday afternoon serial, as corny as Kansas in August—and a masterpiece. Those who analyze its philosophy do so, I imagine, with a smile in their minds. May the Force be with them.

Like "Birth of a Nation" and "Citizen Kane," "Star Wars" was a technical <u>watershed</u> that influenced many of the movies that came after. These films have little in common, except for the way they came along at a crucial moment in cinema history, when new methods were ripe for <u>synthesis</u>. "Birth of a Nation" brought together the developing language and shots and editing. "Citizen Kane" married special effects, advanced sound, a new photographic style and a freedom from linear storytelling. "Star Wars" combined a new generation of special effects with the high-energy action picture; it linked space opera and soap opera, fairy tales and legend,

◆ **Build Vocabulary**

watershed (wô´ tər shed) *n*.: Moment or event after which nothing is the same

synthesis (sin´ thə sis) *n*.: Whole made up of separate elements put together

and packaged them as a wild visual ride.

"Star Wars" effectively brought to an end the golden era of early-1970s personal filmmaking and focused the industry on big-budget special effects blockbusters, blasting off a trend we are still living through. But you can't blame it for what it did; you can only observe how well it did it. In one way or another all the big studios have been trying to make another "Star Wars" ever since (pictures like "Raiders of the Lost Ark," "Jurassic Park" and "Independence Day" are its heirs). It located Hollywood's center of gravity at the intellectual and emotional level of a bright teenager.

It's possible, however, that as we grow older, we retain within the tastes of our earlier selves. How else to explain how much fun "Star Wars" is, even for those who think they don't care for science fiction? It's a good-hearted film in every single frame, and shining through is the gift of a man who knew how to link state-of-the-art technology with a deceptively simple, really very powerful, story. It was not by accident that George Lucas worked with Joseph Campbell, an expert on the world's basic myths, in fashioning a screenplay that owes much to man's oldest stories.

By now the ritual of classic film revival is well established: an older classic is brought out from the studio vaults, restored frame by frame, re-released in the best theaters, and then re-launched on home video. With this "special edition" of the "Star Wars" trilogy (which includes new versions of "Return of the Jedi" and "The Empire Strikes Back"), Lucas has gone one step beyond. His special effects were so advanced in 1977 that they spun off an industry, including his own Industrial Light & Magic Co., the computer wizards who do many of today's best special effects.

Now Lucas has put IL&M to work touching up the effects, including some that his limited 1977 budget left him unsatisfied with. Most of

◆ **Literature and Your Life**

How does *Star Wars* compare and contrast with the types of films you enjoy?

⑤

⑥

Star Wars: Breakthrough Film Still Has the Force ◆ 629

▶Critical Viewing◀

❶ **Analyze** Students may point out that Han looks aggressive—like someone who can stand up for himself, even against the fearsome Jabba the Hut. Jabba's non-human look—his size, wrinkled skin, and reptilian face—make him look frightening and evil.

❷ **Clarify** *2001:A Space Odyssey* is a science-fiction film that begins in the prehistoric past, and ends in the not-too-distant future. Like *Star Wars*, it was highly successful and influential.

◆ Critical Thinking

❸ **Compare and Contrast** Ask students what qualities would make science fiction films seem dated when compared with these two movies. *Students may mention that films, especially older ones, with futuristic technology that is already obsolete would look dated. Films with primitive or cheaply-made special effects also fail to hold up over time.*

▲ **Critical Viewing** This scene between Han Solo and Jabba the Hut was added to the new version of *Star Wars*. What can you learn about these characters from this picture? [Analyze] ❶

the changes are subtle: you'd need a side-by-side comparison to see that a new shot is a little better. There's about five minutes of new material, including a meeting between Han Solo and Jabba the Hut that was shot for the first version but not used. (We learn that Jabba is not immobile, but sloshes along in a kind of spongy undulation.) There's also an improved look to the city of Mos Eisley ("A wretched hive of scum and villainry," says Obi-Wan Kanobi). And the climactic battle scene against the Death Star has been rehabbed.[1]

The improvements are well done, but they point up how well the effects were done to begin with: If the changes are not obvious,

that's because "Star Wars" got the look of the film so right in the first place. The obvious comparison is with Kubrick's "2001: A Space Odyssey," made 10 years earlier, in 1967, ❷ which also holds up perfectly well today. ❸ (One difference is that Kubrick went for realism, trying to imagine how his future world would really look, while Lucas cheerfully plundered the past; Han Solo's Millennium Falcon has a gun turret with a hand-operated weapon that would be at

---

1. **rehabbed** (rē´ hab´´d) *v.:* Rehabilitated.

630 ◆ Nonfiction

 Speaking and Listening Mini-Lesson

Skit

This mini-lesson supports the second Speaking and Listening activity in the Idea Bank on page 635.

Introduce the Concept Ask students if they have ever seen the TV show on which Roger Ebert and Gene Siskel discuss new films, sometimes agreeing, sometimes not. Let students know they will pair off to improvise the same type of conversation, but as typical film-goers rather than critics.

Develop Information Have students brainstorm for specific topics they can bring up: plot, dialogue, acting, music, effects, costumes. Remind them that they should back up their opinions, positive or negative, with reasons.

Apply the Information Students can jot down points they plan to make before improvising.

Assess the Outcome Hold a class discussion in which students can evaluate how well each "critic" expressed his or her opinion and supported it with evidence.

◆ **Build Vocabulary**

❹ **Connotations** With students, consider the connotations of the word *inspirations*. Why did Ebert choose this particular word rather than ideas or notions? *The word* inspirations *connotes not simply ideas but brilliant or entirely unique ideas. Ebert is praising Lucas by using the word* inspirations.

◆ **Literary Focus**

❺ **Critical Review** Have students identify the persuasive language in this passage. Ask them how Ebert supports his claim. *The phrase* dramatic opening *is persuasive. It tells potential viewers that they are in for something exciting right from the start. Ebert supports this claim by describing how the vast spaceship appears from the top of the screen, and telling that Lucas was willing to pay a fine and lose his membership in the Director's Guild in order to create this dramatic opening.*

Customize for
Visual/Spatial Learners
Play the portions of the *Star Wars* video that Ebert describes. Have these students evaluate his descriptions and opinions after viewing the scenes and settings themselves.

home on a World War II bomber, but too slow to hit anything at space velocities.)

❹ Two Lucas inspirations started the story with a tease: He set the action not in the future but "long ago," and jumped into the middle of it with "Chapter 4: A New Hope." These seemingly innocent touches were actually rather powerful; they gave the saga the aura of an ancient tale, and an ongoing one.

As if those two shocks were not enough for the movie's first moments, I learn from a review by Mark R. Leeper that this was the first film to pan the camera across a star field: "Space scenes had always been done with a fixed camera, and for a very good reason. It was more economical not to create a background of stars large enough to pan through." As the camera tilts up, a vast spaceship appears from the top of the screen and moves overhead, an effect reinforced by the surround sound. It is such a dramatic opening that it's no wonder Lucas paid a fine and resigned from the Directors' Guild rather than obey its demand that he begin with conventional opening credits.

The film has simple, well-defined characters, beginning with the robots R2D2 (childlike, easily hurt) and C3PO (fastidious, a

◆ **Build Vocabulary**
fastidious (fas tid′ ē əs) *adj.*: Not easy to please; discriminating

Star Wars: Breakthrough Film Still Has the Force ◆ 631

❶ Speculate Students might say that all three characters are attractive and courageous; Luke is noble and innocent; Princess Leia, independent and outspoken; Han Solo, a loner and a rebel. The characters' youth may make them appealing to young viewers, who can easily identify with them.

◆ Literary Focus

❷ Critical Review Have students go back to the beginning of the review to find appropriate words and phrases such as the following: *Ebert's use of "masterpiece," his statement that the film has become "part of our memories," and phrases such as "technical watershed." They can also cite Ebert's comparing the film with other great film classics such as* Birth of a Nation *and* Citizen Kane.

❸ Clarify Chesley Bonestell (1888–1986) was an artist who specialized in naturalistic paintings of other worlds, based on the most recent scientific data. He also worked on many science-fiction films, such as *War of the Worlds* and *Destination, Moon.*

❶ ▲ **Critical Viewing** Which traits of the characters of "Star Wars" do you think helped to make them popular with viewers? **[Speculate]**

little <u>effete</u>). The evil Empire has all but triumphed in the galaxy, but rebel forces are preparing an assault on the Death Star. Princess Leia (pert, sassy Carrie Fisher) has information pinpointing the star's vulnerable point, and feeds it into R2D2's computer; when her ship is captured, the robots escape from the Death Star and find themselves on Luke Skywalker's planet, where soon Luke (Mark Hamill as an idealistic youngster) meets the wise, old, mysterious Ben Kanobi (Alec Guinness) and they hire the freelance space jockey Han Solo (Harrison Ford, already <u>laconic</u>) to carry them to Leia's rescue.

The story is advanced with spectacularly effective art design, set decoration and effects. Although the scene in the intergalactic bar is

famous for the menagerie of alien drunks, there is another scene, when the two robots are thrown into a hold with other used droids, which equally fills the scene with fascinating throwaway details. And a scene in the Death Star's garbage bin (inhabited by a snake with head curiously shaped like E.T.'s) is also well done.

Many of the planetscapes are startlingly beautiful, and owe something to Chesley Bonestell's imaginary drawings of other worlds. The final assault on the Death Star, when the fighter rockets speed between parallel walls, is a nod in the direction of "2001," with its light trip into another dimension: Kubrick showed, and Lucas learned, how to make the audience feel it is hurtling headlong through space.

Lucas fills his screen with loving touches.

◆ **Literary Focus**
What words and phrases does Ebert use to advance his notion that *Star Wars* is a modern-day film classic? ❷

❸

Cross-Curricular Connection: Science

Robots The robots known as R2D2 and C3PO in *Star Wars* are historic and futuristic at the same time; they are yesterday's vision of what a robot looked like and what it could do.

The word *robot* originated in the Czech writer Karel Capek's 1921 play "R.U.R." (Rossum's Universal Robots). In that play, mechanical beings who were manufactured to be slaves for humanity stage a rebellion and kill their creators. Robots of early science fiction manifest people's fears

that they will be overtaken by mechanization. Today, it is difficult to distinguish robots from other forms of automation. However, robots are being used in some factories, and they are being developed to help people who have lost the use of their limbs.

Suggest that interested students research the modern application of robots in science, industry, and as a tool to help the physically challenged.

There are little alien rats hopping around the desert, and a chess game played with living creatures. Luke's weather-worn "Speeder" vehicle, which hovers over the sand, reminds me uncannily of a 1965 Mustang. And consider the details creating the presence, look and sound of Darth Vader, whose fanged face mask, black cape and hollow breathing are the setting for James Earl Jones's cold voice of doom.

Seeing the film the first time, I was swept away, and have remained swept ever since. Seeing this restored version, I tried to be more objective, and noted that the gun battles on board the space ships go on a bit too long; it is remarkable that the empire marksmen never hit anyone important; and the fighter rain on the enemy ship now plays like the computer games it predicted. I wonder, too, if Lucas could have come up with a more challenging philosophy behind the Force. As Kenobi explains it, it's basically just going with the flow. What if Lucas had pushed a little further to include elements of nonviolence or ideas about intergalactic conservation? (It's a great waste of resources to blow up star systems.)

The films that will live forever are the simplest-seeming ones. They have profound depths, but their surfaces are as clear to an audience as a beloved old story. The way I know this is because the stories that seem immortal—the "Odyssey," the "Tale of Genji," "Don Quixote," "David Copperfield," "Huckleberry Finn"—are all the same: a brave but flawed hero, a quest, colorful people and places, sidekicks, the discovery of life's underlying truths. If I were asked to say with certainty which movies will still be widely known a century or two from now, I would list "2001," and "The Wizard of Oz," and Keaton and Chaplin, and Astaire and Rogers, and probably "Casablanca" . . . and "Star Wars," for sure.

♦ **Build Vocabulary**

effete (e fēt´) adj.: Lacking vigor; overrefined

laconic (lə kän´ ik) adj.: Terse; using few words

♦ **Build Vocabulary**

❹ **Connotations** Ask students what words in this sentence suggest the evil nature of Darth Vader. *The adjective* fanged *connotes a deadly and immoral quality. The reference to James Earl Jones's cold voice of doom also carries an implication of menace.*

❺ **Clarify** Lady Murasaki Shikibus' *The Tale of Genji,* an eleventh-century A.D. novel, is thought to be one of the greatest works of Japanese literature. The hero, Prince Genji, exemplifies the virtues of courtliness and sensitivity to nature.

❻ **Clarify** Buster Keaton made some of the greatest silent film comedies. Charlie Chaplin created some of the greatest films ever, in both the silent and sound eras. Fred Astaire and Ginger Rogers were a song-and-dance team in movie musicals of the 1930's and '40's. *Casablanca* (1942), with Humphrey Bogart and Ingrid Bergman, is one of the most popular movies ever made.

Guide for Responding

♦ Literature and Your Life

Reader's Response What aspect of *Star Wars* did you find most interesting or surprising in either review?

Thematic Focus What are some ways in which Roger Ebert thinks of *Star Wars* as a film legacy for future movie viewers?

☑ Check Your Comprehension

1. According to Ebert, what quality does *Star Wars* as a film have in common with *Birth of a Nation* and *Citizen Kane?*
2. Give two examples of aspects of the newer version of the film that differ from the original.

♦ Critical Thinking

INTERPRET

1. The title of Ebert's review is "Breakthrough Film Still Has the Force." What makes *Star Wars* a breakthrough, original film? [Analyze]
2. In what ways does *Star Wars* fit Ebert's statement that "The films that will live forever are the simplest-seeming ones. They have profound depths, but their surfaces are as clear to an audience as a beloved old story"?

EVALUATE

3. After reading both these reviews, why do you think George Lucas decided to re-release *Star Wars* in 1997? [Evaluate]
4. What movies do you think will be widely known a century or two from now? Explain why. [Make a Judgment]

Star Wars: Breakthrough Film Still Has the Force ♦ 633

Reinforce and Extend

Answers

♦ **Literature and Your Life**

Reader's Response Some students may be most interested in reading about the special effects, while others will be interested in the plot or characterizations.

Thematic Response Ebert thinks everything about the technical production is so effective, and works so well with other film elements, that viewers in future generations will be influenced by it.

☑ **Check Your Comprehension**

1. Like these films, it was a technical watershed.
2. There's a meeting between Han Solo and Jabba the Hut that was not in the original version; an improved look at the city of Mos Eisely; and a rehabilitated climactic battle scene.

♦ **Critical Thinking**

1. Sample response: *Star Wars* was a breakthrough film because it effectively utilized new and invented technology, combining unprecedented special effects with an engaging plot and characters.

2. *Star Wars* meets the criteria Ebert expresses because it has simple, well-defined characters and because, more important, the philosophy behind it is strong and skillfully evoked.

3. The timeless appeal would probably make the movie profitable again.

4. Students might mention films that they consider breakthroughs in terms of their technology or how effectively their messages were communicated.

633

Answers

◆ Reading Strategy

1. He supports his claim particularly by citing the Laurel-and-Hardy quality of the two robots.
2. He cites similar types of stories with simple plots and powerful themes.
3. Students should cite Ebert's descriptions of R2D2 and C3PO.

◆ Build Vocabulary

Using Connotations

1. The slightly humorous connotation of the word *facetiousness* gives it an added dimension over *sarcasm,* which is more straightforward in meaning "harsh or bitter."
2. *Adroit* implies manual dexterity, while *cunning* is mental dexterity.

Using the Word Bank

1. b 2. c 3. a 4. a 5. c 6. c 7. b
8. a 9. c 10. b 11. a

◆ Literary Focus

1. His main points are that *Star Wars* combined new-generation special effects with high-energy action, linked space drama with human-scale drama, and made the whole experience a visual sensation.
2. Students might be particularly persuaded by Canby's final statement that the movie convinced a skeptical 8-year-old sci fi buff.

◆ Build Grammar Skills

Practice

1. This film, I am sure, will survive technical innovations over the next decade.
2. *Star Wars,* in my opinion, is a classic movie.
3. The talents of the special effect crew, everyone can agree, are admirable.
4. Many people, of course, are familiar with characters from *Star Wars.*
5. *Star Wars* was the first film, interestingly, to pan the camera across a star field.

 Writer's Solution

For additional instruction and practice, use the Commas lesson in the **Language Lab CD-ROM** and pages 99–101 on Commas in the *Writer's Solution Grammar Practice Book.*

Guide for Responding (continued)

◆ Reading Strategy

IDENTIFY EVIDENCE

As a conscientious and critical reader, you **identify the evidence** writers provide to support their opinions. The evidence may be facts, observations, examples, statements from authorities, or statistics.

When Roger Ebert praises the changes in special effects in the 1997 re-release of *Star Wars,* he cites examples of some of those changes, such as "an improved look to the city of Mos Eisley."

1. How does Vincent Canby support his claim that "The way definitely not to approach 'Star Wars,' though, is to expect a film of cosmic implications ... It's fun and funny"?
2. What evidence does Roger Ebert give to support his claim that *Star Wars* presents a "deceptively simple, really very powerful, story"?
3. How does Roger Ebert support his claim that "the film has simple, well-defined characters"?

◆ Build Vocabulary

USING CONNOTATIONS

The connotation of a word is the thing or idea that the word suggests. The following pairs of words have similar meanings. On your paper, explain how the connotations of the words make them slightly different.

1. facetiousness, sarcasm
2. adroit, cunning

USING THE WORD BANK

On your paper, write the letter of the word that is the best antonym, or opposite, of the first word.

1. condescension: (a) criticism, (b) praise, (c) pride
2. eclectic: (a) varied, (b) boring, (c) consistent
3. apotheosis: (a) scorn, (b) acclaim, (c) flattery
4. laconic: (a) talkative, (b) quiet, (c) reticent
5. effete: (a) soft, (b) weak, (c) strong
6. fastidious: (a) finicky, (b) critical, (c) obliging
7. synthesis: (a) unification, (b) separation, (c) fusion
8. watershed: (a) trifle, (b) breakthrough, (c) river
9. piously: (a) religiously, (b) carelessly, (c) jokingly
10. adroit: (a) skillful, (b) clumsy, (c) practiced
11. facetiousness: (a) solemnity, (b) humor, (c) playfulness

634 ◆ Nonfiction

◆ Literary Focus

CRITICAL REVIEW

In a **critical review**, the writer makes a recommendation and tries to persuade you to accept that recommendation.

Critical reviews, which frequently appear in newspapers or magazines, are a type of persuasive essay that helps people make informed choices about the movies on which to spend their entertainment dollars.

1. What are the main points that Roger Ebert uses to back up his assertion that *Star Wars* was a breakthrough film?
2. What is it about Vincent Canby's review that persuades you most—either positively or negatively—about *Star Wars*?

◆ Build Grammar Skills

PARENTHETICAL INTERRUPTERS

Parenthetical interrupters make Ebert's and Canby's reviews sound more conversational. Because parenthetical interrupters are not essential to the sentence, they are set off with commas.

Practice Rewrite each sentence, adding the parenthetical interrupter in parentheses. Remember to include commas.

1. This film will survive technical innovations over the next decade. (*I am sure*)
2. *Star Wars* is a classic movie. (*in my opinion*)
3. The talents of the special effects crew are admirable. (*everyone can agree*)
4. Many people are familiar with characters from *Star Wars.* (*of course*)
5. *Star Wars* was the first film to pan the camera across a star field. (*interestingly*)

Writing Application Write sentences using each of the following parenthetical interrupters.

1. after all
2. by the way
3. incidentally
4. I believe
5. in fact

 Beyond the Reviews

FURTHER READING

Other Works by the Authors
Roger Ebert's Book of Film, Roger Ebert
Unnatural Scenery, Vincent Canby

Other Film Criticism:
Agee on Film, James Agee
Kiss Kiss Bang Bang, Pauline Kael
When the Lights Go Down, by Pauline Kael

We suggest that you preview these works before recommending them to students.

INTERNET

Students can find more information about Roger Ebert and also read film reviews from other critics at the following Web sites. Please be aware that the sites may have changed since we published this information.

http://208.218.3.83/BuenaVista/SiskelAnd Ebert/Text/Biography_RogerEbertG.html

http://www.tisd.net/~pvp/MovieReviews.html

We *strongly recommend* that you preview the sites before you send students to them.

Build Your Portfolio

Idea Bank

Writing

1. **Press Release** Imagine that your school is going to have a special showing of *Star Wars*. Write a press release about the movie that explains why the film is worth seeing.

2. **Speech** Write a brief speech a person on the special effects crew of *Star Wars* might give upon winning an award for his or her work.

3. **Interview** Imagine that you could talk to Roger Ebert or Vincent Canby about reviewing movies. Write the interview questions and responses from that imaginary conversation.

Speaking and Listening

4. ***Star Wars* Recording** Play an excerpt from the *Star Wars* theme by composer John Williams. Then, give an explanation to your class about how the music enhances the mood of specific scenes from the movie.

5. **Skit** With a partner, improvise a skit in which two people come out of a theater after seeing the re-release of *Star Wars* and share their initial impressions. **[Performing Arts Link]**

Projects

6. **Movie Collage** Create a collage of quotations, images, and advertisements showing the types of movies you enjoy. Explain your collage to the class. **[Art Link]**

7. **Science-Fiction Exhibit** Design a *Star Wars* exhibit for a science-fiction museum. Create your own illustrations or use *Star Wars* souvenirs you might already have. Write display tags that explain or describe the items. Then organize them to exhibit for the class. **[Art Link]**

Writing Mini-Lesson

Movie Review

A **movie review** influences people's opinions and choices of movies to see. The title of a review and the first paragraph should hook the reader and promote the reviewer's point of view. The body of the review supports the opinion with summaries of the movie, facts, examples, and observations. The last paragraph repeats the initial opinions in a new and interesting way. Choose a movie you have recently seen and write a review to persuade a reader to see it—or not to see it.

Writing Skills Focus: Use Specific Examples

Include **specific examples** so that your readers will be able to picture aspects of the movie in their mind's eye. For each statement or claim you make about a movie, refer to a specific detail or scene to support your opinion. For instance, if you say, "This movie is guaranteed to make you cry," give an example of what happens in a sad scene or discuss background music that evokes a feeling of sorrow.

Prewriting Create an idea web to organize your ideas and find specific examples for your review. Start with your overall opinion. Then create branches for aspects of the movie that support that opinion. Cite specific examples for each aspect.

Drafting State your opinion at the beginning of the review, then support it with specific examples. You might include parenthetical interrupters to keep your tone conversational.

Revising Have a partner read your review for specific examples to back up your opinion. If necessary, you might include more examples or details to back up your opinion. Then check to see that your last paragraph interestingly restates your opinion.

Star Wars: A Trip to a Galaxy . . . /Star Wars: Breakthrough Film Still . . . ◆ 635

Idea Bank

Customizing for
Performance Levels
Following are suggestions for matching Idea Bank topics with your students' performance levels:
- Less Advanced Students: 6
- Average Students: 2, 3, 4, 5
- More Advanced Students: 7

Customizing for
Learning Modalities
Following are suggestions for matching Idea Bank topics with your students' learning modalities:
- Visual/Spatial: 6
- Verbal/Linguistic: 4, 5
- Rhythmic/Musical: 4
- Interpersonal: 5

Writing Mini-Lesson
Refer students to the Writing Handbook, page 965, for instruction on the writing process and page 969 for further information on response to literature.

Writer's Solution

Writers at Work Videodisc
Have students view the videodisc segment for Chapter 7 in which Miguel Algarín discusses the process of preparing a literary response. Ask students what he means by "entertaining the world that is being presented," and how students can apply Algarín's ideas to writing their movie reviews.

Play frames 26321 to 29738

Writing Lab CD-ROM
Have students complete the tutorial on Response to Literature. Follow these steps:
1. Have students use Response Wheels to explore combinations of literary elements and response methods they may be able to use in their movie reviews.
2. Suggest that students also use the Evaluation Word Bin to select from among four groups of adjectives and adverbs that they might use in their movie reviews.

Sourcebook
Have students use Chapter 7, Response to Literature (pp. 195–221), for additional support.

☑ ASSESSMENT OPTIONS

Formal Assessment, Selection Test, pp. 157–159, and Assessment Resources Software. The selection test is designed so that it can be easily customized to the performance levels of your students.
Alternative Assessment, p. 45, includes options for less advanced students, more advanced students, musical/rhythmic learners, logical/mathematical learners, and bodily/kinesthetic learners.

PORTFOLIO ASSESSMENT
Use the following rubrics in the *Alternative Assessment* booklet to assess student writing:
Press Release: Persuasion Rubric, p. 105
Speech: Expression Rubric, p. 94
Interview: Fictional Narrative Rubric, p. 95

Guide for Reading

1. To read, comprehend, and interpret a visual essay
2. To relate a visual essay to personal experience
3. To interpret pictures
4. To understand the elements of a visual essay
5. To build vocabulary in context and learn related words describing color
6. To use semicolons in a series that contains commas
7. To write an introduction to an art exhibit using elaboration
8. To respond to the visual essay through writing, speaking and listening, and projects

SKILLS INSTRUCTION

Vocabulary:
Related Words: Words Describing Color

Grammar:
Semicolons in a Series

Reading Strategy:
Interpret Pictures

Literary Focus:
Visual Essay

Writing:
Elaboration

Speaking and Listening:
Award Panel (teacher edition)

Critical Viewing:
Interpret; Infer; Analyze; Speculate; Draw Conclusions

PORTFOLIO OPPORTUNITIES

Writing: Descriptive Paragraph; Interview; Poem

Writing Mini-Lesson: Introduction to an Art Exhibit

Speaking and Listening: Award Panel; Dramatic Reading

Projects: Parent-and-Child Encyclopedia; Parent-and-Child Video

More About the Author
Tillie Olsen was born in Omaha, Nebraska. The daughter of Russian immigrants, she grew up poor and had to drop out of school to work after the eleventh grade, but she continued to read widely. At 19, she wrote her first novel, titled *Yonnondio*—a Native American term meaning "lament for the lost." Olsen has explored the subject of mothers, daughters, and family relationships her memoir *Silences*, and *Mother to Daughter, Daughter to Mother*, a collection of women's writings, published in 1984.

Tillie Olsen *(1912–   )*

Tillie Olsen knows about mothers and daughters as the mother of four daughters, one of whom is Julie Olsen Edwards, co-author of the essay from *Mothers & Daughters*. In addition to raising four daughters, Tillie Olsen has written fiction as well as nonfiction. She won the O. Henry first prize for her story "Tell Me a Riddle" in 1961. A well-known Canadian writer, Margaret Atwood, said about Tillie Olsen in a review: "Among women writers in the United States 'respect' is too pale a word: 'reverence' is more like it." Olsen's perceptive insights into the mother-daughter relationship have earned her such deserved praise by fellow women authors.

Estelle Jussim *(1927–   )*

An expert on photography can help you understand or appreciate this art form. Estelle Jussim —a professor at Simmons College and an expert on photography, film, and popular imagery —is just such an expert and writer. Dr. Jussim is author of the award-winning books *Landscape as Photograph* (1985), *Slave to Beauty* (1981), *Frederic Remington, the Camera and the Old West* (1983), and *Visual Communication and the Graphic Arts* (1974). In her essay for the book *Mothers & Daughters*, Jussim conveys the unique relationships that mothers and daughters share.

◆ Build Vocabulary

RELATED WORDS: WORDS DESCRIBING COLOR

When Tillie Olsen uses the word *hue*, she is using just one of many words that refer to differences in a color. You can also refer to a color's *shade* or *tint*. *Hue* is a particular shade of a color that distinguishes it from other shades. The word *shade* refers to the degree of darkness of a particular color. A *tint* is a pale or delicate shade of a color.

WORD BANK

hue
sullenness
fervor
rapture
implicit

As you read the excerpt from *Mothers & Daughters*, you will encounter the words on this list. Each word is defined on the page where it first appears.

◆ Build Grammar Skills

SEMICOLONS IN A SERIES

In order to make long sentences clear, writers use **semicolons** to separate a series of items in which one or more of the items contain commas.

Notice that the semicolons in this sentence from *Mothers & Daughters* separate groups of words that already contain commas:

Here are daughters and mothers of every shape and human hue; in every age and stage from mother and infant, to old daughter and old, old mother; and here is the family resemblance in face, expression, stance, body.

636 ◆ *Nonfiction*

Prentice Hall Literature Program Resources

REINFORCE / RETEACH / EXTEND

Selection Support Pages
Build Vocabulary: Related Words: Words Describing Color, p. 188
Build Grammar Skills: Semicolons in a Series, p. 189
Reading Strategy: Interpret Pictures, p. 190
Literary Focus: Visual Essay, p. 191

Strategies for Diverse Student Needs, p. 46

Beyond Literature
Workplace Skills: *Effective Listening*, p. 46

Formal Assessment Selection Test, pp. 160-162; Assessment Resources Software

Alternative Assessment, p. 46

Resource Pro CD-ROM
"Mothers & Daughters"—includes all resource materials and customizable lesson plan

Listening to Literature Audiocassettes
"Mothers & Daughters"

Mothers & Daughters

◆ *Literature and Your Life*

CONNECT YOUR EXPERIENCE

Countless films, books, and documentaries have offered glimpses into the relationship between mothers and daughters. You probably have formed your own ideas about the mother-daughter relationship from mothers and daughters you've known or from your own experiences. This essay will give you further insight into the unique relationship that mothers and daughters share.

THEMATIC FOCUS: LEGACIES

These mothers and daughters present a legacy for the future: The mothers will become grandmothers and the daughters will become mothers of a new generation of daughters.

Journal Writing Write what you think makes a good mother-daughter relationship.

◆ Background for Understanding

ART

One of the most exciting visual arts is also one of the newest—photography. Although the principles of photography were known for centuries, scientists and inventors produced the first portrait photographs in the 1820's. Americans took hold of this new visual art, and people like Mathew Brady amazed the world by photographically documenting historical events like the Civil War. By 1888, George Eastman produced a roll of paper film and a simple box camera for ordinary Americans to use—the Kodak camera and film. The photographs in *Mothers & Daughters* owe their existence to these early photography pioneers.

◆ Literary Focus

VISUAL ESSAY

Like a written essay, a **visual essay** presents information or makes a point about a subject, but a visual essay conveys its point through photographs or other visual forms as well as written text.

In *Mothers & Daughters,* Tillie Olsen and Estelle Jussim have combined written passages, from a variety of authors, with photographs to convey the relationship between mothers and daughters. The writers Tillie Olsen and her daughter Julie Olsen Edwards, Sage Sohier, Eudora Welty, and Estelle Jussim offer their insights on this relationship. Their words work with the photos to give different perspectives on a single theme.

◆ Reading Strategy

INTERPRET PICTURES

You've heard the saying that a picture is worth a thousand words. When you look at a picture, instead of reading words to get meaning, you **interpret** it by "reading" the elements of the picture.

In this visual essay, much of the message is communicated visually. To interpret these pictures, and to understand the relationship between the mothers and daughters, look at these elements in the pictures: the facial expressions and other body language, the closeness or distance between people, the backgrounds, and any other details in each photo that seem to give it particular meaning.

Guide for Reading ◆ 637

Interest Grabber
Raise students' interest in this selection with a quick journal-writing activity. Have them visualize their favorite family photograph. Each student should then write a description of that photo along with some thoughts on what makes it meaningful. Follow up by letting students know that photographs can reveal unique aspects of interpersonal relationships. In this visual essay, they will read, text and photographs collaborate to create brief (and yet full) portraits of mothers and daughters together.

Customize for
Less Proficient Readers
The stylistic variation among these texts may pose difficulties for less proficient readers. Guide these students to see that the texts represent different voices, just as the photographs represent different visions. Also encourage them to paraphrase the points that each writer makes.

Customize for
More Advanced Students
Encourage more advanced students to evaluate and describe the texts and the photographs in terms of purpose and tone. For example, which works would they describe as intimate? Which are more formal? Which text is the most analytical? Students can gather in small groups to discuss their choices.

Customize for
English Language Learners
This selection presents a good opportunity to review a variety of verb tenses with these students. Point out the present tense "the eye seeks deeper vision" from Olsen's piece; the past tense "I learned"; and the past-perfect tense "I'd (I had) got in my own bed" from Welty's piece. Help students to see why each tense was used.

Customize for
Visual/Spatial Learners
Suggest that these students write captions for each picture in this visual essay. Encourage them to consider these questions before writing: Who are these people? What are they doing? What do the details in each picture reveal about the people's lives?

 Preparing for Standardized Tests

Grammar and Language Students can use the grammar skill for this selection, semicolons in a series, in the essay portions of standardized tests. Naming items in a series can make students' ideas more complete, while using semicolons as needed will make their sentences clearer. Write the following sentence on the chalkboard and point out that it uses semicolons to help clarify sentences in which a series of items already contain commas:

> Photographs can be informative, explanatory, and journalistic; artistic, sensitive, and revealing; or simply memorable and fun.

The Build Grammar Skills lesson focuses on this topic. For additional practice, use the Build Grammar Skills page on Semicolons in a Series, p. 189, in **Selection Support.**

One-Minute Insight The photographs and text in this visual essay combine to evoke the rich complexity of its theme. Five photographers and four writers explore the relationship between mothers and daughters from different perspectives. The overall multi-faceted approach is fitting for a relationship that cannot be summed up by a single image or statement—a relationship that is, in Tillie Olsen's words, "Multi, multiform."

◆ Build Grammar Skills

❶ Semicolons in a Series Call students' attention to the semicolons in this sentence. Encourage them to explain their function. *They separate items within the sentence that already contain commas.*

▶Critical Viewing◀

❷ Interpret Some students may say that the photo shows "sullenness" and "estrangement"—they may cite the expressions on the people's faces and the distance between them. Others may say that it shows "admiration" and "wordless closeness," arguing that the daughters and mother feel secure enough within themselves to stand on their own.

◆ Literary Focus

❸ Visual Essay Tillie Olsen's text refers to "a welter of images," and she calls these photographic images "Multi, multi-form." Ask students how Olsen's text is itself a multiform welter of images describing the mother-daughter relationship.

Suggested responses: Olsen captures the "multiform" nature of the images by naming a wide variety of emotions, conditions, and circumstances; she conveys that every person and every mother-daughter relationship is unique.

Mothers & Daughters

Tillie Olsen and Estelle Jussim

August, New Mexico, 1979, Danny Lyon, Magnum Photos, Inc.

Observations by Tillie Olsen and Julie Olsen Edwards

❶ Here are daughters and mothers of every shape and human <u>hue</u>; in every age and stage from mother and infant, to old daughter and old, old mother; and here is the family resemblance in face, expression, stance, body.

Here are mothers and daughters of lack and of privilege, in various dress, settings, environments; posing for photographs or (unconcerned with the camera) sharing tasks, ease, occasions, activities; holding, embracing, touching; or in terrible isolation.

Here is <u>sullenness</u>, anger or controlled anger, resentment; admiration, distaste; playfulness, pride; joy, joy, joy in each other; estrangement; wordless closeness or intense communion.

A welter[1] of images. Multi, multi-form. ❸
The eye seeks deeper vision.

 ▲ Critical Viewing Which feelings described in the text do you think are shown in this photo? **[Interpret]**

1. **welter** (wel′ tər) *n.*: Hodge-podge; number of things tossed and tumbled about.

638 ◆ *Nonfiction*

Block Scheduling Strategies

Consider these suggestions to take advantage of extended class time:

• Use the information in Background for Understanding (p. 637) as the basis of a class discussion on the history of photography. Then have students do research to learn more about one of the people or developments mentioned in the feature.

• Have students work in discussion groups to interpret the photos in this selection. Then have them answer the Reading Strategy questions on page 644.

• Encourage interested students to do the Mood Palette activity in *Alternative Assessment,* p. 46. If necessary, explain that a painter's palette is a thin board used by painters for holding and mixing colors. Students can discuss the group of colors that convey the mood of each photo.

• Have students complete the Writing Mini-Lesson (p. 645). Before students start, have a class discussion on the use of elaboration in the text with the photographs.

Observations by Sage Sohier

A photograph is a sort of daughter: conceived one hopes (but not necessarily) in rapture, it must come to life on its own. One's relationship to it in the beginning largely consists of carting it around and having hopes for it. And *if* it is a successful one, it develops a personality, goes off alone, leads a life of which its mother might not be the best interpreter.

④

◆ **Build Vocabulary**

hue (hū) *n.*: Color; tint

sullenness (sul´ ən nəs) *n.*: Gloom; sadness

rapture (rap´chər) *n.*: State of being filled with joy

Untitled, Brookline, Massachusetts, 1986, Sage Sohier, Courtesy of the artist

▲ Critical Viewing Why do you think the photographer chose to capture the mother hugging a cat instead of her daughter in this photograph? [Infer]

⑤

Mothers & Daughters ◆ 639

  Beyond the Classroom

Career Connection

Photography The photographs in this selection demonstrate that photography is a rich art form. Photography also plays an important role in many other fields, including fashion, real estate, medical and scientific research, advertising, and journalism.

Just as photographs are taken for a wide variety of purposes, photographers are employed in a wide variety of settings. These include magazines and news organizations, advertising agencies, tourist boards, and institutions such as museums and universities, which often employ staff photographers. Some photographers work on a freelance basis; they may work for several different companies, or they may make a living photographing weddings and other special events. In addition to photography skills, these professionals may use writing, marketing, and research skills in order to sell their work.

Have interested students identify and choose one specialized area of photography, such as wildlife photography, portrait photography, or news photography, to research and report on for the class.

❶ Visual Essay Have students contrast Welty's text with Olsen's. How do the two differ in perspective and focus? What purpose does each serve in the visual essay? *Students should note that Olsen's text deals with a broad subject—the many aspects of the mother-daughter relationship, while Welty's text offers an intimate look at one relationship—her own with her mother. They should also note that Olsen's text serves as an introduction to the essay, while Welty's text is one of the contributions to the essay.*

◆ Literature and Your Life

❷ What legacies does Welty acknowledge as she pays tribute to her mother? Do students think that these legacies are valuable in all parent-child relationships? *Students may say that Welty's mother taught her a love of reading and taught her about the power of love and emotion; both these legacies would be extremely important and valuable in any parent-child relationship.*

►Critical Viewing◄

❸ Analyze The mother's expression is proud, pleased, and forthright; she seems happy and comfortable about being photographed. The daughter's expression is more apprehensive and questioning. Students might note that the mother probably made their matching dresses and that the mother and daughter might feel differently about being photographed in them.

Observations by Eudora Welty

❶ I learned from the age of two or three that any room in our house, at any time of day, was there to read in, or to be read to. My mother read to me. She'd read to me in the big bedroom in the mornings, when we were in her rocker together, which ticked in rhythm as we rocked, as though we had a cricket accompanying the story. She'd read to me in the diningroom on winter afternoons in front of the coal fire, with our cuckoo clock ending the story with "Cuckoo," and at night when I'd got in my own bed. I must have given her no peace. Sometimes she'd read to me in the kitchen while she sat churning, and the churning sobbed along with *any* story. . . . She could still recite [the poems in McGuffey's Readers] in full when she was lying helpless and nearly blind, in her bed, an old lady. Reciting, her voice took on resonance and firmness, it rang with the old <u>fervor</u>, with ferocity even. She was **❷** teaching me one more, almost her last, lesson: emotions do not grow old. I knew that I would feel as she did, and I do.

Nellie G. Morgan and Tammie Pruitt Morgan, Bicentennial Celebration, Philadelphia, Mississippi, 1976, Roland Freeman, Courtesy of the artist

◆ Build Vocabulary
fervor (fur′ vər) *n.*: Passion; zeal

◄ **Critical Viewing** What word or words would you use to describe the mother's expression in this photograph? The daughter's? [Analyze] **❸**

 Beyond the Classroom

Community Connection
Local Artistry "Mothers and Daughters" showcases the work of several distinguished photographers. Most communities offer places and opportunities for local artists to show their work.

In a class discussion, have students share information about any places they know of that exhibit or publicize the work of local artists. (Possibilities include schools, libraries, the Town Hall, restaurants, community centers, senior citizen centers, and churches and synagogues.)

Encourage students to follow up by consulting the events listings in your local newspaper and interviewing community members to learn more about local artists and art exhibits. Students can then share the information that they gathered by creating a guide to the art scene in their community.

❹ Speculate Students should note that the photograph was most likely taken by surprise. Although the two young women are posing, they are posing for their mother's camera, and not that of the photographer who captured this family moment. They might also note that the older woman is aware the second photographer is taking a picture, but she does not quite seem to be posing.

Customize for
Bodily/Kinesthetic Learners
Encourage these students to interpret the body language of the two young women being photographed. What do their poses reveal about their personalities and their relationship to each other? *Students might conclude from observing their somewhat stiff poses and careful grooming that the young women want to be perceived as proper or formal in some way; at the same time, their close poses and smiles indicate they are close and comfortable with each other.*

Tang Chung, Lisa Lu, Lucia and Loretta, Los Angeles, California, 1986, Carla Weber, Courtesy of the artist

 ▲ **Critical Viewing** Do you think this photograph was posed or taken by surprise? Explain your answer. **[Speculate]**

Speaking and Listening Mini-Lesson

Award Panel
This mini-lesson supports the Speaking and Listening activity in the Idea Bank on p. 645.

Introduce the Concept Explain to students that they will act as one judge on an award panel charged with choosing the best photograph of the year. Their task is to explain to fellow judges exactly why they think their choice should win the award.

Develop Background Have students choose a photograph to be given the award.

They may choose one in this selection or find another that they think deserves an award. Then have them identify the points they should include in their presentation to the other judges:

• State their choice to receive the award
• Make a statement explaining and supporting their choice of the best photograph
• Elaborate by discussing in detail the reason for the choice. Point out the visual and emotional elements that make the

photograph effective or powerful.

Apply the Information Have students divide into small groups of "judges." Each judge can use the tips in Develop Background to present and support his or her choice to the other judges.

Assess the Outcome Have students evaluate the presentations. Were the judges' reasons clearly stated? Did their presentations help the other judges to see the photos in a new light?

641

Observations by Estelle Jussim
from "The Heart of the Ineffable"

① It has been widely recognized that even the greatest portrait can capture only so much of an individual's personality and character, not all of that person's physical attributes, and certainly not a permanently ascribable[2] mood. An attempt by a photographer to convey not only one, but two persons and their relationship, might seem to be exceedingly difficult, if not impossible. To portray two persons defined as mother and daughter is to define a relationship fraught[3] with cultural and emotional overtones. Such intensity of meaning would seem to demand skillful decoding. Perhaps, also, it requires a grasp of visual language that not all of us possess. Even if we did possess such a visual language, it might prove to be so ethnocentric and tempocentric[4] as to defy our desires for significant universal meanings. This collection makes no pretense of offering more than an intelligent sifting of contemporary imagery, which, upon examination, can reveal much about contemporary life and our implicit ideologies[5] concerning motherhood. **②**

---

2. **ascribable** (ə skrīb′ ə bəl) *adj.*: Assignable; attributable.
3. **fraught** (frôt) *v.*: Filled; loaded.

4. **ethnocentric** (eth′ nō sen′ trik) **and tempocentric** (tem′ pō sen′ trik): Excessively concerned with race and time.
5. **ideologies** (ī′ dē äl′ ə jēz) *n.*: Ways of thinking; doctrines.

◆ Build Vocabulary

implicit (im plis′ it) *adj.*: Essentially a part of; inherent

Untitled, Wilmington, Delaware, 1983, Bruce Horowitz, Courtesy of the artist

Beyond Literature

Career Connection

Careers in the Visual Arts There are many career opportunities available in the field of visual arts. Photographers may work for themselves or for magazines or advertising agencies. Other visual artists might create logos for products, design graphics for computer games, or design the layout of magazine pages. Media researchers find photos, video, and artwork, and they set up photo shoots for textbooks, advertising agencies, and magazines. What career in visual arts interests you most?

◀ **Critical Viewing** What does this woman's body language and expression suggest about her? [Draw Conclusions] **③**

Some of our most vivid memories come from special times in our childhood. Perhaps your fondest memory is of building sand castles at the beach with your best friend or a special day shared with family. This song, like the photos in "Mothers & Daughters," captures special moments like these.

In the song "These Are Days," the speaker is reminding us that there are certain times in our lives that we will always remember. These precious memories will fill you "with laughter until you break" and make you feel "blessed and lucky." As you grow older, you'll encounter many more days you'll remember forever.

These Are Days
Robert Buck & Natalie Merchant

These are days you'll remember.
Never before and never since,
I promise, will the whole world be warm
    as this.
And as you feel it, you'll know it's true
    that you are blessed and lucky.
It's true that you are touched by some-
    thing that will grow and bloom in you.

These are days you'll remember.
When May is rushing over you with desire
to be part of the miracle you see in every
    hour.
You'll know it's true that you are blessed
    and lucky.
It's true that you are touched by some-
    thing that will grow and bloom in you.

These are days.

These are the days you might fill with
    laughter until you break.
These days you might feel a shaft of light
    make its way across your face.
And when you do you'll know how it was
    meant to be.
See the signs and know their meaning.
It's true, you'll know how it was meant to
    be.
Hear the signs and know they're speaking
    to you, to you.

1. In what ways do the photographs in *Mothers & Daughters* recall days to remember?
2. What line from this song best describes a mother-daughter relationship?
3. Do you think this is an appropriate song to accompany these photos? Why or why not?

Guide for Responding

◆ Literature and Your Life

Reader's Response Which photograph do you like best? What is it that interested you most in it?

Thematic Focus Which photograph do you think best represents a future legacy? How and why?

☑ Check Your Comprehension

1. What fond childhood memory does Eudora Welty share?
2. To what does Sage Sohier compare a photograph?

Mothers & Daughters/These Are Days ◆ 643

Beyond the Selection

FURTHER READING
Other Works by the Authors
Silences, Tillie Olsen
Landscape as Photograph, Estelle Jussim

Other Works About Mothers and Daughters
The Joy Luck Club, Amy Tan
The Glass Menagerie, Tennessee Williams
We suggest that you preview these works before recommending them to students.

INTERNET
For more information about Tillie Olsen, go to:
http://mockingbird.creighton.edu/NCW/olsen.htm
Please be aware that the sites may have changed since we published this information.
We *strongly recommend* that you preview the sites before you send students to them.

Answers

◆ Critical Thinking

1. This photograph shows "A welter of images. Multi, multi-form" in that it seems to present two mother-daughter relationships (the older woman and the photographer; the photographer and her two daughters), and suggests various emotions and aspects of their relationships.

2. Some students might use the evidence of conflict between the mother and daughter to predict a future relationship of conflict; others will predict that the mother and daughter will resolve their conflict and go on to have a close future relationship.

3. Students might say that "visual language" means the ability to capture the poses and facial expressions that suggest deep or hidden parts of a relationship.

4. Students might mention journalism, advertising, or careers related to nature or the environment.

◆ Reading Strategy

1. It is possible that the girl is the mother's only daughter, since they are dressed alike and photographed alone.

2. Students might say that the mother is having proud thoughts about her daughter or that she is thinking about something entirely independent of their relationship.

3. She is probably amused that someone is taking a picture of the mother photographing the young women.

◆ Literary Focus

1. The text and the photographs each contribute a different kind of language to make a whole picture. The text is analytical, reflective, and metaphoric, while the photos capture revealing details about people's lives.

2. Sohier's detail about going off alone to lead a life of which the mother might not be the best interpreter might help students to understand the mood of disharmony in the photo.

◆ Build Vocabulary

Using Colorful Words
1. Many houses in Bermuda are painted in pastel <u>hues</u>.
2. As night approached, the forest around them became darker and

644

◆ Critical Thinking

INTERPRET

1. How does "Tang Chung, Lisa Lu, Lucia, and Loretta" by Carla Weber, on p. 641 show what Tillie Olsen considers "A welter of images. Multi, multi-form"? **[Support]**

2. Sage Sohier says that a successful photograph, like a daughter, "develops a personality, goes off alone, leads a life of which its mother might not be the best interpreter." What kind of future relationship do you think the mother and daughter in Sohier's photograph on p. 639 will have? **[Interpret]**

EVALUATE

3. What do you think Estelle Jussim means by the "visual language" needed to portray a complex relationship? **[Interpret]**

EXTEND

4. In what careers could you use skill in photography? **[Career Link]**

◆ Reading Strategy

INTERPRET PICTURES

When you **interpret pictures**, you "read" their message from the elements within the pictures.

1. What do you think is the relationship between the mother and daughter in "Bicentennial Celebration" on p. 640?

2. What do you think is on the mother's mind in the photograph by Bruce Horowitz on p. 642?

3. Why do you think the oldest woman is smiling in "Tang Chung, Lisa Lu, Lucia, and Loretta" by Carla Weber on p. 641?

◆ Literary Focus

VISUAL ESSAY

A **visual essay** presents information on a subject through photographs or other visual forms along with written text.

1. Why do you need both the photography and writing to understand the relationships between mothers and daughters presented in this essay?

2. What details in Sage Sohier's text added to your understanding of her photograph? Explain.

644 ◆ *Nonfiction*

◆ Build Vocabulary

USING COLORFUL WORDS

The words *hue, shade,* and *tint* have specific meanings related to color. On your paper, complete the following sentences using these words.

1. Many houses in Bermuda are painted in pastel ____?____.

2. As night approached, the forest around them became darker and darker ____?____ of green.

3. Dust particles in the air sometimes give the sunset a pinkish ____?____.

USING THE WORD BANK

On your paper, write the word from the Word Bank that best completes each sentence.

1. Although the football team's skill was limited, its ____?____ was enough to win the game.

2. The car commercial's ____?____ message was that the car would make you popular.

3. The meat had a slightly greenish ____?____, so I decided to throw it away.

4. The angry young boy could not hide his ____?____ during his sister's recital.

5. The joyful woman's face filled with ____?____ as she watched her son receive his diploma.

◆ Build Grammar Skills

SEMICOLONS IN A SERIES

Use **semicolons** to separate items in a series when the items already contain commas.

Practice On your paper, rewrite the following sentences, placing semicolons where needed to separate items in series.

1. Mothers and daughters can be happy, playful, joyous, they can be distraught, sad, forlorn, they can stare, stare, stare into the camera lens and still be a mystery.

2. This collection includes photographs by Sage Sohier, Nellie Morgan, and Tang Chung; observations by Tillie Olsen, Estelle Jussim, Sage Sohier, and Eudora Welty, and moments from the lives of several mothers and daughters.

Writing Application List your impressions of these photographs in several series. Use semicolons to separate the items in a series that already use commas.

---

darker <u>shades</u> of green.

3. Dust particles in the air sometimes give the sunset a pinkish <u>tint</u>.

Using the Word Bank
1. fervor;   2. implicit;   3. hue;
4. sullenness;   5. rapture

◆ Build Grammar Skills

Practice

1. Mothers and daughters can be happy, playful, joyous; they can be distraught, sad,

forlorn; they can stare, stare, stare into the camera lens and still be a mystery.

2. This collection includes photographs by Sage Sohier, Nellie Morgan, and Tang Chung; observations by Tillie Olsen, Estelle Jussim, Sage Sohier, and Eudora Welty; and moments from the lives of several mothers and daughters.

Writer's Solution

For additional instruction and practice, use the Semicolons, Colons, and Quotation Marks lesson in the **Language Lab CD-ROM** and pages 102–103 on Semicolons and Colons in the *Writer's Solution Grammar Practice Book*.

Build Your Portfolio

Idea Bank

Writing

1. **Descriptive Paragraph** Write a paragraph describing one of the photographs from *Mothers & Daughters*. Explain what may be happening and how the people feel.

2. **Interview** Write three questions and responses that are part of an interview between a magazine writer and a mother or daughter in one of the photos in this essay.

3. **Poem** Write a poem—with or without rhyme—that describes the mother-and-daughter relationship you observe in one of the photographs.

Speaking and Listening

4. **Award Panel** As a judge on a panel awarding a prize for best photograph of the year, state your choice for this prize and give your reasons.

5. **Dramatic Reading** Read aloud a poem or excerpt from a story about a mother and daughter. Tell how it relates to the relationships presented in this visual essay. **[Performing Arts Link]**

Projects

6. **Parent-and-Child Encyclopedia** Brainstorm for a list of terms related to relationships between parents and children. Write a brief entry for each term, and organize them alphabetically into a parent-and-child encyclopedia. **[Health Link]**

7. **Parent-and-Child Video** If a video camera is available, work with a group to develop a video on how children can better relate to parents and vice versa. You can use narration, dramatic scenes, and photographs. **[Art Link; Performing Arts Link]**

Writing Mini-Lesson

Introduction to an Art Exhibit

Certain kinds of programs, nonfiction books, or events may have an introduction that provides background or other information to give readers or viewers a context for what they are to read or see. For example, the passage by Tillie Olsen and Julie Olsen Edwards introduces the visual essay *Mothers & Daughters* by giving an overview of what readers will see in the essay. Write an **introduction** for a real or imagined art exhibit. The exhibit might be of work by art students in your school or by a group of local artists.

Writing Skills Focus: Elaboration

Elaboration is the development of details about an idea that will help readers see it or understand it fully. In your exhibit introduction, decide on the main points you want to make. Then think of details or personal information that will elaborate on these ideas so that your introduction is both engaging and helpful to those who attend the exhibit.

Prewriting In the left column of a two-column chart, list the main points you want to make in your introduction. In the right column, list the details you can use to elaborate each idea. Your details might include the reasons behind the purpose or goals of the exhibit, biographical details about the artists, details about the style of art or the medium, and anything else that will help exhibit-goers understand and enjoy the show.

Drafting Present each of your ideas in a topic sentence. Then elaborate on the idea using the relevant details from your chart.

Revising Have a writing partner read your introduction and give you feedback on your development of main ideas and details. Elaborate further on any ideas that are not developed enough.

Mothers & Daughters ◆ 645

Idea Bank

Customizing for *Performance Levels*
Following are suggestions for matching Idea Bank topics with your students' performance levels:

    Less Advanced Students: 1
    Average Students: 2, 4, 3, 5, 6
    More Advanced Students: 7

Customizing for *Learning Modalities*
Following are suggestions for matching Idea Bank topics with your students' learning modalities:

    Visual/Spatial: 7
    Verbal/Linguistic: 4, 5
    Logical/Mathematical: 6
    Interpersonal: 2
    Intrapersonal: 3

Writing Mini-Lesson
Refer students to the Writing Handbook, page 965, for instruction on the writing process and page 967 for further information on exposition.

Writing Lab CD-ROM
Have students complete the Tutorial on exposition. Follow these steps:

1. Have students get interactive instruction on gathering details and then use a note cards activity to gather and order their details.

2. Suggest that students play the video tip in which writer N. Scott Momaday discusses paragraph organization, and main ideas and details.

3. Have students use an interactive self-evaluation checklist to help them evaluate and revise their introductions to an art exhibit.

Sourcebook
Have students use Chapter 3, Exposition (pp. 63–89) for additional support.

✓ ASSESSMENT OPTIONS

Formal Assessment, Selection Test, pp. 160–162, and Assessment Resources Software. The selection test is designed so that it can be easily customized to the performance levels of your students. *Alternative Assessment,* p.46, includes options for less advanced students, more advanced students, visual/spatial learners, intrapersonal learners, musical/rhythmic learners, and bodily/kinesthetic learners.

PORTFOLIO ASSESSMENT
Use the following rubrics in the *Alternative Assessment* booklet to assess student writing:
Descriptive Paragraph: Description Rubric, p. 97
Interview: Fictional Narrative Rubric, p. 95
Poem: Poetry Rubric, p. 108
Writing Mini-Lesson: Definition/Classification Rubric, p. 99

*G*uide for Reading

Paul O'Neil *(1909–1988)*

After thirty years as a staff writer for the magazines *Time, Sports Illustrated,* and *Life,* Paul O'Neil became a freelance writer. He's the author of three volumes in the Time-Life series *The Old West,* and more recently wrote *Barnstormers and Speed Kings* in the *Epic of Flight* series. "Imitating Nature's Mineral Artistry" comes from the Time-Life book *Gemstones.*

Ernesto Ruelas Inzunza *(1968–   )*

Author of "Work That Counts," Ernesto Ruelas Inzunza is the executive director of Pronatura-Vera Cruz, a conservation organization in Vera Cruz, Mexico. Pronatura is raising money to meet a challenge grant from the National Fish and Wildlife Foundation and the Agency of International Development. The money will be used to build a nature center and bird observatory in Cardel, one of the monitoring stations mentioned in Inzunza's article. Contributors to this effort are dubbed "Friends of River of Raptors."

◆ Build Vocabulary

PREFIXES: *syn-*

In "Imitating Nature's Mineral Artistry," author Paul O'Neil describes the process used to make synthetic gems. *Synthetic* contains the prefix *syn-*, which comes from the Greek *syn* and means "together with." A *synthetic* gem is one that is produced by bringing parts together chemically as opposed to a gem that is formed naturally.

synthetic
constituents
synthesized
metamorphosis
divulge
saturated
fortuitous
vigilance
myriad
topography

WORD BANK

As you read these essays, you will encounter the words on this list. Each word is defined on the page where it first appears. Preview the list before you read.

◆ Build Grammar Skills

VARIED SENTENCE BEGINNINGS: ADVERB PHRASES

Good writing exhibits variety in sentence structure. To create variety and interest, writers sometimes begin their sentences with **adverb phrases**—prepositional phrases that modify a verb, adjective, or an adverb:

In laboratories and in factories, technicians can now create conditions . . .

In this example, two introductory prepositional phrases modify the verb *create*. *In laboratories* and *in factories* answer the question, Where can technicians create conditions?

646 ◆ Nonfiction

Imitating Nature's Mineral Artistry
◆ Work That Counts ◆

◆ *Literature and Your Life*

CONNECT YOUR EXPERIENCE

Have you ever tasted a tomato that came from a scientist's lab? Chemists, biogeneticists, and other scientists are experimenting to create products that until recently were found only in nature. When you read "Imitating Nature's Mineral Artistry," think about why people try to imitate nature and about the pros and cons of their ongoing effort.

THEMATIC FOCUS: NATURAL FORCES

The chemists in "Imitating Nature's Mineral Artistry" try to imitate forces of nature to make diamonds and other gemstones. Do you think this is a worthwhile effort? Explain.

Journal Writing Write a paragraph describing something in nature you'd like to be able to produce yourself, and why.

◆ Background for Understanding

MATH

One indicator of a gemstone's value—whether it is natural or synthetic (like those discussed in "Imitating Nature's Mineral Artistry")—is the number of carats (or karats). In ancient times, the word *carats* originally meant "seeds" or "beans," which were used in weighing precious stones. Today, one carat is equivalent to 200 milligrams.

The world's largest cut diamond, the Star of Africa, now in the royal scepter of the British crown jewels, weighs 530.2 carats. Perhaps the most famous cut diamond in the world, the Hope diamond, on view at the Smithsonian Institution in Washington D.C., weighs 44.5 carats.

◆ Literary Focus

TECHNICAL ARTICLE

"Imitating Nature's Mineral Artistry" and "Work That Counts" are **technical articles**—writing that explains procedures, provides instructions, or presents specialized information. Technical articles often use terms associated with a particular field of study. For example, the term *flux growth* relates to chemistry, while *raptors,* which means "birds of prey," is associated with ornithology, the study of birds.

To be as specific as possible in their explanations, technical articles often use visual aids to demonstrate their ideas.

◆ Reading Strategy

RELATE DIAGRAMS TO TEXT

Artists aren't the only ones who think a picture is worth a thousand words. Many technical writers use **diagrams** to communicate their ideas and theories. Think of a diagram as a visual extension of the text. Rather than telling information, a diagram shows it. In "Imitating Nature's Mineral Artistry," the diagram of the flame-fusion growth of a ruby helps you to picture a complicated process. In so doing, it collaborates with the text to give you complete information. As you read, remember:

- A diagram is a drawing, plan, or outline of a thing or process.
- A diagram combines pictures, captions, and labels to present information visually.

Do not ignore or overlook diagrams. Use them as an aid to understanding.

Preparing for Standardized Tests

Grammar and Language Portions of some tests require students to demonstrate their writing abilities through essays. Write on the chalkboard, or read aloud, the following sentences:

1. The scientists reached the ancient ruins on the tenth day of the journey.
2. *On the tenth day of the journey,* the scientists reached the ancient ruins.

Point out that although both of these sentences are correct, a steady stream of sentences constructed like the first would be monotonous. Ask students to identify the adverb phrases that introduces the second sentence. Explain that using adverb phrases to introduce sentences will add variety to their writing. The Build Grammar Skills lesson for this selection focuses on this topic. For additional practice, use the Build Grammar Skills page on Varied Sentence Beginnings: Adverb Phrases, p. 193, in **Selection Support.**

◆ **Reading Strategy**

❶ **Relate Diagrams to Text** Have students look at the diagram on page 649. What key element helps readers to connect it to the concept that is introduced in this portion of the text? *The caption, which includes reference to "flame-fusion growth of ruby."*

◆ **Critical Thinking**

❷ **Identify Cause and Effect** Have students explain in their own words why emeralds and certain other gems cannot be manufactured using the flame-fusion method. *Students should note that, unlike the flux growth method, the flame-fusion method involves extremely high temperatures. The ingredients that make up some gems are destroyed at such temperatures, while the ingredients that make up certain others fail to melt.*

▶ **Critical Viewing** ◀

❸ **Contrast** Students should note that the opal differs in color, in brilliance, or brightness, and in texture —whereas other gemstones have solid, smooth surfaces, the opal has a fragmented surface. Although it is solid, it resembles a sponge.

◆ **Reading Strategy**

❹ **Relate Diagrams to Text** Point out that the diagram on page 649 that explains the flame-fusion method also provides information about what a *Verneuil furnace* and *boules* are. Have students refer to the diagram to explain these terms. *A Verneuil furnace is the device in which the chemical components of synthetic gems melt and then solidify; a boule is the solidified mass that forms when the melted chemicals cool down.*

648

Imitating Nature's Mineral Artistry

Paul O'Neil

In laboratories and factories, technicians can now create conditions of heat and chemical activity similar to those that give birth to gemstones deep within the earth. The result is synthetic gems, identical to their natural counterparts in chemistry and crystalline structure, and so similar in appearance that a microscope is often needed to tell them apart.

The chemical ingredients for a man-made gem are easy to obtain, since most gems consist of relatively common chemical compounds. The art of gem synthesis lies in the technique by which the gem material is liquefied, in a melt or a solution, and then allowed to crystallize slowly and evenly.

The so-called flame-fusion method, based on melting and gradual cooling, has been used to grow crystals of about 100 minerals and gems, including ruby, sapphire and spinel.

◆ **Reading Strategy**
Here you're introduced to a concept that is further explained by a diagram.

❶

❷

But the ingredients of some gems decompose during the fierce heating needed to melt them, and others have extraordinarily high melting points. Such gems—among them emerald—are often manufactured by another process, called flux growth. In this process, the gem is crystallized from a solution of its <u>constituents</u> in a molten bath of a solvent, or flux—such

as lead fluoride, boron oxide or lithium oxide.

Because of peculiarities in their internal structure, some gems cannot be <u>synthesized</u> by ordinary crystal growth. Opal, an orderly arrangement of minute, closely packed spheres of silica, is created in the laboratory by precipitating silica spheres through a chemical reaction, allowing them to settle to the bottom of the reaction vessel and then compressing and bonding them to form a compact and sturdy matrix.[1]

▲ **Critical Viewing** In what ways is the structure of this opal different from that of the emerald shown on p. 651? [Contrast] ❸

Artful as they are, synthetic gems nevertheless bear hallmarks of their laboratory origin: an array of microscopic inclusions and growth marks that contrast tellingly with the blemishes and inclusions of natural gems.

One of the gaudier uses of the Verneuil furnace is to make synthetic rutile[2] by sifting pure titanium dioxide through the flame. The boules thus produced—black in color because of oxygen deficiency—are then reheated in a jet of oxygen. As the rutile grows hotter, it oxidizes and changes in color to deep blue followed by light blue, green and, finally, a pale yellow. The color <u>metamorphosis</u> can be stopped at any stage by removing the heat source. Sold since 1948 under a profusion of names, including astryl and titania, the gems are soft, with a hardness of 6 to 6.5, but are ❹

---

1. **matrix** (mā′ triks) *n*.: Framework.
2. **rutile** (roo′ təl) *n*.: Dark-red mineral.

Block Scheduling Strategies

Consider these suggestions to take advantage of extended class time:

- Have students complete the journal activity in Literature and Your Life (p. 647) and discuss their entries in small groups.
- Extend the discussion in the Reading Strategy (p. 647): Ask students to describe diagrams they have encountered in their science, math, or general reading. Follow up with the Reading Strategy page in **Selection Support**, p. 194.

- Have students work in small groups to answer the Critical Thinking questions (pp. 651 and 653).
- Provide an alternative activity, found in **Alternative Assessment** (p. 47), to assess the progress of students with varying performance levels or learning modalities.
- Have students complete the Writing Mini-Lesson (p. 655). Use the Cubing Organizer on page 87 in **Writing and Language Transparencies** to demonstrate how students might develop ideas to include in their product descriptions.

Verneuil Furnace
Flame-Fusion
Growth of Ruby

The chemical ingredients of ruby—aluminum oxide with a chromium coloring agent—sift from a hopper at the top of the apparatus shown above into a jet of oxygen. In a combustion chamber, the oxygen combines with hydrogen in a 4,000° F flame—hot enough to melt the powdered ingredients, which shower onto a ceramic rod at the base of the furnace. There the material solidifies and accumulates in a rounder crystalline mass known as a boule.

Oxygen — Powdered Chemicals

Hydrogen —

Combustion Chamber

Boule

Diagram A

even flashier than strontium titanate, with seven times the fire of diamond.

Since diamonds consist of only one element, synthesizing them would seem to be relatively uncomplicated. The difficulty is one of technique, of creating—and containing—the enormous pressures and temperatures needed to pack carbon atoms tight enough to form diamond. Not surprisingly, many early attempts to synthesize diamond ended disastrously. Of the 80 experiments conducted in the late 19th Century by a Glasgow chemist named James Hannay, all but three were cut short by explosions, several of which wrecked the laboratory. Hannay was convinced that his pains had paid off: After several attempts, he discovered tiny flecks of diamond in his apparatus. But it is now thought that natural diamond dust from another of Hannay's projects had contaminated the experiment.

In the early 1950s, scientists at the General Electric Research Laboratories in Schenectady, New York, began experimenting with techniques for multiplying the force exerted by a hydraulic press. Using a pair of tapered pistons driven from opposite sides into the hole in a doughnut-shaped ring of tungsten carbide, they were able to subject the tiny

intervening space to pressures of more than 1.5 million pounds per square inch. In a series of experiments directed by a chemist named H. Tracy Hall, the apparatus was loaded with a mixture of graphite powder and an iron compound, pressurized and heated with an electric current to more than 4,800° F.—hot enough to melt the iron and dissolve some of the graphite. The dissolved carbon, scientists hoped, would then crystallize out of the molten iron as diamond. Finally, on December 16, 1954, Hall removed a sample from the press and broke it open along a plate of tantalum, a rare element used to conduct electric current. Hall later recalled the moment: "My hands began to tremble; my heart beat rapidly; my knees weakened and no longer gave support. My eyes had caught the flashing light from dozens of tiny triangular faces of octahedral crystals that were stuck to the tantalum and I knew that diamonds had finally been made by man."

Today, the same basic method that yielded Hall's initial success annually produces some 44,000 pounds of industrial diamonds—small diamonds of no particular quality used as an industrial abrasive. Only a few minutes of high temperature and pressure are required to manufacture several hundred carats of

◆ Build Vocabulary

synthetic (sin thet′ ik) *adj.*: Artificially made

constituents (kən stich′ o͞o ənts) *n.*: Components; parts

synthesized (sin′ thə sīzd′) *v.*: Made by bringing together different elements

metamorphosis (met′ ə môr′ fə sis) *n.*: Change of form

Imitating Nature's Mineral Artistry ◆ 649

Beyond the Classroom

Career Connection
Geology As Paul O'Neil's article points out, nature's mineral artistry takes place deep within the earth, as heat and pressure act on various elements to produce precious gemstones.

Scientists who study gem formation and other earth processes are known as geologists. Many geologists apply their knowledge within various industries, studying and locating resources such as oil, gas, coal, precious minerals, and building stone.

Others work in academic and research institutions, studying issues that range from predicting volcanic eruptions to determining the age of the earth.

Have interested students do research to learn more about the practical applications of geology as well as important scientific questions that geologists investigate. Encourage students to share their findings with the class.

◆ Reading Strategy

❶ Relate Diagrams to Text Point out that the process of emerald synthesis through flux growth is further explained in the diagram on this page. Ask students to study the diagram and its caption carefully, then identify the additional details that it provides. *The diagram names the chemical raw materials (beryllium, aluminum, and silicone) that are dissolved in the flux; it shows the electric furnace in which emeralds are synthesized; it specifies how (precipitation while cooling) and where (the bottom of the platinum crucible) the clusters of emeralds form.*

◆ Literary Focus

❷ Technical Articles Call students' attention to the specialized terms *specific gravity, refractive indices,* and *inclusions.* Have them use context clues to determine the approximate meanings of these terms. *Specific gravity and refractive indices—the plural of index—are standards or measures used to evaluate gems; inclusions in this context are bits of other minerals. Also, have students explain where they might go to find the exact technical meanings of the terms. Students might mention an encyclopedia, a book on gems and minerals, or web sites devoted to gemology or geology.*

◆ Critical Thinking

❸ Compare and Contrast Have students draw on the details in this paragraph to name two differences between natural and synthetic rubies. *Natural rubies have straight growth lines, whereas synthetic rubies have curved ones; unlike natural rubies, synthetic rubies contain gas-filled bubbles.*

---

diamond grit from almost any carbon-containing material— paraffin, moth flakes, even sugar and peanuts. But the synthesis of gem-quality diamonds is another matter. In 1970, a painstaking variant of the General Electric method, using synthetic diamond grit as the feed material and maintaining the conditions of high temperature and pressure for stretches of a week, yielded a few gem-quality diamonds weighing up to a carat. But the cost of producing them was so high that it remains cheaper to mine gem diamonds.

Perhaps the finest products of humanity's age-old attempt to imitate nature in the creation of gemstones are synthetic emeralds. Beginning in the late 1930s, two pioneers, Carroll F. Chatham, a San Francisco chemist, and Pierre Gilson of France, succeeded in making emerald so close to the genuine article that it is worth several hundred dollars per carat—although that is still just 1/10 the price of natural emerald of similar quality. Chatham and Gilson did **❶** not <u>divulge</u> the details of their processes, but it is believed that both depend on a technique called flux growth, in which crystals are formed from raw materials dissolved in a flux—a substance that acts as a powerful solvent. In one type of flux growth, the chemical ingredients of emerald, in the form of natural beryl, are added to a 1,500° F. bath of flux to create a <u>saturated</u> solution, which circulates continuously through

Cover

Crucible

Solution

Crystals   **Furnace**

Diagram B

Flux Growth of Emerald

A saturated solution of emerald's chemical ingredients is produced by combining compounds of beryllium, aluminum, and silicone with a flux, or solvent, and heating the mixture to 1,500° F. in an electric furnace. As the mixture cools, gem crystals begin to precipitate out at the bottom of the platinum crucible containing the solution, eventually forming clusters of emeralds.

cooler parts of the container. There, the flux deposits crystals of emerald—so slowly that growth must continue for seven months to produce an emerald one quarter of an inch thick.

It is not easy to distinguish synthetic and natural emeralds, though the synthetic variety is often more transparent, richer in hue and in some ways more perfectly formed than natural emeralds. In addition, the synthetics **❷** have lower specific gravity and refractive indices. But the most telling test is usually a microscopic examination. Magnification of synthetic emeralds reveals fine, lacelike patterns formed by intersecting channels containing liquid flux. Natural emeralds, the <u>fortuitous</u> products of geologic turmoil, ordinarily display much coarser inclusions of pyrite, calcite, actinolite or other minerals. Another detection method is to expose the gems to ultraviolet light: The radiation has little effect on natural emeralds but causes Chatham emeralds to glow with a dull red fluorescence and Gilson synthetics to display an orange hue.

In synthetic rubies and sapphires, specific gravity and the refractive index are the same as in natural corundum. But visible under a microscope in natural gems are straight lines, called growth lines, set at definite angles. In Verneuil synthetics, the growth lines are curved, and spots, which are in

◆ Literary Focus **❸**
These precise details help you to clarify the difference between natural and synthetic rubies.

◆ Build Vocabulary

divulge (də vulj´) *v.*: Reveal

saturated (sach´ ə rāt´ id) *v.*: Completely filled; thoroughly soaked

fortuitous (fôr too͞´ ə təs) *adj.*: Accidental and beneficial at the same time

vigilance (vij´ ə ləns) *n.*: Watchfulness; alertness

650 ◆ *Nonfiction*

Cross-Curricular Connection: Science

"Imitating Nature's Mineral Artistry" contains several terms used in the fields of gemology and geology. Groups of students can work together to research the meanings of these terms as well as answer some basic questions related to these fields.

Suggest that students choose from among the following activities and questions.

- What is a rock? a mineral? a gem?
- What does *specific gravity* mean? What does *refractive index* (sometimes called *index of refraction*) mean?
- What is an *inclusion*? What are *growth marks* and *growth lines*?
- The author mentions that stones made from synthetic rutile have a hardness of 6 to 6.5. Find out the name of the scale that

is used to measure the hardness of gems and minerals. Name three minerals that are harder than synthetic rutile and three that are softer.

- Compile a bibliography for classmates interested in learning more about gems.

Suggest that students present their findings to the class, along with any diagram or visual aid that clarifies the concepts being discussed.

fact gas-filled bubbles, may be seen. Synthetic spinel, which masquerades as any of several species, can be detected by its differing refractive index.

Still, distinguishing between synthetic and natural gemstones calls for vigilance, and sometimes even experts lower their guard. One Manhattan dealer who specializes in colored gemstones, Abraham Nassi, was offered three large red rubies while on an expedition to Burma. "They looked good," he remembered later, and he was prepared to pay the equivalent of $160,000 for the lot. But before any money changed hands, a fourth ruby was offered.

"I had an idea that the four might be worth a half a million dollars," he said, "but wanted to have them in New York and give them a real inspection before I paid." Nassi suggested a total price of $300,000—but only if the stones could first be examined in New York.

The Burmese refused his condition. "That seemed funnier yet. I found a Bangkok dealer who had a microscope and began looking at the stones under magnification. Their color

was wonderful but their crystal structure was peculiar. I spent $200 to telephone the Gemological Institute of America in New York and described what I had seen. They told me what I'd been looking at: This gang had somehow gotten their hands on synthetic Kashan rubies, made in Texas for about $100 a carat, taken them into the jungle and had almost sold them to me as the real thing."

▲ **Critical Viewing** How can you tell from this picture, and from clues in the text, that the emerald is real and not synthetic? **[Analyze]** ❹

Guide for Responding

◆ Literature and Your Life

Reader's Response What are one or two techniques you know of that people have used to imitate nature? Explain.

Thematic Focus How would you determine if a natural product, such as oil or diamonds, was valuable?

Debate Divide into small teams, with each team taking a pro or con position to debate this statement: Scientists should not try to imitate nature.

✓ **Check Your Comprehension**

1. What two kinds of natural gem-producing conditions have scientists learned to imitate?
2. What is the difference in appearance between a synthetic and a real emerald?
3. Contrast the process for making industrial diamonds with that of producing gem-quality diamonds.

◆ Critical Thinking

INTERPRET

1. a) What is the difference between flame-fusion and flux growth? b) Why are rubies made from the flame-fusion method, but emeralds from the flux growth method? **[Compare and Contrast]**
2. What is the major application today of G.E's 1954 experiment led by chemist H. Tracy Hall? **[Analyze]**
3. What characteristic of the diamond led early scientists to think that imitating it would be simple? **[Infer]**

APPLY

4. What might have happened if Abraham Nassi had bought the rubies from the Burmese? **[Speculate]**

EXTEND

5. What kind of knowledge is a gemologist likely to have? **[Career Link]**

Imitating Nature's Mineral Artistry ◆ 651

▶Critical Viewing◀

❹ **Analyze** According to the article, the "imperfections" of this emerald would indicate it is real.

Reinforce and Extend

Answers

◆ **Literature and Your Life**

Reader's Response Examples include virtual reality and cloning.

Thematic Focus Students might mention the concept of supply and demand, or they might talk about putting dollar values on beauty.

✓ **Check Your Comprehension**

1. Scientists have learned to create the (1) necessary temperatures and (2) chemical activity.
2. In general, synthetic gems have growth marks that natural gems don't have. In the case of emeralds, synthetic ones are often more transparent, richer in hue and more perfectly formed.
3. Industrial diamonds can be made from exposing any carbon-containing material to a few minutes of heat and pressure. For gem-quality diamonds, heat and pressure must be maintained for a week.

◆ **Critical Thinking**

1. a) Flame fusion is based on melting and gradual cooling. In the flux growth method, a gem is crystallized from a solution of its constituents in a molten bath of solvent, or flux. b) The chemical ingredients of rubies can take the 4,000° F heat, but the chemical ingredients of emeralds decompose during the heating needed to melt them. The temperature for flux growth is only 1,500 °F.
2. Hall's basic method is now used to make industrial diamonds.
3. It has only one element—carbon.
4. Possible response: He would have lost a lot of money.
5. Gemologists should have expertise in the process of growth of natural gems, where they're found, what their properties are, and how to authenticate them.

Speaking and Listening Mini-Lesson

Oral Demonstration

This mini-lesson supports the Speaking and Listening activity in the Idea Bank on page 655.

Introduce the Concept Tell students that in an oral demonstration, students can use words and actions to show a process or skill.

Develop Background Alert students to the criteria on which their oral demonstrations will be evaluated. Presentations should be clear, with appropriate visual aids or illustrations; steps

should be presented in a logical order and connected with transitions such as first, then, until, after. Discuss these criteria with students and have them suggest other guidelines for an effective demonstration.

Apply the Information Have students prepare and deliver their oral presentations.

Assess the Outcome Use the criteria listed in the Develop Background section when evaluating students' presentations.

In "Work That Counts," author Ernesto Ruelas Inzunza combines the elements of a technical article with his sense of enthusiasm for his field to give readers an exciting account of an important project in the field of wildlife biology.

◆ **Build Grammar Skills**

❶ **Varied Sentence Beginnings: Adverb Phrases** Have students identify the adverb phrase that begins this sentence. *The phrase is At eight this morning.* What question does this prepositional phrase answer? *When were the Swainson's hawks taking off?*

◆ **Literary Focus**

❷ **Technical Articles** Students should note that at the end of the next paragraph, the author explains that the topography and atmospheric conditions of the area provide the birds with winds and updrafts that help them in their migrations.

Work That Counts

Ernesto Ruelas Inzunza

After sunset, I finally have time to sit peacefully and tell my friend Jeros, who is new to hawk watching, the story of the discovery of the River of Raptors.

It is the end of a long day of watching and counting birds of prey in the small town of Chichicaxtle in the state of Veracruz, Mexico. At eight this morning, as Jeros and I climbed the observation tower, about forty-five Swainson's hawks were just taking off from the nearby canyon where they had spent the night. Shortly afterward, we saw hundreds of them turning circles in the thermal columns of hot air, effortlessly gaining altitude. By

❶

◆ **Literary Focus**
What details clarify why so many birds fly along this pathway?

eleven, the Swainson's had joined smaller numbers of broad-winged hawks and turkey vultures, forming long streams of migrants. ❷ Such large flocks, totaling more than 20,000 birds at times, can take up to thirty minutes to pass overhead. Resembling myriad moving organisms in a plankton sample, the raptors filled our binoculars' field of view. We watched the avian river continue north until it disappeared.

Each spring and fall, the spectacle of raptor

◆ **Build Vocabulary**

myriad (mir´ ē əd) *adj.*: Huge number; seemingly countless

topography (tə päg´ rə fē) *n.*: Surface features of a place, such as rivers, lakes, mountains, and so on

---

Beyond the Classroom

Community Connection
Community Bird Counts In "Work That Counts," Ernesto Ruelas Inzunza quotes an 1897 account of the River of Raptors written by Frank M. Chapman. Chapman, who was curator of birds at the American Museum of Natural History, was also the founder of a bird count in which your students can participate—the annual Christmas Bird count, now sponsored by the National Audubon Society.

Every year, about 50,000 people take part in this nationwide event by spending one day between December 17 and January 3 identifying and counting birds within a designated area. The participants report their findings to the Audubon Society, which analyzes and publishes the data and also uses it for long-term research on bird populations and ranges.

Interested students can learn more about the Christmas Bird Count by contacting their local chapter of the Audubon Society.

migration fills the skies of Veracruz in eastern Mexico as the birds funnel through a narrow geographic corridor and above our monitoring stations at Chichicaxtle and Cardel. This bottleneck is formed where the Mexican central volcanic belt reaches the Gulf of Mexico and almost cuts the lowlands of the coastal plain in two. The topography and atmospheric conditions of the lowlands provide birds of prey and many other migrants with the conditions needed for migrating with the least expenditure of energy: tail winds and warm thermal updrafts.

Among the migrating raptors are turkey vultures; ospreys; swallow-tailed, Mississippi, and plumbeous kites; northern harriers; sharp-shinned, Cooper's, Harris's, red-shouldered, broad-winged, Swainson's, zone-tailed, and red-tailed hawks; and falcons, including kestrels, merlins, and peregrines. The migrations of a few other species—hook-billed kites, golden eagles and ferruginous hawks—are less well documented in Veracruz and are currently being studied. Five species of swallows, scissor-tailed flycatchers, white-winged and mourning doves, wood storks, white pelicans, cormorants, and white-faced and white ibises are also among the list of more than 220

species of migratory birds recorded at Veracruz. In fall, the count totals range between 2.5 million and 4 million birds, the highest count anywhere in the world, as birds journeying from eastern, central, and western North America converge here in Veracruz.

After five in the evening, when the temperature dropped down to 82° F and the thermals ceased to form, the pace slowed. Now I can respond in more detail to Jeros's question about the discovery of the River of Raptors. I read him a paragraph written in the spring of 1897 by ornithologist Frank M. Chapman, of the American Museum of Natural History: "On April 6 and 16, flights of hawks—I was unable to determine the species—were observed passing northward, exceeding in number any migration of these birds I have before seen." Almost a hundred years passed before bird counts were organized at Veracruz and Chapman's statements were borne out. Yet as long as these lowlands have been inhabited, the migration must have been seen and accepted by the local inhabitants as an autumn phenomenon. I conclude by telling my friend that perhaps the River of Raptors has always been known. And, he adds, admired.

Guide for Responding

◆ Literature and Your Life

Reader's Response Describe any bird migrations that you've observed. Where were you? What formation did the birds fly in? Could you identify the species?

Thematic Focus What observations have you made about the effect of natural forces, such as storms and droughts, upon birds?

☑ Check Your Comprehension

1. What is Inzunza's work as described in this article?
2. What conditions allow birds to migrate with the least expenditure of energy?
3. (a) Who discovered the River of Raptors? (b) Why was it unique at the time?

◆ Critical Thinking

INTERPRET
1. Explain how the title of this article has a double meaning. **[Analyze]**
2. Why do so many birds converge where the Mexican central volcanic belt reaches the Gulf of Mexico? **[Draw Conclusions]**
3. Why does Veracruz have the highest count of migrating birds of anywhere in the world? **[Analyze]**

APPLY
4. Why is Inzunza's job important? **[Synthesize]**

EXTEND
5. Birds of prey are carnivorous, or flesh eating. Name some other creatures that are carnivorous. Explain. **[Science Link]**

Work That Counts ◆ 653

◆ Literary Focus

❸ **Technical Article** Encourage students to explain what *tail winds* are. *Tail winds are winds that blow in the same direction as the course of a flock of birds, a plane, a ship, and so on. Then point out the term* thermal updrafts—*which means rising columns of warm air. Ask students what sources they could access to learn more about these phenomena. Possibilities include printed or online encyclopedia; meteorology books, or web sites dealing with meteorology.*

◆ Critical Thinking

❹ **Support** Have students cite one or more details in this passage to support the conclusion that the observatory in Veracruz is important to areas well beyond Veracruz. *The observatory is linked to bird life throughout North America; the author states that migrating birds from eastern, central and western North America converge in Veracruz.*

◆ Critical Thinking

❺ **Interpret** What point do students think that the author is making in the last sentence? *Possible responses: He shows that the River of Raptors has a significance that is more than purely scientific; he is expressing the idea that people have an innate connection to nature.*

Reinforce and Extend

Answers

◆ Literature and Your Life

Reader's Response Sample response: I was in the local park and I saw a flock of Canada geese flying in a V-formation.

Thematic Focus Students may have observed birds temporarily disappear in a storm or die off in a severe drought.

☑ Check Your Comprehension

1. Inzunza observes and counts birds of prey for a conservation organization in Veracruz, Mexico.
2. Tail winds and warm thermal updrafts allow them to migrate with the least expenditure of energy.
3. (a) The American ornithologist Frank M. Chapman discovered it (but didn't necessarily name it) in 1897. (b) It was unique because the number of birds migrating far exceeded any Chapman had seen.

◆ Critical Thinking

1. Students should see that the title is literal—counting birds—and figurative—work that is meaningful.
2. Students should realize that so many birds converge there because the topographic and atmospheric conditions are ideal for easy migrating.
3. Students will probably say that Veracruz has such a high number of migrating birds because birds from eastern, central and western North America converge there.

4. Inzunza's work is important because by counting and tracking the number of birds migrating each year scientists can determine which species might be endangered.
5. Possible examples of carnivorous creatures are sharks, people, bears, insectivorous plants.

Answers

◆ Reading Strategy

1. Powdered chemical ingredients of a gem sift from a hopper into a combustion chamber where the chemicals are melted. The melted powder falls onto a ceramic rod at the base of the chamber and accumulate into the mass known as a boule.
2. A solution of emeralds' chemical ingredients is produced by combining a chemical compound with a flux; the solution is heated in an electric furnace; gem crystals precipitate out as they cool.
3. Students' diagrams should use arrows to show tail winds and warm thermal updrafts.

◆ Literary Focus

1. Examples include synthetic diamonds, emeralds and rubies.
2. Sample response: A raptor is a bird of prey; students could check a dictionary or ornithology text to find out about a raptor.
3. Inzunza compares the large migration of birds to moving organisms in a plankton sample.

◆ Build Vocabulary

Using the Prefix syn-
1. b 2. a 3. c

Using the Word Bank
1. divulge; 2. myriad; 3. vigilance; 4. constituents; 5. synthetic; 6. topography; 7. fortuitous; 8. saturated; 9. metamorphosis; 10. synthesized

◆ Build Grammar Skills

Writing Application
1. *After sunset*, I finally have time to tell my friend the story of the River of Raptors.
2. *At the monitoring station*, hawk counting is serious business.
3. *Shortly afterward*, we saw hundreds of Swainson's hawks climbing the thermals.
4. *In the strong tailwinds and warm thermals*, the hawks fly easily.

Writer's Solution

For additional instruction and practice, use the Varying Sentence Structure lesson in the **Language Lab CD-ROM** and pages 121–123, Varying Your Sentences, *Writer's Solution Grammar Practice Book*.

654

Guide for Responding (continued)

◆ Reading Strategy

RELATE DIAGRAMS TO TEXT

Because diagrams can explain something visually, they have many different applications. Working with text, diagrams are often included in instructions and manuals and in articles explaining a process. In "Imitating Nature's Mineral Artistry," O'Neil uses both text and diagrams to give a clear picture of how synthetic gems are formed.

1. Using Diagram A, explain, in sequential order, the process by which powdered chemicals become a boule, such as a ruby boule.
2. Use Diagram B to identify the stages of flux growth.
3. Create a simple diagram that shows how the geographic bottleneck described in "Work That Counts" creates favorable flight conditions. Use a map of Mexico to locate the central volcanic belt, the Gulf of Mexico, and the lowlands of the coastal plain.

◆ Literary Focus

TECHNICAL ARTICLES

These two technical articles differ in the complexity of their ideas and in the way these ideas are demonstrated, but—like all technical articles—they both explain a process.

O'Neil includes diagrams with "Imitating Nature's Mineral Artistry" to help explain visually the complex process of creating synthetic gems. He also uses examples to demonstrate the processes he explains. In "Work That Counts," Inzunza uses comparisons and statistics to clarify his points.

1. Identify an example that O'Neil uses to demonstrate the synthetic creation of gems in "Imitating Nature's Mineral Artistry."
2. Give two examples of specialized language in "Work That Counts." Tell what the terms mean or where you could go to find out.
3. Explain the comparison Inzunza uses in "Work That Counts" to clarify the enormous number of birds that have been counted traveling past the monitoring stations at Chichicaxtle and Cardel.

654 ◆ Nonfiction

◆ Build Vocabulary

USING THE PREFIX syn-

The prefix *syn-* means "together with." On your paper, match each word with its corresponding definition.

1. synchronize   a. number of symptoms occurring together
2. syndrome   b. to move at the same time
3. synthesize   c. make by putting parts together

USING THE WORD BANK

On your paper, complete each analogy using the words from the Word Bank.

1. *Hide* is to *conceal* as ___?___ is to *tell*.
2. *Scarcity* is to *one* as ___?___ is to *one million*.
3. *Concentration* is to *relaxation* as ___?___ is to *sleep*.
4. *Ingredients* is to *recipe* as ___?___ is to *whole*.
5. *Nature* is to *natural* as ___?___ is to *man-made*.
6. *Nose* is to *face* as *mountain* is to ___?___.
7. *Unlucky* is to *accident* as ___?___ is to *bonus*.
8. *Sold out* is to *concert* as ___?___ is to *solution*.
9. *Oxidation* is to *decay* as *heat* is to ___?___.
10. *Grow* is to *plant* as ___?___ is to *form*.

◆ Build Grammar Skills

VARIED SENTENCE BEGINNINGS: ADVERB PHRASES

Adverb phrases are prepositional phrases that modify a verb, adjective, or another adverb. Placing an adverb phrase at the beginning of a sentence is one way to achieve sentence variety.

Writing Application Identify the adverb phrase in the following sentences. Then, on your paper, rewrite each sentence moving the adverb phrase to the beginning. Make any other adjustments required in the sentence.

1. I finally have time after sunset to tell my friend the story of the River of Raptors.
2. Hawk counting at the monitoring station is serious business.
3. We saw hundreds of Swainson's hawks shortly afterward climbing the thermals.
4. The hawks fly easily in the strong tailwinds and warm thermals.

Beyond the Selection

FURTHER READING

Other Works by Paul O'Neil
Gemstones
Barnstormers and Speed Kings

Other Works About Imitating Natural Forces
Rappacini's Daughter, Nathaniel Hawthorne
Frankenstein, Mary Shelley

We suggest that you preview these works before recommending them to students.

INTERNET

Students can learn more at the following Web sites. Please be aware that the sites may have changed since we published this information.

To find out more about natural and synthetic gems, go to **http://micro.magnet.fsu.edu/micro/gallery/presious/precious.html**

To find out more about hawks and birds of prey, go to **http://www.execpc.con/~laurag/raptor/raptor.html**

We *strongly recommend* that you preview the sites before you send students to them.

Build Your Portfolio

Idea Bank

Writing

1. **Persuasive Letter** Suppose you're Ernesto Inzunza, and you're raising money to continue your work. Write a three-paragraph introductory letter to a funding source describing the importance of studying and protecting birds.

2. **Comparison-and-Contrast Essay** Choose two species of raptor, such as osprey and turkey vulture. Write one or two pages comparing their eating, migratory, and nesting habits.

3. **Technical Article** Write a detailed explanation of a process that you take for granted, such as making toast or opening your locker. Create diagrams that clarify your explanation.

Speaking and Listening

4. **Bird-Cast** Imagine you're witnessing the greatest bird migration in history. As if it were a sports event, give a play-by-play description. What birds are passing now? How fast? **[Performing Arts]**

5. **Oral Demonstration** In detailed steps, explain and demonstrate for the class a process with which you're especially familiar, such as how to play your favorite computer game. **[Speech Link]**

Projects

6. **Conservation Update** Using pictures and research material from books or the Internet, prepare an update on efforts to preserve the status of endangered birds worldwide. **[Science Link]**

7. **Diamond Weighing** You know the Star of Africa weighs 530.2 mg. and the Hope diamond weighs 44.5. mg. Using an equivalency table for U.S. and metric measurements, calculate the weight in ounces of these diamonds. **[Math Link]**

Writing Mini-Lesson

Product Description

Product descriptions are important pieces of writing because they introduce a particular product to consumers who will decide whether or not to purchase the product. Write a two-page description of the product of your choice for a consumer magazine. Include important information such as price and color choice, and technical details such as measurements and operating requirements.

Writing Skills Focus: Precise Details

In describing your product, give **precise details**. Instead of saying, "Cruiser has great safety features," say: "Cruiser has dual air bags and two three-point safety belts in the front, two in the rear. The front shoulder mounts have a height adjustment. All doors come equipped with child safety locks."

Prewriting Make a chart labeling the categories your product description will cover. Under each category, jot down precise details.

Design	Safety	Maneuverability
1.	1.	1.
2.	2.	2.

Drafting You might want to organize your report according to the categories you've chosen. If so, devote a paragraph to each category. Make a general statement or a point about each category and then support it with details from your chart. Make sure all details relate to the category.

Revising Review your description by asking yourself: What more would I need to know if I were buying this product? Is every detail specific and completely accurate? Add any further details needed to make your description complete.

Idea Bank

Customizing for *Performance Levels*

Following are suggestions for matching Idea Bank topics with your students' performance levels:

Less Advanced Students: 1, 4
Average Students: 2, 5, 6, 7
More Advanced Students: 3

Customizing for *Learning Modalities*

Following are suggestions for matching Idea Bank topics with your students' learning modalities:

Visual/Spatial: 6
Verbal/Linguistic: 4, 5
Logical/Mathematical: 5, 7

Writing Mini-Lesson

Refer students to the Writing Handbook, page 965, for instruction on the writing process and page 967 for further information on description.

Writing and Language Transparencies Use the Cubing Organizer transparency (p. 87) to demonstrate a way students can develop details for their product descriptions.

Writer's Solution

Writers at Work Videodisc

Have students view the videodisc segment for Chapter 1 in which Colleen McElroy talks about her strategy for gathering details. Discuss how her strategy may be applied to all forms or descriptive writing.

Play frames 3324 to 4292

Writing Lab CD-ROM

Have students complete the Tutorial on description. Follow these steps:

1. Have students consult an audio-annotated student model of a first draft of a student's description. The student comments on the choices she made in drafting the piece.

2. Suggest that students refer to tips for peer editors to learn about peer review strategies for improving a description.

Sourcebook

Have students use Chapter 3, Description (pp. 1–24), for additional support.

✓ ASSESSMENT OPTIONS

Formal Assessment, Selection Test, pp. 163–165, and Assessment Resources Software. The selection test is designed so that it can be easily customized to the performance levels of your students. *Alternative Assessment*, p. 47, includes options for less advanced students, more advanced students, intrapersonal learners, logical/mathematical learners, verbal/linguistic learners, and visual/spatial learners.

PORTFOLIO ASSESSMENT

Use the following rubrics in the *Alternative Assessment* booklet to assess student writing:
Persuasive Letter: Persuasion Rubric, p. 105
Comparison-and-Contrast Essay: Comparison-and-Contrast Rubric, p. 103
Technical Article: Technical Description/Explanation Rubric, p. 115

Establish Writing Guidelines
Before students begin, review the following key characteristics of a consumer report:

- It presents important, up-to-date information about a product, supported by survey and test results, so that potential buyers can make an informed purchasing decision

- It makes recommendations for the consumer.

- You may want to distribute the scoring rubric for a consumer report (p. 658) to make students aware before they begin of the criteria on which they will be evaluated.

Refer students to the Writing Handbook, p. 965, for instruction in the writing process, and page 967 for further information on exposition.

Writing Lab CD-ROM
If your students have access to computers, you may want to have them work on the tutorial on Exposition to complete all or part of their consumer reports. Follow these steps:

1. Have students review the interactive model of a consumer report.
2. Suggest students look at the examples of broad and narrowed topics.
3. Have students draft on the computer.
4. Encourage students to use the Revision checker for unity and coherence.
5. Have students use the Revision checker for homophones.

Sourcebook
Students can find additional support, including topic ideas, models, audience and purpose profiles, and graphic organizers, in the chapter on Exposition (pp. 62–95).

Students may have read consumer reports on items such as electronic equipment, bicycles, cars, and other items in the magazines they read. Invite students to examine a particular report they have read and describe problems or strengths in the examples; they can either offer suggestions for improvement or use the article as a model for their own report.

Consumer Report

Writing Process Workshop

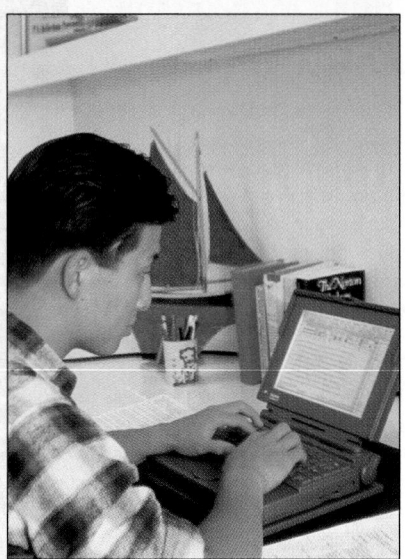

The movie reviews you read in this section were written to help the reader make an informed choice about whether or not to see a particular film. In the same way, a consumer report presents information about a particular product or service, so that potential customers can make an informed choice about whether to buy the product or use the service. A consumer report may include expert opinions, user surveys, or reports from performance tests. It often concludes with a recommendation or rating of the product or service.

The following skills, introduced in this section's Writing Mini-Lessons, will help you develop your consumer report.

Writing Skills Focus

▶ **Give specific examples.** If you say, "This printer is slow," include an example, such as, "It only prints one page per minute." (See p. 635.)

▶ **Elaborate,** or develop details so that the reader can clearly picture what you are saying. (See p. 645.)

▶ **Give precise details.** Instead of saying, "This computer has many features," say "The Orion 5200 has a 233 MHz CPU, 32 MB of memory, and a 24X CD." (See p. 655.)

The following excerpt from a consumer report demonstrates these skills.

① The writer gives specific examples of the features of the Galileo 2000.

② The writer elaborates on "loaded with features" by listing the features.

③ The writer will give precise details on each feature in the remainder of the essay.

WRITING MODEL

In this computer age, the latest product to come along and make all our lives easier is the Galileo 2000.

The Galileo 2000 ① is compact but loaded with features: ② 20 MB of RAM, a World Wide Web browser, calculator, word processor, address book, spreadsheet, and e-mail capability.

The first component I tested was the word processor . . . ③

Prewriting

Choose a Topic: Shop Around Professional writers of consumer reports often conduct extensive investigations of the products or services about which they plan to write. For your own consumer report, do some comparison shopping for products you may be interested in buying, such as shoes, a backpack, or a CD player. Visit several stores to investigate the features of different brands, and jot down details in a notebook. Select one of the items as the subject of your report.

Gather Details You'll need to gather details about the product or products you're testing. Use the following strategies for gathering details:

▶ **Make observations.** Closely examine the product or products. If appropriate, conduct tests and take detailed notes about your observations.

▶ **Conduct a poll or survey.** Get reactions from people who have used the product. Prepare questions in advance, and phrase them to be as unbiased as possible. Instead of questions that can be answered "yes" or "no," have respondents rate their level of agreement or disagreement on a scale of one to ten.

▶ **Get expert advice or knowledge** by consulting with a teacher or an expert on the topic. Other sources of information are newspapers, magazines, and reference books.

Drafting

Use Transition Words To make your consumer report fit together, you'll need to show how your ideas work with one another. Use a Transition Word Bin like the one below to find transition words that will express the relationship between your ideas.

Transition Word Bin

Spatial	Cause and Effect	Compare and Contrast
behind	because	identically
at the center	as a result	in the same way
alongside	consequently	different from
within	side effect	more, less, most
on top of	outcome	similarly, equally

APPLYING LANGUAGE SKILLS: Eliminating Unnecessary Words

Needless words weigh down your writing and may confuse your readers. **Eliminate unnecessary words** in your report.

Wordy:

The Sierra Avalanche is more or less a pretty decent value in those fun things we love to call snowboards. As a matter of fact, I believe that I'll hop right on down to the store and buy one for my little old self.

Streamlined:

The Sierra Avalanche is such a decent value in snowboards, I think I'll buy one myself.

Practice Eliminate unnecessary words in the following:

Past history shows that computers get ever more powerful and increasingly less expensive financially with each and every passing year.

Writing Application Make sure that your consumer report has no unnecessary words.

Writer's Solution Connection Language Lab

For more practice streamlining your sentences, complete the Language Lab lesson on Eliminating Unnecessary Words.

Prewriting

Have students do comparison shopping for products which they may be interested in buying, such as shampoo, a backpack, or a pair of shoes or sneakers. Have them visit several stores to investigate the features of different styles and brands of various items, jot down details in a notebook, and then select one item as the basis for a report. Remind students that it is not necessary to buy a product, such as a pair of sneakers, to evaluate its features though it may be necessary for a product such as shampoo.

Customize for
English Language Learners

These students may find it easier to write a consumer report in which they compare two brands of the same product. They could shop for two types of shoes, for example, and take notes on each brand. Have them list the features of each shoe in a Venn diagram, and then write a comparison of the two. If their oral skills are better than their written ones, have them present their report orally.

 Writer's Solution

Writing Lab CD-ROM
The Gathering Details section of the tutorial on Exposition contains a Notecards activity. Have students complete this activity to develop efficiency in using notecards.

Drafting

Encourage students to incorporate transitions as they draft. The transitions will help them arrange details in an appropriate sequence.

Applying Language Skills

Eliminating Unnecessary Words Remind students that needless words will confuse readers; redundant ones bore them.

Suggested Answer
History shows that computers get more powerful and less expensive with each passing year.

 Writer's Solution

For additional instruction and practice, have students complete the **Language Lab CD-ROM** lesson on Eliminating Unnecessary Words and the practice page (p. 119) on Using Words Concisely in the *Writer's Solution Grammar Practice Book*.

Revising

Have students work with peer reviewers to revise their consumer reports. The peer reviewers should apply the points on the checklist to the writer's draft and offer concrete suggestions for improvement.

 Writer's Solution

Writing Lab CD-ROM

The Revising and Editing section of the tutorial on Exposition contains the following screens to help students revise their consumer reports:

- Interactive self-evaluation checklists
- Revision checkers for transitions and language variety
- Tips for peer editors

Publishing

In addition to the publishing suggestions offered, students might publish their consumer reports in a school newspaper.

Applying Language Skills
Infinitives and Infinitive Phrases

Suggested Answer

To record music from CDs is this tape deck's main function.

 Writer's Solution

For additional instruction and practice, have students complete the practice page 46 on Infinitives and Infinitive Phrases in the *Writer's Solution Grammar Practice Book*.

Reinforce and Extend

Have students reflect on the critical evaluation skills they developed in doing a consumer review. They might discuss or write in their journals in what other situations they might apply these skills.

APPLYING LANGUAGE SKILLS:
Infinitives and Infinitive Phrases

An **infinitive** is the base form of a verb, usually preceded by *to*; it can be used as a noun, adjective, or adverb. An **infinitive phrase** contains an infinitive and all the words that go with it.

Infinitive:

To connect is this modem's goal.

Infinitive Phrase:

To connect you to the Internet speedily is this modem's goal.

Practice On your paper, change the following sentence into one with an infinitive.

> Recording music from CDs is this tape deck's main function.

Writing Application Review your consumer report. Add infinitives where they would make your sentence structure more interesting.

Writer's Solution Connection
Writing Lab

To help you revise your consumer report, see the Revising and Editing screen of the Writing Lab tutorial on Exposition.

Revising

Use a Checklist Use the following checklist to improve your consumer report:

- ▶ What details can I add to strengthen my comparisons and contrasts?
- ▶ How can I improve my language to better suit my audience?
- ▶ Have I used enough transitional words?
- ▶ Have I eliminated any unnecessary words or phrases?
- ▶ Is my organization clear?
- ▶ Have I elaborated on my details to make them clear to the reader?

Publishing

- ▶ **Publish a Consumer Guide** If you have access to a desktop publishing program and someone who knows how to use it, you can create a magazine-style consumer guide easily and inexpensively. Gather the consumer reports of your classmates, and publish them in the guide.
- ▶ **Give an Informative Speech** A good way to share a consumer report is to present it orally. Use charts, maps, illustrations, or diagrams to illustrate your report. If possible, demonstrate your points with a sample of the product.

REVISION MODEL

① 5000-800-liter internal frame
Of all the ~~big~~ backpacks I tested, the Cascade

Designs "Rainier" was by far, ~~completely~~ ②, the best.

It's big, comfortable, convenient, and a pretty good value.

③ It has a 7,200 liter capacity, fully adjustable straps on both the shoulders and hips, and detachable side and top pockets. It's also half the price of other bags in its range.

① The writer changes this detail to specify what "big" means.

② The writer eliminates this unnecessary word.

③ The writer elaborates on his last sentence to make it much more detailed and accurate.

✓ ASSESSMENT		4	3	2	1
PORTFOLIO ASSESSMENT Use these criteria rubric to assess students' writing.	**Organization and Style**	The report is very well organized and all assertions are supported.	The report is organized and most assertions are supported.	Organization needs some improvement. Few points are supported.	The report is poorly organized and support for points is lacking.
	Grammar, Usage, and Mechanics	There are few or no errors in grammar, usage, or mechanics.	There are some but not significant errors in grammar, usage, or mechanics.	There are significant errors in grammar, usage, or mechanics that interfere with the reading.	There are many serious errors in grammar, usage, or mechanics.

Real-World Reading Skills Workshop

Recognizing Bias

Strategies for Success

A biased writer is not neutral; he or she is inclined to favor or oppose a particular situation or viewpoint. Sometimes writers intentionally present a bias in their writing; for example, editorial writing is biased: It takes a position for or against something. Sometimes, however, bias can slip into writing that is supposed to be objective.

Recognizing Bias To be an informed and intelligent consumer of information, it's important that you recognize bias. Don't accept the statements or viewpoints of others uncritically.

Sometimes bias is obvious in a writer's choice of words, but sometimes it's more subtle. You expect a reporter to be neutral, but a reporter who refers to a defendant as a "criminal," obviously is biased against the defendant.

"Loaded" Words Loaded words carry a positive or negative connotation. The word *home,* for instance, has warm, positive connotations, but the word *house* is more neutral.

Stereotypes Stereotypes label all members of a group with the same qualities, ignoring individual differences among them. The statement that "all politicians are crooks" creates a particular stereotype of politicians that reflects a bias against them.

Slanted Arguments Bias is often reflected in a slanted argument—one that promotes only one side of an issue. A slanted argument often omits facts or information that would weaken the argument.

> ✔ Here are other forms of writing in which bias may be present:
> ▶ Campaign literature
> ▶ Editorials
> ▶ Petitions

Apply the Strategy

Answer the questions about this article.

Vote NO for Sunday Shopping

Proposal 232 is asking that the county law that prohibits shopping malls and retail stores from conducting business on Sundays be lifted. I say we vote NO on this proposal. The area is already overcrowded. Sunday shopping would increase local and highway traffic by as much as 80 percent. Furthermore, keeping stores closed on a weekend encourages families and friends to spend time together, instead of shopping at the malls. Aren't six shopping days a week enough? Finally, closed stores on Sundays allow the proprietors of small, family-run businesses to take a day off rather than stay open to compete with money-hungry retail chains. I urge you to vote NO on Proposal 232 for the sake of our county.

1. What loaded words appear in this article? What kind of bias do they indicate?
2. Cite an example of stereotyping from this article.
3. What might be the point of view of someone in favor of Proposal 232?

Real-World Reading Skills Workshop ◆ 659

Introduce the Strategy

Remind students that just because they see something on television, that does not automatically make it the truth. Remind them that the producers of television reports are often severely constrained by broadcast time and may therefore have to omit potentially important details or facts.

Apply the Strategy

For each of these activities, evaluate students' work based on detail and support that they provide in their critical evaluations.

Career Connection: Workplace Skills

Critical Evaluation Point out to students that the ability to review and analyze material critically is beneficial in almost any workplace situation. Workplace responsibilities often call on employees to review reports, proposals, requests, or other materials. Being able to evaluate the quality, purpose, and possible bias of a text or message gives insight into what's behind it and enables them to adjust their approach and response to it.

Viewing Television Reports Critically

Speaking and Listening Workshop

In our fast-paced world, one of the quickest ways to find out about current events is to turn on a television set to get news and other reports. Don't be in a hurry to accept everything you see, however. Think of the report as a product; examine it for quality before accepting it. Consider all the factors that contribute to the way news is presented.

Identify What You're Seeing Identify the type of report you are viewing. Be aware that each type of report has its own emphasis, and adjust your approach and response.

Straightforward news reports are meant to recount information factually and objectively—that is, without the newscaster's or the station's opinion. For example, a report on a political campaign would present the results of popularity polls, but the reporters would not share their own feelings about the candidates.

Feature stories offer in-depth exploration of a topic, often with a more personal and less objective slant. A feature story on overcrowding in homeless shelters might include interviews with homeless people or a tour of a shelter, as well as facts and statistics.

Editorials offer an opinion, often persuasively, and usually on a controversial topic. Editorials are usually accompanied by an announcement that the views presented are the opinions of one individual and that opposing views may also be broadcast. An editorial that proposes raising the speed limit might offer personal opinions supported by facts and statistics.

Tips for Viewing Reports Critically

▶ Identify the type of report you are seeing.
▶ Pay close attention to language and word choice that might cause you to react in a certain way.

Listen to the Language Pay close attention to the language used in a report. Listen for words that are intended to sway you to think a certain way or change your point of view.

A wild grizzly terrorized a group of unsuspecting Boy Scouts camping in the wilderness.

A group of Boy Scouts were surprised by an unexpected visitor to their campsite—a grizzly bear!

Notice how different word choices completely change the news report.

Apply the Strategies

Choose one or more of these activities. Apply the strategies you have learned for critically viewing television reports.

1. Watch a report on television. Identify the type of report, and list factors that influence your approach and response.

2. Prepare two types of mock reports on the same issue. For example, you might do a straightforward news report and an editorial on an election.

3. Compare and contrast a television report on a specific issue with one you've read in a newspaper.

660 ◆ Nonfiction

Extended Reading Opportunities

The defining characteristic of nonfiction is that the events described actually happened. The following works demonstrate that the truth is just as compelling as fiction.

Suggested Titles

My Left Foot
Christy Brown

In this poignant and inspiring autobiography, Irish author and artist Christy Brown tells how he faced and overcame the obstacles in a life disabled by cerebral palsy. Told with great humor and affection, Brown recalls his early days growing up in the slums of Dublin, his teenage years being tossed about from hospital to hospital, and finally his adult years when he found happiness and success as an author.

Death Be Not Proud
John Gunther

In 1947, when he was only seventeen years old, John Gunther, Jr., died of a brain tumor. Rather than spend his final months in despair and anger, John inspired all those around him with his courage, wit, friendliness, and patience. This memoir, written by his father, chronicles those final months of agony and false hope in a candid and unsentimental tone. Far from depressing, this tale of a spirited boy's struggle against death is moving, and ultimately, inspiring.

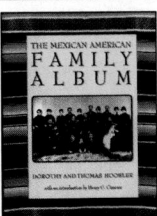

The American Family Albums
Dorothy and Thomas Hoobler

Each of the books in this acclaimed series chronicles the story of an American immigrant group, largely through the newcomers' own words and pictures. Original documents, including diaries, letters, and newspapers, bring the immigrant experience to life. The series includes *The Mexican American Family Album, The Italian American Family Album,* and *The Chinese American Family Album,* among others.

Other Possibilities

Silent Spring	Rachel Carson
Periodic Table	Primo Levi
Pilgrim at Tinker Creek	Annie Dillard

Planning Students' Extended Reading

The nonfiction works on this page provide a variety of nonfiction reading experiences. The following information may help you choose which to assign.

Customize for *Varying Student Needs*

When assigning the selections in this part to your students, keep in mind the following factors:

My Left Foot
- High-interest narrative and connection to popular and critically acclaimed film will interest students.

Death, Be Not Proud
- A short, accessible memoir

The American Family Albums
- Provides multicultural insight into the American population
- Tales of immigrants' stories will appeal to English language learners

Sensitive Issues

Christy Brown's story of his life in *My Left Foot* contains some mature language and situations.

Resources for Teaching Novels and Plays

This resource contains graphic organizers, teaching strategies, and transparencies that will be invaluable in teaching these works.

Planning Instruction and Assessment

Unit Objectives

1. To read plays that exemplify classic Greek drama and Shakespearean drama

2. To apply a variety of reading strategies, particularly strategies for reading drama, appropriate for reading these plays

3. To recognize the literary elements in ancient Greek and Shakespearean tragedy.

4. To increase vocabulary

5. To learn elements of grammar and usage

6. To write in a variety of modes and about situations based on the plays.

7. To develop speaking and listening skills by doing proposed activities

Meeting the Objectives

With each selection you will find instructional material and portfolio opportunities through which students can meet these objectives. Further, you will find additional practice pages for reading strategies, literary elements, vocabulary, and grammar in the **Selection Support** booklet in the Teaching Resources box.

Setting Goals Work with your students at the beginning of the unit to set goals for unit outcomes. Plan what skills and concepts you wish students to acquire. You may individualize according to students' performance levels or learning modalities.

Portfolios You may have students keep portfolios of their work or of their work in progress. The activities and prompts on the Build Your Portfolio page of each selection provide opportunities for students to apply the concepts presented with the selection.

UNIT 8

$\mathcal{D}$*rama*

$\mathcal{D}$rama is one of our earliest literary forms. Ancient people would act out great triumphs, deep fears, or heartfelt wishes in religious rites. Since then, drama has evolved into its modern forms, which range from lively musicals to biting satires. It is the doing or acting quality that makes drama unique in literature. As you read the dramas in this unit, see and hear the action being performed on the stage in your mind.

Commedia dell'arte, Andre Rouillard

Assessing Student Progress

The following tools are available to measure the degree to which students meet the unit objectives:

Informal Assessment

The questions on the Guide for Responding sections are a first level of response to the concepts and skills presented with the selection. Students' responses are a brief informal measure of their grasp of the material. Their responses on this level can indicate where further instruction and practice are needed. You may then follow up with the practice pages in the *Selection Support* booklet.

You will find literature and reading guides in the *Alternative Assessment* booklet, which you may give students on an individual basis for informal assessment of their performance.

Formal Assessment

In the *Formal Assessment* booklet, you will find selection tests and the unit test.

Selection Tests The selection tests measure comprehension and skills acquisition for each selection or group of selections.

Unit Test The unit test applies the unit skills on a broader level. The Critical Reading section measures Unit Objectives 1, 2, and 3. The Vocabulary and Grammar section measures Objectives 4 and 5. The Essay section measures Objectives 1 and 6.

♦ 663

 Humanities: Art

Commedia dell'Arte by Andre Rouillard.

Although the title of this painting indicates a specific dramatic form, the figures show gestures, expressions, and costumes. The masked figures have exaggerated comic costumes and features. The harlequin is a comic character well-known in drama. The man in the hat wears a mask with an exaggerated fake-nose caricature. The man and the woman on the left of the stage are

more realistic types. The young man sitting center stage wears a mask, but with a subtle expression of sorrow.

Have students link this painting with the focus of Unit 8, Drama, by answering the following questions:

1. How might these characters be similar to those in a television situation comedy? *The actors play fixed characters in situations that basically do not change.*

2. Why do you think the artist portrayed a group performing with only one person watching? *With the single viewer in the darkened window the artist suggests that while performance is often judged based on audience reaction, the performance has a value that is separate from the audience reaction. In other words, it's what we do that counts, not what others think of it.*

The Reading for Success page in each unit presents a set of problem-solving procedures to help readers understand authors' words and ideas on multiple levels. Good readers develop a bank of strategies from which they can draw as needed and apply to a variety of reading situations.

Unit 8 presents strategies for reading drama. Students will have encountered most of these strategies earlier. Here, however, they apply them to a very specific situation: reading plays.

How to Use the Reading for Success Page

- Have students preview the Reading for Success page, identifying which strategies they have used before and which are new to students. Then present each strategy as a problem-solving procedure as it applies to drama. For instance, most students have envisioned the action of short stories. Using stage directions to envision the action, however, is a specific way to apply this strategy to drama. Be sure students understand what each strategy involves and under what circumstances to apply it.

- Before reading, have student preview these plays, looking at the annotations in the green boxes that model the strategies.

Reading for Success

Strategies for Reading Drama

While plays share many elements with prose, fiction, and poetry, the greatest difference is that a drama is designed to be acted out on a stage before an audience. The story is told mostly through dialogue and action. Stage directions indicate when and how the actors move and sometimes suggest sound and lighting effects. When you read a play, you are reading a script; you must always keep in mind that it was written to be performed.

The following strategies will help you interact with the text of a drama and imagine the action and characters in performance.

Envision the action.

Reading a play without envisioning the action is like watching a movie with your eyes shut. Use the stage directions and other details to create the scene in your mind. How and where do the actors move? What do they sound like? What goes on between the characters?

Predict.

As the action develops, make predictions about what you think will happen. Look for hints in the dialogue or action that seem to suggest a certain outcome. As you read on, you will see whether your predictions are correct.

Question.

Note the questions that come to mind as you read. For example, why do the characters act as they do? What causes events to happen? Why does the author include certain information? Look for answers to your questions as you read.

Be aware of the historical context.

When does the action of the drama occur? What conditions exist during the times? If the drama takes place in a historical or foreign setting, you may have to consider that customs and accepted conduct may differ from that to which you are accustomed.

Summarize.

Dramas are often broken into acts or scenes. These natural breaks give you an opportunity to review the action. What is the conflict? What happens to move it toward its resolution? Put the characters' actions and words together as you summarize.

When you read the plays in this unit, use these general strategies, as well as those specifically suggested with each drama. They will help you understand the conflict and resolution of the dramas and gain insight into the themes.

664 ◆ *Drama*

Reading Strategies: Support and Reinforcement

Appropriate Reading Strategies Students are given a reading strategy to apply in each act of the plays. Each reading strategy is appropriate to the content of the act.

Reading Prompts To encourage application of the given strategy, there are occasional prompts, within green boxes, at appropriate and significant points.

In addition, there are red boxes prompting application of the Literary Focus concept and maroon boxes prompting students to connect with their lives.

Using the Boxed Annotations and Prompts
The material in the green, red, and maroon boxes along the sides of selections is intended to help stu-

dents apply the literary element and the reading strategy and to make a connection with their lives.

You may use the boxed material in several ways:

- When you introduce the Literary Focus, Reading Strategy, or the Literature and Your Life connection, have students preview the appropriate prompts in the selection to get an overview of how the skill or concept will be developed.

- Have students pause when they come to a box and respond to its prompt before they continue reading. If your students keep reading journals, encourage them to record in the journal the page number, the question or idea proposed in the prompt, and their response.

PART **1** *Dramatic Beginnings*

Theatre of Herodes Atticus, Acropolis, Odeon, Athens, Greece

Dramatic Beginnings ◆ 665

 One-Minute Planning Guide

The two sections of *Antigone* in this unit present a range of emotions, characters, and dramatic techniques and elements that will help students understand the classic beauty of ancient Greek drama. The special feature on the Greek theater gives students background on how plays were presented as well as providing information about the Oedipus myth, which will be vital to their understanding of *Antigone.* Part 1 of *Antigone* introduces two tragic characters making decisions and taking stands that will have profound consequences. Part 2 explores Greek beliefs on the balance between fate and individual choice.

Customize for
Varying Student Needs
When assigning the selections in Part 1 to your students, keep in mind the following factors:

• Without an understanding of the Oedipus myth, students will be confused by frequent references to characters and events from the myth.

• The formal, stylized language may be problematic for your less proficient readers or for students learning English.

• More advanced students will appreciate the footnotes that give more detail about allusions to other Greek myths and historical events.

🎼 Humanities: Art

Theatre of Herodes Atticus, Acropolis—Odeon, Athens, Greece.
This photograph shows a theater built on the Acropolis in Athens, near the site of the older Theater of Dionysos, where *Antigone* and the other plays of Sophocles were originally performed. The theater shown here was built in A.D. 161 by Herodes Atticus, a wealthy Roman who constructed the theater in memory of his dead wife; it follows the classical Roman rather than the Greek model and seats about 5,000 spectators (the Theater of Dionysos could seat about 14,000). Herodes Atticus' Theater is now used for an annual summer festival of music and drama.

Have students link the painting to the focus of Part 1, "Dramatic Beginnings," by answering the following question:

Ancient Greek drama used such non-realistic elements as masks and a chorus, a group of people who spoke in unison. Why might this type of drama be better suited to this theater than a contemporary realistic play, with naturalistic sets and costumes? *Most students will probably say that it would be difficult to create the illusion of a closed, realistic space in an open theater like this.*

Enrichment

Greek Tragedy A Greek tragedy is usually centered on the suffering of a major character and ends in disaster. The origins of tragedy are obscure, but by the time Sophocles wrote, tragedy was a highly developed dramatic form, strongly linked with both religious ritual and artistic performance. It used poetic language, as well as song, and never completely abandoned its sacred origins.

Students living in secular societies will have some difficulty understanding the degree to which religion informed daily life in ancient Greece. The Greeks believed that the good will of the gods determined the city's welfare. Reverence, the fulfillment of religious duty, and patriotism were often synonymous.

Characters had human traits but were actually larger than life. Students accustomed to characters with personality and used to seeing cameras focus in on minute revealing muscular twitches on the faces of tragic characters will miss these aspects in Greek drama. Although characters have their assigned traits, these characteristics are so universal that the personages represent examples or types rather than unique personalities.

Finally, tragedies were usually presented as part of a trilogy. Much of the content was based on myths familiar to the ancient Greeks. This inherited and familiar cultural background made it possible for the playwright to include pungent and subtle allusions whose importance could be understood by ancient Greek audiences without the benefit of explanation.

THE GREEK THEATER

Theater was a celebration in ancient Greece. The Athenians of the fifth century B.C. held festivals to honor Dionysos (dī′ ə nī səs), their god of wine. During these holidays, citizens gathered to watch competitions between playwrights, who presented plays derived from well-known myths. These plays depicted events that exposed arrogance and that emphasized reverence for the gods.

Thousands of Athenians saw the plays. In an outdoor theater like the one shown on page 667, seats rose away in a semicircle from a level orchestral area. The plays performed in these theaters had limited numbers of characters, and scenes were interspersed with songs. There were no curtains to allow for changes of scenery between acts. No violence or irreverence was depicted on stage, although such matters were central to the plots of many plays. Such events occurred offstage and were reported in dialogue.

THE PRESENTATION OF THE PLAYS

Ancient Greek playwrights used a consistent format for most of their productions. Plays opened with a prologue, or exposition, which presented the background to situate the conflict. The entering chorus then sang a parados (par′ əd əs), or opening song. This was followed by the first scene. The chorus's song, called an ode, divided scenes, thus serving the same purpose as a curtain does in modern theater.

The Chorus. The role of the chorus was central to the production and important in interpreting the meaning of the plays. During the odes, a leader called the choragos (kō rā′ gəs) might exchange thoughts with the group in a dialogue. During that recital, the group

rotated first from right to left, singing the strophe (strō′ fē). Then the chorus members moved in the opposite direction during the antistrophe. An epode was included in some odes as a sort of final stanza. At the conclusion, there was a paean (pē′ ən) of thanksgiving to Dionysos and an exodos (ek′ sə dəs), or final exiting scene. Clearly, the chorus played an essential part in any play's success.

THE OEDIPUS MYTH

Sophocles wrote three tragedies about the royal family of Thebes, a city in northeastern Greece. Called the Theban plays, these tragedies were *Oedipus the King*, *Oedipus at Colonus*, and *Antigone*. The stories of these plays were as familiar to the audience as the story of Noah and the Ark or Jonah and the Whale is to many people today.

Abandoned at Birth. Oedipus (ed′ ə pəs) was abandoned at birth by his parents, the Theban king Laios (lā′ yəs) and his wife, Iocaste (yō kas′ tə). A fortuneteller proclaimed in an oracle that the infant would kill his father and marry his mother. Wishing to avoid that fate, the couple had Oedipus taken off to be abandoned on a mountaintop by a servant who was to ensure the baby's death. The parents assumed that this mission was completed. In fact, however, the servant pitied the newborn and gave him to a childless couple in a distant city who raised the boy without ever mentioning his adoption.

A Famous Riddle. When Oedipus left that city to start his adult life, he still did not know that his real father was Laios and that his mother was Iocaste. His travels took him toward Thebes, where he killed a man without knowing it was Laios. Oedipus' fame grew

Drama and the Dionysian Festivals

In Athens, dramatic competitions were held at festivals honoring Dionysos, the Greek god of wine and fertile crops. (Theatrical competitions were never held at festivals honoring other gods.) Of the four annual festivals, the festival City Dionysia was the most prestigious. It was an elaborate festival, extending over several days, at which Athens showed off its wealth and culture to attendees from all over ancient Greece.

Before a festival officially began, the playwrights appeared before public officials and the sponsors of the plays and announced the subjects of their plays. Processions and sacrifices marked the official opening of the festival, after which five days were devoted to performances. Tragedies, comedies, and satyr plays (bawdy comedies that often lampooned the stories of gods and heroes) were performed. In addition, choral recitations were performed and judged.

▲ Critical Viewing What might be some advantages and disadvantages to watching a performance in a theater like this one? [Assess]

►Critical Viewing◄

Assess The majestic mountains surrounding the theater make a natural backdrop that enhances the power of the drama. Some students may enjoy watching a performance in the fresh air. Others may express concern over whether the actors could be seen or heard.

after he confronted the Sphinx, a monster that killed those unable to answer its riddle. The riddle was this: What creature walks on four legs at dawn, two legs at noon, and three legs in the evening? Oedipus answered that the creature was man, a being who crawls as an infant on all fours, walks erect in midlife, and uses a third leg in the form of a cane during old age. The Sphinx leaped into the sea after Oedipus gave the correct answer, and Oedipus was received in the city as a hero.

A Royal Marriage. Iocaste, now a widow, agreed to marry the unknown champion. The couple lived happily for years and raised four children of their own. Then a plague befell the city. The priests claimed the plague was punishment for some unknown sin. During an investigation of his own background, Oedipus learned the facts of his birth. In horror at this revelation, Iocaste committed suicide and Oedipus blinded himself. Iocaste's brother, Creon (krē än), took control of the city and allowed one of Oedipus' children, Antigone (an tig´ ə nē), to lead Oedipus into exile where he died.

A Daughter Mourns. After her return to Thebes, Antigone was deeply troubled by her experience. Her sister, Ismene (is mē´ nē), and brothers, Eteocles (ē tē´ ə klēz) and Polyneices (päl´ ə nī´ sēz) were also burdened by their family background. They were haunted by the curse that caused their father to fulfill his own prophecy and condemned his sons to kill each other for the control of Thebes.

Order Restored. By the time *Antigone* opens, Creon has restored some order to Thebes. The civil war between the brothers has just ended. Eteocles and Polyneices have killed each other in combat. Eteocles had supported Creon's established order and was buried with honors. Polyneices had rebelled with the forces of Argos against Thebes, and Creon ordered that his corpse be left to rot. Antigone's decision to disobey that command is central to the play.

The Greek Theater ◆ 667

Enrichment

The Big Three The main contenders for the tragedy prize at the dramatic competitions were Aeschylus, Euripedes, and Sophocles. Our knowledge of Greek tragedy is based mainly on the work of these three playwrights of the fifth century.

The oldest, Aeschylus, was born to an aristocratic family. As a young man, he earned fame as a soldier fighting against the Persians. He won his first prize for tragedy at approximately forty years of age. (He had been writing for sixteen years.) He won his last prize for tragedy when he was past sixty, with the *Orestia,* a trilogy considered by many to be his masterpiece. Although Aeschylus wrote ninety plays, only seven of them have survived to the present day.

At the age of twenty-seven, Sophocles defeated Aeschylus in the playwright's contest with his first tragedy. Like Aeschylus, Sophocles had served in the military. He held political positions as well, and was a priest of Asclepius, the Greek god of healing. He was the most conservative of the three great tragedians, both socially and religiously.

Euripedes, the youngest of the three, had surprisingly modern attitudes. His characters had greater psychological depth and were more human than the characters of the other two tragedians. In addition, his language was simpler and more colloquial. He disapproved of the prevailing Greek attitudes that subordinated women and glorified war. These beliefs, embedded in the social criticism in his plays, may account for the limited popularity of his plays in ancient Greece. (He won only four prizes in his lifetime.) Today, he is acknowledged as one of the most powerful dramatists in history.

The Development of Actors

Until the fifth century, tragic dramatists acted their own works—alone—with only the chorus to back them up. Early in his career, Aeschylus introduced a second actor. Dialogue could now occur between two characters. Playwrights continued to act in their own tragedies, however, until the early part of fourth century B.C., when Sophocles introduced a third actor. He did not act in his own plays, and eventually, other playwrights followed his example.

When awards for actors were introduced into the competitions (approximately 450 B.C.), the separation between actor and playwright was complete. The number of actors remained fixed at three, requiring a single actor to play many roles. The logistics of some plays even required that the same role be played by different actors in different scenes. Elaborate masks and costumes helped the audience identify each character, no matter which actor played the role.

Guide for Reading

OBJECTIVES

1. To read, comprehend, and interpret a Greek drama.
2. To relate a Greek drama to personal experience
3. To question characters' motives while reading
4. To identify the protagonist and antagonist in a play
5. To build vocabulary in context and learn the word root *-trans-*
6. To use coordinating conjunctions effectively
7. To respond to the play through writing, speaking, and listening

SKILLS INSTRUCTION

Vocabulary:
Word Roots: *-trans-*

Grammar:
Coordinating Conjunctions

Reading Strategy:
Question the Characters' Motives

Literary Focus:
Protagonist and Antagonist

Speaking and Listening:
Readers Theater (teacher edition)

PORTFOLIO OPPORTUNITIES

Writing: Newspaper Article; Letter
Speaking and Listening: Readers Theater

More About the Author

What we now know about Sophocles comes from a combination of anecdotal folklore, inferences from his poetry, and some documented information. He lived long, enjoyed good health, and died before Athens fell from glory. Of the three major Greek tragedy writers of the fifth century (Aeschylus, Sophocles, and Euripedes), Sophocles was the only one not mocked in the comedies of Aristophanes, another important fifth-century playwright.

Sophocles (c. 496–406 B.C.)

The ancient Greek dramatist Sophocles (säf´ ə klēz) wrote one hundred plays, but only seven remain in existence. His most famous are the three dealing with Oedipus and his children: *Oedipus Rex* (Oedipus the King), *Oedipus at Colonus*, and *Antigone*. This trilogy was written over a span of forty years. Born in Kolonos, near Athens, Sophocles was one of the most respected Greek dramatists of his time. He was admired not only for his poetic and dramatic skills but also for his good looks and musical talent. Sophocles frequently won first place in the competitions of plays performed in the Dionysian festivals. With his first tragedy, written at age twenty-seven, he defeated the highly respected Aeschylus (es´ kə ləs). Sophocles made some changes to the traditions of Greek theater. One of the most important changes was to increase the size of the chorus.

In his dramas, Sophocles was mainly concerned with the search for truth and self-understanding—even when the search leads to tragedy. His ability to see current values in old myths thrilled his contemporaries. Audiences since have continued to appreciate the freshness and vitality of his world view.

In *Antigone*, King Creon reaches an understanding of his own faults only after paying a very high price.

◆ Build Vocabulary

WORD ROOTS: *-trans-*

In Act I of *Antigone*, the chorus asks "What mortal arrogance *transcends* the wrath of Zeus?" The root *-trans-*, which means "through," "across," or "over" will help you to define *transcends* as "to go above or beyond limits." As you read *Antigone*, you will be *transported* to another time and place.

WORD BANK

As you read this drama, you will encounter the words on this list. Each word is defined on the page where it first appears. Preview the list before you read. Though you may not know the words, you may still be able to identify the part of speech of each word, which will give you a clue to the word's use. In your notebook, write the words and their parts of speech.

sated
anarchists
sententiously
sultry
transcends

◆ Build Grammar Skills

COORDINATING CONJUNCTIONS

A **coordinating conjunction** links two or more words or groups of words of equal importance. Many sentences in *Antigone* consist of two clauses of equal rank joined by a coordinating conjunction. The conjunction not only joins the clauses but shows the relationship between the ideas in the clauses. Look at these examples from *Antigone*.

The conjunction *and* shows addition:
Our temples shall be sweet with hymns of praise,
And the long night shall echo with our chorus.

The conjunctions *but* and *yet* show contrast or exception:
No one values friendship more highly than I; *but* we must remember . . .

The conjunction *or* shows alternatives:
Find that man, bring him here to me, *or* your death / Will be the least of your problems. . . .

668 ◆ *Drama*

Prentice Hall Literature Program Resources

REINFORCE / RETEACH / EXTEND

Selection Support Pages
Build Vocabulary: Word Roots: *-trans-*, p. 196
Build Grammar Skills: Conjunctions, p. 197
Reading Strategy: Characters' Motives, p.198
Literary Focus: Protagonist and Antagonist, p. 199

Strategies for Diverse Students' Needs, p. 48

Beyond Literature, The Greek Theater, p. 48

Daily Language Practice
Week 11, Greek Drama, p. 26

Formal Assessment Selection Test, pp. 170–172;

Assessment Resources Software
Alternative Assessment, p. 48

Resource Pro CD-ROM *Antigone,* Part 1—
includes all resource materials and customizable lesson plan

Listening to Literature Audiocassettes
Antigone, Part 1

Looking at Literature Videodisc
Chapter 8: *Antigone*

Literature CD-ROM
How to Read and Understand Drama

Antigone

◆ Literature and Your Life

CONNECT YOUR EXPERIENCE

History is full of instances where political situations create family conflicts. In American history, the Civil War is often noted for pitting brother against brother. In this play, a young woman must decide whether to act on loyalty to her family or to follow the law of the land.

THEMATIC FOCUS: CHOICES AND CONSEQUENCES

Not every conflict has a clear winner and loser. Notice the ways in which Creon and Antigone, the main characters in this play, experience both victory and defeat.

Journal Entry Jot down a list of issues on which you would be willing to take a stand. Next to each issue, write down under what circumstances, if any, you might choose *not* to take a stand.

◆ Background for Understanding

LITERATURE

The chorus is an essential element of Greek drama. This group comments on and may explain the action of the play. Sometimes the chorus speaks in a single voice as a group, sometimes in dialogue between two sections of the group.

In an opening song—the *parados* (par´ əd əs), the chorus explains the central conflict of the play. Between scenes, the chorus recites an *ode*. During the ode, the group moves from right to left, singing the *strophe* (strō´ fē). Then the chorus members move in the opposite direction during the *antistrophe*.

◆ Literary Focus

PROTAGONIST AND ANTAGONIST

When you describe a movie to a friend, you probably relate the story in terms of the main character and what happens to him or her. A movie is usually written so that you side with one of the characters more than the others and hope that he or she succeeds. In a literary work, the main character is called the **protagonist**. The protagonist is the main character, the one at the center of the action. The **antagonist** is the character or force in conflict with the protagonist.

In this play, Antigone is the protagonist; she is in conflict with the antagonist, her uncle—Creon the king.

◆ Reading Strategy

QUESTION THE CHARACTERS' MOTIVES

When you decide to do something, what causes you to act? The inner drive or impulse that makes you act is called your motive. When you read about a character like Antigone, you wonder why she acts the way she does and makes the decisions she does. To understand the conflict and resolution in any play, **question the characters' motives.**

At the beginning of the play, Antigone says to her sister, Ismene:

> And now you can prove
> what you are:
> A true sister, or a traitor to
> your family.

What do you think is Antigone's motive in confronting her sister so harshly? Is Antigone a strong, ethical character testing her sister's strength or is she too proud, too willful, too full of her own self-worth? Your questioning of her motives and the motives of the king, Creon, will help you better understand and appreciate the forces at work in the play.

Guide for Reading ◆ 669

Preparing for Standardized Tests

Grammar and Language The Build Grammar Skills lesson for this selection reviews coordinating conjunctions, showing a specific relationship each conjunction expresses between the independent clauses of a compound sentence. Sections of some standardized tests may ask students to improve sentences by choosing the best revision of a sentence, as in the following example:

Choose the best revision of the given sentence. Choose Answer (D) if you think the underlined word in the original sentence needs no revision. *(B)*

I would walk barefoot, <u>and</u> the sand is too hot.
(A) I would walk barefoot, for the sand is too hot.
(B) I would walk barefoot, but the sand is too hot.
(C) I would walk barefoot, so the sand is too hot.
(D) No revision needed.

For additional practice, use the Build Grammar Skills page on Coordinating Conjunctions, p. 197, in **Selection Support.**

Develop Understanding

One-Minute Insight In the first part of this play Sophocles establishes the main characters and the conflict. Proud and reckless, the fiery princess of Thebes, Antigone, breaks the law to bury her brother, who has been labeled a traitor by the king, her uncle. By so doing, she embarks on an course toward her own destruction and the destruction of those around her. As the play opens, the audience is invited to contrast Antigone with her sister, Ismene, who begs Antigone to be reasonable and accept the law. This contrast is a major thread that runs throughout the play.

When Antigone argues her actions with Creon, her uncle and the king, the conflict between human law and divine law is firmly established.

1 Enrichment Point out to students that these stage directions were not written by Sophocles, but were added by the translators to help modern audiences envision and understand the action. The "assault on Thebes," which is given as a time reference, would have been a historic battle familiar to Greeks watching this play in the fifth century.

◆ **Background for Understanding**

2 Explain that the prologue to a Greek tragedy is an introductory scene, which may be a monologue or a dialogue. In the prologue, the playwright sets up the situation. In this case, the prologue alerts readers that the sisters have lost two brothers who fought on opposite sides in a battle. One brother has been buried with honors, and the other is left unburied by the king's orders.

ANTIGONE

PROLOGUE THROUGH SCENE 2

Sophocles

Translated by Dudley Fitts and Robert Fitzgerald

1 **Scene.** *Before the palace of* CREON, *King of Thebes. A central double door, and two lateral doors. A platform extends the length of the facade, and from this platform three steps lead down into the "orchestra," or chorus-ground.*

Time. *Dawn of the day after the repulse of the Argive[1] army from the assault on Thebes.*

2 **Prologue**

[ANTIGONE *and* ISMENE *enter from the central door of the Palace.*]

ANTIGONE. Ismene, dear sister.
You would think that we had already suffered enough
For the curse on Oedipus:[2]

1. **Argive** (är´ gïv): From Argos, the capital of a section of ancient Greece.
2. **curse on Oedipus:** This curse refers to the fate of Oedipus, who was doomed by a decree of the gods to kill his father and marry his mother while ignorant of their true identities.

PERSONS REPRESENTED

ANTIGONE (an tig´ ə nē´), daughter of Oedipus, former King of Thebes

ISMENE (is mē´ nē), another daughter of Oedipus

EURYDICE (yoo rid´ ə sē´), wife of Creon

CREON (krē´ än), King of Thebes, uncle of Antigone and Ismene

HAIMON (hī´ mən), Creon's son, engaged to Antigone

TEIRESIAS (tī rē´ sē əs), a blind prophet

A SENTRY

A MESSENGER

CHORUS

CHORAGOS (kō rā´ gəs), leader of the chorus

A BOY, who leads Teiresias

GUARDS

SERVANTS

▲ Critical Viewing What does this temple, dedicated to Poseidon, the god of the sea, suggest about the importance of the gods in Greek life? [Draw Conclusions]

670 ◆ Drama

Block Scheduling Strategies

Consider these suggestions to take advantage of extended class time:

• Introduce students to the conventions of Greek theater with the Looking at Literature Videodisc, Chapter 8.

• Have students read Background for Understanding (p. 668) for information about the role of the chorus in Greek drama. Discuss what students know about modern play structure—acts, scenes, and so on.

• Use Daily Language Practice for Week 11. You may either use the transparency on the overhead and have students write the passages correctly, or you may dictate the passsages and have students write them.

• Use *Listening to Literature Audiocassettes* to play portions of the play aloud.

• Allow time for groups of students to act out scenes from the play.

• Suggest that students work in groups to brainstorm for a list of words containing the root *-trans-*. Point out that *-trans-* is often used as a prefix. Then have them complete the Build Grammar Skills page on the Word Root *-trans-*, p. 196 in *Selection Support.*

❸ The temple appears majestic and important. It indicates that the gods were important and honored at the time this temple was built.

Customize for
English Language Learners
Explain the stage directions that describe the time and the place in simpler terms. Help these students understand that a "platform that extends the length of the facade" means that the acting platform is as wide as the front of the palace. Explain that the time is the day after the Theban army has beaten the attacking Argive army.

Customize for
Logical/Mathematical Learners
These students especially will benefit from creating a family tree that indicates the relationships between Oedipus, Creon, Antigone, Ismene, the dead brothers, and Iocaste. Students can annotate the tree as they discover new information. For instance, later in the story, students will learn that Antigone accompanied her father, Oedipus, into exile. Students can add a note next to Antigone's name that indicates this aspect of the relationship.

Looking at Literature Videodisc
To provide students with background and motivate them to read *Antigone*, play Chapter 8 of the Videodisc. This segment provides an overview of the conventions of ancient Greek theater. Have students compare the conventions of Greek theater with those of contemporary theater.

Chapter 8

Antigone   671

Temple of Poseidon at Sounion.

This photograph shows the Temple of Poseidon at Sounion. Built around 440 B.C., the temple sits on a promontory overlooking the sea and visible by the ships that passed beneath. It is a ruin now, but once it had six columns at each end, and thirteen on each side. Archaeologists have found fragments of sculpture near the site that suggest the front of the temple was decorated with a carved frieze depicting a battle against the Centaurs—wild mythical creatures that had the body of a horse and the arms, chest, and head of a man.

Explain to students that Greek temples fall into three categories based on how the capitals, or tops, of their columns were designed. This temple of Poseidon is *Doric;* that is, each column has a flat rectangular slab on top. Other temples are *Ionic,* with capitals carved in a ram's-horn design, while a third type, *Corinthian,* has capitals carved with a leaf or floral design.

Encourage interested students to do further research to find out more about Greek art and architecture.

◆ Literary Focus

❶ Protagonist and Antagonist
Antigone sets the action in motion and shows love for her brothers by wanting them both to receive the honors of burial. Because she instigates the action and elicits readers, sympathy through her determination to "do the right thing," students can begin to identify her as the protagonist.

❷ Clarification Antigone's strong statement may be clearer to students if they understand that the Greeks believed that the dead had to be buried before the soul could be at rest. If Ismene won't help bury her brother, she is condemning him to eternal unrest.

◆ Reading Strategy

❸ Ask students how this statement helps clarify Antigone's motives.
Although Antigone is motivated by her desire to honor divine law, her love for her brother is also a powerful motive.

◆ Critical Thinking

❹ Speculate Have students speculate what Creon might do to the women if they disobey his edict.
Some students may suggest that he will have them stoned according to the penalty that has been announced. Others may feel that his family relationship with the women will lead him to be more lenient.

❺ Enrichment In this statement, Antigone is exhibiting hubris—excessive pride that will contribute to her downfall.

I cannot imagine any grief
That you and I have not gone through.
5   And now—
Have they told you of the new decree of
    our King Creon?

ISMENE. I have heard nothing: I know
That two sisters lost two brothers, a
    double death
In a single hour; and I know that the Argive
    army
10 Fled in the night; but beyond this, nothing.

ANTIGONE. I thought so. And that is why I
    wanted you
To come out here with me. There is
    something we must do.

ISMENE. Why do you speak so strangely?

ANTIGONE. Listen, Ismene:
15 Creon buried our brother Eteocles
With military honors, gave him a soldier's
    funeral,
And it was right that he should;
        but Polyneices,
Who fought as bravely
        and died as miserably,—
                    They say that Creon has
                        sworn
No one shall bury him,
                no one mourn for him,
But his body must lie in
    the fields, a
    sweet treasure

> ◆ **Literary Focus**
> What qualities does Antigone show here that help you identify her as the **protagonist?**

❶ 20

For carrion birds[3] to find as they search
    for food.
That is what they say, and our good Creon
    is coming here
    To announce it publicly; and the
        penalty—
Stoning to death in the public square!
25   There it is,
And now you can prove what you are:
A true sister, or a traitor to your family. ❷

ISMENE. Antigone, you are mad! What could
    I possibly do?

ANTIGONE. You must decide whether you will
    help me or not.

ISMENE. I do not understand you. Help you
30 in what?

ANTIGONE. Ismene, I am going to bury him.
    Will you come?

ISMENE. Bury him! You have just said the
    new law forbids it.

ANTIGONE. He is my brother. And he is your
    brother, too. ❸

ISMENE. But think of the danger! Think what
    Creon will do! ❹

ANTIGONE. Creon is not strong enough to
35 stand in my way. ❺

ISMENE. Ah sister!
Oedipus died, everyone hating him ❻

---

3. **carrion** (kar′ ē ən) **birds:** Scavenger birds, such as vultures, that eat the decaying leftovers of another animal's kill.

672 ◆ *Drama*

672

For what his own search brought to light,
  his eyes
Ripped out by his own hand; and Iocaste
40 died,
His mother and wife at once: she twisted
  the cords
That strangled her life; and our two
  brothers died,
Each killed by the other's sword. And we
  are left:
But oh, Antigone,
Think how much more terrible than these
Our own death would be if we should go
45 against Creon
And do what he has forbidden! We are only
  women,
We cannot fight with men, Antigone!
The law is strong, we must give in to the
  law
In this thing, and in worse. I beg the Dead
To forgive me, but I am helpless: I must
50 yield
To those in authority. And I think it is
  dangerous business
To be always meddling.

ANTIGONE.   If that is what you think,
I should not want you, even if you asked to
  come.
You have made your choice and you can be
  what you want to be.
55 But I will bury him; and if I must die,
I say that this crime is holy: I shall lie
  down
With him in death, and I
                    shall be as dear
To him as he to me.
                    It is the dead,
Not the living, who make
       the longest demands:
We die for ever . . .
            You may do as you like,
60 Since apparently the laws of the gods mean
  nothing to you.

ISMENE. They mean a great deal to me; but I
  have no strength
To break laws that were made for the public
  good.

ANTIGONE. That must be your excuse, I

◆ Reading Strategy
What is Antigone's motive for wanting to bury her brother?

suppose. But as for me,
I will bury the brother I love.

65 **ISMENE.**   Antigone,
I am so afraid for you!

ANTIGONE.   You need not be:
You have yourself to consider, after all.

ISMENE. But no one must hear of this, you
  must tell no one!
I will keep it a secret, I promise!

ANTIGONE.   Oh tell it! Tell everyone!
Think how they'll hate you when it all
70 comes out
If they learn that you knew about it all the
  time!

ISMENE. So fiery! You should be cold with
  fear.

ANTIGONE. Perhaps. But I am doing only
  what I must.

ISMENE. But can you do it? I say that you
  cannot.

ANTIGONE. Very well: when my strength
75 gives out, I shall do no more.

ISMENE. Impossible things should not be
  tried at all.

ANTIGONE. Go away, Ismene:
I shall be hating you soon, and the dead
  will too,
For your words are hateful. Leave me my
  foolish plan:
I am not afraid of the danger; if it means
80 death,
It will not be the worst of deaths—death
  without honor.

ISMENE. Go then, if you feel that you must.
You are unwise.
But a loyal friend indeed to those who love
  you.

[*Exit into the Palace.* ANTIGONE *goes off, left.
Enter the* CHORUS.]

Parodos

CHORUS.   [STROPHE 1]

Now the long blade of the sun, lying

Antigone ◆ 673

---

❻ Clarification Tell students that the story of Oedipus, Iocaste, and their sons would have been so familiar to Greek audiences that these brief references would have been easily understood. Contemporary readers, however, may need some background information. Refer students to pages 666 and 667 for background on Oedipus.

◆ **Critical Thinking**

❼ Analyze Invite students to identify personality traits Ismene reveals in this speech. *She is fearful of death, she believes women are weak and subordinate to men, and she is frightened of authority.*

◆ **Build Grammar Skills**

❽ Coordinating Conjunctions Have students identify the conjunctions in this passage and identify the relationships between the clauses joined by the conjunctions. *The conjunction* and *joins the clauses "You have made your choice," "you can be what you want to be." It adds one idea to another. The conjunction* but *shows the contrast between what Ismene might do or be ("you can be what you want to be") and what Antigone will do ("I will bury him.")*

◆ **Reading Strategy**

❾ Question the Characters' Motives Students may suggest that Antigone wants to bury her brother out of family loyalty. She loved Polyneices and wants his body to have an honorable burial. Students should note Antigone's words, "this crime is holy," and her reference to "the laws of the gods." Divine law is also one of her motives.

◆ **Critical Thinking**

❿ Contrast Based on this exchange, have students identify the fundamental difference between Ismene and Antigone. *Antigone is active—she tries to affect events through her actions, even when it seems futile. Ismene is passive. She allows circumstances to rule her actions.*

Cross-Curricular Connection: History

The battle known as "Seven Against Thebes" is renowned in legend and forms the basis for plays by Aeschylus and Euripedes. According to legend, Oedipus' sons had agreed to occupy the throne on alternate years. To get around the agreement, during his year of reign, Eteocles banished his brother to Argos, where Polyneices married the daughter of the king. He gathered an army, which he led with six Argive heroes and returned to attack Thebes.

Each of the seven Argive leaders stationed himself at one of the seven gates that led to Thebes. In response, Eteocles sent six generals to man each of six gates, while he himself went to the the the gate where Polyneices waited. In the ensuing battle, six of the seven against Thebes were slain, including Polyneices, who killed his brother before succumbing himself.

673

Ask students to summarize what they have learned from the Prologue. *Antigone and Ismene had two brothers who killed each other in battle. One was buried with honors, but their uncle, King Creon, will not allow the other to be buried. Antigone wants to bury him herself, but her sister, Ismene, is afraid to break the law.*

◆ **Critical Thinking**

1 Analyze Sophocles uses a metaphor to characterize Polyneices in battle. Discuss the metaphor, and ask students to explain how the image helps them imagine the kind of leader Polyneices was. Then ask students why Sophocles might have portrayed Polyneices this way. *An eagle is usually associated with freedom, nobility, strength, and bold action. These qualities can help students recognize the qualities in Polyneices that made him a fearless and inspirational leader. By portraying Polyneices this way, Sophocles makes Creon look worse for not allowing his burial.*

◆ **Critical Thinking**

2 Connect The Chorus explains that the bragging and swaggering of the seemingly triumphant troops with Polyneices led the gods to turn against them and bring about their defeat. Encourage students to connect this fact to the current action of the play. *The Chorus's explanation reveals the Greek belief that excessive pride would bring on the wrath of the gods and lead to a reversal of fortune. Students should keep this in mind as they read on, looking for evidence of excessive pride in both Antigone and Creon.*

Customize for
More Advanced Students

3 Ask these students to explain the irony of Antistrophe 2. *The chorus is announcing the beginning of an era of peace and prosperity. In fact, even more catastrophes are about to occur.*

Level east to west, touches with glory
Thebes of the Seven Gates.[4] Open,
unlidded
Eye of golden day! O marching light
5 Across the eddy and rush of Dirce's
stream,[5]
Striking the white shields of the enemy
Thrown headlong backward from the blaze
of morning!

CHORAGOS. Polyneices their commander
10 Roused them with windy phrases,
He the wild eagle screaming
Insults above our land,
His wings their shields of snow,
His crest their marshalled helms.

CHORUS. [ANTISTROPHE 1]
Against our seven gates in a yawning ring
15 The famished spears came onward in the
night;
But before his jaws were sated with our
blood,
Or pinefire took the garland of our towers,
He was thrown back; and as he turned,
great Thebes—
No tender victim for his noisy power—
20 Rose like a dragon behind him, shouting
war.

CHORAGOS. For God hates utterly
The bray of bragging tongues;
And when he beheld their smiling,
Their swagger of golden helms,
25 The frown of his thunder blasted
Their first man from our walls.

CHORUS. [STROPHE 2]
We heard his shout of triumph high in the
air
Turn to a scream; far out in a flaming arc
He fell with his windy torch, and the earth
struck him.
And others storming in fury no less than
30 his
Found shock of death in the dusty joy of
battle.

---

4. **Seven Gates:** The city of Thebes was defended by walls containing seven entrances.
5. **Dirce's** (dʉr´ sēz) **stream:** Small river near Thebes into which the body of Dirce, one of the city's early queens, was thrown after her murder.

674 ◆ Drama

CHORAGOS. Seven captains at seven gates
Yielded their clanging arms to the god
That bends the battle-line and breaks it.
35 These two only, brothers in blood,
Face to face in matchless rage,
Mirroring each the other's death,
Clashed in long combat.

CHORUS. [ANTISTROPHE 2]
But now in the beautiful morning of
victory
Let Thebes of the many chariots sing for
40 joy!
With hearts for dancing we'll take leave of
war:
Our temples shall be sweet with hymns of
praise,
And the long night shall echo with our
chorus.

Scene 1

CHORAGOS. But now at last our new King is
coming:
Creon of Thebes, Menoikeus'[6] son.
In this auspicious dawn of his reign
What are the new complexities
5 That shifting Fate has woven for him?
What is his counsel? Why has he
summoned
The old men to hear him?

[*Enter* CREON *from the Palace, center. He addresses the* CHORUS *from the top step.*]

CREON. Gentlemen: I have the honor to inform
you that our Ship of State, which
10 recent storms have threatened to destroy,
has come safely to harbor at last, guided
by the merciful wisdom of Heaven. I have
summoned you here this morning because
I know that I can depend upon you: your
15 devotion to King Laïos was absolute; you
never hesitated in your duty to our late
ruler Oedipus; and when Oedipus died,
your loyalty was transferred to his children.
Unfortunately, as you know, his two sons,

---

6. **Menoikeus** (me noi´ kē əs)

◆ **Build Vocabulary**

sated (sāt´ əd) : Satisfied or pleased

Humanities: Literature

Aristotle's Definition of Tragedy

Aristotle was a Greek philosopher. Born two decades after Socrates' death, he developed an aesthetic, or artistic, philosophy that set up a definition for tragedy and rules that dramatists should follow when writing tragedies.

According to Aristotle's definition, tragedy is an "imitation of an action that is serious, complete, and has sufficient size, in a language that is made sweet . . . exciting pity and fear, bringing about the catharsis of such emotions" (trans. Gudeman). In other words, tragedy is drama about a serious and lofty subject, written in poetic language. Its purpose is to elicit a strong, purifying, emotional response on the part of the audience.

Every tragedy, according to Aristotle, must have six elements: plot, character, thought, diction, music, and spectacle. Furthermore, a tragedy must reflect unity of action and time. In other words, the action should be continuous, with no time lapses or secondary plots. It must take place within a single day.

Challenge students to show how *Antigone* exemplifies Aristotle's elements of tragedy.

20 the princes Eteocles and Polyneices,
have killed each other in battle;
and I, as the next in blood, have succeeded
to the full power of the throne.
I am aware, of course, that no Ruler can
25 expect complete loyalty from his subjects
until he has been tested in office. Nevertheless, I say to you at the very outset that
I have nothing but contempt for the kind
of Governor who is afraid, for whatever
30 reason, to follow the course that he knows
is best for the State; and as for the man
who sets private friendship above the pub-
❹ lic welfare—I have no use for him,
either. I call God to witness that if I saw
35 my country headed for ruin, I should not
be afraid to speak out plainly; and I need
hardly remind you that I would never have
any dealings with an enemy of the people.
No one values friendship more highly than
40 I; but we must remember that friends
made at the risk of wrecking our Ship are
not real friends at all.
These are my principles, at any rate, and that
is why I have made the following
45 decision concerning the sons of Oedipus:
Eteocles, who died as a man should die,
fighting for his country, is to be buried
with full military honors, with all the
❺ ceremony that is usual when the greatest
50 heroes die; but his brother Polyneices, who
broke his exile to come back with fire and
sword against his native city and the
shrines of his fathers' gods, whose one
idea was to spill the blood of his blood and
55 sell his own people into slavery—Polyneices, I say, is to have no burial:
no man is to touch him or say the least
prayer for him; he shall lie on the plain,
unburied; and the birds and the scaveng-
60 ing dogs can do with

◆ Literary Focus
How do Creon's
❻ words reveal him
as the **antagonist**
in this play?

him whatever they like.
This is my command
and you can see the
wisdom behind it. As
long as I am King, no
traitor is going to be honored with the loyal
65 man. But whoever shows by word and
deed that he is on the side of the State—he

shall have my respect while he is living,
and my reverence when he is dead.

CHORAGOS. If that is your will, Creon son of
Menoikeus,
You have the right to enforce it: we are
70 yours.

CREON. That is my will. Take care that you
do your part.

CHORAGOS. We are old men: let the younger
ones carry it out.

CREON. I do not mean that: the sentries
have been appointed.

CHORAGOS. Then what is it that you would
have us do?

CREON. You will give no support to whoever
75 breaks this law.

CHORAGOS. Only a crazy man is in love with
death!

CREON. And death it is; yet money talks,
and the wisest
Have sometimes been known to count a
few coins too many. **❼**

[Enter SENTRY from left.]

SENTRY. I'll not say that I'm out of breath from
80 running, King, because every time I
stopped to think about what I have to tell
you, I felt like going back. And all the time
a voice kept saying, "You fool, don't you
know you're walking straight into trouble?";
85 and then another voice: "Yes, but if you let
somebody else get the news to Creon first,
it will be even worse than that for you!" But
good sense won out, at least I hope it was
good sense, and here I am with a story that
90 makes no sense at all; but I'll tell it anyhow, because, as they say, what's going to
happen's going to happen, and—

CREON. Come to the point. What have you to
say?

SENTRY. I did not do it. I did not see who did
95 it. You must not punish me for what
someone else has done.

CREON. A comprehensive defense! More

Antigone ◆ 675

❽

◆ Critical Thinking

❹ Predict Based on these words,
how do students predict Creon will
react to Antigone's disobedience?
*Most students will probably predict that
Creon will treat Antigone as harshly as he
would any other disobedient subject. His
words "the man who sets private friendship above the public welfare—I have no
use for him" and "friends made at the
risk of wrecking our Ship are not real
friends at all" are indications that he
does not allow his personal relationships
to influence his official decisions.*

◆ Reading Strategy

**❺ Question the Characters'
Motives** What motives does Creon
reveal in this speech? *Some students
may say that Creon is concerned with
the public good; others may feel that he
is only trying to strengthen his power by
making an example of Polyneices and
creating fear in those who would oppose
him.*

◆ Literary Focus

❻ Protagonist and Antagonist
Creon's cold words put him in opposition to Antigone, with whom most
readers will sympathize because of
her noble ideals and love for her
brother.

◆ Critical Thinking

❼ Analyze What do these words
reveal about Creon's character?
*Creon's first thought is that someone
might disobey him for financial gain. He
does not even consider that someone
might be motivated by love, honor, or
respect for religious law. This reveals that
his character is not very noble.*

◆ Background for Understanding

❽ Literature Explain to students
that another convention of theater in
ancient Greece was that much of the
action was imagined to have occurred
offstage and was reported through
dialogue. This led to extensive use of
messengers like this sentry. Although
the sentry is a minor role, he plays an
important function in the play.

Cross-Curricular Connection: Social Studies

The Golden Age of Greece
Sophocles lived during the "Golden Age of Greece"
(461–431 B.C.). During this time, Athens was
Greece's cultural center and its most powerful
state. Many Athenians were wealthy and had
leisure time to pursue interests such as philosophy and the arts. Many of the great art treasures
created during this period may still be seen in
museums throughout the world.

The Athenian political structure was based on
the city state, or *polis*. The governing body consisted of nine rulers called *archons*, ten generals, a cit-

izen assembly, and ten executive committees.
People's law courts administered justice.

In 431 B.C., surrounding city-states led by Sparta,
challenged Athenian power. The resulting conflict,
the Peloponnesian Wars, resulted in the defeat of
Athens. Sparta became Greece's most powerful
city-state, but Athens remained Greece's intellectual center.

Discuss with students which cities are the
intellectual and cultural centers in the United
States and Europe. Suggest they choose cities to
research.

◆ **Critical Thinking**

❶ **Draw Conclusions** Ask students why Creon assumes that a man has defied him. *Students should recall Ismene's earlier words about the weakness of women. These words will help them draw the conclusion that the subordinate position of women in ancient Greece leads Creon to assume that only a man would have the courage or strength to commit an act of defiance against him.*

❷ **Clarification** Here, Sophocles restates the Greek belief that the soul cannot rest when the body remains unburied. Having the sentry describe the burial in terms of the ghost's peace reinforces the conflict between Creon's law and divine law.

◆ **Critical Thinking**

❸ **Infer** What can you infer from the drastic action the soldiers are willing to take to prove they did not bury Polyneices? *Students can infer that the soldiers fear the wrath of Creon; Creon's threats are not idle.*

◆ *Literature and Your Life*

❹ Suggested responses: It is difficult to admit that a position you've strongly defended could be wrong because it means the courage or sacrifice involved in taking the stand was for nothing. Some students may suggest that it's difficult to admit an error because it is embarrassing.

◆ **Reading Strategy**

❺ **Question the Characters' Motives** What does Creon reveal in this speech about his motives? *In this speech, Creon reveals that he fears plots against him. This may be a motive for his inflexible stand against anyone burying Polyneices: Creon is trying to intimidate any others who would rise against him.*

effective, perhaps,
If I knew its purpose. Come: what is it?

SENTRY. A dreadful thing . . . I don't know
how to put it—

CREON. Out with it!

100 **SENTRY.**   Well, then;
The dead man—

                    Polyneices—

[*Pause. The* SENTRY *is overcome, fumbles for words.* CREON *waits impassively.*]

                              out there—
                         someone,—

New dust on the slimy flesh!

[*Pause. No sign from* CREON.]

Someone has given it burial that way, and
105 Gone . . .

[*Long pause.* CREON *finally speaks with deadly control.*]

❶ **CREON.** And the man who dared do this?

SENTRY.   I swear I
Do not know! You must believe me!

                                    Listen:
The ground was dry, not a sign of digging,
no,
Not a wheeltrack in the dust, no trace of
anyone.
It was when they relieved us this morning:
110   and one of them,
The corporal, pointed to it.

                              There it was,
The strangest—
          Look:
The body, just mounded over with light
dust: you see?
❷ Not buried really, but as if they'd covered
it
Just enough for the ghost's peace. And no
115   sign
Of dogs or any wild animal that had been there.
And then what a scene there was! Every man
of us
Accusing the other: we all proved the other
man did it,
We all had proof that we could not have done
it.

676 ◆ *Drama*

120 We were ready to take hot iron in our hands,
Walk through fire, swear by all the gods,
It was not I!
I do not know who it was, but it was not I!

[CREON'S *rage has been mounting steadily, but the* SENTRY *is too intent upon his story to notice it.*]

And then, when this came to nothing,
someone said
125 A thing that silenced us and made us stare
Down at the ground: you had to be told the
news,
And one of us had to do it! We threw the
dice,
And the bad luck fell to me. So here I am,
No happier to be here than you are to have
me:
Nobody likes the man who brings bad
130   news.

CHORAGOS. I have been wondering, King:
can it be that the gods have done this?

CREON. [*Furiously*] Stop!
Must you doddering
wrecks
Go out of your heads
entirely? "The gods!"
135 Intolerable!
The gods favor this
corpse? Why? How
had he served them?
Tried to loot their temples, burn their
images,
Yes, and the whole State, and its laws with
it!
Is it your senile opinion that the gods love
to honor bad men?
A pious thought!—
140   No, from the very beginning
There have been those who have whispered
together,

◆ *Literature
and Your Life*

Why is it difficult
to accept that a
stand you've taken
could be wrong?

◆ **Build Vocabulary**

anarchists (an´ ər kists) *n.*: Those who disrespect laws or rules

sententiously (sen ten´ shəs lē) *adv.*: Pointed; expressing much in few words

Beyond the Classroom

Career Connection
Sentry A sentry's job is to keep watch and to prevent unauthorized persons from passing. It is a job that still exists in the military, and it has many parallels in nonmilitary life as well. Have students explain the role of sentries, or security guards, in department stores, in retirement communities, at busy intersections, and in public parks. Students may be able to suggest other places where sentries are used.

Community Connection
Cemeteries Different cultures have different ways of honoring and housing the dead. At one time, it was customary to bury people on their own property, but now most communities have special places where the dead are buried or entombed. Many of these cemeteries are affiliated with particular religions. Students may use the Yellow Pages or a local map to determine how many such sites exist in their community.

Stiff-necked <u>anarchists</u>, putting their heads
    together,
Scheming against me in alleys. These are
    the men,
And they have bribed my own guard to do
    this thing.

145 Money!   [*Sententiously*]
There's nothing in the world so
    demoralizing as money.
Down go your cities,
Homes gone, men gone, honest hearts
    corrupted,
Crookedness of all kinds, and all for
    money!

[*To* SENTRY]

                     But you—!
150 I swear by God and by the throne of God,
The man who has done this thing shall
    pay for it!
Find that man, bring him here to me, or
    your death
Will be the least of your problems: I'll
    string you up
Alive, and there will be certain ways to
    make you
155 Discover your employer before you die;
And the process may teach you a lesson
    you seem to have missed:

The dearest profit is sometimes all too
    dear:
That depends on the source. Do you
    understand me?
A fortune won is often misfortune.

SENTRY. King, may I speak?

160 CREON.   Your very voice distresses me.

SENTRY. Are you sure that it is my voice,
    and not your conscience?

CREON. By God, he wants to analyze me
    now!

SENTRY. It is not what I say, but what has
    been done, that hurts you.

CREON. You talk too much.

SENTRY.   Maybe; but I've done nothing.

CREON. Sold your soul for some silver: that's
165   all you've done.

SENTRY. How dreadful it is when the right
    judge judges wrong!

CREON. Your figures of speech
May entertain you now; but unless you
    bring me the man,
You will get little profit from them in the
    end.

[*Exit* CREON *into the Palace.*]

170 SENTRY. "Bring me the man"—!
I'd like nothing better than bringing him
    the man!
But bring him or not, you have seen the
    last of me here.
At any rate, I am safe!

[*Exit* SENTRY.]

Ode 1

CHORUS.   [STROPHE 1]
Numberless are the world's wonders, but
    none
More wonderful than man; the stormgray
    sea
Yields to his prows, the huge crests bear
    him high;
Earth, holy and inexhaustible, is graven
With shining furrows where his plows
5   have gone

Antigone ◆ 677

❻ Clarification Explain that in ancient Greek mythology, a group of gods ruled heaven and earth, which is why the sentry swears by all the gods. When characters speak of a single "God," they mean Zeus, king of the gods.

◆ **Critical Thinking**

❼ Relate Ask students to explain why people sometimes blame the messenger for the bad news he or she brings, as Creon does here. *Because Creon cannot punish the person who actually did the burying, he takes out his anger on the messenger. A rational man would realize that the messenger would not report his own disobedience. Encourage students to give examples from books, movies, television programs, or personal experience when a messenger was blamed for his or her message.*

◆ **Literary Focus**

❽ Protagonist and Antagonist Ask students how the sentry's question reinforces Creon's character as the antagonist. *The sentry's question, as well as the chorus's earlier version of the same question, indicates that the public sides with the person who buried Polyneices*

◆ **Critical Thinking**

❾ Analyze What is significant about the sentry's statement? *The sentry's statement captures the heart of the conflict; it also lends support to Creon as a tragic figure. Although he is usually a "right judge," or rational man, he is allowing his fear and pride to lead him into rash decisions.*

Speaking and Listening Mini-Lesson

Readers Theater
This mini-lesson supports the Speaking and Listening activity in the Idea Bank on page 683.

Introduce the Concept Explain that in a Readers Theater presentation, dialogue is read rather than memorized, and the physical action is not staged.

Develop Background Have students brainstorm for a list of qualities that make an oral presentation impressive. These might include expressive voices, clear diction, and dramatic facial expressions.

Apply the Information Help groups assign roles, and let any extras act as the chorus. Provide time for students to rehearse their scenes. You may choose to have the chorus's lines assigned to individual chorus members, rather than have them read in unison.

Assess the Outcome Once groups have presented their scenes, ask students to assess one another's scenes on the basis of clear speech and dramatic presentation. You may want to use the Peer Assessment guidelines for Oral Interpretation in *Alternative Assessment,* p. 119.

Customize for
Less Proficient Readers
1 Help these students recognize that the chorus's ode does not advance the action, but is a speech in honor of humans' superiority over the world of nature. Clarify the achievements listed: People sail over the seas, they use the earth and animals to fulfill their needs, and, above all, they have reason and intellect.

Customize for
More Advanced Students
2 Have these students add some modern achievements to the chorus's ode. Then encourage students to discuss the achievements and the cost. How is the ancient Greek view of humans' relationship to the natural world similar to and different from a contemporary view?

◆ Critical Thinking
3 Analyze Ask students to name the character who would most agree with this sentiment on the part of the chorus and to explain their answers. *Creon would agree with these words. He is the leader of the state and, above all, upholds the state and its laws. To Creon, breaking the law is an act of anarchy, the worst possible crime.*

◆ Reading Strategy
4 Question the Characters' Motives Ask students what Antigone's motive might be for burying Polyneices a second time. *Her motive for burying him the first time was sisterly love; she wanted his soul to rest. When her work was undone, the same motives drove her to rebury him.*

Customize for
Bodily/Kinesthetic Learners
The Greek tragedies have inspired other artists through the ages. Students who excel at dance might like to choose a scene from the play to choreograph and perform (with or without words or music) for the class.

Year after year, the timeless labor of
  stallions.
[ANTISTROPHE 1]
The lightboned birds and beasts that cling
  to cover,
The lithe fish lighting their reaches of
  dim water,
All are taken, tamed in the net of his
  mind;
10 The lion on the hill, the wild horse
  windy-maned,
Resign to him; and his blunt yoke has
  broken
The <u>sultry</u> shoulders of the mountain bull.
[STROPHE 2]
Words also, and thought as rapid as air,
He fashions to his good use; statecraft is his,
And his the skill that deflects the arrows
  of snow,
15 The spears of winter rain: from every wind
He has made himself secure—from all but
  one:
In the late wind of death he cannot stand.
[ANTISTROPHE 2]
O clear intelligence, force beyond all measure!
20 O fate of man, working both good and evil!
When the laws are kept, how proudly his
  city stands!
When the laws are broken, what of his city
  then?
Never may the anarchic man find rest at
  my hearth,
Never be it said that my thoughts are his
  thoughts.

Scene 2
[*Re-enter* SENTRY *leading* ANTIGONE.]

CHORAGOS. What does this mean? Surely
  this captive woman
Is the Princess, Antigone. Why should she
  be taken?

SENTRY. Here is the one who did it! We
  caught her
In the very act of burying him.—Where is
Creon?

CHORAGOS. Just coming from the house.

[*Enter* CREON, *center.*]

5 **CREON.** What has happened?

678 ◆ Drama

Why have you come back so soon?

SENTRY. [*Expansively*] O King,
A man should never be too sure of anything:
  I would have sworn
That you'd not see me here again: your
  anger
Frightened me so, and the things you
10 threatened me with;
But how could I tell then
That I'd be able to solve the case so soon?
No dice-throwing this time: I was only too
  glad to come!

Here is this woman. She is the guilty one:
15 We found her trying to bury him.
Take her, then; question her; judge her as
  you will.
I am through with the whole thing now,
  and glad of it.

CREON. But this is Antigone! Why have you
  brought her here?

SENTRY. She was burying him, I tell you!

20 **CREON.** [*Severely*] Is this the truth?

SENTRY. I saw her with my own eyes. Can I
  say more?

CREON. The details: come, tell me quickly!

SENTRY. It was like this:
After those terrible threats of yours, King,
We went back and brushed the dust away
  from the body.
25 The flesh was soft by now, and stinking,
So we sat on a hill to windward and kept
  guard.
No napping this time! We kept each other
  awake.
But nothing happened until the white
  round sun
Whirled in the center of the round sky over
  us:
30 Then, suddenly,
A storm of dust roared up from the earth,
  and the sky
Went out, the plain vanished with all its trees

◆ Build Vocabulary
sultry (sul´ trē) *adj.*: Oppressively hot or moist; inflamed

---

Humanities: Theater

The Greek Theater Remind students that all the characters they have met so far would have been played by only three actors (all men) in the original ancient Greek performances. Have students review the play to this point and realize that, excepting the chorus, there are usually only two characters on stage at a time. Encourage students to examine the play to see how the parts might have been broken up. For instance, point out that the actor who plays Antigone cannot also play Creon, since they are on stage at the same time. For more on Greek theater, use the page on Greek theater in *Beyond Literature*, p. 48. You can also use the Literature CD-ROM *How to Read and Understand Drama,* Feature 4 on the Greek chorus.

⑤
In the stinging dark. We closed our eyes
    and endured it.
The whirlwind lasted a long time, but it
    passed;
And then we looked, and there was
35 Antigone!
I have seen
A mother bird come back to a stripped
    nest, heard
Her crying bitterly a broken note or two
For the young ones stolen. Just so, when
    this girl
⑥
Found the bare corpse, and all her love's
40 work wasted,
She wept, and cried on heaven to damn
    the hands
That had done this thing.
            And then she brought more dust
And sprinkled wine three times for her
    brother's ghost.
We ran and took her at once. She was not
    afraid,
⑦
Not even when we charged her with what
45 she had done.
She denied nothing.
            And this was a comfort to me,
And some uneasiness: for it is a good thing
To escape from death, but it is no great
    pleasure
To bring death to a friend.
                Yet I always say
There is nothing so comfortable as your
50 own safe skin!

CREON. [*Slowly, dangerously*] And you,
    Antigone,
You with your head hanging,—do you
    confess this thing?

ANTIGONE. I do. I deny nothing.

CREON. [*To* SENTRY]   You may go.

[*Exit* SENTRY.]

⑧
[*TO* ANTIGONE] Tell me, tell me briefly:
Had you heard my proclamation touching
55 this matter?

ANTIGONE. It was public. Could I help
    hearing it?

CREON. And yet you dared defy the law.

ANTIGONE.   I dared.
It was not God's proclamation. That final
    Justice
That rules the world below makes no such
    laws.

60 Your edict, King, was strong,
But all your strength is weakness itself
    against
The immortal unrecorded laws of God.
They are not merely now: they were, and
    shall be,
Operative forever, beyond man utterly.

I knew I must die, even without your
65 decree:
I am only mortal. And if I must die
Now, before it is my time to die,
Surely this is no hardship: can anyone
Living, as I live, with evil all about me,
Think Death less than a friend? This death
70 of mine
Is of no importance; but if I had left my
    brother
Lying in death unburied, I should have
    suffered.
Now I do not.
            You smile at me. Ah Creon,
Think me a fool, if you like; but it may well
    be   **⑨**
75 That a fool convicts me of folly.

CHORAGOS. Like father, like daughter: both
    headstrong, deaf to reason!
She has never learned to yield.

CREON.   She has much to learn.
The inflexible heart breaks first, the
    toughest iron
Cracks first, and the wildest horses bend
    their necks.
At the pull of the smallest curb.
80   Pride? In a slave?   **⑩**
This girl is guilty of a double insolence,
Breaking the given laws and boasting of it.
Who is the man here,
She or I, if this crime goes unpunished?
85 Sister's child, or more than sister's child,
Or closer yet in blood—she and her sister
Win bitter death for this!

[*TO* SERVANTS]   Go, some of you,

Antigone ◆ 679

Beyond the Classroom

Arrest Ismene. I accuse her equally.
Bring her: you will find her sniffling in the
    house there.

90 Her mind's a traitor: crimes kept in the dark
Cry for light, and the guardian brain
    shudders;
But how much worse than this
Is brazen boasting of barefaced anarchy!

  ANTIGONE. Creon, what more do you want
    than my death?

  CREON.   Nothing.
  That gives me everything.

95 ANTIGONE.   Then I beg you: kill me.
  This talking is a great weariness: your
    words
  Are distasteful to me, and I am sure that
    mine
  Seem so to you. And yet they should not
    seem so:
  I should have praise and honor for what I
    have done.
100 All these men here would praise me
  Were their lips not frozen shut with fear of
    you.

  [*Bitterly*]
  Ah the good fortune of kings,
  Licensed to say and do whatever they
    please!

  CREON. You are alone here in that opinion.

  ANTIGONE. No, they are with me. But they
105   keep their tongues in leash.

  CREON. Maybe. But you are guilty, and they
    are not.

680 ◆ Drama

  ANTIGONE. There is no guilt in reverence for
    the dead.

  CREON. But Eteocles—was he not your
    brother too?

  ANTIGONE. My brother too.

  CREON.   And you insult his memory?

  ANTIGONE. [*Softly*] The dead man would not
110   say that I insult it.

  CREON. He would: for you honor a traitor as
    much as him.

  ANTIGONE. His own brother, traitor or not,
    and equal in blood.

  CREON. He made war on his country.
    Eteocles defended it.

  ANTIGONE. Nevertheless, there are honors
    due all the dead.

  CREON. But not the same for the wicked as
115   for the just.

  ANTIGONE. Ah Creon, Creon,
  Which of us can say what the gods hold
    wicked?

  CREON. An enemy is an enemy, even dead.

  ANTIGONE. It is my nature to join in love, not
    hate.

  CREON. [*Finally losing patience*] Go join
120   them, then; if you must have your love,
  Find it in hell!

  CHORAGOS. But see, Ismene comes:

  [*Enter* ISMENE, *guarded.*]

 Humanities: Architecture

Sophocles' tragedies were formally performed in *amphitheaters,* open-air structures built expressly for public performances. (See the photograph on page 667.) *Amphi-* means "on both sides," or "around," and an amphitheater is designed to place the audience on tiers of seats around the action of a play. The bowl-like structure of Greek amphitheaters resulted in remarkable acoustic properties; audiences could hear the actors' voices clearly, even when they spoke quietly.

  A typical amphitheater might seat the audience in a semicircle facing the *proscenium,* or the front of the stage. At either side between audience and stage would be a corridor called a *parodos,* through which the chorus might enter.

  The most famous amphitheater in the world, the Coliseum, is Roman, not Greek.

Roman amphitheaters were often built to house gladiatorial contests rather than dramas. The stages of Roman amphitheaters were raised above the level on which the chorus performed; those of Greek theaters were set at the same level as the chorus's acting area, or *orchestra.*

  Have students describe any experiences they have had with outdoor performances, either dramatic or musical.

Those tears are sisterly, the cloud
That shadows her eyes rains down gentle
   sorrow.

CREON. You too, Ismene,
Snake in my ordered house, sucking my
125 blood
Stealthily—and all the time I never knew
That these two sisters were aiming at my
   throne!
       Ismene,
Do you confess your share in this crime, or
   deny it?
Answer me.

ISMENE. Yes, if she will let me say so. I am
130 guilty.

ANTIGONE. [*Coldly*] No, Ismene. You have no
   right to say so.
You would not help me, and I will not have
   you help me.

ISMENE. But now I know what you meant;
   and I am here
To join you, to take my share of punishment.

ANTIGONE. The dead man and the gods who
135 rule the dead
Know whose act this was. Words are not
   friends.

ISMENE. Do you refuse me, Antigone? I want
   to die with you:
I too have a duty that I must discharge to
   the dead.

ANTIGONE. You shall not lessen my death by
   sharing it.

ISMENE. What do I care for life when you are
140 dead?

ANTIGONE. Ask Creon. You're always hanging
   on his opinions.

ISMENE. You are laughing at me. Why,
   Antigone?

ANTIGONE. It's a joyless laughter, Ismene.

ISMENE.   But can I do nothing?

ANTIGONE. Yes. Save yourself. I shall not
   envy you.
There are those who will praise you; I shall
145 have honor, too.

ISMENE. But we are equally guilty!

ANTIGONE.   No more, Ismene.
You are alive, but I belong to Death.

CREON. [*To the* CHORUS] Gentlemen, I beg
   you to observe these girls:
One has just now lost her mind; the other,
150 It seems, has never had a mind at all.

ISMENE. Grief teaches the steadiest minds to
   waver, King.

CREON. Yours certainly did, when you
   assumed guilt with the guilty!

ISMENE. But how could I go on living
   without her?

CREON.   You are.
She is already dead.

ISMENE.   But your own son's bride!

CREON. There are places enough for him to
155 push his plow.
I want no wicked women for my sons!

ISMENE. O dearest Haimon, how your father
   wrongs you!

CREON. I've had enough of your childish
   talk of marriage!

CHORAGOS. Do you really intend to steal this
   girl from your son?

CREON. No; Death will do that for me.

160 **CHORAGOS.**   Then she must die?

CREON. [*Ironically*] You dazzle me.
         —But enough of this talk!

[*To* GUARDS] You, there, take them away and
   guard them well:
For they are but women, and even brave
   men run
When they see Death coming.

[*Exit* ISMENE, ANTIGONE, *and* GUARDS.]

Antigone ◆ 681

◆ **Literary Focus**

❺ **Protagonist and Antagonist**
Ask students why Creon thinks
Antigone and Ismene have betrayed
him. *He thinks they are trying to take
power away from him.*

◆ **Reading Strategy**

❻ **Question the Characters'
Motives** Have students speculate on
the possible reasons that Antigone
will not allow Ismene to help her.
*Students may say that Antigone is
offended because Ismene is offering her
help too late, that Antigone wants to
protect Ismene, or that Antigone wants
all the glory of defiance for herself.*

◆ **Reading Strategy**

❼ **Question the Characters'
Motives** Ismene feared death earlier
in the play. Discuss with students
why, now, she wants to die, even
though she is innocent of any crime
against the state. *Students may say
that Ismene feels guilty for not supporting her sister, or perhaps she feels guilty
for not obeying the law of the gods.*

❽ **Interpret** Which of the sisters
does Creon think "lost her mind"?
Which "never had a mind"? *Suggested
answer: Creon is saying that Ismene has
just lost her mind when she decided to
join Antigone. To Creon, Antigone's actions
have been mad all along, so she "never
had a mind."*

◆ **Critical Thinking**

❾ **Make Judgments** Creon feels
that the women require guarding
because they will naturally try to
escape their fate. Ask students: How
accurate is Creon's assessment of
Antigone and Ismene? *He may be
right about Ismene, but Antigone has no
fear of death; she is braver than the
"brave men" Creon mentions.*

Humanities: Literature

Tragedy Then and Now While
Sophocles fulfilled the requirements for
tragedy set forth by Aristotle in his *Poetics*,
drama evolved and changed over history, so
that modern dramatists do not now feel
they must remain within the confines of
Aristotle's famous definition. Willy Loman in
Arthur Miller's *Death of a Salesman,* and
Blanche Dubois in Tennessee Williams's *A*
Streetcar Named Desire, for example, are
neither of noble birth nor character. They
are, on the other hand, very ordinary characters with whom the audience can more
easily identify.

Two other requirements for tragedy,
however, do survive in modern drama: that
the audience be made to feel "pity and terror," and that at the end, a "catharsis," a
cleansing, purification, or purging of the
emotions, takes place. In other words, the
audience sympathizes with and fears for the
protagonist, and then feels emotionally
drained or exhausted at the end of the play.

Lead students to identify the sources of
pity, terror, and catharsis in tragic plots of
movies they have seen, and in *Antigone,* as
they progress through the play.

Customize for
Less Proficient Readers
Review with these students
Antigone's family background to
make sure they grasp that Antigone
has died not only because she defied
Creon, but because her family is
cursed by her father's unwitting
crimes against the gods.

Customize for
*Logical/Mathematical
Learners*
Have these students order the
events leading up to Antigone's arrest
and sentencing on a timeline. Remind
students that even events that occur
offstage must be included.

Answers

◆ *Literature and Your Life*

Reader's Response Possible
answers: Those students who agree
with Antigone might respond that to
bury a beloved brother is to obey a
higher order, which is only decent
and natural, regardless of the consequences. Those who agree with
Ismene may say that nothing is
accomplished by disobeying Creon's
order so why take the risk?

Thematic Focus Although students will recall that the proclaimed
punishment was stoning, they may
feel there is still time for Creon to
relent. Most students will probably
feel that Antigone's courage will
enable her to face whatever consequences Creon chooses.

☑ **Check Your Comprehension**

1. Polyneices fought as bravely as his
   honored brother, Eteocles.
   Antigone feels that burying him
   would be a holy crime, obeying
   the supreme authority of the
   gods.
2. Creon reacts in a violent rage,
   threatening to kill the very messenger who brought him the
   news, unless he finds the man
   who did it.

Ode II

CHORUS. [STROPHE 1]

Fortunate is the man who has never tasted
  God's vengeance!
Where once the anger of heaven has struck,
  that house is shaken
Forever: damnation rises behind each child
Like a wave cresting out of the black
  northeast,
5 When the long darkness undersea roars up
And bursts drumming death upon the
  windwhipped sand.

[ANTISTROPHE 1]

I have seen this gathering sorrow from time
  long past
Loom upon Oedipus' children: generation
  from generation
Takes the compulsive rage of the enemy
  god.
10 So lately this last flower of Oedipus' line
Drank the sunlight! but now a passionate
  word
And a handful of dust have closed up all its
  beauty.

◆ **Build Vocabulary**

transcends (tran sendz´) *v.*: Goes above or
beyond limits; exceeds

[STROPHE 2]

What mortal arrogance
Transcends the wrath of Zeus?[7]
Sleep cannot lull him, nor the effortless
15 long months
Of the timeless gods: but he is young
  forever,
And his house is the shining day of high
  Olympos.[8]
All that is and shall be,
And all the past, is his.
No pride on earth is free of the curse of
20 heaven.

[ANTISTROPHE 2]

The straying dreams of men
May bring them ghosts of joy:
But as they drowse, the waking embers
  burn them;
Or they walk with fixed eyes, as blind men
  walk.
But the ancient wisdom speaks for our
25 own time:
  *Fate works most for woe
  With Folly's fairest show.*
Man's little pleasure is the spring of sorrow.

7. **Zeus** (zōōs): King of all Greek gods, he was
believed to throw lightning bolts when angry.
8. **Olympos** (ō lim´ pes): Mountain in Greece, also
known as Olympus, where the gods were believed to
live in ease and splendor.

Guide for Responding

◆ *Literature and Your Life*

Reader's Response Antigone and Ismene disagree over the burial of Polyneices. With whom do
you agree?
Thematic Focus Antigone chooses to do what
she thinks is right, rather than give in to Creon's
law. What consequences do you think she will face
as a result of her choices?

☑ **Check Your Comprehension**

1. Why does Antigone feel that her brother
   should get a proper burial?
2. How does Creon react to the news of
   Polyneices' burial?

◆ **Critical Thinking**

INTERPRET
1. Explain what Ismene means when she says,
   "We are only women,/We cannot fight with
   men, Antigone!" [Interpret]
2. How might Ismene's advice to her sister seem
   cowardly to some readers? [Analyze]
3. In his argument with Antigone, Creon declares
   "An enemy is an enemy, even dead." What
   does he mean? Do you agree? [Interpret]

EXTEND
4. Compare and contrast the government of
   Creon in Thebes with a modern-day government. [Social Studies Link]

682 ◆ *Drama*

◆ **Critical Thinking**

1. Sample response: Ismene
   means that women are not
   as physically strong as men,
   nor are they trained as soldiers. In addition, her
   words reflect that women
   were seen as lower than
   men in ancient Greek society.
2. While some students may
   understand Ismene's fear,

others may feel that for
some beliefs, no price is
too high.
3. Suggested responses: This
   statement shows Creon's
   inflexibility and lack of judgment as a new ruler. To
   demonstrate his power, he
   is willing to punish someone even after the person
   is dead. Some students may
   argue that the dead can

have no enemies.
4. Sample responses: In
   Thebes, Creon governed by
   his will, whether it be good
   or ill. A modern (democratic) government is set up
   with laws to restrain and
   balance the powers that
   affect its citizens.

Guide for Responding (continued)

◆ Reading Strategy

QUESTION THE CHARACTERS' MOTIVES

To fully understand the action of the play, **question the characters' motives.**

1. What was Ismene's motive for not going along with Antigone at first?
2. What is Antigone's motive for burying Polyneices?
3. What is Creon's motive for insisting on Antigone's death?

◆ Literary Focus

PROTAGONIST AND ANTAGONIST

A **protagonist** is the main character of a literary work, and an **antagonist** is a character or force in conflict with the main character.

1. Describe the conflict between Antigone and Creon.
2. What qualities of each character contribute to the conflict?
3. Give examples of actions and feelings that show that Antigone is the protagonist and Creon is the antagonist.

◆ Build Vocabulary

USING THE ROOT -trans-

Knowing that the root -trans- means "through," "above," or "across" will help you define other words that contain -trans-. On your paper, match each word with its appropriate definition.

1. transparent   a. send through the air
2. transmit   b. lift up and move
3. transplant   c. pierce through
4. transfix   d. lets light shine through

USING THE WORD BANK

Copy the words from Column A into your notebook. Next to each word, write the letter of its definition from Column B.

Column A	Column B
1. sated	a. pointedly
2. anarchists	b. oppressively hot or moist
3. sententiously	c. go above or beyond the limit
4. sultry	d. satisfied or pleased
5. transcend	e. those who disrespect rules

◆ Build Grammar Skills

COORDINATING CONJUNCTIONS

A **coordinating conjunction** links two words or grammatical structures of equal importance.

Practice Rewrite each pair of sentences as one sentence, with the coordinating conjunction *but, for, or,* or *and.* Choose the conjunction based on the way ideas are linked.

1. Antigone wants to bury her brother. Ismene is afraid to break the law that Creon decreed.
2. Oedipus learned the truth of what he had done. Antigone accompanied her father into exile.
3. Both Antigone and Ismene grieved. Their brothers killed each other during battle.
4. Ismene could choose to stand up to Creon. She could accept scorn from her sister, Antigone.

Writing Application Write a summary of *Antigone* from the Prologue through Scene 2. Combine clauses using each of the following coordinating conjunctions at least once: *yet, for, and,* and *but.*

Idea Bank

Writing

1. **Newspaper Article** Write a brief newspaper article with a headline that would have appeared in a Thebes newspaper (if newspapers existed then) the day after Polyneices was buried. Answer the questions *who? what? where? when? why?* in your article.

2. **Letter** Imagine that you are Ismene. Write a letter to your sister, Antigone, before her arrest by the sentry. What would you tell her about her plans to bury Polyneices? How would you present this delicate situation?

Speaking and Listening

3. **Readers Theater** With a small group, rehearse and present a scene from *Antigone* in a readers theater performance for your class. Have a group of students perform as the chorus and assign individuals for the other roles. **[Performing Arts Link]**

Antigone ◆ 683

Answers

◆ Reading Strategy

1. Ismene's motive is fear for her life.
2. Antigone's motives are love for her brother, honor and loyalty to the gods, and a belief in divine law.
3. As a new ruler he must establish himself as all powerful.

◆ Literary Focus

1. The conflict centers on which is more important: human, civil law or divine law and family loyalty.
2. Antigone's loyalty to her brother, her strong character, and her refusal to compromise her ideals contribute to her conflict with Creon, who is inflexible, proud, and fearful of any challenge to his authority.
3. Antigone is a sympathetic character who readers want to see succeed because her actions seem admirable and noble. Creon's character is not sympathetic because his actions seem cruel and self-promoting.

◆ Build Vocabulary

Using the Root -trans-
1. d.   2. a.   3. b.   4. c.

Using the Word Bank
1. d.   2. e.   3. a.   4. b.   5. c.

◆ Build Grammar Skills

Practice
1. Antigone wants to bury her brother, *but* Ismene is afraid to break the law that Creon decreed.
2. Oedipus learned the truth of what he had done, *and* Antigone accompanied her father into exile.
3. Both Antigone and Ismene grieved, *for* their brothers killed each other during battle.
4. Ismene could choose to stand up to Creon, *or* she could accept scorn from her sister, Antigone.

 Idea Bank

Customizing for
Performance Levels
Following are suggestions for matching Idea Bank topics with your students' performance levels:
   Less Advanced: 2
   Average: 1
   More Advanced: 1, 3

Customizing for
Learning Modalities
Following are the suggestions for matching Idea Bank topics with your students' learning modalities:
   Verbal/Linguistic: 1, 2, 3
   Interpersonal: 1, 2
   Intrapersonal: 3

✓ ASSESSMENT OPTIONS

Formal Assessment Selection Test, pp. 170–172, Assessment Resources Software. The selection test is designed so that it can be easily customized to the ability levels of your students.

PORTFOLIO ASSESSMENT
Use the following rubrics in *Alternative Assessment* to assess student writing:
Newspaper Article: Summary Rubric
Letter: Expression Rubric

Writer's Solution

For additional instruction and practice, use the lesson in the **Writing Lab CD-ROM** on Eight Parts of Speech, and page 22 on Conjunctions and Interjections and page 120 on Sentence Combining in *Writer's Solution Grammar Practice Book.*

Guide for Reading

OBJECTIVES

1. To read, comprehend, and interpret a Greek drama
2. To relate a Greek drama to personal experience
3. To identify with a character in a play
4. To recognize a tragic character
5. To build vocabulary in context and learn the word root -chor-
6. To use the correct pronoun case in incomplete clauses
7. To write a scene of conflict using correct format for a screenplay
8. To respond to the drama through writing, speaking and listening, and projects

SKILLS INSTRUCTION

Vocabulary:
Word Roots: -chor-
Grammar:
Pronoun Case in Incomplete Clauses
Reading Strategy:
Identify With a Character
Literary Focus:
Tragic Character

Writing:
Format for a Screenplay
Speaking and Listening:
Mock Trial (teacher edition)
Critical Viewing:
Infer

PORTFOLIO OPPORTUNITIES

Writing: Introduction; Final Speech; Editorial
Writing Mini-Lesson: Scene of Conflict
Speaking and Listening: Mock Trial; Film Response
Project: Multimedia Presentation

Interest Grabber Ask students, now that they have read the first part of *Antigone,* whether they would prefer to have Antigone or Ismene for a friend, and to explain their answers. Which qualities in each would make that person a more valuable friend? After discussing this question, ask students which character they would prefer to have as a sister. If their response to the second question is different, ask students why they might look for qualities in a friend different from the qualities they would value in a close relative.

◆ Review and Anticipate

In Scenes 1 and 2, Antigone decides to give her brother Polyneices a proper burial, defying the orders of her uncle Creon, the ruler of Thebes. When Creon finds out, he orders her put to death, claiming that he cannot allow her to disobey him just because she is his niece. Both Creon and Antigone seem locked in a course of action by circumstances and their beliefs. As Scene 2 ends, the Chorus sings, "*Fate works most for woe / With Folly's fairest show. / Man's little pleasure is the spring of sorrow.*" Notice how the events in the remainder of the play carry out the statement that Fate works most for woe.

◆ Literary Focus

TRAGIC CHARACTER

In this play, two strong-willed people, Creon and Antigone, can both be seen as tragic. A **tragic character** is a significant person who experiences a reversal of fortune as a result of fate or a flaw or weakness in his or her character. Critics debate who the tragic hero is in *Antigone*. Some claim Creon fits the definition better, although Antigone's name has been used in the title. The exchanges between Creon and Antigone lead to an irreversible point from which Creon's pride will not allow him to retreat. His actions bring about the tragic events that follow. Others see the flaw in Antigone. To them, her determination is a form of pride, which makes her unyielding and leads to her doom.

◆ Build Grammar Skills

PRONOUN CASE IN INCOMPLETE CLAUSES

In certain kinds of English constructions, some words are omitted because they are understood. When a pronoun occurs in an **incomplete clause,** its case is what it would be if the construction were complete. Clauses beginning with *than* or *as* are often incomplete. Look at this line from Scene 3:

Let's lose to a man, at least! Is a woman stronger than we?

The understood word in this line is *are*. The completed clause therefore would be "Is a woman stronger than *we are*?" When you complete the clause, you can see that *we* is the correct pronoun; you would not say, "Is a woman stronger than *us are?*"

684 ◆ Drama

◆ Reading Strategy

IDENTIFY WITH A CHARACTER

When you **identify with a character**, you put yourself in the character's place. Because you take on his or her feelings or issues, and you experience what he or she does, you sympathize with that character. You may even feel as if you *are* that character. For example, you may suffer with Antigone as she struggles to do what she thinks is right, or you may feel Ismene's fear of punishment. Putting yourself in a character's place can give you greater insight into that character's motives and the events of the play.

◆ Build Vocabulary

WORD ROOTS: -chor-

An important feature of Greek tragedy is the chorus; a member of the chorus is called a *chorister*. The root of *chorister* and *chorus* is -chor-, which comes from Terpsichore (terp sik´ ə rē), the Greek Muse of dance and song.

WORD BANK

Before you read, preview this list of words from the play.

deference
vile
piety
blasphemy
lamentation
chorister

 Prentice Hall Literature Program Resources

REINFORCE / RETEACH / EXTEND

Selection Support
Build Vocabulary: Word Roots: -chor-, p. 200
Build Grammar Skills: Pronoun Case, p. 201
Reading Strategy: Identify With a Character, p. 202
Literary Focus: Tragic Character, p. 203

Strategies for Diverse Students Needs, p. 49

Beyond Literature Government in Ancient Greece, p. 49
Daily Language Practice Week 12, Greek Theater, p. 28

Formal Assessment Selection Test, pp. 173–175; Assessment Resources Software

Alternative Assessment, p. 49

Writing and Language Transparencies
Daily Language Practice, Week 12, p. 123

Art Transparencies Transparency 15

Resource Pro CD-ROM *Antigone,* Part 2— includes all resource materials and customizable lesson plan

Listening to Literature Audiocassettes
Antigone, Part 2

ANTIGONE

SCENES 3 THROUGH 5

Sophocles

Translated by Dudley Fitts
and Robert Fitzgerald

Scene 3

CHORAGOS. But here is Haimon, King, the
last of all your sons.
Is it grief for Antigone that brings him here,
And bitterness at being robbed of his bride?

[*Enter* HAIMON.]

CREON. We shall soon see, and no need of
diviners.[1]
  —Son,
You have heard my final judgment on that
5 girl:
Have you come here hating me, or have you
come
With <u>deference</u> and with love, whatever I
do?

HAIMON. I am your son, father. You are my
guide.
You make things clear for me, and I obey
you.
No marriage means more to me than your
10 continuing wisdom.

CREON. Good. That is the way to behave:
subordinate
Everything else, my son, to your father's
will.

This is what a man prays for, that he may
get
Sons attentive and dutiful in his house,
15 Each one hating his father's enemies,
Honoring his father's friends. But if his
sons
Fail him, if they turn out unprofitably,
What has he fathered but trouble for
himself
And amusement for the malicious?
  So you are right
20 Not to lose your head over this woman.
Your pleasure with her would soon grow
cold, Haimon,
And then you'd have a hellcat in bed and
elsewhere.
Let her find her husband in Hell!
Of all the people in this city, only she
25 Has had contempt for my law and broken it.

Do you want me to show myself weak before
the people?
Or to break my sworn word? No, and I will
not.
The woman dies.
I suppose she'll plead "family ties." Well,
let her.

◆ **Build Vocabulary**

deference (def′ ər əns) *n.*: Yielding in thought

Antigone ◆ 685

---

1. **diviners** (də vin′ erz): Those who forecast the
future.

◆ **Preparing for Standardized Tests**

Grammar and Language The Build Grammar
Skills for this selection helps students to understand a special case that may come up in their
own writing or on the writing skills portions of
standardized tests: In an incomplete clause, the
case of a pronoun should be the same as it would
be if the construction were complete. Students
may be asked to choose the best way of expressing the underlined portion of a sentence, as in the
following:

No one regrets losing the game <u>more than
me</u>. *(B)*
(A) more than me
(B) more than I
(C) more than myself
(D) more than my self

Students will perform better on such items if
they learn to supply the *understood,* or left-out
word(s) in such sentences: No one regrets losing
the game more than I *do.*

Literary Focus

① Tragic Character Ask students to identify a quality in Creon's character, suggested in this passage, that might drive him into a conflict that cannot be resolved. *Lead students to point out Creon's rigidity and tendency to see any deviation from submission to his will as "anarchy," and a threat to the state.*

Reading Strategy

② Identify With a Character Ask students to put themselves in Haimon's place and indicate, based on what they know of his character, what they think his concerns are as he speaks, and to explain their answers. Is he more concerned with Antigone or with public opinion toward his father? *Haimon seems more concerned about his father's reputation. However, he is probably using this argument to achieve his real purpose—saving Antigone.*

Literary Focus

③ Tragic Character Haimon points out that Creon has a temper and that he is not willing to listen rationally to the opinions of others.

---

30 If I permit my own family to rebel,
How shall I earn the world's obedience?
Show me the man who keeps his house in hand,
He's fit for public authority.
           I'll have no dealings
With lawbreakers, critics of the government:
Whoever is chosen to govern should be
35 obeyed—
Must be obeyed, in all things, great and small,
Just and unjust! O Haimon,
The man who knows how to obey, and that man only,
Knows how to give commands when the time comes.
40 You can depend on him, no matter how fast
The spears come: he's a good soldier, he'll stick it out.

Anarchy, anarchy! Show me a greater evil!
This is why cities tumble and the great houses rain down,
This is what scatters armies!

No, no: good lives are made so by
45 discipline.
We keep the laws then, and the lawmakers,
And no woman shall seduce us. If we must lose,
Let's lose to a man, at least! Is a woman stronger than we?

CHORAGOS. Unless time has rusted my wits,
What you say, King, is said with point and
50 dignity.

HAIMON. [*Boyishly earnest*] Father:
Reason is God's crowning gift to man, and you are right
To warn me against losing mine. I cannot say—
I hope that I shall never want to say!—that you
Have reasoned badly. Yet there are other
55 men
Who can reason, too; and their opinions might be helpful.
You are not in a position to know everything
That people say or do, or what they feel:
Your temper terrifies them—everyone

686 ◆ Drama

Will tell you only what
60 you like to hear.
But I, at any rate, can listen; and I have heard them
Muttering and whispering in the dark about this girl.
They say no woman has ever, so unreasonably,
Died so shameful a death for a generous act:
"She covered her brother's body. Is this
65 indecent?
She kept him from dogs and vultures. Is this a crime?
Death?—She should have all the honor that we can give her!"

This is the way they talk out there in the city.

You must believe me:
Nothing is closer to me than your
70 happiness.
What could be closer? Must not any son
Value his father's fortune as his father does his?
I beg you, do not be unchangeable:
Do not believe that you alone can be right.
75 The man who thinks that,
The man who maintains that only he has the power
To reason correctly, the gift to speak, the soul—
A man like that, when you know him, turns out empty.

It is not reason never to yield to reason!

In flood time you can see how some trees
80 bend,
And because they bend, even their twigs are safe,
While stubborn trees are torn up, roots and all.
And the same thing happens in sailing:
Make your sheet fast, never slacken—and

◆ Literary Focus
What traits does Haimon point out to Creon that make the king a tragic character? ③

◆ Build Vocabulary
vile (vīl) *adj.*: Extremely disgusting

Block Scheduling Strategies

Consider these suggestions to take advantage of extended class time:

- Invite students to listen to part or all of the selection on audiocassette. Hold a discussion in which they explain how hearing the dialogue spoken aloud enhanced their appreciation of the drama.
- Allow time for students to visit an electronic museum exhibit of life in ancient Greece. For Internet address, see p. 698.
- Use Daily Language Practice for Week 12. You may put the transparency on an overhead projector and have studnets write the passages correctly or you may dictate the passages to students.
- As a class, complete the Literary Focus page on tragic character in *Selection Support*, p. 203. After students have read the selection, allow them to meet in groups to complete the Literary Focus questions on page 699.
- Organize discussion groups in which students can explore the strengths and weaknesses of Haimon's and Creon's arguments.

686

over you go,
Head over heels and under: and there's
85 your voyage.
Forget you are angry! Let yourself be
moved!
I know I am young; but please let me say
this:
The ideal condition
Would be, I admit, that men should be
right by instinct;
90 But since we are all too likely to go astray,
The reasonable thing is to learn from those
who can teach.

CHORAGOS. You will do well to listen to him,
King,
If what he says is sensible. And you,
Haimon,
Must listen to your father.—Both speak
well.

CREON. You consider it right for a man of
95 my years and experience
To go to school to a boy?

HAIMON.   It is not right
If I am wrong. But if I am young, and right,
What does my age matter?

CREON. You think it right to stand up for an
anarchist?

HAIMON. Not at all. I pay no respect to
100 criminals.

CREON. Then she is not a criminal?

HAIMON. The City would deny it, to a man.

CREON. And the City proposes to teach me
how to rule?

HAIMON. Ah. Who is it that's talking like a
boy now?

CREON. My voice is the one voice giving
105 orders in this City!

HAIMON. It is no City if it takes orders from
one voice.

CREON. The State is the King!

HAIMON.   Yes, if the State is a desert.

[*Pause*]

CREON. This boy, it seems, has sold out to a
woman.

HAIMON. If you are a woman: my concern is
only for you.

CREON. So? Your "concern"! In a public
110 brawl with your father!

HAIMON. How about you, in a public brawl
with justice?

CREON. With justice, when all that I do is
within my rights?

HAIMON. You have no right to trample on
God's right.

CREON. [*Completely out of control*] Fool,
adolescent fool! Taken in by a woman!

HAIMON. You'll never see me taken in by
115 anything vile.

CREON. Every word you say is for her!

HAIMON. [*quietly, darkly*]   And for you.
And for me. And for the gods under the
earth.

CREON. You'll never marry her while she
lives.

HAIMON. Then she must die.—But her death
will cause another.

120 **CREON.** Another?
Have you lost your senses? Is this an open
threat?

HAIMON. There is no threat in speaking to
emptiness.

CREON. I swear you'll regret this superior
tone of yours!
You are the empty one!

HAIMON.   If you were not my
father,
125 I'd say you were perverse.

CREON. You girlstruck
fool, don't play at
words with me!

HAIMON. I am sorry.
You prefer silence.

> ◆ **Reading Strategy**
> In what ways can you
> identify with Haimon
> in this scene?

Antigone ◆ 687

◆ Critical Thinking

❹ Make Judgments Invite students to summarize Creon's and
Haimon's arguments in this passage.
Then present them with a choice:
Who presents the more convincing
argument? *Creon implies that a man's
judgment will always be better than a
boy's. Then he argues that Antigone
broke the law; she is a criminal, and
therefore Haimon should not stand up
for her. Haimon argues that age is
immaterial; what counts is who is right.
He then implies that, if most people in
the city deny that Antigone is a criminal,
she must not be one. Students should
note that, while Haimon makes a good
point about the irrelevance of age in an
argument, Creon's argument against
Antigone is stronger than Haimon's
argument in her favor.*

◆ Critical Thinking

❺ Compare and Contrast Ask
students to compare the political
positions expressed by Creon and
Haimon. *Students may say that Creon
represents a tyrannical position—that a
city must be ruled by one person.
Haimon believes that no one person can
rule without the consent of his or her
subjects.*

◆ Critical Thinking

❻ Compare and Contrast Ask
students to indicate what concepts of
"justice" Creon and Haimon argue
for. *Elicit answers to the effect that
Creon speaks of "justice" in purely legal
or civic terms, while Haimon claims to
represent divine justice, that set down by
the gods.*

◆ Critical Thinking

❼ Interpret Ask students to
explain how Creon has interpreted
Haimon's previous statement.
*Students should explain that Creon sees
the statement that Antigone's "death will
cause another" as a threat on Haimon's
part; that Haimon will take Creon's life.*

◆ Reading Strategy

❽ Identify With a Character
Students will probably identify with
the frustration Haimon feels at being
unable to reason with his father; this
has led him to abandon attempts at
persuasion and fall into name-calling.

687

❶ **Tragic Character** Have students discuss what they think Creon hopes to achieve if he carries out this threat. Do they think his motive is revenge and anger or something else? Remind students to base their answers on what they know of Creon. *Based on what students have learned about Creon, they should say that Creon needs to show the city of Thebes that no act against the state will go unpunished. He is making an example of Antigone. His pride and stubbornness blind him to the potential consequences Haimon warns him against.*

◆ **Critical Thinking**

❷ **Evaluate** Encourage students to evaluate the significance of providing food to the condemned person. *Students should recognize that in a society as bound by ritual and convention as ancient Greek society is, the providing of food is a symbol that indicates that the state did not actually kill the condemned person, but that some other force intervened. This is consistent with the Greek concept of fate.*

CREON.   Now, by God—!
I swear, by all the gods in heaven above us,
You'll watch it, I swear you shall!

❶ [*To the* SERVANTS]   Bring her out!
      Bring the woman out! Let her die before
130   his eyes!
      Here, this instant, with her bridegroom
        beside her!

HAIMON. Not here, no; she will not die here,
      King.
And you will never see my face again.
Go on raving as long as you've a friend to
      endure you.

[*Exit* HAIMON.]

135 CHORAGOS. Gone, gone.
Creon, a young man in a rage is dangerous!

CREON. Let him do, or dream to do, more
      than a man can.
He shall not save these girls from death.

CHORAGOS.   These girls?
You have sentenced them both?

CREON.   No, you are right.
I will not kill the one whose hands are
140   clean.

CHORAGOS. But Antigone?

❷ CREON. [*Somberly*] I will carry her far away
Out there in the wilderness, and lock her
Living in a vault of stone. She shall have
      food,
As the custom is, to absolve the State of her
      death.
145 And there let her pray to the gods of hell:

They are her only gods:
Perhaps they will show her an escape from
      death,
Or she may learn,
              though late,
That <u>piety</u> shown the dead is pity in vain.

[*Exit* CREON.]

Ode III

CHORUS.   [STROPHE]
Love, unconquerable
Waster of rich men, keeper
Of warm lights and all-night vigil
In the soft face of a girl:
5 Sea-wanderer, forest-visitor!
Even the pure Immortals cannot escape
     you,
And mortal man, in his one day's dusk,
Trembles before your glory.

              [ANTISTROPHE]
Surely you swerve upon ruin
10 The just man's consenting heart,
As here you have made bright anger
Strike between father and son—
And none has conquered but Love!
A girl's glance working the will of heaven:
15 Pleasure to her alone who mocks us,
Merciless Aphrodite.[2]

---

2. Aphrodite (af rə dīt′ ē): Goddess of beauty and love, who is sometimes vengeful in her retaliation for offenses.

◆ **Build Vocabulary**
piety (pī′ ə tē) *n.*: Holiness; respect for the divine
blasphemy (blas′ fə mē) *n.*: Disrespectful action or speech against a deity

Scene 4

CHORAGOS. [*As* ANTIGONE *enters guarded*] But
      I can no longer stand in awe of this,
Nor, seeing what I see, keep back my tears.
Here is Antigone, passing to that chamber
Where all find sleep at last.

ANTIGONE.   [STROPHE 1]
5 Look upon me, friends, and pity me
Turning back at the night's edge to say
Good-by to the sun that shines for me no
      longer;
❸ Now sleepy Death
Summons me down to Acheron,[3] that cold
      shore:
10 There is no bridesong there, nor any music.

CHORUS. Yet not unpraised, not without a
      kind of honor,
You walk at last into the underworld;
❹ Untouched by sickness, broken by no
      sword.
What woman has ever found your way to
      death?

ANTIGONE.   [ANTISTROPHE 1]
15 How often I have heard the story of Niobe,[4]
Tantalos'[5] wretched daughter, how the
      stone
Clung fast about her, ivy-close: and they
      say
The rain falls endlessly
And sifting soft snow; her tears are never
      done.
20 I feel the loneliness of her death in mine.

CHORUS. But she was born of heaven, and
      you

---

3. **Acheron** (akʹ ər än'): River in the underworld over which the dead are ferried.
4. **Niobe** (nīʹ ə bē'): A queen of Thebes who was turned to stone while weeping for her slain children. Her seven sons and seven daughters were killed by Artemis and Apollo, the divine twins of Leto. These gods ruined Niobe after Leto complained that Niobe insulted her by bragging of maternal superiority. It was Zeus who turned the bereaved Niobe to stone, but her lament continued and her tears created a stream.
5. **Tantalos** (tanʹ tə ləs): Niobe's father, who was condemned to eternal frustration in the underworld because he revealed the secrets of the gods. Tantalos was tormented by being kept just out of reach of the water and food that was near him but which he could never reach to enjoy.

Are woman, woman-born. If her death is
      yours,
A mortal woman's, is this not for you
Glory in our world and in the world
      beyond?

ANTIGONE.   [STROPHE 2]
25 You laugh at me. Ah, friends, friends,
Can you not wait until I am dead? O
      Thebes,
O men many-charioted, in love with
      Fortune,
Dear springs of Dirce, sacred Theban
      grove,
Be witnesses for me, denied all pity,
30 Unjustly judged! and think a word of love
For her whose path turns
Under dark earth, where there are no more
      tears.

CHORUS. You have passed beyond human
      daring and come at last
Into a place of stone where Justice sits. **❺**
35 I cannot tell
What shape of your father's guilt appears
      in this.

ANTIGONE.   [ANTISTROPHE 2]
You have touched it at last: that bridal bed
Unspeakable, horror of son and mother
      mingling:
Their crime, infection of all our family!
40 O Oedipus, father and brother!
Your marriage strikes from the grave to
      murder mine.
I have been a stranger here in my own land:
All my life
The blasphemy of my birth has followed me.

45 CHORUS. Reverence is a
      virtue, but strength
Lives in established
      law: that must prevail.
You have made your
      choice,
Your death is the doing of your conscious
      hand.

> ◆ **Literary Focus**
> What flaw in Antigone does the chorus point out? **❻**

ANTIGONE.   [EPODE]
Then let me go, since all your words are
      bitter,
50 And the very light of the sun is cold to me.

Antigone ◆ 689

◆ **Reading Strategy**

❸ Identify With a Character
Have students try to imagine themselves in Antigone's position in this scene and to interpret her feelings. Then ask them why they think Antigone makes no attempt to escape or rally public opinion to her side to oppose Creon's death sentence. *Basing their thoughts on what they have already learned about Antigone, students may infer that she wants to be a martyr.*

Comprehension Check ☑

❹ Ask students to paraphrase what the chorus says to Antigone in this passage. *Lead students to respond that the chorus points out that for Antigone, a mortal woman, to suffer the same fate as Niobe, who was descended from a god, raises Antigone to a more exalted stature.*

◆ **Literary Focus**

❺ Tragic Character Ask students what the Chorus implies about the character of Antigone when they say that she has "passed beyond human daring . . . into a place of stone where Justice sits." *Students may say that the chorus sees Antigone's resolve and determination as far greater than that of most people, but she must still be subject to the laws of the state.*

◆ **Literary Focus**

❻ Tragic Character The Chorus points out that although reverence for the dead is admirable, Antigone made her choice when she opposed human law. Her unwillingness to recognize human law leads to her downfall.

 Humanities: Mythology

Antigone's reference to Niobe would have been very familiar to ancient Greek audiences. They would have known that Niobe was the daughter of Tantalus, who tried to humiliate the gods. As punishment, the gods placed Tantalus in a pool of water he could never drink in the midst of fruit trees he could never reach. Because he offended the gods so seriously, Tantalus' descendents were cursed as well.

Niobe, Tantalus' daughter ruled Thebes with her husband Amphion. When she, like her father,

challenged the gods, the gods struck down her seven children. In her grief, Niobe is said to have turned to stone—a stone forever wet with her tears.

Ask students to identify the connections between the stories of Tantalus and Niobe and Antigone. *Students should notice that Niobe ruled Thebes, where Antigone lives. Like Niobe and her children, Antigone belongs to a cursed family. Excessive pride plays a role in both stories as well.*

❶ The fact that a battle scene is used as decoration for an object meant to be both beautiful and useful suggests that war is a significant facet of life in Greek city-states.

◆ Reading Strategy

❷ **Identify With a Character**
Ask students to put themselves in Creon's place and explain why he is motivated to say what he does in this passage. *Students can note that Creon will be responsible for Antigone's death, even if he does not kill her with his own hands; he is paying only lip service to the law of the gods, who may or may not approve of his actions. He still places his own law above divine law.*

◆ Reading Strategy

❸ **Identify With a Character**
Ask students to explain Antigone's feelings at this point. *While she is certain she is right and feels justified as she goes to her death, she can't help wishing that Creon will be punished for what he is doing to her.*

◆ Literary Focus

❹ **Tragic Character** In what way is having a passionate, unyielding heart a fatal flaw? *Antigone's passion and unwillingness to compromise draw her into the conflict that results in her death.*

Art Transparencies Use Art Transparency 15, *Actors Preparing for a Performance* to give students a context for envisioning ancient drama performances. Place the transparency on the overhead projector. Point out that although this scene was discovered in Pompeii, there are many similarities to classic Greek performances. For instance, draw students' attention to the exaggerated masks and the fact that all the players are men. (The "woman" in the dress is a man with a mask.) The activities include a writing assignment that links Greek drama to a modern parody and a mosaic assignment that can be customized to create a scene from *Antigone*.

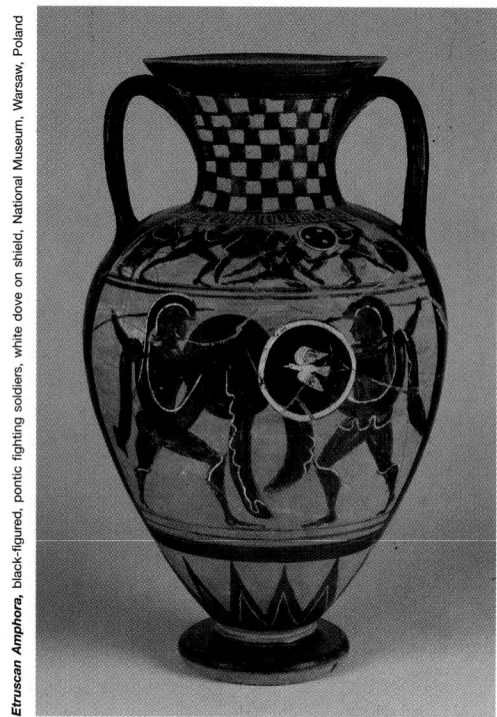

Etruscan Amphora, black-figured, pontic fighting soldiers, white dove on shield, National Museum, Warsaw, Poland

❶ ▲ **Critical Viewing** What does the art on this vessel indicate about the significance of warfare in ancient Greece? **[Infer]**

Lead me to my vigil, where I must have
Neither love nor <u>lamentation</u>; no song, but silence.

[CREON *interrupts impatiently.*]

CREON. If dirges and planned lamentations could put off death,
Men would be singing forever.

[*To the* SERVANTS]   Take her, go!
55 You know your orders: take her to the vault
And leave her alone there. And if she lives
❷ or dies,
That's her affair, not ours: our hands are clean.

◆ Build Vocabulary

lamentation (lam′ ən tā′ shən) *n.*: An expression of grief; weeping

690 ◆ Drama

ANTIGONE. O tomb, vaulted bride-bed in eternal rock,
Soon I shall be with my own again
Where Persephone[6] welcomes the thin
60   ghosts underground:
And I shall see my father again, and you, mother,
And dearest Polyneices—
                              dearest indeed
To me, since it was my hand
That washed him clean and poured the ritual wine:
65 And my reward is death before my time!

And yet, as men's hearts know, I have done no wrong,
I have not sinned before God. Or if I have,
I shall know the truth in death. But if the guilt
Lies upon Creon who judged me, then, I pray,
May his punishment equal my own. **❸**

70 **CHORAGOS.**   O passionate heart,
Unyielding, tormented still by the same winds! **❹**

CREON. Her guards shall have good cause to regret their delaying.

ANTIGONE. Ah! That voice is like the voice of death!

CREON. I can give you no reason to think you are mistaken.

ANTIGONE. Thebes, and you my fathers'
75   gods,
And rulers of Thebes, you see me now, the last
Unhappy daughter of a line of kings,
Your kings, led away to death. You will remember
What things I suffer, and at what men's hands,
Because I would not transgress the laws of
80   heaven.

[*To the* GUARDS, *simply*]

Come: let us wait no longer.

[*Exit* ANTIGONE, *left, guarded.*]

6. **Persephone** (pər sef′ ə nē): Queen of the underworld.

 Humanities: Art

Etruscan Amphora Most of the ancient Greek painting that survives today is found on vases. The vase itself is made of red clay. The artist then covered sections with a black glaze to create the figures and patterns. Vase painters captured the myths, legends, wars, Olympic games, and domestic affairs of ancient Greece. One of the most popular vessels artists chose to paint on was the amphora—a two handled jar such as the one seen here.

Help students connect the art to the play with the following questions:
1. What events from *Antigone* might the scene on this vase portray? *The scene could be showing the battle in which Antigone's two brothers were killed.*
2. Why might an artist choose to capture a scene such as this one? *Battles and heroic deeds were important to the ancient Greeks; capturing them in a painting was one way to tell the stories and preserve their history.*

Ode IV

CHORUS. [STROPHE 1]

All Danae's beauty[7] was locked away
In a brazen cell where the sunlight could
    not come:
A small room, still as any grave, enclosed
    her.
Yet she was a princess too,
And Zeus in a rain of gold poured love
5   upon her.
O child, child,
No power in wealth or war
Or tough sea-blackened ships
Can prevail against untiring Destiny!

[ANTISTROPHE 1]

10 And Dryas' son[8] also, that furious king,
Bore the god's prisoning anger for his pride:
Sealed up by Dionysos[9] in deaf stone,
His madness died among echoes.
So at the last he learned what dreadful
    power
15 His tongue had mocked:
For he had profaned the revels,
And fired the wrath of the nine
Implacable Sisters[10] that love the sound of
    the flute.

[STROPHE 2]

And old men tell a half-remembered tale
Of horror done where a dark ledge splits
20   the sea

---

7. **Danae's** (dan′ ā ēz′) **beauty:** Danae was imprisoned in a brazen, dark tower when it was foretold that she would mother a son who would kill her father. Her beauty attracted Zeus, who visited her in the form of a shower of gold. Perseus was born of the union, and Danae was exiled with the child over stormy seas from which Zeus saved them. Years later, as prophesied, the boy did kill the man he failed to recognize as his grandfather.
8. **Dryas'** (drī′ əs) **son:** Lycorgos (lī kur′ gəs), whose opposition to the worship of Dionysos was severely punished by the gods. He drove the followers of the god from Thrace and was driven insane for having done so. Lycorgos recovered from his madness while imprisoned in a cave, but he was later blinded by Zeus as additional punishment for his offense.
9. **Dionysos** (dī ə nī′ səs): God of wine, in whose honor the Greek plays were performed.
10. **nine Implacable Sisters:** Nine muses, or goddesses, of science and literature. They are the daughters of Zeus and Mnemosyne (ne mas′ ə ne′)—Memory—who inspired invention and influenced the production of art. They are called implacable (im plak′ ə bəl) because they were unforgiving and denied inspiration to anyone who offended them.

And a double surf beats on the gray shores:
How a king's new woman, sick
With hatred for the queen he had
    imprisoned,
Ripped out his two sons' eyes with her
    bloody hands
25 While grinning Ares[11] watched the shuttle
    plunge
Four times: four blind wounds crying for
    revenge,

[ANTISTROPHE 2]

Crying, tears and blood mingled.
    —Piteously born,
Those sons whose mother was of heavenly
    birth!
Her father was the god of the North Wind
30 And she was cradled by gales,
She raced with young colts on the
    glittering hills
And walked untrammeled in the open light:
But in her marriage deathless Fate found
    means
To build a tomb like yours for all her joy.

Scene 5

[*Enter blind* TEIRESIAS, *led by a boy. The opening speeches of* TEIRESIAS *should be in singsong contrast to the realistic lines of* CREON.]

TEIRESIAS. This is the way the blind man
    comes, Princes, Princes,
Lock-step, two heads lit by the eyes of one.

CREON. What new thing have you to tell us,
    old Teiresias?

TEIRESIAS. I have much to tell you: listen to
    the prophet, Creon.

CREON. I am not aware that I have ever
5   failed to listen.

TEIRESIAS. Then you have done wisely, King,
    and ruled well.

CREON. I admit my debt to you.[12] But what
    have you to say?

---

11. **Ares** (er′ ēz): God of war.
12. **my debt to you:** Creon is here admitting that he would not have acquired the throne if Teiresias had not moved the former king, Oedipus, to an investigation of his own background that led eventually to his downfall. The news of his personal history, uncovered with help from Teiresias, forced Oedipus into exile.

Antigone ◆ 691

◆ Critical Thinking

❺ Make Inferences Ask students to explain why the power of Fate is shown to be especially strong in the cases of Danae and Antigone. *Both Danae and Antigone were princesses of royal blood, whose high station did not shield them from their fates. Lead students to see the similarity in all the tales told by the Chorus in this strophe and antistrophe.*

◆ Background for Understanding

❻ The Chorus refers to the story of King Phineus of Salmydessus in Thrace. Phineus imprisoned his first wife, Cleopatra (not the Egyptian Queen) after marrying a second wife, Idaea. Out of jealousy, Idaea made false accusations of treachery against Cleopatra's sons, Plexippus and Pandion, and put out their eyes with a weaver's shuttle. Remind students that Oedipus' eyes were put out by his own hand.

Speaking and Listening Mini-Lesson

Mock Trial

This mini-lesson supports the Speaking and Listening activity in the Idea Bank on page 700.

Introduce the Concept Explain that a mock trial is like a play. Students play the parts of Antigone, attorneys, witnesses, judge, and jury.

Develop Information The defense attorney and "Antigone" should plan their testimony while the prosecutor meets with witnesses. Each

lawyer should prepare an opening statement.

Apply the Information The trial should begin with the opening statements, then testimony and cross-examination, and the lawyers' final arguments. Then the jury can convene and vote. Students should speak clearly and use standard English.

Assess the Outcome Have students use Peer Assessment: Dramatic Performance in *Alternative Assessment,* p. 120.

TEIRESIAS. This, Creon: you stand once more on the edge of fate.

CREON. What do you mean? Your words are a kind of dread.

10 **TEIRESIAS.** Listen, Creon:
I was sitting in my chair of augury,[13] at the place
Where the birds gather about me. They were all a-chatter,
As is their habit, when suddenly I heard
A strange note in their jangling, a scream, a
Whirring fury; I knew that they were
15   fighting,
Tearing each other, dying
In a whirlwind of wings clashing. And I was afraid.
I began the rites of burnt-offering at the altar,
But Hephaistos[14] failed me: instead of bright flame,
There was only the sputtering slime of the fat thigh-flesh
20 **❶** Melting: the entrails dissolved in gray smoke,
The bare bone burst from the welter. And no blaze!

This was a sign from heaven. My boy described it,
Seeing for me as I see for others.

25 I tell you, Creon, you yourself have brought
This new calamity upon us. Our hearths and altars
Are stained with the corruption of dogs and carrion birds
That glut themselves on the corpse of Oedipus' son.
The gods are deaf when we pray to them, their fire
Recoils from our offering, their birds of omen
30 Have no cry of comfort, for they are gorged

---

13. chair of augury: The seat near the temple from which Teiresias would deliver his predictions about the future. Augury was the skill of telling such fortunes from a consideration of omens, like the flight of birds or the position of stars.

14. Hephaistos (he fes' təs): God of fire and the forge. He would be invoked, as he is here by Teiresias, for aid in the starting of ceremonial fires.

692 ◆ Drama

With the thick blood of the dead.
                              O my son,
These are no trifles! Think: all men make mistakes,
But a good man yields when he knows his course is wrong,
35 And repairs the evil. The only crime is pride. **❷**

Give in to the dead man, then: do not fight with a corpse—
What glory is it to kill a man who is dead?
Think, I beg you:
It is for your own good that I speak as I do.
You should be able to yield for your own
40   good.

CREON. It seems that prophets have made me their especial province.
All my life long
I have been a kind of butt for the dull arrows **❸**
Of doddering
    fortunetellers!
        No, Teiresias:

If your birds—if the great eagles of God himself
45 Should carry him stinking bit by bit to heaven,
I would not yield. I am not afraid of pollution:

No man can defile the gods.
                    Do what you will,
Go into business, make money, speculate
In India gold or that synthetic gold from
50   Sardis,[15]
Get rich otherwise than by my consent to
    bury him.
Teiresias, it is a sorry thing when a wise man
Sells his wisdom, lets out his words for
    hire!

TEIRESIAS. Ah Creon! Is there no man left in
    the world—

CREON. To do what?—Come, let's have the
55   aphorism![16]

TEIRESIAS. No man who knows that wisdom
    outweighs any wealth?

CREON. As surely as bribes are baser than
    any baseness.

TEIRESIAS. You are sick, Creon! You are
    deathly sick!

CREON. As you say: it is not my place to
    challenge a prophet.

TEIRESIAS. Yet you have said my prophecy is
60   for sale.

CREON. The generation of prophets has
    always loved gold.

TEIRESIAS. The generation of kings has
    always loved brass.

❹ CREON. You forget yourself! You are
    speaking to your King.

TEIRESIAS. I know it. You are a king because
    of me.

❺ CREON. You have a certain skill; but you
65   have sold out.

TEIRESIAS. King, you will drive me to words
    that—

CREON.   Say them, say them!
Only remember: I will not pay you for them.

15. **Sardis** (sär´ dis): Capital of ancient Lydia, which produced the first coins made from an alloy of gold and silver.
16. **aphorism** (af´ ə riz´ əm): Brief, insightful saying.
Creon is taunting the prophet and suggesting that the old
man is capable only of relying on trite, meaningless
expressions instead of any original thinking.

TEIRESIAS. No, you will find them too costly.

CREON.   No doubt. Speak:
Whatever you say, you will not change my
will.

TEIRESIAS. Then take this, and take it to
70   heart!
The time is not far off when you shall pay
    back
Corpse for corpse, flesh of your own flesh.
You have thrust the child of this world into
    living night,
You have kept from the gods below the
    child that is theirs:
The one in a grave before her death, the
75   other,
Dead, denied the grave. This is your crime:
And the Furies[17] and the dark gods of Hell
Are swift with terrible punishment for you.

Do you want to buy me now, Creon?

                    Not many days,
And your house will be full of men and
80   women weeping,
And curses will be hurled at you from far
Cities grieving for sons unburied, left to rot
Before the walls of Thebes.

These are my arrows, Creon: they are all
    for you.

85 But come, child: lead me home.   [*To* BOY]
Let him waste his fine anger upon younger
    men.
Maybe he will learn at last
To control a wiser tongue in a better head.

[*Exit* TEIRESIAS.]

CHORAGOS. The old man has gone, King, but
    his words
90 Remain to plague us. I am old, too,
But I cannot remember
that he was ever false.

CREON. That is true. . . . It
troubles me.
Oh it is hard to give in! but
    it is worse

◆ **Reading Strategy**
What details help
you identify with
Creon's refusal to
yield?

17. **Furies** (fyo͝or´ ēz): Goddesses of vengence, who
made insane those whose crimes were unpunished, especially those who had sinned against their own families.

◆ **Literary Focus**
❹ **Tragic Character** Ask students
what character trait this statement
reveals in Creon, and how it might
lead him to disaster. *Creon shows himself here to be both rigid and extreme in
his position. When logic fails, he falls
back on his authority as king.*

◆ **Critical Thinking**
❺ **Analyze** Ask students what
Creon's insistence that Teiresias has
been corrupted suggests about
Creon's thinking. *Students may say
that Creon is not capable of considering
any viewpoint opposed to his, and will
entertain even a far-fetched rationale to
discredit it. Students may also recall that
Creon first suspected even Antigone of
acting for money rather than principles.*

Comprehension Check ☑
❻ What does Teiresias mean,
"Corpse for corpse, flesh of your
own flesh"? Who is the "child of this
world"? Who is the child that Creon
has "kept from the gods below"?
*Teiresias means that by sentencing
Antigone to death, Creon will also cause
his son's death. The "child of this world"
is Antigone, whom Creon has entombed;
the other child is Polyneices, whom
Creon refused proper burial.*

◆ **Reading Strategy**
❼ **Identify With a Character** Ask
students to imagine themselves in
Creon's place, and suggest a motive
for Creon's change of attitude
toward Teiresias. *Elicit answers to the
effect that Creon has committed himself
so totally to his course of action regarding Antigone that he cannot bring himself to change his mind, and must try to
discredit the prophet instead.*

🎵 **Humanities: Theater**

Students may be interested in the ways in
which Greek theater differs from modern
theater. Point out these differences:
• The ancient Greeks used little scenery.
  Scenes were painted on the three sides of
  pyramid-shaped structures called *periaktoi*
  (pe rē av´ toi). These structures could be
  swiveled around by "stage hands" to show
  changes of setting.
• Since no violence was supposed to appear
  on stage, if a character was killed, a

"tableau," or wheeled platform with an
actor playing the part of the dead character, would be pushed forward onto the
stage.
• In some Greek dramas, gods appeared
  "flying" in baskets hung from cranes called
  machina (mä´ ke nä), or "machines."
• All actors were male, with boys playing
  female roles. Actors wore masks with
  voice amplifiers, like small megaphones,
  built into the mouth openings. Some wore

platform shoes called *kothurnoi* to make
them look taller and more imposing.

Encourage students to apply these facts
to *Antigone,* where appropriate. For example, tableaus would have been used in the
scene in which Eurydice kills herself; the
actor playing Creon might have worn
kothurnoi to indicate Creon's importance;
Antigone would have been played by a boy.

693

◆ **Critical Thinking**

1 Make Judgments Ask students why they think Creon finds it so hard to give in now, even though he is clearly wavering. *Students might explain that Creon has made his position regarding Antigone's punishment a symbol of his authority in Thebes. He believes that to give ground in any way would raise doubts about his effectiveness as a ruler.*

◆ **Reading Strategy**

2 Identify With a Character Ask students to put themselves in Creon's place at this moment in the play, and to suggest reasons, based on the events of the play and on what they know of him, for his sudden change of heart. *Students might say that Creon has always feared what the gods can do to those who offend them. That is why he had claimed that Antigone's death would not be his fault. When the Choragos reminds him that Teiresias is never wrong about such matters, Creon suddenly senses that he might be in serious trouble.*

To risk everything for stubborn pride.

1 CHORAGOS. Creon: take my advice.

95 **CREON.** What shall I do?

2 CHORAGOS. Go quickly: free Antigone from her vault
And build a tomb for the body of Polyneices.

CREON. You would have me do this?

CHORAGOS. Creon, yes!
And it must be done at once: God moves
100 Swiftly to cancel the folly of stubborn men.

CREON. It is hard to deny the heart! But I
Will do it: I will not fight with destiny.

CHORAGOS. You must go yourself, you cannot leave it to others.

CREON. I will go.
—Bring axes, servants:
105 Come with me to the tomb. I buried her, I
Will set her free.
Oh quickly!
My mind misgives—
The laws of the gods are mighty, and a man must serve them
To the last day of his life!

[*Exit* CREON.]

Pæan

CHORAGOS. [STROPHE 1]
God of many names

CHORUS. O Iacchos[18]
son
of Kadmeian Semele[19]
O born of the Thunder!
Guardian of the West
Regent
of Eleusis' plain[20]

18. **Iacchos** (ē′ ə kəs): One of several alternate names for Dionysos.
19. **Kadmeian Semele** (sem′ ə lē′): Semele was a mortal and the mother of Dionysos. She was the daughter of Thebes' founder, Kadmos.
20. **Eleusis'** (i lo̅o̅′ sis) **plain:** Located north of Athens, this plain was a site of worship for Dionysos and Demeter, gods who protected the harvests of grapes and corn, respectively.

694 ◆ Drama

O Prince of maenad Thebes[21]
and the Dragon Field by rippling
5 Ismenos:[22]

CHORAGOS. [ANTISTROPHE 1]
God of many names

CHORUS. the flame of torches
flares on our hills
the nymphs of Iacchos
dance at the spring of Castalia:[23]

from the vine-close mountain
come ah come in ivy:
Evohe evohe![24] sings through the streets of
10 Thebes

CHORAGOS. [STROPHE 2]
God of many names

CHORUS. Iacchos of Thebes
heavenly Child
of Semele bride of the Thunderer!
The shadow of plague is upon us:
15 come
with clement feet[25]
oh come from Parnasos[26]
down the long slopes
across the lamenting water

CHORAGOS. [ANTISTROPHE 2]
Io[27] Fire! Chorister of the throbbing stars!

21. **maenad** (mē′ nad) **Thebes:** The city is here compared to a maenad, one of Dionysos' female worshipers. Such a follower would be thought of as uncontrolled or disturbed, much as Thebes was while being upset by the civil war.
22. **Dragon Field . . . Ismenos** (is mē′ nas): The Dragon Field was located by the banks of Ismenos, a river sacred to Apollo that flows near Thebes. The Dragon Field was where Kadmos miraculously created warriors by sowing the teeth of the dragon he killed there. Those men helped him establish the city.
23. **Castalia** (kas tā′ lē ə): Location of a site sacred to Apollo, where his followers would worship.
24. **Evohe** (ē vō′ ē): Triumphant shout of affirmation (like "Amen") used at ceremonies dedicated to Dionysos.
25. **clement feet:** *Clement* means "kind" or "favorable." The chorus is here asking Dionysos to step gently into the troubled path and to intervene in a healing manner.
26. **Parnasos** (pär nas′ əs): Mountain that was sacred to both Dionysos and Apollo, located in central Greece.
27. **Io** (ē′ ō): Greek word for "Behold" or "Hail."

◆ **Build Vocabulary**
chorister (kôr′ is tər) *n.:* Member of a chorus

20   O purest among the voices of the night!
     Thou son of God, blaze for us!

CHORUS. Come with choric rapture of
       circling Maenads
     Who cry *Io Iacche!*[28]
                         God of many names!

Exodus

[Enter MESSENGER, *left.]*

MESSENGER. Men of the line of Kadmos,[29]
       you who live
     Near Amphion's citadel:[30]
                         I cannot say
     Of any condition of human life "This is
       fixed,
     This is clearly good, or bad." Fate raises up,
     And Fate casts down the happy and
5   unhappy alike:
     No man can foretell his Fate.
                         Take the case of Creon:
     Creon was happy once, as I count
       happiness:
     Victorious in battle, sole governor of the
       land,
     Fortunate father of children nobly born.
     And now it has all gone from him! Who
10   can say
     That a man is still alive when his life's joy
       fails?
     He is a walking dead man. Grant him rich,
     Let him live like a king in his great house:
     If his pleasure is gone, I would not give
     So much as the shadow of smoke for all he
15   owns.

CHORAGOS. Your words hint at sorrow: what
     is your news for us?

MESSENGER. They are dead. The living are
     guilty of their death.

CHORAGOS. Who is guilty? Who is dead?
     Speak!

---

28. **Io Iacche** (ē ō ē´ ə ke): Cry of celebration used by
Dionysian worshipers.
29. **Kadmos** (kad´ məs): Founder of the city of Thebes,
whose daughter, Semele, gave birth to Dionysos.
30. **Amphion's** (am fī´ ənz) **citadel:** Amphion was a king
of Thebes credited with erecting the walls of the fortress,
or citadel, by using his lyre so magically that its music
caused the stones to move themselves into proper place.

MESSENGER. Haimon.
     Haimon is dead; and the hand that killed
       him
     Is his own hand.

20   **CHORAGOS.**   His father's? or his own?

MESSENGER. His own, driven mad by the
     murder his father had done.

CHORAGOS. Teiresias, Teiresias, how clearly
     you saw it all!

MESSENGER. This is my news: you must
     draw what conclusions you can from it.

CHORAGOS. But look: Eurydice, our Queen:
25   Has she overheard us?

[Enter EURYDICE *from the Palace, center.]*

EURYDICE. I have heard something, friends:
     As I was unlocking the gate of Pallas'[31]
       shrine,
     For I needed her help today, I heard a voice
     Telling of some new sorrow. And I fainted
     There at the temple with all my maidens
30   about me.
     But speak again: whatever it is, I can bear
       it:
     Grief and I are no strangers.

MESSENGER.   Dearest Lady,
     I will tell you plainly all that I have seen.
     I shall not try to comfort you: what is the use,
     Since comfort could lie only in what is not
35   true?
     The truth is always best.
                         I went with Creon
     To the outer plain where Polyneices was
       lying,
     No friend to pity him, his body shredded by
       dogs.
     We made our prayers in that place to
       Hecate[32]
     And Pluto,[33] that they would be merciful.
40   And we bathed
     The corpse with holy water, and we brought
     Fresh-broken branches to burn what was

---

31. **Pallas** (pal´ əs): Pallas Athena, the goddess of
wisdom.
32. **Hecate** (hek´ ə tē): Goddess of the underworld.
33. **Pluto** (plōōt´ ō)**:** God of the underworld who managed the souls of the departed.

Antigone ◆ 695

---

❸ Interpret Ask students to
explain the significance of a person's
wealth or social status in determining
his or her happiness, according to
what the Messenger says. *The
Messenger says that a person's wealth
or social status has no bearing at all on
what finally becomes of him or her.*

◆ **Critical Thinking**

❹ Make Inferences Ask students
to infer what has happened, based on
the Messenger's words. *By saying that
happiness "has all gone from" Creon,
and that "life's joy fails," the Messenger
implies that Antigone is dead, and probably Haimon as well.*

Customize for
Less Proficient Readers
Help these students to summarize
what has happened. They should
understand that Antigone is dead and
that Haimon has killed himself.

Cross-Curricular Connection: Social Studies

The Greek legacy to the Western World compris-
es a great deal more than drama. Every four
years, athletes from around the world meet to
participate in the Olympic games which originated in Greece in 776 B.C. Greek ideas about law,
freedom, justice, and government have influenced
political thinking to the present day. In the arts
and sciences, Greek works became a standard of

excellence for the later people of Europe. In fact,
the word *museum* literally means "house of the
Muses." (The Muses were nine Greek goddesses
who presided over the arts and sciences.) The
achievements of the Greeks were especially
remarkable because they were produced by a
scattering of tiny city-states whose bitter rivalries
eventually cost them their freedom.

◆ Reading Strategy

❷ Identify With a Character
Ask students to put themselves in Creon's place, and to suggest why Creon asks if he is now a prophet. *Students may say that Creon had been afraid that he would find something awful at Antigone's vault, and he now fears that his misgivings will be justified.*

◆ Critical Thinking

❸ Analyze Ask students to imagine why Antigone might have hanged herself. *Students may suggest that she preferred to die quickly by her own hand rather than gradually starve to death.*

◆ Reading Strategy

❹ Identify With a Character
Although it is difficult to identify with a character in such a tragic situation, encourage students to try to identify with Haimon. Then have them explain why Haimon cannot forgive his father, even though Creon begs his forgiveness. *Suggested response: Haimon is mad with grief over the death of Antigone, and he sees his father as her murderer. What Creon has done is beyond forgiveness.*

❶ left of it,
And upon the urn we heaped up a towering barrow
Of the earth of his own land.
⠀⠀⠀⠀⠀⠀⠀⠀⠀When we were done, we ran
45⠀To the vault where Antigone lay on her couch of stone.
One of the servants had gone ahead,
And while he was yet far off he heard a voice
Grieving within the chamber, and he came back
And told Creon. And as the King went closer,
50⠀The air was full of wailing, the words lost,
❷ And he begged us to make all haste. "Am I a prophet?"
He said, weeping, "And must I walk this road,
The saddest of all that I have gone before?
My son's voice calls me on. Oh quickly, quickly!
55⠀Look through the crevice there, and tell me
If it is Haimon, or some deception of the gods!"

We obeyed; and in the cavern's farthest corner
We saw her lying:
She had made a noose of her fine linen veil
❸60⠀And hanged herself. Haimon lay beside her,
His arms about her waist, lamenting her,
His love lost underground, crying out
That his father had stolen her away from him.

When Creon saw him the tears rushed to his eyes
And he called to him: "What have you done, child? Speak to me.
65⠀What are you thinking that makes your eyes so strange?
O my son, my son, I come to you on my knees!"
But Haimon spat in his face. He said not a word,
❹ Staring—
⠀⠀⠀⠀⠀⠀⠀And suddenly drew his sword

And lunged. Creon shrank back, the blade
70⠀missed; and the boy,
Desperate against himself, drove it half its length
Into his own side, and fell. And as he died
He gathered Antigone close in his arms again,
Choking, his blood bright red on her white cheek.
And now he lies dead with the dead, and
75⠀she is his
At last, his bride in the houses of the dead.

[*Exit* EURYDICE *into the Palace.*]

CHORAGOS. She has left us without a word. What can this mean?

MESSENGER. It troubles me, too; yet she knows what is best,
Her grief is too great for public lamentation,
And doubtless she has gone to her
80⠀chamber to weep
For her dead son, leading her maidens in his dirge.

CHORAGOS. It may be so: but I fear this deep silence.

[*Pause*]

MESSENGER. I will see what she is doing. I will go in.

[*Exit* MESSENGER *into the Palace.*]

[*Enter* CREON *with attendants, bearing* HAIMON'S *body.*]

CHORAGOS. But here is the King himself: oh look at him,
85⠀Bearing his own damnation in his arms.

CREON. Nothing you say can touch me any more.
My own blind heart has brought me
From darkness to final darkness. Here you see
The father murdering, the murdered son—
90⠀And all my civic wisdom!

Haimon my son, so young, so young to die,
I was the fool, not you; and you died for me.

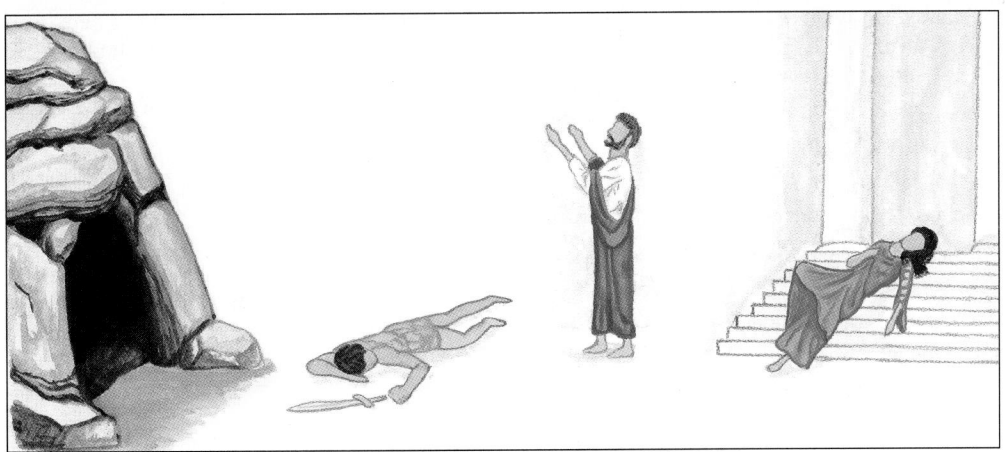

❺

CHORAGOS. That is the truth; but you were late in learning it.

CREON. This truth is hard to bear. Surely a god
95 Has crushed me beneath the hugest weight of heaven,
And driven me headlong a barbaric way
To trample out the thing I held most dear.

The pains that men will take to come to pain!

[*Enter* MESSENGER *from the Palace.*]

MESSENGER. The burden you carry in your hands is heavy,
100 But it is not all: you will find more in your house.

CREON. What burden worse than this shall I find there?

MESSENGER. The Queen is dead.

CREON. O port of death, deaf world,
Is there no pity for me? And you, Angel of evil,
105 I was dead, and your words are death again.
Is it true, boy? Can it be true?
Is my wife dead? Has death bred death?

MESSENGER. You can see for yourself.

[*The doors are opened, and the body of* EURYDICE *is disclosed within.*]

CREON. Oh pity!
110 All true, all true, and more than I can bear!

O my wife, my son!

MESSENGER. She stood before the altar, and her heart
Welcomed the knife her own hand guided,
And a great cry burst from her lips for Megareus[34] dead,
And for Haimon dead, her sons; and her
115 last breath
Was a curse for their father, the murderer of her sons.
And she fell, and the dark flowed in through her closing eyes.

CREON. O God, I am sick with fear.
Are there no swords here? Has no one a blow for me?

MESSENGER. Her curse is upon you for the
120 deaths of both.

CREON. It is right that it should be. I alone am guilty.
I know it, and I say it. Lead me in,
Quickly, friends.
I have neither life nor substance. Lead me in.

❻

CHORAGOS. You are right, if there can be
125 right in so much wrong.
The briefest way is best in a world of sorrow.

---

34. **Megareus** (mə ga′ rē əs): Oldest son of Creon and Eurydice, who was killed in the civil war by Argive forces invading Thebes.

Antigone ◆ 697

 Speaking and Listening Mini-Lesson

❶ **Tragic Character** Ask students whether they believe that Creon or Antigone is the more tragic figure in this drama, and to explain their choices. *Students may choose Antigone because she appears more blameless and sympathetic, having acted in accordance with the principles of divine justice. They may choose Creon because of the way in which a flaw in his character has brought him down from such a height to such a depth of loss and despair.*

Reinforce and Extend

Answers

◆ *Literature and Your Life*

Reader's Response Some students might point out that Creon will seem weak if he backs down, yet many will agree with Haimon, who maintains that his father will lose the respect of the entire city if he remains inflexible, and that "It is not reason never to yield to reason!"

Thematic Focus They choose to remain rigid in their beliefs, are unwilling to appear weak, and refuse to reason or compromise.

☑ **Check Your Comprehension**

1. Teiresias predicts that Creon's house will be full of tears and that his own flesh (Haimon) shall pay back "corpse for corpse."
2. Creon sets out to bury Polyneices and free Antigone.
3. The Messenger tells Eurydice that Creon was too late to save Antigone, and that her son, Haimon, is dead.
4. Antigone hangs herself. In his raging grief, Haimon tries to kill his father, misses, but then mortally wounds himself, dying next to Antigone. Cursing her husband, Eurydice kills herself.

◆ **Critical Thinking**

1. Haimon is more concerned with divine law. He listens to the people, and overhears their sympathy for Antigone—that what she did for her brother was no crime, but a decent act. He begs his father to listen to reason, "God's crowning gift to man," and exclaims that Creon has "no right to trample on God's right."

CREON. Let it come,
Let death come quickly, and be kind to me.
I would not ever see the sun again.

CHORAGOS. All that will come when it will;
but we, meanwhile,
130 Have much to do. Leave the future to itself.

CREON. All my heart was in that prayer!

CHORAGOS. Then do not pray any more: the sky is deaf.

❶ **CREON.** Lead me away. I have been rash and foolish.
135 I have killed my son and my wife.

I look for comfort; my comfort lies here dead.
Whatever my hands have touched has
come to nothing.
Fate has brought all my pride to a thought
of dust.

[*As* CREON *is being led into the house, the* CHORAGOS *advances and speaks directly to the audience.*]

CHORAGOS. There is no happiness where
there is no wisdom;
140 No wisdom but in submission to the gods.
Big words are always punished,
And proud men in old age learn to be wise.

Guide for Responding

◆ *Literature and Your Life*

Reader's Response In Scene 3, Creon and Haimon express sharply different points of view. With which character do you most agree? Why?

Thematic Focus What choices do Creon and Antigone make that lead to their downfall?

Journal Activity List the reasons you think Creon should or should not have changed his mind. Explain which reason you feel is most compelling.

☑ **Check Your Comprehension**

1. Why do Creon and Haimon argue?
2. According to Teiresias, what terrible punishment awaits Creon?
3. What action does Creon take after Teiresias's prophecy?
4. What does the Messenger tell Eurydice before she leaves the stage during the Exodos?
5. What finally happens to Antigone? Haimon? Eurydice?

◆ **Critical Thinking**

INTERPRET
1. Explain the conflicts that drive Haimon to take extreme measures. Does he seem more concerned with divine law, to which Antigone turns for her justification, or with human law? Support your answer. **[Analyze]**
2. Why does Creon say "I have neither life nor substance" in the Exodus? **[Infer]**
3. How great a role do you think fate plays in dictating the outcome of the story? **[Support]**

EVALUATE
4. Both Antigone and Creon are unwilling to appear weak. How could this trait influence a person's outlook on life? **[Evaluate]**

APPLY
5. Explain how this play demonstrates the tension that sometimes exists between individual conscience and designated authority. **[Analyze]**
6. Near the end of the play, Creon says, "The pains that men will take to come to pain!" How do his words apply to contemporary society? **[Relate]**

698 ◆ Drama

2. Creon has lost his beloved son and wife; his rigid pride has destroyed his power to rule.
3. Sample responses: The choices people make dictate the course of their own lives, not fate—fate changes as choice changes; the main characters didn't change, thus they were stuck with their fate. Others may say that fate is fixed

from birth, the sum total of innate pattern of behavior and destiny, which we are unable to alter.
4. Students might respond that people who are afraid of appearing to be weak, indeed are; they resort to trying to control others and usually end up out of control.
5. Suggested response: The entire play is based on the

tension between individual, divine conscience (Antigone), and civil, human authority (Creon), with the potential for human reason (Haimon) to save the day.
6. Students can offer examples from contemporary literature, television programs, and current movies in addition to real-life examples.

Guide for Responding (continued)

◆ Literary Focus

TRAGIC CHARACTER

A **tragic character** is one who suffers a downfall. This character is marked with a tragic flaw that contributes to his or her doom.

1. (a) In your opinion, who is brought down most completely at the conclusion of the action? (b) Give evidence to support your answer.
2. (a) What is this character's tragic flaw? (b) How does this flaw lead to the character's downfall?
3. What role, if any, does fate play in leading to the downfall?

◆ Reading Strategy

IDENTIFY WITH A CHARACTER

When you **identify with a character** in a drama, you sympathize with his or her struggles or experiences.

1. With which character did you most identify? Why?
2. Which actions, events, or lines in the play led you to identify with that character?
3. How did your identification with a character draw you into the action of the play?

Beyond Literature

Cultural Connection

Burial Customs Different societies and cultures have different "burial" customs, some of which are not burials at all! Antigone "buries" her brother by sprinkling his corpse with wine and dust. The Vikings placed kings and great warriors on barges and then set them on fire. Some Aborigines in Australia leave bodies in trees. In Tibet a sky burial returns the body to nature by exposing it to birds and the elements on a high mountain.
Activity Find out more about a burial custom and write a brief explanation of how it reflects the needs and beliefs of a culture.

◆ Build Grammar Skills

PRONOUN CASE IN INCOMPLETE CLAUSES

In **incomplete clauses** introduced by *than* or *as,* a pronoun takes the case that it would have if the understood words were present.

Practice On your paper, write the correct pronoun to complete each sentence. Then write the words that are needed to complete each sentence.

1. The Chorus members see all; no one sees more than (*they/them*) ___?___.
2. When Haimon heard of Antigone's sentence, no one was more enraged than (*he/him*) ___?___.
3. The rest of the group was as certain as (*I/me*) ___?___ about the outcome of the play.
4. Though Ismene avoids her sister's fate, most people believe that Antigone is a much stronger character than (*she/her*) ___?___.
5. Although the details of her problems are different, Antigone faces some of the same issues as ____. (*we/us*)

◆ Build Vocabulary

USING THE ROOT -*chor*-

The root -*chor*- comes from Terpsichore, the Muse of dance and song. Match each of the words in Column A with its definition in Column B.

Column A	Column B
1. choral	a. creating dance
2. choir	b. group of singers
3. choreography	c. sung or performed by a chorus

USING THE WORD BANK

On your paper, write the letter of the word that is the best synonym of the first word.

1. deference: (a) indignity, (b) respect, (c) irony
2. vile: (a) corrupt, (b) honorable, (c) edible
3. piety: (a) atheism, (b) reverence, (c) solitude
4. blasphemy: (a) violence, (b) vandalism, (c) disrespect
5. lamentation: (a) mourning, (b) cheer, (c) glee
6. chorister: (a) warden, (b) singer, (c) lawgiver

Antigone ◆ 699

Beyond the Selection

FURTHER READING

Other Ancient Greek Tragedies
Oedipus Rex, Sophocles
The Seven Against Thebes, Aeschylus

Other Books About Ancient Greek Myths
The Greek Way, Edith Hamilton
Hercules, My Shipmate, Robert Graves
We suggest that you preview these works before recommending them to students.

INTERNET

Students can find information about *Antigone* and ancient Greece at the following Web sites:
http://www.temple.edu/classics/antigone.html
http://www.museum_upenn.edu/Greek_World/Intro.html
Please be aware that addresses may have changed since we published this information. We *strongly recommend* that you preview the sites before you send students to them.

699

Idea Bank

Customizing for
Learning Modalities

Following are suggestions for matching Idea Bank topics with your students' learning modalities:

Interpersonal: 4, 5
Visual/Spatial: 5,6
Bodily /Kinesthetic: 4

Customizing for
Performance Levels

Following are suggestions for matching Idea Bank topics with your students' ability levels:

Less Advanced: 1, 5
Average: 2, 4,5,6
More Advanced: 3, 4, 6

Writing Mini-Lesson

Refer students to the Writing Handbook, page 965, for instruction on the writing process, and page 968 for further information on drama.

Writer's Solution

Writing Lab CD-ROM

Have students complete the tutorial on Creative Writing. Follow these steps:

1. Use the instruction on formatting a script.
2. Use the stage directions Word Bin to get ideas for how characters will move, sound, and act.
3. Use the revision guidelines for making dialogue realistic.

Sourcebook

Have students use Chapter 6, Creative Writing (pp. 165–193), for additional support. The chapter includes specific instruction on using stage directions and writing dialogue (p. 185).

Build Your Portfolio

Idea Bank

Writing

1. **Introduction** Imagine that you are the director of a student theater group in your school. Write a brief introduction to present to an audience before they see a performance of *Antigone.*

2. **Final Speech** Create a brief final speech in which the messenger has one last chance to comment on the action. You might begin with the line "I shall go now over the world's paths to tell the sad story of . . .''

3. **Editorial** Imagine that you are an editor for a Thebes newspaper. Write an editorial on whether Creon's response to Antigone's action was appropriate.

Speaking and Listening

4. **Mock Trial** Hold a mock trial in which both sides of Antigone's case are argued before the class. Have the class act as a jury to determine which argument is more convincing.

5. **Film Response** If possible, see a video version of a few scenes of *Antigone.* With other classmates, compare and contrast your ideas about the characters from reading the play with the interpretations on the video.

Projects

6. **Multimedia Presentation** Create a multimedia presentation on ancient Greek theater. Include illustrations or labeled diagrams, tape recordings of excerpts from *Antigone,* historical maps, timelines, and other items. **[Social Studies Link]**

Writing Mini-Lesson

Scene of Conflict

In Scene 2, as the Sentry hands over to Creon the person arrested for burying Polyneices, Creon exclaims: "But this is Antigone! Why have you brought her here?" That moment captures the major conflict in the play. Think of a conflict from a story, play, or novel that would make a gripping scene for a movie. Who are the characters? What is the reason for their confrontation? Focus on this moment and use it to write a **scene of conflict** for a screenplay.

Writing Skills Focus: Format

The **format** for a screenplay is similar to that of other kinds of drama. The characters' words are set in blocks following the characters' names and special directions are printed in italics, often enclosed in parentheses. Use the format for *Antigone* as a model. Your directions will include information about lights, sound, and camera angles, which are obviously not a part of this ancient Greek script.

Prewriting Draw a picture to get a sense of the setting of the scene for which you will give directions. Indicate where the characters will be seen, and jot down notes about how they might move or what kind of background music to play.

Drafting Write out what the characters say and do as they act out their conflict. Include directions about character movement, camera shots, and background sounds or music within parentheses, separate from the dialogue.

Revising Ask a partner to read your scene and tell you whether your conflict conveys suspense or tension. Your partner may help you sharpen the characters' lines or clarify and expand descriptions that help the reader envision the background.

✓ ASSESSMENT OPTIONS

Formal Assessment, Selection Test, pp. 173–174, and Assessment Resources Software. The selection test is designed so that it can be easily customized to the ability levels of your students.
Alternative Assessment, p. 49, includes options for less advanced students, more advanced students, logical /mathematical learners, bodily/kinesthetic learners, and visual/spatial learners.

PORTFOLIO ASSESSMENT

Use the following rubrics in the *Alternative Assessment* booklet to assess student writing:
Introduction: Expression Rubric, p. 94
Final Speech: Summary Rubric, p. 98
Editorial: Persuasion Rubric, p. 105
Writing Mini-Lesson: Drama Rubric, p. 109

Writing Process Workshop

Video Script

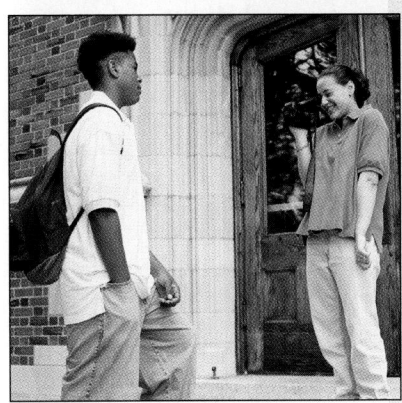

When you watch actors in a movie or television show, have you ever wondered how they know what to say and when to say it? They work from a **video script,** which has all the lines with directions for how to say them and how to move. Write a video script for a scene for a contemporary version of *Antigone*. In addition to the dialogue, include the directions for actors' movements, sound, lighting, and camera angles.

The following skills, introduced in this section's Writing Mini-Lessons, will help you write a video script.

Writing Skills Focus

▶ **Use the proper format** to make your video script easy to understand. The characters' words should be set in blocks following the characters' names. Directions should be in italics, if you are working on a computer; otherwise, enclose them in parentheses. (Use the format for *Antigone* as a model.) In the directions, include information about lights, sound, and camera angles. (See p. 700.)

▶ **Concentrate on dialogue.** Dialogue is the heart of a drama. It is what breathes life into the characters. Your first priority should be to make your dialogue realistic and interesting.

The following excerpt from *Antigone* shows some of the features of the format for drama.

MODEL FROM LITERATURE

from *Antigone* by Sophocles

① **Scene 5**
② [Enter blind ③ TEIRESIAS, led by a boy. The opening speeches of TEIRESIAS should be in singsong in contrast to the lines of CREON.]

    TEIRESIAS. This is the way the blind man comes, Princes, Princes,
Lock step, two heads lit by the eyes of one.

    CREON. What new thing have you to tell us, old Teiresias?

    TEIRESIAS. ④ I have much to tell you: listen to the prophet Creon.

① Indicate the scene number.
② Stage directions and camera directions are set off with brackets or parentheses
③ Names of characters are printed in capitals—even in the stage directions. This way, actors can easily find any dialogue or directions that relate to them.
④ Each character's lines follow the character's name.

 Beyond the Classroom

Career Connection

As they write their scripts, students will make a variety of decisions that would be made by a number of different people in the theater or movie business. Although only a few students may be interested in pursuing careers as script writers, students can use this assignment as a springboard to consider which aspects of the entertainment industry do interest them. Remind students that movie and video studios employ electricians as well as lighting designers, administrative assistants as well as directors, tailors as well as costume designers, and personal trainers as well as dancers. For every production, a medical technician is hired to provide on-the-spot health care and caterers are hired to feed the actors and crew. Have students make a list of the many tasks besides acting that would need to be done if their video scripts were really being produced.

Prepare and Engage

Establish Writing Guidelines
Before students begin, review the following characteristics of a video script:

• A video script uses the proper format to make stage directions and dialogue easy to distinguish and understand,

• It concentrates on dialogue to create interesting, believable characters.

You may distribute copies of the Scoring Rubric for Drama (page 109) in *Alternative Assessment* to make students aware before they begin of the criteria on which they will be evaluated. See the suggestions on page 703 for ways to customize the rubric for this workshop.

Refer students to the Writing Handbook, p. 965, for instruction in the writing process, and p. 968 for further information on drama.

Writer's Solution

Writing Lab CD-ROM

If your students have access to computers, you may want to have them work on the tutorial on Creative Writing to complete all or part of their video script. Follow these steps:

1. Have students use the interactive model of a dramatic scene.
2. Encourage students to use the word bins for drama and view the video clips about gathering details for drama.
3. Have students draft on the computer.
4. Suggest that students review the audio-annotated writing models for drama before they complete their drafts.
5. Have pairs of students complete the peer evaluation checklists for plays.

Sourcebook
Students can find additional support, including models, character trait charts, and specific instruction on writing dialogue, in the chapter on Creative Writing (pp. 165–193).

Prewriting

You can use the Grid Organizer to help your students develop character traits. Place the organizer on the overhead projector. Write the character's name in the vertical box on the left. List the categories of traits in the first column of boxes. Then ask students to suggest details to fill in the appropriate boxes for each category.

Customize for
English Language Learners

Rephrase the character trait categories as questions for these students to answer. For instance, instead of listing "appearance" ask "What does the character look like?" Then, make sure these students understand the meaning of drama-related terms and expressions, such as dialogue, stage directions, character development, costume, sound effects, and others.

Customize for
Less Proficient Writers

These students especially will benefit from using the Character Trait Word Bin or brainstorming in a group for character traits before beginning to draft.

Customize for
More Advanced Students

Challenge these students to relate their updated characters to famous political or entertainment figures who have qualities and issues similar to those of Creon and Antigone. Ask students to include an explanation of the parallels between their characters and the celebrities that served as character models.

Customize for
Bodily/Kinesthetic Learners

These students can role-play the scene before writing their contemporary dialogues. The acting out of the scene and the "trying on" of the role will help these students find updated language for these ancient characters.

Writing Process Workshop

APPLYING LANGUAGE SKILLS: Spoken and Written Language

Spoken language is usually more casual and conversational than **written language**. When you write dialogue—the words characters speak—you should use words and expressions that imitate natural speech and that reveal the personality of the character speaking.

from Antigone:

ISMENE. Antigone, you are mad! What could I possibly do?

ANTIGONE. You must decide whether you will help me or not.

ISMENE. I do not understand you. Help you in what?

ANTIGONE. Ismene, I am going to bury him. Will you come?

ISMENE. Bury him! You have just said the new law forbids it.

Practice Write a short conversation that you and a friend might have.

Writer's Solution Connection Writing Lab

To help you write dialogue that reflects the personalities of your characters, use the section on Developing Characters and Plots in the Creative Writing Tutorial on the Writer's Solution Writing Lab.

702 ◆ *Drama*

Prewriting

Choose a Conflict At the heart of every drama is a conflict. Choose a moment of conflict from the play to use as the basis for your video script.

Develop Character Traits In a dramatic scene, you reveal the personalities of the characters through their dialogue and actions, as well as through the comments and behavior of other characters. Gather details about your characters from the text of *Antigone* to bring them to life. Review the play and update details. For example, a contemporary Antigone might wear jeans; a contemporary Haimon's goal might be to sing in a band. Fill in a chart like the one below to identify and describe important character traits for each of your characters. Use these details to help you imagine how your characters will look, sound, and act.

Character's	Appearance	
	Personality Traits	
	Habits and Abilities	
	Goals	

Drafting

Write the Dialogue Review the format of the dialogue in *Antigone,* and use it as the model for formatting your dialogue.

Use the dialogue itself, rather than the stage directions, to advance the action. For example, when Eurydice kills herself, have another character describe what happened, rather than describing it in the stage directions as something that the audience will see.

Use contemporary language in your updated scene. Give the dialogue a modern-day feel by using words, phrases, and expressions such as you and your friends might use.

Use Stage Directions How will the actors in your video scene know how to speak particular lines? How will they know when to move or stand still? Provide stage directions that give a clear and complete picture to performers and to people who are reading the play.

Writer's Solution

Writing Lab CD-ROMs

If possible, have students use the interactive Character Traits Word Bin of the Creative Writing tutorial. Students can print the list of words they select and refer the list during drafting.

Drafting

Encourage students to refer to their lists or charts of character traits while they are drafting. Students should choose words and use expressions that will reveal these traits through dialogue. Remind students, however, that they should not labor over word choice at this point. If a particular section is giving them difficulty, they should draft the rest of the scene and return later to the difficult portion.

Applying Language Skills

Spoken and Written Language

If time permits, encourage students to prepare for writing their dialogues by spending a day paying special attention to the way they speak. Students should jot down notes for a day on expressions and phrasings that they hear that they think they might use to give the sense of spoken language to their dialogues.

Revising

Use a Revision Checklist Use the following checklist to help you revise your video script.

► What is your scene's main conflict? How might it be possible to make this conflict stronger?
► How well does dialogue develop your characters? How can you improve the way the dialogue reveals the personalities of your characters? How can you make the dialogue sound more like natural speech?
► How thorough and clear are your stage directions? What can you add or change that will make the action even clearer to a reader or an actor?

REVISION MODEL

ISMENE: ① I'm
          ∧I am not sure what I can do, Antigone.
          ② It's crazy!
          ∧It is not wise.
          ③ Choose!
ANTIGONE: ∧Won't you please help me?
ISMENE: ① I'm   ④ What can I do?
          ∧I am confused. ∧In what way would you like

          me to help you?

① The writer changes *I am* to the contraction *I'm* to make the dialogue sound more conversational.
② The writer replaces this formally written sentence with a colloquial expression that reflects natural speech.
③ The writer makes Antigone's words more forceful to reflect the strength of her character.
④ The writer changes Ismene's question to sound more natural.

Publishing

Perform Your Scene Using the dialogue and stage directions in your video script, stage a performance of your scene. Have the actors rehearse the scene, and review any parts of the script that seem difficult or confusing. Appoint a technical director to take care of things such as lighting, sound, and camera angles.

APPLYING LANGUAGE SKILLS: Punctuating Words of Direct Address

When one character speaks directly to another using the listener's name or other identifier, the speaker is using *direct address*. Nouns of direct address should be set off with commas, as in the following examples:

Everything else, my son, to your father's will.

Antigone, are you mad?

Practice Add a character's name or other identifier to indicate to whom each character is speaking.

1. You must decide. (Antigone to Ismene)

2. What can I do? (Ismene to Antigone)

Writing Application Add nouns of direct address to some of your dialogue. Set off words of direct address with commas.

Writer's Solution Connection Language Lab

For more on nouns of direct address, see the lesson on Commas in the Writer's Solution Language Lab.

Revising

You might have students work in pairs to discuss the Revision Model on this page and suggest similar revisions to each other's work. After reading the scenes aloud together, students can use the revision guidelines to revise their own work and to offer constructive criticism of their partner's work.

Writer's Solution

Writing Lab CD-ROM
Students can view the video tips for peer editors and use peer evaluation checklists on-line. The proofreading section also offers an audio-annotated literary model for formatting a play.

Publishing

If students choose to perform their scenes, they can evaluate one another using the Peer Assessment for a Dramatic Performance on page 120 in *Alternative Assessment*.

Applying Language Skills

Point out to students that nouns of direct address can sometimes be used to add emphasis or urgency to a character's words. In other cases, they can create a personal, immediate tone.

Suggested answers:
1. Ismene, you must decide.
2. What can I do, sister?

PORTFOLIO ASSESSMENT Use the rubric for Drama in *Alternative Assessment* (p. 109) to assess students' writing. Use these criteria to customize the rubric to the assignment.		4	3	2	1
	Spoken and Written Language	All dialogue reflects the patterns and expressions of natural speech.	Most dialogue reflects the patterns and expressions of natural speech.	Some dialogue reflects the patterns and expressions of natural speech.	Little or no dialogue reflects the patterns and expressions of natural speech.
	Punctuating Words of Direct Address	Words of direct address are used effectively and always punctuated correctly.	Words of direct address are used and usually punctuated correctly.	Words of direct address are seldom punctuated correctly.	Words of direct address are not used or punctuated correctly.

Introduce the Strategy

Many students will already be familiar with a number of information sites on the Internet. Ask these students to describe how they find information on the Internet. Then ask these same students to share with the class their answer to the following question: How much of the information you have found on the Internet do you think is accurate and reliable? (All, most, some, little)

Keep in mind that not all sites are appropriate for students. We strongly recommend that you monitor all Internet activity in your classroom and discuss with students the need to use caution whenever accessing the Internet at home.

Customize for
Verbal/Linguistic Learners
These students may wish to write out the steps they would follow to find information on the Internet for each of the situations suggested on this page. They can refer to and revise their self-made manual as they actually do the search.

Apply the Strategy

Encourage students to think of other situations for which an Internet search would be the best primary source for finding information. Discuss situations for which the Internet would be only a secondary source. For example, although many people search for medical information on the Internet, a doctor is the most reliable and appropriate source of health information.

Answers
1. The retail sales page posted the information to boost sales. The entertainment magazine page wants to offer readers an informed opinion.
2. The entertainment magazine page is probably more objective.
3. The retail sales page is more useful to someone who wants to order the CD because it will probably have ordering information attached.
4. The retail sales page has details about the range of musical styles, the type of music, and the qualities the artist is known for. The entertainment magazine page offers details about vocal quality

---

Sorting Information on the Internet

Real-World Reading Skills Workshop

Strategies for Success

Up-to-the-minute information on virtually any topic in the world can be found on the Internet! The Internet is the world's largest library—available to all by simply clicking on buttons and typing in key words. With so much information available, you have to learn to discriminate between what's reliable and what's not. Use the following tips to help you sort the information.

Concentrate on Professional Sources
Anyone with a computer and Internet access can set up a Web page, but these amateur sites may not contain reliable or relevant information. Choose Web sites run by professional organizations. If you are looking for reliable information for your visit to New York City, it's probably better to navigate to the New York Tourism Board Home Page than to fifteen-year-old Jimmy Buma's "Ode to the Big Apple" Web page.

Determine Why the Information Was Posted
Many organizations post information for the sake of education; however, some companies and individuals use the Internet to promote products or services. For example, an electronics company will most likely promote its own products on its Web site, without providing information about other brands. Thus, if you are shopping for stereo equipment, it is better to check out the Consumer Reports Web site than a Web site created by a company that manufactures the product. Consider the source of your information, and think about the goals the Web site may have.

> ✔ Here are situations in which sorting information on the Internet can be helpful:
> ▶ Planning a vacation
> ▶ Purchasing electronic equipment
> ▶ Reconnecting with a childhood friend
> ▶ Learning today's news

Apply the Strategy

You're curious about the latest CD from a young country music star. Read the two portions of reviews, then evaluate the information.

> **From an on-line CD retail sales page:**
> This new CD has all the best elements of good country music. From the piano-based ballad to the roadhouse rock and roll, her passion and character make each selection a gem.

> **From an entertainment magazine page:**
> While her voice is strong and powerful, it is questionable whether her latest album would make such an impact if not for the fact that the artist is still in her early teens. A few powerful numbers make this CD worth a listen, but its greatest appeal will be for the old-school country music fans.

1. Based on what you know about the sources, what do you think is the reason each source posted the information?
2. Which review do you think is more objective? Why?
3. Which source is more useful to someone who wants to order the CD? Why?
4. Compare and contrast the kinds of details included in these two reviews.

You can get more information about the reliability of a Web site by consulting a review guide that evaluates Web sites. Here is one you might want to try:

> **Evaluating Quality on the Net**
> http://www.tiac.net/users/hope/findqual.html

---

and ability, possible reasons of the album's popularity, and a projection of who might best enjoy the music.

Please be aware that the address for the suggested Web site may have changed since we published this information. We recommend that you preview the site before sending students to it.

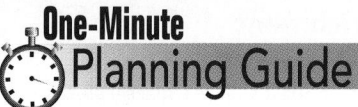
PART 2 *History and Tradition*

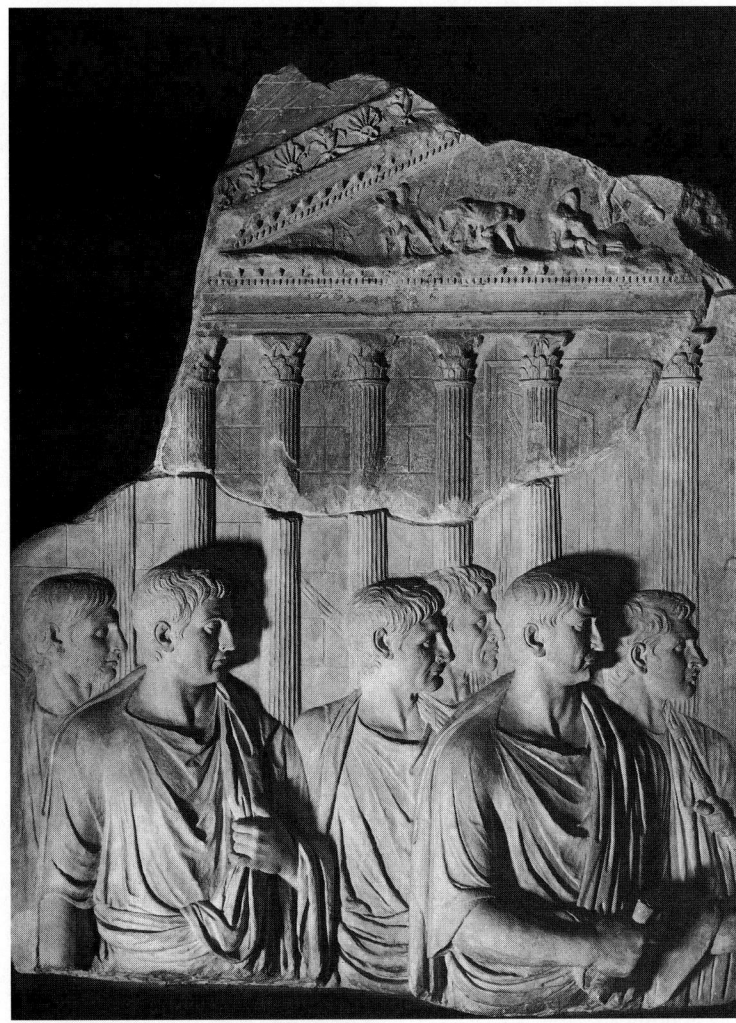

Roman senators at the Imperial Court,
Museo Nazionale Romano delle Terme, Rome, Italy

History and Tradition ◆ 705

The acts in this play cover a variety of dramatic elements that will give students insight into the history and tradition of the theater—especially the work of William Shakespeare. Each of the five acts in *The Tragedy of Julius Caesar* develops an aspect of drama or tragedy while exploring the consequences of each character's actions. Act I introduces a power struggle—a theme so timeless that directors have used *The Tragedy of Julius Caesar* to portray the political situations of many countries and ages. In Act II, students watch Caesar ignore warnings and signs as he walks into the assassination trap. In Act III, in some of the most stirring and memorable soliloquies in drama, Brutus and Antony expound on the choices made.

Act IV develops Brutus' internal conflict through his external conflict with Cassius, a character whose base motives highlight Brutus' noble ones. Act V brings the action to a close with a battle. Antony's triumph in this battle brings about the resolution of all individual, public, and political conflicts.

Customize for
Varying Student Needs
When assigning this play to your students, keep in mind the following factors:

Act I
• The list of unfamiliar character names may intimidate some students.
• Glosses in a text may be unfamiliar to many students.

Act II
• Some students may have difficulty reading blank verse for meaning.

Act III
• More advanced students will enjoy reading the full text of the famous soliloquies in this act.
• Some students may need help understanding the irony in Antony's persuasive speech to the crowd.

Act IV
• This act focuses much more on dialogue than action. Events are referred to or implied rather than described. Students may need help with reading between the lines.

Act V
• The action in this act is fast-paced and students may need help to identify changes in location.

 Humanities: Art

Roman Senators at the Imperial Court.
During the five centuries of the Roman republic, the Senate was the most powerful body in the government; made up largely of aristocrats, it is today considered a model of orderly government. The republic was destroyed by the civil war that followed the assassination of Julius Caesar. When the republic was finally replaced by empire during the reign of Augustus, the Senate was kept on, like the other institutions of government, but it became the tool of the emperor, not the independent body that had ruled during the days of the republic.

Help students link this art with the focus of Part 2, "History and Tradition," by answering the following question:
How does art help society preserve history and tradition? *Art often reflects or comments on important issues or people. Art like this sculpture provides a concrete clue about people who lived thousands of years ago.*

Enrichment

Shakespeare's Globe Theater

Most of Shakespeare's masterpieces were performed at the Globe theater. It was built by Richard and Cuthbert Burbage, sons of James Burbage, who had constructed London's first theater (named, simply, The Theater). Theater people occupied an odd position in London society. Although the city fathers looked down on actors, the common people clamored to see them perform in plays. Men like Shakespeare and the Burbages enjoyed a reputation somewhat like that of a rock star today.

The popularity of plays meant that Shakespeare's Globe, while small enough to allow actors to be heard, had to house audiences as large as 2,500 to 3,000 people. These "packed" houses must have been quite uncomfortable at times, especially when you consider that people didn't bathe or change their clothes very often. Those who paid an admission price of a penny stood throughout the performance. The second most expensive seats in the house were located in a gallery behind the performers. Although these audience members could see only the actors' backs and probably couldn't hear very well, they were willing to pay the extra price to ensure that they themselves would be seen by the rest of the audience.

Modern technology such as lighting and special sound effects was not available to Shakespeare and his contemporaries. For this reason, indications of light, sound, and setting, were often written into the script. Characters are likely to announce "'Tis dark!" as they enter a scene.

The first Globe burned to the ground in 1613, when a cannon fired in a performance of *Henry VIII* ignited the theater's thatched roof. The theater was rebuilt, and it is the foundation of this second Globe that was discovered in 1990.

The Globe Theater

The Tragedy of Julius Caesar, like most of Shakespeare's plays, was produced in a public theater. Public theaters were built around roofless courtyards having no artificial light. Performances, therefore, were given only during daylight hours. Surrounding the courtyard were three levels of galleries with benches where wealthier playgoers sat. Poorer spectators, called groundlings, stood and watched a play from the courtyard, which was called the pit.

Most of Shakespeare's plays were performed in the Globe theater. No one is certain exactly what the Globe looked like, though Shakespeare tells us it was round or octagonal. We know that it was open to the sky and that it held between 2,500 and 3,000 people. (This knowledge was the basis for the reconstruction of the Globe theater that began in 1988.) Its foundation was discovered in 1990; its excavation has revealed clues about the plays, the actors, and the audience. The tiny part of the foundation initially uncovered yielded a great number of hazelnut shells. Hazelnuts were Elizabethan "popcorn"; people munched on them all during a performance.

The stage was a platform that extended into the pit. Actors entered and left the stage from doors located behind the platform. The portion of the galleries behind and above the stage was used primarily as dressing and storage rooms. The second-level gallery right above the stage, however, was used as an upper stage.

There was no scenery in the theaters of Shakespeare's day. Settings were indicated by references in the dialogue. As a result, one scene could follow another in rapid succession. The actors wore elaborate clothing— typical Elizabethan clothing, not costuming.

▲ The new Globe Theater under construction.

▼ Below, visitors enjoy the newly constructed Globe at the International Shakespeare Globe Centre in Southwark, England.

THEATER

Thus, the plays produced in Shakespeare's day were fast-paced, colorful productions that usually lasted two hours.

An important difference between Shakespeare's theater and theater of today is that acting companies of the sixteenth century were made up only of men and boys. Women did not perform on the stage, as it was not considered proper. Boys aged eleven, twelve, or thirteen—before their voices changed—performed the female roles.

Reconstructing the Globe

In 1988, on April 23 (believed to be Shakespeare's birthday), years of fund-raising and effort resulted in a remarkable birthday present for the playwright. Work began on a reconstruction of his Globe theater. The design is based on

archaeological evidence and a drawing by Wendeslas Hollar. A contract drawn up in 1600 for the Fortune playhouse (built by the same carpenter who built the Globe) provides additional details.

The new Globe, like the first two, is made of wood. Traditional sixteenth-century carpentry techniques were used for much of the construction. A thatched roof protects the stage and galleries and lime plaster covers the walls. After long years of fund-raising and construction, the theater opened to its first full season on June 8, 1997, with a production of *Henry V.*

▼ This drawing shows the features of the Globe theater. Notice the stage, the doors through which actors enter and exit, the "upper stage," the galleries where wealthy people sit, and the pit where the groundlings stand.

The Globe Theater ◆ 707

Internet

For additional information, see *Shakespeare and the Globe: Then and Now* on the Internet at this address: **http://shakespeare.eb.com/shakespeare/index2.html**

We recommend that you preview this site before sending students to it. Be aware that addresses may have changed since we published this information.

The site includes biographies, videos, articles, and images related to the works of Shakepeare and the reconstructed Globe theater.

Enrichment

The Globe Today London's new Globe theater is considered a remarkable replica of Shakespeare's original. Located on the Thames, a short distance from the site of the original, it retains the characteristics of the original—including the circular shape, open center, and thatched roof. Since few details of the original remain, the builders relied on the building contracts, which are extant, for the rival theaters, the Rose and the Fortune. These theaters were built by the same carpenter as the Globe.

The new Globe seats 1,000. Because the seats curve around the stage, everyone has a different view of the action; for some, the view is blocked by pillars, but no audience member is more than fifty feet from the stage. The yard, or pit, has room for 450 groundlings, some of whom rest their arms on the edge of the stage. As in Elizabethan times, the audience tends to join in the proceedings, commenting on the action.

Plays are performed as they would have been in Shakespeare's time, with little or no scenery, people moving around in the yard, and vendors circulating to sell refreshments. The experience is a contrast to performances in modern theaters—even performances of Shakespeare's plays—which take place in a darkened, quiet theater with an attentive and respectful audience.

Customize for
Bodily/Kinesthetic Learners
Encourage these students to construct a model of the Globe or an Elizabethan theater. They may use the sketch on this page or do research to discover further details about the theater's construction.

Customize for
Visual/Spatial Learners
Encourage these students to refer to the diagram as they read *The Tragedy of Julius Caesar,* determining where various parts of the action would best be staged.

More About the Author

Shakespeare lived in the intellectual world of the Renaissance, the religious world of the Reformation, and the widening geographic world of the Age of Exploration. Although Shakespeare and his contemporaries did not apply these labels to their time, they were profoundly influenced by the climate of change and adventure.

Ironically, the more that boundaries and traditions were challenged, the more fiercely Elizabethans clung to them. For this reason, rank, social status, and rules of propriety were extremely important to the people of Shakespeare's day. So fanatic were the Elizabethans about social order that Clothing Acts were passed— clothing laws that specified the clothing that could be worn by different classes of people. Not surprisingly, the Clothing Acts were largely ignored, but they reflect the sentiment of the times. Students will notice at the opening of Act I of *The Tragedy of Julius Caesar* that the working class are chided for going about in public without the proper attire that indicates their station and function.

Literature CD-R⊕M To acquaint students with William Shakespeare's life, use *The Time, Life, and Works of Shakespeare* CD-ROM. In Feature 2, students can learn about Shakespeare's early life. Shakespeare's career as an actor is described in Feature 3. Feature 4 documents Shakespeare's rise as a playwright. Feature 5 focuses on the historical context that shaped Shakespeare's later work, and includes information about the Essex rebellion, the ascent to the throne of James I, other major dramatists of Shakespeare's day, and the publication of the first folio of Shakespeare's plays.

To build background on drama, use the CD-ROM *How to Read and Understand Drama,* Feature 3. This feature focuses on the ways in which stage directions suggest dramatic elements, how scenery and lighting indicate transitions in time and place, and how stage devices and conventions help to reveal a character's inner thoughts.

William Shakespeare
(1564–1616)

William Shakespeare is regarded as the greatest writer in the English language. Nearly 400 years after his death, Shakespeare's plays continue to be read widely and produced throughout the world. They have the same powerful impact on today's audiences as they had when they were first staged.

What's Past Is Prologue Based on records showing that Shakespeare was baptized on April 26, 1564, scholars estimate the date of his birth as April 23 of the same year. He was born in Stratford-on-Avon, northwest of London. Shakespeare's father, John, was a successful glove maker and businessman. He was a respected man and a leader in the community. Shakespeare's mother, whose maiden name was Mary Arden, was the daughter of his father's landlord. No written evidence of Shakespeare's boyhood exists, but given his father's status, it is probable that young Will attended the Stratford Grammar School, where he acquired a knowledge of Latin. In addition to Latin grammar, Shakespeare and his classmates would have read Latin dramas by Plautus and Terence, Latin poetry by Ovid, Horace, and Virgil, and studied logic, history, natural history, and some Greek. When Shakespeare left school, he had a solid foundation of classical literature and other subjects.

In late November or early December 1582, Shakespeare married Anne Hathaway. Records show that she was twenty-six and he was eighteen. The couple had a daughter, Susanna, in 1583, and twins, Judith and Hamnet, in 1585. Some scholars believe that for a brief time after his marriage, Shakespeare served as a country schoolmaster.

All the World's a Stage It's uncertain how Shakespeare came to be connected with the theater in the 1580's. Perhaps he was influenced by seeing the traveling performers who stopped and performed in Stratford on their way to London. At the age of eighteen or nineteen, he is believed to have been acting in plays in London. Friends in London helped him financially and professionally. Soon, he was well established in social and theatrical circles. By 1594, he was part owner and principal playwright of the Lord Chamberlain's Men, one of the most successful theater companies in London. In 1599, the company built the famous Globe theater, where most of Shakespeare's plays were performed. When James I became king in 1603, following the death of Elizabeth I, he took control of the Lord Chamberlain's Men and renamed the company The King's Men. A major stockholder in the company, Shakespeare continued to write for and act with this company.

Parting Is Such Sweet Sorrow In about 1610, Shakespeare retired to Stratford, a prosperous middle-class man, having profited from his share in a successful theater company. He moved into the second largest house in Stratford, invested in grain and farmland, and continued to write plays.

Shakespeare wrote his will on March 25, 1616. He left the bulk of his property to his oldest daughter Susanna, and a smaller sum to his other daughter Judith. (Hamnet had died in 1596.) According to the laws of the time, his widow automatically received a lifetime income from one-third of his estate. Although Susanna and Judith both had children, none lived to have children of their own. For this reason, Shakespeare has no living descendants. On April 23 (his birthday, if scholars are correct), 1616, Shakespeare died.

The Tragedy of Julius Caesar

from *Shakespeare Alive!*
Joseph Papp and Elizabeth Kirkland

Joseph Papp, the founder and producer of the New York Shakespeare festival, devoted his life to making Shakespeare accessible to all. In Shakespeare Alive! *he recreates the England in which Shakespeare lived and worked.*

Pounds of flesh in Venice; ambitious king-killers in Scotland; star-crossed lovers in Verona; daughterly ingratitude in ancient Britain; whimsical courtships in the Forest of Arden; sultry love and stern politics in ancient Egypt—Shakespeare's imagination appears to have cornered the market on exciting, inventive plot making. It seems there's no story he hasn't thought of. But how could all of these intriguing plots and stirring adventures possibly come from a single brain?

The answer is simple—they didn't. When it came to plots, Shakespeare was a borrower, not an inventor. It is astonishing to realize that not a single one of the stories in his plays was his own creation. Rather than growing his plots himself, he plucked them from the plentiful orchards of other authors.

Yet before we start suspecting Shakespeare of plagiarism, we'd better take a look at what everyone else was doing in the literary world. Although this business of outright lifting from other writers' work might seem dubious to us, it wasn't unusual in Shakespeare's time. Without copyright laws to protect an author's works,the business of writing and publishing was truly a "free trade" affair,

and everyone's works were saleable commodities. Furthermore, the authors' originality just wasn't an issue; in fact, they were openly encouraged to imitate certain writing styles and literary models, especially, but not exclusively, the classical ones. The upshot of all this was that sixteenth-century authors and playwrights regularly raided both their predecessors and their colleagues, without giving it a second thought; one contemporary of Shakespeare's boasts proudly, "I have so written, as I have read."

In his far-flung borrowing, then, Shakespeare was a product of his times; and yet in this, as in so much else, he flew high above his contemporaries. Shakespeare's ultimate source was the broad spirit of the age, which he drew on in his own unique fashion. The great literary works available in the Elizabethan time mingled in his mind with cheap ballads and penny-pamphlets on sale in Saint Paul's Churchyard, with tavern jokes, church sermons, and the constant influx of new information about foreign lands.All of this jostled up against the phrases and sounds of the everyday work and play of tanners, alehouse keepers, sailors, merchants, constables, nobles, and foreigners in London. Shakespeare imbibed the rich Elizabethan atmosphere as he walked the streets of London, and it was this atmosphere that he converted magically into theater.

Familiar Expressions from Shakespeare

You've probably quoted Shakespeare without even realizing it! Look for familiar expressions and phrases in the following list. You may be surprised at how much Shakespeare you already know!

"Eaten out of house and home," *Henry IV Part 2,* Act 2, Scene 1
"Cruel to be kind," *Hamlet,* Act 3, Scene 4
"Knock,/ knock! Who's there?" *Macbeth,* Act 2, Scene 3
"Too much of a good thing," *As You Like It,* Act 4, Scene 1
"Neither a borrower nor a lender be," *Hamlet,* Act 1, Scene 3
"Something wicked this way comes," *Macbeth,* Act 4, Scene 1
"To thine own self be true," *Hamlet,* Act 1, Scene 3
"A tower of strength," *Richard III,* Act 5, Scene 3

Guide for Reading ◆ 709

◆ **Background for Understanding**

***The Tragedy of Julius Caesar* in Performance** In 1988, Joseph Papp's New York Shakespeare Festival produced *The Tragedy of Julius Caesar.* The performance starred Al Pacino as Mark Antony and Martin Sheen as Brutus. This was not the first time popular actors played these prestigious roles. Marlon Brando played Mark Antony in Metro-Goldwyn-Mayer's 1953 movie production of the play. Both Papp's and Metro's productions were traditional interpretations, with classic settings and period costumes. Others, however, have used the political themes in the play as a comment on contemporary social and political issues. In 1937, Orson Welles staged a production in which Antony's "Friends, Romans, countrymen" funeral oration was delivered amidst searchlights and symbols suggesting a Nazi rally. A 1993 production portrays Cassius as an ambitious businessman and Mark Antony as a contemporary military leader. One of the first plays to be performed at the newly constructed Globe theater in 1599, *The Tragedy of Julius Caesar* has remained a vital and relevant production piece for more than four centuries.

Enrichment Shakespeare's plays have not only had a powerful impact on audiences over the centuries, but they have also had a powerful impact on everyday contemporary English. Dozens of familiar words and phrases were invented by Shakespeare— "catch cold," "laugh it off," "disgraceful conduct," "fair play," and the slang word "lousy," to name just a few. As critic Christopher Morley has written, "Everyone is a Shakespeare scholar unconsciously. You yourself have probably quoted him today."

 Humanities: Theater

Like Hollywood screenwriters, playwrights of the sixteenth century were subject in large part to the whims of the public. Plays were not judged successful based on their literary merit; they were assessed on the size of the audience they drew. And, like movie theaters, sixteenth-century theaters were constantly changing their offerings. This demand for fresh, new material in short order is part of what earned playwrights their reputations as hacks. With a demand for quick turnover, the playwrights couldn't afford to be particularly careful about creating perfect plays.

Like today's entertainment industry, sixteenth-century drama was a ratings game.

After a theater company bought a play from the playwright, they registered it with the office of the Master of Revels. Originally set up to organize court entertainment, the office of the Master of Revels became a powerful department through which government regulations were carried out. This power extended to censorship; in 1589 the Master of Revels was given power to "strike out such part and matters as they shall find unfit and undecent to be handled in plays."

Guide for Reading

OBJECTIVES

1. To read, comprehend, and interpret a play
2. To relate a play to personal experience
3. To use text aids in reading
4. To identify and analyze exposition in drama
5. To build vocabulary in context and learn forms of the word *portent*
6. To learn the use of the subjunctive mood
8. To respond to the play through writing and speaking and listening

SKILLS INSTRUCTION

Vocabulary:
Related Words:
Forms of *Portent*

Grammar:
Subjunctive Mood

Reading Strategy:
Use Text Aids

Critical Viewing:
Infer, Speculate

Literary Focus:
Exposition in Drama

Speaking and Listening:
Enactment (teacher edition)

PORTFOLIO OPPORTUNITIES

Writing: Journal Entry; Speech
Speaking and Listening: Enactment

Interest Grabber Tell students that this play deals with the issues of power and ambition. Use a cluster diagram on an overhead projector to help students explore the feelings people associate with power, control, and authority. Place the organizer on the overhead. In the center circle, write "power." Ask students to suggest words and feelings they associate with power. Write these words in the ovals extending from the center of the organizer. Then lead students in a discussion of why power leads to the feelings and associations they've identified.

◆ Background for Understanding

HISTORY

In 60 B.C., Gaius Julius Caesar joined forces with Marcus Licinius Crassus and Gnaeus Pompey to rule Rome as the First Triumvirate. Although he was trained as a politician, Caesar demonstrated his skill as a warrior with military victories in Gaul and Britain. When his growing strength and popularity began to make Pompey nervous, Pompey allied himself with Caesar's conservative rivals and ordered Caesar to give up his army. Caesar's response was fast and forceful. With his army, he led his troops against Pompey, forcing Pompey and the conservatives to flee to the Balkans. Within sixty days, Caesar became master of Italy. He continued to war with and pursue Pompey, following him to Egypt, where Caesar discovered Pompey had been murdered.

Pompey's forces reorganized after the death of their leader. Caesar defeated these forces once and for all in Spain, where he triumphed over the sons of Pompey. (It is from this final battle that Caesar is returning at the opening of the play.) Soon after, Julius Caesar was assassinated by a group of aristocrats led by Marcus Junius Brutus and Caius Cassius.

The characters in this play are real people who acted in the real-life drama of this episode in Roman history. Marcus Brutus lived from 85–45 B.C. He was a quiet, idealistic man. He had fought against Caesar in support of Pompey, but when Pompey was defeated, Caesar pardoned Brutus and the two resumed the friendship they had before the conflict. Brutus' father-in-law, however, killed himself rather than submit to Caesar's rule. Cassius, who was married to Brutus' sister Junia, also had supported Pompey and was pardoned when Pompey was defeated.

These details from history helped set the stage for the hidden resentments and suspicions that fill *The Tragedy of Julius Caesar.*

LITERATURE

Julius Caesar was a great general, a gifted speaker, and a popular ruler—so why would anyone want to kill him? Shakespeare didn't make up this tragic tale of power and betrayal. He based his play on real people and real events. Shakespeare read about Caesar (and his friends and enemies) in the chronicles of Plutarch, a Greek biographer who delved into the psychological as well as the factual details of his subjects' lives. Shakespeare and other people of his time were able to read Plutarch's *Lives of the Noble Greeks and Romans* translated from Latin into English by Sir Thomas North.

Some Common Elizabethan Words

The English language was somewhat different during Shakespeare's time. As you read *The Tragedy of Julius Caesar,* most of the unfamiliar words and phrases you will encounter are explained in footnotes. The following, however, appear so frequently that learning them will make your reading of the play easier.

anon: Soon
aye: Yes
betimes: Right now
e'en: Even
e'er: Ever
hence: Away, from here
hie: Hurry

hither: Here
marry: Indeed
prithee: Pray thee
sooth: Truly
withal: In addition
wont: Accustomed

710 ◆ Drama

Prentice Hall Literature Program Resources

REINFORCE / RETEACH / EXTEND

Selection Support Pages
Build Vocabulary: Forms of *Portent,* p. 204
Build Grammar Skills: Subjunctive Mood, p. 205
Reading Strategy: Use Text Aids, p. 206
Literary Focus: Exposition in Drama, p. 207

Strategies for Diverse Student Needs, p. 50

Beyond Literature The Globe Theater, p. 51

Formal Assessment Selection Test, pp. 176–178;
Assessment Resources Software

Alternative Assessment, p. 50

Writing and Language Transparencies
Daily Language Practice, Week 13, p. 124
Context Chart, pp. 59–64

Resource Pro CD-ROM
The Tragedy of Julius Caesar, Act I—includes all resource materials and customizable lesson plan

Listening to Literature Audiocassettes
The Tragedy of Julius Caesar, Act I

Literature CD-ROM
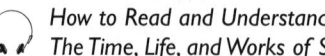
How to Read and Understand Drama
The Time, Life, and Works of Shakespeare

The Tragedy of Julius Caesar, Act I

◆ Literature and Your Life

CONNECT YOUR EXPERIENCE
Have you ever persuaded someone to do or believe something by the way you spoke and what you said, or been persuaded by someone else? The art of persuasion plays an important role early in this play.

Journal Writing List three things you have recently been persuaded to do, or ideas you have been persuaded to consider valid. For each, explain how you were persuaded.

THEMATIC FOCUS: FACING THE CONSEQUENCES
Although political powers sometimes try to persuade one another with words, often they try to "persuade" one another by force. Why do you think political forces so often go to war rather than settle differences through peaceful means?

◆ Literary Focus

EXPOSITION IN DRAMA
The **exposition** of a drama is the opening part of the work that introduces the characters, the setting, the situation, and any other details crucial to an understanding of the work. For example, in the opening of *The Tragedy of Julius Caesar,* a man in the crowd states, "We make holiday to see Caesar and to rejoice in his triumph." The response of the tribunes indicates that they fear Caesar's growing power. In just a few lines of dialogue, Shakespeare has revealed the basic situation: Caesar is returning victorious, the public loves him, and some in the government resent him. The scenes that follow build on the information presented in the exposition.

◆ Build Grammar Skills

THE SUBJUNCTIVE MOOD
The **subjunctive mood** of a verb is used in two situations. It is used to express a condition that is contrary to fact:

If I *were* Brutus now, and he *were* Cassius . . .

In this situation, the verb form is always *were*.

The subjunctive mood is also used in clauses beginning with *that* to express indirectly a demand, recommendation, suggestion, or statement of necessity.

Antony requested that Caesar *take* the crown.

Here, the verb is always the base form. It does not change, regardless of the subject.

◆ Reading Strategy

USE TEXT AIDS
Playwrights provide **text aids** for actors, which can help readers as well. The stage directions that tell actors where and how to move can help you to picture what is happening on the stage. Pay attention to the stage directions (enclosed in brackets in the text) to help you follow the stage action.

Elizabethan plays prepared for a modern reading audience provide another aid: Notes and glosses along the sides of text lines explain the meanings of words and phrases that are no longer in use. Refer to these notes to clarify unfamiliar language.

◆ Build Vocabulary

RELATED WORDS: FORMS OF *PORTENT*
In Act I, much is made of the *portentous* signs that something bad is about to happen. The adjective *portentous* comes from the verb *portend*, which means "to be an omen or warning of." The noun form is *portent.* There will be many *portents* in the acts that follow.

WORD BANK
Before you read, preview this list of words from the selection.

replication
spare
infirmity
surly
portentous
prodigious

One-Minute Insight
Based on historical events in ancient Rome, Shakespeare's *The Tragedy of Julius Caesar* is a brilliant study of character and conflict set in a political arena. Much of the plot hinges on the character and internal conflicts of Caesar's friend Brutus, who is drawn, at first reluctantly, into an assassination conspiracy against Caesar. The choices Brutus makes—and the consequences of these choices—make for a rich portrait of the conflicts between loyalty and ambition; between friendship and what Brutus comes to perceive as his patriotic duty.

Customize for
Less Proficient Readers
To familiarize these students with the plot and characters of the play before they begin reading, you may want to play the portion of a video version through the events in Act I. The version featuring Marlon Brando as Antony is available in most video stores.

Customize for
More Advanced Students
Suggest that these students form a discussion group to talk about the conflicts introduced in Act I of the play: the external conflict between the conspirators and Caesar and the internal conflict within Brutus. Suggest that they watch how these conflicts change and develop throughout the play.

Customize for
English Language Learners
These students will have the most difficulty with Shakespeare's language. You may want to summarize the act for them and have them read only selected key speeches, focusing on the exposition of the plot and the techniques Cassius uses to persuade Brutus to join his conspiracy.

Customize for
Interpersonal Learners
These students will enjoy meeting in groups to analyze and debate the behavior of the major characters after reading each scene. Each member of the group could choose a different character to role-play or defend during the meetings.

Preparing for Standardized Tests

Grammar and Language The Build Grammar Skills lesson for this selection focuses on the use of the subjunctive mood. By familiarizing themselves with the subjunctive mood, students may be able to improve performance on the composition and grammar sections of standardized tests. For example, test items similar to the following ask students to find the error in a sentence.

Although many young people <u>dream of</u> becoming
A

professional <u>athletes</u>, few of even the most
B

<u>talented</u> achieve that goal; therefore, if <u>I was</u>
C   D

planning such a career, I might reconsider.

<u>No Error</u>
E

The correct answer is D because the contrary-to-fact condition requires the subjunctive *were*.

For additional practice, use the Build Grammar Skills page on The Subjunctive Mood, p. 205, in *Selection Support.*

Infer The man standing is looking down at the other two men who have to raise their eyes to see him. The way the men are positioned suggests that the standing man is figuratively as well as literally elevated above the others.

Humanities: Film

On stage, an actor is usually separated from even the closest members of the audience by a space of at least five feet. In many theaters, the stage is raised from two to five feet above the seating area as well. For this reason, subtle facial expressions and small gestures are not the most effective means of communicating a character's emotions. In a movie, however, every twitch of an actor's eyebrow is visible to the audience. The smallest motion of an actor's hand can be used to indicate purpose, indecision, or tension. For instance, close-ups in the MGM version of *Julius Caesar* show the anxiety the conspirators feel before the assassination attempt. In addition to close-ups, camera angles and techniques can be used to enhance the mood of a scene. Ask students to answer the following questions about this still from the MGM version of *Julius Caesar*:

1. How does the camera angle contribute to the sense of Caesar's authority over the kneeling men? *By shooting from over Caesar's shoulder, the director highlights Caesar's physical position over the men.*

2. Describe the expressions on the faces of the characters. *Caesar's expression is calm and confident. He is unaware of the plot against him. The expressions of the kneeling men betray some of their nervousness. Cassius, kneeling at center, wears an expression of repressed anticipation.*

The Tragedy of
JULIUS CAESAR

William Shakespeare

 ▲ **Critical Viewing** How can you tell that the man standing is a man of power? [Infer]

712 ◆ Drama

Block Scheduling Strategies

Consider these suggestions to take advantage of extended class time:

- Invite students to view Feature 2 on the CD-ROM, *The Time, Life, and Works of Shakespeare.* This feature focuses on Shakespeare's early life and Elizabethan London.

- As an alternative to a silent reading of the play, assign roles and have groups act out selected scenes. Encourage students to act the stage directions.

- Make the audiocassette available to students who would like to listen to all or part of the selection.

- Have students work individually or in groups to complete the Critical Thinking questions on page 730.

- Have students complete Reading Strategy: *Use Text Aids* in **Selection Support,** p. 206.

CHARACTERS

Julius Caesar
Octavius Caesar ⎫
Marcus Antonius ⎬ triumvirs* after the death of Julius Caesar
M. Aemilius Lepidus ⎭

Cicero ⎫
Publius ⎬ senators
Popilius Lena ⎭

Marcus Brutus ⎫
Cassius ⎪
Casca ⎪
Trebonius ⎬ conspirators against Julius Caesar
Ligarius ⎪
Decius Brutus ⎪
Metellus Cimber ⎪
Cinna ⎭

Flavius ⎫
Marullus ⎬ tribunes

Artemidorus of Cnidos, a teacher of rhetoric

A Soothsayer
Cinna, a poet
Another Poet

Lucilius ⎫
Titinius ⎪
Messala ⎬ friends to Brutus and Cassius
Young Cato ⎪
Volumnius ⎭

Varro ⎫
Clitus ⎪
Claudius ⎬ servants to Brutus
Strato ⎪
Lucius ⎪
Dardanius ⎭

Pindarus, servant to Cassius
Calpurnia, wife to Caesar
Portia, wife to Brutus
Senators, Citizens, Guards, Attendants, and so on

Scene: During most of the play, at Rome; afterward near Sardis, and near Philippi.

─────────────────────────────

triumvirs (trī um´ vẹrz) n.: In ancient Rome, a group of three rulers who share authority equally.

Act I

Scene i. *Rome. A street.*

[*Enter* FLAVIUS, MARULLUS, *and certain* COMMONERS[1] *over the stage.*]

2

FLAVIUS. Hence! Home, you idle creatures, get you home!
　　Is this a holiday? What, know you not,
　　Being mechanical,[2] you ought not walk
　　Upon a laboring day without the sign
5　　Of your profession?[3] Speak, what trade art thou?

　　CARPENTER. Why, sir, a carpenter.

1. **commoners** (käm´ ən ẹrz) *n.:* People not of the nobility or upper classes.

2. **mechanical:** Of the working class.

3. **sign/Of your profession:** Work clothes and tools.

The Tragedy of Julius Caesar, Act I, Scene i ◆ 713

Humanities: Theater

This opening scene and Caesar's entrance have been staged in a variety of ways to set the scene for a variety of directors' interpretations of the play. The MGM film has Caesar entering in a military procession being cheered by a crowd larger than any theater would accommodate. The emphasis is on pomp and pageantry. In a later production, mounted by the Royal Shakespeare company in England, Caesar is strikingly silhouetted against a simple background of pillars, lending dignity and stature to his character. Trevor Nunn (who also directed *Cats* and *Les Miserables*)

dressed Caesar in black leather and had him enter on a red carpet, flanked by soldiers dressed in gray uniforms. Ask students how each of these entrances might affect their feelings at the beginning of the play. Students should recognize that the choice a director makes about Caesar's entrance will create an emotional response in the audience. The audience's emotional response to Caesar will affect their view of all subsequent events in the play.

1 Use Text Aids Direct students to *gloss* 5 and explain how the two different meanings of the word *cobbler* lead to a misunderstanding between Marullus and the cobbler.

Marullus thinks the tradesman is describing himself as a clumsy worker, when in fact the man is identifying his trade as a mender of shoes.

◆ **Literary Focus**

2 Exposition in Drama Marullus' speech reveals that, recently, the common people were loyal to Pompey, the general defeated by Caesar, and celebrated his triumphs. Now that Pompey has been defeated by Caesar, the people have abruptly shifted their loyalty to Caesar.

Customize for
English Language Learners
Guide these students to understand the figurative language "you blocks, you stones" and "hard hearts" in Marullus' address to the crowd.

MARULLUS. Where is thy leather apron and thy rule?
What dost thou with thy best apparel on?
You, sir, what trade are you?

10   **COBBLER.** Truly, sir, in respect of a fine workman,[4] I am but, as you would say, a cobbler.[5]

❶ MARULLUS. But what trade art thou? Answer me directly.

COBBLER. A trade, sir, that, I hope, I may use with a safe conscience, which is indeed, sir, a mender of bad
15   soles.

FLAVIUS. What trade, thou knave?[6] Thou naughty knave what trade?

COBBLER. Nay, I beseech you, sir, be not out with me: yet, if you be out,[7] sir, I can mend you.[8]

MARULLUS. What mean'st thou by that? Mend me, thou saucy fellow?

20   **COBBLER.** Why, sir, cobble you.

FLAVIUS. Thou art a cobbler, art thou?

COBBLER. Truly, sir, all that I live by is with the awl:[9] I meddle with no tradesman's matters, nor women's matters; but withal, I am indeed, sir, a surgeon to old
25   shoes: when they are in great danger, I recover them. As proper men as ever trod upon neat's leather[10] have gone upon my handiwork.

FLAVIUS. But wherefore art not in thy shop today? Why dost thou lead these men about the streets?

30   **COBBLER.** Truly, sir, to wear out their shoes, to get myself into more work. But indeed, sir, we make holiday to see Caesar and to rejoice in his triumph.[11]

MARULLUS. Wherefore rejoice? What conquest brings he home?

    What tributaries[12] follow him to Rome,
35   To grace in captive bonds his chariot wheels?
You blocks, you stones, you worse than senseless things!
O you hard hearts, you cruel men of Rome,
Knew you not Pompey?[13] Many a time and oft
Have you climbed up to walls and battlements,
40   To tow'rs and windows, yea, to chimney tops,

4. in respect of a fine workman: In relation to a skilled worker.
5. cobbler: Mender of shoes or a clumsy, bungling worker.

6. knave (nāv) *n.*: Tricky rascal; rogue.

7. be not out . . . if you be out: Be not angry . . . if you have worn-out shoes.
8. mend you: Mend your shoes or improve your disposition.

9. awl (ôl) *n.*: Small, pointed tool for making holes in leather.

10. neat's leather: Leather made from the hides of cattle.

11. triumph (trī´ əmf) *n.*: In ancient Rome, a procession celebrating the return of a victorious general and his army.
12. tributaries (trib´ yōō ter´ ēz) *n.*: Captives.

◆ **Literary Focus**
What background do you learn from Marullus' speech? **❷**

13. Pompey (päm´ pē): A Roman general and triumvir defeated by Caesar in 48 B.C. and later murdered.

Cross-Curricular Connection: Social Studies

Marullus asks the mob, "Knew you not Pompey?" He is referring to the Roman general Pompey the Great (106–48 B.C.), once an ally of Caesar, and later, the last obstacle Caesar had to overcome in his rise to power.

Pompey grew up in a wealthy Roman family, in a time of warfare between two generals, Gaius Marius and Lucius Sulla. Still in his twenties, he raised an army of three legions, allied himself with Sulla, and beat Marius. The Senate sent him to Spain, where he defeated Marius' followers.

A string of victories made Pompey a hero to the public but a threat to the Senate, which feared that they could not control such a hero. In 60 B.C., Pompey, Julius Caesar, and Marcus Crassus, formed what became known as the First Triumvirate, to resist the Senate's antimilitarism.

Pompey started to worry about Caesar's growing power and broke with him, leading to civil war. Pompey's army lost two battles to Caesar. After the second, in 48 B.C., Pompey escaped to Egypt, but was killed by order of the Roman-dominated Egyptian government.

<table>
<tr><td></td><td>Your infants in your arms, and there have sat</td></tr>
<tr><td></td><td>The livelong day, with patient expectation,</td></tr>
<tr><td></td><td>To see great Pompey pass the streets of Rome.</td></tr>
<tr><td></td><td>And when you saw his chariot but appear,</td></tr>
<tr><td>45</td><td>Have you not made an universal shout,</td></tr>
<tr><td></td><td>That Tiber[14] trembled underneath her banks</td></tr>
<tr><td></td><td>To hear the replication of your sounds</td></tr>
<tr><td></td><td>Made in her concave shores?[15]</td></tr>
<tr><td></td><td>And do you now put on your best attire?</td></tr>
<tr><td>50</td><td>And do you now cull out[16] a holiday?</td></tr>
<tr><td></td><td>And do you now strew flowers in his way</td></tr>
<tr><td></td><td>That comes in triumph over Pompey's blood?[17]</td></tr>
<tr><td></td><td>Be gone!</td></tr>
<tr><td></td><td>Run to your houses, fall upon your knees,</td></tr>
<tr><td>55</td><td>Pray to the gods to intermit the plague[18]</td></tr>
<tr><td></td><td>That needs must light on this ingratitude.</td></tr>
</table>

FLAVIUS. Go, go, good countrymen, and, for this fault,
Assemble all the poor men of your sort;
Draw them to Tiber banks and weep your tears

60 Into the channel, till the lowest stream
Do kiss the most exalted shores of all.[19]

[All the COMMONERS *exit.]*

❸

See, whe'r their basest mettle[20] be not moved,
They vanish tongue-tied in their guiltiness.
Go you down that way toward the Capitol;

65 This way will I. Disrobe the images,
If you do find them decked with ceremonies.[21]

MARULLUS. May we do so?
You know it is the feast of Lupercal.[22]

FLAVIUS. It is no matter; let no images

70 Be hung with Caesar's trophies. I'll about
And drive away the vulgar[23] from the streets;
So do you too, where you perceive them thick.

❹

These growing feathers plucked from Caesar's wing
Will make him fly an ordinary pitch,[24]

75 Who else would soar above the view of men
And keep us all in servile fearfulness. *[Exit]*

Scene ii. *A public place.*

[Enter CAESAR, ANTONY *(for the course),*[1] CALPURNIA, PORTIA, DECIUS, CICERO, BRUTUS, CASSIUS, CASCA, *a* SOOTHSAYER; *after them,* MARULLUS *and* FLAVIUS.]

14. Tiber (tī′ bər): River that flows through Rome.

15. concave shores: Hollowed-out banks; overhanging banks.

16. cull out: Pick out; select.

17. Pompey's blood: Pompey's sons, whom Caesar has just defeated.

18. intermit the plague (plāg): Stop the calamity or trouble.

19. the most exalted shores of all: The highest banks.

20. whe'r their basest mettle: Whether the most inferior material of which they are made.

21. Disrobe the images . . . decked with ceremonies: Strip the statues . . . covered with decorations.

22. feast of Lupercal (lōō′ pər kal): Ancient Roman festival celebrated on February 15.

23. vulgar (vul′ gər) *n.*: Common people.

24. pitch: Upward flight of a hawk.

1. for the course: Ready for the foot race that was part of the Lupercal festivities.

◆ **Build Vocabulary**
replication (rep′ lə kā′ shən) *n.*: Echo or reverberation

◆ **Reading Strategy**

❸ **Use Text Aids** Students should note when Flavius stops addressing the crowd and begins speaking to Marullus. Ask how they can tell when this change occurs. *He begins addressing Marullus in line 62. Students can tell when the change begins because the stage directions after line 61 indicate that the Commoners exit the stage at that point and Marullus is the only other person left on stage.*

◆ **Literary Focus**

❹ **Exposition in Drama** Lead students to identify the reason Flavius gives for removing Caesar's trophies from public places. What information does this passage provide about Caesar? *Flavius is afraid that all the tributes will make Caesar feel too powerful and encourage him to be tyrannical. The passage introduces Caesar as potentially dangerous to the Roman republic and its citizens.*

Writing and Language Transparencies Use the Context Chart, pp. 107–109, in *Writing and Language Transparencies.* The chart offers suggestions for several ways the chart can be used to enhance your students' understanding of the play.

Literature CD-ROM *The Life, Time, and Works of Shakespeare* Use feature 5 to support students' exploration of the historical and social context in which this play was written.

◆ **Reading Strategy**

2 Use Text Aids Students should explain how the glosses helped them understand the unfamiliar language. For instance, without gloss 4, students might not have known whether the ides of March were things like winds, animals, or frogs, or a specific date, as the note clarifies.

Customize for
Interpersonal Learners

Have two interpersonal learners read aloud the important dialogue between Cassius and Brutus that begins here with line 25 and continues through line 177. Stop them occasionally and ask them to explain to the class how Cassius is trying to win Brutus over to his point of view and how Brutus is responding.

CAESAR. Calpurnia!

CASCA.   Peace, ho! Caesar speaks.

CAESAR.   Calpurnia!

CALPURNIA. Here, my lord.

CAESAR. Stand you directly in Antonius' way
    When he doth run his course. Antonius!

5 **ANTONY.** Caesar, my lord?

CAESAR. Forget not in your speed, Antonius,
    To touch Calpurnia; for our elders say
    The barren, touchèd in this holy chase,
    Shake off their sterile curse.²

ANTONY.   I shall remember:

10   When Caesar says "Do this," it is performed.

CAESAR. Set on, and leave no ceremony out.

SOOTHSAYER. Caesar!

CAESAR. Ha! Who calls?

CASCA. Bid every noise be still; peace yet again!

15 **CAESAR.** Who is it in the press³ that calls on me?
    I hear a tongue, shriller than all the music,
    Cry "Caesar." Speak; Caesar is turned to hear.

SOOTHSAYER. Beware the ides of March.⁴

 CAESAR.   What man is that?

BRUTUS. A soothsayer bids you beware the ides of March.

20 **CAESAR.** Set him before me; let me see his face.

CASSIUS. Fellow, come from the throng; look upon Caesar.

CAESAR. What say'st thou to me now? Speak once again.

SOOTHSAYER. Beware the ides of March.

CAESAR. He is a dreamer, let us leave him. Pass.

    [*A trumpet sounds. Exit all but* BRUTUS *and* CASSIUS.]

25 **CASSIUS.** Will you go see the order of the course?⁵

BRUTUS. Not I.

CASSIUS. I pray you do.

BRUTUS. I am not gamesome:⁶ I do lack some part
    Of that quick spirit⁷ that is in Antony.

716 ◆ Drama

---

2. barren . . . sterile curse: It was believed that women who were unable to bear children (such as Calpurnia), if touched by a runner during this race, would then be able to bear children.

3. press *n.*: Crowd.

4. ides (īdz) **of March:** March 15.

◆ **Reading Strategy**
Which glosses on this page did you use to clarify unfamiliar language? **2**

5. order of the course: The race.

6. gamesome (gām′ səm) *adj.*: Having a liking for sports.
7. quick spirit: Lively disposition.

Cross-Curricular Connection: Mathematics

Caesar is warned to beware "the ides of March." Explain that the *ides* came near the middle of each month in the old Roman calendar.

The earliest known Roman calendar consisted of ten months and a 304-day year. The ten months were called Martius, Aprilis, Maius, Junius, Quintilis, Sextilis, September, October, November, and December. The last six names were taken from the Latin words for the numbers five through ten.

By the time of Julius Caesar, about 700 years later, the calendar was about three months ahead of the natural cycle of seasons. In 46 B.C., Julius Caesar asked an astronomer to create a more accurate calendar. A 365-day year was divided into twelve months of thirty-one or thirty days each, except for February, which had only twenty-nine days. Every fourth year, it would

have thirty days. Quintilius was renamed July to honor Julius Caesar. Sextilis was later renamed August to honor the emperor Augustus. Tradition has it that Augustus moved a day from February to August to make his month as long as Caesar's.

Encourage students to research the Gregorian calendar, which we now use, and compare it to the early Roman calendar.

►Critical Viewing◄

❸ Speculate The guarded expressions and alert body language of Caesar and Antony suggest that they are looking at someone or something they do not completely like or trust. Students may suggest that this is one or more of the conspirators, people in the crowd, or a statue from which Caesar's trophies have been removed.

◆ Critical Thinking

❹ Analyze Guide students to use the side notes for this passage to paraphrase what Brutus is saying about himself. Then ask what kind of conflict Brutus might be feeling as his friend Caesar rises to power. *Brutus is saying that he has been experiencing inner conflict lately. Because he has been so preoccupied with his own thoughts, he has not been paying much attention to his friends. Students may speculate that Brutus is torn by his feelings of love for Caesar and his fears that Caesar is becoming too powerful.*

❸|▲ Critical Viewing At what or whom do you think Caesar and Antony are looking? [Speculate]

30   Let me not hinder, Cassius, your desires;
        I'll leave you.

        CASSIUS. Brutus, I do observe you now of late;
        I have not from your eyes that gentleness
        And show of love as I was wont⁸ to have;
35   You bear too stubborn and too strange a hand⁹
        Over your friend that loves you.

        BRUTUS.   Cassius,
        Be not deceived: if I have veiled my look,
        I turn the trouble of my countenance
        Merely upon myself.¹⁰ Vexèd I am
40   Of late with passions¹¹ of some difference,¹²
        Conceptions only proper to myself,¹³
        Which give some soil,¹⁴ perhaps, to my behaviors;
        But let not therefore my good friends be grieved

8. **wont** (wōnt): Accustomed.

9. **bear . . . hand:** Treat too harshly and too like a stranger.

10. **if I . . . upon myself:** If I have been less open, my troubled face is due entirely to personal matters.

11. **passions:** Feelings; emotions.

12. **of some difference:** In conflict.

13. **Conceptions . . . myself:** Thoughts that concern only me.

14. **soil:** Blemish.

The Tragedy of Julius Caesar, Act I, Scene ii ◆ 717

❶ What does Cassius mean when he asks if Brutus can see his own face and his own shadow? *He is suggesting that Brutus cannot see his own inner self, the noble qualities that other people can see in him.*

❷ Clarification Explain that *glass* is another word for mirror. By offering to be Brutus' "glass," Cassius is saying that he will help Brutus see himself more clearly, that he will reveal Brutus' noble qualities, which Brutus himself seems not to see.

◆ *Literature and Your Life*

❸ Some students may suggest that they appreciate the insights these friends are able to give them. Others may say that it's annoying to have someone presume they know how you think or feel.

---

45   (Among which number, Cassius, be you one)
      Nor construe any further my neglect
      Than that poor Brutus, with himself at war,
      Forgets the shows of love to other men.

      CASSIUS. Then, Brutus, I have much mistook your passion;
      By means whereof this breast of mine hath buried[15]
50   Thoughts of great value, worthy cogitations.[16]
      Tell me, good Brutus, can you see your face?

      BRUTUS. No, Cassius; for the eye sees not itself
      But by reflection, by some other things.

      CASSIUS. 'Tis just.[17]
55 ❶ And it is very much lamented,[18] Brutus,
      That you have no such mirrors as will turn
      Your hidden worthiness into your eye,
      That you might see your shadow.[19] I have heard
      Where many of the best respect[20] in Rome
60   (Except immortal Caesar), speaking of Brutus,
      And groaning underneath this age's yoke,[21]
      Have wished that noble Brutus had his eyes.

      BRUTUS. Into what dangers would you lead me, Cassius,
      That you would have me seek into myself
65   For that which is not in me?

      CASSIUS. Therefore, good Brutus, be prepared to hear;
      And since you know you cannot see yourself
 ❷   So well as by reflection, I, your glass
      Will modestly discover to yourself
70   That of yourself which you yet know not of.[22]
      And be not jealous on[23] me, gentle Brutus:
      Were I a common laughter,[24] or did use
      To stale with ordinary oaths my love
      To every new protester;[25] if you know
75   That I do fawn on men and hug them hard,
      And after scandal[26] them; or if you know
      That I profess myself in banqueting
      To all the rout,[27] then hold me dangerous.

                    [*Flourish of trumpets and shout*]

      BRUTUS. What means this shouting? I do fear the people
      Choose Caesar for their king.

80   **CASSIUS.**   Ay, do you fear it?
      Then must I think you would not have it so.

      BRUTUS. I would not, Cassius, yet I love him well.

---

15. By means . . . buried: Because of which I have kept to myself.
16. cogitations (kaj ə tā´ shənz) *n.*: Thoughts.

17. 'Tis just: It is true.

18. lamented (lə men´ t'd) *v.*: Regretted.

19. turn . . . shadow: Reflect your hidden noble qualities so you could see their image.
20. the best respect: Most respected people.
21. this age's yoke: The tyranny of Caesar.

◆ *Literature and Your Life*
❸ Cassius claims to know Brutus better than Brutus knows himself. How do you deal with friends who think they know what you want or what you think?

22. Will modestly . . . know not of: Will without exaggeration make known to you the qualities you have that you are unaware of.
23. be not jealous on: Do not be suspicious of.
24. common laughter: Object of ridicule.
25. To stale . . . new protester: To make cheap my friendship to anyone who promises to be my friend.
26. scandal: Slander; gossip about.
27. profess myself . . . rout: Declare my friendship to the common crowd.

Cross-Curricular Connection: Social Studies

The Roman Republic The Roman Republic was founded in 509 B.C. when the harsh Etruscan king Tarquinius Superbus was overthrown. Until 27 B.C., Rome remained a republic; that is, there was no king or emperor. Two consuls, elected each year by an assembly called the *Comitia Centuriata,* governed as chief executives, each having the right to veto decisions of the other. The Senate consisted of 300 senators chosen for life

by the consuls. Because the *patricians,* or nobility, controlled the Comitia Centuriata, the *plebeians,* or common people, set up their own assembly, the *Concilium Plebis.* In addition, there were *praetors,* or judicial officials, *quaestors,* or financial officials, and *censors,* supervisors of public morals.

Invite students to find parallels between the structure of the Roman republic and our own government.

But wherefore do you hold me here so long?
What is it that you would impart to me?
85   If it be aught toward the general good,[28]
Set honor in one eye and death i' th' other,
And I will look on both indifferently;[29]
For let the gods so speed[30] me, as I love
The name of honor more than I fear death.

90   **CASSIUS.** I know that virtue to be in you, Brutus,
As well as I do know your outward favor.[31]
Well, honor is the subject of my story.
I cannot tell what you and other men
Think of this life, but for my single self,
95   I had as lief not be,[32] as live to be
In awe of such a thing as I myself.[33]
I was born free as Caesar; so were you:
We both have fed as well, and we can both
Endure the winter's cold as well as he:
100   For once, upon a raw and gusty day,
The troubled Tiber chafing with[34] her shores,
Caesar said to me "Darest thou, Cassius, now
Leap in with me into this angry flood,
And swim to yonder point?" Upon the word,
105   Accout'red[35] as I was, I plungèd in
And bade him follow: so indeed he did.
❹ The torrent roared, and we did buffet[36] it
With lusty sinews,[37] throwing it aside
And stemming it with hearts of controversy.[38]
110   But ere we could arrive the point proposed,
Caesar cried "Help me, Cassius, or I sink!"
I, as Aeneas,[39] our Great ancestor,
Did from the flames of Troy upon his shoulder
The old Anchises bear, so from the waves of Tiber
115 ❺ Did I the tired Caesar. And this man
Is now become a god, and Cassius is
A wretched creature, and must bend his body
If Caesar carelessly but nod on him.
He had a fever when he was in Spain,
120   And when the fit was on him, I did mark
How he did shake: 'tis true, this god did shake.
His coward lips did from their color fly,[40]
❻ And that same eye whose bend[41] doth awe the world
did lose his[42] luster: I did hear him groan;
125   Ay, and that tongue of his, that bade the Romans
Mark him and write his speeches in their books,

The Tragedy of Julius Caesar, Act I, Scene ii ◆ *719*

28. aught . . . good:
Anything to do with the
public welfare.
29. indifferently: Without
preference or concern.
30. speed: Give good
fortune to.

31. favor: Face;
appearance.

32. as lief not be: Just
as soon not exist.
**33. such a thing as I
myself:** Another human
being (Caesar).

34. chafing with: Raging
against.

35. Accout'red: Dressed
in armor.
36. buffet (buf' it) *v*.:
Struggle against.
37. lusty sinews (sin'
yōōz): Strong muscles.
**38. stemming it . . .
controversy:** Making
progress against it with
our intense rivalry.
39. Aeneas (ē nē' es):
Trojan hero of the poet
Virgil's epic poem *Aeneid*,
who carried his old father,
Anchises, from the burn-
ing city of Troy and later
founded Rome.

**40. His coward lips . . .
fly:** Color fled from his
lips, which were like cowardly soldiers fleeing from
a battle.
41. bend *n*.: Glance.
42. his: Its.

Comprehension Check ☑

❷ Who or what does Cassius say is to blame for the tyrannical rule that Romans are suffering? *He says that the people themselves are to blame for putting up with Caesar and not fighting back.*

◆ *Literature and Your Life*

❸ Cassius uses flattery to try to win Brutus over to his side. Ask students if they think flattery and compliments are usually effective in persuading people to do something. Do students tend to trust people who flatter them? *Students should note the importance of distinguishing between flattery as a persuasive tool and a sincere compliment.*

Alas, it cried, "Give me some drink, Titinius,"
As a sick girl. Ye gods! It doth amaze me,
A man of such a feeble temper[43] should
130   So get the start of[44] the majestic world,
❶   And bear the palm[45] alone.

　　　　　　　　　　　　[*Shout. Flourish of trumpets*]

BRUTUS. Another general shout?
　　I do believe that these applauses are
　　For some new honors that are heaped on Caesar.

135   **CASSIUS.** Why, man, he doth bestride the narrow world
　　Like a Colossus,[46] and we petty men
　　Walk under his huge legs and peep about
❷   To find ourselves dishonorable[47] graves.
　　Men at some time are masters of their fates:
140   The fault, dear Brutus, is not in our stars,[48]
　　But in ourselves, that we are underlings.[49]
　　Brutus and Caesar: what should be in that "Caesar"?
　　Why should that name be sounded[50] more than
　　　　yours?
　　Write them together, yours is as fair a name;
145   Sound them, it doth become the mouth as well;
　　Weigh them, it is as heavy; conjure[51] with 'em,
　　"Brutus" will start[52] a spirit as soon as "Caesar."
　　Now, in the names of all the gods at once,
　　Upon what meat doth this our Caesar feed,
150   That he is grown so great? Age, thou art shamed!
❸   Rome, thou hast lost the breed of noble bloods!
　　When went there by an age, since the great flood,[53]
　　But it was famed with[54] more than with one man?
　　When could they say (till now) that talked of Rome,
155   That her wide walks encompassed but one man?
　　Now is it Rome indeed, and room enough,
　　When there is in it but one only man.
　　O, you and I have heard our fathers say,
　　There was a Brutus[55] once that would have brooked[56]
160   Th' eternal devil to keep his state in Rome
　　As easily as a king.

　　BRUTUS. That you do love me, I am nothing jealous;[57]
　　What you would work me to,[58] I have some aim;[59]
　　How I have thought of this, and of these times,
165   I shall recount hereafter. For this present,
　　I would not so (with love I might entreat you)
　　Be any further moved. What you have said
　　I will consider; what you have to say

---

43. **feeble temper:** Weak physical constitution.
44. **get the start of:** Become the leader of.
45. **palm:** Symbol of victory; victor's prize.

46. **Colossus** (kə läs´ əs) *n.*: Gigantic statue of Apollo, a god of Greek and Roman mythology, which was set at the entrance to the harbor of Rhodes about 280 B.C. and was included among the seven wonders of the ancient world.
47. **dishonorable** (dis än´ ər ə b'l) *adj.*: Shameful (because they will not be of free men).
48. **stars:** Destinies. The stars were thought to control people's lives.
49. **underlings:** Inferior people.
50. **sounded:** Spoken or announced by trumpets.
51. **conjure** (kän jər) *v.*: Summon a spirit by a magic spell.
52. **start:** Raise.
53. **great flood:** In Greek mythology, a flood that drowned everyone except Deucalion and his wife Pyrrha who were saved by the god Zeus because of their virtue.
54. **But it was famed with:** Without the age being made famous by.
55. **Brutus:** Lucius Junius Brutus had helped expel the last king of Rome and had helped found the Republic in 509 B.C.
56. **brooked:** Put up with.
57. **nothing jealous:** Not at all doubting.
58. **work me to:** Persuade me of.
59. **aim:** Idea.

720 ◆ *Drama*

170 I will with patience hear, and find a time
Both meet to hear and answer such high things.
Till then, my noble friend, chew upon[60] this:
Brutus had rather be a villager
Than to repute himself a son of Rome
Under these hard conditions as this time
Is like to lay upon us.

175 **CASSIUS.**   I am glad
That my weak words have struck but thus much
  show
Of fire from Brutus.

[*Enter* CASSIUS *and his* TRAIN.]

BRUTUS. The games are done, and Caesar is returning.

CASSIUS. As they pass by, pluck Casca by the sleeve,
180 And he will (after his sour fashion) tell you
What hath proceeded worthy note today.

BRUTUS. I will do so. But look you, Cassius,
The angry spot doth glow on Caesar's brow,
And all the rest look like a chidden train:[61]
185 Calpurnia's cheek is pale, and Cicero
Looks with such ferret[62] and such fiery eyes
As we have seen him in the Capitol,
Being crossed in conference[63] by some senators.

CASSIUS. Casca will tell us what the matter is.

190 **CAESAR.** Antonius.

ANTONY. Caesar?

CAESAR. Let me have men about me that are fat,
Sleek-headed men, and such as sleep a-nights.
Yond Cassius has a lean and hungry look;
195 He thinks too much: such men are dangerous.

ANTONY. Fear him not, Caesar, he's not dangerous;
He is a noble Roman, and well given.[64]

CAESAR. Would he were fatter! But I fear him not.
Yet if my name were liable to fear,
200 I do not know the man I should avoid
So soon as that spare Cassius. He reads much,
He is a great observer, and he looks
quite through the deeds of men.[65] He loves no plays,
As thou dost, Antony; he hears no music;
205 Seldom he smiles, and smiles in such a sort[66]

The Tragedy of Julius Caesar, Act I, Scene ii ◆ 721

60. chew upon: Think about.

◆ **Reading Strategy**
How do the stage directions here help you understand the action?   ④

61. chidden train: Scolded attendants.

62. ferret (fer´ it) *n.*: Small animal, like a weasel, with reddish eyes.

63. crossed in conference: Opposed in debate.

64. well given: Well disposed.
65. looks . . . deeds of men: Sees through people's actions to their motives.
66. sort: Way.

◆ **Build Vocabulary**
spare (sper) *adj.*: Lean or thin

Cross-Curricular Connection: Social Studies

The Roman Empire The year 27 B.C. marked the end of the Roman republic. In that year, Octavius became princeps, or ruler, of Rome, and took the name Augustus. After that, supreme authority rested with the emperor, who was aided and advised by the Senate. The emperor was chosen either by his predecessor or by the army. As time went on, the Senate lost power, and Rome became an absolute monarchy.

Rome controlled many provinces; in fact, in A.D. 117, the Roman empire stretched from northern Britain to the shores of the Red Sea and the Persian Gulf. It included Hibernia (Scotland), Britannia (England), Gallia (France), Hispania (Spain), Achaia (Greece), and Aegyptus (Egypt), among many others. The provinces were governed by Roman governors, aided by a staff of military assistants. Local officials, however, were allowed to manage local affairs.

❶ Infer Cassius, in the picture, has very lean, angular features and Caesar says he distrusts a man with a "lean and hungry look." Also, Cassius' facial expression is unfriendly and threatening.

◆ Critical Thinking

❷ Make Judgments Have students evaluate how accurate they find Caesar's view of Cassius as a threat. *Caesar has a very clear idea of Cassius' motives for opposing him.*

Writing and Language Transparencies Use Daily Language Practice for Week 13. You can display the sentences on the overhead projector and have students make corrections or you can dictate the sentences and have students write them correctly.

◄ **Critical Viewing** What details of Cassius' appearance can you see in this picture that might make Caesar distrust him? [Infer] ❶

As if he mocked himself, and scorned his spirit
That could be moved to smile at anything.
Such men as he be never at heart's ease
Whiles they behold a greater than themselves,
210 And therefore are they very dangerous.
I rather tell thee what is to be feared
Than what I fear; for always I am Caesar.
Come on my right hand, for this ear is deaf,
And tell me truly what thou think'st of him.

[*A trumpet sounds.* CASCA *and his* TRAIN *exit.*]

CASCA. You pulled me by the cloak; would you speak
215   with me?

Humanities: Literature

Plutarch, a Greek biographer, wrote biographies of famous Greek and Roman statesmen and generals. Shakespeare's characterizations of the principals in *Julius Caesar* are based largely on what he learned from reading Plutarch's *The Lives of the Noble Grecians and Romans.* The following excerpt from the Dryden translation gives a clear indication of the character of the real-life Cassius: "Cassius, a man of fierce disposition, and

one that out of private malice, rather than love of public, hated Caesar, not the tyrant, continually fired and stirred him up. Brutus felt the rule an oppression, but Cassius hated the ruler; and among other reasons on which he grounded his quarrel against Caesar, the loss of his lions which he had procured . . . for Caesar, finding these . . . seized them for himself."

Ask students the following questions:

1. How well does Shakespeare's portrayal of Cassius fit with this description? *Shakespeare's characterization is consistent with Plutarch's description.*

2. How does this description affect your interpretation of Cassius' stories about Caesar? *This insight into Cassius' character will lead most students to question his motives in plotting against Caesar.*

◆ **Literary Focus**

❸ **Exposition in Drama** The passage (lines 220–222) describes in detail what was referred to in more general terms earlier in the scene.

BRUTUS. Ay, Casca; tell us what hath chanced[67] today, That Caesar looks so sad.

CASCA. Why, you were with him, were you not?

BRUTUS. I should not then ask Casca what had chanced.

220 ❸ **CASCA.** Why, there was a crown offered him; and being offered him, he put it by[68] with the back of his hand, thus; and then the people fell a-shouting.

BRUTUS. What was the second noise for?

CASCA. Why, for that too.

225 **CASSIUS.** They shouted thrice; what was the last cry for?

CASCA. Why, for that too.

BRUTUS. Was the crown offered him thrice?

CASCA. Ay, marry, was't, and he put it by thrice, every time gentler than other; and at every putting-by 230 mine honest neighbors shouted.

CASSIUS. Who offered him the crown?

CASCA. Why, Antony.

BRUTUS. Tell us the manner of it, gentle Casca.

CASCA. I can as well be hanged as tell the manner of it: it 235 was mere foolery; I did not mark it. I saw Mark Antony offer him a crown—yet 'twas not a crown neither, 'twas one of these coronets[69]—and, as I told you, he put it by once; but for all that, to my thinking, he would fain[70] have had it. Then he offered it to him 240 again; then he put it by again; but to my thinking, he was very loath to lay his fingers off it. And then he offered it the third time. He put it the third time by; and still as he refused it, the rabblement[71] hooted, and clapped their chopt[72] hands, and threw up their 245 sweaty nightcaps,[73] and uttered such a deal of stinking breath because Caesar refused the crown, that it had, almost, choked Caesar; for he swounded[74] and fell down at it. And for mine own part, I durst not laugh, for fear of opening my lips and receiving the 250 bad air.

CASSIUS. But, soft,[75] I pray you; what, did Caesar swound?

CASCA. He fell down in the market place, and foamed at mouth, and was speechless.

The Tragedy of Julius Caesar, Act I, Scene ii ◆ 723

67. hath chanced: Has happened.

68. put it by: Pushed it away.

◆ **Literary Focus**
How does this dialogue develop the situation set up in the exposition?

❹

69. coronets (kôr´ ə nets´) *n.*: Ornamental bands used as crowns.
70. fain (fān) *adv.*: Gladly.

71. rabblement (rāb´ əl mənt) *n.*: Mob.
72. chopt (chäpt) *adj.*: Chapped.
73. nightcaps: Workers' caps.
74. swounded: Swooned; fainted.

75. soft: Slowly.

◆ **Literary Focus**

❹ **Exposition in Drama** This dialogue develops the public's love for Caesar, which was revealed in the exposition.

Customize for
Bodily/Kinesthetic Learners
Have these students act out the offering of the crown, the refusals, and the reactions of the crowd each time. Tell students to use slightly exaggerated body language and facial expressions to indicate the characters' emotions.

Speaking and Listening Mini-Lesson

Enacting an Improvised Scene
This mini-lesson supports the Speaking and Listening activity in the Idea Bank on page 731.

Introduce the Concept Explain that in an enactment, students must see themselves as the characters they play, think how events would look to them as those characters, and how the characters would react.

Develop Background Reread with students the part of Scene ii when Casca tells of the offer of the crown to Caesar. Students can think about how they might react as crowd members.

Apply the Information Students can work in pairs with one partner describing an event and commenting, and the other replying in character. Invite pairs of students to perform their enactments.

Assess the Outcome An excellent enactment will use lively dialogue and body language and incorporate many details from the play. An average enactment will use some body language as well as dialogue and will incorporate some details from the play. A poor enactment will use only dialogue and will include few, if any, details from the play. You may also wish to use Peer Assessment: Dramatic Performance on page 120 in *Alternative Assessment.*

◆ Reading Strategy

❶ Use Text Aids Ask students how notes 76 and 77 clarify what Brutus and Cassius are saying. *Brutus and Cassius use the term falling sickness in two very different ways, which readers might not be able to figure out. Brutus is referring to a physical illness that Caesar might have. Cassius uses the term metaphorically to describe the humiliating position of the Roman people under Caesar's rule.*

Comprehension Check ☑

❷ Why was Caesar sad and angry after the people offered him the crown three times? *His act of refusing the crown did not work out the way he planned: Instead of continuing to beg him to accept it, the crowd was happy that he refused and they stopped asking him. Caesar now feels betrayed by the people.*

❸ Clarification Ask students if they are familiar with the expression "It was Greek to me," meaning that something was incomprehensible.

◆ Literary Focus

❹ Exposition in Drama Ask students what important information is revealed here about increasing tensions between Caesar and other Roman leaders. *The tribunes Marullus and Flavius have been exiled or killed by Caesar, which will increase the fear and resentment that other Roman leaders feel toward Caesar.*

BRUTUS. 'Tis very like he hath the falling-sickness.[76]

255 ❶ **CASSIUS.** No, Caesar hath it not; but you, and I,
And honest Casca, we have the falling-sickness.[77]

CASCA. I know not what you mean by that, but I am sure
Caesar fell down. If the tag-rag people[78] did not clap
him and hiss him, according as he pleased and
260 displeased them, as they use[79] to do the players in the
theater, I am no true man.

BRUTUS. What said he when he came unto himself?

CASCA. Marry, before he fell down, when he perceived
the common herd was glad he refused the crown, he
265 plucked me ope his doublet[80] and offered them his
throat to cut. An I had been a man of any occupation,[81] if I would not have taken him at a word, I
would I might go to hell among the rogues. And so he
❷ fell. When he came to himself again, he said,
270 if he had done or said anything amiss, he desired their
worships to think it was his infirmity.[82] Three or four
wenches,[83] where I stood, cried "Alas, good soul!"
and forgave him with all their hearts; but there's no
heed to be taken of them; if Caesar had stabbed their
275 mothers, they would have done no less.

BRUTUS. And after that, he came thus sad away?

CASCA. Ay.

CASSIUS. Did Cicero say anything?

CASCA. Ay, he spoke Greek.

280 **CASSIUS.** To what effect?

CASCA. Nay, an I tell you that, I'll ne'er look you i' th' face
❸ again. But those that understood him smiled at one
another and shook their heads; but for mine own
part, it was Greek to me. I could tell you more news
285 too: Marullus and Flavius, for pulling scarfs off Cae-
❹ sar's images, are put to silence.[84] Fare you well. There
was more foolery yet, if I could remember it.

CASSIUS. Will you sup with me tonight, Casca?

CASCA. No, I am promised forth.[85]

290 **CASSIUS.** Will you dine with me tomorrow?

CASCA. Ay, if I be alive, and your mind hold,[86] and your
dinner worth the eating.

724 ◆ *Drama*

76. falling-sickness: Epilepsy.

77. We have the falling-sickness: We are becoming helpless under Caesar's rule.

78. tag-rag people: The rabble.

79. use: Are accustomed.

80. doublet (dub' lit) *n.*: Close-fitting jacket.

81. An I . . . occupation: If I had been a working-man (or a man of action).

82. infirmity *n.*: Caesar's illness is epilepsy.

83. wenches (wench' əz) *n.*: Young women.

84. for pulling . . . silence: For taking decorations off statues of Caesar, have been silenced (by being forbidden to take part in public affairs, exiled, or perhaps even executed).

85. am promised forth: Have a previous engagement.

86. hold: Does not change.

◆ Build Vocabulary

infirmity (in fur' mə tē) *n.*: Illness; physical defect

Cross-Curricular Connection: Science

Some historical sources claim that Julius Caesar suffered from epilepsy, the condition to which Brutus refers as "the falling sickness" (line 254). Epilepsy is a general term used to cover a variety of chronic neurological disorders. Epileptics can suffer from seizures that involve muscle spasms and loss of consciousness. Some forms of epilepsy are known to be caused by injury or infection of the brain, while the cause of other forms is unknown. Today, epileptic seizures can be controlled by drugs and sometimes by diet.

Have students contact a local medical center for more information on epilepsy and other chronic disorders of the brain and nervous system.

CASSIUS. Good; I will expect you.

CASCA. Do so. Farewell, both. *[Exit]*

295 **BRUTUS.** What a blunt[87] fellow is this grown to be!
     He was quick mettle[88] when he went to school.

CASSIUS. So is he now in execution[89]
     Of any bold or noble enterprise,
     However he puts on this tardy form.[90]
300 This rudeness is a sauce to his good wit,[91]
     Which gives men stomach to disgest[92] his words
     With better appetite.

BRUTUS. And so it is. For this time I will leave you.
     Tomorrow, if you please to speak with me,
305 I will come home to you; or if you will,
     Come home to me, and I will wait for you.

CASSIUS. I will do so. Till then, think of the world.[93]

[Exit BRUTUS.]

     Well, Brutus, thou art noble; yet I see
     Thy honorable mettle may be wrought
310 From that it is disposed;[94] therefore it is meet
     That noble minds keep ever with their likes;
     For who so firm that cannot be seduced?
     Caesar doth bear me hard,[95] but he loves Brutus.
     If I were Brutus now, and he were Cassius,
315 He should not humor me.[96] I will this night,
     In several hands,[97] in at his windows throw,
     As if they came from several citizens,
     Writings, all tending to the great opinion[98]
     That Rome holds of his name; wherein obscurely
320 Caesar's ambition shall be glancèd at.[99]
     And after this, let Caesar seat him sure;[100]
     For we will shake him, or worse days endure. *[Exit]*

Scene iii. A street.

[Thunder and lightning. Enter from opposite sides, CASCA and CICERO.]

CICERO. Good even, Casca; brought you Caesar home?
     Why are you breathless? And why stare you so?

CASCA. Are not you moved, when all the sway of earth[1]

---

87. blunt: Dull; not sharp.
88. quick mettle: Of a lively disposition.
89. execution (ek´ sə kyōō´shən) *n.*: Carrying out; doing.
90. tardy form: Sluggish appearance.
91. wit: Intelligence.
92. disgest: Digest.

93. the world: Present state of affairs.

♦ **Reading Strategy**
Use the glosses to clarify unfamiliar terms. Then explain what Cassius means in lines 308–310. ❺

94. wrought . . . is disposed: Shaped (like iron) in a way different from its usual form.
95. bear me hard: Dislikes me.
96. humor me: Win me over.
97. several hands: Different handwritings.
98. tending to the great opinion: Pointing out the great respect.
99. glancèd at: Hinted at.
100. seat him sure: Establish himself securely.

1. all the sway of earth: The stable order of Earth.

---

❺ **Use Text Aids** The gloss, side note 94, helps students understand the pun of *mettle* and *metal*. Without the text aid explaining how metal is wrought, students might comprehend only the literal meaning of Cassius' words.

Comprehension Check ☑

❻ How does Cassius plan to use Brutus' concern for the public welfare to win Brutus over to the conspiracy against Caesar? *He plans to write phony letters to Brutus, supposedly from concerned citizens worried about the effects of Caesar's rule.*

Customize for
Verbal/Linguistic Learners
Have these students draft a brief note they might write if they were Cassius. Encourage them to choose the details they will include based on what they have learned about Brutus and how he might be influenced. Tell students they can compare their notes to Cassius' in the beginning of Act II.

The Tragedy of Julius Caesar, Act I, Scene iii ◆ 725

◆ Reading Strategy

❶ Use Text Aids Note 2 helps students envision the trees splitting in two. Notes 9 and 10 help students envision the women. Note 11 clarifies what kind of bird students should picture in their minds.

◆ Build Vocabulary

❷ Forms of *Portent* Challenge students to analyze the word *portentous*. What is the noun form of the word, and what does it mean? What is the suffix, and what is its function? Then ask why Casca describes the strange sights he has seen as "portentous things." *The noun form is portent, which means "omen" or "warning." The suffix is -ous, which changes a noun to an adjective. Casca believes the strange sights are signs or warnings from the gods that something bad is about to happen.*

◆ Literary Focus

❸ Exposition in Drama Ask students what important information is developed in Cicero's words. *Students may say that the speech is included to remind readers or audience members that Caesar is coming to the Capitol the next day. The reminder builds suspense as it supplies information.*

5

Shakes like a thing unfirm? O Cicero,
I have seen tempests, when the scolding winds
Have rived[2] the knotty oaks, and I have seen
Th' ambitious ocean swell and rage and foam,
To be exalted with[3] the threat'ning clouds;

10

But never till tonight, never till now,
Did I go through a tempest dropping fire.
Either there is a civil strife in heaven,
Or else the world, too saucy[4] with the gods,
Incenses[5] them to send destruction.

   CICERO. Why, saw you anything more wonderful?

15

   CASCA. A common slave—you know him well by sight—
Held up his left hand, which did flame and burn
Like twenty torches joined, and yet his hand,
Not sensible of[6] fire, remained unscorched.
Besides—I ha' not since put up my sword—

20

Against[7] the Capitol I met a lion,
Who glazed[8] upon me and went surly by
Without annoying me. And there were drawn
Upon a heap[9] a hundred ghastly[10] women,
Transformèd with their fear, who swore they saw

25

Men, all in fire, walk up and down the streets.
And yesterday the bird of night[11] did sit
Even at noonday upon the market place,
Hooting and shrieking. When these prodigies[12]
Do so conjointly meet,[13] let not men say,

30

"These are their reasons, they are natural,"
❷ For I believe they are portentous things
Unto the climate that they point upon.[14]

   CICERO. Indeed, it is a strange-disposèd[15] time:

35

❸ But men may construe things after their fashion,[16]
Clean from the purpose[17] of the things themselves.
Comes Caesar to the Capitol tomorrow?

   CASCA. He doth; for he did bid Antonius
Send word to you he would be there tomorrow.

   CICERO. Good night then, Casca; this disturbèd sky
Is not to walk in.

40

   CASCA.   Farewell, Cicero. [*Exit* CICERO.]

[*Enter* CASSIUS.]

   CASSIUS. Who's there?

   CASCA.   A Roman.

726 ◆ *Drama*

---

2. Have rived: Have split.

3. exalted with: Lifted up to.

4. saucy: Rude; impudent.

5. Incenses: Enrages.

◆ **Reading Strategy**
Which notes helped you envision Casca's experiences? **❶**

6. sensible of: Sensitive to.

7. Against: Opposite or near.
8. glazed: Stared.
9. were drawn . . . heap: Huddled together.
10. ghastly (gast´ lē) *adj.*: Ghostlike; pale.
11. bird of night: Owl.
12. prodigies (präd´ ə jēz) *n.*: Extraordinary happenings.
13. conjointly meet: Occur at the same time and place.

14. portentous (pôr ten´ təs) **. . . upon:** Bad omens for the country they point to.
15. strange-disposèd: Abnormal.
16. construe . . . fashion: Explain in their own way.
17. Clean from the purpose: Different from the real meaning.

Cross-Curricular Social Studies

Hierarchy Hierarchy and order were very important in Elizabethan times. Animals, the planets, angels, and society were all organized according to rigid rules of rank and classification. The same applied to the political organization of a country. The king or queen was at the top of the ladder, and very definite strata were set below the ruler. The Elizabethan educational system focused on order and obedience. Any break in the natural, social, religious, or political order was unthinkable. Elizabethans believed that such a transgression set off violent disturbances in the heavens and in nature. This belief is manifested in the storms and unusual events described by Casca in this scene. Some break in order has brought on storms and unnatural events.

CASSIUS. Casca, by your voice.

CASCA. Your ear is good. Cassius, what night is this?

CASSIUS. A very pleasing night to honest men.

CASCA. Who ever knew the heavens menace so?

CASSIUS. Those that have known the earth so full of
45   faults.
        For my part, I have walked about the streets,
        Submitting me unto the perilous night,
❹   And thus unbracèd,[18] Casca, as you see,
        Have bared my bosom to the thunder-stone;[19]
50   And when the cross[20] blue lightning seemed to open
        The breast of heaven, I did present myself
        Even in the aim and very flash of it.

CASCA. But wherefore did you so much tempt the
           heavens?
        It is the part[21] of men to fear and tremble
55   When the most mighty gods by tokens send
        Such dreadful heralds to astonish[22] us.

CASSIUS. You are dull, Casca, and those sparks of life
        That should be in a Roman you do want,[23]
        Or else you use not. You look pale, and gaze,
60   And put on fear, and cast yourself in wonder,[24]
        To see the strange impatience of the heavens;
        But if you would consider the true cause
        Why all these fires, why all these gliding ghosts,
        Why birds and beasts from quality and kind,[25]
65   Why old men, fools, and children calculate,[26]
        Why all these things change from their ordinance,[27]
❺   Their natures and preformèd faculties,
        To monstrous quality,[28] why, you shall find
        That heaven hath infused them with these spirits[29]
70   To make them instruments of fear and warning
        Unto some monstrous state.[30]
        Now could I, Casca, name to thee a man
        Most like this dreadful night,
        That thunders, lightens, opens graves, and roars
75 ❻   As doth the lion in the Capitol;
        A man no mightier than thyself, or me,
        In personal action, yet prodigious grown
        And fearful,[31] as these strange eruptions are.

CASCA. 'Tis Caesar that you mean, is it not, Cassius?

18. **unbracèd:** With jacket open.
19. **thunder-stone:** Thunderbolt.
20. **cross:** Zigzag.

21. **part:** Role.

22. **by tokens . . . to astonish:** By portentous signs send such awful announcements to frighten and stun.
23. **want:** Lack.
24. **put on . . . in wonder:** Show fear and are amazed.

25. **from quality and kind:** Acting contrary to their nature.
26. **calculate:** Make predictions.
27. **ordinance:** Regular behavior.
28. **preformèd . . . quality:** Established function to unnatural behavior.
29. **infused . . . spirits:** Filled them with supernatural powers.
30. **monstrous state:** Abnormal condition of government.

31. **fearful:** Causing fear.

◆ **Build Vocabulary**

surly (sur′ lē) *adv.*: In a proud, commanding way

portentous (pôr ten′ təs) *adj.*: Foreboding; full of unspecified meaning

prodigious (prə dij′ əs) *adj.*: Impressively forceful

The Tragedy of Julius Caesar, Act I, Scene iii ◆ *727*

◆ **Critical Thinking**

❹ **Evaluate** Ask students what qualities Cassius reveals by his behavior during the storm. Do they find his behavior admirable or foolish? *Some students may say that Cassius' behavior shows his courage and is admirable. Others may say that Cassius is a show-off and braggart who foolishly goes looking for trouble and seeking out danger.*

Comprehension Check ☑

❺ According to Cassius, how is Caesar like the stormy night? *Like a dangerous storm, Caesar has become very powerful and is using his power to frighten people into submission.*

◆ **Critical Thinking**

❻ **Interpret** Cassius claims that the storms are a result of Caesar's revolt against the order. Ask students to suggest another explanation based on Elizabethan beliefs. *The conspirators' plot against their ruler would be seen as a revolt against political order.*

Enrichment

Shakespeare wrote in a time when plagiarism was not as well defined as it is today. Playwrights and authors freely borrowed from one another's works and often adapted classic works. This loose attitude toward intellectual ownership has led some scholars to suggest that Shakespeare is not the sole author of all the works attributed to him. Although this theory is no longer widely accepted, students should be familiar with the theory and the reasons for it. The following Elizabethan men of letters have been considered as potential "ghostwriters" of the plays we now call Shakespeare's:

Christopher Marlowe is thought to have died in a tavern brawl in 1594—but perhaps he did not. He may have survived and written the plays we attribute to Shakespeare.

Francis Bacon, scientist and philosopher, was a prolific writer. His advocates argue that he might have been embarrassed to admit to writing such frivolous material as plays, and arranged to credit them to Shakespeare.

Lord Oxford was a nobleman in Queen Elizabeth's court. It would have been beneath Oxford's dignity to write for the theater. He would have sought out an obscure, lower-born person to take credit of authorship—someone like Shakespeare.

Have students find out more about Shakespeare's contemporaries and the theories surrounding an alternative authorship of some plays.

80   CASSIUS. Let it be who it is; for Romans now
       Have thews[32] and limbs like to their ancestors;
       But, woe the while![33] Our fathers' minds are dead,
       And we are governed with our mothers' spirits;
       Our yoke and sufferance[34] show us womanish.

85   CASCA. Indeed, they say the senators tomorrow
       Mean to establish Caesar as a king;
       And he shall wear his crown by sea and land,
       In every place save here in Italy.

     CASSIUS. I know where I will wear this dagger then;
90   Cassius from bondage will deliver[35] Cassius.
       Therein,[36] ye gods, you make the weak most strong;
       Therein, ye gods, you tyrants do defeat.
       Nor stony tower, nor walls of beaten brass,
       Nor airless dungeon, nor strong links of iron,
95 ❶   Can be retentive to[37] the strength of spirit;
       But life, being weary of these worldly bars,
       Never lacks power to dismiss itself.
       If I know this, know all the world besides,
       That part of tyranny that I do bear
       I can shake off at pleasure.   [*Thunder still*]

100 CASCA.   So can I;
       So every bondman in his own hand bears
       The power to cancel his captivity.

     CASSIUS. And why should Caesar be a tyrant then?
       Poor man, I know he would not be a wolf
105   But that he sees the Romans are but sheep;
   ❷   He were no lion, were not Romans hinds.[38]
       Those that with haste will make a mighty fire
       Begin it with weak straws. What trash is Rome,
       What rubbish and what offal,[39] when it serves
110   For the base matter[40] to illuminate
       So vile a thing as Caesar! But, O grief,
       Where hast thou led me? I, perhaps, speak this
       Before a willing bondman; then I know
       My answer must be made.[41] But I am armed,
115   And dangers are to me indifferent.
   ❸
     CASCA. You speak to Casca, and to such a man
       That is no fleering tell-tale.[42] Hold, my hand.
       Be factious[43] for redress of all these griefs,[44]
       And I will set this foot of mine as far
       As who goes farthest.   [*They clasp hands.*]

32. thews (thyo͞oz) *n.:* Muscles or sinews; strength.
33. woe the while: Alas for the times.
34. yoke and sufferance: Slavery and meek acceptance of it.

35. will deliver: Will set free.
36. Therein: In that way (by using his dagger on himself).

37. be retentive to: Confine.

38. hinds (hīndz) *n.:* Female deer; peasants; servants.
39. offal (ôf′ əl) *n.:* Garbage.
40. base matter: Inferior or low material; foundation materials.

♦ **Literary Focus**
Explain how Cassius' speech echoes the sentiments expressed by the tribunes in the exposition in Scene i.

41. speak this . . . answer must be made: Say this before a willing servant of Caesar's; then I know I will have to answer for my words.
42. fleering tell-tale: Sneering tattletale.
43. factious (fak′ shəs) *adj.:* Active in forming a faction or a political party.
44. redress (rē′ dres) **of all these griefs:** Setting

728 ♦ *Drama*

120 **CASSIUS.**   There's a bargain made.
Now know you, Casca, I have moved already
Some certain of the noblest-minded Romans
To undergo[45] with me an enterprise
Of honorable dangerous consequence;[46]
125 And I do know, by this[47] they stay for me
In Pompey's porch;[48] for now, this fearful night,
There is no stir or walking in the streets,
And the complexion of the element[49]
In favor's like[50] the work we have in hand,
130 Most bloody, fiery, and most terrible.

[*Enter* CINNA.]

CASCA. Stand close[51] awhile, for here comes one in
haste.

CASSIUS. 'Tis Cinna; I do know him by his gait;[52]
He is a friend. Cinna, where haste you so?

CINNA. To find out you. Who's that? Metellus Cimber?

135 **CASSIUS.** No, it is Casca, one incorporate[53]
To our attempts. Am I not stayed[54] for, Cinna?

CINNA. I am glad on't.[55] What a fearful night is this!
There's two or three of us have seen strange sights.

CASSIUS. Am I not stayed for? Tell me.

CINNA.   Yes, you are.
140 O Cassius, if you could
But win the noble Brutus to our party—

CASSIUS. Be you content. Good Cinna, take this paper,
And look you lay it in the praetor's chair,[56]
Where Brutus may but find it;[57] and throw this
145 In at his window: set this up with wax
Upon old Brutus'[58] statue. All this done,
Repair to Pompey's porch, where you shall find us.
Is Decius Brutus and Trebonius there?

CINNA. All but Metellus Cimber, and he's gone
150 To seek you at your house. Well, I will hie,
And so bestow these papers as you bade me.

CASSIUS. That done, repair to Pompey's Theater.

[*Exit* CINNA.]

Come, Casca, you and I will yet ere day

The Tragedy of Julius Caesar, Act I, Scene iii ◆ *729*

---

**Side notes:**

right all these grievances.
45. undergo: Undertake.
46. consequence (kän´ sə kwens´) *n.*: Importance.
47. by this: By this time.
48. Pompey's porch: Portico of Pompey's Theater.
49. complexion of the element: Condition of the sky; weather.
50. In favor's like: In appearance is like.
51. close: Hidden.

52. gait (gāt) *n.*: Way of moving.

53. incorporate (in kôr´ pər it) *adj.*: United.
54. stayed: Waited.
55. on't: Of it.

56. praetor's (prē´ tərz) **chair:** Roman magistrate's (or judge's) chair.
57. Where . . . find it: Where only Brutus (as the chief magistrate) will find it.
58. old Brutus': Lucius Junius Brutus, the founder of Rome.

◆ **Literary Focus**

❹ **Exposition in Drama** Ask students how Cassius' plan connects to the public sentiment revealed in the exposition. *In the exposition, readers learn that the public loves Caesar. This love does not support Cassius' plan and will make it more difficult for him to convince Brutus that Caesar should not rule. Therefore, he is setting in motion a plan to make Brutus believe that public sentiment has changed.*

Customize for
Less Proficient Readers
Help these students to paraphrase Cassius' words to Casca. Then ask for volunteers to read the speech aloud with appropriate portentous expression.

Customize for
English Language Learners
Help these students match up the names of every character mentioned on this page with their names in the character list at the start of the act. Lead them to establish that every character on the page is loyal to Cassius and not to Caesar.

Cross-Curricular Connection: Art and Architecture

Horace, the Roman poet, proclaimed, "Conquered Greece led the conqueror captive." He was referring to the fact that when Rome conquered Greece, shiploads of Greek statues were brought to Rome, and, when the supply was exhausted, Roman copies were made. Later, Rome developed its own styles of art and architecture.

Graceful paintings decorated the walls of wealthy Roman homes; the basilica, which provided the basic form for later Christian churches, was developed; the Roman arch made it possible to enclose vast areas of space under one roof. Have students research and report on Rome's achievements in art and architecture. You might

suggest they look up famous Roman structures such as the Colosseum, the Arch of Titus, the Baths of Caracalla, and the Pantheon. A good art history book will provide photographs of Roman statues such as the Bust of Hadrian, the Emperor Augustus Addressing His Army, and the reliefs from Trajan's Column.

◆ Critical Thinking

❶ Interpret Ask students to explain Casca's reason for wanting Brutus to join the conspiracy. *Because the common people love and trust Brutus, they will support the overthrow of Caesar if Brutus says it is the right thing to do.*

Reinforce and Extend

Customize for
Less Proficient Readers
Help these students identify the most significant information in each scene.

Answers

Reader's Response Students will probably respond to the frightening, ominous nature of the sights.

Thematic Focus Responses include Caesar's decision to refuse the crown, Brutus' decision to consider Cassius' proposal, and Cassius' decision to approach the other conspirators.

☑ Check Your Comprehension

1. The tribunes are contemptuous of the common people because they are fickle in their allegiance.
2. (a) The soothsayer warns, "Beware the ides of March." (b) Caesar dismisses the warning, calling the soothsayer a dreamer.
3. Casca reports that Julius Caesar was offered the crown three times, and each time (though more and more reluctantly) Caesar refused it. As the people cheered his refusal, Caesar swooned and fell.
4. During a severe thunderstorm, Casca is frightened by a man whose hand is on fire and the reports of men walking burning through the streets.
5. Casca and Cassius are going to see Brutus.

◆ Critical Thinking

1. (a) Cassius is envious of Caesar and bitter about his success. (b) Caesar fears that Cassius has too "lean and hungry look"; Cassius thinks too much and Caesar believes such men are dangerous.
2. Brutus is different from Cassius because he is honorable and is trusted by his noble peers.
3. Brutus' participation will sway others to accept the assassination.

4. Brutus represents honor and integrity; Cassius represents envy and discord; Caesar represents ambition and power.
5. Suggested response: Lawlessness and disorder (anarchy) may be resolved by adopting a harsh, restrictive, oppressive form of government (tyranny). A system of law is needed to avoid both.

6. Sample response: Throughout the world, and in American politics, self-serving power vs. power for the good of many is a neverending struggle.

---

155 See Brutus at his house; three parts of him
Is ours already, and the man entire
Upon the next encounter yields him ours.

CASCA. O, he sits high in all the people's hearts;
And that which would appear offense[59] in us,
His countenance,[60] like richest alchemy,[61]
160 Will change to virtue and to worthiness.

CASSIUS. Him, and his worth, and our great need of him,
You have right well conceited.[62] Let us go,
For it is after midnight, and ere day
We will awake him and be sure of him.   [*Exit*]

59. offense (ə fens´) *n.*: Crime.
60. countenance (koun´ tə nəns) *n.*: Support.
61. alchemy (al´ kə mē) *n.*: An early form of chemistry in which the goal was to change metals of little value into gold.
62. conceited (kən sēt´ id): Understood.

Guide for Responding

◆ Literature and Your Life

Reader's Response What is your reaction to the sight that Cassius, Casca, and Cinna observe during a stormy night in Scene iii?
Thematic Focus Several characters make choices during this act. Which do you think is the most important? Explain.

☑ Check Your Comprehension

1. Explain why the tribunes have only contempt for the common people of Rome.
2. (a) What warning does the soothsayer give? (b) What is Caesar's reaction to this warning?
3. Summarize Casca's report of what happened at the games.
4. What frightens Casca before he meets Cassius at night?
5. Where are Casca and Cassius going as the act closes?

◆ Critical Thinking

INTERPRET
1. (a) How does Cassius feel about Caesar? (b) Why does Caesar fear Cassius? **[Infer]**
2. In what important ways is Brutus different from Cassius? **[Compare and Contrast]**
3. Why is Brutus' participation in the plot essential to Cassius? **[Draw Conclusions]**

APPLY
4. Explain how Brutus, Cassius and Caesar represent qualities that can be found in people of any time period.
5. The philosopher Jeremy Bentham has written, "Tyranny and anarchy are never far asunder." Explain the meaning of this quotation. Then explain how it relates to this play. **[Synthesize]**

EXTEND
6. In what ways are the issues surrounding Julius Caesar of ancient Rome reflected in modern political issues and controversies? **[Social Studies Link]**

730 ◆ Drama

Guide for Responding (continued)

◆ Reading Strategy

USE TEXT AIDS

Notes and stage directions help you to understand the action in *The Tragedy of Julius Caesar*. For example, the directions at the opening of Act I help you to envision the vitality and frenzy of the crowd scene that opens the act. The side notes help you understand that a "mechanical" is not a robot, but a common working man.

1. What information is provided in the side note for Act I, Scene i, line 11, that helps readers to understand the dialogue that follows?
2. The stage directions in Act I, Scene ii, indicate a flourish of trumpets and shouts offstage during the conversation between Brutus and Cassius. Why is it necessary that readers know about these offstage noises?

◆ Literary Focus

EXPOSITION IN DRAMA

The **exposition** is the part of the plot (usually the beginning) that lays the groundwork for the rest of the drama by revealing information about the basic situation.

1. What important information does Marullus reveal in Act I, Scene i, in his speech beginning with line 33?
2. How do you learn that some in the government are resentful of Caesar?

◆ Build Grammar Skills

THE SUBJUNCTIVE MOOD

The subjunctive mood expresses either a condition that is contrary to fact or a wish, suggestion, demand, or request.

Practice In your notebook, rewrite each sentence to express the subjunctive mood.

1. If only I was king, things would be different.
2. He spoke as though he was the only one to tell the truth.
3. The curtain stirred as if it was a ghost moving on stage.
4. Caesar orders that Antony touches Calpurnia during the race.
5. Cassius requests that Brutus joins the conspirators.

◆ Build Vocabulary

RELATED WORDS: FORMS OF *PORTENT*

Complete the following sentences in your notebook, using *portend, portent,* or *portentous.*

1. I fear these to be ___?___ dreams.
2. The ___?___ Casca spoke of frightened him.
3. The storms ___?___ that something terrible will happen.

USING THE WORD BANK

Copy each of the following words in your notebook, and write the letter of the word that is its synonym next to it.

1. replication: (a) original, (b) copy, (c) absence of sound
2. spare: (a) frightened, (b) thin, (c) muscular
3. infirmity: (a) strength, (b) weakness, (c) temper
4. surly: (a) bold, (b) timid, (c) polite
5. portentous: (a) optimistic, (b) unclear, (c) foreboding
6. prodigious: (a) passive, (b) forceful, (c) awkward

Idea Bank

Writing

1. **Journal Entry** Write a journal entry that Caesar might have written following the afternoon at the races during which Antony presented him with a crown three times.

2. **Speech** As Cassius, write an interior monologue—the words that might go through his mind—if Caesar did accept the crown that Anthony offered.

Speaking and Listening

3. **Enactment** Suppose that you and a partner are spectators in the stands at the races when Caesar is invited to accept the crown as king of Rome. Have a conversation with your neighbor about what is going on.

The Tragedy of Julius Caesar, Act I ◆ 731

◆ Reading Strategy

1. The entire dialogue cleverly revolves around double meaning. The side note about the dual usages of *cobbler* illuminates this.
2. The offstage noises indicate that something significant and official is occurring offstage.

◆ Literary Focus

1. Marullus introduces the fact that not everyone is rejoicing over Caesar's power and popularity.
2. Through statements made in conversations between characters, readers learn that Marullus, Flavius, Cassius, Brutus, and Casca resent (in varying degrees) Caesar's rise to power.

◆ Build Grammar Skills

1. If only I *were* king, things would be different.
2. He spoke as though he *were* the only one to tell the truth.
3. The curtain stirred as if it *were* a ghost moving on stage.
4. Caesar orders that Antony *touch* Calpurnia during the race.
5. Cassius requests that Brutus *join* the conspirators.

◆ Build Vocabulary

Related Words: Forms of *Portent*

1. I fear these to be *portentous* dreams.
2. The *portent* Casca spoke of frightened him.
3. The storms *portend* that something terrible will happen.

Using the Word Bank

1. b 2. b 3. b 4. a 5. c 6. b

Guide for Reading, Act II

OBJECTIVES

1. To read, comprehend, and interpret a play
2. To relate a play to personal experience
3. To read blank verse for meaning
4. To recognize iambic pentameter in blank verse
5. To build vocabulary in context and learn the word root -spir-
6. To use correctly the words *affect* and *effect*
7. To respond to the play through writing, speaking, and listening

SKILLS INSTRUCTION

Vocabulary: Word Roots: -spir-

Grammar: Commonly Confused Words: *Affect* and *Effect*

Reading Strategy: Read Blank Verse

Literary Focus: Blank Verse

Speaking and Listening: Debate (teacher edition)

Critical Viewing: Speculate; Connect

PORTFOLIO OPPORTUNITIES

Writing: Editorial; Monologue
Speaking and Listening: Debate

Interest Grabber

Introduce the second act by sharing with students some background about political assassinations in more recent times. You may want to spark students' interest in the classic conspiracy of *The Tragedy of Julius Caesar* by discussing the controversy over the conspiracy theory surrounding John F. Kennedy's assassination. If you think it's appropriate, start by showing a portion of the Oliver Stone movie *JFK*. After viewing the video, or discussing assassinations in general, ask students to suggest reasons why a political leader's enemies might form a conspiracy against the leader. *Reasons include shared resentment against a leader's popularity, shared disagreement with a leader's policies, fear of acting alone, or the possibility that the logistics of the assassination require more than one person.* Have students record the suggestions in a notebook or reading journal and refer to them during the reading of this act. Students will probably find that many of the reasons they suggest for a contemporary conspiracy apply to the ancient Roman conspiracy.

◆ Review and Anticipate

As Caesar returns triumphantly from his war against Pompey's sons, he dismisses a warning to "beware the ides of March." The common people have turned their loyalty from Pompey to Caesar, and they cry out for Caesar to accept the emperor's crown. Although Caesar refuses three times, some still doubt his sincerity. Cassius, whom Caesar distrusts because of his "lean and hungry look," persuades Casca to join a conspiracy against Caesar. Brutus, although he is Caesar's friend, worries about Caesar's ambition. The conspirators plant letters that they hope will bring Brutus to their side. As Act II opens, on the eve of the ides of March, Brutus receives both the letters and a visit from Casca and Cassius. As the act progresses, notice the warnings that Caesar ignores and the shift of power within the group of conspirators.

◆ Literary Focus

BLANK VERSE

Blank verse is a poetic unrhymed iambic pentameter. **Iambic** means that an unaccented or unstressed syllable is followed by an accented or stressed one. **Pentameter** means that there are five feet per line. (A foot is one set in the pattern of accented and unaccented syllables. In this case, a foot is one iamb.)

By alĺ | thĕ gŏds | thăt Rŏ́|măns bŏ́w | bĕfŏ́re,
Ĭ herĕ́ | dĭscărd | mў sĭ́ck|nĕ́ss! Sŏ́ul | ŏf Rŏ́me,

The Tragedy of Julius Caesar is written mainly in blank verse. Shakespeare uses blank verse for important or aristocratic characters, but his minor characters speak in ordinary prose.

◆ Build Grammar Skills

COMMONLY CONFUSED WORDS: *AFFECT* AND *EFFECT*

When Portia says "Hoping it was but an effect of humor, Which sometime hath his hour with every man," she uses a word that is frequently misused: *effect.* Most often, as in this sentence, *effect* is a noun meaning "the result." *Effect* can also be a verb meaning "to bring about" or "to cause." *Affect* is always a verb meaning "to influence." Look at these examples:

Cassius' letters *affected* Brutus' decision.
The *effect* of the letters was significant.

732 ◆ Guide for Reading

◆ Reading Strategy

READ BLANK VERSE

The blank verse structure of Shakespeare's plays should not stand in the way of your understanding. In reading *The Tragedy of Julius Caesar*, don't confuse a line with a sentence. A sentence may continue through several lines. Each line may begin with a capital letter, but that is a poetic convention. A capital letter at the beginning of a line doesn't necessarily indicate the beginning of a sentence. To read for meaning, read in sentences. Though you may pause over a comma at the end of a line, don't stop until you come to a period.

◆ Build Vocabulary

WORD ROOTS: -spir-

In Act II of *The Tragedy of Julius Caesar*, a number of Romans *conspire* to overthrow Caesar. The word root -spir- means "to breathe"; thus *conspire* means "to breathe together" or, in other words, "to unite." *Spir-* is also the root of *conspiracy*, a secret agreement to perform together a treacherous act.

WORD BANK

augmented
entreated
conspiracy
resolution
exploit
imminent

Before you read, preview this list of words from this act.

Prentice Hall Literature Program Resources

REINFORCE / RETEACH / EXTEND

Selection Support Pages
Build Vocabulary: Word Roots: -spir-, p. 208
Build Grammar Skills: Commonly Confused Words: *Affect* and *Effect*, p. 209
Reading Strategy: Read Blank Verse, p. 210
Literary Focus: Blank Verse, p.211

Strategies for Diverse Student Needs, p. 51

Beyond Literature
Multicultural Connection: Omens and Portents, p. 51

Formal Assessment Selection Test, pp. 179–181; Assessment Resources Software

Alternative Assessment, p. 51

Resource Pro CD-ROM
Julius Caesar, Act II—includes all resource material and customizable lesson plan

Listening to Literature Audiocassettes
Julius Caesar, Act II

Literature CD-ROM *The Time, Life, and Works of Shakespeare*

The Tragedy of
JULIUS CAESAR

William Shakespeare

Act II

Scene i. *Rome.*

[*Enter* BRUTUS *in his orchard.*]

BRUTUS. What, Lucius, ho!
    I cannot, by the progress of the stars,
    Give guess how near to day. Lucius, I say!
    I would it were my fault to sleep so soundly.
5   When, Lucius, when? Awake, I say! What, Lucius!

 [*Enter* LUCIUS.]

LUCIUS. Called you, my lord?

BRUTUS. Get me a taper in my study, Lucius.
    When it is lighted, come and call me here.

LUCIUS. I will, my lord.   [*Exit*]

10 **BRUTUS.** It must be by his death; and for my part,
    I know no personal cause to spurn at[1] him,
    But for the general.[2] He would be crowned.
    How that might change his nature, there's the question.
    It is the bright day that brings forth the adder,[3]
15   And that craves[4] wary walking. Crown him that,
    And then I grant we put a sting in him
    That at his will he may do danger with.
    Th' abuse of greatness is when it disjoins
    Remorse from power;[5] and, to speak truth of Caesar,
20   I have not known when his affections swayed[6]
    More than his reason. But 'tis a common proof[7]
    That lowliness[8] is young ambition's ladder,
    Whereto the climber upward turns his face;
    But when he once attains the upmost round,
25   He then unto the ladder turns his back,
    Looks in the clouds, scorning the base degrees[9]
    By which he did ascend. So Caesar may;
    Then lest he may, prevent.[10] And, since the quarrel
    Will bear no color[11] for the thing he is,

◆ Literary Focus
Read lines 10–20 of Brutus' speech aloud to hear the stressed and unstressed syllables of the iambs. **❷**

---

1. spurn at: Kick against; rebel.
2. the general: The public good.
3. adder (ad´ ər) *n.:* Poisonous snake.
4. craves: Requires.
5. disjoins . . . power: Separates mercy from power.
6. affections swayed: Emotions ruled.
7. proof: Experience.
8. lowliness: Humility.
9. base degrees: Low steps or people in lower positions.
10. lest . . . prevent: In case he may, we must stop him.
11. the quarrel . . . no color: Our complaint cannot be justified in view of what he now is.

The Tragedy of Julius Caesar, Act II, Scene i ◆ *733*

One-Minute Insight Act II of *The Tragedy of Julius Caesar* focuses on Brutus' internal conflict. His intense self-examination and struggle with himself over issues of duty, honor, and loyalty are a sharp contrast to Caesar's lack of awareness. Caesar misses the subtle indications and the outright warnings that he is in danger. In this act, an inexorable shift in power (both public and among the conspirators) begins.

Customize for
Musical/Rhythmic Learners
Have these students lead groups in tapping out the iambic pentameter of the poetry in this act and finding the exceptions to the rule. You may wish to suggest specific passages, such as Brutus' first monologue beginning on page 733, or the dialogue between Brutus and Cassius in lines 86–89.

Customize for
More Advanced Students
Ask these students to identify dialogue in which a line of iambic pentameter is begun by one character and completed by another. You can show students examples in lines 76–77 and lines 95–98.

◆ Literary Focus

❶ Blank Verse Begin the act by having students scan a few lines spoken by Brutus and the lines spoken by Lucius. How do they differ, and why? *Brutus speaks in blank verse, except in the first line, in which he calls his servant. Lucius speaks in brief answers that are not in blank verse. Shakespeare uses blank verse for aristocratic or important characters, whereas servants and minor characters usually speak in prose. (Emphasize "usually," as Lucius' speech, lines 35–38, is in blank verse.)*

◆ Literary Focus

❷ Blank Verse Remind students that iambic pentameter reflects the natural rhythm of speech. While they should exaggerate the stresses to identify the rhythm, Shakespeare did not intend for the lines to be spoken in a sing-song pattern.

✎ Preparing for Standardized Tests

Grammar and Language The Build Grammar lesson for this selection focuses on the distinction between *affect* and *effect,* two words often confused by students. This lesson will give students practice in distinguishing between the two. Proficiency in this area will help students perform better on standardized test sections that evaluate students' grasp of English usage by having them identify sentence errors, as in the following example: (A)

Some experts say that a movie can seriously
<u>effect</u> <u>viewers</u>' attitudes and even their
  A   B

actions, but others believe that <u>films have no</u>
                       C

such <u>effects</u>. <u>No error</u>
     D   E

For additional practice, use the Build Grammar Skills page in *Selection Support,* page 209.

❶ Interpret Lead students to consider why Brutus compares Caesar to a serpent's egg, rather than to a serpent or snake. *Brutus doesn't compare Caesar to a snake, because Caesar hasn't actually done any harm yet. Like a snake's egg, though, Caesar has the potential to become something dangerous.*

Customize for
Less Proficient Readers

❷ Remind students who are confused by this passage that in Act I Caesar is advised by the soothsayer to beware the ides of March. Help them recall that the ides fall on the fifteenth of the month.

◆ **Critical Thinking**

❸ Make Inferences Ask students why they think Brutus interprets this portion of the letter as he does. *He is looking for a reason to support his inclination to join the conspirators.*

🎧 **Listening to Literature Audiocassettes** Play this portion of the recording while students follow the text. Listening while reading will help them reinforce the two speakers of the dialogue. It will also help students hear the natural pauses that occur as Brutus reads the letter and thinks about its ramifications.

---

30 Fashion it[12] thus: that what he is, <u>augmented</u>
Would run to these and these <u>extremities</u>;[13]
❶ And therefore think him as a serpent's egg
Which hatched, would as his kind grow mischievous,
And kill him in the shell.

[*Enter* LUCIUS.]

35 LUCIUS. The taper burneth in your closet,[14] sir.
Searching the window for a flint,[15] I found
This paper thus sealed up, and I am sure
It did not lie there when I went to bed.

[*Gives him the letter*]

BRUTUS. Get you to bed again; it is not day.
40 ❷ Is not tomorrow, boy, the ides of March?

LUCIUS. I know not, sir.

BRUTUS. Look in the calendar and bring me word.

LUCIUS. I will, sir.   [*Exit*]

BRUTUS. The <u>exhalations</u>[16] whizzing in the air
45 Give so much light that I may read by them.

[*Opens the letter and reads*]

"Brutus, thou sleep'st; awake, and see thyself.
Shall Rome, &c.[17] Speak, strike, redress.
Brutus, thou sleep'st; awake."

Such <u>instigations</u>[18] have been often dropped
50 Where I have took them up.
"Shall Rome, &c." Thus must I piece it out:[19]
❸ Shall Rome stand under one man's awe?[20] What,
    Rome?
My ancestors did from the streets of Rome
The Tarquin[21] drive, when he was called a king.
55 "Speak, strike, redress." Am I <u>entreated</u>
To speak and strike? O Rome, I make thee promise,
If the redress will follow, thou receivest
Thy full petition at the hand of[22] Brutus!

[*Enter* LUCIUS.]

LUCIUS. Sir, March is wasted fifteen days. [*Knock within*]

60 BRUTUS. 'Tis good. Go to the gate; somebody knocks.

[*Exit* LUCIUS.]

Since Cassius first did whet[23] me against Caesar,
I have not slept.
Between the acting of a dreadful thing
And the first motion,[24] all the interim is

12. Fashion it: State the case.
13. extremities (ek strem´ ə tēz) *n.*: Extremes (of tyranny).

14. closet: Study.
15. flint: Stone used to start a fire.

16. exhalations (eks´ hə lā´ shənz) *n.*: Meteors.

17. &c.: *et cetera*, Latin for "and so forth."

18. instigations (in´ stə gā´ shənz) *n.*: Urgings, incitements, or spurs to act.
19. piece it out: Figure out the meaning.
20. under one man's awe: In fearful reverence of one man.
21. Tarquin (tär´ kwin): King of Rome driven out by Lucius Junius Brutus, Brutus' ancestor.
22. Thy full . . . hand of: All you ask from.

23. whet (hwet) *v.*: Sharpen; incite.

24. motion: Idea; suggestion.

Block Scheduling Strategies

Consider these suggestions to take advantage of extended class time:

• Invite students to view Feature 2 on the CD-ROM *The Time, Life, and Works of Shakespeare.* This feature focuses on the Elizabethan Age and Elizabethan theater.

• Students can work in small groups to read portions of the play aloud. Encourage them to note the rhythm of the blank verse as they read.

• After completing the Reader's Response question on page 748 of the Guide for Responding,

students may enjoy holding a debate between those who would have joined the conspiracy and those who would not.

• Have students complete the Literary Focus page on blank verse in **Selection Support**, p. 211.

• Students may work individually or in groups to answer the Critical Thinking questions on page 748.

• Have students work in pairs to complete the Monologue in the Idea Bank on page 749 and read their monologues aloud to the class.

65　　Like a phantasma,[25] or a hideous dream.
　　　The genius and the mortal instruments[26]
　　　Are then in council, and the state of a man,
　　　Like to a little kingdom, suffers then
　　　The nature of an insurrection.[27]

[*Enter* LUCIUS.]

70　LUCIUS. Sir, 'tis your brother[28] Cassius at the door,
　　　Who doth desire to see you.

　　BRUTUS.　　　　　　　　　　Is he alone?

　　LUCIUS. No, sir, there are moe[29] with him.

　　BRUTUS.　　　　　　　　　Do you know them?

　　LUCIUS. No, sir; their hats are plucked about their ears,
　　　And half their faces buried in their cloaks,
75　　That by no means I may discover them
　　　By any mark of favor.[30]

　　BRUTUS.　　　　　　　Let 'em enter.　　　[*Exit* LUCIUS.]

　　　They are the faction. O conspiracy,
❹　　Sham'st thou to show thy dang'rous brow by night,
　　　When evils are most free? O, then by day
80　　Where wilt thou find a cavern dark enough
　　　To mask thy monstrous visage? Seek none,
　　　　　conspiracy;
　　　Hide it in smiles and affability:
　　　For if thou path, thy native semblance on,[31]
　　　Not Erebus[32] itself were dim enough
85　　To hide thee from prevention.[33]

[*Enter the conspirators,* CASSIUS, CASCA, DECIUS, CINNA, METELLUS
CIMBER, *and* TREBONIUS.]

　　CASSIUS. I think we are too bold upon[34] your rest.
　　　Good morrow, Brutus; do we trouble you?

　　BRUTUS. I have been up this hour, awake all night.
　　　Know I these men that come along with you?

❻
90　CASSIUS. Yes, every man of them; and no man here
　　　But honors you; and every one doth wish
　　　You had but that opinion of yourself
　　　Which every noble Roman bears of you.
　　　This is Trebonius.

　　BRUTUS.　　　　　　　He is welcome hither.

　　CASSIUS. This, Decius Brutus.

95　BRUTUS.　　　　　　　He is welcome too.

The Tragedy of Julius Caesar, Act II, Scene i ◆ 735

25. all the . . . a
phantasma: All the time
between seems like a
nightmare.
26. mortal instruments:
Bodily powers.
27. insurrection (in′ sə
rek′ shən) *n.*: Revolt.
28. brother: Brother-in-
law (Cassius was married
to Brutus' sister).

29. moe: More.

30. discover . . . favor:
Identify them by their
appearance.

◆ **Literary Focus**
What exclamation
does Shakespeare
include that helps
him maintain the
iambic pentameter
of lines 77 and 79?

❺

31. path . . . semblance
on: Walk looking as you
normally do.
32. Erebus (er′ ə bəs):
Dark place between Earth
and Hades.
33. prevention: Being
discovered and stopped.
34. upon: In interfering
with.

◆ **Build Vocabulary**
augmented (ôg ment′ id)
v.: Made greater

entreated (in trēt′ id) *v.*:
Begged; pleaded with

conspiracy (kən spir′ ə sē)
n.: Group plotting a harmful
act or the plot itself

◆ **Reading Strategy**
❹ **Read Blank Verse** Have
students determine how many sentences these six lines, starting with
"Let 'em enter" and ending with "visage," contain. Then ask a student to
read the lines aloud, pausing only
where the sentences end. *The lines
contain four sentences, ending with
"enter," "faction," "free," and "visage."*

◆ **Literary Focus**
❺ **Blank Verse** The exclamation
"O" is used twice and it helps to
maintain the rhythm of lines 77
and 79.

◆ **Critical Thinking**
❻ **Draw Conclusions** Guide students to consider why Cassius speaks
to Brutus in this flattering way. What
does Cassius hope to achieve? *He is
flattering Brutus, hoping to draw him
into the conspiracy.*

Customize for
English Language Learners
Students whose first language is not
English may be confused by the use
of the words *thee, thy,* and *thou.*
Explain that these are old ways of
saying *you* (*thee* and *thou*) and *your*
(*thy*).

❶ Clarification Explain to students that Casca is drawing an analogy between the sun and Caesar. He points out that just as the sun will change its course as the year progresses, so will Caesar change as his power increases.

❷ Enrichment Point out to students that Casca's knowledge of astronomy would have been based on theories of Hipparchus and other Greeks, who claimed that the planets and sun circled the Earth. Shakespeare, however, would have been acquainted with the ideas of Copernicus, who believed that the planets traveled around the sun. Copernicus also developed the theory of axle tilt, which explained the change in seasons by changes in the angle of the Earth's tilt toward the sun—an idea that Casca mentions here.

Comprehension Check ☑

❸ Why doesn't Brutus want to swear an oath? *He wants to believe that he and the other conspirators are such honorable men that their lives are already sworn to truthfulness; an oath would be unnecessary.*

CASSIUS. This, Casca; this, Cinna; and this, Metellus Cimber.

BRUTUS. They are all welcome.
What watchful cares do interpose themselves
Betwixt your eyes and night?[35]

100 **CASSIUS.** Shall I entreat[36] a word?   [*They whisper.*]

DECIUS. Here lies the east; doth not the day break here?

CASCA. No.

CINNA. O, pardon, sir, it doth; and yon gray lines
That fret[37] the clouds are messengers of day.

❶
105 **CASCA.** You shall confess that you are both deceived.
❷   Here, as I point my sword, the sun arises,
Which is a great way growing on[38] the south,
Weighing[39] the youthful season of the year.
Some two months hence, up higher toward the north
110 He first presents his fire; and the high[40] east
Stands as the Capitol, directly here.

BRUTUS. Give me your hands all over, one by one.

CASSIUS. And let us swear our <u>resolution</u>.

❸ **BRUTUS.** No, not an oath. If not the face of men,
115 The sufferance of our souls, the time's abuse[41]—
If these be motives weak, break off betimes,[42]
And every man hence to his idle bed.
So let high-sighted[43] tyranny range on
Till each man drop by lottery.[44] But if these
120 (As I am sure they do) bear fire enough
To kindle cowards and to steel with valor
The melting spirits of women, then, countrymen,
What need we any spur but our own cause
To prick us to redress?[45] What other bond
125 Than secret Romans, that have spoke the word,
And will not palter?[46] And what other oath
Than honesty to honesty engaged[47]
That this shall be, or we will fall for it?
Swear priests and cowards and men cautelous,[48]
130 Old feeble carrions[49] and such suffering souls
That welcome wrongs; unto bad causes swear
Such creatures as men doubt; but do not stain
The even[50] virtue of our enterprise,
Nor th' insuppressive mettle[51] of our spirits,
135 To think that or our cause or[52] our performance
Did need an oath; when every drop of blood
That every Roman bears, and nobly bears,

35. watchful . . . night: Worries that keep you from sleep.
36. entreat (in trēt´) *v.*: Speak.

37. fret (fret) *v.*: Decorate with a pattern.

38. growing on: Tending toward.
39. Weighing: Considering.
40. high: Due.

41. the face . . . time's abuse: The sadness on men's faces, the suffering of our souls, the present abuses.
42. betimes: Quickly.
43. high-sighted: Arrogant (as a hawk about to swoop down on its prey).
44. by lottery: By chance or in his turn.
45. prick us to redress: Goad or spur us on to correct these evils.
46. palter (pôl´ tər): Talk insincerely.
47. honesty engaged: Personal honor pledged.
48. cautelous: Cautious.
49. carrions (kar´ ē ənz) *n.*: Decaying flesh.
50. even: Constant.
51. insuppressive mettle: Uncrushable courage.
52. or . . . or: Either our cause or.

◆ **Build Vocabulary**
resolution (rez´ ə loo´ shən) *n.*: Strong determination

736 ◆ *Drama*

Cross-Curricular Connection: Social Studies

Brutus says that "not Erebus itself were dim enough" (Scene 1, line 84) to hide the conspiracy to assassinate Caesar. Explain to students that Erebus was, in Greek mythology, the part of the underworld (Hades) through which the dead first pass. By the time of Julius Caesar, the Romans had taken for their own many of the gods of the Greeks, but given them Roman names. Hermes, messenger of the gods, was called Mercury; Aphrodite, goddess of love and beauty, Venus; Hera, queen of the gods, Juno; and the king of the Gods, Zeus, was called Jupiter by the Romans. Interested students might list the Roman names of other Greek gods such as Hades (Pluto), Athena (Minerva), Poseidon (Neptune), and Artemis (Diana).

►Critical Viewing◄

④ **Speculate** Logical answers include the greetings beginning with line 86, the discussion of the sunrise beginning with line 100. Some students may suggest that Brutus is speaking to the others, delivering his monologue beginning with line 114.

◆ **Critical Thinking**

⑤ **Make Inferences** Ask students to suggest another reason Brutus might have for not wanting to include Cicero. *He may not want to confide in Cicero because he knows Cicero's honor and will not go along with the plot. He may also fear that Cicero will betray them.*

◆ *Literature and Your Life*

⑥ Encourage students to support their individual responses with examples from literature, movies, television programs, and, if they wish, from personal experience.

④ ▲ **Critical Viewing** What do you think the group is saying to Brutus here? [Speculate]

Is guilty of a several bastardy[53]
If he do break the smallest particle
140 Of any promise that hath passed from him.

CASSIUS. But what of Cicero? Shall we sound him?[54]
I think he will stand very strong with us.

CASCA. Let us not leave him out.

CINNA.   No, by no means.

METELLUS. O, let us have him, for his silver hairs
145 Will purchase us a good opinion,
And buy men's voices to commend our deeds.
It shall be said his judgment ruled our hands;
Our youths and wildness shall no whit[55] appear,
But all be buried in his gravity.

150 **BRUTUS.** O, name him not! Let us not break with him;[56]
⑤ For he will never follow anything
That other men begin.

CASSIUS.   Then leave him out.

CASCA. Indeed, he is not fit.

DECIUS. Shall no man else be touched but only Caesar?

155 **CASSIUS.** Decius, well urged. I think it is not meet

53. guilty . . . bastardy: Is no true Roman.

54. sound him: Find out his opinion.

◆ *Literature and Your Life*

Metellus is saying that Cicero's age and reputation for wisdom will lead people to accept the actions of the conspirators more rapidly. Explain why you think people should or should not be judged by the company they keep.

⑥

55. no whit (hwit) *n.*: Not the least bit.

56. break with him: Confide in him.

The Tragedy of Julius Caesar, Act II, Scene i ◆ 737

Cross-Curricular Connection: History

Tell students that Marcus Tullius Cicero was one of the great speakers and writers of Rome. He studied philosophy and rhetoric in Greece, and after returning to Rome was elected praetor (an administrator of civil justice) in 66 B.C., and then consul in 63 B.C.

Cicero, who believed in a republican form of government, supported Pompey in the struggle between Pompey and Caesar, and approved of Caesar's murder. In 43 B.C., when Caesar's supporters Octavius (later the emperor Augustus), Mark Antony, and Marcus Aemilius Lepidus came to power as the Second Triumvirate, Cicero was one of the many they condemned to death. He was slain trying to escape from his home in Tuscany.

Cicero's prose became the model for literary expression in Europe, and his orations are still among the most commonly studied Latin works.

① Word Roots: -spir- Students can easily locate the word root -spir- in this passage. Challenge them to define the word *spirit*, using the meaning of the word root ("to breathe"). *Spirit means "breath of life."*

◆ **Critical Thinking**

② Analyze Have students determine why it is important to Brutus that Caesar be killed "boldly, but not wrathfully." *For Brutus, it would be dishonorable if Caesar were killed in anger.*

Literature CD-R♦M Use the Literature CD-ROM feature 4 to give students background on Elizabethan staging conventions. After using the feature, lead a class discussion applying what students have learned to *The Tragedy of Julius Caesar.*

Mark Antony, so well beloved of Caesar,
Should outlive Caesar; we shall find of[57] him
A shrewd contriver;[58] and you know, his means;
If he improve[59] them, may well stretch so far
160 As to annoy[60] us all; which to prevent,
Let Antony and Caesar fall together.

BRUTUS. Our course will seem too bloody, Caius Cassius,
To cut the head off and then hack the limbs,
Like wrath in death and envy afterwards;[61]
165 For Antony is but a limb of Caesar.
Let's be sacrificers, but not butchers, Caius.
① We all stand up against the spirit of Caesar,
And in the spirit of men there is no blood.
O, that we then could come by Caesar's spirit,[62]
170 And not dismember Caesar! But, alas,
Caesar must bleed for it. And, gentle[63] friends,
Let's kill him boldly, but not wrathfully;
Let's carve him as a dish fit for the gods,
Not hew him as a carcass fit for hounds.
175 And let our hearts, as subtle masters do,
Stir up their servants[64] to an act of rage,
And after seem to chide 'em.[65] This shall make
② Our purpose necessary, and not envious;
Which so appearing to the common eyes,
180 We shall be called purgers,[66] not murderers.
And for Mark Antony, think not of him;
For he can do no more than Caesar's arm
When Caesar's head is off.

CASSIUS.   Yet I fear him;
For in the ingrafted[67] love he bears to Caesar—

185 **BRUTUS.** Alas, good Cassius, do not think of him.
If he love Caesar, all that he can do
Is to himself—take thought[68] and die for Caesar.
And that were much he should,[69] for he is given
To sports, to wildness, and much company.

190 **TREBONIUS.** There is no fear in him; let him not die,
For he will live and laugh at this hereafter.

[*Clock strikes.*]

BRUTUS. Peace! Count the clock.

CASSIUS.   The clock hath stricken three.

TREBONIUS. 'Tis time to part.

CASSIUS.   But it is doubtful yet
Whether Caesar will come forth today or no;

57. **of:** In.
58. **contriver** (kən trīv′ ər) *n.*: Schemer.
59. **improve:** Increase.
60. **annoy:** Harm.

61. **Like . . . envy afterwards:** As if we were killing in anger with hatred afterward.

62. **come by Caesar's spirit:** Get hold of the principles of tyranny for which Caesar stands.
63. **gentle:** Honorable; noble.

64. **servants:** Their hands.
65. **chide 'em:** Scold them.

66. **purgers:** Healers.

67. **ingrafted:** Deeply rooted.

68. **take thought:** Become melancholy.
69. **that were much he should:** It is unlikely he would do that.

Humanities: Literature

Much of the information that Shakespeare used in creating *The Tragedy of Julius Caesar* came from one source, familiarly known as Plutarch's *Lives,* written by the Greek writer Plutarch (A.D. 46?–A.D. 120?).

The book contains a series of paired biographies, each pair comparing one Greek and one Roman statesman. Shakespeare, like other playwrights of his time, used translations of Plutarch by Sir Thomas North when writing about Greece or Rome.

Every character in *Julius Caesar* is found in Plutarch, except for Brutus' servant Lucius. Even details such as Cassius' leanness, Brutus' studiousness, and Caesar's "falling sickness" are found in Plutarch's work.

Let students know that Shakespeare didn't plagiarize or steal Plutarch's work. He just used Plutarch as a springboard for his own creative genius.

Ask students to name contemporary novels or movies that are based on the lives of real people. What sources do students think contemporary writers might use to find background on their real-life characters? *Students will probably suggest that information can be found in magazines, newspapers, on the Internet, and for some people, in biographies or autobiographies.*

195　For he is superstitious grown of late,
　　　Quite from the main[70] opinion he held once
　　　Of fantasy, of dreams, and ceremonies.[71]
　　　It may be these apparent prodigies,
　　　The unaccustomed terror of this night,
200　And the persuasion of his augurers[72]
　　　May hold him from the Capitol today.

DECIUS. Never fear that. If he be so resolved,
　　　I can o'ersway him;[73] for he loves to hear
　　　That unicorns may be betrayed with trees,[74]
205　And bears with glasses,[75] elephants with holes,[76]
　　　Lions with toils,[77] and men with flatterers;
　　　But when I tell him he hates flatterers
　　　He says he does, being then most flatterèd.
　　　Let me work;
210　For I can give his humor the true bent,[78]
　　　And I will bring him to the Capitol.

CASSIUS. Nay, we will all of us be there to fetch him.

BRUTUS. By the eighth hour; is that the uttermost?[79]

CINNA. Be that the uttermost, and fail not then.

215　**METELLUS.** Caius Ligarius doth bear Caesar hard,[80]
　　　Who rated[81] him for speaking well of Pompey.
　　　I wonder none of you have thought of him.

BRUTUS. Now, good Metellus, go along by him.
　　　He loves me well, and I have given him reasons;
220　Send him but hither, and I'll fashion[82] him.

CASSIUS. The morning comes upon 's; we'll leave you,
　　　　Brutus.
　　　And, friends, disperse yourselves; but all remember
　　　What you have said, and show yourselves true
　　　　Romans.

BRUTUS. Good gentlemen, look fresh and merrily.
225　Let not our looks put on[83] our purposes,
　　　But bear it[84] as our Roman actors do,
　　　With untired spirits and formal constancy.[85]
　　　And so good morrow to you every one.

[*Exit all but* BRUTUS.]

　　　Boy! Lucius! Fast asleep? It is no matter;
230　Enjoy the honey-heavy dew of slumber.
　　　Thou hast no figures nor no fantasies
　　　Which busy care draws in the brains of men;
　　　Therefore thou sleep'st so sound.

The Tragedy of Julius Caesar, Act II, Scene i ◆ *739*

70. Quite from the main: Quite changed from the strong.
71. ceremonies: Omens.

72. augurers (ô′ gər ərz) *n.:* Officials who interpreted omens to decide if they were favorable or unfavorable for an undertaking.
73. I can o'ersway him: I can change his mind.
74. unicorns . . . trees: Story that tells how standing in front of a tree and stepping aside at the last moment cause a charging unicorn to bury his horn in the tree and be caught.
75. glasses: Mirrors.
76. holes: Pitfalls.
77. toils: Nets; snares.
78. give his humor the true bent: Bend his feelings in the right direction.
79. uttermost: Latest.
80. doth bear Caesar hard: Has a grudge against Caesar.
81. rated: Berated.

82. fashion: Mold.

83. put on: Show.
84. bear it: Carry it off.
85. formal constancy: Consistent dignity.

◆ **Literary Focus**

❸ **Blank Verse** Students should be able to locate the line in Decius' speech that is not in iambic pentameter. Invite them to conjecture about why Shakespeare included the short line "Let me work." *It is important that Decius convince Caesar to come to the Capitol—his "work" is a vital part of the plot. Therefore, it is reasonable to conjecture that Shakespeare set the statement off to call attention to it.*

❹ **Clarification** Remind students of the struggle between Caesar and Pompey. Caius Ligarius is one who supported Pompey; therefore, he and Caesar have been enemies since the revolt.

Customize for
Bodily/Kinesthetic Learners
Allow these students to act out the conversation beginning on page 737 with line 141, in which the conspirators discuss the potential participants and the nature of the assassination. Encourage them to use body language, gestures, and facial expressions to indicate the feelings and attitudes of each character.

739

◆ Reading Strategy

1 Read Blank Verse There are seven complete sentences in Portia's speech. Remind students that a semicolon separates two independent clauses. Pausing at the semicolon will help students identify the ideas expressed in the longer sentences in this speech.

◆ Reading Strategy

2 Read Blank Verse With students, determine where a reader should pause in Scene i, lines 245–251. Analyze the passage for meaning. Then ask a volunteer to read the passage aloud. *There are pauses: after "insisted," "not," "you," "did," "enkindled," and "humor." Read for meaning, the passage could be restated as follows: I insisted (that you tell me your problem), but instead of answering, you waved me away with your hand. I left, not wanting to make you even more impatient, and hoping that your impatience with me was just the result of an ordinary bad mood.*

Comprehension Check ☑

3 Does Portia believe Brutus' explanation? What does she think is wrong with him? *No, she knows he is not sick. She believes he is troubled in his mind.*

[*Enter* PORTIA.]

PORTIA.   Brutus, my lord.

BRUTUS. Portia, what mean you? Wherefore rise you now
235 It is not for your health thus to commit
     Your weak condition to the raw cold morning.

PORTIA. Nor for yours neither. Y'have ungently, Brutus,
     Stole from my bed; and yesternight at supper
     You suddenly arose and walked about,
240 Musing and sighing, with your arms across;
     And when I asked you what the matter was,
     You stared upon me with ungentle looks.
     I urged you further; then you scratched your head,
     And too impatiently stamped with your foot.
245 Yet I insisted, yet you answered not,
     But with an angry wafter[86] of your hand
     Gave sign for me to leave you. So I did,
     Fearing to strengthen that impatience
     Which seemed too much enkindled, and withal
250 Hoping it was but an effect of humor,
     Which sometime hath his[87] hour with every man.
     It will not let you eat, nor talk, nor sleep,
     And could it work so much upon your shape
     As it hath much prevailed on your condition,[88]
255 I should not know you[89] Brutus. Dear my lord,
     Make me acquainted with your cause of grief.

BRUTUS. I am not well in health, and that is all.

PORTIA. Brutus is wise and, were he not in health,
     He would embrace the means to come by it.

260 **BRUTUS.** Why, so I do. Good Portia, go to bed.

PORTIA. Is Brutus sick, and is it physical[90]
     To walk unbracèd and suck up the humors[91]
     Of the dank morning? What, is Brutus sick,
     And will he steal out of his wholesome bed,
265 To dare the vile contagion of the night,
     And tempt the rheumy and unpurgèd air[92]
     To add unto his sickness? No, my Brutus:
     You have some sick offense[93] within your mind.
     Which by the right and virtue of my place
270 I ought to know of; and upon my knees
     I charm[94] you, by my once commended[95] beauty,
     By all your vows of love, and that great vow[96]
     Which did incorporate and make us one,
     That you unfold to me, your self, your half,
275 Why you are heavy,[97] and what men tonight

◆ **Reading Strategy**
How many complete sentences are in Portia's speech? **1**

86. **wafter:** Waving.

87. **his:** Its.

88. **condition:** Disposition.
89. **I should not know you:** I would not recognize you as.

90. **physical:** Healthy.
91. **humors:** Dampness.

92. **tempt . . . air:** Risk exposing himself to the air that is likely to cause rheumatism and air that has not been purified by the sun.
93. **sick offense:** Harmful sickness.
94. **charm:** Beg.
95. **commended:** Praised.
96. **great vow:** Marriage vow.
97. **heavy:** Sorrowful.

740 ◆ *Drama*

📜 **Cross-Curricular Connection: History**

Julius Caesar's Life
Julius Caesar is dead before the play that bears his name is even half over. For those who are curious to know more about this great leader, share the following information. Interested students may want to research a particular period in Caesar's life or read some of his writings and speeches.

Gaius Julius Caesar (100?–44 B.C.), a Roman general and statesman, was a brilliant military leader who helped make Rome the center of an empire that stretched across Europe. Caesar also won fame as an orator, politician, and writer. He began his political career as director of public works and games in 65 B.C. In 62, he became *praetor,* the office next in rank to consul, and in 60, joined with Marcus Licinius Crassus and Gaeus Pompey in the *First Triumvirate,* an alliance that ruled Rome. The three took power when Caesar was elected consul in 59, the same year in which he married

Calpurnia. Also that year, Pompey married Caesar's daughter, Julia (from Caesar's first marriage, to Cornelia, who had died about ten years earlier). In 58, knowing he needed military fame and a loyal army in order to gain more power, Caesar began a campaign to conquer Gaul (France). A military genius, Caesar drove the Germans out of Gaul and invaded Britain twice, in 55 and 54.

(continues on page 741)

Have had resort to you; for here have been
Some six or seven, who did hide their faces
Even from darkness.

    BRUTUS.   Kneel not, gentle Portia.

    PORTIA. I should not need, if you were gentle Brutus.
280   Within the bond of marriage, tell me, Brutus,
Is it excepted[98] I should know no secrets
That appertain[99] to you? Am I your self
But, as it were, in sort or limitation,[100]
To keep with you at meals, comfort your bed,
And talk to you sometimes? Dwell I but in the
285   suburbs[101]
Of your good pleasure? If it be no more,
Portia is Brutus' harlot, not his wife.

    BRUTUS. You are my true and honorable wife,
As dear to me as are the ruddy drops[102]
290   That visit my sad heart.

    PORTIA. If this were true, then should I know this secret.
I grant I am a woman; but withal
A woman that Lord Brutus took to wife.
I grant I am a woman; but withal
295   A woman well reputed, Cato's daughter.[103]
Think you I am no stronger than my sex,
Being so fathered and so husbanded?
Tell me your counsels,[104] I will not disclose 'em.
I have made strong proof of my constancy,
300   Giving myself a voluntary wound
Here in the thigh; can I bear that with patience,
And not my husband's secrets?

    BRUTUS.   O ye gods,
Render[105] me worthy of this noble wife!   [*Knock*]
Hark, hark! One knocks. Portia, go in a while,
305   And by and by thy bosom shall partake
The secrets of my heart.
All my engagements[106] I will construe to thee,
All the charactery of my sad brows.[107]
Leave me with haste.   [*Exit* PORTIA.]

[*Enter* LUCIUS *and* CAIUS LIGARIUS.]

          Lucius, who's that knocks?

310 **LUCIUS.** Here is a sick man that would speak with you.

    BRUTUS. Caius Ligarius, that Metellus spake of.
Boy, stand aside. Caius Ligarius! How?

    CAIUS. Vouchsafe good morrow from a feeble tongue.

The Tragedy of Julius Caesar, Act II, Scene i ◆ *741*

---

98. excepted: Made an exception.
99. appertain (ap′ ər tān′) *v.*: Belong.
100. in sort or limitation: Within a limited way.
101. suburbs: Outskirts.

102. ruddy drops: Blood.

103. Cato's daughter: Marcus Porcius Cato had been an ally of Pompey and enemy of Caesar. He killed himself rather than be captured by Caesar.
104. counsels: Secrets.

105. Render (ren′ dər) *v.*: Make.

106. engagements: Commitments.
107. All the charactery of my sad brows: All that is written on my face.

◆ *Literature and Your Life*

4 Ask students how they feel when they know someone like a friend or family member is keeping a secret from them. How do they feel when they know they have to keep a secret? Lead a discussion in which students apply their own feelings to Portia's position. After students have analyzed the situation, have them offer opinions on whether or not Brutus should or should not have told Portia what's going on.

◆ **Critical Thinking**

5 **Analyze** Draw students' attention to Scene i, line 303: "Render me worthy of this noble wife!" Ask students what Brutus' words reveal about his character. *Brutus admires the qualities of loyalty, discretion, courage, and strength that Portia displays. His admiration for these qualities reinforces that he is, essentially, an honorable man.*

◆ **Literary Focus**

6 **Blank Verse** Call students' attention to line 309. Point out that the line continues after the stage directions for characters to exit and enter. Brutus would not pause, but would continue speaking as actors moved around him.

(continued)
    In 49, Pompey, both alarmed and jealous at Caesar's huge success, allied himself with a group who ordered Caesar to give up his army. Rather than comply, Caesar led 5,000 men against Pompey, whose troops surrendered, forcing Pompey and his cohorts to flee Rome. He again defeated Pompey's army in Greece and followed him to Egypt, to find that Pompey had been murdered. In Egypt, Caesar met and fell in love with Cleopatra, and before returning to Rome, won a war that made her ruler of Egypt. After winning two more battles against Pompey's forces, Caesar became the unrivaled ruler of the Roman empire. He pardoned the followers of Pompey, and was granted the powers of dictator for ten years by the Roman people. Later, he was made dictator for life. At a public festival, Mark Antony tested popular feeling by offering Caesar the crown of a king. Because the Romans hated kings, Caesar refused the crown.

Comprehension Check ☑

❶ What piece of work does Brutus mean? Why will it make sick men whole? *Brutus refers to the killing of Caesar, which will make Rome whole again, after being sick with Caesar's tyranny.*

◆ Critical Thinking

❷ Interpret In this passage, Caesar's words are aimed at two different people. Have a volunteer read the lines so that it is clear that Caesar is first talking to himself, then calling to a servant to ask who is there. *The reader should change her or his tone of voice before addressing the servant. She or he might choose to pause before "Who's within?" or to make these words follow "They murder Caesar!" very quickly, as if he had been startled by the sound of a possible intruder.*

◆ Literary Focus

❸ Blank Verse The first two lines technically have an extra syllable. In line 1, however, the rhythm leads "heaven" to be pronounced as one syllable (heav'n) while in line 2, the last two syllables of "Calpurnia" slide together, as if they were one unstressed syllable. (cal purn´ yä)

BRUTUS. O, what a time have you chose out,[108] brave Caius,

315   To wear a kerchief![109] Would you were not sick!

CAIUS. I am not sick, if Brutus have in hand
Any <u>exploit</u> worthy the name of honor.

BRUTUS. Such an exploit have I in hand, Ligarius,
Had you a healthful ear to hear of it.

320 **CAIUS.** By all the gods that Romans bow before,
I here discard my sickness! Soul of Rome,
Brave son, derived from honorable loins,[110]
Thou, like an exorcist,[111] hast conjured up
My mortifièd spirit.[112] Now bid me run,

325   And I will strive with things impossible.
Yea, get the better of them. What's to do?

❶ BRUTUS. A piece of work that will make sick men whole.

CAIUS. But are not some whole that we must make sick?

BRUTUS. That must we also. What it is, my Caius,

330   I shall unfold[113] to thee, as we are going
To whom it must be done.

CAIUS.   Set on[114] your foot,
And with a heart new-fired I follow you,
To do I know not what; but it sufficeth[115]
That Brutus leads me on.   [*Thunder*]

BRUTUS.   Follow me, then.   [*Exit*]

Scene ii. Caesar's house.

[*Thunder and lightning. Enter* JULIUS CAESAR *in his nightgown.*]

❷ CAESAR. Nor heaven nor earth have been at peace tonight:
Thrice hath Calpurnia in her sleep cried out,
"Help, ho! They murder Caesar!" Who's within?

[*Enter a* SERVANT.]

SERVANT. My lord?

5   **CAESAR.** Go bid the priests do present[1] sacrifice,
And bring me their opinions of success.

SERVANT. I will, my lord.   [*Exit*]

[*Enter* CALPURNIA.]

CALPURNIA. What mean you, Caesar? Think you to walk forth?
You shall not stir out of your house today.

742 ▸ *Drama*

---

108. chose out: Picked out.

109. To wear a kerchief: Caius wears a scarf to protect him from drafts because he is sick.

110. derived from honorable loins: Descended from Lucius Junius Brutus, founder of Rome.

111. exorcist (ek´ sôr sist) *n.*: One who calls up spirits.

112. mortifièd spirit: Paralyzed, as if dead, spirit.

113. unfold: Disclose.

114. Set on: Advance.

115. sufficeth (se fis´ eth) *v.*: Is enough.

◆ **Literary Focus**
Which of these lines (1–4) have an extra unaccented syllable? Why doesn't the extra syllable disrupt the rhythm of the iambs? **❸**

1. present: Immediate.

◆ **Build Vocabulary**
exploit (eks´ ploĭt) *n.*: Act or deed, especially a heroic achievement

---

 Beyond the Classroom

Workplace Skills

Cutting Costs Students who know that movies made today have budgets that run into many millions may be surprised to learn that the MGM film of *Julius Caesar* was produced with a budget of only 1.7 million. This included the salaries of several big stars (John Gielgud, Marlon Brando, Deborah Kerr, and Greer Garson) as well as cos-

tumes, sets, lighting, salaries for the crew, feeding the cast and crew during production, and insurance. To stay within this budget, which was tight even by 1950's standards, sets and costumes from another movie were used! Togas, armor, and columns from *Quo Vadis*, another MGM film set in Rome during Nero's reign, were recycled in this film about Caesar's reign. Point

out to students that the producers of *Julius Caesar* probably made this decision by balancing the cost of the costumes against the importance of having big stars. Encourage students to find out as much as possible about the budget of a recent blockbuster film. Encourage them to discuss the information with others in class and to suggest realistic cost-saving measures.

CAESAR. Caesar shall forth. The things that threatened
10 me
Ne'er looked but on my back; when they shall see
The face of Caesar, they are vanishèd.

❹ **CALPURNIA.** Caesar, I never stood on ceremonies,[2]
Yet now they fright me. There is one within,
15 Besides the things that we have heard and seen,
Recounts most horrid sights seen by the watch.[3]
A lioness hath whelpèd[4] in the streets,
And graves have yawned, and yielded up their dead;
Fierce fiery warriors fought upon the clouds
20 In ranks and squadrons and right form of war,[5]
❺ Which drizzled blood upon the Capitol;
The noise of battle hurtled[6] in the air,
Horses did neigh and dying men did groan,
And ghosts did shriek and squeal about the street.
25 O Caesar, these things are beyond all use,[7]
And I do fear them.

CAESAR.   What can be avoided
❻ Whose end is purposed[8] by the mighty gods?
Yet Caesar shall go forth; for these predictions
Are to the world in general as to Caesar.[9]

30 **CALPURNIA.** When beggars die, there are no comets seen;
The heavens themselves blaze forth[10] the death of
princes.

❼ **CAESAR.** Cowards die many times before their deaths;
The valiant never taste of death but once.
Of all the wonders that I yet have heard,
35 It seems to me most strange that men should fear,
Seeing that death, a necessary end,
Will come when it will come.

[*Enter a* SERVANT.]

                    What say the augurers?

SERVANT. They would not have you to stir forth today.
Plucking the entrails of an offering forth,[11]
40 They could not find a heart within the beast.

CAESAR. The gods do this in shame of[12] cowardice:
Caesar should be a beast without a heart
If he should stay at home today for fear.
No, Caesar shall not; Danger knows full well
45 That Caesar is more dangerous than he.
We are two lions littered[13] in one day,
And I the elder and more terrible,
And Caesar shall go forth.

The Tragedy of Julius Caesar, Act II, Scene ii ◆ 743

---

2. stood on ceremonies: Paid attention to omens.

3. Recounts . . . watch: Tells about the awful sights seen by the watchman.

4. whelpèd: Given birth.

5. right form of war: Proper military formation of war.

6. hurtled: (hurt′ əld) *v.*: Clashed together.

7. beyond all use: Contrary to all experience.

8. is purposed: Is intended.

9. for these . . . as to Caesar: Because these predictions apply to the rest of the world as much as they apply to Caesar.

10. blaze forth: Proclaim with meteors and comets.

11. Plucking . . . forth: Pulling out the insides of a sacrificed animal.

12. in shame of: In order to shame.

13. littered: Born.

Cross-Curricular Connection: Social Studies

Soothsayers Explain to students that, in the fourth century B.C., the Romans overcame the Etruscans, who had ruled Rome along with most of what is now Italy. The Romans retained some features of the Etruscan religion, which placed a great deal of importance upon prophesy and divination. Soothsayers predicted the future by studying the flight of birds and the intestines of animals.

When Caesar asks, "What say the augurers?" (Scene ii, line 38), and the reply is, "Plucking entrails of an offering forth,/ They could not find a heart within the beast," Shakespeare is referring to such soothsayers' rituals, adapted by the Romans from the older Etruscan religion.

Suggest that interested students research the history of the Etruscans and the influence of their culture on Rome.

◆ **Reading Strategy**

❶ **Read Blank Verse** With students, determine where a reader would pause in Calpurnia's speech. Then have a volunteer read the passage aloud. *There should be pauses after "confidence," "today," "own," "House," "today." There should be no pause after "fear." It is the last word in a line, but the sense of the lines would not indicate a pause.*

◆ **Critical Thinking**

❷ **Interpret** Ask students why Caesar changes his mind and won't let Decius give illness as a reason for Caesar's not going to the Senate House. *He does not want to lie in front of Decius. It would make him seem weak. A powerful person doesn't have to make excuses.*

◆ **Critical Thinking**

❸ **Analyze** Remind students that Decius is one of the conspirators. What is his motive for interpreting Caesar's dream in a positive way? On what need of Caesar's is he playing? *Decius is trying to get Caesar to go to the Senate House because that is where the conspirators plan to kill him. Decius knows that Caesar needs to feel powerful. He knows his interpretation of the dream will appeal to this need.*

CALPURNIA.   Alas, my lord,
Your wisdom is consumed in confidence.[14]
50   Do not go forth today. Call it my fear
That keeps you in the house and not your own.
We'll send Mark Antony to the Senate House,
And he shall say you are not well today.
Let me, upon my knee, prevail in this.

55   **CAESAR.** Mark Antony shall say I am not well,
And for thy humor,[15] I will stay at home.

[*Enter* DECIUS.]

Here's Decius Brutus, he shall tell them so.

DECIUS. Caesar, all hail! Good morrow, worthy Caesar;
I come to fetch you to the Senate House.

60   **CAESAR.** And you are come in very happy time[16]
To bear my greeting to the senators,
And tell them that I will not come today.
Cannot, is false; and that I dare not, falser:
I will not come today. Tell them so, Decius.

CALPURNIA. Say he is sick.

65   **CAESAR.**   Shall Caesar send a lie?
Have I in conquest stretched mine arm so far
To be afeard to tell graybeards[17] the truth?
Decius, go tell them Caesar will not come.

DECIUS. Most mighty Caesar, let me know some cause,
70   Lest I be laughed at when I tell them so.

CAESAR. The cause is in my will: I will not come.
That is enough to satisfy the Senate.
But for your private satisfaction,
Because I love you, I will let you know.
75   Calpurnia here, my wife, stays me at home.
She dreamt tonight she saw my statue,
Which, like a fountain with an hundred spouts,
Did run pure blood, and many lusty Romans
Came smiling and did bathe their hands in it.
And these does she apply for[18] warnings and
80   portents
And evils <u>imminent</u>, and on her knee
Hath begged that I will stay at home today.

DECIUS. This dream is all amiss interpreted;
It was a vision fair and fortunate:
85   Your statue spouting blood in many pipes,
In which so many smiling Romans bathed,
Signifies that from you great Rome shall suck

14. confidence: Overconfidence.

15. humor: Whim.

16. in very happy time: At just the right moment.

17. afeard to tell graybeards: Afraid to tell old men (the senators).

◆ **Literary Focus**
What is the pattern of stressed and unstressed syllables in lines 71–75?

18. apply for: Consider to be.

◆ **Build Vocabulary**
imminent (im´ ə nənt)
adj.: About to happen

744 ◆ *Drama*

3 Reviving blood, and that great men shall press
90   For tinctures, stains, relics, and cognizance.[19]
      This by Calpurnia's dream is signified.

CAESAR. And this way have you well expounded[20] it.

DECIUS. I have, when you have heard what I can say;
      And know it now, the Senate have concluded
95   To give this day a crown to mighty Caesar.
      If you shall send them word you will not come,
      Their minds may change. Besides, it were a mock
4   Apt to be rendered,[21] for someone to say
5   "Break up the Senate till another time,
      When Caesar's wife shall meet with better dreams."
100   If Caesar hide himself, shall they not whisper
      "Lo, Caesar is afraid"?
      Pardon me, Caesar, for my dear dear love
      To your proceeding[22] bids me tell you this,
      And reason to my love is liable.[23]

105 **CAESAR.** How foolish do your fears seem now, Calpurnia!
      I am ashamèd I did yield to them.
      Give me my robe,[24] for I will go.

[*Enter* BRUTUS, LIGARIUS, METELLUS CIMBER, CASCA, TREBONIUS, CINNA, *and* PUBLIUS.]

      And look where Publius is come to fetch me.

PUBLIUS. Good morrow, Caesar.

CAESAR.   Welcome, Publius.
110   What, Brutus, are you stirred so early too?
      Good morrow, Casca. Caius Ligarius.
      Caesar was ne'er so much your enemy[25]
      As that same ague[26] which hath made you lean.
      What is't o'clock?

BRUTUS.   Caesar, 'tis strucken eight.

115 **CAESAR.** I thank you for your pains and courtesy.

[*Enter* ANTONY.]

      See! Antony, that revels[27] long a-nights,
      Is notwithstanding up. Good morrow, Antony.

ANTONY. So to most noble Caesar.

CAESAR.   Bid them prepare[28] within.
      I am to blame to be thus waited for.
120   Now, Cinna; now, Metellus; what Trebonius,
      I have an hour's talk in store for you;
      Remember that you call on me today;

The Tragedy of Julius Caesar, Act II, Scene ii ◆ 745

---

19. shall press . . . cognizance: Decius interprets Calpurnia's dream with a double meaning. To Caesar he suggests that people will beg for badges to show they are Caesar's servants. To the audience, that people will seek remembrances of his death.
20. expounded (ik spound´ əd) *v.*: Interpreted; explained.
21. mock . . . rendered: Jeering comment likely to be made.

22. proceeding: Advancing in your career.
23. reason . . . liable: My judgment is not as strong as my affection for you is.

24. robe: Toga.

25. Caius Ligarius . . . your enemy: Caesar had recently pardoned Ligarius for supporting Pompey during the civil war.
26. ague (ā gyo̅o̅) *n.*: Fever.

27. revels (rev´ əlz) *v.*: Makes merry.

28. prepare: Set out refreshments.

◆ **Critical Thinking**

4 Interpret Invite volunteers to try saying Decius' speech in contemporary, informal English. *Sample answer: Hey Caesar, the Senate was going to give you a crown today, but they'll probably change their minds if you're too chicken to go because of a silly dream your wife had. Too bad, Caesar. Chicken!*

◆ **Reading Strategy**

5 Read Blank Verse Ask volunteers to read lines 92–104, emphasizing the iambic pentameter; then read as they think the lines should be read on a stage. *The first reading will have a sing-song sound; the second should sound natural, yet bring out the underlying meter of the verse.*

Workplace Skills Mini-Lesson

Leadership

Introduce the Concept The characters of Caesar, Cassius, Brutus, and Antony display a variety of leadership qualities. Tell students to identify and evaluate the leadership qualities of each character and describe ways in which a contemporary person might demonstrate the qualities.

Develop Background Have students meet in groups to identify two or three leadership qualities for each of the four characters. Remind students that the different personalities of the characters will mean that they will possess different leadership qualities.

Apply the Information Have students use an Analysis Map to explore each quality they've identified. The examples section of the map will help students identify current situations in which a person might display the leadership quality or skill. You will find the Analysis Map, and instructions for its use, on pages 71–73 of *Transparencies for Writing*. After students have completed the Maps, have students share their conclusions with the class.

Assess the Outcome You may want to collect the Analysis Maps to evaluate the extent to which students explored each quality.

►Critical Viewing◄

❶ Connect The men are merely pretending to be loyal; they actually intend to kill Caesar.

Comprehension Check ☑

❷ What does Trebonius mean when he says "your best friends shall wish I had been further"? *He means that he will be close enough to Caesar to aid in his murder. When the deed is done, any friends of Caesar's will wish Trebonius and the other assassins had not stood so close.*

◆ **Literary Focus**

❸ Blank Verse Point out that Artemidorus' note to Caesar is not in blank verse. Ask students why they think the playwright made this choice. *The uneven rhythm of the note gives it added importance; the sharp, emphatic sound of the warnings strikes the listener or reader more strongly than it would in blank verse.*

❶ ▲ Critical Viewing Based on what you've read so far, how sincere do you think these men are in kneeling before Caesar? [Connect]

Be near me, that I may remember you.

❷ **TREBONIUS.** Caesar, I will [*aside*] and so near will I be,
125   That your best friends shall wish I had been further.

CAESAR. Good friends, go in and taste some wine with me,
And we (like friends) will straightway go together.

BRUTUS. [*Aside*] That every like is not the same,²⁹ O Caesar,
The heart of Brutus earns³⁰ to think upon.   [*Exit*]

29. **That every like . . . the same:** That everyone who seems to be a friend may actually be an enemy.
30. **earns:** Sorrows.

Scene iii. A street near the Capitol, close to Brutus' house.

[*Enter* ARTEMIDORUS, *reading a paper.*]

❸ **ARTEMIDORUS.** "Caesar, beware of Brutus; take heed of Cassius; come not near Casca; have an eye to Cinna; trust not Trebonius; mark well Metellus Cimber; Decius Brutus loves thee not; thou hast wronged Caius Ligarius. There is but one mind in all these men, and it is bent against Caesar. If thou beest not immortal, look about you: security gives way to conspiracy.¹ The mighty gods defend thee!
                                Thy lover,² ARTEMIDORUS."
10   Here will I stand till Caesar pass along,
And as a suitor³ will I give him this.

1. **security . . . conspiracy:** Overconfident carelessness allows the conspiracy to proceed.
2. **lover:** Devoted friend.
3. **suitor** (sō͞ot′ ər) *n.*: Person who requests, petitions, or entreats.

746 ◆ *Drama*

Speaking and Listening Mini-Lesson

Debate

This mini-lesson supports the Speaking and Listening activity in the Idea Bank on page 749.

Introduce the Concept Review that, in a debate, each of two teams supports the pro or con side of a statement, in this case, "Brutus is an honorable man." Team members will alternate giving arguments, and at the end, have a chance to answer, or *rebut*, the opposing arguments.

Develop Background Each group can find Brutus' words and actions that support its position. Suggest that students consider the following in preparing their arguments:

• Brutus' feelings about Caesar
• his feelings about himself
• his feelings on the conspiracy and his part in it

Apply the Information Groups can take turns holding their debates before the rest of the class.

Assess the Outcome Evaluate students' debates based on the relevance of the examples students choose, the consistency of the position they take, and the effectiveness of the delivery.

My heart laments that virtue cannot live
Out of the teeth of emulation.
If thou read this, O Caesar, thou mayest live;
15 **❹** If not, the Fates with traitors do contrive.[4]   [*Exit*]

4. **contrive:** Conspire.

Scene iv. *Another part of the street.*

[*Enter* PORTIA *and* LUCIUS.]

PORTIA. I prithee, boy, run to the Senate House;
Stay not to answer me, but get thee gone.
Why dost thou stay?

LUCIUS.   To know my errand, madam.

PORTIA. I would have had thee there and here again
5   Ere I can tell thee what thou shouldst do there.
O constancy,[1] be strong upon my side;
Set a huge mountain 'tween my heart and tongue!
I have a man's mind, but a woman's might.[2]
How hard it is for women to keep counsel![3]
Art thou here yet?

10 **LUCIUS.**   Madam, what should I do?
Run to the Capitol, and nothing else?
And so return to you, and nothing else?

PORTIA. Yes, bring me word, boy, if thy lord look well,
For he went sickly forth; and take good note
15   What Caesar doth, what suitors press to him.
Hark, boy, what noise is that?

LUCIUS. I hear none, madam.

PORTIA.   Prithee, listen well.
I heard a bustling rumor like a fray,[4]
And the wind brings it from the Capitol.

20 **LUCIUS.** Sooth, madam, I hear nothing.

[*Enter the* SOOTHSAYER.]

PORTIA. Come hither, fellow. Which way hast thou been?

SOOTHSAYER. At mine own house, good lady.

PORTIA. What is't o'clock?

SOOTHSAYER.   About the ninth hour, lady.

PORTIA. Is Caesar yet gone to the Capitol?

25 **SOOTHSAYER.** Madam, not yet; I go to take my stand,
To see him pass on the Capitol.

❼ **PORTIA.** Thou hast some suit[5] to Caesar, hast thou not?

1. **constancy** (kän´ stən sē)
n.: Firmness of mind or
purpose; resoluteness.
2. **might:** Strength.
3. **counsel:** Secret.

4. **fray** (frā) *n.*: Fight or
brawl.

5. **suit** (so͞ot) *n.*: Petition.

◆ **Reading Strategy**
Where should you
pause when reading
these lines? Why?
❻

The Tragedy of Julius Caesar, Act II, Scene iv ◆ *747*

---

❹ Clarification Explain that the
Fates were three goddesses who
controlled human life. One spun the
web of life, one measured it, and one
cut it at the end.

◆ **Critical Thinking**

❺ Relate Portia's anxiety makes
her talk to herself and give partial
instructions to the boy Lucius. Ask
students to suggest other ways that
anxiety can affect a person's behavior.
*Anxiety or nervousness might cause
someone to behave impatiently, to cry,
or to perform poorly on a test or in a
sport.*

◆ **Reading Strategy**

❻ Read Blank Verse The punctuation indicates that the reader should
pause after "Yes," "well," "forth,"
"doth," and "him" to communicate
the sense of Portia's words. Point out
to students that a less emphatic
pause might be used to set off the
two uses of direct address, "boy."

◆ **Critical Thinking**

❼ Draw Conclusions What can
students conclude that Portia is trying to discover through her questions? *Based on Portia's discussion with
Brutus, students can conclude that she is
trying to discover anything to do with
Caesar that might involve Brutus.*

◆ **Beyond the Classroom**

Community Connection
Local Government Explain to students that
the Roman government was, at this time, run by a
group of senators who made the laws for Rome.
Have students talk about how their community is
governed. Is there a town or city council? Is it run
by a mayor, a town supervisor, or a group of
council persons? Encourage them to find out how
local rules and regulations are made, and discuss
with them how power is divided so no one person is all-powerful.

◆ Critical Thinking

1 Predict Have students predict what the soothsayer will tell Caesar and, based on his reaction to Calpurnia's dream, how Caesar will respond. *The soothsayer will predict Caesar's death, but Caesar, not wanting to appear superstitious or weak, will probably ignore the warning.*

Reinforce and Extend

Customize for
More Advanced Students

Discuss with these students the fact that the delivery of Shakespeare's blank verse has been a source of controversy in modern times. Some actors and critics feel that the poetry is the most important aspect of the work, and that the lines should be "classically declaimed," with a strong emphasis on the rhythm and line length (sometimes at the expense of "realism"). Many actors in modern times, however, choose to deliver Shakespeare's lines completely for sense, leading to a prose reading. Encourage students to read reviews of performances by contemporary actors, such as Mel Gibson, Tracy Ullman, Glenn Close, James Earl Jones, and look for comments on the way each actor chooses to deliver the lines.

Answers
◆ *Literature and Your Life*

Reader's Response Students should base their decision upon the times and what they would stand to gain or lose.

Thematic Focus Examples: Caesar's choice avoids or risks death; Brutus' choice will safeguard the republic of Rome or affect his reputation and honor.

☑ Check Your Comprehension

1. Brutus fears that once Caesar is crowned, he will abuse his power.
2. Cassius, Casca, Decius, Cinna, Metellus Cimber, and Trebonius meet at Brutus' house to plan Caesar's assassination.
3. Brutus recommends that Caesar should be killed boldly, but not wrathfully, and that Mark Antony should not be killed.
4. Calpurnia tells Caesar about the unnatural omens seen by the guards, and of her dream in which

748

SOOTHSAYER. That I have, lady; if it will please Caesar
To be so good to Caesar as to hear me,
30   I shall beseech him to befriend himself.

PORTIA. Why, know'st thou any harm's intended towards him?

SOOTHSAYER. None that I know will be, much that I fear
may chance.
Good morrow to you. Here the street is narrow;
The throng that follows Caesar at the heels,.
35   Of senators, of praetors, common suitors,
Will crowd a feeble man almost to death.
I'll get me to a place more void,[6] and there
Speak to great Caesar as he comes along.   [*Exit*]

PORTIA. I must go in. Ay me, how weak a thing
40   The heart of woman is! O Brutus,
The heavens speed[7] thee in thine enterprise![8]
Sure, the boy heard me—Brutus hath a suit
That Caesar will not grant—O, I grow faint.
Run, Lucius, and commend me[9] to my lord;
45   Say I am merry; come to me again,
And bring me word what he doth say to thee.

[*Exit separately*]

6. void: Empty.

7. speed: Prosper.
8. enterprise (en´ tər prīz´) *n*.: Undertaking; project.

9. commend me (kə mend´) *v*.: Give my kind regards.

Guide for Responding

◆ *Literature and Your Life*

Reader's Response If you had been a Roman citizen, would you have joined the conspirators? Why or why not?

Thematic Focus Whose choices in this act do you think will have the most significant consequences?

☑ Check Your Comprehension

1. In Scene i, lines 10–28, what reasons does Brutus give for killing Caesar?
2. Why is a meeting held at Brutus' house, and who attends the meeting?
3. Explain the two changes in the assassination plan that Brutus recommends.
4. What reasons does Calpurnia, Caesar's wife, give for wanting him to stay home?
5. Who persuades Caesar to go to the Capitol and how?

748 ◆ Drama

◆ Critical Thinking
INTERPRET
1. (a) Why do you think the writer leaves gaps in the letter that Lucius finds? (b) What inferences do you draw from the way Brutus fills in these gaps? **[Infer]**
2. Brutus justifies his actions by comparing Caesar to a serpent's egg in Scene i, lines 32–34. Explain how this is an example of a false analogy (a comparison that is not logical). **[Analyze]**
3. (a) Why does Brutus decide to go along with the conspirators? (b) Explain whether you think his decision proves him honorable. **[Support]**

EVALUATE
4. Which of Brutus' reasons for joining the conspirators do you find most convincing? Explain. **[Assess]**
APPLY
5. How might unwillingness to seem weak lead people to take unnecessary risks? **[Relate]**

---

a statue of Caesar was bleeding.
5. Decius convinces Caesar to go to the Capitol by convincing him that Calpurnia's dream was a sign of Caesar's power and popularity.

◆ Critical Thinking

1. (a) Brutus' own misgivings about Caesar fill in the gaps more effectively than anything the writer could have invented. (b) A reader can infer that

Brutus feels honor-bound to strike and redress the injustice of Caesar's supreme power.
2. A snake's egg cannot hatch into anything but a snake. Caesar as ruler may develop in any number of ways; the outcome is not as certain as it is with a snake's egg.
3. (a) Brutus fears Caesar will abuse his power and, because of the letter he reads, believes that the public opposes Caesar's rule. (b) His decision may be seen as that of an hon-

orable man struggling to do something that is difficult to achieve, a public good; or it may be seen as the ignoble betrayal of a disloyal friend.
4. Remind students that they must identify one of Brutus' reasons. Encourage students to explain how Brutus' reasons fit into their own philosophy.
5. Students should be able to relate their answers to this question to the issue of peer pressure.

Guide for Responding (continued)

◆ Literary Focus

BLANK VERSE

Blank verse is written in iambic pentameter—ten-syllable lines in which every second syllable is stressed. Shakespeare often departs from the pattern to avoid monotony, to imitate the rhythms of real speech, or to vary the "music" of the verse. You might see such a departure in this exercise.

Copy the following passages on a separate piece of paper, and indicate the pattern of unaccented and accented syllables. Using the ˘ mark for an unaccented syllable and the mark ´ for an accented one.
1. Act II, Scene i, lines 162–165
2. Act II, Scene ii, lines 33–37

◆ Build Grammar Skills

COMMONLY CONFUSED WORDS:
EFFECT AND *AFFECT*

In Act II, the *effect* of Cassius' letters is that Brutus, who is deeply *affected* by them, agrees to help overthrow Caesar.

Practice Copy these sentences and add the correct form of *affect* or *effect* in the space provided.
1. Calpurnia's dreams ___?___ her deeply.
2. The ___?___ of Decius' interpretation of Portia's dream is that Caesar decides to go out.
3. The soothsayer's remarks to the ___?___ that Caesar was in danger worried Portia.
4. How will Caesar's assassination ___?___ the people of Rome?

◆ Reading Strategy

READ BLANK VERSE

In reading Shakespearean verse, let the sentence structure rather than the lines guide you to meaning.
1. Read lines 162–174 in Act II, Scene i. How many sentences are in this passage?
2. Copy lines 162–174 as a paragraph. Read your paragraph aloud and mark it to indicate where it is natural to take a breath or pause.

◆ Build Vocabulary

USING THE ROOT -*spir*-

You will recognize the word root -*spir*-, meaning "to breathe," in the following words: *inspire*, *expire*, *spirit*, and *respiration*. Use these words to complete the following sentences on your paper.
1. To ___?___ is to breathe one's last breath.
2. To ___?___ is to breathe confidence into another.
3. ___?___ is the act of breathing.
4. The ___?___ of patriotism breathes patriotic feelings into people.

USING THE WORD BANK

Copy the words from Column A into your notebook. Next to each word, write the letter of its definition from Column B.

Column A	Column B
1. augmented	a. heroic or difficult deed
2. entreated	b. plot
3. conspiracy	c. about to happen
4. resolution	d. begged
5. exploit	e. made greater
6. imminent	f. determination

Idea Bank

Writing

1. **Editorial** As one of the tribunes, write a letter to the editor of *The Roman Times* expressing your feelings about the changing loyalties of the common people.

2. **Monologue** Write a brief monologue in contemporary language that Brutus might give, expressing his mixed feelings about Caesar.

Speaking and Listening

3. **Debate** As a group, debate the following question: Is Brutus an honorable man?

Answers
◆ Literary Focus

1. **Brutus.** Ŏur coŭrse wĭll seém
   tŏo blóodў, Caĭŭs Cassĭús,
   Tŏ cŭt thĕ heăd óff ănd thĕn
   háck thĕ límbs,
   Lĭke wráth ĭn deáth ănd énvў
   áftĕrwărds;
   Fŏr Ántŏnў ĭs bŭt ă límb ŏf
   Cáesăr.
2. **Caesar.** Cówărds díe mánў tímes
   befŏre theĭr deáths;
   Thĕ valĭănt névĕr taste ŏf deáth
   bŭt oŏnce.
   Ŏf all thĕ wóndĕrs thát Ĭ yét
   hăve heárd,
   Ĭt seéms tŏ me móst strange
   thăt men shŏuld feár,
   Seéĭng thăt deáth, ă necéssarў
   énd,
   Wĭll come whĕn ĭt wĭll come.

◆ Build Grammar Skills

1. affect; 2. effect; 3. effect; 4. affect

◆ Reading Strategy

1. There are six sentences.
2. Suggested answer: Our course will seem too bloody,/Caius Cassius,/to cut the head off and then hack the limbs, like wrath in death and envy afterwards;/for Antony is but a limb of Caesar./Let's be sacrificers, but not butchers, Caius./We all stand up against the spirit of Caesar, and in the spirit of men there is no blood./O, that we could come by Caesar's spirit, and not dismember Caesar!/But, alas, Caesar must bleed for it./And, gentle friends, let's kill him boldly, but not wrathfully;/let's carve him as a dish fit for the gods, not hew him as a carcass fit for hounds.

◆ Build Vocabulary

Using the Root -*spir*-
1. To *expire* is to breathe one's last breath.
2. To *inspire* is to breathe confidence into another.
3. *Respiration* is the act of breathing.
4. The *spirit* of patriotism breathes patriotic feelings into people.

Using the Word Bank
1. e   2. d   3. b   4. f   5. a   6. c

Idea Bank

Customizing for
Learning Modalities

Following are suggestions for matching Idea Bank topics with your students' learning modalities:

Intrapersonal Learners: 2
Interpersonal Learners: 3
Verbal/Linguistic Learners: 1,2

Customizing for
Performance Levels

Following are suggestions for matching Idea Bank topics with your students' ability levels:

Less Advanced: 1; Average: 3; More Advanced: 2

Guide for Reading, Act III

OBJECTIVES

1. To read, comprehend, and interpret a drama
2. To relate a drama to personal experience
3. To paraphrase characters' thoughts and words
4. To identify dramatic speeches as asides, soliloquies, or monologues
5. To build vocabulary in context and learn the word root -ora-
6. To identify and use parallel structure
7. To respond to the play through writing and speaking and listening

SKILLS INSTRUCTION

Vocabulary: Word Roots: -ora-

Grammar: Parallel Structure

Reading Strategy: Paraphrase

Literary Focus: Dramatic Speeches

Speaking and Listening: Background Music (teacher edition)

Critical Viewing: Connect

PORTFOLIO OPPORTUNITIES

Writing: Obituary; Reaction to Speeches

Speaking and Listening: Background Music

Interest Grabber If possible, show the assassination scene from the movie version of *Julius Caesar* through Caesar's line "Et tu, Brute? Then fall, Caesar." Use this to spark a discussion on books and movies in which trust, loyalty, and betrayal are the major themes. In this act, each character shows where he stands on the issues mentioned above.

◆ Review and Anticipate

Having ignored the warnings of both the soothsayer in Act I and of his wife, Calpurnia, in Act II, Caesar proceeds to the capitol on the ides of March. Decius has told him that the Senate has decided this day to confer a crown upon Caesar, in effect making him the emperor. Accompanying Caesar to the capitol are the conspirators, led by Cassius and Brutus, as well as Caesar's friend Mark Antony.

As the events in this act unfold, more warnings are ignored and the common people, accused in Act I of being fickle, once again show how easily their loyalties are swayed. This act is the turning point that sets irreversible wheels in motion.

◆ Literary Focus

DRAMATIC SPEECHES

In Shakespearean drama, characters often make special kinds of speeches. An **aside** is a brief comment a character makes that reveals his or her thoughts to the audience or another character. An aside is heard only by the audience or the character to whom it is directed. A **soliloquy** is a longer speech in which a character speaks as if to himself or herself. During a soliloquy, the speaker is usually alone onstage, but even if other characters are on stage, they do not hear the character speaking. Cassius' speech in Act I, Scene ii, lines 308–322, is an example of a soliloquy. Similar to a soliloquy is a monologue. A **monologue** is a long, uninterrupted speech by one character. Antony's famous speech in Act III, Scene ii, beginning with "Friends, Romans, countrymen . . ." is a monologue.

◆ Build Grammar Skills

PARALLEL STRUCTURE

Parallel structure is the use of similar grammatical forms to express similar ideas. The similarity in form emphasizes the similarity in content. Speakers often use parallel structure to make their speeches rhythmic and memorable. In Brutus' speech in Act III, Scene ii, he uses parallel clauses and sentence patterns.

As Caesar loved me, I weep for him; as he was fortunate, I rejoice at it; as he was valiant, I honor him; but as he was ambitious, I slew him.

The repetition of *as . . . I . . .* builds up to an effective climax, making Brutus' reasons for slaying Caesar readily apparent.

◆ Reading Strategy

PARAPHRASE

To modern readers, Shakespeare's writing can appear dense and difficult to understand. One way to approach Shakespeare's passages is to **paraphrase,** or restate, them in your own words.

Shakespeare's Version

Yet in the number I do know but one / That unassailable holds on his rank, / Unshaked of motion; and that I am he . . .

Paraphrased Version

I'm the only person I know who can neither be harmed nor moved by others' desires.

As you read, paraphrase any difficult passages you encounter.

◆ Build Vocabulary

WORD ROOTS: -ora-

Act III of *The Tragedy of Julius Caesar* is noted for its orations. An oration is a speech given at a formal ceremony, such as a graduation or a funeral. *Oration* has as its root the Latin verb *-orare-*, which means "to speak."

WORD BANK

Before you read, preview this list of words from Act III.

suit
spurn
confounded
mutiny
malice
oration
discourse
vile

750 ◆ Drama

Prentice Hall Literature Program Resources

REINFORCE / RETEACH / EXTEND

Selection Support Pages
Build Vocabulary: Word Roots: -ora-, p. 212
Build Grammar Skills: Parallel Structure, p. 201
Reading Strategy: Paraphrase, p. 214
Literary Focus: Dramatic Speeches, p. 215

Strategies for Diverse Student Needs, p. 52

Beyond Literature
Community Connection: Eulogies, p. 52

Formal Assessment Selection Test, p. 182, Assessment Resources Software

Alternative Assessment, p. 52

Writing and Language Transparencies
Cause-and-Effect Organizer, p. 99

Resource Pro CD-ROM
The Tragedy of Julius Caesar, Act III—includes all resource materials and customizable lesson plan

Listening to Literature Audiocassettes
The Tragedy of Julius Caesar, Act III

Literature CD-ROM
How to Read and Understand Drama
The Time, Life, and Works of Shakespeare

The Tragedy of

JULIUS CAESAR

William Shakespeare

Act III

Scene i. *Rome. Before the Capitol.*

[*Flourish of trumpets. Enter* CAESAR, BRUTUS, CASSIUS, CASCA, DECIUS, METELLUS CIMBER, TREBONIUS, CINNA, ANTONY, LEPIDUS, ARTEMIDORUS, PUBLIUS, POPILIUS, *and the* SOOTHSAYER.]

CAESAR. The ides of March are come.

SOOTHSAYER. Ay, Caesar, but not gone.

ARTEMIDORUS. Hail, Caesar! Read this schedule.[1]

DECIUS. Trebonius doth desire you to o'er-read,
5   At your best leisure, this his humble <u>suit</u>.

ARTEMIDORUS. O Caesar, read mine first; for mine's a suit
    That touches Caesar nearer. Read it, great Caesar.

CAESAR. What touches us ourself shall be last served.

ARTEMIDORUS. Delay not, Caesar; read it instantly.

CAESAR. What, is the fellow mad?

10 **PUBLIUS.**   Sirrah, give place.[2]

CASSIUS. What, urge you your petitions in the street?
    Come to the Capitol.

[CAESAR *goes to the Capitol, the rest following.*]

POPILIUS. I wish your enterprise today may thrive.

CASSIUS. What enterprise, Popilius?

POPILIUS.   Fare you well.

              [*Advances to* CAESAR]

15 **BRUTUS.** What said Popilius Lena?

CASSIUS. He wished today our enterprise might thrive.
    I fear our purpose is discoverèd.

BRUTUS. Look how he makes to[3] Caesar; mark him.

CASSIUS. Casca, be sudden,[4] for we fear prevention.
20   Brutus, what shall be done? If this be known,
    Cassius or Caesar never shall turn back,[5]
    For I will slay myself.

1. **schedule** (skej′ ool) *n.*: Paper.

2. **give place:** Get out of the way.

3. **makes to:** Approaches.

4. **be sudden:** Be quick.

5. **Cassius . . . back:** Either Cassius or Caesar will not return alive.

◆ **Build Vocabulary**

suit (sōōt) *n.*: Old word meaning "petition"

The Tragedy of Julius Caesar, Act III, Scene i ◆ 751

◆ Reading Strategy

❶ Paraphrase Ask students to paraphrase the exchange that takes place as the conspirators prepare for the assassination. *Suggested paraphrase:*

CASSIUS: Trebonius knows what to do. Look, Brutus—he's getting Mark Antony out of the way.

DECIUS: Where is Metellus Cimber? It's time for him to present his petition to Caesar.

BRUTUS: He's ready. Stay with him and back him up.

CINNA: Casca, you will strike first.

◆ Reading Strategy

❷ Paraphrase Caesar says that others, who are not as strong as he is, might be influenced by flattery and pleading. Caesar is so strong, though, that his mind will not be changed so easily and he has only contempt for people who think he would be.

◆ Critical Thinking

❸ Analyze Point out to students that in order to get into position, the conspirators quickly follow one after the other in their petitions for Publius Cimber, in effect, "ganging up" on Caesar. This emotional tactic foreshadows the physical ganging up that is soon to occur.

BRUTUS.   Cassius, be constant.[6]
Popilius Lena speaks not of our purposes;
For look, he smiles, and Caesar doth not change.[7]

25 **CASSIUS.** Trebonius knows his time; for look you, Brutus,
He draws Mark Antony out of the way.

[*Exit* ANTONY *and* TREBONIUS.]

DECIUS. Where is Metellus Cimber? Let him go
And presently prefer his suit[8] to Caesar.

BRUTUS. He is addressed.[9] Press near and second[10] him.

30 **CINNA.** Casca, you are the first that rears your hand.

CAESAR. Are we all ready? What is now amiss
That Caesar and his Senate must redress?[11]

METELLUS. Most high, most mighty, and most puissant[12] Caesar,
Metellus Cimber throws before thy seat
An humble heart.   [*Kneeling*]

35 **CAESAR.**   I must prevent thee, Cimber.
These couchings and these lowly courtesies[13]
Might fire the blood of ordinary men,
And turn preordinance and first decree
Into the law of children.[14] Be not fond[15]

40 To think that Caesar bears such rebel blood
That will be thawed from the true quality[16]
With that which melteth fools—I mean sweet words,
Low-crookèd curtsies, and base spaniel fawning.[17]
Thy brother by decree is banishèd.

45 If thou dost bend and pray and fawn for him,
I spurn thee like a cur out of my way.
Know, Caesar doth not wrong, nor without cause
Will he be satisfied.

METELLUS. Is there no voice more worthy than my own,
50 To sound more sweetly in great Caesar's ear
For the repealing of my banished brother?

BRUTUS. I kiss thy hand, but not in flattery, Caesar,
Desiring thee that Publius Cimber may
Have an immediate freedom of repeal.

CAESAR. What, Brutus?

55 **CASSIUS.**   Pardon, Caesar; Caesar, pardon!
As low as to thy foot doth Cassius fall
To beg enfranchisement[18] for Publius Cimber.

CAESAR. I could be well moved, if I were as you;
If I could pray to move,[19] prayers would move me;
60 But I am constant as the Northern Star,

6. **constant:** Firm; calm.

7. **change:** Change the expression on his face.

8. **presently prefer his suit:** Immediately present his petition.
9. **addressed:** Ready.
10. **second:** Support.

11. **amiss . . . redress:** Wrong that Caesar and his Senate must correct.
12. **puissant** (pyo͞o´ i sənt) *adj.:* Powerful.

13. **couchings . . . courtesies:** Low bowings and humble gestures of reverence.
14. **And turn . . . law of children:** And change what has already been decided as children might change their minds.
15. **fond** *adj.:* Foolish.
16. **rebel . . . quality:** Unstable disposition that will be changed from firmness.
17. **base spaniel fawning:** Low doglike cringing.

◆ **Reading Strategy**
Paraphrase Caesar's disdainful words to Metellus.

18. **enfranchisement** (en fran´ chiz mənt) *n.:* Freedom.

19. **pray to move:** Beg others to change their minds.

752 ◆ *Drama*

Block Scheduling Strategies

Consider these suggestions to take advantage of extended class time:

- Suggest that students view feature 4 of the CD-ROM *The Time, Life, and Works of Shakespeare.* They will learn more about Shakespeare's later life, Shakespeare's Stratford, and the Globe theater.
- Use a video of the movie *Julius Caesar* and the **Listening to Literature Audiocassette** recording to support the text. Encourage stu-

dents to identify how each approach enhanced their appreciation of a particular scene.

- Have students work with partners to find examples of parallel structure in Act III; then have them complete the Practice activity in Build Grammar Skills (p. 771).
- Students can choose and complete one of the writing assignments in the Idea Bank (p. 771).
- Ask students to complete Literary Focus: Dramatic Speeches in *Selection Support,* p. 215.

Of whose true-fixed and resting²⁰ quality
There is no fellow²¹ in the firmament.²²
The skies are painted with unnumb'red sparks,
They are all fire and every one doth shine;
65 But there's but one in all doth hold his²³ place.
So in the world; 'tis furnished well with men,
And men are flesh and blood, and apprehensive;²⁴
Yet in the number I do know but one
That unassailable holds on his rank,²⁵
70 Unshaked of motion;²⁶ and that I am he,
Let me a little show it, even in this—
That I was constant. Cimber should be banished,
And constant do remain to keep him so.

CINNA. O Caesar—

CAESAR. Hence! Wilt thou lift up Olympus?²⁷

DECIUS. Great Caesar—

75 **CAESAR.** Doth not Brutus bootless²⁸ kneel?

CASCA. Speak hands for me! [*They stab* CAESAR.]

CAESAR. *Et tu, Brutè?*²⁹ Then fall, Caesar. [*Dies*]

CINNA. Liberty! Freedom! Tyranny is dead!
Run hence, proclaim, cry it about the streets.

80 **CASSIUS.** Some to the common pulpits,³⁰ and cry out
"Liberty, freedom, and enfranchisement!"

BRUTUS. People, and senators, be not affrighted.
Fly not; stand still; ambition's debt is paid.³¹

CASCA. Go to the pulpit, Brutus.

DECIUS. And Cassius too.

85 **BRUTUS.** Where's Publius?

CINNA. Here, quite confounded with this mutiny.

METELLUS. Stand fast together, lest some friend of
Caesar's
Should chance—

BRUTUS. Talk not of standing. Publius, good cheer;
90 There is no harm intended to your person,
Nor to no Roman else. So tell them, Publius.

CASSIUS. And leave us, Publius, lest that the people
Rushing on us should do your age some mischief.

BRUTUS. Do so; and let no man abide³² this deed
95 But we the doers.

[*Enter* TREBONIUS.]

CASSIUS. Where is Antony?

---

20. **resting:** Immovable.
21. **fellow:** Equal.
22. **firmament** (fur´ mə mənt) *n.*: Sky.

23. **his:** Its.

24. **apprehensive** (ap´ rə hen´ siv) *adj.*: Able to understand.
25. **unassailable . . . rank:** Unattackable maintains his position.
26. **Unshaked of motion:** Unmoved by his own or others' impulses.

27. **Olympus** (ō lim´ pəs): Mountain in northern Greece that was, in Greek mythology, the home of the gods.
28. **bootless:** Uselessly.

29. ***Et tu, Brutè?*:** Latin for *And you, Brutus?*

30. **pulpits** (pool´ pits) *n.*: Speakers' platforms.

31. **ambition's . . . paid:** Ambition received what it deserved.

32. **let no man abide:** Let no man take responsibility for.

The Tragedy of Julius Caesar, Act III, Scene i ◆ 753

◆ **Reading Strategy**

❹ **Paraphrase** Challenge students to paraphrase these lines, in which Caesar continues to compare himself to the Northern Star. *Suggested paraphrase: "This is also how it is in the world. The world is full of men, and they all show signs of life; but there is only one that cannot be knocked out of place."* You might then encourage students to comment on what the speech reveals about Caesar. *Students may say that it confirms some of the conspirators' beliefs. Caesar shows himself to be haughty and inflexible; he holds himself above others.*

Customize for
Less Proficient Readers
Point out that a play's stage directions, which appear within brackets and in italics, contain essential information for both actors and readers. Have students identify the critical action named in the stage directions that accompany lines 76 and 77. *The conspirators stab Caesar; Caesar dies.*

◆ **Build Vocabulary**

spurn (spurn) *v.*: Old word meaning "to kick disdainfully"
confounded (kən found´ id) *adj.*: Confused
mutiny (myoot´ ən ē) *n.*: Open rebellion against authority

Cross-Curricular Connection: Science

When Caesar insists that he cannot be moved by prayers or entreaties as other men can, he compares himself to the North Star:

But I am constant as the Northern Star,
Of whose true-fixed and resting quality
There is no fellow in the firmament.
(Scene i, lines 60–63)

Invite a group of students to prepare a brief presentation in which they explain the scientific significance behind this image. In their presenta-

tions, students can use a globe, diagrams, or other visual aids to help answer the following questions:

• Why does the North Star appear "constant," or stationary, throughout the year?

• Why do other stars seem to move through the sky during the course of a year?

• What is another name for the North Star? Will this star always be the North Star, or will it eventually be replaced by another?

▶Critical Viewing◀

❶ Analyze The conspirators' actions make them seem submissive to Caesar and intimidated by him. They appear to be honoring Caesar but, in fact, are getting in position to kill him.

◆ Reading Strategy

❷ Paraphrase Sample paraphrase: We have done Caesar a favor, because everyone fears death, and now Caesar won't have to fear it any longer.

Customize for
Less Proficient Readers

Work with these students to begin identifying the causes and effects of Caesar's assassination. Use the page on Cause and Effect, *Strategies for Diverse Needs,* p. 52.

Customize for
Visual/Spatial Learners

These students might benefit from using the Cause-and-Effect organizer found in *Writing and Language Transparencies,* pp. 99–101.

❶ ▲ **Critical Viewing** Explain how this picture captures the deception of the conspirators. [**Analyze**]

TREBONIUS. Fled to his house amazed.[33]	**33. amazed:** Astounded.
Men, wives, and children stare, cry out and run,	
As[34] it were doomsday.	**34. As:** As if.

BRUTUS.   Fates, we will know your pleasures.
That we shall die, we know; 'tis but the time,
100   And drawing days out, that men stand upon.[35]

35. drawing . . . upon: Prolonging life that people care about.

CASCA.   Why, he that cuts off twenty years of life
Cuts off so many years of fearing death.

BRUTUS.   Grant that, and then is death a benefit.
So are we Caesar's friends, that have abridged
105   His time of fearing death. Stoop, Romans, stoop,
And let us bathe our hands in Caesar's blood
Up to the elbows, and besmear our swords.
Then walk we forth, even to the market place,
And waving our red weapons o'er our heads,
110   Let's all cry "Peace, freedom, and liberty!"

◆ **Reading Strategy**
Paraphrase Brutus' justifications for killing Caesar. ❷

754 ◆ *Drama*

 Speaking and Listening Mini-Lesson

Background Music

This mini-lesson supports the Speaking and Listening activity in the Idea Bank on page 771.

Introduce the Concept Have students discuss movies, television shows, or plays in which background music was an effective enhancement. Invite them to list moods that background music can suggest.

Develop Background Have groups of students talk about the assassination scene and the moods the music should support.

- What is the mood of the opening?
- What kind of music would emphasize the horror of the assassination?
- How would the crowd react after the assassination, and what music might be most effective in emphasizing their mood?

Apply the Information Allow students time to select their music, and, if possible, to tape it. One member of each group can explain what is happening in the scene as the music plays.

Assess the Outcome After each presentation, the class may evaluate the choice of music on the basis of how well they felt the music enhanced the scene.

CASSIUS. Stoop then, and wash. How many ages hence
Shall this our lofty scene be acted over
In states unborn and accents yet unknown!

❸

BRUTUS. How many times shall Caesar bleed in sport,[36]
115 That now on Pompey's basis lies along[37]
No worthier than the dust!

CASSIUS.   So oft as that shall be,
So often shall the knot[38] of us be called
The men that gave their country liberty.

DECIUS. What, shall we forth?

CASSIUS.   Ay, every man away.
120 Brutus shall lead, and we will grace his heels[39]
With the most boldest and best hearts of Rome.

[*Enter a* SERVANT.]

BRUTUS. Soft, who comes here? A friend of Antony's.

SERVANT. Thus, Brutus, did my master bid me kneel;
Thus did Mark Antony bid me fall down;
125 And, being prostrate, thus he bade me say:
Brutus is noble, wise, valiant, and honest;
Caesar was mighty, bold, royal, and loving.
Say I love Brutus and I honor him;
Say I feared Caesar, honored him, and loved him.
130 If Brutus will vouchsafe that Antony
May safely come to him and be resolved[40]
How Caesar hath deserved to lie in death,
Mark Antony shall not love Caesar dead
So well as Brutus living; but will follow
135 The fortunes and affairs of noble Brutus
Thorough the hazards of this untrod state[41]
With all true faith. So says my master Antony.

❹

❺

BRUTUS. Thy master is a wise and valiant Roman;
I never thought him worse.
140 Tell him, so[42] please him come unto this place,
He shall be satisfied and, by my honor,
Depart untouched.

SERVANT.   I'll fetch him presently.

[*Exit* SERVANT]

BRUTUS. I know that we shall have him well to friend.[43]

CASSIUS. I wish we may. But yet have I a mind
145 That fears him much; and my misgiving still
Falls shrewdly to the purpose.[44]

❻

[*Enter* ANTONY.]

BRUTUS. But here comes Antony. Welcome, Mark Antony.

---

36. **in sport:** In plays.

37. **on Pompey's basis lies along:** By the pedestal of Pompey's statue lies stretched out.

38. **knot:** Group.

39. **grace his heels:** Honor him by following him.

◆ **Reading Strategy**
The servant carries a message from Mark Antony to Brutus. Paraphrase the message only.

40. **be resolved:** Have it explained.

41. **Thorough . . . state:** Through the dangers of this new state of affairs.

42. **so:** If it should.

43. **to friend:** As a friend.

44. **my misgiving . . . to the purpose:** My doubts always turn out to be justified.

The Tragedy of Julius Caesar, Act III, Scene i ◆ 755

Comprehension Check ☑

❸ Invite students to summarize the thoughts that Cassius and Brutus express in these lines. *They will go down in history as liberators of Rome.*

◆ **Build Grammar Skills**

❹ Parallel Structure Point out the parallel elements in lines 126–127 and 128–129. Encourage students to explain the purpose that these parallel elements serve within the servant's speech. *They are meant to express Mark Antony's dual feelings and loyalties; they emphasize that Mark Antony does not honor Caesar more than he honors Brutus.*

◆ **Reading Strategy**

❺ Paraphrase Students may paraphrase the message in the following way: Antony says that he honors both Brutus and Caesar. Antony would like to come to Brutus to hear his reasons for killing Caesar, but Antony wants to be assured of his own safety. If Brutus' reasons seem sound to Antony, he will cooperate with Brutus in all future endeavors.

◆ **Critical Thinking**

❻ Contrast Ask students the following question: How does Brutus' attitude toward Mark Antony contrast with Cassius' attitude? Then encourage students to explain how this contrast helps create suspense within the scene. *Students should note that Brutus is inclined to trust Mark Antony, while Cassius strongly distrusts him. This contrast creates suspense because it is yet to be revealed which of the two is right.*

❶ In his first speech to Antony, what does Brutus acknowledge about the conspirators' act? How does he go on to justify it? *He acknowledges that it was bloody and cruel but insists that the conspirators acted for the general good of Rome.*

◆ **Literary Focus**

❷ **Dramatic Speeches** Point out that in this long speech, Antony addresses first the conspirators and then Caesar's corpse. Then ask students if they would classify the speech as a soliloquy or a monologue. *Students should identify it as a monologue, since it is addressed to other onstage performers.*

ANTONY. O mighty Caesar! Dost thou lie so low?
Are all thy conquests, glories, triumphs, spoils,
150 Shrunk to this little measure? Fare thee well.
I know not, gentlemen, what you intend,
Who else must be let blood,[45] who else is rank.[46]
If I myself, there is no hour so fit
As Caesar's death's hour, nor no instrument
155 Of half that worth as those your swords, made rich
With the most noble blood of all this world.
I do beseech ye, if you bear me hard,[47]
Now, whilst your purpled hands[48] do reek and smoke,
Fulfill your pleasure. Live[49] a thousand years,
160 I shall not find myself so apt[50] to die;
No place will please me so, no mean of death,[51]
As here by Caesar, and by you cut off,
The choice and master spirits of this age.

BRUTUS. O Antony, beg not your death of us!
165 Though now we must appear bloody and cruel,
As by our hands and this our present act
You see we do, yet see you but our hands
And this the bleeding business they have done.
Our hearts you see not; they are pitiful;[52]
170 And pity to the general wrong of Rome—
As fire drives out fire, so pity pity[53]—
Hath done this deed on Caesar. For your part,
To you our swords have leaden[54] points, Mark
    Antony:
Our arms in strength of malice, and our hearts
175 Of brothers' temper,[55] do receive you in
With all kind love, good thoughts, and reverence.

CASSIUS. Your voice[56] shall be as strong as any man's
In the disposing of new dignities.[57]

BRUTUS. Only be patient till we have appeased
180 The multitude, beside themselves with fear,
And then we will deliver[58] you the cause
Why I, that did love Caesar when I struck him,
Have thus proceeded.

ANTONY.   I doubt not of your wisdom.
Let each man render me his bloody hand.
185 First, Marcus Brutus, will I shake with you;
Next, Caius Cassius, do I take your hand;
Now, Decius Brutus, yours; now yours, Metellus;
Yours, Cinna; and, my valiant Casca, yours;
Though last, not least in love, yours, good Trebonius.
190 Gentlemen all—alas, what shall I say?
My credit[59] now stands on such slippery ground

45. **be let blood:** Be killed.
46. **rank:** Too powerful; in need of bloodletting.

47. **bear me hard:** Have a grudge against me.
48. **purpled hands:** Bloody hands.
49. **Live:** If I live.
50. **apt:** Ready.
51. **mean of death:** Way of dying.

52. **pitiful:** Full of pity.

53. **pity pity:** Pity for Rome drove out pity for Caesar.
54. **leaden:** Dull; blunt.

55. **Of brothers' temper:** Filled with brotherly feelings.
56. **voice:** Vote.
57. **dignities:** Offices.

58. **deliver:** Tell to.

59. **credit:** Reputation.

◆ **Build Vocabulary**

malice (mal´ is) *n.*: Desire to harm or see harm done to others

---

Cross-Curricular Connection: Social Studies

Assassinations The word *assassination* usually means the murder of a politically prominent person. The word comes from *Hashshashun* ("hemp-eaters"), a band of Muslims in Persia and Asia Minor in the 1100's. They smoked a drug called *hashish,* which is made from the hemp plant, and killed their enemies while under its influence.

History is dotted with other assassinations in addition to that of Julius Caesar. Saint Thomas à Becket was murdered in Canterbury Cathedral in 1170. The assassination of Archduke Ferdinand of Austria in 1914 was one cause of World War I. The series of assassinations committed by the Black Dragon Society in Japan during the 1930's threw control of the government

into the hands of the Japanese army. Four Presidents of the United States have been assassinated: Lincoln in 1865, Garfield in 1881, McKinley in 1901, and Kennedy in 1963.

Suggest that students research the assassination of a politically prominent person in history.

That one of two bad ways you must conceit[60] me,
Either a coward or a flatterer.
That I did love thee, Caesar, O, 'tis true!
195 If then thy spirit look upon us now,
Shall it not grieve thee dearer[61] than thy death
To see thy Antony making his peace,
Shaking the bloody fingers of thy foes,
Most noble, in the presence of thy corse?[62]
200 Had I as many eyes as thou hast wounds,
❷ Weeping as fast as they stream forth thy blood,
It would become me better than to close[63]
In terms of friendship with thine enemies.
Pardon me, Julius! Here wast thou bayed,[64] brave
hart;[65]
205 Here didst thou fall, and here thy hunters stand,
Signed in thy spoil[66] and crimsoned in thy Lethe.[67]
O world, thou wast the forest to this hart;
And this indeed, O world, the heart of thee.
How like a deer, stroken[68] by many princes.
210 Dost thou here lie!

CASSIUS. Mark Antony—

ANTONY.   Pardon me, Caius Cassius.
The enemies of Caesar shall say this;
Then, in a friend, it is cold modesty.[69]

CASSIUS. I blame you not for praising Caesar so;
215 But what compact[70] mean you to have with us?
Will you be pricked[71] in number of our friends,
Or shall we on,[72] and not depend on you?

❸ ANTONY. Therefore I took your hands, but was indeed
Swayed from the point by looking down on Caesar.
220 Friends am I with you all, and love you all,
Upon this hope, that you shall give me reasons
Why, and wherein, Caesar was dangerous.

BRUTUS. Or else were this a savage spectacle.
Our reasons are so full of good regard[73]
225 That were you, Antony, the son of Caesar,
You should be satisfied.

ANTONY.   That's all I seek;
And am moreover suitor that I may
Produce[74] his body to the market place,
And in the pulpit, as becomes a friend,
230 Speak in the order[75] of his funeral.

BRUTUS. You shall, Mark Antony.

❹ CASSIUS.   Brutus, a word with you.
[Aside to BRUTUS] You know not what you do; do not

60. **conceit** (kən sēt′) v.: Think of.

61. **dearer:** More deeply.

62. **corse:** Corpse.

63. **close** (clōz) v.: Reach an agreement.

64. **bayed:** Cornered.
65. **hart** (härt) n.: Deer.

66. **Signed in thy spoil:** Marked by signs of your decaying parts.
67. **Lethe** (lēth′ ē): River in Hades, but in this case a river of blood.
68. **stroken:** Struck down.

69. **cold modesty:** Calm, moderate speech.

70. **compact** (käm′ pakt) n.: Agreement.
71. **pricked:** Marked.
72. **on:** Proceed.

73. **so full of good regard:** So carefully considered.
74. **Produce:** Bring forth.
75. **order:** Course of the ceremonies.

◆ **Reading Strategy**

❸ **Paraphrase** Encourage students to paraphrase Cassius' questions and Antony's reply. *Suggested paraphrase:*

CASSIUS: *How do you see yourself in relation to us? Can we count on you as a friend or not?*

ANTONY: *As a friend—that's why I shook hands with each of you, but then I got carried away because of Caesar's corpse. I will be friends with you all and love you all on the condition that you explain to me why Caesar was dangerous.*

◆ **Literary Focus**

❹ **Dramatic Speeches** Cassius does not want Antony to hear what he has to say because he doesn't want to destroy the illusion of trust between Antony and the conspirators. Although Brutus is convinced of Antony's good intentions, Cassius remains suspicious.

◆ **Literary Focus**
Why doesn't Cassius want the other characters to hear what he says to Brutus in this aside?

The Tragedy of Julius Caesar, Act III, Scene i ◆ 757

◆ **Critical Thinking**

❶ **Contrast** Point out that once again Brutus and Cassius show different views of Mark Antony. Invite students to identify their contrasting opinions as well as the reasons behind them. *Students should note that Cassius believes that it would be a great mistake to allow Antony to speak at Caesar's funeral because he is liable to turn public opinion against the conspirators. Brutus, on the other hand, continues to believe that Mark Antony poses no threat; in fact, he believes that Antony's presence at the funeral will strengthen the conspirators' position and help bring about reconciliation.*

◆ **Literary Focus**

❷ **Dramatic Speeches** Antony reveals that he intends to avenge Caesar's death.

◆ **Critical Thinking**

❸ **Draw Conclusions** Encourage students to draw conclusions about Mark Antony based on this speech. For example: How does it help to explain his behavior earlier in this scene? Does it confirm Brutus' or Cassius' view of Antony? *Students should note that in this speech Antony reveals his true self and true motives; his efforts to win the trust of the conspirators were part of a plot for revenge. As it turns out, Cassius was right to suspect him of deceit.*

◆ **Literary Focus**

❹ **Dramatic Speeches** Would students classify this speech as an aside, a soliloquy, or a monologue? Encourage them to explain their answers. *The speech is a soliloquy—it is a long speech, and Antony is alone on stage.*

consent
That Antony speak in his funeral.
Know you how much the people may be moved
By that which he will utter?

235 **BRUTUS.**   By your pardon:
I will myself into the pulpit first,
And show the reason of our Caesar's death.
What Antony shall speak, I will protest[76]
He speaks by leave and by permission,
240 And that we are contented Caesar shall
Have all true rites and lawful ceremonies.
It shall advantage more than do us wrong.[77]

CASSIUS. I know not what may fall;[78] I like it not.

BRUTUS. Mark Antony, here, take you Caesar's body.
245 You shall not in your funeral speech blame us,
But speak all good you can devise of Caesar,
❶ And say you do't by our permission;
Else shall you not have any hand at all
About his funeral. And you shall speak
250 In the same pulpit whereto I am going,
After my speech is ended.

ANTONY.   Be it so;
I do desire no more.

BRUTUS. Prepare the body then, and follow us.

[*Exit all but* ANTONY.]

ANTONY. O pardon me, thou bleeding piece of earth,
255 That I am meek and gentle with these butchers!
Thou art the ruins of the noblest man
That ever livèd in the tide of times.[79]
Woe to the hand that shed this costly blood!
Over thy wounds now do I prophesy
260 (Which like dumb mouths do ope their ruby lips
To beg the voice and utterance of my tongue),
A curse shall light upon the limbs of men;
❸ Domestic fury and fierce civil strife
❹ Shall cumber[80] all the parts of Italy;
265 Blood and destruction shall be so in use,[81]
And dreadful objects so familiar,
That mothers shall but smile when they behold
Their infants quartered with the hands of war,
All pity choked with custom of fell deeds;[82]
270 And Caesar's spirit, ranging[83] for revenge,
With Ate[84] by his side come hot from hell,
Shall in these confines[85] with a monarch's voice
Cry "Havoc,"[86] and let slip[87] the dogs of war,

76. **protest:** Declare.

77. **advantage . . . wrong:** Benefit us more than hurt us.
78. **what may fall:** What may happen.

79. **tide of times:** Course of all history.
80. **cumber** (kum´ bər) *v.*: Distress; burden.
81. **in use:** Customary.
82. **fell deeds:** Cruel acts.
83. **ranging:** Roaming like a wild beast in search of prey.
84. **Ate** (ā´ tē): Greek goddess personifying reckless ambition in man.
85. **confines** (kän´ finz) *n.*: Boundaries.

◆ **Literary Focus**
What does Antony's soliloquy reveal that other characters do not know? ❷

86. **Havoc:** Latin for *no quarter,* signal for general slaughter.
87. **slip:** Loose.

◆ **Build Vocabulary**

oration (ô rā´ shən) *n.*: Formal speech, especially one given at a state occasion, ceremony, or funeral

discourse (dis kôrs´) *v.*: Speak formally and at length

758 ◆ *Drama*

❸
❹ 275
That this foul deed shall smell above the earth
With carrion[88] men, groaning for burial.

[*Enter* OCTAVIUS' SERVANT.]

You serve Octavius Caesar, do you not?

SERVANT. I do, Mark Antony.

ANTONY. Caesar did write for him to come to Rome.

SERVANT. He did receive his letters and is coming,
280   And bid me say to you by word of mouth—
O Caesar!   [*Seeing the body*]

ANTONY. Thy heart is big;[89] get thee apart and weep.
Passion, I see, is catching, for mine eyes,
Seeing those beads of sorrow stand in thine,
285   Began to water. Is thy master coming?

SERVANT. He lies tonight within seven leagues[90] of Rome.

ANTONY. Post[91] back with speed, and tell him what hath
chanced.[92]
Here is a mourning Rome, a dangerous Rome,
No Rome of safety for Octavius yet.
290   Hie hence and tell him so. Yet stay awhile;
❺ Thou shalt not back till I have borne this corse
Into the market place; there shall I try[93]
In my <u>oration</u> how the people take
The cruel issue[94] of these bloody men;
295   According to the which, thou shalt <u>discourse</u>
To young Octavius of the state of things.
Lend me your hand.   [*Exit*]

Scene ii. *The Forum*

[*Enter* BRUTUS *and goes into the pulpit, and* CASSIUS, *with the*
PLEBEIANS.[1]]

PLEBEIANS. We will be satisfied![2] Let us be satisfied!

BRUTUS. Then follow me, and give me audience, friends.
Cassius, go you into the other street
And part the numbers.[3]
❻ 5   Those that will hear me speak, let 'em stay here;
Those that will follow Cassius, go with him;
And public reasons shall be renderèd
Of Caesar's death.

FIRST PLEBEIAN.   I will hear Brutus speak.

SECOND PLEBEIAN. I will hear Cassius, and compare their
reasons,
10   When severally[4] we hear them renderèd.

[*Exit* CASSIUS, *with some of the* PLEBEIANS.]

The Tragedy of Julius Caesar, Act III, Scene ii ◆ *759*

---

88. carrion (kar′ ē ən)
adj.: Dead and rotting.

89. big: Swollen with grief.

90. lies . . . seven leagues: Is camped tonight within twenty-one miles.
91. Post: Hasten.
92. hath chanced: Has happened.

93. try: Test.

94. cruel issue: Outcome of the cruelty.

1. Plebeians (ple bē′ enz) *n.*: Commoners; members of the lower class.
2. be satisfied: Get an explanation.

3. part the numbers: Divide the crowd.

4. severally (sev′ ər əl ē) *adv.*: Separately.

Enrichment

Shakespeare has the assassination of Caesar take place at the Capitol, in the area called the *Roman Forum* (though the killing actually happened in the Senate House). Mark Antony delivers his funeral oration at the same site. This is apt, because the Roman Forum was Rome's administrative and legal center. The word *forum* originally meant "marketplace," and Rome had several such areas. But the Roman Forum was the true center of the city, and the Roman world. Among the buildings there were the Senate House or *Curia,* the Temples of Saturn and Concord, and the *Tabularium* (Hall of Records).

Because most Roman streets were narrow, the Forum, with its open space, was an ideal setting for important official events, like triumphal processions for victorious generals. Often, it was the scene of occurrences of major consequence throughout the world, such as the crowning of Octavius Caesar as the first Roman emperor, Augustus.

Archaeologists have excavated much of the Forum, allowing modern visitors to see the remains of several imposing structures and get a sense of the grandeur of ancient Rome.

Critical Viewing

❶ Connect Point out to students that Antony is probably speaking his soliloquy in this picture. The text for his speech appears on page 762. Based on his stance and gestures, Antony is probably near the end of his soliloquy when he incites the crowd to action.

◆ Build Grammar Skills

❷ Parallel Structure Point out that Brutus uses parallel structure at several points in this speech. Encourage students to point out each instance. *Students should point out parallel elements in the following sections: . . . hear me...that you may better judge; As Caesar loved me, . . . I slew him; There is tears, . . . for his ambition; Who is here so base, . . . for him I have offended.* Also encourage students to describe the effect of the parallel elements within the speech. *Responses may include: They make the speech more powerful and memorable; they help Brutus to hold the audience's attention.*

◆ Literary Focus

❸ Brutus is trying to convince the crowd that he loved Caesar but that there was a higher duty than his loyalty to Caesar. He knows that if he starts off by denegrating Caesar, the crowd will not listen to anything else he says. By saying he loves Caesar, he draws the crowd in so that they will listen to his reasons.

▲ **Critical Viewing** Based on his stance and his gestures, which words of his speech do you think Antony is speaking? [Connect]

THIRD PLEBEIAN. The noble Brutus is ascended. Silence!

BRUTUS. Be patient till the last.

Romans, countrymen, and lovers,[5] hear me for my cause, and be silent, that you may hear. Believe me
15 for mine honor, and have respect to mine honor, that you may believe. Censure[6] me in your wisdom, and awake your senses,[7] that you may the better judge. If there be any in this assembly, any dear friend of Caesar's, to him I say that Brutus' love to Caesar was
20 no less than his. If then that friend demand why Brutus rose against Caesar, this is my answer: Not that I loved Caesar less, but that I loved Rome more. Had you rather Caesar were living, and die all slaves, than that Caesar were dead, to live all free men? As
25 Caesar loved me, I weep for him; as he was fortunate, I rejoice at it; as he was valiant, I honor him; but, as he was ambitious, I slew him. There is tears, for his love; joy, for his fortune; honor, for his valor; and death, for his ambition. Who is here so base,[8] that
30 would be a bondman?[9] If any, speak; for him have I offended. Who is here so rude,[10] that would not be a Roman? If any, speak; for him have I offended. Who is

5. **lovers:** Dear friends.

6. **Censure** (sen´ shər) *v.*: Condemn as wrong; criticize.
7. **senses:** Powers of reason.

◆ **Literary Focus**
What is Brutus trying to accomplish with this monologue?

8. **base:** Low.
9. **bondman:** Slave.
10. **rude:** Ignorant.

760 ◆ *Drama*

760

here so <u>vile</u>, that will not love his country? If any,
speak; for him have I offended. I pause for a reply.

35 **ALL.** None, Brutus, none!

BRUTUS. Then none have I offended. I have done no more
to Caesar than you shall do to Brutus. The question
of his death is enrolled in the Capitol;[11] his glory not
extenuated,[12] wherein he was worthy, nor his offens-
40 es enforced,[13] for which he suffered death.

[*Enter* MARK ANTONY, *with* CAESAR'S *body.*]

Here comes his body, mourned by Mark Antony,
who, though he had no hand in his death, shall
receive the benefit of his dying, a place in the com-
❹ monwealth, as which of you shall not? With
45 this I depart, that, as I slew my best lover for the good
of Rome, I have the same dagger for myself, when it
shall please my country to need my death.

ALL. Live, Brutus! Live, live!

FIRST PLEBEIAN. Bring him with triumph home unto his
house.

50 **SECOND PLEBEIAN.** Give him a statue with his ancestors.

❺ **THIRD PLEBEIAN.** Let him be Caesar.

FOURTH PLEBEIAN. Caesar's better parts[14]
Shall be crowned in Brutus.

FIRST PLEBEIAN. We'll bring him to his house with shouts
and clamors.

BRUTUS.   My countrymen—

SECOND PLEBEIAN. Peace! Silence! Brutus speaks.

55 **FIRST PLEBEIAN.**   Peace, ho!

BRUTUS. Good countrymen, let me depart alone,
And, for my sake, stay here with Antony.
Do grace to Caesar's corpse, and grace his speech
Tending to Caesar's glories,[15] which Mark Antony
60 By our permission, is allowed to make.
I do entreat you, not a man depart,
Save I alone, till Antony have spoke.   [*Exit*]

FIRST PLEBEIAN. Stay, ho! And let us hear Mark Antony.

THIRD PLEBEIAN. Let him go up into the public chair;
65 We'll hear him. Noble Antony, go up.

ANTONY. For Brutus' sake, I am beholding[16] to you.

FOURTH PLEBEIAN. What does he say of Brutus?

THIRD PLEBEIAN.   He says, for Brutus' sake,
He finds himself beholding to us all.

11. The question . . . in the Capitol: The whole matter of his death is on record in the Capitol.
12. extenuated (ik sten´ yoo wāt id) *v.:* Underrated.
13. enforced (en fôrsd´) *v.:* Given force to.

14. parts: Qualities.

15. Do grace . . . glories: Honor Caesar's body and the speech telling of Caesar's achievements.

16. beholding: Indebted.

◆ **Build Vocabulary**

vile (vīl) *adj.:* Depraved; ignoble

The Tragedy of Julius Caesar, Act III, Scene ii ◆ 761

Beyond the Classroom

Community Connection
Public Forums The main events of Act III take place at the *Forum,* a large public square that was the seat of the Roman government. Among the buildings clustered there were several temples; the *Tabularium,* or Hall of Records; and the Capitol, or Senate House, where Caesar's assassination occurs. Many illustrious speakers addressed the citizens of Rome from a permanent platform that faced the center of the square.

In a class discussion, have students identify buildings in your community that serve public functions and/or serve as public gathering places. Students might then do research to learn more about the roles that these buildings play. For example, students might focus on such questions as: What types of records are kept at your Town or City Hall? Where would someone go to look up a local law or ordinance? What community-wide events are held at local schools or libraries?

Comprehension Check ☑️

1 How did Brutus' speeches affect the crowd of plebeians? *Brutus has won them over—they are convinced that Caesar was a tyrant and deserved to die.*

◆ Build Grammar Skills

2 Parallel Structure Point out the repeated statements within Antony's speech. *Brutus is an honorable man; Brutus says he (Caesar) was ambitious.* Encourage students to comment on the effect that this repetition creates. *Students may say that it helps make the speech rhythmic and compelling. They may also point out that through the rest of his words, Mark Antony casts increasing doubt on both these statements with each repetition.*

◆ Literary Focus

3 Dramatic Speeches Would students classify this speech as a soliloquy or a monologue? Why? *Monologue—in this speech, Mark Antony addresses other characters.*

◆ Literary Focus

4 Dramatic Speeches Both men begin by asking for the audience's attention in almost the same way; both use the technique of asking the audience questions (rhetorical questions); both mention Caesar's ambition. Antony's speech, however, is meant to achieve the opposite effect of Brutus'.

◆ Reading Strategy

5 Paraphrase Sample paraphrase: I am so overcome with sorrow at Caesar's death that I can't speak.

FOURTH PLEBEIAN. 'Twere best he speak no harm of Brutus here!

FIRST PLEBEIAN. This Caesar was a tyrant.

1 70 **THIRD PLEBEIAN.** Nay, that's certain.
We are blest that Rome is rid of him.

SECOND PLEBEIAN. Peace! Let us hear what Antony can say.

ANTONY. You gentle Romans—

ALL. Peace, ho! Let us hear him.

ANTONY. Friends, Romans, countrymen, lend me your ears;
75   I come to bury Caesar, not to praise him.
  The evil that men do lives after them,
  The good is oft interrèd with their bones;
  So let it be with Caesar. The noble Brutus
  Hath told you Caesar was ambitious.
80   If it were so, it was a grievous fault,
  And grievously hath Caesar answered[17] it.
  Here, under leave of Brutus and the rest
  (For Brutus is an honorable man,
  So are they all, all honorable men),
85   Come I to speak in Caesar's funeral.
  He was my friend, faithful and just to me;
  But Brutus says he was ambitious,
  And Brutus is an honorable man.
  He hath brought many captives home to Rome,
2   Whose ransoms did the general coffers fill;
3   Did this in Caesar seem ambitious?
  When that the poor have cried, Caesar hath wept;
  Ambition should be made of sterner stuff.
  Yet Brutus says he was ambitious;
95   And Brutus is an honorable man.
  You all did see that on the Lupercal
  I thrice presented him a kingly crown,
  Which he did thrice refuse. Was this ambition?
  Yet Brutus says he was ambitious;
100   And sure he is an honorable man.
  I speak not to disprove what Brutus spoke,
  But here I am to speak what I do know.
  You all did love him once, not without cause;
  What cause withholds you then to mourn for him?
105   O judgment, thou art fled to brutish beasts,
  And men have lost their reason! Bear with me;
  My heart is in the coffin there with Caesar,
  And I must pause till it come back to me.

17. answered: Paid the penalty for.

◆ **Literary Focus**
Notice how Antony's monologue reflects the style and structure of Brutus' monologue. **4**

◆ **Reading Strategy**
Paraphrase the reason Antony gives for pausing in his speech. **5**

762 ◆ *Drama*

Enrichment

If students look back at the cast of characters at the beginning of the play, they will see that Artemidorus, the citizen who tries to warn Caesar of danger in Scene i, lines 3–8, is identified as a teacher of rhetoric—the art of public speaking. Artemidorus' profession, along with Brutus' and Mark Antony's eloquent speeches before the crowd of plebeians, illustrates the importance of rhetoric in ancient Rome.

The Romans learned a great deal about rhetoric from the Greeks, whose most famous orators and teachers of rhetoric included Pericles, Demosthenes, and Aristotle. In both ancient Greece and Rome, post-secondary education emphasized rhetoric in order to prepare young men for careers in law and politics.

As students read Act III, have them discuss whether they think Brutus or Mark Antony is the better orator and why.

FIRST PLEBEIAN. Methinks there is much reason in his
    sayings.

110 **SECOND PLEBEIAN.** If thou consider rightly of the matter,
    Caesar has had great wrong.

THIRD PLEBEIAN.   Has he, masters?
    I fear there will a worse come in his place.

FOURTH PLEBEIAN. Marked ye his words? He would not
    take the crown,
    Therefore 'tis certain he was not ambitious.

115 **FIRST PLEBEIAN.** If it be found so, some will dear abide
    it.[18]

SECOND PLEBEIAN. Poor soul, his eyes are red as fire with
    weeping.

THIRD PLEBEIAN. There's not a nobler man in Rome than
    Antony.

FOURTH PLEBEIAN. Now mark him, he begins again to
    speak.

ANTONY. But yesterday the word of Caesar might
120   Have stood against the world; now lies he there,
    And none so poor to[19] do him reverence.

18. dear abide/it: Pay
dearly for it.

19. to: As to.

◀ Critical Viewing
How does this
actor portray
Antony's passion in
delivering Caesar's
eulogy? [Connect] ❽

The Tragedy of Julius Caesar, Act III, Scene ii ◆ *763*

▶Critical Viewing◀

❻ **Connect** Call students' attention
to the fact that, as in the opening
scene and during Brutus' speech, the
plebeians are changing their minds
again. Now, they are turning against
Brutus and doubting his claim that
Caesar was ambitious. Moments ago,
they wanted to erect a monument to
Brutus.

Customize for
Logical/Mathematical
Learners

❼ After Brutus' and Antony's monologues have been read, allow your
logical/mathematical learners to conduct a survey or hold a class vote
about which of the two men makes a
more convincing case. Students may
represent the results on a graph.
Follow up with a discussion on the
reasons why students (and plebeians)
might be swayed by the words of
these men.

▶Critical Viewing◀

❽ **Connect** His tense body language and intense facial expression
convey his passion.

Listening to Literature
Audiocassettes Play the
audiocassette recording of Brutus'
and Antony's monologues. Encourage
students to listen without following
the text. Have students discuss the
difference between reading the
speeches and hearing them.

◆ **Beyond the Classroom**

Workplace Skills

Public Speaking Discuss with students that
many careers involve some form of public speaking. Some jobs may involve presenting an idea,
demonstrating a product, or reporting results to a
large group. Other jobs may use public speaking
skills on a smaller scale, for instance, in conducting a meeting. Even a telephone conversation
involves some public speaking skills! In life, students may use public speaking skills when they
attend town council meetings or other group sit-

uations in which attendees are encouraged to
voice their opinion.
    Outline for students the qualities of an effec-
tive speaker: projection, diction, eye contact, and
variety. Have them practice these skills by delivering a short portion of either of the monologues.
For more instruction and activities that will develop students' public speaking skills, use the lessons
on Expressing Disagreement, p. 298, Telephone
Conversation, p. 808, Body Language, p. 876, and
Running a Meeting, p. 950.

Connections to Today's World

The granddaughter of Yitzhak Rabin, the slain Israeli leader, delivers a eulogy for her grandfather. Noa Ben Artzi-Pelossof's eulogy is no funeral oration like Mark Antony's for Caesar, but it is every bit as moving, as she says a final farewell to the man she simply called *Saba,* the Hebrew word for grandfather.

Genre Connection

Traditionally, the eulogy, or funeral speech, is an opportunity for the family and loved ones of the deceased to talk publicly about the person's good, admirable, or lovable qualities.

Discuss with students whether there are more similarities or more differences between Antony's funeral oration for Caesar and this moving speech. Are there more similarities or more differences between the feelings of the speaker for the person who was killed?

Thematic Connection

Ask students to state the theme of each speech—Antony's funeral oration for Caesar and Noa Ben Artzi-Pelossof's eulogy for her grandfather Yitzhak Rabin. What part does revenge play in either speech?

O masters! If I were disposed to stir
Your hearts and minds to mutiny and rage,
I should do Brutus wrong and Cassius wrong,
125   Who, you all know, are honorable men.
I will not do them wrong; I rather choose
To wrong the dead, to wrong myself and you,
Than I will wrong such honorable men.
But here's a parchment with the seal of Caesar;
❶ 130   I found it in his closet; 'tis his will.
Let but the commons[20] hear this testament,
Which, pardon me, I do not mean to read,
And they would go and kiss dead Caesar's wounds,
And dip their napkins[21] in his sacred blood;
135   Yea, beg a hair of him for memory,
And dying, mention it within their wills,
Bequeathing it as a rich legacy
Unto their issue.[22]

FOURTH PLEBEIAN. We'll hear the will; read it, Mark Antony.

140   **ALL.** The will, the will! We will hear Caesar's will!

ANTONY. Have patience, gentle friends, I must not read it.

20. **commons:** Plebeians; commoners.

21. **napkins:** Handkerchiefs.

22. **issue:** Heirs.

CONNECTIONS TO TODAY'S WORLD

All leaders live in some danger of violence against them by groups or individuals who do not agree with their policies. Like Caesar, Yitzhak Rabin's life was cut short by an assassination.

Noa Ben Artzi-Pelossof (1977–   ) is the granddaughter of Yitzhak Rabin, the Prime Minister of Israel from 1974 to 1977 and 1993 to 1995. A celebrated soldier and statesman, he was the first Prime Minister born in Israel. In 1994, Rabin received the Nobel Peace Prize for his efforts toward peace. He was assassinated on November 5, 1995.

In her eulogy at his funeral, Artzi-Pelossof expressed her personal feelings about this public man.

Eulogy for a Fallen Leader—
Yitzhak Rabin

Noa Ben Artzi-Pelossof

"Grandfather, you were the pillar of fire in front of the camp and now we are left in the camp alone, in the dark; and we are so cold and so sad.

"I know that people talk in terms of a national tragedy, and of comforting an entire nation, but we feel the huge void that remains in your absence when grandmother doesn't stop crying.

"Few people really knew you. Now they will talk about you for quite some time, but I feel that they really don't know just how great the pain is, how great the tragedy is; something has been destroyed.

"Grandfather, you were and still are our hero. I want you

It is not meet you know how Caesar loved you.
You are not wood, you are not stones, but men;
And being men, hearing the will of Caesar,
145 It will inflame you, it will make you mad.
'Tis good you know not that you are his heirs;
For if you should, O, what would come of it?

FOURTH PLEBEIAN. Read the will! We'll hear it, Antony!
You shall read us the will, Caesar's will!

150 **ANTONY.** Will you be patient? Will you stay awhile?
I have o'ershot myself[23] to tell you of it.
I fear I wrong the honorable men
Whose daggers have stabbed Caesar; I do fear it.

FOURTH PLEBEIAN. They were traitors. Honorable men!

155 **ALL.** The will! The testament!

SECOND PLEBEIAN. They were villains, murderers! The
will! Read the will!

ANTONY. You will compel me then to read the will?
Then make a ring about the corpse of Caesar,
160 And let me show you him that made the will.
Shall I descend? And will you give me leave?

23. o'ershot myself:
Gone too far.

◆ **Critical Thinking**

❷ Interpret Point out that the common people, who had just moments ago cheered and supported Brutus, now call the conspirators "traitors," "villains," and "murderers." Have students identify the immediate cause of the crowd's change of heart. Also encourage students to comment on what the people's behavior reveals about their traits and motives.

Students should note that the plebeians turn against the conspirators upon hearing about Caesar's will. They may conclude that the plebeians are fickle and unpredictable in their loyalties and that they are motivated by greed and self-interest.

to know that every time I did anything, I saw you in front of me.

"Your appreciation and your love accompanied us every step down the road, and our lives were always shaped by your values. You, who never abandoned anything, are now abandoned. And here you are, my ever-present hero, cold, alone, and I cannot do anything to save you. You are missed so much.

"Others greater than I have already eulogized you, but none of them ever had the pleasure I had to feel the caresses of your arms, your soft hands, to merit your warm embrace that was reserved only for us, to see your half-smile that always told me so much, that same smile which is no longer, frozen in the grave with you.

"I have no feelings of revenge because my pain and feelings of loss are so large, too large. The ground has been swept out from below us, and we are groping now, trying to wander about in this empty void, without any success so far.

"I am not able to finish this; left with no alternative, I say goodbye to you, hero, and ask you to rest in peace, and think about us, and miss us, as down here we love you so very much. I imagine angels are accompanying you now, and I ask them to take care of you because you deserve their protection.

"We will love you, Saba, forever."

1. Compare and contrast the message of Noa Ben Artzi-Pelossof's eulogy for her grandfather with Antony's eulogy for Caesar.
2. (a) How does Artzi-Pelossof help her listeners know her grandfather? (b) How does Antony help his listeners know Caesar?
3. Why do you think some people choose violence to express their disagreement with a leader's policies?

The Tragedy of Julius Caesar, Act III, Scene ii ◆ 765

Answers to Connections to Today's World

1. Both speakers admire their subjects but Antony uses irony to make his points about Caesar's death. Artzi-Pelossof speaks in a more straightforward manner about her feelings. Both speakers express sorrow at the loss of the subject. Antony uses his eulogy to place blame and stir up a conflict. Artzi-Pelossof does not have feelings of revenge.

2. (a) She describes the kind of man he was in terms of their personal relationship. (b) He describes the public good Caesar achieved.
3. People who are unable or unwilling to go through peaceful, public means to express their disagreement with a leader may feel they need to use violence to make a point. In their answers, students should identify some of the peaceful means a person might use to express his or her disagreement.

Customize for
Bodily/Kinesthetic Learners

❶ Have a volunteer perform Antony's speech, lines 170–198, using appropriate gestures and a coat or jacket to represent Caesar's body and toga. Ask other members of the class to act out the plebeians' reactions by reading aloud lines 199–206. Afterward, discuss what makes Antony's speech so effective. Lead students to see that by vividly describing Caesar's death, Antony appeals to the people's emotions; he portrays the assassination as a crime against an individual rather than as an abstract political act.

◆ Reading Strategy

❷ Paraphrase One paraphrase might be "If you have any feelings, you will be moved by what you are about to see and hear. You all recognize Caesar's cloak—I'll never forget the first time he wore it."

ALL. Come down.

SECOND PLEBEIAN. Descend. [ANTONY *comes down.*]

THIRD PLEBEIAN. You shall have leave.

165 **FOURTH PLEBEIAN.** A ring! Stand round.

FIRST PLEBEIAN. Stand from the hearse,[24] stand from the body!

SECOND PLEBEIAN. Room for Antony, most noble Antony!

ANTONY. Nay, press not so upon me; stand far off.

ALL. Stand back! Room! Bear back.

170 **ANTONY.** If you have tears, prepare to shed them now.
You all do know this mantle;[25] I remember
The first time ever Caesar put it on:
'Twas on a summer's evening, in his tent,
That day he overcame the Nervii.
175 Look, in this place ran Cassius' dagger through;
See what a rent[26] the envious[27] Casca made;
Through this the well-belovèd Brutus stabbed,
And as he plucked his cursèd steel away,
Mark how the blood of Caesar followed it,
180 As[28] rushing out of doors, to be resolved[29]
If Brutus so unkindly knocked, or no;
For Brutus, as you know, was Caesar's angel.
Judge, O you gods, how dearly Caesar loved him!
This was the most unkindest cut of all;
185 For when the noble Caesar saw him stab,
Ingratitude, more strong than traitors' arms,
Quite vanquished him. Then burst his mighty heart;
And, in his mantle muffling up his face,
Even at the base of Pompey's statue
190 (Which all the while ran blood) great Caesar fell.
O, what a fall was there, my countrymen!
Then I, and you, and all of us fell down,
Whilst bloody treason flourished[30] over us.
O, now you weep, and I perceive you feel
195 The dint[31] of pity; these are gracious drops.
Kind souls, what[32] weep you when you but behold
Our Caesar's vesture[33] wounded? Look you here,
Here is himself, marred as you see with[34] traitors.

FIRST PLEBEIAN. O piteous spectacle!

200 **SECOND PLEBEIAN.** O noble Caesar!

THIRD PLEBEIAN. O woeful day!

FOURTH PLEBEIAN. O traitors, villains!

24. hearse (hʉrs) *n.*: Coffin.

25. mantle (man´ təl) *n.*: Cloak; toga.

26. rent (rent) *n.*: Torn place.
27. envious (en´ vē əs) *adj.*: Spiteful.

28. As: As if.
29. to be resolved: To learn for certain.

◆ Reading Strategy
Paraphrase Antony's words to the crowd. **❷**

30. flourished (flʉr´ ishd) *v.*: Grew; triumphed.

31. dint (dint) *n.*: Force.
32. what: Why.
33. vesture (ves´ chər) *n.*: Clothing.
34. with: By.

FIRST PLEBEIAN. O most bloody sight!

SECOND PLEBEIAN. We will be revenged.

205   **ALL.** Revenge! About!³⁵ Seek! Burn! Fire! Kill! Slay!
        Let not a traitor live!

ANTONY. Stay, countrymen.

FIRST PEBEIAN. Peace there! Hear the noble Antony.

SECOND PLEBEIAN. We'll hear him, we'll follow him, we'll
210   die with him!

ANTONY. Good friends, sweet friends, let me not stir you up
     To such a sudden flood of mutiny.
     They that have done this deed are honorable.
     What private griefs³⁶ they have, alas, I know not,
215   That made them do it. They are wise and honorable,
     And will, no doubt, with reasons answer you.
     I come not, friends, to steal away your hearts;
     I am no orator, as Brutus is;
     But (as you know me all) a plain blunt man
❸ 220 That love my friend, and that they know full well
❹   That gave me public leave³⁷ to speak of him.
❺   For I have neither writ, nor words, nor worth,
     Action, or utterance,³⁸ nor the power of speech
     To stir men's blood; I only speak right on.³⁹
225   I tell you that which you yourselves do know,
     Show you sweet Caesar's wounds, poor poor dumb
        mouths,
     And bid them speak for me. But were I Brutus,
     And Brutus Antony, there were an Antony
     Would ruffle up your spirits, and put a tongue
230   In every wound of Caesar's that should move
     The stones of Rome to rise and mutiny.

ALL. We'll mutiny.

FIRST PLEBEIAN.   We'll burn the house of Brutus.

THIRD PLEBEIAN. Away, then! Come, seek the conspirators.

ANTONY. Yet hear me, countrymen. Yet hear me speak.

235   **ALL.** Peace, ho! Hear Antony, most noble Antony!

ANTONY. Why, friends, you go to do you know not what:
     Wherein hath Caesar thus deserved your loves?
     Alas, you know not; I must tell you then:
     You have forgot the will I told you of.

240   **ALL.** Most true, the will! Let's stay and hear the will.

ANTONY. Here is the will, and under Caesar's seal.
     To every Roman citizen he gives,
     To every several man, seventy-five drachmas.

The Tragedy of Julius Caesar, Act III, Scene ii ◆ 767

35. About: Let's go.

36. griefs (grēfs) *n.*: Grievances.

37. leave: Permission.

38. neither writ . . . utterance (ut′ ər əns): Neither written speech, nor fluency, nor reputation, nor gestures, nor style of speaking.
39. right on: Directly.

◆ **Literary Focus**

❸ **Dramatic Speeches** Encourage students to comment on the tactics that Antony uses as he continues to address and manipulate the crowd. *Students may point out the following: He cleverly plants the idea of mutiny in people's minds when he says that he does not want to stir up mutiny; he casts doubt on the reasons behind the assassination by saying that they are a mystery to him; he swears that his only motive is to speak his mind.*

Customize for
More Advanced Students
❹ Point out that Mark Antony's speech is brimming with ironies. Encourage students to cite specific lines and explain the sources of irony within them. For example, what would students say is ironic about Antony's statement that "I have neither writ, nor words . . . /. . . nor the power of speech/To stir men's blood" (lines 222–224)?

◆ **Build Vocabulary**

❺ **Word Roots: *-ora-*** Point out that *orator* (line 218) contains the word root *-ora-*, which comes from the Latin verb *orare*, which means "to speak." Have students determine the meaning of *orator*. *Students should connect the word root ora—having to do with speaking—with the suffix -tor-one who does or performs an action, and determine that "orator" means a speaker—in particular, a public speaker.*

Cross-Curricular Connection: Social Studies

Roman Society Roman society was divided into two main groups: citizens and noncitizens. About ten percent of people in Rome were citizens. This group included the ruling class, or *aristocracy;* wealthy businessmen; and *plebeians,* or the lower classes. People from all over the Roman empire were granted Roman citizenship. Noncitizens included foreigners who had not become Roman citizens and slaves, who might be prisoners of war,

children sold by needy parents, or condemned criminals. Slaves, who ranged from cultured Greek teachers to uneducated laborers, had no rights whatsoever. Some slaves, however, were able to buy their freedom, or were granted it by their owners.

Roman women had no legal rights, although they were held in high esteem, and encouraged to attend public functions, unlike their counterparts in Greece.

However, they could not vote.

Children began their education at home. The sons of wealthy families were sent to school from the age of six, and took on the responsibilities of adults at about sixteen. The education of most girls was limited to domestic concerns. Once they had reached sixteen, they were considered to be ready for marriage.

◆ Literary Focus

① Dramatic Speeches Suggested response: In this brief speech, Antony reveals his thoughts to the audience. By the word "mischief," the audience knows that Antony meant to subvert the conspirators' plot.

◆ Critical Thinking

② Predict Have students predict what Antony wants to discuss with Octavius. *Based on Antony's actions, and his earlier discussion with Octavius' servant, Antony probably wants to discuss an alliance formed for the purpose of driving out the conspirators.*

Customize for
English Language Learners

③ The archaic language in this section may pose difficulties for students acquiring proficiency in English. Preview words like *afoot, thither, rid, beliked* and help students discover contemporary synonyms.

SECOND PLEBEIAN. Most noble Caesar! We'll revenge his death!

245 **THIRD PLEBEIAN.** O royal Caesar!

ANTONY. Hear me with patience.

ALL. Peace, ho!

ANTONY. Moreover, he hath left you all his walks,
His private arbors, and new-planted orchards,[40]
250 On this side Tiber; he hath left them you,
And to your heirs forever: common pleasures,[41]
To walk abroad and recreate yourselves.
Here was a Caesar! When comes such another?

FIRST PLEBEIAN. Never, never! Come, away, away!
255 We'll burn his body in the holy place,
And with the brands[42] fire the traitors' houses.
Take up the body.

SECOND PLEBEIAN. Go fetch fire.

THIRD PLEBEIAN. Pluck down benches.

260 **FOURTH PLEBEIAN.** Pluck down forms, windows, anything!

[*Exit* PLEBEIANS *with the body.*]

ANTONY. Now let it work: Mischief, thou art afoot,
Take thou what course thou wilt.

[*Enter* SERVANT.]

How now, fellow?

SERVANT. Sir, Octavius is already come to Rome.

ANTONY. Where is he?

265 **SERVANT.** He and Lepidus are at Caesar's house.

ANTONY. And thither[43] will I straight to visit him;
He comes upon a wish. Fortune is merry,
And in this mood will give us anything.

SERVANT. I heard him say, Brutus and Cassius
270 Are rid[44] like madmen through the gates of Rome.

ANTONY. Belike[45] they had some notice of the people,[46]
How I had moved them. Bring me to Octavius. [*Exit*]

Scene iii. A street.

[*Enter* CINNA THE POET, *and after him the* PLEBEIANS.]

CINNA. I dreamt tonight that I did feast with Caesar,
And things unluckily charge my fantasy.[1]
I have no will to wander forth of doors,[2]
Yet something leads me forth?

40. walks . . . orchards: Parks, his private trees, and newly planted gardens.
41. common pleasures: Public places of recreation.

42. brands: Torches.

◆ **Literary Focus**
How does this aside indicate the true intentions behind Antony's monologue? ❶

43. thither: There.

44. Are rid: Have ridden.

45. Belike: Probably.
46. notice of the people: Word about the mood of the people.

1. things . . . fantasy: The events that have happened weigh heavily on my imagination.
2. of doors: Outdoors.

768 ◆ *Drama*

Cross-Curricular Connection: History

The Emperors of Rome In 27 B.C., Octavius, with whom Antony hopes to join forces in the third act, took the name of Augustus and became the first emperor of Rome. Rome was then no longer a republic, but a monarchy, as Brutus, Cassius, and the other conspirators had feared. The reign of Augustus, however, marked the beginning of the *Pax Romana* (Roman peace), which lasted for 200 years, during which commerce flourished and the standard of living rose.
Among other emperors of this period were Tiberius (14–37 A.D.), Caligula (37–41), Claudius (41–54), Nero (54–68), Trajan (98–117), Hadrian, and Marcus Aurelius (161–180). Suggest that students choose one of these Roman emperors to research, and report on the emperor's life and events in Rome during his reign.

Customize for
Musical/Rhythmic Learners
5 This passage (lines 5–12), with its short, repetitive question-and-response lines, might be fun for these students to read aloud. Encourage them to experiment with different voices, accents, tones, and so on. If possible, make a cassette recorder available so they can tape their readings and decide which they like best.

Extispicium relief (inspection of entrails) from the Forum of Trajan, Rome, Louvre, Paris, France

4 ▲ **Critical Viewing** Why do you think ancient Roman sculptors portrayed political scenes such as this one? [Speculate]

5   **FIRST PLEBEIAN.** What is your name?

      SECOND PLEBEIAN. Whither are you going?

      THIRD PLEBEIAN. Where do you dwell?

5   **FOURTH PLEBEIAN.** Are you a married man or a bachelor?

      SECOND PLEBEIAN. Answer every man directly.

10   **FIRST PLEBEIAN.** Ay, and briefly.

      FOURTH PLEBEIAN. Ay, and wisely.

      THIRD PLEBEIAN. Ay, and truly, you were best.

      CINNA. What is my name? Whither am I going? Where do
        I dwell? Am I a married man or a bachelor? Then, to
15   answer every man directly and briefly, wisely and
        truly: wisely I say, I am a bachelor.

      SECOND PLEBEIAN. That's as much as to say, they are
        fools that marry; you'll bear me a bang[3] for that, I
        fear. Proceed directly.

20   **CINNA.** Directly, I am going to Caesar's funeral.

      FIRST PLEBEIAN. As a friend or an enemy?

      CINNA. As a friend.

      SECOND PLEBEIAN. That matter is answered directly.

3. bear me a bang: Get a blow from me.

The Tragedy of Julius Caesar, Act III, Scene iii ◆ 769

❶ Ask students: What does the crowd's attack on Cinna and the exclamations that follow reveal about the situation in Rome as Act III ends?

The plebeians have become irrational and bloodthirsty as a result of Antony's speeches; they mean to riot and take revenge on the conspirators.

🎧 **Listening to Literature Audiocassettes** Now that students have read Act III, you might have them listen to some or all of the scenes within it on the **Listening to Literature Audiocassettes.**

Reinforce and Extend

Answers

◆ *Literature and Your Life*

Reader's Response To activate students' thinking, have them isolate words or phrases that make a strong impression on them. Then ask them to focus on these impressions as they answer the questions.

Thematic Focus Sample response: Even though Caesar was warned about his fate and he had a choice, his egotistical character actually made the prediction come true. Fate and character seemed to be linked.

☑ Check Your Comprehension

1. Trebonius presents Caesar with a petition and Artemidorus presents him with a letter of warning, but Caesar does not read either.
2. Brutus tells the people that his love for Rome caused him to turn against Caesar.
3. Antony repeatedly refers to Brutus as an "honorable" man.
4. Antony's speech enrages the common people.

◆ Critical Thinking

1. Antony befriends the conspirators to protect himself, to determine who are the assassins, and to position himself to speak at Caesar's funeral.
2. Brutus allows Antony to speak at Caesar's funeral because Brutus plans to speak first and because he mistakenly believes Antony's speaking will be more an advantage than a disadvantage.
3. The contents of Caesar's will enrage the citizens even more against the conspirators.

770

FOURTH PLEBEIAN. For your dwelling, briefly.

25 CINNA. Briefly, I dwell by the Capitol.

THIRD PLEBEIAN. Your name, sir, truly.

CINNA. Truly, my name is Cinna.

FIRST PLEBEIAN. Tear him to pieces! He's a conspirator.

❶ CINNA. I am Cinna the poet! I am Cinna the poet!

30 FOURTH PLEBEIAN. Tear him for his bad verses! Tear him for his bad verses!

CINNA. I am not Cinna the conspirator.

FOURTH PLEBEIAN. It is no matter, his name's Cinna; pluck but his name out of his heart, and turn him

35 going.[4]

THIRD PLEBEIAN. Tear him, tear him! [*They attack him.*] Come, brands, ho! Firebrands![5] To Brutus', to Cassius'! Burn all! Some to Decius' house, and some to Casca's; some to Ligarius'! Away, go!

[*Exit all the* PLEBEIANS *with* CINNA.]

4. turn him/going: Send him on his way.

5. Firebrands: People who stir up others to revolt.

Guide for Responding

◆ *Literature and Your Life*

Reader's Response If you had been in the crowd at Caesar's funeral in Scene ii, how would you have responded to Antony's speech?

Thematic Focus What role do you think fate plays in the death of Caesar? What role do you think Caesar's own character plays?

☑ Check Your Comprehension

1. What petition is presented to Caesar, and how does he respond to it?
2. What justification for Caesar's assassination does Brutus give to the people?
3. How does Antony repeatedly refer to Brutus during the funeral oration?
4. What effect does Antony's oration have on the common people?

◆ Critical Thinking

INTERPRET
1. Why does Antony befriend the conspirators immediately after the assassination? **[Interpret]**
2. Why does Brutus allow Antony to speak at Caesar's funeral? **[Analyze]**
3. How does Caesar's will affect the people? **[Interpret]**

APPLY
4. Antony convinces the crowd to accept his view of Caesar and the conspirators. Think of a modern leader who tries to influence public opinion. What techniques does he or she use? **[Relate]**

EXTEND
5. Identify at least three careers in which public speaking skills would be an asset. Explain. **[Career Link]**

---

4. Sample responses: Persuasive speakers utilize repetition and parallel structure; use simple, memorable themes; choose words carefully; build to a conclusive conviction; and connect to their audience in a meaningful way.

5. Examples of careers in which public speaking skills would be an asset are politician, lawyer, minister, teacher, television or radio news broadcaster, salesman, fund-raiser.

◆ Build Grammar Skills

1. Caesar is described with three parallel superlative adjectives, all starting with *most.*
2. Brutus is described with four adjectives; then Caesar is described with the same number.
3. Brutus uses parallel clauses.
4. Antony speaks with two parallel infinitive phrases.
5. Brutus poses two parallel questions.

◆ Build Vocabulary

Using the Root *-ora-*
1. c 2. a 3. b

Using the Word Bank
1. mutiny
2. oration
3. vile
4. malice
5. suit
6. discourse
7. spurn
8. confounded

Guide for Responding (continued)

◆ Reading Strategy

PARAPHRASE

Paraphrasing, or restating in your own words, is an effective way to clarify and understand Shakespeare's verse.

On your paper, paraphrase the following passages from Act III.

1. Caesar's speech, Scene i, lines 58–73.
2. The servant's speech, Scene i, lines 123–137.
3. Mark Antony's speech, Scene ii, lines 74–108.

◆ Literary Focus

DRAMATIC SPEECHES

Dramatic speeches, such as asides, soliloquys, and monologues, are some of the most famous and memorable parts of Shakespearean dramas.

1. Contrast what Antony says to the other characters in Act III, Scene i, lines 218–222, with what he says in his soliloquy, lines 254–275.
2. Examine Brutus' monologue in Act III, Scene ii, lines 12–34. Do you think Brutus is speaking his true feelings? Explain.
3. What does Antony's aside in Act III, Scene iii, lines 262–263, reveal about the true purpose of his speech to the crowd?

◆ Build Grammar Skills

PARALLEL STRUCTURE

Parallel structure, the expression of similar ideas in similar grammatical form, can make ordinary prose more poetic and a speech more powerful.

Practice In your notebook, identify and explain the parallel elements in each of the following examples.

1. Most high, most mighty, most puissant, Caesar . . .
2. Brutus is noble, wise, valiant, and honest; / Caesar was mighty, bold, royal, and loving.
3. Not that I loved Caesar less, but that I loved Rome more.
4. I come to bury Caesar, not to praise him.
5. Who is here so base, that/would be a bondman? . . .Who is here so rude, that would not be a/Roman?

◆ Build Vocabulary

USING THE ROOT -ora-

The Latin root -ora-, meaning "to speak," is found in a number of English words. In Act III of *The Tragedy of Julius Caesar*, when Mark Antony claims, "I am no *orator*, as Brutus is," do you believe him?

On your paper, match each of the following words, with -ora- as a root, with its definition.

1. oral   **a.** a skilled speaker
2. orator   **b.** skill in public speaking
3. oratory   **c.** spoken

USING THE WORD BANK

On your paper, complete each analogy using the words from the Word Bank.

1. *Riot* is to *prison* as _____?_____ is to *ship*.
2. *Eulogy* is to *funeral* as _____?_____ is to *graduation*.
3. *Helpful* is to *nurse* as _____?_____ is to *liar*.
4. *Goodwill* is to *volunteer* as _____?_____ is to *murderer*.
5. *Application* is to *job* as _____?_____ is to *favor*.
6. *Running* is to *motion* as _____?_____ is to *communication*.
7. *Punch* is to *fight* as _____?_____ is to *insult*.
8. *Wise* is to *enlightened* as _____?_____ is to *ignorant*.

 Idea Bank

Writing

1. **Obituary** Write a newspaper obituary to announce Caesar's death. An obituary contains facts about a person's life and the circumstances of his or her death. Use details about Caesar from Acts I–III to write the obituary.

2. **Reaction to Speeches** Imagine that you are a visitor to Rome who has just heard both Brutus' and Mark Antony's speeches. Write a commentary in which you explain which is more persuasive and why.

Speaking and Listening

3. **Background Music** Select a piece of background music that would be appropriate for the assassination scene. Play the music for the class and explain why you chose it. **[Music Link]**

The Tragedy of Julius Caesar, Act III ◆ 771

◆ Reading Strategy

1. I am not easily swayed to change my mind—I am unmoved and I maintain my position. Cimber stays banished.
2. Brutus, Mark Antony told me to humble myself before you and tell you that Antony admires and respects you and feared Caesar. Will you allow Antony to come here safely, so you can explain why you killed Caesar? Antony shall not mourn Caesar, but will faithfully follow Brutus through the dangers of this new state of affairs.
3. Listen: I'm here to bury Caesar, not to praise him. Let's just forget about Caesars' good deeds. Brutus says Caesar was ambitious. If that's so, Caesar was wrong, and he has paid the price. Brutus and the rest gave me permission to speak here. Caesar was my friend but if Brutus says Caesar was ambitious, I guess he was. Caesar made money for all of us and cried over the needs of the poor, but Brutus wouldn't say he was ambitious if he weren't. I tried to give Caesar the crown, but he turned it down. I don't mean to contradict Brutus, but Caesar can't have been all bad: You loved him once; what happened? This is crazy. I can't talk anymore I'm too upset.

◆ Literary Focus

1. Antony tells the conspirators that they are his friends. In his soliloquy, Antony mourns Caesar and calls the conspirators butchers.
2. Brutus frankly explains his part in Caesar's death when he says that he loved Caesar, but he loved the Roman people more. He is probably sincere. There are many earlier examples of Brutus' love for Caesar, and his concern for Rome.
3. Antony wished to set the crowd against Brutus and the conspirators.

 Idea Bank

Customizing for
Learning Modalities
Verbal/Linguistic: 1, 2
Musical/Rhythmic: 3
Interpersonal: 2

Customizing for
Performance Levels
Less Advanced: 2
Average: 1, 2, 3
More Advanced: 1

Guide for Reading, Act IV

OBJECTIVES

1. To read, comprehend, and interpret a drama
2. To relate a play to personal experience
3. To read between the lines
4. To analyze conflict in drama
5. To build vocabulary in context and learn the root *-phil-*
6. To identify noun clauses
7. To respond to the play through writing, speaking and listening, and projects

SKILLS INSTRUCTION

Vocabulary: Word Roots: *-phil-*

Grammar: Noun Clauses

Reading Strategy: Read Between the Lines

Literary Focus: Conflict in Drama

Speaking and Listening: Musical Score (teacher edition)

Critical Viewing: Draw Conclusions; Analyze

PORTFOLIO OPPORTUNITIES

Writing: Character Profile; Rewrite a Scene

Speaking and Listening: Musical Score

Interest Grabber
Write the following job description on the chalkboard.

Wanted: Strong leader for battle. Must be willing to die and to lead others into death. Position offers no job security and co-workers cannot be trusted.

Discuss with students whether they would take such an undesirable position. Then point out to students that this job description outlines the situation in which Brutus finds himself in Act IV. You may wish to have students write brief job descriptions for other main characters to identify their situations as the act opens.

◆ Review and Anticipate

After the conspirators assassinate Caesar, both Brutus and Mark Antony give funeral speeches. Brutus, using logic and reason, explains to the crowd that Caesar's death was necessary to keep all Romans free. The crowd at first wholeheartedly accepts Brutus' speech. Then, Mark Antony takes the stage and persuades the crowd that Caesar was a great man and Brutus is a traitor. The crowd, having been worked to a frenzy, rushes off to find and destroy the conspirators.

As Act IV opens, Antony, Lepidus (a general), and Octavius Caesar (Julius Caesar's nephew) are planning which of their political opponents must be killed. The remainder of the act reveals the growing conflict between Cassius and Brutus. As the act closes, a mysterious visitor foreshadows Brutus' fate.

◆ Literary Focus

CONFLICT IN DRAMA

Conflict, the struggle between two forces, is what creates drama. The conflict may be **external**—between two characters or groups—or it can be **internal**—involving a character's struggle to decide between two opposing ideas or values. The climax of the play is the point at which the internal and external conflicts are greatest. Usually the action rises to the climax—the moment of highest tension—and then falls as the conflicts are resolved.

What makes conflicts in drama especially compelling is that often the audience can see the outcome of events before the characters themselves can. In Act IV, as the conflict between the two armies nears, it becomes more and more obvious to the audience how the battle will turn out. There is a grisly fascination in watching the characters move inevitably toward their fates.

◆ Build Grammar Skills

NOUN CLAUSES

A **noun clause** is a subordinate clause (a group of words with a subject and verb that cannot stand alone as a sentence) that functions as a noun in a sentence. It may act as a subject, direct or indirect object, or object of a preposition.

> **Subject:** *That you have wronged me* doth appear in this.
> **Direct Object:** You know *that you are Brutus that speaks this.*
> **Object of Preposition:** The common people are swayed by *whoever speaks most persuasively.*

772 ◆ *Drama*

◆ Reading Strategy

READ BETWEEN THE LINES
People and situations in drama—as in life—are not always what they appear to be on the surface. Though you must read line by line to follow the action, by **reading between the lines** you can discover a deeper or different meaning to a character's words or actions.

For example, at the opening of Act IV, Mark Antony describes Lepidus as "meet to be sent on errands." The implication is that Lepidus is capable of little more. You must read between the lines to understand Octavius' reply as well. Octavius points out that Antony "took his voice who should be pricked to die." By this, Octavius is implying that he thought that Antony valued Lepidus' judgment.

◆ Build Vocabulary

WORD ROOTS: *-phil-*
In Act IV, a tragedy befalls Brutus, and he finds his philosophy fails to comfort him. A *philosophy* is a system of principles or beliefs. The root of the word is the Latin *-phil-,* which means "love." A related meaning of *philosophy,* is "love of wisdom."

WORD BANK
Before you read, preview this list of words from Act IV.

| legacies |
| slanderous |
| covert |
| chastisement |
| philosophy |

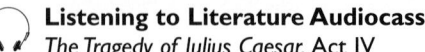
Prentice Hall Literature Program Resources

REINFORCE / RETEACH / EXTEND

Selection Support Pages
Build Vocabulary: Word Roots: *-phil-,* p. 216
Build Grammar Skills: Noun Clauses, p. 217
Reading Strategy: Read Between the Lines, p. 218
Literary Focus: Conflict in Drama, p. 219

Strategies for Diverse Student Needs, p. 53

Beyond Literature
Career Connection: Political Science, p. 53

Formal Assessment Selection Test, pp. 185–187; Assessment Resources Software

Alternative Assessment, p. 53

Resource Pro CD-ROM
The Tragedy of Julius Caesar, Act IV—includes all resource materials and customizable lesson plan

🎧 **Listening to Literature Audiocassettes**
The Tragedy of Julius Caesar, Act IV

The Tragedy of
JULIUS CAESAR

William Shakespeare

Act IV

Scene i. *A house in Rome.*

[*Enter* ANTONY, OCTAVIUS, *and* LEPIDUS.]

ANTONY. These many then shall die; their names are
pricked.

OCTAVIUS. Your brother too must die; consent you,
Lepidus?

LEPIDUS. I do consent—

OCTAVIUS.   Prick him down, Antony.

❶ LEPIDUS. Upon condition Publius shall not live,
5   Who is your sister's son, Mark Antony.

ANTONY. He shall not live; look, with a spot I damn him.[1]
But, Lepidus, go you to Caesar's house;
Fetch the will hither, and we shall determine
How to cut off some charge in <u>legacies</u>.

10 **LEPIDUS.** What, shall I find you here?

OCTAVIUS. Or[2] here or at the Capitol.   [*Exit* LEPIDUS.]

ANTONY. This is a slight unmeritable[3] man,
Meet to be sent on errands; is it fit,
The threefold world[4] divided, he should stand
One of the three to share it?

15 **OCTAVIUS.**   So you thought him,
And took his voice[5] who should be pricked to die
In our black sentence and proscription.[6]

❷ ANTONY. Octavius, I have seen more days[7] than you;
And though we lay these honors on this man,
❸
20   To ease ourselves of divers <u>sland'rous</u> loads,[8]
He shall but bear them as the ass bears gold,
To groan and sweat under the business,
Either led or driven, as we point the way;
And having brought our treasure where we will,
25   Then take we down his load, and turn him off,
(Like to the empty ass) to shake his ears
And graze in commons.[9]

The Tragedy of Julius Caesar, Act IV, Scene i ◆ *773*

---

1. with a spot . . . him:
With a mark on the tablet,
I condemn him.
2. Or: Either.
3. slight unmeritable:
Insignificant and without
merit.
4. threefold world: Three
areas of the Roman
empire—Europe, Asia, and
Africa.
5. voice: Vote; opinion.
6. proscription: List of
those sentenced to death
or exile.
7. have seen more days:
Am older.
**8. divers sland'rous
loads:** Various burdens of
blame.
9. in commons: On
public pasture.

◆ **Build Vocabulary**

legacies (leg´ ə sēz) *n.*:
Money, property, or
position left in a will to
someone
slanderous (slan´ dər əs)
adj.: Damaging to a
person's reputation

Develop Understanding

One-Minute Insight Act IV takes
place as the tri-
umvirate
(Antony, Octavius, and Lepidus) and
the conspirators (Cassius and Brutus)
prepare for battle. In this act
Shakespeare gives us a new perspective on the principal characters.
Antony's cold, calculating side is
revealed as he expresses his plan to
divide power between himself and
Octavius, leaving Lepidus out. Brutus'
emotional side is shown as he lashes
out at Cassius, then apologizes, citing
as an excuse his grief at Portia's
death.

Customize for
More Advanced Students
Suggest that advanced students
choose a passage in which reading
between the lines is necessary to get
the speaker's full meaning. Suggest
they rewrite the passage in "plain
English"—words that explicitly
express its meaning. Invite students
to contrast the two versions and discuss why Shakespeare chose language
that required more of an effort on
the part of the reader.

◆ **Background for
Understanding**

❶ Students might be interested to
know that Shakespeare compressed
time in order to make his play work.
Octavius did not arrive in Rome until
six weeks after Caesar's death, and he
did not ally himself with Antony and
Lepidus until eighteen months later.

◆ **Literary Focus**

❷ **Conflict in Drama** Ask students to summarize the conflict
between Antony and Octavius. *Is the
conflict internal or external? Antony
speaks to Octavius behind Lepidus'
back, plotting to leave Lepidus out,
should they win the battle, but letting
him remain for the present to share any
blame. Octavius argues in favor of
Lepidus. The conflict is external.*

◆ **Critical Thinking**

❸ **Make Inferences** Encourage
students to think about the new
character traits Shakespeare reveals
about Antony and Octavius. *Readers
learn that Antony has a deceitful side,
and that Octavius is more loyal and honest than Antony.*

Preparing for Standardized Tests

Grammar and Language Understanding noun
clauses, the focus of the Build Grammar Skills lesson for this selection, will help students with the
sections of standardized tests that deal with sentence structure. Students may be asked to indicate the function of a noun clause in a sentence:

Which of the following sentences has a noun
clause as the subject? *(D)*

(A) We found to our dismay <u>that the road
was flooded</u>.

(B) <u>If the road is flooded</u>, we'll have to turn
back.

(C) If we had known <u>that the road was flooded</u>,
we would have gone a different way.

(D) <u>That the road is flooded</u> is our main
problem.

(E) <u>We asked</u> whether the road was flooded.

Students should choose *D* as the correct
answer because the entire noun clause is the subject of the verb *is*.

For practice with noun clauses, students can
use the Build Grammar Skills page on Noun
Clauses in *Selection Support,* p. 217.

►Critical Viewing◄

1 Draw Conclusions Students can draw the conclusion that these are powerful, important men by noticing the elegant clothing, the sumptuous food, the confident postures and expressions.

Customize for
Less Proficient Readers

These students may need assistance in recognizing that the discussion between Octavius and Antony concerns the man who just left the room. Help students to understand that Antony compares Lepidus to a horse to highlight Lepidus' inability and unworthiness to think and act as one of the triumverate.

◆ Critical Thinking

2 Make Inferences Antony and Octavius disagreed about Lepidus, but now move on to more important matters. Ask: What can you infer about both Antony and Octavius from this abrupt change of topic? *The two men are intelligent and practical. They recognize the need to put aside their personal differences and focus on how best to counteract the threat from Cassius and Brutus.*

1 ▲ **Critical Viewing** What details in this picture indicate that these are important, powerful men? [Draw Conclusions]

OCTAVIUS.   You may do your will;
    But he's a tried and valiant soldier.

    ANTONY. So is my horse, Octavius, and for that
30   I do appoint him store of provender.[10]
    It is a creature that I teach to fight,
    To wind,[11] to stop, to run directly on,
    His corporal motion governed by my spirit.[12]
    And, in some taste,[13] is Lepidus but so.
35   He must be taught, and trained, and bid go forth.
    A barren-spirited[14] fellow; one that feeds
    On objects, arts, and imitations,[15]
    Which, out of use and staled[16] by other men,
    Begin his fashion.[17] Do not talk of him
40   But as a property. And now, Octavius,
    Listen great things. Brutus and Cassius
    Are levying powers;[18] we must straight make head.[19]
    Therefore let our alliance be combined,
    Our best friends made, our means stretched;[20]
45   And let us presently go sit in council
2   How <u>covert</u> matters may be best disclosed,
    And open perils surest answerèd.[21]

    OCTAVIUS. Let us do so; for we are at the stake,[22]
    And bayed about with many enemies;
50   And some that smile have in their hearts, I fear,
    Millions of mischiefs.[23]   [*Exit*]

10. appoint . . . provender: Give him a supply of food.
11. wind (wind) *v.:* Turn.
12. His . . . spirit: His body movements governed by my mind.
13. taste: Degree.
14. barren-spirited: Without ideas of his own.
15. feeds/On objects, arts, and imitations: Enjoys curiosities, arts, and styles.
16. staled: Cheapened.
17. Begin his fashion: He begins to use. (He is hopelessly behind the times.)
18. levying powers: Enlisting troops.
19. straight make head: Quickly gather soldiers.
20. stretched: Used to the fullest advantage.
21. How . . . answerèd: How secrets may be discovered and dangers met.
22. at the stake: Like a bear tied to a stake and set upon by many dogs.
23. mischiefs: Plans to injure us.

774 ◆ *Drama*

◈ Block Scheduling Strategies

Consider these suggestions to take advantage of extended class time:

• Students may enjoy viewing feature 5 of the CD-ROM *The Time, Life, and Works of Shakespeare*. They will be introduced to other Elizabethan dramatists.

• As a class, analyze the internal and external conflicts Brutus faces. Then have students complete Literary Focus: Conflict in Drama in **Selection Support**, p. 219.

• Invite students to listen to Act IV of the play on audiocassette. Then discuss how the actors' presentation affected students' understanding of the conflicts between Antony and Octavius and between Brutus and Cassius.

• Suggest that students work in small groups to complete the Critical Thinking questions (p. 786).

• Encourage students to choose an idea from the Idea Bank (p. 787). After students complete their writing, suggest they trade papers with partners and evaluate each other's writing on the basis of how well they have interpreted the characters of Brutus or Portia.

Scene ii. *Camp near Sardis.*

[*Drum. Enter* BRUTUS, LUCILIUS, LUCIUS, *and the* ARMY. TITINIUS *and* PINDARUS *meet them.*]

BRUTUS. Stand ho!

LUCILIUS. Give the word, ho! and stand.

BRUTUS. What now, Lucilius, is Cassius near?

LUCILIUS. He is at hand, and Pindarus is come
5   To do you salutation[1] from his master.

BRUTUS. He greets me well. Your master, Pindarus,
In his own change, or by ill officers,
Hath given me some worthy cause to wish
Things done undone;[2] but if he be at hand,
I shall be satisfied.

10 **PINDARUS.**   I do not doubt
But that my noble master will appear
Such as he is, full of regard and honor.

BRUTUS. He is not doubted. A word, Lucilius,
How he received you; let me be resolved.[3]

15 **LUCILIUS.** With courtesy and with respect enough,
But not with such familiar instances,[4]
Nor with such free and friendly conference[5]
As he hath used of old.

BRUTUS.   Thou hast described
A hot friend cooling. Ever note, Lucilius,
20 When love begins to sicken and decay
It useth an enforcèd ceremony.[6]
There are no tricks in plain and simple faith;
But hollow[7] men, like horses hot at hand,[8]
Make gallant show and promise of their mettle;

[*Low march within*]

25 But when they should endure the bloody spur,
They fall their crests, and like deceitful jades
Sink in the trial.[9] Comes his army on?

LUCILIUS. They mean this night in Sardis to be
quartered;
The greater part, the horse in general,[10]
Are come with Cassius.

[*Enter* CASSIUS *and his Powers.*]

30 **BRUTUS.**   Hark! He is arrived.
March gently[11] on to meet him.

CASSIUS. Stand, ho!

The Tragedy of Julius Caesar, Act IV, Scene ii ◆ 775

◆ **Literary Focus**
How does the greeting between Brutus and Lucilius indicate the increasing tension of the conflict?

1. **To do you salutation:** To bring you greetings.

2. **In his own . . . done undone:** Has changed in his feelings toward me or has received bad advice from subordinates and has made me wish we had not done what we did.

3. **resolved:** Fully informed.

4. **familiar instances:** Marks of friendship.
5. **conference:** Conversation.

6. **enforcèd ceremony:** Forced formality.

7. **hollow:** Insincere.
8. **hot at hand:** Full of spirit when reined in.

9. **They fall . . . the trial:** They drop their necks, and like worn-out worthless horses, fail the test.

10. **horse in general:** Cavalry.

11. **gently:** Slowly.

◆ **Build Vocabulary**
covert (kuv´ ərt) *adj.*: Hidden; secret

◆ **Literary Focus**

❸ **Conflict in Drama** Make sure students understand that Brutus speaks first to his own servant, Lucilius, about Cassius' servant, Pindarus ("*He greets me well*"). Then he speaks directly to Pindarus, referring to Cassius ("*Your master . . .*") Ask: What does Brutus suspect Cassius of doing? What is the source of Brutus' internal conflict? *The line "In his own change, or by ill officers" implies that Brutus suspects Cassius of being involved in some sort of corruption. Because Brutus can justify his own part in the conspiracy only if he believes that each conspirator was honorable, he is deeply disturbed by his suspicions about Cassius.*

◆ **Reading Strategy**

❹ **Read Between the Lines** Ask: By reading between the lines in this passage, what can you infer about the relationship between Brutus and Cassius? *The relationship is not as strong as it once was. Brutus has already told Lucilius that he suspects Cassius of dishonesty. What he interprets as coolness on the part of Cassius makes him think either that Cassius is angry with him or that Cassius has something to hide.*

Remind students that if they read
between the lines, they can often
learn how characters perceive themselves. Ask: How does Brutus view
himself? *Brutus perceives himself as
one who is fair to everyone, even to his
enemies.*

◆ **Reading Strategy**

❷ **Read Between the Lines**
Suggest that, by reading between the
lines, students can find Brutus' reason
for wanting to speak with Cassius
privately, where the troops cannot
hear. *Brutus says that the armies
"should perceive nothing but love"
between himself and Cassius because he
understands the demands of leadership.
Good leaders should present a united
front to their subordinates.*

◆ **Literary Focus**

❸ **Conflict in Drama** This passage (lines 1–12) explains Cassius' ill-
feeling toward Brutus. Have students
work with partners, using the notes
in the text, to paraphrase it. *Sample
answer:*
CASSIUS: *The reason I'm angry is that
you denounced Lucius for taking bribes,
even though I had written you a letter
in his defense.*
BRUTUS: *You shouldn't have written a
letter defending a dishonest man.*
CASSIUS: *At a time like this, you should-
n't be so critical of every little thing.*
BRUTUS: *You, yourself, have a reputation
for taking bribes.*

◆ **Reading Strategy**

❹ **Read Between the Lines** Ask
students what they can determine
about Cassius' personality by reading
between the lines. *Responses can
include this: Cassius is saying that if others besides Brutus accused him of dishonesty he would kill them. These are
the words of a hot-tempered, aggressive
man.*

BRUTUS. Stand, ho! Speak the word along.

FIRST SOLDIER. Stand!

35 **SECOND SOLDIER.** Stand!

THIRD SOLDIER. Stand!

CASSIUS. Most noble brother, you have done me wrong.

❶ **BRUTUS.** Judge me, you gods! Wrong I mine enemies?
And if not so, how should I wrong a brother?

40 **CASSIUS.** Brutus, this sober form[12] of yours hides
wrongs;
And when you do them—

BRUTUS.   Cassius, be content.[13]
Speak your griefs softly; I do know you well.
Before the eyes of both our armies here
❷ (Which should perceive nothing but love from us)
45 Let us not wrangle. Bid them move away;
Then in my tent, Cassius, enlarge[14] your griefs,
And I will give you audience.

CASSIUS.   Pindarus,
Bid our commanders lead their charges[15] off
A little from this ground.

50 **BRUTUS.** Lucilius, do you the like, and let no man
Come to our tent till we have done our conference.
Let Lucius and Titinius guard our door.

[*Exit all but* BRUTUS *and* CASSIUS]

Scene iii. *Brutus' tent.*

CASSIUS. That you have wronged me doth appear in this:
You have condemned and noted[1] Lucius Pella
For taking bribes here of the Sardians;
Wherein my letters, praying on his side,[2]
5 Because I knew the man, was slighted off.[3]

BRUTUS. You wronged yourself to write in such a case.

❸ **CASSIUS.** In such a time as this it is not meet
That every nice offense should bear his comment.[4]

BRUTUS. Let me tell you, Cassius, you yourself
10 Are much condemned to have an itching palm,[5]
To sell and mart[6] your offices for gold
To undeservers.

CASSIUS.   I an itching palm?
❹ You know that you are Brutus that speaks this,
Or, by the gods, this speech were else your last.

15 **BRUTUS.** The name of Cassius honors[7] this corruption,

---

12. **sober form:** Serious manner.

13. **be content:** Be patient.

14. **enlarge:** Freely express.

15. **charges:** Troops.

1. **noted:** Publicly denounced.

2. **praying on his side:** Pleading on his behalf.
3. **slighted off:** Disregarded.

4. **every . . . comment:** Every petty fault should receive its criticism.

5. **condemned . . . palm:** Accused of having a hand eager to accept bribes.
6. **mart:** Trade.

7. **honors:** Gives respectability to.

And <u>chastisement</u> doth therefore hide his head.

CASSIUS. Chastisement!

BRUTUS. Remember March, the ides of March remember.
Did not great Julius bleed for justice' sake?

20
What villain touched his body, that did stab,
And not[8] for justice? What, shall one of us,
That struck the foremost man of all this world

❺ But for supporting robbers,[9] shall we now
Contaminate our fingers with base bribes,

25
And sell the mighty space of our large honors[10]
For so much trash[11] as may be grasped thus?
I had rather be a dog, and bay[12] the moon,
Than such a Roman.

CASSIUS.   Brutus, bait[13] not me;
I'll not endure it. You forget yourself

❻ 30
To hedge me in.[14] I am a soldier, I,
Older in practice, abler than yourself
To make conditions.[15]

❼ **BRUTUS.**   Go to! You are not, Cassius.

CASSIUS. I am.

BRUTUS. I say you are not.

35
CASSIUS. Urge[16] me no more, I shall forget myself;
Have mind upon your health;[17] tempt me no farther.

BRUTUS. Away, slight[18] man!

❽ **CASSIUS.** Is't possible?

BRUTUS.   Hear me, for I will speak.
Must I give way and room to your rash choler?[19]

40
Shall I be frighted when a madman stares?

CASSIUS. O ye gods, ye gods! Must I endure all this?

BRUTUS. All this? Ay, more: fret till your proud heart
   break.
Go show your slaves how choleric[20] you are,
And make your bondmen tremble. Must I budge?[21]

45
Must I observe you?[22] Must I stand and crouch
Under your testy humor?[23] By the gods,
You shall digest the venom of your spleen,[24]
Though it do split you; for, from this day forth,
I'll use you for my mirth,[25] yea, for my laughter,
When you are waspish.[26]

50
CASSIUS.   Is it come to this?

BRUTUS. You say you are a better soldier:
Let it appear so; make your vaunting[27] true,

8. **And not:** Except.

9. **But . . . robbers:** Here Brutus says, for the first time, that Caesar's officials were also involved in taking bribes and that this was a motive in his assassination.
10. **honors:** Offices.
11. **trash:** Dirty money.
12. **bay:** Howl at.
13. **bait:** Harass (as a bear tied to a stake is harassed by dogs).
14. **hedge me in:** Restrict my actions.
15. **conditions:** Decisions.

16. **Urge:** Drive.
17. **health:** Safety.
18. **slight:** Insignificant.
19. **choler** (käl´ ər) n.: Anger.
20. **choleric** (käl´ ər ik) adj.: Quick-tempered.
21. **budge:** Flinch away from you.
22. **observe you:** Show reverence toward you.
23. **testy humor:** Irritability.
24. **digest . . . spleen:** Eat the poison of your spleen. (The spleen was thought to be the source of anger.)
25. **mirth:** Amusement.
26. **waspish:** Bad-tempered.
27. **vaunting** (vônt´ iŋ) n.: Boasting.

◆ **Build Vocabulary**
chastisement (chas tīz´ mənt) n.: Punishment; severe criticism

The Tragedy of Julius Caesar, Act IV, Scene iii ◆ 777

◆ Build Grammar Skills

❶ Noun Clauses Have students identify the noun clause in line 64 and explain its function. *The clause is "that I shall be sorry for"; it is the direct object of the verb phrase "may do" and answers the question "may do what?"*

◆ Reading Strategy

❷ Read Between the Lines Cassius' strong reaction to Brutus' accusations suggests that he is very sensitive about being thought weak or cowardly. He has a similar reaction when he is accused of taking bribes. Students can read between the lines that Brutus is probably not the first person to accuse him of weakness and dishonesty.

◆ Literary Focus

❸ Conflict in Drama Suggested response: In addition to accusing Cassius of accepting bribes, Brutus expresses anger at Cassius for refusing to help with gold to pay his legions.

And it shall please me well. For mine own part,
I shall be glad to learn of[28] noble men.

CASSIUS. You wrong me every way; you wrong me,
55   Brutus;
I said, an elder soldier, not a better.
Did I say, better?

BRUTUS.   If you did, I care not.

CASSIUS. When Caesar lived, he durst not thus have
moved[29] me.

BRUTUS. Peace, peace, you durst not so have tempted
him.

60 **CASSIUS.** I durst not?

BRUTUS. No.

CASSIUS. What? Durst not tempt him?

BRUTUS.   For your life you durst not.

CASSIUS. Do not presume too much upon my love;
❶ I may do that I shall be sorry for.

65 **BRUTUS.** You have done that you should be sorry for.
There is no terror, Cassius, in your threats;
For I am armed so strong in honesty
That they pass by me as the idle wind,
Which I respect not. I did send to you
70   For certain sums of gold, which you denied me;
For I can raise no money by vile means.
By heaven, I had rather coin my heart
And drop my blood for drachmas than to wring
From the hard hands of peasants their vile trash
75   By any indirection.[30] I did send
To you for gold to pay my legions,
Which you denied me. Was that done like Cassius?
Should I have answered Caius Cassius so?
When Marcus Brutus grows so covetous[31]
80   To lock such rascal counters[32] from his friends.
Be ready, gods, with all your thunderbolts,
Dash him to pieces!

CASSIUS.   I denied you not.

BRUTUS. You did.

CASSIUS.   I did not. He was but a fool
That brought my answer back. Brutus hath rived[33]
my heart.
85   A friend should bear his friend's infirmities;

28. learn of: Hear about; learn from.

29. moved: Irritated.

◆ **Reading Strategy**
What can you read between the lines that would help you explain why Cassius is so offended by Brutus' words? ❷

◆ **Literary Focus**
How does this conflict between Brutus and Cassius reflect Brutus' internal conflict over his participation in the conspiracy? ❸

30. indirection: Irregular methods.

31. covetous (kuv′ it əs) *adj.*: Greedy.
32. rascal counters: Worthless coins.

33. rived (rīv'd) *v.*: Broken.

778 ◆ Drama

Beyond the Classroom

Workplace Skills

Expressing Disagreement In the heat of the moment, Brutus and Cassius express their disagreement with each other in very hostile terms. If they had expressed their disagreement differently, the conflict between them may have been avoided. Tell students that there are appropriate and constructive ways to express disagreement in life and in the workplace. As a class, come up with some guidelines for expressing disagree-

ment. Elicit from students the following points:

- Use a calm, respectful tone.
- Present your reasons and offer evidence.
- Listen to what the other person has to say and consider his or her point of view before responding.

For more instruction and activities that will develop students' ability to express disagreement effectively and appropriately, use the Speaking and Listening Workshop on page 298.

But Brutus makes mine greater than they are.

BRUTUS. I do not, till you practice them on me.

CASSIUS. You love me not.

BRUTUS.   I do not like your faults.

CASSIUS. A friendly eye could never see such faults.

90 **BRUTUS.** A flatterer's would not, though they do appear
As huge as high Olympus.

CASSIUS. Come, Antony, and young Octavius, come,
Revenge yourselves alone[34] on Cassius,
For Cassius is aweary of the world:

95 Hated by one he loves; braved[35] by his brother;
Checked like a bondman;[36] all his faults observed,
Set in a notebook, learned and conned by rote[37]
To cast into my teeth. O, I could weep
My spirit from mine eyes! There is my dagger,

100 And here my naked breast; within, a heart
Dearer than Pluto's mine,[38] richer than gold;
If that thou be'st a Roman, take it forth.

❹ I, that denied thee gold, will give my heart.
Strike as thou didst at Caesar; for I know,
When thou didst hate him worst, thou lovedst him

105   better
Than ever thou lovedst Cassius.

BRUTUS.   Sheathe your dagger.
Be angry when you will, it shall have scope.[39]
Do what you will, dishonor shall be humor.[40]
O Cassius, you are yokèd[41] with a lamb

110 That carries anger as the flint bears fire,
Who, much enforcèd,[42] shows a hasty spark,
And straight is cold again.

CASSIUS.   Hath Cassius lived
To be but mirth and laughter to his Brutus
When grief and blood ill-tempered vexeth him?

❺
115 **BRUTUS.** When I spoke that, I was ill-tempered too.

CASSIUS. Do you confess so much? Give me your hand.

BRUTUS. And my heart too.

CASSIUS.   O Brutus!

BRUTUS.   What's the matter?

CASSIUS. Have not you love enough to bear with me
When that rash humor which my mother gave me
Makes me forgetful?

The Tragedy of Julius Caesar, Act IV, Scene iii ◆ *779*

34. alone: Only.

35. braved: Bullied.
36. Checked like a bondman: Scolded like a slave.
37. conned by rote: Memorized.

38. Pluto's mine: Mythological Roman god of the underworld and of riches symbolized by his mine.

39. scope: Free play.
40. dishonor . . . humor: Any dishonorable acts will be considered just your irritable disposition.
41. yokèd: In partnership.
42. enforcèd: Provoked.

◆ **Reading Strategy**

❹ **Read Between the Lines**
Cassius makes a dramatic gesture in this passage, offering Brutus his dagger to kill him. Ask students whether or not they believe Cassius is wholly sincere. If not, why does he make the gesture? *Students may say that both Cassius and Brutus know that the dagger will not be accepted. If Cassius thought it would, he would not have offered it. He is trying to end the argument because he needs Brutus, and he wants to take Brutus' mind off the bribery issue.*

◆ **Reading Strategy**

❺ **Read Between the Lines** You may want to point out that although this play was written almost 500 years ago, Cassius and Brutus both make use of what have become standard contemporary excuses. See if students can identify these excuses for hurting someone's feelings. *Cassius offers being "ill tempered" as an excuse (I was in a bad mood). Brutus offers the same excuse (". . . I was ill-tempered too"). Then Cassius adds that his mother gave him his "rash humor" (I can't help it; it's in my genes).*

►Critical Viewing◄

❶ Analyze Suggested answer: The two men are looking directly at each other, standing very erect, and scowling. Cassius' hand is on his dagger.

◆ Reading Strategy

❷ Read Between the Lines Ask students to venture guesses about the purpose of this passage. Why did Shakespeare include it? *Students may say that it draws Brutus and Cassius together after their argument. Now they can both take out their anger on the poet!*

◀ **Critical Viewing** How do the expressions and body language of these actors playing Brutus and Cassius indicate conflict? [Analyze] ❶

120 **BRUTUS.**   Yes, Cassius, and from henceforth,
When you are overearnest with your Brutus,
He'll think your mother chides, and leave you so.[43]

[*Enter a* POET, *followed by* LUCILIUS, TITINIUS, *and* LUCIUS.]

POET. Let me go in to see the generals;
There is some grudge between 'em; 'tis not meet
125   They be alone.

LUCILIUS. You shall not come to them.

POET. Nothing but death shall stay me.

CASSIUS. How now? What's the matter?

POET. For shame, you generals! What do you mean?
130   Love, and be friends, as two such men should be;
❷   For I have seen more years, I'm sure, than ye.

CASSIUS. Ha, ha! How vilely doth this cynic[44] rhyme!

BRUTUS. Get you hence, sirrah! Saucy fellow, hence!

CASSIUS. Bear with him, Brutus, 'tis his fashion.

135 **BRUTUS.** I'll know his humor when he knows his time.[45]
What should the wars do with these jigging[46] fools?
Companion,[47] hence!

CASSIUS.   Away, away, be gone!   [*Exit* POET.]

780 ◆ *Drama*

43. your mother . . . so: It is just your inherited disposition and let it go at that.

44. cynic: Rude fellow.

45. I'll know . . . time: I'll accept his eccentricity when he chooses a proper time to exhibit it.
46. jigging: Rhyming.
47. Companion: Fellow (used to show contempt).

 Beyond the Classroom

Career Connection
Poet Toward the end of Scene iii, a poet appears. No one seems to pay much attention to him, and we might wonder why Shakespeare, himself a poet, included this minor character.

Some students in the class may read and/or write poetry, or even aspire to becoming poets. Lead students to recognize that most poets have jobs, often as English teachers or college professors, in addition to writing poetry—at least when they start out. Encourage interested students to investigate the "second" professions of poets whom they admire. Suggest that they also investigate how a student interested in poetry writing can get training and practice, and how a beginning poet gets his or her poems published. Young poets in your class might enjoy getting together to read and discuss one another's poems. They could form a poetry club at school to lend one another support.

BRUTUS. Lucilius and Titinius, bid the commanders
Prepare to lodge their companies tonight.

CASSIUS. And come yourselves, and bring Messala with
140   you
   Immediately to us.   [*Exit* LUCILIUS *and* TITINIUS.]

BRUTUS.   Lucius, a bowl of wine. [*Exit* LUCIUS.]

❸ **CASSIUS.** I did not think you could have been so angry.

BRUTUS. O Cassius, I am sick of many griefs.

CASSIUS. Of your <u>philosophy</u> you make no use,
145   If you give place to accidental evils.[48]

BRUTUS. No man bears sorrow better. Portia is dead.

CASSIUS. Ha? Portia?

BRUTUS. She is dead.

CASSIUS. How scaped I killing when I crossed you so?[49]
150   O insupportable and touching loss!
   Upon[50] what sickness?

BRUTUS.   Impatient of my absence,
   And grief that young Octavius with Mark Antony
❹   Have made themselves so strong—for with her death
   That tidings[51] came—with this she fell distract,[52]
155   And (her attendants absent) swallowed fire.

CASSIUS. And died so?

BRUTUS.   Even so.

CASSIUS.   O ye immortal gods!
❺
[*Enter* LUCIUS, *with wine and tapers.*]

BRUTUS. Speak no more of her. Give me a bowl of wine
   In this I bury all unkindness, Cassius.   [*Drinks*]

CASSIUS. My heart is thirsty for that noble pledge.
160   Fill, Lucius, till the wine o'erswell the cup;
   I cannot drink too much of Brutus' love.

                         [*Drinks. Exit* LUCIUS.]

[*Enter* TITINIUS *and* MESSALA.]

BRUTUS. Come in, Titinius! Welcome, good Messala.
   Now sit we close about this taper here,
   And call in question[53] our necessities.

CASSIUS. Portia, art thou gone?

165 **BRUTUS.**   No more, I pray you.
   Messala, I have here receivèd letters

The Tragedy of Julius Caesar, Act IV, Scene iii ◆ 781

48. Of your philosophy . . . accidental evils: Brutus' philosophy was Stoicism. As a Stoic he believed that nothing evil would happen to a good man.

49. How scaped . . . you so?: How did I escape being killed when I opposed you so?
50. Upon: As a result of.

51. tidings: News.
52. fell distract: Became distraught.

53. call in question: Examine.

◆ **Build Vocabulary**
philosophy (fil äs´ ə fē) *n.*: System of principles or beliefs

◆ **Build Grammar Skills**
❸ **Noun Clauses** Draw students' attention to Cassius' words. Ask them to identify the noun clause and its function in the sentence. *The clause is "you could have been so angry"; it is the direct object of "did think."* You may want to point out that the relative pronoun *that* has been omitted.

❹ **Clarification** According to the Roman historian Plutarch, Portia committed suicide by swallowing burning coals.

◆ **Critical Thinking**
❺ **Compare and Contrast** Invite discussion about how this scene might have been different if Brutus had informed Cassius of Portia's death at the beginning. *Possible responses: Cassius would have been less likely to speak his mind because he would not have wanted to upset Brutus; Cassius would have blamed Brutus' anger on the death of Portia and might not have taken Brutus' insulting words seriously.*

781

1 Tell students that Cicero was a distinguished Roman orator and statesman. Because he believed in a republican form of government, he was one of the many Antony, Octavius, and Lepidus condemned to death. He was killed trying to escape from his home. (For more information on Cicero, see Cross-Curricular Connection note in Act II, p. 737.)

2 Clarification Some scholars believe that Shakespeare meant to delete either Messala's telling Brutus of Portia's death or Brutus' telling Cassius previously of her death. Otherwise, it appears that either Brutus is pretending not to know of Portia's death, or that Shakespeare made a mistake.

◆ **Reading Strategy**

3 Read Between the Lines
Suggested response: *Brutus shows little emotion in front of his friend Messala, but his reaction was quite different with Cassius. Perhaps this is because, in this passage, he really knows about her death already, and so is not shocked.*

◆ **Critical Thinking**

4 Make Inferences Students have seen Antony and Octavius putting aside personal matters to discuss matters of war. Ask students which character is like Antony and Octavius in this respect. Have them contrast Cassius with Brutus. *Brutus is able to stop thinking about his wife's death to concentrate on the impending battle ("our work alive"). Cassius says he would not be able to suppress his feelings as Brutus does (". . . my nature could not bear it so").*

That young Octavius and Mark Antony
Come down upon us with a mighty power,[54]
Bending their expedition toward Philippi.[55]

170   **MESSALA.** Myself have letters of the selfsame tenure.[56]

  BRUTUS. With what addition?

  MESSALA. That by proscription and bills of outlawry
Octavius, Antony, and Lepidus
Have put to death an hundred senators.

175   **BRUTUS.** Therein our letters do not well agree.
Mine speak of seventy senators that died
By their proscriptions, Cicero being one.

1   **CASSIUS.** Cicero one?

  MESSALA.   Cicero is dead,
And by that order of proscription.
180   Had you your letters from your wife, my lord?

  BRUTUS. No, Messala.

  MESSALA. Nor nothing in your letters writ of her?

  BRUTUS. Nothing, Messala.

  MESSALA.   That methinks is strange.

  BRUTUS. Why ask you? Hear you aught[57] of her in yours?

185   **MESSALA.** No, my lord.

  BRUTUS. Now as you are a Roman, tell me true.

2   **MESSALA.** Then like a Roman bear the truth I tell,
For certain she is dead, and by strange manner.

  BRUTUS. Why, farewell, Portia. We must die, Messala.
190   With meditating that she must die once,
I have the patience to endure it now.

  MESSALA. Even so great men great losses should endure.

  CASSIUS. I have as much of this in art[58] as you,
But yet my nature could not bear it so.

4 195   **BRUTUS.** Well, to our work alive.[59] What do you think
Of marching to Philippi presently?

  CASSIUS. I do not think it good.

  BRUTUS.   Your reason?

  CASSIUS.   This it is:
'Tis better that the enemy seek us;
So shall he waste his means, weary his soldiers,
200   Doing himself offense,[60] whilst we, lying still,

54. power: Army.
55. Bending . . . Philippi (fi lip´ī): Directing their rapid march toward Philippi.
56. selfsame tenure: Same message.

57. aught (ôt) *n.*: Anything at all.

◆ **Reading Strategy**
What can you learn about Brutus' feelings for Portia by reading between the lines? **3**

58. have . . . art: Have as much Stoicism in theory.

59. to our work alive: Let us go about the work we have to do as living men.

60. offense: Harm.

782 ◆ *Drama*

Are full of rest, defense, and nimbleness.

BRUTUS. Good reasons must of force[61] give place to
better.
The people 'twixt Philippi and this ground
Do stand but in a forced affection;[62]
205 For they have grudged us contribution.[63]
The enemy, marching along by them,
By them shall make a fuller number up,[64]
Come on refreshed, new-added[65] and encouraged;
From which advantage shall we cut him off
210 If at Philippi we do face him there,
These people at our back.

❺ CASSIUS. Hear me, good brother.

BRUTUS. Under your pardon.[66] You must note beside
That we have tried the utmost of our friends,
Our legions are brimful, our cause is ripe.
215 The enemy increaseth every day;
We, at the height, are ready to decline.
There is a tide in the affairs of men
Which, taken at the flood, leads on to fortune;
Omitted,[67] all the voyage of their life
220 Is bound[68] in shallows and in miseries.
On such a full sea are we now afloat,
And we must take the current when it serves,
Or lose our ventures.

❻ CASSIUS. Then, with your will,[69] go on;
We'll along ourselves and meet them at Philippi.

225 **BRUTUS.** The deep of night is crept upon our talk,
And nature must obey necessity,
Which we will niggard with a little rest.[70]
There is no more to say?

CASSIUS. No more. Good night.
Early tomorrow will we rise and hence.[71]

[*Enter* LUCIUS.]

BRUTUS. Lucius, my gown.[72] [*Exit* LUCIUS.]
230 Farewell, good Messala.
Good night, Titinius. Noble, noble Cassius,
Good night, and good repose.

CASSIUS. O my dear brother,
This was an ill beginning of the night.
Never come[73] such division 'tween our souls!
Let it not, Brutus.

[*Enter* LUCIUS, *with the gown.*]

The Tragedy of Julius Caesar, Act IV, Scene iii ◆ *783*

61. of force: Of necessity.

**62. Do stand . . .
affection:** Support us only
by fear of force.
63. grudged us contribution: Given us aid and
supplies grudgingly.
64. shall make . . . up:
Will add more to their
numbers.
65. new-added:
Reinforced.

66. Under your pardon:
Excuse me.

67. Omitted: Neglected.
68. bound: Confined.

69. with your will:
As you wish.

70. niggard . . . rest:
Satisfy stingily with a short
sleep.

71. hence: Leave.

72. gown: Nightgown.

73. Never come: May
there never come.

**Customize for
*Less Proficient Readers***
❺ Help these students summarize
Cassius' plan for battle, and then
Brutus' plan. *Cassius suggests that they
should stay where they are and be fresh
for battle, while the enemy will be tired
from marching. Brutus thinks they
should march to Philippi because the
enemy may pick up more forces as they
are on the march.* Encourage discussion about which plan is best. Direct
them to lines 223–224 to find out
which plan will be adopted.

◆ **Reading Strategy**
❻ **Read Between the Lines**
Encourage students to find out what
they can determine about the relationship between Cassius and Brutus
by reading between the lines as they
argue their points about different battle strategies. *Students might say that,
because Cassius gives in to Brutus, Brutus
has more power in the relationship.*

◆ **Workplace Skills Mini-Lesson**

Providing Input for Decisions
Introduce the Concept Refer students
to Brutus' and Cassius' conversation about
the merits of attacking at Philippi or waiting
to be attacked (on this page). Draw attention to the manner in which each man presents his points for consideration.

Develop Background Let students know
that the more responsible a person's job,

the more she or he will be asked to express
opinions that will affect important decisions.
Discuss ways to express opinions in such a
situation. Lead students to consider these
points:
• When stating an opinion, always have
  strong reasons that support the opinion.
• Speak in a respectful and rational tone of
  voice.

Apply the Information Present this scenario: You work for a small store. Your boss
tells you she is considering opening on
Sundays. She asks for your opinion. Have
students work in small groups to provide
imput into the decision.

Assess the Outcome Students should
evaluate one another on the strength of
their opinion, supporting facts, and tone.

❶ **Read Between the Lines** This
passage reveals the complexity of
Brutus' personality. Have students
explain the complexity. *Only a short
time ago, Brutus was the man who
could put his wife's death out of his
mind to discuss a battle plan. In this
passage, we see a kinder, gentler side of
Brutus' personality.*

Customize for
Less Proficient Readers
These students may benefit from acting out portions of these scenes with
students taking individual parts. Use
the **Strategies for Diverse Student
Needs** page on Preparing a Reader's
Theater, p. 53, to assist these students in preparing.

Customize for
More Advanced Students
Have these students improvise a
monologue or write a journal entry
that captures Brutus' thoughts and
feelings at this point in the play.
Encourage students to reference
details from the play that affect his
situation and his feelings about it.

235 **BRUTUS.**   Everything is well.

CASSIUS. Good night, my lord.

BRUTUS.   Good night, good brother.

TITINIUS, MESSALA. Good night, Lord Brutus.

BRUTUS.   Farewell, every one.

[*Exit*]

Give me the gown. Where is thy instrument?[74]

LUCIUS. Here in the tent.

BRUTUS.   What, thou speak'st drowsily?
❶ 240   Poor knave,[75] I blame thee not; thou art
o'erwatched.[76]
Call Claudius and some other of my men;
I'll have them sleep on cushions in my tent.

LUCIUS. Varro and Claudius!

[*Enter* VARRO *and* CLAUDIUS.]

VARRO. Calls my lord?

245 **BRUTUS.** I pray you, sirs, lie in my tent and sleep.
It may be I shall raise[77] you by and by
On business to my brother Cassius.

VARRO. So please you, we will stand and watch your
pleasure.

250 **BRUTUS.** I will not have it so; lie down, good sirs;
It may be I shall otherwise bethink me.[78]

[VARRO *and* CLAUDIUS *lie down.*]

Look. Lucius, here's the book I sought for so;
I put it in the pocket of my gown.

LUCIUS. I was sure your lordship did not give it me.

BRUTUS. Bear with me, good boy, I am much forgetful.
255   Canst thou hold up thy heavy eyes awhile,
And touch[79] thy instrument a strain or two?

LUCIUS. Ay, my lord, an't[80] please you.

BRUTUS.   It does, my boy.
I trouble thee too much, but thou art willing.

LUCIUS. It is my duty, sir.

260 **BRUTUS.** I should not urge thy duty past thy might;
I know young bloods[81] look for a time of rest.

74. instrument: Lute
(probably).

75. knave (nāv) *n.*:
Servant.
76. o'erwatched: Weary
with too much
watchfulness.

77. raise: Wake.

**78. otherwise bethink
me:** Change my mind.

79. touch: Play.

80. an't: If it.

81. young bloods: Young
bodies.

LUCIUS. I have slept, my lord, already.

BRUTUS. It was well done, and thou shalt sleep again;
I will not hold thee long. If I do live,
265   I will be good to thee.

[*Music, and a song*]

This is a sleepy tune. O murd'rous[82] slumber!
Layest thou thy leaden mace[83] upon my boy,
That plays thee music? Gentle knave, good night;
I will not do thee so much wrong to wake thee.
270   If thou dost nod, thou break'st thy instrument;
I'll take it from thee; and, good boy, good night.
Let me see, let me see; is not the leaf[84] turned down
Where I left reading? Here it is, I think.

[*Enter the* GHOST OF CAESAR.]

❷ | How ill this taper burns. Ha! Who comes here?
275   I think it is the weakness of mine eyes
That shapes this monstrous apparition.[85]
It comes upon[86] me. Art thou anything?
Art thou some god, some angel, or some devil,
That mak'st my blood cold, and my hair to stare?[87]
280   Speak to me what thou art.

GHOST. Thy evil spirit, Brutus.

BRUTUS.   Why com'st thou?

GHOST. To tell thee thou shalt see me at Philippi.

BRUTUS. Well; then I shall see thee again?

GHOST. Ay, at Philippi.

285   **BRUTUS.** Why, I will see thee at Philippi then.
❸
                         [*Exit* GHOST.]

Now I have taken heart thou vanishest.
Ill spirit, I would hold more talk with thee.
Boy! Lucius! Varro! Claudius! Sirs, awake!
Claudius!

290   **LUCIUS.** The strings, my lord, are false.[88]

BRUTUS. He thinks he still is at his instrument.
Lucius, awake!

LUCIUS. My lord?

BRUTUS. Didst thou dream, Lucius, that thou so criedst
out?

---

82. murd'rous: Deathlike.

83. mace (mās) *n.*: Staff of office (an allusion to the practice of tapping a person on the shoulder with a mace when arresting him).

84. leaf: Page.

85. monstrous apparition: Ominous ghost.
86. upon: Toward.

87. stare: Stand on end.

◆ **Reading Strategy**
What warning can you discover by reading between the lines?

---

88. false: Out of tune.

The Tragedy of Julius Caesar, Act IV, Scene iii ◆ 785

---

❷ **Clarification** Brutus remarks that the candle burns "ill." Explain that candles were thought to dim in the presence of ghosts.

◆ **Critical Thinking**

❸ **Make Inferences** The ghost of Caesar appears to Brutus. Ask: Why does the ghost appear to Brutus? Do you think that Brutus understands the ghost's message? *The ghost is telling Brutus that disaster awaits him at Philippi. Students may suggest that Brutus does not understand the message at first because his response ("Why, I will see thee at Philippi then") seems matter-of-fact. When the ghost vanishes, Brutus realizes that he should have asked for an explanation.*

Customize for
Visual/Spatial Learners
Encourage these students to consider how best to represent the ghost on stage. Invite them to share their ideas with classmates.

Beyond the Classroom

Career Connection
Music Careers Students who are interested in careers in music should explore the many "backstage" roles in the industry. Sound technicians, electricians, agents, business managers, and others who perform behind the scenes are able to work in an exciting field that interests them, even if they can't sing or play an instrument. Have interested students do research and create a chart showing the many opportunities available in the music industry.

Political Science The events in this play give a negative view of politics and politicians. Point out to students, however, that many people seek public office to do good—to change policy or improve the quality of life in their area. Under our system of government, however, these people can't just take an office; they must be elected or appointed. Have students do research to find the political positions available at the local, state, and national level. Follow up with the Career Connection: Political Science, p. 53, in *Beyond Literature*.

Answers

◆ *Literature and Your Life*

Reader's Response Ask students if there is anything about either man that elicits sympathy. Is either one kind, considerate, compassionate, merciful, or worthy of sympathy?

Thematic Focus Example: Brutus will most likely die.

☑ **Check Your Comprehension**

1. Antony, Octavius, and Lepidus are in control of Rome after the death of Caesar. Antony is the oldest and the stongest personality; Octavius is his right-hand man; Lepidus is only fit for running errands.
2. Cassius is angry because Brutus has condemned Lucius Pella. Cassius defends himself by telling Brutus to kill him, thus putting himself at Brutus' mercy.
3. Portia committed suicide. Brutus accepts her death fatalistically, but Cassius expresses grief.
4. The candle dims, and the ghost of Julius Caesar appears and speaks to Brutus. Brutus speaks with the ghost and asks it not to leave because he wants to talk to it more.

◆ **Critical Thinking**

1. The argument between Brutus and Cassius is much more emotional in tone than the argument between Octavius and Antony.
2. Brutus may not want Cassius' pity to cloud their discussion, or he may not want to let Cassius know that he is mourning and potentially more vulnerable than usual.
3. The ghost of Caesar is portending the death of Brutus.
4. Students should base their predictions on events that have occurred so far as well as on character traits.
5. Although students may not agree with the actions of each character, they may be able to recognize the leadership qualities in each. Have students explain the qualities that led them to make their choice.

---

295   LUCIUS. My lord, I do not know that I did cry.

     BRUTUS. Yes, that thou didst. Didst thou see anything?

     LUCIUS. Nothing, my lord.

     BRUTUS. Sleep again, Lucius. Sirrah Claudius!
     [*To* VARRO] Fellow thou, awake!

300   VARRO. My lord?

     CLAUDIUS. My lord?

     BOTH. Why did you so cry out, sirs, in your sleep?

     BRUTUS. Did we, my lord?

     BRUTUS.   Ay. Saw you anything?

     VARRO. No, my lord, I saw nothing.

     CLAUDIUS.   Nor I, my lord.

305   BRUTUS. Go and commend me[89] to my brother Cassius;
     Bid him set on his pow'rs betimes before,[90]
     And we will follow.

     BOTH.   It shall be done, my lord.   [*Exit*]

89. commend me: Carry my greetings.
90. set on . . . before: Advance his troops.

Guide for Responding

◆ *Literature and Your Life*

Reader's Response With whom do you sympathize more in Act IV—Brutus or Cassius? Why?
Thematic Focus What consequences do you think Brutus will face for the choices he has made?

☑ **Check Your Comprehension**

1. What three men rule Rome after Caesar's death? Describe each of them.
2. What is the immediate cause of the quarrel between Brutus and Cassius? How does Cassius defend himself?
3. How does Portia die? Describe Brutus' and Cassius' reactions to the death.
4. What supernatural event occurs at the end of the act? Describe Brutus' reaction to the event.

786 ◆ Drama

◆ **Critical Thinking**

INTERPRET

1. How is the argument between Brutus and Cassius different from the one between Octavius and Antony in Scene i? **[Contrast]**
2. Why do you think Brutus delays telling Cassius of Portia's death? **[Infer]**
3. What does the ghost mean when he says to Brutus, "Thou shalt see me at Philippi"? **[Draw Conclusions]**
4. Who do you think will be the victor in the upcoming battle? Explain. **[Speculate]**

EVALUATE

5. Which character in this act do you feel would make the best leader for Rome? Explain. **[Assess]**

☑ **ASSESSMENT OPTIONS**

Formal Assessment, Selection Test, pp. 185–187, and Assessment Resources Software. The selection test is designed so that it can be easily customized to the ability levels of your students.

PORTFOLIO ASSESSMENT
Use the following rubrics in *Alternative Assessment* to assess student writing.
Character Profile: Description Rubric, p. 97
Rewrite a Scene: Drama Rubric, p. 109

Guide for Responding (continued)

◆ Reading Strategy

READ BETWEEN THE LINES

Shakespeare provides clues that indicate a deeper meaning to some lines—but you have to **read between the lines** to find the clues.

For instance, in the middle of the act, when Brutus and Cassius are arguing, Brutus says, "Remember March, the ides of March remember." What he is really referring to is the assassination of Caesar, though he does not say so explicitly in this line.

1. In Scene iii, Brutus says to Cassius, "You yourself / Are much condemned to have an itching palm, / To sell and mart your offices for gold / To undeservers." What is Brutus saying about Cassius' character?

2. By reading between the lines of the conversations between Brutus and Cassius, what hints can you find that they will probably be defeated at Philippi?

◆ Build Vocabulary

USING THE ROOT -*phil*-

The root -*phil*- means "love," and is a common root of English words. On your paper, write the word with the root -*phil*- that correctly completes each sentence.

1. _____?_____ could be called a "love of wisdom."
2. A _____?_____ is a person who donates money to one or more charitable organizations.
3. _____?_____ is a city whose name means "city of brotherly love."

USING THE WORD BANK

Copy the following sentences into your notebook, and complete each sentence with a word from the Word Bank.

1. In an atmosphere of suspicion, Antony and Octavius make _____?_____ plans.
2. Cassius denies the _____?_____ accusations that Brutus reports have been made against Cassius.
3. Antony requests to see Caesar's will to begin sorting and carrying out Caesar's _____?_____.
4. Stoicism was the _____?_____ Brutus followed.
5. Brutus' _____?_____ of Cassius for allowing bribery leads to a bitter argument.

◆ Literary Focus

CONFLICT IN DRAMA

As Brutus and Cassius prepare for battle, it becomes increasingly clear that their efforts are doomed. The outcome of the battle will resolve the **conflict** between the two political forces.

1. What have you known about Cassius that Brutus just begins to realize in this act?
2. How does the conflict between Cassius and Brutus heighten the tension of the larger conflict to come?

◆ Build Grammar Skills

NOUN CLAUSES

A **noun clause** is a subordinate clause used as a noun. It can function as a subject, predicate noun, direct object, indirect object, or object of a preposition.

Practice On your paper write these sentences and underline the noun clause in each one. Then identify its function in the sentence.

1. Brutus says that he is Caesar's friend.
2. What he does is shocking to Caesar.
3. Do what you will.
4. You must note beside / That we have tried the utmost of our friends.

Idea Bank

Writing

1. **Character Profile** Write a profile of Brutus as if for a magazine-style news program. Include interviews with friends, "coworkers," and family members.

2. **Rewrite a Scene** Write another scene for Act IV, in which Portia's ghost confronts Brutus.

Speaking and Listening

3. **Musical Score** With a partner, choose background music for the quarrel between Brutus and Cassius in Scene iii. Play the music while you read the scene aloud for the class. [**Music Link**]

◆ Reading Strategy

1. He is saying that Cassius has a reputation for taking bribes. Students might read between the lines that Brutus is inclined to believe what he has heard.

2. The unstated message that students can read between the lines is that the public doesn't support the two men, that each of the men has doubts about their ability to succeed, that the men have doubts about each other that will make it difficult for them to present a united front.

◆ Build Vocabulary

Using the Root -*phil*-

1. Philosophy could be called a love of wisdom.
2. A philanthropist is a person who donates money to one or more charitable organizations.
3. Philadelphia is a city whose name means "city of brotherly love."

Using the Word Bank

1. covert
2. slanderous
3. legacies
4. philosophy
5. chastisement

◆ Literary Focus

1. Students probably recognized long before Brutus did that Cassius is not noble; he is a devious man motivated by self-promotion and preservation.

2. The conflict between Cassius and Brutus heightens the sense that everything is falling apart. Even the conspirators are fighting with one another.

◆ Build Grammar Skills

1. that he is Caesar's friend: direct object
2. What he does: subject
3. What you will: direct object
4. That we have tried: direct object

Idea Bank

Customizing for
Learning Modalities

The following suggestions will help you match Idea Bank topics to your students' learning modalities:

Musical Rhythmic: 3
Verbal/Linguisitic: 1, 2
Interpersonal: 1

Customizing for
Performance Levels

Following are suggestions for matching Idea Bank topics with your students' performance levels:

Less Advanced: 1, 3
Average: 1, 2, 3
More Advanced: 2

Guide for Reading, Act V

OBJECTIVES

1. To read, comprehend, and interpret a drama
2. To relate a drama to personal experience
3. To identify cause-and-effect relationships
4. To identify the characteristics of tragedy
5. To build vocabulary in context and learn the prefix -mis
6. To use and correctly punctuate words of direct address
7. To write a speech making use of connotations
8. To respond to the play through writing, speaking and listening, and projects

SKILLS INSTRUCTION

Vocabulary:
Prefixes: -mis

Grammar: Words of Direct Address

Reading Strategy: Identify Cause and Effect

Literary Focus: Tragedy

Writing: Connotation

Speaking and Listening: Respond to Shakespearean English; Sound Effects (teacher edition)

Critical Viewing: Analyze

PORTFOLIO OPPORTUNITIES

Writing: Epitaph; Response; Take a Side
Writing Mini-Lesson: Speech
Speaking and Listening: Sound Effects; Respond to Shakespearean English
Projects: Model of the Globe; Elizabethan Faire

Interest Grabber

Write on the chalkboard the following headings for three columns: "Good Guys," "Bad Guys," and "Undecided." With the class, go through the cast of characters on page and decide under which heading to write each character's name. After they read Act V, students may be able to reclassify the characters in the "Undecided" column, or they may decide to leave several names in that column. Discuss why some characters are difficult to classify.

Tell students they are now coming to the climax of the play—the final act. Which side do they predict will win the battle? What do they think will happen to the central characters, Brutus, Cassius, and Antony?

◆ Review and Anticipate

In Act IV, the alliance between Brutus and Cassius begins to fall apart. Brutus accuses Cassius of accepting bribes, and Cassius criticizes Brutus' abilities as a leader in war. After they resolve their differences, Brutus is visited by Caesar's ghost, who promises he will see him at Philippi.

Act V opens on the plains of Philippi with the armies of Octavius and Antony amassed against those of Brutus and Cassius. As the defenders of Caesar's legacy prepare to battle his assassins, nothing less than the future of Rome is at stake.

◆ Literary Focus

TRAGEDY

Tragedy is a dramatic form that was first defined around 330 B.C. by the Greek philosopher Aristotle. The main character in a tragedy is involved in a struggle that ends in disaster. This character is always a person of high rank whose ruin is caused by a tragic flaw or weakness. The tragic flaw may be excessive ambition, pride, jealousy, or some other common human frailty. The flaw inevitably leads to the character's downfall. As this play unfolds, Brutus' blindness to the true motives of the other conspirators leads him into disastrous alliances and actions. His downfall is tragic because he is a noble man (as stated by Antony at the end of this act) who did the wrong thing for the right reason.

◆ Build Grammar Skills

WORDS OF DIRECT ADDRESS

Dialogue is the backbone of any drama: With the exceptions of asides and soliloquies, the characters are always speaking to one another. When the playwright wants to emphasize to whom a character is speaking, he or she will set off these **words of direct address** with commas and occasionally an exclamation point. Look at these examples from Act V:

> Now, *Antony,* our hopes are answered . . .

> Stand fast, *Titinius,* we must out and talk . . .

> *Villains!* You did not do so, when your vile daggers / Hacked . . .

Notice the words of direct address that clarify to whom a character is speaking.

788 ◆ Drama

◆ Reading Strategy

IDENTIFY CAUSE AND EFFECT

Dramatic situations have both causes and effects. A **cause** is what makes something occur; an **effect** is the result. Plays are carefully constructed with a chain of causes and effects that lead to the final tragic outcome.

Caesar's actions, which Brutus perceives as showing too much ambition, are the cause of Brutus' decision to join the conspiracy. The effect is Caesar's death.

You can track interlocking causes and effects in *The Tragedy of Julius Caesar* with a graphic organizer like the following:

◆ Build Vocabulary

PREFIXES: mis-

In this act you will encounter the word *misconstrue*. *Misconstrue* contains the prefix *mis-,* which means "wrong" or "bad." *Misconstrue* means "make the wrong interpretation."

WORD BANK

Before you read, preview this list of words from Act V.

presage
ensign
consorted
demeanor
disconsolate
misconstrued
envy

 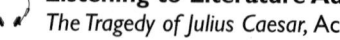

The Tragedy of
JULIUS CAESAR

William Shakespeare

Act V

Scene i. *The plains of Philippi.*

[*Enter* OCTAVIUS, ANTONY, *and their Army.*]

❶

OCTAVIUS. Now, Antony, our hopes are answerèd;
You said the enemy would not come down,
But keep the hills and upper regions.
It proves not so; their battles¹ are at hand;
5 They mean to warn² us at Philippi here,
Answering before we do demand of them.³

ANTONY. Tut, I am in their bosoms,⁴ and I know
Wherefore⁵ they do it. They could be content
To visit other places, and come down
10 With fearful bravery,⁶ thinking by this face⁷
To fasten in our thoughts⁸ that they have courage;
But 'tis not so.

1. **battles:** Armies.
2. **warn:** Challenge.
3. **Answering . . . of them:** Appearing in opposition to us before we challenge them.
4. **am in their bosoms:** Know what they are thinking.
5. **Wherefore:** Why.
6. **fearful bravery:** Awesome show of bravery covering up their fear.
7. **face:** Appearance.
8. **fasten in our thoughts:** Convince us.

❷ ▼ **Critical Viewing** What details in this sculpture indicate that the subjects are preparing for battle? [**Analyze**]

Relief of Domitius Ahenobarbus, Louvre, Paris, France

The Tragedy of Julius Caesar, Act V, Scene i ◆ *789*

Develop Understanding

One-Minute Insight Act V of *Julius Caesar* resolves the conflict between the triumvirate (Octavius Caesar, Antony, and Lepidus) and Brutus and Cassius at the battle of Philippi. Although his tragic flaw—poor judgment—leads to his downfall, Brutus maintains his nobility and courage to the end.

Customize for
Less Proficient Readers
Many new minor characters are introduced in this final act. Keeping all the names straight may be challenging for these students. Suggest that they make an alphabetical "Cast of Characters" to keep as they read.

Customize for
English Language Learners
Have these students listen to Act V on the **Listening to Literature Audiocassettes** as they follow along in the text. Help them summarize the action in each scene.

◆ Critical Thinking

❶ Make Judgments Based on this passage, who do students now think was right about the plan of attack—Cassius or Brutus? How do students think the battle will turn out? *Because Octavius says "our hopes are answered," and Antony says that he knows what Cassius and Brutus are thinking, one can assume that Brutus' plan—the one they adopted—was wrong. Antony and Octavius will probably win the battle.*

▶**Critical Viewing**◀
❷ Analyze Suggested response: The shields, swords, armor, and helmets suggest preparation for battle.

 Preparing for Standardized Tests

Reading and Vocabulary In the critical reading portions of many standardized tests, students are asked to read a passage and answer questions about what they have read. The relationships between ideas are not always stated in the passage; students must make the connections through inference, deduction, and other critical reading strategies. For instance, after reading a passage about *The Tragedy of Julius Caesar,* students may be asked to answer a question like the following:

The most significant factors contributing to the conspirators downfall were (B)
(A) The defeat of Pompey and Caesar's ambition
(B) Antony's influence over the crowds and Antony's alliance with Octavius
(C) The crowd's fickleness and Cassius' lean and hungry look
(D) Brutus' alliance with Cassius and Cassius' lean and hungry look

The correct answer is B. The other details, though accurately drawn from the play, do not have a significant cause-and-effect relationship with the conspirators' downfall.

Practice in identifying cause-and-effect relationships will help students improve their performance on Critical Reading and Reading Comprehension test items. For further instruction and practice, use the Reading Strategy page on Cause and Effect in *Selection Support,* p. 222.

Build Grammar Skills

❶ Words of Direct Address Ask students: To whom is the messenger speaking? How do you know? *The messenger is addressing the generals. Readers know this because the word "generals," set off by commas, is included in the sentence.*

Literary Focus

❷ Tragedy Sample answer: Brutus' words are tragic because he did not use words with Caesar; Antony heightens the tragedy by reminding Brutus how Caesar trusted his loving and loyal words.

Critical Thinking

❸ Infer Discuss with the class how Antony feels toward Brutus and why he feel this way. *Anthony is angry with Brutus for his part in assassinating Caesar. He points out the fatal hypocrisy of Brutus, who appeared to honor Caesar right up to the moment he stabbed him.*

[*Enter a* MESSENGER.]

❶ MESSENGER.   Prepare you, generals,
The enemy comes on in gallant show;
Their bloody sign[9] of battle is hung out,
15   And something to be done immediately.

ANTONY. Octavius, lead your battle softly[10] on
Upon the left hand of the even[11] field.

OCTAVIUS. Upon the right hand I; keep thou the left.

ANTONY. Why do you cross me in this exigent?[12]

20   **OCTAVIUS.** I do not cross you; but I will do so.   [*March*]

[*Drum. Enter* BRUTUS, CASSIUS, *and their Army;*
LUCILIUS, TITINIUS, MESSALA, *and others.*]

BRUTUS. They stand, and would have parley.[13]

CASSIUS. Stand fast, Titinius, we must out and talk.

OCTAVIUS. Mark Antony, shall we give sign of battle?

ANTONY. No, Caesar, we will answer on their charge.[14]
25   Make forth;[15] the generals would have some words.

OCTAVIUS. Stir not until the signal.

BRUTUS. Words before blows; is it so, countrymen?

OCTAVIUS. Not that we love words better, as you do.

BRUTUS. Good words are better than bad strokes, Octavius.

❸ ANTONY. In your bad strokes, Brutus, you give good
30   words;
Witness the hole you made in Caesar's heart,
Crying "Long live! Hail, Caesar!"

CASSIUS.   Antony,
The posture[16] of your blows are yet unknown;
But for your words, they rob the Hybla bees,[17]
And leave them honeyless.

35   **ANTONY.**   Not stingless too.

BRUTUS. O, yes, and soundless too;
For you have stol'n their buzzing, Antony,
And very wisely threat before you sting.

ANTONY. Villains! You did not so, when your vile daggers
40   Hacked one another in the sides of Caesar.
You showed your teeth[18] like apes, and fawned like hounds,

9. **bloody sign:** Red flag.

10. **softly:** Slowly.
11. **even:** Level.

12. **exigent:** Critical situation.

13. **parley:** Conference between enemies.

14. **answer on their charge:** Meet their advance.
15. **Make forth:** Go forward.

◆ Literary Focus
Why are Brutus' words in line 29 tragic? How does Antony's reply highlight the tragedy? **❷**

16. **posture:** Quality.
17. **Hybla bees:** Bees, from the town of Hybla in Sicily, noted for their sweet honey.

18. **showed your teeth:** Grinned.

790 ◆ Drama

Block Scheduling Strategies

Consider these suggestions to take advantage of extended class time:

- Treat students to readings from Shakespeare's sonnets and plays included in Feature 3 on the CD-ROM *The Time, Life, and Works of Shakespeare.*
- Have students research Shakespeare on the Internet either before or after they complete the play. See pages 707 and 800 for an Internet address they can access.

- Students can pair up to complete the Build Grammar Skills lesson on page 802.
- A group can listen to all or part of this act on the audiocassette. Suggest that students discuss how hearing the play performed affected their appreciation and their ability to follow the language of the play.

790

And bowed like bondmen, kissing Caesar's feet;
Whilst damnèd Casca, like a cur, behind
Struck Caesar on the neck. O you flatterers!

45 **CASSIUS.** Flatterers! Now, Brutus, thank yourself;
This tongue had not offended so today,
If Cassius might have ruled.[19]

OCTAVIUS. Come, come, the cause.[20] If arguing make us
sweat,
The proof[21] of it will turn to redder drops.

50 Look,
I draw a sword against conspirators.
When think you that the sword goes up[22] again?
Never, till Caesar's three and thirty wounds
Be well avenged; or till another Caesar

55 Have added slaughter to the sword of traitors.[23]

BRUTUS. Caesar, thou canst not die by traitors' hands,
Unless thou bring'st them with thee.

OCTAVIUS.   So I hope.
I was not born to die on Brutus' sword.

BRUTUS. O, if thou wert the noblest of thy strain,[24]

60 Young man, thou couldst not die more honorable.

CASSIUS. A peevish[25] schoolboy, worthless of such
honor,
Joined with a masker and a reveler.[26]

ANTONY. Old Cassius still!

OCTAVIUS.   Come, Antony; away!
Defiance, traitors, hurl we in your teeth.

65 If you dare fight today, come to the field;
If not, when you have stomachs.[27]

[*Exit* OCTAVIUS, ANTONY, *and Army.*]

CASSIUS. Why, now blow wind, swell billow, and swim
bark![28]
The storm is up, and all is on the hazard.[29]

BRUTUS. Ho, Lucilius, hark, a word with you.

[LUCILIUS *and* MESSALA *stand forth.*]

LUCILIUS.   My lord?

[BRUTUS *and* LUCILIUS *converse apart.*]

CASSIUS. Messala.

MESSALA.   What says my general?

19. **If Cassius might have ruled:** If Cassius had had his way when he urged that Antony be killed.
20. **cause:** Business at hand.
21. **proof:** Test.

22. **goes up:** Goes into its scabbard.

23. **till another Caesar . . . traitors:** Until I, another Caesar, have also been killed by you.

24. **noblest of thy strain:** Best of your family.

25. **peevish:** Silly.

26. **a masker and a reveler:** One who takes part in masquerades and festivities.

27. **stomachs:** Appetites for battle.

28. **bark:** Ship.
29. **on the hazard:** At stake.

◆ **Reading Strategy**

❹ **Identify Cause and Effect**
Recall with students Brutus' earlier decision not to kill Antony as well as Caesar. Invite them to conjecture how the opposite decision would have changed the course of events. *The effect of not killing Antony is the battle that is about to be fought. If the conspirators had gotten Antony out of the way, they may have "gotten away" with killing Caesar.*

◆ **Literary Focus**

❺ **Tragedy** Lead students to contrast Brutus with Cassius. What difference in their personalities led Cassius to suggest killing Antony, while Brutus would not agree? Why is Brutus considered a tragic hero, but not Cassius? *By contrast with Cassius, Brutus is more honorable and noble, and therefore more tragic. Brutus' acceptance of Cassius is a sign of Brutus' tragic flaw—he is blind to Cassius' envious and self-serving nature.*

Comprehension Check ☑

❻ What does Octavius mean by these lines? *"Let's get to the point. If arguing makes us sweat, fighting it out will make us bleed."*

◆ **Literary Focus**

❼ **Tragedy** Help students understand the significance of these lines, in which Brutus says that Octavius cannot be killed by a traitor because neither Brutus nor Cassius is a traitor. Discuss with students why Shakespeare keeps reminding readers that Brutus does not consider himself a traitor. *If Brutus had killed Caesar for any other but a patriotic reason, he would not stand up as a tragic hero. He would be a traitor and a murderer.*

Customize for
English Language Learners

❶ Guide students to see that Cassius is using metaphors—literary comparisons—to suggest the fierce battle to come. Be sure students understand that his words are not to be taken literally. Students may wish to share some metaphors or idioms from their native languages.

◆ Reading Strategy

❷ Identify Cause and Effect
Sample answer: Cassius is nervous because he has seen a bad omen. Students may suggest that the effects of his nervousness include his conflict with Brutus and a potentially poor performance on the battlefield.

◆ Build Grammar Skills

❸ Words of Direct Address Ask students: To whom is Cassius speaking? How do the commas help you know how to read the lines aloud?
Cassius is speaking to Brutus. The commas signal a pause before and after "most noble Brutus."

❹ Clarification Explain that Brutus is saying he does not believe in taking his own life, rather than waiting for death as ordained by fate. However, if the only alternative is to walk back to Rome as a captive, he would take his life.

❺ Clarification Explain that Cato (Portia's father) was on Pompey's side during the civil war between Caesar and Pompey. Cato committed suicide at the battle of Utica in 46 B.C. rather than fall into captivity.

70

CASSIUS.   Messala,
This is my birthday; as this very day
Was Cassius born. Give me thy hand, Messala:
Be thou my witness that against my will
(As Pompey was)[30] am I compelled to set[31]

75
Upon one battle all our liberties.
You know that I held Epicurus strong,[32]
And his opinion; now I change my mind.
And partly credit things that do presage.

❶ Coming from Sardis, on our former[33] ensign

80
Two mighty eagles fell,[34] and there they perched,
Gorging and feeding from our soldiers' hands,
Who to Philippi here consorted us.
This morning are they fled away and gone,
And in their steads do ravens, crows, and kites[35]

85
Fly o'er our heads and downward look on us
As we were sickly prey; their shadows seem
A canopy most fatal,[36] under which
Our army lies, ready to give up the ghost.

MESSALA. Believe not so.

CASSIUS.   I but believe it partly,

90
For I am fresh of spirit and resolved
To meet all perils very constantly.[37]

BRUTUS. Even so, Lucilius.

CASSIUS.   Now, most noble Brutus,

❸
The gods today stand friendly, that we may,
Lovers in peace, lead on our days to age!

95
But since the affairs of men rest still incertain,[38]
Let's reason with the worst that may befall.[39]
If we do lose this battle, then is this
The very last time we shall speak together.
What are you then determinèd to do?

100
BRUTUS. Even by the rule of that philosophy
By which I did blame Cato for the death
Which he did give himself; I know not how,

❹
But I do find it cowardly and vile,

❺
For fear of what might fall, so to prevent

105
The time of life,[40] arming myself with patience
To stay the providence[41] of some high powers
That govern us below.

CASSIUS.   Then, if we lose this battle,
You are contented to be led in triumph[42]
Thorough[43] the streets of Rome?

110
BRUTUS. No, Cassius, no; think not, thou noble Roman,

---

30. As Pompey was: Against his own judgment, Pompey was urged to do battle against Caesar. The battle resulted in Pompey's defeat and murder.
31. set: Stake.
32. held Epicurus strong: Believed in Epicurus' philosophy that the gods do not interest themselves in human affairs and that omens are merely superstitions.
33. former: Foremost.
34. fell: Swooped down.

◆ Reading Strategy
What is the cause of Cassius' nervousness? What might its effect be? **❷**

---

35. ravens . . . kites: Birds that are bad omens.
36. A canopy most fatal: A rooflike covering foretelling death.
37. very constantly: Most resolutely.
38. rest still incertain: Always remain uncertain.
39. befall: Happen.

40. so to prevent . . . life: Thus to anticipate the natural end of life.
41. stay the providence: Await the ordained fate.

42. in triumph: As a captive in the victor's procession.
43. Thorough: Through.

---

792 ◆ *Drama*

792

That ever Brutus will go bound to Rome;
He bears too great a mind. But this same day
Must end that work the ides of March begun;
And whether we shall meet again I know not.

115   Therefore our everlasting farewell take.
Forever, and forever, farewell, Cassius!
If we do meet again, why, we shall smile;
If not, why then this parting was well made.

    CASSIUS. Forever, and forever, farewell, Brutus!

120   If we do meet again, we'll smile indeed;
If not, 'tis true this parting was well made.

    BRUTUS. Why then, lead on. O, that a man might know
The end of this day's business ere it come!
But it sufficeth that the day will end,

125   And then the end is known. Come, ho! Away!   [*Exit*]

Scene ii. *The field of battle.*

[*Call to arms sounds. Enter* BRUTUS *and* MESSALA.]

    BRUTUS. Ride, ride, Messala, ride, and give these bills[1]
Unto the legions on the other side.[2]

                              [*Loud call to arms*]

Let them set on at once; for I perceive
But cold <u>demeanor</u>[3] in Octavius' wing,

5   And sudden push gives them the overthrow,[4]
Ride, ride, Messala! Let them all come down.[5]   [*Exit*]

Scene iii. *The field of battle.*

[*Calls to arms sound. Enter* CASSIUS *and* TITINIUS.]

    CASSIUS. O, look, Titinius, look, the villains[1] fly!
Myself have to mine own turned enemy.[2]
This ensign here of mine was turning back;
I slew the coward, and did take it[3] from him.

5   **TITINIUS.** O Cassius, Brutus gave the word too early,
Who, having some advantage on Octavius,
Took it too eagerly; his soldiers fell to spoil,[4]
Whilst we by Antony are all enclosed.

[*Enter* PINDARUS.]

    PINDARUS. Fly further off, my lord, fly further off!

10   Mark Antony is in your tents, my lord.
Fly, therefore, noble Cassius, fly far off!

    CASSIUS. This hill is far enough. Look, look, Titinius!
Are those my tents where I perceive the fire?

    TITINIUS. They are, my lord.

1. bills: Written orders.
2. other side: Wing of the army commanded by Cassius.

3. cold demeanor: (di mēn´ ər): Lack of spirit in their conduct.
4. sudden push . . . overthrow: Sudden attack will defeat them.
5. Let . . . down: Attack all at once.

1. villains: His own men.
2. Myself . . . enemy: I have become an enemy to my own soldiers.
3. it: Banner or standard.

4. fell to spoil: Began to loot.

◆ Build Vocabulary

presage (prē sāj´) *v.:* Warn of a future event

ensign (en´ s'n) *n.:* Old word for a standard bearer; one who carries a flag

consorted (kän sôr tid) *v.:* Joined; accompanied

demeanor (di mēn ər) *n.:* Behavior

◆ *Literature and Your Life*

6 Encourage students to support their answers with examples from movies, literature, and life. Some students may not be comfortable sharing personal details. Make clear to students that they can use examples from fiction.

Customize for
Visual/Spatial Learners
Remind students that a play is meant to be seen. Readers who cannot view the action may have trouble keeping track of who is—and is not—on stage at any given time. Suggest to students that they can sketch simple diagrams indicating the placement and movement of onstage characters.

Comprehension Check ☑

7 What mistake did Brutus make?
Brutus gave the victory signal to his men too soon. Having overcome Octavius, they began plundering the enemy camp instead of coming to the aid of Cassius' men when they were surrounded by Antony's forces.

◆ *Literature and Your Life*
Do you think people should prepare for the worst or expect the best? **6**

🗞 Cross-Curricular Connection: History

Pompey Early in *Julius Caesar*, Marullus asks a mob, "Knew you not Pompey?" He means the Roman general Pompey the Great (106-48 B.C.), once an ally of Caesar, and later, the last obstacle Caesar had to overcome in his rise to power.

Pompey grew up in a wealthy Roman family, in a time of warfare between two generals, Gaius Marius and Lucius Sulla. Still in his twenties, he raised an army of three legions, allied himself with Sulla, and beat Marius. The Senate sent him to Spain, where he defeated Marius' followers.

A string of victories made Pompey a hero to the public, but a threat to the Senate, which feared that they could not control such a hero. In 60 B.C., Pompey, Julius Caesar, and Marcus Crassus formed what became known as the First Triumvirate, to resist the Senate's antimilitarism.

Pompey started to worry about Caesar's growing power and broke with him, leading to civil war. Pompey's army lost two battles to Caesar. After the second, in 48 B.C., Pompey escaped to Egypt, but was killed by order of the Roman-dominated Egyptian government.

◆ **Critical Thinking**

❶ Interpret Ask students to explain the point Cassius is making in this short speech. *Cassius says that he is going to die on his birthday. He compares his life to a journey at the end of which he has returned to the spot where he began. The image of a journey is strengthened by Brutus' mention of a compass.*

◆ **Reading Strategy**

❷ Identify Cause and Effect Have students explain what causes Cassius to order Pindarus to kill him. *Cassius believes he has caused his friend Titinius to be captured by Antony's legions.*

◆ **Literary Focus**

❸ Tragedy Invite students to discuss why they do, or do not, view Cassius' death as tragic. *Students should note that Cassius' death is not tragic because Cassius is not a tragic figure. In Act IV, Shakespeare deliberately shows that he was involved in shady dealings, and earlier in the play he was shown as being scheming and envious. His nature is not noble enough for his death to be considered tragic.*

CASSIUS. Titinius, if thou lovest me,
15   Mount thou my horse and hide⁵ thy spurs in him
    Till he have brought thee up to yonder troops
    And here again, that I may rest assured
    Whether yond troops are friend or enemy.

TITINIUS. I will be here again even with a thought.⁶ [*Exit*]

CASSIUS. Go, Pindarus, get higher on that hill;
20   My sight was ever thick.⁷ Regard⁸ Titinius,
    And tell me what thou not'st about the field.

                    [*Exit* PINDARUS.]

❶   This day I breathèd first. Time is come round,
    And where I did begin, there shall I end.
    My life is run his compass.⁹ Sirrah, what news?
25

PINDARUS. [*Above*] O my lord!

CASSIUS. What news?

PINDARUS. [*Above*] Titinius is enclosèd round about
    With horsemen that make to him on the spur;¹⁰
    Yet he spurs on. Now they are almost on him.
30   Now, Titinius! Now some light.¹¹ O, he lights too!
    He's ta'en!¹² [*Shout*] And, hark! They shout for joy.

CASSIUS. Come down; behold no more.
    O, coward that I am, to live so long,
    To see my best friend ta'en before my face!

35 [*Enter* PINDARUS.]

    Come hither, sirrah.
    In Parthia did I take thee prisoner;
    And then I swore thee, saving of thy life,
    That whatsoever I did bid thee do,
40   Thou shouldst attempt it. Come now, keep thine
      oath.
❸   Now be a freeman, and with this good sword,
    That ran through Caesar's bowels, search¹³ this
      bosom.
    Stand not¹⁴ to answer. Here, take thou the hilts,
    And when my face is covered, as 'tis now,
45   Guide thou the sword—Caesar, thou art revenged,
    Even with the sword that killed thee.   [*Dies*]

PINDARUS. So, I am free; yet would not so have been,
    Durst I have done my will. O Cassius!
    Far from this country Pindarus shall run,
50   Where never Roman shall take note of him.   [*Exit*]

5. hide: Sink.

6. even with a thought: As quick as a thought.

7. thick: Dim.
8. Regard: Observe.

9. his compass: Its full course.

10. make . . . spur: Ride toward him at top speed.

11. light: Dismount from their horses.
12. ta'en: Taken; captured.

◆ **Reading Strategy**
What is the cause of Cassius' request? What might be some effects of Pindarus fulfilling the request? **❷**

13. search: Penetrate.

14. Stand not: Do not wait.

794 ◆ *Drama*

Speaking and Listening Mini-Lesson

Sound Effects

This mini-lesson supports the Speaking and Listening activity in Idea Bank on page 803.

Introduce the Concept Lead students to note that sound effects add color and realism to a scene, but should not distract the audience's attention from the dialogue, or drown out dialogue.

Develop Background Invite discussion about how sound effects add to enjoyment and appreciation of a performance. Students can consider these questions:

• Where can the text use sound effects?

• How will each sound effect be created?

Apply the Information Students can experiment with sound effects while other students read portions of the play aloud. For presentations, sound effects may be live or recorded on tape. If possible, record all readings with sound effects.

Assess the Outcome Have students evaluate how well the sound effects enhanced the scenes. They should point out places where the effects distracted from or drowned out the reading.

4 ▲ **Critical Viewing** This battle is the outcome of events that were set in motion
5 earlier in the play. What is the original cause that leads to this battle? **[Analyze]**

[*Enter* TITINIUS *and* MESSALA.]

> **MESSALA.** It is but change,[15] Titinius; for Octavius
> Is overthrown by noble Brutus' power,
> As Cassius' legions are by Antony.

6 **TITINIUS.** These tidings will well comfort Cassius.

> **MESSALA.** Where did you leave him?

55 **TITINIUS.**   All <u>disconsolate</u>,
> With Pindarus his bondman, on this hill.

15. **change:** An exchange.

◆ **Build Vocabulary**

disconsolate (dis kän´ sə lit) *adj*.: So unhappy that nothing will comfort

The Tragedy of Julius Caesar, Act V, Scene iii ◆ 795

►Critical Viewing◄

❹ **Analyze** Suggested response: The ultimate cause of the battle is the conflict between two factions: those who believe in the republic and those who were in favor of making Caesar emperor.

Customize for
Visual/Spatial Learners
❺ Use the picture on this page to help visual/spatial learners understand what a confusing scene a battle is and how Cassius misinterpreted the action he viewed. Ask students if they can tell who is winning the battle pictured here. *Most students will not be able to find details to support the claim that either side is winning. They should be able to relate their own confusion to Cassius' misinterpretation of events.*

Comprehension Check ☑

❻ How was Pindarus' report false?
Titinius has returned; therefore, there was no reason for Cassius to die.

 Cross-Curricular Connection: History

Julius Caesar failed to become the first Roman emperor; that honor fell to his chosen heir, *Octavius Caesar* (63 B.C.–A.D. 14), in 27 B.C. He took the name *Augustus* (Latin for "The Exalted").

When Julius was assassinated in 44 B.C., Octavius, nineteen, hurried to Rome to assert his rights as Julius' heir. He joined forces with Julius' former chief lieutenant, Mark Antony, who had taken control of Rome after the assassination.

They ruled with general Marcus Lepidus as a triumvirate, which controlled Rome after their forces beat those of Brutus and Cassius in 42 B.C.

The triumvirate fell apart. Lepidus was made to retire. Antony, who ruled Rome's eastern provinces, joined with the queen of Egypt, Cleopatra, to fight Octavius for domination of Rome, but their fleet was sunk in 31 B.C., in the Battle of Actium, leaving Octavius in complete control.

As Emperor Augustus, Octavius was an energetic ruler, who expanded the empire, strengthened the army, and built up the city of Rome. He himself said, "I found Rome brick and left it marble."

◆ Build Vocabulary

❶ Prefixes: mis- Point out that *mistrust* contains the prefix *mis-*. Ask students: What does this prefix add to your understanding of the meaning of the word *mistrust*? *Added to the root "trust," "mistrust" means "do not trust," as in "I mistrust (do not trust) him."*

◆ Reading Strategy

❷ Identify Cause and Effect Ask students to predict what effect Pindarus' false report might have on Titinius. *Pindarus' report that Titinius had been captured caused Cassius to kill himself, believing Titinius' capture to be his fault. Students may say that Cassius' death, in turn may cause Titinius to kill himself, knowing that Cassius died for his sake.*

◆ Build Grammar Skills

❸ Words of Direct Address Ask students: What dual purpose does the direct address "brave Cassius" serve? *The phrase identifies the person to whom Titinius is speaking and emphasizes how Titinius regards Cassius.*

MESSALA. Is not that he that lies upon the ground?

TITINIUS. He lies not like the living. O my heart!

MESSALA. Is not that he?

TITINIUS.   No, this was he, Messala,
60   But Cassius is no more. O setting sun,
     As in thy red rays thou dost sink to night,
     So in his red blood Cassius' day is set.
     The sun of Rome is set. Our day is gone;
     Clouds, dews, and dangers come; our deeds are done!
65   Mistrust of my success[16] hath done this deed.

❶ MESSALA. Mistrust of good success hath done this deed.
     O hateful Error, Melancholy's child,[17]
     Why dost thou show to the apt thoughts of men
     The things that are not?[18] O Error, soon conceived,[19]
70   Thou never com'st unto a happy birth,
     But kill'st the mother that engend'red thee![20]

TITINIUS. What, Pindarus! Where art thou, Pindarus?

MESSALA. Seek him, Titinius, whilst I go to meet
     The noble Brutus, thrusting this report
75   Into his ears. I may say "thrusting" it;
❷ For piercing steel and darts envenomèd[21]
     Shall be as welcome to the ears of Brutus
     As tidings of this sight.

TITINIUS.   Hie you, Messala,
     And I will seek for Pindarus the while.   [*Exit* MESSALA.]

80   Why didst thou send me forth, brave[22] Cassius?
❸ Did I not meet thy friends, and did not they
     Put on my brows this wreath of victory,
     And bid me give it thee? Didst thou not hear their shouts?
     Alas, thou hast misconstrued everything!
85   But hold thee,[23] take this garland on thy brow;
     Thy Brutus bid me give it thee, and I
     Will do his bidding. Brutus, come apace,[24]
     And see how I regarded[25] Caius Cassius.
     By your leave,[26] gods. This is a Roman's part:[27]
90   Come, Cassius' sword, and find Titinius' heart.   [*Dies*]

[*Call to arms sounds. Enter* BRUTUS, MESSALA, YOUNG CATO, STRATO, VOLUMNIUS, *and* LUCILIUS.]

BRUTUS. Where, where, Messala, doth his body lie?

MESSALA. Lo, yonder, and Titinius mourning it.

BRUTUS. Titinius' face is upward.

16. Mistrust . . . success: Fear that I would not succeed.

17. Melancholy's child: One of despondent temperament.

18. Why dost . . . are not?: Why do you (despondent temperament) fill easily impressed men's thoughts with imagined fears?
19. conceived: Created.
20. mother . . . thee: Cassius (in this case), who conceived the error.

21. envenomèd: Poisoned.

22. brave: Noble.

23. hold thee: Wait a moment.

24. apace: Quickly.
25. regarded: Honored.
26. By your leave: With your permission.
27. part: Role; duty.

◆ Build Vocabulary

misconstrued (mis kän strood´) *v.*: Misunderstood; misinterpreted

CATO.   He is slain.

BRUTUS. O Julius Caesar, thou art mighty yet!
95   Thy spirit walks abroad, and turns our swords
        In our own proper entrails.[28]   [*Low calls to arms*]

CATO.   Brave Titinius!
        Look, whe'r[29] he have not crowned dead Cassius.

BRUTUS. Are yet two Romans living such as these?
        The last of all the Romans, fare thee well!
100   It is impossible that ever Rome
        Should breed thy fellow.[30] Friends, I owe moe tears
        To this dead man than you shall see me pay.
        I shall find time, Cassius; I shall find time.
        Come, therefore, and to Thasos[31] send his body;
105   His funerals shall not be in our camp,
        Lest it discomfort us.[32] Lucilius, come,
        And come, young Cato; let us to the field.
        Labeo and Flavius set our battles[33] on.
        'Tis three o'clock; and, Romans, yet ere night
110   We shall try fortune in a second fight.   [*Exit*]

Scene iv. *The field of battle.*

[*Call to arms sounds. Enter* BRUTUS, MESSALA, YOUNG CATO,
LUCILIUS, *and* FLAVIUS.]

BRUTUS. Yet, countrymen, O, yet hold up your heads!

                              [*Exit, with followers*]

CATO. What bastard[1] doth not? Who will go with me?
        I will proclaim my name about the field.
        I am the son of Marcus Cato,[2] ho!
5   A foe to tyrants, and my country's friend.
        I am the son of Marcus Cato, ho!

[*Enter* SOLDIERS *and fight.*]

LUCILIUS. And I am Brutus, Marcus Brutus, I;
        Brutus, my country's friend; know me for Brutus![3]

                              [YOUNG CATO *falls.*]

        O young and noble Cato, art thou down?
10   Why, now thou diest as bravely as Titinius,
        And mayst be honored, being Cato's son.

FIRST SOLDIER. Yield, or thou diest.

LUCILIUS.   Only I yield to die.[4]
        There is so much that thou wilt kill me straight;[5]
        Kill Brutus, and be honored in his death.

15   **FIRST SOLDIER.** We must not. A noble prisoner!

---

28. **own proper entrails:** Very own inner organs.
29. **whe'r:** Whether.

30. **fellow:** Equal.

31. **Thasos:** An island not far from Philippi.

32. **discomfort us:** Discourage our soldiers.

33. **battles:** Armies.

1. **bastard:** Person who is not a true Roman.

2. **Marcus Cato:** Brutus' wife's father.

3. **And I am . . . Brutus:** Lucilius impersonates Brutus in order to protect him and confuse the enemy.

4. **Only . . . die:** I will surrender only to die.
5. **much . . . straight:** Much honor in it that you will kill me immediately.

The Tragedy of Julius Caesar, Act V, Scene iv ◆ *797*

◆◆ **Speaking and Listening Mini-Lesson**

Respond to Shakespearean English
This mini-lesson supports the second Speaking and Listening activity in the Idea Bank on page 803.
Introduce the Concept With students, compare and contrast Shakespearean with modern English. Create a chart displaying Shakespearean words or expressions with modern ones with similar meanings.

Develop Background Play the excerpt for the class. Then, with students, explore ways to improvise the scene in contemporary English. Lead students to include these strategies:
• Use suitable gestures and expressions.
• Speak as if you were your character.
• Stick to the original ideas.

Apply the Information Invite students to improvise their modern-English scenes for the class.
Assess the Outcome Have students evaluate skits according to how well they communicated the same ideas as Shakespeare's scene. You may choose to give students the Peer Assessment: Dramatic Performance sheet on page 120 of the *Alternative Assessment* booklet.

◆ Reading Strategy

❶ Identify Cause and Effect
Sample answer: Antony respects Brutus, and therefore Lucilius, because he is Brutus' friend. He does not want to make an enemy of Lucilius.

Comprehension Check ☑

❷ What does Brutus want Clitus and Dardanius to do? Why? *Brutus wants his men to kill him so he will not be taken prisoner.*

◆ Literary Focus

❸ Cause and Effect Students may identify several causes of Brutus' despair including his almost certain defeat to come in the battle, his death predicted by Caesar's ghost, a realization that he aligned himself with dishonorable men, or the fact that he killed Caesar, a man who trusted him.

[*Enter* ANTONY.]

SECOND SOLDIER. Room, ho! Tell Antony, Brutus is ta'en.

FIRST SOLDIER. I'll tell thee news. Here comes the
    general.
  Brutus is ta'en, Brutus is ta'en, my lord.

ANTONY. Where is he?

20 **LUCILIUS.** Safe, Antony; Brutus is safe enough.
  I dare assure thee that no enemy
  Shall ever take alive the noble Brutus.
  The gods defend him from so great a shame!
  When you do find him, or alive or dead,
25 He will be found like Brutus, like himself.[6]

ANTONY. This is not Brutus, friend, but, I assure you,
  A prize no less in worth. Keep this man safe;
  Give him all kindness. I had rather have
  Such men my friends than enemies. Go on,
30 And see whe'r Brutus be alive or dead,
  And bring us word unto[7] Octavius' tent
  How everything is chanced.[8]   [*Exit*]

Scene v. *The field of battle.*

[*Enter* BRUTUS, DARDANIUS, CLITUS, STRATO, *and* VOLUMNIUS.]

BRUTUS. Come, poor remains[1] of friends, rest on this
    rock.

CLITUS. Statilius showed the torchlight,[2] but, my lord,
  He came not back; he is or ta'en or slain.

BRUTUS. Sit thee down, Clitus. Slaying is the word;
    It is a deed in fashion. Hark thee, Clitus. [*Whispers*]
5 ❷
❸ **CLITUS.** What, I, my lord? No, not for all the world!

BRUTUS. Peace then, no words.

CLITUS.   I'll rather kill myself.

BRUTUS. Hark thee, Dardanius.   [*Whispers*]

DARDANIUS.   Shall I do such a deed?

CLITUS. O Dardanius!

10 **DARDANIUS.** O Clitus!

CLITUS. What ill request did Brutus make to thee?

DARDANIUS. To kill him, Clitus. Look, he meditates.

CLITUS. Now is that noble vessel[3] full of grief,
  That it runs over even at his eyes.

798 ◆ Drama

---

6. **like himself:** Behaving in a noble way.

◆ **Reading Strategy**
Identify why Antony treats Lucilius the way he does. **❶**

7. **unto:** In.
8. **is chanced:** Has happened.

1. **poor remains:** Pitiful survivors.

2. **showed the torchlight:** Signaled with a torch.

◆ **Reading Strategy**
What is the cause of Brutus' despair? What is the effect?

3. **vessel:** Human being.

Beyond the Classroom

Career Connection
Military Careers Military battles play important roles in Shakespeare's tragedies, *Julius Caesar, Antony and Cleopatra, Macbeth,* and *Hamlet.* While the United States has not been involved in a major war for decades, more than 500,000 U.S. Army personnel are on active duty today. Women as well as men pursue careers in the army, navy, marines, and air force. Have students find out about career opportunities in the military, including training, education, pay, benefits, and years of service required.

Community Connection
War Memorials Monuments have been erected around the world to honor war heroes. Encourage students to survey their town to find memorials to local war heroes. Students can then search town records to find out more about each soldier's life and death.

15   **BRUTUS.** Come hither, good Volumnius; list[4] a word.

VOLUMNIUS. What says my lord?

BRUTUS.   Why, this, Volumnius:
The ghost of Caesar hath appeared to me
Two several[5] times by night; at Sardis once,
And this last night here in Philippi fields.
I know my hour is come.

20 ❹ **VOLUMNIUS.**   Not so, my lord.

❺ **BRUTUS.** Nay, I am sure it is, Volumnius.
Thou seest the world, Volumnius, how it goes;
Our enemies have beat us to the pit.[6]

                [*Low calls to arms*]

It is more worthy to leap in ourselves
25 Than tarry till they push us.[7] Good Volumnius,
Thou know'st that we two went to school together;
Even for that our love of old, I prithee
Hold thou my sword-hilts whilst I run on it.

VOLUMNIUS. That's not an office[8] for a friend, my lord.

                [*Call to arms still*]

30 **CLITUS.** Fly, fly, my lord, there is no tarrying here.

BRUTUS. Farewell to you; and you; and you, Volumnius.
Strato, thou hast been all this while asleep;
Farewell to thee too, Strato. Countrymen,
My heart doth joy that yet in all my life
35 ❻ I found no man but he was true to me.
I shall have glory by this losing day
More than Octavius and Mark Antony
By this vile conquest shall attain unto.[9]
So fare you well at once, for Brutus' tongue
40 Hath almost ended his life's history.
Night hangs upon mine eyes; my bones would rest,
That have but labored to attain this hour.[10]

          [*Call to arms sounds. Cry within*, "Fly, fly, fly!"]

CLITUS. Fly, my lord, fly!

BRUTUS.   Hence! I will follow.

          [*Exit* CLITUS, DARDANIUS, *and* VOLUMNIUS.]

I prithee, Strato, stay thou by thy lord,
45 Thou art a fellow of a good respect.[11]
Thy life hath had some smatch[12] of honor in it;
Hold then my sword, and turn away thy face,
While I do run upon it. Wilt thou, Strato?

The Tragedy of Julius Caesar, Act V, Scene v ◆ *799*

---

4. list: Hear.

5. several: Separate.

6. pit: Trap or grave.

7. tarry . . . us: Wait until they kill us.

8. office: Task.

9. By this . . . unto: By this evil victory shall gain. (Brutus sees the victory of Octavius and Antony as causing the downfall of Roman freedom.)
10. this hour: Time of death.

11. respect: Reputation.
12. smatch: Smack or taste.

---

❶ Analyze Conflict is indicated by the drawn sword and the war helmet. Triumph may be indicated by the expression on the face of the man wearing the helmet, by the fact that he is still wearing his helmet, and by the fact that his head is placed above the other man's. Defeat may be indicated by the missing helmet, by the pained expression of the man with the sword, and by the fact that he seems almost to be sinking out of the picture.

◆ Critical Thinking

❷ Interpret Invite interpretation of Brutus' final words. How do they reveal his essential nobility? *By saying that he is more ready to die than he was to murder Caesar, Brutus shows that he did not want to kill Caesar for selfish reasons.*

◆ Reading Strategy

❸ Identify Cause and Effect Guide the class in tracing the chain of causes and effects that begins with the conspirators' plan to kill Caesar and ends with Brutus' death. Have students note how each effect became a cause for the next effect. *Brutus, Cassius, and the other conspirators kill Caesar; Antony and Octavius, who supported Caesar, oppose Brutus and Cassius in the battle of Philippi; Octavius' legions defeat Brutus'; Brutus takes his own life.*

◆ Literary Focus

❹ Tragic Hero Some students may identify Caesar as the tragic hero while others will indentify Brutus as the tragic hero.

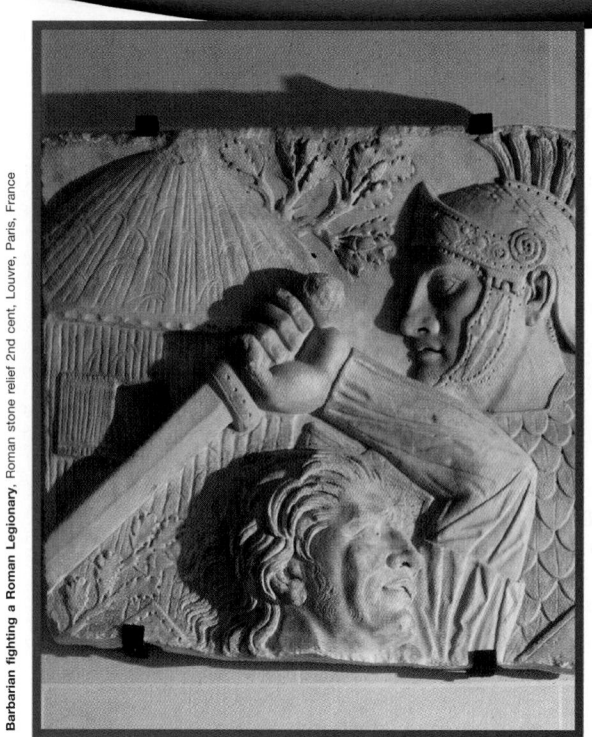

Barbarian fighting a Roman Legionary, Roman stone relief 2nd cent, Louvre, Paris, France

◄ **Critical Viewing** What details in this sculpture indicate conflict, triumph, and defeat? [Analyze] ❶

STRATO. Give me your hand first. Fare you well, my lord.

50 ❷ **BRUTUS.** Farewell, good Strato—Caesar, now be still;
❸ I killed not thee with half so good a will. [*Dies*]

[*Call to arms sounds. Retreat sounds. Enter* ANTONY, OCTAVIUS, MESSALA, LUCILIUS, *and the Army.*]

OCTAVIUS. What man is that?

MESSALA. My master's man.[13] Strato, where is thy master?

STRATO. Free from the bondage you are in, Messala;
55 The conquerors can but make a fire of him
For Brutus only overcame himself,
And no man else hath honor[14] by his death.

LUCILIUS. So Brutus should be found. I thank thee, Brutus,
That thou hast proved Lucilius' saying[15] true.

60 **OCTAVIUS.** All that served Brutus, I will entertain them.[16]
Fellow, wilt thou bestow[17] thy time with me?

STRATO. Ay, if Messala will prefer[18] me to you.

◆ **Literary Focus** Considering Antony's words, ask yourself who the real tragic hero in this play is. ❹

13. man: Servant.

14. no man else hath honor: No other man gains honor.

15. Lucilius' saying: See Act V, Scene iv, line 25.
16. entertain them: Take them into my service.
17. bestow: Spend.
18. prefer: Recommend.

 Beyond the Selection

FURTHER READING

Other Works by William Shakespeare
The Tragedy of Hamlet, Prince Of Denmark
The Tragedy of Othello
The Comedy of Errors

Other Works About Choices and Consequences
For Whom the Bell Tolls, Ernest Hemingway
Catch-22, Joseph Heller
The Red Badge of Courage, Stephen Crane

INTERNET

For information about the complete works of William Shakespeare, the Globe theater, and the Elizabethan era, go to **http://pc1.fhs.weber.k12.ut.us/academ /English/marler/shakes/william.htm**

Please be aware, however, that sites may have changed from the time we published this information. We *strongly recommend* that you preview sites before you send students to them.

OCTAVIUS. Do so, good Messala.

MESSALA. How died my master, Strato?

65 STRATO. I held the sword, and he did run on it.

MESSALA. Octavius, then take him to follow thee,
That did the latest service to my master.

ANTONY. This was the noblest Roman of them all.
All the conspirators save[19] only he
70 Did that[20] they did in envy of great Caesar;
He, only in a general honest thought
❺ And common good to all, made one of them.[21]
His life was gentle,[22] and the elements
So mixed[23] in him that Nature might stand up
75 And say to all the world, "This was a man!"

OCTAVIUS. According to his virtue,[24] let us use[25] him
With all respect and rites of burial.
❻ Within my tent his bones tonight shall lie,
Most like a soldier ordered honorably.[26]
80 So call the field[27] to rest, and let's away
To part[28] the glories of this happy day.   [Exit all.]

19. save: Except.
20. that: What.

21. made one of them:
Became one of the
conspirators.
22. gentle: Noble.
23. so mixed: Well balanced.

24. virtue: Excellence.
25. use: Treat.

26. ordered honorably:
Treated with honor.
27. field: Army.
28. part: Share.

◆ Build Vocabulary

envy (en′ vē) n.: Feeling
of desire for another's
possessions or qualities
and jealousy at not
having them

Guide for Responding

◆ *Literature and Your Life*

Reader's Response What insights did you gain
from the play?
Thematic Focus Explain how the choices some
characters made in this act were the inevitable consequences of events that occurred much earlier in
the play.
Group Discussion In a small group, develop a
treaty or contract to which the two sides might have
agreed instead of going to battle.

☑ **Check Your Comprehension**

1. On whose birthday does the battle take place,
and how does that person feel about the battle?
2. Explain the misunderstanding that leads to Cassius' death.
3. Why does Brutus think it is time to die?
4. Who does Antony say is the noblest Roman of all?

◆ **Critical Thinking**

INTERPRET

1. What does Cassius mean in Act V, Scene i, lines
45–47? **[Analyze]**
2. What does Brutus mean by his final words,
"Caesar, now be still; / I killed not thee with half
so good a will"? **[Interpret]**
3. How and why does Antony's attitude toward
Brutus change during this act? **[Infer]**

APPLY

4. Now that Octavius and Antony have triumphed,
what do you think will become of the Roman
republic? Do you think this is a good or bad
thing? **[Speculate]**

EXTEND

5. Compare another defeated leader from history
to Brutus. Explain how the circumstances,
possible motives, and outcomes are similar and
different. **[Social Studies Link]**

The Tragedy of Julius Caesar, Act V, Scene v ◆ 801

◆ **Critical Thinking**

1. Cassius says that Antony would
not be able to speak such insults if
Brutus had listened to Cassius'
advice to kill Antony.
2. Brutus is more ready to die than
he was to murder Caesar.
3. At the beginning of Act V, Antony
see Brutus as a villain for his part
in the assassination of Caesar. At
the end, Antony finally realizes that
Brutus was the only conspirator

who killed out of an honest concern for the common good, not
for envy or power.
4. Sample response: The Roman
republic will die, but the people
helped to let it happen. They, too,
made a choice and must suffer the
consequences.
5. Example: Robert E. Lee would be
an example of a noble leader who,
because of his deep sense of
honor, aligned himself with the
wrong side and was defeated.

◆ **Critical Thinking**

❺ **Infer** Ask students: Why does
Antony praise his enemy, Brutus?
*Antony has come to see Brutus as a
truly honorable man. He realizes that
Brutus thought he was acting for the
good of Rome, not for personal gain.*

◆ **Critical Thinking**

❻ **Speculate** Lead a discussion
about Rome's future following the
action of the play. What does the
phrase "part the glories of this happy
day" suggest? *Students may suggest
that "happy day" suggests a hopeful
future—at least for Antony and Octavius.
Since Antony and Octavius were battling
those who fought to save the republic
(Brutus and Cassius), students might predict that Rome will become a monarchy.*

Reinforce and Extend

Answers
◆ *Literature and Your Life*

Reader's Response Students may
respond: If a good person does
something wrong for the right reason, it still turns out bad. Beware of
whose company you keep. Watch out
for flatterers. Never underestimate
your enemy.

Thematic Focus Suggested
answer: Brutus' defeat is the
inevitable consequence of his joining
men with selfish motives.

☑ **Check Your Comprehension**

1. The battle takes place on Cassius'
birthday, and he feels it is one of
many bad omens.
2. When Cassius saw Titinius unseat-
ed from his horse, he assumed
that everything was lost.
3. Brutus thinks it is time to die
because he feels that the victory
of Antony and Octavius marks the
end of Roman freedom.
4. Anthony says that Brutus is the
noblest Roman of all.

◆ Reading Strategy

1. The effects that result in this act from Caesar's assassination include the battle, which in conjunction with other events causes the deaths of Cassius and Brutus. Antony and Octavius become rulers of Rome.
2. Brutus committed suicide because the threat of defeat and surrender meant he would be led bound through the streets of Rome in disgrace. The effect of his suicide is that the fighting will stop and Brutus will have an honorable funeral.

◆ Literary Focus

1. Example: Brutus' tragic flaw is error in judgment—he misjudged Cassius, Antony, and the Roman people.
2. Once Brutus joined the conspirators, he could not turn back, because even if he turned them in, he would be accused of being part of the plot, lose the trust of Caesar, and still lose the republic.
3. Examples: In V, v, lines 36–38, Brutus states, "I shall have glory by losing day/More the Octavius and Mark Antony/By this vile conquest shall attain unto." In lines 50–51, Brutus says, ". . . Caesar, now be still;/I killed not thee with half so good a will." In V, v, lines 13–14, Clitus says of Brutus: "Now is that noble vessel full of grief,/That it runs over even at his eyes."

◆ Build Vocabulary

Using the Prefix mis-
1. b 2. a 3. c

Using the Word Bank
1. a 2. c 3. c 4. b
5. b 6. a 7. b

◆ Build Grammar Skills

Practice
1. Prepare, you generals, the enemy comes on in a gallant show.
2. Octavius, lead your battle softly on.
3. In your bad strokes, Brutus, you give good words.
4. Young man, thou couldst not die more honorable.
5. Mark Antony, shall we give sign of battle?
6. No Caesar, we will answer on their charge.

Guide for Responding (continued)

◆ Reading Strategy

IDENTIFY CAUSE AND EFFECT

When you **identify the causes and effects** of actions in this drama, you see the relationships between events that bring about the ultimate tragedy.
1. List three effects of Caesar's death that occur in Act V. Explain the chain of events that lead to the final result.
2. What is the immediate cause of Brutus' suicide? What do you think its effect will be?

◆ Literary Focus

TRAGEDY

The last act of *The Tragedy of Julius Caesar* depicts the downfall of Brutus. His death is the inevitable consequence of a chain of events set in motion when he joined the conspirators in Act I.
1. In your own words, what is Brutus' tragic flaw?
2. Once Brutus has joined the conspirators, can he turn back? Why or why not?
3. Find two passages that show that Brutus is essentially a noble man.

Beyond Literature

Media Connection

Shakespeare Goes to Hollywood The timeless themes of Shakespeare's works have made them popular subjects for filmmakers as well as producers of plays. Movie adaptations have been made of *Hamlet, Macbeth, Much Ado About Nothing, Richard III,* and others. Actors such as Kenneth Branagh, Mel Gibson, Leonardo Di Caprio, Claire Danes and Glenn Close have played roles in movies of Shakespeare's plays.

Activity Watch a recent film adaptation of one of Shakespeare's plays. Give a brief oral report explaining why the theme is still of interest to audiences today.

◆ Build Vocabulary

USING THE PREFIX mis-

The prefix *mis-* means "wrong" or "bad." On your paper, match each word that begins with *mis-* with its definition.
1. misnomer
2. misanthrope
3. misconduct

  a. one who thinks badly of people
  b. a wrong name
  c. bad behavior

USING THE WORD BANK

On your paper, write the letter of the word that is a synonym for the word from the Word Bank.
1. misconstrued: (a) confused, (b) angered, (c) understood
2. presage: (a) help, (b) review, (c) predict
3. disconsolate: (a) joyful, (b) angry, (c) cheerless
4. consorted: (a) abandoned, (b) accompanied, (c) served
5. demeanor: (a) feelings, (b) behavior, (c) anger
6. ensign: (a) flag-bearer, (b) signature, (c) janitor
7. envy: (a) sympathy, (b) jealousy, (c) sadness

◆ Build Grammar Skills

WORDS OF DIRECT ADDRESS

Writers set off **words of direct address** with commas and occasionally an exclamation point.

Practice On your paper, write the following passages. Underline the word or words of direct address and insert the proper punctuation.
1. Prepare you generals the enemy comes on in a gallant show.
2. Octavius lead your battle softly on.
3. In your bad strokes Brutus you give good words.
4. Young man thou couldst not die more honorable.
5. Mark Antony shall we give sign of battle?
6. No Caesar we will answer on their charge.

Writing Application Write a brief dialogue between two or more characters that could be part of a play. In the dialogue, have the characters address each other directly. Punctuate their words of direct address properly.

Writing Application
Sample Response: "Adam, you and I have to talk when I come home over the holidays."
"I'll be working most days, Jennifer, but we'll figure something out."

Build Your Portfolio

 Idea Bank

Writing

1. **Epitaph** Write an epitaph for Brutus. An epitaph is brief, gives birth and death dates, and often includes an appropriate inspiring verse.

2. **Response** In Act V, Scene i, lines 39–44, Antony launches a bitter verbal attack against Brutus and Cassius. Brutus makes no attempt to respond. Write a short speech in which Brutus *does* respond to Antony's criticism.

3. **Take a Side** Throughout the play, Brutus gives his reasons for killing Caesar. Antony just as eloquently states why Caesar should not have been killed. With whom do you agree? Write a position paper taking either Brutus' or Antony's side. Support any assertions you make.

Speaking and Listening

4. **Sound Effects** With classmates, create sound effects for the final act of the play. Make a recording of the effects and play them for the class.

5. **Respond to Shakespearean English** Find a recording of a play by Shakespeare. Play an excerpt for the class, then improvise a performance of the same scene in contemporary language.

Projects

6. **Model of the Globe** Research to find out more about the Globe theater. Create a model of the theater to better understand how plays like *The Tragedy of Julius Caesar* were performed during Shakespeare's day.

7. **Elizabethan Faire** With a group, organize an "Elizabethan Faire," incorporating costumes, music, art, and, if possible, food to give your classmates a flavor of the period in which Shakespeare lived and wrote.

 Writing Mini-Lesson

Speech

When Antony presented the crown to Caesar, he probably spoke to the spectators with a prepared talk, or speech. Most likely, he said something at the beginning of the speech to grab the attention of the listeners. Then he probably presented supporting facts and anecdotes to show why Caesar was worthy of the crown. Write your own speech to honor a special person or event.

Writing Skills Focus: Connotation

Shakespeare chose carefully the words he put into the mouths of his characters. He was aware that words carry **connotations**—associations that give them deeper meaning than their literal definitions. For instance, the word *valiant* has associations that are not communicated by simply saying *brave*. The word *integrity* paints a more vivid picture of a person's character than *honesty* does. Use words with positive connotations to lend power to your speech.

Prewriting Brainstorm for qualities and impressions of the person or event that is the subject of your speech. Using a dictionary or thesaurus, make a list of words that have both a literal and connotative meaning that will help you express these ideas.

Drafting Use lively, specific verbs in your speech. Choose verbs connotative for their meanings. A word like *sizzle* literally means "extremely hot." Its connotation, however, suggests more—someone or something that is very exciting and energetic.

Revising Read your speech aloud to a small group. Does your first sentence grab their attention? Are your verbs lively and energetic with connotative as well as literal meanings? Ask the group for suggestions and make revisions you feel will improve your speech.

The Tragedy of Julius Caesar, Act V ◆ 803

Customizing for *Learning Modalities*

Following are suggestions for matching Idea Bank topics with your students' learning modalities.

Musical/Rhythmic: 4
Interpersonal: 5, 7
Bodily/Kinesthetic: 6, 7
Visual/Spatial: 6, 7

Customizing for *Performance Levels*

Following are suggestions for matching Idea Bank topics with your students' performance levels:

Less Advanced: 1, 4
Average: 2, 5, 7
More Advanced: 3, 5, 6, 7

 Writer's Solution

Writing Lab CD-ROM

Have students write their speeches using the tutorial on Persuasion. Follow these steps:

1. Use the note cards activity to organize ideas.
2. Have students draft on the computer.
3. Use the revision checker for double comparisons.

Sourcebook

Have students use Chapter 4, Persuasion (pp. 97–127), for additional support. The chapter includes in-depth instruction on writing for different audiences (p.113).

✓ ASSESSMENT OPTIONS

Formal Assessment, Selection Test, pp. 188–189, Assessment Resources Software. The selection test is designed so that it can be easily customized to the ability levels of your students. *Alternative Assessment,* p. 54, includes options for less advanced students and more advanced students.

PORTFOLIO ASSESSMENT
Use the following rubrics in the *Alternative Assessment* booklet to assess student writing:
Epitaph: Response to Literature Rubric. p.110
Response: Expression Rubric, p. 94
Take a Side: Persuasion Rubric, p. 105
Writing Mini-Lesson: Persuasion Rubric, p. 105

Establish Writing Guidelines

Before students begin, review the following key characteristics of a critical evaluation

- A critical evaluation is written with words that have appropriate connotations.

- It provides examples from the text for support.

You may distribute copies of the Scoring Rubric for Response to Literature (p. 110) in *Alternative Assessment* to make students aware before they begin of the criteria on which they will be evaluated. See the suggestions on page 808 for ways you can customize the rubric for this workshop.

Refer students to the Writing Handbook, page 965, for instruction in the writing process, and page 969 for further information on response to literature.

 Writer's Solution

Writers at Work Videodisc

Play the videodisc segment on Response to Literature (Ch. 7) in which Miguel Algarín discusses the process of preparing a literary response.

Play frames 26321 to 29738

Writing Lab CD-ROM

If your students have access to computers, you may want to have them work on the tutorial on Response to Literature to complete all or part of their critical reviews. Follow these steps:

1. Encourage students to use the Response Wheel activity in the Prewriting section.
2. Suggest that students write to the purpose by completing an audience profile and then using the instruction on writing for different purposes.
3. Have students draft on computer.
4. Tell students to use the revision checkers for varied language and for pronoun and antecedents.
5. Have students review the instruction on punctuating literary titles.

Critical Evaluation

Writing Process Workshop

When you're deciding whether or not to see a new movie, you may look at television or newspaper reviews of the movie to see what the critics think. A movie review is one type of critical evaluation—a written or spoken examination of what is and is not effective in a literary work, television program, or movie. Most often, a critical evaluation includes a brief summary of the work, comments upon its merits or weaknesses, and recommendations to readers or viewers.

Write a critical evaluation of *The Tragedy of Julius Caesar* or another literary work you've read. The following skills, introduced in this section's Writing Mini-Lesson, will help you.

Writing Skills Focus

▶ **Choose words with appropriate connotations.** Choosing words that have strong connotations—feelings and ideas associated with them—will give your evaluation more punch. (See p. 803.)

▶ **Provide examples** from the text for support. For example, if you say, "Antony is a skilled orator," follow that with a sentence such as, "In Act III, Scene ii, he stirs up the crowd with his 'Friends, Romans, countrymen . . .' speech."

The following is an excerpt from Ben Okri's critical evaluation of *Clear Light of Day*, a novel by Anita Desai.

① The writer offers an opinion about the effect of silence in Desai's novel.

② The writer gives an indication of the mood of the book.

③ The writer uses a word with connotations that create an image in readers' minds.

MODEL FROM LITERATURE

① Silence is clarity and white heat in Anita Desai's *Clear Light of Day*, a novel about a family reunion, its unease, and the ② disturbing remembrances that accompany it. Tara, now married to a diplomat, revisits her childhood home in Old Delhi and finds that, on the ③ shabby surface, nothing has changed.

804 ◆ Drama

Sourcebook

Students can find additional support including topic ideas, models, word bins, and graphic organizers in the chapter on Response to Literature (pp. 194–227)

Prewriting

Choose a Topic To which selection in this book have you had the strongest reaction? That selection will make the best subject for a critical evaluation. Scan the table of contents, or flip through the book to spark your memory.

Clarify Your Opinions Once you've chosen your selection, collect your thoughts about it. Create a chart like this one, listing what you liked about the selection and what you didn't like about it.

What I Liked	What I Didn't Like
_____	_____
_____	_____

Identify Your Purpose Review your list of likes and dislikes. Decide whether you will or will not recommend the work to other readers.

Summarize Your Opinions Begin by jotting down a brief summary of the selection. Then list your opinions about various aspects of the work, as well as the work as a whole. Next, jot down details from the story that will help support each opinion.

Drafting

Follow a Format Using the details you've gathered, draft your evaluation. Start with a paragraph that reveals your general opinion of the selection. Follow with a brief summary of the key details. Then elaborate on your opinion of the work, providing examples and details for support. End with a recommendation to readers.

Use Evaluative Modifiers Present your opinions forcefully and clearly by using precise adjectives to either praise or criticize the work. Look at these examples:

Precise Adjectives

Mild Praise	High Praise	Mild Disapproval	Strong Disapproval
readable	imaginative	dull	awful
expressive	hilarious	unfocused	tactless
solid	inspired	vague	tedious
mildly amusing	stimulating	inconsistent	painfully boring
informative	original	melodramatic	useless

APPLYING LANGUAGE SKILLS: Quotation Marks and Underlining

Place quotation marks around any examples that you quote directly from the text. If you are evaluating a poem or short story, place its title in quotation marks. If you are evaluating a novel or play, underline the title (if you are writing by hand) or enter it in italics (if you are working on a computer).

Plays and Novels:
The Tragedy of Julius Caesar
The Catcher in the Rye

Poems and Short Stories:
"Reapers"
"The Monkey's Paw"

Practice On your paper, write the following passage, placing quotation marks or underlining where necessary.

> In Shakespeare's play Hamlet, the famous lines To be or not to be show Prince Hamlet's classic moment of indecision.

Writer's Solution Connection Language Lab

For more practice with quotation marks, complete the Language Lab lesson on Semicolons, Colons, and Quotation Marks.

Prewriting

To help students choose a topic, you might suggest that they brainstorm in groups for a list of literary works they have read recently. Tell them to jot down notes as they share ideas. They can use their notes to choose a literary work about which to write.

Customize for
English Language Learners
Students learning English may have trouble using a variety of evaluative words. Help these students make lists of synonyms for words such as *like, dislike, good,* and *bad* that they can use to add variety to their critical evaluations.

Customize for
Less Proficient Writers
These students might need some guidance in choosing details to put into their critical evaluations. Work with them to create a set of questions that can guide them as they draft, such as "What was the best feature of this literary work? What specific examples of this feature do you find in the work?"

Customize for
More Advanced Students
Challenge these students to write about a longer work, and to incorporate specific literary terms in their critical reviews.

Writer's Solution

Writing Lab CD-ROM
The Gathering Details section of the Response to Literature tutorial contains a Word Bin of evaluation words. Have students use this activity to generate ideas for different words they can use to express their assessment of a work.

Drafting

Encourage students to draft their critical evaluations in a single sitting, getting all their ideas down on paper without laboring over word choice. Once students have completed a draft, they can go back into their work and make revisions.

Applying Language Skills

Quotation Marks and Underlining Remind students that in an analysis evaluating a literary work, and possibly comparing it to others, it will be especially important for students to use quotation marks and underlining correctly.

Answer
In Shakespeare's play, *Hamlet,* the famous lines "To be or not to be" show Prince Hamlet's classic moment of indecision.

Writer's Solution

For additional practice, use the **Language Lab CD-ROM** on Semicolons, Colons, and Quotation Marks.

Answers
In the end, perhaps, it is Caesar's belief in his own immortality that proves to be his downfall: Just before he dies, he tells the senators, "But I am as constant as the Northern Star."

Revising

Have students check their work for variety in evaluation words and for supporting examples. If they feel they need more supporting examples, encourage them to go back into the story to find some before creating a final draft.

Writer's Solution

Writing Lab CD-ROM

The revising screen contains information on going back to the selection for more information. Have students review this screen before creating a final draft.

Reinforce and Extend

Review the Writing Guidelines

After students have completed their assignments, review the characteristics of critical evaluations. Encourage students to come up with additional criteria for an effective evaluation based on what they learned by completing the assignment.

Applying Language Skills

Practice Answer In the end, perhaps, it is Caesar's belief in his own immortality that proves to be his downfall: Just before he dies he tells the senators, "But I am constant as the Northern Star."

APPLYING LANGUAGE SKILLS: Capitalization

Observe the following rules of capitalization of sentence beginnings:

1. Capitalize the first word of a direct quotation that can stand alone as a sentence: *The soothsayer says to Caesar, "Beware the ides of March."*

2. Capitalize the first word of a sentence in parentheses if that sentence stands alone: *Caesar made a show of refusing the crown. (In fact, he had arranged with Brutus to offer it to him.)*

3. Capitalize the first word of a sentence after a colon: *Brutus has a quality that makes Antony admire him: He is honest.*

Practice In your notebook, capitalize the proper words in the following sentence.

In the end, perhaps, it is caesar's belief in his own immortality that proves to be his downfall: just before he dies, he tells the senators, "but I am constant as the northern star."

Writer's Solution Connection Writing Lab

For more help using quotations in your literary analysis, see Using Quotations in the Writing Lab tutorial on Response to Literature.

806 ◆ Drama

Offer Precise Details It's not enough to simply say that you found a story humorous; you must back up your opinions. Explain *why* you found the story humorous, and cite specific examples of details that contributed to the humor.

Revising

Use a Checklist Use this checklist to guide your revision.
  ▶ Have you summarized the selection in a way that will enable readers to follow what you're saying?
  ▶ Have you clearly expressed your opinion of the work?
  ▶ Do your evaluative modifiers express the appropriate degree of praise or disappointment?
  ▶ What can you do to strengthen your support for your opinion?

Use a Model Look at the revisions made in this paragraph from a review of Shakespeare's poem *The Tragedy of Julius Caesar.*

REVISION MODEL

In the ①*Tragedy of Julius Caesar,* Cassius is one of the conspirators against Caesar. Cassius believes that the gods do not interest themselves in human affairs. ②*and that omens are merely superstitions* Now he credits his fate to bad omens. He thinks that when eagles follow their armies to Philippi, it is a good sign. However, when the eagles are replaced by ravens and crows, this foreshadows death to him. ③*"Their shadows seem a canopy most fatal," says Cassius.*

① The writer changes the quotation marks to underscore because a play is a full-length work.
② The writer adds information that clarifies her point.
③ This quotation from the text supports the writer's point.

Publishing

▶ **Create a Class Publication** With some classmates, create a class magazine of critical reviews.
▶ **Create a Book Group on the Internet** Post your critical evaluation on a bulletin board. Invite other readers to share their responses to your evaluation and to share evaluations of books they have enjoyed.

✓ ASSESSMENT		4	3	2	1
PORTFOLIO ASSESSMENT Use the rubric on Response to Literature in the *Alternative Assessment* booklet (p. 110) to assess students' writing. Add these criteria to customize the rubric to this assignment.	**Choose words with appropriate connotations**	All words used convey connotations appropriate to purpose.	Most words used convey connotations appropriate to purpose.	Some words do not have appropriate connotations.	Few, if any, words have appropriate connotations.
	Provide examples	All assertions are supported with examples.	Most assertions are supported with examples.	Some of the examples do not directly support the assertion being made.	Few appropriate examples are used.

Real-World Reading Skills Workshop

Adjust Your Reading Rate

When you are reading the Sunday comics, you'll read much faster than you would if you were reading your biology textbook. You don't have to read everything the same way. You can skim, scan, or read thoroughly; it's wise to adjust your reading rate to suit the material and your reading goals.

Identify Your Reading Purpose You'll approach different kinds of reading material with different purposes. Your reading rate should reflect your purpose for reading. If you pick up a television guide looking for something to watch, you'll probably just skim the contents to see what's on. If you are researching a particular type of product before deciding what to purchase or if you are you reading *The Tragedy of Julius Caesar* for an upcoming literature test, you'll read more slowly and carefully.

To acquire in-depth knowledge of a topic, you read slowly and closely; if you need only an overview of a specific piece of information, you can skim or scan. When you skim, you read or glance through quickly. When you scan, you read through quickly but looking for main points or specific information.

Slow Down, Speed Up Adjust your reading rate for the different parts of a single work. For example, you can read introductions, overviews,

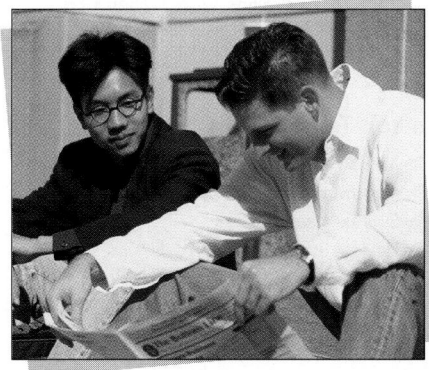

and summaries fairly quickly because they usually do not contain detailed information. You should read sections that explain complex ideas or that contain facts, dates, or statistics more closely. You may even want to takes notes on these sections.

Use the Clues When reading a textbook, highlighted words within the text are a clue that a term or idea is important. Slow down to make sure you understand the definition or concept.

Footnotes and glosses (notes in the side margin) are more of a choice. Use them as needed to aid your understanding. Don't stop to read footnotes that explain words or references that you already understand.

Apply the Strategy

Describe how you might adjust your reading rate in the following situations:

1. You are reading a letter from your friend who is studying in Europe for a month.
2. You are reading *Celebrity Stories* magazine.
3. You are reading an encyclopedia article on the history of India and its people.
4. You are reading an instruction manual that explains how to hook up your new stereo speakers.
5. You are reviewing a chapter in your science textbook to prepare for a possible quiz.

✔ Here are other situations in which you would use different reading rates.
- ▶ Reading a business letter
- ▶ Reading the different parts of a newspaper
- ▶ Reading a nonfiction article on a topic unfamiliar to you
- ▶ Reading a novel or play
- ▶ Looking up a number in a telephone directory

Real-World Reading Skills Workshop ◆ 807

3. You will read closely and slowly, possibly even taking notes on special vocabulary and cultural terms.
4. You will read carefully, pausing between reading steps to carry out the instructions.
5. You will not read as closely as the first time you read the chapter. Instead, you will skim or scan, looking for main ideas and taking notes on details that support those ideas.

Ask students to list all the reasons they use the telephone. Besides "visiting with friends" answers should include, ordering products, getting information, sharing information, making appointments, and getting directions. Point out that in all these cases, it is especially important to be heard and understood. Since they cannot be judged on their appearance during a telephone call, the person on the other end of the line will form an opinion based on their telephone conversation skills.

Suggested Answers:

1. Sample answers: (a) My name is Max Field and I'm calling to report an accident on the corner of Main and Third. Two cars collided, and it looks like one of the drivers is unconscious. (b) Hello, my name is Tanya Corrin. I'm calling about the receptionist job advertised in The Journal. I'd like to make an appointment for an interview.
2. The language and tone of voice students use should reflect the age and relationship of the person with whom they are speaking. However, even in the casual conversation with the friend, students must be clear and precise about the time and place of the meeting.

Telephone Conversation | Speaking and Listening Workshop

The telephone is one of our most valuable means of communication. You can use the telephone to visit with friends, get information, make appointments, or order products. Your telephone transaction will go smoothly if you use good sense and good manners.

Get Off to a Good Start When you're making a personal or professional call, begin by identifying yourself and your purpose. "Hello, my name is Keisha Jones. I'm calling in response to your ad in Friday's paper." "Hi, Mrs. Flynn, this is Tom. Is Mary at home?"

When you are calling to request information or order a product, it is not necessary to identify yourself at the beginning, but if you're ordering something, you will need to give your name and other information at some point during the conversation.

Speak Up Whether you realize it or not, when you speak face to face, you read body language. These visual cues help you to "hear" what is being said. However, when you're on the telephone, those visual cues are not available, so it's especially important to speak clearly. The person on the other end of the line is dependent solely on your voice message.

Say It Again Repeating information ensures that you have heard the other person correctly. When you are receiving phone numbers, addresses, directions, name spellings, or the date and time of appointments, repeat them to verify their accuracy.

End on a Good Note At the end of a business call, thank the other person and confirm future contact. For instance, "Thank you for your time, Mrs. Goetz. I'll call you next week to confirm our appointment."

Apply the Strategies

Develop your telephone style and skill. Practice the following telephone conversations:
1. Work out what you would say to open a telephone conversation in the following situations.
   a. You've just witnessed a terrible car accident and call to report it.
   b. You are calling to inquire about a part-time position at a dentist's office.
2. With a partner, role-play the following telephone conversations:
   a. You are calling to thank your grandmother for a birthday present you received in the mail.
   b. You are making plans with a friend to meet at the movies.

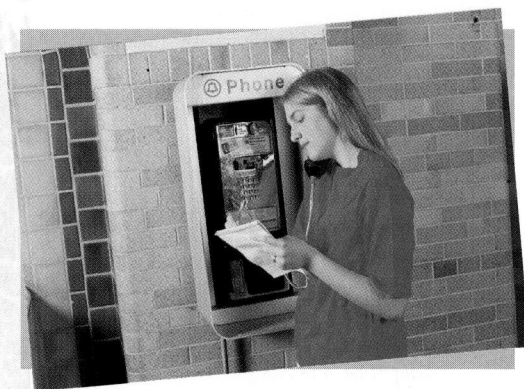

Tips for Telephone Conversations
▶ Identify yourself
▶ Communicate your purpose
▶ Speak clearly
▶ Review information

808 ◆ *Drama*

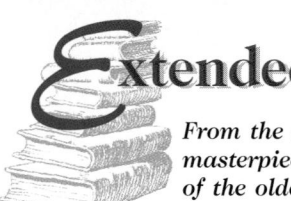

Extended Reading Opportunities

From the ancient Greek tragedies to Shakespeare's masterpieces to contemporary plays, drama is one of the oldest and most respected forms of literature. These plays will show you why.

Suggested Titles

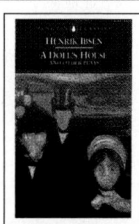

Antigone
Jean Anouilh

If ever there were an argument to prove the timelessness of the great Greek tragedies, it would include Jean Anouilh's *Antigone*. Anouilh (1910–1987), a French playwright, rewrites Sophocles' classic with twentieth-century dialogue. He also makes Sophocles' characters more human, delving into their thoughts and feelings. A brilliant and enjoyable play in its own right, this *Antigone* will also enrich your understanding and appreciation of Sophocles' original.

Twelfth Night
William Shakespeare

A twin brother and sister separated in their youth, a rich countess looking for a husband, a young duke looking for a wife, and a scheming steward ... these are the principal characters of *Twelfth Night, or What You Will*, one of William Shakespeare's most delightful comedies. In addition to being a classic "screwball comedy," this play also introduces one of Shakespeare's most memorable heroines, the beautiful and intelligent Viola.

A Doll's House
Henrik Ibsen

This well-known and popular play by Norwegian playwright Henrik Ibsen tells the story of Nora Helmer, a woman who lives an apparently comfortable life as the wife of a bank manager. Her husband, however, treats her like a plaything, rather than as a mature adult. When a crisis threatens to destroy the family, Nora comes into her own as a responsible person—though her actions have consequences of their own.

Other Possibilities

Witness for the Prosecution	Agatha Christie
Fools	Neil Simon
Two Gentlemen of Verona	William Shakespeare

Planning Students' Extended Reading

All the works on this page are good choices for extending students' understanding of and appreciation for dramas. The following information may help you choose which to assign.

Customize for *Varying Student Needs*

- *Antigone* is a challenging play that will appeal to your more advanced students.
- *Twelfth Night,* while challenging, has high appeal due to its humor. You can use the movie version of the play to help students understand it.
- *A Doll's House* is a shorter play. The conflict is easy to understand, and the vocabulary is not too challenging for your less advanced students.

Sensitive Issues

- *Antigone* and *A Doll's House* both portray characters challenging authority.
- The characters in *Twelfth Night* drink alcohol in several scenes. The dialogue contains sexual innuendoes.

Resources for Teaching Novels and Plays
This booklet contains graphic organizers, teaching strategies, and transparencies that will be invaluable in teaching any of these novels.

Planning Instruction and Assessment

Unit Objectives

1. To read a variety of poems
2. To apply reading strategies appropriate for reading poetry
3. To recognize literary elements used in poems
4. To increase vocabulary
5. To learn elements of grammar and usage
6. To write in a variety of modes and about situations based on the poems
7. To develop speaking and listening skills, by doing proposed activities

Meeting the Objectives

With each selection, you will find instructional material and portfolio opportunities through which students can meet these objectives. Further, you will find additional practice pages for reading strategies, literary elements, vocabulary, and grammar in the **Selection Support** booklet in the Teaching Resources box.

Setting Goals Work with your students at the beginning of the unit to set goals for unit outcomes. Plan what skills and concepts you wish students to acquire. You may individualize according to students' performance levels or learning modalities.

Portfolios You may have students keep portfolios of their work or of their work in progress. The activities and prompts on the Build Your Portfolio page of each selection provide opportunities for students to apply the concepts presented with the selection.

Awaiting Spring, Scott Burdick

 Humanities: Art

Awaiting Spring by Scott Burdick.

Call attention to the elements of balance in this painting. Students might note the two figures, one carved, one living, poised at either end of the staircase. Help them see, in addition, the balance between the heavily carved staircase and the delicate bare tree and cloudy sky above it. There is also the balance between what is fixed—the carved figure and staircase—and what can change—the living woman, the tree about to bud, and the sky about to rain.

Have students link this painting with the focus of Unit 9, Poetry, by answering the following questions:

1. Poems are memorable for their vivid images and figures of speech. What vivid description or figure of speech (imaginative comparison) would you use to describe this painting? *Students might say that the sky looks like a smoky blue marble or the tree reaches its arms to the stone angel.*

2. If you were to write a poem about this painting, what sort of emotion would it express, and what images in the painting contribute to that emotion? *Sample answer: My poem would be melancholy; the cloudy sky and the woman whose face is turned away contribute to that emotion.*

Poetry

There are almost as many definitions of poetry as there are poets. Poetry can appear in neat stanzas, or it can look almost like prose on a page. Sometimes, it might even form a picture with the words. It can tell a story, express an idea, define a character, convey an emotion, describe a setting, or examine a situation. The poems in this unit will give you a sense of the wide range of literature that we call poetry.

Assessing Student Progress

The following tools are available to measure the degree to which students meet the unit objectives:

Informal Assessment

The questions on the Guide for Responding sections are a first level of response to the concepts and skills presented with the selection. Students' responses are a brief informal measure of their grasp of the material. Their responses on this level can indicate where further instruction and practice are needed. You may then follow up with the practice pages in *Selection Support.*

You will find literature and reading guides in the *Alternative Assessment* booklet, which you may give students on an individual basis for informal assessment of their performance.

Formal Assessment

In the *Formal Assessment* booklet, you will find selection tests and a unit test.

Selection Tests The selection tests measure comprehension and skills acquisition for each selection or group of selections.

Unit Test The unit test, which calls on students to read a passage of literature they have not previously seen, applies the unit skills on a broader level. The Critical Reading section measures Unit Objectives 1, 2, and 3. The Vocabulary and Grammar section measures Objectives 4 and 5. The Essay section measures Objectives 1 and 6.

Both the Critical Reading and the Vocabulary and Grammar sections use formats similar to those found on many standardized tests, including the SAT.

◆ 811

Alternative Assessment

Portfolios As you review individual pieces or the collected work in students' portfolios, you will find assessment sheets available in the portfolio section of the *Alternative Assessment* booklet.

Scoring Rubrics You will find scoring rubrics for writing modes in the *Alternative Assessment* booklet. You can apply these to Writing Mini-Lessons and to Writing Process Workshop lessons.

Speaking and Listening The *Alternative Assessment* booklet contains assessment sheets for speaking and listening activities.

Learning Modalities The *Alternative Assessment* contains activities that appeal to different learning styles. You may use these to as an alternative measurement of students' growth

Guide for Reading

OBJECTIVES

1. To read, comprehend, and interpret a poem
2. To relate a poem to personal experience
3. To use strategies for reading poetry to read for success
4. To recognize atmosphere in poetry
5. To build vocabulary in context and learn words with multiple meanings
6. To recognize and use inverted word order
7. To write a crime report with a clear, consistent purpose
8. To respond to the poem through writing, speaking and listening, and projects

SKILLS INSTRUCTION

Vocabulary:
Words With Multiple Meanings

Grammar:
Inverted Word Order

Reading for Success:
Strategies for Reading Poetry

Literary Focus:
Atmosphere

Writing:
Clear, Consistent Purpose

Speaking and Listening:
Folk Music (teacher edition)

Critical Viewing:
Infer; Draw Conclusions

PORTFOLIO OPPORTUNITIES

Writing: Journal Entry; Editorial; Alternate Chorus

Writing Mini-Lesson: Crime Report

Speaking and Listening: Paired Reading; Folk Music

Projects: Irish Writers Timeline; Encyclopedia of Folklore

More About the Author

William Butler Yeats and Lady Augusta Gregory, the founders of the Irish literary revival, were fascinated by the stories of fairies and the supernatural in Irish folklore. Together, they traveled through western Ireland investigating and collecting the tales and beliefs of the Irish people. They gathered the stories into a volume called *The Celtic Twilight*.

William Butler Yeats
(1865–1939)

A father who believes in the "religion of art" can leave an unusual legacy for a son inclined to be an artist. William Butler Yeats was the son of John Butler Yeats, a well-known Irish painter. William studied painting for three years, and art remained one of the three main concerns of his life. The other two were Irish nationalism and the study of the supernatural. These concerns are central issues in much of Yeats's poetry and drama. "The Stolen Child" reflects his fascination with Irish folklore, a source he used frequently in his early work.

The "First Irish Poet" Yeats's poetry broke new ground. His writing was simple, natural, and more closely linked to the voice of Irish people, their folklore traditions, and their national concerns than that of previous Irish poets. His interest in Irish politics and nationalism led him to help found the Irish National Theater in 1899.

For a time, Yeats moved to England because of political conflicts between people in Ireland of English and Irish ancestry. (His father was of English ancestry, and his mother was of Irish ancestry.) When he returned, he resided in Thoor Ballylee, a countryside tower that became an important symbol in his later poems. Yeats is considered one of the greatest twentieth-century poets in the English language.

Yeats was awarded the Nobel Prize for Literature in 1922. In one of his most famous poems, "Under Ben Bulben," he provides his own epitaph in the last lines of the poem. These lines are carved on Yeats's tombstone:

> *Cast a cold eye*
> *On life, on death,*
> *Horseman, pass by!*

◆ Build Vocabulary

WORDS WITH MULTIPLE MEANINGS

When Yeats says, "Where the wave of moonlight *glosses* / The dim grey sands with light," he is describing the moonlight shining or polishing each grain of sand with its rays of light. *Gloss* is one of many words in English that has multiple meanings. In this poem, it means "to shine; make lustrous"; *gloss* can also be a noun meaning an explanation inserted in a text to make it more understandable, similar to an annotation or a footnote.

herons	
glosses	**WORD BANK**
slumbering	Before you read, preview this list of words from the poem.

◆ Build Grammar Skills

INVERTED WORD ORDER

"The Stolen Child" begins with the line "Where dips the rocky highland . . ." What makes the clause sound unusual is the **inverted word order.** Usually, English word order falls into a subject-verb-complement pattern. In the clause from Yeats's poem, the verb, *dips*, precedes the subject, *the rocky highland*. Yeats intentionally uses inverted word order to give a mysterious, chantlike quality to his poem. When you see other instances of inverted word order, read the sentence in normal order for sense.

Prentice Hall Literature Program Resources

REINFORCE / RETEACH / EXTEND

Selection Support Pages
Build Vocabulary: Words With Multiple Meanings, p. 224
Build Grammar Skills: Inverted Word Order, p. 225
Reading for Success: Strategies for Reading Poetry, pp. 226–227
Literary Focus: Atmosphere, p. 228

Strategies for Diverse Student Needs, p. 55

Beyond Literature
Cultural Connection: *Celtic Folklore,* p. 55

Formal Assessment Selection Test, pp. 195–197; Assessment Resources Software

Alternative Assessment, p. 55

Resource Pro CD-R⊘M
"The Stolen Child"—includes all resource materials and customizable lesson plan

 Listening to Literature Audiocassette
"The Stolen Child"

Literature CD-R⊘M *How to Read and Understand Poetry,* Feature 2

The Stolen Child

◆ Literature and Your Life

CONNECT YOUR EXPERIENCE

In almost any culture around the world, you can hear tales of little people who, through their supernatural powers, can make a person rich, beautiful, or powerful. Fairies, elves, sprites, pixies—these are just a few of the names by which these magical folk are known. As you may know from fairy tales, getting their help is not always as easy as it seems. There's usually a hidden price to pay. "The Stolen Child" tells the story of fairies who offer a world of pleasant delights—but at a very high price.

Journal Writing Jot down what you know about fairies and other magical little people from folklore and fairy tales.

THEMATIC FOCUS: MAKING CHOICES

The fairies in "The Stolen Child" offer compelling reasons for the child to follow them. At the end of the poem, notice the suggestion of what is lost in exchange for this choice. Next time you face a choice, you may ask yourself not only what you will gain, but what you may lose.

◆ Background for Understanding

CULTURE

Some call them pixies or sprites, others call them fairies; each of these creatures comes from folklore and legend. They are human in shape with magical powers. In Irish, or Celtic, folklore, these spirit creatures are called fairies. They live in a place called Avalon, which means "place of apples."

According to folklore, if you find a circle of dark green grass or a circle of mushrooms, you may have stumbled onto a fairy ring—a place where fairies have danced. If you see a glow come from decaying wood, it is believed you have seen a fairy spark. In reality, the first phenomenon is created by fungus and the second from phosphorous (which glows) produced in decaying wood.

◆ Literary Focus

ATMOSPHERE

Picture the following setting as the first scene in a movie: Nightfall. Large birds flap their long wings, creating shadows on a lonely lake. Water rats wake from sleep and begin to scamper in circles. The dew glistens in the moonlight.

These images create a tranquil, slightly mysterious or even magical atmosphere. **Atmosphere** is the mood or the overall feeling that a story or poem conveys. A writer establishes atmosphere through details of the setting or action. In poetry, rhyme, meter, and other sound devices can also create atmosphere. Together, all these elements create the effect the poet wants.

The following lines from "The Stolen Child" create a mysterious, mystical atmosphere in which a meeting takes place between fairies and a human child.

> Where the wave of moonlight glosses
> The dim grey sands with light,
> Far off by the furthest Rosses . . .

Guide for Reading ◆ 813

Preparing for Standardized Tests

Reading and Vocabulary Identifying words with multiple meanings is a skill that will help students perform better on the vocabulary and reading comprehension sections of standardized tests. Students may be given questions such as the following:

In which sentence does the underlined word have the same meaning as the underlined word in the first sentence? *(C)*

The bird was able to light on the tiny twig.
(A) I need more light in order to read.
(B) The canoe looks heavy, but it's light.
(C) A helicopter can light on the roof.
(D) I left the light on all night.
(E) The moon will light your way.

By noting that *light* is used as a verb and that the more common meanings of *light*, "illumination" and "of little weight," make no sense in the context, students can determine that item C is the correct answer. For additional practice in identifying and defining words with multiple meanings, use the Build Vocabulary page in **Selection Support,** p. 224.

813

The Reading for Success page in each unit presents a set of problem-solving procedures to help readers understand authors' words and ideas on multiple levels. Good readers develop a bank of strategies from which they can draw as needed.

Unit 9 introduces strategies for reading poetry. These strategies give readers an approach to understand poetry through its distinguishing qualities, including figurative language, images, and sound elements. By using these strategies as they read, students will be better able to analyze the material presented in this selection.

These strategies for reading poetry are modeled with "The Stolen Child." Each green box shows an example of the thinking process involved in applying one of these strategies.

How to Use the Reading for Success Page

- Introduce the strategies for reading poetry, presenting each as a problem-solving procedure. Be sure students understand what each strategy involves and under what circumstances to apply it.

- Before students read the poem, have them preview it, looking at the annotations in the green boxes that model the strategies.

- To reinforce these strategies after students have read "The Stolen Child," have students do the Reading for Success pages in *Selection Support,* pp. 226–227. This activity gives students an opportunity to read a selection and practice strategies for reading poetry by writing their own annotations.

Reading for Success

Strategies for Reading Poetry

Poetry is a very distinctive kind of writing. It differs from other forms of writing in its appearance, its use of language, and its sound. Poets' imaginative use of language can sometimes make a poem seem complex or hard to understand. Here are strategies to help you read poetry successfully and enjoy it as well.

Identify the speaker.

When you read a poem, you are hearing the voice of the poem's speaker. The speaker is not necessarily the poet, although it can be or it can be a part of the poet's personality. The speaker may be a character created by the poet. Determine who you think is "telling" the poem, and try to determine his or her perspective on the situation in the poem. Recognizing the speaker and his or her perspective will give you an insight into the meaning of the poem.

Envision images and figures of speech.

Use your senses to experience the pleasures of a poem. For instance, see the dim gray sands bathed in moonlight; feel the frothy bubbles of the trout stream; hear the mooing of the cows on the nearby hillside.

Read according to punctuation.

Keep in mind that even if a poem is shaped to fit a particular rhythm and rhyme, a poem's words are put together and punctuated as sentences. For example, when you read "The Stolen Child," notice that each stanza is a complete sentence, expressing a complete thought. When you read a poem, don't stop at the end of each line unless a punctuation mark (period, comma, colon, semicolon, or dash) stops you.

Listen to the poem.

One of the things that distinguishes poetry from prose is its sound. Poetry is meant to be read aloud; only by doing so will you hear the music of the poet's words.

Paraphrase.

Restate the speaker's experiences and feelings in your own words. Restating the lines or stanzas will help you clarify their meaning.

Respond to what you read.

Think about what the speaker has said. How do the images in the poem affect you? What does the poem say to you?

As you read "The Stolen Child," look at the notes in the boxes. These notes demonstrate how to apply these strategies to a poem.

Reading Strategies: Support and Reinforcement

Appropriate Reading Strategies Students are given a reading strategy to apply in reading each selection. Each reading strategy in this unit will help them gain insight into the poems to which they apply it.

Reading Prompts To encourage application of the given reading strategy, there are occasional prompts, within green boxes, at appropriate and significant points.

In addition, there are red boxes prompting application of the Literary Focus concept and maroon boxes prompting students to connect with their lives.

Using the Boxed Annotations and Prompts

The material in the green, red, and maroon boxes along the sides of selections is intended to help students apply the literary element and the reading strategy and to make a connection with their lives.

You may use the boxed material in these ways:

- Have students pause when they come to a box and respond to its prompt before they continue reading.

- Urge students to read through the selection ignoring the boxes. After they have read the selection completely, they may go back and review the selection, responding to the prompts.

THE STOLEN CHILD

MODEL

WILLIAM BUTLER YEATS

Where dips the rocky highland
Of Sleuth Wood in the lake,
There lies a leafy island
Where flapping <u>herons</u> wake
5 The drowsy water rats;
There we've hid our faery[1] vats,
Full of berries
And of reddest stolen cherries.
Come away, O human child!
10 *To the waters and the wild*
With a faery, hand in hand,
For the world's more full of weeping
    than you can understand.

❶

Where the wave of moonlight <u>glosses</u>
The dim grey sands with light,
15 Far off by furthest Rosses[2]

---

1. **faery:** A different spelling of fairy.
2. **Rosses:** Marshes.

◆ Build Vocabulary

herons (her′ ənz) *n.:* Birds with long necks, legs, and bills that live along riverbanks and marshes

glosses (glôs′ əs) *v.:* Shines

◀ **Critical Viewing** In what way does this picture contribute to the dreamlike atmosphere of "The Stolen Child"? [Infer]

❷

Notice that the **speakers** *of this poem are the fairies. Their point of view affects your view of events.*

Use your senses to envision the grains of sand glowing in the moonlight.

The Stolen Child ◆ 815

Develop Understanding

Literature CD-ROM To introduce students to poetry you might use the **Literature CD-ROM**, Feature 4, which introduces poetry, discusses reader response to poetry, and provides quotations from several well-known poets.

One-Minute Insight

In this poem, fairies are tempting a child to come away from his life as a human, with all its attendant suffering, and join them in a fairyland where nature is friendly and benign. In the last stanza, however, the fairies reveal that the child will also leave the good things in human life and go to the unknown, the wild world of the fairies. Readers are left to contemplate the price that must be paid for escaping the trials and responsibilities of the real world.

◆ Reading for Success

❶ **Identify the Speaker** Ask students who the speakers are and what word or words reveal the speakers' identity. *The speakers are fairies, and the words "we've" and "our" together with their descriptions reveal their identity.*

Listening to Literature Audiocassettes You may wish to play the audiocassette of the poem as students read through it for the first time.

▶Critical Viewing◀

❷ **Infer** This misty photograph of a forest contributes to the magical, dreamlike tone of Yeats's poem; it's easy to imagine the fairies leaping "to and fro" and chasing bubbles in this scene.

Block Scheduling Strategies

Consider these suggestions to take advantage of extended class time:

- Have students view Feature 2 on the **Literature CD-ROM.** This section discusses the definition of poetry and oral tradition.
- Introduce the strategies for reading poetry on page 811. Have students examine the application of these strategies in the boxed annotations. After they have read the poem, have them answer the Reading for Success questions on page 819.

- Let students work in small groups to discuss and answer the questions in the Connections to Today's World feature on page 818. Encourage students to find other popular songs that have themes related to the themes in "The Stolen Child" and "Cats in the Cradle." Allow time for students to present their choices to the class.
- Ask students to work in small groups to complete the Alternate Chorus in the Writing section in the Idea Bank on page

820. Then groups can read the poem and their choruses into a tape recorder and play the recording for the class.
- Students who are interested in the Irish Writers Timeline in the Projects section of the Idea Bank on page 820 might enjoy creating an Irish History Timeline for the nineteenth and twentieth centuries, showing the historical events that influenced Yeats and his writing.

❶ Words With Multiple Meanings
Ask students what the word *foot* can mean as both a noun and a verb. *Foot as a noun is a body part; foot as a verb means to move quickly or dance.* Which meaning of the word is used here? *Foot here means to move quickly or dance.*

◆ **Reading for Success**

❷ Envision Images and Figures of Speech Ask students to describe the image they envision when they read the lines, "While the world is full of troubles/And is anxious in its sleep." To what does Yeats compare "the world"? *Students should envision the world as a person tossing and turning in his or her sleep. Some students may identify the figure of speech as "personification."*

◆ **Reading for Success**

❸ Listen to the Poem; Respond Have volunteers read aloud the chorus of the poem. Ask students how this part of the poem affects them. *Students may indicate that the chorus makes them feel uneasy, or that they find it magical and appealing.*

◆ **Literary Focus**

❹ Atmosphere Ask students to describe the atmosphere that is created by the repetition of this chorus. *The chantlike quality of the chorus and the images in it create a magical, mysterious atmosphere.*

◆ **Reading for Success**

❺ Paraphrase Have students restate this portion of the stanza in their own words. *Suggested paraphrase: Where the water runs from the hills above Glen-Car, we whisper in the ears of sleeping fish and make them uneasy.*

◆ **Reading for Success**

❻ Read According to Punctuation Have students read this stanza aloud, pausing where punctuation indicates, rather than at the ends of lines. *Students should pause after going "solemn-eyed" and "breast."*

816

---

❶ We foot it all the night,
Weaving olden dances
Mingling hands and mingling glances
Till the moon has taken flight;
20 To and fro we leap
❷ And chase the frothy bubbles,
While the world is full of troubles
And is anxious in its sleep.
Come away, O human child!
25 *To the waters and the wild*
❸ *With a faery, hand in hand,*
❹ *For the world's more full of weeping*
than you can understand.

Where the wandering water gushes
From the hills above Glen-Car,
30 In pools among the rushes
❺ That scarce could bathe a star,
We seek for <u>slumbering</u> trout
And whispering in their ears
Give them unquiet dreams;
35 Leaning softly out
From ferns that drop their tears
Over the young streams.

◆ **Build Vocabulary**

slumbering (slum′ bər iŋ) *v.*: Sleeping

Come away, O human child!
To the waters and the wild
40 *With a faery, hand in hand,*
For the world's more full of weeping
than you can understand.

Away with us he's going,
The solemn-eyed:
He'll hear no more the lowing[3]
45 Of the calves on the warm hillside
Or the kettle on the hob[4]
Sing peace into his breast,
Or see the brown mice bob
Round and round the oatmeal chest.

50 *For he comes, the human child,*
To the waters and the wild
With a faery, hand in hand,
From a world more full of weeping
than he can understand.

6

Respond by identifying your feelings about the fairies' triumph.

3. lowing (lō′ iŋ) *n.*: Mooing.
4. hob (häb) *n.*: Ledge on a fireplace used for keeping a kettle or pan warm.

Guide for Responding

◆ *Literature and Your Life*

Reader's Response Do you agree with the line repeated in "The Stolen Child" that "the world's more full of weeping than you can understand"? Why or why not?

Thematic Focus What do you think will be the consequence of a human child choosing to go with fairies rather than staying with humans?

✓ **Check Your Comprehension**

1. Who is the speaker of this poem?
2. Where have the fairies hidden vats full of berries?
3. Why do the fairies say the human child should go with them?
4. Summarize what happens in the poem.

Reinforce and Extend

Answers

◆ *Literature and Your Life*

Reader's Response Students' answers will depend upon their personal experience, but they should support their opinion with examples or evidence.

Thematic Focus Some students might indicate that the child's human nature will arise and cause conflicts; others might indicate that the child will betray the earthly world.

✓ **Check Your Comprehension**

1. A fairy (or group of fairies) is the speaker of the poem.
2. They have hidden the vats of berries on a lake island.
3. They say the child should come with them because the world is full of sadness.
4. Fairies try to lure a child to come with them; they tempt it with berries and descriptions of carefree, mischievous activities. In the end, the child goes with the fairies, leaving behind the earthly world.

"The Stolen Child" tells of a child lost through fairies' magical powers. "Cat's in the Cradle" tells of a lost childhood. Not until the child is grown does the father realize all the precious moments he has lost.

An artist in the American folk tradition of Woody Guthrie and Bob Dylan, Harry Chapin wrote songs that are essentially short stories set to music. A true humanitarian, over the course of his career he raised more than five million dollars for various causes. He died in 1981 in a car crash, while on the way to perform at a benefit concert.

Cat's in the Cradle

Harry Chapin and Sandy Chapin

My child arrived just the other day,
He came to the world in the usual way.
But there were planes to catch, and bills
   to pay.
He learned to walk while I was away.
And he was talking 'fore I knew it, and
   as he grew,
He'd say, "I'm gonna be like you, Dad.
You know I'm gonna be like you."

And the cat's in the cradle and the silver
   spoon,
Little boy blue and the man in the moon.
"When you coming home, Dad?" "I don't
   know when,
But we'll get together then.
You know we'll have a good time then."

My son turned ten just the other day.
He said, "Thanks for the ball, Dad, come
   on let's play.
Can you teach me to throw?" I said, "Not
   today,
I got a lot to do." He said, "That's ok."

And he walked away but his smile,
   lemme tell you,
Said, "I'm gonna be like him, yeah.
You know, I'm gonna be like him."

And the cat's in the cradle and the silver
   spoon,
Little boy blue and the man in the moon.
"When you coming home, Dad?" "I don't
   know when,
But we'll get together then.
You know we'll have a good time then."

Well, he came from college just the other
   day,
So much like a man I just had to say,
"Son, I'm proud of you. Can you sit for a
   while?"
He shook his head, and he said with a
   smile,
"What I'd really like, Dad, is to borrow
   the car keys.
See you later. Can I have them please?"

Cat's in the Cradle ◆ 817

Like "The Stolen Child," Harry Chapin's song "Cat's in the Cradle" tells the story of a lost child. The child in the song, however, is not lost through magical means. The everyday cares and worries of the real word eventually create a void between father and son that cannot be crossed.

More About the Author
Singer/songwriter Harry Chapin (1942–1981) was a social activist as well as an artist. He committed time and money to the cause of ending world hunger, founding World Hunger Year in 1975. Besides being a songwriter, Chapin was a filmmaker (nominated for an Academy Award) and the author of a musical play (nominated for two Tony Awards). Chapin died in a car accident on July 16, 1981.

Customize for
English Language Learners
Students whose first language is not English may not be familiar with the nursery rhymes from which these lines are taken. Have volunteers recite the rhymes and discuss why the writer chose to include them.

Thematic Connection
Ask students how the child in Chapin's song is learning to realize that the world is "full of weeping," just as it is for the stolen child. *As he asks for his father's company and is denied, he learns to adjust to not having his father's companionship.*

Customize for
More Advanced Students
Advanced readers can be challenged to explain how the narrative turns around in the third verse. In what way has the son become like his father?

Speaking and Listening Mini-Lesson

Folk Music
This mini-lesson supports the Speaking and Listening activity in the Idea Bank on page 820.

Introduce the Concept Many folk songs tell stories. Because these songs come from cultures all over the world, many have references that listeners will not understand. If students choose songs from unfamiliar cultures, they may have to do some research to understand and explain such references.

Develop Background When looking for songs, students should consider these questions:

- From which culture does the song come?
- On what story is the song based?
- What references will have to be explained?
- In what ways does the song differ from, or add to, the story?

Apply the Information Many libraries have song books and recordings of folk songs. Encourage students to use these sources. Students should take notes on the stories, list and research their references, then give their presentations.

Assess the Outcome Students should answer all the questions in Develop Background. Assess presentations based on how thoroughly each question was addressed. You may wish to allow students to revise their presentations based on your feedback.

◆ Critical Thinking

Compare and Contrast Ask students how this song and Yeat's poem are similar and how they are different. *They both use rhythm and rhyme and both include a verse/refrain, or chorus. They treat the theme of loss and the troubles faced in the real world. In Yeats's poem, a child is lost when he leaves the real world. In Chapin's song, a child is lost when he becomes part of the real world.*

◆ Critical Thinking

Draw Conclusions The father and the son in the picture, unlike the father and the son in the song, are spending time together on an activity they are enjoying. They find time to "escape" from the trials of the world together; they are forming an emotional bond.

Answers

1. Students may point out that the theme (demanding modern life swallowing up people's time), language ("my new job's a hassle") and details (college, car keys) of Chapin's song could all make it a modern version of the story in Yeat's poem.
2. Yeat's poem and Chapin's song are both told in stanzas that alternate between pieces of a story in progress and a chorus, or refrain.
3. The moral to this song might be "Enjoy the people you love before it's too late."
4. Sample advice: (a) Devote some attention to your son before it's too late; (b) Be forgiving toward your father even though he was not always there for you.

CONNECTIONS TO TODAY'S WORLD

And the cat's in the cradle and the silver
spoon,
Little boy blue and the man in the moon.
"When you coming home, son?" "I don't
know when,
But we'll get together then, Dad.
You know we'll have a good time then."

I've long since retired and my son's
moved away.
I called him up just the other day.
I said, "I'd like to see you if you don't
mind."
He said, "I'd love to, Dad, if I could
find the time.
You see, my new job's a hassle and
the kid's got the flu,
But it's sure nice talking to you,
Dad.

▲ **Critical Viewing** What details in this picture indicate that this father and son are closer to each other than the father and son in "Cat's in the Cradle"? [Draw Conclusions]

It's been sure nice talking to you."
And as I hung up the phone, it occurred
to me,
He'd grown up just like me.
My boy was just like me.

And the cat's in the cradle and the silver
spoon,
Little boy blue and the man in the moon.
"When you coming home, son?" "I don't
know when,
But we'll get together then, Dad.
You know we'll have a good time
then."

1. In what way is the story told in "Cat's in the Cradle" a modern version of "The Stolen Child"?
2. Explain how the structure of "The Stolen Child" is similar to the structure of this song.
3. If there were a moral to this song, what would it be?
4. (a) What advice would you give to the father in this song? (b) What advice would you give to the son?

818 ◆ Poetry

 Beyond the Selection

FURTHER READING

Other Works by William Butler Yeats
Collected Poems
Collected Plays

Other Works by Harry Chapin
Heads and Tails
Short Stories

Other Works With the Theme of Choices and Consequences

"The Road Not Taken," Robert Frost
"anyone lived in a pretty how town,"
E.E. Cummings
"Richard Corey," Edward Arlington Robinson

We suggest that you preview these works before recommending them to students.

INTERNET

The Internet provides an excellent opportunity for students to learn more about William Butler Yeats and Harry Chapin at the following Web sites. Please be aware, however, that the sites may have changed from the time we published this information.

For more information on William Butler Yeats's life and works, go to **http://www.nadn.navy.mil/EnglishDept/ILV/yeats.htm**

To learn more about Harry Chapin and his work, go to his fan page at **http://www.littlejason.com/chapin/index.html**

We *strongly recommend* that you preview the sites before you send students to them.

Guide for Responding (continued)

◆ Critical Thinking

INTERPRET

1. What details in the setting of this poem create a sense of mystery and magic? **[Analyze]**
2. (a) Which events in the poem could occur in real life? (b) Which could occur only in fantasy stories? **[Classify]**

EVALUATE

3. The fairies list the features of the human world that the child must leave behind. Do you think the fairies promise enough to make such a sacrifice worthwhile? **[Assess]**

EXTEND

4. Which art form—film, theater, music, dance, painting, photography, or sculpture—do you think would be the best to interpret this poem? Explain. **[Career Link]**

◆ Reading for Success

STRATEGIES FOR READING POETRY

Review the reading strategies and the notes describing how to read poetry. Then apply these strategies to answer the following questions.

1. How does knowing the speaker of the poem help you understand what is happening?
2. Which sense(s) do you use most in reading this poem? Explain your answer.
3. Paraphrase the following lines from the fifth stanza: "We seek for slumbering trout/And whispering in their ears/Give them unquiet dreams."
4. Explain how reading each stanza as a sentence helps you understand the story in the poem.

◆ Literary Focus

ATMOSPHERE

Atmosphere is the feeling created by a story or poem. Descriptive details, word choice, and the rhythm and rhyme create the atmosphere in "The Stolen Child."

1. What is the atmosphere of this poem? Which words, images, or techniques establish this atmosphere?
2. In what way does the atmosphere affect your expectations of how the poem will turn out?

◆ Build Vocabulary

USING WORDS WITH MULTIPLE MEANINGS

Many words in English, such as *gloss*, have different meanings. Read the following sentence sets. Identify the word in each set that is used with different meanings. In your notebook, explain the different meanings.

1. The glosses helped me understand the play.
   The sunlight glosses the trees with gold.
2. The small plane climbed until it was just a dot in the sky.
   My mother used a plane to level the top of the door.
   The haughty woman thought she existed on a higher plane than the common people.
3. We caught more than one hundred fish in our net.
   You must calculate your budget on your net income.

USING THE WORD BANK

On your paper, answer each question.

1. Where would you expect to see a heron?
2. What kind of item from your home would you gloss?
3. Would you want to drive a truck while slumbering? Why or why not?

◆ Build Grammar Skills

INVERTED WORD ORDER

Poets sometimes use **inverted word order** to emphasize words or to make their writing fit a rhyme or rhythm pattern. In the line, "Where dips the rocky highland," Yeats inverts the word order to create a sense of other-worldliness—of creatures who do not speak in the same speech patterns as people do.

> **Inverted word order** changes the usual subject-verb-complement pattern of word order in English.

Practice Find three other examples of inverted word order in "The Stolen Child." Identify the pattern of each. Then, in each case, explain the effect Yeats created by inverting word order.

The Stolen Child ◆ 819

Using the Word Bank

1. You might expect to see a heron near water.
2. You might gloss a tabletop or a mirror.
3. You would not want to drive a truck while slumbering, or sleeping, because you could get into an accident.

◆ Build Grammar Skills

Examples: (1) "To and fro we leap" is a adverb/subject/verb structure which creates a dance-like effect; (2) "Where the wandering water gushes" is an adverb/subject/verb structure, a repeated construction in the poem that creates a musical effect; (3) "Away with us he's going" is a complement/subject/verb structure that creates a musical, jaunty effect.

✎ Writer's Solution

For additional instruction and practice, use the Special Problems in Agreement lesson in the **Language Lab CD-ROM** and page 121 on Varying Your Sentences in the *Writer's Solution Grammar Practice Book.*

Answers

◆ Critical Thinking

1. Mysterious or magical setting details include the leafy island waves of moonlight gray sands and dripping ferns.
2. (a) Some events that could occur in real life are flapping herons waking water rats, calves lowing on a hillside, and mice running around the oatmeal chest; (b) fantasy events include fairies dancing in the moonlight and whispering in the ears of fish.
3. Students may think the fairies' promises are too ambiguous to take the risk.
4. Some students may mention dance because the poem features an evocative moonlight dance.

◆ Reading for Success

1. Knowing that the speaker of the poem is a fairy or group of fairies helps to highlight the choice between magic and reality.
2. Students will probably say they use the sense of sight the most because there are many vivid set images they can mentally picture.
3. Example: We look for sleeping fish and whisper disturbing thoughts in their ears so they will sleep poorly.
4. Reading each stanza as a sentence helps to clarify complete thoughts.

◆ Literary Focus

1. Sample response: The poem has a magical, mysterious atmosphere, supported by images such as *wave of moonlight; dim gray sands with light* and *bathe a star.*
2. Students might say the magical atmosphere of the poem suggests that the child might be taken off by the fairies, which in fact happens.

◆ Build Vocabulary

Words With Multiple Meanings

1. First sentence: *glosses* means "a marginal explanation"; second sentence: *glosses* means "to put a shine upon."
2. First sentence: *plane* means airplane; second sentence: *plane* means a "woodworking instrument used for paring and smoothing"; third sentence: *plane* means a level of dignity.
3. First sentence: *net* means "a fabric with an open mesh"; second sentence: *Net* means "remaining after deductions, as for expenses."

819

Idea Bank

Customizing for *Performance Levels*

Following are suggestions for matching Idea Bank topics with your students' performance levels:

Less Advanced Students: 1, 4
Average Students: 2, 3, 5, 6,
More Advanced Students: 7

Customizing for *Learning Modalities*

Following are suggestions for matching Idea Bank topics with your students' learning modalities:

Verbal/Linguistic: 4, 5
Interpersonal: 4
Visual/Spatial: 7
Musical/Rhythmic 3, 4, 5

Writing Mini-Lesson

Refer students to the Writing Handbook, page 965, for instruction on the writing process and page 969 for further information on practical and technical writing.

Writers at Work Videodisc

Have students view the videodisc segment for Chapter 8 in which Larry Cataldo talks about the importance of gathering precise details for the type of practical writing that his work calls for.

Writing Lab CD-ROM

Have students complete the tutorial on Practical and Technical Writing. Follow these steps:

1. Have students consult a Purpose Profile to answer questions aimed at helping them to achieve their intended purpose.

2. Encourage students to use Transition Word bins to select words that suggest chronological and spatial relationships that they can use in their crime report.

3. Have students use a Proofreading Checklist to pinpoint possible errors in their drafts.

Sourcebook

Have students use Chapter 8, Practical and Technical Writing (pp. 229–257), for additional support.

Build Your Portfolio

Idea Bank

Writing

1. **Journal Entry** Imagine that you are the child the fairies stole. Write a postcard home. Tell your family what life with the fairies is like.

2. **Editorial** Imagine that you live in the area where the child was stolen by fairies. Write an editorial for the local newspaper. In it share your opinion on what happened and how the community should respond to the kidnapping.

3. **Alternate Chorus** Write lyrics for a chorus that a group of humans might whisper to the child to persuade him to remain in the human world. You may use rhythm and rhyme similar to that in "The Stolen Child."

Speaking and Listening

4. **Paired Reading** With a partner, read "The Stolen Child" aloud. One person should read the regular print and the other the italicized portions. Be expressive to convey the atmosphere of the poem. **[Performing Arts Link]**

5. **Folk Music** Choose a song that tells a story from folklore. Learn the story on which the song is based. Play the song for your class, and explain the references they don't understand. **[Music Link]**

Projects

6. **Irish Writers Timeline** Create a timeline that shows Yeats's place in the spectrum of Irish authors. Annotate the timeline to indicate any authors who influenced or were influenced by Yeats.

7. **Encyclopedia of Folklore** Research how other cultures besides the Irish perceive the magical people in folklore. Create a mini-encyclopedia. Include an explanation and illustration for each culture. **[Social Studies Link]**

Writing Mini-Lesson

Crime Report

What W. B. Yeats describes in "The Stolen Child" is a kidnapping. Imagine that you are a detective who investigates the crime of the child stolen. Write a **crime report** describing what you found at a crime scene, including evidence or possible clues for solving the crime. In your crime report, you would include interviews with witnesses to the crime as well as people who may have seen or heard anything out of the ordinary on the night of the crime.

Writing Skills Focus: Clear, Consistent Purpose

Your purpose determines the details, tone, and language you use when writing. A crime report has a **clear, consistent purpose:** to describe all information available about a crime in an orderly, logical fashion with as much detail as possible so that the crime can eventually be solved. Keep this purpose in mind as you write. Be thorough, but don't wander off in directions that have no bearing on the case.

Prewriting Review the poem to gather details about the fairies' habits and the setting. Use these details to create a diagram of the crime scene, using labels to identify each important object. As you draw, you may think of more details about the crime scene to include in your report. Refer to the diagram as you draft.

Drafting Use exact nouns and vivid verbs to help readers picture the scene the way you encountered it. If you include information from eyewitnesses, use direct quotations from them.

Revising Show your crime scene diagram and report draft to a classmate. Ask your classmate to match the labeled objects in the sketch with details in your report. This will help you identify any details that need to be added to your report.

✓ ASSESSMENT OPTIONS

Formal Assessment, Selection Test, pp. 195–197, and Assessment Resources Software. The selection test is designed so that it can be easily customized to the performance levels of your students.

Alternative Assessment, p. 55, includes options for less advanced students, more advanced students, musical/rhythmic learners, visual/spatial learners, interpersonal learners, and verbal/linguistic learners.

PORTFOLIO ASSESSMENT

Use the following rubrics in the *Alternative Assessment* booklet to assess student writing:
Journal Entry: Description Rubric, p. 97
Editorial: Persuasion Rubric, p. 105
Alternate Chorus: Poetry Rubric, p. 108
Writing Mini-Lesson: Technical Description/ Explanation Rubric, p. 115

PART **1** *Meaning and Sound*

Untitled, O. S. Eguchi

Meaning and Sound ◆ *821*

Part 1 focuses on the language of poetry—the way that poets create meaning and effects through words. The poems provide examples of musical devices and figures of speech. The first group of poems—ranging from formal, structured poems, like Robert Browning's "Meeting at Night" to traditional chants like the Navajo "Prayer of First Dancers"—illustrates sound devices. The second group, illustrating simile, metaphor, and personification, includes classic poems by Emily Dickinson and Eve Merriam and contemporary poems by Yehuda Amichai and Philip Fried.

Customize for
Varying Student Needs
When assigning the poems in this part, keep in mind these factors:
• All of the poems except "Prayer of First Dancers" are very short.
• The following poems contain vocabulary that may challenge less proficient readers or English language learners:
  "The Kraken"
  "Right Hand"
• The following poems contain abstract concepts:
  "A Pace Like That"
  "Right Hand"
• Students will benefit from having a context for "Prayer of First Dancers," a longer poem with much repetition
• The following poems contain sharp, accessible images:
  "Reapers"
  "Metaphor"
• Dickinson's irregularities of capitalization and punctuation in "The Wind—tapped like a tired Man" may confuse some readers

Humanities: Art

Untitled by O. S. Eguchi.
This untitled photograph superimposes a stalk of flowers on a page of sheet music. Explain to students that the photographer develops two separate negatives on the same sheet of paper to achieve this effect. Combining the images in this way suggests a relationship between them.

Have students link the painting to the focus of Part 1, "Meaning and Sound," by answering the following questions:

1. What relationship between a flower and a song might the photographer be suggesting? *The pho-*

tographer might be suggesting that songs, like flowers, have a certain symmetry, that the beauty in both seems simple but is actually quite complex, and perhaps that both increase in beauty upon reflection.

2. Poetry is the type of literature closest to music. What are songlike features in poetry?
Songlike features in poetry include rhythm, the sounds of various words, the use of rhyme, the use of repeated patterns of sound.

OBJECTIVES

1. To read, comprehend, and interpret poems
2. To relate poems to personal experience
3. To listen to sounds and rhythms in poetry
4. To identify musical devices in poetry
5. To build vocabulary in context and learn the prefix *mil-*
6. To recognize and use concrete and abstract nouns
7. To write a proposal for a poetry anthology using specific examples
8. To respond to five poems through writing, speaking and listening, and projects

SKILLS INSTRUCTION

Vocabulary:
Prefixes: *mil-*

Grammar:
Concrete and Abstract Nouns

Reading Strategy:
Listen

Literary Focus:
Musical Devices

Speaking and Listening:
Oral Report (teacher edition)

Critical Viewing:
Speculate; Compare and Contrast; Connect; Support

PORTFOLIO OPPORTUNITIES

Writing: Letter to Editor; City Chant; Musical Devices

Writing Mini-Lesson: Proposal for a Poetry Anthology

Speaking and Listening: Medieval Chants; Oral Report

Projects: Creatures Across Cultures; World War I

More About the Authors

John McCrae wrote "In Flanders Fields" in twenty minutes, as he sat in an ambulance, thinking of a friend whose grave was nearby. **Alfred, Lord Tennyson** was fascinated with myth and legend. His most famous work, *Idylls of the King,* tells the story of King Arthur and the knights of the Round Table. **Jean Toomer** was headmaster of an African American school in rural Georgia in 1941. This exposure became the inspiration for *Cane,* his most influential work. **Robert Browning's** extensive knowledge of literature and mythology came in large part from his father's 6,000-volume library. The **Navajo** live in Arizona, New Mexico, and Utah.

Guide for Reading

John McCrae (1872–1918)

A physician working as a medical officer in France during World War I, McCrae saw firsthand the war about which he wrote. "In Flanders Fields" was published by the British magazine *Punch* in 1915. The poem was reprinted in the United States to boost the morale of soldiers and to encourage civilians to join the service.

Alfred, Lord Tennyson (1809–1892)

No artist can ever know how time will view his or her achievements. The most popular English poet of the nineteenth century and the first English writer ever to be made a baron, Alfred, Lord Tennyson lost favor with the public shortly after his death. Today, however, he is again known as the greatest Victorian poet and perhaps the most lyrical poet in the history of the English language.

Jean Toomer (1894–1967)

French, Dutch, Welsh, German, Jewish, African, and Indian: Jean Toomer was descended from all these ethnicities and races. "Because of these," he said, "my position in America has been a curious one." In 1923, Toomer became famous at a young age with the publication of his book *Cane,* which includes short stories, poems, and a short novel.

Robert Browning (1812–1889)

Browning worked for more than thirty years before his talent was acknowledged, devoting his time to the care of his more famous wife, Elizabeth Barrett Browning. Yet it was his development of the dramatic monologue that had a greater influence on twentieth-century poetry. He is now considered a more significant poet than his wife.

Navajo

The Navajo today constitute the largest Native American tribe in the United States. Chants and sand paintings are part of a the Navajo's complex system of ceremonials. "Prayer of First Dancers" from *The Night Chant* comes from that tradition of holy ceremonies.

822 ◆ *Poetry*

◆ Build Vocabulary

PREFIXES: *mil-*

When Alfred, Lord Tennyson wants to emphasize the incredible size and age of the Kraken and its surroundings, he describes the "Huge sponges of *millennial* growth and height" that surround it. *Millennial,* which means "of or relating to a thousand-year period," contains the prefix *mil-* and comes from the Latin *mille,* which means "one thousand." The sponges in Tennyson's poem, therefore, are so old that they've been growing for literally a thousand years.

WORD BANK

Before you read, preview these words from the poems.

| abysmal |
| millennial |

◆ Build Grammar Skills

CONCRETE AND ABSTRACT NOUNS

A **concrete noun** names something physical that can be directly perceived by one of the five senses, while an **abstract noun** names an idea, belief, quality or concept—something that cannot be seen, heard, smelled, tasted, or touched.

You can see, touch, and smell the *poppies* (a concrete noun) in "In Flanders Fields," but you cannot directly perceive *speed* (an abstract noun) in "Meeting at Night."

Poets rely on concrete nouns to create sensory images. You will notice far more concrete nouns in these and other poems than abstract nouns.

Prentice Hall Literature Program Resources

REINFORCE / RETEACH / EXTEND

Selection Support Pages
Build Vocabulary: Prefixes: *mil-*, p. 229
Build Grammar Skills: Abstract Nouns, p. 230
Reading Strategy: Listen, p. 231
Literary Focus: Musical Devices, p. 232

Strategies for Diverse Student Needs, p. 56

Beyond Literature *Art,* p. 56

Formal Assessment Selection Test, pp. 198–200; Assessment Resources Software

Alternative Assessment, p. 56

Resource Pro CD-ROM "In Flanders Fields," "The Kraken," "Reapers," "Meeting at Night," "Prayer of First Dancers"—includes all resource materials and customizable lesson plan

Listening to Literature Audiocassettes "In Flanders Fields," "The Kraken," "Reapers," "Meeting at Night," "Prayer of First Dancers"

Looking at Literature Videodisc Chapter 9: "In Flanders Fields"

Literature CD-ROM *How to Read and Understand Poetry*

In Flanders Fields ◆ The Kraken
Reapers ◆ Meeting at Night ◆ Prayer of First Dancers

◆ *Literature and Your Life*

CONNECT YOUR EXPERIENCE

A story read aloud, a moving speech, a dramatic proclamation: When you hear any of these, you may have the impression that you are hearing music. Similarly, when you read poetry, your inner voice can turn the lines into a song in your head. Think about the songs you like, and what it is about them that appeals to you. As you read these poems, try to hear them as songs.

Journal Writing Write down the lyrics to one of your favorite songs, and read the lyrics aloud without music. Do the words themselves suggest music? Why or why not?

THEMATIC FOCUS: FROM THE PAST

Poets and songwriters are influenced by the poems and songs of previous generations. Think about how the poems and songs you know relate in structure and subject matter to the poems in this group.

◆ Background for Understanding

HISTORY

Many factors led to World War I (1914–1918), the backdrop of John McCrae's poem "In Flanders Fields." Principal among them were the territorial and economic rivalries between Germany, France, and Great Britain on one side and Russia and Austria-Hungary on the other. These conflicts had been brewing since the late nineteenth century. Northern France, including Flanders fields, was a chief battlefield of the war. Many towns were destroyed, and once-productive farmland was blighted with miles of bomb craters, trenches—and bodies.

◆ Reading Strategy

LISTEN

Listening is an important skill for appreciating all literature, but especially for poetry, which is created for the ear, as well as for the eye. To appreciate the sound of a poem, listen to it as it is read aloud. Listen to the rhythm of the lines, and pay attention to rhymes and other repeated sounds. For example, the first four lines of "The Kraken" end with alternating rhymes. Often, the rhythms and sounds of a poem suggest a mood or reflect an idea. "In Flanders Fields" has a regular repetitive beat, suggesting the regularity of rows of grave markers repeating and repeating. Notice the effect when the regular rhythm is broken, and how the broken rhythm calls attention to certain lines.

◆ Literary Focus

MUSICAL DEVICES

One of the things that distinguishes poetry from prose is the former's use of **musical devices,** the tools of language that a poet uses to make a poem sound a certain way.

Alliteration is the repetition of the first sound of several words. In "Reapers," for instance, the men "start their silent swinging." Each repetition of the s sound echoes the swish of the blades.

Onomatopoeia is the use of words to imitate actual sounds—*bang, tap,* and *swish* sound like what they mean.

Assonance is the repetition of similar vowel sounds. In "The Kraken," Tennyson repeats the long e sound in a number of words: *deep, beneath, dreamless, sleep,* and *see.*

Consonance is the repetition of similar consonant sounds at the end of accented syllables. In "Meeting at Night," notice the repeated t and ch sounds in "blue spurt of a lighted match." This repetition strengthens the impression these words create.

Meter is the formal organization of rhythms in a poem. You can hear the pattern of alternating stressed and unstressed syllables in the first two lines of "In Flanders Fields."

Repetition and **rhyme** also give a poem the sound of a song.

Guide for Reading ◆ 823

Preparing for Standardized Tests

Reading and Vocabulary Deducing word meaning through understanding the derivation and meaning of prefixes will enable students to improve performance on the portions of standardized tests that test students' ability to identify the meaning of vocabulary in context. Using prefixes, students will be able to narrow their choices on items like the following.

We look forward to the changes that may occur in the new millenium.

The word *millenium* means
(A) large group of people

(B) theater with one hundred seats
(C) period of a thousand years
(D) decade

With no prior knowledge of the word, choices B, C, and D all make sense. However, because students know that the meaning of the prefix *mil-* is "one thousand," they can elimate choices B and D, making C the correct choice.

The Build Vocabulary lesson focuses on deducing word meaning through the use of the prefix *mil-*. For additional practice, use the Build Vocabulary page in *Selection Support,* p. 229.

One-Minute Insight

This poem, in its stark simplicity, calls on the living to acknowledge our bond with the dead—and our debt to those who gave their lives. The dead, the speakers of the poem, call upon us to take up the fight for a better world.

◆ Build Grammar Skills

❶ Concrete and Abstract Nouns Ask students to identify the nouns in this passage and to tell whether they are concrete or abstract. *The following nouns are all concrete: fields, poppies, crosses, row.* Invite students to speculate about why the poet has chosen only concrete nouns. *Concrete nouns can be perceived with the senses, so they create vivid, sensory images.*

◆ Critical Thinking

❷ Interpret Ask students what the torch in this passage represents. *Suggested response: The torch represents the cause for which the soldiers fought.*

▶Critical Viewing◀

❸ Speculate The poet seemed to like simple things, as evidenced by the simple, straightforward language of his poem. He would probably want a simple marker.

Looking at Literature Videodisc

To establish the relevance of the idea of honoring those who died fighting for their countries, play Chapter 9 of the videodisc. This segment focuses on war memorials and other public monuments in the United States. Ask students why they think it is important to commemorate significant people and events.

Chapter 9

In Flanders Fields

John McCrae

In Flanders fields the poppies blow
Between the crosses, row on row,
    That mark our place; and in the sky
    The larks, still bravely singing, fly
5 Scarce heard amid the guns below.

We are the Dead. Short days ago
We lived, felt dawn, saw sunset glow,
    Loved and were loved, and now we lie
    In Flanders fields.

10 Take up our quarrel with the foe:
To you from failing hands we throw
    The torch; be yours to hold it high.
    If ye break faith with us who die
We shall not sleep, though poppies grow
    In Flanders fields.

▲ Critical Viewing How do you think the poet would feel about this simple marker? [Speculate]

824 ◆ Poetry

THE KRAKEN
Alfred, Lord Tennyson

❹
Below the thunders of the upper deep;
Far, far beneath in the abysmal sea,
His ancient, dreamless, uninvaded sleep
The Kraken[1] sleepeth: faintest sunlights flee

5 About his shadowy sides: above him swell
❺ Huge sponges of millennial growth and height;
And far away into the sickly light,
From many a wondrous grot[2] and secret cell
Unnumbered and enormous polypi[3]

10 Winnow[4] with giant arms the slumbering green.
There hath he lain for ages and will lie
Battening[5] upon huge seaworms in his sleep,
❻ Until the latter fire[6] shall heat the deep;
Then once by man and angels to be seen,

15 In roaring he shall rise and on the surface die.

---

1. **Kraken** (krä′ kən) *n.*: Sea monster resembling a giant squid; from Scandinavian folklore.
2. **grot** (grät) *n.*: Grotto; an underwater cave.
3. **polypi** (päl′ ip ē) *n.*: Corallike creatures with long, waving tentacles.
4. **winnow** (win′ ō) *v.*: To fan; to move wings or tentacles.
5. **Battening** (bat′ ən in) *v.*: Feeding on; growing fat on.
6. **the latter fire**: The apocalypse.

❼
▶ Critical Viewing
How does this rendition of the Kraken compare and contrast with the impression of the Kraken in Tennyson's poem? [Compare and Contrast]

In Flanders Fields / The Kraken   825

♦ **Build Vocabulary**

abysmal (ə biz′ məl) *adj.*: Bottomless; too deep for measurement; profoundly deep

millennial (mi len′ ē əl) *adj.*: Lasting one thousand years

The poet's imagination is captured by the mythical sea monster that lives at the bottom of the ocean. An elemental force of nature, the Kraken dies only when the world ends. Like all creations of the imagination, the Kraken thrives in an unexplored world, but loses its power when brought to light and examined.

♦ Literary Focus

❹ **Musical Devices** Ask students to identify the use of repetition and rhyme. *Students should see that "far" and forms of "sleep" are repeated; there are rhymes between "deep" and "sleep," "sea" and "flee."*

♦ Build Vocabulary

❺ **The Prefix *mil-*** Point out that millennial contains the prefix *mil-*. Ask what the prefix and the word mean. Then ask how this particular word adds to the effect of the poem. *Students should know that mil- means "one thousand," and that millennial means "lasting one thousand years." The word contributes to the image of an ancient creature.*

♦ Literary Focus

❻ **Musical Devices** Invite students to identify the musical device here. *Students should identify assonance: in the single-syllable words* deep *and* seen, *the vowel sounds are repeated but followed by different consonants.*

▶ Critical Viewing ◀

❼ **Compare and Contrast** *Students may say that the many arms reflect the Kraken's "unnumbered polypi" and that the partially seen creature is mysterious like the Kraken.*

🎵 Humanities: Art

Nineteenth-century wood engraving of a Kraken.

This wood engraving shows the Scandinavian sea monster, Kraken, attacking a ship. The illustration presents the Kraken as a threatening and destructive creature. The rough lines indicating turmoil in the scene contribute to a mood of fear and horror.

   Use these questions for discussion:

1. Does the picture of the Kraken match the mental image you formed from reading

Tennyson's poem? Explain. *Some students may say that the Kraken in the picture does match their mental images; others may find the Kraken in the picture stylized and even graceful, compared with the huge, age-old monster Tennyson describes.*

2. According to the last line of the poem, what should happen to the Kraken in the picture? Explain your answer. *The Kraken should die, because the last line indicates that when he rises to the surface of the sea he will die.*

One-Minute Insight The reapers in this poem are too busy to notice the field rat injured by the blade of one of their mowers. Or, perhaps the impersonal, repetitive nature of their job has dulled their sense of pity for a small animal.

◆ Literary Focus

❶ Musical Devices Ask students to identify the musical devices in these lines. *Students should note the alliteration of* start, silent, *and* swinging, *as well as of* thing, that's *and* their. *They should also note the rhyme of the end-of-line words* done *and* one.

▶Critical Viewing◀

❷ Connect The farmer is dwarfed by the land and the animals: birds, sky, clouds, and furrows all appear large and looming. Students could generalize from this picture that the land is the master of farmers.

Humanities: Art

Ploughing by Nancy Smith.

All the major forms in this bold and graphic representation of a man ploughing a field—the birds flying helter skelter, the farmer, the draft horses—are rendered in silhouette, accenting the starkness of the vast country landscape.

Use this question for discussion. What line from "Reapers" does this picture most closely illustrate? Why? *Students might cite the line "Black horses drive a mower through the weeds," because this, and not the reapers with scythes, is closest to what is shown.*

Reapers
Jean Toomer

Black reapers with the sound of steel on stones
Are sharpening scythes. I see them place the hones[1]
In their hip-pockets as a thing that's done,
And start their silent swinging, one by one.
5   Black horses drive a mower through the weeds,
And there, a field rat, startled, squealing bleeds,
His belly close to ground. I see the blade,
Blood-stained, continue cutting weeds and shade.

---

1. **hones** (hōnz) *n.*: Hard stones used to sharpen cutting tools.

Ploughing, Nancy Smith, Stapleton Collection

The Countryman has to live by faith.

▶ Critical Viewing Based on this picture, describe the relationship between farmers and the land. [Connect]

Speaking and Listening Mini-Lesson

Oral Report

This mini-lesson supports the Speaking and Listening activity in the Idea Bank on page 831.

Introduce the Concept An oral report is a brief oral presentation that conveys information in a lively way. In a good oral report, the speaker uses clear, simple language, speaks audibly and with expression at an even pace, and occasionally uses visual aids to help listeners understand and remember what they hear.

Develop Background Help students identify research sources where they can find both mythical creatures and the various arguments people have had about their existence. Tell students that ideally, both "believers" and "non-believers" should feel the student's report was fair and complete.

Apply the Information Students' reports should include a description of the creature, its history, and the beliefs about it. Remind students to use a lively, engaging tone of voice and to use visual aids if they will add needed information or enhance their reports.

Assess the Outcome Have students evaluate each report based on its content, how clearly the material was organized and presented, and how much they enjoyed the delivery. Students might use Self-Assessment or the Peer Assessment for a Speaker/Speech, pages 118 and 119 in *Alternative Assessment.*

Meeting at Night
Robert Browning

1

The gray sea and the long black land;
And the yellow half-moon large and low;
And the startled little waves that leap
In fiery ringlets from their sleep,
5 As I gain the cove with pushing prow,
And quench its speed i' the slushy sand.

2

Then a mile of warm sea-scented beach;
Three fields to cross till a farm appears;
A tap at the pane, the quick sharp scratch
10 And blue spurt of a lighted match,
And a voice less loud, through its joys and fears,
Than the two hearts beating each to each!

Atlantic Moon, Jane Wilson, Fischbach Gallery, New York

❸ ▶ Critical Viewing Identify the elements of this picture that reflect the setting and atmosphere of "Meeting at Night." [Support]

Guide for Responding

◆ *Literature and Your Life*

Reader's Response Which of these four poems seems most relevant to your life? Why?

Thematic Focus Which of these poems do you think focuses the most on handing down something from the past? Explain.

☑ Check Your Comprehension

1. In "The Kraken," what is the Kraken doing, and how do you know?
2. Who are the speakers of "In Flanders Fields"? How do you know?
3. In "Reapers," what do the reapers do before they start swinging their scythes?
4. Describe the journey of the speaker of "Meeting at Night."

◆ Critical Thinking

INTERPRET
1. What would be the far-reaching effect of "the latter fire" that could cause the Kraken's death? [Analyze]
2. The speakers of "In Flanders Fields" deliver an urgent message to the poem's audience. What is this message? [Interpret]
3. What is the central message of "The Reapers"? [Speculate]
4. At the end of "Meeting at Night," what is the reason for the "tap at the pane"?

EVALUATE
5. Explain whether you think the speakers of "In Flanders Fields" are justified in requesting others to take up the torch. [Make a Judgment]

Reapers/Meeting at Night ◆ 827

◆ Critical Thinking

1. An apocalypse ("the latter fire") would end the world.
2. The urgent message the speakers deliver is that their deaths will be in vain unless their successors, the audience of the poem, fight for the same principles they did. "If ye break faith with us who die" indicates a moral pact between soldiers dead and alive.
3. Students might say that the central message is that even death or pain cannot stop the forward movement of progress.
4. The tap on the window pane announces to one lover the arrival of the other.
5. Students might suggest that the dead have a right to ask the living to carry on their legacy, at any cost, if they are fighting for a worthy principle. Or, they might say that no one has the right to ask another to die.

One-Minute Insight "Prayer of First Dancers" conveys the Navajo people's profound sense of connection with nature. Like all chants, this one relies on the rhythmical repetition of phrases; it produces an effect of gathering momentum in praise and a request for spiritual and physical healing.

◆ Literary Focus

❶ Musical Devices Invite students to identify the musical device in these lines. Then ask what impact this device has. *Students may say that repetition induces a prayerful, reverent attitude; that it conveys a sense of wonder; or that it creates a strong rhythm for dancing.*

◆ Reading Strategy

❷ Listen Remind students of the poem's traditional uses as a chant and a prayer. Ask one or two students to read the passage aloud, reminding them that they are addressing "he-rain." Then discuss the differences between reading the poem silently and hearing it read aloud. *Students will probably say that hearing the poem makes its repetition more powerful and conveys its emotion more fully.*

◆ Build Grammar Skills

❸ Concrete and Abstract Nouns Ask students to identify the concrete nouns in this passage. *Concrete nouns are rainbow, head, darkness, cloud, ends, wings, he-rain, mist, she-rain. Then ask students to describe the effect of so many concrete with no abstract nouns. Students should realize that the poem celebrates nature—the concrete, material world that can be experienced with the senses. The poem is not concerned with ideas or abstractions.*

▶ Critical Viewing ◀

❹ Connect Suggested response: Both the painting and the poem use repetition.

PRAYER OF FIRST DANCERS
from The Night Chant

Our Home and Native Land, 1983, Dannielle B. Hayes

Navajo

In Tse'gíhi,
In the house made of the dawn,
In the house made of the evening twilight,
In the house made of the dark cloud,
5   In the house made of the he-rain,
In the house made of the dark mist,
In the house made of the she-rain,
In the house made of pollen,
In the house made of grasshoppers,
10   Where the dark mist curtains the doorway,
The path to which is on the rainbow,
Where the zigzag lightning stands high on top,
Where the he-rain stands high on top,
Oh, male divinity!
15   With your moccasins of dark cloud, come to us.
With your leggings of dark cloud, come to us.
With your shirt of dark cloud, come to us.
With your head-dress of dark cloud, come to us.
With your mind enveloped in dark cloud, come to us.
20   With the dark thunder above you, come to us soaring.
With the shapen cloud at your feet, come to us soaring.

▲ **Critical Viewing** What technique used in this picture reflects a technique in "Prayer of First Dancers"? Explain. **[Connect]**

828 ◆ Poetry

With the far darkness made of the dark cloud over your head, come to us soaring.
With the far darkness made of the he-rain over your head, come to us soaring.
With the far darkness made of the dark mist over your head, come to us soaring.
25   With the far darkness made of the she-rain over your head, come to us soaring.
With the zigzag lightning flung out on high over your head, come to us soaring.
With the rainbow hanging high over your head, come to us soaring.
With the far darkness made of the dark cloud on the ends of your wings, come to us soaring.
With the far darkness made of the he-rain on the ends of your wings, come to us soaring.
30   With the far darkness made of the dark mist on the ends of your wings, come to us soaring.
With the far darkness made of the she-rain on the ends of your wings, come to us soaring.
With the zigzag lightning flung out on high on the ends of your wings, come to us soaring.
With the rainbow hanging high on the ends of your wings, come to us soaring.
With the near darkness made of the dark

 Humanities: Art

Our Home and Native Land, 1983, by Danielle Hayes.

This gouache and pencil work emphasizes repetition both in the way the six Native American figures seem to echo one another and in its use of color—bright orange—repeated in various parts of the picture.

Use the following question for discussion: Both the poem and the dance portrayed here use repetition. Why do you think repetition is an important part of this religious ceremony? *Students may say that repetition in dance conveys a sense that all are working in unison to celebrate nature. Repetition in the poem is a way of celebrating each aspect of nature.*

◆ Critical Thinking

❺ **Infer** Ask students what the speaker doing? What does the speaker ask for in return? *The speaker is preparing a sacrifice in honor of the divinity. In return, he asks for health.*

◆ Critical Thinking

❻ **Draw Conclusions** Ask students why the speaker refers to beauty so often in this passage. *Students should see that the speaker loves the beauty of nature and is able to appreciate it now that the sacrifice and the ceremony have been performed.*

cloud, of the he-rain, of the dark mist
and of the she-rain, come to us.
35 With the darkness on the earth, come to
us.
With these I wish the foam floating on
the flowing water over the roots of the
great corn.
I have made your sacrifice.
I have prepared a smoke for you.
❺
40 My feet restore for me.
My limbs restore for me.
My body restore for me.
My mind restore for me.
My voice restore for me.

✳ ✳ ✳ ✳

Happily the old men will regard you.
45 Happily the old women will regard you.
Happily the young men will regard you.
Happily the young women will regard you.
Happily the boys will regard you.

Happily the girls will regard you.
50 Happily the children will regard you.
Happily the chiefs will regard you.
Happily, as they scatter in different
directions, they will regard you.
Happily, as they approach their homes,
they will regard you.
Happily may their roads home be on the
trail of pollen.
55 Happily may they all get back.
In beauty I walk.
With beauty before me, I walk.
With beauty behind me, I walk.
With beauty below me, I walk.
60 With beauty above me, I walk.
With beauty all around me, I walk.
It is finished again in beauty,
It is finished in beauty,
It is finished in beauty,
It is finished in beauty.
❻

Guide for Responding

◆ *Literature and Your Life*

Reader's Response Which elements of this poem did you find most musical? Why?
Thematic Focus Based on your reading of "Prayer of First Dancers," what important legacy do you think the Navajo have handed down to their children? Explain.

☑ Check Your Comprehension

1. Identify three images from nature that are repeated throughout "Prayer of First Dancers."
2. What is the speaker's request?

◆ Critical Thinking

INTERPRET
1. What attitude does the speaker of "Prayer of First Dancers" have toward the "you" being addressed in the chant? **[Draw Conclusions]**
2. What details indicate a strong sense of community? **[Support]**

APPLY
3. What does "Prayer of First Dancers" reveal about the Navajos' attitude toward nature? **[Generalize]**
4. Identify a contemporary song that contains images and ideas similar to those found in "Prayer of First Dancers." **[Relate]**

Prayer of First Dancers ◆ 829

| | Reinforce and Extend

Answers
◆ *Literature and Your Life*

Reader's Response Students might mention the repetition, which contributes to its lulling, chant-like quality.

Thematic Focus Students are likely to mention a deep reverence for nature.

☑ **Check Your Comprehension**

1. Three images are the darkness, a rainbow, and lightning.
2. The speaker's request is for the divinity to restore his health.

◆ **Critical Thinking**

1. The attitude of the speaker toward "you" is one of reverence.
2. The constant repetition of the pronoun *us* indicates a community feeling; the refrain beginning *Happily* includes mention of all different group members of the community.
3. The Navajos hold nature in high esteem and feel humble before it.
4. Students should mention a song that conveys nature's power.

Beyond the Selection

FURTHER READING
Other Works by the Authors
In Flanders Fields, and Other Poems, John McCrae
"Ulysses," Alfred, Lord Tennyson
Cane, Jean Toomer
"My Last Duchess," Robert Browning
Other Works With the Theme of "From the Past"
Spoon River Anthology, Edgar Lee Masters
"Kubla Khan," Samuel Taylor Coleridge
  We suggest that you preview these works before recommending them to students.

INTERNET
Students can find more information at the following Web sites. Please be aware that sites may have changed since we published this information. For information on McCrae: **http://www.IAEhv.np/users/robr/poppies.html**
On Tennyson: **http://www.stg.brown.edu/projects...w/victorian/tennyson/tennybio.html**
On Toomer: **http://micket.la.psu.edu/~jselzer/burke/toom.doc**
On Browning: **http://mirrors.org.sg./victorian/rb/rbbio.html**
  We *strongly recommend* that you preview the sites before you send students to them.

Answers
◆ Reading Strategy

1. There are ten syllables in each line of "The Kraken." Rhyming word pairs include deep/sleep; sea/flee; swell/cell; height/light; lie/die; green/seen.

2. "In Flanders Fields" breaks the rhythm and creates a jolting effect which pulls the reader's focus to these lines.

3. Alliteration is the sound effect of the first two lines in "Reapers"; the sound reflects the swishing motion of the blades through the grass.

4. Repetition is the principal sound effect in "Prayer of First Dancers," and it creates the rhythm of a chant.

◆ Literary Focus

1. The combination of assonance and consonance creates a feeling of depth and mystery.

2. The meter of "In Flanders Field" has the quality of a march, and the poem stresses the importance of marching on.

3. Alliteration is the most prominent musical device: sound/steel/stones/ sharpening/scythes/silent/swinging/startled/squealing/shades; close/continued/cutting

4. Alliteration: long/land/large/low/ leap; Onomatopoeia: quench; slushy; scratch; Consonance: beach; scratch

5. (a) Repetition is most prominent. (b) The repetition makes it perfect for a chant, which is characterized by repetition and a lulling rhythm.

◆ Build Vocabulary

Using the Prefix *mil-*
1. b   2. c   3. d   4. a

Using the Word Bank
1. It would be very difficult because the pool would be too deep for measurement.

2. You would have to wait one thousand years.

Guide for Responding (continued)

◆ Reading Strategy

LISTEN
Listening to the sounds and rhythms of these poems is part of the poetic experience. The sound of a poem gives you insight into the poet's intent.

1. Listen to the rhyme and rhythm of "The Kraken." How many syllables are in each line? Identify three pairs of rhyming words.

2. The rhythm of "In Flanders Fields" is a regular beat that occasionally breaks. Identify the lines where the rhythm is broken, and explain how it affects the way you listen to those lines.

3. What sound do you hear repeated in the first two lines of "Reapers"? What action from the poem does this sound reflect?

4. (a) What sounds and rhythms do you hear in "Prayer of First Dancers"? (b) What effect do these sounds create?

◆ Literary Focus

MUSICAL DEVICES
Just as a composer of music must know harmony and melody in order to create the effects he or she desires, poets use various language tools, or **musical devices,** to create effects in their poems.

1. In the first five lines of "The Kraken," Tennyson combines both assonance and consonance. What is the effect of this combination of musical devices?

2. How does the meter of "In Flanders Fields" relate to the purpose of the poem?

3. What musical device is most prominent in "Reapers"? Give examples.

4. Cite an example of alliteration, onomatopoeia, and consonance in "Meeting at Night."

5. (a) What musical device is most prominent in "Prayer of First Dancers"? (b) How does this device lend itself to the way in which the poem is traditionally used?

◆ Build Vocabulary

USING THE PREFIX *mil-*
The prefix *mil-* comes from the Latin *mille,* meaning "one thousand." On your paper, match each word beginning with *mil-* with its definition.

1. millennium   **a.** one thousand thousands
2. millipede   **b.** a period of one thousand years
3. millimeter   **c.** an insect with many legs
4. million   **d.** one one-thousandth of a meter

USING THE WORD BANK
On your paper, answer the following questions.

1. If a pool were *abysmal,* how easy would it be for you to retrieve your sunglasses if you dropped them in it? Explain.

2. If you planted *millennial* roses, how long would you have to wait to see them bloom?

◆ Build Grammar Skills

CONCRETE AND ABSTRACT NOUNS
Concrete nouns name specific things that can be perceived by the senses. **Abstract nouns** name ideas or concepts that cannot be seen, heard, felt, tasted, or smelled. The word *moccasins* from "Prayer of First Dancers" is a concrete noun because it names something you can see and feel. *Beauty,* on the other hand, is a concept that cannot be directly perceived by the senses. It is an abstract noun.

Practice On your paper, identify each noun as *concrete* or *abstract*.

1. poppies   5. ringlets   9. rainbow
2. hope   6. joy   10. beauty
3. dawn   7. voice   11. conflict
4. scythes   8. fears   12. hearts

Writing Application On your paper, write a paragraph about these poems from the point of view of an enthusiastic critic. Use at least four of the following abstract and concrete nouns: *beauty, battleground, mountains, clouds, spirituality, seaworms, thrill, faith, scythes, herbs,* and *sea.* Underline the concrete nouns, and circle the abstract nouns.

◆ Build Grammar Skills

Practice
Concrete Nouns: 1. poppies;
3. dawn;   4. scythes;
5. ringlets;   7. voice;
9. rainbow;   12. hearts

Abstract Nouns: 2. hope;
6. joy;   8. fears;   10. beauty;   11. conflict

✎ Writer's Solution

For additional instruction and practice, use the Types of Nouns lesson in the **Language Lab CD-ROM** and page 5 on Nouns in the *Writer's Solution Grammar Practice Book.*

Build Your Portfolio

 ### Idea Bank

Writing

1. **Letter to Editor** It is 1917 and World War I is raging. You've just read "In Flanders Fields." Write a letter to the editor saying why you do or don't agree with the poem.

2. **City Chant** "Prayer of First Dancers" praises many aspects of nature. Write a chant (with variations on a repeated phrase) in which you praise aspects of a city or town.

3. **Musical Devices** Compare two of these poems in terms of the musical devices used in them.

Speaking and Listening

4. **Medieval Chants** Several early music groups have recorded chants recited by monks since medieval times. Find and play a recording for the class. Explain how it is similar to "Prayer of First Dancers" from "The Night Chant." **[Music Link]**

5. **Oral Report** Find out more about mythical creatures like the Kraken, such as the Yeti or the Loch Ness Monster. Give an oral report explaining the reasons some people think these creatures exist and the reasons some people don't. **[Science Link]**

Projects

6. **Creatures Across Cultures** Create a poster or other visual presentation showing mythological monsters, such as the Kraken, from various cultures. Provide pictures and detailed descriptions. **[Social Studies Link]**

7. **World War I** Up until World War II broke out, World War I was known as "The Great War." Why is this? Research the death toll from each country participating in World War I. Present your statistics in a table. **[Math Link]**

 ### Writing Mini-Lesson

Proposal for a Poetry Anthology

Because many poems are fairly short, poetry is a form of literature well suited to anthologies. An anthology is a collection of works that have something in common, either in form or theme. Write a **proposal for a poetry anthology** that you would like to create. Choose a number of poems that you feel belong together. You can arrange them by form, such as an anthology of sonnets or haiku; by theme, such as love, individuality, or hope; or by poetic element.

Writing Skills Focus: Specific Examples

Once you've decided on the common element that will link the poems in your anthology, make sure that you give **specific examples** of each in your proposal. For example, if you plan to organize your anthology by musical devices, show examples of alliteration, consonance, and repetition in the poems you suggest.

Prewriting Think of how you would like to arrange your poems. For example, if you're going to make an anthology based on musical devices, you might make a chart like this one:

Musical Device	Title	Example
Alliteration	"Reapers"	Steel on stones
Onomatopoeia	"Meeting . . ."	Slushy sand

Drafting Begin by explaining the concept or organization of the anthology you propose. Then introduce the specific examples you have chosen.

Revising Ask a friend to review your proposal. Have you included specific examples of each form or genre of poem? Is it clear why you want to include each poem? If not, revise your proposal to make it more complete and clear.

 ### Idea Bank

Customizing for *Performance Levels*
Following are suggestions for matching Idea Bank topics with your students' performance levels:
Less Advanced Students: 1, 4
Average Students: 2, 3, 5, 6,
More Advanced Students: 7

Customizing for *Learning Modalities*
Following are suggestions for matching Idea Bank topics with your students' learning modalities:
Musical/Rhythmic: 2, 3
Verbal/Linguistic: 4, 5
Logical/Mathematical: 7
Visual/Spatial: 6

Writing Mini-Lesson

Refer students to the Writing Handbook, page 965, for instruction on the writing process and page 967 for further information on descriptive writing.

Writing Lab CD-ROM
Have students complete the tutorial on Descriptive Writing. Follow these steps:

- Encourage students to complete the Audience Profile to help them focus on their intended audience.

- Have students use the interactive instruction on ways they can organize their proposal.

- Tell students to use the revision checkers for vague or overused adjectives before completing their final revision.

Sourcebook
Have students use Chapter 1, Description (pp. 1–24), for additional support. The chapter includes an annotated student model of a remembrance (p. 24).

✓ ASSESSMENT OPTIONS

Formal Assessment, Selection Test, pp. 198–200, and Assessment Resources Software. The selection test is designed so that it can be easily customized to the performance levels of your students. *Alternative Assessment,* p. 56, includes options for less advanced students, more advanced students, verbal/linguistic learners and bodily/kinesthetic learners.

PORTFOLIO ASSESSMENT
Use the following rubrics in the *Alternative Assessment* booklet to assess student writing:
Letter to Editor: Persuasion Rubric, p. 105
City Chant: Poetry Rubric, p. 108
Musical Devices: Comparison/Contrast Rubric, p. 103
Writing Mini-Lesson: Description Rubric, p. 97

Guide for Reading

Emily Dickinson (1830–1886)

Emily Dickinson was born in Amherst, Massachusetts. As she grew older, she rarely left her house. In fact, during the last ten years of her life, she dressed only in white and would not allow anyone to see her. When her health failed, she permitted her doctor to examine her only by observing her from a distance. In 1886, Emily Dickinson died in the house in which she was born. (To learn more about Emily Dickinson, see pp. 414 and 415.)

Yehuda Amichai (1924–)

Although born in Germany, Yehuda Amichai (yə hoō' də ä' mi khī) emigrated with his family to Palestine, the region that became Israel in 1948. He was a soldier in the Israeli defense forces and fought in several wars.

In addition to poetry, Amichai has also written short stories, a novel, and a play. He writes in Hebrew, using this ancient language to write about timeless themes and contemporary topics. Amichai's poetry has been translated into more than thirty languages.

Eve Merriam (1916–1992)

Eve Merriam was born in Philadelphia. Because her family was always interested in books and reading, Merriam began her lifelong fascination with poetry at an early age. She has written books of poetry for children, including *There Is No Rhyme for Silver,* and adults, including *Family Circle.* Merriam calls poetry the most immediate and richest form of communication.

Philip Fried (1945–)

Philip Fried, a poet and editor, is the founder of *The Manhattan Review,* an international poetry journal, as well as the author of two collections of poetry, *Mutual Trespasses* and *Quantum Genesis. The Manhattan Review* features interviews with poets from around the world as well as translations of their work. Fried has also collaborated with his wife, photographer Lynn Saville, on *Acquainted With the Night,* a collection of poems selected by him and photographs taken by her.

◆ Build Vocabulary

WORD ROOTS: *-tac-*
In "Right Hand" the speaker recalls watching his grandfather iron "countless *taciturn* trousers."

Taciturn has as its root *-tac-*. This root and its variation *-tic-* mean "silent." *Taciturn* means "silent; uncommunicative." A *tacit* agreement is one that is understood; it does not need to be spoken.

countenance
tremulous
flurriedly
decipher
taciturn
eloquent
guttural
diffused
garrulity

WORD BANK
Before you read, preview this list of words from the poems.

◆ Build Grammar Skills

ELLIPTICAL CLAUSES
In an **elliptical clause**, one or more words are omitted because they are understood. Often, in adjective clauses, the relative pronoun *that* is not written or spoken.

I'm looking at the lemon tree [that] I planted.

The complete clause is *that I planted,* but the word *that* is understood.

Elliptical clauses in which the relative pronoun is not stated have an informal, conversational tone.

Prentice Hall Literature Program Resources

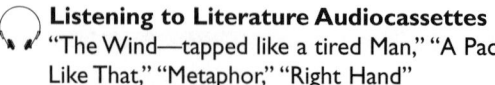

The Wind—tapped like a tired Man
A Pace Like That ◆ Metaphor
◆ Right Hand ◆

◆ *Literature and Your Life*

CONNECT YOUR EXPERIENCE
Some days just don't go the way we'd like. Fortunately, there is always a new day to make a fresh start and right a wrong or accomplish a goal. If you appreciate the possibilities of each new day, you'll be surprised how much you can accomplish!

THEMATIC FOCUS: FROM THE PAST
The speakers in these poems realize the importance of each day and the effect of the large and small choices they make.

Journal Writing Jot down choices that you are currently facing in your life—such as what classes to take or whether to take an after-school job. Indicate the hopes for and concerns about the outcomes of your choices.

◆ Background for Understanding

CULTURE
In "A Pace Like That" Amichai makes a comparison to a Torah scroll. A Torah scroll is a long, rolled parchment. On this parchment, the first five books of the Bible are written in Hebrew. The Torah relates centuries of Jewish history. Particular readings from the Torah are assigned to each day; the entire cycle of readings takes a year to complete.

◆ Literary Focus

FIGURATIVE LANGUAGE
Figurative language is writing or speech not meant to be interpreted literally. Writers use a variety of figures of speech to help readers see things in new ways.

A **simile** compares unlike things using the word *like* or *as*. In "Right Hand," Fried uses a simile when he says his grandfather's hand moves "back and forth *like* a Greek chorus." A **metaphor** also makes a comparison, by writing or speaking about one thing as if it were another. In her poem "Metaphor," Merriam writes about a day as if it were a sheet of paper. **Personification** is a figure of speech in which an object, animal, or idea is described as if it had human characteristics. For instance, "The Wind—tapped like a tired Man" describes the wind as a guest in a home.

◆ Reading Strategy

PARAPHRASE
A poet's style and word choice are intended to create a particular mood or convey a feeling in a poem, but because of the concise nature of poetry, you may not see the intended meaning right away. It's helpful to **paraphrase** the lines of a poem, using your own words to restate what the lines say. When you read these poems, pause occasionally to paraphrase complicated lines or stanzas. If the poet makes a comparison, express the similarities in your own words. For example, after you read the first four lines of Amichai's poem "A Pace Like That," you can paraphrase them like this:

> I realized when I was looking at the lemon tree I planted last year that I'd like to slow down. I'd like to take the time to appreciate things like the tree growing in my yard.

Keep a chart on which you paraphrase passages from the poems.

Poet's Words	Paraphrase

Guide for Reading ◆ 833

Preparing for Standardized Tests

Reading and Vocabulary Comprehension sections of standardized tests might call upon students to answer questions like the following. Choose the answer that best expresses the meaning of the first two lines of Robert Frost's "Nothing Gold Can Stay." *(B)*

> *Nature's first green is gold,*
> *Her hardest hue to hold.*

(A) People don't see that green is really gold.
(B) The first color nature offers is the most valuable, but it's the hardest to hold on to.
(C) Nature's many colors are never still.

(D) Nature's first leaves are green, then gold, but then all color fades.

Lead students to see that a paraphrase captures the main ideas in a piece of writing by rephrasing them in language that can be easily understood. The correct paraphrase is B, because it retells the lines of poetry in simple language, without adding or interpreting meaning. The Reading Strategy for these poems gives students practice in paraphrasing lines of poetry. For additional practice, use the Reading Strategy page in *Selection Support,* p. 235.

One-Minute Insight

By personifying a gentle wind blowing through the speaker's room, Emily Dickinson conveys a sense of connection with nature and the importance of the everyday events of the natural world. In "A Pace Like That," Yehuda Amichai expresses this same sense of connection and stresses the importance of taking time to enjoy each day.

◆ Literary Focus

❶ Figurative Language This line contains two types of figurative language. Ask students to identify them. *Simile—the wind is being compared to a man; personification—in "tapping," the wind is taking on human characteristics.*

◆ Literary Focus

❷ Figurative Language Ask students what human characteristics the speaker gives to the wind to personify it. *She says the wind has speech, a countenance (face), and fingers.*

◆ Critical Thinking

❸ Interpret Ask students what simile in this stanza helps convey the speaker's impression of the wind in her room. Then ask what impression the simile conveys. *She says the wind is "like a timid Man," suggesting that the wind is a gentle, tentative visitor that doesn't stay long. Perhaps the speaker wants the wind to stay, since she says she "became alone."*

►Critical Viewing◄

❹ Relate The picture seems to relate best to "The Wind—tapped like a tired Man" since it pictures a window and a room that is a likely setting for the poem.

The Wind—tapped like a tired Man

Emily Dickinson

❶ The Wind—tapped like a tired Man—
And like a Host—"Come in"
I boldly answered—entered then
My Residence within

5   A Rapid—footless Guest—
To offer whom a Chair
Were as impossible as hand
A Sofa to the Air—

No Bone had He to bind Him—
10   His Speech was like the Push
❷ Of numerous Humming Birds at once
From a superior Bush—

His Countenance—a Billow—
His Fingers, as He passed
15   Let go a music—as of tunes
Blown tremulous in Glass—

He visited—still flitting—
Then like a timid Man
❸ Again, He tapped—'twas flurriedly—
20   And I became alone—

◆ Build Vocabulary

countenance (koun′ tə nəns) *n.*: The face; facial features
tremulous (trem′ yoo ləs) *adj.*: Trembling; quivering
flurriedly (flur′ əd lē) *adv.*: In a flustered, agitated way

▲ **Critical Viewing** Explain to which poem you think this picture best relates. [Relate] **❹**

834 ◆ Poetry

 Block Scheduling Strategies

Consider these suggestions to take advantage of extended class time:

- Introduce or review the types of figurative language presented in Literary Focus on page 833. Reinforce students' understanding of figurative language by having them suggest similes and metaphors based on the pictures accompanying these selections.
- After students have read "The Wind" and "A Pace Like That," have them look out the window or sit outside to observe a plant, a tree, an animal, or a force of nature such as sunshine, shadow, or wind. Have them make notes about details of the natural force or object that suggest human characteristics. This activity will prepare students for the Writing Mini-Lesson on personification (p. 840).
- Direct students to gather into small groups to discuss and then answer the Critical Thinking questions on pages 835, 837, and 838.

- Introduce elliptical clauses. Have students read the explanation in Build Grammar Skills on page 832 and complete the exercise on page 839. You may also have students complete Build Grammar Skills in *Selection Support,* p. 234.
- Provide an alternative activity, such as the discussion or presentation found in *Alternative Assessment,* to assess the progress of students with varying performance levels or learning modalities.

A PACE LIKE THAT

Yehuda Amichai

I'm looking at the lemon tree I planted.
A year ago. I'd need a different pace, a slower one,
to observe the growth of its branches, its leaves as they open.
I want a pace like that.

5   Not like reading a newspaper
    but the way a child learns to read,
    or the way you quietly <u>decipher</u> the inscription
    on an ancient tombstone.

    And what a Torah scroll takes an entire year to do
10 as it rolls its way from Genesis to the death of Moses,
    I do each day in haste
    or in sleepless nights, rolling over from side to side.

    The longer you live, the more people there are
    who comment on your actions. Like a worker
15 in a manhole: at the opening above him
    people stand around giving free advice
    and yelling instructions,
    but he's all alone down there in his depths.

◆ **Build Vocabulary**

decipher (dē sī´ fər) v.:
Translate; make out the
meaning

Guide for Responding

◆ *Literature and Your Life*

Reader's Response What kind of pace would
you like to keep in your own life?

Thematic Focus Each of these poems reflects its
poet's perspective on life by showing a response to
day-to-day events. What "day-to-day" choices have
you made that indicate your approach to life?

☑ **Check Your Comprehension**

1. In "The Wind—tapped like a tired Man," who is
   the "Guest" who enters the speaker's residence?
2. What does the speaker in "A Pace Like That"
   say happens more the longer you live?

◆ Critical Thinking

INTERPRET

1. What impression of the wind does Emily Dickinson present through her poem? **[Interpret]**
2. In "A Pace Like That," why might the speaker want a slower pace in which to live? **[Infer]**
3. Why is the Torah scroll a good image for a slow pace? **[Support]**

APPLY

4. Describe the pace at which you think life should be lived. **[Relate]**

EXTEND

5. What are some health benefits of a relaxed approach to life? **[Science Link]**

The Wind—tapped like a tired Man/A Pace Like That ◆ 835

◆ Build Grammar Skills

❺ **Elliptical Clauses** Have students identify the two elliptical clauses in this passage and tell what missing word is understood in each clause. *Line 6 contains the elliptical clause "a child learns to read." The relative pronoun "that" is understood. Lines 7–8 include the elliptical clause "you quietly decipher the inscription on an ancient tombstone." Once again, the relative pronoun "that" is understood.*

◆ Reading Strategy

❻ **Paraphrase** To help students paraphrase these lines, remind them that it takes a year to read the Torah scroll. The Torah helps people understand the meaning of life and their place in the universe. Then ask students to restate the entire stanza in their own words. *Sample answer: I struggle every day to find quick answers to the meaning of life, instead of slowing down and exploring these questions at a leisurely pace.*

◆ Literary Focus

❼ **Figurative Language** Ask students what two things are compared in the simile in the last stanza. Then ask how the things are different and how they are similar. *The simile compares a person who has lived a long time with a worker in a manhole. They are different because the person who has lived a long time does not literally work down in a manhole. They are similar because both receive unwanted advice and both are ultimately on their own.*

Reinforce and Extend

Answers

◆ *Literature and Your Life*

Reader's Response Some students may wish for a slow, meditative pace, but most students will probably want to meet the fast pace of modern life.

Thematic Focus Possible response: I decided not to try out for a second sport because I don't want that much pressure.

☑ **Check Your Comprehension**

1. The guest is the wind.
2. The longer you live, the more advice you get.

◆ Critical Thinking

1. She offers the impression of a nervous, timid character.
2. The speaker wants a slower pace to appreciate life more and to analyze things with more care.

3. It is a good image because it takes a year to read the Torah scroll, but the year-long reading repays the reader with insights.
4. Students might describe a pace that alternates busy activity with time for reflection.
5. Relaxation helps people lose their tension, which can cause health problems.

One-Minute Insight Through an extended metaphor comparing each new morning to a blank sheet of paper, Eve Merriam conveys an optimistic view of life: that each new day is important because it brings an opportunity for a fresh start.

◆ Literary Focus

❶ Figurative Language Ask students to identify the figurative expression in this stanza and tell what type of figurative language it is. *"Morning is/a new sheet of paper" is a metaphor.* Why is morning like a new sheet of paper? *Both a new sheet of paper and a new day offers a fresh start.*

◆ Critical Thinking

❷ Interpret Ask students what the used "sheet of paper" might represent and where it might be filed away each day. *Suggested response: The used sheet of paper is the person's experience that day. The consequences of that experience are filed away in the person's memory, as a resource to be mined in the future.*

►Critical Viewing◄

❸ Analyze The photograph may have been chosen because the colors of dawn and the freshness of the scene emphasize the newness of morning. Also, the climbing figure suggests the effort and accomplishment that are possible with each new day.

Customize for
Intrapersonal Learners
Have these students imagine that it is first thing in the morning and their journals are "a new sheet of paper." Suggest they write something that reflects their sense of freshness—it might be a brief poem, a scene from a story, or a description of an insight they had recently.

Metaphor
Eve Merriam

❶
Morning is
a new sheet of paper
for you to write on.

Whatever you want to say,
5 all day,
until night
❷ folds it up
and files it away.

The bright words and the dark words
10 are gone
until dawn
and a new day
to write on.

▼ **Critical Viewing** Why do you think this photograph was chosen to accompany "Metaphor"? [Analyze]
❸

836 ◆ Poetry

Workplace Skills Mini-Lesson

Being Focused
Observing the slow growth of a lemon tree and studying the Torah, two activities Amichai refers to in his poem, require that a person be focused, a skill that is important in many jobs.

Introduce the Concept Discuss what it means to be focused: applying close attention to the task at hand, the ability to cancel out distractions, the desire to carry a project through to completion.

Develop Background Review some ways in which students apply focus in their own lives; for

example, concentrating on learning the complete rules of a new game, studying for an important test in the middle of a bustling room, or exceeding their personal best in a track sport.

Apply the Information Have students list three jobs or careers they would be interested in, and explain how the ability to focus might help them succeed in each one.

Assess the Outcome Have individuals share their ideas aloud. Assess based on how well students demonstrate the need for focus in the jobs they list.

Guide for Responding

◆ Literature and Your Life

Reader's Response To what would you compare the morning? Why?

Thematic Focus Each new day provides an opportunity to make choices that will have positive consequences. What are some possible effects of a positive approach to each new day?

Journal Writing Jot down a few sentences about a choice you made that did not have the results you wanted. What might you do differently if given the same choice again?

☑ Check Your Comprehension

1. To what is morning compared?
2. What does dawn bring?

◆ Critical Thinking

INTERPRET

1. What does "files it away" in line 8 suggest? **[Infer]**
2. What do you think the poet means by "The bright words and the dark words" in line 9? **[Interpret]**

EVALUATE

3. What makes this metaphor so effective? **[Evaluate]**

Metaphor ◆ 837

This mini-lesson supports the Speaking and Listening activity in the Idea Bank on page 840.

Reinforce and Extend

Customize for
Verbal/Linguistic Learners
Encourage verbal/linguistic learners to brainstorm for as many metaphors as they can for a new day; for example, "morning is a seedling sprouting out of fertile soil." Encourage them to choose the one they feel is the strongest and expand it into a poem with an extended metaphor.

Answers
◆ Literature and Your Life

Reader's Response Sample response: I would compare the morning to a child's first steps because it is a time of day to be moved into slowly.

Thematic Focus A positive approach to each new day will lead people to accept new challenges and gather exciting or important new experience.

☑ Check Your Comprehension

1. Morning is compared to a new sheet of paper.
2. Dawn brings a new day.

◆ Critical Thinking

1. "Files it away" suggests storing it (experience) for future use.
2. "The bright words and the dark words" might represent good and bad feelings, moods, and experiences that people accumulate throughout the day.
3. Comparing morning to a new sheet of paper is an effective metaphor because it holds up to all of Merriam's examples: morning is like new paper because it gets used, stored away, and replaced by a new fresh opportunity to start.

 ### Speaking and Listening Mini-Lesson

This mini-lesson supports the Speaking and Listening activity in the Idea Bank on page 840.

Introduce the Concept A dialogue is a conversation that reflects the personalities and ideas of the characters involved, in this case, the speakers of two poems. Before students role-play a dialogue, they need to analyze the poems for clues to the speakers' ideas and attitudes.

Develop Background Have partners choose which speaker each will portray. Then have them explore each speaker's character. Lead students to consider these questions:

• What is each character's attitude toward life?

• How would the character react to being stuck in an elevator?

• What insights can each speaker offer the other?

Apply the Information After answering the questions above, students should outline the conversation in the elevator. Allow them to rehearse and then present their role-played conversation for the class.

Assess the Outcome Evaluate each role play, based on how well each dialogue reflects the differing personalities and points of view of the two speakers.

In this touching poem, the speaker pays tribute to his grandfather, a Jewish immigrant whose right hand—"seamed," "eloquent," and "self-assured"—reveals his character and the quality of his days. In this characterization, Fried celebrates the importance of an "ordinary" (yet extraordinary) man whose experience is informed by the place where he lives and the place from which he comes.

◆ Literary Focus

❶ Figurative Language Ask students to identify the personification in these lines. *The hand is compared to a smiling person.*

❷ Clarification Explain that Yiddish is a language that was spoken by many Eastern European Jews when they immigrated to the United States. A variation of the German language, with many original words of its own, the language has many guttural, rasping sounds. Yiddish is a lively language full of colorful expressions. Yiddish speakers often use their hands to emphasize the meaning of their words.

❸ Clarification Make sure students understand that a Greek chorus was a group of actors or singers used to comment from the sidelines on the significance of the action in an ancient Greek play. The chorus moved first to one side of the stage and then to the other as they recited their lines.

◆ Reading Strategy

❹ Paraphrase Ask students to explain the meaning of this line in their own words. *Sample answer: Although Grandpa hadn't said much in a long time, his hand was very expressive.*

Reinforce and Extend

Answers
◆ Literature and Your Life

Reader's Response Some students might feel they would not be able to communicate with him, while others will be intrigued by his unique character.

RIGHT HAND

Philip Fried

Grandfather carried his voice in the seamed
palm of his right hand, the one
that had ironed countless <u>taciturn</u> trousers.

❶
5 What an <u>eloquent</u> hand, it broke into grins
and self-assured narration whenever
it opened—how could a hand carry nothing,
bear away nothing from its nation?
❷
When it entered a room, even the corners
10 mumbled in Yiddish, the very dust
had sifted from consonants' <u>guttural</u> rubbing.

❸
The poems this hand had proclaimed to shirts
as it moved back and forth like a Greek chorus
across the stage of the ironing board—
these poems had <u>diffused</u> in clouds of steam.

❹
15 Grandpa himself had long been struck dumb
by the <u>garrulity</u> of this hand,
but sometimes he'd thrust it deep in his pocket
and, straightening up, display an uncanny
knack for spelling English words.

◆ Build Vocabulary

taciturn (tas´ ə tʉrn) *adj.*: Silent; uncommunicative

eloquent (el´ ə kwənt) *adj.*: Vividly expressive

guttural (gut´ ər əl) *adj.*: Produced from the throat; harsh; rasping

diffused (di fyo͞ozd´) *v.*: Spread out; dispersed

garrulity (gə ro͞o´ lə tē) *n.*: Talkativeness

Guide for Responding

◆ Literature and Your Life

Reader's Response Would you like to spend time with the man described in this poem? Why or why not?

Thematic Focus What are some significant choices the grandfather has made in his life?

☑ **Check Your Comprehension**

1. What does Grandfather's hand do as it irons shirts?
2. Describe two ways in which Grandfather's hand expresses itself.

◆ Critical Thinking

INTERPRET

1. Explain the contrast between Grandfather's hand and Grandfather himself. **[Analyze]**
2. Why do you think Grandfather puts his hand in his pocket when he spells English words? **[Infer]**
3. Explain the meaning of the lines "When it entered a room, even the corners/mumbled in Yiddish . . ."

APPLY

4. Describe a friend's personality through his or her hands, eyes, or smile. **[Relate]**

Thematic Focus He has chosen to immigrate to this country; he has chosen to commune with himself rather than talk a lot to others.

☑ **Check Your Comprehension**

1. It "speaks" to the shirts.
2. It "broke into grins/and self-assured narration" and "proclaimed poems."

◆ Critical Thinking

1. Grandfather's hand is eloquent and garrulous, while he is as taciturn as the trousers he presses.
2. He is self-conscious; he does not want his Yiddish self (the hand) to emerge.
3. These lines indicate that the personality embodied in the hand is a strong Yiddish presence, one that necessarily evokes a response, thus "even the corners/mumbled in Yiddish."
4. Sample response: His eyes dart all around, quickly, trying to keep pace with the flow of his ideas.

Guide for Reponding (continued)

◆ Reading Strategy

PARAPHRASE

Paraphrasing—restating in your own words—is one way to clarify the meaning of complex or abstract lines or sections of these poems.

1. Paraphrase the first and last stanzas of "The Wind—tapped like a tired Man."
2. (a) Choose words that describe the speed of each event or activity in the first two stanzas of "A Pace Like That." (b) Use these words to paraphrase what Amichai says about the kind of pace he wants to achieve.
3. The poem "Metaphor" is written in three sentences. Paraphrase each sentence.
4. (a) Identify two words Fried uses to describe his grandfather's hand, and give a synonym for each. (b) Paraphrase the description using the synonyms you have chosen.

◆ Literary Focus

FIGURATIVE LANGUAGE

Figurative language is speech or writing that presents ideas in a way not meant to be interpreted literally. Specific types of figurative language are called figures of speech. Common figures of speech are **simile, metaphor,** and **personification.** Poets and other writers use figurative language to create vivid word pictures, to make their writing emotionally intense and concentrated, and to state their ideas in new and unusual ways.

1. (a) What simile does Amichai use in "A Pace Like That" to describe the way people comment on his actions? (b) Explain how this comparison clarifies his meaning.
2. What qualities of the wind might lead Emily Dickinson to describe it as a rapid, footless guest?
3. Identify the simile Fried uses in "Right Hand" to describe the movement of his grandfather's hand ironing shirts.
4. Explain the metaphor in "Metaphor."
5. Which poem uses the most vivid personification? Use examples to support your answer.

◆ Build Vocabulary

USING THE ROOT -tac-

Knowing that the root -tac- and its variant -tic- mean "silent," describe the following people or things in your notebook.

1. a taciturn judge
2. a reticent witness
3. a tacit understanding

USING THE WORD BANK

Practice In your notebook, respond to each of the numbered items using words from the Word Bank. Use each word only once.

1. List four words that deal with speech or speaking.
2. Write one adjective and one adverb that could be used to describe the actions or attitude of a high-strung, excited person.
3. Write a synonym for the word *face*.
4. Write the word that names what a shade or thin curtain does to light shining through it.
5. Identify the word you would most likely find in a story about a secret code.

◆ Build Grammar Skills

ELLIPTICAL CLAUSES

In an **elliptical clause,** words that are understood or implied are omitted.

Practice Copy the following sentences in your notebook. Underline the elliptical clause in each; then write the omitted word or words.

1. I don't understand the way you decipher the inscription.
2. I admire the way he writes.
3. Do you remember the year he came to live here?
4. He is the one I need to help me.
5. The poems this hand had proclaimed to shirts . . .

The Wind—tapped like a tired Man/A Pace Like That/Metaphor/Right Hand ◆ 839

Answers

◆ Reading Strategy

1. (1) The Wind came to my window and I boldly invited It in, so the Wind entered. (2) It visited but then It nervously asked to be excused, after which I was left alone.
2. (a) Sample response: Looking at the lemon tree—leisurely; sleeping and dreaming—hurriedly. (b) He wants to observe things in a leisurely way.
3. Morning is a new opportunity. You choose what to do with it and in the evening it's all filed away. A new day brings new opportunities.
4. (a) eloquent: expressive; garrulity: talkativeness; (b) My grandfather's hand was expressive and talkative.

◆ Literary Focus

1. (a) He says they're like people standing around a manhole yelling down advice. (b) This comparison conveys the speaker's sense of being observed.
2. The wind is stealthy and quick; it doesn't leave a trace.
3. It moved back and forth like a Greek Chorus moves across a stage.
4. A clean sheet of paper is a new start; so is a new day.
5. Sample response: "The Wind" because it makes the wind seem just like a quick, nervous person.

◆ Build Vocabulary

Using the Word Root -tac-
1. one who doesn't talk much
2. a witness who is reluctant to speak
3. an unspoken understanding

Using the Word Bank
1. taciturn, eloquent, guttural, garrulity;   2. tremulous, flurriedly;
3. countenance;   4. diffused;
5. decipher

◆ Build Grammar Skills

1. I don't understand <u>the way</u> (that) <u>you decipher the inscription</u>.
2. I admire the way (that) <u>he writes</u>.
3. Do you remember the year (that) <u>I came to live here</u>?
4. He is the one (who) <u>I need to help me</u>.
5. The poems (that) <u>this hand had proclaimed to shirts</u>.

 Beyond the Selection

FURTHER READING

Other Works by the Poets
"A Light Exists in Spring," Emily Dickinson
"This Is My Mother's House," Yehuda Amichai
Family Circle, Eve Merriam
"Sunday," Philip Fried

Other Works About Daily Choices
"Ballad of the Morning Streets," Amiri Baraka
"Reveille," A. E. Housman

We suggest that you preview these works before recommending them to students.

INTERNET

Students can visit the following Web sites for more information. Please be aware that sites may have changed since we published this information.

Dickinson: **http://www.learner.org/channel/previews/multimedia.html**

Merriam: **http://mbhs.bergtraum.k12.ny.us/cybereng/poetry/eatpoem.html**

We *strongly recommend* that you preview sites before you send students to them.

Idea Bank

Customizing for
Performance Levels

Following are suggestions for matching Idea Bank topics with your students' performance levels:

Less Advanced Students: 1, 6
Average Students: 2, 4, 5
More Advanced Students: 3, 7

Customizing for
Learning Modalities

Following are suggestions for matching Idea Bank topics with your students' learning modalities:

Interpersonal: 4, 5
Verbal/Linguistic: 3, 4, 5
Logical/Mathematical: 7
Visual/Spatial: 6

Writing Mini-Lesson

Refer students to the Writing Handbook, page 965, for instruction on the writing process and page 967 for further information on descriptive writing.

Writing Lab CD-ROM

Have students complete the tutorial on Descriptive Writing. Follow these steps:

1. Have students Use a Character Trait Word Bin to see examples of words they might want to use in creating their characters. Allow time for students to draft on the computer.
2. Encourage students to use Revision Checkers to find any overused or vague adjectives in their descriptions.

Sourcebook

Have students use Chapter 1, Description (pp. 1–24), for additional support. The chapter includes techniques on gathering details (p. 18).

Build Your Portfolio

Idea Bank

Writing Ideas

1. **Most Admired** "Right Hand" is a celebration of a person the poet admires. Write a paragraph about someone you admire. Describe his or her admirable qualities and physical features.

2. **Perfect Day Directions** The poem "Metaphor" describes a day as a sheet of paper on which you can write anything you choose. Write the "directions" for your perfect day.

3. **Metaphor Poem** Eve Merriam uses the metaphor of a sheet of paper to describe the possibilities of each new day. Write a brief poem in which you use one central metaphor to describe "choices."

Speaking and Listening

4. **Wind Interview** With a partner, prepare and act out an interview with the speaker of "The Wind—tapped like a tired Man."

5. **Dialogue** Imagine that the speakers of "A Pace Like That" and "Metaphor" have been stuck on an elevator together for three hours. Role-play the conversation that might be taking place between them as they head into hour four.

Projects

6. **Visual Biography** Fried associates ironing, Yiddish, and spelling with his grandfather. Create a collage biography of a relative or friend. Arrange pictures and objects on a paper to show the things you associate with this person. **[Art Link]**

7. **Hurricane Statistics** The wind in Dickinson's poem is a much friendlier wind than one you'd encounter in a hurricane. Find statistics about hurricanes' wind speeds, frequency, and duration. Present your findings to the class using charts and graphs. **[Math Link; Science Link]**

Writing Mini-Lesson

Character Creation

In "The Wind—tapped like a tired Man," Emily Dickinson brings the wind to life with personification; she describes the wind's movements as the actions of a person. Use techniques similar to Dickinson's to create a character from an object (such as a computer), a plant (such as a tree outside your window), or a weather condition (such as rain). Write a description of how this character acts and sounds, giving the subject of your description human qualities.

> **Writing Focus: Consistent Focus**
>
> In describing your character, keep a **consistent focus.** If you begin by characterizing an object as an energetic three-year-old, use comparisons that suggest this image throughout your description. In "The Wind—tapped like a tired Man," Dickinson keeps a consistent focus; all her comparisons and details create a unified image of the nervous movements of a "tremulous" "flitting" visitor.

Prewriting Begin by listing the qualities of the thing you are describing. Ask yourself questions about how your subject moves, looks, and sounds. Based on these details, determine the type of character your subject is. The details may suggest a gentle elderly person or a cranky child.

Drafting Organize your description around a specific moment. For instance, Emily Dickinson describes a moment when the wind blows through her house. You might describe a moment when a tree is scratching on your window or your computer is "waking up."

Revising Ask a partner to read your description and tell you the general impression he or she gets from it. Together, look for any details that do not contribute to the general impression or central focus. Revise to create a more unified picture of your subject.

✓ ASSESSMENT OPTIONS

Formal Assessment, Selection Test, pp. 201–203, and Assessment Resources Software. The selection test is designed so that it can be easily customized to the performance levels of your students.
Alternative Assessment, p. 57, includes options for less advanced students, more advanced students, interpersonal learners, verbal/linguistic learners and visual/spatial learners.

PORTFOLIO ASSESSMENT
Use the following rubrics in the *Alternative Assessment* booklet to assess student writing:
Most Admired: Description Rubric, p. 97
Perfect Day Directions: How-to/Explanation Rubric, p. 100
Metaphor Poem: Poetry Rubric, p. 108
Writing Mini-Lesson: Description, p. 97

Writing Process Workshop

Literary Analysis

Have you ever seen a movie with a friend and then afterwards had a deep discussion in which you picked apart every aspect of the film? Literary critics, teachers, and students do the same with a work of literature when they write a literary analysis.

Write a **literary analysis** of one of the works in this section. Closely examine the work of literature by taking it apart and discussing its various elements. A literary analysis provides the opportunity for you to explain how the author has used particular literary elements and how those elements work together to convey the author's message.

The following skills will help you write a keen literary analysis.

Writing Skills Focus

▶ **Be consistent in your purpose.** For example, if your purpose is to explain the use of nature words in haiku, then don't discuss sound devices. (See p. 820.)

▶ **Use specific examples.** Every time you make an assertion about the work, back it up with an example from the text. (See p. 831.)

▶ **Paraphrase** specific passages to further describe images or explain details.

The following excerpt from a literary analysis about imagery in haiku shows these skills.

Ploughing (detail), Nancy Smith, Stapleton Collection

WRITING MODEL

Haiku by Issa

A gentle spring rain.
Look, a rat is lapping
Sumida River. ①

Issa, the writer of this haiku, knew well how important it is to use seasonal words in haiku. Although this haiku contains a scarce 15 syllables, because of the poet's choice of words it conveys a lasting image of a peaceful scene of a creature by a river in the rain.

By briefly describing a riverside scene in a soft spring rain, ② Issa creates a clear image in our minds. "Lapping" further clarifies that image. ③ We are reminded . . .

① The writer uses a specific example of a haiku.

② The writer paraphrases to describe the image.

③ The writer sticks to the purpose: to explain the importance of imagery in haiku.

Writing Process Workshop ◆ 841

 Cross-Curricular Connection: Science

Explain to students that literary analysis and scientific analysis share similar critical thinking processes. When medical researchers write up their findings, their technical reports must withstand the critical analysis of the worldwide scientific community. While readers analyze literary works in terms of their literary elements and how they fit together, readers analyze technical reports in terms of scientific method, validity in comparison with other scientific data, and possible flaws.

Writing Lab CD-ROM

If students have access to computers, have them work in the tutorial on Response to Literature to complete all or part of their literary analysis. Follow these steps:

1. Students can review the interactive model of a response to literature.
2. Have students use the Response Wheels to focus their response.
3. Have students use the Evaluation Word Bins to improve word choice.
4. After drafting, students can use the Interactive Self-Evaluation Checklist to guide revision.

Establish Writing Guidelines
Review the following key characteristics of a literary analysis:

- A literary analysis takes apart a work of literature and discusses its elements.
- The analysis explains how the author uses particular literary elements.
- It explains how the author puts the elements together to convey a message.

Before students begin, you may want to share with them the Scoring Rubric for Literary Analysis/Interpretation (p. 112 in *Alternative Assessment*) so students see the criteria by which they will be evaluated. Suggestions on page 843 customize the rubric to this workshop.

Writing and Language Transparencies You may wish to use Writing Process Model 8: Interpreting a Work of Literature (pp. 53–59) to model the writing process and to provide students with a model literary analysis.

Connect to Literature Unit 7, Nonfiction, includes two examples of critical reviews: Vincent Canby's "Star Wars—A Trip to a Far Galaxy That's Fun and Funny" (p. 631) and Roger Ebert's "Star Wars: Breakthrough Film Still Has the Force" (p. 626). Ask students to compare how the authors supported their main ideas. Point out that critical reviews of films are a type of literary analysis.

 Writer's Solution

Writers at Work Videodisc
To introduce students to the key elements of a literary response and to let them hear teacher and poet Miguel Algarín discuss response to literature, play the videodisc segment on Response to Literature (Ch. 7). Have students discuss how Algarín uses response to literature.

Play frames 22209 to 31154

Sourcebook
Students can find additional support, including guidelines for gathering details and organizing their analyses, in Chapter 7, Response to Literature (pp. 194–227).

841

Develop Student Writing

Prewriting

You may want to have students use an Analysis Map graphic organizer (*Writing and Language Transparencies*, p. 71) to help organize their thoughts.

Customize for
English Language Learners

Because these students may not have yet developed a wide range of evaluative words, work with them to create a list of precise descriptors.

 Writer's Solution

Writing Lab CD-ROM

The Self-Interview Checklist will help students recall recently-read works and answer a series of questions to find an appropriate topic for a literary analysis.

Drafting

Remind students that to support the main idea of a literary analysis they must use specific details, including quoted phrases and sentences, from the literary work.

Applying Language Skills

Run-on Sentences Explain to students that run-on sentences confuse readers and blur ideas. A literary analysis aims to show clear relationships among the literary elements a writer uses. Run-on sentences, however, run ideas together and thus blur the clear relationships the analysis should establish.

Answers

Suggested response: Repetition is a common sound device, and the Navajo often used it in their poetry. It gives the poetry a ceremonial, almost sacred feeling.

 Writer's Solution

For additional instruction and practice, use the **Language Lab CD-ROM** lesson on Fragments and Run-on Sentences and the practice page on Fragments and Run-ons, p. 59, in the *Writer's Solution Grammar Practice Book*.

APPLYING LANGUAGE SKILLS: Run-on Sentences

Avoid run-on sentences— sentences that have two main clauses not separated by adequate punctuation.

Run-on Sentence:

Emily Dickinson frequently punctuates her poems with dashes, they give the poems a unique feel and style.

Corrected With a Conjunction:

Emily Dickinson frequently punctuates her poems with dashes, <u>and</u> they give the poems a unique feel and style.

Corrected With a Semicolon:

Emily Dickinson frequently punctuates her poems with dashes<u>;</u> they give the poems a unique feel and style.

Practice On your paper, correct the following run-on sentence.

> Repetition is a common sound device, the Navajo often used it in their poetry, it gives the poetry a ceremonial, almost sacred feeling.

Writer's Solution Connection Language Lab

For more practice correcting run-on sentences, complete the Language Lab lesson on Run-on Sentences and Fragments.

842 ◆ Poetry

Prewriting

Interview Yourself Review works of literature you've read during the past year. Then answer the following questions:

- ▶ What were the most enjoyable, interesting, and frustrating literary works I encountered this year?
- ▶ Why did the works strike me this way?
- ▶ What was especially memorable about the subjects or stories?
- ▶ Which characters come to mind in an especially vivid way?
- ▶ What was special about any of the settings of the works or about the author's use of language?
- ▶ Would I want to reread any of these literary works? Why or why not?

Take notes as you conduct your self-interview, and use these notes to help you choose a topic for a literary analysis.

Consider the Meaning If you're writing a literary analysis of a poem, ask yourself how the poet used language to get his or her message across. Think about the use of figurative language. What images has the poet created to convey ideas to the reader? If you are analyzing a lyric poem, look for details the poet uses to suggest mood or feeling.

Focus Your Topic Explore your reactions to the work you've chosen. You won't be able to include everything you think and feel about the work, so concentrate on one of its literary elements—setting, theme, or mood, for example. Make a chart like the following one to further help you focus your topic:

Literary Work	Broad Topic	Focused Topic
"The Monkey's Paw"	Suspense	The author's use of foreshadowing to build suspense
Julius Caesar	Soliloquy	Cassius' speech in Act I, ii, 308–322
"Meeting at Night"	Sound Devices	How alliteration and onomatopoeia add to the poem's meaning

Drafting

Write the Introduction Your introduction is the place to capture your readers' attention and tell them the purpose of your paper. Include the title and author of the work you'll be evaluating. Open with a statement that will intrigue your readers. Then clearly state your main idea.

Write the Body and Conclusion Develop your main idea in the **body** of your analysis. Present each main idea in a **separate paragraph,** and include specific details to support each main idea. In the **conclusion,** restate your main idea and make a final, compelling point.

Revising

Use a Checklist The following checklist will help you revise your literary analysis:

▶ Do you grab the reader's attention in the first paragraph?
▶ Is your main idea clearly presented? Does the body of your analysis support and develop your main idea?
▶ Are your introduction, body, and conclusion clearly organized?
▶ Do you use specific examples and quotations?

REVISION MODEL

① alliteration and onomatopoeia

In "Meeting at Night," Robert Browning uses ~~lots of~~

~~musical devices~~ to make the poem more vivid. When the

② the terms "pushing prow" and "slushy sand" let the reader

narrator is in the boat, ~~you can~~ feel his exertion. ~~Also,~~

② In the second stanza, the

words "Tap at the pane" are themselves like a hand striking a window.

~~when he knocks on the window it sounds really vivid.~~

① *Alliteration and onomatopoeia are more specific than lots of musical devices.*

② *The writer replaces vague statements with direct quotations from the text.*

Publishing

Create a Library Display With your classmates and the librarian, create a library display of your literary analyses.

▶ Set up the display so that it attracts students' attention.
▶ Bind and mount the analyses to make them accessible and attractive.
▶ Use posters, photos, or other illustrations to make the display visually appealing.

APPLYING LANGUAGE SKILLS: Adjective Clauses

An adjective clause is a subordinate clause (a clause that contains a subject and a verb, but cannot stand alone as a sentence) that modifies a noun or pronoun in a sentence's main clause. The following words commonly introduce adjective clauses:

that, which, who, whom, whose, whoever, where, when

The adjective clause in the following sentence modifies *figurative device:*

Simile is the figurative device that Tennyson uses most.

Practice On your paper, identify the adjective clauses in the following sentences and indicate which word in the main clause it modifies.

1. The object to which Emily Dickinson compares the wind is a tired man.
2. The man who wrote that poem lived a long time ago.

Writer's Solution Connection Writing Lab

For more help using quotations in your literary analysis, see Using Quotations in the Writing Lab tutorial on Response to Literature.

Revising

After discussing the Revision Model, you may want also to use the Revision Overlay for Writing Process Model 8: Interpreting a Work of Literature (*Writing and Language Transparencies,* p. 55) to model the revising process further.

Publishing

Remind students that literary analyses are often published in newspapers and magazines as well as on the Internet. They may want to pursue these sources of publishing.

Applying Language Skills
Adjective Clauses Discuss with students how they can, by using adjective clauses, combine short, choppy sentences into more mature sentences. You might model this process for them.

Answers

1. The adjective clause *to which Emily Dickinson compares the wind* modifies *object.*
2. The adjective clause *who wrote that poem* modifies *man.*

Writer's Solution

For additional instruction and practice, use the practice pages on Adjective Clauses, p. 51, in the *Writer's Solution Grammar Practice Book.*

Reinforce and Extend

Applying Knowledge After students have completed their papers, ask them to discuss how literary analysis skills might be applied in other curricular areas. Ask them to identify the elements that might be important—for instance, in the analysis of a history or science book.

✓ ASSESSMENT		4	3	2	1
PORTFOLIO ASSESSMENT Use the rubric on Literary Analysis/Interpretation (p. 112) to assess students' writing. Add these criteria to customize the rubric to this assignment.	**Reference to Specific Literary Elements**	The literary analysis addresses all significant literary elements and shows how the author uses them to convey purpose.	The analysis addresses most of the literary elements and shows in part how the author uses them to convey purpose.	The analysis addresses few of the literary elements and shows in part how the author uses them to convey purpose.	The analysis addresses few of the literary elements and fails to show how the author uses them to convey purpose.
	Sentence Structure	The writer uses a variety of sentence structures, including complex sentences with adjective clauses.	The writer uses a variety of sentence structures but only limited use of complex sentences.	The literary analysis shows some sentence variety but no complex sentences.	The literary analysis shows no sentence variety.

Real-World Reading Skills Workshop

Strategies for Success

Photographs, paintings, charts, and diagrams are all different types of visuals that enhance and complement the text in a book. They provide you with information not available in the written text. These strategies will help you use visuals to your benefit.

Visuals in Combination With Text To get the most from illustrations and photographs, look at them in combination with the text and the captions. Consider how the visuals relate to the written text. Don't make an assumption about the visuals that isn't supported in the text.

Charts, Diagrams, and Graphs Charts, diagrams, and graphs are different ways of presenting or summarizing information visually. Diagrams usually show a process, while graphs and charts show relationships within the information being represented. (See p. 920 for further information on reading charts.)

Captions and Labels Captions provide information about or direct your attention to a part of the visual. If there is more than one visual on a page, all the captions may be clustered together. Look for clues such as arrows or phrases to match each caption to its visual. A visual may contain labels—either within the visual or connected to it by lines—that identify the parts of the visual.

> ✔ Here are other situations in which visual cues may provide additional information:
> ▶ Instruction manuals
> ▶ Textbooks
> ▶ Cookbook recipes
> ▶ Illustrated magazine articles

PREHISTORIC ART TREASURE IS FOUND IN FRENCH CAVE

by Marlise Simons

Paris, Jan. 18—In the mountains of southern France, where human beings have habitually hunted, loved, and produced art, explorers have discovered an underground cave full of Stone Age paintings, so beautifully made and well preserved that experts are calling it one of the archaeological finds of the century.

The enormous underground cavern, which was found on December 18, 1994, in a gorge near the town of Vallon-Pont-d'Arc in the Ardäche region, is studded with more than 300 vivid images of animals and human hands that experts believe were made some 20,000 years ago.

Apply the Strategy

Refer to the picture and its accompanying text as you answer the questions.

1. What visual clues helped you determine the topic of the article?
2. What word in the headline suggests the importance of the archaeological find?
3. What information does the photograph provide that the text does not?

844 ◆ *Poetry*

Cross-Curricular Connection: Science and Math

To convey critical information, science and math textbooks rely heavily on visual clues like charts, graphs, diagrams, drawings, formulas, labels, photos, captions, headings, and footnotes. These visuals often provide information that would be unwieldy or nearly impossible to convey concisely in text. Have students bring in sample pages from science or math textbooks to analyze visual clues and the information they convey.

PART 2 *Structure*

Helicon Desk, Cathleen Toelke

One-Minute Planning Guide

The poems in this section illustrate the art of poetry. Structure, or verbal design, provides a framework within which poets work. These poems illustrate categories of poetry—narrative, dramatic, and lyric—and tightly structured forms—sonnet, villanelle, tanka, and haiku.

Customize for *Varying Student Needs*

- All of the poems, except "La Belle Dame sans Merci" are short. "La Belle Dame sans Merci" is two pages.
- The following poems contain vocabulary that may challenge less proficient readers or English language learners.

Sonnet 18

"Danny Deever" (dialect)

- The following poems contain simple language and clear images and messages:

"Making a Fist"

"Jade Flower Palace"

"The Moon at the Fortified Pass"

"What Are Friends For"

Tanka

Haiku

- Students may be intrigued by the clever arrangement of words in "Some Like Poetry"

 Humanities: Art

Helicon Desk by Cathleen Toelke.

Explain that "Helicon" has several meanings, but the most likely one for this painting comes from Greek mythology, in which the Helicon Mountains were the home of the Muses, the divine figures who inspired writers, artists, and performers. Help students see how a writing desk could be compared to the home of the Muses. The whole painting invites the imagination to play with associations. Call attention to the way the items in the painting resemble folded pieces of paper, like origami—the folding screen, the sharp-edged shadows, and the oddly jutting desk.

Help students link this art with the focus of Part 2, Structure, by answering the following questions:

1. What kind of poetry do you think this artist would write? *Students may feel that the angular, structured images in the painting indicate that the artist would write highly structured poetry.*

2. A poem is an arrangement of words structured to arouse emotion and convey meaning. Look at the way the items in this painting are arranged. Which item do you think the artist wants you to notice first, and what has she done to make you notice it? *Students should note that the item they choose has other items pointing at it, or is a brighter color, or is placed at a focal point.*

845

Guide for Reading

OBJECTIVES

1. To read, comprehend, and interpret poetry
2. To relate poems to personal experience
3. To identify the speaker in two poems
4. To recognize the elements of narrative and dramatic poetry
5. To build vocabulary in context and learn the word root *-journ-*
6. To use hyphens appropriately in writing
7. To write a news bulletin with a climax and resolution
8. To respond to the poems through writing, speaking and listening, and projects

SKILLS INSTRUCTION

Vocabulary:
Word Roots: *-journ-*

Grammar:
Hyphens

Reading Strategy:
Identify the Speaker

Literary Focus:
Narrative and Dramatic Poetry

Writing:
Climax and Resolution

Speaking and Listening:
Story in Music (teacher edition)

Critical Viewing:
Support; Analyze

PORTFOLIO OPPORTUNITIES

Writing: Diary Entry; Letter to the Knight; Mock Narrative

Writing Mini-Lesson: News Bulletin Based on Poem

Speaking and Listening: Oral Reading; Story in Music

Projects: Dialect Chart; Art

More About the Authors

After **John Keats's** first poems were published, his work was severely attacked by critics. Some people, including the English poet Percy Bysshe Shelley, felt that the harsh criticism hastened Keats's death, but Keats continued writing, producing his best work in the next two years. Though he died at the age of 25, he is considered among the greatest of the English romantic poets.

Much of **Rudyard Kipling's** work focuses on the life of the soldier. He strongly supported the British colonial system. As readers began to oppose colonialism, Kipling's popularity waned, but modern critics recognize his work for its evocative imagery and vivid use of language.

John Keats (1795–1821)

John Keats was born in England. Both of his parents died while he was still a boy, and his guardian sent Keats to school in London. Later, Keats studied surgery. He decided, however, to devote his life to writing poetry.

In 1816, Keats met Leigh Hunt, an editor who published Keats's first sonnet, "On First Looking Into Chapman's Homer." Hunt also introduced Keats to Shelley and Wordsworth. Like them, he emphasized feeling and imagination over reason and logic in his poetry.

Although he died young, Keats left a surprisingly large body of work. His poems, including the narrative poem "La Belle Dame sans Merci," communicate an appreciation of beauty and a sadness at its impermanence.

Rudyard Kipling (1865–1936)

Rudyard Kipling was born in India to English parents. He grew up speaking both Hindustani and English until the age of six, when he was sent to England for a formal education.

Returning to India at eighteen, Kipling worked as a journalist. Many of his early poems and stories first appeared in newspapers. "Danny Deever" was included in a collection of Kipling's poems called *Barracks Room Ballads*.

In 1907, he became the first English author to win the Nobel Prize for Literature. He produced a vast body of work, including stories, poems, and novels.

◆ Build Vocabulary

WORD ROOTS: *-journ-*

In "La Belle Dame sans Merci," the speaker laments "And this is why I *sojourn* here . . ." The word *sojourn* contains the root *-journ-*, which means "day." It's easy to understand how the current meaning of *sojourn*, "stay temporarily," could evolve from "a day's stay."

Other words that contain the root, such as *journal* and *adjourn*, also have meanings that have evolved from the meaning of "day."

WORD BANK

sedge
thrall
sojourn
whimpers
quickstep

As you read these poems, you will encounter the words on this list. Each word is defined on the page where it first appears. Preview the list before you read.

◆ Build Grammar Skills

HYPHENS

These poems contain examples of **hyphens**—used to connect two or more words that function as a single word. Notice the use of hyphens in the following examples from the poems:

Pale Warriors, *death-pale* were they all

"What makes that *front-rank* man fall down?"

The hyphens used in these lines from the poems form compound modifiers. Hyphens are not used in compound modifiers that include words ending in *-ly* (*poorly* trusted, for example) or with compound proper adjectives. (*Native American* customs for instance). Hyphens are used, however, in many compound nouns, such as mother-in-law.

Prentice Hall Literature Program Resources

REINFORCE / RETEACH / EXTEND

Selection Support Pages
Build Vocabulary: Word Roots: *-journ-*, p. 237
Build Grammar Skills: Hyphens, p. 238
Reading Strategy: Identify the Speaker, p. 239
Literary Focus: Narrative and Dramatic Poetry, p. 240

Strategies for Diverse Student Needs, p. 58

Beyond Literature *The Military,* p. 58

Formal Assessment Selection Test, pp. 204–206; and Assessment Resources Software

Alternative Assessment, p. 58

Writing and Language Transparencies
Graphic Organizer: Story Map, pp. 83–86

Resource Pro CD-ROM "La Belle Dame sans Merci" and "Danny Deever"—includes all resource materials and customizable lesson plan

Listening to Literature Audiocassettes
"La Belle Dame sans Merci" and "Danny Deever"

Literature CD-ROM
How to Read and Understand Poetry, Feature 4

La Belle Dame sans Merci
◆ Danny Deever ◆

◆ *Literature and Your Life*

CONNECT YOUR EXPERIENCE

Our choices in life are based on what we want and need. Sometimes, we want what we can't have. "La Belle Dame sans Merci" relates the tale of a knight who cannot have the love of the beautiful woman he serves. "Danny Deever" shows the consequences of one man's rash action, but it does not reveal the wants or needs that led to his choice.

THEMATIC FOCUS: FACING THE CONSEQUENCES

In both "La Belle Dame sans Merci" and "Danny Deever," characters must face the consequences of choices they have made. Think about whether the price they pay is too high.

Journal Writing Outline the standards on which you make choices.

◆ Background for Understanding

HISTORY

In "La Belle Dame sans Merci," a knight pines for a beautiful woman who is forever out of his reach. This unattainable desire is at the heart of courtly love, a medieval code of attitudes and conduct followed by noble lords and ladies, especially knights.

In the tradition of courtly love, a knight focuses his adoration on a beautiful, intelligent, high-minded woman. Whether or not the woman loves him is immaterial. This love is believed too noble and pure to be corrupted by physical affection. The knight performs great deeds to honor the lady, but he suffers terribly in the knowledge that his affection can never be returned.

◆ Literary Focus

NARRATIVE AND DRAMATIC POETRY

A **narrative poem** tells a story and is usually longer than other types of poems. Like any story, a narrative poem has one or more characters, a setting, a conflict, and a series of events that come to a conclusion. Most narrative poems are divided into stanzas—or groups of lines that have the same pattern of rhythm and rhyme.

Dramatic poetry is poetry in which one or more characters speak. By using the words of one or more speakers to tell directly what is happening, dramatic poetry creates the illusion that the reader is actually witnessing a dramatic event.

◆ Reading Strategy

IDENTIFY THE SPEAKER

Whenever you read a poem, **identify its speaker** as an important first step in gaining insight into the poem. The speaker of the poem may be the poet or a fictitious character created by the poet. Even when a poet uses the pronoun *I* in a poem, the speaker may be fictional and not the poet himself or herself.

For example, in "La Belle Dame sans Merci," Keats uses the characters themselves as the speakers, and by doing so, is able to delve deeply into the characters' minds. We are able to feel the knight's anguish and emotions.

Like other fictional characters, the speaker in a narrative poem may reveal information about himself or herself directly, through forthright statements, or indirectly, through hints and implications.

Guide for Reading ◆ 847

 Preparing for Standardized Tests

Reading and Vocabulary The Build Vocabulary lesson for this selection focuses on using the word root *-journ-* to determine the meaning of words such as *sojourn.* Students can apply their word-building skills when matching words with their correct definitions on standardized tests. For additional practice, use the Build Vocabulary page in **Selection Support**, p. 237.

Critical Reading portions of many standardized tests require students to evaluate a writer's

points and make judgments about how the writer's point of view influences the information included in a work. Identifying the speaker in poetry will give students practice in recognizing the different perspectives from which information can be presented. For further instruction and practice, use the Reading Strategy page, Identify the Speaker, in **Selection Support,** page 239.

One-Minute Insight

"La Belle Dame sans Merci" (literally, "The Beautiful Woman Without Pity") is a character who appears in world literature under different names—Circe or Morgan le Fay, for example. In English, she is the *beldame*, a word for a witch or enchantress who takes pleasure in destroying the unlucky men whom she enthralls. In this poem, a young man comes under her spell, only to find his life drained away after an enchanted night. Students might relate to the broader theme of this poem—things that seem attractive can sometimes disappoint or even endanger a person.

▶Critical Viewing◀

❶ Support Suggested response: She is pulling him towards her by tugging at a wrapping about his neck; she looks relaxed and seductive, and he is not resisting her.

◆ Literary Focus

❷ Narrative and Dramatic Poetry Ask students to identify the character and details of setting introduced in this first stanza. Ask students to identify the season these details seem to indicate. *The knight-at-arms is the character; details of setting include the withered grass by a lake that is silent and barren. The season seems to be late autumn or perhaps early winter—seasons of dormancy and death.*

❸ Clarification Explain to students that the image of the lily and the fading rose both suggest death. Students may be interested to know that, at the time he wrote this poem, Keats was nursing his brother, who was dying of tuberculosis.

◆ Reading Strategy

❹ Identify the Speaker Lead students to see that in these two stanzas a new speaker is established. Ask them to identify the speaker of the first stanza and the one here and to predict which will be the main character in the story that is about to unfold. *The first speaker is a minor character who finds the knight by the lake. The second speaker is the knight. Students should note that the knight is the main character; he tells his story.*

848

La Belle Dame sans Merci[1]

John Keats

La Belle Dame sans Merci, John W. Waterhouse, Hessisches Landes Museum, Darmstadt

 ▲ **Critical Viewing** What evidence indicates that the lady has the knight "in thrall"? [Support]

848 ◆ *Poetry*

O what can ail thee, knight-at-arms,
 Alone and palely loitering?
The sedge has withered from the lake,   ❷
 And no birds sing.

5 O what can ail thee, knight-at-arms,
 So haggard and so woe-begone?
The squirrel's granary is full,
 And the harvest's done.

I see a lily on thy brow,
10 With anguish moist and fever dew,   ❸
And on thy cheeks a fading rose
 Fast withereth too.

I met a lady in the meads,[2]
 Full beautiful—a faery's child,
15 Her hair was long, her foot was light,
 And her eyes were wild.

I made a garland for her head,
 And bracelets too, and fragrant zone;[3]
She looked at me as she did love,
20 And made sweet moan.   ❹

I set her on my pacing steed,
 And nothing else saw all day long,
For sidelong would she bend, and sing
 A faery's song.

---

1. **La Belle Dame sans Merci:** "The Beautiful Lady Without Pity" (French).
2. **meads** (mēdz) *n.*: Old-fashioned form of meadow.
3. **fragrant zone:** Sweet-smelling plant.

✦ Block Scheduling Strategies

Consider these suggestions to take advantage of extended class time:

- Invite students to view Feature 4 on the CD-ROM, which features narrative poetry.
- Interested students can do further research on the subject of courtly love and the Middle Ages, discussed in Background for Understanding on page 847. They might find books such as the following useful: *The Art of Courtly Love* by Andreas Cappellanus and *French Chivalry* by Sidney Painter.

- After you have explained narrative and dramatic poetry, have students work in small groups to discuss and answer the Literary Focus questions on page 852. Have them then complete Literary Focus: Narrative and Dramatic Poetry in *Selection Support*, p. 240.
- Allow time for students to work in groups, reading the poems aloud. The have them listen to the **Listening to Literature Audiocassette** recordings of the poems. Students can analyze and evaluate the recorded readings as well as their own.

25 She found me roots of relish sweet,
    And honey wild, and manna dew,[4]
And sure in language strange she said—
    'I love thee true.'

She took me to her elfin grot,[5]
30   And there she wept, and sighed full sore,
And there I shut her wild wild eyes
    With kisses four.

And there she lullèd me asleep,
    And there I dreamed—Ah! woe betide!
35 The latest dream I ever dreamed
    On the cold hill's side.

❺

I saw pale kings and princes too,
    Pale warriors, death-pale were they all;
They cried—'La Belle Dame sans Merci

───────────────────

4. **manna** (man′ ə) **dew** (dōō): Sweet substance obtained from the bark of certain ash trees.
5. **elfin** (el′ fən) **grot:** Cave belonging to a fairy.

40   Hath thee in thrall!'

I saw their starved lips in the gloam,
    With horrid warning gapèd wide,
And I awoke and found me here,
    On the cold hill's side.

45 And this is why I sojourn here,
    Alone and palely loitering,
Though the sedge has withered from the
    lake,   ❻
    And no birds sing.

◆ **Build Vocabulary**

sedge (sej) *n.*: Grassy plant that grows in wet areas

thrall (thrôl) *n.*: Complete control; slavery

sojourn (sō′ jʉrn) *v.*: Stay temporarily

Guide for Responding

◆ *Literature and Your Life*

Reader's Response What word or words would you use to describe the knight? Explain your answer.

Thematic Focus What choices did the knight make that brought about his current condition?

Group Discussion Discuss the reasons that the knight might have had for making the choices he did. Could he have made different choices? Explain your conclusion to the class.

☑ **Check Your Comprehension**

1. What is the setting of the poem?
2. Describe the lady the knight meets.
3. Describe the knight's dream.

◆ **Critical Thinking**

INTERPRET
1. Explain how the people in the knight's dream relate to his present condition. **[Analyze]**
2. Why is the knight "alone and palely loitering"? **[Draw Conclusions]**
3. In what way does the autumn setting reinforce the meaning and the mood of the poem? **[Connect]**

APPLY
4. In ancient myths, the fertility of the land is tied to the health of a heroic figure. The land can be bountiful again only when the spell put on the heroic figure is broken. Explain how "La Belle Dame sans Merci" incorporates elements of a myth. **[Apply]**

La Belle Dame sans Merci ◆ 849

◆ Critical Thinking

❺ **Infer** Ask students what the knight's dream is telling him about his own fate. *His dream is telling him that he too will become a victim of La Belle Dame.*

◆ Literary Focus

❻ **Narrative Poetry** Have students explain the resolution of the conflict. *The knight is doomed to pine away for the lady until he dies.*

Reinforce and Extend

Answers

◆ *Literature and Your Life*

Reader's Response Some students may describe the knight as weak or lacking in valor because he allows himself to be taken in.

Thematic Focus He lets himself fall in love with the lady, and he lets her lead him into the elfin grot.

☑ **Check Your Comprehension**

1. The setting is the countryside, by a lake, in late autumn.
2. The lady is beautiful, with long hair, a light step, and wild eyes.
3. The knight dreams of death-pale kings, princes, and warriors warning him that La Belle Dame sans Merci has him in her thrall.

◆ Critical Thinking

1. The people in the knight's dream had all fallen victim to La Belle Dame in the past.
2. The knight has now lost his vigor and sense of purpose.
3. The late autumn setting reinforces the meaning and mood of the poem because in late autumn nature is barren and depleted of vigor in much the way the lady has left the knight.
4. The repetition of the phrase "the sedge has withered from the lake" reinforces the notion that the land, like the heroic knight, has fallen weak. This connection between fertility of land and health of hero is a concept borrowed from myth.

🎵 **Humanities: Art**

La Belle Dame sans Merci by John W. Waterhouse.

English painter John William Waterhouse (1849–1917) was inspired by the poetry of Keats and Tennyson. His distinctive style—dreamy and romantic—perfectly captures the mood of Keats's poem.

This painting sets "La Belle Dame" and the knight in a dark and mysterious forest. The rich detail of the painting shows the flowers of the forest and the patterns and textures of the woman's clothing and the knight's armor. Her luminous skin and appealing face draw the knight to her.

Use this question for discussion:
1. How would you compare the lady in the picture to the one described in Keats's poem, "La Belle Dam sans Merci"? *Students might observe the lady is similar because she has long hair, a mysterious air, and an intent expression.*

One-Minute Insight

In Kipling's poem, young soldiers about to witness the hanging of one of their ranks are "dreadin'" what they've "got to watch." Kipling never reveals the reasons behind Danny's crime. Instead he focuses on the reactions of the men who lived, worked, ate, and drank with him.

Listening to Literature Audiocassettes "Danny Deever" is a rhythmic poem spoken in dialect. Students might enjoy listening to the audiocassette as they read the poem so they can hear the sound of the dialect for themselves.

◆ Reading Strategy

❶ **Identify the Speaker** Ask students to identify the two speakers of this dramatic poem. *Files-on-Parade and Color-Sergeant are the speakers.*

◆ Build Grammar Skills

❷ **Hyphens** Ask students to identify the part of speech of each hyphenated word in lines 9–11. *Rear-rank—noun; Files-on-Parade—noun; front-rank— adjective; Color-Sergeant—noun.* Ask: Why are these words hyphenated? *They connect two or more words that function as a single word.*

◆ Literary Focus

❸ **Narrative and Dramatic Poetry** Ask: How does this passage help readers feel they are actually witnessing the events being described? *Sample response: The presentation through conversation creates a sense of immediacy, as if the reader were standing near the two speakers hearing them.*

Danny Deever

Rudyard Kipling

❶ "What are the bugles blowin' for?" said Files-on-Parade.[1]
"To turn you out, to turn you out," the Color-Sergeant[2] said.
"What makes you look so white, so white?" said Files-on-Parade.
"I'm dreadin' what I've got to watch," the Color-Sergeant said.
5   For they're hangin' Danny Deever, you can hear the Dead March play,
    The regiment's in 'ollow square[3] —they're hangin' him today;
    They've taken of his buttons off an' cut his stripes away,
    An' they're hangin' Danny Deever in the mornin'.

❷ "What makes the rear-rank breathe so 'ard?" said Files-on-Parade.
10 "It's bitter cold, it's bitter cold," the Color-Sergeant said.
"What makes that front-rank man fall down?" says Files-on-Parade.
"A touch o' sun, a touch o' sun," the Color-Sergeant said.
    They are hangin' Danny Deever, they are marchin' of 'im round,
    They 'ave 'alted Danny Deever by 'is coffin on the ground;
15   An' 'e'll swing in 'arf a minute for a sneakin' shootin' hound—
    O they're hangin' Danny Deever in the mornin'!

"'Is cot was right-'and cot to mine," said Files-on-Parade.
"'E's sleepin' out an' far tonight," the Color-Sergeant said.
"I've drunk 'is beer a score o' times," said Files-on-Parade.
20 "'E's drinkin' bitter beer alone," the Color-Sergeant said.
❸   They are hangin' Danny Deever, you must mark 'im to 'is place,
    For 'e shot a comrade sleepin'—you must look 'im in the face;
    Nine 'undred of 'is county an' the regiment's disgrace,
    While they're hangin' Danny Deever in the mornin'.

25 "What's that so black agin the sun?" said Files-on-Parade.
"It's Danny fightin' 'ard for life," the Color-Sergeant said.
"What's that that whimpers over'ead?" said Files-on-Parade.
"It's Danny's soul that's passin' now," the Color-Sergeant said.
    For they're done with Danny Deever, you can 'ear the quickstep play,
30   The regiment's in column, an' they're marchin' us away;
    Ho! the young recruits are shakin', an' they'll want their beer to-day,
    After hangin' Danny Deever in the mornin'.

---

1. **Files-on-Parade:** Soldier who directs marching formation.
2. **Color-Sergeant:** Flag-bearer.
3. **'ollow square:** For a hanging, soldiers' ranks form three sides of a square; the fourth side is the gallows.

◆ Build Vocabulary

whimpers (hwim´ pərz) v.: Makes a low, whining sound, as in crying or fear

quickstep (kwik´ step´) n.: Pace used in normal military marching, as contrasted with the slower pace of the dead march

---

Speaking and Listening Mini-Lesson

Story in Music
This mini-lesson supports the Speaking and Listening activity in the Idea Bank on page 853.

Introduce the Concept Explain to students that they are going to choose three songs that tell a story—one from each of three musical genres. In each case, they will explain the song's storytelling techniques, such as having a speaker or narrator, or explaining the rhythmical pattern.

Develop Background Point out that ballads, country music, folk songs, and the blues often tell a story. Have students consider these questions as they choose their three songs.
• What happens in the story? Who are the characters? Where does it take place?
• What techniques does the songwriter use? Is there a refrain or chorus? Does the song contain a strong rhythm? Does it rhyme?

Apply the Information Students can play the songs they have chosen for the class. Encourage them to introduce each song by explaining what it is about and what techniques help make it effective. Allow time for questions after each presentation.

Assess the Outcome Assess students' explanations on the basis of how clearly the speaker explained the storytelling techniques in the songs. Students may use the Peer Assessment for Speaker/Speech, page 118 in *Alternative Assessment*.

The Battle of Bunker Hill, Howard Pyle, Delaware Art Museum

▲ Critical Viewing Compare the method of fighting depicted in this painting with the way battles are fought today. [Analyze] | ❹

❹ **Analyze** Sample answer: The soldiers in the painting are marching in straight lines with muskets as their weapons. If they met an enemy, they would fight face-to-face. Today, much fighting is done at a distance. Weapons are more sophisticated, and land soldiers rarely march.

Reinforce and Extend

Answers

◆ *Literature and Your Life*

Reader's Response Students are likely to respond that they would find it painful or uncomfortable to watch the hanging; some might also say they would identify with Danny Deever and feel afraid.

Thematic Response Students might respond that Danny Deever was a reckless person who did not consider consequences before acting.

☑ **Check Your Comprehension**

1. "Danny Deever" is set on a battlefield or on the way to a battlefield; the regiment is marching.
2. The Color-Sergeant and Files-on-Parade relate the events.
3. The Color-Sergeant has experience with military executions.
4. Danny Deever killed a comrade who was sleeping.

◆ **Critical Thinking**

1. He means that he and Danny Deever were friends—or at least they had drinks together many times.
2. The Color-Sergeant seems wiser, and perhaps more hardened, to the ways of the military; Files-on-Parade is more naive and innocent.
3. The conflicting explanations are not believable; it's obvious that the Color-Sergeant is covering up the soldiers' horrified reaction at the brutal act they are witnessing—the hanging of Danny Deever.
4. Many students will say that the lack of information makes them more sympathetic to Deever because Deever's side of the story is never heard, and he might be unjustly accused.

Guide for Responding

◆ *Literature and Your Life*

Reader's Response If you were in the regiment, how would you feel about having to watch the hanging? Explain.

Thematic Focus What might lead someone like Danny Deever to make a choice that he must have known would result in his execution?

Journal Entry Write a journal entry exploring your response to this poem.

☑ **Check Your Comprehension**

1. Describe the setting of "Danny Deever."
2. Who are the two soldiers who relate the event through their dialogue?
3. Of the two speakers in the poem, which has some prior experience with military executions?
4. For what crime is Danny Deever being executed?

◆ **Critical Thinking**

INTERPRET
1. What does Files-on-Parade mean when he says, "I've drunk 'is beer a score o' times"? [Infer]
2. Compare and contrast Files-on-Parade and the Color-Sergeant. [Compare and Contrast]
3. The Color-Sergeant explains one soldier's hard breathing by saying it is "bitter cold." He explains another soldier's fainting as the result of a "touch o' sun." Are these conflicting explanations believable? What really accounts for the physical problems of the men? [Draw Conclusions]

EVALUATE
4. The poem gives few facts about Danny Deever or his crime. Explain whether this lack of information makes you more or less sympathetic to him. [Evaluate]

Danny Deever ◆ 851

✎ Humanities: Art

The Battle of Bunker Hill by Howard Pyle.

A writer as well as an artist, Howard Pyle (1853–1911) is particularly known for his magnificent illustrations of such children's classics as *The Merry Adventures of Robin Hood*. His consistent use of rich color created a dramatic lifelike world.

Use these questions for discussion:

1. Which details in the painting are similar to details in the poem? Which details are different? *Possible similarities: The army is marching in*

formation. The uniforms suggest a historical setting. Possible differences: There is no flag bearer in the painting. In Pyle's picture the battle is raging, although there's no indication this is the case in the poem.

2. Does the illustration glorify war? *Some students may say that the painting suggests that war is heroic and noble; others may say that the dead bodies indicate the horrible reality of any war.*

◆ Reading Strategy

1. He reveals that the lady is a beautiful lady without pity, and suggests that she cast a spell on him. A speaker who had not had direct experience with the lady could not have revealed this.
2. Students might say that "Danny Deever" would have been more effective if told exclusively by the speakers because their dialogue is already effective, and it seems as if they have the perspective to tell the whole story.

◆ Literary Focus

1. The first two stanzas reveal the setting and introduce the main character, a knight-at-arms.
2. The speaker in stanzas 1–3 is someone who encounters the knight and asks him what's wrong. From stanza 4 on, the knight tells his story of what has happened to him. This shift from one speaker to another sets up the flashback into the knight's story.
3. The last stanza ties the story together because it makes it clear that the knight has answered the first speaker's question.
4. The dialect in "Danny Deever" creates the effect of authenticity.
5. Students might say another soldier is speaking because the dialect is the same and because he says "you can 'ear the quick-step play," as if he were present on the scene.

◆ Build Vocabulary

Using the Word Root -journ-
1. adjourned; 2. journal;
3. journalist

Using the Word Bank
1. sedge   4. thrall
2. quickstep   5. whimpers
3. sojourn

◆ Build Grammar Skills

The British army was based on <u>well-built</u> traditions and <u>rock-solid</u> rules that would not allow for leniency for Danny Deever. <u>Files-on-Parade</u> had the cot on the <u>left-hand</u> side of Deever.

Writer's Solution

For additional practice, use page 109 on Hyphens in the *Writer's Solution Grammar Practice Book*.

Guide for Responding (continued)

◆ Reading Strategy

IDENTIFY THE SPEAKER

The **speaker** is the voice of a poem. The speaker may be the poet, or it may be a fictional character or even an inanimate object. It is up to you, the reader, to identify the speaker in a poem.

1. What does the speaker of "La Belle Dame sans Merci" reveal about the lady? How would this poem be different if Keats had used a different speaker?
2. Tell whether you think "Danny Deever" would have been more effective if all the action had been revealed through the words of Files-on-Parade and the Color-Sergeant. Explain your answer.

◆ Literary Focus

NARRATIVE AND DRAMATIC POETRY

"La Belle Dame sans Merci" is a **narrative poem**—a poem that tells a story. Like a short story, it has a plot, characters, and a setting.

"Danny Deever" is a **dramatic poem**—a poem in which one or more characters tell what is happening through dialogue.

1. In "La Belle Dames sans Merci," which stanzas describe the setting and introduce the main character?
2. The speaker from stanza 4 to the end of "La Belle Dame sans Merci" is different from the speaker of stanzas 1–3. How does this shift help communicate what is happening in the story?
3. How does the last stanza of "La Belle Dame sans Merci" tie the story together?
4. In "Danny Deever," what effect is created by having Files-on-Parade and the Color-Sergeant speak in dialect?
5. The last half of each stanza of "Danny Deever" employs the same distinctive speech patterns used by Files-on-Parade and the Color-Sergeant. These lines, however, are not enclosed in quotation marks. Who do you think is speaking those words—another soldier, the poet, or some other observer?

◆ Build Vocabulary

USING THE ROOT -journ-

Knowing that the root -journ- means "day," fill in each blank with a word that contains the root.
1. At the end of the day, the meeting was ___?___.
2. Each day, I write my thoughts and impressions in my ___?___.
3. One aspect of the career of ___?___ is gathering facts about and reporting on the day's events.

USING THE WORD BANK

Practice Copy the following sentences in your notebook, and fill in the blanks with the appropriate word from the Word Bank.
1. The ground near the pond was covered with ___?___.
2. The kindergarten class drew laughs from the crowd as they marched on stage in ___?___.
3. While in London, we had a ___?___ at a quaint bed-and-breakfast.
4. The beautiful woman held the enchanted knight in ___?___.
5. We could hear the ___?___ of the child who had been scolded and sent to his room.

◆ Build Grammar Skills

HYPHENS

Hyphens are used to separate the parts of some compound nouns and adjectives. Hyphens are not used in compound modifiers that include words ending in -ly or with compound proper adjectives. Hyphens are used, however, in many compound nouns.

Practice Copy the paragraph below into your notebook. Insert hyphens where necessary.

The British army was based on well built traditions and rock solid rules that would not allow for leniency for Danny Deever. Files on Parade had the cot on the left hand side of Deever.

Beyond the Selection

FURTHER READING

Other Works by the Authors
"Ode on a Grecian Urn," John Keats
Barrack-Room Ballads, Kim, Rudyard Kipling

Other Works About Choices and Consequences
"Ozymandias," Percy Bysshe Shelley
"Lucy Grey," William Wordsworth
  We suggest that you preview these works before recommending them.

INTERNET

You and your students may learn more about Keats and Kipling at the following Web sites. Please be aware that the sites may have changed since we published this information.
  Keats: **http://utl1.library.utoronto.ca/utel/rp/authors/keats.html**
  Kipling: **http://www.kipling.org.uk/rudyard.htm**
  We *strongly recommend* that you preview the sites before you send students to them.

Build Your Portfolio

Idea Bank

Writing

1. **Diary Entry** As Files-on-Parade or the Color-Sergeant, write a diary entry relating your reactions to the events of the day.

2. **Letter to the Knight** As an advice columnist, respond to a letter from the knight in "La Belle Dame sans Merci." Tell him whether you think his "courtly love" is worth the price he's paying and what you think he should do.

3. **Mock Narrative** Write a mock narrative poem about a silly or insignificant event. Use rhythm and repetition as Kipling does in "Danny Deever."

Speaking and Listening

4. **Oral Reading** In small groups, practice reading "Danny Deever" aloud, experimenting with ways of making each speaker sound natural but different from the other. When you are ready, give a reading of "Danny Deever" for your class.

5. **Story in Music** Like poems, the lyrics of songs often tell a story. Stories can be found in a wide variety of musical styles, including ballads, country, pop, rap, and the blues. Choose an example from each of three styles. Play them for the class and explain the techniques, such as rhythm and repetition, that each uses. **[Music Link]**

Projects

6. **Dialect Chart** Create a chart that would help readers of "Danny Deever" understand the dialect and special language. Show how some words and expressions, such as "'arf a minute" and "score o' times" would be expressed by you and your friends. **[Social Studies Link]**

7. **Art** Depict either of the poems in art form. Use any medium to capture the mood of the poem and represent your interpretation. **[Art Link]**

Writing Mini-Lesson

News Bulletin Based on Poem

Imagine that you are a news reporter present at the hanging of Danny Deever. Your job is to get the story on Deever and be ready to go on the air live from the scene. Write a **news bulletin** that will inform your listeners about the circumstances leading up to the hanging and the mood of the soldiers.

Writing Skills Focus: Climax and Resolution

In a news bulletin, the **climax**—or high point of conflict—is usually mentioned right away to grab the viewer's or listener's attention. For instance, in your report about Danny Deever, you might lead with "Just moments ago, an execution took place here at Rudyard Kipling army base." Once your listeners are hooked, you can fill in the details. Report on the **resolution** (Danny's death) and the events that follow the resolution.

Prewriting Review the poem to gather details about the mood of the soldiers. Look also for statements in the poem by Files-on-Parade and the Color-Sergeant that could be used as quotations in your report.

Drafting Begin your broadcast with a sensational lead-in, guaranteed to "hook" the viewer. Then, start at the beginning of the story and lead listeners through the series of events that led to the climax you reported at the opening of your report. Conclude with a description of the atmosphere following the event.

Revising Read over your report and identify the exciting lead-in, the sequence of events leading to the climax, quotations from observers, and a wrap-up. If you cannot identify any one of these parts, revise your report to include it.

La Belle Dame sans Merci/Danny Deever ◆ 853

Idea Bank

Customizing for *Performance Levels*

Following are suggestions for matching Idea Bank topics with your students' performance levels:

Less Advanced Students: 1, 4
Average Students: 2, 5, 6, 7
More Advanced Students: 3

Customizing for *Learning Modalities*

Following are suggestions for matching Idea Bank topics with your students' learning modalities:

Musical/Rhythmic: 5
Verbal/Linguistic: 4, 5
Logical/Mathematical: 6
Visual/Spatial: 7

Writing Mini-Lesson

Refer students to the Writing Handbook, page 965, for instruction on the writing process and page 967 for further information on narration.

Writing and Language Transparencies You might have students use the Story Map, pp. 83–86, to work out the climax and resolution in their news bulletins.

Writing Lab CD-ROM Have students complete the tutorial on Narrative Writing. Follow these steps:

1. Have students use a Chain of Events chart to map out the sequence of events for their news bulletins describing what led up to Danny Deever's hanging.

2. Encourage students to consult interactive tips on better word choice to learn how to revise dull statements by adding strong verbs and precise nouns.

Sourcebook Have students use Chapter 2, Narration (pp. 31–56), for additional support.

✓ ASSESSMENT OPTIONS

Formal Assessment, Selection Test, pp. 204–206, and Assessment Resources Software. The selection test is designed so that it can be easily customized to the performance levels of your students.

Alternative Assessment, p. 58, includes options for less advanced students, more advanced students, musical/rhythmic learners, logical/mathematical learners, visual/spatial learners, intrapersonal learners, and verbal/linguistic learners.

PORTFOLIO ASSESSMENT

Use the following rubrics in *Alternative Assessment* to assess student writing:

Diary Entry: Expression Rubric, p. 94
Letter to the Knight: Problem-Solution Rubric, p. 101
Mock Narrative: Poetry Rubric, p. 108
Writing Mini-Lesson: Summary Rubric, p. 98

OBJECTIVES

1. To read, comprehend, and interpret six short lyric poems
2. To relate the poems to personal experience
3. To read poetry in sentences
4. To recognize the characteristics of lyric poetry
5. To build vocabulary in context and learn the root -path-
6. To recognize adjectival modifiers
7. To write a lyric poem using setting and mood
8. To respond to the poems through writing, speaking and listening, and projects

SKILLS INSTRUCTION

Vocabulary:
Word Roots: -path-
Grammar:
Adjectival Modifiers
Reading Strategy:
Read in Sentences
Literary Focus:
Lyric Poetry

Writing:
Setting and Mood
Speaking and Listening:
Newscast (teacher edition)
Critical Viewing:
Infer; Make a Judgment; Analyze

PORTFOLIO OPPORTUNITIES

Writing: Remembrance; Statement Poem; Story
Writing Mini-Lesson: Lyric Poem
Speaking and Listening: Reading to Music; Newscast
Projects: Painting/Drawing; Profile of a People

More About the Authors
Federico García Lorca was also a playwright, director, and musician who founded a traveling theater in Spain. **Naomi Shihab Nye** won a Guggenheim Fellowship in 1997; she has edited a book of poetry for teens, *I Feel A Little Jumpy Around You.* **Tu Fu** failed his civil service exams and thus spent many years as an impoverished wanderer. His friend **Li Po** was successful at court in his youth, but was later banished for political reasons. **Rosellen Brown** has been a professor of English at the University of Houston since 1982. **Wisława Szymborska** (vēs wä′ wä shēm bor′ skä) said, when she learned she had won the Nobel Prize, "I am very happy, stunned, and frightened. I'm afraid I will not have a quiet life now."

Guide for Reading

Federico García Lorca (1898–1936)

Federico García Lorca wrote many of his poems shortly after World War I, a culturally vibrant time in his homeland of rural Andalusia, outside Granada, Spain. Although García Lorca didn't intend his work to be political, Nationalist forces found it offensive, and they assassinated him at the beginning of the Spanish Civil War.

Naomi Shihab Nye (1952–)

Poet, songwriter, short-story writer, and children's book author, Naomi Shihab Nye now lives in San Antonio, Texas. Her perception, imaginative sense of language, and ability to keep you close to an experience are evident in "Making a Fist."

Tu Fu (712–770)

Chinese poet Tu Fu of the Tang Dynasty was little known and for the most part unappreciated during his lifetime. Today, however, he is regarded as a supreme craftsman. His poems are admired as much for their form as for their content. Tu Fu's poems celebrate nature, condemn the senselessness of war, and, as in "Jade Flower Palace," lament the passage of time.

Li Po (702–762)

A major Chinese classical poet of the Tang Dynasty, Li Po was a romantic who wrote about the joys of nature, love, friendship, and solitude. Although he was influenced by Taoist thought, he did not embrace the simple lifestyle this philosophy encouraged.

Rosellen Brown (1939–)

Besides being a poet, Rosellen Brown is an accomplished novelist and short-story writer. Her novel *Tender Mercies* was a national best-seller and became a major motion picture. Her latest book of poetry, *Cora Frye's Pillow Book,* was published in 1994.

Wisława Szymborska (1923–)

The author of sixteen collections of poetry, Wisława Szymborska of Poland has said, "No questions are of such significance as those that are naive." Her poetry asks direct questions about the meaning of life and death. Upon granting her the 1996 Nobel Prize for Literature, the Swedish Academy called her the "Mozart of poetry."

854 ◆ Poetry

◆ Build Vocabulary

WORD ROOTS: -path-
As the ancient poet sits and views the even more ancient ruins in Tu Fu's "Jade Flower Palace," the pathos of the scene overcomes him. *Pathos* contains the Greek root -path- which means "feelings; suffering." *Pathos* itself describes the quality in an object or situation that evokes stong feelings of sorrow, compassion, or *sympathy*.

WORD BANK
Before you read, preview this list of words from the poems.

| monotonously |
| pathos |
| wistful |

◆ Build Grammar Skills

ADJECTIVAL MODIFIERS
Several types of structures act as adjectives. Among the structures that may be **adjectival modifiers** are prepositional phrases, participial phrases, and adjective clauses. Here are examples from these poems:

Prepositional Phrase:
Now begins the cry / *Of the guitar*
The prepositional phrase *of the guitar* modifies *cry.*

Participial Phrase:
I felt the life *sliding out of me*
The participial phrase *sliding out of me* modifies *life.*

Adjectival Clause:
I *who did not die*
The adjectival clause *who did not die* modifies the pronoun *I.*

Prentice Hall Literature Program Resources

REINFORCE / RETEACH / EXTEND
Selection Support Pages
Build Vocabulary: Word Roots: -path-, p. 241
Build Grammar Skills: Adjectival Modifiers, p. 242
Reading Strategy: Read in Sentences, p. 243
Literary Focus: Lyric Poetry, p. 244
Strategies for Diverse Student Needs, p. 59
Beyond Literature
Cross-Curricular Connection: Social Studies: *The Great Wall of China,* p. 59
Formal Assessment Selection Test, pp. 207–209;

Assessment Resources Software
Alternative Assessment, p. 59
Resource Pro CD-ROM
"The Guitar"; "Making a Fist"; "Jade Flower Palace"; "The Moon at the Fortified Pass"; "What Are Friends For"; "Some Like Poetry"—includes all resource materials and customizable lesson plan

Listening to Literature Audiocassettes
"The Guitar"; "Making a Fist"; "Jade Flower Palace"; "The Moon at the Fortified Pass"; "What Are Friends For"; "Some Like Poetry"

The Guitar ◆ Making a Fist
Jade Flower Palace ◆ The Moon at the Fortified Pass
What Are Friends For ◆ Some Like Poetry

◆ *Literature and Your Life*

CONNECT YOUR EXPERIENCE

If you've ever reflected upon the meaning of friendship, beauty, war, or death, you already have something in common with these poets. Questioning issues such as these is often where poetry begins.

Look for important themes in these poems, and compare the poets' reflections with your own.

Journal Writing Jot down several themes that you might want to explore in a poem. Note several of your reflections on each theme.

THEMATIC FOCUS: TO THE FUTURE

The poems in this group span the time from the eighth through the twentieth centuries. Because the poets' thoughts are timeless, people of future generations can read the poems and reflect on them, just as you are doing.

◆ Background for Understanding

LITERATURE

Certain poems are classified as "lyric" poems because of their highly musical qualities. Originally, in ancient Greece, poems were recited or sung to the accompaniment of a lyre, a small stringed, harp-like instrument. Even today, lyrics are associated with music: The words to songs are called lyrics.

◆ Literary Focus

LYRIC POETRY

Lyric poetry is poetry expressing the observations and feelings of a single speaker. It was originally written to be accompanied by music; its musicality is one of its distinctive features.

A lyric poem may follow a traditional form, such as a sonnet, or it may be written in *free verse*—verse not written in a formal rhythmical pattern. "Making a Fist" and "What Are Friends For" are written in free verse.

While reading, you'll notice that a lyric poem, unlike a narrative poem, never tells a full story. Rather, it zeros in on an experience or creates and explores a single effect. Use an organizer like the one shown to explore how the details in each poem contribute to the main effect.

◆ Reading Strategy

READ IN SENTENCES

One way that poetry is different from prose is that poetry is written in lines and stanzas, while prose is written in sentences and paragraphs. Yet poetry, like prose, achieves its meaning through sentences. In poetry, a sentence may extend over several lines or it may even end in the middle of a line.

To get the literal meaning of a poem, **read** it **according to its sentences,** not its lines. Don't stop at the end of a line unless there is a period, comma, colon, semicolon, or dash. Notice where the stops are in the following lines from Federico García Lorca's "The Guitar":

> Now begins the cry
> Of the guitar,
> Breaking down the vaults
> Of dawn.
> Now begins the cry
> Of the guitar.

Preparing for Standardized Tests

Grammar and Language Identifying modifiers and understanding their function is a skill students can apply to the verbal portions of standardized tests. Students might be given an adjectival modifier and asked to identify which word in the sentence the phrase or clause modifies, as in the following:

Selena was moved by the sight of the setting sun.

Which word does of the setting sun modify: *(C)*

(A) moved
(B) Selena
(C) sight

Lead students to see that in this example the modifier, of the setting sun, is a prepositional phrase. It modifies the noun sight. For practice in identifying these types of modifiers, use the Build Grammar Skills page on Adjectival Modifiers, p. 242, in **Selection Support**.

Write the word *poetry* in large block letters at the center of the chalkboard. Around it, write the words *Friendship, Beauty, Sadness, War,* and *Death*. Circle each word, and connect it to the word *poetry*. Let students know this is a cluster diagram showing some major themes of lyric poetry. Invite students to suggest words and phrases of their own. *Sample answers: love, youth, age, growing up, nature.* Emphasize that a lyric poem can express anything a human being feels or observes. Tell students that they are going to read six lyric poems on six different themes, and that each one is like a snapshot of the poet's feelings at a certain time. Urge students to "see" this snapshot as they read each poem.

Customize for
Less Proficient Readers
Ask these students to say the main idea of each poem in one sentence. If students have trouble, suggest that they look again at the cluster diagram on the chalkboard for clues.

Customize for
More Advanced Readers
Invite students to describe the setting of each poem and to discuss how the setting affects the poem's mood, or atmosphere.

Customize for
English Language Learners
Ask these students to skim the poems and look at the illustrations on the page. Have them write down two or more difficult words or phrases in the poems and two or more easy ones. Encourage students to explain the easy words; then work with them to find the meanings of the hard ones by using such aids as cognates and picture clues from accompanying illustrations.

Customize for
Intrapersonal Learners
These students might be interested in expressing the theme and spirit of one of these poems in a different form; for example, a journal entry, a brief musical interpretation, a painting, or a dance. Suggest that they begin by jotting down the theme, then decide which art form would best express the feelings they associate with that theme.

One-Minute Insight

In "The Guitar," the speaker compares the mournful notes of a guitar to a wounded heart. A fist becomes the central image in "Making a Fist"; the speaker's mother answers her fearful question about death by saying that you know you are going to die "when you can no longer make a fist." These poems are united in their use of single powerful images to encompass strong and complicated emotions.

Listening to Literature Audiocassettes Have students listen to the taped reading of "The Guitar" as they read silently. When they are finished listening, ask students to suggest alternative ideas for oral readings, perhaps using music and different tones of voice.

▶Critical Viewing◀

❶ Infer The position of the man's head, the expression on his face and the dark colors indicate that he is probably playing a mournful song.

◆ **Critical Thinking**

❷ Interpret Ask students to identify the mood of the poem and to cite specific words that convey that mood. *The mood of the poem is mournful, or melancholic. The repetition of the words* cry *and* weeps *convey that mood.*

◆ **Build Grammar Skills**

❸ Adjectival Modifiers Ask students to identify the adjectival modifier in line 21 to identify its structure and to identify the noun it modifies. *"Without a target" is a prepositional phrase modifying the noun "arrow."*

▶Critical Viewing◀

❹ Make a Judgment Students who appreciate impressionistic artwork will probably find the painting effective because it shows both open hands and fists, both of which embody the message of "Making a Fist."

The Guitar
Federico García Lorca
Translated by Elizabeth du Gué Trapier

The Old Guitarist, 1903, Pablo Picasso, Art Institute of Chicago

▲ Critical Viewing What kind of song do you think the man in this painting is playing? Explain your answer. [Infer]

Now begins the cry
Of the guitar,
Breaking the vaults
Of dawn.
5   Now begins the cry
Of the guitar.
Useless
To still it.
Impossible
10 To still it.
It weeps <u>monotonously</u>
As weeps the water,
As weeps the wind
Over snow.
15 Impossible
To still it.
It weeps
For distant things,
Warm southern sands
20 Desiring white camellias.[1]
It mourns the arrow without a
     target,
The evening without morning.
And the first bird dead
Upon a branch.
25 O guitar!
A wounded heart,
Wounded by five swords.

❷

❸

---
1. **camellias** (kə mēl´ yəz): Flowers of the camellia, a type of evergreen tree and shrub that grows mainly in the Far East.

◆ **Build Vocabulary**

monotonously (mə nät´ən əs lē) *adv.*: Going on and on without variation

856 ◆ Poetry

Humanities: Art

The Old Guitarist, 1903, by Pablo Picasso.
   Bearded, bent, and barefoot, the old guitarist in this famous painting from Picasso plucks out notes that are undoubtedly as sad as the guitar in Garcia Lorca's poem.
   Spanish-born Pablo Picasso (1881–1973) is generally considered the most important visual artist of the twentieth century. During his career Picasso went through numerous periods. In his

Blue Period, which occurred early in his career, he painted alienated blue figures in a dark, sorrowful, and pessimistic mood. This period is epitomized by *The Old Guitarist.*
   Use this questions for discussion:
   How do you think Garcia Lorca would have responded to Picasso's painting? *He would probably have liked it as it expresses in visual medium much of what he was expressing in words in "The Guitar."*

Making a Fist

Naomi Shihab Nye

Impressions of Hands, 1969, Antoni Tapies, Museum of Modern Art, New York

▲ Critical Viewing Do you think this is an effective painting to accompany this poem? Why or why not? [Make a Judgment]

For the first time, on the road north of Tampico,[1]
I felt the life sliding out of me,
a drum in the desert, harder and harder to hear.
I was seven, I lay in the car
5   watching palm trees swirl a sickening pattern
      past the glass.
My stomach was a melon split wide inside my skin.

"How do you know if you are going to die?"
I begged my mother.
We had been traveling for days.
10   With strange confidence she answered,
"When you can no longer make a fist."

Years later I smile to think of that journey,
the borders we must cross separately,
stamped with our unanswerable woes.
15   I who did not die, who am still living,
still lying in the backseat behind all my questions,
clenching and opening one small hand.

1. **Tampico** (tam pē kō´): Seaport in eastern Mexico.

Guide for Responding

◆ *Literature and Your Life*

Reader's Response What single image in these two poems did you find most striking? Why?

Thematic Focus Which of these poems would you include in a time capsule? Why?

☑ Check Your Comprehension

1. To what does García Lorca compare the weeping of the guitar?
2. (a) What does the speaker ask in "Making a Fist"? (b) What answer does the mother give?

◆ Critical Thinking

INTERPRET
1. What emotions does García Lorca give the guitar in his poem? [Infer]
2. What does the poet's childhood journey represent in "Making a Fist"? [Interpret]

EVALUATE
3. Which of these poems more effectively communicates the speaker's reaction to a single event? Explain. [Criticize]

EXTEND
4. What musical instrument seems most like a person to you? Why? [Music Link]

The Guitar/Making a Fist ◆ 857

◆ Reading Strategy

❺ Read in Sentences Invite a volunteer to read the second stanza aloud in sentence form, stopping in the appropriate places in order to make it sound natural.

◆ Literary Focus

❻ Lyric Poetry Lyric poetry zeroes in on an experience in order to express feelings. What feelings are reflected in these lines? *Suggested response: As an adult, the speaker is still like a child with a painful curiosity about (and fear of) death.*

Reinforce and Extend

Answers
◆ *Literature and Your Life*

Reader's Response Encourage students to cite details that contribute to the strength of the impression.

Thematic Focus Sample response: "The Guitar," because it expresses a representative and universal feeling of mourning and loss.

☑ Check Your Comprehension

1. He compares it to the weeping sound of water and wind.
2. (a) The speaker asks, "How do you know when you are going to die?" (b) The mother answers, "When you can no longer make a fist."

◆ Critical Thinking

1. He gives it sorrow and longing.
2. Possible response: The childhood journey in "Making a Fist" stands for the journey of life.
3. Students might respond that "Making a Fist" more effectively communicates the speaker's reaction to a single event because the "event"—personalizing death for the first time—is made more explicit in that poem.
4. Sample response: A piano seems most like a person because it can express many moods.

857

Develop Understanding

One-Minute Insight

"Jade Flower Palace" is a lyric poem that expresses the speaker's feeling about the impermanence of power and glory. The setting includes images of scurrying rats, ruins, and ghost fires that convey the message that power and glory are fleeting. In contrast, the setting of "The Moon at the Fortified Pass" is an active kingdom—its people alive and its armies on the move. Yet it is in a lonely moment in time in the mountain setting that the speaker portrays the soldiers' homesickness and fear of death in order to emphasize the senselessness of war.

◆ Reading Strategy

❶ Read in Sentences Ask a student to read from "The stream ..." to "tiles" in order to notice the stops and to emphasize the short, simple sentences.

◆ Build Grammar Skills

❷ Adjectival Modifiers Ask students to find a participial phrase used as an adjectival modifier in lines 4–5. What noun does it modify? *"Standing in ruins" is a participial phrase modifying the noun "palace."*

◆ Critical Thinking

❸ Infer Ask students which images in this passage convey the idea that things are not permanent. *The images of ghost fires and shattered pavements that are all washed away convey the idea of impermanence.*

◆ Reading Strategy

❹ Read in Sentences Point out that the word "Only" (line 14) begins a sentence that crosses a stanza break. Ask a volunteer to read the sentence aloud.

◆ Literary Focus

❺ Lyric Poetry Encourage students to suggest what feelings the speaker in this lyric poem expresses. *Suggested answers: This speaker expresses the feelings of sadness, wistfulness, loneliness, and perhaps a sense of resignation.*

Jade Flower Palace

Tu Fu

Translated by Kenneth Rexroth

❶ The stream swirls. The wind moans in
The pines. Gray rats scurry over
Broken tiles. What prince, long ago,
❷ Built this palace, standing in
5 Ruins beside the cliffs? There are
Green ghost fires in the black rooms.
❸ The shattered pavements are all
Washed away. Ten thousand organ
Pipes whistle and roar. The storm
10 Scatters the red autumn leaves.
His dancing girls are yellow dust.
Their painted cheeks have crumbled
Away. His gold chariots
And courtiers are gone. Only
❹
15 A stone horse is left of his
Glory. I sit on the grass and
Start a poem, but the pathos of
It overcomes me. The future
❺ Slips imperceptibly away.
20 Who can say what the years will bring?

◆ Build Vocabulary

pathos (pā´ thäs) *n.*: Quality in something experienced or observed that arouses feelings of pity, sorrow, sympathy, or compassion
wistful (wist´ fəl) *adj.*: Expressing longing

858 ◆ Poetry

Block Scheduling Strategies

Consider these suggestions to take advantage of extended class time:

- Have students complete the journal activity in Literature and Your Life (p. 855). After they read the poems, ask them to search for ways in which the poems illuminate the themes they jotted down.

- Allow time for students to look for other poems that deal with the themes addressed in

these two poems. Have students share poems they've found with the rest of the class.

- Invite students to work in groups to prepare and present the newscast suggested in the Idea Bank on page 863. Use the Speaking and Listening Mini-Lesson on page 859 to get students started.

The Moon
at the Fortified Pass

Li Po
Translated by
Lin Yutang

The bright moon lifts from the Mountain of Heaven
In an infinite haze of cloud and sea,
And the wind, that has come a thousand miles, ❻
Beats at the Jade Pass[1] basements. . . .
5 China marches its men down Po-teng Road
While Tartar[2] troops peer across blue waters of the
    bay. . . . ❼
And since not one battle famous in history
Sent all its fighters back again,
The soldiers turn round, looking toward the border, ❽
10 And think of home, with <u>wistful</u> eyes,
And of those tonight in the upper chambers
Who toss and sigh and cannot rest.

---

1. **Jade Pass:** Gap in the Great Wall in northeastern China.
2. **Tartar** (tär´ tər): Tartars were nomadic tribes who originally lived in Mongolia, Manchuria, and Siberia. From A.D. 200 through 400, the Tartars were almost constantly at war with the Chinese. A thousand years later, under the leadership of Genghis Khan, the Tartars conquered China as well as a number of European and Asian countries.

◀ **Critical Viewing** Imagine this picture as a setting for "The Moon at the Fortified Pass." What might make the soldiers "wistful"? [Analyze] ❾

Jade Flower Palace/The Moon at the Fortified Pass ◆ 859

◆ **Literary Focus**

❼ **Lyric Poetry** Point out that since this is a lyric poem, its historical situation is described in only two lines. In a narrative poem, much more about the history of this conflict would have been explained. Ask students to describe the setting for this event. *Sample answer: The place is the Jade Pass, a fortified gap in the Great Wall in northeastern China. The setting is moonlit, hazy, windy, and far from home.*

◆ **Critical Thinking**

❽ **Infer** What descriptive words in this passage indicate the soldiers' feeling, and what is that feeling? *The phrases "looking toward the border," "And think of home," reflect the soldiers' feeling, which is one of homesickness.*

▶ **Critical Viewing** ◀

❾ **Analyze** Suggested response: These aspects of the setting would make the soldiers wistful: the darkness of night; the beauty of the moon; the loneliness of the mountains; the distance from home.

Speaking and Listening Mini-Lesson

Newscast
This mini-lesson supports the Speaking and Listening activity in the Idea Bank on page 863.
Introduce the Concept Newscasts are radio and television broadcasts that report current events.
Develop Background Let students know that an effective newscast has these qualities:

- It begins with a gripping "lead," or opening, that attracts interest and provides the most important facts. Details are provided in later sentences.
- It relates the facts in a simple, straightforward way, always maintaining accuracy. Opinions are inappropriate to a newscast.
- Interviews are often included in a newscast; it concludes with a brief wrap-up or summary.

Apply the Information Invite students to work in pairs or small groups, with one member as the newscaster and others as interviewees. Have them prepare a list of interviewees and questions, then present their newscasts to the class.
Assess the Outcome Assess newscasts based on the points discussed in Develop Background and for how well students interpret the poem.

One-Minute Insight "What Are Friends For" examines a contrast of opinions about friendship. The speaker presents her mother's cynical view of friendship. The daughter, in contrast, expresses the positive attitude that friends offer emotional support, not material things. In "Some Like Poetry," the speaker expresses her feelings about poetry. Each stanza of the poem examines one of the words in the title: *Some, Like,* and *Poetry.* In the end, the reader discovers that for the poet *like* is a vast understatement.

◆ **Critical Thinking**

❶ **Speculate** Ask students what occurrences might have contributed to the mother's pessimistic view of friendship. *Suggested response: In the past friends have forgotten duties, failed to visit, and not baked a casserole for a sick friend. The mother has experienced other disappointments from friends, too. Someone "has just made her bitter."*

◆ **Critical Thinking**

❷ **Analyze** Ask students to express the speaker's view of friendship. *Friends are extremely important for emotional reasons (they "touch" you and "fill you with music"). The speaker may be suggesting that if friends occasionally disappoint by not fulfilling small obligations, they are "there" in the most meaningful ways—they give of themselves.*

▶**Critical Viewing**◀

❸ **Analyze** Suggested answer: The artist has captured the qualities of closeness and trust, and the feeling of sharing an experience.

What Are Friends For

Rosellen Brown

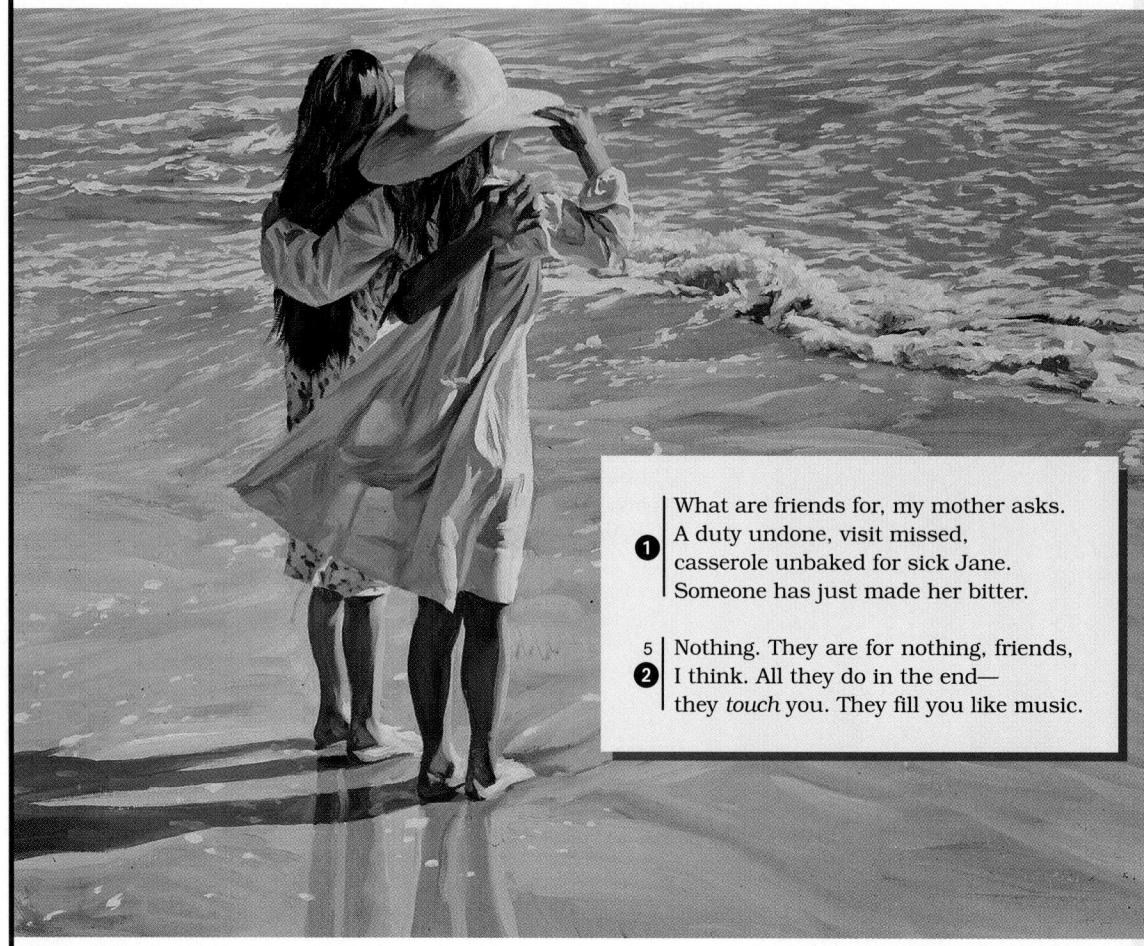

Best Friends, Craig Nelson/Bernstein & Andriulli, Inc.

❶ What are friends for, my mother asks.
A duty undone, visit missed,
casserole unbaked for sick Jane.
Someone has just made her bitter.

5 ❷ Nothing. They are for nothing, friends,
I think. All they do in the end—
they *touch* you. They fill you like music.

❸ ▲ **Critical Viewing** What qualities of friendship has the artist captured? **[Analyze]**

860 ◆ *Poetry*

◆ **Workplace Skills Mini-Lesson**

Developing a Positive Attitude

Introduce the Concept Having a positive attitude toward co-workers and tasks is important in almost any job.

Develop Background Let students know that they can use these strategies to help develop a positive attitude about tasks for which they have negative feelings:

• Keep in mind the long view. What will they gain by completing the task? *They might*

prove themselves responsible to complete tasks that interest them more; they might earn the trust and respect of others.

• Emphasize positive aspects of the task. For example, it may be a source of satisfaction to complete an unpleasant task well and speedily.

Apply the Information Ask students to think of a job or task that they dislike. On the left side of a page divided into two

columns, they should jot down at least three things they do not like about the task. On the right side they should note a believable positive strategy to combat each negative thought.

Assess the Outcome Let students assess their own work for this activity after they have applied the strategies and can evaluate their effectiveness.

Some Like Poetry

Wisława Szymborska
Translated by Joanna Trzeciak

Some—
that means not all.
Not even the majority of all but the minority.
Not counting school, where one must,
5 and poets themselves,
there will be perhaps two in a thousand.

Like—
but one also likes chicken-noodle soup,
one likes compliments and the color blue,
10 one likes an old scarf,
one likes to prove one's point,
one likes to pet a dog.

Poetry—
but what sort of thing is poetry?
15 More than one shaky answer
has been given to this question.
But I do not know and do not know and clutch on to it,
as to a saving bannister.

Guide for Responding

◆ Literature and Your Life

Reader's Response With which speaker would you most like to have a conversation? Why?

Thematic Focus What do these poems draw from the past?

☑ Check Your Comprehension

1. Where does the speaker of "Jade Flower Palace" sit, and what does he do?
2. Identify the event on which Li Po focuses in "The Moon at the Fortified Pass."
3. What answer is given by the speaker to the title question, "What Are Friends For"?
4. Identify two examples in "Some Like Poetry" of different meanings of the word *like*.

◆ Critical Thinking

INTERPRET

1. Explain the statement in "Jade Flower Palace," "The future/slips imperceptively away." **[Draw Conclusions]**
2. How does Li Po feel toward the soldiers going into battle? **[Interpret]**
3. In "What Are Friends For," how do the speaker's feelings contrast with her mother's? **[Contrast]**
4. What is the speaker's point in "Some Like Poetry"? **[Interpret]**

EXTEND

5. Name another work of literature that deals with war and compare its central message with that of "The Moon at the Fortified Pass." **[Literature Link]**

What Are Friends For/Some Like Poetry ◆ 861

◆ Critical Thinking

❹ Interpret Ask students what statement the speaker is making about "some" in relation to poetry. *Sample answer: Poetry is not to everyone's taste; only some people like it.*

◆ Literary Focus

❺ Lyric Poetry Ask students to summarize the speaker's feelings about poetry. *For the speaker, poetry is lifesaving.*

Reinforce and Extend

Answers

◆ Literature and Your Life

Reader's Response Sample response: I would most like to have a conversation with the speaker of "What Are Friends For" because she clearly respects people.

Thematic Focus These poems draw upon feelings and experiences of the poets' pasts.

☑ Check Your Comprehension

1. He sits on the grass and begins to write a poem.
2. The event is a confrontation between the Tartars and the Chinese.
3. Friends fill an emotional need.
4. Examples: One likes chicken soup; one likes to pet a dog.

◆ Critical Thinking

1. The future will become the past and slip away.
2. Li Po knows the soldiers might not come back from battle, and he seems to sympathize with them.
3. The mother's feelings are cynical; the speaker's feelings are generous and optimistic.
4. Her point is that it is hard to evaluate who likes poetry and how much they like it, but that she places an ultimate value on poetry.
5. Students might mention such works as "In Flanders Fields," "Conscientious Objector," "Desert Exile," or "There Will Come Soft Rains."

Beyond the Selection

FURTHER READING

Other Works by the Poets
The Poet in New York, Lorca; *Words Under the Words*, Nye; *A Rosellen Brown Reader*, Brown; *View with a Grain of Sand*, Szymborska

Other Works About Legacies
"Ozymandias" Percy Bysshe Shelley
Leaves of Grass, Walt Whitman

    We suggest that you preview these works before recommending them to students.

INTERNET

Students can learn more about the poets at the following Web site. Please be aware that the sites may have changed since we published this information.
    Naomi Shaib Nye: **http://www.mme.wsu.edu/~lau**
    Tu Fu: **http://mirrors.org.sg/hyperhistory...n2/ people_n2/persons4_n2/tufu.html**
    For a news release reporting Szymborska's Nobel Prize go to **http://www.poland.net/siec.polska/03**
    We *strongly recommend* that you preview the sites before you send students to them.

Answers

◆ Reading Strategy

1. The reader pauses at the comma on the first sentence, then reads a further description. The second sentence is read as a simple statement, ending with a period.
2. The short sentences of "Jade Flower Palace" give the poem a staccato rhythm, while "The Moon at the Fortified Pass" has longer sentences, marked by commas and ellipses, that create a more flowing rhythm.
3. The brief sentence is "Some like poetry."

◆ Literary Focus

1. The central emotion is one of melancholy or mournfulness.
2. (a) It focuses on how people feel about poetry. (b) The speaker has a passionate and life-sustaining love for poetry.

◆ Build Vocabulary

Use the Root -path-
1. (b) pathos;   2. (c) pathology;
3. (b) antipathy;   4. (b) sympathy;
5. (c) empathy

Using the Word Bank
1. wistful;   2. pathos;
3. monotonously

◆ Build Grammar Skills

Practice

1. It mourns the **arrow** without a target.
2. The **soldiers** turn around, looking toward the border.
3. And the **wind**, that has come a thousand miles.
4. …While Tartar **troops** peer across blue waters of the bay.
5. ….Warm southern **sands**/Desiring white camellias.

Writer's Solution

For additional instruction and practice, use page 51 on Adjective Clauses in the *Writer's Solution Grammar Practice Book*.

Guide for Responding (continued)

◆ Reading Strategy

READ IN SENTENCES

Reading poetry in sentences, not necessarily by line, is a key to understanding a poem's literal meaning. The punctuation can guide you through a poem's structure.

1. The second sentence in "The Guitar" is a repetition of part of the first sentence. Explain how the punctuation leads you to read the two sentences differently.
2. Contrast the sentences in "Jade Flower Palace" and "The Moon at the Fortified Pass" based on the use of commas and periods.
3. "Some Like Poetry" interrupts one short sentence with elaboration about each word. What is the brief sentence "hidden" in Szymborska's poem?

◆ Literary Focus

LYRIC POETRY

A **lyric poem** takes a sharp-eyed and concentrated look at a single incident or experience, and in doing so, reveals the feelings of the poem's speaker. Some of these lyric poems—"What Are Friends For" for example—suggest a story beneath the surface, but they don't actually tell that story.

1. What would you say is the central emotion conveyed in "The Guitar"?
2. (a) On what single subject does "Some Like Poetry" focus? (b) What is the speaker's personal feeling about the subject?

Beyond Literature

Community Connection

Community Gatherings The speaker in Rosellen Brown's poem suggests that friends make life more enjoyable. Many communities host events where people gather to share friendship and good times. Parades, block parties, town picnics, and concerts in the park are just a few types of gatherings that are sponsored by communities. What events or gatherings does your community offer?

◆ Build Vocabulary

USING THE ROOT -path-

The Greek root -path- means "feeling; suffering." On your paper, write the word you would most closely associate with the person or thing in each numbered item.

1. A very sad movie: (a) pathology, (b) pathos, (c) antipathy
2. A medical researcher: (a) pathos, (b) sympathy, (c) pathology
3. An enemy: (a) sympathy, (b) antipathy, (c) empathy
4. A suffering animal: (a) empathy, (b) sympathy, (c) pathos
5. A very close friend: (a) antipathy, (b) pathology, (c) empathy

USING THE WORD BANK

On your paper, write the word from the Word Bank suggested by each book title.

1. *A Film Critic's Guide to the 100 Saddest Movies of All Time*
2. *The Odyssey*
3. *Games to Play on Long Car Trips*

◆ Build Grammar Skills

ADJECTIVAL MODIFIERS

These poems use several different types of word groups as **adjectival modifiers** to describe or limit the meaning of nouns or pronouns.

Practice Copy each of the following items in your notebook. Underline the modifier in each, and draw a line to the word that it modifies.

1. It mourns the arrow without a target.
2. The soldiers turn round, looking toward the border.
3. And the wind, that has come a thousand miles …
4. …While Tartar troops peer across blue waters of the bay.
5. …Warm southern sands/Desiring white camellias.

Build Your Portfolio

 Idea Bank

Writing

1. **Remembrance** In "Making a Fist," Naomi Shihab Nye focuses on an emotionally powerful moment. Write a paragraph describing such a moment experienced by a character in a book or movie you enjoyed.

2. **Statement Poem** Each section of "Some Like Poetry" elaborates on one of the three words in the poem's title. Write a simple three- or four-word statement and create a poem around the words, using Szymborska's poem as a model.

3. **Story** Write a short story using the mother and speaker of "What Are Friends For" as your main characters. Create a plot, conflict, and resolution.

Speaking and Listening

4. **Reading to Music** Find and play for the class a recording of classical Spanish guitar music. Play the recording a second time, softly, as you read "The Guitar." Explain why you chose the music you did. **[Performing Arts Link]**

5. **Newscast** As a reporter standing at the fortified pass in ancient China, describe for viewers the positions and actions of the Chinese and Tartar armies. **[Social Studies Link]**

Projects

6. **Painting/Drawing** Imagine that the speaker of "Jade Flower Palace" sits on the grass to paint rather than to write. In your favorite medium, draw or paint what the speaker sees. **[Art Link]**

7. **Profile of a People** Who were the Tartars? Research their role in history and their conflict with the Chinese. Present your findings to the class in a report with illustrations. **[Social Studies Link]**

 Writing Mini-Lesson

Lyric Poem

Think about an experience or moment in time that left a particularly strong impression on you. Watching the ocean during a storm, the first time you heard the song that became your favorite, the sight of a shooting star streaking across the night sky—the possibilities are limitless. Write a **lyric poem** in which you enable your readers to experience the moment as you did.

Writing Skills Focus: Setting and Mood

A poem's **setting,** the time and place in which the experience occurred, and its **mood,** the feeling you get while reading, are often closely related. In "Jade Flower Palace," the setting of the forsaken and decrepit palace creates a desolate mood. Focus on a setting that will create a distinct mood.

Prewriting Where did your memorable moment occur? What did the place look like, and what feelings did it give you? Before you write, make a chart like this one:

Place	Descriptive Words	Feelings I Got
lake at night	clear, cool, mysterious	calm, awe, delight

Drafting Write your impressions and feelings using vivid descriptive language to capture the mood of the setting. Although you may use partial sentences or break sentences over several lines, use punctuation to indicate pauses and stops.

Revising It's useful to read a poem aloud to yourself when you're revising it. Trust your ear to pick up any awkward rhythms or clunky word choices, then revise to correct these problems. Add modifiers where more detail is needed to describe the setting or create a mood. For more on adjectival modifiers, see pp. 854 and 862.

 Idea Bank

Customizing for *Performance Levels*
Following are suggestions for matching Idea Bank topics with your students' performance levels:
- Less Advanced Students: 1, 4
- Average Students: 2, 3, 6
- More Advanced Students: 5, 7

Customizing for *Learning Modalities*
Following are suggestions for matching Idea Bank topics with your students' learning modalities:
- Musical/Rhythmic: 4
- Verbal/Linguistic: 4, 5
- Bodily/Kinesthetic 5
- Visual/Spatial: 6

 Writing Mini-Lesson

Refer students to the Writing Handbook, page 965, for instruction on the writing process and page 968 for further information on creative writing.

 Writer's Solution

Writers at Work Videodisc
Have students view the videodisc segment for Chapter 6 in which Naomi Shihab Nye talks about gathering details for creative writing. Discuss with students how her words apply to gathering details of setting and mood for a lyric poem.

Play frames 20514 to 20978

Writing Lab CD-ROM
Have students complete the tutorial on Creative Writing. Follow these steps:
1. Ask students go to use Word Bins for Poetry to see words or phrases they might use in their poems. These word bins feature rhyming words, sensory details, colors, and places.
2. Have students select a video tip from Naomi Shihab Nye to hear her thoughts on revising a draft.
3. Ask students to go to Guide for Publishing and Presenting where they will follow checklists designed to help them plan a class poetry reading.

Sourcebook
Have students use Chapter 6, Creative Writing (pp. 165–189), for additional support. The chapter includes an annotated student model of a lyric poem (p. 189).

✓ ASSESSMENT OPTIONS

Formal Assessment, Selection Test, pp. 207–209, and Assessment Resources Software. The selection test is designed so that it can be easily customized to the performance levels of your students.

Alternative Assessment, p. 59, includes options for less advanced students, more advanced students, verbal/linguistic learners, interpersonal learners, logical/mathematical learners, intrapersonal learners, musical/rhythmical learners and bodily/kinesthetic learners.

PORTFOLIO ASSESSMENT
Use the following rubrics in the *Alternative Assessment* booklet to assess student writing:
Remembrance: Description Rubric, p. 97
Statement Poem: Poetry Rubric, p. 108
Story: Fictional Narrative Rubric, p. 95
Lyric Poem: Poetry Rubric, p. 108

*G*uide for Reading

OBJECTIVES

1. To read, comprehend, and interpret a group of poems
2. To relate poems to personal experience
3. To envision the imagery in poems
4. To recognize poetic forms: haiku, tanka, sonnet, villanelle
5. To build vocabulary in context and learn related words that are forms of *temperate*
6. To identify noun clauses
7. To write a consumer report of poetic forms, using techniques to grab the reader's attention
8. To respond to the poems through writing, speaking and listening, and projects

SKILLS INSTRUCTION

Vocabulary:
Related Words: Forms of *Temperate*
Grammar:
Noun Clauses
Reading Strategy:
Envision the Imagery
Literary Focus:
Poetic Forms

Writing:
Grab Readers' Attention
Speaking and Listening:
Poetry Reading (teacher edition)
Critical Viewing:
Compare and Contrast; Analyze

PORTFOLIO OPPORTUNITIES

Writing: Villanelle Opener; Haiku; Essay
Writing Mini-Lesson: Consumer Report of Poetic Forms
Speaking and Listening: Rhyme Scheme; Poetry Reading
Projects: Oral Report; Japanese Poetry

More About the Authors
 William Shakespeare composed 154 sonnets between 1593 and 1601. He began writing poetry when London authorities closed public theaters for a period to avoid outbreaks of the plague.
 Theodore Roethke (reht kē) was greatly influenced by his childhood as the son of a greenhouse owner. He found images for the developing self in the rooting, blossoming, and dying of his father's plants.
 Matsuo Bashō wrote travel sketches based on his wanderings through rural Japan. These sketches trace his inward quest for the simple life.

William Shakespeare *(1564–1616)*

Shakespeare's skill in writing English sonnets is one of the reasons his name has remained famous through the ages. Today, the English sonnet is also known as the Shakespearean sonnet. If mastering a poetic form wasn't enough for a life achievement, Shakespeare owned a theater and worked as an actor. These outstanding accomplishments stand beside the thirty-eight plays he wrote within about twenty years. (To learn more about Shakespeare, turn to pp. 710 and 711.)

Theodore Roethke *(1908–1963)*

American poet Theodore Roethke is known for his affectionate portrayals of children and the elderly. He had a talent for a wide variety of poetic styles—his poems range from witty, realistic poems in strict form to free-form verse with exotic imagery. In 1948, Roethke received a Pulitzer Prize for his *Collected Poems,* which ends with the poem "The Waking."

Ki no Tsurayuki *(872–945)*

Ki no Tsurayuki (kē nō tsoō rä yoō kē) was the chief aide to Emperor Daigo and one of the leading poets, critics, and diarists of his time. He helped assemble, and wrote the preface to, the *Kōkin Wakashū*—a major anthology of Japanese poetry of the time.

Priest Jakuren *(1139?–1202)*

Jakuren entered the Buddhist priesthood at the age of twenty-three. He spent his time traveling the countryside, writing poetry, and seeking spiritual fulfillment.

Matsuo Bashō *(1644–1694)*

Matsuo Bashō was a master of *renga*, a type of collaborative poem. Haiku evolved from the starting verse of this type of poem. A master of poetic forms, Bashō traveled the countryside teaching others.

Kobayashi Issa *(1762–1826)*

Banished from his rural home as a teenager, Kobayashi Issa (kō bä yä shē ē sä) lived his life in urban poverty. His difficult circumstances created in him an appreciation for the fleeting lives of small creatures.

◆ Build Vocabulary

RELATED WORDS: FORMS OF *TEMPERATE*
 You will encounter the word *temperate,* which means "not extreme," in Sonnet 18. Other forms of the word *temperate* also indicate moderation. For instance, *temperance* is "restrained or moderate behavior." To *temper* something is "to bring it to the right consistency—to remove its extremes."

WORD BANK
 Before reading, preview these words from the poems.

| temperate |
| eternal |

◆ Build Grammar Skills

NOUN CLAUSES
 A **noun clause** is a subordinate clause used as a noun in a sentence. (A subordinate clause is a group of words that contains a subject and a verb but cannot stand alone as a sentence.) Like a noun, a noun clause can function as a subject, object, or a predicate noun.

Subject:
 What falls away is always.

Direct Object:
 One cannot ask loneliness / *How or where it starts.*

Object of a Preposition:
 I feel my fate in *what I cannot fear.*

Predicate Noun:
 Japanese poets' belief was *that poems should be brief.*

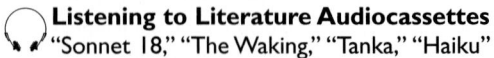

Sonnet 18 ◆ The Waking ◆ Tanka ◆ Haiku

◆ *Literature and Your Life*

CONNECT YOUR EXPERIENCE

When you participate in a sport or play a game, you agree to follow certain rules. The rules exist, in part, to create a challenge—to test a player's skill. In the same way, the rules governing certain forms of poetry challenge the poets' skills. Some poets choose to "play the game" of the sonnet, the haiku, or the villanelle.

THEMATIC FOCUS: HUMANS AND NATURE

The many images from nature in these poems may lead you to ask: Why do poets frequently focus on nature?

Journal Writing Jot down an image from nature that you might use as the basis for a poem.

◆ Background for Understanding

LITERATURE

Poetry has many forms. For centuries, the tanka was the only form used by Japanese poets. The popularity of the tanka and the haiku shows the Japanese preference for simplicity and for suggestion over elaboration.

Sonnets developed from Italian songs in the Middle Ages. (The word *sonnet* comes from the Italian word *sonetto*, which means "little sound or song.") Villanelles originated in the "round" songs of medieval French farm workers. The repetition that comes from the round songs is a major feature of villanelles.

◆ Literary Focus

POETIC FORMS

To express their ideas, poets can choose from a variety of **poetic forms**, or structures. The following are a few examples.

A **haiku** is a lyric, unrhymed poem of three lines of five, seven, and five syllables. A **tanka** consists of five unrhymed lines of five, seven, five, seven, seven syllables. Both forms include simple, straightforward images. Traditionally, a haiku always includes an image from nature.

A **sonnet** is a fourteen-line poem written in iambic pentameter (five unaccented syllables each followed by an accented one). There are two types, Shakespearean (English) and Petrarchan (Italian). A Shakespearean sonnet contains three quatrains (which rhyme *abab cdcd efef*) followed by a rhymed couplet (*gg*).

A **villanelle** is a lyric poem written in three-line stanzas, ending with a four-line stanza. It has two refrains formed by repeating line 1 in lines 6, 12, and 18 and line 3 in lines 9, 15, and 19.

◆ Reading Strategy

ENVISION THE IMAGERY

To appreciate the images that the poets use, create a mental picture. When you **envision,** you use your memory and imagination to *see, feel, hear, smell,* and *taste* what the poets describe. For example, when you read Tsurayuki's image of a winter night, feel the bitter wind blowing off the river and hear the birds' mournful calls. Use associations to help you. For example, although you may have never heard a plover cry, you have probably heard some bird that makes a sad sound. Comparisons will also help you. Shakespeare compares the qualities of a particular woman to those of a summer day. Envisioning the summer day helps you appreciate some of the feelings Shakespeare associates with the woman of his sonnet.

Use a graphic organizer like the one shown to help you envision the imagery in these poems.

Image	Association
"darling buds of May"	warm sun, bright colors
spring rain	freshness, renewal

Guide for Reading ◆ 865

Preparing for Standardized Tests

Vocabulary Vocabulary development will enable students to improve performance on both reading comprehension and vocabulary items. The Build Vocabulary lesson in this selection focuses on forms of *Temperate*. Recognizing how different parts of speech are formed from the same word may help students on the verbal section of standardized tests which might ask students to complete analogies based on their understanding of related words. Write the following example on the chalkboard:

TEMPERATE : TEMPERANCE

  (A) indulgent : indulgence
  (B) grateful : gratify
  (C) temperate : moderate
  (D) temperate : temperature
  (E) eternity : eternal

Ask students which word pair matches the relationship between temperate / temperance. Lead them to see that *(A) indulgent*

: indulgence is the correct choice because the words are related in the same way as the example—their meanings are similar and they are both adjective / noun forms of the same word.

The Build Vocabulary lesson accompanying these selections focuses on forms of the word "temperate." For additional practice, use the Build Vocabulary page on Related Words: Forms of *Temperate*, p. 245, in **Selection Support**.

One-Minute Insight Shakespeare's famous sonnet begins by praising the beauty and temperance of his beloved as surpassing those of a summer day. It ends by testifying to the power of poetry to immortalize the person the poet loves.

"The Waking" reflects upon our daily process of waking up—literally and figuratively—the process of becoming "awake" to the world of nature and the meaning of life.

◆ Literary Focus

❶ Poetic Forms Ask students to identify the end rhymes that help unify the sonnet. *The end rhymes "day" and "May" (lines 1 and 3) and "temperate" and "date" (lines 2 and 4) unify the first four lines, giving them an abab rhyme scheme. The rhyme scheme for the rest of the poem is cdcd, efef, gg.*

Comprehension Check ☑

❷ Be sure students understand the meaning of "the eye of heaven." *It is the sun.*

◆ Critical Thinking

❸ Interpret Ask students why the beloved's "eternal summer" (beauty) will never fade, unlike the beauty of an actual summer day. *The beloved's "eternal summer" will never fade because it will be kept alive by those who read Shakespeare's sonnet.*

♫ Humanities: Art

Frances Howard by Isaac Oliver.
Isaac Oliver (1564–1617) was one of the chief portrait miniaturists at the courts of Elizabeth I and James I in England. A miniaturist is an artist who paints very small, detailed paintings. Ask students: What objective does Oliver's portrait share with Shakespeare's Sonnet 18? *Suggested response: Isaac Oliver's miniature portrait attempts to do in paint what Shakespeare's sonnet does in words—to commit its subject, a young woman, to immortality.*

►Critical Viewing◄
❹ Compare and Contrast
Students should include details of hairstyles, clothing, and jewelry.

866

Sonnet 18

William Shakespeare

Frances Howard, Isaac Oliver, Victoria and Albert Museum

❶ Shall I compare thee to a summer's day?
Thou art more lovely and more <u>temperate</u>:
Rough winds do shake the darling buds of May,
And summer's lease hath all too short a date:
5 **❷** Sometime too hot the eye of heaven shines,
And often is his gold complexion dimmed;
❸ And every fair from fair sometime declines,
By chance or nature's changing course untrimmed;[1]
But thy eternal summer shall not fade,
10 Nor lose possession of that fair thou owest;[2]
Nor shall Death brag thou wander'st in his shade,
When in eternal lines to time thou grow'st:
    So long as men can breathe, or eyes can see,
    So long lives this, and this gives life to thee.

---

1. **untrimmed:** (un trimd´) *v.*: Not made or kept neat; disordered.
2. **owest:** (o´ ist) *v.*: Own.

◆ Build Vocabulary
temperate (tem´ pər it) *adj.*: Moderate in degree or quality

▲ **Critical Viewing** Notice the formal pose of this late sixteenth- century portrait. In what ways have fashions and perceptions of beauty changed since this portrait was painted? [**Compare and Contrast**] **❹**

Block Scheduling Strategies

Consider these suggestions to take advantage of extended class time:

• Lead a class discussion based on the Thematic Focus question in Literature and Your Life: "Why do poets frequently focus on nature?" Help students to understand that urban environments are also affected by elements of nature, including seasons and weather conditions.

• Use the Speaking and Listening Mini-Lesson (p. 867) to develop students' skill and appreciation in reading poetry aloud.

• Before students write their haiku from the Idea Bank (p. 871), have them divide into small groups to brainstorm for themes and scenes from nature that would be suitable to the haiku form. Group members can read their haiku aloud to one another.

• Use Daily Language Practice for Week 24. You may display the practice sentences on an overhead projector and have students write them correctly, or you may dictate the sentences to students.

The Waking

Theodore Roethke

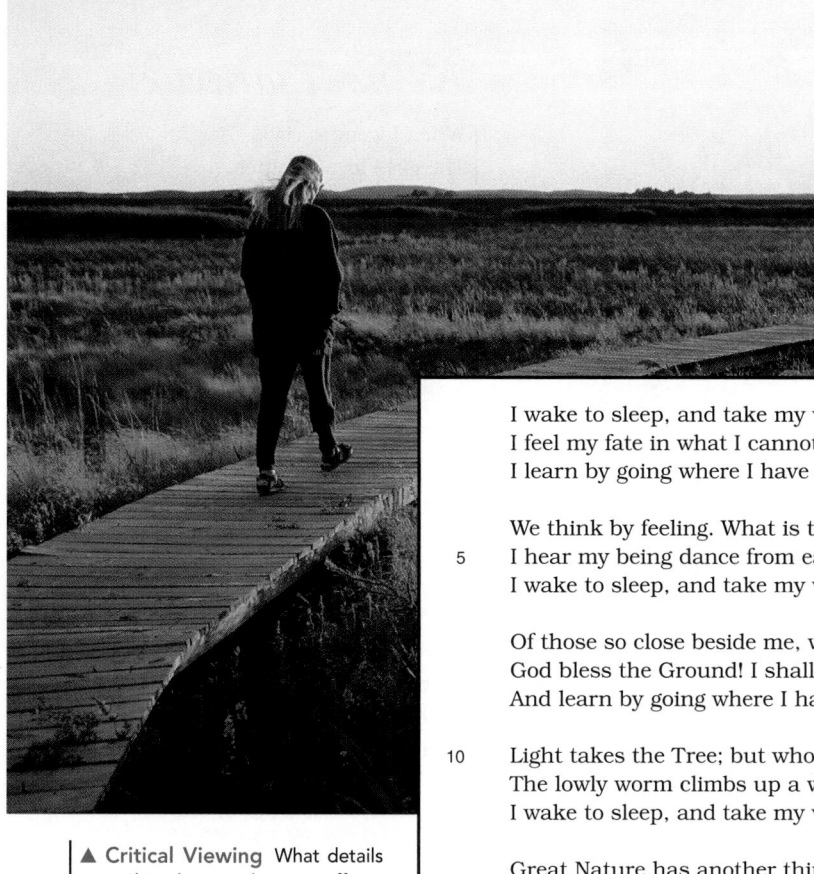

▲ Critical Viewing What details
in this photo make it an effective picture to accompany "The
Waking"? [Analyze]

⑤

I wake to sleep, and take my waking slow.
I feel my fate in what I cannot fear.
I learn by going where I have to go.

5   We think by feeling. What is there to know?
I hear my being dance from ear to ear.
I wake to sleep, and take my waking slow.

Of those so close beside me, which are you?
God bless the Ground! I shall walk softly there,
And learn by going where I have to go.

10   Light takes the Tree; but who can tell us how?
The lowly worm climbs up a winding stair; **⑥**
I wake to sleep, and take my waking slow.

Great Nature has another thing to do
To you and me; so take the lively air, **⑦**
15   And, lovely, learn by going where to go.

This shaking keeps me steady. I should know.
What falls away is always. And is near.
I wake to sleep, and take my waking slow.
I learn by going where I have to go. **⑧**

►Critical Viewing◄
⑤ Analyze Possible response: The
woman in the photo appears to take
her waking slow; she seems contem-
plative, and she is possibly appreciating nature.

◆ **Reading Strategy**

⑥ Envision the Imagery To help
students envision the imagery in this
stanza, have them close their eyes
and imagine morning sunlight shining
on a tree that they know well.
Encourage them to imagine as many
details as possible, and ask for volunteers to describe what they envision.

◆ **Critical Thinking**

⑦ Interpret Ask students what is
meant by the lines "Great Nature has
another thing to do / To you and me:
so take the lively air." *Some students
might think that these lines are asking
us to be aware of our feelings because
nature teaches us to appreciate the
beauty of life; others might think that
"another thing to do / to you and me"
refers to death. Still, the advice of these
lines is to appreciate nature in the
present.*

◆ **Literary Focus**

⑧ Poetic Forms Point out the
scheme of stanzas and refrains in a
villanelle as described on page 865.
Ask students to find where these
two refrain lines appear earlier in the
poem. Then ask why Roethke might
have chosen these two lines as the
refrain. *The refrain lines appear in lines
1, 3, 6, and 12. Variations on them
appear in lines 9 and 15. These lines
express the central meaning of the
poem: that waking up to life and learning about life represent a gradual
process that cannot be rushed or
planned.*

 Speaking and Listening Mini-Lesson

Poetry Reading

This mini-lesson supports the Speaking and
Listening activities in the Idea Bank on page
871.

Introduce the Concept Reading poetry
aloud enhances enjoyment and understanding, but it is a skill that requires practice.

Develop Background Play the audiocassette recording of the six poems in this
group. Lead students to recognize these

points:

• Poetry should not be read in a singsong
voice, and the rhymes should not be over-
emphasized.

• Readers of poetry must convey both the
meaning of the poem and the feelings
behind the words. They should choose a
pace and a tone of voice that suit the
mood of each poem.

Apply the Information Have students

practice reading their poems aloud in pairs
or small groups. Then provide class time for
their final performances.

Assess the Outcome Students should
evaluate each other's performances based
on how well each reader used his or her
voice to convey the meaning and mood of
each poem. Suggest they use Peer
Assessment: Oral Interpretation, p. 119, in
Alternative Assessment.

One-Minute Insight

These four Japanese poems, tanka and haiku, reflect a traditional Buddhist emphasis on contemplation of nature as a path to wisdom and understanding of life. Vivid, fleeting images from nature are used to express important ideas and feelings about human experience.

◆ Critical Thinking

❶ Interpret Ask students to explain the connection between the winter scene, the girl, and the writer's feelings. *Suggested response: The description of the cold winter night and the crying plover suggests that the girl has been coldhearted or unfriendly to the writer, and as a result, he feels sad.*

◆ Literature and Your Life

❷ Ask students to remember a fall evening from their own experience and to jot down any sensory details and feelings they remember from that evening. Then have them compare their associations of a fall evening with those expressed by the speaker of this poem.

►Critical Viewing◄

❸ Compare and Contrast Elicit these ideas from students: The painting conveys a lonely nighttime feeling similar to the mood of the two tankas. The painting conveys a peaceful feeling of quiet contentment and solitude, unlike the lonely feelings expressed by the poems.

Customize for
English Language Learners

If you have students in your class whose first language is Japanese, they might enjoy translating the English version of the tanka back into the Japanese, concentrating on trying to achieve the right number of syllables per line. They can then explain their translation to the class.

The Monkey Bridge in Koshu Province, 1841, Hiroshige Hitsu, Christie's, New York

868 ◆ Poetry

Tanka

Translated by
Geoffrey Bownas

Ki no Tsurayuki

❶
When I went to visit
The girl I love so much,
That winter night
The river blew so cold
That the plovers[1] were crying.

---

1. **plovers** (pluv´ ərz) *n.*: Wading shore birds with short tails, long, pointed wings, and short, stout beaks.

Priest Jakuren

❷
One cannot ask loneliness
How or where it starts.
On the cypress-mountain,[1]
Autumn evening.

---

1. **cypress-mountain:** Cypress trees are cone-bearing evergreen trees, native to North America, Europe, and Asia.

❸ ◀ Critical Viewing Compare the mood of this painting with the mood or feelings evoked in these tankas. **[Compare and Contrast]**

 Humanities: Art

The Monkey Bridge in Koshu Province, 1841, by Hiroshige Hitsu.

The prolific Japanese artist and printmaker Hiroshige Hitsu (1797–1858) is widely admired and his work is collected all over the world today. Hiroshige was a great master of Japanese wood block printing. His restful, reflective landscapes were very popular in Japan during his lifetime and influenced western artists Whistler, Cezanne, and Van Gogh. Capturing the mysterious and profound moods of nature, Hiroshige often executed prints to illustrate haiku.

Use this question for discussion:
Many of Hitsu's paintings and prints feature bridges like the one in this picture. Why do you think Hitsu was interested in bridges as a painting subject? *Students might point out that bridges are an evocative symbol because they enable people to go from one part of nature to another, as well as to interact with other people, or they might observe that bridges in the time Hiroshige painted blended into the environment, reflecting the Japanese respect for nature.*

Haiku

Translated by
Daniel C. Buchanan

落お
ちざ
ざま
水みに
こ
ぼ
花はし
椿つばけ
り

Bashō

Falling upon earth,
Pure water spills from the cup
Of the camellia.

Issa

A gentle spring rain.
Look, a rat is lapping
Sumida River.

春はる
雨さめ
鼠ねずみや
隅すみの
田だな
川がわめ
る

Guide for Responding

◆ Literature and Your Life

Reader's Response Which poetic form did you like most? What about it did you most enjoy?

Thematic Focus Which poetic form would you like to write in? What would be the form's advantages and disadvantages?

Activity Choose a poetic form for students in the tenth grade to use. Present your choice with reasons to a small group.

✓ Check Your Comprehension

1. To what does the speaker of Sonnet 18 refer that "shall not fade"?
2. What dances "from ear to ear" in "The Waking"?
3. (a) What does Bashō describe in his haiku? (b) What creature is the subject of Issa's haiku?
4. What real-life situation makes the plovers cry in the tanka by Ki no Tsurayuki?
5. What does the word "it" refer to in the line by Priest Jakuren, "How or where it starts"?

◆ Critical Thinking

INTERPRET

1. In Sonnet 18, does the beloved fare better or worse than a summer's day? Explain how you know. **[Draw Conclusions]**
2. What does the speaker of "The Waking" mean by, "I wake to sleep, and take my waking slow"? **[Interpret]**
3. What is the connection between loneliness and the cypress-mountain in the tanka by Priest Jakuren? **[Connect]**
4. To which senses do the haiku appeal? **[Analyze]**

APPLY

5. Choose one of these poems, and explain how you might experience the ideas and feelings in it if the poem were not written in its particular form. **[Speculate]**

EVALUATE

6. Which form do you think is most challenging for a poet to use? Explain. **[Assess]**

Tanka/Haiku ◆ 869

869

Answers

◆ Reading Strategy

1. Students might associate these sensory details with hot summer days in which the temperature was very hot and the sky was hazy rather than bright.
2. Students might feel anticipation or curiosity.
3. Answers may include the following images: the plovers crying; the cypress mountain; water spilling from a camellia; rat lapping river water.

◆ Literary Focus

1. The message is that the beloved is fairer than a summer's day.
2. The first "fair" refers to one who is attractive, and the second "fair" refers to a temporary condition.
3. The third quatrain contrasts the woman's fairness with summer by saying her fairness will not fade. The earlier quatrains identified similar ties.
4. "Eternal lines" refers to immortality.
5. "This" refers to the poem.
6. The final couplet states that all the good qualities listed will live forever in this poem.
7. "I wake to sleep and take my waking slow" and "I learn by going where I have to go."
8. Both the tanka and the haiku include simple, straightforward images that relate to nature.

◆ Build Vocabulary

Using Forms of *Temperate*
1. temperate; 2. temperance;
3. intemperate; 4. tempered

Using the Word Bank
1. intemperate; 2. eternal;
3. moderate; 4. eternity

◆ Build Grammar Skills

1. <u>whoever was interested</u> (indirect object)
2. <u>what I cannot fear.</u> (object of preposition)
3. <u>Whoever reads these poems</u> (subject)
4. <u>thou wander'st in his shade.</u> (direct object)
5. <u>that the refrain must repeat in a particular line</u> (predicate noun)

Guide for Responding (continued)

◆ Reading Strategy

ENVISION THE IMAGERY

Associations and details help you **envision the imagery** in these poems. The imagery, in turn, helps you understand the poet's message.
1. In Sonnet 18, what sensory details do you associate with "Sometime too hot the eye of heaven shines, / And often is his gold complexion dimmed"?
2. What feelings do you experience when you envision the "winding stair" in Roethke's "The Waking"?
3. Identify one image from each tanka and haiku.

◆ Literary Focus

POETIC FORMS

The poets in this section wrote in a variety of **poetic forms,** each using rules to structure poems with certain patterns of lines, syllables, rhythms, and rhymes. These poems are examples of sonnet, villanelle, tanka, and haiku.

The Shakespearean sonnet contains four quatrains (four-line groups) followed by one rhymed couplet (a two-line group). Usually, each quatrain explores a different aspect of the poem's idea. The couplet sums up the poem or comments on what is said in the quatrains.
1. What is the message of the first two quatrains of Sonnet 18?
2. To what does the first "fair," in line 7 refer? The second?
3. How does the third quatrain relate to the first two?
4. What are the "eternal lines" of line 12?
5. To what does "this" refer in the final line?
6. How does the final couplet sum up Sonnet 18?
7. What are the two refrain lines in "The Waking"?
8. Because a Japanese word may have a different number of syllables in English, haiku and tanka do not always have the standard number of syllables or lines in their English translations. Even in translation, however, the poems retain other features of the form. Explain how the tanka and haiku in this section fit the form.

◆ Build Vocabulary

USING FORMS OF *TEMPERATE*

Copy the following sentences in your notebook. Complete each sentence with one of these words: *tempered, temperate, intemperate, temperance*.
1. Priest Jakuren lived a _____?_____ life.
2. He practiced _____?_____ in his activities.
3. A rash, _____?_____, act would be unthinkable for him.
4. Like metal that has been _____?_____ in a furnace, his character was strengthened by his simple life.

USING THE WORD BANK

Notice the relationship between the first pair of words in each numbered item. In your notebook, complete the second pair of words by supplying a word that indicates a similar relationship.
1. *Foolish* is to *thoughtful* as _____?_____ is to *temperate*.
2. *Mortal* is to _____?_____ as *solar* is to *lunar*.
3. *Compassionate* is to *kind* as _____?_____ is to *temperate*.
4. *Earth* is to *earthly* as _____?_____ is to *eternal*.

◆ Build Grammar Skills

NOUN CLAUSES

A **noun clause** is a subordinate clause that functions as a noun. A noun clause can be a subject, predicate noun, direct object, indirect object, or object of a preposition.

Practice Copy the following sentences in your notebook. Underline the noun clause in each, and identify how it is used (subject, predicate noun, direct object, indirect object, or object of a preposition).
1. Bashō taught whoever was interested the form of *renga*.
2. "I feel my fate in what I cannot fear."
3. Whoever reads these poems will be enriched.
4. "Nor shall Death brag thou wander'st in his shade, . . ."
5. One difficulty of writing a villanelle is that the refrain must repeat in a particular line.

  Beyond the Selection

FURTHER READING

Other Works by the Poets
"Sonnet 29," William Shakespeare
"Child on Top of a Greenhouse," Theodore Roethke; "Autumn," Matsuo Bashō

Other Works About Nature
"Spring Is Like a Perhaps Hand," E.E. Cummings
"Wind and Water and Stone," Octavio Paz
"After Apple Picking" and "Birches," Robert Frost
We suggest that you preview these works before recommending them to students.

INTERNET

Students can learn more about these poets and forms of poetry at the following Web sites. Please be aware that the sites may have changed since we published this information.

To learn more about haiku, go to **http:// awaweb.co.jp/~kunikiyo/ indexj.html**

To learn more about Bashō, go to **http://www. stonebridge.com/basho.html**

We *strongly recommend* that you preview these sites before you send students to them.

Build Your Portfolio

Idea Bank

Writing

1. **Villanelle Opener** Write a three-line stanza to begin a villanelle, using "The Waking" as a model. In the first and third lines, express ideas you would want to repeat throughout the poem.

2. **Haiku** Choose a theme or scene from nature and write a haiku. Follow the 5-7-5 syllable pattern of haikus.

3. **Essay** Write a "how-to" essay explaining how to tell the difference between a sonnet and a villanelle. Use "The Waking" and Sonnet 18 as examples.

Speaking and Listening

4. **Rhyme Scheme** With a partner, read aloud Sonnet 18 or "The Waking." Experiment with alternating and combining your voices. Perform your reading for the class. **[Performing Arts Link]**

5. **Poetry Reading** With a few classmates arrange a group poetry reading. Choose and read aloud different poems in different forms—either from this section or another source. **[Performing Arts Link]**

Projects

6. **Oral Report** Find out more about William Shakespeare. Present your findings in an oral report to the class. Include a reading of a sonnet other than Sonnet 18. **[Performing Arts Link]**

7. **Japanese Poetry** Create a poster that would spark student interest in Japanese poetry. Present information about major poetic forms, old and new. Include poems or excerpts from poems. **[Social Studies Link]**

Writing Mini-Lesson

Consumer Report of Poetic Forms

A consumer report outlines the features of a product or service. The report focuses on the subject's strengths and weaknesses. The information is presented in such a way that a consumer or "shopper" can decide for himself or herself. Imagine that your classmates are shopping for a poetic form to read. Write a **consumer report** of the poetic forms in this section. In your report, discuss the advantages and disadvantages of each form and conclude with a recommendation.

Writing Skills: Grab Readers' Attention

In order to capture and keep the attention of readers, introduce your report with a lively statement that tells an important finding or conclusion. That is how you **grab a reader's attention.** You can use a direct quotation from a survey, an image, or a bold statement. For example, a consumer report about haiku might begin: "Haiku delivers images strong enough to last three centuries."

Prewriting Use a three-column chart to classify the features of each form into advantages and disadvantages. Focus on the high and low points for a reader. For instance, you might see the length of a haiku as a drawback—"not much poem for your money."

Drafting Be specific about what you see as noteworthy in each poetic form. Support the claims you make by including examples from the poems in this section.

Revising Try out your introductory sentence on a partner. Does it grab his or her attention? Is the rest of your report clearly written and accurate? Consider your partner's suggestions, and make the necessary revisions.

Sonnet 18/The Waking/Tanka/Haiku ◆ 871

Idea Bank

Customizing for *Performance Levels*
Following are suggestions for matching Idea Bank topics with your students' performance levels:

    Less Advanced Students: 1, 4
    Average Students: 2, 5, 6, 7
    More Advanced Students: 3

Customizing for *Learning Modalities*
Following are suggestions for matching Idea Bank topics with your students' learning modalities:

    Intrapersonal: 2
    Verbal/Linguistic: 4, 5, 6
    Visual/Spatial: 7

Writing Mini-Lesson

Refer students to the Writing Handbook, page 965, for instruction on the writing process and page 967 for further information on exposition.

Writing Lab CD-ROM
Have students complete the tutorial on Exposition. Follow these steps:

1. Have students view a video clip and see an example of a comparison-and-contrast essay and a product evaluation. Have them discuss how these essays include techniques that they might apply to their consumer report of poetic forms.

2. Suggest that students use the notecard activity to help them organize their ideas for their consumer report.

Sourcebook
Have students use Chapter 3, Exposition (pp. 63–89), for additional support. The chapter contains specific instruction on considering audience and purpose (p. 79).

✓ ASSESSMENT OPTIONS

Formal Assessment, Selection Test, pp. 210–212, and Assessment Resources Software. The selection test is designed so that it can be easily customized to the performance levels of your students.

Alternative Assessment, p. 60, includes options for less advanced students, more advanced students, logical/mathematical learners, visual/spatial learners, and interpersonal learners.

PORTFOLIO ASSESSMENT

Use the following rubrics in the *Alternative Assessment* booklet to assess student writing:
Villanelle Opener: Poetry Rubric, p. 108
Haiku: Poetry Rubric, p. 108
Essay: How-to/Process Explanation Rubric, p. 100
Writing Mini-Lesson: Comparison/Contrast Rubric, p. 103; Technical Description/Explanation Rubric, p. 115

Establish Writing Guidelines
Review the following key characteristics of a narrative poem:

- A narrative poem tells a story and is usually longer than other poetry.

- Like a story, it has characters who face a conflict and resolve it.

- Most narrative poems have multiple stanzas, all with the same rhyme pattern.

Before students begin, you may want to share with them the Scoring Rubric for Poetry (page 108 in *Alternative Assessment*) so that students see the criteria by which they will be evaluated. Suggestions on page 874 customize the rubric to this workshop.

Connect to Literature Refer students to Alexander Pushkin's narrative poem "The Bridegroom" (p. 54) in Unit 1. Have students review the poem for characterization and conflict.

Writer's Solution

To introduce students to the key elements of poetry and to show how poet Naomi Shihab Nye uses them, play the videodisc segment on Creative Writing (Ch. 6).

Play frames 11043 to 20512

Writing Lab CD-ROM
If students have access to computers, have them work in the tutorial on Creative Writing to complete all or part of their narrative poems.
Follow these steps:

1. Students can review the interactive model of a poem.

2. To help students choose a topic, have them watch the author video to learn how poet Nye finds ideas for poems.

3. Students can draft their narrative poems on computer.

4. Have students use the Audio-annotated Student Model to compare the first draft with a revision to see how and why one writer revised his poem.

Sourcebook
Students can find additional support, including topic ideas, models, and graphic organizers, in the chapter on Creative Writing (pp. 164–193).

Narrative Poem

Writing Process Workshop

La Belle Dame sans Merci, John W. Waterhouse, Hessisches Landes Museum, Darmstadt

One of the poems in this section is a narrative poem. A **narrative poem** tells a story; it is usually longer than other types of poems. Like a story, a narrative poem has one or more characters, a conflict, and a series of events that come to a conclusion. Most narrative poems are divided into stanzas, or groups of lines that have the same rhyme pattern.

Write a narrative poem. The following skills, introduced in this unit's Writing Mini-Lessons, will help you write a narrative poem.

Writing Skills Focus

▶ **Grab the reader's attention.** Begin your poem with a dramatic statement or scene. Next, introduce a conflict. Build up that conflict to a **climax,** and then end the poem with the resolution of the climax. (See pp. 853 and 871.)

▶ **Use musical devices** such as alliteration, onomatopoeia, and consonance to give your narrative poem a musical quality.

▶ **Pay attention to setting and mood.** Establish a setting that lets your reader envision the action. Use vivid verbs, adjectives, adverbs, and exact nouns to set the proper mood. (See p. 863.)

The following stanzas from John Keats's narrative poem show these skills at work.

MODEL FROM LITERATURE

from "La Belle Dame sans Merci" by John Keats

① The poet grabs the reader's attention with a mysterious question.

② The poet creates a somber mood with these images.

③ The poet uses alliteration in this stanza, repeating the s and sh sounds with *She . . . she . . . sighed . . . sore . . . shut.*

O what can ail thee, knight-at-arms,
    Alone and palely loitering? ①
The sedge has withered from the lake,
    And no birds sing. ②
       * * *
I met a lady in the meads,
    Full beautiful—a faery's child,
Her hair was long, her foot was light,
    And her eyes were wild.
       * * *
She took me to her elfin grot,
  ③ And there she wept, and sighed full sore,
And there I shut her wild wild eyes
    With kisses four. . .

872 ◆ *Poetry*

 Beyond the Classroom

Workplace Skill
Elements of Advertising Although the advertising world rarely uses narrative poems, the elements employed in writing them are widely applied. Advertisers must grab the audience's attention and introduce some element with which the viewer or listener can identify as a problem, such as how to stay trim, which car to buy, or where to find the best bargains. Musical devices, especially rhyme and rhythm, help audiences remember the message long after seeing or hearing the ad. Finally, the setting and mood of a visual ad also conveys a strong message. Ask students to analyze a print ad in terms of the elements of a narrative poem.

Prewriting

Choose a Topic A narrative poem tells a story. Think of a story that will be the basis for your poem. You can use your imagination or you can write about a real-life event or experience. Use the following suggestions to help you come up with a story for your narrative poem:

▶ **Examine photos, newspapers, or magazines.** Most pictures and articles have a story behind them. Look for those that will stimulate your imagination.

▶ **Create a Conflict Word Bin.** Create two lists, like the ones below. The first should have main characters; the second, a person, group, force, or problem that the main character must face. Mix and match the two columns until you find a suitable combination for your narrative poem.

Conflict Word Bin	
Character	**Conflict**
A knight	searching for an answer
A teenager	struggling with a decision
A detective	preparing for a challenge
An athlete	searching for a criminal

▶ **Use sensory images**—words that appeal to the senses of sight, sound, smell, taste, and touch—to make your narrative poem more vivid. Before drafting, make a list of words relevant to your narrative that appeal to each of these senses. Refer to this list as you write.

▶ **Think of a climax and resolution.** The plot of your narrative poem must eventually lead to a climax, the high point of the action. After the conflict, the action falls and a resolution is reached, in which the conflict is settled and loose ends are tied up.

Drafting

Use Musical Devices In poetry, sound is often as important as meaning. Use one or all of the following musical devices to enhance the mood and meaning of your poem:

Rhyme is the most commonly used sound device:

This darksome burn, horseback <u>brown</u>,
His rollrock highroad roaring <u>down</u> . . .

APPLYING LANGUAGE SKILLS: Punctuating Poetry

Use commas, semicolons, quotation marks, and end punctuation according to the same rules you use for prose. You will notice that lines of some poems begin with a capital letter, regardless of the punctuation at the end of the previous line. Place punctuation at the end of a line only if you want to indicate a pause or a stop.

From "La Belle Dame sans Merci":

I saw pale kings and princes too,
Pale warriors, death pale were they all;
They cried—'La Belle Dame sans Merci
Hath thee in thrall!'

Writing Application Identify places in your narrative poem where punctuation should be used to indicate pauses.

Writer's Solution Connection Writing Lab

To help you with your story line, refer to the Story Line Diagram in the Writing Lab tutorial on Creative Writing.

Prewriting

Since a narrative poem tells a story, you may want students to use a Story Map graphic organizer (*Writing and Language Transparencies*, page 83) to organize the elements of their narration.

Customize for
More Advanced Students
Have these students concentrate on a story that introduces symbolic meaning. Suggest that they choose some object, such as an item from nature, a utensil, or an article of clothing, that will play a symbolic role in the story-poem.

 Writer's Solution

Writing Lab CD-ROM
A Poetry Topic Wheel and a Conflict Wheel are included in the Choosing a Topic section of the tutorial on Creative Writing. Students can use these to select a topic for a narrative poem and save the activities to their Activity Drawer.

Drafting

As they write, encourage students to use musical devices that enhance meaning. For instance, they might choose a staccato rhythm for fast-paced dramatic parts or choose soothing vowel sounds along with alliteration to suggest quiet moments in the narrative.

Applying Language Skills

Punctuating Poetry Suggest to students that they write the poem as prose in order to punctuate accurately. That process will help them avoid rote end-of-line punctuation.

 Writer's Solution

For additional explanation and examples of poetic devices and narrative elements, use the On-line Writing Handbook on the **Language Lab CD-ROM.**

Revising

You may want to have students work with a three-member editorial board to revise their narrative poems. One board member should respond to the story line; another to the musical devices; another to the punctuation.

Writer's Solution

The Interactive Self-Evaluation Checklists in the Revision section of the tutorial on Creative Writing will help students judge the subject, images, form, and sound devices in their narrative poems.

Publishing

Remind students that the dramatic readings and performances can be done live or on audio or video tape.

Applying Language Skills

Problems with Modifiers
Remind students that problems with modifiers can alter meaning in writing, including in a narrative poem.

Reinforce and Extend

Review the Writing Process
After students have completed their papers, review the characteristics of narrative poems. Ask students to identify the most difficult part of creating the poems. Then ask them to analyze how they would approach a similar assignment differently.

APPLYING LANGUAGE SKILLS: Problems With Modifiers

Avoid the following **problems with modifiers** as you draft your poem:

Double Negative:
There weren't no stars out.

Double Comparison:
Bullet was a more faster horse.

Improper Use of *Here*:
This here car is my favorite.

Confusing Adjective and Adverb:
That cat moves slow.
(correct: slowly)

Practice On your paper, correct the problems with modifiers in the following poem.

> And as I stared
> The most greatest beast
> Leaped quick to my side
> "Don't fear nothing!"
> I said to myself . . .

Writing Application Review your narrative poem and correct any problems with modifiers.

Writer's Solution Connection Language Lab

For more practice with modifiers, complete the Language Lab lesson on Problems With Modifiers.

Rhythm and Meter Rhythm is the pattern of accented and unaccented syllables in a line of poetry. Meter is the number of beats per line. Experiment with different rhythms and meters to create different moods.

Alliteration is the repetition of consonant sounds at the beginning of words:
> The *long light* shakes across the *lakes* . . .

Onomatopoeia is the use of words that imitate the sounds they name. Examples include *whirr*, *buzz* and *bang*.

Revising

Have a Peer Check Your Work Use the following checklist with a peer to help you revise your narrative poem.
- ▶ Is the story easy to follow? How can the writer clarify what happens?
- ▶ Are the images striking and vivid? How might the images be made more effective?
- ▶ Does the author use musical devices?

REVISION MODEL

As I recall, the night was clear,
And scarcely a whisper could I ①hear discern,

From the people on the street below,
②Shuffling about
Walking around in the evening snow.

① The writer changes this word to preserve the rhyme and meter.
② Shuffling is more descriptive and onomatopoetic than walking.

Publishing

- ▶ **Give a Dramatic Reading** With a group of classmates, arrange to have a reading of your narrative poems. You might wish to have another student serve as host of the reading and introduce each poet. When you present your poem, speak clearly and with emotion.
- ▶ **Perform Your Poem** Stage a performance of your narrative poem. Act as the director, and use classmates as actors.

✓ ASSESSMENT		4	3	2	1
PORTFOLIO ASSESSMENT Use the rubric on Poetry in *Alternative Assessment* (p. 108) to assess students' writing. Add these criteria to customize the rubric to this assignment.	**Narrative Element: Character**	The writer develops a character who is consistent in what he says and does.	The writer develops a character who shows somewhat consistent behavior.	The writer develops a character who behaves somewhat inconsistently.	The writer develops a totally inconsistent character.
	Narrative Element: Conflict and Resolution	The poem builds a series of conflicts and reaches a resolution of all of them.	The poem builds a series of conflicts and reaches a partial resolution of them.	The poem builds few conflicts but resolves them.	The poem builds few or no conflicts and resolves none of them.

Real-World Reading Skills Workshop

Reading Directions

Strategies for Success

Whether you're programming your VCR, using a computer program, or taking your SAT's, you will do much better if you read the directions. Directions tell you what to do and in what order. Some directions will tell you specifically what not to do. Don't make assumptions and add steps that are not specified in the directions. The following tips will help you:

Note Every Detail Directions specify an order of steps. Look for words that clue you in to the order of steps, such as *first*, *before*, *next*, *while* and *after*. In addition, some directions require specific measurements, amounts, and times. Double-check that you are following these as the directions indicate.

Read and Reread Directions often include a sequence of steps. Before you start to follow them, read all the directions through once so that you know everything that's required. If there are any parts you don't understand, reread to try to clarify them or, if possible, ask someone for help.

Rely on Diagrams Some directions may include diagrams. For example, directions for assembling a piece of furniture or hooking up an appliance such as a VCR will usually be accompanied by diagrams or sketches. These are an important part of the directions. Study all diagrams carefully, and refer to them as they outline how to assemble what you are building.

> ✔ Here are other situations in which reading directions is important:
> ► Setting the alarm on an alarm clock
> ► Recording an outgoing message on an answering machine
> ► Taking a test in school

Apply the Strategy

Read the following directions for reattaching a car's rearview mirror. Then answer the following questions.

> First, prepare the surface by cleaning the inside of the windshield with alcohol. When the windshield is dry, apply a thin layer of activator to the point of attachment. Wait 5 minutes.
>
> Next, apply a single drop of glue to the windshield and a single drop of glue to the mounting clip. Allow 2 minutes for glue to become tacky. Do not touch the glue.
>
> Place mounting clip on windshield. Hold in place for 10 minutes. Before attaching mirror to mounting clip, check that clip is secure by pushing up and down. If clip does not move, attach the mirror. If clip moves, wait 5 more minutes before attaching mirror.

1. What is the first step in attaching the mirror?
2. How long should you wait after applying the activator before applying the glue?
3. What must you do before attaching the mirror to the mounting clip?

Introduce the Strategy

Remind students that body language is part of everyday life, from home to classroom to social event. You may want to ask students to make a list of the kinds of body language they can see in the classroom at the moment.

Apply the Strategy

Remind students that body language includes the movement and position of the whole body: head, face, arms, hands, torso, legs, feet.

You may want students to extend the application to other situations such as social situations or job or scholastic interviews.

Customize for
Visual/Spatial Learners

You may wish to demonstrate for these students the postures and signals described in the text. After students have seen the body language, they can complete the activities with a partner.

Customize for
English Language Learners

Ask these students if the same "signals" have the same indications in their native country. Have a volunteer demonstrate the body language described in the text and ask students how they would respond to it. Encourage these students to share their responses with the class in a discussion of communication styles of different cultures.

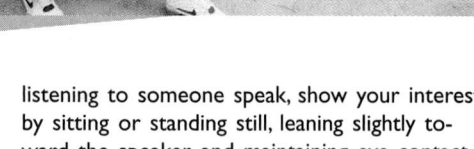

Understanding Body Language
Speaking and Listening Workshop

In addition to using words, people can "speak" with the rest of their body. The way a person sits, stands, gestures, and looks as he or she talks can communicate almost as much as what he or she is saying. You should be aware of the unspoken messages others communicate through their body language.

Reading the Signals

There's a new student in your biology class. As the teacher introduces her, she slumps with her arms folded across her chest and gazes toward the floor. What message does she communicate through her body language? You would be correct in suggesting that she may be lacking in confidence.

Notice what people say through body language in different situations. Sitting or standing straight generally shows confidence, while slouching or slumping tends to suggest insecurity, shyness, or even fear. Standing with hands on hips or standing too close to someone suggests aggressiveness. A person who crosses his or her arms across the chest may be defensive about something.

Warning Signs
When you're speaking, you may notice that you don't have your listener's full attention. Check for these signs: Your listener drums fingers or taps a foot, checks a watch, or looks around instead of looking at you.

Sending Signals
What you notice about other people's body language applies to you as well. Let your body language communicate confidence and a positive attitude. If you are listening to someone speak, show your interest by sitting or standing still, leaning slightly toward the speaker, and maintaining eye contact.

Apply the Strategy
With a partner role-play the following situations, using body language to show silent messages in each situation.

1. A shy older person gets directions from a helpful teenager.
2. A store clerk handles the complaint of an angry shopper returning a broken product.
3. A person who is late for an appointment runs into an old friend who won't stop talking.

876 ◆ *Poetry*

 Beyond the Classroom

Workplace Skills Mini-Lesson
Using Body Language Body language, often called nonverbal communication, plays a large role in the workplace. For example, the personnel director watches an interviewee's body language during a job interview; the boss watches an employee's body language during a briefing; employees watch the boss's body language during a sales review. Likewise, sales people watch customers' body language for cues about reactions to products or services.

Have students brainstorm to list other workplace situations in which body language is part of the communication process.

Extended Reading Opportunities

Poetry is the oldest literary form. For thousands of years, it was also considered the highest. The following collections provide opportunities to appreciate this literary form.

Suggested Titles

How to Read a Poem
Burton Raffel

Poetry can be difficult and intimidating to read. To the unsuspecting reader, it can seem like a garble of words with an impossibly hidden message. In this book, the author skillfully guides the reader through all the facets of poetry—from forms and meter to sound devices and metaphors. After reading this book, you'll see poetry not as an inscrutable maze of words and sounds, but as a celebration of the richness and variety of language.

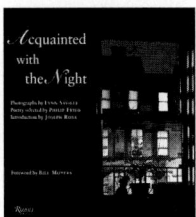

Acquainted With the Night
Lynn Saville and Philip Fried

This unique book pairs evocative black-and-white photographs by the photographer Lynn Saville with classic and contemporary poems and poetic excerpts about the night. Some of the featured poets include Robert Frost, Walt Whitman, William Wordsworth, and Emily Dickinson.

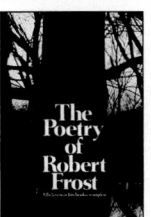

The Poetry of Robert Frost

This is the definitive volume of Robert Frost's poetry. Throughout his long and distinguished literary career, Frost brought to life the rhythm and beauty of rural New England life like no other poet before or since. More than just beautiful imagery, however, his poems also display irony, depth of meaning, and subtle humor that make them classics.

Other Possibilities

Voices of Poetry	Allen Kerschner, Editor
Black Out Loud: An Anthology of Modern Poems by Black Americans	Arnold Adoff, Editor
Sprints and Distances: Sports in Poetry and the Poetry in Sports	Lillian Morrison, Editor
Words Under the Words	Naomi Shihab Nye

Planning Students' Extended Reading

All the works on this page are good choices for extending student's appreciation for and understanding of poetry. The following information may help you choose which to assign.

Customize for *Varying Student Needs*

When assigning these works to your students, keep in mind the following factors.

- *How to Read a Poem* is a good choice for students who view poetry as difficult and inaccessible. Points are illustrated with brief examples from good poetry.

- The black-and-white photos in *Acquainted With the Night* will provide your visual learners with visual images to start discussion on the imagery in the poetry. Each poem is accompanied by a photograph that students can evaluate in terms of its appropriateness for the poem.

- *The Poetry of Robert Frost* will appeal especially to your more advanced students with a special interest in the poet who wrote "Mowing" and "After Apple Picking."

Sensitive Issues

Some of the poems in *Acquainted With the Night* contain sexual and religious references. In the same collection, an image of the roof garden on the Metropolitan Museum of Art shows a silhouette of a naked woman's form.

Planning Instruction and Assessment

Unit Objectives

1. To read epic and legendary stories from around the world
2. To apply a variety of reading strategies appropriate ffor these selections
3. To recognize literary elements used in these epics and legends
4. To increase vocabulary
5. To learn elements of grammar and usage
6. To write in a variety of modes and about situations based on the selections
7. To develop speaking and listening skills, by doing proposed activities

Meeting the Objectives

With each selection, you will find instructional material and portfolio opportunities through which students can meet these objectives. Further, you will find additional practice pages for reading strategies, literary elements, vocabulary, and grammar in **Selection Support** in the Teaching Resources box.

Setting Goals Work with your students at the beginning of the unit to set goals for unit outcomes. Plan what skills and concepts you wish students to acquire. You may individualize according to students' performance levels or learning modalities.

Portfolios You may have students keep portfolios of their work or of their work in progress. The activities and prompts on the Build Your Portfolio page of each selection provide opportunities for students to apply the concepts presented with the selection.

Knights About to Depart on the Quest for the Holy Grail, Tapestry designed by Sir E. Burne-Jones, woven by William Morris & Co., Birmingham Museums and Art Gallery

 Humanities: Art

Knights About to Depart on the Quest for the Holy Grail, designed by Sir Edward Burne-Jones, tapestry woven by William Morris and Company.

This tapestry represents the collaborative effort of two great Victorian artists: Edward Coley Burne-Jones (1833–1898) and William Morris (1834–1896). The two men met at Oxford, where they were both divinity students. Burne-Jones was a painter

and designer; Morris, besides being a painter, wrote brilliant poetry and designed furniture and wallpaper.

The subject of King Arthur and his knights exerted a strong hold over the imaginations of the Victorians, inspiring many beautiful works of art. The lady with the crown on the left is probably Queen Guinevere, who appears to be handing a shield to King Arthur, her husband.

Use this question for discussion: Why do you think stories about legendary figures like King Arthur continue to hold such an attraction for people? *Such stories contain exciting adventures; the heroes they tell about embody qualities that are widely admired.*

878

Epics and Legends

Great legends develop in every culture, reflecting the history and beliefs of the people who create them. These stories serve two purposes: They explain important events in the history of a people, and they shape these events into a heroic and memorable form. The various tales of different cultures have become identifying marks of these cultures; other people can read these stories and sense how the culture was shaped and what figures and issues are central to its history.

Within each of these stories, the customs, folklore, and history of a particular culture are revealed, sometimes in an entertaining manner.

◆ *879*

Assessing Student Progress

The following tools are available to measure the degree to which students meet the unit objectives:

Informal Assessment

The questions on the Guide for Responding sections are a first level of response to the concepts and skills presented with the selection. Students' responses are a brief informal measure of their grasp of the material. Their responses on this level can indicate where further instruction and practice are needed. You may then follow up with the practice pages in the *Selection Support* booklet.

You will find literature and reading guides in the *Alternative Assessment* booklet, which you may give students on an individual basis for informal assessment of their performance.

Formal Assessment

In the *Formal Assessment* booklet, you will find selection tests and a unit test.

Selection Tests The selection tests measure comprehension and skills acquisition for each selection or group of selections.

Unit Test The unit test, which calls on students to read a passage of literature they have not previously seen, applies the unit skills on a broader level. The Critical Reading section measures Unit Objectives 1, 2, and 3. The Vocabulary and Grammar section measures Objectives 4 and 5. The Essay section measures Objectives 1 and 6.

Both the Critical Reading and the Vocabulary and Grammar sections use formats similar to those found on many standardized tests, including the SAT.

Alternative Assessment

Portfolios As you review individual pieces or the collected work in students' portfolios, you will find assessment sheets available in the portfolio section of the *Alternative Assessment* booklet.

Scoring Rubrics You will find scoring rubrics for writing modes in the *Alternative Assessment* booklet. You can apply these to Writing Mini-Lessons and to Writing Process Workshop lessons.

Speaking and Listening The *Alternative Assessment* booklet contains assessment sheets for speaking and listening activities.

Learning Modalities The *Alternative Assessment* booklet contains activities that appeal to different learning styles. You may use these as an alternative measurement of students' growth.

The Reading for Success page in each unit presents a set of problem-solving procedures to help readers understand authors' words and ideas on multiple levels. Good readers develop a bank of strategies from which they can draw as needed and apply in a variety of reading situations.

Unit 10 presents strategies for reading epics and legends. Students will have encountered these strategies earlier. Here, however, they apply them to a specific kind of literature.

How to Use the Reading for Success Page

- Introduce the strategies for reading epics and legends, presenting each as a problem-solving procedure. Be sure students understand what each strategy involves and under what circumstances to apply it.

- Before students read the selections in this unit, point out that these selections represent legendary stories from a variety of world cultures. They should be open to the cultural context; they may encounter attitudes and customs different from what they might expect. Accepting these differences is an important part of the reading process.

Reading for Success

Strategies for Reading Epics and Legends

Every culture has its epics and legends—stories of heroes who embody the values, strengths, and traditions of that culture. While the legends may differ from culture to culture, the feature they have in common is a hero who achieves fame through great deeds. Because the legendary stories in this unit come from widely different time periods and cultures, you need to be open to differences in style and structure. The following strategies will help you read epics and legends effectively.

Reread or read ahead.

If you don't understand a passage, reread it, looking for connections among the words or sentences. It might also help you to read ahead, because a word or idea may be clarified further on. Try to follow the plot line.

Summarize.

As you read, pause periodically to restate in your own words what you have read. By doing this in your mind, you can check your understanding of the key events and their significance.

Be aware of the historical and cultural context.

The heroic tales in this unit took place long ago and far away. Customs and attitudes are very different from those that you know, and places may be unfamiliar. It's important to be open to these differences and not to impose preset expectations. Before you begin the following selections, familiarize yourself with the names of the characters.

Look for the writer's purpose and attitude.

Most epics and legends were passed on from generation to generation to preserve the history and values of a culture. The stories you will read here have other purposes as well. For instance, the purpose of *Don Quixote* is to poke fun at the values of the culture in which Cervantes lived. The writer's purpose in *Arthur Becomes King of Britain* is to bring some humanity and humor to the legendary hero.

You will read heroic tales more effectively if you actively use these strategies. You will be better able to follow the plot and apply your understanding to your own world.

Reading Strategies: Support and Reinforcement

Appropriate Reading Strategies Students are given a reading strategy to apply with each selection. Applying the strategies will give them insight into each selection.

Reading Prompts To encourage application of the given reading strategy, there are occasional prompts, within green boxes, at appropriate and significant points.

In addition, there are red boxes prompting application of the Literary Focus concept and maroon boxes prompting students to connect with their lives.

Using the Boxed Annotations and Prompts

The material in the green, red, and maroon boxes along the sides of selections is intended to help students apply the literary element and the reading strategy and to make a connection with their lives. You may use the boxed material in several ways:

- Have students pause when they come to a box and respond to its prompt before they continue reading.

- Urge students to read through the selection ignoring the boxes. After they have read the selection completely, they may go back and review the selection, responding to the prompts.

PART 1 *European Traditions*

Sir Galahad, George Frederic Watts,
The Fogg Art Museum, Harvard University

The first part of Unit 10 begins with an excerpt from *Don Quixote* that mocks the medieval romance. Tennyson's "Morte d'Arthur" tells the story of Arthur's death and the return of Excalibur to the Lady of the Lake. In his elegant poetry, Tennyson captures the grandeur of this classic legend. The excerpt from T. H. White's *The Once and Future King*, "Arthur Becomes King of Britain," takes a less reverent tone as it tells how young Arthur became king. White's gently comic prose version of the Arthurian legend was the inspiration for the stage and movie musical *Camelot*.

Customize for
Varying Student Needs
When assigning the selections in this part, keep in mind these factors:

from Don Quixote
- Students who are less proficient in reading may be put off at first by the elaborate style. Have them preview the picture on page 887 and be sure they know that Cervantes was making fun of flowery books about knights and their adventures.

"Morte d'Arthur"
- English language learners may have trouble deciphering Tennyson's meaning. Summarize passages for them and then play the section of the audiocassette where the passage is read.

"Arthur Becomes King of Britain"
- The story may seem so foreign to less advanced students that they may not at first catch its humorous tone. Before they read it, tell them the "straight" version of the same events.

 Humanities: Art

Sir Galahad by George Frederic Watts.
George Frederic Watts (1817–1904) was a successful English painter and sculptor. He studied at the Royal Academy and then spent some time in Italy, where he was influenced by the work of the great Italian Renaissance painter Titian.

Ask students what they know about Sir Galahad. *The son of Sir Lancelot, Galahad surpassed his father in virtue; in some versions of the Arthurian legend, Galahad, the only truly pure knight, succeeds in finding the Holy Grail.*

Use these questions for discussion:
1. The knight who fights for justice and virtue has been the prime hero in the European tradition for centuries. Modern versions include the cowboy and good soldier. What has the painter done to make Galahad look heroic in this painting? *He has painted Galahad with an ideal beauty and strength, in brilliantly gleaming armor, accompanied by a beautiful white*

horse. *Galahad's head is surrounded by a halo-like cloud.*

2. What would a contemporary Galahad look like? In particular, how would this person differ from the hero shown in this painting? *Students may propose figures who resemble such heroes as Luke Skywalker or Batman. They should explain what the hero would be wearing, what—if any—weapons he or she carries, and what animal or vehicle—if any—he or she rides.*

881

Guide for Reading

More About the Author
Many critics and historians regard Miguel de Cervantes's Don Quixote as the first novel in western literature. Others disagree, associating the birth of the novel with earlier or later works. Most critics do agree, however, that Cervantes was a great innovator in terms of psychological realism and sophistication. Although the "knights in shining armor" whom Don Quixote tries to imitate are rather one-dimensional figures, Don Quixote himself is a complex, contradictory, and touchingly human hero.

Miguel de Cervantes
(1547–1616)

As the creative genius behind *Don Quixote*, Miguel de Cervantes is counted among the world's greatest writers. His masterpiece *Don Quixote* has been translated into more than sixty languages and continues to be studied, critiqued, and debated even today. A poet and playwright as well as a novelist, Cervantes was born in a small town outside Madrid, Spain. Little is known about the author's early life—except the misfortunes he experienced.

A Life Full of Adventure As a young soldier in Turkey, Cervantes was wounded and permanently lost the use of his left arm and hand. Sailing home from the war, he was captured and enslaved by pirates. They took him to Algiers, where he was held prisoner for five years. Finally, he was freed when the Trinitarian friars paid a five-hundred-ducat ransom for him.

Settling Down Back in Spain, Cervantes married and took a job as a purchasing agent for the navy. His misfortunes continued, however; problems with work and finances resulted in fines and imprisonment. His luck finally turned when he published the first part of *Don Quixote*. He settled in Madrid and devoted his last years to writing. Wildly popular when it was first published, *Don Quixote* later became the model for a new type of fiction: that of the hero who does not conform to his times.

◆ Build Vocabulary

WORD ROOT: -son-

In this selection, Don Quixote decides to name his horse Rocinante because he believes it is a "lofty, sonorous name." *Sonorous* has the root -son-, which comes from the Latin *sonorus*, meaning "a sound." Knowing this root helps you to see that *sonorous* means "having a powerful, rich sound." You can also see this root in words such as *sonic*, which means "having to do with sound."

lucidity
adulation
interminable
affable
sallying
requisite
sonorous
veracious
vanquish
extolled

WORD BANK

As you read this story, you will encounter the words in this list. Each word is defined on the page where it first appears. Preview the list before you read.

◆ Build Grammar Skills

GERUNDS AND GERUND PHRASES

As you read *Don Quixote*, look for examples of gerunds and gerund phrases. A **gerund** is a verb form ending in -ing that acts as a noun. A **gerund phrase** includes all the words that go with a gerund. Like nouns, gerunds and gerund phrases can perform all the roles of a noun in a sentence: subject, direct or indirect object, object of a preposition, and appositive. In this example, the gerund *hunting* is used as the object of the preposition *of*:

Don Quixote was an early riser and fond of *hunting*.

In the following example, the gerund phrase *reading books of chivalry* acts as the object of the preposition *to*:

... the above named gentleman devoted his leisure ... to *reading books of chivalry* ...

from Don Quixote

◆ Literature and Your Life

CONNECT YOUR EXPERIENCE

You're reading the latest suspense or adventure novel and have encountered a devious villain. As the conflict intensifies, you find yourself silently shouting at the pages. You know they're just words on the page, but in the excitement of the tale you get a little carried away. The main character in *Don Quixote* gets carried away by the excitement of the romantic stories he reads about knights and battles. His overactive imagination creates some humorous scenes and situations.

Journal Writing Briefly describe the last book, movie, or video game that "carried you away."

THEMATIC FOCUS: OVERCOMING OBSTACLES

Don Quixote's imagination is a powerful force. You may wonder, as you follow his adventures, whether his imagination helps him or hurts him.

◆ Background for Understanding

CULTURE

Cervantes was born at the peak of Spain's Golden Age, a time when Spanish power and influence in Europe and the Western Hemisphere were greater than ever before or since. By the time Cervantes wrote *Don Quixote*, however, Spain's fortunes were fast declining because of a series of disastrous wars, bad economic policies, and the stunning defeat of the Spanish Armada by the British Navy in 1588. This last event signaled the end of Spain's rule of the seas and the beginning of England's. To some extent, Spain's transition from great confidence to deep despair is echoed in the novel, as Don Quixote takes refuge in chivalry from the realities of an unfriendly world.

◆ Literary Focus

PARODY

A **parody** is a comical piece of writing that mocks the characteristics of a specific literary form. By exaggerating or humorously imitating the ideas, language, tone, or action in a work of literature, a parody calls attention to the ridiculous qualities of its subject. A parody works best when the object of its ridicule is a usually serious topic. *Don Quixote* is a parody that ridicules knights and the literature of chivalry. By exaggerating Don Quixote's behavior, Cervantes entertains his audience while making fun of the traditional "knight in shining armor."

◆ Reading Strategy

COMPARE AND CONTRAST

Much of the humor in *Don Quixote* comes from the sharp difference between the ideal knight and Don Quixote's version of a knight. **Comparing and contrasting** the two versions will highlight the humor of Don Quixote, a mock "knight in shining armor." To help you identify the similarities and differences between Don Quixote and an "ideal knight," make a chart with three columns. In the first column, list the qualities or things that you associate with real knights—a war horse, armor, a squire, a lady love, bold adventures, and so on. Label the second column, "Ideal Knight" and list details about the ideal knight's horse, armor, and so on. Label the third column Don Quixote. Then, as you read the selection, jot down details that compare and contrast Don Quixote's knightly attributes and possessions with the ideal.

Qualities or Things	Ideal Knight	Don Quixote
armor		
squire		
war horse		
adventures		
opponents		
motivation		

Guide for Reading ◆ 883

Interest Grabber

Ask students to describe some of the superheroes they've seen in films. Then invite them to brainstorm for episodes in a film that makes fun of superheroes. Encourage them to use exaggeration and distortion to heighten the humor of their invented scenes. Finally, point out that they are using techniques similar to those that Cervantes uses in his parody.

Customize for
Less Proficient Readers
Less proficient readers may have difficulty filling in the Reading Strategy chart that compares and contrasts Don Quixote with an "ideal knight." Model the process by helping students identify relevant passages. Then encourage them to jot down details that apply to each of the headings— *Ideal Knight; Don Quixote.*

Customize for
More Advanced Students
Encourage students to keep track of specific words and phrases that help them to identify this selection as a parody. Students might then use *Don Quixote* as a basis to discuss the qualities of parody in general, identifying other familiar literary works as parodies.

Customize for
English Language Learners
Recognizing and using gerund phrases can significantly increase fluency, since gerunds can perform all the functions in sentences that nouns can. Provide language learners with extra instruction in this skill. Then have them complete Build Grammar Skills: Gerund Phrases, p. 250 in **Selection Support**.

Customize for
Visual/Spatial Learners
Let these students know that some artists specialize in caricature, exaggerated depiction of people to create a humorous effect. A caricature is much like a parody. Have students find examples of caricatures by classic or contemporary artists. Invite them to give talks in which they explain the elements of parody in the works they chose.

✎ Preparing for Standardized Tests

Grammar and Language Portions of some standardized tests require students to demonstrate their mastery of English in written essays. Using gerunds and gerund phrases effectively can make a piece of writing more fluent and mature:

As a knight-errant, Don Quixote devotes himself to *helping people in distress.*

Lead students to recognize that *helping people in distress* is a gerund phrase (they can recognize *helping* as the gerund because it is a verb form ending in *-ing*) and that it functions as the object of the preposition *to* in this sentence. The Build Grammar Skills lesson focuses on this topic. For additional practice, use the Build Grammar Skills page on Gerund Phrases, p. 250, in **Selection Support**.

One-Minute Insight

"...enchantments, quarrels, battles, challenges, wounds, wooings, loves, agonies...." This list summarizes the "impossible nonsense" found in the stories of knights that Cervantes parodies. His main character is Don Quixote, an old gentleman who has gone crazy reading books of chivalry and now tries to emulate the knights of former times. He dons some rusty armor, mounts a tired old horse, and calls a farm-girl his Lady. Later, he attacks a windmill that he believes is a giant, ignoring the warnings of his "squire," Sancho Panza. Through Quixote, Cervantes humorously and touchingly contrasts romantic ideals with life's realities.

▶**Critical Viewing**◀

❶ Evaluate Don Quixote's heroic qualities are shown through his upright posture. He is prepared to do heroic battle should the need arise. However, his emaciated horse and the fact that he is pictured without a face make him seem ridiculous.

◆ **Critical Thinking**

❷ Infer Have students reach conclusions about Quixote. *He is an impoverished gentleman who must spend all of his income to maintain an upper-class lifestyle.*

◆ **Critical Thinking**

❸ Evaluate Ask students how these remarks add humor. *Cervantes adds an element of humor and irony by seeming to take his fictional hero very seriously.*

The First Part of The Ingenious Gentleman Don Quixote of La Mancha[1]

from Don Quixote

Miguel de Cervantes
Translated by John Ormsby

CHAPTER I

Which Treats of the Character and Pursuits of the Famous Gentleman Don Quixote of La Mancha

In a village of La Mancha, which I prefer to leave unnamed, there lived not long ago one of those gentlemen that keep a lance in the lance-rack, an old shield, a lean hack, and a greyhound for hunting. A stew of rather more beef than mutton, hash on most nights, bacon and eggs on Saturdays, lentils on Fridays, and a pigeon or so extra on Sundays consumed three quarters of his income. The rest went for a coat of fine cloth and velvet breeches and shoes to match for holidays, while on weekdays he cut a fine figure in his best homespun. He had in his house a housekeeper past forty, a niece under twenty, and a lad for the field and marketplace, who saddled the hack as well as handled the pruning knife. The age of this gentleman of ours was bordering on fifty. He was of a hardy constitution, spare, gaunt-featured, a very early riser, and fond of hunting. Some say that his surname was Quixada or Quesada (for there is no unanimity among those who write on the subject), although reasonable conjectures tend to show that he was called Quexana. But this scarcely affects our story; it will be enough not to stray a hair's breadth from the truth in telling it.

Don Quixote, Honoré Daumier, Neue Pinakothek, Munich

 ▲ **Critical Viewing** What heroic qualities of Don Quixote are captured in this picture? What ridiculous qualities? **[Evaluate]**

---

1. **La Mancha:** Province in south central Spain.

884 ◆ *Epics and Legends*

◈ **Block Scheduling Strategies**

Consider these suggestions to take advantage of extended class time:

- Use the information and examples in Build Grammar Skills (p. 882) to introduce gerunds. Suggest that students review their own writing for more examples of gerunds and gerund phrases. Have students do the Build Grammar Skills exercise on page 890.

- Introduce the concept of parody in the Literary Focus on page 883. You may wish to use the Literary Focus page on parody in **Selection Support**, page 252, for further instruction. Then have students answer the Literary Focus questions on page 890.

- Have students gather in small groups to discuss and complete the Critical Thinking questions on page 890.

- Use Daily Language Practice for Weeks 31 and 32. You may display the practice sentences on an overhead projector and have students write them correctly, or you may dictate the sentences to students.

- Arrange for students to watch a video performance or listen to the soundtrack of the musical *Man of La Mancha.* The viewing or listening experience will help students complete one of the Speaking and Listening projects in the Idea Bank (p. 891).

You must know that the above-named gentleman devoted his leisure (which was mostly all the year round) to reading books of chivalry—and with such ardor and avidity that he almost entirely abandoned the chase and even the management of his property. To such a pitch did his eagerness and infatuation go that he sold many an acre of tillage land to buy books of chivalry to read, bringing home all he could find.

But there were none he liked so well as those written by the famous Feliciano de Silva, for their <u>lucidity</u> of style and complicated conceits[2] were as pearls in his sight, particularly when in his reading he came upon outpourings of <u>adulation</u> and courtly challenges. There he often found passages like *"the reason of the unreason with which my reason is afflicted so weakens my reason that with reason I complain of your beauty"*; or again, *"the high heavens, that of your divinity divinely fortify you with the stars, render you deserving of the desert your greatness deserves."*

◆ **Literary Focus**
Read this italicized passage aloud. What qualities of writing does it appear to mock?

Over this sort of folderol[3] the poor gentleman lost his wits, and he used to lie awake striving to understand it and worm out its meaning; though Aristotle[4] himself could have made out or extracted nothing, had he come back to life for that special purpose. He was rather uneasy about the wounds which Don Belianís gave and received, because it seemed to him that, however skilled the surgeons who had cured him, he must have had his face and body covered all over with seams and scars. He commended, however, the author's way of ending his book, with a promise to go on with that <u>interminable</u> adventure, and many a time he felt the urge to take up his pen and finish it just as its author had promised. He would no doubt have done so, and succeeded with it too, had he not been occupied with greater and more absorbing thoughts.

Many an argument did he have with the

---

2. **conceits** (kən sēts′) *n.*: Elaborate comparisons or metaphors.
3. **folderol** (fäl′ də räl′) *n.*: Mere nonsense.
4. **Aristotle** (ar′ is tät′əl): Ancient Greek philosopher.

---

priest of his village (a learned man, and a graduate of Sigüenza[5]) as to which had been the better knight, Palmerín of England or Amadís of Gaul. Master Nicolás, the village barber, however, used to say that neither of them came up to the Knight of Phœbus, and that if there was any that could compare with *him* it was Don Galaor, the brother of Amadís of Gaul, because he had a spirit equal to every occasion, and was no wishy-washy knight or a crybaby like his brother, while in valor he was not a whit behind him.

In short, he became so absorbed in his books that he spent his nights from sunset to sunrise, and his days from dawn to dark, poring over them; and what with little sleep and much reading his brain shriveled up and he lost his wits. His imagination was stuffed with all he read in his books about enchantments, quarrels, battles, challenges, wounds, wooings, loves, agonies, and all sorts of impossible nonsense. It became so firmly planted in his mind that the whole fabric of invention and fancy he read about was true, that to him no history in the world was better substantiated. He used to say the Cid Ruy Díaz[6] was a very good knight but that he was not to be compared with the Knight of the Burning Sword who with one backstroke cut in half two fierce and monstrous giants. He thought more of Bernardo del Carpio because at Roncesvalles he slew Roland in spite of enchantments, availing himself of Hercules' trick when he strangled Antæus the son of Terra in his arms. He approved highly of the giant Morgante, because, although of the giant breed which is always arrogant and

---

5. **Sigüenza** (sē gwän′ sä): One of a group of "minor universities" granting degrees that were often laughed at by Spanish humorists.
6. **Cid Ruy Díaz** (sēd roo′ ē dē′ äs): Famous Spanish soldier Ruy Diaz de Vivar: called the Cid, a derivation of the Arabic word for lord.

◆ **Build Vocabulary**

lucidity (loo sid′ ə tē) *n.*: Clarity; ability to be understood

adulation (a′ joo lā′ shən) *n.*: Excessive praise or admiration

interminable (in tʉr′ mi nə bəl) *adj.*: Lasting, or seeming to last forever

from *Don Quixote* ◆ 885

◆ **Critical Thinking**

❹ **Draw Conclusions** Based on this passage, what conclusions can students draw about Don Quixote's interest in books of chivalry? *Suggested responses: It is taking over his life; it is making him neglect his responsibilities.*

◆ **Literary Focus**

❺ **Parody** Students should note the mock loftiness of the passage and the absurd repetitions within it. They may say that Cervantes is using exaggeration to ridicule the artificiality and triteness of the typical heroic novel.

◆ **Reading Strategy**

❻ **Compare and Contrast** Point out that in this passage Cervantes pokes fun at certain customs and attitudes of his day. Have students identify those customs and attitudes. *Suggested responses: Cervantes might be mocking people's preoccupation with books of chivalry and their heroes.* **Ask students to identify conventions of our culture that compare to the ones Cervantes mocks in this passage.** *Students might observe that many people talk about film, television, and pop stars in the same way as these characters talk about knights.*

◆ **Critical Thinking**

❼ **Interpret** Have students express in their own words the main idea that this passage conveys. *Responses may include the following: Don Quixote can no longer distinguish between fantasy and reality; he talks about fictional characters as if they were real people.*

Humanities: Art

Don Quixote by Honoré Daumier.

The caricaturist, painter, and sculptor Honoré Daumier (1808–1879) is best known for his cartoons satirizing the politics and society of nineteenth century France. He found a wide audience for his cartoons attacking certain public figures and aspects of society. After 1850 Daumier produced a series of works based on *Don Quixote*. This image of Don Quixote on his horse is very loosely rendered and almost appears incomplete when compared to earlier, more detailed versions of the painting. Nevertheless, his lively use of line and texture captures the essence of the gentleman of La Mancha.

Use these questions for discussion:
1. Why do you think Daumier painted Don Quixote as a faceless figure? *Sample response: In reality, Don Quixote was simply masquerading as a knight. By painting him as faceless Daumier revealed the truth about him.*

2. If you were painting a portrait of Don Quixote on his horse, how would your painting compare to this one? *Some students might exaggerate details to show Quixote's foolishness; others might paint Quixote as he saw himself—a regal and heroic figure.*

◆ Build Grammar Skills

❶ Gerund Phrases Have students identify the gerund phrase in this sentence. *Students should identify the phrase* kicking at that traitor of a Ganelon. *Then have them explain its function in the sentence. It is the object of the preposition of.*

◆ Literary Focus

❷ Parody Have students use this passage to describe the author's attitude toward his "hero," Don Quixote. Encourage them to cite specific phrases to support their responses. *Students may say that the author views Don Quixote as an outlandish, deluded, and somewhat pitiful character. In support, they may cite such phrases as "his wits being quite gone," "strangest notion," "madman," and "poor man."*

◆ Reading Strategy

❸ Compare and Contrast Students may note that a traditional knight's helmet is polished, impressive-looking, fully closed, and able to withstand cuts and blows. Don Quixote's helmet, on the other hand, is a crude and improvised piece of old armor, with "a kind of half-helmet of pasteboard."

Comprehension Check ☑

❹ Suggest that students carefully reread this difficult sentence. Then have them explain what Cervantes is saying about Don Quixote and his horse. *Although the horse is in reality a broken-down and pitiful-looking creature, in Don Quixote's eyes, it is more magnificent than the most celebrated horses from history.*

◆ Critical Thinking

❺ Connect Ask: In what ways is Don Quixote's approach to naming his horse similar to his approach to outfitting himself with armor? *Elicit the following: In both cases, he uses his imagination to transform something shabby into something heroic; in both cases, he does all he can to model himself on the famous knights whom he admires.*

---

ill-mannered, he alone was <u>affable</u> and well-bred. But above all he admired Reinaldos of Montalbán, especially when he saw him <u>sallying</u> forth from his castle and robbing everyone he met, and when beyond the seas he stole that image of Mohammed which, as his history says, was entirely of gold. To have a bout of kicking ❶ at that traitor of a Ganelon he would have given his housekeeper, and his niece into the bargain.

In a word, his wits being quite gone, he hit upon the strangest notion that ever madman in this world hit upon. He fancied it was right and <u>requisite</u>, no less for his own greater renown than in the service of his country, that he ❷ should make a knight-errant of himself, roaming the world over in full armor and on horseback in quest of adventures. He would put into practice all that he had read of as being the usual practices of knights-errant: righting every kind of wrong, and exposing himself to peril and danger from which he would emerge to reap eternal fame and glory. Already the poor man saw himself crowned by the might of his arm Emperor of Trebizond[7] at least. And so, carried away by the intense enjoyment he found in these pleasant fancies, he began at once to put his scheme into execution.

The first thing he did was to clean up some armor that had belonged to his ancestors and had for ages been lying forgotten in a corner, covered with rust and mildew. He scoured and polished it as best he could, but the one great defect he saw in it was that it had no closed helmet, nothing but a simple morion.[8] This deficiency, however, his ingenuity made good, for he contrived a kind of half-helmet of pasteboard which, fitted on to the morion, looked like a whole one. It is true that, in order to see if it was strong and fit to withstand a cut, he drew his sword and gave it a couple of slashes, the first of which undid in an instant what had taken him a week to do. The ease with which he had knocked it to pieces

> ◆ **Reading Strategy**
> ❸ Compare and contrast Don Quixote's armor with that of a traditional knight's.

---

7. **Trebizond** (treb´ i zänd´): In medieval times, a Greek empire off the southeast coast of the Black Sea.
8. **morion** (môr´ ē än´) *n.*: Old-fashioned soldier's helmet with a brim, covering the top part of the head.

886 ◆ *Epics and Legends*

---

disconcerted him somewhat, and to guard against the danger he set to work again, fixing bars of iron on the inside until he was satisfied with its strength. Then, not caring to try any more experiments with it, he accepted and commissioned it as a helmet of the most perfect construction.

He next proceeded to inspect his nag, which, with its cracked hoofs and more blemishes than the steed of Gonela, that "*tantum pellis et ossa* ❹ *fruit*,"[9] surpassed in his eyes the Bucephalus of Alexander or the Babieca of the Cid.[10] Four days were spent in thinking what name to give him, because (as he said to himself) it was not right that a horse belonging to a knight so famous, and one with such merits of its own, should be without some distinctive name. He strove to find something that would indicate what it had been before belonging to a knight-errant, and what it had now become. It was only reasonable that it should be given a new name to match the new ❺ career adopted by its master, and that the name should be a distinguished and full-sounding one, befitting the new order and calling it was about to follow. And so, after having composed, struck out, rejected, added to, unmade, and re-made a multitude of names out of his memory and fancy, he decided upon calling it Rocinante. To his thinking this was a lofty, <u>sonorous</u> name that nevertheless indicated what the hack's[11]

---

9. *"tantum pellis et ossa fruit"* (tän´ tum pel´ is et äs´ ə frōō´ it): "It was nothing but skin and bones" (Latin).
10. **Bucephalus** (byōō sef´ ə les) **of Alexander or the Babieca** (bäb ē ā´ kä) **of the Cid:** Bucephalus was Alexander the Great's war horse; Babieca was the Cid's war horse.
11. **hack's:** Horse's.

◆ Build Vocabulary

affable (af´ ə bəl) *adj.*: Pleasant; friendly

sallying (sal´ ē in) *v.*: Rushing forth suddenly

requisite (rek´ wə zit) *adj.*: Required by circumstances

sonorous (sə nôr´ əs) *adj.*: Having a powerful, impressive sound

veracious (və rā´ shəs) *adj.*: Truthful; accurate

vanquish (van´ kwish) *v.*: Conquer; force into submission

extolled (eks tōld´) *adj.*: Praised

Cross-Curricular Connection: Social Studies

The first thing that Don Quixote does after deciding to become a knight-errant is to clean up some old and rusty armor that had belonged to his ancestors. The outfit that he restores would have dated from the period in which the manufacturing and use of armor reached it peak in Europe—the 1300's to the mid-1500's. After this time, gunpowder was increasingly used in battle and the production of armor, useful in hand-to-hand combat, declined.

Have students discuss how the description of Don Quixote's armor reinforces his identity as a hero who does not conform to his times. You might also have groups of students do research and then report on the use and design of armor in various periods and cultures, ranging from ancient Greece to Spain of the 1500's.

status had been before it became what now it was, the first and foremost of all the hacks in the world.

Having got a name for his horse so much to his taste, he was anxious to get one for himself, and he spent eight days more pondering over this point. At last he made up his mind to call himself Don Quixote—which, as stated above, led the authors of this <u>veracious</u> history to infer that his name quite assuredly must have been Quixada, and not Quesada as others would have it. It occurred to him, however, that the valiant Amadís was not content to call himself Amadís and nothing more but added the name of his kingdom and country to make it famous and called himself Amadís of Gaul. So he, like a good knight, resolved to add on the name of his own region and style himself Don Quixote of La Mancha. He believed that this accurately described his origin and country, and that he did it honor by taking its name for his own.

So then, his armor being furbished, his morion turned into a helmet, his hack christened, and he himself confirmed, he came to the conclusion that nothing more was needed now but to look for a lady to be in love with, for a knight-errant without love was like a tree without leaves or fruit, or a body without a soul.

"If, for my sins, or by my good fortune," he said to himself, "I come across some giant hereabouts, a common occurrence with knights-errant, and knock him to the ground in one onslaught, or cleave him asunder at the waist, or, in short, <u>vanquish</u> and subdue him, will it not be well to have someone I may send him to as a present, that he may come in and fall on his knees before my sweet lady, and in a humble, submissive voice say, 'I am the giant Caraculiambro, lord of the island of Malindrania, vanquished in single combat by the never sufficiently <u>extolled</u> knight Don Quixote of La Mancha, who has commanded me to present myself before your grace, that your highness may dispose of me at your pleasure'?"

Oh, how our good gentleman enjoyed the delivery of this speech, especially when he had thought of someone to call his lady! There was, so the story goes, in a village near his own a very good-looking farm-girl with whom he had been at one time in love, though, so far as is

Don Quixote and the Windmill, c.1900, Francisco J. Torrome

▲ **Critical Viewing** How does this picture illustrate the effects of the "shriveled brain" of the hero? [Connect] **⑧**

from *Don Quixote* ◆ 887

Customize for
Less Proficient Readers

⑥ Point out that the author provides a brief summary at this point in the tale. Invite students to expand upon this summary by making their own general statements about Don Quixote and his actions so far.
Possible summary: Obsessed by romantic tales of chivalry, Don Quixote, a man who had led a quiet and ordinary life, prepares to embark upon new adventures as a knight-errant.

◆ **Literary Focus**

⑦ Parody Encourage students to identify and discuss ways in which Cervantes parodies tales of chivalry in this passage. *Responses may include: Quixote refers to encounters with giants as "common occurrences" within such tales; he imitates the absurdly flowery style of speech in these tales when he recounts the words of the giant Caraculiambro, and he finds a pretext to refer to himself immodestly and ridiculously as "the never sufficiently extolled knight Don Quixote of La Mancha."*

▶**Critical Viewing**◀

⑧ Connect Students should connect the question to the earlier passage in which Cervantes reveals that the main effect of Don Quixote's "shriveled brain" is a failure to distinguish between fantasy and reality. Subsequently, they should also connect it to the adventure in which Don Quixote mistakes a windmill for a giant and receives a painful blow.

 Humanities: Art

Don Quixote and the Windmill, 1900, by Francisco J. Torrome.

Over the centuries, many artists have been inspired by Don Quixote and his exploits. This artwork by Francisco J. Torrome captures the decisive moment in the "Terrible and Undreamed-of Adventure of the Windmills." Torrome captures the comedy of this episode. Don Quixote loses his battle with the windmill and is dashed to the ground while a dismayed Sancho Panza clutches his head in the distance. The downward slant of the blades of the windmill emphasize the forward thrust of the man and the horse as they fall. The idyllic landscape behind Sancho contrasts with the chaotic scene in the foreground. This artist's interpretation of the famous windmill scene is skillfully rendered.

Use these questions for discussion:
1. Based on this illustration, what predictions can you make about the adventures on which Don Quixote will embark? *Students may predict that Don Quixote and his horse will meet with many mishaps.*
2. How does this illustration contrast Don Quixote and Sancho Panza? *Quixote perceives the windmills as monsters, while Panza—a realist—sees them for what they are. Quixote pays for his folly, while Panza is dismayed but unharmed.*

◆ Literary Focus

❶ Parody Students may note that the object of a knight's love is traditionally a princess, queen, or other noble lady. Don Quixote's love, however, is described as a "farm-girl."

◆ Critical Thinking

❷ Compare and Contrast Encourage students to point out the differences between Sancho Panza and Don Quixote that are brought out in this passage. *Students may describe Sancho Panza as realistic, practical, or straightforward; Don Quixote by contrast, may be described as unrealistic, overly romantic, or totally deluded. Students may also note that Sancho's traits help him to avoid danger, while Don Quixote's traits tend to put him in danger.*

◆ Reading Strategy

❸ Compare and Contrast In what way is the outcome of Don Quixote's battle different from the outcome a "real" knight would experience? *Students should note that Don Quixote comes away defeated and humiliated; a traditional knight would fight capably against a real foe.*

Comprehension Check ☑

❹ Point out that the "sage Freston" to whom Don Quixote refers was introduced in a chapter that precedes this episode. Then encourage students to use context clues to explain who this person is. *He is an evil magician and Don Quixote's enemy.*

◆ Build Grammar Skills

❺ Gerund Phrases Have students identify the gerund phrase in this passage. *Students should identify the phrase* vanquishing them. *What is its function in the sentence in which it appears? It is the object of the preposition* of.

---

❶ **◆ Literary Focus**
How is Don Quixote's lady love a parody of the traditional fair maiden that is the object of a knight's love?

known, she never knew it nor gave a thought to the matter. Her name was Aldonza Lorenzo, and upon her he thought fit to confer the title of Lady of his Thoughts. Searching for a name not too remote from her own, yet which would aim at and bring to mind that of a princess and great lady, he decided upon calling her Dulcinea del Toboso, since she was a native of El Toboso. To his way of thinking, the name was musical, uncommon, and significant, like all those he had bestowed upon himself and his belongings.

CHAPTER VIII

Of the Good Fortune Which the Valiant Don Quixote Had in the Terrible and Undreamed-of Adventure of the Windmills, With Other Occurrences Worthy to Be Fitly Recorded

At this point they came in sight of thirty or forty windmills that are on that plain.

"Fortune," said Don Quixote to his squire, as soon as he had seen them, "is arranging matters for us better than we could have hoped. Look there, friend Sancho Panza,[12] where thirty or more monstrous giants rise up, all of whom I mean to engage in battle and slay, and with whose spoils we shall begin to make our fortunes. For this is righteous warfare, and it is God's good service to sweep so evil a breed from off the face of the earth."

"What giants?" said Sancho Panza.

"Those you see there," answered his master, "with the long arms, and some have them nearly two leagues[13] long."

❷ "Look, your worship," said Sancho. "What we see there are not giants but windmills, and what seem to be their arms are the vanes that turned by the wind make the millstone go."

"It is easy to see," replied Don Quixote,

---

12. Sancho Panza: A simple country man whom Don Quixote takes as his squire. In contrast to Don Quixote, Panza is practical and has common sense.
13. leagues: A league is about three miles.

888 ◆ Epics and Legends

"that you are not used to this business of adventures. Those are giants, and if you are afraid, away with you out of here and betake yourself to prayer, while I engage them in fierce and unequal combat."

❷ So saying, he gave the spur to his steed Rocinante, heedless of the cries his squire Sancho sent after him, warning him that most certainly they were windmills and not giants he was going to attack. He, however, was so positive they were giants that he neither heard the cries of Sancho, nor perceived, near as he was, what they were.

"Fly not, cowards and vile beings," he shouted, "for a single knight attacks you."

A slight breeze at this moment sprang up, and the great vanes began to move.

"Though ye flourish more arms than the giant Briareus, ye have to reckon with me!" exclaimed Don Quixote, when he saw this.

So saying, he commended himself with all his heart to his lady Dulcinea, imploring her to support him in such a peril. With lance braced and covered by his shield, he charged at Rocinante's fullest gallop and attacked the first mill that stood in front of him. But as he drove his lance-point into the sail, the wind whirled it ❸ around with such force that it shivered the lance to pieces. It swept away with it horse and rider, and they were sent rolling over the plain, in sad condition indeed.

Sancho hastened to his assistance as fast as the animal could go. When he came up he found Don Quixote unable to move, with such an impact had Rocinante fallen with him.

"God bless me!" said Sancho. "Did I not tell your worship to watch what you were doing, because they were only windmills? No one could have made any mistake about it unless he had something of the same kind in his head."

"Silence, friend Sancho," replied Don Quixote. "The fortunes of war more than any other are liable to frequent fluctuations. Moreover I think, and it is the truth, that that same sage Frestón ❹ who carried off my study and books, has turned these giants into mills in order to rob me of the glory of vanquishing them, such is the enmity ❺ he bears me. But in the end his wicked arts will avail but little against my good sword."

Speaking and Listening Mini-Lesson

Role Play

This mini-lesson supports the Speaking and Listening activity in the Idea Bank on page 891.

Introduce the Concept Point out that although Don Quixote and Sancho Panza go in quest of adventures together, the two have very different views of the world. Let students know that they will express the two characters' contrasting attitudes as they role play the scene in which Sancho tries to talk Don Quixote out of attacking the windmills.

Develop Background Have students review and analyze the conversation that the two characters have before Don Quixote charges at the windmills. Suggest that students identify the main points that each character makes as well as the traits that each shows.

Apply the Information Have students work in pairs to prepare their scenes. Encourage the partners to create their own original versions of the scene by elaborating on the points and traits they identified. Encourage them also to use both facial expressions and gestures to help communicate the personality traits of the characters.

Assess the Outcome Let students evaluate their own and their classmate's work. After each performance you might ask: Did the scene bring out the contrasts between the two characters? How did it show these contrasts?

"God's will be done," said Sancho Panza, and helping him to rise got him up again on Rocinante, whose shoulder was half dislocated. Then, discussing the adventure, they followed the road to Puerto Lápice, for there, said Don Quixote, they could not fail to find adventures in abundance and variety, as it was a well-traveled thoroughfare. For all that, he was much grieved at the loss of his lance, and said so to his squire.

♦ *Literature and Your Life*

6 How has Don Quixote let his books "go to his head"? Can you relate to his feelings?

"I remember having read," he added, "how a Spanish knight, Diego Pérez de Vargas by name, having broken his sword in battle, tore from an oak a ponderous bough or branch. With it he did such things that day, and pounded so many Moors, that he got the surname of Machuca, and he and his descendants from that day forth were called Vargas y Machuca. I mention this because from the first oak I see I mean to tear such a branch, large and stout. I am determined and resolved to do such deeds with it that you may deem yourself very fortunate in being found worthy to see them and be an eyewitness of things that will scarcely be believed."

"Be that as God wills," said Sancho, "I believe it all as your worship says it. But straighten yourself a little, for you seem to be leaning to one side, maybe from the shaking you got when you fell."

"That is the truth," said Don Quixote, "and if I make no complaint of the pain it is because knights-errant are not permitted to complain of any wound, even though their bowels be coming out through it."

"If so," said Sancho, "I have nothing to say. But God knows I would rather your worship complained when anything ailed you. For my part, I confess I must complain however small the ache may be, unless this rule about not complaining applies to the squires of knights-errant also."

Don Quixote could not help laughing at his squire's simplicity, and assured him he might complain whenever and however he chose, just as he liked. So far he had never read of anything to the contrary in the order of knighthood.

Sancho reminded him it was dinner time, to which his master answered that he wanted nothing himself just then, but that Sancho might eat when he had a mind. With this permission Sancho settled himself as comfortably as he could on his beast, and taking out of the saddlebags what he had stowed away in them, he jogged along behind his master munching slowly. From time to time he took a pull at the wineskin with all the enjoyment that the thirstiest tavernkeeper in Málaga might have envied. And while he went on in this way, between gulps, he never gave a thought to any of the promises his master had made him, nor did he rate it as hardship but rather as recreation going in quest of adventures, however dangerous they might be.

♦ *Literature and Your Life*

6 Students may say that Don Quixote has let his books "go to his head" to the point that he models his life on them. They may be able to relate to his fascination with an idealized fictional world and its heroes but not to the extremes to which he goes.

♦ **Critical Thinking**

7 **Infer** Encourage students to use this passage to make inferences about Sancho Panza. *Inferences may include these: He is a realist; he has no illusions about being heroic or extraordinary; he is a down-to-earth person; he is sympathetic and respectful toward Don Quixote.*

Reinforce and Extend

Answers
♦ *Literature and Your Life*

Reader's Response Students might find it most ridiculous when Don Quixote confuses the windmills for monsters that must be vanquished, and he charges at them.

Thematic Focus On the one hand, Quixote's imagination causes him to imagine unreal threats, making windmills into monsters. However, he overcomes "obstacles" with imaginative explanations as when he says sage Freston (the magician) turned the monsters into windmills to humiliate him.

✓ **Check Your Comprehension**

1. He reads tales of chivalry.
2. He decides to become a knight-errant.
3. He pierced a windmill sail with his lance and the wind whirled it around with such force that Don Quixote and his horse went flying.

Guide for Responding

♦ *Literature and Your Life*

Reader's Response Which aspect of Don Quixote's appearance or behavior do you think is most ridiculous? Why?

Thematic Focus How does Don Quixote's imagination both create obstacles and help him overcome them?

✓ **Check Your Comprehension**

1. What sorts of books does Don Quixote read?
2. What unusual decision does Don Quixote make as a result of his reading?
3. What sent Don Quixote and his horse rolling across the plain?

from *Don Quixote* ♦ 889

Beyond the Selection

FURTHER READING
Other Works by Miguel de Cervantes
La Galatea
Exemplary Novels
Eight Comedies and Eight Entremeses
Other Works About the Power of Imagination
"The Secret Life of Walter Mitty," James Thurber
"Ode on a Grecian Urn," John Keats
"The Legend of Sleepy Hollow," Washington Irving
    We suggest that you preview these works before recommending them to students.

INTERNET
The Internet provides an excellent opportunity for students to learn more about Don Quixote. Encourage students to visit the following Web site for information. Please be aware, however, that the site may have changed from the time we published this information.
    For background information on Don Quixote, a "tour" of historic editions, and a collection of illustrations, go to: **http://milton.mse.jhu.edu:8003/quixote/index/html**
    We *strongly recommend* that you preview the site before you send students to it.

Answers

◆ Critical Thinking

1. Reading books about chivalry has filled Don Quixote's mind with delusions about himself.
2. By using special names for people and things Don Quixote inflates their status.
3. He sees the windmills as giants because he is delusional and his need to perform a chivalrous act is so great.
4. Seeing things as they are, he keeps his master from even greater danger.
5. This approach enables one to be happy in one's own world, however, it is also unrealistic and dangerous.
6. Students are likely to refer to career guides, course catalogues, books or Web sites that focus on a particular field.

◆ Reading Strategy

1. Sample response: In his own mind, Quixote was like the knights of old in that he was well-bred, honorable, and adventurous.
2. Don Quixote is older, more pretentious, and certainly less sane than his idealized image of a knight.
3. The contrast tells us that Cervantes took an ironic and cynical view of chivalry—he probably thought it a pompous and outdated medieval convention.

◆ Literary Focus

1. Through his detailed description of Don Quixote dressing in rusty armor, Cervantes pokes fun at the way knights dressed.
2. It is an example of parody because it shows how a real knight would attack a real monster, but the effort becomes a mockery when the monster turns out to be a windmill.
3. Cervantes parodies knights' names by having Don Quixote call himself Don Quixote of la Mancha; he parodies knights' fine horses by giving the delusional Quixote an emaciated nag; he parodies the social status of knights' ladies by making Quixote's lady a farm-girl; he parodies knights' battles by putting Quixote in battle with a windmill.

890

Guide for Responding (continued)

◆ Critical Thinking

INTERPRET
1. How has reading books about chivalry affected Don Quixote's mind? [Analyze]
2. Why does Don Quixote like to use special names for people and things? [Infer]
3. What makes Don Quixote see the windmills as giant monsters? [Speculate]
4. Why is Sancho Panza a particularly helpful squire to Don Quixote? [Deduce]

EVALUATE
5. Don Quixote makes the world fit his illusions. What are the advantages and dangers of such an approach to life? [Evaluate]

EXTEND
6. Don Quixote tries to learn about being a knight from reading romantic, fictional accounts. What sources would you use to find out about a career that interested you? [Career Link]

◆ Reading Strategy

COMPARE AND CONTRAST
To see the humor of *Don Quixote*, **compare and contrast** the elements of the parody with the original. Look for similarities and differences between Don Quixote and the "ideal knight."
1. In what ways is Don Quixote, at least in his own mind, similar to the knights of old?
2. In what general ways does Don Quixote contrast with his idealized image of a knight?
3. What does this contrast tell us about Cervantes's view of chivalry?

◆ Literary Focus

PARODY
Cervantes creates a **parody** of the literature of chivalry by ridiculing the behavior of knights and suggesting that chivalrous ideals are pure illusion.
1. How does Cervantes poke fun at the way knights dressed?
2. How is the incident with the windmills an example of parody?
3. What specific aspects of chivalry does Cervantes parody? Give examples.

890 ◆ Epics and Legends

◆ Build Vocabulary

USING THE ROOT -son-
Knowing that the root -son- means "hearing or sound," match each word with its definition. On your paper, write the correct definition next to each numbered word.
1. sonic   a. unity of sound
2. consonance   b. not in harmony
3. dissonant   c. having to do with sound
4. unison   d. harmony of musical tones

USING THE WORD BANK
On your paper, write the word from the Word Bank whose meaning is closest to that of the words below.
1. necessary   6. unending
2. dashing forth   7. honest
3. friendly   8. conquer
4. resonant   9. clearness
5. praised   10. excessive praise

◆ Build Grammar Skills

GERUNDS AND GERUND PHRASES
A **gerund** is a verb form ending in -ing used as a noun. A **gerund phrase** includes all the words that go with the gerund. Gerunds and gerund phrases perform all the same roles in a sentence that a noun does: subject, direct or indirect object, object of preposition, and appositive.

Practice Copy the following sentences in your notebook. Underline the gerunds or gerund phrases. Identify the function of each gerund or gerund phrase in the sentence.
1. It will be enough not to stray from the truth in telling it.
2. He commends the author's way of ending his books.
3. He follows the usual practice of knights: righting wrongs and exposing himself to all kinds of danger.
4. On his journey, Don Quixote tries attacking windmills.
5. Eating is one of Sancho's greatest pleasures.

◆ Build Vocabulary

Using the Root -son-
1. c   2. d   3. b   4. a

Using the Word Bank
1. requisite   6. interminable
2. sallying   7. veracious
3. affable   8. vanquish
4. sonorous   9. lucidity
5. extolled   10. adulation

◆ Build Grammar Skills

1. It will be enough not to stray from the truth in <u>telling it</u>. (object of preposition *in*)
2. He commends the author's way of <u>ending his books</u>. (object of preposition *of*)
3. He follows the usual practice of knights: <u>righting wrongs and exposing himself</u> to all kinds of danger. (appositive—further explains "the usual practice of knights")
4. On his journey, Don Quixote tries <u>attacking windmills</u>. (direct object)
5. <u>Eating</u> is one of Sancho's greatest pleasures. (subject)

Writer's Solution

For additional instruction and practice, use pages 44–45 on Gerunds and Gerund Phrases in the *Writer's Solution Grammar Practice Book*.

Build Your Portfolio

 ## Idea Bank

Writing

1. **Definition of a Hero** Write a definition of a modern hero. Include the qualities that you think people of today admire. Give examples from movies, sports, or entertainment to illustrate your points.

2. **Don Quixote in America** Suppose Don Quixote were to wander into your community for his next adventure. Write one or two paragraphs describing problems he might encounter.

3. **Create a Scene** In another scene from the novel, Don Quixote decides a flock of sheep is an enemy army and charges! Write the dialogue Don Quixote and Sancho might have had before or after the charge.

Speaking and Listening

4. **Role Play** Role-play the scene in which Sancho tries to talk Don Quixote out of attacking the windmills. **[Performing Arts Link]**

5. **Musical** The musical *Man of La Mancha* is based on the character Don Quixote. Watch a video performance or listen to the soundtrack. Then discuss what the songs reveal about the hero's infatuation with romantic ideals. Share your conclusions with the class. **[Music Link]**

Projects

6. **Cartoon** Reread the description of Don Quixote's armor and horse. Then draw a cartoon of the forlorn-looking knight astride Rocinante as they joust the windmill. **[Art Link]**

7. **Visual Essay** Create a visual essay on the theme of heroes. Use photos from magazines and newspapers. Write captions that illustrate how your examples and opinions relate to a central message about heroes. **[Social Studies Link]**

 ## Writing Mini-Lesson

Sketch of a Comic Hero

The typical hero of a work of literature—whether warrior, political leader, great athlete, or something else—usually has one defining characteristic: He or she is very serious. The quest or challenge that the hero undertakes is also one of the gravest import. Cervantes, however, turned the entire genre of the heroic tale on its head when he created his comic hero Don Quixote. In the spirit of Cervantes, create a comic hero and write a **sketch** of that hero. Describe your hero's character traits and achievements.

Writing Skills Focus: Clear and Logical Organization

To present your hero in a sketch, you'll need a **clear and logical organization**. For instance, you might want to describe the hero's life and exploits chronologically. Or you may discuss your hero's attributes in order of importance, starting from the least important and moving to the most. Whatever method you choose, use it consistently for the entire sketch.

Prewriting Start by creating a character chart like the one below, showing the various character traits of your hero. Underneath each trait, give an example that you can use in your draft.

Trait:	Example:
Nearsighted	Attempts to slay windmills
Absorbed in heroic books	Thinks of himself as a great hero

Drafting Begin your profile with a catchy introduction, such as a quotation, question, or anecdote that illustrates a humorous quality of your hero. Then discuss qualities of your hero and give examples of each.

Revising Ask a peer whether your sketch conveys the comic qualities of your hero. If not, add further details to show those qualities.

from Don Quixote ◆ 891

 ## Idea Bank

Customizing for *Performance Levels*

Following are suggestions for matching Idea Bank topics with your students' performance levels:
 Less Advanced Students: 1, 4
 Average Students: 2, 5, 6
 More Advanced Students: 3, 7

Customizing for *Learning Modalities*

Following are suggestions for matching Idea Bank topics with your students' learning modalities:
 Musical/Rhythmic: 5
 Verbal/Linguistic: 1, 2, 3, 4, 5
 Visual/Spatial: 6, 7

 ## Writing Mini-Lesson

Refer students to the Writing Handbook, page 965, for instruction on the writing process and page 967 for further information on description.

Writing Lab CD-ROM

Have students complete the tutorial on Descriptive Writing. Follow these steps:
1. Have students use the Word Bins activity to see examples of character trait words they might use in their sketch of a comic hero.
2. Have students compose their sketches on the computer.
3. Have students refer to the peer review guidelines and checklist when having a peer check their sketch.

Sourcebook

Have students use Chapter 1, Description (pp. 1–25), for additional support.

✓ ASSESSMENT OPTIONS

Formal Assessment, Selection Test, pp. 217–219, and Assessment Resources Software. The selection test is designed so that it can be easily customized to the performance levels of your students.
Alternative Assessment, p. 61, includes options for less advanced students, more advanced students, intrapersonal learners and verbal/linguistic learners.

PORTFOLIO ASSESSMENT

Use the following rubrics in the *Alternative Assessment* booklet to assess student writing:
Definition of a Hero: Definition/Classification Rubric, p. 99
Don Quixote in America: Problem-Solution Rubric, p. 101
Create a Scene: Fictional Narrative Rubric, p. 95
Writing Mini-Lesson: Description Rubric, p. 97

Guide for Reading

1. To read, comprehend, and interpret a legend
2. To relate a legend to personal experience
3. To recognize an author's attitude
4. To identify the features of a legend
5. To build vocabulary in context and learn the suffix -ous
6. To recognize and use the subjunctive mood
7. To write a letter of recommendation using clear and consistent purpose
8. To respond to the legend through writing, speaking and listening, and projects

SKILLS INSTRUCTION

Vocabulary:
Suffixes -ous

Grammar:
Subjunctive Mood

Reading Strategy:
Recognize an Author's Attitude

Literary Focus:
Legend

Writing:
Clear and Consistent Purpose

Speaking and Listening:
Oral Reading (teacher edition)

Critical Viewing:
Infer; Interpret; Draw Conclusions

PORTFOLIO OPPORTUNITIES

Writing: List; Epic Essay; Local Legends
Speaking and Listening: Music; Oral Reading
Projects: Art; Feudalism Chart

More About the Authors

Alfred, Lord Tennyson, who became Britain's Poet Laureate in 1850, also wrote about current events. One of his most famous poems, "The Charge of the Light Brigade," celebrated a British cavalry unit that made a brave but futile charge against Russians in the Battle of Balaclava during the Crimean War.

T. H. White's *The Sword and the Stone* (1938), was the first of five books that became *The Once and Future King,* the basis of a cartoon, a musical, and a film. The fifth book in the tetralogy, *The Book of Merlyn,* was published in 1977, thirteen years after T.H. White died. White's other works include the autobiographical *England Have My Bones* (1936).

Alfred, Lord Tennyson
(1809–1892)

The fourth son of twelve children, Tennyson was born in Lincolnshire, England. After preparing for college at his clergyman father's home, he attended Cambridge University for a few years, but strained family finances forced him to withdraw before receiving a degree. Living at home, he perfected his craft as a poet, experimenting with different poetic forms. From 1850 to his death, he enjoyed a popular and enthusiastic following for his exquisite short lyrics and powerful longer works. The subjects of his poems are widely drawn from the biblical and classical eras as well as events of his time. The "Morte d'Arthur" is the most famous excerpt from his epic *Idylls of the King,* a set of twelve narrative poems based on the Arthurian legends.

T. H. White
(1906–1964)

Terence Hanbury White's interesting life began in Bombay, India. At the age of thirty, he resigned his teaching position to devote himself to his many interests. These included flying airplanes, deep-sea diving, falconry, knitting, jumping horses, and, of course, writing. Many of these skills and hobbies later found their way into his writing. His most famous work, from which "Arthur Becomes King of Britain" is taken, is the four-part novel *The Once and Future King* (1958), a comic retelling of the Arthurian legends originally written down 500 years earlier by Sir Thomas Malory. *The Once and Future King* inspired the musical *Camelot* (1960) as well as the movie *Monty Python and the Holy Grail* (1974).

◆ Build Vocabulary

SUFFIXES: -OUS

In "Arthur Becomes King of Britain," one of the characters, a young man named Kay, in his preparations to be knighted, takes a *sumptuous* bath. *Sumptuous* combines the Latin word *sumptus,* meaning "expense," with the suffix -ous, which means "like" or "pertaining to." *Sumptuous,* which means "magnificent; splendid," pertains to the expense of something. There are dozens of other words with the suffix -ous, such as *slanderous* (relating to slander) and *adventurous* (relating to adventure).

WORD BANK

lamentation
swarthy
stickler
sumptuous
palfrey

As you read these selections, you will encounter the words in this list. Each word is defined on the page where it first appears. Preview the list before you read.

◆ Build Grammar Skills

SUBJUNCTIVE MOOD

As you read "Arthur Becomes King of Britain" and "Morte d'Arthur," you'll see examples of verbs in the **subjunctive mood**. The subjunctive mood has two purposes. The first is to state a wish or condition that is contrary to fact, usually in clauses beginning with *if, as if,* or *as though.*

The past subjunctive of the verb *be* is always *were,* not *was,* regardless of the subject:

> The Wart went as pale as Sir Kay was, and looked as if he *were* going to strike him.

The subjunctive mood is also used in clauses beginning with *that* to express, indirectly, a demand, recommendation, suggestion, or statement of necessity:

> To prove his worth, it was required that Wart *remove* the sword.

Here, the verb is always the base form. It does not change, regardless of the subject.

Prentice Hall Literature Program Resources

REINFORCE / RETEACH / EXTEND

Selection Support Pages
Build Vocabulary: Suffixes -ous, p. 253
Build Grammar Skills: Subjunctive Mood, p. 254
Reading Strategy: Author's Attitude, p. 255
Literary Focus: Legend, p. 256

Strategies for Diverse Students Needs
"Morte d'Arthur," "Arthur Becomes King," p. 62

Beyond Literature
Courage, Honesty, and Compassion, p. 62

Formal Assessment Selection Test, pp. 220–222;

Assessment Resources Software
Alternative Assessment, p. 62

Writing and Language Transparencies
Writing Process Model 9: Business Letter, pp. 61–64

Resource Pro CD-ROM "Morte d'Arthur," "Arthur Becomes King"—includes all resource materials and customizable lesson plan

Listening to Literature Audiocassettes
"Morte d'Arthur," "Arthur Becomes King"

Looking at Literature Videodisc
Chapter 10: "Morte d'Arthur"

Morte d'Arthur ◆ Arthur Becomes King of Britain

◆ *Literature and Your Life*

CONNECT YOUR EXPERIENCE
The heroes you admire reveal a great deal about what's important to you. Arthur's legend has made him a hero to many people to whom courage, honesty, and compassion are important.

Journal Writing List three people you see as heroes. Give at least two reasons why you consider each a hero.

THEMATIC FOCUS: FROM THE PAST
According to the legend, before Arthur formed the Round Table, knights went around fighting for the sake of fighting. The Arthurian tradition has given following generations a model for using strength for a good cause.

◆ Background for Understanding

HISTORY
The real King Arthur was most likely a British chieftain who defeated the Saxons in a decisive battle in A.D. 518. For years afterward, bards across England and Wales sang about his exploits. In 1138, Geoffrey of Monmouth celebrated Arthur's real and imagined triumphs in his *History of the Kings of Britain.* Around the same time, French troubadours elaborated on the tales by adding Lady Guinevere and the Knights of the Round Table. The enriched legends then returned to England, where Thomas Malory (1400–1471) reworked them in his *Le Morte d'Arthur* (French for "The Death of Arthur").

◆ Literary Focus

LEGEND
A **legend** is a popular story handed down for generations. Most legends have some basis in historical fact, which usually has become obscured or lost through centuries of retelling and embellishment. Artists, poets, screenwriters, and novelists often turn to legends for inspiration. T. H. White, for example, based his novel *The Once and Future King* on the Arthurian legends, and Alfred, Lord Tennyson uses the same source for his epic poem *The Idylls of the King.*

◆ Reading Strategy

RECOGNIZE AN AUTHOR'S ATTITUDE
All writers have a particular attitude toward their subjects. Recognizing the **author's attitude** will give you an insight into the work.

The author's attitude is the way he or she feels about the subject. This attitude is reflected in the way the author interprets and presents characters and events. If the author admires and respects the subject, for example, then the author will present the details in such a way that you, the reader, will also admire and respect the subject.

To recognize an author's attitude, notice the details and events the author chooses to present, and think about the message the author conveys—either directly or indirectly—through this information.

As you read "Morte d'Arthur" look for clues that show the author's serious and respectful attitude toward his subject. Then, as you read "Arthur Becomes King of Britain" consider how White's attitude is quite different.

Guide for Reading ◆ 893

Preparing for Standardized Tests

Grammar and Language The sentence completion portions of some standardized tests may contain items that are best completed in the subjunctive mood. For example, students may encounter a question like the following.

Choose the word or pair of words which, when substituted for the blank space, best completes the meaning of the sentence.

The dog, although friendly, looked as though it _____ aggressive. *(C)*

(A) was   (C) were

(B) was not   (D) were not

Lead students to understand that because the sentence is expressing a condition contrary to fact, answer C, which expresses the subjunctive mood, is correct.

Students who can recognize and understand the use of the subjunctive mood will be able to answer these types of questions correctly. For additional practice, use the Build Grammar Skills page in **Selection Support,** p. 254.

One-Minute Insight

A legend works on many levels. Readers may see the story of King Arthur as a saga of knights and battles or as a fantasy of wizards and magic. Tennyson stressed the affirmation of ageless moral principals such as goodness, honor, loyalty, honesty, and bravery. He lived when scientific speculation had cast doubts on religious matters. To him, it was important that Arthur shine forth as a beacon of moral goodness in an increasingly skeptical world.

He ties this ancient legend to his world by telling a story within a story: Several friends, while sitting around the fire on Christmas Eve, prevail upon the poet in the group to share his retelling of the Arthur legend. The poet finally agrees to share one portion of the story. He then tells the story of Arthur's death, and Sir Bedivere's obedience to the dying king's last request. Like the men around the fire, Bedivere mourns the passing of an age, the death of all that seems noble and true. As the tale winds to a close, Arthur's funeral barge floats away and the friends are roused from their rapt involvement in the tale. Tennyson ends on an optimistic note, with bells singing out a return of Arthur and what he represented.

❶ Clarification The author frames the telling of "Morte d'Arthur" in his own era. The poem opens late on Christmas Eve after the festivities are done. A group of friends is sad that in modern times the serious aspects of Christmas are neglected in favor of games and lighter interests. The friends include the narrator (Tennyson), Francis (Frank) Allen (the host), Holmes (a parson), and Everard Hall (the poet who will read his tale of King Arthur).

Comprehension Check ☑

❷ What reason does Hall give for thinking his books are of little value?
Styles and forms in poetry change over time, just as the creations of nature do. Hall thinks that his poems are old-fashioned and therefore not worth saving.

Morte d'Arthur

Alfred, Lord Tennyson

The Epic

At Francis Allen's on the Christmas eve—
The game of forfeits[1] done—the girls all kissed
Beneath the sacred bush[2] and passed away—
❶ The parson Holmes, the poet Everard Hall,
5   The host, and I sat round the wassail bowl,[3]
Then halfway ebbed; and there we held a talk,
How all the old honor had from Christmas gone,
Or gone or dwindled down to some odd games
In some odd nooks like this; till I, tired out
10 With cutting eights[4] that day upon the pond,
Where, three times slipping from the outer edge,
I bumped the ice into three several stars,
Fell in a doze; and half-awake I heard
The parson taking wide and wider sweeps,
15 Now harping on the church commissioners,
Now hawking at geology and schism;[5]
Until I woke, and found him settled down
Upon the general decay of faith
Right through the world: "at home was little left,
20 And none abroad; there was no anchor, none,
To hold by." Francis, laughing, clapped his hand
On Everard's shoulder, with "I hold by him."
"And I," quoth Everard, "by the wassail-bowl."
"Why yes," I said, "we knew your gift that way
25 At college; but another which you had—
I mean of verse (for so we held it then),
What came of that?" "You know," said Frank, "he burnt
His epic, his King Arthur, some twelve books"—
And then to me demanding why: "O, sir,
30 He thought that nothing new was said, or else
Something so said 'twas nothing—that a truth
Looks freshest in the fashion of the day;
God knows; he has a mint of reasons; ask.
It pleased *me* well enough." "Nay, nay," said Hall,
35 "Why take the style of those heroic times?
❷ For nature brings not back the mastodon,[6]
Nor we those times; and why should any man
Remodel models? these twelve books of mine

1. **forfeits** (fôr´ fits) *n*.: Game in which something is taken away as a penalty for making a mistake.
2. **sacred bush:** Mistletoe.
3. **wassail bowl** (wäs´ əl bōl´) *n*.: Punch bowl.

4. **cutting eights:** Ice-skating so that skates cut figure eights in the ice.

5. **schism** (siz´ əm) *n*.: Division within an organization, especially a church, because of a difference of opinion.

6. **mastodon** (mas´ tə dän) *n*.: Extinct animal resembling the elephant but larger.

Block Scheduling Strategies

Consider these suggestions to take advantage of extended class time:

- Before students begin reading, have them form discussion groups to exchange ideas on the attributes of a hero. They may then work on the Journal Writing activity in Literature and Your Life (p. 893). Encourage them to think of ways in which heroes are similar.
- Use the **Looking at Literature Videodisc**, Ch. 10, to give students medieval context in which to read these works.

- Suggest that students apply the Reading Strategy, Recognize an Author's Attitude, to these pages. Have them answer the Reading Strategy questions on page 915 and follow up with the Reading Strategy page in *Selection Support*, page 255.
- Show portions of *A Connecticut Yankee in King Arthur's Court, Camelot,* and *Monty Python and the Holy Grail*. Encourage students to compare plot details and authors' attitudes.

The Dream of Arthur in Avalon (detail), Sir Edward Burne-Jones, The Museo de Arte de Ponce, The Luis A. Ferré Foundation, Inc. Ponce, Puerto Rico

❸ Infer Elicit responses such as the following: *Arthur is mourned by several stately women, several of whom wear royal crowns. Their positions and expressions show grief, but they are formal, rather than natural. Arthur's passing appears as a ritual.*

Customize for
More Advanced Students
Ask students to suggest why a mid-nineteenth century parson might tie "geology" to a "decay of faith" (lines 13–22). *Students should recognize that geology represents science, which is often, but not necessarily, seen as being in opposition to religion and faith.*

 Looking at Literature Videodisc To provide students with background on medieval castles, play Chapter 10 of the videodisc. This segment provides an overview of the purpose and uses of castles during the Middle Ages. Have students discuss how castles function in the legend of King Arthur.

Chapter 10

❸ ▲ Critical Viewing What does this picture tell you about the circumstances of Arthur's death? [Infer]

Morte d'Arthur ◆ 895

🎵 **Humanities: Art**

The Dream of Arthur in Avalon by Sir Edward Burne-Jones.

It is not surprising that the British Pre-Raphaelite painter Sir Edward Coley Burne-Jones (1833–1898) chose this scene from Arthurian legend as a painting subject—he was known for his enthusiasm for the medieval. The subject of this painting is taken from Book xxi, Chapters 5 and 6, of Malory's *Morte d'Arthur*, in which Arthur,

mortally wounded, is transported into the vale of Avalon by the three queens, who are seen around Arthur's bed playing a Welsh harp.

Burne-Jones's dreamy, romantic "literary" style, executed in a flat technique, was effective not only in painting but in stained glass, tapestry, mosaic, and relief—all media that interested medieval artists as well.

Use this question for discussion:

What seems to be happening to King Arthur in this picture? How do you know? *Students might say that King Arthur is asleep or wounded and being tended by the queens, or they might answer more figuratively that he is about to embark on a journey to eternity. The concerned people surrounding him suggest that he is on his death bed. His dream might be of paradise.*

❶ Ask students to paraphrase this passage. *At the narrator's request Francis, the host, gets Hall's poem. Hall is persuaded to read his work aloud. After expressing doubt on the quality, Hall reads in a clear, resonant voice.*

◆ Reading Strategy

❷ Recognize an Author's Attitude Suggested response: The formal language and dramatic images seem to indicate that Tennyson's attitude toward this subject is reverent and respectful. The image of the broken cross in a ruined chapel is the author's way of creating the feeling that Arthur's defeat is also the defeat of goodness and virtue.

◆ Critical Thinking

❸ Speculate Invite students to conjecture why Arthur doubts that there shall be no "talk of knightly deeds" in the future. *All of Arthur's knights have been killed except for Sir Bedivere. With Arthur himself mortally wounded, the ways of preserving a world of brave and noble acts are about to vanish.*

◆ Critical Thinking

❹ Evaluate Invite students to consider how the use of modern words, like "wounded" and "helmet" in place of old-fashioned words such as "smitten" and "helm," would have affected this passage. *Suggested response: The old-fashioned words stress the gulf in time between the story of King Arthur and today. This kind of language gives the poem a solemn, serious tone.*

40　Were faint Homeric echoes,[7] nothing-worth,
　　Mere chaff and draff,[8] much better burnt." "But I,"
　　Said Francis, "picked the eleventh from this hearth,
　　And have it; keep a thing, its use will come.
　　I hoard it as a sugarplum for Holmes."
45　He laughed, and I, though sleepy, like a horse
　　That hears the corn-bin open, pricked my ears;
　　For I remembered Everard's college fame
　　When we were Freshmen. Then at my request
　　He brought it; and the poet, little urged,

❶
　　But with some prelude of disparagement,
50　Read, mouthing out his hollow o's and a's,
　　Deep-chested music, and to this result.

Morte d'Arthur

　　So all day long the noise of battle rolled
　　Among the mountains by the winter sea,
　　Until King Arthur's table, man by man,
55　Had fallen in Lyonnesse[9] about their lord,
　　King Arthur; then, because his wound was deep,
　　The bold Sir Bedivere uplifted him,
　　Sir Bedivere, the last of all his knights,
　　And bore him to a chapel nigh the field,
60　A broken chancel[10] with a broken cross,
　　That stood on a dark strait of barren land.
　　On one side lay the ocean, and on one
　　Lay a great water, and the moon was full.
　　Then spake King Arthur to Sir Bedivere:

❸
65　"The sequel of today unsolders[11] all
　　The goodliest fellowship of famous knights
　　Whereof this world holds record. Such a sleep
　　They sleep—the men I loved. I think that we
　　Shall never more, at any future time,
70　Delight our souls with talk of knightly deeds,
　　Walking about the gardens and the halls
　　Of Camelot, as in the days that were.
　　I perish by this people which I made—
　　Though Merlin sware that I should come again
75　To rule once more—but let what will be be,

❹
　　I am so deeply smitten through the helm[12]
　　That without help I cannot last till morn.
　　Thou therefore take my brand[13] Excalibur,
　　Which was my pride; for thou rememberest how
80　In those old days, one summer noon, an arm
　　Rose up from out the bosom of the lake,
　　Clothed in white samite,[14] mystic, wonderful,
　　Holding the sword—and how I rowed across
　　And took it, and have worn it, like a king;
85　And, wheresoever I am sung or told

896 ◆ *Epics and Legends*

7. Homeric echoes (hō mer´ ik ek´ ōs): Imitations of the poems of the Greek poet Homer (of about the eighth century B.C.).
8. chaff and draff: Anything worthless; dregs.

◆ Reading Strategy
❷ What is Tennyson's attitude toward his subject? How can you tell?

9. Lyonnesse (lī´ ə nes´): Legendary country off the southwestern coast of England, supposed to have sunk beneath the sea.
10. chancel (chan´ səl) *n.*: Part of a church around the altar.
11. unsolders (un säd´ ərs) *v.*: Separates.

12. helm: Helmet.

13. brand: Sword.

14. samite (sam´ īt) *n.*: Heavy silk fabric.

Speaking and Listening Mini-Lesson

Oral Reading
This mini-lesson supports the Speaking and Listening activity in the Idea Bank on page 916.

Introduce the Concept Ask students if they have heard poetry read aloud. Discuss elements of the reading that made it effective. Have students select a passage from "Morte d'Arthur" to present as an oral reading.

Develop Background To help students develop their oral readings, suggest that they do the following:

• Work by themselves in front of a mirror to polish gestures and expressions.

• Record their readings so they may listen for awkward spots to be improved for their final presentations.

• Work with partners, listening to each other's work and making suggestions to improve the presentations.

Apply the Information Have students present their readings. You might record the readings on audiotape so that students may listen to their own work and that of other class members.

Assess the Outcome Suggest that students assess their readings by using the Peer Assessment: Oral Interpretation on page 119 in the **Alternative Assessment** booklet.

In aftertime, this also shall be known.
But now delay not; take Excalibur,
And fling him far into the middle mere;[15]
Watch what thou seest, and lightly[16] bring me word."

90   To him replied the bold Sir Bedivere:
"It is not meet,[17] Sir King, to leave thee thus,
Aidless, alone, and smitten through the helm.
A little thing may harm a wounded man.
Yet I thy hest will all perform at full,[18]
95   Watch what I see, and lightly bring thee word."

        So saying, from the ruined shrine he stepped
And in the moon athwart the place of tombs,
Where lay the mighty bones of ancient men,
Old knights, and over them the sea wind sang
100   Shrill, chill, with flakes of foam. He, stepping down
By zigzag paths and juts of pointed rock,
Came on the shining levels of the lake.

        There drew he forth the brand Excalibur,
And o'er him, drawing it, the winter moon,
105   Brightening the skirts of a long cloud, ran forth
And sparkled keen with frost against the hilt;
For all the haft[19] twinkled with diamond sparks,
Myriads[20] of topaz lights, and jacinth work[21]
Of subtlest jewelry. He gazed so long
110   That both his eyes were dazzled, as he stood,
This way and that dividing the swift mind,
In act to throw; but at the last it seemed
Better to leave Excalibur concealed
There in the many-knotted water flags,[22]
115   That whistled still and dry about the marge.[23]
So strode he back slow to the wounded king.

        Then spake King Arthur to Sir Bedivere:
"Hast thou performed my mission which I gave?
What is it thou hast seen, or what hast heard?"
120   And answer made the bold Sir Bedivere:
"I heard the ripple washing in the reeds,
And the wild water lapping on the crag."

        To whom replied King Arthur, faint and pale:
"Thou hast betrayed thy nature and thy name,
125   Not rendering[24] true answer, as beseemed[25]
Thy fealty, nor like a noble knight;
For surer sign had followed, either hand,
Or voice, or else a motion of the mere.
This is a shameful thing for men to lie.
130   Yet now, I charge thee, quickly go again
As thou art lief and dear, and do the thing
I bade thee, watch, and lightly bring me word."

        Then went Sir Bedivere the second time
Across the ridge, and paced beside the mere,

15. mere (mir) *n.*: Lake.
16. lightly *adv.*: Quickly.

◆ Literary Focus

❺ How does Arthur's command add mystery to the legend?

17. meet *adj.*: Proper.
18. I thy hest will all perform at full: I will carry out your order completely.

19. haft *n.*: Handle or hilt of a sword.
20. myriads (mir′ e ədz) *n.*: Large numbers.
21. topaz (to′ paz) . . . **work**: Yellow and reddish-orange jewels.

22. water flags: Marsh plants.
23. marge (marj) *n.*: Edge.

24. rendering (ren′ dər iŋ) *v.*: Giving.
25. beseemed (bi sēməd′) *v.*: Was suitable to.

◆ **Literary Focus**

❺ Suggested response: *Arthur commands that he be told what happens after the sword is thrown into the lake. Readers' interest is heightened because his command indicates something unusual might happen.*

◆ **Critical Thinking**

❻ **Infer** Ask students what quality of Excalibur the author focuses on in this passage and what effect that quality has on Sir Bedivere. *Tennyson focuses on the bright colors of the jewels on the handle of the sword and describes the hypnotic effect the jewels have on Sir Bedivere.*

❼ **Clarification** King Arthur makes a play on words here. The name "Bedivere" means "of truth," or "truthful." Thus when Sir Bedivere lies about what he did with the sword, Arthur accuses him of betraying his name.

Customize for
English Language Learners
These students will need assistance with the style and wording of this poem. Help these students discover unfamiliar words that are repeated throughout the poem, such as *hast, wouldst, thou,* and *thee.* Lead students to use context clues and similarities to known words to recognize that that these words mean *has, would,* and *you.*

Morte d'Arthur ◆ 897

Cross-Curricular Connection: Social Studies

Chivalry in Medieval Times King Arthur and his retinue are thought of as advocates of *chivalry*—the code of behavior that was supposed to govern the actions of knights and nobles in the Middle Ages. The word comes from the French *chevalerie,* or mounted soldiers. The English word *cavalry* is derived from the same root.

The primary sources on the nature of chivalry are poems by eleventh and twelfth century minstrels in England and Europe.

These epics celebrated the deeds and character of idealized heroes. These heroes were deeply devout and ever ready to defend their faith, even with their lives. They protected the weak and helpless and fought evil and injustice. Most were devoted to particular women, in whose names they performed their gallantries.

Have interested students research the code of chivalry by which King Arthur and his knights lived. Then have them rewrite

and update that code to fit our times. Suggest to students that their revised codes of chivalry encompass the noblest human characteristics while also reflecting the realities of the time and place in which students live.

◆ Critical Thinking

❶ Compare and Contrast Have students explain how Bedivere's rationale for disobeying King Arthur's command differs from his previous one. *Previously Sir Bedivere had been too dazzled by the jeweled sword to speak at all. This time he can speak and says that it would be wrong to deprive the world of such a splendid object as Excalibur.*

◆ Build Grammar Skills

❷ Subjunctive Mood Ask students how many examples of the subjunctive mood occur in this passage (lines 143–147), what verb is used, and why the subjunctive mood is employed in each case. *There are three uses of the subjunctive mood: "if this were done," "Were it well to obey," "if a king demand." The first two uses describe situations that are contrary to fact; the third use expresses a demand.*

◆ *Literature and Your Life*

❸ Suggested response: *Societies preserve things that belonged to a hero as a way of cherishing his or her memory. People like to see things that belonged to heroes because it gives them a sense of being close to, or touched by, heroism themselves.*

◆ Literary Focus

❹ Legend Ask students if they have heard a different account of how Arthur acquired Excalibur. *Many students will have heard that they young Arthur discovered the sword lodged in a stone.* Ask students why the details of a legend may vary in different tellings. *Students should recognize that as legends are passed along, often orally, each new teller changes the story to one degree or another. If a story is told throught the generations, one area may end up with a version that is very different from the version in another area.*

---

135 Counting the dewy pebbles, fixed in thought;
But when he saw the wonder of the hilt,
How curiously and strangely chased,[26] he smote
His palms together, and he cried aloud:
    "And if indeed I cast the brand away;
140 Surely a precious thing, one worthy note,
Should thus be lost forever from the earth,
Which might have pleased the eyes of many men.
What good should follow this, if this were done?
What harm, undone? deep harm to disobey,
145 Seeing obedience is the bond of rule.
Were it well to obey then, if a king demand
An act unprofitable, against himself?
The king is sick, and knows not what he does.
What record, or what relic of my lord
150 Should be to aftertime, but empty breath
And rumors of a doubt? but were this kept,
Stored in some treasure-house of mighty kings,
Some one might show it at a joust of arms,
Saying, 'King Arthur's sword, Excalibur,
155 Wrought by the lonely maiden of the lake;
Nine years she wrought it, sitting in the deeps
Upon the hidden bases of the hills.'
So might some old man speak in the aftertime
To all the people, winning reverence;
160 But now much honor and much fame were lost."
    So spake he, clouded with his own conceit,
And hid Excalibur the second time,
And so strode back slow to the wounded king.
    Then spoke King Arthur, breathing heavily:
165 "What is it thou hast seen, or what hast heard?"
    And answer made the bold Sir Bedivere:
"I heard the water lapping on the crag,
And the long ripple washing in the reeds."
    To whom replied King Arthur, much in wrath:
170 "Ah, miserable and unkind, untrue,
Unknightly, traitor-hearted! Woe is me!
Authority forgets a dying king,
Laid widowed of the power in his eye
That bowed the will. I see thee what thou art,
175 For thou, the latest-left of all my knights,
In whom should meet the offices[27] of all,
Thou wouldst betray me for the precious hilt;
Either from lust of gold, or like a girl
Valuing the giddy pleasure of the eyes.
180 Yet, for a man may fail in duty twice,
And the third time may prosper, get thee hence;
But, if thou spare to fling Excalibur,
I will arise and slay thee with my hands."

898 ◆ *Epics and Legends*

---

26. chased *v.:* Decorated by engraving or embossing.

> ◆ *Literature and Your Life*
> Why do you think societies preserve the things that belong to a hero? Why do people like to see things that belonged to their heroes?

27. offices *n.:* Duties.

Humanities: Literature

The *Round Table* is a name that is used both as a designation for King Arthur's court and for a table where Arthur would sit with his knights. The earliest reference to this table is in a twelfth century historical chronicle in verse, *Le Roman de Brut*, by Wace, a Norman poet. He wrote that the king wanted the table to be round to prevent fighting among the knights for the seats of highest honor. At a round table, all seats were equal in prestige.

A description of the Round Table by an English priest, Layamon, says that it could seat 1,600 men and could be folded up and carried on horseback. Another version says that the table sat twelve and that one seat, the *siege perilous* (*siege* is French for "seat") was left empty. It was reserved for a knight who was pure enough to find the Holy Grail, the cup used by Jesus at the Last Supper. Suddenly, this legend has it, the name of Sir Galahad appeared on this chair, and he occupied it from then on. Galahad was one of the three knights who found the Grail. The others were Sir Bors and Sir Perceval (also known as Parsifal) Students might be interested in researching one of these three men and reporting their findings to the class.

Then quickly rose Sir Bedivere, and ran,
185 And, leaping down the ridges lightly, plunged
Among the bulrush beds,[28] and clutched the sword,
And strongly wheeled and threw it. The great brand
Made lightnings in the splendor of the moon,
And flashing round and round, and whirled in an arch,
190 Shot like a streamer of the northern morn,[29]
Seen where the moving isles of winter shock[30]
By night, with noises of the northern sea.
So flashed and fell the brand Excalibur;
But ere he dipped the surface, rose an arm
195 Clothed in white samite, mystic, wonderful,
And caught him by the hilt, and brandished him
Three times, and drew him under in the mere.
And lightly went the other to the king.
    Then spoke King Arthur, drawing thicker breath:
200 "Now see I by thine eyes that this is done.
Speak out; what is it thou hast heard, or seen?"
    And answer made the bold Sir Bedivere:
"Sir King, I closed mine eyelids, lest the gems
Should blind my purpose, for I never saw,
205 Nor shall see, here or elsewhere, till I die,
Not though I live three lives of mortal men,
So great a miracle as yonder hilt.
Then with both hands I flung him, wheeling him;
But when I looked again, behold an arm,
210 Clothed in white samite, mystic, wonderful,
That caught him by the hilt, and brandished him
Three times, and drew him under in the mere."
    And answer made King Arthur, breathing hard:
"My end draws nigh; 'tis time that I were gone.
215 Make broad thy shoulders to receive my weight,
And bear me to the margin,[31] yet I fear
My wound hath taken cold, and I shall die."
    So saying, from the pavement he half rose,
Slowly, with pain, reclining on his arm,
220 And looking wistfully with wide blue eyes
As in a picture. Him Sir Bedivere
Remorsefully regarded through his tears,
And would have spoken, but he found not words,
Then took with care, and kneeling on one knee,
225 O'er both his shoulders drew the languid hands,
And rising bore him through the place of tombs.
    But, as he walked, King Arthur panted hard,
Like one that feels a nightmare on his bed
When all the house is mute. So sighed the king,
230 Muttering and murmuring at his ear, "Quick, quick!
I fear it is too late, and I shall die."
But the other swiftly strode from ridge to ridge,

28. **bulrush** (bo͠ol´
rush) **beds:** Growth of
marsh plants.

29. **a streamer of the
northern morn:** North-
ern lights; the aurora
borealis.
30. **the moving isles
of winter shock:**
Icebergs crash.

◆ Literary Focus
6 What aspects of Sir
Bedivere's act are
typical of legends?

31. **margin** (mar´ jen)
n.: Edge.

Morte d'Arthur ◆ *899*

◆ Literary Focus

❶ Legend How do these details reflect Arthur's legendary status?

These mysterious women on a barge that appears on the lake from which Excalibur came create a sense of mystery and wonder. They must have some magical power to know of Arthur's death. His affiliation with these magical women makes Arthur seem larger than life.

◆ Build Grammar Skills

❷ Subjunctive Mood Ask students which verb in this passage (lines 251–253) indicates the use of the subjunctive mood and why the mood is employed here. *The verb is "were." The subjunctive mood is used here to state a condition that is contrary to fact. "As it were one voice" should be understood as "As if it were one voice, but it isn't."*

Customize for
Visual/Spatial Learners

❸ The passage that describes King Arthur being placed in the barge with three queens to attend him uses many phrases, including "his brow / striped with dark blood; his face was white / And colorless, and like the withered moon" that appeal to the sense of sight. Invite these students to create notes for a film version of this scene, in which they describe camera angles, lighting, and other approaches that would heighten the visual effects of this scene.

◆ Critical Thinking

❹ Connect Ask students to connect Sir Bedivere's lament to the conversation between the friends at the opening of the poem. *The friends at the beginning of the poem complain that the times have changed, that nothing is sacred anymore. Bedivere mourns the passing away of a noble, honorable time. He feels that all that is good and true has died with Arthur.*

Clothed with his breath, and looking, as he walked,
Larger than human on the frozen hills.
235　He heard the deep behind him, and a cry
Before. His own thought drove him like a goad.[32]
Dry clashed his harness[33] in the icy caves
And barren chasms, and all to left and right
The bare black cliff clanged round him, as he based
240　His feet on juts of slippery crag that rang
Sharp-smitten with the dint of armèd heels—
And on a sudden, lo! the level lake,
And the long glories of the winter moon.
　　　Then saw they how there hove a dusky barge,
245　Dark as a funeral scarf from stem to stern,
Beneath them; and descending they were ware
❶ That all the decks were dense with stately forms
Black-stoled,[34] black-hooded, like a dream—by these
Three queens with crowns of gold—and from them rose
250　A cry that shivered to the tingling stars,
And, as it were one voice, an agony
❷ Of lamentation, like a wind that shrills
All night in a waste land, where no one comes,
Or hath come, since the making of the world.
255　　　Then murmured Arthur, "Place me in the barge,"
And to the barge they came. There those three queens
Put forth their hands, and took the king, and wept.
But she that rose the tallest of them all
And fairest laid his head upon her lap,
260　And loosed the shattered casque,[35] and chafed his hands,
And called him by his name, complaining loud,
And dropping bitter tears against his brow
Striped with dark blood; for all his face was white
And colorless, and like the withered moon
265　Smote by the fresh beam of the springing east;
❸ And all his greaves and cuisses dashed with drops
Of onset;[36] and the light and lustrous curls—
That made his forehead like a rising sun
High from the dais-throne—were parched with dust;
270　Or, clotted into points and hanging loose,
Mixed with the knightly growth that fringed his lips.
So like a shattered column lay the king;
Not like that Arthur who, with lance in rest,
From spur to plume a star of tournament,
275　Shot through the lists at Camelot, and charged
Before the eyes of ladies and of kings.
　　　Then loudly cried the bold Sir Bedivere:
"Ah! my Lord Arthur, whither shall I go?
❹ Where shall I hide my forehead and my eyes?
280　For now I see the true old times are dead,
When every morning brought a noble chance,

900　◆　*Epics and Legends*

---

32. goad (gōd) *n.*: Sharp pointed stick used to drive oxen.
33. harness (har´ nis) *n.*: Armor.

34. black-stoled: Wearing long black scarves around their shoulders.

35. casque (kask) *n.*: Helmet.

36. greaves (grevz) **and cuisses** (kwis´ es) . . . **onset:** Armor for the legs below the knee and for the thigh spattered with blood from the battle.

◆ Build Vocabulary
lamentation (lam´ ən tā´ shən) *n.*: Mourning

Humanities: Art

Coats of Arms.

In the eleventh century, around the time when the Arthurian legend is supposed to have taken place, knights and nobles began to display coats of arms on shields and flags. These were symbolic identifications of themselves and their families. The original purpose of these coats of arms was to allow the knights' followers to identify them in battle.

Coats of arms, which often carried mottoes, were handed down over generations, and developed into an elaborate system. The study of coats of arms is called heraldry because it was the heralds, originally message bearers, who regulated and registered coats of arms in huge books called armorials. No two families could use the same design. Britain is the only country still to make use of these designs today.

Interested students might want to make a chart comparing coats of arms of some prominent medieval families. They can chart such information as the meaning of the symbols used, the mottoes carried, the colors used, and ways in which the coats of arms were personally connected to the families they identified. Encourage students to create their own coats of arms with symbols and colors that reflect their talents and abilities.

How Sir Bedivere Cast the Sword Excalibur Into the Water,
Aubrey Beardsley, Houghton Library, Harvard University

⑤ ▲ **Critical Viewing** This illustration depicts a significant moment in the Arthurian legend. What symbolic details does the illustrator include? What is their significance? **[Interpret]**

Morte d'Arthur ◆ 901

⑤ Interpret Elicit responses such as the following: *The illustration depicts the silk-clad arm taking the sword Excalibur into the lake. Sir Bedivere stands in a formal posture with his arm raised in a farewell salute. The darkness surrounding the scene suggests the serious and somber nature of this mysterious event.*

🎼 **Humanities: Art**

How Sir Bedivere Cast the Sword Excalibur Into the Water by Aubrey Beardsley.

Aubrey Beardsley (1872–1898) was a major figure in the 1890's art movement *Art Nouveau*, which was marked by the use of an elegant style, featuring flowing curves and elaborate decorative elements. Beardsley had a strong influence on this movement, a particularly high achievement considering he died of tuberculosis at the age of 25.

This illustration is one of 500 drawings by Beardsley for an edition of Sir Thomas Malory's fifteenth-century book, *Le Morte D'Arthur*, the source used by Tennyson for "The Idylls of the King."

Use this question for discussion:

How does this picture contrast with Tennyson's description of the event?

Students may say that Tennyson emphasizes *action and movement while the illustration presents a stylized, motionless scene. Also Tennyson's setting seems wilder, colder, and more barren than Beardsley's quiet lake surrounded by reeds and plants.*

◆ Critical Thinking

❶ Infer Invite students to suggest explanations for Sir Bedivere's gloomy forecast of his future. *Suggested response: Sir Bedivere had been part of a fellowship. Now that he is the last remaining Knight of the Round Table, he doubts that he can maintain their values and way of life by himself. He fears that he will be isolated in a world whose beliefs that are foreign to him.*

◆ Critical Thinking

❷ Interpret Ask: What does Arthur's answer mean, particularly the line "Lest one good custom should corrupt the world?" *Arthur sees that God has many ways of guiding people to a good, virtuous life. "...Lest one good custom should corrupt the world" means that God recognizes that even by following a good custom, people would get stuck and become unable to grow.*

◆ Critical Thinking

❸ Interpret Challenge students to interpret Arthur's words to Sir Bedivere. What does Arthur believe that Sir Bedivere should do in times to come? *Arthur advises Sir Bedivere to continue to practice the beliefs that the Round Table stood for by praying for his own soul and for those of his friends. This desire to pray is what distinguishes human beings from beasts.*

◆ Build Vocabulary

❹ Using the Suffix -ous Ask students how they would determine the meaning of the word "grievous." *The root of "grievous" is related to the word "grief." The suffix -ous means "like" or "pertaining to." Therefore, "grievous" means "pertaining to grief."*

◆ Literary Focus

❺ Legend Elicit responses like the following: *Like other legendary paradises, Avilion offers an escape from daily worries and pain; it is a place where all is fair and mild, a nurturing environment free of conflict.*

❻ Clarification The poet Everard Hall's retelling of the King Arthur legend ends here. The narrator switches to the original Christmas Eve setting at the beginning of the poem.

And every chance brought out a noble knight.
Such times have been not since the light that led
The holy Elders with the gift of myrrh.[37]
285   But now the whole ROUND TABLE is dissolved
Which was an image of the mighty world;
❶ And I, the last, go forth companionless,
And the days darken round me, and the years,
Among new men, strange faces, other minds."
290   And slowly answered Arthur from the barge:
❷ "The old order changeth, yielding place to new,
And God fulfills himself in many ways,
Lest one good custom should corrupt the world.
Comfort thyself: what comfort is in me?
295 I have lived my life, and that which I have done
May He within himself make pure! but thou,
If thou shouldst never see my face again,
Pray for my soul. More things are wrought by prayer
Than this world dreams of. Wherefore, let thy voice
300 Rise like a fountain for me night and day.
For what are men better than sheep or goats
❸ That nourish a blind life within the brain,
If, knowing God, they lift not hands of prayer
Both for themselves and those who call them friend?
305 For so the whole round earth is every way
Bound by gold chains about the feet of God.
But now farewell. I am going a long way
With these thou seest—if indeed I go—
For all my mind is clouded with a doubt—
310 To the island-valley of Avilion;[38]
Where falls not hail, or rain, or any snow,
Nor ever wind blows loudly, but it lies
Deep-meadowed, happy, fair with orchard lawns
And bowery[39] hollows crowned with summer sea,
315 **❹** Where I will heal me of my grievous wound."
     So said he, and the barge with oar and sail
Moved from the brink, like some full-breasted swan
that, fluting a wild carol ere her death,
Ruffles her pure cold plume, takes the flood
320 With swarthy webs. Long stood Sir Bedivere
Revolving many memories, till the hull
Looked one black dot against the verge of dawn,
And on the mere the wailing died away.

     Here ended Hall, and our last light, that long
325 **❻** Had winked and threatened darkness, flared and fell;
At which the parson, sent to sleep with sound,
And waked with silence, grunted "Good!" but we
Sat rapt:[40] it was the tone with which he read—
Perhaps some modern touches here and there

37. the light . . . of myrrh (mur): Star that guided the three Kings (the holy Elders) with their gift of incense (myrrh) to Bethlehem at the birth of Jesus.

38. island-valley of Avilion: Island paradise of Avalon where heroes were taken after death, according to Celtic mythology and medieval romances.

◆ Literary Focus
❺ How is Avilion similar to other legendary paradises?

39. bowery (bou´ ər ē) *adj.*: Enclosed by overhanging boughs of trees or by vines.

40. rapt *adj.*: Completely absorbed; engrossed.

◆ Build Vocabulary
swarthy (swôr´ *th*ē) *adj.*: Having a dark complexion

Cross-Curricular Connection: History

During the Middle Ages, types of armor changed as different kinds of warfare developed. In the twelfth century, the time of King Arthur, a knight's main protection was chain mail, or tiny metal rings, linked together. A coat of chain mail deflected arrows, swords, and lances. Metal helmets protected the head and face.

Chain mail, however, was vulnerable to thirteenth century weapons like longbows, maces, crossbows, and battle-axes. As a result, plate armor was introduced. It was designed to cover the entire body and included armored *gauntlets*, or gloves, and *sollerets*, or shoes. Although full-plate armor was secure, it had disadvantages. It severely limited movement. It was very expensive, costing as much as a farm. It was also heavy; a knight in full armor had to be hoisted onto his horse by a machine.

The invention of guns made plate armor obsolete. During the sixteenth century, only breastplates and helmets were still worn.

902

330 Redeemed[41] it from the charge of nothingness—
Or else we loved the man, and prized his work;
I know not; but we sitting, as I said,
The cock crew loud, as at that time of year
The lusty bird takes every hour for dawn.
335 Then Francis, muttering, like a man ill-used,
"There now—that's nothing!" drew a little back,
And drove his heel into the smoldered log,
That sent a blast of sparkles up the flue.
And so to bed, where yet in sleep I seemed
340 To sail with Arthur under looming shores,
Point after point; till on to dawn, when dreams
Begin to feel the truth and stir of day,
❼ To me, methought, who waited with the crowd,
There came a bark that, blowing forward, bore
345 King Arthur; like a modern gentleman
Of stateliest port;[42] and all the people cried,
"Arthur is come again: he cannot die."
Then those that stood upon the hills behind
Repeated—"Come again, and thrice as fair";
350 And, further inland, voices echoed—"Come
With all good things, and war shall be no more."
At this a hundred bells began to peal,
That with the sound I woke, and heard indeed
The clear church bells ring in the Christmas morn.

41. Redeemed
(ri dēmd') v.: Rescued
or saved.

42. of stateliest port:
Who carried himself in
a most majestic or
dignified manner.

❽ **◆ Reading Strategy**
Hall's story ends on
Christmas morning.
What does this tell
you about Tennyson's
attitude toward
Arthur?

Guide for Responding

◆ *Literature and Your Life*

Reader's Response What is your opinion
of Sir Bedivere's actions in response to Arthur's
request? Explain.

Thematic Focus How do Arthur's actions
in his final hours create a legacy of courage and
honor for the generations that follow?

☑ Check Your Comprehension

1. What occasion is being celebrated at the
start of the poem?
2. In the poem within the poem, what has
happened to King Arthur?
3. What does Arthur specifically request of
Sir Bedivere? How does Bedivere react?
4. Describe Arthur's departure.

◆ Critical Thinking
INTERPRET

1. What does Arthur say will soon be lost forever?
How, in lines 277–289, does Sir Bedivere echo
Arthur's feelings? **[Connect]**
2. What are Sir Bedivere's reasons for not throwing Excalibur into the lake? **[Interpret]**
3. Interpret Arthur's final words to Sir Bedivere.
[Interpret]

EVALUATE

4. Would this selection have a different effect if it
had been written in prose? Explain. **[Assess]**

APPLY

5. The modern novelist F. Scott Fitzgerald has
written, "Show me a hero and I will write you a
tragedy." Do you think that the Arthurian legend
is a tragedy? Explain your answer. **[Define]**

Morte d'Arthur ◆ *903*

903

One-Minute Insight

Legends are very adaptable. Where Tennyson sees Arthur as a heroic embodiment of ancient goodness and virtue, T.H. White views young Arthur in a more accessible way. Even figures of legend, he seems to say, are recognizably human. The characters in White's version of the Arthurian story are not stiff figures in an old-fashioned, still-life tableau. They live, breathe, and blunder. In fact, this excerpt from "The Once and Future King" tells how Arthur became king becasue Sir Kay forgot his sword.

◆ Reading Strategy

❶ Author's Attitude Recognizing the speech styles of the characters will help understand White's attitude toward them and toward his subject. Some of White's characters have speech patterns that reflect mannerisms of provincial English nobles of modern times, especially those with little education or culture. King Pellinore's constant use of "what" as an interjection is one example. Another is Sir Ector's habit of dropping the final g in words like "comin'" or "anythin.'" White seems to be poking fun at these characters.

❷ Clarification King Pellinore is the king of a northern part of Britain. He is describing the death of the renowned King Uther Pendragon, the Conqueror (Arthur's father and predecessor as King of England). The boy Wart is the young Arthur. Sir Ector is one of Uther's knights, and Sir Kay is his son.

Customize for
English Language Learners

Assist students in translating the Sergeant's dialect: "Nah" (Now), "fer" (for), "'is" (his), "lite" (late, or recently deceased), "awai" (away).

Arthur Becomes King of Britain

from The Once and Future King

T. H. White

King Pellinore arrived for the important weekend in a high state of flurry.

"I say," he exclaimed, "do you know? Have you heard? Is it a secret, what?"

❶ "Is what a secret, what?" they asked him.

"Why, the King," cried his majesty. "You know, about the King?"

"What's the matter with the King?" inquired Sir Ector. "You don't say he's comin' down to hunt with those darned hounds of his or anythin' like that?"

❷ "He's dead," cried King Pellinore tragically. "He's dead, poor fellah, and can't hunt any more."

Sir Grummore stood up respectfully and took off his cap.

"The King is dead," he said. "Long live the King."

Everybody else felt they ought to stand up too, and the boys' nurse burst into tears.

"There, there," she sobbed. "His loyal highness dead and gone, and him such a respectful gentleman. Many's the illuminated picture I've cut out of him, from the Illustrated Missals, aye, and stuck up over the mantel. From the time when he was in swaddling bands,[1] right through them world towers till he was a-visiting the dispersed areas as the world's Prince Charming, there

---

1. **swaddling bands:** Long, narrows bands of cloths wrapped around a newborn baby in former times.

904 ◆ *Epics and Legends*

wasn't a picture of 'im but I had it out, aye, and give 'im a last thought o' nights."

"Compose yourself, Nannie," said Sir Ector.

"It is solemn, isn't it?" said King Pellinore, "what? Uther the Conqueror, 1066 to 1216."

"A solemn moment," said Sir Grummore. "The King is dead. Long live the King."

"We ought to pull down the curtains," said Kay, who was always a <u>stickler</u> for good form, "or half-mast[2] the banners."

"That's right," said Sir Ector. "Somebody go and tell the sergeant-at-arms."

It was obviously the Wart's duty to execute this command, for he was now the junior nobleman present, so he ran out cheerfully to find the sergeant. Soon those who were left in the solar[3] could hear a voice crying out, "Nah then, one-two, special mourning fer 'is lite majesty, lower awai on the command Two!" and then the flapping of all the standards, banners, pennons, pennoncells, banderolls, guidons, streamers and cognizances[4] which made gay the

---

2. **half-mast** (haf mast´) *v.*: Hang a flag at half-mast.
3. **solar** (so´ lər) *n.*: Here, sun room. Solar is often used as an adjective.
4. **standards . . . cognizances** (kag´ nə zən´ səz) *n.*: Banners or flags.

◆ Build Vocabulary

stickler (stik´ lər) *n.*: Person who insists uncompromisingly on the observance of something specified

---

Cross-Curricular Connection: History

During the Middle Ages, if a young boy of good family wished to be a *knight* (boys of the lower classes could not hope for this honor), he left home at the age of seven to serve in another noble household as a *page*. He studied the rules of knightly behavior and the use of small weapons. At the age of fifteen, he became a *squire* (Arthur is Sir Kay's squire), serving as a knight's valet and learning to fight on horseback. He would accompany his knight into battle and fight by his side. After five years, the squire would be eligible for knighthood.

Knighthood could be conferred by any knight. There was little ceremony involved at first. The knight helped the squire into his armor and proclaimed his new status. The ceremony later grew more elaborate. Two knights took part, and a new knight was tapped on the back with a sword. Later still, knighthood took on more of a religious character, and knights-to-be had to keep an all-night vigil in church, fasting and praying, and swearing to follow the dictates of the Church.

▶**Critical Viewing**◀
❹ **Draw Conclusions** Suggested response: *Judging from T.H. White's attitude towards the formality of court life to this point, which he mocks by giving events an absurd twist, he would probably poke fun of the stateliness of the occasion.*

◆ **Reading Strategy**

❺ **Recognize an Author's Attitude** First, be sure that students are aware of malapropisms like "hair" (for heir) and "next of skin" (for next of kin) and the confusion caused by the constant interjection of "what." Then elicit responses such as the following: *The comic use of language suggests that White has a humorous attitude and does not take his subject terribly seriously at this point.*

❻ **Clarification** "Gramarye" is another name for England.

The Crowning of Arthur, Royal MS, by permission of the British Library

snowy turrets of the Forest Sauvage.

"How did you hear?" asked Sir Ector.

"I was pricking through the purlieus[5] of the forest after that Beast, you know, when ❸ I met with a solemn friar of orders gray, and he told me. It's the very latest news."

"Poor old Pendragon," said Sir Ector.

"The King is dead," said Sir Grummore solemnly. "Long live the King."

"It is all very well for you to keep on mentioning that, my dear Grummore," exclaimed King Pellinore petulantly, "but who is this King, what, that is to live so long, what, accordin' to you?"

"Well, his heir," said Sir Grummore, rather taken aback.

"Our blessed monarch," said the Nurse tearfully, "never had no hair. Anybody that

---

5. **purlieus** (pur′ lōōz) *n*.: Outlying part of a forest, exempted from forest laws.

▲ **Critical Viewing** Based on what you've read so far, how do you think T. H. White would feel about the formality and ceremony of this coronation scene? **[Draw Conclusions]** ❹

studied the loyal family knowed that."

"Good gracious!" exclaimed Sir Ector. "But he must have had a next-of-kin?"

"That's just it," cried King Pellinore in high excitement. "That's the excitin' part of it, what? No hair and no next of skin, and who's to succeed to the throne? That's what my friar was so excited about, what, and why he was asking who could succeed to what, what? What?"

"Do you mean to tell me," exclaimed Sir Grummore indignantly, "that there ain't no King of Gramarye?" ❻

◆ **Reading Strategy**
What does Pellinore's way of speaking tell you about the author's attitude toward him? ❺

Arthur Becomes King of Britain ◆ 905

Humanities: Art

The Crowning of Arthur (Royal MS).

This page of an illuminated manuscript shows Arthur being crowned. Although the drawing style is simple, even somewhat cartoonish, the illustration depicts a stately occasion. The most important figure, next to Arthur himself, is a Bishop. The Bishop is recognized by his pointed headdress, or miter, and his robes. Thus, one important aspect of the coronation is that it is approved by the Church. Arthur holds a scepter, which symbolizes his authority over worldly affairs. The other

onlookers represent the acceptance of Arthur by his new subjects.

Use this question for discussion: Does this illustration show what you would expect to see at a coronation ritual? Why or why not? *Students might respond that they would expect to see more luxurious clothing and jewels at a coronation, but the ritual of the Bishop placing the crown upon the king, who is holding a scepter, and the expressions of the eager onlookers would all probably be what students would expect to see.*

1 Clarification Characters sometimes lapse into old-fashioned, stylized language, like "signs and wonders of no mean might." This suggests that King Pellinore may be repeating something he has heard from someone else, possibly from a "solemn friar of orders grey." This formal language suggests the importance of the news.

◆ **Reading Strategy**

2 Recognize an Author's Attitude Ask student show this description of the sword in the stone shows the author's attitude toward King Pellinore. *Suggested response: Pellinore's muddled description is a sign that the author wants to portray Pellinore as a comic character, somewhat limited in brain power.*

◆ **Critical Thinking**

3 Infer Invite students to suggest what the effect is of Sir Grummore's reaction to the description of the sword in the stone. *Sir Grummore's indignant response—that the appearance of the sword is possibly the work of "agitators"—is a humorous device that gently pokes fun at the image of Excalibur, which is usually shown in a more solemn way.*

◆ **Build Vocabulary**

4 Using the Suffix -ous Challenge students to explain how they would figure out the meaning of the word piteously. *First drop the second suffix -ly (they will add it again at the end). Then note that the root of the word is pity. The suffix -ous means "like" or "pertaining to." Thus "piteous" means "pertaining to pity," or "pathetic," and "piteously" means "pathetically."*

◆ **Literary Focus**

5 Legend *Suggested response: The formal, old-fashioned language points up the ancient origin of the legend, and creates an amusing contrast to the everyday, comic world that most of the characters inhabit.*

1 "Not a scrap of one," cried King Pellinore, feeling important. "And there have been signs and wonders of no mean might."

"I think it's a scandal," said Sir Grummore. "God knows what the dear old country is comin' to."

"What sort of signs and wonders?" asked Sir Ector.

2 "Well, there has appeared a sort of sword in a stone, what, in a sort of a church. Not in the church, if you see what I mean, and not in the stone, but that sort of thing, what, like you might say."

"I don't know what the Church is coming to," said Sir Grummore.

"It's in an anvil,"[6] explained the King.

"The Church?"

"No, the sword."

"But I thought you said the sword was in the stone?"

"No," said King Pellinore. "The stone is outside the Church."

"Look here, Pellinore," said Sir Ector. "You have a bit of a rest, old boy, and start again. Here, drink up this horn of mead[7] and take it easy."

"The sword," said King Pellinore, "is stuck through an anvil which stands on a stone. It goes right through the anvil and into the stone. The anvil is stuck to the stone. The stone stands outside a church. Give me some more mead."

3 "I don't think that's much of a wonder," remarked Sir Grummore. "What I wonder at is that they should allow such things to happen. But you can't tell nowadays, what with all these Saxon agitators."[8]

"My dear fellah," cried Pellinore, getting excited again, "it's not where the stone is, what, that I'm trying to tell you, but what is written on it, what, where it is."

"What?"

---

6. **anvil** (an´ vəl) *n.*: Iron or steel block.
7. **mead** (mēd) *n.*: Drink made of fermented honey and water, often with spices or fruit added.
8. **Saxon** (sak´ sən) **agitators**: Ancient Germanic people who conquered parts of England.

906 ◆ *Epics and Legends*

"Why, on its pommel."[9]

"Come on, Pellinore," said Sir Ector. "You just sit quite still with your face to the wall for a minute, and then tell us what you are talkin' about. Take it easy, old boy. No need for hurryin'. You sit still and look at the wall, there's a good chap, and talk as slow as you can."

4 "There are words written on this sword in this stone outside this church," cried King Pellinore piteously, "and these words are as follows. Oh, do try to listen to me, you two, instead of interruptin' all the time about nothing for it makes a man's head go ever so."

"What are these words?" asked Kay.

"These words say this," said King Pellinore, "so far as I can understand from that old friar of orders gray."

"Go on, do," said Kay, for the King had come to a halt.

"Go on," said Sir Ector, "what do these words on this sword in this anvil in this stone outside this church, say?"

King Pellinore closed his eyes tight, extended his arms in both directions, and announced in capital letters, "Whoso Pulleth Out This Sword of this Stone and Anvil, is Rightwise King Born of All England."

◆ **Literary Focus**
What do formal words like these contribute to the legend?

5

"Who said that?" asked Sir Grummore.

"But the sword said it, like I tell you."

"Talkative weapon," remarked Sir Grummore skeptically.

"It was written on it," cried the King angrily. "Written on it in letters of gold."

"Why didn't you pull it out then?" asked Sir Grummore.

"But I tell you that I wasn't there. All this that I am telling you was told to me by that friar I was telling you of, like I tell you."

---

9. **pommel** (pum´ əl) *n.*: Round knob on the end of the hilt of some swords.

 Humanities: Literature

The first known reference to King Arthur appeared in *Gododdin*, a seventh-century Welsh poem. The reference was noted by Nennius, a Welsh chronicler, in his *Historia Britonum* (A.D. 900). In the next few centuries, Arthur became a popular figure in Britain and Brittany in France. His stature grew in French Breton tales until he was seen as a great ruler and warlord. By the twelfth century, Britain had made him a national folk hero.

In Geoffrey of Monmouth's *Historia regum Britanniae* (1137), Arthur is shown as the master of a great empire. Tales of Arthur and his court spread all over Europe. A French poet, Chretien de Troyes, wrote romances focusing on Sir Lancelot and Sir Perceval. German poets added more Arthurian literature. Wolfram von Eschenbach wrote *Parzifal*, and Gottfried von Strassburg created the story of Tristan and Isolde.

In writing *Le Morte D'Arthur*, Sir Thomas Malory used these different stories to create the first comprehensive account of the legend in English. Malory's work has served as the basis for most Arthurian literature since that time.

"Has this sword with this inscription been pulled out?" inquired Sir Ector.

"No," whispered King Pellinore dramatically. "That's where the whole excitement comes in. They can't pull this sword out at all, although they have all been tryin' like fun, and so they have had to proclaim a tournament all over England, for New Year's Day, so that the man who comes to the tournament and pulls out the sword can be King of all England forever, what, I say."

"Oh, father," cried Kay. "The man who pulls the sword out of the stone will be the King of England. Can't we go to the tournament, father, and have a shot?"

"Couldn't think of it," said Sir Ector.

"Long way to London," said Sir Grummore, shaking his head.

"My father went there once," said King Pellinore.

Kay said, "Oh, surely we could go? When I am knighted I shall have to go to a tournament somewhere, and this one happens at just the right date. All the best people will be there, and we should see the famous knights and great kings. It does not matter about the sword, of course, but think of the tournament, probably the greatest there has ever been in Gramarye, and all the things we should see and do. Dear father, let me go to this tourney, if you love me, so that I may bear away the prize of all, in my maiden fight."

❻

"But, Kay," said Sir Ector, "I have never been to London."

"All the more reason to go. I believe that anybody who does not go for a tournament like this will be proving that he has no noble blood in his veins. Think what people will say about us, if we do not go and have a shot at that sword. They will say that Sir Ector's family was too vulgar and knew it had no chance."

"We all know the family has no chance," said Sir Ector, "that is, for the sword."

"Lot of people in London," remarked Sir Grummore, with a wild surmise. "So they say."

He took a deep breath and goggled at his host with eyes like marbles.

"And shops," added King Pellinore suddenly, also beginning to breathe heavily.

"Dang it!" cried Sir Ector, bumping his horn mug on the table so that it spilled. "Let's all go to London, then, and see the new King!"

❼

They rose up as one man.

"Why shouldn't I be as good a man as my father?" exclaimed King Pellinore.

"Dash it all," cried Sir Grummore. "After all, it is the capital!"

"Hurray!" shouted Kay.

"Lord have mercy," said the nurse.

At this moment the Wart came in with Merlyn, and everybody was too excited to notice that, if he had not been grown up now, he would have been on the verge of tears.

"Oh, Wart," cried Kay, forgetting for the moment that he was only addressing his squire, and slipping back into the familiarity of their boyhood. "What do you think? We are all going to London for a great tournament on New Year's Day!"

"Are we?"

"Yes, and you will carry my shield and spears for the jousts, and I shall win the palm[10] of everybody and be a great knight!"

"Well, I am glad we are going," said the Wart, "for Merlyn is leaving us too."

"Oh, we shan't need Merlyn."

"He is leaving us," repeated the Wart.

"Leavin' us?" asked Sir Ector. "I thought it was we that were leavin'?"

"He is going away from the Forest Sauvage."

Sir Ector said, "Come now, Merlyn, what's all this about? I don't understand all this a bit."

"I have come to say Goodbye, Sir Ector,"

❽

---

10. **win the palm:** Be the winner. A palm leaf is a symbol of victory.

Arthur Becomes King of Britain ◆ 907

1 Infer Have students explain why they think White has Sir Ector suggest that Merlyn remain and become a librarian. *Sample answer: Ector is shown to be shallow because he cannot appreciate Merlyn's unusual powers. Thus he suggests that Merlyn take up a limited clerical job.*

▶**Critical Viewing**◀

2 Suggested answer: *The responses of the surrounding people, pointing and raising their hands in surprise, indicate the young man is performing an amazing feat.*

Gallahad's Sword in Stone, Royal MS, by permission of the British Library

said the old magician. "Tomorrow my pupil Kay will be knighted, and the next week my other pupil will go away as his squire. I have outlived my usefulness here, and it is time to go."

"Now, now, don't say that," said Sir Ector. "I think you're a jolly useful chap whatever happens. You just stay and teach me, or be the librarian or something. Don't you leave an

▲ Critical Viewing How can you tell that the young man in this picture is performing an amazing feat? [Infer] **2**

old man alone, after the children have flown."

"We shall all meet again," said Merlyn. "There is no cause to be sad."

"Don't go," said Kay.

"I must go," replied their tutor. "We have had a good time while we were young, but it

908 ◆ *Epics and Legends*

Humanities: Art

Gallahad's Sword in Stone (Royal MS).

This illuminated manuscript shows the act of pulling a sword from a stone, one element of the legendary story. In the selection, Arthur becomes King after he removes the sword from the stone. Therefore, students may wonder why Galahad is portrayed here as removing the sword. In legend, Galahad (Lancelot's son) successfully

repeated Arthur's feat. The circumstances were slightly different for Galahad's attempt, as the stone was floating in a river when he removed the sword. The drama of the moment is highlighted by an attentive audience, including a king and queen.

Use this question for discussion: Does the character pulling the sword from the stone seem aware of the magnitude of

his feat? What features of this picture help you to answer this question? *Students might observe that the character has a mild, even casual expression on his face, indicating he is not aware of the magnitude of his feat. Although he is pulling the sword with both hands, he does not appear to be expending huge amounts of strength or energy.*

◆ **Reading Strategy**

❸ **Recognize an Author's Attitude** Invite students to describe the author's attitude toward Merlyn in this passage. *Suggested response: Even though Merlyn shows his magical powers by vanishing, the author downplays Merlyn's feat as if it were an everyday occurrence. His attitude toward Merlyn seems distant and matter-of-fact.*

is in the nature of Time to fly. There are many things in other parts of the kingdom which I ought to be attending to just now, and it is a specially busy time for me. Come, Archimedes, say Goodbye to the company.'

"Goodbye," said Archimedes tenderly to the Wart.

"Goodbye," said the Wart without looking up at all.

"But you can't go," cried Sir Ector, "not without a month's notice."

"Can't I?" replied Merlyn, taking up the position always used by philosophers who propose to dematerialize. He stood on his toes, while Archimedes held tight to his shoulder—began to spin on them slowly like a top—spun faster and faster till he was only a blur of grayish light— and in a few seconds there was no one there at all.

"Goodbye, Wart," cried two faint voices outside the solar window.

"Goodbye," said the Wart for the last time— and the poor fellow went quickly out of the room.

◆ *Literature and Your Life*

❹ What qualities do you admire in Wart? What qualities do you not admire?

The knighting took place in a whirl of preparations. Kay's sumptuous bath had to be set up in the box room, between two towel-horses and an old box of selected games which contained a worn-out straw dart-board—it was called fléchette in those days—because all the other rooms were full of packing. The nurse spent the whole time constructing new warm pants for everybody, on the principle that the climate of any place outside the Forest Sauvage must be treacherous to the ex-

◆ **Build Vocabulary**

sumptuous (sump´ chōō əs) *adj.*: Magnificent

treme, and, as for the sergeant, he polished all the armor till it was quite brittle and sharpened the swords till they were almost worn away.

At last it was time to set out.

Perhaps, if you happen not to have lived in the Old England of the twelfth century, or whenever it was, and in a remote castle on the borders of the Marshes at that, you will find it difficult to imagine the wonders of their journey.

The road, or track, ran most of the time along the high ridges of the hills or downs, and they could look down on either side of them upon the desolate marshes where the snowy reeds sighed, and the ice crackled, and the duck in the red sunsets quacked loud on the winter air. The whole country was like that. Perhaps there would be a moory marsh on one side of the ridge, and a forest of a hundred thousand acres on the other, with all the great branches weighted in white. They could sometimes see a wisp of smoke among the trees, or a huddle of buildings far out among the impassable reeds, and twice they came to quite respectable towns which had several inns to boast of, but on the whole it was an England without civilization. The better roads were cleared of cover for a bow-shot on either side of them, lest the traveler should be slain by hidden thieves.

They slept where they could, sometimes in the hut of some cottager who was prepared to welcome them, sometimes in the castle of a brother knight who invited them to refresh themselves, sometimes in the firelight and fleas of a dirty little hovel with a bush tied to a pole outside it—this was the signboard used at that time by inns—and once or twice on the open ground, all huddled together for warmth between their grazing chargers. Wherever they went and wherever they slept, the east wind whistled in the reeds, and the geese went over high in the starlight, honking at the stars.

◆ *Literature and Your Life*

❹ Some students may admire Wart's sensitivity, others may see it as a sign of weakness. Encourage students to identify Wart's goodbye to Merlyn with a difficult parting they have experienced.

◆ **Build Vocabulary**

❺ **The Suffix -ous** Challenge students to explain how they can determine the definition of the word *treacherous*. *The word root is related to the word treachery. The suffix -ous means "like," or "pertaining to." "Treacherous," then, means "pertaining to treachery," or, in this context, "untrustworthy."*

◆ **Reading Strategy**

❻ **Recognize an Author's Attitude** What attitude is revealed by this description of the places where the travelers stayed? *An author may show his or her attitude toward a subject through contrast. Here there is a huge contrast between images commonly associated with a group of nobles on a journey, such as luxurious housing and fine food and the barren, scruffy, even squalid images the author presents. The contrast makes it clear that the author is making fun of the crude conditions that he sees as common in the provinces of Britain of that time.*

Looking at Literature Videodisc Follow up on the Enrichment note at the bottom of this page by showing Chapter 10 of the Looking at Literature Videodisc. This feature gives background on the uses and purposes of medieval castles.

Enrichment

At the time when the story of King Arthur takes place, kings lived in *castles*, fortified structures that housed the king and his retainers, stored food and arms, served as a prison, and protected the local population in the event of an attack.

A castle sat on high ground. If the land was flat, an artificial hill, or *motte*, was built. It was ringed by a water-filled ditch, or *moat*, crossed by a *drawbridge* that could be raised from inside the castle. The high stone walls were up to thirty feet thick, with platforms on top from which defenders could fight off attackers. Inside the outer wall was a courtyard, or *bailey*. Within the bailey

stood a tall tower known as a *keep*, or *donjon*— the strongest point.

Attackers might attempt a *siege* and starve a castle's occupants into surrender. They could try to tunnel under the walls or knock the heavy wooden doors down with a battering ram. Tall wooden towers might be pushed against the castle walls to enable soldiers to swarm onto the platforms. A stone castle was nearly invulnerable to attack, however, until the appearance of guns during the 1400's, at which point stone fortifications ceased to be effective.

ondon was full to the brim. If Sir Ector had not been lucky enough to own a little land in Pie Street, on which there stood a respectable inn, they would have been hard put to it to find a lodging. But he did own it, and as a matter of fact drew most of his dividends from that source, so they were able to get three beds between the five of them. They thought themselves fortunate.

On the first day of the tournament, Sir Kay managed to get them on the way to the lists at least an hour before the jousts could possibly begin. He had lain awake all night, imagining how he was going to beat the best barons in England, and he had not been able to eat his breakfast. Now he rode at the front of the cavalcade, with pale cheeks, and Wart wished there was something he could do to calm him down.

For country people, who only knew the dismantled tilting ground[11] of Sir Ector's castle, the scene which met their eyes was ravishing. It was a huge green pit in the earth, about as big as the arena of a football match. It lay ten feet lower than the surrounding country, with sloping banks, and the snow had been swept off it. It had been kept warm with straw, which had been cleared off that morning, and now the close-worn grass sparkled green in the white landscape. Round the arena there was a world of color so dazzling and moving and twinkling as to make one blink one's eyes. The wooden grandstands were painted in scarlet and white. The silk pavilions of famous people, pitched on every side, were azure and green and saffron and checkered. The pennons and pennoncells which floated everywhere in the sharp wind were flapping with every color of the rainbow, as they strained and slapped at their flagpoles, and the barrier down the middle of the arena

itself was done in chessboard squares of black and white. Most of the combatants and their friends had not yet arrived, but one could see from those few who had come how the very people would turn the scene into a bank of flowers, and how the armor would flash, and the scalloped sleeves of the heralds jig in the wind, as they raised their brazen trumpets to their lips to shake the fleecy clouds of winter with joyances[12] and fanfares.

"Good heavens!" cried Sir Kay. "I have left my sword at home."

"Can't joust without a sword," said Sir Grummore. "Quite irregular."

"Better go and fetch it," said Sir Ector. "You have time."

"My squire will do," said Sir Kay. "What an awful mistake to make! Here, squire, ride hard back to the inn and fetch my sword. You shall have a shilling[13] if you fetch it in time."

The Wart went as pale as Sir Kay was, and looked as if he were going to strike him. Then he said, "It shall be done, master," and turned his ambling <u>palfrey</u> against the stream of newcomers. He began to push his way toward their hostelry[14] as best he might.

"To offer me money!" cried the Wart to himself. "To look down at this beastly little donkey-affair off his great charger and to call me Squire! Oh, Merlyn, give me patience with the brute, and stop me from throwing his filthy shilling in his face."

When he got to the inn it was closed. Everybody had thronged to see the famous tournament, and the entire household had followed after the mob. Those were lawless days and it was not safe to leave your house—or even to go to sleep in it—unless you were certain that it was impregnable.[15]

---

11. **tilting ground:** Ground on which a joust takes place.

12. **joyances** (joi´ əns iz) *n.:* Old word for *rejoicing.*
13. **shilling** (shil´ in) *n.:* British silver coin.
14. **hostelry** (has´ təl rē) *n.:* Inn.
15. **impregnable** (im preg´ nə bəl) *adj.:* Not capable of being entered by force.

910 ◆ *Epics and Legends*

Cross-Curricular Connection: History

A tournament such as the one to which Arthur and his companions go in this story is quite different from the tournaments staged by knights in the 1100's. In these events, a large number of knights would form two "armies" that would fight each other, often for several days, and over large expanses of territory. Often, large sums of money were wagered on the outcome.

Kings grew to dislike these tournaments; when a number of armed knights gathered together, there was always a possibility of rebellion. Also, such mock battles usually resulted in the destruction of property, and people might be injured or even killed.

By the 1200's, a milder kind of tournament evolved, like the one in which Sir Kay hopes to compete. Knights would *joust*, or

fight with blunted weapons. They also engaged in *tilting*. In this competition, two mounted knights with lances would charge each other in narrow lanes, or *lists*, on either side of a wooden barrier and attempt to knock each other from their horses. Injuries and deaths might occur, but the newer form of tournament proved to be very popular, and considerably safer.

The wooden shutters bolted over the downstairs windows were two inches thick, and the doors were double-barred.

"Now what do I do," asked the Wart, "to earn my shilling?"

He looked ruefully at the blind little inn, and began to laugh.

"Poor Kay," he said. "All that shilling stuff was only because he was scared and miserable, and now he has good cause to be. Well, he shall have a sword of some sort if I have to break into the Tower of London.

"How does one get hold of a sword?" he continued. "Where can I steal one? Could I waylay some knight even if I am mounted on an ambling pad, and take his weapons by force? There must be some swordsmith or armorer in a great town like this, whose shop would be still open."

He turned his mount and cantered off along the street. There was a quiet churchyard at the end of it, with a kind of square in front of the church door. In the middle of the square there was a heavy stone with an anvil on it, and a fine new sword was stuck through the anvil.

"Well," said the Wart, "I suppose it is some sort of war memorial, but it will have to do. I am sure nobody would grudge Kay a war memorial, if they knew his desperate straits"

He tied his reins round a post of the lych gate,[16] strode up the gravel path, and took hold of the sword.

"Come, sword," he said. "I must cry your mercy and take you for a better cause.

"This is extraordinary," said the Wart. "I feel strange when I have hold of this sword, and I notice everything much more clearly."

___

16. **lych** (lich) **gate:** Roofed gate at the entrance to a churchyard.

◆ Build Vocabulary

palfrey (pôl′ frē) *n*.: Saddle horse, especially one for a woman

Look at the beautiful gargoyles[17] of the church, and of the monastery which it belongs to. See how splendidly all the famous banners in the aisle are waving. How nobly that yew[18] holds up the red flakes of its timbers to worship God. How clean the snow is. I can smell something like sweet briar—and is it music that I hear?"

It was music, whether of pan-pipes or of recorders, and the light in the churchyard was so clear, without being dazzling, that one could have picked a pin out twenty yards away.

"There is something in this place," said the Wart. "There are people. Oh, people, what do you want?"

Nobody answered him, but the music was loud and the light beautiful.

"People," cried the Wart, "I must take this sword. It is not for me, but for Kay. I will bring it back."

There was still no answer, and Wart turned back to the anvil. He saw the golden letters, which he did not read, and the jewels on the pommel, flashing in the lovely light.

"Come, sword," said the Wart.

He took hold of the handles with both hands, and strained against the stone. There was a melodious consort[19] on the recorders, but nothing moved.

The Wart let go of the handles, when they were beginning to bite into the palms of his hands, and stepped back, seeing stars.

"It is well fixed," he said.

He took hold of it again and pulled with all his might. The music played more strongly, and the light all about the churchyard glowed like amethysts; but the sword still stuck.

"Oh, Merlyn," cried the Wart, "help me to get this weapon."

___

17. **gargoyles** (gar′ goilz) *n*.: Gotesquely carved animals or fantastic creatures, on a building.
18. **yew** (yo͞o) *n*.: Type of evergreen tree with red cones.
19. **consort** (kan′ sort) *n*.: Harmony of sounds.

Arthur Becomes King of Britain ◆ *911*

❹ Clarification "Pad" in this context is a derogatory word for a horse that is old, infirm, or otherwise unimpressive.

◆ Critical Thinking

❺ Infer Ask students what Wart's feelings when he holds the sword suggest about the sword itself.
Suggested response: Wart's feeling strange and noticing everything more clearly suggests that the sword has some kind of extraordinary power.

◆ Critical Thinking

❻ Interpret Invite students' explanations for the presence of the people who do not answer and the otherworldly music in this passage.
Suggested response: The people's not answering Wart may suggest that they are not flesh-and-blood onlookers, but possibly ghosts or magicians. The music, which comes from nowhere, is not made by human beings. Something mysterious and magical is taking place.

◆ Build Vocabulary

❼ The Suffix -ous Ask students how they would determine the meaning of the word "melodious."
Students should see that the root of the word is related to melody. The suffix -ous means "like" or "pertaining to." Therefore, melodious means "pertaining to, or like, melody."

◆ Literary Focus

❽ Legend Ask students how anyone but Wart could know what sounds were heard at that moment? Why would the author include these details? Students should recognize that these details cannot be verified by witnesses, but were probably added to enhance the significance of this legendary moment.*

❶ Clarification Students should know that in an earlier section of *The Once and Future King*, Merlyn had used his powers to temporarily transform young Arthur into various animals, including a fish and a bird, so that he could learn their wisdom and communicate with them. These animals make a reappearance here and repeat advice that they had given him previously.

◆ **Critical Thinking**

❷ Infer Have students explain how the love that the animals have for Arthur helps him pull out the sword. How does the presence of the animals add to the occasion? *Suggested response: Because of the special bond Arthur has with these animals, he is aware of a "power" within him. The presence of the animals adds to the mystery and magic of the occasion.*

▶ **Critical Viewing** ◀

❸ Infer Elicit responses such as the following: *By representing the Round Table and its knights and the Holy Grail in such detail, art such as this helps the viewer to create a mental image of important scenes from legends, thus preserving them in the viewer's mind.*

❹ Clarification A merlin is a variety of hawk. Hawks depend on the gripping power of their taloned feet to capture prey. The merlin offers Arthur advice on how to grip the sword. Like the advice of the other animals, it is based on its own experience.

The name of the wizard, here given as "Merlyn," is also spelled "Merlin," and he may be named after the bird.

The Round Table and the Holy Grail, Musée Condé, Chantilly, France

These was a kind of rushing noise, and a long chord played along with it. All round the churchyard there were hundreds of old friends. They rose over the church wall all together, like the Punch-and-Judy[20] ghosts of remembered days, and there were badgers and nightingales and vulgar crows and hares and wild geese and falcons and fishes and dogs and dainty unicorns and solitary wasps and hedgehogs and griffins and the thousand other animals he had met. They loomed round the church wall, the lovers and helpers of the Wart, and they all spoke solemnly in turn. Some of them had come from the banners in the church, where they were painted in heraldry, some from the waters and the sky and the fields about—but all, down to the smallest shrew mouse, had come to help on account of love. Wart felt

---

20. Punch-and-Judy: Puppets of the quarrelsome Punch and his wife, Judy, who constantly fight in a comical way.

912 ◆ *Epics and Legends*

▲ **Critical Viewing** Explain how art, like the painting shown here, can preserve a legend visually. [Infer] **❸**

his power grow.

"Put your back into it," said a luce (or pike) off one of the heraldic banners, "as you once did when I was going to snap you up. Remember that power springs from the nape of the neck."

"What about those forearms," asked a badger gravely, "that are held together by a chest? Come along, my dear embryo,[21] and find your tool."

A merlin sitting at the top of the yew tree cried out, "Now then, Captain Wart, what is the first law of the foot? I thought I once heard something about never letting go." **❹**

"Don't work like a stalling woodpecker," urged a tawny owl affectionately. "Keep up

---

21. embryo: (em´ brē ō) *n.*: Anything in an early stage of development.

Humanities: Art

The Round Table and the Holy Grail.

This illustration shows the round table, twelve knights in various positions and rooms near the table, and the Holy Grail, the cup believed to have been used by Jesus at the Last Supper.

Use this question for discussion:

1. How is the style of this illustration different from the ones on pages 905 and 908? *Students*

should recognize that this illustration is more colorful and shows more detail than the others; it also features motifs of flowers, handwriting from what is probably an illuminated manuscript, and other details and symbols meaningful to the legend. Students may also notice that there are other frames partially shown. This artwork probably tells a story in the same way a comic strip or storyboard might.

a steady effort, my duck, and you will have it yet."

A white-front said. "Now, Wart, if you were once able to fly the great North Sea, surely you can coordinate a few little wing-muscles here and there? Fold your powers together, with the spirit of your mind, and it will come out like butter. Come along, Homo sapiens,[22] for all we humble friends of yours are waiting here to cheer."

The Wart walked up to the great sword for the third time. He put out his right hand softly and drew it out as gently as from a scabbard.

There was a lot of cheering, a noise like a hurdy-gurdy[23] which went on and on. In the middle of this noise, after a long time, he saw Kay and gave him the sword. The people at the tournament were making a frightful row.

"But this is not my sword," said Sir Kay.

"It was the only one I could get," said the Wart. "The inn was locked."

"It is a nice-looking sword. Where did you get it?"

"I found it stuck in a stone, outside a church."

Sir Kay had been watching the tilting nervously, waiting for his turn. He had not paid much attention to his squire.

"That is a funny place to find one," he said.

"Yes, it was stuck through an anvil."

"What?" cried Sir Kay, suddenly rounding upon him. "Did you just say this sword was stuck in a stone?"

"It was," said the Wart. "It was a sort of war memorial."

Sir Kay stared at him for several seconds in amazement, opened his mouth, shut it again, licked his lips, then turned his back and plunged through the crowd. He was

looking for Sir Ector, and the Wart followed after him.

"Father," cried Sir Kay, "come here a moment."

"Yes, my boy," said Sir Ector. "Splendid falls these professional chaps do manage. Why, what's the matter, Kay? You look as white as a sheet."

"Do you remember that sword which the King of England would pull out?"

"Yes."

"Well, here it is. I have it. It is in my hand. I pulled it out."

Sir Ector did not say anything silly. He looked at Kay and he looked at the Wart. Then he stared at Kay again, long and lovingly, and said, "We will go back to the church."

"Now then, Kay," he said, when they were at the church door. He looked at his first-born kindly, but straight between the eyes. "Here is the stone, and you have the sword. It will make you the King of England. You are my son that I am proud of, and always will be, whatever you do. Will you promise me that you took it out by your own might?"

Kay looked at his father. He also looked at the Wart and at the sword.

Then he handed the sword to the Wart quite quietly.

He said, "I am a liar. Wart pulled it out."

As far as the Wart was concerned, there was a time after this in which Sir Ector kept telling him to put the sword back into the stone—which he did—and in which Sir Ector and Kay then vainly tried to take it out. The Wart took it out for them, and stuck it back again once or twice. After this, there was another time which was more painful.

He saw that his dear guardian was looking quite old and powerless, and that he was kneeling down with difficulty on a gouty[24] knee.

"Sir," said Sir Ector, without looking up, although he was speaking to his own boy.

---

22. **Homo sapiens** (hō′ mo sā′ pe enz′): Human being.

23. **hurdy-gurdy** (hur′ de gur′ de) *n.*: Musical instrument, like a barrel organ, played by turning a crank.

24. **gouty** (gout′ e) *adj.*: Having gout, a disease causing swelling and severe pain in the joints.

Arthur Becomes King of Britain ◆ *913*

❶ Infer Ask students why Wart reacts as he does to the last developments in the story. *Suggested response: The relationships between Wart and those he has thought of as his family have abruptly changed. Deprived of these family ties, Wart may suddenly feel isolated, and fearful of a strange and unlooked-for future.*

Reinforce and Extend

Answers

♦ *Literature and Your Life*

Reader's Response Students might say young Arthur (or Wart) because he is sensible and honorable and, as revealed by the final scene, very human.

Thematic Focus Students might say that perhaps Wart is a new kind of hero—one who is softer and who pays attention to the needs of others rather than placing ultimate emphasis on showing his prowess.

☑ **Check Your Comprehension**

1. He brings the news that the King is dead.
2. Whoever can pull the sword out of the anvil and the stone will be the next King of England.
3. Sir Kay left his sword at home.
4. He removes the sword from the anvil and stone.
5. They realize that he pulled the sword from the stone, which was the object of the tournament.

♦ **Critical Thinking**

1. Magical forces of nature seem to unite to help Wart draw the sword from the stone; talking animals coax him to success.
2. His explanations, at first, reveal that he is shallow and ambitious.
3. Wart is ambivalent about becoming King; he seems fearful and does not want to rise above his friends.
4. Sample response: White's dialogue for his characters is crude and unbecoming of knights; he uses malapropisms like "next of skin"; he puts the knights in undignified situations, such as how he describes their lodging in London.

"Please do not do this, father," said the Wart, kneeling down also. "Let me help you up, Sir Ector, because you are making me unhappy."

"Nay, nay, my lord," said Sir Ector, with some very feeble old tears. "I was never your father nor of your blood, but I wote[25] well ye are of an higher blood than I wend[26] ye were."

"Plenty of people have told me you are not my father," said the Wart, "but it does not matter a bit."

"Sir," said Sir Ector humbly, "will ye be my good and gracious lord when ye are King?"

"Don't!" said the Wart.

"Sir," said Sir Ector, "I will ask no more of you but that you will make my son, your foster-brother, Sir Kay, seneschal[27] of all your lands."

Kay was kneeling down too, and it was more than the Wart could bear.

"Oh, do stop," he cried. "Of course he can be seneschal, if I have got to be this King, and, oh, father, don't kneel down like that, because it breaks my heart. Please get up, Sir Ector, and don't make everything so horrible. Oh, dear, oh, dear, I wish I had never seen that filthy sword at all."

And the Wart also burst into tears.

---

25. **wote** (wot) *v.*: Old word meaning know.
26. **wend** (wend) *v.*: Here, old word meaning *thought.*

27. **seneschal** (sen´ ə shəl) *n.*: Steward in the house of a medieval noble.

Guide for Responding

♦ *Literature and Your Life*

Reader's Response Which character is your favorite? Why?

Thematic Focus Is the Wart the type of courageous hero you expect to meet in a traditional tale of heroism? What qualities might a humble character like the Wart model for future generations?

Discussion With a group, discuss why the Wart bursts into tears at the end and wishes he had never seen "the filthy sword" in the stone.

☑ **Check Your Comprehension**

1. What significant news does King Pellinore bring?
2. Explain how the new king of England is to be chosen.
3. Why does Sir Kay ask the Wart to hurry back to the inn from the arena?
4. What extraordinary feat does the Wart perform in the churchyard?
5. What do Sir Ector and Sir Kay realize when the Wart returns to the arena?

♦ **Critical Thinking**

INTERPRET

1. In what ways is the Wart's drawing of the sword from the stone a moment of magic and mystery? **[Support]**
2. What do Sir Kay's explanations to Sir Ector about pulling the sword reveal about Sir Kay's character? **[Analyze]**
3. How does the Wart feel about becoming king? **[Draw Conclusions]**

EVALUATE

4. Give some examples of how T. H. White pokes fun at the Arthurian legends with a light and humorous attitude. **[Evaluate]**

APPLY

5. Reread the words of encouragement given by the luce, the badger, the merlin, the tawny owl, and the white-front. How might their advice be pertinent to life in general? **[Apply]**

---

5. The animals' words are relevant to many challenges in life; if one is persistent, focused, and goal-oriented, success is more likely.

Guide for Responding (continued)

◆ Reading Strategy

RECOGNIZE AN AUTHOR'S ATTITUDE

Recognizing an **author's attitude** toward his or her subject will help you appreciate a piece of writing. Authors T. H. White and Alfred, Lord Tennyson have strikingly different attitudes toward their common subject, Arthur.

1. Find three examples of words, phrases, and situations in "Arthur Becomes King of Britain" that show T. H. White's light and humorous attitude toward the Arthurian legends.
2. (a) What is Tennyson's attitude toward his subject? (b) Cite three passages in "Morte d'Arthur" that show Tennyson's attitude.

◆ Literary Focus

LEGEND

A **legend** is an imaginative story handed down for generations and believed, but not proved, to have a historical basis. Legends also provide information about the culture that created them.

1. Do you think warfare was a common occurrence during this period? Support your opinion.
2. What values or qualities do the Arthurian legends illustrate that indicate that the legend will continue through future generations?
3. Why do you think the details of a legend, such as how Arthur acquires Excalibur, differ from version to version?

Beyond Literature

Media Connection

Hollywood's Portrayal of Camelot
The movie *Camelot* captures the warm humor of T. H. White's *The Once and Future King*. In this 1967 movie adaptation of the 1960 Lerner and Loewe musical, Hollywood presents a lavish and lively interpretation of this legendary place. The film won Academy Awards for art direction, music direction, and costumes.
Activity Watch the video of *Camelot* and compare the characters and dialogue to those of "Arthur Becomes King of Britain" and "Morte d'Arthur."

◆ Build Vocabulary

USING THE SUFFIX *-ous*

The common suffix *-ous* means "like" or "pertaining to." On your paper, write the word from the following list that best completes each sentence.

a. sumptuous **b.** adventurous **c.** slanderous

1. To hurt his reputation, his opponents spread ___?___ stories about him.
2. White and Tennyson both tell ___?___ tales.
3. The king prepared a ___?___ banquet for his guests.

USING THE WORD BANK

On your paper, write the word from the Word Bank that best defines each statement.

1. Sounds of this are heard at funerals.
2. Things that are this are usually expensive as well.
3. You'd better practice before riding one of these.
4. A fastidious person is probably this also.
5. Spending too much time in the sun will make your skin look this way.

◆ Build Grammar Skills

SUBJUNCTIVE MOOD

Writers use the **subjunctive mood** of the verb to state a condition that is contrary to fact, usually in clauses beginning with *if, as if,* or *as though,* or to express indirectly a demand, suggestion, or statement of necessity. The most commonly used subjunctive form is the past subjunctive of *be,* which is always *were.*

Practice In your notebook, correct each sentence by writing the correct subjunctive form.

1. Sir Bedivere acted as if Excalibur was more important than Arthur's command.
2. My end draws nigh; 'tis time that I am gone.
3. What heroes would be in Avilion, if there really was such a place?
4. If King Arthur was to come again, would war really end?
5. Arthur demanded that Bedivere should cast Excalibur into the lake.

Morte d'Arthur/Arthur Becomes King of Britain ◆ 915

Beyond the Selection

FURTHER READING
The complete book The Once and Future King.
More Books by T. H. White
The Book of Merlyn (the end of the Arthur story)
The Book of Beasts.
Other Books About King Arthur
The Acts of King Arthur and His Noble Knights, John Steinbeck
A Connecticut Yankee in King Arthur's Court, Mark Twain
We suggest that you preview these works.

INTERNET
The Internet provides an excellent opportunity for students to learn more about Tennyson, T. H. White, and the King Arthur legends. Encourage students to visit the following Web site for information. Please be aware, however, that the site may have changed from the time we published this information.
For more information about Alfred, Lord Tennyson, go to **http://charon. sfus.edu/TENNYSON/tennyson.html**
For more information about T.H. White, go to **http://www2netdoor.com/~moulder/thwhite.html**
We *strongly recommend* that you preview the sites.

Idea Bank

Customizing for
Performance Levels

Following are suggestions for matching Idea Bank topics with your students' performance levels:

Less Advanced Students: 1, 5
Average Students: 2, 4, 6
More Advanced Students: 3, 7

Customizing for
Learning Modalities

Following are suggestions for matching Idea Bank topics with your students' learning modalities:

Musical/Rhythmic: 4
Verbal/Linguistic: 4, 5
Bodily/Kinesthetic: 5
Visual/Spatial: 6
Logical/Mathematical: 7

Writing Mini-Lesson

Refer students to the Writing Handbook, page 965, for instruction on the writing process and page 969 for further information on practical writing.

Writing and Language Transparencies Use the set of transparencies for Writing Process Model 9: Business Letter, pp. 61–64, to provide a model of a business letter and to guide students through the writing and revising process.

Writing Lab CD-ROM

Have students complete the tutorial on practical and technical writing. Follow these steps:

1. Refer students to the Purpose Profile, where they can answer a series of questions to help them achieve their intended purpose.

2. Suggest that students use the Letter Shell to help them correctly format their letter of recommendation.

3. Have students use a Revision Checker for Vague Language. This tool will help them replace vague terms with more precise ones.

Sourcebook

Have students use Chapter 8, Practical and Technical Writing (pp. 229–257), for additional support. The chapter includes tips for gathering details from personal experience (p. 247).

Build Your Portfolio

Idea Bank

Writing

1. **List** Based on these two selections, make a list of Arthur's heroic qualities. Explain which actions or words indicate each quality.

2. **Epic Essay** Write an essay analyzing the qualities of "Morte d'Arthur" that make it an epic. Mention the values expressed in the selection, the qualities that make Arthur a hero, and the ways in which the actions and events are larger than life.

3. **Local Legends** Choose a legend with which you are familiar and write a short scene that might be used in a stage or screen version of the legend.

Speaking and Listening

4. **Music** The musical *Camelot* is based on *The Once and Future King*. With several classmates, watch a videotape or listen to the soundtrack of *Camelot*. As a panel, discuss how the film or lyrics depict the Arthurian legend. Each panel member can present a different aspect. **[Music Link]**

5. **Oral Reading** Read aloud your favorite section of "Morte d'Arthur" to classmates. Use hand gestures, facial expressions, and vocal expression to give meaning to your oral reading.

Projects

6. **Art** Create a painting or drawing to illustrate an important event in "Arthur Becomes King of Britain." **[Art Link]**

7. **Feudalism Chart** Feudalism was an economic, political, and social system in medieval England. Feudalism was also practiced in Japan and other European countries. Research feudalism at the library. Make a chart to compare and contrast the practice of feudalism in different countries. **[Social Studies Link]**

Writing Mini-Lesson

Letter of Recommendation

Is there someone from history, from fiction, or from your own life who deserves the title "Sir" in the grand land of Camelot? Write a **letter of recommendation** to King Arthur. Explain how this person meets the qualifications for knighthood and describe the talents or abilities he or she would contribute to Arthur's court.

As you plan and write the letter of recommendation, keep this point in mind:

Writing Skills Focus: Clear and Consistent Purpose

Open with a **clear statement of your purpose**, telling your recommendation for knighthood and your reasons. In the body of your letter, you must develop your purpose-setting statement in a clear and consistent way. That means each detail or example you give should show why your candidate is fit to sit at the Round Table.

Prewriting Write the name of your candidate and list as many facts, details, and examples about his or her life as you can recall. Choose the information that most supports your claim that he or she is qualified for knighthood; for example, honorable, brave, honest, and trustworthy.

Drafting As you write your letter, use the information you have listed. You may want to organize your points by order of importance, leading up to the most important.

Revising Reread your draft. Does every detail support your purpose in a clear and consistent way? Have you made clear how your candidate meets the qualifications? Have you followed the correct form for a business letter? Revise to strengthen your letter's content, consistency, and format.

✓ ASSESSMENT OPTIONS

Formal Assessment, Selection Test, pp. 220–222, and Assessment Resources Software. The selection test is designed so that it can be easily customized to the performance levels of your students.
Alternative Assessment, p. 62, includes options for less advanced students, more advanced students, visual/spatial learners, bodily/kinesthetic learners, and interpersonal learners.

PORTFOLIO ASSESSMENT

Use the following rubrics in the ***Alternative Assessment*** booklet to assess student writing:
List: Definition/Classification Rubric, p. 99
Epic Essay: Response to Literature Rubric, p. 110
Local Legends: Fictional Narrative Rubric, p. 95
Writing Mini-Lesson: Business Letter/Memo Rubric, p. 113

Writing Process Workshop

Research Paper

When you present factual information on a topic you've researched—such as the Arthurian Legends—you're writing a **research paper**. A research paper usually includes an introduction that states the main idea, a body that develops and elaborates on the main idea, and a conclusion that summarizes the points you have made. When you refer to information you've found through your research, you need to give credit to the source in a footnote or parenthetical citation. At the end of the paper, include a bibliography that lists all the sources you used.

Write a research paper on a topic that interests you. The following skills, introduced in this section's Writing Mini-Lessons, will help.

Writing Skills Focus

▶ **Use clear and logical organization** for your paper. Whether you choose order of importance, chronological, or compare-and-contrast, stick with that method of organization for the body of your research paper. (See p. 891.)

▶ **Have a clear, consistent purpose** for your research paper. State your purpose in your opening paragraph, and develop it in the body of the paper. (See p. 916.)

The following introduction from a paper on the effect of CDs on the music industry shows these skills at work.

WRITING MODEL

① CDs have had a dramatic impact on the music industry. Although music has always been big business, CDs have made it even more so.

Since the 1983 introduction of CD technology, the music industry has increased sales by $100 million annually. The new technology created consumer demand in nearly every category. From pop to jazz to rock to rap, the instant popularity of CDs created a revolution in how music is delivered. ②

① The purpose of this report is to describe the influence of CDs on the music industry. The writer sticks to this point in his introduction.

② The writer uses point-by-point organization: He makes an observation or comment about CDs and then backs it up with an example.

Writing Process Workshop ◆ *917*

Develop Student Writing

Prewriting

Writing and Language Transparencies You may want students to organize their thoughts by using a Comparison-and-Contrast (p. 95), Cause-and Effect (p. 99), or Outline graphic organizer (p. 103), depending on the organizational pattern they have chosen.

Customize for
Visual/Spatial Learners

Encourage these students to include visuals in their research papers: graphs, charts, maps, photographs, and diagrams.

 Writer's Solution

Writing Lab CD-ROM
The Gathering Information section in the Research Writing tutorial gives tips for using library resources, using on-line services, and taking notes.

Drafting

You may want to designate the documentation form you prefer students use—parenthetical, footnote, or endnote—but remind them that all three forms are valid means of citing sources.

Remind students that every supporting detail will have come from some source and therefore must be documented.

Applying Language Skills

Topic Sentence and Support
Remind students that every paragraph has a topic sentence; together, the topic sentences equal the thesis statement. If students prepare an outline, each lettered item in the outline (A, B, C, etc.) should be reflected in a topic sentence and, therefore, a paragraph.

Answer

Suggested response: Fiber-rich foods contribute to good health.

 Writer's Solution

For additional instruction and practice, use "Understanding Research Papers," and "Writing a Research Paper," pp. 135–136, in the *Writer's Solution Grammar Practice Book.*

918

Applying Language Skills:
Topic Sentence and Support

Each of your paragraphs has a main idea that is stated in a **topic sentence**. The **supporting sentences** further develop the main idea with details, explanations, and examples. Notice the topic sentence (the first sentence) and supporting sentences in the following paragraph:

A medieval feast was designed to appeal to the senses. The dishes were colorful, such as green eel stew, and highly spiced, such as rabbit seasoned with ginger and nutmeg. Regarding flavor, most dishes were a bit sour and salty.

Practice On your paper, add a topic sentence to the following paragraph.

One of the ways in which fiber-rich foods help is by reducing the risk of heart disease. Another is by cleansing the digestive system of infection.

Writer's Solution Connection
Language Lab

For more help writing effective topic sentences, complete the Language Lab lesson on Topic Sentence and Support.

Prewriting

Choose a Topic The topic you choose for your research paper should be one for which there is a good amount of information available. If you can't think of a topic, consider one of the topic ideas listed here.

Topic Ideas
- A famous writer
- An endangered animal or plant
- A recent invention or discovery
- The source of a famous myth or legend

Find Appropriate Sources In a library, locate the resources that will help you. These may include history books, newspapers, and magazines. Use the most up-to-date resources, because they may contain information not included in older materials.

Take Accurate Notes Use note cards and source cards to record your information. Here are some tips:

Note Cards
- Enter only one piece of information on each card.
- Include the page number from which you obtained the information.
- Write a head at the top of each card telling on which aspect of your topic the note focuses.

Source Cards
- Create one source card for each source you use.
- List all the information you will need for crediting the source: author, title, publisher, date, and so on.

Drafting

Organize Your Ideas Write a thesis statement, which indicates the main point you want to make about your topic. All of the information in your paper should support your thesis statement. Include your thesis statement in your introduction. Follow with a series of body paragraphs, each focusing on a single subpoint and providing supporting details. End with a conclusion that drives home your main idea.

Work With Your Notes Use your note cards as you draft your research paper. Work the information from your note cards into your draft. Copy facts, dates, and page references accurately. However, you should rephrase other information in your own words.

 Cross-Curricular Connection: Science

Explain to students that research is the backbone of the scientific community. However, instead of beginning with a thesis sentence, scientists begin with a hypothesis that they prove or disprove. Scientists write in scientific language, beginning with a review of the literature and then turning to primary research, discussing control and experimental groups, variables, and results. Nevertheless, the scientist must, like any other academic, document his findings and credit his sources. Have students check scientific journals for examples.

Document Your Sources You are required to document, or give credit to, your sources in the following situations:
• When you use another person's exact words
• When you use another person's idea, even if you rephrase it in your own words

Failure to do so is called plagiarism—presenting someone else's ideas as your own. Plagiarism is a serious offense.

Quote Your Sources Accurately At some points in your paper, you will wish to quote a source directly. Be sure that you record those passages word for word.

Revising

Use a Checklist The following checklist will help you revise.

▶ Do all the body paragraphs support my thesis statement?
As you revise, make sure that you've actually made a point about your topic in each paragraph, rather than just restating information you've gathered. For example, if you're writing a paper about Peter the Great, you wouldn't simply state the facts of his life, you'd want to draw some conclusions about why he was a great leader.

▶ Is my information accurate?
Invite a peer to read your draft. If the reader questions the accuracy of any information, go back to your notes and check them.

▶ Have I accurately cited my sources of information?
Make sure that every source that you rephrase and every passage that you quote directly are marked with a footnote or a parenthetical citation. If you have omitted one, use your note cards to identify the source. Then add a citation.

▶ Is my paper clearly organized?
Read through your paper from start to finish, looking for any places where it seems to jump around or where one idea doesn't seem to flow logically from the previous one. Rearrange your ideas to make the organization clear, and add transitions to make connections from one idea to the next.

Publishing

▶ **Classroom** Share your research paper by presenting it to classmates as a special news report.
▶ **Audio Corner** Make a recording of your report. Create a classroom corner where classmates can listen to your recording.

APPLYING LANGUAGE SKILLS: Citing Sources

When you quote a passage directly and when you paraphrase an idea from a source, **cite the source** in a parenthetical citation or in a footnote. A parenthetical citation immediately follows the quoted information. A footnote appears at the bottom of the page.

Parenthetical Citation:

Astronomers suspected that supernovas "might serve as stellar forges." (Murdin 119)

Footnote:

1. Paul Murdin, *Supernovae* (Cambridge: Cambridge University Press, 1985), 119.

Writing Application Add quotations to your research paper. Then document those quotations.

Writer's Solution Connection Writing Lab

For additional help in crediting sources, use the Citing and Crediting Sources section of the Writing Lab tutorial on Research Writing.

Revising

As a guide for peer editors, you may want students to use the Scoring Rubric for Research Report/Paper (*Alternative Assessment*, p. 106) along with the customized rubrics on this page.

Publishing

If students interviewed someone in preparation for completing the research paper, they may want to send the interviewee a completed copy.

Applying Language Skills

Citing Sources
Remind students that to use someone else's ideas or words is to commit plagiarism. Thus, to avoid literary theft, they must cite sources for paraphrased as well as quoted ideas.

 Writer's Solution

For additional instruction and practice, see Crediting Sources in the *Writer's Solution Sourcebook*, pp. 160–161.

Reinforce and Extend

Applying Knowledge
After students have completed their papers, ask them to discuss the logical processes involved in gathering, organizing, and presenting information. Ask how these logical processes apply to other kinds of writing.

✓ ASSESSMENT		4	3	2	1
PORTFOLIO ASSESSMENT Use the rubric on Description in *Alternative Assessment* (p. 106) to assess students' writing. Add these criteria to customize the rubric to this assignment.	**Topic Sentences**	The research paper includes and supports a topic sentence in every paragraph.	The research paper includes and supports a topic sentence in most paragraphs.	The research paper supports topic sentences.	The research paper includes few topic sentences and little or no support.
	Research Process	The writer completed the research process using exemplary sources evidenced by exemplary note cards.	The writer completed the research process using adequate sources evidenced by adequate note cards.	The writer partly completed the research process using some sources evidenced by some note cards.	The writer did not complete the research process.

Customize for
Linguistic Learners
To help linguistic learners understand the visual, shade in the row and column of a sample chart, circling where they intersect. Then ask these students to write a sentence giving the information found in that block.

Apply the Strategy

Have students study the chart. Focus attention first on the title, then the four headings. Ask students to respond to the four questions. Then with the class, discuss the thought process used in answering the questions. Ask which column they scanned first to acquire each answer.

Answers
1. Vitamin C prevents scurvy.
2. Vitamin A promotes good vision.
3. Vitamin C functions to aid immunity and help connective tissue growth.
4. Night blindness is one symptom of vitamin A deficiency.

Reading Charts

Real-World Reading Skills Workshop

Strategies for Success

Charts present information in a visual form. You'll find various kinds of charts in your textbooks, but you'll also find charts all around you in your daily life—in informational articles in newspapers and magazines, on product labels, in manuals, in schedules. If you need to check the times on a bus schedule, for example, or locate sources of vitamin C, you'll probably need to read a chart.

Examine the Chart When you first look at a chart, examine it closely to determine its organization. Information usually appears in columns and rows. Notice how the columns and rows are labeled. Usually one type of information appears in the columns and another type in the rows. Read across the rows and down the columns. To find a specific piece of information, note where the relevant column and row intersect.

Find What You Need A chart may offer more information than you need. Know exactly what you do need. For example, a bus schedule may offer weekend travel times in a separate chart or column. If you are traveling during a weekday, make sure you look under the correct column. Also, if the bus departs from two different stations in your town, read the schedule for the station you want.

> ✔ Here are other situations in which information is presented in a chart:
> ▶ Correct clothing size according to height and weight
> ▶ Mileage between cities on a road map
> ▶ Bus, train, or airline schedules
> ▶ Sports teams' schedules
> ▶ Class schedules

Apply the Strategy

Use the vitamin chart to answer the questions that follow.

Vitamin Sources and Functions			
Vitamin	**Source**	**Function**	**Deficiency Disease**
A	green and yellow vegetables	promotes bone growth and vision	night blindness
B_1	grains, liver, legumes	metabolizes carbohydrates	beriberi
C	citrus fruits, potatoes, tomatoes	aids immunity, helps connective tissue growth	scurvy
D	milk, yeast	regulates bone formation	rickets, bowlegs

1. What vitamin prevents scurvy?
2. What vitamin promotes good vision?
3. What is the function of vitamin C?
4. What is one symptom of a vitamin A deficiency?

 Beyond the Classroom

Workplace Skill
Creating Charts and Graphs The workplace is filled with charts and graphs. While virtually every word processing program includes chart- and graph-making capabilities, the user must know how to create them before he or she can use the software. Graphs always show relationships: sales dollars by the year, production by the product number, phone calls by the month. Thus, to make a graph, you must know what relationship you are trying to explain. Ask students to find examples of graphs and charts from the work-place. Compare them and discuss other ways the information could be presented.

PART 2 *World Heroes*

Rama and Lakshman Confer With the Animal Armies, from the *Adventures of Rama,* Freer Gallery of Art, Smithsonian Institution, Washington, D.C.

Dipankara Buddha, 17th Century A.D., Nepal, Asian Art Museum of San Francisco, The Avery Brundage Collection

World Heroes ◆ 921

One-Minute Planning Guide

In Part 2, students will meet heroes from India and old Mali, as well as some modern movie characters who will help them understand that epics tell timeless tales in any age. In "Rama's Initiation," the adventures of the young epic hero Rama provide an exciting story and provides students with a context to understand Indian cultural beliefs. "Sundiata: An Epic of Old Mali" is a classic tale of an underdog. Based on a historical figure, it relates how the physically disabled boy Mari Djata overcomes obstacles to become a powerful and respected hero. The elements of epics are connected to modern culture in the high-interest essay "Star Wars: An Epic for Today." The author shows how the writer of the Star Wars trilogy incorporates storytelling techniques that have been used since before people had a written history.

Customize for *Varying Student Needs*

When assigning the selections in this part, keep in mind these factors.

"Rama's Initiation"
- The unfamiliar names of characters may prove difficult for less advanced readers.
- Most students will need assistance appreciating the cultural details.
- The vocabulary is challenging.

from *Sundiata*
- Less advanced students and English language learners will need assistance with the unusual and formal diction.
- Some characters have more than one name, which may confuse some students.
- Cultural references will need to be explained.

 Humanities: Art

Rama and Lakshman Confer With the Animal Armies, from *Adventures of Rama.*

Rama, hero of the Indian epic *The Ramayana,* was the human form of the god Vishnu. He is usually portrayed with dark skin (here blue); Lakshman is his half-brother.

Dipankara Buddha (17th century Nepal). Dipankara, also called Atisa, was an Indian Buddhist whose traveled to Tibet and whose reforms became the basis for a Tibetan Buddhist sect.

Figure of a drummer seated on a folding stool, Ashanti brass.

The Ashanti people live in the west African countries of Ghana, Togo, and the Ivory Coast. This brass figure is used for weighing quantities of gold.

Help students link this art with the focus of Part 2, "World Heroes," by answering the following question:

Imagine a truly global hero, for a united Earth. What problems might such a hero combat and what qualities would he or she need? *Students are likely to envision the hero battling problems such as an alien invasion or environmental crisis. The hero might need such traditional qualities as bravery and intelligence, as well as less traditional skills, such as the ability to adapt to bizarre or rapidly changing situations and to unite very different allies.*

*G*uide for Reading

1. To read, comprehend, and interpret an epic
2. To relate an epic to personal experience
3. To make inferences about culture when reading an epic
4. To identify the qualities of an epic hero
5. To build vocabulary in context and learn the word root *-min-*
6. To identify and punctuate restrictive and nonrestrictive appositives
7. To write a script treatment proposal using language appropriate to the purpose
8. To respond to the epic through writing, speaking and listening, and projects

SKILLS INSTRUCTION

Vocabulary:
Word Roots: *-min-*

Grammar:
Restrictive and Nonrestrictive Appositives

Reading Strategy:
Make Inferences About Culture

Literary Focus:
The Epic Hero

Writing:
Appropriate Language for Purpose

Speaking and Listening:
Oral Tales (teacher edition)

Critical Viewing:
Speculate, Connect, Support, Analyze

PORTFOLIO OPPORTUNITIES

Writing: Letter; Personal Narrative; Opening Argument

Writing Mini-Lesson: Script Treatment Proposal

Speaking and Listening: Oral Tales; Indian Music

Projects: Painting; Dance

More About the Author

R. K. Narayan is considered one of the best Indian authors writing in English. Having completed his education in 1930, Narayan at first became a teacher. However, he soon left to devote his full time to writing. Narayan's first novel, *Swami and Friends,* was published in 1935. Set in the fictitious Indian town of Malgudi (as are all his later works), *Swami and Friends* narrates the adventures of a group of schoolboys. One of Narayan's favorite themes is the clash between old traditions and contemporary urban life in India.

About the Ramayana

The great Indian epic, the *Ramayana,* written by the poet Valmike, consists of twenty-four thousand stanzas. Parts of the *Ramayana* date from 500 B.C.

The epic tells how Prince Rama wins his bride, Sita, by proving his strength. Just as he is about to inherit the throne, evil plots result in his banishment from the kingdom. For fourteen years, he wanders in exile with his wife, Sita, and his brother, Lakshmana. Sita is kidnapped, and Rama rescues her with the help of Manuman, the monkey god. After the rescue, Rama is welcomed back to the kingdom.

The excerpt you are about to read tells of adventures from Rama's childhood, before his banishment. Even as boys, Rama and his brother Lakshmana show extraordinary strength and ability.

R. K. Narayan (1906–)

For the writer R. K. Narayan (nə rī´ en), the *Ramayana* and *Mahabharata* played a significant role in fostering a love for literature. He often cites the importance of oral literature in traditional Indian society: "The storyteller who has studied the epics, the *Ramayana* and the *Mahabharata*, may take up any of the thousand episodes in them, create a narrative with his individual stamp on it, and hold the attention of an audience, numbering thousands, for hours."

Born into the Hindu Brahmin caste, Narayan spoke Tamil at home, used English at school, and was taught traditional Indian melodies and prayers in Sanskrit, India's ancient classical language. In addition to his contemporary versions of Indian epics, R. K. Narayan has published dozens of novels and short story collections.

◆ Build Vocabulary

WORD ROOTS *-min-*

The character Agasthya in this episode from the *Ramayana* is referred to as *diminutive*. The root *-min-* in *diminutive* comes from the Latin *minutus* meaning "small." Therefore, when Agasthya is described as being *diminutive,* it means he is tiny in size.

WORD BANK

austerities
decrepitude
sublime
august
secular
obeisance
exuberance
diminutive
esoteric

As you read "Rama's Initiation" from the *Ramayana,* you will encounter the words on this list. Each word will be defined on the page where it first appears. Before you read, list in your notebook any words or word parts that you think you recognize. Then, as you read, check whether the words mean what you thought they did.

◆ Build Grammar Skills

RESTRICTIVE AND NONRESTRICTIVE APPOSITIVES

An appositive is a noun or pronoun placed next to another noun or pronoun to identify, rename, or explain it. An appositive phrase is a noun or pronoun with modifiers, placed next to a noun or pronoun to add information or details. An appositive is **restrictive** when it is necessary to clarify or identify the noun to which it refers. Commas are not used with restrictive appositives.

Restrictive: Send your son *Rama* with me.

Since the king has more than one son, the appositive *Rama* is necessary to identify which son.

An appositive is **nonrestrictive** if it provides additional, but not necessary, information. Nonrestrictive appositives are set off with commas.

Nonrestrictive: This Thataka is more dreadful than Yama, *the god of death,* who takes a life only when the time is ripe.

Since there is only one Yama, the appositive phrase adds information, but it is not necessary.

922 ◆ *Epics and Legends*

Prentice Hall Literature Program Resources

REINFORCE / RETEACH / EXTEND

Selection Support Pages
Build Vocabulary: Word Roots: *-min-,* p. 257
Build Grammar Skills: Restrictive and Nonrestrictive Appositives, p. 258
Reading Strategy: Make Inferences About Culture, p. 259
Literary Focus: The Epic Hero, p. 260

Strategies for Diverse Student Needs, p. 63

Beyond Literature
Cultural Connection: *Hinduism in India,* p. 63

Formal Assessment Selection Test, pp. 223–225, Assessment Resources Software

Alternative Assessment, p. 63

Writing and Language Transparencies Art Transparency 14

Resource Pro CD-ROM
"Rama's Initiation"—includes all resource materials and customizable lesson plan

 Listening to Literature Audiocassettes
"Rama's Initiation"

Rama's Initiation *from the* Ramayana

◆ *Literature and Your Life*

CONNECT YOUR EXPERIENCE

What qualities do you think a hero possesses? As you read this episode from the *Ramayana,* you might be surprised to note that ancient heroes have much in common with contemporary superheroes; heroes have always combatted evil, and as you'll see in the *Ramayana,* they have respected the land that nurtures all people.

Journal Writing All over the world, young people prove their mental, spiritual, and physical strength to themselves, to their peers, and to adults. Choose a young person who you believe has heroic qualities. In your journal, jot down some notes upon which you could base an epic focusing on this person.

THEMATIC FOCUS: FROM THE PAST

The *Ramayana* has influenced nearly every aspect of Indian culture —from children's bedtime stories to religious studies. Ask yourself what Rama's adventures reveal about Indian culture.

◆ Background for Understanding

CULTURE

Hinduism, one of the oldest living religions in the world, is the major religion of India. While it has no single book that outlines all its doctrines and beliefs, there are many sacred writings. These include the *Vedas,* which contain prayers, hymns, explanations, and philosophy; the *Puranas,* which tell the tales of Hindu gods and goddesses; the Hindu epics *Mahabharata* and the *Ramayana* and the *Manu-Smitri,* a code of religious and social law. The *Ramayana* tells of Prince Rama, believed by many to be another incarnation of the Hindu god Krishna.

◆ Literary Focus

THE EPIC HERO

The **epic hero** possesses certain qualities—bravery, great strength, and a desire to achieve immortality through heroic deeds. The hero is based on a legendary or historic person who travels on a long and challenging journey, during which he proves his heroic qualities: He fights evil, falls in love, protects his honor, and rescues people in distress.

This episode from the *Ramayana* puts Rama in a situation in which he must prove some of his heroic qualities.

◆ Reading Strategy

MAKE INFERENCES ABOUT CULTURE

You can use information revealed in sources such as epics to **make inferences about a culture.** Chances are, you don't know a great deal about life in India 2,000 years ago. However, if you draw upon the details in the *Ramayana* in combination with your own experiences, you can make some strong inferences about this ancient culture. In particular, the experiences of the hero Rama will reveal the customs and values of his culture.

To help you make inferences about a culture, use a chart like the one below to jot down cultural details from the epic, details from your own background and experience, and the resulting cultural inferences.

Details from the epic

↓

Relationship to my experience

↓

Cultural inferences

Guide for Reading ◆ *923*

Make the statement that super heroes from all times and cultures possess certain traits in common. Enlist students' help in generating a representative list of super heroes from ancient to present times—for example, Zeus, King Arthur, Robin Hood, and Xena, Warrior Princess. Together with students, discuss the characteristics that some of these heroes hold in common, such as courage, bravery, loyalty, and integrity. Let them know that in reading this selection about a young Indian boy, they will get an opportunity to witness the making of a hero.

Customize for
Less Proficient Readers
Use the art on page 924 to introduce students to the setting of the court of King Dasaratha. Then, to help avoid confusion, draw attention to "Thataka's Story" (p. 927). Explain that "Thataka's Story" is a story within a story, a common narrative technique in epics.

Customize for
English Language Learners
So that students will not spend too much time on the pronunciation of characters' names at the expense of fluency, write on the board the names of the main characters: King Dasaratha and his sons Rama and Lakshmana; Viswamithra, the sage; Vasishtha, the king's adviser; and Thataka, a she-demon. Use the phonetic spelling on pages 924, 925, and 926 to pronounce the names for students. If any of your students are from India, encourage them to pronounce the names for the class.

Customize for
Intrapersonal Learners
Explain that in this story Rama makes perhaps the most significant journey of his life. Encourage these students to write in their journals the various thoughts, impressions, and feelings Rama has as he passes along on this journey.

✎ Preparing for Standardized Tests

Grammar and Language Some standardized tests contain sections on standard written English. One type of item tested might be the use of commas with appositives. To give students practice for this type of item, write the following sentence on the chalkboard, and ask students to correctly punctuate it.

The bouquet of flowers yellow and pink roses looked lovely on the kitchen table.

Verify for students that commas should be placed between *flowers* and *yellow* and between

roses and looked because *yellow and pink roses* is a nonrestrictive phrase; it provides additional but not necessary information and should be set off by commas. Let students know that on standardized tests they may encounter a similar sentence punctuated in various ways, and they will be asked to identify the one with the nonrestrictive appositive phrase that has been correctly punctuated.

For additional practice, use the Build Grammar Skills page in **Selection Support,** p. 258.

923

One-Minute Insight

In "Rama's Initiation," the young man Rama accepts his calling to help defend a sage and perform a sacrifice in a far-away sacred place. He proves himself by defeating a demon and thus begins his adventures as an epic hero. His adventures demonstrate the importance of bravery, strength, and respect for wisdom in Indian culture.

◆ Critical Thinking

❶ Infer The writer states that Viswamithra was a dreaded name. Ask students what they can infer about Viswamithra's actions as king. *Suggested response: He was probably feared because he is described as a conqueror and as quick-tempered. He might have used his authority to harm people who displeased him.*

►Critical Viewing◄

❷ Speculate Suggested response: Because there are so many people in the picture, the meeting might be about something that involves the whole community, such as a how to confront a common problem or threat. It might also be a spiritual meeting.

Humanities: Art

Persian translation of the Ramayana of Valmiki (detail).

This piece, by an unknown artist, illustrates a scene from the *Ramayana.* The picture plane is divided by the architectural elements of the columns, a device often used in Indian painting to suggest depth. The columns and hanging floral garlands between them are highly detailed and give a rich, decorative effect.

Use this question for discussion: What might be the difference between the people sitting on the canopied platform and those in the foreground of the picture? *Students might speculate the people on the platform belong to a ruling or governing class. They might comment on the distance between the platform and the people surrounding it, and observe that it might symbolize the distance between two classes.*

Rama's Initiation

from the Ramayana

R. K. Narayan

The new assembly hall, Dasaratha's[1] latest pride, was crowded all day with visiting dignitaries, royal emissaries, and citizens coming in with representations or appeals for justice. The King was always accessible, and fulfilled his duties as the ruler of Kosala without grudging the hours spent in public service.

On a certain afternoon, messengers at the gate came running in to announce, "Sage Viswamithra."[2] When the message was relayed to the King, he got up and hurried forward to receive the visitor. Viswamithra, once a king, a conqueror, and a dreaded name until he renounced his kingly role and chose to become a sage (which he accomplished through severe austerities), combined in himself the sage's eminence and the king's authority and was quick tempered and positive. Dasaratha led him to a proper seat and said, "This is a day of glory for us; your gracious presence is most welcome. You must have come from afar. Would you first rest?"

"No need," the sage replied simply. He had complete mastery over his bodily needs through inner discipline and austerities, and

---

1. **Dasaratha's** (dä sä rä′ täz)
2. **Viswamithra** (vish wä′ mē trä): Teacher of Rama, the main character of the Ramayana.

924 ◆ *Epics and Legends*

Persian Translation of the Ramayana of Valmiki (detail), Mughal, school of Akbar, Freer Gallery of Art, Smithsonian Institution, Washington, D.C.

▲ **Critical Viewing** What do you think is the topic of this public meeting? [Speculate] **❷**

was above the effects of heat, cold, hunger, fatigue, and even decrepitude. The King later asked politely, "Is there anything I can do?" Viswamithra looked steadily at the King and answered, "Yes. I am here to ask of you a favor. I wish to perform, before the next full moon, a

Block Scheduling Strategies

Consider these suggestions to take advantage of extended class time.

- Allow time for students to share other stories that tell the adventures of a hero. Use these examples to help students construct a definition of an epic hero.
- Introduce the concept of making inferences about a culture with the Reading Strategy feature (p. 923). Lead students to see how they can combine the notes they write in the first two boxes on the chart to come up with

general inferences about a culture. Then direct students to complete the Reading Strategy questions on page 930.

- Both projects in the Idea Bank (p. 931) involve the arts. You might want to plan ahead so that students can use class time to work on their projects. Students choosing the art project will need to bring their supplies with them. Students choosing the dance project will need to select their music in advance.

yagna[3] at Sidhasrama[4]. Doubtless you know where it is?"

"I have passed that sacred ground beyond the Ganges[5] many times."

The sage interrupted. "But there are creatures hovering about waiting to disturb every holy undertaking there, who must be overcome in the same manner as one has to conquer the five-fold evils[6] within before one can realize holiness. Those evil creatures are endowed with immeasurable powers of destruction. But it is our duty to pursue our aims undeterred. The yagna I propose to perform will strengthen the beneficial forces of this world, and please the gods above."

"It is my duty to protect your sublime effort. Tell me when, and I will be there."

The sage said, "No need to disturb your august self. Send your son Rama with me, and he will help me. He can."

"Rama!" cried the King, surprised, "When I am here to serve you."

Viswamithra's temper was already stirring. "I know your greatness," he said, cutting the King short. "But I want Rama to go with me. If you are not willing, you may say so."

The air became suddenly tense. The assembly, the ministers and officials, watched in solemn silence. The King looked miserable. "Rama is still a child, still learning the arts and practicing the use of arms." His sentences never seemed to conclude, but trailed away as he tried to explain. "He is a boy, a child, he is too young and tender to contend with demons."

"But I know Rama," was all that Viswamithra said in reply.

"I can send you an army, or myself lead an army to guard your performance. What can a

stripling[7] like Rama do against those terrible forces . . .? I will help you just as I helped Indra[8] once when he was harassed and deprived of his kingdom."

Viswamithra ignored his speech and rose to leave. "If you cannot send Rama, I need none else." He started to move down the passage.

The King was too stricken to move. When Viswamithra had gone half way, he realized that the visitor was leaving unceremoniously and was not even shown the courtesy of being escorted to the door. Vasishtha,[9] the King's priest and guide, whispered to Dasaratha, "Follow him and call him back," and hurried forward even before the King could grasp what he was saying. He almost ran as Viswamithra had reached the end of the hall and, blocking his way, said, "The King is coming; please don't go. He did not mean . . ."

A wry smile played on Viswamithra's face as he said without any trace of bitterness, "Why are you or anyone agitated? I came here for a purpose; it has failed: no reason to prolong my stay."

"Oh, eminent one, you were yourself a king once."

"What has that to do with us now?" asked Viswamithra, rather irked, since he hated all

---

7. **stripling** (strip´ liŋ) n.: Young boy passing into manhood.
8. **Indra** (in´ drə): Hindu god associated with rain and thunderclouds.
9. **Vasishtha** (vä sē´ sh tä): King's priest and guide.

◆ **Build Vocabulary**

austerities (ô ster´ ə tēz) n.: Self-denials

decrepitude (dē krep´ ə tо̄о̄d) n.: State of being worn out by old age or illness

sublime (sə blīm´) adj.: Noble; admirable

august (ô gust´) adj.: Worthy of respect because of age and dignity

Rama's Initiation ◆ 925

---

3. **yagna** (yäg nä´) n.: Sacrifice.
4. **Sidhasrama** (sēd häs rä´ mä)
5. **Ganges** (gan´ jēz): River in northern India.
6. **five-fold evils:** Lust, anger, miserliness, egoism, and envy.

925

reference to his <u>secular</u> past and wanted always to be known as a Brahma Rishi.[10]

① Vasishtha answered mildly, "Only to remind you of an ordinary man's feelings, especially a man like Dasaratha who had been childless and had to pray hard for an issue . . ."

"Well, it may be so, great one; I still say that I came on a mission and wish to leave, since it has failed."

"It has not failed," said Vasishtha, and just then the King came up to join them in the passage; the assembly was on its feet.

Dasaratha made a deep <u>obeisance</u> and said, "Come back to your seat, Your Holiness."

"For what purpose, Your Majesty?" Viswamithra asked.

"Easier to talk seated . . ."

"I don't believe in any talk," said Viswamithra; but Vasishtha pleaded with him until he returned to his seat.

② When they were all seated again, Vasishtha addressed the King: "There must be a divine purpose working through this seer, who may know but will not explain. It is a privilege that Rama's help should be sought. Do not bar his way. Let him go with the sage."

"When, oh when?" the King asked anxiously.

"Now," said Viswamithra.

The King looked woebegone and desperate, and the sage relented enough to utter a word of comfort. "You cannot count on the physical proximity of someone you love, all the time. A seed that sprouts at the foot of its parent tree remains stunted until it is transplanted. Rama will be in my care, and he will be quite well. But ultimately, he will leave me too. Every human being, when the time comes, has to depart and seek his fulfillment in his own way."

"Sidhasrama is far away . . .?" began the King.

----

10. **Brahma Rishi** (brä′ mä rǐ′ shē): Enlightened sage.

926 ◆ Epics and Legends

"I'll ease his path for him, no need for a chariot to take us there," said Viswamithra reading his mind.

"Rama has never been separated from his brother Lakshmana.[11] May he also go with him?" pleaded the King, and he looked relieved when he heard Viswamithra say, "Yes, I will look after both, though their mission will be to look after me. Let them get ready to follow me; let them select their favorite weapons and prepare to leave."

Dasaratha, with the look of one delivering hostages into the hand of an enemy, turned to his minister and said, "Fetch my sons."

Following the footsteps of their master like his shadows, Rama and Lakshmana went past the limits of the city and reached the Sarayu River, which bounded the capital on the north. When night fell, they rested at a wooded grove and at dawn crossed the river. When the sun came over the mountain peak, they reached a pleasant grove over which hung, like a canopy, fragrant smoke from numerous sacrificial fires. Viswamithra explained to Rama, "This is where God Shiva[12] meditated once upon a time and reduced to ashes the god of love when he attempted to spoil his meditation. From time immemorial saints praying to Shiva come here to perform their sacrifices, and the pall of smoke you notice is from their sacrificial fires." **④**

A group of hermits emerged from their seclusion, received Viswamithra, and invited him and his two disciples to stay with them for the night. Viswamithra resumed his journey at dawn and reached a desert region at midday. The mere expression "desert" hardly conveys the absolute aridity of this land. Under a relentless sun, all vegetation had dried and turned to dust, stone and rock crumbled into powdery sand, which lay in vast dunes, stretching away to the horizon.

----

11. **Lakshmana** (läks mä′ nä)
12. **God Shiva** (shē′ və): Hindu god of destruction.

Cross-Curricular Connection: Social Studies

Hinduism The major religion of India, Hinduism, is the oldest religion in the world. One of the important teachings of Hinduism is reincarnation. Hindus believe that when the body dies, the soul is reborn in a continuous process. The soul of someone who lives a good personal life and performs pious deeds will be reborn into a higher status, possibly one of wealth and high standing in society. The soul of a person who lives a bad personal life and performs evil deeds will be reborn into a lower condition, such as that of a pig or a cockroach.

Another major aspect of Hinduism in the past was the *caste system*, a strict system of hereditary social classes. Members of one caste could not mix with members of the other castes. In recent times, however, different castes do intermingle. These are four traditional castes: the *Brahmans*, or priests; the *Kishatryas*, nobles and military leaders; the *Vaisyas*, business people and landowners; and the *Sudras*, farmers, workers, and servants. *Untouchables* were considered so low that they were outside the caste system. "Untouchability" was outlawed in 1950.

Here every inch was scorched and dry and hot beyond imagination. The ground was cracked and split, exposing enormous fissures everywhere. The distinction between dawn, noon, and evening did not exist here, as the sun seemed to stay overhead and burn the earth without moving. Bleached bones lay where animals had perished, including those of monstrous serpents with jaws open in deadly thirst; into these enormous jaws had rushed (says the poet) elephants desperately seeking shade, all dead and fossilized, the serpent and the elephant alike. Heat haze rose and singed the very heavens. While traversing this ground, Viswamithra noticed the bewilderment and distress on the faces of the young men, and transmitted to them mentally two *mantras*[13] (called "Bala" and "Adi-Bala").

◆ Reading Strategy
What inferences can you make about the role of meditation and incantations in Indian culture and religion?

When they meditated on and recited these incantations, the arid atmosphere was transformed for the rest of their passage and they felt as if they were wading through a cool stream with a southern summer breeze blowing in their faces. Rama, ever curious to know the country he was passing through, asked, "Why is this land so terrible? Why does it seem accursed?"

"You will learn the answer if you listen to this story—of a woman fierce, ruthless, eating and digesting all living creatures, possessing the strength of a thousand mad elephants."

---

13. *mantras* (män´träz): Sacred syllables.

◆ **Build Vocabulary**

secular (sek´ yə lər) *adj.*: Not sacred or religious

obeisance (ō bā´ səns) *n.*: Gesture of respect

exuberance (eg zōō´ bər əns) *n.*: State of high spirits and good health

diminutive (də min´ yōō tiv) *adj.*: Smaller than average

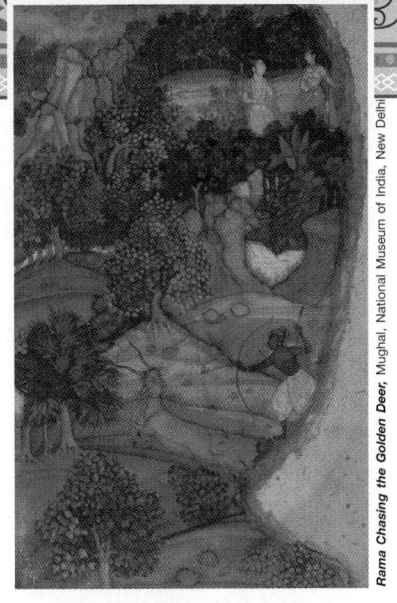

Rama Chasing the Golden Deer, Mughal, National Museum of India, New Delhi

▲ **Critical Viewing** What details in this painting support inferences you've made from reading this epic? [Connect; Support]

Thataka's Story

The woman I speak of was the daughter of Suketha[14] a *yaksha,* a demigod of great valor, might, and purity. She was beautiful and full of wild energy. When she grew up she was married to a chieftain named Sunda. Two sons were born to them—Mareecha and Subahu[15]—who were endowed with enormous supernatural powers in addition to physical strength; and in their conceit and exuberance they laid waste their surroundings. Their father, delighted at their pranks and infected by their mood, joined in their activities. He pulled out ancient trees by their roots and flung them about, and he slaughtered all creatures that came his way. This depredation came to the notice of the great savant Agasthya[16] (the diminutive saint who

---

14. **Suketha** (sōō kā´ tä)
15. **Mareecha** (mä´ rē chä) **and Subahu** (sä bä´ hōō)
16. **savant** (sə vänt´) **Agasthya** (ä gus tē yä´): Learned man named Agasthya.

Rama's Initiation ◆ 927

Comprehension Check ☑

❺ Have students describe the desert region. *The plants had turned to dust, and stones had crumbled into sand. The ground was dry and cracked. Always overhead, the sun was constantly shining. The bleached, white bones of dead animals lay on the ground where they had died.*

◆ **Reading Strategy**

❻ **Make Inferences About Culture** Elicit responses such as the following: *Sample answer: The Indian people use meditation and incantations to help free the human spirit to rise beyond the demands and discomforts of the human body.*

◆ **Reading Strategy**

❼ **Make Inferences About Culture** Rama asks Viswamithra why the land is so terrible. What two inferences can students make about ancient Indian culture from Viswamithra's response? *(1) Storytelling is an important way to impart history or lessons. (2) Humans—or rather demigods and demons in human form—can possess supernatural powers.*

▶ **Critical Viewing** ◀

❽ **Connect; Support** Suggested response: Students might comment that the scene shows that Rama is brave and adventurous, and that Lakshmana helps Rama in his endeavors.

◆ **Build Grammar Skills**

❾ **Restrictive and Nonrestrictive Appositives** Have students identify the appositive here, say whether it is restrictive or nonrestrictive, and why. *The appositive is Agasthya. It is restrictive because it is necessary to the meaning of the sentence. Otherwise, the audience would not know to which savant Viswamithra is referring.*

 Humanities: Language and Literature

The *Sanskrit language* is considered part of the Indo-European family of languages, which includes English, German, Latin, and Farsi (spoken in ancient Persia and modern Iran). The beginnings of Sanskrit can be traced to approximately 1500 B.C. when the Aryans invaded India, bringing their language with them. This language evolved into Vedic Sanskrit, the language of the Indian upper classes. Gradually, Vedic Sanskrit fell out of use as a spoken language but became a standard form of written language, referred to now as classical Sanskrit. The Sanskrit literature began orally and was passed down through many generations before the stories were written down. Two of the most important works of classical Sanskrit are the *Ramayana* and the *Mahabharata.*

Encourage interested students to learn more about the Sanskrit language and literature. For example, students might find out about the sacred syllable "om." (It is a word of assent comparable to the English "amen.") "Om" is used as a way to help meditation. Students might be interested in finding out the meaning of other Sanskrit words that are commonly used in meditation and yogic practice.

► Critical Viewing ◄

❶ Analyze Sample answer: *In this piece of art, Rama is admired for his prowess as a hunter.*

◆ **Critical Thinking**

❷ Synthesize Draw attention to the physical change in Thataka and her sons. Ask how this change is related to their actions. *Sample answer: They were superior beings, or demigods. However, they did not use their great powers to do good; instead they behaved worse than wild animals. Their changed appearance reflects the evil ways in which they acted.*

◆ **Build Vocabulary**

❸ Word Roots: -min- Have students identify the word with the root *-min-*. *The word is* minutest. *Ask students what the root* -min- *means. It means "small." What does* minutest *mean in this context?* Thataka is saying that she has gotten rid of everything—even the smallest bit of life.

◆ **Critical Thinking**

❹ Draw Conclusions Point out that Rama hesitates to kill Thataka when she confronts him. Ask students what they can conclude about Rama. *Suggested response: Apparently Rama has been taught to respect women and not to harm them.*

◆ **Build Grammar Skills**

❺ Restrictive and Nonrestrictive Appositives Have students identify the appositive phrase and explain whether it is restrictive or nonrestrictive. *"The god of death" is the appositive. It is nonrestrictive because it is not necessary to the meaning of the sentence but gives added information about Yama.*

Rama Chases a Demon Disguised as a Golden Deer, Fazl, Freer Gallery of Art, Smithsonian Institution, Washington, D.C.

❶ ▲ **Critical Viewing** What details in this painting indicate Rama's importance? **[Analyze]**

once, when certain demoniac beings hid themselves at the bottom of the sea and Indra appealed for his help to track them, had sipped off the waters of the ocean). Agasthya had his hermitage in this forest, and when he noticed the destruction around, he cursed the perpetrator of this deed and Sunda fell dead. When his wife learned of his death, she and her sons stormed in, roaring revenge on the saint. He met their challenge by cursing them. "Since you are destroyers of life, may you become *asuras*[17] and

17. *asuras* (ä sōō´ räz)

◆ **Build Vocabulary**

esoteric (es´ ə ter´ ik) *adj.:* Beyond the understanding of most people

928 ◆ *Epics and Legends*

dwell in the nether worlds." (Till now they had been demigods. Now they were degraded to demonhood.) The three at once underwent a transformation; their features and stature became forbidding, and their natures changed to match. The sons left to seek the company of superdemons. The mother was left alone and lives on here, breathing fire and wishing everything ill. Nothing flourishes here; only heat and sand remain. She is a scorcher. She carries a trident with spikes; a cobra entwined on her arm is her armlet. The name of this fearsome creature is Thataka.[18] Just as the presence of a little *loba* (meanness) dries up and disfigures a whole human personality, so does the presence of this monster turn into desert a region which was once fertile. In her restlessness she constantly harasses the hermits at their prayers; she gobbles up anything that moves and sends it down her entrails.

Touching the bow slung on his shoulder, Rama asked. "Where is she to be found?"

Before Viswamithra could answer, she arrived, the ground rocking under her feet and a storm preceding her. She loomed over them with her eyes spitting fire, her fangs bared, her lips parted revealing a cavernous mouth; and her brows twitching in rage. She raised her trident and roared, "In this my kingdom, I have crushed out the minutest womb of life and you have been sent down so that I may not remain hungry."

Rama hesitated; for all her evil, she was still a woman. How could he kill her? Reading his thoughts, Viswamithra said, "You shall not consider her a woman at all. Such a monster must receive no consideration. Her strength, ruthlessness, appearance, rule her out of that category. Formerly God Vishnu himself killed Kyathi, the wife of Brigu,[19] who harbored the

18. **Thataka** (tä tä´ kä)
19. **Vishnu** (vēsh´ nōō) . . . **Kyathi** (kyä´ tē) . . . **Brigu** (brē´gōō)

 Humanities: Art

Rama Chases a Demon Disguised as a Golden Deer.

This visual interpretation of a scene from the *Ramayana* is in the collection of the Freer Gallery, a gift made to the nation by Charles Lang Freer (1856–1919), a United States financier and art collector with a particular interest in Asian art.

Use these questions for discussion:

1. How might Rama know that the golden deer he is hunting is actually a demon? *Students* might respond that since ancient Indians believed that the body could be transformed and forces of evil could assume other physical identities, the prospect of a demonic force disguising itself as an innocent animal was one that Rama was free to consider.

2. For what purpose might Rama be hunting the golden deer? *He might be hunting it for the purpose of killing it, and thus ridding the empire of an evil force.*

asuras fleeing his wrath, when she refused to yield them. Mandorai[20] a woman bent upon destroying all the worlds, was vanquished by Indra and he earned the gratitude of humanity. These are but two instances. A woman of demoniac tendencies loses all consideration to be treated as a woman. This Thataka is more dreadful than Yama, the god of death, who takes a life only when the time is ripe. But this monster, at the very scent of a living creature, craves to kill and eat. Do not picture her as a woman at all. You must rid this world of her. It is your duty."

Rama said, "I will carry out your wish."

Thataka threw her three-pronged spear at Rama. As it came flaming, Rama strung his bow and sent an arrow which broke it into fragments. Next she raised a hail of stones under which to crush her adversaries. Rama sent up

his arrows, which shielded them from the attack. Finally Rama's arrow pierced her throat and ended her career; thereby also inaugurating Rama's life's mission of destroying evil and demonry in this world. The gods assembled in the sky and expressed their joy and relief and enjoined Viswamithra, "Oh, adept and master of weapons, impart without any reserve all your knowledge and powers to this lad. He is a savior." Viswamithra obeyed this injunction and taught Rama all the esoteric techniques in weaponry. Thereafter the presiding deities of various weapons, *asthras*,[21] appeared before Rama submissively and declared, "Now we are yours: command us night or day."

> ◆ *Literature and Your Life*
>
> **6** How does Rama compare to most contemporary superheros?

---

20. **Mandorai** (mänd rä′ ē)

21. *asthras* (äs′ träz)

Guide for Responding

◆ *Literature and Your Life*

Reader's Response Do you think Viswamithra did the right thing by persuading Rama to overcome his hesitation about killing Thataka? Why or why not?

Thematic Focus At the time Viswamithra asked for Rama, Dasaratha was still trying to pass down to his son the qualities that would equip him to be a hero. If you had been in Dasaratha's place, would you have let Rama go? Explain your answer.

Group Discussion Was Viswamithra acting in Rama's best interests by insisting that only he accompany Viswamithra to Sidhasrama? In a small group of classmates, respond to this question.

☑ Check Your Comprehension

1. Why does the sage Viswamithra want Rama to accompany him to Sidhasrama?
2. Why is King Dasaratha at first reluctant to grant the sage's request?
3. Why is the region through which Rama, Lakshmana, and Viswamithra pass so inhospitable?
4. (a) Why is Rama reluctant to fight Thataka at first? (b) How does Viswamithra persuade him to fight?
5. What are the outcomes of Rama's first battle?

Rama's Initiation ◆ 929

 Beyond the Selection

FURTHER READING

Other Works by R. K. Narayan
Under the Banyan Tree and Other Stories, *Grandmother's Tale*, *Waiting for the Mahatma*

Other Works About Heroes of the Past
The *Odyssey*, Homer
The *Aeneid*, Virgil
Idylls of the King, Alfred, Lord Tennyson
Poetic Edda (Unknown)

We suggest that you preview these works before recommending them to students.

INTERNET

You and your students can visit the following Web sites for more information. Please be aware that the sites may have changed since we published this information. For a lesson plan on the *Ramayana* accompanied by the story and a teaching guide, go to **http://www.askasia.org/frclasrom/lessplan/1000054.htm** For more information on R.K. Narayan, go to **http://members.aol.com/mohangk/narayan.htm**

We *strongly recommend* that you preview the sites before you send students to them.

Answers

◆ Critical Thinking

1. Viswamithra, a sage, knew that by challenging Rama in this way he would help the boy to prove his prowess and heroic qualities.
2. He has found enlightenment and probably wants no reminder of his worldly ways and, perhaps, of his past failings.
3. They undergo physical transformation as a result of Agasthya's curse so that their appearance will reflect their internal evil.
4. Viswamithra is wise, worldly, and self-disciplined, and he can impart valuable lessons to Rama about the difference between how things appear and their true nature.
5. A child could be compared to a seed in any time period because the principle still applies: like a seed growing into a tree, a child is small and needs nurturing to develop into a healthy adult.
6. Students might compare Rama with a super hero from a comic book, science fiction series, or a film in which the hero exhibits prowess to vanquish evil.

◆ Literary Focus

1. Rama's journey with Viswamithra, on which he is introduced to the workings of evil, begin his passage from childhood to adulthood.
2. Rama shows his heroic powers by overcoming his reservations and killing Thataka, an evil force.
3. The people recognized Rama's heroism and asked Viswamithra to prepare him to lead them in all they would do.

◆ Reading Strategy

1. The *Ramayana* shows that the wisdom and spiritual powers of the sage can overcome worldly trials.
2. The *Ramayana* reveals that kings had great respect for sages in ancient India; they accepted their counsel and followed their recommendations.
3. Readers can infer that ancient Indians honored and protected women.

◆ Build Vocabulary

Using the Root -min-

1. minimum—small amount;
2. minority—smaller number of two parts;   3. small or brief amount of

---

Guide for Responding (continued)

◆ Critical Thinking

INTERPRET

1. Explain why Viswamithra chose the young and inexperienced Rama to help him perform such a dangerous task. **[Infer]**
2. Why do you think Viswamithra dislikes all references to his nonreligious past? **[Interpret]**
3. Why do you think Thataka and her two sons undergo a physical transformation as one result of Agasthya's curse? **[Draw Conclusions]**
4. Explain why Viswamithra is a worthy teacher to Rama in his quest to be a hero. **[Interpret]**

APPLY

5. Explain how Viswamithra's comparison of a child to a seed could apply in any time period. **[Relate]**

EXTEND

6. Compare and contrast Rama with a popular superhero in a story, book, or film with which you are familiar. **[Literature Link]**

◆ Literary Focus

THE EPIC HERO

The **epic hero** is the central character of an epic. In his adventures, the hero demonstrates extraordinary skills and special qualities.

1. How does Rama begin the passage from childhood to adulthood?
2. How does Rama show his heroic powers?
3. How do the events that follow Rama's battle with Thataka indicate that Rama is an epic hero?

◆ Reading Strategy

MAKE INFERENCES ABOUT CULTURE

The *Ramayana* presents a picture of Indian culture 2,000 years ago. From the stories told and the details given, you can **infer** beliefs, values, and customs of the period.

1. How does the *Ramayana* show the importance of the sage in Indian culture?
2. What does the *Ramayana* reveal about the relationship between kings and sages in ancient India?
3. Rama hesitates before killing Thataka because she is a woman. What can you infer from this about Indian culture and society?

◆ Build Vocabulary

USING THE ROOT -min-

The root *-min-* means "small." Use this knowledge to help you define each of the following words:

1. minimum   2. minority   3. minute   4. diminish

USING THE WORD BANK

On your paper, write the word whose meaning is closest to that of the first word.

1. austerities: (a) savings, (b) deprivations, (c) blows
2. decrepitude: (a) weariness, (b) unconcern, (c) fear
3. sublime: (a) pleasant, (b) tragic, (c) noble
4. august: (a) overheated, (b) dignified, (c) confused
5. secular: (a) nonreligious, (b) expansive, (c) serious
6. obeisance: (a) anger, (b) shallowness, (c) respect
7. exuberance: (a) excitement, (b) gloom, (c) conceit
8. diminutive: (a) foolish, (b) little, (c) showy
9. esoteric: (a) mysterious, (b) accessible, (c) haughty

◆ Build Grammar Skills

RESTRICTIVE AND NONRESTRICTIVE APPOSITIVES

Restrictive appositives and appositive phrases are essential to the meaning of the sentence; they are not set off by commas. **Nonrestrictive** appositives are not essential to the sentence's meaning; these are set off with commas.

Practice In your notebook, write the following sentences. Underline the appositive or appositive phrase in each. If the appositive is nonrestrictive, set it off with commas.

1. Viswamithra a sage of great understanding entered the king's assembly hall.
2. King Dasaratha the father of two young sons greeted the sage warmly.
3. "Send your son Rama with me, and he will help me," said the sage.
4. Vasishtha the king's priest and guide urged Dasaratha to agree to the sage's demand.
5. In the end, the brothers Rama and Lakshmana accompanied the holy man on his quest.

---

time;   4. diminish—to make smaller

Using the Word Bank

1. deprivations;   2. weariness;
3. pleasant;   4. dignified;
5. nonreligious;   6. respect;
7. excitement;   8. little;
9. mysterious

◆ Build Grammar Skills

1. Viswamithra, <u>a sage of great understanding</u>, entered the king's assembly hall.

2. King Dasaratha, <u>the father of two young sons</u>, greeted the sage warmly.
3. "Send your son <u>Rama</u> with me, and he will help me," said the sage.
4. Vasishtha, <u>the king's priest and guide</u>, urged Dasaratha to agree to the sage's demand.
5. In the end the brothers <u>Rama and Lakshmana</u> accompanied the holy man on his quest.

 Writer's Solution

For additional instruction and practice, use the Commas lesson in the **Language Lab CD-ROM** and page 40 on Appositive and Appositive Phrases in the *Writer's Solution Grammar Practice Book*.

*B*uild *Y*our *P*ortfolio

 ## Idea Bank

Writing

1. Letter As Viswamithra, write a letter to Dasaratha asking permission for Rama to accompany you on a dangerous mission. Explain why the mission will be a growth experience.

2. Personal Narrative Rama's initiation into adulthood was characteristic for an epic hero. What experience has helped prepare you for adulthood? Write a brief personal narrative relating this experience and its impact on you.

3. Opening Argument You are a lawyer called upon to defend Thataka. Write an opening argument in which you detail how you will prove that Thataka was grossly misjudged. Your objective is to restore Thataka to her status as a demigod.

Speaking and Listening

4. Oral Tales Prepare a version of this episode for an audience of young children. Make an audiotape to give to young relatives or friends. **[Performing Arts Link]**

5. Indian Music In your library, research classical Indian music, particularly music featuring the stringed instruments sitar and tamboura. Give an oral report or demonstration to your class. If possible, find recordings associated with the *Ramayana*. Play them for the class. **[Music Link]**

Projects

6. Painting Reread the description of the devouring creature Thataka and the desert domain she inhabited. Create a painting that expresses the terrifying mood of this scene. **[Art Link]**

7. Dance With a group of classmates, reenact the heroic journey and battle of Rama as a dance. Incorporate classical Indian music into your performance. **[Performing Arts Link]**

 ## Writing Mini-Lesson

Script Treatment Proposal

The *Ramayana* has all the ingredients for a summer blockbuster—exotic settings, a fearless superhero, an old sage with magical powers. Think what a special effects artist could do with an evil creature like Thataka! Write a **script treatment** outlining how you propose to tell the story, cast the film, and use special effects and music to create a box-office success.

> **Writing Skills Focus: Appropriate Language for Your Purpose**
>
> Your script treatment has to show its readers that you're onto a great film idea. To do this, you'll have to make every word count. Use vivid words and phrases to express the excitement and suspense of key scenes. Also, use **language** that appeals to the emotions, such as a *stirring* scene, and *sympathetic* and *inspiring* characters.

Prewriting Before you begin writing, envision your film in your mind. To help you plan your script treatment, make an outline with headings such as story events, cast, special effects, and music. For each heading, list ideas and suggestions that you think will keep the attention of a large audience.

Events	Cast	Special Effects	Music

Drafting As you draft your treatment, draw on the information in your outline. Add to it as you envision new and better scene ideas. Use vivid and precise terms and language that will appeal to your readers' emotions.

Revising Reread your draft. Ask: Have I left out any information the backers of the film will want to know? Is my persuasive language convincing and emotional? Is it *too* emotional? Revise accordingly.

Rama's Initiation ◆ 931

OBJECTIVES

1. To read, comprehend, and interpret, an epic
2. To relate an epic to students' personal experience
3. To recognize the storyteller's purpose in an epic
4. To identify epic conflict
5. To build vocabulary in context and learn the word root *-firm-*
6. To develop skill in using sentence variety
7. To write an outline for a storytelling notes considering audience knowledge
8. To respond to the epic through writing, speaking and listening, and projects

SKILLS INSTRUCTION

Vocabulary:
Word Roots: *-firm-*
Grammar:
Sentence Variety
Reading Strategy:
Storyteller's Purpose
Literary Focus:
Epic Conflict

Writing:
Audience Knowledge
Speaking and Listening:
Oral Tales (teacher edition)
Critical Viewing:
Analyze, Infer, Relate

PORTFOLIO OPPORTUNITIES

Writing: News Article; Writing in the Heroic Tradition; Critical Evaluation

Writing Mini-Lesson: Storytelling as a Griot

Speaking and Listening: Oral Tales; Role Play

Projects: Documentary; Herb Research

More About Griots

In the time of Sundiata, griots tutored princes and gave council to kings. They were wise and educated, and they used their wide knowledge of history to shed light on problems of the day. Wealthy families of Mali had their own griot to advise them. Griots served as mediators in disputes and they arranged the terms of marriages. Later, griots became the official musicians of the society, playing the *ngoni*, a lute, and the *kora*, a 21-string cross. These griots, known as *jelis*, sang proudly of their history. The great majority of today's *jelis* are women—and they have become some of the leading pop music stars of Mali, Guinea, Senegal, and the Gambia.

Guide for Reading

Sundiata

Although the original author is not known, the story of Sundiata has been told by the storytellers, or griots (grē´ ōz), of Mali—an African republic—for many centuries. Many African ethnic groups rely on the memories of their griots, rather than on written accounts, to preserve a record of the past.

Griots are both storytellers and historians. They call themselves the memory of the people, and they travel from village to village, teaching the history and legends of their ancestors to the new generations. Thus, the griots preserve their history and culture orally.

D. T. Niane

After listening to the stories told by Mamadou Kouyate (mä´ mä dōō kōō ya´ te), a griot of the Keita clan, Djibril Tamsir Niane (dyē´ bril täm´ sēr nī´ yan) wrote *Sundiata: An Epic of Old Mali* in his Malinke language. Niane's work was translated into English and other languages, and now people all over the world profit from the griot's wisdom.

Niane's own ancestors were griots. In addition to *Sundiata*, D. T. Niane has collected and retold many other ancient legends of Mali. His translations of the ancient oral histories is one way he affirms their value. A noted historian, his specific area of interest is medieval African empires. This expertise has helped him to create the background for *Sundiata* and other works.

◆ Build Vocabulary

WORD ROOT: *-firm-*

The hero in this selection, Mari Djata, is said to have an *infirmity*. The word root *-firm-* is derived from the Latin word *firmare*, "to strengthen." By combining this meaning with the meaning of the prefix *in-*, "lacking" or "without," you can figure out that *infirmity* means "without strength" or "physical weakness."

WORD BANK

fathom
taciturn
malicious
infirmity
innuendo
diabolical
estranged
affront

As you read this selection from *Sundiata*, you will encounter the words on this list. Each word is defined on the page where it first appears.

With a partner, read the words aloud. Share the meaning of any of the words you already know.

◆ Build Grammar Skills

SENTENCE VARIETY

Writers use **sentence variety** to create an interesting rhythm in their writing. They vary their sentences in several ways. D. T. Niane uses a mix of sentence lengths and structures. He also varies his sentence types, using declarative, interrogative, and exclamatory sentences:

Declarative: *Malicious tongues began to blab.*
Interrogative: *What three-year-old has not yet taken his first steps?*
Exclamatory: *How impatient man is!*

Using different sentence beginnings also adds variety:

Begins With an Adverb: *Now he was resting on nothing …*
Begins With a Prepositional Phrase: *At the age of three he still crawled along on all-fours …*
Begins With a Participial Phrase: *Having become all-powerful, Sassouma Bérété persecuted Sogolon …*

As you read from *Sundiata*, notice the effect of the sentence variety.

932 ◆ Epics and Legends

 Prentice Hall Literature Program Resources

REINFORCE / RETEACH / EXTEND

Selection Support Pages
Build Vocabulary: Word Roots: *-firm-*, p. 261
Build Grammar Skills: Sentence Variety, p. 262
Reading Strategy: Storyteller's Purpose, p. 263
Literary Focus: Epic Conflict, p. 264

Strategies for Diverse Students' Needs, p. 64

Beyond Literature
Cross Curricular Connection: *Geography*, p. 64

Formal Assessment Selection Test, pp. 226–228;
Assessment Resources Software

Alternative Assessment, p. 64

Writing and Language Transparencies
Week 28, p. 139

Resource Pro CD-ROM
"Sundiata"—includes all resource materials and customizable lesson plan

 Listening to Literature Audiocassettes
"Sundiata"

from Sundiata: An Epic of Old Mali

◆ *Literature and Your Life*

CONNECT YOUR EXPERIENCE

If you've ever been ridiculed—even over something as trivial as a bad haircut or a botched basketball shot—you know that the temptation to strike back can be strong. While it may not always be appropriate to strike back, often there are other ways to put a stop to ridicule. In this episode, the much-belittled Mari Djata finds a noble way to not only stop the ridicule, but also to become a hero.

Journal Writing Write about a time when, like Mari Djata in this story, you were unfairly compared with another. Describe the situation and how you felt.

THEMATIC FOCUS: FROM THE PAST

Ideally, the legacy handed down from king to king encompasses wisdom, prudence, courage, and great strength. What are the results when one of these qualities is absent? How do people respond? Think about these questions as you read this selection.

◆ Background for Understanding

HISTORY

Almost 1,000 years ago, the area of west Africa that includes present-day Ghana and Mali was highly unstable. Rival kings fought for control of the salt and gold caravan trade that passed through their territory. Eventually, Sumanguru, a warrior king of Ghana, gained control of the region and cruelly oppressed the Mandinka people of Mali. Although weak and scattered, the Mandinka rebelled against Sumanguru. Just when Mali needed a leader most, against all odds, the hero Sogolon-Diata rose to power. (In rapidly spoken Mandinka, "Sogolon-Diata" became "Sundiata.") A member of the Keita clan which had ruled Mali for centuries, Sundiata united his people, fought off Sumanguru, and ushered in a glorious period of peace and prosperity.

◆ Literary Focus

EPIC CONFLICT

At the heart of any epic is an **epic conflict**—a situation in which the hero struggles against an obstacle or set of obstacles. Part of an epic conflict may be a difficult situation in childhood. In the traditional epic, the hero surmounts difficulties, conquers enemies, and finally emerges triumphant. Through these struggles, the hero passes from childhood to adulthood, proving his wisdom, bravery, and power.

As you read from the folk epic *Sundiata*, take note of the obstacles that confront Mari Djata, blocking his path on the way to achieving heroism.

◆ Reading Strategy

STORYTELLER'S PURPOSE

Griots have a **purpose,** or reason for relating their stories. The griots who told and retold the story of Sundiata for centuries had several purposes. First, they wanted to inform their people about important historical events. In addition, they intended to entertain their listeners with an exciting account of a hero's adventures. Further, by recounting the positive and negative results of various actions, the griots instructed the people in appropriate or expected behavior. Thinking about these different purposes will give you greater insight into the epic *Sundiata*.

To help you keep track of the storyteller's purposes, make a chart like the one shown. As you read the selection, list events, passages, or other aspects of the epic that illustrate each of the purposes.

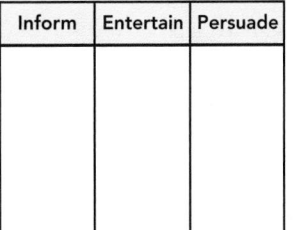

Inform	Entertain	Persuade

Interest Grabber

Make the statement that most political leaders use brain, not brawn, to settle most problems. Action heroes, however, often use more brawn than brain to fight evil. Ask students for examples of each, such as politicians who think out problems, and fictional super heroes who use extraordinary physical powers to make their impact on the world. Then let students know that the storytellers, or griots, of Mali told of political leaders that were like action heroes. The excerpt from *Sundiata* they are about to read describes a person who is both is a great leader and the possessor of superhuman powers.

Customize for
Less Proficient Readers
Ask students to pause at the end of each page to ask themselves: "What is Mari Djata's (Sogolon's son's) problem? What might happen to solve that problem?" When they finish reading, have them go back and review their predictions to see which were most nearly correct.

Customize for
More Advanced Students
These students might enjoy creating an epic that tells the (fictionalized) tale of an American leader. Have them pattern their epic after this one by providing a problem and its solution, supporting characters who create obstacles to the hero's success, and a hero who is able to overcome those obstacles.

Customize for
English Language Learners
Remind students that the hero Sundiata is also called Sogolon's son, Sogolon Djata, and Mari Djata. Write these names on the chalkboard, along with their pronunciations, for these students to refer to as they read. This quick-reference chart will help them keep track of Sundiata's actions throughout the epic.

✏️ Preparing for Standardized Tests

Reading and Vocabulary The Build Vocabulary lesson here introduces a common root, *-firm-* and its use in word building. Succeeding on the vocabulary sections of standardized tests requires a solid understanding of the meaning of prefixes, suffixes, roots, and base words. A vocabulary test might include a question like this:

Choose the synonym.
　VERIFY *(A)*
　(A) confirm　(B) conform　(C) retract
Knowing that the root *-firm-* means "to strengthen" would enable students to select *confirm* even

if they were unfamiliar with all three choices. For additional practice, use the Build Vocabulary page in *Selection Support,* p. 261.

Grammar and Language The Build Grammar Skills lesson for this selection reviews sentence variety, a skill students will draw upon as they write essays on standardized tests. For additional practice, use the Build Grammar Skills page on Sentence Variety, p. 262, in *Selection Support*.

Develop Understanding

In this translation of an African legend, future king Mari Djata (also known as Sogolon Djata and as Sundiata), seems a most unlikely hero, with his huge head and his inability to stand upright. How Mari Djata overcomes his infirmity and regains his honor is an exciting and instructive tale. Students will learn the dangers of jealousy and intolerance as they hear about one of West Africa's renowned ancient rulers.

Humanities: Art

Senegalese Glass Painting.

In urban areas of modern Senegal, painting on glass is a popular art form. What originally began as a way to make inexpensive and durable advertising signs for businesses and trucks has become an art form with striking results.

This work is painted in vivid primary colors that are flatly applied. The artist makes little attempt to show depth with gradations of color or shadows. The result is a bright pattern that is bold and decorative in the manner of African fabric. At the same time, it tells a story.

You might ask the following question:

What do you learn about the people in the painting from the details of the work? *The people seem to value music and culture based on the instruments being played. There is probably a social hierarchy, based on the elegant outfit worn by the central figure and the simpler clothing worn by the others.*

---

from SUNDIATA:
An Epic of Old Mali

D. T. Niane

Senegalese Glass Painting Used on Sundiata, collection of Professor Donal Cruise-O'Brien, Courtesy of Longman International Education

CHARACTERS IN *SUNDIATA*

Balla Fasséké (bä´ lä fä sä´ kä): Griot and counselor of Sundiata.

Boukari (bo͞o kä´ rē): Son of the king and Namandjé, one of his wives; also called Manding (män´ diŋ) Boukari.

Dankaran Touman (dän´ kä rän   to͞o´ män): Son of the king and his first wife, Sassouma, who is also called Sassouma Bérété.

Djamarou (jä mä´ ro͞o): Daughter of Sogolon and the king; sister of Sundiata and Kolonkan.

Farakourou (fä rä ko͞o´ ro͞o): Master of the forges.

Gnankouman Doua (nän ko͞o´ män   do͞o´ ə) The king's griot; also called simply, Doua.

Kolonkan (kō lōn´ kən): Sundiata's eldest sister.

Namandjé (nä män´ jē): One of the king's wives.

Naré Maghan (nä´ rä   mäg´ hän): Sundiata's father.

Nounfaïri (no͞on´ fä e̅´ rē): Soothsayer and smith; father of Farakourou.

Sassouma Bérété (sä so͞o´ mä   be´ re te): The king's first wife.

Sogolon (sô gô lōn´): Sundiata's mother; also called Sogolon Kedjou (kä´ jo͞o).

Sundiata (so͞on dyä´ tä): Legendary king of Mali; referred to as Djata (dyä´ tä) and Sogolon Djata, which means "son of Sogolon." Sundiata is also called Mari (mä´ rē) Djata.

Block Scheduling Strategies

Consider these suggestions to take advantage of extended class time:

- Ask students to work in groups to brainstorm for a list of words containing the root -*firm*- introduced in Build Vocabulary on page 932. Allow time for groups to compare their lists.
- As you review the information in Background for Understanding (p. 933), display a map and have students share

facts about West Africa that they have learned in social studies classes.

- Introduce the Reading Strategy: Storyteller's Purpose on page 933. Have students fill out a chart as they read the story and then answer the Reading Strategy questions on page 940. You may follow up with the Reading Strategy page in **Selection Support,** p. 263.

- Students may work in pairs or small groups to answer the Critical Thinking questions on page 940. Reconvene the class to discuss the answers.
- Use the audiotape version of "Sundiata" to explore the difference between reading and hearing a story. Discuss the fact that the art of the griots was in taking a historic event and rendering it as oral history with a dramatic flair.

CHILDHOOD

God has his mysteries which none can <u>fathom</u>. You, perhaps, will be a king. You can do nothing about it. You, on the other hand, will be unlucky, but you can do nothing about that either. Each man finds his way already marked out for him and he can change nothing of it.

Sogolon's son had a slow and difficult childhood. At the age of three he still crawled along on all-fours while children of the same age were already walking. He had nothing of the great beauty of his father Naré Maghan. He had a head so big that he seemed unable to support it; he also had large eyes which would open wide whenever anyone entered his mother's house. He was <u>taciturn</u> and used to spend the whole day just sitting in the middle of the house. Whenever his mother went out he would crawl on all-fours to rummage about in the calabashes[1] in search of food, for he was very greedy.

<u>Malicious</u> tongues began to blab. What three-year-old has not yet taken his first steps? What three-year-old is not the despair of his parents through his whims and shifts of mood? What three-year-old is not the joy of his circle through his backwardness in talking? Sogolon Djata (for it was thus that they called him, prefixing his mother's name to his), Sogolon Djata,

---

1. **calabashes** (kal´ ə bash´ iz) n.: Dried, hollow shells of gourds, used as bowls.

◀ Critical Viewing How does the artist show which is the most important character in this painting? [Analyze]

◆ Build Vocabulary

fathom (fath´ əm) v.: Understand thoroughly

taciturn (tas´ ə tʉrn) adj.: Uncommunicative

malicious (mə lish´ əs) adj.: Intentionally harmful

infirmity (in fʉr´ mə tē) n.: Physical weakness

innuendo (in´ yo͞o en´ dō) n.: Insinuation

diabolical (dī ə bäl´ ik əl) adj.: Wicked; cruel

estranged (e strānjd´) adv.: Removed from; at a distance

---

then, was very different from others of his own age. He spoke little and his severe face never relaxed into a smile. You would have thought that he was already thinking, and what amused children of his age bored him. Often Sogolon would make some of them come to him to keep him company. These children were already walking and she hoped that Djata, seeing his companions walking, would be tempted to do likewise. But nothing came of it. Besides, Sogolon Djata would brain the poor little things with his already strong arms and none of them would come near him any more.

The king's first wife was the first to rejoice at Sogolon Djata's <u>infirmity</u>. Her own son, Dankaran Touman, was already eleven. He was a fine and lively boy, who spent the day running about the village with those of his own age. He had even begun his initiation in the bush.[2] The king had had a bow made for him and he used to go behind the town to practice archery with his companions. Sassouma was quite happy and snapped her fingers at Sogolon, whose child was still crawling on the ground. Whenever the latter happened to pass by her house, she would say, "Come, my son, walk, jump, leap about. The jinn[3] didn't promise you anything out of the ordinary, but I prefer a son who walks on his two legs to a lion that crawls on the ground." She spoke thus whenever Sogolon went by her door. The <u>innuendo</u> would go straight home and then she would burst into laughter, that <u>diabolical</u> laughter which a jealous woman knows how to use so well.

Her son's infirmity weighed heavily upon Sogolon Kedjou; she had resorted to all her talent as a sorceress to give strength to her son's legs, but the rarest herbs had been useless. The king himself lost hope.

How impatient man is! Naré Maghan became imperceptibly <u>estranged</u> but Gnankouman

---

2. **initiation in the bush:** Education in tribal lore given to twelve-year-old West African boys so they can become full members of the tribe.

3. **jinn** (jin) n.: Supernatural beings that influence human affairs. Their promise was that the son of Sogolon would make Mali a great empire.

---

from *Sundiata: An Epic of Old Mali* ◆ 935

◆ Reading Strategy

① Storyteller's Purpose Point out the use of the pronoun *you* in this opening paragraph. Ask what the storyteller's purpose is in this section. *His purpose is to teach each person a lesson: your fate is predetermined, or established in advance. You cannot change it. By using the pronoun you, the storyteller makes direct contact with the listener.*

◆ Build Grammar Skills

② Sentence Variety Have students notice the rhythm created by the storyteller's use of questions here. Ask students to consider how the use of questions gets listeners involved in the story. *Suggested response: The questions allow listeners to respond directly to the story.*

▶ Critical Viewing ◀

③ Analyze The artist places one figure at the center of the painting and makes him larger than the others. This man is also shown to have more elaborate clothing than the others. He also holds a staff, which often indicates a ruler or wise man. The attention of all the other figures is focused on the central figure. In these ways, the artist indicates that this character is the most important one in the painting.

◆ Reading Strategy

④ Storyteller's Purpose What is the storyteller's purpose in telling you this? What does he want you to believe about Sogolon? *The storyteller's purpose is to emphasize the extent of the infirmity that Mari Djata (Sogolon Djata) must overcome. He also wants people to understand how cruel Sassouma, Mari Djata's enemy, can be.*

🎵 Humanities: Literature

Oral Tradition

Long before there were books and libraries, people shared their history and fantasies through oral literature. Information was passed from generation to generation in song, poem, or story form. These oral histories recounted the culture of a people through plots and characters that everyone could understand and remember. The themes of oral literature centered on the beginning of the world, love, and tragedy. Oral histories included epic tales of heroism, ballads, folk tales, fables, and proverbs.

These oral tales often followed people as they moved from place to place, telling the stories they knew. That is why we find stories of a great flood in the literature of many different cultures, and why certain fairy tales reappear with differently-named characters in a variety of countries.

Much later, when written works became more common, many of these oral tales were recorded in writing. That is how *The Epic of Gilgamesh*, Greek myths, the *Ramayana*, and Sundiata remain with us today.

Students may enjoy speculating on how the electronic age might change the nature of the passage of literature from one generation to the next.

◆ Reading Strategy

2 Storyteller's Purpose Story-tellers often use metaphor to teach a lesson. What is the metaphor, or comparison, that the Griot Doua is using here? What lesson is he teaching? *Sample answer: Doua is comparing Mari Djata (Sogolon's son) to a silk cotton tree. The tree emerges from a tiny seed (as a baby does) and develops slowly and with difficulty (like the boy Mari Djata). The lesson is to have patience. While a boy may develop slowly and with infirmities, in time he will grow up to be a strong man.*

◆ Literary Focus

3 Epic Conflict In this paragraph, the storyteller foreshadows the struggle to follow. Ask students what three things mentioned here appear to stand in the way of Mari Djata's success? *The obstacles that stand in the way of Mari Djata's success are his failure to walk, the fact that the king is aging and will no longer be able to protect him, and the growth of the son of his enemy, Sassouma.*

◆ Build Grammar Skills

4 Sentence Variety The author changes the rhythm of his words when the old king speaks. Ask students how sentence variety makes the king's speech sound impressive. *Suggested response: (1) He uses long sentences to list the griots of his family, to tell what Mari Djata will learn, and to say what he will inherit. (2) To emphasize his power as king, he injects two imperative sentences: "Be inseparable . . ." and "May your destiny be. . . ." (3) To add a poetic quality to his words, the king starts some sentences with prepositional phrases: "In Mali . . ." and "From his mouth. . . ." (4) He begins several sentences with I to highlight what he personally has done as king.*

Comprehension Check ☑

5 Be sure students know who "the lion" represents. *It is Mari Djata. In one of her insults, Sassouma called him "a lion that crawls on the ground."*

Doua never ceased reminding him of the hunter's words. Sogolon became pregnant again. The king hoped for a son, but it was a daughter called Kolonkan. She resembled her mother and had nothing of her father's beauty. The disheartened king debarred Sogolon from his house and she lived in semi-disgrace for a while. Naré Maghan married the daughter of one of his allies, the king of the Kamaras. She was called Namandjé and her beauty was legendary. A year later she brought a boy into the world. When the king consulted soothsayers[4] on the destiny of this son, he received the reply that Namandjé's child would be the right hand of some mighty king. The king gave the newly-born the name of Boukari. He was to be called Manding Boukari or Manding Bory later on.

1 Naré Maghan was very perplexed. Could it be that the stiff jointed son of Sogolon was the one the hunter soothsayer had foretold?

"The Almighty has his mysteries," Gnankouman Doua would say and, taking up the hunter's words, added, "The silk cotton tree emerges from a tiny seed."

2 One day Naré Maghan came along to the house of Nounfaïri, the blacksmith seer of Niani. He was an old, blind man. He received the king in the anteroom which served as his workshop. To the king's question he replied, "When the seed germinates growth is not always easy; great trees grow slowly but they plunge their roots deep into the ground."

"But has the seed really germinated?" said the king.

"Of course," replied the blind seer. "Only the growth is not as quick as you would like it; how impatient man is."

This interview and Doua's confidence gave the king some assurance. To the great displeasure of Sassouma Bérété the king restored Sogolon to favor and soon another daughter was born to her. She was given the name of Djamarou.

3 However, all Niani talked of nothing else but the stiff-legged son of Sogolon. He was now seven and he still crawled to get about. In spite

---

4. **soothsayers** (sōōth′ sā′ ərz) *n*.: People who can foretell the future.

---

of all the king's affection, Sogolon was in despair. Naré Maghan aged and he felt his time coming to an end. Dankaran Touman, the son of Sassouma Bérété, was now a fine youth.

One day Naré Maghan made Mari Djata come to him and he spoke to the child as one speaks to an adult. "Mari Djata, I am growing old and soon I shall be no more among you, but before death takes me off I am going to give you the present each king gives his successor. In Mali every prince has his own griot. Doua's father was my father's griot, Doua is mine and the son of Doua, Balla Fasséké here, will be your griot. Be inseparable friends from this day forward. From his mouth you will hear the history of your ancestors, you will learn the art of governing Mali according to the principles which our ancestors have bequeathed to us. I have served my term and done my duty too. I have done everything which a king of Mali ought to do. I am handing an enlarged kingdom over to you and I leave you sure allies. May your destiny be accomplished, but never forget that Niani is your capital and Mali the cradle of your ancestors."

The child, as if he had understood the whole meaning of the king's words, beckoned Balla Fasséké to approach. He made room for him on the hide he was sitting on and then said, "Balla, you will be my griot."

"Yes, son of Sogolon, if it pleases God," replied Balla Fasséké.

The king and Doua exchanged glances that radiated confidence.

The Lion's Awakening **5**

A short while after this interview between Naré Maghan and his son the king died. Sogolon's son was no more than seven years old. The council of elders met in the king's palace. It was no use Doua's defending the king's will which reserved the throne for Mari Djata, for the council took no account of Naré Maghan's wish. With the help of Sassouma Bérété's intrigues, Dankaran Touman was proclaimed king and a regency council was formed in which the queen mother was all-powerful. A short time after, Doua died.

As men have short memories, Sogolon's son

was spoken of with nothing but irony and scorn. People had seen one-eyed kings, one-armed kings, and lame kings, but a stiff-legged king had never been heard tell of. No matter how great the destiny promised for Mari Djata might be, the throne could not be given to someone who had no power in his legs; if the jinn loved him, let them begin by giving him the use of his legs. Such were the remarks that Sogolon heard every day. The queen mother, Sassouma Bérété, was the source of all this gossip.

Having become all-powerful, Sassouma Bérété persecuted Sogolon because the late Naré Maghan had preferred her. She banished Sogolon and her son to a back yard of the palace. Mari Djata's mother now occupied an old hut which had served as a lumber-room of Sassouma's.

The wicked queen mother allowed free passage to all those inquisitive people who wanted to see the child that still crawled at the age of seven. Nearly all the inhabitants of Niani filed into the palace and the poor Sogolon wept to see herself thus given over to public ridicule. Mari Djata took on a ferocious look in front of the crowd of sightseers. Sogolon found a little consolation only in the love of her eldest daughter, Kolonkan. She was four and she could walk. She seemed to understand all her mother's miseries and already she helped her with the housework. Sometimes, when Sogolon was attending to the chores, it was she who stayed beside her sister Djamarou, quite small as yet.

6 Sogolon Kedjou and her children lived on the queen mother's leftovers, but she kept a little garden in the open ground behind the village. It was there that she passed her brightest moments looking after her onions and gnougous.[5] One day she happened to be short of condi-

◆ *Literature and Your Life*
Why do you think people ridicule others even when they know the pain and hurt it causes?

ments and went to the queen mother to beg a little baobab leaf.[6]

"Look you," said the malicious Sassouma, "I have a calabash full. Help yourself, you poor woman. As for me, my son knew how to walk at seven and it was he who went and picked these baobab leaves. Take them then, since your son is unequal to mine." Then she laughed derisively with that fierce laughter which cuts through your flesh and penetrates right to the bone.

Sogolon Kedjou was dumbfounded. She had never imagined that hate could be so strong in a human being. With a lump in her throat she left Sassouma's. Outside her hut Mari Djata, sitting on his useless legs, was blandly eating out of a calabash. Unable to contain herself any longer, Sogolon burst into sobs and seizing a piece of wood, hit her son.

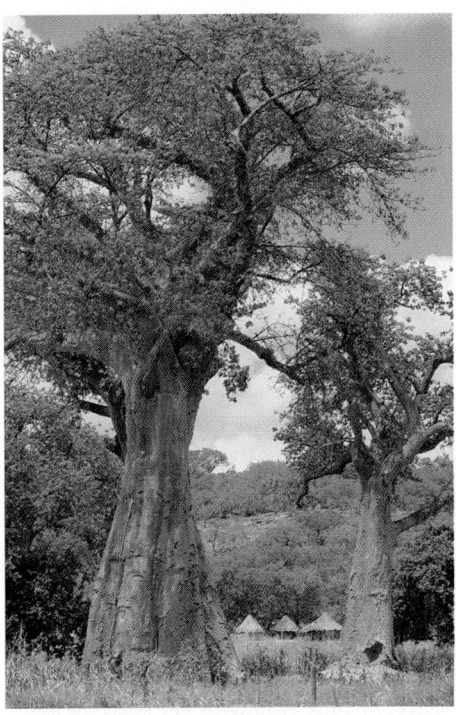

▲ **Critical Viewing** What skills might be needed to gather leaves from these baobab trees? [Infer] **8**

---

5. **gnougous** (noo′ goo′z) *n.*: Root vegetables.
6. **baobab** (bä′ ō bab′) leaf *n.*: Baobab is a thick-trunked tree; its leaves are used to flavor foods.

from Sundiata: An Epic of Old Mali ◆ 937

◆ *Literature and Your Life*

6 To help students respond to this question, point out that one of the purposes of this legend is to teach a lesson. *Sample answer: Some people ridicule others to cover up their own insecurities.*

◆ **Critical Thinking**

7 **Interpret** Point out that Sassouma, who has mercilessly ridiculed Sogolon and her Mari Djata, allows them to eat her leftovers. Ask: What does this fact say about Sassouma? *Most students will recognize that by feeding Sogolon and Mari Djata leftovers, Sassouma has found yet another way to humiliate them.*

▶**Critical Viewing**◀

8 **Infer** Sample answer: *To gather leaves from the baobab trees, one would need to be a good climber, and to be strong and agile.*

Cross-Curricular Connection: Social Studies

The empire of Mali, which Sundiata formed in the thirteenth century, is in the region now known as the Republic of Mali. It is the largest country in West Africa.

This empire was a very rich state and one of the world's major producers of gold, but it has a history of instability. It was taken over in the fifteenth century by the Songhai empire, but that empire declined rapidly, and the region became a jumble of small states. In the nineteenth century,

Mali became part of the French empire. It broke from the French in 1960 under the leadership of Modibo Keita, a man from the same Keita tribe as Sundiata. Keita became the first president of the republic, but he was overthrown in 1968 by General Moussa Traoré, who in turn was overthrown in 1991.

Locate Mali on a map and discuss with students how its location made it an important crossroads in Sundiata's times.

◆ Literary Focus

❶ Epic Conflict Sample response: *Because Sogolon's great humiliation has led her to attack her son, Mari Djata is suddenly awakened to the obstacles he needs to overcome to create a better life for his mother and to fulfill his potential. This realization heightens the epic conflict.*

◆ Critical Thinking

❷ Infer Have students explain how they can tell that the smith and the griot know why Mari Djata wants the iron bar. *They refer to this as "the great day." In addition, the smith is identified as a soothsayer, or fortune teller, who would know what the future will bring.*

◆ Reading Strategy

❸ Storyteller's Purpose Have students determine whether the purpose of this passage is to instruct or to entertain. What technique does the griot use to keep the audience interested? *Some students will suggest that the use of suspense indicates the storyteller's wish to entertain. Others may feel that by focusing on Sundiata's strenuous effort, the storyteller is teaching a lesson about determination.*

"Oh son of misfortune, will you never walk? Through your fault I have just suffered the greatest <u>affront</u> of my life! What have I done, God, for you to punish me in this way?"

Mari Djata seized the piece of wood and, looking at his mother, said, "Mother, what's the matter?"

"Shut up, nothing can ever wash me clean of this insult."

"But what then?"

"Sassouma has just humiliated me over a matter of a baobab leaf. At your age her own son could walk and used to bring his mother baobab leaves."

"Cheer up, Mother, cheer up."

"No. It's too much. I can't."

"Very well then, I am going to walk today," said Mari Djata. "Go and tell my father's smiths to make me the heaviest possible iron rod. Mother, do you want just the leaves of the baobab or would you rather I brought you the whole tree?"

◆ Literary Focus
In what way does this event contribute to the epic conflict?

"Ah, my son, to wipe out this insult I want the tree and its roots at my feet outside my hut."

Balla Fasséké, who was present, ran to the master smith, Farakourou, to order an iron rod.

Sogolon had sat down in front of her hut. She was weeping softly and holding her head between her two hands. Mari Djata went calmly back to his calabash of rice and began eating again as if nothing had happened. From time to time he looked up discreetly at his mother, who was murmuring in a low voice, "I want the whole tree, in front of my hut, the whole tree."

All of a sudden a voice burst into laughter behind the hut. It was the wicked Sassouma telling one of her serving women about the scene of humiliation and she was laughing loudly so that Sogolon could hear. Sogolon fled into the hut and hid her face under the blankets so as not to have before her eyes this heedless boy, who was more preoccupied with eating than with anything else. With her head buried in the bedclothes Sogolon wept and her body shook violently. Her daughter, Sogolon Djamarou, had come and sat down beside her and

938 ◆ Epics and Legends

she said, "Mother, Mother, don't cry. Why are you crying?"

Mari Djata had finished eating and, dragging himself along on his legs, he came and sat under the wall of the hut for the sun was scorching. What was he thinking about? He alone knew.

The royal forges were situated outside the walls and over a hundred smiths worked there. The bows, spears, arrows and shields of Niani's warriors came from there. When Balla Fasséké came to order the iron rod, Farakourou said to him, "The great day has arrived then?"

"Yes. Today is a day like any other, but it will see what no other day has seen."

The master of the forges, Farakourou, was the son of the old Nounfaïri, and he was a soothsayer like his father. In his workshops there was an enormous iron bar wrought by his father, Nounfaïri. Everybody wondered what this bar was destined to be used for. Farakourou called six of his apprentices and told them to carry the iron bar to Sogolon's house.

When the smiths put the gigantic iron bar down in front of the hut the noise was so frightening that Sogolon, who was lying down, jumped up with a start. Then Balla Fasséké, son of Gnankouman Doua, spoke.

"Here is the great day, Mari Djata. I am speaking to you, Maghan, son of Sogolon. The waters of the Niger can efface the stain from the body, but they cannot wipe out an insult. Arise, young lion, roar, and may the bush know that from henceforth it has a master."

The apprentice smiths were still there, Sogolon had come out, and everyone was watching Mari Djata. He crept on all-fours and came to the iron bar. Supporting himself on his knees and one hand, with the other hand he picked up the iron bar without any effort and stood it up vertically. Now he was resting on nothing but his knees and held the bar with both his hands. A deathly silence had gripped all those present. Sogolon Djata closed his eyes, held tight, the muscles in his arms tensed. With a violent jerk he threw his weight on to it and his knees left the ground. Sogolon Kedjou was all eyes and watched her son's legs,

---

🎙 Speaking and Listening Mini-Lesson

Oral Tales

This mini-lesson supports the Speaking and Listening activity in the Idea Bank on page 941.

Introduce the Concept A family's oral tale might be the story of how the family came to live where they do now, how they got into the business for which they are known, or how they achieved something special in their lives.

Develop Background Point out that an interesting oral tale would tell details in chronological order. Students might make outlines or timelines to help them organize their thoughts. They should consider the use of suspense and humor to hold the audience's attention. Remind students that by using sentence variety in their oral tales, they will help to keep listeners engaged.

Apply the Information Have students practice their tales by recording them, listening, and then revising them. Suggest that they use an appropriate tone of voice when relating suspenseful or humorous events. Have them deliver the polished tales to the class.

Assess the Outcome Evaluate students' work for clarity, use of sentence variety, appropriate tone of voice, and ability to hold an audience.

which were trembling as though from an electric shock. Djata was sweating and the sweat ran from his brow. In a great effort he straightened up and was on his feet at one go—but the great bar of iron was twisted and had taken the form of a bow!

④ Then Balla Fasséké sang out the "Hymn to the Bow," striking up with his powerful voice:

"Take your bow, Simbon.
Take your bow and let us go.
Take your bow, Sogolon Djata."

When Sogolon saw her son standing she stood dumb for a moment, then suddenly she sang these words of thanks to God, who had given her son the use of his legs:

"Oh day, what a beautiful day,
Oh day, day of joy;
Allah[7] Almighty, you never created a finer day.
So my son is going to walk!"

Standing in the position of a soldier at ease, Sogolon Djata, supported by his enormous rod, was sweating great beads of sweat. Balla Fasséké's song had alerted the whole palace and people

◆ **Reading Strategy**
⑤ For what purposes might the griot have included songs in this story?

7. **Allah** (al' ə): Muslim name for God.

came running from all over to see what had happened, and each stood bewildered before Sogolon's son. The queen mother had rushed there and when she saw Mari Djata standing up she trembled from head to foot. After recovering his breath Sogolon's son dropped the bar and the crowd stood to one side. His first steps were those of a giant. Balla Fasséké fell into step and pointing his finger at Djata, he cried:

"Room, room, make room!
The lion has walked;
Hide antelopes,
Get out of his way."

Behind Niani there was a young baobab tree and it was there that the children of the town came to pick leaves for their mothers. With all his might the son of Sogolon tore up the tree and put it on his shoulders and went back to his mother. He threw the tree in front of the hut and said, "Mother, here are some baobab leaves for you. From henceforth it will be outside your hut that the women of Niani will come to stock up."

◆ **Build Vocabulary**

affront (ə frunt') *n.*: Intentional insult

Guide for Responding

◆ *Literature and Your Life*

Reader's Response Were you surprised when Sogolon struck Mari Djata toward the end of the epic? Explain why you were or were not surprised.

Thematic Focus As part of his legacy, King Naré Maghan passed down to Mari Djata "an enlarged kingdom" and "sure allies." Do you think Mari Djata is qualified to build upon that legacy? Explain.

Group Discussion Discuss the qualities that make a hero. Does Mari Djata possess those qualities? Why or why not?

☑ Check Your Comprehension

1. What is the attitude of Sassouma Bérété and other people in the kingdom toward Mari Djata?
2. What prediction does the soothsayer make about the king's son?
3. What happens to Sogolon and her son after the king dies?
4. What surprising announcement does Mari Djata make after Sassouma Bérété insults his mother?
5. What extraordinary feat does seven-year-old Mari Djata accomplish?

from *Sundiata: An Epic of Old Mali* ◆ 939

Beyond the Selection

FURTHER READING

Another Work by D. T. Niane
Africa from the Twelfth to the Sixteenth Century

Other Works About Heroic Struggles
"The Labors of Hercules," *Handbook of Greek Mythology*, H.J. Rose
"David and Goliath" I Samuel 17, the Bible
The War of the Worlds, H.G. Wells
The Eyes of the Dragon, Stephen King
   We suggest that you preview these works before recommending them to students.

INTERNET

The Internet provides an opportunity to learn more about *Sundiata* at the following Web site. Please be aware, however, that the site may have changed from the time we published this information. To read the story of the *Sundiata* and learn more about Mali culture and about griots, go to **http://artsedge.kennedy-center.org/aoi/html/mali.html**
   We *strongly recommend* that you preview the sites before you send students to them.

◆ **Literary Focus**

④ **Epic Conflict** The great iron bar might have been twisted into a variety of shapes. Have students speculate on why the storyteller insists that it formed the shape of a bow. *The bow represents Mari Djata's strength and his ability to fight against his enemies.*

◆ **Reading Strategy**

⑤ **Storyteller's Purpose** Suggested response: One role of griots was to pass along their wisdom and knowledge in the form of song. Here the griot sings songs of praise: they herald the phenomenal rise of King Sogolon Djata (Mari Djata), who has overthrown his enemies and, most of all, overcome obstacles that would have daunted most men.

Reinforce and Extend

Customize for
Verbal/Linguistic Learners
Today we would call Mari Djata an "underdog." The underdog as hero is a common theme in modern times. Have students discuss movies about underdogs who ultimately triumph over obstacles.

Answers
◆ *Literature and Your Life*

Reader's Response Some students might have been surprised that Sogolon struck the son whom she loved and protected, but others will not be surprised that mounting pressures caused Sogolon to resort to this unjust act.

Thematic Focus Students might say that Mari Djata's ingenuity and spectacular rise at the end of the epic show he has the strength and character to build upon his father's legacy.

☑ **Check Your Comprehension**

1. They gossip about him, belittle him, and are completely unsupportive.
2. The soothsayer says the king's son, Namandjé's child, will be the right hand to some mighty king.
3. They occupy an old hut on Sassouma's property.
4. He says, "I am going to walk today."
5. He pulled a baobab tree up from the roots and presented it to his mother.

◆ Critical Thinking

1. The soothsayer means that it takes a long time to nurture the qualities of greatness; Mari Djata is growing slowly now to become great later.
2. Some students might say that Mari Djata seems to be above insult, while others will respond that he knows he will eventually prove his superiority over the crowds.
3. Through the triumph of Mari Djata, the epic shows that cruel words and deeds must not be allowed free reign, and that those with honor must protect those with little power; in a good world, honor will prevail.
4. Students might compare this monarchy with that of King Arthur's court or the court of King Dasaratha from the *Ramayana*.

◆ Reading Strategy

1. The storyteller's main purpose in telling this epic was probably to prove that qualities of greatness can be found anywhere, including within those people society sees as infirm.
2. It is part of the Muslim culture to praise Allah, or God, who is regarded as responsible for shaping events.

◆ Literary Focus

1. Mari Djata seems unruffled by people's reaction to his disability. On one occasion he "brains" other children who are walking near him.
2. Mari Djata's disability has enabled him to see people for what they truly are. He knows people as both loyal and cruel, and insight into people will make him an effective leader.

◆ Build Vocabulary

Using the Root *-firm-*

1. to strongly establish;   2. to say with strength that sometime is true;   3. expanse of the heavens

Using the Word Bank

1. understand;   2. tight-lipped;   3. harmful;   4. illness;   5. hint;   6. evil;   7. removed;   8. insult

◆ Build Grammar Skills

Example sentences:

1. Using potions and herbs, Sogolon tried in vain to heal her son.

Guide for Responding (continued)

◆ Critical Thinking

INTERPRET
1. What does the soothsayer mean when he tells the king, "great trees grow slowly"? **[Interpret]**
2. Why doesn't Mari Djata respond to the crowds who torment and tease him? **[Infer]**
3. In what specific ways does this epic illustrate the importance of honor? **[Support]**

EXTEND
4. Compare the monarchy of this epic with another one that you know about. **[Social Studies Link]**

◆ Reading Strategy

STORYTELLER'S PURPOSE
The griots of ancient Mali had different purposes in mind as they retold the story of Sundiata.
1. What do you think was the storyteller's main purpose for telling this epic? Explain.
2. Why do you think the storyteller includes praises to Allah at the end of the epic?

◆ Literary Focus

EPIC CONFLICT
Mari Djata's confrontation of his physical disability creates the **epic conflict** in this tale.
1. How does Mari Djata respond to the way people react to his disability?
2. In what specific ways does Mari Djata's disability contribute to his effectiveness as a leader?

Beyond Literature

Community Connection

Preserving History Through Stories
Most cultures owe a great deal of their preserved history to storytellers. The *griots* of Mali preserved the epic tale of Sundiata. Celtic history was passed on by the *bards;* their Anglo-Saxon counterparts were called *scops.* Storytellers captured attitudes and customs of a time and preserved the names of important historical figures. Find out more about the function of storytellers in a culture that interests you. Share what you learn with your class.

◆ Build Vocabulary

USING THE ROOT *-firm-*
The root *-firm-* means "to strengthen." Incorporate the meaning of "strengthen" in the definitions of each of the following words:

1. confirm   2. affirm   3. firmament

USING THE WORD BANK
On your paper, write the word whose meaning is closest to that of the first word.
1. fathom: (a) confuse, (b) understand, (c) remove
2. taciturn: (a) angry, (b) gracious, (c) tight-lipped
3. malicious: (a) mournful, (b) harmful, (c) changeable
4. infirmity: (a) sadness, (b) illness, (c) fear
5. innuendo: (a) style, (b) hint, (c) allowance
6. diabolical: (a) evil, (b) passionate, (c) extreme
7. estranged: (a) removed, (b) indecent, (c) plentiful
8. affront: (a) coverup, (b) accident, (c) insult

◆ Build Grammar Skills

SENTENCE VARIETY
It's important to vary the structure and kinds of sentences you use. **Sentence variety** means more than using sentences of different length. Beginning sentences with different constructions is also an effective way to achieve sentence variety.

Practice In your notebook, rewrite the following sentences so that each begins with either an adverb, prepositional phrase, participial phrase (Verb form, acting as an adjective, along with the words that complete it), or subordinate clause (A group of words, containing a subject and a verb, that cannot stand alone as a sentence).
1. Sogolon tried in vain to heal her son using potions and herbs.
2. The stiff-legged son of Sogolon still crawled about although he was now seven.
3. The young prince slowly straightened up and was on his feet in one go.
4. Mari Djata tore up the tree with all his might and went back to his hut.
5. Sogolon wept with her head buried in the bedclothes, and her body shook violently.

---

2. Although he was now seven, the stiff-legged son of Sogolon still crawled about.
3. In one go, the young prince slowly straightened up and was on his feet.
4. With all his might, Mari Djata tore up the tree, and then he went back to his hunt.
5. With her head buried in the bedclothes, Sologon wept and her body shook violently.

✒ Writer's Solution

For additional instruction and practice, use the Varying Sentence Structure and Varying Sentence Lengths and Structures lessons in the **Language Lab CD-ROM.** You may also use pages 121–123 on Varying Your Sentences in the *Writer's Solution Grammar Practice Book.*

Build Your Portfolio

Idea Bank

Writing

1. News Article You are an eyewitness to Mari Djata's extraordinary feat. Write an account of this event for a newspaper. Answer the questions *who? what? when? where? why?* and *how?*

2. Writing in the Heroic Tradition Write a brief episode in the later life of Mari Djata. Show how he fulfills the heroic tradition. Include cultural details revealed in *Sundiata*.

3. Critical Evaluation In an essay, evaluate the central conflict in *Sundiata*. Keeping in mind the characteristics of an epic, is the conflict believable and engaging? Support your points with examples from the epic.

Speaking and Listening

4. Oral Tales Many families keep their histories alive in the same way that Mali villages do. Share a family story that focuses on your family's origins or on a milestone, such as a birth, death, or a special achievement. **[Social Studies Link]**

5. Role Play Imagine that Sogolon and Sassouma Bérété meet each other right after Sundiata tears up the baobab tree. Role-play a conversation between them. **[Performing Arts Link]**

Projects

6. Documentary Do research to learn about the arts in the country of Mali. Present your findings to the class in the form of a mini-documentary. **[Art Link; Social Studies Link]**

7. Herb Research Sogolon used the rarest herbs in an effort to cure her son. Write a research report on the different ways herbs have been used as healing agents in ancient and current times. **[Science Link; Social Studies Link]**

Writing Mini-Lesson

Storytelling Notes

Although the griots of ancient Mali presented epics from memory, a modern storyteller might want to work from a good set of notes. Combine the old and the new to write the outline for a storytelling of the *Sundiata* epic today. The following tip will help you write effective notes.

**Writing Skills Focus:
Audience Knowledge**

Considering your **audience's knowledge** is an important part of storytelling. You can't assume, for example, that your listeners know where Mali is. They may not know what a baobab, a calabash, or even a soothsayer is either. In your notes, be sure to identify and define the terms with which a general audience may be unfamiliar.

Prewriting Make a chart that lists the characters and events you will include. Under each heading, jot down ideas for what might best enrich your telling of the story. Remember, you don't have to develop a finished piece of writing, only notes.

Drafting In your draft, elaborate on the thoughts and notes you compiled in prewriting. Account for all the parts of a story: an introduction to characters and setting, a conflict, a climax, and a resolution. Also, make sure you consider the knowledge level of your audience. For example, for a general audience of any age, define unfamiliar terms. You might also want to compare ancient practices with contemporary ones.

Revising Read through your notes to be sure they will serve you well when you go to tell your story. Ask: Did I account for all parts of the story? Did I provide enough background information to keep my audience informed?

from *Sundiata: An Epic of Old Mali* ◆ 941

The movie trilogy known as *Star Wars* is a modern epic. It is the tale of a young hero and his battle to overcome obstacles and to fight evil. As Mari Djata had to learn leadership skills from his griot and his father, young Luke Skywalker learns the skills he will need to save the universe from the Jedi knights (from Obi-Wan Kenobi, in particular).

In this selection, the origins of the names of the characters in the *Star Wars* epic are explained. Students will see that the sound and the background of each name help reflect the personality and the role of the character.

Extension Many students will have seen one or all of the *Star Wars* films, but the details of the film may not be fresh in their minds. As an optional activity, you may wish to have interested students rent and watch the *Star Wars* videos and then present a report to the class in which they identify and explain the elements of *Star Wars* that are characteristic an epic.

Customize for
More Advanced Students
Have these students find out more about some of the references used in this essay, such as J.R.R. Tolkien's *Lord of the Rings,* the John Carter of Mars tales by Edgar Rice Burroughs, and Frank Herbert's *Dune.* Students can present relevant information to the rest of the class to enhance their understanding of this essay.

Enrichment
Influenced by the heroes of epics and legends, George Lucas set a traditional hero tale in a futuristic setting. In *Star Wars, The Empire Strikes Back,* and *The Return of the Jedi,* as Lucas traces the adventures of Luke Skywalker, he draws on the traditional stages in the life of a hero. In addition, the pitting of the youthful Skywalker against the experienced Darth Vader and the conflict between the small rebel force and the powerful Empire are examples of the battle between the underdog and the bully.

CONNECTIONS TO TODAY'S WORLD

The epics in this section reflect the values and traditions of the cultures from which they come. In "Star Wars: An Epic for Today," Eric Nash explores the ways in which the *Star Wars* trilogy brings together elements of contemporary American society with references to epics of the world.

George Lucas's science-fiction *Star Wars* trilogy includes *Star Wars* (1977), *The Empire Strikes Back* (1980), and *Return of the Jedi* (1983). These films were so popular that upon re-release in 1996, they drew larger crowds than any other films released at the same time.

Star Wars is widely viewed as a modern epic. It contains many of the elements of a classic epic: It chronicles the adventures of a hero; it vividly describes battles between good and evil; and it reflects the values of a culture.

Star Wars: An Epic for Today

Eric P. Nash

Twenty years ago, the film maker George Lucas expanded everybody's notion of how fast a movie could really move with the first installment of his "Star Wars" trilogy. A new generation of moviegoers will be introduced to "Star Wars" on Friday, when the film returns to the big screen with a digitally remastered soundtrack, new scenes (including a meeting between Han Solo and the gelatinous Jabba the Hutt) and some visually enhanced effects. Part of what makes the "Star Wars" universe such fun is that the characters seem to emerge from their own complex cultures. Then there is the ear-tickling felicity of the names. It's hard to resist saying Boba Fett, Bounty Hunter, out loud just to try it on the lips. Just where did George Lucas come up with all these weird names?

"Basically, I developed the names for the characters phonetically," Mr. Lucas

942 ◆ *Epics and Legends*

Like other epic heroes, Skywalker has his weaknesses as well as his strengths. As the hero matures, he has to overcome the fears and disadvantages that come with beginning as an ordinary human being. The origin of the hero is frequently marked by an unusual circumstance, such as Sundiata's slow progress in walking. Skywalker, raised by foster parents, is ignorant of his true heritage.

Like other epic heroes, Skywalker is not alone on his journey. In addition to his trustworthy friends, Han Solo, Princess Leia, Chewbacca, C-3PO, and R2D2, Skywalker receives the gifts of the Force and his light saber from his spiritual guide, Obi-Wan Kenobi. Students may draw parallels to King Arthur here.

As often happens in epics, Skywalker is separated from his companions. As the lone hero, he must seek out a spiritual teacher on a long journey or quest. When he returns, he is prepared to confront the forces and temptations that would defeat an ordinary man. Therefore, when he confronts Darth Vader, who is both enemy and father, Skywalker is strong enough to suffer serious injury rather than give up the struggle for his cause.

❶ ▲ Critical Viewing What details make the subject of this picture look like a legendary hero? [**Analyze**]

said. "I obviously wanted to telegraph a bit of the character in the name. The names needed to sound unusual but not spacey. I wanted to stay away from the kind of science fiction names like Zenon and Zorba. They had to sound indigenous and have consistency between their names and their culture."

Much has been made of the director's use of world myths from Joseph Campbell's "Hero With a Thousand Faces," but "Star Wars" is also a synthesis of the treasure trove of American pop culture—everything from comic strips, pulp fiction and films ranging from John Ford's "Searchers" to Victor Fleming's "Wizard of Oz" to Akira Kurosawa's "Hidden Fortress."

"Star Wars" in turn has spawned a galaxy of sub-industries—more than two dozen novels, trading cards, action figures, role-playing games, scores of websites and guides specializing in intergalactic arcana—many of which

The Names Came From Earth ◆ *943*

►Critical Viewing◄

❶ Relate Students might cite King Kong or the yeti.

◆ Critical Thinking

❷ Infer Characters' names may reflect their personalities and may telegraph their roles in a story. Ask students why they think the name Darth Vader is appropriate and what his role is in the epic. *Sample answer: The origin of the name Darth Vader from the Dutch "Dark Father" suits Darth Vader who is a wicked person. He represents the forces of evil that Luke must overcome.*

◆ Critical Thinking

❸ Relate Have students explain how the origin of Luke Skywalker's name relates to his role in the epic. *Suggested response: Luke comes from the Greek "leukos" meaning light. Skywalker is the name of Loki, the Norse god of fire. Thus Luke Skywalker will be the hero who uses the power of "the Force" (fire) to fight on the side of good (light) against the evil represented by Darth Vader.*

ONNECTIONS TO TODAY'S WORLD

▲ Critical Viewing What other mythical creatures does this Wookiee bring to mind? [Relate]

have been consulted in preparing this interstellar who's who.

Darth Vader: Mr. Lucas went back to the Dutch root for father to arrive at a name that approximates "Dark Father." Vader's original name is Anakin Skywalker. Anakin is a variation on a race of giants in Genesis, and Skywalker is an appellation for Loki, the Norse god of fire and mischief. The inspiration for Vader's face mask was in all likelihood the grille of a '56 Chevy.

Luke Skywalker: The name of the character played by Mark Hamill derives from the Greek leukos, or light, an interesting contrast to Darth Vader. Luke of the Gospels was a gentile who converted to Christianity, an appropriate name for a boy who discovers the power of the Force.

Tatooine is the name of Luke's home planet, derived from the town of Tataouine in Tunisia, the country where the desert scenes in "Star Wars" were filmed. An early draft of the script was called "The Adventures of Luke Starkiller." It's easy to read Luke S. as a stand-in for Lucas.

Princess Leia Organa (Carrie Fisher) has braids that resemble dinner rolls, but her name evokes the lovely Dejah Thoris in the

944 ◆ *Epics and Legends*

944

John Carter of Mars tales by Edgar Rice Burroughs, as well as Lady Galadriel of Lothlorien in J. R. Tolkien's "Lord of the Rings." The surname Organa reflects the conflict of nature and technology seen in the forest-dwelling heroes pitted against the machines of the Empire, according to Lucas's biographer, Dale Pollock.

The name **Han Solo** (Harrison Ford) capitalizes on the archaic sound of Han, a variation of John, to set us in a mythical world. The name Solo addresses his key character issue. Solo is a lone gun who must learn to trust others and identify with a greater cause. The swashbuckler's name also recalls one of the great pop culture adventurers, Napoleon Solo, "The Man from U.N.C.L.E." Napoleon Solo, by the way, first appeared as a minor hood in the James Bond novel "Goldfinger."

R2-D2 According to Mr. Lucas, the robot who resembles a whistling Hoover vacuum cleaner got his name from a sound editor's shorthand for "Reel Two, Dialogue Two" during the making of his earlier hit, "American Graffiti."

Chewbacca, the towering Wookiee, was a name inspired by Indiana, Mr. Lucas's rambunctious malamute. (The dog also lent his name to the hero of the film maker's Indiana Jones series.) Wookiee comes from an ad lib in "THX 1138," the film maker's first feature film: "I think I ran over a Wookiee back there."

Jedi, the name of the ancient knighthood, is a tip of the hat to Burroughs's Barsoom, where lords bear the title of Jed or Jeddak.

Obi-Wan Kenobi (Alec Guinness), also known as old Ben Kenobi, is revealed to us as a Jedi knight and introduces Luke to the power of the Force. Obi is the Japanese word for the sash used to tie a kimono; it may connote the Jedi knight's status as a martial arts master. Similarly, Wan sounds like the Japanese honorific suffix san. "OB" is also short for Old Ben, but there is chatter on the Internet that his name is really OB-1, a

cryptic reference to Mr. Lucas's much anticipated history of the Clone Wars in future "Star Wars" installments.

Ewoks, those almost unbearably cute, highly marketable teddy-bear characters who saved the day in "The Return of the Jedi" inhabit the forest moon of Endor (the witch in the Book of Samuel hailed from a similarly named locale). Their name may sound like a variant of Wookiee, but it is taken from Miwok, the Indian tribe indigenous to San Rafael, California, the location of Mr. Lucas's Skywalker ranch.

Boba Fett, at least according to one fan on the World Wide Web, is a sly reference to another hotshot jockey, Bob Falfa, the drag racer played by none other than Mr. Ford in "American Graffiti."

Banthas, the shaggy, screw-horned mounts of the honking **Sand People,** are a variation on banth, a beast found on Barsoom. The Sand People bear similarities to nomadic tribes in the science fiction writer Frank Herbert's desert classic "Dune." The diminutive **Jawas,** who chatter like the cartoon chipmunks Chip 'n Dale, call to mind Indonesian Islam. Their name is perhaps echoic of Moroccan Gnawa trance music.

1. Why do you think George Lucas looked to world myths, literature, and popular culture for the characters' names for *Star Wars*?
2. Name three sources Lucas used for names and explain how the names and their sources are significant in terms of world cultures.
3. What does *Star Wars* reveal about contemporary American culture?
4. In what ways is the *Star Wars* trilogy a modern-day epic?

④ Literature Connection
George Lucas borrowed freely from many other works of fantasy and science fiction. Have students who have read *Lord of the Rings* explain how it fits into the epic genre. *It is the tale of an unlikely hero and an epic conflict between good and evil.*

◆ **Critical Thinking**

⑤ Make Judgments Han Solo's last name recalls Napoleon Solo from the popular espionage series "The Man from U.N.C.L.E.," and R2-D2's name came from a movie sound editor's words. Ask: How do these two names reflect what the writer George Lucas thinks about contemporary American culture? *Suggested response: These names point out the important role of television and movies in creating the heroes of contemporary culture.*

⑥ Literature Connection The Jedi knights are reminiscent of warriors in a number of epics and legends. Ask students to name famous knights from literature. *Students will probably mention knights of the Round Table, such as Lancelot, Tristram, Gawain, and Galahad.*

◆ **Critical Thinking**

⑦ Infer Invite students to consider how Obi-Wan Kenobi's name reflects his role in Star Wars. *Suggested response: The word obi brings to mind a martial arts master and wan sounds like a Japanese title of honor. Thus Obi-Wan Kenobi is an honored person who teaches Luke Sky-walker how to battle using the power of "the Force."*

Answers

1. He may have looked to world myths and literature to connect his epic tale to the epic tradition. He may have included elements of popular culture because he knew that all epics reflect aspects of the culture from which they come.
2. Lucas uses names from Norse mythology, which connects his characters to world myths; he uses biblical references that tie to the religious beliefs of much of the Western world; he uses Moroccan Gnawan music, which ties his story to Eastern cultures.
3. The Millenium Falcon's resemblance to a souped-up car reflects an admiration for an enterprising mind, the plot reflects an appreciation for pure adventure, and the unusual characters and names reflect diversity.
4. The epic qualities of *Star Wars* include a hero overcoming enormous odds, a hero with special abilities and powers, and a reflection of the culture from which it comes.

Establish Writing Guidelines
Review the following key characteristics about a multimedia presentation:

- A multimedia presentation uses a variety of media.
- It can address any subject in any mode through any effective organization.
- It uses media appropriate for the subject.

Before students begin, you may want to share with them the Scoring Rubric for Multimedia Report (p. 107 in *Alternative Assessment*) so students see the criteria by which they will be evaluated. Suggestions on page 948 customize the rubric to this workshop.

Connect to Literature You might refer students to the selection from "Rare Air: Michael on Michael" (page 359) in Unit 4. Have students discuss the multimedia presentation that could spring from it.

 Writer's Solution

Sourcebook
To introduce students to the key elements of a multimedia presentation, have them review Multimedia Presentation, page 136 in Chapter 5 in the *Writer's Solution Sourcebook*. Ask students to identify the media included in the model.

Writing Lab CD-ROM
If students have access to computers, have them work in the Research Writing tutorial, the multimedia presentation segments, to complete all or part of their presentations. Follow these steps:

1. Students can see an audio-annotated model of a multimedia presentation.
2. Have students study video tips from writers about how audience shapes a presentation.
3. Have students study writing tips for using maps, charts, and graphs.

Sourcebook
Students can find additional support, including topic ideas, models, and graphic organizers, in Chapter 5 on Research Writing (pp. 128–163).

Multimedia Presentation	# Writing Process Workshop

When epics and legends were told in ancient times, the storytellers had only their voices to bring the tales to life for their audiences. You have many other resources available for presentations. Create a **multimedia presentation** on a subject that interests you. A multimedia presentation supplies information through a variety of media. Among the media you may use are written materials, slides, videos, music, maps, charts, graphs, photos, drawings, and fine art reproductions.

The following skills from this section's Writing Mini-Lessons will help you make an interesting multimedia presentation.

Writing Skills Focus

▶ **Use an appropriate medium** for the subject. For instance, if you're discussing the effect of television on how we get the news, include video clips.

▶ **Use language appropriate for your purpose.** For example, if your purpose is to share the beauty and excitement of diving, use words such as *exhilarating* or *graceful* to help your audience envision the experience. (See p. 931.)

▶ **Consider audience knowledge.** Don't "talk down" to your audience but do define technical terms that may be unfamiliar. Use visual aids to help them understand aspects of your topic that are outside their experience. (See p. 941.)

The following excerpt from the written portion of a multimedia presentation on scuba diving shows these skills.

WRITING MODEL

① Since the audience consists of classmates who may not have done scuba diving before, the presenter explains what a regulator is.

② The writer uses language that helps convey her feelings about the dive.

③ Since the most prominent sensations experienced in diving are visual ones, the presenter uses photographs and video in her presentation.

When I first arrived in scuba class, I was frightened and had second thoughts. My teacher, however, dispelled those fears when she showed me how the regulator, or breathing device, ① worked. (*Listen to this part of an interview with her as she describes the concept of the regulator.*)

Diving exposed me to a larger world than I could ever have imagined. For instance, seeing a stingray on a dive is an exhilarating ② and slightly frightening experience. Here is some video footage of some stingrays that we had the pleasure of diving with. ③

 Beyond the Classroom

Workplace Skill
Multimedia in the Workplace The workplace relies heavily on multimedia for almost all presentations. Multimedia in the workplace, however, usually refers to high-tech, connected to computer technology. Presentation software allows the presenter to use full color, sound, and motion along with text and visual displays, some of which may be scanned into the presentation program. If students have access to the technology, suggest they consider using it for their own multimedia presentation.

They should save the presentation on disc and make it part of their job portfolio.

Prewriting

Use a Topic Web If you're not assigned a topic, choose one that interests you and that you can develop with multimedia. You can use a topic web like the one shown to help narrow your topic.

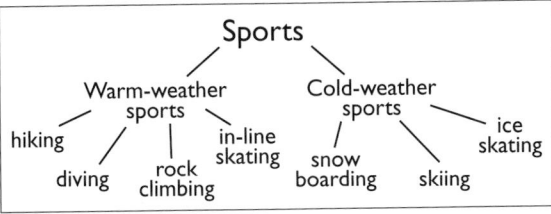

Sports
- Warm-weather sports
  - hiking
  - diving
  - rock climbing
  - in-line skating
- Cold-weather sports
  - snow boarding
  - skiing
  - ice skating

Find Multimedia Support Visual aids and other types of media will significantly enliven your presentation. Indicate how the media will enhance your audience's understanding of the topic. For instance, your written report may indicate that readers should press "play" to hear a recording of music from a particular country. If you are giving an oral presentation, explain why you are showing a visual.

Maps can clarify historical or geographical information.

Graphs and Charts can make complicated information easier to understand.

Pictures can illustrate objects, scenes, and other details.

Diagrams can show the relationships of parts to a whole.

Audio and Video can bring your subject to life for your audience.

Drafting

Write a Strong Introduction A strong introduction grabs the audience's attention and tells them what to expect in your multimedia presentation. To make the topic clear, include your main idea in the introduction. To capture your audience's interest, you might open with a question, an anecdote, a quotation from an expert, a startling fact, or a piece of media. Use the following introduction as an example:

"Good morning, Chicagoans. The temperature on this January morning is a lovely 75 degrees. Traffic's blocked up due to a burst dike on the lake. There's also a monsoon warning for this afternoon . . ."

A scene from a sci-fi thriller? Hardly. As this graph shows, this could be a typical forecast from fifty years in the future if we continue to deplete the ozone layer at current levels . . .

APPLYING LANGUAGE SKILLS: Semicolons and Colons

In the written portion of your report, use a **semicolon** to form a compound sentence when the two ideas being joined are closely related and are not joined by a conjunction:

The palace of Versailles is near Paris; it was built by Louis XIV.

Also use semicolons to separate items on a list that already contain commas:

Attractions in and around Paris include churches like Notre Dame; the palace at Versailles, just outside Paris; and the Louvre, an art museum.

You might also need to create lists or cite long quotations. Use **colons** to introduce a list of items after words like *the following* or a long, block-indented quotation.

Notre Dame's architectural details include the following: flying buttresses, two lofty towers, and numerous gargoyles.

Writer's Solution Connection Language Lab

For more practice with colons and semicolons, complete the Language Lab lesson on Semicolons, Colons, and Quotation Marks.

Prewriting

Writing and Language Transparencies You may want students to use a Herringbone Organizer (p. 76) to organize their thoughts and connect the various media to a central idea.

Customize for *More Advanced Students*

Have these students plan from the beginning that they will make their multimedia presentations to a community audience. Have them choose topics that target a specific audience.

Writer's Solution

Writing Lab CD-ROM

For students who work best in groups, have them use the Group Projects in the Inspirations in the Research Writing tutorial to find topics for their multimedia presentations.

Drafting

As they write, encourage students to be creative as they introduce and present information. Remind them that the many literary devices they have studied can be effectively applied to a multimedia presentation: alliteration, personification, analogy, symbolism, foreshadowing, flashback, and so on.

Applying Language Skills

Semicolons and Colons

Remind students that as they show more mature writing style, they will use phrases and clauses to enhance sentence structures. Semicolons and colons will thus become essential to their writing accuracy.

Writer's Solution

For additional explanation and practice on semicolons and colons, use the Semicolons and Colons worksheet, p. 102, in the *Writer's Solution Grammar Practice Book.*

Revising

You may want to have peer editors work in groups made up of multiple learning styles. Visual learners can respond to visuals; verbal/linguistic learners to auditory and text. A fourth member of the group should focus on how the pieces fit together.

 Writer's Solution

Students can use the Organization Outliner tool in the Revising and Editing section of the Research Writing tutorial to help them highlight the relationships among the parts in the presentations.

They can then use the Revision Checker for Unity and Coherence to refine the text portion of the presentation.

Publishing

You may want to suggest that students save the multimedia report for their job portfolios.

Applying Language Skills

Concise Language

Remind students that the most powerful language springs from specific nouns and verbs, not a series of adjectives and adverbs.

Answer

Possible revision: As I descended through the crystal-clear water, hundreds of fish swam below.

Reinforce and Extend

Review the Writing Process

After students have completed their multimedia presentations, ask them to brainstorm a list of workplace uses for multimedia presentations. Ask how those presentations might differ from the ones they have just completed.

Writing Process Workshop

APPLYING LANGUAGE SKILLS: Concise Language

Use **concise language**—exact nouns, vivid verbs, the right adjectives and adverbs (as opposed to many adjectives and adverbs). Eliminate unnecessary words and phrases.

Vague and Wordy:
As you may or may not know, the coral reef has many colors and hues. An immense number and lots of different kinds of various fish and food live in and around one small piece of the reef.

Concise:
The coral reef is an explosion of color. A single section of reef can support more than 200 varieties of fish.

Practice In your notebook, make the following sentence concise.

> As I descended through the blue clear, bright, and rather warm water, I saw a whole bunch of fish moving below me somewhere.

Writer's Solution Connection Writing Lab

For more help on giving your presentation, see Tips on Presenting Work Orally in the Publishing and Presenting section of the Writing Lab tutorial on Research.

Write the Body Develop your main idea in the body of the written portion of your presentation. Back up assertions with solid facts. Use multimedia examples to illustrate points or observations that you make.

Write an Effective Conclusion A strong conclusion underscores your main points and encourages the audience to keep thinking about your presentation. Consider ending your presentation with an entertaining or startling fact or quotation. Accompany it with a visual or audio segment that will remain in the audience's mind after your presentation has ended.

Revising

Use a Checklist The following checklist will help you revise your multimedia presentation:

▶ Do you use the appropriate language for your audience?
▶ Do you use the appropriate medium or media for your subject?
▶ Is there a clear connection between your words and the visuals you use?
▶ Is your language concise?

REVISION MODEL

On a dive, we used a special camera to take underwater

① Here is a picture of such a camera.
photos. ~~Listen to my teacher talking about the camera.~~

② , or buoyancy control device,
We also had to use a BCD to keep us from sinking

to the bottom or rising to the surface too quickly.

① The presenter changes the medium from audio to a picture to better illustrate an underwater camera.

② Because the audience may be unfamiliar with the term BCD, the presenter defines it.

Publishing

▶ **Present Your Report** Present your multimedia presentation to the class. Make sure that you arrange beforehand for any equipment that you will need, such as an overhead projector or television and VCR. During the presentation, remember to speak loudly and clearly.

☑ ASSESSMENT		4	3	2	1
PORTFOLIO ASSESSMENT Use the rubric on Multimedia Report in *Alternative Assessment* (p. 107) to assess student writing. Add these criteria to customize the rubric to this assignment.	**Introduction**	The multimedia presentation opens with a vibrant attention getter.	The presentation opens with a attention getter.	The presentation opens with an attempt at gaining audience attention.	The presentation omits any introductory attention getter.
	Concise Language	The verbal portions, both written and oral, of the multimedia presentation exhibit consistently concise language.	The verbal portions usually exhibit concise language.	The verbal portions sometimes exhibit concise language.	The verbal portions rarely exhibit concise language.

Real-World Reading Skills Workshop

Reading a Map

Strategies for Success

Imagine that you went to a new city alone and the only thing you had to guide you was a map. You'd soon know how important it is to be able to read maps! To navigate your way through a city or town, you would use a street map. Street maps of cities often show buildings, parks, and other landmarks, in addition to streets.

Identify Your Purpose First, clarify why you're looking at a street map. Are you looking for a particular street or do you just want an overall layout of a neighborhood? Do you want to visit a specific landmark or museum? Sometimes a specific section, such as the downtown area of a big city, will be blown up in a separate, more detailed box. If you are looking for a location that falls in this section, you can find it more easily if you use the more detailed map.

Get an Overview After you identify your purpose, determine whether the street map meets your needs.

- Does it show the entire area or just a section?
- Are all streets shown on the map or just major ones?
- Which way is north on the map?
- What is the scale of centimeters or inches to a kilometer or a mile?
- Does the map include landmarks and buildings?

Read the Map Start by finding your location on the map. Next, locate your destination. Finally, plan a route from your location to your destination by identifying the direction you need to travel, the streets you need to take, and the places where you will need to make turns.

Apply the Strategy

You're visiting London and staying in a hotel on Page Street. Use the map to answer the questions.

1. What direction must you travel to get from Page Street to Westminster Cathedral?
2. What is the most direct route from Westminster Cathedral to the entrance of St. James's Park on King Charles Street?
3. In what order would you visit Westminster Cathedral, St. James's Park, and Parliament Square starting from where you are staying? Why?

Introduce the Strategy

Point out to students that reading a map is an essential skill for both personal and business life. You may also want to point out that some automobiles now come equipped with computerized maps that pinpoint the car's location and gives directions from there to a specific destination. Likewise, maps on the Internet pinpoint directions to virtually any address in the United States.

Customize for
Bodily/Kinesthetic Learners
Explain to these students that they may better be able to follow a map if they hold the map to correspond to the direction they are facing.

Apply the Strategy

Have students study the map carefully. You may want to suggest that they reposition the map as they make left or right turns.

Answers
1. You must travel northwest to get from Page Street to Westminster Cathedral.
2. The most direct route is Victoria Street to Smith Street to King Charles Street.
3. Suggested answers: the best order is either Parliament Square, St. James Park, and then Westminster Cathedral or Westminster Cathedral, St. James Park, and Parliament Square. Both these routes avoid backtracking.

Introduce the Strategy

Remind students that in the workplace, meetings are part of daily life. To make them aware of the frequency of meetings, ask students to make a list of meetings—formal or informal—they have attended recently.

Apply the Strategy

Remind students before they role-play that preparation must precede the activity. Then, when groups meet, remind students to first appoint a note-taker, then to develop an agenda. Have groups review the Tips for Running a Meeting before they begin role-play.

Reinforce and Extend

After students have completed the role-playing activities, hold a class discussion in which they assess their meeting skills. Encourage students to offer constructive criticism to one another on skills that could be improved. You may wish to have interested students hold meetings to plan the budget and logistics for a class outing. Other groups might plan fund-raisers to raise the money for the outing.

Running a Meeting

Speaking and Listening Workshop

Meetings may be large and official, such as a student government meeting with representatives from each homeroom, or small and informal, like a meeting with friends to plan a party. All meetings have one thing in common—they have a purpose: There is a goal (or goals) to be met. If you are in charge, run your meetings efficiently so that the goals can be achieved.

Get Organized Start by planning the meeting. Plan an agenda—a list of the topics to be addressed—to keep group members focused on essential points. For a formal meeting, make copies of the agenda and distribute it to all who attend the meeting. For an informal meeting, you might make a list of the meeting's goals and share these goals with the group at the beginning of the meeting. In either case, all members of the group should understand and agree to the meeting goals.

Follow Through As you proceed through the questions and issues on the agenda, it's a good idea to have someone take notes. The note-taker can record decisions made, responsibilities assigned, or other questions that need to be resolved. At the end of the meeting, you or the note-taker should summarize the plans or decisions that were made and any future actions to be taken.

950 ◆ *Epics and Legends*

Tips for Running a Meeting

✔ *These strategies can help you to conduct an efficient and successful meeting:*
  ▶ Plan ahead—develop and distribute an agenda
  ▶ Arrange to have any display items or media equipment you may need, such as a slide projector
  ▶ Speak clearly, confidently, and loudly enough so that everyone in the room can hear you
  ▶ Appoint a note-taker to record the main points of the discussion
  ▶ Summarize at the end

Use Meeting Manners As a meeting leader, your job is to keep the meeting on track and to have it run smoothly. If group members begin discussing topics unrelated to the meeting's goals, politely call their attention back to the agenda.

Apply the Strategies

In small groups, role-play one of the following meetings. Use the strategies you've learned to run the meeting.

1. The prom is coming up. Plan several meetings that are necessary to organize the event.

2. You've just started a band. Plan the band's first meeting, in which you will discuss where and when practice sessions will be held and work out details about upcoming gigs.

3. You're concerned about the lack of recycling in your town. Organize a meeting to discuss starting a recycling program in your school.

 Beyond the Classroom

Workplace Skills Mini-Lesson

Participating in a Meeting Life in the workplace sometimes seems controlled by meetings. Although the person running the meeting should be in control and keep everyone on track, sometimes meetings go astray. Remind students that even though someone else may be in charge, participants can help keep the meeting on target. First, they can think before they speak, refraining when their ideas are unrelated to the meeting's purpose. Second, they can make oral transitions to tie together what has transpired and prepare others to move on. Third, they can help soothe others by watching for nonverbal clues that communicate frustration or anger. Ask students what other roles participants might take, positive or negative.

Extended Reading Opportunities

Heroes, battles, quests, monsters: These are the elements of epics and legends. The following books offer a sample of these timeless themes and situations.

Suggested Titles

Cuchulain of Muirthemne: The Story of the Men of the Red Branch of Ulster
Lady Augusta Gregory

Irish author Lady Augusta Gregory tells the story of Cuchulain, "The Achilles of Ireland," in this retelling of the great Irish epic, the *Ulster Cycle*. In this spectacular tale, the heroic Cuchulain single-handedly deters the invading army of the evil Queen Maeve until the Red Branch warriors awake from enchantment.

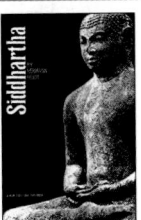

Siddhartha
Hermann Hesse

This book tells of Siddhartha, a young man living in India around the sixth century B.C. Born to wealthy and intelligent parents, Siddhartha nonetheless is dissatisfied with his existence and embarks on a quest for wisdom and the meaning of life. His insatiable thirst for wisdom and knowledge takes him through all areas of Indian society. Besides being an enjoyable story, this tale will undoubtedly also teach you something about yourself and your place in the world.

The Hollow Hills
Mary Stewart

The Hollow Hills, Mary Stewart's second novel in her Arthurian trilogy, tells the story of how Merlin helps Arthur become king of all Britain. The story takes place in the fifth century, a time of danger and fear, where no law is stable and no ride through the countryside is without peril. Sudden battles amidst the misty mountains and quick retreats into mysterious caves within the hollow hills set the backdrop for this exciting tale of medieval action and romance.

Other Possibilities

Gilgamesh
American Indian Myths and Legends
The Norse Myths

Translated by David Ferry
Richard Erdoes, Editor
Kevin Crossly-Holland

Planning Student's Extended Reading

All the works on this page are good choices for extending students understanding of and appreciation for epics and legends.

Customize for *Varying Student Needs*

When assigning these works to your students, keep in mind the following factors.

- *Cuchulain of Muirthemne* is an adaptation of the Irish epic, the *Tain*. More advanced students may wish to read portions of Thomas Kinsella's translation of the original *Tain Bo Cuilnge*.

- *Siddhartha* is a challenging tale of growth and self-discovery. The parallels to the life of Buddha give the work a legendary and symbolic quality.

- *The Hollow Hills* is a contemporary classic that will make the Arthurian legend come alive for all your students. The romance and adventure are played out by very human and realistic characters, rather than lofty, untouchable heroes.

Sensitive Issues

These books contain some issues and references that you may find sensitive in your classroom:

- *Cuchulain of Muirthemne* contains references to drinking. The battles, while not described in great detail, are violent, with many casualties.

- *Siddartha* contains sexual references. It also deals with themes that may be sensitive, such as challenging authority and spiritualism versus materialism.

Literature Study Guides

A study guide is available for *Siddhartha*. It includes section summaries, discussion questions, and activities.

Resources for Teaching Novels and Plays

This guide contains graphic organizers, teaching strategies and transparencies that will be invaluable in teaching any of these novels.

Access Guide to Vocabulary

KEY TO PRONUNCIATION SYMBOLS USED

Symbol	Key Words						
		i	is, hit, mirror	yōō	use, cute, few	ə	a in ago
a	asp, fat, parrot	ī	ice, bite, high	yŏŏ	united, cure, globule		e in agent
ā	ape, date, play	ō	open, tone, go	oi	oil, point, toy		i in sanity
ä	ah, car, father	ô	all, horn, law	ou	out, crowd, plow		o in comply
e	elf, ten, berry	ōō	ooze, tool, crew	u	up, cut, color		u in focus
ē	even, meet, money	ŏŏ	look, pull, moor	ʉr	urn, fur, deter	ər	perhaps, murder

Symbol	Key Words						
		k	kill, tackle, bake	t	top, cattle, hat	th	thin, nothing, truth
b	bed, fable, dub	l	let, yellow, ball	v	vat, hovel, have	*th*	then, father, lathe
d	dip, beadle, had	m	met, camel, trim	w	will, always, swear	zh	azure, leisure
f	fall, after, off	n	not, flannel, ton	y	yet, onion, yard	ŋ	ring, anger, drink
g	get, haggle, dog	p	put, apple, tap	z	zebra, dazzle, haze		
h	he, head, hotel	r	red, port, dear	ch	chin, catcher, arch		
j	joy, agile, badge	s	sell, castle, pass	sh	she, cushion, dash		

Foreign Sounds

à — This symbol, representing the *a* in French *salle*, can best be described as intermediate between (a) and (ä).

ë — This symbol represents the sound of the vowel cluster in French *coeur* and can be approximated by rounding the lips as for (ō) and pronouncing (e).

ö — This symbol variously represents the sound of *eu* in French *feu*, or of *ö* or *oe* in German *blöd* or *Geothe*, and can be approximated by rounding lips as for (ō) and pronouncing (ā).

ô — This symbol represents a range of sounds between (ô) and (u); it occurs typically in the sound of the *o* in French *tonne* or German *korrekt*; in Italian *poco* and Spanish *torero*, it is almost like English (ô), as in *horn*.

ü — This symbol variously represents the sound of *u* in French *duc* and in German *grun* and can be approximated by rounding the lips as for (ō) and pronouncing (ē).

kh — This symbol represents the voiceless velar or uvular fricative as in the *ch* of German *doch* or Scots English *loch*. It can be approximated by placing the tongue as for (k) but allowing the breath to escape in a stream, as in pronouncing (h).

H — This symbol represents a sound similiar to the preceding but formed by friction against the forward part of the palate, as in German *ich*. It can be made by placing the tongue as for English (sh) but with the tip pointing downward.

n — This symbol indicates that the vowel sound immediately preceding it is nasalized; that is, the nasal passage is left open so that the breath passes through both the mouth and nose in voicing the vowel, as in French *mon* (mōn). The letter *n* itself is not pronounced unless followed by a vowel.

r — This symbol represents any of the various sounds used in languages other than English for the consonant *r*. It may represent the tongue-point trill or uvular trill of the *r* in French *reste* or *sur*, German *Reuter*, Italian *ricotta*, Russian *gorod*, etc.

' — The apostrophe is used after final *l* and *r*, in certain French pronunciations, to indicate that they are voiceless after an unvoiced consonant as in lettre (let′r′). In Russian words the "soft sign" in Cyrillic spelling is indicated by (y′). The sound can be approximated by pronouncing an unvoiced (y) directly after the consonant involved, as in *Sevastopol* (se′väs tô′pel y′).

Access Guide to Vocabulary ◆ *953*

953

Literary Terms Handbook

ACT *See Drama.*

ALLITERATION *Alliteration* is the repetition of initial consonant sounds. Writers use alliteration to give emphasis to words, to imitate sounds, and to create musical effects. Notice, in the following lines from Jean Toomer's "Reapers," how the *s* sounds suggest the sound of the blades sliding against stones to be sharpened.

> "Black reapers with the sound of steel on stones/Are sharpening scythes—"

See Assonance, Consonance, and Rhyme.

ALLUSION An *allusion* is a reference to a well-known person, place, event, literary work, or work of art. Writers often make allusions to famous works such as the Bible or William Shakespeare's plays. They also make allusions to mythology, politics, or current events. For example, the title of Stephen Vincent Benét's story "By the Waters of Babylon," p. 500, is an allusion to Psalm 137 in the Bible.

ANECDOTE An *anecdote* is a brief story about an interesting, amusing, or strange event. Anecdotes are told to entertain or to make a point. James Thurber, for example, fills "The Dog That Bit People," p. 234, with humorous anecdotes about his family and their dog, Muggs.

See Narrative.

ANTAGONIST The *antagonist* of a work is the character who opposes the protagonist (the character whom readers want to see succeed). Creon is the antagonist in the play *Antigone*, p. 670.

See Character and Protagonist.

ANTICLIMAX Like a climax, an *anticlimax* is the turning point in a story. However, an anticlimax is always a letdown. It's the point at which you learn that the story will not turn out the way you'd expected.

APHORISM An *aphorism* is a brief, memorable saying that expresses a basic truth. Many cultures pass on wisdom in the form of aphorisms, such as the aphorisms from Confucius' *The Analects*, p. 204.

ASIDE An *aside* is a short speech delivered by an actor in a play, expressing the character's thoughts.

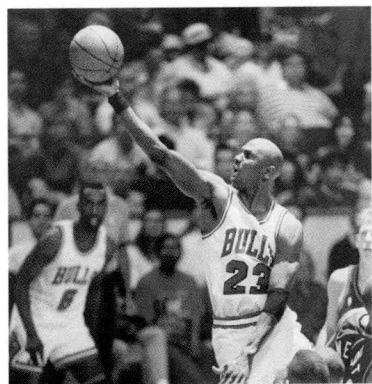

In his autobiography, "Rare Air: Michael on Michael," Michael Jordan shares his experiences through words and photographs.

Traditionally, the aside is directed to the audience and is presumed to be inaudible to the other actors.

ASSONANCE *Assonance* is the repetition of vowel sounds followed by different consonants in two or more stressed syllables. In "The Kraken," p. 825, Tennyson repeats the long e sound in the following lines:

> Below the thunders of the upper *deep*;
> Far, far beneath in the abysmal *sea*,
> His ancient, dreamless, uninvaded *sleep*
> The Kraken sleepeth: faintest sunlights *flee*

See Consonance.

ATMOSPHERE *Atmosphere*, or *mood*, is the feeling created in a reader by a literary work or passage. The atmosphere is often suggested by descriptive details. The following lines from "The Stolen Child," p. 815, create a mysterious, mystical atmosphere in which a meeting takes place between fairies and a human child:

> Where the wave of moonlight glosses
> The dim grey sands with light

AUTOBIOGRAPHY An *autobiography* is a form of nonfiction in which a person tells his or her own life story. An autobiography may tell about the person's whole life or only a part of it. "A Child's Christmas in Wales," p. 596, is an autobiographical incident from writer Dylan Thomas.

See Biography and Nonfiction.

BIOGRAPHY A *biography* is a form of nonfiction in which a writer tells the life story of another person. Biographies have been written about many famous people, historical and contemporary, but they can also be written about "ordinary" people. "Marion Anderson: Famous Concert Singer," p. 602, is a brief biography by Langston Hughes.

See Autobiography and Nonfiction.

BLANK VERSE *Blank verse* is poetry written in unrhymed iambic pentameter lines. This verse form was widely used by Elizabethan dramatists like William Shakespeare. *The Tragedy of Julius Caesar*, p. 712, is written mostly in blank verse.

See Meter.

CHARACTER A *character* is a person or an animal who takes part in the action of a literary work. The *main character*, or *protagonist*, is the most important character in a story. This character often changes in some important way as a result of the story's events.

The *antagonist* opposes the main character. Characters are sometimes classified as round or flat, dynamic or static. A round character shows many different traits—faults as well as virtues. Annie John's mother in *A Walk to the Jetty* is an example of a round character. At times she is kind and loving to Annie; at other times she is stern and overbearing. Annie's father is a flat character. We see him only as a quiet, nonconfrontational man. A dynamic character develops and grows during the course of the story, as does Tom Benecke in Jack Finney's "Contents of the Dead Man's Pocket" on p. 5. A static character does not change. Scoresby in Mark Twain's "Luck," p. 520, is a static character.

See Antagonist, Characterization, Motivation, and Protagonist.

CHARACTERIZATION *Characterization* is the act of creating and developing a character. In *direct characterization*, the author directly states a character's traits. For example, in William Melvin Kelley's "A Visit to Grandmother," on p. 166, GL is described as "part con man, part practical joker and part Don Juan." A writer uses *indirect characterization* when showing a character's personality through his or her actions, thoughts, feelings, words, and appearance, or through another character's observations and reactions. In the same story, Kelley presents Chig's observations and memories of his father. Kelley also shows the actions and words of Chig's father during the emotional scene with Chig's grandmother. Such indirect characterization relies on the reader to put together the clues that will designate the character's personality.

See Character.

CLIMAX The *climax* of a story, novel, or play is the high point of interest or suspense. The events that make up the rising action lead up to the climax. The events that make up the falling action follow the climax. The climax of "Damon and Pythias," p.102, occurs when the deadline has been reached and Pythias has not yet returned.

See Conflict, Plot, and Anticlimax.

CONFLICT A *conflict* is a struggle between opposing forces. Characters in conflict form the basis of stories, novels, and plays.

There are two kinds of conflict: external and internal. In an *external conflict*, the main character struggles against an outside force, as in Carl Stephenson's "Leiningen Versus the Ants," p. 480, in which Leiningen and his men struggle against an army of ants. The outside force may be nature itself, in a person-against-nature conflict. Edmund Hillary and Tenzing Norgay face such a conflict in "The Final Assault."

An *internal conflict* involves a character in conflict with himself or herself. For example, in Doris Lessing's "Through the Tunnel," p. 221, Jerry faces a struggle between his desire to swim through the tunnel and his fear of the danger involved

A story may have more than one conflict. In addition to his internal conflict, Jerry also faces external conflicts—the tunnel's length and the oppressive water pressure.

See Plot.

CONNOTATION The *connotation* of a word is the set of ideas associated with it in addition to its explicit meaning. For example, the title "The Bean Eaters" refers literally to people who eat beans. The phrase connotes simplicity and poverty.

The connotation of a word can be personal, based on individual experiences, but more often, cultural connotations—those recognizable by most people in a group—determine a writer's word choices.

See Denotation.

CONSONANCE *Consonance* is the repetition of similar consonant sounds at the end of accented syllables. In "Meeting at Night," p. 827, the repeated *t* and *ch* sounds in "the spurt of a lighted match" create consonance. Consonance is used to create musical effects, to link ideas, and to emphasize particular words.

See Assonance.

COUPLET A *couplet* is a pair of rhyming lines, usually of the same length and meter. A couplet generally expresses a single idea. Shakespeare's Sonnet 18, on p. 866, ends with the following couplet:

> So long as men can breathe, or eyes can see
> So long lives this, and this gives life to thee.

See Stanza.

CRITICAL REVIEW A *critical review* offers one person's judgment of a movie, play, or other performance. In the review, the reviewer discusses the various elements of the performance and makes a recommendation. Critical reviews tend to be persuasive.

See Persuasion.

DENOTATION The *denotation* of a word is its dictionary meaning, independent of other associations that the word may have. The denotation of the word *lake*, for example, is an inland body of water.

See *Connotation.*

DENOUEMENT See Plot.

DESCRIPTION A *description* is a portrait in words of a person, place, or object. Descriptive writing uses sensory details—those that appeal to the senses: sight, hearing, taste, smell, and touch. Description can be found in all types of writing. Annie Dillard's essay "Flood," on p. 610, contains descriptive passages.

DEVELOPMENT See Plot.

DIALECT *Dialect* is the form of language spoken by people in a particular region or group. Pronunciation, vocabulary, and sentence structure are affected by dialect. Writers use dialect to make their characters sound realistic and to create local color. In Chinua Achebe's "Civil Peace," on p. 396, some of the characters speak in a Nigerian dialect of English.

DIALOGUE A *dialogue* is a conversation between characters. Writers use dialogue to reveal character, to present events, to add variety to a narrative, and to interest readers.

DICTION *Diction* is word choice. To discuss a writer's diction is to consider the vocabulary used, the appropriateness of the words, and the vividness of the language. Both the *denotation*, or literal meaning, and the *connotation*, or associations, of words contribute to the overall effect. Diction can be formal, as in this excerpt from Edgar Allan Poe's "The Masque of the Red Death," which begins on p. 78:

> It was a voluptuous scene, that masquerade.

But first let me tell of the rooms in which it was held. There were seen—an imperial suite."

Diction can also be informal and conversational, as in these lines from "Flood" by Annie Dillard, on p. 610:

> Women are bringing coffee in mugs to the road crew . . . Some kid starts doing tricks on a skateboard; I head home.

See Connotation and Denotation.

DIRECT CHARACTERIZATION
See Characterization.

DRAMA A *drama* is a story written to be performed by actors. The script of a drama is made up of dialogue—the words the actors say—and stage directions, which are comments on how and where action happens.

The drama's setting is the place where the action occurs. It is indicated by one or more sets that suggest interior or exterior scenes. Props are objects, such as a sword or a cup of tea, that are used onstage.

At the beginning of most plays, a brief exposition gives the audience some background information about the characters and the situation. Just as in a story or novel, the plot of a drama is built around characters in conflict.

Dramas are divided into large units called *acts* and into smaller units called *scenes.* A long play may include many sets that change with the scenes or it may indicate a change of scene with lighting.

See Genre, Stage Directions, and Tragedy.

DRAMATIC IRONY See Irony.

DRAMATIC POETRY *Dramatic poetry* is poetry that uses the techniques of drama. A dramatic poem is a verse that presents the speech of one or more characters. Dramatic poems are like little plays and usually involve many narrative elements, such as setting, conflict, and plot. Such elements may be found in Rudyard Kipling's "Danny Deever," on p. 850.

EPIC An *epic* is a long narrative or narrative poem about the deeds of gods or heroes. Because of its length and its loftiness of theme, an epic usually presents a telling portrait of the culture in which it was produced. The ancient *folk epics* like the *Ramayana* and *Sundiata* were recited aloud as entertainment at feasts and were not written down until long after they were composed.

See Narrative Poem.

ESSAY An *essay* is a short nonfiction work about a particular subject. In an *analytical essay,* the author breaks down a large idea into parts. By explaining how the parts of a concept or object fit together, the essay helps readers understand the whole idea or thing.

A *descriptive* essay seeks to convey an impression about a person, place, or object. In "Flood," p. 610, Annie Dillard describes the effects of a terrible storm.

An *expository* essay gives information, discusses ideas, or explains a process. In Rachel Carson's "The Marginal World," the author presents examples and facts that share information about the mysterious sea in a personal and entertaining way.

A *humorous essay* presents the author's thoughts on a subject in a amusing way that is intended to make readers laugh. James Thurber's "The Dog That Bit People," p. 234, is a humorous essay.

A *narrative essay* tells a true story. In the narrative essay from "Speak, Memory," on p. 305, Nabokov tells a true story from his childhood.

In a *reflective essay*, a writer shares his or her thoughts about and impressions of an idea or experience. In the excerpt from *The Way to Rainy Mountain*, p. 582, N. Scott Momaday reflects on the death of his grandmother.

A *persuasive essay* attempts to convince readers to adopt a particular opinion or course of action. The excerpt from Solzhenitsyn's Nobel lecture, p. 587, and "Keep Memory Alive," p. 591, are persuasive essays.

A *visual essay* presents information or makes a point about a subject through photographs and other visual forms as well as through text. One of the visual essays in this book is "Mothers & Daughters," p. 638.

This classification of essays is loose at best. Most essays contain passages that could be classified differently from the essay as a whole. For example, a descriptive passage may be found in a narrative essay, or a factual, expository section may be used to support a persuasive argument.

See Description, Exposition, Genre, Narration, Nonfiction, Persuasion.

EXPOSITION *Exposition* is writing or speech that explains a process or presents information. In the plot of a story or drama, the exposition is the part of the work that introduces the characters, the setting, and the basic situation.

EXTENDED METAPHOR In an *extended metaphor*, as in a regular metaphor, a subject is spoken or written of as though it were something else. However, an extended metaphor differs from a regular metaphor in that several comparisons are made. All extended metaphors sustain the comparison for several lines or for an entire poem. Eve Merriam uses an extended metaphor in her poem "Metaphor," on p. 836, to compare morning to "a new sheet of paper."

See Figurative Language and Metaphor.

FALLING ACTION See Plot.

FANTASY A *fantasy* is highly imaginative writing that contains elements not found in real life. Examples of fantasy include stories that involve supernatural elements, stories that resemble fairy tales, and stories that deal with imaginary places and creatures. Many science-fiction stories, such as Ray Bradbury's "There Will Come Soft Rains," on p. 534, contain elements of fantasy.

See Science Fiction.

FICTION *Fiction* is prose writing that tells about imaginary characters and events. The term is usually used for novels and short stories, but it also applies to dramas and narrative poetry. Some writers rely on their imaginations alone to create their works of fiction. Others base their fiction on actual events and people, to which they add invented characters, dialogue, and plot situations.

See Genre, Narrative, and Nonfiction.

FIGURATIVE LANGUAGE *Figurative language* is writing or speech not meant to be interpreted literally.

Figurative language is often used to create vivid impressions by setting up comparisons between dissimilar things.

Look, for example, at this description from Emily Dickinson's "The Wind tapped like a tired Man":

His Countenance—a Billow—
His Fingers, as He passed
Let go a music—as of tunes
Blown tremulous in Glass—

Some frequently used figures of speech are *metaphors, similes,* and *personification.*

See Literal Language, Metaphors, Personification, and Similes.

FOOT See Meter.

FORESHADOWING *Foreshadowing* is the use in a literary work of clues that suggest events that have yet to occur. Use of this technique helps to create suspense, keeping readers wondering and speculating about what will happen next. There are many instances of foreshadowing in W. W. Jacobs's "The Monkey's Paw," on p. 46. For example, Mr. White's son says that he bets he never will see the money wished for by his father. This proves true and foreshadows his death.

See Suspense.

FREE VERSE *Free verse* is poetry not written in a regular rhythmical pattern, or meter. Free verse seeks to capture the rhythms of speech. It is the dominant form of contemporary poetry. "What Are Friends For" by Rosellen Brown, p. 857, and "Making a Fist" by Naomi Shihab Nye, p. 860, are examples of free verse.

See Meter.

GENRE A *genre* is a category or type of literature. Literature is commonly divided into three major genres: poetry, prose, and drama. Each major genre is in turn divided into smaller genres, as follows:

1. Poetry: Lyric Poetry, Concrete Poetry, Dramatic Poetry, Narrative Poetry, and Epic Poetry
2. Prose: Fiction (Novels and Short Stories) and Nonfiction (Biography, Autobiography, Letters, Essays, and Reports)
3. Drama: Serious Drama and Tragedy, Comic Drama, Melodrama, and Farce

See Drama, Poetry, and Prose.

HAIKU The *haiku* is a three-line verse form. The first and third lines of a haiku each have five syllables. The second line has seven syllables. A haiku seeks to convey a single vivid emotion by means of images from nature. The poems on p. 869 are haiku.

Translators of Japanese haiku try to maintain the syllabic requirements. Western writers, however, sometimes use the form more loosely.

IAMB *See Meter.*

IMAGE An *image* is a word or phrase that appeals to one or more of the five senses—sight, hearing, touch, taste, or smell. Writers use images to re-create sensory experiences in words.

See Description.

IMAGERY *Imagery* is the descriptive or figurative language used in literature to create word pictures for the reader. These pictures, or images, are created by details of sight, sound, taste, touch, smell, or movement.

INDIRECT CHARACTERIZATION *See* Characterization.

IRONY *Irony* is the general term for literary techniques that portray differences between appearance and reality, expectation and result, or meaning and intention. In *verbal irony*, words are used to suggest the opposite of what is meant. In *dramatic irony*, there is a contradiction between what a character thinks and what the reader or audience knows to be true. In *irony of situation*, an event occurs that directly contradicts the expectations of the characters, the reader, or the audience.

During the funeral in William Shakespeare's *The Tragedy of Julius Caesar*, p. 712, Antony calls Brutus "an honorable man" when, in fact, he wants the people to think just the opposite. This is an example of verbal irony.

In the same play, dramatic irony occurs when the audience, knowing that Caesar will be assassinated, watches him set out on the ides of March.

In W. W. Jacob's "The Monkey's Paw," p. 46, the Whites expect the paw to bring them happiness; instead, it brings them nothing but grief. This is an example of irony of situation.

LEGEND A *legend* is a widely told story about the past, which may or may not have a foundation in fact. One example, retold in many versions, is the legend of King Arthur. A legend often reflects a people's identity or cultural values. It generally has more historical truth and less emphasis on the supernatural than does a myth.

See Myth.

LITERAL LANGUAGE *Literal language* uses words in their ordinary senses. It is the opposite of *figurative language*. If you tell someone standing on a diving board to jump in, you are speaking literally. If you tell someone standing on the street corner to jump in the lake, you are speaking figuratively.

See Figurative Language.

LYRIC POEM A *lyric poem* is a highly musical verse that expresses the observations and feelings of a single speaker. In ancient times, lyric poems were sung to the accompaniment of the lyre, a type of stringed instrument. Modern lyric poems are not usually sung. However, they still have a musical quality that is achieved through rhythm and such other devices as alliteration and rhyme. Federico García Lorca's "The Guitar," on p. 856, is a lyric poem expressing the wailing and crying sound of a guitar.

METAPHOR A *metaphor* is a figure of speech in which one thing is spoken of as though it were something else. Unlike a simile, which compares two things using *like* or *as,* a metaphor implies a comparison between them. In "Making a Fist," on p. 857, Naomi Shihab Nye uses this metaphor:

My stomach was a melon
split wide inside my skin.

See Extended Metaphor and Figurative Language.

METER The *meter* of a poem is its rhythmical

Mark Antony's "Friends, Romans, countrymen . . ." monologue from *The Tragedy of Julius Caesar* is one of the most famous dramatic speeches in literature.

pattern. This pattern is determined by the number and types of stresses, or beats, in each line. To describe the meter of a poem, you must scan its lines. *Scanning* involves marking the stressed and unstressed syllables. Each strong stress is marked with a slanted accent mark (´) and each unstressed syllable with a curved accent mark (˘). The stressed and unstressed syllables are then divided by vertical lines (|) into groups called *feet*. The following types of feet are common in English poetry:

1. *Iamb:* a foot with one unstressed syllable followed by a stressed syllable, as in the word "again"

2. *Trochee:* a foot with a stressed syllable followed by an unstressed syllable, as in the word "wonder"

3. *Anapest:* a foot with two unstressed syllables followed by one strong stress, as in the phrase "on the beach"

4. *Dactyl:* a foot with one strong stress followed by two unstressed syllables, as in the word "wonderful"

5. *Spondee:* a foot with two strong stresses, as in the word "spacewalk"

Depending on the type of foot that is most common in them, lines of poetry are described as *iambic, trochaic, anapestic,* and so forth.

Lines are also described in terms of the number of feet that occur in them, as follows:

1. *Monometer:* one foot
   Ăll thíngs
   Áre ă
   Bĕcómĭng.

2. *Dimeter:*
   Ă búyĕr | fŏr thém
   Ă hándsŏme | yŏŭng mán
   —"The Bridegroom," p. 54

3. *Trimeter:*
   Sŭccéss ĭs | cóuntĕd | swéetĕst
   Bў thóse| whŏ ne´er | sŭccéed.
   —"Success is Counted Sweetest," p. 148

4. *Tetrameter:* verse written in four-foot lines

5. *Pentameter:* verse written in five-foot lines

6. *Hexameter:* verse written in six-foot lines

7. *Heptameter:* verse written in seven-foot lines

Blank verse is poetry written in unrhymed iambic pentameter. Poetry that does not have a regular meter is called *free verse.*

MONOLOGUE A *monologue* is a speech by one character in a play, story, or poem. A monologue may be addressed to another character or to the audience, or it may be a *soliloquy*—a speech that presents the character's thoughts as though the character were overheard when alone. In Act II, Scene i, of *The Tragedy of Julius Caesar,* p. 712, Brutus delivers an impassioned monologue citing reasons to assassinate Caesar.

See Drama and Soliloquy.

MOOD *See* Atmosphere.

MORAL A *moral* is a lesson taught by a literary work. A fable usually ends with a moral that is directly stated.

MOTIVATION *Motivation* is a reason that explains or partially explains why a character thinks, feels, acts, or behaves in a certain way. Motivation results from a combination of the character's personality and the situation that confronts the character.

See Character and Characterization.

MYTH A *myth* is a fictional tale that explains the actions of gods or the causes of natural phenomena. Unlike legends, myths have little historical truth and involve supernatural elements. Every culture has its collections of myths. Among the most familiar are the myths of the ancient Greeks and Romans. "Damon and Pythias," on p.102, is a classic Greek myth about the unbreakable bond of friendship.

See Oral Tradition.

NARRATION *Narration* is writing that tells a story. The act of telling a story in speech is also called narration. Novels and short stories are fictional narratives. Nonfiction works such as news stories, biographies, and autobiographies are also narratives. A narrative poem tells a story in verse.

See Anecdote, Essay, Narrative Poem, Nonfiction, Novel, and Short Story.

NARRATIVE A *narrative* is a story told in fiction, nonfiction, poetry, or drama.

See Narration.

NARRATIVE POEM A *narrative poem* is one that tells a story. "La Belle Dame sans Merci," on p. 842, is an example of a narrative poem. It tells the story of a knight driven to despair because he loves a pitiless woman.

See Dramatic Poetry, Epic, and Narration.

NARRATOR A *narrator* is a speaker or character who tells a story. The narrator may be either a character in the story or an outside observer. The writer's choice of narrator determines the story's *point of view,* which in turn determines the type and amount of information the writer can reveal.

See Speaker and Point of View.

NONFICTION *Nonfiction* is prose writing that presents and explains ideas or that tells about real people, places, objects, or events. Nonfiction narratives are about actual people, places, and events, unlike fictional narratives, which present imaginary characters and events. To be classed as nonfiction, a work must be true.

Among nonfiction forms are essays, newspaper and magazine articles, journals, travelogues, biographies, and autobiographies. Historical, scientific, technical, political, and philosophical writings are also nonfiction.

See Autobiography, Biography, and Essay.

NOVEL A *novel* is a long work of fiction. Like a short story, a novel has a plot that explores characters in conflict. However, a novel is much longer than a short story and may have one or more subplots, or minor stories, and several themes.

OCTAVE See Stanza.

ONOMATOPOEIA *Onomatopoeia* is the use of words that imitate sounds. *Whirr, thud, sizzle,* and *hiss* are typical examples. Writers can deliberately choose words that contribute to a desired sound effect.

ORAL TRADITION The *oral tradition* is the passing of songs, stories, and poems from generation to generation by word of mouth. Many folk songs, ballads, fairy tales, legends, and myths originated in the oral tradition.

See Myth.

PARABLE A *parable* is simple, brief narrative that teaches a lesson by using characters and events to stand for abstract ideas. The parable "How Much Land Does a Man Need?" p. 130, teaches a lesson about greed.

PARODY A *parody* is a comical piece of writing that mocks the characteristics of a specific literary form. Through exaggeration of the types of ideas, language, tone, or action in a type of literature or a specific work, a parody calls attention to the ridiculous aspects of its subject. The excerpt from *Don Quixote,* p. 884, is a parody of the romantic literature that was popular in the late sixteenth century.

PENTAMETER See Meter.

PERSONIFICATION *Personification* is a type of figurative language in which a nonhuman subject is given human characteristics. Emily Dickinson personifies the wind when she describes it as tapping like a tired Man.

See Figurative Language.

PERSUASION *Persuasion* is writing or speech that attempts to convince the reader to adopt a particular opinion or course of action. A newspaper editorial that says a city council decision was wrong is an example of persuasive writing attempting to mold opinion. Critical reviews, such as the reviews of the movie *Star Wars,* pp. 626 and 629, are a form of persuasive writing.

See Critical Review and Essay.

PLOT *Plot* is the sequence of events in a literary work. In most novels, dramas, short stories, and narrative poems, the plot involves both characters and a central conflict. The plot usually begins with an *exposition* that introduces the setting, the characters, and the basic situation. This is followed by the *inciting incident,* which introduces the central conflict. The conflict then increases during the *development* until it reaches a high point of interest or suspense, the *climax.* All the events leading up to the climax make up the *rising action.* The climax is followed by the *falling action,* which leads to the *resolution,* or end, of the central conflict. Any events that occur after the resolution make up the *denouement.*

POETRY *Poetry* is one of the three major types of literature, the others being prose and drama. Most poems make use of highly concise, musical, and emotionally charged language. Many also make use of imagery, figurative language, and special devices of sound such as rhyme. Poems are often divided into lines and stanzas and often employ regular rhythmical patterns, or meters. However, some poems are written out just like prose, and some poems are written in free verse.

See Free Verse, Genre, Meter, Rhyme, Rhythm.

POINT OF VIEW The *point of view* is the perspective, or vantage point, from which the story is told. If the narrator is part of the action, the story is told from the *first-person* point of view. We see and know only what the character telling the story knows. "By the Waters of Babylon," p. 500, is told from the first-person point of view. In a story told by a *third person*, the narrator is someone outside the action. An *omniscient third-person* narrator is all-knowing; the narrator knows more about the characters and events than any one character can know. The third-person omniscient narrator of "The Street of the Canon," on p. 40, reveals the thoughts and feelings of several characters. A *limited third-person* narrator tells only the thoughts and feelings of one character. "A Visit to Grandmother," p. 166, is told by a third-person limited narrator.

See Narrator.

PROSE *Prose* is the ordinary form of written language. Most writing that is not poetry, drama, or song is considered prose. Prose is one of the major genres of literature and occurs in two forms: fiction and nonfiction.

See Fiction, Genre, and Nonfiction.

PROTAGONIST The main character in a work of fiction, the character reader's would like to see succeed, is the *protagonist*. Antigone is the protagonist of the play *Antigone.*

See Antagonist and Character.

REPETITION *Repetition* is the use of any element of language—a sound, a word, a phrase, a clause, or a sentence—more than once. In "Prayers From the First Dancers" from *The Night Chant,* on p. 822, the words "in the house made" are repeated eight times, each time in connection with a different image.

Poets use many kinds of repetition. Alliteration, assonance, rhyme, and rhythm are repetitions of certain sounds and sound patterns.

A refrain is a repeated line or group of lines. In both prose and poetry, repetition is used for musical effects and for emphasis.

See Alliteration, Assonance, Consonance, Rhyme, and Rhythm.

RESOLUTION *See Plot.*

RHYME *Rhyme* is the repetition of sounds at the ends of words. *End rhyme* occurs when the rhyming words come at the ends of lines, as in "The Kraken," by Alfred, Lord Tennyson, p. 825:

> Below the thunders of the upper *deep;*
> Far, far beneath in the abysmal **sea,**
> His ancient, dreamless, uninvaded *sleep*
> The Kraken sleepeth: faintest sunlights **flee**

Internal rhyme occurs when the rhyming words fall within a line.

See Repetition and Rhyme Scheme.

RHYME SCHEME A *rhyme scheme* is a regular pattern of rhyming words in a poem. The rhyme scheme of a poem is indicated by using different letters of the alphabet for each new rhyme. In an *aabb* stanza, for example, line 1 rhymes with line 2 and line 3 rhymes with line 4.

Many poems use the same pattern of rhymes, though not the same rhymes, in each stanza.

See Rhyme.

RHYTHM *Rhythm* is the pattern of *beats,* or stresses, in spoken or written language. Some poems have a very specific pattern, or meter, whereas prose and free verse use the natural rhythms of everyday speech.

See Meter.

RISING ACTION *See Plot.*

SCENE *See Drama.*

SCIENCE FICTION *Science fiction* is writing that tells about imaginary events that involve science or technology. Many science-fiction stories are set in the future. The setting can be on Earth, in space, on other planets, or in a totally imaginary place. Ray Bradbury's "There Will Come Soft Rains," on p. 534, is an example of science fiction.

See Fantasy.

SENSORY LANGUAGE Sensory language is writing or speech that appeals to one or more of the senses.

See Image.

SESTET *See Stanza.*

SETTING The *setting* of a literary work is the time

and place of the action. Time can include not only the historical period—past, present, or future—but also a specific year, season, or time of day. Place may involve not only the geographical place—a region, country, state, or town—but also the social, economic, or cultural environment.

In some stories, setting serves merely as a backdrop for action, a context in which the characters move and speak. In others, however, setting is a crucial element. The setting functions as the "main character" in Ray Bradbury's "There Will Come Soft Rains," on p. 534.

Description of the setting often helps establish the mood of a story. For example, in Edgar Allan Poe's "The Masque of the Red Death," on p. 78, the setting contributes to the growing horror.

See Mood.

SHORT STORY A *short story* is a brief work of fiction. The short story resembles the longer novel but generally has a simpler plot and setting. In addition, the short story tends to reveal character at a crucial moment rather than to develop it through many incidents. For example, Doris Lessing's "Through the Tunnel," p. 221, concentrates on what happens as Jerry learns to swim through the tunnel.

See Fiction, Genre, and Novel.

SIMILE A *simile* is a figure of speech in which *like* or *as* is used to make a comparison between two basically unlike ideas. "Alexandra is as bright as Jason" is a comparison, not a simile. "Alexandra is as bright as a bulb" is a simile.

Poets often use similes. The following example from Philip Fried's "Right Hand," on p. 838, compares a hand to a Greek chorus:

> . . . as it moved back and forth like a Greek chorus across the stage of the ironing board

By drawing together different elements, effective similes make vivid and meaningful comparisons that enrich what the writer has to say.

See Figurative Language.

SOLILOQUY A *soliloquy* is a long speech expressing the thoughts of a character alone on stage. In William Shakespeare's *The Tragedy of Julius Caesar*, p. 712, Brutus begins a soliloquy while he is alone in his orchard. This soliloquy reveals Brutus' fears about how Caesar might change were he crowned king.

See Monologue.

SONNET A *sonnet* is a fourteen-line lyric poem, usually written in rhymed iambic pentameter. The *English*, or *Shakespearean*, *sonnet* consists of three quatrains (four-line stanzas) and a couplet (two lines), usually rhyming *abab cdcd efef gg*.

The couplet usually comments on the ideas contained in the preceding twelve lines. The sonnet is usually not printed with the stanzas divided, but a reader can see distinct ideas in each. See Sonnet 18 by William Shakespeare on p. 866.

The *Italian*, or *Petrarchan*, *sonnet* consists of an octave (eight-line stanza) and a sestet (six-line stanza). Often the octave rhymes *abbaabba* and the sestet rhymes *cdecde*. The octave states a theme or asks a question. The sestet comments on or answers the question.

The Petrarchan sonnet took its name from Petrarch, a fourteenth-century Italian poet. Once the form was introduced in England, it underwent change. The Shakespearean sonnet is, of course, named after William Shakespeare.

See Lyric Poem, Meter, and Stanza.

SPEAKER The *speaker* is the imaginary voice assumed by the writer of a poem. In many poems, the speaker is not identified by name. When reading a poem, remember that the speaker within the poem may be a person, an animal, a thing, or an abstraction. The speaker in Gabriela Mistral's "Fear," on p. 889, is a woman who fears for her daughter's future.

STAGE DIRECTIONS *Stage directions* are notes included in a drama to describe how the work is to be performed or staged. These instructions are printed in italics and are not spoken aloud. They are used to describe sets, lighting, sound effects, and the appearance, personalities, and movements of characters.

See Drama.

STANZA A *stanza* is a formal division of lines in a poem, considered as a unit. Often the stanzas in a poem are separated by spaces.

Stanzas are sometimes named according to the number of lines found in them. A *couplet*, for example, is a two-line stanza. A *tercet* is a stanza with three lines. Other types of stanzas include the following:

1. *Quatrain*: four-line stanza
2. *Cinquain*: five-line stanza
3. *Sestet*: six-line stanza
4. *Heptastich*: seven-line stanza
5. *Octave*: eight-line stanza

Sonnets, limericks, and haiku all have distinct stanza forms. A *sonnet* is a fourteen-line poem that is made up

Literary Terms Handbook ◆ 963

either of three quatrains and a couplet or of an octave followed by a sestet. A *limerick* consists of a single five-line stanza with a particular pattern of rhymes. A *haiku* is made up of a single three-line stanza.

See Haiku and Sonnet.

SURPRISE ENDING A *surprise ending* is a conclusion that violates the expectations of the reader but in a way that is both logical and believable. O. Henry's "Hearts and Hands," on p. 264, and Saki's "The Open Window," on p. 471, have surprise endings. Both authors were masters of this form.

SUSPENSE *Suspense* is a feeling of curiosity or uncertainty about the outcome of events in a literary work. Writers create suspense by raising questions in the minds of their readers.

SYMBOL A *symbol* is anything that stands for or represents something else. An object that serves as a symbol has its own meaning, but it also represents abstract ideas. Marks on paper can symbolize spoken words. A flag symbolizes a country. A flashy car may symbolize wealth. Writers sometimes use such conventional symbols in their work, but sometimes they also create symbols of their own through emphasis or repetition.

In Edgar Allan Poe's "The Masque of the Red Death," on p. 78, the masked figure symbolizes death, and the clock symbolizes the passage of time.

TANKA A tanka consists of five unrhymed lines with a pattern of five, seven, five, seven, seven syllables. Tankas appear on p. 868.

TECHNICAL ARTICLE A *technical article* is a type of expository writing that explains a procedure, provides instructions, or represents specialized information. Often, specialized vocabulary is used. Sometimes, diagrams or charts illustrate complicated structures or steps. The technical article "Imitating Nature's Mineral Artistry," p. 648, explains how technology is used to create synthetic gems.

TETRAMETER *See Meter.*

THEME A *theme* is a central message or insight into life revealed through the literary work. The theme is not a condensed summary of the plot. Instead, it is a generalization about people or about life that is communicated through the literary work.

The theme of a literary work may be stated directly or implied. In "The Princess and All the Kingdom," on p. 552, the moral is clearly and simply stated by the old chancellor who explains to the prince that his conquests have brought him new responsibilities. In "The

Censors," on p. 554, a powerful message is also delivered, but no one states exactly what it is. The theme of Valenzuela's short story is not stated—it's implied.

When the theme of a work is *implied*, readers think about what the work seems to say about the nature of people or about life. The story or poem can be viewed as a specific example of the generalization the writer is trying to communicate.

Note that there is usually no single correct statement of a work's theme, though there can be incorrect ones. Also, a long work, like a novel or a full-length play, may have several themes. Finally, not all literary works have themes. A work meant only to entertain may have no theme at all.

TONE The *tone* of a literary work is the writer's attitude toward his or her audience and subject. The tone can often be described by a single adjective, such as *formal* or *informal, serious* or *playful, bitter* or *ironic.* Rachel Carson's awed and respectful tone in "The Marginal World," on p. 571, expresses her intensity as she seeks the meaning behind the beauty of the natural world.

TRAGEDY A *tragedy* is a work of literature, especially a play, that results in a catastrophe for the main character. In ancient Greek drama, the main character was always a significant person, a king or a hero, and the cause of the tragedy was a tragic flaw, or weakness, in his or her character. In modern drama, the main character can be an ordinary person and the cause of the tragedy can be some evil in society itself. The purpose of tragedy is not only to arouse fear and pity in the audience, but also, in some cases, to convey a sense of the grandeur and nobility of the human spirit.

Shakespeare's *The Tragedy of Julius Caesar,* on p. 714, is a tragedy. Brutus is a brave and noble figure whose tragic flaw is assuming that honorable ends justify dishonorable means.

See Drama.

TRIMETER *See Meter.*

VERBAL IRONY *See Irony.*

VILLANELLE A *villanelle* is a lyric poem written in three-line stanzas, ending with a four-line stanza. It has two refrain lines that appear initially in the first and third lines of the first stanza; then they appear alternately as the third line of subsequent stanzas, and finally, as the last two lines of the poem. Theodore Roethke's "The Waking," on p. 867, is an example of a villanelle.

WRITING HANDBOOK

THE WRITING PROCESS

A polished piece of writing can seem to have been effortlessly created, but most good writing is the result of a process of writing, rethinking, and rewriting. The process can be roughly divided into a series of stages: prewriting, drafting, revising, editing, proofreading, and publishing.

It's important to remember that the writing process is one that moves backward as well as forward. Even while you are moving forward in the creation of your composition, you may still return to a previous stage—to rethink or rewrite.

Following are stages of the writing process, with key points to address during each stage.

Prewriting

In this stage you plan out the work to be done. You prepare to write by exploring ideas, gathering information, and working out an organization. Following are the key steps to take at this stage.

Step 1: Analyze the writing situation. Start by clarifying your assignment, so that you know exactly what you are supposed to do.

- *Focus your topic.* If you need to, narrow the topic—the subject you are writing about—so that you can write about it fully in the space you have.
- *Know your purpose.* What is your goal for this paper? What do you want to accomplish? Your purpose will determine what you include in it.
- *Know your audience.* Who will read your paper influences what you say and how you say it.

Step 2: Gather ideas and information. You can do this in a number of ways:

- *Brainstorm.* When you brainstorm, either alone or with others, you come up with possible ideas to use in your paper. Not all of your brainstormed ideas will be useful or suitable. You'll need to evaluate them later.
- *Consult other people about your subject.* Speaking informally with others may suggest an idea or approach you did not see at first.
- *Make a list of questions about your topic.* Then find the answers to your questions.

- *Do research.* Your topic may require information that you don't have, so you will need to go to other sources to find information. There are numerous ways to find information on a topic. See the Research Handbook on p. 979 for suggestions.

The ideas and information you gather will become the content of your paper. Not all of the information you gather will be needed. As you develop and revise your paper, you will make further decisions about what to include and what to leave out.

Step 3: Organize. First, make a rough plan for how you want to present your information. Sort your ideas and notes; decide what goes with what, and which points are the most important. You can make an outline to show the order of ideas, or you can use some other organizing plan that works for you.

There are many ways in which you can organize and develop your material. Use a method that works for your topic. Following are common methods of organizing information in the development of a paper.

- *Chronological Order* In this method, events are presented in the order in which they occurred. This organization works best for presenting narrative material or explaining in a "how to."
- *Spatial Order* In spatial order, details are presented as seen in space, for example, from left to right or from foreground to background. This order is good for descriptive writing.
- *Order of Importance* This order helps readers see the relative importance of ideas. You present ideas from most to least important or from least to most important.
- *Main Idea and Details* This logical organization works well to support an idea or opinion.

Drafting

When you draft, you put down your ideas on paper in rough form. Working from your prewriting notes and your outline or plan, you develop and present your ideas in sentences and paragraphs.

Don't worry about getting everything perfect at the drafting stage. Concentrate on getting your ideas down.

Draft in a way that works for you. Some writers work best by writing a quick draft—putting down all their ideas without stopping to evaluate them. Other writers prefer to develop each paragraph carefully and thoughtfully, making sure each main idea is supported by details.

As you are developing a draft, keep in mind your purpose and your audience. These determine what you say and how you say it.

Don't be afraid to change your original plans during drafting. Some of the best ideas are those that were not planned at the beginning. Write as many drafts as you like. You can draft over and over until you've got it the way you like.

Most papers, regardless of the topic, are developed with an introduction, a body, and a conclusion. Here are tips for developing these parts.

Introduction In the introduction to a paper, you want to engage your readers' attention and let them know the purpose of your paper. You may use the following strategies in your introduction:

- State your main idea.
- Take a stand.
- Use an anecdote.
- Quote someone.
- Startle your readers.

Body of the paper In the body of your paper, you present your information and make your points. Your **organization** is an important factor in leading readers through your ideas. Your elaboration on your main ideas is also important. **Elaboration** is the development of ideas to make your written work precise and complete. You can use the following kinds of details to elaborate your main ideas:

- Facts and statistics
- Anecdotes
- Sensory details
- Examples
- Explanation and definition
- Quotations

Conclusion The ending of your paper is the final impression you leave with your readers. Your conclusion should give readers the sense that you have pulled everything together. Following are some effective ways to end your paper:

- Summarize and restate.
- Ask a question.
- State an opinion.
- Tell an anecdote.
- Call for action.

Revising

Once you have a draft, you can look at it critically or have others review it. This is the time to make changes—on many levels. Revising is the process of reworking what you have written to make it as good as it can be. You may change some details so that your ideas flow smoothly and are clearly supported. You may discover that some details don't work and you'll need to discard them. Two strategies may help you start the revising process:

1. Read your work aloud. This is an excellent way to catch any ideas or details that have been left out and to notice errors in logic.
2. Ask someone else to read your work. Choose someone who can point out its strengths as well as suggest how to improve it.

How do you know what to look for and what to change? Here is a checklist of major writing issues. If the answer to any of these questions is no, then that is an area that needs revision.

1. Does the writing achieve your purpose?
2. Does the paper have unity? That is, does it have a single focus, with all details and information contributing to that focus?
3. Is the arrangement of information clear and logical?
4. Have you elaborated enough to give your audience adequate enough information?

Editing

When you edit, you look more closely at the language you have used, so that the way you express your ideas is most effective.

- Replace dull language with vivid, precise words.
- Cut or change redundant expressions (unnecessary repetition).
- Cut empty words and phrases, those that do not add anything to the writing.
- Check passive voice. Usually active voice is more effective.
- Replace wordy expressions with shorter, more precise ones.

Proofreading

After you finish your final draft, the last step is to proofread the draft to make it ready for a reader. You may do this on your own or with the help of a partner.

It's useful to have handy both a dictionary and a usage handbook to help you check for correctness. Here are the tasks in proofreading:

- Correct errors in grammar and usage.
- Correct errors in punctuation and capitalization.
- Correct errors in spelling.

THE MODES OF WRITING

Description

Description is writing that creates a vivid picture for readers, draws readers into a scene, and makes readers feel as if they are meeting a character or experiencing an event firsthand. A description may stand on its own or be part of a longer work, such as a short story.

When you write a description, bring it to life with sensory details, which tell how your subject looks, smells, sounds, tastes, or feels. You'll want to choose your details carefully so that you create a single main impression of your subject. Avoid language and details that don't contribute to this main impression. Keep these guidelines in mind whenever you are assigned one of the following types of description:

Observation In an observation, you describe an event that you have witnessed firsthand, often over an extended period of time. You may focus on an aspect of daily life or on a scientific phenomenon, such as a storm or an eclipse.

Remembrance When you write a remembrance, you use vivid descriptive details to bring to life memorable people, places, or events from your past.

Description of a Place Often used to set the scene in a story or drama, your description of a place should convey the physical look and atmosphere of a scene—either interior or exterior.

Character Profile In a character profile, you capture a person's appearance and personality traits and reveal information about his or her life. Your subject may be a real person or a fictional character.

Narration

Whenever writers tell any type of story, they are using **narration**. While there are many kinds of narration, most narratives share certain elements—characters, a setting, a sequence of events (or plot, in fiction), and, often, a theme. You might be asked to try your hand at one of these types of narration:

Anecdote An anecdote, which may be oral or written, is a brief and often humorous narrative that is true or based on the truth. You may use an anecdote both to entertain and to make a general point about life.

Personal Narrative A personal narrative is a true story about a memorable experience or period in your life. In a personal narrative, your feelings about events shape the way you tell the story—even the way you describe people and places.

Firsthand Biography A firsthand biography tells about the life (or a period in the life) of a person whom you know personally. You can use your close relationship with the person to help you include personal insights not found in biographies based solely on research.

Short Story Short stories are short fictional, or made-up, narratives in which a main character faces a conflict that is resolved by the end of the story. In planning a short story, you focus on developing the plot, the setting, and the characters. You must also decide on a point of view: Will your story be told by a character who participates in the action, or by someone who describes the action as an outside observer?

Exposition

Exposition is writing that informs or explains. The information you include in expository writing is factual or (when you're expressing an opinion) based on fact.

Your expository writing should reflect a well-thought-out organization—one that includes a clear introduction, body, and conclusion and is appropriate for the type of exposition you are writing. Here are some types of exposition you may be asked to write:

Cause-and-Effect Essay In a cause-and-effect essay, you consider the reasons something did happen or might happen. You may examine several causes of a single effect or several effects of a single cause.

Comparison-and-Contrast Essay When you write a comparison-and-contrast essay, you consider the similarities and differences between two or more subjects. You may organize your essay point by point—discussing each aspect of your subject in turn—or subject by subject—discussing all the qualities of one subject first, then the qualities of the next subject.

Problem-and-Solution Essay In a problem-and-solution essay, you identify a conflict or problem and offer a resolution. Begin with a clear statement of the problem and follow with a reasoned path to a solution.

Summary To write a summary or synopsis of an event or a literary work, you include only the details that your readers will need in order to understand the key features of the event or the literary work. Omit any personal opinions; include only factual details.

How-to Instructions You use how-to instructions

to explain the steps involved in doing a particular task. In writing instructions it is also important to anticipate and answer questions the reader may have about why a particular procedure is being recommended.

Persuasion

Persuasion is writing or speaking that attempts to convince people to agree with a position or take a desired action. When used effectively, persuasive writing has the power to change people's lives. As a reader and a writer, you will find yourself engaged in many forms of persuasion. Here are a few of them:

Persuasive Essay In writing a persuasive essay, you build an argument, supporting your opinions with a variety of evidence: facts, statistics, examples, statements from experts. You also anticipate and develop counterarguments to opposing opinions.

Advertisement When you write an advertisement, you present information in an appealing way to make the product or service seem desirable.

Position Paper In a position paper, you try to persuade readers to accept your views on a controversial issue. Most often, your audience will consist of people who have some power to shape policy related to the issue. Your views in a position paper should be supported with evidence.

Persuasive Speech A persuasive speech is a piece of persuasion that you present orally instead of in writing. As a persuasive speaker, you use a variety of techniques, such as repetition of key points, to capture your audience's interest and to add force to your argument.

Letter to the Editor When you write a letter to the editor, you may be responding to an article or an editorial published earlier, or you may be writing to express concern on an issue of importance to the community. Your letter should describe the issue briefly, present your views supported with evidence, and state any action you think should be taken.

Research Writing

Writers often use outside research to gather information and explore subjects of interest. The product of that research is called **research writing.** In connection with your reading, you may occasionally be assigned one of the following types of research writing:

Biographical Report In a biographical report, you examine a person's life and achievements. You include the dates and details of the main events in the person's life and, at times, make educated guesses about the reasons behind those events. For your biographical report, you may need to research not only the life of an individual but also the times in which he or she lived.

Research Paper A research paper uses information gathered from a variety of outside sources to explore a topic. In your research paper, you will usually include an introduction, in which your thesis, or main point, is stated; a body, in which you present support for the thesis; and a conclusion that summarizes, or restates, your main points. You should credit the sources of information, using footnotes or other types of citation, and include a bibliography, or general list of sources, at the end.

Multimedia Presentation In preparing a multimedia presentation, you will gather and organize information in a variety of media, or means of communication. You may use written materials, slides, videos, audiocassettes, sound effects, art, photographs, models, charts, and diagrams.

Creative Writing

Creative writing blends imagination, ideas, and emotions, and allows you to present your own unique view of the world. Poems, plays, short stories, dramas, and even some cartoons are examples of creative writing. All are represented in this anthology and may provide inspiration for you to produce your own creative works, such as the following:

Lyric Poem In a lyric poem, you use sensory images, figurative language, and sound devices to express deep thoughts and feelings about a subject. To give your lyric poem a musical quality, employ sound devices, such as rhyme, rhythm, alliteration, and onomatopoeia.

Narrative Poem Writing a narrative poem is similar to writing a short story, with a plot, characters, and a theme. However, your narrative poem, unlike a story, will be divided into stanzas (groups of lines that form a unit) usually composed of rhyming lines that have a definite rhythm, or beat.

Song Lyrics In writing lyrics, or words, for a song, you use many elements of poetry—rhyme, rhythm, repetition, and imagery. In addition, your song lyrics should convey emotions, as well as interesting ideas.

Drama When you write a drama or a dramatic scene, you are writing a story that is intended to be performed. Since a drama consists almost entirely of the words and actions of the characters, be sure to write dialogue that clearly shows the characters' personalities, thoughts, and emotions, and stage directions that convey your ideas about sets, props, sound effects, and the speaking style and movements of the characters.

Response to Literature

In a **response to literature,** you express your thoughts and feelings about a work and often, in so doing, gain a better understanding of what the work is all about. Your response to literature can take many forms—oral or written, formal or informal. During the course of your reading, you may be asked to respond to a work of literature in one of these forms:

Literary Analysis In a literary analysis, you take a critical look at various important elements in the work. You then attempt to explain how the author has used those elements and how they work together to convey the author's message.

Retelling of a Fairy Tale Most fairy tales—stories about good and evil characters, giants, and magic deeds—have been handed down from generation to generation, and often the original authors are unknown. When you retell a fairy tale in your own way, you can add to the original or change it. For example, you might set it in another place or time period or write it as a poem or a drama.

Reader's Response Journal Entry Your reader's response journal is a record of your thoughts and feelings about works you have read. Use it to remind yourself of writers and works that you particularly liked or disliked, or to provide a source of writing ideas.

Letter to an Author People sometimes respond to a work of literature by writing a letter to the author. You can praise the work, ask questions, or offer constructive criticism.

Critical Review In a critical review of a literary work, you discuss various elements in the work and offer opinions about them. You may also give a summary of the work and a recommendation to readers.

Practical and Technical Writing

Practical writing is fact-based writing that people do in the workplace or in their day-to-day lives. Business letters, memos, school forms, and job applications are examples of practical writing. **Technical writing**, which is also based on facts, explains procedures, provides instructions, or presents specialized information. You encounter technical writing every time you read a manual or a set of instructions.

In the following descriptions, you'll find tips for tackling several types of practical and technical writing.

Letter Requesting Information In a letter requesting information, you state the information you're searching for and ask any specific questions you have. In your letter, include your name and address so that you can receive a response. Include the date, which can help you or the recipient keep track of correspondence. It is also customary to include the address of the party to whom you are writing. Use a formal greeting followed by a colon. Keep the body of the letter as brief and clear as possible. Use a polite closing, and remember to sign as well as type or print your name.

News Release News releases announce factual information about upcoming events. Also called press releases, they are usually sent to local newspapers, local radio stations, and other media. When you write a news release, use this format: Position your name and phone number in the upper right corner. Then capture your main point in a centered headline, which will allow the recipient to see at a glance what the news release is about. In the body, present factual information in a concise way. You may begin with an opening location tag that tells in which town or city the news release originated. The numeral 30 or number signs (###) customarily indicate the end of the news release.

Guidelines When you write guidelines, you give information about how people should act or you provide tips on how to do something. List guidelines one by one, using somewhat formal language. Your guidelines may or may not be numbered. In addition to factual information, which should be complete and accurate, guidelines may contain your opinions.

Process Explanation In a process explanation, you offer a step-by-step explanation of how to do something. Your explanation should be specific, using headings, labels, or numbers to make the process clear. You may also include diagrams or other illustrations to further clarify the process.

GRAMMAR AND MECHANICS HANDBOOK

Nouns A **noun** is the name of a person, place, or thing. A **common noun** names any one of a class of people, places, or things. A **proper noun** names a specific person, place, or thing.

Common Noun	Proper Noun
city	Washington, D.C.

Pronouns A **pronoun** is a word that stands for a noun or for a word that takes the place of a noun.

A **personal pronoun** refers to (1) the person speaking, (2) the person spoken to, or (3) the person, place, or thing spoken about.

	Singular	Plural
First Person	I, me, my, mine	we, us, our, ours
Second Person	you, your, yours	you, your, yours
Third Person	he, him, his, she, her, hers, it, its	they, them, their, theirs

A **reflexive pronoun** ends in -*self* or -*selves* and adds information to a sentence by pointing back to a noun or a pronoun earlier in the sentence.

> I was saying to *myself*, "Ed, my boy, this Everest—you've got to push it a bit harder!"
>
> —"The Final Assault," Edmund Hillary, p. 29

An **intensive pronoun** ends in -*self* or -*selves* and simply adds emphasis to a noun or a pronoun in the same sentence.

> After a time, I *myself* was allowed to go into the dead houses and search for metal.
>
> —"By the Waters of Babylon," Stephen Vincent Benét, p. 500

A **demonstrative pronoun** directs attention to a specific person, place, or thing.

> this   these   that   those
>
> *These* are the juiciest pears I've ever tasted.

A **relative pronoun** begins a subordinate (relative) clause and connects it to another idea in the sentence.

> The poet *who* wrote "Fear" is Gabriela Mistral.

An **indefinite pronoun** refers to a person, place, or thing, often without specifying which one.

> And then, for a moment, *all* is still, . . .
>
> —"The Masque of the Red Death," Edgar Allan Poe, p. 81

Verbs A **verb** is a word that expresses time while showing an action, a condition, or the fact that something exists.

An **action verb** indicates the action of someone or something.

An action verb is **transitive** if it directs action toward someone or something named in the same sentence.

> He *dusted* his hands, muttering.
>
> —"Contents of the Dead Man's Pocket," Jack Finney, p. 5

An action verb is **intransitive** if it does not direct action toward something or someone named in the same sentence.

> I *waved* and *shouted*, then as suddenly *stopped* as I realized my foolishness.
>
> —"The Final Assault," Edmund Hillary, p. 31

A **linking verb** is a verb that connects the subject of a sentence with a noun or pronoun that renames or describes the subject. All linking verbs are intransitive.

> Romance at short notice *was* her specialty.
>
> —"The Open Window," Saki, p. 474

A **helping verb** is a verb that can be added to another verb to make a verb phrase.

> Nor *did* I suspect that these experiences could be part of a novel's meaning.

Adjectives An **adjective** describes a noun or a pronoun or gives a noun or a pronoun a more specific meaning. Adjectives answer these questions:

What kind?	*blue* lamp, *large* tree
Which one?	*this* table, *those* books
How many?	*five* stars, *several* buses
How much?	*less* money, *enough* votes

The articles *the, a,* and *an* are adjectives. *An* is used before a word beginning with a vowel sound.

A noun may sometimes be used as an adjective.

> *diamond* necklace   *summer* vacation

Adverbs An **adverb** modifies a verb, an adjective, or another adverb. Adverbs answer the questions *where? when? in what way? to what extent?*

> He could stand *there.* (modifies verb *stand*)
> He was *blissfully* happy. (modifies adjective *happy*)
> It ended *too* soon. (modifies adverb *soon*)

Prepositions A **preposition** relates a noun or a pronoun that appears with it to another word in the sentence.

before the end   *near* me   *inside* our fence

Conjunctions A **conjunction** connects other words or groups of words.

A **coordinating conjunction** connects similar kinds or groups of words.

mother *and* father   simple *yet* stylish

Correlative conjunctions are used in pairs to connect similar words or groups of words.

both Sue *and* Meg   *neither* he *nor* I

A **subordinating conjunction** connects two complete ideas by placing one idea below the other in rank or importance.

You would know him *if* you saw him.

Sentences A **sentence** is a group of words with a subject and a predicate. Together, these parts express a complete thought.

A **fragment** is a group of words that does not express a complete thought.

Subject and Verb Agreement To make a subject and verb agree, make sure that both are singular or both are plural.

Many *storms are* the cause of beach erosion.
Either the *cats* or the *dog is* hungry.
Neither *Angie* nor her *sisters were* present.
The *conductor*, as well as the soloists, *was applauded*.

Phrase A **phrase** is a group of words, without a subject and a verb, that functions in a sentence as one part of speech.

A **prepositional phrase** is a group of words that includes a preposition and a noun or a pronoun that is the object of the preposition.

outside my window   below the counter

An **adjective phrase** is a prepositional phrase that modifies a noun or a pronoun by telling *what kind* or *which one*.

The wooden gates *of that lane* stood open.

An **adverb phrase** is a prepositional phrase that modifies a verb, an adjective, or an adverb by pointing out *where, when, in what way,* or *to what extent*.

On a sudden impulse, he got to his feet.
—"Contents of the Dead Man's Pocket,"
Jack Finney, p. 8

An **appositive phrase** is a noun or a pronoun with modifiers, placed next to a noun or a pronoun to identify it or add information and details.

M. Morissot, *watchmaker by trade but local militiaman for the time being*, stopped short . . .
—"Two Friends," Guy de Maupassant, p. 96

A **participial phrase** is a participle with its modifiers or complements. The entire phrase acts as an adjective.

Choosing such a tide, I hoped for a glimpse of the pool.
—"The Marginal World," Rachel Carson, p. 572

A **gerund phrase** is a gerund with modifiers or a complement, all acting together as a noun.

. . . *moving along the ledge* was quite as easy as he thought it would be.
—"Contents of the Dead Man's Pocket,"
Jack Finney, p. 9

An **infinitive phrase** is an infinitive with modifiers, complements, or a subject, all acting together as a single part of speech.

To be alive to hear this song is a victory . . .
—"Old Song," Traditional, p. 202

Clauses A **clause** is a group of words with a subject and a verb.

An **independent clause** has a subject and a verb and can stand by itself as a complete sentence.

A **subordinate clause** has a subject and a verb but cannot stand by itself as a complete sentence; it can only be part of a sentence.

An **adjective clause** is a subordinate clause that modifies a noun or a pronoun by telling *what kind* or *which one*.

For country people, *who only knew the dismantled tilting ground of Sir Ector's castle,* the scene which met their eyes was ravishing.
—"Arthur Becomes King of Britain,"
T. H. White, p. 910

An **adverb clause** modifies a verb, an adjective, an adverb, or a verbal by telling *where, when, in what way, to what extent, under what condition,* or *why*.

She took up that magazine *when her daughter-in-law came in* . . .
—"The Good Deed," Pearl S. Buck, p. 342

A **noun clause** is a subordinate clause that acts as a noun.

That you have wronged me doth appear in this.

—*The Tragedy of Julius Caesar,*
William Shakespeare, p. 228

Summary of Capitalization and Punctuation

CAPITALIZATION

Capitalize the first word of a sentence and also the first word in a quotation if the quotation is a complete sentence.

"Mummy," he said, "I can stay under water for two minutes—..."

—"Through the Tunnel," Doris Lessing, p. 281

Capitalize all proper nouns and adjectives.

W. W. Jacobs   Flanders Fields   African writers

Capitalize a person's title when it is followed by the person's name or when it is used in direct address.

Reverend Tallboys   Mrs. Prothero   Major Moberly

Capitalize titles showing family relationships when they refer to a specific person, unless they are preceded by a possessive noun or pronoun.

Grandmother   his father

Capitalize the first word and all other key words in the titles of books, periodicals, poems, stories, plays, paintings, and other works of art.

The Way to Rainy Mountain   "Spring and All"

PUNCTUATION

End Marks Use a **period** to end a declarative sentence, an imperative sentence, an indirect question, and most abbreviations.

She broke off with a little shudder.

—"The Open Window," Saki, p. 472

Use a **question mark** to end a direct question, an incomplete question, or a statement that is intended as a question.

"Monkey's paw?" said Mrs. White curiously.

—"The Monkey's Paw," W. W. Jacobs, p. 48

Use an **exclamation mark** after a statement showing strong emotion, an urgent imperative sentence, or an interjection expressing strong emotion.

"Bring him in! Bring him in now!"

—"The Dog That Bit People,"
James Thurber, p. 238

Commas Use a **comma** before the coordinating conjunction to separate two independent clauses in a compound sentence.

His arms had begun to tremble from the steady strain of clinging to his narrow perch, and he did not know what to do now ...

—"Contents of the Dead Man's Pocket,"
Jack Finney, p. 16

Use commas to separate three or more words, phrases, or clauses in a series.

Animals took shape: yellow giraffes, blue lions, pink antelopes, lilac panthers cavorting in crystal substance.

—"There Will Come Soft Rains,"
Ray Bradbury, p. 537

Use commas to separate adjectives of equal rank. Do not use commas to separate adjectives that must stay in a specific order.

I was immediately transported to the foot of mountains, with narrow defiles twisting in and out amongst their *towering, arid* peaks.

—"The Cabuliwallah,"
Rabindranath Tagore, p. 287

Use a comma after an introductory word, phrase, or clause.

When Marian Anderson again returned to America, she was a seasoned artist.

—"Marian Anderson: Famous Concert Singer,"
Langston Hughes, p. 604

Use commas to set off parenthetical and nonessential expressions.

All of these works, *of course*, had earlier left their marks ...

—"Star Wars: A Trip to a Galaxy ...,"
Vincent Canby, p. 626

Use commas with places, dates, and titles.

Poe was raised in Richmond, Virginia.
August 4, 2026
Alfred, Lord Tennyson

Use a comma to indicate words left out of an elliptical sentence, to set off a direct quotation, and to prevent a sentence from being misunderstood.

Vincent Canby writes for *The New York Times*, Roger Ebert, for the *Chicago Sun Times*.

Semicolons Use a **semicolon** to join independent clauses that are not already joined by a conjunction.

They could find no buffalo; *they had to hang an old hide from the sacred tree.*

—*The Way to Rainy Mountain*,
N. Scott Momaday, p. 585

Use a semicolon to join independent clauses separated by either a conjunctive adverb or a transitional expression.

James Thurber wrote many books; moreover, he was a cartoonist and a journalist.

Use semicolons to avoid confusion when independent clauses or items in a series already contain commas.

There were the Useful Presents: engulfing mufflers of the old coach days, and mittens made for giant sloths; zebra scarfs of a substance like silky gum that could be tug-o'-warred down to the galoshes; . . .

—"A Child's Christmas in Wales,"
Dylan Thomas, p. 598

Colons Use a **colon** in order to introduce a list of items following an independent clause.

The authors we are reading include a number of poets: Robert Frost, Octavio Paz, and Emily Dickinson.

Use a colon to introduce a formal quotation.

The next day Howard Taubman wrote enthusiastically in *The New York Times:*
Marian Anderson has returned to her native land one of the great singers of our time . . .

—"Marian Anderson: Famous Concert Singer,"
Langston Hughes, p. 604

Quotation Marks A **direct quotation** represents a person's exact speech or thoughts and is enclosed in quotation marks.

"Clara, my mind is made up."

—"With All Flags Flying," Anne Tyler, p. 472

An **indirect quotation** reports only the general meaning of what a person said or thought and does not require quotation marks.

She rattled on cheerfully about the shooting and the scarcity of birds, . . .

—"The Open Window," Saki, p. 472

Always place a comma or a period inside the final quotation mark.

"There are ceremonies going on," I said, "and I am busy."

—"The Cabuliwallah,"
Rabindranath Tagore, p. 290

Place a question mark or an exclamation mark inside the final quotation mark if the end mark is part of the quotation; if it is not part of the quotation, place it outside the final quotation mark.

"If you only cleared the house, you'd be quite happy, wouldn't you?"

—"The Monkey's Paw," W. W. Jacobs, p. 49

Have you ever read the poem "Africa"?

Use single quotation marks for a quotation within a quotation.

Use quotation marks around the titles of short written works, episodes in a series, songs, and titles of works mentioned as parts of a collection.

"Making a Fist"   "These Are Days"

Underline or italicize titles of longer works, such as plays, movies, or novels.

Dashes Use **dashes** to indicate an abrupt change of thought, a dramatic interrupting idea, or a summary statement.

It made her so mad to see Muggs lying there, oblivious of the mice—they came running up to her—that she slapped him and he slashed at her, but he didn't make it.

—"The Dog That Bit People,"
James Thurber, p. 236

Parentheses Use **parentheses** to set off asides and explanations only when the material is not essential or when it consists of one or more sentences.

Automatically I looked at our pressure gauges—just over 2,900 pounds (2,900 pounds was just over 700 liters; 180 into 700 was about 4) . . .

—"The Final Assault," Edmund Hillary, p. 31

Hyphens Use a **hyphen** with certain numbers, after certain prefixes, with two or more words used as one word, and with a compound modifier coming before a noun.

fifty-two   greenish-blue water

Apostrophes Add an **apostrophe** and -s to show the possessive case of most singular nouns.

Prospero's castle   the playwright's craft

Add an apostrophe to show the possessive case of plural nouns ending in -s and -es.

the sailors' ships   the babies' mothers

Add an apostrophe and -s to show the possessive case of plural nouns that do not end in -s or -es.

the children's games   the people's friend

Use an apostrophe in a contraction to indicate the position of the missing letter or letters.

I *didn't* love any one of you more than the other.

—"A Visit to Grandmother,"
William Melvin Kelley, p. 174

GLOSSARY OF COMMON USAGE

among, between

Among is usually used with three or more items. *Between* is generally used with only two items.

Among the poems we read this year, Eve Merriam's "Metaphor" was my favorite.

"Like the Sun" tells of one man's conflict *between* telling the truth and telling white lies.

amount, number

Amount refers to a mass or a unit, whereas *number* refers to individual items that can be counted. Therefore, *amount* generally appears with a singular noun, and *number* appears with a plural noun.

Being able to climb Mount Everest requires a huge *amount* of training.

In his story "The Masque of the Red Death," Poe uses a *number* of intriguing symbols.

any, all

Any should not be used in place of *any other* or *all*.

Rajika liked Anne Tyler's "With All Flags Flying" better than *any other* short story.

Of *all* W. W. Jacobs's short stories, "The Monkey's Paw" is one of the most famous.

around

In formal writing, *around* should not be used to mean *approximately* or *about*. These usages are allowable, however, in informal writing or in colloquial dialogue.

Shakespeare's *Romeo and Juliet* had its first performance in *approximately* 1595.

Shakespeare was *about* thirty when he wrote this play.

as, because, like, as to

The word *as* has several meanings and can function as several parts of speech. To avoid confusion, use *because* rather than *as* when you want to indicate cause and effect.

Because Cyril was interested in the history of African American poetry, he decided to write his report on Langston Hughes.

Do not use the preposition *like* to introduce a clause that requires the conjunction *as*.

James Thurber conversed *as* he wrote—wittily.

The use of *as to* for *about* is awkward and should be avoided.

Rosa has an interesting theory *about* Edgar Allan Poe's choice of subject matter.

bad, badly

Use the predicate adjective *bad* after linking verbs such as *feel, look,* and *seem*. Use *badly* whenever an adverb is required.

Sara Teasdale's poem "There Will Come Soft Rains" shows clearly that the author felt *bad* about the destruction of the war.

In "Through the Tunnel," Jerry *badly* wants to be able to swim the length of the tunnel.

because of, due to

Use *due to* if it can logically replace the phrase *caused by*. In introductory phrases, however, *because of* is better usage than *due to*.

The popularity of the mystery is largely *due to* the works of Edgar Allan Poe.

Because of lack of oxygen, Edmund Hillary and

Tenzing Norgay moved more and more lethargically as they made their way up Everest.

being as, being that

Avoid these expressions. Use *because* or *since* instead.

Because the protagonist of Anton Chekhov's "A Problem" is a static character, he changes little in the course of the story.

Since there was a question about who reached the summit of Everest first, Tenzing Norgay decided to answer that question once and for all in his biography.

beside, besides

Beside is a preposition meaning "at the side of" or "close to." Do not confuse *beside* with *besides*, which means "in addition to." *Besides* can be a preposition or an adverb.

As the three men cross the lawn and approach the open window, a brown spaniel trots *beside* them.

There are many other Indian oral epics *besides* the *Ramayana*.

can, may

The verb *can* generally refers to the ability to do something. The verb *may* generally refers to permission to do something.

Dylan Thomas describes his childhood Christmases so vividly that most readers *can* visualize the scene.

Creon's edict states that no one *may* bury Polyneices.

different from, different than

The preferred usage is *different from*.

The structure and rhyme scheme of a Shakespearean sonnet are *different from* the organization of a Petrarchan sonnet.

farther, further

Use *farther* when you refer to distance. Use *further* when you mean "to a greater degree" or "additional."

The *farther* the ants travel, the more ominous and destructive they seem.

The storm at the end of Act I of *The Tragedy of Julius Caesar further* hints at the ominous deeds to come.

fewer, less

Use *fewer* for things that can be counted. Use *less* for amounts or quantities that cannot be counted.

Poetry often uses *fewer* words than prose to convey ideas and images.

It takes *less* time to perform a Greek tragedy than to perform a Shakespearean play.

good, well

Use the adjective *good* after linking verbs such as *feel, look, smell, taste,* and *seem.* Use *well* whenever you need an adverb, or as an adjective describing health.

Caesar remarks that Cassius does not look *good*; on the contrary, his appearance is "lean" and "hungry."

Twain wrote especially *well* when he described eccentric characters.

hopefully

You should not attach this adverb to a sentence loosely, as in "*Hopefully*, the rain will stop by noon." Rewrite the sentence so that *hopefully* modifies a specific verb. Other possible ways of revising such sentences include using the adjective *hopeful* or a phrase such as *everyone hopes that*.

Dr. Martin Luther King, Jr., wrote and spoke *hopefully* about his dream of racial harmony.

Mr. White was *hopeful* that the monkey's paw would bring him good fortune.

Everyone *hopes* that the class production of *Antigone* will be a big success.

its, it's

Do not confuse the possessive pronoun *its* with the contraction *it's*, used in place of "it is" or "it has."

In *its* very first lines, "The Stolen Child" establishes an eerie mood.

In "The Street of the Cañon," Pepe knows that *it's* dangerous to attend Don Romeo's party.

just, only

When you use *just* as an adverb meaning "no more than," be sure you place it directly before the word it logically modifies. Likewise, be sure you place *only* before the word it logically modifies.

Just one wish changed the Whites' lives forever.

A short story can usually develop *only* a few characters, whereas a novel can include many.

kind of, sort of

In formal writing, you should not use these colloquial expressions. Instead, use a word such as *rather* or *somewhat*.

> Poe portrays Prince Prospero as *rather* arrogant.

> The tone of Tenzig Norgay's biography is *somewhat* defensive.

lay, lie

Do not confuse these verbs. *Lay* is a transitive verb meaning "to set or put something down." Its principal parts are *lay, laying, laid, laid. Lie* is an intransitive verb meaning "to recline." Its principal parts are *lie, lying, lay, lain.*

> The monkey's paw *lay* on the table in the living room for a while before anyone dared to pick it up.

> La belle dame sans merci enchants the knight as he *lies* in her "elfin grot."

leave, let

Be careful not to confuse these verbs. *Leave* means "to go away" or "to allow to remain." *Let* means "to permit."

> Threatening *Antigone* not to disobey his orders, Creon angrily *leaves* the stage.

> At first Mr. Carpenter's family does not want to *let* him enter the retirement home.

raise, rise

Raise is a transitive verb that usually takes a direct object. *Rise* is an intransitive verb and never takes a direct object.

> In his speech, Antony unexpectedly *raises* the subject of Caesar's will.

> When the Cabuliwallah comes to call, Mini *rises* from her chair and runs to greet him.

set, sit

Do not confuse these verbs. *Set* is a transitive verb meaning "to put (something) in a certain place." Its principal parts are *set, setting, set, set. Sit* is an intransitive verb meaning "to be seated." Its principal parts are *sit, sitting, sat, sat.*

> Antigone's conduct *sets* a high standard for all those who believe that conscience must be our ultimate guide.

> Jerry's mother *sits* in her beach chair while Jerry swims in the ocean.

so, so that

Be careful not to use the coordinating conjunction *so* when your context requires *so that. So* means "accordingly" or "therefore" and expresses a cause-and-effect relationship. *So that* expresses purpose.

> He wanted to do well on the test, *so* he read *The Tragedy of Julius* Caesar again.

> Antony uses eloquent rhetoric to stir up the people *so that* they will turn against the conspirators.

than, then

The conjunction *than* is used to connect the two parts of a comparison. Do not confuse *than* with the adverb *then*, which usually refers to time.

> I enjoyed "The Marginal World" more *than* "The Flood."

> Marian Anderson gave a triumphant singing recital in New York that evening, and she *then* embarked on a coast-to-coast American tour.

that, which, who

Use the relative pronoun *that* to refer to things or people. Use *which* only for things and *who* only for people.

> The poem *that* Cheryl liked the most was "The Street."

> Haiku, *which* consists of only seventeen syllables, is often built around one or two vivid images.

> The assassin *who* strikes Caesar first is Casca.

unique

Because *unique* means "one of a kind," you should not use it carelessly to mean "interesting" or "unusual." Avoid such illogical expressions as "most unique," "very unique," and "extremely unique."

> Emily Dickinson's unconventional themes and bold experiments with form make her *unique* in the history of nineteenth-century American poetry.

when, where

Do not directly follow a linking verb with *when* or *where*. Be careful not to use *where* when your context requires *that*.

> **Faulty:** The exposition is *when* an author provides the reader with important background information.

> **Revised:** In the exposition, an author provides the reader with important background information.

> **Faulty:** Madras, India, is *where* R. K. Narayan was born.

> **Revised:** R. K. Narayan was born in Madras, India.

Speaking and Listening Handbook

Language is both spoken and written. The literature in this book is written, which is one form of communication, but most of your communication is probably oral. Oral communication involves both speaking and listening. Having strong speaking and listening skills benefits you both in your school life and your life outside of school.

Many of the assignments accompanying the literature in this textbook involve speaking and listening. This handbook identifies some of the terminology related to speaking and listening, both the oral communication you experience every day and the assignments you may do in conjunction with the literature in this book.

Oral Communication

You use many different kinds of oral communication each day. When you communicate with your friends, when you communicate with your teachers or your parents, when you interact with a cashier in a store, you are communicating orally. In addition to ordinary, everyday conversation, oral communication includes class discussions, speeches, interviews, presentations, debates. When you communicate face to face, you usually use more than your voice to get your message across. If you communicate by telephone, however, you must rely solely on your verbal skills.

The following terms will give you a better understanding of the many elements that are part of oral communication.

ARTICULATION is the process of forming sounds into words; it is the way in which the tongue, teeth, lower jaw, and soft palate are used to produce speech sounds.

BODY LANGUAGE refers to the use of facial expressions, eye contact, gestures, posture, and movement to communicate a feeling or idea.

CONNOTATION is the set of associations a word calls to mind. The connotations of the words you choose influence the message you send. For example, most people respond more favorably to being described as "slim" rather than as "skinny." The connotation of *slim* is more appealing than that of *skinny.*

EYE CONTACT is direct visual contact with another person's eyes.

FEEDBACK is the set of verbal and nonverbal reactions that indicate to a speaker that a message has been received and understood.

GESTURES are the movements made with arms, hands, face, and fingers to communicate.

INFLECTION refers to the rise and fall in the pitch of the voice in speaking; it is also called **intonation.**

LISTENING is understanding and interpreting sound in a meaningful way. You listen differently for different purposes.

Listening for key information: For example, when a teacher gives an assignment, or when someone gives you directions to a place, you listen for key information.

Listening for main points: In a classroom exchange of ideas or information, or while watching a television documentary, you listen for main points.

Listening critically: When you evaluate a performance, song, or a persuasive or political speech, you listen critically, questioning and judging the speaker's message.

NONVERBAL COMMUNICATION is communication without the use of words. People communicate nonverbally through gestures, facial expressions, posture, and body movements. Sign language is an entire language based on nonverbal communication.

PROJECTION is speaking in such a way that the voice carries clearly to an audience. It's important to project your voice when speaking in a large space like a classroom or auditorium.

VOCAL DELIVERY is the way in which you present a message. Your vocal delivery involves all of the following elements:

Volume: the loudness or quietness of your voice
Pitch: the high or low quality of your voice
Rate: the speed at which you speak; also called pace
Stress: the amount of emphasis placed on different syllables in a word or on different words in a sentence

All of these elements individually, and the way in which they are combined, contribute to the meaning of a spoken message.

Speaking and Listening Situations

The following are some of the many types of situations in which you apply your speaking and listening skills.

AUDIENCE Your audience in any situation refers to the person or people to whom you direct your message. An audience can be a group of people sitting in a classroom or auditorium observing a performance or just one person to whom you address a question or a comment. When preparing for any speaking situation, it's useful to analyze your audience, learning what you can about their background, interests, and attitudes so that you can tailor your message to them.

DEBATE A debate is a formal public-speaking situation in which participants prepare and present arguments on opposing sides of a question, stated as a **proposition.** The proposition must be controversial: It must concern an issue that may be solved in two different, valid ways.

The two sides in a debate are the *affirmative* (pro) and the *negative* (con). The affirmative side argues in favor of the proposition, while the negative side argues against it. The affirmative side begins the debate, since it is seeking a change in belief or policy. The opposing sides take turns presenting their arguments, and each side has an opportunity for *rebuttal,* in which they may challenge or question the other side's argument.

GROUP DISCUSSION results when three or more people meet to solve a common problem, arrive at a decision, or answer a question of mutual interest. Group discussion is one of the most widely used forms of interpersonal communication in modern society. **Meetings** are a kind of organized group discussion for a specific purpose.

INTERVIEW An interview is a form of interaction in which one person, the interviewer, asks questions of another person, the interviewee. Interviews may take place for many purposes: to obtain information, to discover a person's suitability for a job or a college, or to inform the public of a notable person's opinions.

ORAL INTERPRETATION is the reading or speaking of a piece of literature aloud for an audience. Oral interpretation involves giving expression to the ideas, meaning, or even the structure of a piece of literature. The speaker interprets the piece through his or her vocal delivery. **Storytelling,** in which a speaker reads or tells a story expressively, is a form of oral interpretation.

PANEL DISCUSSION is a group discussion on a topic of interest common to all members of a panel and to a listening audience. A panel is usually composed of four to six experts on a particular topic who are brought together to share information and opinions.

PANTOMINE is a form of nonverbal communication in which an idea or a story is communicated completely through the use of gesture, body language, and facial expressions, without any words at all.

PARLIAMENTARY PROCEDURE refers to the set of rules used to conduct a meeting in an orderly manner. Parliamentary procedure makes discussions at meetings more efficient and productive, and protects the rights of individuals attending the meeting.

All of the business conducted according to parliamentary procedure is handled through motions. Motions are proposals for action made by members of the meeting. For example, beside main motions that set forth the items of business that will be considered, a motion can be made to adjourn—or end the meeting—or to amend, or alter the wording of a motion.

The following are the main principles of parliamentary procedure:

1. Only one item of business may be considered at a time.

2. Everyone has a right to express an opinion, and each opinion is treated as valuable.

3. Every member of the group has the right to vote, and each vote is counted as equal.

4. The group always follows the decision of the majority.

READERS' THEATER is a dramatic reading of a piece of literature in which participants take parts from a story or play and read aloud in expressive voices. Unlike a play, however, sets and costumes are not part of the performance, and the participants remain seated as they deliver their lines.

ROLE PLAY To role-play is to take the role of a person or character and, as that character, act out a given situation, speaking, acting, and responding in the manner of the character.

SPEECH A speech is a talk or address given to an audience. A speech may be **impromptu**—delivered on the spur of the moment with no preparation—or formally prepared and delivered for a specific purpose or occasion.

- *Purposes:* The most common purposes of speeches are to persuade (for example, political speeches), to entertain, to explain, and to inform.
- *Occasions:* Different occasions call for different types of speeches. Speeches given on these occasions could be persuasive, entertaining, or informative, as appropriate. The following are common occasions for speeches.
  Introduction: Introducing a speaker or presenter at a meeting or assembly
  Presentation: Giving an award or acknowledging the contributions of someone
  Acceptance: Accepting an award or tribute
  Keynote: Giving an inspirational address at a large meeting or convention
  Commencement: Honoring the graduates of a school or university

RESEARCH HANDBOOK

Many of the assignments and activities in this literature book require you to find out more about your topic. Whenever you need ideas, details, or information, you must conduct research. You can find information by using library resources and computer resources, as well as by interviewing experts in a field.

Before you begin, create a research plan that lists the questions you want answered about your topic. Then decide which sources will best provide answers to those questions. When gathering information, it is important to use a variety of sources and not to rely on one main source of information. It is also important to document where you find different pieces of information you use so that you can cite those sources in your work.

The suggestions that follow can help you locate your sources.

Library Resources

Libraries contain many sources of information in both print and electronic form. You'll save time if you plan your research before actually going to the library. Make a list of the information you think you will need, and for each item list possible sources for the information. Here are some sources to consider:

NONFICTION BOOKS An excellent starting point for researching your topic, nonfiction books can provide either broad coverage or specific details, depending on the book. To find appropriate nonfiction books, use the library catalog, which may be in card files or in electronic form on computers. In either case, you can search by author, title, or subject; in a computer catalog, you can also search by key word. When you find the listing for a book you want, print it out or copy down the title, author, and call number. The call number, which also appears on the book's spine, will help you locate the book in the library.

NEWSPAPERS AND MAGAZINES Books are often not the best places for finding up-to-the-minute information. Instead, you might try newspapers and magazines. To find information about an event that occurred on a specific date, go directly to newspapers and magazines for that date. To find articles on a particular topic, use indexes like the *Readers' Guide to Periodical Literature*, which lists magazine articles under subject headings. For each article that you want, jot down the title, author (if given), page number or numbers, and the name and date of the magazine in which the article appears. If your library does not have the magazine you need, either as a separate issue or on microfilm, you may still be able to obtain photocopies of the article through an interlibrary loan.

REFERENCE WORKS The following important reference materials can also help you with your research.

- *General encyclopedias* have articles on thousands of topics and are a good starting point for your research, although they shouldn't be used as primary sources.
- *Specialized encyclopedias* contain articles in particular subject areas, such as science, music, or art.
- *Biographical dictionaries and indexes* contain brief articles on people and often suggest where to find more information.
- *Almanacs* provide statistics and data on current events and act as a calendar for the upcoming year.
- *Atlases*, or books of maps, usually include geographical facts and may also include information like population and weather statistics.
- *Indexes and bibliographies*, such as the *Readers' Guide to Periodical Literature*, tell you in what publications you can find specific information, articles, or shorter works (such as poems or essays).
- *Vertical files* (drawers in file cabinets) hold pamphlets, booklets, and government publications that often provide current information.

Computer Research

The Internet Use the Internet to get up-to-the-minute information on virtually any topic. The Internet provides access to a multitude of resource-rich sources such as news media, museums, colleges and universities, and government institutions. There are a number of indexes and directories organized by subject to help you locate information on the Internet, including Yahoo!, the World Wide Web Virtual Library, the Kids Web, and the Webcrawler. These indexes and directories will help you find direct links to information related to your topic.

Internet Sources and Addresses

- **Yahoo! Directory** allows you to do word searches or link directly to your topic by clicking on such subjects as the arts, computers, entertainment, or government.
http://www.yahoo.com
- **World Wide Web Virtual Library** is a comprehensive and easy-to-use subject catalog that provides direct links to academic subjects in alphabetical order.
http://celtic.stanford.edu/vlib/Overview.html
- **Kids Web** supplies links to reference materials, such as dictionaries, *Bartlett's Familiar Quotations*, a thesaurus, and a world fact book.
http://www.npac.syr.edu/textbook/kidsweb/
- **Webcrawler** helps you to find links to information about your topic that are available on the Internet when you type in a concise term or key word.
http://www.webcrawler.com

CD-ROM References

Other sources that you can access using a computer are available on CD-ROM. The Wilson Disk, Newsquest, the *Readers' Guide to Periodical Literature*, and many other useful indexes are available on CD-ROM, as are encyclopedias, almanacs, atlases, and other reference works. Check your library to see which are available.

Interviews as Research Sources

People who are experts in their field or who have experience or knowledge relevant to your topic are excellent sources for your research. If such people are available to you, the way to obtain information from them is through an interview. Follow these guidelines to make your interview successful and productive:

- Make an appointment at a time convenient to the person you want to interview, and arrange to meet in a place where he or she will feel comfortable talking freely.
- If necessary, do research in advance to help you prepare the questions you will ask.
- Before the interview, list the questions you will ask, wording them so that they encourage specific answers. Avoid questions that can be answered simply with *yes* or *no*.

- Make an audiotape or videotape of the interview if possible. If not, write down the answers as accurately as you can.
- Include the date of the interview at the top of your notes or on the tape.
- Follow up with a thank-you note or phone call to the person you interviewed.

Sources for a Multimedia Presentation

When preparing a multimedia presentation, keep in mind that you'll need to use some of your research findings to illustrate or support your main ideas when you actually give the presentation. Do research to find media support, such as visuals, CD's, and so on—in addition to those media you might create yourself. Here are some media that may be useful as both sources and illustrations:

- Musical recordings on audio cassette or compact disk (CD) (often available at libraries)
- Videos that you prepare yourself
- Fine art reproductions (often available at libraries and museums)
- Photographs that you or others have taken
- Computer presentations using slide shows, graphics, and so on
- Video or audio cassette recordings of interviews that you conduct.

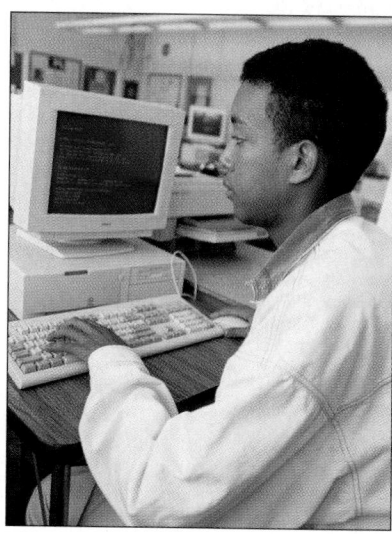

INDEX OF AUTHORS AND TITLES

INDEX OF SKILLS

LITERARY TERMS

READING STRATEGIES

VOCABULARY

CRITICAL THINKING AND VIEWING

WRITING

Writing Opportunities

Index of Skills ◆ 985

Art Credits

Index of Fine Art/Art Credits ◆ 991

600, 601: © 1997 Estate of Fritz Eichenberg/Licensed by VAGA, New York, NY; **602:** UPI/Corbis-Bettmann; **608:** Thomas Victor; **610-611 & 613:** Steve Proehl/The Image Bank; **619:** (top) Lisa Quinones/Black Star/PNI; (bottom) Hiroyuki Matsumoto/Black Star/PNI; **623:** Courtesy of the artist; **624:** (left) © Frank Capri/Saga/Archive Photos; (right) Lisa Rose/Globe Photos; **626, 630-631, 632:** Photofest; **638:** Danny Lyon/Magnum Photos, Inc.; **639:** *Brookline, Massachusetts,* 1986, Photograph by Sage Sohier © 1986; **640:** (left) *Nellie G. Morgan and Tammie Pruitt Morgan, Bicentennial Celebration, Philadelphia, Mississippi, 1976.* Photo © 1997, Roland L. Freeman; **640-641 & 642:** Courtesy of the photographer; **646:** (left) Ralph Morese/Life Magazine © Time Inc.; (center) Andy Caulfield/The Image Bank; (right) Photo by Scott Weidensaul; **648:** (rc) © Photo Researchers, Inc.; **648-649 & 650-651:** (background) Andy Caulfield/The Image Bank; **651:** (rc) © Carl Frank/Photo Researchers, Inc.; **652:** Scott Weidensaul; **656:** David Young-Wolff/PhotoEdit; **659:** Rwoda Sydney/PhotoEdit; **660:** Paul Conklin/PhotoEdit; **661:** (left) Taken from the front cover of *My Left Foot* by Christy Brown, a Minerva paperback, published in 1990. © Hulton Deutsch. Hand coloured by Helena Zakrewska-Rucinska. Design Lucy Bennett. Photograph courtesy of Hulton Getty/Tone Stone Images; (center) Full unabridged cover from *Death Be Not Proud* by John Gunther. © 1949 by John Gunther. Selection reprinted by permission of HarperCollins Publishers; (right) From THE MEXICAN AMERICAN FAMILY ALBUM by Dorothy and Thomas Hoobler. © 1994 by Dorothy and Thomas Hoobler. Reprinted by permission of Oxford University Press, Inc.; **662-663:** Superstock; **665:** Richard Barnet/Omni-Photo Communications, Inc.; **667:** © Uniphoto, Inc. **668:** Vatican Museum/Scala/Art Resource, NY; **670-671:** (background) Fotopic/Omni-Photo Communications, Inc.; **685:** (background) Fotopic/Omni-Photo Communications, Inc.; **690:** Etruscan Amphora, Black-figured, pontic fighting soldiers, white dove on shield, National Museum, Warsaw, Poland, Erich Lessing/Art Resource, NY; **701:** Ken Karp Photography; **705:** *Roman Senators at the Imperial Court,* Roman relief. Museo Nazionale Romano delle Terme, Rome Italy, Alinari/Art Resource, NY; **706:** (top) & (bottom) Robert Harding Picture Library; **707:** Illustration by Hugh Dixon from "Shakespeare in Performance," courtesy of Salmander Books, London; **708:** *William Shakespeare* (detail), Artist Unknown, courtesy of the National Portrait Gallery, London; **710:** © Michael Holford/Collection of the British Museum; **712:** Culver Pictures, Inc.; **717 & 722:** Photofest; **737 & 746:** Culver Pictures, Inc.; **754, 760, 763:** Photofest; **764 & 765:** (background) NASA; **769:** Extispicium Relief (inspection of entrails) from the Forum of Trajan, Rome. Early Hadrianic. Louvre, Paris, France, Alinari/Art Resource, NY; **774 & 780:** Photofest; **789:** Relief of *Domitius Ahenobarbus,* scene of a census, Louvre, Paris, France, Erich Lessing/Art Resource, NY; **795:** Photofest; **800:** Erich Lessing/Art Resource, NY; **804:** Photofest; **807:** Kopstein/Monkmeyer; **808:** Ken Karp Photography; **809:** (left) Book cover of *Antigone,* adapted by Lewis Galantiere from the plays by Jean Anouilh, Reprinted by special arrangement with Samuel French Inc.; (center) From *Twelfth Night* by William Shakespeare. Published by Penguin Books Ltd.; (right) From *A Doll's House* by Henrik Ibsen. Published by Penguin Books Ltd.; **810-811:** *Awaiting Spring,* Scott Burdick, watercolor, 20"x 30", courtesy of the artist; **812:** The Granger Collection, New York; **815 & 816:** Corel Professional Photos CD-ROM™; **817 & 818:** (background) NASA; (top) Michael W. Nelson/PNI; **821:** O. S. Eguchi/Photonica; **822:** (top) & (bottom) The Granger Collection, New York; (tc) *Alfred, Lord Tennyson,* c.1840, S. Laurence,

courtesy of the National Portrait Gallery, London; (bc) *Jean Toomer* (detail), c.1925, Winold Reiss, gift of Laurence A. Fleischman and Howard Garfinkle with a matching grant from the National Endowment of the Arts, National Portrait Gallery, Smithsonian Institution, Washington, D. C./Art Resource, New York; **824:** Lorette Moureau; **825:** The Granger Collection, New York; **826:** *Ploughing,* transport poster, Nancy Smith (fl.1940–50) Stapleton Collection/The Bridgeman Art Library International Ltd., London/New York; **827:** *Atlantic Moon,* Jane Wilson, oil on linen 18" x 18", courtesy Fischbach Gallery, New York; **828:** *Our Home and Native Land,* 1983, Dannielle B. Hayes, work print, gouache and pencil, 22" x 30", Omni-Photo Communications, Inc.; **832:** (tl) The Granger Collection, New York; (tr) Photo by Bachrach; (bl) Inge Morath/Magnum Photos, Inc.; (br) Photo by Lynn Saville; **834:** Catherine Karnow/Woodfin Camp & Associates; **836-837:** Corel Professional Photos CD-ROM™; **841:** *Ploughing,* transport poster, Nancy Smith (fl.1940–50) Stapleton Collection/The Bridgeman Art Library International Ltd., London/New York; **844:** AP/Wide World Photos; **845:** © 1989 Cathleen Toelke; **846:** (left) The Granger Collection, New York; (right) *Rudyard Kipling* (detail), 1899, P. Burne-Jones, courtesy of the National Portrait Gallery, London; **848:** *La Belle Dame sans Merci,* John W. Waterhouse, Hessiches Landes Museum, Darmstadt; **850:** Corel Professional Photos CD-ROM™; **851:** *The Battle of Bunker Hill,* Howard Pyle, Delaware Art Museum, Howard Pyle Collection; **854:** (top) By permission of the heirs of Federico Garcia Lorca, Rogelio Robelis Saavedra and Courtney Jose Choin Castro; (center) photo by Michael Nye; (bottom) AP/Wide World Photos; **856:** *The Old Guitarist,* 1903, Pablo Picasso, Spanish, 1881–1973, oil on panel 112.9 cm x 82.6 cm, Helen Birch Bartlett Memorial Collection, 1926.253 photograph courtesy of The Art Institute of Chicago. All rights reserved, © 1997 estate of Pablo Picasso/Artists Rights Society (ARS), New York; **857:** *Impressions of Hands,* 1969, Antoni Tapies, soft-ground etching, printed in black and aquatint, printed in medium red-brown, Plate: $19^{9}/16$" x $15^{1}/2$", Collection, The Museum of Modern Art, New York, Donald Karshan Fund; **858-859:** Corel Professional Photos CD-ROM™; **860:** *Best Friends,* Craig Nelson/ Bernstein & Andriulli, Inc.; **864:** (top) *William Shakespeare,* (detail), artist unknown, Courtesy of the National Portrait Gallery, London; (bottom) AP/Wide World Photos; **866:** *Frances Howard,* Isaac Oliver, Victoria and Albert Museum/Art Resource, NY; **867:** Frank Siteman/Stock, Boston; **868:** *The Monkey Bridge in Koshu Province,* 1841, Hiroshige Hitsu, Christie's, New York; **872:** *La Belle Dame sans Merci,* John W. Waterhouse, Hessiches Landes Museum, Darmstadt; **875:** Billy E. Barnes/PhotoEdit; **876:** Tony Freeman/PhotoEdit; **877:** (left) Cover from *How to Read a Poem* by Burton Raffel. Published by Meridian, the Penguin Group, a division of Penguin Books USA Inc.; (center) book cover of *Acquainted with the Night* by Lynn Saville. Reprinted by permission of Rizzoli International Publications, Inc.; (right) From THE POETRY OF ROBERT FROST, edited by Edward Connery Lathem. Reprinted by permission of Henry Holt & Company, Inc.; **878-879:** *Knights About to Depart on the Quest for the Holy Grail,* Tapestry designed by Sir E. Burne-Jones, woven by William Morris & Co., (129'07) Birmingham Museums and Art Gallery; **881:** *Sir Galahad,* by George Frederick Watts, (1817–1904) The Fogg Art Museum, Harvard University/Bridgeman Art Library International Ltd., London/New York; **882:** The Granger Collection, New York; **884:** *Don Quixote,* Honoré Daumier, Neue Pinakothek, Munich, Giraudon/Art Resource, New York; **887:** *Don Quixote and the Windmill,* c. 1900, Francisco J. Torrome, Bonhams, London/Bridgeman Art

Library International, London/New York; **892:** (left) *Alfred, Lord Tennyson*, c.1840, S. Laurence, courtesy of the National Portrait Gallery, London; (right) Thomas Victor; **895:** *The Dream of Arthur in Avalon*, detail, Sir Edward Burne-Jones, The Museo de Arte de Ponce, The Luis A. Ferré Foundation, Inc. Ponce, Puerto Rico; **901:** By permission of the Houghton Library, Harvard University; **905:** *The Crowning of Arthur*, Royal MS, By permission of the British Library; **908:** *Gallahad's Sword in the Stone*, Royal MS, by permission of the British Library; **912:** *The Round Table and the Holy Grail*, miniature from the Romand de Tristan. Ms. 645-647/315-317 v.3 fol. 1, 2nd half of 15th c., Musee Condee, Chantilly, France. Giraudon/Art Resource, NY; **917 & 920:** Ken Karp Photography; **921:** (tr) The Granger Collection, New York; (lc) *Rama and Lakshman Confer With the Animal Armies*, from *The Adventures of Rama*, courtesy of the Freer Gallery of Art, Smithsonian Institution, Washington, D.C., fol. 194v, full view; (br) *Dipankara Buddha*, gilt copper repousse, 17th century A.D., 27^1/2" x 9^3/4", Asian Art Museum of San Francisco, The Avery Brundage Collection; **922:** AP/Wide World Photos; **924:** Persian translation of the *Ramayana of Valmiki* (detail), Mughal, school of Akbar, late 16th century, Indian manuscript, miniatures in opaque colors and gold: average leaf - 27.5 cm x 15.2 cm, courtesy of the Freer Gallery of Art, Smithsonian Institution, Washington, D. C., 07.271 24r; **927:** *Rama Chasing the Golden Deer*, from the *Ramayana*, Sanskrit text on the reverse, 1600, Mughal, National Museum of India, New Delhi/The Bridgeman Art Library International Ltd., London/New York; **928:** *Rama Chases a Demon Disguised as a Golden Deer*, Fazl, courtesy of the Freer Gallery of Art, Smithsonian Institution, Washington, D. C., fol. 128v; **932 & 934:** Senegalese glass painting used on *Sundiata*, from the collection of Professor Donal Cruise-O'Brien, Courtesy of Longman International Education; **937:** Michael Melford/The Image Bank; **942:** (background) NASA; **943 & 944:** (top) Photofest; **944-945:** (background) NASA; **946:** © The Stock Market/Norbert Wu 1996; **950:** Tony Freeman/PhotoEdit; **951:** (left) Avenel Books, Crown Publishers, Inc., Affilliate of Random House, Inc.; (center) book cover of *Siddhartha* by Herman Hesse. Designed by Alvin Lustig; Reprinted by permission of New Directions Publishing Corp.; (right) From *The Hollow Hills* by Mary Stewart. ©1973 by Mary Stewart. Reprinted by permission of Ballantine Books, a division of Random House, Inc. **955:** UPI/Corbis-Bettmann; **960:** Photofest.

ACKNOWLEDGMENTS (continued)

The Asia Society and Nguyen Ngoc Bich
"Thoughts of Hanoi" by Nguyen Thi Vinh from *A Thousand Years of Vietnamese Poetry*, edited by Nguyen Ngoc Bich. Copyright 1962, 1967, 1968, 1969, 1970, 1971, 1974 by The Asia Society and Nguyen Ngoc Bich.

Bancroft Library
Excerpt from *Desert Exile: The Uprooting of a Japanese-American Family* by Yoshiko Uchida. Copyright © 1982 by Yoshiko Uchida. Reprinted courtesy of the Bancroft Library, University of California, Berkeley.

Elizabeth Barnett, Literary Executor of the Estate of Norma Millay Ellis
"Conscientious Objector" by Edna St. Vincent Millay, from *Collected Poems*, HarperCollins. Copyright © 1934, 1962 by Edna St. Vincent Millay and Norma Millay Ellis. All rights reserved. Reprinted by permission of Elizabeth Barnett, literary executor.

Susan Bergholz Literary Services, and Henry Dunow Literary Agency
"The Censors" by Luisa Valenzuela. Copyright 1976 by Luisa Valenzuela, renewed 1988. Translation copyright © 1982 by David Unger, first published in *Short Stories*, ed. Howe, David Godine. Translation reprinted by permission of Susan Bergholz Literary Services, New York, underlying rights by Henry Dunow Literary Agency. All rights reserved.

Chana Bloch
"Pride" by Dahlia Ravikovitch, translated by Chana Bloch and Ariel Bloch from *The Window*, Sheep Meadow Press, 1989. Reprinted by permission of Chana Bloch.

Brandt & Brandt Literary Agents, Inc.
"By the Waters of Babylon" by Stephen Vincent Benet, from *The Selected Works of Stephen Vincent Benet*, Holt, Rhinehart & Winston, Inc. Copyright 1937 by Stephen Vincent Benet. Copyright renewed © 1964 by Thomas C. Benet, Stephanie B. Mahin and Rachel Benet Lewis. Reprinted by permission of Brandt & Brandt Literary Agents, Inc.

Columbia Records
"Old Friends" by Paul Simon. Copyright © 1968 by Paul Simon. All rights reserved.

Don Congdon Associates, Inc.
"Contents of the Dead Man's Pocket" by Jack Finney, published in *Collier's*, 1956. Copyright © 1957 by Crowell Collier Publishing, renewed 1984 by Jack Finney. "There Will Come Soft Rains" by Ray Bradbury, published in *Collier's Weekly*, 1950. Copyright © 1950 by Crowell-Collier Publishing, renewed 1977 by Ray Bradbury. Reprinted by permission of Don Congdon Associates, Inc.

Crown Publishers, Inc., a division of Random House, Inc.
"Damon and Pythias" from *Classic Myths to Read Aloud* by William Russell. Copyright © 1988 by William F. Russell. Reprinted by permission of Crown Publishers, Inc.

Darhansoff & Verrill Literary Agency
"I Am Not One of Those Who Left the Land" by Anna Akhmatova from *Poems of Akhmatova*, selected, translated and introduced by Stanley Kunitz and Max Hayward, Copyright © 1973. Reprinted by permission of Darhansoff & Verrill Literary Agency.

Doubleday, a division of Bantam Doubleday Dell Publishing Group, Inc.
"Shakespeare's Reading List" from *Shakespeare Alive!* by Joseph Papp and Elizabeth Kirkland. Copyright © 1988 by New York Shakespeare Festival. "A Visit to Grandmother," copyright © 1964 by William Melvin Kelley, from *Dancers on the Shore* by William Melvin Kelley. "The Bridge" by Leopold Staff, from *Postwar Polish Poetry*, selected and translated by Czeslaw Milosz. Translation copyright 1965 by Czeslaw Milosz. "The Waking", copyright 1953 by Theodore Roethke, from *The Collected Poems of Theodore Roethke* by Theodore Roethke. Used by permission of Doubleday, a division of Bantam Doubleday Dell Publishing Group, Inc.

Doubleday, a division of Bantam Doubleday Dell Publishing Group, Inc., and Harold Ober Associates, Inc.
"Civil Peace" from *Girls at War and Other Stories* by Chinua Achebe. Copyright © 1972, 1973 by Chinua Achebe. Used by permission of Doubleday, a division of Bantam Doubleday Dell Publishing Group, Inc., and Harold Ober Associates, Inc.

Henry Dunow Literary Agency
"The Censors" from *Open Door* by Luisa Valenzuela; Copyright © 1976, renewed 1988 by Luisa Valenzuela.

Roger Ebert
"'Star Wars' Breakthrough Film Still Has the Force" by Roger Ebert. First published in January 1997, *Chicago Sun Times.* © 1977 The Ebert Co., Ltd. Used by permission of the author.

Editions Robert Laffont
From *In the Name Of Sorrow and Hope* by Noa Ben Artzi-Pelossof. Copyright © 1996 by Editions Robert Laffont.

Ann Elmo Agency, Inc.
"Leiningen Versus the Ants" by Carl Stephenson. Reprinted by permission of Ann Elmo Agency, Inc., 60 East 42nd Street, New York, NY 10165.

EMI Blackwood Music Inc.
"Yesterday," words and music by John Lennon and Paul McCartney. Copyright © 1965, 1966, Renewed 1993, 1994 Sony/ATV Songs LLC. Administered by EMI Blackwood Music Inc. (BMI). All rights reserved. International Copyright Secured. Used by Permission.

Farrar, Straus & Giroux, Inc.
"What are Friends For" by Rosellen Brown. From *Cora Fry's pillow book* by Rosellen Brown. Copyright © 1994. "All" by Bei Dao, translated by Donald Finkel and Xueliang Chen, and "Also All" by Shu Ting, translated by Donald Finkel and Jinsheng Yi, from *A Splintered Mirror: Chinese Poetry from the Democracy Movement,* translated by Donald Finkel, additional translations by Carolyn Kizer, © 1991 by Donald Finkel. "A Walk to the Jetty" from *Annie John* by Jamaica Kincaid. Copyright © 1985 by Jamaica Kincaid. "The Fish" from *The Complete Poems 1927-1979* by Elizabeth Bishop. Copyright © 1979, 1983 by Alice Helen Methfessel. Excerpt from *Nobel Lecture* by Alexander Solzhenitsyn, translated by F. D. Reeve. Copyright © 1972 by the Nobel Foundation. Translation copyright © 1972 by Farrar, Straus & Giroux, Inc. "A Storm in the Mountains" from *Stories and Prose Poems* by Alexander Solzhenitsyn, translated by Michael Glenny. Translation copyright © 1970, 1971 by Michael Glenny. Reprinted by permission of Farrar, Straus & Giroux, Inc.

Frankfurt, Garbus, Klein & Selz
Lyrics from "Cats in the Cradle" by Sandy and Harry Chapin. Copyright © 1974 Story Songs Ltd. Used with permission. All Rights Reserved.

Harcourt Brace & Company
"Jazz Fantasia" from *Smoke and Steel* by Carl Sandburg, copyright 1920 by Harcourt Brace & Company and renewed 1948 by Carl Sandburg. "How to React to Familiar Faces" from *How to Travel With a Salmon & Other Essays* by Umberto Eco, copyright © Gruppo Editoriale Fabbi, Bompiani, Sonzogno, Estas S.p.A., English translation by William Weaver, copyright © 1994 by Harcourt Brace & Company. "Antigone" from *Sophocles: The Oedipus Cycle, An English Version* by Dudley Fitts and Robert Fitzgerald, copyright 1939 by Harcourt Brace & Company and renewed 1967 by Dudley Fitts and Robert Fitzgerald. CAUTION: All rights, including professional, amateur, motion picture, recitation, lecturing, performance, public reading, radio broadcasting, and television are strictly reserved. Inquiries on all rights should be addressed to Harcourt Brace & Company, Permissions Department, Orlando, FL 32887-6777. Reprinted by permission of Harcourt Brace & Company.

Harcourt Brace and Company, and The Hogarth Press, an imprint of Random House UK.
"The Widow and the Parrot" from *The Complete Shorter Fiction of Virginia Woolf,* copyright © 1985 by Quentin Bell and Angelica Garnett. Reprinted by permission.

Harcourt Brace and Company, and The Wylie Agency, Inc.
"The Garden of Stubborn Cats" from *Marcovaldo or the Seasons in the City* by Italo Calvino, English translation copyright © 1983 by Harcourt Brace & Company and Martin Secker & Warburg, Ltd. Reprinted by permission.

HarperCollins Publishers, Inc.
Excerpts from *Rare Air* by Michael Jordan. Photographs by Walter Looss, Jr. Edited by Mark Vancil. Copyright © 1993 Rare Air, Ltd. Text © 1993 Michael Jordan. Photos © 1993 Walter Looss, Jr. "Flood" from *Pilgrim At Tinker Creek* by Annie Dillard. Copyright © 1974 by Annie Dillard. Reprinted by permission of HarperCollins Publishers, Inc.

HarperCollins Publishers Inc., and Jonathan Clowes Ltd.
"Through the Tunnel" from *The Habit of Loving* by Doris Lessing. Copyright © 1954, 1955 by Doris Lessing. Originally appeared in *The New Yorker.* Copyright renewed. Reprinted by kind permission of HarperCollins Publishers, Inc., and Jonathan Clowes Ltd., London, on behalf of Doris Lessing.

HarperCollins Publishers Ltd.
From *The Analects of Confucius,* translated by Arthur Waley. Reprinted by permission of HarperCollins Publishers Ltd.

Harvard University Press
Excerpts from *One Writer's Beginnings* by Eudora Welty. Reprinted by permission of the publisher, Cambridge, Mass.: Harvard University Press, Copyright © 1983, 1984 by Eudora Welty.

Harvard University Press and the Trustees of Amherst College
"The Wind-Tapped Like a Tired Man" (#436), "I dwell in Possibility—" (#657), and "Success if Counted Sweetest" (poem #67) by Emily Dickinson. Reprinted by permission of the publishers and the Trustees of Amherst College from *The Poems of Emily Dickinson,* Thomas J. Johnson, ed., Cambridge, Mass.: The Belknap Press of Harvard University Press, Copyright © 1951, 1955, 1979, 1983 by the President and Fellows of Harvard College.

Hill and Wang, a division of Farrar, Straus & Giroux, Inc., and Albert Bonniers Forlag AB
"The Princess and all the Kingdom" from *The Marriage Feast* by Pär Lagerkvist, translated by Alan Blair. Translation copyright © 1954 by Random House. Reprinted by permission of Hill and Wang, a division of Farrar, Straus & Giroux, Inc., and Albert Bonniers Forlag AB.

Hispanic Society of America
"The Guitar" by Federico García Lorca from *Translations From Hispanic Poets,* edited by Elizabeth du Gue Trapier. Reprinted by permission of the Hispanic Society of America.

Hodder and Stoughton Limited
"The Final Assault" from *High Adventure* by Edmund Hillary. Copyright 1955. Reproduced by permission of Hodder and Stoughton Limited.

Henry Holt & Co.
"Mowing" and "After Apple Picking" from *The Poetry of Robert Frost,* edited by Edward Connery Lathem. Published by Holt, Rinehart and Winston.

Houghton Mifflin Company
"The Marginal World" from *The Edge of the Sea* by Rachel Carson. Copyright © 1955 by Rachel L. Carson, © renewed 1983 by Roger Christie. Reprinted by permission of Houghton Mifflin Company. All rights reserved.

Japan Publications, Inc.
"Falling upon earth" by Basho and "A gentle spring rain" by Issa, reprinted from *One Hundred Famous Haiku,* translated by Daniel C. Buchanan, with permission from Japan Publications, Inc., ©1973

John Johnson Ltd., and Penguin Books Ltd.
"The Bridegroom," from *The Bronze Horseman and Other Poems* by Alexander Pushkin, translated by D. M. Thomas (Penguin Books 1982). Translation copyright © D. M. Thomas, 1982. Reprinted by permission of John Johnson (Authors' Agent) Limited, and Penguin Books Ltd.

The Johns Hopkins University Press
"Fear" from *Selected Poems of Gabriela Mistral,* translated and edited by Doris Dana. Copyright © 1961, 1964, 1970, 1971 by Doris Dana. Reprinted by permission of The Johns Hopkins University Press.

Alfred A. Knopf, Inc.
"The Apple Tree" from *The Scrapbook of Katherine Mansfield* by Katherine Mansfield, edit., J. Middleton Murray. Copyright 1939 by Alfred A. Knopf, Inc. and renewed 1967 by Mrs. Mary Middleton Murray. "The Weary Blues" from *Selected Poems* by Langston Hughes. Copyright 1926 by Alfred A. Knopf, Inc. and renewed 1954 by Langston Hughes. Reprinted by permission of the publisher.

Jon Krakauer
From "Into Thin Air" by Jon Krakauer from the September 1996 issue of *Outside Magazine.* Reprinted by permission of the author.

John Landau Management
"These Are Days" by Natalie Merchant, from *Our Time in Eden,* copyright © 1992 ASCAP. Reprinted by permission of John Landau Management.

Library of America
"Prayer of First Dancers," Navajo, from *The Night Chant,* by permission of the Library of America.

Liveright Publishing Corporation
"Reapers" from Cane by Jean Toomer. Copyright 1923 by Boni & Liveright, renewed 1951 by Jean Toomer. Reprinted by permission of Liveright Publishing Corporation.

Macmillan Publishing Company
"The Stolen Child" from *The Collected Works of W. B. Yeats, Volume I: The Poems,* Revised and edited Richard J. Finneran. Copyright 1906 by Macmillan Publishing Company, renewed 1934 by William Butler Yeats.

Martin Secker & Warburg, Ltd.
Excerpt from *My Left Foot* by Christy Brown. Copyright © 1954 by Christy Brown. Reprinted by permission of Martin Secker & Warburg, Ltd.

Natural History Magazine
"Work That Counts" by Ernest Ruelas Inzunza from *Natural History,* October 1996, Volume 105, Number 10. Copyright © the American Museum of Natural History, 1996. Reprinted by permission of Natural History Magazine.

NAL Penguin, a division of Penguin Books USA Inc.
From *The Tragedy of Julius Caesar* by William Shakespeare, edited by William and Barbara Rosen. Copyright © 1963 by William and Barbara Rosen.

NBA Properties, Inc., and Frank Deford
"NBA: The Greatest Ever" by Frank DeFord which aired on NBC, November 2, 1996. Reprinted with the permission of NBA Properties, Inc. and Frank Deford.

New Directions Publishing Corp.
"A Tree Telling of Orpheus" by Denise Levertov, from *Poems 1968-1972.* Copyright © 1970 by Denise Levertov. "The Street" by Octavio Paz, from *Selected Poems.* Copyright © 1973 by Octavio Paz and Muriel Rukeyser. "Spring and All" by of William Carlos Williams, from *Collected Poems: 1909-1939, Volume I.* Copyright © 1938 by New Directions Publishing Corp. "Jade Blossom Palace" by Tu Fu, translated by David Hinton, from *The Selected Poems of Tu Fu.* Copyright © 1989 by David Hinton. Reprinted by permission of New Directions Publishing Corp.

New Directions Publishing Corporation, and David Higham Associates Ltd.
Dylan Thomas, *A Child's Christmas in Wales.* Copyright © 1952 by Dylan Thomas; Copyright © 1954 New Directions Publishing Corporation. Reprinted by permission of New Directions Publishing Corporation, and David Higham Associates Ltd.

New Orleans Poetry Journal Press, Inc.
"Columbus Dying" from *Adam's Footprint* by Vassar Miller, Copyright © 1956 by Vassar Miller. Reprinted by permission of New Orleans Poetry Journal Press, Inc.

The New Yorker
"Some Like Poetry" by Wislawa Szymborska, translated by Joanna Trzeciak, first appeared in *The New Yorker Special Politics Issue,* October 1996. Used by permission of the translator.

The New York Times Co.
"Star Wars: An Epic For Today" (The Names Came From Earth) by Eric Nash, published in *The New York Times,* January 26, 1997. Copyright © 1997 by The New York Times Company. "Star Wars—A Trip to a Far Galaxy" by Vincent Canby, published in *The New York Times,* May 16, 1977. Copyright © 1977 by The New York Times Co. Reprinted by permission of The New York Times Co.

The Nobel Foundation
"Keep Memory Alive," excerpt from Elie Wiesel's Nobel Prize Acceptance Speech. Copyright © 1986 by the Nobel Foundation. Used by permission of the Nobel Foundation, Oslo, Norway.

W. W. Norton & Company, Inc.
From *Don Quixote,* A Norton Critical Edition, The Ormsby Translation, Revised by Miguel de Cervantes, edited by Joseph Jones & Kenneth Douglas. Copyright © 1981 by W. W. Norton & Company, Inc. Reprinted by permission of W. W. Norton & Company, Inc.

Naomi Shihab Nye
"Making a Fist" from *Hugging the Jukebox* by Naomi Shihab Nye. Copyright © Naomi Shihab Nye, 1982. Reprinted by permission of the author.

Harold Ober Associates, Inc.
"The Good Deed" by Pearl S. Buck. Copyright 1953 by Pearl S. Buck. Copyright renewed 1981. "Marian Anderson: Famous Concert Singer" by Langston Hughes. Copyright © 1954 by Langston Hughes, renewed 1982 by George Houston Bass. Reprinted by permission of Harold Ober Associates Incorporated.

Peter Owen Ltd.
"A Man" by Nina Cassian, translated by Roy MacGregor-Hastie. Reprinted by permission of Peter Owen Ltd, London.

Pantheon Books, a division of Random House, Inc.
"The Orphan Boy and the Elk Dog", from *American Indian Myths and Legends* by Richard Erdoes and Alfonso Ortiz,

editors. Copyright © 1984 by Richard Erdoes and Alfonso Ortiz. Reprinted by permission of Pantheon Books, a division of Random House, Inc.

Penguin Books Ltd.
"One Cannot ask loneliness" by Priest Jakuren, from *The Penguin Book of Japanese Verse* edited and translated by Geoffrey Bownas and Anthony Thwaite (Penguin Books, 1964). Translation copyright © Geoffrey Bownas and Anthony Thwaite, 1964. Reprinted by permission of Penguin Books Ltd.

Présence Africaine
"Africa" from *Coups de Pilon* by David Diop, published by Présence Africaine, 1956. "Childhood" and "The Lion's Awakening" from *Sundiata: An Epic of Old Mali* by D.T. Niane, translated by G. D. Pickett. © Présence Africaine 1960 (original French version: Soundjata, ou L'Epopée Mandingue). © Longman Group Ltd. (English Version) 1965. Reprinted by permission of Présence Africaine.

Reynolds Price
"What's in a Picture," retitled "A Picture From the Past" by Reynolds Price from the September/October 1996 issue of *Civilization Magazine,* copyright © 1996. Reprinted by permission of the author.

The Putnam Publishing Group
"In Flanders Fields" reprinted by permission of The Putnam Publishing Group from *In Flanders Fields* by John McCrae. Copyright © 1919 by G. P. Putnam's Sons, Renewed.

The Putnam Publishing Group, and David Higham Associates
"Arthur Becomes King" from *The Once and Future King* by T. H. White. Copyright © 1939, 1940 by T. H. White; Renewed © 1958 by T. H. White Proprietor. Reprinted by permission of The Putnam Publishing Group, and David Higham Associates.

Random House, Inc.
"The Moon at the Fortified Pass" by Li Po, translated by Wytter Bynner, from The Wisdom of China and India edited by Lin Yutang. Copyright 1942 and renewed 1970 by Random House, Inc. "At Harvest Time" and "Style" from *Wouldn't Take Nothing For My Journey Now* by Maya Angelou. Copyright © 1993 by Maya Angelou. Reprinted by permission of Random House, Inc.

Real World Music and Lipservices
"Biko" by Peter Gabriel. © 1980 by Real World Music Ltd. Reproduced with kind permission of Real World Music and Lipservices. All Rights Reserved. International Copyright Secured.

Marian Reiner
"Metaphor" from *It Doesn't Always Have to Rhyme* by Eve Merriam. Copyright © 1964 by Eve Merriam. Copyright renewed 1992 Eve Merriam. Reprinted by permission of Marian Reiner.

Russell & Volkening
"Uncoiling" from *Daughters of the Fifth Sun* by Pat Mora. Copyright © 1995 by Pat Mora. Published by Riverside Books. "With All Flags Flying" by Anne Tyler, published by *Redbook Magazine,* June 1971. Copyright © 1971 by Anne Tyler. Reprinted by the permission of Russell & Volkening as agents for the authors.

Schocken Books, distributed by Pantheon Books, a division of Random House, Inc.
"Before the Law," from *Franz Kafka: The Complete Stories* by Franz Kafka, edited by Nahum N. Glatzer. Copyright © 1946, 1947, 1948, 1949, 1954, 1958, 1971 by Schocken Books, Inc. Reprinted by permission of Schocken Books, distributed by Pantheon Books, a division of Random House, Inc.

Simon & Schuster Inc.
"The Stolen Child" from *The Collected Poems of W. B. Yeats, Volume I: The Poems,* Revised and edited Richard J. Finneran. Copyright 1906 by Macmillan Publishing Company, renewed 1934 by William Butler Yeats.

The Society of Authors as the literary representative of the Estate of W. W. Jacobs
"The Monkey's Paw" from *The Lady of the Barge* by W. W. Jacobs. Reprinted by permission.

Sage Sohier
Sage Sohier, *Untitled,* text and photograph © Sage Sohier, Brookline, Massachusetts, 1986. Published in *Mothers & Daughters* by Tillie Olsen with Julie Olsen Edwards and Estelle Jussim. Reprinted by permission of the author.

The Estate of Rabindranath Tagore
"The Cabuliwallah" from *A Tagore Reader* by Rabindranath Tagore, copyright © 1945.

Third World Press
"The Bean Eaters" from *Blacks* by Gwendolyn Brooks. Copyright © 1991 by Gwendolyn Brooks. Reprinted by permission of the publisher, Third World Press, Chicago, IL

Rosemary A. Thurber
"The Dog That Bit People" copyright 1933, © 1961 by James Thurber. From *My Life and Hard Times,* published by Harper & Row. Reprinted by permission of Rosemary A. Thurber.

Time-Life Books, Inc.
"Imitating Natures Mineral Artistry" from *Planet Earth: Gemstones* by Paul O'Neil and the Editors of Time-Life Books. Copyright © 1983 Time-Life Books Inc. Reprinted by permission of Time-Life Books, Inc.

The University of California Press
"A Pace Like That" translated by Chana Bloch, from *The Selected Poetry of Yehuda Amichai,* edited and translated by Chana Bloch and Stephen Mitchell. Copyright © 1996 The Regents of the University of California. Reprinted by permission of The University of California Press.

University of New Mexico Press
Reprinted from *The Way to Rainy Mountain* by N. Scott Momaday. First published in The Reporter, January 26, 1967. © 1969 The University of New Mexico Press and reprinted with their permission.

The University of North Carolina Press
"The Street of Cañon" from *Mexican Village* by Josephina Niggli. Copyright 1945 The University of North Carolina Press. Reprinted by permission of the publisher.

Viking Penguin, a division of Penguin Books USA Inc.
"Like the Sun" from *Under the Banyan Tree* by R. K. Narayan. Copyright © 1985 by R. K. Narayan. From *What Makes a Degas a Degas* by Richard Muhlberger. Copyright © 1993 by The Metropolitan Museum of Art. Used by permission of Viking Penguin, a division of Penguin Books USA Inc. "The Open Window" from The Complete Short Stories of Saki (H. H. Munro), published by Viking Press, Inc.

Vintage Books, a division of Random House, Inc.
From *Speak, Memory* by Vladimir Nabokov. Copyright © 1966 by Vladimir Nabokov. Reprinted by permission of Vintage Books, a Division of Random House, Inc.

Wallace Literary Agency for R. K. Narayan
"Rama's Initiation" from *The Ramayana: A Shortened Modern Prose Version of the Indian Epic* by R. K. Narayan. Published by

Acknowledgments ◆ *997*

Penguin Books. Copyright © 1972 by R. K. Narayan. Reprinted by permission of the author.

A. P. Watt Ltd.
From *A Problem* by Anton Chekhov, translated from Russian by Constance Garnett. Reprinted by permission of A. P. Watt Ltd. on behalf of The Executors of the Estate of Constance Garnett.

Wieser & Wieser, Inc.
"Auto Wreck" from *Collected Poems 1940-1978* by Karl Shapiro. Copyright 1942 and renewed 1970 by Karl Shapiro. Reprinted by permission of Wieser & Wieser, Inc.

Zohar Press
Grateful acknowledgment to Zohar Press for permission to reprint "Right Hand" by Philip Fried from his book *Quantum*

Genesis and Other Poems (Zohar, 1997).

Note: Every effort has been made to locate the copyright owner of material reprinted in this book. Omissions brought to our attention will be corrected in subsequent editions.

ILLUSTRATION CREDITS

23, 72, 87, 95, 147, 165, 178, 201, 219, 251, 263, 271, 283, 297, 303, 336, 339, 357, 363, 375, 381, 395, 424, 469, 479, 513, 528, 533, 622, 625, 649, 650, 659, 702, 704, 833, 855, 863, 920, 947: Ernest Albanese.

26, 61, 117, 291, 313, 949: Ortelius Design.

47, 51: S.I. International representing Allen Davis.

79, 80-81: S.I. International representing Jordi Torres.

ADDITIONAL CREDITS

Editorial: Tim Callahan, Elaine Goldman, Gregory Lynch, Laura Ring

Media Resources: Diane Alimena, Katty Gavilanes, Suzi Myers

Permissions: Rosalyn Arcilla, Jeanette Myers

Photo Research Service: Omni-Photo Communications, Inc.

PrePress Production: James D. Gwyn

Production: Claudia Dukeshire, Deborah O'Connell

Design and Page Layout: Ernest Albanese, Robert Aleman, Jane Alexander, Lisa Ann Arcuri, Penelope Baker, Anthony Barone, Linda Berniak, Elizabeth Bostwick, Emily Buckley, Chris Calloway, Rui Camarinha, Tara Campbell, Carlos Crespo, Thomas Davidson, Paul DelSignore, Robert Dobasczewski, Irene Ehrmann, Jeffrey Engel, Frederic Joe Galka, Diane Gerard, Pat Gilbanks, Florrie Gladson, Julie Goldstein, Alison Grabow, Leslie Greenberg, Greg Harrison, Ralph Henriquez, Kathleen Kennedy, Gregory Ludwig, Laura Maggio, Lynn Mandarino, John McClure, Deirdre Mitchell, Thomas Mitchell, Rebecca Myers, Karolyn Necco, Evelyn O'Shea, Harry Phillips, Linda Punskovsky, Ken Rosenblat, David Rosenthal, Phyllis Rosinsky, Janelle Roth, Irene Schwartz, Jan Schwartz, Rose Sievers, Dakota Smith, Scott Steinhardt, Tom Tedesco, Frances Turcott, Karen Vignola, Wendy Wolf